KT-441-861

Additional praise for *Romanticism: An Anthology*, Third Edition

'In the third edition of his groundbreaking *Romanticism*: *An Anthology*, Duncan Wu has made a very good text even better.'

David Latane, Virginia Commonwealth University

'The third edition of Duncan Wu's *Romanticism* is an outstanding anthology, an excellent choice for advanced undergraduate courses on the Romantic era. I look forward to using this edition of *Romanticism* for years to come.'

Kim Wheatley, College of William and Mary

'I have chosen it for my elective "British Romantic Poetry" as this text is superior to any other available in its combination of essential canonical poetry with an astute selection of other literature, including extensive representation of women writers.'

Paul Betz, Georgetown University

OTHER BOOKS BY DUNCAN WU

Wordsworth's Reading 1770–1799
Wordsworth's Reading 1800–1815
Making Plays: Interviews with Contemporary British Dramatists and Directors
Wordsworth: An Inner Life
Wordsworth's Poets
Six Contemporary Dramatists: Bennett, Potter, Gray, Brenton, Hare, Ayckbourn

William Wordsworth: Selected Poems (co-edited with Stephen Gill)
Romanticism: A Critical Reader (editor)
William Wordsworth: The Five-Book Prelude (editor)
Women Romantic Poets: An Anthology (editor)
A Companion to Romanticism (editor)
William Hazlitt, The Plain Speaker: Key Essays (editor)
The Selected Writings of William Halitt, nine volumes (editor)
British Romanticism and the Edinburgh Review (co-edited with Massimiliano Demata)
William Wordsworth: The Earliest Poems 1785–1790 (editor)
Metaphysical Hazlitt (co-edited with Uttara Natarajan and Tom Paulin)

ENGLAND, WALES and the BORDERS
in the 19th Century
N
Glasgow
Edinburgh
Lammermuir Hills
Holy Island
SCOTLAND
Abbotsford
Arran
Ayr
Cheviot Hills
Gretna Green
Dumfries
Hadrian's Wall
Cockermouth
Penrith
Keswick
Grasmere
Rydal Mt
Hawkshead
Kendal
Isle of Man
Wensleydale
Pennines
Holderness
Manchester
Liverpool
Newstead Abbey
Lincoln
Gwyrch
Mt Snowdon
Shrewsbury
Eastwood
The Fens
Wem
Nottingham
Mts
ENGLAND
WALES
Cambrian
Birmingham
Coventry
Forest of Arden
Rugby
Cambridge
Malvern Hills
Tintern Abbey
Chiltern Hills
Swansea
Cotswold Hills
Oxford
Marlow
London
Eton
Windsor
Clevedon
North Downs
Cobham
Salisbury Plain
Mendip Hills
Bath
Valley of the Rocks
The Weald
Canterbury
Stonehenge
Field Place
Tunbridge Wells
Porlock
Nether Stowey
Winchester
Dover
Salisbury
Alfoxden House (Holford)
South Downs
Dorset Downs
Felpham
Brighton
New Forest
Ottery St Mary
Bournemouth
Isle of Wight
Portland Bill
Blackmoor
Land's End
100 miles

ROMANTICISM

AN ANTHOLOGY

Third Edition

EDITED BY **DUNCAN WU**

© 1994, 1998, 2006 by Blackwell Publishing
except for editorial material and organization © 1994, 1998, 2006 by Duncan Wu

BLACKWELL PUBLISHING
350 Main Street, Malden, 02148-5020, USA
108 Cowley Road, Oxford OX4 1JF, UK
550 Swanston Street, Carlton, Victoria 3053, Australia

The right of Duncan Wu to be identified as the Author of this Work has been asserted in accordance with the UK Copyright, Designs, and Patents Act 1988.

All rights reserved. No part of this publication may be reproduced, stored in a retrieval system, or transmitted, in any form or by any means, electronic, mechanical, photocopying, recording or otherwise, except as permitted by the UK Copyright, Designs, and Patents Act 1988, without the prior permission of the publisher.

First edition published 1994
Second edition published 1998
Third edition published 2006 by Blackwell Publishing Ltd

3 2007

Library of Congress Cataloging-in-Publication Data

Romanticism: an anthology / edited by Duncan Wu.– 3rd ed.
p. cm.— (Blackwell anthologies)
Includes bibliographical references and index.
ISBN: 978-1-4051-2085-2 (pbk.: alk. paper)
1. English literature—19th century. 2. English literature—18th century. 3. Romanticism—Great Britain. I. Wu, Duncan. II. Series.

PR1139.R66 2005
820.8′0145—dc22
2004018665

A catalogue record for this title is available from the British Library.

Set in 9 on 10.5pt Dante
by SPI Publisher Services, Pondicherry, India
Printed and bound in the United Kingdom
by TJ International Ltd, Padstow, Cornwall

The publisher's policy is to use permanent paper from mills that operate a sustainable forestry policy, and which has been manufactured from pulp processed using acid-free and elementary chlorine-free practices. Furthermore, the publisher ensures that the text paper and cover board used have met acceptable environmental accreditation standards.

For further information on
Blackwell Publishing, visit our website:
www.blackwellpublishing.com

Contents

Illustrations

Plates

Plates fall between pages 694 and 695

Abbreviations

Blake, *Early Illuminated Books*	William Blake, *The Early Illuminated Books* ed. Morris Eaves, Robert N. Essick, and Joseph Viscomi (London, 1993).
CC *Table Talk*	S. T. Coleridge, *Table Talk* ed. Carl Woodring (2 vols., Princeton, 1990).
FN	*The Fenwick Notes of William Wordsworth* ed. Jared Curtis (London, 1993).
Grasmere Journals	Dorothy Wordsworth, *The Grasmere and Alfoxden Journals* ed. Pamela Woof (Oxford, 2002).
Griggs	*The Collected Letters of Samuel Taylor Coleridge* ed. E. L. Griggs (6 vols, Oxford, 1956–71).
Howe	*The Works of William Hazlitt*, ed. P. P. Howe (21 vols, London, 1930–4).
Jones	*The Letters of Percy Bysshe Shelley* ed. F. L. Jones (2 vols, Oxford, 1964).
Keats Circle	*The Keats Circle: Letters and Papers 1816–1878* ed. Hyder E. Rollins (2 vols. Cambridge, Mass., 1948).
Lindop	*The Works of Thomas de Quincey* ed. Grevel Lindop et al. (21 vols., London, 2000–3).
LY	*The Letters of William and Dorothy Wordsworth: The Later Years 1821–53* ed. Ernest de Selincourt, rev. Alan G. Hill (4 vols, Oxford, 1978–88).
Marchand	*Byron's Letters and Journals* ed. Leslie A. Marchand (12 vols, London, 1973–82).
Marrs	*The Letters of Charles and Mary Anne Lamb* ed. Edwin W. Marrs, Jr (3 vols, Ithaca, NY, 1975–8).
Medwin	Thomas Medwin, *Conversations of Lord Byron* (London, 1824).
Morley (1927)	*The Correspondence of Crabb Robinson with the Wordsworth Circle* ed. Edith J. Morley (2 vols, Oxford, 1927).
Morley (1938)	*Henry Crabb Robinson on Books and Their Writers* ed. Edith J. Morley (3 vols, London, 1938).

MY	*The Letters of William and Dorothy Wordsworth: The Middle Years* ed. Ernest de Selincourt, *i: 1806–11*, rev. Mary Moorman (Oxford, 1969); *ii: 1812–20*, rev. Mary Moorman and Alan G. Hill (Oxford, 1970).
Notebooks	*The Notebooks of Samuel Taylor Coleridge* ed. Kathleen Coburn and Anthony Harding (5 vols, New York, 1957–2003).
Owen and Smyser	*The Prose Works of William Wordsworth* ed. W. J. B. Owen and Jane Worthington Smyser (3 vols, Oxford, 1974).
RES	*Review of English Studies.*
Rollins	*The Letters of John Keats, 1814–1821* ed. Hyder E. Rollins (2 vols, Cambridge, Mass., 1958).
Romanticism: A Critical Reader	*Romanticism: A Critical Reader* ed. Duncan Wu (Oxford, 1995).
SC	*Shelley and his Circle 1773–1822* ed. K. N. Cameron and D. H. Reiman (10 vols, Cambridge, Mass, 1961–2002).
Shelley Journals	*The Journals of Mary Shelley 1814–1844* ed. Paula R. Feldman and Diana Scott-Kilvert (2 vols, Oxford, 1987).
TWC	*The Wordsworth Circle.*
Wu	*Selected Writings of William Hazlitt* ed. Duncan Wu (9 vols, London, 1998).

Introduction

I perceive that in Germany as well as in Italy there is a great struggle about what they call Classical *and* Romantic, *terms which were not subjects of Classification in England – at least when I left it four or five years ago.*

(Byron, in the rejected Dedication to *Marino Faliero*, dated 14 August 1820)

When *Lyrical Ballads* first appeared in 1798 the word 'Romantic' was no compliment. It meant 'fanciful', 'light', even 'inconsequential'.[1] Wordsworth and Coleridge would have resisted its application; twenty years later, the new generation of writers would recognize it only as the counter in a debate conducted among European intellectuals, hardly relevant to what they were doing. And that, after all, is the nature of theoretical discourse: even when conducted by practitioners, it may not bear greatly on the creative process.

Romance was originally a descriptive term, used to refer to the verse epics of Tasso and Ariosto. Eighteenth-century critics like Thomas Warton used it in relation to fiction, often European, and it was in that context that Novalis applied it to German literature. The idea didn't take flight until August Wilhelm Schlegel used it in a lecture course at Berlin, 1801–4, when he made the distinction mentioned by Byron. Romantic literature, he argued, appeared in the Middle Ages with the work of Dante, Petrarch and Boccaccio; in reaction to Classicism it was identified with progressive and Christian views. In another course of lectures in Vienna, 1808–9, he went further: Romanticism was 'organic' and 'plastic', as against the 'mechanical' tendencies of Classicism. By 1821, when Byron dedicated *Marino Faliero* to Goethe, the debate was in full flood: Schlegel's ideas had been picked up and extrapolated by Madame de Staël, and in 1818 Stendhal became the first Frenchman to claim himself *un romantique* – for Shakespeare and against Racine; for Byron and against Boileau. Within a year Spanish and Portuguese critics too were wading in.

Having originated in disagreement, and largely in academe, the concept has remained fluid ever since, and although many definitions are suggested, none command universal agreement. In that respect Romanticism is distinct from movements formed by artists, which tend to be coherent in their objectives, at least to begin with. When the Pre-

Notes

[1] It is in this sense that Thomas Paine uses it in his comments 'On Revolution', p. 25, below.

Raphaelite Brotherhood turned themselves into a school, they knew exactly how they wanted to challenge received notions about pictorial representation; the Imagists published a manifesto of sorts in *Blast* that represented an agreed line of attack. The British Romantic poets could not have done this. Blake, Wordsworth, Coleridge, Byron, Shelley and Keats never met in the same place and, had they done so, would probably have fallen out immediately.

One factor was the generation gap. Byron, Shelley and Keats might have enjoyed the company of Wordsworth as he was in his later twenties and early thirties, but by the time they reached artistic maturity – *c.*1816 for Shelley and Byron, 1819 for Keats – he was well into middle age, had accepted the job of Distributor of Stamps for Westmorland, and appeared to have abandoned the religious and political views of his youth. His support for the Tory Lord Lonsdale in the 1818 general election confirmed his allegiance to a conservatism they despised. So far as they were concerned, he had betrayed the promise of *Tintern Abbey* for a sinecure. All this makes it doubly unfortunate that they were unable to read *The Prelude*, unpublished till 1850. Had they done so, they would have seen him differently.

Byron caught up with the critical debate surrounding the concept of Romanticism in 1821, but Coleridge beat him to it by a year. In 1820 the sage of Highgate compiled a list of 'Romantic' writers in which the only English poets of the day were Southey, Scott and Byron.[2] The oddity of this serves to underline the inbuilt resistance of the concept to satisfactory definition – something that guarantees its usefulness as a critical and pedagogical tool. Critics continue to adapt it to their various needs while teachers use it to make connections between sometimes disparate writers of the period.

The pre-eminence of Blake, Wordsworth, Coleridge, Keats, Byron and Shelley was largely the invention of the twentieth century, and is now superseded by a widespread acceptance that Charlotte Smith, Hannah More, Anna Laetitia Barbauld, Helen Maria Williams, Felicia Dorothea Hemans and Letitia Landon be read alongside them. In this introduction, I want to address ways in which they might be considered part of a community for which the concept of Romanticism, however ill-defined, has meaning.

Romanticism: Culture and Society

The Romantic period has an immediacy which earlier ones tend to lack. This is because so many of our values and preoccupations derive from it. For one thing, it coincides with the moment at which Britain industrialized itself. Factories sprang up in towns and cities across the country, and the old agrarian lives people had known for centuries stopped being taken for granted. Instead labourers began to move into urban conurbations, working long hours in close proximity to each other. This had a number of consequences, not least that they began to fight for their 'rights'. We take our rights for granted, forgetting the length of the intellectual journey working people had to make merely to understand they had such things. For many, the feudal system of medieval times continued to dictate their understanding of their place in society.

Notes

[2] He includes Goethe, Tieck, Southey, Scott and Byron among poets, and himself, Schlegel, and Campbell among critics.

The process by which people were awakened to a sense of self-determination was global. It began with the American Revolution and continued with that in France. And the impact of those upheavals cannot be overstated. Whole populations began to question the legitimacy of hereditary monarchs whose right to rule had once been accepted without question. It was not surprising that struggles elsewhere to do away with monarchical government affected the British; in fact, the real surprise is their failure to take the same step – a grim testament to the determination with which the government stifled unrest. By the summer of 1817, it had in place a sophisticated network of spies instrumental in thwarting popular uprisings in Yorkshire, Derbyshire and Nottinghamshire. A favoured technique was for *agents provocateurs* to incite revolutionary activity, and for the government to execute its supporters.[3]

Revolution in America and France generated conflict because of the knock-on effect on international trade. By the time Wordsworth was in his mid-twenties, Britain was embroiled in nothing less than world war which, unlike those in the twentieth century, would last not for years but decades. From 1793 to 1802, and then from 1803 until 1815, Britain grappled with France across the globe, often fighting single-handedly against a well-equipped and resourceful enemy who, for much of that time, had the advantage. To an island-bound people like the British, the constant threat of invasion over more than two decades was bound to have a powerful effect. Whatever one's sympathies with the ideals of the American and French Revolutions, it became difficult to express anything other than support for the national cause. Patriotic feeling in its most jingoistic form ran high, something vividly indicated by the caricatures of James Gillray. In *The French Invasion; or John Bull bombarding the Bum-boats* (1793), he depicts George III, transformed into a map of England and Wales, excreting onto a swarm of French gunboats. In this context the King's evacuations are heroic and patriotic. Gillray thus turns a scatological image into an emblem of British defiance – one that reveals both contempt for Europe as well as the centuries-old tendency to insularity.[4] (See Plates 1 and 2)

All the same, war even on a global scale could not of itself suppress the desire for just government. Wars are expensive, and in order to pay its bills, the government had to levy higher taxes, principally from working people. On 14 June 1815, the additional expenditure arising from Napoleon's escape from Elba and its consequences led Nicholas Vansittart, Chancellor of the Exchequer, to raise £79 million (£3,330 million / US$6.1 billion today) largely through tax revenues. This generated intense resentment, particularly at a time of bad harvests and record unemployment. Nor did that hardship cease when the war ended; the following years were no better.

International conflict, the threat of invasion by Napoleon, social and political discontent – the writers in this book lived with these things, and were shaped by them. To that extent, it is helpful to consider Barbauld, Wordsworth, Williams, Coleridge, Smith, Blake, Keats, Byron, Hemans and Shelley as war poets, surrounded by upheaval and conflict, and passionately engaged with it. That engagement was made possible by another important development: the rise of the media.

Notes

[3] When these tactics were discovered, they inspired some classic radical journalism; see for instance Leigh Hunt, 'Informers', *The Examiner* (29 June 1817) and Hazlitt, 'On the Spy-System' (Wu iv 194–5).

[4] For more on Gillray, see the Gillray Gallery: http://users.ox.ac.uk/~scat1492/gillray.htm

This period was the first in history in which the population could keep abreast of political developments through newsprint. Historians have long acknowledged that the French press played an important part in the Revolution, enjoying unprecedented freedom between the fall of the Bastille in July 1789 and that of the monarchy in August 1792.[5] It was not for nothing that J. L. Carra and Antoine-Joseph Gorsas, both journalists, were among those guillotined by Robespierre. The inventions of the steam-press (by which *The Times* was produced from 1814 onwards) and the paper-making machine (in 1803) meant that it was easier than ever to produce newspapers on an industrial scale. And from around 1810 the boom of the mail-coach, which travelled at the hitherto unimaginable speed of 12 miles per hour, enabled publishers to distribute on a nationwide scale. For the first time, it was possible for Coleridge in Keswick to receive the papers the day after their publication before sending them on to Wordsworth in Grasmere;[6] there is no sense in which those living in the provinces were necessarily cut off.

Nor was it only well-educated poets in the Lake District who kept up with the news: it was now available to the illiterate and the poor. In 1807 the *Morning Chronicle* cost sixpence – £1.02 / US$2 today; Cobbett sold his *Political Register* at a price that made it accessible to the labouring folk he sought to address – twopence (34 pence / US$0.60 today), which led Tory wags to call it the 'twopenny trash'.[7] Groups of men would club together and buy a single copy which would be read aloud. This is the subject of David Wilkie's masterpiece, The *Chelsea Pensioners Reading the Waterloo Dispatch*,[8] which portrays retired soldiers at a haunt near the Chelsea Royal Hospital, one of their number reading to them from the Waterloo gazette (see Plate 3). It's difficult to imagine such a scene from an earlier time, but by 1822 it seemed so precisely to capture the historical moment that the painting was besieged when put on show, forcing the Royal Academy to place rails in front of it.

In so far as it derived from technological developments, the new-found influence of the press was uncontrollable, but the government did its utmost to suppress unfavourable comment: Peter Finnerty was imprisoned in October 1797 for his report of the trial and execution of William Orr, which criticized Lord Castlereagh;[9] Cobbett was imprisoned in June 1810 for having condemned the flogging of five English militia-men by German mercenaries; in 1813 John and Leigh Hunt were imprisoned for comments on the indulgent lifestyle of the Prince Regent in *The Examiner* (see p. 792). All of them received sentences of two years. It could have been worse. There were calls for even stiffer penalties such as transportation, not least from such erstwhile revolutionary sympathizers as Robert Southey, regular contributor to the *Quarterly Review.* In an article published in February 1817, less than a month prior to the suspension of habeas corpus, he asked:

Notes

[5] See J. Gilchrist and W. J. Murray, *The Press in the French Revolution* (London, 1971).

[6] See pp. 823–4.

[7] On 16 August 1817, Cobbett wrote that Tory journalists such as Gifford and Southey, 'Corruption's forlorn-hope, came, at last, about a month before the Parliament met, to call for *new laws* to protect the Constitution against the "Two-penny *Trash*". New Laws to protect a Constitution against *trash!*' (*Cobbett's Weekly Political Pamphlet* 32, 20 (16 August 1817), col. 616).

[8] It was commissioned by the Duke of Wellington and is now at Apsley House, London.

[9] After his release he departed with the Walcheren Expedition as a reporter, but was summoned back to London by Castlereagh. When he wrote of this in the *Morning Chronicle*, he was immediately arrested and sentenced to another two years' imprisonment.

THE EXAMINER.

No. 520. SUNDAY, DEC. 14, 1817.

THE POLITICAL EXAMINER.

Party is the madness of many for the gain of a few. POPE.

No. 505.

LIBERTY OF THE PRESS.

[CONTINUED FROM LAST WEEK.]

THE reader was presented in our last with an extract from the *Courier* announcing certain " measures" that were " in contemplation" for suppressing what it called " audacious libels" and for " the *extinction* of those writings, which aim," it tells us, " only to unsettle all our notions in religion, morals, and politics." He also had a pretty little aiding and abetting paragraph brought before him

this energy was sufficient, and the late troubles in the manufacturing districts were owing, as was asserted, to these very writings, why were the former not prevented and the latter silenced long ago?

The *Courier* replies, that " the impunity" with which " the publications of COBBETT and others were sent forth" last year, and " the inactivity of the law at that period, it must confess, *did astonish it*."

But the law, as the public well remembers, was not inactive. It was expounded in circular letters, and inflicted, where it could be, in ex-officio informations; and yet in the midst of all this, and of every other possible symptom of a vigour not only within the pale of the law but beyond it, the Ministers themselves told us, that the Crown Lawyers had in vain examined the writings in question,—nay, " had been unable, *after the most dili-*

Figure 1 Leigh Hunt's *Examiner* for 14 December 1817, showing the paper's motto which appeared on the front page of every issue: 'Party is the madness of many for the gain of a few'. That Sunday, Hunt wrote about press freedom, increasingly circumscribed by a government anxious about public hostility.

> Why is it that this convicted incendiary [Cobbett], and others of the same stamp, are permitted week after week to sow the seeds of rebellion, insulting the government, and defying the laws of the country? . . . Men of this description, like other criminals, derive no lessons from experience. But it behoves the Government to do so, and curb sedition in time; lest it should be called upon to crush rebellion and to punish treason.[10]

Not content with this public plea that liberal journalists be arrested when the suspension of babeas corpus allowed it, Southey took it upon himself to write a private memorandum to the Prime Minister, Lord Liverpool, telling him that laws, however repressive, are 'altogether nugatory while such manifestoes as those of Cobbett, Hone, and the *Examiner*, &c., are daily and weekly issued, fresh and fresh, and read aloud in every alehouse where the men are quartered, or where they meet together'.[11] This was supported by a typically convoluted letter by that other distinguished former revolutionary, Samuel Taylor Coleridge – but, as Liverpool wrote, 'I cannot well understand him.'[12] He certainly felt less threatened by the liberal press than his correspondents, as he decided not to take the steps they favoured. Cobbett, however, was taking no risks: believing that suspension of habeas corpus in March 1817 was passed as a means of licensing his detention, and not relishing the prospect of another spell in prison, he fled to America where he remained for two years.

Time and again, newspaper and journal reports were the means by which authors in this volume learnt of developments at home and abroad: it was how Wordsworth kept up with events in France when he returned from Paris in late 1792, and how Shelley heard of the Peterloo Massacre in 1819. Not only that; many of these writers published their poems (some of which dealt with current events) in newspapers – including Barbauld, Robinson, Coleridge, Southey, Wordsworth, Seward, Williams, Keats and Shelley.

Notes

[10] *Quarterly Review* 16 (for October 1816, though actually published 11 February 1817), 225–78, pp. 275–6.

[11] Charles Duke Yonge, *The Life and Administration of Robert Banks, Second Earl of Liverpool, K.G.* (3 vols, London, 1868), ii 298.

[12] For Coleridge's letter of 28 July 1817, see Griggs iv 757–63.

Coleridge was invited to write for the *Morning Chronicle* in early July 1796, and possibly to edit it.[13] In June 1794, avowing his disapproval 'of monarchical and aristocratical governments', Wordsworth proposed to his friend William Mathews that they co-edit a journal addressed to 'the dispassionate advocates of liberty and discussion'.[14] Not only were the writers in this book shaped by their historical moment – they helped to shape it themselves.

The most obvious evidence of the media's effect on the populace was the new-found hunger for scandal. As is the case today, the press became particularly excited when sex and politics were entwined. Mary Anne Clarke hit the headlines in early 1809 when it was revealed that she had been paid by army officers to recommend them to her lover for promotion – he was Frederick Augustus, Duke of York and Albany, second son of George III, and the army's commander-in-chief. The matter was raised in the Commons and referred to a select committee which found the Duke culpable, precipitating his resignation (though he was reappointed in 1811). Eight years later Hazlitt could refer in passing to 'the droll affair of Mrs Clarke',[15] confident that his readers would remember how droll it had been.

Another symptom was the cult of celebrity, the first and biggest beneficiary being one of the authors in this volume – Byron. He was colourful enough not to have required the assistance of gossip-columnists, but he had it anyway, and during his years in London, 1812–16, day-to-day reports of his affairs and adventures filled their pages. It is hard to imagine a poet now generating such speculation, or crowds of people following him through the streets. The world, as Samuel Rogers observed, went 'stark mad' about him. Byron found fame both intoxicating and tiresome. And not surprisingly: he was sufficiently indiscreet about his incestuous passion for his half-sister for London to have been ablaze with it in the weeks prior to his exile from Britain. When he died, helping Greece in its fight for independence, scenes of mass hysteria greeted his coffin as it journeyed from London to Nottinghamshire, the like of which had not previously been seen.

The new mass society even had its own entertainment industry – which, more than the media, gripped the imaginations of the writers in this book. Another century would pass before radio would enable performers to address the nation, but in the meantime, the two main theatres in London – Drury Lane and Covent Garden – were capable of accommodating audiences of over 3,000, more than three times the size of the Olivier Theatre in London today. And every night of the working week these theatres held capacity crowds from across the social spectrum. Those crowds learnt quickly how to exercise a collective influence: when the management attempted to increase admission prices in September 1809, they orchestrated sixty-seven nights of riots, making performances impossible – a state of affairs that ended only with negotiation.

Should there be any doubt as to the importance of theatre to the Romantics, it is worth recalling that one of the distinctions of which Byron was most proud was his seat on the committee of management of Drury Lane theatre. Along with Keats, Hazlitt and Lamb, he was an enthusiastic playgoer. Hazlitt collected his theatre reviews into a memorable book – *A View of the English Stage* (1818). Lamb, Godwin, More, Hemans, Coleridge, Shelley, Wordsworth and Byron wrote for the stage. And Mary Robinson was one of the finest Shakespearean actresses of her day.

Notes

[13] See Griggs i 226.

[14] *EY* 123, 126.

[15] Wu iv 181.

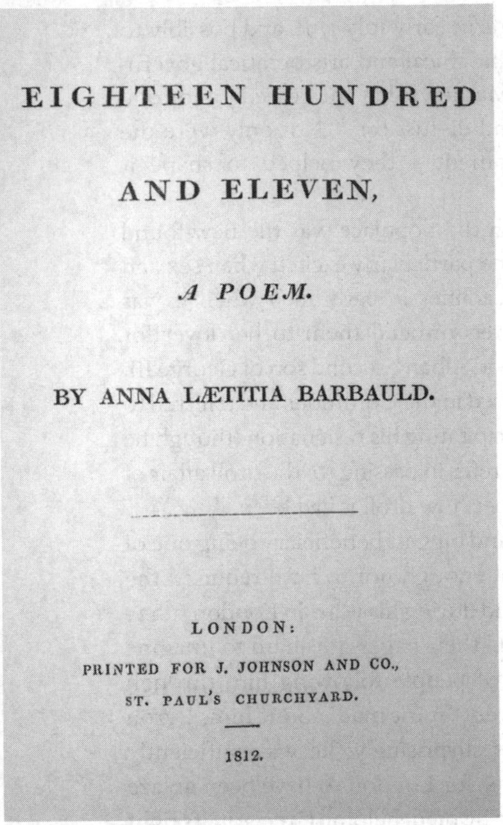

EIGHTEEN HUNDRED

AND ELEVEN,

A POEM.

BY ANNA LÆTITIA BARBAULD.

LONDON:

PRINTED FOR J. JOHNSON AND CO.,

ST. PAUL'S CHURCHYARD.

1812.

Figure 2 The title-page of Anna Laetitia Barbauld's *Eighteen Hundred and Eleven* (1812) which drew hostile reviews that effectively ended her career as a poet (see p. 34)

Romantic Poets

For all this, there were reasons for being cynical about the affairs of the world during the Romantic period. The everyday squalor of the lives of working people made it all but impossible to believe that they could revolt against the conservative interests that kept them in their place. To Burke, they were 'a swinish multitude' (p. 13), while for Shelley, who believed in change, the Dublin poor was 'one mass of animated filth' (p. 1044). Extreme poverty and lack of education meant that social and political justice were many years in the making, with no political reform until 1832 (after the deaths of Barbauld, Blake, Smith, Keats, Shelley and Byron). In the meantime there were obstacles aplenty, one being the inherent instability of the monarchy. George III, to whom the British looked for leadership, was subject (from 1788 onwards) to periodic fits of insanity, and he was judged totally mad from 1811. This was more serious than it would be today, when the monarch is little more than a figurehead; in those days he had the power to dissolve Parliament, appoint and dismiss governments, and declare wars. Without his consent laws could not be passed. When he suffered relapses, his administration was effectively suspended, arousing the power-hungry tendencies of his son, the Prince of Wales, who though not himself insane, was a byword for volatility and over-indulgence.

Perhaps we have seen too much in our lifetimes to feel much hope. If so, that is where we differ from the Romantics, whose capacity for belief defines them. They were optimists for human nature. Some were activists, seeking to foment revolution where they could – Shelley during his stay in Ireland, or Byron, willing to die in the cause of Greek independence; others, though not activists, sided with revolution – Helen Maria Williams, who exiled herself to France in 1791; Wordsworth, who lived in France, 1791–2; Paine, who became a member of the French National Assembly in 1791; or Charlotte Smith, who visited Paris to witness the Revolution for herself. Even those who seem to us conservative, such as Hannah More, were prepared to fight the slave trade – a cause that aligned her with such radical temperaments as Barbauld, Coleridge and Wordsworth.

They were products of their time in believing in a more just world than that in which they lived. When Williams wrote that philosophy would 'renovate the gladdened earth' (see p. 301), she was thinking first and foremost of the writings of Voltaire and Rousseau, but also of Paine and Price. And if philosophy could generate revolution, so too could poetry. Such a faith cannot have been easy to maintain, especially after the Terror gave rise to the Revolutionary Wars, when it became virtually impossible to hold fast to radical principles without being seen as a traitor. There is little doubt that political (as much as moral) intolerance made Williams, Shelley and Byron reluctant to return home.

For those who remained, the government had ways of making life unpleasant: Thelwall was harassed on his lecture-tours by spies and hecklers. When he proposed settling in Somerset in August 1797, Coleridge told him they would be accused of creating 'plot and damned conspiracy – a school for the propagation of demagogy and atheism'.[16] Even after the Napoleonic Wars, the government did not relax its grip: the Ely and Littleport bread-riots of 1816 resulted in the execution of five ringleaders; 600 starving weavers set out from Manchester in March 1817 to petition for help for the ailing cotton trade, but they were rounded up by government forces as they crossed from Staffordshire into Derbyshire; and in August 1819, in the worst example, armed militiamen cut down hundreds of men, women and children demonstrating peacefully at St Peter's Fields, Manchester – a measure that won the public endorsement of the Prince Regent.

In spite of this, the writers in this book refused to succumb to despair, preferring to hope and, in some cases, to fight. It is not just their capacity for optimism that distinguishes them, but the kind of belief to which they clung. Where earlier generations looked to an afterlife, the Romantics tended to reject formalized religion. This was partly because the Church of England then wielded a degree of political power it no longer possesses, and was complicit in the injustice the writers opposed. Typical of this is the reference by Blake's chimney-sweeper to 'God and his Priest and King / Who make up a heaven of our misery'.[17] Instead, they thought they could create, through their writing, a promised land in which property was of no consequence and people would live in harmony. It lay neither in the distant future nor in the abstract; to them it was attainable, imminently, in the here and now. Wordsworth's philosophical epic, *The Recluse*, was supposed to describe how it would be made real.[18] Although he sometimes discussed it in biblical terms, he tends at this stage of his career (1797–9) to betray little commitment to Christian theism; instead, he writes of

> A presence that disturbs me with the joy
> Of elevated thoughts, a sense sublime
> Of something far more deeply interfused,
> Whose dwelling is the light of setting suns,
> And the round ocean, and the living air,
> And the blue sky, and in the mind of man –
> A motion and a spirit that impels
> All thinking things, all objects of all thought,
> And rolls through all things.
>
> (*Tintern Abbey* 95–103)

The feeling he has while standing on the banks of the Wye is in itself divine, created by a 'presence' that will redeem humanity from the post-lapsarian 'weariness' encountered earlier in the poem. Wordsworth is famous for having said that he had no need of a redeemer;[19] when he wrote *Tintern Abbey*, he had little need of God, at least in the generally accepted sense.[20] For him, mankind is capable of redemption through an act of self-realization – something that explains the appeal of *Tintern Abbey* to Shelley and Keats.

Notes

16 Griggs i 344.

17 'The Chimney Sweeper' (*Experience*) 11–12.

18 For more on *The Recluse*, see pp. 413–15.

19 'I recollect Wordsworth saying to me: "I have no need of a Redeemer"; but I believe his religion to be like [that] of the German metaphysicians, a sentimental and metaphysical mysticism in which the language of Christianity is used, which is a sort of analogy to this poetical and philosophical religion' (*Henry Crabb Robinson on Books and their Writers* ed. Edith J. Morley (3 vols, London, 1938), i 158).

20 In May 1796 Coleridge told Thelwall that Wordsworth 'is a republican, and at least a semi-atheist' (Griggs i 216).

What excited them was its faith – not in formalized religion, but in the redemptive potential of the mind. It can be traced to *The Eolian Harp* (1795), in which Coleridge had asked himself whether all living things might be

> organic harps diversely framed,
> That tremble into thought, as o'er them sweeps,
> Plastic and vast, one intellectual breeze,
> At once the soul of each, and God of all?
> (*ll.* 37–40)

The answer Coleridge receives from his wife-to-be is 'no', reflecting his awareness of the radical nature of what he asks. Although as a Unitarian he could not accept many aspects of the Anglican faith, Coleridge was emphatically Christian in his poetry, more so than Wordsworth. What they shared was a profound belief in the power of the mind to change the world. The conceit that human beings were instruments waiting to be struck by the divine afflatus of the universe is precisely such a notion, valuable for affirming our susceptibility *en masse* to God's will. This was what revolution meant to Coleridge: he reconceived it as a religious event on a universal scale, by which God's 'intellectual' (spiritual) influence would redeem the fallen world.

Recent critics have accused Wordsworth of suppressing his knowledge of the hardships of working people in his poetry, particularly *Tintern Abbey.*[21] This is not the occasion for a refutation of that view, but it is worth saying that Wordsworth thought his work engaged fully with life as it was lived; indeed, it was on those grounds that he was attacked by reviewers.[22] He considered that his millenarian aspirations had to be grounded in an awareness of suffering – the 'still, sad music of humanity' (l. 92). When Keats raved about Wordsworth to John Hamilton Reynolds in May 1818, it was to commend his ability to sharpen 'one's vision into the heart and nature of man, of convincing one's nerves that the world is full of misery and heartbreak, pain, sickness, and oppression'.[23] In that respect, Wordsworth was a crucial influence on how Keats conceived *Hyperion: A Fragment* – a poem about the aspirations that spring out of dispossession (see p. 1337).

Though in some ways more abstract than Wordsworth, Shelley was no less conscious of the conditions in which people laboured. Perhaps more than any other writer of his class (he was heir to baronet), he wanted to speak to the disenfranchised poor of a near future similar to that described by Wordsworth:

> Man, oh not men! a chain of linked thought,
> Of love and might to be divided not . . .
>   Man, one harmonious soul of many a soul,
>   Whose nature is its own divine control,
> Where all things flow to all, as rivers to the sea . . .
> (*Prometheus Unbound* IV 394–5, 400–2)

In Shelley's promised land, humanity is a 'harmonious soul' redeemed from hatred and hostility by the Christ-like quality of pity and forgiveness. The difference is that where

Notes

[21] For a review of the various arguments see Nicholas Roe, *The Politics of Nature: William Wordsworth and Some Contemporaries* (Basingstoke, 2002), chapter 7, and Thomas McFarland, *William Wordsworth: Intensity and Achievement* (Oxford, 1992), chapter 1.

[22] See, for instance, Jeffrey's comments on the Pedlar in his review of *The Excursion*, p. 719–20.

[23] See p. 1353.

Coleridge needed a Unitarian God, and Wordsworth demanded only an unspecific 'presence', Shelley reduces the deity to the 'divine control' deep within the self. God has been so circumscribed he almost doesn't exist. Such scepticism is typical. At the end of *Mont Blanc*, he admits that one possibility inspired by the mountain, besides the 'still and solemn Power' that inheres within it, is that 'Silence and solitude were vacancy.' He does not flinch at the thought of spiritual absence.

Byron shared the radical aspirations expressed by Wordsworth and Coleridge in their youth, but flatly rejected their philosophizing. For him, the word 'metaphysical' was an insult. He was more practical, something underlined by his readiness to die in the Greek War of Independence (for which he remains a national hero in Greece, with streets and squares named after him). But even he is capable of expressing, in *Childe Harold's Pilgrimage* Canto III, something of Wordsworth's pantheist conviction in the redemptive power of nature:

> I live not in myself, but I become
> Portion of that around me; and to me
> High mountains are a feeling, but the hum
> Of human cities torture. . . .
> (ll. 680–3)

If these lines sound unpersuasive, Byron remained true to himself in that he knew that the Wordsworthian response to nature affirmed something he took seriously – inner potential. Frustration with the restrictions of our earthly state permeates his poetry, compelling him to aspire to a level of existence beyond the merely human. Hence his ambiguous praise for that arch-overreacher Napoleon,[24] the divinations of Manfred, who can command the spirits, and his enduring admiration for Prometheus, in some sense the archetype of the Byronic hero. As Wordsworth put it, 'We feel that we are greater than we know.'[25]

Blake is sometimes considered the exception to virtually anything one might want to say about other writers of the time – and so, in a sense, he is. He was born in 1757 – and thus is as much an eighteenth-century writer as a Romantic one. And if, like his contemporaries, he read Wordsworth, it was late in life, and without much pleasure.[26] However, it was he who, in 1789, on the brink of tumult in France, described the 'son of fire':

> Spurning the clouds written with curses, stamps the stony law to dust, loosing the eternal horses from the dens of night, crying, 'Empire is no more! And now the lion and wolf shall cease.' (p. 217)

Revolution as apocalypse: to Blake, events in France were the harbingers not merely of political liberation, but of the spiritual millennium predicted in the Bible. And in this he was no less Romantic than the writers who were to follow. For him, as for them, the fallen world was a conundrum the resolution of which led back to paradise. He would spend much of his creative life explaining to the world, in his own distinctive manner, how paradise had been lost, and how it might be reclaimed. And never without grief at the 'Marks of weakness' and 'marks of woe'[27] on the faces of those around him.

Notes

[24] See pp. 862–4.

[25] 'Afterthought' to *The River Duddon* 14.

[26] A particularly memorable marginal note in Blake's copy of Wordsworth's *Poems* (1815) reads: 'I see in Wordsworth the natural man rising up against the spiritual man continually – and then he is no poet but a heathen philosopher at enmity against all true poetry or inspiration' (see *The Complete Poetry and Prose of William Blake* ed. David V. Erdman, commentary by Harold Bloom (2nd edn, New York, 1982), p. 665).

[27] *London* 4.

It would be remarkable were the poetry of female Romantics not to reflect their natural pragmatism – an inevitable by-product of the fact that they were often (as in the cases of Charlotte Smith and Felicia Hemans) single mothers providing for their children. And yet their work is permeated by the same aspirations to be found in their male contemporaries. After all, Smith's natural milieu is her beloved Sussex Downs, where she draws strength from the flora and fauna that surround her. In *Beachy Head* she does so in a manner that transcends a purely taxonomic urge, ranging across millennia to speculate on the 'strange ferment' that produced the hills (l. 387), after attempting to recreate the more recent past.

> Haunts of my youth!
> Scenes of fond daydreams, I behold ye yet,
> Where 'twas so pleasant by thy northern slopes
> To climb the winding sheep-path . . .
>
> (*Beachy Head* 297–300)

These lines exemplify the larger project of Smith's poetry – to reclaim childhood happiness as a means of understanding the troubled context of the present. Her distant relative Wordsworth was attempting something similar in *The Prelude*, written at around the same time.

None of this is to underestimate the sexual politics of female poetry. Hemans's *Records of Woman* sequence is a serious attempt to explore the experience of women within a male-dominated society. Some critics have suggested that her concerns are primarily 'domestic', but that hardly establishes the terms in which we might speak of a 'female romanticism' – which could be as much the invention of commentators as 'Romanticism' itself. It is true that *Records of Woman* is concerned with the plight of those lumbered with feckless, unreliable, weak or ineffectual men: Seymour saves himself, but fails to save Arabella Stuart; Werner Stauffacher is saved only by 'the entreaties of his wife, a woman who seems to have been of an heroic spirit'; Properzia Rossi lavishes her love and art on a man unworthy of her; the Indian Woman is deserted by her husband for another woman, and so forth. To that extent the sequence presents the female perspective, but it would be a mistake to describe Hemans's as a purely feminist agenda, at least in the sense we understand the term.

Critics tend to downplay the value she places on the relationship between the sexes. *Gertrude, or Fidelity till Death* describes how Gertrude nurses her husband in his final tormented hours with what Hemans calls 'the most heroic devotedness', to become the exemplar for a mode of behaviour that, despite her own experience, Hemans valued. Even Juana, notwithstanding the neglect of her husband, is praised for wifely devotion after his death: 'Surely that humble, patient love *must* win back love at last!'[28] These women are models of heroic conduct. It is true that Hemans has her own distinctive preoccupation: the limits of human (often female) endeavour. But that cannot of itself be held to define such an all-embracing concept as 'female romanticism', even if it does reflect Hemans's own perspective.

Gender is one factor among many taken into account as we look at a writer's work. Were we to argue that it determines subject-matter, genre and poetic form, it would be necessary

Notes

[28] *Juana* 32.

also to prove that certain subjects, genres and forms were selected only, or at least predominantly, by women. But that is not the case. After all, Southey chose to write about Joan of Arc and her sufferings (one of the subjects of *Records of Woman*), as did other male writers before him, while More, Yearsley, Barbauld and Williams composed anti-slavery poems alongside those of Cowper, Blake, Southey and Coleridge.[29] The obvious conclusion is that Hemans and her contemporaries saw themselves as participating in a literary forum with male writers against whom they sought to prove themselves. And when it came to visionary experience, Hemans could describe it with as much conviction as Blake:

And then a glorious mountain-chain uprose,
  Height above spiry height!
A soaring multitude of woods and snows
  All steeped in golden light!
(*Despondency and Aspiration* 75–8)

RECORDS OF WOMAN:

WITH OTHER POEMS.

BY

FELICIA HEMANS.

——Mightier far
Than strength of nerve or sinew, or the sway
Of magic potent over sun and star,
Is love, though oft to agony distrest,
And though his favourite seat be feeble woman's breast.
WORDSWORTH.

Das ist das Loos des Schönen auf der Erde!
SCHILLER

THE SECOND EDITION

WILLIAM BLACKWOOD, EDINBURGH:
AND T. CADELL, LONDON.
MDCCCXXVIII.

Figure 3 The title-page of Felicia Hemans's *Records of Woman,* the complete sequence of which appears on pp. 1249–1308. The two epigraphs are from Wordsworth's 'Laodamia' and Schiller's *Wallenstein*: 'Das ist das Los des Schönen auf der Erde!' ('That is the lot of the beautiful on earth!')

It has been argued that 'male' romanticism is characterized by a preoccupation with the sublime, but female writers could be just as persuasive in their understanding of it – as in Hemans's 'Second Sight' and 'The Spirit's Mysteries', Barbauld's 'A Summer Evening's Meditation', or 'Mrs Robinson to the Poet Coleridge', all of which are included here. Of course women brought to their art insights deriving from female experience, but it is our duty as readers to appreciate those insights in their historical context, rather than exploit them as vehicles for political agendas of our own.

The central aim of the third edition of *Romanticism: An Anthology* is to provide readers with a comprehensive guide to one of the richest periods in literary history, from its eighteenth-century beginnings to the point at which younger writers transformed it into something distinct. I hope that it contains almost everything required for a wide-ranging course on Romantic poetry.

Texts are freshly edited for this volume from both manuscript and early printed sources. Typically, readers are not restricted to highlights but have access to complete works, with all their fluctuations of tone, mood and rhythm. The work of essayists such as Hazlitt and Lamb is presented in full, as far as possible. Limitations of space compel

Notes

[29] Besides the various examples in this book, see *The Poetry of Slavery: An Anglo-American Anthology 1764–1865* ed. Marcus Wood (Oxford, 2003).

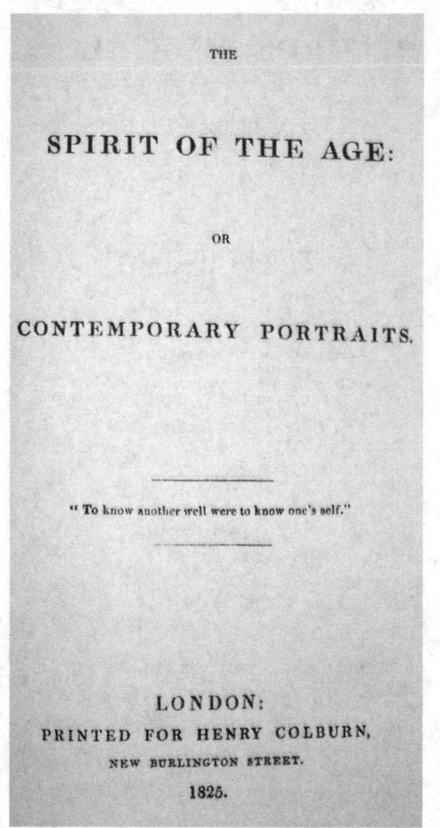
THE

SPIRIT OF THE AGE:

OR

CONTEMPORARY PORTRAITS.

"To know another well were to know one's self."

LONDON:
PRINTED FOR HENRY COLBURN,
NEW BURLINGTON STREET.
1825.

Figure 4 The title-page of Hazlitt's *The Spirit of the Age*, one of the first (and best) books about Romanticism, published as early as 1825. Its epigraph, 'To know another well were to know one's self', is from *Hamlet* V ii 139–40.

me to extract from *Confessions of an English Opium-Eater* and *Suspiria de Profundis*, although 'On the Knocking at the Gate in *Macbeth*' is presented whole. No attempt can be made in a book of this size to encompass the rich and extensive corpus of Romantic novel-writing; they are best digested whole, and there is in any case no way of extracting from the complete works of Jane Austen within an anthology that encapsulates other genres. As with earlier editions, I have therefore excluded fiction.

For this edition, headnotes have been completely rewritten so as to incorporate recent debate and provide introductions to selected texts. Lists of 'Further Reading', introduced in the second edition, have been updated to reflect current scholarship. They aim to provide a representative selection of critical works, but make no claim to be definitive or exhaustive. Footnotes are revised from those in the second edition, providing new points of information and interpretive comment.

I hope that readers will find this book helpful in their study of one of the richest periods in literature.

Further reading

M. H. Abrams, *The Mirror and the Lamp: Romantic Theory and the Critical Tradition* (New York, 1953).
M. H. Abrams *Natural Supernaturalism: Tradition and Revolution in Romantic Literature* (New York, 1971).
M. H. Abrams, *The Correspondent Breeze: Essays on English Romanticism* (New York, 1984).
Walter Jackson Bate, *From Classic to Romantic: Premises of Taste in Eighteenth-Century England* (New York, 1961).
Aidan Day, *Romanticism* (London, 1996).
English Romantic Poets ed. M. H. Abrams (Oxford, 1975).
Seamus Perry, 'Romanticism: The Brief History of a Concept', in *A Companion to Romanticism* ed. Duncan Wu (Oxford, 1998).

Editorial Principles

This edition adopts the policy advocated by Coleridge on New Year's Day 1834 widely accepted as the basis for contemporary scholarly editions: 'After all you can say, I think the chronological order is the best for arranging a poet's works. All your divisions are in particular instances inadequate, and they destroy the interest which arises from watching the progress, maturity, and even the decay of genius.'[1] Authors are introduced successively by their dates of birth; works are placed in order of composition where known and, when not known, by date of publication.

The edition is designed for the use of students and general readers, and textual procedures are geared accordingly. Except for works in dialect or in which archaic effects were deliberately sought, punctuation and orthography are normalized, pervasive initial capitals and italics removed, and contractions expanded except where they are of metrical significance (for instance, Keats's 'charact'ry' is demanded by the exigencies of metre, but 'thro'' is expanded to 'through'). Although the accidental features of late eighteenth- and early nineteenth-century printed texts have their own intrinsic interest, and are of importance in considering the evolution of any given work, it should be noted that most poets were content to leave such matters to the printers or their collaborators. In many cases, therefore, accidental features of early printed texts cannot be assumed to be disposed according to the author's wishes. Conversely, I have taken the view that, on those occasions when capitalization is demonstrably authorial, and consistently applied, it should be allowed to stand – as in the case of Shelley's *Adonais* and *The Mask of Anarchy.* The punctuation applied by writers to their own works is another matter, as styles vary from one author to another, are sometimes eccentric, and can often mislead the modern reader. I have treated authorial punctuation as a good (though not infallible) guide as to emphasis, meaning and sentence structure, but have not followed it unquestioningly.

For this third edition I have checked and double-checked many editorial decisions that I once took for granted, making occasional adjustments – most notably in the case of William Blake. The strangeness and power of his work are derived to some extent from

Notes

[1] *CC Table Talk* i 453

his peculiar systems of capitalization and punctuation. In seeking to present his texts to a student readership I have sought to preserve some of that power, while emending his pointing so as to guide the reader through the text. I hope that in returning to the copy-texts, and reinstating many of their incidental features, I have reached some kind of medium.

All texts have been edited for this anthology. I have followed procedures designed to produce a clear reading text. In editing from manuscript, I have aimed to present each draft as it stood on completion. Deletions are accepted only when alternative readings are provided; where they are not, the original is retained. Alternative readings are accepted only when the original has been deleted; where they are not, the original is retained. Where the original reading is deleted but legible, and the alternative fragmentary, illegible or inchoate, the original has been retained. Where, in the rush of composition, words are omitted, they have been supplied from adjacent drafts or manuscripts. As a rule, I have silently corrected scribal errors. Ampersands are expanded to 'and' throughout.

There is, perhaps inevitably, an exception to this: John Clare, for whose texts I am indebted to the editorial labours of Eric Robinson. It should be noted that Robinson's policy of transcribing 'exactly what Clare wrote' with minimal intervention, leaving his spelling and punctuation intact, is at present the subject of debate.

Dates of composition, where they can be verified, are indicated alongside titles with details of publication. Copy-text details are provided alongside titles, whether early printed sources (usually presented in small capitals over the title of the work), or manuscript. Headnotes are provided for each author, including biographical materials, critical comments on the selection and useful secondary reading. Annotations gloss archaisms, difficult constructions, allusions, echoes, other verbal borrowings, and provide points of information where necessary. On occasion they direct the reader to secondary materials with a particular bearing on the work in question.

Acknowledgements

First Edition (1994)

Work on the this volume began with consultation of numerous colleagues, who kindly offered advice on the anthology they wished to use. For that and help of various kinds it is a pleasure to thank Jonathan Bate, Shahin Bekhradnia, J. Drummond Bone, Geoffrey Brackett, Richard W. Clancey, David Fairer, Richard Gravil, Jack Haeger, Keith Hanley, Anthony Harding, Brooke Hopkins, M. C. Howatson, Kenneth Johnston, Grevel Lindop, Jerome J. McGann, Philip Martin, Michael O'Neill, Roy Park, Janice Patten, Tom Paulin, Cecilia Powell, Roger Robinson, Nicholas Roe, the late William Ruddick, Charles Rzepka, William S. Smith, Jane Stabler, David Stewart, Tim Trengove-Jones, J. R. Watson, Mary Wedd, Pamela Woof and Jonathan Wordsworth. I wish also to thank the advisers consulted by Blackwell for comments and advice.

This anthology is more dependent than most on original research for its texts, and in the course of editing I have incurred debts of many kinds to various librarians and archivists whom it is a pleasure to thank here: B. C. Barker-Benfield and the staff of the Upper Reading Room, Bodleian Library, Oxford; Elaine Scoble of the Wolfson Library, St Catherine's College, Oxford; the staff of the English Faculty Library, Oxford; Deborah Hedgecock of the Guildhall Library, London; and Jeff Cowton of the Wordsworth Library, Grasmere. It was my good fortune to have been a Fellow of St Catherine's College, Oxford, during work on this book, and among friends and colleagues there I acknowledge the generous help of Richard Parish, J. Ch. Simopoulos and J. B. McLaughlin. Nicola Trott was my collaborator at an early stage of work, and played a crucial part in formulating its aims and procedures, and in seeking advice from colleagues. My work has been expedited by the rapid and accurate typing of Pat Wallace; James Price of Woodstock Books kindly provided me with early printed texts of a number of works included; and Andrew McNeillie, my editor, offered enthusiastic help and advice throughout. For a retreat in the Cotswolds where much of the editing was completed during the summer of 1993, and for assistance of many kinds I thank Caroline Cochrane.

This book was produced during tenure of a British Academy post-doctoral Fellowship; I am deeply grateful to the Academy for its kind support.

Second Edition (1998)

Since this anthology was first published, I have received suggestions for revision from many people; I thank them all. I owe a particular debt to those students with whom I have used it as a course text, and who have helped determine the various ways in which revision might be implemented.

For expert advice and information I thank Douglas Gifford, Bonnie Woodbery, Nicholas Roe, Jane Stabler, Edwin Moïse, Nelson Hilton, Suzanne Gilbert, Bob Cummings, Richard W. Clancey, David Pirie, Roger Robinson, R. E. Cavaliero, Zachary Leader, David Fairer, David Birkett, Peter Cochran, Richard Cronin, Charles Branchini, Susan Castillo, E. A. Moignard, Michael O'Neill, Jonathan Wordsworth and Constance Parrish.

In researching many of the new texts for this anthology, I am grateful once again to Jeff Cowton of the Wordsworth Library, Grasmere, and the staff of the Upper Reading Room, Bodleian Library, Oxford, and the British Library, London. I am particularly indebted to my proof-reader, Henry Maas, and Alison Truefitt, my copy-editor, for the care they have taken over a challenging typescript. Once again, Andrew McNeillie has proved a patient and supportive editor, and Caroline Cochrane has provided much encouragement along the way. I thank them both.

Third Edition (2004)

I thank all those who have suggested ways in which *Romanticism: An Anthology* might be revised. The NASSR-List continues to be an invaluable means of communicating with fellow Romanticists, and I am grateful to its subscribers for sending me information on their respective courses, in particular Kevin Binfield, Dan White, Brad Sullivan, Sara Guyer, SueAnn Schatz, Richard Matlak, Charles Snodgrass, Mary Waters, David Latane, Ann R. Hawkins and Patricia Matthew. I wish also to thank the many university professors who responded to the survey conducted by Blackwell Publishers into how this book might be revised. For specific help I thank Jane Stabler, Nicholas Roe, Susan J. Wolfson, Leslie Brisman, Nanora L. Sweet, Lucy Newlyn, Simon Kövesi, Jacqueline M. Labbe, Judith Pascoe, Ronald Tetreault, Hans Werner Breunig, Essaka Joshua, Grant Scott, Monika Class and Kim Wheatley. It has not been possible to adopt all suggestions, but the wealth of information and advice provided by all parties has been the most important single influence on the shape of this new edition. Those using this book as a course text should feel free to address their comments directly to me: duncan.wu@stcatz.ox.ac.uk

At Blackwell Publishers I wish for the last time to thank Andrew McNeillie, who commissioned the first edition of this anthology over a decade ago, and who was responsible for commissioning this one. I am indebted to his successors, Al Bertrand and Emma Bennett, for the care they have taken in guiding this edition to the press, and to copy-editor Sandra Raphael and proof-reader Henry Maas, who have saved me from infelicities too numerous to mention.

The editor and publishers wish to thank the following for permission to quote material in copyright:

Curtis Brown on behalf of Eric Robinson for material from John Clare, *The Shepherd's Calendar* ed. Eric Robinson and Geoffrey Summerfield, Oxford University Press, 1964;

John Clare ed. Eric Robinson and David Powell, The Oxford Authors, Oxford University Press, 1984, copyright © 1964 and 1984 Eric Robinson; Harvard University Press for material from John Keats, *The Letters of John Keats* ed. Hyder Edward Rollins, vols 1–2 copyright © 1958 by the President and Fellows of Harvard College; the Houghton Library, Harvard University, for material from texts of John Keats MS transcripts; and manuscript material by Mary Shelley, MS Eng 822, 2r–2v, and Percy Bysshe Shelley, MS Eng 258.3, 2r–3r; the London Borough of Camden for the Collections at Keats House, Hampstead, for John Keats holograph texts, 'On Sitting Down to Read *King Lear* Once Again' and 'Bright Star, Would I Were Steadfast as Thou Art'; John Murray Publishers, Ltd, for material from Lord Byron's letters from *Byron's Letters and Journals* ed. Leslie A. Marchand; Oxford University Press for material from William Blake, *The Letters of William Blake* ed. Geoffrey Keynes, 3rd edn, Clarendon Press, 1980; Robert Burns, *The Letters of Robert Burns* ed. J. De Lancey Ferguson, 2nd edn, ed. G. Ross Roy, vols 1–2, Clarendon Press, 1985; Dorothy Wordsworth, *The Grasmere Journals* ed. Pamela Woof, Clarendon Press, 1991; Samuel Taylor Coleridge, *The Letters of Samuel Taylor Coleridge* ed. Earl Leslie Griggs, vols 1–6, Clarendon Press, 1956–71; George Gordon Byron, 6th Baron Byron, *The Complete Poetical Works of Lord Byron* ed. Jerome J. McGann and Barry Weller, vols 1–7, Clarendon Press, 1980–93; and Percy Bysshe Shelley, *The Letters of Percy Bysshe Shelley* ed. Frederick L. Jones, vols 1–2, Clarendon Press, 1964; Routledge for material from Samuel Taylor Coleridge, *Table Talk* ed. Carl Woodring, vols 1–2, 1990; the Bodleian Library, Oxford, for material from MS texts of John Clare, George Dyer, Mary Shelley and Percy Bysshe Shelley; the Wordsworth Trust, Grasmere, for material from MS texts of Samuel Taylor Coleridge, Dorothy Wordsworth and William Wordsworth; the British Library, for material from MS texts of Samuel Taylor Coleridge and John Thelwall; Lord Abinger, for material from MS texts of Mary Shelley.

Every effort has been made to trace copyright holders; if any have been inadvertently overlooked the publishers will be pleased to make the necessary arrangement at the first opportunity.

A Romantic Timeline 1770–1851

Current affairs	Date		Science and the Arts
Boston massacre	1770	5 March	
		7 April	Wordsworth born, Cockermouth, Cumbria
		20th May	Hölderlin born
		24 August	Chatterton poisons himself in London, aged 17 Hegel born, Stuttgart
		16 December	Beethoven born, Bonn
	1771	25 December	Dorothy Wordsworth born, Cockermouth, Cumbria
Emmanuel Swedenborg dies	1772	29 March	
William Murray, Lord Mansfield, rules that there is no legal basis for slavery in England, giving a stimulus to the movement to abolish the slave trade in the colonies		14 May	
Lord Mansfield delivers judgement in the case of James Somersett, a runaway slave, ruling that no one has the right 'to take a slave by force to be sold abroad' – often regarded as the beginning of the end of slavery in England		22 June	
		4 August	Blake apprenticed to the antiquarian engraver James Basire
		9 October	Mary Tighe born, Dublin
		21 October	Coleridge born, Ottery St Mary, Devon
		December	Anna Laetitia Aikin publishes her *Poems* (dated 1773 on title-page), including 'A Summer Evening's Meditation' (p. 35)
	1773	May	Hannah More publishes *The Search after Happiness*
		September	Anna Laetitia Aikin and John Aikin publish *Miscellaneous Pieces in Prose*
Boston Tea Party		16 December	
	1774	4 April	Goldsmith dies, London
		12 August	Southey born, Bristol
	1775	10 February	Lamb born, London
		23 April	Turner born, London
		16 December	Jane Austen born, Steventon, Hampshire
	1776	17 February	Gibbon publishes first volume of *Decline and Fall of the Roman Empire*
		10 June	Garrick's last appearance on stage as Don Felix in Centlivre's *The Wonder!*
		11 June	Constable born, Suffolk
American Declaration of Independence		4 July	

Current affairs	Date		Science and the Arts
		25 August	David Hume dies
		10 December	Mary Robinson makes her debut as Juliet at Drury Lane Theatre
	1777	8 May	Sheridan's *School for Scandal* opens at Drury Lane Theatre
		10 December	Hannah More's *Percy* opens at Covent Garden theatre
		25 December	Sydney Owenson, Lady Morgan, born on the Dublin packet-boat in the Irish Sea
	1778	29 January	Fanny Burney publishes *Evelina*
		8 March	Wordsworth's mother dies
		10 April	Hazlitt born, Maidstone, Kent
		29 May	Sheridan's *The Critic* opens at Drury Lane
		30 May	Voltaire dies, Paris
		2 July	Rousseau dies, Paris
	1779	20 January	Garrick dies, London
Captain Cook dies, Hawaii		14 February	
		29 April	Goethe's *The Sorrows of Werther* first published in London
		8 October	Blake admitted to study at the Royal Academy schools
		3 December	Mary Robinson's performance as Perdita is attended by the Prince of Wales, whose mistress she becomes shortly after
Gordon Riots in London	1780	2–8 June	
		6 June	Blake involved in the attack on Newgate Prison
		29 August	Ingres born
Cornwallis surrenders to Washington at Yorktown	1781	19 October	Fuseli paints *The Nightmare*
	1782	January	Hannah More publishes *Sacred Dramas* (including 'Sensibility')
		18 August	Blake marries Catherine Boucher (b. 1762)
		September	Coleridge goes to school at Christ's Hospital in London, where he meets Charles Lamb
	1783	5 June	Montgolfier brothers give first public demonstration of their hot-air balloon
Treaty of Paris, confirming American Independence		3 September	
Pitt becomes Prime Minister at the age of 24 (until 1801)		19 December	
		30 December	Wordsworth's father dies

Current affairs	Date	Science and the Arts
	1784 June	Charlotte Smith publishes first edition of *Elegiac Sonnets* (p. 83)
	19 October	Leigh Hunt born, Southgate
	13 December	Dr Johnson dies, London, aged 75
	1785 June	Ann Yearsley publishes *Poems, on Several Occasions*
	July	Cowper publishes *The Task* (p. 18)
	15 August	De Quincey born, Manchester
	18 October	Thomas Love Peacock born, Weymouth, Dorset
	1786 25 January	Benjamin Robert Haydon born, Plymouth
	1 May	Mozart's *Marriage of Figaro* first performed in Prague
	7 June	Beckford's *Vathek* published, unauthorized
	25 June	Goya appointed painter to the King of Spain
	1787 1 April	Wordsworth's first published poem, a sonnet addressed to Helen Maria Williams, appears in the *European Magazine* (for March)
Warren Hastings impeached by Burke in House of Commons for maladministration and corruption in Bengal	May	
Committee for the Abolition of the Slave-Trade, composed mainly of Quakers, formed in London	22 May	
American Constitution drafted and signed	17 September	
	1788 22 January	Byron born, London
	8 February	Hannah More publishes *Slavery: A Poem* (p. 66)
	22 February	Schopenhauer born, Danzig
Charles Wesley dies	28 March	
Sir William Dolben proposes a Bill to the House of Commons limiting the number of slaves who could be transported from Africa to British colonies in the West Indies (it is passed on 26 May, despite much opposition)	21 May	
	2 August	Gainsborough dies, London
George III suffers mental collapse	November	Ann Yearsley publishes *Poem on the Inhumanity of the Slave-Trade* (p. 160)
Three Estates assemble at Versailles	**1789** 4 May	
The Third estate names itself the National Assembly	17 June	
Storming of the Bastille	14 July	
March on Versaille; French royal family escorted to Paris	6 October	

Current affairs	Date		Science and the Arts
Price addresses the London Revolution Society		4 November	Blake completes *Songs of Innocence* (p. 179) and begins *The Book of Thel* (1789–90) (p. 176)
President Washington delivers the first 'State of the Union' address	1790	8 January	
Fletcher Christian and fellow mutineers settle on the Pitcairn Islands		15 January	
		26 January	Mozart's *Cosi fan tutte* first performed in Vienna
Benjamin Franklin dies, Philadelphia, aged 84		17 April	
		June	Blake publishes the *Marriage of Heaven and Hell* (p. 206)
		13 July	Wordsworth arrives in France on his first trip to the Continent
Louis XVI swears oath of loyalty to the new constitution		14 July	
Suspension of habeas corpus		October	
Slaves revolt in Haiti		23 October	
General election: Pitt returned with increased majority		November	Helen Maria Williams publishes *Letters written in France in summer of 1790* (p. 296)
		1 November	Burke publishes *Reflections on the Revolution in France* (p. 10)
		29 November	Wollstonecraft publishes *A Vindication of the Rights of Men,* in response to Burke
Congress moves from New York City to Philadelphia		6 December	Kant publishes *The Critique of Pure Reason*
	1791	1 January	Haydn arrives in England
		22 February	Paine publishes *The Rights of Man* Part 1 (p. 24)
The French royal family is prevented from leaving Paris by the National Guard		18 April	
French royal family flees, only to be captured at Varennes the following day		20 June	
Anti-Dissenter riots in Birmingham during which Joseph Priestley's house burned down by Church-and-King mob		14 July	
Louis XVI suspended from office until he agrees to ratify the constitution (which he does on 13 September)		16 July	
Slave riots in San Domingo		August	
		22 September	Michael Faraday born, London (inventor of the dynamo and the electric motor)
		30 September	Mozart's *The Magic Flute* first performed in Vienna
French Legislative Assembly established		1 October	
United Irishmen founded by Wolfe Tone in Belfast to fight for Irish nationalism		14 October	

Current affairs	Date		Science and the Arts
	1791	November	Wordsworth visits Charlotte Smith in Brighton
		5 December	Mozart dies, aged 35, in Vienna
		17 December	Ann Radcliffe publishes *The Romance of the Forest*
		December	Wordsworth's second visit to France (for a year)
			Burns publishes 'Tam O'Shanter' (p. 270)
	1792	January	Mary Wollstonecraft publishes *A Vindication of the Rights of Woman*
		16 February	Paine publishes *The Rights of Man* Part II
		18 February	Thomas Holcroft's *The Road to Ruin* successfully performed at Covent Garden theatre
		23 February	Joshua Reynolds dies, London
France declares war on Austria		20 April	
Paine charged with sedition		21 May	Paine's *Rights of Man* banned
		4 August	Shelley born, Field Place, Sussex
Tuileries stormed by Paris mob; French royal family placed in detention three days later		10 August	
September Massacres of royalist and other prisoners in Paris		3–7 September	
Robespierre elected to the National Assembly		5 September	
Paine flees to France		13 September	
France proclaims itself a Republic		22 September	
		December	Mary Wollstonecraft in Paris
Louis XVI tried for treason by the National Assembly		11 December	
		15 December	Anne-Caroline Wordsworth, Wordsworth's natural daughter, born
Paine sentenced to death by British courts for seditious libel (*Rights of Man* Part II)		18 December	
		30 December	Hannah More publishes *Village Politics* (counterrevolutionary propaganda)
Louis XVI sentenced to death	1793	19 January	
Louis XVI executed		21 January	
France declares war on Britain and Holland		1 February	
		14 February	Godwin publishes *Political Justice* (see p. 151)
Suspension of habeus corpus		March	Publication of William Frend's *Peace and Union Recommended*
Committee of Public Safety formed, led by Danton, Robespierre, Saint-Just and Couthon		6 April	

Current affairs	Date	Science and the Arts
	June	Smith publishes *The Emigrants* (p. 100)
Marat murdered in his bath by Charlotte Corday, heralding the Terror	13 July	John Clare born Helpstone, Northamptonshire
	25 September	Felicia Dorothea Browne born, Liverpool
France institutes a new calendar	7 April	
	10 October	Blake advertises *Songs of Experience* (p. 191)
Marie Antoinette executed	16 October	
	2 December	Coleridge enlists in the King's Regiment, 15th Light Dragoons, as Silas Tomkyn Comberbache
Paine imprisoned in the Luxembourg jail	28 December	Blake begins to produce copies of *Visions of the Daughters of Albion* (p. 217)
	1794 April	Joseph Priestley emigrates to America
	10 May	Ann Radcliffe publishes *The Mysteries of Udolpho*
Arrest of Thomas Hardy and other radicals including John Thelwall	12 May	
Pitt's Bill to suspend habeas corpus receives royal assent	23 May	
	26 May	Godwin publishes *Caleb Williams*
	17 June	Coleridge's first meeting with Southey, Balliol College, Oxford
Robespierre executed; end of the Terror	28 July	
	20 October	Godwin publishes 'Cursory Strictures' in the *Morning Chronicle*, leading to acquittal of some defendants in the treason trials
Treason trials begin in London with the trial of Thomas Hardy	28 October	
Paine released from Luxembourg jail, having excaped execution by an oversight	4 November	
Thomas Hardy found not guilty	5 November	
Thelwall found not guilty at the treason trials	5 December	
France invades Holland (winter 1794–5)	15 December	
Release of remaining defendants at treason trials		
France abolishes slavery in its territories, conferring citizenship on former slaves	**1795** 4 February	
	27 February	Wordsworth begins regular meetings with Godwin in London (until July)
	March	Hannah More launches the Cheap Repository tracts (2 million distributed by the end of the year)
Prince of Wales marries his cousin, Caroline-Amelia of Brunswick-Wolfenbüttel, at St James's Palace	8 April	
	19 May	James Boswell dies, London
	4 October	Coleridge marries Sara Fricker at St Mary Redcliffe, Bristol, followed by a six-week honeymoon in Clevedon

Current affairs	Date		Science and the Arts
King's coach stoned at opening of Parliament by crowd demanding bread and Pitt's resignation	1795	29 October	
		31 October	Keats born, London
Pitt and Grenville introduce Bills outlawing treasonable practices and unlawful assemblies (they become law on 18 December)		6 November	
		December	Southey publishes *Joan of Arc* (which includes passages by Coleridge)
			Helen Maria Williams publishes *Letters containing a Sketch of the Politics of France*
	1796	12 March	Matthew Lewis publishes *The Monk*
Napoleon commands Italian campaign, defeating Austrians in sequence of battles leading to the Peace of Leoben		April	
		16 April	Coleridge publishes his first volume of *Poems*
		May	Edward Jenner discovers vaccine against smallpox
		21 July	Burns dies
Washington's farewell address		18 September	
		19 September	Hartley Coleridge born
		22 September	Mary Lamb stabs her mother to death and badly injures her father
Catherine the Great, Empress of Russia, dies		17 November	
		December	Coleridge moves to Nether Stowey, Somerset
			Anna Seward publishes *Llangollen Vale with Other Poems*
			Anna Yearsley publishes *The Rural Lyre*
	1797	31 January	Schubert born, Vienna
John Adams elected second President in America; his Vice-President is Jefferson		4 March	
		15 April	Hölderlin begins to publish *Hyperion*
		7 July	Burke dies; Lamb arrives at Nether Stowey and goes walking with the Wordsworths, leaving Coleridge behind (see p. 612)
		16 July	Wordsworth and his sister move into Alfoxden House near Coleridge at Nether Stowey
		17 July	Thelwall arrives at Nether Stowey (where he remains until the end of the month)
		29 August	Joseph Wright of Derby dies
		30 August	Mary Godwin born
		10 September	Mary Wollstonecraft dies; funeral on 15 September

Current affairs	Date		Science and the Arts
		October	Southey publishes 'Hannah, A Plaintive Tale' in the *Monthly Magazine* (see p. 724)
		16 October	Coleridge sends a copy of the recently completed *Osorio* to Sheridan at Drury Lane theatre, but it is rejected
		28 October	Coleridge publishes second edition of his *Poems*
		20 November	Wordsworth's play *The Borderers* sent to Covent Garden theatre, but rejected as unperformable the following month
		10 December	Ann Radcliffe publishes *The Italian*
	1798	14 January	Coleridge preaches at the Unitarian chapel in Shrewsbury and is heard by Hazlitt, aged 17 (see p. 772)
		25 January	Wordsworth composes 'A Night-Piece', initiating a spate of composition including 'The Ruined Cottage', 'The Pedlar', and most of the 1798 *Lyrical Ballads*
		February	Coleridge writes *Frost at Midnight* and (until April) *Christabel*
		19 March	Wordsworth begins writing 'The Thorn' (see p. 375)
		14 April	Coleridge, 'France: An Ode' published in the *Morning Post* (see p. 630)
		20 May	Hazlitt visits Nether Stowey and is brought to Alfoxden where he reads the manuscript of *Lyrical Ballads* (p. 779)
Uprising of the United Irishmen, led by Lord Edward Fitzgerald and Wolfe Tone		23 May	
		7 June	Malthus publishes *Essay on Population*
		11 June	Hazlitt leaves Nether Stowey after a visit of three weeks
Napoleon invades Egypt		July	
		10 July	Wordsworth and his sister depart from Bristol on a walking-tour of the Wye Valley in the course of which he will compose 'Tintern Abbey' (returning to Bristol 13 July)
Battle of the Nile; Nelson victorious over the French		1 August	
		18 September	*Lyrical Ballads* published anonymously
		19 September	Coleridge and the Wordsworths arrive at Hamburg
		October	Wordsworth in Germany, begins *The Two-Part Prelude* (p. 448)
		1 November	Southey's review of *Lyrical Ballads* appears in the *Critical Review* (October issue) (p. 730)
			Haydn composes *The Creation*
			Joanna Baillie publishes the first volume of her *Series of Plays*

Current affairs	Date		Science and the Arts
Napoleon invades Syria	**1799**	5 February	
		11 February	Berkeley Coleridge dies (b. 14 May 1798)
		12 February	Coleridge arrives at Göttingen
		19 February	Constable enrols at Royal Academy
		4 April	Coleridge hears of Berkeley Coleridge's death (in a letter from Poole, posted 15 March)
		21 April	The Wordsworths return to England
		23 May	Thomas Hood born, London
		6 June	Pushkin born, Moscow
Napoleon becomes First Consul		10 November	
		24 November	Coleridge's first meeting with Sara Hutchinson, Sockburn
		2 December	Godwin, *St Leon* published
Washington dies, Mount Vernon		14 December	
		20 December	Wordsworth and his sister move into Dove Cottage, Grasmere
			Wordsworth completes *The Two-Part Prelude* (p. 448)
		24 December	Wordsworth begins writing 'The Brothers' (p. 483)
			Goya begins etching his *Caprichos*, including 'The Sleep of Reason Begets Monsters'
First soup-kichens in London to relieve the hungry and homeless	**1800**	January	Maria Edgeworth publishes *Castle Rackrent* anonymously
		28 February	Mary Robinson publishes 'The Haunted Beach' in the *Morning Post* (p. 250)
		2 April	Beethoven, *Symphony No. 1* first performed
		25 April	Cowper dies
		29 April	Joanna Baillie's *De Monfort* produced at Drury Lane theatre by John Philip Kemble
		24 July	Coleridge and family take up residence at Greta Hall, Keswick
		14 September	Derwent Colleridge born, Keswick
		20 November	Mary Robinson publishes *Lyrical Tales*
		26 December	Mary Robinson dies, Englefield Green, Surrey
			Volta invents galvanic cell (first electric battery)
Toussaint L'Ouverture takes command of Haiti, liberates black slaves	**1801**	25 January	*Lyrical Ballads* (1800) published as by Wordsworth
Pitt resigns and is succeeded by Henry Addington in March		February	
Jefferson delivers inaugral address as third US President		4 March	
First census in England and Wales compiled by John Rickman (published in December)		10 March	
Battle of Copenhagen		2 April	

Current affairs	Date		Science and the Arts
General Enclosure Act, standardizing procedures for obtaining permission to enclose land		June	
Truce between Britain and France		1 October	
Cobbett's *Weekly Political Register* begins publishing (till 1835)	1802	January	
		24 February	Scott publishes *Minstrelsy of the Scottish Border*
Peace of Amiens, bringing a temporary respite to the war between France and Britain (until May 1803)		27 March	
		4 April	Coleridge composes 'A Letter to Sara Hutchinson' (see p. 663)
		18 April	Erasmus Darwin dies
Napoleon becomes Life Consul of France		2 August	
		August	Wordsworth and his sister in Calais to meet Annette Vallon and her daughter, Anne-Caroline
		14 August	Letitia Landon born
		October	Foundation of *Edinburgh Review*
		4 October	Wordsworth marries Mary Hutchinson at Brompton Church
			Coleridge publishes 'Dejection: An Ode' in the *Morning Post* (see p. 673)
		19 October	Coleridge, 'The Daydream' published in the *Morning Post* (see p. 658)
		2 December	Harris Bigg-Wither proposes marriage to Jane Austen; she accepts, but changes her mind and formally retracts the following day
Toussaint L'Ouverture dies in prison	1803	7 April	
Britain declares war on France, ending the Peace of Amiens		18 May	
		24 May	Beethoven, *Sonata in A for Violin* (Kreutzer) first performed
		25 May	Emerson born, Boston
		30 June	Thomas Lovell Beddoes born, Clifton
Emmet leads an uprising in Ireland which fails due to lack of French support		July	Hazlitt visits Lake District to paint portraits of Coleridge and Wordsworth
		August	Keats starts to attend the Revd John Clarke's school at Enfield
		12 August	Coleridge and the Wordsworths set out from Grasmere on their tour of Scotland
			Warrant issued for arrest of Blake on charges of sedition
		5 September	Coleridge arrested in Fort Augustus as a spy; soon released
		10 September	Coleridge sends 'The Pains of Sleep' to Southey (see p. 680)
Execution of Robert Emmet		20 September	Mary Tighe composes *Psyche* (privately published, 1805)

Current affairs	Date		Science and the Arts
	1804	11–12 January	Blake tried and acquitted for sedition at Chichester Quarter Sessions
		6 February	Joseph Priestley dies, Pennsylvania
		12 February	Kant dies, Königsberg, Prussia
		21 February	Richard Trevithick's steam locomotive (the first to be built) makes its first run, Penydarren ironworks in Wales
		6 April	Coleridge sets sail on the *Speedwell* for the Mediterranean, in search of better health (returns August 1806)
		15 April	Keats's father dies after falling from his horse
Pitt's second ministry begins (until January 1806)		10 May	
Napoleon proclaimed Emperor (coronation 2 December)		18 May	
		4 July	Hawthorne born, Salem, Mass.
	1805	12 January	Scott's *Lay of the Last Minstrel* published (sells 44,000 copies)
		27 January	Samuel Palmer born, London
		5 February	John Wordsworth (the poet's brother) dies at sea
Jefferson inaugurated as US President for a second term		4 March	
		7 April	Beehoven, *Symphony No. 3* (*Eroica*) first performed
		9 May	Schiller dies, Weimar
		19 May	Wordsworth completes *The Prelude* in thirteen Books
Napoleon declared King of Italy in Milan		26 May	
		19 July	Hazlitt publishes his first book, *An Essay on the Principles of Human Action*
Napoleon decides not to invade England		September	
Battle of Trafalgar, Nelson mortally wounded		21 October	
Napoleon defeats Russian and Austrian armies at Austerlitz		2 December	
Pitt dies; Baron Grenville becomes head of the Coalition Ministry of All the Talents (until 26 March 1807)	1806	23 January	
		6 March	Elizabeth Barrett Browning born, Durham
		9 April	Brunel born, Portsmouth
		May	Charlotte Dacre publishes *Zofloya*
		20 May	John Stuart Mill born, Pentonville
Francis II decrees an end to the Holy Roman Empire		6 August	
		17 August	Coleridge returns to England after Mediterranean sojourn
		13 September	James Fox dies, Devon

Current affairs	Date		Science and the Arts
		9 October	Joseph Grimaldi, clown, makes his first appearance at Covent Garden theatre
Napoleon defeats Prussians at Jena and occupies Berlin		14 October	
Napoleon declares blockade of Great Britain		21 November	
	1807	January	Charles and Mary Lamb, *Tales from Shakespeare* first published
		7 January	Coleridge writes 'To William Wordsworth', inspired by reading of *The Prelude* (p. 686)
		February	Charlotte Smith's *Beachy Head* published posthumously (see p. 122)
Abolition Act receives royal assent, abolishing the slave trade		25 March	
		8 May	Wordsworth publishes *Poem in Two Volumes*
Peninsular War begins		December	
America prohibits slave-trade	1808	January	
		3 January	Leigh Hunt founds *The Examiner*
		15 January	Coleridge lectures on 'Poetry and Principles of Taste' at the Royal Institution, London (till June)
		22 February	Scott publishes *Marmion* (2,000 copies sell in two months)
Spain invaded by France; Bonaparte made King		March	
		May	Felicia Dorothea Browne (later Hemans) publishes her first book of *Poems*
		1 May	Hazlitt marries Sarah Stoddart
		1 June	Coleridge begins to publish *The Friend*
		September	Blake completes *Milton*
		20 September	Covent Garden theatre burns to the ground
		December	Hannah More publishes *Coelebs in Search of a Wife* (which becomes a best-seller)
			Goethe publishes *Faust* Part 1
	1809	19 January	Poe born, Boston
Quarterly Review founded as a Tory response to the Whig *Edinburgh Review*		February	
Lincoln Born, Kentucky		12 February	Darwin born, Shrewsbury
Madison inaugarated as fourth US President		4 March	
Byron takes his seat in the House of Lords		13 March	
		16 March	Byron publishes *English Bards and Scotch Reviewers*
Napoleon takes Vienna		12 May	
		15 May	Blake exhibits his paintings in London (till September), visited by Crabb Robinson and Southey

Current affairs	Date		Science and the Arts
Papal States annexed to France	1809	17 May	
		31 May	Haydn dies, Vienna
Pope Pius VII excommunicates Napoleon		10 June	
Paine dies, New York State		8 June	
Napoleon arrests and imprisons Pope Pius VII		July	
		2 July	Byron sails for the Mediterranean with Hobhouse
		18 September	Covent Garden theatre reopens after being burnt down, with a new scale of ticket prices, precipitating the O.P. (or old price) riots which last 67 nights
		20 December	Joseph Johnson, bookseller and publisher, dies in London
	1810	1 March	Chopin born, Warsaw
		24 March	Mary Tighe dies, Woodstock
Sir John Burdett imprisoned in the Tower of London for libellous article against the House of Commons in the *Weekly Political Register*; riots in London		April	
		3 May	Byron swims the Hellespont
		8 May	Scott's *The Lady of the Lake* published (sells 20,300 copies)
Cobbett sentenced to two years' imprisonment for an article against the flogging of five English militia-men by German mercenaries in his *Political Register*		9 July	
		28 October	Basil Montagu tells Coleridge of remarks made by Wordsworth about Coleridge's opium addiction, suggesting that Wordsworth had commissioned him to do so, resulting in an irreparable breach
			Goya etching *The Disasters of War*
Prince of Wales declared Regent, his father having been recognized as insane	1811	5 February	
First Luddite riots in Nottingham		11 March	
		25 March	Shelley expelled from Oxford for having co-written the *Necessity of Atheism*
		14 July	Byron Returns to England
		18 July	Thackeray born, Calcutta
		25 August	Shelley elopes with Harriet Westbrook
		22 October	Liszt born, Raiding, Hungary
		30 October	Austen's *Sense and Sensibility* published
		18 November	Coleridge lectures on Shakespeare and Milton at Scot's Corporation Hall (until 17 January 1812)

Current affairs	Date		Science and the Arts
	1812	January	Anna Laetitia Barbauld publishes *Eighteen Hundred and Eleven* (see p. 44)
		7 February	Dickens born, Portsmouth
		27 February	Byron delivers maiden speech in the Lords on behalf of the Luddites
		10 March	Byron publishes *Childe Harold's Pilgrimage* Cantos I and II (500 copies sell in three days)
Leigh Hunt attacks the Prince Regent in *The Examiner*		22 March	
		21 April	Byron's second speech in the Lords
		7 May	Browning born, Camberwell
Assassination of the Prime Minister, Spencer Perceval, precipitating Liverpool's administration		11 May	
		4 June	Catherine Wordsworth dies in Grasmere (less than 4 years old)
America declares war on Britain		18 June	
Napoleon declares war on Russia		22 June	
Cobbett released from prison after two years, a ruined man		9 July	
Napoleon enters Moscow		September	
		4 October	Shelley and Godwin meet in London
French begin retreat from Moscow		19 October	
		3 November	Coleridge lectures on Shakespeare, Surrey Institution (till 26 January 1813)
		11 November	Shelley meets Mary Godwin
		1 December	Thomas Wordsworth dies, Grasmere (6 years old)
	1813	23 January	Coleridge's *Remorse* opens at Drury Lane theatre in London, to widespread acclaim
		28 January	Austen's *Pride and Prejudice* published
Leigh Hunt sentenced to two years' imprisonment for libelling the Prince Regent		3 February	
		1 May	Wordsworth moves into Rydal Mount
		5 May	Søren Kierkegaard born
		18 May	Wordsworth assumes duties of his new office, Distributor of Stamps for Westmorland
		22 May	Wagner born, Leipzig
		June	Shelley publishes *Queen Mab* privately (250 copies only); it was pirated in 1821
		11 August	Henry James Pye, Poet Laureate, dies
Napoleon's last major victory at Dresden		27 August	
Napoleon defeated at Leipzig		19 October	
		October	Madame de Staël, *De l'Allemagne* published in French and English

Current affairs	Date		Science and the Arts
	1813	4 November	Southey takes oath as Poet Laureate
Metternich, with reluctant approval of Russia and Prussia, offers peace to Napoleon (proposal withdrawn by 2 December)		9 November	
Allies begin invasion of France	1814	1 January	
		26 January	Edmund Kean makes his debut on the London stage as Shylock at Drury Lane theatre (Hazlitt is in the audience)
		1 February	Byron publishes *The Corsair* (10,000 copies sell in a day)
		March	Burney, *The Wanderer* published
		24 March	Shelley marries Harriet Westbrook
Allies take Paris (news reaches London 5 April)		31 March	
Napoleon defeated at Toulouse; exiled to Elba		10 April	
		9 May	Austen's *Mansfield Park* published
		7 July	Scott's *Waverley* published anonymously
		28 July	Shelley elopes with Mary Godwin and her half-sister, Jane (later Claire) Clairmont, to the continent
		17 August	Wordsworth publishes *The Excursion*
Washington DC captured by the British		September	
		14 September	Shelley, Mary Godwin and Jane Clairmont return from the continent
		October	J.C. Spurzheim, phrenologist, visits Britain
		November	John Walter, proprietor of *The Times*, introduces the steam-press
Peace of Ghent ends war between America and Britain		24 December	
		29 December	Jeffrey's hostile review of *The Excursion* appears in the *Edinburgh Review* for November (p. 715)
	1815	2 January	Byron marries Annabella Milbanke (separated 1816)
Battle of New Orleans, in which General Jackson defeats British troops		8 January	
Leigh Hunt released from prison		3 February	
		24 February	Scott publishes *Guy Mannering* (entire edition sells out the day after publication)
Napoleon escapes from Elba (news of which reaches London on 10 March)		1 March	
		7 April	Byron first meets Walter Scott at offices of John Murray, London
		27 April	Wordsworth publishes his first collected *Poems*
		12 May	Wordsworth publishes *The White Doe of Rylstone*, late May

Current affairs	Date		Science and the Arts
			Byron appointed to the sub-committee of management at Drury Lane theatre
		30 May	Coleridge writes to Wordsworth expressing disappointment with *The Excursion* (see p. 689)
		1 June	James Gillray dies, London (aged 58)
Napoleon defeated at Waterloo; exiled to St Helena in August		18 June	
		1 October	Keats enrols as medical student at Guy's Hospital, Southwark
		December	Austen publishes *Emma* (dedicated to the Prince Regent)
			Peacock publishes *Headlong Hall*
		17 December	Indian jugglers perform at Olympic New Theatre, Strand, London, precipitating Hazlitt's essay 'The Indian Jugglers'
	1816	15 February	Leigh Hunt publishes *Rimini* (see p. 796)
		10 February	Shelley's *Alastor* published in London (see 1053)
		10 April	Coleridge recites Kubla Khan to Byron at his home in London
		15 April	Coleridge becomes house-guest and patient of Dr and Mrs Gillman, Highgate, London
		21 April	Charlotte Brontë born
		25 April	Byron sets out for the Continent from London
		2 May	Shelley, Mary Godwin and Claire Clairmont leave London for Geneva
		4 May	Byron visits the battlefield at Waterloo
			Scott's *The Antiquary* published (sells 6,000 copies in six days)
		5 May	Keats' 'To Solitude' (his first published poem) appears in the *Examiner*
		9 May	Maturin's *Bertram* opens at Drury Lane theatre, to wild acclaim
		25 May	Byron and Shelley meet at the Hotel Angleterre in Sécheron near Geneva
			Coleridge publishes *Kubla Khan, Christabel* and *The Pains of Sleep* to unfavourable reviews
		10 June	Byron moves into Villa Diodati, only a few hundred yards up the hill from the Shelleys at Montalègre
		17 June	Mary Godwin begins writing the story that will turn into *Frankenstein*
		7 July	Sheridan dies
		6 August	Austen completes *Persuasion*
		8 September	Shelley, Mary Godwin and Claire Clairmont return to England
		5 October	Byron leaves Geneva for Milan

Current affairs	Date		Science and the Arts
	1816	9 November	Harriet Shelley conmmits suicide, her body discovered 10 December
		18 November	Byron publishes *Childe Harold's Pilgrimage* Canto III (see p. 852)
		1 December	Hunt praises 'Young Poets' (including Shelley and Keats) in *The Examiner*
Spa Fields riots in London		2 December	
		30 December	Shelley marries Mary Godwin
	1817	19 January	Shelley's *Hymn to Intellectual Beauty* published in *The Examiner* (see p. 1071)
Southey publishes an article in the *Quarterly* for October 1816 saying that radical journalists should be prevented from 'insulting the government, and defying the laws of the country'		11 February	
		13 February	Southey's *Wat Tyler* published
		14 February	Hazlitt and Hunt publish *The Round Table*
		1 March	Keats's *Poems* published
Suspension of habeas corpus, which precipitates Cobbett's flight to America		4 March	
Monroe becomes fifth President of US			
Southey writes to Lord Liverpool asking for more repressive laws to control the press		19 March	
Blackwood's Edinburgh Magazine founded		April	
Popular uprisings in the provinces		June	
William Hone (radical publisher) tried for publishing 'blasphemous parodies'		18 June	
		23 June	John Philip Kemble's farewell performance as Coriolanus at Covent Garden theatre
		3 July	Byron publishes *Manfred* (see p. 896)
		9 July	Hazlitt publishes *Characters of Shakespeare's Plays*
		11 July	Coleridge publishes *Biographia Literaria* and *Sibylline Leaves*
		12 July	Thoreau born, Concord, Mass.
		14 July	Madame de Staël dies, Paris
		18 July	Austen dies, Winchester; buried Winchester Cathedral 24 July
		October	Lockhart publishes the first of the Cockney School attacks in *Blackwood's* (see p. 1324)
Princess Charlotte dies in childbirth		6 November	
		December	Austen's *Northanger Abbey* and *Persuasion* published posthumously
William Hone finally acquitted		20 December	
		26–8 December	Shelley writes 'Ozymandias' in a competition with Horace Smith at Marlow; it is published in *The Examiner*, 11 January 1818 (see p. 1079)
		28 December	Haydon hosts 'the immortal dinner' (see p. 834)

Current affairs	Date		Science and the Arts
	1818	1 January	Mary Shelley publishes *Frankenstein* anonymously
		12 January	Shelly publishes *The Revolt of Islam*
		13 January	Hazlitt begins to lecture on English Poetry at the Surrey Institution (till March)
		27 January	Coleridge begins lecturing on Poetry and Drama at Flower-de-Luce Court, Fetter Lane (till March)
Habeas corpus restored		28 January	
		31 January	Scott published *Rob Roy*
		6 February	Coleridge begins to lecture on Shakespeare in London
		16 February	Fuseli as Professor of Painting begins a course of lectures at the Royal Academy, Somerset House
		28 February	Byron publishes *Beppo*
		28 April	Byron publishes *Childe Harold* Canto IV (4,000 copies sold)
		29 April	Hazlitt publishes *A View of the English Stage*
		30 April	Emily Brontë born, Thornton
		5 May	Karl Marx born, Trier, Rhine Province, Prussia
		18 May	Lamb publishes his *Works* (2 vols) with C. and J. Ollier
		19 May	Keats publishes *Endymion*
		22 June	Keats and Charles Brown depart for their walking tour of the Lake District and Scotland
		18 August	Keats returns to London from Inverness (by boat)
		1 September	Lockhart's attack on Keats, 'The Cockney School of Poetry' No. IV (signed 'Z'), published in *Blackwood's* (for August) (see p. 1327)
		27 September	Croker publishes a hostile review of Keats's *Endymion* in the April number of the *Quarterly Review*
		15 November	Thomas Love Peacock publishes *Nightmare Abbey*
			Shelley arrives in Rome (until 22 November)
Queen Charlotte dies		17 November	
University of Virginia founded by Jefferson	1819	25 January	
		8 February	Ruskin born, London
		1 April	Polidori publishes 'The Vampyre: A Tale by Lord Byron' in the *New Monthly Magazine*
		15 April	John Hamilton Reynolds publishes *Peter Bell. A Lyrical Ballad*
		22 April	Wordsworth's *Peter Bell* published

Current affairs	Date		Science and the Arts
Princess Victoria born	1819	24 May	
		31 May	Whitman born
		15 July	Byron's *Don Juan* Cantos I and II published anonymously by Murray (see p. 933)
		1 August	Melville born, New York
		14 August	Hazlitt publishes *Political Essays*
Peterloo Massacre takes place, St Peter's Fields, Manchester		16 August	
		Early September	Shelley prints *The Cenci* in Livorno
		5 September	Shelley composes 'The Mask of Anarchy' (until 23 September) (see p. 1164)
Trial of Richard Carlile, radical publisher, for criticizing the Government over the Peterloo Massacre and publishing Paine's *The Age of Reason*, critical of the Church of England (he is sentenced 21 November)		12 October	
		25 October	Shelley composes 'Ode to the West Wind' (see p. 1175)
Richard Carlile imprisoned for 3 years and fined £1,500 (£62,500/US$116,000 today)		21 November	
		26 November	William Hone and George Cruikshank publish *The Political House that Jack Built*
		December	Shelley composes 'England in 1819' (see p. 1180)
Bolivar becomes President and military dictator of Colombia		17 December	
Military insurrection at cadiz precipitates revolution in Spain, leading to restoration of 1812 constitution in March	1820	1 January	*London Magazine* begins publishing
		16 January	Hunt publishes *The Indicator*
			Clare, *Poems Descriptive of Rural Life and Scenery* published; it runs to four editions and sells over 3,500 copies
		28 January	Southey's *Poetical Works* (14 vols) published
George III dies at Windsor Castle, to be succeeded by his son, Prince Regent since 1811, as George IV		29 January	
		3 February	Keats has his first haemorrhage indicating that he is suffering from tubercolosis
Cato Street Conspiracy foiled (plan to blow up Cabinet); the principals are executed on 1 May		23 February	
		25 March	Haydon's *Christ's Entry into Jerusalem* exhibited in London
		May	Hartley Coleridge deemed to have forfeited his Fellowship at Oriel College, Oxford

Current affairs	Date		Science and the Arts
		June	Shelley composes 'To a Skylark' (see p. 1181)
		Late June	Peacock publishes 'The Four Ages of Poetry' in *Ollier's Literary Miscellany*, No. 1
		1 July	Keats publishes *Lamia, Isabella, The Eve of St Agnes, and Other Poems*
		6 July	Wordsworth publishes *The River Duddon*
Start of the trial of Queen Caroline to prove her infidelities so that George IV can divorce her; she is eventually acquitted		17 August	
		14 August	Shelley's *Prometheus Unbound . . . with Other Poems* published in London
		September	Blake finishes work on the first illuminated copy of Jerusalem
		1 September	Lamb publishes the first of his *Elia* essays, 'Recollections of the South Sea House', in the *London Magazine* (for August)
		17 September	Keats sails for Rome
		13 October	Wordsworth meets Helen Maria Williams for the first time in Paris (they meet again 20 October)
		15 November	Keats and Severn move into 26 Piazza di Spagna, Rome
	1821	February	Shelley writing 'A Defence of Poetry' (not published till 1840)
		23 February	Keats dies, Rome
		27 February	John Scott, editor of the *London Magazine*, killed in a duel
		6 April	Hazlitt, *Table Talk* volume 1 published
Napoleon dies, St Helena		5 May	
		July	Shelley publishes *Adonais* in Pisa (p. 1199)
Coronation of George IV		19 July	
Queen Caroline (wife of George IV) dies		7 August	
		September	Clare, *The Village Minstrel* published (sells 800 copies in three months)
		October	Cobbett sets out on the rural rides
		1 October	De Quincey's *Confessions of an English Opium-Eater* Part I appears in the *London Magazine*, followed by Part II in November
		1 November	Byron moves to Pisa
		11 November	Dostoyevsky born, Moscow
		11 December	Fight between Tom Hickman (the Gas-man) and Bill Neat at Hungerford, Berkshire, attended by Hazlitt (see p. 759)
		12 December	Flaubert born, Rouen
		19 December	Byron publishes *Sardanapalus, The Two Foscari, and Cain*

Current affairs	Date		Science and the Arts
	1822	February	Hazlitt's 'The Fight' published in *New Monthly Magazine* (p. 759)
		15 June	Hazlitt, *Table Talk* volume 2 published
		8 July	Shelley drowned off Livorno
Castlereagh commits suicide by slitting his own throat; succeeded as Foreign Secretary by Canning		12 August	
		16 August	Shelley cremated on beach not far from Viareggio, Italy
		October	De Quincey publishes *Confessions of an English Opium-Eater* in book form
			Schubert composes Symphony No. 8
		14 October	*The Liberal* No. 1 published
		December	Lamb's *Elia* published – the first collected volume of *Elia* essays
		24 December	Matthew Arnold born
	1823	February	Mary Shelley publishes *Valperga*.
		23 April	Hazlitt's 'My First Acquaintance with Poets' published in *The Liberal* (see p. 771)
		9 May	Hazlitt publishes *Liber Amoris*
		June	Hemans publishes *The Siege of Valencia*
		28 July	Richard Brinsley Peake's *Presumption, or the fate of Frankenstein* opens at the Lyceum, London, for a run of 37 performances – the first of many adaptations
		25 August	Mary Shelley returns to England
Monroe Doctrine enunciated in America		2 December	
		12 December	Heman's *The Vespers of Palermo* performed at Covent Garden theatre
	1824	4 January	Byron lands at Missolonghi to great welcome
		22 January	Byron composes 'On this day I completed my thirty-sixth year'
		March	Coleridge elected Fellow of the Royal Society
		19 April	Byron dies, Missolonghi, from marsh fever and excessive bleeding
		7 May	Beethoven, *Symphony No. 9 in D minor* first performed
		June	Shelley's *Posthumous Poems* published, edited by Mary Shelley
		12 July	James Hogg's *Private Memoirs and Confessions of a Justified Sinner* published in London
		September	Shelley's *Posthumous Poems* suppressed, at the insistence of Sir Timothy Shelley

Current affairs	Date		Science and the Arts
	1825	11 January	Hazlitt, *The Spirit of the Age* published anonymously
John Quincy Adams elected sixth US President		4 March	
		9 March	Anna Laetitia Barbauld dies, Stoke Newington
		16 April	Fuseli dies
		May	Hemans publishes *The Forest Sanctuary and Other Poems*
		June	Barbauld's *Works* posthumously published by her niece, Lucy Aikin
		September	Stockton to Darlington railway becomes the first line open to the public
		7 November	Charlotte Dacre dies, London
	1826	14 January	Constable (publisher) bankrupted, precipitating financial ruin for Sir Walter Scott and others
		23 January	Mary Shelley publishes *The Last Man*
		March	Blake publishes *Job*
		28 April	Hazlitt publishes *The Plain Speaker* anonymously
Jefferson dies, Monticello, Va		4 July	
	1827	26 March	Beethoven dies, Vienna
		April	Clare, *The Shepherd's Calendar, with Village Stories and Other Poems* published (sells only 425 copies over two and a half years)
Lord Liverpool, Prime Minister since 1811, succeeded by Canning		30 April	
Canning dies		8 August	
		12 August	Blake dies, London
		15 December	Helen Maria Williams dies
Wellington becomes Prime Minister	1828	January	First two volumes of Hazlitt's *Life of Napoleon Buonaparte* published
		16 April	Goya dies in Spain, but is buried in France
Repeal of Test and Corporation Act that kept non-Anglicans from holding office		28 April	
		May	Hemans publishes *Records of Woman* (see p. 1249); goes into a second edition in October
		12 May	D.G. Rossetti born, London
		21 June	Coleridge, Wordsworth and Dora Wordsworth tour the Netherlands and the Rhine (till 7 August)
		19 November	Schubert dies, Vienna

Current affairs	Date		Science and the Arts
Jackson elected seventh President of the US	1829	4 March	
Catholic Emancipation Act		4 April	
Metropolitan Police Act puts 'Peelers' on the streets of London		June	
		December	Coleridge publishes *On the Constitution of Church and State*
	1830	May	Hazlitt's *Life of Napoleon Buonaparte* volumes 3 and 4 published
George IV dies; accession of William IV, his brother		25 June	
'Captain Swing' agrarian riots		August	
		18 September	Hazlitt dies, Frith Street, Soho
The Whig, Earl Grey, succeeds Wellington (Tory) as Prime Minister, bringing an era of reform		16 November	
		5 December	Christina Rossetti born, London
		10 December	Emily Dickinson born, Amherst, Mass.
Bolivar dies, Colombia		17 December	
Lord John Russell introduces Reform Bill	1831	1 March	
Government defeated on Reform Bill; Parliament dissolved		10 April	
		8 June	Sarah Siddons dies
New Parliament with Whig majority		14 June	
Reform Bill defeated in Lords		8 October	
		31 October	Mary Shelley publishes revised edition of *Frankenstein*
		14 November	Hegel dies, Berlin
	1832	23 January	Manet born, Paris
		3 February	Crabbe dies
		22 March	Goethe dies in Weimar
Revised Reform Bill defeated in Lords; Grey resigns as Prime Minister 9 May; recalled 15 May		7 May	
		6 June	Bentham dies
Reform Bill receives royal assent		7 June	
		21 September	Scott dies, Abbotsford
		October	Hunt publishes Shelley's *The Mask of Anarchy*
		December	Posthumous publication of Goethe's *Faust* Part 2
	1833	15 March	Edmund Kean dies
Emancipation Act receives its final reading, abolishing slavery in British colonies		26 July	
Wilberforce dies, London		29 July	

Current affairs	Date		Science and the Arts
		5 August	Emerson visits Coleridge at Highgate
		7 September	Hannah More dies, leaving her sizeable fortune to a range of charities and religious institutions
	1834	17 February	John Thelwall dies
Hunt begins publishing *Leigh Hunt's London Journal* (till December 1835)		2 April	
		19 July	Degas born, Paris
		25 July	Coleridge dies, Highgate
Poor Law Reform Act		14 August	
Slaves throughout the British Empire become legally free		August	
Fire destroys Houses of Parliament		16 October	
		23 December	Malthus dies
		27 December	Lamb dies (buried 3 January, Edmonton)
	1835	March	Mary Shelley publishes Lodore
		16 May	Felicia Hemans dies, Dublin
		July	Clare's *The Rural Muse* published
		15 October	Marx enrolled as a student at the University of Bonn
Siege of the Alamo; Davy Crockett killed	1836	March	
		7 April	William Godwin dies
Madison dies, Montpelier, Va.		28 June	
	1837	10 February	Pushkin dies, St Petersburg
Van Buren elected eighth US President		4 March	
William IV dies, succeeded by his 17-year-old niece as Queen Victoria		June	
Charter presented to Parliament by National Convention of Chartists; rejection leads to riots in Birmingham and elsewhere in July	1838	13 May	
		15 October	Letitia Landon dies, Gold Coast
Outbreak of Opium War with China		November	
	1839	January	Shelley's collected *Poetical Works* (4 vols) edited by Mary Shelley begins publishing (until May)
		1 February	De Quincey begins his 'Lake Reminiscences' in *Tait's Edinburgh Magazine* (for January) with the first part of his essay on Wordsworth
	1840	6 January	Fanny Burney dies, London
Queen Victoria marries her first cousin, Albert of Saxe-Coburg-Gotha, St James's Palace London		10 February	

Current affairs	Date		Science and the Arts
	1840	2 June	Thomas Hardy born, Upper Bockhampton, Dorset
		14 November	Monet born, Paris
	1841	25 February	Renoir born, Limoges
Harrison elected ninth President of the US		4 March	
		31 March	Schumann, *Symphony No. 1* first performed
	1843	21 March	Southey dies
		4 April	Wordsworth accepts the post of Poet Laureate in a letter to Sir Robert Peel
	1844	2 May	William Beckford dies, after a severe attack of influenza
		28 July	Gerard Manley Hopkins born, Stratford, Essex
		15 October	Friedrich Nietzsche born
Polk elected eleventh President of US	**1845**	4 March	
		1 April	De Quincey begins *Suspiria de Profundis* in *Blackwood's* (for March), which continues in issues for April, June and July
	1846	May	Brontë sisters publish *Poems by Currer, Ellis and Acton Bell*
		22 June	Benjamin Robert Haydon commits suicide
		12 September	Robert Browning marries Elizabeth Barrett
	1847	20 May	Mary Lamb dies, aged 82
		19 October	Charlotte Brontë publishes *Jane Eyre*
		December	Emily Brontë publishes *Wuthering Heights*
Gold discovered in California; beginning of the gold rush	**1848**	24 January	
Second Republic proclaimed in France		February	Marx and Engels publish *Communist Manifesto*
June Days (until 26 June), bloody civil war in Paris		23 June	
Louis Napoleon Bonaparte elected President of France		December	
		19 December	Emily Brontë dies
	1849	6 January	Hartley Coleridge dies
Roman Republic is established		5 February	
Taylor elected twelfth President of US		4 March	
		22 May	Maria Edgeworth dies, Edgeworthstown
		7 October	Poe dies, Baltimore
		17 October	Chopin dies, Paris

Current affairs	Date		Science and the Arts
		1 November	Wordsworth's *Poetical Works* (6 vols), last edition in his lifetime, begins publishing De Quincey publishes 'The English Mail-Coach', anonymously, in *Blackwood's* (for October)
American Express founded	**1850**	18 March	
		23 April	Wordsworth dies, aged 80
		July	*The Prelude* first published, posthumously
Taylor dies, to be succeeded as US President by Fillmore		9 July	
		18 August	Balzac dies, Paris
California admitted to the Union		September	
	1851	1 February	Mary Shelley dies, Chester Square, London, aged 53

Romanticism

Richard Price (1723–1791)

No man was more thoroughly a product of the Enlightenment than Richard Price – except, perhaps, his friend, Thomas Jefferson. Philosopher, theologian, mathematician, he became an expert on insurance and advised the newly founded Society for Equitable Assurances on Lives and Survivorships on actuarial matters. He also suggested to the Prime Minister, William Pitt the younger, ways in which to reduce the national debt. A leading Dissenter, he campaigned vigorously for legal recognition of the right to freedom of worship.

It is as a political pamphleteer that Price bears most on our understanding of the Romantics. A believer in liberty and representative government, he supported the American Revolution, and discussed with John Adams and Thomas Jefferson ways in which they might consolidate its achievements. He found the French Revolution no less inspiring and, shortly after the fall of the Bastille (14 July 1789), described it as 'the commencement of a general reformation in the governments of the world which hitherto have been little better than usurpations on the rights of mankind, impediments to the progress of human improvement, and contrivances for enabling a few grandees to oppress and enslave the rest of mankind'.

Price's famous *Discourse* was delivered as a sermon to the London Revolution Society, 4 November 1789, founded in honour not of the recent uprisings in France or America, but of the Glorious Revolution of 1688 (the expulsion of James II from England, and the transfer of sovereignty to the Protestant William and Mary). The Society contained members of the established church, and 'many persons of rank and consequence from different parts of the kingdom'. At annual anniversary meetings it held a religious service in the morning, followed by a more festive gathering at a tavern; it was at the religious service that Price delivered his *Discourse*. For Price, the Glorious Revolution had established the principles of just and stable government: the right to liberty of conscience in religious matters; the right to resist power when abused; and the right of the people to choose their own governors. His *Discourse*, with its praise for the French, was received with acclaim by the Society, whose members voted immediately to encourage the establishment of similar groups throughout the country, and to congratulate the National Assembly in Paris on the Revolution. It was sent to the Assembly and read out there on 25 November, when it was greeted with equal enthusiasm. To many in Britain this was an incendiary act, establishing Price as the hate-figure of choice for the Tories, making him the subject of scurrilous caricatures, most famously James Gillray's brilliant (and funny) *Smelling Out a Rat* (3 December 1790).

The *Discourse* sparked off a pamphlet war that inspired some of the most important political works in the language. It began with a scorching response from the great Whig orator Edmund Burke, who offered a conservative reaction in *Reflections on the Revolution in France* (1790), arguing in support of the monarchy and the existing system of government (see pp. 10–16). Articulated with characteristic brilliance, his *Reflections* was nonetheless the work of an old man, motivated in part by fear of revolutionary change. It drew responses from a host of younger writers: within a month Mary Wollstonecraft had published her *Vindication of the Rights of Men*; her *Vindication of the Rights of Woman* followed in 1792 (pp. 276–85). Thomas Paine, who was old enough to have fought in the American War of Independence, would publish his great apology for republicanism, *The Rights of Man*, in 1791–2 (pp. 24–7).

If there was a literary event at the end of the eighteenth century that heralded the cultural, political and social change of the Romantic period, this was it. No one realized that at the time, of course; anxiety about war with the French was uppermost, and would remain so for the next two decades. All the same, Price's declaration of a new world in prospect would be the rallying cry not just for radical fellow-travellers, but for the visionaries who would shortly precipitate a literary renaissance the effects of which would resonate for many decades to come. Among those following the pamphlet war as it unfolded was a young Cambridge undergraduate called William Wordsworth who, years later in *The Thirteen-Book Prelude*, would recall having read 'the master pamphlets of the day' (ix 97).

Price was treading dangerously; a few years later his 'ardour for liberty' would have led him and his publisher to be tried for sedition. These two brief extracts from the *Discourse* offer something of its remarkable courage and energy. When they were composed the storming of the Bastille was still news; less than a month before, 20,000 people had stormed Versailles and 'escorted' the King and Queen to Paris in what many saw as one of the most sinister developments in the Revolution so far. Louis's execution would wait until January 1793, but for many it was prefigured in the events of the summer and autumn of 1789.

Further reading

Richard Price, *A Discourse on the Love of our Country 1789* (Spelsbury, 1992).

D. O. Thomas, *The Honest Mind: The Thought and Work of Richard Price* (Oxford, 1977).

P. M. Zall, 'The Cool World of Samuel Taylor Coleridge: The American Connection: Dr Richard Price (1723–91)', *TWC* 7 (1976), 95–100.

[*On Representation*]

From A Discourse on the Love of our Country (1789)

When the representation is fair and equal, and at the same time vested with such powers as our House of Commons possesses, a kingdom may be said to govern itself, and consequently to possess true liberty. When the representation is partial, a kingdom possesses liberty only partially; and if extremely partial, it only gives a *semblance* of liberty. But if not only extremely partial, but corruptly chosen, and under corrupt influence after being chosen, it becomes a *nuisance*, and produces the worst of all forms of government: a government by corruption, a government carried on and supported by spreading venality and profligacy through a kingdom.

May heaven preserve this kingdom from a calamity so dreadful! It is the point of depravity to which abuses under such a government as ours naturally tend, and the last stage of national unhappiness. We are at present, I hope, at a great distance from it. But it cannot be pretended that there are no advances towards it, or that there is no reason for apprehension and alarm.

The inadequateness of our representation has been long a subject of complaint.[1] This is, in truth, our fundamental grievance, and I do not think that anything is much more our duty (as men who love their country and are grateful for the Revolution)[2]

Notes

On Representation

[1] *The inadequateness . . . complaint* Few working people, and no women, had the vote.

[2] *Revolution* the Glorious Revolution of 1688, when the Protestant William of Orange displaced the Stuart dynasty that dated back to James I.

than to unite our zeal in endeavouring to get it redressed. At the time of the American war, associations were formed for this purpose in London and other parts of the kingdom, and our present Minister himself has, since that war, directed to it an effort which made him a favourite with many of us.[3] But all attention to it seems now lost, and the probability is that this inattention will continue and that nothing will be done towards gaining for us this essential blessing till some great calamity again alarms our fears, or till some great abuse of power again provokes our resentment – or perhaps till the acquisition of a pure and equal representation by other countries (while we are mocked with the shadow)[4] kindles our shame.

Prospects for Reform[1]

From A Discourse on the Love of our Country (1789)

What an eventful period is this! I am thankful that I have lived to see it, and I could almost say, 'Lord, now lettest thou thy servant depart in peace, for mine eyes have seen thy salvation.'[2] I have lived to see a diffusion of knowledge which has undermined superstition and error; I have lived to see the rights of men better understood than ever, and nations panting for liberty which seemed to have lost the idea of it. I have lived to see *thirty millions* of people,[3] indignant and resolute, spurning at slavery, and demanding liberty with an irresistible voice, their King led in triumph, and an arbitrary monarch surrendering himself to his subjects.[4]

After sharing in the benefits of one revolution, I have been spared to be a witness to two other revolutions, both glorious.[5] And now, methinks, I see the ardour for liberty catching and spreading; a general amendment beginning in human affairs; the dominion of kings changed for the dominion of laws, and the dominion of priests giving way to the dominion of reason and conscience.

Be encouraged, all ye friends of freedom, and writers in its defence! The times are auspicious. Your labours have not been in vain. Behold kingdoms admonished by you, starting from sleep, breaking their fetters, and claiming justice from their oppressors! Behold the light you have struck out, after setting America free,[6] reflected to France

Notes

[3] *At the time . . . us* In the early 1780s the Prime Minister, William Pitt the Younger ('our present Minister'), advocated peace with the American colonies, economic reform, and reform of parliamentary representation. Such organizations as the Constitutional Society (established 1780) lobbied for parliamentary reform.

[4] 'A representation chosen principally by the Treasury, and a few thousands of the dregs of the people, who are generally paid for their votes' (Price's footnote).

PROSPECTS FOR REFORM

[1] This was one of the most celebrated parts of Price's Discourse, thanks to the fact that the first paragraph of it was quoted by Burke in his *Reflections*, with the following introduction:

> Plots, massacres, assassinations seem to some people a trivial price for obtaining a revolution. Cheap, bloodless reformation, a guiltless liberty appear flat and vapid to their taste. There must be a great change of scene; there must be a magnificent stage effect; there must be a grand spectacle to rouse the imagination grown torpid with the lazy enjoyment of sixty years' security and the still unanimating repose of public prosperity. The preacher found them all in the French Revolution. This inspires a juvenile warmth through his whole frame. His enthusiasm kindles as he advances; and when he arrives at his peroration it is in a full blaze. Then viewing, from the Pisgah of his pulpit, the free, moral, happy, flourishing and glorious state of France as in a bird's-eye landscape of a promised land, he breaks out into the following rapture . . .

[2] *Lord . . . thy salvation* from Luke 2:29–30.

[3] *thirty millions of people* the population of France.

[4] *their King . . . subjects* A reference to the storming of Versailles by 20,000 people, and compelled 'escort' of the French Royal family to Paris, less than a month before.

[5] *After sharing . . . glorious* Price sees himself as a beneficiary of the Glorious Revolution; he also witnessed (and supported) both the American Revolution, which resulted in independence from Britain in 1776, and the French Revolution.

[6] *setting America free* The Treaty of Paris, confirming the independence of America, was signed on 3 September 1783. Washington was elected first President of the Republic in 1789 (until 1797).

and there kindled into a blaze that lays despotism in ashes, and warms and illuminates Europe!

Tremble all ye oppressors of the world! Take warning all ye supporters of slavish governments and slavish hierarchies! Call no more (absurdly and wickedly) reformation, innovation. You cannot now hold the world in darkness. Struggle no longer against increasing light and liberality. Restore to mankind their rights, and consent to the correction of abuses, before they and you are destroyed together.

Thomas Warton (1728–1790)

'Thomas Warton was a man of taste and genius,' Hazlitt wrote. 'His sonnets I cannot help preferring to any in the language.'[1] Given the distinguished tradition of sonneteering in English poetry, which embraced Surrey, Shakespeare, Sidney, Donne, Daniel and Wyatt, to say nothing of the poets of his own time, Hazlitt's endorsement of Warton may seem odd to us, if not downright eccentric, but it stands as a reminder of Warton's standing among the Romantics.

The son of Thomas Warton the elder (*c.*1688–1745), Warton the Younger was to become one of the foremost poets and literary historians of his time. He studied at Trinity College, Oxford, where he remained as Fellow and Tutor (1751 onwards), Professor of Poetry (1757–67), and Camden Professor of History (1785). Though appointed Poet Laureate in 1785 much of his best verse was by then behind him – and in many ways his most enduring achievement turned out to be his *History of Poetry* (1774–81). Three volumes were published by the time he died, and although 88 pages of a fourth were printed during his lifetime they were not to be published until it was finished by others in 1824. The *History* revived interest in medieval and sixteenth-century poetry, and anticipated the Romantic movement in its shift away from the neo-classicism of earlier periods.

Wordsworth and Coleridge were not 21 at his death (Wordsworth was up at Cambridge, Coleridge a schoolboy at Christ's Hospital in London), but they knew his poetry, and like many other young writers found their interest in the sonnet aroused by his efforts. They recognized the influence of *To the River Lodon* on Bowles's *To the Itchin* and Smith's *To the River Arun* (see pp. 95–6), a tradition which would inform Coleridge's *To the River Otter* (pp. 598–9) and Wordsworth's address to the Derwent in the *Two-Part Prelude*.

Further reading

The Correspondence of Thomas Warton ed. David Fairer (Athens, Ga., 1995).

David Fairer, 'Thomas Warton, Thomas Gray, and the Recovery of the Past', in *Thomas Gray: Contemporary Essays* ed. W. B. Hutchings and William Ruddick (Liverpool, 1993), pp. 146–70.

A. Harris Fairbanks, ' "Dear Native Brook": Coleridge, Bowles, and Thomas Warton the Younger', *TWC* 6 (1975) 313–15.

Notes

1 Howe ix 242.

Sonnet IX. To the River Lodon[1]

From Poems (1777)

Ah! what a weary race my feet have run
  Since first I trod thy banks with alders crowned,
  And thought my way was all through fairy ground
  Beneath thy azure sky and golden sun,
Where first my muse to lisp her notes begun.[2]
  While pensive memory traces back the round
  Which fills the varied interval between,
  Much pleasure, more of sorrow, marks the scene.
Sweet native stream, those skies and suns so pure
No more return to cheer my evening road;
  Yet still one joy remains – that not obscure,
Nor useless, all my vacant days have flowed,
  From youth's gay dawn to manhood's prime mature,
  Nor with the muse's laurel[3] unbestowed.

Edmund Burke (1729–1797)

Burke founded modern Conservative thought in Britain, and has an important place in the intellectual history of Romanticism. He was raised in an atmosphere of religious tolerance – his father was a Protestant, his mother a Catholic. A native of Dublin, he was brought up as a Protestant and graduated from Trinity College (1747–8) before moving to London where he studied law at the Middle Temple in 1750. But he would never be called to the bar because literary work was always more to his taste than academic study.

He was only 19 when he composed one of his most influential and important works, *A Philosophical Enquiry into the Origin of our Ideas of the Sublime and Beautiful* (1757), which explores the nature of 'negative' pleasures – the mixed experience of pleasure and pain, attraction and terror. Its central innovation was to question the classical ideal of clarity, arguing that vagueness and obscurity were more evocative of the unknown and the infinite. Fear (a desirable sensation for Burke) is diminished by knowledge, but heightened by veiled intimations – something he demonstrates by citing Milton's description of Death, where 'all is dark, uncertain, confused, terrible and sublime to the last degree'. This was nothing less than a revolution in artistic and literary thought, and besides providing a licence for the popular cult of the Gothic would have a tremendous impact on the Romantic poets; see, for instance, Wordsworth's climbing of Snowdon (pp. 566–70), De Quincey's account of opium

Notes

To the River Lodon

[1] The River Loddon runs through Basingstoke, where Warton was born, and where his father was vicar and headmaster of the Grammar School.

[2] *Where first . . . begun* Warton lived in Basingstoke until 1744, when he matriculated at Trinity College, Oxford, and his earliest poems were composed there. His earliest known poem is *Birds Nesting in Dunsfold Orchard*, written when he was seven or eight.

[3] *muse's laurel* i.e. poetic fame. Warton was well established as a major poet by the time he became Professor of Poetry at Oxford in 1757.

addiction (pp. 812–18), Byron's *Childe Harold* Canto III (pp. 852–87) and Shelley's *Hymn to Intellectual Beauty* (pp. 1071–3).

In 1765 Burke was appointed secretary to the Marquis of Rockingham, then Prime Minister, entering Parliament in the same year as MP for Wendover. A Whig, he was not afraid to champion liberal causes. He favoured liberty of commerce and defended the rights of the colonies, especially America – a subject on which he published. He opposed the control exercised over Parliament by allies of George III; supported the cause of Irish Catholics; campaigned for the emancipation of British India and the abolition of the slave-trade. His efforts to halt slavery in British colonies won him the admiration and friendship of Hannah More and the Bluestockings. By this time he had acquired the reputation of an orator; it was said that 'he was the most eloquent man of his time: his wisdom was greater than his eloquence.'[1]

He was 60 by the time the Bastille fell in July 1789. The storming of Versailles in October, and Price's *Discourse* (see pp. 4–6) led him to compose *Reflections on the Revolution in France* (1790). The selections below include quintessential passages from it, including his lament for the age of chivalry and his paean to Marie Antoinette, 'glittering like the morning star, full of life and splendour and joy'. It is interesting to compare his view of her with that of Charlotte Smith in her poem, *The Emigrants* (see p. 100).

His Whig colleagues (particularly Charles James Fox) were horrified by his abandonment of liberal politics, and *Reflections* alienated him from them. In subsequent works, he would go further, advising the government to suppress free opinions at home. This apparent inconsistency can be explained by the fact that the American Revolution (which he supported) was, as he saw it, fought on behalf of traditional rights and liberties which the English government had infringed. The new French Revolution was intended to introduce a new order of things based on a bogus rationalistic philosophy. To him, it seemed that liberty was championed as a metaphysical abstraction; equality was contrary to nature and therefore impossible to achieve; while fraternity was so much 'cant and gibberish'.

Unlike Rousseau, Burke saw man as essentially evil. In his view society had to depend on safeguards which had stood the test of time; hence his support of Englishness, and his view that the English form of government, for all its faults, was divinely sanctioned. If this seems eccentric, it is worth remembering that the *Reflections* has remained an enduringly popular work. Priced at three shillings (the equivalent of £10 or US$18 today), it sold 30,000 copies in the first two years of publication. It was quickly translated into both French and German, and its arguments became common currency in ideological discourse of the 1790s. It was in response that Thomas Paine composed his manifesto for republicanism, *The Rights of Man* (1791–2).

At the time *Reflections* appeared, Wordsworth was (as he later recalled) 'hot' in the radical cause, and reacted with outrage, composing among other things a defence of regicide entitled 'A Letter to the Bishop of Llandaff', which fortunately for him was not published. (Had it been, it would have precipitated his arrest and imprisonment.) In later years he came to revise his judgement, valuing Burke for his achievement as a conservative philosopher, and he inserted a tribute to him in *The Prelude* (see p. 579). Though Coleridge seems not to have held Burke in particularly high regard, his later prose works, *Lay Sermons* (1816–17) and *On the Constitution of Church and State* (1830), were strongly influenced by him.

Notes

1 This phrase is quoted by Hazlitt in his 1807 essay on Burke, but no source has ever been traced.

Of all the Romantics, Hazlitt was perhaps one of the most openly admiring: Burke was one of his heroes, along with Rousseau. He loved him for his oratory and subtlety of thought, even if he did not always agree with what he said. 'I cannot help looking upon him as the chief boast and ornament of the English House of Commons', he wrote, adding that he was a 'man of clear understanding, of strong sense, and subtle reasoning'.[2]

Further reading

David Bromwich, *A Choice of Inheritance: Self and Community from Edmund Burke to Robert Frost* (Cambridge, Mass., 1989), chapter 3.

David Bromwich, 'Edmund Burke, *Reflections on the Revolution in France*', in *A Companion to Romanticism* ed. Duncan Wu (Oxford, 1998), pp. 113–21.

Tom Furniss, *Edmund Burke's Aesthetic Ideology: Language, Gender, and Political Economy in Revolution* (Cambridge, 1993).

William Hazlitt, 'Character of Mr Burke, 1807', *Political Essays* (1819).

Conor Cruise O'Brien, *The Great Melody: A Thematic Biography and Commented Anthology of Edmund Burke* (London, 1992).

Jane Stabler, *Burke to Byron, Barbauld to Baillie, 1790–1830* (Basingstoke, 2002), pp. 16–30.

Obscurity

From A Philosophical Enquiry into the Origins of our Ideas of the Sublime and Beautiful (1757)

To make anything very terrible,[1] obscurity seems in general to be necessary. When we know the full extent of any danger, when we can accustom our eyes to it, a great deal of the apprehension vanishes. Everyone will be sensible of this who considers how greatly night adds to our dread in all cases of danger, and how much the notions of ghosts and goblins (of which none can form clear ideas) affect minds, which give credit[2] to the popular tales concerning such sorts of beings.

Those despotic governments which are founded on the passions of men – and principally upon the passion of fear – keep their chief as much as may be from the public eye. The policy has been the same in many cases of religion; almost all the heathen temples were dark. Even in the barbarous temples of the Americans[3] at this day, they keep their idol in a dark part of the hut, which is consecrated to his worship. For this purpose too the druids performed all their ceremonies in the bosom of the darkest woods, and in the shade of the oldest and most spreading oaks.[4]

No person seems better to have understood the secret of heightening, or of setting terrible things (if I may use the expression) in their strongest light by the force of a judicious obscurity, than Milton. His description of Death in the second Book is admirably studied; it is astonishing with what a gloomy pomp, with what a significant and expressive uncertainty of strokes and colouring he has finished the portrait of the king of terrors.

Notes

[2] Wu iv 280–1. For more on Hazlitt's fascination with Burke, see David Bromwich, *Hazlitt: The Mind of a Critic* (New Haven, 1999).

OBSCURITY

[1] *terrible* terrifying.

[2] *credit* credibility.

[3] *the Americans* Red Indians.

[4] *For this purpose . . . spreading oaks* In the 18th century it was believed, erroneously, that druids performed human sacrifices in woods. They were frequently described doing so in antiquarian or poetic works.

The other shape
(If shape it might be called) that shape had none
Distinguishable in member, joint, or limb;
Or substance might be called that shadow seemed,
For each seemed either. Black he stood as night,
Fierce as ten furies, terrible as hell,
And shook a deadly dart. What seemed his head
The likeness of a kingly crown had on.
(*Paradise Lost* ii 666–73)

In this description all is dark, uncertain, confused, terrible and sublime to the last degree.

History will record . . . [1]

From Reflections on the Revolution in France (1790)

History will record that on the morning of the 6th of October 1789, the King and Queen of France, after a day of confusion, alarm, dismay, and slaughter, lay down, under the pledged security of public faith, to indulge nature in a few hours of respite, and troubled, melancholy repose. From this sleep the queen was first startled by the sentinel at her door, who cried out to her to save herself by flight – that this was the last proof of fidelity he could give – that they were upon him, and he was dead. Instantly he was cut down. A band of cruel ruffians and assassins, reeking with his blood, rushed into the chamber of the Queen and pierced with a hundred strokes of bayonets and poniards the bed, from whence this persecuted woman had but just time to fly almost naked and, through ways unknown to the murderers, had escaped to seek refuge at the feet of a King and husband not secure of his own life for a moment.

This King, to say no more of him, and this Queen, and their infant children (who once would have been the pride and hope of a great and generous people) were then forced to abandon the sanctuary of the most splendid palace in the world, which they left swimming in blood, polluted by massacre and strewed with scattered limbs and mutilated carcasses. Thence they were conducted into the capital of their kingdom.

Two had been selected from the unprovoked, unresisted, promiscuous slaughter, which was made of the gentlemen of birth and family who composed the king's bodyguard. These two gentlemen, with all the parade of an execution of justice, were cruelly and publicly dragged to the block and beheaded in the great court of the palace. Their heads were stuck upon spears and led the procession, whilst the royal captives who followed in the train were slowly moved along, amidst the horrid yells, and shrilling screams, and frantic dances, and infamous contumelies, and all the unutterable abominations of the furies of hell in the abused shape of the vilest of women. After they had been made to taste, drop by drop, more than the bitterness of death in the slow torture of a journey of twelve miles, protracted to six hours, they were, under a guard composed of those very soldiers who had thus conducted them through this famous triumph, lodged in one of the old palaces of Paris, now converted into a bastille for kings.[2]

Notes

History will Record

[1] This lurid account of what took place at Versailles, when a mob stormed the royal palace and escorted Louis XVI and Marie Antoinette to Paris, is vividly recounted by Burke.

[2] *one of the . . . for kings* the Tuileries.

Is this a triumph to be consecrated at altars? to be commemorated with grateful thanksgiving? to be offered to the divine humanity with fervent prayer and enthusiastic ejaculation? These Theban and Thracian orgies,[3] acted in France and applauded only in the Old Jewry,[4] I assure you, kindle prophetic enthusiasm in the minds but of very few people in this kingdom, although a saint and apostle, who may have revelations of his own and who has so completely vanquished all the mean superstitions of the heart, may incline to think it pious and decorous to compare it with the entrance into the world of the Prince of Peace, proclaimed in a holy temple by a venerable sage, and not long before not worse announced by the voice of angels to the quiet innocence of shepherds.

The age of chivalry is gone

From Reflections on the Revolution in France (1790)

I hear that the august person[1] who was the principal object of our preacher's triumph,[2] though he supported himself, felt much on that shameful occasion. As a man, it became him to feel for his wife and his children, and the faithful guards of his person that were massacred in cold blood about him; as a prince, it became him to feel for the strange and frightful transformation of his civilized subjects, and to be more grieved for them than solicitous for himself. It derogates little from his fortitude, while it adds infinitely to the honour of his humanity. I am very sorry to say it, very sorry indeed, that such personages are in a situation in which it is not unbecoming in us to praise the virtues of the great.

I hear, and I rejoice to hear, that the great lady,[3] the other object of the triumph, has borne that day (one is interested that beings made for suffering should suffer well), and that she bears all the succeeding days, that she bears the imprisonment of her husband, and her own captivity, and the exile of her friends, and the insulting adulation of addresses, and the whole weight of her accumulated wrongs, with a serene patience, in a manner suited to her rank and race, and becoming the offspring of a sovereign distinguished for her piety and her courage; that, like her, she has lofty sentiments; that she feels with the dignity of a Roman matron; that in the last extremity she will save herself from the last disgrace; and that, if she must fall, she will fall by no ignoble hand.

It is now sixteen or seventeen years[4] since I saw the Queen of France, then the dauphiness,[5] at Versailles, and surely never lighted on this orb, which she hardly seemed to touch, a more delightful vision. I saw her just above the horizon, decorating and cheering the elevated sphere she just began to move in – glittering like the morning star, full of life and splendour and joy. Oh what a revolution! and what a heart must I have to contemplate without emotion that elevation and that fall! Little did I dream when she added titles of veneration to those of enthusiastic, distant, respectful love, that she should ever be obliged to carry the sharp antidote against disgrace concealed in that bosom; little did I dream that I should have lived to see such

Notes

[3] *Theban and Thracian orgies* Thebes, the principal city of Boeotia, was associated in Greek legend with Dionysiac orgies, which were commonly believed to have been imported from Thrace. The orgiastic rites of Cotys were also introduced to Athens from Thrace.

[4] *applauded only in the Old Jewry* where Richard Price delivered his sermon and discourse.

THE AGE OF CHIVALRY IS GONE

[1] *the august person* Louis XVI.

[2] *our preacher's triumph* a tart reference to Richard Price's discourse.

[3] *the great lady* Marie Antoinette.

[4] *sixteen or seventeen years* Burke visited France in 1773.

[5] *dauphiness* wife of the dauphin (eldest son of the King of France).

disasters fallen upon her in a nation of gallant men, in a nation of men of honour and of cavaliers. I thought ten thousand swords must have leaped from their scabbards to avenge even a look that threatened her with insult. But the age of chivalry is gone.

That of sophisters,[6] economists, and calculators[7] has succeeded; and the glory of Europe is extinguished forever. Never, never more shall we behold that generous loyalty to rank and sex, that proud submission, that dignified obedience, that subordination of the heart which kept alive, even in servitude itself, the spirit of an exalted freedom. The unbought grace of life, the cheap defence of nations, the nurse of manly sentiment and heroic enterprise, is gone! It is gone, that sensibility of principle, that chastity of honour which felt a stain like a wound, which inspired courage whilst it mitigated ferocity, which ennobled whatever it touched, and under which vice itself lost half its evil by losing all its grossness.

This mixed system of opinion and sentiment had its origin in the ancient chivalry; and the principle, though varied in its appearance by the varying state of human affairs, subsisted and influenced through a long succession of generations even to the time we live in. If it should ever be totally extinguished, the loss I fear will be great. It is this which has given its character to modern Europe. It is this which has distinguished it under all its forms of government, and distinguished it to its advantage, from the states of Asia and possibly from those states which flourished in the most brilliant periods of the antique world.[8] It was this which, without confounding ranks, had produced a noble equality and handed it down through all the gradations of social life. It was this opinion which mitigated kings into companions and raised private men to be fellows with kings. Without force or opposition, it subdued the fierceness of pride and power, it obliged sovereigns to submit to the soft collar of social esteem, compelled stern authority to submit to elegance, and gave a domination, vanquisher of laws, to be subdued by manners.

But now all is to be changed. All the pleasing illusions which made power gentle and obedience liberal, which harmonized the different shades of life, and which, by a bland assimilation, incorporated into politics the sentiments which beautify and soften private society, are to be dissolved by this new conquering empire of light and reason. All the decent drapery of life is to be rudely torn off. All the super-added ideas, furnished from the wardrobe of a moral imagination, which the heart owns and the understanding ratifies as necessary to cover the defects of our naked, shivering nature, and to raise it to dignity in our own estimation, are to be exploded as a ridiculous, absurd, and antiquated fashion.

On this scheme of things, a king is but a man, a queen is but a woman; a woman is but an animal, and an animal not of the highest order. All homage paid to the sex in general as such, and without distinct views, is to be regarded as romance and folly. Regicide, and parricide,[9] and sacrilege are but fictions of superstition, corrupting jurisprudence[10] by destroying its simplicity. The murder of a king, or a queen, or a bishop, or a father are only common homicide; and if the people are by any chance or in any way gainers by it, a sort of homicide much the most pardonable, and into which we ought not to make too severe a scrutiny . . .

We are but too apt to consider things in the state in which we find them, without sufficiently adverting to the causes by which they have been produced and possibly may be upheld. Nothing is more certain than that our manners, our civilization, and

Notes

[6] *sophisters* specious philosophers (such as Rousseau).

[7] *calculators* mathematicians.

[8] *the antique world* Burke looks back to Ancient Greece and Rome.

[9] *parricide* murder of one's ruler.

[10] *jurisprudence* the legal system.

all the good things which are connected with manners and with civilization have, in this European world of ours, depended for ages upon two principles and were, indeed, the result of both combined: I mean the spirit of a gentleman and the spirit of religion. The nobility and the clergy, the one by profession, the other by patronage, kept learning in existence, even in the midst of arms and confusions, and whilst governments were rather in their causes than formed. Learning paid back what it received to nobility and to priesthood, and paid it with usury, by enlarging their ideas and by furnishing their minds. Happy if they had all continued to know their indissoluble union and their proper place! Happy if learning, not debauched by ambition, had been satisfied to continue the instructor, and not aspired to be the master! Along with its natural protectors and guardians, learning will be cast into the mire and trodden down under the hoofs of a swinish multitude.[11]

On Englishness

From Reflections on the Revolution in France (1790)

I almost venture to affirm that not one in a hundred amongst us participates in the 'triumph' of the Revolution Society.[1] If the King and Queen of France and their children were to fall into our hands by the chance of war in the most acrimonious of all hostilities (I deprecate such an event, I deprecate such hostility), they would be treated with another sort of triumphal entry into London. We formerly have had a king of France in that situation;[2] you have read how he was treated by the victor in the field, and in what manner he was afterwards received in England. Four hundred years have gone over us, but I believe we are not materially changed since that period.

Thanks to our sullen resistance to innovation, thanks to the cold sluggishness of our national character, we still bear the stamp of our forefathers. We have not (as I conceive) lost the generosity and dignity of thinking of the fourteenth century, nor as yet have we subtilized[3] ourselves into savages.[4] We are not the converts of Rousseau; we are not the disciples of Voltaire; Helvetius has made no progress amongst us.[5] Atheists are not our preachers; madmen are not our lawgivers. We know that *we* have made no discoveries, and we think that no discoveries are to be made in morality – nor many in the great principles of government, nor in the ideas of liberty which were understood long before we were born, altogether as well as they will be after the grave has heaped its mould upon our presumption, and the silent tomb shall have imposed its law on our pert loquacity.[6]

Notes

[11] *the hoofs of a swinish multitude* This was a particularly inflammatory remark, the inspiration of many angry responses in satirical pamphlets and periodicals. Thomas Spence called one of his periodicals *Pig's Meat or Lessons for the Swinish Multitude*, each bearing a frontispiece showing a pig trampling on the orb and sceptre.

On Englishness

[1] *the 'triumph' of the Revolution Society* Richard Price delivered his *Discourse* to the London Revolution Society on 4 November 1789 (see pp. 4–6).

[2] *We formerly have had . . . situation* John II of France, captured by the Black Prince at the Battle of Poitiers in 1356, died in captivity, London, 1364.

[3] *subtilized* refined.

[4] *savages* Jean-Jacques Rousseau (1712–78) had written in praise of primitive man for living according to innate need, unspoilt by the inequality and over-refinement found in 'civilized' societies.

[5] The writings of Rousseau, François-Marie Arouet de Voltaire (1694–78), and Claude-Adrien Helvétius (1715–71) strongly influenced revolutionary thought and action in the eighteenth century.

[6] *pert loquacity* impudent chatter.

In England we have not yet been completely embowelled of our natural entrails; we still feel within us, and we cherish and cultivate, those inbred sentiments[7] which are the faithful guardians, the active monitors[8] of our duty, the true supporters of all liberal and manly[9] morals. We have not been drawn and trussed[10] in order that we may be filled, like stuffed birds in a museum, with chaff and rags and paltry blurred shreds of paper about the rights of man. We preserve the whole of our feelings still native and entire, unsophisticated[11] by pedantry and infidelity. We have real hearts of flesh and blood beating in our bosoms. We fear God. We look up with awe to kings, with affection to parliaments, with duty to magistrates, with reverence to priests, and with respect to nobility. Why? Because when such ideas are brought before our minds, it is *natural* to be so affected; because all other feelings are false and spurious, and tend to corrupt our minds, to vitiate our primary morals, to render us unfit for rational liberty, and (by teaching us a servile, licentious, and abandoned insolence) to be our low sport for a few holidays, to make us perfectly fit for, and justly deserving of slavery, through the whole course of our lives.

You see, sir,[12] that in this enlightened age I am bold enough to confess that we are generally men of untaught[13] feelings, that instead of casting away all our old prejudices, we cherish them to a very considerable degree and, to take more shame to ourselves, we cherish them because they *are* prejudices. And the longer they have lasted, and the more generally they have prevailed, the more we cherish them.

We are afraid to put men to live and trade each on his own private stock of reason,[14] because we suspect that this stock in each man is small, and that the individuals would do better to avail themselves of the general bank and capital of nations and of ages. Many of our men of speculation,[15] instead of exploding general prejudices, employ their sagacity to discover the latent wisdom which prevails in them. If they find what they seek (and they seldom fail), they think it more wise to continue the prejudice, with the reason involved, than to cast away the coat of prejudice, and to leave nothing but the naked reason – because prejudice, with its reason, has a motive to give action to that reason, and an affection which will give it permanence. Prejudice is of ready application in the emergency; it previously engages the mind in a steady course of wisdom and virtue, and does not leave the man hesitating in the moment of decision – sceptical, puzzled and unresolved. Prejudice renders a man's virtue his habit, and not a series of unconnected acts. Through just prejudice, his duty becomes a part of his nature.

Society is a Contract

From Reflections on the Revolution in France (1790)

Society is indeed a contract.[1] Subordinate contracts for objects of mere occasional interest may be dissolved at pleasure, but the state ought not to be considered as

Notes

7 *inbred sentiments* innate feelings.
8 *monitors* reminders.
9 *manly* humane.
10 *drawn and trussed* After disembowelling (drawing) a bird, its wings were pinned to its sides with skewers (trussing).
11 *unsophisticated* uncontaminated.
12 *sir* Richard Price.
13 *untaught* natural, spontaneous.
14 *reason* Radicals placed their faith in the redemptive power of reason; the culmination of that argument would be Godwin's *Political Justice* (see pp. 153–5).
15 *speculation* intelligence, wisdom.

Society is a Contract
1 *Society is indeed a contract* In his *Contrat social* (1762), Rousseau had argued that genuine political society could only be formed through a social pact, or free association of intelligent human beings who choose the kind of government to which they will owe allegiance. Burke invokes Rousseau's notion so as to revise it.

nothing better than a partnership agreement in a trade of pepper and coffee, calico or tobacco, or some other such low concern, to be taken up for a little temporary interest, and to be dissolved by the fancy of the parties. It is to be looked on with other reverence because it is not a partnership in things subservient only to the gross animal existence of a temporary and perishable nature.

It is a partnership in all science,[2] a partnership in all art,[3] a partnership in every virtue and in all perfection. As the ends[4] of such a partnership cannot be obtained in many generations,[5] it becomes a partnership not only between those who are living, but between those who are living, those who are dead, and those who are to be born. Each contract of each particular state is but a clause in the great primeval contract of eternal society, linking the lower with the higher natures, connecting the visible and invisible world[6] according to a fixed compact sanctioned by the inviolable oath which holds all physical and all moral natures each in their appointed place. This law is not subject to the will of those who, by an obligation above them and infinitely superior, are bound to submit their will to that law. The municipal corporations of that universal kingdom[7] are not morally at liberty at their pleasure, and on their speculations of a contingent improvement wholly to separate and tear asunder the bands of their subordinate community, and to dissolve it into an unsocial, uncivil, unconnected chaos of elementary principles.

It is the first and supreme necessity only, a necessity that is not chosen but chooses, a necessity paramount to deliberation, that admits no discussion and demands no evidence, which alone can justify a resort to anarchy. This necessity is no exception to the rule because this necessity itself is a part too of that moral and physical disposition of things to which man must be obedient by consent or force. But if that which is only submission to necessity should be made the object of choice, the law is broken, nature is disobeyed, and the rebellious are outlawed, cast forth, and exiled from this world[8] of reason, and order, and peace, and virtue, and fruitful penitence, into the antagonist world of madness, discord, vice, confusion, and unavailing sorrow.

These, my dear sir, are, were, and I think long will be the sentiments of not the least learned and reflecting part of this kingdom. They who are included in this description form their opinions on such grounds as such persons ought to form them; the less enquiring receive them from an authority which those whom providence dooms to live on trust need not be ashamed to rely on. These two sorts of men move in the same direction, though in a different place. They both move with the order of the universe. They all know or feel this great ancient truth: 'Quod illi principi et praepotenti deo qui omnem hunc mundum regit, nihil eorum quae quidem fiant in terris acceptius quam concilia et caetus hominum jure sociati quae civitates appellantur.'[9] They take this tenet of the head and heart not from the great name which it immediately bears, nor from the greater from whence it is derived, but from that which alone can give true weight and sanction to any learned opinion: the common nature and common relation of men.

Notes

[2] *science* knowledge.

[3] *art* skill.

[4] *ends* aims, objectives.

[5] *in many generations* i.e. it takes many generations.

[6] *the visible and invisible world* i.e. earth and heaven.

[7] *The municipal corporations of that universal kingdom* i.e. the universe (heaven as well as earth).

[8] *nature is disobeyed . . . world* Burke's parallel is with Adam and Eve, cast out of Eden for eating the fruit of the tree of knowledge.

[9] 'To the great and all-powerful God who rules this entire universe, nothing is more pleasing than the unions and gatherings of men bound together by laws that are called states' (Cicero, *Dream of Scipio* III 5 [13]).

Persuaded that all things ought to be done with reference, and referring all to the point of reference to which all should be directed,[10] they think themselves bound (not only as individuals in the sanctuary of the heart, or as congregated in that personal capacity) to renew the memory of their high origin and caste; but also in their corporate character to perform their national homage to the institutor and author and protector of civil society, without which civil society man could not by any possibility arrive at the perfection of which his nature is capable, nor even make a remote and faint approach to it.

They conceive that He who gave our nature to be perfected by our virtue willed also the necessary means of its perfection. He willed therefore the state; He willed its connection with the source and original archetype of all perfection. They who are convinced of this His will (which is the law of laws and the sovereign of sovereigns) cannot think it reprehensible that this our corporate fealty and homage, that this our recognition of a signiory paramount[11] (I had almost said this oblation[12] of the state itself), as a worthy offering on the high altar of universal praise, should be performed as all public solemn acts are performed – in buildings, in music, in decoration, in speech, in the dignity of persons, according to the customs of mankind, taught by their nature; that is, with modest splendour, with unassuming state, with mild majesty and sober pomp.

For those purposes they think some part of the wealth of the country is as usefully employed as it can be, in fomenting[13] the luxury of individuals. It is the public ornament; it is the public consolation; it nourishes the public hope. The poorest man finds his own importance and dignity in it, whilst the wealth and pride of individuals at every moment makes the man of humble rank and fortune sensible of his inferiority, and degrades and vilifies his condition. It is for the man in humble life – and to raise his nature, and to put him in mind of a state[14] in which the privileges of opulence will cease, when he will be equal by nature, and may be more than equal by virtue – that this portion of the general wealth of his country is employed and sanctified.

I assure you I do not aim at singularity.[15] I give you opinions which have been accepted amongst us from very early times to this moment, with a continued and general approbation, and which indeed are so worked into my mind that I am unable to distinguish what I have learned from others from the results of my own meditation.

William Cowper (1731–1800)

The loss of his mother when he was 6, and persecution by an older boy at school, led to a mental imbalance from which Cowper (pronounced 'Cooper') was to suffer for the rest of his life. For a while in early manhood he was set for a successful career as a lawyer or politician, but though called to the bar in 1754, he made no attempt to practise. His tendency to depression was exacerbated when his father forbade him to marry Theodora Cowper, his cousin. When he was

Notes

[10] *the point of reference to which all should be directed* God.
[11] *signiory paramount* executive authority.
[12] *oblation* devotional offering.
[13] *fomenting* encouraging.
[14] *a state* heaven.
[15] *singularity* eccentricity.

32, a well-meaning uncle nominated him for the job of Clerk of Journals of the House of Lords, but the prospect of a formal examination for the post led to near-suicide.

After a religious conversion while at Dr Cotton's St Albans asylum in 1765, he lived in retirement in rural Huntingdon, where he befriended Morley Unwin, a retired evangelical clergyman, and his wife Mary. After Unwin's death in 1767 Cowper moved to Olney in Buckinghamshire with Mrs Unwin and her children, where he came under the influence of the former slave-trader turned evangelical pastor John Newton.[1] An abortive engagement to Mrs Unwin led to another bout of depression in 1773 (not helped by his association with Newton), which now entailed the belief that he was eternally damned.

Composed in the ornate couplet style favoured by Pope's successors, a good deal of Cowper's poetry now sounds very much of its time, but *The Task* (1785) is a different matter. Originally conceived as a sort of a joke, when a friend suggested he write a mock-heroic poem in blank verse on the subject of 'the sofa', it grew into an extended blank verse meditation on all manner of subjects close to Cowper's heart, such as the virtues of a rural existence and the evils of the education system. He explained its purpose as being 'to discountenance the modern enthusiasm after a London life, and to recommend rural ease and leisure as friendly to piety and virtue'. One important factor that made this poem of six books and 5,000 lines innovatory was its unabashed preoccupation with the self.

'The Winter Evening' was one of the first celebrations in verse of 'The mind contemplative'. Distinguished by a refusal to make the kind of claims to which the Romantics would be prone (his is 'a soul that does not always think'), Cowper provides a setting, a state of mind, and an account of the fancy that are reworked in Coleridge's *Frost at Midnight* (pp. 624–9). Crazy Kate from *The Task* Book I is the archetype for madwomen in Romantic poetry, including Southey's Hannah (pp. 724–5) and Margaret in Wordsworth's *The Ruined Cottage* (pp. 422–35).

Cowper was deeply troubled by slavery – a hot issue towards the end of the eighteenth century, when the abolitionist campaign was gaining widespread support, including that of MPs on both sides in the House of Commons. At first he resisted the idea of writing poems on the subject, but after repeated requests from friends in the movement wrote a series of ballads designed for a popular audience of which 'Sweet Meat has Sour Sauce' is the most successful. Written in the persona of the captain of a slave ship, it is inspired by a particular set of circumstances. On 21 May 1788 the House of Commons passed a Bill proposed by Sir William Dolben, MP for the University of Oxford. It aimed to restrict the number of slaves who could be transported from Africa to British colonies in the West Indies. Five days later, merchants and inhabitants of Liverpool presented a petition to the House, complaining that the Bill would put them out of business. They were supported by MPs with slave-owning interests. Fortunately, the Bill was passed in both Houses: the move towards abolition had begun. Cowper's detestation of slavery was shared by Hannah More, Anna Laetitia Barbauld and Ann Yearsley.

In the same year that he published *The Task* Cowper began to translate Homer, starting with a blank verse rendering of *The Iliad* (1791). But after Mary Unwin's death in 1794 he became a mental and physical invalid, and remained so until his death. (See Plate 4 for a portrait of Cowper aged 61.)

Notes

[1] For more on this interesting character, see Bernard Martin, *John Newton: A Biography* (London, 1950).

Further reading

Vincent Newey, *Cowper's Poetry: A Critical Study and Reassessment* (Liverpool, 1982).

Martin Priestman, *Cowper's* Task: *Structure and Influence* (Cambridge, 1983).

[*Crazy Kate*]

From The Task (1785) (Book I)

There often wanders one whom better days
Saw better clad, in cloak of satin trimmed
With lace, and hat with splendid ribbon bound.
A serving-maid was she, and fell in love
With one who left her, went to sea, and died.
Her fancy followed him through foaming waves
To distant shores, and she would sit and weep
At what a sailor suffers; fancy too
(Delusive most where warmest wishes are)
Would oft anticipate his glad return
And dream of transports[1] she was not to know.
She heard the doleful tidings of his death
And never smiled again. And now she roams
The dreary waste, there spends the livelong day,
And there, unless when Charity forbids,[2]
The livelong night. A tattered apron hides,
Worn as a cloak, and hardly hides a gown
More tattered still, and both but ill conceal
A bosom heaved with never-ceasing sighs.
She begs an idle pin of all she meets
And hoards them in her sleeve, but needful food,
Though pressed with hunger oft, or comelier clothes,
Though pinched with cold, asks never. Kate is crazed.

[*On Slavery*]

From The Task (1785) (Book II)

Oh for a lodge in some vast wilderness,
Some boundless contiguity[1] of shade,
Where rumour of oppression and deceit,
Of unsuccessful or successful war
Might never reach me more! My ear is pained,
My soul is sick with ev'ry day's report

Notes

CRAZY KATE

[1] *transports* pleasures.

[2] *unless . . . forbids* Charity (in the form of a householder) might save Kate from wandering at night and provide her with accommodation.

ON SLAVERY

[1] *contiguity* proximity.

Of wrong and outrage with which earth is filled.
There is no flesh in man's obdurate heart –
It does not feel for man. The nat'ral bond
Of brotherhood is fevered as the flax
That falls asunder at the touch of fire.
He finds his fellow guilty of a skin
Not coloured like his own, and having pow'r
T' enforce the wrong, for such a worthy cause[2]
Dooms and devotes[3] him as his lawful prey.
Lands intersected by a narrow frith[4]
Abhor each other. Mountains interposed
Make enemies of nations who had else
Like kindred drops been mingled into one.
Thus man devotes his brother, and destroys;
And worse than all, and most to be deplored
As human nature's broadest, foulest blot,
Chains him, and tasks him, and exacts his sweat
With stripes that Mercy with a bleeding heart
Weeps when she sees inflicted on a beast.
  Then what is man? And what man seeing this,
And having human feelings, does not blush
And hang his head to think himself a man?
I would not have a slave to till my ground,
To carry me, to fan me while I sleep
And tremble when I wake, for all the wealth
That sinews bought and sold have ever earned.
No, dear as freedom is, and in my heart's
Just estimation prized above all price,
I had much rather be myself the slave
And wear the bonds, than fasten them on him.
We have no slaves at home – then why abroad?
And they themselves, once ferried o'er the wave
That parts us, are emancipate and loosed.[5]
Slaves cannot breathe in England; if their lungs
Receive our air, that moment they are free,
They touch our country and their shackles fall.
That's noble, and bespeaks a nation proud
And jealous of the blessing. Spread it then,
And let it circulate through ev'ry vein
Of all your Empire, that where Britain's power
Is felt, mankind may feel her mercy too.

Notes

[2] *a worthy cause* ironic; the cause is completely unworthy.

[3] *devotes* condemns.

[4] *frith* estuary – perhaps a reference to the English Channel.

[5] *And they . . . loosed* At the trial of the slave James Somerset in 1772 it was deemed that 'as soon as any slave sets his foot upon English territory, he becomes free.' This meant that a former slave who arrived in England could not be forcibly removed and returned to slavery elsewhere, and it was seen by many as a step towards complete abolition.

[*The Winter Evening*]

From The Task (Book IV)

Just when our drawing-rooms begin to blaze
With lights by clear reflection multiplied
From many a mirror (in which he of Gath,
Goliath,[1] might have seen his giant bulk
Whole without stooping, tow'ring crest and all),
My pleasures too begin. But me perhaps
The glowing hearth may satisfy awhile
With faint illumination that uplifts
The shadow to the ceiling, there by fits
Dancing uncouthly[2] to the quiv'ring flame.
  Not undelightful[3] is an hour to me
So spent in parlour twilight; such a gloom
Suits well the thoughtful or unthinking mind,
The mind contemplative, with some new theme
Pregnant,[4] or indisposed alike to all.
Laugh ye, who boast your more mercurial pow'rs
That never feel a stupor, know no pause
Nor need one. I am conscious, and confess
Fearless, a soul that does not always think.
Me oft has fancy ludicrous and wild
Soothed with a waking dream of houses, tow'rs,
Trees, churches, and strange visages expressed
In the red cinders, while with poring eye
I gazed, myself creating what I saw.
Nor less amused have I quiescent watched
The sooty films that play upon the bars –
Pendulous, and foreboding in the view
Of superstition, prophesying still,
Though still deceived, some stranger's near approach.[5]
  'Tis thus the understanding takes repose
In indolent vacuity of thought,
And sleeps and is refreshed. Meanwhile the face
Conceals the mood lethargic with a mask
Of deep deliberation, as[6] the man
Were tasked to his full strength, absorbed and lost.
Thus oft reclined at ease, I lose an hour
At evening, till at length the freezing blast

Notes

THE WINTER EVENING

[1] *he of Gath, / Goliath* The story of how young David slew the giant Goliath is told at 1 Samuel 17.

[2] *uncouthly* strangely.

[3] *Not undelightful* The double negative (see also line 317) is symptomatic of Cowper's relaxed manner and was used also by Wordsworth; see for instance 'Not useless do I deem' (pp. 444–7).

[4] *pregnant* inspired. The usage is Miltonic, recalling *Paradise Lost* Book I, where the Holy Spirit 'Dovelike satst brooding on the vast abyss / And mad'st it pregnant' (ll. 21–2).

[5] Cowper alludes to the belief that the films of soot that form on the bars of log fires portend the arrival of an unexpected guest – which Coleridge's *Frost at Midnight* also recalls (see p. 624n3).

[6] *as* i.e. as if.

That sweeps[7] the bolted shutter summons home
The recollected powers and, snapping short
The glassy threads with which the fancy weaves
Her brittle toys, restores me to myself.
How calm is my recess, and how the frost
Raging abroad, and the rough wind, endear
The silence and the warmth enjoyed within.
  I saw the woods and fields at close of day,
A variegated show; the meadows green
Though faded, and the lands where lately waved
The golden harvest, of a mellow brown,
Upturned so lately by the forceful share.[8]
I saw far off the weedy fallows[9] smile
With verdure not unprofitable, grazed
By flocks fast-feeding and selecting each
His fav'rite herb; while all the leafless groves
That skirt th' horizon wore a sable hue
Scarce noticed in the kindred dusk of eve.
Tomorrow brings a change, a total change
Which even now – though silently performed,[10]
And slowly, and by most unfelt – the face
Of universal nature undergoes.
  Fast falls a fleecy show'r. The downy flakes
Descending, and with never-ceasing lapse
Softly alighting upon all below,
Assimilate all objects. Earth receives
Gladly the thick'ning mantle, and the green
And tender blade that feared the chilling blast
Escapes unhurt beneath so warm a veil.

Sweet Meat has Sour Sauce, or The Slave-Trader in the Dumps (composed 1788)[1]

From Works ed. Robert Southey (15 vols, 1835–7)

A trader I am to the African shore,
But since that my trading is like to be o'er,
I'll sing you a song that you ne'er heard before,
    Which nobody can deny, deny,
    Which nobody can deny.

Notes

[7] *sweeps* sweeps [across].
[8] *share* ploughshare.
[9] *weedy fallows* fields lying fallow, full of weeds.
[10] *silently performed* The starting-point for Coleridge's *Frost at Midnight*: 'The frost performs its secret ministry / Unhelped by any wind.'

SWEET MEAT HAS SOUR SAUCE
[1] For the circumstances that inspired this poem, see headnote p. 17.

When I first heard the news it gave me a shock,
Much like what they call an electrical knock,
And now I am going to sell off my stock,
Which nobody can deny.

'Tis a curious assortment of dainty regales,[2]
To tickle the Negroes with when the ship sails –
Fine chains for the neck, and a cat with nine tails,
Which nobody can deny.

Here's supple-jack plenty, and store of rattan[3]
That will wind itself round the sides of a man
As close as a hoop round a bucket or can,
Which nobody can deny.

Here's padlocks and bolts, and screws for the thumbs
That squeeze them so lovingly till the blood comes;
They sweeten the temper like comfits[4] or plums,
Which nobody can deny.

When a Negro his head from his victuals withdraws
And clenches his teeth and thrusts out his paws,
Here's a notable engine to open his jaws,[5]
Which nobody can deny.

Thus going to market, we kindly prepare
A pretty black cargo of African ware,
For what they must meet with when they get there,
Which nobody can deny.

'Twould do your heart good to see 'em below
Lie flat on their backs all the way as we go,
Like sprats[6] on a gridiron, scores in a row,[7]
Which nobody can deny.

But ah! if in vain I have studied an art
So gainful to me, all boasting apart,
I think it will break my compassionate heart,
Which nobody can deny.

For oh, how it enters my soul like an awl;[8]
This pity, which some people self-pity call,
Is sure the most heart-piercing pity of all,
Which nobody can deny.

So this is my song, as I told you before;
Come buy off my stock, for I must no more
Carry Caesars and Pompeys[9] to sugar-cane shore,
Which nobody can deny, deny,
Which nobody can deny.

Notes

[2] *dainty regales* choice gifts (ironic).

[3] *Here's supple-jack plenty . . . rattan* Canes, switches and ropes were made out of supple-jack (stems of creeping or twining shrubs found in the West Indies) and rattan.

[4] *comfits* sweetmeat made of some fruit, root, etc., preserved with sugar.

[5] *to open his jaws* clamp designed to open the mouths of lockjaw sufferers, used for force-feeding slaves who attempted to starve themselves to death.

[6] *sprats* small sea-fish.

[7] *scores in a row* Plans showing how slaves were crammed into slave-ships were a powerful weapon in the abolitionist campaign. Hannah More carried one with her, showing it to horrified guests at dinner parties.

[8] *awl* small tool for making holes in leather.

[9] *Caesars and Pompeys* Slaves were often named after Roman rulers.

Thomas Paine (1737–1809)

Writer, deist and American revolutionary leader, Tom Paine was one of the foremost political thinkers of his time. A former corset-maker and customs officer, he emigrated to America at the age of 37 in 1774 to be swept up in what was to become the American War of Independence. Two years later he published *Common Sense*, the first appeal for independence, to popular acclaim, selling 120,000 copies within three months. His forthright account of British government as a 'monarchical tyranny' marked him out as a republican: 'it is the pride of kings which throws mankind into confusion,' he wrote.

After America's victory, he returned briefly to England (May–September 1789), and went from there to France, where he became an associate of Thomas Jefferson and member of the Lafayette circle. Burke having published *Reflections on the Revolution in France* in 1790, Paine composed what was to be one of the most effective responses to it, *The Rights of Man* (1791–2). Beginning with the idea that good government is founded on reason, Paine argued that democracy – a society in which all men have equal rights and in which leadership depends on talent and wisdom – is better than aristocracy. In the course of his argument he demonstrates that a hereditary monarchy is prone to 'ignorance and incapacity'; establishes republicanism as the only logical and fair method of government; champions the American experience on the grounds that 'the nation, through its constitution, controls the whole government'; and proposes the institution of welfare support for the elderly, sick and impoverished.

The Rights of Man is a passionate argument for humane, fair and democratic government, but it is hard not to be struck by how much remains controversial within a British context. If that is so now, it must have seemed rebarbative to Pitt's increasingly repressive government, particularly given its immediate popularity: it sold 200,000 copies in 1791–3, many in cheap editions designed for working people. Not surprisingly, the government banned *The Rights of Man* in September 1792 and issued an order for Paine's arrest. He narrowly escaped and fled to Paris; he was charged with sedition in his absence and sentenced to death in December – a sentence that would have been carried out had he returned.

Already a member of the National Assembly, he took an active part in the governmental affairs of France. Significantly, he voted against the execution of Louis in January 1793, an act that earned him no friends among those responsible for the Reign of Terror that summer. In December he was imprisoned in the Luxembourg gaol to await execution, where his health declined. Eluding the guillotine by chance, he was released in November 1794 and remained in France for several years before returning to America in 1802. He died at his home in New Rochelle in 1809 from a fever contracted in prison; the whereabouts of his remains are unknown.

Paine's prose, written with a clarity and conviction that surpasses anything to be found in the work of his contemporaries, rings out as an articulate and well-reasoned defence of republicanism. In 'Freedom of Posterity' he refutes Burke's argument that the English are bound to the constitutional monarchy established by their forefathers at the time of the Glorious Revolution of 1688. 'On Revolution' argues that a revolution is needed to abolish 'Monarchical sovereignty' and shift power to the hands of the people. 'Republicanism' argues for what Paine felt to be the only system 'established and conducted for the interest of the public'.

Further reading

Thomas Paine, *Common Sense* ed. Isaac Kramnick (2nd edn, Harmondsworth, 1976).

Thomas Paine, *Rights of Man* introduced by Eric Foner (Harmondsworth, 1984).

The Thomas Paine Reader ed. Michael Foot and Isaac Kramnick (Harmondsworth, 1987).

Of the Origin and Design of Government in General

From Common Sense (Philadelphia, 1776)

Some writers have so confounded[1] society with government as to leave little or no distinction between them – whereas they are not only different, but have different origins. Society is produced by our wants, and government by our wickedness; the former promotes our happiness positively by uniting our affections, the latter negatively by restraining our vices. The one encourages intercourse, the other creates distinctions.[2] The first is a patron, the last a punisher.

Society in every state is a blessing, but government even in its best state is but a necessary evil – in its worst state an intolerable one. For when we suffer, or are exposed to the same miseries by a government which we expect in a country without government, our calamity is heightened by reflecting that we furnish the means by which we suffer.

Government, like dress, is the badge of lost innocence; the palaces of kings are built on the ruins of the bowers of paradise.[3] For were the impulses of conscience clear, uniform, and irresistibly obeyed, man would need no other lawgiver. But that not being the case, he finds it necessary to surrender up a part of his property[4] to furnish means for the protection of the rest – and this he is induced to do by the same prudence which in every other case advises him out of two evils to choose the least. Wherefore, security being the true design and end of government, it unanswerably follows that whatever form thereof appears most likely to ensure it to us, with the least expense and greatest benefit, is preferable to all others.

[*Freedom of Posterity*]

From The Rights of Man Part I (1791)

The English Parliament of 1688 did a certain thing[1] which, for themselves and their constituents, they had a right to do, and which it appeared right should be done. But, in addition to this right (which they possessed by delegation), they set up another right by assumption: that of binding and controlling posterity to the end of time. The case, therefore, divides itself into two parts – the right which they possessed by delegation, and the right which they set up by assumption. The first is admitted but with respect to the second I reply:

There never did, there never will, and there never can, exist a parliament, or any description of men, or any generation of men, in any country, possessed of the right or the power of binding and controlling posterity to the 'end of time', or of commanding for ever how the world shall be governed, or who shall govern it. And therefore all such clauses, acts or declarations by which the makers of them attempt to do what they have neither the right nor the power to do – nor the power to execute – are in

Notes

GOVERNMENT IN GENERAL

[1] *confounded* confused.

[2] *The one . . . distinctions* Society encourages social intercourse; government promotes the social hierarchy.

[3] *the palaces of kings . . . paradise* an idea deriving from Rousseau's concept of the noble savage, outlined in his *Discourse on Inequality*.

[4] *surrender up a part of his property* in taxes – one cause of the American Revolution.

FREEDOM OF POSTERITY

[1] *a certain thing* i.e. replace the Catholic James II with the Protestant William of Orange. The Glorious Revolution was seen by English radicals as the forerunner of the revolutions in America and, subsequently, France.

themselves null and void. Every age and generation must be as free to act for itself, in all cases, as the ages and generations which preceded it.

The vanity and presumption of governing beyond the grave is the most ridiculous and insolent of all tyrannies. Man has no property in man, neither has any generation a property in the generations which are to follow. The parliament or the people of 1688, or of any other period, had no more right to dispose of the people of the present day, or to bind or to control them *in any shape whatever,* than the parliament or the people of the present day have to dispose of, bind or control those who are to live a hundred or a thousand years hence. Every generation is and must be competent to all the purposes which its occasions require. It is the living, and not the dead, that are to be accommodated. When man ceases to be, his power and his wants cease with him, and having no longer any participation in the concerns of this world, he has no longer any authority in directing who shall be its governors, or how its government shall be organized, or how administered.

[*On Revolution*]

From The Rights of Man Part I (1791)

When we survey the wretched condition of man under the monarchical and hereditary systems of government, dragged from his home by one power, or driven by another, and impoverished by taxes more than by enemies, it becomes evident that those systems are bad, and that a general revolution in the principle and construction of governments is necessary.

What is government more than the management of the affairs of a nation? It is not, and from its nature cannot be, the property of any particular man or family, but of the whole community at whose expense it is supported. And though by force or contrivance it has been usurped into an inheritance, the usurpation cannot alter the right of things. Sovereignty, as a matter of right, appertains to the nation only, and not to any individual; and a nation has at all times an inherent indefeasible[1] right to abolish any form of government it finds inconvenient, and establish such as accords with its interest, disposition and happiness. The romantic[2] and barbarous distinction of men into kings and subjects, though it may suit the condition of courtiers, cannot that of citizens – and is exploded by the principle upon which governments are now founded. Every citizen is a member of the sovereignty, and as such can acknowledge no personal subjection, and his obedience can be only to the laws.

When men think of what government is, they must necessarily suppose it to possess a knowledge of all the objects and matters upon which its authority is to be exercised. In this view of government, the republican system as established by America and France operates to embrace the whole of a nation, and the knowledge necessary to the interest of all the parts is to be found in the centre, which the parts by representation form. But the old governments are on a construction that excludes knowledge as well as happiness – government by monks who know nothing of the world beyond the walls of a convent is as consistent as government by kings.

Notes

On Revolution

[1] *indefeasible* undeniable.

[2] *romantic* impractical, fanciful. It is interesting to find Paine using this word. Unaware of the revolution in literature that would take place within the next decade, he is thinking of Burke's claims that medieval codes of honour were the best means by which human conduct might be regulated.

What were formerly called revolutions were little more than a change of persons or an alteration of local circumstances. They rose and fell like things of course,[3] and had nothing in their existence or their fate that could influence beyond the spot that produced them. But what we now see in the world, from the revolutions of America and France, are a renovation of the natural order of things, a system of principles as universal as truth and the existence of man, and combining moral with political happiness and national prosperity.

I. Men are born and always continue free and equal in respect of their rights. Civil distinctions, therefore, can be founded only on public utility.
II. The end[4] of all political associations is the preservation of the natural and imprescriptible rights of man; and these rights are liberty, property, security, and resistance of oppression.
III. The nation is essentially the source of all sovereignty; nor can any individual or any body of men be entitled to any authority which is not expressly derived from it.

In these principles there is nothing to throw a nation into confusion by inflaming ambition. They are calculated to call forth wisdom and abilities, and to exercise them for the public good, and not for the emolument[5] or aggrandizement of particular descriptions of men or families. Monarchical sovereignty – the enemy of mankind and the source of misery – is abolished, and sovereignty itself is restored to its natural and original place: the nation. Were this the case throughout Europe, the cause of wars would be taken away.

[*Republicanism*]

From The Rights of Man Part II (1792)

What is called a republic is not any particular form of government. It is wholly characteristical of the purport,[1] matter or object for which government ought to be instituted, and on which it is to be employed: 'res-publica' (the public affairs, or the public good – or, literally translated, the public thing). It is a word of a good original,[2] referring to what ought to be the character and business of government, and in this sense it is naturally opposed to the word 'monarchy', which has a base original signification – it means arbitrary power in an individual person, in the exercise of which *himself* (and not the 'res-publica') is the object.

Every government that does not act on the principle of a republic – or, in other words, that does not make the res-publica its whole and sole object – is not a good government. Republican government is no other than government established and conducted for the interest of the public, as well individually as collectively. It is not necessarily connected with any particular form, but it most naturally associates with the representative form, as being best calculated to secure the end for which a nation is at the expense of supporting it.

Notes

[3] *of course* as a matter of course; over a course of time.
[4] *end* aim.
[5] *emolument* financial benefit.

Republicanism
[1] *purport* purpose, intention.
[2] *original* meaning, referent.

Various forms of government have affected to style themselves a republic. Poland calls itself a republic, which is an hereditary aristocracy with what is called an elective[3] monarchy. Holland calls itself a republic, which is chiefly aristocratical with an hereditary stadtholdership.[4] But the government of America, which is wholly on the system of representation, is the only real republic in character and in practice that now exists. Its government has no other object than the public business of the nation, and therefore it is properly a republic; and the Americans have taken care that *this* and no other shall always be the object of their government, by their rejecting everything hereditary, and establishing government on the system of representation only . . . What Athens was in miniature, America will be in magnitude: the one was the wonder of the ancient world, the other is becoming the admiration, the model of the present. It is the easiest of all the forms of government to be understood, and the most eligible in practice – and excludes at once the ignorance and insecurity of the hereditary mode, and the inconvenience of the simple democracy.

Anna Seward (1742–1809)

Seward was born in Eyam, Derbyshire, the daughter of Thomas Seward and Elizabeth Hunter, of Lichfield. Her father was headmaster of Lichfield Grammar School, and had taught Samuel Johnson. Under his tutelage she was reading Milton at 2, and composing religious verse by the age of 10. An accident lamed her in childhood. In 1750 her father became a Canon of Lichfield Cathedral, and from 1754 the family resided in the Bishop's Palace. Partly, no doubt, because her brother and two sisters died in infancy, she enjoyed an intensely close relationship with Honora Sneyd, adopted by the Sewards as a child, and their close relationship is the subject of some of her finest verse. Honora's marriage to Richard Lovell Edgeworth in 1773 caused Anna profound unhappiness.

Her literary reputation was established with the *Elegy on Captain Cook* (1780), which had entered its fourth edition by 1784. The hanging of Major André, a suitor of Honora Sneyd, in the American War, provided the occasion for her *Monody on Major André* (1781), a success both at home and in America. And her popularity was consolidated by *Poem to the Memory of Lady Miller* (1782) and *Louisa, a Poetical Novel, in Four Epistles* (1784).

Seward held forth in literary circles as the Swan of Lichfield, unafraid to pass judgement on her contemporaries in print. She wrote a series of letters signed 'Benvolio' to the *Gentleman's Magazine* in 1786, designed to deflate Dr Johnson's posthumous reputation. Despite her own earlier support for the French Revolution, she reprimanded Helen Maria Williams for her radical attachments, and expressed strong reservations about Charlotte Smith's advocacy of suicide in her translations from Petrarch and Goethe.

Her visit to Lady Eleanor Butler and Sarah Ponsonby, the Ladies of Llangollen, was the occasion for the title poem in *Llangollen Vale, and Other Poems* (1796); two of the poems here, 'To Time Past' and 'Eyam', are taken from that volume. 'To Time Past', composed in 1788, is one of her finest love poems to Honora Sneyd. Written in anticipation of Sneyd's impending marriage to

Notes

[3] *elective* elected.

[4] *stadtholdership* magistrate-general (abolished 1802).

Edgeworth, it brings anxiety at her own future into painfully sharp focus; the prospect before her is one of loneliness among the 'bare bleak fields' of winter. In the event, Seward's life was a comfortable one; unlike other women writers, she was not compelled to write out of financial necessity. After her father's death in 1790 she lived comfortably on £400 per annum (the equivalent of about £34,000 today). Perhaps because 'Eyam' is about memory, it reminds us of *The Prelude*; like that work it is confessional, and attempts to describe the emotional attachments of places known to her. But this selection begins with a sonnet of April 1771, edited from manuscript, in which Seward declares how much more she loves Honora when illness increases her concern for her well-being.

Further reading

Margaret Eliza Ashmun, *The Singing Swan* (London, 1931).

Daniel Robinson, 'Reviving the Sonnet: Women Romantic Poets and the Sonnet Claim', *ERR* 6 (1995) 98–127.

Sonnet written from an Eastern Apartment in the Bishop's Palace at Lichfield, which commands a view of Stowe Valley. April 1771 (edited from MS)[1]

In this chill morning of a wintry spring
I look into the gloomed and rainy vale;
The sullen clouds, the whistling winds assail,
Lour on the fields, and with their ruffling wing
Disturb the lake. But love and memory cling
To their *known* scene in this cold influence pale;
Yet *prized*, as when it bloomed in summer's gale,
Tinged by his setting sun. And thus, when fling
The powers of sickness o'er some beauteous form
Their shadowy languors (form devoutly dear
As thine to me, Honora[2]), with more warm
And anxious gaze the eyes of Love sincere
Bend on the charms, dim in their tintless snow,
Than when with health's purpureal[3] grace they glow.

To Time Past. Written Dec. 1772

From Llangollen Vale, with Other Poems (1796)

Return, blessed years, when not the jocund spring,
Luxuriant summer, nor the amber hours
Calm autumn gives, my heart invoked to bring

Notes

Sonnet written from an Eastern Apartment

[1] This sonnet is edited from a manuscript in the Bodleian Library entitled 'Unpublished Verses Written by Anna Seward'. It is not in her hand, and may date from around 1800. Seward's note to the poem runs as follows: 'The energetic spirit of Milton's sonnets, and the majestic grace of their varied pauses undulating through the lines, induced the author of these to adopt their model rather than the more facile measures of the modern sonnet, viz. three stanzas closing with a couplet.'

[2] Honora Sneyd, adopted as a child by Seward's parents, with whom Seward enjoyed a close attachment.

[3] *purpureal* a purple colour that, to Seward, indicates good health.

Joys whose rich balm o'er all the bosom pours! –
When ne'er I wished might grace the closing day
One tint purpureal[1] or one golden ray;
When the loud storms that desolate the bowers
Found dearer welcome than favonian[2] gales,
And winter's bare bleak fields, than summer's flowery vales!

Yet not to deck pale hours with vain parade
Beneath the blaze of wide-illumined dome;
Not for the bounding dance; not to pervade
And charm the sense with music; nor, as roam
The mimic passions o'er theatric scene,
To laugh or weep – oh not for these, I ween,
But for delights that made the *heart* their home
Was the grey night-frost on the sounding plain
More than the sun invoked, that gilds the grassy lane.

Yes, for the joys that trivial joys excel,
My loved Honora,[3] did we hail the gloom
Of dim November's eve; and, as it fell,
And the bright fires shone cheerful round the room,
Dropped the warm curtains with no tardy hand,
And felt our spirits and our hearts expand,
Listening their steps, who still, where'er they come,
Make the keen stars that glaze the settled snows,
More than the sun invoked, when first he tints the rose.

Affection, friendship, sympathy – your throne
Is winter's glowing hearth, and ye were ours;
Thy smile, Honora, made them all our own.
Where are they *now*? Alas, their choicest powers
Faded at thy retreat, for thou art gone!
And many a dark long eve I sigh alone
In thrilled remembrance of the vanished hours,
When storms were dearer than the balmy gales,
And winter's bare bleak fields than green luxuriant vales.

Advice to Mrs Smith. A Sonnet.[1]

From Gentleman's Magazine (1786)

Muse of the south, whose soul-enchanting shell
With mournful notes can melt the softened heart,
And to each breast of sympathy impart
The tender sorrow thou describ'st so well!
Ah, never let thy lyre superior dwell

Notes

To Time Past

[1] *purpureal* purple.

[2] *favonian* from the west wind – therefore favourable, gentle.

[3] Honora Sneyd.

Advice to Mrs Smith

[1] This sonnet was written in response to the translations from Petrarch and Goethe that appeared for the first time in the third edition of Charlotte Smith's *Elegiac Sonnets* (1786) (pp. 90–1, 93–5).

On themes thy better judgement must disdain!
It ill befits that verse like thine should tell
Of Petrarch's love, or Werther's frantic pain!
Let not or foreign taste or tales enchain
The genuine freedom of thy flowing line;
Nor the dark dreams of suicide[2] obtain
Deceitful lustre from such tones as thine;
But still, to nature and to virtue given,
Thy heavenly talent dedicate to heaven!

Eyam[1] (composed August 1788)

From Llangollen Vale, with Other Poems (1796)

For one short week I leave, with anxious heart,
Source of my filial cares, the FULL OF DAYS,
Lured by the promise of harmonic art
To breathe her Handel's[2] soul-exalting lays.
Pensive I trace the Derwent's amber wave,[3]
Foaming through sylvan banks, or view it lave
The soft, romantic vallies, high o'er-peered
By hills and rocks, in savage grandeur reared.

Not two short miles from thee, can I refrain
Thy haunts, my native Eyam, long unseen?
Thou and thy loved inhabitants again
Shall meet my transient gaze. Thy rocky screen,
Thy airy cliffs, I mount, and seek thy shade,
Thy roofs that brow the steep, romantic glade;
But while on me the eyes of Friendship glow,
Swell my pained sighs, my tears spontaneous flow.

In scenes paternal, not beheld through years,
Nor viewed till *now* but by a father's side,
Well might the tender, tributary tears
From keen regrets of duteous fondness glide!
Its pastor, to this human flock no more
Shall the long flight of future days restore;
Distant he droops, and that once-gladdening eye
Now languid gleams, e'en when his friends are nigh.[4]

Notes

[2] Goethe's hero, Werther, commits suicide. Seward's concern was not an over-reaction. The popularity of Goethe's novel led to a rash of suicides throughout Europe.

EYAM

[1] 'This poem was written August 1788, on a journey through Derbyshire, to a music meeting at Sheffield. The author's father was Rector of Eyam, an extensive village that runs along a mountainous terrace in one of the highest parts of the Peak. She was born there, and there passed the first seven years of her life, visiting the place often with her father in future periods. The middle part of this village is built on the edge of a deep dell, which has very picturesque and beautiful features' (Seward's note).

[2] George Frederic Handel (1685–1759), who became a British subject in 1726 having arrived in London in 1711.

[3] 'From the peculiar nature of the clay on the mountains from which it descends, the River Derwent has a yellow tint, that well becomes the dark foliage on its banks, and the perpetual foam produced by a narrow, and rocky channel' (Seward's note). The River Derwent to which she refers is different from that apostrophized by Wordsworth in *The Two-Part Prelude*.

[4] Thomas Seward (1708–90) was senile by the time this poem was composed.

Through this known walk, where weedy gravel lies,
Rough and unsightly, by the long, coarse grass
Of the once smooth and vivid green, with sighs
To the deserted rectory I pass,
Stray through the darkened chamber's naked bound
Where childhood's earliest, liveliest bliss I found:
How changed since erst, the lightsome walls beneath,
The social joys did their warm comforts breathe!

Ere yet I go, who may return no more,
That sacred pile, mid yonder shadowy trees,
Let me revisit. Ancient, massy door,
Thou gratest hoarse! My vital spirits freeze,
Passing the vacant pulpit, to the space
Where humble rails the decent altar grace,
And where my infant sister's ashes sleep,[5]
Whose loss I left the childish sport to weep.

Now the low beams, with paper garlands hung,[6]
In memory of some village youth or maid,
Draw the soft tear from thrilled remembrance sprung;
How oft my childhood marked that tribute paid.
The gloves, suspended by the garland's side,
White as its snowy flowers, with ribbands tied;
Dear village, long these wreaths funereal spread,
Simple memorials of thy early dead!

But oh, thou blank and silent pulpit! – thou
That with a father's precepts, just and bland,
Didst win my ear, as reason's strength'ning glow
Showed their full value, now thou seemst to stand
Before my sad, suffused,[7] and trembling gaze,
The dreariest relic of departed days;
Of eloquence paternal, nervous, clear,
DIM APPARITION THOU – and bitter is my tear.

Anna Laetitia Barbauld (*née* Aikin) (1743–1825)

Barbauld was born at Kibworth, Leicester, the elder child of Dr John Aikin, a schoolmaster, and Jane Jennings. In 1758 her father became a teacher at the Warrington Academy for Dissenters, where one of his colleagues, Joseph Priestley (friend of Benjamin Franklin, discoverer of oxygen and founder of modern Unitarianism), encouraged her poetic talents. With her brother John (1747–1822), a physician and accomplished author, she published *Miscellaneous*

Notes

[5] Seward's brother and two sisters died in infancy.

[6] 'The ancient custom of hanging a garland of white roses, made of writing paper, and a pair of white gloves, over the pew of the unmarried villagers, who die in the flower of their age, is observed to this day in the village of Eyam, and in most other villages and little towns in the Peak' (Seward's note).

[7] *suffused* tearful.

Pieces in Prose in 1773, the year which also saw publication of her *Poems* (which included 'A Summer Evening's Meditation'). They were an immediate success, the *Poems* reaching a fifth edition by 1777.

Despite well-founded doubts, in 1774 she married Rochemont Barbauld, a Dissenting minister educated at the Warrington Academy, with whom she ran a boys' school in Palgrave, Suffolk. They had no children, but in 1777 adopted her nephew, Charles Rochemont Aikin, for whom she composed her popular *Lessons for Children* (1778) and *Hymns in Prose for Children* (1781). Visits to London put her in touch with the Bluestocking circle, among whom she is celebrated in More's *Sensibility* (see pp. 56–66). Despite the success of their school, her husband felt increasingly overwhelmed, and it closed in 1785, allowing them to travel in France and Switzerland for a year.

On their return to England the Barbaulds settled in Hampstead, where she devoted herself to pamphleteering, most notably in defence of Dissenters (1790), democratic government and popular education (1792), and an attack on the newly declared war with France in 1793. Political concerns were never far from her mind, and one of the finest testaments to her convictions is her *Epistle to William Wilberforce* (1791) (see pp. 38–41), one of the most eloquent antislavery poems of the day. It was composed at a moment when the campaign against slavery faltered: on 18 April 1791 Wilberforce (1759–1833) proposed his first Bill urging abolition. Although it had the support of Charles James Fox and the Prime Minister, William Pitt, it was defeated two days later. He tried again a year later, and although that Bill was passed by the House of Commons, it was thrown out by the Lords the following year (this is the struggle recalled by Wordsworth at *Thirteen-Book Prelude* x 201–10). The slave trade was not outlawed until February 1807.

From 1796 her brother took over editorship of the *Monthly Magazine*, an important periodical issued under the imprint of the radical publisher, Joseph Johnson, and read by Wordsworth and Coleridge among others. She contributed a good deal of poetry to it, including her poem *To Mr Coleridge* (1797) (see pp. 42–3). Composed shortly after their meeting in Bristol, August 1797, it is distinguished by early recognition of his talents, and her shrewd warning against the 'metaphysic lore' which was to embroil him in later years. Such was her eminence by 1800 that Wordsworth sent her a complimentary copy of the new two-volume *Lyrical Ballads*, and George Dyer included three of her poems in an anthology of *Odes*.[1]

In 1802 the Barbaulds moved to Stoke Newington. By this time her husband's mental health was increasingly fragile, and in 1808, after several fits of violence, he committed suicide by drowning. Released from the obligation of tending him, she enjoyed a period of vigorous productivity, editing Akenside and Collins, the *Letters* of Richardson, *The British Novelists* (50 vols, 1810), and reviewing fiction for the *Monthly Review* (1809–15). She died in Stoke Newington in 1825.

In addition to the works mentioned above, Barbauld is represented by a complete text of *Eighteen Hundred and Eleven* (1812) – a passionate, perceptive work about the disastrous state in which the country found itself. Britain had been at war with France since 1793, with a brief hiatus during the Treaty of Amiens in 1802. By the time she was writing, most of Britain's allies had capitulated to the French, whose control over Europe was almost total. As both sides had widespread economic interests, the conflict effectively amounted to a world war, entailing what we would now call economic sanctions – blockades, in fact – and by 1810 Britain's economy was near collapse. The result was to impoverish civilian

Notes

1 *Odes* ed. George Dyer (Ludlow, 1800) includes her poems *To Content, To Wisdom* and *To Spring*.

Figure 5 Anna Laetitia Barbauld (1743–1825), engraved by Chapman after an unknown artist, published 1798. She was hailed by the Bluestockings as an important new talent in the early 1770s and remained prominent in the literary world until her death. (National Portrait Gallery, London.)

populations, who bore the brunt of scarcity and high prices, the effects of which were exacerbated by bankruptcies, layoffs, labour revolts and cuts in production. When in 1811 George III declined into permanent dementia, the argument for a negotiated settlement became overwhelming. All the same, the country would remain at war until May 1814.

Eighteen Hundred and Eleven, with its plea for an end to the conflict, constituted a bold statement that made her a prime target of Tory reviewers. Writing anonymously in June 1812, John Wilson Croker[2] of the *Quarterly Review* began his attack with two sentences that set the tone for what was to come: 'Our old acquaintance Mrs Barbauld turned satirist! The last thing we should have expected, and, now that we have seen her satire, the last thing that we could have desired.'[3] In those days it was acceptable to attack female poets on the grounds of their sex, as Croker proceeded to do:

> We had hoped, indeed, that the empire might have been saved without the intervention of a lady-author: we even flattered ourselves that the interests of Europe and of humanity would in some degree have swayed our public councils, without the descent of (dea ex machina) Mrs Anna Laetitia Barbauld in a quarto, upon the theatre where the great European tragedy is now performing. Not such, however, is her opinion; an irresistible impulse of public duty – a confident sense of commanding talents – have induced her to dash down her shagreen spectacles and her knitting needles, and to sally forth, hand in hand with her renowned compatriot,[4] in the magnanimous resolution of saving a sinking state, by the instrumentality of a pamphlet in prose and a pamphlet in verse.[5]

Croker concluded by 'warning her to desist from satire, which indeed is satire on herself alone; and of entreating, with great earnestness, that she will not, for the sake of this ungrateful generation, put herself to the trouble of writing any more party pamphlets in verse'.[6] As this was the most influential of the hostile reviews, some of its specific criticisms are quoted in my annotations. Although it's impossible not to be struck by their chauvinism today – and there's no doubt that Barbauld's male reviewers deliberately used her gender as one of many sticks with which to beat her – it's worth remembering that their primary motivation was political. She was by this time well known as a radical Dissenter, and the fact that she was a woman made them all the more determined to respond with the criticism always directed at those who stand up for the poor and disadvantaged in times of war – that she was a traitor. The anonymous reviewer in the *Eclectic Review* attacked Barbauld's poem for being 'in a most extraordinary degree unkindly and unpatriotic', adding: 'It seems hardly possible that such a poem as this could have been produced, without the concurrence of a peculiarly frigid temperament.'[7]

Although it has been suggested that none of the reviews were positive, the Unitarian *Monthly Repository* was the exception, whose reviewer, 'M.', commended *Eighteen Hundred and Eleven* in fulsome terms: 'We lament that this poem is not more extended . . . Many more reflections of the most impressive nature might, on such a subject, have flowed from the pen of an author, whom every man of poetic and moral taste reveres as a

Notes

[2] Croker was a menace where radical poets were concerned; he was also responsible for one of the harshest attacks on Keats.

[3] *Quarterly Review* 7 (1812) 309–13, p. 309.

[4] William Roscoe, books by whom were reviewed in the same number of the *Quarterly*, and who is mentioned in the poem.

[5] *Quarterly Review* 7 (1812) 309–13, p. 309.

[6] Ibid., p. 313.

[7] *Eclectic Review* 8 (1812) 474–8, pp. 474–5.

poet, a patriot and a Christian.'[8] But this was not enough, on its own, to mitigate the ferocity of the onslaught and the pain it must have caused. Perhaps for that reason Barbauld resolved not to publish any more poetry during her lifetime; doubtless those close to her encouraged her to remain silent. Lucy Aikin recalled in her memoir: 'Who indeed, that knew and loved her, could have wished her to expose again that honoured head to the scorns of the unmanly, the malignant, and the base? . . . She even laid aside the intention which she had entertained of preparing a new edition of her Poems, long out of print and often enquired for in vain.'[9]

Further reading

Anna Laetitia Barbauld: Selected Poetry and Prose ed. William McCarthy and Elizabeth Kraft (Peterborough, Ontario, 2002).

Anna Laetitia Barbauld, *Poems 1773* ed. Lisa Vargo and Allison Muri

http://www.rc.umd.edu/editions/contemps/barbauld/poems1773/

William Keach, 'A Regency Prophecy and the End of Anna Barbauld's Career', *SIR* 33 (1994) 569–77.

Jon Mee, *Romanticism, Enthusiasm and Regulation: Poetics and the Policing of Culture in the Romantic Period* (Oxford, 2003), chapter 4.

Lucy Newlyn, *Reading, Writing, and Romanticism: The Anxiety of Reception* (Oxford, 2000), pp. 164–9.

A Summer Evening's Meditation

From Poems (1773)

One sun by day, by night ten thousand shine.
(Young)[1]

'Tis passed! – the sultry tyrant of the south[2]
Has spent his short-lived rage. More grateful hours
Move silent on; the skies no more repel
The dazzled sight, but with mild maiden beams
Of tempered light invite the cherished eye
To wander o'er their sphere, where, hung aloft,
Dian's bright crescent,[3] like a silver bow
New-strung in heaven, lifts high its beamy horns
Impatient for the night, and seems to push
Her brother down the sky. Fair Venus shines
Even in the eye of day – with sweetest beam
Propitious shines, and shakes a trembling flood
Of softened radiance from her dewy locks.
The shadows spread apace, while meekened Eve,
Her cheek yet warm with blushes, slow retires
Through the Hesperian gardens of the west,[4]
And shuts the gates of day. 'Tis now the hour
When Contemplation from her sunless haunts

Notes

8 *Monthly Repository* 7 (1812) 108.

9 *The Works of Anna Laetitia Barbauld. With a Memoir by Lucy Aikin* (2 vols, 1825), i. lii–liii.

A Summer Evening's Meditation

1 Edward Young, *Night Thoughts* ix 748. Though little read today, Young was tremendously influential in the late eighteenth century.

2 *the sultry tyrant of the south* the sun.

3 *Dian's bright crescent* the moon, of which Diana was goddess.

4 *the Hesperian gardens of the west* In Greek myth, the daughters of Hesperus (the evening star) guarded the garden in which golden apples grew in the Isles of the Blessed, at the western extremity of the earth.

(The cool damp grotto or the lonely depth
Of unpierced woods, where, wrapped in solid shade,
She mused away the gaudy hours of noon
And fed on thoughts unripened by the sun)[5]
Moves forward, and with radiant finger points
To yon blue concave swelled by breath divine,
Where, one by one, the living eyes of heaven[6]
Awake, quick kindling o'er the face of ether
One boundless blaze – ten thousand trembling fires
And dancing lustres – where th' unsteady eye,
Restless and dazzled, wanders unconfined
O'er all this field of glories: spacious field,
And worthy of the Master![7] – He whose hand
With hieroglyphics older than the Nile
Inscribed the mystic tablet[8] hung on high
To public gaze, and said, 'Adore, oh man,
The finger of thy God!' From what pure wells
Of milky light, what soft o'erflowing urn
Are all these lamps so filled – these friendly lamps
For ever streaming o'er the azure deep
To point our path and light us to our home?
How soft they slide along their lucid spheres,
And, silent as the foot of time, fulfil
Their destined courses! Nature's self is hushed
And, but[9] a scattered leaf which rustles through
The thick-wove foliage, not a sound is heard
To break the midnight air – though the raised ear,
Intensely listening, drinks in every breath.
How deep the silence, yet how loud the praise!
But are they silent all, or is there not
A tongue in every star that talks with man
And woos him to be wise – nor woos in vain?
    This dead of midnight is the noon of thought,
And wisdom mounts her zenith with the stars.
At this still hour the self-collected soul
Turns inward, and beholds a stranger there
Of high descent, and more than mortal rank:
An embryo God, a spark of fire divine
Which must burn on for ages, when the sun
(Fair transitory creature of a day!)
Has closed his golden eye and, wrapped in shades,
Forgets his wonted journey through the east.
    Ye citadels of light and seats of gods!
Perhaps my future home from whence the soul,
Revolving periods past, may oft look back

Notes

[5] *fed on thoughts unripened by the sun* cf. Wordsworth, 'These chairs they have no words to utter' 13: 'I have thoughts that are fed by the sun.' Their common source is *Paradise Lost* iii 37.

[6] *the living eyes of heaven* the stars.

[7] *the Master* God.

[8] *the mystic tablet* on which were written the Ten Commandments.

[9] *but* except.

With recollected tenderness on all
The various busy scenes she left below,
Its deep-laid projects and its strange events,
As on some fond and doting tale that soothed
Her infant hours. Oh be it lawful now
To tread the hallowed circle of your courts,
And with mute wonder and delighted awe
Approach your burning confines!
Seized in thought,
On fancy's wild and roving wing I sail,[10]
From the green borders of the peopled earth
And the pale moon, her duteous fair attendant;
From solitary Mars; from the vast orb
Of Jupiter, whose huge gigantic bulk
Dances in ether like the lightest leaf;
To the dim verge, the suburbs of the system[11]
Where cheerless Saturn midst her wat'ry moons,
Girt with a lucid zone,[12] majestic sits
In gloomy grandeur, like an exiled queen
Amongst her weeping handmaids. Fearless thence
I launch into the trackless deeps of space
Where, burning round, ten thousand suns appear
Of elder beam, which ask no leave to shine
Of our terrestrial star, nor borrow light
From the proud regent of our scanty day[13] –
Sons of the morning, first-born of creation,
And only less than Him who marks their track
And guides their fiery wheels. Here must I stop,
Or is there aught beyond? What hand unseen
Impels me onward through the glowing orbs
Of habitable nature far remote,
To the dread confines of eternal night,
To solitudes of vast unpeopled space,
The deserts of creation, wide and wild,
Where embryo systems and unkindled suns
Sleep in the womb of chaos?
Fancy droops,
And thought astonished stops her bold career;
But oh, thou mighty mind, whose powerful word
Said, 'Thus let all things be', and thus they were –
Where shall I seek thy presence? How unblamed[14]
Invoke thy dread perfection?[15]

Notes

[10] McCarthy and Kraft suggest an antecedent in Hume, *Enquiry Concerning Human Understanding*: 'the thought can in an instant transport us into the most distant regions of the universe; or even beyond the universe, into the unbounded chaos, where nature is supposed to lie in total confusion.'

[11] *suburbs of the system* outskirts of the solar system.

[12] *zone* belt; a reference to the rings around Saturn.

[13] *the proud regent of our scanty day* the sun.

[14] *unblamed* uncensured (i.e. without doing God an injustice).

[15] *How unblamed . . . perfection* McCarthy and Kraft note the allusion to *Paradise Lost* iii 3: 'May I express thee unblamed?'

Have the broad eyelids of the morn[16] beheld thee,
Or does the beamy shoulder of Orion[17]
Support thy throne? Oh, look with pity down
On erring, guilty man – not in thy names
Of terror clad; not with those thunders armed
That conscious Sinai felt,[18] when fear appalled
The scattered tribes: Thou hast a gentler voice
That whispers comfort to the swelling heart
Abashed, yet longing to behold her maker.
   But now my soul, unused to stretch her powers
In flight so daring, drops her weary wing
And seeks again the known accustomed spot
Dressed up with sun and shade, and lawns and streams,
A mansion fair and spacious for its guest,
And full replete with wonders. Let me here,
Content and grateful, wait th' appointed time
And ripen for the skies: the hour will come
When all these splendours bursting on my sight
Shall stand unveiled, and to my ravished sense
Unlock the glories of the world unknown.

Epistle to William Wilberforce, Esq.,[1] on the Rejection of the Bill for Abolishing the Slave Trade[2] (composed by 17 June 1791)

***From* Poems (1792)**

Cease, Wilberforce, to urge thy generous aim –
Thy country knows the sin and stands the shame!
The preacher, poet, senator,[3] in vain
Has rattled in her sight the Negro's chain,
With his deep groans assailed her startled ear
And rent the veil that hid his constant tear,
Forced her averted eyes his stripes to scan,
Beneath the bloody scourge laid bare the man,
Claimed pity's tear, urged conscience' strong control
And flashed conviction on her shrinking soul.

Notes

[16] *eyelids of the morn* a biblical expression, as McCarthy and Kraft note; cf. Job 41:18.

[17] *Orion* giant hunter who sprang from the urine of Jupiter, Neptune and Mercury. Anna refers to the constellation of Orion into which he was turned at his death.

[18] *those thunders . . . felt* Jehovah delivered the Ten Commandments to Moses on Mount Sinai amidst 'thunders and lightnings', Exodus 19.

Epistle to William Wilberforce, Esq.,

[1] William Wilberforce (1759–1833), leader of the movement for the abolition of the slave trade in Parliament.

[2] The Society for the Abolition of the Slave Trade was founded by Thomas Clarkson and a group of Quakers in 1787; Wilberforce was its representative in the House of Commons, and the cause was taken up by a number of Bluestockings, including Hannah More and Barbauld. Wilberforce proposed abolition of the slave trade in the House in April 1791, but despite support from Edmund Burke, Charles James Fox and the Prime Minister, his motion was rejected. This poem was composed soon after, and certainly by 17 June.

[3] *senator* politician.

The muse, too soon awaked, with ready tongue
At mercy's shrine applausive[4] paeans rung,
And freedom's eager sons in vain foretold
A new Astrean[5] reign, an age of gold!
She knows and she persists – still Afric bleeds;
Unchecked, the human traffic still proceeds;
She stamps her infamy to future time
And on her hardened forehead seals the crime.
  In vain, to thy white standard gathering round,
Wit, worth, and parts and eloquence are found;[6]
In vain to push to birth thy great design
Contending chiefs and hostile virtues join;[7]
All from conflicting ranks, of power possessed
To rouse, to melt, or to inform the breast.
Where seasoned tools of avarice[8] prevail,
A nation's eloquence, combined, must fail.
Each flimsy sophistry by turns they try –
The plausive[9] argument, the daring lie,
The artful gloss that moral sense confounds,
Th' acknowledged thirst of gain[10] that honour wounds
(Bane of ingenuous minds!), th' unfeeling sneer
Which sudden turns to stone the falling tear.
They search assiduous with inverted skill
For forms of wrong, and precedents of ill;
With impious mockery wrest the sacred page,[11]
And glean up crimes from each remoter age;
Wrung nature's tortures, shuddering, while you tell,
From scoffing fiends bursts forth the laugh of hell;[12]
In Britain's senate, misery's pangs give birth
To jests unseemly, and to horrid mirth –
Forbear! thy virtues but provoke our doom
And swell th' account of vengeance yet to come.
For (not unmarked in Heaven's impartial plan)
Shall man, proud worm, contemn his fellow man?
And injured Afric, by herself redressed,
Darts her own serpents at her tyrant's breast.
Each vice, to minds depraved by bondage known,
With sure contagion fastens on his own;[13]

Notes

[4] *applausive* applauding.

[5] *Astrean* Astrea, goddess of justice in the Golden Age, abandoned the earth in disgust at the crimes of humanity.

[6] *Wit, worth, and parts and eloquence are found* a tribute to those in the House of Commons who supported the Abolitionist cause.

[7] *Contending chiefs and hostile virtues join* Leaders on both sides of the House supported the measure.

[8] *seasoned tools of avarice* a reference to those who for years had supported the slave-trade out of greed.

[9] *plausive* specious.

[10] *thirst of gain* As in the debate of 1788, a central argument of those opposed to abolition was that the slave trade was a lucrative industry.

[11] *the sacred page* According to some opponents of the bill, slavery was divinely sanctioned.

[12] *From scoffing fiends . . . hell* McCarthy and Kraft note that when William Smith, one of the Abolitionist MPs, described how an African woman had been forced to throw her murdered child from a ship, some of his colleagues in the House of Commons burst into laughter.

[13] *Darts her own serpents . . . breast* a reference, as McCarthy and Kraft suggest, to the argument that Britons degraded themselves by their participation in the slave trade.

In sickly languors melts his nerveless frame,
And blows to rage impetuous passion's flame;
Fermenting swift, the fiery venom gains
The milky innocence of infant veins;
There swells the stubborn will, damps learning's fire,
The whirlwind wakes[14] of uncontrolled desire,
Sears the young heart to images of woe
And blasts the buds of virtue as they blow.
  Lo! where reclined, pale Beauty courts the breeze,
Diffused on sofas of voluptuous ease;
With anxious awe, her menial train around
Catch her faint whispers of half-uttered sound.
See her, in monstrous fellowship, unite
At once the Scythian and the Sybarite;[15]
Blending repugnant vices, misallied,
Which frugal nature purposed to divide;
See her, with indolence to fierceness joined,
Of body delicate, infirm of mind,
With languid tones imperious mandates urge,
With arm recumbent wield the household scourge,[16]
And with unruffled mien, and placid sounds,
Contriving torture and inflicting wounds.
  Nor in their palmy walks and spicy groves
The form benign of rural pleasure roves;
No milkmaid's song or hum of village talk
Soothes the lone poet in his evening walk;
No willing arm the flail unwearied plies
Where the mixed sounds of cheerful labour rise;
No blooming maids and frolic swains are seen
To pay gay homage to their harvest queen;
No heart-expanding scenes their eyes must prove[17]
Of thriving industry and faithful love:
But shrieks and yells disturb the balmy air,
Dumb sullen looks of woe announce despair
And angry eyes through dusky features glare.
Far from the sounding lash the muses fly
And sensual riot drowns each finer joy.
  Nor less from the gay east[18] on essenced wings,
Breathing unnamed perfumes, contagion springs;[19]
The soft luxurious plague alike pervades
The marble palaces and rural shades;
Hence thronged Augusta[20] builds her rosy bowers
And decks in summer wreaths her smoky towers;[21]

Notes

[14] *wakes* trails.

[15] *The Scythian and the Sybarite* the savage and the sensualist. The ancient Scythians were notorious for savagery; the citizens of Sybaris, an ancient Greek city of southern Italy, were renowned for effeminacy and debauchery.

[16] *pale Beauty . . . scourge* The pale, beautiful mistress of the house reclines lies down ('recumbent') as she whips (scourges) her servants into action.

[17] *prove* experience, witness.

[18] *east* the East Indies, or India.

[19] *contagion springs* it was believed that disease was carried by the wind.

[20] *Augusta* London.

[21] *decks . . . towers* Pollution generated by the burning of fossil fuels was a major problem in 18th-century London.

And hence in summer bow'rs Art's costly hand
Pour courtly splendours o'er the dazzled land.
The manners melt, one undistinguished blaze
O'erwhelms the sober pomp of elder days;
Corruption follows with gigantic stride
And scarce vouchsafes his shameless front to hide;
The spreading leprosy taints ev'ry part,
Infects each limb, and sickens at the heart.
Simplicity, most dear of rural maids,
Weeping resigns her violated shades;
Stern Independence from his glebe[22] retires
And anxious Freedom eyes her drooping fires;
By foreign wealth are British morals changed,
And Afric's sons, and India's, smile avenged.
For you whose tempered ardour long has borne
Untired the labour, and unmoved the scorn,
In virtue's fasti[23] be inscribed your fame,
And uttered yours with Howard's honoured name.[24]
Friends of the friendless – hail, ye generous band
Whose efforts yet arrest Heaven's lifted hand,
Around whose steady brows in union bright
The civic wreath and Christian's palm unite!
Your merit stands, no greater and no less,
Without or with the varnish of success;
But seek no more to break a nation's fall,
For ye have saved yourselves, and that is all.
Succeeding times your struggles, and their fate,
With mingled shame and triumph shall relate,
While faithful history in her various page,
Marking the features of this motley age,
To shed a glory, and to fix a stain,
Tells how you strove, and that you strove in vain.

The Rights of Woman (composed *c.*1795)[1]

From Works (1825)

Yes, injured woman, rise, assert thy right!
Woman! too long degraded, scorned, oppressed;
Oh born to rule in partial law's despite,
Resume thy native empire o'er the breast!

Notes

[22] *glebe* field.
[23] *fasti* annals.
[24] John Howard (1726–90), prison reformer and philanthropist.

THE RIGHTS OF WOMAN

[1] Apparently an angry response to Mary Wollstonecraft's criticism of Barbauld's poem *To a Lady, with some painted Flowers* in *Vindication of the Rights of Woman* (1792), chapter 4. Wollstonecraft's central argument was that a male discourse created a 'false system of female manners, which robs the whole sex of its dignity, and classes the brown and fair with the smiling flowers that only adorn the land'. As proof that 'even women of superior sense' have adopted it, she quoted Barbauld's poem in its entirety. Barbauld's answer is complex and subtle; critics remain in doubt as to where it is ironic and where in earnest.

Go forth arrayed in panoply[2] divine,
That angel pureness which admits no stain;
Go bid proud man his boasted rule resign
And kiss the golden sceptre of thy reign.

Go gird thyself with grace, collect thy store
Of bright artillery glancing from afar –
Soft melting tones thy thundering cannon's roar,
Blushes and fears thy magazine[3] of war.

Thy rights are empire: urge no meaner claim –
Felt, not defined, and, if debated, lost;
Like sacred mysteries which, withheld from fame,
Shunning discussion, are revered the most.

Try all that wit and art suggest to bend
Of thy imperial foe the stubborn knee;
Make treacherous man thy subject, not thy friend –
Thou mayst command, but never canst be free.

Awe the licentious and restrain the rude;
Soften the sullen, clear the cloudy brow;
Be more than princes' gifts, thy favours sued –
She hazards all, who will the least allow.

But hope not, courted idol of mankind,
On this proud eminence secure to stay;
Subduing and subdued, thou soon shalt find
Thy coldness soften, and thy pride give way.

Then, then, abandon each ambitious thought,
Conquest or rule thy heart shall feebly move,
In Nature's school, by her soft maxims taught
That separate rights are lost in mutual love.

To Mr Coleridge[1] (composed *c.*1797)

From The Monthly Magazine (1799)

Midway the hill of science,[2] after steep
And rugged paths that tire the unpractised feet,
A grove extends, in tangled mazes wrought,
And filled with strange enchantment: dubious shapes

Notes

[2] *panoply* armour for spiritual warfare.

[3] *magazine* munitions.

To Mr Coleridge

[1] Barbauld met Coleridge in August 1797, on a visit to their mutual friend John Prior Estlin, a fellow Unitarian, in Bristol.

[2] *science* knowledge. As McCarthy and Kraft observe, this recalls Coleridge's own *Effusion XXXV*, in which its author describes himself 'on the midway slope / Of yonder hill' (ll. 26–7), and is based on the Hill Difficulty in Bunyan's *Pilgrim's Progress*.

Flit through dim glades, and lure the eager foot
Of youthful ardour to eternal chase;
Dreams hang on every leaf; unearthly forms
Glide through the gloom, and mystic visions swim
Before the cheated sense.[3] Athwart the mists,
Far into vacant space, huge shadows stretch
And seem realities; while things of life,
Obvious to sight and touch, all glowing round,
Fade to the hue of shadows. Scruples[4] here,
With filmy net, most like the autumnal webs
Of floating gossamer, arrest the foot
Of generous enterprise, and palsy[5] hope
And fair ambition with the chilling touch
Of sickly hesitation and blank fear.
Nor seldom Indolence these lawns among
Fixes her turf-built seat, and wears the garb
Of deep philosophy, and museful sits
In dreamy twilight of the vacant mind,
Soothed by the whispering shade – for soothing soft
The shades, and vistas lengthening into air
With moonbeam rainbows tinted. Here each mind
Of finer mould,[6] acute and delicate,
In its high progress to eternal truth[7]
Rests for a space in fairy bowers entranced,
And loves the softened light and tender gloom,
And, pampered with most unsubstantial food,
Looks down indignant on the grosser world
And matter's cumbrous shapings.
                                                    Youth beloved
Of science, of the muse beloved: not here,
Not in the maze of metaphysic lore
Build thou thy place of resting! Lightly tread
The dangerous ground, on noble aims intent;
And be this Circe[8] of the studious cell
Enjoyed but still subservient. Active scenes
Shall soon with healthful spirit brace thy mind,
And fair exertion, for bright fame sustained,
For friends, for country, chase each spleen-fed fog[9]
That blots the wide creation:
Now Heaven conduct thee with a parent's love!

Notes

[3] *A grove extends . . . sense* Barbauld correctly discerned in the young Coleridge a tendency to abstract thought; as late as 1800 he concurred with her judgement in a letter to Estlin: 'The more I see of Mrs Barbauld the more I admire her – that wonderful propriety of mind! She has great acuteness, very great . . . My own subtleties too often lead me into strange (though, God be praised) transient out-of-the-way-nesses' (Griggs i 578).

[4] *Scruples* intellectual conundrums.

[5] *palsy* paralyse.

[6] *mould* substance.

[7] *its high progress . . . truth* Coleridge believed that mankind was 'progressive' – constantly improving, morally and spiritually.

[8] *Circe* Greek enchantress who changed men into pigs. Barbauld warns Coleridge not to become a slave of 'metaphysic lore', but to subordinate it to his quest for knowledge and poetic talent.

[9] *spleen-fed fog* mood of depression.

Eighteen Hundred and Eleven, A Poem
(composed by 1 December 1811; published February 1812)

Still the loud death drum, thundering from afar,
O'er the vexed nations pours the storm of war:[1]
To the stern call still Britain bends her ear,
Feeds the fierce strife, the alternate hope and fear –
Bravely, though vainly, dares to strive with fate,
And seeks by turns to prop each sinking state.[2]
Colossal Power[3] with overwhelming force
Bears down each fort of Freedom in its course;
Prostrate she lies beneath the despot's sway,
While the hushed nations curse him – and obey.
  Bounteous in vain, with frantic man at strife,
Glad nature pours the means – the joys of life;
In vain with orange-blossoms scents the gale,
The hills with olives clothes, with corn the vale;
Man calls to Famine, nor invokes in vain,
Disease and Rapine follow in her train;
The tramp of marching hosts disturbs the plough,
The sword, not sickle, reaps the harvest now,
And where the soldier gleans the scant supply,
The helpless peasant but retires to die;[4]
No laws his hut from licensed outrage shield,
And war's least horror is the ensanguined field.
  Fruitful in vain, the matron counts with pride
The blooming youths that grace her honoured side;
No son returns to press her widowed hand,
Her fallen blossoms strew a foreign strand.
Fruitful in vain, she boasts her virgin race,
Whom cultured arts adorn and gentlest grace;
Defrauded of its homage, Beauty mourns,[5]
And the rose withers on its virgin thorns.
Frequent, some stream obscure, some uncouth name
By deeds of blood is lifted into fame;
Oft o'er the daily page some soft one bends
To learn the fate of husband, brothers, friends,
Or the spread map with anxious eye explores
Its dotted boundaries and pencilled shores,
Asks *where* the spot that wrecked her bliss is found,
And learns its name but to detest the sound.

Notes

EIGHTEEN HUNDRED AND ELEVEN

[1] *Still the loud . . . of war* Britain and France had been at war for 17 of the previous 19 years (since 1793); see headnote, pp. 32–4 above.

[2] *each sinking state* Britain had failed to prevent Russia (1807), Spain (1808) and Austria (1809) from making peace with France.

[3] *Colossal Power* Napoleon.

[4] *The helpless peasant but retires to die* Famine was widespread throughout Europe thanks to the disruption of agriculture by armies (l. 17), and seizures of crops to feed them (l. 19).

[5] No young men survive to marry the beautiful young women who mourn their deaths.

And think'st thou, Britain, still to sit at ease,
An island queen amidst thy subject seas,
While the vexed billows, in their distant roar,
But soothe thy slumbers, and but kiss thy shore?
To sport in wars, while danger keeps aloof,
Thy grassy turf unbruised by hostile hoof?
So sing thy flatterers – but, Britain, know,
Thou who hast shared the guilt must share the woe.[6]
Nor distant is the hour; low murmurs spread,
And whispered fears, creating what they dread;
Ruin, as with an earthquake shock, is here,
There, the heart-witherings of unuttered fear,
And that sad death,[7] whence most affection bleeds,
Which sickness, only of the soul, precedes.
Thy baseless wealth[8] dissolves in air away
Like mists that melt before the morning ray:
No more on crowded mart or busy street
Friends, meeting friends, with cheerful hurry greet;
Sad on the ground thy princely merchants bend
Their altered looks, and evil days portend,
And fold their arms, and watch with anxious breast
The tempest blackening in the distant west.[9]
Yes, thou must droop; thy Midas dream is o'er;
The golden tide of commerce leaves thy shore,
Leaves thee to prove the alternate ills that haunt
Enfeebling Luxury and ghastly Want;
Leaves thee, perhaps, to visit distant lands,
And deal the gifts of Heaven with equal hands.
Yet, oh my country – name beloved, revered,
By every tie that binds the soul endeared,
Whose image to my infant senses came
Mixed with Religion's light and Freedom's holy flame!
If prayers may not avert, if 'tis thy fate
To rank amongst the names that once were great,
Not like the dim, cold crescent[10] shalt thou fade,
Thy debt to Science and the Muse unpaid;
Thine are the laws surrounding states revere,
Thine the full harvest of the mental year,
Thine the bright stars in glory's sky that shine,
And arts that make it life to live are thine.
If westward streams the light that leaves thy shores,
Still from thy lamp the streaming radiance pours.

Notes

[6] *but, Britain, know . . . woe* Nonetheless, Britain did not experience invasion.

[7] *that sad death* McCarthy and Kraft suggest a reference to the suicide of the financier Abraham Goldsmid in 1810; there were numerous other bankruptcies at this time. A ruined merchant was responsible for the assassination of the Prime Minister, Spencer Perceval, only months after this poem's publication.

[8] *baseless wealth* The government had issued paper currency in excess of its gold reserves, thus rendering it worthless.

[9] *The tempest blackening in the distant west* impending conflict with the United States. Though not declared until June 1812, it had been brewing for years. In large part it was a by-product of the war with France, specifically the damage wrought to American trade, Britain's impressment of American seamen and the Chesapeake affair.

[10] *the dim, cold crescent* The Ottoman empire had been in decline for years.

Wide spreads thy race from Ganges to the pole,
O'er half the western world thy accents roll;
Nations beyond the Appalachian hills
Thy hand has planted and thy spirit fills;
Soon as their gradual progress shall impart
The finer sense of morals and of art,
Thy stores of knowledge the new states shall know,
And think thy thoughts, and with thy fancy glow;
Thy Lockes, thy Paleys[11] shall instruct their youth,
Thy leading star direct their search for truth;
Beneath the spreading Platan's[12] tent-like shade,
Or by Missouri's rushing waters laid,
'Old father Thames' shall be the poet's theme,
Of Hagley's woods[13] the enamoured virgin dream,
And Milton's tones the raptured ear enthrall,
Mixed with the roar of Niagara's fall;
In Thomson's glass[14] the ingenuous youth shall learn
A fairer face of Nature to discern;
Nor of the bards that swept the British lyre
Shall fade one laurel, or one note expire.
Then, loved Joanna,[15] to admiring eyes
Thy storied groups in scenic pomp shall rise;
Their high-souled strains and Shakespeare's noble rage
Shall with alternate passion shake the stage.
Some youthful Basil from thy moral lay
With stricter hand his fond desires shall sway;
Some Ethwald, as the fleeting shadows pass,
Start at his likeness in the mystic glass;
The tragic Muse resume her just control,
With pity and with terror purge the soul,
While wide o'er transatlantic realms thy name
Shall live in light, and gather *all* its fame.
    Where wanders Fancy down the lapse of years,
Shedding o'er imaged woes untimely tears?
Fond moody power! As hopes, as fears prevail,
She longs, or dreads, to lift the awful veil;
On visions of delight now loves to dwell,
Now hears the shriek of woe or Freedom's knell.
Perhaps, she says, long ages past away,
And set in western waves our closing day,
Night, Gothic night, again may shade the plains
Where Power is seated and where Science reigns;
England, the seat of arts, be only known
By the grey ruin and the mouldering stone,

Notes

[11] *Thy Lockes, thy Paleys* Intellectuals. John Locke (1632–1704) and William Paley (1743–1805) were important philosophers.

[12] *the spreading Platan's* sycamore, plane tree.

[13] *Hagley's woods* Hagley was the estate of George, Lord Lyttelton (1709–73), in Worcestershire, near Birmingham; it is praised by James Thomson in *Spring* (1728) 904 ff. In the 1740s Lyttelton turned it into one of the most admired, and renowned, landscape gardens of the 18th century.

[14] *Thomson's glass* his poem, *The Seasons* (1730).

[15] *loved Joanna* Joanna Baillie (1762–1851), whose *Plays on the Passions* (1798–1812) met with success (see pp. 307–8); Barbauld refers specifically to *Count Basil* and *Ethwald*.

That Time may tear the garland from her brow,
And Europe sit in dust, as Asia now.
Yet then the ingenuous youth whom Fancy fires
With pictured glories of illustrious sires,
With duteous zeal their pilgrimage shall take
From the Blue Mountains or Ontario's lake,[16]
With fond adoring steps to press the sod
By statesmen, sages, poets, heroes trod;
On Isis'[17] banks to draw inspiring air,
From Runnymede[18] to send the patriot's prayer;
In pensive thought, where Cam's slow waters wind,[19]
To meet those shades that ruled the realms of mind;
In silent halls to sculptured marbles bow
And hang fresh wreaths round Newton's awful brow.[20]
Oft shall they seek some peasant's homely shed
Who toils unconscious of the mighty dead,
To ask where Avon's winding waters stray[21]
And thence a knot of wildflowers bear away;
Anxious enquire where Clarkson,[22] friend of man,
Or all-accomplished Jones[23] his race began;
If of the modest mansion aught remains
Where Heaven and nature prompted Cowper's strains;[24]
Where Roscoe,[25] to whose patriot breast belong
The Roman virtue and the Tuscan song,
Led Ceres[26] to the black and barren moor
Where Ceres never gained a wreath before[27] –
With curious search their pilgrim steps shall rove
By many a ruined tower and proud alcove,
Shall listen for those strains that soothed of yore

Notes

[16] Barbauld knew of Lake Ontario, the Niagara Falls and the Blue Mountains of Pennsylvania through William Winterbotham's *View of the American United States* (1795).

[17] *Isis* poetic name for the River Thames in Oxford.

[18] *Runnymede* In 1215 in Runnymede, King John signed the Magna Carta, a major statement of liberties in England.

[19] *where Cam's slow waters wind* The Cam rises in Hertfordshire, flows past Cambridge into the Isle of Ely, and there joins the Ouse.

[20] *Newton's awful brow* Sir Isaac Newton was a Fellow of Trinity College, Cambridge, and Lucasian Professor of Mathematics. He is commemorated by a statue in the antechapel of Trinity, mentioned by Wordsworth, *Thirteen-Book Prelude* iii 58–9.

[21] *where Avon's winding waters stray* Stratford-on-Avon, Shakespeare's birthplace.

[22] Thomas Clarkson (1760–1846), a 'friend of man' in that he was a prominent campaigner for abolition of the slave trade. He was born in Wisbech.

[23] Sir William Jones (1746–94), linguist and orientalist. Born in London, he became a Judge at the High Court in Calcutta, and published widely on the law and oriental languages. His authoritative translations did much to introduce oriental elements into western literature.

[24] William Cowper (1731–1800), author of *The Task* (1785); see pp. 16–17.

[25] William Roscoe (1753–1831), botanist, historian, banker, and (like Barbauld) a prominent Unitarian. He had been opposed to the war with France from its outset.

[26] *Ceres* Roman goddess of the growth of food plants.

[27] 'The Historian of the age of Leo has brought into cultivation the extensive tract of Chatmoss' (Barbauld's note). She refers to Roscoe's experiments at Chat Moss in Lancashire in which he reclaimed moorland for the cultivation of high-quality crops. Croker's review in the *Quarterly* was scathing about this reference; quoting lines 147–50, he commented: 'O the unequal dispensations of this poetical providence! Chatham and Nelson empty names! Oxford and Cambridge in ruins! London a desert, and the Thames a sedgy brook! while Mr Roscoe's barns and piggeries are in excellent repair, and objects not only of curiosity but even of reverence and enthusiasm' (*Quarterly Review* 7 (1812) 311–12).

Thy rock, stern Skiddaw, and thy fall, Lodore;[28]
Feast with Dun Edin's[29] classic brow their sight,
And 'visit Melross by the pale moonlight'.[30]
But who their mingled feelings shall pursue
When London's faded glories rise to view?
The mighty city, which by every road,
In floods of people poured itself abroad;
Ungirt by walls, irregularly great,
No jealous drawbridge, and no closing gate;
Whose merchants (such the state which commerce brings)
Sent forth their mandates to dependent kings;
Streets, where the turbaned Moslem, bearded Jew,
And woolly Afric, met the brown Hindu;
Where through each vein spontaneous plenty flowed,
Where Wealth enjoyed, and Charity bestowed.
Pensive and thoughtful shall the wanderers greet
Each splendid square, and still, untrodden street;
Or of some crumbling turret, mined by time,
The broken stair with perilous step shall climb,
Thence stretch their view the wide horizon round,
By scattered hamlets trace its ancient bound,
And, choked no more with fleets, fair Thames survey –
Through reeds and sedge pursue his idle way.
With throbbing bosoms shall the wanderers tread
The hallowed mansions of the silent dead,
Shall enter the long isle and vaulted dome[31]
Where Genius and where Valour find a home;
Awestruck, midst chill sepulchral marbles breathe,
Where all above is still as all beneath;
Bend at each antique shrine, and frequent turn
To clasp with fond delight some sculptured urn,
The ponderous mass of Johnson's form to greet,
Or breathe the prayer at Howard's sainted feet.[32]
Perhaps some Briton, in whose musing mind
Those ages live which Time has cast behind,
To every spot shall lead his wondering guests
On whose known site the beam of glory rests:
Here Chatham's[33] eloquence in thunder broke,
Here Fox persuaded, or here Garrick spoke;[34]
Shall boast how Nelson, fame and death in view,
To wonted victory led his ardent crew,

Notes

[28] *Thy rock, stern Skiddaw, and thy fall, Lodore* Skiddaw mountain and the Lodore falls in the Lake District were popular tourist attractions.

[29] *Dun Edin* poetical name for Edinburgh.

[30] *visit Melross by the pale moonlight* An allusion to Scott's popular poem, *The Lay of the Last Minstrel* (1805), ii 1–2: 'If thou wouldst view fair Melrose aright, / Go visit it by the pale moonlight.' Then as now, Melrose Abbey was popular with tourists.

[31] *the long isle and vaulted dome* of St Paul's cathedral.

[32] *The ponderous mass . . . feet* Statues of Samuel Johnson and John Howard (prison reformer) stand in the nave of St Paul's.

[33] *Chatham* Pitt the elder, first Earl of Chatham (1708–78), Prime Minister during the Seven Years War.

[34] *Here Fox persuaded, or here Garrick spoke* Charles James Fox (1749–1806), Whig leader, and a focus for liberal opinion, particularly during the ministries of Pitt the younger (1783–1801, 1804–6); David Garrick (1717–79), actor-manager.

In England's name enforced, with loftiest tone,[35]
Their duty – and too well fulfilled his own;
How gallant Moore,[36] as ebbing life dissolved,
But hoped his country had his fame absolved;
Or call up sages whose capacious mind
Left in its course a track of light behind;
Point where mute crowds on Davy's lips[37] reposed,
And Nature's coyest secrets were disclosed;
Join with their Franklin, Priestley's injured name,[38]
Whom, then, each continent shall proudly claim.
Oft shall the strangers turn their eager feet
The rich remains of ancient art to greet,
The pictured walls with critic eye explore,
And Reynolds[39] be what Raphael was before.
On spoils from every clime their eyes shall gaze,
Egyptian granites and the Etruscan vase;
And when midst fallen London, they survey
The stone where Alexander's ashes lay,[40]
Shall own with humbled pride the lesson just
By Time's slow finger written in the dust.
There walks a spirit[41] o'er the peopled earth –
Secret his progress is, unknown his birth;
Moody and viewless[42] as the changing wind,
No force arrests his foot, no chains can bind;
Where'er he turns, the human brute awakes,
And, roused to better life, his sordid hut forsakes;
He thinks, he reasons, glows with purer fires,
Feels finer wants, and burns with new desires.
Obedient Nature follows where he leads –
The steaming marsh is changed to fruitful meads;
The beasts retire from man's asserted reign,
And prove his kingdom was not given in vain.

Notes

35 'Every reader will recollect the sublime telegraphic dispatch, "England expects every man to do his duty" ' (Barbauld's note). Admiral Lord Nelson issued this order prior to the Battle of Trafalgar (21 October 1805), in which he was killed, despite a British victory.

36 ' "I hope England will be satisfied", were the last words of General Moore' (Barbauld's note). General Sir John Moore led the army that failed to prevent Napoleon from taking Madrid. He evacuated his troops at the Battle of Corunna at the expense of his own life.

37 *Davy's lips* Sir Humphry Davy (1778–1829), the foremost scientist of his day, lectured on chemistry and physics at the Royal Institution.

38 *Join with their Franklin, Priestley's injured name* Benjamin Franklin and Joseph Priestley experimented with electricity in the 1790s. They were also radicals, and Priestley was hounded out of England by a mob drummed up by Tory opponents, because of his support for the French Revolution. He emigrated to America in 1794.

39 Sir Joshua Reynolds was the most distinguished and successful portrait-painter of his day, and had been, from 1768 to 1792, President of the Royal Academy. He published his *Discourses* from 1769 to 1791, and in 1784 was made Painter-in-Ordinary to the King – an honour which, as he ruefully observed, brought him a stipend less than that of the King's rat-catcher.

40 *The stone where Alexander's ashes lay* Barbauld has in mind the granite sarcophagus on display at the British Museum from 1802 onwards, believed to be that of Alexander the Great.

41 *spirit* perhaps that of civilization, or at least the spirit that makes civilization possible. In this account of the rise and fall of civilizations Barbauld is probably inspired by Comte de Volney's *The Ruins, or A Survey of the Revolutions of Empires* (1792). The 'spirit' was a gift to Croker in the *Quarterly*; quoting lines 215–18, he commented: 'This extraordinary personage is prodigiously wise and potent, but withal a little fickle, and somewhat, we think, for so wise a being, unjust and partial. He has hitherto resided in this country, and chiefly in London; Mrs Barbauld, however, foresees that he is beginning to be tired of us, and is preparing to go out of town' (*Quarterly Review* 7 (1812) 312).

42 *viewless* invisible.

Then from its bed is drawn the ponderous ore,
Then Commerce pours her gifts on every shore,
Then Babel's towers and terraced gardens rise,
And pointed obelisks invade the skies;
The prince commands, in Tyrian purple[43] dressed,
And Egypt's virgins weave the linen vest.
Then spans the graceful arch the roaring tide,
And stricter bounds the cultured fields divide.
Then kindles Fancy, then expands the heart,
Then blow the flowers of Genius and of Art;
Saints, heroes, sages, who the land adorn,
Seem rather to descend than to be born;
Whilst History, midst the rolls consigned to fame,
With pen of adamant inscribes their name.
  The genius now forsakes the favoured shore,
And hates, capricious, what he loved before;
Then empires fall to dust, then arts decay,
And wasted realms enfeebled despots sway;
Even Nature's changed; without his fostering smile
Ophir[44] no gold, no plenty yields the Nile;
The thirsty sand absorbs the useless rill,
And spotted plagues from putrid fens distil.
In desert solitudes then Tadmor[45] sleeps,
Stern Marius then o'er fallen Carthage weeps;[46]
Then with enthusiast love the pilgrim roves
To seek his footsteps in forsaken groves,
Explores the fractured arch, the ruined tower,
Those limbs disjointed of gigantic power;
Still at each step he dreads the adder's sting,
The Arab's javelin, or the tiger's spring;
With doubtful caution treads the echoing ground,
And asks where Troy or Babylon[47] is found.
  And now the vagrant Power no more detains
The Vale of Tempe[48] or Ausonian[49] plains;
Northward he throws the animating ray,
O'er Celtic nations bursts the mental day –
And, as some playful child the mirror turns,
Now here, now there, the moving lustre burns;
Now o'er his changeful fancy more prevail
Batavia's[50] dykes than Arno's purple vale,
And stinted suns, and rivers bound with frost,

Notes

[43] *Tyrian purple* In ancient times, a purple or crimson dye was made at Phoenicia from molluscs.

[44] *Ophir* the land from which Solomon's navy fetched gold; see 1 Kings 9: 26–8.

[45] *Tadmor* a biblical name for the oasis of Palmyra between Syria and Babylon.

[46] *Stern Marius then o'er fallen Carthage weeps* Plutarch relates that, on being denied entry to Carthage by its Roman governor, Sextilius, Gaius Marius remarked: 'Tell him, then, that thou hast seen Gaius Marius a fugitive, seated amid the ruins of Carthage.'

[47] *Troy or Babylon* major cities of ancient times which are no longer to be found. The point is that London will share the same fate.

[48] *The Vale of Tempe* a valley in Thessaly celebrated as a rural paradise; effectively Greece.

[49] *Ausonian* Italian; effectively Rome.

[50] *Batavia* Holland.

Than Enna's plains[51] or Baia's viny coast;
Venice the Adriatic weds in vain,
And Death sits brooding o'er Campania's plain;[52]
O'er Baltic shores and through Hercynian groves,[53]
Stirring the soul, the mighty impulse moves;
Art plies his tools, and Commerce spreads her sail,
And wealth is wafted in each shifting gale.
The sons of Odin[54] tread on Persian looms,
And Odin's daughters breathe distilled perfumes;
Loud minstrel bards, in Gothic halls, rehearse
The Runic rhyme, and 'build the lofty verse';[55]
The Muse, whose liquid notes were wont to swell
To the soft breathings of the Aeolian shell,
Submits, reluctant, to the harsher tone,
And scarce believes the altered voice her own.
And now, where Caesar saw with proud disdain
The wattled hut and skin of azure stain,[56]
Corinthian columns rear their graceful forms,
And light verandas brave the wintry storms,
While British tongues the fading fame prolong
Of Tully's eloquence and Maro's song.[57]
Where once Bonduca whirled the scythed car,[58]
And the fierce matrons raised the shriek of war,
Light forms beneath transparent muslins float,
And tutored voices swell the artful note.
Light-leaved acacias and the shady plane
And spreading cedar grace the woodland reign;
While crystal walls[59] the tenderer plants confine,
The fragrant orange and the nectared pine;[60]
The Syrian grape there hangs her rich festoons,
Nor asks for purer air, or brighter noons;
Science and Art urge on the useful toil,
New mould a climate and create the soil,
Subdue the rigour of the northern bear,[61]
O'er polar climes shed aromatic air,
On yielding Nature urge their new demands,
And ask not gifts but tribute at her hands.
London exults – on London Art bestows
Her summer ices and her winter rose;
Gems of the east her mural crown adorn,

Notes

[51] *Enna's plains* Enna was a town in the middle of Sicily surrounded by plains of wheat. Baiae was a Roman resort in the Bay of Naples associated with the wines of Campania.

[52] *Campania's plain* Not the Roman *campagna* but the province of Naples, a centre of bubonic plague.

[53] *Hercynian groves* the Black Forest in Germany.

[54] *sons of Odin* northern Europeans – Danes, Swedes, Germans.

[55] *build the lofty verse* an allusion to Milton's *Lycidas*: 'Who would not sing for Lycidas? he knew / Himself to sing, and build the lofty rhyme' (ll. 10–11).

[56] *azure stain* Julius Caesar described how the Britons painted themselves with blue war-paint in his *Gallic Wars*.

[57] *Tully* Cicero; *Maro* Virgil.

[58] *scythed car* The native British queen, Boudicca, fixed knives to the wheels of her chariot.

[59] *crystal walls* greenhouse.

[60] *pine* pineapple.

[61] *the northern bear* the constellation of the Great Bear, which contains the north star.

And Plenty at her feet pours forth her horn;
While even the exiles her just laws disclaim,
People a continent, and build a name.[62]
August she sits, and with extended hands
Holds forth the Book of Life to distant lands.[63]
    But fairest flowers expand but to decay;
The worm is in thy core, thy glories pass away;
Arts, arms and wealth destroy the fruits they bring;
Commerce, like beauty, knows no second spring.
Crime walks thy streets, Fraud earns her unblessed bread,
O'er want and woe thy gorgeous robe is spread,
And angel charities in vain oppose:
With grandeur's growth the mass of misery grows.
For see, to other climes the genius soars,
He turns from Europe's desolated shores;
And lo! even now, midst mountains wrapped in storm,
On Andes' heights he shrouds his awful form;
On Chimborazo's summits[64] treads sublime,
Measuring in lofty thought the march of Time;
Sudden he calls, ''Tis now the hour!' he cries,
Spreads his broad hand, and bids the nations rise.
La Plata[65] hears amidst her torrents' roar;
Potosi[66] hears it, as she digs the ore:
Ardent, the genius fans the noble strife,
And pours through feeble souls a higher life,
Shouts to the mingled tribes from sea to sea,
And swears thy world, Columbus, shall be free.[67]

Hannah More (1745–1833)

For Dr Johnson, she was 'the most powerful versificatrix in the English language'; in purely financial terms, Hannah More was one of the most successful writers of her day, having made £30,000 by her publications by 1825 (£1.3 million / US$2,385,000 today). Born at Fishponds in the parish of Stapleton, near Bristol, she was the fourth of five daughters of Mary Grace and Jacob More (d. 1783), a teacher who (unusually for the time) was determined to ensure that his daughters were capable of making an independent living. By the age of 4 she astonished the local clergyman with her recital of the catechism. Her father was apparently 'frightened by his

Notes

[62] *While even . . . name* Those exiled and disowned by Britain's (un)just and oppressive laws leave for other countries – Australia or America.

[63] *Holds forth the Book of Life to distant lands* a reference to the work of the British and Foreign Bible Society (founded 1804), which distributed cheap bibles at home and abroad.

[64] *Chimborazo's summits* Chimborazo is the highest peak in the Andes, in present-day Ecuador; first scaled in June 1797.

[65] *La Plata* a large river in South America, formed by the union of the great rivers Parana and Uruguay.

[66] *Potosi* St Luis de Potosi is a city in Mexico situated in the midst of rich gold mines.

[67] *free* Barbauld's optimism about South America stems from news of independence movements among the Spanish colonies there.

own success' at teaching her Latin and mathematics, but the entreaties of his family encouraged him to continue.

She began her career as a playwright, winning praise from the poet John Langhorne for *The Search after Happiness* (1773). It was through him that she met David Garrick, who would compose the epilogue for her tragedy *The Inflexible Captive* (1774). He in turn introduced her to Burke, Johnson, Reynolds and, crucially, Elizabeth Montagu, queen of the Bluestockings, of which More quickly became a member. Never as close-knit and exclusive as they are sometimes thought, the group included at various times Anna Laetitia Barbauld, Elizabeth Carter, Mrs Boscawen, the Duchess of Beaufort, Mrs Leveson, Mrs Walsingham and the Duchess of Portland, and received visits from Reynolds, Johnson, Walpole and Lord Lyttelton.

On visits to London More stayed with Garrick and his wife Eva Marie at their riverside villa in Hampton. On one of these visits he encouraged her to work on a new tragedy, *Percy*, about a woman misjudged and murdered by a jealous husband. It opened in London in 1777 to immediate acclaim and sold 4,000 copies in a fortnight. Mrs Siddons's performance is said to have reduced Charles James Fox, the Whig leader, to tears. But after Garrick died in January 1779 More stopped writing for the stage, his death having prompted her to reassess her future.

Garrick was famous as an exponent of the drama of sensibility, which he must have discussed with her. As a tribute to him, she composed *Sensibility*, presented here complete in its earliest (and best) text of 1782 (see p. 56). Later versions depersonalize its contents, which has tended to blind readers to the fact that it was written for, and inspired by, a small coterie – among whom it had been circulating for at least a year prior to publication. As such, it contains many in-jokes, as well as a tribute to Garrick that in later versions was toned down and, ultimately, eliminated. Its air of light-heartedness enshrines something of the good humour that made the Bluestockings such a congenial group, but it is useful to bear in mind that they were famous partly for the moral and religious works that several of their number (notably Hester Chapone and Catherine Macaulay) had published, and for campaigning on behalf of universal education. Moreover, as Sylvia Harcstark Myers has argued, Elizabeth Carter claimed that it was 'unfair to women to keep them from rational conversation with men because it kept them from developing their intellectual capacities':[1] this is the feminist subtext that underlies More's portrayal of this group of educated women who wished to rid society of card-playing in exchange for polite conversation. Accordingly, More portrays Sensibility as a female deity, 'the melancholy muse' (l. 206) capable of generating pleasure – 'The sacred rapture of a pain like this!' (l. 170). In its central passage (ll. 239ff.), she discounts the writings of male writers such as Otway, Rowe and Richardson, arguing that sensibility is the preserve of Bluestockings such as Frances Boscawen, Elizabeth Carter, Hester Chapone, Frances Walsingham, Mary Delany and Anna Laetitia Barbauld. Her view of psychology and literature is gendered: she thinks women have a way of thinking and feeling that better disposes them to sensibility:

> . . . where bright imagination reigns,
> The fine-wrought spirit feels acuter pains:
> Where glow exalted sense, and taste refined,
> There keener anguish rankles in the mind;
> There feeling is diffused through every part,
> Thrills in each nerve, and lives in all the heart.
> (ll. 65–70)

Notes

[1] *The Bluestocking Circle: Women, Friendship, and the Life of the Mind in Eighteenth-Century England* (Oxford, 1990), p. 262.

Reviews were largely favourable; critics rightly saw that its central point was its critique of debased forms of sentiment. The *Monthly Review* approved:

> In a book 'chiefly intended for young persons',[2] it is not with impropriety that Miss More has introduced the concluding composition, *Sensibility*, there being nothing of which they are more apt to form mistaken ideas than of that sympathetic tenderness which is supposed to have its source in the amiable affections of the heart. From these mistaken ideas it is that so many, by giving way to the immoderate indulgence of sensibility, destroy their own peace, while a still greater number, by its affectation, render themselves disgusting.[3]

For similar reasons the *European Magazine* commended it: 'It displays a considerable portion of that quality which gives name to the poem, and shows the writer in a very amiable point of view, as an individual. Her candour, friendship, gratitude, and taste, are eminently conspicuous in several parts of the poem.'[4]

More retired to a cottage in Cowslip Green, Somerset, devoting herself to didactic and educational works, one of the most important of which was *Slavery: A Poem* (1788). The year before, she had written to Elizabeth Carter to tell her of 'the great object I have so much at heart – the project to abolish the slave trade in Africa. This most important cause has very much occupied my thoughts this summer; the young gentleman who has embarked in it with the zeal of an apostle has been much with me, and engaged all my little interest, and all my affections in it. It is to be brought before parliament in the spring. Above one hundred members have promised their votes.' The 'young gentleman' was William Wilberforce, then in his twenties; she was in her forties. Despite the age difference, and the fact that he was a liberal and she a conservative, they had much in common, and became firm friends. Both were disciples of the reformed slave-trader John Newton, and that no doubt helped bring them together. At the age of 28, Wilberforce was already campaigning in Parliament for measures to be taken to eliminate slavery at home and in the colonies. More believed that slavery was an abomination, and was advising her friends to boycott the use of West Indian sugar in their tea. She even carried about with her Clarkson's plan of an African slave-ship, showing it to interested and horrified guests at dinner parties.

She was following events closely when on 21 May 1788 Sir William Dolben proposed a Bill to the House of Commons aimed at restricting the number of slaves who could be transported from Africa to British colonies in the West Indies. Though a comparatively small measure, it was the first step towards abolition, and aroused the well-funded opposition of business interests. On 26 May merchants and inhabitants of Liverpool presented a petition to the House, arguing that Dolben's Bill would cause them financial ruin; fortunately the Bill was passed in both Houses. *Slavery: A Poem* was written in anticipation, within two weeks ('too short and too much hurried', More said), and articulates its author's impatience with the caution of the proposed measures, arguing instead for complete abolition. One of the most favourable of its reviews appeared in the *New Annual Register*, which remarked that 'The sentiments which she expresses are humane and just; her descriptions pathetic and affecting; and her indignation against those who degrade the sable race in the scale of being is delivered in language that is poetical and spirited.'[5] William Cowper also wrote a poem on the occasion of Dolben's Bill, satirizing the pleas of those in the

Notes

[2] A reference to the full title of the volume in which *Sensibility* was first published; see p. 56.

[3] *Monthly Review* 67 (1782) 31–5, p. 32.

[4] *European Magazine* 1 (1782) 205–6, p. 205.

[5] *New Annual Register* 9 (1788) 260.

Figure 6 Hannah More (1745–1833) painted by Henry William Pickersgill, 1822. One of the most successful female writers of the period, beginning with success as a dramatist in the early 1770s. (National Portrait Gallery, London.)

slave trade who claimed that it would make them destitute (see pp. 21–2).

One of More's biggest successes, the Cheap Repository tracts, was the idea of her friend Bishop Porteus. By late 1791 the political radicalism that had crossed the Channel from France was alarming to those who, like Porteus, feared working-class insurrection or, worse still, French invasion. He suggested to More that she 'write some little thing tending to open their eyes under their present wild impressions of liberty and equality'. The declared agenda of the Cheap Repository was thus to deradicalize working people, encouraging them to accept their lot.

To this end a range of writers composed moral tales and ballads that were published, individually, on single sheets (called 'broadsides') under the Cheap Repository imprint; in the end More wrote over fifty. The secret of their success lay partly in their design: each was decked out with rakish titles and woodcuts in the manner of the bawdy songsheets sold in alehouses. As More observed, 'It is as vulgar as heart can wish, but it is only designed for the most vulgar class of readers.'

The first was published on 3 March 1795; over 300,000 copies were sold by 18 April, and two million within the year. In the event few copies were sold to working people, most being purchased in bulk by philanthropic committees and distributed free of charge in schools, workhouses, hospitals and prisons. *The Story of Sinful Sally*, published in February 1796, is typical: the text is interspersed by woodcuts, each showing its protagonist at a different stage in her journey. The series came to an end when, in 1799, More was compelled to give it up due to ill health.

In later years she enjoyed success with *Coelebs in Search of a Wife* (1809) which, though published anonymously, went into eleven editions within the year. The enduring popularity of her work during the nineteenth century drew many pilgrims to her door, and she was compelled to reserve two days a week for visitors so that she could spend the remainder in peace. She died peacefully on 7 September 1833, at the age of 88, leaving her fortune to a range of charitable institutions and religious societies.

Further reading

Selected Writings of Hannah More ed. Robert Hole (London, 1996).

Sylvia Harcstark Myers, *The Bluestocking Circle: Women, Friendship, and the Life of the Mind in Eighteenth-Century England* (Oxford, 1990).

Ann Stott, *Hannah More: The First Victorian* (Oxford, 2003).

Sensibility: A Poetical Epistle to the Hon. Mrs Boscawen[1]

From Sacred Dramas: chiefly intended for young persons: the subjects taken from the Bible. To which is added, Sensibility, A Poem (1782)

Spirits are not finely touched but to fine issues.[2]
(Shakespeare)

The following little poem was sent several years ago, as an epistle to the honoured friend to whom it is inscribed. It has since been enlarged, and several passages have been added, or altered, as circumstances required.[3]

Notes

SENSIBILITY

[1] Sensibility was a preoccupation central to the Bluestocking coterie of which More was part. It is the subject also of poems by Ann Yearsley (p. 155) and Anna Laetitia Barbauld (p. 31). Frances, daughter of William Evelyn Glanville, Esq., married Admiral Edward Boscawen, Viscount Falmouth, in 1742. He was a national hero, having thwarted a French invasion in an important battle in Lagos Bay in August 1759. He died of typhoid fever, 10 January 1761. In 1775, More told her sister that 'Mrs Boscawen's life has been a continued series of afflictions that may almost bear a parallel with those of the righteous man of Uz.'

[2] *Measure for Measure* I i 35–6.

[3] More continued to revise the poem through successive editions.

Accept, Boscawen, these unpolished lays,
Nor blame too much the verse you cannot praise;
For you, far other bards have waked the string,
Far other bards for you were wont to sing.
Yet on the gale their parting music steals;
Yet your charmed ear the loved impression feels;
You heard the lyres of Lyttelton and Young,[4]
And this a grace, and that a seraph strung.
These are no more! But not with these decline
The Attic chasteness and the flame divine:
Still sad Elfrida's poet[5] shall complain,
And either Warton breathe his classic strain.[6]
Nor fear lest genuine poesy expire
While tuneful Beattie wakes old Spenser's lyre.[7]
His sympathetic lay his soul reveals,
And paints the perfect bard from what he feels.
  Illustrious Lowth![8] For him the muses wove
The fairest garland from their greenest grove.
Though Latian[9] bards had gloried in his name,
When in full brightness burnt the Latian flame,
Yet fired with nobler hopes than transient bays,
He scorned the meed of perishable praise,
Spurned the cheap wreath by human science won,
Borne on the wing sublime of Amos' son;[10]
He seized his mantle as the prophet flew,[11]
And caught some portion of his spirit too.
  To snatch bright beauty from devouring fate
And bid it boast with him a deathless date;
To show how genius fires, how taste restrains,
While what both are, his pencil best explains,
Have we not Reynolds?[12] Lives not Jenyns yet,
To prove his lowest title was a wit?[13]
Though purer flames thy hallowed zeal inspire

Notes

[4] *Lyttelton and Young* At the behest of Elizabeth Montagu and Elizabeth Carter, Edward Young (1683-1765) composed *Resignation* to console Mrs Boscawen for her husband's death. George, Lord Lyttelton (1709–73), was introduced to Mrs Boscawen by Mrs Montagu. He had addressed a poem to her husband in September 1747 ('To the Memory of Capt. Grenville').

[5] *sad Elfrida's poet* William Mason (1725–97), author of *Elfrida: a dramatic poem* (1752). 'Milton calls Euripedes "sad Electra's poet"' (More's note); see Milton's *Sonnet VIII. When the assault was intended to the City* 13.

[6] *And either Warton breathe his classic strain* Joseph Warton (1722–1800) and his brother Thomas Warton the younger (1728–90) were distinguished classicists. Joseph translated and edited Virgil in 1753; Thomas composed poems in Latin.

[7] *tuneful Beattie wakes old Spenser's lyre* More refers to *The Minstrel* (1771–4) by James Beattie (1735–1803), written in Spenserian stanzas.

[8] Robert Lowth, Bishop of London (1710–87), a skilled Latinist and Hebrew scholar. His most famous work was *De Sacra Poesi Hebraeorum* (1753), translated by Gregory in 1787 as *Lectures on the Sacred Poetry of the Hebrews*.

[9] *Latian* Latin.

[10] *Amos' son* Isaiah.

[11] *He seized his mantle as the prophet flew* More alludes to Elijah's casting of his mantle (cloak) on Elisha (1 Kings 19: 19).

[12] 'See his Discourses to the Academy' (More's note). Sir Joshua Reynolds (1723–92), was the most renowned portrait-painter of the age. His first discourse was delivered in 1769, and subsequent lectures became yearly fixtures at the Royal Academy. He met More in 1775, when she described his most recent discourse as 'a masterpiece for matter as well as style'.

[13] Later editions of *Sensibility* carried the note: 'Mr Soame Jenyns had just published his work *On the internal Evidence of the Christian Religion.*' Soame Jenyns (1704–87), poet and pamphleteer, was much admired by More; she claimed to know someone converted to Christianity by his *View of the Internal Evidence of the Christian Religion* (1776).

Than ere were kindled at the muse's fire,
Thee, mitred Chester,[14] all the Nine[15] shall boast,
And is not Johnson theirs, himself an host?[16]
Yes: still for you your gentle stars dispense
The charm of friendship and the feast of sense;
Yours is the bliss, and Heav'n no dearer sends
To call the wisest, brightest, best, your friends.
With Carter trace the wit to Athens known,[17]
Or find in Montagu[18] that wit our own;
Or, pleased, attend Chapone's instructive page,[19]
Which charms her own, and forms the rising age;
Or boast in Walsingham[20] the various pow'r
To soothe the lonely, grace the lettered hour –
To polished life its highest charm she gives,
Whose song is music, and whose canvas lives.
Delany shines, in worth serenely bright,
Wisdom's strong ray, and virtue's milder light;
And she who blessed the friend, and graced the page
Of Swift, still lends her lustre to our age:[21]
Long, long protract thy light, oh star benign,
Whose setting beams with added brightness shine!
Oh much-loved Barbauld,[22] shall my heart refuse
Its tribute to thy virtues and thy muse?
While round thy brow the poet's wreath I twine,
This humble merit shall at least be mine,
In all thy praise to take a gen'rous part,
Thy laurels bind thee closer to my heart.
My verse thy merits to the world shall teach,
And love the genius it despairs to reach.
Yet what is wit, and what the poet's art?
Can genius shield the vulnerable heart?
Ah no, where bright imagination reigns,

Notes

[14] 'See the Bishop's admirable Poem on Death' (More's note). Beilby Porteus, Bishop of Chester and, later, London (1731–1808), first published the popular *Death: A Poetical Essay* in 1759. His response to this allusion was an appreciative quatrain:

How potent is thy Muse, oh More,
Whose vivifying breath
Can do what Muse ne'er did before:
Give life and fame to – *death*!

[15] *Nine* the Muses.

[16] *And is not Johnson theirs, himself an host?* More was a friend of Dr Johnson, whom she met in 1774.

[17] *With Carter trace the wit to Athens known* Elizabeth Carter's translation, *All the Works of Epictetus which are now extant* (1758), was a considerable success in its day.

[18] Elizabeth Montagu, 'Queen of the Blue-stockings' (1720–1800). 'She is not only the finest genius, but the finest lady I ever saw,' More wrote in 1775.

[19] *Chapone's instructive page* Hester Chapone (1727-1801), friend and collaborator of Richardson, who called her 'a little spitfire'. Her best-known work, to which More refers here, was *Letters on the Improvement of the Mind* (1773), dedicated to Mrs Montagu. It was enormously popular, being reprinted 16 times by the end of the century.

[20] Mrs Boyle Walsingham was a Bluestocking and close friend of More's.

[21] *And she who blessed . . . to our age* Mary Delany (1700–88), Bluestocking, had known Pope and Swift. She met Swift in 1733, and enjoyed a correspondence with him. In a letter of 1788, Burke told More that Mrs Delany 'was almost the only person he ever saw who, at eight-eight, blushed like a girl'. She is now best known for nearly a thousand perfectly accurate plant pictures made from cut paper in her old age, preserved in the Print Room of the British Museum, London. See Ruth Hayden, *Mrs Delany and her Flower Collages* (2nd edn, London, 1992).

[22] *Oh much-loved Barbauld* In 1782 Anna Laetitia Barbauld was best known for her first volume of poems, which included *Corsica* (1773), of which Mrs Montagu was a keen admirer.

The fine-wrought spirit feels acuter pains:
Where glow exalted sense, and taste refined,
There keener anguish rankles in the mind;
There feeling is diffused through every part,
Thrills in each nerve, and lives in all the heart;
And those whose gen'rous souls each tear would keep
From others' eyes, are born themselves to weep.
Say, can the boasted pow'rs of wit and song
Of life one pang remove, one hour prolong?
Presumptuous hope, which daily truths deride –
For you, alas, have wept, and Garrick died![23]
Ne'er shall my heart his loved remembrance lose,
Guide, critic, guardian, glory of my muse!
Oh shades of Hampton,[24] witness, as I mourn,
Could wit or song elude *his* destined urn?
Though living virtue still your haunts endears,
Yet buried worth shall justify my tears.
Garrick! Those pow'rs which form a friend were thine;
And let me add, with pride, that friend was mine –
With pride! At once the vain emotion's fled,
Far other thoughts are sacred to the dead.
Who now with spirit keen, yet judgement cool,
Th' unequal wand'rings of my muse shall rule?
Whose partial praise my worthless verse ensure?
For Candour smiled when Garrick would endure.
If harsher critics were compelled to blame,
I gained in friendship what I lost in fame;
And friendship's fost'ring smiles can well repay
What critic rigour justly takes away.
With keen acumen how his piercing eye
The fault concealed from vulgar view would spy!
While with a gen'rous warmth he strove to hide –
Nay, vindicate – the fault his judgement spied.
So pleased, could he detect a happy line,
That he would fancy merit ev'n in mine.
Oh gen'rous error, when by friendship bred!
His praises flattered me, but not misled.
No narrow views could bound his lib'ral mind;
His friend was man, his party humankind.
Agreed in this, opposing statesmen strove
Who most should gain his praise, or court his love.
His worth all hearts as to one centre drew;
Thus Tully's Atticus was Caesar's too.[25]
His wit so keen, it never missed its end,
So blameless too, it never lost a friend;
So chaste, that modesty ne'er learned to fear,
So pure, religion might unwounded hear.

Notes

[23] *and Garrick died!* David Garrick (1717-79), actor-manager, was More's principal mentor.

[24] *Oh shades of Hampton* Garrick's house, Hampton Villa in Middlesex.

[25] Atticus, though Cicero's friend and confidant, was politically neutral and remained friendly with Cicero's adversaries, Caesar and his followers.

How his quick mind, strong pow'rs, and ardent heart,
Impoverished nature, and exhausted art,
A brighter bard records,[26] a deathless muse!
But I his talents in his virtues lose:
Great parts are nature's gift; but that he shone
Wise, moral, good and virtuous, was his own.
Though Time his silent hand across has stole,
Soft'ning the tints of sorrow on the soul,
The deep impression long my heart shall fill,
And every mellowed trace be perfect still.
Forgive, Boscawen, if my sorrowing heart,
Intent on grief, forget the rules of art;
Forgive, if wounded recollection melt –
You best can pardon who have oft'nest felt.
You who for many a friend and hero mourn,
Who bend in anguish o'er the frequent urn;
You who have found how much the feeling heart
Shapes its own wound, and points itself the dart;
You who from tender sad experience feel
The wound such minds receive can never heal;
That grief a thousand entrances can find,
Where parts superior dignify the mind;
Would you renounce the pangs those feelings give,
Secure in joyless apathy to live?
For though in souls where taste and sense abound,
Pain through a thousand avenues can wound;
Yet the same avenues are open still,
To casual blessings as to casual ill.
Nor is the trembling temper more awake
To every wound which misery can make,
Than is the finely-fashioned nerve alive
To every transport pleasure has to give.
For if, when home-felt[27] joys the mind elate,
It mourns in secret for another's fate;
Yet when its own sad griefs invade the breast,
Abroad, in others' blessings, see it blessed!
Ev'n the soft sorrow of remembered woe,
A not unpleasing sadness may bestow.
Let not the vulgar read this pensive strain,
Their jests the tender anguish would profane.
Yet these some deem the happiest of their kind,
Whose low enjoyments never reached the mind;
Who ne'er a pain but for themselves have known,
Nor ever felt a sorrow but their own;
Who call romantic every finer thought

Notes

[26] 'Mr Sheridan's Monody' (More's note). Sheridan's *Verses to the Memory of Garrick, spoken as a monody* was read at Drury Lane theatre and published in 1779.

[27] *Home-felt* experienced inwardly. The phrase derives from Milton, *Comus* 262: 'a sacred, and *home-felt* delight'. It occurs also in Pope's *Essay on Man* ii 256, and Warton's translation of Virgil:

Yet calm content, secure from guilty cares,
Yet *home-felt pleasure*, peace, and rest, are theirs . . .
(Warton, *Georgics* ii 566–7)

Conceived by pity, or by friendship wrought.
Ah, wherefore happy? Where's the kindred mind?
Where the large soul that takes in humankind?
Where the best passions of the mortal breast?
Where the warm blessing when another's blessed?
Where the soft lenitives of others' pain,
The social sympathy, the sense humane,
The sigh of rapture and the tear of joy,
Anguish that charms, and transports that destroy?
For tender Sorrow has her pleasures too,
Pleasures which prosp'rous Dullness never knew.
She never knew, in all her coarser bliss,
The sacred rapture of a pain like this!
Nor think the cautious only are the just;
Who never was deceived I would not trust.
Then take, ye happy vulgar, take your part
Of sordid joy which never touched the heart.
Benevolence, which seldom stays to choose,
Lest pausing Prudence teach her to refuse;
Friendship which, once determined, never swerves,
Weighs ere it trusts, but weighs not ere it serves;
And soft-eyed Pity, and Forgiveness bland,
And melting Charity with open hand;
And artless Love, believing and believed,
And gen'rous Confidence which ne'er deceived;
And Mercy stretching out, ere Want can speak,
To wipe the tear from pale Affliction's cheek:
These ye have never known – then take your part
Of sordid joy, which never touched the heart.
  You who have melted in bright glory's flame
Or felt the spirit-stirring breath of fame;
Ye noble few, in whom her promised meed
Wakes the great thought, and makes the wish the deed;
Ye who have tasted the delight to give,
And, God's own agents, bid the wretched live;
Who the chill haunts of Desolation seek,
Raise the sunk heart, and flush the fading cheek;
Ye who with pensive Petrarch love to mourn,
Or weave fresh chaplets for Tibullus' urn;
Who cherish both in Hammond's plaintive lay,[28]
The Provence myrtle, and the Roman bay;
Ye who divide the joys, and share the pains
Which merit feels, or Heav'n-born Fancy feigns;
Would you renounce such joys, such pains as these,
For vulgar pleasures, or for selfish ease?
Would you, to 'scape the pain, the joy forego,

Notes

[28] *Hammond's plaintive lay* James Hammond (1710–42), poet and politician, whose posthumously published *Love Elegies* (1743) were an instant success.

And miss the transport to avoid the woe?
Would you the sense of real sorrow lose,
Or cease to woo the melancholy muse?
No, Greville,[29] no! Thy song, though steeped in tears,
Though all thy soul in all thy strain appears,
Yet wouldst thou all thy well-sung anguish choose,
And all th' inglorious peace thou begg'st, refuse.
  Or you, Boscawen, when you fondly melt
In raptures none but mothers ever felt;
And view, enamoured, in your beauteous race,
All Leveson's sweetness, and all Beaufort's grace;[30]
Yet think what dangers each loved child may share,
The youth if valiant, and the maid if fair;
That perils multiply as blessings flow,
And constant sorrows on enjoyments grow;
You who have felt how fugitive is joy,
That while we clasp the phantom we destroy;
That life's bright sun is dimmed by clouded views,
And who have most to love have most to lose;
Yet from these fair possessions would you part,
To shield from future pain your guarded heart?
Would your fond mind renounce its tender boast,
Or with their opening bloom of promise lost?
Yield the dear hopes which break upon your view,
For all the quiet Dullness ever knew?
Debase the objects of your tend'rest prayer
To save the dangers of a distant care?
Consent, to shun the anxious fears you prove,
They less should merit, or you less should love?
  Yet while I hail the sympathy divine,
Which makes, oh man, the wants of others thine;
I mourn heroic Justice, scarcely owned,
And principle for sentiment dethroned.
While Feeling boasts her ever-tearful eye,
Stern Truth, firm Faith, and manly Virtue fly.
  Sweet sensibility, thou soothing pow'r
Who shedd'st thy blessings on the natal hour
Like fairy favours! Art can never seize,
Nor affectation catch thy pow'r to please:
Thy subtle essence still eludes the chains
Of definition, and defeats her pains.
Sweet sensibility, thou keen delight!
Thou hasty moral, sudden sense of right!
Thou untaught goodness! Virtue's precious seed!
Thou sweet precursor of the gen'rous deed!
Beauty's quick relish! Reason's radiant morn,

Notes

29 'Beautiful Ode to Indifference' (More's note). Frances Macartney (?1726–89), was the wife of Richard Fulke Greville, godmother of Fanny Burney, and author of 'A Prayer for Indifference'.

30 Leveson and Beaufort are Mrs Boscawen's daughters. Frances married Admiral John Leveson-Gower in 1773; Elizabeth married Henry, 5th Duke of Beaufort, in 1766.

Which dawns soft light before Reflection's born!
To those who know thee not, no words can paint,
And those who know thee, know all words are faint!
'Tis not to mourn because a sparrow dies,
To rave in artificial ecstasies;
'Tis not to melt in tender Otway's fires;
'Tis not to faint when injured Shore expires;
'Tis not because the ready eye o'erflows
At Clementina's or Clarissa's woes.[31]
 Forgive, oh Richardson, nor think I mean,
With cold contempt, to blast thy peerless scene;
If some faint love of virtue glow in me,
Pure spirit, I first caught that flame from thee.
 While soft Compassion silently relieves,
Loquacious Feeling hints how much she gives;
Laments how oft her wounded heart has bled,
And boasts of many a tear she never shed.
 As words are but th' external marks to tell
The fair ideas in the mind that dwell;
And only are of things the outward sign,
And not the things themselves they but define;
So exclamations, tender tones, fond tears,
And all the graceful drapery Pity wears;
These are not Pity's self, they but express
Her inward sufferings by their pictured dress;
And these fair marks, reluctant I relate,
These lovely symbols may be counterfeit.
Celestial Pity, why must I deplore
Thy sacred image stamped on basest ore?
There are, who fill with brilliant plaints the page,
If a poor linnet meet the gunner's rage;
There are, who for a dying fawn display
The tend'rest anguish in the sweetest lay;[32]
Who for a wounded animal deplore,
As if friend, parent, country, were no more;
Who boast quick rapture trembling in their eye,
If from the spider's snare they save a fly;
Whose well-sung sorrows every breast inflame,
And break all hearts but his from whom they came;
Yet scorning life's *dull* duties to attend,
Will persecute a wife, or wrong a friend;
Alive to every woe by fiction dressed,
The innocent he wronged, the wretch distressed,
May plead in vain; their suff'rings come not near,
Or he relieves them cheaply with a tear.[33]

Notes

[31] More refers to Catullus' poem in which Lesbia mourns her dead sparrow; Thomas Otway's *Venice Preserved* (1682); Nicholas Rowe's tragedy, *Jane Shore* (1714); Richardson's *Clarissa* (1747–8), and *Sir Charles Grandison* (1754), the heroine of which is called Clementina Porretta.

[32] More apparently disapproved of Marvell's *The Nymph complaining for the death of her faun*.

[33] More attacks a kind of sensibility that she and the other Bluestockings regarded as debased. In 1782, shortly after *Sensibility* had been published, she told her sister:

Not so the tender moralist of Tweed;
His Man of Feeling is a man indeed.[34]
Oh blessed Compassion! Angel Charity!
More dear one genuine deed performed for thee
Than all the periods Feeling e'er can turn,
Than all thy soothing pages, polished Sterne![35]
Not that by deeds alone this love's expressed,
If so, the affluent only were the blessed;
One silent wish, one prayer, one soothing word,
The precious page of Mercy shall record;
One soul-felt sigh by pow'rless Pity giv'n,
Accepted incense, shall ascend to heav'n!
Since trifles make the sum of human things,
And half our mis'ry from our foibles springs;
Since life's best joys consist in peace and ease,
And few can save or serve, but all may please:
Oh let th' ungentle spirit learn from hence,
A small unkindness is a great offence.
Large bounties to bestow we wish in vain,
But all may shun the guilt of giving pain.
To bless mankind with tides of flowing wealth,
With pow'r to grace them or to crown with health
Our little lot denies; but Heav'n decrees
To all, the gift of minist'ring to ease.
The gentle offices of patient love,
Beyond all flatt'ry, and all price above;
The mild forbearance at another's fault,
The taunting word, suppressed as soon as thought;
On these Heav'n bade the bliss of life depend,
And crushed ill-fortune when he made a friend.
A solitary blessing few can find,
Our joys with those we love are intertwined;
And he, whose helpful tenderness removes
Th' obstructing thorn which wounds the breast he loves,
Smooths not another's rugged path alone,
But scatters roses to adorn his own.
The hint malevolent, the look oblique,
The obvious satire, or implied dislike;
The sneer equivocal, the harsh reply,
And all the cruel language of the eye;
The artful injury whose venomed dart
Scarce wounds the hearing while it stabs the heart;
The guarded phrase whose meaning kills, yet told,
The list'ner wonders how you thought it cold;
Small slights, contempt, neglect unmixed with hate,
Make up in number what they want in weight.

Notes

'Mrs Montagu, Mrs Chapone, and Mrs Carter, are mightily pleased that I have attacked that mock feeling and sensibility which is at once the boast and disgrace of these times, and which is equally deficient in taste and truth.'

[34] Henry Mackenzie (1745–1831), native of Edinburgh, published his sentimental novel, *The Man of Feeling*, in 1771.

[35] Later versions of the poem read 'perverted Sterne'. Her attack is probably on *A Sentimental Journey* (1768).

These, and a thousand griefs minute as these,
Corrode our comfort and destroy our ease.
As this strong feeling tends to good or ill,
It gives fresh pow'r to vice or principle;
'Tis not peculiar to the wise and good;
'Tis passion's flame, the virtue of the blood.
But to divert it to its proper course,
There Wisdom's pow'r appears, there Reason's force;
If, ill-directed, it pursues the wrong,
It adds new strength to what before was strong;
Breaks out in wild irregular desires,
Disordered passions and illicit fires.
But if the virtuous bias rule the soul,
This lovely feeling then adorns the whole;
Sheds its sweet sunshine on the moral part,
Nor wastes on fancy what should warm the heart.
Cold and inert the mental pow'rs would lie
Without this quick'ning spark of deity.
To draw the rich materials from the mine,
To bid the mass of intellect refine,
To melt the firm, to animate the cold,
And Heav'n's own impress stamp on nature's gold;
To give immortal Mind its finest tone,
Oh sensibility, is all thy own!
This is th' ethereal flame which lights and warms,
In song transports us, and in action charms.
'Tis *this* that makes the pensive strains of Gray[36]
Win to the open heart their easy way;
Makes the touched spirit glow with kindred fire,
When sweet Serena's[37] poet wakes the lyre.
'Tis *this*, though nature's hidden treasures lie
Bare to the keen inspection of her eye,
Makes Portland's[38] face its brightest rapture wear,
When her large bounty smooths the bed of care;
'Tis *this* that breathes through Sevigné's sweet page,[39]
That nameless grace which soothes a second age;
'Tis *this* whose charms the soul resistless seize,
And gives Boscawen half her pow'r to please.
Yet why those terrors? Why that anxious care,
Since your last hope[40] the deathful war will dare?
Why dread that energy of soul which leads

Notes

[36] 'This is meant of the *Elegy in a Country Churchyard*, of which exquisite poem *sensibility* is, perhaps, the characteristic beauty' (More's note).

[37] 'Triumphs of Temper' (More's note). Serena is the principal character in William Hayley's *The Triumphs of Temper* (1781), admired by the Bluestockings.

[38] Lady Margaret Cavendish Harley, 2nd Duchess of Portland, prominent among the Bluestockings. She died in 1785.

[39] Marie de Rabutin-Chantal, marquise de Sévigné (1626–96), whose letters are an indispensable source of information on life under Louis XIV. Her equally remarkable, but more personal, letters to her daughter were first translated into English in 1727, and gained immediate popularity. These are the ones most admired by More who, in a letter of 1786, commended their 'excess of maternal tenderness'.

[40] 'Admiral Boscawen's only remaining son was then in America, and at the Battle of Lexington' (More's note). George Evelyn Boscawen, 3rd Viscount Falmouth, born in 1758, survived the American War and died in 1808.

To dang'rous glory by heroic deeds?
Why tremble lest his ardent soul aspire?
You fear the son because you knew the sire.
Hereditary valour you deplore
And dread, yet wish to find one hero more.

Slavery: A Poem (1788)[1]

Oh great design!
Ye sons of mercy! Oh complete your work;
Wrench from Oppression's hand the iron rod,
And bid the cruel feel the pains they give.
(Thomson's *Liberty*)[2]

If Heaven has into being deigned to call
Thy light, oh liberty, to shine on all,
Bright intellectual[3] sun, why does thy ray
To earth distribute only partial day?
Since no resisting cause from spirit flows,
Thy penetrating essence to oppose;
No obstacles by nature's hand impressed,
Thy subtle and ethereal beams arrest;
Nor motion's laws can speed thy active course,
Nor strong repulsion's pow'rs obstruct thy force –
Since there is no convexity in mind,
Why are thy genial beams to parts confined?
While the chill north with thy bright ray is blessed
Why should fell darkness half the south invest?
Was it decreed, fair Freedom, at thy birth,
That thou shouldst ne'er irradiate *all* the earth?
While Britain basks in thy full blaze of light,
Why lies sad Afric quenched in total night?
   Thee only, sober goddess, I attest,
In smiles chastised, and decent graces dressed;
Not that unlicensed monster of the crowd
Whose roar terrific bursts in peals so loud,
Deaf'ning the ear of Peace; fierce Faction's tool
Of rash Sedition born, and mad Misrule,

Notes

Slavery: A Poem

[1] More's poem was composed in anticipation of the passing of Sir William Dolben's Bill restricting the number of slaves who could be transported from Africa to British colonies in the West Indies; see headnote, p. 54. It was published at the same time as Yearsley's *Poem on the Inhumanity of the Slave-Trade* (p. 160).

[2] More is recalling, though inaccurately, a passage from Thomson's *Winter*, which celebrates the labours of a Parliamentary Committee that investigated allegations of torture in prisons in 1729:

O great design! if executed well,
With patient care, and wisdom-tempered zeal.
Ye sons of mercy! yet resume the search;
Drag forth the legal monsters into light,
Wrench from their hands Oppression's iron rod,
And bid the cruel feel the pains they give.
(ll. 376–81)

[3] *intellectual* spiritual.

Whose stubborn mouth, rejecting Reason's rein,
No strength can govern, and no skill restrain;
Whose magic cries the frantic vulgar draw,
To spurn at order, and to outrage law;
To tread on grave Authority and Pow'r,
And shake the work of ages in an hour.
Convulsed her voice, and pestilent her breath,
She raves of mercy while she deals out death –
Each blast is fate; she darts from either hand
Red conflagration o'er th' astonished land;
Clamouring for peace, she rends the air with noise,
And to reform a part, the whole destroys.
   Oh plaintive Southerne,[4] whose impassioned strain
So oft has waked my languid muse in vain!
Now, when congenial themes her cares engage,
She burns to emulate thy glowing page;
Her failing efforts mock her fond desires,
She shares thy feelings, not partakes thy fires.
Strange pow'r of song – the strain that warms the heart
Seems the same inspiration to impart;
Touched by the kindling energy alone,
We think the flame which melts us is our own;
Deceived, for genius we mistake delight;
Charmed as we read, we fancy we can write.
   Though not to me, sweet bard, thy pow'rs belong,
Fair Truth, a hallowed guide, inspires my song!
Here art would weave her gayest flow'rs in vain,
For Truth the bright invention would disdain.
For no fictitious ills these numbers flow,
But living anguish and substantial woe;
No individual griefs my bosom melt,
For millions feel what Oroonoko felt:[5]
Fired by no single wrongs, the countless host
I mourn, by rapine dragged from Afric's coast.
   Perish th' illiberal thought which would debase
The native genius of the sable race!
Perish the proud philosophy which sought
To rob them of the pow'rs of equal thought!
Does then th' immortal principle within
Change with the casual colour of a skin?
Does matter govern spirit, or is mind
Degraded by the form to which 'tis joined?
   No; they have heads to think, and hearts to feel,
And souls to act, with firm though erring zeal;
For they have keen affections, kind desires,
Love strong as death, and active patriot fires;
All the rude energy, the fervid flame

Notes

[4] 'Author of the tragedy of Oroonoko' (More's note). Thomas Southerne's *Oroonoko* (1695–6), an adaptation of Aphra Behn's anti-slavery novel (1688), was enormously popular.

[5] *what Oroonoko felt* The heir to an African king, Oroonoko is taken as a slave to Surinam, an English colony.

Of high-souled passion and ingenuous shame –
Strong but luxuriant virtues boldly shoot
From the wild vigour of a savage root.
    Nor weak their sense of honour's proud control,
For pride is virtue in a pagan soul;
A sense of worth, a conscience of desert,
A high, unbroken haughtiness of heart;
That self-same stuff which erst proud empires swayed,
Of which the conquerors of the world were made.
Capricious fate of man! That very pride
In Afric scourged, in Rome was deified.
    No muse, oh Qua-shi,[6] shall thy deeds relate,
No statute snatch thee from oblivious fate!
For thou wast born where never gentle muse
On valour's grave the flow'rs of genius strews;
And thou wast born where no recording page
Plucks the fair deed from time's devouring rage.
Had fortune placed thee on some happier coast,
Where polished souls heroic virtue boast,
To thee, who sought'st a voluntary grave,
Th' uninjured honours of thy name to save,
Whose generous arm thy barbarous master spared,
Altars had smoked, and temples had been reared.
    Whene'er to Afric's shores I turn my eyes,
Horrors of deepest, deadliest guilt arise;
I see, by more than fancy's mirror shown,
The burning village and the blazing town,
See the dire victim torn from social life,
The shrieking babe, the agonizing wife!
She, wretch forlorn, is dragged by hostile hands,
To distant tyrants sold, in distant lands!
Transmitted miseries and successive chains
The sole sad heritage her child obtains!
Ev'n this last wretched boon their foes deny:
To weep together, or together die.
By felon hands, by one relentless stroke,
See the fond links of feeling nature broke!
The fibres twisting round a parent's heart,
Torn from their grasp, and bleeding as they part.

Notes

[6] ' "It is a point of honour among negroes of a high spirit to die rather than to suffer their glossy skin to bear the mark of the whip. Qua-shi had somehow offended his master, a young planter with whom he had been bred up in the endearing intimacy of a playfellow. His services had been faithful; his attachment affectionate. The master resolved to punish him, and pursued him for that purpose. In trying to escape, Qua-shi stumbled and fell; the master fell upon him. They wrestled long with doubtful victory. At length, Qua-shi got uppermost, and being firmly seated on his master's breast, he secured his legs with one hand, and with the other drew a sharp knife; then said, 'Master, I have been bred up with you from a child; I have loved you as myself; in return, you have condemned me to a punishment, of which I must ever have borne the marks – thus only I can avoid them.' So saying, he drew the knife with all his strength across his own throat, and fell down dead, without a groan, on his master's body." Ramsay's *Essay on the Treatment of African Slaves*' (More's note). More refers to James Ramsay (1733–89), *An Essay on the Treatment and Conversion of African Slaves in the British Sugar Colonies* (1784).

Hold, murderers, hold! Nor aggravate distress;
Respect the passions you yourselves possess!
Ev'n you, of ruffian heart and ruthless hand,
Love your own offspring, love your native land.
Ah, leave them holy freedom's cheering smile,
The Heav'n-taught fondness for the parent soil;
Revere affections mingled with our frame,
In every nature, every clime the same;
In all, these feelings equal sway maintain;
In all, the love of home and freedom reign –
And Tempe's vale[7] and parched Angola's sand
One equal fondness of their sons command.
Th' unconquered savage laughs at pain and toil,
Basking in freedom's beams which gild his native soil.
Does thirst of empire, does desire of fame
(For these are specious crimes), our rage inflame?
No; sordid lust of gold their fate controls –
The basest appetite of basest souls;
Gold, better gained by what their ripening sky,
Their fertile fields, their arts[8] and mines supply.
What wrongs, what injuries does Oppression plead,
To smooth the horror of th' unnatural deed?
What strange offence, what aggravated sin?
They stand convicted of a darker skin!
Barbarians, hold! Th' opprobrious commerce spare,
Respect His sacred image which they bear.
Though dark and savage, ignorant and blind,
They claim the common privilege of kind;
Let malice strip them of each other plea,
They still are men, and men should still be free.
Insulted reason loathes th' inverted trade –
Dire change! The agent is the purchase made!
Perplexed, the baffled muse involves the tale;
Nature confounded, well may language fail!
The outraged goddess, with abhorrent eyes,
Sees man the traffic, souls the merchandise!
Plead not, in reason's palpable abuse,
Their sense of feeling callous and obtuse;[9]
From heads to hearts lies nature's plain appeal –
Though few can reason, all mankind can feel.
Though wit may boast a livelier dread of shame,
A loftier sense of wrong, refinement claim;
Though polished manners may fresh wants invent,
And nice[10] distinctions nicer souls torment –

Notes

7 *Tempe's vale* idyllic valley in Thessaly, praised by Virgil, *Georgics* ii 469.

8 'Besides many valuable productions of the soil, cloths and carpets of exquisite manufacture are brought from the coast of Guinea' (More's note).

9 'Nothing is more frequent than this cruel and stupid argument, that they do not *feel* the miseries inflicted on them as Europeans would do' (More's note). This was one of the arguments of the merchants who claimed that regulation of the slave-trade would put them out of business; see headnote p. 54.

10 *nice* subtle.

Though these on finer spirits heavier fall,
Yet natural evils are the same to all.
Though wounds there are which reason's force may heal,
There needs no logic sure to make us feel.
The nerve, howe'er untutored, can sustain
A sharp, unutterable sense of pain,
As exquisitely fashioned in a slave
As where unequal fate a sceptre gave.
Sense is as keen where Congo's sons preside
As where proud Tiber rolls his classic tide.
Rhetoric or verse may point the feeling line –
They do not whet sensation, but define.
Did ever slave less feel the galling chain,
When Zeno[11] proved there was no ill in pain?
Their miseries philosophic quirks[12] deride;
Slaves groan in pangs disowned by Stoic pride.
  When the fierce sun darts vertical his beams,
And thirst and hunger mix their wild extremes;
When the sharp iron wounds his inmost soul,[13]
And his strained eyes in burning anguish roll –
Will the parched negro find, ere he expire,
No pain in hunger, and no heat in fire?
  For him, when fate his tortured frame destroys,
What hope of present fame or future joys?
For this have heroes shortened nature's date;
For that have martyrs gladly met their fate;
But him, forlorn, no hero's pride sustains,
No martyr's blissful visions soothe his pains;
Sullen, he mingles with his kindred dust,
For he has learned to dread the Christian's trust.
To him what mercy can that pow'r display,
Whose servants murder, and whose sons betray?
Savage, thy venial error I deplore –
They are *not* Christians who infest thy shore!
  Oh thou sad spirit, whose preposterous yoke
The great deliverer death at length has broke!
Released from misery, and escaped from care,
Go meet that mercy man denied thee here.
In thy dark home, sure refuge of th' oppressed,
The wicked vex not, and the weary rest.
And if some notions, vague and undefined,
Of future terrors have assailed thy mind;
If such thy masters have presumed to teach,
As terrors only they are prone to preach
(For should they paint eternal mercy's reign,

Notes

[11] *Zeno* Zeno of Citium (*c.* 335–*c.* 263 BC) founded the Stoic school of philosophy.

[12] *quirks* quibbles, subtle or evasive arguments.

[13] 'This is not said figuratively. The writer of these lines has seen a complete set of chains, fitted to every separate limb of these unhappy, innocent men, together with instruments for wrenching open the jaws, contrived with such ingenious cruelty as would shock the humanity of an inquisitor' (More's notes).

Where were th' oppressor's rod, the captive's chain?);
If, then, thy troubled soul has learned to dread
The dark unknown thy trembling footsteps tread
On Him, who made thee what thou art, depend:
He, who withholds the means, accepts the end.
Not *thine* the reckoning dire of light abused,
Knowledge disgraced, and liberty misused;
On *thee* no awful judge incensed shall sit
For parts perverted, and dishonoured wit.
Where ignorance will be found the surest plea,
How many learned and wise shall envy *thee*!
   And thou, white savage, whether lust of gold
Or lust of conquest ruled thee uncontrolled –
Hero or robber – by whatever name
Thou plead thy impious claim to wealth or fame;
Whether inferior mischiefs be thy boast,
A petty tyrant rifling Gambia's coast;
Or bolder carnage track thy crimson way,
Kings dispossessed, and provinces thy prey,
Panting to tame wide earth's remotest bound,
All Cortez[14] murdered, all Columbus found;
O'er plundered realms to reign, detested lord,
Make millions wretched, and thyself abhorred;
In reason's eye, in wisdom's fair account,
Your sum of glory boasts a like amount;
The means may differ, but the end's the same:
Conquest is pillage with a nobler name.
Who makes the sum of human blessings less,
Or sinks the stock of general happiness,
No solid fame shall grace, no true renown,
His life shall blazon, or his memory crown.
   Had those advent'rous spirits who explore
Through ocean's trackless wastes the far-sought shore;
Whether of wealth insatiate, or of pow'r,
Conquerors who waste, or ruffians who devour –
Had these possessed, oh Cook,[15] thy gentle mind,
Thy love of arts, thy love of humankind;
Had these pursued thy mild and liberal plan,
Discoverers had not been a curse to man!
Then, blessed philanthropy, thy social hands
Had linked dissevered worlds in brothers' bands,
Careless if colour or if clime divide;
Then, loved and loving, man had lived and died.
   The purest wreaths which hang on glory's shrine,
For empires founded, peaceful Penn,[16] are thine;

Notes

[14] Hernán Cortez (1485–1547), Spanish conquistador, overthrew the Aztec empire, killing and enslaving its people, winning Mexico for Spain.

[15] James Cook (1728–79) circumnavigated the world in the *Endeavour*, 1768–71.

[16] William Penn (1644–1718), Quaker and founder of Pennsylvania.

No bloodstained laurels crowned thy virtuous toil,
No slaughtered natives drenched thy fair-earned soil.
   Still thy meek spirit in thy flock survives,[17]
Consistent still, *their* doctrines rule their lives;
Thy followers only have effaced the shame
Inscribed by Slavery on the Christian name.
   Shall Britain, where the soul of Freedom reigns,
Forge chains for others she herself disdains?
Forbid it, Heaven! Oh let the nations know
The liberty she loves she will bestow;
Not to herself the glorious gift confined,
She spreads the blessing wide as humankind;
And, scorning narrow views of time and place,
Bids all be free in earth's extended space.
   What page of human annals can record
A deed so bright as human rights restored?
Oh may that godlike deed, that shining page,
Redeem *our* fame, and consecrate *our* age!
   And see, the cherub Mercy from above,
Descending softly, quits the sphere of love!
On feeling hearts she sheds celestial dew,
And breathes her spirit o'er th' enlightened few;
From soul to soul the spreading influence steals,
Till every breast the soft contagion feels.
She bears, exulting, to the burning shore,
The loveliest office angel ever bore:
To vindicate the pow'r in heaven adored;
To still the clank of chains, and sheathe the sword;
To cheer the mourner, and with soothing hands
From bursting hearts unbind th' oppressor's bands;
To raise the lustre of the Christian name,
And clear the foulest blot that dims its fame.
   As the mild spirit hovers o'er the coast,
A fresher hue the withered landscapes boast;
Her healing smiles the ruined scenes repair,
And blasted Nature wears a joyous air.
She spreads her blessed commission from above,
Stamped with the sacred characters of love;
She tears the banner stained with blood and tears,
And, Liberty, thy shining standard rears!
As the bright ensign's glory she displays,
See pale Oppression faints beneath the blaze!
The giant dies, no more his frown appals;
The chain, untouched, drops off; the fetter falls.
Astonished Echo tells the vocal shore,
'Oppression's fall'n, and Slavery is no more!'

Notes

[17] 'The Quakers have emancipated all their slaves throughout America' (More's note).

The dusky myriads crowd the sultry plain,
And hail that mercy long invoked in vain;
Victorious pow'r! She bursts their two-fold bands,
And Faith and Freedom spring from Mercy's hands.

Cheap Repository: The Story of Sinful Sally. Told by Herself (1796)

Showing how, from being Sally of the Green, she was first led to become Sinful Sally, and afterwards Drunken Sal, and how at last she came to a most melancholy and almost hopeless end, being therein a warning to all young women both in town and country. Price one halfpenny.

Come each maiden lend an ear,
  Country lass and London belle!
Come and drop a mournful tear
  O'er the tale that I shall tell!

I that ask your tender pity,
  Ruined now and all forlorn,
Once like you was young and pretty,
  And as cheerful as the morn.

In yon distant cottage sitting,
  Far away from London town,
Once you might have seen me knitting
  In my simple kersey[1] gown.

Where the little lambkins leap,
  Where the meadow looks so gay,
Where the drooping willows weep,
  Simple Sally used to stray.

Then I tasted many a blessing,
  Then I had an honest fame;
Father, mother, me caressing,
  Smiled and thought me free from blame.

Then amid my friends so dear,
  Life it speeded fast away;
Oh, it moves a tender tear
  To think how peaceful was the day!

From the villages surrounding,
  Ere I well had reached eighteen,
Came the modest youths abounding,
  All to Sally of the Green.

Notes

Cheap Repository

[1] *kersey* coarse cloth woven from wool.

Courting days were thus beginning,
And I soon had proved a wife;
Oh, if I had kept from sinning,
Now how blessed had been my life!

Come each maiden, lend an ear,
Country lass and London belle!
Come ye now and deign to hear
How poor sinful Sally fell.

Where the hill begins inclining,
Half a furlong from the road,
O'er the village white and shining
Stands Sir William's great abode.

Near his meadow I was tripping,
Vainly[2] wishing to be seen,
When Sir William met me skipping,
And he spoke me on the Green;

Bid me quit my cloak of scarlet,[3]
Blamed my simple kersey gown,
Eyed me then, so like a varlet
Such as live in London town.

With his presents I was loaded,
And bedecked in ribbons gay;
Thus my ruin was foreboded –
Oh how crafty was his way!

Vanished now from cottage lowly,
My poor parents' heart I break,
Enter on a state unholy,
Turn a mistress to a rake.

Now no more by morning light
Up to God my voice I raise;
Now no shadows of the night
Call my thoughts to prayer and praise.

Hark! A well known sound I hear!
'Tis the church's Sunday bell;
No, I dread to venture near;
No, I'm now the child of hell.

Notes

[2] *Vainly* Sally's troubles begin with the sin of vanity.

[3] *scarlet* Sally is a scarlet woman even before her sinful career begins. The obvious comparison is with the whore of Babylon, Revelation 17: 3–6.

Now I lay my Bible by,
   Choose that impious book so new;
Love the bold blaspheming lie,
   And that filthy novel too.

Next to London town I pass
   (Sinful Sally is my name),
There to gain a front of brass[4]
   And to glory in my shame.

Powdered well, and puffed, and painted,
   Rivals all I there outshine;
With skin so white and heart so tainted,
   Rolling in my chariot fine.

In the park I glitter daily,
   Then I dress me for the play,
Then to masquerade so gaily,
   All London hears me tear away.

When I meet some meaner[5] lass,
   Then I toss with proud disdain;
Laugh and giggle as I pass,
   As if I never knew a pain.

But amidst my peals of laughter
   Horror seizes oft my frame;
Pleasure now, damnation after,
   And a never-dying flame.[6]

'Save me, save me, Lord!' I cry,
   'Save my soul from Satan's chain!'
Now I see salvation nigh,
   Now I turn to sin again.

By a thousand ills o'ertaken
   See me now quite sinking down,
Till so lost and so forsaken
   Sal is cast upon the town.

At the dusk of evening grey,
   Forth I step from secret cell,
Roaming like a beast of prey
   Or some hateful imp of hell.

Ah, how many youths so blooming
   By my wanton looks I've won;
Then by vices all consuming
   Left them ruined and undone!

Notes

[4] *brass* unblushing impudence.

[5] *meaner* poorer.

[6] *a never-dying flame* a reference to the flames of hell.

Thus the cruel spider stretches
  Wide his web for every fly;
Then each victim that he catches
  Straight he poisons till he die.

Now no more by conscience troubled,
  Deep I plunge in every sin;
True, my sorrows are redoubled,
  But I drown them all in gin.

See me next with front so daring
  Band of ruffian rogues among;
Fighting, cheating, drinking, swearing –
  And Sal's the vilest of the throng.

Mark that youngest of the thieves;
  Taught by Sal he ventures further;
What he filches Sal receives –
  'Tis for Sal he does the murder.

See me then attend my victim
  To the fatal gallows tree,
Pleased to think how I have nicked[7] him,
  Made him swing while I am free.

Jack I laughing see depart,
  While with Dick I drink and sing;
Soon again I'll fill the cart,
  Make this present lover swing.

But while thus with guilt surprising,
  Sal pursues her bold career,
See God's dreadful wrath arising
  And the day of vengeance near.

Fierce disease my body seizes,
  Racking pain afflicts my bones;[8]
Dread of death my spirit freezes,
  Deep and doleful are my groans.

Here with face so shrunk and spotted
  On the clay-cold ground I lie;
See how all my flesh is rotted –
  Stop, oh stranger, see me die!

Conscience, as my breath's departing,
  Plunges too his arrow deep,
With redoubled fury starting
  Like some giant from his sleep.

Notes

[7] *nicked* tricked, cheated.

[8] *Racking pain afflicts my bones* symptomatic of venereal disease.

In this pit of ruin lying
Once again before I die,
Fainting, trembling, weeping, sighing –
Lord, to thee I'll lift mine eye.

Thou canst save the vilest harlot,
Grace I've heard is free and full,
Sins that once were red as scarlet
Thou canst make as white as wool.

Saviour, whom I've pierced so often,
Deeper still my guilt imprint!
Let thy mighty spirit soften
This my hardened heart of flint!

Vain, alas, is all my groaning,
For I fear the die is cast;
True, thy blood is all atoning,
But my day of grace is past.

Saviour, hear me or I perish!
None who lives is quite undone;
Still a ray of hope I'll cherish
Till eternity's begun.

Charlotte Smith (*née* Turner) (1749–1806)

Wordsworth was one of her greatest admirers. In 1836 he remembered her as 'my old friend . . . who was the first *Modern* distinguished in that composition'[1] (that is, the sonnet), and when acknowledging her influence on his late poem, 'Stanzas Suggested in a Steamboat off St Bees' Heads', he said that 'She wrote little, and that little unambitiously, but with true feeling for rural nature, at a time when nature was not much regarded by English poets.'[2]

Charlotte Smith was born in London on 4 May 1749, the elder daughter of Nicholas Turner of Stoke House, Guildford, and Bignor Park, Sussex, and Anna Towers. She and her sister were brought up by a kindly aunt after their mother's death when she was 3, spending time at their father's estate of Bignor Park, on the banks on the River Arun in Sussex, as she recalled in *The Emigrants* (1793):

> There (where from hollows fringed with yellow broom,
> The birch with silver rind, and fairy leaf,
> Aslant the low stream trembles) I have stood
> And meditated how to venture best
> Into the shallow current, to procure

Notes

[1] *LY* iii 149.

[2] *PW* iv 403

> The willow-herb of glowing purple spikes,
> Or flags whose sword-like leaves concealed the tide,
> Startling the timid reed-bird from her nest,
> As with aquatic flowers I wove the wreath,
> Such as, collected by the shepherd girls,
> Deck in the villages the turfy shrine,
> And mark the arrival of propitious May.
> (*The Emigrants* ii 335–46)

The freshness and intensity of these recollections are validated by their precise detail. Smith's ability to perceive nature in this way was partly a gift, but also a skill taught to her at the age of 6 by the landscape painter George Smith, then in his early forties, who lived in Chichester. He encouraged her to think of landscapes as greater than the mere sum of their parts – possessing atmosphere even to the point of being enchanted. Short sight led her to specialize in painting botanical specimens, with which the South Downs were (and still are) well provided. The precise, sensitive documentation of the flora around her was to be a consistent feature of her poems.

Unusually for the time, she enjoyed for several years a good education at boarding-school in Kensington, London, where she first learnt to read Italian and write sonnets. Her father's career as a gambler was going badly, however, and she was withdrawn at the age of 12 because of his increasing debt. Within a few years, things were so bad that Turner was compelled to marry a rich heiress, Miss Henrietta Meriton. And when that had happened, he arranged for his eldest daughter to marry a wealthy West India merchant of his acquaintance, Benjamin Smith. Two months short of 16, she was (in her words) 'sold, a legal prostitute', and began a child-bearing career that would span the next twenty-two years, producing twelve children. To make matters worse, her new husband was not what he appeared: besides turning out to be a spendthrift, he would behave abusively and violently towards wife and daughters. The first sign of real trouble came in December 1783 when litigation over his father's will led to his imprisonment at the King's Bench prison in London for embezzlement. He was there for seven months, some of which his wife shared, as was customary. It was at this time that she decided to publish a book in order to raise funds, and began writing sonnets.

She contributed to the *European Magazine* from 1782 onwards; two years later, with the encouragement of William Hayley (friend of Cowper and patron of Blake), she published her *Elegiac Sonnets*. It was an immediate success, perhaps because readers identified with the resigned melancholy of its author. By the time it reached its third edition in 1786, reviewers were openly expressing concern on her behalf. 'We are sorry to see the eye which can shine with so much poetic fire sullied with a tear,' wrote the *Critical Review*, 'and we hope the soothings of the favoured muse may wipe it from her cheek.'[3] For its part, the *Gentleman's Magazine* proclaimed her a better sonneteer than either Shakespeare or Milton, before continuing:

> We cannot, however, forbear expressing a hope that the misfortunes she so often hints at, are all imaginary. We must have perused her very tender and exquisite effusions with diminished pleasure, could we have supposed her sorrows to be real. It would be hard indeed if a lady, who has so much contributed to the delight of others, should feel any want of happiness herself.[4]

Her poems are distinctive for the way in which her hardships, though never detailed, colour her observations, producing an intriguing blend of the confessional and the sentimental. It is a poetry that gives a remarkably precise account of the

Notes

3 *Critical Review* 61 (1786) 467–8.

4 *Gentleman's Magazine* 56.1 (1786) 333–4, p. 333.

author's inner and outer worlds. The sonnet was a fashionable form in which to be writing, and Smith had a happy knack of exploiting popular taste, not least with translations from Goethe's *Werther*, which was enjoying immense popularity; in so doing, she aroused the envious criticisms of Anna Seward, who accused her of promoting 'dark dreams of suicide' (see pp. 29–30). This volume contains the complete text of *Elegiac Sonnets* (3rd edn, 1786).

Despite literary success, the debts were huge, and creditors still knocking at the door. In summer 1784 the family was forced into exile in Normandy for six months, where they rented a ruined château. This cannot have been easy for someone who, like Smith, loved her native countryside, and helps explain her sympathy with the exiles from Revolutionary France whom she saw wandering Brighton beach eight years later: 'I mourn your sorrows, for I too have known / Involuntary exile.'[5] During these months she became increasingly impatient with her abusive, unfaithful husband, and decided to leave him as soon as she could.

In 1785, leaving her husband in France, she took her children back to Sussex to settle at Woolbeding House. Here she continued to write sonnets, including the translations from Petrarch and Metastasio that would appear in the third edition. Benjamin returned to England and for a while continued to make a nuisance of himself – partly because he had a legal entitlement to his wife's earnings, and was not above demanding them from her publishers. He finally announced in early 1788 that he was leaving for Barbados: at last, she was free.

His departure was a relief, but she remained in debt and had no choice but to keep writing. In 1788 she worked hard on a successful novel, *Emmeline*, and a fifth edition of *Elegiac Sonnets*, one of the subscribers to which was the young William Wordsworth, then an undergraduate at St John's College, Cambridge. It was symptomatic of the *Sonnets'* popularity that the fifth edition, published New Year's Day 1789, made her £180 (£12,600 / US$23,500 today).

Later that year she moved to the fashionable Regency town of Brighton, where she wrote more best-selling novels, most notably *Ethelinde* (1790) and *Celestina* (1791) – the second of which earned £200 (£14,000 / US$25,600 today) from its first edition alone. During 1791, partly out of solidarity with the Revolution, she visited Paris, where she met Helen Maria Williams (p. 285). The 21-year-old William Wordsworth was aware of that connection when he visited Smith in Brighton in November, Paris-bound, requesting a letter of introduction to Williams. His interest in Smith, which dated from his schooldays,[6] stemmed partly from the fact that they were distant relations.[7] At this moment he was on his way to France where he would remain until late 1792, and meet other Revolutionary sympathizers. Smith took a shine to the young man with the Cumbrian accent, and showed him two poems in manuscript which he copied into the back of his copy of *Elegiac Sonnets*.[8] 'She received me in the politest manner,' Wordsworth told his brother Richard, 'and showed me every possible civility.'[9]

With the execution of Louis XVI in January 1793, and the resulting outbreak of war, radicals at home found themselves torn between outrage inspired by events in Paris and loyalty to the Revolution. This is evident in *The Emigrants* which is in the first place a political work. For Smith, the point about the French clergy and nobility who found safety from the horrors of

Notes

[5] *The Emigrants* 155–6.

[6] He read *Elegiac Sonnets* when it was first published, having been lent a copy by his schoolteacher, Thomas Bowman.

[7] John Robinson (1727–1802), politician, was descended from Wordsworth's grandfather, Richard Wordsworth of Sockbridge; he was the husband of Mary Crowe, the stepdaughter of Charlotte Smith's father-in-law, Richard Smith.

[8] The transcriptions are published in *Wordsworth's Poets* ed. Duncan Wu (Manchester, 2003), pp. 142–3.

[9] *EY* 68.

the Revolution through exile in rural Sussex is that experience has revealed to them the injustice of both their former conduct towards the poor, and the assumptions on which it was based (i 244–95). Smith's point is that the injustices of which they were guilty continue in England (i 315–46). In Book II her radical indignation is offset by horror at the execution of Louis and uncertain fate of his family (Marie Antoinette had not been guillotined at the time Smith was writing). His execution in January 1793 led Smith to reassess her earlier sympathies, a reaction experienced by many who nonetheless shared its republican aims.

Though provided both in her preface and the poem itself with an immediate historical and political context, *The Emigrants* is a personal work. Smith knew many of the French emigrants, not just from having seen them in Brighton, but because she offered them shelter for several months in her own home, and helped find them long-term accommodation elsewhere. Her sympathy for them is evident from the way in which she writes (see i 153–61); with Marie Antoinette she identifies as a 'mother, petrified with grief' (ii 152):

> Ah, who knows,
> From sad experience, more than I, to feel
> For thy desponding spirit, as it sinks
> Beneath procrastinated fears for those
> More dear to thee than life!
> (ii 169–73)

Smith's mastery of the strict form of the sonnet stood her in good stead when it came to blank verse: she avoids monotony by constant variation of tone and rhythm, run-on lines, and stretching the rules of syntax to the limit (see for instance i 169–95). Her frequent use of personification should not blind us to her passion, most notably in the culminating account of her sufferings, making this autobiographical poem a worthy precursor of *The Prelude*.

One reason why Wordsworth was reluctant to publish *The Prelude* was that autobiography was even in his day a largely undiscovered genre liable to cause bemusement, if not hostility, among readers. That's one factor that makes *The Emigrants* such a forward-looking work; the other is its author's evident radicalism. For reviewers in such conservative journals as the *British Critic*, these were compelling obstacles to a sympathetic reading.

> As philanthropists, we feel compassion at the sad allusion to sorrows, which the writer, in her own person, tells us she has suffered: but as critics, we cannot approve of the egotism which occupies too large a portion of her present work. In sonnets, and elegy, the poet is allowed to pour forth his complaints, and may appear as the principal person: in a poem like *The Emigrants*, the writer should have brought forward a greater number of other characters, and have been herself more concealed.
>
> To genius we pay the most unbounded tribute of admiration and respect, when it is employed on subjects that become a good and great mind: but when fine talents descend to propagate popular cant against order, tending to excite discontent; or when they become the instruments by which 'to stab at once the morals of a land' (Cowper) . . . by treating with petulant and unseasonable scoffs the institutions of religion, we lament that the gifted powers of imagination should be so grossly perverted . . . The virtuous and pious, no less than ingenious Cowper, is everywhere the advocate of the Christian religion and its sacred ordinances: and it is an indecency ill-becoming Mrs Smith to sneer at usages manifestly tending to public utility and general piety.[10]

Notes

[10] *British Critic* I (1793) 403–6, p. 405.

Figure 7 Charlotte Smith (1749–1806) engraved by Pierre Condé from a portrait by John Opie, published 1797. Of this engraving, made for the eighth edition of her *Elegiac Sonnets* (1797), Smith remarked: 'I think Mr Condé has done all that could be done save only that my family say what I do not venture to suggest myself: that there is a want of spirit in the eyes.' (National Portrait Gallery, London.)

The reviewer could not have known it, but Smith had some cause for resenting some of the practices of Catholic clerics in France: while resident there during the 1780s, one of her children had been forcibly taken away in deep snow for baptism. The point, though, is that the reviewer had difficulty accepting Smith's 'egotistical' perspective; this criticism was reiterated by the *Critical Review*:

> We will not say that we are entirely disappointed: there is in this poem good scenery and well-discriminated groups of figures, but there is too much of mere reflection, verging towards humble prose, and the pathos is weakened by the author's adverting too often to perplexities in her own situation . . . Herself, and not the French emigrant, fills the foreground; begins and ends the piece; and the pity we should naturally feel for those overwhelming and uncommon distresses she describes, is lessened by their being brought into parallel with the inconveniences of a narrow income or a protracted law-suit.[11]

Smith would have found little cheer in the *European Magazine* which commended the poem as a whole but criticized it on the grounds that 'some of the expressions are very *hazardées*'.[12] A page was then taken up with enumerating some of the usages and constructions that offended the reviewer – Charlotte's use of 'innumerous' for 'innumerable' (line 5), for instance, and the elision of the particle in 'cause thy creatures [to] cease' (line 422).

Despite literary success, Smith faced constant pressure to provide for her large family (which included nine people by 1794), and produced books at a breathtaking rate: *The Old Manor House* (1793), *D'Arcy* (1793), *The Banished Man* (1794), *Rural Walks* (1795), *Montalbert* (1795), *Rambles Farther* (1796), *Marchmont* (1796), *The Young Philosopher* (1798), *What is she?* (1799), *Letters of a Solitary Wanderer* (1799), *History of England* (1806) and *The Natural History of Birds* (1807). Such a pace of work took a calamitous toll. Rheumatism was a severe problem by 1794, when she was induced to visit Bath in the hope that the waters might help. By 1804 she was suffering from pleurisy and an accelerated heartbeat that woke her in the night, leaving her unable to breathe. Shortly after, she contracted the uterine cancer that was to kill her late in 1806.

She was buried at St John's Church, Stoke, near Guildford, close to her family home, leaving behind a mass of manuscripts, many of which were promptly burnt. Of the few that survived, most seemed to have provided copy for *Beachy Head, and Other Poems* (1807). *Beachy Head* is an extraordinary, heroic work, all of which is included here (pp. 122–41). It is an attempt to preserve the life and times of the region in a manner similar to White's *Natural History of Selborne* (1789). The fact that she did not live to complete it cannot detract from what Stuart Curran calls its 'multitudinous, uncanny particularity'[13] – the sharp and sensitive detail with which she describes the natural world. That 'particularity' extends beyond a close knowledge of local flora and fauna to include an intense and pervasive awareness of the history of south-east England from prehistoric times onwards, local traditions and folklore, and notable inhabitants. Its achievement resides in its unpredictability and inventiveness, the product of many years' labour, her imagination as vigorous as ever. It is also her testament.

Reviewers used its posthumous appearance as an opportunity to pay tribute to its author. The *Universal Magazine* found in it 'the quaint moralizing of Cowper, and the plaintive tenderness of Gray',[14] while the *Literary Panorama* commended

Notes

[11] *Critical Review* 9 (1793) 299–302, pp. 299–300.

[12] *European Magazine* 24 (1793) 41–5, p. 42.

[13] *The Poems of Charlotte Smith* ed. Stuart Curran (New York, 1993), p. xxvii.

[14] *Universal Magazine* 7 (1807) 228–31, p. 229.

her close observation of the natural world: 'the notes which accompany these poems are proofs of her general attention and accuracy.'[15] Even the *British Critic*, so sniffy about *The Emigrants*, thought *Beachy Head* 'distinguished by great vigour and, by what was the characteristic of the author's mind, a sweet and impressive tenderness of melancholy'.[16] The *Monthly Review* most accurately summarized the critical consensus:

> The same tenderness and sensibility, the same strain of moral reflection, and the same enthusiastic love of nature, pervade all her effusions. It appears also as if the wounded feelings of Charlotte Smith had found relief and consolation, during her latter years, in an accurate observation not only of the beautiful *effect* produced by the endless diversity of natural objects that daily solicit our regard, but also in a careful study of their scientific arrangement, and their more minute variations.[17]

Further reading

The Poems of Charlotte Smith ed. Stuart Curran (New York, 1993).

Stuart Curran, 'The I Altered', in *Romanticism and Feminism* ed. Anne K. Mellor (Bloomington, Ind., 1988), pp. 185–207.

Loraine Fletcher, *Charlotte Smith: A Critical Biography* (Basingstoke, 1998).

Jacqueline Labbe, *Charlotte Smith: Romanticism, Poetry and the Culture of Gender* (Manchester, 2003).

Daniel Robinson, 'Reviving the Sonnet: Women Romantic Poets and the Sonnet Claim', *ERR* 6 (1995) 98–127.

Elegiac Sonnets: the third edition. With twenty additional sonnets (1786)

To William Hayley, Esq.[1]

Sir,

While I ask your protection for these essays, I cannot deny having myself some esteem for them. Yet permit me to say that did I not trust to your candour and sensibility, and hope they will plead for the errors your judgement must discover, I should never have availed myself of the liberty I have obtained – that of dedicating these simple effusions to the greatest modern master of that charming talent, in which I can never be more than a distant copyist.

I am,

Sir,

Your most obedient and obliged servant,
Charlotte Smith

Notes

[15] *Literary Panorama* 2 (1807) 294–5, p. 294.

[16] *British Critic* 30 (1807) 170–4, p. 171.

[17] *Monthly Review* 56 (1808) 99–101, p. 99.

Elegiac Sonnets

[1] William Hayley (1745–1820), poet, biographer, translator, friend of Blake, Anna Seward, Cowper and others. To date his most successful poem, at least in commercial terms, was *The Triumphs of Temper*, to which Smith alludes in *Sonnet XIX*, below. Hayley and Smith were neighbours in Sussex, and Hayley was instrumental in helping her publish the *Elegiac Sonnets* in 1784. On reading the first of the sonnets, he was inspired to write his own 'Sonnet to Mrs Smith':

Thou whose chaste song simplicity inspires,
Attractive poetess of plaintive strain!
Speak not unjustly of poetic fires,
Nor the pure bounty of thy Muse arraign:
No, not the source, the soother she of pain.
If thy soft breast the thorns of anguish knew,
Ah! think what myriads with thy truth complain
Of fortune's thorny paths! and think how few
Of all those myriads know thy magic art,
The fiercer pangs of sorrow to subdue,
By those melodious tears that ease thy heart,
And bid the breath of fame thy life renew;
Sure to excite, till nature's self decays,
Her lasting sympathy, her endless praise!

Preface to the First Edition

The little poems which are here called sonnets have, I believe, no very just claim to that title, but they consist of fourteen lines, and appear to me no improper vehicle for a single sentiment. I am told, and I read it as the opinion of very good judges, that the legitimate sonnet is ill-calculated for our language. The specimens Mr Hayley has given, though they form a strong exception, prove no more than that the difficulties of the attempt vanish before uncommon powers.

Some very melancholy moments have been beguiled by expressing in verse the sensations those moments brought. Some of my friends, with partial indiscretion, have multiplied the copies they procured of several of these attempts, till they found their way into the prints of the day in a mutilated state, which, concurring with other circumstances, determined me to put them into their present form. I can hope for readers only among the few who, to sensibility of heart, join simplicity of taste.

Preface to the Third Edition

The reception given by the public, as well as my particular friends, to the two first editions of these small poems, has induced me to add to the present such other sonnets as I have written since, or have recovered from my acquaintance, to whom I had given them without thinking well enough of them at the time to preserve any copies myself. A few of those last written I have attempted on the Italian model, with what success I know not, but I am persuaded that to the generality of readers those which are less regular will be more pleasing.

As a few notes were necessary, I have added them at the end. I have there quoted such lines as I have borrowed, and, even where I am conscious the ideas were not my own, I have restored them to their original possessors.

Woolbeding,[2] 22 March 1786

Sonnet I

The partial[1] muse has, from my earliest hours,
   Smiled on the rugged path I'm doomed to tread,
And still with sportive hand has snatched wildflowers
   To weave fantastic garlands for my head;
But far, far happier is the lot of those
   Who never learned her dear delusive art,
Which, while it decks the head with many a rose,
   Reserves the thorn to fester in the heart.[2]
For still she bids soft Pity's melting eye
   Stream o'er the ills she knows not to remove,

Notes

[2] *Woolbeding* village in the South Downs in West Sussex; Smith resided at Woolbeding House from early 1785. The house still stands and is owned by the National Trust, though it is not open to the public at the time of writing.

Sonnet I

[1] *partial* friendly, partial to the poet.

[2] Philomel was seduced, according to Ovid, by her brother-in-law, Tereus, King of Thrace. She was turned into a nightingale, and her sad song was said to be caused by a thorn in her breast.

Points every pang, and deepens every sigh
   Of mourning Friendship or unhappy Love.
Ah then, how dear the muse's favours cost
If those paint sorrow best who feel it most![3]

Sonnet II. Written at the Close of Spring

The garlands fade that spring so lately wove –
   Each simple flower, which she had nursed in dew;
Anemonies[1] that spangled every grove,
   The primrose wan, and harebell, mildly blue.
No more shall violets linger in the dell,
   Or purple orchis variegate the plain,
Till spring again shall call forth every bell,
   And dress with humid hands her wreaths again.
Ah, poor humanity! So frail, so fair
   Are the fond visions of thy early day,
Till tyrant Passion and corrosive Care
   Bid all thy fairy colours fade away!
Another May new buds and flowers shall bring;
Ah, why has happiness no second spring?

Sonnet III. To a Nightingale[1]

Poor melancholy bird, that all night long
   Tell'st to the moon thy tale of tender woe;
   From what sad cause can such sweet sorrow flow,
And whence this mournful melody of song?

Thy poet's musing fancy would translate
   What mean the sounds that swell thy little breast,
   When still at dewy eve thou leav'st thy nest,
Thus to the listening night to sing thy fate.

Pale Sorrow's victims wert thou once among,
   Though now released in woodlands wild to rove;
   Say, hast thou felt from friends some cruel wrong,
Or diedst thou – martyr of disastrous love?
Ah, songstress sad, that such my lot might be:
To sigh and sing at liberty, like thee!

Notes

[3] In a note Smith acknowledges an echo of Pope, *Eloisa to Abelard* 365–6: 'The well sung woes shall soothe my pensive ghost; / He best can paint them who shall feel them most.' The italics are Smith's.

Sonnet II

[1] '*Anemone nemorosa*: the wood-anemone' (Smith's note).

Sonnet III

[1] 'The idea from the 43rd sonnet of Petrarch. Seconda parte: *Quel rosignioul, che si soave piagne*' (Smith's note).

Sonnet IV. To the Moon

Queen of the silver bow,[1] by thy pale beam,
  Alone and pensive, I delight to stray
And watch thy shadow trembling in the stream,
  Or mark the floating clouds that cross thy way.
And while I gaze, thy mild and placid light
  Sheds a soft calm upon my troubled breast;
And oft I think, fair planet of the night,
  That in thy orb the wretched may have rest.
The sufferers of the earth perhaps may go,
  Released by death, to thy benignant sphere,
And the sad children of Despair and Woe
  Forget in thee their cup of sorrow here.
Oh, that I soon may reach thy world serene,
Poor wearied pilgrim, in this toiling scene!

Sonnet V. To the South Downs

Ah, hills beloved! – where once, an happy child,
  Your beechen shades, 'your turf, your flowers among',[1]
I wove your bluebells into garlands wild,
  And woke your echoes with my artless song.
Ah, hills beloved! your turf, your flowers remain;
  But can they peace to this sad breast restore,
For one poor moment soothe the sense of pain,
  And teach a breaking heart to throb no more?
And you, Aruna,[2] in the vale below,
  As to the sea your limpid waves you bear,
Can you one kind Lethean[3] cup bestow
  To drink a long oblivion to my care?
Ah no! When all, e'en Hope's last ray, is gone,
There's no oblivion but in death alone!

Sonnet VI. To Hope

Oh Hope, thou soother sweet of human woes!
  How shall I lure thee to my haunts forlorn?
For me wilt thou renew the withered rose,
  And clear my painful path of pointed thorn?
Ah, come, sweet nymph, in smiles and softness dressed,

Notes

Sonnet IV

[1] *Queen of the silver bow* Diana the huntress, goddess of the moon.

Sonnet V

[1] Smith notes a borrowing from Gray's *Ode on a Distant Prospect of Eton College* 8: 'Whose turf, whose shades, whose flowers among'.

[2] 'The River Arun' (Smith's note).

[3] *Lethean* water from the River Lethe, river of forgetfulness in Hades, which enabled souls to forget their previous existence.

Like the young hours[1] that lead the tender year;
Enchantress come, and charm my cares to rest!
Alas, the flatterer flies, and will not hear;
A prey to fear, anxiety, and pain,
Must I a sad existence still deplore?
Lo! the flowers fade, but all the thorns remain,
'For me the vernal garland blooms no more'.[2]
Come then, 'pale Misery's love',[3] be thou my cure,
And I will bless thee, who though slow art sure.

Sonnet VII. On the Departure of the Nightingale

Sweet poet of the woods, a long adieu!
Farewell, soft minstrel of the early year!
Ah, 'twill be long ere thou shalt sing anew
And pour thy music on the 'night's dull ear'.[1]
Whether on spring thy wandering flights await,[2]
Or whether silent in our groves you dwell,
The pensive muse shall own thee for her mate,[3]
And still protect the song she loves so well.
With cautious step, the love-lorn youth shall glide
Through the lone brake[4] that shades thy mossy nest;
And shepherd girls from eyes profane shall hide
The gentle bird, who sings of pity best.
For still thy voice shall soft affections move,
And still be dear to sorrow and to love!

Sonnet VIII. To Spring

Again the wood, and long withdrawing vale,
In many a tint of tender green are dressed,
Where the young leaves unfolding scarce conceal
Beneath their early shade the half-formed nest
Of finch or woodlark; and the primrose pale
And lavish cowslip, wildly scattered round,
Give their sweet spirits to the sighing gale.
Ah, season of delight, could aught be found
To soothe awhile the tortured bosom's pain,
Of sorrow's rankling shaft to cure the wound

Notes

SONNET VI

1 *the young hours* The Horae were three daughters of Jupiter representing spring, summer and winter.

2 *For me the vernal garland blooms no more* Smith notes the borrowing from Pope, *Imitation of the first Ode of the fourth Book of Horace* 32.

3 *pale Misery's love* This is, Smith notes, a borrowing from Shakespeare, *King John* III iv 35.

SONNET VII

1 *night's dull ear* a borrowing, as Smith notes, from Shakespeare, *Henry V* Prologue 11.

2 'Alludes to the supposed migration of the nightingale' (Smith's note).

3 *The pensive muse . . . mate* Smith notes the allusion to Milton, *Sonnet I* 13–14: 'Whether the muse or love call thee his mate, / Both them I serve, and of their train am I.'

4 *brake* bracken.

And bring life's first delusions once again,
'Twere surely met in thee! Thy prospect fair,
Thy sounds of harmony, thy balmy air,
Have power to cure all sadness but despair.[1]

Sonnet IX

Blessed is yon shepherd on the turf reclined,
  Who on the varied clouds which float above
Lies idly gazing, while his vacant mind
  Pours out some tale antique of rural love!
  Ah, *he* has never felt the pangs that move
  Th' indignant spirit when, with selfish pride,
  Friends on whose faith the trusting heart relied
    Unkindly shun th' imploring eye of woe;
  The ills they ought to soothe with taunts deride,
    And laugh at tears themselves have forced to flow!
Nor *his* rude bosom those fine feelings melt,
  Children of Sentiment and Knowledge born,
Through whom each shaft with cruel force is felt,
  Empoisoned by deceit, or barbed with scorn.

Sonnet X. To Mrs G.[1]

Ah, why will Mem'ry with officious care
  The long lost visions of my days renew?
Why paint the vernal landscape green and fair
  When life's gay dawn was opening to my view?
Ah, wherefore bring those moments of delight,
  When with my Anna,[2] on the southern shore,
I thought the future, as the present, bright?
  Ye dear delusions, ye return no more!
Alas, how different does the truth appear
  From the warm picture youth's rash hand portrays!
How fades the scene, as we approach it near,
  And pain and sorrow strike how many ways!
Yet of that tender heart, ah, still retain
A share for me, and I will not complain!

Notes

Sonnet VIII

[1] *all sadness but despair* an allusion, as Smith notes, to *Paradise Lost* iv 155–6: 'Vernal delight and joy, able to drive / All sadness but despair'.

Sonnet X

[1] Mrs G. has not been identified, but was presumably a childhood friend.

[2] *Anna* probably a reference to Catherine Anne Dorset, Smith's sister, who wrote children's stories of animals in human dress.

Sonnet XI. To Sleep

Come, balmy sleep, tired nature's soft resort,
On these sad temples all thy poppies shed,
And bid gay dreams from Morpheus'[1] airy court
Float in light vision round my aching head![2]
Secure of all thy blessings, partial power,
On his hard bed the peasant throws him down;
And the poor sea-boy, in the rudest hour,
Enjoys thee more than he who wears a crown.[3]
Clasped in her faithful shepherd's guardian arms,
Well may the village girl sweet slumbers prove;
And they, oh gentle sleep, still taste thy charms
Who wake to labour, liberty, and love.
But still thy opiate aid dost thou deny
To calm the anxious breast, to close the streaming eye.

Sonnet XII. Written on the Seashore. October 1784[1]

On some rude fragment of the rocky shore,
Where on the fractured cliff the billows break,
Musing, my solitary seat I take,
And listen to the deep and solemn roar.

O'er the dark waves the winds tempestuous howl;
The screaming seabird quits the troubled sea,
But the wild gloomy scene has charms for me,[2]
And suits the mournful temper of my soul.[3]

Already shipwrecked by the storms of fate,
Like the poor mariner methinks I stand,
Cast on a rock; who sees the distant land
From whence no succour comes – or comes too late;
Faint and more faint are heard his feeble cries,
Till in the rising tide th' exhausted sufferer dies.

Notes

Sonnet XI

[1] Morpheus was the Greek god of sleep.

[2] In later editions of *Elegiac Sonnets*, Smith noted the borrowing from William Mason, *Elegy V. On the Death of a Lady* 12: 'Float in light vision round the poet's head'.

[3] As she notes, Smith is recalling *2 Henry IV* III i 18–20:

> Wilt thou upon the high and giddy mast
> Seal up the shipboy's eyes, and rock his brains
> In cradle of the rude impetuous surge?

Sonnet XII

[1] When she composed this, Smith was resident at Bignor Park, West Sussex, about four miles south of Petworth, close to the south coast of England. The house is still to be seen and may be visited.

[2] For echoes by Smith and Wordsworth see *Emigrants* i 157 and n21 below.

[3] 'This line is not my own, but I know not where to look for it' (Smith's note). In later editions of the volume Smith replaced this with the annotation, 'Young'. As Curran notes, her source is in fact Edward Young's *The Revenge* (1721):

> Rage on, ye winds, burst clouds, and waters roar!
> You bear a just resemblance of my fortune,
> And suit the gloomy habit of my soul.
>
> (I i 5–7)

Sonnet XIII. From Petrarch[1]

Oh place me where the burning noon
   Forbids the withered flower to blow;
Or place me in the frigid zone
   On mountains of eternal snow;
Let me pursue the steps of fame,
   Or poverty's more tranquil road;
Let youth's warm tide my veins inflame,
   Or sixty winters chill my blood:
Though my fond soul to heaven were flown,
   Or though on earth 'tis doomed to pine,
Prisoner or free, obscure or known,
   My heart, oh Laura, still is thine.
Whate'er my destiny may be,
That faithful heart still burns for thee!

Sonnet XIV. From Petrarch[1]

Loose to the wind her golden tresses streamed,
   Forming bright waves with amorous Zephyr's sighs;[2]
   And though averted now, her charming eyes
Then with warm love and melting pity beamed.
Was I deceived? Ah surely, nymph divine,
   That fine suffusion on thy cheek was love!
   What wonder then those lovely tints should move,
Should fire this heart, this tender heart of mine?
Thy soft melodious voice, thy air, thy shape,
   Were of a goddess, not a mortal maid;
   Yet though thy charms, thy heavenly charms should fade,
My heart, my tender heart could not escape,
   Nor cure for me in time or change be found:
   The shaft extracted does not cure the wound.

Sonnet XV. From Petrarch[1]

Where the green leaves exclude the summer beam,
   And softly bend as balmy breezes blow,
And where, with liquid lapse, the lucid stream
   Across the fretted rock is heard to flow,
Pensive I lay; when she whom earth conceals,
   As if still living, to my eyes appears,

Notes

SONNET XIII

1 *'Pommi ove 'l sol, occide i fiori e l'erba*. Petrarch, Sonnetto 112. Parte prima' (Smith's note).

SONNET XIV

1 *'Erano i capelli all 'aura sparsi*. Sonnetto 69. Parte prima' (Smith's note).

2 *amorous Zephyr's sighs* Zephyr, the west wind of myth, married Flora, goddess of flowers and gardens, who lived an eternal spring.

SONNET XV

1 *'Se lamentar augelli o verde fronde*. Sonnetto 21. Parte secondo' (Smith's note).

And pitying Heaven her angel form reveals,
To say, 'Unhappy Petrarch, dry your tears!
Ah why, sad lover, thus before your time,
In grief and sadness should your life decay,
And like a blighted flower, your manly prime
In vain and hopeless sorrow fade away?
Ah, wherefore should you mourn, that her you love,
Snatched from a world of woe, survives in bliss above!'

Sonnet XVI. From Petrarch[1]

Ye vales and woods, fair scenes of happier hours!
Ye feathered people,[2] tenants of the grove!
And you, bright stream, befringed with shrubs and flowers,
Behold my grief, ye witnesses of love!

For ye beheld my infant passion rise,
And saw through years unchanged my faithful flame;
Now cold in dust, the beauteous object lies,
And you, ye conscious scenes, are still the same!

While busy Memory still delights to dwell
On all the charms these bitter tears deplore,
And with a trembling hand describes too well
The angel form I shall behold no more,
To heaven she's fled, and nought to me remains
But the pale ashes which her urn contains.

Sonnet XVII. From the Thirteenth Cantata of Metastasio[1]

On thy grey bark, in witness of my flame,
I carve Miranda's cipher, beauteous tree;
Graced with the lovely letters of her name,
Henceforth be sacred to my love and me!

Though the tall elm, the oak, and sombre pine,
With broader arms may noon's fierce ardours break,
To shelter me and her I love, be thine;
And thine to see her smile and hear her speak.

No bird, ill-omened, round thy graceful head
Shall clamour harsh, or wave his heavy wing,

Notes

Sonnet XVI

[1] *'Valle che de lamenti miei se piena.* Sonnetto 33. Parte seconda (Smith's note).

[2] *Ye feathered people* i.e. birds.

Sonnet XVII

[1] *'Scrivo in te l'amato nome / Di colei, per cui, mi moro.* I do not mean this as a translation; the original is much longer, and full of images which could not be introduced in a sonnet – and some of them, though very beautiful in the Italian, would I believe not appear to advantage in an English dress' (Smith's note).

But fern and flowers arise beneath thy shade,
Where the wild bees their lullabies shall sing;
And in thy boughs the murmuring ring-dove rest,
And there the nightingale shall build her nest.

Sonnet XVIII. To the Earl of Egremont[1]

Wyndham, 'tis not thy blood, though pure it runs
Through a long line of glorious ancestry,
Percys and Seymours, Britain's boasted sons,
Who trust the honours of their race to thee;

'Tis not thy splendid domes, where Science loves
To touch the canvas, and the bust to raise;
Thy rich domains, fair fields, and spreading groves –
'Tis not all these the muse delights to praise.

In birth and wealth and honours, great thou art,
But nobler in thy independent mind;
And in that liberal hand and feeling heart
Given thee by Heaven – a blessing to mankind!
Unworthy oft may titled fortune be;
A soul like thine is true nobility!

Sonnet XIX. To Mr Hayley. On Receiving some Elegant Lines from Him[1]

For me the muse a simple band designed
Of 'idle'[2] flowers that bloom the woods among,
Which, with the cypress and the willow joined,
A garland formed as artless as my song;
And little dared I hope its transient hours
So long would last, composed of buds so brief,
Till Hayley's hand, among the vagrant flowers,
Threw from his verdant crown a deathless leaf.
For high in fame's bright fane has judgement placed
The laurel wreath Serena's poet[3] won,
Which, wov'n with myrtles by the hands of Taste,
The muse decreed for this her favourite son.
And those immortal leaves his temples shade,
Whose fair eternal verdure shall not fade!

Notes

SONNET XVIII

[1] Sir George O'Brien Wyndham, third Earl of Egremont (1751–1837), Sussex philanthropist, liberal, and patron of the arts. Smith was introduced to him by William Hayley. In politics he was a Whig. His home, Petworth House, was a nursery of art and a college of agriculture. In later years he was a patron of Turner and Haydon (for whom see p. 833).

SONNET XIX

[1] The 'elegant lines' may have been the sonnet which Hayley was inspired to write on reading the first of the elegiac sonnets, quoted p. 83n1.

[2] *idle* The quotation marks are puzzling; possibly Smith is thinking of the sermon on the mount, Luke 12: 27.

[3] *Serena's poet* Serena is the protagonist of William Hayley's *The Triumphs of Temper* (1781).

Sonnet XX. To the Countess of Abergavenny. Written on the Anniversary of her Marriage[1]

On this blessed day may no dark cloud or shower
With envious shade the sun's bright influence hide;
But all his rays illume the favoured hour
That saw thee, Mary, Henry's lovely bride!

With years revolving may it still arise,
Blessed with each good approving Heaven can lend;
And still with ray serene, shall those blue eyes
Enchant the husband, and attach the friend.

For you, fair friendship's amaranth[2] shall blow,[3]
And love's own thornless roses bind your brow;
And when, long hence, to happier worlds you go,
Your beauteous race shall be what you are now;
And future Nevills through long ages shine,
With hearts as good, and forms as fair as thine.

Sonnet XXI. Supposed to be Written by Werther[1]

Go, cruel tyrant of the human breast,
To other hearts thy burning arrows bear!
Go where fond hope and fair illusion rest –
Ah, why should Love inhabit with Despair?
Like the poor maniac[2] I linger here,
Still haunt the scene where all my treasure lies,
Still seek for flowers where only thorns appear,
And drink delicious poison from her eyes.[3]
Towards the deep gulf that opens on my sight
I hurry forward, Passion's helpless slave,
And, scorning Reason's mild and sober light,
Pursue the path that leads me to the grave:
So round the flame the giddy insect flies,
And courts the fatal fire by which it dies.

Notes

SONNET XX

[1] Mary, Lady Abergavenny (1760–96) married Henry Nevill, Earl of Abergavenny (1755–1843) on 3 October 1781. She was the daughter of Smith's brother-in-law.

[2] *amaranth* a mythical unfading flower.

[3] *blow* bloom.

SONNET XXI

[1] Smith's five sonnets run variations on passages from Goethe's popular novel about Werther, the young man driven to suicide by his love for Charlotte (Lotte in the German). They alarmed Anna Seward, who feared Smith was might encourage similarly suicidal tendencies in her readers; see pp. 29–30.

[2] 'See the story of the lunatic: "Is this the destiny of man? Is he only happy before he possesses his reason, or after he has lost it? Full of hope you go to gather flowers in winter, and are grieved not to find any – and do not know why they cannot be found." *Sorrows of Werther*, Volume 2' (Smith's note).

[3] In later editions Smith added a footnote acknowledging a borrowing from Pope, *Eloisa to Abelard*:

> Still on thy breast enamoured let me lie,
> Still drink delicious poison from thy eye,
> Pant on thy lip, and to thy heart be pressed.
>
> (ll. 121–3)

Sonnet XXII. By the Same. To Solitude[1]

Oh Solitude, to thy sequestered vale
  I come to hide my sorrow and my tears,
And to thy echoes tell the mournful tale
  Which scarce I trust to pitying friendship's ears.
Amidst thy wild woods and untrodden glades,
  No sounds but those of melancholy move;
And the low winds that die among thy shades
  Seem like soft Pity's sighs for hopeless love.
And sure some story of despair and pain
  In yon deep copse thy murm'ring doves relate;
And hark, methinks in that long plaintive strain,
  Thine own sweet songstress[2] weeps my wayward fate;
Ah, nymph, that fate assist me to endure,
And bear awhile what death alone can cure!

Sonnet XXIII. By the Same. To the North Star[1]

Towards thy bright beams I turn my swimming eyes,
  Fair, fav'rite planet,[2] which in happier days
Saw my young hopes (ah, faithless hopes!) arise,
  And on my passion shed propitious rays;
Now nightly wandering mid the tempests drear
  That howl the woods and rocky steeps among,
I love to see thy sudden light appear
  Through the swift clouds driv'n by the wind along;
Or in the turbid[3] water, rude and dark,
  O'er whose wild stream the gust of winter raves,
Thy trembling light with pleasure still I mark,
  Gleam in faint radiance on the foaming waves:
So o'er my soul short rays of reason fly,
Then fade – and leave me to despair and die!

Sonnet XXIV. By the Same

Make there my tomb, beneath the lime-tree's shade,[1]
  Where grass and flowers in wild luxuriance wave;
Let no memorial mark where I am laid,
  Or point to common eyes the lover's grave!

Notes

Sonnet XXII

1 ' "I climb steep rocks, I break my way through copses, among thorns and briars, which tear me to pieces, and I feel a little relief." *Sorrows of Werther*, Volume 1' (Smith's note).

2 *songstress* the nightingale.

Sonnet XXIII

1 ' "The greater bear, favourite of all the constellations; for when I left you of an evening it used to shine opposite your window." *Sorrows of Werther*, Volume 2' (Smith's note).

2 *Fair, fav'rite planet* The planet Venus, the evening star, is the brightest in the sky.

3 *turbid* cloudy, opaque.

Sonnet XXIV

1 ' "At the corner of the churchyard which looks towards the fields, there are two lime-trees. It is there I wish to rest." *Sorrows of Werther*, Volume 2' (Smith's note).

But oft at twilight morn, or closing day,
The faithful friend with falt'ring step shall glide,
Tributes of fond regret by stealth to pay,
And sigh o'er the unhappy suicide.
And sometimes, when the sun with parting rays
Gilds the long grass that hides my silent bed,
The tear shall tremble in my Charlotte's eyes;[2]
Dear, precious drops – they shall embalm the dead.
Yes! Charlotte o'er the mournful spot shall weep,
Where her poor Werther and his sorrows sleep.

Sonnet XXV. By the Same. Just before his Death[1]

Why should I wish to hold in this low sphere
'A frail and feverish being?'[2] Wherefore try
Poorly, from day to day, to linger here,
Against the powerful hand of Destiny?
By those who know the force of hopeless care
On the worn heart, I sure shall be forgiven;
If to elude dark guilt, and dire despair,
I go uncalled to mercy and to heaven!
Oh thou, to save whose peace I now depart,
Will thy soft mind thy poor lost friend deplore,
When worms shall feed on this devoted heart,
Where even thy image shall be found no more?
Yet may thy pity mingle not with pain,
For then thy hapless lover dies in vain.

Sonnet XXVI. To the River Arun

On thy wild banks, by frequent torrents worn,
No glittering fanes or marble domes appear,
Yet shall the mournful muse thy course adorn,
And still to her thy rustic waves be dear.
For with the infant Otway,[1] lingering here,
Of early woes she bade her votary[2] dream,
While thy low murmurs soothed his pensive ear,
And still the poet consecrates the stream.

Notes

[2] Werther was hopelessly in love with Charlotte.

Sonnet XXV

[1] ' "May my death remove every obstacle to your happiness. Be at peace, I entreat you; be at peace." *Sorrows of Werther*, Volume 2' (Smith's note).

[2] *A frail and feverish being* from Milton, *Comus* 8.

Sonnet XXVI

[1] 'Otway was born at Trotten, a village in Sussex. Of Woolbeding, another village on the banks of the Arun (which runs through them both), his father was rector. Here it was, therefore, that he probably passed many of his early years. The Arun is here an inconsiderable stream, winding in a channel deeply worn, among meadow, heath and wood' (Smith's note). Smith moved to Woolbeding House in her native Sussex in 1785, where this sonnet was composed. Thomas Otway (1652–85), dramatist, was known chiefly for his tragedy, *Venice Preserved* (1681).

[2] *votary* ardent follower (of the 'mournful muse').

Beneath the oak and birch that fringe thy side,
The first-born violets of the year shall spring,
And in thy hazels, bending o'er the tide,
The earliest nightingale delight to sing,
While kindred spirits, pitying, shall relate
Thy Otway's sorrows, and lament his fate!

Sonnet XXVII

Sighing I see yon little troop at play,
By Sorrow yet untouched, unhurt by Care,
While free and sportive they enjoy today
'Content and careless of tomorrow's fare!'[1]
Oh happy age, when hope's unclouded ray
Lights their green path, and prompts their simple mirth,
Ere yet they feel the thorns that lurking lay
To wound the wretched pilgrims of the earth,
Making them rue the hour that gave them birth,
And threw them on a world so full of pain
Where prosperous folly treads on patient worth,
And to deaf Pride, Misfortune pleads in vain!
Ah, for their future fate, how many fears
Oppress my heart – and fill mine eyes with tears!

Sonnet XXVIII. To Friendship

Oh thou, whose name too often is profaned,
Whose charms celestial few have hearts to feel!
Unknown to Folly and by Pride disdained,
To thy soft solace may my sorrows steal!
Like the fair moon, thy mild and genuine ray
Through life's long evening shall unclouded last;
While the frail summer friendship fleets away
As fades the rainbow from the northern blast.
'Tis thine, oh nymph, with 'balmy hands to bind'[1]
The wounds inflicted in misfortune's storm,
And blunt severe Affliction's sharpest dart;
'Tis thy pure spirit warms my Anna's mind,
Beams through the pensive softness of her form,
And holds its altar on her spotless heart.

Notes

Sonnet XXVII

[1] 'Thomson' (Smith's note). This line is borrowed from Thomson's *Autumn* 191, where it refers to 'the gay birds that sung them to repose'.

Sonnet XXVIII

[1] *balmy hands to bind* 'Collins' (Smith's note). Collins's *Ode to Pity* begins: 'Oh thou, the friend to man assigned, / With balmy hands his wounds to bind'.

Sonnet XXIX. To Miss C———. On being Desired to Attempt Writing a Comedy[I]

Wouldst thou then have *me* tempt the comic scene
Of laughing Thalia[2] – used so long to tread
The gloomy paths of sorrow's cypress shade,
And the lorn lay with sighs and tears to stain?
Alas, how much unfit her sprightly vein!
Arduous to try and seek the sunny mead,
And bowers of roses, where she loves to lead
The sportive subjects of her golden reign!

Enough for me if still, to soothe my days,
Her fair and pensive sister[3] condescend
With tearful smile to bless my simple lays;
Enough if her soft notes she sometimes lend,
To gain for me, of feeling hearts, the praise,
And chiefly thine, my ever partial friend!

Sonnet XXX. To the River Arun

Be the proud Thames of trade the busy mart!
Arun, to thee will other praise belong;
Dear to the lover's and the mourner's heart,
And ever sacred to the sons of song!

Thy shadowy rocks unhappy love shall seek,
Where mantling loose, the green clematis[I] flaunts,
And sorrow's drooping form and faded cheek
Choose on thy willowed shore her lonely haunts.

Banks which inspired thy Otway's plaintive strain!
Wilds whose lorn echoes learned the deeper tone
Of Collins' powerful shell![2] Yet once again
Another poet, Hayley, is thine own!
Thy classic stream anew shall hear a lay
Bright as its waves and various as its way!

Notes

Sonnet XXIX

[I] Miss C——remains unidentified; a possible contender is the authoress Elizabeth Carter, one of the subscribers to the fifth edition of *Elegiac Sonnets* in 1789.

[2] *Thalia* muse of comedy.

[3] *sister* Erato, muse of lyric poetry.

Sonnet XXX

[I] 'Clematis: the plant bindwith, or virgin's bower, which towards the end of June begins to cover the hedges and sides of rocky hollows with its beautiful foliage, and flowers of a yellowish white and of an agreeable fragrance, which are succeeded by seed-pods, that bear some resemblance to feathers or hair, whence it is sometimes called Old Man's Beard' (Smith's note).

[2] 'Collins, as well as Otway, was a native of this country, and I should imagine at some period of his life an inhabitant of this neighbourhood, since, in his beautiful *Ode on the Death of Colonel Ross*, he says:

> The muse shall still, with social aid,
> Her gentlest promise keep,
> E'en humble Harting's cottaged vale
> Shall learn the sad repeated tale
> And bid her shepherds weep.

And in the *Ode to Pity*:

> Wild Arun too has heard thy strains,
> And Echo, midst my native plains,
> Been soothed with Pity's lute.' (Smith's note)

Sonnet XXXI. Written on Farm Wood, South Downs, in May 1784[1]

Spring's dewy hand on this fair summit weaves
The downy grass with tufts of Alpine flowers,[2]
And shades the beechen slopes with tender leaves,
And leads the shepherd to his upland bowers,
Strewn with wild thyme; while slow-descending showers
Feed the green ear,[3] and nurse the future sheaves.
Ah, blessed the hind[4] whom no sad thought bereaves
Of the gay season's pleasures! All his hours
To wholesome labour given, or thoughtless mirth;
No pangs of sorrow past or coming dread
Bend his unconscious spirit down to earth,
Or chase calm slumbers from his careless head.
Ah, what to me can those dear days restore,
When scenes could charm that now I taste no more!

Sonnet XXXII. To Melancholy. Written on the Banks of the Arun, October 1785

When latest autumn spreads her evening veil,
And the grey mists from these dim waves arise,
I love to listen to the hollow sighs
Through the half-leafless wood that breathes the gale.
For at such hours the shadowy phantom, pale,
Oft seems to fleet before the poet's eyes;
Strange sounds are heard, and mournful melodies,
As of night-wanderers who their woes bewail;
Here, by his native stream, at such an hour,
Pity's own Otway I methinks could meet,
And hear his deep sighs swell the saddened wind.
Oh melancholy, such thy magic power,
That to the soul these dreams are often sweet,
And soothe the pensive visionary mind!

Sonnet XXXIII. To the Naiad of the Arun

Go, rural naiad, wind thy stream along
Through woods and wilds, then seek the ocean caves
Where sea-nymphs meet their coral rocks among,
To boast the various honours of their waves!

Notes

SONNET XXXI

[1] At this period Smith was sharing her husband's incarceration at the King's Bench Prison for debt. As her imprisonment was voluntary, she was able to visit her nine children who remained at Bignor Park. This sonnet must have been written on one such visit.

[2] 'An infinite variety of plants are found on these hills, particularly about this spot. Many sorts of orchis and cistus of singular beauty, with several others with which I am but imperfectly acquainted' (Smith's note).

[3] *green ear* of corn, which in due course will ripen into sheaves.

[4] *hind* peasant.

'Tis but a little, o'er thy shallow tide,
That toiling trade her burdened vessel leads;
But laurels grow luxuriant on thy side,
And letters live along thy classic meads.
Lo, where mid British bards[1] thy natives shine!
And now another poet helps to raise
Thy glory high – the poet of *The Mine*[2] –
Whose brilliant talents are his smallest praise:
And who, to all that genius can impart,
Adds the cool head and the unblemished heart!

Sonnet XXXIV. To a Friend

Charmed by thy suffrage[1] shall I yet aspire
(All inauspicious as my fate appears,
By troubles darkened, that increase with years)
To guide the crayon, or to touch the lyre?
Ah me! the sister muses still require
A spirit free from all intrusive fears,
Nor will they deign to wipe away the tears
Of vain regret that dim their sacred fire.
But when thy sanction crowns my simple lays,
A ray of pleasure lights my languid mind,
For well I know the value of thy praise;
And to how few the flattering meed[2] confined,
That thou, their highly favoured brows to bind,
Wilt weave green myrtle and unfading bays!

Sonnet XXXV. To Fortitude

Nymph of the rock, whose dauntless spirit braves
The beating storm, and bitter winds that howl
Round thy cold breast; and hear'st the bursting waves
And the deep thunder with unshaken soul;
Oh come and show how vain the cares that press
On my weak bosom, and how little worth
Is the false fleeting meteor, Happiness,
That still misleads the wanderers of the earth![1]
Strengthened by thee, this heart shall cease to melt
O'er ills that poor humanity must bear;

Notes

Sonnet XXXIII

[1] *British bards* 'Otway, Collins, Hayley' (Smith's note).

[2] *the poet of The Mine* John Sargent, author of *The Mine* (1785), was MP for Seaford, and a mutual friend of Smith and Hayley.

Sonnet XXXIV

[1] *suffrage* encouragement.

[2] *meed* reward, tribute.

Sonnet XXXV

[1] Smith writes of happiness in these terms in *Beachy Head* 255–8.

Nor friends estranged, or ties dissolved be felt
To leave regret, and fruitless anguish there.
And when at length it heaves its latest sigh,
Thou and mild hope shall teach me how to die!

Sonnet XXXVI

Should the lone wanderer, fainting on his way,
Rest for a moment of the sultry hours,
And though his path through thorns and roughness lay,
Pluck the wild rose, or woodbine's gadding[1] flowers;
Weaving gay wreaths beneath some sheltering tree,
The sense of sorrow he awhile may lose;
So have I sought thy flowers, fair Poesy,
So charmed my way with friendship and the muse!
But darker now grows life's unhappy day,
Dark with new clouds of evil yet to come,
Her pencil sickening Fancy throws away,
And weary Hope reclines upon the tomb;
And points my wishes to that tranquil shore
Where the pale spectre Care pursues no more.

The Emigrants: A Poem in Two Books (1793)

Dedication: To William Cowper, Esq.[1]

Dear Sir,

There is, I hope, some propriety in my addressing a composition to you, which would never perhaps have existed had I not, amid the heavy pressure of many sorrows, derived infinite consolation from your poetry, and some degree of animation and of confidence from your esteem.[2]

The following performance is far from aspiring to be considered as an imitation of your inimitable poem, *The Task*; I am perfectly sensible that it belongs not to a feeble and feminine hand to draw the bow of Ulysses.[3]

The force, clearness, and sublimity of your admirable poem; the felicity, almost peculiar to your genius, of giving to the most familiar objects dignity and effect, I could never hope to reach – yet, having read *The Task* almost incessantly from its first

Notes

SONNET XXXVI

[1] *gadding* straggling. Smith may be recalling William Mason, *The English Garden* (1772):

> There smiles in varied tufts the velvet rose,
> There flaunts the gadding woodbine . . .
>
> (i 432–3)

THE EMIGRANTS

[1] By the time Smith dedicated *The Emigrants* to Cowper, he was a famous author for *The Task*, which was one of the best-selling poems of its time. Having finished an early version of her poem in April 1793, she sent it to Cowper, who suggested some alterations to it. From what she says here, it would appear that he also assured her that it should be published.

[2] *your esteem* Cowper praised Smith's abilities when introduced to her by William Hayley in early August 1792.

[3] *the bow of Ulysses* Ulysses acquired, when young, a bow which he never used, valuing it so highly that he left it at home. The contest to draw its string and win the hand of Penelope forms the culmination of the homecoming which ends *The Odyssey.*

publication[4] to the present time, I felt that kind of enchantment described by Milton when he says

> The angel ended, and in Adam's ear
> So charming left his voice, that he awhile
> Thought him still speaking.
>
> (*Paradise Lost* viii 1–3)

And from the force of this impression, I was gradually led to attempt, in blank verse, a delineation of those interesting objects which happened to excite my attention, and which even pressed upon an heart that has learned, perhaps from its own sufferings, to feel with acute though unavailing compassion the calamity of others.

A dedication usually consists of praises and of apologies; *my* praise can add nothing to the unanimous and loud applause of your country. She regards you with pride as one of the few who, at the present period, rescue her from the imputation of having degenerated in poetical talents; but in the form of apology I should have much to say, if I again dared to plead the pressure of evils, aggravated by their long continuance, as an excuse for the defects of this attempt.

Whatever may be the faults of its execution, let me vindicate myself from those that may be imputed to the design. In speaking of the emigrant clergy,[5] I beg to be understood as feeling the utmost respect for the integrity of their principles, and it is with pleasure I add my suffrage to that of those who have had a similar opportunity of witnessing the conduct of the emigrants of all descriptions during their exile in England – which has been such as does honour to *their* nation, and ought to secure to them in ours the esteem of every liberal mind.[6]

Your philanthropy, dear sir, will induce you, I am persuaded, to join with me in hoping that this painful exile may finally lead to the extirpation of that reciprocal hatred so unworthy of great and enlightened nations; that it may tend to humanize both countries, by convincing each that good qualities exist in the other; and at length annihilate the prejudices that have so long existed to the injury of both.

Yet it is unfortunately but too true that with the body of the English, this national aversion has acquired new force by the dreadful scenes which have been acted in France during the last summer[7] – even those who are the victims of the Revolution have not escaped the odium which the undistinguishing multitude annex to all the natives of a country where such horrors have been acted. Nor is this the worst effect those events have had on the minds of the English: by confounding the original cause with the wretched catastrophes that have followed its ill management, the attempts of public virtue with the outrages that guilt and folly have committed in its disguise – the very name of liberty has not only lost the charm it used to have in British ears, but many who have written or spoken in its defence have been stigmatized as promoters of anarchy, and enemies to the prosperity of their country.[8] Perhaps even the author of

Notes

[4] *The Task* was first published in 1785; like *The Emigrants*, it is written in blank verse.

[5] *the emigrant clergy* On 26 May 1792 the French government decided that priests who refused to join the Constitutional Church were traitors and should be deported. With the end of the monarchy on 10 August that decree became effective, precipitating the exile of many clergymen to England. The presence of 3 bishops and 220 priests among the victims of the September massacres underlined the dangers to the clergy at that moment.

[6] Smith was courageous in writing about the plight of French émigrés. The outbreak of war between England and France (declared in February 1793) led most people to regard French people of any description as 'the enemy'.

[7] *the dreadful scenes . . . last summer* The storming of the Tuileries (10 August 1792) was followed by the imprisonment of the king and his family, and the September massacres of royalist and other prisoners in Paris (2–7 September).

[8] *many who have written . . . their country* Pitt's government had embarked on a campaign to repress radical activity following the outbreak of war with France in February 1793. The most obvious evidence of this was the treason trials of 1794 (see pp. 316–17).

The Task, with all his goodness and tenderness of heart, is in the catalogue of those who are reckoned to have been too warm in a cause which it was once the glory of Englishmen to avow and defend. The exquisite poem, indeed, in which you have honoured liberty by a tribute highly gratifying to her sincerest friends, was published some years before the demolition of regal despotism in France – which, in the fifth Book, it seems to foretell.[9] All the truth and energy of the passage to which I allude must have been strongly felt when, in the Parliament of England, the greatest orator of our time quoted the sublimest of our poets – when the eloquence of Fox[10] did justice to the genius of Cowper.

I am, dear sir,
With the most perfect esteem,
Your obliged and obedient servant,
CHARLOTTE SMITH

Brighthelmstone,[11] 10 May 1793

Book I

Scene: on the cliffs to the eastward of the town of Brighthelmstone in Sussex
Time: a morning in November 1792

Slow in the wintry morn, the struggling light
Throws a faint gleam upon the troubled waves;
Their foaming tops, as they approach the shore,
And the broad surf that, never ceasing, breaks
On the innumerous[1] pebbles, catch the beams
Of the pale sun, that with reluctance gives
To this cold northern isle its shortened day.
Alas, how few the morning wakes to joy!
How many murmur at oblivious night
For leaving them so soon; for bearing thus
Their fancied bliss (the only bliss they taste!)
On her black wings away; changing the dreams
That soothed their sorrows; for calamities
(And every day brings its own sad proportion);
For doubts, diseases, abject dread of death,
And faithless friends, and fame and fortune lost,
Fancied or real wants, and wounded pride
That views the daystar but to curse his beams.
Yet He whose Spirit into being called
This wondrous world of waters; He who bids
The wild wind lift them till they dash the clouds,
And speaks to them in thunder; or whose breath,
Low murmuring o'er the gently heaving tides,
When the fair moon, in summer night serene,
Irradiates with long trembling lines of light

Notes

[9] *Task* Book V includes a passage in praise of liberty (ll. 446ff.), and one contrasting the monarchy in England and France (to the detriment of the latter) (ll. 331–62).

[10] *the eloquence of Fox* Charles James Fox, Whig leader in the House of Commons.

[11] *Brighthelmstone* Smith moved to Brighton in summer 1789, where she would be based for the next three and a half years.

BOOK I

[1] *innumerous* innumerable. A poeticism, to which some reviewers objected; see p. 82.

Their undulating surface; that great Power,
Who, governing the planets, also knows
If but a sea-mew falls,[2] whose nest is hid
In these incumbent cliffs; He surely means
To us, his reasoning creatures, whom He bids
Acknowledge and revere his awful hand,
Nothing but good. Yet man, misguided man,
Mars the fair work that he was bid enjoy,
And makes himself the evil he deplores.
How often, when my weary soul recoils
From proud oppression, and from legal crimes
(For such are in this land, where the vain boast
Of equal law is mockery, while the cost
Of seeking for redress is sure to plunge
Th' already injured to more certain ruin,
And the wretch starves before his counsel[3] pleads) –
How often do I half abjure society
And sigh for some lone cottage, deep embowered
In the green woods that these steep chalky hills
Guard from the strong south-west;[4] where round their base
The beech wide flourishes, and the light ash
With slender leaf half hides the thymy turf!
There do I wish to hide me, well content
If on the short grass, strewn with fairy flowers,
I might repose thus sheltered;[5] or, when eve
In orient crimson lingers in the west,
Gain the high mound, and mark these waves remote
(Lucid though distant), blushing with the rays
Of the far-flaming orb that sinks beneath them.
For I have thought that I should then behold
The beauteous works of God unspoiled by man
And less affected then by human woes
I witnessed not; might better learn to bear
Those that injustice and duplicity
And faithlessness and folly fix on me:
For never yet could I derive relief,
When my swoln heart was bursting with its sorrows,
From the sad thought that others like myself
Live but to swell affliction's countless tribes!
Tranquil seclusion I have vainly sought;
Peace, who delights in solitary shade,
No more will spread for me her downy wings,

Notes

[2] *If but a sea-mew falls* a reference to Matthew 10:29: 'Are not two sparrows sold for a farthing? and one of them shall not fall on the ground without your Father.' The passage was popular among 18th-century writers, thanks perhaps to Pope's *Essay on Man*:

> Who sees with equal eye, as God of all,
> A hero perish, or a sparrow fall . . .
>
> (i 87–8)

[3] *counsel* lawyer. Having spent time in prison with her husband, Smith had a jaundiced view of the legal system.

[4] *the strong south-west* wind.

[5] *I might repose thus sheltered* a reworking of Virgil's topos: 'o qui me gelidis in vallibus Haemi / Sistat, et ingenti ramorum protegat umbra!' (*Georgics* ii 488–9).

But, like the fabled Danaïds or the wretch
Who ceaseless up the steep acclivity
Was doomed to heave the still rebounding rock,[6]
Onward I labour – as the baffled wave
Which yon rough beach repulses, that returns
With the next breath of wind, to fail again.
Ah, mourner, cease these wailings! Cease and learn
That not the cot sequestered where the briar
And woodbine wild embrace the mossy thatch
(Scarce seen amid the forest gloom obscure),
Or more substantial farm, well-fenced and warm,
Where the full barn and cattle foddered round
Speak rustic plenty; nor the statelier dome
By dark firs shaded, or the aspiring pine
Close by the village church (with care concealed
By verdant foliage, lest the poor man's grave
Should mar the smiling prospect of his lord);
Where offices well-ranged, or dovecote stocked,
Declare manorial residence – not these
Or any of the buildings new and trim,
With windows circling towards the restless sea,
Which, ranged in rows,[7] now terminate my walk,
Can shut out for an hour the spectre care
That, from the dawn of reason, follows still
Unhappy mortals, till the friendly grave
(Our sole secure asylum) 'ends the chase'.[8]
    Behold, in witness of this mournful truth
A group approach me, whose dejected looks
(Sad heralds of distress!) proclaim them men
Banished for ever and for conscience sake
From their distracted country, whence the name
Of freedom misapplied, and much abused
By lawless anarchy, has driven them far
To wander – with the prejudice they learned
From bigotry (the tut'ress of the blind)
Through the wide world unsheltered; their sole hope
That German spoilers through that pleasant land
May carry wide the desolating scourge
Of war and vengeance.[9] Yet unhappy men,
Whate'er your errors, I lament your fate;
And, as disconsolate and sad ye hang
Upon the barrier of the rock, and seem

Notes

[6] Lines 68–70 refer to the fifty daughters of Danaus, King of Argos, who ordered them to kill their fifty husbands, whom he suspected of plotting against him. The daughters were punished by having eternally to draw water into leaking pots in Hades. Sisyphus was condemned in hell to roll uphill a huge stone which perpetually rolled down again.

[7] *ranged in rows* recently built Georgian terraces, erected during Brighton's heyday as a social centre.

[8] *ends the chase* 'I have a confused notion that this expression, with nearly the same application, is to be found in Young, but I cannot refer to it' (Smith's note). In fact, Smith is quoting Samuel Cooke, *Simonides on Human Life Paraphrased* (1742): 'Death ends the chase, and all the farce is o'er' (l. 32).

[9] *war and vengeance* Many French emigrants had joined the Prussian army on the borders, which had been attempting to invade France since May 1792.

To murmur your despondence, waiting long
Some fortunate reverse that never comes,
Methinks in each expressive face I see
Discriminated anguish. There droops[10] one
Who in a moping cloister long consumed
This life inactive, to obtain a better,[11]
And thought that meagre abstinence, to wake
From his hard pallet with the midnight bell,
To live on eleemosynary bread,[12]
And to renounce God's works, would please that God.
And now the poor pale wretch receives, amazed,
The pity strangers give to his distress
(Because these strangers are, by his dark creed,
Condemned as heretics), and with sick heart
Regrets his pious prison and his beads.[13]
Another, of more haughty port,[14] declines
The aid he needs not, while in mute despair
His high indignant thoughts go back to France,
Dwelling on all he lost – the Gothic[15] dome
That vied with splendid palaces,[16] the beds
Of silk and down, the silver chalices,
Vestments with gold enwrought for blazing altars,
Where, amid clouds of incense, he held forth
To kneeling crowds the imaginary bones
Of saints supposed, in pearl and gold enchased,[17]
And still with more than living monarchs' pomp
Surrounded; was believed by mumbling bigots
To hold the keys of heaven, and to admit
Whom he thought good to share it. Now, alas,
He to whose daring soul and high ambition
The world seemed circumscribed – who, wont to dream
Of Fleuri, Richelieu, Alberoni,[18] men
Who trod on empire, and whose politics
Were not beyond the grasp of his vast mind –
Is, in a land once hostile, still profaned
By disbelief and rites unorthodox,
The object of compassion. At his side,

Notes

[10] *droops* The diction is Miltonic; cf. *Samson Agonistes* 594: 'So much I feel my genial spirits *droop*.'

[11] *a better* i.e. a better life.

[12] *eleemosynary bread* alms.

[13] 'Lest the same attempts at misrepresentation should now be made, as have been made on former occasions, it is necessary to repeat that nothing is farther from my thoughts than to reflect invidiously on the emigrant clergy, whose steadiness of principle excites veneration, as much as their sufferings compassion. Adversity has now taught them the charity and humility they perhaps wanted when they made it a part of their faith that salvation could be obtained in no other religion than their own' (Smith's note).

[14] *port* demeanour.

[15] *Gothic* used here in the architectural sense, referring to a style common in Western Europe between the 12th and 16th centuries.

[16] 'Let it not be considered as an insult to men in fallen fortune, if these luxuries (undoubtedly inconsistent with their profession) be here enumerated. France is not the only country where the splendour and indulgences of the higher, and the poverty and depression of the inferior clergy, have alike proved injurious to the cause of religion' (Smith's note).

[17] *enchased* set.

[18] *Fleuri, Richelieu, Alberoni* powerful French cardinals.

Lighter of heart than these, but heavier far[19]
Than he was wont, another victim comes –
An Abbé who with less contracted brow
Still smiles and flatters, and still talks of hope,
Which, sanguine as he is, he does not feel,
And so he cheats the sad and weighty pressure
Of evils present. Still, as men misled
By early prejudice (so hard to break),
I mourn your sorrows, for I too have known
Involuntary exile[20] and, while yet
England had charms for me,[21] have felt how sad
It is to look across the dim cold sea
That melancholy rolls its refluent[22] tides
Between us and the dear regretted land
We call our own – as now ye pensive wait
On this bleak morning, gazing on the waves
That seem to leave your shore, from whence the wind
Is loaded to your ears with the deep groans
Of martyred saints and suffering royalty,[23]
While to your eyes the avenging power of Heaven
Appears in awful anger to prepare
The storm of vengeance, fraught with plagues and death.
Even he of milder heart, who was indeed
The simple shepherd in a rustic scene,
And mid the vine-clad hills of Languedoc
Taught to the barefoot peasant, whose hard hands
Produced the nectar he could seldom taste,[24]
Submission to the Lord for whom he toiled –
He, or his brethren, who to Neustria's sons[25]
Enforced religious patience, when, at times,
On their indignant hearts Power's iron hand
Too strongly struck, eliciting some sparks
Of the bold spirit of their native north –
Even these parochial priests, these humbled men
Whose lowly undistinguished cottages
Witnessed a life of purest piety,
While the meek tenants were, perhaps, unknown

Notes

[19] *heavier far* an echo of Michael's consoling words to Adam and Eve, who are told that they shall 'possess / A paradise within thee, happier far' (*Paradise Lost* xii 586–7).

[20] *Involuntary exile* Smith and her family were compelled to live near Dieppe, 1784–5, so as to elude her husband's creditors.

[21] *had charms for me* Smith echoes herself; cf. *Sonnet XII. Written on the Sea Shore* 7: 'But the wild gloomy scene has charms for me'. In later years Wordsworth would echo Smith in his *Lines Left upon a Seat in a Yew-Tree* 21: 'Stranger! these gloomy boughs / Had charms for him.'

[22] *refluent* flowing back.

[23] *suffering royalty* After the storming of the Tuileries by the Paris mob on 10 August 1792 the royal family sought refuge at the Legislative Assembly; they were imprisoned at the Temple on 12 August.

[24] 'See the finely descriptive verses written at Montauban in France in 1750 by Dr Joseph Warton, printed in Dodsley's *Miscellanies* iv. 203' (Smith's note). Warton's *Verses written at Montauban in France, 1750* was published in Robert Dodsley's *Collection of Poems* vol. 4 (1755), pp. 207–8, and reprinted in the *London Magazine* 24 (1755) 183–4. The poem laments that the French peasants pick grapes without being able to afford to taste the wine they produce: 'No cups nectareous shall their toils repay' (l. 5).

[25] *Neustria's sons* inhabitants of Normandy.

Each to the haughty lord of his domain,
Who marked them not (the noble scorning still
The poor and pious priest, as with slow pace
He glided through the dim-arched avenue
Which to the castle led, hoping to cheer
The last sad hour of some laborious life
That hastened to its close) – even such a man
Becomes an exile, staying not to try
By temperate zeal to check his madd'ning flock,
Who at the novel sound of liberty
(Ah, most intoxicating sound to slaves!)
Start into licence. Lo! dejected now,
The wandering pastor mourns, with bleeding heart,
His erring people, weeps and prays for them,
And trembles for the account that he must give
To Heaven for souls entrusted to his care.
Where the cliff, hollowed by the wintry storm,
Affords a seat with matted seaweed strewn,
A softer form reclines; around her run,
On the rough shingles or the chalky bourn,
Her gay unconscious children, soon amused,
Who pick the fretted stone or glossy shell
Or crimson plant marine, or they contrive
The fairy vessel with its ribband sail
And gilded paper pennant; in the pool
Left by the salt wave on the yielding sands,
They launch the mimic navy. Happy age,
Unmindful of the miseries of man!
Alas, too long a victim to distress,
Their mother, lost in melancholy thought,
Lulled for a moment by the murmurs low
Of sullen billows, wearied by the task
Of having here, with swoln and aching eyes,
Fixed on the grey horizon, since the dawn
Solicitously watched the weekly sail
From her dear native land – now yields awhile
To kind forgetfulness, while fancy brings,
In waking dreams, that native land again!
Versailles appears, its painted galleries
And rooms of regal splendour, rich with gold,
Where, by long mirrors multiplied,[26] the crowd
Paid willing homage – and, united there,
Beauty gave charms to empire. Ah! too soon
From the gay visionary pageant roused,
See the sad mourner start, and, drooping, look
With tearful eyes and heaving bosom round
On drear reality, where dark'ning waves,

Notes

[26] *by long mirrors multiplied* The Palace of Versailles has a long chamber lined with mirrors.

Urged by the rising wind, unheeded foam
Near her cold rugged seat. To call her thence
A fellow-sufferer comes: dejection deep
Checks, but conceals not quite, the martial air
And that high consciousness of noble blood
Which he has learned from infancy to think
Exalts him o'er the race of common men.
Nursed in the velvet lap of luxury
And fed by adulation, could *he* learn
That worth alone is true nobility,
And that *the peasant* who, 'amid the sons
Of Reason, Valour, Liberty, and Virtue,
Displays distinguished merit, is a noble
Of Nature's own creation'?[27] If even here,
If in this land of highly-vaunted freedom
Even Britons controvert the unwelcome truth,
Can it be relished by the sons of France –
Men who derive their boasted ancestry
From the fierce leaders of religious wars,
The first in chivalry's emblazoned page,
Who reckon Gueslin, Bayard or De Foix[28]
Among their brave progenitors? *Their* eyes,
Accustomed to regard the splendid trophies
Of heraldry (that with fantastic hand
Mingles, like images in feverish dreams,
'Gorgons and hydras and chimeras dire'[29]
With painted puns, and visionary shapes),
See not the simple dignity of virtue,
But hold all base, whom honours such as these
Exalt not from the crowd[30] – as one who long
Has dwelt amid the artificial scenes
Of populous city[31] deems that splendid shows,
The theatre, and pageant pomp of courts,
Are only worth regard; forgets all taste
For nature's genuine beauty; in the lapse
Of gushing waters hears no soothing sound,
Nor listens with delight to sighing winds
That on their fragrant pinions waft the notes
Of birds rejoicing in the tangled copse;
Nor gazes pleased on ocean's silver breast,

Notes

[27] 'These lines are Thomson's, and are among those sentiments which are now called (when used by living writers) not commonplace declamation but sentiments of dangerous tendency' (Smith's note). Smith quotes from Thomson, *Coriolanus* (1749), III iii.

[28] *Gueslin, Bayard or De Foix* famous French warriors.

[29] *Gorgons and hydras and chimeras dire* from *Paradise Lost* i 628.

[30] 'It has been said, and with great appearance of truth, that the contempt in which the nobility of France held the common people was remembered, and with all that vindictive asperity which long endurance of oppression naturally excites, when, by a wonderful concurrence of circumstances, the people acquired the power of retaliation. Yet let me here add what seems to be in some degree inconsistent with the former charge – that the French are good masters to their servants, and that in their treatment of their negro slaves they are allowed to be more mild and merciful than other Europeans' (Smith's note).

[31] *populous city* cf. Satan in *Paradise Lost*, 'As one who long in populous city pent' (ix 445).

While lightly o'er it sail the summer clouds
Reflected in the wave that, hardly heard,
Flows on the yellow sands: so to *his* mind
That long has lived where Despotism hides
His features harsh, beneath the diadem[32]
Of worldly grandeur, abject slavery seems,
If by that power imposed, slavery no more.
For luxury wreathes with silk the iron bonds,
And hides the ugly rivets with her flowers,
Till the degenerate triflers, while they love
The glitter of the chains, forget their weight.
But more, the men whose ill-acquired wealth[33]
Was wrung from plundered myriads by the means
Too often legalised by power abused,
Feel all the horrors of the fatal change,
When their ephemeral greatness, marred at once
(As a vain toy that Fortune's childish hand
Equally joyed to fashion or to crush),
Leaves them exposed to universal scorn
For having nothing else, not even the claim
To honour, which respect for heroes past
Allows to ancient titles – men like these
Sink even beneath the level whence base arts
Alone had raised them, unlamented sink,
And know that they deserve the woes they feel.
  Poor wand'ring wretches, whosoe'er ye are
That hopeless, houseless, friendless, travel wide
O'er these bleak russet downs, where, dimly seen,
The solitary shepherd shiv'ring tends
His dun discoloured flock (shepherd unlike
Him whom in song the poet's fancy crowns
With garlands, and his crook with vi'lets binds) –
Poor vagrant wretches! Outcasts of the world
Whom no abode receives, no parish owns,
Roving, like nature's commoners, the land
That boasts such general plenty – if the sight
Of wide-extended misery softens yours
Awhile, suspend your murmurs, here behold
The strange vicissitudes of fate, while thus
The exiled nobles from their country driven,
Whose richest luxuries were theirs, must feel
More poignant anguish than the lowest poor,
Who, born to indigence, have learned to brave

Notes

32 *diadem* crown.

33 'The financiers and *fermiers généraux* are here intended. In the present moment of clamour against all those who have spoken or written in favour of the first Revolution of France, the declaimers seem to have forgotten that under the reign of a mild and easy-tempered monarch, in the most voluptuous court in the world, the abuses by which men of this description were enriched had arisen to such height that their prodigality exhausted the immense resources of France, and, unable to supply the exigencies of government, the ministry were compelled to call *le tiers état* – a meeting that gave birth to the Revolution which has since been so ruinously conducted' (Smith's note).

Rigid Adversity's depressing breath!
Ah, rather Fortune's worthless favourites
Who feed on England's vitals – pensioners
Of base corruption, who, in quick ascent
To opulence unmerited, become
Giddy with pride, and as ye rise, forgetting
The dust ye lately left, with scorn look down
On those beneath ye (though your equals once
In fortune, and in worth superior still,
They view the eminence on which ye stand
With wonder, not with envy, for they know
The means by which ye reached it, have been such
As in all honest eyes degrade ye far
Beneath the poor dependent, whose sad heart
Reluctant pleads for what your pride denies) –
Ye venal, worthless hirelings of a court!
Ye pampered parasites whom Britons pay
For forging fetters for them! – rather here
Study a lesson that concerns ye much,
And, trembling, learn that if oppressed too long
The raging multitude, to madness stung,
Will turn on their oppressors and no more
By sounding titles and parading forms
Bound like tame victims, will redress themselves!
Then swept away by the resistless torrent
Not only all your pomp may disappear,
But in the tempest lost, fair Order sink
Her decent head, and lawless Anarchy
O'erturn celestial Freedom's radiant throne –
As now in Gallia, where Confusion, born
Of party rage and selfish love of rule,
Sully the noblest cause that ever warmed
The heart of patriot virtue.[34] There arise
The infernal passions: Vengeance, seeking blood,
And Avarice, and Envy's harpy fangs
Pollute the immortal shrine of Liberty,
Dismay her votaries, and disgrace her name.
Respect is due to principle, and they
Who suffer for their conscience have a claim,
Whate'er that principle may be, to praise.
These ill-starred exiles then who bound by ties
To them the bonds of honour; who resigned
Their country to preserve them, and now seek
In England an asylum, well deserve
To find that (every prejudice forgot
Which pride and ignorance teaches) we for them
Feel as our brethren, and that English hearts

Notes

[34] 'This sentiment will probably *renew* against me the indignation of those who have an interest in asserting that no such virtue anywhere exists' (Smith's note).

Of just compassion ever own the sway
As truly as our element, the deep,
Obeys the mild dominion of the moon.
This they *have* found, and may they find it still!
Thus mayst thou, Britain, triumph! May thy foes,
By Reason's gen'rous potency subdued,
Learn that the God thou worshippest delights
In acts of pure humanity! May thine
Be still such bloodless laurels, nobler far
Than those acquired at Cressy or Poitiers[35] –
Or of more recent growth, those well bestowed
On him[36] who stood on Calpe's blazing height
Amid the thunder of a warring world,
Illustrious rather from the crowds he saved
From flood and fire, than from the ranks who fell
Beneath his valour! Actions such as these,
Like incense rising to the throne of Heaven,
Far better justify the pride that swells
In British bosoms, than the deafening roar
Of victory from a thousand brazen throats,
That tell with what success wide-wasting war
Has by our brave compatriots thinned the world.

Book II

Quippe ubi fas versum atque nefas: tot bella per orbem
Tam multae scelerum facies; non ullus aratro
Dignus honos: squalent abductis arva colonis,
Et curvae rigidum falces conflantur in ensem.
Hinc movet Euphrates, illinc Germania bellum;
Vicinae ruptis inter se legibus urbes
Arma ferunt: saevit toto Mars impius orbe.
(*Virgil, Georgics* i 505–11)[1]

Scene: on an eminence on one of those downs, which afford to the south a view of the sea; to the north of the weald of Sussex
Time: an afternoon in April 1793[2]

Notes

[35] *Cressy or Poitiers* important battles fought by Edward III in his attempt to win the French throne.

[36] *him* George Augustus Eliott, first Baron Heathfield (1717–90), who maintained British rule of Gibraltar throughout a four-year siege, by sea and land, from the Spanish (1779–83). He was a local hero, as Heathfield was in East Sussex, and was buried at the church in the village. Gibraltar was originally a Phoenician trading-post called Calpe.

Book II

[1] 'For here right and wrong are confounded: there are so many wars throughout the world: so many sorts of wickedness: the due honours are not paid to the plough: the husbandmen are carried away and the fields lie neglected, and the crooked sickles are beaten into cruel swords. Here Euphrates, and there Germany, makes war: the neighbouring cities break their leagues, and wage war with each other: impious Mars rages all over the globe' (John Martyn's translation, 1741).

[2] After the execution of Louis XVI, 21 January 1793, violence in Paris intensified. War broke out between Britain and France in February.

Long wintry months are past;[3] the moon that now
Lights her pale crescent even at noon has made
Four times her revolution, since with step
Mournful and slow,[4] along the wave-worn cliff,
Pensive I took my solitary way[5]
Lost in despondence, while contemplating
Not my own wayward destiny alone
(Hard as it is, and difficult to bear!),
But in beholding the unhappy lot
Of the lorn exiles who amid the storms
Of wild disastrous anarchy are thrown,
Like shipwrecked sufferers, on England's coast,
To see, perhaps, no more their native land
Where Desolation riots.[6] They, like me,
From fairer hopes and happier prospects driven,
Shrink from the future, and regret the past.
But on this upland scene, while April comes
With fragrant airs to fan my throbbing breast,
Fain would I snatch an interval from care
That weighs my wearied spirit down to earth,
Courting, once more, the influence of hope
(For 'Hope' still waits upon the flowery prime)[7]
As here I mark Spring's humid hand unfold
The early leaves that fear capricious winds,
While, even on sheltered banks, the timid flowers
Give, half-reluctantly, their warmer hues
To mingle with the primroses' pale stars.
No shade the leafless copses yet afford,
Nor hide the mossy labours of the thrush
That, startled, darts across the narrow path;
But quickly reassured, resumes his task,
Or adds his louder notes to those that rise
From yonder tufted brake, where the white buds
Of the first thorn are mingled with the leaves
Of that which blossoms on the brow of May.[8]
    Ah, 'twill not be! so many years have passed
Since, on my native hills, I learned to gaze
On these delightful landscapes, and those years
Have taught me so much sorrow that my soul
Feels not the joy reviving nature brings,

Notes

[3] *Long wintry months are past* Wordsworth may have been echoing this line when he began *Tintern Abbey*: 'Five years have passed.'

[4] *step / Mournful and slow*

> With how sad steps, ô Moone, thou
> climb'st the skies,
> How silently, and with how wanne a face . . .
> (Sidney, *Astrophil and Stella*, sonnet 31, 1–2)

[5] *my solitary way* A recollection of the closing lines of *Paradise Lost*, in which Adam and Eve 'with wandering steps and slow, / Through Eden took their solitary way'.

[6] *Where Desolation riots* Counter-revolutionary disturbances had been going on in France for a long time; the Vendée was particularly badly affected in March 1793.

[7] 'Shakespeare' (Smith's note). As Curran points out, the allusion is not to Shakespeare but Edmund Waller, *To my young Lady Lucy Sidney* 13: 'Hope waits upon the flowery prime.'

[8] Smith refers firstly to blackthorn, the buds of which appear before the leaves, and secondly to hawthorn (or may-tree), the leaves of which come first, in mid to late May.

But, in dark retrospect, dejected dwells
On human follies, and on human woes.
What is the promise of the infant year,
The lively verdure, or the bursting blooms,
To those who shrink from horrors such as war
Spreads o'er the affrighted world? With swimming eye,
Back on the past they throw their mournful looks,
And see the temple which they fondly hoped
Reason would raise to Liberty, destroyed
By ruffian hands; while, on the ruined mass,
Flushed with hot blood, the fiend of discord sits
In savage triumph, mocking every plea
Of policy and justice, as she shows
The headless corse of one whose only crime
Was being born a monarch.[9] Mercy turns
From spectacle so dire her swoln eyes,
And Liberty, with calm unruffled brow
Magnanimous, as conscious of her strength
In reason's panoply, scorns to distain[10]
Her righteous cause with carnage, and resigns
To fraud and anarchy the infuriate crowd.
  What is the promise of the infant year
To those who (while the poor but peaceful hind
Pens, unmolested, the increasing flock
Of his rich master in this sea-fenced isle)
Survey, in neighbouring countries, scenes that make
The sick heart shudder, and the man who thinks
Blush for his species? *There* the trumpet's voice
Drowns the soft warbling of the woodland choir;
And violets, lurking in their turfy beds
Beneath the flow'ring thorn, are stained with blood.
There fall, at once, the spoiler and the spoiled,
While war, wide-ravaging, annihilates
The hope of cultivation, gives to fiends,
The meagre, ghastly fiends of Want and Woe,
The blasted land. There, taunting in the van[11]
Of vengeance-breathing armies, Insult stalks,
And, in the ranks, 'Famine, and Sword, and Fire,
Crouch for employment.'[12] Lo! the suffering world,
Torn by the fearful conflict, shrinks amazed
From Freedom's name, usurped and misapplied,
And, cow'ring to the purple tyrant's rod,
Deems *that* the lesser ill. Deluded men!
Ere ye profane her ever-glorious name,
Or catalogue the thousands that have bled

Notes

[9] *a monarch* a reference to Louis XVI, beheaded 21 January 1793.

[10] *distain* stain, sully.

[11] *the van* vanguard.

[12] 'Shakespeare' (Smith's note). *Henry V*, Prologue 7–8. Wordsworth has the same allusion in a similar passage of *Descriptive Sketches*, also published in 1793: 'Like lightnings eager for th' almighty word, / Look up for sign of havoc, Fire and Sword' (ll. 802–3).

Resisting her, or those who greatly died
Martyrs to liberty, revert awhile
To the black scroll that tells of regal crimes
Committed to destroy her; rather count
The hecatombs[13] of victims who have fallen
Beneath a single despot, or who gave
Their wasted lives for some disputed claim
Between anointed robbers – monsters both![14]
'Oh polished perturbation – golden care!'[15] –
So strangely coveted by feeble man
To lift him o'er his fellows – toy for which
Such showers of blood have drenched th' affrighted earth.
Unfortunate *his* lot, whose luckless head
Thy jewelled circlet, lined with thorns, has bound;
And who, by custom's laws, obtains from thee
Hereditary right to rule, unchecked,
Submissive myriads: for untempered power,
Like steel ill-formed, injures the hand
It promised to protect. Unhappy France!
If e'er thy lilies, trampled now in dust
And blood-bespotted, shall again revive
In silver splendour, may the wreath be wov'n
By voluntary hands,[16] and freemen, such
As England's self might boast, unite to place
The guarded diadem[17] on *his* fair brow,
Where Loyalty may join with Liberty
To fix it firmly. In the rugged school
Of stern adversity so early trained,
His future life, perchance, may emulate
That of the brave Bernois,[18] so justly called
The darling of his people, who revered
The warrior less than they adored the man!
But ne'er may party rage, perverse and blind,
And base venality, prevail to raise
To public trust a wretch[19] whose private vice
Makes even the wildest profligate recoil,
And who, with hireling ruffians leagued, has burst
The laws of nature and humanity,
Wading beneath the patriot's specious mask
And in equality's illusive name,
To empire through a stream of kindred blood!
Innocent prisoner, most unhappy heir

Notes

[13] *hecatombs* mass graves.

[14] 'Such was the cause of quarrel between the Houses of York and Lancaster, and of too many others with which the page of history reproaches the reason of man' (Smith's note).

[15] 'Shakespeare' (Smith's note). From *2 Henry IV* IV v 23.

[16] *If e'er thy lilies . . . voluntary hands* If France ever again revives the monarchy, let it be voluntary.

[17] *diadem* crown.

[18] 'Henry the Fourth of France. It may be said of this monarch that, had all the French sovereigns resembled him, despotism would have lost its horrors; yet he had considerable failings, and his greatest virtues may be chiefly imputed to his education in the school of adversity' (Smith's note).

[19] *wretch* almost certainly Marat, editor of *L'ami du peuple*, an energetically pro-revolutionary paper; assassinated by Charlotte Corday, 13 July 1793.

Of fatal greatness,[20] who art suffering now
For all the crimes and follies of thy race,
Better for thee, if o'er thy baby brow
The regal mischief never had been held –
Then, in an humble sphere, perhaps content,
Thou hadst been free and joyous on the heights
Of Pyrennean mountains shagged with woods
Of chestnut, pine and oak; as on these hills
Is yonder little thoughtless shepherd lad
Who, on the slope abrupt of downy turf
Reclined in playful indolence, sends off
The chalky ball, quick bounding far below,
While, half-forgetful of his simple task,
Hardly his length'ning shadow, or the bells'
Slow tinkling of his flock, that supping tend
To the brown fallows in the vale beneath,
Where nightly it is folded, from his sport
Recall the happy idler. While I gaze
On his gay vacant countenance, my thoughts
Compare with his obscure, laborious lot,
Thine, most unfortunate, imperial boy –
Who round thy sullen prison daily hear'st
The savage howl of Murder as it seeks
Thy unoffending life; while sad within
Thy wretched mother,[21] petrified with grief,
Views thee with stony eyes, and cannot weep!
Ah, much I mourn thy sorrows, hapless Queen,
And deem thy expiation made to Heaven
For every fault to which prosperity
Betrayed thee when it placed thee on a throne
Where boundless power was thine, and thou wert raised
High (as it seemed) above the envious reach
Of destiny! Whate'er thy errors were,
Be they no more remembered, though the rage
Of party swelled them to such crimes as bade
Compassion stifle every sigh that rose
For thy disastrous lot. More than enough
Thou hast endured, and every English heart,
Ev'n those that highest beat in Freedom's cause,
Disclaim as base, and of that cause unworthy,
The vengeance or the fear that makes thee still
A miserable prisoner! Ah, who knows,
From sad experience, more than I, to feel
For thy desponding spirit, as it sinks
Beneath procrastinated fears for those
More dear to thee than life! But eminence
Of misery is thine, as once of joy;

Notes

[20] *Innocent prisoner . . . greatness* the Dauphin, Louis XVII, then 7 years old, who is thought to have died in June 1795.

[21] *Thy wretched mother* Marie Antoinette, with whom Louis XVII was imprisoned. At the time of writing she was still alive, only to be executed on 16 October 1793.

And as we view the strange vicissitude
We ask anew where happiness is found.
Alas, in rural life, where youthful dreams
See the Arcadia that romance describes,
Not even content resides! In yon low hut
Of clay and thatch, where rises the grey smoke
Of smould'ring turf cut from the adjoining moor,
The labourer, its inhabitant, who toils
From the first dawn of twilight till the sun
Sinks in the rosy waters of the west,
Finds that with poverty it cannot dwell –
For bread, and scanty bread, is all he earns
For him and for his household. Should disease
Born of chill wintry rains arrest his arm,[22]
Then, through his patched and straw-stuffed casement,[23] peeps
The squalid figure of extremest Want,
And from the parish the reluctant dole,
Dealt by th' unfeeling farmer, hardly saves
The ling'ring spark of life from cold extinction;
Then the bright sun of spring, that smiling bids
All other animals rejoice, beholds,
Crept from his pallet, the emaciate wretch
Attempt with feeble effort to resume
Some heavy task above his wasted strength,
Turning his wistful looks (how much in vain!)
To the deserted mansion where no more
The owner (gone to gayer scenes) resides,
Who made even luxury virtue; while he gave
The scattered crumbs to honest Poverty.
But, though the landscape be too oft deformed
By figures such as these, yet peace is here,
And o'er our vallies, clothed with springing corn,
No hostile hoof shall trample, nor fierce flames
Wither the wood's young verdure, ere it form
Gradual the laughing May's luxuriant shade;
For by the rude sea guarded we are safe,
And feel not evils such as with deep sighs
The emigrants deplore, as they recall
The summer past, when nature seemed to lose
Her course in wild distemperature,[24] and aid,
With seasons all reversed, destructive war.
  Shuddering, I view the pictures they have drawn
Of desolated countries where the ground,
Stripped of its unripe produce, was thick strewn
With various death – the warhorse falling there

Notes

[22] *Should disease . . . his arm* i.e. If he should be prevented from working by disease brought on by exposure to wintry rain . . .

[23] *his patched and straw-stuffed casement* Gaps in the window-frame are patched and stuffed with straw to keep out draughts; the poor person ('extremest Want') looks through it.

[24] *distemperature* extreme heat.

By famine, and his rider by the sword.
The moping clouds sailed heavy charged with rain,
And bursting o'er the mountain's misty brow
Deluged, as with an inland sea, the vales;[25]
Where through the sullen evening's lurid gloom,
Rising like columns of volcanic fire,
The flames of burning villages illumed
The waste of water; and the wind that howled
Along its troubled surface brought the groans
Of plundered peasants, and the frantic shrieks
Of mothers for their children; while the brave,
To pity still alive, listened aghast
To these dire echoes, hopeless to prevent
The evils they beheld, or check the rage
Which ever, as the people of one land
Meet in contention, fires the human heart
With savage thirst of kindred blood, and makes
Man lose his nature, rendering him more fierce
Than the gaunt monsters of the howling waste.
  Oft have I heard the melancholy tale
Which, all their native gaiety forgot,
These exiles tell – how hope impelled them on,
Reckless of tempest, hunger or the sword,
Till, ordered to retreat they knew not why
From all their flattering prospects, they became
The prey of dark suspicion and regret:[26]
Then in despondence sunk the unnerved[27] arm
Of gallant Loyalty. At every turn
Shame and Disgrace appeared, and seemed to mock
Their scattered squadrons – which the warlike youth,
Unable to endure, often implored,
As the last act of friendship, from the hand
Of some brave comrade, to receive the blow
That freed the indignant spirit from its pain.
To a wild mountain, whose bare summit hides
Its broken eminence in clouds, whose steeps
Are dark with woods, where the receding rocks
Are worn by torrents of dissolving snow,
A wretched woman, pale and breathless, flies,
And gazing round her, listens to the sound

Notes

[25] 'From the heavy and incessant rains during the last campaign, the armies were often compelled to march for many miles through marshes overflowed, suffering the extremities of cold and fatigue. The peasants frequently misled them and, after having passed these inundations at the hazard of their lives, they were sometimes under the necessity of crossing them a second and a third time. Their evening quarters after such a day of exertion were often in a wood without shelter, and their repast, instead of bread, unripe corn, without any other preparation than being mashed into a sort of paste' (Smith's note).

[26] 'It is remarkable that, notwithstanding the excessive hardships to which the army of the emigrants was exposed, very few in it suffered from disease till they began to retreat; then it was that despondence consigned to the most miserable death many brave men who deserved a better fate, and then despair impelled some to suicide, while others fell by mutual wounds, unable to survive disappointment and humiliation' (Smith's note).

[27] *unnerved* weakened.

Of hostile footsteps. No, it dies away!
Nor noise remains but of the cataract,[28]
Or surly breeze of night that mutters low
Among the thickets where she trembling seeks
A temporary shelter, clasping close
To her hard-heaving heart her sleeping child,
All she could rescue of the innocent group
That yesterday surrounded her. Escaped
Almost by miracle, fear, frantic fear,
Winged her weak feet! Yet half-repentant now
Her headlong haste, she wishes she had stayed
To die with those affrighted Fancy paints
The lawless soldier's victims. Hark, again
The driving tempest bears the cry of Death!
And with deep sudden thunder, the dread sound
Of cannon vibrates on the tremulous earth,
While, bursting in the air, the murderous bomb
Glares o'er her mansion. Where the splinters fall
Like scattered comets, its destructive path
Is marked by wreaths of flame! Then, overwhelmed
Beneath accumulated horror, sinks
The desolate mourner, yet in death itself,
True to maternal tenderness, she tries
To save the unconscious infant from the storm
In which she perishes, and to protect
This last dear object of her ruined hopes
From prowling monsters, that from other hills
More inaccessible, and wilder wastes,
Lured by the scent of slaughter, follow fierce
Contending hosts, and to polluted fields
Add dire increase of horrors. But, alas,
The mother and the infant perish both!
  The feudal chief whose Gothic battlements
Frown on the plain beneath, returning home
From distant lands, alone and in disguise,
Gains at the fall of night his castle walls,
But at the vacant gate no porter sits
To wait his lord's admittance. In the courts
All is drear silence. Guessing but too well
The fatal truth, he shudders as he goes
Through the mute hall where, by the blunted light
That the dim moon through painted casements lends,
He sees that devastation has been there.
Then, while each hideous image to his mind
Rises terrific, o'er a bleeding corse
Stumbling he falls; another interrupts
His staggering feet – all, all who used to rush
With joy to meet him, all his family
Lie murdered in his way! And the day dawns

Notes

[28] *cataract* waterfall.

On a wild raving maniac whom a fate
So sudden and calamitous has robbed
Of reason, and who round his vacant walls
Screams unregarded and reproaches Heaven!
Such are thy dreadful trophies, savage War,
And evils such as these, or yet more dire,
Which the pained mind recoils from – all are thine!
The purple pestilence that to the grave
Sends whom the sword has spared is thine, and thine
The widow's anguish and the orphan's tears!
Woes such as these does man inflict on man,
And by the closet murderers whom we style
Wise politicians are the schemes prepared
Which, to keep Europe's wavering balance even,
Depopulate her kingdoms, and consign
To tears and anguish half a bleeding world!
   Oh could the time return when thoughts like these
Spoiled not that gay delight which vernal suns
Illuminating hills, and woods, and fields,
Gave to my infant spirits! Memory come,
And from distracting cares that now deprive
Such scenes of all their beauty, kindly bear
My fancy to those hours of simple joy,
When, on the banks of Arun, which I see
Make its irriguous[29] course through yonder meads,
I played, unconscious then of future ill!
There (where from hollows fringed with yellow broom,
The birch with silver rind, and fairy leaf,
Aslant the low stream trembles) I have stood
And meditated how to venture best
Into the shallow current, to procure
The willow-herb of glowing purple spikes,
Or flags[30] whose sword-like leaves concealed the tide,
Startling the timid reed-bird from her nest,
As with aquatic flowers I wove the wreath,
Such as, collected by the shepherd girls,
Deck in the villages the turfy shrine,
And mark the arrival of propitious May.
How little dreamed I then the time would come
When the bright sun of that delicious month
Should, from disturbed and artificial sleep,
Awaken me to never-ending toil,
To terror and to tears – attempting still
With feeble hands and cold desponding heart
To save my children from the o'erwhelming wrongs
That have for ten long years been heaped on me![31]

Notes

[29] *irriguous* irrigating. Milton refers to 'the flowery lap / Of some irriguous valley' (*Paradise Lost* iv 254–5).

[30] *flags* wild iris.

[31] *the o'erwhelming wrongs . . . on me!* In thinking of herself as having suffered for a decade Smith is casting her mind back to her husband's imprisonment for debt in December 1783; see headnote, p. 78.

The fearful spectres of chicane and fraud
Have, Proteus-like, still changed their hideous forms
(As the law lent its plausible disguise),
Pursuing my faint steps, and I have seen
Friendship's sweet bonds (which were so early formed,
And once I fondly thought of amaranth[32]
Inwove with silver seven times tried) give way
And fail, as these green fan-like leaves of fern
Will wither at the touch of autumn's frost.
Yet there are those whose patient pity still
Hears my long murmurs, who unwearied try
With lenient hands to bind up every wound
My wearied spirit feels, and bid me go
'Right onward'[33] – a calm votary of the nymph
Who from her adamantine rock points out
To conscious rectitude the rugged path
That leads at length to peace! Ah yes, my friends,
Peace will at last be mine, for in the grave
Is peace – and pass a few short years, perchance
A few short months, and all the various pain
I now endure shall be forgotten there,
And no memorial shall remain of me
Save in your bosoms; while even *your* regret
Shall lose its poignancy, as ye reflect
What complicated woes that grave conceals!
But if the little praise that may await
The mother's efforts should provoke the spleen
Of priest or Levite,[34] and they then arraign
The dust that cannot hear them, be it yours
To vindicate my humble fame, to say
That not in selfish sufferings absorbed
'I gave to misery all I had, my tears.'[35]
And if, where regulated sanctity
Pours her long orisons to heaven, my voice
Was seldom heard, that yet my prayer was made
To him who hears even silence – not in domes
Of human architecture filled with crowds,
But on these hills, where boundless yet distinct,
Even as a map, beneath are spread the fields
His bounty clothes, divided here by woods
And there by commons rude[36] or winding brooks,
While I might breathe the air perfumed with flowers
Or the fresh odours of the mountain turf,
And gaze on clouds above me, as they sailed
Majestic, or remark the reddening north

Notes

[32] *amaranth* imaginary unfading plant.

[33] 'Milton, Sonnet 22d' (Smith's note); see *To Mr Cyriack Skinner Upon his Blindness* 8–9: 'but still bear up and steer / Right onward'.

[34] *Levite* contemptuous term for a clergyman.

[35] 'Gray' (Smith's note); see *Elegy* 123

[36] *commons rude* coarse common land.

When bickering arrows of electric fire
Flash on the evening sky;[37] I made my prayer
In unison with murmuring waves that now
Swell with dark tempests, now are mild and blue
As the bright arch above, for all to me
Declare omniscient goodness, nor need I
Declamatory essays to incite
My wonder or my praise, when every leaf
That spring unfolds, and every simple bud
More forcibly impresses on my heart
His power and wisdom. Ah, while I adore
That goodness, which designed to all that lives
Some taste of happiness, my soul is pained
By the variety of woes that man
For man creates, his blessings often turned
To plagues and curses: saint-like Piety,
Misled by Superstition, has destroyed
More than Ambition, and the sacred flame
Of Liberty becomes a raging fire
When Licence and Confusion bid it blaze.
From thy high throne above yon radiant stars,
Oh power omnipotent, with mercy view
This suffering globe, and cause thy creatures cease,[38]
With savage fangs, to tear her bleeding breast;
Restrain that rage for power that bids a man,
Himself a worm, desire unbounded rule
O'er beings like himself; teach the hard hearts
Of rulers that the poorest hind who dies
For their unrighteous quarrels in thy sight
Is equal to the imperious lord that leads
His disciplined destroyers to the field.
May lovely Freedom in her genuine charms,
Aided by stern but equal Justice, drive
From the ensanguined earth the hell-born fiends
Of Pride, Oppression, Avarice and Revenge
That ruin what thy mercy made so fair!
Then shall these ill-starred wanderers, whose sad fate
These desultory lines lament, regain
Their native country; private vengeance then
To public virtue yield, and the fierce feuds
That long have torn their desolated land
May (even as storms that agitate the air
Drive noxious vapours from the blighted earth)
Serve, all tremendous as they are, to fix
The reign of Reason, Liberty, and Peace!

Notes

[37] *bickering arrows . . . sky* the aurora borealis or northern lights.

[38] *cause thy creatures cease* cause thy creatures [to] cease. Such syntactical liberties irritated some reviewers; see headnote p. 82.

Beachy Head

From Beachy Head: with Other Poems (1807)[1]

On thy stupendous summit, rock sublime,
That o'er the channel reared, halfway at sea
The mariner at early morning hails,[2]
I would recline; while Fancy should go forth
And represent the strange and awful hour
Of vast concussion when the Omnipotent
Stretched forth his arm and rent the solid hills,[3]
Bidding the impetuous main flood rush between
The rifted shores, and from the continent
Eternally divided this green isle.
Imperial lord of the high southern coast,
From thy projecting headland I would mark
Far in the east the shades of night disperse,
Melting and thinned, as from the dark blue wave
Emerging, brilliant rays of arrowy light
Dart from the horizon, when the glorious sun
Just lifts above it his resplendent orb.
Advances now, with feathery silver touched,
The rippling tide of flood; glisten the sands,
While, inmates of the chalky clefts that scar
Thy sides precipitous, with shrill harsh cry,
Their white wings glancing in the level beam,
The terns, and gulls, and tarrocks,[4] seek their food,
And thy rough hollows echo to the voice
Of the gray choughs[5] and ever-restless daws,
With clamour not unlike the chiding hounds,
While the lone shepherd and his baying dog
Drive to thy turfy crest his bleating flock.
  The high meridian[6] of the day is past,
And ocean now, reflecting the calm heaven,
Is of cerulean hue, and murmurs low
The tide of ebb upon the level sands.
The sloop, her angular canvas shifting still,
Catches the light and variable airs

Notes

BEACHY HEAD

[1] The 'Advertisement' to this posthumous volume states: 'The poem entitled *Beachy Head* is not completed according to the original design. That the increasing debility of its author has been the cause of its being left in an imperfect state will, it is hoped, be a sufficient apology.' See also headnote, p. 82.

[2] 'In crossing the Channel from the coast of France, Beachy Head is the first land made' (Smith's note).

[3] 'Alluding to the idea that this island was once joined to the continent of Europe, and torn from it by some convulsion of nature. I confess I never could trace the resemblance between the two countries. Yet the cliffs about Dieppe resemble the chalk cliffs on the southern coast. But Normandy has no likeness whatever to the parts of England opposite to it' (Smith's note).

[4] 'Terns: *Sterna hirundo*, or sea swallow; gulls: *Larus canus*; tarrocks: *Larus tridactylus*' (Smith's note).

[5] 'Gray choughs: *Corvus graculus*. Cornish choughs, or, as these birds are called by the Sussex people, saddle-backed crows, build in great numbers on this coast' (Smith's note).

[6] *high meridian* noon.

That but a little crisp the summer sea,
Dimpling its tranquil surface. Afar off,
And just emerging from the arch immense
Where seem to part the elements, a fleet
Of fishing vessels stretch their lesser sails,[7]
While more remote, and like a dubious spot
Just hanging in the horizon, laden deep,
The ship of commerce, richly freighted, makes
Her slower progress on her distant voyage,
Bound to the orient climates where the sun
Matures the spice within its odorous shell,
And, rivalling the grey worm's filmy toil,
Bursts from its pod the vegetable down,[8]
Which, in long turbaned wreaths,[9] from torrid heat
Defends the brows of Asia's countless castes.
There the earth hides within her glowing breast
The beamy adamant[10] and the round pearl
Enchased[11] in rugged covering, which the slave,
With perilous and breathless toil, tears off
From the rough sea-rock deep beneath the waves.
These are the toys of nature, and her sport
Of little estimate in Reason's eye;
And they who reason, with abhorrence see
Man, for such gauds[12] and baubles, violate
The sacred freedom of his fellow man –
Erroneous estimate! As heaven's pure air,
Fresh as it blows on this aërial height,
Or sound of seas upon the stony strand,
Or inland, the gay harmony of birds,
And winds that wander in the leafy woods,
Are to the unadulterate taste more worth
Than the elaborate harmony brought out
From fretted stop, or modulated airs
Of vocal science.[13] So the brightest gems
Glancing resplendent on the regal crown,
Or trembling in the high-born beauty's ear,
Are poor and paltry to the lovely light
Of the fair star[14] that, as the day declines
Attendant on her queen, the crescent moon
Bathes her bright tresses in the eastern wave.

Notes

[7] *lesser sails* as they drag their nets, the fishing vessels proceed slowly through the sea, dependent only on their smaller sails.

[8] 'Cotton: *Gossypium herbaceum*' (Smith's note).

[9] *long turbaned wreaths* The Indiaman on the horizon carries cotton which will be used in the production of turbans. Lines 41–9 are inspired by *Paradise Lost* ii 636–42.

[10] 'Diamonds, the hardest and most valuable of precious stones. For the extraordinary exertions of the Indians in diving for the pearl oysters, see the account of the pearl fisheries in Percival's *View of Ceylon*' (Smith's note). Robert Percival's *An Account of Ceylon* was first published in 1803.

[11] *Enchased* set.

[12] *gauds* showy ornaments, finery.

[13] Lines 57–68 are an attack on slavery. To reasonable people, the enslavement of men in exchange for jewels is an unequal transaction; just as, to the unadulterated sensibility, the delights of nature are worth more than the elaborate harmonies of music or the sound of the human voice.

[14] *fair star* Venus.

For now the sun is verging to the sea,
And as he westward sinks, the floating clouds
Suspended move upon the evening gale,
And gathering round his orb, as if to shade
The insufferable brightness, they resign
Their gauzy whiteness and, more warmed, assume
All hues of purple. There transparent gold
Mingles with ruby tints and sapphire gleams
And colours such as nature through her works
Shows only in the ethereal canopy.[15]
Thither aspiring fancy fondly soars,
Wandering sublime through visionary vales
Where bright pavilions rise, and trophies fanned
By airs celestial, and adorned with wreaths
Of flowers that bloom amid Elysian bowers.
Now bright and brighter still the colours glow,
Till half the lustrous orb within the flood
Seems to retire, the flood reflecting still
Its splendour, and in mimic glory dressed;
Till the last ray, shot upward, fires the clouds
With blazing crimson, then in paler light
Long lines of tenderer radiance lingering yield
To partial darkness, and on the opposing side
The early moon distinctly rising throws
Her pearly brilliance on the trembling tide.
The fishermen who at set seasons pass
Many a league off at sea their toiling night
Now hail their comrades from their daily task
Returning, and make ready for their own
With the night-tide commencing. The night tide
Bears a dark vessel on, whose hull and sails
Mark her a coaster from the north. Her keel
Now ploughs the sand, and sidelong now she leans,
While with loud clamours her athletic crew
Unload her, and resounds the busy hum
Along the wave-worn rocks. Yet more remote,
Where the rough cliff hangs beetling[16] o'er its base,
All breathes repose; the water's rippling sound
Scarce heard, but now and then the sea-snipe's cry[17]
Just tells that something living is abroad;
And sometimes crossing on the moon-bright line
Glimmers the skiff, faintly discerned awhile,
Then lost in shadow.
Contemplation here,
High on her throne of rock, aloof may sit
And bid recording Memory[18] unfold

Notes

[15] *ethereal canopy* sky.

[16] *beetling* Beetling (overhanging) cliffs recollect Thomson, *Spring* 454, who describes the hawk 'High, in the beetling Cliff'.

[17] 'In crossing the Channel this bird is heard at night, uttering a short cry, and flitting along near the surface of the waves. The sailors call it the sea-snipe, but I can find no species of sea-bird of which this is the vulgar name. A bird so called inhabits the Lake of Geneva' (Smith's note).

[18] *recording Memory* i.e. history.

Her scroll voluminous, bid her retrace
The period when from Neustria's hostile shore[19]
The Norman launched his galleys, and the bay
O'er which that mass of ruin[20] frowns even now
In vain and sullen menace, then received
The new invaders – a proud martial race,
Of Scandinavia the undaunted sons
Whom Dogon, Fier-a-bras, and Humfroi led
To conquest, while Trinacria to their power
Yielded her wheaten garland, and when thou,
Parthenope, within thy fertile bay
Received the victors.[21]
In the mailed ranks
Of Normans landing on the British coast
Rode Taillefer, and with astounding voice
Thundered the war-song daring Roland sang
First in the fierce contention; vainly brave,
One not inglorious struggle England made,
But failing, saw the Saxon heptarchy[22]
Finish for ever. Then the holy pile,

Notes

19 *Neustria's hostile shore* Normandy.

20 *ruin* Pevensey Castle.

21 'The Scandinavians (modern Norway, Sweden, Denmark, Lapland, etc.) and other inhabitants of the north, began towards the end of the eighth century to leave their inhospitable climate in search of the produce of more fortunate countries.

The north-men made inroads on the coasts of France and, carrying back immense booty, excited their compatriots to engage in the same piratical voyages; and they were afterwards joined by numbers of necessitous and daring adventurers from the coasts of Provence and Sicily.

In 844 these wandering innovators had a great number of vessels at sea and, again visiting the coasts of France, Spain, and England, the following year they penetrated even to Paris; and the unfortunate Charles the Bald, King of France, purchased at a high price the retreat of the banditti he had no other means of repelling.

These successful expeditions continued for some time till Rollo (otherwise Raoul) assembled a number of followers and, after a descent on England, crossed the Channel, and made himself master of Rouen, which he fortified. Charles the Simple, unable to contend with Rollo, offered to resign to him some of the northern provinces, and to give him his daughter in marriage. Neustria, since called Normandy, was granted to him, and afterwards Brittany. He added the more solid virtues of the legislator to the fierce valour of the conqueror; converted to Christianity, he established justice, and repressed the excesses of his Danish subjects, till then accustomed to live only by plunder. His name became the signal for pursuing those who violated the laws, as well as the cry of Haro, still so usual in Normandy. The Danes and Francs produced a race of men celebrated for their valour, and it was a small party of these that in 983, having been on a pilgrimage to Jerusalem, arrived on their return at Salerno, and found the town surrounded by Mahometans, whom the Salernians were bribing to leave their coast. The Normans represented to them the baseness and cowardice of such submission and, notwithstanding the inequality of their numbers, they boldly attacked the Saracen camp and drove the infidels to their ships. The Prince of Salerno, astonished at their successful audacity, would have loaded them with the marks of his gratitude but, refusing every reward, they returned to their own country from whence, however, other bodies of Normans passed into Sicily (anciently called Trinacria); and many of them entered into the service of the Emperor of the east, others of the Pope, and the Duke of Naples was happy to engage a small party of them in defence of his newly founded duchy. Soon afterwards three brothers of Coutance, the sons of Tancred de Hauteville – Guillaume Fier-a-bras, Drogon, and Humfroi – joining the Normans established at Aversa, became masters of the fertile island of Sicily and, Robert Guiscard joining them, the Normans became sovereigns both of Sicily and Naples (Parthenope). How William, the natural son of Robert, Duke of Normandy, possessed himself of England, is too well-known to be repeated here. William, sailing from St Valori, landed in the bay of Pevensey and at the place now called Battle met the English forces under Harold – an esquire (ecuyer) called Taillefer, mounted on an armed horse, led on the Normans, singing in a thundering tone the war song of Rollo. He threw himself among the English and was killed on the first onset. In a marsh not far from Hastings, the skeletons of an armed man and horse were found a few years since, which are believed to have belonged to the Normans, as a party of their horse, deceived in the nature of the ground, perished in the morass' (Smith's note).

22 *Saxon heptarchy* the seven kingdoms established by the Angles and Saxons in Britain.

Yet seen upon the field of conquest, rose,[23]
Where to appease Heaven's wrath for so much blood,
The conqueror bade unceasing prayers ascend,
And requiems for the slayers and the slain.
But let not modern Gallia form from hence
Presumptuous hopes that ever thou again,
Queen of the isles, shalt crouch to foreign arms.[24]
The enervate[25] sons of Italy may yield,
And the Iberian,[26] all his trophies torn
And wrapped in Superstition's monkish weed,
May shelter his abasement, and put on
Degrading fetters. Never, never thou,
Imperial mistress of the obedient sea!
But thou, in thy integrity secure,
Shalt now undaunted meet a world in arms.
  England, 'twas where this promontory rears
Its rugged brow above the channel wave,
Parting the hostile nations, that thy fame,
Thy naval fame, was tarnished, at what time
Thou, leagued with the Batavian, gavest to France
One day of triumph – triumph the more loud
Because even then so rare.[27] Oh well redeemed,
Since, by a series of illustrious men
Such as no other country ever reared,
To vindicate her cause. It is a list
Which, as Fame echoes it, blanches[28] the cheek
Of bold Ambition, while the despot feels
The extorted sceptre tremble in his grasp.
  From even the proudest roll by glory filled,
How gladly the reflecting mind returns
To simple scenes of peace and industry
Where, bosomed in some valley of the hills,
Stands the lone farm, its gate with tawny ricks
Surrounded, and with granaries and sheds
Roofed with green mosses, and by elms and ash

Notes

23 'Battle Abbey was raised by the Conqueror, and endowed with an ample revenue, that masses might be said night and day for the souls of those who perished in battle' (Smith's note).

24 *But let not . . . foreign arms* The principal anxiety in Britain at this period was of invasion from France ('Gallia').

25 *enervate* weak, effeminate.

26 Smith is thinking of Spain's defeat at the hands of the French in 1794.

27 'In 1690, King William being then in Ireland, Tourville, the French admiral, arrived on the coast of England. His fleet consisted of 78 large ships, and 22 fire-ships. Lord Torrington, the English admiral, lay at St Helens with only 40 English and a few Dutch ships, and, conscious of the disadvantage under which he should give battle, he ran up between the enemy's fleet and the coast, to protect it. The Queen's Council, dictated to by Russell, persuaded her to order Torrington to venture a battle. The orders Torrington appears to have obeyed reluctantly: his fleet now consisted of 22 Dutch and 34 English ships. Evertson, the Dutch admiral, was eager to obtain glory; Torrington, more cautious, reflected on the importance of the stake. The consequence was that the Dutch rashly sailing on were surrounded, and Torrington, solicitous to recover this false step, placed himself with difficulty between the Dutch and the French. But three Dutch ships were burnt, two of their admirals killed, and almost all their ships disabled. The English and Dutch, declining a second engagement, retired towards the mouth of the Thames. The French, from ignorance of the coast and misunderstanding among each other, failed to take all the advantage they might have done of this victory' (Smith's note).

28 *blanches* whitens.

Partially shaded; and not far removed
The hut of sea-flints built – the humble home
Of one who sometimes watches on the heights
When hid in the cold mist of passing clouds
The flock, with dripping fleeces, are dispersed
O'er the wide down; then from some ridged point
That overlooks the sea, his eager eye
Watches the bark[29] that for his signal waits
To land its merchandise. Quitting for this
Clandestine traffic his more honest toil,
The crook abandoning, he braves himself
The heaviest snowstorm of December's night,
When with conflicting winds the ocean raves,
And on the tossing boat unfearing mounts
To meet the partners of the perilous trade
And share their hazard.[30] Well it were for him
If no such commerce of destruction known,
He were content with what the earth affords
To human labour, even where she seems
Reluctant most. More happy is the hind[31]
Who with his own hands rears on some black moor
Or turbary[32] his independent hut
Covered with heather, whence the slow white smoke
Of smouldering peat arises. A few sheep,
His best possession, with his children share
The rugged shed when wintry tempests blow;
But when with spring's return the green blades rise
Amid the russet heath, the household live
Joint tenants of the waste throughout the day,
And often, from her nest among the swamps,
Where the gemmed sun-dew[33] grows, or fringed buck-bean,[34]
They scare the plover[35] that with plaintive cries
Flutters, as sorely wounded,[36] down the wind.
Rude, and but just removed from savage life,
Is the rough dweller among scenes like these
(Scenes all unlike the poet's fabling dreams
Describing Arcady).[37] But he is free;
The dread that follows on illegal acts
He never feels, and his industrious mate
Shares in his labour. Where the brook is traced

Notes

[29] *bark* ship.

[30] 'The shepherds and labourers of this tract of country, a hardy and athletic race of men, are almost universally engaged in the contraband trade, carried on for the coarsest and most destructive spirits, with the opposite coast. When no other vessel will venture to sea, these men hazard their lives to elude the watchfulness of the Revenue officers, and to secure their cargoes' (Smith's note).

[31] *hind* peasant, farm-labourer.

[32] *turbary* peat bog.

[33] 'sun-dew: *Drosera rotundifolia*' (Smith's note).

[34] 'buck-bean: *Menyanthes trifoliatum*' (Smith's note).

[35] 'plover: *Tringa vanellus*' (Smith's note).

[36] *as sorely wounded* i.e. as if sorely wounded, so as to distract attention from her nest.

[37] *Arcady* the mountainous central Pelopennesus, named after Arcas, son of Zeus, who reigned here; the people were shepherd-musicians. Although the Greeks regarded it as barbaric, the Romans idealized it into a paradise of nymphs and shepherds. The 'poet' Smith has in mind is probably Virgil, who celebrates Arcadia at *Eclogues* x 31ff.

By crowding osiers,[38] and the black coot[39] hides
Among the plashy reeds her diving brood,
The matron wades, gathering the long green rush[40]
That well prepared hereafter lends its light
To her poor cottage, dark and cheerless else
Through the drear hours of winter. Otherwhile
She leads her infant group where charlock[41] grows
'Unprofitably gay',[42] or to the fields
Where congregate the linnet and the finch
That on the thistles so profusely spread
Feast in the desert, the poor family
Early resort, extirpating[43] with care
These and the gaudier mischief of the ground;
Then flames the high-raised heap, seen afar off
Like hostile war-fires flashing to the sky.[44]
Another task is theirs. On fields that show
As[45] angry Heaven had rained sterility
Stony and cold, and hostile to the plough,
Where, clamouring loud, the evening curlew[46] runs
And drops her spotted eggs among the flints,
The mother and the children pile the stones
In rugged pyramids, and all this toil
They patiently encounter, well content
On their flock bed[47] to slumber undisturbed
Beneath the smoky roof they call their own.
Oh little knows the sturdy hind who stands
Gazing, with looks where envy and contempt
Are often strangely mingled, on the car[48]
Where prosperous Fortune sits; what secret care
Or sick satiety is often hid
Beneath the splendid outside. *He* knows not
How frequently the child of luxury,
Enjoying nothing, flies from place to place
In chase of pleasure that eludes his grasp,
And that content is e'en less found by him
Than by the labourer whose pick-axe smooths
The road before his chariot, and who doffs
What *was* an hat; and, as the train pass on,
Thinks how one day's expenditure like this
Would cheer him for long months, when to his toil
The frozen earth closes her marble breast.

Notes

38 *osiers* willow-trees.

39 'coot: *Fulica aterrima*' (Smith's note).

40 *the long green rush* Rushes could be burnt for long periods; they served, effectively, as candles.

41 *charlock* wild mustard.

42 '"With blossomed furze, unprofitably gay", Goldsmith' (*Deserted Village* 194) (Smith's note).

43 *extirpating* rooting out.

44 'The beacons formerly lighted up on the hills to give notice of the approach of an enemy. These signals would still be used in case of alarm, if the telegraph now substituted could not be distinguished on account of fog or darkness' (Smith's note). The semaphore, an upright post with movable arms, was invented in 1792, and a chain of them linked with London in 1795.

45 *As* i.e. as if.

46 'Curlew: *Charadrius oedicnemus*' (Smith's note).

47 *flock bed* mattress stuffed with wool.

48 *car* coach; the peasant looks at a rich man ('Fortune') in the carriage drawn by horses.

Ah, who *is* happy? Happiness! A word
That like false fire[49] from marsh effluvia born
Misleads the wanderer, destined to contend
In the world's wilderness with want or woe.
Yet *they* are happy who have never asked
What good or evil means: the boy
That on the river's margin gaily plays
Has heard that death is there; he knows not death,
And therefore fears it not, and venturing in
He gains a bullrush or a minnow – then,
At certain peril, for a worthless prize,
A crow's or raven's nest, he climbs the boll[50]
Of some tall pine, and of his prowess proud
Is for a moment happy. Are *your* cares,
Ye who despise him, never worse applied?
The village girl is happy who sets forth
To distant fair, gay in her Sunday suit,
With cherry-coloured knots and flourished shawl,
And bonnet newly-purchased. So is he,
Her little brother, who his mimic drum
Beats till he drowns her rural lovers' oaths
Of constant faith and still-increasing love.
Ah, yet a while, and half those oaths believed,
Her happiness is vanished, and the boy,
While yet a stripling, finds the sound he loved
Has led him on till he has given up
His freedom and his happiness together.[51]
I once was happy, when while yet a child,[52]
I learned to love these upland solitudes,
And, when elastic[53] as the mountain air,
To my light spirit care was yet unknown,
And evil unforeseen. Early it came,
And childhood scarcely passed, I was condemned,
A guiltless exile,[54] silently to sigh,
While Memory with faithful pencil drew
The contrast, and, regretting, I compared
With the polluted smoky atmosphere
And dark and stifling streets, the southern hills
That to the setting sun their graceful heads
Rearing, o'erlook the frith[55] where Vecta[56] breaks

Notes

49 *false fire* The *ignis fatuus*, a phosphorescent light seen hovering over marshy ground, believed to be produced by the spontaneous combustion of inflammable gas produced by decaying organic matter; it was often blamed for leading travellers astray. Smith's point is that the pursuit of happiness is similarly perilous.

50 *boll* trunk.

51 *the boy . . . his happiness together* the boy becomes a soldier with a real drum.

52 *I once . . . child* Smith echoes her own *Sonnet V. To the South Downs* 1: 'Ah hills beloved, where once, an happy child . . .' See also line 368.

53 *elastic* buoyant.

54 *A guiltless exile* probably a reference to enforced residence in France during the 1780s, to escape her husband's numerous creditors.

55 *frith* the English Channel.

56 'Vecta: the Isle of Wight, which breaks the force of the waves when they are driven by south-west winds against this long and open coast. It is somewhere described as "Vecta shouldering the western waves" ' (Smith's note).

With her white rocks the strong impetuous tide,
When western winds the vast Atlantic urge
To thunder on the coast. Haunts of my youth!
Scenes of fond daydreams, I behold ye yet,
Where 'twas so pleasant by thy northern slopes
To climb the winding sheep-path, aided oft
By scattered thorns whose spiny branches bore
Small woolly tufts, spoils of the vagrant lamb
There seeking shelter from the noonday sun;
And pleasant, seated on the short soft turf,
To look beneath upon the hollow way
While heavily upward moved the labouring wain
And, stalking slowly by, the sturdy hind,
To ease his panting team,[57] stopped with a stone
The grating wheel.
Advancing higher still
The prospect widens, and the village church
But little, o'er the lowly roofs around
Rears its gray belfry and its simple vane;
Those lowly roofs of thatch are half-concealed
By the rude arms of trees, lovely in spring[58]
When on each bough the rosy-tinctured bloom
Sits thick and promises autumnal plenty.[59]
For even those orchards round the Norman farms
Which, as their owners mark the promised fruit,
Console them for the vineyards of the south,
Surpass not these.
Where woods of ash and beech
And partial copses fringe the green hill-foot,
The upland shepherd rears his modest home,
There wanders by a little nameless stream
That from the hill wells forth, bright now and clear,
Or after rain with chalky mixture gray,
But still refreshing in its shallow course
The cottage garden – most for use designed,
Yet not of beauty destitute. The vine
Mantles the little casement,[60] yet the briar
Drops fragrant dew among the July flowers;
And pansies rayed and freaked,[61] and mottled pinks
Grow among balm, and rosemary and rue;
There honeysuckles flaunt, and roses blow
Almost uncultured – some with dark green leaves
Contrast their flowers of pure unsullied white;
Others, like velvet robes of regal state

Notes

[57] *panting team* of oxen, who are turning a mill-wheel.

[58] 'Every cottage in this country has its orchard, and I imagine that not even those of Herefordshire or Worcestershire exhibit a more beautiful prospect, when the trees are in bloom, and the *Primavera candida e vermiglia* is everywhere so enchanting' (Smith's note). As Curran notes, Smith alludes to Petrarch, Sonnet 310, line 4 ('pure and rosy spring').

[59] *autumnal plenty* as Curran notes, apple harvests.

[60] *casement* window; the vine shelters it from the sun.

[61] *pansies rayed and freaked* a recollection of *Lycidas* 144: 'the pansy freaked with jet' ('freaked' is Milton's coinage).

Of richest crimson, while in thorny moss
Enshrined and cradled, the most lovely, wear
The hues of youthful beauty's glowing cheek.
With fond regret I recollect e'en now
In spring and summer what delight I felt
Among these cottage gardens, and how much
Such artless nosegays, knotted with a rush
By village housewife or her ruddy maid,
Were welcome to me, soon and simply pleased.
　An early worshipper at Nature's shrine,
I loved her rudest scenes – warrens and heaths,
And yellow commons, and birch-shaded hollows,
And hedgerows, bordering unfrequented lanes
Bowered with wild roses, and the clasping woodbine
Where purple tassels of the tangling vetch[62]
With bittersweet[63] and bryony[64] inweave,
And the dew fills the silver bindweed's[65] cups –
I loved to trace the brooks whose humid banks
Nourish the harebell and the freckled pagil,[66]
And stroll among o'ershadowing woods of beech,
Lending in summer, from the heats of noon,
A whispering shade; while haply there reclines
Some pensive lover of uncultured[67] flowers
Who from the tumps[68] with bright green mosses clad
Plucks the wood sorrel[69] with its light thin leaves,
Heart-shaped and triply folded, and its root
Creeping like beaded coral; or who there
Gathers the copse's pride, anémones[70]
With rays like golden studs on ivory laid
Most delicate, but touched with purple clouds –
Fit crown for April's fair but changeful brow.
　Ah, hills so early loved, in fancy still
I breathe your pure keen air, and still behold
Those widely spreading views, mocking alike
The poet and the painter's utmost art.
And still, observing objects more minute,
Wondering remark the strange and foreign forms
Of sea-shells, with the pale calcareous[71] soil
Mingled, and seeming of resembling substance[72] –
Though surely the blue ocean (from the heights

Notes

[62] 'vetch: *Vicia sylvatica*' (Smith's note).

[63] 'bittersweet: *Solanum dulcamara*' (Smith's note).

[64] 'bryony: *Bryonia alba*' (Smith's note).

[65] 'bindweed: *Convolvulus sepium*' (Smith's note).

[66] 'harebell: *Hyacinthus non scriptus*; pagil: *Primula veris*' (Smith's note). The preceding line echoes Wordsworth, 'Ode' 195: 'I love the brooks which down their channels fret.'

[67] *uncultured* uncultivated; i.e. wildflowers.

[68] *tumps* humps.

[69] 'sorrel: *Oxalis acetosella*' (Smith's note).

[70] 'anémones: *Anemóne nemorosa*. It appears to be settled on late and excellent authorities that this word should not be accented on the second syllable, but on the penultima. I have however ventured the more known accentuation as more generally used, and suiting better the nature of my verse' (Smith's note).

[71] *calcareous* containing lime.

[72] 'Among the crumbling chalk I have often found shells, some quite in a fossil state and hardly distinguishable from chalk. Others appeared more recent – cockles, mussels, and periwinkles, I well remember, were among the number, and some whose names I do not know. A great number were like those of small land-snails. It is now many years since I made these observations. The appearance of sea-shells so far from

Where the Downs westward trend,[73] but dimly seen)
Here never rolled its surge. Does Nature then
Mimic, in wanton mood, fantastic shapes
Of bivalves[74] and inwreathed volutes[75] that cling
To the dark sea-rock of the wat'ry world?
Or did this range of chalky mountains once
Form a vast basin where the ocean waves
Swelled fathomless?[76] What time these fossil shells,
Buoyed on their native element, were thrown
Among the embedding calx;[77] when the huge hill
Its giant bulk heaved, and in strange ferment
Grew up a guardian barrier 'twixt the sea
And the green level of the sylvan weald?[78]
  Ah, very vain is Science'[79] proudest boast,
And but a little light its flame yet lends
To its most ardent votaries; since from whence
These fossil forms are seen is but conjecture,
Food for vague theories or vain dispute,
While to his daily task the peasant goes
Unheeding such inquiry – with no care
But that the kindly change of sun and shower
Fit for his toil the earth he cultivates.
As little recks[80] the herdsman of the hill,
Who, on some turfy knoll idly reclined,
Watches his wether[81] flock, that deep beneath
Rest the remains of men, of whom is left
No traces in the records of mankind
Save what these half-obliterated mounds
And half-filled trenches doubtfully impart
To some lone antiquary who on times remote,
Since which two thousand years have rolled away,
Loves to contemplate.[82] He perhaps may trace,
Or fancy he can trace, the oblong square
Where the mailed legions under Claudius[83] reared
The rampire[84] or excavated fossé[85] delved;

Notes

the sea excited my surprise, though I then knew nothing of natural history. I have never read any of the late theories of the earth, nor was I ever satisfied with the attempts to explain many of the phenomena which call forth conjecture in those books I happened to have had access to on this subject' (Smith's note).

[73] *trend* stretch.

[74] *bivalves* double-shelled molluscs; e.g. oyster, mussel.

[75] *volutes* spiral-shelled molluscs; e.g. periwinkles.

[76] 'The theory here slightly hinted at is taken from an idea started by Mr White' (Smith's note). Gilbert White's *Natural History of Selborne* (1789) documents the countryside of south-east England.

[77] *calx* lime.

[78] *sylvan weald* wooded tract between the North and South Downs, including parts of Surrey, Sussex, and Kent.

[79] *Science'* The possessive case is indicated, but Smith elides the final 's' on account of the metre.

[80] *recks* cares.

[81] *wether* castrated male sheep.

[82] 'These Downs are not only marked with traces of encampments, which from their forms are called Roman or Danish, but there are numerous tumuli among them – some of which, having been opened a few years ago, were supposed by a learned antiquary to contain the remains of the original natives of the country' (Smith's note).

[83] 'That the legions of Claudius were in this part of Britain appears certain, since this Emperor received the submission of Cantii, Atrebates, Irenobates, and Regni, in which latter denomination were included the people of Sussex' (Smith's note).

[84] *rampire* rampart, barrier.

[85] *fossé* ditch, trench.

What time the huge unwieldy elephant
Auxiliary reluctant, hither led
From Afric's forest glooms and tawny sands,
First felt the northern blast, and his vast frame
Sunk useless – whence in after-ages found,
The wondering hinds on those enormous bones
Gazed;[86] and in giants dwelling on the hills
Believed and marvelled.[87]
                                        Hither, ambition, come!
Come and behold the nothingness of all
For which you carry through the oppressed earth
War and its train of horrors – see where tread
The innumerous hoofs of flocks above the works
By which the warrior sought to register
His glory, and immortalize his name.
The pirate Dane, who from his circular camp
Bore in destructive robbery fire and sword
Down through the vale,[88] sleeps unremembered here;
And here, beneath the greensward, rests alike
The savage native who his acorn meal
Shared with the herds that ranged the pathless woods,[89]
And the centurion who, on these wide hills
Encamping, planted the Imperial Eagle.[90]
All, with the lapse of time, have passed away,
Even as the clouds, with dark and dragon shapes,[91]
Or, like vast promontories crowned with towers,

Notes

[86] 'In the year 1740 some workmen digging in the park at Burton in Sussex discovered, nine feet below the surface, the teeth and bones of an elephant. Two of the former were seven feet eight inches in length. There were, besides these, tusks, one of which broke in removing it, a grinder not at all decayed, and a part of the jaw-bone, with bones of the knee and thigh, and several others. Some of them remained very lately at Burton House, the seat of John Biddulph, Esq. Others were in possession of the Revd Dr Langrish, minister of Petworth at that period, who was present when some of these bones were taken up, and gave it as his opinion that they had remained there since the universal deluge. The Romans under the Emperor Claudius probably brought elephants into Britain. Milton, in the second Book of his *History*, in speaking of the expedition, says that "He, like a great eastern king, with armed elephants, marched through Gallia." This is given on the authority of Dion Cassius, in his Life of the Emperor Claudius. It has therefore been conjectured that the bones found at Burton might have been those of one of these elephants, who perished there soon after its landing, or, dying on the high downs (one of which, called Duncton Hill, rises immediately above Burton Park), the bones might have been washed down by the torrents of rain and buried deep in the soil. They were not found together but scattered at some distance from each other. The two tusks were twenty feet apart. I had often heard of the elephant's bones at Burton, but never saw them, and I have no books to refer to. I think I saw, in what is now called the National Museum at Paris, the very large bones of an elephant, which were found in North America – though it is certain that this enormous animal is never seen in its natural state, but in the countries under the torrid zone of the old world. I have, since making this note, been told that the bones of the rhinoceros and hippopotamus have been found in America' (Smith's note).

[87] 'The peasants believe that the large bones sometimes found belonged to giants who formerly lived on the hills. The devil also has a great deal to do with the remarkable forms of hill and vale: the Devil's Punchbowl, the Devil's Leaps, and the Devil's Dyke, are names given to deep hollows, or high and abrupt ridges, in this and the neighbouring county.' (Smith's note) The 'neighbouring county' is Surrey.

[88] 'The incursions of the Danes were for many ages the scourge of this island' (Smith's note).

[89] 'The aborigines of this country lived in woods, unsheltered but by trees and caves, and were probably as truly savage as any of those who are now termed so' (Smith's note).

[90] *the Imperial Eagle* emblematic of the Roman Empire. Roman remains are to be found across the south-east of England.

[91] *the clouds, with dark and dragon shapes* There may be a general reminiscence in these lines of Hamlet's discussion with Polonius as to the shapes of the clouds: 'Do you see yonder cloud that's almost in shape of a camel?' (*Hamlet* III ii 376–7).

Cast their broad shadows on the Downs, then sail
Far to the northward, and their transient gloom
Is soon forgotten.
But from thoughts like these,
By human crimes suggested, let us turn
To where a more attractive study courts
The wanderer of the hills; while shepherd girls
Will from among the fescue[92] bring him flowers
Of wondrous mockery, some resembling bees
In velvet vest, intent on their sweet toil;[93]
While others mimic flies that lightly sport
In the green shade, or float along the pool,
But here seem perched upon the slender stalk
And gathering honey-dew;[94] while in the breeze
That wafts the thistle's plumed seed along,
Bluebells wave tremulous. The mountain thyme[95]
Purples the hassock of the heaving mole,[96]
And the short turf is gay with tormentil[97]
And birdsfoot trefoil, and the lesser tribes
Of hawkweed,[98] spangling it with fringed stars.
Near where a richer tract of cultured land
Slopes to the south, and burnished by the sun,
Bend in the gale of August floods of corn;
The guardian of the flock, with watchful care,[99]
Repels by voice and dog the encroaching sheep,
While his boy visits every wired trap[100]
That scars the turf, and from the pitfalls takes
The timid migrants[101] who, from distant wilds,
Warrens, and stone quarries, are destined thus
To lose their short existence. But unsought
By luxury yet, the shepherd still protects
The social bird[102] who, from his native haunts

Notes

[92] 'The grass called sheep's fescue (*Festuca ovina*) clothes these downs with the softest turf' (Smith's note).

[93] '*Ophrys apifera*, bee ophrys, or orchis, found plentifully on the hills, as well as the next' (Smith's note).

[94] '*Ophrys muscifera*, fly orchis. Linnaeus, misled by the variations to which some of this tribe are really subject, has perhaps too rashly esteemed all those which resemble insects as forming only one species, which he terms ophrys insectifera. See *English Botany*' (Smith's note).

[95] 'Bluebells: *Campanula rotundifolia*; mountain thyme: *Thymus serpyllum*. "It is a common notion that the flesh of sheep which feed upon aromatic plants, particularly wild thyme, is superior in flavour to other mutton. The truth is that sheep do not crop these aromatic plants unless, now and then, by accident, or when they are first turned on hungry to downs, heaths, or commons; but the soil and situations favourable to aromatic plants produce a short sweet pasturage, best adapted to feeding sheep, whom nature designed for mountains and not for turnip grounds and rich meadows. The attachment of bees to this, and other aromatic plants, is well known." Martyn's *Miller*' (Smith's note). Smith quotes Thomas Martyn, *The Gardener's and Botanist's Dictionary . . . by the late Philip Miller . . . To which are now added a complete enumeration and description of all plants* (1797–1807).

[96] *hassock of the heaving mole* molehill.

[97] 'Tormentil: *Tormentilla reptans*' (Smith's note).

[98] 'Birdsfoot trefoil: *Trifolium ornithopoides*; hawkweed: *Hieracium*, many sorts' (Smith's note).

[99] 'The Downs, especially to the south, where they are less abrupt, are in many places under the plough, and the attention of the shepherds is there particularly required to keep the flocks from trespassing' (Smith's note).

[100] 'Square holes cut in the turf, into which a wire noose is fixed, to catch wheatears. Mr White says that these birds (*Motacilla oenanthe*) are never taken beyond the River Adur, and Beding Hill – but this is certainly a mistake' (Smith's note).

[101] 'These birds are extremely fearful and, on the slightest appearance of a cloud, run for shelter to the first rut, or heap of stones, that they see' (Smith's note).

[102] 'The yellow wagtail: *Motacilla flava*. It frequents the banks of rivulets in winter, making its nest in meadows

Of willowy current or the rushy pool,
Follows the fleecy crowd,[103] and flirts and skims
In fellowship among them.
Where the knoll
More elevated takes the changeful winds,
The windmill rears its vanes, and thitherward,
With his white load, the master travelling
Scares the rooks rising slow on whispering wings,
While o'er his head, before the summer sun
Lights up the blue expanse, heard more than seen,
The lark sings matins[104] and, above the clouds
Floating, embathes his spotted breast in dew.
Beneath the shadow of a gnarled thorn
Bent by the sea-blast,[105] from a seat of turf
With fairy nosegays[106] strewn, how wide the view![107] –
Till in the distant north it melts away
And mingles indiscriminate with clouds;
But if the eye could reach so far, the mart
Of England's capital, its domes and spires
Might be perceived. Yet hence the distant range
Of Kentish hills[108] appear in purple haze,
And nearer undulate the wooded heights
And airy summits[109] that above the Mole[110]
Rise in green beauty, and the beaconed ridge
Of Blackdown[111] shagged with heath, and swelling rude
Like a dark island from the vale, its brow
Catching the last rays of the evening sun
That gleam between the nearer park's old oaks,
Then lighten up the river and make prominent
The portal and the ruined battlements
Of that dismantled fortress, raised what time
The Conqueror's successors fiercely fought,
Tearing with civil feuds the desolate land.[112]
But now a tiller of the soil dwells there,
And of the turret's looped and raftered halls

Notes

and cornfields. But after the breeding season is over, it haunts downs and sheepwalks, and is seen constantly among the flocks, probably for the sake of the insects it picks up. In France the shepherds call it *la bergeronette*, and say it often gives them, by its cry, notice of approaching danger' (Smith's note).

[103] *the fleecy crowd* of sheep.

[104] *matins* technically, a morning prayer that is sung; in this case it refers to the lark's song at dawn.

[105] 'The strong winds from the south-west occasion almost all the trees, which on these hills are exposed to it, to grow the other way' (Smith's note).

[106] *nosegays* perfumes, scents.

[107] 'So extensive are some of the views from these hills, that only the want of power in the human eye to travel so far, prevents London itself being discerned. Description falls so infinitely short of the reality, that only here and there distinct features can be given' (Smith's note).

[108] 'A scar of chalk in a hill beyond Sevenoaks in Kent is very distinctly seen of a clear day' (Smith's note).

[109] 'The hills about Dorking in Surrey, over almost the whole extent of which county the prospect extends' (Smith's note).

[110] The River Mole rises on the borders of Sussex and flows north to Dorking.

[111] 'This is an high ridge extending between Sussex and Surrey. It is covered with heath and has almost always a dark appearance. On it is a telegraph' (Smith's note).

[112] 'In this country there are several of the fortresses or castles built by Stephen of Blois in his contention for the kingdom, with the daughter of Henry I, the Empress Matilda. Some of these are now converted into farmhouses' (Smith's note).

Has made an humbler homestead where he sees,
Instead of armed foemen, herds that graze
Along his yellow meadows, or his flocks
At evening from the upland driv'n to fold.
In such a castellated mansion once
A stranger chose his home, and where hard by
In rude disorder fallen, and hid with brushwood,
Lay fragments gray of towers and buttresses,
Among the ruins often he would muse.
His rustic meal soon ended, he was wont
To wander forth, listening the evening sounds
Of rushing milldam[113] or the distant team,[114]
Or nightjar chasing fern-flies;[115] the tired hind
Passed him at nightfall, wondering he should sit
On the hilltop so late; they[116] from the coast
Who sought bye-paths with their clandestine load,
Saw with suspicious doubt the lonely man
Cross on their way; but village maidens thought
His senses injured, and with pity say
That he, poor youth, must have been crossed in love –
For often, stretched[117] upon the mountain turf
With folded arms, and eyes intently fixed
Where ancient elms and firs obscured a grange[118]
Some little space within the vale below,
They heard him as complaining of his fate,
And to the murmuring wind of cold neglect
And baffled hope he told. The peasant girls
These plaintive sounds remember, and even now
Among them may be heard the stranger's songs.

Notes

[113] *milldam* dam constructed across a stream so as to raise its level, enabling it to power a mill-wheel.

[114] *the distant team* of horses.

[115] 'Dr Aikin remarks, I believe, in his essay "On the Application of Natural History to the Purposes of Poetry", how many of our best poets have noticed the same circumstance, the hum of the dor beetle (*Scaraboeus stercorarius*) among the sounds heard by the evening wanderer. I remember only one instance in which the more remarkable, though by no means uncommon noise, of the fern owl, or goatsucker, is mentioned. It is called the nighthawk, the jar bird, the churn owl, and the fern owl, from its feeding on the *Scaraboeus solstitialis*, or fern chafer, which it catches while on the wing with its claws, the middle toe of which is long and curiously serrated, on purpose to hold them. It was this bird that was intended to be described in the 42nd sonnet (Smith's *Sonnets*). I was mistaken in supposing it as visible in November; it is a migrant, and leaves this country in August. I had often seen and heard it, but I did not then know its name or history. It is called goatsucker (*Caprimulgus*) from a strange prejudice taken against it by the Italians, who assert that it sucks their goats; and the peasants of England still believe that a disease in the backs of their cattle, occasioned by a fly which deposits its egg under the skin and raises a boil, sometimes fatal to calves, is the work of this bird, which they call a puckeridge. Nothing can convince them that their beasts are not injured by this bird, which they therefore hold in abhorrence' (Smith's note). Smith refers to *An Essay on the Application of Natural History to Poetry* (1777) by John Aikin, brother of Anna Laetitia Barbauld.

[116] *they* smugglers.

[117] *stretched* A verbal echo connects Smith's solitary with the melancholic poet of Gray's *Elegy*: 'His listless length at noontide would he stretch, / And pore upon the brook that babbles by' (ll. 103–4).

[118] *grange* granary.

Were I a shepherd on the hill,
   And ever as the mists withdrew
Could see the willows of the rill
Shading the footway to the mill
   Where once I walked with you;

And as away night's shadows sail,
   And sounds of birds and brooks arise,
Believe that from the woody vale
I hear your voice upon the gale
   In soothing melodies;

And viewing from the Alpine height
   The prospect dressed in hues of air,
Could say, while transient colours bright
Touched the fair scene with dewy light,
   ''Tis that *her* eyes are there!'

I think I could endure my lot
   And linger on a few short years,
And then, by all but you forgot,
Sleep where the turf that clothes the spot
   May claim some pitying tears.

For 'tis not easy to forget
   One who through life has loved you still,
And you, however late, might yet
With sighs to memory giv'n, regret
   The shepherd of the hill.

Yet otherwhile it seemed as if young Hope
Her flattering pencil gave to Fancy's hand,
And in his wanderings reared to soothe his soul
Ideal bowers of pleasure. Then, of solitude
And of his hermit life still more enamoured,
His home was in the forest, and wild fruits
And bread sustained him. There in early spring
The barkmen[119] found him ere the sun arose;
There at their daily toil, the wedgecutters[120]
Beheld him through the distant thicket move.
The shaggy dog following the truffle-hunter[121]
Barked at the loiterer, and perchance at night
Belated villagers from fair or wake,
While the fresh night-wind let the moonbeams in
Between the swaying boughs, just saw him pass –
And then in silence, gliding like a ghost
He vanished, lost among the deepening gloom!
But near one ancient tree, whose wreathed roots
Formed a rude couch, love-songs and scattered rhymes,
Unfinished sentences, or half-erased,
And rhapsodies like this, were sometimes found:

Notes

119 'As soon as the sap begins to rise, the trees intended for felling are cut and barked. At which time the men who are employed in that business pass whole days in the woods' (Smith's note).

120 'The wedges used in ship-building are made of beech wood, and great numbers are cut every year in the woods near the Downs' (Smith's note).

121 'Truffles are found under the beech woods by means of small dogs trained to hunt them by the scent' (Smith's note).

Let us to woodland wilds repair
 While yet the glittering night-dews seem
To wait the freshly-breathing air
 Precursive of the morning beam
That, rising with advancing day,
Scatters the silver drops away.

An elm uprooted by the storm,
 The trunk with mosses gray and green
Shall make for us a rustic form
 Where lighter grows the forest scene;
And far among the bowery shades
Are ferny lawns and grassy glades.

Retiring May to lovely June
 Her latest garland now resigns;
The banks with cuckoo-flowers[122] are strewn,
 The woodwalks blue with columbines,[123]
And with its reeds the wandering stream
Reflects the flag-flower's[124] golden gleam.

There, feathering down the turf to meet,
 Their shadowy arms the beeches spread,
While high above our sylvan seat
 Lifts the light ash its airy head;
And later leaved, the oaks between
Extend their boughs of vernal green.

The slender birch its paper rind
 Seems offering to divided love,
And shuddering even without a wind
 Aspins their paler foliage move
As if some spirit of the air
Breathed a low sigh in passing there.

The squirrel in his frolic mood
 Will fearless bound among the boughs;
Yaffils[125] laugh loudly through the wood,
 And murmuring ring-doves tell their vows;
While we, as sweetest woodscents rise,
Listen to woodland melodies.

And I'll contrive a sylvan room
 Against the time of summer heat,
Where leaves, inwoven in nature's loom,

Notes

[122] 'Cuckoo-flowers: *Lychnis dioica*. Columbines: *Aquilegia vulgaris*. Shakespeare describes the cuckoo buds as being yellow. He probably meant the numerous ranunculi, or March marigolds (*Caltha palustris*) which so gild the meadows in spring; but poets have never been botanists. The cuckoo-flower is the *Lychnis floscuculi*' (Smith's note). Smith refers to *Love's Labour's Lost* V ii 896: 'And cuckoo-buds of yellow hue'.

[123] 'Columbines: *Aquilegia vulgaris*' (Smith's note).

[124] 'Flag-flower: *Iris pseudacorus*' (Smith's note).

[125] 'Yaffils: woodpeckers (*picus*); three or four species in Britain.' (Smith's note).

Shall canopy our green retreat,
And gales that 'close the eye of day'[126]
Shall linger ere they die away.

And when a sear and sallow hue
From early frost the bower receives,
I'll dress the sand rock cave for you,
And strew the floor with heath and leaves,
That you, against the autumnal air
May find securer shelter there.

The nightingale will then have ceased
To sing her moonlight serenade,
But the gay bird with blushing breast[127]
And woodlarks still will haunt the shade,[128]
And by the borders of the spring
Reed-wrens will yet be carolling.[129]

The forest hermit's lonely cave
None but such soothing sounds shall reach,
Or hardly heard, the distant wave
Slow breaking on the stony beach,
Or winds that now sigh soft and low
Now make wild music as they blow.

And then before the chilling north
The tawny foliage falling light
Seems as it flits along the earth
The footfall of the busy sprite
Who, wrapped in pale autumnal gloom,
Calls up the mist-born mushroom.

Oh, could I hear your soft voice there,
And see you in the forest green
All beauteous as you are, more fair
You'd look amid the sylvan scene,
And in a wood-girl's simple guise
Be still more lovely in mine eyes.

Ye phantoms of unreal delight,
Visions of fond delirium born,
Rise not on my deluded sight,
Then leave me drooping and forlorn
To know such bliss can never be,
Unless Amanda[130] loved like me.

Notes

[126] ' "And liquid notes that close the eye of day". Milton. The idea here meant to be conveyed is of the evening wind, so welcome after a hot day of summer, and which appears to soothe and lull all nature into tranquillity' (Smith's note). The quotation is from *Sonnet I* 5.

[127] 'The robin (*Motacilla rubecula*), which is always heard after other songsters have ceased to sing' (Smith's note).

[128] 'The woodlark (*Alauda nemorosa*) sings very late' (Smith's note).

[129] 'Reed-wrens (*Motacilla arundinacea*) sing all the summer and autumn, and are often heard during the night' (Smith's note).

[130] *Amanda* Smith leaves a blank at this point in the printed text; the present reading is conjectural.

The visionary, nursing dreams like these,
Is not indeed unhappy. Summer woods
Wave over him, and whisper as they wave
Some future blessings he may yet enjoy.
And as above him sail the silver clouds,
He follows them in thought to distant climes
Where, far from the cold policy of this,
Dividing him from her he fondly loves,
He in some island of the southern sea
May haply build his cane-constructed bower
Beneath the breadfruit or aspiring palm
With long green foliage rippling in the gale.[131]
Oh, let him cherish his ideal bliss –
For what is life, when Hope has ceased to strew
Her fragile flowers along its thorny way?
And sad and gloomy are his days who lives
Of Hope abandoned!
Just beneath the rock
Where Beachy overpeers the Channel wave,
Within a cavern mined by wintry tides
Dwelt one who, long disgusted with the world
And all its ways, appeared to suffer life
Rather than live;[132] the soul-reviving gale
Fanning the beanfield[133] or the thymy heath
Had not for many summers breathed on him;
And nothing marked to him the season's change
Save that more gently rose the placid sea,
And that the birds which winter on the coast
Gave place to other migrants; save that the fog,
Hovering no more above the beetling cliffs,
Betrayed not then the little careless sheep
On the brink grazing, while their headlong fall[134]
Near the lone hermit's flint-surrounded home
Claimed unavailing pity – for his heart
Was feelingly alive to all that breathed;
And outraged as he was, in sanguine youth,
By human crimes, he still acutely felt
For human misery.

Notes

[131] 'An allusion to the visionary delights of the new discovered islands where it was at first believed men lived in a state of simplicity and happiness, but where, as later enquiries have ascertained, that exemption from toil, which the fertility of the country gives them, produces the grossest vices, and a degree of corruption that late navigators think will end in the extirpation of the whole people in a few years' (Smith's note).

[132] 'In a cavern almost immediately under the cliff called Beachy Head, there lived, as the people of the country believed, a man of the name of Darby, who for many years had no other abode than this cave, and subsisted almost entirely on shellfish. He had often administered assistance to shipwrecked mariners, but venturing into the sea on this charitable mission during a violent equinoctial storm, he himself perished. As it is above thirty years since I heard this tradition of Parson Darby (for so I think he was called), it may now perhaps be forgotten' (Smith's note).

[133] *the soul-reviving gale . . . beanfield* Smith may have in mind Coleridge, *Eolian Harp* 9–10: 'How exquisite the scents / Snatched from yon beanfield!'

[134] 'Sometimes in thick weather the sheep, feeding on the summit of the cliff, miss their footing and are killed by the fall' (Smith's note).

Wandering on the beach,
He learned to augur from the clouds of heaven,
And from the changing colours of the sea
And sullen murmurs of the hollow cliffs,
Or the dark porpoises[135] that near the shore
Gambolled and sported on the level brine
When tempests were approaching; then at night
He listened to the wind, and as it drove
The billows with o'erwhelming vehemence,
He, starting from his rugged couch, went forth
And hazarding a life too valueless
He waded through the waves with plank or pole
Towards where the mariner in conflict dread
Was buffeting for life the roaring surge –
And now just seen, now lost in foaming gulfs,
The dismal gleaming of the clouded moon
Showed the dire peril. Often he had snatched
From the wild billows some unhappy man
Who lived to bless the hermit of the rocks.
But if his generous cares were all in vain,
And with slow swell the tide of morning bore
Some blue-swoln corse to land, the pale recluse
Dug in the chalk a sepulchre – above
Where the dank sea-wrack marked the utmost tide,
And with his prayers performed the obsequies[136]
For the poor helpless stranger.
One dark night
The equinoctial wind[137] blew south by west
Fierce on the shore; the bellowing cliffs were shook
Even to their stony base, and fragments fell
Flashing and thundering on the angry flood.
At daybreak, anxious for the lonely man,
His cave the mountain shepherds visited,
Though sand and banks of weeds had choked their way:
He was not in it, but his drowned corse,
By the waves wafted, near his former home
Received the rites of burial. Those who read,
Chiselled within the rock these mournful lines,
Memorials of his sufferings, did not grieve
That, dying in the cause of charity,
His spirit, from its earthly bondage freed,
Had to some better region fled for ever.

Notes

[135] 'Dark porpoises: *Delphinus phocoena*' (Smith's note). Porpoises are still to be seen in the waters off the south coast of England.

[136] *obsequies* funeral rites.

[137] *equinoctial wind* Smith refers to the winds prevailing at the time of the autumnal equinox (22 or 23 September).

George Crabbe (1754–1832)

A native of Aldeburgh in Suffolk, Crabbe set up in practice as a surgeon in 1775. He decided to try his fortunes as a writer in 1780 and went to London, where he secured the patronage of Edmund Burke. Returning to Aldeburgh as a curate after publication of his poem, *The Library* (1781), he became chaplain to the Duke of Rutland in 1782. He published *The Village* in 1783 and *The Newspaper* in 1785. Then, for twenty-two years, he published nothing until *Poems* (1807), *The Borough* (1810), *Tales* (1812) and *Tales of the Hall* (1819). These works won him the admiration and friendship of a new generation: Jeffrey, Byron, Scott, Rogers, Moore and Campbell. As Byron told Murray in 1817, 'Crabbe's the man' (Marchand v 266).

One reason for this was Crabbe's mastery of the post-Popean manner so popular towards the end of the eighteenth century; Byron and like-minded readers regarded him as free of what they saw as the misguided notions advocated by Wordsworth and Coleridge. And unlike the Romantics, Crabbe saw himself as working in the realist tradition of Shakespeare and Chaucer. These qualities may help to explain his comparative unpopularity now. All the same, the fact that he took little part in the dominant literary movement of the day should not blind us to his genius, seen at its most striking in *Peter Grimes*, a complete text of which appears below. There is no other poem in the canon so persuasive in its analysis of the psychology of the child murderer (and abuser). Its uncompromisingly hard edge would be toned down and sentimentalized in Benjamin Britten's opera (1945), by which it is best known.

Crabbe's most perceptive critic remains Hazlitt who, in *The Spirit of the Age*, described him as 'a repulsive writer':

> He takes the most trite, the most gross and obvious and revolting part of nature for the subject of his elaborate descriptions; but it is Nature still, and Nature is a great and mighty Goddess! It is well for the Reverend Author that it is so . . . . Whoever makes an exact image of any thing on the earth, however deformed or insignificant, according to him, must succeed – and he himself has succeeded.
>
> (Wu vii 148)

In a less sympathetic assessment Wordsworth observed that '19 out of 20 of Crabbe's pictures are mere matters of fact with which the Muses have just about as much to do as they have with a collection of medical reports, or of law cases.' All the same, he liked Crabbe personally, and commemorated him in the 'Extempore Effusion on the Death of James Hogg' (pp. 580–2).

Further reading

George Crabbe: The Complete Poetical Works ed. Nora Dalrymple-Champneys and Arthur Pollard (3 vols, Oxford, 1988).

Jerome J. McGann, 'The Anachronism of George Crabbe', in *The Beauty of Inflections: Literary Investigations in Historical Method and Theory* (Oxford, 1985), pp. 294–312.

Neil Powell, *George Crabbe: An English Life* (London, 2004).

Frank Whitehead, *George Crabbe: A Reappraisal* (London, 1995).

Peter Grimes[1]

From The Borough (1810) Letter XXII: The Poor of the Borough

Old Peter Grimes made fishing his employ;
His wife he cabined with him and his boy,
And seemed that life laborious to enjoy:
To town came quiet Peter with his fish,
And had of all a civil word and wish.
He left his trade upon the Sabbath-day
And took young Peter in his hand to pray;
But soon the stubborn boy from care broke loose –
At first refused, then added his abuse.
His father's love he scorned, his power defied,
But being drunk, wept sorely when he died.
  Yes, then he wept, and to his mind there came
Much of his conduct, and he felt the shame!
How he had oft the good old man reviled,
And never paid the duty of a child;
How when the father in his Bible read,
He in contempt and anger left the shed:
'It is the Word of life!' the parent cried –
'This is the life itself!' the boy replied;
And while old Peter in amazement stood,
Gave the hot spirit to his boiling blood:
How he, with oath and furious speech, began
To prove his freedom and assert the man;
And when the parent checked his impious rage
How he had cursed the tyranny of age –
Nay, once had dealt the sacrilegious[2] blow
On his bare head and laid his parent low!
The father groaned – 'If thou art old', said he,
'And hast a son, thou wilt remember me:
Thy mother left me in an happy time,
Thou kill'dst not her – Heav'n spares the double crime.'
On an inn settle[3] in his maudlin grief,
This he revolved and drank for his relief.
  Now lived the youth in freedom, but debarred
From constant pleasure, and he thought it hard –
Hard that he could not every wish obey,
But must awhile relinquish ale and play –
Hard that he could not to his cards attend,
But must acquire the money he would spend.
With greedy eye he looked on all he saw,

Notes

Peter Grimes

1 'The original of Peter Grimes was an old fisherman of Aldborough while Mr. Crabbe was practising there as a surgeon. He had a succession of apprentices from London, and a certain sum with each. As the boys all disappeared under circumstances of strong suspicion, the man was warned that if another followed in like manner he should certainly be charged with murder' (note in 1834 edition of Crabbe's *Works*).

2 *sacrilegious* because he was disobeying the fifth commandment, to honour thy father and mother.

3 *settle* bench.

He knew not justice, and he laughed at law;
On all he marked, he stretched his ready hand –
He fished by water and he filched by land.
Oft in the night has Peter dropped his oar,
Fled from his boat and sought for prey on shore;
Oft up the hedgerow glided, on his back
Bearing the orchard's produce in a sack,
Or farmyard load tugged fiercely from the stack.
And as these wrongs to greater numbers rose,
The more he looked on all men as his foes.
He built a mud-walled hovel where he kept
His various wealth, and there he oft-times slept;
But no success could please his cruel soul –
He wished for one to trouble and control;
He wanted some obedient boy to stand
And bear the blow of his outrageous hand,
And hoped to find in some propitious hour
A feeling creature subject to his power.
Peter had heard there were in London then
(Still have they being?) workhouse-clearing men
Who, undisturbed by feelings just or kind,
Would parish-boys to needy tradesmen bind.
They in their want a trifling sum would take,
And toiling slaves of piteous orphans make.[4]
Such Peter sought, and when a lad was found,
The sum was dealt him and the slave was bound.
Some few in town observed in Peter's trap
A boy, with jacket blue and woollen cap;
But none enquired how Peter used the rope,
Or what the bruise that made the stripling stoop;
None could the ridges on his back behold,
None sought him shiv'ring in the winter's cold,
None put the question, 'Peter, dost thou give
The boy his food? – What, man? The lad must live!
Consider, Peter, let the child have bread,
He'll serve thee better if he's stroked and fed.'
None reasoned thus – and some, on hearing cries,
Said calmly, 'Grimes is at his exercise.'
Pinned,[5] beaten, cold, pinched, threatened and abused,
His efforts punished and his food refused,
Awake tormented, soon aroused from sleep,
Struck if he wept, and yet compelled to weep,
The trembling boy dropped down and strove to pray,
Received a blow and trembling turned away,
Or sobbed and hid his piteous face, while he,
The savage master, grinned in horrid glee!
He'd now the power he ever loved to show,
A feeling being subject to his blow.

Notes

[4] In order to reduce the poor-rate in London, it was customary towards the end of the 18th century to farm out children of paupers to 'masters' in other parishes, who would be given about £5 in return for maintaining them and teaching them a trade.

[5] *Pinned* pinned down by force.

Thus lived the lad in hunger, peril, pain,
His tears despised, his supplications vain;
Compelled by fear to lie, by need to steal,
His bed uneasy and unblessed his meal.
For three sad years the boy his tortures bore,
And then his pains and trials were no more.
'How died he, Peter?' – when the people said,
He growled, 'I found him lifeless in his bed';
Then tried for softer tone, and sighed, 'Poor Sam is dead.'
Yet murmurs were there and some questions asked –
How he was fed, how punished and how tasked?
Much they suspected but they little proved,
And Peter passed untroubled and unmoved.
Another boy with equal ease was found,
The money granted and the victim bound;
And what his fate? One night it chanced he fell
From the boat's mast and perished in her well
Where fish were living kept, and where the boy
(So reasoned men) could not himself destroy.
'Yes, so it was!', said Peter, 'in his play;
For he was idle both by night and day!
He climbed the main mast and then fell below' –
Then showed his corpse and pointed to the blow.
What said the jury? They were long in doubt,
But sturdy Peter faced the matter out.
So they dismissed him, saying at the time,
'Keep fast your hatchway when you've boys who climb.'
This hit the conscience, and he coloured more
Than for the closest questions put before.
Thus all his fears the verdict set aside,
And at the slave-shop Peter still applied.
Then came a boy, of manners soft and mild –
Our seamen's wives with grief beheld the child;
All thought (though poor themselves) that he was one
Of gentle blood, some noble sinner's son
Who had, belike, deceived some humble maid
Whom he had first seduced and then betrayed.
However this, he seemed a gracious lad,
In grief submissive and with patience sad.
Passive he laboured, till his slender frame
Bent with his loads, and he at length was lame;
Strange that a frame so weak could bear so long
The grossest insult and the foulest wrong.
But there were causes – in the town they gave
Fire, food and comfort to the gentle slave;
And though stern Peter, with a cruel hand
And knotted rope, enforced the rude command,
Yet he considered what he'd lately felt,
And his vile blows with selfish pity dealt.
One day such draughts the cruel fisher made,
He could not vend them in his borough trade

But sailed for London mart: the boy was ill,
But ever humbled to his master's will.
And on the river, where they smoothly sailed,
He strove with terror and awhile prevailed;
But new to danger on the angry sea,
He clung affrightened to his master's knee;
The boat grew leaky and the wind was strong,
Rough was the passage and the time was long;
His liquor failed, and Peter's wrath arose . . .
No more is known – the rest we must suppose
Or learn of Peter. Peter, says he, spied
The stripling's danger and for harbour tried;
Meantime the fish and then th' apprentice died.
The pitying women raised a clamour round,
And weeping said, 'Thou hast thy 'prentice drowned!'
Now the stern man was summoned to the hall,
To tell his tale before the burghers all:
He gave th' account, professed the lad he loved,
And kept his brazen features all unmoved.
The Mayor himself with tone severe replied,
'Henceforth with thee shall never boy abide;
Hire thee a freeman whom thou durst not beat,
But who, in thy despite, will sleep and eat.
Free thou art now! – again shouldst thou appear,
Thou'lt find thy sentence, like thy soul, severe.'
Alas for Peter! not an helping hand,
So was he hated, could he now command;
Alone he rowed his boat, alone he cast
His nets beside, or made his anchor fast;
To hold a rope or hear a curse was none –
He toiled and railed, he groaned and swore alone.
Thus by himself compelled to live each day,
To wait for certain hours the tide's delay;
At the same times the same dull views to see,
The bounding marsh-bank and the blighted tree;
The water only, when the tides were high,
When low, the mud half-covered and half-dry;
The sunburnt tar that blisters on the planks,
And bankside stakes in their uneven ranks;
Heaps of entangled weeds that slowly float
As the tide rolls by the impeded boat.
When tides were neap, and in the sultry day,
Through the tall bounding mud-banks made their way,[6]
Which on each side rose swelling, and below
The dark warm flood ran silently and slow;
There anchoring, Peter chose from man to hide,

Notes

[6] *When tides . . . way* When the tide is neap, the high-water level is at its lowest point, leaving a larger area of mud exposed than at other times.

There hang his head, and view the lazy tide
In its hot slimy channel slowly glide –
Where the small eels that left the deeper way
For the warm shore, within the shallows play;
Where gaping mussels, left upon the mud,
Slope their slow passage to the fallen flood.
Here dull and hopeless he'd lie down and trace
How sidelong crabs had scrawled their crooked race,
Or sadly listen to the tuneless cry
Of fishing gull or clanging golden-eye;[7]
What time the seabirds to the marsh would come,
And the loud bittern, from the bullrush home,
Gave from the salt-ditch side the bellowing boom.
He nursed the feelings these dull scenes produce,
And loved to stop beside the opening sluice,
Where the small stream, confined in narrow bound,
Ran with a dull, unvaried, sad'ning sound –
Where all presented to the eye or ear
Oppressed the soul with misery, grief and fear.
   Besides these objects there were places three
Which Peter seemed with certain dread to see;
When he drew near them he would turn from each,
And loudly whistle till he passed the reach.[8]
   A change of scene to him brought no relief:
In town, 'twas plain, men took him for a thief;
The sailors' wives would stop him in the street
And say, 'Now, Peter, thou'st no boy to beat!'
Infants at play, when they perceived him, ran,
Warning each other, 'That's the wicked man!'
He growled an oath, and in an angry tone
Cursed the whole place and wished to be alone.
Alone he was, the same dull scenes in view,
And still more gloomy in his sight they grew.
Though man he hated, yet employed alone
At bootless labour, he would swear and groan,
Cursing the shoals that glided by the spot,
And gulls that caught them when his arts could not.
   Cold nervous tremblings shook his sturdy frame,
And strange disease (he couldn't say the name);
Wild were his dreams, and oft he rose in fright,
Waked by his view of horrors in the night –
Horrors that would the sternest minds amaze,
Horrors that demons might be proud to raise.
And though he felt forsaken, grieved at heart
To think he lived from all mankind apart,
Yet if a man approached, in terrors he would start.

Notes

[7] *golden-eye* a sea duck.

[8] *reach* portion of the river between two bends.

A winter passed since Peter saw the town,
And summer lodgers were again come down;
These, idly curious, with their glasses spied
The ships in bay as anchored for the tide –
The river's craft, the bustle of the quay,
And sea-port views which landmen love to see.
One, up the river, had a man and boat
Seen day by day – now anchored, now afloat.
Fisher he seemed, yet used no net nor hook;
Of sea fowl swimming by no heed he took,
But on the gliding waves still fixed his lazy look.
At certain stations he would view the stream
As if he stood bewildered in a dream,
Or that some power had chained him for a time
To feel a curse or meditate on crime.
This known, some curious, some in pity went,
And others questioned, 'Wretch, dost thou repent?'
He heard, he trembled, and in fear resigned
His boat: new terror filled his restless mind.
Furious he grew and up the country ran,
And there they seized him – a distempered man.
Him we received, and to a parish bed,
Followed and cursed, the groaning man was led.
Here when they saw him whom they used to shun –
A lost lone man, so harassed and undone –
Our gentle females (ever prompt to feel)
Perceived compassion on their anger steal;
His crimes they couldn't from their memories blot,
But they were grieved and trembled at his lot.
A priest too came to whom his words are told,
And all the signs they shuddered to behold.
'Look, look!' they cried, 'his limbs with horror shake,
And as he grinds his teeth, what noise they make!
How glare his angry eyes, and yet he's not awake!
See what cold drops upon his forehead stand,
And how he clenches that broad bony hand!'
The priest attending found he spoke at times
As one alluding to his fears and crimes:
'It was the fall', he muttered, 'I can show
The manner how – I never struck a blow!'
And then aloud, 'Unhand me, free my chain!
On oath, he fell – it struck him to the brain!
Why ask my father? That old man will swear
Against my life – besides he wasn't there!
What, all agreed? Am I to die today?
My Lord, in mercy, give me time to pray!'
Then as they watched him, calmer he became,
And grew so weak he couldn't move his frame,
But murmuring spake, while they could see and hear
The start of terror and the groan of fear;
See the large dew-beads on his forehead rise

And the cold death-drop glaze his sunken eyes.
Nor yet he died, but with unwonted force
Seemed with some fancied being to discourse.
He knew not us, or with accustomed art
He hid the knowledge, yet exposed his heart;
'Twas part confession and the rest defence –
A madman's tale, with gleams of waking sense.
 'I'll tell you all,' he said, 'the very day
When the old man first placed them in my way –
My father's spirit (he who always tried
To give me trouble when he lived and died)!
When he was gone, he could not be content
To see my days in painful labour spent,
But would appoint his meetings, and he made
Me watch at these, and so neglect my trade.
 'Twas one hot noon – all silent, still, serene;
No living being had I lately seen.
I paddled up and down and dipped my net
But (such his pleasure) I could nothing get;
A father's pleasure! – when his toil was done,
To plague and torture thus an only son.
And so I sat and looked upon the stream,
How it ran on – and felt as in a dream:
But dream it was not. No – I fixed my eyes
On the midstream and saw the spirits rise:
I saw my father on the water stand
And hold a thin pale boy in either hand,
And there they glided ghastly on the top
Of the salt flood, and never touched a drop.
I would have struck them, but they knew th' intent,
And smiled upon the oar, and down they went.
 Now from that day, whenever I began
To dip my net, there stood the hard old man,
He and those boys. I humbled me and prayed
They would be gone – they heeded not but stayed.
Nor could I turn, nor would the boat go by,
But gazing on the spirits, there was I;
They bade me leap to death, but I was loath to die.
And every day, as sure as day arose,
Would these three spirits meet me ere the close:
To hear and mark them daily was my doom,
And "Come", they said with weak sad voices, "come!"
To row away with all my strength I tried,
But there were they, hard by me in the tide,
The three unbodied forms – and "Come", still "come!", they cried.
 Fathers should pity, but this old man shook
His hoary locks and froze me by a look.
Thrice, when I struck them, through the water came
An hollow groan that weakened all my frame.

"Father", said I, "have mercy!" He replied
I know not what – the angry spirit lied:
"Didst thou not draw thy knife?" said he. 'Twas true,
But I had pity and my arm withdrew;
He cried for mercy, which I kindly gave,
But he has no compassion in his grave.
There were three places where they ever rose –
The whole long river has not such as those –
Places accursed where, if a man remain,
He'll see the things which strike him to the brain.
And there they made me on my paddle lean
And look at them for hours – accursed scene!
When they would glide to that smooth eddy space,
Then bid me leap and join them in the place;
And at my groans each little villain sprite
Enjoyed my pains and vanished in delight.
In one fierce summer day, when my poor brain
Was burning hot, and cruel was my pain,
Then came this father-foe, and there he stood
With his two boys again upon the flood.
There was more mischief in their eyes, more glee
In their pale faces when they glared at me.
Still did they force me on the oar to rest,
And when they saw me fainting and oppressed,
He with his hand (the old man) scooped the flood,
And there came flame about him mixed with blood;
He bade me stoop and look upon the place,
Then flung the hot red liquor in my face –
Burning it blazed, and then I roared for pain –
I thought the demons would have turned my brain!
Still there they stood, and forced me to behold
A place of horrors – they cannot be told:
Where the flood opened, there I heard the shriek
Of tortured guilt no earthly tongue can speak.
"All days alike for ever!" did they say,
"And unremitted torments every day!"
Yes, so they said . . .'
But here he ceased and gazed
On all around, affrightened and amazed;
And still he tried to speak and looked in dread
Of frightened females gathering round his bed,
Then dropped exhausted and appeared at rest,
Till the strong foe the vital powers possessed.
Then with an inward, broken voice he cried,
'Again they come!' and muttered as he died.

William Godwin (1756–1836)

When Godwin published *Political Justice* in February 1793, only days after France had declared war on England, the British government was as sensitive to radical dissent as America was to communism during the McCarthy era. For the next decade, he would be regarded as one of the main enemies of the state, and an icon of radical thought.

It was a curious fate for the son of a strict Calvinist clergyman. Only religious texts were read in his father's house, and when he was 11 he was boarded out with a violently puritanical Sandemanian minister, Samuel Newton, who whipped him for the slightest deviation from religious practice or thought. The followers of Robert Sandeman were more extreme than the Scottish Calvinists against whom they were reacting; two central tenets were that religious faith was rational, and should not be 'sullied' by emotion, and that an individual's property should always be at the disposal of the church, because wealth was inherently sinful. Those tenets were to exert a strong influence on Godwin's masterwork, *Political Justice* (1793).

By the time he graduated from the Hoxton Dissenting Academy in 1778, he was a staunch Tory Calvinist. But religion had made his childhood too unremittingly joyless, and he was too intelligent a freethinker to refrain from questioning the assumptions of his teachers. After reading Holbach and Helvétius, the deist thinkers who influenced the French Revolution, Godwin abandoned the church, became an atheist, and went to London to earn his living as a writer. *Political Justice* was ostensibly a reply to Burke, though it came out three years after the *Reflections*, and was considerably more ambitious as a work of philosophy. Godwin was remarkably fortunate in the timing of its publication: on 21 January 1793 Louis XVI was guillotined; on 1 February the French National Assembly declared war on Britain; Britain entered the war on 11 February; and *Political Justice* was published three days later. For radicals it was a welcome rallying-cry just at the moment when they felt most embattled, something that clearly put Godwin at risk of prosecution. But because it was priced at £1.16s.0d. (the equivalent of £120 pounds today), the government decided not to take Godwin to court. As Pitt declared, 'a three guinea book could never do much harm amongst those who had not three shillings to spare.' This was a miscalculation: for all its expense, the first edition was purchased by subscription and read aloud to meetings of working people; cheap pirated editions packed the booksellers' shops.

Godwin founded his vision of a better society in a philosophical belief in the moral perfectibility of mankind, attainable through the exercise of reason. When all were governed by rationality, he believed, human institutions, including that of marriage (which was derived from property laws), would wither away. It was a prospect of a world stripped of property, social inequalities and political strife, which would justify his reputation as one of the first philosophical anarchists and proto-Marxists. His ideas may seem absurd today, but in 1793 they seemed to many radicals to be the only logical response to the derailing of the Revolution under Robespierre. Among them was Wordsworth, recently returned from France; years later, he remembered that Godwinism had been a 'dream':

> flattering to the young ingenuous mind
> Pleased with extremes, and not the least with that
> Which makes the human reason's naked self
> The object of its fervour.
>
> (*Thirteen-Book Prelude* x 815–18)

Wordsworth was for a time strongly attached to the ideas in *Political Justice*, perhaps because of its enormous faith in the powers of the individual (also a feature of his own thought). He regularly breakfasted with Godwin, whose ideas would influence *Adventures on Salisbury Plain* (1795), *The Borderers* (1797–9) and *The Convict* (1796–8), but eventually tired of a creed that so emphatically denied the importance of the emotions. 'There was the rub that made philosophy of so short life,' Hazlitt wrote, 'reason without passion' (Wu vii 90). (Coleridge, by contrast, was consistently hostile to Godwinism because, as a devout Unitarian, he detested its atheism.)

For the moment, however, Godwin was one of the most influential radical thinkers of the day – never more so than during the treason trials of 1794. Increasingly alarmed by unrest at their increasingly repressive measures, the government tried a number of known radical sympathizers for treason – Thomas Hardy, John Horne Tooke and John Thelwall. Had they been found guilty they would have been hanged, drawn and quartered, and the government would have issued as many as 800 more arrest warrants. But Godwin intervened with an anonymous article in the *Morning Chronicle* entitled 'Cursory Strictures on the Charge Delivered by Lord Chief Justice Eyre' that was completely to alter the course of events. It dealt logically and calmly with the case against the beleaguered radicals, exposing it as completely unfounded. At that point it became impossible for the government successfully to pursue the case, and within days the first of the accused had been found not guilty. The others were discharged shortly after. It was a major victory for English radicals in the midst of an ongoing war with Pitt's government.

Ten days after completing *Political Justice*, Godwin began writing a novel, *Caleb Williams* (1794), the plot of which effectively subverted the philosophy he had just explicated. But its achievement lies in that very fact: had it followed its original course, which was intended to illustrate Godwinian rationalism, it would have been a far less compelling and disturbing story. What he cannot have expected as he began it was that the characters would take on their own lives to the point at which they wrested control of the narrative from his grasp, turning it into one of the great fictional works in the language. The first psychological thriller which we would recognize as such, it remains a powerful influence on fiction today – not least his daughter's *Frankenstein* (1818).[1] Godwin's influence as a philosopher would continue into the nineteenth century (even on his son-in-law, Percy Bysshe Shelley), but none of his later writings had an impact equal to those published in the 1790s, and by the time Hazlitt published *The Spirit of the Age* in 1825 it could truly be said of Godwin that 'he is to all intents and purposes dead and buried' (Wu vii 87).

The extracts below come from the first edition of *Political Justice*, the one best known to Wordsworth and Coleridge. 'On Property' provides Godwin's most concise account of the world he would ideally like to live in; 'Love of Justice' outlines his belief that humanity is motivated by an innate sense of moral good; 'On Marriage' observes that marriage is a branch of the property system, and suggests that in a rational society propagation would be motivated not by lust but 'by the dictates of reason and duty'.

Further reading

The Political and Philosophical Writings of William Godwin ed. Mark Philp, Pamela Clemit, Austin Gee and William St Clair (7 vols, London, 1993).

Don Locke, *A Fantasy of Reason: The Life and Thought of William Godwin* (London, 1980).

Nicholas Roe, *Wordsworth and Coleridge: The Radical Years* (Oxford, 1988)

William St Clair, *The Godwins and the Shelleys: The Biography of a Family* (London, 1989).

Notes

[1] Novels of our own time which betray Godwin's influence include Melvyn Bragg, *The Maid of Buttermere* (1987).

[On Property]

From Political Justice (2 vols, 1793)

Accumulated property treads the powers of thought in the dust, extinguishes the sparks of genius, and reduces the great mass of mankind to be immersed in sordid cares – beside depriving the rich (as we have already said) of the most salubrious and effectual motives to activity.

If superfluity were banished, the necessity for the greater part of the manual industry of mankind would be superseded, and the rest (being amicably shared among all the active and vigorous members of the community) would be burdensome to none. Every man would have a frugal yet wholesome diet; every man would go forth to that moderate exercise of his corporal functions that would give hilarity to the spirits – none would be made torpid with fatigue, but all would have leisure to cultivate the kindly and philanthropical[1] affections of the soul, and to let loose his faculties in the search of intellectual improvement.

What a contrast does this scene present us with the present state of human society, where the peasant and the labourer work till their understandings are benumbed with toil, their sinews contracted and made callous by being forever on the stretch, and their bodies invaded with infirmities and surrendered to an untimely grave! What is the fruit of this disproportioned and unceasing toil? At evening they return to a family, famished with hunger, exposed half-naked to the inclemencies of the sky, hardly sheltered, and denied the slenderest instruction (unless in a few instances, where it is dispensed by the hands of ostentatious charity, and the first lesson communicated is unprincipled servility). All this while their rich neighbour – but we visited him before.

[Love of Justice]

From Political Justice (2 vols, 1793)

All men love justice. All men are conscious that man is a being of one common nature, and feel the propriety of the treatment they receive from one another being measured by a common standard. Every man is desirous of assisting another, whether we should choose to ascribe this to an instinct implanted in his nature which renders this conduct a source of personal gratification, or to his perception of the reasonableness of such assistance. So necessary a part is this of the constitution of mind that no man perpetrates any action, however criminal, without having first invented some sophistry, some palliation, by which he proves to himself that it is best to be done.

Hence it appears that offence, the invasion of one man upon the security of another, is a thought alien to mind, and which nothing could have reconciled to us but the sharp sting of necessity. To consider merely the present order of human society, it is evident that the first offence must have been his who began a monopoly, and took advantage of the weakness of his neighbours to secure certain exclusive privileges to himself. The man on the other hand who determined to put an end to this monopoly, and who peremptorily demanded what was superfluous to the possessor and would be of extreme benefit to himself, appeared to his own mind to be

Notes

On Property

[1] *philanthropical* benevolent.

merely avenging the violated laws of justice. Were it not for the plausibleness of this apology, it is to be presumed that there would be no such thing as crime in the world.

[*On Marriage*]

From Political Justice (2 vols, 1793)

It is absurd to expect that the inclinations and wishes of two human beings should coincide through any long period of time. To oblige them to act and to live together is to subject them to some inevitable portion of thwarting, bickering, and unhappiness. This cannot be otherwise so long as man has failed to reach the standard of absolute perfection. The supposition that I must have a companion for life is the result of a complication of vices. It is the dictate of cowardice, and not of fortitude. It flows from the desire of being loved and esteemed for something that is not desert.[1]

But the evil of marriage as it is practised in European countries lies deeper than this. The habit is for a thoughtless and romantic youth of each sex to come together, to see each other for a few times and under circumstances full of delusion, and then to vow to each other eternal attachment.

What is the consequence of this? In almost every instance they find themselves deceived. They are reduced to make the best of an irretrievable mistake. They are presented with the strongest imaginable temptation to become the dupes of falsehood. They are led to conceive it their wisest policy to shut their eyes upon realities, happy if by any perversion of intellect they can persuade themselves that they were right in their first crude opinion of their companion. The institution of marriage is a system of fraud – and men who carefully mislead their judgements in the daily affairs of their life must always have a crippled judgement in every other concern.

We ought to dismiss our mistake as soon as it is detected, but we are taught to cherish it. We ought to be incessant in our search after virtue and worth, but we are taught to check our enquiry and shut our eyes upon the most attractive and admirable objects. Marriage is law, and the worst of all laws. Whatever our understandings may tell us of the person from whose connection we should derive the greatest improvement – of the worth of one woman and the demerits of another – we are obliged to consider what is law, and not what is justice.

Add to this that marriage is an affair of property, and the worst of all properties. So long as two human beings are forbidden by positive institution to follow the dictates of their own mind, prejudice is alive and vigorous. So long as I seek to engross one woman to myself, and to prohibit my neighbour from proving his superior desert and reaping the fruits of it, I am guilty of the most odious of all monopolies. Over this imaginary prize men watch with perpetual jealousy, and one man will find his desires and his capacity to circumvent as much excited, as the other is excited to traverse his projects and frustrate his hopes. As long as this state of society continues, philanthropy will be crossed and checked in a thousand ways, and the still augmenting stream of abuse will continue to flow.

The abolition of marriage will be attended with no evils. We are apt to represent it to ourselves as the harbinger of brutal lust and depravity. But it really happens (in this as in other cases) that the positive laws which are made to restrain our vices, irritate and multiply them – not to say that the same sentiments of justice and happiness

Notes

ON MARRIAGE

1 *desert* deserving.

which in a state of equal property would destroy the relish for luxury, would decrease our inordinate appetites of every kind, and lead us universally to prefer the pleasures of intellect to the pleasures of sense.

The intercourse[2] of the sexes will in such a state fall under the same system as any other species of friendship. Exclusively of all groundless and obstinate attachments, it will be impossible for me to live in the world without finding one man of a worth superior to that of any other whom I have an opportunity of observing. To this man I shall feel a kindness in exact proportion to my apprehension of his worth. The case will be precisely the same with respect to the female sex. I shall assiduously cultivate the intercourse of that woman whose accomplishments shall strike me in the most powerful manner. 'But it may happen that other men will feel for her the same preference that I do': this will create no difficulty. We may all enjoy her conversation, and we shall all be wise enough to consider the sensual intercourse as a very trivial object. This, like every other affair in which two persons are concerned, must be regulated in each successive instance by the unforced consent of either party.

It is a mark of the extreme depravity of our present habits that we are inclined to suppose the sensual intercourse any wise material to the advantages arising from the purest affection. Reasonable men now eat and drink not from the love of pleasure, but because eating and drinking are essential to our healthful existence. Reasonable men then will propagate their species not because a certain sensible pleasure is annexed to this action, but because it is right the species should be propagated. And the manner in which they exercise this function will be regulated by the dictates of reason and duty.

Ann Yearsley (*née* Cromartie) (1756–1806)

In December 1784 the *Gentleman's Magazine* published a letter 'from a gentleman, residing on Clifton Hill near Bristol, to a friend in London, dated 30 November 1784':

> We have a phenomenon upon this hill: a poor woman, about the age of thirty, who has led hitherto the painful life of a milkmaid; has shown the most pious cares to a mother lately deceased; has proved a most excellent wife to a husband of no vice, but of very little capacity; and who has taken, and still takes, the care of her five children. In the midst of so laborious and so anxious a life, her passion for books, that began at the age of five years, has been supported, and has enabled her to show a taste in poetry, particularly in blank verse . . . Her countenance bespeaks sense. She is gifted with a clear voice, and, I believe, of much compass. She warbles wild notes in a style that makes me believe (though, indeed, I am no judge) that, with instruction, she might have become a siren.[1]

Yearsley's passion for books may not have been supported by a formal education, but her brother

Notes

[2] *intercourse* i.e. social intercourse.

ANN YEARSLEY

[1] *Gentleman's Magazine* 54 (1784) 897. A 'siren' in this case is a woman who sings beautifully.

taught her to read, and her mother borrowed books on her behalf. She married John Yearsley in June 1774 by whom, within six years, she had as many children. During this time she managed to read and write poetry, some of which found its way to Hannah More, the leavings from whose table provided scraps for Yearsley's pig. It was as a result of Hannah's patronage that the letter appeared in the *Gentleman's Magazine* and that, in April 1785, one of Yearsley's poems appeared in its pages with the note: 'A collection of the poems of this extraordinary woman has been advertised for publication, by a 5 shilling subscription.'[2] In the preface to Ann's first book, Hannah related her 'discovery', made after visiting Elizabeth Montagu in Berkshire:

> On my return from Sandleford, a copy of verses was shown me, said to be written by a poor illiterate woman in this neighbourhood, who sells milk from door to door. The story did not engage my faith, but the verses excited my attention; for, though incorrect, they breathed the genuine spirit of poetry and were rendered still more interesting by a certain natural and strong expression of misery which seemed to fill the heart and mind of the author.[3]

With Montagu, Hannah organized a subscription list for Yearsley's *Poems, on Several Occasions*. It was an extraordinarily successful enterprise: over a thousand contributors were enrolled, including seven duchesses, sixteen countesses, Reynolds, Walpole, Burney and most of the Bluestocking set. Hannah even sent her protégé on tour to meet her society friends; as she told a correspondent: 'Do you know that my poor milkwoman has been sent for to Stoke, to visit the Duchess of Beaufort and the Duchess of Rutland; and to Bath, to Lady Spencer, Mrs Montagu, etc.? I hope all these honours will not turn her head, and indispose her for her humble occupations.'[4]

Yearsley's first volume was published in June 1785 to considerable acclaim, and it might have stood as an exemplar of the way in which women writers could help each other towards literary distinction in a male world were it not for the rapid souring of their friendship. Hannah had placed the subscription money in a trust fund and appointed herself and Elizabeth Montagu as its trustees in order to prevent Ann's husband from gaining access to it – effectively making Yearsley and her children dependent on More. Within a few months of the book's publication Yearsley's gratitude had turned to resentment. She agreed that she and her husband should not have access to the principal sum that had been collected, but thought they should get the interest, and wanted all the money divided among the children when they reached the age of 21. She told her side of the story in an 'Autobiographical Narrative' added to the fourth edition of her *Poems* in 1786. The literary world was shocked, and reviewers made great play with the hostilities between the two poets; the *European Magazine* reprinted all of the 'Narrative', commenting:

> With good intentions, as we trust, on both sides, something appears to have been wanting. There seems to have been too much hauteur and too little delicacy on the part of the patroness, and perhaps too much jealousy and too little confidence on the part of the client. To use the words of Miss Betty More to Miss Yearsley, 'There is a manner in speaking', and, we may add, in acting, in which both the ladies seem to have erred.[5]

By reprinting all of the 'Narrative', the reviewer implicitly sided with Yearsley, and a number of others gave their support: 'if we are to believe what is here related, and we know not that it has ever been contradicted, Miss More's conduct to the poetical ward, since the first publication of her *Poems*, has cancelled every prior obligation,

Notes

[2] *Gentleman's Magazine* 55 (1785) 305. The poem was *To Stella, on a Visit to Mrs Montagu*, later published in the *Poems* (1785).

[3] Ann Yearsley, *Poems, on Several Occasions* (1785), p. iv.

[4] William Roberts, *Memoirs of the Life and Correspondence of Mrs Hannah More* (3rd edn, 4 vols, London, 1835), i 332.

[5] *European Magazine* 11 (1787) 87–90, p. 87.

and what would otherwise have been deemed base ingratitude, and unwarrantable petulance, now appears a proper spirit, and just resentment.'[6] There was bitterness on both sides. Hannah commented that 'vanity, luxury, idleness, and pride, have entered the cottage the moment poverty vanished',[7] and told Mrs Montagu: 'Mrs Yearsley's conceit that you can envy her talents gives me comfort – for as it convinces me that she is mad, I build upon it a hope that she is not guilty in the all-seeing eye.'[8] She and Montagu hung on as trustees for a while but were eventually persuaded to resign, and the money passed to Yearsley through various intermediaries.

By 1786 she had a new patron, Frederick Augustus Hervey, Bishop of Derry and Earl of Bristol, who contributed £50 towards the costs of the fourth edition of the *Poems*, and to whom she dedicated her *Poem on the Inhumanity of the Slave-Trade* (1788), presented here complete. This was an important moment, as it marked the beginning of the numerous laws that led to abolition. On 21 May 1788, Sir William Dolben proposed a Bill to the House of Commons that limited the number of slaves which could be transported from Africa to British colonies in the West Indies. There was a good deal of opposition even to this comparatively mild proposal. On 26 May merchants and inhabitants of Liverpool presented a petition to the House, saying that Dolben's Bill would cause them financial ruin; all the same, the Bill was passed in both Houses. Yearsley's poem on the slave trade was composed and published in direct competition with Hannah More's *Slavery: A Poem* (see pp. 66–73).

Yearsley had discovered within herself a fierce, passionate, independent voice that felt powerfully the pain of injustice, whether on a domestic or a political level. But the *Poem on the Inhumanity of the Slave-Trade* is also of its time, in so far as it contains many stylistic mannerisms which she had picked up from Milton and Young, whose work she knew well; this is what the *Critical Review* meant when it observed that it is 'frequently rather turgid than sublime, but her sentiments are liberal, and often expressed with peculiar energy'.[9]

Another aspect of Yearsley's political personality emerges in the poems she wrote after the execution of Louis XVI. Wordsworth's response to this important moment in the French Revolution was to write a pamphlet in defence of regicide;[10] Yearsley's was to write a lament on behalf of 'Ill-fated Louis', whose slaughter she regarded as unjust. Shortly after, she composed a similar poem lamenting the imprisonment of Marie Antoinette, who was to be executed in October. Her attitude compares with that of Charlotte Smith in *The Emigrants*, also published in 1793 (see pp. 100–21), as against that of more committed radicals such as Helen Maria Williams. Both poems on the French royal family were sold at Ann's circulating library, which she opened in 1793. Her final volume of poems was *The Rural Lyre* (1796), a sizeable collection which shows her deploying a variety of metres and stanza forms with considerable virtuosity; one of its subscribers was Charlotte Smith.

Further reading

Moira Ferguson, 'The Unpublished Poems of Ann Yearsley', *Tulsa Studies in Women's Literature* 12 (1993) 13–46.

Moira Ferguson, *Eighteenth-Century Women Poets: Nation, Class, and Gender* (Albany, NY, 1995), chapters 4 and 5.

Jerome J. McGann, *The Poetics of Sensibility: A Revolution in Literary Style* (Oxford, 1996), pp. 55–64.

Alan Richardson, 'Darkness Visible: Race and Representation in Bristol Abolitionist Poetry, 1770–1810', *TWC* 27 (1996) 67–72.

Notes

6 *Critical Review* 64 (1787) 435–7, p. 435.

7 William Roberts, *Memoirs of the Life and Correspondence of Mrs Hannah More* (3rd edn., 4 vols, London, 1835), i 368–9.

8 Ibid., i 374.

9 Ibid.

10 *A Letter to the Bishop of Llandaff*, not published in Wordsworth's lifetime

Addressed to Sensibility[1]

From Poems on various subjects (1787)

Oh Sensibility! Thou busy nurse
Of inj'ries once received, why wilt thou feed
Those serpents in the soul, their stings more fell
Than those which writhed round Priam's priestly son?[2]
I feel them here! They rend my panting breast,
But I will tear them thence – ah, effort vain!
Disturbed they grow rapacious, while their fangs
Strike at poor memory; wounded she deplores
Her ravished joys, and murmurs o'er the past.
  Why shrinks my soul within these prison walls[3]
Where wretches shake their chains? Ill-fated youth,
Why does thine eye run wildly o'er my form,
Pointed with fond enquiry? 'Tis not me
Thy restless thought would find; the silent tear
Steals gently down his cheek. Ah, could my arms
Afford thee refuge, I would bear thee hence
To a more peaceful dwelling! Vain the wish;
Thy pow'rs are all unhinged, and thou wouldst sit
Insensible to sympathy: farewell.
Lamented being, ever lost to hope,
I leave thee, yea, despair myself of cure.
  For oh, my bosom bleeds, while griefs like thine
Increase the recent pang. Pensive I rove,
More wounded than the hart whose side yet holds
The deadly arrow. Friendship, boast no more
Thy hoard of joys o'er which my soul oft hung
Like the too-anxious miser o'er his gold.
My treasures all are wrecked; I quit the scene
Where haughty Insult cut the sacred ties
Which long had held us. Cruel Julius, take
My last adieu! The wound thou gav'st is death,
Nor canst e'en thou recall my frighted sense
With friendship's pleasing sound; yet will I clasp
Thy valued image to my aching mind,
And, viewing that, forgive thee; will deplore
The blow that severed two congenial souls!

Notes

ADDRESSED TO SENSIBILITY

[1] Sensibility was a central preoccupation of the Bluestockings, with whom Yearsley became involved through Hannah More, who claimed the credit for discovering 'her wild wood-notes'. Yearsley gave this poem pride of place in her 1787 volume, inviting comparison with More's *Sensibility* (p. 56).

[2] *Priam's priestly son* a reference to Laocoön, Trojan priest of Apollo, who attempted to dissuade the Trojans from admitting the wooden horse. For this, his sons were killed by sea-serpents, and he died in extreme agony while trying to save them.

[3] 'Bedlam' (Yearsley's note). The Hospital of St Mary of Bethlehem in London opened as a hospital for lunatics in 1402. As Yearsley indicates, treatment of the insane was, in the 18th century, little different from that of convicts.

Officious Sensibility, 'tis thine
To give the finest anguish, to dissolve
The dross of spirit till all essence, she
Refines on real woe; from thence extracts
Sad unexisting phantoms, never seen.
Yet, dear ideal mourner, be thou near
When on Lysander's[4] tears I silent gaze;
Then, with thy viewless pencil, form his sigh,
His deepest groan, his sorrow-tinged thought,
Wish immature, impatience, cold despair,
With all the tort'ring images that play,
In sable hue, within his wasted mind.
And when this dreary group shall meet my thought,
Oh throw my pow'rs upon a fertile space
Where mingles ev'ry varied soft relief.
Without thee, I could offer but the dregs
Of vulgar consolation; from her cup
He turns the eye, nor dare it soil his lip!
Raise thou my friendly hand; mix thou the draught
More pure than ether, as ambrosia[5] clear,
Fit only for the soul; thy chalice fill
With drops of sympathy, which swiftly fall
From my afflicted heart: yet – yet beware,
Nor stoop to seize from passion's warmer clime
A pois'nous sweet. Bright cherub, safely rove
Through all the deep recesses of the soul!
Float on her raptures, deeper tinge her woes,
Strengthen emotion, higher waft her sigh,
Sit in the tearful orb, and ardent gaze
On joy or sorrow. But thy empire ends
Within the line of spirit. My rough soul,
Oh Sensibility, defenceless hails
Thy feelings most acute. Yet ye who boast
Of bliss *I* ne'er must reach, ye who can fix
A rule for sentiment, if rules there are
(For much I doubt, my friends, if rule e'er held
Capacious sentiment), ye sure can point
My mind to joys that never touched the heart.
What is this joy? Where does its essence rest?
Ah, self-confounding sophists, will ye dare
Pronounce *that* joy which never touched the heart?
Does education give the transport keen,
Or swell your vaunted grief? No, nature feels
Most poignant, undefended; hails with me
The pow'rs of Sensibility untaught.

Notes

[4] Lysander is a classical name for an inmate of Bedlam.

[5] *ambrosia* in Greek myth, the food of gods and immortals.

A Poem on the Inhumanity of the Slave-Trade (1788)[1]

Go seek the soul refined and strong:
Such aids my wildest pow'r of song:
For those I strike the rustic lyre
Who share the transports they inspire.[2]

To the Right Hon. and Right Revd Frederick, Earl of Bristol, Bishop of Derry,[3] *etc., etc.*

My Lord,

Being convinced that your ideas of justice and humanity are not confined to one race of men,[4] I have endeavoured to lead you to the Indian coast. My intention is not to cause that anguish in your bosom which powerless compassion ever gives; yet my vanity is flattered when I but *fancy* that your Lordship feels as I do.

With the highest reverence, I am,
My Lord,
Your Lordship's much obliged,
And obedient servant,
ANN YEARSLEY

Bristol, thine heart hath throbbed to glory: slaves,
E'en Christian slaves, have shook their chains, and gazed
With wonder and amazement on thee.[5] Hence,
Ye grov'ling souls, who think the term I give
Of Christian slave, a paradox! To *you*
I do not turn, but leave you to conception
Narrow; with that be blessed, nor dare to stretch
Your shackled souls along the course of freedom.
Yet, Bristol, list! nor deem Lactilla's[6] soul
Lessened by distance; snatch her rustic thought,
Her crude ideas, from their panting state,
And let them fly in wide expansion; lend
Thine energy, so little understood
By the rude million, and I'll dare the strain
Of Heav'n-born Liberty till Nature moves
Obedient to her voice. Alas, my friend,
Strong rapture dies within the soul, while pow'r
Drags on his bleeding victims. Custom, law,
Ye blessings and ye curses of mankind,
What evils do ye cause? We feel enslaved,
Yet move in your direction. Custom, thou
Wilt preach up filial piety; thy sons
Will groan, and stare with impudence at heav'n,

Notes

A POEM ON THE INHUMANITY OF THE SLAVE-TRADE

[1] This poem was published in competition with Hannah More's *Slavery: A Poem* (see p. 66), and was inspired by Sir William Dolben's Bill

[2] The source of the epigraph is not known; Yearsley may have written it herself.

[3] Frederick Augustus Hervey, 4th Earl of Bristol and 5th Baron Howard de Walden, Bishop of Derry (1730–1803), very active in Irish politics, was Yearsley's patron.

[4] i.e. the Irish.

[5] Bristol was deeply implicated in the slave trade. For years it had been one of the main ports which handled newly arrived slaves from abroad.

[6] *Lactilla* name for a milkmaid.

As if they did abjure the act, where Sin
Sits full on Inhumanity; the church
They fill with mouthing, vap'rous sighs and tears,
Which, like the guileful crocodile's, oft fall,
Nor fall but at the cost of human bliss.
   Custom, thou hast undone us, led us far
From godlike probity, from truth, and heaven.
   But come, ye souls who feel for human woe,
Though dressed in savage guise! Approach, thou son,
Whose heart would shudder at a father's chains,
And melt o'er thy loved brother as he lies
Gasping in torment undeserved. Oh sight
Horrid and insupportable, far worse
Than an immediate, an heroic death!
Yet to this sight I summon thee. Approach,
Thou slave of avarice, that canst see the maid
Weep o'er her inky sire! Spare me, thou God
Of all-indulgent mercy, if I scorn
This gloomy wretch, and turn my tearful eye
To more enlightened beings. Yes, my tear
Shall hang on the green furze, like pearly dew
Upon the blossom of the morn. My song
Shall teach sad Philomel a louder note,
When Nature swells her woe. O'er suff'ring *man*
My soul with sorrow bends! Then come, ye few
Who feel a more than cold, material essence;
Here ye may vent your sighs, till the bleak north
Find its adherents aided. Ah, no more!
The dingy youth comes on, sullen in chains;
He smiles on the rough sailor who aloud
Strikes at the spacious heav'n, the earth, the sea,
In breath too blasphemous – yet not to *him*
Blasphemous, for *he* dreads not either. Lost
In dear internal imag'ry, the soul
Of Indian Luco rises to his eyes,
Silent, not inexpressive; the strong beams
With eager wildness yet drink in the view
Of his too-humble home where he had left
His mourning father and his Incilanda.
   Curse on the toils spread by a Christian hand
To rob the Indian of his freedom! Curse
On him who from a bending parent steals
His dear support of age, his darling child –
Perhaps a son, or a more tender daughter –
Who might have closed his eyelids as the spark
Of life gently retired. Oh thou poor world,
Thou fleeting good to individuals! See
How much for thee they care, how wide they ope
Their helpless arms to clasp thee! Vapour thou,
More swift than passing wind! Thou leav'st them nought
Amid th' unreal scene, but a scant grave.

I know the crafty merchant will oppose
The plea of nature to my strain, and urge
His toils are for his children; the soft plea
Dissolves my soul – but when I sell a son,
Thou God of nature, let it be my own!
Behold that Christian! See what horrid joy
Lights up his moody features, while he grasps
The wished-for gold, purchase of human blood!
Away, thou seller of mankind! Bring on
Thy daughter to this market, bring thy wife,
Thine aged mother (though of little worth),
With all thy ruddy boys! Sell them, thou wretch,
And swell the price of Luco! Why that start?
Why gaze as thou wouldst fright me from my challenge
With look of anguish? Is it *nature* strains
Thine heart-strings at the image? Yes, my charge
Is full against her, and she rends thy soul,
While I but strike upon thy pitiless ear,
Fearing her rights are violated. Speak,
Astound the voice of Justice! Bid thy tears
Melt the unpitying pow'r, while thus she claims
The pledges of thy love. Oh, throw thine arm
Around thy little ones, and loudly plead
Thou *canst not* sell thy children. Yet beware
Lest Luco's groan be heard; should *that* prevail,
Justice will scorn thee in her turn, and hold
Thine act against thy pray'r. 'Why clasp', she cries,
'That blooming youth? Is it because thou lov'st him?'
Why, Luco was beloved: then wilt thou feel,
Thou selfish Christian, for thy private woe,
Yet cause such pangs to him that is a father?
Whence comes thy right to barter for thy fellows?
Where are thy statutes? Whose the iron pen
That gave thee precedent? Give me the seal
Of virtue or religion for thy trade,
And I will ne'er upbraid thee; but if force
Superior, hard brutality alone
Become thy boast, hence to some savage haunt,
Nor claim protection from my social laws.
Luco is gone; his little brothers weep,
While his fond mother climbs the hoary rock
Whose point o'erhangs the main. No Luco there,
No sound, save the hoarse billows. On she roves,
With love, fear, hope, holding alternate rage
In her too-anxious bosom. Dreary main!
Thy murmurs now are riot, while she stands
List'ning to ev'ry breeze, waiting the step
Of gentle Luco. Ah return, return,
Too hapless mother; thy indulgent arms
Shall never clasp thy fettered Luco more.
See Incilanda – artless maid, my soul

Keeps pace with thee and mourns. Now o'er the hill
She creeps, with timid foot, while Sol embrowns
The bosom of the isle, to where she left
Her faithful lover: here the well-known cave,
By nature formed amid the rock, endears
The image of her Luco; here his pipe,
Formed of the polished cane, neglected lies,
No more to vibrate; here the useless dart,
The twanging bow, and the fierce panther's skin,
Salute the virgin's eye. But where is Luco?
He comes not down the steep though he had vowed,
When the sun's beams at noon should sidelong gild
The cave's wide entrance, he would swift descend
To bless his Incilanda. Ten pale moons
Had glided by, since to his generous breast
He clasped the tender maid and whispered love.
   Oh mutual sentiment, thou dang'rous bliss,
So exquisite that Heav'n had been unjust
Had it bestowed less exquisite of ill;
When thou art held no more, thy pangs are deep,
Thy joys convulsive to the soul; yet all
Are meant to smooth th' uneven road of life.
   For Incilanda, Luco ranged the wild,
Holding her image to his panting heart;
For her he strained the bow, for her he stripped
The bird of beauteous plumage – happy hour,
When with these guiltless trophies he adorned
The brow of her he loved. Her gentle breast
With gratitude was filled, nor knew she aught
Of language strong enough to paint her soul,
Or ease the great emotion, whilst her eye
Pursued the gen'rous Luco to the field
And glowed with rapture at his wished return.
   Ah sweet suspense, betwixt the mingled cares
Of friendship, love, and gratitude – so mixed,
That ev'n the soul may cheat herself. Down, down,
Intruding memory! Bid thy struggles cease
At this soft scene of innate war. What sounds
Break on her ear? She, starting, whispers 'Luco?'
Be still, fond maid; list to the tardy step
Of leaden-footed woe. A father comes,
But not to seek his son who, from the deck,
Had breathed a last adieu; no, he shuts out
The soft, fallacious gleam of hope, and turns
Within upon the mind. Horrid and dark
Are his wild, unenlightened pow'rs; no ray
Of forced philosophy to calm his soul,
But all the anarchy of wounded nature.
Now he arraigns his country's gods, who sit,
In his bright fancy, far beyond the hills,
Unriveting the chains of slaves; his heart

Beats quick with stubborn fury, while he doubts
Their justice to his child. Weeping old man,
Hate not a Christian's God, whose record holds
Thine injured Luco's name. Frighted he starts,
Blasphemes the deity whose altars rise
Upon the Indian's helpless neck, and sinks,
Despising comfort, till by grief and age
His angry spirit is forced out. Oh guide,
Ye angel-forms, this joyless shade to worlds
Where the poor Indian, with the sage, is proved
The work of a Creator. Pause not here,
Distracted maid! Ah, leave the breathless form
On whose cold cheek thy tears so swiftly fall,
Too unavailing! 'On this stone', she cries,
'My Luco sat, and to the wand'ring stars
Pointed my eye, while from his gentle tongue
Fell old traditions of his country's woe.'
Where now shall Incilanda seek him? Hence,
Defenceless mourner, ere the dreary night
Wrap thee in added horror. Oh despair,
How eagerly thou rend'st the heart! She pines
In anguish deep and sullen: Luco's form
Pursues her, lives in restless thought, and chides
Soft consolation. Banished from his arms,
She seeks the cold embrace of death; her soul
Escapes in one sad sigh. Too hapless maid! –
Yet happier far than he thou lov'dst; his tear,
His sigh, his groan avail not, for they plead
Most weakly with a Christian. Sink, thou wretch,
Whose act shall on the cheek of Albion's sons
Throw shame's red blush; thou who hast frighted far
Those simple wretches from thy God, and taught
Their erring minds to mourn his partial love,[7]
Profusely poured on thee, while they are left
Neglected to *thy* mercy. Thus deceived,
How doubly dark must be their road to death!
   Luco is borne around the neighb'ring isles,
Losing the knowledge of his native shore
Amid the pathless wave, destined to plant
The sweet luxuriant cane.[8] He strives to please,
Nor once complains, but greatly smothers grief.
His hands are blistered, and his feet are worn,
Till ev'ry stroke dealt by his mattock[9] gives
Keen agony to life; while from his breast

Notes

[7] 'Indians have been often heard to say, in their complaining moments, "God Almighty no love us well; he be good to buckera; he bid buckera burn us; he no burn buckera" ' (Yearsley's note). 'Buckera', Yearsley explains in a further note, means 'white man'.

[8] *cane* sugar-cane.

[9] *mattock* tool for loosening hard ground.

The sigh arises, burdened with the name
Of Incilanda. Time inures the youth,
His limbs grow nervous, strained by willing toil,
And resignation, or a calm despair
(Most useful either) lulls him to repose.
  A Christian renegade that from his soul
Abjures the tenets of our schools, nor dreads
A future punishment, nor hopes for mercy,
Had fled from England to avoid those laws
Which must have made his life a retribution
To violated justice, and had gained,
By fawning guile, the confidence (ill-placed)
Of Luco's master. O'er the slave he stands
With knotted whip, lest fainting nature shun
The task too arduous, while his cruel soul
Unnat'ral, ever feeds, with gross delight,
Upon his suff'rings. Many slaves there were,
But none who could suppress the sigh and bend
So quietly as Luco. Long he bore
The stripes that from his manly bosom drew
The sanguine stream (too little prized); at length
Hope fled his soul, giving her struggles o'er,
And he resolved to die. The sun had reached
His zenith; pausing faintly, Luco stood,
Leaning upon his hoe, while mem'ry brought,
In piteous imag'ry, his aged father,
His poor fond mother, and his faithful maid.
The mental group in wildest motion set
Fruitless imagination. Fury, grief,
Alternate shame, the sense of insult, all
Conspire to aid the inward storm – yet words
Were no relief; he stood in silent woe.
  Gorgon, remorseless Christian, saw the slave
Stand musing mid the ranks and, stealing soft
Behind the studious Luco, struck his cheek
With a too-heavy whip that reached his eye,
Making it dark for ever. Luco turned
In strongest agony, and with his hoe
Struck the rude Christian on the forehead. Pride,
With hateful malice, seized on Gorgon's soul,
By nature fierce, while Luco sought the beach
And plunged beneath the wave. But near him lay
A planter's barge, whose seamen grasped his hair,
Dragging to life a wretch who wished to die.
  Rumour now spreads the tale, while Gorgon's breath
Envenomed aids her blast. Imputed crimes
Oppose the plea of Luco, till he scorns
Even a just defence, and stands prepared.
The planters, conscious that to fear alone
They owe their cruel pow'r, resolve to blend
New torment with the pangs of death, and hold

Their victims high in dreadful view, to fright
The wretched number left. Luco is chained
To a huge tree, his fellow-slaves are ranged
To share the horrid sight; fuel is placed
In an increasing train, some paces back,
To kindle slowly, and approach the youth,
With more than native terror. See, it burns!
He gazes on the growing flame, and calls
For 'Water, water!' The small boon's denied.
E'en Christians throng each other to behold
The different alterations of his face
As the hot death approaches. (Oh shame, shame
Upon the followers of Jesus! Shame
On him that dares avow a God!) He writhes,
While down his breast glide the unpitied tears,
And in their sockets strain their scorched balls.
'Burn, burn me quick! I cannot die!' he cries,
'Bring fire more close!' The planters heed him not,
But still prolonging Luco's torture, threat
Their trembling slaves around. His lips are dry,
His senses seem to quiver ere they quit
His frame for ever, rallying strong, then driv'n
From the tremendous conflict. Sight no more
Is Luco's, his parched tongue is ever mute;
Yet in his soul his Incilanda stays,
Till both escape together. Turn, my muse,
From this sad scene; lead Bristol's milder soul
To where the solitary spirit roves,
Wrapped in the robe of innocence, to shades
Where pity breathing in the gale dissolves
The mind, when fancy paints such real woe.
   Now speak, ye Christians (who for gain enslave
A soul like Luco's, tearing her from joy
In life's short vale – and if there be a hell,
As ye believe, to *that* ye thrust her down,
A blind, involuntary victim), where
Is your true essence of religion? Where
Your proofs of righteousness, when ye conceal
The knowledge of the Deity from those
Who would adore him fervently? Your God
Ye rob of worshippers, his altars keep
Unhailed, while driving from the sacred font
The eager slave, lest he should hope in Jesus.
   Is this your piety? Are these your laws,
Whereby the glory of the Godhead spreads
O'er barb'rous climes? Ye hypocrites, disown
The Christian name, nor shame its cause; yet where
Shall souls like yours find welcome? Would the Turk,
Pagan, or wildest Arab, ope their arms
To gain such proselytes? No. He that owns

The name of Mussulman[10] would start, and shun
Your worse than serpent touch; *he* frees his slave
Who turns to Mahomet.[11] The Spaniard stands
Your brighter contrast; he condemns the youth
For ever to the mine, but ere the wretch
Sinks to the deep domain, the hand of Faith
Bathes his faint temples in the sacred stream,
Bidding his spirit hope.[12] Briton, dost thou
Act up to this? If so, bring on thy slaves
To Calv'ry's mount, raise high their kindred souls
To him who died to save them:[13] this alone
Will teach them calmly to obey thy rage,
And deem a life of misery but a day,
To long eternity. Ah, think how soon
Thine head shall on earth's dreary pillow lie
With thy poor slaves, each silent, and unknown
To his once furious neighbour. Think how swift
The sands of time ebb out, for him and *thee*.
Why groans that Indian youth, in burning chains
Suspended o'er the beach? The lab'ring sun
Strikes from his full meridian on the slave
Whose arms are blistered by the heated iron
Which, still corroding, seeks the bone. What crime
Merits so dire a death? Another gasps
With strongest agony, while life declines
From recent amputation.[14] Gracious God!
Why thus in mercy let thy whirlwinds sleep
O'er a vile race of Christians, who profane
Thy glorious attributes? Sweep them from earth,
Or check their cruel pow'r; the savage tribes
Are angels when compared to brutes like these.
　Advance, ye Christians, and oppose my strain;
Who dares condemn it? Prove from laws divine,
From deep philosophy, or social love,
That ye derive your privilege. I scorn
The cry of Av'rice, or the trade that drains
A fellow-creature's blood; bid Commerce plead
Her public good, her nation's many wants,
Her sons thrown idly on the beach, forbade

Notes

10 *Mussulman* Muslim.

11 'The Turk gives freedom to his slave on condition that he embraces Mahometism' (Yearsley's note).

12 'The Spaniard, immediately on purchasing an Indian, gives him baptism' (Yearsley's note).

13 *him who died to save them* Christ, crucified on Calvary.

14 'A Coromantin slave in Jamaica (who had frequently escaped to the mountains) was, a few years since, doomed to have his leg cut off. A young practitioner from England (after the surgeon of the estate had refused to be an executioner) undertook the operation, but after the removal of the limb, on the slave's exclaiming, "You buckera! God Almighty made dat leg; you cut it off! You put it on again?" was so shocked, that the other surgeon was obliged to take up the vessels, apply the dressings, etc. The negro suffered without a groan, called for his pipe, and calmly smoked till the absence of his attendant gave him an opportunity of tearing off his bandages, when he bled to death in an instant. Many will call this act of the negro's stubbornness; under *such* circumstances, I dare give it a more glorious epithet, and that is *fortitude*' (Yearsley's note). Coromantin slaves came from the eastern coast of Madras.

To seize the image of their God and sell it.
I'll hear her voice, and Virtue's hundred tongues
Shall sound against her. Hath our public good
Fell rapine[15] for its basis? Must our wants
Find their supply in murder? Shall the sons
Of Commerce shiv'ring stand, if not employed
Worse than the midnight robber? Curses fall
On the destructive system that shall need
Such base supports! Doth England need them? No;
Her laws, with prudence, hang the meagre thief
That from his neighbour steals a slender sum,
Though famine drove him on. O'er *him* the priest,
Beneath the fatal tree,[16] laments the crime,
Approves the law, and bids him calmly die.
Say, doth this law that dooms the thief protect
The wretch who makes another's life his prey,
By hellish force to take it at his will?
Is this an English law, whose guidance fails
When crimes are swelled to magnitude so vast,
That Justice dare not scan them? Or does Law
Bid Justice an eternal distance keep
From England's great tribunal, when the slave
Calls loud on Justice only? Speak, ye few
Who fill Britannia's senate, and are deemed
The fathers of your country! Boast your laws,
Defend the honour of a land so fall'n
That Fame from ev'ry battlement is flown,
And heathens start e'en at a Christian's name.
  Hail, social love![17] True soul of order, hail!
Thy softest emanations – pity, grief,
Lively emotion, sudden joy, and pangs
Too deep for language – are thy own: then rise,
Thou gentle angel! Spread thy silken wings
O'er drowsy man, breathe in his soul, and give
Her godlike pow'rs thy animating force
To banish inhumanity. Oh loose
The fetters of his mind, enlarge his views,
Break down for him the bound of avarice, lift
His feeble faculties beyond a world
To which he soon must prove a stranger! Spread
Before his ravished eye the varied tints
Of future glory; bid them live to Fame
Whose banners wave for ever. Thus inspired,
All that is great, and good, and sweetly mild,
Shall fill his noble bosom. He shall melt –
Yea, by thy sympathy unseen, shall feel

Notes

[15] *rapine* plunder, robbery.
[16] *fatal tree* from which he is to be hanged.
[17] *Hail, social love!* Moira Ferguson suggests that in this final apostrophe to social love, Yearsley implicitly criticizes Hannah More for religious hypocrisy and lack of love.

Another's pang; for the lamenting maid
His heart shall heave a sigh; with the old slave
(Whose head is bent with sorrow) he shall cast
His eye back on the joys of youth, and say,
'Thou once couldst feel, as I do, love's pure bliss;
Parental fondness, and the dear returns
Of filial tenderness were thine, till torn
From the dissolving scene.' Oh, social love,
Thou universal good, thou that canst fill
The vacuum of immensity, and live
In endless void! Thou that in motion first
Set'st the long lazy atoms, by thy force
Quickly assimilating, and restrained
By strong attraction – touch the soul of man;
Subdue him; make a fellow-creature's woe
His own by heartfelt sympathy, whilst wealth
Is made subservient to his soft disease.
 And when thou hast to high perfection wrought
This mighty work, say, 'Such is Bristol's soul.'

William Blake (1757–1827)

He was a native Londoner, one of seven children born to a London hosier, James Blake, and his wife, Catherine Hermitage. They were Dissenting Whigs (James Blake voted for Charles James Fox), and seem to have given Blake and his siblings a pious and devout upbringing. All the same, the Blake children had some odd propensities. His older brother encountered Moses and Abraham, and Blake was almost beaten by his father for claiming to have seen angels in the treetops on Peckham Rye. Parental disapproval made little difference, however, and his visionary propensities continued to flourish.

Blake's formal education began when he was sent to Henry Pars's Drawing School in the Strand to become a draughtsman. Four years later he was apprenticed to James Basire, engraver to the Society of Antiquaries. During this period he was inducted into the English Gothic tradition, partly by drawing the monuments in Westminster Abbey. There he apparently saw a vision of monks, priests, choristers and censer-bearers marching in procession.

For a few years after leaving Basire in 1779 he studied at the Royal Academy but found himself at odds with the orthodoxies laid down by Reynolds and followed at the Academy. He dropped out, married Catherine Boucher in 1782, and set up as an engraver. His principal employer from 1788 onwards was Joseph Johnson,[1] the Unitarian publisher of Tom Paine, Mary Wollstonecraft, William Godwin and the young William Wordsworth, among others. Blake may have met some of them, but he is known to have attended only

Notes

[1] For more on whom see Gerald Tyson, *Joseph Johnson: A Liberal Publisher* (Iowa City, 1979) and Helen Braithwaite, *Romanticism, Publishing and Dissent* (Basingstoke, 2003).

one of Johnson's literary dinners at his rooms at 72 St Paul's Churchyard.

His first volume of poems, *Poetical Sketches* (1783), was the first and last to use traditional letterpress; from then on his books were produced using his own 'infernal' printing method with which he experimented when producing *All Religions Are One* and *There Is No Natural Religion*, etched around 1788. He would inscribe design and text, in reverse, directly onto a copper plate using a varnish resistant to the acid bath into which it would be immersed.[2] Each page would be hand-printed, and then individually water-coloured by him or his wife: by this method no two books were identical. He did not care that they could not be mass-produced; the gain in artistic control was worth it. No other technique would have allowed him so completely to shape the reading experience. Because each character of each word was the work of his own hand, it was susceptible to variation and emphasis as he saw fit. He was also in charge of page layout – integral to the meaning of the work, as it incorporates ornament and illustration that complement or counterpoint the text. Indeed, the interweaving of word and image is essential to a full understanding of his poems and prophecies; serious readers will wish to make use of the Blake Trust / Tate Gallery editions (listed under 'Further Reading', p. 174), which combine colour reproductions of his books with detailed commentaries.

Thel (1789) is a sustained attempt to examine the 'fall' into the physical world and sexual experience. Only Blake would have approached such a subject in this distinctive manner, through a narrative that concerns a girl's encounters with a series of characters – lily, cloud, clod of clay, and worm – loaded with allegorical significance never precisely spelt out. Much hinges on the virgin's return to the Vales of Har, which signifies reluctance to submit to the descent into experience. Some take this to reflect badly on her, while others question the advice dispensed by those she encounters. *Thel* is a good place to begin one's study of Blake's way of thinking: it takes us into a world in which, as in life, judgements as to meaning and morality are anything but straightforward. The parallel world, fall from grace and concern with sexual initiation are revisited in subsequent works.

Songs of Innocence (1789) and its companion volume, *Songs of Experience* (1794), contain Blake's most popular and influential poems. Although their titles imply opposition, Blake was resistant to easy formulations, and it is typical that when producing joint copies of *Songs of Innocence and of Experience*, he sometimes transferred poems from one to the other. Moreover, it is possible to read such works as 'Holy Thursday' (*Innocence*) ironically, just as its corresponding poem in *Experience* can be read with positive connotations. Rather than assuming some kind of opposition (which Blake would have disavowed), it is more appropriate to think of the two groups as engaging in dialogue.

'Every child may joy to hear,' Blake wrote – but though composed for children, the *Songs* contain some highly sophisticated poetry. Blakean innocence entails a complex mixture of qualities including unfettered energy, simplicity, love and spontaneity. Steering clear of sin and divine punishment (often incorporated into didactic works aimed at children), such poems as 'The Lamb' and 'Spring' emphasize the intensity and purity of childhood vision, laying emphasis on the god-like qualities in man. There is a political subtext too: it is worth remembering that publication of *Innocence* in 1789 coincided with the beginning of the Revolution in France; *Experience* with the events that led to the execution of Louis XVI and the Reign of Terror. This is most obvious in 'London',

Notes

[2] The process is fully explained by Joseph Viscomi, *Blake and the Idea of the Book* (Princeton, NY, 1993), part III.

'Holy Thursday' (*Experience*) and 'The Chimney Sweeper' (*Experience*), which are primarily works of social and political protest.

When in the early 1790s he reconceived the two volumes of *Songs* as a single book, he composed a motto for it, which in the end he decided not to use:

The good are attracted by men's perceptions,
And think not for themselves –
Till experience teaches them to catch
And to cage the fairies and elves.

And then the knave begins to snarl,
And the hypocrite to howl –
And all his good friends show their private ends,
And the eagle is known from the owl.

In 1790 Blake moved from central London into the suburb of Lambeth. Three years before, perhaps inspired partly by grief at the death of his brother Robert in 1787, he had studied the writings of Emanuel Swedenborg, the theologian and philosopher who theorized that the spirits of the dead rise from the body and assume physical form in another world. Though Swedish, Swedenborg died in London in 1772, when he was 84 and Blake 14. Such was the popularity of his work that, in the 1780s, his followers formed the New Church, or Church of the New Jerusalem (which continues today). A visionary who conversed with angels and spirits, Swedenborg's brand of religion had a powerful appeal for Blake, who identified with his spiritual experiences. Moreover, Swedenborg was capable of remarking that 'God is a man, all angels and spirits are men in a perfect form' – the kind of sentiment that recurs in Blake's writings (see Plate 5).

As time went on, the Swedenborgian faith became increasingly institutionalized. It ordained ministers with their own robes and rituals, and was taken over by conservatives who pledged loyalty to king and country, adhering to such doctrines as predestination (in favour of which Swedenborg had written). Blake quickly became disillusioned, and a year after joining scribbled in his copy of Swedenborg's *Divine Providence*: 'Lies and Priestcraft', 'Predestination . . . more abominable than Calvin's' and 'Cursed Folly!' He came to loathe the systematizing tendencies of all religious beliefs, and composed a satire on Swedenborgianism, *The Marriage of Heaven and Hell* (which echoes the title of Swedenborg's own *Heaven and Hell*).

The argument of the *Marriage* is that Swedenborg, though pretending to the status of a radical, is really a stooge for the forces of reaction. This is most explicitly articulated in Plate 11, where Blake explains how the systems generated by institutionalized religions exiled the true poets of ancient times who were also, by implication, true priests; the result has been to make people forget that 'All deities reside in the human breast.' Despite appearances to the contrary, he argues, Swedenborg is a type of the kind of clerical impostor. Blake aims to prove this by imitating his literary mannerisms, such as the 'correspondences' and 'memorable relations', to expose the underlying complacency of his thought. To this end, Blake condenses Swedenborgian ideas and literary techniques in a helter-skelter manner, producing a comically distorted version of them. For instance, the title of Blake's work echoes Swedenborg's opposition of heaven and hell, proposing a relationship that most theologians would have found either inappropriate or nonsensical.

Being of an older generation than other major poets of the Romantic period, as well as an exception to many of the defining features singled out by commentators, Blake was for years regarded as a madman operating outside the normal boundaries of literature. As late as the 1950s, it was possible to teach a course on Romanticism without mentioning him. All that has changed, and if Blake has a claim to be regarded not just as a Romantic, but as a herald of the movement, it is never stronger than in the *Marriage*, when he declares his faith in a spiritual world: 'If the doors of perception were cleansed, everything would appear to man as it is: Infinite' (plate 14). Neither Wordsworth nor Coleridge read those words at the time, but had they done so, they would probably have been exhilarated by the politicizing of its message in 'A Song of Liberty' (plate 25), the great apocalyptic finale of the *Marriage*, which some scholars suggest originated as a separate work to it. Even if they are right, it resolves the *Marriage* in a way that could not be more appropriate – extending Blake's argument into the historical moment of its composition, arguing that the 'outing' of such false prophets as Swedenborg (and, more generally, institutionalized religions as a whole) is liberating not just on a spiritual plane but also on the ideological: as the harbinger of worldwide revolution. Imagination is thus seen not just as the agent of artistic creation, but as the vehicle of revolutionary change in the outside world. No wonder Blake was such an icon for the baby-boomers of the 1960s.

In autumn 1790 the Blakes moved to Lambeth in south London, where they produced a series of books, now referred to as the Lambeth prophecies, which include *Visions of the Daughters of Albion* (1793). This work takes us straight into Blake's mythical universe. On her way to her beloved Theotormon, Oothoon is raped by Bromion. Having impregnated her, he casts her off; they are nonetheless bound back to back. Theotormon refuses to marry her, and sits weeping on the threshold of Bromion's cave. The rest of the poem consists of their lamentations. Thematically, it extends Blake's preoccupation with the journey from innocence to experience in *Thel*, but the obvious distinction is that where Thel retreats from the body and all it entails, returning to the vales of Har, Oothoon accepts it. The extent to which Oothoon is a feminist or a tool of the male ideology remains a bone of contention among critics. All the same, it is worth bearing in mind that Blake probably knew Mary Wollstonecraft through the Johnson circle,[3] and would have read her *Vindication of the Rights of Woman* (1792). He may even have been aware of her rejected proposal to Henry Fuseli's wife that she move into their home and form a platonic *ménage à trois*, a scenario that may have inspired aspects of the *Visions*.

While working on *Visions of the Daughters*, Blake continued to pursue his career as an engraver, supplying a number of illustrations to John Gabriel Stedman's *Narrative of a Five Years' Expedition against the Revolted Negroes of Surinam* (1796), one of the best known of which is an image of a captured black man hanging by the ribs from a gallows. Stedman's text left its mark on *Visions of the Daughters*: Bromion is a slave-owner – 'Stamped with my signet are the swarthy children of the sun' (line 29) – and Theotormon hears the 'voice of slaves' (line 39). For Blake the plight of women and slaves was the result of the failure to comprehend fully what the eye sees.

Underlying these works is the nagging question: why did God permit the Fall? Blake attempts an answer in *The Book of Urizen* (1794), which contains the kernel of the mythology elaborated in subsequent works such as *Jerusalem*, *Milton* and *The Four Zoas*. *Urizen* was Blake's first attempt to rewrite the Scriptures,[4] and it is on one level a parody of Genesis. His central innovation is to postulate a primal unity before the act of creation when heaven and earth were one. The Fall thus occurs concurrently with the creation of the known universe, rather than at the later stage claimed by the Bible and Milton. In Blake's retelling, the act of creation – 'An activity unknown and horrible' – cannot avoid destroying an original unity more perfect than anything generated by its breakdown. Creation of the physical world is the first in a series of repressive acts responsible for enslavement of

Notes

[3] Wollstonecraft probably met Blake when he engraved the illustrations for her *Original Stories from Real Life* in 1791.

[4] Blake considered that the Bible was 'a state trick, through which though the people at all times could see they never had the power to throw off'. Its rewriting was therefore a revolutionary act.

the human spirit. It culminates with the imposition of a tyranny Blake's readers understood only too well: 'One king, one God, one law'.

The myth is rehearsed three times. In the first, Urizen's story is told beginning with the moment he splits off from 'eternity' (chapter I). In the second, Urizen recalls the moment before creation as 'The heavens / Awoke' (chapter II). After creation of Los (and Death), the 'changes of Urizen' are codified as a series of 'Ages' in a parody of the Bible. During the course of what follows, time, institutionalized religion, and the human body itself are seen as different kinds of tyranny imposed on humanity in the aftermath of the Fall.

If Blake's sceptical attitude towards the Bible seems extreme, it is as well to bear in mind that he was one of a number of radicals (including Thomas Paine) who questioned the political and social control exercised by government and clergy through Biblical texts. All of which goes to underline David Worrall's contention that *Urizen* is one of Blake's 'most politically interventionist works of the 1790s'.

Blake would compose other visionary works, including *Vala, or the Four Zoas* (first version, 1797, revised 1802, 1807), *Milton* (1804–?8) and *Jerusalem* (1804–?20), but none has the clarity or simplicity of *Urizen*. His final years were revitalized by the friendship of artists such as John Linnell and John Varley. Linnell was an enthusiastic patron and commissioned Blake's *Illustrations of the Book of Job* and watercolours of *Paradise Lost* and *Paradise Regained*. He also introduced Blake to Samuel Palmer in 1824; Palmer was only 19, and the experience was enormously important to him. 'Do you work with fear and trembling?' Blake asked him. When he died, 12 August 1827, Blake was at work on a series of designs illustrating Dante.

The apparent hermeticism of Blakean myth can tempt us to think of Blake as if he lived in a social vacuum, cut off from the maelstrom of activity that surrounded him. But even a cursory glance at his works reveals that no one was more caught up in the ideological, religious and intellectual currents of the day. He emerges out of the bedrock of eighteenth-century culture, well known among the many thousands of writers and artists that thronged metropolitan London. And many of the Romantic writers, once considered as somehow distinct, admired him and his work. 'Blake is a real name, I assure you – and a most extraordinary man, if he be still living,' Charles Lamb told a correspondent in 1824. When he read the *Songs* in 1812, Wordsworth 'considered Blake as having the elements of poetry a thousand times more than either Byron or Scott' – high praise from someone not known for admiring other people's poetry. When he caught up with an illuminated copy of the *Songs* in 1818, Coleridge bestowed on Blake the ultimate compliment:

> He is a man of Genius – and I apprehend, a Swedenborgian – certainly, a mystic *emphatically*. You perhaps smile at *my* calling another Poet, a *Mystic*; but verily I am in the very mire of common-place common-sense compared with Mr Blake, apo- or rather ana-calyptic Poet, and Painter! (Griggs iv 834)

Texts of Blake's work are always problematic. In previous editions of this anthology I have regularized punctuation, spelling and capitalization, as throughout the volume, on the grounds that to do so eases comprehension for the reader. For this third edition I have preferred to reinstate Blake's capitals; although punctuation remains editorial, I have brought it somewhat closer to that used by Blake in his published works, which often allows for nuances and ambiguities which would otherwise be lost. There are several occasions (though not many) on which I have also reinstated Blake's orthography, usually in cases where it might be argued to bear on interpretation – as for instance in the cases of 'Tyger', 'appalls' and 'ecchoing'. I hope that these texts will be no less accessible than those in earlier editions, while retrieving some of the rich textures of the originals. As they have not reached the same finished state as those published by Blake, these works edited from manuscript are treated in the same way as other such works elsewhere in this volume. As ever, I am indebted to the labours of those responsible for the Blake Trust / Tate Gallery editions; their datings and bibliographical observations are accepted here as authoritative, though on occasion I have preferred my own readings and arrangements of the various works.

Further reading

The Blake Trust / Tate Gallery Editions (General Editor: David Bindman):

1. *Jerusalem* ed. Morton D. Paley (1991).
2. *Songs of Innocence and of Experience* ed. Andrew Lincoln (1991).
3. *The Early Illuminated Books* ed. Morris Eaves, Robert N. Essick and Joseph Viscomi (1993).
4. *The Continental Prophecies* ed. D. W. Dörrbecker (1995).
5. *Milton* ed. Robert N. Essick and Joseph Viscomi (1993).
6. *The Urizen Books* ed. David Worrall (1995).

The Illustrated Blake annotated by David V. Erdman (London, 1975).

The Cambridge Companion to William Blake ed. Morris Eaves (Cambridge, 2003).

Peter Ackroyd, *Blake* (London, 1995).

G. E. Bentley, Jr., *The Stranger from Paradise: A Biography of William Blake* (New Haven, 2001).

David V. Erdman, *Blake: Prophet Against Empire* (Princeton, NJ, 1969).

Northrop Frye, *Fearful Symmetry: A Study of William Blake* (Princeton, NJ, 1947).

Zachary Leader, *Reading Blake's Songs* (London, 1981).

Jon Mee, *Dangerous Enthusiasm: William Blake and the Culture of Radicalism in the 1790s* (Oxford, 1992).

Morton Paley, *Energy and the Imagination: A Study of the Development of Blake's Thought* (Oxford, 1970).

E. P. Thompson, *Witness Against the Beast: William Blake and the Moral Law* (Cambridge, 1993).

Joseph Viscomi, *Blake and the Idea of the Book* (Princeton, NJ, 1993).

All Religions Are One (composed *c.*1788)

The voice of one crying in the wilderness.[1]

The Argument. As the true method of knowledge is experiment, the true faculty of knowing must be the faculty which experiences: this faculty I treat of.

Principle 1st. That the Poetic Genius is the true Man, and that the body or outward form of Man is derived from the Poetic Genius. Likewise that the forms of all things are derived from their Genius which, by the Ancients, was called an Angel and Spirit and Demon.

Principle 2d. As all men are alike in outward form, so (and with the same infinite variety) all are alike in the Poetic Genius.

Principle 3d. No man can think, write or speak from his heart, but he must intend truth. Thus all sects of Philosophy are from the Poetic Genius adapted to the weaknesses of every individual.

Principle 4. As none by travelling over known lands can find out the unknown, so, from already acquired knowledge, man could not acquire more. Therefore an universal Poetic Genius exists.

Principle 5. The Religions of all Nations are derived from each Nation's different reception of the Poetic Genius, which is everywhere called the Spirit of Prophecy.

Notes

All Religions Are One

[1] Matthew 5: 5; Mark 1:3; Luke 3: 4; John 1: 23. Blake's illustration shows John the Baptist, prophet of the coming of Christ; by implication, his situation – that of one crying in the wilderness – is one that Blake shares.

Principle 6. The Jewish and Christian Testaments are an original derivation from the Poetic Genius. This is necessary from the confined nature of bodily sensation.

Principle 7th. As all men are alike (though infinitely various), so all Religions and as all similars have one source.

The true Man is the source, he being the Poetic Genius.

There is no Natural Religion (composed *c.*1788)[1]

The Argument. Man has no notion of moral fitness but from Education. Naturally he is only a natural organ subject to Sense.

I Man cannot naturally Perceive but through his natural or bodily organs.
II Man by his reasoning power can only compare and judge of what he has already perceived.
III From a perception of only 3 senses or 3 elements none could deduce a fourth or fifth.
IV None could have other than natural or organic thoughts if he had none but organic perceptions.
V Man's desires are limited by his perceptions; none can desire what he has not perceived.
VI The desires and perceptions of man, untaught by anything but organs of sense, must be limited to objects of sense.

I Man's perceptions are not bounded by organs of perception. He perceives more than sense (though ever so acute) can discover.
II Reason, or the ratio of all we have already known, is not the same that it shall be when we know more.
III [*missing*][2]
IV The bounded is loathed by its possessor. The same dull round, even of a universe, would soon become a mill with complicated wheels.
V If the many become the same as the few when possessed, 'More! More!' is the cry of a mistaken soul; less than all cannot satisfy Man.
VI If any could desire what he is incapable of possessing, despair must be his eternal lot.
VII The desire of man being Infinite, the possession is Infinite, and himself Infinite.

Conclusion. If it were not for the Poetic or Prophetic character, the Philosophic and Experimental would soon be at the ratio of all things, and stand still, unable to do other than repeat the same dull round over again.

Application. He who sees the infinite in all things, sees God. He who sees the Ratio only, sees himself only.

Therefore God becomes as we are, that we may be as He is.

Notes

THERE IS NO NATURAL RELIGION

[1] This has traditionally been presented as two separate and distinct works, featuring the (a) and (b) series of plates; however, recent editorial discoveries have led to its being regarded as one work consisting of two parts, the second answering the first. Accordingly, it is presented here as a single work. The first six principles present apparently straightforward statements of Lockean thought, so that they can be refuted by the seven statements that follow.

[2] The plate etched for proposition III is lost.

The Book of Thel (1789)

[Plate 1]

Thel's Motto

Does the Eagle know what is in the pit?
Or wilt thou go ask the Mole:
Can Wisdom be put in a silver rod?
Or Love in a golden bowl?[1]

[Plate 3]

Thel[2]

I

The daughters of Mne Seraphim[3] led round their sunny flocks,
All but the youngest; she in paleness sought the secret air,
To fade away like morning beauty from her mortal day;
Down by the river of Adona[4] her soft voice is heard,
And thus her gentle lamentation falls like morning dew.
  'Oh life of this our spring! Why fades the lotus of the water?
Why fade these children of the spring, born but to smile and fall?
Ah! Thel is like a wat'ry bow, and like a parting cloud,
Like a reflection in a glass, like shadows in the water,
Like dreams of infants, like a smile upon an infant's face,
Like the dove's voice, like transient day, like music in the air:
Ah! gentle may I lay me down, and gentle rest my head;
And gentle sleep the sleep of death, and gentle hear the voice
Of him that walketh in the garden in the evening time.'[5]
  The Lily of the valley[6] breathing in the humble grass
Answered the lovely maid and said, 'I am a wat'ry weed,
And I am very small, and love to dwell in lowly vales;
So weak, the gilded butterfly scarce perches on my head.
Yet I am visited from heaven, and he that smiles on all
Walks in the valley, and each morn over me spreads his hand
Saying, "Rejoice, thou humble grass, thou new-born lily flower,
Thou gentle maid of silent valleys, and of modest brooks;
For thou shalt be clothed in light and fed with morning manna,[7]

Notes

THE BOOK OF THEL

1 The first two lines of the motto question the perspective from which knowledge can be gained; the second two question the containers of knowledge, either as verbal metaphor or the incarnation of spirit in body. *Silver rod . . . golden bowl* in Ecclesiastes 12: 6 a 'silver cord' and 'golden bowl' are images of mortality.

2 *Thel* Various meanings have been suggested, including 'will', 'wish' or 'desire'.

3 *Mne Seraphim* No one is sure of Blake's meaning. Some suggest that it is an error for 'Bne Seraphim', the sons of the Seraphim. The Seraphim are the order of angels nearest to God, whose duty is to love him.

4 *Adona* related to Adonis, a figure in Greek myth associated with the cycles of the vegetable world.

5 *hear the voice . . . time* cf. Genesis 3: 8: 'And they heard the voice of the Lord God walking in the garden in the cool of the day.'

6 *Lily of the valley* flower of innocence, symbol of Thel's virginity. Cf. Song of Solomon 2: 1: 'the lily of the valleys'.

7 *morning manna* God provided the Israelites with manna (food) in the wilderness, Exodus 16: 14–26.

Till summer's heat melts thee beside the fountains and the springs
To flourish in eternal vales!'' Then why should Thel complain?

[Plate 4]
Why should the mistress of the vales of Har[8] utter a sigh?'
She ceased and smiled in tears, then sat down in her silver shrine.
  Thel answered: 'Oh thou little virgin of the peaceful valley,
Giving to those that cannot crave – the voiceless, the o'ertired;
Thy breath doth nourish the innocent lamb, he smells thy milky garments,
He crops[9] thy flowers while thou sittest smiling in his face,
Wiping his mild and meekin[10] mouth from all contagious taints.
Thy wine doth purify the golden honey; thy perfume,
Which thou dost scatter on every little blade of grass that springs,
Revives the milked cow, and tames the fire-breathing steed.
But Thel is like a faint cloud kindled at the rising sun:
I vanish from my pearly throne, and who shall find my place?'[11]
  'Queen of the vales', the Lily answered, 'ask the tender cloud[12]
And it shall tell thee why it glitters in the morning sky,
And why it scatters its bright beauty through the humid air:
Descend, oh little cloud, and hover before the eyes of Thel.'
  The Cloud descended, and the Lily bowed her modest head
And went to mind her numerous charge among the verdant grass.

[Plate 5]

II

'Oh little Cloud', the virgin said, 'I charge thee tell to me
Why thou complainest not when in one hour thou fade away;
Then we shall seek thee but not find. Ah, Thel is like to thee:
I pass away – yet I complain, and no one hears my voice.'
  The Cloud then showed his golden head and his bright form emerged,
Hovering and glittering on the air before the face of Thel.
  'Oh virgin, know'st thou not our steeds drink of the golden springs[13]
Where Luvah[14] doth renew his horses? Look'st thou on my youth,
And fearest thou because I vanish and am seen no more.
Nothing remains; oh maid, I tell thee, when I pass away,
It is to tenfold life – to love, to peace, and raptures holy;
Unseen descending, weigh my light wings upon balmy flowers,
And court the fair-eyed dew to take me to her shining tent:
The weeping virgin trembling kneels before the risen sun
Till we arise linked in a golden band, and never part,
But walk united, bearing food to all our tender flowers.'

Notes

[8] *Har* another character of Blake's, the father of Tiriel. His valley is a place of innocence.

[9] *crops* eats.

[10] *meekin* meek.

[11] *But Thel . . . place* cf. Job 7: 9: 'As the cloud is consumed and vanisheth away: so he that goeth down to the grave shall come up no more.'

[12] *the tender cloud* the male principle, the fructifier.

[13] *Oh virgin . . . springs* cf. Shakespeare, *Cymbeline* II iii 21–2: 'and Phoebus gins arise, / His steeds to water at those springs.'

[14] *Luvah* god of desire, Prince of Love; one of Blake's Four Zoas (the four principles which rule human life).

'Dost thou, oh little Cloud? I fear that I am not like thee;
For I walk through the vales of Har and smell the sweetest flowers,
But I feed not the little flowers; I hear the warbling birds,
But I feed not the warbling birds – they fly and seek their food.
But Thel delights in these no more because I fade away,
And all shall say, "Without a use this shining woman lived –
Or did she only live to be at death the food of worms." '
The Cloud reclined upon his airy throne and answered thus:
'Then if thou art the food of worms, oh virgin of the skies,
How great thy use, how great thy blessing; everything that lives
Lives not alone, nor for itself: fear not and I will call
The weak worm from its lowly bed, and thou shalt hear its voice.
Come forth, worm of the silent valley, to thy pensive queen.'
The helpless worm arose and sat upon the Lily's leaf,
And the bright Cloud sailed on, to find his partner in the vale.

[Plate 6]

III

Then Thel, astonished, viewed the Worm upon its dewy bed.
'Art thou a Worm? Image of weakness, art thou but a Worm?
I see thee like an infant wrapped in the Lily's leaf;
Ah, weep not, little voice, thou canst not speak[15] but thou canst weep.
Is this a Worm? I see thee lay helpless and naked – weeping,
And none to answer, none to cherish thee with mother's smiles.'
The Clod of Clay[16] heard the Worm's voice and raised her pitying head;
She bowed over the weeping infant, and her life exhaled
In milky fondness, then on Thel she fixed her humble eyes.
'Oh beauty of the vales of Har, we live not for ourselves.
Thou seest me the meanest thing, and so I am indeed;
My bosom of itself is cold, and of itself is dark,

[Plate 7]
But he that loves the lowly pours his oil upon my head,
And kisses me, and binds his nuptial bands around my breast,
And says, "Thou mother of my children, I have loved thee,
And I have given thee a crown that none can take away."[17]
But how this is, sweet maid, I know not and I cannot know;
I ponder and I cannot ponder; yet I live and love.'
The daughter of beauty wiped her pitying tears with her white veil
And said, 'Alas! I knew not this, and therefore did I weep.
That God would love a Worm I knew, and punish the evil foot
That, wilful, bruised its helpless form. But that he cherished it
With milk and oil I never knew; and therefore did I weep,
And I complained in the mild air because I fade away,
And lay me down in thy cold bed, and leave my shining lot.'
'Queen of the vales', the matron Clay answered, 'I heard thy sighs,
And all thy moans flew o'er my roof, but I have called them down.

Notes

[15] *thou canst not speak* a pun on the word 'infant', which means 'without speech' (*in-fans*).

[16] The worm and the clod are the baby and its mother.

[17] *a crown that none can take away* cf. 1 Peter 5:4: 'a crown of glory that fadeth not away'; see also Revelation 3.

Wilt thou, oh Queen, enter my house?[18] 'Tis given thee to enter
And to return; fear nothing, enter with thy virgin feet.'

[Plate 6]

IV

The eternal gate's terrific porter lifted the northern bar;[19]
Thel entered in and saw the secrets of the land unknown;
She saw the couches of the dead, and where the fibrous roots
Of every heart on earth infixes deep its restless twists:
A land of sorrows and of tears where never smile was seen.
She wandered in the land of clouds through valleys dark, list'ning
Dolours and lamentations; waiting oft beside a dewy grave
She stood in silence, list'ning to the voices of the ground,
Till to her own grave-plot she came, and there she sat down[20]
And heard this voice of sorrow breathed from the hollow pit:
'Why cannot the Ear be closed to its own destruction?
Or the glist'ning Eye, to the poison of a smile?
Why are Eyelids stored with arrows ready drawn,
Where a thousand fighting men in ambush lie?
Or an Eye of gifts and graces, show'ring fruits and coined gold?
Why a Tongue impressed with honey from every wind?[21]
Why an Ear, a whirlpool fierce to draw creations in?
Why a Nostril wide inhaling terror, trembling and affright?
Why a tender curb upon the youthful burning boy?
Why a little curtain of flesh[22] on the bed of our desire?'
The virgin started from her seat, and with a shriek
Fled back unhindered till she came into the vales of Har.

The End

Songs of Innocence (1789)

Introduction

Piping down the valleys wild,
Piping songs of pleasant glee,
On a cloud I saw a child
And he laughing said to me:

'Pipe a song about a Lamb!'
So I piped with a merry cheer;
'Piper, pipe that song again!'
So I piped, he wept to hear.

Notes

[18] *my house* cf. Job 17: 13: 'the grave is mine house: I have made my bed in the darkness.'

[19] *The eternal gate's . . . bar* The exact meaning is unclear, although many interpretations have been offered. The porter is variously identified as Pluto, god of the underworld, or as Death, among others.

[20] *there she sat down* cf. Psalm 137: 1: 'By the rivers of Babylon, there we sat down, yea, we wept.'

[21] *Why a Tongue . . . wind* probably a recollection of Spenser, *Faerie Queene* I ix st. 31, 5: 'His subtill tongue, like dropping honny'.

[22] *a little curtain of flesh* the hymen.

'Drop thy pipe, thy happy pipe,
Sing thy songs of happy cheer!'
So I sung the same again
While he wept with joy to hear.

'Piper, sit thee down and write
In a book, that all may read.'
So he vanished from my sight
And I plucked a hollow reed.

And I made a rural pen,
And I stained the water clear,
And I wrote my happy songs
Every child may joy to hear.

Children as an audience.

The Shepherd

How sweet is the Shepherd's sweet lot,
From the morn to the evening he strays;
He shall follow his sheep all the day
And his tongue shall be filled with praise.

For he hears the lambs innocent call,[1]
And he hears the ewes tender reply;
He is watchful while they are in peace,
For they know when their Shepherd is nigh.

The Ecchoing Green

The Sun does arise,
And make happy the skies;
The merry bells ring
To welcome the Spring;
The skylark and thrush,
The birds of the bush,
Sing louder around
To the bells' cheerful sound,
While our sports shall be seen
On the Ecchoing Green.

Old John with white hair
Does laugh away care,
Sitting under the oak
Among the old folk.
They laugh at our play
And soon they all say,

Notes

THE SHEPHERD
[1] *the lambs innocent call* the stray sheep is a biblical symbol; see, for instance, Psalm 119: 176; Isaiah 53: 6; Matthew 18: 12.

'Such, such were the joys
When we all, girls and boys,
In our youth-time were seen
On the Ecchoing Green.'

Till the little ones weary
No more can be merry,
The sun does descend
And our sports have an end:
Round the laps of their mothers,
Many sisters and brothers
Like birds in their nest
Are ready for rest,
And sport no more seen
On the darkening Green.

The Lamb

Little Lamb who made thee?
Dost thou know who made thee?
Gave thee life and bid thee feed
By the stream and o'er the mead;
Gave thee clothing of delight,
Softest clothing woolly bright;
Gave thee such a tender voice,
Making all the vales rejoice:
Little Lamb who made thee?
Dost thou know who made thee?

Little Lamb I'll tell thee,
Little Lamb I'll tell thee;
He is called by thy name,
For he calls himself a Lamb;
He is meek and he is mild,
He became a little child:
I a child and thou a lamb,
We are called by his name,[1]
Little Lamb God bless thee,
Little Lamb God bless thee.

The Little Black Boy[1]

My mother bore me in the southern wild
And I am black, but O! my soul is white.
White as an angel is the English child,
But I am black as if bereaved of light.

Notes

THE LAMB

[1] *I a child . . . his name* Critics note the child's identification with Christ and the lamb.

THE LITTLE BLACK BOY

[1] Blake was aware of the passing of a Bill proposed in the House of Commons on 21 May 1788 by Sir William Dolben MP, which restricted the number of slaves who could be transported from Africa to British colonies in the West Indies.

My mother taught me underneath a tree,
And sitting down before the heat of day,
She took me on her lap and kissed me,
And pointing to the east began to say,

'Look on the rising sun: there God does live[2]
And gives his light, and gives his heat away;
And flowers and trees and beasts and men receive
Comfort in morning, joy in the noonday.

And we are put on earth a little space
That we may learn to bear the beams of love;
And these black bodies and this sunburnt face
Is but a cloud, and like a shady grove.

For when our souls have learned the heat to bear
The cloud will vanish; we shall hear his voice
Saying, "Come out from the grove, my love and care,
And round my golden tent like lambs rejoice."'

Thus did my mother say and kissed me;
And thus I say to little English boy,
When I from black and he from white cloud free,
And round the tent of God like lambs we joy,

I'll shade him from the heat till he can bear
To lean in joy upon our Father's knee;
And then I'll stand and stroke his silver hair,
And be like him, and he will then love me.

The Blossom

Merry Merry Sparrow
Under leaves so green,
A happy Blossom
Sees you swift as arrow;
Seek your cradle narrow
Near my Bosom.

Pretty Pretty Robin
Under leaves so green,
A happy Blossom
Hears you sobbing sobbing,
Pretty Pretty Robin
Near my bosom.

Notes

[2] *Look on the rising sun . . . live* The association of God with the rising sun echoes Isaiah 45: 6; 59: 19: 'So shall they fear the name of the Lord from the west, and his glory from the rising of the sun.'

The Chimney Sweeper[1]

When my mother died I was very young,
And my father sold me while yet my tongue
Could scarcely cry weep weep weep weep,[2]
So your chimneys I sweep, and in soot I sleep.

There's little Tom Dacre, who cried when his head
That curled like a lamb's back, was shaved; so I said,
'Hush Tom never mind it, for when your head's bare
You know that the soot cannot spoil your white hair.'

And so he was quiet, and that very night,
As Tom was a-sleeping he had such a sight,
That thousands of sweepers – Dick, Joe, Ned and Jack –
Were all of them locked up in coffins of black,

And by came an Angel who had a bright key,
And he opened the coffins and set them all free.
Then down a green plain leaping laughing they run
And wash in a river and shine in the Sun.

Then naked and white, all their bags left behind,
They rise upon clouds and sport in the wind;
And the Angel told Tom, if he'd be a good boy;
He'd have God for his father and never want joy.

And so Tom awoke and we rose in the dark
And got with our bags and our brushes to work.
Though the morning was cold, Tom was happy and warm
So if all do their duty, they need not fear harm.

The Little Boy Lost

'Father, father, where are you going?
Oh do not walk so fast.
Speak, father, speak to your little boy
Or else I shall be lost.'

The night was dark, no father was there,
The child was wet with dew;
The mire was deep,[1] and the child did weep,
And away the vapour flew.[2]

Notes

THE CHIMNEY SWEEPER

[1] Blake knew that an attempt was made in 1788 to improve the conditions of child chimney-sweeps: 8 was the proposed minimum age; hours of work would be limited; regulations were proposed to ensure that sweeps were properly washed every week; and a ban proposed on the use of children in chimneys on fire. In the event, the Porter's Act was not passed.

[2] *weep weep weep weep* suggestive of both the child's cry as he touts for work, as well as his grief.

THE LITTLE BOY LOST

[1] *The mire was deep* a biblical image; e.g. Psalm 69: 2: 'I sink in deep mire.'

[2] *away the vapour flew* the boy is led astray by a will-o'-the-wisp.

The Little Boy Found

The little boy lost in the lonely fen,
Led by the wand'ring light,[1]
Began to cry, but God ever nigh,
Appeared like his father in white.[2]

He kissed the child and by the hand led
And to his mother brought,
Who in sorrow pale through the lonely dale
Her little boy weeping sought.

Laughing Song

When the green woods laugh with the voice of joy
And the dimpling stream runs laughing by,
When the air does laugh with our merry wit,
And the green hill laughs with the noise of it.

When the meadows laugh with lively green
And the grasshopper laughs in the merry scene;
When Mary and Susan and Emily
With their sweet round mouths sing, 'Ha, ha, he!'

When the painted birds laugh in the shade
Where our table with cherries and nuts is spread,
Come live and be merry and join with me
To sing the sweet chorus of 'Ha, ha, he!'

A Cradle Song

Sweet dreams form a shade
O'er my lovely infant's head;
Sweet dreams of pleasant streams
By happy silent moony beams.

Sweet sleep with soft down
Weave thy brows an infant crown;
Sweet sleep Angel mild,
Hover o'er my happy child.

Sweet smiles in the night
Hover over my delight;
Sweet smiles, Mother's smiles
All the livelong night beguiles.

Notes

THE LITTLE BOY FOUND

[1] *the wand'ring light* will-o'-the-wisp.

[2] *like his father in white* cf. the transfigured Christ; Matthew 17: 2; Luke 9: 29: 'And as he prayed, the fashion of his countenance was altered, and his raiment was white and glistering.'

Sweet moans, dovelike sighs,
Chase not slumber from thy eyes;
Sweet moans, sweeter smiles,
All the dovelike moans beguiles.

Sleep sleep happy child,
All creation slept and smiled;
Sleep sleep, happy sleep,
While o'er thee thy mother weep.

Sweet babe in thy face,
Holy image I can trace;
Sweet babe once like thee
Thy maker lay and wept for me,

Wept for me, for thee, for all,
When he was an infant small;
Thou his image ever see,
Heavenly face that smiles on thee –

Smiles on thee, on me, on all,
Who became an infant small:
Infant smiles are his own smiles;
Heaven and earth to peace beguiles.[1]

The Divine Image

To Mercy, Pity, Peace and Love
All pray in their distress;
And to these virtues of delight
Return their thankfulness.

For Mercy, Pity, Peace and Love
Is God our Father dear;
And Mercy, Pity, Peace and Love
Is Man his child and care.

For Mercy has a human heart,
Pity a human face;
And Love, the human form divine,
And Peace, the human dress.

Then every man of every clime
That prays in his distress,
Prays to the human form divine
Love, Mercy, Pity, Peace.

Notes

A Cradle Song

[1] *Heaven and earth . . . beguiles* perhaps an echo of Milton's *On the Morning of Christ's Nativity*, where Christ's birth is accompanied by a divine harmony which 'alone / Could hold all heaven and earth in happier union' (ll. 107–8).

And all must love the human form
In heathen, turk or jew;
Where Mercy, Love and Pity dwell
There God is dwelling too.[1]

Holy Thursday[1]

'Twas on a Holy Thursday, their innocent faces clean,
The children walking two and two in red and blue and green,
Grey-headed beadles walked before with wands as white as snow
Till into the high dome of Paul's they like Thames' waters flow.

Oh what a multitude they seemed, these flowers of London town,
Seated in companies they sit with radiance all their own;
The hum of multitudes was there but multitudes of lambs –
Thousands of little boys and girls raising their innocent hands.

Now like a mighty wind they raise to heaven the voice of song,
Or like harmonious thunderings the seats of heaven among;
Beneath them sit the aged men, wise guardians of the poor –
Then cherish pity, lest you drive an angel from your door.

Night

The sun descending in the west,
The evening star does shine;
The birds are silent in their nest
And I must seek for mine.
The moon like a flower
In heaven's high bower
With silent delight
Sits and smiles on the night.

Farewell green fields and happy groves,
Where flocks have took delight;
Where lambs have nibbled, silent moves
The feet of angels bright;
Unseen they pour blessing
And joy without ceasing
On each bud and blossom
And each sleeping bosom.

Notes

The Divine Image

[1] *Where mercy . . . dwelling too* cf. 1 John 4: 16: 'God is love; and he that dwelleth in love dwelleth in God, and God in him.'

Holy Thursday

[1] Blake describes the service for 6,000 or so of the poorest children in the charity schools of London, held in St Paul's Cathedral on the first Thursday in May from 1782 onwards. They would be marched there by their beadles (parish officers) for what Keynes called 'a compulsory exhibition of their piety and gratitude to their patrons'.

They look in every thoughtless nest
Where birds are covered warm,
They visit caves of every beast
To keep them all from harm;
If they see any weeping
That should have been sleeping
They pour sleep on their head
And sit down by their bed.

When wolves and tygers howl for prey
They pitying stand and weep,
Seeking to drive their thirst[1] away
And keep them from the sheep.
But if they rush dreadful,
The angels most heedful
Receive each mild spirit,
New worlds to inherit.

And there the lion's ruddy eyes
Shall flow with tears of gold,
And pitying the tender cries,
And walking round the fold,
Saying, 'Wrath by his[2] meekness,
And by his health sickness
Is driven away
From our immortal day.

And now beside thee bleating lamb,
I can lie down and sleep,
Or think on him who bore thy name,
Graze after thee and weep.
For, washed in life's river,[3]
My bright mane for ever
Shall shine like the gold
As I guard o'er the fold.'

Spring

Sound the flute!
Now it's mute.
Birds delight
Day and Night;
Nightingale
In the dale,
Lark in Sky
Merrily
Merrily Merrily to welcome in the Year.

Notes

NIGHT

[1] *thirst* i.e. for blood.

[2] *his* i.e. Christ's.

[3] *life's river* the River of Life is biblical; see Revelation 22: 1–2.

Little boy
Full of joy;
Little girl
Sweet and small;
Cock does crow,
So do you;
Merry voice,
Infant noise –
Merrily Merrily to welcome in the Year.

Little Lamb
Here I am,[1]
Come and lick
My white neck!
Let me pull
Your soft Wool,
Let me kiss
Your soft face;
Merrily Merrily we welcome in the Year.

Nurse's Song

When the voices of children are heard on the green
And laughing is heard on the hill,
My heart is at rest within my breast
And everything else is still.

'Then come home my children, the sun is gone down
And the dews of night arise;
Come come, leave off play, and let us away
Till the morning appears in the skies.'

'No no let us play, for it is yet day
And we cannot go to sleep;
Besides in the sky, the little birds fly
And the hills are all covered with sheep.'

'Well well, go and play till the light fades away
And then go home to bed.'
The little ones leaped and shouted and laughed
And all the hills ecchoed.

Notes

SPRING

[1] *Here I am* frequently used in the Bible; see Genesis 22: 1, 11; 31: 11.

Infant Joy

'I have no name
I am but two days old.' –
What shall I call thee?
'I happy am,
Joy is my name.' –
Sweet joy befall thee!

Pretty joy!
Sweet joy but two days old,
Sweet joy I call thee;
Thou dost smile,
I sing the while,[1]
Sweet joy befall thee.

A Dream

Once a dream did weave a shade
O'er my Angel-guarded bed,
That an Emmet[1] lost its way
Where on grass methought I lay.

Troubled wildered and forlorn
Dark benighted travel-worn,
Over many a tangled spray,
All heart-broke I heard her say,

'Oh my children! Do they cry,
Do they hear their father sigh?
Now they look abroad to see;
Now return and weep for me.'

Pitying I dropped a tear;
But I saw a glow-worm near
Who replied, 'What wailing wight
Calls the watchman of the night?

I am set to light the ground
While the beetle goes his round;
Follow now the beetle's hum,
Little wanderer hie thee home.'[2]

Notes

Infant Joy

[1] When he read this poem in February 1818, Coleridge marked it as one of his favourites, while proposing a new reading of lines 9–10: 'O smile, O smile! / I'll sing the while' – 'For a babe two days old does not, cannot *smile* – and innocence and the very truth of Nature must go together' (Griggs iv 837).

A Dream

[1] *Emmet* ant.

[2] *Little wanderer, hie thee home* The dor-beetle, which flies after sunset with a humming sound, was known as 'the watchman'. The glow-worm was said, in a folk-song, to light people 'home to bed' on moonless nights.

On Another's Sorrow

Can I see another's woe
And not be in sorrow too?
Can I see another's grief
And not seek for kind relief?

Can I see a falling tear
And not feel my sorrow's share?
Can a father see his child
Weep, nor be with sorrow filled?

Can a mother sit and hear
An infant groan, an infant fear?
No no never can it be,
Never never can it be.

And can he who smiles on all
Hear the wren with sorrows small,
Hear the small bird's grief and care,
Hear the woes that infants bear –

And not sit beside the nest
Pouring pity in their breast?
And not sit the cradle near
Weeping tear on infant's tear?

And not sit both night and day
Wiping all our tears away?
O! no never can it be,
Never never can it be.

He doth give his joy to all,
He becomes an infant small;
He becomes a man of woe,
He doth feel the sorrow too.

Think not thou canst sigh a sigh
And thy maker is not by;
Think not thou canst weep a tear
And thy maker is not near.

O! he gives to us his joy,
That our grief he may destroy;
Till our grief is fled and gone
He doth sit by us and moan.

Songs of Experience (1794)

Introduction

Hear the voice of the Bard!
Who Present, Past and Future sees;
Whose ears have heard
The Holy Word
That walked among the ancient trees

Calling the lapsed Soul,[1]
And weeping in the evening dew;
That might control
The starry pole,
And fallen fallen light renew!

'Oh Earth oh Earth return!
Arise from out the dewy grass;
Night is worn,
And the morn
Rises from the slumberous mass.

Turn away no more:
Why wilt thou turn away?
The starry floor
The wat'ry shore
Is giv'n thee till the break of day.'

Earth's Answer

Earth raised up her head
From the darkness dread and drear;
Her light fled,
Stony dread!
And her locks covered with grey despair.

'Prisoned on wat'ry shore
Starry Jealousy[1] does keep my den
Cold and hoar,
Weeping o'er,
I hear the father of the ancient men.

Notes

Introduction

[1] *Whose ears have heard . . . Soul* cf. Genesis 3: 8, where Adam and Eve, now fallen, 'heard the voice of the Lord God walking in the garden in the cool of the day: and Adam and his wife hid themselves from the presence of the Lord God amongst the trees of the garden.'

Earth's Answer

[1] *Starry Jealousy* The idea of God as jealous is biblical; see Exodus 20: 5; 34: 14, and Deuteronomy 4: 24: 'For the Lord thy God is a consuming fire, even a jealous God.'

Selfish father of men
Cruel jealous selfish fear
Can delight
Chained in night
The virgins of youth and morning bear?

Does spring hide its joy
When buds and blossoms grow?
Does the sower
Sow by night,
Or the ploughman in darkness plough?

Break this heavy chain
That does freeze my bones around!
Selfish! vain!
Eternal bane!
That free Love with bondage bound.'

The Clod and the Pebble

'Love seeketh not Itself to please,
Nor for itself hath any care;
But for another gives its ease
And builds a Heaven in Hell's despair.'

So sung a little Clod of Clay
Trodden with the cattle's feet,
But a Pebble of the brook
Warbled out these metres meet:

'Love seeketh only Self to please,
To bind another to Its delight;
Joys in another's loss of ease,
And builds a Hell in Heaven's despite.'

Holy Thursday

Is this a holy thing to see
In a rich and fruitful land,
Babes reduced to misery,
Fed with cold and usurous hand?

Is that trembling cry a song?
Can it be a song of joy?
And so many children poor?
It is a land of poverty!

And their sun does never shine,
And their fields are bleak and bare,
And their ways are filled with thorns,
It is eternal winter there.

For where'er the sun does shine
And where'er the rain does fall,
Babe can never hunger there,
Nor poverty the mind appall.

The Little Girl Lost[1]

In futurity
I prophetic see
That the earth from sleep
(Grave the sentence deep)

Shall arise and seek
For her maker meek,
And the desert wild
Become a garden mild.

In the southern clime,
Where the summer's prime
Never fades away,
Lovely Lyca lay.

Seven summers old
Lovely Lyca told;
She had wandered long
Hearing wild birds' song.

'Sweet sleep, come to me
Underneath this tree;
Do father, mother weep?
Where can Lyca sleep?

Lost in desert wild
Is your little child;
How can Lyca sleep
If her mother weep?

If her heart does ache
Then let Lyca wake;
If my mother sleep
Lyca shall not weep.

Frowning, frowning night,
O'er this desert bright,
Let thy moon arise
While I close my eyes.'

Notes

THE LITTLE GIRL LOST

[1] This poem, and *The Little Girl Found*, originally appeared in *Songs of Innocence*; in some respects they are counterparts to *The Little Boy Lost* and *The Little Boy Found*.

Sleeping Lyca lay
While the beasts of prey,
Come from caverns deep,
Viewed the maid asleep.

The kingly lion stood
And the virgin viewed,
Then he gambolled round
O'er the hallowed ground.

Leopards, tygers play
Round her as she lay,
While the lion old
Bowed his mane of gold,

And her bosom lick,
And upon her neck
From his eyes of flame
Ruby tears there came;

While the lioness
Loosed her slender dress,
And naked they conveyed
To caves the sleeping maid.[2]

The Little Girl Found

All the night in woe
Lyca's parents go;
Over valleys deep,
While the deserts weep.

Tired and woe-begone,
Hoarse with making moan,
Arm in arm seven days
They traced the desert ways.

Seven nights they sleep
Among shadows deep,
And dream they see their child
Starved in desert wild.

Pale through pathless ways
The fancied image strays –
Famished, weeping, weak,
With hollow piteous shriek.

Notes

[2] The obvious parallel is with Daniel in the lions' den; cf Daniel 6: 16–22, though compare also Isaiah 11: 6: 'The wolf also shall dwell with the lamb, and the leopard shall lie down with the kid; and the calf and the young lion and the fatling together; and a little child shall lead them.'

Rising from unrest,
The trembling woman pressed
With feet of weary woe;
She could no further go.

In his arms he bore
Her, armed with sorrow sore;
Till before their way
A couching lion lay.

Turning back was vain;
Soon his heavy mane
Bore them to the ground:
Then he stalked around

Smelling to his prey.
But their fears allay
When he licks their hands,
And silent by them stands.

They look upon his eyes
Filled with deep surprise,
And wondering behold
A spirit armed in gold.

On his head a crown,
On his shoulders down
Flowed his golden hair;
Gone was all their care.

'Follow me', he said,
'Weep not for the maid;
In my palace deep
Lyca lies asleep.'

Then they followed
Where the vision led,
And saw their sleeping child
Among tygers wild.

To this day they dwell
In a lonely dell;
Nor fear the wolvish howl,
Nor the lion's growl.

The Chimney Sweeper

A little black thing among the snow,
Crying weep, weep, in notes of woe!
'Where are thy father and mother, say?'
'They are both gone up to the church to pray.

Because I was happy upon the heath
And smiled among the winter's snow,
They clothed me in the clothes of death,
And taught me to sing the notes of woe.

And because I am happy and dance and sing,[1]
They think they have done me no injury,
And are gone to praise God and his Priest and King
Who make up a heaven of our misery.'

Nurse's Song

When the voices of children are heard on the green
And whisp'rings are in the dale,
The days of my youth rise fresh in my mind,
My face turns green and pale.

Then come home, my children, the sun is gone down,
And the dews of night arise;
Your spring and your day are wasted in play,
And your winter and night in disguise.

The Sick Rose

Oh Rose thou art sick;
The invisible worm
That flies in the night
In the howling storm

Has found out thy bed
Of crimson joy,
And his dark secret love
Does thy life destroy.

The Fly

Little Fly
Thy summer's play
My thoughtless hand
Has brushed away.[1]

Am not I
A fly like thee?
Or art not thou
A man like me?

Notes

THE CHIMNEY SWEEPER

[1] *And because . . . sing* Erdman suggests a reference to May Day, when sweeps and milkmaids danced in the streets of London in return for alms.

THE FLY

[1] In his notebook, Blake drafted another stanza at this point:

The cut worm
Forgives the plough
And dies in peace
And so do thou.

For I dance
And drink and sing,
Till some blind hand
Shall brush my wing.

If thought is life
And strength and breath,
And the want
Of thought is death,

Then am I
A happy fly,
If I live
Or if I die.

The Angel

I dreamt a Dream! What can it mean?
And that I was a maiden Queen
Guarded by an Angel mild:
Witless woe was ne'er beguiled!

And I wept both night and day,
And he wiped my tears away,
And I wept both day and night,
And hid from him my heart's delight.

So he took his wings and fled,
Then the morn blushed rosy red;
I dried my tears, and armed my fears
With ten thousand shields and spears.

Soon my Angel came again;
I was armed, he came in vain:
For the time of youth was fled
And grey hairs were on my head.

The Tyger[1] (See Plate 6)

Tyger Tyger burning bright
In the forests of the night;
What immortal hand or eye
Could frame thy fearful symmetry?

Notes

THE TYGER

[1] This is regarded as the contrary poem to 'The Lamb' in *Songs of Innocence*. Charles Lamb read it in 1824, and memorized its opening two lines, describing them as 'glorious, but alas! I have not the book; for the man is flown, whither I know not – to Hades or a madhouse. But I must look on him as one of the most extraordinary persons of the age.'

In what distant deeps or skies
Burnt the fire of thine eyes?
On what wings dare he aspire?
What the hand dare seize the fire?

And what shoulder and what art
Could twist the sinews of thy heart?
And when thy heart began to beat,
What dread hand and what dread feet?

What the hammer? What the chain?
In what furnace was thy brain?
What the anvil? What dread grasp
Dare its deadly terrors clasp?

When the stars threw down their spears
And watered heaven with their tears
Did he smile his work to see?
Did he who made the Lamb make thee?

Tyger Tyger burning bright
In the forests of the night:
What immortal hand or eye
Dare frame thy fearful symmetry?

My Pretty Rose-Tree

A flower was offered to me,
Such a flower as May never bore;
But I said, 'I've a Pretty Rose-tree',
And I passed the sweet flower o'er.

Then I went to my Pretty Rose-tree
To tend her by day and by night;
But my Rose turned away with jealousy:
And her thorns were my only delight.

Ah, Sunflower!

Ah, sunflower! weary of time,
Who countest the steps of the Sun,
Seeking after that sweet golden clime
Where the traveller's journey is done;

Where the Youth pined away with desire,
And the pale Virgin shrouded in snow,
Arise from their graves and aspire
Where my Sunflower wishes to go.

The Lily

The modest Rose puts forth a thorn,
The humble Sheep a threat'ning horn;
While the Lily white shall in Love delight,
Nor a thorn nor a threat stain her beauty bright.

The Garden of Love

I went to the Garden of Love
And saw what I never had seen:
A Chapel was built in the midst
Where I used to play on the green.[1]

And the gates of this Chapel were shut,
And 'Thou shalt not' writ over the door;
So I turned to the Garden of Love
That so many sweet flowers bore,

And I saw it was filled with graves
And tombstones where flowers should be;
And Priests in black gowns[2] were walking their rounds,
And binding with briars my joys and desires.

The Little Vagabond

Dear Mother, dear Mother, the Church is cold
But the Alehouse is healthy and pleasant and warm;
Besides I can tell where I am used well –
Such usage in heaven will never do well.

But if at the Church they would give us some Ale,
And a pleasant fire our souls to regale,
We'd sing and we'd pray all the livelong day,
Nor ever once wish from the Church to stray.

Then the Parson might preach and drink and sing,
And we'd be as happy as birds in the spring;
And modest dame Lurch, who is always at Church,
Would not have bandy[1] children nor fasting nor birch.

And God like a father rejoicing to see
His children as pleasant and happy as he,
Would have no more quarrel with the Devil or the Barrel,
But kiss him and give him both drink and apparel.

London

I wander through each chartered[1] street
Near where the chartered Thames does flow,
And mark in every face I meet
Marks of weakness, marks of woe.

Notes

THE GARDEN OF LOVE

[1] *A chapel . . . green* possibly a reference to the building of a chapel on South Lambeth green in 1793. Members of the congregation were required to pay for their places.

[2] *black gowns* In his notebook Blake originally wrote 'black gounds', a Cockney pronunciation, thus giving the line an internal rhyme.

THE LITTLE VAGABOND

[1] *bandy* bandy legs are a symptom of rickets, caused by vitamin deficiency.

LONDON

[1] *chartered* mapped, but also owned by corporations (by the terms of a charter). In Blake's notebook, this originally read, 'dirty'.

Figure 8 Blake's 'London', plate 46 from *Songs of Innocence and Experience* (*c.* 1815–26). On a 'midnight street' a young boy leads an old man on crutches – 'Marks of weakness, marks of woe'. Further down the page, to the right of the text, a naked vagabond warms his hands over a glowing fire. (Fitzwilliam Museum, Cambridge / Bridgeman Art Library.)

In every cry of every Man,
In every Infant's cry of fear,
In every voice, in every ban,
The mind-forged manacles[2] I hear.

How the Chimney-sweeper's cry
Every black'ning church appalls,
And the hapless Soldier's sigh
Runs in blood down Palace walls.

But most through midnight streets I hear
How the youthful Harlot's curse
Blasts the new born Infant's tear,
And blights with plagues the Marriage hearse.[3]

The Human Abstract[1]

Pity would be no more
If we did not make somebody Poor;
And Mercy no more could be,
If all were as happy as we.

And mutual fear brings peace
Till the selfish loves increase;
Then Cruelty knits a snare
And spreads his baits with care.

He sits down with holy fears
And waters the ground with tears;
Then Humility takes its root
Underneath his foot.

Soon spreads the dismal shade
Of Mystery over his head,
And the Caterpillar and Fly
Feed on the Mystery.

And it bears the fruit of Deceit,
Ruddy and sweet to eat;
And the Raven his nest has made
In its thickest shade.

Notes

[2] *mind-forged manacles* The original MS reading is 'German-forged links' – a reference to the House of Hanover, which provided Britain with its monarchs.

[3] *blights with plagues the Marriage hearse* apparently a reference to the passing on of sexually transmitted diseases by mothers to their children.

THE HUMAN ABSTRACT

[1] This song is a counterpart of 'The Divine Image'. Above it in Blake's notebook appear some lines related to it:

How came pride in Man
From Mary it began
How contempt and scorn

The Gods of the earth and sea
Sought through Nature to find this Tree,
But their search was all in vain:
There grows one in the Human Brain.

Infant Sorrow

My mother groaned! my father wept,
Into the dangerous world I leapt:
Helpless, naked, piping loud:
Like a fiend hid in a cloud.

Struggling in my father's hands,
Striving against my swaddling bands,
Bound and weary I thought best
To sulk upon my mother's breast.

A Poison Tree[1]

I was angry with my friend;
I told my wrath, my wrath did end.
I was angry with my foe;
I told it not, my wrath did grow.

And I watered it in fears,
Night and morning with my tears;
And I sunned it with smiles,
And with soft deceitful wiles.

And it grew both day and night
Till it bore an apple bright;
And my foe beheld it shine,
And he knew that it was mine,

And into my garden stole
When the night had veiled the pole –
In the morning glad I see
My foe outstretched beneath the tree.

A Little Boy Lost

'Nought loves another as itself
Nor venerates another so,
Nor is it possible to Thought
A greater than itself to know.

Notes

A Poison Tree

[1] In Blake's notebook this poem was originally entitled 'Christian Forbearance'.

And Father, how can I love you
Or any of my brothers more?
I love you like the little bird
That picks up crumbs around the door.'

The Priest sat by and heard the child,
In trembling zeal he seized his hair;
He led him by his little coat
And all admired the Priestly care.

And standing on the altar high,
'Lo, what a fiend is here!' said he,
'One who sets reason up for judge
Of our most holy Mystery.'

The weeping child could not be heard,
The weeping parents wept in vain;
They stripped him to his little shirt
And bound him in an iron chain,

And burned him in a holy place[1]
Where many had been burned before.
The weeping parents wept in vain –
Are such things done on Albion's shore?

A Little Girl Lost

Children of the future Age
Reading this indignant page,
Know that in a former time
Love! sweet Love! was thought a crime.

In the Age of Gold,
Free from winters cold,
Youth and maiden bright
To the holy light,
Naked in the sunny beams delight.

Once a youthful pair
Filled with softest care
Met in garden bright
Where the holy light
Had just removed the curtains of the night.

There in rising day
On the grass they play;
Parents were afar,
Strangers came not near,
And the maiden soon forgot her fear.

Notes

A LITTLE BOY LOST

[1] *a holy place* biblical name for the sanctuary in the Temple.

Tired with kisses sweet,
They agree to meet
When the silent sleep
Waves o'er heavens deep,
And the weary tired wanderers weep.

To her father white
Came the maiden bright,
But his loving look,
Like the holy book
All her tender limbs with terror shook.

'Ona! pale and weak!
To thy father speak:
Oh the trembling fear!
Oh the dismal care!
That shakes the blossoms of my hoary hair!'

To Tirzah[1]

Whate'er is Born of Mortal Birth
Must be consumed with the Earth
To rise from Generation free;
Then what have I to do with thee?

The Sexes sprung from Shame and Pride –
Blowed in the morn, in evening died;
But Mercy changed Death into Sleep –
The Sexes rose to work and weep.

Thou Mother of my Mortal part,
With cruelty didst mould my Heart
And with false self-deceiving tears
Didst bind my Nostrils Eyes and Ears;

Didst close my Tongue in senseless clay
And me to Mortal Life betray:
The Death of Jesus set me free –
Then what have I to do with thee?[2]
It is Raised
a Spiritual Body[3]

Notes

To Tirzah

[1] This poem does not appear in early copies of the *Songs.* Tirzah was the first capital of the northern kingdom of Israel, a counterpart of Jerusalem in the south; cf. Song of Solomon 6: 4: 'Thou art beautiful, O my love, as Tirzah, comely as Jerusalem, terrible as an army with banners.' See also Numbers 27: 1–11; Blake associated Tirzah with the fallen realm of the senses, a power that confines humanity within a vision of the human body as finite and corrupt.

[2] *Then what . . . thee* cf. Jesus to his mother, John 2: 4: 'what have I to do with thee? Mine hour is not yet come.'

[3] *It is . . . Body* On Blake's plate, these words appear on the garment of an old man ministering to a dead body; they come from 1 Corinthians 15: 44: 'It is sown a natural body; it is raised a spiritual body.'

The Schoolboy[1]

I love to rise in a summer morn
When the birds sing on every tree;
The distant huntsman winds his horn,
And the skylark sings with me –
Oh what sweet company!

But to go to school in a summer morn,
Oh! it drives all joy away;
Under a cruel eye outworn,
The little ones spend the day
In sighing and dismay.

Ah! then at times I drooping sit
And spend many an anxious hour;
Nor in my book can I take delight,
Nor sit in learning's bower,
Worn through with the dreary shower.

How can the bird that is born for joy
Sit in a cage and sing?
How can a child, when fears annoy,
But droop his tender wing
And forget his youthful spring?

Oh! father and mother, if buds are nipped
And blossoms blown away,
And if the tender plants are stripped
Of their joy in the springing day
By sorrow and care's dismay,

How shall the summer arise in joy
Or the summer fruits appear?
Or how shall we gather what griefs destroy,
Or bless the mellowing year
When the blasts of winter appear?

The Voice of the Ancient Bard[1]

Youth of delight come hither
And see the opening morn –
Image of truth new-born;
Doubt is fled and clouds of reason,
Dark disputes and artful teasing.
Folly is an endless maze,
Tangled roots perplex her ways –
How many have fallen there!
They stumble all night over bones of the dead,
And feel they know not what but care,
And wish to lead others, when they should be led.

Notes

THE SCHOOLBOY

[1] This song was originally included in *Songs of Innocence.*

THE VOICE OF THE ANCIENT BARD

[1] This song was originally included in *Songs of Innocence.*

A Divine Image[1]

Cruelty has a Human Heart
And Jealousy a Human Face;
Terror the Human Form Divine,
And Secrecy the Human Dress.

The Human Dress is forged Iron,
The Human Form a fiery Forge,
The Human Face a Furnace sealed,
The Human Heart its hungry Gorge.

The Marriage of Heaven and Hell[1] (1790)[2]

[Plate 2]

The Argument

Rintrah[3] roars and shakes his fires in the burdened air;[4]
Hungry clouds swag[5] on the deep.

Once meek, and in a perilous path,
The just man kept his course along
The vale of death;
Roses are planted where thorns grow,
And on the barren heath
Sing the honey bees.

Then the perilous path was planted;
And a river, and a spring
On every cliff and tomb;
And on the bleached bones[6]
Red clay[7] brought forth.

Notes

A Divine Image

[1] This poem is known to us only through a print made after Blake's death; it appears in one copy of the *Songs*, and was not usually included in the volume. It was apparently composed as a counterpart to 'The Divine Image' in *Songs of Innocence* (p. 185). Blake's design shows a blacksmith hammering at a wall round the sun.

The Marriage of Heaven and Hell

[1] Blake's title alludes to two of Swedenborg's: *De coelo . . . et de inferno* and *De amore conjugali* (*A Treatise Concerning Heaven and Hell* and *Marital Love*). For more on Blake's attitude to Swedenborg, see headnote, p. 171 above.

[2] Various datings have been suggested over the years, but the editors of the Blake Trust/Tate Gallery edition settle on 1790.

[3] *Rintrah* the just wrath of the prophet, presaging revolution.

[4] *Rintrah . . . air* cf. Amos 1: 2: 'The Lord will roar from Zion, and utter his voice from Jerusalem.'

[5] *swag* sway, sag.

[6] *bleached bones* a valley of dry bones symbolizes the exiled 'house of Israel', Ezekiel 37: 3–4.

[7] *Red clay* sometimes taken to mean Adam, the first man, formed from the dust of the ground.

Till the villain left the paths of ease
To walk in perilous paths, and drive
The just man into barren climes.

Now the sneaking serpent walks
In mild humility
And the just man rages in the wilds
Where lions roam.

Rintrah roars and shakes his fires in the burdened air;
Hungry clouds swag on the deep.

[Plate 3]
As a new heaven is begun, and it is now thirty-three years since its advent: the Eternal Hell revives.[8] And lo! Swedenborg is the Angel sitting at the tomb; his writings are the linen clothes folded up.[9] Now is the dominion of Edom,[10] and the return of Adam into Paradise; see Isaiah 34 and 35.[11]

Without Contraries is no progression. Attraction and Repulsion, Reason and Energy, Love and Hate, are necessary to Human existence.[12]

From these contraries spring what the religious call Good and Evil. Good is the passive that obeys Reason. Evil is the active springing from Energy.[13]

Good is Heaven. Evil is Hell.

The Voice of the Devil

All Bibles or sacred codes have been the causes of the following errors.

1. That man has two real existing principles, viz. a Body and a Soul.
2. That Energy,[14] called Evil, is alone from the Body, and that Reason, called Good, is alone from the Soul.
3. That God will torment man in eternity for following his Energies.

But the following Contraries to these are True

1. Man has no Body distinct from his Soul, for that called Body is a portion of Soul discerned by the five Senses (the chief inlets of Soul in this age).
2. Energy is the only life and is from the Body, and Reason is the bound or outward circumference of Energy.
3. Energy is Eternal Delight.

Notes

[8] *As a new heaven . . . revives* In 1790 it was 33 years since 1757, the year of the Swedenborgian Last Judgement and (coincidentally) Blake's birth. Christ was 33 at the time of his crucifixion and resurrection. Thus, Blake identifies his lifetime with Christ's and the eternal hell resurrected.

[9] *his writings . . . folded up* Jesus' body was wrapped in a linen shroud, laid in a sepulchre, and closed with a rock (Mark 15: 46). When three women came to anoint the body, they found the stone rolled aside and the body gone.

[10] *Edom* Esau, cheated of his birthright by his brother Jacob (Genesis 25: 29–34); his dominion is foreseen by his father, Isaac (Genesis 27: 40). The dominion of Edom is a time when the just man has restored to him what is his due – effectively, a time of revolution.

[11] *Isaiah 34 and 35* Isaiah 34 prophesies the 'day of the Lord's vengeance' against the enemies of Israel; Isaiah 35 concerns the restoration of power to Israel. Blake may have interpreted them as being about the French Revolution.

[12] *Without contraries . . . existence* a swipe at Swedenborg's theory of correspondence and equilibrium.

[13] *Good is . . . Energy* cf. Blake's marginalia in Lavater's *Aphorisms*: 'Active evil is better than passive good.'

[14] *Energy* a term associated with revolutionary action, particularly in discussions of current events in Revolutionary France; Burke commented on 'this dreadful and portentous energy' in 1790.

[Plate 5]

Those who restrain desire do so because theirs is weak enough to be restrained; and the restrainer (or Reason) usurps its place and governs the unwilling.

And, being restrained, it by degrees becomes passive, till it is only the shadow of desire.

The history of this is written in *Paradise Lost*, and the Governor (or Reason) is called Messiah.

And the original Archangel, or possessor of the command of the heavenly host, is called the Devil or Satan, and his children are called Sin and Death.[15]

But in the Book of Job, Milton's Messiah is called Satan.[16]

For this history has been adopted by both parties.

It indeed appeared to Reason as if Desire was cast out, but the Devil's account is that the Messi- [Plate 6] -ah fell, and formed a heaven of what he stole from the Abyss.

This is shown in the Gospel, where he prays to the Father to send the comforter, or Desire,[17] that Reason may have Ideas to build on, the Jehovah of the Bible being no other than he[18] who dwells in flaming fire.

Know that after Christ's death he became Jehovah.

But in Milton the Father is Destiny, the Son a Ratio of the five senses, and the Holy Ghost, Vacuum!

Note: The reason Milton wrote in fetters when he wrote of Angels and God, and at liberty when of Devils and Hell, is because he was a true Poet and of the Devil's party without knowing it.

A Memorable Fancy[19] [The Five Senses]

As I was walking among the fires of hell,[20] delighted with the enjoyments of Genius (which to Angels look like torment and insanity), I collected some of their Proverbs, thinking that as the sayings used in a nation mark its character, so the Proverbs of Hell show the nature of infernal wisdom better than any description of buildings or garments.

When I came home,[21] on the abyss of the five senses, where a flat-sided steep frowns over the present world,[22] I saw a mighty Devil[23] folded in black clouds hovering on the sides of the rock; with cor- [Plate 7] -roding fires[24] he wrote the following sentence, now perceived by the minds of men, and read by them on earth.

Notes

[15] *The history . . . Death* a deliberate inversion of the plan of Milton's poem, by which it becomes the story of how desire and energy is usurped by restraint and reason. Blake casts Jesus as Reason and Satan as the hero. In *Paradise Lost* Satan's daughter, Sin, is born from his head, and Death is the product of their incestuous union.

[16] *But in the Book . . . Satan* In Job, Satan accuses and torments Job (as God's agent); likewise, 'Milton's Messiah' accuses and torments Adam and Eve.

[17] *This is shown . . . Desire* a reference to John 14: 16-17, 26, where Jesus tells his disciples that he will pray to the 'Father' to 'give you another Comforter', which is 'the Spirit of truth' and 'the Holy Ghost'.

[18] *he* Blake originally etched 'the Devil'.

[19] The 'Memorable Fancy' parodies Swedenborg's 'Memorable Relations' – short tales used to underline particular ideas.

[20] *As I was walking . . . Hell* parodic of Swedenborg's excursions in the spiritual world.

[21] *home* various interpretations have been suggested: the world of daily business; Blake's workshop; or England.

[22] *on the abyss . . . world* In Blake's metaphor the abyss is the head, where all five senses are located, and the cliff is the face.

[23] *a mighty Devil* Blake himself, who has hell inside his head. He sees himself reflected in the copper plate.

[24] *With corroding fires* acids; Blake etched sentences into copper plates with acids.

How do you know but ev'ry Bird that cuts the airy way,
Is an immense world of delight, closed by your senses five?[25]

Proverbs of Hell[26]

In seed-time learn, in harvest teach, in winter enjoy.
Drive your cart and your plough over the bones of the dead.
The road of excess leads to the palace of wisdom.
Prudence is a rich ugly old maid courted by Incapacity.
He who desires but acts not breeds pestilence.
The cut worm forgives the plough.
Dip him in the river who loves water.
A fool sees not the same tree that a wise man sees.
He whose face gives no light shall never become a star.
Eternity is in love with the productions of time.
The busy bee has no time for sorrow.
The hours of folly are measured by the clock, but of wisdom: no clock can measure.
All wholesome food is caught without a net or a trap.
Bring out number, weight and measure in a year of dearth.
No bird soars too high, if he soars with his own wings.
A dead body revenges not injuries.
The most sublime act is to set another before you.
If the fool would persist in his folly he would become wise.
Folly is the cloak of knavery.
Shame is Pride's cloak.
[Plate 8]
Prisons are built with stones of Law, Brothels with bricks of Religion.
The pride of the peacock is the glory of God.
The lust of the goat is the bounty of God.
The wrath of the lion is the wisdom of God.
The nakedness of woman is the work of God.
Excess of sorrow laughs. Excess of joy weeps.
The roaring of lions, the howling of wolves, the raging of the stormy sea, and the destructive sword, are portions of eternity too great for the eye of man.
The fox condemns the trap, not himself.
Joys impregnate, Sorrows bring forth.
Let man wear the fell[27] of the lion, woman the fleece of the sheep.
The bird a nest, the spider a web, man friendship.
The selfish smiling fool and the sullen frowning fool shall be both thought wise, that they may be a rod.
What is now proved, was once only imagined.
The rat, the mouse, the fox, the rabbit, watch the roots; the lion, the tiger, the horse, the elephant, watch the fruits.
The cistern contains; the fountain overflows.
One thought fills immensity.

Notes

[25] *How do you know . . . five* an echo of Chatterton, *Bristowe Tragedie, or the Dethe of Syr Charles Bawdin* (1768): 'How dydd I knowe thatt ev'ry darte/That cutte the airie waie/Myghte nott fynde passage toe my harte/And close myne eyes for aie?'

[26] The proverb or aphorism was a widely employed literary form; Blake knew the biblical Book of Proverbs and Lavater's *Aphorisms on Man* (1788), among others.

[27] *fell* skin.

Always be ready to speak your mind, and a base man will avoid you.
Every thing possible to be believed is an image of truth.
The eagle never lost so much time as when he submitted to learn of the crow.
[Plate 9]
The fox provides for himself, but God provides for the lion.
Think in the morning, Act in the noon, Eat in the evening, Sleep in the night.
He who has suffered you to impose on him knows you.
As the plough follows words, so God rewards prayers.
The tygers of wrath are wiser than the horses of instruction.
Expect poison from the standing water.
You never know what is enough unless you know what is more than enough.
Listen to the fool's reproach! It is a kingly title!
The eyes of fire, the nostrils of air, the mouth of water, the beard of earth.
The weak in courage is strong in cunning.
The apple tree never asks the beech how he shall grow; nor the lion, the horse how he shall take his prey.
The thankful receiver bears a plentiful harvest.
If others had not been foolish, we should be so.
The soul of sweet delight can never be defiled.
When thou seest an Eagle, thou seest a portion of Genius, lift up thy head!
As the caterpillar chooses the fairest leaves to lay her eggs on, so the priest lays his curse on the fairest joys.[28]
To create a little flower is the labour of ages.
'Damn!' braces; 'Bless!' relaxes.
The best wine is the oldest, the best water the newest.
Prayers plough not! Praises reap not!
Joys laugh not! Sorrows weep not!
[Plate 10]
The head Sublime, the heart Pathos, the genitals Beauty, the hands and feet Proportion.
As the air to a bird or the sea to a fish, so is contempt to the contemptible.
The crow wished everything was black; the owl that everything was white.
Exuberance is Beauty.
If the lion was advised by the fox, he would be cunning.
Improvement makes straight roads, but the crooked roads without improvement are roads of Genius.
Sooner murder an infant in its cradle than nurse unacted desires.
Where man is not nature is barren.
Truth can never be told so as to be understood, and not be believed.
Enough! or Too much.
[Plate 11]

The ancient Poets animated all sensible objects with Gods or Geniuses, calling them by the names and adorning them with the properties of woods, rivers, mountains, lakes, cities, nations, and whatever their enlarged and numerous senses could perceive.

And particularly they studied the genius of each city and country, placing it under its mental deity.

Till a system was formed, which some took advantage of, and enslaved the vulgar by attempting to realize or abstract the mental deities from their objects: thus began Priesthood.

Notes

[28] Cf. 'The Garden of Love' 11–12.

Choosing forms of worship from poetic tales.
And at length they pronounced that the Gods had ordered such things.
Thus men forgot that All deities reside in the human breast.

[Plate 12]

A Memorable Fancy [Isaiah and Ezekiel]

The Prophets Isaiah and Ezekiel dined with me, and I asked them how they dared so roundly to assert that God spake to them, and whether they did not think at the time that they would be misunderstood, and so be the cause of imposition?

Isaiah answered, 'I saw no God, nor heard any, in a finite organical perception.[29] But my senses discovered the infinite in everything, and, as I was then persuaded, and remain confirmed, that the voice of honest indignation[30] is the voice of God, I cared not for consequences, but wrote.'

Then I asked, 'Does a firm persuasion that a thing is so, make it so?'

He replied, 'All poets believe that it does, and in ages of imagination this firm persuasion removed mountains;[31] but many are not capable of a firm persuasion of anything.'

Then Ezekiel said, 'The philosophy of the east taught the first principles of human perception. Some nations held one principle for the origin and some another. We of Israel taught that the Poetic Genius (as you now call it) was the first principle and all the others merely derivative, which was the cause of our despising the Priests and Philosophers of other countries, and prophesying that all Gods would [Plate 13] at last be proved to originate in ours and to be the tributaries of the Poetic Genius. It was this that our great poet King David[32] desired so fervently, and invokes so pathetic'ly,[33] saying by this he conquers enemies and governs kingdoms. And we so loved our God that we cursed in his name all the deities of surrounding nations,[34] and asserted that they had rebelled. From these opinions the vulgar came to think that all nations would at last be subject to the jews.

'This', said he, 'like all firm persuasions, is come to pass, for all nations believe the jews' code and worship the jews' god, and what greater subjection can be?'

I heard this with some wonder, and must confess my own conviction. After dinner I asked Isaiah to favour the world with his lost works; he said none of equal value was lost. Ezekiel said the same of his.

I also asked Isaiah what made him go naked and barefoot three years? He answered, 'The same that made our friend Diogenes the Grecian.'[35]

I then asked Ezekiel why he ate dung, and lay so long on his right and left side?[36] He answered, 'The desire of raising other men into a perception of the infinite: this the

Notes

[29] *I saw no God . . . perception* Though appropriated for the priesthood by the religious, Isaiah is here reclaimed for the just man. The statement is highly subversive of the Bible, where Isaiah is inclined to say such things as 'Moreover the Lord said unto me' (Isaiah 8: 1).

[30] *honest indignation* at, for instance, social or political injustice. In the Bible indignation is attributed, by contrast, to God: 'his lips are full of indignation' (Isaiah 30: 27).

[31] *removed mountains* an allusion to Jesus, who withers a fig tree with his words, and tells his disciples, 'if ye have faith, and doubt not . . . if ye shall say unto this mountain, Be thou removed, and be thou cast into the sea; it shall be done' (Matthew 21: 21).

[32] *our great poet King David* second king of Judah and Israel, author of the Psalms.

[33] *pathetic'ly* movingly.

[34] *And we so loved . . . nations* ironic; Isaiah and Ezekiel curse the deities of other nations, and predict their destruction (Isaiah 19, Ezekiel 29–32).

[35] *Diogenes the Grecian* Greek philosopher of the Cynic school (d. 320 BC), said to have wandered through Athens with a lantern searching for one honest person; also said to have lived in a barrel.

[36] *I then asked Ezekiel . . . side* Ezekiel lay 390 days on his left side, 40 on his right. He did not eat dung but cooked with it (Ezekiel 4).

North American tribes practise, and is he honest who resists his genius or conscience, only for the sake of present ease or gratification?'

[Plate 14]

The ancient tradition that the world will be consumed in fire at the end of six thousand years is true,[37] as I have heard from Hell.

For the cherub with his flaming sword is hereby commanded to leave his guard at the tree of life;[38] and when he does, the whole creation will be consumed and appear infinite and holy, whereas it now appears finite and corrupt.

This will come to pass by an improvement of sensual enjoyment.

But first the notion that man has a body distinct from his soul is to be expunged. This I shall do by printing in the infernal method, by corrosives,[39] which in Hell are salutary and medicinal, melting apparent surfaces away, and displaying the infinite which was hid.

If the doors of perception were cleansed, everything would appear to man as it is: Infinite.

For man has closed himself up till he sees all things through narrow chinks of his cavern.

[Plate 15]

A Memorable Fancy [A Printing-House in Hell][40]

I was in a printing-house in Hell and saw the method in which knowledge is transmitted from generation to generation.

In the first chamber was a Dragon-Man, clearing away the rubbish from a cave's mouth; within, a number of Dragons were hollowing the cave.

In the second chamber was a Viper[41] folding round the rock and the cave, and others adorning it with gold, silver, and precious stones.

In the third chamber was an Eagle with wings and feathers of air[42] – he caused the inside of the cave to be infinite; around were numbers of Eagle-like men, who built palaces in the immense cliffs.

In the fourth chamber were Lions of flaming fire, raging around and melting the metals into living fluids.

In the fifth chamber were unnamed forms, which cast the metals into the expanse.[43]

There they were received by Men who occupied the sixth chamber, and took the forms of books and were arranged in libraries.

[Plate 16]

The Giants who formed this world into its sensual existence and now seem to live in it in chains are, in truth, the causes of its life and the sources of all activity;[44] but the chains are the cunning of weak and tame minds, which have power to resist energy.

Notes

[37] *The ancient tradition . . . true* In the fashion of Swedenborg, Blake predicts the end of the world. It was widely believed, at the end of the 18th century, that the 6,000 year lifespan of the world was about to end.

[38] *For the cherub . . . life* At Genesis 3: 22, 24, cherubim are commanded to guard the way of the tree of life with a flaming sword.

[39] *corrosives* Blake's printing technique involved the use of acid.

[40] This memorable fancy picks up the metaphor of body as cave, in order to show how the 'doors of perception' can be cleansed by 'a printing-house in hell' with five chambers (one for each sense) and a sixth where men receive the products of the first five. The printing-house produces imaginative ('infernal') thoughts.

[41] *Viper* perhaps a brush or pen, or the lines made by such implements.

[42] *feathers of air* Blake used feathers in his printing process, perhaps to stir the acid over his plates.

[43] *cast the metals . . . expanse* probably copper plates 'cast . . . into the expanse' of paper, during the printing process.

[44] *The Giants . . . activity* By contrast, Swedenborg condemned the antediluvian giants at Genesis 6: 4 for self-love and sensuality.

According to the proverb, the weak in courage is strong in cunning.

Thus one portion of being is the Prolific; the other, the Devouring. To the devourer it seems as if the producer was in his chains, but it is not so: he only takes portions of existence and fancies that the whole.

But the Prolific would cease to be Prolific unless the Devourer as a sea received the excess of his delights.

Some will say, 'Is not God alone the Prolific?' I answer, 'God only acts and is in existing beings or men.'

These two classes of men are always upon earth, and they should be enemies; whoever tries [Plate 17] to reconcile them seeks to destroy existence.

Religion is an endeavour to reconcile the two.

Note: Jesus Christ did not wish to unite, but to separate them (as in the parable of sheep and goats[45]), and he says, 'I came not to send Peace but a Sword.'[46]

Messiah or Satan or Tempter was formerly thought to be one of the Antediluvians who are our Energies.

A Memorable Fancy [The Vanity of Angels][47]

An Angel came to me and said, 'Oh pitiable foolish young man! Oh horrible! Oh dreadful state! Consider the hot burning dungeon thou art preparing for thyself to all eternity, to which thou art going in such career.'

I said, 'Perhaps you will be willing to show me my eternal lot, and we will contemplate together upon it and see whether your lot or mine is most desirable.'

So he took me through a stable, and through a church, and down into the church-vault, at the end of which was a mill.[48] Through the mill we went, and came to a cave. Down the winding cavern we groped our tedious way, till a void, boundless as a nether sky, appeared beneath us, and we held by the roots of trees and hung over this immensity. But I said, 'If you please, we will commit ourselves to this void, and see whether providence is here also; if you will not, I will'. But he answered, 'Do not presume, oh young man; but as we here remain, behold thy lot which will soon appear when the darkness passes away.'

So I remained with him, sitting in the twisted [Plate 18] root of an oak. He was suspended in a fungus which hung with the head downward into the deep.

By degrees we beheld the infinite Abyss,[49] fiery as the smoke of a burning city; beneath us, at an immense distance, was the sun, black but shining; round it were fiery tracks on which revolved vast spiders, crawling after their prey, which flew, or rather swum, in the infinite deep, in the most terrific shapes of animals sprung from corruption. And the air was full of them, and seemed composed of them. These are Devils, and are called Powers of the air. I now asked my companion which was my eternal lot? He said, 'Between the black and white spiders.'[50]

Notes

45 Matthew 25: 32–3.

46 Matthew 10: 34. See also Luke 12: 51, where Jesus asks: 'Suppose ye that I am come to give peace on earth? I tell you, nay; but rather division.'

47 This memorable fancy is based on an episode in Swedenborg's *Conjugal Love* in which an angel shows a young man various contrary visions by alternately opening his internal, and closing his external sight. Blake satirizes Swedenborg by giving his narrator the energy and wisdom to challenge his angelic guide.

48 *So he took me . . . mill* The church is entered through a stable of rationalism and leads to the mill of mechanistic philosophy that Blake so thoroughly despised.

49 *the infinite Abyss* presumably hell.

50 *Between the black and white spiders* In Swedenborgian terms, an existence between false reasoners, perhaps between false contraries such as good and evil.

But now, from between the black and white spiders, a cloud and fire burst and rolled through the deep, black'ning all beneath so that the nether deep grew black as a sea, and rolled with a terrible noise: beneath us was nothing now to be seen but a black tempest, till, looking east[51] between the clouds and the waves, we saw a cataract of blood mixed with fire; and, not many stones' throw from us, appeared and sunk again the scaly fold of a monstrous serpent. At last, to the east, distant about three degrees,[52] appeared a fiery crest above the waves. Slowly it reared, like a ridge of golden rocks, till we discovered two globes of crimson fire from which the sea fled away in clouds of smoke. And now we saw it was the head of Leviathan.[53] His forehead was divided into streaks of green and purple, like those on a tiger's forehead; soon we saw his mouth and red gills hang just above the raging foam, tinging the black deep with beams of blood, advancing toward us [Plate 19] with all the fury of a spiritual existence.

My friend the Angel climbed up from his station into the mill; I remained alone, and then this appearance was no more, but I found myself sitting on a pleasant bank beside a river by moonlight, hearing a harper who sung to the harp.[54] And his theme was, 'The man who never alters his opinion is like standing water, and breeds reptiles of the mind.'

But I arose and sought for the mill, and there I found my Angel who, surprised, asked me how I escaped.

I answered, 'All that we saw was owing to your metaphysics. For when you ran away, I found myself on a bank by moonlight hearing a harper. But now we have seen my eternal lot, shall I show you yours?' He laughed at my proposal, but I by force suddenly caught him in my arms, and flew westerly through the night, till we were elevated above the earth's shadow.[55] Then I flung myself with him directly into the body of the sun; here I clothed myself in white, and, taking in my hand Swedenborg's volumes, sunk from the glorious clime, and passed all the planets till we came to Saturn. Here I stayed to rest, and then leaped into the void between saturn and the fixed stars.[56]

'Here', said I, 'is your lot – in this space (if space it may be called[57]).' Soon we saw the stable and the church, and I took him to the altar, and opened the Bible, and lo! it was a deep pit, into which I descended, driving the angel before me. Soon we saw seven houses of brick.[58] One we entered; in it were a [Plate 20] number of monkeys, baboons, and all of that species, chained by the middle, grinning and snatching at one another, but withheld by the shortness of their chains. However, I saw that they sometimes grew numerous, and then the weak were caught by the strong, and, with a grinning aspect, first coupled with, and then devoured, by plucking off first one limb and then another, till the body was left a helpless trunk. This, after grinning and kissing it with seeming fondness, they devoured too. And here and there I saw one savourily picking the flesh off of his own tail. As the stench terribly annoyed us both,

Notes

[51] *east* In Swedenborg the Lord is always 'to the east'.

[52] *distant . . . degrees* Paris, centre of the French Revolution, is three degrees in longitude from London.

[53] *Leviathan* huge sea-dragon associated with eclipses of sun and moon, who threatens the natural order; see Isaiah 27: 1 and Revelation 13: 2, for instance. Blake probably has in mind the prophecy in Revelation that the Leviathan will be cast in a pit for a thousand years before being loosed – effectively turning him into a version of the just man whose time has come (Revelation 11: 7; 20: 1–3).

[54] *and then this . . . harp* The abrupt transition mimics, and to some extent parodies, that at Revelation 13–14, where the vision of the beast suddenly gives way to a vision of the Lamb where John hears 'the voice of harpers harping with their harps' (Revelation 14:2–3).

[55] *I by force . . . shadow* a parody of Swedenborgian space travel.

[56] *into the void . . . stars* i.e. into an intellectual vacuum.

[57] *if space it may be called* The phrasing echoes Milton's description of Death.

[58] *seven houses of brick* houses in Swedenborg signify states of mind; possibly also a reference to the seven churches of Asia castigated by John, Revelation 1:4.

we went into the mill, and I in my hand brought the skeleton of a body, which in the mill was Aristotle's Analytics.[59]

So the Angel said, 'Thy fantasy has imposed upon me and thou oughtest to be ashamed.'

I answered, 'We impose on one another, and it is but lost time to converse with you whose works are only Analytics.'

Opposition is true friendship.

[Plate 21]

I have always found that Angels have the vanity to speak of themselves as the only wise; this they do with a confident insolence sprouting from systematic reasoning.

Thus Swedenborg boasts that what he writes is new, though it is only the contents or index of already published books.

A man carried a monkey about for a show, and, because he was a little wiser than the monkey, grew vain, and conceived himself as much wiser than seven men. It is so with Swedenborg: he shows the folly of churches and exposes hypocrites, till he imagines that all are religious, and himself the single [Plate 22] one on earth that ever broke a net.

Now hear a plain fact: Swedenborg has not written one new truth. Now hear another: he has written all the old falsehoods.

And now hear the reason: he conversed with Angels, who are all religious, and conversed not with Devils who all hate religion, for he was incapable through his conceited notions.

Thus Swedenborg's writings are a recapitulation of all superficial opinions, and an analysis of the more sublime – but no further.

Have now another plain fact: any man of mechanical talents may, from the writings of Paracelsus or Jacob Behmen,[60] produce ten thousand volumes of equal value with Swedenborg's – and, from those of Dante or Shakespeare, an infinite number.

But when he has done this, let him not say that he knows better than his master, for he only holds a candle in sunshine.

A Memorable Fancy [A Devil, My Friend]

Once I saw a Devil in a flame of fire, who arose before an Angel that sat on a cloud, and the Devil uttered these words:

'The worship of God is honouring his gifts in other men, each according to his genius, and loving the [Plate 23] greatest men best. Those who envy or calumniate great men hate God, for there is no other God.'

The Angel hearing this became almost blue; but, mastering himself, he grew yellow, and, at last, white, pink and smiling. And then replied:

'Thou idolater! Is not God One? And is not he visible in Jesus Christ? And has not Jesus Christ given his sanction to the law of ten commandments, and are not all other men fools, sinners and nothings?'

Notes

[59] *Analytics* Aristotle wrote two volumes of *Analytics*, which serve to symbolize an inhuman rationality. Its transformation from the monkey skeleton parodies similar transformations in Swedenborg.

[60] *Paracelsus or Jacob Behmen* Philippus Aureolus Theophrastus Bombastus von Hohenheim, known as Paracelsus (1493–1541), a Swiss-German physician and alchemist; Jakob Boehme (1575–1624), German cobbler and mystic. Blake placed Paracelsus and Boehme alongside Shakespeare among his closest spiritual friends.

The Devil answered, 'Bray a fool in a mortar with wheat, yet shall not his folly be beaten out of him.[61] If Jesus Christ is the greatest man, you ought to love him in the greatest degree; now hear how he has given his sanction to the law of ten commandments. Did he not mock at the Sabbath, and so mock the Sabbath's God? Murder those who were murdered because of him? Turn away the law from the woman taken in adultery? Steal the labour of others to support him? Bear false witness when he omitted making a defence before Pilate? Covet when he prayed for his disciples, and when he bid them shake off the dust of their feet against such as refused to lodge them? I tell you, no virtue can exist without breaking these ten commandments: Jesus was all virtue and acted from impulse, [Plate 24] not from rules.'

When he had so spoken, I beheld the Angel who stretched out his arms embracing the flame of fire, and he was consumed and arose as Elijah.[62]

Note: This Angel, who is now become a Devil, is my particular friend: we often read the Bible together in its infernal or diabolical sense, which the world shall have if they behave well.

I have also the Bible of Hell:[63] which the world shall have whether they will or no.

One law for the lion and ox is oppression.[64]

[Plate 25]

A Song of Liberty[65]

1. The Eternal Female groaned![66] It was heard over all the Earth:
2. Albion's[67] coast is sick, silent; the American meadows faint!
3. Shadows of Prophecy shiver along by the lakes and the rivers, and mutter across the ocean! France, rend down thy dungeon;[68]
4. Golden Spain, burst the barriers of old Rome;[69]
5. Cast thy keys,[70] oh Rome, into the deep down falling, even to eternity down falling,
6. And weep![71]
7. In her trembling hands, she took the new-born terror howling;
8. On those infinite mountains of light now barred out by the Atlantic sea,[72] the new-born fire stood before the starry king![73]
9. Flagged[74] with grey-browed snows and thunderous visages, the jealous wings[75] waved over the deep.
10. The speary hand burned aloft, unbuckled was the shield, forth went the hand of jealousy among the flaming hair, and [Plate 26] hurled the new-born wonder[76] through the starry night.
11. The fire, the fire, is falling!

Notes

[61] *Bray a fool . . . him* cf. Proverbs 27: 22: 'Though thou shouldest bray [crush] a fool in a mortar among wheat with a pestle, yet will not his foolishness depart from him.'

[62] *I beheld . . . Elijah* Elijah is taken up to heaven in a chariot of fire, 2 Kings 2: 11.

[63] *the Bible of Hell* possibly a work projected by Blake, which might have included the Proverbs of Hell and *Urizen*.

[64] Above this motto in Blake's plate, a bearded man, looking at the reader with an expression of anguish, crawls along the ground on all fours, naked.

[65] Some have argued that this originated as a separate work from the *Marriage*.

[66] *The Eternal Female groaned* This momentous birth (of Revolution) heralds an apocalypse.

[67] *Albion* England.

[68] *France, rend down thy dungeon* The Bastille prison was stormed by the mob, and demolished, in July 1789. It was a powerful symbol of liberation.

[69] *Rome* the Roman Catholic Church.

[70] *keys* keys of St Peter, symbolic of papal power.

[71] This line originally read: 'And weep and bow thy reverend locks.'

[72] *On those . . . sea* the mythical ancient kingdom of Atlantis.

[73] *the starry king* Urizen, the primeval priest, in this case a type of the oppressive ruler.

[74] *Flagged* covered.

[75] *the jealous wings* of Urizen; cf. 'Earth's Answer' 7 and n.

[76] *the new-born wonder* Orc, spirit of revolution.

12. Look up! Look up! Oh citizen of London, enlarge thy countenance! Oh Jew, leave counting gold, return to thy oil and wine! Oh African! Black African! (Go, winged thought, widen his forehead.)[77]
13. The fiery limbs, the flaming hair, shot like the sinking sun into the western sea.
14. Waked from his eternal sleep, the hoary element[78] roaring fled away;
15. Down rushed, beating his wings in vain the jealous king;[79] his grey-browed counsellors, thunderous warriors, curled veterans, among helms and shields and chariots, horses, elephants: banners, castles, slings and rocks,
16. Falling, rushing, ruining! buried in the ruins, on Urthona's[80] dens.
17. All night beneath the ruins; then their sullen flames faded emerge round the gloomy king.
18. With thunder and fire: leading his starry hosts through the waste wilderness [Plate 27] he promulgates his ten commands,[81] glancing his beamy eyelids over the deep in dark dismay,
19. Where the son of fire[82] in his eastern cloud, while the morning plumes her golden breast,
20. Spurning the clouds written with curses, stamps the stony law[83] to dust, loosing the eternal horses from the dens of night, crying, 'Empire is no more! And now the lion and wolf shall cease.'[84]

Chorus

Let the priests of the Raven of dawn no longer, in deadly black, with hoarse note, curse the sons of joy; nor his accepted brethren (whom, tyrant, he calls free) lay the bound or build the roof; nor pale religious lechery call that virginity that wishes but acts not!

For everything that lives is Holy.[85]

Visions of the Daughters of Albion (1793)

[Plate 1]

The Eye sees more than the Heart knows.[1]

[Plate 3]

The Argument

I loved Theotormon[2]
And I was not ashamed;
I trembled in my virgin fears
And I hid in Leutha's vale!

Notes

[77] *Oh, citizen . . . forehead* Blake foresees revolution across the world, from England to the Middle East and Africa.

[78] *the hoary element* The sea retreats, in preparation for the re-emergence of Atlantis. The disappearance of the sea is prophesied Revelation 21: 1.

[79] *the jealous king* Urizen, who is falling.

[80] Urthona is the creative, imaginative principle.

[81] *ten commands* cf. God's handing down to Moses of the Ten Commandments, Exodus 20.

[82] *the son of fire* a Christ-like anti-Moses, anti-Jehovah figure, who is to liberate mankind.

[83] *the stony law* The Ten Commandments were inscribed on tablets of stone.

[84] *And now . . . cease* cf. Isaiah's prophecy of a new heaven and new earth where 'the wolf and the lamb shall feed together (Isaiah 65: 25).

[85] *For everything . . . holy* a parodic reversal of Revelation 15: 4: 'For thou [God] only art holy: for all nations shall come and worship before thee.'

VISIONS OF THE DAUGHTERS OF ALBION

[1] The motto appears on the poem's title-page.

[2] *Theotormon* Blake's coinage; the speaker in the argument is Oothoon, who represents thwarted love. The name Theotormon probably means 'tormented of god' or 'tormented of law'.

I plucked Leutha's flower,[3]
And I rose up from the vale;
But the terrible thunders tore
My virgin mantle[4] in twain.

Visions

Enslaved,[5] the Daughters of Albion[6] weep: a trembling lamentation
Upon their mountains, in their valleys, sighs toward America.
For the soft soul of America,[7] Oothoon wandered in woe
Along the vales of Leutha seeking flowers to comfort her;
And thus she spoke to the bright Marigold of Leutha's vale:
'Art thou a flower? Art thou a nymph? I see thee now a flower,
Now a nymph! I dare not pluck thee from thy dewy bed!'
The golden nymph replied, 'Pluck thou my flower, Oothoon the mild;
Another flower shall spring, because the soul of sweet delight
Can never pass away.' She ceased and closed her golden shrine.
Then Oothoon plucked the flower, saying, 'I pluck thee from thy bed,
Sweet flower, and put thee here to glow between my breasts;[8]
And thus I turn my face to where my whole soul seeks.'
Over the waves she went in winged exulting swift delight,
And over Theotormon's reign[9] took her impetuous course.
Bromion rent her with his thunders.[10] On his stormy bed
Lay the faint maid, and soon her woes appalled his thunders hoarse.
Bromion spoke: 'Behold this harlot here on Bromion's bed,
And let the jealous dolphins[11] sport around the lovely maid.
Thy soft American plains are mine, and mine thy north and south.
Stamped with my signet are the swarthy children of the sun[12] –
They are obedient, they resist not, they obey the scourge;
Their daughters worship terrors and obey the violent.
[Plate 5]
Now thou may'st marry Bromion's harlot, and protect the child
Of Bromion's rage that Oothoon shall put forth in nine moons' time.'
Then storms rent Theotormon's limbs; he rolled his waves around
And folded his black jealous waters round the adulterate pair.
Bound back to back in Bromion's caves,[13] terror and meekness dwell.

Notes

[3] *I plucked Leutha's flower* symbolic of an attempt to acquire sexual experience.

[4] *My virgin mantle* the hymen.

[5] *Enslaved* Wollstonecraft had described women as 'the slaves of injustice'.

[6] *Albion* England.

[7] America has been 'raped' by European exploitation.

[8] *between my breasts* In Homer's *Iliad*, Juno places the 'bridle' (girdle) of Venus between her breasts as a sign of sexual awakening.

[9] *Theotormon's reign* the sea.

[10] *Bromion . . . thunders* On her way to her beloved Theotormon, Oothoon is raped by Bromion. Bromion also embodies the cruelty of slave-owners (lines 29–30). His name means 'roarer' in Greek.

[11] *jealous dolphins* representative of the feelings of Theotormon, whom Bromion is addressing.

[12] *Stamped . . . sun* Newly bought slaves were branded with their owner's name.

[13] *Bound back to back . . . caves* Oothoon and Bromion are bound back to back in Theotormon's cave, while he guards its entrance. This is depicted in one of the most famous, and impressive, of Blake's illustrations (see Blake, *Early Illuminated Books* 268–9).

At entrance Theotormon sits wearing the threshold hard
With secret tears; beneath him sound like waves on a desert shore
The voice of slaves beneath the sun, and children bought with money
That shiver in religious caves beneath the burning fires
Of lust, that belch incessant from the summits of the earth.
Oothoon weeps not – she cannot weep! Her tears are locked up
But she can howl incessant writhing her soft snowy limbs,
And calling Theotormon's Eagles to prey upon her flesh.[14]
'I call with holy voice, kings of the sounding air!
Rend away this defiled bosom that I may reflect
The image of Theotormon on my pure transparent breast.'
The Eagles at her call descend and rend their bleeding prey:
Theotormon severely smiles – her soul reflects the smile
As the clear spring mudded with feet of beasts grows pure and smiles.
The Daughters of Albion hear her woes, and echo back her sighs.
'Why does my Theotormon sit weeping upon the threshold,
And Oothoon hovers by his side, persuading him in vain?[15]
I cry, "Arise, oh Theotormon, for the village dog
Barks at the breaking day; the nightingale has done lamenting;
The lark does rustle in the ripe corn, and the Eagle returns
From nightly prey, and lifts his golden beak to the pure east,
Shaking the dust from his immortal pinions to awake
The sun that sleeps too long. Arise, my Theotormon, I am pure
Because the night is gone that closed me in its deadly black."
They told me that the night and day were all that I could see;
They told me that I had five senses to enclose me up,
And they enclosed my infinite brain into a narrow circle,
And sunk my heart into the Abyss, a red round globe hot burning,
Till all from life I was obliterated and erased.
Instead of morn arises a bright shadow like an eye
In the eastern cloud; instead of night, a sickly charnel house,
That Theotormon hears me not! To him the night and morn
Are both alike: a night of sighs, a morning of fresh tears –
[Plate 6]
And none but Bromion can hear my lamentations.
With what sense is it that the chicken shuns the ravenous hawk?
With what sense does the tame pigeon measure out the expanse?
With what sense does the bee form cells? Have not the mouse and frog
Eyes and ears and sense of touch? Yet are their habitations
And their pursuits as different as their forms and as their joys.
Ask the wild ass why he refuses burdens; and the meek camel
Why he loves man – is it because of eye, ear, mouth or skin
Or breathing nostrils? No, for these the wolf and tiger have.

Notes

[14] *And calling . . . flesh* When Zeus chained Prometheus on the mountain-top (when he refused to reveal the prophecy of Zeus' fall), an eagle preyed on Prometheus' liver.

[15] Theotormon's ineffectual response to the rape of Oothoon by Bromion is probably suggested by the behaviour of J. G. Stedman (see headnote, p. 172), who wrote of how he fell in love with Joanna, a slave. After a brief affair, he failed to buy her freedom and returned to England without her. He remembered how 'I fancied I saw her tortured, insulted, and bowing under the weight of her chains, calling aloud, but in vain, for my assistance.' Although he disapproved of the treatment of female slaves, Stedman did nothing to prevent the cruelty he witnessed.

Ask the blind worm the secrets of the grave, and why her spires
Love to curl round the bones of death; and ask the rav'nous snake
Where she gets poison; and the winged eagle why he loves the sun –
And then tell me the thoughts of man that have been hid of old.
  Silent I hover all the night, and all day could be silent
If Theotormon once would turn his loved eyes upon me.
How can I be defiled when I reflect thy image pure?
Sweetest the fruit that the worm feeds on, and the soul preyed on by woe,
The new-washed lamb tinged with the village smoke, and the bright swan
By the red earth of our immortal river! I bathe my wings
And I am white and pure to hover round Theotormon's breast.'
  Then Theotormon broke his silence, and he answered.
'Tell me what is the night or day to one o'erflowed with woe?
Tell me what is a thought, and of what substance is it made?
Tell me what is a joy, and in what gardens do joys grow?
And in what rivers swim the sorrows, and upon what mountains
[Plate 7]
Wave shadows of discontent? And in what houses dwell the wretched
Drunken with woe forgotten, and shut up from cold despair?
Tell me where dwell the thoughts forgotten till thou call them forth?
Tell me where dwell the joys of old, and where the ancient loves?
And when will they renew again, and the night of oblivion past?[16]
That I might traverse times and spaces far remote, and bring
Comforts into a present sorrow and a night of pain.
Where goest thou, oh thought? To what remote land is thy flight?
If thou returnest to the present moment of affliction
Wilt thou bring comforts on thy wings, and dews and honey and balm?
Or poison from the desert wilds, from the eyes of the envier?'
  Then Bromion said (and shook the cavern with his lamentation),
'Thou knowest that the ancient trees seen by thine eyes have fruit,
But knowest thou that trees and fruits flourish upon the earth
To gratify senses unknown? Trees, beasts and birds unknown?
Unknown, not unperceived, spread in the infinite microscope,
In places yet unvisited by the voyager, and in worlds
Over another kind of seas, and in atmospheres unknown.
Ah, are there other wars, beside the wars of sword and fire?
And are there other sorrows, beside the sorrows of poverty?
And are there other joys, beside the joys of riches and ease?
And is there not one law for both the lion and the ox?
And is there not eternal fire, and eternal chains
To bind the phantoms of existence from eternal life?'
  Then Oothoon waited silent all the day and all the night,
[Plate 8]
But when the morn arose, her lamentation renewed –
The Daughters of Albion hear her woes, and echo back her sighs.
'Oh Urizen![17] Creator of men! mistaken Demon of heaven!
Thy joys are tears, thy labour vain – to form men to thine image.

Notes

[16] *And when . . . past* i.e. when will the thoughts, joys, and loves renew; when will the night of oblivion be past?

[17] *Urizen* ('your reason') the creator of the fallen, fragmented world.

How can one joy absorb another? Are not different joys
Holy, eternal, infinite? And each joy is a Love!
Does not the great mouth laugh at a gift, and the narrow eyelids mock
At the labour that is above payment? And wilt thou take the ape
For thy counsellor? Or the dog, for a schoolmaster to thy children?
Does he who contemns poverty, and he who turns with abhorrence
From usury, feel the same passion? Or are they moved alike?
How can the giver of gifts experience the delights of the merchant?
How the industrious citizen the pains of the husbandman?
How different far the fat-fed hireling with hollow drum
Who buys whole cornfields into wastes,[18] and sings upon the heath –
How different their eye and ear! How different the world to them!
With what sense does the parson claim the labour of the farmer?[19]
What are his nets and gins and traps, and how does he surround him
With cold floods of abstraction, and with forests of solitude,
To build him castles and high spires where kings and priests may dwell?
Till she who burns with youth, and knows no fixed lot, is bound
In spells of law to one she loathes. And must she drag the chain
Of life in weary lust?[20] Must chilling murderous thoughts obscure
The clear heaven of her eternal spring? – to bear the wintry rage
Of a harsh terror, driv'n to madness, bound to hold a rod[21]
Over her shrinking shoulders all the day, and all the night
To turn the wheel of false desire? – and longings that wake her womb
To the abhorred birth of cherubs in the human form
That live a pestilence and die a meteor, and are no more?
Till the child dwell with one he hates, and do the deed he loathes,
And the impure scourge force his seed into its unripe birth
Ere yet his eyelids can behold the arrows of the day.
  Does the whale worship at thy footsteps as the hungry dog?
Or does he scent the mountain prey because his nostrils wide
Draw in the ocean? Does his eye discern the flying cloud
As the raven's eye? Or does he measure the expanse like the vulture?
Does the still spider view the cliffs where eagles hide their young?
Or does the fly rejoice because the harvest is brought in?
Does not the eagle scorn the earth and despise the treasures beneath?
But the mole knoweth what is there, and the worm shall tell it thee.
Does not the worm erect a pillar in the mouldering churchyard,
[Plate 9]
And a palace of eternity in the jaws of the hungry grave?
Over his porch these words are written: "Take thy bliss O Man!
And sweet shall be thy taste, and sweet thy infant joys renew!"
  Infancy, fearless, lustful, happy! – nestling for delight
In laps of pleasure; Innocence! honest, open, seeking
The vigorous joys of morning light, open to virgin bliss –

Notes

[18] *cornfields into wastes* Expenditure of harvests and men on war is associated with enclosure and agricultural decline. The enlistment of young men in the army left a dearth of farmers to till the land, which in turn led to food shortages.

[19] *With what sense . . . farmer* a reference to tithes, taxes paid by peasants to the church.

[20] *And must . . . lust* Wollstonecraft probably inspired the notion of marriage as slavery.

[21] *rod* yoke for bearing burdens over the shoulders; though perhaps also the rod or whip of her slave-driving husband.

Who taught thee modesty, subtle modesty, child of night and sleep?
When thou awakest, wilt thou dissemble all thy secret joys
Or wert thou not awake when all this mystery was disclosed?
Then com'st thou forth a modest virgin knowing to dissemble[22]
With nets found under thy night pillow, to catch virgin joy,
And brand it with the name of whore, and sell it in the night[23]
In silence, ev'n without a whisper, and in seeming sleep.
Religious dreams and holy vespers light thy smoky fires;
Once were thy fires lighted by the eyes of honest morn.
And does my Theotormon seek this hypocrite modesty,
This knowing, artful, secret, fearful, cautious, trembling hypocrite?
Then is Oothoon a whore indeed! and all the virgin joys
Of life are harlots, and Theotormon is a sick man's dream,
And Oothoon is the crafty slave of selfish holiness.
  But Oothoon is not so: a virgin filled with virgin fancies,
Open to joy and to delight wherever beauty appears.
If in the morning sun I find it, there my eyes are fixed
[Plate 10]
In happy copulation; if in evening mild, wearied with work,
Sit on a bank and draw the pleasures of this free-born joy.
The moment of desire! the moment of desire! The virgin
That pines for man shall awaken her womb to enormous joys
In the secret shadows of her chamber;[24] the youth shut up from
The lustful joy shall forget to generate, and create an amorous image
In the shadows of his curtains and in the folds of his silent pillow.[25]
Are not these the places of religion? The rewards of continence?
The self-enjoyings of self-denial? Why dost thou seek religion?
Is it because acts are not lovely that thou seekest solitude
Where the horrible darkness is impressed with reflections of desire?
  Father of Jealousy,[26] be thou accursed from the earth!
Why hast thou taught my Theotormon this accursed thing?
Till beauty fades from off my shoulders, darkened and cast out,
A solitary shadow wailing on the margin of nonentity.
  I cry, "Love! Love! Love! happy, happy Love! Free as the mountain wind!"
Can that be Love, that drinks another as a sponge drinks water?
That clouds with jealousy his nights, with weepings all the day?
To spin a web of age around him, grey and hoary, dark,
Till his eyes sicken at the fruit that hangs before his sight?[27]
Such is self-love that envies all! – a creeping skeleton
With lamp-like eyes, watching around the frozen marriage bed.
  But silken nets and traps of adamant will Oothoon spread,
And catch for thee girls of mild silver, or of furious gold;
I'll lie beside thee on a bank and view their wanton play

Notes

[22] *a modest virgin . . . dissemble* Wollstonecraft lamented the tendency of women to spend so much time in front of mirrors, 'for this exercise of cunning is only an instinct of nature to enable them to obtain indirectly a little of that power of which they are unjustly denied a share'.

[23] *sell it in the night* prostitution.

[24] *The virgin . . . chamber* female masturbation.

[25] *the youth . . . pillow* male masturbation.

[26] *Father of jealousy* Urizen.

[27] *Till his eyes . . . sight* cf. Tantalus who, in Hades, has delicious fruit growing just beyond reach in Greek myth.

In lovely copulation, bliss on bliss, with Theotormon;
Red as the rosy morning, lustful as the first-born beam,
Oothoon shall view his dear delight, nor e'er with jealous cloud
Come in the heaven of generous love, nor selfish blightings bring.
  Does the sun walk in glorious raiment on the secret floor
[Plate 11]
Where the cold miser spreads his gold? Or does the bright cloud drop
On his stone threshold? Does his eye behold the beam that brings
Expansion to the eye of pity? Or will he bind himself
Beside the ox to thy hard furrow? Does not that mild beam blot
The bat, the owl, the glowing tiger, and the king of night?
The sea-fowl takes the wintry blast for a cov'ring to her limbs
And the wild snake the pestilence to adorn him with gems and gold;
And trees and birds and beasts and men behold their eternal joy.
Arise, you little glancing wings, and sing your infant joy!
Arise and drink your bliss, for every thing that lives is holy!'
  Thus every morning wails Oothoon, but Theotormon sits
Upon the margined ocean, conversing with shadows dire.
  The Daughters of Albion hear her woes, and echo back her sighs.

The End

The First Book of Urizen[1] (1794)

[Plate 2]

Preludium to the First Book of Urizen

Of the primeval Priest's assumed power,[2]
When Eternals spurned back his[3] religion
And gave him a place in the north –
Obscure, shadowy, void, solitary.

Eternals, I hear your call gladly[4] –
Dictate swift-wingèd words, and fear not
To unfold your dark visions of torment.

Notes

THE FIRST BOOK OF URIZEN

[1] The title is designed to contrast Blake's poem with the title of Genesis in the Authorized Version of the Bible – 'The First Book of Moses'. Perhaps *Urizen* was intended to be the first part of Blake's 'Bible of Hell' mentioned in *The Marriage of Heaven and Hell*. Urizen himself has been aligned in the past with Reason – 'your reason'. Blake was no admirer of reason in its purest state; it is, in the present context, the force of division and separation, responsible for the making of unjust laws.

[2] *Of the . . . power* Blake imitates the usual opening to an epic poem (e.g. 'Of arms and the man I sing . . . ', 'Of man's first disobedience . . . '). It echoes the anticlericalism of *The Marriage of Heaven and Hell*.

[3] *his* Urizen's.

[4] *I hear your call gladly* Blake, the poet, receives the dictation of the Eternals.

[Plate 3]

Chapter I

1. Lo, a shadow of horror is risen
In Eternity! Unknown, unprolific!
Self-closed, all-repelling; what Demon
Hath formed this abominable void,[5]
This soul-shudd'ring vacuum? Some said,
'It is Urizen'.[6] But unknown, abstracted,
Brooding secret,[7] the dark power hid.

2. Times on times he divided,[8] and measured
Space by space in his ninefold darkness,[9]
Unseen, unknown; changes appeared
In his desolate mountains,[10] rifted furious
By the black winds of perturbation.

3. For he strove in battles dire,
In unseen conflictions, with shapes
Bred from his forsaken wilderness,
Of beast, bird, fish, serpent and element,
Combustion, blast, vapour and cloud.[11]

4. Dark, revolving in silent activity,
Unseen in tormenting passions,
An activity unknown and horrible;
A self-contemplating shadow
In enormous labours occupied.

5. But Eternals beheld his vast forests.
Age on ages he lay, closed, unknown,
Brooding, shut in the deep; all avoid
The petrific[12] abominable chaos.

Notes

[5] *What demon . . . void* cf. Genesis 1: 2: 'And the earth was without form, and void.'

[6] *Some said . . . Urizen* the first act of naming in the poem.

[7] *Brooding secret* an allusion to the moment of creation in *Paradise Lost* i 21–2, where the Holy Spirit 'Dove-like sat'st brooding on the vast abyss / And madest it pregnant'.

[8] *divided* The Creation begins with Urizen's splitting away from the Eternals into selfhood.

[9] *ninefold darkness* Milton's Satan lay for nine days in the abyss of hell.

[10] *mountains* Urizen becomes a landscape: Creation and the Fall are one and the same.

[11] *Of beast . . . cloud* The elements (l. 24) are accompanied by emblematic beasts (l. 23).

[12] *petrific* a Miltonic coinage meaning stony, static (see *Paradise Lost* x 294). The point is that chaos is static when compared to all-flexible eternity.

6. His cold horrors silent, dark Urizen
Prepared: his ten thousands of thunders
Ranged in gloomed array stretch out across
The dread world, and the rolling of wheels,
As of swelling seas, sound in his clouds,
In his hills of stored snows, in his mountains
Of hail and ice; voices of terror
Are heard, like thunders of autumn,
When the cloud blazes over the harvests.

Chapter II[13]

1. Earth was not, nor globes of attraction.[14]
The will of the Immortal[15] expanded
Or contracted his all-flexible senses.
Death was not, but eternal life sprung.

2. The sound of a trumpet! The heavens
Awoke, and vast clouds of blood rolled
Round the dim rocks of Urizen (so named
That solitary one in Immensity).

3. Shrill the trumpet, and myriads of Eternity
[Plate 4]
Muster around the bleak deserts
Now filled with clouds darkness and waters
That rolled perplexed, lab'ring, and uttered
Words articulate, bursting in thunders
That rolled on the tops of his mountains.

4. 'From the depths of dark solitude,[16] From
The eternal abode in my holiness,
Hidden, set apart in my stern counsels,
Reserved for the days of futurity,
I have sought for a joy without pain,
For a solid without fluctuation.
Why will you die oh Eternals?[17]
Why live in unquenchable burnings?

Notes

[13] In this chapter Blake tells the story of the Creation a second time.

[14] *globes of attraction* solar systems; planets held together by gravity. In Blake's plate, 'attraction' is split into two parts, 'attrac-/-tion', with the second part hovering above the first, mimicking a gravity-less state.

[15] *the Immortal* Urizen.

[16] Lines 57–91 comprise Urizen's account of the Creation.

[17] *Why will you die, oh Eternals?* an echo of Ezekiel 18: 31: 'why will ye die, oh house of Israel?'

5. First I fought with the fire, consumed
Inwards, into a deep world within:
A void immense, wild dark and deep
Where nothing was; Nature's wide womb.
And self-balanced, stretched o'er the void
I alone, even I! the winds merciless
Bound; but condensing in torrents
They fall and fall; strong, I repelled
The vast waves, and arose on the waters –
A wide world of solid obstruction.

6. Here alone I, in books formed of metals,
Have written the secrets of wisdom,[18]
The secrets of dark contemplation,
By fightings and conflicts dire
With terrible monsters sin-bred,
Which the bosoms of all inhabit,
Seven deadly sins of the soul.

7. Lo! I unfold my darkness: and on
This rock place with strong hand the Book
Of eternal brass, written in my solitude.

8. Laws of peace, of love, of unity,
Of pity,[19] compassion, forgiveness.
Let each choose one habitation,
His ancient infinite mansion.
One command, one joy, one desire,
One curse, one weight, one measure,
One King, one God, one Law.'[20]

Chapter III

1. The voice ended. They saw his pale visage
Emerge from the darkness, his hand
On the rock of eternity unclasping
The Book of brass. Rage seized the strong,

Notes

[18] *Here alone . . . wisdom* parodic of God's handing down to Moses of the Ten Commandments, Exodus 20.

[19] *pity* not, for Blake, a desirable quality, as it consolidates division.

[20] *One King, one God, one Law* Blake regarded the imposition of these things as tyranny.

2. Rage, fury, intense indignation,
In cataracts of fire blood and gall,
In whirlwinds of sulphurous smoke
And enormous forms of energy;
All the seven deadly sins of the soul
[Plate 5]
In living creations appeared
In the flames of eternal fury.

3. Sund'ring, dark'ning, thund'ring!
Rent away with a terrible crash,
Eternity rolled wide apart,
Wide asunder rolling
Mountainous all around
Departing; departing; departing:
Leaving ruinous fragments of life,
Hanging frowning cliffs, and all between
An ocean of voidness unfathomable.

4. The roaring fires ran o'er the heav'ns
In whirlwinds and cataracts of blood,
And o'er the dark deserts of Urizen
Fires pour through the void on all sides
On Urizen's self-begotten armies.

5. But no light from the fires: all was darkness
In the flames of Eternal fury.

6. In fierce anguish and quenchless flames
To the deserts and rocks he ran raging
To hide, but he could not: combining,
He dug mountains and hills in vast strength,
He piled them in incessant labour,
In howlings and pangs and fierce madness
Long periods in burning fires labouring
Till hoary and age-broke and aged,
In despair and the shadows of death.

7. And a roof vast, petrific, around,
On all sides he framed, like a womb
Where thousands of rivers in veins
Of blood pour down the mountains to cool
The eternal fires beating without
From Eternals; and, like a black globe

Viewed by sons of Eternity, standing
On the shore of the infinite ocean,
Like a human heart struggling and beating,
The vast world of Urizen appeared.

8. And Los[21] round the dark globe of Urizen
Kept watch for Eternals to confine
The obscure separation alone;
For Eternity stood wide apart
[Plate 7]
As the stars are apart from the earth.

9. Los wept, howling around the dark Demon
And cursing his lot; for in anguish
Urizen was rent from his side:[22]
And a fathomless void for his feet,
And intense fires for his dwelling.

10. But Urizen laid in a stony sleep
Unorganized, rent from Eternity.

11. The Eternals said: 'What is this? Death.[23]
Urizen is a clod of clay.'

[Plate 9]

12. Los howled in a dismal stupor,
Groaning! Gnashing! Groaning!
Till the wrenching apart was healed.

13. But the wrenching of Urizen healed not;
Cold, featureless, flesh or clay,
Rifted with direful changes
He lay in a dreamless night.

14. Till Los roused his fires, affrighted
At the formless unmeasurable death.

Notes

[21] *Los* the imagination, now separated from Urizen.

[22] *Urizen was rent from his side* cf. the creation of Eve from Adam's rib, Genesis 2: 21.

[23] *What is . . . Death* the second act of naming in the poem.

[Plate 10]

Chapter IVa

1. Los, smitten with astonishment,
Frightened at the hurtling bones,

2. And at the surging sulphureous
Perturbed Immortal mad-raging

3. In whirlwinds and pitch and nitre
Round the furious limbs of Los;

4. And Los formed nets and gins[24]
And threw the nets round about.

5. He watched in shudd'ring fear
The dark changes, and bound every change
With rivets of iron and brass;

6. And these were the changes of Urizen.

[Plate 12]

Chapter IVb

1. Ages on ages rolled over him!
In stony sleep ages rolled over him!
Like a dark waste stretching changeable
By earthquakes riv'n, belching sullen fires,
On ages rolled ages in ghastly
Sick torment; around him in whirlwinds
Of darkness, the Eternal Prophet[25] howled,
Beating still on his rivets of iron,
Pouring sodor[26] of iron, dividing
The horrible night into watches.

2. And Urizen (so his eternal name)
His prolific delight obscured more and more
In dark secrecy, hiding in surging
Sulphureous fluid his fantasies.
The Eternal Prophet heaved the dark bellows

Notes

[24] *gins* snares, traps.

[25] *the Eternal Prophet* Los.

[26] *sodor* solder – which, like rivets, is used to join metal components.

And turned restless the tongs, and the hammer
Incessant beat, forging chains new and new,
Numb'ring with links, hours, days, and years.[27]

3. The Eternal Mind bounded began to roll
Eddies of wrath ceaseless round and round,
And the sulphureous foam surging thick
Settled – a lake, bright and shining clear,
White as the snow on the mountains cold.

4. Forgetfulness, dumbness, necessity!
In chains of the mind locked up
Like fetters of ice shrinking together
Disorganized, rent from Eternity.
Los beat on his fetters of iron,
And heated his furnaces, and poured
Iron sodor and sodor of brass.

5. Restless turned the Immortal enchained,
Heaving dolorous! Anguished! Unbearable
Till a roof shaggy wild enclosed
In an orb[28] his fountain of thought.

6. In a horrible dreamful slumber
Like the linked infernal chain
A vast spine writhed in torment
Upon the winds, shooting pained
Ribs, like a bending cavern,
And bones of solidness froze
Over all his nerves of joy.
And a first Age passed over
And a state of dismal woe.

[Plate 13]

7. From the caverns of his jointed Spine
Down sunk with fright a red
Round globe[29] hot burning, deep
Deep down into the abyss:
Panting, conglobing, trembling,
Shooting out ten thousand branches
Around his solid bones.
And a second Age passed over
And a state of dismal woe.

Notes

[27] *Numb'ring . . . years* Los constructs a calendar.

[28] *an orb* the skull.

[29] *a red / Round globe* the heart.

8. In harrowing fear rolling round;
His nervous brain shot branches
Round the branches of his heart
On high into two little orbs;[30]
And fixed in two little caves
Hiding carefully from the wind,
His eyes beheld the deep,
And a third Age passed over:
And a state of dismal woe.

9. The pangs of hope began,
In heavy pain striving, struggling;
Two Ears in close volutions[31]
From beneath his orbs of vision
Shot spiring out and petrified
As they grew. And a fourth Age passed
And a state of dismal woe.

10. In ghastly torment sick;
Hanging upon the wind;
[Plate 15]
Two Nostrils bent down to the deep.
And a fifth Age passed over,
And a state of dismal woe.

11. In ghastly torment sick;
Within his ribs bloated round,
A craving hungry cavern;
Thence arose his channelled Throat,
And like a red flame a Tongue
Of thirst and of hunger appeared.
And a sixth Age passed over:
And a state of dismal woe.

12. Enraged and stifled with torment,
He threw his right Arm to the north,
His left Arm to the south,
Shooting out in anguish deep;
And his Feet stamped the nether Abyss
In trembling and howling and dismay.
And a seventh Age passed over
And a state of dismal woe.

Notes

30 *two little orbs* the eyes.

31 *close volutions* inner ear.

Chapter V

1. In terrors Los shrunk from his task –
His great hammer fell from his hand;
His fires beheld and, sickening,
Hid their strong limbs in smoke.
For with noises ruinous loud
With hurtlings and clashings and groans
The Immortal endured his chains
Though bound in a deadly sleep.

2. All the myriads of Eternity
All the wisdom and joy of life
Roll like a sea around him,
Except what his little orbs
Of sight by degrees unfold.

3. And now his eternal life,
Like a dream, was obliterated.

4. Shudd'ring, the Eternal Prophet smote
With a stroke, from his north to south region.
The bellows and hammer are silent now,
A nerveless silence; his prophetic voice
Seized; a cold solitude and dark void
The Eternal Prophet and Urizen closed.

5. Ages on ages rolled over them,
Cut off from life and light, frozen
Into horrible forms of deformity.
Los suffered his fires to decay,
Then he looked back with anxious desire,
But the space undivided by existence
Struck horror into his soul.

6. Los wept obscured with mourning;
His bosom earthquaked with sighs;
He saw Urizen, deadly black,
In his chains bound, and Pity began,

7. In anguish dividing and dividing
(For pity divides the soul),[32]

Notes

[32] *For pity divides the soul* Pity is a divisive – and therefore unfavourable – quality for Blake, since it is allied to fear and selfishness. It leads Los to split into two parts, a fallen Los (or Adam) and Enitharmon (or Eve).

In pangs, eternity on eternity,
Life in cataracts poured down his cliffs.
The void shrunk the lymph into Nerves
Wand'ring wide on the bosom of night,
And left a round globe of blood
Trembling upon the void.
[Plate 16]
Thus the Eternal Prophet was divided
Before the death-image of Urizen;
For in changeable clouds and darkness
In a winterly night beneath,
The Abyss of Los stretched immense.
And now seen, now obscured, to the eyes
Of Eternals the visions remote
Of the dark separation appeared.
As glasses discover Worlds
In the endless Abyss of space,
So the expanding eyes of Immortals
Beheld the dark visions of Los,
And the globe of life-blood trembling.

[Plate 18]

8. The globe of life-blood trembled
Branching out into roots:
Fibrous, writhing upon the winds:
Fibres of blood, milk, and tears:[33]
In pangs, eternity on eternity.
At length, in tears and cries embodied,
A female form trembling and pale
Waves before his deathy face.

9. All Eternity shuddered at sight
Of the first female now separate,[34]
Pale as a cloud of snow
Waving before the face of Los.

10. Wonder, awe, fear, astonishment,
Petrify the eternal myriads
At the first female form now separate.
[Plate 19]
They called her Pity, and fled.

Notes

[33] *Fibrous . . . tears* Blake's description of blood seems strange to us, but was up-to-date at the time of writing. Blood was thought to contain fibres and red globules. Other vessels were believed to carry blood, milk, chyle and tears.

[34] *All Eternity . . . separate* The Eternals are horrified at the creation of the first female because it implies infinite human division.

11. 'Spread a tent,[35] with strong curtains around them;
Let cords and stakes bind in the Void,[36]
That Eternals may no more behold them!'

12. They began to weave curtains of darkness;
They erected large pillars round the Void
With golden hooks fastened in the pillars.
With infinite labour the Eternals
A woof wove, and called it 'Science'.

Chapter VI

1. But Los saw the female and pitied;
He embraced her, she wept, she refused.
In perverse and cruel delight
She fled from his arms, yet he followed.

2. Eternity shuddered when they saw
Man begetting his likeness
On his own divided image.

3. A time passed over, the Eternals
Began to erect the tent;
When Enitharmon sick,
Felt a Worm[37] within her womb.

4. Yet helpless it lay like a Worm
In the trembling womb
To be moulded into existence.

5. All day the worm lay on her bosom;
All night within her womb
The worm lay till it grew to a serpent,
With dolorous hissings and poisons
Round Enitharmon's loins folding.

Notes

[35] *a tent* the sky, the firmament.

[36] *Spread a tent . . . Void* Blake recalls Isaiah 54: 2: 'Enlarge the place of thy tent, and let them stretch forth the curtains of thine habitations: spare not, lengthen thy cords, and strengthen thy stakes.'

[37] *a worm* 'seminal worms' were believed to be the seed of the human nervous system.

6. Coiled within Enitharmon's womb,
The serpent grew, casting its scales;
With sharp pangs the hissings began
To change to a grating cry;
Many sorrows and dismal throes,
Many forms of fish, bird and beast,
Brought forth an Infant form[38]
Where was a worm before.

7. The Eternals their tent finished
Alarmed with these gloomy visions,
When Enitharmon groaning
Produced a man Child to the light.

8. A shriek ran through Eternity:
And a paralytic stroke
At the birth of the Human shadow.

9. Delving earth in his resistless way,
Howling, the Child with fierce flames
Issued from Enitharmon.

10. The Eternals closed the tent.
They beat down the stakes, the cords
[Plate 20]
Stretched for a work of eternity;
No more Los beheld Eternity.

11. In his hands he seized the infant,[39]
He bathed him in springs of sorrow,
He gave him to Enitharmon.

Chapter VII

1. They named the child Orc, he grew
Fed with milk of Enitharmon.

Notes

[38] *Brought forth an Infant form* The apocalyptic tone is heightened by the echo of Revelation 12: 5, where the 'woman clothed with the sun' 'brought forth a man child'.

[39] *he seized the infant* cf. the child of the 'woman clothed with the sun' in Revelation, which 'was caught up unto God, and to his throne' (Revelation 12: 5).

2. Los awoke her; oh sorrow and pain!
A tight'ning girdle grew
Around his bosom. In sobbings
He burst the girdle in twain,
But still another girdle
Oppressed his bosom. In sobbings
Again he burst it. Again
Another girdle succeeds;
The girdle was formed by day,
By night was burst in twain.

3. These falling down on the rock
Into an iron chain
In each other link by link locked.

4. They took Orc to the top of a mountain –
Oh how Enitharmon wept!
They chained his young limbs to the rock[40]
With the Chain of Jealousy
Beneath Urizen's deathful shadow.

5. The dead heard the voice of the child
And began to awake from sleep;
All things heard the voice of the child
And began to awake to life.

6. And Urizen craving with hunger
Stung with the odours of Nature
Explored his dens around.

7. He formed a line and a plummet
To divide the Abyss beneath.
He formed a dividing rule;

8. He formed scales to weigh;
He formed massy weights;
He formed a brazen quadrant;
He formed golden compasses
And began to explore the Abyss,
And he planted a garden of fruits.

Notes

[40] *They chained . . . rock* cf. Abraham's binding of Isaac to the altar (Genesis 22: 9); Laius's piercing of Oedipus's ankles when abandoning him to the wolves; and Jupiter's nailing of Prometheus to the rock of the Caucasus.

9. But Los encircled Enitharmon
With fires of Prophecy
From the sight of Urizen and Orc.

10. And she bore an enormous race.

Chapter VIII

1. Urizen explored his dens –
Mountain, moor and wilderness,
With a globe of fire lighting his journey,
A fearful journey, annoyed
By cruel enormities, forms
[Plate 22]
Of life on his forsaken mountains.

2. And his world teemed vast enormities
Fright'ning, faithless, fawning
Portions of life; similitudes
Of a foot, or a hand, or a head,
Or a heart, or an eye, they swam, mischievous
Dread terrors! delighting in blood.

3. Most Urizen sickened to see
His eternal creations appear –
Sons and daughters of sorrow on mountains
Weeping! wailing! First Thiriel appeared,
Astonished at his own existence
Like a man from a cloud born; and Utha
From the waters emerging, laments;
Grodna rent the deep earth howling
Amazed! his heavens immense cracks
Like the ground parched with heat; then Fuzon
Flamed out! – first begotten, last born.[41]
All his eternal sons in like manner,
His daughters from green herbs and cattle,
From monsters and worms of the pit.

Notes

[41] Thiriel (air), Utha (water), Grodna (earth) and Fuzon (fire) correspond to the four elements.

4. He, in darkness closed, viewed all his race
And his soul sickened![42] He cursed
Both sons and daughters, for he saw
That no flesh nor spirit could keep
His iron laws one moment.

5. For he saw that life lived upon death;
[Plate 25]
The ox in the slaughterhouse moans,
The dog at the wintry door.
And he wept, and he called it 'Pity',
And his tears flowed down on the winds.

6. Cold he wandered on high, over their cities
In weeping and pain and woe;
And wherever he wandered in sorrows
Upon the aged heavens
A cold shadow followed behind him
Like a spider's web – moist, cold and dim,
Drawing out from his sorrowing soul
The dungeon-like heaven dividing,
Wherever the footsteps of Urizen
Walked over the cities in sorrow.

7. Till a Web dark and cold throughout all
The tormented element stretched
From the sorrows of Urizen's soul;
And the Web is a Female in embryo.
None could break the Web, no wings of fire,

8. So twisted the cords and so knotted
The meshes: twisted like to the human brain.

9. And all called it The Net of Religion.

Chapter IX

1. Then the inhabitants of those Cities[43]
Felt their Nerves change into Marrow,
And hardening bones began
In swift diseases and torments,

Notes

[42] *He . . . sickened* There is no way the fall from a state of original innocence can be reversed, as Urizen realizes.

[43] *the inhabitants of those Cities* an allusion to the inhabitants of Sodom and Gomorrah, Genesis 19: 25: 'And he overthrew those cities, and all the plain, and all the inhabitants of those cities, and that which grew upon the ground.'

In throbbings and shootings and grindings
Through all the coasts; till weakened
The Senses inward rushed, shrinking,
Beneath the dark net of infection;

2. Till the shrunken eyes, clouded over,
Discerned not the woven hypocrisy.
But the streaky slime in their heavens
Brought together by narrowing perceptions
Appeared transparent air; for their eyes
Grew small like the eyes of a man
And in reptile forms shrinking together
Of seven feet stature they remained.

3. Six days they shrunk up from existence
And on the seventh day they rested;
And they blessed the seventh day, in sick hope,
And forgot their eternal life.

4. And their thirty cities divided
In form of a human heart;
No more could they rise at will
In the infinite void, but bound down
To earth by their narrowing perceptions
[Plate 27]
They lived a period of years
Then left a noisome[44] body
To the jaws of devouring darkness.

5. And their children wept, and built
Tombs in the desolate places,
And formed laws of prudence, and called them
The eternal laws of God.

6. And the thirty cities remained
Surrounded by salt floods, now called
Africa; its name was then Egypt.

7. The remaining sons of Urizen
Beheld their brethren shrink together
Beneath the net of Urizen:
Persuasion was in vain
For the ears of the inhabitants
Were withered and deafened and cold!

Notes

[44] *noisome* noxious, foul, rotten.

And their eyes could not discern
Their brethren of other cities.

8. So Fuzon called all together
The remaining children of Urizen:
And they left the pendulous earth:[45]
They called it Egypt, and left it.[46]

9. And the salt ocean rolled englobed.

The End of the first book of Urizen

Letter from William Blake to the Revd Dr Trusler,[1] *23 August 1799* (extract)

Reverend Sir,
I really am sorry that you are fall'n out with the spiritual world, especially if I should have to answer for it. I feel very sorry that your ideas and mine on moral painting differ so much as to have made you angry with my method of study. If I am wrong, I am wrong in good company. I had hoped your plan comprehended all species of this art, and especially that you would not regret that species which gives existence to every other – namely, visions of eternity. You say that I want somebody to elucidate my ideas, but you ought to know that what is grand is necessarily obscure to weak men. That which can be made explicit to the idiot is not worth my care. The wisest of the ancients considered what is not too explicit as the fittest for instruction because it rouses the faculties to act – I name Moses, Solomon, Aesop, Homer, Plato . . .

I have therefore proved your reasonings ill-proportioned, which you can never prove my figures to be. They are those of Michelangelo, Raphael, and the antique, and of the best living models. I perceive that your eye is perverted by caricature prints, which ought not to abound so much as they do. Fun I love, but too much fun is, of all things, the most loathsome. Mirth is better than fun, and happiness is better than mirth. I feel that a man may be happy in this world. And I know that this world is a world of imagination and vision. I see everything I paint in this world, but everybody does not see alike. To the eyes of a miser, a guinea[2] is more beautiful than the sun, and a bag worn with the use of money has more beautiful proportions than a vine filled with grapes. The tree which moves some to tears of joy is, in the eyes of others, only a green thing that stands in the

Notes

[45] *the pendulous earth* cf. *Paradise Lost* iv 1000: 'The pendulous round earth with balanced air'.

[46] *They called it Egypt, and left it* a reworking of the story of how the Israelites were conducted out of Egypt by God, commemorated in the Passover: 'Remember this day, in which ye came out from Egypt, out of the house of bondage; for by strength of hand the Lord brought you out from this place' (Exodus 18: 3).

Letter from William Blake

[1] Blake had been introduced to John Trusler with a view to his illustrating some of his works, but they fell out when Trusler told him that 'Your fancy seems to be in the other world, or the world of spirits, which accords not with my intentions.' Trusler wrote on this letter the comment: 'Blake, dimmed with superstition'.

[2] *guinea* gold coin worth 21 shillings, not minted since 1813.

way. Some see nature all ridicule and deformity (and by these I shall not regulate my proportions), and some scarce see nature at all. But to the eyes of the man of imagination, nature is imagination itself. As a man is, so he sees; as the eye is formed, such are its powers.

You certainly mistake when you say that the visions of fancy are not be found in this world. To me, this world is all one continued vision of fancy or imagination, and I feel flattered when I am told so. What is it sets Homer, Virgil, and Milton in so high a rank of art? Why is the Bible more entertaining and instructive than any other book? Is it not because they are addressed to the imagination (which is spiritual sensation), and but mediately to the understanding or reason? Such is true painting, and such was alone valued by the Greeks and the best modern artists. Consider what Lord Bacon says: 'Sense sends over to imagination before reason have judged, and reason sends over to imagination before the decree can be acted' (see *Advancement of Learning* Part 2, p. 47 of first edition).[3]

But I am happy to find a great majority of fellow mortals who can elucidate my visions – and particularly they have been elucidated by children, who have taken a greater delight in contemplating my pictures than I even hoped. Neither youth nor childhood is folly or incapacity; some children are fools and so are some old men. But there is a vast majority on the side of imagination or spiritual sensation . . .

The Mental Traveller

From The Pickering Manuscript (composed 1800–4)

I travelled through a land of men,
A land of men and women too,
And heard and saw such dreadful things
As cold earth-wanderers never knew.

For there the babe is born in joy
That was begotten in dire woe;
Just as we reap in joy the fruit
Which we in bitter tears did sow.

And, if the babe is born a boy,
He's given to a woman old
Who nails him down upon a rock,
Catches his shrieks in cups of gold.

She binds iron thorns around his head,
She pierces both his hands and feet,
She cuts his heart out at his side
To make it feel both cold and heat.

Notes

[3] Francis Bacon, Baron Verulam, Viscount St Albans (1561–1626) published his *Of the Advancement of Learning* in 1605.

Her fingers number every nerve
Just as a miser counts his gold,
She lives upon his shrieks and cries,
And she grows young as he grows old.

Till he becomes a bleeding youth
And she becomes a virgin bright;
Then he rends up his manacles
And binds her down for his delight.

He plants himself in all her nerves
Just as a husbandman[1] his mould,[2]
And she becomes his dwelling-place,
And garden fruitful seventy-fold.

An aged shadow soon he fades,
Wand'ring round an earthly cot,[3]
Full filled all with gems and gold
Which he by industry had got.

And these are the gems of the human soul,
The rubies and pearls of a lovesick eye,
The countless gold of the aching heart,
The martyr's groan and the lover's sigh.

They are his meat, they are his drink;
He feeds the beggar and the poor,
And the wayfaring traveller –
Forever open is his door.

His grief is their eternal joy;
They make the roofs and walls to ring,
Till from the fire on the hearth
A little female babe does spring.

And she is all of solid fire,
And gems and gold, that none his hand
Dares stretch to touch her baby form
Or wrap her in his swaddling-band.

But she comes to the man she loves,
If young or old, or rich or poor.
They soon drive out the aged host –
A beggar at another's door.

Notes

THE MENTAL TRAVELLER

[1] *husbandman* farmer.

[2] *mould* soil, earth.

[3] *cot* cottage.

He wanders weeping far away
Until some other take him in;
Oft blind and age-bent, sore distressed,
Until he can a maiden win.

And to allay his freezing age
The poor man takes her in his arms;
The cottage fades before his sight,
The garden and its lovely charms;

The guests are scattered through the land.
For the eye altering, alters all;
The senses roll themselves in fear
And the flat earth becomes a ball;

The stars, sun, moon – all shrink away,
A desert vast without a bound;
And nothing left to eat or drink,
And a dark desert all around.

The honey of her infant lips,
The bread and wine of her sweet smile,
The wild game[4] of her roving eye
Does him to infancy beguile.

For as he eats and drinks he grows
Younger and younger every day,
And on the desert wild they both
Wander in terror and dismay.

Like the wild stag she flees away,
Her fear plants many a thicket wild;
While he pursues her night and day,
By various arts of love beguiled,

By various arts of love and hate;
Till the wide desert planted o'er
With labyrinths of wayward love,
Where roams the lion, wolf, and boar;

Till he becomes a wayward babe
And she a weeping woman old.
Then many a lover wanders here;
The sun and stars are nearer rolled;

Notes

[4] *game* sport.

The trees bring forth sweet ecstasy
To all who in the desert roam –
Till many a city there is built,
And many a pleasant shepherd's home.

But when they find the frowning babe,
Terror strikes through the region wide;
They cry, 'The babe, the babe is born!'
And flee away on every side.

For who dare touch the frowning form –
His arm is withered to its root;
Lions, boars, wolves, all howling flee
And every tree does shed its fruit.

And none can touch that frowning form
Except it be a woman old;
She nails him down upon the rock
And all is done as I have told.

The Crystal Cabinet

***From* The Pickering Manuscript (composed 1800–4)**

The maiden caught me in the wild
Where I was dancing merrily,
She put me into her cabinet
And locked me up with a golden key.

This cabinet is formed of gold
And pearl and crystal, shining bright,
And within it opens into a world
And a little lovely moony night.

Another England there I saw,
Another London with its Tower,
Another Thames and other hills
And another pleasant Surrey bower,

Another maiden like herself,
Translucent, lovely, shining clear –
Threefold each in the other closed:
Oh, what a pleasant trembling fear!

Oh, what a smile, a threefold smile
Filled me that like a flame I burned;
I bent to kiss the lovely maid
And found a threefold kiss returned.

I strove to seize the inmost form
With ardour fierce and hands of flame,
But burst the crystal cabinet
And like a weeping babe became –

A weeping babe upon the wild
And weeping woman, pale, reclined.
And in the outward air again
I filled with woes the passing wind.

[*And did those feet in ancient time*[1]]

From Milton (composed 1803–8)

And did those feet[2] in ancient time
Walk upon England's mountains green?
And was the holy lamb of God
On England's pleasant pastures seen?

And did the countenance divine
Shine forth upon our clouded hills?
And was Jerusalem builded here,
Among these dark Satanic mills?

Bring me my bow of burning gold!
Bring me my arrows of desire!
Bring me my spear – oh clouds unfold!
Bring me my chariot of fire![2]

I will not cease from mental fight
Nor shall my sword sleep in my hand,
Till we have built Jerusalem
In England's green and pleasant land.

Notes

AND DID THOSE FEET IN ANCIENT TIME

[1] This poem is best known today as a hymn, 'Jerusalem', having been set to music by Hubert Parry in 1916 and arranged by Edward Elgar in 1922.

[2] *Bring me my chariot of fire* a reference to the chariot of fire that carried Elijah to heaven, 2 Kings 2: 11.

Mary Robinson (*née* Darby) (1758–1800)

'She is a woman of undoubted genius,' Coleridge told Southey in January 1800, 'She overloads everything, but I never knew a human being with so *full* a mind – bad, good, and indifferent, I grant you, but full and overflowing.'[1] It was not an unfair account, and certainly more charitable than that of many of her contemporaries.

Mary Robinson was born and brought up in Bristol, the younger daughter of John Darby, a whaling captain from America, and Mary Seys. Her first school was that run in Bristol by Hannah More's sisters. When her father absconded to Labrador, ostensibly to set up a whaling station, her mother moved her to a school in Chelsea, where she was taught by the gifted but alcoholic Meribah Lorington. In later years Robinson described her as 'the most extensively accomplished female that I ever remember to have met with. . . . All that I ever learned I acquired from this extraordinary woman.'[2] At a time when women were seldom educated, Lorington was remarkably erudite; besides knowing Latin, French and Italian, she was, according to Robinson, 'a perfect arithmetician and astronomer'.[3]

She concluded her formal education at a finishing school in Marylebone. Her dancing-master introduced her to David Garrick, who encouraged her interest in acting. 'He would sometimes dance a minuet with me, sometimes request me to sing the favourite ballads of the day', she later recalled. She remembered him as tremendously charismatic: 'he appeared to me as one who possessed more power, both to awe and to attract, than any man I ever met with'.[4]

In April 1774 she married Thomas Robinson, an articled clerk at Lincoln's Inn, who was thought to be comfortably off. This was not, alas, the case, and within months he was driven out of the capital to evade his creditors. Robinson gave birth to their daughter, Mary Elizabeth, in Wales, November 1774. In 1775 Robinson was imprisoned for debt and, like Charlotte Smith, Robinson partook of her husband's punishment, nursing her daughter in the cells. During her incarceration she began to write; her first volume, *Poems* (1775), was partly funded by Georgiana Cavendish, Duchess of Devonshire, one of the few women to respond to her requests for assistance. She went on to publish *Captivity: A Poem* (1777).

On release from prison, thanks to Garrick and Sheridan, she found employment as an actress at Drury Lane theatre and became famous overnight for her portrayal of Juliet. Success continued with the roles of Ophelia, Viola, Rosalind, Lady Macbeth and Perdita. It was while playing Perdita, in 1779, that she caught the attention of the 17-year-old Prince of Wales. Their first assignation was, allegedly, in Kew Gardens: 'She had been concealed in the island opposite, and on a signal that the coast was clear, stepped into a boat, and was rowed across.'[5] She became his mistress in return for a promised £20,000 (the equivalent of £1.7 million today), which never materialized. He abandoned her a year later, exposing her to a storm of ridicule that compelled her to retire from the stage. After lengthy negotiations she managed to coax £5,000 out of the royal family. Subsequent lovers included Charles James Fox, who secured an annuity for her of £500, and Colonel Bastre Tarleton, a war hero and veteran of the American War, who became the recipient of many letters and poems. Tarleton

Notes

1 Griggs i 562.
2 *Memoirs of the late Mrs Robinson* (2 vols., 1803), i 32–3.
3 Ibid., i 33.
4 Ibid., i 55.
5 The Hon. Grantley F. Berkeley, *My Life and Recollections* (4 vols, London, 1865–6), iv 34

was the father of the child she was carrying when, at the age of 24, she suffered the miscarriage that left her paralysed from the waist down.

After spending several years on the continent with Tarleton, she returned to England in 1788. By this time she relied increasingly on her writing for income, and in succeeding years her productivity was remarkable. Between 1775 and 1800 she produced six volumes of poetry, eight novels and two plays, with remarkable success. Her Gothic chiller *Vancenza, or The Dangers of Credulity* (1792) sold out in a day. She often published her poetry in newspapers such as the *World* and the *Oracle*, usually under the names of 'Laura' and 'Laura Maria'. Her talent for engaging in poetical dialogues with Hannah Cowley, Hester Piozzi and Robert Merry aligned her for a while with the Della Cruscans – a group known for affected, sentimental, and highly ornamented verse. For a while they were very popular, and her biographer in the *Memoirs* records that 'During her poetical disguise, many complimentary poems were addressed to her: several ladies of the bluestocking club, while Mrs Robinson remained unknown, even ventured to admire – nay, more, to recite her productions in their learned and critical coterie.'[6] But the popularity of the Della Cruscans did not endure, and by the mid-1790s the public had tired of their mannered style.

She was best known to the first-generation Romantics as a contributor of verse to the *Morning Post*, where her poems appeared under the name 'Tabitha Bramble'. Coleridge, Southey and Wordsworth were fellow-contributors, and it was Coleridge who engaged in dialogue with her, in both verse and prose. They met several times in London during January and February 1800, and besides admiring her poetry Coleridge found he had sympathy with her political views. After her death he told her daughter that 'I cultivated your Mother's acquaintance, thrice happy if I could have soothed her sorrows, or if the feeble Lamp of my Friendship could have yielded her one ray of Hope & Guidance.'[7] They kept in touch even after Coleridge moved with his family to Keswick in the Lake District in July 1800. He gave her a manuscript copy of *Kubla Khan*, which prompted *Mrs Robinson to the Poet Coleridge* (p. 254). In addition, her *The Snow-Drop* prompted Coleridge's poem of the same name, and her celebratory ode to the new-born Derwent Coleridge, *Ode Inscribed to the Infant Son of S. T. Coleridge* (p. 252), sent to Coleridge in manuscript, inspired his address to her, *A Stranger Minstrel* (which he later told Robinson's daughter was 'excessively silly'). Her *Lyrical Tales* (1800) were influenced by *Lyrical Ballads*, and almost persuaded Wordsworth to change the title of the second edition of his work.[8]

Robinson's reputation did not die with her. It was kept alive by her daughter, Mary Elizabeth Robinson, who collected together some of her fugitive verses, along with those of other poets, in *The Wild Wreath* (1804), and edited a complete edition of the *Poetical Works* (1806). Mary Robinson is one of the most important poets of her time, and readers seeking a fuller selection of her works should seek out Judith Pascoe's Broadview edition (2000) listed below. Robinson possessed a unique and original voice, and transcended her Della Cruscan roots to create something with the power to impress the up-and-coming Romantics. Even the influence of Wordsworth and Coleridge is transmuted, in *Lyrical Tales*, into something which, though reminiscent of *Lyrical Ballads*, is distinct from it. This is precisely how Coleridge felt when he first read *The Haunted Beach* in the *Morning Post*, where it appeared on 28 February 1800. He wrote immediately to Southey, advising him to include it in his forthcoming *Annual Anthology*: 'if you should not have received that day's paper, write immediately that I may transcribe it – it falls off sadly to the last – wants tale and interest; but the images are new and very distinct – that "silvery carpet" is so *just* that it is unfortunate it should *seem* so bad, for it is *really* good

Notes

[6] *Memoirs of the late Mrs Robinson* (2 vols., 1803), ii 125.

[7] Griggs ii 904.

[8] It is worth noting that *Odes* ed. George Dyer (Ludlow, 1800), published just before her death, contains one of her poems, *To Meditation*.

– but the metre – aye, that woman has an ear!'[9] It is not hard to see why Coleridge enjoyed the poem so much. Like some of his own, it plays on our susceptibility to the uncanny, the sinister, the spooky; the Gothicism is, perhaps, a little crude next to *Christabel* or *The Ancient Mariner*, but it works. The anonymous author of the biography appended to her *Memoirs* recounted the circumstances of its composition:

> On one of these nights of melancholy inspiration, she discovered from her window a small boat struggling in the spray, which dashed against the wall of her garden. Presently two fishermen brought on shore in their arms a burden which, notwithstanding the distance, Mrs Robinson perceived to be a human body, which the fishermen, after covering it with a sail from their boat, left on the land and disappeared. But a short time elapsed before the men returned, bringing with them fuel, with which they vainly endeavoured to reanimate their unfortunate charge. Struck with a circumstance so affecting, which the stillness of the night rendered yet more impressive, Mrs Robinson remained for some time at her window, motionless with horror. At length, recovering her recollection, she alarmed the family, but before they could gain the beach, the men had again departed. The morning dawned, and day broke in upon the tragical scene. The bathers passed and repassed with little concern, while the corpse continued, extended on the shore, not twenty yards from the Steine. During the course of the day many persons came to look on the body, which still remained unclaimed and unknown. Another day wore away, and the corpse was unburied, the lord of the manor having refused to a fellow-being a grave in which his bones might decently repose, alleging as an excuse *that he did not belong to that parish*. Mrs Robinson, humanely indignant at the scene which passed, exerted herself, but without success, to procure by subscription a small sum for performing the last duties to a wretched outcast. Unwilling, by an ostentatious display of her name, to offend the higher and more fastidious powers, she presented to the fishermen her own contribution, and declined further to interfere. The affair dropped, and the body of the stranger, being dragged to the cliff, was covered by a heap of stones without the ceremony of a prayer.
>
> These circumstances made on the mind of Mrs Robinson a deep and lasting impression; even at a distant period she could not repeat them without horror and indignation. This incident gave rise to the poem entitled *The Haunted Beach*, written but a few months before her death.[10]

Further reading

Mary Robinson, *Selected Poems* ed. Judith Pascoe (Peterborough, Ontario, 2000).

Mary Robinson, *A Letter to the Women of England, on the Injustice of Mental Subordination* ed. Adriana Craciun, Anne Irmen Close, Megan Musgrave and Orianne Smith (http://www.rc.umd.edu/editions/contemps/robinson/cover.htm).

Stuart Curran, 'Mary Robinson's *Lyrical Tales* in Context', in *Re-Visioning Romanticism* ed. Carol Shiner Wilson and Joel Haefner (Philadelphia, 1994), pp. 17–35.

Susan Luther, 'A Stranger Minstrel: Coleridge's Mrs Robinson', *SIR* 33 (1994) 391–409.

Jerome J. McGann, *The Poetics of Sensibility: A Revolution in Literary Style* (Oxford, 1996), pp. 94–116.

Jacqueline Labbe, 'Selling One's Sorrows: Charlotte Smith, Mary Robinson, and the Marketing of Poetry, *TWC* 25 (1994) 68–71.

Judith Pascoe, 'Mary Robinson and the Literary Marketplace', in *Romantic Women Writers* ed. Paula R. Feldman and Theresa M. Kelley (Hanover, NH, 1995), pp. 252–68.

Lisa Vargo, 'The Claims of "real life and manners": Coleridge and Mary Robinson', *TWC* 26 (1995) 134–7.

Notes

[9] Griggs i 576. See also Coleridge's letter to Mary Elizabeth Robinson, Griggs ii 903–6.

[10] *Memoirs of the late Mrs Robinson* (2 vols., 1803), ii 121–4.

A London Summer Morning (composed 1794)

From The Wild Wreath (1804)

Who has not waked to list the busy sounds
Of summer morning in the sultry smoke[1]
Of noisy London? On the pavement hot
The sooty chimney-boy, with dingy face
And tattered covering, shrilly bawls his trade,[2]
Rousing the sleepy housemaid. At the door
The milk-pail rattles, and the tinkling bell
Proclaims the dustman's office, while the street
Is lost in clouds imperious.[3] Now begins
The din of hackney coaches,[4] wagons, carts;
While tinmen's shops, and noisy trunk-makers,
Knife-grinders, coopers, squeaking cork-cutters,
Fruit-barrows, and the hunger-giving cries
Of vegetable vendors, fill the air.
Now ev'ry shop displays its varied trade,
And the fresh-sprinkled pavement cools the feet
Of early walkers. At the private door
The ruddy housemaid twirls the busy mop,
Annoying the smart 'prentice,[5] or neat[6] girl
Tripping with bandbox[7] lightly. Now the sun
Darts burning splendour on the glitt'ring pane,
Save where the canvas awning throws a shade
On the gay merchandise. Now spruce and trim
In shops where beauty smiles with industry,
Sits the smart damsel, while the passenger
Peeps through the window, watching ev'ry charm.
Now pastry dainties catch the eyes minute
Of hummy insects, while the slimy snare[8]
Waits to enthral them. Now the lamp-lighter
Mounts the slight ladder, nimbly venturous,
To trim the half-filled lamp,[9] while at his feet
The pot-boy[10] yells discordant. All along
The sultry pavement, the old-clothes man cries
In tone monotonous, and sidelong views
The area for his traffic. Now the bag
Is slily opened, and the half-worn suit

Notes

A London Summer Morning

[1] *sultry smoke* Though not a problem today, smog was a pervasive feature of 18th-century London due to the burning of wood fires and fossil fuels – a necessity even during the summer.

[2] *shrilly bawls his trade* He would have been crying out 'Sweep, sweep', like his colleague in Blake's 'The Chimney Sweep' (p. 183).

[3] *clouds imperious* commanding, or obscuring clouds of dust; the effect is of course mock-heroic. Note the Miltonic inversion of noun and adjective.

[4] *hackney coaches* four-wheeled coaches, drawn by two horses, with seats for six passengers.

[5] *'prentice* apprentice, probably a lawyer's clerk.

[6] *neat* smart, well-dressed.

[7] *bandbox* cardboard box for hats.

[8] *the slimy snare* fly-traps of some kind.

[9] *trim the half-filled lamp* The lamp-lighter's first task, in the morning, is to refill the lamp with fuel and to trim its wick, so that it will burn brightly when it is reignited that evening.

[10] *pot-boy* boy who serves beer to customers in a tavern.

(Sometimes the pilfered treasure of the base
Domestic spoiler) for one half its worth
Sinks in the green abyss. The porter now
Bears his huge load along the burning way,
And the poor poet wakes from busy dreams
To paint the summer morning.

The Haunted Beach[1]

From Lyrical Tales (1800)

Upon a lonely desert beach
    Where the white foam was scattered,
A little shed upreared its head,
    Though lofty barks were shattered.
The seaweeds gath'ring near the door
    A sombre path displayed,
And all around, the deaf'ning roar
Re-echoed on the chalky shore,
    By the green billows made.

Above, a jutting cliff was seen
    Where seabirds hovered, craving,
And all around the crags were bound
    With weeds, forever waving;
And here and there, a cavern wide
    Its shad'wy jaws displayed,
And near the sands, at ebb of tide,
A shivered mast was seen to ride
    Where the green billows strayed.

And often, while the moaning wind
    Stole o'er the summer ocean,
The moonlight scene was all serene,
    The waters scarce in motion;
Then while the smoothly slanting sand
    The tall cliff wrapped in shade,
The fisherman beheld a band
Of spectres gliding hand in hand,
    Where the green billows played.

And pale their faces were as snow,
    And sullenly they wandered;
And to the skies, with hollow eyes,
    They looked, as though they pondered.
And sometimes from their hammock shroud

Notes

THE HAUNTED BEACH

[1] Robinson's biographer relates the story of how this poem came to be written, headnote, p. 248, above.

They dismal howlings made;
And while the blast blew strong and loud
The clear moon marked the ghastly crowd
Where the green billows played.

And then above the haunted hut,
The curlews, screaming, hovered;
And the low door, with furious roar,
The frothy breakers covered.
For in the fisherman's lone shed
A murdered man was laid,
With ten wide gashes on his head;
And deep was made his sandy bed
Where the green billows played.

A shipwrecked mariner was he,
Doomed from his home to sever,
Who swore to be, through wind and sea,
Firm and undaunted ever;
And when the wave resistless rolled,
About his arm he made
A packet rich of Spanish gold,
And, like a British sailor bold,
Plunged where the billows played.

The spectre band, his messmates brave,
Sunk in the yawning ocean,
While to the mast he lashed him fast
And braved the storm's commotion.
The winter moon upon the sand
A silv'ry carpet[2] made,
And marked the sailor reach the land,
And marked his murd'rer wash his hand,
Where the green billows played.

And since that hour the fisherman
Has toiled and toiled in vain;
For all the night, the moony light
Gleams on the spectred main.
And when the skies are veiled in gloom,
The murd'rer's liquid way
Bounds o'er the deeply yawning tomb,
And flashing fires the sands illume
Where the green billows play.

Full thirty years his task has been,
Day after day more weary;
For Heaven designed his guilty mind
Should feed on prospects dreary.

Notes

[2] *silv'ry carpet* For Coleridge's admiring comment on this, see p. 247, above.

Bound by a strong and mystic chain,
He has not pow'r to stray,
But destined mis'ry to sustain,
He wastes, in solitude and pain,
A loathsome life away.

Ode Inscribed to the Infant Son of S.T. Coleridge, Esq. Born 14 September 1800 at Keswick in Cumberland.

From The Poetical Works of the Late Mrs Robinson (1806)

Spirit of Light, whose eye unfolds
The vast expanse of Nature's plan;
And from thy eastern throne[1] beholds
The mazy paths of the lorn traveller – man!
To thee I sing, Spirit of Light, to thee
Attune the varying strain of wood-wild minstrelsy![2]

Oh pow'r creative, but for thee
Eternal chaos all things would enfold,
And black as Erebus[3] this system be,
In its ethereal space, benighted, rolled.
But for thy influence, e'en this day
Would slowly, sadly, pass away;
Nor proudly mark the mother's tear of joy,[4]
The smile seraphic of the baby boy,
The father's eyes, in fondest transport taught
To beam with tender hope, to speak the enraptured thought.

To thee I sing, Spirit of Light, to thee
Attune the strain of wood-wild minstrelsy!
Thou sail'st o'er Skiddaw's[5] heights sublime,
Swift borne upon the wings of joyous time!
The sunny train, with widening sweep,
Rolls blazing down the misty-mantled steep;
And far and wide its rosy ray
Flushes the dewy-silvered breast of day!
Hope-fost'ring day, which Nature bade impart
Heav'n's proudest rapture to the parent's heart.

Day! First ordained to see the baby pressed
Close to its beauteous mother's throbbing breast,
While instinct, in its laughing eyes, foretold

Notes

Ode Inscribed

[1] *eastern throne* the sun rises in the east.

[2] *wood-wild minstrelsy* cf. Shakespeare, who in Milton's *L'Allegro* is said to 'Warble his native wood-notes wild' (l. 134).

[3] *Erebus* In Greek cosmology, Erebus (darkness) and Nyx were the offspring of Chaos.

[4] *the mother's tear of joy* Pascoe notes that Mrs Coleridge was in correspondence with Mrs Robinson.

[5] *Skiddaw* oldest and fourth highest peak in the Lake District (3,053 ft). Robinson never saw the Lakes, and is dependent on Coleridge's descriptions. She had written to him at around the time she composed this poem: 'Oh Skiddaw! I think, if I could but once contemplate thy summit, I should never quit the prospect it would present till my eyes were closed for ever' (Griggs ii 669).

The mind susceptible, the spirit bold,
The lofty soul, the virtues prompt to trace
The wrongs that haunt mankind o'er life's tempestuous space.

Romantic mountains,[6] from whose brows sublime
Imagination might to frenzy turn,
Or to the starry worlds in fancy climb,
Scorning this low earth's solitary bourn;[7]
Bold cataracts,[8] on whose headlong tide
The midnight whirlwinds howling ride;
Calm-bosomed lakes that, trembling, hail
The cold breath of the morning gale,
And on your lucid mirrors wide display,
In colours rich, in dewy lustre gay;
Mountains and woodlands, as the dappled dawn
Flings its soft pearl-drops on the summer lawn;
Or paly moonlight, rising slow,
While o'er the hills the ev'ning zephyrs blow –
Ye all shall lend your wonders, all combine
To bless the baby boy with harmonies divine.

Oh baby, when thy unchained tongue
Shall, lisping, speak thy fond surprise;
When the rich strain thy father sung
Shall from thy imitative accents rise;
When through thy soul rapt Fancy shall diffuse
The mightier magic of his loftier muse –
Thy wakened spirit, wond'ring, shall behold
Thy native mountains capped with streamy gold,
Thy native lakes, their cloud-topped hills among,
Oh hills made sacred by thy parent's song![9]
Then shall thy soul, legitimate,[10] expand,
And the proud lyre quick throb at thy command!
And Wisdom, ever watchful, o'er thee smile,
His white locks waving to the blast the while;
And pensive Reason, pointing to the sky,
Bright as the morning star her clear broad eye,
Unfold the page of Nature's book sublime –
The lore of ev'ry age, the boast of ev'ry clime!

Sweet baby boy, accept a stranger's song;
An untaught minstrel joys to sing of thee!
And, all alone, her forest haunts among,
Courts the wild tone of mazy harmony!
A stranger's song, babe of the mountain wild,

Notes

[6] *Romantic mountains* Robinson had not visited the Lake District, but probably had a good knowledge of it through picturesque guidebooks and engravings.

[7] *bourn* limit, boundary.

[8] *cataracts* waterfalls.

[9] *thy parent's song* probably a reference to *Frost at Midnight* 59–63.

[10] *legitimate* genuine, intense.

Greets thee as Inspiration's darling child!
Oh may the fine-wrought spirit of thy sire
Awake thy soul and breathe upon thy lyre!
And blessed, amid thy mountain haunts sublime,
Be all thy days, thy rosy infant days,
And may the never-tiring steps of time
Press lightly on with thee o'er life's disastrous maze.

Ye hills, coeval[11] with the birth of time!
Bleak summits, linked in chains of rosy light!
Oh may your wonders many a year invite
Your native son the breezy path to climb
Where, in majestic pride of solitude,
Silent and grand, the hermit thought shall trace,
Far o'er the wild infinity of space,
The sombre horrors of the waving wood;
The misty glen; the river's winding way;
The last deep blush of summer's ling'ring day;
The winter storm that, roaming unconfined,
Sails on the broad wings of the impetuous wind.

Oh, whether on the breezy height
Where Skiddaw greets the dawn of light,
Ere the rude sons of labour homage pay
To summer's flaming eye or winter's banner grey;
Whether Lodore[12] its silver torrent flings
The mingling wonders of a thousand springs;
Whether smooth Bassenthwaite,[13] at eve's still hour,
Reflects the young moon's crescent pale,
Or meditation seeks her silent bow'r
Amid the rocks of lonely Borrowdale[14] –
Still may thy name survive, sweet boy, till Time
Shall bend to Keswick's vale thy Skiddaw's brow sublime!

Mrs Robinson to the Poet Coleridge (composed October 1800)[1]

From Memoirs of the Late Mrs Robinson (1801)

Rapt in the visionary theme,
Spirit divine, with thee I'll wander,
Where the blue, wavy, lucid stream
Mid forest glooms shall slow meander!
With thee I'll trace the circling bounds
Of thy new paradise, extended,

Notes

[11] *coeval* the same age as; as old as.

[12] *Lodore* large waterfall on the banks of Derwentwater, near Keswick.

[13] *Bassenthwaite* large lake, at one end of which is Keswick.

[14] *Borrowdale* the valley at the opposite end of Derwentwater from Keswick.

Mrs Robinson to the Poet Coleridge

[1] This poem is a tribute to Coleridge's *Kubla Khan* (see p. 620), and contains numerous allusions to it.

And listen to the varying sounds
Of winds and foamy torrents blended!

Now by the source, which lab'ring heaves
The mystic fountain, bubbling, panting,
While gossamer its network weaves[2]
Adown the blue lawn, slanting –
I'll mark thy 'sunny dome' and view
Thy 'caves of ice',[3] thy fields of dew,
Thy ever-blooming mead, whose flow'r
Waves to the cold breath of the moonlight hour!
Or, when the day-star,[4] peering bright
On the grey wing of parting night;
While more than vegetating pow'r
Throbs, grateful to the burning hour,
As summer's whispered sighs unfold
Her million million buds of gold! –
Then will I climb the breezy bounds
Of thy new paradise, extended,
And listen to the distant sounds
Of winds and foamy torrents blended!

Spirit divine, with thee I'll trace
Imagination's boundless space!
With thee, beneath thy 'sunny dome'
I'll listen to the minstrel's lay
Hymning the gradual close of day;
In 'caves of ice' enchanted roam,
Where on the glitt'ring entrance plays
The moon's beam with its silv'ry rays;[5]
Or when the glassy stream
That through the deep dell flows,
Flashes the noon's hot beam –
The noon's hot beam that midway shows
Thy flaming temple, studded o'er
With all Peruvia's lustrous store![6]
There will I trace the circling bounds
Of thy new paradise, extended,
And listen to the awful sounds
Of winds and foamy torrents blended.

And now I'll pause to catch the moan
Of distant breezes, cavern-pent;
Now, ere the twilight tints are flown,
Purpling the landscape far and wide,

Notes

[2] *While gossamer . . . weaves* fine filmy substance, consisting of cobwebs, spun by small spiders, seen spread over the lawn.

[3] *Kubla Khan* 36.

[4] *day-star* morning star.

[5] *silv'ry rays* As Robinson was aware, Coleridge had admired the 'silv'ry carpet' in 'The Haunted Beach'; see p. 247.

[6] *With all . . . store* Peru had long been celebrated for its natural reserves of gold, silver and precious stones.

On the dark promontory's side
I'll gather wild-flow'rs, dew-besprent,
And weave a crown for thee,
Genius of heav'n-taught poesy!
While, op'ning to my wond'ring eyes,
Thou bid'st a new creation rise,
I'll raptured trace the circling bounds
Of thy rich paradise, extended,
And listen to the varying sounds
Of winds and foamy torrents blended.

And now, with lofty tones inviting,
Thy nymph, her dulcimer swift-smiting,
Shall wake me in ecstatic measures
Far, far removed from mortal pleasures,
In cadence rich, in cadence strong,
Proving the wondrous witcheries of song!
I hear her voice – thy 'sunny dome',
Thy 'caves of ice' aloud repeat –
Vibrations, madd'ning sweet,
Calling the visionary wand'rer home!
She sings of thee, oh favoured child
Of minstrelsy, sublimely wild! –
Of thee whose soul can feel the tone
Which gives to airy dreams a magic all thy own!

The Savage of Aveyron (composed October 1800)[1]

From The Wild Wreath (1804)

'Twas in the mazes of a wood,
The lonely wood of Aveyron,
I heard a melancholy tone:
It seemed to freeze my blood!
A torrent near was flowing fast,
And hollow was the midnight blast
As o'er the leafless woods it passed
While terror-fraught I stood!
Oh mazy woods of Aveyron,
Oh wilds of dreary solitude!
Amid thy thorny alleys rude
I thought myself alone!
I thought no living thing could be
So weary of the world as me,

Notes

THE SAVAGE OF AVEYRON

[1] Pascoe points out that this poem was probably inspired by reports in the *Morning Post* of the wild boy of Aveyron: 'He lived on potatoes, chestnuts, and acorns . . . His features are regular, but without expression; every part of his body is covered with scars; these scars attest the cruelty of the persons by whom, it is presumed, he has been abandoned; or perhaps they are attributable only to the dangers of a solitary existence at a tender age, and in a rude tract of country' (*Morning Post* 3 October 1800).

While on my winding path the pale moon shone.

Sometimes the tone was loud and sad,
And sometimes dulcet, faint, and slow;
And then a tone of frantic woe:
It almost made me mad.
The burden was 'Alone! Alone!'
And then the heart did feebly groan;
Then suddenly a cheerful tone
Proclaimed a spirit glad!
Oh mazy woods of Aveyron,
Oh wilds of dreary solitude!
Amid your thorny alleys rude
I wished myself a traveller alone.

'Alone!' I heard the wild boy say,
And swift he climbed a blasted oak;
And there, while morning's herald woke,
He watched the opening day.
Yet dark and sunken was his eye,
Like a lorn maniac's, wild and shy,
And scowling like a winter sky,
Without one beaming ray!
Then, mazy woods of Aveyron
Then, wilds of dreary solitude,
Amid thy thorny alleys rude
I sighed to be a traveller alone.

'Alone! Alone!' I heard him shriek –
'Twas like the shriek of dying man!
And then to mutter he began,
But oh, he *could not speak*!
I saw him point to heav'n and sigh,
The big drop trembled in his eye;
And slowly from the yellow sky
I saw the pale morn break.
I saw the woods of Aveyron
Their wilds of dreary solitude;
I marked their thorny alleys rude,
And wished to be a traveller alone!

His hair was long and black, and he
From infancy *alone* had been;
For since his fifth year he had seen,
None marked his destiny!
No mortal ear had heard his groan,
For him no beam of hope had shone;
While sad he sighed, 'Alone! Alone!'
Beneath the blasted tree.
And then, oh woods of Aveyron,
Oh wilds of dreary solitude,
Amid your thorny alleys rude
I thought myself a traveller alone.

And now upon the blasted tree
He carved three notches broad and long,
And all the while he sang a song
Of nature's melody!
And though of words he nothing knew,
And though his dulcet tones were few,
Across the yielding bark he drew,
Deep sighing, notches three.
Oh mazy woods of Aveyron,
Oh wilds of dreary solitude,
Amid your thorny alleys rude
Upon this blasted oak no sunbeam shone.

And now he pointed one, two, three;
Again he shrieked with wild dismay;
And now he paced the thorny way,
Quitting the blasted tree.
It was a dark December morn,
The dew was frozen on the thorn,
But to a wretch so sad, so lorn,
All days alike would be!
Yet mazy woods of Aveyron,
Yet wilds of dreary solitude,
Amid your frosty alleys rude
I wished to be a traveller alone.

He followed me along the wood
To a small grot his hands had made,
Deep in a black rock's sullen shade,
Beside a tumbling flood.
Upon the earth I saw him spread
Of withered leaves a narrow bed,
Yellow as gold, and streaked with red –
They looked like streaks of blood!
Pulled from the woods of Aveyron
And scattered o'er the solitude
By midnight whirlwinds strong and rude,
To pillow the scorched brain that throbbed alone.

Wild berries were his winter food,
With them his sallow lip was dyed;
On chestnuts wild he fed beside,
Steeped in the foamy flood.
Chequered with scars his breast was seen,
Wounds streaming fresh with anguish keen,
And marks where other wounds had been
Torn by the brambles rude.
Such was the boy of Aveyron,
The tenant of that solitude,
Where still, by misery unsubdued,
He wandered nine long winters all alone.

Before the step of his rude throne,
The squirrel sported, tame and gay,
The dormouse slept its life away
Nor heard his midnight groan.
About his form a garb he wore,
Ragged it was, and marked with gore,
And yet where'er 'twas folded o'er
Full many a spangle shone!
Like little stars, oh Aveyron,
They gleamed amid thy solitude;
Or like, along thy alleys rude,
The summer dewdrops sparkling in the sun.

It once had been a lady's vest,
White as the whitest mountain's snow,
Till ruffian hands had taught to flow
The fountain of her breast!
Remembrance bade the wild boy trace
Her beauteous form, her angel face,
Her eye that beamed with heavenly grace,
Her fainting voice that blessed,
When in the woods of Aveyron
Deep in their deepest solitude,
Three barb'rous ruffians shed her blood,
And mocked, with cruel taunts, her dying groan.

Remembrance traced the summer bright,
When all the trees were fresh and green,
When lost the alleys long between,
The lady passed the night;
She passed the night, bewildered wild,
She passed it with her fearless child
Who raised his little arms and smiled
To see the morning light.
While in the woods of Aveyron
Beneath the broad oak's canopy,
She marked aghast the ruffians three
Waiting to seize the traveller alone!

Beneath the broad oak's canopy
The lovely lady's bones were laid;
But since that hour no breeze has played
About the blasted tree!
The leaves all withered ere the sun
His next day's rapid course had run,
And ere the summer day was done
It winter seemed to be.
And still, oh woods of Aveyron,
Amid thy dreary solitude
The oak a sapless trunk has stood,
To mark the spot where murder foul was done!

From her the wild boy learned 'Alone!'
She tried to say, 'My babe will die!'
But angels caught her parting sigh,

The babe her dying tone.
And from that hour the boy has been
Lord of the solitary scene,
Wand'ring the dreary shades between,
Making his dismal moan!
Till, mazy woods of Aveyron,
Dark wilds of dreary solitude,
Amid your thorny alleys rude
I thought myself alone.
And could a wretch more wretched be,
More wild or fancy-fraught than he,
Whose melancholy tale would pierce an heart of stone?

Robert Burns (1759–1796)

Scotland's greatest poet did not live to see the birth of the new literary movement (if one dates it from publication of *Lyrical Ballads* in 1798), but his work was such a powerful influence on its authors that many would claim him as its godfather, if not its progenitor – titles he deserves to share with Cowper. His finest single poem, included here in its earliest published form, exemplifies the element of the picaresque that runs through Romanticism, articulated in 'The Idiot Boy', 'Peter Bell', 'The Ancient Mariner' and *Don Juan*; as Wordsworth once said, 'Who but some impenetrable dunce, or narrow-minded puritan in works of art, ever read without delight the picture which [Burns] has drawn of the convivial exaltation of the rustic adventurer, Tam o' Shanter?' (Owen and Smyser iii 124).

Robert Burns was the oldest child of Agnes Broun and William Burnes, a tenant farmer. His father's rejection of Calvinism in favour of a less prescriptive, humanist faith was an act of defiance that helped forge his son's personality. In due course, he took over as chief labourer when his father's health went into decline. William Burnes died in 1784, leaving his son head of a large family at the age of 25. For some reason that event unleashed a period of remarkable creativity, including many of the poems published in his first book-length publication, *Poems Chiefly in the Scottish Dialect* (1786). It was an immediate success: 612 copies were printed and sold at three shillings each (the equivalent of £11 today). It sold out within a month of publication on 31 July 1786.

One of its most successful poems, 'Epistle to J. L*****k, an old Scotch bard', shows Burns's colloquial, lyric style at its most engaging. To gauge its impact, you have to imagine a time when the poetry pages of magazines and newspapers were filled with Popean imitations in decasyllabic couplets; odes to fear, hope and other abstract entities, and versifications of biblical episodes. The idea that someone could write something like the 'Epistle' was shocking enough, but that they should deploy an energetic folk stanza brimming with unfamiliar usages drawn from idiomatic lowland Scots was well nigh unprecedented, at least in polite circles. Not only that, but, as English readers swiftly discovered, Burns had no trouble in turning poems that initially must have seemed alienatingly avant-garde into meditations on the nature of human relationships; in this case its power derives from his kinship with a man he has never met. For some English readers the use of dialect words was an obstacle, but it did not hinder Burns' growing popularity – and certainly not among readers in the north of England, who also used them.

Among these was the 16-year-old William Wordsworth, who borrowed a copy of the Kilmarnock poems from the library in Penrith, close to the border. Burns' newness and freshness struck him immediately, and exerted a strong influence on the new poetic forged by the lyrical ballads just over a decade later; mindful of those qualities, Coleridge once described Burns as 'the only *always-natural* poet in our language'.

Burns's fearless appetite for the everyday must have seemed almost improper to readers brought up on poems that spouted pieties about personified virtues. Instead he writes about working people in taverns or describes detailed observations made at the plough – things as trivial as daisies, for instance, or mice; one is called 'To a Louse, On Seeing one on a Lady's Bonnet at Church'. How did that go down with the literary coteries of London? Very well, if the reviews are anything to go by: the *New London Magazine* remarked: 'We do not recollect to have ever met with a more signal instance of true and uncultivated genius than in the author of these poems.'

Part of his success lay in his versatility, for alongside the 'Epistle' and 'To a Mouse', Burns gave his public 'Man was Made to Mourn', non-dialect meditations on the more melancholy aspects of human existence so beloved of late eighteenth-century readers. It may be less daring than the dialect works, but he excels in it, and in doing so provided readers like Wordsworth with a model on which to base their own excursions in the genre, such as 'Simon Lee', 'The Last of the Flock' and 'Resolution and Independence'.

It is right that 'Tam o' Shanter' remains Burns's most important single work – not just for its obvious merits, but because it best exemplifies his strengths. It has endured both for its comedic appeal (and Burns is one of the funniest poetic talents in the literature) and his expert handling of the mock-Gothic storyline. No one could better have managed the orgiastic excesses of the witches' sabbath into which Tam drunkenly rides:

> The dancers quick and quicker flew –
> They reeled, they set, they crossed, they
> cleekit,
> Till ilka carlin swat and reekit
> And coost her duddies on the wark,
> And linket at it in her sark.
>
> (ll. 150–4)

You don't need to know that this is a description of the 'rigwoodie hags' dancing round a fire in order to find it both funny and compelling. Burns's language is imbued with a momentum of its own that induces laughter and exhilaration – an effect unstaled by familiarity. In his *Lectures on the English Poets* (1818) Hazlitt described it as a 'masterpiece': 'Burns has given the extremes of licentious eccentricity and convivial enjoyment in the story of this scape-grace, and of patriarchal simplicity and gravity in describing the old national character of the Scottish peasantry' (Wu ii 292). When writing to Burns, the critic Alexander Fraser Tytler was no less enthusiastic: 'I have seldom in my life tasted of higher enjoyment from any work of genius than I have received from this composition; and I am much mistaken if this poem alone, had you never written another syllable, would not have been sufficient to have transmitted your name down to posterity with high reputation.'[1]

Further reading

Robert Burns, *The Kilmarnock Poems* ed. Donald A. Low (London, 1985).

Tom Crawford, *Burns: A Study* (Edinburgh, 1960).

David Daiches, *Robert Burns: The Poet* (London, 1950, rev. 1966).

Maurice Lindsay, *The Burns Encyclopaedia* (London, 1959).

James Mackay, *Burns: A Biography* (Edinburgh, 1992).

Carol McGuirk, *Robert Burns and the Sentimental Era* (Athens, Ga., 1985).

Franklyn Snyder, *The Life of Robert Burns* (London, 1932).

Notes

[1] *Robert Burns: The Critical Heritage* ed. Donald A. Low (London, 1974), p. 95.

From Poems, Chiefly in the Scottish Dialect (1786)

Epistle to J. L*****k,[1] an old Scotch bard, 1 April 1785

While briers an' woodbines budding green,
An' paitricks[2] scraichan loud at e'en,
And morning poossie[3] whiddan[4] seen,
Inspire my muse,
This freedom, in an *unknown* frien',
I pray excuse.

On Fasteneen[5] we had a rockin,[6]
To ca' the crack[7] and weave our stockin;
And there was muckle fun and jokin,
Ye need na doubt;
At length we had a hearty yokin,[8]
At sang about.[9]

There was ae sang[10] amang the rest,
Aboon them a' it pleased me best,
That some kind husband had addressed
To some sweet wife:
It thirled the heart-strings through the breast,
A' to the life.

I've scarce heard aught described[11] sae weel
What gen'rous,[12] manly bosoms feel;
Thought I, 'Can this be Pope or Steele
Or Beattie's wark?'[13]
They tald me 'twas an odd kind chiel[14]
About Muirkirk.[15]

It pat me fidgean-fain[16] to hear't,
An' sae about him there I spier't;[17]
Then a' that kent him round declared

Notes

Epistle to J. L*****k

[1] *J. L*****k* John Lapraik (1727–1807) was a tenant farmer imprisoned for debt in Ayr, 1785. He composed poetry in prison, and published his *Poems on Several Occasions* in Kilmarnock, 1788. Burns had not met him at the time he composed this epistolary poem.

[2] *paitricks* partridges.

[3] *poossie* hare.

[4] *whiddan* scudding.

[5] *Fasteneen* Shrove-Tuesday evening.

[6] *rockin* social evening featuring stories and songs.

[7] *ca' the crack* have a chat.

[8] *yokin* set-to.

[9] *sang about* singing in turn.

[10] *ae sang* Lapraik's 'When I upon thy bosom lean', a song addressed to his wife at a time when she was anxious about their misfortunes. It was published in Lapraik's *Poems on Several Occasions* (1788).

[11] *aught described* anything that described.

[12] *gen'rous* kind, sympathetic.

[13] *Can this be . . . wark* all writers skilled at describing tender feelings – Pope in such poems as *Elegy to the Memory of an Unfortunate Lady,* Steele in his essays, James Beattie (1735–1803) in *The Minstrel*, a semi-autobiographical poem in Spenserian stanzas. Burns is almost certainly recalling Beattie's account of Edwin's sensitivity and kindness.

[14] *chiel* man.

[15] *Muirkirk* Lapraik lived at Dalfram, on Ayr Water, near the village of Muirkirk.

[16] *fidgean-fain* fidgeting with eagerness.

[17] *spier't* asked about him.

He had ingine,[18]
That nane excelled it, few cam near't,
It was sae fine.

That set him to a pint of ale,
An' either douse[19] or merry tale,
Or rhymes an' sangs he'd made himsel,
Or witty catches –
'Tween Inverness and Tiviotdale[20]
He had few matches.

Then up I gat, an swoor an aith,[21]
Though I should pawn my pleugh an' graith,[22]
Or die a cadger pownie's[23] death
At some dyke-back,[24]
A pint an' gill I'd gie them baith
To hear your crack.[25]

But first an' foremost, I should tell,
Amaist as soon as I could spell,
I to the crambo-jingle[26] fell,
Though rude an' rough,
Yet crooning to a body's sel[27]
Does weel eneugh.

I am nae poet, in a sense,
But just a rhymer like by chance,
An' hae to learning nae pretence –
Yet what the matter?
Whene'er my muse does on me glance,
I jingle at her.

Your critic-folk may cock their nose
And say, 'How can you e'er propose
You wha ken[28] hardly verse frae prose,
To mak a sang?'
But by your leaves, my learned foes,
Ye're maybe wrang.
What's a' your jargon o' your schools,
Your Latin names for horns an' stools?

Notes

[18] *ingine* genius, ingenuity.
[19] *douse* sweet.
[20] *'Tween Inverness and Tiviotdale* between the north and south of Scotland.
[21] *swoor an aith* swore an oath.
[22] *pleugh an' graith* plough and harness. Throughout his work Burns portrays himself as a humble ploughman. Although he had much experience as a farmer, it was a pose that belied both his education and his long apprenticeship in literary Edinburgh.
[23] *cadger pownie* pony belonging to a hawker.
[24] *dyke-back* behind a wall.
[25] *crack* conversation.
[26] *crambo-jingle* rhyming songs.
[27] *crooning to a body's sel* singing to oneself.
[28] *ken* know.

If honest nature made you fools,
What sairs[29] your Grammars?
Ye'd better taen up spades and shools[30]
Or knappin-hammers.[31]

A set o' dull, conceited hashes[32]
Confuse their brains in College classes!
They gang in stirks[33] and come out asses,[34]
Plain truth to speak;
An' syne[35] they think to climb Parnassus
By dint o' Greek!

Gie me ae spark o' nature's fire,
That's a' the learning I desire;
Then, though I drudge through dub[36] an' mire
At pleugh or cart,
My muse, though hamely in attire,
May touch the heart.[37]

Oh for a spunk[38] o' Allan's glee,
Or Ferguson's, the bauld an' slee,[39]
Or bright Lapraik's, my friend to be,[40]
If I can hit it!
That would be lear[41] eneugh for me,
If I could get it.

Now sir, if ye hae friends enow,
Though real friends I b'lieve are few,
Yet, if your catalogue be fow,[42]
I'se no insist;
But gif ye want ae friend that's true,
I'm on your list.

I winna blaw[43] about mysel,
As ill I like my fauts to tell;
But friends an' folk that wish me well,
They sometimes roose[44] me –
Though I maun own as monie still
As far abuse me.

Notes

[29] *sairs* serves.
[30] *shools* shovels.
[31] *knappin-hammers* hammers for breaking stones or flints.
[32] *hashes* fools.
[33] *stirks* steers.
[34] *asses* young bullocks.
[35] *syne* then.
[36] *dub* puddle.
[37] Wordsworth was so attached to this stanza that he used lines 73–4 and 77–8 as an epigraph to 'The Ruined Cottage' MS.B.
[38] *spunk* spark.
[39] *bauld an' slee* bold and clever.
[40] Allan Ramsay (1686–1758), Scottish poet; Robert Ferguson (1750–74), whose *Poems* (Edinburgh, 1773) strongly influenced Burns; John Lapraik (1727–1807), whose *Poems on Several Occasions* was published at Kilmarnock, 1788.
[41] *lear* learning.
[42] *fow* full.
[43] *blaw* boast.
[44] *roose* praise.

There's ae wee faut they whiles lay to me:
I like the lasses (Gude forgie me!);
For monie a plack[45] they wheedle frae me
At dance or fair –
Maybe some ither thing they gie me
They weel can spare.

But Mauchline Race[46] or Mauchline Fair,
I should be proud to meet you there;
We'se gie ae night's discharge to care
If we forgather,
An' hae a swap o' rhymin-ware
Wi' ane anither.

The four-gill chap,[47] we'se gar him clatter,
An' kirs'n[48] him wi' reekin[49] water;
Syne we'll sit down an' tak our whitter[50]
To cheer our heart;
An' faith, we'se be acquainted better
Before we part.

Awa ye selfish, warly[51] race,
Wha think that havins, sense an' grace,
Ev'n love an' friendship should give place
To 'catch-the-plack'![52]
I dinna like to see your face,
Nor hear your crack.

But ye whom social pleasure charms,
Whose hearts the tide of kindness warms,
Who hold your being on the terms,
'Each aid the others' –
Come to my bowl, come to my arms,
My friends, my brothers!

But to conclude my lang epistle,
As my auld pen's worn to the grissle;[53]
Twa lines frae you wad gar me fissle,[54]
Who am, most fervent,
While I can either sing or whistle,
Your friend and servant.

Notes

[45] *plack* coin.

[46] *Mauchline Race* Horses still race at the course in Mauchline, East Ayrshire.

[47] *chap* cup. A 'gill' is a small measure (of alcohol).

[48] *kirs'n* christen.

[49] *reekin* steaming.

[50] *whitter* draught.

[51] *warly* worldly.

[52] *catch-the-plack* money-making.

[53] *grissle* his quill pen is worn down.

[54] *gar me fissle* make me fidget (with excitement).

Man was Made to Mourn, A Dirge (composed August 1785)

I

When chill November's surly blast
Made fields and forests bare,
One ev'ning, as I wand'red forth
Along the banks of Aire,[1]
I spied a man whose aged step
Seemed weary, worn with care;[2]
His face was furrowed o'er with years
And hoary was his hair.

II

'Young stranger, whither wand'rest thou?'
Began the rev'rend sage,
'Does thirst of wealth thy step constrain,
Or youthful pleasure's rage?
Or haply, pressed with cares and woes,
Too soon thou hast began
To wander forth, with me to mourn
The miseries of man.

III

The sun that overhangs yon moors,
Out-spreading far and wide,
Where hundreds labour to support
A haughty lordling's pride;
I've seen yon weary winter sun
Twice forty times return,
And ev'ry time has added proofs
That man was made to mourn.

IV

Oh man, while in thy early years,
How prodigal of time!
Misspending all thy precious hours,
Thy glorious, youthful prime!
Alternate follies take the sway,
Licentious passions burn,
Which tenfold force gives nature's law
That man was made to mourn.

V

Look not alone on youthful prime
Or manhood's active might;
Man then is useful to his kind,
Supported is his right:

Notes

MAN WAS MADE TO MOURN

[1] The River Ayr rises on the western border of Scotland and flows east to the sea.

[2] *I spied a man . . . care* This solitary was an influence on Wordsworth's leech-gatherer in *Resolution and Independence*.

But see him on the edge of life,
  With cares and sorrows worn,
Then age and want (oh, ill-matched pair!)
  Show man was made to mourn.

VI

A few seem favourites of fate,
  In pleasure's lap caressed;
Yet think not all the rich and great
  Are likewise truly blessed.
But oh! what crowds in ev'ry land,
  All wretched and forlorn,
Through weary life this lesson learn –
  That man was made to mourn!

VII

Many and sharp the num'rous ills
  Enwoven with our frame!
More pointed still we make ourselves
  Regret, remorse and shame!
And man, whose heav'n-erected face
  The smiles of love adorn,
Man's inhumanity to man[3]
  Makes countless thousands mourn!

VIII

See yonder poor, o'erlaboured wight,
  So abject, mean and vile,
Who begs a brother of the earth
  To give him leave to toil;[4]
And see his lordly fellow-worm
  The poor petition spurn –
Unmindful, though a weeping wife
  And helpless offspring mourn.

IX

If I'm designed yon lordling's slave,
  By nature's law designed,
Why was an independent wish
  E'er planted in my mind?
If not, why am I subject to
  His cruelty or scorn?
Or why has man the will and pow'r
  To make his fellow mourn?

Notes

[3] *Man's inhumanity to man* Donald Low notes an allusion to Edward Young, *Night Thoughts* viii 104–5: 'Man's . . . endless inhumanities to man'.

[4] *To give him leave to toil* As Low notes, De Quincey refers to 'those groans which ascended to heaven from [Burns's] over-burdened heart – those harrowing words, "To give him leave to toil", which record almost a reproach to the ordinances of God' (Masson ii 137).

X

Yet let not this too much, my son,
　Disturb thy youthful breast;
This partial view of humankind
　Is surely not the last!
The poor, oppressed, honest man
　Had never, sure, been born,
Had there not been some recompense
　To comfort those that mourn!

XI

Oh death – the poor man's dearest friend,
　The kindest and the best!
Welcome the hour, my aged limbs
　Are laid with thee at rest!
The great, the wealthy, fear thy blow,
　From pomp and pleasure torn;
But oh, a blessed relief for those
　That weary-laden mourn!'

To a Mouse, on turning her up in her nest, with the plough, November 1785[1]

Wee, sleeket,[2] cowran,[3] tim'rous beastie,
Oh what a panic's in thy breastie![4]
Thou need na start awa sae hasty
　Wi' bickering brattle![5]
I wad be laith[6] to rin[7] an' chase thee
　Wi' murd'ring pattle![8]

I'm truly sorry man's dominion
Has broken nature's social union,
An' justifies that ill opinion
　Which makes thee startle
At me, thy poor earth-born companion
　An' fellow mortal!

I doubt na, whyles, but thou may thieve;
What then? Poor beastie, thou maun live!
A daimen-icker in a thrave[9]

Notes

To a Mouse

[1] According to Burns's brother Gilbert, the poem was composed 'while the author was holding the plough'. John Blane, who worked on the plough with Burns, later recalled that he had chased the mouse with the intention of killing it, but was stopped by the poet, who then became 'thoughtful and abstracted'.

[2] *sleeket* smooth, sleek.

[3] *cowran* cowering.

[4] *breastie* little breast.

[5] *bickering brattle* scampering sounds.

[6] *laith* loath.

[7] *rin* run.

[8] *pattle* spade used to clear mud from the plough.

[9] *A daimen-icker in a thrave* the occasional ear of corn in a couple of stooks.

'S a sma' request:
I'll get a blessin wi' the lave,[10]
An' never miss't!

Thy wee-bit housie, too, in ruin!
It's silly wa's[11] the win's are strewin!
An' naething, now, to big[12] a new ane
O' foggage[13] green!
An' bleak December's winds ensuin,
Baith snell[14] an' keen!

Thou saw the fields laid bare an' wast,[15]
An' weary winter comin fast,
An' cozie here, beneath the blast,
Thou thought to dwell;
Till crash! the cruel coulter[16] passed
Out through thy cell.

That wee-bit heap o' leaves an' stibble[17]
Has cost thee monie a weary nibble!
Now thou's turned out, for a' thy trouble,
But[18] house or hald,
To thole[19] the winter's sleety dribble,
An' cranreuch[20] cauld!

But mousie, thou art no thy-lane[21]
In proving foresight may be vain:
The best-laid schemes o' mice an' men
Gang aft agley,[22]
An' lea'e us nought but grief an' pain
For promised joy!

Still, thou art blessed compared wi' me![23]
The present only toucheth thee:
But och! I backward cast my e'e
On prospects drear!
An' forward, though I canna see,
I guess an' fear!

Notes

[10] *lave* rest, remainder. Low notes the allusion to Deuteronomy 24: 19: 'When thou cuttest down thine harvest in thy field, and hast forgot a sheaf in the field, thou shalt not go again to fetch it; it shall be for the stranger, for the fatherless, and for the widow: that the Lord thy God may bless thee in all the work of thine hands.'

[11] *silly wa's* helpless walls.

[12] *big* build.

[13] *foggage* rank grass.

[14] *snell* sharp, severe.

[15] *wast* waste.

[16] *coulter* cutting blade of the plough.

[17] *stibble* stubble.

[18] *But* without.

[19] *thole* endure.

[20] *cranreuch* hoar-frost.

[21] *no thy-lane* not alone.

[22] *agley* awry.

[23] Donald Low notes the allusion to *Rasselas* chapter 2: 'As he passed through the fields, and saw the animals around him, "Ye", said he, "are happy, and need not envy me that walk thus among you, burdened with myself; nor do I, ye gentle beings, envy your felicity, for it is not the felicity of man. I have many distresses from which ye are free; I fear pain when I do not feel it; I sometimes shrink at evils recollected, and sometimes start at evils anticipated. Surely the equity of Providence has balanced peculiar sufferings with peculiar enjoyments."'

Tam o' Shanter. A Tale (composed late 1790)

From Francis Grose, The Antiquities of Scotland (1791)

When chapman billies[1] leave the street,
And drouthy[2] neebors, neebors meet,
As market-days are wearing late,
And folk begin to tak the gate;[3]
While we sit bowsing at the nappy,[4]
And gettin fou, and unco[5] happy,
We think na on the lang Scots miles,[6]
The waters, mosses, slaps[7] and styles
That lie between us and our hame,
Where sits our sulky sullen dame,
Gathering her brows like gathering storm,
Nursing her wrath to keep it warm.
   This truth fand honest Tam o' Shanter,
As he frae Ayr ae night did canter
(Auld Ayr, whom ne'er a town surpasses
For honest men and bonnie lasses).
   Oh Tam, hadst thou but been sae wise
As taen thy ain wife Kate's advice!
She tauld thee weel, thou was a skellum,[8]
A bletherin, blusterin, drunken blellum;[9]
That frae November till October,
Ae market-day thou was na sober;
That ilka melder[10] wi' the miller,
Thou sat as long as thou had siller;[11]
That every naig was ca'd a shoe on,
The smith and thee gat roarin fou[12] on;
That at the L—d's house, even on Sunday,
Thou drank wi' Kirkton Jean till Monday.
She prophesied that late or soon,
Thou wad be found deep drowned in Doon;[13]
Or catched wi' warlocks in the mirk,
By Alloway's auld haunted kirk.
   Ah, gentle dames, it gars me greet,[14]
To think how mony counsels sweet,
How mony lengthened sage advices,
The husband frae the wife despises!

Notes

Tam o'Shanter

[1] *chapman billies* pedlars.
[2] *drouthy* thirsty.
[3] *gate* road.
[4] *nappy* ale.
[5] *fou and unco* full and mighty.
[6] *the lang Scots miles* Scottish miles were longer than English ones; they were also variable. One measurement offered is 1,976 yards (as opposed to 1,760).
[7] *slaps* bogs.
[8] *skellum* good-for-nothing.
[9] *blellum* chatterer.
[10] *melder* meal-grinding.
[11] *siller* silver.
[12] *fou* drunk.
[13] *drowned in Doon* the River Doon runs through Ayrshire to the sea, beyond Burns's birthplace at Alloway.
[14] *gars me greet* makes me weep.

But to our tale: ae market-night
Tam had got planted[15] unco right,
Fast by an ingle bleezing[16] finely,
Wi' reamin swats[17] that drank divinely;
And at his elbow, souter[18] Johnie,
His ancient, trusty, drouthy crony -
Tam lo'ed him like a vera brither,
They had been fou for weeks tegither.
The night drave on wi' sangs and clatter,
And ay the ale was growing better;
The landlady and Tam grew gracious
With favours secret, sweet and precious;
The souter tauld his queerest stories,
The landlord's laugh was ready chorus;
The storm without might rair and rustle,
Tam did na mind the storm a whistle.
Care, mad to see a man sae happy,
E'en drowned himsel amang the nappy;
As bees flee hame wi' lades o' treasure,
The minutes winged their way wi' pleasure –
Kings may be blessed, but Tam was glorious,
O'er a' the ills o' life victorious![19]
But pleasures are like poppies spread:
You seize the flower, its bloom is shed;
Or like the snow-falls in the river,
A moment white, then melts for ever;[20]
Or like the borealis race[21]
That flit ere you can point their place;
Or like the rainbow's lovely form,
Evanishing amid the storm.
Nae man can tether time or tide,
The hour approaches Tam maun[22] ride;
That hour, o' night's black arch the keystane,[23]

Notes

[15] *planted* settled.
[16] *an ingle bleezing* a fire blazing.
[17] *reamin swats* foaming new ale.
[18] *souter* cobbler.
[19] *Kings may be blessed . . . victorious* important lines, as they make a political, as much as a moral, point. Wordsworth was especially keen on them, as Henry Crabb Robinson recalled: 'He praised Burns for his introduction to *Tam o' Shanter.* He had given a poetical apology for drunkenness by bringing together all the circumstances which can serve to render excusable what is in itself disgusting, thus interesting our feelings and making us tolerant of what would otherwise be not endurable' (Morley (1938) i 88).
[20] *Or like . . . ever* In a letter of 1814 Byron described these lines as 'very graceful and pleasing' (Marchand iv 56). Coleridge, in his Lectures on Shakespeare and Milton, described Burns as 'a person who balances sameness with difference – and triteness with novelty – who reconciles judgement with enthusiasm and vehemence with feeling – Art with Nature – the manner with the matter, and our admiration of the poem with the sympathy with the characters and incidents of the poem.'
[21] *borealis race* aurora borealis, the play of (apparently) cosmic light in the night sky.
[22] *maun* must.
[23] *keystane* The keystone is to be an important image (see l. 210).

That dreary hour he mounts his beast in;
And sic a night he taks the road in,
As ne'er poor sinner was abroad in.
  The wind blew as 'twad blawn its last,
The rattling showers rose on the blast,
The speedy gleams the darkness swallowed,
Loud, deep and lang, the thunder bellowed:
That night, a child might understand,
The Deil had business on his hand.
  Weel mounted on his grey mare, Meg
(A better never lifted leg),
Tam skelpit[24] on through dub[25] and mire,
Despising wind and rain and fire,
Whyles[26] holding fast his gude blue bonnet,
Whyles crooning o'er an auld Scots sonnet,
Whyles glowring round wi' prudent cares
Lest bogles[27] catch him unawares:
Kirk Alloway[28] was drawing nigh,
Whare ghaists and houlets nightly cry.
  By this time he was cross the ford
Where in the snaw the chapman smoored,[29]
And past the birks and meikle stane[30]
Where drunken Charlie brak's neck-bane;[31]
And through the whins and by the cairn
Where hunters fand the murdered bairn;
And near the tree aboon the well
Whare Mungo's mither hanged hersel.
Before him, Doon[32] pours all his floods;
The doubling storm roars through the woods;
The lightnings flash from pole to pole;
Near and more near, the thunders roll:
When, glimmering through groaning trees,
Kirk Alloway seemed in a bleeze[33] –
Through ilka bore[34] the beams were glancing,
And loud resounded mirth and dancing.
  Inspiring, bold John Barleycorn,[35]
What dangers thou canst make us scorn!
Wi' tippeny,[36] we fear nae evil;
Wi' usquabae,[37] we'll face the Devil!
The swats sae reamed in Tammie's noddle,

Notes

[24] *skelpit* hurried.
[25] *dub* pool.
[26] *Whyles* sometimes.
[27] *bogles* spectres.
[28] *Kirk Alloway* Alloway Church. By the time this poem was written the church was derelict, having last been used for worship in 1756.
[29] *smoored* was smothered.
[30] *birks and meikle stane* birch trees and large rocks.
[31] *brak's neck-bane* broke his neck.
[32] *Doon* the River Doon.
[33] *bleeze* blaze.
[34] *ilka bore* every gap.
[35] *John Barleycorn* malt whisky.
[36] *tippeny* ale.
[37] *usquabae* whisky.

Fair play, he cared na deils a boddle.[38]
But Maggie stood right sair astonished
Till, by the heel and hand admonished,
She ventured forward on the light,
And, wow, Tam saw an unco sight!
Warlocks and witches in a dance,
Nae cotillon brent new frae France,
But hornpipes, jigs, strathspeys and reels
Put life and mettle in their heels.
A winnock-bunker in the east,[39]
There sat auld Nick in shape o' beast:
A towzie tyke,[40] black, grim and large –
To gie them music was his charge.
He screwed the pipes and gart them skirl[41]
Till roof and rafters a' did dirl![42]
Coffins stood round like open presses
That shawed the dead in their last dresses,
And by some devilish cantraip[43] slight
Each in its cauld hand held a light
By which heroic Tam was able
To note upon the haly table[44]
A murderer's banes in gibbet airns;[45]
Twa span-lang,[46] wee, unchirstened bairns;
A thief new-cutted frae a rape,
Wi' his last gasp his gab did gape;
Five tomahawks, wi' blood red-rusted;
Five scymitars, wi' murder crusted;
A garter which a babe had strangled;
A knife a father's throat had mangled,
Whom his ain son of life bereft,
The grey hairs yet stak to the heft;
Wi' mair of horrible and awefu',
That even to name wad be unlawfu':
Three lawyers' tongues turned inside out,
Wi' lies seamed like a beggar's clout;
Three priests' hearts, rotten, black as muck,
Lay stinking, vile, in every neuk.[47]
  As Tammie glow'red, amazed and curious,
The mirth and fun grew fast and furious.
The piper loud and louder blew;

Notes

[38] *he cared na deils a boddle* He didn't care about devils (a boddle is a worthless copper coin).

[39] *A winnock-bunker in the east* a bunker beneath the small east window, at the far end of the church.

[40] *towzie tyke* shaggy dog.

[41] *He screwed the pipes and gart them skirl* He turned ('screwed') the drones on the bagpipes and made them squeal ('skirl').

[42] *dirl* vibrate (with the sound).

[43] *cantraip* witchcraft.

[44] *the haly table* the holy table – presumably the altar.

[45] *A murderer's banes in gibbet airns* After execution, the corpses of condemned murderers were encased in iron and hung from the gibbet until the flesh was decomposed.

[46] *span-lang* A span was the distance between the tip of the thumb and that of the little finger, commonly assumed to measure about 9 inches.

[47] *Three lawyers' tongues . . . neuk* Lines 143–6 were removed from later versions of the poem. *neuk* corner.

The dancers quick and quicker flew –
They reeled, they set, they crossed, they cleekit,
Till ilka carlin swat and reekit[48]
And coost her duddies[49] on the wark,
And linket[50] at it in her sark.[51]
Now Tam, oh Tam! had thae been queans[52]
A' plump and strappin in their teens,
Their sarks, instead o' creeshie flainen,
Been snaw-white seventeen-hunder linen[53] –
Thir breeks o' mine, my only pair,
That ance were plush, o' gude blue hair,
I wad hae gien them off my hurdies[54]
For ae blink o' the bonie burdies!
But withered beldams, auld and droll,
Rigwoodie[55] hags wad spean a foal,
Loupin and flingin on a crumock –
I wonder didna turn thy stomach.
But Tam kend what was what fu' brawlie,
There was ae winsome wench and walie[56]
That night enlisted in the core
(Lang after kend[57] on Carrick shore,[58]
For mony a beast to dead she shot
And perished mony a bonnie boat,
And shook baith meikle corn and bear,
And kept the countryside in fear);
Her cutty sark o' Paisley harn,[59]
That while a lassie she had worn,
In longitude though sorely scanty,
It was her best, and she was vauntie.[60]
Ah, little thought thy reverend graunie,
That sark she coft[61] for her wee Nannie,
Wi' twa pund Scots ('twas a' her riches)
Should ever graced a dance o' witches!
But here my muse her wing maun cour
(Sic flights are far beyond her power)
To sing how Nannie lap and flang[62] –
A souple jad[63] she was, and strang –

Notes

[48] *They reeled . . . reekit* They whirled round in the reel, faced their partners, passed across the circle of the dance, linked arms, and turned, till every witch sweated and steamed.

[49] *duddies* clothes.

[50] *linket* tripped.

[51] *sark* shirt.

[52] *queans* young girls.

[53] *Their sarks . . . linen* . . . had their shirts, instead of being filthy flannels, been quality linen . . .

[54] *hurdies* buttocks.

[55] *Rigwoodie hags wad spean a foal* ancient hags who would wean a foal.

[56] *ae winsome wench and walie* one choice, handsome wench.

[57] *kend* known.

[58] *Carrick shore* The coastline in this part of south Ayrshire is now a popular tourist attraction.

[59] *Her cutty sark o' Paisley harn* Her shortened undershirt was made of 'harn' (coarse linen).

[60] *vauntie* proud.

[61] *coft* bought.

[62] *lap and flang* leapt and jumped.

[63] *souple jad* supple woman (a jade is actually a horse).

And how Tam stood, like ane bewitched,
And thought his very een enriched;
Even Satan glow'red and fidged fu' fain,
And hotched, and blew wi' might and main;[64]
Till first ae caper – syne anither –
Tam lost his reason a' thegither
And roars out, 'Weel done, Cutty Sark!'
And in an instant all was dark:
And scarcely had he Maggie rallied,
When out the hellish legion sallied.
As bees bizz out wi' angry fyke
When plundering herds assail their byke;[65]
As open pussie's[66] mortal foes,
When, pop! she starts before their nose;
As eager rins the market-croud,
When 'Catch the thief!' resounds aloud;
So Maggie rins, the witches follow,
Wi' mony an eldritch[67] shout and hollo.
Ah Tam, ah Tam, thou'll get thy fairin!
In hell they'll roast thee like a herrin!
In vain thy Kate awaits thy comin,
Kate soon will be a woefu' woman!!!
Now do thy speedy utmost, Meg,
And win the keystane o' the brig;[68]
There at them thou thy tail may toss –
A running stream they dare na cross!
But ere the keystane she could make,
The fient a tail she had to shake;
For Nannie, far before the rest,
Hard upon noble Maggy pressed,
And flew at Tam with furious ettle[69] –
But little kend she Maggy's mettle!
Ae spring brought off her master hale,
But left behind her ain grey tail:
The carlin[70] claught her by the rump
And left poor Maggy scarce a stump.
Now wha this tale o' truth shall read,
Ilk man and mother's son, take heed:
Whene'er to drink you are inclined,
Or cutty sarks rin in your mind –
Think, ye may buy the joys o'er dear,
Remember Tam o' Shanter's mare!

Notes

[64] *glow'red . . . might and main* Satan displays his excitement by fidgeting, jerking and breathing heavily.
[65] *byke* hive.
[66] *pussie's* hare's.
[67] *eldritch* ghostly.
[68] *the keystane of the brig* the keystone of the bridge. 'It is a well-known fact that witches, or any evil spirits, have no power to follow a poor wight any farther than the middle of the next running stream. It may be proper likewise to mention to the benighted traveller, that when he falls in with "bogles", whatever danger may be in his going forward, there is much more hazard in turning back' (Burns's footnote).
[69] *ettle* intent.
[70] *carlin* witch.

Song (composed by November 1793, published 1796, edited from MS)

Oh my love's like the red, red rose,
That's newly sprung in June;
My love's like the melody
That's sweetly played in tune.

As fair art thou, my bonny lass,
So deep in love am I;
And I can love thee still, my dear,
Till a' the seas gang dry.

Till a' the seas gang dry, my dear,
And the rocks melt wi' the sun;
I will love thee still, my dear,
While the sands o' life shall run.

And fare thee weel, my only love,
Oh fare thee weel awhile!
And I will come again, my love,
Though 'twere ten thousand mile.

Mary Wollstonecraft (1759–1797)

Prolific lady of letters, moral writer and novelist, her most influential single work was *A Vindication of the Rights of Woman* (1792), which used the egalitarian ideals of the French Revolution as the basis for a sustained appeal for women's rights. She is now regarded as the mother of modern feminism.

Mary Wollstonecraft was the second of seven children, the first daughter of Edward John Wollstonecraft and Elizabeth Dickson. Home life was difficult: her father was abusive and prone to drink; her mother doted on the eldest of her brothers, Ned. She left home at 19 to support herself as a writer – a remarkably brave and daring decision for a woman at that time.

In 1784, she, her sister Eliza and her 'soulmate' Fanny Blood opened a school in the London suburb of Islington, later moving to Newington Green; two years later it was in financial trouble and closed. By this time Wollstonecraft was becoming known in intellectual circles, and was among those published by the Unitarian, Joseph Johnson (others included Anna Laetitia Barbauld, Blake, Wordsworth, Cowper and Paine); early works include *Thoughts on the Education of Daughters* (1786), *Original Stories from Real Life* (1787) and *Mary: A Fiction* (1788). In 1788 she began contributing to Johnson's periodical, the *Analytical Review*.

A Vindication of the Rights of Men was issued anonymously, 29 November 1790, within a month of Burke's *Reflections*, to which it was the first major response. It was an unflinching attack on the hereditary system on behalf of which Burke had written. In the extract below Wollstonecraft deplores the poverty and oppression that led to the French Revolution, and criticizes Burke's dependence on rhetoric.

A Vindication of the Rights of Woman (1792) argues that true political freedom can only be attained with equality of the sexes. Her principal precursors were the Bluestockings (see

p. 53) – Hannah More, Anna Laetitia Barbauld and Ann Yearsley – but none would have ventured as far as she did. Indeed, she criticizes Barbauld's 'To a Lady, with Some Painted Flowers' for writing, of women, 'Your best and sweetest empire is – to please.' Wollstonecraft observed that femininity was socially constructed – over-refinement, sensibility, concern with appearances, and seductiveness being parts of a false consciousness imposed by a male culture. To prove this she traced the cultivation in women of a series of unnatural and crippling inversions: reputation favoured over genuine modesty; looks over reason and understanding; sensibility over physical and mental vigour; and deceit and cunning over love. Finally, and perhaps most devastatingly, she argues that the legal disempowerment of women encourages them to become social outlaws – the theme of her last novel, *Maria, or the Wrongs of Woman* (1798).

She flouted convention fearlessly in her personal life. Rejected by the painter Fuseli and his wife when she proposed a platonic *ménage*, she went to France in December 1792 to witness the Revolution. There she fell in love with Gilbert Imlay, the traveller and writer, by whom she had a daughter, Fanny, 14 May 1794. The following year she twice attempted suicide on finding that Imlay was now living with an actress. In 1796 she and William Godwin became lovers; despite criticisms of marriage made by them both in their various works, they were married on 29 March 1797. She gave birth to her second daughter Mary (the future Mary Shelley) on 30 August that year, but thanks to inadequate hygiene on the part of those attending her, she contracted an infection and died of puerperal fever on 10 September.

For years afterwards Wollstonecraft remained the target of frequent attacks by Tory critics. A year after her death, Robert Bisset in the *Anti-Jacobin Review* used the appearance of Godwin's *Memoirs of the Author of A Vindication of the Rights of Woman* (1798) as an excuse for remarking that, 'Although they married, yet, as the philosopher himself bears testimony, they lived for several months in a state of illicit commerce.'[1] Bisset went on to criticize *Vindication of the Rights of Woman*, 'which the superficial fancied to be profound, and the profound knew to be superficial: it indeed had very little title to the character of ingenuity.'[2] And the *European Magazine* noted that Godwin's *Memoirs*

> will be read with disgust by every female who has any pretensions to delicacy; with detestation by everyone attached to the interests of religion and morality; and with indignation by anyone who might feel any regard for the unhappy woman whose frailties should have been buried in oblivion. Licentious as the times are, we trust it will obtain no imitators of the heroine in this country.[3]

It has never been easy to be a freethinker in England, and Wollstonecraft had the added disadvantage of being imprisoned within a series of gender-based prejudices of which she was a tireless opponent. Over a century would pass before that achievement would be fully credited (see Plate 7).

Further reading

A Wollstonecraft Anthology ed. Janet Todd (Bloomington, Ind., 1977).

The Collected Letters of Mary Wollstonecraft ed. Janet Todd (London, 2003).

A Routledge Literary Sourcebook on Mary Wollstonecraft's A Vindication of the Rights of Woman ed. Adriana Craciun (London and New York, 2002).

Mary Wollstonecraft, *The Vindications: The Rights of Men and The Rights of Woman* ed. D. L. Macdonald and Kathleen Scherf (Peterborough, Ontario, 1997).

The Cambridge Companion to Mary Wollstonecraft ed. Claudia L. Johnson (Cambridge, 2002).

William Godwin, *Memoirs of the Author of A Vindication of the Rights of Woman* ed. Pamela Clemit and Gina Luria Walker (Peterborough, Ontario, 2001).

Janet Todd, *Mary Wollstonecraft: A Revolutionary Life* (London, 2000).

Notes

1 *Anti-Jacobin Review* I (1798) 94–102, p. 98.

2 Ibid., p. 95.

3 *European Magazine* 33 (1798) 246–51, p. 251.

[*On Poverty*]

From A Vindication of the Rights of Men (1790)

In this great city[1] that proudly rears its head and boasts of its population and commerce, how much misery lurks in pestilential corners, whilst idle mendicants assail, on every side, the man who hates to encourage impostors, or repress, with angry frown, the plaints of the poor! How many mechanics,[2] by a flux of trade or fashion, lose their employment – whom misfortunes (not to be warded off) lead to the idleness that vitiates their character and renders them afterwards averse to honest labour! Where is the eye that marks these evils, more gigantic than any of the infringements of property which you piously deprecate? Are these remediless evils? And is the human heart satisfied in turning the poor over to another world to receive the blessings this could afford?

If society was regulated on a more enlarged plan; if man was contented to be the friend of man, and did not seek to bury the sympathies of humanity in the servile appellation of master; if, turning his eyes from ideal regions of taste and elegance, he laboured to give the earth he inhabited all the beauty it is capable of receiving, and was ever on the watch to shed abroad all the happiness which human nature can enjoy – he who, respecting the rights of men, wishes to convince or persuade society that this is true happiness and dignity, is not the cruel oppressor of the poor, nor a short-sighted philosopher – *he* fears God and loves his fellow-creatures. Behold the whole duty of man! The citizen who acts differently is a sophisticated being.

Surveying civilized life, and seeing with undazzled eye the polished vices of the rich, their insincerity, want of natural affections, with all the specious train that luxury introduces, I have turned impatiently to the poor to look for man undebauched by riches or power. But alas, what did I see? A being scarcely above the brutes over which it tyrannized – a broken spirit, worn-out body, and all those gross vices which the example of the rich, rudely copied, could produce. Envy built a wall of separation that made the poor hate, whilst they bent to their superiors who, on their part, stepped aside to avoid the loathsome sight of human misery.

What were the outrages of a day[3] to these continual miseries? Let those sorrows hide their diminished head before the tremendous mountain of woe that thus defaces our globe! Man preys on man – and you[4] mourn for the idle tapestry that decorated a gothic pile, and the dronish bell that summoned the fat priest to prayer. You mourn for the empty pageant of a name, when slavery flaps her wing, and the sick heart retires to die in lonely wilds far from the abodes of man. Did the pangs you felt for insulted nobility, the anguish that rent your heart when the gorgeous robes were torn off the idol human weakness had set up, deserve to be compared with the long-drawn sigh of melancholy reflection, when misery and vice thus seem to haunt our steps, and swim on the top of every cheering prospect? Why is our fancy to be appalled by terrific perspectives of a hell beyond the grave? Hell stalks abroad: the lash resounds on the slave's naked sides, and the sick wretch, who can no longer earn the sour bread of unremitting labour, steals to a ditch to bid the world a long goodnight – or, neglected in some ostentatious hospital, breathes its last amidst the laugh of mercenary attendants.

Notes

On Poverty

[1] *this great city* London.

[2] *mechanics* manual labourers.

[3] *a day* 6 October 1789, when the people marched on the Palace of Versailles and 'conducted' the king and queen back to Paris. Burke realized that this was a harbinger of the larger threat to the persons of the French royal family, and he had lamented it at length in his *Reflections* (see p. 10).

[4] *you* Wollstonecraft is addressing Burke.

Such misery demands more than tears. I pause to recollect myself, and smother the contempt I feel rising for your rhetorical flourishes and infantine sensibility.

From A Vindication of the Rights of Woman (1792)

Introduction

After considering the historic page, and viewing the living world with anxious solicitude, the most melancholy emotions of sorrowful indignation have depressed my spirits, and I have sighed when obliged to confess that either nature has made a great difference between man and man, or that the civilization which has hitherto taken place in the world has been very partial. I have turned over various books written on the subject of education, and patiently observed the conduct of parents and the management of schools; but what has been the result? – a profound conviction that the neglected education of my fellow-creatures is the grand source of the misery I deplore; and that women in particular are rendered weak and wretched by a variety of concurring causes, originating from one hasty conclusion. The conduct and manners of women, in fact, evidently prove that their minds are not in a healthy state; for, like the flowers which are planted in too rich a soil, strength and usefulness are sacrificed to beauty; and the flaunting leaves, after having pleased a fastidious eye, fade, disregarded on the stalk, long before the season when they ought to have arrived at maturity. One cause of this barren blooming I attribute to a false system of education, gathered from the books written on this subject by men who, considering females rather as women than human creatures, have been more anxious to make them alluring mistresses than wives; and the understanding of the sex has been so bubbled[1] by this specious homage, that the civilized women of the present century, with a few exceptions, are only anxious to inspire love, when they ought to cherish a nobler ambition, and by their abilities and virtues exact respect.

In a treatise, therefore, on female rights and manners, the works which have been particularly written for their improvement must not be overlooked; especially when it is asserted, in direct terms, that the minds of women are enfeebled by false refinement; that the books of instruction, written by men of genius, have had the same tendency as more frivolous productions; and that, in the true style of Mahometanism, they are only considered as females, and not as a part of the human species, when improvable reason is allowed to be the dignified distinction which raises men above the brute creation, and puts a natural sceptre in a feeble hand.

Yet because I am a woman, I would not lead my readers to suppose that I mean violently to agitate the contested question respecting the equality or inferiority of the sex; but as the subject lies in my way, and I cannot pass it over without subjecting the main tendency of my reasoning to misconstruction, I shall stop a moment to deliver, in a few words, my opinion. In the government of the physical world it is observable that the female in point of strength is, in general, inferior to the male. The male pursues, the female yields – this is the law of nature; and it does not appear to be suspended or abrogated in favour of woman. This physical superiority cannot be denied – and it is a noble prerogative! But not content with this natural pre-eminence, men endeavour to sink us still lower, merely to render us alluring objects for a

Notes

FROM A VINDICATION OF THE RIGHTS OF WOMAN

1 *bubbled* deluded.

moment; and women, intoxicated by the adoration which men, under the influence of their senses, pay them, do not seek to obtain a durable interest in their hearts, or to become the friends of the fellow creatures who find amusement in their society.

I am aware of an obvious inference: from every quarter have I heard exclamations against masculine women; but where are they to be found? If by this appellation men mean to inveigh against their ardour in hunting, shooting, and gaming, I shall most cordially join in the cry; but if it be against the imitation of manly virtues or, more properly speaking, the attainment of those talents and virtues, the exercise of which ennobles the human character, and which raises females in the scale of animal being, when they are comprehensively termed mankind; all those who view them with a philosophical eye must, I should think, wish with me, that they may every day grow more and more masculine.

This discussion naturally divides the subject. I shall first consider women in the grand light of human creatures who, in common with men, are placed on this earth to unfold their faculties; and afterwards I shall more particularly point out their peculiar designation.

I wish also to steer clear of an error which many respectable writers have fallen into; for the instruction which has hither been addressed to women, has rather been applicable to *ladies*, if the little indirect advice, that is scattered through *Sandford and Merton* be excepted;[2] but, addressing my sex in a firmer tone, I pay particular attention to those in the middle class, because they appear to be in the most natural state. Perhaps the seeds of false refinement, immorality, and vanity, have ever been shed by the great. Weak, artificial beings, raised above the common wants and affections of their race, in a premature unnatural manner, undermine the very foundation of virtue, and spread corruption through the whole mass of society! As a class of mankind they have the strongest claim to pity; the education of the rich tends to render them vain and helpless, and the unfolding mind is not strengthened by the practice of those duties which dignify the human character. They only live to amuse themselves, and by the same law which in nature invariably produces certain effects, they soon only afford barren amusement.

But as I purpose taking a separate view of the different ranks of society, and of the moral character of women, in each, this hint is, for the present, sufficient; and I have only alluded to the subject, because it appears to me to be the very essence of an introduction to give a cursory account of the contents of the work it introduces.

My own sex, I hope, will excuse me, if I treat them like rational creatures, instead of flattering their *fascinating* graces, and viewing them as if they were in a state of perpetual childhood, unable to stand alone. I earnestly wish to point out in what true dignity and human happiness consists – I wish to persuade women to endeavour to acquire strength, both of mind and body, and to convince them that the soft phrases, susceptibility of heart, delicacy of sentiment, and refinement of taste, are almost synonymous with epithets of weakness, and that those beings who are only the objects of pity and that kind of love, which has been termed its sister, will soon become objects of contempt.

Notes

[2] Thomas Day's didactic novel *Sandford and Merton* (1783) was written for children. A follower of Rousseau, Day believed that children were by nature wilful and disobedient; one way of tutoring them was through moral tales. Harry Sandford is thus a moral exemplar; his playmate Tommy Merton is mischievous, lazy, untruthful, and prone to accidents. Wollstonecraft reviewed Day's novel in the *Analytical Review*.

Dismissing then those pretty feminine phrases, which the men condescendingly use to soften our slavish dependence, and despising that weak elegancy of mind, exquisite sensibility, and sweet docility of manners, supposed to be the sexual characteristics of the weaker vessel, I wish to show that elegance is inferior to virtue, that the first object of laudable ambition is to obtain a character as a human being, regardless of the distinction of sex; and that secondary views should be brought to this simple touchstone.

This is a rough sketch of my plan; and should I express my conviction with the energetic emotions that I feel whenever I think of the subject, the dictates of experience and reflection will be felt by some of my readers. Animated by this important object, I shall disdain to cull my phrases or polish my style; I aim at being useful, and sincerity will render me unaffected; for, wishing rather to persuade by the force of my arguments, than dazzle by the elegance of my language, I shall not waste my time in rounding periods,[3] nor in fabricating the turgid bombast of artificial feelings, which, coming from the head, never reach the heart. I shall be employed about things, not words! – and, anxious to render my sex more respectable members of society, I shall try to avoid that flowery diction[4] which has slided from essays into novels, and from novels into familiar letters and conversation.

These pretty nothings, these caricatures of the real beauty of sensibility, dropping glibly from the tongue, vitiate the taste, and create a kind of sickly delicacy that turns away from simple unadorned truth; and a deluge of false sentiments and over-stretched feelings, stifling the natural emotions of the heart, render the domestic pleasures insipid, that ought to sweeten the exercise of those severe duties, which educate a rational and immortal being for a nobler field of action.

The education of women has, of late, been more attended to than formerly; yet they are still reckoned a frivolous sex, and ridiculed or pitied by the writers who endeavour by satire or instruction to improve them. It is acknowledged that they spend many of the first years of their lives in acquiring a smattering of accomplishments: meanwhile strength of body and mind are sacrificed to libertine notions of beauty, to the desire of establishing themselves – the only way women can rise in the world – by marriage. And this desire making mere animals of them, when they marry they act as such children may be expected to act: they dress; they paint, and nickname God's creatures.[5] Surely these weak beings are only fit for a seraglio! Can they govern a family, or take care of the poor babes whom they bring into the world?

If then it can be fairly deduced from the present conduct of the sex, from the prevalent fondness for pleasure which takes place of ambition and those nobler passions that open and enlarge the soul; that the instruction which women have received has only tended, with the constitution of civil society, to render them insignificant objects of desire – mere propagators of fools! – if it can be proved that in aiming to accomplish them, without cultivating their understandings, they are taken out of their sphere of duties, and made ridiculous and useless when the short-lived bloom of beauty is over,[6] I presume that *rational* men will excuse me for endeavouring to persuade them to become more masculine and respectable.

Notes

[3] *rounding periods* forming polished sentences.

[4] *flowery diction* The obvious target here is Burke, who was accused of having sacrificed logic to rhetoric.

[5] *nickname God's creatures* an allusion to Hamlet's haranguing of Ophelia: 'You jig and amble, and you lisp, you nickname God's creatures and make your wantonness your ignorance' (III i 144–6).

[6] 'A lively writer, I cannot recollect his name, asks what business women turned of forty have to do in the world' (Wollstonecraft's note). She may thinking of Fanny Burney's popular novel *Evelina* (1778), in which the licentious Lord Merton remarks: 'I don't know what the devil a woman lives for after thirty: she is only in other folks' way.'

Indeed the word masculine is only a bugbear: there is little reason to fear that women will acquire too much courage or fortitude; for their apparent inferiority with respect to bodily strength, must render them, in some degree, dependent on men in the various relations of life; but why should it be increased by prejudices that give a sex to virtue, and confound simple truths with sensual reveries?

Women are, in fact, so much degraded by mistaken notions of female excellence, that I do not mean to add a paradox when I assert, that this artificial weakness produces a propensity to tyrannize, and gives birth to cunning, the natural opponent of strength, which leads them to play off those contemptible infantile airs that undermine esteem even whilst they excite desire. Do not foster these prejudices, and they will naturally fall into their subordinate, yet respectable station, in life.

It seems scarcely necessary to say, that I now speak of the sex in general. Many individuals have more sense than their male relatives; and, as nothing preponderates where there is a constant struggle for an equilibrium, without[7] it has naturally more gravity, some women govern their husbands without degrading themselves, because intellect will always govern.

[*On the Lack of Learning*]

Many are the causes that, in the present corrupt state of society, contribute to enslave women by cramping their understandings and sharpening their senses. One, perhaps, that silently does more mischief than all the rest, is their disregard of order.

To do everything in an orderly manner is a most important precept which women who, generally speaking, receive only a disorderly kind of education, seldom attend to with that degree of exactness that men, who from their infancy are broken into method, observe. This negligent kind of guesswork (for what other epithet can be used to point out the random exertions of a sort of instinctive common sense never brought to the test of reason?) prevents their generalizing matters of fact, so they do today what they did yesterday, merely because they did it yesterday.

This contempt of the understanding in early life has more baneful consequences than is commonly supposed, for the little knowledge which women of strong minds attain is, from various circumstances, of a more desultory kind than the knowledge of men, and it is acquired more by sheer observations on real life than from comparing what has been individually observed with the results of experience generalized by speculation. Led by their dependent situation and domestic employments more into society, what they learn is rather by snatches; and as learning is with them, in general, only a secondary thing, they do not pursue any one branch with that persevering ardour necessary to give vigour to the faculties and clearness to the judgement.

In the present state of society, a little learning[8] is required to support the character of a gentleman, and boys are obliged to submit to a few years of discipline. But in the education of women, the cultivation of the understanding is always subordinate to the acquirement of some corporeal accomplishment. Even while enervated by confinement and false notions of modesty, the body is prevented from attaining that grace and beauty which relaxed half-formed limbs never exhibit. Besides, in youth their faculties are not brought forward by emulation, and having no serious scientific study, if they have natural sagacity it is turned too soon on life and manners. They dwell on effects and modifications without tracing them back to causes, and complicated rules to adjust behaviour are a weak substitute for simple principles.

Notes

[7] *without* i.e. without its having.

[8] *a little learning* cf. Pope, *Essay on Criticism* 215: 'A little learning is a dang'rous thing.'

As a proof that education gives this appearance of weakness to females, we may instance the example of military men, who are, like them, sent into the world before their minds have been stored with knowledge or fortified by principles. The consequences are similar: soldiers acquire a little superficial knowledge snatched from the muddy current of conversation; and, from continually mixing with society, they gain what is termed a knowledge of the world; and this acquaintance with manners and customs has frequently been confounded with a knowledge of the human heart.

But can the crude fruit of casual observation, never brought to the test of judgement, formed by comparing speculation and experience, deserve such a distinction? Soldiers, as well as women, practise the minor virtues with punctilious politeness. Where is then the sexual difference, when the education has been the same? All the difference that I can discern arises from the superior advantage of liberty, which enables the former to see more of life.

[*A Revolution in Female Manners*]

Let not men then in the pride of power use the same arguments that tyrannic kings and venal ministers have used, and fallaciously assert that woman ought to be subjected because she has always been so. But when man, governed by reasonable laws, enjoys his natural freedom, let him despise woman if she do not share it with him – and, till that glorious period arrives, in descanting on the folly of the sex, let him not overlook his own.

Women, it is true, obtaining power by unjust means by practising or fostering vice, evidently lose the rank which reason would assign them, and they become either abject slaves or capricious tyrants. They lose all simplicity, all dignity of mind, in acquiring power, and act as men are observed to act when they have been exalted by the same means.

It is time to effect a revolution in female manners, time to restore to them their lost dignity, and make them (as a part of the human species) labour, by reforming themselves, to reform the world. It is time to separate unchangeable morals from local manners. If men be demi-gods, why let us serve them! And if the dignity of the female soul be as disputable as that of animals; if their reason does not afford sufficient light to direct their conduct whilst unerring instinct is denied, they are surely of all creatures the most miserable, and, bent beneath the iron hand of destiny, must submit to be a fair defect in creation.[9] But to justify the ways of providence respecting them,[10] by pointing out some irrefragable reason for thus making such a large portion of mankind accountable and not accountable, would puzzle the subtlest casuist.

[*On State Education*]

When, therefore, I call women slaves, I mean in a political and civil sense, for indirectly they obtain too much power, and are debased by their exertions to obtain illicit sway.

Notes

9 *a fair defect in creation* a recollection of Adam's question in *Paradise Lost* Book X:

> Oh why did God,
> Creator wise, that peopled highest heaven
> With spirits masculine, create at last
> This novelty on earth, this fair defect
> Of nature . . . ? (ll. 888–92)

10 *But to justify . . . them* an ironic allusion to *Paradise Lost* i 25–6: 'I may assert Eternal Providence, / And justify the ways of God to men'.

Let an enlightened nation[1] then try what effect reason would have to bring them back to nature and their duty; and allowing them to share the advantages of education and government with man, see whether they will become better, as they grow wiser and become free. They cannot be injured by the experiment, for it is not in the power of man to render them more insignificant than they are at present.

To render this practicable, day schools for particular ages should be established by government in which boys and girls might be educated together. The school for the younger children, from five to nine years of age, ought to be absolutely free and open to all classes.[2] A sufficient number of masters should also be chosen by a select committee in each parish, to whom any complaint of negligence, etc., might be made, if signed by six of the children's parents.

Ushers[3] would then be unnecessary, for I believe experience will ever prove that this kind of subordinate authority is particularly injurious to the morals of youth. What, indeed, can tend to deprave the character more than outward submission and inward contempt? Yet how can boys be expected to treat an usher with respect, when the master seems to consider him in the light of a servant, and almost to countenance the ridicule which becomes the chief amusement of the boys during the play hours?

But nothing of this kind could occur in an elementary day-school, where boys and girls, the rich and poor, should meet together. And to prevent any of the distinctions of vanity, they should be dressed alike, and all obliged to submit to the same discipline, or leave the school. The schoolroom ought to be surrounded by a large piece of ground in which the children might be usefully exercised, for at this age they should not be confined to any sedentary employment for more than an hour at a time. But these relaxations might all be rendered a part of elementary education, for many things improve and amuse the senses when introduced as a kind of show, to the principles of which, drily laid down, children would turn a deaf ear – for instance, botany, mechanics, and astronomy. Reading, writing, arithmetic, natural history and some simple experiments in natural philosophy might fill up the day, but these pursuits should never encroach on gymnastic plays in the open air. The elements of religion, history, the history of man, and politics, might also be taught by conversations in the socratic form.[4]

After the age of nine, girls and boys intended for domestic employments or mechanical trades ought to be removed to other schools, and receive instruction in some measure appropriated to the destination of each individual, the two sexes being still together in the morning. But in the afternoon, the girls should attend a school where plain-work, mantua-making, millinery,[5] etc., would be their employment.

The young people of superior abilities or fortune might now be taught, in another school, the dead and living languages,[6] the elements of science, and continue the

Notes

ON STATE EDUCATION

[1] *an enlightened nation* 'France' (Wollstonecraft's note).

[2] 'Treating this part of the subject, I have borrowed some hints from a very sensible pamphlet written by the late Bishop of Autun on public education' (Wollstonecraft's note). She refers to Talleyrand's *Rapport sur l'instruction publique* (1791), which argued for universal public education until the age of 8.

[3] *Ushers* assistant masters.

[4] *conversations in the socratic form* Socrates taught a form of enquiry. When his opponents boasted that they knew what justice, piety, temperance, or law was, Socrates would ask them to give an account of it in order to demonstrate that the account offered was inadequate, thus indicating the need to revise accepted ways of thinking. The two sides then entered into dialogue.

[5] *plain-work, mantua-making, millinery* Some might think that this shows a reactionary streak in Wollstonecraft, but she thought of these as life skills. Plain-work is straightforward needlework (as opposed to the more complex acquirements demanded for embroidery); mantuas were loose gowns worn by women during the 18th century; milliners make hats.

[6] *the dead and living languages* i.e. French and German, as well as ancient tongues such as Latin and Greek.

study of history and politics on a more extensive scale, which would not exclude polite literature.

'Girls and boys still together?' I hear some readers ask. Yes.[7] And I should not fear any other consequence than that some early attachment might take place – which, whilst it had the best effect on the moral character of the young people, might not perfectly agree with the views of the parents (for it will be a long time, I fear, before the world is so enlightened that parents, only anxious to render their children virtuous, will let them choose companions for life themselves).

Besides, this would be a sure way to promote early marriages, and from early marriages the most salutary physical and moral effects naturally flow. What a different character does a married citizen assume from the selfish coxcomb who lives but for himself, and who is often afraid to marry lest he should not be able to live in a certain style. Great emergencies excepted, which would rarely occur in a society of which equality was the basis, a man can only be prepared to discharge the duties of public life by the habitual practice of those inferior ones which form the man.

In this plan of education the constitution of boys would not be ruined by the early debaucheries which now make men so selfish, nor girls rendered weak and vain by indolence and frivolous pursuits. But I presuppose that such a degree of equality should be established between the sexes as would shut out gallantry and coquetry, yet allow friendship and love to temper the heart for the discharge of higher duties.

Helen Maria Williams (1761–1827)

Helen Maria Williams was born in London in 1761 to Charles Williams, an army officer, and Helen Hay. When her father died in 1769 she and her mother moved to Berwick-upon-Tweed, where her mother educated her at home. Her formative years were spent in Scotland, a country which she always loved. In exile in France in 1814, she lamented her inability to return:

> Ah, lost to me thy fir-clad hills,
> The music of thy mountain rills,
> Yet ever shall the mem'ry last,
> 'Pleasant and mournful' of the past.[1]

Williams returned to London in 1781 and, with the help of the Dissenting minister Dr Andrew Kippis, published her first poem, *Edwin and Eltruda, A Legendary Tale* (1782). The entire episode, she later recalled, was fortuitous: 'My first production, the Legendary Tale of Edwin and Eltruda, was composed to amuse some solitary hours, and without any view to publication. Being shown to Dr Kippis, he declared that it deserved to be committed to the press, and offered to take upon himself the task of introducing it to the world.'[2] Its success made her well known in literary circles, and within a short time her friends included Fanny Burney, William Hayley, Samuel Johnson, Elizabeth Montagu, Anna Seward, the Wartons, Samuel Rogers, and Charlotte Smith. In 1783 she published *An Ode on the Peace*, and in 1784 *Peru, A Poem. In Six Cantos*, which she dedicated to Elizabeth Montagu. Boswell recounts the story of her first meeting with

Notes

[7] *Yes* Although the norm today, it was rare for boys and girls to be educated together in Wollstonecraft's day. Conservative critics of her book saw it as the recipe for immorality and rebellion.

Helen Maria Williams

[1] *The Travellers in Haste* 11–14, from *Poems on Various Subjects* (1823).

[2] Preface, *Poems* (1786).

Figure 9 Helen Maria Williams (1761–1827), engraved after a painting by an unknown artist, published 1816. Having been a successful poet since the early 1780s, she moved to Paris to witness the French Revolution, where she became acquainted with Thomas Paine and Mary Wollstonecraft. (National Portrait Gallery, London.)

Dr Johnson in May 1784, after the appearance of *An Ode on the Peace*:

> He had dined that day at Mr Hoole's, and Miss Helen Maria Williams being expected in the evening, Mr Hoole put into his hands her beautiful 'Ode on the Peace'. Johnson read it over, and when this elegant and accomplished young lady was presented to him, he took her by the hand in the most courteous manner, and repeated the finest stanza of her poem; this was the most delicate and pleasing compliment he could pay.[3]

More than 1,500 people subscribed to her collected *Poems* of 1786. It was read by, among others, the young William Wordsworth, then a schoolboy of 16 at Hawkshead Grammar School. As she had become known as a poet of sensibility, it was at that moment fashionable to address sentimental sonnets to her in the periodicals of the day.[4] This is precisely what Wordsworth did: his first published poem, *Sonnet on Seeing Miss Helen Maria Williams Weep at a Tale of Distress*, appeared in the *European Magazine* for March 1787. The most successful single poem in the 1786 volume played to the popular appetite for the Gothic: *Part of an Irregular Fragment, Found in a Dark Passage of the Tower* (p. 290). The *European Magazine* observed that it was 'the poem which we esteem the best display of Miss Williams' poetical powers',[5] while the *Monthly Review* reprinted it, with the encomium:

> In the *Irregular Fragment* the writer rises on no feeble wing into the regions of fancy and passion. The piece has so much merit that we cannot deny ourselves the satisfaction of presenting it to our readers entire; after premising that it is founded on the idea of an apartment in the Tower, shut up for ages, in which are assembled the ghosts of all those whom history relates to have been murdered in that state prison, and of a murdered royal family, whose story is lost in the lapse of time.[6]

Even as late as 1823, one of the reviewers of her collected poems judged that 'an *Irregular Fragment* and her sonnets are all that the volume contains of real poetry.'[7] This was not fair, but the *Fragment* is a remarkable work – perhaps the archetypal Gothic poem of the eighteenth-century. Its lurid imagery and skilfully contrived-climax guaranteed its success. But what many of its readers seem not to have noticed were its political implications. In a volume dedicated to the Queen it was odd, to say the least, to find a poem which portrays the English monarchy as a succession of homicidal maniacs. The 1786 collection is, in fact, most notable for its articulation, via conventional literary forms, of a clearly defined radical intelligence.

Williams's *Julia, A Novel; Interspersed with Some Poetical Pieces* (1790) revised Rousseau's *Nouvelle Héloïse*, making the triangle one of a man who dies, leaving two women to bring up a child together. *The Bastille, A Vision* (one of the poetical pieces with which it is 'interspersed') offers a cocktail of Gothicism and radicalism in which her target is the French *ancien régime*, its many injustices symbolized by the Bastille (stormed 14 July 1789). As with the 1786 volume, reviewers missed the novel's politics; the *Monthly Review* commented that 'The pieces of poetry, occasionally introduced, are, in general, elegant, and considerably enhance the value of the volumes.'[8] The *Analytical Review* found the poems 'ingenious and harmonious',[9] and the

Notes

[3] *Boswell's Life of Johnson* ed. George Birkbeck Hill, rev. L. F. Powell (6 vols, Oxford, 1934–40), iv 282.

[4] See, for instance, *To Miss Helen Maria Williams: On her Poem of Peru, Gentleman's Magazine* 54 (1784) 532; Anna Seward's *Sonnet to Miss Williams on her Epic Poem, Peru, Gentleman's Magazine* 54 (1784) 613; and *Sonnet to Miss Helena-Maria Williams* by J. B——o in the *European Magazine* 12 (1787) 144.

[5] *European Magazine* 10 (1786) 89–93, 177–80, p. 180.

[6] *Monthly Review* 75 (1786) 44–9, p. 44.

[7] *Literary Museum* 47 (15 March 1823) 166.

[8] *Monthly Review* 2 (1790) 334–6, p. 335.

[9] *Analytical Review* 7 (1790) 97–100, p. 100.

Critical merely noted that 'The poetry, interspersed, perhaps too frequently interspersed, deserves the character we have already had occasion to give of this lady's works; it is in general tender, pathetic, and pleasing.'[10]

By this time Williams was known for her support of the French Revolution, and it came as no surprise when she visited Paris to witness it for herself – an experience described in her *Letters Written in France in the Summer of 1790* (1790), of which extracts are presented here, including her account of a visit to the Bastille (see p. 296). Back in London she published a new edition of her *Poems* in 1791, before returning to France in July with her mother and two sisters, Cecilia and Persis, explaining her reasons for doing so in *A Farewell, for Two Years, to England. A Poem* (1791). She was going into a kind of political exile, partly because she wanted to support the French Revolution, and partly because she disapproved of the failure of Wilberforce's 1791 Bill to regulate the slave trade. The *Farewell* may not be her best poetical achievement, but it is the product of an intensely felt passion at a particular moment. As the Revolution had not yet resulted in the execution of the king, Williams's convictions garnered admiration from like-minded reviewers, such as that in the *Analytical*: 'The idea of visiting France, now become the first seat of freedom, fires her muse with more than usual ardour. The poem will be read with pleasure by those whose bosoms glow with kindred sentiments.'[11] The *Monthly* also regarded her sympathetically:

> Much of nature gives animation to this poem, much fond recollection of the innocent pleasures of early youth. She has, very properly, introduced her favourite subject, the renovation of Gallic liberty, and has taken occasion, gently and tenderly, to expostulate with those of her countrymen who seem unwilling to allow their neighbours the blessing of that freedom which they so happily enjoy. She also adverts, very pathetically, to the late miscarriage of Mr Wilberforce's slave-bill, and, turning to France, exhorts her generously to espouse the cause of the poor Africans.[12]

Even when reviewers disagreed with her politics, as with the *Critical*, she was indulged: 'Miss Williams' farewell numbers are extremely sweet and musical, and her enthusiasm in the cause of liberty shines with a lustre so bright and ardent as to excite our warm admiration. We cannot say that her principles always coincide with our own, or that her arguments are absolutely incontrovertible, but where they do not convince, we applaud the spirit with which they are delivered, and the numbers in which they are conveyed.'[13]

In Paris she and her lover, John Hurford Stone, were at the centre of expatriate society at White's Hotel. Visitors during this period included Thomas Paine, Mary Wollstonecraft, Charlotte Smith and the 21-year-old Wordsworth, whom she narrowly missed, despite his having procured a letter of introduction to her.

The months following the execution of Louis XVI in January 1793 were difficult ones for English radicals. Williams's support for the Revolution did not waver – a stand that was to cost her dearly. One of the earliest warnings of what was to happen came with an open letter from Anna Seward who, until the execution, had publicly supported events in France. The letter appeared in the *Gentleman's Magazine* for February 1793, prefaced by an explanation of how it was 'sent to Miss Helen Maria Williams a few days before the tidings of that demoniac transaction, the murder of the deposed and blameless Louis, reached this nation'.[14] She proceeded to articulate her

Notes

10 *Critical Review* 69 (1790) 592–3, p. 593.

11 *Analytical Review* 10 (1791) 188.

12 *Monthly Review* 5 (1791) 341–2.

13 *Critical Review* 2 (1791) 232.

14 *Gentleman's Magazine* 63 (1793) 108–10, p. 108.

revulsion at the execution of the King, and advised: 'Oh return while yet you may, to the bosom of your native country, which has fostered your talents and enrolled your fame!'[15] She continued: 'Fly,dear Helen, that land of carnage! from the pernicious influence of that equalizing system which, instead of diffusing universal love, content and happiness, lifts every man's hand against his brother.'[16] It concluded ominously: 'Adieu, my dear friend! Love and respect your country half as well as I love and respect you, and we shall soon cease to view you in a state of cold alienation, and of impending danger!'[17] From the point of view of personal survival this was good advice; the outbreak of war with Britain in February, and the Reign of Terror, which began in October 1793, would make life precarious for foreigners. Williams, her mother and sisters were detained in the Luxembourg prison under the general order of 7 October, placing all British and Hanoverian subjects 'in a state of arrest in houses of security'.

While in confinement she continued to record her impressions of Revolutionary France in the *Letters Containing a Sketch of the Politics of France* (1795). Although her account of the revolution has drawn accusations of inaccuracy, it provides a vivid and credible account of the affairs of the day. She emphasizes the part played by women in the revolution, their efforts to fight tyranny and their fortitude: 'My narratives make a part of that marvellous story which the eighteenth century has to record to future times, and the testimony of a witness will be heard. Perhaps, indeed, I have written too little of events which I have known so well; but the convulsions of states form accumulations of private calamity that distract the attention by overwhelming the heart, and it is difficult to describe the shipwreck when sinking in the storm.'[18] None of this was well received at home: the *British Critic* commented of the 1795 *Letters*: 'As usual, the French are all wise, generous, good, great, etc. etc. etc. and every other nation, her own in particular, contemptible in the balance.'[19] Perhaps the most impressive part of the volume is that dealing with Madame Roland (1754–93), wife of Jean-Marie Roland, prominent in the Girondist faction (see p. 306).

Williams and her family owed their release from prison to Jean Debry, a humane deputy to the Convention, who brought suspicion on himself by pleading their cause. They were released in July 1794, and Williams left her family in Paris to join John Hurford Stone in Switzerland, where they may have married. Stone, a Unitarian and fellow-radical, was separated from his first wife, who had been left behind in England. But these complications led them to be regarded not only as politically unsound, but as morally reprobate.

Hostilities between Britain and France worsened. At the height of the war, in 1798, letters from Williams and Stone to Joseph Priestley in America were intercepted by an English ship and published in London as evidence of her treachery. The *Anti-Jacobin Review* crowed: 'These self-transported *patriots* triumph, by anticipation, in the conquest of England, the downfall of her monarchy, and the consequent establishment of a republic, under which their pious friend, Dr Priestley, may live unmolested by *Kings*, by *tithes* or by *Bishops*.'[20] In the same year Williams's *Tour in Switzerland* was published, to receive equally poisonous coverage. The reviewer in the *British Critic* hardly bothers with the book, instead reviewing her career as a traitor: after she 'caught the infection of Gallic liberty' she became 'the *companion* of a man employed by the French government . . . Miss or Mrs Williams felt no compunction at attending Mr S. on his excursion,

Notes

[15] Ibid., p. 109.
[16] Ibid., p. 110.
[17] Ibid.
[18] *Poems on Various Subjects* (1823), p. x.
[19] *British Critic* 8 (1796) 321.
[20] *Anti-Jacobin Review* 1 (1798) 146–51, p. 150.

who is, we are told, a married man, and has a wife living in this country.'[21]

She continued to express her views in volumes on French history (1815, 1819) and became a naturalized French citizen in 1817. In October 1820, Wordsworth finally caught up with her on a visit to Paris. Nearly three decades after the Revolution, he was able to pay tribute to her by reciting her sonnet 'To Hope' from memory – it had been published only months before his 1791 visit to Paris, when he had unluckily missed her.[22]

When her collected poems were issued in 1823, reviews were surprisingly respectful. 'Anything from the pen of Miss Williams must be important,' declared the *Monthly Literary Register*. 'Without deeply entering into comparisons, we may remark that there appears through all her considerable works a sober and masculine propriety seldom encountered in the pages of her fair contemporaries.'[23] The *European Magazine* concurred: 'We think the volume a very acceptable offering to the public, and it will be valued by many as a reminiscence of a lady whose name was once so familiar to our studies, but whose pen has latterly kept no pace with the promise of her earlier productions.'[24] More grudgingly, the *Monthly Review* described her poetry as 'always above mediocrity though wanting in some of the higher characteristics of genius'.[25]

Still regarded as suspect, she died in Paris in 1827. Her obituarist in the *Monthly* offered the tart judgement: 'She wrote several works connected with France, which obtained for her a considerable degree of popularity in that country, as well as in this; but they have been already forgotten.'[26] She was buried next to John Hurford Stone, who had died in 1818.

Further reading

Helen Maria Williams, *Letters from France* ed. Neil Fraistat and Susan S. Lanser (Peterborough, Ontario, 2001).

Mary A. Favret, *Romantic Correspondence: Women, Politics, and the Fiction of Letters* (Cambridge, 1993).

Deborah Kennedy, *Helen Maria Williams and the Age of Revolution* (Lewisburg, Pa., 2002).

Nicola J. Watson, *Revolution and the Form of the British Novel, 1790-1825* (Oxford, 1994).

Part of an Irregular Fragment, found in a Dark Passage of the Tower

***From* Poems (1786)**

Advertisement

The following poem is formed on a very singular and sublime idea. A young gentleman, possessed of an uncommon genius for drawing, on visiting the Tower of London, passing one door of a singular construction, asked what apartment it led to, and expressed a desire to have it opened. The person who showed the place shook his head and answered, 'Heaven knows what is within that door; it has been shut for ages.' This answer made small impression on the other hearers, but a very deep one on the imagination of this youth. Gracious Heaven! An apartment shut up for ages – and in the Tower!

Notes

[21] *British Critic* 12 (1798) 24–9, p. 24.

[22] This is further discussed in *Wordsworth's Poets* ed. Duncan Wu (Manchester, 2003), pp. 138–40.

[23] *Monthly Literary Register* 3 (1823) 124–6, p. 124.

[24] *European Magazine* 83 (1823) 355–6, p. 356.

[25] *Monthly Review* 102 (1823) 20–31, p. 23.

[26] *Monthly Review* 7 (1828) 139.

Ye Towers of Julius! London's lasting shame,
By many a foul and midnight murder fed.[1]

Genius builds on a slight foundation, and rears beautiful structures on 'the baseless fabric of a vision.' The above transient hint dwelt on the young man's fancy, and conjured into his memory all the murders which history records to have been committed in the Tower: Henry VI, the Duke of Clarence, the two young Princes, sons of Edward IV, Sir Thomas Overbury, etc. He supposes all their ghosts assembled in this unexplored apartment, and to these his fertile imagination has added several others. One of the spectres raises an immense pall of black velvet, and discovers the remains of a murdered royal family whose story is lost in the lapse of time. The gloomy wildness of these images struck my imagination so forcibly that, endeavouring to catch the fire of the youth's pencil, this fragment was produced.

I

Rise, winds of night! Relentless tempests rise!
Rush from the troubled clouds, and o'er me roll;
In this chill pause a deeper horror lies,
A wilder fear appals my shudd'ring soul.
'Twas on this day,[2] this hour accursed,
That Nature, starting from repose,
Heard the dire shrieks of murder burst –
From infant innocence they rose
And shook these solemn towers!
I shudd'ring pass that fatal room,
For ages wrapped in central gloom;
I shudd'ring pass that iron door
Which fate perchance unlocks no more;
Death, smeared with blood, o'er the dark portal lours.

II

How fearfully my step resounds
Along these lonely bounds;
Spare, savage blast, the taper's quiv'ring fires,
Deep in these gath'ring shades its flame expires.
Ye host of heaven! The door recedes;
It mocks my grasp – what unseen hands
Have burst its iron bands?
No mortal force this gate unbarred
Where danger lives, which terrors guard –
Dread powers! Its screaming hinges close
On this dire scene of impious deeds.
My feet are fixed! Dismay has bound
My step on this polluted ground –
But lo! the pitying moon a line of light
Athwart the horrid darkness dimly throws,
And from yon grated window chases night.

Notes

Part of an Irregular Fragment

[1] Williams quotes Gray, *The Bard* 87–8.

[2] 'The anniversary of the murder of Edward V, and his brother Richard, Duke of York' (Williams's note).

III

Ye visions that before me roll,
That freeze my blood, that shake my soul,
Are ye the phantoms of a dream?
Pale spectres, are ye what ye seem?
They glide more near,
Their forms unfold!
Fixed are their eyes, on me they bend –
Their glaring look is cold!
And hark, I hear
Sounds that the throbbing pulse of life suspend!

IV

'No wild illusion cheats thy sight
With shapes that only live in night –
Mark the native glories spread
Around my bleeding brow!
The crown of Albion wreathed my head
And Gallia's lillies[3] twined below;
When my father shook his spear,
When his banner sought the skies,
Her baffled host recoiled with fear,
Nor turned their shrinking eyes.
Soon as the daring eagle springs
To bask in heav'n's empyreal light,
The vultures ply their baleful wings,
A cloud of deep'ning colour marks their flight,
Staining the golden day;
But see, amid the rav'nous brood
A bird of fiercer aspect soar.
The spirits of a rival race[4]
Hang on the noxious blast, and trace
With gloomy joy his destined prey,
Inflame th' ambitious wish that thirsts for blood,
And plunge his talons deep in kindred gore.

V

View the stern form that hovers nigh –
Fierce rolls his dauntless eye
In scorn of hideous death;
Till starting at a brother's[5] name,
Horror shrinks his glowing frame,
Locks the half-uttered groan,

Notes

[3] 'Henry VI was crowned when an infant, at Paris' (Williams's note).

[4] 'Richard III, by murdering so many near relations, seemed to revenge the sufferings of Henry VI and his family, on the House of York' (Williams's note).

[5] 'Richard III, who murdered his brother, the Duke of Clarence' (Williams's note).

And chills the parting breath.
Astonished Nature heaved a moan
When her affrighted eye beheld the hands
She formed to cherish, rend her holy bands.[6]

VI

Look where a royal infant[7] kneels,
Shrieking and agonized with fear;
He sees the dagger pointed near
A much-loved brother's[8] breast,
And tells an absent mother all he feels.
His eager eye he casts around;
Where shall her guardian form be found
On which his eager eye would rest?
On her he calls in accents wild
And wonders why her step is slow
To save her suff'ring child!
Robed in the regal garb, his brother stands
In more majestic woe,
And meets the impious stroke with bosom bare,
Then fearless grasps the murd'rer's hands,
And asks the minister of hell to spare
The child whose feeble arms sustain
His bleeding form from cruel death.
In vain fraternal fondness pleads,
For cold is now his livid cheek,
And cold his last expiring breath.
And now with aspect meek,
The infant lifts its mournful eye,
And asks with trembling voice to die,
If death will cure his heaving heart of pain.
His heaving heart now bleeds!
Foul tyrant, o'er the gilded hour
That beams with all the blaze of power,
Remorse shall spread her thickest shroud;
The furies in thy tortured ear
Shall howl with curses deep and loud,
And wake distracting fear!
I see the ghastly spectre rise,
Whose blood is cold, whose hollow eyes
Seem from his head to start;
With upright hair and shiv'ring heart,
Dark o'er thy midnight couch he bends,
And clasps thy shrinking frame, thy impious spirit rends.'

Notes

[6] i.e. by fratricide, an unnatural act.

[7] 'Richard Duke of York' (Williams's note).

[8] 'Edward V' (Williams's note).

VII

Now his thrilling accents die,
His shape eludes my searching eye;
But who is he,[9] convulsed with pain,
That writhes in every swelling vein?
Yet in so deep, so wild a groan,
A sharper anguish seems to live
Than life's expiring pang can give:
He dies deserted and alone.
If pity can allay thy woes,
Sad spirit, they shall find repose;
Thy friend, thy long-loved friend is near;
He comes to pour the parting tear,
He comes to catch the parting breath.
Ah heaven! no melting look he wears,
His altered eye with vengeance glares;
Each frantic passion at his soul;
'Tis he has dashed that venomed bowl
With agony and death.

VIII

But whence arose that solemn call?
Yon bloody phantom waves his hand
And beckons me to deeper gloom;
Rest, troubled form, I come –
Some unknown power my step impels
To horror's secret cells.
'For thee I raise this sable pall,
It shrouds a ghastly band;
Stretched beneath, thy eye shall trace
A mangled regal race.
A thousand suns have rolled since light
Rushed on their solid night;
See, o'er that tender frame grim Famine hangs
And mocks a mother's pangs!
The last, last drop which warmed her veins
That meagre infant drains,
Then gnaws her fond sustaining breast.
Stretched on her feeble knees, behold
Another victim sinks to lasting rest;
Another yet her matron arms would fold,
Who strives to reach her matron arms in vain,
Too weak her wasted form to raise.

Notes

[9] 'Sir Thomas Overbury, poisoned in the Tower by Somerset' (Williams's note).

On him she bends her eager gaze;
She sees the soft imploring eye
That asks her dear embrace, the cure of pain –
She sees her child at distance die!
But now her steadfast heart can bear
Unmoved the pressure of despair.
When first the winds of winter urge their course
O'er the pure stream, whose current smoothly glides,
The heaving river swells its troubled tides;
But when the bitter blast with keener force
O'er the high wave an icy fetter throws,
The hardened wave is fixed in dead repose.

IX

Say, who that hoary form? Alone he stands,
And meekly lifts his withered hands –
His white beard streams with blood!
I see him with a smile deride
The wounds that pierce his shrivelled side
Whence flows a purple flood;
But sudden pangs his bosom tear –
On one big drop, of deeper dye,
I see him fix his haggard eye
In dark and wild despair!
That sanguine drop which wakes his woe,
Say, spirit, whence its source?'
'Ask no more its source to know –
Ne'er shall mortal eye explore
Whence flowed that drop of human gore,
Till the starting dead shall rise
Unchained from earth, and mount the skies,
And time shall end his fated course.'
'Now th' unfathomed depth behold:
Look but once! A second glance
Wraps a heart of human mould
In death's eternal trance.

X

That shapeless phantom, sinking slow
Deep down the vast abyss below,
Darts through the mists that shroud his frame –
A horror nature hates to name!'
'Mortal, could thine eyes behold
All those sullen mists enfold,
Thy sinews at the sight accursed
Would wither, and thy heart-strings burst;
Death would grasp with icy hand
And drag thee to our grisly band!
Away! the sable pall I spread,

And give to rest th' unquiet dead;
Haste, ere its horrid shroud enclose
Thy form, benumbed with wild affright,
And plunge thee far through wastes of night,
In yon black gulf's abhorred repose!'
As, starting at each step, I fly,
Why backward turns my frantic eye
That closing portal past?
Two sullen shades, half-seen, advance!
On me a blasting look they cast,
And fix my view with dang'rous spells
Where burning frenzy dwells!
Again! their vengeful look – and now a speechless –
* * * * * * *[10]

[*A Visit to the Bastille*]

From Letters written in France in the summer of 1790 (1790)

Before I suffered my friends at Paris to conduct me through the usual routine of convents, churches and palaces, I requested to visit the Bastille, feeling a much stronger desire to contemplate the ruins of that building than the most perfect edifices of Paris. When we got into the carriage, our French servant called to the coachman, with an air of triumph, 'A la Bastille – mais nous n'y resterons pas.'[1]

We drove under that porch which so many wretches have entered never to repass,[2] and alighting from the carriage descended with difficulty into the dungeons, which were too low to admit of our standing upright, and so dark that we were obliged at noonday to visit them with the light of a candle. We saw the hooks of those chains by which the prisoners were fastened round the neck to the walls of their cells – many of which, being below the level of the water, are in a constant state of humidity; and a noxious vapour issued from them, which more than once extinguished the candle, and was so insufferable that it required a strong spirit of curiosity to tempt one to enter. Good God! – and to these regions of horror were human creatures dragged at the caprice of despotic power. What a melancholy consideration, that

Man, proud man,
Dressed in a little brief authority,
Plays such fantastic tricks before high heaven
As make the angels weep.[3]

There appears to be a greater number of these dungeons than one could have imagined the hard heart of tyranny itself would contrive, for, since the destruction of the building, many subterraneous cells have been discovered underneath a piece of

Notes

[10] The row of asterisks was printed at the end as part of the pretence that the manuscript was a newly discovered 'fragment'.

A Visit to the Bastille

[1] 'To the Bastille – but we shall not remain there' (Williams's translation).

[2] *have entered never to repass* because they were tortured and executed there.

[3] *Measure for Measure* II ii 117–20.

ground which was enclosed within the walls of the Bastille, but which seemed a bank of solid earth before the horrid secrets of this prison-house were disclosed. Some skeletons were found in these recesses with irons still fastened on their decaying bones.

After having visited the Bastille, we may indeed be surprised that a nation so enlightened as the French submitted so long to the oppressions of their government. But we must cease to wonder that their indignant spirits at length shook off the galling yoke . . .

When the Bastille was taken, and the old man of whom you have no doubt heard, and who had been confined in a dungeon thirty-five years, was brought into daylight, which had not for so long a space of time visited his eyes, he staggered, shook his white beard, and cried faintly, 'Messieurs, vous m'avez rendu un grand service, rendez m'en un autre, tuez moi! Je ne sais pas où aller.'[4] 'Allons, allons', the crowd answered with one voice. 'La nation te nourrira.'[5]

As the heroes of the Bastille passed along the streets after its surrender, the citizens stood at the doors of their houses loaded with wine, brandy, and other refreshments which they offered to these deliverers of their country. But they unanimously refused to taste any strong liquors, considering the great work they had undertaken as not yet accomplished, and being determined to watch the whole night, in case of any surprise.

[*On Revolution*]

From Letters written in France in the summer of 1790 (1790)

As we came out of La Maison de Ville, we were shown, immediately opposite, the far-famed lantern at which, for want of a gallows, the first victims of popular fury were sacrificed. I own that the sight of La Lanterne chilled the blood within my veins. At that moment, for the first time, I lamented the revolution, and, forgetting the imprudence or the guilt of those unfortunate men, could only reflect with horror on the dreadful expiation they had made. I painted in my imagination the agonies of their families and friends, nor could I for a considerable time chase these gloomy images from my thoughts.

It is forever to be regretted that so dark a shade of ferocious revenge was thrown across the glories of the revolution. But alas! Where do the records of history point out a revolution unstained by some actions of barbarity? When do the passions of human nature rise to that pitch which produces great events, without wandering into some irregularities? If the French Revolution should cost no farther bloodshed, it must be allowed, notwithstanding a few shocking instances of public vengeance, that the liberty of twenty-four millions of people will have been purchased at a far cheaper rate than could ever have been expected from the former experience of the world.[1]

Notes

[4] 'Gentlemen, you have rendered me one great service; render me another: kill me, for I know not where to go' (Williams's translation).

[5] 'Come along, come along, the nation will provide for you' (Williams's translation).

On Revolution

[1] The violence of the Revolution was something that had to be excused by anyone seeking to defend it. None other than William Wordsworth, an admirer of Williams, would address the same subject in his unpublished 'Letter to the Bishop of Llandaff' (1793): 'Alas! the obstinacy and perversion of men is such that she [i.e. Liberty] is too often obliged to borrow the very arms of despotism to overthrow him, and in order to reign in peace must establish herself by violence.'

[*Retrospect from England*]

From Letters written in France in the summer of 1790 (1790)

Every visitor brings me intelligence from France full of dismay and horror. I hear of nothing but crimes, assassinations, torture and death. I am told that every day witnesses a conspiracy, that every town is the scene of a massacre, that every street is blackened with a gallows, and every highway deluged with blood. I hear these things, and repeat to myself: Is this the picture of France? Are these the images of that universal joy which called tears into my eyes and made my heart throb with sympathy? To me, the land which these mighty magicians have suddenly covered with darkness where, waving their evil wand, they have reared the dismal scaffold, have clotted the knife of the assassin with gore, have called forth the shriek of despair and the agony of torture – to me, this land of desolation appeared dressed in additional beauty beneath the genial smile of liberty. The woods seemed to cast a more refreshing shade, and the lawns to wear a brighter verdure, while the carols of freedom burst from the cottage of the peasant, and the voice of joy resounded on the hill and in the valley.

Must I be told that my mind is perverted, that I am become dead to all sensations of sympathy, because I do not weep with those who have lost a part of their superfluities,[1] rather than rejoice that the oppressed are protected, that the wronged are redressed, that the captive is set at liberty, and that the poor have bread? Did the universal parent of the human race implant the feelings of pity in the heart, that they should be confined to the artificial wants of vanity, the ideal deprivations of greatness; that they should be fixed beneath the dome of the palace, or locked within the gate of the chateau; without extending one commiserating sigh to the wretched hamlet, as if its famished inhabitants, though not ennobled by man, did not bear, at least, the ensigns of nobility stamped on our nature by God?

Must I hear the charming societies in which I found all the elegant graces of the most polished manners, all the amiable urbanity of liberal and cultivated minds, compared with the most rude, ferocious, and barbarous levellers that ever existed? Really, some of my English acquaintance (whatever objections they may have to republican principles) do, in their discussions of French politics, adopt a most free and republican style of censure. Nothing can be more democratical than their mode of expression, or display a more levelling spirit, than their unqualified contempt of *all* the leaders of the revolution.

It is not my intention to shiver[2] lances in every society I enter, in the cause of the National Assembly. Yet I cannot help remarking that, since the Assembly does not presume to set itself up as an example to this country, we seem to have very little right to be furiously angry, because they think proper to try another system of government themselves. Why should they not be suffered to make an experiment in politics? I have always been told that the improvement of every science depends upon experiment. But I now hear that, instead of their new attempt to form the great machine of society upon a simple principle of general amity upon the Federation of its members, they ought to have repaired the feudal wheels and springs by which their ancestors directed its movements.

Notes

RETROSPECT FROM ENGLAND

[1] *superfluities* superabundance – in effect, their property.

[2] *shiver* shatter.

Yet if mankind had always observed this retrograde motion, it would surely have led them to few acquisitions in virtue or in knowledge, and we might even have been worshipping the idols of paganism at this moment. To forbid, under the pains and penalties of reproach, all attempts of the human mind to advance to greater perfection, seems to be proscribing every art and science. And we cannot much wonder that the French, having received so small a legacy of public happiness from their forefathers, and being sensible of the poverty of their own patrimony, should try new methods of transmitting a richer inheritance to their posterity.

The Bastille, A Vision[1]

From Julia, A Novel (1790)

I.1
'Drear cell, along whose lonely bounds
Unvisited by light
Chill silence dwells with night,
Save when the clanging fetter sounds!
Abyss where mercy never came,
Nor hope the wretch can find,
Where long inaction wastes the frame,
And half annihilates the mind!

I.2
Stretched helpless in this living tomb,
Oh haste, congenial death!
Seize, seize this ling'ring breath,
And shroud me in unconscious gloom –
Britain, thy exiled son no more
Thy blissful vales shall see;
Why did I leave thy hallowed shore,
Distinguished land, where all are free?'

I.3
Bastille! within thy hideous pile
Which stains of blood defile,
Thus rose the captive's sighs,
Till slumber sealed his weeping eyes –
Terrific visions hover near!
He sees an awful form appear
Who drags his step to deeper cells
Where stranger wilder horror dwells.

Notes

THE BASTILLE, A VISION

[1] This poem is preceded in the novel by the following passage: 'Mr F. called at Mr Clifford's one evening, and finding Charlotte and Julia sitting at work, he desired their permission to read to them a poem written by a friend lately arrived from France, and who, for some supposed offence against the state, had been immured several years in the Bastille, but was at length liberated by the interference of a person in power. The horrors of his solitary dungeon were one night cheered by the following prophetic dream.' The prison of the Bastille had for years symbolized the injustice of the *ancien régime*, and its storming on 14 July 1789 (still celebrated today) was welcomed by many on both sides of the English Channel. Williams visited the ruins of the Bastille when she went to Paris in 1790; see p. 296.

II.1
'Oh tear me from these haunted walls
Or those fierce shapes control,
Lest madness seize my soul;
That pond'rous mask of iron[2] falls,
I see.' 'Rash mortal, ha! Beware,
Nor breathe that hidden name!
Should those dire accents wound the air,
Know death shall lock thy stiff'ning frame.'

II.2
'Hark, that loud bell which sullen tolls!
It wakes a shriek of woe
From yawning depths below;
Shrill through this hollow vault it rolls!
A deed was done in this black cell
Unfit for mortal ear;
A deed was done, when tolled that knell,
No human heart could live and hear!

II.3
Rouse thee from thy numbing trance,
Near yon thick gloom advance,
The solid cloud has shook;
Arm all thy soul with strength to look –
Enough! Thy starting locks have rose,
Thy limbs have failed, thy blood has froze;
On scenes so foul, with mad affright,
I fix no more thy fastened sight.'

III.1
'Those troubled phantoms melt away,
I lose the sense of care!
I feel the vital air –
I see, I *see* the light of day!
Visions of bliss, eternal powers!
What force has shook those hated walls?
What arm has rent those threat'ning towers?
It falls – the guilty fabric[3] falls!'

III.2
'Now favoured mortal, now behold!
To soothe thy captive state
I ope the book of fate –
Mark what its registers unfold!
Where this dark pile in chaos lies,
With nature's execrations hurled,
Shall freedom's sacred temple rise
And charm an emulating world!

Notes

[2] 'Alluding to the prisoner who has excited so many conjectures in Europe' (Williams's note). The man in the iron mask was a state prisoner during the reign of Louis XIV, and was confined in the Bastille. His identity remains a mystery.

[3] *the guilty fabric* i.e. the physical fabric of the building.

III.3
'Tis her awak'ning voice commands
Those firm, those patriot bands,
Armed to avenge her cause
And guard her violated laws!
Did ever earth a scene display
More glorious to the eye of day
Than millions with according mind
Who claim the rights of humankind?

IV.1
Does the famed Roman page sublime
An hour more bright unroll
To animate the soul
Than this, loved theme of future time?
Posterity, with rev'rence meet,
The consecrated act shall hear;
Age shall the glowing tale repeat
And youth shall drop the burning tear!

IV.2
The peasant, while he fondly sees
His infants round the hearth
Pursue their simple mirth
Or emulously climb his knees,
No more bewails their future lot
By tyranny's stern rod oppressed,
While freedom guards his straw-roofed cot
And all his useful toils are blessed.

IV.3
Philosophy,[4] oh share the meed
Of freedom's noblest deed!
'Tis thine each truth to scan,
Guardian of bliss and friend of man!
'Tis thine all human wrongs to heal,
'Tis thine to love all nature's weal,
To give each gen'rous purpose birth
And renovate the gladdened earth.'[5]

A Farewell, for Two Years, to England. A Poem (1791)

Sweet spring, while others hail thy op'ning flowers,
The first young hope of summer's blushing hours,
Me they remind that when her ardent ray

Notes

[4] *Philosophy* The works of numerous philosophers, including Rousseau and Holbach, were credited with having generated an intellectual climate favourable to the Revolution.

[5] *And renovate the gladdened earth* Williams's language in this line is full of millennial optimism; many believed that the French Revolution was the harbinger of a universal spiritual revolution to come.

Shall reach the summit of our lengthened day,
Then, Albion, far from thee, my cherished home,
To foreign climes my pensive steps must roam,
And twice shall spring, dispelling winter's gloom,
Shed o'er thy lovely vales her vernal bloom;
Twice shall thy village-maids, with chaplets gay
And simple carols, hail returning May;
And twice shall autumn, o'er thy cultured plain,
Pour the rich treasures of his yellow grain;
Twice shall thy happy peasants bear along
The lavish store, and wake the harvest-song,
Ere from the bounded deep my searching eye,
Ah, land beloved, shall thy white cliffs descry.
Where the slow Loire, on borders ever gay,
Delights to linger in his sunny way,
Oft, while I seem to count, with musing glance,
The murm'ring waves that near his brink advance,
My wand'ring thoughts shall seek the grassy side,
Parental Thames, where rolls thy ample tide;
Where on thy willowed bank, methinks, appears
Engraved the record of my passing years.
Ah, not like thine, their course is gently led,
By zephyrs fanned, through paths with verdure spread;
They flow, as urged by storms the mountain rill
Falls o'er the fragments of the rocky hill.
   My native scenes! Can aught in time or space
From this fond heart your loved remembrance chase?
Linked to that heart by ties for ever dear,
By joy's light smile, and sorrow's tender tear;
By all that ere my anxious hopes employed,
By all my soul has suffered or enjoyed!
Still blended with those well-known scenes, arise
The varying images the past supplies;
The childish sports that fond attention drew,
And charmed my vacant heart when life was new;
The harmless mirth, the sadness robbed of power
To cast its shade beyond the present hour –
And that dear hope which soothed my youthful breast,
And showed the op'ning world in beauty dressed;
That hope which seemed with bright unfolding rays
(Ah, vainly seemed!) to gild my future days;
That hope which, early wrapped in lasting gloom,
Sunk in the cold inexorable tomb!
And Friendship, ever powerful to control
The keen emotions of the wounded soul,
To lift the suff'ring spirit from despair,
And bid it feel that life deserves a care.
Still each impression that my heart retains
Is linked, dear land, to thee by lasting chains.
   She too, sweet soother of my lonely hours,
Who gilds my thorny path with fancy's flowers,

The muse who early taught my willing heart
To feel with transport her prevailing art,
Who deigned before my infant eyes to spread
Those dazzling visions she alone can shed –
She who will still be found where'er I stray
The loved companion of my distant way;
Midst foreign sounds, her voice that charms my ear,
Breathed in my native tongue, I still shall hear;
Midst foreign sounds, endeared will flow the song
Whose tones, my Albion, will to thee belong!
　And when with wonder thrilled, with mind elate,
I mark the change sublime in Gallia's state,
Where new-born Freedom treads the banks of Seine,
Hope in her eye, and Virtue in her train!
Pours day upon the dungeon's central gloom,
And leads the captive from his living tomb;
Tears the sharp iron from his loaded breast,
And bids the renovated[1] land be blessed –
My thoughts shall fondly turn to that loved isle
Where Freedom long has shed her genial smile.
Less safe in other lands the triple wall
And massy portal of the Gothic hall,
Than in that favoured isle the straw-built thatch
Where Freedom sits, and guards the simple latch.
　Yet, Albion, while my heart to thee shall spring,
To thee its first, its best affections bring;
Yet when I hear exulting millions pour
The shout of triumph on the Gallic shore,
Not without sympathy my pensive mind
The bounds of human bliss enlarged, shall find;
Not without sympathy my glowing breast
Shall hear, on any shore, of millions blessed,
Scorning those narrow souls, whate'er their clime,
Who meanly think that sympathy a crime,
Who, if one wish for human good expand
Beyond the limits of their native land,
And from the worst of ills would others free,
Deem that warm wish, my country, guilt to thee.
Ah, why those blessings to one spot confine,
Which, when diffused, will not the less be thine?
Ah, why repine if far those blessings spread
For which so oft thy gen'rous sons have bled?
Shall Albion mark with scorn the lofty thought,
The love of liberty, herself has taught?
Shall *her* brave sons, in this enlightened age,
Assume the bigot-frown of papal rage,

Notes

A FAREWELL, FOR TWO YEARS

[1] *renovated* This picks up the millennial hope implied in the final line of the preceding poem. Universal spiritual renewal was one of the expected results of the French Revolution.

Nor tolerate the vow to Freedom paid
If diff'ring from the ritual *they* have made?
Freedom, who oft on Albion's fost'ring breast
Has found *her* friends in stars and ermine dressed,
Allows that some among her chosen race
Should there the claim to partial honours trace,
And in the long-reflected lustre shine
That beams through ancestry's ennobled line;
While she, with guardian wing, can well secure
From each proud wrong the undistinguished poor.
On Gallia's coast, where oft the robe of state
Was trailed by those whom Freedom's soul must hate;
Where, like a comet, rank appeared to glow
With dangerous blaze that threatened all below –
There Freedom now, with gladdened eye, beholds
The simple vest that flows in equal folds.
   And though on Seine's fair banks a transient storm[2]
Flung o'er the darkened wave its angry form,
That purifying tempest now has passed –
No more the trembling waters feel the blast;
The bord'ring images, confusedly traced
Along the ruffled stream, to order haste;[3]
The vernal dayspring bursts the partial gloom,
And all the landscape glows with fresher bloom.
   When, far around that bright'ning scene, I view
Objects of gen'ral bliss, to Gallia new,
Then, Albion, shall my soul reflect with pride
Thou wert her leading star, her honoured guide;
That, long in slav'ry sunk, when taught by thee,
She broke her fetters, and has dared be free;
In new-born majesty she seems to rise,
While sudden from the land oppression flies.
So, at the solemn hour of nature's birth,
When brooding darkness[4] veiled the beauteous earth,
Heaven's awful mandate pierced the solid night –
'Let there be light', it said, 'and there was light!'
   Ah, when shall reason's intellectual ray
Shed o'er the moral world more perfect day?
When shall that gloomy world appear no more
A waste, where desolating tempests roar?
Where savage Discord howls in threat'ning form,
And wild Ambition leads the madd'ning storm;
Where hideous Carnage marks his dang'rous way,
And where the screaming vulture scents his prey?
Ah, come, blessed Concord, chase with smile serene
The hostile passions from the human scene.

Notes

[2] *a transient storm* a reference to the storming of the Bastille, 14 July 1789, which initiated its demolition and the execution of its governor and some of its garrison. Williams's views on this event are elucidated in her *Letters*; see pp. 296–7.

[3] *to order haste* hasten to order.

[4] *brooding darkness* Miltonic; cf. *L'Allegro* 6: 'Where brooding darkness spreads his jealous wings'.

May Glory's lofty path be found afar
From agonizing groans and crimson war,
And may the ardent mind that seeks renown
Claim not the martial, but the civic crown,
While pure Benevolence, with happier views
Of bright success, the gen'ral good pursues!
Ah, why, my country, with indignant pain,
Why in thy senate did she plead in vain?
Ah, why in vain enforce the captives' cause,
And urge humanity's eternal laws?
With fruitless zeal the tale of horror trace,
And ask redress for Afric's injured race?
Unhappy race! Ah, what to them availed
That touching eloquence whose efforts failed?
Though in the senate Mercy found combined
All who possess the noblest pow'rs of mind,
On other themes, pre-eminently bright,
They shine, like single stars, with sep'rate light –
Here, only *here*, with intermingled rays,
In one resplendent constellation blaze.
Yes, captive race, if all the force displayed
By glowing Genius, in Compassion's aid,
When with that energy she boasts alone,
She made your wrongs, your ling'ring tortures known,
Bade full in view the bloody visions roll,
Shook the firm nerves, and froze the shudd'ring soul,
As when the sun, in piercing radiance bright,
Dispelling the low mists of doubtful light,
Its lustre on some hideous object throws
And all its hateful horror clearly shows –
If Genius could in Mercy's cause prevail,
When Interest presses the opposing scale,
How swift had Britons torn your galling chain,
And from their country wiped its foulest stain!
But oh, since mis'ry, in its last excess,
In vain from British honour hopes redress,
May other lands the bright example show,
May other regions lessen human woe!
Yes, Gallia, haste! Though Britain's sons decline
The glorious power to save, that power is thine;
Haste, since, while Britain courts that dear-bought gold
For which her virtue and her fame are sold,
And calmly calculates her trade of death,
Her groaning victims yield in pangs their breath;
Then save some portion of that suff'ring race
From ills the mind can scarce endure to trace!
Oh, whilst with mien august thy leaders scan,
And guard with jealous zeal the rights of man,[5]

Notes

[5] *the rights of man* a reference to Thomas Paine's famous republican work (1791–2).

Forget not that to all kind Nature gives
Those common rights, the claim of all that lives.
But yet my filial heart its wish must breathe
That Britain first may snatch this deathless wreath;
First to the earth this act divine proclaim,
And wear the freshest palm of virtuous fame;
May I, in foreign realms, her glories hear,
Catch the loved sounds, and pour th' exulting tear!
And when, the destined hour of exile past,
My willing feet shall reach their home at last;
When, with the trembling hope Affection proves,[6]
My eager heart shall search for those it loves,
May no sharp pang that cherished hope destroy,
And from my bosom tear the promised joy,
Shroud every object, every scene in gloom,
And lead my bleeding soul to Friendship's tomb!
But may that moment to my eyes restore
The friends whose love endears my native shore!
Ah, long may Friendship, like the western ray,
Cheer the sad evening of a stormy day,
And gild my shadowy path with ling'ring light,
The last dear beam that slowly sinks in night.

[Madame Roland][1]

From Letters containing a Sketch of the Politics of France (1795)

At this period one of the most accomplished women that France has produced perished on the scaffold. This lady was Madame Roland, the wife of the late minister. On the 31st of May he had fled from his persecutors, and his wife who remained was carried to prison. The wits observed on this occasion that the body of Roland was missing, but that he had left his soul behind.

Madame Roland was indeed possessed of the most distinguished talents and a mind highly cultivated by the study of literature. I had been acquainted with her since I first came to France, and had always observed in her conversation the most ardent attachment to liberty and the most enlarged sentiments of philanthropy – sentiments which she developed with an eloquence peculiar to herself, with a flow and power of expression which gave new graces and new energy to the French language. With these extraordinary endowments of mind she united all the warmth of a feeling heart and all the charms of the most elegant manners. She was tall and well-shaped, her air was dignified, and although more than thirty five years of age she was still handsome. Her countenance had an expression of uncommon sweetness, and her full dark eyes beamed with the brightest rays of intelligence.

Notes

[6] *proves* experiences.

FROM LETTERS CONTAINING A SKETCH

[1] Manon Jeanne Philipon (1754–93) was an intellectual and writer, and married Jean-Marie Roland in 1781. Although they supported the revolution, both opposed its worst excesses until 1 June 1793, when she was detained in a series of prisons before being executed on 8 November. Her husband had escaped to Rouen and then to Normandy, but committed suicide when he heard of her death.

I visited her in the prison of St Pelagie, where her soul, superior to circumstances, retained its accustomed serenity, and she conversed with the same animated cheerfulness in her little cell as she used to do in the hotel of the minister. She had provided herself with a few books, and I found her reading Plutarch.[2] She told me she expected to die, and the look of placid resignation with which she spoke of it convinced me that she was prepared to meet death with a firmness worthy of her exalted character. . . .

When more than one person is led at the same time to execution, since they can suffer only in succession, those who are reserved to the last are condemned to feel multiplied deaths at the sound of the falling instrument and the sight of the bloody scaffold. To be the first victim was therefore considered as a privilege, and had been allowed to Madame Roland as a woman. But when she observed the dismay of her companion, she said to him, 'Allez le premier: que je vous épargne au moins la douleur de voir couler mon sang.'[3] She then turned to the executioner and begged that this sad indulgence might be granted to her fellow sufferer. The executioner told her that he had received orders that she should perish first.

'But you cannot, I am sure', said she with a smile, 'refuse the last request of a lady.' The executioner complied with her demand. When she mounted the scaffold and was tied to the fatal plank, she lifted up her eyes to the statue of Liberty near which the guillotine was placed, and exclaimed, 'Ah Liberté, comme on t'a jouée!'[4] The next moment she perished. But her name will be recorded in the annals of history as one of those illustrious women whose superior attainments seem fitted to exalt her sex in the scale of being.

Joanna Baillie (1762–1851)

Joanna Baillie was the younger daughter of Dorothea Hunter and James Baillie, a Presbyterian minister of Bothwell, Lanarkshire, later Professor of Divinity at the University of Glasgow. Her mother's family was distinguished: her aunt was Anne Hunter (1742–1821), the poet and Bluestocking; her uncles were the famous surgeons, William and John Hunter. In 1783 William bequeathed his London house in Great Windmill Street to Baillie's brother Matthew, a physician and anatomist. She resided with him from 1784, and on his marriage in 1791 moved to Hampstead, where she was a near neighbour of Anna Laetitia Barbauld.

Her first publication was the little-noticed *Poems; wherein it is attempted to describe certain views of nature and of rustic manners* (1790). The volume has much charm, and is quite experimental, as the various poems not merely evoke different scenes, but different psychological states. They look forward to her *Series of Plays; in which it is attempted to delineate the stronger passions of the mind* (3 vols, 1798–1812), the work that attracts most critical attention today, and for which she was best known in her own day. The first volume contained two plays on hate, two on love. It appeared anonymously, leading to speculation about the identity of its

Notes

[2] Plutarch (*c.* AD 46–*c.*120), Greek biographer and moral philosopher, author of the 'Parallel Lives', relating the lives of eminent Greek and Roman statesmen and soldiers.

[3] 'Go first; let me at least spare you the pain of seeing my blood shed' (Williams's translation).

[4] 'Ah Liberty, how hast thou been sported with!' (Williams's translation); apparently the source of Wordsworth, *Thirteen-Book Prelude* x 352–4. Wordsworth was an admirer of Roland's *Memoirs*.

author. Her authorship was acknowledged in 1800, the year that saw the first performance of *De Monfort* with Sarah Siddons in the starring role.

Her dramas were important because they represented a reaction against the highly mannered and overblown acting favoured in her day; instead she favoured 'the expressions of passion', by which she meant truth to human psychology. The power of drama lay in its immediacy, she believed, and in its ability to show us 'the passions, the humours, the weaknesses, the prejudices of men': 'For who hath followed the great man into his secret closet, or stood by the side of his nightly couch, and heard those exclamations of the soul which heaven alone may hear, that the historian should be able to inform us?' Baillie argues that the historian cannot provide such insights into the mind of great men; the dramatist can. Her 'Introductory Discourse' explains this at length, with particular emphasis on the importance of tragedy. Baillie may have discussed these matters with Wordsworth, whom she came to know, and who seems to echo her in his preface to *Lyrical Ballads.*

Further reading

Catherine B. Burroughs, 'English Romantic Women Writers and Theatre Theory: Joanna Baillie's Prefaces to the *Plays on the Passions*', *RR* 274–96.

Margaret S. Carhart, *The Life and Work of Joanna Baillie* (New Haven, 1923).

Janice Patten, 'Joanna Baillie, *A Series of Plays*', in *A Companion to Romanticism* ed. Duncan Wu (Oxford, 1998), pp. 169–78.

Jane Stabler, *Burke to Byron, Barbauld to Baillie, 1790–1830* (Basingstoke, 2002), pp. 46–64.

Introductory Discourse (extracts)

From A Series of Plays (1798)

Before I explain the plan of this work, I must make a demand upon the patience of my reader, whilst I endeavour to communicate to him those ideas regarding human nature, as they in some degree affect almost every species of moral writings, but particularly the Dramatic, that induced me to attempt it; and, as far as my judgment enabled me to apply them, has directed me in the execution of it.

From that strong sympathy which most creatures, but the human above all, feel for others of their kind, nothing has become so much an object of man's curiosity as man himself. We are all conscious of this within ourselves, and so constantly do we meet with it in others, that like every circumstance of continually repeated occurrence, it thereby escapes observation . . .

Amongst the many trials to which the human mind is subjected, that of holding intercourse, real or imaginary, with the world of spirits: of finding itself alone with a being terrific and awful, whose nature and power are unknown, has been justly considered as one of the most severe. The workings of nature in this situation, we all know, have ever been the object of our most eager enquiry. No man wishes to see the Ghost[1] himself, which would certainly procure him the best information on the subject, but every man wishes to see one who believes that he sees it, in all the agitation and wildness of that species of terror. To gratify this curiosity how many

Notes

Introductory Discourse

[1] *the Ghost* probably a reference to the Ghost in *Hamlet*, who causes such terror in its opening scenes.

people have dressed up hideous apparitions to frighten the timid and superstitious! and have done it at the risk of destroying their happiness or understanding for ever. For the instances of intellect being destroyed by this kind of trial are more numerous, perhaps, in proportion to the few who have undergone it than by any other.

How sensible are we of this strong propensity within us, when we behold any person under the pressure of great and uncommon calamity! Delicacy and respect for the afflicted will, indeed, make us turn ourselves aside from observing him, and cast down our eyes in his presence; but the first glance we direct to him will involuntarily be one of the keenest observation, how hastily soever it may be checked; and often will a returning look of enquiry mix itself by stealth with our sympathy and reserve.

But it is not in situations of difficulty and distress alone, that man becomes the object of this sympathetic curiosity; he is no less so when the evil he contends with arises in his own breast, and no outward circumstance connected with him either awakens our attention or our pity. What human creature is there, who can behold a being like himself under the violent agitation of those passions which all have, in some degree, experienced, without feeling himself most powerfully excited by the sight? I say, all have experienced; for the bravest man on earth knows what fear is as well as the coward; and will not refuse to be interested for one under the dominion of this passion, provided there be nothing in the circumstances attending it to create contempt. Anger is a passion that attracts less sympathy than any other, yet the unpleasing and distorted features of an angry man will be more eagerly gazed upon, by those who are no wise concerned with his fury or the objects of it, than the most amiable placid countenance in the world. Every eye is directed to him; every voice hushed to silence in his presence; even children will leave off their gambols as he passes, and gaze after him more eagerly than the gaudiest equipage. The wild tossings of despair; the gnashing of hatred and revenge; the yearnings of affection, and the softened mien of love; all that language of the agitated soul, which every age and nation understands, is never addressed to the dull nor inattentive.

It is not merely under the violent agitations of passion, that man so rouses and interests us; even the smallest indications of an unquiet mind, the restless eye, the muttering lip, the half-checked exclamation, and the hasty start, will set our attention as anxiously upon the watch, as the first distant flashes of a gathering storm. When some great explosion of passion bursts forth, and some consequent catastrophe happens, if we are at all acquainted with the unhappy perpetrator, how minutely will we endeavour to remember every circumstance of his past behaviour! and with what avidity will we seize upon every recollected word or gesture, that is in the smallest degree indicative of the supposed state of his mind, at the time when they took place. If we are not acquainted with him, how eagerly will we listen to similar recollections from another! Let us understand, from observation or report, that any person harbours in his breast, concealed from the world's eye, some powerful rankling passion of what kind soever it may be, we will observe every word, every motion, every look, even the distant gait of such a man, with a constancy and attention bestowed upon no other. Nay, should we meet him unexpectedly on our way, a feeling will pass across our minds as though we found ourselves in the neighbourhood of some secret and fearful thing. If invisible, would we not follow him into his lonely haunts, into his closet, into the midnight silence of his chamber? There is, perhaps, no employment which the human mind will with so much avidity pursue, as the discovery of concealed passion, as the tracing the varieties and progress of a perturbed soul.

It is to this sympathetic curiosity of our nature, exercised upon mankind in great and trying occasions, and under the influence of the stronger passions, when the grand, the generous, the terrible attract our attention far more than the base and depraved, that the high and powerfully tragic, of every composition, is addressed.

This propensity is universal. Children begin to show it very early; it enters into many of their amusements, and that part of them too, for which they show the keenest relish. It tempts them many times, as well as the mature in years, to be guilty in tricks, vexations and cruelty; yet God Almighty has implanted it within us, as well as all our other propensities and passions, for wise and good purposes. It is our best and most powerful instructor. From it we are taught the proprieties and decencies of ordinary life, and are prepared for distressing and difficult situations. In examining others we know ourselves. With limbs untorn, with head unsmitten, with senses unimpaired by despair, we know what we ourselves might have been on the rack, on the scaffold, and in the most afflicting circumstances of distress. Unless when accompanied with passions of the dark and malevolent kind, we cannot well exercise this disposition without becoming more just, more merciful, more compassionate; and as the dark and malevolent passions are not the predominant inmates of the human breast, it hath produced more deeds – O many more! of kindness than of cruelty. It holds up for our example a standard of excellence, which without its assistance, our inward consciousness of what is right and becoming might never have dictated. It teaches us, also, to respect ourselves, and our kind; for it is a poor mind, indeed, that from this employment of its faculties, learns not to dwell upon the noble view of human nature rather than the mean. . . .

If the study of human nature, then, is so useful to the poet, the novelist, the historian, and the philosopher, of how much greater importance must it be to the dramatic writer? To them it is a powerful auxiliary, to him it is the centre and strength of the battle. If characteristic views of human nature enliven not their pages, there are many excellencies with which they can, in some degree, make up for the deficiency, it is what we receive from them with pleasure rather than demand. But in his works no richness of invention, harmony of language, nor grandeur of sentiment will supply the place of faithfully delineated nature. The poet and the novelist may represent to you their great characters from the cradle to the tomb. They may represent them in any mood or temper, and under the influence of any passion which they see proper, without being obliged to put words into their mouths, those great betrayers of the feigned and adopted. They may relate every circumstance however trifling and minute, that serves to develop their tempers and dispositions. They tell us what kind of people they intend their men and women to be, and as such we receive them. If they are to move us with any scene of distress, every circumstance regarding the parties concerned in it, how they looked, how they moved, how they sighed, how the tears gushed from their eyes, how the very light and shadow fell upon them, is carefully described, and the few things that are given them to say along with all this assistance, must be very unnatural indeed if we refuse to sympathize with them. But the characters of the drama must speak directly for themselves. Under the influence of every passion, humour[2] and impression; in the artificial veilings of hypocrisy and ceremony, in the openness of freedom and confidence, and in the lonely hour of meditation they speak. He who made us hath placed within our breast a judge that judges instantaneously of everything they say. We expect to find them creatures like

Notes

[2] *humour* mood.

ourselves; and if they are untrue to nature, we feel that we are imposed upon; as though the poet had introduced to us for brethren, creatures of a different race, beings of another world.

As in other works deficiency in characteristic truth may be compensated by excellencies of a different kind, in the drama characteristic truth will compensate every other defect. Nay, it will do what appears a contradiction; one strong genuine stroke of nature will cover a multitude of sins even against nature herself. When we meet in some scene of a good play a very fine stroke of this kind, we are apt to become so intoxicated with it, and so perfectly convinced of the author's great knowledge of the human heart, that we are unwilling to suppose that the whole of it has not been suggested by the same penetrating spirit. Many well-meaning enthusiastic critics have given themselves a great deal of trouble in this way; and have shut their eyes most ingeniously against the fair light of nature for the very love of it. They have converted, in their great zeal, sentiments palpably false, both in regard to the character and situation of the persons who utter them, sentiments which a child or a clown would detect, into the most skilful depictments of the heart. I can think of no stronger instance to show how powerfully this love of nature dwells within us.[3]

Formed as we are with these sympathetic propensities in regard to our own species, it is not at all wonderful that theatrical exhibition has become the grand and favourite amusement of every nation into which it has been introduced. Savages will, in the wild contortions of a dance, shape out some rude story expressive of character or passion, and such a dance will give more delight to his companions than the most artful exertions of agility. Children in their gambols will make out a mimic representation of the manners, characters, and passions of grown men and women, and such a pastime will animate and delight them much more than a treat of the daintiest sweetmeats, or the handling of the gaudiest toys. Eagerly as it is enjoyed by the rude and the young, to the polished and the ripe in years it is still the most interesting amusement. Our taste for it is durable as it is universal. Independently of those circumstances which first introduced it, the world would not have long been without it. The progress of society would soon have brought it forth; and men in the whimsical decorations of fancy would have displayed the characters and actions of their heroes, the folly and absurdity of their fellow-citizens, had no priests of Bacchus ever existed.

In whatever age or country the drama might have taken its rise, tragedy would have been the first-born of its children. For every nation has its great men, and its great events upon record; and to represent their own forefathers struggling with those difficulties, and braving those dangers, of which they have heard with admiration, and the effects of which they still, perhaps, experience, would certainly have been the most animating subject for the poet, and the most interesting for his audience, even independently of the natural inclination we all so universally show for scenes of horror and distress, of passion and heroic exertion. Tragedy would have been the first child of the drama, for the same reasons that have made heroic ballad, with all its battles, murders, and disasters, the earliest poetical compositions of every country.

We behold heroes and great men at a distance, unmarked by those small but distinguishing features of the mind, which give a certain individuality to such an

Notes

[3] 'It appears to me a very strong testimony of the excellence of our great national dramatist [Shakespeare], that so many people have been employed in finding out obscure and refined beauties, in what appear to ordinary observation his very defects. Men, it may be said, do so merely to show their own superior penetration and ingenuity. But granting this; what could make other men listen to them, and listen so greedily too, if it were not that they have received from the works of Shakespeare, pleasure far beyond what the most perfect poetical compositions of a different character can afford' (Baillie's note).

infinite variety of similar beings, in the near and familiar intercourse of life. They appear to us from this view like distant mountains, whose dark outlines we trace in the clear horizon, but the varieties of whose roughened sides, shaded with heath and brushwood, and seamed with many a cleft, we perceive not. When accidental anecdote reveals to us any weakness or peculiarity belonging to them, we start upon it like a discovery. They are made known to us in history only, by the great events they are connected with, and the part they have taken in extraordinary or important transactions. Even in poetry and romance, with the exception of some love story interwoven with the main events of their lives, they are seldom more intimately made known to us. To tragedy it belongs to lead them forward to our nearer regard, in all the distinguishing varieties which nearer inspection discovers; with the passions, the humours, the weaknesses, the prejudices of men. It is for her to present to us the great and magnanimous hero, who appears to our distant view as a superior being, as a god, softened down with those smaller frailties and imperfections which enable us to glory in, and claim kindred to his virtues. It is for her to exhibit to us the daring and ambitious man, planning his dark designs, and executing his bloody purposes, marked with those appropriate characteristics which distinguish him as an individual of that class; and agitated with those varied passions, which disturb the mind of man when he is engaged in the commission of such deeds. It is for her to point out to us the brave and impetuous warrior struck with those visitations of nature which, in certain situations, will unnerve the strongest arm, and make the boldest heart tremble. It is for her to show the tender, gentle, and unassuming mind animated with that fire which, by the provocation of circumstances, will give to the kindest heart the ferocity and keenness of a tiger. It is for her to present to us the great and striking characters that are to be found amongst men, in a way which the poet, the novelist, and the historian can but imperfectly attempt. But above all, to her, and to her only it belongs to unveil to us the human mind under the dominion of those strong and fixed passions which, seemingly unprovoked by outward circumstances, will from small beginnings brood within the breast, till all the better dispositions, all the fair gifts of nature are borne down before them. Those passions which conceal themselves from the observation of men; which cannot unbosom themselves even to the dearest friend; and can, often times, only give their fullness vent in the lonely desert, or in the darkness of midnight. For who hath followed the great man into his secret closet, or stood by the side of his nightly couch, and heard those exclamations of the soul which heaven alone may hear, that the historian should be able to inform us? And what form of story, what mode of rehearsed speech will communicate to us those feelings, whose irregular bursts, abrupt transitions, sudden pauses, and half-uttered suggestions, scorn all harmony of measured verse, all method and order of relation?

On the first part of this task her[4] bards have eagerly exerted their abilities: and some amongst them, taught by strong original genius to deal immediately with human nature and their own hearts, have laboured in it successfully. But in presenting to us those views of great characters, and of the human mind in difficult and trying situations which peculiarly belong to tragedy, the far greater proportion, even of those who may be considered as respectable dramatic poets, have very much failed. From the beauty of those original dramas to which they have ever looked back with admiration, they have been tempted to prefer the embellishments of poetry to faithfully delineated nature. They have been more occupied in considering the

Notes

[4] *her* i.e. Tragedy's.

works of the great dramatists who have gone before them, and the effects produced by their writings, than the varieties of human character which first furnished materials for those works, or those principles in the mind of man by means of which such effects were produced. Neglecting the boundless variety of nature, certain strong outlines of character, certain bold features of passion, certain grand vicissitudes, and striking dramatic situations have been repeated from one generation to another; whilst a pompous and solemn gravity, which they have supposed to be necessary for the dignity of tragedy, has excluded almost entirely from their works those smaller touches of nature, which so well develop the mind; and by showing men in their hours of state and exertion only, they have consequently shown them imperfectly. Thus, great and magnanimous heroes, who bear with majestic equanimity every vicissitude of fortune; who in every temptation and trial stand forth in unshaken virtue, like a rock buffeted by the waves; who encompassed with the most terrible evils, in calm possession of their souls, reason upon the difficulties of their state; and, even upon the brink of destruction, pronounce long eulogiums[5] on virtue, in the most eloquent and beautiful language, have been held forth to our view as objects of imitation and interest; as though they had entirely forgotten that it is only from creatures like ourselves that we feel, and therefore, only from creatures like ourselves that we receive the instruction of example.[6] Thus, passionate and impetuous warriors, who are proud, irritable, and vindictive, but generous, daring, and disinterested; setting their lives at a pin's fee for the good of others, but incapable of curbing their own humour of a moment to gain the whole world for themselves; who will pluck the orbs of heaven from their places, and crush the whole universe in one grasp, are called forth to kindle in our souls the generous contempt of everything abject and base; but with an effect proportionably feeble, as the hero is made to exceed in courage and fire what the standard of humanity will agree to.[7] Thus, tender and pathetic lovers, full of the most gentle affections, the most amiable dispositions, and the most exquisite feelings; who present their defenceless bosoms to the storms of this rude world in all the graceful weakness of sensibility, are made to sigh out their sorrows in one

Notes

5 *eulogiums* speeches of praise.

6 'To a being perfectly free from all human infirmity our sympathy refuses to extend. Our Saviour himself, whose character is so beautiful, and so harmoniously consistent; in whom, with outward proofs of his mission less strong than those that are offered to us, I should still be compelled to believe, from being utterly unable to conceive how the idea of such a character could enter into the imagination of man, never touches the heart more nearly than when he says, "Father, let this cup pass from me." Had he been represented to us in all the unshaken strength of these tragic heroes, his disciples would have made fewer converts, and his precepts would have been listened to coldly. Plays in which heroes of this kind are held forth, and whose aim is, indeed, honourable and praiseworthy, have been admired by the cultivated and refined, but the tears of the simple, the applauses of the young and untaught have been wanting' (Baillie's note).

7 'In all burlesque imitations of tragedy, those plays in which this hero is pre-eminent, are always exposed to bear the great brunt of the ridicule; which proves how popular they have been, and how many poets, and good ones too, have been employed upon them. That they have been so popular, however, is not owing to the intrinsic merit of the characters they represent, but their opposition to those mean and contemptible qualities belonging to human nature, of which we are most ashamed. Besides, there is something in the human mind, independently of its love of applause, which inclines it to boast. This is ever the attendant of that elasticity of soul, which makes us bound up from the touch of oppression; and if there is nothing in the accompanying circumstances to create disgust, or suggest suspicions of their sincerity (as in real life is commonly the case), we are very apt to be carried along with the boasting of others. Let us in good earnest believe that a man is capable of achieving all that human courage can achieve, and we will suffer him to talk of impossibilities. Amidst all their pomp of words, therefore, our admiration of such heroes is readily excited (for the understanding is more easily deceived than the heart), but how stands our sympathy affected? As no caution nor foresight, on their own account, is ever suffered to occupy the thoughts of such bold disinterested beings, we are the more inclined to care for them, and take an interest in their fortune through the course of the play: yet, as their souls are unappalled by anything; as pain and death are not at all regarded by them; and as we have seen them very ready to plunge their own swords into their own bosoms, on no very weighty occasion, perhaps, their death distresses us but little, and they commonly fall unwept' (Baillie's note).

unvaried strain of studied pathos, whilst this constant demand upon our feelings makes us absolutely incapable of answering it.[8] Thus, also, tyrants are represented as monsters of cruelty, unmixed with any feelings of humanity; and villains as delighting in all manner of treachery and deceit, and acting upon many occasions for the very love of villainy itself; though the perfectly wicked are as ill fitted for the purposes of warning, as the perfectly virtuous are for those of example.[9] This spirit of imitation, and attention to effect, has likewise confined them very much in their choice of situations and events to bring their great characters into action; rebellions, conspiracies, contentions for empire, and rivalships in love have alone been thought worthy of trying those heroes; and palaces and dungeons the only places magnificent or solemn enough for them to appear in.

They have, indeed, from this regard to the works of preceding authors, and great attention to the beauties of composition, and to dignity of design, enriched their plays with much striking, and sometimes sublime imagery, lofty thoughts, and virtuous sentiments; but in striving so eagerly to excel in those things that belong to tragedy in common with many other compositions, they have very much neglected those that are peculiarly her own. As far as they have been led aside from the first labours of a tragic poet by a desire to communicate more perfect moral instruction, their motive has been respectable, and they merit our esteem. But this praiseworthy end has been injured instead of promoted by their mode of pursuing it. Every species of moral writing has its own way of conveying instruction, which it can never, but with disadvantage, exchange for any other. The drama improves us by the knowledge we acquire of our own minds, from the natural desire we have to look into the thoughts, and observe the behaviour of others. Tragedy brings to our view men placed in those elevated situations, exposed to those great trials, and engaged in those extraordinary transactions, in which few of us are called upon to act . . .

From this general view, which I have endeavoured to communicate to my reader, of tragedy, and those principles in the human mind upon which the success of her efforts depends, I have been led to believe, that an attempt to write a series of tragedies, of simpler construction, less embellished with poetical decorations, less constrained by that lofty seriousness which has so generally been considered as necessary for the support of tragic dignity, and in which the chief object should be to delineate the progress of the higher passions in the human breast, each play exhibiting a particular passion, might not be unacceptable to the public. And I have been the more readily induced to act upon this idea, because I am confident, that tragedy, written upon this plan, is fitted to produce stronger moral effect than upon any other. I have said that tragedy in representing to us great characters struggling with difficulties, and placed

Notes

8 'Were it not that in tragedies where these heroes preside, the same soft tones of sorrow are so often repeated in our ears, till we are perfectly tired of it, they are more fitted to interest us than any other: both because in seeing them, we own the ties of kindred between ourselves and the frail mortals we lament; and sympathize with the weakness of mortality unmixed with any thing to degrade or disgust; and also, because the misfortunes, which form the story of the play, are frequently of the more familiar and domestic kind. A king driven from his throne will not move our sympathy so strongly as a private man torn from the bosom of his family' (Baillie's note).

9 'I have said nothing here in regard to female character, though in many tragedies it is brought forward as the principal one of the piece, because what I have said of the above characters is likewise applicable to it. I believe there is no man that ever lived, who has behaved in a certain manner, on a certain occasion, who has not had amongst women some corresponding spirit, who on the like occasion, and every way similarly circumstanced, would have behaved in the like manner. With some degree of softening and refinement, each class of the tragic heroes I have mentioned has its corresponding one amongst the heroines. The tender and pathetic no doubt has the most numerous, but the great and magnanimous is not without it, and the passionate and impetuous boasts of one by no means inconsiderable in numbers, and drawn sometimes to the full as passionate and impetuous as itself' (Baillie's note).

in situations of eminence and danger, in which few of us have any chance of being called upon to act, conveys its moral efficacy to our minds by the enlarged views which it gives to us of human nature, by the admiration of virtue, and execration of vice which it excites, and not by the examples it holds up for our immediate application. But in opening to us the heart of man under the influence of those passions to which all are liable, this is not the case. Those strong passions that, with small assistance from outward circumstances, work their way in the heart, till they become the tyrannical masters of it, carry on a similar operation in the breast of the monarch, and the man of low degree. It exhibits to us the mind of man in that state when we are most curious to look into it, and is equally interesting to all. Discrimination of character is a turn of mind, though more common than we are aware of, which everybody does not possess; but to the expressions of passion, particularly strong passion, the dullest mind is awake; and its true unsophisticated language the dullest understanding will not misinterpret . . .

William Lisle Bowles (1762–1851)

Born into a clergy family at Kings Sutton, Northamptonshire, William Lisle Bowles was the pupil of Joseph Warton at Winchester, and Thomas Warton at Trinity College, Oxford, where he matriculated in 1781 (graduated 1792). Rejected in love by the niece of Sir Samuel Romilly, he went on a walking tour of northern England, Scotland and the Continent, during which he composed his *Fourteen Sonnets* (1789). The edition of 100 copies sold out immediately, and a second, containing twenty-one sonnets, was published within weeks. They reached a ninth edition by 1805. He published much else, but nothing as popular and influential as the sonnets. Wordsworth and Coleridge read them in 1789, and in *Biographia Literaria* Coleridge praised 'the genial influence of a style of poetry, so tender, and yet so manly, so natural and real, and yet so dignified, and harmonious, as the sonnets, etc., of Mr Bowles!'[1] True, it was the combination of the same melancholy as that found in the sonnets of his Oxford tutor, Thomas Warton, with a sophisticated sense of the picturesque and sublime, that made his sonnets distinctive and, in their day, fashionable. His sonnet to the Itchin looks back to Warton's 'To the River Lodon' (see p. 7), and forward to Coleridge's 'To the River Otter' (pp. 598–9).

Further reading

Bill Ruddick, ' "Genius of the Sacred Fountain of Tears": A Bicentenary Tribute to the Sonnets of William Lisle Bowles', *Charles Lamb Bulletin* NS 72 (1990) 276–84.

A. Harris Fairbanks, ' "Dear Native Brook": Coleridge, Bowles, and Thomas Warton the younger', *TWC* 6 (1975) 313–15.

From Fourteen Sonnets (1789)

Sonnet VIII. To the River Itchin,[1] near Winton

Itchin, when I behold thy banks again,
    Thy crumbling margin, and thy silver breast
    On which the self-same tints still seem to rest,

Notes

[1] CC *Biographia* i 17. He also included three of Bowles's sonnets in his *Sonnets from Various Authors* (1796).

To The River Itchin

[1] The Itchen (as it is spelled now) runs through Winchester, where Bowles went to school; the Itchen runs behind the school.

Why feels my heart the shiv'ring sense of pain?
  Is it that many a summer's day has passed
Since in life's morn I carolled[2] on thy side?
Is it that oft since then my heart has sighed
  As youth, and hope's delusive gleams, flew fast?
Is it that those who circled on thy shore,
Companions of my youth, now meet no more?
  Whate'er the cause, upon thy banks I bend
Sorrowing, yet feel such solace at my heart,
  As at the meeting of some long-lost friend
  From whom, in happier hours, we wept to part.

John Thelwall (1764–1834)

'Citizen John Thelwall had something good about him,' Coleridge recalled in 1830, 'We were once sitting in Somersetshire in a beautiful recess. I said to him, "Citizen John! This is a fine place to talk treason in!" "Nay, Citizen Samuel!", replied he, "it is a place to make a man forget that there is any necessity for treason." ' As one of the defendants at the treason trials of 1794, Thelwall had good reason to want to forget.

The son of a silk mercer in London, he had been involved in the theatre, the law and the family business before becoming a journalist. His interest in politics was stimulated by involvement in the Society for Free Debate at Coachmakers' Hall in Southwark. In autumn 1793 he joined the London Corresponding Society and on 21 October became a member of the General Committee. The Society had been founded by Thomas Hardy, a Scottish cobbler, on 25 January 1792, as a means of agitating among those wishing for political reform. The low subscription fee of one penny a week was intended to encourage the involvement of tradesmen and artisans. Thelwall came to the fore at a crowded general meeting on 20 January 1794, which was followed by an anniversary dinner at the Globe Tavern in Fleet Street. By this time he had already begun to prove his extraordinary talents as a political orator, poet and publicist. After the dinner he took the chair to propose the toasts, including one to *The Rights of Man*, after which he sang republican songs of his own composition, copies of which were later sold to members of the society and the audiences at his political lectures.

At a time of comparative political freedom it is not easy to imagine how dangerous it was to be a radical in 1794. England had been at war with France for a year (and would remain so until 1815), and Pitt's government was increasingly intolerant of French sympathizers at home. By the spring of 1794 the Terror in Paris was at its height: Robespierre executed Danton and other eminent French politicians in March and April 1794. Undaunted, the London Corresponding Society held a mass meeting on the bowling green at Chalk Farm on 14 April, at which Thelwall acted as master of ceremonies. By this time he was under constant surveillance by government spies, who reported that, when quenching his thirst after the five-hour meeting, he had removed the froth from his tankard with a knife, remarking, 'So should all tyrants be served!' That meeting, and another, of the radical Society for Constitutional Information on 2 May, sent alarm through Pitt's increasingly anxious wartime government. Fears of a French invasion

Notes

[2] *carolled* sang and, by implication, wrote poetry.

made it imperative that the government stifle dissident voices. Ten days later Thomas Hardy, secretary of the London Corresponding Society, and Daniel Adams, secretary of the Society for Constitutional Information, were arrested at home on the charge of treason. Thelwall and the Revd Jeremiah Joyce were arrested the following day; Horne Tooke, John Lovett, John Richter and John Augustus Bonney on 16 May. Pitt then sus pended habeas corpus, allowing him to detain the prisoners in the Tower of London for up to eight months without trial. The Tower was not then the tourist attraction it is today: its cells were cold, unhygienic, brutal places, where the prisoners quickly became ill. The punishment they faced for treason was centuries old: hanging, drawing and quartering. Thelwall distracted himself by composing his *Poems Written in Close Confinement* (1795).

A few days before the trials, Godwin published an attack on the government case under the title *Cursory Strictures on the Charge delivered by Lord Chief Justice Eyre to the Grand Jury.* It appeared in the *Morning Chronicle* for 21 October, and had an immediate impact. The treason trials began on 25 October; one by one, the accused were either acquitted or had their charges dropped, thanks largely to the devastating effect of Godwin's pamphlet.

A committed freethinker, Thelwall continued to agitate and lecture in spite of the fact that government spies followed him everywhere, often paying stooges to heckle or break up his meetings by force. His lectures, delivered in Beaufort Buildings off the Strand, were published in his periodical, the *Tribune*. They attracted audiences of 400–500, who paid the relatively high entrance fee of one shilling and sixpence (just over £4 or US$7.50 in today's currency), among whom were a number of 'aristocrats'.

The government was constantly seeking excuses for suppressing political dissent; their chance came on 29 October 1795, when the king was attacked by a mob on his way to open Parliament. This, and a large meeting of the London Corresponding Society in the fields near Copenhagen House, Islington, in which Thelwall was involved, provided the government with the excuse they needed: in early November the government introduced two Bills to Parliament, the first extending the definition of treason, and the second forbidding meetings of fifty or more without the consent of local magistrates. The Two Bills, or 'Gagging Acts', as they were known, became law on 18 December. Thelwall warned in the *Tribune* that they would give rise to even worse problems, and in its last issue he published his moving *Civic Oration*, announcing his decision to retire from politics (see pp. 320–1). There were many protests by societies across the land, but the government was implacable.

In summer 1796 he left London for Norwich, where he delivered a course of twenty-two lectures, admitting no more than forty-nine people to each one, on the subject of 'Classical History, and particularly the Laws and Revolutions of Rome', a cover under which he commented on current affairs. Later that year he lectured at Great Yarmouth, where the third meeting was broken up by ninety sailors armed with bludgeons. The three remaining lectures were safely delivered, and Thelwall went on to speak at King's Lynn and Wisbech. Throughout these times he was subject to constant harassment by government agents. Lectures at Derby, Stockport and Norwich were broken up by soldiers, and he was chased fifteen miles out of Ashby-de-la-Zouch when passing through on private business.

He was finally driven out of political agitation altogether. When he set off, on 29 June 1797, for a pedestrian tour of the west of England and Wales, he was on the lookout for a suitable retreat. Among those who welcomed him were Coleridge, Wordsworth and his sister Dorothy, whom he met at Nether Stowey. Coleridge, whose own political lectures were curtailed by the two Bills, had begun a correspondence with him in late April 1796, with the words: 'Pursuing the same end by the same means we ought not to be strangers to each other.' He enclosed a copy of his *Poems* (1796), which Thelwall analysed in his letter of 10 May 1796 (see pp. 321–2). He criticized Coleridge's ornate manner, reminding him of the need to write simply and lucidly; the principles he prescribed were close to those that would be espoused in the preface to *Lyrical Ballads*, and which are followed in Thelwall's proto-conversation poems, 'Lines written at Bridgwater' and 'To the Infant Hampden'. As 'Lines written at Bridgwater' reveals, Thelwall was at ease among the poets, and for a while entertained the possibility of settling among them. But they were already under surveillance by a government spy, and the landlord of Alfoxden House was sufficiently alarmed to deny the Wordsworths occupation for a further year.

Thelwall moved on, returned to Bristol, Gloucestershire and finally Wales, where he found a small farm in the hamlet of Llys Wen, on the banks of the Wye, to which he retired with his family. This proved disastrous; the locals harassed him, his efforts at farming failed and his beloved daughter, Maria, died. In later years he returned to lecturing, but this time on the subject of elocution. Years after his death, Wordsworth recalled: 'He really was a man of extraordinary talent, an affectionate husband and a good father. Though brought up in the city on a tailor's board he was truly sensible of the beauty of natural objects.'

Further reading

C. Cestre, *John Thelwall: A Pioneer of Democracy in England* (London, 1906).

Nicholas Roe, 'Coleridge and John Thelwall: The Road to Nether Stowey', in *The Coleridge Connection* ed. Richard Gravil and Molly Lefebure (Basingstoke, 1990), pp. 60–80.

E. P. Thompson, 'Disenchantment or Default? A Lay Sermon', in *Power and Consciousness* ed. Conor Cruise O'Brien and William Dean Vanech (London and New York, 1969), pp. 149–81.

E. P. Thompson, 'Hunting the Jacobin Fox', in *The Romantics: England in a Revolutionary Age* (Woodbridge, 1997), pp. 156–220.

Stanzas on hearing for certainty that we were to be tried for high treason (composed 28 September 1794)

From Poems Written in Close Confinement in the Tower and Newgate upon a Charge of Treason (1795)

Short is perhaps our date of life,[1]
But let us while we live be gay –
To those be thought and anxious care
Who build upon the distant day.

Though in our cup tyrannic power[2]
Would dash the bitter dregs of fear,
We'll gaily quaff the mantling draught,[3]
While patriot toasts the fancy cheer.

Notes

STANZAS ON HEARING FOR CERTAINTY

[1] *Short is perhaps . . . life* The penalty for treason was death (see headnote).

[2] *tyrannic power* Thelwall had cause to regard Pitt's government as tyrannical. They had arrested him and his radical friends without specific cause, and had confiscated their possessions.

[3] *mantling draught* The draught of beer is 'mantled' by a head of foam. But the implicit comparison is with the cloak (or mantle) worn by monarchs.

Sings not the seaman, tempest-tossed,
When surges wash the riven shroud,[4]
Scorning the threat'ning voice of fate
That pipes in rocking winds aloud?

Yes, he can take his cheerful glass,
And toast his mistress in the storm,
While duty and remembered joys
By turns his honest bosom warm.

And shall not we, in storms of state,
At base oppression's fury laugh,
And while the vital spirits flow,
To freedom fill, and fearless quaff?

Short is perhaps our date of life,
But let us while we live be gay –
To those be thought and anxious care
Who build upon the distant day.

Tower, 28 *September* 1794

Dangerous tendency of the attempt to suppress political discussion (published 21 March 1795)

From The Tribune (1795)

While prudent and moderate measures leave the door open to peaceful investigation, men of talents and moral character step forward into the field of politics, and never fail to take the lead in popular meetings and associations, for which nature seems to have intended them.

While this continues, all is peaceful and rational enquiry, and the people, though bold, are orderly. Nor even when persecution inflames their passions, are they easily provoked to actual intemperance. But when words are construed into treason, and men can no longer unbosom themselves to their friends at a tavern, or associate together for the diffusion of political information, but at the peril of their lives, the benevolent and moderate part of mankind retire from the scene of action, to brood, with prophetic anxiety, over the melancholy prospect.[1]

Enquiry is thus, it is true, in some degree suppressed, and the counsellors of these overbearing measures are apt to congratulate themselves on their supposed success. But the calm is more dreadful than the hurricane they pretended to apprehend. In the ferment of half-smothered indignation, feelings of a more gloomy complexion are generated, and characters of a very different stamp are called into action.

Notes

[4] *riven shroud* severed rigging.

Dangerous Tendency of the Attempt

[1] *melancholy prospect* Thelwall writes in anticipation of the Gagging Acts of December 1795, which banned 'seditious meetings' and aimed to ensure the 'safety of his majesty's person' (see headnote).

Men who have neither genius nor benevolence succeed those who had both, and, with no other stimulus than fury, and no other talent than hypocrisy and intrigue, embark in projects which every friend of humanity must abhor – and which, while the free, open, and manly character of the species was yet uncrushed by the detestable system of persecuting opinions, never could have entered the imagination.

Whoever will consult the page of history will find that in every country on the earth where liberty has been alternately indulged and trampled, this has been but too uniformly the progress of the human mind.

Let us ask then this serious question: is it possible for any person to be a more dangerous enemy to the peace and personal safety of the sovereign, than he who advises the persecution of opinion and the suppression of peaceable associations?

Civic oration on the anniversary of the acquittal of the lecturer[1] *(5 December*[2]*), being a vindication of the principles, and a review of the conduct, that placed him at the bar of the Old Bailey. Delivered Wednesday 9 December 1795* (extracts)

From The Tribune (1795)

I was born near this place.[3] My residence can be traced with ease during every part of my life, and if there had been any disgraceful particulars in my history, the industrious malice of faction need not have been confined to general abuses. There have been times in which poverty and misfortune frowned upon my youth, and in which I had to struggle with the bitterest disadvantages to which an independent spirit could be subjected; when without a profession (for I could not eat the bread of legal peculation), I had to support an aged mother and a brother robbed of every faculty of reason.

Yet upon all these embarrassments, when a debating society and a magazine brought me together but about £50 or £60 a year,[4] I look back with the proud consciousness of never having stooped even to a mean action. Search then, probe me to the quick, and if you can find one stain upon my character, think me in reality a plunderer and an assassin. But if you cannot, what will you think of a profligate administration, with more vices upon their heads than I have words to speak them? What will you think of their assassins, and the black epithets and calumnies with which they have so incessantly pursued me? . . .

When our beloved associates – when those men of mind and virtue, whose names I will cherish with veneration so long as 'memory holds her seat'[5] – when Gerrald, Margarot, Muir, Palmer and Skirving[6] were doomed to Botany Bay without having

Notes

Civic Oration on the Anniversary

[1] Thelwall lectured at Beaufort Buildings off the Strand, and published his texts in *The Tribune*.

[2] This is a reference to Thelwall's acquittal at the treason trials in 1794.

[3] *this place* Beaufort Buildings, off the Strand; Thelwall was born in Chandos Street, Covent Garden (about 5 minutes' walk away), 27 July 1764

[4] *about £50 or £60 a year* roughly equivalent to £2700–£3300 / US$5000–6000 today.

[5] *Hamlet* I v 96.

[6] Scottish radicals who fell foul of the oppressive policies of the government: Joseph Gerrald, a delegate to Edinburgh of the London Corresponding Society, was tried for sedition in March 1794 and sentenced to 14 years' transportation to Botany Bay, where he died in 1796; Maurice Margarot, the first chairman of the LCS, was tried for sedition in January 1794 and sentenced to transportation (he was returned in 1809, and died in 1815); Thomas Muir (1765–98) was tried in August 1793, sentenced to 14 years' transportation, but escaped to France, where he died; the Revd Thomas Fyshe Palmer (1747–1802), a Unitarian minister, was found guilty of sedition and sentenced to 7 years' transportation (after serving his time he died on the journey home); William Skirving was sentenced to 14 years' transportation in January 1794 but died in Botany Bay, 1796.

violated one law or principle of our constitution, it was natural (though it was not wise) for men who revered their talents and their virtues to indulge the British vice of intemperance – for it is a British vice, and we are too apt to be proud of it. It was natural that under such circumstances, our blood should boil, and that we should say angry things, and pass vapouring, intemperate resolutions. But the minister knew that the 'very head and jut of our offending went but to this – no further!'[7]

What, then, is that administration, which wishes to hang every man who makes use of an intemperate word against them?

But they have been disappointed – and what do they now attempt? They attempt to pass laws which will make all those things treason which they endeavoured to make treason before without any law whatever.

The minister introduces Two Bills.[8] What are they? Bills that subject a man to all the penalties of High Treason who shall publish, or even write, *without publishing*, any dissertation which approves any form of government but the existing government of the country. . . .

I cannot be ignorant that these acts are made in a very considerable degree with a view to my destruction. I know also that the time will come when – in consequence of the persecutions I have endured, and the temper (permit me to say) with which I have faced those persecutions – I may be an instrument of some service to the liberties and happiness of my country. I shall not therefore give the minister an opportunity to destroy me upon any trifling contest. I have here maintained myself in decency, and cleared away the encumbrances which former persecutions had brought upon me. With something less than £100[9] in my pocket I shall retire from this place, for the cultivation of my mind, and, carrying the consciousness of my own integrity into retirement, maintain myself by the labours of my pen.

Having been so long seeking for my country, and having endured so much persecution in that search, I think I shall not be accused either of selfishness or pusillanimity, when I say that I shall now wait till my country seeks for me, and that when my country does seek for me, she shall find me ready for my post, whatever may be the difficulty or the danger.

Letter from John Thelwall to Samuel Taylor Coleridge, 10 May 1796 (extract) (edited from MS)

Of your favourite poem I fear I shall speak in terms that will disappoint you. There are passages most undoubtedly in the *Religious Musings* of very great merit, and perhaps there is near half of the poem that no poet in our language need have been ashamed to own. But this praise belongs almost exclusively to those parts that are not at all religious. As for the generality of those passages which are most so, they are certainly anything in the world rather than poetry (unless indeed the mere glowing rapidity of the blank verse may entitle them to that distinction).

They are the very acme of abstruse, metaphysical, mystical rant, and all ranting abstraction, metaphysics and mysticism are wider from true poetry than the equator from the poles. The whole poem also is infected with inflation and turgidity . . . 'a vision *shadowy* of truth', '*wormy* grave', and a heap of like instances might be selected

Notes

[7] *Othello* I iii 80–1.

[8] The Two Bills were introduced in November 1795 and became law on 18 December.

[9] *something less than £100* something less, therefore, than the equivalent of £5500 / US$10,100 today.

worthy of Blackmore[1] himself. ('Ye petrify th' *imbrothelled atheist's* heart' is one of those illiberal and unfounded calumnies with which Christian meekness never yet disdained to supply the want of argument – but this by the way.) '*Lovely* was the *death* of him whose life was love' is certainly enough to make any man sick whose taste has not been corrupted by the licentious (I mean 'pious') nonsense of the conventicle.[2]

You may, if you please, 'lay the flattering unction to your soul'[3] that my irreligious principles dictate the severity of this criticism, and, though it may strengthen you in the suspicion, I must confess that your religious verses approach much nearer to poetry than those of Milton on the same subject. In short, while I was yet a Christian, and a very zealous one (i.e. when I was about your age),[4] I became thoroughly convinced that Christian poetry was very vile stuff – that religion was a subject which none but a rank infidel could handle poetically.

Before I wipe the gall from my pen, I must notice an affectation of the Della Crusca[5] school which blurs almost every one of your poems – I mean the frequent accent upon the adjectives and weak words. . . . 'For chiefly in the oppressed *good* man's face' etc.

Having dwelt thus largely upon the defects, I shall proceed to prove my qualifications to set up for a critic by running very slightly over the numerous beauties with which it abounds. 'The *thought-benighted sceptic*' is very happy, as is also 'Mists dim-floating of idolatry – misshaped the omnipresent sin'. (The word 'Split' appears to me ill-chosen and unpoetical.) The whole passage 'Thus from the elect' . . . (ll. 102–18), though not quite free either from mysticism or turgidity, is upon the whole very grand and very poetical. Lines 133–5 and 138–44 are also equally fine in sentiment, conception and expression. And though '*connatural* mind', '*tortuous* folds', '*savagery* of holy zeal', 'at his mouth *im*breathe', and '*fiendish* deeds', offend me not a little as being affected and pedantic (and therefore of course unpoetical), yet the whole passage, lines 181–255, delights me very much. The satire is dignified, the poetry sublime and ardent. Of the ensuing paragraph, 'In the primeval age' etc., the first and third lines are bad; but the ensuing passage consisting of 144 lines beginning with 'soon imagination conjured up a host of new desires', and ending at line 364 breathes a rapture and energy of mind seldom to be met with among modern bards. I must however in sincerity add that, according to my judgement, all that follows hangs like a dead weight upon the poem.

Lines written at Bridgwater in Somersetshire, on 27 July 1797, during a long excursion in quest of a peaceful retreat[1]

From Poems Written Chiefly in Retirement (1801)

Day of my double birth! who gave me first
To breathe life's troubled air, and, kindlier far,
Gave all that makes life welcome – gave me her[2]

Notes

LETTER FROM JOHN THELWALL TO COLERIDGE

[1] Sir Richard Blackmore (1654–1729), author of indifferent epics including *Creation: A Philosophical Poem* (1712).

[2] *conventicle* Dissenting religious gathering (or chapel).

[3] Hamlet to his mother: 'Lay not that flattering unction to your soul, / That not your trespass but my madness speaks' (*Hamlet* III iv 145–6).

[4] *your age* Coleridge was 24; Thelwall is looking back to *c*.1788.

[5] The Della Cruscans of the late 18th century advocated an affected, ornamented sentimentality, and are probably in Wordsworth's mind when he mentions the 'gaudiness and inane phraseology of many modern writers' in the Advertisement to *Lyrical Ballads* (1798), p. 331, below.

LINES WRITTEN AT BRIDGWATER IN SOMERSETSHIRE

[1] Thelwall was at this point walking to Bristol from Nether Stowey, where he had been Coleridge's guest.

[2] *Day of my double birth! . . . her* Thelwall was born on 27 July 1764; his second birthday was 27 July 1797, when he wrote this poem; *her* Susan Thelwall (née Vellum), who married him on 27 July 1791.

Who now, far distant,[3] sheds, perchance, the tear
In pensive solitude, and chides the hours
That keep her truant wanderer from her arms –
Hers and our smiling babies; eventful day!
How shall I greet thee now, at thy return,
So often marked with sadness? Art thou, say,
Once more arrived a harbinger of woes,
Precursor of a year of miseries,
Of storms and persecutions, of the pangs
Of disappointed hope, and keen regrets,
Wrung from the bosom by a sordid world
That kindness pays with hatred, and returns
Evil for good? – a world most scorpion-like
That stings what warms it, and the ardent glow
Of blessed benevolence too oft transmutes
To sullen gloom and sour misanthropy,
Wounding, with venomed tooth, the fostering breast
That her milk turns to gall. Or art thou come,
In most unwonted guise, oh fateful day,
With cheering prophecy of kindlier times?
Of hours of sweet retirement, tranquil joys
Of friendship, and of love – of studious ease,
Of philosophic thought – poetic dreams
In dell romantic, or by bubbling brook,
High wood, or rocky shore; where fancy's train,
Solemn or gay, shall in the sunbeam sport,
Or murmur in the gloom, peopling earth, air,
Ocean, and woodland haunt, mountain and cave
With wildest fantasies – wild, but not vain,
For, but for dreams like these, Meonides[4]
Had never shook the soul with epic song,
Nor Milton, slumbering underneath the shade
Of fancy-haunted oak, heard the loud strain
Of heavenly minstrelsy – nor yet had he,
Shakespeare (in praise of whom smooth Avon still
Flows eloquent to every Briton's ear),
Pierced the dark womb of nature with keen glance,
Tracing the embryo passions ere their birth,
And every mystic movement of the soul
Baring to public ken. Oh bards, to whom
Youth owes its emulation, age the bliss
Of many a wintry evening, dull and sad
But for your cheering aid! Ye from whose strains,
As from a font of inspiration, oft
The quickening mind, else stagnant, learns to flow
In tides of generous ardour, scattering wide
Smiling fertility, fresh fruits and flowers

Notes

[3] *far distant* Thelwall had left his family in Derby while on a walking tour of the west of England and Wales, in search of a suitable retreat from politics.

[4] *Meonides* Homer, author of the *Iliad* and the *Odyssey.*

Of intellectual worth![5] Oh might my soul
Henceforth with yours hold converse, in the scenes
Where nature cherishes poetic thought,
Best cradled in the solitary haunts
Where bustling cares intrude not, nor the throng
Of cities or of courts. Yet not for aye
In hermit-like seclusion would I dwell
(My soul estranging from my brother man)
Forgetful and forgotten; rather oft,
With some few minds congenial, let me stray
Along the muses' haunts, where converse, meet
For intellectual beings, may arouse
The soul's sublimer energies, or wing
The fleeting time most cheerily – the time
Which, though swift-fleeting, scatters, as he flies,
Seeds of delight, that, like the furrowed grain,
Strewed by the farmer as he onward stalks
Over his well-ploughed acres, shall produce,
In happy season, its abundant fruits.
    Day of my double birth,[6] if such the year
Thou usherest in, most welcome! For my soul
Is sick of public turmoil[7] – ah, most sick
Of the vain effort to redeem a race
Enslaved, because degenerate; lost to hope
Because to virtue lost – wrapped up in self,
In sordid avarice, luxurious pomp,
And profligate intemperance – a race
Fierce without courage, abject and yet proud,
And most licentious, though most far from thee.
    Ah, let me then, far from the strifeful scenes
Of public life (where reason's warning voice
Is heard no longer, and the trump of truth
Who blows but wakes The Ruffian Crew of Power
To deeds of maddest anarchy and blood) –
Ah, let me, far in some sequestered dell,
Build my low cot! Most happy might it prove,
My Samuel,[8] near to thine, that I might oft
Share thy sweet converse, best-beloved of friends,
Long-loved ere known[9] – for kindred sympathies
Linked (though far distant) our congenial souls!
Ah! 'twould be sweet, beneath the neighb'ring thatch,[10]

Notes

[5] *Ye from whose strains . . . worth* The 'strains' of Milton and Shakespeare inspire the young poet.

[6] *Day of my double birth* see p. 322 n 2.

[7] *public turmoil* Thelwall had been persecuted by government agents, his lectures broken up by force; he was chased out of towns, and caballed against even by other radicals.

[8] *My Samuel* Coleridge, whom Thelwall described in February 1797 as 'one of the most extraordinary geniuses and finest scholars of the age'.

[9] *Long-loved ere known* Their earliest contact was the letter of April 1796 (see above); they seem not to have met until summer 1797.

[10] *beneath the neighb'ring thatch* It was hoped that Thelwall and his family might move in next door to Coleridge at Nether Stowey, but animosity towards radicalism made that impossible.

In philosophic amity to dwell,
Inditing moral verse, or tale, or theme,
Gay or instructive.[11] And it would be sweet,
With kindly interchange of mutual aid,
To delve our little garden plots, the while
Sweet converse flowed, suspending oft the arm
And half-driven spade, while, eager, one propounds,
And listens one, weighing each pregnant word,
And pondering fit reply that may untwist
The knotty point – perchance of import high –
Of moral truth, of causes infinite
(Creating power, or uncreated worlds
Eternal and uncaused!), or whatsoe'er
Of metaphysic or of ethic lore
The mind with curious subtlety[12] pursues,
Agreeing or dissenting – sweet alike,
When wisdom, and not victory, the end.
  And 'twould be sweet, my Samuel (ah, most sweet!),
To see our little infants[13] stretch their limbs
In gambols unrestrained, and early learn
Practical love, and – wisdom's noblest lore –
Fraternal[14] kindliness, while rosiest health
Bloomed on their sunburnt cheeks. And 'twould be sweet
(When what to toil was due, to study what,[15]
And literary effort, had been paid)[16]
Alternate in each other's bower to sit,
In summer's genial season. Or, when bleak,
The wintry blast had stripped the leafy shade,
Around the blazing hearth, social and gay,
To share our frugal viands, and the bowl
Sparkling with home-brewed beverage – by our sides
Thy Sara and my Susan,[17] and, perchance,
Alfoxden's musing tenant, and the maid
Of ardent eye who with fraternal love
Sweetens his solitude. With these should join
Arcadian Poole,[18] swain of a happier age
When Wisdom and Refinement loved to dwell
With rustic Plainness, and the pastoral vale
Was vocal to the melodies of verse,
Echoing sweet minstrelsy.
                    With such, my friend –
With such, how pleasant to unbend awhile,

Notes

[11] *Inditing . . . instructive* Thelwall worked for years on an epic poem, 'The Hope of Albion' that, he believed, would establish him as one of the finest poets of the age.

[12] *The mind with curious subtlety* perhaps the source of Coleridge's phrase, 'the self-watching subtilizing mind' ('Frost at Midnight' 27).

[13] *our little infants* Hartley Coleridge (b. 1796), Algernon Sydney Thelwall (b. 1795), Maria Thelwall (b. 1794).

[14] *Fraternal* One of the objects of the French Revolution was *fraternité*.

[15] *to study what* what was due to study.

[16] *When what . . . paid* when we had fully laboured, studied and written . . .

[17] Sara Fricker married Coleridge, 4 October 1795; Susan Vellum married Thelwall, 27 July 1791.

[18] *Alfoxden's . . . solitude* William and Dorothy Wordsworth, who were living at Alfoxden House not far away. 'Arcadian Poole' refers to Thomas Poole (1765–1837), Coleridge's friend and next-door neighbour in Nether Stowey.

Winging the idle hour with song or tale,
Pun or quaint joke or converse, such as fits
Minds gay, but innocent. And we would laugh
(Unless, perchance, Pity's more kindly tear
Check the obstreperous mirth) at such who waste
Life's precious hours in the delusive chase
Of wealth and worldly gewgaws, and contend
For honours emptier than the hollow voice
That rings in echo's cave, and which, like that,
Exists but in the babbling of a world
Creating its own wonder. Wiselier we
To intellectual joys will thus devote
Our fleeting years, mingling Arcadian sports
With healthful industry. Oh, it would be
A golden age revived! Nor would we lack
Woodnymph, or naiad,[19] to complete the group
Of classic fable; for, in happy time,
Sylvanus, Chester,[20] in each hand should bring
The sister nymphs, Julia of radiant eye
And stately tread, the dryad[21] of the groves,
And she, of softer mien, the meek-eyed maid,
Pensively sweet, whom Fancy well might deem
The fairy of the brooks that bubble round.
    Ah, fateful day! what marvel if my soul
Receive thy visits awfully,[22] and fain[23]
With fancy's glowing characters would trace
Thy yet to me blank legend, painting most
What most my bosom yearns for – friendship's joys,
And social happiness, and tranquil hours
Of studious indolence? Or, sweeter far,
The high poetic rapture that becalms
Even while it agitates? Ah, fateful day,
If that the year thou lead'st (as fain my soul
Would augur, from some hours of joy late passed,
And friendships unexpected) – if the year
Thou usherest in, has aught, perchance, in store
To realize this vision, welcome most –
Ah most, most welcome! for my soul, at peace,
Shall to its native pleasures then return,
And in my Susan's arms, each pang forgot,
Nightly will I repose – yielding my soul
(Unshared, unharrassed, by a thankless world)
To the domestic virtues, calm and sweet,
Of husband and of father – to the joys
Of relative affiance; its mild cares

Notes

19 *naiad* water-nymph.

20 *Sylvanus, Chester* John Chester, a nearby farmer who encouraged Coleridge in his quest for agricultural knowledge, is cast as Sylvanus, Roman god of the country (usually represented as half-man, half-goat). For more on Chester see Hazlitt, 'My First Acquaintance with Poets', p. 781.

21 *dryad* wood-nymph.

22 *awfully* with awe.

23 *fain* willingly.

And stingless ecstasies; while gentlest sleep,
Unwooed, uncalled, on the soft pillow waits
Of envyless obscurity. Ah, come!
Hours of long wished tranquillity, ah come!
Snatch from my couch the thorn of anxious thought,
That I may taste the joys my soul best loves,
And find, once more, 'that Being is a Bliss!'

William Wordsworth and Samuel Taylor Coleridge, *Lyrical Ballads* (1798)

Lyrical Ballads (1798) is arguably the most important single volume of the period. It signalled a revolution in literary history, and has generated a vast amount of critical literature in the two centuries since its first publication. It is presented here in its entirety, separately from the author selections, so that readers can experience it in something approaching the shape in which it was first published.

It sprang directly out of the *annus mirabilis* of 1797–8. Its authors spent many days in each other's company, from the moment the Wordsworths moved into Alfoxden House in June 1797, four miles' walk from Coleridge's cottage at Nether Stowey, to the following summer when they moved out. That year was to change the lives and careers of both men forever. Wordsworth was 27, Coleridge 25 and Dorothy 26. In some ways Coleridge was the more innovatory: he would compose his three greatest poems – *The Ancient Mariner*, *Kubla Khan* and *Christabel* (Part I) – and concoct the plan for the poem that would help precipitate the millennium (Christ's thousand-year rule on earth), *The Recluse*, persuading Wordsworth that he was the only poet able to write it. Together they would plan, write and publish the *Lyrical Ballads*. Dorothy played an indispensable part in all this, through her record of this period in the Alfoxden journal, which describes the experiences and observations that fuelled the poetry of that moment, and served as a source for much of Wordsworth's poetry (see, for instance, 'A Night-Piece' and 'The Discharged Soldier', pp. 418–22). Its precise descriptions of the natural world constitute a major literary achievement in their own right.

The proposal for a joint volume was already in the air when, on 20 November 1797, Dorothy noted that *The Ancient Mariner* was to be published 'with some pieces of William's'. In those days poetry tended to be written in ornate rhyming couplets, festooned with a repertoire of devices which had been in fashion since Pope's day. With the exception of such writers as Cowper and Burns, there were few poets with a serious interest in the workings of the human mind or who wrote in a relaxed, colloquial style about human relationships. Such subjects were important to Wordsworth and Coleridge because of 'The Recluse'. It was to set out the vision of a world in which a life-force could enter into the lives of ordinary people through an enlightened perception of nature, improving them morally, and leading ultimately to a kind of non-violent political and social revolution. This is the belief that underpins 'Tintern Abbey', one of the finest of the poems in the collection, as well as 'Goody Blake and Harry Gill', 'The Thorn' and 'The Idiot Boy'.

It is worth considering these works in that light. In 'Goody Blake and Harry Gill' Wordsworth is concerned to explore a scientifically documented case-history (see p. 363 n 1) that demonstrates how words are capable of altering the physical constitution of an individual. In this case they are delivered in the form of a curse, but the argument of the poem is that blessings have an equal and opposite potency. It was Shelley who would write that 'Poets are the unacknowledged legislators of the world' (p. 1199), but 'Goody Blake and Harry Gill' anticipates that by arguing that if an utterance can render a grown man permanently cold, it should be able to change our intellectual and moral disposition for the better. In his 'Essays upon Epitaphs' (1810), Wordsworth argued precisely that: 'Words are too awful an instrument for good and evil to be trifled with: they hold above all other external powers a dominion over thoughts.' The spell Goody Blake casts over Harry Gill is proof of the power of words. Wordsworth does not explain why Gill is stricken by them – presumably it is due to an unconscious awareness that he has behaved unjustly – but that is not what concerns him. The point of the poem is to acknowledge the power of words as an instrument for both good and evil, and thus legitimize the idea of a poem that could precipitate revolution.

'The Thorn' is daring because Wordsworth provides so little commentary on the retired sea-captain who narrates it[1] – for its true subject, disclosed only in passing, is not Martha Ray but the 'adhesive' sensibility of the man who has become obsessed with her. Did she smother her child? Did she bury its corpse? The answers are irrelevant because Martha Ray, who appears to be the subject of the poem, is nothing of the kind. She is a vector for the captain's prurient inquisitiveness, which prevents him from responding in a compassionate manner to her continuing grief. Rather than offer her shelter and sustenance, he prefers to spy on her through his telescope. Nor is he the only one. Despite being aware of her suffering, the village allows her to remain on the hillside, using her as the focus for lurid speculation. And that, rather than the conjectured history of Martha Ray, is Wordsworth's subject. 'The Thorn' is about a village (and, by implication, a world) that has forgotten how to be human – a far cry from the ideal place to which he wanted to take readers of 'The Recluse'. As with 'Goody Blake and Harry Gill', Wordsworth believed that it was only by confronting the fallen world, with all its injustices and cruelties, that paradise could be regained.

In this context, 'The Idiot Boy' is one of the most daring poems in the volume. One of its earliest readers was the Scottish man of letters John Wilson, then a student at the University of Glasgow, who told Wordsworth that Johnny Foy generated feelings only of 'disgust and contempt': 'it appears almost unnatural that a person in a state of complete idiotism, should excite the warmest feelings of attachment in the breast even of his mother.'[2] Perhaps like many of Wordsworth's readers, Wilson would have found it easier to accept Johnny Foy as the protagonist of a poem such as Southey's 'The Idiot', written at the same period (see p. 725). But he was missing the point. As Wordsworth answered, 'I have often applied to Idiots, in my own mind, that sublime expression of scripture that, "their life is hidden with God." They are worshipped, probably from a feeling of this sort, in several parts of the East.'

This was an extraordinary thing to say. Far from attempting to compromise with Wilson, Wordsworth insists that Johnny Foy is closer to God, even true visionary enlightenment, than those around him. And the poem is designed to bear that out. His mother's fears, though indicative of her love, are shown to be unfounded; it is as if the natural forces to which he surrendered guarantee his well-being, returning him to Betty at the end of the poem. And his uncanny ability to transcend the physical limitations of the world is heightened by transfiguration first into a fairy-tale wanderer riding the night skies, then into a

Notes

1 Wordsworth attempted to remedy this in his 'Note to "The Thorn" '; see pp. 507–9.

2 The complete text of Wilson's letter is published by Philip Dundas, 'John Wilson to William Wordsworth (1802): A New Text', *WC* 34: 2 (Spring 2003) 111–15.

'silent horseman-ghost' and finally into a 'fierce and dreadful' sheep-hunter. He is all of those things and none of them. It is as if these possibilities, fantastic though they sound, are incapable of containing him for more than the instant it takes us to envisage them. 'Mighty prophet! Seer blessed!' Wordsworth would write of Hartley Coleridge in 1804 (p. 540); Johnny Foy's disability, in so far as he has one, manifests itself not in the kind of violent or bizarre behaviour that John Wilson expected, but in precisely the kind of exalted status attributed to Hartley. Of all the characters in the volume, Johnny Foy is closest to the protagonist of 'The Recluse'.

Although Coleridge was an inspirational force at the time of this collaboration, he had difficulty writing poems to order for *Lyrical Ballads*. Originally it was hoped that *Christabel* would appear in the volume, but he got no further than Part I. 'The Nightingale' was not written specifically for it, while *The Dungeon* and *The Foster Mother's Tale* were quarried from *Osorio*, the play he completed in 1797. All the same, 'The Ancient Mariner' remains one of the most enduringly popular of his poems, and makes an important statement by being the first poem in the book. Wordsworth would come to regret that, and in later editions moved it so that it was not the first thing readers saw when they opened the volume. For the 1800 edition he wrote a 'note' apologizing for the poem's 'great defects' (see p. 509).

Coleridge may not have composed as many poems as he hoped, but his influence is found throughout, permeating Wordsworth's writing more strongly than at any other time in their respective careers. His pantheist beliefs strongly colour 'Lines Written at a Small Distance from my House' and the central statement of 'Tintern Abbey':

And I have felt
A presence that disturbs me with the joy
Of elevated thoughts, a sense sublime
Of something far more deeply interfused,
Whose dwelling is the light of setting suns,
And the round ocean, and the living air,
And the blue sky, and in the mind of man –
A motion and a spirit that impels
All thinking things, all objects of all thought,
And rolls through all things.
(ll. 94–103)

The peculiarly Coleridgean element is the way in which love of nature has been incorporated into a spiritual vision of all-embracing unity, for Wordsworth is recalling *Religious Musings* (see p. 608), in which ''tis God / Diffused through all that doth make all one whole' (ll. 144–5).

No one recognized the significance of *Lyrical Ballads* when it first appeared in early October 1798. Sales were respectable[3] (such that by 1807 Francis Jeffrey could remark that 'The Lyrical Ballads were unquestionably popular'[4]) but few copies sold at first, and along with one or two good reviews it attracted some bad ones, including one by Robert Southey (see pp. 730–1). 'If he could not conscientiously have spoken differently of the volume,' Wordsworth said, 'he ought to have declined the task of reviewing it.' But then, Southey and Wordsworth had been in competition for some time, and it was not surprising that Southey wished to dampen interest in the work of the man he regarded as his nearest rival. His main argument was that Wordsworth and Coleridge are bad storytellers: having written off *The Idiot Boy* as 'bald in story' he comments that the other ballads 'are not so highly embellished in narration'.[5] Southey exemplifies the reader invited, in the Advertisement, to cast away his 'pre-established codes of decision', and respond

Notes

[3] See W. J. B. Owen, 'Costs, Sales, and Profits of Longman's Editions of Wordsworth', *The Library* ser. 5, 12 (1957) 93–107.

[4] In his review of *Poems, in Two Volumes* (1807), *Edinburgh Review* 11 (1807).

[5] See p. 731.

to a new kind of poetry concerned with 'a natural delineation of human passions, human characters, and human incidents' – one that dispensed with traditional narrative technique in favour of a concentration on emotional or psychological states.

This was way ahead of its time, and entailed the unreal expectation that the poetry-reading public re-educate itself. That couldn't happen overnight, and if in 1798 Wordsworth and Coleridge hoped that it would, they had changed their minds by 1815, by which time they had both received a good deal of criticism for what many regarded as the strangeness and obscurity of their work. It was with the benefit of that experience that Wordsworth observed that 'every author, as far as he is great and at the same time original, has had the task of creating the taste by which he is to be enjoyed: so has it been, so will it continue to be.'[6] He was right. In due course, *Lyrical Ballads* changed completely the way in which people read and interpreted poetry. And though sales were not spectacular, they were sufficiently good for it to be enlarged in 1800 by a second volume (consisting of poems by Wordsworth only), and for revised editions to appear in 1802 and 1805.

Constituent poems are presented *in the order in which they first appeared* in *Lyrical Ballads* (1798) – not chronologically as is the case elsewhere in this anthology. Dates of composition and attribution are provided at the beginning of each work. Readers should bear in mind that this information was not available to readers of the first edition, which appeared anonymously (although the authors' identities were widely known in literary circles).

Further reading

This brief list does not include articles about individual poems.

Coleridge: The Ancient Mariner and Other Poems ed. Alun R. Jones and William M. Tydeman (London, 1973).

Wordsworth: Lyrical Ballads ed. Alun R. Jones and William M. Tydeman (London, 1972).

Neil Fraistat, *The Poem and the Book: Interpreting Collections of Romantic Poetry* (Chapel Hill, NC, 1985), chapter 3.

William Hazlitt, 'My First Acquaintance with Poets', pp. 771–84 below.

Mary Jacobus, *Tradition and Experiment in Wordsworth's Lyrical Ballads 1798* (Oxford, 1976).

Scott McEathron, 'Wordsworth and Coleridge, *Lyrical Ballads*', in *A Companion to Romanticism* ed. Duncan Wu (Oxford, 1998), pp. 144–56.

Stephen M. Parrish, *The Art of the Lyrical Ballads* (Cambridge, Mass., 1973).

Jane Stabler, *Burke to Byron, Barbauld to Baillie, 1790–1830* (Basingstoke, 2002), pp. 104–14.

Mark Storey, *The Problem of Poetry in the Romantic Period* (Basingstoke, 2000), chapter 1.

The Language of men!

Lyrical Ballads, with A Few Other Poems.[1]

Advertisement (by Wordsworth,[2] composed June 1798)

It is the honourable characteristic of poetry that its materials are to be found in every subject which can interest the human mind. The evidence of this fact is to be sought not in the writings of critics, but in those of poets themselves.

Notes

[6] *Prose Works* iii 80.

Lyrical Ballads

[1] The text is that of the edition published by J. and A. Arch, London, 1798. I have been guided in my editing of these works by the editorial decisions of James A. Butler and Karen Green, editors of the Cornell Wordsworth volume of *Lyrical Ballads*.

[2] Throughout this text of *Lyrical Ballads*, I have provided the reader with authorship details for each work. It should be borne in mind that the volume was published anonymously, so that its first readers were unaware not only of who wrote what, but of the fact that it contained the work of more than one person. Though by Wordsworth, the Advertisement and its ideas would have been worked out with Coleridge.

The majority of the following poems are to be considered as experiments. They were written chiefly with a view to ascertain how far the language of conversation in the middle and lower classes of society is adapted to the purposes of poetic pleasure. Readers accustomed to the gaudiness and inane phraseology of many modern writers,[3] if they persist in reading this book to its conclusion, will perhaps frequently have to struggle with feelings of strangeness and awkwardness: they will look round for poetry, and will be induced to enquire by what species of courtesy these attempts can be permitted to assume that title. It is desirable that such readers, for their own sakes, should not suffer the solitary word 'poetry' (a word of very disputed meaning) to stand in the way of their gratification, but that while they are perusing this book, they should ask themselves if it contains a natural delineation of human passions, human characters and human incidents; and, if the answer be favourable to the author's wishes, that they should consent to be pleased in spite of that most dreadful enemy to our pleasures: our own pre-established codes of decision.[4]

Readers of superior judgement may disapprove of the style in which many of these pieces are executed. It must be expected that many lines and phrases will not exactly suit their taste. It will perhaps appear to them that, wishing to avoid the prevalent fault of the day,[5] the author has sometimes descended too low, and that many of his expressions are too familiar, and not of sufficient dignity. It is apprehended that the more conversant the reader is with our elder writers, and with those in modern times who have been the most successful in painting manners[6] and passions,[7] the fewer complaints of this kind will he have to make.

An accurate taste in poetry and in all the other arts, Sir Joshua Reynolds[8] has observed, is an acquired talent which can only be produced by severe thought, and a long continued intercourse with the best models of composition. This is mentioned not with so ridiculous a purpose as to prevent the most inexperienced reader from judging for himself, but merely to temper the rashness of decision, and to suggest that if poetry be a subject on which much time has not been bestowed, the judgement may be erroneous, and that in many cases it necessarily will be so.

The tale of 'Goody Blake and Harry Gill' is founded on a well-authenticated fact which happened in Warwickshire.[9] Of the other poems in the collection, it may be proper to say that they are either absolute inventions of the author, or facts which took place within his personal observation or that of his friends.

The poem of 'The Thorn', as the reader will soon discover, is not supposed to be spoken in the author's own person: the character of the loquacious narrator will sufficiently show itself in the course of the story. 'The Rime of the Ancyent Marinere' was professedly written in imitation of the style, as well as of the spirit, of the elder poets. But with a few exceptions, the author believes that the language adopted

Notes

[3] *the gaudiness . . . writers* based on Hugh Blair's attack on modern poetry in his *Lectures on Rhetoric and Belles Lettres* (1783): 'In after ages, when poetry became a regular art, studied for reputation and for gain, authors began to affect what they did not feel. Composing coolly in their closets, they endeavoured to imitate passion, rather than to express it' (ii 323).

[4] *pre-established codes of decision* prejudices.

[5] *the prevalent fault of the day* gaudy and inane phraseology.

[6] *manners* in a letter of 1799, Wordsworth commends the appearance, in Burns's poetry, of 'manners connected with the permanent objects of nature, and partaking of the simplicity of those objects' (*EY* 255–6).

[7] *elder writers . . . passions* Wordsworth probably has in mind Milton and Shakespeare ('elder writers'), and Burns, Cowper and Joanna Baillie (see p. 307) ('those in modern times').

[8] Sir Joshua Reynolds (1723–92), was the most renowned portrait-painter of the age. His first discourse was delivered in 1769, and subsequent lectures became yearly fixtures at the Royal Academy. For further details see my *Wordsworth's Reading 1770–1799* (1993), p. 116.

[9] It was a case-history in a medical text, Erasmus Darwin's *Zoönomia* (1794–6). Wordsworth borrowed it from his friend, Joseph Cottle, in early March 1798.

in it has been equally intelligible for these three last centuries. The lines entitled 'Expostulation and Reply', and those which follow, arose out of conversation with a friend[10] who was somewhat unreasonably attached to modern books of moral philosophy.

The Rime of the Ancyent Marinere, in seven parts (by Coleridge, composed November 1797–March 1798)[1]

Argument

How a ship, having passed the line,[2] was driven by storms to the cold country towards the South Pole, and how from thence she made her course to the tropical latitude of the great Pacific Ocean; and of the strange things that befell, and in what manner the ancyent marinere came back to his own country.

I

It is an ancyent marinere,
And he stoppeth one of three:
'By thy long grey beard and thy glittering eye
Now wherefore stoppest me?

The bridegroom's doors are opened wide,
And I am next of kin;
The guests are met, the feast is set –
Mayst hear the merry din.'

But still he holds the wedding-guest:
'There was a ship', quoth he –
'Nay, if thou'st got a laughsome tale,
Marinere, come with me!'

He holds him with his skinny hand,
Quoth he, 'There was a ship –'
'Now get thee hence, thou grey-beard loon,
Or my staff shall make thee skip!'

He holds him with his glittering eye –
The wedding-guest stood still,
And listens like a three years' child:
The marinere hath his will.[3]

Notes

[10] *a friend* William Hazlitt; see Hazlitt's account of the 'conversation', p. 781.

The Rime of the Ancyent Marinere

[1] For circumstances of composition see Fenwick Note to 'We are Seven', p. 583, below. From 1800 to 1817 this poem was subtitled 'A Poet's Reverie'.

[2] *line* equator.

[3] Lines 19–20 are by Wordsworth; see p. 583 below.

The wedding-guest sat on a stone,
He cannot choose but hear;
And thus spake on that ancyent man,
The bright-eyed marinere:

'The ship was cheered, the harbour cleared,
Merrily did we drop
Below the kirk, below the hill,
Below the lighthouse top.

The sun came up upon the left,
Out of the sea came he;
And he shone bright, and on the right
Went down into the sea.

Higher and higher every day,
Till over the mast at noon –'
The wedding-guest here beat his breast,
For he heard the loud bassoon.[4]

The bride hath paced into the hall,
Red as a rose is she;
Nodding their heads before her goes
The merry minstrelsy.[5]

The wedding-guest he beat his breast,
Yet he cannot choose but hear;
And thus spake on that ancyent man,
The bright-eyed marinere.

'Listen, stranger! Storm and wind,
A wind and tempest strong!
For days and weeks it played us freaks –
Like chaff we drove along.

Listen, stranger! Mist and snow,
And it grew wondrous cauld:
And ice mast-high came floating by
As green as emerauld.

And through the drifts[6] the snowy clifts[7]
Did send a dismal sheen;
Ne shapes of men ne beasts we ken –
The ice was all between.

Notes

[4] *the loud bassoon* Coleridge's friend, Thomas Poole, had given a bassoon to the church at Nether Stowey.

[5] *before her . . . minstrelsy* cf. Chaucer, *Squire's Tale* 268: 'Toforn hym gooth the loude mynstralcye.'

[6] *drifts* floating ice.

[7] *clifts* clefts.

The ice was here, the ice was there,
  The ice was all around;
It cracked and growled, and roared and howled
  Like noises of a swound.[8]

At length did cross an albatross,
  Thorough the fog it came;
And an[9] it were a Christian soul,[10]
  We hailed it in God's name.

The marineres gave it biscuit-worms,[11]
  And round and round it flew:
The ice did split with a thunder-fit;
  The helmsman steered us through.

And a good south wind sprung up behind,
  The albatross did follow;
And every day, for food or play,
  Came to the marineres' hollo!

In mist or cloud, on mast or shroud,
  It perched for vespers[12] nine,
Whiles all the night, through fogsmoke white,
  Glimmered the white moonshine.'

'God save thee, ancyent marinere,
  From the fiends that plague thee thus!
Why look'st thou so?' 'With my crossbow
  I shot the albatross.[13]

II

The sun came up upon the right,
  Out of the sea came he;
And broad as a weft[14] upon the left
  Went down into the sea.

Notes

[8] *swound* swoon.

[9] *an* as if.

[10] *a Christian soul* i.e. a human being.

[11] This detail was removed from later versions of the poem.

[12] *vespers* evenings.

[13] No explanation for the action is given; it was suggested by Wordsworth after reading Shelvocke's *Voyage Round the World* (1726): 'we had continual squalls of sleet, snow and rain, and the heavens were perpetually hid from us by gloomy dismal clouds. In short, one would think it impossible that any thing living could subsist in so rigid a climate; and, indeed, we all observed, that we had not had the sight of one fish of any kind, since we were come to the southward of the straits of le Mair, nor one seabird, except a disconsolate black albatross, who accompanied us for several days, hovering about us as if he had lost himself, till Hatley (my second Captain), observing, in one of his melancholy fits, that this bird was always hovering near us, imagined, from his colour, that it might be some ill omen. That which, I suppose, induced him the more to encourage his superstition, was the continued series of contrary tempestuous winds, which had oppressed us ever since we had got into this sea. But be that as it would, he, after some fruitless attempts, at length, shot the albatross, not doubting (perhaps) that we should have a fair wind after it. I must own that this navigation is truly melancholy, and was the more so to us, who were by ourselves without a companion, which would have somewhat diverted our thoughts from the reflection of being in such a remote part of the world' (pp. 72–3). In 1804 Coleridge witnessed the shooting of a hawk during his sea-voyage to Malta, and commented in his notebook: 'Poor hawk! Oh strange lust of murder in man! It is not cruelty; it is mere non-feeling from non-thinking' (*Notebooks* ii 2090).

[14] *weft* signal-flag.

And the good south wind still blew behind,
But no sweet bird did follow,
Ne any day for food or play
Came to the marineres' hollo!

And I had done an hellish thing
And it would work 'em woe:
For all averred[15] I had killed the bird
That made the breeze to blow.

Ne dim ne red, like God's own head
The glorious sun uprist:
Then all averred I had killed the bird
That brought the fog and mist.
"'Twas right", said they, "such birds to slay,
That bring the fog and mist."

The breezes[16] blew, the white foam flew,
The furrow followed free:
We were the first that ever burst
Into that silent sea.

Down dropt the breeze, the sails dropt down,
'Twas sad as sad could be,
And we did speak only to break
The silence of the sea.

All in a hot and copper sky
The bloody sun at noon
Right up above the mast did stand,
No bigger than the moon.

Day after day, day after day,
We stuck, ne breath ne motion,
As idle as a painted ship
Upon a painted ocean.

Water, water, everywhere,
And all the boards did shrink;
Water, water, everywhere,
Ne any drop to drink.

The very deeps did rot: oh Christ,
That ever this should be!
Yea, slimy things did crawl with legs
Upon the slimy sea.

About, about, in reel and rout
The death-fires danced at night;
The water, like a witch's oils,
Burnt green and blue and white.

Notes

[15] *averred* maintained that.

[16] *breezes* trade winds.

And some in dreams assured were
Of the spirit that plagued us so;
Nine fathom deep he had followed us
From the land of mist and snow.

And every tongue, through utter drouth,[17]
Was withered at the root;
We could not speak, no more than if
We had been choked with soot.

Ah wel-a-day! what evil looks
Had I from old and young!
Instead of the cross the albatross
About my neck was hung.

III

I saw a something in the sky
No bigger than my fist;
At first it seemed a little speck
And then it seemed a mist;
It moved and moved, and took at last
A certain shape, I wist.[18]

A speck, a mist, a shape, I wist!
And still it nered and nered:
And an it dodged a water-sprite,
It plunged and tacked and veered.

With throat unslaked, with black lips baked,
Ne could we laugh, ne wail;
Then while through drouth all dumb they stood,
I bit my arm, and sucked the blood,
And cried, "A sail! A sail!"

With throat unslaked, with black lips baked,
Agape they heard me call:
Gramercy![19] they for joy did grin
And all at once their breath drew in
As they were drinking all.

She doth not tack from side to side
Hither to work us weal;[20]
Withouten wind, withouten tide
She steddies with upright keel.

Notes

[17] *drouth* dryness.
[18] *wist* was aware of.
[19] *Gramercy!* mercy on us!
[20] *weal* harm.

The western wave was all aflame,
  The day was well nigh done!
Almost upon the western wave
  Rested the broad bright sun;
When that strange shape[21] drove suddenly
  Betwixt us and the sun.

And strait the sun was flecked with bars
  (Heaven's Mother send us grace!),
As if through a dungeon-grate he peered
  With broad and burning face.

Alas! thought I, and my heart beat loud,
  How fast she neres and neres!
Are those *her* sails that glance in the sun
  Like restless gossameres?

Are these *her* naked ribs, which flecked
  The sun that did behind them peer?
And are these two all, all the crew,
  That woman and her fleshless pheere?[22]

His bones were black with many a crack,
  All black and bare, I ween;
Jet black and bare, save where with rust
Of mouldy damps and charnel crust
  They're patched with purple and green.

Her lips are red, *her* looks are free,
  Her locks are yellow as gold;
Her skin is as white as leprosy,
And she is far liker death than he,
  Her flesh makes the still air cold.

The naked hulk alongside came,
  And the twain were playing dice;
"The game is done! I've won! I've won!"
  Quoth she, and whistled thrice.

A gust of wind sterte up behind
  And whistled through his bones;
Through the holes of his eyes and the hole of his mouth
  Half-whistles and half-groans.

Notes

[21] *strange shape* According to Wordsworth, the ghost-ship was suggested by a dream of Coleridge's friend and neighbour John Cruikshank, who is said to have seen 'a skeleton ship with figures in it'.

[22] *pheere* companion.

With never a whisper in the sea
  Off darts the spectre-ship;
While clombe[23] above the eastern bar
The horned moon, with one bright star
  Almost atween the tips.[24]

One after one by the horned moon
  (Listen, oh stranger, to me!)
Each turned his face with a ghastly pang
  And cursed me with his ee.

Four times fifty living men,
  With never a sigh or groan,
With heavy thump, a lifeless lump,
  They dropped down one by one.

Their souls did from their bodies fly,
  They fled to bliss or woe;
And every soul, it passed me by
  Like the whiz of my crossbow.'

IV

'I fear thee, ancyent marinere,
  I fear thy skinny hand;
And thou art long and lank and brown
  As is the ribbed sea-sand.[25]

I fear thee and thy glittering eye,
  And thy skinny hand so brown –'
'Fear not, fear not, thou wedding-guest,
  This body dropt not down.

Alone, alone, all all alone,
  Alone on the wide wide sea;
And Christ would take no pity on
  My soul in agony.

The many men so beautiful,
  And they all dead did lie!
And a million million slimy things
  Lived on – and so did I.

I looked upon the rotting sea
  And drew my eyes away;
I looked upon the eldritch[26] deck,
  And there the dead men lay.

Notes

[23] *clombe* climbed; still used in everyday speech at the time of writing.

[24] *The horned moon . . . tips* In a copy of *Lyrical Ballads* (1798) now at Trinity College, Cambridge, Coleridge explained: 'It is a common superstition among sailors that something evil is about to happen whenever a star dogs the moon.'

[25] *And thou art long . . . sea-sand* These two lines are by Wordsworth (see p. 701n22).

[26] *eldritch* ghostly.

I looked to heaven and tried to pray
   But or ever a prayer had gusht,
A wicked whisper came and made
   My heart as dry as dust.

I closed my lids and kept them close
   Till the balls like pulses beat;
For the sky and the sea, and the sea and the sky
Lay like a load on my weary eye,
   And the dead were at my feet.

The cold sweat melted from their limbs,
   Ne rot, ne reek did they;
The look with which they looked on me
   Had never passed away.

An orphan's curse would drag to hell
   A spirit from on high;
But oh! more horrible than that
   Is the curse in a dead man's eye!
Seven days, seven nights, I saw that curse
   And yet I could not die.

The moving moon went up the sky
   And nowhere did abide;
Softly she was going up
   And a star or two beside;

Her beams bemocked the sultry main
   Like morning frosts yspread;
But where the ship's huge shadow lay
The charmed[27] water burnt alway
   A still and awful red.

Beyond the shadow of the ship
   I watched the water-snakes;
They moved in tracks of shining white,
And when they reared, the elfish light
   Fell off in hoary flakes.

Within the shadow of the ship
   I watched their rich attire:
Blue, glossy green, and velvet black,
They coiled and swam, and every track
   Was a flash of golden fire.

Oh happy living things! no tongue
   Their beauty might declare:
A spring of love gusht from my heart
   And I blessed them unaware!
Sure my kind saint took pity on me,
   And I blessed them unaware.

Notes

[27] *charmed* dead calm.

The self-same moment I could pray,
And from my neck so free
The albatross fell off and sank
Like lead into the sea.

V

Oh sleep, it is a gentle thing
Beloved from pole to pole!
To Mary Queen[28] the praise be yeven;[29]
She sent the gentle sleep from heaven
That slid into my soul.

The silly[30] buckets on the deck
That had so long remained,
I dreamt that they were filled with dew
And when I awoke it rained.

My lips were wet, my throat was cold,
My garments all were dank;
Sure I had drunken in my dreams
And still my body drank.

I moved and could not feel my limbs,
I was so light, almost
I thought that I had died in sleep
And was a blessed ghost.

The roaring wind – it roared far off,
It did not come anear;
But with its sound it shook the sails
That were so thin and sere.[31]

The upper air bursts into life
And a hundred fire-flags sheen,[32]
To and fro they are hurried about;
And to and fro, and in and out
The stars dance on between.[33]

The coming wind doth roar more loud,
The sails do sigh like sedge;
The rain pours down from one black cloud,
And the moon is at its edge.

Notes

28 *Mary Queen* the Virgin Mary.

29 *yeven* given.

30 *silly* plain, rustic, homely.

31 *sere* worn.

32 *sheen* shining.

33 *The upper air . . . between* the aurora borealis, which also features in Wordsworth's 'The Complaint of a Forsaken Indian Woman'.

Hark, hark! The thick black cloud is cleft
 And the moon is at its side;
Like waters shot from some high crag,
The lightning falls with never a jag,
 A river steep and wide.

The strong wind reached the ship, it roared
 And dropped down like a stone!
Beneath the lightning and the moon
 The dead men gave a groan.

They groaned, they stirred, they all uprose,
 Ne spake, ne moved their eyes;
It had been strange, even in a dream,
 To have seen those dead men rise.

The helmsman steered, the ship moved on,
 Yet never a breeze up-blew;
The marineres all 'gan work the ropes
 Where they were wont to do;
They raised their limbs like lifeless tools –
 We were a ghastly crew.

The body of my brother's son
 Stood by me, knee to knee;
The body and I pulled at one rope
 But he said nought to me –
And I quaked to think of my own voice,
 How frightful it would be!

The daylight dawned, they dropped their arms
 And clustered round the mast;
Sweet sounds rose slowly through their mouths
 And from their bodies passed.

Around, around, flew each sweet sound
 Then darted to the sun;
Slowly the sounds came back again,
 Now mixed, now one by one.

Sometimes a-dropping from the sky
 I heard the lavrock[34] sing;
Sometimes all little birds that are,
How they seemed to fill the sea and air
 With their sweet jargoning![35]

And now 'twas like all instruments,
 Now like a lonely flute,
And now it is an angel's song
 That makes the heavens be mute.

Notes

[34] *lavrock* lark.

[35] *jargoning* birdsong.

It ceased, yet still the sails made on
  A pleasant noise till noon,
A noise like of a hidden brook
  In the leafy month of June,
That to the sleeping woods all night
  Singeth a quiet tune –

Listen, oh listen, thou wedding-guest!'
  'Marinere, thou hast thy will!
For that which comes out of thine eye doth make
  My body and soul to be still.'

'Never sadder tale was told
  To a man of woman born;
Sadder and wiser thou wedding-guest
  Thou'lt rise tomorrow morn!

Never sadder tale was heard
  By a man of woman born;
The marineres all returned to work
  As silent as beforne.

The marineres all 'gan pull the ropes,
  But look at me they n'old;[36]
Thought I, I am as thin as air –
  They cannot me behold.

Till noon we silently sailed on,
  Yet never a breeze did breathe;
Slowly and smoothly went the ship,
  Moved onward from beneath.

Under the keel nine fathom deep,
  From the land of mist and snow,
The spirit slid, and it was he
  That made the ship to go.
The sails at noon left off their tune
  And the ship stood still also.

The sun right up above the mast
  Had fixed her to the ocean;
But in a minute she 'gan stir
  With a short uneasy motion –
Backwards and forwards half her length,
  With a short uneasy motion.

Then like a pawing horse let go,
  She made a sudden bound;
It flung the blood into my head,
  And I fell into a swound.

Notes

[36] *n'old* would not.

How long in that same fit I lay,
 I have not to declare;
But ere my living life returned,
I heard and in my soul discerned
 Two voices in the air.

"Is it he?" quoth one, "Is this the man?
 By him who died on cross,
With his cruel bow he laid full low
 The harmless albatross.

The spirit who bideth by himself
 In the land of mist and snow,
He loved the bird that loved the man
 Who shot him with his bow."

The other was a softer voice,
 As soft as honey-dew;
Quoth he, "The man hath penance done
 And penance more will do." '

VI

First Voice
But tell me, tell me! speak again,
 Thy soft response renewing –
What makes that ship drive on so fast?
 What is the ocean doing?

Second Voice
 Still as a slave before his lord,
 The ocean hath no blast;
His great bright eye most silently
 Up to the moon is cast –

If he may know which way to go,
 For she guides him smooth or grim.
See, brother, see – how graciously
 She looketh down on him!

First Voice
But why drives on that ship so fast
 Withouten wave or wind?
Second Voice
The air is cut away before
 And closes from behind.

Fly, brother, fly! more high, more high,
 Or we shall be belated;
For slow and slow that ship will go
 When the marinere's trance is abated.

'I woke, and we were sailing on
As in a gentle weather;
'Twas night, calm night, the moon was high –
The dead men stood together.

All stood together on the deck,
For a charnel-dungeon[37] fitter;
All fixed on me their stony eyes
That in the moon did glitter.

The pang, the curse, with which they died
Had never passed away;
I could not draw my een from theirs
Ne turn them up to pray.

And in its time the spell was snapt
And I could move my een;
I looked far forth but little saw
Of what might else be seen –

Like one that on a lonely road
Doth walk in fear and dread,
And having once turned round walks on
And turns no more his head,
Because he knows a frightful fiend
Doth close behind him tread.

But soon there breathed a wind on me,
Ne sound ne motion made;
Its path was not upon the sea,
In ripple or in shade.

It raised my hair, it fanned my cheek,
Like a meadow-gale of spring –
It mingled strangely with my fears,
Yet it felt like a welcoming.

Swiftly, swiftly flew the ship,
Yet she sailed softly too;
Sweetly, sweetly blew the breeze –
On me alone it blew.

Oh dream of joy! Is this indeed
The lighthouse top I see?
Is this the hill? Is this the kirk?
Is this mine own countrée?

Notes

37 *charnel-dungeon* a dungeon containing dead bodies.

We drifted o'er the harbour-bar,[38]
And I with sobs did pray,
"Oh let me be awake, my God!
Or let me sleep alway!"

The harbour-bay was clear as glass,[39]
So smoothly it was strewn![40]
And on the bay the moonlight lay
And the shadow of the moon.

The moonlight bay was white all o'er
Till rising from the same,
Full many shapes that shadows were
Like as of torches came.

A little distance from the prow
Those dark red shadows were;
But soon I saw that my own flesh
Was red as in a glare.

I turned my head in fear and dread
And by the holy rood,[41]
The bodies had advanced, and now
Before the mast they stood.

They lifted up their stiff right arms,
They held them strait and tight;
And each right arm burnt like a torch,
A torch that's borne upright.
Their stony eyeballs glittered on
In the red and smoky light.

I prayed and turned my head away
Forth looking as before;
There was no breeze upon the bay,
No wave against the shore.

The rock shone bright, the kirk no less
That stands above the rock;
The moonlight steeped in silentness
The steady weathercock.

And the bay was white with silent light,
Till rising from the same
Full many shapes that shadows were
In crimson colours came.

Notes

[38] *harbour-bar* bank of silt across the mouth of the harbour.

[39] The five stanzas from here to line 502 were omitted from later versions of the poem; they describe the bizarre sight of the resurrected sailors lifting their 'stiff right arms' burning brightly 'like a torch'. Accusations of strangeness from reviewers, and perhaps even distaste from Wordsworth, may have led Coleridge to remove them.

[40] *strewn* levelled.

[41] *rood* cross.

A little distance from the prow
   Those crimson shadows were;
I turned my eyes upon the deck –
   Oh Christ! what saw I there?

Each corse lay flat, lifeless and flat,
   And by the holy rood
A man all light, a seraph-man[42]
   On every corse there stood.

This seraph-band, each waved his hand –
   It was a heavenly sight!
They stood as signals to the land,
   Each one a lovely light;

This seraph-band, each waved his hand,
   No voice did they impart –
No voice, but oh! the silence sank
   Like music on my heart.

Eftsones I heard the dash of oars,
   I heard the pilot's cheer;
My head was turned perforce away
   And I saw a boat appear.

Then vanished all the lovely lights,
   The bodies rose anew;
With silent pace each to his place
   Came back the ghastly crew.
The wind that shade nor motion made,
   On me alone it blew.

The pilot and the pilot's boy,
   I heard them coming fast –
Dear Lord in heaven! it was a joy
   The dead men could not blast.

I saw a third, I heard his voice –
   It is the hermit good![43]
He singeth loud his godly hymns
   That he makes in the wood.
He'll shrieve my soul, he'll wash away
   The albatross's blood.

VII

This hermit good lives in that wood
   Which slopes down to the sea;
How loudly his sweet voice he rears!
He loves to talk with marineres
   That come from a far countrée.

Notes

[42] *seraph-man* The seraphim were the highest order of angels, whose purpose was to glow with the love of God.

[43] *It is the hermit good!* J. C. C. Mays compares the hermit with Wordsworth's Pedlar (see pp. 435–44).

He kneels at morn, and noon and eve,
He hath a cushion plump;
It is the moss that wholly hides
The rotted old oak-stump.

The skiff-boat nered, I heard them talk:
"Why, this is strange, I trow!
Where are those lights so many and fair,
That signal made but now?"

"Strange, by my faith!" the hermit said,
"And they answered not our cheer!
The planks look warped, and see those sails,
How thin they are and sere!
I never saw aught like to them
Unless perchance it were

The skeletons of leaves that lag
My forest brook along,
When the ivy-tod[44] is heavy with snow
And the owlet whoops to the wolf below
That eats the she-wolf's young."

"Dear Lord! it has a fiendish look,"
The pilot made reply,
"I am a-feared." "Push on, push on!"
Said the hermit cheerily.

The boat came closer to the ship
But I ne spake ne stirred;
The boat came close beneath the ship
And strait a sound was heard!

Under the water it rumbled on,
Still louder and more dread;
It reached the ship, it split the bay –
The ship went down like lead.

Stunned by that loud and dreadful sound
Which sky and ocean smote,
Like one that hath been seven days drowned,
My body lay afloat;
But swift as dreams, myself I found
Within the pilot's boat.

Upon the whirl where sank the ship
The boat spun round and round,
And all was still, save that the hill
Was telling of the sound.

Notes

[44] *ivy-tod* ivy-bush.

I moved my lips – the pilot shrieked
   And fell down in a fit;
The holy hermit raised his eyes
   And prayed where he did sit.

I took the oars; the pilot's boy,
   Who now doth crazy go,
Laughed loud and long, and all the while
   His eyes went to and fro:
"Ha! ha!" quoth he, "full plain I see
   The Devil knows how to row."

And now all in my own countrée
   I stood on the firm land!
The hermit stepped forth from the boat,
   And scarcely he could stand.

"Oh shrieve me, shrieve me, holy man!"
   The hermit crossed his brow.
"Say quick," quoth he, "I bid thee say
   What manner man art thou?"

Forthwith this frame of mine was wrenched
   With a woeful agony,
Which forced me to begin my tale –
   And then it left me free.

Since then, at an uncertain hour,
   Now oft-times and now fewer,
That anguish comes and makes me tell
   My ghastly aventure.

I pass, like night, from land to land,
   I have strange power of speech;
The moment that his face I see
I know the man that must hear me –
   To him my tale I teach.

What loud uproar bursts from that door!
   The wedding-guests are there;
But in the garden bower the bride
   And bridemaids singing are;
And hark, the little vesper bell[45]
   Which biddeth me to prayer.

Oh wedding-guest! this soul hath been
   Alone on a wide wide sea;
So lonely 'twas, that God himself
   Scarce seemed there to be.

Notes

[45] *vesper bell* bell used to summon the congregation for vespers, evensong.

Oh sweeter than the marriage-feast,
'Tis sweeter far to me
To walk together to the kirk
With a goodly company!

To walk together to the kirk
And all together pray,
While each to his great Father bends,
Old men, and babes, and loving friends,
And youths and maidens gay.

Farewell, farewell! but this I tell
To thee, thou wedding-guest!
He prayeth well who loveth well
Both man and bird and beast.

He prayeth best who loveth best
All things both great and small,
For the dear God who loveth us,
He made and loveth all.'[46]

The marinere, whose eye is bright,
Whose beard with age is hoar,
Is gone; and now the wedding-guest
Turned from the bridegroom's door.

He went like one that hath been stunned
And is of sense forlorn:
A sadder and a wiser man[47]
He rose the morrow morn.

The Foster-Mother's Tale: A Dramatic Fragment (by Coleridge, extracted from Osorio, composed April–September 1797)[1]

FOSTER-MOTHER. I never saw the man whom you describe.
MARIA. 'Tis strange! He spake of you familiarly
As mine and Albert's common foster-mother.
FOSTER-MOTHER. Now blessings on the man, whoe'er he be,

Notes

[46] *For the dear God . . . all* The failure of the moral satisfactorily to account for the events of the poem, and the mariner's continuing penance, has been noted by many critics, not least Coleridge himself, as Henry Nelson Coleridge recalled: 'Mrs Barbauld, meaning to be complimentary, told our poet, that she thought *The Ancient Mariner* very beautiful, but that it had the fault of containing no moral. "Nay, madam," replied the poet, "if I may be permitted to say so, the only fault in the poem is that there is *too much!* In a work of such pure imagination I ought not to have stopped to give reasons for things, or inculcate humanity to beasts" ' (CC *Table Talk* i 273n7; see also ii 272–3).

[47] *A sadder and a wiser man* Wordsworth's 'The Ruined Cottage', which Coleridge would have known by the time he wrote this poem, originally ended:

> I turned to the old man and said, 'My friend,
> Your words have consecrated many things
> And for the tale which you have told I think
> I am a better and a wiser man.

THE FOSTER-MOTHER'S TALE

[1] In editions of *Lyrical Ballads* after 1798, Coleridge added the subtitle 'A Narration in Dramatic Blank Verse', omitting ll. 4–15, 69–71.

That joined your names with mine! Oh my sweet lady,
As often as I think of those dear times
When you two little ones would stand at eve
On each side of my chair, and make me learn
All you had learnt in the day; and how to talk
In gentle phrase, then bid me sing to you –
'Tis more like heaven to come than what *has* been!
MARIA. Oh my dear mother! This strange man has left me
Troubled with wilder fancies than the moon
Breeds in the lovesick maid who gazes at it,
Till, lost in inward vision, with wet eye
She gazes idly! But that entrance,[2] Mother!
FOSTER-MOTHER. Can no one hear? It is a perilous tale.
MARIA. No one.
FOSTER-MOTHER. My husband's father told it me,
Poor old Leoni! (Angels rest his soul!)
He was a woodman, and could fell and saw
With lusty[3] arm. You know that huge round beam
Which props the hanging wall of the old chapel?
Beneath that tree, while yet it was a tree,
He found a baby wrapped in mosses lined
With thistle-beards[4] and such small locks of wool
As hang on brambles. Well, he brought him home
And reared him at the then Lord Velez's cost.
And so the babe grew up a pretty boy –
A pretty boy, but most unteachable,
And never learnt a prayer, nor told a bead,[5]
But knew the names of birds, and mocked[6] their notes,
And whistled as he were a bird himself.
And all the autumn 'twas his only play
To get the seeds of wild-flowers, and to plant them
With earth and water on the stumps of trees.
A friar who gathered simples[7] in the wood,
A grey-haired man, he loved this little boy,
The boy loved him. And when the friar taught him,
He soon could write with the pen, and from that time
Lived chiefly at the convent or the castle.
So he became a very learned youth.
    But oh, poor wretch – he read, and read, and read,
Till his brain turned! And ere his twentieth year
He had unlawful thoughts of many things,

Notes

[2] *entrance* the entrance to a dungeon, the existence of which has to be explained by the play.

[3] *lusty* strong.

[4] *thistle-beards* the down or pappus which crowns the 'seeds' of the thistle, and by which they are carried along by the wind.

[5] *told a bead* i.e. counted a bead on a rosary.

[6] *mocked* imitated.

[7] *simples* medicinal herbs.

And though he prayed, he never loved to pray
With holy men, nor in a holy place.
But yet his speech – it was so soft and sweet,
The late Lord Velez ne'er was wearied with him.
And once, as by the north side of the chapel
They stood together, chained in deep discourse,
The earth heaved under them with such a groan
That the wall tottered, and had well-nigh fallen
Right on their heads. My Lord was sorely frightened;
A fever seized him, and he made confession
Of all the heretical and lawless talk
Which brought this judgement: so the youth was seized
And cast into that hole. My husband's father
Sobbed like a child – it almost broke his heart.
And once as he was working in the cellar,
He heard a voice distinctly: 'twas the youth's,
Who sung a doleful song about green fields,
How sweet it were on lake or wild savannah[8]
To hunt for food and be a naked man,[9]
And wander up and down at liberty.
He always doted on the youth and now
His love grew desperate; and, defying death,
He made that cunning entrance I described –
And the young man escaped.
MARIA. 'Tis a sweet tale,
Such as would lull a listening child to sleep,
His rosy face besoiled with unwiped tears.
And what became of him?
FOSTER-MOTHER. He went on shipboard
With those bold voyagers who made discovery
Of golden lands.[10] Leoni's younger brother
Went likewise, and when he returned to Spain,
He told Leoni that the poor mad youth,
Soon after they arrived in that new world,
In spite of his dissuasion, seized a boat,
And all alone set sail by silent moonlight
Up a great river, great as any sea,
And ne'er was heard of more. But 'tis supposed
He lived and died among the savage men.

Notes

[8] *savannah* treeless plain in tropical America.
[9] *naked man* i.e. savage.
[10] *golden lands* South and Central America.

Lines left upon a seat in a Yew-Tree which stands near the Lake of Esthwaite, on a desolate part of the shore, yet commanding a beautiful prospect[1] (by Wordsworth, composed April–May 1797)

Nay, traveller, rest! This lonely yew-tree stands
Far from all human dwelling. What if here
No sparkling rivulet spread the verdant herb?[2]
What if these barren boughs the bee not loves?
Yet, if the wind breathe soft, the curling waves
That break against the shore shall lull thy mind,
By one soft impulse saved from vacancy.
Who he was
That piled these stones, and with the mossy sod
First covered o'er, and taught this aged tree,
Now wild, to bend its arms in circling shade,[3]
I well remember. He was one who owned
No common soul. In youth by genius nursed,
And big with[4] lofty views, he to the world
Went forth, pure in his heart, against the taint
Of dissolute tongues, 'gainst jealousy and hate
And scorn, against all enemies prepared –
All but neglect. And so his spirit damped
At once, with rash disdain he turned away,
And with the food of pride sustained his soul
In solitude. Stranger, these gloomy boughs
Had charms for him[5] – and here he loved to sit,
His only visitants a straggling sheep,
The stonechat or the glancing sandpiper;
And on these barren rocks, with juniper
And heath and thistle thinly sprinkled o'er,
Fixing his downward eye, he many an hour
A morbid pleasure nourished, tracing here
An emblem of his own unfruitful life.
And lifting up his head, he then would gaze
On the more distant scene – how lovely 'tis
Thou seest – and he would gaze till it became
Far lovelier, and his heart could not sustain
The beauty still more beauteous. Nor, that time,
Would he forget those beings to whose minds,

Notes

Lines left upon a seat in a Yew-Tree

[1] Wordsworth had in mind a particular place near Esthwaite Water; the solitary he describes is partly based on the Revd William Braithwaite, who built a yew-tree seat there. Charles Lamb heard this poem read (probably by Wordsworth) when he visited Nether Stowey in early July 1797, and afterwards asked Coleridge to send him a copy, saying: 'But above all, *that Inscription*! – it will recall to me the tones of all your voices.'

[2] *spread the verdant herb* help the grass to grow.

[3] *to bend . . . shade* In his *Unpublished Tour* Wordsworth recalled how 'the boughs had been trained to bend round the seat and almost embrace the person who might occupy the seat within, allowing only an opening for the beautiful landscape' (*Prose Works* ii 336).

[4] *big with* full of.

[5] *Had charms for him* an echo of Charlotte Smith's *Sonnet XII. Written on the Sea Shore* 7: 'But the wild gloomy scene has charms for me.'

Warm from the labours of benevolence,
The world, and man himself, appeared a scene
Of kindred loveliness: then he would sigh
With mournful joy, to think that others felt
What he must never feel. And so, lost man,
On visionary views would fancy feed,
Till his eye streamed with tears. In this deep vale
He died, this seat his only monument.
   If thou be one whose heart the holy forms
Of young imagination have kept pure,
Stranger, henceforth be warned – and know that pride,
Howe'er disguised in its own majesty,
Is littleness; that he who feels contempt
For any living thing hath faculties
Which he has never used; that thought with him
Is in its infancy. The man whose eye
Is ever on himself doth look on one
The least of nature's works – one who might move
The wise man to that scorn which wisdom holds
Unlawful ever. Oh be wiser thou!
Instructed that true knowledge leads to love,
True dignity abides with him alone
Who, in the silent hour of inward thought,
Can still suspect, and still revere himself,
In lowliness of heart.

The Nightingale; A Conversational Poem, written in April 1798 (by Coleridge, composed April–May 1798)

No cloud, no relic of the sunken day
Distinguishes the west,[1] no long thin slip
Of sullen[2] light, no obscure trembling hues.
Come, we will rest on this old mossy bridge.
You see the glimmer of the stream beneath
But hear no murmuring: it flows silently
O'er its soft bed of verdure. All is still,
A balmy night, and though the stars be dim
Yet let us think upon the vernal showers
That gladden the green earth, and we shall find
A pleasure in the dimness of the stars.
And hark, the nightingale begins its song –
'Most musical, most melancholy' bird![3]

Notes

THE NIGHTINGALE

[1] *the west* The sun sets in the west.

[2] *sullen* dim.

[3] *'Most musical, most melancholy' bird* Milton, *Il Penseroso* 62. 'This passage in Milton possesses an excellence far superior to that of mere description: it is spoken in the character of the melancholy man, and has therefore a *dramatic* propriety. The author makes this remark to rescue himself from the charge of having alluded with levity to a line in Milton – a charge than which none could be more painful to him, except perhaps that of having ridiculed his Bible' (Coleridge's note).

A melancholy bird? Oh idle thought!
In nature there is nothing melancholy.
But some night-wandering man whose heart was pierced
With the remembrance of a grievous wrong
Or slow distemper[4] or neglected love
(And so, poor wretch, filled all things with himself
And made all gentle sounds tell back the tale
Of his own sorrows) – he, and such as he,
First named these notes a melancholy strain,
And many a poet echoes the conceit[5] –
Poet who hath been building up the rhyme
When he had better far have stretched his limbs
Beside a brook in mossy forest-dell[6]
By sun or moonlight, to the influxes[7]
Of shapes and sounds and shifting elements
Surrendering his whole spirit, of his song
And of his fame forgetful! So his fame
Should share in nature's immortality
(A venerable thing!), and so his song
Should make all nature lovelier, and itself
Be loved, like nature! But 'twill not be so;
And youths and maidens most poetical[8]
Who lose the deep'ning twilights of the spring
In ballrooms and hot theatres, they still,
Full of meek sympathy, must heave their sighs
O'er Philomela's[9] pity-pleading strains.
My friend, and my friend's sister,[10] we have learnt
A different lore; we may not thus profane
Nature's sweet voices always full of love
And joyance! 'Tis the merry nightingale
That crowds and hurries and precipitates
With fast thick warble his[11] delicious notes,
As he were fearful that an April night
Would be too short for him to utter forth
His love-chant, and disburden his full soul
Of all its music! And I know a grove
Of large extent, hard by a castle huge[12]
Which the great lord inhabits not – and so
This grove is wild with tangling underwood,
And the trim walks are broken up, and grass,

Notes

[4] *distemper* depression.

[5] *conceit* thought, fancy.

[6] *stretched his limbs . . . forest-dell* cf. Gray, *Elegy* 103: 'His listless length at noontide would he stretch, / And pore upon the brook that babbles by.'

[7] *influxes* perceptions entering the mind.

[8] *poetical* immersed in poetical conventions.

[9] *Philomela* Most poets of the time identified the nightingale with Philomela, raped by her brother-in-law, Tereus, King of Thrace. When she revealed what had happened to her sister, she was saved from his rage by being turned into a nightingale.

[10] *My friend, and my friend's sister* William and Dorothy Wordsworth.

[11] *his* Despite the traditional identification of the nightingale with Philomela, Coleridge is technically correct; male nightingales sing as part of the courtship ritual.

[12] *a castle huge* Coleridge probably has in mind Enmore Castle, home of Lord Egmont. It was demolished in 1834.

Thin grass and king-cups grow within the paths.
But never elsewhere in one place I knew
So many nightingales. And far and near
In wood and thicket over the wide grove,
They answer and provoke each other's songs
With skirmish and capricious passagings,[13]
And murmurs musical and swift jug jug
And one low piping sound more sweet than all,
Stirring the air with such an harmony,
That should you close your eyes, you might almost
Forget it was not day. On moonlight bushes
Whose dewy leafits are but half-disclosed,
You may perchance behold them on the twigs,
Their bright, bright eyes, their eyes both bright and full,
Glist'ning, while many a glow-worm in the shade
Lights up her love-torch.[14]
A most gentle maid[15]
Who dwelleth in her hospitable home
Hard by the castle, and at latest eve
(Even like a lady vowed and dedicate
To something more than nature in the grove)
Glides through the pathways. She knows all their notes,
That gentle maid, and oft, a moment's space,
What time the moon was lost behind a cloud,
Hath heard a pause of silence; till the moon
Emerging hath awakened earth and sky
With one sensation, and those wakeful birds
Have all burst forth in choral minstrelsy,
As if one quick and sudden gale had swept
An hundred airy harps![16] And she hath watched
Many a nightingale perch giddily
On blos'my twig still swinging from the breeze,
And to that motion tune his wanton song,
Like tipsy joy that reels with tossing head.
Farewell, oh warbler, till tomorrow eve!
And you, my friends – farewell, a short farewell!
We have been loitering long and pleasantly,
And now for our dear homes. That strain again!
Full fain it would delay me! My dear babe[17]
Who, capable of no articulate sound,
Mars all things with his imitative lisp –
How he would place his hand beside his ear,

Notes

[13] *passagings* of music.

[14] *Lights up her love-torch* technically correct; the female glow-worm emits a green light to attract males.

[15] *A most gentle maid* Various real-life counterparts have been suggested, including Dorothy Wordsworth and Ellen Cruikshank, whose father was agent to the Earl of Egmont.

[16] *airy harps* i.e. Aeolian harps.

[17] *My dear babe* Hartley Coleridge. In a notebook entry for 1797, Coleridge describes how Hartley 'fell down and hurt himself. I caught him up crying and screaming, and ran out of doors with him. The moon caught his eye, he ceased crying immediately, and his eyes and the tears in them – how they glittered in the moonlight!' (*Notebooks* i 219).

His little hand, the small forefinger up,
And bid us listen! And I deem it wise
To make him nature's playmate. He knows well
The evening star; and once, when he awoke
In most distressful mood (some inward pain
Had made up that strange thing, an infant's dream)
I hurried with him to our orchard-plot
And he beholds the moon, and hushed at once
Suspends his sobs and laughs most silently,
While his fair eyes that swam with undropped tears
Did glitter in the yellow moonbeam! Well,
It is a father's tale. But if that Heaven
Should give me life, his childhood shall grow up
Familiar with these songs, that with the night
He may associate joy. Once more farewell,
Sweet nightingale! Once more, my friends, farewell!

The Female Vagrant (by Wordsworth, derived from 'Salisbury Plain', initially composed late summer 1793 and revised for inclusion in Lyrical Ballads, 1798)

'By Derwent's side[1] my father's cottage stood',
The woman thus her artless story told,
'One field, a flock, and what the neighbouring flood
Supplied, to him were more than mines of gold.
Light was my sleep, my days in transport[2] rolled;
With thoughtless joy I stretched along the shore
My father's nets, or watched (when from the fold
High o'er the cliffs I led my fleecy store[3]),
A dizzy depth below, his boat and twinkling oar.

My father was a good and pious man,
An honest man by honest parents bred,
And I believe that, soon as I began
To lisp, he made me kneel beside my bed,
And in his hearing there my prayers I said;
And afterwards, by my good father taught,
I read, and loved the books in which I read –
For books in every neighbouring house I sought,
And nothing to my mind a sweeter pleasure brought.

Can I forget what charms did once adorn
My garden, stored with peas and mint and thyme,
And rose and lily for the Sabbath morn?

Notes

THE FEMALE VAGRANT

[1] *By Derwent's side* Her father was a fisherman on Derwentwater.

[2] *transport* happiness.

[3] *fleecy store* sheep.

The Sabbath bells, and their delightful chime;
The gambols and wild freaks at shearing time;
My hen's rich nest through long grass scarce espied;
The cowslip-gathering at May's dewy prime;
The swans that, when I sought the waterside,
From far to meet me came, spreading their snowy pride.

The staff I yet remember, which upbore
The bending body of my active sire;
His seat beneath the honeyed sycamore
When the bees hummed, and chair by winter fire;
When market-morning came, the neat attire
With which, though bent on haste, myself I decked;
My watchful dog, whose starts of furious ire
When stranger passed, so often I have checked;
The redbreast known for years, which at my casement[4] pecked.

The suns of twenty summers danced along –
Ah, little marked, how fast they rolled away!
Then rose a mansion proud our woods among,
And cottage after cottage owned its sway;[5]
No joy to see a neighbouring house, or stray
Through pastures not his own, the master took.
My father dared his greedy wish gainsay:
He loved his old hereditary nook,
And ill could I the thought of such sad parting brook.

But when he had refused the proffered gold,
To cruel injuries he became a prey –
Sore traversed[6] in whate'er he bought and sold.
His troubles grew upon him day by day
Till all his substance fell into decay:
His little range of water was denied,[7]
All but the bed where his old body lay,
All, all was seized, and weeping side by side
We sought a home where we uninjured might abide.

Can I forget that miserable hour
When from the last hilltop my sire surveyed,
Peering above the trees, the steeple tower
That on his marriage-day sweet music made?
Till then he hoped his bones might there be laid
Close by my mother in their native bowers.
Bidding me trust in God, he stood and prayed;
I could not pray – through tears that fell in showers
Glimmered our dear loved home: alas, no longer ours!

Notes

[4] *casement* window.

[5] *owned its sway* yielded to its power, i.e. was abandoned by its inhabitants.

[6] *traversed* thwarted.

[7] 'Several of the lakes in the north of England are let out to different fishermen, in parcels marked out by imaginary lines drawn from rock to rock' (Wordsworth's note).

There was a youth whom I had loved so long
That when I loved him not I cannot say.
Mid the green mountains many and many a song
We two had sung like little birds in May.
When we began to tire of childish play
We seemed still more and more to prize each other:
We talked of marriage and our marriage-day,
And I in truth did love him like a brother,
For never could I hope to meet with such another.

His father said that to a distant town
He must repair to ply the artist's[8] trade:
What tears of bitter grief till then unknown!
What tender vows our last sad kiss delayed!
To him we turned – we had no other aid.
Like one revived, upon his neck I wept,
And her whom he had loved in joy, he said
He well could love in grief: his faith he kept,
And in a quiet home once more my father slept.

Four years each day with daily bread was blessed,
By constant toil and constant prayer supplied.
Three lovely infants lay upon my breast,
And often, viewing their sweet smiles, I sighed
And knew not why. My happy father died
When sad distress reduced the children's meal –
Thrice happy, that from him the grave did hide
The empty loom,[9] cold hearth and silent wheel,[10]
And tears that flowed for ills which patience could not heal.

'Twas a hard change, an evil time was come:
We had no hope, and no relief could gain.
But soon with proud parade, the noisy drum
Beat round to sweep the streets of want and pain.[11]
My husband's arms now only served to strain
Me and his children hungering in his view.
In such dismay my prayers and tears were vain;
To join those miserable men he flew,
And now to the sea-coast, with numbers more we drew.

There foul neglect for months and months we bore,
Nor yet the crowded fleet its anchor stirred.
Green fields before us and our native shore,
By fever, from polluted air incurred,[12]

Notes

[8] *artist* craftsman, artisan.

[9] *empty loom* Her husband was a weaver, and can no longer find work.

[10] *wheel* spinning-wheel, which, in former times, she would have used when work was to be found.

[11] *the noisy drum . . . pain* Soldiers were enlisted for the American War of Independence in exactly this manner: drummer-boys would parade round provincial towns, followed by conscription officers promising relief from poverty and hunger if men signed up for war. In 1793, when this poem was written, Wordsworth would have seen this process taking place in aid of the war with Revolutionary France (declared February 1793).

[12] *incurred* caught.

Ravage was made for which no knell was heard.[13]
Fondly we wished and wished away, nor knew
Mid that long sickness, and those hopes deferred,
That happier days we never more must view.
The parting signal streamed,[14] at last the land withdrew,

But from delay the summer calms were passed.
On as we drove, the equinoctial[15] deep
Ran mountains high before the howling blast.
We gazed with terror on the gloomy sleep
Of them that perished in the whirlwind's sweep,
Untaught that soon such anguish must ensue,
Our hopes such harvest of affliction reap,
That we the mercy of the waves should rue.
We reached the western world,[16] a poor devoted[17] crew.

Oh dreadful price of being to resign
All that is dear *in* being: better far
In Want's most lonely cave till death to pine,
Unseen, unheard, unwatched by any star;
Or, in the streets and walks where proud men are,
Better our dying bodies to obtrude,[18]
Than dog-like, wading at the heels of war,
Protract a cursed existence with the brood
That lap (their very nourishment) their brother's blood.

The pains and plagues that on our heads came down –
Disease and famine, agony and fear,
In wood or wilderness, in camp or town –
It would thy brain unsettle even to hear.
All perished; all, in one remorseless year,
Husband and children! One by one, by sword
And ravenous plague, all perished. Every tear
Dried up, despairing, desolate, on board
A British ship I waked, as from a trance restored.

Peaceful as some immeasurable plain
By the first beams of dawning light impressed,[19]
In the calm sunshine slept the glittering main.
The very ocean has its hour of rest
That comes not to the human mourner's breast.
Remote from man and storms of mortal care,
A heavenly silence did the waves invest;[20]

Notes

[13] *Ravage . . . heard* Those who died from fever were not given a church funeral.

[14] *streamed* the signal flag streamed in the wind.

[15] *equinoctial* equatorial.

[16] *the western world* America, where the female vagrant's husband was to fight in the War of Independence on the British side. Wordsworth later recalled that 'All that relates to her sufferings as a soldier's wife in America, and her condition of mind during her voyage home, were faithfully taken from the report made to me of her own case by a friend who had been subjected to the same trials and affected in the same way' (*FN* 62).

[17] *devoted* doomed.

[18] *Better . . . obtrude* Very poor people did starve to death in the streets of London at this time.

[19] *impressed* imprinted, as when, in *Paradise Lost*, the sun 'impressed his beams' on Eden (iv 150).

[20] *the waves invest* cf. Milton's invocation to 'holy light', which 'as with a mantle didst invest / The rising world of waters' (*Paradise Lost* iii 10–11).

I looked and looked along the silent air,
Until it seemed to bring a joy to my despair.

Ah, how unlike those late terrific[21] sleeps!
And groans, that rage of racking[22] famine spoke,
Where looks inhuman dwelt on festering heaps![23]
The breathing pestilence that rose like smoke![24]
The shriek that from the distant battle broke!
The mine's[25] dire earthquake, and the pallid host[26]
Driven by the bomb's incessant thunderstroke
To loathsome vaults[27] where heartsick anguish tossed,
Hope died, and fear itself in agony was lost!

Yet does that burst of woe congeal my frame
When the dark streets appeared to heave and gape,
While like a sea the storming army[28] came,
And Fire from hell reared his gigantic shape,
And Murder, by the ghastly gleam, and Rape
Seized their joint prey – the mother and the child!
But from these crazing thoughts, my brain, escape!
For weeks the balmy air breathed soft and mild,
And on the gliding vessel heaven and ocean smiled.

Some mighty gulf of separation passed,
I seemed transported to another world:
A thought resigned with pain, when from the mast
The impatient mariner the sail unfurled,
And, whistling, called the wind that hardly curled
The silent sea. From the sweet thoughts of home
And from all hope I was forever hurled.
For me, farthest from earthly port to roam
Was best, could I but shun the spot where man might come.

And oft, robbed of my perfect mind,[29] I thought
At last my feet a resting-place had found.
Here will I weep in peace (so fancy wrought),
Roaming the illimitable waters[30] round;
Here watch, of every human friend disowned,
All day, my ready tomb the ocean flood.
To break my dream the vessel reached its bound,
And homeless near a thousand homes I stood,
And near a thousand tables pined, and wanted[31] food.

Notes

21 *terrific* terrifying.

22 *racking* Hunger racks the body with pain.

23 *Where looks . . . heaps* The image is of heaps of decomposing, unburied corpses, dead from hunger.

24 *The breathing . . . smoke* Disease was thought to be airborne; there is a hint that the 'festering heaps' of corpses mentioned in the preceding line were the source of disease.

25 *mine* tunnel in which explosives, once detonated, would cause the ground to give way.

26 *the pallid host* The host (of soldiers) are 'pallid' (wan, pale) because they are starving.

27 *loathsome vaults* Soldiers blown up by mines would be buried alive by the 'dire earthquake'.

28 *the storming army* American troops storm the town occupied by the British.

29 *robbed of . . . mind* cf. *King Lear* IV vii 62: 'I fear I am not in my perfect mind.'

30 *the illimitable waters* The sea is like Chaos, 'a dark / Illimitable ocean without bound' (*Paradise Lost* ii 891–2).

31 *wanted* needed.

By grief enfeebled was I turned adrift,
Helpless as sailor cast on desert rock;
Nor morsel to my mouth that day did lift,
Nor dared my hand at any door to knock.
I lay where, with his drowsy mates, the cock
From the cross timber of an outhouse[32] hung.
How dismal tolled that night the city clock!
At morn my sick heart-hunger scarcely stung,
Nor to the beggar's language could I frame my tongue.

So passed another day, and so the third.
Then did I try (in vain) the crowd's resort;
In deep despair by frightful wishes stirred,
Near the seaside I reached a ruined fort.
There pains which nature could no more support,
With blindness linked, did on my vitals fall;
Dizzy my brain, with interruption short
Of hideous sense.[33] I sunk, nor step could crawl,
And thence was borne away to neighbouring hospital.

Recovery came with food. But still my brain
Was weak, nor of the past had memory.
I heard my neighbours in their beds complain
Of many things which never troubled me:
Of feet still bustling round with busy glee,
Of looks where common kindness had no part,
Of service done with careless cruelty,
Fretting the fever round the languid heart,
And groans which, as they said, would make a dead man start.

These things just served to stir the torpid sense,
Nor pain nor pity in my bosom raised;
Memory, though slow, returned with strength; and thence
Dismissed, again on open day I gazed
At houses, men and common light, amazed.
The lanes I sought and, as the sun retired,
Came where beneath the trees a faggot blazed.
The wild brood saw me weep, my fate enquired,
And gave me food and rest – more welcome, more desired.

My heart is touched to think that men like these,
The rude earth's tenants, were my first relief.
How kindly did they paint their vagrant ease!
And their long holiday[34] that feared not grief –
For all belonged to all, and each was chief.
No plough their sinews strained; on grating road
No wain they drove; and yet the yellow sheaf
In every vale for their delight was stowed:
For them in nature's meads the milky udder flowed.[35]

Notes

[32] *outhouse* barn.

[33] *hideous sense* When conscious she was in severe pain.

[34] *their long holiday* Life, to them, was a holiday from care.

[35] *and yet the yellow sheaf . . . flowed* They took milk and corn wherever they found it.

Semblance, with straw and panniered ass, they made
Of potters wandering on from door to door.
But life of happier sort to me portrayed,
And other joys my fancy to allure:
The bagpipe dinning on the midnight moor
In barn uplighted, and companions boon
Well-met from far with revelry secure
In depth of forest glade, when jocund June
Rolled fast along the sky his warm and genial moon.

But ill it suited me, in journey dark
O'er moor and mountain, midnight theft to hatch;
To charm the surly housedog's faithful bark,
Or hang on tiptoe at the lifted latch.
The gloomy lantern and the dim blue match,
The black disguise, the warning whistle shrill,
And ear still busy on its nightly watch,
Were not for me, brought up in nothing ill.
Besides, on griefs so fresh my thoughts were brooding still.

What could I do, unaided and unblessed?
Poor father, gone was every friend of thine!
And kindred of dead husband are at best
Small help, and after marriage such as mine,
With little kindness would to me incline.
Ill was I then for toil or service fit:
With tears whose course no effort could confine,
By highway-side forgetful would I sit
Whole hours, my idle arms in moping sorrow knit.[36]

I lived upon the mercy of the fields,
And oft of cruelty the sky accused;
On hazard, or what general bounty yields[37] –
Now coldly given, now utterly refused.
The fields I for my bed have often used.
But what afflicts my peace with keenest ruth[38]
Is that I have my inner self abused,
Foregone the home[39] delight of constant truth
And clear and open soul, so prized in fearless youth.

Three years a wanderer, often have I viewed,
In tears, the sun towards that country tend[40]
Where my poor heart lost all its fortitude.
And now across this moor my steps I bend –
Oh tell me whither, for no earthly friend
Have I!' She ceased and, weeping, turned away,
As if because her tale was at an end.
She wept because she had no more to say
Of that perpetual weight which on her spirit lay.

Notes

[36] *knit* folded.

[37] *On hazard . . . yields* She lived on charity or what she chanced to find.

[38] *ruth* remorse.

[39] *home* inner.

[40] *the sun . . . tend* the sun sets in the west.

Goody Blake and Harry Gill: A True Story (by Wordsworth, composed 7–13 March 1798)[1]

Oh what's the matter? What's the matter?
What is't that ails young Harry Gill,
That evermore his teeth they chatter,
Chatter, chatter, chatter still?
Of waistcoats Harry has no lack,
Good duffle grey, and flannel fine;
He has a blanket on his back,
And coats enough to smother nine.

In March, December, and in July,[2]
'Tis all the same with Harry Gill;
The neighbours tell, and tell you truly,
His teeth they chatter, chatter still.
At night, at morning, and at noon,
'Tis all the same with Harry Gill;
Beneath the sun, beneath the moon,
His teeth they chatter, chatter still.

Young Harry was a lusty drover,[3]
And who so stout of limb as he?
His cheeks were red as ruddy clover,
His voice was like the voice of three.
Auld Goody[4] Blake was old and poor,
Ill fed she was, and thinly clad;
And any man who passed her door
Might see how poor a hut she had.

All day she spun in her poor dwelling,
And then her three hours' work at night –
Alas, 'twas hardly worth the telling,
It would not pay for candlelight.
This woman dwelt in Dorsetshire,[5]

Notes

GOODY BLAKE AND HARRY GILL: A TRUE STORY

[1] This poem has a source in a medical treatise, Erasmus Darwin's *Zoönomia* (1794–6), which Wordsworth read in early March 1798: 'A young farmer in Warwickshire, finding his hedges broke, and the sticks carried away during a frosty season, determined to watch for the thief. He lay many cold hours under a haystack, and at length an old woman, like a witch in a play, approached and began to pull up the hedge. He waited till she had tied up her bottle of sticks and was carrying them off, that he might convict her of the theft; and then, springing from his concealment, he seized his prey with violent threats. After some altercation, in which her load was left upon the ground, she kneeled upon her bottle of sticks, and raising her arms to heaven, beneath the bright moon, then at the full, spoke to the farmer (already shivering with cold): "Heaven grant that thou never mayest know again the blessing to be warm!" He complained of cold all the next day, and wore an upper coat – and in a few days another – and in a fortnight took to his bed, always saying nothing made him warm. He covered himself with very many blankets, and had a sieve over his face as he lay; and from this one insane idea he kept his bed above twenty years for fear of the cold air, till at length he died' (ii 359).

[2] *July* stressed on the first syllable.

[3] *drover* cattle farmer.

[4] *Goody* 'goodwife'; traditional address for a countrywoman, often implying age.

[5] *Dorsetshire* Although Erasmus Darwin (Wordsworth's source) had located the story in Warwickshire, Wordsworth places it in Dorset, where he and Dorothy lived, 1795–7.

Her hut was on a cold hillside,
And in that country[6] coals are dear,[7]
For they come far by wind and tide.

By the same fire to boil their pottage,[8]
Two poor old dames (as I have known)
Will often live in one small cottage,
But she, poor woman, dwelt alone.
'Twas well enough when summer came,
The long, warm, lightsome summer day;
Then at her door the canty[9] dame
Would sit, as any linnet gay.

But when the ice our streams did fetter,[10]
Oh, then how her old bones would shake!
You would have said, if you had met her,
'Twas a hard time for Goody Blake.
Her evenings then were dull and dead –
Sad case it was, as you may think,
For very cold to go to bed,
And then for cold not sleep a wink.

Oh joy for her, whene'er in winter
The winds at night had made a rout,[11]
And scattered many a lusty splinter,
And many a rotten bough about.
Yet never had she, well or sick
(As every man who knew her says),
A pile beforehand, wood or stick,
Enough to warm her for three days.

Now when the frost was past enduring
And made her poor old bones to ache,
Could anything be more alluring
Than an old hedge to Goody Blake?
And now and then, it must be said,
When her old bones were cold and chill,
She left her fire or left her bed
To seek the hedge of Harry Gill.

Now Harry he had long suspected
This trespass of old Goody Blake,
And vowed that she should be detected,
And he on her would vengeance take.

Notes

6 *country* region.
7 *coals are dear* Coal was shipped from Wales; it was of poor quality and expensive.
8 *pottage* soup.
9 *canty* cheerful.
10 *fetter* chain, bind. The 1790s was a decade notorious for the coldness of its winters; it has been described as a mini ice age.
11 *rout* party.

And oft from his warm fire he'd go,
And to the fields his road would take,
And there at night, in frost and snow,
He watched to seize old Goody Blake.

And once, behind a rick[12] of barley,
Thus looking out did Harry stand;
The moon was full and shining clearly,
And crisp with frost the stubble-land.
He hears a noise, he's all awake –
Again? On tiptoe down the hill
He softly creeps: 'tis Goody Blake,
She's at the hedge of Harry Gill.

Right glad was he when he beheld her:
Stick after stick did Goody pull.
He stood behind a bush of elder
Till she had filled her apron full.
When with her load she turned about,
The by-road back again to take,
He started forward with a shout
And sprang upon poor Goody Blake.

And fiercely by the arm he took her,
And by the arm he held her fast,
And fiercely by the arm he shook her,
And cried, 'I've caught you then at last!'
Then Goody, who had nothing said,
Her bundle from her lap let fall,
And kneeling on the sticks she prayed
To God that is the judge of all.

She prayed, her withered hand uprearing,
While Harry held her by the arm:
'God, who art never out of hearing –
Oh may he never more be warm!'[13]
The cold, cold moon above her head,
Thus on her knees did Goody pray,
Young Harry heard what she had said,
And icy cold he turned away.

He went complaining all the morrow
That he was cold and very chill;
His face was gloom, his heart was sorrow –

Notes

[12] *rick* corn-stack; barley and other grain was cut with a scythe and bound into sheaves, which were stacked and thatched to await threshing.

[13] *Oh may . . . warm* Joseph Cottle recalled how this line gave particular pleasure to Hannah More when she heard the poem: 'she said, "I must hear *Harry Gill* once more". On coming to the words, "Oh may he never more be warm!", she lifted up her hands in smiling horror' (*Reminiscences of Samuel Taylor Coleridge and Robert Southey* (London, 1847), p. 260).

Alas that day for Harry Gill!
That day he wore a riding-coat
But not a whit the warmer he;
Another was on Thursday brought,
And ere the Sabbath he had three.
'Twas all in vain, a useless matter,

And blankets were about him pinned;
Yet still his jaws and teeth they clatter
Like a loose casement[14] in the wind.
And Harry's flesh it fell away,
And all who see him say 'tis plain
That, live as long as live he may,
He never will be warm again.

No word to any man he utters,
Abed or up, to young or old,
But ever to himself he mutters,
'Poor Harry Gill is very cold.'[15]
Abed or up, by night or day,
His teeth they chatter, chatter still:
Now think, ye farmers all, I pray,
Of Goody Blake and Harry Gill.

Lines written at a small distance from my house,[1] and sent by my little boy[2] to the person to whom they are addressed (by Wordsworth, composed 1–9 March 1798)[3]

It is the first mild day of March,
Each minute sweeter than before,
The redbreast sings from the tall larch
That stands beside our door.

There is a blessing in the air
Which seems a sense of joy to yield
To the bare trees and mountains bare,[4]
And grass in the green field.

Notes

[14] *casement* window.

[15] *Poor . . . cold* cf. *King Lear* III iv 147: 'Poor Tom's a-cold.'

LINES WRITTEN AT A SMALL DISTANCE

[1] *my house* Alfoxden House, where the Wordsworths resided, June 1797–July 1798.

[2] *my little boy* Basil Montagu Jr., whose mother had died, and whose father, a friend of Wordsworth's, was unable to look after him.

[3] Wordsworth later exchanged the cumbersome original title for 'To my Sister'.

[4] *mountains bare* an exaggeration; the Quantock Hills in which Alfoxden House is located do not compare with the mountains of the Lake District, where Wordsworth grew up.

My sister, 'tis a wish of mine
Now that our morning meal is done –
Make haste, your morning task resign,
Come forth and feel the sun!

Edward[5] will come with you – and pray
Put on with speed your woodland dress,
And bring no book, for this one day
We'll give to idleness.

No joyless forms[6] shall regulate
Our living calendar;
We from today, my friend, will date
The opening of the year.[7]

Love, now an universal birth,
From heart to heart is stealing,
From earth to man, from man to earth –
It is the hour of feeling.

One moment now may give us more
Than fifty years of reason;
Our minds shall drink at every pore
The spirit of the season.

Some silent laws[8] our hearts may make
Which they shall long obey;
We for the year to come may take
Our temper[9] from today.

And from the blessed power that rolls
About, below, above,
We'll frame the measure[10] of our souls –
They shall be tuned to love.[11]

Then come, my sister, come, I pray,
With speed put on your woodland dress;
And bring no book, for this one day
We'll give to idleness.

Notes

[5] *Edward* Basil Montagu Jr.

[6] *forms* rules, conventions.

[7] *We from . . . year* In 1793 the French completely reorganized their calendar to begin from the birth of the republic (22 September 1792) rather than that of Christ.

[8] *silent laws* effectively, New Year's resolutions.

[9] *temper* constitution.

[10] *measure* rhythm, harmony.

[11] *And from . . . love* a memorable expression of the pantheistic credo that was imparted to Wordsworth by Coleridge, also to be found in *Tintern Abbey* 94–103.

Simon Lee, the old Huntsman, with an incident in which he was concerned (by Wordsworth, composed between March and 16 May 1798)

In the sweet shire of Cardigan[1]
Not far from pleasant Ivor Hall,
An old man dwells, a little man,
I've heard he once was tall.
Of years he has upon his back,
No doubt, a burden weighty;
He says he is three score and ten,
But others say he's eighty.

A long blue livery-coat[2] has he
That's fair behind and fair before;
Yet meet him where you will, you see
At once that he is poor.
Full five and twenty years he lived
A running huntsman[3] merry,
And though he has but one eye left,
His cheek is like a cherry.

No man like him the horn could sound,
And no man was so full of glee;
To say the least, four counties round
Had heard of Simon Lee.
His master's dead, and no one now
Dwells in the Hall of Ivor,
Men, dogs, and horses – all are dead;
He is the sole survivor.

His hunting feats have him bereft
Of his right eye, as you may see;
And then, what limbs those feats have left
To poor old Simon Lee!
He has no son, he has no child;
His wife, an aged woman,
Lives with him near the waterfall,
Upon the village[4] common.

And he is lean and he is sick,
His little body's half awry,[5]
His ankles they are swoln and thick,
His legs are thin and dry.

Notes

Simon Lee, the old Huntsman

[1] *Cardigan* Cardiganshire is on the west coast of Wales; however, Simon Lee's real-life counterpart was Christopher Tricky, the huntsman who lived in a cottage on the common near Alfoxden Park.

[2] *livery-coat* as worn by a retainer of an aristocratic family.

[3] *running huntsman* Simon would have hunted on foot, running alongside the gentry who rode on horseback.

[4] *village* Holford.

[5] *awry* twisted, bent.

When he was young he little knew
Of husbandry or tillage,[6]
And now he's forced to work, though weak –
The weakest in the village.

He all the country[7] could outrun,
Could leave both man and horse behind;
And often, ere the race was done,
He reeled and was stone-blind.[8]
And still there's something in the world
At which his heart rejoices,
For when the chiming[9] hounds are out
He dearly loves their voices![10]

Old Ruth works out of doors with him
And does what Simon cannot do;
For she, not over-stout of limb,
Is stouter of the two.
And though you with your utmost skill
From labour could not wean them,
Alas, 'tis very little, all
Which they can do between them!

Beside their moss-grown hut of clay
Not twenty paces from the door,
A scrap of land they have, but they
Are poorest of the poor.
This scrap of land he from the heath
Enclosed when he was stronger,
But what avails the land to them
Which they can till no longer?

Few months of life has he in store
As he to you will tell,
For still, the more he works, the more
His poor old ankles swell.
My gentle reader, I perceive
How patiently you've waited,
And I'm afraid that you expect
Some tale will be related.

Oh reader, had you in your mind
Such stores as silent thought[11] can bring –
Oh gentle reader, you would find
A tale in every thing.[12]

Notes

6 *tillage* cultivation of the land.

7 *country* region.

8 *stone-blind* totally blind.

9 *chiming* barking together.

10 *He dearly . . . voices* Wordsworth later recalled: 'The expression when the hounds were out, "I dearly love their voice", was word for word from his own lips' (*FN* 37).

11 *silent thought* cf. Shakespeare, *Sonnet 30*: 'When to the sessions of sweet silent thought . . .'

12 *A tale in every thing* cf. *As You Like It* II i 15–17, where Duke Senior remarks that his life in Arden 'Finds tongues in trees, books in the running brooks, / Sermons in stones, and good in every thing'.

What more I have to say is short,
I hope you'll kindly take it;
It is no tale, but, should you think,
Perhaps a tale you'll make it.

One summer day I chanced to see
This old man doing all he could
About the root of an old tree,
A stump of rotten wood.
The mattock[13] tottered in his hand;
So vain was his endeavour,
That at the root of the old tree
He might have worked forever.

'You're overtasked, good Simon Lee,
Give me your tool,' to him I said;[14]
And at the word, right gladly he
Received my proffered aid.[15]
I struck, and with a single blow
The tangled root I severed,
At which the poor old man so long
And vainly had endeavoured.

The tears into his eyes were brought,
And thanks and praises seemed to run
So fast out of his heart, I thought
They never would have done.
I've heard of hearts unkind, kind deeds
With coldness still returning;
Alas, the gratitude of men
Has oft'ner left me mourning.[16]

Anecdote for Fathers, showing how the art of lying may be taught (by Wordsworth, composed between April and 16 May 1798)

I have a boy of five years old,[1]
His face is fair and fresh to see,
His limbs are cast in beauty's mould,
And dearly he loves me.

Notes

[13] *mattock* tool for tilling the ground.

[14] *You're overtasked . . . said* a response to Burns, *Man was Made to Mourn* 57–60 (see p. 266).

[15] *right gladly . . . aid* Critics have seen this poem as a response to Godwin who, in *Political Justice*, attacked gratitude as an unjust and degrading sentiment, having its origin in the unequal distribution of wealth and influence.

[16] *Alas, the gratitude . . . mourning* a highly inventive reworking of the conclusion to Burns's *Man was Made to Mourn*: 'Man's inhumanity to man / Makes countless thousands mourn.'

Anecdote for Fathers

[1] *a boy of five years old* Basil Montagu Jr, the son of Wordsworth's friend Basil Montagu, who was a lawyer in London, and whose wife was dead.

One morn we strolled on our dry walk,
Our quiet house all full in view,
And held such intermitted talk
As we are wont[2] to do.

My thoughts on former pleasures ran;
I thought of Kilve's[3] delightful shore –
My pleasant home when spring began
A long long year before.

A day it was when I could bear
To think, and think, and think again;
With so much happiness to spare
I could not feel a pain.

My boy was by my side, so slim
And graceful in his rustic dress!
And oftentimes I talked to him
In very idleness.

The young lambs ran a pretty race,
The morning sun shone bright and warm;
'Kilve', said I, 'was a pleasant place,
And so is Liswyn farm.[4]

My little boy, which like you more?'
I said and took him by the arm,
'Our home by Kilve's delightful shore,
Or here at Liswyn farm?

And tell me, had you rather be
(I said and held him by the arm)
At Kilve's smooth shore by the green sea
Or here at Liswyn farm?'

In careless mood he looked at me
While still I held him by the arm
And said, 'At Kilve I'd rather be
Than here at Liswyn farm.'

'Now, little Edward, say why so,
My little Edward, tell me why.'
'I cannot tell, I do not know.'
'Why this is strange!' said I.

Notes

[2] *wont* used.

[3] *Kilve* small village on the Somersetshire coast, not far from Alfoxden. It is pronounced as a single syllable. See Berta Lawrence, 'Kilve by the Green Sea', *Charles Lamb Bulletin* NS 91 (1995) 157–8. It is generally agreed that by Kilve Wordsworth means Racedown, and that by Liswyn he means Alfoxden.

[4] *Liswyn farm* John Thelwall, who visited Wordsworth and Coleridge in Somerset in July 1797, had retreated to Llys Wen farm in Wales. Dorothy and William went there for the first time in early August 1798. For more on Thelwall see pp. 316–18.

'For here are woods and green hills warm;
There surely must some reason be
Why you would change sweet Liswyn farm
For Kilve by the green sea.'

At this, my boy, so fair and slim,
Hung down his head, nor made reply,
And five times did I say to him,
'Why? Edward, tell me why?'

His head he raised; there was in sight –
It caught his eye, he saw it plain –
Upon the house-top, glittering bright,
A broad and gilded vane.[5]

Then did the boy his tongue unlock
And thus to me he made reply;
'At Kilve there was no weathercock,
And that's the reason why.'

Oh dearest, dearest boy! my heart
For better lore would seldom yearn,
Could I but teach the hundredth part
Of what from thee I learn.

We are seven (by Wordsworth, composed between April and 16 May 1798)

A simple child, dear brother Jim,[1]
That lightly draws its breath,
And feels its life in every limb –
What should it know of death?

I met a little cottage girl,[2]
She was eight years old, she said;
Her hair was thick with many a curl
That clustered round her head.

She had a rustic woodland air
And she was wildly clad;
Her eyes were fair, and very fair –
Her beauty made me glad.

'Sisters and brothers, little maid,
How many may you be?'
'How many? Seven in all', she said,
And wondering looked at me.

Notes

[5] *vane* weather-cock.

WE ARE SEVEN

[1] *Jim* James Tobin, a friend of Wordsworth and Coleridge's. The first line of the poem was written impromptu by Coleridge.

[2] *I met . . . girl* The poem is based on Wordsworth's meeting with a child near Goodrich Castle on the River Wye in summer 1793.

'And where are they, I pray you tell?'
She answered, 'Seven are we,
And two of us at Conway[3] dwell,
And two are gone to sea.

Two of us in the churchyard lie
(My sister and my brother),
And in the churchyard cottage I
Dwell near them with my mother.'

'You say that two at Conway dwell
And two are gone to sea,
Yet you are seven – I pray you tell,
Sweet maid, how this may be?'

Then did the little maid reply,
'Seven boys and girls are we;
Two of us in the churchyard lie
Beneath the churchyard tree.'

'You run about, my little maid,
Your limbs they are alive;
If two are in the churchyard laid,
Then ye are only five.'

'Their graves are green, they may be seen',[4]
The little maid replied,
'Twelve steps or more from my mother's door,
And they are side by side.

My stockings there I often knit,
My kerchief[5] there I hem,
And there upon the ground I sit,
I sit and sing to them.

And often after sunset, sir,
When it is light and fair,
I take my little porringer[6]
And eat my supper there.

The first that died was little Jane,
In bed she moaning lay,
Till God released her of her pain
And then she went away.

Notes

[3] *Conway* a sea-port in North Wales, about 120 miles north of Goodrich Castle.

[4] *Their graves . . . seen* The child regards the graves as proof that her siblings are alive.

[5] *kerchief* headscarf.

[6] *porringer* wooden soup-bowl.

So in the churchyard she was laid
And all the summer dry,
Together round her grave we played,
My brother John and I.

And when the ground was white with snow,
And I could run and slide,
My brother John was forced to go,
And he lies by her side.'

'How many are you then', said I,
'If they two are in heaven?'
The little maiden did reply,
'Oh master, we are seven!'

'But they are dead – those two are dead!
Their spirits are in heaven!'
'Twas throwing words away, for still
The little maid would have her will
And said, 'Nay, we are seven!'

Lines written in early spring (by Wordsworth, composed *c.* 12 April 1798)[1]

I heard a thousand blended notes[2]
While in a grove I sat reclined
In that sweet mood when pleasant thoughts
Bring sad thoughts to the mind.

To her fair works did nature link
The human soul that through me ran,
And much it grieved my heart to think
What man has made of man.[3]

Through primrose-tufts, in that sweet bower,
The periwinkle[4] trailed its wreaths;
And 'tis my faith that every flower
Enjoys the air it breathes.[5]

Notes

LINES WRITTEN IN EARLY SPRING

[1] According to Wordsworth this poem was 'composed while I was sitting by the side of the brook that runs down the coomb (in which stands the village of Holford), through the grounds of Alfoxden. It was a chosen resort of mine. The brook fell down a sloping rock so as to make a waterfall considerable for that country, and, across the pool below, had fallen a tree, an ash if I rightly remember, from which rose perpendicularly boughs in search of the light intercepted by the deep shade above' (*FN* 36).

[2] *notes* pronounced so as to rhyme with 'thoughts', as Wordsworth, with his Cumbrian accent, would have done.

[3] *And much . . . man* Wordsworth has in mind the conclusion to Burns's *Man was Made to Mourn*: 'Man's inhumanity to man / Makes countless thousands mourn.'

[4] *periwinkle* evergreen trailing plant with light blue flowers (US myrtle).

[5] *And 'tis . . . breathes* Wordsworth was up-to-date in his botanical knowledge; in 1791 Erasmus Darwin had written, in *The Economy of Vegetation*, that leaves function as lungs.

The birds around me hopped and played,
Their thoughts I cannot measure,
But the least motion which they made –
It seemed a thrill of pleasure.

The budding twigs spread out their fan
To catch the breezy air;
And I must think, do all I can,
That there was pleasure there.

If I these thoughts may not prevent,
If such be of my creed[6] the plan,
Have I not reason to lament
What man has made of man?

The Thorn (by Wordsworth, composed between 19 March and 20 April 1798)[1]

I

'There is a thorn, it looks so old,
In truth you'd find it hard to say
How it could ever have been young,
It looks so old and grey.
Not higher than a two years' child,
It stands erect, this aged thorn;
No leaves it has, no thorny points –
It is a mass of knotted joints,
A wretched thing forlorn.
It stands erect and, like a stone,
With lichens[2] it is overgrown.

II

Like rock or stone, it is o'ergrown
With lichens to the very top,
And hung with heavy tufts of moss,
A melancholy crop;
Up from the earth these mosses creep,
And this poor thorn they clasp it round
So close, you'd say that they were bent
With plain and manifest intent
To drag it to the ground –
And all had joined in one endeavour
To bury this poor thorn for ever.

Notes

[6] *creed* credo, belief.

THE THORN

[1] Wordsworth recalled that this poem 'arose out of my observing, on the ridge of Quantock Hill, on a stormy day, a thorn which I had often passed in calm and bright weather without noticing it. I said to myself, "Cannot I by some invention do as much to make this thorn permanently an impressive object as the storm has made it to my eyes at this moment?" I began the poem accordingly, and composed it with great rapidity' (*FN* 14). See also the 'Note to "The Thorn" ' (1800), pp. 507–9 below. The poem is in the form of a dialogue; an interlocutor enters at ll. 78–88, 100–3, and 210–13. For Southey's hostile comments, see p. 731.

[2] *lichens* slow-growing grey-green plants encrusting the surface of old walls, trees and thorn bushes.

III

High on a mountain's highest ridge
Where oft the stormy winter gale
Cuts like a scythe, while through the clouds
It sweeps from vale to vale;
Not five yards from the mountain path
This thorn you on your left espy,
And to the left, three yards beyond,
You see a little muddy pond
Of water, never dry.
I've measured it from side to side;
'Tis three feet long and two feet wide.

IV

And close beside this aged thorn
There is a fresh and lovely sight,
A beauteous heap, a hill of moss,
Just half a foot in height.
All lovely colours there you see,
All colours that were ever seen,
And mossy net-work[3] too is there,
As if by hand of lady fair
The work had woven been,
And cups,[4] the darlings of the eye,
So deep is their vermilion dye.

V

Ah me, what lovely tints are there
Of olive-green and scarlet bright!
In spikes, in branches, and in stars,
Green, red, and pearly white.
This heap of earth o'ergrown with moss,
Which close beside the thorn you see,
So fresh in all its beauteous dyes,
Is like an infant's grave in size,
As like as like can be;
But never, never, anywhere
An infant's grave was half so fair.

VI

Now would you see this aged thorn,
This pond and beauteous hill of moss,
You must take care and choose your time
The mountain when to cross.

Notes

[3] *net-work* embroidery.

[4] *cups* blooms.

For oft there sits, between the heap
That's like an infant's grave in size
And that same pond of which I spoke,
A woman in a scarlet cloak,[5]
And to herself she cries,
"Oh misery! Oh misery!
Oh woe is me! Oh misery!"

VII

At all times of the day and night
This wretched woman thither goes,
And she is known to every star
And every wind that blows;
And there beside the thorn she sits
When the blue daylight's in the skies,
And when the whirlwind's on the hill,
Or frosty air is keen and still,
And to herself she cries,
"Oh misery! Oh misery!
Oh woe is me! Oh misery!" '

VIII

'Now wherefore thus, by day and night,
In rain, in tempest, and in snow,
Thus to the dreary mountain-top
Does this poor woman go?
And why sits she beside the thorn
When the blue daylight's in the sky,
Or when the whirlwind's on the hill,
Or frosty air is keen and still,
And wherefore does she cry?
Oh wherefore, wherefore, tell me why
Does she repeat that doleful cry?'

IX

'I cannot tell, I wish I could;
For the true reason no one knows.
But if you'd gladly view the spot,
The spot to which she goes –
The heap that's like an infant's grave,
The pond, and thorn so old and grey –
Pass by her door ('tis seldom shut),

Notes

[5] *a scarlet cloak* traditionally associated with guilt and sin; cf. the whore of Babylon 'arrayed in purple, and scarlet colour' (Revelation 17: 4).

And if you see her in her hut,[6]
Then to the spot away!
I never heard of such as dare
Approach the spot when she is there.'

X

'But wherefore to the mountain-top
Can this unhappy woman go,
Whatever star is in the skies,
Whatever wind may blow?'
'Nay rack your brain, 'tis all in vain –
I'll tell you everything I know;
But to the thorn, and to the pond
Which is a little step beyond,
I wish that you would go.
Perhaps when you are at the place
You something of her tale may trace.

XI

I'll give you the best help I can:
Before you up the mountain go,
Up to the dreary mountain-top,
I'll tell you all I know.
'Tis now some two and twenty years
Since she (her name is Martha Ray[7])
Gave with a maiden's true goodwill
Her company to Stephen Hill,
And she was blithe and gay,
And she was happy, happy still
Whene'er she thought of Stephen Hill.

XII

And they had fixed the wedding-day,
The morning that must wed them both,
But Stephen to another maid
Had sworn another oath,
And with this other maid to church
Unthinking Stephen went –
Poor Martha! On that woeful day
A cruel, cruel fire, they say,
Into her bones was sent:
It dried her body like a cinder
And almost turned her brain to tinder.

Notes

6 *hut* cottage.

7 *Martha Ray* the mother of Wordsworth's friend Basil Montagu, and grandmother of Basil Montagu Jr, whom he and Dorothy were looking after at Alfoxden (featured in *Anecdote for Fathers*). Ray had been the mistress of the 4th Earl of Sandwich, and on 7 April 1779 had been shot dead on the steps of Covent Garden Theatre by a jealous lover, the Revd James Hackman. Why Wordsworth should have used a name with such painful associations remains unexplained.

XIII

They say full six months after this,
While yet the summer leaves were green,
She to the mountain-top would go,
And there was often seen;
'Tis said a child was in her womb,
As now to any eye was plain –
She was with child and she was mad,
Yet often she was sober-sad
From her exceeding pain.
Oh me! Ten thousand times I'd rather
That he had died, that cruel father!

XIV

Sad case for such a brain to hold
Communion with a stirring child!
Sad case (as you may think) for one
Who had a brain so wild!
Last Christmas when we talked of this,
Old Farmer Simpson did maintain
That in her womb the infant wrought
About its mother's heart, and brought
Her senses back again;
And when at last her time drew near,
Her looks were calm, her senses clear.

XV

No more I know – I wish I did,
And I would tell it all to you.
For what became of this poor child
There's none that ever knew;
And if a child was born or no,
There's no one that could ever tell;
And if 'twas born alive or dead,
There's no one knows, as I have said.
But some remember well
That Martha Ray about this time
Would up the mountain often climb.

XVI

And all that winter, when at night
The wind blew from the mountain-peak,
'Twas worth your while, though in the dark,
The churchyard path to seek:
For many a time and oft were heard
Cries coming from the mountain-head.
Some plainly living voices were,

And others, I've heard many swear,
Were voices of the dead.
I cannot think, whate'er they say,
They had to do with Martha Ray.

XVII

But that she goes to this old thorn,
The thorn which I've described to you,
And there sits in a scarlet cloak,
I will be sworn is true.
For one day with my telescope,[8]
To view the ocean wide and bright,
When to this country[9] first I came,
Ere I had heard of Martha's name,
I climbed the mountain's height;
A storm came on, and I could see
No object higher than my knee.

XVIII

'Twas mist and rain, and storm and rain,
No screen, no fence could I discover;[10]
And then the wind – in faith, it was
A wind full ten times over!
I looked around, I thought I saw
A jutting crag, and off I ran
Head-foremost through the driving rain,
The shelter of the crag to gain;
And, as I am a man,
Instead of jutting crag, I found
A woman seated on the ground.

XIX

I did not speak – I saw her face,
Her face it was enough for me;
I turned about and heard her cry,
"Oh misery! Oh misery!"
And there she sits, until the moon
Through half the clear blue sky will go,
And when the little breezes make
The waters of the pond to shake,
As all the country know,
She shudders and you hear her cry,
"Oh misery! Oh misery!" '

Notes

[8] *my telescope* the one piece of evidence to corroborate Wordsworth's later assertion that the speaker of the poem was the retired 'captain of a small trading vessel' (see p. 507).

[9] *country* area, district.

[10] *discover* see.

XX

'But what's the thorn? And what's the pond?
And what's the hill of moss to her?
And what's the creeping breeze that comes
The little pond to stir?'
'I cannot tell, but some will say
She hanged her baby on the tree;
Some say she drowned it in the pond
Which is a little step beyond;
But all and each agree
The little babe was buried there,
Beneath that hill of moss so fair.

XXI

I've heard the scarlet moss is red
With drops of that poor infant's blood –
But kill a new-born infant thus?
I do not think she could.
Some say, if to the pond you go,
And fix on it a steady view,
The shadow of a babe you trace,
A baby and a baby's face,
And that it looks at you;
Whene'er you look on it, 'tis plain
The baby looks at you again.

XXII

And some had sworn an oath that she
Should be to public justice brought,
And for the little infant's bones
With spades they would have sought.
But then the beauteous hill of moss
Before their eyes began to stir,
And for full fifty yards around,
The grass it shook upon the ground.
But all do still aver[11]
The little babe is buried there,
Beneath that hill of moss so fair.

XXIII

I cannot tell how this may be,
But plain it is, the thorn is bound
With heavy tufts of moss that strive
To drag it to the ground.
And this I know, full many a time

Notes

[11] *aver* maintain.

When she was on the mountain high,
By day, and in the silent night,
When all the stars shone clear and bright,
That I have heard her cry,
"Oh misery! Oh misery!
Oh woe is me! Oh misery!" '

The Last of the Flock (by Wordsworth, composed between March and 16 May 1798)[1]

In distant countries I have been,
And yet I have not often seen
A healthy man, a man full grown,
Weep in the public roads alone.
But such a one on English ground
And in the broad highway, I met;
Along the broad highway he came,
His cheeks with tears were wet.
Sturdy he seemed, though he was sad,
And in his arms a lamb he had.

He saw me and he turned aside
As if he wished himself to hide;
Then with his coat he made essay[2]
To wipe those briny tears away.
I followed him, and said, 'My friend,
What ails you? Wherefore weep you so?'
'Shame on me, sir! This lusty lamb,
He makes my tears to flow;
Today I fetched him from the rock –
He is the last of all my flock.

When I was young, a single man,
And after youthful follies ran,
Though little given to care and thought,
Yet so it was a ewe I bought;
And other sheep from her I raised,
As healthy sheep as you might see.

Notes

THE LAST OF THE FLOCK

[1] In later years Wordsworth recalled that the encounter described here 'occurred in the village of Holford, close by Alfoxden' (*FN* 9). It was apparently relayed to him by one of those who had taken part: 'I never in my whole life saw a man weep alone in the roads; but a friend of mine did see this poor man weeping alone, with the lamb, the last of the flock, in his arms' (*LY* iii 292). Critics observe that this poem refutes the Godwinian argument that 'property was the cause of every vice, and the source of all the wretchedness, of the poor.' It also illustrates the disastrous effects of the 'Speenhamland system' for paying from parish rates the difference between what a man earned and what he needed to live. Wages were so low that a man could not live without supplementing his earnings from the parish. But if he possessed anything, even a few pounds saved over the years, he was refused both help and employment.

[2] *made essay* tried.

And then I married, and was rich
As I could wish to be;
Of sheep I numbered a full score,[3]
And every year increased my store.

Year after year my stock it grew,
And from this one, this single ewe,
Full fifty comely sheep I raised –
As sweet a flock as ever grazed!
Upon the mountain did they feed,
They throve, and we at home did thrive.
This lusty lamb of all my store
Is all that is alive;
And now I care not if we die
And perish all of poverty.

Ten children, sir, had I to feed –
Hard labour in a time of need!
My pride was tamed, and in our grief
I of the parish asked relief.
They said I was a wealthy man;
My sheep upon the mountain fed
And it was fit that thence I took
Whereof to buy us bread.
"Do this. How can we give to you"
They cried, "what to the poor is due?"

I sold a sheep as they had said,
And bought my little children bread,
And they were healthy with their food;
For me it never did me good.
A woeful time it was for me
To see the end of all my gains,
The pretty flock which I had reared
With all my care and pains,
To see it melt like snow away!
For me it was a woeful day.

Another still, and still another!
A little lamb and then its mother!
It was a vein that never stopped,
Like blood-drops from my heart they dropped
Till thirty were not left alive;
They dwindled, dwindled, one by one,
And I may say that many a time
I wished they all were gone:
They dwindled one by one away –
For me it was a woeful day.

Notes

[3] *a full score* twenty.

To wicked deeds I was inclined,
And wicked fancies crossed my mind,
And every man I chanced to see,
I thought he knew some ill of me.
No peace, no comfort could I find,
No ease, within doors or without,
And crazily, and wearily,
I went my work about.
Oft-times I thought to run away;
For me it was a woeful day.

Sir, 'twas a precious flock to me,
As dear as my own children be;
For daily with my growing store
I loved my children more and more.
Alas, it was an evil time,
God cursed me in my sore distress;
I prayed, yet every day I thought
I loved my children less;
And every week, and every day
My flock, it seemed to melt away.

They dwindled, sir, sad sight to see,
From ten to five, from five to three –
A lamb, a wether,[4] and a ewe;
And then at last, from three to two.
And of my fifty, yesterday
I had but only one,
And here it lies upon my arm –
Alas, and I have none!
Today I fetched it from the rock;
It is the last of all my flock.'

The Dungeon (by Coleridge, extracted from Osorio, composed April-September 1797)[1]

And this place our forefathers made for man!
This is the process of our love and wisdom
To each poor brother who offends against us;
Most innocent, perhaps – and what if guilty?
Is this the only cure, merciful God?
Each pore and natural outlet shrivelled up
By ignorance and parching poverty,
His energies roll back upon his heart

Notes

[4] *wether* castrated male sheep.

THE DUNGEON

[1] In Coleridge's play, this was part of a soliloquy by the protagonist, Albert, when jailed by the Inquisition. Like Wordsworth's 'The Convict' (pp. 405–6), this poem is a plea for penal reform.

And stagnate and corrupt; till, changed to poison,
They break out on him like a loathsome plague-spot.
Then we call in our pampered mountebanks
And this is their best cure: uncomforted
And friendless solitude, groaning and tears
And savage faces at the clanking hour,
Seen through the steams and vapour of his dungeon,
By the lamp's dismal twilight. So he lies
Circled with evil, till his very soul
Unmoulds its essence, hopelessly deformed
By sights of ever more deformity!
With other ministrations, thou, oh nature,
Healest thy wandering and distempered child:
Thou pourest on him thy soft influences,
Thy sunny hues, fair forms, and breathingsweets,
Thy melodies of woods, and winds, and waters,
Till he relent, and can no more endure
To be a jarring and a dissonant thing
Amid this general dance and minstrelsy;
But, bursting into tears, wins back his way,
His angry spirit healed and harmonized
By the benignant touch of love and beauty.[2]

The Mad Mother (by Wordsworth, composed between March and 16 May 1798)[1]

Her eyes are wild, her head is bare,
The sun has burnt her coal-black hair,
Her eyebrows have a rusty stain,
And she came far from over the main.[2]
She has a baby on her arm,
Or else she were alone;
And underneath the haystack warm,
And on the greenwood stone,
She talked and sung the woods among –
And it was in the English tongue.

'Sweet babe, they say that I am mad,
But nay, my heart is far too glad;
And I am happy when I sing
Full many a sad and doleful thing.

Notes

[2] *Till he relent . . . beauty* The experience of being harmonized and healed by nature is celebrated in 'This Lime-Tree Bower my Prison' and 'Frost at Midnight'; conversely, 'The Ancient Mariner' and 'Christabel' are concerned with the suffering of those alienated from nature's healing power.

THE MAD MOTHER

[1] In later years, Wordsworth recalled that 'The subject was reported to me by a lady of Bristol who had seen the poor creature' (*FN* 11). In a letter of 1836 he remarked: 'though she came from far, English was her native tongue – which shows her either to be of these islands, or a North American. On the latter supposition, while the distance removes her from us, the fact of her speaking our language brings us at once into close sympathy with her' (*LY* iii 293).

[2] *main* sea.

Then, lovely baby, do not fear!
I pray thee, have no fear of me,
But safe as in a cradle, here
My lovely baby, thou shalt be;
To thee I know too much I owe,
I cannot work thee any woe.

A fire was once within my brain,
And in my head a dull, dull pain;
And fiendish faces – one, two, three,
Hung at my breasts, and pulled at me.
But then there came a sight of joy,
It came at once to do me good;
I waked and saw my little boy,
My little boy of flesh and blood –
Oh joy for me that sight to see!
For he was here, and only he.

Suck, little babe, oh suck again!
It cools my blood, it cools my brain;
Thy lips I feel them, baby, they
Draw from my heart the pain away.
Oh, press me with thy little hand,
It loosens something at my chest;
About that tight and deadly band
I feel thy little fingers pressed.
The breeze I see is in the tree,
It comes to cool my babe and me.[3]

Oh love me, love me, little boy!
Thou art thy mother's only joy;
And do not dread the waves below,
When o'er the sea-rock's edge[4] we go.
The high crag cannot work me harm,
Nor leaping torrents when they howl;
The babe I carry on my arm,
He saves for me my precious soul.
Then happy lie, for blessed am I –
Without me my sweet babe would die.

Then do not fear, my boy, for thee
Bold as a lion I will be;
And I will always be thy guide
Through hollow snows and rivers wide.
I'll build an Indian bower;[5] I know

Notes

[3] *The breeze . . . me* In *Biographia Literaria* Coleridge described these lines as 'so expressive . . . of that deranged state, in which from the increased sensibility the sufferer's attention is abruptly drawn off by every trifle, and in the same instant plucked back again by the one despotic thought, and bringing home with it, by the blending, fusing power of imagination and passion, the alien object to which it had been so abruptly diverted, no longer an alien but an ally and an inmate' (CC *Biographia* ii 150–1).

[4] *o'er the sea-rock's edge* along the cliff-top.

[5] *I'll build . . . bower* The mad mother was either an American Indian, or lived among them.

The leaves that make the softest bed;
And if from me thou wilt not go,
But still be true till I am dead –
My pretty thing, then thou shalt sing,
As merry as the birds in spring.

Thy father cares not for my breast;
'Tis thine, sweet baby, there to rest,
'Tis all thine own! And if its hue
Be changed, that was so fair to view,
'Tis fair enough for thee, my dove!
My beauty, little child, is flown;
But thou wilt live with me in love –
And what if my poor cheek be brown?
'Tis well for me; thou canst not see
How pale and wan it else would be.

Dread not their taunts, my little life!
I am thy father's wedded wife,
And underneath the spreading tree
We two will live in honesty.
If his sweet boy he could forsake,
With me he never would have stayed;
From him no harm my babe can take,
But he, poor man, is wretched made;
And every day we two will pray
For him that's gone and far away.

I'll teach my boy the sweetest things,
I'll teach him how the owlet sings.
My little babe, thy lips are still,
And thou hast almost sucked thy fill.
Where art thou gone, my own dear child?
What wicked looks are those I see?
Alas, alas! that look so wild,
It never, never came from me;
If thou art mad, my pretty lad,
Then I must be forever sad.

Oh smile on me, my little lamb,
For I thy own dear mother am.
My love for thee has well been tried;
I've sought thy father far and wide.
I know the poisons of the shade,
I know the earth-nuts fit for food;
Then, pretty dear, be not afraid –
We'll find thy father in the wood.
Now laugh and be gay, to the woods away,
And there, my babe, we'll live for aye.'

The Idiot Boy (by Wordsworth, composed between March and 16 May 1798)[1]

'Tis eight o'clock, a clear March night,
The moon is up, the sky is blue,
The owlet[2] in the moonlight air –
He shouts from nobody knows where,
He lengthens out his lonely shout:
Halloo, halloo! A long halloo!

Why bustle thus about your door?
What means this bustle, Betty Foy?
Why are you in this mighty fret?
And why on horseback have you set
Him whom you love, your idiot boy?

Beneath the moon that shines so bright,
Till she is tired, let Betty Foy
With girt[3] and stirrup fiddle-faddle;
But wherefore set upon a saddle
Him whom she loves, her idiot boy?

There's scarce a soul that's out of bed –
Good Betty, put him down again!
His lips with joy they burr at you,
But, Betty, what has he to do
With stirrup, saddle, or with rein?

The world will say 'tis very idle –
Bethink you of the time of night?
There's not a mother – no not one,
But when she hears what you have done,
Oh Betty, she'll be in a fright!

But Betty's bent on her intent,
For her good neighbour, Susan Gale
(Old Susan, she who dwells alone)
Is sick and makes a piteous moan
As if her very life would fail.

There's not a house within a mile,
No hand to help them in distress,
Old Susan lies abed in pain,
And sorely puzzled are the twain,
For what she ails[4] they cannot guess.

Notes

THE IDIOT BOY

[1] According to Wordsworth this poem was 'composed in the groves of Alfoxden almost extempore; not a word, I believe, being corrected, though one stanza was omitted. I mention this in gratitude to those happy moments, for, in truth, I never wrote anything with so much glee' (*FN* 10). For Southey's less than charitable comments on the poem, see p. 730.

[2] *owlet* full-grown owl.

[3] *girt* saddle-girth.

[4] *what she ails* what ails her.

And Betty's husband's at the wood
Where by the week he doth abide,
A woodman in the distant vale;
There's none to help poor Susan Gale –
What must be done? What will betide?

And Betty from the lane has fetched
Her pony that is mild and good
Whether he be in joy or pain,
Feeding at will along the lane,
Or bringing faggots[5] from the wood.

And he is all in travelling trim,[6]
And by the moonlight, Betty Foy
Has up upon the saddle set
(The like was never heard of yet)
Him whom she loves, her idiot boy.

And he must post[7] without delay
Across the bridge that's in the dale,
And by the church and o'er the down
To bring a Doctor from the town,
Or she will die, old Susan Gale.

There is no need of boot or spur,
There is no need of whip or wand,[8]
For Johnny has his holly-bough,
And with a hurly-burly now
He shakes the green bough in his hand.

And Betty o'er and o'er has told
The boy who is her best delight
Both what to follow, what to shun,
What do, and what to leave undone,
How turn to left, and how to right,

And Betty's most especial charge[9]
Was, 'Johnny, Johnny! Mind that you
Come home again, nor stop at all,
Come home again whate'er befall –
My Johnny do, I pray you do.'

To this did Johnny answer make
Both with his head and with his hand,
And proudly shook the bridle too,
And then! his words were not a few,
Which Betty well could understand.

Notes

[5] *faggots* bundles of sticks for fuel.
[6] *in travelling trim* i.e. saddled.
[7] *post* travel quickly.
[8] *wand* stick, cane.
[9] *charge* instruction.

And now that Johnny is just going,
Though Betty's in a mighty flurry,
She gently pats the pony's side
On which her idiot boy must ride,
And seems no longer in a hurry.

But when the pony moved his legs –
Oh then for the poor idiot boy!
For joy he cannot hold the bridle,
For joy his head and heels are idle,
He's idle all for very joy.

And while the pony moves his legs,
In Johnny's left hand you may see
The green bough's motionless and dead;
The moon that shines above his head
Is not more still and mute than he.

His heart it was so full of glee
That till full fifty yards were gone
He quite forgot his holly whip
And all his skill in horsemanship –
Oh happy, happy, happy John!

And Betty's standing at the door,
And Betty's face with joy o'erflows,[10]
Proud of herself and proud of him,
She sees him in his travelling trim;
How quietly her Johnny goes!

The silence of her idiot boy -
What hopes it sends to Betty's heart!
He's at the guide-post,[11] he turns right,
She watches till he's out of sight,
And Betty will not then depart.

Burr, burr, now Johnny's lips they burr[12]
As loud as any mill or near it;
Meek as a lamb the pony moves,
And Johnny makes the noise he loves,
And Betty listens, glad to hear it.

Away she hies to Susan Gale,
And Johnny's in a merry tune;[13]
The owlets hoot, the owlets curr,
And Johnny's lips they burr, burr, burr,
And on he goes beneath the moon.

Notes

[10] *And . . . o'erflows* Defending this poem in a letter to John Wilson, Wordsworth remarked that 'I have indeed often looked upon the conduct of fathers and mothers of the lower classes of society towards idiots as the great triumph of the human heart. It is there that we see the strength, disinterestedness, and grandeur of love' (*EY* 357).

[11] *guide-post* signpost.

[12] *Burr . . . burr* Coleridge attacked the poem in *Biographia Literaria*, on the grounds of its 'disgusting images of ordinary morbid idiocy'; Wordsworth 'has even, by the "burr, burr, burr" . . . assisted in recalling them' (CC *Biographia* ii 48–9).

[13] *tune* mood.

His steed and he right well agree,
For of this pony there's a rumour
That should he lose his eyes and ears,
And should he live a thousand years,
He never will be out of humour.

But then he is a horse that thinks!
And when he thinks his pace is slack;
Now, though he knows poor Johnny well,
Yet for his life he cannot tell
What he has got upon his back.

So through the moonlight lanes they go
And far into the moonlight dale,
And by the church and o'er the down
To bring a Doctor from the town
To comfort poor old Susan Gale.

And Betty, now at Susan's side,
Is in the middle of her story,
What comfort Johnny soon will bring,
With many a most diverting thing
Of Johnny's wit and Johnny's glory.[14]

And Betty's still at Susan's side –
By this time she's not quite so flurried;
Demure with porringer[15] and plate
She sits, as if in Susan's fate
Her life and soul were buried.

But Betty (poor good woman!), she –
You plainly in her face may read it –
Could lend out of that moment's store
Five years of happiness or more
To any that might need it.

But yet I guess that now and then
With Betty all was not so well,
And to the road she turns her ears,
And thence full many a sound she hears,
Which she to Susan will not tell.

Poor Susan moans, poor Susan groans;
'As sure as there's a moon in heaven',
Cries Betty, 'he'll be back again –
They'll both be here, 'tis almost ten;
They'll both be here before eleven.'

Notes

[14] *Johnny's glory* Defending this poem in a letter to John Wilson, Wordsworth remarked that, 'I have often applied to idiots, in my own mind, that sublime expression of scripture that, "their life is hidden with God"' (*EY* 357).

[15] *porringer* wooden soup-bowl.

Poor Susan moans, poor Susan groans,
The clock gives warning for eleven –
'Tis on the stroke. 'If Johnny's near',
Quoth Betty, 'he will soon be here,
As sure as there's a moon in heaven.'

The clock is on the stroke of twelve
And Johnny is not yet in sight;
The moon's in heaven, as Betty sees,
But Betty is not quite at ease –
And Susan has a dreadful night.

And Betty, half an hour ago,
On Johnny vile reflections cast;
'A little idle sauntering thing!'
With other names, an endless string,
But now that time is gone and past.

And Betty's drooping at the heart,
That happy time all past and gone;
'How can it be he is so late?
The Doctor, he has made him wait –
Susan, they'll both be here anon!'

And Susan's growing worse and worse,
And Betty's in a sad quandary,[16]
And then there's nobody to say
If she must go or she must stay –
She's in a sad quandary.

The clock is on the stroke of one,
But neither Doctor nor his guide
Appear along the moonlight road;
There's neither horse nor man abroad,
And Betty's still at Susan's side.

And Susan, she begins to fear
Of sad mischances not a few;
That Johnny may perhaps be drowned,
Or lost perhaps, and never found –
Which they must both forever rue.

She prefaced half a hint of this
With, 'God forbid it should be true!'
At the first word that Susan said,
Cried Betty, rising from the bed,
'Susan, I'd gladly stay with you;

Notes

[16] *quandary* stressed on the second syllable.

I must be gone, I must away.
Consider, Johnny's but half-wise;
Susan, we must take care of him,
If he is hurt in life or limb –'
'Oh God forbid!' poor Susan cries.

'What can I do?' says Betty, going,
'What can I do to ease your pain?
Good Susan tell me, and I'll stay;
I fear you're in a dreadful way,
But I shall soon be back again.'

'Good Betty go, good Betty go,
There's nothing that can ease my pain.'
Then off she hies, but with a prayer
That God poor Susan's life would spare
Till she comes back again.

So through the moonlight lane she goes
And far into the moonlight dale;
And how she ran and how she walked
And all that to herself she talked
Would surely be a tedious tale.

In high and low, above, below,
In great and small, in round and square,
In tree and tower was Johnny seen,
In bush and brake, in black and green,
'Twas Johnny, Johnny, everywhere.

She's past the bridge that's in the dale,
And now the thought torments her sore –
Johnny perhaps his horse forsook
To hunt the moon that's in the brook,
And never will be heard of more.

And now she's high upon the down,
Alone amid a prospect wide;
There's neither Johnny nor his horse
Among the fern or in the gorse;
There's neither Doctor nor his guide.

'Oh saints! What is become of him?
Perhaps he's climbed into an oak
Where he will stay till he is dead;
Or sadly he has been misled
And joined the wandering gipsy-folk;

Or him that wicked pony's carried
To the dark cave, the goblin's hall;
Or in the castle he's pursuing,
Among the ghosts, his own undoing,
Or playing with the waterfall.'

At poor old Susan then she railed,
While to the town she posts away;
'If Susan had not been so ill,
Alas! I should have had him still,
My Johnny, till my dying day.'

Poor Betty, in this sad distemper,
The Doctor's self would hardly spare;
Unworthy things she talked, and wild –
Even he, of cattle[17] the most mild,
The pony had his share.

And now she's got into the town
And to the Doctor's door she hies;
'Tis silence all on every side –
The town so long, the town so wide
Is silent as the skies.

And now she's at the Doctor's door,
She lifts the knocker – rap, rap, rap!
The Doctor at the casement[18] shows
His glimmering eyes that peep and doze,
And one hand rubs his old nightcap.

'Oh Doctor, Doctor! Where's my Johnny?'
'I'm here, what is't you want with me?'
'Oh sir, you know I'm Betty Foy
And I have lost my poor dear boy –
You know him, him you often see;

He's not so wise as some folks be.'
'The devil take his wisdom!' said
The Doctor, looking somewhat grim,
'What, woman, should I know of him?'
And grumbling, he went back to bed.

'Oh woe is me! Oh woe is me!
Here will I die, here will I die;
I thought to find my Johnny here,
But he is neither far nor near –
Oh what a wretched mother I!'

She stops, she stands, she looks about,
Which way to turn she cannot tell.
Poor Betty, it would ease her pain
If she had heart to knock again;
The clock strikes three – a dismal knell!

Notes

[17] *cattle* animals.

[18] *casement* window.

Then up along the town she hies,
No wonder if her senses fail,
This piteous news so much it shocked her
She quite forgot to send the Doctor
To comfort poor old Susan Gale.

And now she's high upon the down
And she can see a mile of road;
'Oh cruel! I'm almost threescore;
Such night as this was ne'er before,
There's not a single soul abroad.'

She listens, but she cannot hear
The foot of horse, the voice of man;
The streams with softest sound are flowing,
The grass you almost hear it growing,
You hear it now if e'er you can.

The owlets through the long blue night
Are shouting to each other still,
Fond lovers, yet not quite hob-nob,
They lengthen out the tremulous sob
That echoes far from hill to hill.

Poor Betty now has lost all hope,
Her thoughts are bent on deadly sin;
A green-grown pond she just has passed
And from the brink she hurries fast
Lest she should drown herself therein.

And now she sits her down and weeps,
Such tears she never shed before;
'Oh dear, dear pony! My sweet joy!
Oh carry back my idiot boy
And we will ne'er o'erload thee more.'

A thought is come into her head;
'The pony he is mild and good
And we have always used him well;
Perhaps he's gone along the dell
And carried Johnny to the wood.'

Then up she springs as if on wings –
She thinks no more of deadly sin;
If Betty fifty ponds should see,
The last of all her thoughts would be
To drown herself therein.

Oh reader, now that I might tell
What Johnny and his horse are doing,
What they've been doing all this time –
Oh could I put it into rhyme,
A most delightful tale pursuing!

Perhaps (and no unlikely thought)
He with his pony now doth roam
The cliffs and peaks so high that are,
To lay his hands upon a star
And in his pocket bring it home.

Perhaps he's turned himself about,
His face unto his horse's tail,
And still and mute, in wonder lost,
All like a silent horseman-ghost
He travels on along the vale.

And now, perhaps, he's hunting sheep,
A fierce and dreadful hunter he!
Yon valley that's so trim and green,
In five months' time, should he be seen,
A desert wilderness will be.

Perhaps, with head and heels on fire,
And like the very soul of evil,
He's galloping away, away,
And so he'll gallop on for aye,
The bane of all that dread the devil.

I to the muses have been bound
These fourteen years by strong indentures;[19]
Oh gentle muses, let me tell
But half of what to him befell,
For sure he met with strange adventures.

Oh gentle muses, is this kind?
Why will ye thus my suit repel?
Why of your further aid bereave[20] me?
And can ye thus unfriended leave me,
Ye muses, whom I love so well?

Who's yon, that, near the waterfall
Which thunders down with headlong force,
Beneath the moon, yet shining fair,
As careless as if nothing were,
Sits upright on a feeding horse?

Unto his horse that's feeding free
He seems, I think, the rein to give;
Of moon or stars he takes no heed,
Of such we in romances read –
'Tis Johnny, Johnny, as I live!

Notes

[19] *indentures* contract by which apprentice is bound to a master who will teach him a trade. Wordsworth's apprenticeship to the muses of poetry, by his reckoning, began in 1784, when he was 14.

[20] *bereave* deprive.

And that's the very pony too!
Where is she, where is Betty Foy?
She hardly can sustain her fears;
The roaring waterfall she hears,
And cannot find her idiot boy.

Your pony's worth his weight in gold,
Then calm your terrors, Betty Foy!
She's coming from among the trees,
And now, all full in view, she sees
Him whom she loves, her idiot boy,

And Betty sees the pony too.
Why stand you thus, good Betty Foy?
It is no goblin, 'tis no ghost –
'Tis he whom you so long have lost,
He whom you love, your idiot boy.

She looks again, her arms are up,
She screams, she cannot move for joy;
She darts as with a torrent's force,
She almost has o'erturned the horse,
And fast she holds her idiot boy.

And Johnny burrs and laughs aloud –
Whether in cunning or in joy
I cannot tell; but while he laughs,
Betty a drunken pleasure quaffs
To hear again her idiot boy.

And now she's at the pony's tail,
And now she's at the pony's head,
On that side now, and now on this,
And almost stifled with her bliss,
A few sad tears does Betty shed.

She kisses o'er and o'er again
Him whom she loves, her idiot boy;
She's happy here, she's happy there,
She is uneasy everywhere;
Her limbs are all alive with joy.

She pats the pony, where or when
She knows not, happy Betty Foy!
The little pony glad may be,
But he is milder far than she,
You hardly can perceive his joy.

'Oh Johnny, never mind the Doctor;
You've done your best, and that is all.'
She took the reins when this was said,
And gently turned the pony's head
From the loud waterfall.

By this the stars were almost gone,
The moon was setting on the hill
So pale you scarcely looked at her;
The little birds began to stir,
Though yet their tongues were still.

The pony, Betty, and her boy,
Wind slowly through the woody dale;
And who is she, betimes abroad,
That hobbles up the steep rough road?
Who is it but old Susan Gale?

Long Susan lay deep lost in thought
And many dreadful fears beset her,
Both for her messenger and nurse;
And as her mind grew worse and worse,
Her body it grew better.

She turned, she tossed herself in bed,
On all sides doubts and terrors met her,
Point after point did she discuss,
And while her mind was fighting thus,
Her body still grew better.

'Alas, what is become of them?
These fears can never be endured –
I'll to the wood.' The word scarce said,
Did Susan rise up from her bed,
As if by magic cured.

Away she posts up hill and down,
And to the wood at length is come,
She spies her friends, she shouts a greeting –
Oh me, it is a merry meeting
As ever was in Christendom!

The owls have hardly sung their last
While our four travellers homeward wend;
The owls have hooted all night long,
And with the owls began my song,
And with the owls must end.

For while they all were travelling home,
Cried Betty, 'Tell us Johnny, do,
Where all this long night you have been,
What you have heard, what you have seen –
And Johnny, mind you tell us true.'

Now Johnny all night long had heard
The owls in tuneful concert strive;
No doubt too he the moon had seen,
For in the moonlight he had been
From eight o'clock till five.

And thus to Betty's question he
Made answer like a traveller bold
(His very words I give to you):
'The cocks did crow to-whoo, to-whoo,
And the sun did shine so cold.'[21]
Thus answered Johnny in his glory,
And that was all his travel's story.

Lines written near Richmond, upon the Thames, at Evening (by Wordsworth, derived from a sonnet written 1789, complete in this form by 29 March 1797)[1]

How rich the wave in front, impressed
With evening twilight's summer hues,
While, facing thus the crimson west,
The boat her silent path pursues![2]
And see how dark the backward stream,
A little moment past, so smiling!
And still, perhaps, with faithless gleam,
Some other loiterer beguiling.[3]

Such views the youthful bard allure,
But heedless of the following gloom,
He deems their colours shall endure
Till peace go with him to the tomb.
And let him nurse his fond deceit;
And what if he must die in sorrow?
Who would not cherish dreams so sweet,
Though grief and pain[4] may come tomorrow?

Glide gently, thus forever glide,
Oh Thames! that other bards may see
As lovely visions by thy side
As now, fair river; come to me!

Notes

[21] *The cocks . . . cold* According to Wordsworth, these words were spoken by a local idiot and reported to him at Alfoxden by his friend Thomas Poole. They provided the starting-point for the poem (*FN* 10).

Lines written near Richmond

[1] The title was concocted for the poem's appearance in *Lyrical Ballads*: 'The title is scarcely correct. It was during a solitary walk on the banks of the Cam that I was first struck with this appearance, and applied it to my own feelings in the manner here expressed, changing the scene to the Thames, near Windsor' (*FN* 36).

[2] *How rich . . . beguiling* The poem begins with a picturesque sunset, described in the manner of the picturesque theorist, William Gilpin, whose *Observations on the Lakes* (1786) Wordsworth admired from his schooldays onwards. Gilpin had described such a scene in exactly this manner: 'its fires, glowing in the west, light up a new radiance through the landscape; and spread over it, instead of sober light and shade, all the colours of nature, in one bright, momentary gleam' (i 91).

[3] *Some . . . beguiling* The brilliant sky at sunset draws the loiterer's attention away from the darkness coming up behind. Wordsworth is imitating Bowles's *Sonnet VIII. On Leaving a Village in Scotland*:

> Yet still your brightest images shall *smile*,
> To charm the lingering stranger, and *beguile*
> His way . . .
>
> (ll. 10–12)

[4] *grief and pain* a comment that anticipates the doleful judgement of *Resolution and Independence* 48–9: 'We poets in our youth begin in gladness, / But thereof comes in the end despondency and madness.'

Oh glide, fair stream, forever so;
Thy quiet soul on all bestowing,
Till all our minds forever flow,
As thy deep waters now are flowing.

Vain thought! Yet be as now thou art,
That in thy waters may be seen
The image of a poet's heart,
How bright, how solemn, how serene!
Such heart did once the poet[5] bless
Who, pouring here a *later* ditty,
Could find no refuge from distress
But in the milder grief of pity.

Remembrance! as we glide along,
For him suspend the dashing oar,[6]
And pray that never child of song
May know his freezing sorrows[7] more.
How calm, how still! the only sound
The dripping of the oar suspended!
The evening darkness gathers round
By virtue's holiest powers attended.

Expostulation and Reply (by Wordsworth, composed probably 23 May 1798)[1]

'Why, William, on that old grey stone,
Thus for the length of half a day,
Why, William, sit you thus alone
And dream your time away?

Where are your books that light bequeathed
To beings else forlorn and blind?
Up, up, and drink the spirit breathed
From dead men to their kind!

Notes

[5] 'Collins's "Ode on the Death of Thomson" – the last written, I believe, of the poems which were published during his lifetime. This Ode is also alluded to in the next stanza' (Wordsworth's note). William Collins (1721–59) actually published the 'Ode' in June 1749, a year before *The Passions* in 1750. James Thomson (1700–48), poet and author of *The Seasons*, was buried in Richmond Church. Wordsworth was a lifelong admirer of both.

[6] *For him . . . oar* cf. Collins, 'Ode on the Death of Mr. Thomson' 13–16:

> Remembrance oft shall haunt the shore
> When Thames in summer wreaths is dressed,
> And oft suspend the dashing oar
> To bid his gentle spirit rest!

[7] *his freezing sorrows* Collins suffered spells of insanity and poverty.

Expostulation and Reply

[1] See Advertisement to *Lyrical Ballads* (1798) above, for Wordsworth's explanation of the poem. It is based on a conversation which took place on a walk at Alfoxden with William Hazlitt. Hazlitt was 20, and was writing his *Essay on the Principles of Human Action* (1805). For Hazlitt's recollection, see p. 781.

You look round on your mother earth
As if she for no purpose bore you;
As if you were her first-born birth,
And none had lived before you!'

One morning thus, by Esthwaite Lake,[2]
When life was sweet I knew not why,
To me my good friend Matthew spake,
And thus I made reply.

'The eye it cannot choose but see,
We cannot bid the ear be still;
Our bodies feel where'er they be,
Against or with our will.

Nor less I deem that there are powers[3]
Which of themselves our minds impress,
That we can feed this mind of ours
In a wise passiveness.[4]

Think you, mid all this mighty sum
Of things forever speaking,
That nothing of itself will come,
But we must still[5] be seeking?

Then ask not wherefore, here, alone,
Conversing as I may,[6]
I sit upon this old grey stone
And dream my time away.'

The Tables Turned: an evening scene, on the same subject (by Wordsworth, composed probably 23 May 1798)[1]

Up, up, my friend, and clear your looks!
Why all this toil and trouble?[2]
Up, up, my friend, and quit your books,
Or surely you'll grow double!

The sun above the mountain's head
A freshening lustre mellow
Through all the long green fields has spread,
His first sweet evening yellow.

Notes

[2] *Esthwaite Lake* Wordsworth attended school at Hawkshead, on Esthwaite Water in the Lake District. Although this poem was inspired by a discussion with William Hazlitt at Alfoxden in 1798, Wordsworth locates it in the Lakes, and characterizes Matthew as his schoolmaster.

[3] *powers* i.e. external to us; natural forces.

[4] *wise passiveness* 'Oh how few can transmute activity of mind into emotion,' Coleridge exclaimed in a notebook entry of 1804, 'yet there are [those] who, active as the stirring tempest and playful as a May blossom in a breeze of May, can yet for hours together remain with hearts broad awake, and the understanding asleep in all but its retentiveness and receptivity' (*Notebooks* i 1834).

[5] *still* always.

[6] *Conversing . . . may* i.e. with the natural world.

THE TABLES TURNED

[1] The speaker is William from the preceding poem, who simply continues his argument.

[2] *toil and trouble* an echo of the witches in *Macbeth*: 'Double, double, toil and trouble' (IV i 10–11).

Books! 'tis a dull and endless strife;
Come hear the woodland linnet –
How sweet his music! On my life,
There's more of wisdom in it.

And hark, how blithe the throstle[3] sings!
And he is no mean preacher;
Come forth into the light of things,
Let nature be your teacher.

She has a world of ready wealth,
Our minds and hearts to bless –
Spontaneous wisdom breathed by health,
Truth breathed by cheerfulness.

One impulse from a vernal wood
May teach you more of man,
Of moral evil and of good
Than all the sages can.

Sweet is the lore which nature brings,
Our meddling intellect
Misshapes the beauteous forms of things –
We murder to dissect.[4]

Enough of science[5] and of art,[6]
Close up these barren leaves;[7]
Come forth, and bring with you a heart
That watches and receives.

Old Man Travelling; Animal Tranquillity and Decay, A Sketch (by Wordsworth, composed by June 1797)

The little hedgerow birds
That peck along the road, regard him not.
He travels on, and in his face, his step,
His gait, is one expression; every limb,
His look and bending figure, all bespeak
A man who does not move with pain, but moves
With thought. He is insensibly subdued
To settled quiet; he is one by whom
All effort seems forgotten, one to whom
Long patience has such mild composure given,
That patience now doth seem a thing of which
He hath no need. He is by nature led

Notes

[3] *throstle* thrush.

[4] *We murder to dissect* i.e. in analysing what we perceive, we destroy it.

[5] *science* knowledge.

[6] *art* skill, artfulness.

[7] *barren leaves* pages of books.

To peace so perfect that the young behold
With envy what the old man hardly feels.
   I asked him whither he was bound, and what
The object of his journey; he replied:
'Sir, I am going many miles to take
A last leave of my son, a mariner,
Who from a sea-fight has been brought to Falmouth,
And there is dying in an hospital.'[1]

The Complaint of a Forsaken Indian Woman (by Wordsworth, composed between early March and 16 May 1798)

When a Northern Indian, from sickness, is unable to continue his journey with his companions, he is left behind, covered over with deer-skins, and is supplied with water, food, and fuel, if the situation of the place will afford it. He is informed of the track which his companions intend to pursue, and, if he is unable to follow or overtake them, he perishes alone in the desert (unless he should have the good fortune to fall in with some other tribes of Indians). It is unnecessary to add that the females are equally, or still more, exposed to the same fate; see that very interesting work, Hearne's *Journey from Hudson's Bay to the Northern Ocean*.[1] When the Northern Lights[2] (as the same writer informs us) vary their position in the air, they make a rustling and a crackling noise. This circumstance is alluded to in the first stanza of the following poem.

Before I see another day
Oh let my body die away!
In sleep I heard the northern gleams,[3]
The stars they were among my dreams;
In sleep did I behold the skies,
I saw the crackling flashes drive,
And yet[4] they are upon my eyes,
And yet I am alive.
Before I see another day
Oh let my body die away!

My fire is dead[5] – it knew no pain,
Yet is it dead, and I remain.
All stiff with ice the ashes lie,

Notes

OLD MAN TRAVELLING

[1] Lines 15–20 may have been a late addition to the poem and were removed from texts published after 1815.

THE COMPLAINT OF A FORSAKEN

[1] A reference to Samuel Hearne's *Journey from Prince of Wales' Fort in Hudson Bay, to the Northern Ocean* (1795), which describes the plight of a sick Indian woman left behind by her tribe: 'The poor woman . . . came up with us three several times, after having been left in the manner described. At length, poor creature, she dropped behind, and no one attempted to go back in search of her' (p. 203).

[2] *Northern Lights* the aurora borealis.

[3] *northern gleams* Hearne writes: 'I do not remember to have met with any travellers into high northern latitudes, who remarked their having heard the Northern Lights make any noise in the air as they vary their colours or position – which may probably be owing to the want of perfect silence at the time they made their observations on those meteors. I can positively affirm that in still nights I have frequently heard them make a rustling and crackling noise, like the waving of a large flag in a fresh gale of wind' (*Journey*, p. 224).

[4] *yet* still.

[5] *My fire is dead* According to Hearne, members of the tribe abandoned to die were left with some provisions: 'the friends or relations of the sick generally leave them some

And they are dead, and I will die.
When I was well, I wished to live,
For[6] clothes, for warmth, for food and fire;
But they to me no joy can give,
No pleasure now, and no desire.
Then here contented will I lie,
Alone I cannot fear to die.

Alas, you might have dragged me on
Another day, a single one!
Too soon despair o'er me prevailed,
Too soon my heartless[7] spirit failed;
When you were gone my limbs were stronger –
And oh, how grievously I rue
That afterwards, a little longer,
My friends, I did not follow you!
For strong and without pain I lay,
My friends, when you were gone away.

My child, they gave thee to another,
A woman who was not thy mother;
When from my arms my babe they took,
On me how strangely did he look!
Through his whole body something ran,
A most strange something did I see –
As if he strove to be a man,
That he might pull the sledge for me.
And then he stretched his arms, how wild!
Oh mercy, like a little child!

My little joy! My little pride!
In two days more I must have died.
Then do not weep and grieve for me;
I feel I must have died with thee.
Oh wind, that o'er my head art flying
The way my friends their course did bend,
I should not feel the pain of dying
Could I with thee a message send.
Too soon, my friends, you went away,
For I had many things to say.

I'll follow you across the snow,
You travel heavily and slow;
In spite of all my weary pain,
I'll look upon your tents again.
My fire is dead, and snowy white

Notes

victuals and water, and, if the situation of the place will afford it, a little firing. When those articles are provided, the person to be left is acquainted with the road which the others intend to go, and then, after covering them well up with deer-skins, etc., they take their leave, and walk away crying' (*Journey*, pp. 202–3).

[6] *For* i.e. I wished for . . .

[7] *heartless* disheartened.

The water which beside it stood;
The wolf has come to me tonight
And he has stolen away my food.
Forever left alone am I,
Then wherefore should I fear to die?

My journey will be shortly run,[8]
I shall not see another sun,
I cannot lift my limbs to know
If they have any life or no.
My poor forsaken child, if I
For once could have thee close to me,
With happy heart I then would die
And my last thoughts would happy be.
I feel my body die away,
I shall not see another day.

The Convict (by Wordsworth, composed between 21 March and October 1796)[1]

The glory of evening was spread through the west –
  On the slope of a mountain I stood;
While the joy that precedes the calm season of rest[2]
  Rang loud through the meadow and wood.

'And must we then part from a dwelling so fair?'
  In the pain of my spirit I said,
And with a deep sadness I turned to repair
  To the cell where the convict is laid.

The thick-ribbed walls that o'ershadow the gate
  Resound, and the dungeons unfold;
I pause,[3] and at length through the glimmering grate[4]
  That outcast of pity behold.

His black matted head on his shoulder is bent,
  And deep is the sigh of his breath,
And with steadfast dejection his eyes are intent
  On the fetters that link him to death.

'Tis sorrow enough on that visage to gaze,
  That body dismissed from his care;
Yet my fancy has pierced to his heart, and portrays[5]
  More terrible images there.

Notes

[8] *My journey will be shortly run* cf. *Samson Agonistes* 597–8: 'My race of glory run, and race of shame, / And I shall shortly be with them that rest.'

THE CONVICT

[1] Prison reform was a topical issue at the time this poem was first composed, thanks partly to Godwin, who had argued, in the second edition of *Political Justice* (1796), that it was wrong to punish someone 'for what is past and irrecoverable' (ii 322).

[2] *the calm season of rest* i.e. night-time.

[3] *I pause* i.e. to allow his eyes to adjust to the darkness.

[4] *grate* barred window to the prison cell.

[5] *portrays* visualizes.

His bones are consumed and his life-blood is dried,
With wishes the past to undo;
And his crime, through the pains that o'erwhelm him, descried,
Still[6] blackens and grows on his view.

When from the dark synod[7] or blood-reeking field,[8]
To his chamber the monarch is led,
All soothers of sense their soft virtue shall yield,
And quietness pillow his head.

But if grief, self-consumed, in oblivion would doze,
And conscience her tortures appease,
Mid tumult and uproar this man must repose
In the comfortless vault of disease.

When his fetters at night have so pressed on his limbs
That the weight can no longer be borne,
If, while a half-slumber his memory bedims,
The wretch on his pallet should turn;

While the jail-mastiff howls at the dull-clanking chain,
From the roots of his hair there shall start
A thousand sharp punctures of cold-sweating pain,
And terror shall leap at his heart.

But now he half-raises his deep-sunken eye,
And the motion unsettles a tear;
The silence of sorrow it seems to supply,
And asks of me why I am here.

'Poor victim! No idle intruder has stood
With o'erweening complacence our state to compare –
But one whose first wish is the wish to be good
Is come as a brother thy sorrows to share.[9]

At thy name, though Compassion her nature resign,
Though in Virtue's proud mouth thy report be a stain,[10]
My care, if the arm of the mighty were mine,
Would plant thee where yet thou might'st blossom again.'[11]

Notes

[6] *Still* continually.

[7] *dark synod* secret council.

[8] *blood-reeking field* the battlefield that literally stinks of blood. The monarch is, by implication, far more culpable than the convict. Britain had been at war with France since 1798.

[9] *No idle . . . share* The narrator tells the convict that he comes not to gloat over, but to share his grief.

[10] *At thy . . . stain* Compassionate people feel nothing for convicts, while the virtuous cannot mention them without feeling tainted.

[11] *My care . . . again* perhaps a plea for the humane transportation of convicts, though it is just as likely that Wordsworth is just suggesting that they be given a second chance.

Lines written a few miles above Tintern Abbey, on revisiting the banks of the Wye during a tour, 13 July 1798 (by Wordsworth, composed 10–13 July 1798)[1] (see Plate 8)

Five years have passed; five summers, with the length
Of five long winters![2] And again I hear
These waters, rolling from their mountain springs
With a sweet inland murmur.[3] Once again
Do I behold these steep and lofty cliffs,
Which on a wild secluded scene impress
Thoughts of more deep seclusion, and connect
The landscape with the quiet of the sky.[4]
The day is come when I again repose
Here, under this dark sycamore, and view
These plots of cottage-ground, these orchard-tufts,
Which, at this season, with their unripe fruits,
Among the woods and copses lose themselves,
Nor, with their green and simple hue, disturb
The wild green landscape. Once again I see
These hedgerows – hardly hedgerows, little lines
Of sportive wood run wild; these pastoral farms[5]
Green to the very door; and wreaths of smoke
Sent up in silence from among the trees,
With some uncertain notice,[6] as might seem,
Of vagrant dwellers in the houseless woods,
Or of some hermit's cave, where by his fire
The hermit sits alone.[7]
                                        Though absent long,
These forms of beauty[8] have not been to me
As is a landscape to a blind man's eye;
But oft, in lonely rooms, and mid the din
Of towns and cities, I have owed to them,

Notes

LINES WRITTEN A FEW MILES ABOVE TINTERN ABBEY

[1] 'No poem of mine was composed under circumstances more pleasant for me to remember than this: I began it upon leaving Tintern, after crossing the Wye, and concluded it just as I was entering Bristol in the evening, after a ramble of four or five days, with my sister. Not a line of it was altered, and not any part of it written down till I reached Bristol. It was published almost immediately after in the little volume of which so much has been said in these notes' (*FN* 15). In conversation and correspondence Wordsworth and his circle usually referred to the poem as 'Tintern Abbey'.

[2] *Five years . . . winters* Wordsworth's first visit to the Wye was in August 1793.

[3] 'The river is not affected by the tides a few miles above Tintern' (Wordsworth's note). Wordsworth later commented: 'The Wye is a stately and majestic river from its width and depth, but never slow and sluggish; you can always hear its murmur. It travels through a woody country, now varied with cottages and green meadows, and now with huge and fantastic rocks' (Christopher Wordsworth, *Memoirs of William Wordsworth* (2 vols, London, 1851), i 117).

[4] *connect . . . sky* The fusing of landscape and sky is a picturesque touch derived from William Gilpin, *Observations on the River Wye* (1782): 'Many of the furnaces on the banks of the river consume charcoal which is manufactured on the spot, and the smoke (which is frequently seen issuing from the sides of the hills, and spreading its thin veil over a part of them) beautifully breaks their lines, and unites them with the sky' (p. 12).

[5] *pastoral farms* sheep farms.

[6] *With some uncertain notice* faintly discernible.

[7] *as might seem . . . alone* The 'vagrant dwellers' (gypsies) and hermit are figments of the imagination; the smoke comes from the charcoal-furnaces (see note 4 above).

[8] *forms of beauty* natural objects, impressed on the mind in the manner described at *Pedlar* 27–43.

In hours of weariness, sensations sweet,
Felt in the blood, and felt along the heart,
And passing even into my purer mind[9]
With tranquil restoration;[10] feelings too
Of unremembered pleasure – such, perhaps,
As may have had no trivial influence
On that best portion of a good man's life,
His little, nameless, unremembered acts
Of kindness and of love. Nor less, I trust,
To them I may have owed another gift,
Of aspect more sublime; that blessed mood
In which the burden of the mystery,[11]
In which the heavy and the weary weight
Of all this unintelligible world
Is lightened – that serene and blessed mood
In which the affections gently lead us on
Until the breath of this corporeal frame[12]
And even the motion of our human blood
Almost suspended, we are laid asleep
In body, and become a living soul,[13]
While with an eye made quiet by the power
Of harmony, and the deep power of joy,[14]
We see into the life of things.[15]
If this
Be but a vain belief – yet oh, how oft
In darkness, and amid the many shapes
Of joyless daylight, when the fretful stir
Unprofitable,[16] and the fever of the world,
Have hung upon the beatings of my heart,
How oft, in spirit, have I turned to thee,
Oh sylvan[17] Wye! Thou wanderer through the woods,
How often has my spirit turned to thee!
And now, with gleams of half-extinguished thought,
With many recognitions dim and faint
And somewhat of a sad perplexity,[18]
The picture of the mind revives again;
While here I stand, not only with the sense

Notes

[9] *my purer mind* i.e. the spiritual element of his being.

[10] *restoration* The memory of the 'forms of beauty' is spiritually restorative, like the spots of time, *Two-Part Prelude* i 294, by which the mind is 'nourished and invisibly repaired'.

[11] *the burden of the mystery* Life is burdensome because the affairs of the world are so often 'unintelligible' (l. 41).

[12] *corporeal frame* the physical body.

[13] *become a living soul* alluding to the moment at which Adam was created by God: 'And the Lord God formed man of the dust of the ground, and breathed into his nostrils the breath of life; and man became a living soul' (Genesis 2:7).

[14] *the deep power of joy* 'Joy', during the Alfoxden period, is the name given by Coleridge and Wordsworth to the pantheist perception of Nature as unified by a universal life force; see *Pedlar* 217–18: 'in all things / He saw one life, and felt that it was joy.'

[15] *Until the breath . . . things* The 'forms of beauty' induce a mystic state in which the poet is released from the confines of the body and instead engages, in a completely spiritual manner, with the life-force of the universe.

[16] *Unprofitable* probably an echo of *Hamlet*: 'How . . . unprofitable / Seem to me all the uses of this world' (I ii 133–4).

[17] *sylvan* wooded.

[18] *sad perplexity* due to the fact that the 'recognitions' are only 'dim and faint'; the memorized 'forms of beauty' do not match up to what is before the poet as he looks down at the same scene five years later.

Of present pleasure, but with pleasing thoughts
That in this moment there is life and food
For future years.[19] And so I dare to hope,
Though changed, no doubt, from what I was when first
I came among these hills, when like a roe[20]
I bounded o'er the mountains[21] by the sides
Of the deep rivers and the lonely streams
Wherever nature led, more like a man
Flying from something that he dreads than one
Who sought the thing he loved.[22] For nature then
(The coarser pleasures of my boyish days
And their glad animal movements all gone by)
To me was all in all.
I cannot paint
What then I was. The sounding cataract
Haunted me like a passion;[23] the tall rock,
The mountain, and the deep and gloomy wood,
Their colours and their forms, were then to me
An appetite, a feeling and a love
That had no need of a remoter charm
By thought supplied, or any interest
Unborrowed from the eye. That time is past,
And all its aching joys are now no more,
And all its dizzy raptures. Not for this
Faint I, nor mourn, nor murmur; other gifts
Have followed – for such loss, I would believe,
Abundant recompense. For I have learned
To look on nature not as in the hour
Of thoughtless youth, but hearing oftentimes
The still, sad[24] music of humanity,
Not harsh nor grating, though of ample power
To chasten and subdue. And I have felt
A presence that disturbs me with the joy
Of elevated thoughts, a sense sublime
Of something[25] far more deeply interfused,
Whose dwelling is the light of setting suns,
And the round ocean, and the living air,
And the blue sky, and in the mind of man[26] –

Notes

[19] *pleasing thoughts . . . future years* In the five years since his first visit he has derived pleasure from recollections of the Wye Valley; he hopes that the present visit will provide similar benefits in future. The habit of storing mental pictures is described, months before, in *Pedlar* 30–43.

[20] *roe* small deer.

[21] *like a roe . . . mountains* from Song of Solomon 2: 8–9: 'The voice of my beloved! Behold, he cometh leaping upon the mountains, skipping upon the hills. My beloved is like a roe, or a young hart.'

[22] *more like . . . loved* In August 1793 Wordsworth was wandering across the countryside in a state of severe emotional distress, as the newly declared war on France prevented him from returning to Annette Vallon who, in December 1792, had given birth to their illegitimate daughter, Caroline.

[23] *The sounding . . . passion* cf. *Pedlar* 31–4, where images of landscape 'almost seemed / To haunt the bodily sense'.

[24] *still, sad* Wordsworth alludes to the 'still, small' voice of God that speaks to Elijah, 1 Kings 19: 12.

[25] *something* Wordsworth is deliberately unspecific, but there is little doubt that he is thinking in terms of a universal, pantheistic life force – the One Life.

[26] *the light . . . man* probably, as critics argue, a recollection of Virgil, *Aeneid* vi 724–7 (translated): 'an inner spirit sustains the sky and the earth and the sea, the bright globe of the moon, the sun and the stars, and mind activates the whole frame, pervading all its members, and blends with the great body.'

A motion and a spirit that impels
All thinking things, all objects of all thought,
And rolls through all things.[27] Therefore am I still
A lover of the meadows and the woods
And mountains, and of all that we behold
From this green earth, of all the mighty world
Of eye and ear (both what they half-create[28]
And what perceive) – well-pleased to recognize
In nature and the language of the sense,[29]
The anchor of my purest[30] thoughts, the nurse,
The guide, the guardian of my heart, and soul
Of all my moral being.
Nor, perchance,
If I were not thus taught, should I the more
Suffer my genial spirits[31] to decay;
For thou[32] art with me,[33] here, upon the banks
Of this fair river – thou, my dearest friend,
My dear, dear friend, and in thy voice I catch
The language of my former heart, and read
My former pleasures in the shooting lights
Of thy wild eyes. Oh, yet a little while
May I behold in thee what I was once,
My dear, dear sister! And this prayer I make,
Knowing that Nature never did betray
The heart that loved her;[34] 'tis her privilege,
Through all the years of this our life, to lead
From joy to joy, for she can so inform[35]
The mind that is within us, so impress
With quietness and beauty, and so feed
With lofty thoughts, that neither evil tongues,[36]
Rash judgements, nor the sneers of selfish men,
Nor greetings where no kindness is, nor all
The dreary intercourse of daily life,
Shall e'er prevail against us, or disturb
Our cheerful faith that all which we behold
Is full of blessings. Therefore let the moon
Shine on thee in thy solitary walk,
And let the misty mountain-winds be free
To blow against thee. And in after-years,
When these wild ecstasies shall be matured

Notes

[27] *And I have felt . . . things* This remarkable affirmation of the pantheist One Life should be compared with *Pedlar* 204–22, composed only months before.

[28] *half-create* Wordsworth notes a borrowing from Young, *Night Thoughts* vi 427: 'And half-create the wondrous world they [the senses] see'.

[29] *the language of the sense* what the senses perceive.

[30] *purest* most spiritual.

[31] *genial spirits* creative energies, vitality. Cf. *Samson Agonistes* 594: 'So much I feel my genial spirits droop.'

[32] *thou* Dorothy Wordsworth.

[33] *For thou art with me* an allusion to the most famous of the Psalms: 'Yea, though I walk through the valley of the shadow of death, I will fear no evil: for thou art with me; thy rod and thy staff, they comfort me' (23: 4).

[34] *that Nature . . . her* probably an allusion to Samuel Daniel, *The Civil Wars* ii 225–6: 'Here have you craggy rocks to take your part, / That never will betray their faith to you.'

[35] *inform* imbue.

[36] *evil tongues* Milton describes himself as 'On evil times though fallen, and evil tongues' (*Paradise Lost* vii 26).

Into a sober pleasure, when thy mind
Shall be a mansion[37] for all lovely forms,
Thy memory be as a dwelling-place
For all sweet sounds and harmonies – oh then
If solitude, or fear, or pain, or grief
Should be thy portion,[38] with what healing thoughts
Of tender joy wilt thou remember me,
And these my exhortations! Nor perchance,
If I should be where I no more can hear
Thy voice, nor catch from thy wild eyes these gleams
Of past existence, wilt thou then forget
That on the banks of this delightful stream
We stood together; and that I, so long
A worshipper of nature, hither came
Unwearied in that service – rather say
With warmer love, oh with far deeper zeal
Of holier love! Nor wilt thou then forget
That, after many wanderings, many years
Of absence, these steep woods and lofty cliffs
And this green pastoral landscape, were to me
More dear, both for themselves, and for thy sake.

William Wordsworth (1770–1850)

William Wordsworth was born on 7 April 1770, the second son of John Wordsworth Sr (1741–83), legal agent for Sir James Lowther, later Earl of Lonsdale, the most powerful landowner in the Lake District. The family was relatively well off, and lived in the grandest house in the main street of the small town of Cockermouth; he attended the local school with Fletcher Christian (later famous for his role in the mutiny on the *Bounty*). In March 1778 Wordsworth's mother Ann died of pneumonia. He was sent to Hawkshead Grammar School in May 1779, on the other side of the Lake District. Here he received an excellent education in the English grammar-school tradition, acquiring expertise in Latin, Greek and mathematics.[1] He lodged with the kindly Ann Tyson in Colthouse, and prospered under two teachers, William Taylor and Thomas Bowman, recent graduates from Cambridge University. They loved contemporary poetry, and with their encouragement Wordsworth became an early reader, and admirer, of Cowper, Charlotte Smith, Helen Maria Williams and Anna Laetitia Barbauld.[2]

When he was 13 his father died, leaving him and his siblings (Richard, Christopher, John and Dorothy) orphans. It was a devastating event in emotional and psychological terms, but its most

Notes

[37] *mansion* home, resting-place.
[38] *portion* lot, fate.

William Wordsworth

[1] For more on Wordsworth's education, see Richard W. Clancey, *Wordsworth's Classical Undersong: Education, Rhetoric, and Poetic Truth* (Basingstoke, 2000).

[2] Contrary to the observations of some critics, Wordsworth was throughout his life a keen admirer of the work of women writers.

immediate effect was to render the Wordsworth children homeless and at the mercy of relatives, not all of whom were happy to spend money on their upbringing and education. This would be a problem throughout the next decade, as the sums necessary for Wordsworth's university years were stinted, and pressure exerted to compel him to become a clergyman.

His good relationships with friends and teachers at school seem to have insulated him from the full impact of his parents' deaths. It was at Hawkshead, when he was 15, that he began to compose poetry; his teachers quickly recognized that he was producing something better than what was being published at the time. When he was 16, one of his sonnets appeared in a major periodical of the day, the *European Magazine*. By the time he left Hawkshead he had written a long poem, 'The Vale of Esthwaite', which included an early version of the spot of time in which he waited for the horses to take him home to see his dying father.[3]

'Beside the pleasant mills of Trompington / I laughed with Chaucer,'[4] he would write in *The Prelude* – and Wordsworth's Cambridge years seem to have been happy ones. He continued to write poetry but after his first year failed to distinguish himself in his academic studies. The University syllabus was concerned chiefly with the work of the Greek mathematician Euclid, which he had mastered at Hawkshead;[5] in later years he suggested that the level of proficiency he had reached at school was so high that he felt unchallenged by the Cambridge course. Nonetheless, he did better in College examinations on Latin and Greek literature, which he translated in his spare time. His relatives were impatient for him to enter the church and become financially independent, and it may have been partly in reaction to them that he went to France for a lengthy walking tour in 1790 with a College friend, Robert Jones.

France was in the grip of Revolution, and Wordsworth and Jones were swept up in it. Wordsworth returned on his own in 1791–2, and stayed for a time at Blois, near Orléans. Here he met Michel Beaupuy, the soldier who was to serve as a mentor (see p. 559, below), and had an affair with a French girl, Annette Vallon. She gave birth to a child, Caroline Wordsworth, in December 1792. By then he was back in London, publishing his poems, *An Evening Walk* and *Descriptive Sketches*, as a means of raising money before returning to France to join his family. Although he succeeded in getting the poems into print (they appeared in late January 1793), his return to France was delayed by the execution of Louis XVI in February, which led almost immediately to Britain's declaration of war on France.

His failure to return to Annette and their child caused Wordsworth profound distress – a response that strengthened his attachment to the French cause. One symptom of this was the composition in spring 1793 of a pamphlet defending regicide, *A Letter to the Bishop of Llandaff*. It argued from a republican position, and suggested that popular violence was an inevitable (and excusable) by-product of revolution. This was the poet who would later become famous for writing about celandines and primroses! Had it been published at the time it was composed, Wordsworth would almost certainly have been locked up and tried for treason. Fortunately for him, it did not appear in print until 1876. The angry, frustrated pamphleteer went on a walking tour that took him to Portsmouth, where he saw the British fleet preparing to fight the French; Salisbury Plain, which he crossed in a hallucinatory state

Notes

[3] A full text may be found in *Wordsworth: The Earliest Poems 1785–1790* ed. Duncan Wu (Manchester and New York, 2002). For Wordsworth's explanation of spots of time see p. 455.

[4] See *Five-Book Prelude* iii 279–80;

[5] The Pedlar, too, is a mathematician (*Pedlar* 146–53). Euclid makes an appearance in Book V of the *Thirteen-Book Prelude* (p. 551).

(recalled in *Thirteen-Book Prelude* xii 312ff.); Tintern Abbey, which he saw for the first time (see *Tintern Abbey*, especially ll. 76–84), and finally Wales, where he stayed with Robert Jones.

At this period the radical philosophy of Godwin's *Political Justice* (see pp. 151–5) had a strong appeal for him in its non-violent affirmation of revolutionary ideals, and when he returned to London in 1795 the two men became friends, breakfasting together with other young rationalists. What he liked about Godwinism was its uncompromising imposition of justice on a society that was (in his view) corrupt; in Godwin's system there was no escape – the process by which reason would take over the running of society was inescapable. But Wordsworth would soon tire of it, because Godwin outlawed emotion. And as he matured in his early twenties, Wordsworth began to come to terms with the grief stemming from the early loss of his parents.

By 1796 he had rejected the strictures of Godwinian rationalism and was living with Dorothy at Racedown Lodge in Dorset. In this obscure country retreat he nurtured his continuing interest in radical politics while continuing to write poetry – though at this stage he published very little. The closeness of their adult years owed much to grief at their parents' loss in 1783; they loved each other – but as brother and sister, not lovers (as some misguided critics have suggested). They lived together as early as 1794, at Windy Brow near Keswick in the Lake District, and it seemed natural that they set up house together in Dorset. Dorothy had no one else with whom she could live, and in those days it was not respectable for single women to live on their own. Her healing and kindly influence provided the environment in which Wordsworth was able to compose the earliest version of *The Ruined Cottage*, which Coleridge probably heard when he visited the Wordsworths at Racedown in June 1797.

The Ruined Cottage is Wordsworth's first indisputably great poem. It has been aptly described by its first editor, Jonathan Wordsworth, as a 'tragedy'; what distinguishes the version presented here (completed in the spring of 1798) is the profound optimism of its conclusion, in which, confronted by the pain and suffering of the ill-fated Margaret, we are directed to feel consolation at the sight of the spear-grass and other plants in her garden:

> I well remember that those very plumes,
> Those weeds, and the high speargrass on that wall,
> By mist and silent raindrops silvered o'er,
> As once I passed did to my mind convey
> So still an image of tranquillity,
> So calm and still, and looked so beautiful
> Amid the uneasy thoughts which filled my mind,
> That what we feel of sorrow and despair
> From ruin and from change, and all the grief
> The passing shows of being leave behind,
> Appeared an idle dream that could not live
> Where meditation was.
>
> (ll. 513–24)

This is a central statement in English Romantic poetry: life is indeed full of sorrow and despair, but surrounded by the spear-grass and weeds that are all that remain of Margaret's garden, such 'grief' becomes no more than an 'idle dream'. Why is this 'Romantic'? Not because it minimizes Margaret's tragic life, but because it places her suffering in the context of an optimistic philosophy that sees it as part of a cosmic process of becoming. In another poem, written in late 1798, Wordsworth would describe a girl whose dead body was 'Rolled round in earth's diurnal course / With rocks and stones and trees!' (see p. 478). As with Margaret, the attitude is one of acceptance and equanimity. Grief is a powerful force throughout Wordsworth's poetry – as it was throughout his life – but in the great work of 1797–8 he attempts to accommodate it into a vision of transcendence.

This reflects Coleridge's influence, and his plans for a philosophical poem called 'The Recluse', of which *The Ruined Cottage* was to have been part. Seeing around them the continuing hardship and suffering which the French Revolution was intended to counteract, Wordsworth and Coleridge asked themselves how the poet might improve the human condition. The answer incorporated elements of both men's thought. Its central tenet (later to be the subject of *Prelude* Book VIII) was that love of Nature led to love of mankind; that is to say, the intensely perceived, and imaginatively enhanced, engagement with the pantheist life-force running through the natural world could lead, in turn, to a sympathy and compassion for all things, including other members of the human race. Essentially, 'The Recluse' would argue that if everyone was 'converted' by imaginative process, the world would be improved, and a sort of Utopia created in which humanity could live without strife.

The emphasis on the role of Nature was distinctively Wordsworthian, and is attributed to him when it appears for the first time in Coleridge's poetry, in 'This Lime-Tree Bower my Prison', in July 1797 (pp. 612–17); the pantheism came from Coleridge, who had espoused his conviction in a unifying, all-embracing divinity since 1794, when he wrote the first version of *Religious Musings* (see pp. 608–10). A poem that explained how love of Nature could lead to universal brotherhood would, Wordsworth and Coleridge believed, precipitate the process. Like Godwin, they foresaw a world in which, filled with the love that flowed through nature, people would come to love one other. It was something they had already experienced for themselves.

> And from the blessed power that rolls
> About, below, above,
> We'll frame the measure of our souls –
> They shall be tuned to love.
> ('Lines Written at a Small Distance from My House' 33–6)

They believed that this would lead to the millennium – Christ's thousand-year rule on earth. This was not as mad as it now sounds. It was widely believed, as the eighteenth century came to an end, that the American and French Revolutions were harbingers of universal betterment, and that the scriptural prophecies of St John the Divine were about to be fulfilled. 'The ancient tradition that the world will be consumed in fire at the end of six thousand years is true, as I have heard from hell,' Blake had written in *The Marriage of Heaven and Hell* (1790). Neither Wordsworth nor Coleridge would have declared their convictions quite so nakedly, but a millennial brotherhood was in their sights as they devised 'The Recluse'. Coleridge had wanted to write such a poem himself (he wanted to call it *The Brook*), but he so idolized Wordsworth that he persuaded him that he was the only poet fitted to compose it. What more noble aim than to write the poem that would, in effect, precipitate the end of the world? It would dominate Wordsworth's poetic ambitions for the next forty years.

Despite Wordsworth's initial enthusiasm for the concept of pantheism – the belief that the God is all, and all is God – it virtually disappeared from his poetry after 1798. Perhaps that was symptomatic of the fact that he found it hard to sustain a belief in the optimistic philosophy they formulated in 1797–8. And perhaps that, in turn, was why he never completed 'The Recluse'. Not that he didn't try. 'Home at Grasmere', Part I, Book I of 'The Recluse' was probably composed in 1800; 'A Tuft of Primroses' was written in 1806; and *The Excursion*, a lengthy preliminary to 'The Recluse', was published in 1814. But Wordsworth of all people was aware that none of these works, which contain poetry worthy of our attention, fulfilled the ambitions of the work originally mapped out in 1797–8. Nor did they amount to a complete poem. Claims that his entire published output constituted 'The Recluse' were symptomatic of a growing desperation at the knowledge that the great epic that would justify his career as a poet was slipping from his grasp.

When Coleridge expressed his disappointment with *The Excursion* in a letter of 1815 (see pp. 689–91), Wordsworth seems to have lost any real conviction that he could continue with 'The Recluse', although he would make spasmodic but unpersuasive attempts to return to it. In truth, as readers of Coleridge's letter may suspect, the original scheme for 'The Recluse' was so unrealistic, so insanely grandiose, that no human being could ever have composed it. However, for a short while in 1798, Wordsworth's belief in it enabled him to write a number of works that he would not otherwise have been able to write, now regarded as among his finest, all of which are included here: *The Ruined Cottage, The Pedlar, There is an Active Principle, Not Useless do I Deem* and *The Discharged Soldier.*

Besides 'The Recluse', Wordsworth and Coleridge spent their remarkable year of creative work together planning and writing the first volume of *Lyrical Ballads* (pp. 327–411), designed to help them raise money to visit Germany – then the intellectual hub of Europe, and the perfect place for the author of 'The Recluse'. They travelled to Germany in early autumn 1798. Held up in Goslar, a small medieval market-town in the Harz mountains, by what he believed to be the severest winter of the eighteenth century, Wordsworth began a six-week period of intense creative activity which included composition of most of the first Part of what we now call 'The Two-Part Prelude'. Perhaps he could not get on with 'The Recluse', but *The Prelude* was the epic poem he was destined to write. It demanded no special academic study, as 'The Recluse' was expected to; its subject-matter was mined from within – something for which Wordsworth had a special talent. This was his great work, even if he did not know it yet.

'The Two-Part Prelude' begins with a despairing question – 'Was it for this . . . ?' – because he had lost hope of continuing with 'The Recluse'. And yet the clear, lucid poetry of *The Prelude* poured out of him. It was not essentially philosophical, as 'The Recluse' was to be, but surveyed his teenage years in Hawkshead, during and after the death of his father. Throughout the intervening years those powerful memories had acquired layers of reflection and meditation, and the changes wrought by time on what seems to be an unshakeable hold on the past are an important part of the subject of *The Prelude*. At first we may not notice how our first glance of the woman with the pitcher on her head in the second of the concluding spots of time in Part I has altered, however subtly, when we see her the second time, so that it is not the pitcher, but 'her garments vexed and tossed' that strike us (see p. 456). What is going on? Wordsworth wants to be faithful to the way in which the mind works constantly, perhaps without our being aware of it, on the past – rewriting it in the light of the powerful emotions trapped in the texture of the memory itself. We may not be fully aware of those emotions (in this case fear and apprehension), but they are present nonetheless.

Part II of the poem was finished in late 1799, just as the Wordsworths, back in England, moved into Dove Cottage in Grasmere. Wordsworth thought of *The Prelude* as an autobiographical poem addressed to Coleridge – out of guilt, largely, because it was not 'The Recluse'. He intended to write a third Part, and attempted it in 1801. In early 1804 he completely reorganized it, revising what he had done in 1799, adding such passages as the description of the ascent of Snowdon (p. 566), the Winander boy (p. 474) and the infant prodigy (p. 543), to produce the *Five-Book Prelude*. Not satisfied with that, he continued work throughout 1804–5, until completion of *The Thirteen-Book Prelude* in early 1806. It still had no title – those of the various versions are attributed to it by editors. He could not leave it alone and returned to it periodically until he died. Editors have uncovered no less than sixteen distinct versions in his manuscripts, the most important of which are now in print. When he died it was further altered by his executors before publication in 1850. So it was that one of the greatest masterpieces of the Romantic period was known at first hand only to a small coterie – Coleridge, Dorothy, De Quincey and the poet's immediate circle. Byron, Shelley and Keats knew of it only by repute. Had they had the opportunity to read it, their regard for its author might have been higher.

Though available to the Victorians, *The Prelude* had little appeal to Victorian readers. Its success has come in the last hundred years. We should not be surprised. The story it tells – of promise under constant threat; of a man scarred by loss; of a poetic sensibility and its long, arduous journey to maturity – is of our own time, one that speaks to our own preoccupation with the individual psyche and the perilous course we must all trace from youth to adulthood. It is Wordsworth's victory, for it possesses an enduring relevance that 'The Recluse' would never have had.

Today Wordsworth is regarded as one of the foremost of the Romantics; during the early 1800s, however, his poetry was not widely known and often misunderstood – in particular, 'The Thorn', 'We Are Seven' and 'The Excursion' came in for vitriolic attack and ridicule. By the 1820s he had acquired the status of a father-figure to the second-generation writers such as Keats, Byron and Shelley, who accused him of having betrayed the radical leanings of earlier work (see for instance 'To Wordsworth', p.1052, and the dedication to *Don Juan*, pp. 933–7). It is true that he became more conservative, as the apostrophe to Burke in the *Fourteen-Book Prelude* (see p. 579) reveals. In 1821, in his defence, he told a correspondent:

> If I were addressing those who have dealt so liberally with the words 'renegado', 'apostate', etc., I should retort the charge upon them, and say, *you* have been deluded by places and persons, while I have stuck to principles – I abandoned France and her rulers when they abandoned the struggle for Liberty, gave themselves up to Tyranny, and endeavoured to enslave the world. I disapproved of the war against France at its commencement, thinking (which was perhaps an error) that it might have been avoided. But after Buonaparte had violated the independence of Switzerland, my heart turned against him and the nation that could submit to be the instrument of such an outrage. (*LY* i 97)

Politics aside, Wordsworth (see Plate 9) is sometimes said to have become a worse poet as he got older. That is unfair, though his verse naturally reflected changes in him. All the same, the conclusion to *The River Duddon* (1820) is one of the finest sonnets he ever composed – a meditation on the past, and the damage wrought by time on human potential (p. 578). *Airey-Force Valley* (p. 580) is as good as anything in *The Prelude*, while the *Extempore Effusion Upon the Death of James Hogg* stands as one of the most impressive elegies of the Romantic period, if only for the remarkable stanza at its heart:

> Like clouds that rake the mountain-summits,
> Or waves that own no curbing hand,
> How fast has brother followed brother,
> From sunshine to the sunless land!
> (ll. 21–4)

By 1843, when he was appointed Poet Laureate, Wordsworth's reputation was at its height. At the age of 73, he had outlived all the other major Romantic writers and was still composing and revising. In his final years he was awarded honorary degrees from Durham and Oxford and supervised the final lifetime edition of his poetry in 1849–50. He remains the most highly regarded, and enduringly popular, of the Romantics.

Further reading

Wordsworth's complete poetical works are available in the Cornell Wordsworth Series under the general editorship of Stephen M. Parrish. *The Wordsworth Circle*, a quarterly journal edited by Marilyn Gaull, publishes articles on Wordsworth and his contemporaries.

Jonathan Bate, *The Song of the Earth* (London, 2000).

David Bromwich, *Disowned by Memory: Wordsworth's Poetry of the 1790s* (Chicago, 1998).

The Cambridge Companion to Wordsworth ed. Stephen Gill (Cambridge, 2003).

Richard W. Clancey, *Wordsworth's Classical Undersong: Education, Rhetoric, and Poetic Truth* (Basingstoke, 2000).

Stephen Gill, *William Wordsworth: A Life* (Oxford, 1989).

Stephen Gill, *Wordsworth and the Victorians* (Oxford, 1998).

Geoffrey Hartman, *Wordsworth's Poetry 1787–1814* (New Haven, 1964).

Herbert Lindenberger, *On Wordsworth's Prelude* (Princeton, NJ, 1963).

Alan Liu, *Wordsworth: The Sense of History* (Stanford, Calif., 1989).

Lucy Newlyn, *Coleridge, Wordsworth, and the Language of Allusion* (Oxford, 1986).

Michael O'Neill, *Romanticism and the Self-Conscious Poem* (Oxford, 1997), chapter 2.

Richard Onorato, *The Character of the Poet: Wordsworth in The Prelude* (Princeton, NJ, 1971).

W. J. B. Owen, *Wordsworth as Critic* (Oxford, 1969).

Stephen M. Parrish, *The Art of the Lyrical Ballads* (Cambridge, Mass., 1973).

Nicholas Roe, *Wordsworth and Coleridge: The Radical Years* (Oxford, 1988).

Jonathan Wordsworth, *William Wordsworth: The Borders of Vision* (Oxford, 1982).

Duncan Wu, *Wordsworth: An Inner Life* (Oxford, 2002).

A Night-Piece (composed by 25 January 1798; edited from MS)[1]

The sky is overspread
With a close veil of one continuous cloud
All whitened by the moon, that just appears
A dim-seen orb, yet chequers not the ground
With any shadow – plant, or tower, or tree.
At last, a pleasant gleam breaks forth at once,
An instantaneous light; the musing man
Who walks along with his eyes bent to earth
Is startled. He looks about, the clouds are split
Asunder, and above his head he views
The clear moon, and the glory of the heavens.
There in a black-blue vault she sails along,
Followed by multitudes of stars, that small,
And bright, and sharp, along the gloomy vault
Drive as she drives. How fast they wheel away,
Yet vanish not! The wind is in the trees,
But they are silent;[2] still they roll along
Immeasurably distant, and the vault
Built round by those white clouds, enormous clouds,
Still deepens its interminable depth.

Notes

A NIGHT-PIECE

[1] This poem was, Wordsworth recalled many years after its composition, 'Composed upon the road between Nether Stowey and Alfoxden, extempore. I distinctly recollect the very moment I was struck, as described, "He looks up at the clouds, etc." ' (*FN* 13). Critics note that it reworks a number of images and expressions from a journal entry by Dorothy of 25 January 1798: 'The sky spread over with one continuous cloud, whitened by the light of the moon, which, though her dim shape was seen, did not throw forth so strong a light as to chequer the earth with shadows. At once the clouds seemed to cleave asunder, and left her in the centre of a black-blue vault. She sailed along, followed by multitudes of stars, small, and bright, and sharp. Their brightness seemed concentrated (half-moon)' (*DWJ* i 2).

[2] *But they are silent* David Chandler suggests that this is a reply to the question posed by Mrs Barbauld in 'A Summer Evening's Meditation': 'But are they silent all? Or is there not / A tongue in every star that talks with man . . . ?' (ll. 48–9)

At length the vision closes, and the mind,
Not undisturbed by the deep joy it feels,
Which slowly settles into peaceful calm,
Is left to muse upon the solemn scene.

The Discharged Soldier (composed late January 1798; edited from MS)[1]

I love to walk
Along the public way, when, for the night
Deserted in its silence, it assumes
A character of deeper quietness
Than pathless solitudes. At such a time
I slowly mounted up a steep ascent[2]
Where the road's watery surface, to the ridge
Of that sharp rising, glittered in the moon,
And seemed before my eyes another stream[3]
Stealing with silent lapse[4] to join the brook[5]
That murmured in the valley.
On I passed
Tranquil, receiving in my own despite
Amusement as I slowly passed along,
From such near objects as from time to time
Perforce disturbed the slumber of the sense
Quiescent[6] and disposed to sympathy,
With an exhausted mind worn out by toil
And all unworthy of the deeper joy
Which waits on distant prospect – cliff or sea,
The dark blue vault, and universe of stars.
Thus did I steal along that silent road,
My body from the stillness drinking in
A restoration like the calm of sleep,
But sweeter far. Above, before, behind,
Around me, all was peace and solitude:
I looked not round, nor did the solitude
Speak to my eye, but it was heard and felt.
Oh happy state, what beauteous pictures now
Rose in harmonious imagery! They rose
As from some distant region of my soul
And came along like dreams; yet such as left
Obscurely mingled with their passing forms

Notes

The Discharged Soldier

[1] This poem constituted part of Wordsworth's never-completed epic poem, *The Recluse* (see pp. 413–14), before being incorporated first into *Five-Book Prelude* iv 185–321, and then into *Thirteen-Book Prelude* iv 363–504.

[2] *a steep ascent* Briers Brow, above the ferry on the western shore of Windermere.

[3] *And seemed . . . stream* A few days before this line was composed, 31 January 1798, Dorothy had written: 'The road to the village of Holford glittered like another stream' (*DWJ* i 5).

[4] *lapse* flow; cf. *Paradise Lost* viii 263: 'And liquid lapse of murmuring streams'.

[5] *brook* Sawrey Brook.

[6] *Quiescent* at repose, inert.

A consciousness of animal delight,
A self-possession felt in every pause
And every gentle movement of my frame.[7]
While thus I wandered, step by step led on,
It chanced a sudden turning of the road
Presented to my view an uncouth shape,[8]
So near that, stepping back into the shade
Of a thick hawthorn, I could mark him well,
Myself unseen. He was in stature tall,
A foot above man's common measure tall,
And lank, and upright. There was in his form
A meagre stiffness. You might almost think
That his bones wounded him. His legs were long,
So long and shapeless that I looked at them
Forgetful of the body they sustained.
His arms were long and lean, his hands were bare;
His visage, wasted though it seemed, was large
In feature, his cheeks sunken, and his mouth
Showed ghastly[9] in the moonlight; from behind
A milestone propped him,[10] and his figure seemed
Half-sitting and half-standing. I could mark
That he was clad in military garb,
Though faded yet entire. His face was turned
Towards the road, yet not as if he sought
For any living object. He appeared
Forlorn and desolate, a man cut off
From all his kind, and more than half detached
From his own nature.
He was alone,
Had no attendant, neither dog, nor staff,
Nor knapsack; in his very dress appeared
A desolation, a simplicity
That appertained[11] to solitude. I think
If but a glove had dangled in his hand,
It would have made him more akin to man.
Long time I scanned him with a mingled sense
Of fear and sorrow. From his lips meanwhile
There issued murmuring sounds, as if of pain
Or of uneasy thought, yet still his form
Kept the same fearful steadiness. His shadow
Lay at his feet and moved not.
In a glen
Hard by, a village stood,[12] whose silent doors

Notes

[7] *self-possession . . . frame* awareness of physical well-being diffused through the body and its activity.

[8] *an uncouth shape* perhaps a reminiscence of *Paradise Lost* ii 666, which describes Death: 'The other shape, / If shape it might be called that shape had none'. Wordsworth would have known Burke's comments on the lines (see pp. 9–10 above).

[9] *ghastly* ghost-like, pale.

[10] *A milestone propped him* the third milestone from Hawkshead, just beyond Far Sawrey; the milestone has since disappeared from that spot.

[11] *appertained* belonged.

[12] *a village stood* Far Sawrey.

Were visible among the scattered trees,
Scarce distant from the spot an arrow's flight.[13]
I wished to see him move, but he remained
Fixed to his place, and still from time to time
Sent forth a murmuring voice of dead[14] complaint,
A groan scarce audible. Yet all the while
The chained mastiff in his wooden house
Was vexed, and from among the village trees
Howled, never ceasing. Not without reproach
Had I prolonged my watch, and now, confirmed,
And my heart's specious cowardice[15] subdued,
I left the shady nook where I had stood
And hailed the stranger. From his resting-place
He rose, and with his lean and wasted arm
In measured gesture lifted to his head
Returned my salutation. A short while
I held discourse on things indifferent
And casual matter. He meanwhile had ceased
From all complaint, his station he resumed,
Propped by the milestone as before. And when, erelong,
I asked his history, he in reply
Was neither slow nor eager; but, unmoved,[16]
And with a quiet uncomplaining voice,
A stately air of mild indifference,
He told a simple fact – that he had been
A soldier, to the tropic isles[17] had gone,
Whence he had landed now some ten days past;
That on his landing he had been dismissed,
And with the little strength he yet had left
Was travelling to regain his native home.
At this I turned and through the trees looked down
Into the village. All were gone to rest,
Nor smoke nor any taper[18] light appeared,
But every silent window to the moon
Shone with a yellow glitter. 'No one there',
Said I, 'is waking; we must measure back
The way which we have come. Behind yon wood
A labourer dwells, an honest man and kind;
He will not murmur should we break his rest,
And he will give you food (if food you need)
And lodging for the night.' At this he stooped
And from the ground took up an oaken staff
By me yet unobserved – a traveller's staff

Notes

[13] *an arrow's flight* approximately 300 yards.
[14] *dead* muffled, deadened.
[15] *my heart's specious cowardice* he was motivated by fear rather than kindness.
[16] *unmoved* without emotion.
[17] *tropic isles* West Indies. An anachronism: Wordsworth has in mind the campaigns against the French that occurred in the mid-1790s, although the encounter took place during the long vacation of 1788. Conditions were bad – 40,000 British troops had died of yellow fever by 1796. Survivors were often diseased, and had no alternative but to beg in the streets.
[18] *taper* candle.

Which I suppose from his slack hand had dropped,
And, such the languor of the weary man,
Had lain till now neglected in the grass,
But not forgotten.
Back we turned and shaped
Our course toward the cottage. He appeared
To travel without pain, and I beheld
With ill-suppressed astonishment his tall
And ghostly figure moving at my side.
As we advanced I asked him for what cause
He tarried there, nor had demanded rest
At any inn or cottage. He replied,
'My weakness made me loath to move; in truth
I felt myself at ease, and much relieved,
But that the village mastiff fretted me,
And every second moment rang a peal
Felt at my very heart. I do not know
What ailed him, but it seemed as if the dog
Were howling to the murmur of the stream.'
While thus we travelled on I did not fail
To question him of what he had endured
From war, and battle, and the pestilence.[19]
He all the while was in demeanour calm,
Concise in answer. Solemn and sublime
He might have seemed, but that in all he said
There was a strange half-absence, and a tone
Of weakness and indifference, as of one
Remembering the importance of his theme
But feeling it no longer. We advanced
Slowly, and ere we to the wood were come,
Discourse had ceased. Together on we passed
In silence through the shades gloomy and dark;
Then, turning up along an open field,
We gained the cottage. At the door I knocked,
And called aloud, 'My friend, here is a man
By sickness overcome. Beneath your roof
This night let him find rest, and give him food –
The service if need be I will requite.'
Assured that now my comrade would repose
In comfort, I entreated that henceforth
He would not linger in the public ways
But at the door of cottage or of inn
Demand the succour which his state required,
And told him, feeble as he was, 'twere fit
He asked relief or alms. At this reproof,
With the same ghastly mildness in his look,
He said, 'My trust is in the God of Heaven,
And in the eye of him that passes me.'

Notes

[19] *the pestilence* yellow fever.

By this the labourer had unlocked the door,
And now my comrade touched his hat again
With his lean hand, and in a voice that seemed
To speak with a reviving interest
Till then unfelt, he thanked me; I returned
The blessing of the poor unhappy man,
And so we parted.

The Ruined Cottage (composed 1797–8; edited from MS)[1]

First Part

'Twas summer and the sun was mounted high;
Along the south the uplands feebly glared
Through a pale steam, and all the northern downs,
In clearer air ascending, showed far off
Their surfaces with shadows dappled o'er
Of deep embattled clouds.[2] Far as the sight
Could reach those many shadows lay in spots
Determined and unmoved, with steady beams
Of clear and pleasant sunshine interposed –
Pleasant to him who on the soft cool moss
Extends his careless limbs beside the root
Of some huge oak whose aged branches make
A twilight[3] of their own, a dewy shade
Where the wren warbles while the dreaming man,
Half-conscious of that soothing melody,
With sidelong eye looks out upon the scene,
By those impending branches made more soft,
More soft and distant.
Other lot was mine.
Across a bare wide common I had toiled
With languid feet which by the slippery ground
Were baffled still; and when I stretched myself
On the brown earth my limbs from very heat
Could find no rest, nor my weak arm disperse
The insect host which gathered round my face
And joined their murmurs to the tedious noise

Notes

THE RUINED COTTAGE

[1] In its brief original form, which does not survive, *The Ruined Cottage* was read to Coleridge on 5 June 1797. This version stems from work of February–March 1798, when it was lengthened and given a more formal structure by the addition of the opening section (ll. 1–54), the central transition (ll. 185–237), and the final lines of reconciliation (ll. 493–538). Wordsworth also added, with Coleridge's encouragement, a long philosophical account of the narrator's life which, though important, had the effect of unbalancing the poem. Wordsworth therefore removed it and until 1804 regarded it as a separate work, *The Pedlar* (see pp. 435–44). *The Ruined Cottage* meanwhile was the compact and tightly constructed poem printed here. It was later revised with *The Pedlar* for *The Excursion* (1814).

[2] *deep embattled clouds* an allusion to Charlotte Smith, *Sonnet LIX* 3–4: 'Sudden, from many a deep embattled cloud / Terrific thunders burst.'

[3] *twilight* The 'twilight' in the midst of sunshine is highly reminiscent of Milton's 'darkness visible', and looks back to Virgil's 'ingenti ramorum protegat umbra' (*Georgics* ii 489).

Of seeds of bursting gorse that crackled round.
I rose and turned towards a group of trees
Which midway in that level stood alone;
And thither come at length, beneath a shade
Of clustering elms[4] that sprang from the same root
I found a ruined house, four naked walls[5]
That stared upon each other. I looked round,
And near the door I saw an aged man
Alone and stretched upon the cottage bench;
An iron-pointed staff lay at his side.
With instantaneous joy I recognized
That pride of nature and of lowly life,
The venerable Armytage, a friend
As dear to me as is the setting sun.[6]
Two days before
We had been fellow-travellers. I knew
That he was in this neighbourhood, and now
Delighted found him here in the cool shade.
He lay, his pack of rustic merchandise
Pillowing his head. I guess he had no thought
Of his way-wandering life. His eyes were shut,
The shadows of the breezy elms above
Dappled his face. With thirsty heat oppressed
At length I hailed him, glad to see his hat
Bedewed with water-drops, as if the brim
Had newly scooped a running stream. He rose
And pointing to a sunflower, bade me climb
The [ ][7] wall where that same gaudy flower
Looked out upon the road.
It was a plot
Of garden-ground now wild, its matted weeds
Marked with the steps of those whom as they passed,
The gooseberry-trees that shot in long lank slips,
Or currants hanging from their leafless stems
In scanty strings, had tempted to o'erleap
The broken wall. Within that cheerless spot,
Where two tall hedgerows of thick willow boughs
Joined in a damp cold nook, I found a well
Half covered up with willow-flowers and weeds.
I slaked my thirst and to the shady bench

Notes

[4] *clustering elms* Elms tend to grow in clusters as groups of them spring from a single root; they are now a rare sight in England thanks to the ravages of Dutch elm disease in the 1970s.

[5] *four naked walls* The nakedness of the walls tends to humanize them and emphasize their vulnerability; cf. *Two-Part Prelude* i 343.

[6] *a friend . . . sun* In the original *Ruined Cottage* of summer 1797 the Pedlar had addressed the poet as 'stranger'. By February 1798 he was the mouthpiece for Wordsworth's new philosophy of redemption (see p. 444), and the two protagonists had been made old friends as a way of increasing the reader's confidence in what he had to say. It was daring to make the protagonist a Pedlar; when the poem was revised and published in 1814 critics like Francis Jeffrey disapproved of a lower-class character being given such an exalted role: 'Did Mr Wordsworth really imagine that his favourite doctrines were likely to gain anything in point of effect or authority by being put into the mouth of a person accustomed to higgle about tape, or brass sleeve-buttons?' For Jeffrey's comments, see p. 719.

[7] There is a gap in the MS at this point.

Returned, and while I stood unbonneted[8]
To catch the motion of the cooler air
The old man said, 'I see around me here
Things which you cannot see. We die, my friend,
Nor we alone, but that which each man loved
And prized in his peculiar nook of earth
Dies with him, or is changed, and very soon
Even of the good is no memorial left.
The poets, in their elegies and songs
Lamenting the departed, call the groves,
They call upon the hills and streams to mourn,
And senseless rocks – nor idly, for they speak
In these their invocations with a voice
Obedient to the strong creative power
Of human passion. Sympathies there are
More tranquil, yet perhaps of kindred birth,
That steal upon the meditative mind
And grow with thought. Beside yon spring I stood,
And eyed its waters till we seemed to feel
One sadness, they and I. For them a bond
Of brotherhood is broken: time has been
When every day the touch of human hand
Disturbed their stillness, and they ministered
To human comfort. When I stooped to drink
A spider's web hung to the water's edge,
And on the wet and slimy footstone lay
The useless fragment of a wooden bowl;[9]
It moved my very heart.
The day has been
When I could never pass this road but she
Who lived within these walls, when I appeared,
A daughter's welcome gave me, and I loved her
As my own child. Oh sir! The good die first,
And they whose hearts are dry as summer dust
Burn to the socket.[10] Many a passenger[11]
Has blessed poor Margaret for her gentle looks
When she upheld the cool refreshment drawn
From that forsaken spring, and no one came
But he was welcome, no one went away
But that it seemed she loved him. She is dead,
The worm is on her cheek,[12] and this poor hut,
Stripped of its outward garb of household flowers,

Notes

[8] *unbonneted* without his hat.

[9] *The useless . . . bowl* cf. the final chapter of Ecclesiastes, 'Remember now thy Creator in the days of thy youth . . . Or ever the silver cord be loosed, or the golden bowl be broken, or the pitcher be broken at the fountain, or the wheel broken at the cistern. Then shall the dust return to the earth as it was: and the spirit shall return unto God who gave it.'

[10] *Burn to the socket* The image is of a candle burning down to its socket in a candlestick.

[11] *passenger* passer-by.

[12] *The worm is on her cheek* cf. Viola, in *Twelfth Night* II iv 110–12: 'she never told her love, / But let concealment, like a worm in the bud, / Feed on her damask cheek.'

Of rose and sweetbriar, offers to the wind
A cold bare wall whose earthy top is tricked[13]
With weeds and the rank speargrass. She is dead,
And nettles rot and adders sun themselves
Where we have sat together while she nursed
Her infant at her breast. The unshod colt,
The wandering heifer and the potter's ass,
Find shelter now within the chimney-wall
Where I have seen her evening hearthstone blaze
And through the window spread upon the road
Its cheerful light. You will forgive me, sir,
But often on this cottage do I muse
As on a picture, till my wiser mind
Sinks, yielding to the foolishness of grief.
   She had a husband, an industrious man,
Sober and steady. I have heard her say
That he was up and busy at his loom
In summer ere the mower's scythe had swept
The dewy grass, and in the early spring
Ere the last star had vanished. They who passed
At evening, from behind the garden-fence
Might hear his busy spade, which he would ply
After his daily work till the daylight
Was gone, and every leaf and flower were lost
In the dark hedges. So they passed their days
In peace and comfort, and two pretty babes
Were their best hope next to the God in heaven.
You may remember, now some ten years gone,
Two blighting seasons when the fields were left
With half a harvest. It pleased heaven to add
A worse affliction in the plague of war;[14]
A happy land was stricken to the heart –
'Twas a sad time of sorrow and distress.
A wanderer among the cottages,
I with my pack of winter raiment[15] saw
The hardships of that season. Many rich
Sunk down as in a dream among the poor,
And of the poor did many cease to be,
And their place knew them not. Meanwhile, abridged
Of daily comforts, gladly reconciled
To numerous self-denials, Margaret
Went struggling on through those calamitous years
With cheerful hope. But ere the second autumn,
A fever seized her husband. In disease
He lingered long, and when his strength returned
He found the little he had stored to meet
The hour of accident, or crippling age,

Notes

[13] *tricked* decked.

[14] *war* England had been at war with France for five years as Wordsworth was writing in 1798; it should be borne in mind, however, that the poem is set during the aftermath of the American War, which had ended in 1783.

[15] *winter raiment* warm clothes to sell to cottagers.

Was all consumed. As I have said, 'twas now
A time of trouble: shoals of artisans[16]
Were from their daily labour turned away
To hang for bread on parish charity,[17]
They and their wives and children – happier far
Could they have lived as do the little birds
That peck along the hedges, or the kite[18]
That makes her dwelling in the mountain rocks.
Ill fared it now with Robert, he who dwelt
In this poor cottage. At his door he stood
And whistled many a snatch of merry tunes
That had no mirth in them, or with his knife
Carved uncouth[19] figures on the heads of sticks;
Then idly sought about through every nook
Of house or garden any casual task
Of use or ornament, and with a strange,
Amusing but uneasy novelty
He blended where he might the various tasks
Of summer, autumn, winter, and of spring.
But this endured not; his good humour soon
Became a weight in which no pleasure was,
And poverty brought on a petted[20] mood
And a sore temper. Day by day he drooped,[21]
And he would leave his home, and to the town
Without an errand would he turn his steps,
Or wander here and there among the fields.
One while he would speak lightly of his babes
And with a cruel tongue; at other times
He played with them wild freaks of merriment,
And 'twas a piteous thing to see the looks
Of the poor innocent children. "Every smile",
Said Margaret to me here beneath these trees,
"Made my heart bleed."'
At this the old man paused,
And looking up to those enormous elms
He said, ''Tis now the hour of deepest noon.
At this still season of repose and peace,
This hour when all things which are not at rest
Are cheerful, while this multitude of flies
Fills all the air with happy melody,
Why should a tear be in an old man's eye?
Why should we thus with an untoward[22] mind,
And in the weakness of humanity,
From natural wisdom turn our hearts away,
To natural comfort shut our eyes and ears,
And feeding on disquiet, thus disturb
The calm of Nature with our restless thoughts?'

Notes

[16] *shoals of artisans* crowds of workmen.
[17] *parish charity* Until the early part of the century, the poor were the responsibility of their local parish, which received no government funding to help them.
[18] *kite* large hawk.
[19] *uncouth* grotesque, ugly.
[20] *petted* peevish.
[21] *he drooped* an echo of Milton, *Samson Agonistes* 594: 'So much I feel my genial spirits droop.'
[22] *untoward* stubborn, perverse.

Second Part

He spake with somewhat of a solemn tone,
But when he ended there was in his face
Such easy cheerfulness, a look so mild,
That for a little time it stole away
All recollection, and that simple tale
Passed from my mind like a forgotten sound.
A while on trivial things we held discourse,
To me soon tasteless.[23] In my own despite
I thought of that poor woman as of one
Whom I had known and loved. He had rehearsed
Her homely tale with such familiar power,
With such an active countenance, an eye
So busy, that the things of which he spake
Seemed present, and, attention now relaxed,
There was a heartfelt chillness in my veins.
I rose, and turning from that breezy shade
Went out into the open air, and stood
To drink the comfort of the warmer sun.
Long time I had not stayed ere, looking round
Upon that tranquil ruin, I returned
And begged of the old man that for my sake
He would resume his story.
He replied,
'It were a wantonness,[24] and would demand
Severe reproof, if we were men whose hearts
Could hold vain dalliance with[25] the misery
Even of the dead, contented thence to draw
A momentary pleasure, never marked
By reason, barren of all future good.
But we have known that there is often found
In mournful thoughts, and always might be found,
A power to virtue friendly; were't not so
I am a dreamer among men, indeed
An idle dreamer. 'Tis a common tale
By moving accidents uncharactered,
A tale of silent suffering, hardly clothed
In bodily form, and to the grosser sense
But ill adapted – scarcely palpable
To him who does not think. But at your bidding
I will proceed.

Notes

[23] *tasteless* without taste, insipid.
[24] *wantonness* self-indulgence.
[25] *hold vain dalliance with* draw entertainment from.

While thus it fared with them
To whom this cottage till that hapless year
Had been a blessed home, it was my chance
To travel in a country far remote;
And glad I was when, halting by yon gate
That leads from the green lane, again I saw
These lofty elm-trees. Long I did not rest –
With many pleasant thoughts I cheered my way
O'er the flat common. At the door arrived,
I knocked, and when I entered, with the hope
Of usual greeting, Margaret looked at me
A little while, then turned her head away
Speechless, and sitting down upon a chair
Wept bitterly. I wist[26] not what to do,
Or how to speak to her. Poor wretch! At last
She rose from off her seat – and then, oh sir!
I cannot tell how she pronounced my name:
With fervent love, and with a face of grief
Unutterably helpless, and a look
That seemed to cling upon me, she enquired
If I had seen her husband. As she spake
A strange surprise and fear came to my heart,
Nor had I power to answer ere she told
That he had disappeared – just two months gone.
He left his house: two wretched days had passed,
And on the third by the first break of light,
Within her casement[27] full in view she saw
A purse of gold.[28] "I trembled at the sight",
Said Margaret, "for I knew it was his hand
That placed it there. And on that very day
By one, a stranger, from my husband sent,
The tidings came that he had joined a troop
Of soldiers going to a distant land.[29]
He left me thus. Poor man, he had not heart
To take a farewell of me, and he feared
That I should follow with my babes, and sink
Beneath the misery of a soldier's life."
This tale did Margaret tell with many tears,
And when she ended I had little power
To give her comfort, and was glad to take
Such words of hope from her own mouth as served
To cheer us both. But long we had not talked
Ere we built up a pile of better thoughts,
And with a brighter eye she looked around
As if she had been shedding tears of joy.
We parted. It was then the early spring;

Notes

[26] *wist* knew.

[27] *casement* window.

[28] *A purse of gold* A 'bounty' of three guineas was paid to men when they enlisted – a strong incentive for poor men with starving families.

[29] *a distant land* America.

I left her busy with her garden tools,
And well remember, o'er that fence she looked,
And, while I paced along the footway path,
Called out and sent a blessing after me,
With tender cheerfulness, and with a voice
That seemed the very sound of happy thoughts.
  I roved o'er many a hill and many a dale
With this my weary load, in heat and cold,
Through many a wood and many an open ground,
In sunshine or in shade, in wet or fair,
Now blithe, now drooping, as it might befall;
My best companions now the driving winds
And now the "trotting brooks"[30] and whispering trees,
And now the music of my own sad steps,
With many a short-lived thought that passed between
And disappeared. I came this way again
Towards the wane of summer, when the wheat
Was yellow, and the soft and bladed grass
Sprang up afresh and o'er the hayfield spread
Its tender green. When I had reached the door
I found that she was absent. In the shade
Where we now sit, I waited her return.
Her cottage in its outward look appeared
As cheerful as before, in any show
Of neatness little changed – but that I thought
The honeysuckle crowded round the door
And from the wall hung down in heavier wreaths,
And knots of worthless stonecrop started out
Along the window's edge, and grew like weeds
Against the lower panes. I turned aside
And strolled into her garden. It was changed.
The unprofitable bindweed spread his bells
From side to side, and with unwieldy wreaths
Had dragged the rose from its sustaining wall
And bent it down to earth.[31] The border tufts,
Daisy, and thrift, and lowly camomile,
And thyme, had straggled out into the paths
Which they were used to deck.
                                        Ere this an hour
Was wasted. Back I turned my restless steps,
And as I walked before the door it chanced
A stranger passed, and guessing whom I sought,
He said that she was used to ramble far.

Notes

[30] *trotting brooks* an allusion to Burns's *To William Simpson*, about the poet and his relationship to nature:

> The Muse, nae poet ever fand her,
> Till by himsel he learned to wander
> Adown some trottin burn's meander . . .
>
> (ll. 85–7)

[31] *the rose . . . earth* a symbol of Margaret herself, without the support of her husband.

The sun was sinking in the west, and now
I sat with sad impatience. From within
Her solitary infant cried aloud.
The spot though fair seemed very desolate,
The longer I remained more desolate;
And looking round I saw the corner-stones,
Till then unmarked, on either side the door
With dull red stains discoloured, and stuck o'er
With tufts and hairs of wool, as if the sheep
That feed upon the commons thither came
Familiarly, and found a couching-place
Even at her threshold.
                                        The house-clock struck eight:
I turned and saw her distant a few steps.
Her face was pale and thin, her figure too
Was changed. As she unlocked the door she said,
"It grieves me you have waited here so long,
But in good truth I've wandered much of late,
And sometimes – to my shame I speak – have need
Of my best prayers to bring me back again."
While on the board[32] she spread our evening meal
She told me she had lost her elder child,
That he for months had been a serving-boy,
Apprenticed by the parish.[33] "I perceive
You look at me, and you have cause. Today
I have been travelling far, and many days
About the fields I wander, knowing this
Only, that what I seek I cannot find.
And so I waste my time: for I am changed,
And to myself", said she, "have done much wrong,
And to this helpless infant. I have slept
Weeping, and weeping I have waked. My tears
Have flowed as if my body were not such
As others are, and I could never die.
But I am now in mind and in my heart
More easy, and I hope", said she, "that Heaven
Will give me patience to endure the things
Which I behold at home."
                                                It would have grieved
Your very soul to see her. Sir, I feel
The story linger in my heart. I fear
'Tis long and tedious, but my spirit clings
To that poor woman. So familiarly
Do I perceive her manner and her look
And presence, and so deeply do I feel
Her goodness, that not seldom in my walks
A momentary trance comes over me

Notes

[32] *board* table.

[33] *Apprenticed by the parish* Margaret has allowed her son to become an apprentice because she would no longer be responsible for clothing and feeding him.

And to myself I seem to muse on one
By sorrow laid asleep or borne away,
A human being destined to awake
To human life, or something very near
To human life, when he shall come again
For whom she suffered. Sir, it would have grieved
Your very soul to see her: evermore
Her eyelids drooped, her eyes were downward cast,
And when she at her table gave me food
She did not look at me. Her voice was low,
Her body was subdued. In every act
Pertaining to her house-affairs appeared
The careless stillness which a thinking mind
Gives to an idle matter. Still she sighed,
But yet no motion of the breast was seen,
No heaving of the heart. While by the fire
We sat together, sighs came on my ear –
I knew not how, and hardly whence, they came.
I took my staff, and when I kissed her babe
The tears stood in her eyes. I left her then
With the best hope and comfort I could give:
She thanked me for my will, but for my hope
It seemed she did not thank me.
                                        I returned
And took my rounds along this road again
Ere on its sunny bank the primrose flower
Had chronicled the earliest day of spring.
I found her sad and drooping. She had learned
No tidings of her husband. If he lived,
She knew not that he lived: if he were dead,
She knew not he was dead. She seemed the same
In person or appearance, but her house
Bespoke a sleepy hand of negligence.
The floor was neither dry nor neat, the hearth
Was comfortless,[34]
The windows too were dim, and her few books,[35]
Which one upon the other heretofore
Had been piled up against the corner-panes
In seemly order, now with straggling leaves
Lay scattered here and there, open or shut,
As they had chanced to fall. Her infant babe
Had from its mother caught the trick[36] of grief,
And sighed among its playthings. Once again
I turned towards the garden-gate, and saw
More plainly still that poverty and grief
Were now come nearer to her. The earth was hard,

Notes

[34] Line defective in the MS.

[35] *her few books* Margaret is literate; this was unusual. In 1795 60% of the female population was unable to read or write. Most received little, if any, formal education.

[36] *trick* habit.

With weeds defaced and knots of withered grass;
No ridges there appeared of clear black mould,[37]
No winter greenness. Of her herbs and flowers
It seemed the better part were gnawed away
Or trampled on the earth. A chain of straw,
Which had been twisted round the tender stem
Of a young apple-tree, lay at its root;
The bark was nibbled round by truant sheep.
Margaret stood near, her infant in her arms,
And, seeing that my eye was on the tree,
She said, "I fear it will be dead and gone
Ere Robert come again."
Towards the house
Together we returned, and she enquired
If I had any hope. But for her babe,
And for her little friendless boy, she said,
She had no wish to live – that she must die
Of sorrow. Yet I saw the idle loom
Still in its place. His Sunday garments hung
Upon the self-same nail, his very staff
Stood undisturbed behind the door. And when
I passed this way beaten by autumn winds,
She told me that her little babe was dead
And she was left alone. That very time,
I yet remember, through the miry lane
She walked with me a mile, when the bare trees
Trickled with foggy damps, and in such sort
That any heart had ached to hear her, begged
That wheresoe'er I went I still would ask
For him whom she had lost. We parted then,
Our final parting; for from that time forth
Did many seasons pass ere I returned
Into this tract[38] again.
Five tedious years[39]
She lingered in unquiet widowhood,
A wife and widow. Needs must it have been
A sore heart-wasting. I have heard, my friend,
That in that broken arbour she would sit
The idle length of half a sabbath day –
There, where you see the toadstool's lazy head –
And when a dog passed by she still would quit
The shade and look abroad. On this old bench
For hours she sat, and evermore her eye
Was busy in the distance, shaping things
Which made her heart beat quick. Seest thou that path? –
The greensward now has broken its grey line –

Notes

[37] *mould* earth.

[38] *tract* district.

[39] *Five tedious years* ll. 446–92 were the first to be written. They were inspired by Southey's account of a war widow in *Joan of Arc* (1797), Book VII, who is described as 'tortured with vain hope' for her absent husband.

There to and fro she paced through many a day
Of the warm summer, from a belt of flax
That girt her waist, spinning the long-drawn thread
With backward steps.[40] Yet ever as there passed
A man whose garments showed the soldier's red,[41]
Or crippled mendicant[42] in sailor's garb,
The little child who sat to turn the wheel
Ceased from his toil, and she, with faltering voice,
Expecting still[43] to learn her husband's fate,
Made many a fond enquiry; and when they
Whose presence gave no comfort were gone by,
Her heart was still more sad. And by yon gate
Which bars the traveller's road, she often stood,
And when a stranger horseman came, the latch
Would lift, and in his face look wistfully,
Most happy if from aught discovered there
Of tender feeling she might dare repeat
The same sad question.
                                        Meanwhile her poor hut
Sunk to decay; for he was gone, whose hand
At the first nippings of October frost
Closed up each chink, and with fresh bands of straw
Chequered the green-grown thatch. And so she lived
Through the long winter, reckless[44] and alone,
Till this reft[45] house, by frost, and thaw, and rain,
Was sapped; and when she slept, the nightly damps
Did chill her breast, and in the stormy day
Her tattered clothes[46] were ruffled by the wind
Even at the side of her own fire. Yet still
She loved this wretched spot, nor would for worlds
Have parted hence; and still that length of road,
And this rude bench, one torturing hope endeared,
Fast rooted at her heart. And here, my friend,
In sickness she remained; and here she died,
Last human tenant of these ruined walls.'[47]
   The old man ceased; he saw that I was moved.
From that low bench, rising instinctively,
I turned aside in weakness, nor had power
To thank him for the tale which he had told.
I stood, and leaning o'er the garden gate
Reviewed that woman's sufferings; and it seemed
To comfort me while with a brother's love
I blessed her in the impotence of grief.
At length towards the cottage I returned

Notes

[40] *from a belt . . . steps* Robert had been a weaver, and Margaret supports herself in her last years by spinning flax.

[41] *the soldier's red* The British army wore red uniforms, making them easy targets on the battlefield.

[42] *mendicant* beggar.

[43] *still* always.

[44] *reckless* not caring (i.e. for herself).

[45] *reft* bereft (i.e. without Robert).

[46] *Her tattered clothes* a detail picked up from Cowper's Crazy Kate (see p. 18).

[47] The poem originally ended at this point. All that follows was composed in spring 1798.

Fondly, and traced with milder interest
That secret spirit of humanity
Which, mid the calm oblivious[48] tendencies
Of Nature, mid her plants, her weeds and flowers,
And silent overgrowings, still survived.
The old man, seeing this, resumed, and said,
'My friend, enough to sorrow have you given,
The purposes of wisdom ask no more:
Be wise and cheerful, and no longer read
The forms of things with an unworthy eye:
She sleeps in the calm earth, and peace is here.
I well remember that those very plumes,
Those weeds, and the high speargrass on that wall,
By mist and silent raindrops silvered o'er,
As once I passed did to my mind convey
So still an image of tranquillity,
So calm and still, and looked so beautiful
Amid the uneasy thoughts which filled my mind,
That what we feel of sorrow and despair
From ruin and from change, and all the grief
The passing shows of being leave behind,
Appeared an idle dream that could not live
Where meditation was. I turned away,
And walked along my road in happiness.'[49]
He ceased. By this the sun declining shot
A slant and mellow radiance, which began
To fall upon us where beneath the trees
We sat on that low bench. And now we felt,
Admonished thus, the sweet hour coming on:
A linnet warbled from those lofty elms,
A thrush sang loud, and other melodies
At distance heard peopled the milder air.
The old man rose and hoisted up his load;
Together casting then a farewell look

Notes

[48] *oblivious* Nature carries on oblivious to human affairs.

[49] *happiness* an astonishing conclusion, all things considered. The philosophy of consolation and, ultimately, redemption, that underlies this work requires that we regard injustice and suffering as an 'idle dream', mere shadows of a higher and brighter reality to come – an insight delivered, crucially, by the 'forms of things'. This is even clearer in the early version of these lines, found in Wordsworth's notebook:

> And waking from the silence of my grief
> I looked around. The cottage and the elms,
> The road, the pathway and the garden wall
> Which old and loose and mossy o'er the road
> Hung bellying, all appeared – I know not how
> But to some eye within me – all appeared
> Colours and forms of a strange discipline.
> The trouble which they sent into my thought
> Was sweet. I looked and looked again, and to myself
> I seemed a better and a wiser man.

The concept that grief might be an 'idle dream' originated with Bishop Berkeley, whose ideas informed Coleridge's *Religious Musings*:

> Believe thou, oh my soul,
> Life is a vision shadowy of truth,
> And vice, and anguish, and the wormy grave,
> Shapes of a dream. The veiling clouds retire,
> And lo! – the throne of the redeeming God . . .
> (ll. 396–400)

Unlike Coleridge (and many others at this period), Wordsworth did not expect a Christian apocalypse, but the Pedlar's meditation asks us to see Margaret's life and death in terms of universal harmony.

Upon those silent walls, we left the shade,
And ere the stars were visible attained
A rustic inn, our evening resting-place.

The Pedlar (composed February–March 1798, edited from MS)[1]

Him had I seen the day before, alone
And in the middle of the public way,
Standing to rest himself. His eyes were turned
Towards the setting sun, while, with that staff
Behind him fixed, he propped a long white pack
Which crossed his shoulders, wares for maids who live
In lonely villages or straggling huts.[2]
I knew him[3] – he was born of lowly race
On Cumbrian hills, and I have seen the tear
Stand in his luminous[4] eye when he described
The house in which his early youth was passed,
And found I was no stranger to the spot.
I loved to hear him talk of former days
And tell how when a child, ere[5] yet of age
To be a shepherd, he had learned to read
His bible in a school that stood alone,
Sole building on a mountain's dreary edge,
Far from the sight of city spire, or sound
Of minster clock. From that bleak tenement[6]
He many an evening to his distant home
In solitude returning saw the hills
Grow larger in the darkness, all alone
Beheld the stars come out above his head,
And travelled through the wood, no comrade near
To whom he might confess the things he saw.
So the foundations of his mind were laid.
In such communion, not from terror free,[7]

Notes

THE PEDLAR

[1] *The Pedlar* begins abruptly because it was composed originally as part of *The Ruined Cottage*. It is Wordsworth's earliest piece of autobiographical and philosophical poetry, and was to be a dry run for both *The Recluse* and *The Prelude* (though Wordsworth had no idea, as he composed it, that he would soon be writing an autobiographical poem; see *Two-Part Prelude* headnote, p. 448 n 1). He decided within the year that these verses were too long for incorporation into *The Ruined Cottage* and by October 1800 had turned them into an independent work entitled *The Pedlar*. For a time it was planned to publish the poem with *Christabel*, and it was revised in 1801–2 with this in mind. However, it remained unpublished (as did *Christabel*) when, in spring 1804, Wordsworth planned *The Excursion*, in which the Pedlar, renamed the Wanderer, would be a central character. *The Pedlar* and *The Ruined Cottage* were once again brought together and revised as a single entity for *The Excursion*, published in 1814. *The Pedlar* remained in manuscript in this early form until 1969.

[2] *huts* cottages.

[3] *I knew him* 'At Hawkshead also, while I was a schoolboy, there occasionally resided a packman . . . with whom I had frequent conversations upon what had befallen him, and what he had observed during his wandering life, and, as was natural, we took much to each other' (*FN* 79).

[4] *luminous* shining.

[5] *ere* before.

[6] *tenement* building.

[7] *not from terror free* Burke had celebrated the importance of fear in aesthetic terms in his *Sublime and Beautiful* (1757) (see pp. 9–10). For Wordsworth, fear is important as it stimulates and intensifies imaginative thought; cf. *Two-Part Prelude* i 67–80.

While yet a child, and long before his time,
He had perceived the presence and the power
Of greatness, and deep feelings had impressed
Great objects on his mind with portraiture
And colour so distinct that on his mind
They lay like substances, and almost seemed
To haunt the bodily sense.[8] He had received
A precious gift, for as he grew in years
With these impressions would he still compare
All his ideal stores, his shapes and forms,
And, being still unsatisfied with aught
Of dimmer character, he thence attained
An *active* power to fasten images
Upon his brain, and on their pictured lines
Intensely brooded, even[9] till they acquired
The liveliness of dreams.[10] Nor did he fail,
While yet a child, with a child's eagerness
Incessantly to turn his ear and eye
On all things which the rolling seasons brought
To feed such appetite. Nor this alone
Appeased his yearning – in the after-day[11]
Of boyhood, many an hour in caves forlorn
And in the hollow depths of naked crags
He sate, and even in their fixed lineaments,
Or[12] from the power of a peculiar eye,[13]
Or by creative feeling[14] overborne,
Or by predominance of thought[15] oppressed,
Even in their fixed and steady lineaments
He traced an ebbing and a flowing mind,
Expression ever varying.[16]
Thus informed,
He had small need of books; for many a tale
Traditionary round the mountains hung,[17]
And many a legend peopling the dark woods
Nourished imagination in her growth,
And gave the mind that apprehensive power
By which she is made quick to recognize

Notes

[8] *deep feelings . . . sense* Sublime natural forms are literally stamped ('impressed') on the child's mind as mental 'images', thanks partly to strong feelings (of fear, pain, pleasure) that he experienced in their presence.

[9] *even* to be scanned as a single syllable, 'e'en'.

[10] *he thence . . . dreams* Recollections of landscape are valued because they can be compared with the imaginary ('ideal') scenes that the child creates and stores in his head. The process by which the mind thinks about remembered landscapes ('Intensely brooded'), giving them more and more vividness, was especially important, and underlies the pantheist claims of *Tintern Abbey* 23–50, and much of the poetry in the *Two-Part Prelude.*

[11] *after-day* later time.

[12] *Or* either.

[13] *the power of a peculiar eye* especially sharp observation.

[14] *creative feeling* imaginative sympathy.

[15] *predominance of thought* dominance of thought over other kinds of response.

[16] *Even in . . . varying* Even in the solid and unmovable rocks, the Pedlar perceived the ebb and flow of a pantheistic life-force.

[17] *for many a tale . . . hung* Legends and folklore nourish the imagination as well as fear. Wordsworth presumably has in mind the kind of story that inspired *The Brothers.*

The moral properties[18] and scope of things.
But greedily he read and read again
Whate'er the rustic vicar's shelf supplied:
The life and death of martyrs who sustained
Intolerable pangs,[19] and here and there
A straggling volume, torn and incomplete,
Which left half-told the preternatural tale,
Romance of giants, chronicle of fiends,
Profuse in garniture of wooden cuts[20]
Strange and uncouth, dire faces, figures dire,
Sharp-kneed, sharp-elbowed, and lean-ankled too,
With long and ghostly shanks, forms which once seen
Could never be forgotten[21] – things though low,
Though low and humble, not to be despised
By such as have observed the curious links
With which the perishable hours of life
Are bound together, and the world of thought
Exists and is sustained.[22] Within his heart
Love was not yet, nor the pure joy of love,[23]
By sound diffused, or by the breathing air,
Or by the silent looks of happy things,
Or flowing from the universal face –
Of earth and sky. But he had felt the power
Of Nature, and already was prepared
By his intense conceptions to receive
Deeply the lesson deep of love, which he
Whom Nature, by whatever means, has taught
To feel intensely, cannot but receive.
   Ere his ninth year he had been sent abroad[24]
To tend his father's sheep; such was his task
Henceforward till the later day of youth.
Oh then, what soul was his, when on the tops
Of the high mountains he beheld the sun
Rise up and bathe the world in light! He looked,
The ocean and the earth beneath him lay
In gladness and deep joy. The clouds were touched,
And in their silent faces he did read
Unutterable love. Sound needed none,
Nor any voice of joy: his spirit drank

Notes

[18] *moral properties* It was important to Wordsworth and Coleridge that a natural education be not merely creative, but provide the individual with an understanding ('apprehensive power') of the relationships between people, and enable him to see his relationship to the world around him.

[19] *The life and death . . . pangs* Wordsworth read Foxe's *Book of Martyrs* as a schoolboy at Hawkshead.

[20] *Profuse in garniture of wooden cuts* with many woodcut illustrations.

[21] *the preternatural tale . . . forgotten* Coleridge and Wordsworth believed that children should read fairy-tales as they did when young; see Coleridge's letter to Poole, pp. 618–19.

[22] *the curious links . . . sustained* a reference to the associationist philosophy of David Hartley, which informs much of Wordsworth's thinking at this moment. The 'links' that connect the 'perishable hours of life' are emotions (arising, in this case, out of the romances of giants and chronicles of fiends) that confirm the underlying unity and order of the imaginative mind.

[23] *Within his heart . . . love* Although he can see it in the rocks (ll. 56–7) the boy cannot yet feel within himself the pantheist life-force ('love').

[24] *abroad* out.

The spectacle. Sensation, soul, and form,
All melted into him; they swallowed up
His animal being. In them did he live,
And by them did he live – they were his life.[25]
In such access of mind,[26] in such high hour
Of visitation from the living God,[27]
He did not feel the God, he felt his works.
Thought was not; in enjoyment it expired.
Such hour by prayer or praise was unprofaned;
He neither prayed, nor offered thanks or praise;
His mind was a thanksgiving to the power
That made him. It was blessedness and love.
  A shepherd on the lonely mountain-tops,
Such intercourse[28] was his, and in this sort
Was his existence oftentimes possessed.
Oh *then* how beautiful, how bright, appeared
The written promise.[29] He had early learned
To reverence the volume which displays
The mystery, the life which cannot die,
But in the mountains did he FEEL his faith,
There did he see the writing. All things there
Breathed immortality, revolving life,
And greatness still revolving, infinite.
There littleness was not, the least of things
Seemed infinite, and there his spirit shaped
Her prospects – nor did he *believe;* he saw.
What wonder if his being thus became
Sublime and comprehensive?[30] Low desires,
Low thoughts, had there no place; yet was his heart
Lowly, for he was meek in gratitude
Oft as he called to mind those ecstacies,
And whence they flowed; and from them he acquired
Wisdom which works through patience – thence he learned
In many a calmer hour of sober thought
To look on Nature with an humble heart,
Self-questioned where it did not understand,
And with a superstitious[31] eye of love.
  Thus passed the time, yet to the neighbouring town
He often went with what small overplus
His earnings might supply, and brought away
The book which most had tempted his desires

Notes

[25] *The clouds . . . life* Wordsworth draws on Coleridge's *Reflections on Having left a Place of Retirement* 26–42 (see pp. 606–7), in which the poet enjoys a similar pantheistic experience atop a hill.

[26] *access of mind* the boy is incorporated into the larger consciousness of 'the living God'. 'Mind' in this case probably means 'spirit'.

[27] *in such high hour . . . God* cf. Charles Lloyd's *London* 82, which celebrates the visionary who 'holds high converse with the present God'.

[28] *intercourse* communion.

[29] *The written promise* This phrase, and the reference to 'the writing' at l. 123, show that Wordsworth is recalling Bishop Berkeley's theory that the natural world is the symbolic language of God's thought. In the same month as *The Pedlar* Coleridge composed *Frost at Midnight* 63–7 (see pp. 626, 628).

[30] *Sublime and comprehensive* noble, lofty or well-balanced.

[31] *superstitious* conscientious.

While at the stall he read. Among the hills
He gazed upon that mighty orb[32] of song,
The divine Milton.[33] Lore of different kind,
The annual savings of a toilsome life,
The schoolmaster supplied – books that explain
The purer elements of truth involved
In lines and numbers, and by charm severe,
Especially perceived where Nature droops
And feeling is suppressed, preserve the mind
Busy in solitude and poverty.[34]
And thus employed he many a time o'erlooked[35]
The listless hours when in the hollow vale,
Hollow and green, he lay on the green turf
In lonesome idleness. What could he do?
Nature was at his heart, and he perceived,
Though yet he knew not how, a wasting[36] power
In all things which from her sweet influence
Might tend to wean[37] him. Therefore with her hues,
Her forms, and with the spirit of her forms,
He clothed the nakedness of austere truth.[38]
While yet he lingered in the elements
Of science, and among her simplest laws,
His triangles they were the stars of heaven,
The silent stars; his altitudes[39] the crag
Which is the eagle's birthplace, or some peak
Familiar with forgotten years which shows
Inscribed, as with the silence of the thought,
Upon its bleak and visionary[40] sides
The history of many a winter storm,
Or obscure records of the path of fire.[41]
Yet with these lonesome sciences he still
Continued to amuse the heavier hours
Of solitude. Yet not the less he found
In cold elation, and the lifelessness
Of truth by oversubtlety dislodged
From grandeur and from love, an idle toy,[42]
The dullest of all toys. He saw in truth
A holy spirit and a breathing soul;[43]

Notes

[32] *orb* world.

[33] *Milton* a favourite poet with young Wordsworth.

[34] *books . . . poverty* Mathematics is here regarded as inhumane, constricted and deadly. In later years Wordsworth admitted to being so good at it that he was put in the fast stream: 'When at school, I, with the other boys of the same standing, was put upon reading the first six books of Euclid, with the exception of the fifth; and also in algebra I learnt simple and quadratic equations' (*Prose Works* iii 373).

[35] *o'erlooked* didn't notice, whiled away.

[36] *wasting* destructive, consuming.

[37] *wean* A child is 'weaned' from its mother when she ceases to breastfeed it. Nature will wean the boy away from the destructive tendency of geometrical analysis.

[38] *Therefore . . . truth* The boy clothes the 'austere truth' of geometry with the colours and shapes of the landscape he loves.

[39] *altitudes* in geometrical terms, the height of a triangle measured by a perpendicular from the peak to the base.

[40] *visionary* embodying truth.

[41] *the path of fire* an apocalyptic and tumultuous event in the past, to which the mountains bear witness by their markings.

[42] *toy* hobby.

[43] *A holy spirit and a breathing soul* Nature rather than God.

He reverenced her and trembled at her look,
When with a moral beauty in her face
She led him through the worlds.
But now, before his twentieth year was passed,
Accumulated feelings pressed his heart
With an increasing weight; he was o'erpowered
By Nature, and his spirit was on fire
With restless thoughts. His eye became disturbed,[44]
And many a time he wished the winds might rage
When they were silent. Far more fondly now
Than in his earlier season did he love
Tempestuous nights, the uproar and the sounds
That live in darkness. From his intellect,
And from the stillness of abstracted thought,
He sought repose in vain. I have heard him say
That at this time he scanned the laws of light
Amid the roar of torrents, where they send
From hollow clefts up to the clearer air
A cloud of mist, which in the shining sun
Varies its rainbow hues.[45] But vainly thus,
And vainly by all other means he strove
To mitigate[46] the fever of his heart.
From Nature and her overflowing soul
He had received so much that all his thoughts
Were steeped in feeling.[47] He was only then
Contented when with bliss ineffable[48]
He felt the sentiment of being spread
O'er all that moves, and all that seemeth still,[49]
O'er all which, lost beyond the reach of thought
And human knowledge, to the human eye
Invisible, yet liveth to the heart;
O'er all that leaps, and runs, and shouts, and sings,
Or beats the gladsome air; o'er all that glides
Beneath the wave, yea, in the wave itself,
And mighty depth of waters. Wonder not
If such his transports[50] were; for in all things
He saw one life, and felt that it was joy.[51]
One song they sang, and it was audible –
Most audible then when the fleshly ear,
O'ercome by grosser prelude of that strain,[52]
Forgot its functions, and slept undisturbed.[53]

Notes

[44] *disturbed* i.e. with intense passion and creative thought.

[45] *I have heard . . . hues* The Pedlar attempts to reconcile Newtonian optics with his perceptions of Nature.

[46] *mitigate* reduce.

[47] *steeped in feeling* filled with emotion. For Wordsworth and Coleridge profound thought was possible only for those capable of deep feeling.

[48] *ineffable* indescribable.

[49] *He felt . . . still* The Pedlar is aware of some divine presence, not unlike the Platonic world soul, infused throughout the natural world.

[50] *transports* raptures.

[51] *He saw one life, and felt that it was joy* This is a primary statement of Wordsworth's pantheistic belief, arrived at under Coleridge's influence in 1798. It recurs in some of the 1798 lyrical ballads (including *Tintern Abbey*), but virtually disappears from his writing after that year.

[52] *grosser prelude of that strain* The 'music' of ordinary sense experience – so intense that it leads to loss of bodily awareness and a perception of the mystic 'song' of the one life.

[53] *From Nature . . . undisturbed* ll. 204–22 were transferred to the *Two-Part Prelude* in autumn 1799, to describe the poet's own feelings when he was 16; see *Two-Part Prelude* ii 446–64.

These things he had sustained[54] in solitude
Even till his bodily strength began to yield
Beneath their weight.[55] The mind within him burnt,
And he resolved to quit his native hills.
The father strove to make his son perceive
As clearly as the old man did himself
With what advantage he might teach a school
In the adjoining village. But the youth,
Who of this service made a short essay,[56]
Found that the wanderings of his thought were then
A misery to him, that he must resign
A task he was unable to perform.
He asked his father's blessing, and assumed
This lowly occupation. The old man
Blessed him and prayed for him, yet with a heart
Foreboding[57] evil.
                    From his native hills
He wandered far. Much did he see of men,
Their manners,[58] their enjoyments and pursuits,
Their passions and their feelings, chiefly those
Essential and eternal in the heart,
Which mid the simpler forms of rural life
Exist more simple in their elements,
And speak a plainer language.[59] Many a year
Of lonesome meditation and impelled
By curious thought he was content to toil
In this poor[60] calling, which he now pursued
From habit and necessity. He walked
Among the impure haunts of vulgar men
Unstained; the talisman[61] of constant thought
And kind sensations in a gentle heart
Preserved him. Every show of vice to him
Was a remembrancer[62] of what he knew,
Or a fresh seed of wisdom, or produced
That tender interest[63] which the virtuous feel
Among the wicked, which when truly felt
May bring the bad man nearer to the good,

Notes

[54] *sustained* suffered.

[55] *These things . . . weight* The transcendent experiences are so intense that they sap his strength.

[56] *essay* trial.

[57] *Foreboding* anticipating.

[58] *manners* way of life.

[59] *chiefly those . . . language* Partly in reaction to the ornamented and overwrought diction of much late eighteenth-century verse, Wordsworth composed a poetry reflecting the less 'sophisticated' language and experiences of country folk, which he regarded as truer to the emotions. Cf. Preface to *Lyrical Ballads* (1800): 'Low and rustic life was generally chosen because in that situation the essential passions of the heart find a better soil in which they can attain their maturity, are less under restraint, and speak a plainer and more emphatic language' (see p. 497).

[60] *poor* humble. When *The Pedlar* was published as part of *The Excursion* in 1814, Francis Jeffrey attacked the poem for the lowly origins of its protagonist (see pp. 719–20).

[61] *talisman* The Pedlar's thoughts act as a charm that protects him.

[62] *remembrancer* reminder.

[63] *tender interest* compassion.

But, innocent of evil, cannot sink
The good man to the bad.
Among the woods
A lone enthusiast, and among the hills,
Itinerant[64] in this labour he had passed
The better portion of his time, and there
From day to day had his affections[65] breathed
The wholesome air of Nature; there he kept
In solitude and solitary thought,
So pleasant were those comprehensive views,
His mind in a just equipoise[66] of love.
Serene it was, unclouded by the cares
Of ordinary life – unvexed, unwarped
By partial bondage.[67] In his steady course
No piteous revolutions[68] had he felt,
No wild varieties of joy or grief.
Unoccupied by sorrow of its own,
His heart lay open; and, by Nature tuned
And constant disposition of his thoughts
To sympathy with man,[69] he was alive
To all that was enjoyed where'er he went,
And all that was endured; and, in himself
Happy, and quiet in his cheerfulness,
He had no painful pressure from within
Which made him turn aside from wretchedness
With coward fears. He could afford to suffer
With those whom he saw suffer. Hence it was
That in our best experience he was rich,
And in the wisdom of our daily life.
For hence, minutely, in his various rounds
He had observed the progress and decay
Of many minds, of minds and bodies too –
The history of many families,
And how they prospered, how they were o'erthrown
By passion or mischance, or such misrule
Among the unthinking masters of the earth
As makes the nations groan. He was a man,
One whom you could not pass without remark[70] –
If you had met him on a rainy day
You would have stopped to look at him. Robust,
Active, and nervous,[71] was his gait; his limbs
And his whole figure breathed intelligence.
His body, tall and shapely, showed in front
A faint line of the hollowness of age,
Or rather what appeared the curvature

Notes

[64] *Itinerant* travelling.
[65] *affections* feelings.
[66] *equipoise* balance.
[67] *partial bondage* i.e. to the cares of daily life.
[68] *revolutions* reversals, changes.
[69] *by Nature tuned . . . man* Wordsworth's first statement of the belief that love of Nature leads to love of mankind, the central tenet of *The Recluse.*
[70] *without remark* without noticing.
[71] *nervous* vigorous.

Of toil; his head looked up steady and fixed.
Age had compressed the rose upon his cheek
Into a narrower circle of deep red,
But had not tamed his eye, which, under brows
Of hoary grey, had meanings which it brought
From years of youth, which, like a being made
Of many beings, he had wondrous skill
To blend with meanings of the years to come,
Human, or such as lie beyond the grave.
Long had I loved him. Oh, it was most sweet
To hear him teach in unambitious style
Reasoning and thought, by painting as he did
The manners[72] and the passions. Many a time
He made a holiday and left his pack
Behind, and we two wandered through the hills
A pair of random travellers. His eye
Flashing poetic fire he would repeat
The songs of Burns,[73] or many a ditty wild
Which he had fitted to the moorland harp –
His own sweet verse – and, as we trudged along,
Together did we make the hollow grove
Ring with our transports.
                                        Though he was untaught,
In the dead lore of schools[74] undisciplined,
Why should he grieve? He was a chosen son.
He yet retained an ear which deeply felt
The voice of Nature in the obscure wind,
The sounding mountain, and the running stream.
From deep analogies by thought supplied,
Or consciousnesses not to be subdued,
To every natural form, rock, fruit, and flower,
Even the loose stones that cover the highway,
He gave a moral life;[75] he saw them feel,
Or linked them to some feeling. In all shapes
He found a secret and mysterious soul,
A fragrance and a spirit of strange meaning.
Though poor in outward show, he was most rich:
He had a world about him – 'twas his own,
He made it – for it only lived to him,
And to the God who looked into his mind.
Such sympathies would often bear him far
In outward gesture, and in visible look,
Beyond the common seeming[76] of mankind.
Some called it madness; such it might have been,

Notes

[72] *manners* way of life.

[73] *The songs of Burns* Wordsworth praised 'the simplicity, the truth and the vigour of Burns' (*FN* 170); see also 331n7.

[74] *the dead lore of schools* philosophy.

[75] *To every . . . life* He attributed to natural things the ability to act as independent moral agents; effectively, he endowed them with human emotions.

[76] *seeming* conduct, behaviour.

But that he had an eye which evermore
Looked deep into the shades of difference[77]
As they lie hid in all exterior forms,
Near or remote, minute or vast – an eye
Which from a stone, a tree, a withered leaf,
To the broad ocean and the azure heavens
Spangled with kindred multitudes of stars,
Could find no surface where its power might sleep –
Which spake perpetual logic to his soul,
And by an unrelenting agency
Did bind his feelings even as in a chain.[78]

[*Not useless do I deem*] (composed February–March 1798; edited from MS)[1]

'Not useless do I deem
These quiet sympathies with things that hold
An inarticulate language,[2] for the man
Once taught to love such objects as excite
No morbid passions, no disquietude,
No vengeance and no hatred, needs must feel[3]
The joy of that pure principle of love
So deeply that, unsatisfied with aught
Less pure and exquisite,[4] he cannot choose
But[5] seek for objects of a kindred love
In fellow natures, and a kindred joy.
Accordingly he by degrees perceives
His feelings of aversion softened down,
A holy tenderness pervade his frame.[6]
His sanity of reason not impaired
(Say rather all his thoughts now flowing clear,
From a clear fountain flowing), he looks round,
He seeks for good, and finds the good he seeks –

Notes

[77] *shades of difference* small and subtle differences perceptible only to the trained mind.

[78] *such it might . . . chain* Not satisfied with 'exterior forms' (l. 348), or with any single 'surface' or outward appearance (l. 353), the Pedlar's eye is trained to perceive the essential – the 'perpetual logic' of existence. Because it sees through to what is permanent, it is continously active ('unrelenting' in its 'agency'), and has the effect of regulating his feelings, linking them into a chain of beneficial associations.

Not useless do I deem

[1] This was originally composed as part of 'The Pedlar', and is meant to be spoken by him. Though fragmentary, it is important because it articulates the philosophy of Wordsworth's ambitious, never-completed epic poem, *The Recluse*, describing in detail the means by which love of Nature leads to love of mankind. Years later it was revised and incorporated into *The Excursion* Book IV (ll. 1198–1292).

[2] *Not useless . . . language* In the background is the notion, derived from Bishop Berkeley, that all natural things are part of a mental 'language' spoken by God.

[3] *needs must feel* Wordsworth's language indicates that the process he is describing is necessitarian. The individual has no choice but to feel 'the joy of that pure principle of love' emanating from natural objects.

[4] *exquisite* refined.

[5] *he cannot choose / But* Once again, the language indicates that Wordsworth is talking about a necessitarian process; having felt the pantheist impulse of pure love passing through him from the natural world, the individual has no choice but to seek out 'objects of a kindred love' – that is, other people.

[6] *Accordingly . . . frame* One of the effects of the pure principle of love is to dissolve petty feelings of dislike or hostility, allowing a reciprocal love of other people to 'pervade' his spirit.

Till execration[7] and contempt are things
He only knows by name, and if he hears
From other mouth the language which they speak
He is compassionate, and has no thought,
No feeling, which can overcome his love.
And further, by contemplating these forms
In the relations which they bear to man,
We shall discover what a power is theirs
To stimulate our minds, and multiply
The spiritual presences of absent things.[8]
Then weariness[9] will cease: we shall acquire
The [ ] habit by which sense is made
Subservient still to moral purposes[10] –
A vital essence and a saving power.
Nor shall we meet an object but may read
Some sweet and tender lesson[11] to our minds
Of human suffering or of human joy.
All things shall speak of man, and we shall read
Our duties[12] in all forms; and general laws
And local accidents[13] shall tend alike
To quicken and to rouse,[14] and give the will
And power by which a [ ] chain of good[15]
Shall link us to our kind. No naked hearts,
No naked minds, shall then be left to mourn
The burden of existence.[16] Science then
Shall be a precious visitant; and then,
And only then, be worthy of her name.[17]
For then her heart shall kindle, her dull eye –
Dull and inanimate – no more shall hang
Chained to its object in brute slavery;
But better taught and mindful of its use
Legitimate, and its peculiar power
While with a patient interest it shall watch
The processes of things, and serve the cause
Of order and distinctness; not for this

Notes

[7] *execration* hatred.

[8] *And further . . . things* A central belief behind *The Recluse*: as in *Tintern Abbey*, memories of natural forms are impressed on the mind so that the individual can contemplate them at will. Their effect is to 'stimulate' or refresh the mind (cf. the 'tranquil restoration' of *Tintern Abbey* 31), and place the individual in contact, on a spiritual level, with natural objects that are not physically present. Essentially Wordsworth is claiming that everyone may experience what is described at *Tintern Abbey* 26–50.

[9] *weariness* cf. 'the heavy and the weary weight / Of all this unintelligible world', *Tintern Abbey* 40–1.

[10] *The [ ] habit . . . purposes* i.e. the way in which perceived natural forms ('sense') make us habitually 'seek for objects of a kindred love / In fellow natures' (ll. 10–11, above). Nature compels us to love our fellow man.

[11] *lesson* sermon.

[12] *Our duties* i.e. the moral duty to love our fellow man.

[13] *and general laws / And local accidents* i.e. the general laws by which love of nature leads to love of man, and unforeseen incidents ('local accidents') which bring us into contact with natural forms.

[14] *To quicken and to rouse* i.e. stimulate the mind, as at l. 27 above.

[15] *chain of good* a chain of association – that is, the beneficial chain that inspires love of mankind through love of nature.

[16] *No naked hearts . . . burden of existence* The ills of mankind – disease, war, poverty, and other social ills – will be alleviated.

[17] *Science . . . worthy of her name* Science will then be worthy of its original meaning, 'knowledge' (from Latin *scientia*).

Shall it forget that its most noble end,
Its most illustrious province, must be found
In ministering to the excursive power
Of intellect and thought. So build we up
The being that we are. For was it meant
That we should pore, and dwindle as we pore
Forever dimly pore on things minute,
On solitary objects, still beheld
In disconnection, dead and spiritless;
And still dividing, and dividing still,[18]
Break down all grandeur, still unsatisfied
With our unnatural toil while littleness
May yet become more little, waging thus
An impious warfare[19] with the very life
Of our souls? Or was it ever meant
That this majestic imagery, the clouds,
The ocean, and the firmament of heaven
Should be a barren picture on the mind?[20]
Never for ends[21] of vanity and pain
And sickly wretchedness were we endued
Amid this world of feeling and of life
With apprehension, reason, will and thought,
Affections,[22] organs, passions. Let us rise
From this oblivious sleep, these fretful dreams
Of feverish nothingness. Thus disciplined
All things shall live in us, and we shall live
In all things that surround us.[23] This I deem
Our tendency, and thus shall every day
Enlarge our sphere of pleasure and of pain.
For thus the senses and the intellect
Shall each to each supply a mutual aid,
Invigorate and sharpen and refine
Each other with a power that knows no bound,

Notes

[18] *solitary objects . . . dividing still* The kind of sterile, forensic thinking typical of some kinds of philosophy or science was regarded by Wordsworth and Coleridge as opposed to the visionary ambitions of 'The Recluse'. See, for instance, Coleridge's letter to John Thelwall of October 1797:

> I can at times feel strongly the beauties you describe, in themselves and for themselves, but more frequently all things appear little . . . the universe itself, what but an immense heap of little things? I can contemplate nothing but parts, and parts are all little! My mind feels as if it ached to behold and know something great – something one and indivisible. And it is only in the faith of this that rocks or waterfalls, mountains or caverns give me the sense of sublimity or majesty! (Griggs i 349)

[19] *impious warfare* Wordsworth is recalling the 'impious war' raised by Satan at *Paradise Lost* i 43.

[20] *Or was it ever meant . . . on the mind* Wordsworth's account of lack of imagination is inspired by Hamlet's avowal of depression:

> this most excellent canopy, the air, look you, this brave o'erhanging firmament, this majestical roof fretted with golden fire, why, it appeareth nothing to me but a foul and pestilent congregation of vapours. What a piece of work is a man, how noble in reason, how infinite in faculties, in form and moving, how express and admirable in action, how like an angel in apprehension, how like a god! – the beauty of the world; the paragon of animals; and yet to me what is this quintessence of dust? (II ii 299–308)

[21] *ends* aims.

[22] *Affections* emotions.

[23] *Thus disciplined . . . that surround us* A reiteration of the pantheist conviction that underpins much of the Alfoxden poetry, as for instance at *Pedlar* 105–6, 'In them did he live, / And by them did he live – they were his life', or 217–18: 'in all things / He saw one life, and felt that it was joy.'

And forms and feelings acting thus, and thus
Reacting, they shall each acquire
A living spirit and a character
Till then unfelt, and each be multiplied,
With a variety that knows no end.
Thus deeply drinking in[24] the soul of things
We shall be wise perforce, and we shall move
From strict necessity[25] along the path
Of order and of good. Whate'er we see,
Whate'er we feel, by agency direct
Or indirect, shall tend to feed and nurse
Our faculties and raise to loftier height
Our intellectual soul.'
The old man ceased.
The words he uttered shall not pass away;[26]
They had sunk into me, but not as sounds
To be expressed by visible characters,
For while he spake my spirit had obeyed
The presence of his eye, my ear had drunk
The meanings of his voice. He had discoursed
Like one who in the slow and silent works,
The manifold conclusions of his thought,
Had brooded till Imagination's power
Condensed them to a passion whence she drew
Herself new energies, resistless force.

[*Away, away – it is the air*] (composed between 20 April and 16 May 1798; first published 1947)[1]

Away, away – it is the air
That stirs among the withered leaves;
Away, away, it is not there,
Go hunt among the harvest sheaves.
There is a bed in shape as plain
As form of hare or lion's lair;
It is the bed where we have lain
In anguish and despair.

Away and take the eagle's eyes,
The tyger's smell,

Notes

[24] *drinking in* cf. the Pedlar, who 'drank / The spectacle' (*Pedlar* 102–3).

[25] *perforce . . . strict necessity* This passage is necessitarian. The individual has no choice but to be acted upon by 'forms and feelings', which acquire their 'living spirit' that brings wisdom to the individual, irrespective of his or her will. The phrase 'strict necessity' alludes to *Paradise Lost* v 528.

[26] *The words . . . pass away* Throughout Wordsworth's poetry, he is ambitious to formulate a poetry calculated to interest mankind permanently – a poetry that articulates ultimate and immutable truths.

Away, away – it is the air

[1] This fragmentary poem is widely thought to be associated with 'The Thorn'.

Ears that can hear the agonies
And murmurings of hell;
And when you there have stood
By that same bed of pain –
The groans are gone, the tears remain –
Then tell me if the thing be clear,
The difference betwixt a tear
Of water and of blood.

[*The Two-Part Prelude*]
(Part I composed October 1798–February 1799; Part II, autumn 1799; edited from MS)[1]

First Part

Was it for this
That one, the fairest of all rivers, loved
To blend his murmurs with my nurse's song,
And from his alder shades and rocky falls,
And from his fords and shallows, sent a voice
That flowed along my dreams?[2] For this didst thou,
Oh Derwent, travelling over the green plains
Near my 'sweet birthplace',[3] didst thou, beauteous stream,
Make ceaseless music through the night and day,
Which with its steady cadence tempering
Our human waywardness, composed my thoughts
To more than infant softness, giving me,
Among the fretful dwellings of mankind,
A knowledge, a dim earnest[4] of the calm
Which nature breathes among the fields and groves?
Beloved Derwent, fairest of all streams,
Was it for this that I, a four years' child,
A naked boy, among thy silent pools,
Made one long bathing of a summer's day,
Basked in the sun, or plunged into thy streams
Alternate all a summer's day, or coursed[5]
Over the sandy fields, and dashed the flowers
Of yellow grunsel;[6] or, when crag and hill,

Notes

The Two-Part Prelude

[1] This is the earliest complete version of Wordsworth's masterpiece, *The Prelude*. There were to be three further versions: one in Five Books (completed February 1804); one in Thirteen (completed early 1806); and one in Fourteen (published posthumously in 1850). It was known only to Wordsworth's close friends, including Coleridge and De Quincey. No one expected Wordsworth to write an autobiographical poem; he began it in Germany in the winter of 1798–9, which he believed to be the coldest of the century, in a state of despair at not managing to get on with *The Recluse*, the great millennial epic poem proposed by Coleridge (see pp. 414–15).

[2] *Was it for this . . . dreams* This question expresses Wordsworth's disappointment at being unable to compose *The Recluse*. The river is the Derwent which, as present-day visitors can see, flows along the far side of the garden wall of the Wordsworth house in Cockermouth.

[3] *sweet birthplace* The quotation marks, which appear in the manuscript, refer the reader to Coleridge's *Frost at Midnight* 28; it is particularly appropriate that *The Prelude*, which is addressed to Coleridge, should allude to his work.

[4] *earnest* foretaste, pledge.

[5] *coursed* run.

[6] *grunsel* ragwort.

The woods, and distant Skiddaw's lofty height[7]
Were bronzed with a deep radiance, stood alone,
A naked savage in the thunder shower?
  And afterwards, 'twas in a later day,
Though early,[8] when upon the mountain-slope
The frost and breath of frosty wind had snapped
The last autumnal crocus, 'twas my joy
To wander half the night among the cliffs
And the smooth hollows where the woodcocks ran
Along the moonlight turf. In thought and wish
That time, my shoulder all with springes[9] hung,
I was a fell destroyer. Gentle powers
Who give us happiness and call it peace,
When scudding on from snare to snare I plied
My anxious visitation – hurrying on,
Still hurrying, hurrying onward – how my heart
Panted among the scattered yew-trees and the crags
That looked upon me, how my bosom beat
With expectation! Sometimes strong desire,
Resistless, overpowered me, and the bird
Which was the captive of another's toils[10]
Became my prey; and when the deed was done
I heard among the solitary hills
Low breathings coming after me, and sounds
Of undistinguishable motion, steps
Almost as silent as the turf they trod.[11]
  Nor less in springtime, when on southern banks
The shining sun had from his knot of leaves
Decoyed the primrose flower, and when the vales
And woods were warm, was I a rover then
In the high places, on the lonesome peaks
Among the mountains and the winds. Though mean
And though inglorious were my views, the end
Was not ignoble.[12] Oh, when I have hung
Above the raven's nest, by knots of grass
Or half-inch fissures in the slipp'ry rock
But ill sustained, and almost (as it seemed)
Suspended by the blast which blew amain,[13]
Shouldering the naked crag[14] – oh, at that time,

Notes

[7] *distant Skiddaw's lofty height* Skiddaw is the fourth highest peak in the Lake District at 3,053 feet.

[8] *And . . . early* Wordsworth jumps forward to his time at Hawkshead Grammar School, which he joined in May 1779; he left Hawkshead for Cambridge in the autumn of 1787.

[9] *springes* traps; Wordsworth is thinking of *Hamlet* I iii 115: 'Aye, springes to catch woodcocks.'

[10] *toils* a pun, meaning both 'trap' and 'labours'.

[11] *and when . . . trod* Wordsworth's guilt might be explained partly by the fact that woodcock were a delicacy and fetched a good price for those who could catch them – sixteen or twenty pence a couple on the spot before being sent to London on the Kendal stagecoach. They were trapped by snares set at the end of narrowing avenues of stones which the birds would not jump over.

[12] *the end . . . ignoble* ravens preyed on lambs and anyone who destroyed their eggs was rewarded by the parish. The 'end' (aim) was not, in Wordsworth's case, monetary.

[13] *amain* strongly.

[14] *Shouldering the naked crag* The slightly inflated diction suggests that Wordsworth is recalling Atlas, the Titan of myth, who bore the world on his shoulders.

While on the perilous ridge I hung alone,[15]
With what strange utterance did the loud dry wind
Blow through my ears! The sky seemed not a sky
Of earth, and with what motion moved the clouds!
 The mind of man is fashioned and built up
Even as a strain of music; I believe
That there are spirits which, when they would form
A favoured being, from his very dawn
Of infancy do open out the clouds
As at the touch of lightning, seeking him
With gentle visitation – quiet powers,
Retired and seldom recognized, yet kind
And to the very meanest not unknown.
With me, though rarely, in my early days,
They communed; others too there are who use,
Yet haply aiming at the self-same end,
Severer interventions, ministry[16]
More palpable – and of their school was I.
 They guided me. One evening, led by them,
I went alone into a shepherd's boat,
A skiff that to a willow-tree was tied
Within a rocky cave, its usual home.
The moon was up, the lake was shining clear
Among the hoary mountains; from the shore
I pushed, and struck the oars, and struck again
In cadence, and my little boat moved on
Just like a man who walks with stately step
Though bent on speed.[17] It was an act of stealth
And troubled pleasure; not without the voice
Of mountain-echoes did my boat move on,
Leaving behind her still on either side
Small circles glittering idly in the moon
Until they melted all into one track
Of sparkling light.[18] A rocky steep uprose
Above the cavern of the willow-tree,
And now, as suited one who proudly rowed
With his best skill, I fixed a steady view
Upon the top of that same craggy ridge,
The bound of the horizon, for behind
Was nothing but the stars and the grey sky.
She was an elfin pinnace;[19] twenty times
I dipped my oars into the silent lake,
And, as I rose upon the stroke, my boat
Went heaving through the water like a swan –

Notes

[15] *I hung alone* See Wordsworth's comments in the 1815 Preface, pp. 575–6.

[16] *ministry* guidance.

[17] *Just like . . . speed* Wordsworth recalls the description of Michael from *Paradise Lost* xii 1–2: 'As one who in his journey bates at noon, / Though bent on speed'.

[18] *sparkling light* probably a recollection of the 'tracks of shining white' made by the water-snakes in Coleridge's *Ancient Mariner* (1798) 266.

[19] *elfin pinnace* The language embodies the child's imaginative absorption; the boat seems to be enchanted.

When, from behind that rocky steep (till then
The bound of the horizon), a huge cliff,[20]
As if with voluntary power instinct,[21]
Upreared its head. I struck and struck again,
And, growing still in stature, the huge cliff
Rose up between me and the stars, and still,
With measured motion, like a living thing
Strode after me. With trembling hands I turned,
And through the silent water stole my way
Back to the cavern of the willow-tree.
There in her mooring-place I left my bark,
And through the meadows homeward went with grave
And serious thoughts; and after I had seen
That spectacle, for many days my brain
Worked with a dim and undetermined sense
Of unknown modes of being.[22] In my thoughts
There was a darkness – call it solitude
Or blank desertion; no familiar shapes
Of hourly objects,[23] images of trees,
Of sea or sky, no colours of green fields,
But huge and mighty forms that do not live
Like living men moved slowly through my mind
By day, and were the trouble of my dreams.[24]
Ah, not in vain, ye beings of the hills,
And ye that walk the woods and open heaths
By moon or starlight, thus from my first dawn
Of childhood did ye love to intertwine
The passions that build up our human soul,
Not with the mean and vulgar works of man,
But with high objects, with eternal things,
With life and nature, purifying thus
The elements of feeling and of thought,
And sanctifying by such discipline
Both pain and fear, until we recognize
A grandeur in the beatings of the heart.[25]
Nor was this fellowship vouchsafed to me
With stinted kindness.[26] In November days,
When vapours rolling down the valleys made
A lonely scene more lonesome, among woods

Notes

[20] *a huge cliff* Glenridding Dodd, the stepped-back summit of which causes its peak to make a sudden delayed appearance above the 'craggy steep' of Stybarrow Crag as one rows out from the shores of Patterdale (see Grevel Lindop, *A Literary Guide to the Lake District* (1993), pp. 317–18).

[21] *instinct* imbued, filled.

[22] *unknown modes of being* forms of life beyond human experience. The vagueness and imprecision is meant to evoke the child's fear.

[23] *hourly objects* objects that can be depended on to be the same from one hour to the next.

[24] *But huge . . . dreams* As the alien mountain-forms take hold of his imagination, the boy is 'deserted' by the reassuring memories of ordinary things.

[25] *Ah, not in vain . . . heart* The feelings and thoughts of Wordsworth's childhood were purer for having been associated not with man-made things (as in a town), but the enduring forms of Nature. This natural education has sanctified – that is to say, given value to – the otherwise unpleasant sensations of pain and fear; thus, when his heart beat with terror, he recognized the 'grandeur' of the experience.

[26] *Nor was . . . kindness* This special relationship with Nature ('fellowship') was not given grudgingly.

At noon, and mid the calm of summer nights
When by the margin of the trembling lake
Beneath the gloomy hills I homeward went
In solitude, such intercourse[27] was mine.
   And in the frosty season, when the sun
Was set, and visible for many a mile,
The cottage windows through the twilight blazed,
I heeded not the summons;[28] clear and loud
The village clock tolled six; I wheeled about,
Proud and exulting like an untired horse
That cares not for its home. All shod with steel
We hissed along the polished ice[29] in games
Confederate,[30] imitative of the chase
And woodland pleasures – the resounding horn,
The pack loud bellowing, and the hunted hare.
So through the darkness and the cold we flew,
And not a voice was idle. With the din,
Meanwhile, the precipices rang aloud,
The leafless trees and every icy crag
Tinkled like iron, while the distant hills
Into the tumult sent an alien sound
Of melancholy not unnoticed – while the stars
Eastward were sparkling clear, and in the west
The orange sky of evening died away.
   Not seldom from the uproar I retired
Into a silent bay, or sportively
Glanced sideway, leaving the tumultuous throng,
To cut across the shadow[31] of a star
That gleamed upon the ice. And oftentimes,
When we had given our bodies to the wind,
And all the shadowy banks on either side
Came sweeping through the darkness, spinning still
The rapid line of motion – then at once
Have I, reclining back upon my heels,
Stopped short: yet still the solitary cliffs
Wheeled by me, even as if the earth had rolled
With visible motion her diurnal[32] round;
Behind me did they stretch in solemn train[33]
Feebler and feebler, and I stood and watched
Till all was tranquil as a summer sea.
   Ye powers of earth, ye genii of the springs!
And ye that have your voices in the clouds
And ye that are familiars of the lakes

Notes

[27] *intercourse* companionship (with Nature).

[28] *The cottage . . . summons* Candle- and fire-light through the cottage windows tell the boy that it is time to go home.

[29] *We hissed . . . ice* Wordsworth's phrasing recalls Erasmus Darwin's *Botanic Garden*, 'Hang o'er the sliding steel, and hiss along the ice' (*Economy of Vegetation* iii 570).

[30] *Confederate* collective; games played in groups.

[31] *shadow* reflection; altered to 'image' in the *Thirteen-Book Prelude*, and 'reflex' for *Fourteen-Book Prelude*.

[32] *diurnal* daily, as in *A slumber did my spirit seal*, in which Lucy is 'Rolled round in earth's diurnal course / With rocks and stones and trees' (ll. 7–8).

[33] *train* sequence, succession.

And of the standing pools,[34] I may not think
A vulgar hope was yours when ye employed
Such ministry[35] – when ye through many a year
Thus by the agency of boyish sports
On caves and trees, upon the woods and hills,
Impressed[36] upon all forms the characters[37]
Of danger or desire, and thus did make
The surface of the universal earth
With meanings of delight, of hope and fear,
Work like a sea.[38]
                    Not uselessly employed,
I might pursue this theme through every change
Of exercise and sport to which the year
Did summon us in its delightful round.
We were a noisy crew; the sun in heaven
Beheld not vales more beautiful than ours,
Nor saw a race in happiness and joy
More worthy of the fields where they were sown.
I would record with no reluctant voice
Our home amusements by the warm peat-fire
At evening, when with pencil and with slate,
In square divisions parcelled out, and all
With crosses and with cyphers scribbled o'er,[39]
We schemed and puzzled, head opposed to head,
In strife too humble to be named in verse;
Or round the naked table, snow-white deal,
Cherry or maple, sat in close array,
And to the combat, loo or whist,[40] led on
A thick-ribbed army[41] – not (as in the world)
Discarded and ungratefully thrown by
Even for the very service they had wrought,[42]
But husbanded[43] through many a long campaign.
Oh with what echoes on the board they fell!
Ironic diamonds, hearts of sable hue,
Queens gleaming through their splendour's last decay,
Knaves wrapped in one assimilating gloom,
And kings indignant at the shame incurred
By royal visages. Meanwhile abroad

Notes

[34] *Ye powers . . . pools* The tutelary spirits have their source in Shakespeare, *Tempest* V i 33: 'Ye elves of hills, brooks, standing lakes and groves'.

[35] *ministry* guidance

[36] *Impressed* stamped, printed.

[37] *characters* signs, marks.

[38] *Work like a sea* See Cowper, *Task* vi 737–8: 'this tempestuous state of human things, / Is merely as the working of a sea.' Their association with 'boyish sports' has given the impression of movement to the poet's recollection of the landscape in which he grew up.

[39] *With crosses . . . o'er* noughts and crosses (tick-tack-toe). The line echoes *Paradise Lost*, where man is ridiculed for attempting to map the heavens, 'With centric and eccentric scribbled o'er' (viii 83).

[40] *loo or whist* The description of these eighteenth-century card-games recalls the game of ombre in Pope's *Rape of the Lock* iii. See J. R. Watson, 'Wordsworth's Card Games', *TWC* 6 (1975) 299–302.

[41] *A thick-ribbed army* The cards' edges have thickened through use.

[42] *not . . . wrought* cf. for example, the discharged soldier (see p. 418).

[43] *husbanded* saved up; they were survivors.

The heavy rain was falling, or the frost
Raged bitterly with keen and silent tooth,[44]
Or, interrupting the impassioned game,[45]
Oft from the neighbouring lake the splitting ice,
While it sank down towards the water, sent
Among the meadows and the hills its long
And frequent yellings,[46] imitative some
Of wolves that howl along the Bothnic main.[47]
  Nor with less willing heart would I rehearse
The woods of autumn and their hidden bowers
With milk-white clusters[48] hung, the rod and line
(True symbol of the foolishness of hope)
Which with its strong enchantment led me on
By rocks and pools where never summer star
Impressed its shadow,[49] to forlorn cascades
Among the windings of the mountain-brooks;
The kite, in sultry calms from some high hill
Sent up, ascending thence till it was lost
Among the fleecy clouds, in gusty days
Launched from the lower grounds, and suddenly
Dashed headlong – and rejected by the storm.
All these and more with rival claims demand
Grateful acknowledgement. It were a song
Venial, and such as if I rightly judge
I might protract unblamed, but I perceive
That much is overlooked, and we should ill
Attain our object if from delicate fears
Of breaking in upon the unity
Of this my argument[50] I should omit
To speak of such effects as cannot here
By regularly classed, yet tend no less
To the same point, the growth of mental power
And love of nature's works.
                              Ere I had seen
Eight summers[51] – and 'twas in the very week
When I was first entrusted to thy vale,
Beloved Hawkshead! – when thy paths, thy shores
And brooks, were like a dream of novelty
To my half-infant mind, I chanced to cross

Notes

[44] *keen and silent tooth* 'Thy tooth is not so keen,' Amiens tells the winter wind in *As You Like It* II vii 177. But as Owen *WC* 107 points out, ll. 225–7 are based on Cowper's *Winter Evening*: 'how the frost / Raging abroad, and the rough wind, endear / The silence and the warmth enjoyed within' (*Task* iv 308–10; see pp. 20–1).

[45] *the impassioned game* a particularly persuasive detail; the game fully engages the players' emotions ('passions').

[46] *its long . . . yellings* The ice makes a yelling noise as it breaks up; Coleridge had used this detail in *The Ancient Mariner* (1798) 57–60.

[47] *Bothnic main* the northern Baltic.

[48] *milk-white clusters* hazel nuts. 'Nutting', composed for *The Two-Part Prelude*, was discarded immediately and published in *Lyrical Ballads* (1800) as an independent work; see pp. 475–6.

[49] *shadow* reflection.

[50] *argument* theme; cf. *Paradise Lost* i 24: 'the height of this great argument'.

[51] *Ere I had . . . summers* Despite Wordsworth's claims, he went to Hawkshead Grammar School in May 1779 at the age of 9.

One of those open fields which, shaped like ears,[52]
Make green peninsulas on Esthwaite's Lake.
Twilight was coming on, yet through the gloom
I saw distinctly on the opposite shore,
Beneath a tree and close by the lakeside,
A heap of garments, as if left by one
Who there was bathing. Half an hour I watched
And no one owned them; meanwhile the calm lake
Grew dark with all the shadows on its breast,
And now and then a leaping fish disturbed
The breathless stillness. The succeeding day
There came a company, and in their boat
Sounded with iron hooks and with long poles.
At length the dead man,[53] mid that beauteous scene
Of trees and hills and water, bolt upright
Rose with his ghastly face. I might advert[54]
To numerous accidents in flood or field,[55]
Quarry or moor, or mid the winter snows,
Distresses and disasters, tragic facts
Of rural history that impressed my mind
With images to which, in following years,
Far other feelings were attached, with forms
That yet exist with independent life,
And, like their archetypes, know no decay.[56]
    There are in our existence spots of time
Which with distinct pre-eminence retain
A fructifying[57] virtue, whence, depressed
By trivial occupations and the round
Of ordinary intercourse, our minds
(Especially the imaginative power)
Are nourished, and invisibly repaired.[58]
Such moments chiefly seem to have their date
In our first childhood.
                                    I remember well
('Tis of an early season that I speak,
The twilight of rememberable life)
While I was yet an urchin,[59] one who scarce
Could hold a bridle, with ambitious hopes
I mounted, and we rode towards the hills.

Notes

[52] *shaped like ears* There are three such peninsulas on the map; the one Wordsworth has in mind is Strickland Ees.

[53] *the dead man* John Jackson, village schoolmaster from Sawrey, was drowned while bathing in Esthwaite Water, 18 June 1779.

[54] *advert* refer.

[55] *To numerous . . . field* an echo of *Othello* I iii 134–5: 'Wherein I spake of most disastrous chances, / Of moving accidents by flood and field'.

[56] *tragic facts . . . decay* A change has taken place in Wordsworth's thought since *The Pedlar* and *Tintern Abbey* (composed only months before). As in those works, he is concerned with the storing-up of visual memories in the mind as a result of deep emotional response. However, the images are now treasured not for their permanence but because of quite distinct new feelings that have become attached to them over the years.

[57] *fructifying* the power to make fruitful.

[58] *repaired* As in *Tintern Abbey* 40–2, the essential characteristic of these remembered 'spots of time' is to restore the mind.

[59] *an urchin* Wordsworth was 5 at the time this incident took place. He was staying with his grandparents at Penrith.

We were a pair of horsemen: honest James[60]
Was with me, my encourager and guide.
We had not travelled long ere some mischance
Disjoined me from my comrade and, through fear
Dismounting, down the rough and stony moor
I led my horse, and, stumbling on, at length
Came to a bottom where in former times
A man, the murderer of his wife, was hung
In irons; mouldered was the gibbet-mast,
The bones were gone, the iron and the wood,
Only a long green ridge of turf remained
Whose shape was like a grave.[61] I left the spot
And, reascending the bare slope, I saw
A naked pool that lay beneath the hills,
The beacon on the summit,[62] and, more near,
A girl who bore a pitcher on her head
And seemed with difficult steps to force her way
Against the blowing wind. It was in truth
An ordinary sight, but I should need
Colours and words that are unknown to man
To paint the visionary dreariness[63]
Which, while I looked all round for my lost guide,
Did at that time invest the naked pool,
The beacon on the lonely eminence,
The woman and her garments vexed and tossed
By the strong wind.
Nor less I recollect,
Long after, though my childhood had not ceased,
Another scene which left a kindred power
Implanted in my mind. One Christmas-time,
The day before the holidays began,[64]
Feverish and tired and restless, I went forth
Into the fields, impatient for the sight
Of those three horses which should bear us home,
My brothers and myself.[65] There was a crag,[66]

Notes

[60] *honest James* identified in the *Fourteen-Book Prelude* as being 'An ancient Servant of my Father's house' (xii 229).

[61] *Mouldered was the gibbet-mast . . . like a grave* The valley-bottom was Cowdrake Quarry, east of Penrith, where Thomas Nicholson was hanged in 1767 for having murdered a butcher. However, *The Prelude* is not a record of fact, and it is worth noting that Nicholson's gibbet had not 'mouldered down' in 1775, and a 5-year-old would not have ridden that far. Wordsworth may also have in mind a rotted gibbet in the water-meadows near Ann Tyson's cottage, the last remains of Thomas Lancaster, hanged in 1672 for poisoning his wife.

[62] *The beacon on the summit* built in 1719 to warn of invasion from Scotland; it is still to be seen, a short building with a pointed roof on the hill above Penrith.

[63] *visionary dreariness* an oxymoron that has generated much critical commentary. Wordsworth's point is that in spite of the ordinariness and bleakness of the scene, it was impressed on his mind with all the intensity and power of a vision. At the back of his mind is Milton's hell, a 'dismal situation waste and wild', where there was no light, 'but rather darkness visible' (*Paradise Lost* i 60, 63).

[64] *One Christmas-time . . . began* probably 19 December 1783, when Wordsworth was 13.

[65] *My brothers and myself* Wordsworth's brothers, Richard (1768–1816) and John (1772–1805), also attended Hawkshead Grammar School. The horses were to take them home to Cockermouth; it was a fairly lengthy journey as Hawkshead and Cockermouth were at opposite ends of the Lake District. Whether they chose to go round the coastal route or towards the east, to Keswick, through Ambleside and thence to Hawkshead, it was necessary to travel around the central mountains. The horses were in fact delayed.

[66] *a crag* probably the ridge north of Borwick Lodge, a mile and a half from Hawkshead Grammar School.

An eminence which from the meeting-point
Of two highways ascending, overlooked
At least a long half-mile of those two roads,
By each of which the expected steeds might come,
The choice uncertain. Thither I repaired
Up to the highest summit. 'Twas a day
Stormy, and rough, and wild, and on the grass
I sat, half-sheltered by a naked wall;
Upon my right hand was a single sheep,
A whistling hawthorn on my left, and there,
Those two companions at my side, I watched,
With eyes intensely straining, as the mist
Gave intermitting prospects of the wood
And plain beneath. Ere I to school returned
That dreary time, ere I had been ten days
A dweller in my father's house, he died,[67]
And I and my two brothers, orphans then,
Followed his body to the grave. The event,
With all the sorrow which it brought, appeared
A chastisement,[68] and when I called to mind
That day so lately past, when from the crag
I looked in such anxiety of hope,
With trite reflections of morality,
Yet with the deepest passion, I bowed low
To God, who thus corrected my desires.[69]
And afterwards the wind and sleety rain
And all the business of the elements,
The single sheep, and the one blasted tree,
And the bleak music of that old stone wall,
The noise of wood and water, and the mist
Which on the line of each of those two roads
Advanced in such indisputable shapes[70] –
All these were spectacles and sounds to which
I often would repair, and thence would drink
As at a fountain.[71] And I do not doubt
That in this later time, when storm and rain
Beat on my roof at midnight, or by day
When I am in the woods, unknown to me
The workings of my spirit thence are brought.[72]
    Nor, sedulous[73] as I have been to trace
How nature by collateral[74] interest

Notes

[67] *he died* John Wordsworth Sr died on 30 December 1783 after spending a shelterless night lost during his return from the Seignory of Millom two weeks before. His wife, Ann, had died five years previously, just before Wordsworth's eighth birthday.

[68] *chastisement* (stressed on the first syllable) punishment.

[69] *I bowed low to God . . . desires* The child believes he has been punished for looking forward too eagerly to the Christmas holidays – in effect, he has killed his father.

[70] *indisputable shapes* De Selincourt notes an interesting echo of Hamlet addressing his father's ghost: 'Thou com'st in such a questionable shape / That I will speak to thee' (I iv 43–4).

[71] *fountain* stream or well.

[72] *unknown to me . . . brought* Spots of time mould the adult mind by the power of association, though it remains unaware of their workings.

[73] *sedulous* careful, anxious.

[74] *collateral* indirect, sideways.

And by extrinsic passion[75] peopled first
My mind with forms or beautiful or grand[76]
And made me love them, may I well forget
How other pleasures have been mine, and joys
Of subtler origin – how I have felt,
Not seldom, even in that tempestuous time,
Those hallowed and pure motions of the sense
Which seem in their simplicity to own
An intellectual[77] charm, that calm delight
Which, if I err not, surely must belong
To those first-born affinities[78] that fit
Our new existence to existing things,
And in our dawn of being constitute
The bond of union betwixt life and joy.
   Yes, I remember when the changeful earth
And twice five seasons on my mind had stamped
The faces of the moving year; even then,
A child, I held unconscious intercourse
With the eternal beauty, drinking in
A pure organic[79] pleasure from the lines
Of curling mist, or from the level plain
Of waters coloured by the steady clouds.
   The sands of Westmorland, the creeks and bays
Of Cumbria's rocky limits, they can tell
How when the sea threw off his evening shade
And to the shepherd's hut beneath the crags
Did send sweet notice of the rising moon,
How I have stood, to images like these
A stranger, linking with the spectacle
No body of associated forms[80]
And bringing with me no peculiar sense
Of quietness or peace – yet I have stood,
Even while my eye has moved o'er three long leagues[81]
Of shining water, gathering, as it seemed,
Through the wide surface of that field of light
New pleasure like a bee among the flowers.
   Thus often in those fits of vulgar[82] joy
Which through all seasons on a child's pursuits
Are prompt attendants, mid that giddy bliss
Which like a tempest works along the blood
And is forgotten – even then I felt
Gleams like the flashing of a shield. The earth
And common face of nature spake to me

Notes

[75] *extrinsic passion* emotions not directly related to the natural scenes that were to 'educate' the poet. Nature operated on the boy without his being aware of it.

[76] *or . . . or* either . . . or.

[77] *intellectual* spiritual – the sense in which Wordsworth often uses the word.

[78] *first-born affinities* affinities with which the child is born.

[79] *organic* sensuous, bodily.

[80] *linking . . . forms* Wordsworth emphasizes that he has enjoyed these things in and for themselves, rather than for any association they may have with other things. He has been a 'stranger' to them in so far as he has not seen them before and sees them freshly.

[81] *three long leagues* at least nine miles (a league is a varying measure of about three miles).

[82] *vulgar* ordinary, unremarkable.

Rememberable things – sometimes, 'tis true,
By quaint associations, yet not vain
Nor profitless if haply they impressed
Collateral objects and appearances,[83]
Albeit lifeless then, and doomed to sleep
Until maturer seasons called them forth
To impregnate and to elevate the mind.
And if the vulgar joy by its own weight
Wearied itself out of the memory,
The scenes which were a witness of that joy
Remained in their substantial lineaments
Depicted on the brain,[84] and to the eye
Were visible, a daily sight. And thus,
By the impressive agency of fear,[85]
By pleasure, and repeated happiness,
So frequently repeated, and by force
Of obscure feelings representative
Of joys that were forgotten, these same scenes
So beauteous and majestic in themselves,
Though yet the day was distant, did at length
Become habitually dear, and all
Their hues and forms were by invisible links[86]
Allied to the affections.[87]
I began
My story early, feeling, as I fear,
The weakness of a human love for days
Disowned by memory, ere the birth of spring
Planting my snowdrops among winter snows.
Nor will it seem to thee, my friend,[88] so prompt
In sympathy, that I have lengthened out
With fond and feeble tongue a tedious tale.
Meanwhile my hope has been that I might fetch
Reproaches from my former years, whose power
May spur me on, in manhood now mature,
To honourable toil.[89] Yet should it be
That this is but an impotent desire,
That I by such enquiry am not taught
To understand myself, nor thou to know
With better knowledge how the heart was framed

Notes

[83] *sometimes . . . appearances* The 'associations' (or juxtapositions) are quaint, but not vain or without benefit if indirectly ('collaterally') they impress natural objects and appearances on the mind.

[84] *in their substantial lineaments . . . brain* The storing up of visual images is described in similar terms at *Pedlar* 32–4: 'on his mind / They lay like substances, and almost seemed / To haunt the bodily sense.'

[85] *the impressive agency of fear* fear's ability to stamp 'impressions' on the memory.

[86] *invisible links* associative links in the mind. Wordsworth draws on the theory of the mind's association of ideas derived from sense-experience, as expounded by David Hartley (1705–57) in his *Observations of Man* (1749) – a strong influence on Coleridge.

[87] *And thus . . . affections* Fear, pleasure and repeated happiness all work to make the natural world constantly precious ('habitually dear'), and to connect its colours and shapes to the poet's emotions ('affections').

[88] *my friend* Coleridge, to whom the poem is addressed.

[89] *honourable toil* When he composed these lines in February 1799, Wordsworth expected to go on with *The Recluse.*

Of him thou lovest, need I dread from thee
Harsh judgements if I am so loath to quit
Those recollected hours that have the charm
Of visionary things,[90] and lovely forms
And sweet sensations that throw back our life
And make our infancy a visible scene
On which the sun is shining?

Second Part

Thus far, my friend, have we retraced the way
Through which I travelled when I first began
To love the woods and fields. The passion yet
Was in its birth, sustained (as might befall)
By nourishment that came unsought;[1] for still
From week to week, from month to month, we lived
A round of tumult. Duly were our games
Prolonged in summer till the daylight failed;
No chair remained before the doors; the bench
And threshold steps were empty; fast asleep
The labourer, and the old man who had sat
A later lingerer – yet the revelry
Continued, and the loud uproar! At last,
When all the ground was dark, and the huge clouds
Were edged with twinkling stars, to bed we went,
With weary joints and with a beating mind.[2]
  Ah, is there one who ever has been young
And needs a monitory voice to tame
The pride of virtue and of intellect?[3]
And is there one, the wisest and the best
Of all mankind, who does not sometimes wish
For things which cannot be, who would not give,
If so he might, to duty and to truth
The eagerness of infantine desire?
A tranquillizing spirit presses now
On my corporeal frame,[4] so wide appears
The vacancy between me and those days
Which yet have such self-presence[5] in my heart
That sometimes, when I think of them, I seem
Two consciousnesses – conscious of myself
And of some other being. A grey stone

Notes

[90] *Missionary things* things seen imaginatively.

SECOND PART

[1] *nourishment that came unsought* Where in Part I Wordsworth discussed his unconscious reponse to the influence of nature, he aims to show in Part II how nature in adolescence was 'sought / For her own sake'.

[2] *a beating mind* cf. *The Tempest* IV i 162–3: 'A turn or two I'll walk, / To still my beating mind.'

[3] *Ah, is . . . intellect* 'How can anyone who remembers what it was like to be young need a warning ("monitory voice") not to overrate the achievements of maturity?'

[4] *corporeal frame* body; the effect is similar to that described in *Tintern Abbey* 44–6.

[5] *self-presence* presence to himself – actuality, immediacy.

Of native rock, left midway in the square
Of our small market-village, was the home
And centre of these joys; and when, returned
After long absence, thither I repaired,
I found that it was split, and gone to build
A smart assembly-room[6] that perked and flared
With wash and rough-cast, elbowing the ground
Which had been ours. But let the fiddle scream
And be ye happy! Yet I know, my friends,[7]
That more than one of you will think with me
Of those soft starry nights, and that old dame
From whom the stone was named, who there had sat
And watched her table with its huckster's wares,
Assiduous for the length of sixty years.[8]
We ran a boisterous race, the year span round
With giddy motion. But the time approached
That brought with it a regular desire
For calmer pleasures, when the beauteous scenes
Of nature were collaterally attached
To every scheme of holiday delight
And every boyish sport – less grateful[9] else,
And languidly pursued.[10]
When summer came
It was the pastime of our afternoons
To beat along the plain[11] of Windermere
With rival oars, and the selected bourn[12]
Was now an island musical with birds
That sang for ever; now a sister isle
Beneath the oak's umbrageous[13] covert, sown
With lilies-of-the-valley like a field;
And now a third small island[14] where remained
An old stone table and one mouldered cave –
A hermit's history. In such a race,
So ended, disappointment could be none,
Uneasiness, or pain, or jealousy;
We rested in the shade, all pleased alike,
Conquered and conqueror. Thus our selfishness
Was mellowed down, and thus the pride of strength
And the vainglory of superior skill
Were interfused[15] with objects which subdued
And tempered them, and gradually produced

Notes

[6] *A smart assembly-room* Hawkshead Town Hall, built 1790, covered with gravel stucco ('rough-cast') and whitewash. Wordsworth didn't like white buildings because of the way they stuck out in the landscape.

[7] *my friends* An address to Coleridge and John Wordsworth (the poet's brother), with whom the poet visited Hawkshead on 2 November 1799.

[8] *that old dame . . . years* Ann Holme, who set out her wares – cakes, pies and sweets – on the large stone at the end of the market square in Hawkshead

[9] *grateful* pleasing.

[10] *languidly pursued* Natural beauty is still only an additional ('collateral') pleasure, though it is beginning to be valued.

[11] *plain* flat surface of the lake.

[12] *bourn* aim, destination.

[13] *umbrageous* shady.

[14] *a third small island* Lady Holm, where there was once a chapel to the Virgin Mary.

[15] *interfused* mingled; cf. *Tintern Abbey* 97.

A quiet independence of the heart.
And to my friend who knows me, I may add,
Unapprehensive of reproof, that hence
Ensued a diffidence and modesty,
And I was taught to feel, perhaps too much,
The self-sufficing power of solitude.
No delicate viands[16] sapped our bodily strength;
More than we wished we knew the blessing then
Of vigorous hunger, for our daily meals
Were frugal, Sabine fare;[17] and then, exclude
A little weekly stipend,[18] and we lived
Through three divisions of the quartered year
In penniless poverty. But now, to school
Returned from the half-yearly holidays,
We came with purses more profusely filled,[19]
Allowance which abundantly sufficed
To gratify the palate with repasts
More costly than the dame of whom I spake,
That ancient woman,[20] and her board, supplied.
Hence inroads into distant vales, and long
Excursions far away among the hills;
Hence rustic dinners on the cool green ground,
Or in the woods, or by a riverside
Or fountain[21] – festive banquets that provoked
The languid action of a natural scene
By pleasure of corporeal appetite.
Nor is my aim neglected if I tell
How twice in the long length of those half-years
We from our funds perhaps with bolder hand
Drew largely – anxious for one day, at least,
To feel the motion of the galloping steed.
And with the good old innkeeper,[22] in truth,
I needs must say that sometimes we have used
Sly subterfuge, for the intended bound
Of the day's journey was too distant far
For any cautious man – a structure famed
Beyond its neighbourhood, the antique walls
Of that large abbey with its fractured arch,[23]
Belfry, and images, and living trees,
A holy scene! Along the smooth green turf

Notes

[16] *delicate viands* decorative delicacies of no nutritional value.

[17] *Sabine fare* The Roman poet Horace had a Sabine farm and recommended a frugal diet, although Ann Tyson, Wordsworth's landlady, fed the poet pasties, cakes, dumplings, eggs and porridge for breakfast.

[18] *A little weekly stipend* In 1787, the year he left Hawkshead, Wordsworth received sixpence a week.

[19] *But now . . . filled* When Wordsworth returned to school in January 1787, after the half-yearly holiday, he had an extra guinea (worth 42 'weekly stipends').

[20] *That ancient woman* Ann Tyson was 73 in January 1787.

[21] *fountain* spring or stream.

[22] *innkeeper* who hired out the horses.

[23] *that large abbey with its fractured arch* Furness Abbey is about 20 miles south of Hawkshead, near Barrow-in-Furness. It was founded by Cistercian monks in 1127 and dissolved by Henry VIII in 1539. The fractured arch is still to be seen. Its roof-timbers, stripped of their valuable lead, had long since fallen by Wordsworth's day.

Our horses grazed. In more than inland peace
Left by the winds that overpass the vale
In that sequestered ruin trees and towers,
Both silent and both motionless alike,
Hear all day long the murmuring sea that beats
Incessantly upon a craggy shore.
Our steeds remounted, and the summons given,
With whip and spur we by the chantry[24] flew
In uncouth[25] race, and left the cross-legged knight,
And the stone abbot,[26] and that single wren
Which one day sang so sweetly in the nave
Of the old church that, though from recent showers
The earth was comfortless, and, touched by faint
Internal breezes from the roofless walls,
The shuddering ivy dripped large drops, yet still
So sweetly mid the gloom the invisible bird
Sang to itself that there I could have made
My dwelling-place, and lived for ever there
To hear such music.[27] Through the walls we flew
And down the valley, and, a circuit made
In wantonness of heart, through rough and smooth
We scampered homeward. Oh, ye rocks and streams,
And that still spirit of the evening air,
Even in this joyous time I sometimes felt
Your presence, when with slackened step we breathed[28]
Along the sides of the steep hills, or when,
Lightened by gleams of moonlight from the sea,
We beat with thundering hoofs the level sand.[29]
There was a row of ancient trees, since fallen,
That on the margin of a jutting land
Stood near the lake of Coniston, and made
With its long boughs above the water stretched
A gloom through which a boat might sail along
As in a cloister. An old hall[30] was near,
Grotesque and beautiful, its gavel-end[31]
And huge round chimneys to the top o'ergrown
With fields of ivy. Thither we repaired,
'Twas even a custom with us, to the shore
And to that cool piazza.[32] They who dwelt
In the neglected mansion-house supplied
Fresh butter, tea-kettle, and earthenware,
And chafing-dish with smoking coals,[33] and so

Notes

[24] *chantry* chapel where masses were once said for the dead.

[25] *uncouth* unseemly, indecorous (because of their surroundings).

[26] *the cross-legged knight . . . abbot* The stone figures of several cross-legged knights and an abbot may still be seen in the museum at Furness Abbey.

[27] *So sweetly . . . music* cf. Shakespeare, Sonnet 73: 'Bare ruined choirs, where late the sweet birds sang'.

[28] *breathed* i.e. let the horses get their breath back.

[29] *the level sand* The return journey took them along Levens Sands from Rampside to Greenodd.

[30] *An old hall* Coniston Hall, dating from 1580, was the seat of the wealthy Le Fleming family.

[31] *gavel-end* gable.

[32] *cool piazza* the shady colonnade formed by the branches of the sycamore trees.

[33] *chafing-dish with smoking coals* portable charcoal stove used to cook trout, or char, from the lake.

Beneath the trees we sat in our small boat
And in the covert[34] ate our delicate meal
Upon the calm smooth lake. It was a joy
Worthy the heart of one who is full-grown
To rest beneath those horizontal boughs
And mark the radiance of the setting sun,
Himself unseen, reposing on the top
Of the high eastern hills. And there I said,
That beauteous sight before me, there I said
(Then first beginning in my thoughts to mark
That sense of dim similitude which links
Our moral feelings with external forms)
That in whatever region I should close
My mortal life I would remember you,
Fair scenes, that dying I would think on you,
My soul would send a longing look to you,
Even as that setting sun while all the vale
Could nowhere catch one faint memorial gleam
Yet with the last remains of his last light
Still lingered, and a farewell lustre threw
On the dear mountain-tops where first he rose.[35]
'Twas then my fourteenth summer, and these words
Were uttered in a casual access
Of sentiment, a momentary trance
That far outran the habit of my mind.
    Upon the eastern shore of Windermere
Above the crescent of a pleasant bay,
There was an inn[36] – no homely-featured shed,
Brother of the surrounding cottages,
But 'twas a splendid place, the door beset
With chaises,[37] grooms, and liveries,[38] and within
Decanters, glasses, and the blood-red wine.[39]
In ancient times, or ere the hall was built
On the large island,[40] had this dwelling been

Notes

[34] *covert* shade.

[35] *Even as . . . rose* In later years Wordsworth recalled that this image 'suggested itself to me while I was resting in a boat along with my companions under the shade of a magnificent row of sycamores, which then extended their branches from the shore of the promontory upon which stands the ancient, and at that time the more picturesque, Hall of Coniston, the seat of the Le Flemings, from very early times' (*FN* 6).

[36] *an inn* the White Lion at Bowness, now the Royal Hotel.

[37] *chaises* light carriages.

[38] *liveries* uniforms.

[39] *the blood-red wine* an echo of the anonymous ballad, *Sir Patrick Spens*: 'The king sits in Dunfermling toune, / Drinking the blude-reid wine' (ll. 1–2). Wordsworth knew it from Percy's *Reliques of Ancient English Poetry* (1765), a copy of which he purchased in Hamburg shortly before starting work on the *Two-Part Prelude*.

[40] *the hall . . . island* The first and finest of the neoclassical villas in the Lakes was the circular mansion on Belle Isle in Windermere, designed by John Plaw in 1774 for Thomas English, but not completed until the early 1780s when John Christian Curwen had become its owner. Wordsworth follows the guidebook writers of the day – Hutchinson, West and Gilpin – in deploring the changes that had taken place, including the felling of many trees and the demolition of the old buildings (including, perhaps, the 'hut' mentioned here). Dorothy had harsh words for the circular mansion in June 1802: ' . . . & that great house! Mercy upon us! If it *could* be concealed it would be well for all who are not pained to see the pleasantest of earthly spots deformed by man' (*Grasmere Journals* 107; her italics).

More worthy of a poet's love, a hut[41]
Proud of its one bright fire and sycamore shade.
But though the rhymes were gone which once inscribed
The threshold, and large golden characters[42]
On the blue-frosted signboard had usurped
The place of the old lion, in contempt
And mockery of the rustic painter's hand,
Yet to this hour the spot to me is dear
With all its foolish pomp. The garden lay
Upon a slope surmounted by the plain
Of a small bowling-green; beneath us stood
A grove, with gleams of water through the trees
And over the tree-tops – nor did we want
Refreshment, strawberries and mellow cream.
And there, through half an afternoon, we played
On the smooth platform, and the shouts we sent
Made all the mountains ring. But ere the fall
Of night, when in our pinnace we returned
Over the dusky lake, and to the beach
Of some small island steered our course, with one,[43]
The minstrel of our troop, and left him there,
And rowed off gently while he blew his flute
Alone upon the rock – oh then the calm
And dead still water lay upon my mind
Even with a weight of pleasure, and the sky,
Never before so beautiful, sank down
Into my heart, and held me like a dream.

Thus day by day my sympathies increased,
And thus the common range of visible things
Grew dear to me. Already I began
To love the sun – a boy I loved the sun
Not as I since have loved him (as a pledge
And surety[44] of our earthly life, a light
Which while I view I feel I am alive),
But for this cause: that I had seen him lay
His beauty on the morning hills, had seen
The western mountain touch his setting orb
In many a thoughtless hour, when from excess
Of happiness my blood appeared to flow
With its own pleasure, and I breathed with joy.
And from like feelings, humble though intense
(To patriotic and domestic love
Analogous[45]), the moon to me was dear,

Notes

[41] *hut* cottage.

[42] *characters* letters.

[43] *one* Robert Greenwood, another of Ann Tyson's boarders, who was elected Fellow of Trinity College, Cambridge in 1792. Wordsworth remained in touch with him for many years.

[44] *surety* guarantee.

[45] *To patriotic . . . analogous* His love for the moon was like love of country and family ('domestic love') because it gave him pleasure in the region where he lived.

For I would dream away my purposes,
Standing to look upon her while she hung
Midway between the hills, as if she knew
No other region, but belonged to thee –
Yea, appertained by a peculiar right
To thee and thy grey huts,[46] my native vale.
　Those incidental charms which first attached
My heart to rural objects day by day
Grew weaker, and I hasten on to tell
How Nature – intervenient till this time,
And secondary[47] – now at length was sought
For her own sake. But who shall parcel out[48]
His intellect by geometric rules,
Split like a province into round and square?
Who knows the individual hour in which
His habits were first sown, even as a seed?
Who that shall point as with a wand, and say,
'This portion of the river of my mind
Came from yon fountain'? Thou, my friend,[49] art one
More deeply read in thy own thoughts, no slave
Of that false secondary power[50] by which
In weakness we create distinctions, then
Believe our puny boundaries are things
Which we perceive, and not which we have made.
To thee, unblinded by these outward shows,
The unity of all has been revealed;[51]
And thou wilt doubt with me, less aptly skilled
Than many are to class the cabinet
Of their sensations,[52] and in voluble[53] phrase
Run through the history and birth of each
As of a single independent thing.
Hard task[54] to analyse a soul, in which
Not only general habits and desires,
But each most obvious and particular thought –
Not in a mystical[55] and idle sense,
But in the words of reason deeply weighed –
Hath no beginning.

Notes

[46] *grey huts* cottages built of grey stone.

[47] *intervenient . . . secondary* Nature had been experienced in the midst of other distractions.

[48] *parcel out* divide up, categorize, analyse.

[49] *my friend* Wordsworth turns once more to Coleridge, to whom this poem is dedicated.

[50] *that false secondary power* the power of rational analysis, as opposed to the imaginative perception of unity.

[51] *To thee . . . revealed* Coleridge was a Unitarian, and capable of writing: ''tis God / Diffused through all that doth make all one whole' (*Religious Musings* 144–5).

[52] *to class . . . sensations* classify sensations as if they were exhibits in a cabinet. The metaphor is borrowed from Locke's *Essay on Human Understanding*: 'The senses at first let in particular ideas, and furnish the yet empty cabinet.'

[53] *voluble* glib, fluent.

[54] *Hard task* a deliberate echo of Milton, who speaks of having to describe the war in heaven as 'Sad task and hard' (*Paradise Lost* v 564); describing the growth of the mind is just as worthy of epic treatment for Wordsworth.

[55] *mystical* mysterious, occult.

Blessed the infant babe[56]
(For with my best conjectures I would trace
The progress of our being[57]) – blessed the babe
Nursed in his mother's arms, the babe who sleeps
Upon his mother's breast, who when his soul
Claims manifest kindred with an earthly soul,
Doth gather passion from his mother's eye![58]
Such feelings pass into his torpid[59] life
Like an awakening breeze, and hence his mind,
Even in the first trial of its powers,
Is prompt and watchful, eager to combine
In one appearance all the elements
And parts of the same object, else detached
And loath to coalesce.[60] Thus day by day
Subjected to the discipline of love,
His organs and recipient faculties[61]
Are quickened,[62] are more vigorous; his mind spreads,
Tenacious of the forms which it receives.[63]
In one beloved presence – nay and more,
In that most apprehensive habitude[64]
And those sensations which have been derived
From this beloved presence, there exists
A virtue which irradiates and exalts
All objects through all intercourse of sense.[65]
No outcast he, bewildered and depressed:
Along his infant veins are interfused
The gravitation and the filial bond
Of nature that connect him with the world.[66]
Emphatically such a being lives
An inmate of this *active* universe.
From nature largely he receives, nor so
Is satisfied, but largely[67] gives again –
For feeling has to him imparted strength;
And, powerful in all sentiments of grief,
Of exultation, fear and joy, his mind,
Even as an agent of the one great mind

Notes

[56] *Blessed the infant babe* The Infant Babe passage was inspired partly by the death of Coleridge's baby son Berkeley, news of which reached Coleridge in Germany in April 1799, several months after it had taken place; for Coleridge's reaction see his letter to Poole of 6 April 1799, p. 656.

[57] *The progress of our being* Just as Milton charted progress from the Garden of Eden, Wordsworth will trace that of the growing mind.

[58] *who when . . . eye* When his soul first forms a relationship with another, the baby learns to love by seeing its mother's love in her eyes.

[59] *torpid* dormant.

[60] *loath to coalesce* reluctant to come together, making wholes. Inspired by its mother's love, the baby becomes able to form parts into wholes, ordering what he perceives; in other words, his mind is working imaginatively.

[61] *recipient faculties* senses.

[62] *quickened* enlivened.

[63] *Tenacious . . . receives* The mind retains visual images; cf. *Tintern Abbey* 23–50.

[64] *most apprehensive habitude* A relationship ('habitude') best suited to learning ('most apprehensive').

[65] *this beloved presence . . . sense* The mother's love is a power ('virtue') that infuses all objects which the child perceives, exalting them; cf. *Tintern Abbey* 101–2: 'A motion and a spirit that impels / All thinking things, all objects of all thought'.

[66] *Along his infant veins . . . world* The child's loving relationship with his mother is what connects him to natural objects.

[67] *largely* abundantly.

Creates, creator and receiver both,[68]
Working but in alliance with the works
Which it beholds. Such, verily, is the first
Poetic spirit of our human life,
By uniform control of after-years
In most abated and suppressed, in some
Through every change of growth or of decay
Pre-eminent till death.
From early days,
Beginning not long after that first time
In which, a babe, by intercourse of touch,
I held mute dialogues with my mother's heart,
I have endeavoured to display the means
Whereby the infant sensibility,
Great birthright of our being, was in me
Augmented and sustained. Yet is a path
More difficult before me, and I fear
That in its broken windings we shall need
The chamois'[69] sinews and the eagle's wing.
For now a trouble came into my mind
From unknown causes: I was left alone,
Seeking this visible world, nor knowing why.
The props of my affections were removed,
And yet the building stood, as if sustained
By its own spirit.[70] All that I beheld
Was dear to me, and from this cause it came:
That now to nature's finer influxes[71]
My mind lay open to that more exact
And intimate communion which our hearts
Maintain with the minuter properties[72]
Of objects which already are beloved,
And of those only.
Many are the joys
Of youth, but oh what happiness to live
When every hour brings palpable access[73]
Of knowledge, when all knowledge is delight,
And sorrow is not there! The seasons came,
And every season brought a countless store
Of modes and temporary qualities[74]
Which, but for this most watchful power of love,
Had been neglected – left a register
Of permanent relations,[75] else unknown.
Hence life, and change, and beauty, solitude

Notes

[68] *Creates . . . both* The child's mind becomes creative as well as receptive; it is imaginative – working in harmony with Nature. In doing so it acts as an agent of God.

[69] *chamois* mountain antelope which Wordsworth may have seen on his 1790 walking tour which took him through the Alps.

[70] *The props . . . spirit* The 'props' of the boy's feelings are the 'incidental charms which first attached / My heart to rural objects day by day' (ll. 237–8); they are no longer required for his love of nature to exist in its own right.

[71] *influxes* influences.

[72] *minuter properties* qualities known only to those who possess a well-established love of nature.

[73] *palpable access* perceptible increase.

[74] *modes and temporary qualities* short-lived weather or seasonal conditions.

[75] *register . . . relations* permanent recollection in the mind of changing scenes in nature.

More active even than 'best society',[76]
Society made sweet as solitude
By silent inobtrusive sympathies
And gentle agitations of the mind
From manifold distinctions (difference
Perceived in things where to the common eye
No difference is) – and hence, from the same source,
Sublimer joy.[77] For I would walk alone[78]
In storm and tempest, or in starlight nights
Beneath the quiet heavens, and at that time
Would feel whate'er there is of power in sound
To breathe[79] an elevated mood, by form
Or image unprofaned. And I would stand
Beneath some rock, listening to sounds that are
The ghostly language of the ancient earth
Or make their dim abode in distant winds:
Thence did I drink the visionary power.
I deem not profitless these fleeting moods
Of shadowy exultation – not for this,
That they are kindred to our purer mind[80]
And intellectual life, but that the soul,
Remembering how she felt, but what she felt
Remembering not, retains an obscure sense
Of possible sublimity, to which
With growing faculties she doth aspire,
With faculties still growing, feeling still
That whatsoever point they gain they still
Have something to pursue.
                                        And not alone
In grandeur and in tumult, but no less
In tranquil scenes, that universal power
And fitness[81] in the latent qualities
And essences of things, by which the mind
Is moved with feelings of delight, to me
Came strengthened with a superadded soul,[82]
A virtue not its own. My morning walks
Were early; oft before the hours of school[83]
I travelled round our little lake, five miles

Notes

[76] *best society* Wordsworth alludes to *Paradise Lost*, where Adam in Eden says: 'For solitude sometimes is best society' (ix 249).

[77] *sublimer joy* A series of things follows from the permanently impressed features of Nature on the poet's mind: change, beauty, solitude more active than society, society as sweet as solitude and the 'gentle agitations' produced by noticing many distinctions not observable to the untrained eye. From this last feature is produced 'sublimer joy'.

[78] Lines 351–71 were composed in January–February 1798, as part of a passage describing the narrator of *The Ruined Cottage*. While boarding with the Tysons at Colthouse, Wordsworth often went for walks at 1 a.m.

[79] *breathe* inspire.

[80] *kindred to our purer mind* of a spiritual nature.

[81] *fitness* harmony.

[82] *superadded soul* The 'superadded soul' is presumably an element of the 'visionary power' of l. 360. It is additional to natural objects, and is not conferred on them by the perceiving mind: it comes from beyond.

[83] *oft before the hours of school* School began at 6 or 6.30 a.m. during the summer; the five-mile walk would have taken Wordsworth round Esthwaite Water – although that seems a generous estimate for a lake which is little more than a mile long. The friend was John Fleming, who went up to Cambridge in 1785.

Of pleasant wandering – happy time more dear
For this, that one was by my side, a friend
Then passionately loved. With heart how full
Will he peruse these lines, this page (perhaps
A blank to other men), for many years
Have since flowed in between us, and, our minds
Both silent to each other, at this time
We live as if those hours had never been.
Nor seldom did I lift our cottage latch
Far earlier, and before the vernal[84] thrush
Was audible, among the hills I sat
Alone upon some jutting eminence
At the first hour of morning, when the vale
Lay quiet in an utter solitude.
How shall I trace the history, where seek
The origin of what I then have felt?
Oft in those moments such a holy calm
Did overspread my soul, that I forgot
The agency of sight, and what I saw
Appeared like something in myself – a dream,
A prospect[85] in my mind.
'Twere long to tell
What spring and autumn, what the winter snows,
And what the summer shade, what day and night,
The evening and the morning, what my dreams
And what my waking thoughts supplied, to nurse
That spirit of religious love in which
I walked with nature. But let this at least
Be not forgotten – that I still retained
My first creative sensibility,
That by the regular action of the world
My soul was unsubdued. A plastic[86] power
Abode with me, a forming hand,[87] at times
Rebellious, acting in a devious mood,
A local spirit of its own, at war
With general tendency, but for the most
Subservient strictly to the external things
With which it communed.[88] An auxiliar[89] light
Came from my mind, which on the setting sun
Bestowed new splendour; the melodious birds,
The gentle breezes, fountains that ran on
Murmuring so sweetly in themselves, obeyed
A like dominion, and the midnight storm
Grew darker in the presence of my eye.

Notes

[84] *vernal* spring-time.

[85] *prospect* landscape, view.

[86] *plastic* shaping, forming.

[87] *forming hand* an allusion to the creation of Eve at *Paradise Lost* viii 470: 'Under his forming hands a creature grew.'

[88] *at times . . . communed* The imagination sometimes behaves with a will of its own, but is usually subordinate to the natural world (i.e. prepared to enhance it).

[89] *auxiliar* enhancing; the 'auxiliar light' is the imagination.

Hence my obeisance, my devotion hence,
And *hence* my transport.[90]
Nor should this perchance
Pass unrecorded, that I still had loved
The exercise and produce of a toil
Than analytic industry to me
More pleasing, and whose character I deem
Is more poetic, as resembling more
Creative agency – I mean to speak
Of that interminable building[91] reared
By observation of affinities
In objects where no brotherhood exists
To common minds. My seventeenth year was come,
And, whether from this habit[92] rooted now
So deeply in my mind, or from excess
Of the great social principle of life[93]
Coercing all things into sympathy,
To unorganic natures I transferred
My own enjoyments,[94] or, the power of truth
Coming in revelation, I conversed
With things that really are; I at this time
Saw blessings spread around me like a sea.
Thus did my days pass on, and now at length
From Nature and her overflowing soul[95]
I had received so much that all my thoughts
Were steeped in feeling.
I was only then
Contented when with bliss ineffable[96]
I felt the sentiment of being spread
O'er all that moves, and all that seemeth still,
O'er all that, lost beyond the reach of thought
And human knowledge, to the human eye
Invisible, yet liveth to the heart;
O'er all that leaps and runs, and shouts and sings,
Or beats the gladsome air; o'er all that glides
Beneath the wave, yea in the wave itself
And mighty depth of waters. Wonder not
If such my transports[97] were, for in all things
I saw one life, and felt that it was joy.
One song they sang, and it was audible –

Notes

[90] *transport* ecstasy. It is because the mind is believed to be 'lord and master' over what it perceives that the poet devotes himself to Nature.

[91] *interminable building* mental structure.

[92] *this habit* the 'observation of affinities' (l. 433).

[93] *the great social principle of life* love, which might have led Wordsworth to see his feelings reflected in inanimate objects ('unorganic natures').

[94] *or, from excess . . . own enjoyments* Wordsworth has in mind Coleridge's lines in the 1798 text of *Frost at Midnight*:

> But still the living spirit in our frame
> That loves not to behold a lifeless thing,
> Transfuses into all its own delights
> Its own volition . . . (ll. 21–4)

[95] Lines 446–64 comprise *Pedlar* 204–22, incorporated here in autumn 1799, with the necessary change of pronoun from 'he' to 'I'.

[96] *ineffable* indescribable.

[97] *transports* raptures.

Most audible then when the fleshly ear,
O'ercome by grosser prelude of that strain,[98]
Forgot its functions and slept undisturbed.
If this be error,[99] and another faith
Find easier access to the pious mind,
Yet were I grossly destitute of all
Those human sentiments which make this earth
So dear, if I should fail with grateful voice
To speak of you, ye mountains and ye lakes
And sounding cataracts, ye mists and winds
That dwell among the hills where I was born.
If in my youth I have been pure in heart,
If, mingling with the world, I am content
With my own modest pleasures, and have lived
With God and nature communing, removed
From little enmities and low desires,
The gift is yours; if in these times of fear,
This melancholy waste[100] of hopes o'erthrown,
If, mid indifference and apathy
And wicked exultation, when good men
On every side fall off we know not how,
To selfishness, disguised in gentle names
Of peace and quiet and domestic love,
Yet mingled not unwillingly with sneers
On visionary minds[101] – if in this time
Of dereliction and dismay I yet
Despair not of our nature, but retain
A more than Roman confidence,[102] a faith
That fails not, in all sorrow my support,
The blessing of my life, the gift is yours,
Ye mountains! – thine, oh nature! Thou hast fed
My lofty speculations, and in thee,
For this uneasy heart of ours, I find
A never-failing principle[103] of joy
And purest passion.

Notes

[98] *grosser prelude of that strain* sensual joy preceding the more refined pleasures of response to the pantheist one life.

[99] *If this be error* Wordsworth sometimes sounds certain, but it is characteristic of him sometimes to express doubt; cf. *Tintern Abbey* 50ff.: 'If this / Be but a vain belief . . . ' The phrasing is in fact borrowed from Shakespeare, Sonnet 116, l. 13.

[100] *waste* desert.

[101] *when good men . . . minds* Wordsworth is reacting to Coleridge's exhortation to incorporate into *The Recluse* an address to 'those, who, in consequence of the complete failure of the French Revolution, have thrown up all hopes of the amelioration of mankind, and are sinking into an almost epicurean selfishness, disguising the same under the soft titles of domestic attachment and contempt for visionary *philosophes*' (Griggs i 527). The most obvious example is that of James Mackintosh, a former apologist for the French Revolution who, in a series of notorious lectures of February–June 1799, attacked the progressive causes he had once advocated. His apostasy drew comments in Hazlitt's essay on Mackintosh in *The Spirit of the Age* (1825), an uncharacteristically harsh epigram by Lamb and a notebook entry by Coleridge: 'Did Mackintosh change his opinions, with a cold clear predetermination, formed at one moment, to make £5000 a year by that change?' (*Notebooks* i 947).

[102] *more than Roman confidence* Although Maxwell adduced the example of the Roman general, Varro, commended after his defeat by Hannibal at Cannae (216 BC) for not despairing of the republic, Wordsworth may simply be recommending Stoicism. His admiration for Roman history and thought is analysed by Jane Worthington, *Wordsworth's Reading of Roman Prose* (1946).

[103] *principle* source.

Thou, my friend, wast reared
In the great city, mid far other scenes,[104]
But we by different roads at length have gained
The self-same bourn. And from this cause to thee
I speak unapprehensive of contempt,
The insinuated scoff of coward tongues,
And all that silent language which so oft
In conversation betwixt man and man
Blots from the human countenance all trace
Of beauty and of love. For thou hast sought
The truth in solitude, and thou art one,
The most intense of nature's worshippers,
In many things my brother, chiefly here
In this my deep devotion.
Fare thee well![105]
Health and the quiet of a healthful mind
Attend thee, seeking oft the haunts of men,
And yet more often living with thyself,
And for thyself. So haply shall thy days
Be many, and a blessing to mankind.

End of the Second Part[106]

[*There is an active principle*] (extract) (composed between 6 October 1798 and late April 1799; edited from MS)[1]

There is an active principle alive
In all things[2] – in all natures, in the flowers
And in the trees, in every pebbly stone
That paves the brooks, the stationary rocks,
The moving waters, and the invisible air.
All beings have their properties which spread[3]
Beyond themselves, a power by which they make
Some other being conscious of their life –
Spirit that knows no insulated spot,
No chasm, no solitude. From link to link

Notes

[104] *Thou, my friend . . . other scenes* In *Frost at Midnight*, Coleridge had written: 'For I was reared / In the great city, pent mid cloisters dim' (ll. 56–7).

[105] *Fare thee well!* Coleridge in November 1799 was about to go south to become a journalist in London; the Wordsworths were about to move into Dove Cottage.

[106] *End of the Second Part* entered by Dorothy when she copied the poem. She thought it would be continued, and Wordsworth indeed attempted to write a third Part at the end of 1801. However, when he next made a serious start on the poem, in January 1804 he decided to reorganize the work completely, and ended up creating the *Five-Book Prelude*.

There is an active principle

[1] Had Wordsworth been able to complete *The Recluse* in 1798–9, this would have comprised one of its central statements, along with 'Not Useless do I Deem' (pp. 444–7). Its overt pantheism looks back to the Alfoxden poetry, especially the central episode of *The Pedlar* (ll. 204–22). In later years it was revised to form the opening of *Excursion* Book IX (1814).

[2] *In all things* cf. *Pedlar* 217–18: 'in all things / He saw one life, and felt that it was joy.'

[3] *spread* cf. *Pedlar* 208–9: 'He felt the sentiment of being spread / O'er all that moves, and all that seemeth still.'

It circulates, the soul of all the worlds.[4]
This is the freedom of the universe,
Unfolded still the more, more visible
The more we know[5] – and yet is reverenced least,
And least respected, in the human mind,
Its most apparent home.

[*There was a boy*] (composed between 6 October and early December 1798)

From Lyrical Ballads (2nd edn, 2 vols, 1800)

There was a boy – ye knew him well,[1] ye cliffs
And islands of Winander![2] Many a time
At evening, when the stars had just begun
To move along the edges of the hills,
Rising or setting, would he stand alone
Beneath the trees or by the glimmering lake,
And there, with fingers interwoven, both hands
Pressed closely palm to palm and to his mouth
Uplifted, he, as through an instrument,
Blew mimic hootings to the silent owls
That they might answer him. And they would shout
Across the watery vale, and shout again
Responsive to his call, with quivering peals
And long halloos, and screams, and echoes loud
Redoubled and redoubled – a wild scene
Of mirth and jocund din! And when it chanced
That pauses of deep silence mocked his skill,
Then sometimes in that silence while he hung
Listening, a gentle shock of mild surprise
Has carried far[3] into his heart the voice
Of mountain torrents; or the visible scene
Would enter unawares[4] into his mind
With all its solemn imagery, its rocks,
Its woods, and that uncertain heaven, received
Into the bosom of the steady lake.[5]

Notes

[4] *the soul of all the worlds* Wordsworth has in mind the Platonic world soul.

[5] *Unfolded . . . know* The divine spirit becomes more evident to us as we acquire experience.

There was a boy

[1] When first composed, this poem was sent to Coleridge, who told Wordsworth on 10 December 1798 that the lines 'are very beautiful, and leave an affecting impression' (Griggs i 452). In early 1804 this poem was incorporated into *Five-Book Prelude* iv 472–505, and then into *Thirteen-Book Prelude* v 389–422. It was originally composed in the first person, with all the experiences attributed to the poet.

[2] *Winander* Windermere.

[3] 'The very expression, "far", by which space and its infinities are attributed to the human heart, and to its capacities of re-echoing the sublimities of nature, has always struck me as with a flash of sublime revelation,' wrote De Quincey of this passage in 1839; see p. 825.

[4] *unawares* unconsciously; it is important to Wordsworth and Coleridge that moments of vision occur spontaneously – cf. *The Ancient Mariner* (1798): 'A spring of love gusht from my heart / And I blessed them unaware!' (ll. 276–7).

[5] After reading 'There was a boy' in December 1798, Coleridge wrote of ll. 24–5: 'I should have recognised [them] any where; and had I met these lines running wild in the deserts

Fair are the woods, and beauteous is the spot,
The vale where he was born. The churchyard hangs
Upon a slope above the village school,
And there, along that bank, when I have passed
At evening, I believe that near his grave
A full half-hour together I have stood
Mute – for he died when he was ten years old.[6]

Nutting (composed between 6 October and 28 December 1798)[1]

From Lyrical Ballads (2nd edn, 2 vols, 1800)

It seems a day,
One of those heavenly days which cannot die,
When forth I sallied from our cottage-door,
And with a wallet o'er my shoulder slung,
A nutting-crook in hand, I turned my steps
Towards the distant woods, a figure quaint,
Tricked out in proud disguise of beggar's weeds[2]
Put on for the occasion, by advice
And exhortation of my frugal dame.[3]
Motley accoutrement! of power to smile
At thorns, and brakes, and brambles, and, in truth,
More ragged than need was. Among the woods,
And o'er the pathless rocks, I forced my way
Until, at length, I came to one dear nook
Unvisited, where not a broken bough
Drooped with its withered leaves (ungracious sign
Of devastation), but the hazels rose
Tall and erect, with milk-white clusters hung,
A virgin scene! A little while I stood,
Breathing with such suppression of the heart
As joy delights in; and, with wise restraint
Voluptuous, fearless of a rival, eyed
The banquet, or beneath the trees I sate
Among the flowers, and with the flowers I played;

Notes

of Arabia, I should have instantly screamed out "Wordsworth!" ' (Griggs i 453). Wordsworth offered a gloss on ll. 21–5 in his 1815 Preface: 'The Boy, there introduced, is listening, with something of a feverish and restless anxiety, for the recurrence of the riotous sounds which he had previously excited; and, at the moment when the intenseness of his mind is beginning to remit, he is surprised into a perception of the solemn and tranquillizing images which the Poem describes' (*Prose Works* iii 35n).

[6] Although, as Wordsworth later recalled, the boy who hooted at the owls was a conflation of himself and a schoolfriend called William Raincock, the grave he has in mind is that of his schoolfriend John Tyson, who died in 1782 at the age of 12.

NUTTING

[1] 'Written in Germany, intended as part of a poem on my own life [*The Two-Part Prelude*], but struck out as not being wanted there. Like most of my schoolfellows I was an impassioned nutter . . . These verses arose out of the remembrance of feelings I had often had when a boy, and particularly in the extensive woods that still stretch from the side of Esthwaite Lake towards Graythwaite, the seat of the ancient family of Sandys' (*FN* 13).

[2] *weeds* clothes.

[3] *my frugal dame* Ann Tyson, Wordsworth's landlady at Hawkshead. Cf. *Two-Part Prelude* ii 88–90.

A temper known to those who, after long
And weary expectation, have been blessed
With sudden happiness beyond all hope.
  Perhaps it was a bower beneath whose leaves
The violets of five seasons reappear
And fade, unseen by any human eye,
Where fairy water-breaks[4] do murmur on
For ever; and I saw the sparkling foam,
And, with my cheek on one of those green stones
That, fleeced with moss, beneath the shady trees,
Lay round me scattered like a flock of sheep,
I heard the murmur and the murmuring sound,
In that sweet mood when pleasure loves to pay
Tribute to ease; and, of its joy secure,
The heart luxuriates with indifferent[5] things,
Wasting its kindliness on stocks[6] and stones,
And on the vacant air. Then up I rose,
And dragged to earth both branch and bough, with crash
And merciless ravage, and the shady nook
Of hazels, and the green and mossy bower,
Deformed and sullied, patiently gave up
Their quiet being; and, unless I now
Confound my present feelings with the past,
Even then, when from the bower I turned away,
Exulting, rich beyond the wealth of kings,
I felt a sense of pain when I beheld
The silent trees, and the intruding sky.
  Then, dearest maiden,[7] move along these shades
In gentleness of heart; with gentle hand
Touch – for there is a spirit in the woods.

[*Strange fits of passion I have known*] (composed between 6 October and 28 December 1798)[1]

From Lyrical Ballads (2nd edn, 2 vols, 1800)

Strange fits of passion I have known,
And I will dare to tell,
But in the lover's ear alone,
What once to me befell.

Notes

[4] *water-breaks* stretches of rapid water.

[5] *indifferent* not insensible but neutral, impartial, disinterested.

[6] *stocks* tree-stumps, dead wood.

[7] *dearest maiden* The anonymous 'maiden' (perhaps associated with Wordsworth's sister Dorothy) is bidden to establish contact with a wood-spirit.

STRANGE FITS OF PASSION I HAVE KNOWN

[1] This poem, the three that follow it and 'I travelled among unknown men' (p. 522), comprise what have come to be known as the Lucy poems. 'She was a phantom of delight' is often classed among them. Much ink has been expended on the question of Lucy's identity; for Coleridge's explanation, which remains the most plausible, see his letter to Poole, 6 April 1799, p. 656.

When she I loved was strong and gay
And like a rose in June,
I to her cottage bent my way
Beneath the evening moon.

Upon the moon I fixed my eye,
All over the wide lea;[2]
My horse trudged on, and we drew nigh
Those paths so dear to me.

And now we reached the orchard-plot,
And as we climbed the hill,
Towards the roof of Lucy's cot
The moon descended still.

In one of those sweet dreams I slept,
Kind nature's gentlest boon!
And all the while my eyes I kept
On the descending moon.

My horse moved on; hoof after hoof
He raised and never stopped:
When down behind the cottage roof
At once the planet dropped.

What fond[3] and wayward thoughts will slide
Into a lover's head;
'Oh mercy!' to myself I cried,
'If Lucy should be dead!'

Song (composed between 6 October and 28 December 1798)

From Lyrical Ballads (2nd edn, 2 vols, 1800)

She dwelt among th' untrodden ways
Beside the springs of Dove,[1]
A maid whom there were none to praise
And very few to love.

A violet by a mossy stone
Half-hidden from the eye,
Fair as a star when only one
Is shining in the sky!

Notes

[2] *lea* meadow.

[3] *fond* meaning either 'foolish' or 'loving, affectionate'.

Song

[1] *Dove* There are three English rivers with this name. Wordsworth probably meant the one in Derbyshire, rather than those in Yorkshire or Cumbria.

She lived unknown, and few could know
  When Lucy ceased to be;
But she is in her grave, and oh!
  The difference to me.

[*A slumber did my spirit seal*] (composed between 6 October and 28 December 1798)[1]

From Lyrical Ballads (2nd edn, 2 vols, 1800)

A slumber did my spirit seal,[2]
  I had no human fears;
She seemed a thing that could not feel
  The touch of earthly years.

No motion has she now, no force;
  She neither hears nor sees;
Rolled round in earth's diurnal[3] course
  With rocks and stones and trees!

[*Three years she grew in sun and shower*] (composed between 6 October and 28 December 1798)

From Lyrical Ballads (2nd edn, 2 vols, 1800)

Three years she grew in sun and shower,
Then Nature said, 'A lovelier flower
On earth was never sown;
This child I to myself will take,
She shall be mine, and I will make
A lady of my own.

Myself will to my darling be
Both law and impulse, and with me
The girl in rock and plain,
In earth and heaven, in glade and bower,
Shall feel an overseeing power
To kindle or restrain.

Notes

A SLUMBER DID MY SPIRIT SEAL

[1] When first composed, this poem was sent to Coleridge. In a letter to his friend Thomas Poole of 6 April 1799, Coleridge remarked: 'Oh, this strange, strange, strange scene-shifter, Death! that giddies one with insecurity, and so unsubstantiates the living things that one has grasped and handled! Some months ago Wordsworth transmitted to me a most sublime Epitaph. Whether it had any reality, I cannot say. Most probably, in some gloomier moments he had fancied the moment in which his sister might die' (Griggs i 479). Critics ever since have speculated as to the identity of the woman lamented in this poem.

[2] *seal* contain, lock up.

[3] *diurnal* daily; cf. *Two-Part Prelude* i 182.

She shall be sportive as the fawn
That wild with glee across the lawn
Or up the mountain springs,
And hers shall be the breathing balm
And hers the silence and the calm
Of mute insensate things.

The floating clouds their state shall lend
To her, for her the willow bend,
Nor shall she fail to see
Even in the motions of the storm
A beauty that shall mould her form
By silent sympathy.

The stars of midnight shall be dear
To her, and she shall lean her ear
In many a secret place
Where rivulets dance their wayward round,
And beauty born of murmuring sound
Shall pass into her face.

And vital feelings of delight
Shall rear her form to stately height,
Her virgin bosom swell,
Such thoughts to Lucy I will give
While she and I together live
Here in this happy dell.

Thus Nature spake – the work was done –
How soon my Lucy's race was run!
She died and left to me
This heath, this calm and quiet scene,
The memory of what has been,
And never more will be.

[*The Prelude: Glad Preamble*]
(composed late November 1799; edited from MS)[1]

Oh there is blessing in this gentle breeze
That blows from the green fields, and from the clouds,
And from the sky: it beats against my cheek,
And seems half-conscious of the joy it gives.
Oh welcome messenger, oh welcome friend!
A captive greets thee, coming from a house
Of bondage, from yon city's walls set free,

Notes

THE PRELUDE: GLAD PREAMBLE

[1] Wordsworth began work on this passage while walking from Ullswater to Grasmere, 18 November 1799, and completed it soon after moving into Dove Cottage two days later. It was used as the opening to *Prelude* Book I in all versions of the poem after January 1804

A prison where he hath been long immured.[2]
Now I am free, enfranchised and at large,
May fix my habitation where I will.
What dwelling shall receive me? In what vale
Shall be my harbour? Underneath what grove
Shall I take up my home, and what sweet stream
Shall with its murmur lull me to my rest?
The earth is all before me:[3] with a heart
Joyous, nor scared at its own liberty,
I look about, and should the guide I choose
Be nothing better than a wandering cloud,[4]
I cannot miss my way. I breathe again;
Trances of thought and mountings of the mind
Come fast upon me. It is shaken off,
As by miraculous gift 'tis shaken off,
The heavy weight of many a weary day
Not mine, and such as were not made for me.
Long months of peace (if such bold word accord
With any promises of human life),
Long months of ease and undisturbed delight
Are mine in prospect – whither shall I turn?
By road or pathway, or through open field,
Or shall a twig or any floating thing
Upon the river, point me out my course?
   Enough that I am free, embrace today
An uncontrolled enfranchisement; for months
To come may live a life of chosen tasks,
May quit the tiresome sea and dwell on shore –
If not a settler on the soil, at least
To drink wild waters, and to pluck green herbs,
And gather fruits fresh from their native tree.
Nay more: if I may trust myself, this hour
Hath brought a gift that consecrates my joy,
For I, methought, while the sweet breath of heaven
Was blowing on my body, felt within
A corresponding mild creative breeze,[5]
A vital breeze which travelled gently on
O'er things which it had made, and is become
A tempest, a redundant[6] energy

Notes

[2] *immured* confined, walled up. The city from which Wordsworth has been released is probably a mixture of Goslar in Germany (where he spent the cold winter of 1798–9) and London.

[3] *The earth is all before me* an allusion to the conclusion of *Paradise Lost*, as Adam and Eve are expelled from Eden:

> Some natural tears they dropped, but wiped them soon;
> The world was all before them, where to choose
> Their place of rest, and Providence their guide.
> They hand in hand, with wandering steps and slow,
> Through Eden took their solitary way.

Wordsworth's poem begins where Milton leaves off. He too is making a new start, but does so in a spirit of profound optimism.

[4] Providence guided Adam and Eve out of Eden (see the preceding note).

[5] *A corresponding mild creative breeze* the subject of much comment among recent critics; see, most notably, M. H. Abrams's title essay in *The Correspondent Breeze: Essays on English Romanticism* (New York and London, 1984).

[6] *redundant* overflowing, exuberant.

Vexing its own creation. 'Tis a power
That does not come unrecognized, a storm
Which, breaking up a long-continued frost,
Brings with it vernal promises, the hope
Of active days, of dignity and thought,
Of prowess in an honourable field,[7]
Pure passion, virtue, knowledge, and delight,
The holy life of music and of verse.

[*Prospectus to 'The Recluse'*] (composed probably November or December 1799; edited from MS)[1]

On man, on nature, and on human life,
Thinking in solitude, from time to time
I find sweet passions traversing my soul
Like music;[2] unto these, where'er I may,
I would give utterance in numerous verse.[3]
Of truth, of grandeur, beauty, love, and hope,
Of joy in various commonalty[4] spread,
Of the individual mind that keeps its own
Inviolate retirement, and consists[5]
With being limitless – the one great life[6] –
I sing: fit audience let me find, though few!
'Fit audience find, though few!'[7] Thus prayed the bard,
Holiest of men. Urania,[8] I shall need
Thy guidance, or a greater muse (if such
Descend to earth, or dwell in highest heaven),
For I must tread on shadowy ground, must sink
Deep, and ascend aloft, and breathe in worlds
To which the heaven of heavens[9] is but a veil.
All strength, all terror, single or in bands,
That ever was put forth by personal forms[10] –
Jehovah with his thunder, and the choir
Of shouting angels, and th' empyreal thrones[11] –
I pass them unalarmed. The darkest pit
Of the profoundest hell,[12] night, chaos, death,
Nor aught of blinder vacancy scooped out

Notes

[7] *prowess in an honourable field* a reference to the composition of *The Recluse*; see p. 414.

PROSPECTUS TO 'THE RECLUSE'

[1] Composed soon after arrival in Grasmere, 19 November 1799, published in a much revised form in *The Excursion* (1814), as an announcement of the plan of *The Recluse*.

[2] *I find . . . music* Passions (emotions) play across the poet's soul just as the winds cross the strings on an Aeolian harp.

[3] *numerous verse* poetic metre.

[4] *commonalty* community.

[5] *consists* coexists.

[6] *the one great life* the pantheist perception of *Pedlar* 204–22 and *Tintern Abbey* 94–103.

[7] *Paradise Lost* vii 31.

[8] Urania, muse of astronomy, is invoked by Milton, *Paradise Lost* Book VII.

[9] *the heaven of heavens is but a veil* cf. *Paradise Lost* vii 553.

[10] *personal forms* celestial beings to whom individual forms are usually attributed.

[11] *empyreal thrones* high-ranking angels, as at *Paradise Lost* ii 430.

[12] *profoundest hell* an echo of *Paradise Lost* i 251.

By help of dreams, can breed such fear and awe
As fall upon me often when I look
Into my soul, into the soul of man –
My haunt, and the main region of my song.
   Beauty, whose living home is the green earth,
Surpassing far what hath by special craft[13]
Of delicate[14] poets been culled forth and shaped
From earth's materials, waits upon my steps,
Pitches her tents before me as I move,
My hourly neighbour. Paradise and groves
Elysian,[15] blessed islands in the deep
Of choice seclusion – wherefore need they be
A history, or but a dream, when minds
Once wedded to this outward frame of things
In love, finds these the growth of common day?[16]
   Such pleasant haunts foregoing, if my song
Must turn elsewhere, and travel near the tribes
And fellowships of man, and see ill sights
Of passions ravenous from each other's rage,[17]
Insult and injury, and wrong and strife;
Must hear humanity in fields and groves
Pipe solitary anguish; or must hang
Brooding above the fierce confederate[18] storm
Of sorrow, barricadoed[19] evermore
Within the walls of cities,[20] to these sounds
Let me find meaning more akin to that
Which to God's ear they carry, that even these
Hearing, I be not heartless[21] or forlorn.
   Come thou, prophetic spirit, soul of man,
Thou human soul of the wide earth, that hast
Thy metropolitan temple[22] in the hearts
Of mighty poets, unto me vouchsafe[23]
Thy foresight, teach me to discern, and part
Inherent things from casual, what is fixed
From fleeting,[24] that my soul may live, and be
Even as a light hung up in heaven to cheer
The world in times to come. And if with this
I mingle humbler matter – with the thing
Contemplated describe the mind and man
Contemplating, and who he was, and what
The transitory being that beheld
This vision, when and where and how he lived

Notes

[13] *craft* skill.
[14] *delicate* fastidious.
[15] *groves Elysian* the Elysian fields, where the souls of the blessed were believed to live in an eternal spring.
[16] *Paradise . . . day* Paradise materializes in different forms before the poet in everyday sights.
[17] *passions ravenous from each other's rage* emotions stirred up by the sight of passion in other people.
[18] *confederate* leagued, allied.
[19] *barricadoed* cf. *Paradise Lost* viii 241.
[20] *the fierce . . . cities* Those confined within the hell of city life are united in misery.
[21] *heartless* unhappy.
[22] *metropolitan temple* throne.
[23] *vouchsafe* grant.
[24] *part . . . fleeting* Innate qualities will be separated from the random, the permanent from the ephemeral.

With all his little realities of life
(In part a fellow-citizen, in part
An outlaw and a borderer of his age) –
Be not this labour useless.
Oh great God!
To less than thee I cannot make this prayer;
Innocent mighty spirit, let my life
Express the image of a better time,
Desires more wise and simpler manners, nurse
My heart in genuine freedom, all pure thoughts
Be with me and uphold me to the end.

The Brothers: A Pastoral Poem (composed December 1799-early March 1800)[1]

From Lyrical Ballads (2nd edn, 2 vols, 1800)

'These tourists,[2] Heaven preserve us, needs must live
A profitable life! Some glance along,
Rapid and gay, as if the earth were air,
And they were butterflies to wheel about
Long as their summer lasted; some, as wise,
Upon the forehead of a jutting crag
Sit perched with book and pencil on their knee,
And look and scribble, scribble on and look,
Until a man might travel twelve stout miles[3]
Or reap an acre of his neighbour's corn.
But, for that moping[4] son of idleness –
Why can he tarry yonder? In our churchyard
Is neither epitaph nor monument,
Tombstone nor name,[5] only the turf we tread
And a few natural graves.' To Jane, his wife,
Thus spake the homely priest of Ennerdale.
It was a July evening, and he sat
Upon the long stone-seat beneath the eaves
Of his old cottage – as it chanced that day,
Employed in winter's work. Upon the stone

Notes

THE BROTHERS: A PASTORAL POEM

[1] *The Brothers* is based on a story told to Wordsworth and Coleridge while on a walking tour of the Lakes in 1799. They heard about Jerome Bowman (who broke his leg near Scale Force, crawled three miles at night on hands and knees, and then died from his injuries) and his son who 'broke his neck before this, by falling off a crag', as Coleridge put it. The son was believed 'to have laid down and slept, but walked in his sleep, and so came to this crag and fell off. This was at Proud Knot on the mountain called Pillar up Ennerdale. His pike-staff stuck midway and stayed there till it rotted away' (*Notebooks* i 540). In 1800 Wordsworth appended the following note to the title: 'This poem was intended to be the concluding poem of a series of pastorals the scene of which was laid among the mountains of Cumberland and Westmorland. I mention this to apologise for the abruptness with which the poem begins.'

[2] *tourists* Even in 1800, the Lake District was a popular tourist resort.

[3] *stout miles* the old English 'long mile' of 2,428 yards.

[4] *moping* aimless, purposeless.

[5] *neither epitaph . . . name* Several Lake District churchyards had no tombstones.

His wife sat near him, teasing matted wool,
While from the twin cards[6] toothed with glittering wire,
He fed the spindle of his youngest child,
Who turned her large round wheel in the open air
With back and forward steps.[7] Towards the field
In which the parish chapel stood alone
Girt round with a bare ring of mossy wall,
While half an hour went by, the priest had sent
Many a long look of wonder; and at last,
Risen from his seat, beside the snowy ridge
Of carded wool which the old man had piled
He laid his implements with gentle care,
Each in the other locked, and down the path
Which from his cottage to the churchyard led
He took his way, impatient to accost
The stranger whom he saw still lingering there.
'Twas one well known to him in former days:
A shepherd-lad, who ere his thirteenth year[8]
Had changed his calling – with the mariners
A fellow-mariner – and so had fared
Through twenty seasons; but he had been reared
Among the mountains, and he in his heart
Was half a shepherd on the stormy seas.
Oft in the piping shrouds[9] had Leonard heard
The tones of waterfalls, and inland sounds
Of caves and trees. And when the regular wind
Between the tropics[10] filled the steady sail
And blew with the same breath through days and weeks,
Lengthening invisibly its weary line
Along the cloudless main, he, in those hours
Of tiresome indolence, would often hang
Over the vessel's side, and gaze and gaze;
And while the broad green wave and sparkling foam
Flashed round him images and hues that wrought
In union with the employment of his heart,
He – thus by feverish passion overcome –
Even with the organs of his bodily eye,
Below him in the bosom of the deep
Saw mountains, saw the forms of sheep that grazed

Notes

[6] *twin cards* a pair of combs used for teasing out the hairs of wool before they are spun into thread.

[7] *Upon the stone . . . steps* In the Fenwick Notes of 1843, Wordsworth recalled: 'I could write a treatise of lamentation upon the changes brought about among the cottages of Westmorland by the silence of the spinning wheel. During long winter nights and wet days, the wheel upon which wool was spun gave employment to a great part of a family. The old man, however infirm, was able to card the wool, as he sate in the corner by the fireside; and often, when a boy, have I admired the cylinders of carded wool which were softly laid upon each other by his side. Two wheels were often at work on the same floor, and others of the family, chiefly the little children, were occupied in teasing and cleaning the wool to fit it for the hand of the carder. So that all except the smallest infants were contributing to mutual support' (*FN* 20).

[8] *ere his thirteenth year* John Wordsworth, the poet's younger brother, also decided early on that he would be a sailor.

[9] *shrouds* ropes supporting the mast of a ship, climbed when changing sails. The wind plays ('pipes') through them.

[10] *the regular wind . . . tropics* trade winds blowing towards the equator from the tropics of Cancer and Capricorn.

On verdant hills, with dwellings among trees,
And shepherds clad in the same country grey
Which he himself had worn.[11]
And now at length,
From perils manifold, with some small wealth
Acquired by traffic in the Indian Isles,[12]
To his paternal home he is returned
With a determined purpose to resume
The life which he lived there – both for the sake
Of many darling[13] pleasures, and the love
Which to an only brother he has borne
In all his hardships, since that happy time
When, whether it blew foul or fair, they two
Were brother shepherds on their native hills.
They were the last of all their race;[14] and now,
When Leonard had approached his home, his heart
Failed in him, and not venturing to enquire
Tidings of one whom he so dearly loved,
Towards the churchyard he had turned aside[15]
That (as he knew in what particular spot
His family were laid) he thence might learn
If still his brother lived, or to the file[16]
Another grave was added. He had found
Another grave, near which a full half-hour
He had remained; but as he gazed there grew
Such a confusion in his memory
That he began to doubt, and he had hopes
That he had seen this heap of turf before –
That it was not another grave, but one
He had forgotten. He had lost his path
As up the vale he came that afternoon
Through fields which once had been well known to him,
And oh, what joy the recollection now
Sent to his heart! He lifted up his eyes,
And looking round he thought that he perceived
Strange alteration wrought on every side
Among the woods and fields, and that the rocks,
And the eternal hills themselves, were changed.

Notes

[11] 'This description of the calenture is sketched from an imperfect recollection of an admirable one in prose, by Mr Gilbert, author of *The Hurricane*' (Wordsworth's note). The calenture was defined by Johnson as 'a distemper peculiar to sailors in hot climates, wherein they imagine the sea to be green fields, and will throw themselves into it'. Gilbert's *Hurricane* (1796) may have been read by Wordsworth in the year of its publication; in later years at Rydal Mount he owned a copy.

[12] *traffic in the Indian Isles* trade in the East Indies.

[13] *darling* dearly loved.

[14] *They were the last of all their race* As in *Michael*, Wordsworth is concerned in this poem with the dying-out of small landowners – 'statesmen', whose small plots of land had descended through the same families for generations. Wordsworth made this point when he sent the Whig leader, Charles James Fox, a copy of *Lyrical Ballads* (1800); see p. 516n36.

[15] *When Leonard . . . aside* probably based on John Wordsworth's arrival in Grasmere at the end of January 1800; according to Dorothy, 'twice did he approach the door and lay his hand upon the latch, and stop, and turn away without the courage to enter (we had not met for several years). He then went to the inn and sent us word that he was come' (*EY* 649).

[16] *file* row, line.

By this the priest, who down the field had come
Unseen by Leonard, at the churchyard gate
Stopped short; and thence, at leisure, limb by limb
He scanned him with a gay complacency.[17]
'Aye', thought the vicar, smiling to himself,
''Tis one of those who needs must leave the path
Of the world's business, to go wild alone –
His arms have a perpetual holiday.
The happy man will creep about the fields
Following his fancies by the hour, to bring
Tears down his cheek, or solitary smiles
Into his face, until the setting sun
Write Fool upon his forehead.' Planted thus
Beneath a shed[18] that overarched the gate
Of this rude churchyard, till the stars appeared
The good man might have communed with himself,
But that the stranger, who had left the grave,
Approached. He recognized the priest at once,
And after greetings interchanged (and given
By Leonard to the vicar as to one
Unknown to him), this dialogue ensued.

LEONARD
You live, sir, in these dales, a quiet life.
Your years make up one peaceful family,
And who would grieve and fret, if – welcome come
And welcome gone – they are so like each other
They cannot be remembered? Scarce a funeral
Comes to this churchyard once in eighteen months;
And yet, some changes must take place among you.
And you who dwell here, even among these rocks
Can trace the finger of mortality,[19]
And see that with our threescore years and ten[20]
We are not all that perish. I remember
(For many years ago I passed this road)
There was a footway all along the fields
By the brook-side; 'tis gone. And that dark cleft –
To me it does not seem to wear the face
Which then it had.

Notes

[17] *complacency* self-satisfaction.
[18] *shed* porchway, roof.
[19] *the finger of mortality* signs of death or change.
[20] *threescore years and ten* seventy years, man's allotted life-span: 'the days of our years are threescore years and ten' (Psalm 90: 10).

PRIEST

Why, sir, for aught I know,
That chasm is much the same.

LEONARD

But surely, yonder –

PRIEST

Aye, there indeed your memory is a friend
That does not play you false. On that tall pike
(It is the loneliest place of all these hills)
There were two springs which bubbled side by side
As if they had been made that they might be
Companions for each other! Ten years back,
Close to those brother fountains, the huge crag
Was rent with lightning – one is dead and gone,
The other, left behind, is flowing still.[21]
For accidents and changes such as these,
Why, we have store[22] of them! A water-spout
Will bring down half a mountain – what a feast
For folks that wander up and down like you,
To see an acre's breadth of that wide cliff
One roaring cataract! A sharp May storm
Will come with loads of January snow
And in one night send twenty score of sheep
To feed the ravens; or a shepherd dies
By some untoward death among the rocks;
The ice breaks up, and sweeps away a bridge;
A wood is felled. And then, for our own homes –
A child is born or christened, a field ploughed,
A daughter sent to service,[23] a web spun,[24]
The old house-clock is decked with a new face[25]–
And hence, so far from wanting facts or dates
To chronicle the time, we all have here
A pair of diaries: one serving, sir,
For the whole dale, and one for each fireside.[26]
Yours was a stranger's judgment[27] – for historians
Commend me to these vallies!

LEONARD

Yet your churchyard
Seems (if such freedom may be used with you)
To say that you are heedless of the past:

Notes

[21] 'The impressive circumstance here described actually took place some years ago in this country, upon an eminence called Kidstow Pike, one of the highest of the mountains that surround Hawes Water. The summit of the Pike was stricken by lightning, and every trace of one of the fountains disappeared, while the other continued to flow as before' (Wordsworth's note).

[22] *store* a good store, plenty.

[23] *sent to service* put to work as a servant.

[24] *a web spun* a piece of cloth woven.

[25] *decked with a new face* repainted.

[26] *we all . . . fireside* Time is measured by the public events, shared by the community, and private ones, known to each family.

[27] *Yours was a stranger's judgement* painfully ironic; the priest is still unaware of Leonard's identity.

An orphan could not find his mother's grave.
Here's neither head nor foot-stone, plate of brass,
Cross-bones or skull, type of our earthly state
Or emblem of our hopes. The dead man's home
Is but a fellow to that pasture field.[28]

PRIEST

Why there, sir, is a thought that's new to me.
The stonecutters, 'tis true, might beg their bread
If every English churchyard were like ours;
Yet your conclusion wanders from the truth.
We have no need of names and epitaphs,
We talk about the dead by our firesides.
And then for our immortal part[29] – we want
No symbols, sir, to tell us that plain tale.
The thought of death sits easy on the man
Who has been born and dies among the mountains.[30]

LEONARD

Your dalesmen, then, do in each other's thoughts
Possess a kind of second life. No doubt
You, sir, could help me to the history
Of half these graves?

PRIEST

For eight-score winters past[31] –
With what I've witnessed, and with what I've heard –
Perhaps I might; and on a winter's evening,
If you were seated at my chimney's nook,
By turning o'er these hillocks one by one
We two could travel, sir, through a strange round,
Yet all in the broad highway of the world.[32]
Now there's a grave – your foot is half upon it –
It looks just like the rest, and yet that man
Died broken-hearted.

LEONARD

'Tis a common case –
We'll take another. Who is he that lies
Beneath yon ridge, the last of those three graves? –
It touches on that piece of native[33] rock
Left in the churchyard wall.

Notes

[28] *The dead . . . field* The graveyard looks the same as the meadow.

[29] *our immortal part* i.e. the soul.

[30] 'There is not anything more worthy of remark in the manners of the inhabitants of these mountains, than the tranquillity – I might say indifference – with which they think and talk upon the subject of death. Some of the country churchyards, as here described, do not contain a single tombstone, and most of them have a very small number' (Wordsworth's note).

[31] *eight-score winters past* i.e. the last 160 years (a score is twenty).

[32] *By turning . . . world* The life-stories of those buried before them comprise a wide range ('strange round') of experience, which, taken as a whole, would be revealed as entirely normal ('in the broad highway of the world').

[33] *native* a piece of rock embedded in the ground even before the graveyard was put there.

PRIEST

That's Walter Ewbank.
He had as white a head and fresh a cheek
As ever were produced by youth and age
Engendering in the blood of hale fourscore.[34]
For five long generations had the heart
Of Walter's forefathers o'erflowed the bounds
Of their inheritance[35] – that single cottage
(You see it yonder), and those few green fields.
They toiled and wrought, and still, from sire[36] to son,
Each struggled, and each yielded as before
A little – yet a little. And old Walter –
They left to him the family heart, and land
With other burdens than the crop it bore.
Year after year the old man still preserved
A cheerful mind, and buffeted with bond,
Interest and mortgages, at last he sank,
And went into his grave before his time.[37]
Poor Walter – whether it was care that spurred him
God only knows, but to the very last
He had the lightest foot in Ennerdale.
His pace was never that of an old man –
I almost see him tripping down the path
With his two grandsons after him. But you,
Unless our landlord be your host tonight,[38]
Have far to travel, and in these rough paths
Even in the longest day of midsummer –

LEONARD

But these two orphans . . .

PRIEST

Orphans – such they were,
Yet not while Walter lived. For though their parents
Lay buried side by side as now they lie,
The old man was a father to the boys –
Two fathers in one father – and if tears
Shed when he talked of them where they were not,
And hauntings from the infirmity of love,
Are aught of what makes up a mother's heart,
This old man in the day of his old age
Was half a mother to them. If you weep, sir,
To hear a stranger talking about strangers,[39]

Notes

[34] *He had . . . fourscore* Walter was 80, but he was healthy and vigorous ('hale') thanks to his combination of youth and age.

[35] *the heart . . . inheritance* The Ewbanks were more generous than they could afford.

[36] *sire* father.

[37] *buffeted . . . time* The cost of Walter's independence was that the land he inherited was burdened by mortgages and debt.

[38] *Unless our landlord be your host tonight* unless you plan to stay at the inn.

[39] *If you weep . . . strangers* again, painfully ironic. The Priest is still unaware that the story he has been telling is that of Leonard's family.

Heaven bless you when you are among your kindred!
Aye, you may turn that way – it is a grave
Which will bear looking at.

LEONARD

These boys, I hope
They loved this good old man?

PRIEST

They did, and truly –
But that was what we almost overlooked,
They were such darlings of each other. For
Though from their cradles they had lived with Walter,
The only kinsman near them in the house,
Yet he being old they had much love to spare,
And it all went into each other's hearts.
Leonard, the elder by just eighteen months,
Was two years taller – 'twas a joy to see,
To hear, to meet them! From their house the school
Was distant three short miles; and in the time
Of storm, and thaw, when every water-course
And unbridged stream (such as you may have noticed,
Crossing our roads at every hundred steps)
Was swoln into a noisy rivulet,
Would Leonard then, when elder boys perhaps
Remained at home, go staggering through the fords[40]
Bearing his brother on his back. I've seen him
On windy days, in one of those stray brooks –
Aye, more than once I've seen him mid-leg deep,
Their two books lying both on a dry stone
Upon the hither side. And once I said,
As I remember, looking round these rocks
And hills on which we all of us were born,
That God who made the great book of the world[41]
Would bless such piety.[42]

LEONARD

It may be then –

PRIEST

Never did worthier lads break English bread:
The finest Sunday that the autumn saw,
With all its mealy[43] clusters of ripe nuts,
Could never keep these boys away from church
Or tempt them to an hour of sabbath breach.[44]
Leonard and James! I warrant, every corner

Notes

[40] *fords* A ford is a shallow place in a river where people and animals can wade across.

[41] *the great book of the world* i.e. the natural world.

[42] *piety* virtue.

[43] *mealy* meal-coloured.

[44] *sabbath breach* violating the command not to work on the Sabbath (Sunday).

Among these rocks, and every hollow place
Where foot could come, to one or both of them
Was known as well as to the flowers that grow there.
Like roebucks they went bounding o'er the hills;[45]
They played like two young ravens on the crags.
Then they could write, aye, and speak too, as well
As many of their betters.[46] And for Leonard –
The very night before he went away,
In my own house I put into his hand
A bible, and I'd wager twenty pounds
That if he is alive he has it yet.

LEONARD

It seems these brothers have not lived to be
A comfort to each other?

PRIEST

That they might
Live to that end, is what both old and young
In this our valley all of us have wished –
And what for my part I have often prayed.
But Leonard –

LEONARD

Then James still is left among you?

PRIEST

'Tis of the elder brother I am speaking –
They had an uncle (he was at that time
A thriving man and trafficked[47] on the seas[48]),
And but for this same uncle, to this hour
Leonard had never handled rope or shroud.
For the boy loved the life which we lead here;
And, though a very stripling, twelve years old,
His soul was knit[49] to this his native soil.
But, as I said, old Walter was too weak
To strive with such a torrent. When he died,
The estate and house were sold, and all their sheep –
A pretty flock, and which, for aught I know,
Had clothed the Ewbanks for a thousand years.
Well – all was gone, and they were destitute;
And Leonard, chiefly for his brother's sake,
Resolved to try his fortune on the seas.
'Tis now twelve years since we had tidings from him.
If there was one among us who had heard
That Leonard Ewbank was come home again,

Notes

[45] *Like roebucks . . . hills* cf. *Tintern Abbey* 68–9.

[46] *betters* social superiors.

[47] *trafficked* traded.

[48] *he was . . . seas* The poet's cousin, another John Wordsworth, was a successful captain working for the East India Company. Wordsworth's brother John succeeded him as captain of the *Earl of Abergavenny.*

[49] *knit* joined, attached.

From the Great Gavel, down by Leeza's Banks,
And down the Enna, far as Egremont,[50]
The day would be a very festival,
And those two bells of ours, which there you see
Hanging in the open air – but oh, good sir,
This is sad talk; they'll never sound for him,
Living or dead. When last we heard of him
He was in slavery among the Moors
Upon the Barbary Coast.[51] 'Twas not a little
That would bring down his spirit, and no doubt
Before it ended in his death, the lad
Was sadly crossed.[52] Poor Leonard, when we parted
He took me by the hand and said to me
If ever the day came when he was rich
He would return, and on his father's land
He would grow old among us.

LEONARD

If that day
Should come, 'twould needs be a glad day for him;
He would himself, no doubt, be then as happy
As any that should meet him.

PRIEST

Happy, sir –

LEONARD

You said his kindred were all in their graves,
And that he had one brother . . .

PRIEST

That is but
A fellow[53] tale of sorrow. From his youth
James, though not sickly, yet was delicate;
And Leonard being always by his side
Had done so many offices about him[54]
That, though he was not of a timid nature,
Yet still the spirit of a mountain boy
In him was somewhat checked. And when his brother
Was gone to sea and he was left alone,
The little colour that he had was soon
Stolen from his cheek; he drooped, and pined and pined . . .

Notes

[50] 'The Great Gavel, so called, I imagine, from its resemblance to the gable end of a house, is one of the highest of the Cumberland mountains. It stands at the head of the several vales of Ennerdale, Wastdale, and Borrowdale. The Leeza is a river which flows into the Lake of Ennerdale; on issuing from the Lake, it changes its name and is called the End, or Eyne, or Enna. It falls into the sea a little below Egremont' (Wordsworth's note).

[51] *Barbary Coast* north coast of Africa.

[52] *crossed* grieved.

[53] *fellow* similar.

[54] *Had done so many offices about him* had looked after him so much.

LEONARD

But these are all the graves of full grown men . . .

PRIEST

Aye, sir, that passed away. We took him to us –
He was the child of all the dale. He lived
Three months with one, and six months with another,
And wanted neither food, nor clothes, nor love;
And many, many happy days were his.
But, whether blithe or sad, 'tis my belief
His absent brother still was at his heart.
And when he lived beneath our roof, we found
(A practice till this time unknown to him)
That often, rising from his bed at night,
He in his sleep would walk about, and sleeping
He sought his brother Leonard. You are moved;
Forgive me, sir – before I spoke to you
I judged you most unkindly.

LEONARD

But this youth,
How did he die at last?

PRIEST

One sweet May morning
(It will be twelve years since, when spring returns)
He had gone forth among the new-dropped lambs
With two or three companions, whom it chanced
Some further business summoned to a house
Which stands at the dale-head.[55] James, tired perhaps,
Or from some other cause, remained behind.
You see yon precipice? It almost looks
Like some vast building made of many crags,
And in the midst is one particular rock
That rises like a column from the vale,
Whence by our shepherds it is called the Pillar.[56]
James pointed to its summit, over which
They all had purposed to return together,
Informed them that he there would wait for them.
They parted, and his comrades passed that way
Some two hours after, but they did not find him
At the appointed place – a circumstance
Of which they took no heed. But one of them,
Going by chance, at night, into the house
Which at this time was James' home, there learned
That nobody had seen him all that day.
The morning came, and still he was unheard of;
The neighbours were alarmed, and to the brook
Some went, and some towards the lake. Ere noon

Notes

[55] *dale-head* head of the valley.

[56] *the Pillar* a mountain in Ennerdale.

They found him at the foot of that same rock,
Dead, and with mangled limbs. The third day after,
I buried him, poor lad, and there he lies.

LEONARD
And that then *is* his grave. Before his death
You said that he saw many happy years?

PRIEST
Aye, that he did.

LEONARD
And all went well with him?

PRIEST
If he had one, the lad had twenty homes.

LEONARD
And you believe then, that his mind was easy?

PRIEST
Yes, long before he died he found that time
Is a true friend to sorrow; and unless
His thoughts were turned on Leonard's luckless fortune,
He talked about him with a cheerful love.

LEONARD
He could not come to an unhallowed end![57]

PRIEST
Nay, God forbid! You recollect I mentioned
A habit which disquietude and grief
Had brought upon him; and we all conjectured
That as the day was warm he had lain down
Upon the grass, and waiting for his comrades
He there had fallen asleep – that in his sleep
He to the margin of the precipice
Had walked, and from the summit had fallen headlong.
And so no doubt he perished. At the time
We guess that in his hands he must have had
His shepherd's staff; for midway in the cliff
It had been caught, and there for many years
It hung – and mouldered there.

The priest here ended.
The stranger would have thanked him, but he felt
Tears rushing in. Both left the spot in silence,
And Leonard, when they reached the churchyard gate,
As the priest lifted up the latch, turned round,

Notes

[57] *an unhallowed end* In 1800 suicide was still regarded as a sin.

And looking at the grave he said, 'My brother'.
The vicar did not hear the words; and now,
Pointing towards the cottage, he entreated
That Leonard would partake his homely fare.
The other thanked him with a fervent voice,
But added that, the evening being calm,
He would pursue his journey. So they parted.
It was not long ere Leonard reached a grove
That overhung the road. He there stopped short,
And sitting down beneath the trees, reviewed
All that the priest had said.
His early years
Were with him in his heart – his cherished hopes,
And thoughts which had been his an hour before,
All pressed on him with such a weight that now
This vale where he had been so happy seemed
A place in which he could not bear to live.
So he relinquished all his purposes.
He travelled on to Egremont; and thence
That night addressed a letter to the priest
Reminding him of what had passed between them,
And adding – with a hope to be forgiven –
That it was from the weakness of his heart
He had not dared to tell him who he was.
This done, he went on shipboard, and is now
A seaman, a grey-headed mariner.

Preface to Lyrical Ballads (complete text; composed September 1800)[1]

From Lyrical Ballads (2 vols, 1800)

The first volume of these Poems[2] has already been submitted to general perusal. It was published as an experiment which, I hoped, might be of some use to ascertain how far, by fitting to metrical arrangement a selection of the real language of men[3] in a state of vivid sensation, that sort of pleasure and that quantity of pleasure may be imparted, which a Poet may rationally endeavour to impart.

I had formed no very inaccurate estimate of the probable effect of those Poems: I flattered myself that they who should be pleased with them would read them with more than common pleasure: and on the other hand I was well aware that by those who should

Notes

Preface to Lyrical Ballads

[1] This Preface, Wordsworth's most important critical work, was first published in this form in 1800, and revised for the 1802 edition of *Lyrical Ballads*. Extracts from the 1802 version are presented at pp. 525–7. The Preface was written at Coleridge's insistence, and drew on ideas conceived or gathered by him; as he told Southey, 29 July 1802, 'Wordsworth's Preface is half a child of my own brain' (Griggs ii 830). Throughout this essay, Wordsworth tends to capitalize such words as 'Poem' and 'Reader', and I have tended to preserve those typographical features.

[2] *The first volume of these Poems* Wordsworth refers to *Lyrical Ballads* (1798), included in this anthology in its entirety; see pp. 330–411.

[3] *the real language of men* Wordsworth's use of this phrase brought him much criticism, because many people responded that no one spoke as people did in his poems. The idea was clearly endorsed by Coleridge in 1800, and probably originated with him. All the same, that didn't stop him from describing it as 'an equivocal expression' in *Biographia Literaria* (1817); see p. 693.

dislike them they would be read with more than common dislike. The result has differed from my expectation in this only, that I have pleased a greater number than I ventured to hope I should please.

For the sake of variety and from a consciousness of my own weakness, I was induced to request the assistance of a Friend, who furnished me with the Poems of the 'Ancient Mariner', 'The Foster-Mother's Tale', 'The Nightingale', and the Poem entitled 'Love'.[4] I should not, however, have requested this assistance, had I not believed that the Poems of my Friend would in a great measure have the same tendency as my own, and that, though there would be found a difference, there would be found no discordance in the colours of our style as our opinions on the subject of poetry do almost entirely coincide.

Several of my Friends are anxious for the success of these Poems from a belief that, if the views with which they were composed were indeed realized, a class of Poetry would be produced well adapted to interest mankind permanently, and not unimportant in the multiplicity, and in the quality of its moral relations: and on this account they have advised me to prefix a systematic defence of the theory upon which the poems were written.[5] But I was unwilling to undertake the task because I knew that on this occasion the Reader would look coldly upon my arguments, since I might be suspected of having been principally influenced by the selfish and foolish hope of *reasoning* him into an approbation of these particular Poems: and I was still more unwilling to undertake the task because adequately to display my opinions and fully to enforce my arguments would require a space wholly disproportionate to the nature of a preface. For to treat the subject with the clearness and coherence of which I believe it susceptible, it would be necessary to give a full account of the present state of the public taste in this country, and to determine how far this taste is healthy or depraved: which again could not be determined without pointing out in what manner language and the human mind act and react on each other, and without retracing the revolutions not of literature alone but likewise of society itself. I have therefore altogether declined to enter regularly upon this defence; yet I am sensible that there would be some impropriety in abruptly obtruding upon the Public, without a few words of introduction, Poems so materially different from those upon which general approbation is at present bestowed.

It is supposed, that by the act of writing in verse an Author makes a formal engagement that he will gratify certain known habits of association, that he not only thus apprizes the Reader that certain classes of ideas and expressions will be found in his book, but that others will be carefully excluded. This exponent or symbol held forth by metrical language must in different eras of literature have excited very different expectations: for example, in the age of Catullus, Terence, and Lucretius, and that of Statius or Claudian;[6] and in our own country, in the age of Shakespeare and

Notes

[4] *a friend . . . 'Love'* 'Love' did not appear in *Lyrical Ballads* 1798, but was added in 1800. The 'friend' is Coleridge. As for 'The Ancient Mariner', it appeared in the 1800 volume with a sort of apology, written by Wordsworth – see p. 509.

[5] *they have advised . . . written* The 'friends' consist of Coleridge. 'I never cared a straw about the theory,' Wordsworth told Barron Field, 'and the Preface was written at the request of Coleridge out of sheer good nature. I recollect the very spot, a deserted quarry in the vale of Grasmere, where he pressed the thing upon me, and but for that it would never have been thought of.'

[6] Catullus (?84–?54 BC) was a Roman poet, remembered for a range of work including elegies, epigrams and love poems to his beloved 'Lesbia'; Terence (BC 195–159) wrote comedies, a polished and urbane writer; Lucretius (99–55 BC), Roman philosophic poet, author of *De rerum natura* ('On the nature of things'); Statius (*c.* 45–*c.* 96) was the author of the *Thebaid*, an epic in the manner of Virgil. Claudian (4th–5th century) was the last notable Latin classical poet. He is regarded as a vigorous, skilful, imaginative writer, the author of several epics including *The Rape of Proserpine*. The latter two authors use a more inflated manner than the earlier ones, and date from a period of general decline. Similarly, Wordsworth contrasts the writing of Dryden and Pope unfavourably with that of earlier times because he thinks of the Augustans as

Beaumont and Fletcher, and that of Donne and Cowley, or Dryden, or Pope. I will not take upon me to determine the exact import of the promise which by the act of writing in verse an Author in the present day makes to his Reader; but I am certain it will appear to many persons that I have not fulfilled the terms of an engagement thus voluntarily contracted. I hope therefore the Reader will not censure me if I attempt to state what I have proposed to myself to perform, and also (as far as the limits of a preface will permit) to explain some of the chief reasons which have determined me in the choice of my purpose: that at least he may be spared any unpleasant feeling of disappointment, and that I myself may be protected from the most dishonourable accusation which can be brought against an Author – namely, that of an indolence which prevents him from endeavouring to ascertain what is his duty, or, when his duty is ascertained, prevents him from performing it.

The principal object, then, which I proposed to myself in these Poems, was to make the incidents of common life interesting by tracing in them (truly,[7] though not ostentatiously) the primary laws of our nature,[8] chiefly as far as regards the manner in which we associate ideas[9] in a state of excitement.[10] Low and rustic life was generally chosen because in that condition the essential passions of the heart find a better soil in which they can attain their maturity, are less under restraint, and speak a plainer and more emphatic language;[11] because in that situation our elementary feelings coexist in a state of greater simplicity, and consequently may be more accurately contemplated and more forcibly communicated; because the manners of rural life germinate from those elementary feelings,[12] and (from the necessary character of rural occupations) are more easily comprehended and are more durable; and lastly, because in that condition the passions of men are incorporated[13] with the beautiful and permanent forms of nature.[14]

The language too of these men is adopted (purified indeed from what appear to be its real defects – from all lasting and rational causes of dislike or disgust) because such men hourly communicate with the best objects[15] from which the best part of language is originally derived, and because, from their rank in society and the sameness and narrow circle of their intercourse being less under the influence of social vanity, they convey their feelings and notions in simple and unelaborated expressions. Accordingly, such a language, arising out of repeated experience and regular feelings, is a more permanent and a far more philosophical language[16] than that which is frequently substituted for it by poets who think that they are conferring honour upon themselves and their art, in proportion as they separate themselves from the

Notes

having been guilty of using a form of 'poetic diction' that took them away from life as experienced by ordinary people. It was because of such sentiments that Byron took issue with Wordsworth; he preferred the writing of Pope and Dryden, and believed that everything since had been a deviation from the 'correct' path of literature; see p. 838.

[7] *truly* truthfully.

[8] *the primary laws of our nature* i.e. (in this context) the workings of the mind.

[9] *we associate ideas* The association of ideas – that is to say, the way in which emotions are connected with, for instance, memories, is an important element in Wordsworth's thinking. See *Pedlar* 78–81, *Two-Part Prelude* i 418–24, 432–42.

[10] *a state of excitement* i.e. emotional excitement, when we feel intensely.

[11] *Low and rustic . . . language* a belief first expressed in February 1798, *Pedlar* 239–45.

[12] *the manners of rural life . . . feelings* There is an implied comparison with the social life ('manners') of the city, which has become detached from 'elementary' human emotion.

[13] *incorporated* interfused, united, blended.

[14] *the passions . . . nature* as, for instance, in the way that Michael's unfinished sheepfold becomes a symbol of his tragedy, or that Margaret's ruined cottage embodies hers. The search for permanence – of language and symbol – is fundamental to Wordsworth's aesthetic.

[15] *the best objects* for example, natural objects.

[16] *philosophical language* i.e. fit for philosophical discourse.

sympathies of men and indulge in arbitrary and capricious habits of expression, in order to furnish food for fickle tastes and fickle appetites[17] of their own creation.[18]

I cannot, however, be insensible to the present outcry against the triviality and meanness both of thought and language which some of my contemporaries have occasionally introduced into their metrical compositions. And I acknowledge that this defect, where it exists, is more dishonourable to the writer's own character than false refinement or arbitrary innovation (though I should contend at the same time that it is far less pernicious in the sum of its consequences).

From such verses the poems in these volumes will be found distinguished at least by one mark of difference – that each of them has a worthy *purpose*. Not that I mean to say that I always began to write with a distinct purpose formally conceived, but I believe that my habits of meditation have so formed my feelings, as that my descriptions of such objects as strongly excite those feelings will be found to carry along with them a *purpose*. If in this opinion I am mistaken, I can have little right to the name of a poet; for all good poetry is the spontaneous overflow of powerful feelings.[19] But though this be true, poems to which any value can be attached were never produced on any variety of subjects but by a man who, being possessed of more than usual organic[20] sensibility, had also thought long and deeply.[21] For our continued influxes of feeling[22] are modified and directed by our thoughts, which are indeed the representatives of all our past feelings.[23] And, as by contemplating the relation of these general representatives[24] to each other, we discover what is really important to men, so by the repetition and continuance of this act, feelings connected with important subjects will be nourished, till at length (if we be originally possessed of much organic sensibility) such habits of mind will be produced that, by obeying blindly and mechanically[25] the impulses of those habits, we shall describe objects and utter sentiments of such a nature, and in such connection with each other, that the understanding of the being to whom we address ourselves – if he be in a healthful state of association[26] – must necessarily be in some degree enlightened, his taste exalted, and his affections ameliorated.[27]

I have said that each of these poems has a purpose. I have also informed my Reader what this purpose will be found principally to be: namely, to illustrate the manner in which our feelings and ideas are associated in a state of excitement.[28] But (speaking in less general language) it is to follow the fluxes and refluxes[29] of the mind when agitated by the great and simple affections of our nature. This object I have endeavoured in these short essays[30] to attain by various means: by tracing the maternal

Notes

[17] *fickle tastes and fickle appetites* tastes and appetites governed by literary fashion.

[18] 'It is worthwhile here to observe that the affecting parts of Chaucer are almost always expressed in language pure and universally intelligible even to this day' (Wordsworth's note). Wordsworth believed that 'every great and original writer, in proportion as he is great or original, must himself create the taste by which he is to be relished' (*MY* i 150).

[19] *all good poetry . . . feelings* one of Wordsworth's best-known pronouncements; note, however, the sentence that follows, frequently omitted or forgotten.

[20] *organic* innate, inherent.

[21] *If in this opinion . . . deeply* Wordsworth's championing of 'powerful feelings' is strongly modified by the insistence on long and profound thought.

[22] *influxes of feeling* i.e. 'flowing-in' of emotion; cf. the Pedlar's 'access of mind' (*Pedlar* 107).

[23] *For our . . . feelings* Emotions in the past work in the present, as thoughts, to alter continuing influxes of emotion in the present.

[24] *these general representatives* thoughts deriving from feelings in the past.

[25] *by obeying blindly and mechanically* It is crucial to the creative act that the poet completely surrender to associations, and habits of thought and feeling.

[26] *a healthful state of association* i.e. a state of mind in which the reader is receptive, and does not impose on the poetry irrelevant prejudices or assumptions.

[27] *ameliorated* improved. Poetry should be emotionally uplifting.

[28] *the manner . . . excitement* the way in which emotions and ideas interact associatively when the mind is stimulated.

[29] *fluxes and refluxes* ebb and flow.

[30] *essays* attempts.

passion through many of its more subtle windings (as in the poems of 'The Idiot Boy' and 'The Mad Mother'); by accompanying the last struggles of a human being at the approach of death, cleaving in solitude to life and society (as in the poem of the forsaken Indian);[31] by showing, as in the stanzas entitled 'We are Seven', the perplexity and obscurity which in childhood attend our notion of death – or rather our utter inability to admit that notion; or by displaying the strength of fraternal or (to speak more philosophically) of moral attachment when early associated with the great and beautiful objects of nature (as in 'The Brothers'); or, as in the incident of 'Simon Lee', by placing my Reader in the way of receiving from ordinary moral sensations another and more salutary impression than we are accustomed to receive from them.[32]

It has also been part of my general purpose to attempt to sketch characters under the influence of less impassioned feelings, as in the 'Old Man Travelling', 'The Two Thieves', etc. – characters of which the elements are simple, belonging rather to nature than to manners,[33] such as exist now and will probably always exist, and which from their constitution may be distinctly and profitably contemplated. I will not abuse the indulgence of my Reader by dwelling longer upon this subject, but it is proper that I should mention one other circumstance which distinguishes these Poems from the popular poetry of the day. It is this – that the feeling therein developed gives importance to the action and situation, and not the action and situation to the feeling.[34] My meaning will be rendered perfectly intelligible by referring my reader to the poems entitled 'Poor Susan' and 'The Childless Father'[35] (particularly to the last stanza of the latter Poem).

I will not suffer a sense of false modesty to prevent me from asserting that I point my Reader's attention to this mark of distinction far less for the sake of these particular Poems than from the general importance of the subject. The subject is indeed important![36] For the human mind is capable of excitement without the application of gross and violent stimulants,[37] and he must have a very faint perception of its beauty and dignity who does not know this, and who does not further know that one being is elevated above another in proportion as he possesses this capability.[38]

It has therefore appeared to me that to endeavour to produce or enlarge this capability is one of the best services in which (at any period) a Writer can be engaged – but this service, excellent at all times, is especially so at the present day. For a multitude of causes, unknown to former times, are now acting with a combined force to blunt the discriminating powers of the mind and, unfitting it for all voluntary exertion, to reduce it to a state of almost savage torpor.[39] The most effective of these causes are the great national events[40] which are daily taking place, and the increasing accumulation of men in cities, where the uniformity of their occupations produces a

Notes

31 *the poem of the forsaken Indian* i.e. 'The Complaint of a Forsaken Indian Woman', p. 403.

32 *by placing . . . them* The initial pity, which leads the narrator to offer to help Simon Lee, gives way to the more complex sentiment expressed in the final lines of the poem.

33 *manners* customs.

34 *the feeling . . . feeling* a crucial distinction between Wordsworth's poetry and that of many of his more fashionable contemporaries: his poetry is inspired primarily by the emotion behind it rather than by the incidents or the social class of those it describes.

35 *'Poor Susan' and 'The Childless Father'* These poems, first published in *Lyrical Ballads* (1800), are not included in this anthology, but Wordsworth's point is borne out just as well by 'Simon Lee', 'The Last of the Flock', 'Complaint of a Forsaken Indian Woman', 'The Thorn' and 'The Idiot Boy'.

36 In view of his stylistic conservatism when it came to prose, it is worth noting that the exclamation mark at this point is Wordsworth's.

37 *gross and violent stimulants* a reference to the sort of violent or salacious detail often found in Gothic chillers of the day.

38 *this capability* imaginative sympathy.

39 *savage torpor* barbaric laziness.

40 *national events* Britain had been at war with France since 1793.

craving for extraordinary incident which the rapid communication[41] of intelligence hourly gratifies. To this tendency of life and manners the literature and theatrical exhibitions[42] of the country have conformed themselves. The invaluable works of our elder writers (I had almost said the works of Shakespeare and Milton) are driven into neglect by frantic novels, sickly and stupid German tragedies, and deluges of idle and extravagant stories in verse.[43]

When I think upon this degrading thirst after outrageous[44] stimulation, I am almost ashamed to have spoken of the feeble effort with which I have endeavoured to counteract it. And, reflecting upon the magnitude of the general evil, I should be oppressed with no dishonourable melancholy had I not a deep impression of certain inherent and indestructible qualities of the human mind (and likewise of certain powers in the great and permanent objects[45] that act upon it which are equally inherent and indestructible), and did I not further add to this impression a belief that the time is approaching when the evil will be systematically opposed by men of greater powers and with far more distinguished success.

Having dwelt thus long on the subjects and aim of these poems, I shall request the Reader's permission to apprise him of a few circumstances relating to their *style*, in order (among other reasons) that I may not be censured for not having performed what I never attempted. The Reader will find no personifications of abstract ideas in these volumes, not that I mean to censure such personifications: they may be well fitted for certain sorts of composition, but in these Poems I propose to myself to imitate – and, as far as is possible, to adopt – the very language of men, and I do not find that such personifications make any regular or natural part of that language. I wish to keep my Reader in the company of flesh and blood, persuaded that by so doing I shall interest him. Not but that I believe that others who pursue a different track may interest him likewise. I do not interfere with their claim; I only wish to prefer a different claim of my own.

There will also be found in these volumes little of what is usually called 'poetic diction':[46] I have taken as much pains to avoid it as others ordinarily take to produce it. This I have done for the reason already alleged – to bring my language near to the language of men, and, further, because the pleasure which I have proposed to myself to impart is of a kind very different from that which is supposed by many persons to be the proper object of poetry. I do not know how, without being culpably particular,[47] I can give my Reader a more exact notion of the style in which I wished these poems to be written than by informing him that I have at all times endeavoured to look steadily at my subject. Consequently, I hope that there is in these Poems little falsehood of description, and that my ideas are expressed in language fitted to their respective importance.[48] Something I must have gained by this practice, as it is friendly to one property of all good poetry – namely, good sense. But it has necessarily cut me off from a large portion of phrases and figures of speech which, from father to son, have long been regarded as the common inheritance of Poets. I have also thought it expedient to restrict myself still further, having abstained from the use of many

Notes

[41] *rapid communication* the semaphore telegraph (invented 1792) and the stagecoach.

[42] *exhibitions* performances.

[43] *frantic novels . . . verse* Gothic novels, and plays by sentimental writers like Kotzebue, were popular. Many 'stories in verse' appeared in contemporary periodicals; see Robert Mayo, 'The Contemporaneity of the *Lyrical Ballads*', *PMLA* 69 (1954) 486–522.

[44] *outrageous* excessive.

[45] *the great and permanent objects* i.e. primarily the internalized images of objects in the natural world, such as mountains, lakes, trees.

[46] *poetic diction* Two years later, when revising *Lyrical Ballads* for a further edition, Wordsworth expanded on what he meant by this phrase in an Appendix, excerpts from which are included at pp. 522–5.

[47] *culpably particular* too meticulously detailed.

[48] *fitted to their respective importance* i.e. by the weight of emotion behind them.

expressions in themselves proper and beautiful, but which have been foolishly repeated by bad Poets till such feelings of disgust are connected with them as it is scarcely possible by any art of association to overpower.

If in a Poem there should be found a series of lines, or even a single line, in which the language, though naturally arranged and according to the strict laws of metre, does not differ from that of prose, there is a numerous class of critics who, when they stumble upon these prosaisms as they call them, imagine that they have made a notable discovery, and exult over the Poet as over a man ignorant of his own profession. Now these men would establish a canon of criticism which the Reader will conclude he must utterly reject if he wishes to be pleased with these volumes. And it would be a most easy task to prove to him that not only the language of a large portion of every good poem, even of the most elevated character, must necessarily, except with reference to the metre, in no respect differ from that of good prose, but likewise that some of the most interesting parts of the best poems will be found to be strictly the language of prose when prose is well written. The truth of this assertion might be demonstrated by innumerable passages from almost all the poetical writings, even of Milton himself. I have not space for much quotation; but, to illustrate the subject in a general manner, I will here adduce a short composition of Gray, who was at the head of those who by their reasonings[49] have attempted to widen the space of separation betwixt prose and metrical composition, and was more than any other man curiously elaborate in the structure of his own poetic diction.

In vain to me the smiling mornings shine,
And reddening Phoebus lifts his golden fire:
The birds in vain their amorous descant join,
Or cheerful fields resume their green attire:
These ears alas! for other notes repine;
A different object do these eyes require;
My lonely anguish melts no heart but mine;
And in my breast the imperfect joys expire;
Yet Morning smiles the busy race to cheer,
And new-born pleasure brings to happier men;
The fields to all their wonted tribute bear;
To warm their little loves the birds complain.
I fruitless mourn to him that cannot hear
And weep the more because I weep in vain.

It will easily be perceived that the only part of this sonnet which is of any value is the lines printed in italics: it is equally obvious that, except in the rhyme, and in the use of the single word 'fruitless' for 'fruitlessly', which is so far a defect, the language of these lines does in no respect differ from that of prose.

Is there, then, it will be asked, no essential difference between the language of prose and metrical composition? I answer that there neither is nor can be any essential difference. We are fond of tracing the resemblance between poetry and painting, and, accordingly, we call them sisters.[50] But where shall we find bonds of connection sufficiently strict to typify the affinity betwixt metrical and prose composition? They

Notes

[49] *reasonings* Wordsworth was probably aware of Gray's dictum in his correspondence that 'the language of the age is never the language of poetry.' The poem is Gray's 'Sonnet on the Death of Richard West'.

[50] *we call them sisters* This was a commonplace of eighteenth-century aesthetic theory.

both speak by and to the same organs; the bodies in which both of them are clothed may be said to be of the same substance, their affections are kindred and almost identical, not necessarily differing even in degree;[51] poetry sheds no tears 'such as angels weep',[52] but natural and human tears; she can boast of no celestial ichor[53] that distinguishes her vital juices from those of prose; the same human blood circulates through the veins of them both.

If it be affirmed that rhyme and metrical arrangement of themselves constitute a distinction which overturns what I have been saying on the strict affinity of metrical language with that of prose, and paves the way for other distinctions which the mind voluntarily admits, I answer that the distinction of rhyme and metre is regular and uniform, and not like that which is produced by what is usually called 'poetic diction'[54] – arbitrary, and subject to infinite caprices upon which no calculation whatever can be made. In the one case, the Reader is utterly at the mercy of the Poet respecting what imagery or diction he may choose to connect with the passion, whereas in the other the metre obeys certain[55] laws, to which the Poet and Reader both willingly submit because they are certain, and because no interference is made by them with the passion but such as the concurring testimony of ages has shown to heighten and improve the pleasure which co-exists with it.

It will now be proper to answer an obvious question, namely, why, professing these opinions, have I written in verse? To this in the first place I reply, because, however I may have restricted myself, there is still left open to me what confessedly constitutes the most valuable object of all writing whether in prose or verse, the great and universal passions of men,[56] the most general and interesting of their occupations, and the entire world of nature, from which I am at liberty to supply myself with endless combinations of forms and imagery.[57] Now, granting for a moment that whatever is interesting in these objects may be as vividly described in prose, why am I to be condemned, if to such description I have endeavoured to superadd the charm which, by the consent of all nations, is acknowledged to exist in metrical language? To this, it will be answered, that a very small part of the pleasure given by Poetry depends upon the metre, and that it is injudicious to write in metre, unless it be accompanied with the other artificial distinctions of style with which metre is usually accompanied, and that by such deviation more will be lost from the shock which will be thereby given to the Reader's associations, than will be counterbalanced by any pleasure which he can derive from the general power of numbers. In answer to those who thus contend for the necessity of accompanying metre with certain appropriate colours of style in order to the accomplishment of its appropriate end, and who also, in my opinion, greatly underrate the power of metre in itself, it might perhaps be almost sufficient to observe, that poems are extant, written upon more humble subjects, and in a more

Notes

[51] 'I here use the word "poetry" (though against my own judgement) as opposed to the word "prose", and synonymous with metrical composition. But much confusion has been introduced into criticism by this contradistinction of poetry and prose, instead of the more philosophical one of poetry and science. The only strict antithesis to prose is metre' (Wordsworth's note).

[52] *such as angels weep* from *Paradise Lost* i 620, where Satan is lachrymose.

[53] *celestial ichor* the blood of the gods in Greek myth.

[54] *poetic diction* The phrase is discussed at further length in the Appendix Wordsworth added to the Preface for the 1802 edition of *Lyrical Ballads*; see pp. 522–5.

[55] *certain* fixed.

[56] *the great and universal passions of men* For 'passions' think of emotions, or psychological twists and turns. The task of understanding how the human mind worked prior to the existence of a 'science' of psychology, in the sense in which it now exists, is Wordsworth's main project. See also the 'Note to "The Thorn" ', pp. 507–9.

[57] *imagery* Wordsworth defined imagery as 'sensible objects really existing, and felt to exist'.

naked and simple style than what I have aimed at, which poems have continued to give pleasure from generation to generation. Now, if nakedness and simplicity be a defect, the fact here mentioned affords a strong presumption that poems somewhat less naked and simple are capable of affording pleasure at the present day; and all that I am now attempting is to justify myself for having written under the impression of this belief.

But I might point out various causes why, when the style is manly, and the subject of some importance, words metrically arranged[58] will long continue to impart such a pleasure to mankind as he who is sensible of the extent of that pleasure will be desirous to impart. The end of Poetry is to produce excitement in coexistence with an overbalance of pleasure. Now, by the supposition, excitement is an unusual and irregular state of the mind; ideas and feelings do not in that state succeed each other in accustomed order. But, if the words by which this excitement is produced are in themselves powerful, or the images and feelings have an undue proportion of pain connected with them, there is some danger that the excitement may be carried beyond its proper bounds. Now the co-presence of something regular, something to which the mind has been accustomed when in an unexcited or a less excited state, cannot but have great efficacy in tempering and restraining the passion by an intertexture of ordinary feeling. This may be illustrated by appealing to the Reader's own experience of the reluctance with which he comes to the re-perusal of the distressful parts of *Clarissa Harlowe*, or *The Gamester*.[59] While Shakespeare's writings, in the most pathetic scenes, never act upon us as pathetic beyond the bounds of pleasure – an effect which is in a great degree to be ascribed to small but continual and regular impulses of pleasurable surprise[60] from the metrical arrangement. On the other hand (what it must be allowed will much more frequently happen) if the Poet's words should be incommensurate with the passion, and inadequate to raise the Reader to a height of desirable excitement, then (unless the Poet's choice of his metre has been grossly injudicious) in the feelings of pleasure which the Reader has been accustomed to connect with metre in general, and in the feeling, whether cheerful or melancholy, which he has been accustomed to connect with that particular movement of metre, there will be found something which will greatly contribute to impart passion to the words, and to effect the complex end which the Poet proposes to himself.

If I had undertaken a systematic defence of the theory upon which these poems are written, it would have been my duty to develop the various causes upon which the pleasure received from metrical language depends. Among the chief of these causes is to be reckoned a principle which must be well known to those who have made any of the Arts the object of accurate reflection; I mean the pleasure which the mind derives from the perception of similitude in dissimilitude.[61] This principle is the great spring of the activity of our minds and their chief feeder. From this principle the direction of

Notes

[58] *words metrically arranged* Wordsworth would probably have been aware of Johnson's claim that metre 'shackles attention and governs passions' (*Rambler* 88).

[59] Wordsworth refers to Samuel Richardson's *Clarissa* (1747–8), about the noble but doomed heroine Clarissa Harlowe and the aristocratic rake Robert Lovelace; and Edward Moore's prose drama of family life, *The Gamester* (1753).

[60] *surprise* It is worth comparing Coleridge's later notebook entry, dating from March 1805:

> Two kinds of pleasure are procured in the two master-movements and impulses of man, the gratification of the love of variety with the gratification of the love of uniformity – and that by a recurrence, delightful as a painless and yet exciting act of memory, tiny breezelets of surprise, each one destroying the ripplets which the former had made, yet all together keeping the surface of the mind in a bright dimple-smile! (*Notebooks* ii 2515)

[61] *the perception of similitude in dissimilitude* The pleasure derived from the combination of uniformity and variety in a work of art was another commonplace of eighteenth-century aesthetics.

the sexual appetite, and all the passions connected with it take their origin: It is the life of our ordinary conversation; and upon the accuracy with which similitude in dissimilitude, and dissimilitude in similitude are perceived, depend our taste and our moral feelings. It would not have been a useless employment to have applied this principle to the consideration of metre, and to have shown that metre is hence enabled to afford much pleasure, and to have pointed out in what manner that pleasure is produced. But my limits will not permit me to enter upon this subject, and I must content myself with a general summary.

I have said that Poetry is the spontaneous overflow of powerful feelings: it takes its origin from emotion recollected in tranquillity:[62] the emotion is contemplated till by a species of reaction the tranquillity gradually disappears, and an emotion similar to that which was before the subject of contemplation is gradually produced, and does itself actually exist in the mind.[63] In this mood successful composition generally begins, and in a mood similar to this it is carried on; but the emotion, of whatever kind and in whatever degree, from various causes is qualified by various pleasures, so that in describing any passions whatsoever (which are voluntarily described) the mind will upon the whole be in a state of enjoyment.[64]

Now, if Nature be thus cautious in preserving in a state of enjoyment a being thus employed, the Poet ought to profit by the lesson thus held forth to him, and ought especially to take care, that whatever passions he communicates to his Reader, those passions, if his Reader's mind be sound and vigorous, should always be accompanied with an overbalance of pleasure. Now the music of harmonious metrical language,[65] the sense of difficulty[66] overcome, and the blind association of pleasure which has been previously received from works of rhyme or metre of the same or similar construction – all these imperceptibly make up a complex feeling of delight, which is of the most important use in tempering[67] the painful feeling, which will always be found intermingled with powerful descriptions of the deeper passions.[68] This effect is always produced in pathetic[69] and impassioned poetry while, in lighter compositions, the ease and gracefulness with which the Poet manages his numbers[70] are themselves confessedly a principal source of the gratification of the Reader.

I might perhaps include all which it is *necessary* to say upon this subject by affirming what few persons will deny, that of two descriptions, either of passions, manners, or characters, each of them equally well-executed, the one in prose and the other in verse, the verse will be read a hundred times where the prose is read once. We see that Pope, by the power of verse alone, has contrived to render the plainest common sense interesting, and even frequently to invest it with the appearance of passion. In consequence of these convictions I related in metre the tale of 'Goody Blake and Harry Gill', which is one of the rudest[71] of this collection. I wished to draw attention to the truth that the power of the human imagination is sufficient to produce such changes even in our physical nature as might almost appear miraculous. The truth is an important one; the fact (for it is a *fact*)[72] is a valuable illustration of it. And I have

Notes

[62] *emotion recollected In tranquillity* In August–September 1800 Coleridge recorded in his notebook that poetry was a 'recalling of passion in tranquillity' (*Notebooks* i 787).

[63] *The emotion . . . in the mind* What the poet experiences is related to the original emotion, rather than the original emotion itself.

[64] *so that . . . enjoyment* Wordsworth emphasizes that we gain aesthetic pleasure even from reading poetry that is tragic in theme.

[65] *harmonious metrical language* poetry.

[66] *the sense of difficulty* i.e. that of disciplining the 'language of prose' into metrical form.

[67] *tempering* modifying.

[68] *deeper passions* serious, darker emotions, such as grief.

[69] *pathetic* passionate, deeply felt.

[70] *numbers* i.e. verse, metre.

[71] *rudest* less sophisticated.

[72] It was important to Wordsworth to make clear that 'Goody Blake and Harry Gill' was not invented, but a true story; see p. 331.

the satisfaction of knowing that it has been communicated to many hundreds of people[73] who would never have heard of it, had it not been narrated as a Ballad, and in a more impressive metre than is usual in Ballads.

Having thus adverted to a few of the reasons why I have written in verse, and why I have chosen subjects from common life, and endeavoured to bring my language near to the real language of men, if I have been too minute[74] in pleading my own cause, I have at the same time been treating a subject of general interest; and it is for this reason that I request the Reader's permission to add a few words with reference solely to these particular poems, and to some defects which will probably be found in them. I am sensible that my associations must have sometimes been particular instead of general, and that, consequently, giving to things a false importance, sometimes from diseased impulses I may have written upon unworthy subjects; but I am less apprehensive on this account, than that my language may frequently have suffered from those arbitrary connections of feelings and ideas with particular words, from which no man can altogether protect himself. Hence I have no doubt that, in some instances, feelings even of the ludicrous may be given to my Readers by expressions which appeared to me tender and pathetic. Such faulty expressions, were I convinced they were faulty at present, and that they must necessarily continue to be so, I would willingly take all reasonable pains to correct. But it is dangerous to make these alterations on the simple authority of a few individuals, or even of certain classes of men; for where the understanding of an Author is not convinced, or his feelings altered, this cannot be done without great injury to himself: for his own feelings are his stay and support,[75] and if he sets them aside in one instance, he may be induced to repeat this act till his mind loses all confidence in itself and becomes utterly debilitated. To this it may be added, that the Reader ought never to forget that he is himself exposed to the same errors as the Poet, and perhaps in a much greater degree: for there can be no presumption in saying, that it is not probable he will be so well acquainted with the various stages of meaning through which words have passed, or with the fickleness or stability of the relations of particular ideas to each other; and above all, since he is so much less interested in the subject, he may decide lightly and carelessly.

Long as I have detained my Reader, I hope he will permit me to caution him against a mode of false criticism which has been applied to Poetry in which the language closely resembles that of life and nature. Such verses have been triumphed over in parodies of which Dr Johnson's stanza is a fair specimen.

I put my hat upon my bead,
And walked into the Strand,
And there I met another man
Whose hat was in his hand.

Immediately under these lines I will place one of the most justly admired stanzas of *The Babes in the Wood*.

Notes

[73] *it has been . . . people* 'Goody Blake and Harry Gill' was in 1800 the most reprinted of the 1798 *Lyrical Ballads*, having appeared in the *Edinburgh Magazine* 14 (1799) 387–9, the *Ipswich Magazine* (1799) 118–19, *New Annual Register* 19 (1799) 200–3 and the *Universal Magazine* 105 (1799) 270–1.

[74] *minute* detailed.

[75] *stay and support* cf. 'Resolution and Independence' 144: ' "God", said I, 'be my help and stay secure.'

These pretty babes with hand in hand
Went wandering up and down;
But never more they saw the man
Approaching from the town.

In both these stanzas the words, and the order of the words, in no respect differ from the most unimpassioned conversation. There are words in both – for example, 'the Strand' and 'the town' – connected with none but the most familiar ideas; yet the one stanza we admit as admirable, and the other as a fair example of the superlatively contemptible. Whence arises this difference? Not from the metre, not from the language, not from the order of the words; but the *matter* expressed in Dr Johnson's stanza is contemptible. The proper method of treating trivial and simple verses to which Dr Johnson's stanza would be a fair parallelism is not to say this is a bad kind of poetry, or this is not poetry; but this wants sense; it is neither interesting in itself, nor can *lead* to anything interesting; the images neither originate in that sane state of feeling which arises out of thought, nor can excite thought or feeling in the Reader. This is the only sensible manner of dealing with such verses: Why trouble yourself about the species till you have previously decided upon the genus? Why take pains to prove that an ape is not a Newton when it is self-evident that he is not a man?[76]

I have one request to make of my Reader, which is, that in judging these Poems he would decide by his own feelings genuinely, and not by reflection upon what will probably be the judgement of others. How common is it to hear a person say, 'I myself do not object to this style of composition, or this or that expression, but to such and such classes of people it will appear mean or ludicrous.' This mode of criticism, so destructive of all sound unadulterated judgement, is almost universal. I have therefore to request that the Reader would abide independently by his own feelings, and that if he finds himself affected he would not suffer such conjectures to interfere with his pleasure.

If an Author by any single composition has impressed us with respect for his talents, it is useful to consider this as affording a presumption that, on other occasions where we have been displeased, he nevertheless may not have written ill or absurdly. And further, to give him so much credit for this one composition as may induce us to review what has displeased us with more care than we should otherwise have bestowed upon it. This is not only an act of justice but, in our decisions upon poetry especially, may conduce in a high degree to the improvement of our own taste. For an *accurate* taste in poetry, and in all the other arts (as Sir Joshua Reynolds[77] has observed) is an *acquired* talent which can only be produced by thought and a long-continued intercourse with the best models of composition. This is mentioned not with so ridiculous a purpose as to prevent the most inexperienced Reader from judging for himself (I have already said that I wish him to judge for himself), but merely to temper the rashness of decision, and to suggest that if poetry be a subject on which much time has not been bestowed, the judgement may be erroneous, and that in many cases it necessarily will be so.

Notes

[76] *Why take pains . . . not a man?* Wordsworth alludes to Pope's *Essay on Man*:

Superior beings, when of late they saw
A mortal man unfold all Nature's law,
Admired such wisdom in an earthly shape
And showed a Newton as we show an ape.
(ii 31–4)

[77] Sir Joshua Reynolds (1723–92), was the most renowned portrait-painter of the age. His first discourse was delivered in 1769, and subsequent lectures became yearly fixtures at the Royal Academy.

I know that nothing would have so effectually contributed to further the end[78] which I have in view, as to have shown of what kind the pleasure is, and how the pleasure is produced which is confessedly produced by metrical composition essentially different from that which I have here endeavoured to recommend. For the Reader will say that he has been pleased by such composition, and what can I do more for him?

The power of any art is limited, and he will suspect that, if I propose to furnish him with new friends, it is only upon condition of his abandoning his old friends. Besides, as I have said, the Reader is himself conscious of the pleasure which he has received from such composition – composition to which he has peculiarly attached the endearing name of Poetry – and all men feel an habitual gratitude and something of an honourable bigotry for the objects which have long continued to please them. We not only wish to be pleased, but to be pleased in that particular way in which we have been accustomed to be pleased.

There is a host of arguments in these feelings, and I should be the less able to combat them successfully, as I am willing to allow that, in order entirely to enjoy the Poetry which I am recommending, it would be necessary to give up much of what is ordinarily enjoyed. But would my limits have permitted me to point out how this pleasure is produced, I might have removed many obstacles and assisted my Reader in perceiving that the powers of language are not so limited as he may suppose, and that it is possible that poetry may give other enjoyments – of a purer, more lasting, and more exquisite nature. But this part of my subject I have been obliged altogether to omit: as it has been less my present aim to prove that the interest excited by some other kinds of poetry is less vivid and less worthy of the nobler powers of the mind, than to offer reasons for presuming that, if the object which I have proposed to myself were adequately attained, a species of poetry would be produced which is genuine poetry, in its nature well-adapted to interest mankind permanently, and likewise important in the multiplicity and quality of its moral relations.

From what has been said, and from a perusal of the Poems, the Reader will be able clearly to perceive the object which I have proposed to myself. He will determine how far I have attained this object and (what is a much more important question) whether it be worth attaining. And upon the decision of these two questions will rest my claim to the approbation of the public.

Note to 'The Thorn' (composed late September 1800)[1]

From Lyrical Ballads (2 vols, 1800)

This poem ought to have been preceded by an introductory poem which I have been prevented from writing by never having felt myself in a mood when it was probable that I should write it well.

The character which I have here introduced speaking is sufficiently common. The reader will perhaps have a general notion of it if he has ever known a man (a captain of a small trading vessel, for example[2]) who, being past the middle age of life, had retired

Notes

[78] *end* objective.

Note to 'The Thorn'

[1] *The Thorn* (see pp. 375–82) was originally published in *Lyrical Ballads* (1798) without any explanation. This essay, significant both for what it says about its subject as well as what it says about tautology, was published in the second edition of *Lyrical Ballads* (1800), in anticipation of the widespread misunderstanding of the poem that was to follow.

[2] *a captain . . . example* The telescope at line 181 of the poem is the only piece of evidence that supports this suggestion.

upon an annuity or small independent income to some village or country town of which he was not a native, or in which he had not been accustomed to live. Such men, having little to do, become credulous and talkative from indolence. And from the same cause (and other predisposing causes by which it is probable that such men may have been affected) they are prone to superstition. On which account it appeared to me proper to select a character like this to exhibit some of the general laws by which superstition acts upon the mind. Superstitious men are almost always men of slow faculties and deep feelings. Their minds are not loose but adhesive.[3] They have a reasonable share of imagination, by which word I mean the faculty which produces impressive effects out of simple elements. But they are utterly destitute of fancy – the power by which pleasure and surprise are excited by sudden varieties of situation and by accumulated imagery.

It was my wish in this poem to show the manner in which such men cleave[4] to the same ideas, and to follow the turns of passion (always different, yet not palpably different) by which their conversation is swayed. I had two objects to attain: first, to represent a picture which should not be unimpressive, yet consistent with the character that should describe it; secondly (while I adhered to the style in which such persons describe), to take care that words – which in their minds are impregnated with passion[5] – should likewise convey passion to readers who are not accustomed to sympathize with men feeling in that manner, or using such language. It seemed to me that this might be done by calling in the assistance of lyrical and rapid metre. It was necessary that the poem, to be natural, should in reality move slowly. Yet I hoped that by the aid of the metre, to those who should at all enter into the spirit of the poem, it would appear to move quickly. (The reader will have the kindness to excuse this note, as I am sensible that an introductory poem is necessary to give this poem its full effect.)

Upon this occasion I will request permission to add a few words closely connected with 'The Thorn', and many other poems in these volumes. There is a numerous class of readers who imagine that the same words cannot be repeated without tautology. This is a great error. Virtual tautology is much oftener produced by using different words when the meaning is exactly the same. Words – a poet's words more particularly – ought to be weighed in the balance of feeling, and not measured by the space which they occupy upon paper. For the reader cannot be too often reminded that poetry is passion: it is the history or science of feelings. Now every man must know that an attempt is rarely made to communicate impassioned feelings without something of an accompanying consciousness of the inadequateness of our own powers, or the deficiencies of language. During such efforts there will be a craving[6] in the mind, and as long as it is unsatisfied the speaker will cling to the same words, or words of the same character.

There are also various other reasons why repetition and apparent tautology are frequently beauties of the highest kind. Among the chief of these reasons is the interest which the mind attaches to words not only as symbols of the passion, but as *things*, active and efficient, which are of themselves part of the passion. And further, from a spirit of fondness, exultation, and gratitude, the mind luxuriates in the repetition of words which appear successfully to communicate its feelings.

The truth of these remarks might be shown by innumerable passages from the Bible, and from the impassioned poetry of every nation.

Notes

[3] *adhesive* persevering, tending to worry at certain ideas. Wordsworth is talking about the psychology of obsession.

[4] *cleave* cling, stick.

[5] *passion* emotion.

[6] *craving* i.e. an emotional craving, or frustration.

Awake, awake, Deborah! Awake, awake, utter a song!
Arise, Barak, and lead thy captivity captive, thou son of Abinoam!
At her feet he bowed, he fell, he lay down. At her feet he bowed, there he fell
down dead.
Why is his chariot so long in coming? Why tarry the wheels of his chariot?
(Judges 12: 27, and part of 28; see also the
whole of that tumultuous and wonderful poem)

Note to Coleridge's 'The Rime of the Ancient Mariner'[1]

From Lyrical Ballads (2nd edn, 2 vols, 1800)

I cannot refuse myself the gratification of informing such readers as may have been pleased with this poem, or with any part of it, that they owe their pleasure in some sort to me, as the author[2] was himself very desirous that it should be suppressed. This wish had arisen from a consciousness of the defects of the poem, and from a knowledge that many persons had been much displeased with it.[3] The poem of my friend has indeed great defects: first, that the principal person has no distinct character, either in his profession of mariner, or as a human being who having been long under the control of supernatural impressions might be supposed himself to partake of something supernatural; secondly, that he does not act, but is continually acted upon; thirdly, that the events having no necessary connection do not produce each other; and lastly, that the imagery is somewhat too laboriously accumulated. Yet the poem contains many delicate touches of passion, and indeed the passion is everywhere true to nature; a great number of the stanzas present beautiful images and are expressed with unusual felicity of language; and the versification, though the metre is itself unfit for long poems, is harmonious and artfully varied, exhibiting the utmost powers of that metre, and every variety of which it is capable. It therefore appeared to me that these several merits (the first of which, namely that of the passion, is of the highest kind[4]) gave to the poem a value which is not often possessed by better poems. On this account I requested of my friend to permit me to republish it.

Notes

NOTE TO COLERIDGE'S RIME

[1] Wordsworth appended this note to Coleridge's poem when it appeared in the second edition of *Lyrical Ballads* (1800), sending it to the printer a few days before the decision not to include *Christabel*. His doubts about *The Ancient Mariner* may have been reinforced by Southey's comments in the *Critical Review* (see p. 731). The note must have contributed to the 'change' in the relationship between the two men, lamented in Wordsworth's 'A Complaint' (p. 572). It certainly embittered Coleridge in later years; in 1818 he recalled the Wordsworths' 'cold praise and effective discouragement of every attempt of mine to roll onward in a distinct current of my own – who admitted that the Ancient Mariner and the Christabel . . . were not without merit, but were abundantly anxious to acquit their judgements of any blindness to the very numerous defects' (Griggs i 631n2).

[2] *the author* Coleridge.

[3] *many persons . . . with it* probably a reference to Southey's damning comment that it was a 'poem of little merit' (see p. 731).

[4] *the first of which . . . kind* a comment consistent with Wordsworth's *Note to 'The Thorn'*, which states that 'poetry is passion; it is the history or science of feelings' (see p. 508).

Michael: A Pastoral Poem (composed October–December 1800)

From Lyrical Ballads (2nd edn, 2 vols, 1800)

If from the public way you turn your steps
Up the tumultuous brook of Greenhead Gill[1]
You will suppose that with an upright path
Your feet must struggle, in such bold ascent
The pastoral mountains front you, face to face.
But courage! for beside that boisterous brook
The mountains have all opened out themselves,
And made a hidden valley of their own.
No habitation there is seen; but such
As journey thither find themselves alone
With a few sheep, with rocks and stones, and kites[2]
That overhead are sailing in the sky.[3]
　It is in truth an utter solitude,
Nor should I have made mention of this dell
But for one object which you might pass by –
Might see and notice not. Beside the brook
There is a straggling heap of unhewn stones;
And to that place a story appertains,
Which, though it be ungarnished with events,
Is not unfit, I deem, for the fireside
Or for the summer shade. It was the first,
The earliest of those tales that spake to me
Of shepherds, dwellers in the vallies, men
Whom I already loved – not verily
For their own sakes, but for the fields and hills
Where was their occupation and abode.
And hence this tale, while I was yet a boy –
Careless of books, yet having felt the power
Of nature – by the gentle agency
Of natural objects, led me on to feel
For passions that were not my own, and think
(At random and imperfectly indeed)
On man, the heart of man, and human life.[4]
Therefore, although it be a history[5]
Homely and rude,[6] I will relate the same
For the delight of a few natural hearts[7] –

Notes

MICHAEL: A PASTORAL POEM

[1] *Greenhead Gill* Greenhead Gill (a gill is a Lake District term for a mountain stream) is in the Vale of Grasmere, Cumbria. Wordsworth later recalled that this poem was based on memories of a family who once owned Dove Cottage.

[2] *kite* small bird of prey.

[3] *but such . . . sky* lines indebted to Dorothy's account of her walk with her brother to the sheepfold on 11 October 1800: 'Kites sailing in the sky above our heads – sheep bleating and in lines and chains and patterns scattered over the mountains' (*Grasmere Journals* 26).

[4] *man, the heart of man, and human life* the subject of Wordsworth's never-completed epic, *The Recluse*; see 'Prospectus to "The Recluse" ', p. 481.

[5] *history* story.

[6] *rude* unsophisticated, simple.

[7] *a few natural hearts* Wordsworth is painfully aware that in relating a story about poor country folk he is working against public taste. The 'few' for whom he saw himself writing would have included, primarily, Dorothy and Coleridge. ' "Fit audience find, though few!" Thus prayed the bard, / Holiest of men' ('Prospectus to "The Recluse" ' 12–13).

Figure 10 Dove Cottage, Grasmere, home of William and Dorothy Wordsworth, 1799–1809, as seen by Harry Goodwin in 1887.

And with yet fonder feeling, for the sake
Of youthful poets who among these hills
Will be my second self when I am gone.
Upon the forest-side in Grasmere vale
There dwelt a shepherd, Michael was his name,
An old man, stout of heart and strong of limb.
His bodily frame had been from youth to age
Of an unusual strength; his mind was keen,
Intense, and frugal, apt for all affairs;[8]
And in his shepherd's calling he was prompt
And watchful more than ordinary men.
Hence he had learned the meaning of all winds,
Of blasts of every tone; and oftentimes
When others heeded not, he heard the south
Make subterraneous music, like the noise
Of bagpipers on distant Highland hills.
The shepherd, at such warning, of his flock
Bethought him, and he to himself would say,
'The winds are now devising work for me!'
And truly at all times the storm that drives
The traveller to a shelter, summoned him
Up to the mountains: he had been alone
Amid the heart of many thousand mists
That came to him and left him on the heights.
So lived he till his eightieth year was passed;
And grossly that man errs who should suppose
That the green valleys, and the streams and rocks,
Were things indifferent to the shepherd's thoughts.[9]
Fields, where with cheerful spirits he had breathed
The common air, the hills which he so oft
Had climbed with vigorous steps – which had impressed
So many incidents upon his mind
Of hardship, skill or courage, joy or fear;
Which like a book preserved the memory
Of the dumb animals whom he had saved,
Had fed or sheltered, linking to such acts,
So grateful in themselves, the certainty
Of honourable gains – these fields, these hills,
Which were his living being even more
Than his own blood (what could they less?), had laid
Strong hold on his affections, were to him
A pleasurable feeling of blind love,
The pleasure which there is in life itself.
He had not passed his days in singleness:
He had a wife, a comely matron – old,
Though younger than himself full twenty years.
She was a woman of a stirring life,

Notes

[8] *apt for all affairs* suitable for all kinds of work.

[9] *And grossly . . . thoughts* Wordsworth told the Whig leader, Charles James Fox, that this poem and *The Brothers* 'were written with a view to show that men who do not wear fine clothes can feel deeply'.

Whose heart was in her house. Two wheels she had
Of antique form – this, large for spinning wool,
That, small for flax – and if one wheel had rest
It was because the other was at work.[10]
The pair had but one inmate[11] in their house,
An only child, who had been born to them
When Michael telling[12] o'er his years began
To deem that he was old – in shepherd's phrase,
With one foot in the grave. This only son,
With two brave sheep dogs tried in many a storm
(The one of an inestimable worth),
Made all their household. I may truly say
That they were as a proverb in the vale
For endless industry. When day was gone,
And from their occupations out of doors
The son and father were come home, even then
Their labour did not cease, unless when all
Turned to their cleanly supper-board, and there
Each with a mess of pottage[13] and skimmed milk,
Sat round their basket piled with oaten cake,[14]
And their plain home-made cheese. Yet when their meal
Was ended, Luke (for so the son was named)
And his old father both betook themselves
To such convenient work as might employ
Their hands by the fireside – perhaps to card[15]
Wool for the housewife's spindle, or repair
Some injury done to sickle, flail, or scythe,[16]
Or other implement of house or field.
   Down from the ceiling by the chimney's edge
(Which in our ancient uncouth country style
Did with a huge projection overbrow[17]
Large space beneath) as duly as the light
Of day grew dim, the housewife hung a lamp,
An aged utensil which had performed
Service beyond all others of its kind.
Early at evening did it burn, and late,
Surviving comrade of uncounted[18] hours
Which going by from year to year had found
And left the couple neither gay perhaps
Nor cheerful, yet with objects[19] and with hopes
Living a life of eager industry.
And now, when Luke was in his eighteenth year,
There by the light of this old lamp they sat,

Notes

[10] *Two wheels . . . work* see Wordsworth's comment on the cottage industry of spinning, p. 484n7.

[11] *inmate* dependent.

[12] *telling* counting.

[13] *pottage* porridge.

[14] *oaten cake* a kind of bread eaten by local statesmen (for statesmen see p. 485n14).

[15] *card* comb out.

[16] *sickle, flail, or scythe* implements that reveal Michael's other labours: growing hay (cut with the scythe) and corn (cut with the scythe or sickle and threshed with the flail).

[17] *overbrow* overhang.

[18] *uncounted* countless.

[19] *objects* objectives, aims.

Father and son, while late into the night
The housewife plied her own peculiar[20] work,
Making the cottage through the silent hours
Murmur as with the sound of summer flies.
Not with a waste of words, but for the sake
Of pleasure which I know that I shall give
To many living now, I of this lamp
Speak thus minutely; for there are no few
Whose memories will bear witness to my tale.
The light was famous in its neighbourhood,
And was a public symbol of the life
The thrifty pair had lived. For as it chanced
Their cottage on a plot of rising ground
Stood single, with large prospect north and south,
High into Easedale, up to Dunmail Raise,
And westward to the village near the lake.
And from this constant light so regular
And so far-seen, the house itself by all
Who dwelt within the limits of the vale,
Both old and young, was named The Evening Star.
  Thus living on through such a length of years
The shepherd, if he loved himself, must needs
Have loved his helpmate;[21] but to Michael's heart
This son of his old age was yet more dear –
Effect which might perhaps have been produced
By that instinctive tenderness, the same
Blind[22] spirit which is in the blood of all,
Or that a child more than all other gifts,
Brings hope with it, and forward-looking thoughts,
And stirrings of inquietude,[23] when they
By tendency of nature[24] needs must fail.
From such, and other causes, to the thoughts
Of the old man his only son was now
The dearest object that he knew on earth.
Exceeding was the love he bare to him,
His heart and his heart's joy! For oftentimes
Old Michael, while he was a babe in arms,
Had done him female service,[25] not alone
For dalliance[26] and delight, as is the use
Of fathers, but with patient mind enforced
To acts of tenderness; and he had rocked
His cradle with a woman's gentle hand.
  And in a later time, ere yet the boy
Had put on boy's attire,[27] did Michael love

Notes

[20] *peculiar* particular.
[21] *helpmate* wife.
[22] *Blind* unquestioning.
[23] *inquietude* anxiety about Luke.
[24] *tendency of nature* age.
[25] *Old Michael . . . female service* Michael tended his baby son as if he had been his mother.
[26] *For dalliance* for playfulness.
[27] *ere yet . . . attire* Until well into the nineteenth century, boys and girls were dressed in frocks until, between the ages of 3 and 7, boys were 'breeched'.

(Albeit of a stern unbending mind)
To have the young one in his sight when he
Had work by his own door, or when he sat
With sheep before him on his shepherd's stool
Beneath that large old oak, which near their door
Stood, and from its enormous breadth of shade
Chosen for the shearer's covert[28] from the sun,
Thence in our rustic dialect was called
The Clipping[29] Tree – a name which yet it bears.
There, while they two were sitting in the shade
With others round them, earnest all and blithe,
Would Michael exercise his heart with looks
Of fond correction and reproof, bestowed
Upon the child if he disturbed the sheep
By catching at their legs, or with his shouts
Scared them while they lay still beneath the shears.
And when by Heaven's good grace the boy grew up
A healthy lad, and carried in his cheek
Two steady roses that were five years old,
Then Michael from a winter coppice[30] cut
With his own hand a sapling, which he hooped
With iron, making it throughout in all
Due requisites a perfect shepherd's staff,
And gave it to the boy; wherewith equipped,
He as a watchman oftentimes was placed
At gate or gap, to stem[31] or turn the flock;
And, to his office[32] prematurely called,
There stood the urchin, as you will divine,
Something between a hindrance and a help –
And for this cause not always, I believe,
Receiving from his father hire[33] of praise,
Though nought was left undone which staff, or voice,
Or looks, or threatening gestures, could perform.
But soon as Luke, now ten years old, could stand
Against the mountain blasts, and to the heights,
Not fearing toil, nor length of weary ways,
He with his father daily went, and they
Were as companions – why should I relate
That objects which the shepherd loved before
Were dearer now? – that from the boy there came
Feelings and emanations, things which were
Light to the sun and music to the wind,
And that the old man's heart seemed born again?
Thus in his father's sight the boy grew up
And now when he had reached his eighteenth year,
He was his comfort and his daily hope.

Notes

[28] *covert* shade.
[29] 'Clipping is the word used in the north of England for shearing' (Wordsworth's note).
[30] *coppice* a small wood.
[31] *stem* stop.
[32] *office* job, work.
[33] *hire* reward.

While this good household thus were living on
From day to day, to Michael's ear there came
Distressful tidings. Long before the time
Of which I speak, the shepherd had been bound
In surety for his brother's son,[34] a man
Of an industrious life and ample means,
But unforeseen misfortunes suddenly
Had pressed upon him, and old Michael now
Was summoned to discharge the forfeiture –
A grievous penalty, but little less
Than half his substance.[35] This unlooked-for claim,
At the first hearing, for a moment took
More hope out of his life than he supposed
That any old man ever could have lost.
As soon as he had gathered so much strength
That he could look his trouble in the face,
It seemed that his sole refuge was to sell
A portion of his patrimonial fields.[36]
Such was his first resolve; he thought again,
And his heart failed him. 'Isabel', said he,
Two evenings after he had heard the news,
'I have been toiling more than seventy years,
And in the open sunshine of God's love
Have we all lived, yet if these fields of ours
Should pass into a stranger's hand, I think
That I could not lie quiet in my grave.
Our lot is a hard lot;[37] the sun itself
Has scarcely been more diligent than I,
And I have lived to be a fool at last
To my own family. An evil man
That was, and made an evil choice, if he
Were false to us; and if he were not false,
There are ten thousand to whom loss like this
Had been no sorrow. I forgive him – but
'Twere better to be dumb than to talk thus.
When I began, my purpose was to speak
Of remedies and of a cheerful hope.

Notes

[34] *In surety for his brother's son* Michael made himself liable for his nephew's debt.

[35] *Long before . . . substance* The failure of his nephew to pay off the loan Michael had guaranteed, using his land as security, means that he is now forced to pay the penalty – a sum amounting to only slightly less than half his entire capital.

[36] *patrimonial fields* the land he had inherited from his forefathers. This poem is preoccupied with the plight of small landowners – families who passed the same small plot of land from one generation to the next over many centuries. When Wordsworth sent Charles James Fox, the Whig leader, a copy of *Lyrical Ballads* in 1801, he drew his attention to this poem: 'The domestic affections will always be strong amongst men who live in a country not crowded with population, if these men are placed above poverty. But if they are proprietors of small estates, which have descended to them from their ancestors, the power which these affections will acquire amongst such men is inconceivable by those who have only had an opportunity of observing hired labourers, farmers, and the manufacturing poor. Their little tract of land serves as a kind of permanent rallying point for their domestic feelings, as a tablet upon which they are written, which makes them objects of memory in a thousand instances when they would otherwise be forgotten. It is a fountain fitted to the nature of social man from which supplies of affection, as pure as his heart was intended for, are daily drawn. This class of men is rapidly disappearing' (*EY* 314–15).

[37] *lot* way of life.

Our Luke shall leave us, Isabel; the land
Shall not go from us, and it shall be free –
He shall possess it, free as is the wind
That passes over it. We have, thou knowest,
Another kinsman; he will be our friend
In this distress. He is a prosperous man,
Thriving in trade, and Luke to him shall go
And with his kinsman's help and his own thrift
He quickly will repair this loss, and then
May come again to us. If here he stay
What can be done? Where everyone is poor
What can be gained?'[38]
At this the old man paused
And Isabel sat silent, for her mind
Was busy looking back into past times.
'There's Richard Bateman', thought she to herself,
'He was a parish-boy[39] – at the church door
They made a gathering for him, shillings, pence,[40]
And halfpennies, wherewith the neighbours bought
A basket which they filled with pedlar's wares,
And with this basket on his arm the lad
Went up to London, found a master[41] there,
Who out of many chose the trusty boy
To go and overlook his merchandise
Beyond the seas, where he grew wondrous rich
And left estates and monies to the poor,
And at his birthplace built a chapel, floored
With marble which he sent from foreign lands.'[42]
These thoughts, and many others of like sort,
Passed quickly through the mind of Isabel,
And her face brightened. The old man was glad,
And thus resumed: 'Well, Isabel, this scheme
These two days has been meat and drink to me:
Far more than we have lost is left us yet.
We have enough – I wish indeed that I
Were younger, but this hope is a good hope.
Make ready Luke's best garments; of the best
Buy for him more, and let us send him forth
Tomorrow, or the next day, or tonight –
If he could go, the boy should go tonight.'
Here Michael ceased, and to the fields went forth
With a light heart. The housewife for five days
Was restless morn and night, and all day long
Wrought on with her best fingers[43] to prepare

Notes

[38] *Where everyone . . . gained* No one in the village has enough money to employ Luke.

[39] *parish-boy* supported by the parish.

[40] *shillings, pence* before decimalization in 1970, there were 12 pence to the shilling, and 20 shillings to the pound.

[41] *master* employer.

[42] 'The story alluded to here is well known in the country. The chapel is called Ings Chapel, and is on the right hand side of the road leading from Kendal to Ambleside' (Wordsworth's note). Bateman's marble floor is still to be seen.

[43] *Wrought on with her best fingers* idiomatic; she worked as hard as she possibly could.

Things needful for the journey of her son.
But Isabel was glad when Sunday came
To stop her in her work; for when she lay
By Michael's side, she for the last two nights
Heard him, how he was troubled in his sleep;
And when they rose at morning she could see
That all his hopes were gone. That day at noon
She said to Luke, while they two by themselves
Were sitting at the door: 'Thou must not go,
We have no other child but thee to lose,
None to remember – do not go away,
For if thou leave thy father he will die.'
The lad made answer with a jocund[44] voice,
And Isabel, when she had told her fears,
Recovered heart. That evening her best fare
Did she bring forth, and all together sat
Like happy people round a Christmas fire.
　Next morning Isabel resumed her work,
And all the ensuing week the house appeared
As cheerful as a grove in spring. At length
The expected letter from their kinsman came,
With kind assurances that he would do
His utmost for the welfare of the boy –
To which requests were added that forthwith
He might be sent to him. Ten times or more
The letter was read over; Isabel
Went forth to show it to the neighbours round;
Nor was there at that time on English land
A prouder heart than Luke's. When Isabel
Had to her house returned the old man said,
'He shall depart tomorrow.' To this word
The housewife answered, talking much of things
Which, if at such short notice he should go,
Would surely be forgotten – but at length
She gave consent, and Michael was at ease.
　Near the tumultuous brook of Greenhead Gill
In that deep valley, Michael had designed
To build a sheepfold,[45] and before he heard
The tidings of his melancholy loss
For this same purpose he had gathered up
A heap of stones, which close to the brook-side
Lay thrown together, ready for the work.
With Luke that evening thitherward[46] he walked,
And soon as they had reached the place he stopped,
And thus the old man spake to him: 'My son,

Notes

[44] *jocund* happy.

[45] 'It may be proper to inform some readers that a sheepfold in these mountains is an unroofed building of stone walls, with different divisions. It is generally placed by the side of a brook for the convenience of washing the sheep; but it is also useful as a shelter for them, and as a place to drive them into, to enable the shepherds conveniently to single out one or more for any particular purpose' (Wordsworth's note).

[46] *thitherward* in that direction, to that place.

Tomorrow thou wilt leave me. With full heart
I look upon thee, for thou art the same
That wert a promise to me ere thy birth,
And all thy life hast been my daily joy.
I will relate to thee some little part
Of our two histories; 'twill do thee good
When thou art from me, even if I should speak
Of things thou canst not know of. After thou
First cam'st into the world, as it befalls
To new-born infants, thou didst sleep away
Two days, and blessings from thy father's tongue
Then fell upon thee. Day by day passed on,
And still I loved thee with increasing love.
Never to living ear came sweeter sounds
Than when I heard thee by our own fireside
First uttering without words a natural tune –
When thou, a feeding babe, didst in thy joy
Sing at thy mother's breast. Month followed month,
And in the open fields my life was passed,
And in the mountains, else I think that thou
Hadst been brought up upon thy father's knees.
But we were playmates, Luke; among these hills,
As well thou know'st, in us the old and young
Have played together – nor with me didst thou
Lack any pleasure which a boy can know.'
　Luke had a manly heart, but at these words
He sobbed aloud. The old man grasped his hand,
And said, 'Nay do not take it so – I see
That these are things of which I need not speak.
Even to the utmost I have been to thee
A kind and a good father; and herein
I but repay a gift which I myself
Received at others' hands, for, though now old
Beyond the common life of man,[47] I still
Remember them who loved me in my youth.
Both of them sleep together – here they lived
As all their forefathers had done; and when
At length their time was come, they were not loath
To give their bodies to the family mould.[48]
I wished that thou should'st live the life they lived;
But 'tis a long time to look back, my son,
And see so little gain from sixty years.
These fields were burdened when they came to me;[49]
Till I was forty years of age, not more
Than half of my inheritance was mine.
I toiled and toiled; God blessed me in my work,

Notes

[47] *the common life of man* the usual lifespan of a man (three-score years and ten); he is 84.

[48] *mould* the earth from which man was formed, and to which he returns in the grave.

[49] *These fields were burdened when they came to me* Michael inherited his land with the burden of a mortgage.

And till these three weeks past the land was free –
It looks as if it never could endure
Another master. Heaven forgive me, Luke,
If I judge ill for thee, but it seems good
That thou should'st go.'
At this the old man paused,
Then pointing to the stones near which they stood,
Thus after a short silence he resumed:
'This was a work for us, and now, my son,
It is a work for me. But lay one stone –
Here, lay it for me, Luke, with thine own hands –
I for the purpose brought thee to this place.
Nay, boy, be of good hope: we both may live
To see a better day. At eighty-four
I still am strong and stout; do thou thy part,
I will do mine. I will begin again
With many tasks that were resigned to thee;
Up to the heights, and in among the storms,
Will I without thee go again, and do
All works which I was wont to do alone
Before I knew thy face. Heaven bless thee, boy;
Thy heart these two weeks has been beating fast
With many hopes. It should be so – yes, yes,
I knew that thou could'st never have a wish
To leave me, Luke – thou hast been bound to me
Only by links of love. When thou art gone
What will be left to us? But I forget
My purposes. Lay now the corner-stone
As I requested, and hereafter, Luke,
When thou art gone away, should evil men
Be thy companions, let this sheepfold be
Thy anchor and thy shield. Amid all fear
And all temptation, let it be to thee
An emblem of the life thy fathers lived,
Who, being innocent,[50] did for that cause
Bestir them in good deeds. Now fare thee well.
When thou return'st, thou in this place wilt see
A work which is not here. A covenant[51]
'Twill be between us – but whatever fate
Befall thee, I shall love thee to the last,
And bear thy memory with me to the grave.'
The shepherd ended here, and Luke stooped down
And as his father had requested, laid
The first stone of the sheepfold. At the sight
The old man's grief broke from him; to his heart
He pressed his son, he kissed him and wept –
And to the house together they returned.

Notes

[50] *innocent* uncorrupted.

[51] *covenant* an echo of the biblical covenant made by God with Abraham, Genesis 17: 19.

Next morning, as had been resolved, the boy
Began his journey; and when he had reached
The public way he put on a bold face,
And all the neighbours as he passed their doors
Came forth with wishes and with farewell prayers
That followed him till he was out of sight.
   A good report did from their kinsman come
Of Luke and his well-doing; and the boy
Wrote loving letters, full of wondrous news,
Which, as the housewife phrased it, were throughout
The prettiest letters that were ever seen.
Both parents read them with rejoicing hearts.
So many months passed on, and once again
The shepherd went about his daily work
With confident and cheerful thoughts; and now
Sometimes when he could find a leisure hour
He to that valley took his way, and there
Wrought at the sheepfold. Meantime Luke began
To slacken in his duty, and at length
He in the dissolute city gave himself
To evil courses; ignominy and shame
Fell on him, so that he was driven at last
To seek a hiding-place beyond the seas.
   There is a comfort in the strength of love,
'Twill make a thing endurable which else
Would break the heart – old Michael found it so.
I have conversed with more than one who well
Remember the old man, and what he was
Years after he had heard this heavy news.
His bodily frame had been from youth to age
Of an unusual strength. Among the rocks
He went, and still looked up upon the sun,
And listened to the wind, and, as before,
Performed all kinds of labour for his sheep
And for the land, his small inheritance.
And to that hollow dell from time to time
Did he repair, to build the fold of which
His flock had need. 'Tis not forgotten yet
The pity which was then in every heart
For the old man; and 'tis believed by all
That many and many a day he thither went,
And never lifted up a single stone.
   There by the sheepfold sometimes was he seen
Sitting alone, with that his faithful dog –
Then old – beside him, lying at his feet.
The length of full seven years from time to time
He at the building of this sheepfold wrought,
And left the work unfinished when he died.[52]

Notes

[52] *when he died* Michael would have been 91 or 92.

Three years, or little more, did Isabel
Survive her husband; at her death the estate
Was sold, and went into a stranger's hand.
The cottage which was named The Evening Star
Is gone; the ploughshare has been through the ground
On which it stood. Great changes have been wrought
In all the neighbourhood; yet the oak is left
That grew beside their door, and the remains
Of the unfinished sheepfold may be seen
Beside the boisterous brook of Greenhead Gill.

[*I travelled among unknown men*] (composed *c.* 29 April 1801)

From Poems in Two Volumes (1807)

I travelled among unknown men
  In lands beyond the sea;[1]
Nor, England, did I know till then
  What love I bore to thee.

'Tis passed, that melancholy dream!
  Nor will I quit thy shore
A second time, for still I seem
  To love thee more and more.

Among thy mountains did I feel
  The joy of my desire;
And she I cherished turned her wheel
  Beside an English fire.

Thy mornings showed, thy nights concealed
  The bowers where Lucy played;
And thine is, too, the last green field
  Which Lucy's eyes surveyed!

Appendix to the Preface to Lyrical Ballads: On Poetic Diction (extracts) (composed early 1802)[1]

From Lyrical Ballads (2 vols, 1802)

As perhaps I have no right to expect from a reader of an introduction to a volume of poems that attentive perusal without which it is impossible, imperfectly as I have been compelled to express my meaning, that what I have said in the preface should

Notes

I TRAVELLED AMONG UNKNOWN MEN

[1] *I travelled . . . sea* Wordsworth is probably recalling his visit to Germany, 1798–9.

APPENDIX TO THE PREFACE TO LYRICAL BALLADS

[1] Wordsworth added this Appendix to his earlier Preface to *Lyrical Ballads* (1800) when preparing a further edition in early 1802. In the Preface he said that his poems contained 'little of what is usually called "poetic diction" ' before proceeding to criticize its use in the poetry of Gray and Pope; see p. 500. It was clearly something that required explanation.

throughout be fully understood, I am the more anxious to give an exact notion of the sense in which I use the phrase 'poetic diction'. And for this purpose I will here add a few words concerning the origin of the phraseology which I have condemned under that name.

The earliest poets of all nations generally wrote from passion excited by real events.[2] They wrote naturally, and as men. Feeling powerfully as they did, their language was daring and figurative. In succeeding times, poets and men ambitious of the fame of poets, perceiving the influence of such language and desirous of producing the same effect without having the same animating passion, set themselves to a mechanical adoption of those figures of speech, and made use of them, sometimes with propriety, but much more frequently applied them to feelings and ideas with which they had no natural connection whatsoever. A language was thus insensibly produced, differing materially from the real language of men *in any situation*.

The reader or hearer of this distorted language found himself in a perturbed and unusual state of mind; when affected by the genuine language of passion he had been in a perturbed and unusual state of mind also. In both cases he was willing that his common judgement and understanding should be laid asleep, and he had no instinctive and infallible perception of the true[3] to make him reject the false; the one served as a passport for the other.[4] The agitation and confusion of mind were in both cases delightful, and no wonder if he confounded the one with the other, and believed them both to be produced by the same, or similar, causes. Besides, the poet spake to him in the character of a man to be looked up to, a man of genius and authority.

Thus, and from a variety of other causes, this distorted language was received with admiration, and poets (it is probable) who had before contented themselves for the most part with misapplying only expressions which at first had been dictated by real passion, carried the abuse still further, and introduced phrases composed apparently in the spirit of the original figurative language of passion, yet altogether of their own invention, and distinguished by various degrees of wanton deviation from good sense and nature.

It is indeed true that the language of the earliest poets was felt to differ materially from ordinary language because it was the language of extraordinary occasions – but it was really spoken by men, language which the poet himself had uttered when he had been affected by the events which he described, or which he had heard uttered by those around him. To this language it is probable that metre of some sort or other was early superadded. This separated the genuine language of poetry still further from common life, so that whoever read or heard the poems of these earliest poets felt himself moved in a way in which he had not been accustomed to be moved in real life, and by causes manifestly different from those which acted upon him in real life. This was the great temptation to all the corruptions which have followed. Under the protection of this feeling, succeeding poets constructed a phraseology which had one thing, it is true, in common with the genuine language of poetry – namely, that it was not heard in ordinary conversation, that it was unusual. But the first poets, as I have said, spake a language which, though unusual, was still the language of men. This circumstance, however, was disregarded by their successors. They found that they could please by easier means. They became proud of a language which they themselves had invented, and which was uttered only by themselves. And, with the spirit of

Notes

[2] *passion excited by real events* cf. Wordsworth's insistence that the proper object of poetry is truth, p. 497 above.

[3] *the true* i.e. the real – real emotions, real objects.

[4] *the one . . . other* in other words, language became detached from reality.

a fraternity, they arrogated[5] it to themselves as their own. In process of time metre became a symbol or promise of this unusual language, and whoever took upon him to write in metre, according as he possessed more or less of true poetic genius, introduced less or more of this adulterated phraseology into his compositions, and the true and the false became so inseparably interwoven that the taste of men was gradually perverted, and this language was received as a natural language – and at length, by the influence of books upon men, did to a certain degree really become so.[6] Abuses of this kind were imported from one nation to another, and with the progress of refinement this diction became daily more and more corrupt, thrusting out of sight the plain humanities of nature by a motley masquerade of tricks, quaintnesses, hieroglyphics,[7] and enigmas . . .

Perhaps I can in no way, by positive example, more easily give my reader a notion of what I mean by the phrase 'poetic diction' than by referring him to a comparison between the metrical paraphrases which we have of passages in the Old and New Testament, and those passages as they exist in our common translation; see Pope's 'Messiah' throughout; Prior's 'Did sweeter sounds adorn my flowing tongue', etc., etc.; 'Though I speak with the tongues of men and of angels', etc., etc; see 1 Corinthians 13.

By way of immediate example, take the following of Dr Johnson:

Turn on the prudent ant thy heedless eyes,
Observe her labours, sluggard, and be wise!
No stern command, no monitory voice
Prescribes her duties, or directs her choice;
Yet, timely provident, she hastes away
To snatch the blessings of a plenteous day.
When fruitful summer loads the teeming plain,
She crops the harvest and she stores the grain.
How long shall sloth usurp thy useless hours,
Unnerve thy vigour, and enchain thy powers?
While artful shades thy downy couch enclose,
And soft solicitation courts repose,
Amidst the drowsy charms of dull delight
Year chases year with unremitted flight;
Till want now following, fraudulent and slow,
Shall spring to seize thee, like an ambushed foe.

(*The Ant*)

From this hubbub of words pass to the original: 'Go to the ant, thou sluggard, consider her ways and be wise – which having no guide, overseer, or ruler, provideth her meat in the summer, and gathereth her food in the harvest. How long wilt thou sleep, oh sluggard? When wilt thou arise out of thy sleep? Yet a little sleep, a little slumber, a little folding of the hands to sleep. So shall thy poverty come as one that travaileth, and thy want as an armed man' (Proverbs 6).

One more quotation and I have done. It is from Cowper's 'Verses Supposed to be Written by Alexander Selkirk'.

Notes

[5] *arrogated* claimed.

[6] *by the influence . . . so* The artificial, distorted language of poets was picked up in colloquial speech and thus, to some extent, became the 'natural language'.

[7] *hieroglyphics* words of unknown or mysterious meaning.

Religion – what treasure untold
Resides in that heavenly word!
More precious than silver and gold
Or all that this earth can afford.
But the sound of the church-going bell
These valleys and rocks never heard,
Ne'er sighed at the sound of a knell,
Or smiled when a sabbath appeared.

Ye winds that have made me your sport,
Convey to this desolate shore
Some cordial endearing report
Of a land I must visit no more.
My friends, do they now and then send
A wish or a thought after me?
Oh tell me I yet have a friend,
Though a friend I am never to see.

I have quoted this passage as an instance of three different styles of composition. The first four lines are poorly expressed. Some critics would call the language prosaic; the fact is it would be bad prose – so bad that it is scarcely worse in metre. The epithet 'church-going' applied to a bell (and that by so chaste a writer as Cowper) is an instance of the strange abuses which poets have introduced into their language till they and their readers take them as matters of course, if they do not single them out expressly as objects of admiration. The two lines 'Ne'er sighed at the sound', etc., are in my opinion an instance of the language of passion wrested from its proper use, and, from the mere circumstance of the composition being in metre, applied upon an occasion that does not justify such violent expressions – and I should condemn the passage (though perhaps few readers will agree with me) as vicious poetic diction.

The last stanza is throughout admirably expressed. It would be equally good whether in prose or verse, except that the reader has an exquisite pleasure in seeing such natural language so naturally connected with metre. The beauty of this stanza tempts me here to add a sentiment which ought to be the pervading spirit of a system, detached parts of which have been imperfectly explained in the preface – namely, that in proportion as ideas and feelings are valuable, whether the composition be in prose or in verse, they require and exact one and the same language.

Preface to Lyrical Ballads (extracts) (revised text composed January to April 1802)[1]

From Lyrical Ballads (2 vols, 1802)

Taking up the subject, then, upon general grounds, I ask what is meant by the word poet? What is a poet? To whom does he address himself? And what language is to be expected from him? He is a man speaking to men – a man (it is true) endued[2] with more lively sensibility, more enthusiasm and tenderness, who has a greater knowledge

Notes

PREFACE TO LYRICAL BALLADS

[1] In addition to preparing an Appendix to the Preface originally composed for *Lyrical Ballads* in 1800, Wordsworth revised the Preface itself. As well as adjusting some of the phrasing, he added this passage on the topic, 'What is a poet?' It is one of his most important comments on his craft and vocation.

[2] *endued* endowed.

of human nature, and a more comprehensive[3] soul, than are supposed to be common among mankind; a man pleased with his own passions and volitions,[4] and who rejoices more than other men in the spirit of life that is in him, delighting to contemplate similar volitions and passions as manifested in the goings-on of the universe,[5] and habitually impelled to create them where he does not find them.

To these qualities he has added a disposition to be affected more than other men by absent things as if they were present,[6] an ability of conjuring up in himself passions which are indeed far from being the same as those produced by real events, yet (especially in those parts of the general sympathy which are pleasing and delightful) do more nearly resemble the passions produced by real events than anything which, from the motions of their own minds merely, other men are accustomed to feel in themselves – whence, and from practice, he has acquired a greater readiness and power in expressing what he thinks and feels, and especially those thoughts and feelings which, by his own choice, or from the structure of his own mind, arise in him without immediate external excitement.

But whatever portion of this faculty we may suppose even the greatest poet to possess, there cannot be a doubt but that the language which it will suggest to him must in liveliness and truth fall far short of that which is uttered by men in real life under the actual pressure of those passions – certain shadows of which the poet thus produces, or feels to be produced, in himself.

However exalted a notion we would wish to cherish of the character of a poet, it is obvious that, while he describes and imitates passions, his situation is altogether slavish and mechanical compared with the freedom and power of real and substantial action and suffering. So that it will be the wish of the poet to bring his feelings near to those of the persons whose feelings he describes – nay, for short spaces of time, perhaps, to let himself slip into an entire delusion, and even confound[7] and identify his own feelings with theirs, modifying only the language which is thus suggested to him by a consideration that he describes for a particular purpose: that of giving pleasure. Here, then, he will apply the principle on which I have so much insisted – namely, that of selection. On this he will depend for removing what would otherwise be painful or disgusting in the passion; he will feel that there is no necessity to trick out[8] or elevate nature.[9] And the more industriously he applies this principle, the deeper will be his faith that no words which his fancy or imagination can suggest will be compared with those which are the emanations of reality and truth. . . .

Aristotle, I have been told,[10] hath said that poetry is the most philosophic of all writing.[11] It is so. Its object is truth,[12] not individual and local, but general and operative;[13] not standing upon external testimony, but carried alive into the heart by

Notes

[3] *more comprehensive* more intense, profound, and all-embracing.

[4] *volitions* impulses, good deeds.

[5] *the universe* the created world.

[6] *To these qualities . . . present* So vividly does the poet recall natural objects, which have 'impressed' themselves on his mind, that they seem to be present; the process is described in *Tintern Abbey* 23–50, and elucidated for the first time in 'Not Useless do I Deem' 24–8:

And further, by contemplating these forms
In the relations which they bear to man,
We shall discover what a power is theirs
To stimulate our minds, and multiply
The spiritual presences of absent things . . .

[7] *confound* confuse; effectively, the poet cannot tell the difference between his own feelings and those of his subject.

[8] *trick out* dress up.

[9] *nature* natural utterance.

[10] *I have been told* probably by Coleridge, who had been a Grecian (a boy in the highest class) at Christ's Hospital.

[11] *Aristotle . . . writing* Wordsworth aimed to compose the great philosophical epic of his day – *The Recluse* (see pp. 413–15). Aristotle thought poetry the most philosophical genre because it shows men not as they are but as they should be.

[12] *truth* effectively, the real world – real people and real things, as opposed to abstract personifications.

[13] *operative* practical.

passion – truth which is its own testimony, which gives strength and divinity to the tribunal to which it appeals, and receives them from the same tribunal.

Poetry is the image of man and nature. The obstacles which stand in the way of the fidelity of the biographer and historian (and of their consequent utility) are incalculably greater than those which are to be encountered by the poet who has an adequate notion of the dignity[14] of his art. The poet writes under one restriction only – namely, that of the necessity of giving immediate pleasure to a human being possessed of that information which may be expected from him, not as a lawyer, a physician, a mariner, an astronomer, or a natural philosopher, but as a man.[15] Except this one restriction, there is no object standing between the poet and the image of things; between this, and the biographer and historian, there are a thousand.

Nor let this necessity of producing immediate pleasure be considered as a degradation of the poet's art; it is far otherwise. It is an acknowledgement of the beauty of the universe, an acknowledgement the more sincere because it is not formal, but indirect; it is a task light and easy to him who looks at the world in the spirit of love. Further, it is a homage paid to the native and naked dignity of man, to the grand elementary principle of pleasure[16] by which he knows, and feels, and lives, and moves. . . .

To H.C., Six Years Old (composed probably between 4 March and 4 April 1802)[1]

From Poems in Two Volumes (1807)

Oh thou, whose fancies from afar are brought,
Who of thy words dost make a mock apparel,
And fittest to unutterable thought
The breeze-like motion and the self-born carol;
Thou fairy voyager, that dost float
In such clear water, that thy boat
May rather seem
To brood on air than on an earthly stream,[2]
Suspended in a stream as clear as sky,
Where earth and heaven do make one imagery;
Oh blessed vision, happy child,

Notes

[14] *dignity* high status.

[15] *not as . . . man* i.e. the poet is concerned with fidelity to psychological truth, rather than with facts.

[16] *pleasure* positive sensations (spiritual and physical) deriving from our involvement with the external world.

To H.C., Six Years Old

[1] Hartley Coleridge (b. 1796) had already featured in Coleridge's *Frost at Midnight*, *Christabel*, *The Nightingale*, and would appear again in Wordsworth's 'Ode' (pp. 538–42). Lucy Newlyn has observed that this poem is 'close to the rhythms and language' of Marvell's *On a Drop of Dew* (see *Coleridge, Wordsworth, and the Language of Allusion* (Oxford, 1986), p. 146).

[2] 'See Carver's description of his situation upon one of the lakes of America' (Wordsworth's note). Wordsworth has in mind Carver's account of Lake Superior: 'The water in general appeared to lie on a bed of rocks. When it was calm, and the sun shone bright, I could sit in my canoe, where the depth was upwards of six fathoms, and plainly see huge piles of stones at the bottom, of different shapes, some of which appeared as if they were hewn. The water at this time was as pure and transparent as air; and my canoe seemed as if it hung suspended in that element. It was impossible to look attentively through this limpid medium at the rocks below, without finding, before many minutes were elapsed, your head swim, and your eyes no longer able to behold the dazzling scene' (Jonathan Carver, *Travels through the interior parts of North America* (1778), pp. 132–3).

That art so exquisitely wild,
I think of thee with many fears
For what may be thy lot in future years.

I thought of times when Pain might be thy guest,
Lord of thy house and hospitality;
And Grief, uneasy lover, never rest
But when she sate within the touch of thee.
Oh too industrious folly!
Oh vain and causeless melancholy!
Nature will either end thee quite,
Or, lengthening out thy season of delight,
Preserve for thee, by individual right,
A young lamb's heart among the full-grown flocks.
What hast thou to do with sorrow
Or the injuries of tomorrow?
Thou art a dew-drop, which the morn brings forth,
Not doomed to jostle with unkindly shocks,
Or to be trailed along the soiling earth;
A gem that glitters while it lives,
And no forewarning gives;
But, at the touch of wrong, without a strife,
Slips in a moment out of life.

The Rainbow (composed probably 26 March 1802)

From **Poems in Two Volumes** (1807)

My heart leaps up when I behold
  A rainbow in the sky;
So was it when my life began,
So is it now I am a man,
So be it when I shall grow old
  Or let me die!
The child is father of the man,
And I could wish my days to be
Bound each to each by natural piety.

[*These chairs they have no words to utter*] (composed *c.* 22 April 1802; edited from MS)[1]

These chairs they have no words to utter,
No fire is in the grate to stir or flutter,
The ceiling and floor are mute as a stone,
My chamber is hushed and still,
    And I am alone,
    Happy and alone.

Notes

THESE CHAIRS THEY HAVE NO WORDS TO UTTER

[1] These two poems should be read in the light of Dorothy Wordsworth's journal entry of 29 April 1802, p. 587 below.

Oh, who would be afraid of life,
The passion, the sorrow, and the strife,
    When he may lie
    Sheltered so easily –
May lie in peace on his bed,
Happy as they who are dead?

Half an hour afterwards

I have thoughts that are fed by the sun;[2]
  The things which I see
  Are welcome to me,
  Welcome every one;
  I do not wish to lie
    Dead, dead,
Dead, without any company.[3]
  Here alone on my bed,
With thoughts that are fed by the sun
And hopes that are welcome every one,
  Happy am I.

Oh life, there is about thee
A deep delicious peace;
I would not be without thee –
  Stay, oh stay!
Yet be thou ever as now,
Sweetness and breath with the quiet of death,
  Peace, peace, peace.

Resolution and Independence (composed probably 3 May–4 July 1802)[1]

From Poems in Two Volumes (1807)

There was a roaring in the wind all night,
The rain came heavily and fell in floods;
But now the sun is rising calm and bright,
The birds are singing in the distant woods;
Over his own sweet voice the stockdove broods,[2]
The jay makes answer as the magpie chatters,
And all the air is filled with pleasant noise of waters.

Notes

[2] *I have thoughts that are fed by the sun* an echo of Anna Laetitia Barbauld's *A Summer Evening's Meditation*, in which Contemplation 'fed on thoughts unripened by the sun' (l. 22).

[3] *without any company* Wordsworth echoes Arcite's dying speech in Chaucer's *Knight's Tale*:

> What is this world? What askest men to have?
> Now with his love, now in his colde grave
> Allone, withouten any compaignye?
> (ll. 2777–9)

RESOLUTION AND INDEPENDENCE

[1] The incident which inspired this poem is recounted by Dorothy Wordsworth, p. 587.

[2] *Over . . . broods* See Wordsworth's comments on this line in the 1815 Preface, p. 576.

All things that love the sun are out of doors,
The sky rejoices in the morning's birth,
The grass is bright with raindrops, on the moors
The hare is running races in her mirth
And with her feet she from the plashy earth
Raises a mist which, glittering in the sun,
Runs with her all the way, wherever she doth run.

I was a traveller then upon the moor;[3]
I saw the hare that raced about with joy;
I heard the woods and distant waters roar,
Or heard them not, as happy as a boy –
The pleasant season did my heart employ.
My old remembrances went from me wholly,
And all the ways of men, so vain and melancholy.

But as it sometimes chanceth, from the might
Of joy in minds that can no farther go,
As high as we have mounted in delight
In our dejection do we sink as low –
To me that morning did it happen so,
And fears and fancies thick upon me came,
Dim sadness, and blind thoughts I knew not nor could name.

I heard the skylark singing in the sky,[4]
And I bethought me of the playful hare;
Even such a happy child of earth am I,
Even as these blissful creatures do I fare;
Far from the world I walk, and from all care.
But there may come another day to me –
Solitude, pain of heart, distress, and poverty.

My whole life I have lived in pleasant thought
As if life's business were a summer mood,
As if all needful things would come unsought
To genial faith, still rich in genial good;
But how can he expect that others should
Build for him, sow for him, and at his call
Love him, who for himself will take no heed at all?

I thought of Chatterton,[5] the marvellous boy,
The sleepless soul that perished in its pride;
Of him[6] who walked in glory and in joy

Notes

[3] *I was then . . . moor* In the Fenwick Notes, Wordsworth recalls: 'This old man I met a few hundred yards from my cottage at Town End, Grasmere, and the account of him is taken from his own mouth' (*FN* 14). As in *The Prelude*, he is not concerned with factual truth, but with truth to the emotions.

[4] *I heard . . . sky* cf. *The Ancient Mariner* (1798) 347–8: 'Sometimes a-dropping from the sky / I heard the lavrock sing.'

[5] During his short life, Thomas Chatterton (1752–70) composed a number of forged medieval poems supposedly by the 15th-century poet, Thomas Rowley. Wordsworth and Coleridge both admired these works as schoolboys. It is often noted that this poem imitates the metre of Chatterton's *Excellent Ballade of Charitie*.

[6] Robert Burns.

Behind his plough[7] upon the mountainside.
By our own spirits are we deified;[8]
We poets in our youth begin in gladness,
But thereof comes in the end despondency and madness.

Now whether it were by peculiar grace,[9]
A leading from above, a something given,
Yet it befell that, in this lonely place,
When up and down my fancy thus was driven,
And I with these untoward thoughts had striven,
I saw a man before me unawares –
The oldest man he seemed that ever wore grey hairs.

My course I stopped as soon as I espied
The old man in that naked wilderness;
Close by a pond, upon the further side,
He stood alone. A minute's space I guess
I watched him, he continuing motionless.
To the pool's further margin then I drew,
He being all the while before me full in view.

As a huge stone is sometimes seen to lie[10]
Couched on the bald top of an eminence,
Wonder to all who do the same espy
By what means it could thither come, and whence;
So that it seems a thing endued with sense,
Like a sea-beast crawled forth, which on a shelf
Of rock or sand reposeth, there to sun itself –

Such seemed this man, not all alive nor dead,
Nor all asleep, in his extreme old age.
His body was bent double, feet and head
Coming together in their pilgrimage,
As if some dire constraint of pain, or rage
Of sickness felt by him in times long past,
A more than human weight upon his frame had cast.

Himself he propped, his body, limbs, and face,
Upon a long grey staff of shaven wood;
And still as I drew near with gentle pace,
Beside the little pond or moorish flood,
Motionless as a cloud the old man stood
That heareth not the loud winds when they call,
And moveth altogether, if it move at all.

Notes

[7] *Behind his plough* Burns was a farmer, and in some of his poems, such as 'To a Mouse' (pp. 268–9), described himself at the plough.

[8] *deified* made god-like, divine.

[9] *grace* divine influence.

[10] For Wordsworth's important comments on ll.64–84 see pp. 577–8.

At length, himself unsettling, he the pond
Stirred with his staff, and fixedly did look
Upon the muddy water, which he conned[11]
As if he had been reading in a book.
And now such freedom as I could I took,
And drawing to his side, to him did say,
'This morning gives us promise of a glorious day.'

A gentle answer did the old man make
In courteous speech which forth he slowly drew,
And him with further words I thus bespake,
'What kind of work is that which you pursue?
This is a lonesome place for one like you.'
He answered me with pleasure and surprise,
And there was, while he spake, a fire about his eyes.

His words came feebly, from a feeble chest,
Yet each in solemn order followed each,
With something of a lofty utterance dressed,
Choice word and measured phrase, above the reach
Of ordinary men – a stately speech
Such as grave livers[12] do in Scotland use,
Religious men, who give to God and man their dues.

He told me that he to this pond had come
To gather leeches, being old and poor –
Employment hazardous and wearisome![13]
And he had many hardships to endure;
From pond to pond he roamed, from moor to moor,
Housing, with God's good help, by choice or chance;
And in this way he gained an honest maintenance.[14]

The old man still stood talking by my side,
But now his voice to me was like a stream
Scarce heard, nor word from word could I divide;
And the whole body of the man did seem
Like one whom I had met with in a dream,
Or like a man from some far region sent
To give me human strength, and strong admonishment.

My former thoughts returned: the fear that kills,
The hope that is unwilling to be fed,
Cold, pain, and labour, and all fleshly ills,
And mighty poets in their misery dead.
And now, not knowing what the old man had said,
My question eagerly did I renew,
'How is it that you live, and what is it you do?'

Notes

[11] *conned* studied.

[12] *livers* folk.

[13] *He told me . . . wearisome* Leeches were widely used in medical treatment. Many illnesses, including fevers, were thought to be caused by an excess of blood; leeches were applied to bleed the patient.

[14] *maintenance* living.

He with a smile did then his words repeat,
And said that gathering leeches far and wide
He travelled, stirring thus about his feet
The waters of the ponds where they abide.
'Once I could meet with them on every side
But they have dwindled long by slow decay;
Yet still I persevere, and find them where I may.'

While he was talking thus, the lonely place,
The old man's shape and speech, all troubled me;
In my mind's eye I seemed to see him pace
About the weary moors continually,
Wandering about alone and silently.
While I these thoughts within myself pursued,
He, having made a pause, the same discourse renewed.

And soon with this he other matter blended,
Cheerfully uttered, with demeanour kind,
But stately in the main; and when he ended,
I could have laughed myself to scorn to find
In that decrepit man so firm a mind.
'God', said I, 'be my help and stay[15] secure;
I'll think of the leech-gatherer on the lonely moor.'

[*I grieved for Buonaparte*] (composed 21 May 1802)[1]

From Poems in Two Volumes (1807)

I grieved for Buonaparte,[2] with a vain
And an unthinking grief! The vital blood
Of that man's mind, what can it be? What food
Fed his first hopes? What knowledge could *he* gain?

Notes

[15] *stay* support.

I GRIEVED FOR BUONAPARTE

[1] On the afternoon of 21 May 1802 at Dove Cottage, Dorothy read Milton's sonnets to her brother. He later recalled that 'I was particularly struck on that occasion with the dignified simplicity and majestic harmony that runs through most of them – in character so totally different from the Italian, and still more so from Shakespeare's fine sonnets. I took fire, if I may be allowed to say so, and produced three sonnets the same afternoon' (*FN* 19). This poem is one of the three composed that afternoon. It was among the first of many remarkable sonnets which Wordsworth would write over the coming months, the best of which are presented in the pages following. This sonnet was a favourite of Wordsworth's brother John, who would perish in the wreck of the *Earl of Abergavenny* in 1805. In December 1802, having seen it in manuscript, he wrote to Dorothy: 'I am much pleased with William's sonnet to Bonaparte. I think it is well written. It is like the rest of his sonnets which I have seen not much likely to please *common* people at the first sight, but I think they are very good.' Helpful critical comment on this poem, and other aspects of Wordsworth's feelings towards Napoleon, may be found in Simon Bainbridge, *Napoleon and English Romanticism* (Cambridge, 1995), chapter 2.

[2] *Buonaparte* Wordsworth kept abreast of current affairs (including Britain's conflict with France) through the newspapers. He was well aware that Napoleon had been made First Consul in 1799, and that his military campaign had been so successful that Britain was the only country from the original alliance to remain independent of French rule. However, war had been going on for nearly a decade, and all sides had tired of it, so that on 27 March 1802 a peace was agreed that would permit Wordsworth to visit France during the summer and be reunited with Annette Vallon. He would then meet their daughter, Caroline, for the first time.

'Tis not in battles[3] that from youth we train
The Governor who must be wise and good,
And temper with the sternness of the brain
Thoughts motherly, and meek as womanhood.
Wisdom doth live with children round her knees:
Books, leisure, perfect freedom, and the talk
Man holds with weekday man in the hourly walk
Of the mind's business: these are the degrees
By which true Sway doth mount; this is the stalk
True Power doth grow on; and her rights are these.

[*The world is too much with us*] (composed late May 1802)

From Poems in Two Volumes (1807)

The world is too much with us; late and soon,
Getting and spending, we lay waste our powers:
Little we see in nature that is ours;
We have given our hearts away, a sordid boon!
This sea that bares her bosom to the moon;
The winds that will be howling at all hours
And are up-gathered now like sleeping flowers;
For this, for every thing, we are out of tune;
It moves us not. Great God! I'd rather be
A Pagan suckled in a creed outworn;
So might I, standing on this pleasant lea,[1]
Have glimpses that would make me less forlorn;
Have sight of Proteus coming from the sea;[2]
Or hear old Triton blow his wreathed horn.[3]

Composed upon Westminster Bridge, 3 September 1802 (composed probably 31 July 1802, possibly revised early September 1802)[1]

From Poems in Two Volumes (1807)

Earth has not any thing to show more fair:
Dull would he be of soul who could pass by
A sight so touching in its majesty:
This city now doth like a garment wear

Notes

[3] *'Tis not in battles* Wordsworth was aware that Napoleon's education had been almost exclusively in the army: five years at the military college of Brienne, and a year at the military academy of Paris, before (at the age of 16) becoming second lieutenant of artillery in the regiment of La Fère, a kind of training school for young artillery officers.

The world is too much with us

[1] *lea* meadow.

[2] *Have sight . . . sea* cf. *Paradise Lost* iii 603–4: 'call up unbound / In various shapes old Proteus from the sea'.

[3] *Have sight . . . horn* cf. Spenser, *Colin Clouts Come Home Againe* 245–8: 'Triton blowing loud his wreathed horne . . . And Proteus eke with him does drive his heard.'

Composed upon Westminster Bridge

[1] This famous sonnet was inspired by the view from Westminster Bridge, at about 5.30 or 6.30 on the morning of 31 July 1802, as Dorothy and William were heading out of London to France (where Wordsworth would be reunited with Annette Vallon and meet, for the first time, their daughter Caroline). Dorothy described the view in her

The beauty of the morning; silent, bare,
Ships, towers, domes, theatres, and temples lie
Open unto the fields, and to the sky;
All bright and glittering in the smokeless air.
Never did sun more beautifully steep[2]
In his first splendour valley, rock, or hill;
Ne'er saw I, never felt, a calm so deep!
The river glideth at his own sweet will:[3]
Dear God! the very houses seem asleep;
And all that mighty heart is lying still!

To Toussaint L'Ouverture[1] (composed August 1802)

From Poems in Two Volumes (1807)

Toussaint, the most unhappy man of men!
Whether the rural milkmaid by her cow
Sing in thy hearing, or thou liest now
Alone in some deep dungeon's earless den –
Oh miserable chieftain, where and when
Wilt thou find patience? Yet die not! Do thou
Wear rather in thy bonds a cheerful brow;
Though fallen thyself, never to rise again,
Live, and take comfort. Thou hast left behind
Powers that will work for thee – air, earth, and skies;
There's not a breathing of the common wind
That will forget thee; thou hast great allies;
Thy friends are exultations, agonies,
And love, and man's unconquerable mind.

Notes

journal: 'It was a beautiful morning. The City, St Paul's, with the river and a multitude of little boats, made a most beautiful sight as we crossed Westminster Bridge. The houses were not overhung by their cloud of smoke and they were spread out endlessly, yet the sun shone so brightly, with such a pure light, that there was even something like the purity of one of Nature's own grand spectacles. We rode on cheerfully.' Many years later, Wordsworth suggested that the sonnet was written 'on the roof of a coach, on my way to France' (*FN* 23), which would make the date of composition 31 July 1802, rather than 3 September, though it is possible that he revised his draft on returning to London in early September. For detailed discussion see Pamela Woof's fine essay in *'Earth has not any thing to shew more fair'*, ed. Peter Oswald, Alice Oswald and Robert Woof (Grasmere, 2002).

[2] *steep* bathe, envelop.

[3] *own sweet will* Shakespeare, Sonnet 16, l.14: 'And you must live, drawn by your own sweet will.'

To Toussaint L'Ouverture

[1] François Dominique Toussaint L'Ouverture (1746–1803), son of a Negro slave, became governor of San Domingo (Haiti), then a French colony, in 1801. He resisted Napoleon's attempts to reintroduce slavery, leading a popular uprising. All slaves were freed, and non-blacks were amazed by his magnanimity. Toussaint made himself governor-general for life, and dictated a constitution that gave him absolute power. He attempted to convince Napoleon of his loyalty while remaining aware that Napoleon did not trust him and would attempt to reassert French rule as soon as he could. As Wordsworth was aware, Napoleon invaded Haiti in January 1802 with a much larger force than expected. After fierce fighting, Toussaint surrendered in May, and by the time Wordsworth composed this sonnet was in France, where he was imprisoned and tortured at the Fort-de-Joux in the French Alps. He would die there, April 1803. His heroic life and death aroused sympathy in England, where the movement for the Abolition of the Slave-Trade was gathering pace.

[*It is a beauteous evening, calm and free*] (composed 1–29 August 1802)[1]

From Poems in Two Volumes (1807)

It is a beauteous evening, calm and free;
The holy time is quiet as a nun
Breathless with adoration; the broad sun
Is sinking down in its tranquillity;
The gentleness of heaven is on the sea:
Listen! The mighty Being is awake
And doth with his eternal motion make
A sound like thunder – everlastingly.
Dear Child![2] Dear Girl! that walkest with me here,
If thou appear'st untouched by solemn thought,
Thy nature is not therefore less divine:
Thou liest in Abraham's bosom[3] all the year;
And worshipp'st at the Temple's inner shrine,
God being with thee when we know it not.

1 September 1802 (composed 29 August–1 September 1802)[1]

From Poems in Two Volumes (1807)

We had a fellow-passenger who came
From Calais with us, gaudy in array –
A Negro woman, like a lady gay,
Yet silent as a woman fearing blame;
Dejected, meek – yea, pitiably tame
She sat, from notice turning not away,
But on our proffered kindness still did lay
A weight of languid speech, or at the same
Was silent, motionless in eyes and face.
She was a Negro woman driv'n from France,

Notes

It is a beauteous evening, calm and free

[1] This poem was composed on the beach at Calais. William and Dorothy took advantage of the Peace of Amiens in the summer of 1802 to visit France to meet his former French girlfriend, Annette Vallon, and their daughter, Caroline Wordsworth, whom he had not previously seen. Dorothy recorded in her journal for August: 'The weather was very hot. We walked by the sea-shore almost every evening with Annette and Caroline, or William and I alone . . . The reflections in the water were more beautiful than the sky itself, purple waves brighter than precious stones for ever melting away upon the sands. The fort, a wooden building at the entrance of the harbour at Calais, when the evening twilight was coming on, and we could not see anything of the building but its shape which was far more distinct than in perfect daylight, seemed to be reared upon pillars of ebony, between which pillars the sea was seen in the most beautiful colours that can be conceived. Nothing in Romance was ever half so beautiful.' Wordsworth wrote several other sonnets at Calais that August – 'Fair star of evening, splendour of the west', 'Is it a reed that's shaken by the wind', and 'Jones! when from Calais southward you and I', all published in *Poems in Two Volumes* (1807).

[2] *Dear child* Wordsworth's daughter, Caroline.

[3] *Abraham's bosom* see Luke 16: 22: 'And it came to pass that the beggar died, and was carried by the angels into Abraham's bosom.'

1 September 1802

[1] Composed during Wordsworth's brief visit to France during the Treaty of Amiens, 1802. In 1827, he added a headnote: 'Among the capricious acts of tyranny that disgraced these times was the chasing of all Negroes from France by decree of the government. We had a fellow-passenger who was one of the expelled.' In the wake of the disastrous San Domingo campaign, Napoleon banned all colonial blacks from the French mainland.

Rejected like all others of that race,
Not one of whom may now find footing there;
This the poor outcast did to us declare,
Nor murmured at the unfeeling ordinance.

London 1802 (composed September 1802)

From Poems in Two Volumes (1807)

Milton, thou shouldst be living at this hour,
England hath need of thee! She is a fen
Of stagnant waters. Altar, sword, and pen,
Fireside, the heroic wealth of hall and bower,
Have forfeited their ancient English dower
Of inward happiness. We are selfish men;
Oh raise us up, return to us again,
And give us manners, virtue, freedom, power!
Thy soul was like a star and dwelt apart;
Thou hadst a voice whose sound was like the sea,
Pure as the naked heavens, majestic, free –
So didst thou travel on life's common way,
In cheerful godliness, and yet thy heart
The lowliest duties on itself did lay.

[*Great men have been among us*] (composed summer 1802)

From Poems in Two Volumes (1807)

Great men have been among us; hands that penned
And tongues that uttered wisdom, better none:
The later Sidney, Marvell, Harrington,
Young Vane,[1] and others who called Milton friend.
These moralists could act and comprehend:
They knew how genuine glory was put on;
Taught us how rightfully a nation shone
In splendour; what strength was, that would not bend
But in magnanimous meekness. France, 'tis strange,
Hath brought forth no such souls as we had then.
Perpetual emptiness! Unceasing change!
No single volume paramount, no code,
No master spirit, no determined road;
But equally a want of books and men!

Notes

GREAT MEN HAVE BEEN AMONG US

[1] *Great men . . . Vane* English republicans of the civil war period. Algernon Sidney was a distinguished republican executed for complicity in the Rye House plot, 1683; he was the author of a republican tract, *Discourse concerning Civil Government* (1698), which Wordsworth probably read while an undergraduate. Wordsworth had also read the work of Andrew Marvell (1621–78), poet, friend and secretary to Milton, by 1795. James Harrington (1611–77) was the author of the republican classic, *Commonwealth of Oceana* (1656); Wordsworth is likely to have read it during his time in France, 1791–2. Wordsworth admired Milton's sonnet *To Henry Vane the Younger*, beginning: 'Vane, young in years, but in sage counsel old'. Vane was executed on 14 January 1662.

entitled Ode. Intimations of Immortality from ns of Early Childhood) (composed between March 1802 and 6 March 1804)[1]

rom Poems in Two Volumes (1807)

Paulò majora canamus.[2]

when meadow, grove, and stream,
, and every common sight,
To me did seem
Apparelled in celestial light,
The glory and the freshness of a dream.
It is not now as it has been of yore;
Turn wheresoe'er I may
By night or day
The things which I have seen I now can see no more.

The rainbow comes and goes
And lovely is the rose,
The moon doth with delight
Look round her when the heavens are bare;
Waters on a starry night
Are beautiful and fair;
The sunshine is a glorious birth;
But yet I know, where'er I go,
That there hath passed away a glory from the earth.

Now while the birds thus sing a joyous song,
And while the young lambs bound
As to the tabor's[3] sound,
To me alone there came a thought of grief;
A timely utterance gave that thought relief
And I again am strong.
The cataracts blow their trumpets from the steep –
No more shall grief of mine the season wrong;
I hear the echoes through the mountains throng,
The winds come to me from the fields of sleep
And all the earth is gay;
Land and sea
Give themselves up to jollity,
And with the heart of May
Doth every beast keep holiday.
Thou child of joy
Shout round me, let me hear thy shouts, thou happy shepherd-boy!

Notes

ODE

[1] Probably some or all of stanzas 1–4 (ll. 1–57) composed 27 March 1802. Further composition – possibly including some or, less probably, all of stanzas 5–8 – on 17 June 1802. Most of the last seven stanzas probably composed, and the poem completed, early 1804, by 6 March. See also the Fenwick Note to this poem, p. 582.

[2] 'Let us sing of somewhat more exalted things' (Virgil, *Eclogue* iv 1).

[3] *tabor* a small drum.

Ye blessed creatures, I have heard the call
Ye to each other make; I see
The heavens laugh with you in your jubilee;
My heart is at your festival,
My head hath its coronal[4] –
The fullness of your bliss, I feel, I feel it all.
Oh evil day! if I were sullen
While the earth herself is adorning
This sweet May morning,
And the children are pulling
On every side
In a thousand valleys far and wide
Fresh flowers, while the sun shines warm
And the babe leaps up on his mother's arm –
I hear, I hear, with joy I hear!
But there's a tree, of many one,
A single field which I have looked upon,
Both of them speak of something that is gone;
The pansy at my feet
Doth the same tale repeat:
Whither is fled the visionary gleam?
Where is it now, the glory and the dream?

Our birth is but a sleep and a forgetting.
The soul that rises with us, our life's star,
Hath had elsewhere its setting
And cometh from afar.[5]
Not in entire forgetfulness,
And not in utter nakedness,
But trailing clouds of glory do we come
From God, who is our home.
Heaven lies about us in our infancy!
Shades of the prison-house begin to close
Upon the growing boy,[6]
But he beholds the light and whence it flows,
He sees it in his joy;
The youth who daily farther from the east
Must travel, still is nature's priest,
And by the vision splendid
Is on his way attended:
At length the man perceives it die away
And fade into the light of common day.

Earth fills her lap with pleasures of her own;
Yearnings she hath in her own natural kind,
And even with something of a mother's mind
And no unworthy aim,

Notes

[4] *coronal* small garland of flowers worn on the head.

[5] *The soul . . . afar* Wordsworth suggests that we exist, before birth, in spiritual form. For his later comments on pre-existence, see p. 582.

[6] *Shades . . . boy* Wordsworth probably has in mind Coleridge's recollection of his schooldays at Christ's Hospital: 'For I was reared / In the great city, pent mid cloisters dim' (*Frost at Midnight* 56–7).

The homely nurse doth all she can
To make her foster-child, her inmate man,
Forget the glories he hath known
And that imperial palace whence he came.

Behold the child[7] among his new-born blisses,
A four years' darling of a pygmy size!
See where mid work of his own hand he lies,
Fretted by sallies of his mother's kisses
With light upon him from his father's eyes!
See at his feet some little plan or chart,
Some fragment from his dream of human life
Shaped by himself with newly-learned art –
A wedding or a festival,
A mourning or a funeral;
And this hath now his heart,
And unto this he frames his song.
Then will he fit his tongue
To dialogues of business, love, or strife;
But it will not be long
Ere this be thrown aside,
And with new joy and pride
The little actor cons[8] another part,
Filling from time to time his 'humorous stage'[9]
With all the persons down to palsied Age
That Life brings with her in her equipage[10] –
As if his whole vocation
Were endless imitation.

Thou[11] whose exterior semblance doth belie
Thy soul's immensity;
Thou best philosopher who yet dost keep
Thy heritage; thou eye among the blind
That, deaf and silent, read'st the eternal deep,
Haunted for ever by the eternal mind;
Mighty prophet! Seer blessed!
On whom those truths do rest
Which we are toiling all our lives to find;
Thou, over whom thy immortality
Broods like the day, a master o'er a slave,
A presence which is not to be put by,
To whom the grave
Is but a lonely bed without the sense or sight
Of day or the warm light,

Notes

[7] *the child* Hartley Coleridge, who had already been celebrated as a gifted being by Wordsworth in *To H.C., Six Years Old* (pp. 527–8), and by Coleridge in *Frost at Midnight*, *Christabel* 644–65 and *The Nightingale* 91–105.

[8] *cons* learns.

[9] *humorous stage* The theatre is peopled by characters with different moods ('humours'). The quotation is from Samuel Daniel's dedicatory sonnet to *Musophilus*, *To the Right Worthy and Judicious Favourer of Virtue, Mr Fulke Grevill* 1–2: 'I do not here upon this hum'rous stage / Bring my transformed verse.' Wordsworth is also recalling the seven ages of man speech, *As You Like It* II vii 139–66.

[10] *equipage* retinue, attendant following.

[11] *Thou* Hartley Coleridge.

A place of thought where we in waiting lie;[12]
Thou little child, yet glorious in the might
Of untamed pleasures, on thy being's height –
Why with such earnest pains dost thou provoke
The years to bring the inevitable yoke,
Thus blindly with thy blessedness at strife?
Full soon thy soul shall have her earthly freight,
And custom lie upon thee with a weight
Heavy as frost, and deep almost as life.

Oh joy! that in our embers
Is something that doth live,
That nature yet remembers
What was so fugitive!
The thought of our past years in me doth breed
Perpetual benedictions, not indeed
For that which is most worthy to be blessed –
Delight and liberty, the simple creed
Of childhood, whether fluttering or at rest,
With new-born hope forever in his breast –
Not for these I raise
The song of thanks and praise;
But for those obstinate questionings
Of sense and outward things,[13]
Fallings from us, vanishings,[14]
Blank misgivings of a creature
Moving about in worlds not realized,
High instincts before which our mortal nature
Did tremble like a guilty thing surprised;[15]
But for those first affections,
Those shadowy recollections
Which, be they what they may,
Are yet the fountain-light of all our day,
Are yet a master-light of all our seeing;
Uphold us, cherish us, and make
Our noisy years seem moments in the being
Of the eternal silence – truths that wake
To perish never,
Which neither listlessness nor mad endeavour,
Nor man nor boy,
Nor all that is at enmity with joy
Can utterly abolish or destroy!

Notes

[12] *To whom . . . lie* See Dorothy Wordsworth's journal, p. 587 below, and 'These chairs, they have no words to utter' 11–12. Lines 121–4 were cut from versions of the poem after 1815.

[13] *obstinate . . . things* The soul constantly challenges the notion that the outward, material reality of the physical world might be all there is.

[14] *vanishings* Years later, Wordsworth is reported to have said, 'There was a time in my life when I had to push against something that resisted, to be sure that there was anything outside me. I was sure of my own mind; everything else fell away and vanished into thought' (*WPW* iv 467); see also Fenwick Note to this poem, p. 582 below.

[15] *like a guilty thing surprised* cf. Horatio talking about the ghost at *Hamlet* I i 148–9: 'And then it started like a guilty thing / Upon a fearful summons.'

Hence, in a season of calm weather,
Though inland far we be,
Our souls have sight of that immortal sea
Which brought us hither,
Can in a moment travel thither
And see the children sport upon the shore,
And hear the mighty waters rolling evermore.

Then sing, ye birds; sing, sing a joyous song!
And let the young lambs bound
As to the tabor's sound!
We in thought will join your throng,
Ye that pipe and ye that play,
Ye that through your hearts today
Feel the gladness of the May!
What though the radiance which was once so bright
Be now for ever taken from my sight?
Though nothing can bring back the hour
Of splendour in the grass, of glory in the flower,
We will grieve not, rather find
Strength in what remains behind,
In the primal sympathy
Which having been must ever be,
In the soothing thoughts that spring
Out of human suffering,
In the faith that looks through death,
In years that bring the philosophic mind.

And oh, ye fountains, meadows, hills and groves,
Think not of any severing of our loves!
Yet in my heart of hearts I feel your might;
I only have relinquished one delight
To live beneath your more habitual sway.
I love the brooks which down their channels fret[16]
Even more than when I tripped lightly as they;
The innocent brightness of a new-born day
Is lovely yet;
The clouds that gather round the setting sun
Do take a sober colouring from an eye
That hath kept watch o'er man's mortality;
Another race hath been, and other palms are won.
Thanks to the human heart by which we live,
Thanks to its tenderness, its joys and fears,
To me the meanest flower[17] that blows can give
Thoughts that do often lie too deep for tears.

Notes

[16] *fret* move in an agitated manner.

[17] *the meanest flower* borrowed from Gray, *Ode on the Pleasure Arising from Vicissitude* 49: 'The meanest flowret of the vale'.

From The Five-Book Prelude (February–March 1804; edited from MS)[1]
[The Infant Prodigy] (from Book IV)

Rarely, and with reluctance, would I stoop
To transitory themes,[2] yet I rejoice –
And, by these thoughts admonished, must speak out
Thanksgivings from my heart – that I was reared
Safe from an evil which these days have laid
Upon the children of the land, a pest[3]
That might have dried me up, body and soul.
Let few words paint it: 'tis a child – no child,
But a dwarf man – in knowledge, virtue, skill,
In what he is not and in what he is,
The noontide shadow of a man complete;
A worshipper of worldly seemliness,
Not quarrelsome (for that were far beneath
His dignity), with gifts he bubbles o'er
As generous as a fountain. Selfishness
May not come near him, gluttony or pride;
The wandering beggars propagate his name,
Dumb creatures find him tender as a nun.[4]
Yet deem him not for this a naked dish
Of goodness merely, he is garnished out:
Arch are his notices,[5] and nice his sense
Of the ridiculous; deceit and guile
He can look through and through in pleasant spleen,[6]
At the broad follies of the licensed world;[7]
Though shrewd, yet innocent himself withal,
And can read lectures upon innocence.[8]

Notes

From The Five-Book Prelude

[1] In February–March 1804, Wordsworth returned to *The Prelude* with the aim of turning it into a poem consisting of Five Books. He reorganized the *Two-Part Prelude*, placing the spots of time at the end of the poem, and used the 'glad preamble', composed in 1799 (pp. 479–81), as an introduction to the poem. Among the various passages he composed towards the five-Book version was this satirical attack on educational theorists of the day. It was followed immediately by 'There was a boy', which had been published as an independent poem in *Lyrical Ballads* (1800) (pp. 474–5). In early March Wordsworth abandoned the five-Book poem, dismembered it, and began working towards a new version in thirteen Books. This passage was later revised to form *Thirteen-Book Prelude* v 223–9, 294–388.

[2] *transitory themes* Wordsworth rightly recognized the controversy over different ways of educating children to be of its time.

[3] *pest* plague. Wordsworth's target is the tradition of educationalists who followed in the wake of Locke's *Some thoughts concerning education* (1693). These include Rousseau's *Emile* (1762) – which Wordsworth had read by 1796; Richard and Maria Edgeworth's *Practical Education* (1798) (read by Coleridge shortly after publication) and Thomas Day's *Sandford and Merton* (1783–6). See also James Chandler, 'Wordsworth, Rousseau and the Politics of Education', in *Romanticism: A Critical Reader*, ed. Duncan Wu (1995), pp. 57–83, and Alan Richardson, *Literature, Education and Romanticism* (Cambridge, 1994), pp. 51–8.

[4] *Selfishness . . . nun* Thomas Day's protagonist, Harry Sandford, is 'brave, generous to beggars, kind to animals, even cockchafers, calm in the presence of an angry bull. Even the cattle were glad when he came back after an absence.' The literary model is Chaucer's portrait of the prioress (*General Prologue* 118–62).

[5] *Arch are his notices* His observations are clever, crafty, even mischievous.

[6] *pleasant spleen* amusement, as at *Twelfth Night* III ii 68–9: 'If you desire the spleen, and will laugh yourselves into stitches, follow me.'

[7] *He can . . . world* He is licensed to ignore deceit and guile, and other 'follies'.

[8] *And can read . . . innocence* richly ironic. The child's sophistication belies his 'goodness'. He is in no position to speak learnedly on the subject of innocence.

He is fenced round – nay armed, for aught we know,
In panoply complete;[9] and fear itself,
Unless it leap upon him in a dream,
Touches him not.[10] In brief, the moral part
Is perfect; in learning and in books
He is a prodigy. His discourse moves slow,
Massy and ponderous as a prison door,
Tremendously embossed with terms of art;[11]
With propositions are the younker's[12] brains
Filled to the brim; the path in which he treads
Is choked with grammars; cushion of divine
Was never such a type of thought profound
As is the pillow where he rests his head.[13]
The ensigns of the empire which he holds,
The globe and sceptre of his royalties,
Are telescopes and crucibles and maps.[14]
Ships he can guide across the pathless sea,
And tell you all their cunning;[15] he can read
The inside of the earth, and spell the stars;
He knows the policies of foreign lands,
Can string you names of districts, cities, towns
The whole world over,[16] tight as beads of dew
Upon a gossamer thread! His teachers stare,
The country people pray for God's good grace
And shudder at his deep experiments.[17]
He sifts, he weighs, takes nothing upon trust –
All things are put to question.[18] He must live
Knowing that he grows wiser every day
Or else not live at all[19] – and seeing too

Notes

[9] *panoply complete* full armour; cf. Cowper's satirical portrait of the clergyman, 'armed himself in panoply complete' (*Task* ii 345).

[10] *fear itself . . . touches him not* Without fear, the infant prodigy is deprived of a principal formative influence; cf. *The Two-Part Prelude* i 139–41.

[11] *terms of art* technical jargon.

[12] *younker's* youngster's.

[13] *cushion of divine . . . head* The prodigy's pillow is a better symbol ('type') of profound thought than the cushion on which the parson rests his Bible in front of a pulpit. The image is suggested by the Cowper's 'plump convivial parson' who 'lays'

> His rev'rence and his worship both to rest
> On the same cushion of habitual sloth.
> (*Task* iv 597–8)

[14] *maps* The scientific instruments and maps indicate the prodigy's intellectual authority, just as flags ('ensigns'), orb and sceptre symbolize a king's sovereignty.

[15] *cunning* secrets (of their operation).

[16] *He knows . . . over* cf. John Locke, *Some Thoughts Concerning Education*: 'I now live in the house with a child . . . [who] knew the limits of the four parts of the world, could readily point, being asked, to any country upon the globe . . . and could find the longitude and latitude of any place, before he was six years old.'

[17] The country people, in their ignorance, fear the prodigy may be seeking forbidden knowledge.

[18] *he sifts . . . trust* cf. Coleridge's outrage at this tendency, in a letter to Poole, 16 October 1797: 'I have known some who have been *rationally* educated, as it is styled. They were marked by a microscopic acuteness; but when they looked at great things, all became a blank and they saw nothing – and denied (very illogically) that any thing could be seen . . . [they] called the want of imagination Judgment, and the never being moved to rapture Philosophy!' (Griggs i 354–5).

[19] *He must live . . . at all* Wordsworth regarded knowledge, as opposed to understanding, as redundant: 'Lastly comes that class of objects which are interesting almost solely because they are known, and the knowledge may be displayed; and this unfortunately comprehends three fourths of what, according to the plan of modern education, children's heads are stuffed with, that is, minute remote or trifling facts in geography, topography, natural history, chronology etc., or acquisitions in art, or accomplishments which the child makes by rote and which are quite beyond its age' (*MY* i 287).

Each little drop of wisdom as it falls
Into the dimpling cistern[20] of his heart.[21]
Meanwhile old Grandam Earth is grieved to find
The playthings which her love designed for him
Unthought of: in their woodland beds the flowers
Weep, and the riversides are all forlorn.
   Now this is hollow, 'tis a life of lies
From the beginning, and in lies must end.
Forth bring him to the air of common sense,
And, fresh and showy as it is, the corpse
Slips from us into powder. Vanity,
That is his soul, there lives he, and there moves –
It is the soul of everything he seeks;
That gone, nothing is left which he can love.
Nay, if a thought of purer birth should rise
To carry him towards a better clime,
Some busy helper still is on the watch
To drive him back, and pound[22] him like a stray
Within the pinfold[23] of his own conceit,
Which is his home, his natural dwelling-place.
Oh, give us once again the wishing-cap
Of Fortunatus, and the invisible coat
Of Jack the giant-killer, Robin Hood,
And Sabra in the forest with St George![24]
The child whose love is here at least does reap
One precious gain – that he forgets himself.[25]
   These mighty workmen of our latter age[26]
Who with a broad highway have overbridged
The froward[27] chaos of futurity,[28]
Tamed to their bidding; they who have the art
To manage books, and things, and make them work
Gently on infant minds as does the sun
Upon a flower – the tutors of our youth,
The guides, the wardens of our faculties

Notes

[20] *dimpling cistern* The surface of the water in the barrel ('cistern') dimples with each drop that falls into it.

[21] Cf. the manner in which the Wordsworths reared Basil Montagu at Alfoxden: 'You ask to be informed of our system respecting Basil; it is a very simple one, so simple that in this age of systems you will hardly be likely to follow it. We teach him nothing at present but what he learns from the evidence of his senses. He has an insatiable curiosity which we are always careful to satisfy to the best of our ability. It is directed to everything he sees, the sky, the fields, trees, shrubs, corn, the making of tools, carts, etc., etc., etc. He knows his letters, but we have not attempted any further step in the path of *book learning*. Our grand study has been to make him *happy*' (*EY* 180).

[22] *pound* impound.

[23] *pinfold* enclosure for stray animals.

[24] Fortunatus' hat took him wherever he wanted; Jack's coat made him invisible while killing giants; St George married Sabra, daughter of the King of Egypt, after rescuing her from a dragon.

[25] Wordsworth recommended that children be allowed to read 'fairy tales, romances, the best biographies and histories, and such parts of natural history relating to the powers and appearances of the earth and elements, and the habits and structures of animals, as belong to it not as an art or science, but as a magazine of form and feeling' (*MY* i 287). See also Coleridge on fairy-tales, p. 618.

[26] Lines 452–70 derive from a fragment probably composed in Goslar during the winter of 1798–9, intended as an introduction to 'There was a boy'.

[27] *froward* wayward, uncontrollable.

[28] *Who with a broad highway . . . futurity* Educationalists are compared to Milton's Sin and Death who in *Paradise Lost* build a bridge over Chaos to their new empire on earth (x 282–305).

And stewards of our labour, watchful men
And skilful in the usury of time,
Sages who in their prescience would control
All accidents, and to the very road which they
Have fashioned would confine us down
Like engines[29] – when will they be taught
That in the unreasoning progress of the world
A wiser spirit is at work for us,
A better eye than theirs, most prodigal
Of blessings and most studious of our good,
Even in what seem our most unfruitful hours?

Daffodils ['*I wandered lonely as a cloud*'] (composed March 1804–April 1807)[1]

From Poems (1815)[2]

I wandered lonely as a cloud
That floats on high o'er vales and hills,
When all at once I saw a crowd,
A host of golden daffodils;[3]
Beside the lake, beneath the trees,
Fluttering and dancing in the breeze.

Continuous as the stars that shine
And twinkle on the milky way,
They stretched in never-ending line
Along the margin of a bay:
Ten thousand saw I at a glance,
Tossing their heads in sprightly dance.

The waves beside them danced, but they
Outdid the sparkling waves in glee: –
A Poet could not but be gay
In such a jocund company:
I gazed – and gazed – but little thought
What wealth the show to me had brought:

For oft when on my couch I lie
In vacant or in pensive mood,

Notes

[29] *engines* Educational theories are as imprisoning as manufacturing machines – machine-looms, for instance – which were just coming into use.

Daffodils

[1] For the incident that inspired this poem see Dorothy Wordsworth's journal, p. 586 below. In 1815 Wordsworth attached a note: 'The subject of these stanzas is rather an elementary feeling and simple impression (approaching to the nature of an ocular spectrum) upon the imaginative faculty, than an *exertion* of it.' For further discussion of the poem and its background see Pamela Woof and Madeline Harley, *The Wordsworths and the Daffodils* (Grasmere, 2002).

[2] *Daffodils* was first published in *Poems in Two Volumes* (1807), without the second stanza, which was added for its appearance in *Poems* (1815). It is considered to be one of Wordsworth's most felicitous additions to any of his works. Wordsworth never published it with a title, although he referred to it privately as *Daffodils* from May 1807 onwards.

[3] *daffodils* not the garden daffodils of today but the small, pale and wild *Narcissus pseudonarcissus*.

They flash upon that inward eye
Which is the bliss of solitude,[4]
And then my heart with pleasure fills,
And dances with the daffodils.

Stepping Westward (composed 3 June 1805)

From Poems in Two Volumes (1807)

While my fellow-traveller and I were walking by the side of Loch Ketterine one fine evening after sunset,[1] *in our road to a hut*[2] *where, in the course of our tour, we had been hospitably entertained some weeks before, we met in one of the loneliest parts of that solitary region two well-dressed women, one of whom said to us by way of greeting, 'What you are stepping westward?'*

'What you are stepping westward?' 'Yea.'
'Twould be a wildish destiny
If we, who thus together roam
In a strange land, and far from home,
Were in this place the guests of Chance –
Yet who would stop, or fear to advance,
Though home or shelter he had none,
With such a sky to lead him on?

The dewy ground was dark and cold;
Behind, all gloomy to behold;
And stepping westward seemed to be
A kind of *heavenly* destiny.
I liked the greeting – 'twas a sound
Of something without place or bound,
And seemed to give me spiritual right
To travel through that region bright.

The voice was soft, and she who spake
Was walking by her native lake;
The salutation had to me
The very sound of courtesy:
Its power was felt, and while my eye
Was fixed upon the glowing sky,
The echo of the voice enwrought[3]
A human sweetness with the thought
Of travelling through the world that lay
Before me in my endless way.

Notes

[4] *They flash . . . solitude* These two lines were written by Wordsworth's wife, Mary. Coleridge commented in his notebook, 1808–11: ' "To flash upon that inward eye / Which is the bliss of solitude' – and to make every thing present by a series of images – this an absolute essential of poetry, and of itself would form a poet, though not of the highest class' (*Notebooks* iii 3247).

Stepping Westward

[1] *While . . . sunset* Wordsworth and Dorothy toured Scotland in 1803.

[2] *hut* cottage.

[3] *enwrought* interwove, combined.

The Solitary Reaper (composed 5 November 1805)[1]

From Poems in Two Volumes (1807)

Behold her, single in the field,
Yon solitary highland lass!
Reaping and singing by herself –
Stop here, or gently pass!
Alone she cuts, and binds the grain,
And sings a melancholy strain;
Oh listen! for the vale profound
Is overflowing with the sound.

No nightingale did ever chaunt
So sweetly to reposing bands
Of travellers in some shady haunt
Among Arabian sands;
No sweeter voice was ever heard
In springtime from the cuckoo-bird,
Breaking the silence of the seas
Among the farthest Hebrides.

Will no one tell me what she sings?
Perhaps the plaintive numbers flow
For old, unhappy, far-off things
And battles long ago;
Or is it some more humble lay,
Familiar matter of today?
Some natural sorrow, loss, or pain
That has been, and may be again?

Whate'er the theme, the maiden sang
As if her song could have no ending;
I saw her singing at her work
And o'er the sickle bending;
I listened till I had my fill,
And as I mounted up the hill,
The music in my heart I bore
Long after it was heard no more.

Notes

The Solitary Reaper

[1] 'This poem was suggested by a beautiful sentence in a MS tour in Scotland written by a friend, the last line being taken from it verbatim' (Wordsworth's note). Thomas Wilkinson, the Lake District poet, was a friend of Wordsworth, and his *Tours to the British Mountains* was published in 1824. The sentence that inspired Wordsworth runs as follows: 'Passed a female who was reaping alone: she sung in Erse as she bended over her sickle; the sweetest human voice I ever heard: her strains were tenderly melancholy, and felt delicious, long after they were heard no more' (p. 12).

From The Thirteen-Book Prelude (composed 1804–6; edited from MS)[1]

[*The Arab Dream*] (*from Book V*)[2]

Hitherto
In progress through this verse, my mind hath looked
Upon the speaking face of earth and heaven[3]
As her prime teacher, intercourse with man
Established by the sovereign intellect
Who through that bodily image hath diffused
A soul divine which we participate,[4]
A deathless spirit. Thou also, man, hast wrought,
For commerce of thy nature with itself,
Things worthy of unconquerable life;[5]
And yet we feel, we cannot choose but feel
That these must perish. Tremblings of the heart
It gives to think that the immortal being
No more shall need such garments; and yet man,
As long as he shall be the child of earth,
Might almost 'weep to have'[6] what he may lose,
Nor be himself extinguished, but survive
Abject, depressed, forlorn, disconsolate.[7]
A thought is with me sometimes, and I say:
'Should earth by inward throes be wrenched throughout,
Or fire[8] be sent from far to wither all
Her pleasant habitations, and dry up
Old ocean in his bed, left singed and bare,
Yet would the living presence still subsist
Victorious, and composure would ensue,
And kindlings like the morning – presage sure
(Though slow perhaps) of a returning day.
But all the meditations of mankind,
Yea, all the adamantine holds[9] of truth

Notes

FROM THE THIRTEEN-BOOK PRELUDE

[1] Wordsworth began work on the *Thirteen-Book Prelude* as soon as he abandoned and dismembered the five-Book version of the poem in early March 1804. As it happens, the Arab dream was originally composed at the same time as the five-Book poem, about February 1804 but not apparently included in it. Evidently, Wordsworth knew exactly where he wished to place it when he expanded the poem in March.

[2] The title of Book V is 'Books', though in fact Wordsworth is preoccupied less with the literary works that have most influenced him than with explaining the purpose of artistic endeavour, and its place within the larger scheme of things.

[3] *the speaking face of earth and heaven* Wordsworth has in mind Coleridge's account of the nature as 'The lovely shapes and sounds intelligible / Of that eternal language which thy God / Utters' (*Frost at Midnight* 64–6).

[4] *intercourse . . . participate* God has diffused his divine soul through the medium of the natural world (his 'bodily image'), and is thus enabled to engage in converse with man.

[5] *Things worthy of unconquerable life* i.e. works of art that deserve to be immortal.

[6] *weep to have* Shakespeare, Sonnet 64: 'This thought is as a death, which cannot choose / But weep to have that which it fears to lose' (ll. 13–14).

[7] *yet man . . . disconsolate* Man, while still living ('unextinguished'), must regret possession of earthly achievements that he fears losing, and live on, abject, and disconsolate.

[8] *fire* Some of Wordsworth's ideas here may derive from Thomas Burnet's *Sacred Theory of the Earth*, Book III of which is entitled 'Concerning the Conflagration'; Wordsworth owned a copy of Burnet at Rydal Mount.

[9] *adamantine holds* indestructible fortresses.

By reason built, or passion[10] (which itself
Is highest reason in a soul sublime),
The consecrated works of bard and sage,[11]
Sensuous or intellectual, wrought by men,
Twin labourers and heirs of the same hopes –
Where would they be? Oh, why hath not the mind
Some element to stamp her image on
In nature somewhat nearer to her own?[12]
Why, gifted with such powers to send abroad
Her spirit, must it lodge in shrines so frail?'[13]
One day, when in the hearing of a friend[14]
I had given utterance to thoughts like these,
He answered with a smile that in plain truth
'Twas going far to seek disquietude;[15]
But on the front[16] of his reproof confessed
That he at sundry seasons had himself
Yielded to kindred hauntings[17] – and forthwith
Added that once upon a summer's noon
While he was sitting in a rocky cave
By the sea-side (perusing, as it chanced,
The famous history of the errant knight
Recorded by Cervantes[18]), these same thoughts
Came to him, and to height unusual rose
While listlessly he sat, and, having closed
The book, had turned his eyes towards the sea.
On poetry and geometric truth
(The knowledge that endures), upon these two
And their high privilege of lasting life
Exempt from all internal injury,[19]
He mused; upon these chiefly – and at length,
His senses yielding to the sultry air,
Sleep seized him and he passed into a dream.
He saw before him an Arabian waste,
A desert, and he fancied that himself
Was sitting there in the wide wilderness
Alone upon the sands. Distress of mind
Was growing in him when, behold, at once
To his great joy a man was at his side,
Upon a dromedary mounted high!
He seemed an Arab of the bedouin tribes;
A lance he bore,[20] and underneath one arm

Notes

10 *passion* emotion; 'Poetry is passion: it is the history or science of feelings' (Note to *The Thorn*, p. 508).

11 *The consecrated . . . sage* works of the imagination and the intellect.

12 *Oh why . . . own* Wordsworth laments the fact that there is no substance as durable as the mind itself (which he regards as immortal), on which its thoughts might be recorded.

13 *shrines so frail* i.e. books.

14 *a friend* Coleridge; though in the *Fourteen-Book Prelude* the dreamer becomes Wordsworth.

15 *disquietude* anxiety.

16 *on the front* immediately after.

17 *kindred hauntings* similar anxieties.

18 *The famous history . . . Cervantes* Miguel de Cervantes Saavedra, *Don Quixote*, which Wordsworth and Coleridge knew from early childhood.

19 *Exempt . . . injury* Poetry and geometry may be subject to external injury (that is to say, books can be damaged), but are perfect in themselves.

20 *A lance he bore* shades of the Don, who famously used his lance to tilt at windmills.

A stone, and in the opposite hand a shell
Of a surpassing brightness. Much rejoiced
The dreaming man that he should have a guide
To lead him through the desert, and he thought –
While questioning himself what this strange freight
Which the newcomer carried through the waste
Could mean – the Arab told him that the stone
(To give it in the language of the dream)
Was Euclid's *Elements*.[21] ' "And this", said he,
"This other", pointing to the shell, "this book,
Is something of more worth." And at the word
The stranger', said my friend continuing,
'Stretched forth the shell towards me, with command
That I should hold it to my ear. I did so,
And heard that instant in an unknown tongue,
Which yet I understood, articulate sounds,
A loud prophetic blast of harmony,
An ode in passion uttered, which foretold
Destruction to the children of the earth
By deluge now at hand.'
No sooner ceased
The song, but with calm look the Arab said
That all was true, that it was even so
As had been spoken, and that he himself
Was going then to bury those two books –
The one that held acquaintance with the stars
And wedded man to man by purest bond
Of nature, undisturbed by space or time;
The other that was a god – yea, many gods,
Had voices more than all the winds, and was
A joy, a consolation, and a hope.
My friend continued, 'Strange as it may seem,
I wondered not, although I plainly saw
The one to be a stone, the other a shell,
Nor doubted once but that they both were books,
Having a perfect faith in all that passed.
A wish was now engendered[22] in my fear
To cleave unto[23] this man, and I begged leave
To share his errand with him. On he passed
Not heeding me; I followed, and took note
That he looked often backward with wild look,
Grasping his twofold treasure to his side.
Upon a dromedary, lance in rest
He rode, I keeping pace with him; and now
I fancied that he was the very knight
Whose tale Cervantes tells, yet not the knight,

Notes

[21] *Euclid's Elements* Euclid was a Greek mathematician of the third century BC, whose *Elements* was the basic textbook of geometry used by Wordsworth at Hawkshead and Cambridge.

[22] *engendered* created.

[23] *cleave unto* stick to.

But was an Arab of the desert too –
Of these was neither, and was both at once.
His countenance meanwhile grew more disturbed,
And, looking backwards when he looked, I saw
A glittering light, and asked him whence it came.
"It is", said he, "the waters of the deep
Gathering upon us." Quickening then his pace,
He left me. I called after him aloud;
He heeded not, but with his twofold charge[24]
Beneath his arm, before me, full in view,
I saw him riding o'er the desert sands
With the fleet waters of the drowning world
In chase of him. Whereat I waked in terror,
And saw the sea before me, and the book
In which I had been reading at my side.'
   Full often, taking from the world of sleep
This Arab phantom which my friend beheld,
This semi-Quixote, I to him have given
A substance, fancied him a living man,
A gentle dweller in the desert, crazed
By love and feeling and internal thought
Protracted among endless solitudes –
Have shaped him, in the oppression of his brain,[25]
Wandering upon this quest, and thus equipped.
And I have scarcely pitied him, have felt
A reverence for a being thus employed,
And thought that in the blind and awful lair
Of such a madness, reason did lie couched.
Enow[26] there are on earth to take in charge
Their wives, their children, and their virgin loves,
Or whatsoever else the heart holds dear –
Enow to think of these; yea, will I say,
In sober contemplation of the approach
Of such great overthrow, made manifest
By certain evidence, that I methinks
Could share that maniac's anxiousness, could go
Upon like errand. Oftentimes, at least,
Me hath such deep entrancement half possessed
When I have held a volume in my hand
(Poor earthly casket of immortal verse[27]) –
Shakespeare or Milton, labourers divine!

Notes

[24] *charge* burden.
[25] *oppression of his brain* derangement, anxiety.
[26] *Enow* enough.
[27] *Poor earthly casket of immortal verse* a paradox: verse, which is immortal, is contained within the casket, or coffin, of the book.

[*Crossing the Alps*] (from The Thirteen-Book Prelude Book VI)[1]

That day we first
Beheld the summit of Mont Blanc, and grieved
To have a soulless image on the eye
Which had usurped upon a living thought
That never more could be.[2] The wondrous Vale
Of Chamouny did on the following dawn,
With its dumb cataracts and streams of ice,
A motionless array of mighty waves,
Five rivers broad and vast, make rich amends,
And reconciled us to realities.
There small birds warble from the leafy trees,
The eagle soareth in the element;
There doth the reaper bind the yellow sheaf,
The maiden spread the haycock in the sun,
While winter like a tamed lion walks,
Descending from the mountain to make sport
Among the cottages by beds of flowers.
Whate'er in this wide circuit we beheld
Or heard was fitted to our unripe state
Of intellect and heart. By simple strains
Of feeling, the pure breath of real life,
We were not left untouched. With such a book[3]
Before our eyes we could not choose but read
A frequent lesson of sound tenderness,
The universal reason of mankind,
The truth of young and old. Nor, side by side
Pacing, two brother pilgrims, or alone
Each with his humour, could we fail to abound
(Craft this which hath been hinted at before)
In dreams and fictions pensively composed,
Dejection taken up for pleasure's sake,
And gilded sympathies. The willow wreath,
Even among those solitudes sublime,
And sober posies of funereal flowers
Culled from the gardens of the Lady Sorrow,
Did sweeten many a meditative hour.[4]
Yet still in me, mingling with these delights,
Was something of stern mood, an under-thirst[5]
Of vigour never utterly asleep.
Far different dejection once was mine,

Notes

CROSSING THE ALPS

[1] Wordsworth is recounting his tour of the Continent in summer 1790, which he undertook with his College friend, Robert Jones.

[2] *That day . . . be* The actual image of the mountain displaced, in the mind, the image of the unseen mountain, which was more 'alive' because it was imaginatively generated.

[3] *book* the book of nature.

[4] *The willow wreath . . . hour* The somewhat artificial manner of all this indicates that Wordsworth is affectionately mocking his youthful self, preoccupied with poetic sorrows.

[5] *under-thirst* a typically original way of talking about his inner world.

A deep and genuine sadness then I felt,
The circumstances I will here relate
Even as they were. Upturning with a band
Of travellers, from the Valais we had clomb[6]
Along the road that leads to Italy;
A length of hours, making of these our guides
Did we advance, and having reached an inn
Among the mountains, we together ate
Our noon's repast, from which the travellers rose
Leaving us at the board. Erelong we followed,
Descending by the beaten road that led
Right to a rivulet's edge, and there broke off.
The only track now visible was one
Upon the further side, right opposite,
And up a lofty mountain. This we took
After a little scruple[7] and short pause,
And climbed with eagerness – though not, at length
Without surprise and some anxiety
On finding that we did not overtake
Our comrades gone before. By fortunate chance,
While every moment now increased our doubts,
A peasant met us, and from him we learned
That to the place which had perplexed[8] us first
We must descend, and there should find the road
Which in the stony channel of the stream
Lay a few steps, and then along its banks –
And further, that thenceforward all our course
Was downwards with the current of that stream.
Hard of belief, we questioned him again,
And all the answers which the man returned
To our enquiries, in their sense and substance,
Translated by the feelings which we had,
Ended in this – that we had crossed the Alps.
   Imagination! lifting up itself
Before the eye and progress of my song
Like an unfathered vapour; here that power,
In all the might of its endowments, came
Athwart me. I was lost as in a cloud,
Halted without a struggle to break through,
And now, recovering, to my soul I say,
'I recognize thy glory'.[9] In such strength
Of usurpation,[10] in such visitings
Of awful promise, when the light of sense

Notes

6 *clomb* climbed.

7 *scruple* moment.

8 *perplexed* confused.

9 *Imagination . . . glory* Against the moment in August 1790 when his imagination had been disappointed, Wordsworth places the 'glory' of the present (i.e. the moment of composition, spring 1804).

10 *usurpation* another usurpation (cf. l. 455 above). This time, however, the usurpation proves the strength, rather than the weakness, of the imagination; it may sound forced, but Wordsworth needs to believe that the imagination can overcome the deadening influences of reality.

Goes out in flashes that have shown to us
The invisible world, doth greatness make abode,
There harbours whether we be young or old.
Our destiny, our nature, and our home,
Is with infinitude, and only there –
With hope it is, hope that can never die,
Effort, and expectation, and desire,
And something evermore about to be.[11]
The mind beneath such banners militant[12]
Thinks not of spoils or trophies, nor of aught
That may attest its prowess, blessed in thoughts
That are their own perfection and reward –
Strong in itself, and in the access of joy
Which hides it like the overflowing Nile.
   The dull and heavy slackening which ensued
Upon those tidings by the peasant given
Was soon dislodged. Downwards we hurried fast,
And entered with the road which we had missed
Into a narrow chasm. The brook and road
Were fellow-travellers in this gloomy pass,
And with them did we journey several hours
At a slow step. The immeasurable height
Of woods decaying, never to be decayed,
The stationary blasts of waterfalls,
And everywhere along the hollow rent[13]
Winds thwarting winds, bewildered and forlorn,
The torrents shooting from the clear blue sky,
The rocks that muttered close upon our ears,
Black drizzling crags that spake by the wayside
As if a voice were in them, the sick[14] sight
And giddy prospect of the raving stream,
The unfettered clouds and region of the heavens,
Tumult and peace, the darkness and the light,
Were all like workings of one mind, the features
Of the same face, blossoms upon one tree,
Characters[15] of the great Apocalypse,[16]
The types[17] and symbols of eternity,
Of first, and last, and midst, and without end.[18]

Notes

[11] *something evermore about to be* Few phrases more succinctly characterize Wordsworth's literary personality; in his poetry sublimity is always beyond reach.

[12] *such banners militant* i.e. effort, expectation, and desire, and something evermore about to be.

[13] *rent* ravine.

[14] *sick* probably means 'sickening', given the 'giddy prospect' in the next line.

[15] *Characters* letters.

[16] *Characters . . . Apocalypse* Contemporary geological theory held that all but the highest Alpine peaks were created by the retreating waters of the Flood. Thus the features of the landscape would indeed have been engraved ('charactered') by the first apocalyptic event in the history of mankind. They also function as a reminder of the apocalypse to come.

[17] *types* letters, as in typeface.

[18] *The unfettered clouds . . . without end* Wordsworth's source is Pope, *Essay on Man* ii 266–72:

> All are but parts of one stupendous whole,
> Whose body nature is, and God the soul,
> That (changed through all, and yet in all the same) . . .
> Warms in the sun, refreshes in the breeze,
> Glows in the sun, and blossoms in the trees . . .

Line 571 echoes Milton's description of God, *Paradise Lost* v 165: 'Him first, Him last, Him midst, and without end'.

[*The London Beggar*] (*From* The Thirteen-Book Prelude Book VII)[1]

Oh friend,[2] one feeling was there which belonged
To this great city by exclusive right:
How often in the overflowing streets
Have I gone forwards with the crowd, and said
Unto myself, 'The face of everyone
That passes by me is a mystery!'
Thus have I looked, nor ceased to look, oppressed
By thoughts of what and whither, when and how,
Until the shapes before my eyes became
A second-sight[3] procession, such as glides
Over still mountains, or appears in dreams,
And all the ballast of familiar life –
The present and the past, hope, fear, all stays,[4]
All laws, of acting, thinking, speaking man –
Went from me, neither knowing me, nor known.
And once, far travelled in such mood, beyond
The reach of common indications, lost
Amid the moving pageant, 'twas my chance
Abruptly to be smitten with the view
Of a blind beggar who, with upright face,
Stood propped against a wall, upon his chest
Wearing a written paper to explain
The story of the man and who he was.
My mind did at this spectacle turn round
As with the might of waters, and it seemed
To me that in this label was a type
Or emblem of the utmost that we know
Both of ourselves and of the universe;
And, on the shape of this unmoving man,
His fixed face and sightless eyes, I looked
As if admonished[5] from another world.

[London and the Den of Yordas] (*from* The Thirteen-Book Prelude Book VIII)

Preceptress[1] stern, that didst instruct me next –
London, to thee I willingly return!
Erewhile[2] my verse played only with the flowers
Enwrought upon thy mantle,[3] satisfied

Notes

THE LONDON BEGGAR

[1] Book VII is about Wordsworth's residence in London during the 1790s.

[2] *Oh friend* Coleridge.

[3] *second sight* mystic; second sight is the power by which occurrences in the future are perceived as though they were present.

[4] *stays* emotional and psychological support.

[5] *admonished* cf. other admonitions in Wordsworth – *Ruined Cottage* 530 and *Resolution and Independence* 119.

LONDON AND THE DEN OF YORDAS

[1] *Preceptress* teacher.

[2] *Erewhile* in the past.

[3] *Enwrought upon thy mantle* In Milton's *Lycidas*, the River Cam has a 'mantle hairy . . . Inwrought with figures dim' (ll. 104–5).

With this amusement, and a simple look
Of childlike inquisition[4] now and then
Cast upwards on thine eye to puzzle out
Some inner meanings which might harbour there.
Yet did I not give way to this light mood
Wholly beguiled, as one incapable
Of higher things, and ignorant that high things
Were round me. Never shall I forget the hour,[5]
The moment rather say, when, having thridded
The labyrinth of suburban villages,
At length I did unto myself first seem
To enter the great city. On the roof
Of an itinerant vehicle[6] I sat,
With vulgar[7] men about me, vulgar forms
Of houses, pavement, streets, of men and things,
Mean shapes on every side, but at the time
When to myself it fairly might be said
(The very moment that I seemed to know)
'The threshold now is overpassed' – great God!
That aught external to the living mind
Should have such mighty sway, yet so it was.
A weight of ages[8] did at once descend
Upon my heart – no thought embodied, no
Distinct remembrances, but weight and power,
Power growing with the weight. Alas, I feel
That I am trifling; 'twas a moment's pause,
All that took place within me came and went
As in a moment, and I only now
Remember that it was a thing divine.
  As when a traveller hath from open day
With torches passed into some vault of earth,
The grotto of Antiparos[9] or the den
Of Yordas among Craven's mountain tracts;[10]
He looks and sees the cavern spread and grow,
Widening itself on all sides, sees, or thinks
He sees,[11] erelong the roof above his head,
Which instantly unsettles and recedes –
Substance and shadow, light and darkness, all
Commingled, making up a canopy

Notes

[4] *inquisition* enquiry.

[5] *the hour* i.e. of Wordsworth's first sight of London.

[6] *an itinerant vehicle* i.e. a vehicle that travels around, a stagecoach, probably from Cambridge to London (Wordsworth was probably an undergraduate when he first visited London).

[7] *vulgar* ordinary.

[8] *A weight of ages* Effectively, Wordsworth was conscious of the history of the city.

[9] *The grotto of Antiparos* famous cave on the island of Antiparos in the Aegean. As Wordsworth never went there he must have read about it, possibly in John Ozell's 1718 translation of Joseph Pitton de Tournefort's *Relation d'un voyage au Levant* (1717), which describes a torchlit procession and mass in the grotto on Christmas Day 1673.

[10] *the den . . . tracts* limestone cave near Ingleton in West Yorkshire, visited by Wordsworth and his brother John in May 1800. It is the subject of a description by Thomas West in his *Guide to the Lakes* (3rd edn, 1784), which Wordsworth owned and read.

[11] *sees, or thinks / He sees* from Virgil, *Aeneid* vi 454: 'aut videt, aut vidisse putat', borrowed also by Milton, *Paradise Lost* i 783–4.

Of shapes and forms and tendencies to shape
That shift and vanish, change and interchange
Like spectres, ferment quiet and sublime
Which after a short space works[12] less and less,
Till, every effort, every motion gone,
The scene before him lies in perfect view,
Exposed and lifeless as a written book.
But let him pause awhile and look again
And a new quickening[13] shall succeed, at first
Beginning timidly, then creeping fast
Through all which he beholds. The senseless mass,
In its projections, wrinkles, cavities,
Through all its surface, with all colours streaming
Like a magician's airy pageant,[14] parts,
Unites, embodying everywhere some pressure[15]
Or image, recognized or new, some type
Or picture of the world; forests and lakes,
Ships, rivers, towers, the warrior clad in mail,
The prancing steed, the pilgrim with his staff,
The mitred bishop and the throned king –
A spectacle to which there is no end.

[*Paris, December 1791*] (*from* The Thirteen-Book Prelude Book IX)[1]

Where silent zephyrs[2] sported with the dust
Of the Bastille[3] I sat in the open sun,
And from the rubbish gathered up a stone
And pocketed the relic in the guise
Of an enthusiast; yet, in honest truth,
Though not without some strong incumbences[4]
And glad[5] (could living man be otherwise?),
I looked for something which I could not find,
Affecting more emotion than I felt.
For 'tis most certain that the utmost force
Of all these various objects which may show
The temper of my mind as then it was
Seemed less to recompense the traveller's pains –
Less moved me, gave me less delight – than did

Notes

[12] *works* seethes.
[13] *quickening* invigoration.
[14] *magician's airy pageant* cf. Prospero's 'insubstantial pageant faded', *Tempest* IV i 155.
[15] *pressure* imprint.

Paris, December 1791

[1] Wordsworth is remembering his visit to Paris in December 1791. It was on this residence in France that he met Annette Vallon, with whom he had a child, Caroline, born in December 1792. His immediate excuse for visiting Revolutionary France was to perfect his command of the language so as to qualify as a gentleman's travelling companion or tutor.
[2] *zephyrs* small breezes.
[3] *the dust / Of the Bastille* the dust was all that was left of it. The Bastille, a large prison in the centre of Paris, symbol of the tyranny of the *ancien régime*, had been stormed by the Paris mob on 14 July 1789, and then demolished.
[4] *incumbences* feelings of obligation – presumably to the Revolutionary cause (in spite of his posturing as an 'enthusiast').
[5] *glad* i.e. about the Revolution.

A single picture merely, hunted out
Among other sights: the 'Magdalene' of Le Brun,[6]
A beauty exquisitely wrought, fair face
And rueful, with its ever-flowing tears.

[*Blois, Spring 1792*] (*from* The Thirteen-Book Prelude Book IX)[1]

A knot of military officers
That to a regiment appertained which then
Was stationed in the city[2] were the chief
Of my associates; some of these wore swords
Which had been seasoned in the wars, and all
Were men well-born[3] – at least laid claim to such
Distinction, as the chivalry of France.
In age and temper differing, they had yet
One spirit ruling in them all, alike
(Save only one, hereafter to be named[4])
Were bent upon undoing what was done.
This was their rest, and only hope; therewith
No fear had they of bad becoming worse,
For worst to them was come – nor would have stirred,
Or deemed it worth a moment's while to stir,
In anything, save only as the act
Looked thitherward. One, reckoning by years,
Was in the prime of manhood, and erewhile
He had sat lord in many tender hearts,
Though heedless of such honours now, and changed:
His temper[5] was quite mastered by the times,
And they had blighted him, had eat away
The beauty of his person, doing wrong
Alike to body and to mind. His port,[6]
Which once had been erect and open, now
Was stooping and contracted, and a face,
By nature lovely in itself, expressed
As much as any that was ever seen
A ravage out of season, made by thoughts
Unhealthy and vexatious. At the hour,
The most important of each day, in which
The public news was read, the fever came,
A punctual visitant, to shake this man,

Notes

[6] *the 'Magdalene' of Le Brun* Charles le Brun (1616–90) painted a picture of St Mary Magdalene (the repentant prostitute who washed Christ's feet with her tears). Wordsworth would have seen it at the Carmelite convent in the rue d'Enfer. It is now in the Louvre.

BLOIS, SPRING 1792

[1] Wordsworth moved to Blois, near Orléans, early in 1792.

[2] *city* Blois.

[3] *men well-born* In spring 1792 the French army was staffed largely by royalist officers.

[4] *Save . . . named* Wordsworth's friend, Michel Beaupuy, who converted Wordsworth to the Revolutionary cause.

[5] *temper* character.

[6] *port* bearing.

Disarmed his voice and fanned his yellow cheek
Into a thousand colours. While he read,
Or mused, his sword was haunted by his touch
Continually, like an uneasy place
In his own body.
'Twas in truth an hour
Of universal ferment. Mildest men
Were agitated, and commotions, strife
Of passion and opinion, filled the walls
Of peaceful houses with unquiet sounds.
The soil of common life was at that time
Too hot to tread upon! Oft said I then,
And not then only, 'What a mockery this
Of history, the past and that to come!
Now do I feel how I have been deceived,
Reading of nations and their works in faith –
Faith given to vanity and emptiness;
Oh, laughter for the page that would reflect
To future times the face of what now is!'[7]
The land all swarmed with passion, like a plain
Devoured by locusts – Carra, Gorsas[8] – add
A hundred other names forgotten now,
Nor to be heard of more. Yet were they powers
Like earthquakes, shocks repeated day by day,
And felt through every nook of town and field.

[*Beaupuy*] (*from* The Thirteen-Book Prelude Book IX)

Among that band of officers was one,[1]
Already hinted at, of other mould[2] –
A patriot, thence rejected by the rest,
And with an oriental loathing spurned
As of a different caste.[3] A meeker man
Than this lived never, or a more benign,
Meek though enthusiastic to the height
Of highest expectation. Injuries
Made him more gracious, and his nature then
Did breathe its sweetness out most sensibly,[4]
As aromatic flowers on Alpine turf
When foot hath crushed them. He through the events
Of that great change[5] wandered in perfect faith

Notes

[7] *Oh laughter . . . is* He who would attempt to record the events of the Revolution for posterity would only bring mockery upon himself, so complex have things become.

[8] *Carra, Gorsas* journalist deputies in the French National Assembly, and members of the Girondin faction with which Beaupuy and Wordsworth consorted. They were probably known to Wordsworth. Carra was guillotined on 31 October 1793, Gorsas on the 7th.

BEAUPUY

[1] *one* Michel Beaupuy (1755–96).

[2] *mould* clay, substance.

[3] *And with . . . caste* He was spurned by the others with the same kind of loathing shown by Indians towards those of a lower caste.

[4] *sensibly* perceptibly.

[5] *that great change* the Revolution.

As through a book, an old romance or tale
Of fairy,[6] or some dream of actions wrought
Behind the summer clouds. By birth he ranked
With the most noble,[7] but unto the poor
Among mankind he was in service bound
As by some tie invisible, oaths professed
To a religious order. Man he loved
As man, and to the mean and the obscure,
And all the homely in their homely works,
Transferred a courtesy which had no air
Of condescension, but did rather seem
A passion and a gallantry, like that
Which he, a soldier, in his idler day
Had paid to woman. Somewhat vain he was,
Or seemed so; yet it was not vanity
But fondness, and a kind of radiant joy
That covered him about when he was bent
On works of love or freedom, or revolved
Complacently[8] the progress of a cause
Whereof he was a part – yet this was meek
And placid, and took nothing from the man
That was delightful. Oft in solitude
With him did I discourse about the end[9]
Of civil government, and its wisest forms,
Of ancient prejudice and chartered[10] rights,
Allegiance, faith, and laws by time matured,
Custom and habit, novelty and change –
Of self-respect and virtue in the few
For patrimonial honour set apart,
And ignorance in the labouring multitude.
For he, an upright man and tolerant,
Balanced these contemplations in his mind;
And I, who at that time was scarcely dipped
Into the turmoil, had a sounder judgement
Than afterwards,[11] carried about me yet
With less alloy to its integrity
The experience of past ages, as (through help
Of books and common life) it finds its way
To youthful minds, by objects over-near
Not pressed upon, nor dazzled or misled
By struggling with the crowd for present ends. . . .
And when my friend
Pointed upon occasion to the site
Of Romorantin,[12] home of ancient kings;

Notes

[6] *fairy* magic.

[7] *By birth . . . noble* Beaupuy was an aristocrat, descended on his mother's side from Montaigne. Many French aristocrats were in favour of the Revolution, though his rank separated him from his fellow-soldiers in Blois. He was 36 when he befriended the 22-year-old Wordsworth.

[8] *Complacently* with pleasure.

[9] *end* aim, objective.

[10] *chartered* legislated.

[11] *a sounder . . . afterwards* i.e. in 1793–5, during his flirtation with Godwinian thought (see next extract).

[12] *Romorantin* small town in the Loire, once a provincial capital.

To the imperial edifice of Blois;
Or to that rural castle, name now slipped
From my remembrance (where a lady lodged,
By the first Francis[13] wooed, and, bound to him
In chains of mutual passion, from the tower,
As a tradition of the country tells,
Practised to commune with her royal knight
By cressets[14] and love-beacons, intercourse
'Twixt her high-seated residence and his
Far off at Chambord[15] on the plain beneath) –
Even here, though less than with the peaceful house
Religious, mid these frequent monuments
Of kings, their vices or their better deeds,
Imagination, potent to inflame
At times with virtuous wrath and noble scorn,
Did also often mitigate the force
Of civic prejudice, the bigotry
(So call it) of a youthful patriot's mind;
And on these spots with many gleams I looked
Of chivalrous delight. Yet not the less,
Hatred of absolute rule, where will of one
Is law for all, and of that barren pride
In those who, by immunities unjust,
Betwixt the sovereign and the people stand
(His helpers and not theirs), laid stronger hold
Daily upon me – mixed with pity too
And love, for where hope is, there love will be
For the abject multitude. And when we chanced
One day to meet a hunger-bitten girl,
Who crept along, fitting her languid self
Unto a heifer's motion, by a cord
Tied to her arm, and picking thus from the lane
Its sustenance, while the girl with her two hands
Was busy knitting in a heartless[16] mood
Of solitude – and at the sight my friend
In agitation said ''Tis against that
Which we are fighting', I with him believed
Devoutly that a spirit was abroad
Which could not be withstood; that poverty,
At least like this, would in a little time
Be found no more; that we should see the earth
Unthwarted in her wish to recompense
The industrious and the lowly child of toil,
All institutes[17] for ever blotted out
That legalized exclusion, empty pomp
Abolished, sensual state and cruel power,
Whether by edict of the one or few;

Notes

[13] *the first Francis* Francis I (1515–57); attempts to identify the château and the mistress have been unsuccessful.
[14] *cressets* torches.
[15] *Chambord* a château in the Loire Valley, built by Francis I.
[16] *heartless* despondent, without heart.
[17] *institutes* laws, edicts, judgements.

And finally, as sum and crown of all,
Should see the people having a strong hand
In making their own laws, whence better days
To all mankind.[18]

[*Godwinism*] (*from* The Thirteen-Book Prelude Book X)[1]

This was the time when all things tended fast
To depravation; the philosophy
That promised to abstract the hopes of man
Out of his feelings,[2] to be fixed thenceforth
For ever in a purer element[3]
Found ready welcome. Tempting region that
For Zeal to enter and refresh herself,
Where passions had the privilege to work,
And never hear the sound of their own names![4]
But (speaking more in charity) the dream
Was flattering to the young ingenuous mind
Pleased with extremes, and not the least with that
Which makes the human reason's naked self
The object of its fervour. What delight!
How glorious, in self-knowledge and self-rule,
To look through all the frailties of the world!
And, with a resolute mastery shaking off
The accidents of nature, time and place,
That make up the weak being of the past,
Build social freedom on its only basis,
The freedom of the individual mind,
Which (to the blind restraint of general laws
Superior) magisterially adopts
One guide, the light of circumstances, flashed
Upon an independent intellect.[5]

Notes

[18] *To all mankind* Like many supporters of the Revolution, Wordsworth believed that the rest of the world would follow France's example.

Godwinism

[1] For an outline of Godwin's life and ideas, see pp. 151–2. Wordsworth's attachment to Godwinian rationalism occurred in 1794–5, when he and Godwin met frequently in London.

[2] *Out of his feelings* Godwin put forward a philosophy by which, true to his origins as a Sandemanian (by which religious belief was completely intellectual), political aspiration was divorced from the emotions.

[3] *a purer element* ironic. At the time of writing, ten years after the event, he certainly does not believe in anything purer than the emotions; it seemed at the time, however, to him and many other believers in Godwin's system, that radical aspirations could be justified through a completely anti-emotional philosophy.

[4] *Where passions . . . names* Wordsworth points out that Godwin was essentially repressive; emotion was involved in one's commitment to his philosophy, but it was not recognized as such.

[5] *What delight . . . intellect* These lines are all heavily ironic, and satirize Wordsworth's younger self.

[*Confusion and Recovery; Racedown, spring 1796*] (*from* The Thirteen-Book Prelude Book X)[1]

Time may come
When some dramatic story may afford
Shapes livelier to convey to thee, my friend,
What then[2] I learned, or think I learned, of truth,
And the errors into which I was betrayed
By present objects, and by reasonings false
From the beginning, inasmuch as drawn
Out of a heart which had been turned aside
From nature by external accidents,
And which was thus confounded[3] more and more,
Misguiding and misguided. Thus I fared,
Dragging all passions, notions, shapes of faith,
Like culprits to the bar;[4] suspiciously
Calling the mind to establish in plain day
Her titles and her honours;[5] now believing,
Now disbelieving; endlessly perplexed
With impulse, motive, right and wrong, the ground
Of moral obligation, what the rule
And what the sanction – till, demanding proof,
And seeking it in everything, I lost
All feeling of conviction, and (in fine[6])
Sick, wearied out with contrarieties,[7]
Yielded up moral questions in despair,
And for my future studies, as the sole
Employment of the enquiring faculty,
Turned towards mathematics, and their clear
And solid evidence.[8]
Ah, then it was
That thou, most precious friend,[9] about this time
First known to me,[10] didst lend a living help

Notes

Confusion and Recovery

[1] From London, where his attachment to Godwinism peaked in 1795, Wordsworth retreated to Racedown Lodge in Dorset, where he lived with Dorothy and made his first serious attempts to write poetry. It was here that, according to *The Prelude*, he had an emotional crisis precipitated jointly by a disillusionment with Godwin and disappointment at the failure of the Revolution. On 21 March 1796 he described the second edition of *Political Justice* in terms that indicate his distaste: 'Such a piece of barbarous writing I have not often seen. It contains scarce one sentence decently written' (*EY* 170–1).

[2] *then* i.e. during his experience of the Revolution, and in the years following it.

[3] *confounded* confused.

[4] *bar* the barrier or wooden rail marking off the immediate precinct of the judge's seat, at which prisoners are stationed for arraignment, trial or sentence. In Wordsworth's simile, he analysed his former beliefs and emotions as rigorously as a lawyer cross-examining a witness in a courtroom.

[5] *Calling the mind . . . honours* Wordsworth's crisis involved a doubt over the value of imaginative thought.

[6] *in fine* in the end.

[7] *contrarieties* unresolved, opposing arguments.

[8] *Turned . . . evidence* Against the continual doubt that seemed to surround the morality of, for instance, regicide, or the suppression of emotion by false prophets like Godwin, Wordsworth turns to mathematics which provides the solace of 'clear / And solid evidence', with no moral ambiguity.

[9] *most precious friend* Coleridge.

[10] *about this time . . . me* not true; Wordsworth met Coleridge in September 1795, and no doubt kept in touch in ensuing months, but close contact did not occur until June 1797.

To regulate my soul. And then it was
That the beloved woman[11] in whose sight
Those days were passed (now speaking in a voice
Of sudden admonition, like a brook
That does but cross a lonely road; and now
Seen, heard and felt, and caught at every turn,
Companion never lost through many a league[12])
Maintained for me a saving intercourse
With my true self. For, though impaired and changed
Much, as it seemed, I was no further changed
Than as a clouded, not a waning moon.
She, in the midst of all, preserved me still
A poet, made me seek beneath that name
My office[13] upon earth, and nowhere else.
And lastly Nature's self, by human love
Assisted, through the weary labyrinth
Conducted me again to open day,
Revived the feelings of my earlier life,
Gave me that strength and knowledge full of peace,
Enlarged and never more to be disturbed,
Which through the steps of our degeneracy,
All degradation of this age, hath still
Upheld me, and upholds me at this day[14]
In the catastrophe (for so they dream,
And nothing less) when finally to close
And rivet up[15] the gains of France, a Pope
Is summoned in to crown an Emperor[16] –
This last opprobrium,[17] when we see the dog
Returning to his vomit;[18] when the sun
That rose in splendour, was alive, and moved
In exultation among living clouds,
Hath put his function and his glory off,[19]
And, turned into a gewgaw,[20] a machine,
Sets like an opera phantom.[21]

Notes

[11] *the beloved woman* Dorothy, with whom Wordsworth resided at Racedown Lodge from September 1795 to June 1797.

[12] *league* about three miles; by 'many a league', Wordsworth just means over a long time.

[13] *office* role, vocation.

[14] *this day* Wordsworth moves forward from 1796 to the time of writing, December 1804.

[15] *to close . . . up* Wordsworth's language underlines his dismay; all the gains of the Revolution have now been imprisoned – effectively thrown away.

[16] *a Pope . . . Emperor* Napoleon had been emperor since May 1804 but summoned Pope Pius VII to crown him on 2 December.

[17] *opprobrium* disgrace.

[18] *the dog . . . vomit* The French returned to a monarchy – something of which, as a good republican, Wordsworth disapproved. The allusion is to Proverbs 26: 11: 'As a dog returneth to his vomit, so a fool returneth to his folly.'

[19] *put . . . off* cast . . . away.

[20] *gewgaw* worthless toy.

[21] *the sun . . . phantom* The sun of the French Republic, that once rose in glory, now sets, looking more like a clumsy theatrical effect ('opera phantom').

[*The Climbing of Snowdon*] (*from* The Thirteen-Book Prelude Book XIII)[1]

In one of these excursions, travelling then
Through Wales on foot and with a youthful friend,
I left Bethgelert's huts[2] at couching-time[3]
And westward took my way to see the sun
Rise from the top of Snowdon. Having reached
The cottage at the mountain's foot, we there
Roused up the shepherd who by ancient right
Of office is the stranger's usual guide,
And after short refreshment sallied forth.
It was a summer's night, a close warm night,
Wan, dull and glaring,[4] with a dripping mist
Low-hung and thick that covered all the sky,
Half threatening storm and rain; but on we went
Unchecked, being full of heart and having faith
In our tried pilot.[5] Little could we see,
Hemmed round on every side with fog and damp,
And, after ordinary travellers' chat
With our conductor, silently we sunk
Each into commerce with his private thoughts.
Thus did we breast the ascent, and by myself
Was nothing either seen or heard the while
Which took me from my musings, save that once
The shepherd's cur did to his own great joy
Unearth a hedgehog in the mountain crags
Round which he made a barking turbulent.
This small adventure (for even such it seemed
In that wild place and at the dead of night)
Being over and forgotten, on we wound
In silence as before.
With forehead bent
Earthward, as if in opposition set
Against an enemy, I panted up
With eager pace, and no less eager thoughts.
Thus might we wear perhaps an hour away,
Ascending at loose distance each from each,
And I, as chanced, the foremost of the band –
When at my feet the ground appeared to brighten,
And with a step or two seemed brighter still;
Nor had I time to ask the cause of this,
For instantly a light upon the turf
Fell like a flash.[6] I looked about, and lo!

Notes

THE CLIMBING OF SNOWDON

[1] For the final episode of *The Prelude*, Wordsworth goes back in time to June–August 1791, when he made a walking tour of north Wales with his Welsh College friend, Robert Jones. The account of the climb was composed for the final Book of the *Five-Book Prelude* in February 1804, and revised the following year for the *Thirteen-Book Prelude*.

[2] *Bethgelert's huts* the cottages of Beddgelert, a village at the foot of Snowdon.

[3] *couching-time* bed-time.

[4] *glaring* Maxwell suggests that this word is used in the dialect sense of dull, rainy, sticky, clammy.

[5] *tried pilot* experienced guide.

[6] *a light . . . flash* cf. the central event described in *A Night-Piece* (pp. 417–18).

The moon stood naked in the heavens at height
Immense above my head, and on the shore
I found myself of a huge sea of mist,
Which meek and silent rested at my feet.
A hundred hills their dusky backs upheaved
All over this still ocean;[7] and beyond,
Far, far beyond, the vapours shot themselves
In headlands, tongues, and promontory shapes,
Into the sea – the real sea, that seemed
To dwindle and give up its majesty,
Usurped[8] upon as far as sight could reach.
Meanwhile, the moon looked down upon this show
In single glory, and we stood, the mist
Touching our very feet. And from the shore
At distance not the third part of a mile
Was a blue chasm, a fracture in the vapour,
A deep and gloomy breathing-place through which
Mounted the roar of waters, torrents, streams
Innumerable, roaring with one voice.
The universal spectacle throughout
Was shaped for admiration and delight,
Grand in itself alone, but in that breach
Through which the homeless voice of waters rose,
That dark deep thoroughfare, had nature lodged
The soul, the imagination of the whole.[9]
  A meditation rose in me that night[10]
Upon the lonely mountain when the scene
Had passed away, and it appeared to me
The perfect image of a mighty mind,
Of one that feeds upon infinity,
That is exalted by an under-presence,
The sense of God, or whatsoe'er is dim
Or vast in its own being.[11] Above all,
One function of such mind had nature there
Exhibited by putting forth,[12] in midst
Of circumstance most awful and sublime:
That domination which she[13] oftentimes
Exerts upon the outward face of things,
So moulds them, and endues, abstracts, combines,[14]

Notes

[7] *A hundred hills their dusky backs upheaved . . . ocean* borrowed from Milton's account of Creation, *Paradise Lost* vii 285–7:

> the mountains huge appear
> Emergent, and their broad backs upheave
> Into the clouds . . .

[8] *Usurped* cf. other imaginative usurpations at Book VI, ll. 455 and 533 (pp. 553, 554).

[9] *The soul, the imagination of the whole* The revelation offered on Snowdon is of the identity of soul and imagination.

[10] *that night* The 'meditation' took place in May 1805, as he composed these lines, fourteen months after describing the climbing of Snowdon itself.

[11] *it appeared . . . being* The experience has been internalized: what is remembered becomes a symbol of the imaginative mind itself, which contains an 'under-presence' of power, whether divine or otherwise. Infinity and vastness exist within the poet's mind.

[12] *Exhibited by putting forth* demonstrated by analogy.

[13] *she* the mind (from l. 74).

[14] *So moulds them, and endues, abstracts, combines* The mist transforms the slopes of the mountain into a sea; in the same way, the imagination is capable of transforming any object it recalls. Cf. Wordsworth's comments on the imagination in the 1815 Preface (pp. 575–8).

Or by abrupt and unhabitual influence
Doth make one object so impress itself
Upon all others, and pervade them so,
That even the grossest minds must see and hear
And cannot choose but feel.[15]
The power which these
Acknowledge when thus moved, which Nature thus
Thrusts forth upon the senses, is the express
Resemblance, in the fullness of its strength
Made visible, a genuine counterpart
And brother, of the glorious faculty
Which higher minds[16] bear with them as their own.
This is the very spirit in which they deal
With all the objects of the universe;
They from their native selves can send abroad
Like transformation, for themselves create
A like existence, and, whene'er it is
Created for them, catch it by an instinct.[17]
Them the enduring and the transient both
Serve to exalt. They build up greatest things
From least suggestions,[18] ever on the watch,
Willing to work and to be wrought upon.
They need not extraordinary calls
To rouse them: in a world of life they live,
By sensible impressions not enthralled,
But quickened, roused, and made thereby more fit
To hold communion with the invisible world.[19]
Such minds are truly from the Deity
For they are Powers,[20] and hence the highest bliss
That can be known is theirs – the consciousness
Of whom they are,[21] habitually infused
Through every image and through every thought,
And all impressions. Hence religion, faith,
And endless occupation for the soul,
Whether discursive or intuitive;[22]
Hence sovereignty within[23] and peace at will,
Emotion which best foresight need not fear,
Most worthy then of trust when most intense;

Notes

[15] *That even . . . feel* It is crucial to the millennial scheme of *The Recluse* that all people, however insensitive to the lure of the metaphysical, should be susceptible to the improving effects of imaginative thought.

[16] *higher minds* Wordsworth believes that some people are particularly prone to imaginative vision.

[17] *whene'er it is . . . instinct* The imagination is both creative and receptive; on occasion, the transformation occurs outside the individual, and is 'caught' by the perceiving mind.

[18] *They build . . . suggestions* a crucial element in Wordsworth's thinking. Reviewers of the day criticized him for writing about subjects they considered trivial, but for him the imagination was 'the faculty that produces impressive effects out of simple elements' (p. 508).

[19] *By sensible . . . world* Wordsworth's elect are not imprisoned by their senses (the view of some Enlightenment thinkers), but are enlivened imaginatively and enabled to perceive the higher world that lies beyond them.

[20] *Powers* divinely empowered beings.

[21] *the consciousness . . . are* Because the imaginative mind creates and perceives, the very act of perception confirms its individual identity.

[22] *Whether discursive or intuitive* Wordsworth is thinking of the distinction made by Milton between discursive reason (belonging to man), and a higher, 'intuitive' reason, to which man may aspire, which is possessed by angels (*Paradise Lost* v 487–90).

[23] *sovereignty within* complete spiritual mastery.

Hence cheerfulness in every act of life;
Hence truth in moral judgements, and delight
That fails not in the external universe.[24]
Oh, who is he that hath his whole life long
Preserved, enlarged, this freedom in himself? –
For this alone is genuine liberty.[25]
Witness, ye solitudes where I received
My earliest visitations,[26] careless then
Of what was given me, and where now I roam
A meditative, oft a suffering, man,
And yet I trust with undiminished powers –
Witness – whatever falls[27] my better mind,
Revolving with the accidents of life,
May have sustained – that, howsoe'er misled,
I never, in the quest of right and wrong,
Did tamper with myself from private aims;[28]
Nor was in any of my hopes the dupe
Of selfish passions; nor did wilfully
Yield ever to mean cares and low pursuits,
But rather did with jealousy[29] shrink back
From every combination that might aid
The tendency, too potent in itself,
Of habit to enslave the mind – I mean
Oppress it by the laws of vulgar sense
And substitute a universe of death,[30]
The falsest of all worlds, in place of that
Which is divine and true.
To fear and love
(To love as first and chief, for there fear ends[31])
Be this ascribed, to early intercourse
In presence of sublime and lovely forms
With the adverse principles of pain and joy –
Evil as one is rashly named by those
Who know not what they say.[32] From love (for here
Do we begin and end) all grandeur comes,
All truth and beauty – from pervading love;
That gone, we are as dust. Behold the fields
In balmy[33] springtime full of rising flowers
And happy creatures! See that pair, the lamb

Notes

[24] *delight . . . universe* unfailing pleasure at beholding natural objects.

[25] *liberty* one of the primary objectives of the (now failed) French Revolution. Wordsworth is implicitly revising this political term, turning it into a spiritual one. The 'liberty' of the Wordsworthian visionary is interior, a freedom of the soul.

[26] *ye solitudes . . . visitations* the landscape of the Lakes. The 'visitations' are from the life-force within the natural world – effectively, God (cf. *Pedlar* 108).

[27] *falls* befalls.

[28] *never . . . from private aims* This is made clearer in the revised *Fourteen-Book Prelude*:

> Never did I, in quest of right and wrong,
> Tamper with conscience from a private aim . . .
> (xiv 150–1)

[29] *with jealousy* scrupulously.

[30] *a universe of death* in which the individual is enslaved by unimaginative reliance on the senses; the phrase is from *Paradise Lost* ii 622.

[31] *To love . . . ends* Fear leads to love of nature, and thence to love of mankind. Cf. *Thirteen-Book Prelude* i 305–6: 'Fair seedtime had my soul, and I grew up / Fostered alike by beauty and by fear.'

[32] *Evil . . . say* Neither fear nor pain are evil, because they play their part in shaping the imaginative mind.

[33] *balmy* mild, fragrant.

And the lamb's mother, and their tender ways
Shall touch thee to the heart. In some green bower
Rest, and be not alone, but have thou there
The one who is thy choice of all the world –
There linger, lulled and lost, and rapt away –
Be happy to thy fill! Thou call'st this love,
And so it is, but there is higher love
Than this, a love that comes into the heart
With awe and a diffusive sentiment;[34]
Thy love is human merely – this proceeds
More from the brooding soul,[35] and is divine.
  This love more intellectual[36] cannot be
Without imagination, which in truth
Is but another name for absolute strength
And clearest insight, amplitude of mind[37]
And reason[38] in her most exalted mood.
This faculty hath been the moving soul
Of our long labour: we have traced the stream
From darkness and the very place of birth
In its blind cavern, whence is faintly heard
The sound of waters; followed it to light
And open day, accompanied its course
Among the ways of nature; afterwards
Lost sight of it bewildered and engulfed,
Then given it greeting as it rose once more
With strength, reflecting in its solemn breast
The works of man and face of human life;
And lastly, from its progress have we drawn
The feeling of life endless,[39] the great thought
By which we live, infinity and God.

Elegiac Stanzas, Suggested by a Picture of Peele Castle[1] in a Storm, Painted by Sir George Beaumont[2] (composed between 20 May and 27 June 1806)

From Poems in Two Volumes (1807)

I was thy neighbour once, thou rugged pile![3]
Four summer weeks I dwelt in sight of thee;
I saw thee every day, and all the while
Thy form was sleeping on a glassy sea.

Notes

[34] *diffusive sentiment* a love that comes from outside the individual, and spreads from soul to soul ('diffusive').

[35] *the brooding soul* i.e. that of God, as suggested by the allusion to the moment of creation in *Paradise Lost* i 21–2, where the Holy Spirit 'Dove-like sat'st brooding on the vast abyss / And madest it pregnant'.

[36] *intellectual* spiritual.

[37] *amplitude of mind* effectively, greatness of soul.

[38] *reason* i.e. intuitive reason, the theme of Book XIII.

[39] *life endless* the afterlife.

Elegiac Stanzas

[1] Piel Castle is in northern Lancashire, on a promontory opposite Rampside, where Wordsworth spent the summer of 1794. Beaumont's painting is now at the Wordsworth Museum, Grasmere.

[2] Sir George Howland Beaumont, 7th Baronet (1753–1827), of Coleorton Hall, near Ashby-de-la-Zouch, Leicestershire. He had sketched in the Lakes in 1798, and given Wordsworth a farmstead at Applethwaite, less than two miles north of Greta Hall at the foot of Skiddaw, in 1803.

[3] *thou rugged pile* Piel Castle.

So pure the sky, so quiet was the air!
So like, so very like, was day to day!
Whene'er I looked, thy image still was there –
It trembled, but it never passed away.

How perfect was the calm; it seemed no sleep,
No mood which season takes away, or brings;
I could have fancied that the mighty deep
Was even the gentlest of all gentle things.

Ah *then*, if mine had been the painter's hand
To express what then I saw, and add the gleam,
The light that never was, on sea or land,
The consecration, and the poet's dream,

I would have planted thee, thou hoary pile,
Amid a world how different from this! –
Beside a sea that could not cease to smile,
On tranquil land, beneath a sky of bliss;

Thou shouldst have seemed a treasure-house, a mine
Of peaceful years, a chronicle of heaven –
Of all the sunbeams that did ever shine
The very sweetest had to thee been given.

A picture had it been of lasting ease,
Elysian quiet,[4] without toil or strife;
No motion but the moving tide, a breeze,
Or merely silent nature's breathing life.

Such, in the fond delusion of my heart,
Such picture would I at that time have made;
And seen the soul of truth in every part –
A faith, a trust that could not be betrayed.

So once it would have been – 'tis so no more;
I have submitted to a new control:
A power is gone, which nothing can restore –
A deep distress hath humanized my soul.[5]

Not for a moment could I now behold
A smiling sea[6] and be what I have been;
The feeling of my loss will ne'er be old –
This, which I know, I speak with mind serene.

Then, Beaumont, friend! who would have been the friend,
If he had lived, of him[7] whom I deplore,[8]
This work of thine[9] I blame not, but commend;
This sea in anger, and that dismal shore.

Notes

[4] *Elysian quiet* i.e. as peaceful as the Elysian fields, where in Greek myth the souls of dead heroes enjoyed eternal life.

[5] *A deep distress . . . soul* the drowning of Wordsworth's brother John (b.1773) in the wreck of the *Earl of Abergavenny*, of which he was Captain, 25 February 1805.

[6] *Not for a moment . . . sea* cf. Wordsworth's comment in a letter: 'since the loss of my dear brother, we have all had such painful and melancholy thoughts connected with the ocean that nothing but a paramount necessity could make us live near it' (*MY* i 212).

[7] *him* John Wordsworth.

[8] *deplore* lament.

[9] *This work of thine* Sir George Beaumont's *A Storm: Peele Castle* was exhibited at the Royal Academy, 2 May 1806, where Wordsworth probably saw it.

Oh 'tis a passionate work! – yet wise and well,
Well-chosen is the spirit that is here;
That hulk which labours in the deadly swell,
This rueful sky, this pageantry of fear!

And this huge castle, standing here sublime,
I love to see the look with which it braves,
Cased in the unfeeling armour of old time,
The lightning, the fierce wind, and trampling waves.

Farewell, farewell the heart that lives alone,
Housed in a dream, at distance from the kind![10]
Such happiness, wherever it be known,
Is to be pitied, for 'tis surely blind.

But welcome fortitude, and patient cheer,
And frequent sights of what is to be borne!
Such sights, or worse, as are before me here –
Not without hope we suffer and we mourn.[11]

A Complaint (composed between 30 October 1806 and April 1807)[1]

From Poems in Two Volumes (1807)

There is a change – and I am poor;
Your love hath been, nor long ago,
A fountain at my fond heart's door
Whose only business was to flow –
And flow it did, not taking heed
Of its own bounty,[2] or my need.

What happy moments did I count!
Blessed was I then all bliss above!
Now, for this consecrated fount
Of murmuring, sparkling, living love,
What have I? Shall I dare to tell?
A comfortless and hidden well.

A well of love – it may be deep –
I trust it is, and never dry;
What matter if the waters sleep
In silence and obscurity?
Such change, and at the very door
Of my fond heart, hath made me poor.

Notes

[10] *kind* humankind.

[11] *Not without hope . . . mourn* Edward Wilson notes that this line echoes the Book of Common Prayer's 'Order for the Burial of the Dead': 'Oh merciful God . . . who also hath taught us, by his holy Apostle St Paul, not to be sorry, as men without hope, for them that sleep in him' ('An Echo of St. Paul and Words of Consolation in Wordsworth's "Elegiac Stanzas" ', *RES* 43 (1992) 75–80).

A Complaint

[1] 'Suggested by a change in the manners of a friend' (*FN* 9). The friend was Coleridge. Strains had been developing between the Wordsworths and Coleridge since around 1802, the period of *Dejection*.

[2] *bounty* its gift of love.

Star Gazers (composed November 1806)[1]

From Poems in Two Volumes (1807)

What crowd is this? What have we here? We must not pass it by;
A telescope upon its frame and pointed to the sky,
Long is it as a barber's pole, or mast of little boat,
Some little pleasure-skiff that doth on Thames's waters float.

The showman chooses well his place – 'tis Leicester's busy Square;
And he's as happy in his night, for the heavens are blue and fair;
Calm, though impatient, are the crowd, each is ready with the fee,
And envies him that's looking – what an insight it must be!

Now, showman, where can lie the cause? Shall thy implement have blame –
A boaster that, when he is tried, fails and is put to shame?
Or is it good as others are, and be their eyes at fault?
Their eyes or minds? Or finally, is this resplendent vault?[2]

Is nothing of that radiant pomp so good as we have here?
Or gives a thing but small delight that never can be dear?
The silver moon with all her vales, and hills of mightiest fame,
Do they betray us when they're seen? And are they but a name?

Or is it rather that conceit[3] rapacious[4] is and strong?
And bounty[5] never yields so much but it seems to do her wrong?
Or is it that when human souls a journey long have had
And are returned into themselves they cannot but be sad?

Or does some deep and earnest thought the blissful mind employ[6]
Of him who gazes, or has gazed – a grave and steady joy
That doth reject all show of pride, admits no outward sign,
Because not of this noisy world, but silent and divine?

Or is it (last unwelcome thought!) that these spectators rude,
Poor in estate, of manners base, men of the multitude,
Have souls which never yet have risen, and therefore prostrate[7] lie,
Not to be lifted up at once to power and majesty?

Whate'er the cause, 'tis sure that they who pry and pore
Seem to meet with little gain, seem less happy than before;
One after one they take their turns, nor have I one espied
That does not slackly go away as if dissatisfied.

Notes

STAR GAZERS

[1] 'Observed by me in Leicester Square as here described, 1806' (*FN* 14). Wordsworth probably saw the showman charging customers to look through his telescope when walking through Leicester Square with Charles Lamb during a visit to London, April–May 1806.

[2] *resplendent vault* the sky; cf. the vault in *A Night-Piece* (pp. 417–18).

[3] *conceit* conception, expectation of what we will see down the telescope.

[4] *rapacious* greedy; i.e. people expect too much.

[5] *bounty* i.e. the reward of seeing the moon down the telescope.

[6] *employ* preoccupy.

[7] *prostrate* overcome, defeated.

[*St Paul's*] (composed 1808; edited from MS)[1]

Pressed[2] with conflicting thoughts of love and fear,
I parted from thee, friend,[3] and took my way
Through the great city, pacing with an eye
Downcast, ear sleeping, and feet masterless,
That were sufficient guide unto themselves,
And step by step went pensively. Now, mark
Not how my trouble was entirely hushed
(That might not be), but how by sudden gift,[4]
Gift of imagination's holy power,
My soul in her uneasiness received
An anchor of stability. It chanced
That, while I thus was pacing, I raised up
My heavy eyes and instantly beheld,
Saw at a glance in that familiar spot
A visionary scene: a length of street
Laid open[5] in its morning quietness,
Deep, hollow, unobstructed, vacant, smooth,
And white with winter's purest white, as fair,
As fresh and spotless as he ever sheds
On field or mountain. Moving form was none,
Save here and there a shadowy passenger,
Slow, shadowy, silent, dusky, and beyond
And high above this winding length of street,
This noiseless and unpeopled avenue,
Pure, silent, solemn, beautiful, was seen
The huge majestic temple of St Paul
In awful sequestration,[6] through a veil,
Through its own sacred veil of falling snow.

Notes

St Paul's

[1] This poem was never published by Wordsworth. It was inspired by his departure early on the morning of 3 April 1808 from Coleridge's lodgings above the *Courier* offices in the Strand to start his journey back to Grasmere. On 8 April he described it to Sir George Beaumont: 'I left Coleridge at 7 o'clock on Sunday morning; and walked towards the city in a very thoughtful and melancholy state of mind. I had passed through Temple Bar and by St Dunstan's, noticing nothing, and entirely occupied by my own thoughts, when, looking up, I saw before me the avenue of Fleet Street, silent, empty, and pure white, with a sprinkling of new-fallen snow, not a cart or carriage to obstruct the view, no noise, only a few soundless and dusky foot-passengers here and there; you remember the elegant curve of Ludgate Hill in which this avenue would terminate, and beyond and towering above it was the huge and majestic form of St Paul's, solemnized by a thin veil of falling snow. I cannot say how much I was affected at this unthought-of sight in such a place, and what a blessing I felt there is in habits of exalted imagination. My sorrow was controlled, and my uneasiness of mind, not quieted and relieved altogether, seemed at once to receive the gift of an anchor of security' (*MY* i 209).

[2] *Pressed* oppressed.

[3] *friend* Coleridge.

[4] *by sudden gift* cf. *Resolution and Independence* 50–1: 'Now whether it were by peculiar grace, / A leading from above, a something given . . . '

[5] *Laid open* cf. *Composed upon Westminster Bridge, 3 September 1802*, in which 'Ships, towers, domes, theatres, and temples lie / Open unto the fields, and to the sky.'

[6] *awful sequestration* awe-inspiring seclusion.

[*Surprised by joy – impatient as the wind*] (composed between 1812 and 1814)[1]

From Poems (1815)

Surprised by joy – impatient as the wind
I wished to share the transport[2] – oh, with whom
But thee,[3] long buried in the silent tomb,
That spot which no vicissitude[4] can find?
Love, faithful love recalled thee to my mind –
But how could I forget thee? Through what power,
Even for the least division of an hour,
Have I been so beguiled[5] as to be blind
To my most grievous loss? That thought's return
Was the worst pang that sorrow ever bore,
Save one, one only, when I stood forlorn,
Knowing my heart's best treasure was no more;
That neither present time, nor years unborn
Could to my sight that heavenly face restore.

Preface (extract)[1]

From Poems (1815)

Imagination (in the sense of the word as giving title to a class[2] of the following poems) has no reference to images that are merely a faithful copy existing in the mind of certain external objects, but is a word of higher import, denoting operations of the mind upon those objects, and processes of creation or of composition governed by certain fixed laws. I proceed to illustrate my meaning by instances.

A parrot *hangs* from the wires of his cage by his beak or by his claws, or a monkey from the bough of a tree by his paws or his tail: each creature does so literally and actually. In the first *Eclogue* of Virgil, the shepherd, thinking of the time when he is to take leave of his farm, thus addresses his goats:

Non ego vos posthac viridi projectus in antro
Dumosa *pendere* procul de rupe videbo . . . [3]

. . . half way up
Hangs one who gathers samphire[4]

Notes

SURPRISED BY JOY

[1] 'This was in fact suggested by my daughter Catherine long after her death' (*FN* 21). Catherine Wordsworth died 4 June 1812.

[2] *transport* ecstasy.

[3] *thee* his dead daughter Catherine.

[4] *vicissitude* change, development in human affairs.

[5] *beguiled* deceived.

PREFACE

[1] *Poems* (1815) was Wordsworth's first attempt to collect his shorter poems. For the occasion he composed an important Preface that outlines his ideas about the imagination.

[2] *a class* In *Poems* (1815) Wordsworth divided his collected works into 'classes' or categories, one of which was 'Imagination'.

[3] Virgil, *Eclogue* i 76–7: 'No more, stretched in some mossy grot, shall I watch you in the distance hanging from a bushy crag.'

[4] *King Lear* IV vi 15–16.

is the well-known expression of Shakespeare, delineating an ordinary image upon the cliffs of Dover. In these two instances is a slight exertion of the faculty which I denominate[5] imagination, in the use of one word. Neither the goats nor the samphire-gatherer[6] do literally hang (as does the parrot or the monkey), but, presenting to the senses something of such an appearance, the mind in its activity, for its own gratification, contemplates them as hanging.

> As when far off at sea a fleet descried
> *Hangs* in the clouds, by equinoxial winds
> Close sailing from Bengala or the Isles
> Of Ternate or Tydore, whence merchants bring
> Their spicy drugs; they on the trading flood
> Through the wide Ethiopian to the Cape
> Ply, stemming nightly toward the pole – so seemed
> Far off the flying fiend.[7]

Here is the full strength of the imagination involved in the word *hangs* and exerted upon the whole image. First the fleet (an aggregate of many ships) is represented as one mighty person whose track, we know and feel, is upon the waters; but, taking advantage of its appearance to the senses, the poet dares to represent it as *hanging in the clouds*, both for the gratification of the mind in contemplating the image itself, and in reference to the motion and appearance of the sublime object to which it is compared.[8]

From images of sight we will pass to those of sound: 'Over his own sweet voice the stock-dove *broods* . . . '[9] Of the same bird:

> His voice was *buried* among trees,
> Yet to be come at by the breeze . . . [10]
> Oh cuckoo! shall I call thee *bird*
> Or but a wandering *voice*?[11]

The stock-dove is said to *coo*, a sound well imitating the note of the bird. But by the intervention of the metaphor *broods*, the affections[12] are called in by the imagination to assist in marking the manner in which the bird reiterates and prolongs her soft note, as if herself delighting to listen to it, and participating of a still and quiet satisfaction like that which may be supposed inseparable from the continuous process of incubation.

Notes

5 *denominate* call.

6 *samphire-gatherer* one who gathers, a plant that grows on rocks by the sea, the leaves of which were used in pickles. Wordsworth was probably referring to true samphire (*Crithmum maritimum*), though the leaves of marsh samphire (species of *Salicornia*) are also eaten.

7 *Paradise Lost* ii 636–43.

8 Wordsworth first discussed his ideas relating to Milton's image in a letter to Sir George Beaumont, 28 August 1811:

> We had another fine sight one evening, walking along a rising ground about two miles distant from the shore. It was about the hour of sunset, and the sea was perfectly calm, and in a quarter where its surface was indistinguishable from the western sky, hazy and luminous with the setting sun, appeared a tall sloop-rigged vessel, magnified by the atmosphere through which it was viewed, and seeming rather to hang in the air than to float upon the waters. Milton compares the appearance of Satan to a *fleet* descried far off at sea; the visionary grandeur and beautiful form of this *single* vessel, could words have conveyed to the mind the picture which Nature presented to the eye, would have suited his purpose as well as the largest company of vessels that ever associated together with the help of a trade wind. (*MY* i 508)

9 *Resolution and Independence* 5.

10 'Oh nightingale' 13–14.

11 *To the Cuckoo* 3–4.

12 *affections* feelings.

'His voice was buried among trees': a metaphor expressing the love of seclusion by which this bird is marked, and characterizing its note as not partaking of the shrill and the piercing, and therefore more easily deadened by the intervening shade – yet a note so peculiar, and withal so pleasing, that the breeze, gifted with that love of the sound which the poet feels, penetrates the shade in which it is entombed, and conveys it to the ear of the listener.

. . . shall I call thee bird
Or but a wandering voice?

This concise interrogation[13] characterizes the seeming ubiquity of the voice of the cuckoo, and dispossesses the creature almost of a corporeal existence – the imagination being tempted to this exertion of her power by a consciousness in the memory that the cuckoo is almost perpetually heard throughout the season of spring, but seldom becomes an object of sight.

Thus far of images independent of each other, and immediately endowed by the mind with properties that do not inhere in them,[14] upon an incitement[15] from properties and qualities the existence of which is inherent and obvious. These processes of imagination are carried on either by conferring additional properties upon an object, or abstracting[16] from it some of those which it actually possesses, and thus enabling it to react upon the mind which hath performed the process, like a new existence.

I pass from the imagination acting upon an individual image to a consideration of the same faculty employed upon images in a conjunction[17] by which they modify each other. The reader has already had a fine instance before him in the passage quoted from Virgil, where the apparently perilous situation of the goat hanging upon the shaggy precipice is contrasted with that of the shepherd contemplating it from the seclusion of the cavern in which he lies stretched at ease and in security. Take these images separately, and how unaffecting the picture compared with that produced by their being thus connected with, and opposed to, each other!

As a huge stone is sometimes seen to lie
Couched on the bald top of an eminence,
Wonder to all who do the same espy
By what means it could thither come, and whence;
So that it seems a thing endued with sense,
Like a sea-beast crawled forth, which on a shelf
Of rock or sand reposeth, there to sun himself –

Such seemed this man, not all alive nor dead,
Nor all asleep, in his extreme old age . . .
Motionless as a cloud the old man stood
That heareth not the loud winds when they call
And moveth altogether, if it move at all.[18]

In these images, the conferring, the abstracting, and the modifying powers of the imagination, immediately and mediately acting, are all brought into conjunction.[19] The stone is endowed with something of the power of life to approximate it to the

Notes

[13] *interrogation* question.

[14] *do not inhere in them* i.e. qualities and properties not actually possessed by the objects themselves.

[15] *incitement* stimulus.

[16] *abstracting* removing.

[17] *conjunction* combination.

[18] *Resolution and Independence* 64–72, 82–4.

[19] *brought into conjunction* i.e. act together.

sea-beast, and the sea-beast stripped of some of its vital qualities to assimilate it to the stone – which intermediate image is thus treated for the purpose of bringing the original image (that of the stone) to a nearer resemblance to the figure and condition of the aged man, who is divested of so much of the indications of life and motion as to bring him to the point where the two objects unite and coalesce in just comparison. After what has been said, the image of the cloud need not be commented upon.

Thus far of an endowing or modifying power. But the imagination also shapes and *creates* – and how? By innumerable processes, and in none does it more delight than in that of consolidating numbers into unity, and dissolving and separating unity into number – alternations proceeding from, and governed by, a sublime consciousness of the soul in her own mighty and almost divine powers. Recur to the passage already cited from Milton.[20] When the compact fleet, as one person, has been introduced 'sailing from Bengala', 'they' (i.e. the 'merchants' representing the fleet resolved into a multitude of ships) 'Ply' their voyage towards the extremities of the earth; 'so' (referring to the word 'As' in the commencement) 'seemed the flying fiend' – the image of his person acting to recombine the multitude of ships into one body, the point from which the comparison set out.

'So seemed': and to whom 'seemed'? To the heavenly muse who dictates the poem, to the eye of the poet's mind, and to that of the reader, present at one moment in the wide Ethiopian, and the next in the solitudes, then first broken in upon, of the infernal regions!

Conclusion (composed 1818–20)[1]

From The River Duddon (1820)

I thought of thee,[2] my partner and my guide,
As being past away. Vain sympathies!
For *backward*, Duddon, as I cast my eyes,
I see what was, and is, and will abide;
Still glides the stream, and shall for ever glide;
The form remains, the function never dies,
While *we*, the brave, the mighty, and the wise,[3]
We men who, in our morn of youth, defied
The elements, must vanish; be it so!
Enough, if something from our hands have power
To live, and act, and serve the future hour;
And if, as tow'rd the silent tomb we go,
Through love, through hope, and faith's transcendent dower,[4]
We feel that we are greater than we know.

Notes

[20] *the passage . . . Milton* i.e. *Paradise Lost* ii 636–43, quoted p. 576.

CONCLUSION

[1] Wordsworth composed a sequence of sonnets describing the Duddon Valley, which he published in 1820. This concluding sonnet is probably the most famous, and the best. The River Duddon springs from the top of the Wrynose Pass and then descends through one of the most picturesque valleys in the Lake District.

[2] *thee* the River Duddon.

[3] *While we . . . wise* borrowed from Wordsworth's early translation of Moschus' *Lament for Bion* (1789) 5: 'But we, the great, the mighty and the wise'. Shelley, who frequently alludes to Moschus' *Lament*, also echoes the line at *Mont Blanc* 82.

[4] *dower* gift.

[*Genius of Burke!*] (composed by 1832; edited from MS)[1]

From The Fourteen-Book Prelude (1850), Book VII (extract)

Genius of Burke! forgive the pen seduced
By specious wonders,[2] and too slow to tell
Of what the ingenuous, what bewildered men
Beginning to mistrust their boastful guides,[3]
And wise men, willing to grow wiser, caught
(Rapt auditors!) from thy most eloquent tongue –
Now mute, for ever mute, in the cold grave.[4]
I see him, old but vigorous in age,
Stand, like an oak whose stag-horn branches start
Out of its leafy brow, the more to awe
The younger brethren of the grove. But some –
While he forewarns, denounces, launches forth,
Against all systems built on abstract rights,[5]
Keen ridicule; the majesty[6] proclaims
Of institutes and laws hallowed by time;[7]
Declares the vital power of social ties
Endeared by custom, and with high disdain
Exploding upstart theory, insists
Upon the allegiance to which men are born –
Some (say at once a froward[8] multitude)
Murmur (for truth is hated where not loved)
As the winds fret within the Eolian cave,
Galled by their monarch's chain.[9] The times[10] were big
With ominous change which, night by night, provoked
Keen struggles, and black clouds of passion raised;
But memorable moments intervened
When Wisdom, like the goddess from Jove's brain,[11]
Broke forth in armour of resplendent words,
Startling the synod.[12] Could a youth, and one

Notes

GENIUS OF BURKE

[1] This is one of the best-known instances of how Wordsworth's political views had altered since his republican youth. Burke's *Reflections on the Revolution in France* (1790) had argued eloquently against the revolution (pp. 10–16), and Wordsworth did not approve of it at the time of its publication. By 1832, however, he had become an adherent of the liberal conservatism with which Burke was associated.

[2] *specious wonders* i.e. the work of radical writers like Paine, Wollstonecraft and Godwin.

[3] *the ingenuous . . . guides* young men taken in by radical ideologues like Thomas Paine – of whom Wordsworth had been one.

[4] Burke died in 1797.

[5] *abstract rights* an allusion to Paine's *Rights of Man* (1791–2), written in response to Burke (p. 23).

[6] *the majesty* Burke.

[7] *Of institutes . . . time* One of Burke's central arguments in the *Reflections* was that society and its laws constituted 'a partnership not only between those who are living, but between those who are living, those who are dead, and those who are to be born' (p. 15).

[8] *froward* wayward, undisciplined.

[9] *As the winds . . . chain* Aeolus, god of the winds, was given command of the winds by Zeus, and kept them in a cave, releasing them at will.

[10] *The times* Wordsworth is looking back to the French Revolution, 1789–95.

[11] *the goddess . . . brain* Minerva, daughter of Zeus, was born without a mother, springing fully armed from her father's head when it was split open by the axe of Prometheus.

[12] *synod* House of Commons, where Burke was known for his passionate oratory.

In ancient story versed, whose breast had heaved
Under the weight of classic eloquence,
Sit, see, and hear, unthankful, uninspired?[13]

Airey-Force Valley (composed September 1835)[1]

From Yarrow Revisited, and Other Poems (1835)

Not a breath of air
Ruffles the bosom of this leafy glen.
From the brook's margin, wide around, the trees
Are steadfast as the rocks; the brook itself,
Old as the hills that feed it from afar,
Doth rather deepen than disturb the calm
Where all things else are still and motionless.
And yet, even now, a little breeze, perchance
Escaped from boisterous winds that rage without,
Has entered, by the sturdy oaks unfelt,
But to its gentle touch how sensitive
Is the light ash that, pendent from the brow
Of yon dim cave, in seeming silence makes
A soft eye-music of slow-waving boughs,
Powerful almost as vocal harmony
To stay the wanderer's steps and soothe his thoughts.

Extempore Effusion upon the Death of James Hogg[1] (composed between 21 November and 3 December 1835)

From Poetical Works (1836)

When first,[2] descending from the moorlands,
I saw the Stream of Yarrow glide
Along a bare and open valley,
The Ettrick Shepherd[3] was my guide.

When last[4] along its banks I wandered,
Through groves that had begun to shed

Notes

[13] *Could a youth . . . uninspired?* Wordsworth in youth was no admirer of Burke, and would not, presumably, have confessed to feeling inspired by his words.

AIREY-FORCE VALLEY

[1] Aira Force is a waterfall on the north shore of Ullswater. This poem celebrates the gorge that rises above it.

EXTEMPORE EFFUSION UPON THE DEATH OF JAMES HOGG

[1] James Hogg, poet, novelist and man of letters, died 21 November 1835. Wordsworth later commented: 'These verses were written extempore immediately after reading a notice of the Ettrick Shepherd's death in the Newcastle paper, to the editor of which I sent a copy for publication. The persons lamented in these verses were all either of my friends or acquaintance' (*FN* 58). For a cogent line-by-line analysis of the poem, see William Ruddick's 'Subdued Passion and Controlled Emotion: Wordsworth's "Extempore Effusion upon the Death of James Hogg" ', *Charles Lamb Bulletin* NS 87 (1994) 98–110.

[2] *When first* Wordsworth first walked along the banks of the River Yarrow in September 1814.

[3] *The Ettrick Shepherd* the name under which Hogg often published. After his father went bankrupt when he was 6, he was removed from school and spent most of his life as a shepherd.

[4] *When last* Wordsworth returned to the Yarrow in September–October 1831, when his guide was Sir Walter Scott, a friend since the early 1800s.

Their golden leaves upon the pathways,
My steps the Border Minstrel[5] led.

The mighty Minstrel breathes no longer,
Mid mouldering ruins[6] low he lies;
And death upon the braes of Yarrow
Has closed the Shepherd-poet's eyes:

Nor has the rolling year twice measured,
From sign to sign, its steadfast course,
Since every mortal power of Coleridge[7]
Was frozen at its marvellous source;

The rapt One of the godlike forehead,
The heaven-eyed creature sleeps in earth:
And Lamb,[8] the frolic and the gentle,
Has vanished from his lonely hearth.

Like clouds that rake the mountain-summits,
Or waves that own no curbing hand,
How fast has brother followed brother,
From sunshine to the sunless land!

Yet I, whose lids from infant slumbers
Were earlier raised, remain to hear
A timid voice that asks in whispers,
'Who next will drop and disappear?'

Our haughty life is crowned with darkness,
Like London with its own black wreath,[9]
On which with thee, oh Crabbe![10] forth-looking,
I gazed from Hampstead's breezy heath.

As if but yesterday departed,
Thou too art gone before; but why
O'er ripe fruit, seasonably gathered,
Should frail survivors[11] heave a sigh?

Mourn rather for that holy Spirit,[12]
Sweet as the spring, as ocean deep;
For Her who, ere her summer faded,
Has sunk into a breathless sleep.

Notes

5 *the Border Minstrel* Sir Walter Scott, died 21 September 1832. His earliest literary success had come with *The Minstrelsy of the Scottish Border* (1802–3).

6 *Mid mouldering ruins* Scott was buried at Dryburgh Abbey, 26 September 1832.

7 Samuel Taylor Coleridge died 25 July 1834.

8 Charles Lamb died 27 December 1834. Lamb remained a friend of Wordsworth from the time of their first meeting at Nether Stowey in June 1797. It is appropriate that he follows Coleridge in this list, as they had been friends since their time together at Christ's Hospital.

9 *Like London . . . wreath* a reference to the pall of black smoke hanging over London, produced by the burning of household fires.

10 George Crabbe died 3 February 1832; see p. 142.

11 *frail survivors* Wordsworth was 65 at the time of composition.

12 *that holy Spirit* Felicia Dorothea Hemans, who became a friend of Wordsworth during her visit to the Lake District in 1830, and corresponded with him until the end of her life, shortened by many years' hard work (see pp. 1241–7). She was the most recently deceased of those celebrated here, having died on 16 May 1835.

No more of old romantic[13] sorrows,
For slaughtered youth and love-lorn maid!
With sharper grief is Yarrow smitten,
And Ettrick[14] mourns with her their Poet dead.

[*On the 'Ode'*] (extract)

From The Fenwick Notes (dictated 1843)

Nothing was more difficult for me in childhood than to admit the notion of death as a state applicable to my own being. I have said elsewhere: 'A simple child . . . that lightly draws its breath, / And feels its life in every limb – / What should it know of death?'[1] But it was not so much from [excess[2]] of animal vivacity that *my* difficulty came, as from a sense of the indomitableness[3] of the spirit within me. I used to brood over the stories of Enoch and Elijah, and almost to persuade myself that, whatever might become of others, I should be translated in something of the same way to heaven.

With a feeling congenial to this, I was often unable to think of external things as having external existence, and I communed with all that I saw as something not apart from, but inherent in, my own immaterial nature.[4] Many times while going to school have I grasped at a wall or tree to recall myself from this abyss of idealism to the reality. At that time I was afraid of such processes. In later periods of life I have deplored (as we have all reason to do) a subjugation of an opposite character, and have rejoiced over the remembrances, as is expressed in the lines, 'obstinate questionings',[5] etc. To that dreamlike vividness and splendour which invest objects of sight in childhood, everyone (I believe, if he would look back) could bear testimony, and I need not dwell upon it here.

But having in the poem regarded it as presumptive evidence of a prior state of existence, I think it right to protest against a conclusion which has given pain to some good and pious persons that I meant to inculcate such a belief. It is far too shadowy a notion to be recommended to faith as more than an element in our instincts of immortality. But let us bear in mind that, though the idea is not advanced in revelation, there is nothing there to contradict it, and the fall of man presents an analogy in its favour. Accordingly, a pre-existent state has entered into the popular creeds of many nations, and among all persons acquainted with classic literature is known as an ingredient in Platonic philosophy.

Archimedes said that he could move the world if he had a point whereon to rest his machine. Who has not felt the same aspirations as regards the world of his own mind? Having to wield some of its elements when I was impelled to write this poem on the immortality of the soul, I took hold of the notion of pre-existence as having sufficient foundation in humanity for authorizing me to make for my purpose the best use of it I could as a poet.

Notes

[13] *romantic* i.e. from old medieval romances, which provided much of Scott's subject-matter.

[14] *Ettrick* the village of Ettrick, where Hogg lived, worked and is buried, is in the Scottish lowlands.

On the 'Ode'

[1] 'We are Seven' 1-4.

[2] *excess* editorial conjecture, necessary to fill a gap left in the MS.

[3] *indomitableness* effectively, strength, power.

[4] *my own immaterial nature* spirit.

[5] *obstinate questionings* See *Ode* 144 ff.

[*On 'We are Seven'*] (extract)

From The Fenwick Notes (dictated 1843)

In reference to this poem, I will here mention one of the most remarkable facts in my own poetic history and that of Mr Coleridge.

In the spring of the year 1798,[1] he, my sister and myself started from Alfoxden, pretty late in the afternoon, with a view to visit Lynton and the Valley of Stones near it. And as our united funds were very small, we agreed to defray the expense of the tour by writing a poem to be sent to the new *Monthly Magazine* set up by Phillips the bookseller, and edited by Dr Aikin.[2] Accordingly we set off and proceeded along the Quantock Hills towards Watchet, and in the course of this walk was planned the poem of 'The Ancient Mariner', founded on a dream (as Mr Coleridge said) of his friend Mr Cruikshank.[3] Much the greatest part of the story was Mr Coleridge's invention, but certain parts I myself suggested; for example, some crime was to be committed which should bring upon the Old Navigator (as Coleridge afterwards delighted to call him) the spectral persecution, as a consequence of that crime and his own wanderings.

I had been reading in Shelvocke's *Voyages*[4] a day or two before, that while doubling Cape Horn they frequently saw albatrosses – in that latitude the largest sort of seafowl, some extending their wings 12 or 13 feet. 'Suppose', I said, 'you represent him as having killed one of these birds on entering the South Sea, and that the tutelary spirits of these regions take upon them to avenge the crime?' The incident was thought fit for the purpose, and adopted accordingly. I also suggested the navigation of the ship by the dead men, but do not recollect that I had anything more to do with the scheme of the poem.

The gloss with which it was subsequently accompanied was not thought of by either of us at the time – at least, not a hint of it was given to me – and I have no doubt it was a gratuitous afterthought.[5] We began the composition together on that (to me) memorable evening; I furnished two or three lines at the beginning of the poem, in particular:

> And listened like a three years' child:
> The mariner had his will.[6]

These trifling contributions all but one (which Mr Coleridge has with unnecessary scrupulosity recorded[7]) slipped out of his mind – as they well might. As we endeavoured to proceed conjointly[8] (I speak of the same evening), our respective manners[9] proved so widely different that it would have been quite presumptuous in me to do anything but separate from an undertaking upon which I could only have been a clog.

Notes

On 'We are Seven'

[1] *In the year . . . 1798* The walking tour took place not in spring 1798 but in mid-November 1797.

[2] *The Monthly Magazine*, an influential radical periodical founded in 1796 by Richard Phillips and edited by Dr John Aikin (1747–1822), brother of Mrs Barbauld.

[3] John Cruikshank, land agent to Lord Egmont at Nether Stowey, and Coleridge's neighbour there. He was the brother of Ellen Cruikshank, the 'most gentle maid' of Coleridge's 'The Nightingale' 69.

[4] George Shelvocke, *Voyage round the World, by the way of the Great South Sea* (1726); for the passage to which Wordsworth refers, see p. 334n14.

[5] *The gloss . . . afterthought* The 1817 text of 'The Ancient Mariner' carries a series of marginal glosses; see pp. 694–711.

[6] *The Ancient Mariner* (1798) 19–20.

[7] *which Mr Coleridge . . . recorded* See note to the 1817 text of 'The Ancient Mariner' 227, p. 701.

[8] *conjointly* together.

[9] *manners* literary styles.

Dorothy Wordsworth (1771–1855)

Dorothy Wordsworth was born in Cockermouth in 1771. When she was 6 her mother died, and she moved away from the Lake District, to Halifax in Yorkshire, where she was brought up by her mother's cousin, Elizabeth Threlkeld. The ensuing years were not all unhappy, but she very much missed her brothers. When in December 1783 her father died, she was unable to attend his funeral. Between the ages of 15 and 17 she was brought up by her grandmother in Penrith, and from 1788 to 1794 by her kindly uncle, William Cookson, at Forncett Rectory in Norfolk. By then a young woman, she spent time with a variety of people in various places: with Elizabeth Threlkeld in Halifax, in Newcastle with the Misses Griffiths (other cousins of her mother), with the Hutchinson family at Sockburn and at Rampside with more cousins (this time on her father's side).

Her life changed when, in the summer of 1795, for the first time since childhood, she was able to live with her brother William at Racedown Lodge in Dorset. Here they lived a settled, domestic existence which neither had known in adulthood. This continued at Alfoxden House in Somerset, where they moved to be close to Coleridge, four miles away in Nether Stowey. She had already written many letters which reveal a precocious literary talent, but it was at Alfoxden that her abilities blossomed with the writing of a journal. The manuscripts of the Alfoxden journal are now lost, but transcripts show that her close, detailed observations of the natural world were the inspiration for much of her brother's poetry, and constitute a significant literary achievement in themselves.

She went to Germany with her brother in 1798 and settled with him at Dove Cottage on 20 December 1799. It was probably the most important event in her life. Here she was to write the Grasmere journals which, besides continuing to provide the source for much of Wordsworth's poetry, documented the goings-on of life over the first three years of their lives at Dove Cottage. It was her masterpiece. As Pamela Woof has written:

> There is simply nothing like it anywhere else. This Journal calls out to us directly across some two hundred years, and its writer and her world come alive. It sometimes moves in little rushes when days can be noted with a staccato speed; it sometimes slows down to linger on a single figure: a beggar woman, a leech-gatherer, a child catching hailstones at a cottage door, a bow-bent postman with his little wooden box at his back, an old seaman with a beard like grey plush; it sometimes slows to linger on a whole scene: a funeral, or children with their mother by a fire, or a lakeshore on a windy day with daffodils, or a man with carts going up a hill and a little girl putting stones behind the wheels . . . The Journal conveys directly the unpremeditated rhythms; they seem comfortable with Dorothy's nature; they reflect her wholehearted acceptance of the experience of living.[1]

The most important thing about the journals is, of course, that their naturalness and unliterariness depend on the fact that Dorothy never intended them to be published; they were private documents, intended only for her eyes and those of her brother. And yet it is the same perspective as that of the great poet of *The Prelude*, for here are the same characters, the same village folk, the same sharp observation of the natural world. They are guileless, undeceived, full of compassion and wisdom about the ways of the world. I am indebted in my work on the journals to Pamela

Notes

[1] *Grasmere Journals* ix.

Woof's exemplary paperback edition, which contains the most accurate text and the most helpful notes of any thus far published.

Some of Dorothy's poetry was published during her lifetime, mainly alongside her brother's in his collected works. She began writing in about 1805, and seems to have continued writing, very occasionally until after the onset of dementia in 1829. Her last years were marked by a sad and slow decline; she survived her brother by five years, and was nursed until her death by Mary Wordsworth. A selection of her verse is presented here, edited from Dorothy's Commonplace Book at Dove Cottage.

Further reading

Dorothy Wordsworth, *The Grasmere and Alfoxden Journals* ed. Pamela Woof (Oxford, 2002).

Dorothy Wordsworth, *Journal of my Second Tour in Scotland, 1822* ed. Jiro Nagasawa (Tokyo, 1989).

Pamela Woof, *Dorothy Wordsworth, Writer* (Grasmere, 1988).

Pamela Woof, 'Dorothy Wordsworth and Mary Lamb, Writers', *Charles Lamb Bulletin* NS 66–7 (1989) 41–53, 82–93.

From The Grasmere Journals

Wednesday 3 September 1800

Coleridge, William and John[1] went from home to go upon Helvellyn[2] with Mr Simpson. They set out after breakfast. I accompanied them up near the blacksmith's – a fine, coolish morning. I ironed till half past three, now very hot. I then went to a funeral at John Dawson's[3] – about ten men and four women. Bread, cheese and ale; they talked sensibly and cheerfully about common things. The dead person, 56 years of age, buried by the parish; the coffin was neatly lettered and painted black and covered with a decent cloth. They set the corpse down at the door and, while we stood within the threshold, the men with their hats off sang with decent and solemn countenances a verse of a funeral psalm. The corpse was then borne down the hill and they sang till they had got past the Town End.[4]

I was affected to tears while we stood in the house, the coffin lying before me. There were no near kindred, no children. When we got out of the dark house, the sun was shining and the prospect looked so divinely beautiful as I never saw it. It seemed more sacred than I had ever seen it, and yet more allied to human life. The green fields, neighbours of the churchyard, were green as possible and, with the brightness of the sunshine, looked quite gay. I thought she was going to a quiet spot and I could not help weeping very much.

When we came to the bridge, they began to sing again and stopped during four lines before they entered the churchyard. The priest[5] met us – he did not look as a man ought to do on such an occasion (I had seen him half-drunk the day before in a pothouse[6]). Before we came with the corpse one of the company observed he wondered what sort of cue[7] 'our parson would be in'? N.B. It was the day after the fair.[8] I had not finished ironing till 7 o'clock. The wind was now high and I did not walk. Writing my journal now at 8 o'clock. William and John came home at 10 o'clock.

Notes

WEDNESDAY 3 SEPTEMBER 1800

1 John Wordsworth (1773–1805), brother of William and Dorothy, a sea-captain, visited Dove Cottage, January–September 1800.

2 Helvellyn is a large mountain (3116 ft) that towers above Grasmere.

3 John Dawson's farm was on the Rydal road at the top of the hill behind Dove Cottage. The funeral was that of a pauper, Susan Shacklock.

4 *Town End* the small cluster of cottages (including Dove Cottage) just off the main road to Keswick, half a mile from the village of Grasmere.

5 *The priest* Edward Rowlandson, curate of Grasmere for more than forty years. He was notorious for getting drunk.

6 *pothouse* ale-house, tavern.

7 *cue* condition.

8 *the fair* Grasmere fair is held yearly in the meadows between Town End and the village of Grasmere.

Friday 3 October 1800 (extract)[1]

When William and I returned from accompanying Jones, we met an old man almost double. He had on a coat thrown over his shoulders above his waistcoat and coat. Under this he carried a bundle and had an apron on and a nightcap. His face was interesting. He had dark eyes and a long nose (John, who afterwards met him at Wythburn, took him for a Jew). He was of Scotch parents but had been born in the army. He had had a wife, 'and a good woman, and it pleased God to bless us with ten children'; all these were dead but one of whom he had not heard for many years, a sailor. His trade was to gather leeches,[2] but now leeches are scarce and he had not strength for it. He lived by begging and was making his way to Carlisle where he should buy a few godly books to sell. He said leeches were very scarce partly owing to this dry season, but many years they have been scarce. He supposed it owing to their being much sought-after, that they did not breed fast, and were of slow growth. Leeches were formerly *2s. 6d.* per 100; they are now *30s.* He had been hurt in driving a cart: his leg broke, his body driven over, his skull fractured. He felt no pain till he recovered from his first insensibility;[3] it was then 'late in the evening, when the light was just going away.'

Thursday 15 April 1802[1]

It was a threatening misty morning, but mild. We set off after dinner from Eusemere; Mrs Clarkson[2] went a short way with us but turned back. The wind was furious and we thought we must have returned. We first rested in the large boathouse, then under a furze-bush opposite Mr Clarkson's; saw the plough going in the field. The wind seized our breath, the lake was rough. There was a boat by itself floating in the middle of the bay below Water Millock; we rested again in the Water Millock lane. The hawthorns are black and green, the birches here and there greenish but there is yet more of purple to be seen on the twigs. We got over into a field to avoid some cows – people working, a few primroses by the roadside, woodsorrel flowers, the anemone, scentless violets, strawberries, and that starry yellow flower which Mrs Clarkson calls pilewort.[3]

When we were in the woods beyond Gowbarrow Park[4] we saw a few daffodils[5] close to the waterside. We fancied that the lake had floated the seeds ashore and that the little colony had so sprung up. But as we went along there were more and yet more, and at last, under the boughs of the trees, we saw that there was a long belt of them along the shore, about the breadth of a country turnpike road. I never saw daffodils so beautiful. They grew among the mossy stones, about and about them; some rested their heads upon these stones as on a pillow for weariness, and the rest tossed and reeled and danced, and seemed as if they verily laughed with the wind that blew upon them over the lake. They looked so gay – ever-glancing, ever-changing.

Notes

FRIDAY 3 OCTOBER 1800

[1] This entry was written a week after the encounter had taken place; it is a source for Wordsworth's 'Resolution and Independence', composed eighteen months later.

[2] *leeches* blood-letting was the usual method of treating physical ailments such as fevers, and a favoured means of performing this operation was to apply leeches to the patient's skin.

[3] *insensibility* unconsciousness.

THURSDAY 15 APRIL 1802

[1] This entry is a source for Wordsworth's 'Daffodils'.

[2] *Mrs Clarkson* Catherine Clarkson (1772–1856), wife of Thomas Clarkson (1760–1846), agitator for abolition of the slave trade, from about 1785 onwards. After his health collapsed in 1794 he built a house, Eusemere, on Ullswater. Dorothy had been friendly with the Clarksons since meeting them in September 1800.

[3] *pilewort* the lesser celandine.

[4] *beyond Gowbarrow Park* on the western shore of Ullswater, the Park belonged to the Duke of Norfolk.

[5] *daffodils* not the garden daffodils of today but the small, pale and wild *Narcissus pseudonarcissus.*

This wind blew directly over the lake to them. There was, here and there, a little knot, and a few stragglers a few yards higher up – but they were so few as not to disturb the simplicity and unity and life of that one busy highway. We rested again and again.

The bays were stormy, and we heard the waves at different distances and in the middle of the water like the sea. Rain came on; we were wet when we reached Luff's but we called in. Luckily all was cheerless and gloomy, so we faced the storm – we *must* have been wet if we had waited; put on dry clothes at Dobson's. I was very kindly treated by a young woman, the landlady looked sour but it is her way. She gave us a goodish supper, excellent ham and potatoes. We paid 7*s.* when we came away. William was sitting by a bright fire when I came downstairs; he soon made his way to the library piled up in a corner of the window. He brought out a volume of Enfield's *Speaker*,[6] another miscellany, and an odd volume of Congreve's plays. We had a glass of warm rum and water; we enjoyed ourselves and wished for Mary.[7] It rained and blew when we went to bed. N.B. Deer in Gowbarrow Park like to skeletons.

Thursday 29 April 1802

A beautiful morning. The sun shone and all was pleasant. We sent off our parcel to Coleridge by the wagon. Mr Simpson heard the cuckoo today. Before we went out, after I had written down 'The Tinker', which William finished this morning, Luff[1] called. He was very lame, limped into the kitchen (he came on a little pony).

We then went to John's Grove,[2] sat a while at first. Afterwards William lay and I lay in the trench under the fence – he with his eyes shut and listening to the waterfalls and the birds. There was no one waterfall above another – it was a sound of waters in the air, the voice of the air. William heard me breathing and rustling now and then, but we both lay still and unseen by one another. He thought that it would be as sweet thus to lie so in the grave, to hear the *peaceful* sounds of the earth and just to know that one's dear friends were near.[3] The lake was still; there was a boat out. Silver How[4] reflected with delicate purple and yellowish hues as I have seen [in] spar.[5] Lambs on the island[6] and running races together by the half-dozen in the round field near us. The copses green*ish*, hawthorn green.

Came home to dinner, then went to Mr Simpson.[7] We rested a long time under a wall. Sheep and lambs were in the field – cottages smoking. As I lay down on the grass, I observed the glittering silver line on the ridges of the backs of the sheep, owing to their situation respecting the sun, which made them look beautiful but with something of strangeness, like animals of another kind – as if belonging to a more splendid world. Met old Mr Simpson at the door; Mrs Simpson poorly. I got mullens[8] and pansies. I was sick and ill and obliged to come home soon. We went to bed immediately – I slept upstairs. The air coldish where it was felt somewhat frosty.

Notes

[6] *Enfield's Speaker* William Enfield, *The Speaker; or Miscellaneous Pieces Selected from the Best English Writers* (1774), popular anthology, frequently reprinted. Dorothy had met Enfield in 1788.

[7] *Mary* Mary Hutchinson, who would marry Wordsworth in October.

THURSDAY 29 APRIL 1802

[1] Capt. Charles Luff (or Lough), d. 1815. He and his wife Letitia, friends of the Wordsworths, resided in Patterdale but occasionally (as here) lodged in Ambleside.

[2] *John's Grove* formerly a small grove of fir trees almost opposite the Wishing Gate beyond How Top on the old Rydal Road beyond Dove Cottage. The firs had been cut down in 1801.

[3] These remarks provide a context for 'These chairs they have no thoughts to utter', composed a week before, p. 528, above. See also 'Ode' 120–3.

[4] *Silver How* mountain on the western side of Grasmere lake, opposite Town End.

[5] *spar* crystalline mineral.

[6] *the island* in the middle of Grasmere lake.

[7] *Mr Simpson* Revd. Joseph Simpson of High Broadraine, Grasmere, vicar of the small church at Wythburn. He died on 27 June 1807 at the age of 92.

[8] *mullens* the mullein is a plant with a spike of yellow flowers and hairy leaves.

4 October 1802

On Monday 4 October 1802, my brother William was married to Mary Hutchinson.[1] I slept a good deal of the night and rose fresh and well in the morning. At a little after 8 o'clock I saw them go down the avenue towards the church.[2] William had parted from me upstairs. I gave him the wedding ring – with how deep a blessing! I took it from my forefinger where I had worn it the whole of the night before; he slipped it again onto my finger and blessed me fervently.[3]

When they were absent, my dear little Sara[4] prepared the breakfast. I kept myself as quiet as I could, but when I saw the two men[5] running up the walk, coming to tell us it was over, I could stand it no longer and threw myself on the bed where I lay in stillness, neither hearing or seeing anything till Sara came upstairs to me and said, 'They are coming'. This forced me from the bed where I lay, and I moved I knew not how straightforward, faster than my strength could carry me, till I met my beloved William and fell upon his bosom. He and John Hutchinson led me to the house and there I stayed to welcome my dear Mary. As soon as we had breakfasted we departed.[6] It rained when we set off. Poor Mary was much agitated when she parted from her brothers and sisters and her home.

A Cottage in Grasmere Vale (composed *c.* 1805, edited from MS)

Peaceful our valley, fair and green,
And beautiful her cottages,
Each in its nook, its sheltered hold,
Or guarded by its tuft of trees –

Many and beautiful they are,
But there is *one* that I love best,
A lowly shed in truth it is,
A brother of the rest.

Yet when I sit on rock or hill,
Down looking on the valley fair,
That cottage with its clustering trees
Summons my heart – it settles there.

Others there are whose small domain
Of fertile fields and hedgerows green
Might more entice a wanderer's mind
To wish that *there* his home had been.

Notes

4 October 1802

[1] Wordsworth had known Mary Hutchinson since early childhood, when they attended Ann Birkett's dame school together.

[2] Wordsworth was married at All Saints Church, Brompton-by-Sawdon, Yorkshire, a mile or so down the road from Gallow Hill (today called Gallows Hill), where the Hutchinson family resided. Only five people were present at the service: besides the couple, Mary's siblings, Thomas, John and Joanna.

[3] Pamela Woof comments: 'That Dorothy wore the ring the night before denotes her full acceptance of Mary Hutchinson and the marriage, and that Wordsworth slipped it for a moment back on to her finger was surely a pledge that the marriage would not exclude her' (*Grasmere Journals* 265). The ring may be seen in the Wordsworth Museum, Grasmere.

[4] Sara Hutchinson, Mary's sister.

[5] *the two men* John and Thomas Hutchinson, Mary's brothers, were witnesses.

[6] *we departed* for Dove Cottage.

Such wish be his! I blame him not,
My fancy is unfettered, wild!
I love that house because it is
The very mountains' child.

Fields hath it of its own, green fields,
But they are craggy, steep and bare;
Their fence is of the mountain stone
And moss and lichen flourish there.

And when the storm comes from the north
It lingers near that pastoral spot,
And piping through the mossy walls,
It seems delighted with its lot.

And let it take its own delight,
And let it range the pastures bare;
Until it reach that group of trees
It may not enter there.

A green unfading grove it is,
Skirted with many a lesser tree –
Hazel and holly, beech and oak –
A bright and flourishing company!

Precious the shelter of those trees,
They screen the cottage that I love;
The sunshine pierces to the roof
And the tall pine-trees tower above.

After-recollection at sight of the same cottage (edited from MS)

When first I saw that dear abode
It was a lovely winter's day;[1]
After a night of perilous storm
The west wind ruled with gentle sway –

A day so mild it might have been
The first day of the gladsome spring;
The robins warbled, and I heard
One solitary throstle[2] sing.

A Sketch (composed by 1826; edited from MS)

There is one cottage in our dale,
In naught distinguished from the rest,
Save by a tuft of flourishing trees,
The shelter of that little nest.

Notes

After-recollection at sight of the same cottage

[1] *When first . . . day* 20 November 1799, when the Wordsworths moved into Dove Cottage.

[2] *throstle* thrush.

The public road through Grasmere vale
Winds close beside that cottage small,
And there 'tis hidden by the trees
That overhang the orchard wall.

You lose it there – its serpent line
Is lost in that close household grove;
A moment lost – and then it mounts
The craggy hills above.

Thoughts on my Sickbed (composed *c.* 1831; edited from MS)[1]

And has the remnant of my life
Been pilfered of this sunny spring?
And have its own prelusive sounds[2]
Touched in my heart no echoing string?

Ah, say not so! The hidden life,
Couchant[3] within this feeble frame,
Hath been enriched by kindred gifts
That undesired, unsought-for, came

With joyful heart in youthful days,
When fresh each season in its round
I welcomed the earliest celandine
Glittering upon the mossy ground.

With busy eyes I pierced the lane
In quest of known and unknown things;
The primrose a lamp on its fortress rock,
The silent butterfly spreading its wings,

The violet betrayed by its noiseless breath,
The daffodil dancing in the breeze,
The carolling thrush on his naked perch,
Towering above the budding trees.

Our cottage-hearth no longer our home,
Companions of nature were we;
The stirring, the still, the loquacious, the mute –
To all we gave our sympathy.

Notes

THOUGHTS ON MY SICKBED

[1] In 1829 Dorothy developed a serious illness, apparently presenile dementia, from which she never fully recovered. From 1830 to 1835 she experienced shorter and shorter remissions until being permanently debilitated.

[2] *its own prelusive sounds* i.e. sounds that herald the spring, such as birdsong, etc.

[3] *Couchant* lying.

Yet never in those careless days
When springtime in rock, field, or bower
Was but a fountain of earthly hope
A promise of fruits and the *splendid* flower –

No! – then I never felt a bliss
That might with *that* compare,
Which, piercing to my couch of rest,
Came on the vernal air.

When loving friends an offering brought,
The first flowers of the year,
Culled from the precincts of our home,
From nooks to memory dear,

With some sad thoughts the work was done,
Unprompted and unbidden,
But joy it brought to my *hidden* life,
To consciousness no longer hidden.

I felt a power unfelt before,
Controlling weakness, languor, pain;
It bore me to the terrace-walk,[4]
I trod the hills again.

No prisoner in this lonely room,
I *saw* the green banks of the Wye,[5]
Recalling thy prophetic words –
Bard, brother, friend from infancy!

No need of motion or of strength
Or even the breathing air,
I thought of nature's loveliest scenes,
And with memory I was there.

Notes

[4] *the terrace-walk* at Rydal Mount, where the Wordsworths lived at this time, there was a terrace leading from the house along the side of the mountain overlooking Rydal Water and Windermere. It can still be seen today.

[5] *I saw . . . Wye* Dorothy visited the Wye Valley with her brother in July 1798; she is addressed in *Tintern Abbey* (pp. 407–11).

Samuel Taylor Coleridge (1772–1834)

While preparing the manuscript of his *Lectures on the English Poets* (1818) for publication, Hazlitt scribbled a note about a former friend that would not make it into the printed text:

> He is the earliest friend I ever had, and I will add to increase the obligation, that he is the only person from whom I ever learnt anything in conversation. He was the only person I ever knew who answered to my idea of a man of genius, and that idea at the time I first became acquainted with Mr. Coleridge was somewhat higher than it is at present. (Wu ii 379)

When he first met Coleridge in January 1798, Hazlitt fell in love with his intellect. He was always to feel let down by Coleridge's inability to fulfil his potential, almost as if it were one they were doomed to share. What he cannot have foreseen was that posterity would judge Coleridge to be one of the finest poets of their time, for just three remarkable works – 'The Ancient Mariner', 'Kubla Khan' and 'Christabel'.

Samuel Taylor Coleridge was the tenth and last child of the Reverend John Coleridge, the vicar of the village of Ottery St Mary and headmaster of the local grammar school. Although he died when his youngest son was only 8, John Coleridge had by then filled him with an unquenchable love of ideas and books (see Coleridge's letter to Poole, pp. 618–19). Shortly after his father's death, Coleridge was sent to Christ's Hospital in the City of London, where he was to meet his lifelong friend, Charles Lamb (see *This Lime-Tree Bower my Prison* and headnote to Lamb, pp. 735–9). As a Grecian (a member of the highest class), he benefited from an excellent education in the classics, although the techniques used to impart such skills were by modern standards less than humane.[1]

Coleridge had a turbulent time at Jesus College, Cambridge, where he matriculated in 1791 at the age of 19. It was here that he began to espouse republicanism and became interested in the brand of Unitarianism promoted by the Reverend Joseph Priestley, more famous today for his scientific experiments with electricity and gases than for his theological writings. (Among other things, his experiments with what he called 'phlogiston' led to the discovery of oxygen.) While he was at Cambridge Coleridge became a supporter of William Frend, whose *Peace and Union* (1793), a pamphlet advocating parliamentary reform and increased suffrage, led to its author's expulsion from the University. In the midst of this, Coleridge joined the King's Light Dragoons under the name Silas Tomkyn Comberbache (S.T.C.). It took six weeks and the strenuous efforts of his brother George to gain his release – by no means a straightforward procedure, one for which certain formalities had to be observed. After an unofficial payment of 25 guineas, the Regimental Muster Roll recorded: 'discharged S. T. Comberbache, Insane; 10 April 1794.'

In June Coleridge met Robert Southey, at that time an undergraduate at Balliol College, Oxford.

Notes

1 His teacher, the Revd James Boyer (or Bowyer) was an enthusiastic flogger; see Rosemary Ashton, *The Life of Samuel Taylor Coleridge* (1996), pp. 20–1.

Southey's achievements included having edited *The Flagellant*, an anti-flogging journal, at Westminster School, which had led swiftly to his expulsion. He was now engaged on *Joan of Arc*, an epic poem of which 10,000 lines had already been consigned to the fire for being so bad. Together they devised a radical political scheme called 'pantisocracy' – a word deriving from the Greek *pant-isocratia*, an all-equal society.[2] Together with Southey's College friend Robert Lovell, they planned to establish a commune on the banks of the Susquehanna, where Priestley had emigrated in April 1794. Coleridge and Southey hoped that twelve married couples could be converted to pantisocratic ideals, and would embark from Bristol for America in April 1795. In this society owning no property, the men would each contribute £125 to a common fund, and labour on a land-holding for two or three hours a day. As a first step it was decided that they would get married. Lovell had already married Mary Fricker, whose widowed mother kept a dress-shop in Bristol. Mary had two sisters; Southey would marry the third sister, Edith, while Coleridge would marry the eldest, Sara.

Pantisocracy was a product of the moment. It would not survive the pressure of the adult world, and the much hoped-for emigration to America never took place. All the same, Coleridge married Sara on 4 October 1795, something he would later regret. They were temperamentally ill-suited; she took no part in his intellectual life, and resented the increasing amounts of time he devoted to his work, much of which was conducted away from home. All the same, they were happy at the outset, Coleridge recording in a letter to his friend Thomas Poole that he was 'united to the woman whom I love best of all created beings . . . Mrs Coleridge – MRS COLERIDGE!! – I like to *write* the name' (Griggs ii 160). She is a key figure in Coleridge's poems of this period, notably *The Eolian Harp, Reflections on Having Left a Place of Retirement* and *This Lime-Tree Bower my Prison* (see pp. 600–5, 606–8, 612–17).

The mid-1790s were a period of frenetic activity. Coleridge delivered lectures expounding his philosophical and religious beliefs in Bristol in 1795, and founded and largely wrote his own periodical, *The Watchman*, in 1796. A cornerstone of his thesis was that the millennium – Christ's thousand-year rule on earth – was nigh, and that the French Revolution was a herald of it: 'Speed it, oh Father! Let thy Kingdom come!' he wrote in the final line of *Reflections on Having Left a Place of Retirement.* Humanity would not be able to resist these redemptive forces, and all would be united in a common apprehension of good. In times as cynical as our own, it is hard to understand how anyone could invent theories so wildly idealistic, but Coleridge was typical of his generation in wishing to do so. They had watched the French Revolution, which had promised so much, go sour; now they wanted to see whether there were other, non-violent means by which its ideals of *liberté, egalité* and *fraternité* might be achieved.

His year of intense association with Wordsworth and Dorothy began in July 1797 when Coleridge brought them from Dorset to live a few miles down the road from his cottage in Nether Stowey at Alfoxden House near Holford (see p. 612). Wordsworth's influence registered immediately in *This Lime-Tree Bower my Prison,* which contains an element new to Coleridge's writing: love of nature. At its conclusion he is no longer the self-pitying solitary, 'Lamed by the scathe of fire' (as he has it in the earliest text), but is solaced by the awareness of natural

Notes

[2] For more on the origins of this, see Nicholas Roe, *The Politics of Nature: William Wordsworth and Some Contemporaries* (2nd edn, Basingstoke, 2002), chapter 2.

beauty even in that most unlovely of birds, 'the last rook', on which he bestows a blessing. The emotional arc from pensiveness to consolation is traced also in 'Frost at Midnight' and 'Dejection: An Ode'.

'Fears in Solitude' (the title of which aptly describes the usual starting-point of the conversation poems) brings together the joint concerns of politics and morality. Its central preoccupation is the fear that the British have become, as Coleridge puts it, 'A selfish, lewd, effeminated race', and that in their decadence they have declared war not merely on Revolutionary France, but on God and the natural world. As an emblem of this, he imagines:

> Boys and girls,
> And women that would groan to see a child
> Pull off an insect's leg – all read of war,
> The best amusement for our morning meal!
> (ll. 101–4)

At a time of national emergency, this was tantamount to announcing one's support for the enemy, and it is little wonder, given the repressiveness of Pitt's government, that a spy was sent to investigate the possibility that Coleridge and the Wordsworths were in league with them.[3]

By the time he composed 'Fears in Solitude', Coleridge knew that it was written in the same manner as 'The Eolian Harp', 'Reflections on Having Left a Place of Retirement' and 'This Lime-Tree Bower' – *sermoni propiora*, ('more like conversation'), as he puts it in the epigraph of 'Reflections'. These 'conversation poems' were written as 'a sort of middle thing between poetry and oratory' – unabashed about moralizing in a style that was almost prosaic. Although he sometimes sounds apologetic about them, they are now regarded as among his finest work.

It is a mark of his versatility that at the time he was writing them, he was also capable of writing

Figure 11 Samuel Taylor Coleridge (1772–1834) by Peter Vandyke, 1795. At the time this portrait was made, Coleridge was delivering radical lectures in Bristol, and was shortly to form the most important friendship of his life, with Wordsworth. (National Portrait Gallery, London.)

three great poems that have a distinct rhetorical style, and which take an utterly different view of our place in the cosmos. The first of them, 'The Ancient Mariner', is presented here in both the 1798 version (published in *Lyrical Ballads*, see pp. 332–49) and that of 1817 – the first to introduce the marginal glosses which serve as both a commentary and a counterpoint to the narrative (see pp. 694–711). Its protagonist continues to fascinate because he is such a potent emanation of our darker side. What is the cause of his woes? A thoughtless, random act of the kind committed by millions every day. The consequence is that his shipmates, none of whom is implicated, perish; he becomes the plaything of arbitrary forces beyond his comprehension; and when recounting these

Notes

[3] For more on this, see Nicholas Roe, *Wordsworth and Coleridge: The Radical Years* (Oxford, 1988), pp. 257–62.

events he brings misery upon whoever he meets. It is hard not to see it as a tale of everlasting damnation, set in an anarchic world dominated by chance and irrationality – that which the twentieth century was to make its own, in other words. At its conclusion Coleridge offers a platitude that is meant to reassure – 'And the dear God who loveth us, / He made and loveth all' (ll. 649–50) – leaving us with the challenge of reconciling it with what we have witnessed.

'Kubla Khan' is presented both in its earliest manuscript text and in the form in which it was published in 1816, with Coleridge's preface. It is like no other work either by Coleridge or any of his contemporaries. The Khan Kubla yearns for repose and peace, building a paradise to which he can retire – and yet, for all his worldly power, he cannot cleanse his garden of such unsettling elements as 'Ancestral voices prophesying war!' A poem that went no further would be remarkable enough, but it proceeds to step outside the narrative framework established at the outset to describe its author aspiring to build another kind of pleasure-dome, this time in air, inspired by 'an Abyssinian maid'.

When he published it Coleridge apologized for not having finished it, presenting it 'rather as a psychological curiosity than on the ground of any supposed *poetic* merits' (p. 619); in truth, it could never have been more complete than it is. Whatever his ambitions for it, 'Kubla Khan' stands as one of the most powerful poems of the Romantic period about the nature of creativity.

From Coleridge's perspective (and that of his contemporaries) 'Christabel' was also defective in being fragmentary. Only Part I was written in 1798; the remainder of what survives was completed by 1801. Its author had plans to conclude his strange adult fairy-tale, and it was on that basis that 'Christabel' was at one stage to have been included in *Lyrical Ballads* (1800). But he could not bring it to a resolution, and in any case, finished or not, it was too weird for Wordsworth. It remained in manuscript for years, being read by Coleridge to horrified social gatherings, until Byron, having attended one such reading, instructed his publisher John Murray to put it into print immediately. Anxious to keep the most lucrative best-seller in the stable happy, Murray obliged. It was almost universally panned, perhaps not surprisingly. No one quite knew how to take such a dark tale, particularly one that lacked 'an ending'.

'Christabel' is a masterpiece. Its plot does not need resolving – at least not in the heavy-handed manner Coleridge proposed (see p. 655n45) – because it depends not on the intricacies of narrative, but on the powerful forces that drive its characters. It is no accident that the poem's protagonist has a name bringing together two suffering innocents from the Bible (Christ/Abel), nor that the 'hissing sound' she emits in Part II indicates her possession by whatever evil spirit Geraldine represents. Its key event is the stripping of Geraldine before she gets into bed with Christabel:

> Behold! her bosom and half her side –
> A sight to dream of, not to tell!
> And she is to sleep by Christabel.
>
> (ll. 246–8)

Christabel is not to be saved; the reader can only bear witness to a sexual act held by the poem to be unspeakable. The nature of what Coleridge is trying to discuss is clearer in the manuscript, where we are told that Geraldine's side is 'lean and old and foul of hue', a detail excised in the published text. It was none other than Hazlitt who pointed out in his review that this line 'is necessary to make common sense of the first and second part'.[4] What he meant was that Coleridge's focus is less on the sexual element (although that is not glossed over) as on the fact that Geraldine is a contaminating, snake-like presence that is to take another victim.

In some ways the most important product of 1797–8 was another fragmentary work: *The Recluse*. It was the most ambitious poem Coleridge would never write. For some time he had planned an epic poem about man, nature and society entitled *The Brook*, an amplification and development of *Religious Musings* (1794–6). But his love and regard for Wordsworth was such that he 'gave' it to him, believing him the only person capable of writing it. Many of its central theories – such as its reworking of the idealist philosophy of Berkeley and the associationist thought of Hartley – went straight into Wordsworth's poems of that moment; see for instance 'The Ruined Cottage', 'The Pedlar' and 'Not Useless do I Deem' (pp. 422–35, 435–44, 444–7). But the tragedy of Wordsworth's career was that he would never be able to complete it. He hoped, when he published *The Excursion* (1814), that it would be understood to be 'the second part of a long and laborious work, which is to consist of three parts'[5] (that is, *The Recluse*), but Coleridge was disappointed with it, and his letter to Wordsworth of 1815 (pp. 689–91) explicates the mind-boggling ambitions of the poem that would never be – far too grandiose for anyone, however gifted, to have written.

Though an exhilarating period, the year of close association with the Wordsworths was precarious. Coleridge lived on very little, with a growing family to support. In December 1797 the Wedgwood brothers sent him a gift of £100, but Coleridge returned it, saying that he needed a secure income. Instead, he took the post of a Unitarian minister and travelled to Shrewsbury, where he delivered a sermon on 14 January 1798. Here he met the young William Hazlitt, who describes their first meeting in 'My First Acquaintance with Poets' (pp. 771–84). A career as a clergyman might have brought the close working relationship with Wordsworth to a premature conclusion had it not been for the Wedgwoods. Having spent the night at Hazlitt's home in Wem, Coleridge received a letter from them offering him an annuity of £150 a year for life (£9000 / US$16,500 today) were he to devote himself to poetry and philosophy. Two days later he wrote to accept, and returned to Stowey, via the Wedgwoods, in early February.

With Wordsworth, Coleridge devised the *Lyrical Ballads* principally as a means of raising money to visit Germany, which they believed to be the centre of the intellectual world and therefore the most appropriate place for the poet of 'The Recluse' to gather his materials. At first Coleridge expected to write as many poems for it as Wordsworth, but he could not write them. Instead he quarried two extracts from his play, *Osorio*, and sent them to Wordsworth with 'The Ancient Mariner' and 'The Nightingale', neither of which was written specifically for *Lyrical Ballads*.

Despite this bout of writer's block, his close association with Wordsworth during 1797–8 was euphoric, as the high quality of Coleridge's poetry testifies. It could not last. His worsening addiction to opium, a marriage in decline and increasing emotional frustration would first destroy his creativity, then his friendship with the Wordsworths.

When he composed 'A Letter to Sara Hutchinson' in April 1802, Coleridge was at odds with his wife and hopelessly in love with Sara Hutchinson (who would become Wordsworth's sister-in-law); within hours of its composition, he would sit up all night encouraging Wordsworth

Notes

[4] Wu ix 24.

[5] *Prose Works* iii 5.

to propose marriage to Mary Hutchinson. That would always pain him because he could not help but feel jealous at his inability to take the same step with regard to Sara. The enduring misery of his 'coarse domestic life' made him increasingly bitter. That, combined with frequent bouts of illness and dependence on opium, led him increasingly to resent Wordsworth's stable and satisfying home life. He solaced himself with the thought of how, in happier times he, Sara and Mary sat together in front of the fire – an incident recalled in 'The Day-Dream', 'A Letter to Sara Hutchinson' and 'A Day-Dream'. But as the years passed even that memory failed to compensate him for the suspicion that Wordsworth had cheated him of happiness, and in December 1806 he would believe he had seen him and Sara Hutchinson in bed together: 'An hour and more with [Wordsworth] in bed – O agony!'[6] Whether or not this horrific vision was opium-induced, his response was typically extreme, and it served only to deepen his resentment over time. Even before this, the strains between them are evident in such poems as 'Spots in the Sun' (p. 684) and Wordsworth's 'A Complaint' (p. 572).

Coleridge's last conversation poem is a final, valiant attempt to resist the various enemies that were destroying both the friendship and his ability to write poetry. 'To William Wordsworth', edited here from the earliest complete manuscript, is his immediate response to the *Thirteen-Book Prelude,* which he heard its author recite in January 1807. He was one of the few to have read it in its entirety, as it would remain unpublished until after Wordsworth's death. For all the mutual distrust, Coleridge was profoundly impressed by it, and he poured all the energy he could into this celebration of poetic vigour, in an attempt to do justice to 'A tale divine of high and passionate thoughts / To their own music chaunted!' (ll. 39–40). *The Prelude* is hailed as ultimate proof, were any needed, that Wordsworth was truly the author of 'The Recluse'. Coleridge could not have been more wrong. Wordsworth had probably never been capable of writing 'The Recluse', except perhaps for a few optimistic weeks or months in 1798. Neither of them could accept that, and only with the passing of many years would the painful truth begin to dawn.

Given the complications that crept into their friendship, it is remarkable that they remained on close terms for as long as they did. In 1810 a mutual friend, Basil Montagu, falsely told Coleridge that Wordsworth had asked him to say that he had been a complete nuisance to his family because he was a 'rotten drunkard'. Wordsworth disclaimed the remark as soon as he heard of it, but the misunderstandings of earlier years made it impossible for Coleridge either to forget or forgive. Wordsworth visited London in 1812 to effect a reconciliation, but without success. Despite the intercession of several mutual acquaintances, frequent meetings in London and a joint tour of the continent in 1822, they would never recapture the closeness they had once enjoyed.

Coleridge's later years were mitigated by the generosity of James Gillman, a doctor, and his wife, who took him in as a house guest at their Highgate home from April 1816 until his death in 1834. Their aim was to regulate his intake of opium and thus help him become more productive. They succeeded. Their loving care prolonged his life, helping to give him the time and energy with which to work. A series of long prose works followed, many of which he dictated to amanuenses: *The Statesman's Manual* (1816), lectures on Shakespeare, Milton, Dante, Spenser, Ariosto,and Cervantes (1819), lectures on philosophy (1818–19), *Aids to Reflection* (1825) and *On the Constitution of Church and State* (1829). This was a remarkable achievement for someone

Notes

[6] *Notebooks* iii 3328.

whose health was so fragile. In addition, Coleridge continued his correspondence and notebooks, and even found time to dictate his extensive *Opus Maximum*, the crowning achievement of his later years. And amidst all this, he managed to compose short poems that rank with his best, such as 'Constancy to an Ideal Object' (pp. 711–12).[7] Contrary to his being the underachiever ridiculed by Hazlitt, Coleridge managed to produce numerous works of prose and poetry on a scale realized only with completion of the Collected Coleridge Edition in 2002.

Further reading

The Collected Works of Samuel Taylor Coleridge is Bollingen Series LXXV, published by Princeton University Press and Routledge in 2002.

Coleridge: The Ancient Mariner and Other Poems ed. Alun R. Jones and William M. Tydeman (London, 1973).

Samuel Taylor Coleridge: Poems ed. John Beer (2nd edn, London, 1993).

Rosemary Ashton, *The Life of Samuel Taylor Coleridge: A Critical Biography* (Oxford, 1996).

Walter Jackson Bate, *Coleridge* (London, 1968).

John Beer, *Coleridge the Visionary* (London, 1959).

John Beer, *Coleridge's Poetic Intelligence* (London, 1977).

The Cambridge Companion to Coleridge ed. Lucy Newlyn (Cambridge, 2002).

Richard Holmes, *Coleridge: Early Visions* (London, 1982).

Richard Holmes, *Coleridge: Darker Reflections* (London, 1998).

Molly Lefebure, *Samuel Taylor Coleridge: A Bondage of Opium* (London, 1974).

Thomas McFarland, *Coleridge and the Pantheist Tradition* (Oxford, 1969).

Samuel Taylor Coleridge and the Sciences of Life ed. Nicholas Roe (Oxford, 2001).

Seamus Perry, *Coleridge and the Uses of Division* (Oxford, 1999).

Nicholas Roe, *Wordsworth and Coleridge: The Radical Years* (Oxford, 1988).

Susan J. Wolfson, *Formal Charges: The Shaping of Poetry in British Romanticism* (Stanford, Calif., 1997), chapter 3.

A journal dedicated to Coleridge, *The Coleridge Bulletin*, is published twice a year by the Friends of Coleridge.

Sonnet V. To the River Otter[1] (composed between 1793 and 1796)

From Sonnets from Various Authors (1796)[2]

Dear native brook, wild streamlet of the west![3]
 How many various-fated years have passed,
 What blissful and what anguished hours, since last
I skimmed the smooth thin stone along thy breast,
 Numbering its light leaps! Yet so deep impressed
 Sink the sweet scenes of childhood, that mine eyes
I never shut amid the sunny blaze,
 But straight with all their tints thy waters rise,
Thy crossing plank, thy margin's willowy maze,
 And bedded sand that, veined with various dyes,

Notes

[7] For useful commentary on this poem, see Susan Wolfson, *Formal Charges: The Shaping of Poetry in British Romanticism* (1997), pp. 92–5.

Sonnet V. To the River Otter

[1] Coleridge was born at Ottery St Mary in Devon on the River Otter.

[2] In 1796 Coleridge published a short pamphlet of sonnets by himself, Charlotte Smith, Bowles and Warton, among others. This sonnet is indebted to nativity sonnets by two eighteenth-century poets: Warton's 'To the River Lodon' and Bowles's 'To the Itchin'.

[3] *the west* i.e. the west of England.

Gleamed through thy bright transparence to the gaze!
Visions of childhood, oft have ye beguiled
Lone manhood's cares, yet waking fondest sighs –
Ah, that once more I were a careless child!

Letter from S. T. Coleridge to George Dyer,[1] *10 March 1795* (extract)

There is one sentence in your last letter which affected me greatly: 'I feel a degree of languor, etc. etc., and, by seeing and frequently feeling much illiberality, acquire something of misanthropy'! It is melancholy to think that the best of us are liable to be shaped and coloured by surrounding objects – and a demonstrative proof that man was not made to live in great cities![2] Almost all the physical evil in the world depends on the existence of moral evil, and the long-continued contemplation of the latter does not tend to meliorate[3] the human heart. The pleasures which we receive from rural beauties are of little consequence compared with the moral effect of these pleasures;[4] beholding constantly the best possible, we at last become ourselves the best possible. In the country, all around us smile good and beauty, and the images of this divine καλοκἀγαθοῦ[5] are miniatured on the mind of the beholder as a landscape on a convex mirror.[6] Thomson,[7] in that most lovely poem, *The Castle of Indolence*, says,

I care not, Fortune, what you me deny –
You cannot rob me of free nature's grace!
You cannot shut the windows of the sky
Through which the morning shows her dewy face;
You cannot bar my constant feet to rove
Through wood and vale by living stream at eve . . . [8]

Alas, alas! She *can* deny us all this, and can force us, fettered and handcuffed by our dependencies and wants, to *wish* and *wish* away the bitter little of life in the felon-crowded dungeon of a great city!

God love you, my very dear sir! I would that we could form a pantisocracy[9] in England and that you could be one of us! The finely-fibred heart that, like the statue of Memnon,[10] trembles into melody on the sunbeam touch of benevolence, is most easily jarred into the dissonance of misanthropy. But you will never suffer your feelings to be benumbed by the torpedo touch of that fiend – I know you, and know that you will drink of every mourner's sorrows even while your own cup is trembling over its brink!

Notes

LETTER FROM S. T. COLERIDGE TO GEORGE DYER

[1] Coleridge met Dyer in London in August 1794, when he persuaded him of the merits of pantisocracy ('he was enraptured – pronounced it impregnable' Griggs i 98).

[2] *man was not made . . . cities* Dyer lived in London.

[3] *meliorate* improve.

[4] *The pleasures . . . pleasures* It was always important to Coleridge that love of nature had an improving moral effect on the individual. It would be amplified and reworked by Wordsworth into the central principle of *The Recluse*: that love of nature leads to love of mankind (see Wordsworth, 'Not Useless do I Deem', pp. 444–7).

[5] καλοκἀγαθῦ nobility and beauty.

[6] *as a landscape on a convex mirror* The Claude Lorraine Glass was a dark or coloured hand-mirror, used by picturesque tourists to reflect the features of the landscape in subdued tones.

[7] James Thomson (1700–48), author of *The Seasons*, a loco-descriptive poem.

[8] *The Castle of Indolence* ii 19–24.

[9] *pantisocracy* Coleridge and Southey wished to go to America and set up an ideal society in which everyone was equal and all possessions were shared (see p. 593).

[10] *like the statue of Memnon* The statue of Memnon at Thebes in Egypt was believed to give forth a musical sound when touched by the dawn or the setting sun.

Effusion XXXV. Composed 20 August 1795, at Clevedon, Somersetshire[1]

From Poems on Various Subjects (1796)

My pensive Sara,[2] thy soft cheek reclined
Thus on mine arm, most soothing sweet it is
To sit beside our cot, our cot o'ergrown
With white-flowered jasmine and the broad-leaved myrtle[3]
Meet emblems they of innocence and love),
And watch the clouds that late were rich with light
Slow-sad'ning round, and mark the star of eve
Serenely brilliant (such should wisdom be)
Shine opposite! How exquisite the scents
Snatched from yon bean-field! And the world *so* hushed!
The stilly murmur of the distant sea
Tells us of silence. And that simplest lute
Placed lengthways in the clasping casement – hark
How by the desultory breeze caressed![4]
Like some coy maid half-yielding to her lover,
It pours such sweet upbraidings as must needs
Tempt to repeat the wrong. And now its strings
Boldlier swept, the long sequacious[5] notes
Over delicious surges sink and rise,
Such a soft floating witchery of sound
As twilight elfins make when they at eve
Voyage on gentle gales from fairyland,
Where melodies round honey-dropping flowers
Footless and wild, like birds of paradise,
Nor pause nor perch, hov'ring on untamed wing.

Notes

[1] This has come to be regarded as the first of the conversation poems. It is presented here alongside its much later, canonical version, entitled 'The Eolian Harp'. When first published in 1796 it was called 'Effusion XXXV' because Coleridge wanted to number his poems as 'effusions' (inspired outpourings); it was not published under that title again.

[2] *Sara* Sara Fricker, with whom Coleridge was in love. He was to marry her less than two months after this poem was composed, on 4 October 1795. In early August he told Southey that 'Domestic happiness is the greatest of things sublunary – and of things celestial it is perhaps impossible for unassisted man to believe anything greater' (Griggs i 158).

[3] *white-flowered jasmine and the broad-leaved myrtle* In Milton's poem Adam and Eve's 'blissful bower' also contains jasmine and myrtle (see *Paradise Lost* iv 694 698).

[4] The Aeolian harp is a stringed instrument placed in front of an open window so as to catch the breeze; it is not unlike modern wind-chimes.

[5] *sequacious* following one another in unvarying regularity of order.

The Eolian Harp. Composed at Clevedon, Somersetshire[1]

From Poetical Works (1834)

My pensive Sara, thy soft cheek reclined
Thus on mine arm, most soothing sweet it is
To sit beside our cot, our cot o'ergrown
With white-flowered jasmine and the broad-leaved myrtle
(Meet emblems they of innocence and love),
And watch the clouds that late were rich with light
Slow-sad'ning round, and mark the star of eve
Serenely brilliant (such should wisdom be)
Shine opposite! How exquisite the scents
Snatched from yon bean-field! And the world so hushed!
The stilly murmur of the distant sea
Tells us of silence.
And that simplest lute
Placed lengthways in the clasping casement – hark
How by the desultory breeze caressed!
Like some coy maid half-yielding to her lover,
It pours such sweet upbraidings as must needs
Tempt to repeat the wrong. And now its strings
Boldlier swept, the long sequacious notes
Over delicious surges sink and rise,
Such a soft floating witchery of sound
As twilight elfins make when they at eve
Voyage on gentle gales from fairyland,
Where melodies round honey-dropping flowers
Footless and wild, like birds of paradise,
Nor pause nor perch, hovering on untamed wing.
Oh the one life within us and abroad,[2]
Which meets all motion and becomes its soul,
A light in sound, a sound-like power in light,
Rhythm in all thought, and joyance everywhere –
Methinks it should have been impossible
Not to love all things in a world so filled,
Where the breeze warbles, and the mute still air
Is Music slumbering on its instrument![3]

Notes

[1] It is worth noting that *c.*1800 Coleridge meditated the image of the Aeolian harp in a marginal note to his copy of Kant's *Critik der reinen Vernunft*:

> The mind does not resemble an Eolian harp, nor even a barrel-organ turned by a stream of water, conceive as many tunes mechanized in it as you like – but rather, as far as objects are concerned, a violin, or other instrument of few strings yet vast compass, played on by a musician of genius.

[2] *Oh the one life . . . abroad* it is perhaps surprising to find that ll. 26–33 were written not in 1795 but in 1817 (see next note). Coleridge's celebration of the pantheist One Life echoes Wordsworth, *The Pedlar* 217–18: 'for in all things / He saw one life, and felt that it was joy'.

[3] Lines 26–33 comprise the most substantial addition to this version of the poem; they were first published in the errata to *Sibylline Leaves* (1817). Lines 32–3 as published in 1817, uncorrected by the errata, read: 'Where even the breezes, and the common air, / Contain the power and spirit of Harmony.'

And thus, my love, as on the midway slope
Of yonder hill I stretch my limbs at noon,
Whilst through my half-closed eyelids I behold
The sunbeams dance, like diamonds, on the main,
And tranquil muse upon tranquillity,
Full many a thought uncalled and undetained,
And many idle flitting fantasies
Traverse my indolent and passive brain –
As wild and various as the random gales
That swell or flutter on this subject lute!
And what if all of animated nature
Be but organic harps diversely framed,
That tremble into thought, as o'er them sweeps,
Plastic[6] and vast, one intellectual[7] breeze,
At once the soul of each, and God of all?[8]

Notes

[6] *Plastic* shaping, formative, creative. It is important to Coleridge that God's spiritual influence shape the sensibility of the beings it enters.

[7] *intellectual* spiritual.

[8] *And what if all . . . all* A major pantheist declaration: 'And what if all natural things are like Aeolian harps, each unique and individual in itself ("diversely framed"), receiving, just as the harps receive the breeze, the spiritual ("intellectual") apprehension of the one God?' An early MS of the poem contains a more detailed and explicit version of ll. 36–40:

And what if all of animated life
Be but as instruments diversely framed,
That tremble into thought, while through them breathes
One infinite and intellectual breeze,
And all in different heights so aptly hung
That murmurs indistinct and bursts sublime,
Shrill discords and most soothing melodies,
Harmonious form Creation's vast concért?
Thus God would be the universal soul,
Mechanized matter as th' organic harps,
And each one's tunes be that which each calls 'I'.

And thus, my love, as on the midway slope
Of yonder hill I stretch my limbs at noon,
Whilst through my half-closed eyelids I behold
The sunbeams dance, like diamonds, on the main,
And tranquil muse upon tranquillity,
Full many a thought uncalled and undetained,
And many idle flitting fantasies
Traverse my indolent and passive brain –
As wild and various as the random gales
That swell and flutter on this subject lute!
And what if all of animated nature
Be but organic harps diversely framed,
That tremble into thought, as o'er them sweeps,
Plastic and vast, one intellectual breeze,
At once the soul of each, and God of all?

But thy more serious eye a mild reproof
Darts, oh beloved woman![9] – nor such thoughts
Dim and unhallowed dost thou not reject,
And biddest me walk humbly with my God.
Meek daughter in the family of Christ,[10]
Well hast thou said and holily dispraised[11]
These shapings of the unregenerate mind,
Bubbles that glitter as they rise and break
On vain philosophy's aye-babbling spring.[12]
For never guiltless may I speak of Him,
Th' INCOMPREHENSIBLE! save when with awe
I praise him, and with faith that inly[13] *feels* –
Who with his saving mercies healed me,
A sinful and most miserable man
Wildered and dark, and gave me to possess
Peace, and this cot,[14] and thee, heart-honoured maid!

Notes

[9] *But thy . . . woman* Referring to these lines, Lamb told Coleridge that he and his sister enjoyed the 'pleasing picture of Mrs C. checking your wild wanderings, which we were so fond of hearing you indulge when among us. It has endeared us more than anything to your good lady, and your own self-reproof that follows delighted us' (Marrs i 12).

[10] *Meek daughter . . . Christ* Coleridge's language is, of course, figurative. Sara's father was a Bristol manufacturer who died bankrupt in 1786, leaving his wife and six children penniless. Sara's mother ran a dress shop.

[11] *holily dispraised* piously attacked. Coleridge's unease about the pantheist experience of ll. 36–40 is transferred completely to Sara.

[12] *Bubbles . . . spring* Can Sara really have thought all this so early in her relationship with Coleridge? He attributes to her the criticisms that he is 'vain' (impractical) and 'aye-babbling'.

[13] ' "L'athée n'est point à mes yeux un faux esprit; je puis vivre avec lui aussi bien et mieux qu'avec le dévot, car il raisonne davantage, mais il lui manque un sens, et mon âme ne se fond point entièrement avec la sienne: il est froid au spectacle le plus ravissant, et il cherche un syllogisme lorsque je rends une action de grâce." *Appel à l'impartiale postérité, par la Citoyenne Roland*, troisième partie, p. 67' (Coleridge's note to the 1796 text, dropped from versions of the poem after 1803). 'The atheist is not, to my eyes, deceived; I can live with him as well as – if not better than with – the zealot, because he reasons more. But he is lacking in a certain sense, and my soul does not entirely combine with his: he is untouched by the most ravishing spectacle, and searches for a syllogism when I thank God.' French copies of Madame Roland's memoirs were available in England by late July 1795; their popularity led to an English translation later that year, published by Joseph Johnson (who had published Wordsworth's *An Evening Walk* in 1793, and who would publish *Frost at Midnight* in 1798).

[14] *cot* cottage.

But thy more serious eye a mild reproof
Darts, oh beloved woman! – nor such thoughts
Dim and unhallowed dost thou not reject,
And biddest me walk humbly with my God.
Meek daughter in the family of Christ,
Well hast thou said and holily dispraised
These shapings of the unregenerate mind,
Bubbles that glitter as they rise and break
On vain philosophy's aye-babbling spring.
For never guiltless may I speak of Him,
Th' Incomprehensible! save when with awe
I praise him, and with faith that inly feels –
Who with his saving mercies healed me,
A sinful and most miserable man
Wildered and dark, and gave me to possess
Peace, and this cot, and thee, heart-honoured maid!

Reflections on having left a Place of Retirement (composed March–April 1796)[1]

From Poems (1797)

'Sermoni propiora'. – Horace.[2]

Low was our pretty cot;[3] our tallest rose
Peeped at the chamber-window. We could hear
At silent noon, and eve, and early morn,
The sea's faint murmur. In the open air
Our myrtles blossomed, and across the porch
Thick jasmines twined;[4] the little landscape round
Was green and woody and refreshed the eye.[5]
It was a spot which you might aptly call
The Valley of Seclusion. Once I saw
(Hallowing his sabbath-day by quietness)
A wealthy son of commerce saunter by,
Bristowa's[6] citizen; methought it calmed
His thirst of idle gold, and made him muse
With wiser feelings – for he paused and looked
With a pleased sadness, and gazed all around,
Then eyed our cottage, and gazed round again,
And sighed, and said it was a blessed place.
And we *were* blessed. Oft with patient ear,
Long-listening to the viewless skylark's note
(Viewless, or haply for a moment seen
Gleaming on sunny wing), in whispered tones
I've said to my beloved, 'Such,[7] sweet girl,
The inobtrusive song of happiness,
Unearthly minstrelsy – then only heard
When the soul seeks to hear, when all is hushed
And the heart listens!'
                                        But the time when first
From that low dell, steep up the stony mount
I climbed with perilous toil and reached the top –
Oh, what a goodly scene! *Here* the bleak mount,

Notes

REFLECTIONS ON HAVING LEFT A PLACE OF RETIREMENT

[1] During the spring of 1796 Coleridge was working industriously on *The Watchman*, his own journal, for which he wrote much of its contents. He had married Sara Fricker the previous October, and honeymooned with her at a cottage in Clevedon, Somerset. When first published this poem was entitled *Reflections on entering into active life. A poem which affects not to be poetry.*

[2] From *Satires* I iv 42. In a note to *Fears in Solitude* (1798), Coleridge was to write: 'The above is perhaps not poetry but rather a sort of middle thing between poetry and oratory – *sermoni propiora*. Some parts are, I am conscious, too tame even for animated prose.'

[3] *cot* cottage.

[4] *myrtles . . . jasmines* 'Meet emblems they of innocence and love', *Eolian Harp* 5.

[5] *the little landscape . . . eye* cf. Coleridge's letter to Poole, 7 October 1795: 'The prospect around us is perhaps more various than any in the kingdom – Mine Eye gluttonizes. – The Sea – the distant Islands! – the opposite Coasts! – I shall assuredly write Rhymes' (Griggs i 160).

[6] *Bristowa's* Bristol's.

[7] *Such* i.e. similar to this (the skylark's song).

The bare bleak mountain speckled thin with sheep;
Grey clouds, that shadowing spot the sunny fields;
And river, now with bushy rocks o'erbrowed,
Now winding bright and full with naked banks;
And seats, and lawns, the abbey and the wood,
And cots, and hamlets, and faint city-spire;
The channel *there*, the islands and white sails,
Dim coasts, and cloudlike hills, and shoreless ocean –
It seemed like Omnipresence![8] God, methought,
Had built him there a temple: the whole world
Seemed *imaged* in its vast circumference.
No wish profaned my overwhelmed heart[9] –
Blessed hour! It was a luxury – to be!
   Ah, quiet dell, dear cot, and mount sublime!
I was constrained to quit you. Was it right,
While my unnumbered brethren toiled and bled,[10]
That I should dream away the trusted hours
On rose-leaf beds, pamp'ring the coward heart
With feelings all too delicate for use?
Sweet is the tear that from some Howard's[11] eye
Drops on the cheek of one he lifts from earth;
And he that works me good with unmoved face
Does it but half – he chills me while he aids –
My benefactor, not my brother man.[12]
Yet even this, this cold beneficence
Seizes my praise, when I reflect on those
(The sluggard pity's vision-weaving tribe!)
Who sigh for wretchedness, yet shun the wretched,
Nursing in some delicious solitude
Their slothful loves and dainty sympathies!
I therefore go and join head, heart and hand,
Active and firm, to fight the bloodless fight
Of Science,[13] Freedom, and the Truth in Christ.[14]
   Yet oft when after honourable toil
Rests the tired mind, and waking loves to dream,
My spirit shall revisit thee, dear cot!
Thy jasmine and thy window-peeping rose,

Notes

[8] *Omnipresence* the god-like perspective granted Coleridge from the top of the 'stony mount' is comparable with that of the visionary of *Religious Musings*, who 'Views all creation, and he loves it all / And blesses it' (ll. 126–7). This is the first poem by either Coleridge or Wordsworth to present the ascent of a mountain as a meeting with divine forces; compare the ascent of Snowdon, *Prelude* Book XIII (pp. 566–70).

[9] *No wish . . . heart* Any materialistic ambitions at such a moment of divine apprehension would be a kind of profanity.

[10] *While my . . . bled* Britain had been at war with France since 1793.

[11] John Howard (1726–90), prison reformer and philanthropist.

[12] *My benefactor . . . man* A spiritual affirmation of brotherhood is more desirable on its own than a good deed without it.

[13] *Science* knowledge, which would have included such things as chemistry.

[14] *I therefore . . . Christ* Coleridge was not actually going to sign up as a soldier; the 'bloodless fight' will consist of his editing of a new journal dedicated to the causes of Unitarianism and radical politics: *The Watchman*.

And myrtles fearless of the mild sea-air;
And I shall sigh fond wishes, sweet abode!
Ah, had none greater, and that all had such!
It might be so, but the time is not yet:
Speed it, oh Father! Let thy Kingdom come![15]

Religious Musings (extract) (composed 1794–6)[1]

From Poems (1797)

There is one Mind,[2] one omnipresent Mind
Omnific.[3] His most holy name is LOVE –
Truth of subliming[4] import! with the which
Who feeds and saturates his constant soul,
He from his small particular orbit flies
With blessed outstarting![5] From himself he flies,
Stands in the sun, and with no partial gaze[6]
Views all creation, and he loves it all
And blesses it,[7] and calls it very good![8]
This is indeed to dwell with the most high –
Cherubs and rapture-trembling seraphim
Can press no nearer to th' Almighty's throne.
But that we roam unconscious, or with hearts
Unfeeling of our universal Sire,
And that in his vast family no Cain[9]
Injures uninjured (in her best-aimed blow
Victorious murder a blind suicide[10]),

Notes

[15] *Speed it . . . come* Coleridge looks forward to the millennium (Christ's thousand-year rule on earth), when all people will share his love of nature, and 'fond wishes'.

RELIGIOUS MUSINGS

[1] In this important poem the young Coleridge set out, though in very dense and frequently obscure terms, his central religious and political beliefs. He presents the French Revolution in terms of his expectation of the millennium (Christ's thousand-year rule on earth, thought to be nigh) and in this important extract explicates his Unitarian principles.

[2] *There is one Mind* Coleridge was a fervent Unitarian, and this opening remark expresses the central Unitarian belief in the absolute unity of the godhead.

[3] *Omnific* all-creating, as at *Paradise Lost* vii 217: ' "Silence, ye troubled waves, and thou Deep, peace", / Said then th' Omnific Word.'

[4] *subliming* exalting.

[5] *Who feeds . . . outstarting* He who feeds and saturates his soul in the truth that God is Love may transcend (outstart) his earthly state ('particular orbit').

[6] *with no partial gaze* i.e. with a vision as universal and all-embracing as that of God.

[7] *And blesses it* other Coleridgean blessings can be found in *The Ancient Mariner* (1798) 277 and *Frost at Midnight* (1798) 49 ff.

[8] *Views all . . . good* from Genesis 1: 31: 'And God saw every thing that he had made, and behold, it was very good.'

[9] *Cain* the son of Adam and Eve, who killed his brother Abel and brought murder into the world; see Genesis 4: 8.

[10] *Victorious murder a blind suicide* Because we are united in a common humanity, murder is as destructive of the aggressor as it is of the victim.

Haply for this some younger angel now
Looks down on human nature – and behold!
A sea of blood[11] bestrewed with wrecks where mad
Embattling interests on each other rush
With unhelmed rage![12]
'Tis the sublime of man,
Our noontide majesty,[13] to know ourselves
Parts and proportions of one wondrous whole;
This fraternizes[14] man, this constitutes
Our charities and bearings – but 'tis God
Diffused through all that doth make all one whole.[15]
This the worst superstition: Him except,
Aught to desire,[16] supreme reality,
The plenitude and permanence of bliss!
Oh fiends of superstition![17] – not that oft
Your pitiless rites have floated with man's blood
The skull-piled temple, not for this shall wrath
Thunder against you from the Holy One!
But (whether ye, th' unclimbing bigot, mock
With secondary gods, or if more pleased
Ye petrify th' imbrothelled atheist's heart[18] –
The atheist your worst slave) I o'er some plain
Peopled with death, and to the silent sun
Steaming with tyrant-murdered multitudes,
Or where mid groans and shrieks loud-laughing trade[19]
More hideous packs his bales of living anguish –
I will raise up a mourning, oh ye fiends,
And curse your spells that film the eye of faith,[20]
Hiding the present God, whose presence lost,
The moral world's cohesion, we become

Notes

[11] *A sea of blood* The image is from Revelation 16: 3.

[12] *A sea of blood . . . rage* During the period in which this poem was written, the Reign of Terror had come to an end with Robespierre's execution, and had given way to full-scale war as France had taken on the European allies (1793 onwards). As a committed republican, Coleridge was horrified by what he saw.

[13] *Our noontide majesty* the height of our spiritual existence.

[14] *fraternizes 'Fraternité'* was one of the ideals of the French Revolution. Coleridge believes our brotherhood to be affirmed by a collective perception of ourselves as part of the godhead.

[15] *'tis God . . . whole* a reiteration of the pantheist belief in a single divinity diffused through the universe; cf. *Eolian Harp* 36–40.

[16] *This the . . . desire* i.e the worst superstition is to desire anything except Him.

[17] *fiends of superstition* an attack on European Christians, who are responsible for using superstition as a means of perpetuating the slave trade.

[18] *th' imbrothelled atheist's heart* the atheist is, effectively, in the brothel of hell; for Thelwall's view of this phrase, see p. 322 above.

[19] *trade* the slave trade.

[20] *I o'er some plain . . . faith* It is not clear whether Coleridge has some specific event in mind, but in general terms he is saying that the present war between France and the allies is leading people to lose faith in God. The image of a film over the eyes echoes the conversion of Saul, the persecutor of the Christians, when 'there fell from his eyes as it had been scales' (Acts 9: 18).

An anarchy of spirits! Toy-bewitched,[21]
Made blind by lusts, disherited of soul,
No common centre man, no common sire
Knoweth![22] A sordid solitary thing,
Mid countless brethren with a lonely heart,
Through courts and cities the smooth savage roams
Feeling himself, his own low self the whole,
When he by sacred sympathy might make
The whole one self![23] Self, that no alien knows!
Self, far diffused as fancy's wing can travel!
Self, spreading still, oblivious of its own,
Yet all of all possessing! This is faith![24]
This the Messiah's destined victory!

Letter from S. T. Coleridge to John Thelwall,[1] *19 November 1796* (extract)

Your portrait of yourself interested me. As to me, my face, unless when animated by immediate eloquence, expresses great sloth and great (indeed almost idiotic) good nature. 'Tis a mere carcass of a face – fat, flabby, and expressive chiefly of inexpression. Yet I am told that my eyes, eyebrows, and forehead are physiognomically good,[2] but of this the deponent[3] knoweth not. As to my shape, 'tis a good shape enough if measured – but my gait is awkward, and the walk and the whole man indicates *indolence capable of energies*. I am, and ever have been, a great reader, and have read almost everything – a library-cormorant. I am deep in all out of the way books, whether of the monkish times or of the puritanical era.[4] I have read and digested most of the historical writers but I do not *like* history. Metaphysics and poetry and 'facts of mind' (i.e. accounts of all the strange phantasms that ever possessed your philosophy-dreamers[5] from Thoth the Egyptian[6] to Taylor the English pagan[7]) are my darling studies.

Notes

[21] *Toy-bewitched* seduced by idle pastimes.

[22] *An anarchy . . . Knoweth* Coleridge is attacking Godwinian thought, which he despised for its atheism and disapproval of marriage.

[23] *A sordid . . . self* Instead of enjoying the Unitarian perception of himself as part of the godhead, the Godwinian is a selfish moral degenerate.

[24] *Self, far diffused . . . Faith* Faith consists of self diffused through the world, integrated with the Unitarian God.

Letter from S. T. Coleridge to John Thelwall

[1] For Thelwall, see pp. 316–18. Coleridge first wrote to Thelwall in late April 1796, with the words: 'Pursuing the same end by the same means we ought not to be strangers to each other' (Griggs i 204). Coleridge probably meant their shared antipathy to private property, and their republicanism.

[2] *physiognomically good* i.e. that they indicate good character traits.

[3] *deponent* witness.

[4] *monkish times . . . era* i.e. from the Middle Ages to the seventeenth century.

[5] *philosophy-dreamers* visionaries.

[6] *Thoth the Egyptian* Thoth is the Greek name for Hermes Trismegistus, a mythological figure said to have founded the art of alchemy.

[7] *Taylor the English pagan* Thomas Taylor (1758–1835), classical scholar and Neoplatonist. Coleridge's copy of Taylor's translation of Plato's *Cratylus* (1793) was retained at Rydal Mount in later years.

In short, I seldom read except to amuse myself, and I am almost always reading. Of useful knowledge, I am a so-so chemist, and I love chemistry.[8] All else is blank, but I *will* be (please God) an horticulturist and a farmer.[9] I compose very little and I absolutely hate composition. Such is my dislike that even a sense of duty is sometimes too weak to overpower it.

I cannot breathe through my nose, so my mouth, with sensual thick lips, is almost always open. In conversation I am impassioned, and oppose what I deem error with an eagerness which is often mistaken for personal asperity[10] – but I am ever so swallowed up in the *thing*, that I perfectly forget my opponent. Such am I.

Notes

[8] *chemistry* One of Coleridge's greatest mentors, Joseph Priestley (1733–1804), the founder of modern Unitarianism, was an accomplished chemist and discovered oxygen.

[9] *an horticulturalist and a farmer* Coleridge enjoyed the theory, rather than the practice, of farming. He was a regular reader of the *Letters and Papers on Agriculture, Planting, etc., Selected from the Correspondence of the Bath and West of English Society.*

[10] *asperity* roughness, boisterousness.

Letter from S. T. Coleridge to Robert Southey, 17 July 1797 (including early version of *This Lime-Tree Bower My Prison*)[1] (extract)

. . . I am as much a Pangloss as ever – only less *contemptuous*, than I used to be, when I argue how unwise it is to feel contempt for any thing.[2]

I had been on a visit to Wordsworth's at Racedown near Crewkerne[3] – and I brought him and his sister back with me and here[4] I have settled them. By a combination of curious circumstances a gentleman's seat,[5] with a park and woods, elegantly and completely furnished, with nine lodging rooms, three parlours and a hall, in a most beautiful and romantic situation by the sea-side, four miles from Stowey – this we have got for Wordsworth at the rent of £23 *a year, taxes included*!! The park and woods are *his* for all purposes he wants them – i.e. he may walk, ride, and keep a horse in them, and the large gardens are altogether and entirely his. Wordsworth is a very great man – the only man to whom *at all times* and in *all modes of excellence* I feel myself inferior – the only one, I mean, whom I have yet met with[6] (for the London literati appear to me to be very much like little potatoes – i.e. no great things, a compost of nullity and dullity!).

Charles Lamb[7] has been with me for a week; he left me Friday morning. The second day after Wordsworth came to me, dear Sara accidentally emptied a skillet of boiling milk on my foot, which confined me during the whole time of C. Lamb's stay and still prevents me from all walks longer than a furlong. While Wordsworth, his sister, and C. Lamb were out one evening, sitting in the arbour of T. Poole's garden,[8] which communicates with mine, I wrote these lines, with which I am pleased.

Well, they are gone; and here must I remain,
Lamed by the scathe of fire,[9] lonely and faint,
This lime-tree bower my prison. They, meantime,
My friends, whom I may never meet again,[10]

Notes

LETTER FROM S. T. COLERIDGE TO ROBERT SOUTHEY,

[1] The earliest extant text of *This Lime-Tree Bower My Prison* survives in this revealing letter to Coleridge's former mentor, Robert Southey. The poem was first published in Southey's *Annual Anthology* (1800), as *This Lime-Tree Bower My Prison, A Poem Addressed to Charles Lamb of the India House, London*, but probably the best-known version is that in Coleridge's collected poetical works of 1834; see pp. 613–17. By this time some bitterness existed between Coleridge and Southey, thanks largely to the collapse of pantisocracy (see p. 593).

[2] *I am as much . . . thing* Pangloss was the eternal optimist of Voltaire's *Candide* (1759). Coleridge's emphatic respect for natural things represents a distinctively Wordsworthian way of thinking; he even echoes Wordsworth's *Lines Left Upon a Seat in A Yew-Tree* (composed by July 1797): 'he who feels contempt / For any living thing, hath faculties / Which he has never used' (ll. 48–50).

[3] *I had been . . . Crewkerne* Wordsworth and his sister had been resident at Racedown Lodge in Dorset since July 1795. Coleridge visited them there in June 1797.

[4] *here* i.e. at Alfoxden House, four miles away from where Coleridge lived at Nether Stowey, Somerset. It was here that Wordsworth's close association with Coleridge began to bear fruit: *The Ruined Cottage* (completed February 1798); *Lyrical Ballads* (composed spring–summer 1798); and blank verse fragments which later contributed to *The Prelude* and *The Excursion*.

[5] *seat* residence.

[6] *Wordsworth . . . met with* A loaded comment, as Coleridge had, only a few years before, idolized Southey in much the same way (see pp. 592–3).

[7] *Charles Lamb* Coleridge's friend since their shared schooldays at Christ's Hospital; for more on Lamb, see pp. 735–9.

[8] The incompatibility that was to ruin his marriage with Sara Fricker is evident even at this early moment: the claim that his injury had been accidental is questionable. The garden attached to Tom Poole's house adjoins that of Coleridge Cottage, as visitors can still observe today.

[9] *Lamed . . . fire* an interesting phrase, eliminated from subsequent versions of the poem, which prompts comparison of Coleridge with Vulcan, whose leg was broken when he was flung out of Olympus.

[10] *whom I may never meet again* an exaggeration; as he has just told Southey, Wordsworth and his sister had moved into Alfoxden House only days before. They would certainly remain for at least a year.

This Lime-Tree Bower My Prison[1]

From Poetical Works (1834)

In the June of 1797, some long-expected friends paid a visit to the author's cottage, and on the morning of their arrival he met with an accident which disabled him from walking during the whole time of their stay. One evening, when they had left him for a few hours, he composed the following lines in the garden bower.

Well, they are gone, and here must I remain,
This lime-tree bower my prison! I have lost
Beauties and feelings, such as would have been
Most sweet to my remembrance even when age
Had dimmed mine eyes to blindness! They, meanwhile,
Friends whom I never more may meet again,

Notes

THIS LIME-TREE BOWER MY PRISON

[1] This is the version of the poem that has entered the canon.

On springy[11] heath, along the hilltop edge,[12]
Wander delighted, and look down, perchance,
On that same rifted dell, where many an ash
Twists its wild limbs beside the ferny rock,
Whose plumy ferns[13] forever nod and drip
Sprayed by the waterfall. But chiefly thou,
My gentle-hearted Charles![14] – thou who hast pined
And hungered after nature many a year
In the great city pent, winning thy way,
With sad yet bowed soul, through evil and pain
And strange calamity.[15] Ah, slowly sink
Behind the western ridge, thou glorious sun!
Shine in the slant beams of the sinking orb,
Ye purple heath-flowers! Richlier burn, ye clouds!
Live in the yellow light, ye distant groves!
And kindle, thou blue ocean! So my friend,
Struck with joy's deepest calm, and gazing round
On the wide view, may gaze till all doth seem
Less gross than bodily,[16] a living thing
That acts upon the mind, and with such hues
As clothe the Almighty Spirit, when he makes
Spirits perceive His presence![17]

Notes

[11] 'Elastic, I mean' (Coleridge's note) – meaning, simply, that the furze and heather reassumes its original shape after having been trodden on. In the course of the poem the poet himself will reassume his original mood, having been depressed by the 'accident' and its consequences.

[12] *the hilltop edge* The Wordsworths and Lamb would have climbed up the Quantock Hills behind Coleridge's cottage.

[13] 'The ferns that grow in moist places, grow five or six together and form a complete "Prince of Wales' feather" – i.e. plumy' (Coleridge's note).

[14] *My gentle-hearted Charles!* 'For God's sake,' Lamb wrote to Coleridge, when the poem was published in 1800, 'don't make me ridiculous any more by terming me gentle-hearted in print, or do it in better verses . . . the meaning of "gentle" is equivocal at best, and almost always means "poor-spirited" ' (Marrs i 217–18).

[15] *strange calamity* In September 1796 Lamb's sister Mary stabbed their mother to death in a fit of insanity; see p. 737. Lamb had been working in East India House in the City of London since 1792.

[16] *Less gross than bodily* a difficult phrase, meaning, presumably, that the world becomes more spiritualized as Lamb gazes upon it, granting him the experience described in *Reflections upon Having Left a Place of Retirement* 26–42.

[17] 'You remember, I am a Berkeleian' (Coleridge's note). George Berkeley, Bishop of Cloyne (1685–1753), denied the existence of the material world in favour of an invisible world created by God, perceptible by human beings in moments of heightened vision.

On springy heath, along the hilltop edge,
Wander in gladness, and wind down, perchance,
To that still roaring dell of which I told;
The roaring dell, o'erwooded, narrow, deep,
And only speckled by the midday sun;
Where its slim trunk the ash from rock to rock
Flings arching like a bridge – that branchless ash,
Unsunned and damp, whose few poor yellow leaves
Ne'er tremble in the gale, yet tremble still,
Fanned by the waterfall! And there my friends
Behold the dark green file of long lank weeds,[2]
That all at once (a most fantastic sight!)
Still nod and drip beneath the dripping edge
Of the blue clay-stone.
Now, my friends emerge
Beneath the wide wide heaven – and view again
The many-steepled tract magnificent
Of hilly fields and meadows, and the sea,
With some fair bark, perhaps, whose sails light up
The slip of smooth clear blue betwixt two isles
Of purple shadow! Yes, they wander on
In gladness all – but thou, methinks, most glad,
My gentle-hearted Charles! For thou hast pined
And hungered after nature many a year
In the great city pent, winning thy way,
With sad yet patient soul, through evil and pain
And strange calamity! Ah, slowly sink
Behind the western ridge, thou glorious sun!
Shine in the slant beams of the sinking orb,
Ye purple heath-flowers! Richlier burn, ye clouds!
Live in the yellow light, ye distant groves!
And kindle, thou blue ocean! So my friend,
Struck with deep joy, may stand, as I have stood,
Silent with swimming sense; yea, gazing round
On the wide landscape, gaze till all doth seem
Less gross than bodily, and of such hues
As veil the Almighty Spirit, when yet he makes
Spirits perceive His presence.

Notes

[2] 'The Asplenium scolopendrium, called in some countries the Adder's tongue, in others the Hart's tongue; but Withering gives the Adder's tongue as the trivial name of the Ophioglossum only' (Coleridge's note). Coleridge and Wordsworth acquired copies of William Withering's *Arrangement of British Plants* (4 vols, 1796) in August 1800.

A delight
Comes sudden on my heart, and I am glad
As I myself were there! Nor in this bower
Want I sweet sounds or pleasing shapes. I watched
The sunshine of each broad transparent leaf
Broke by the shadows of the leaf or stem
Which hung above it; and that walnut tree
Was richly tinged; and a deep radiance lay
Full on the ancient ivy which usurps
Those fronting elms, and now with blackest mass
Makes their dark foliage gleam a lighter hue
Through the last twilight. And though the rapid bat
Wheels silent by, and not a swallow twitters,
Yet still the solitary humble-bee[18]
Sings in the bean-flower. Henceforth I shall know
That nature ne'er deserts the wise and pure;
No scene so narrow but may well employ
Each faculty of sense, and keep the heart
Awake to love and beauty.[19] And sometimes
'Tis well to be bereaved of promised good,
That we may lift the soul and contemplate
With lively joy the joys we cannot share.
My sister and my friends! when the last rook
Beat its straight path along the dusky air
Homewards, I blessed it, deeming its black wing
Crossed, like a speck, the blaze of setting day,
While ye stood gazing; or when all was still,
Flew creaking o'er your heads, and had a charm
For you, my sister and my friends, to whom
No sound is dissonant which tells of Life!

Notes

[18] *humble-bee* Against a copy of the 1817 printed text, Coleridge entered the following note: 'Cows without horns are called Hummel cows, in the country as the Hummel bee, as stingless (unless it be a corruption of *humming*, from the sound observable).'

[19] *Awake to love and beauty* at around this time Coleridge would describe how the 'wandering and distempered child' would be 'healed and harmonized / By the benignant touch of love and beauty' (*The Dungeon* 29–30).

A delight
Comes sudden on my heart, and I am glad
As I myself were there! Nor in this bower,
This little lime-tree bower, have I not marked
Much that has soothed me. Pale beneath the blaze
Hung the transparent foliage; and I watched
Some broad and sunny leaf, and loved to see
The shadow of the leaf and stem above
Dappling its sunshine! And that walnut tree
Was richly tinged, and a deep radiance lay
Full on the ancient ivy which *usurps*
Those fronting elms, and now with blackest mass
Makes their dark branches gleam a lighter hue
Through the late twilight; and though now the bat
Wheels silent by, and not a swallow twitters,
Yet still the solitary humble-bee
Sings in the bean-flower! Henceforth I shall know
That nature ne'er deserts the wise and pure –
No scene so narrow but may well employ
Each faculty of sense, and keep the heart
Awake to love and beauty! And sometimes
'Tis well to be bereaved of promised good,
That we may lift the soul, and contemplate
With lively joy the joys we cannot share.
My gentle-hearted Charles! when the last rook
Beat its straight path along the dusky air
Homewards, I blessed it, deeming its black wing
(Now a dim speck, now vanishing in the light)
Had crossed the mighty orb's dilated glory
While thou stoodst gazing; or, when all was still,
Flew creaking[3] o'er thy head, and had a charm
For thee, my gentle-hearted Charles! to whom
No sound is dissonant which tells of Life.

Notes

[3] 'Some months after I had written this line, it gave me pleasure to find that Bartram had observed the same circumstance of the Savanna crane. "When these birds move their wings in flight, their strokes are slow, moderate and regular; and even when at a considerable distance or high above us, we plainly hear the quill-feathers; their shafts and webs upon one another creak as the joints or working of a vessel in a tempestuous sea" ' (Coleridge's note). Coleridge was reading William Bartram's *Travels through North and South Carolina* (1794) by summer 1797, and quickly communicated his enthusiasm for the work to Wordsworth.

Letter from S. T. Coleridge to John Thelwall, 14 October 1797 (extract)

I can at times feel strongly the beauties you describe – in themselves and for themselves. But more frequently all things appear little – all the knowledge that can be acquired, child's play; the universe itself, what but an immense heap of *little* things? I can contemplate nothing but parts, and parts are all little! My mind feels as if it ached to behold and know something *great*, something *one* and *indivisible*[1] – and it is only in the faith of this that rocks or waterfalls, mountains or caverns, give me the sense of sublimity or majesty! But in this faith *all things* counterfeit infinity! 'Struck with the deepest calm of joy', I stand

Silent, with swimming sense, and gazing round
On the wide landscape, gaze till all doth seem
Less gross than bodily, a living thing
Which acts upon the mind, and with such hues
As clothe th' Almighty Spirit, when he makes
Spirits perceive his presence![2]

Letter from S. T. Coleridge to Thomas Poole,[1] *16 October 1797* (extract)

I read every book that came in my way without distinction. And my father was fond of me, and used to take me on his knee, and hold long conversations with me.[2] I remember that at eight years old I walked with him one winter evening from a farmer's house a mile from Ottery, and he told me the names of the stars, and how Jupiter was a thousand times larger than our world, and that the other twinkling stars were suns that had worlds rolling round them. And when I came home, he showed me how they rolled round. I heard him with a profound delight and admiration, but without the least mixture of wonder or incredulity. For, from my early reading of fairy tales and genii etc. etc., my mind had been habituated *to the Vast* – and I never regarded my senses in any way as the criteria of my belief. I regulated all my creeds by my conceptions – not by my sight, even at that age.

Should children be permitted to read romances, and relations of giants and magicians and genii? I know all that has been said against it, but I have formed my faith in the affirmative. I know no other way of giving the mind a love of 'the Great' and 'the Whole'.[3] Those who have been led to the same truths step by step through the constant testimony of their senses, seem to me to want a sense which I possess: they contemplate nothing but *parts*, and all parts are necessarily little. And the universe to them is but a mass of *little things*. It is true that the mind *may* become credulous and prone to

Notes

LETTER FROM S. T. COLERIDGE TO JOHN THELWALL

[1] *My mind feels . . . indivisible* Coleridge yearns for the transcendental experience described in *Religious Musings* 140–2.

[2] See the preceding text of 'This Lime-Tree Bower My Prison' 21–6.

LETTER FROM S. T. COLERIDGE TO THOMAS POOLE,

[1] Thomas Poole (1765–1837) was a well-to-do tanner of Nether Stowey. He encouraged and materially helped Coleridge from about 1794 onwards. He found Coleridge a cottage in Nether Stowey which adjoined his own back garden, funded Coleridge's magazine, *The Watchman*, and looked after Sara Coleridge and the children during Coleridge's many absences.

[2] *And my father . . . me* Coleridge was the youngest of John Coleridge's many children, and probably the favourite. John Coleridge was headmaster of the King Henry VII Grammar School at Ottery St Mary and vicar of St Mary's, until his death in 1781.

[3] *Should children . . . Whole* cf. Wordsworth's views on education as expressed in the passage on the infant prodigy in the *Five-Book Prelude* (pp. 543–6).

superstition by the former method – but are not the experimentalists[4] credulous even to madness in believing any absurdity rather than believe the grandest truths, if they have not the testimony of their own senses in their favour? I have known some who have been *rationally* educated, as it is styled. They were marked by a microscopic acuteness, but when they looked at great things, all became a blank and they saw nothing – and denied (very illogically) that anything could be seen, and uniformly put the negation of a power for the possession of a power, and called the want of imagination 'judgement', and the never being moved to rapture 'philosophy'!

Of the Fragment of 'Kubla Khan'[1]

From Christabel; Kubla Khan: A Vision; The Pains of Sleep (1816)

The following fragment is here published at the request of a poet of great and deserved celebrity,[2] and as far as the author's own opinions are concerned, rather as a psychological curiosity than on the ground of any supposed *poetic* merits.

In the summer of the year 1797,[3] the author, then in ill health, had retired to a lonely farmhouse between Porlock and Lynton on the Exmoor confines of Somerset and Devonshire. In consequence of a slight indisposition, an anodyne had been prescribed,[4] from the effects of which he fell asleep in his chair at the moment that he was reading the following sentence, or words of the same substance, in *Purchas's Pilgrimage*: 'Here the Khan Kubla commanded a palace to be built, and a stately garden thereunto. And thus ten miles of fertile ground were enclosed with a wall.'[5]

The author continued for about three hours in a profound sleep (at least of the external senses) during which time he has the most vivid confidence that he could not have composed less than from two to three hundred lines – if that indeed can be called composition in which all the images rose up before him as *things*, with a parallel production of the correspondent expressions, without any sensation or consciousness of effort. On awaking he appeared to himself to have a distinct recollection of the whole, and taking his pen, ink, and paper, instantly and eagerly wrote down the lines that are here preserved. At this moment he was unfortunately called out by a person on business from Porlock and detained by him above an hour, and on his return to his room, found to his no small surprise and mortification that though he still retained some vague and dim recollection of the general purpose of the vision, yet, with the exception of some eight or ten scattered lines and images, all the rest had passed away like the images on the surface of a stream into which a stone has been cast – but, alas! without the after-restoration of the latter:

Notes

[4] *experimentalists* those who base their religious faith and beliefs only on what is perceived by the five senses, and on the reason.

Of the Fragment of 'Kubla Khan'

[1] This short essay was prefaced to 'Kubla Khan' on its first publication in 1816. It is followed by two texts: the manuscript text (which is the closest we can get to the poem as written in 1797) and the published text of 1816, which is now regarded as canonical.

[2] *a poet of great and deserved celebrity* Lord Byron, who described it as 'a fine wild poem' (Marchand v 108). 'Kubla Khan' and 'Christabel' circulated in MS in literary circles for years before they were formally published. Other early readers included Charles Lamb, Walter Scott and Mary Robinson.

[3] *In the summer . . . 1797* The correct date is early November 1797.

[4] *an anodyne . . . prescribed* Opium was generally used for the treatment of dysentery at this time.

[5] 'In Xaindu did Cublai Can build a stately pallace, encompassing sixteene miles of plaine ground with a wall, wherein are fertile meddowes, pleasant springs, delightfull streames, and all sorts of beasts of chase and game, and in the middest thereof a sumptuous house of pleasure, which may be removed from place to place' (Samuel Purchas, *Purchas his Pilgrimage* (1613), p. 350).

Then all the charm
Is broken – all that phantom-world so fair
Vanishes, and a thousand circlets spread,
And each misshapes the other. Stay awhile,
Poor youth, who scarcely dar'st lift up thine eyes –
The stream will soon renew its smoothness, soon
The visions will return! And lo, he stays,
And soon the fragments dim of lovely forms
Come trembling back, unite, and now once more
The pool becomes a mirror.[6]

Yet from the still-surviving recollections in his mind, the author has frequently purposed to finish for himself what had been originally, as it were, given to him. *Αὔριον ἅδιον ἄσω*,[7] but the tomorrow is yet to come.

As a contrast to this vision, I have annexed a fragment of a very different character, describing with equal fidelity the dream of pain and disease.[8]

[*Kubla Khan*] (composed early November 1797;[1] edited from MS)[2]

In Xannadù did Cubla Khan
A stately pleasure-dome decree,
Where Alph, the sacred river, ran
Through caverns measureless to man
Down to a sunless sea.
So twice six miles of fertile ground
With walls and towers were compassed round;
And here were gardens bright with sinuous rills
Where blossomed many an incense-bearing tree;
And here were forests ancient as the hills,
Enfolding sunny spots of greenery.
But oh, that deep romantic chasm that slanted
Down a green hill athwart a cedarn cover!
A savage place, as holy and enchanted
As e'er beneath a waning moon was haunted
By woman wailing for her demon-lover!
And from this chasm, with hideous turmoil seething,
As if this earth in fast thick pants were breathing,
A mighty fountain momently was forced
Amid whose swift half-intermitted burst

Notes

[6] Coleridge quotes own *The Picture* 69–78.

[7] *Αὔριον ἅδιον ἄσω* 'Tomorrow I shall sing more sweetly'; Theocritus, *Idyll* i 145.

[8] *a fragment . . . disease The Pains of Sleep*; see pp. 680–3.

Kubla Khan

[1] The exact date of composition is unknown. If, as seems likely, Coleridge's retirement to a farmhouse occurred during the walking tour to the Valley of the Rocks with the Wordsworths, the probable date is early November 1797.

[2] This text is edited from the earliest surviving MS in Coleridge's hand, which dates from before February 1804 It is not given a title and may at that stage have been thought of as a 'fragment'. The published text, which differs in a number of particulars, is presented here as a parallel text for ease of comparison. For comment on the two versions see John Beer, 'The Languages of *Kubla Khan*', in *Coleridge's Imagination* ed. Richard Gravil, Lucy Newlyn and Nicholas Roe (1985), pp. 218–62.

Kubla Khan

From Christabel; Kubla Khan: a vision; The Pains of Sleep (1816)

In Xanadu did Kubla Khan
A stately pleasure-dome decree,
Where Alph, the sacred river, ran
Through caverns measureless to man
   Down to a sunless sea.
So twice five miles of fertile ground
With walls and towers were girdled round;
And here were gardens bright with sinuous rills
Where blossomed many an incense-bearing tree;
And here were forests ancient as the hills,
And folding sunny spots of greenery.

But oh, that deep romantic chasm which slanted
Down the green hill athwart a cedarn cover!
A savage place, as holy and enchanted
As e'er beneath a waning moon was haunted
By woman wailing for her demon-lover!
And from this chasm, with ceaseless turmoil seething,
As if this earth in fast thick pants were breathing,
A mighty fountain momently was forced
Amid whose swift half-intermitted burst

suggests the mind taken over by a semi-automatic composition.

Huge fragments vaulted like rebounding hail,
Or chaffy grain beneath the thresher's flail!
And mid these dancing rocks at once and ever,
It flung up momently the sacred river.
Five miles meandering with a mazy motion
Through wood and dale the sacred river ran,
Then reached the caverns measureless to man
And sank in tumult to a lifeless ocean.
And mid this tumult Cubla heard from far
Ancestral voices prophesying war![3]
  The shadow of the dome of pleasure
  Floated midway on the wave,
  Where was heard the mingled measure
  From the fountain and the cave;
It was a miracle of rare device,
A sunny pleasure-dome with caves of ice!

  A damsel with a dulcimer
  In a vision once I saw:
It was an Abyssinian maid
And on her dulcimer she played,
Singing of Mount Amara.[4]
Could I revive within me
Her symphony and song,
To such a deep delight 'twould win me
That with music loud and long,
I would build that dome in air,
That sunny dome, those caves of ice!
And all who heard should see them there,
And all should cry, 'Beware, beware!
His flashing eyes, his floating hair!
Weave a circle round him thrice,
And close your eyes in holy dread –
For he on honey-dew hath fed
And drank the milk of paradise.'

This fragment with a good deal more, not recoverable, composed in a sort of reverie brought on by two grains of opium taken to check a dysentery,[5] at a farm-house between Porlock and Lynton, a quarter of a mile from Culbone Church, in the fall of the year 1797.
S. T. Coleridge

Notes

[3] *Ancestral voices prophesying war* presumably the voices of ancestors looking forward to war in the present; though another way of reading it would be to regard the ancestral voices as speaking to the individual psyche. In March 1798 Coleridge told his brother George: 'I believe most steadfastly in original sin; that from our mothers' wombs our understandings are darkened; and even where our understandings are in the light, that our organization is depraved, and our volitions imperfect' (Griggs i 396).

[4] *Mount Amara* Coleridge originally wrote 'Amora' in the MS. Mount Amara alludes to *Purchas his Pilgrimage*, in which it is said to be 'situate as the navel of the Ethopian body, and centre of their empire, under the equinoctial line where the sun may take his best view thereof, as not encountering in all his long journey with the like theatre . . . the sun himself so in love with the sight, that the first and last thing he vieweth in all those parts is this hill.' See also *Paradise Lost* iv 281.

[5] *two grains . . . dysentery* It is worth bearing in mind that the only available treatment for stomach disorders and pains of various kinds (including toothache) was opium or its derivatives. Many people consumed it for entirely legitimate medicinal purposes, and became addicted as a result.

Huge fragments vaulted like rebounding hail,
Or chaffy grain beneath the thresher's flail!
And mid these dancing rocks at once and ever,
It flung up momently the sacred river.
Five miles meandering with a mazy motion
Through wood and dale the sacred river ran,
Then reached the caverns measureless to man
And sank in tumult to a lifeless ocean.
And mid this tumult Kubla heard from far
Ancestral voices prophesying war!
  The shadow of the dome of pleasure
  Floated midway on the waves,
  Where was heard the mingled measure
  From the fountain and the caves;
It was a miracle of rare device,
A sunny pleasure-dome with caves of ice!

  A damsel with a dulcimer
  In a vision once I saw:
  It was an Abyssinian maid
  And on her dulcimer she played,
  Singing of Mount Abora.
  Could I revive within me
  Her symphony and song,
  To such a deep delight 'twould win me
That with music loud and long,
I would build that dome in air,
That sunny dome, those caves of ice!
And all who heard should see them there,
And all should cry, 'Beware, beware!
His flashing eyes, his floating hair!
Weave a circle round him thrice,
And close your eyes with holy dread –
For he on honey-dew hath fed
And drank the milk of paradise.'

Frost at Midnight (composed February 1798)[1]

From Fears in Solitude, written in 1798 during an alarm of an invasion; to which are added France: An Ode; and Frost at Midnight (1798)

The frost performs its secret ministry
Unhelped by any wind. The owlet's cry
Came loud – and hark, again! loud as before.
The inmates of my cottage, all at rest,
Have left me to that solitude which suits
Abstruser musings, save that at my side
My cradled infant[2] slumbers peacefully.
'Tis calm indeed! – so calm that it disturbs
And vexes meditation with its strange
And extreme silentness. Sea, hill, and wood,
This populous village! Sea, and hill, and wood,
With all the numberless goings-on of life,
Inaudible as dreams! The thin blue flame
Lies on my low-burnt fire, and quivers not;
Only that film[3] which fluttered on the grate
Still flutters there, the sole unquiet thing.
Methinks its motion in this hush of nature
Gives it dim sympathies with me who live,
Making it a companionable form
With which I can hold commune. Idle thought!
But still the living spirit in our frame
That loves not to behold a lifeless thing,
Transfuses into all its own delights
Its own volition – sometimes with deep faith
And sometimes with fantastic playfulness.[4]

Notes

FROST AT MIDNIGHT

[1] This is the earliest version, presented here alongside the better-known text of 1834. The main difference is the conclusion to this text, ll. 80–5, eliminated in later revisions. Coleridge's literary source is Cowper's description of a winter evening in *The Task*, p. 20.

[2] *My cradled infant* Hartley Coleridge, born 19 September 1796. He was one and a half years old. This is the first of his numerous appearances in the poetry of Wordsworth and Coleridge, including *The Nightingale* 91–105, *Christabel* 644–65, *To H.C., Six Years Old* and *Ode* 85–131.

[3] 'In all parts of the kingdom these films are called "strangers", and supposed to portend the arrival of some absent friend' (Coleridge's note). The same detail turns up in Cowper's description of a winter evening, p. 20.

[4] *But still . . . playfulness* Coleridge's language indicates that the mind, when it infers the existence of an inner life in external objects, is engaging in an essentially fanciful act – it is making patterns (in the terms of Coleridge's much later definition of fancy, p. 692) out of fixities and definites. This is emphasized in ll. 20–5 which, in versions of the poem from 1812 to 1817, were expanded:

With which I can hold commune. Haply hence,
That still the living spirit in our frame
Which loves not to behold a lifeless thing,
Transfuses into all things its own Will
And its own pleasures; sometimes with deep faith,
And sometimes with a wilful playfulness,
That stealing pardon from our common sense
Smiles, as self-scornful, to disarm the scorn
For these wild relics of our childish thought,
That flit about, oft go, and oft return
Not uninvited. Ah, there was a time,
When oft, amused by no such subtle toys
Of the self-watching mind, a child at school,
With most believing superstitious wish . . .

The 1817 text was briefer:

Making it a companionable form,
To which the living spirit in our frame,
That loves not to behold a lifeless thing,
Transfuses its own pleasures, it own will.
How oft, at school, with most believing mind,
Presageful, have I gazed upon the bars
To watch that fluttering stranger! And as oft . . .

In 1834 this passage was replaced by a formulation even more sceptical of the charms of fancy.

Frost at Midnight

From Poetical Works (1834)

The frost performs its secret ministry
Unhelped by any wind. The owlet's cry
Came loud – and hark, again! loud as before.
The inmates of my cottage, all at rest,
Have left me to that solitude which suits
Abstruser musings, save that at my side
My cradled infant slumbers peacefully.
'Tis calm indeed! – so calm that it disturbs
And vexes meditation with its strange
And extreme silentness. Sea, hill, and wood,
This populous village! Sea, and hill, and wood,
With all the numberless goings-on of life,
Inaudible as dreams! The thin blue flame
Lies on my low-burnt fire, and quivers not;
Only that film which fluttered on the grate
Still flutters there, the sole unquiet thing.
Methinks its motion in this hush of nature
Gives it dim sympathies with me who live,
Making it a companionable form
Whose puny flaps and freaks the idling spirit
By its own moods interprets, everywhere
Echo or mirror seeking of itself,
And makes a toy of thought.

suggests a Wordsworthian sense of transcendental reality of natural phenomena.

Ah me! amused by no such curious toys
Of the self-watching subtilizing[5] mind,
How often in my early schoolboy days,[6]
With most believing superstitious wish
Presageful have I gazed upon the bars,
To watch the *stranger* there! – and oft belike,
With unclosed lids, already had I dreamt
Of my sweet birthplace, and the old church-tower
Whose bells, the poor man's only music, rang
From morn to evening all the hot fair-day,
So sweetly that they stirred and haunted me
With a wild pleasure, falling on mine ear
Most like articulate sounds of things to come!
So gazed I till the soothing things I dreamt
Lulled me to sleep, and sleep prolonged my dreams!
And so I brooded all the following morn,
Awed by the stern preceptor's[7] face, mine eye
Fixed with mock study on my swimming book;
Save if the door half-opened, and I snatched
A hasty glance, and still my heart leaped up,
For still I hoped to see the *stranger's* face –
Townsman, or aunt, or sister more beloved,
My playmate when we both were clothed alike![8]
Dear babe,[9] that sleepest cradled by my side,
Whose gentle breathings heard in this dead calm
Fill up the interspersed vacancies
And momentary pauses of the thought;
My babe so beautiful, it fills my heart
With tender gladness thus to look at thee,
And think that thou shalt learn far other lore
And in far other scenes! For I was reared
In the great city, pent mid cloisters dim,[10]
And saw nought lovely but the sky and stars.
But *thou*, my babe, shalt wander like a breeze
By lakes and sandy shores, beneath the crags
Of ancient mountain, and beneath the clouds
Which image in their bulk both lakes and shores
And mountain crags;[11] so shalt thou see and hear
The lovely shapes and sounds intelligible

Notes

[5] *subtilizing* given to subtle reasoning.

[6] *my early schoolboy days* a reference to Coleridge's time at Christ's Hospital in the City of London, 1782–91. His lack of enthusiasm for those years may owe something to the use of violence by the masters at the school.

[7] *preceptor* teacher.

[8] *sister . . . alike* Until well into the 19th century, small boys and girls were dressed in frocks until boys were breeched. Coleridge was deeply attached to his sister Anne (1767–91), whose early death from consumption distressed him greatly. In September 1794 he told Edith Fricker that Anne had been 'beautiful and accomplished – like you, she was lowly of heart. Her eye beamed with meekest sensibility' (Griggs i 102).

[9] *Dear babe* Coleridge turns again to his son Hartley.

[10] *pent mid cloisters dim* cf. Charles Lamb who in 'This Lime-Tree Bower My Prison' 'hungered after nature many a year / In the great city pent' (ll. 29–30). Coleridge is alluding to Satan in *Paradise Lost*, 'one who long in populous city pent' (ix 445).

[11] *But thou . . . crags* Coleridge had not actually seen the Lake District in February 1798, when these lines were written; Cumbrian lakes do not have 'sandy shores'. He is no doubt thinking of the account of the mountains and lakes in Wordsworth's *The Pedlar*, which was being written at the same time as this poem.

But oh, how oft,
How oft at school, with most believing mind,
Presageful, have I gazed upon the bars,
To watch that fluttering stranger! And as oft
With unclosed lids, already had I dreamt
Of my sweet birthplace, and the old church-tower
Whose bells, the poor man's only music, rang
From morn to evening all the hot fair-day,
So sweetly that they stirred and haunted me
With a wild pleasure, falling on mine ear
Most like articulate sounds of things to come!
So gazed I till the soothing things I dreamt
Lulled me to sleep, and sleep prolonged my dreams!
And so I brooded all the following morn,
Awed by the stern preceptor's face, mine eye
Fixed with mock study on my swimming book;
Save if the door half opened, and I snatched
A hasty glance, and still my heart leaped up,
For still I hoped to see the stranger's face –
Townsman, or aunt, or sister more beloved,
My playmate when we both were clothed alike!
Dear babe, that sleepest cradled by my side,
Whose gentle breathings heard in this deep calm
Fill up the interspersed vacancies
And momentary pauses of the thought;
My babe so beautiful, it fills my heart
With tender gladness thus to look at thee,
And think that thou shalt learn far other lore
And in far other scenes! For I was reared
In the great city, pent mid cloisters dim,
And saw nought lovely but the sky and stars.
But thou, my babe, shalt wander like a breeze
By lakes and sandy shores, beneath the crags
Of ancient mountain, and beneath the clouds
Which image in their bulk both lakes and shores
And mountain crags; so shalt thou see and hear
The lovely shapes and sounds intelligible

Of that eternal language which thy God
Utters,[12] who from eternity doth teach
Himself in all, and all things in himself.
Great universal teacher! He shall mould[13]
Thy spirit, and by giving make it ask.
   Therefore all seasons shall be sweet to thee,
Whether the summer clothe the general earth
With greenness, or the redbreasts sit and sing
Betwixt the tufts of snow on the bare branch
Of mossy apple-tree, while all the thatch
Smokes in the sun-thaw; whether the eave-drops fall
Heard only in the trances[14] of the blast,
Or whether the secret ministry of cold
Shall hang them up in silent icicles,
Quietly shining to the quiet moon;
Like those, my babe, which ere tomorrow's warmth
Have capped their sharp keen points with pendulous drops,
Will catch thine eye, and with their novelty
Suspend thy little soul; then make thee shout
And stretch and flutter from thy mother's arms,
As thou would'st fly for very eagerness.[15]

Notes

[12] *so shalt . . . utters* a reference to Bishop Berkeley's theory that the natural world is the symbolic language of God's thought. At more or less the same time that this was written, Wordsworth was describing the Pedlar's perception of the 'written promise' (*Pedlar* 119).

[13] *mould* The pantheist perception Coleridge confers on Hartley is formative of the individual; cf. the intellectual breeze of *The Eolian Harp* (1795), which is 'Plastic' (l. 39).

[14] *trances* moments of suspension, when the blast stills.

[15] Lines 80–5 were removed from subsequent versions of the poem, as Coleridge explained in a marginal note made in a copy of the 1798 volume: 'The six last lines I omit because they destroy the rondo, and return upon itself of the poem. Poems of this kind of length ought to lie coiled with its tail round its head. S.T.C.' For Hartley's sensitivity to natural things, see Coleridge's notebook entry, p. 355n17 above.

Of that eternal language which thy God
Utters, who from eternity doth teach
Himself in all, and all things in himself.
Great universal teacher! He shall mould
Thy spirit, and by giving make it ask.
   Therefore all seasons shall be sweet to thee,
Whether the summer clothe the general earth
With greenness, or the redbreast sit and sing
Betwixt the tufts of snow on the bare branch
Of mossy apple-tree, while the nigh thatch
Smokes in the sun-thaw; whether the eave-drops fall
Heard only in the trances of the blast,
Or if the secret ministry of frost
Shall hang them up in silent icicles,
Quietly shining to the quiet moon.

France: An Ode (composed March–early April 1798)[1]

From Fears in Solitude, written in 1798 during an alarm of an invasion; to which are added France: an ode; and Frost at Midnight (1798)

I

Ye clouds, that far above me float and pause,
Whose pathless march no mortal may control!
Ye ocean waves, that, wheresoe'er ye roll,
Yield homage only to eternal laws!
Ye woods, that listen to the night-bird's singing,
Midway the smooth and perilous steep reclined;
Save when your own imperious branches swinging
Have made a solemn music of the wind!
Where, like a man beloved of God,
Through glooms which never woodman trod,
How oft, pursuing fancies holy,
My moonlight way o'er flow'ring weeds I wound,
Inspired beyond the guess of folly
By each rude[2] shape, and wild unconquerable sound!
Oh ye loud waves, and oh ye forests high,
And oh ye clouds, that far above me soared!
Thou rising sun! Thou blue rejoicing sky!
Yea, every thing that is and will be free,
Bear witness for me wheresoe'er ye be,
With what deep worship I have still adored
The spirit of divinest liberty.

Notes

FRANCE: AN ODE

[1] This poem is Coleridge's response to the suppression of the Swiss cantons by the French government. It was an important moment for radicals in Britain, because it was the first time that the French had acted contrary to the principles of the Revolution. When published in the *Morning Post*, 16 April 1798 (under the title *The Recantation: An Ode*), it was prefaced by a brief note by the paper's editor, Daniel Stuart: 'The following excellent Ode will be in unison with the feelings of every friend to liberty and foe to oppression; of all who, admiring the French Revolution, detest and deplore the conduct of France towards Switzerland. It is very satisfactory to find so zealous and steady an advocate for freedom as Mr Coleridge concur with us in condemning the conduct of France towards the Swiss Cantons.' When reprinted with corrections by the same paper in 1802, it was accompanied by an Argument:

> *First stanza*: An invocation to those objects in nature the contemplation of which had inspired the poet with a devotional love of liberty. *Second stanza*: The exultation of the poet at the commencement of the French Revolution, and his unqualified abhorrence of the Alliance against the Republic. *Third stanza*: The blasphemies and horrors during the domination of the Terrorists regarded by the poet as a transient storm, and as the natural consequence of the former despotism and of the foul superstition of Popery. Reason, indeed, began to suggest many apprehensions; yet still the poet struggled to retain the hope that France would make conquests by no other means than by presenting to the observation of Europe a people more happy and better instructed than under other forms of government. *Fourth stanza*: Switzerland, and the poet's recantation. *Fifth stanza*: An address to Liberty, in which the poet expresses his conviction that those feelings and that grand ideal of freedom which the mind attains by its contemplation of its individual nature, and of the sublime surrounding objects (see stanza the first) do not belong to men, as a society, nor can possibly be either gratified or realized, under any form of human government; but belong to the individual man, so far as he is pure, and inflamed with the love and adoration of God in nature.

[2] *rude* rough.

II

When France in wrath her giant limbs upreared,[3]
And with that oath[4] which smote earth, air, and sea,
Stamped her strong foot and said she would be free,
Bear witness for me, how I hoped and feared!
With what a joy, my lofty gratulation[5]
Unawed, I sung amid a slavish band;
And when to whelm the disenchanted nation,
Like fiends embattled by a wizard's wand,
The monarchs marched in evil day,
And Britain joined the dire array[6] –
Though dear her shores, and circling ocean,
Though many friendships, many youthful loves
Had swoln the patriot emotion,
And flung a magic light o'er all her hills and groves;
Yet still my voice unaltered sang defeat
To all that braved the tyrant-quelling lance,[7]
And shame too long delayed, and vain retreat!
For ne'er, oh Liberty! with partial[8] aim
I dimmed thy light, or damped thy holy flame;
But blessed the paeans of delivered France,
And hung my head, and wept at Britain's name!

III

'And what', I said, 'though blasphemy's loud scream
With that sweet music of deliv'rance strove;
Though all the fierce and drunken passions wove
A dance more wild than ever maniac's dream;[9]
Ye storms, that round the dawning east assembled,
The sun was rising, though ye hid his light!'
And when to soothe my soul, that hoped and trembled,
The dissonance ceased, and all seemed calm and bright;
When France, her front deep-scarred and gory,
Concealed with clust'ring wreaths of glory;
When insupportably advancing,[10]
Her arm made mock'ry of the warrior's ramp,
While, timid looks of fury glancing,
Domestic treason, crushed beneath her fatal stamp,

Notes

[3] *When France . . . upreared* i.e. when the Revolution began.

[4] *that oath* When the French Revolution was in its early days, 20 June 1789, the commoners were barred from the meeting-place of the Estates General and instead took an oath in a nearby tennis court, vowing to stand firm until reform of the constitution.

[5] *gratulation* pleasure, exultation.

[6] *And Britain . . . array* England joined the alliance of Austria and Prussia against France shortly after the execution of Louis XVI, February 1793.

[7] *the tyrant-quelling lance* i.e. of Revolutionary France, with whose interests the young Coleridge identified.

[8] *partial* selfish.

[9] *And what . . . dream* During Robespierre's Reign of Terror (October 1793 to July 1794) the clergy were persecuted and executed, along with the aristocrats, politicians of all colours, foreigners and anyone identifiable as alien to the interests of the state.

[10] *When insupportably advancing* Coleridge alludes to Milton, *Samson Agonistes* 136: 'When insupportably his foot advanced'.

Writhed like a wounded dragon in his gore –
Then I reproached my fears that would not flee,
'And soon', I said, 'shall wisdom teach her lore
In the low huts of them that toil and groan!
And conqu'ring by her happiness alone,
Shall France compel the nations to be free,[11]
Till love and joy look round, and call the earth their own!'

IV

Forgive me, Freedom! Oh forgive these dreams!
I hear thy voice, I hear thy loud lament
From bleak Helvetia's[12] icy caverns sent –
I hear thy groans upon her bloodstained streams!
Heroes, that for your peaceful country perished,
And ye, that fleeing spot the mountain snows
With bleeding wounds – forgive me, that I cherished
One thought that ever blessed your cruel foes![13]
To scatter rage and trait'rous guilt
Where Peace her jealous home had built;
A patriot race to disinherit
Of all that made their stormy wilds so dear,
And with inexpiable[14] spirit
To taint the bloodless freedom of the mountaineer.
Oh France! that mockest heav'n, adult'rous,[15] blind,
And patriot only in pernicious toils! –
Are these thy boasts, champion of humankind?
To mix with kings in the low lust of sway,[16]
Yell in the hunt, and share the murd'rous prey;
T' insult the shrine of liberty with spoils
From freemen torn; to tempt and to betray![17]

V

The sensual and the dark rebel in vain,
Slaves by their own compulsion! In mad game
They burst their manacles, and wear the name
Of freedom graven on a heavier chain![18]
Oh Liberty! with profitless endeavour
Have I pursued thee many a weary hour:

Notes

[11] *Shall France . . . free* It was believed that Revolution would spread to other countries.

[12] *Helvetia* Switzerland.

[13] *your cruel foes* i.e. France.

[14] *inexpiable* unpardonable, unforgivable.

[15] *adult'rous* France has adulterated the principle of liberty.

[16] *sway* power – in this case, over Switzerland.

[17] *T' insult . . . to betray!* Coleridge said that this was a reference to the ceding of Belgium and parts of the Venetian Republic by Austria to France, October 1797.

[18] *wear the name . . . chain!* Coleridge noted that 'At Genoa the word "Liberty" is engraved on the chains of the galley-slaves and the doors of prisons.'

But thou nor swell'st the victor's strain, nor ever
Didst breathe thy soul in forms of human pow'r.[19]
Alike from all, howe'er they praise thee
(Nor pray'r, nor boastful name delays thee),
Alike from priesthood's harpy minions
And factious blasphemy's obscener slaves,
Thou speedest on thy subtle pinions,
To live amid the winds, and move upon the waves![20]
And then I felt thee on the sea-cliff's verge,
Whose pines, scarce travelled by the breeze above,
Had made one murmur with the distant surge!
Yes, while I stood and gazed, my temples bare,
And shot my being through earth, sea, and air,
Possessing all things with intensest love,
Oh Liberty, my spirit felt thee there![21]

Fears in Solitude. Written April 1798, During the Alarm of an Invasion[1] (composed 20 April 1798)[2]

From Fears in Solitude, written in 1798 during the alarm of an invasion; to which are added France: an ode; and Frost at Midnight (1798)

A green and silent spot amid the hills![3]
A small and silent dell! O'er stiller place
No singing skylark ever poised himself!
The hills are heathy, save that swelling slope
Which hath a gay and gorgeous covering on,
All golden with the never-bloomless furze,
Which now blooms most profusely; but the dell,
Bathed by the mist, is fresh and delicate
As vernal cornfield, or the unripe flax,
When through its half-transparent stalks, at eve,

Notes

[19] *But thou . . . pow'r* Coleridge felt a general disillusionment with those in power at this moment; in March 1798 he told his brother George: 'As to the rulers of France, I see in their views, speeches, and actions, nothing that distinguishes them to their advantage from other animals of the same species. History has taught me that rulers are much the same in all ages and under all forms of government: they are as bad as they dare to be' (Griggs i 395).

[20] *Alike from all . . . waves* The point of the poem is that true liberty is found neither with institutionalized religion ('priesthood's harpy minions') nor with atheistic revolutionaries ('factious blasphemy's obscener slaves'); it is found in nature.

[21] *And shot . . . love* the poem culminates in another moment of god-like apprehension (cf. *Reflections upon Having left a Place of Retirement* 26–42). In this case, Coleridge claims that his investment of love in the landscape enabled him to perceive the pantheist life-force in nature – which he regards as representing true liberty.

Fears in Solitude

[1] In February 1797 the French had landed no less than 1,200 men at Fishguard in preparation for an invasion of England; it was widely feared that they would try again in spring 1798, and that the West Country would be their landing-point. For discussion of this poem see Peter Larkin, ' "Fears in Solitude": Reading (from) the Dell', *TWC* 22 (1991) 11–14.

[2] The central argument of the poem is the fear that, in declaring war on himself, man has, like the ancient mariner, declared war on God. In an early MS, Coleridge comments: 'The above is perhaps not poetry, but rather a sort of middle thing between poetry and oratory – *sermoni propiora*. Some parts are, I am conscious, too tame even for animated prose.' The phrase *sermoni propiora* means 'more like conversation'. As an anti-war poem, *Fears in Solitude* might be compared with Wordsworth's *The Female Vagrant*, being prepared at this moment for *Lyrical Ballads* (1798); see pp. 356–62.

[3] *the hills* the Quantock hills in Somerset, close to Nether Stowey.

The level sunshine glimmers with green light.
Oh 'tis a quiet, spirit-healing nook,
Which all, methinks, would love – but chiefly he,
The humble man, who in his youthful years
Knew just so much of folly as had made
His early manhood more securely wise;
Here he might lie on fern or withered heath,
While from the singing lark (that sings unseen –
The minstrelsy which solitude loves best),
And from the sun, and from the breezy air,
Sweet influences trembled o'er his frame;[4]
And he with many feelings, many thoughts,
Made up a meditative joy, and found
Religious meanings in the forms of nature!
And so, his senses gradually wrapped
In a half-sleep, he dreams of better worlds,
And dreaming hears thee still, oh singing lark,
That singest like an angel in the clouds!
  My God! it is a melancholy thing
For such a man, who would full fain preserve
His soul in calmness, yet perforce must feel
For all his human brethren; oh my God,
It is indeed a melancholy thing,
And weighs upon the heart, that he must think
What uproar and what strife may now be stirring
This way or that way o'er these silent hills –
Invasion, and the thunder and the shout,
And all the crash of onset; fear and rage
And undetermined conflict – even now,
Ev'n now, perchance, and in his native isle,
Carnage and screams beneath this blessed sun!
We have offended, oh my countrymen!
We have offended very grievously,
And have been tyrannous. From east to west
A groan of accusation pierces heaven!
The wretched plead against us, multitudes
Countless and vehement, the sons of God,
Our brethren! Like a cloud that travels on,
Steamed up from Cairo's swamps of pestilence,
Ev'n so, my countrymen, have we gone forth
And borne to distant tribes slavery and pangs –
And, deadlier far, our vices, whose deep taint
With slow perdition murders the whole man,
His body and his soul! Meanwhile, at home,
We have been drinking with a riotous thirst
Pollutions from the brimming cup of wealth –
A selfish, lewd, effeminated race,

Notes

[4] *Sweet influences . . . frame* the humble man is responsive to the influence of nature, as recommended in *The Eolian Harp* 36–40.

Contemptuous of all honourable rule,
Yet bartering freedom, and the poor man's life,
For gold, as at a market! The sweet words
Of Christian promise (words that even yet
Might stem destruction, were they wisely preached)
Are muttered o'er by men, whose tones proclaim
How flat and wearisome they feel their trade.
Rank scoffers some, but most too indolent
To deem them falsehoods, or to *know* their truth.
Oh blasphemous! the book of life is made
A superstitious instrument on which
We gabble o'er the oaths we mean to break,[5]
For all must swear – all, and in every place,
College and wharf, council and justice-court,
All, all must swear, the briber and the bribed,
Merchant and lawyer, senator and priest,
The rich, the poor, the old man, and the young,
All, all make up one scheme of perjury,
That faith doth reel; the very name of God
Sounds like a juggler's charm; and bold with joy,
Forth from his dark and lonely hiding-place
(Portentous sight!), the owlet Atheism,
Sailing on obscene wings athwart the noon,
Drops his blue-fringed lids, and holds them close,
And, hooting at the glorious sun in heaven,
Cries out, 'Where is it?'
                                        Thankless too for peace
(Peace long preserved by fleets and perilous seas),
Secure from actual warfare, we have loved
To swell the war-whoop, passionate for war![6]
Alas! for ages ignorant of all
Its ghastlier workings (famine or blue plague,
Battle, or siege, or flight through wintry snows),
We, this whole people, have been clamorous
For war and bloodshed, animating sports,
The which we pay for,[7] as a thing to talk of –
Spectators and not combatants! No guess
Anticipative of a wrong unfelt,
No speculation on contingency,[8]
However dim and vague, too vague and dim
To yield a justifying cause – and forth
(Stuffed out with big preamble, holy names,
And adjurations of[9] the God in heaven)

Notes

[5] *We gabble . . . break* Coleridge's target is subscription to the Thirty-nine Articles, the practice whereby Dissenters from the established church were compelled to swear allegiance to its founding principles. As a Unitarian he had an interest in seeing the Test and Corporation Acts repealed.

[6] *passionate for war* Coleridge's target is popular support for the war with France.

[7] *animating sports . . . pay for* This is a pious attack on such sports as boxing, cockfighting and the like. The obvious comparison is with gladiatorial combat in ancient Rome.

[8] *No guess . . . contingency* i.e. there is no attempt to anticipate the harm that will come to those fighting on our behalf.

[9] *adjurations of* appeals to.

We send our mandates[10] for the certain death
Of thousands and ten thousands! Boys and girls,
And women that would groan to see a child
Pull off an insect's leg – all read of war,
The best amusement for our morning meal!
The poor wretch, who has learnt his only prayers
From curses,[11] who knows scarcely words enough
To ask a blessing of his heavenly Father,
Becomes a fluent phraseman, absolute
And technical in victories and defeats,
And all our dainty terms for fratricide,
Terms which we trundle smoothly o'er our tongues
Like mere abstractions, empty sounds to which
We join no feeling and attach no form,
As if the soldier died without a wound,
As if the fibres of this godlike frame
Were gored without a pang, as if the wretch,
Who fell in battle doing bloody deeds,
Passed off to heaven, *translated* and not killed,
As though he had no wife to pine for him,
No God to judge him! Therefore evil days
Are coming on us, oh my countrymen!
And what if all-avenging Providence,
Strong and retributive, should make us know
The meaning of our words, force us to feel
The desolation and the agony
Of our fierce doings?[12]
Spare us yet awhile,
Father and God! Oh spare us yet awhile!
Oh let not English women drag their flight
Fainting beneath the burden of their babes,
Of the sweet infants, that but yesterday
Laughed at the breast! Sons, brothers, husbands, all
Who ever gazed with fondness on the forms
Which grew up with you round the same fireside,
And all who ever heard the sabbath bells
Without the infidel's scorn, make yourselves pure!
Stand forth! Be men! Repel an impious foe,
Impious and false, a light yet cruel race
That laugh away all virtue, mingling mirth
With deeds of murder; and still promising
Freedom, themselves too sensual to be free,
Poison life's amities,[13] and cheat the heart
Of Faith and quiet Hope, and all that soothes
And all that lifts the spirit! Stand we forth;

Notes

[10] *mandates* orders.

[11] *prayers / From curses* probably a recollection of Caliban in *The Tempest*: 'You taught me language, and my profit on't / Is, I know how to curse' (I ii 363–4). I am grateful to Essaka Joshua for this note.

[12] *And what if . . . doings* Coleridge's point is that God will punish English people for the way in which they have become hardened to the reality of war.

[13] *amities* friendships.

Render them back upon th' insulted ocean,
And let them toss as idly on its waves
As the vile seaweeds which some mountain blast
Swept from our shores! And oh! may we return
Not with a drunken triumph, but with fear,
Repenting of the wrongs with which we stung
So fierce a foe to frenzy!
                                        I have told,
Oh Britons! Oh my brethren! I have told
Most bitter truth, but without bitterness.
Nor deem my zeal or factious[14] or mistimed;
For never can true courage dwell with them
Who, playing tricks with conscience, dare not look
At their own vices. We have been too long
Dupes of a deep delusion![15] Some, belike,
Groaning with restless enmity, expect
All change from change of constituted power –
As if a government had been a robe
On which our vice and wretchedness were tagged
Like fancy-points and fringes,[16] with the robe
Pulled off at pleasure.[17] Fondly these attach
A radical causation to a few
Poor drudges of chastising Providence,
Who borrow all their hues and qualities
From our own folly and rank wickedness,
Which gave them birth, and nurse them.[18]
                                                            Others, meanwhile,
Dote with a mad idolatry; and all
Who will not fall before their images
And yield them worship, they are enemies
Ev'n of their country! Such have I been deemed.[19]
But oh dear Britain! Oh my mother isle!
Needs must thou prove a name most dear and holy
To me, a son, a brother, and a friend,
A husband and a father, who revere
All bonds of natural love, and find them all
Within the limits of thy rocky shores.

Notes

[14] *factious* Coleridge was disillusioned with politics; as he told his brother George in March 1798, 'I am of no party. It is true, I think the present ministry weak and perhaps unprincipled men, but I could not with a safe conscience vote for their removal' (Griggs i 396).

[15] *a deep delusion* namely, the radical hope that the French Revolution would lead to a new era of justice and enlightenment in human affairs.

[16] *fancy-points and fringes* buttons and bows. As his mother-in-law ran a dress shop, Coleridge would have known that fancy-points were ornate laces used for fastening clothes; their undoing would allow a robe to be 'pulled off'. The fringes would have consisted of lace edgings.

[17] *As if . . . pleasure* The vice and wretchedness of the *ancien régime* is compared with a robe that has been removed; Coleridge is saying that vice and wretchedness are not so easily done away with – they are endemic in humanity.

[18] *Fondly . . . nurse them* It is a foolish (fond) delusion to ascribe radicalism to those responsible for destroying the *ancien régime*; they are really the servants (drudges) of God, empowered by the inherent evil of those who gave them power – the people.

[19] *Such have I been deemed* During his support of France in the war against England, Coleridge was considered an enemy of the state. He has now, of course, changed his mind (see preceding poem), though it is worth noting that Pitt's spies were watching both Wordsworth and Coleridge at this moment.

Oh native Britain! Oh my mother isle!
How shouldst thou prove aught else but dear and holy
To me, who from thy lakes and mountain-hills,
Thy clouds, thy quiet dales, thy rocks, and seas,
Have drunk in all my intellectual[20] life,
All sweet sensations, all ennobling thoughts,
All adoration of the God in nature,
All lovely and all honourable things,
Whatever makes this mortal spirit feel
The joy and greatness of its future being?[21]
There lives nor form nor feeling in my soul
Unborrowed from my country! Oh divine
And beauteous island, thou hast been my sole
And most magnificent temple, in the which
I walk with awe, and sing my stately songs,
Loving the God that made me!
May my fears,
My filial fears, be vain! and may the vaunts
And menace of the vengeful enemy
Pass like the gust that roared and died away
In the distant tree, which heard, and only heard;
In this low dell bowed not the delicate grass.
But now the gentle dew-fall sends abroad
The fruitlike perfume of the golden furze;
The light has left the summit of the hill,
Though still a sunny gleam lies beautiful
On the long-ivied beacon.[22] Now farewell,
Farewell awhile, oh soft and silent spot!
On the green sheep-track, up the heathy hill,
Homeward I wind my way; and lo! recalled
From bodings, that have well-nigh wearied me,
I find myself upon the brow, and pause
Startled! And after lonely sojourning
In such a quiet and surrounded scene,
This burst of prospect (here the shadowy main,
Dim-tinted, there the mighty majesty
Of that huge amphitheatre of rich
And elmy fields) seems like society
Conversing with the mind, and giving it
A livelier impulse, and a dance of thought;
And now, beloved Stowey, I behold
Thy church-tower, and (methinks) the four huge elms
Clust'ring, which mark the mansion of my friend;[23]
And close behind them, hidden from my view,
Is my own lowly cottage, where my babe

Notes

[20] *intellectual* spiritual.

[21] *How shouldst thou prove . . . being* The point is that Coleridge's moral and spiritual being has been shaped by the English countryside – by nature, in fact.

[22] *the long-ivied beacon* A chain of beacons were built across the countryside to warn of threats of invasion from France.

[23] *the mansion of my friend* Alfoxden House, four miles from Nether Stowey, where Coleridge had lodged the Wordsworths (see p. 612).

And my babe's mother[24] dwell in peace! With light
And quickened footsteps thitherward I tend,
Rememb'ring thee, oh green and silent dell!
And grateful that by nature's quietness
And solitary musings all my heart
Is softened, and made worthy to indulge
Love, and the thoughts that yearn for humankind.

Christabel (Part I composed February–April 1798; Part II composed by August–October 1800; Conclusion to Part II composed *c.* 6 May 1801)[1]

From Christabel; Kubla Khan: a vision; The Pains of Sleep (1816)

Preface

The first part of the following poem was written in the year 1797, at Stowey, in the county of Somerset. The second part, after my return from Germany, in the year 1800, at Keswick, Cumberland. It is probable that if the poem had been finished at either of the former periods, or if even the first and second part had been published in the year 1800, the impression of its originality would have been much greater than I dare at present expect. But for this I have only my own indolence to blame. The dates are mentioned for the exclusive purpose of precluding charges of plagiarism or servile imitation from myself.[2] For there is amongst us a set of critics, who seem to hold that every possible thought and image is traditional; who have no notion that there are such things as fountains in the world, small as well as great; and who would therefore charitably derive every rill they behold flowing, from a perforation made in some other man's tank. I am confident, however, that as far as the present poem is concerned, the celebrated poets whose writings I might be suspected of having imitated, either in particular passages, or in the tone and the spirit of the whole, would be among the first to vindicate me from the charge, and who, on any striking coincidence, would permit me to address them in this doggerel version of two monkish Latin hexameters.

'Tis mine and it is likewise yours;
But an if this will not do;
Let it be mine, good friend! for I
Am the poorer of the two.

I have only to add that the metre of *Christabel* is not, properly speaking, irregular, though it may seem so from its being founded on a new principle: namely, that of counting in each line the accents, not the syllables. Though the latter may vary

Notes

[24] *my babe . . . mother* Hartley Coleridge and Sara, who was pregnant with Berkeley Coleridge (see next letter, p. 656).

CHRISTABEL

[1] *Christabel* was not published until 1816, but came close to appearing in *Lyrical Ballads* (1800). Coleridge even sent a copy of Part I to the printers in early September 1800; it seems to have been his inability to complete the poem that led to its being cancelled from the volume.

[2] *plagiarism or servile imitation from myself* Walter Scott's poem *The Lay of the Last Minstrel* (1805) borrowed from *Christabel*, Scott having been shown a manuscript copy by a mutual acquaintance, John Stoddart, in September–October 1802.

from seven to twelve, yet in each line the accents will be found to be only four. Nevertheless, this occasional variation in number of syllables is not introduced wantonly, nor for the mere ends of convenience, but in correspondence with some transition in the nature of the imagery or passion.

Part I

'Tis the middle of night by the castle clock,
And the owls have awakened the crowing cock;
Tu-whit!——Tu-whoo!
And hark, again! the crowing cock,
How drowsily it crew.

Sir Leoline, the Baron rich,
Hath a toothless mastiff bitch;
From her kennel beneath the rock
She makes answer to the clock,
Four for the quarters and twelve for the hour,
Ever and aye, moonshine or shower,
Sixteen short howls, not overloud;
Some say she sees my lady's shroud.

Is the night chilly and dark?
The night is chilly but not dark.
The thin grey cloud is spread on high,
It covers but not hides the sky.
The moon is behind, and at the full,
And yet she looks both small and dull.
The night is chill, the cloud is grey:
'Tis a month before the month of May,
And the spring comes slowly up this way.

The lovely lady, Christabel,
Whom her father loves so well,
What makes her in the wood so late
A furlong[3] from the castle gate?
She had dreams all yesternight
Of her own betrothed knight –
Dreams that made her moan and leap
As on her bed she lay in sleep;
And she in the midnight wood will pray
For the weal[4] of her lover that's far away.

She stole along, she nothing spoke,
The breezes they were still also;
And nought was green upon the oak
But moss and rarest mistletoe;
She kneels beneath the huge oak tree
And in silence prayeth she.

Notes

[3] *A furlong* an eighth of a mile (220 yards).

[4] *weal* welfare.

The lady leaps up suddenly,
The lovely lady, Christabel!
It moaned as near as near can be,
But what it is, she cannot tell:
On the other side it seems to be
Of the huge, broad-breasted, old oak tree.

The night is chill, the forest bare –
Is it the wind that moaneth bleak?
There is not wind enough in the air
To move away the ringlet curl
From the lovely lady's cheek;
There is not wind enough to twirl
The one red leaf, the last of its clan,
That dances as often as dance it can,
Hanging so light and hanging so high
On the topmost twig that looks up at the sky.

Hush, beating heart of Christabel!
Jesu Maria,[5] shield her well!

She folded her arms beneath her cloak
And stole to the other side of the oak:
    What sees she there?

There she sees a damsel bright
Dressed in a silken robe of white;
Her neck, her feet, her arms were bare,
And the jewels disordered in her hair.
I guess 'twas frightful there to see
A lady so richly clad as she –
    Beautiful exceedingly!

'Mary mother, save me now!'
Said Christabel, 'And who art thou?'

The lady strange made answer meet
And her voice was faint and sweet.
'Have pity on my sore distress,
I scarce can speak for weariness!
Stretch forth thy hand, and have no fear –'

Said Christabel, 'How cam'st thou here?'
And the lady, whose voice was faint and sweet,
Did thus pursue her answer meet:

'My sire is of a noble line
And my name is Geraldine.

Notes

[5] *Jesu Maria* an oath used by Friar Lawrence at *Romeo and Juliet* II iii 69.

Five warriors seized me yestermorn –
Me, even me, a maid forlorn;
They choked my cries with force and fright
And tied me on a palfrey[6] white.
The palfrey was as fleet as wind,
And they rode furiously behind.
They spurred amain,[7] their steeds were white,
And once we crossed the shade of night.
As sure as Heaven shall rescue me,
I have no thought what men they be;
Nor do I know how long it is
(For I have lain in fits, I wis)
Since one, the tallest of the five,
Took me from the palfrey's back,
A weary woman scarce alive.
Some muttered words his comrades spoke,
He placed me underneath this oak,
He swore they would return with haste;
Whither they went I cannot tell –
I thought I heard, some minutes past,
Sounds as of a castle-bell.
Stretch forth thy hand (thus ended she)
And help a wretched maid to flee.'

Then Christabel stretched forth her hand
And comforted fair Geraldine,
Saying that she should command
The service of Sir Leoline,
And straight be convoyed,[8] free from thrall,[9]
Back to her noble father's hall.

So up she rose and forth they passed
With hurrying steps, yet nothing fast;
Her lucky stars the lady blessed,
And Christabel, she sweetly said,
'All our household are at rest,
Each one sleeping in his bed.
Sir Leoline is weak in health
And may not well awakened be,
So to my room we'll creep in stealth
And you tonight must sleep with me.'

They crossed the moat, and Christabel
Took the key that fitted well –
A little door she opened straight
All in the middle of the gate,
The gate that was ironed[10] within and without
Where an army in battle array had marched out.

Notes

[6] *palfrey* a saddle-horse for ordinary riding, as opposed to a war-horse.

[7] *amain* at full speed.

[8] *convoyed* escorted.

[9] *thrall* captivity.

[10] *ironed* reinforced with iron.

The lady sank, belike through pain,
And Christabel with might and main
Lifted her up, a weary weight,
Over the threshold of the gate;
Then the lady rose again
And moved as she were not in pain.

So free from danger, free from fear,
They crossed the court – right glad they were.
And Christabel devoutly cried
To the lady by her side,
'Praise we the Virgin all divine
Who hath rescued thee from thy distress!'
'Alas, alas,' said Geraldine,
'I cannot speak for weariness.'
So free from danger, free from fear,
They crossed the court – right glad they were.

Outside her kennel, the mastiff old
Lay fast asleep in moonshine cold.
The mastiff old did not awake,
Yet she an angry moan did make.
And what can ail the mastiff bitch?
Never till now she uttered yell
Beneath the eye of Christabel.
Perhaps it is the owlet's scritch,
For what can ail the mastiff bitch?

They passed the hall that echoes still,
Pass as lightly as you will.
The brands[11] were flat, the brands were dying,
Amid their own white ashes lying;
But when the lady passed, there came
A tongue of light, a fit of flame,
And Christabel saw the lady's eye,
And nothing else saw she thereby
Save the boss of the shield of Sir Leoline tall
Which hung in a murky old nitch[12] in the wall.
'Oh softly tread', said Christabel,
'My father seldom sleepeth well.'

Sweet Christabel, her feet she bares
And they are creeping up the stairs,
Now in glimmer and now in gloom,
And now they pass the Baron's room,
As still as death with stifled breath;
And now have reached her chamber door,
And now with eager feet press down
The rushes of her chamber floor.

Notes

[11] *brands* wood burnt in the hearth.

[12] *nitch* niche.

The moon shines dim in the open air
And not a moonbeam enters here.
But they without its light can see
The chamber carved so curiously,
Carved with figures strange and sweet
All made out of the carver's brain
For a lady's chamber meet;
The lamp with twofold silver chain
Is fastened to an angel's feet.

The silver lamp burns dead and dim,
But Christabel the lamp will trim.[13]
She trimmed the lamp and made it bright
And left it swinging to and fro,
While Geraldine in wretched plight
Sank down upon the floor below.

'Oh weary lady Geraldine,
I pray you, drink this cordial[14] wine.
It is a wine of virtuous powers –
My mother made it of wild-flowers.'

'And will your mother pity me,
Who am a maiden most forlorn?'

Christabel answered, 'Woe is me!
She died the hour that I was born.
I have heard the grey-haired friar tell
How on her deathbed she did say
That she should hear the castle bell
Strike twelve upon my wedding day.
Oh mother dear, that thou wert here!'
'I would', said Geraldine, 'she were.'

But soon with altered voice said she,
'Off, wandering mother! Peak and pine!
I have power to bid thee flee.'[15]
Alas, what ails poor Geraldine?
Why stares she with unsettled eye?
Can she the bodiless dead espy?
And why with hollow voice cries she,
'Off, woman, off! this hour is mine –
Though thou her guardian spirit be,
Off, woman, off! – 'tis given to me'?

Then Christabel knelt by the lady's side,
And raised to heaven her eyes so blue;
'Alas!' said she, 'this ghastly ride –

Notes

[13] *trim* to clean the wick of a lamp for fresh burning.

[14] *cordial* reviving, restorative.

[15] *Off . . . flee* In a marginal note entered in a copy of the 1816 printed text, Coleridge explained: 'The mother of Christabel, who is now her guardian spirit, appears to Geraldine, as in answer to her wish. Geraldine fears the spirit, but yet has power over it for a time.'

Dear lady, it hath wildered[16] you!'
The lady wiped her moist cold brow,
And faintly said, ''Tis over now!'

Again the wild-flower wine she drank;
Her fair large eyes 'gan[17] glitter bright,
And from the floor whereon she sank,
The lofty lady stood upright:
She was most beautiful to see,
Like a lady of a far countrée.

And thus the lofty lady spake:
'All they who live in the upper sky
Do love you, holy Christabel!
And you love them, and for their sake,
And for the good which me befell,
Even I, in my degree will try,
Fair maiden, to requite you well.
But now unrobe yourself, for I
Must pray, ere yet in bed I lie.'

Quoth Christabel, 'So let it be!'
And as the lady bade, did she.
Her gentle limbs did she undress,
And lay down in her loveliness.

But through her brain, of weal and woe
So many thoughts moved to and fro
That vain it were her lids to close;
So halfway from the bed she rose,
And on her elbow did recline
To look at the lady Geraldine.

Beneath the lamp the lady bowed
And slowly rolled her eyes around;
Then drawing in her breath aloud
Like one that shuddered, she unbound
The cincture[18] from beneath her breast:
Her silken robe and inner vest
Dropped to her feet, and full in view,
Behold! her bosom and half her side –
A sight to dream of, not to tell!
And she is to sleep by Christabel.[19]

Notes

[16] *wildered* perplexed, bewildered.

[17] *'gan* began to.

[18] *cincture* belt.

[19] *Behold . . . Christabel* The MS text of 1800, in the Christabel notebook at the Wordsworth Library, Grasmere, make Geraldine less human:

Behold! her bosom and half her side
Are lean and old and foul of hue –
A sight to dream of, not to tell,
And she is to sleep with Christabel.

In a MS version of 1816, Geraldine's side is 'dark and rough as the sea-wolf's hide'.

She took two paces and a stride,
And lay down by the maiden's side;
And in her arms the maid she took,
Ah wel-a-day!
And with low voice and doleful look
These words did say:

'In the touch of this bosom there worketh a spell
Which is lord of thy utterance, Christabel![20]
Thou knowest tonight, and wilt know tomorrow,
This mark of my shame, this seal of my sorrow;
But vainly thou warrest,
For this is alone in
Thy power to declare,
That in the dim forest
Thou heard'st a low moaning,
And found'st a bright lady surpassingly fair,
And didst bring her home with thee in love and in charity,
To shield her and shelter her from the damp air.'

The Conclusion to Part I

It was a lovely sight to see
The lady Christabel, when she
Was praying at the old oak tree.
Amid the jagged shadows
Of mossy leafless boughs,
Kneeling in the moonlight
To make her gentle vows;
Her slender palms together pressed,
Heaving sometimes on her breast;
Her face resigned to bliss or bale,
Her face – oh call it fair, not pale!
And both blue eyes more bright than clear,
Each about to have a tear.

With open eyes (ah woe is me!)
Asleep, and dreaming fearfully,
Fearfully dreaming, yet I wis,
Dreaming that alone, which is –
Oh sorrow and shame! Can this be she,
The lady who knelt at the old oak tree?
And lo! the worker of these harms
That holds the maiden in her arms,
Seems to slumber still and mild,
As a mother with her child.

Notes

[20] *In the touch . . . Christabel* A marginal note to a copy of the 1816 printed text by Coleridge reads: 'As soon as the wicked bosom, with the mysterious sign of evil stamped thereby, touches Christabel, she is deprived of the power of disclosing what had occurred.'

A star hath set, a star hath risen,
Oh Geraldine, since arms of thine
Have been the lovely lady's prison!
Oh Geraldine, one hour was thine –
Thou'st had thy will! By tairn[21] and rill
The night-birds all that hour were still;
But now they are jubilant anew,
From cliff and tower, tu-whoo! tu-whoo!
Tu-whoo! tu-whoo! from wood and fell!

And see! the lady Christabel
Gathers herself from out her trance;
Her limbs relax, her countenance
Grows sad and soft; the smooth thin lids
Close o'er her eyes, and tears she sheds –
Large tears that leave the lashes bright;
And oft the while she seems to smile
As infants at a sudden light!

Yea she doth smile and she doth weep
Like a youthful hermitess
Beauteous in a wilderness,
Who praying always, prays in sleep.

And if she move unquietly,
Perchance 'tis but the blood so free
Comes back and tingles in her feet.
No doubt she hath a vision sweet:
What if her guardian spirit 'twere?
What if she knew her mother near?
But this she knows – in joys and woes,
That saints will aid if men will call,
For the blue sky bends over all!

Part II

'Each matin bell',[22] the Baron saith,
'Knells us back to a world of death.'
These words Sir Leoline first said
When he rose and found his lady dead;
These words Sir Leoline will say
Many a morn to his dying day.

And hence the custom and law began
That still at dawn the sacristan[23]
Who duly pulls the heavy bell

Notes

[21] *tairn* The earliest MS version of the poem has a note: 'Tairn or tarn (derived by Lye from the Icelandic *tiorn*, stagnum, palus) is rendered in our dictionaries as synonymous with mere or lake; but it is properly a large pool or reservoir in the mountains, commonly the feeder of some mere in the valleys. Tarn Watling and Blellum Tarn, though on lower ground than other tarns, are yet not exceptions – for both are on elevations, and Blellum Tarn feeds the Winander mere.' This is the first clear indication that the poem is set in the Lake District.

[22] *matin bell* sounded at midnight or 2 a.m.

[23] *sacristan* sexton of a parish church.

Five and forty beads must tell[24]
Between each stroke – a warning knell
Which not a soul can choose but hear
From Bratha Head[25] to Windermere.[26]

Saith Bracy the bard, 'So let it knell!
And let the drowsy sacristan[27]
Still count as slowly as he can!
There is no lack of such, I ween,
As well fill up the space between.
In Langdale Pike[28] and Witch's Lair[29]
And Dungeon Ghyll[30] (so foully rent),
With ropes of rock and bells of air
Three sinful sextons' ghosts are pent,
Who all give back, one after t'other,
The death-note to their living brother;
And oft too, by the knell offended,
Just as their one! – two! – three! is ended,
The Devil mocks the doleful tale
With a merry peal from Borrowdale.'[31]

The air is still – through mist and cloud
That merry peal comes ringing loud;
And Geraldine shakes off her dread
And rises lightly from the bed,
Puts on her silken vestments white
And tricks her hair in lovely plight,[32]
And nothing doubting of her spell
Awakens the lady Christabel.

'Sleep you, sweet lady Christabel?
I trust that you have rested well.'

And Christabel awoke and spied
The same who lay down by her side –
Oh rather say, the same whom she
Raised up beneath the old oak tree!
Nay, fairer yet, and yet more fair,
For she belike hath drunken deep
Of all the blessedness of sleep!
And while she spake, her looks, her air
Such gentle thankfulness declare,
That (so it seemed) her girded vests
Grew tight beneath her heaving breasts.

Notes

24 *tell* count.

25 *Bratha Head* i.e. the length of Langdale, through which the River Brathay runs until it reaches Windermere.

26 *Windermere* Windermere lake.

27 *sacristan* (or sexton) officer responsible for the fabric of the church; his main duties were ringing bells and digging graves.

28 *Langdale Pike* consists of two mountains of over 2,300 ft each, called Harrison Stickle and Pike of Stickle.

29 *Witch's Lair* probably the cave on Pike of Stickle.

30 *Dungeon Ghyll* stream going up between the two Langdale Pikes to a height of 2,400 ft.

31 *Borrowdale* the valley of Borrowdale is due north of the Langdale Pikes.

32 *plight* fashion.

'Sure I have sinned!' said Christabel,
'Now heaven be praised if all be well!'
And in low faltering tones, yet sweet,
Did she the lofty lady greet
With such perplexity of mind
As dreams too lively leave behind.[33]

So quickly she rose, and quickly arrayed
Her maiden limbs, and having prayed
That He who on the cross did groan
Might wash away her sins unknown,
She forthwith led fair Geraldine
To meet her sire, Sir Leoline.

The lovely maid and the lady tall
Are pacing both into the hall,
And pacing on through page and groom,
Enter the Baron's presence-room.[34]

The Baron rose, and while he pressed
His gentle daughter to his breast,
With cheerful wonder in his eyes
The lady Geraldine espies,
And gave such welcome to the same,
As might beseem so bright a dame!

But when he heard the lady's tale,
And when she told her father's name,
Why waxed[35] Sir Leoline so pale,
Murmuring o'er the name again –
Lord Roland de Vaux of Tryermaine?

Alas, they had been friends in youth,
But whispering tongues can poison truth,
And constancy lives in realms above;
And life is thorny, and youth is vain,
And to be wroth[36] with one we love
Doth work like madness in the brain.
And thus it chanced, as I divine,
With Roland and Sir Leoline;
Each spake words of high disdain
And insult to his heart's best brother –
They parted, ne'er to meet again!
But never either found another
To free the hollow heart from paining –
They stood aloof, the scars remaining
Like cliffs which had been rent asunder.

Notes

[33] *With such . . . behind* In a MS marginal note to a copy of the 1816 printed text, Coleridge wrote: 'Christabel is made to believe that the fearful sight had taken place only in a dream.'

[34] *presence-room* room where Sir Leoline receives guests; reception room.

[35] *waxed* became.

[36] *wroth* angry.

A dreary sea now flows between,
But neither heat, nor frost, nor thunder
Shall wholly do away, I ween,
The marks of that which once hath been.

Sir Leoline a moment's space
Stood gazing on the damsel's face,
And the youthful Lord of Tryermaine
Came back upon his heart again.

Oh then the Baron forgot his age,
His noble heart swelled high with rage;
He swore by the wounds in Jesu's side
He would proclaim it far and wide
With trump and solemn heraldry,
That they who thus had wronged the dame
Were base as spotted infamy!
'And if they dare deny the same,
My herald shall appoint a week,
And let the recreant traitors seek
My tournay court[37] – that there and then
I may dislodge their reptile souls
From the bodies and forms of men!'
He spake – his eye in lightning rolls!
For the lady was ruthlessly seized, and he kenned[38]
In the beautiful lady the child of his friend!

And now the tears were on his face,
And fondly in his arms he took
Fair Geraldine, who met th' embrace,
Prolonging it with joyous look,
Which when she viewed, a vision fell
Upon the soul of Christabel –
The vision of fear, the touch and pain!
She shrunk and shuddered, and saw again
(Ah woe is me! Was it for thee,
Thou gentle maid, such sights to see?[39]) –
Again she saw that bosom old,
Again she felt that bosom cold,
And drew in her breath with a hissing sound.
Whereat the knight turned wildly round,
And nothing saw but his own sweet maid
With eyes upraised, as one that prayed.

The touch, the sight, had passed away,
And in its stead that vision blessed,

Notes

[37] *My tournay court* The sheriff's county court usually met twice a year.

[38] *kenned* recognized.

[39] *Which when she viewed . . . to see* Coleridge's MS note in a copy of the 1816 volume reads: 'Christabel then recollects the whole, and knows that it was not a dream, but yet cannot disclose the fact that the strange lady is a supernatural being with the stamp of the Evil Ones on her.'

Which comforted her after rest,[40]
While in the lady's arms she lay,
Had put a rapture in her breast,
And on her lips and o'er her eyes
Spread smiles like light!
With new surprise,
'What ails then my beloved child?'
The Baron said. His daughter mild
Made answer, 'All will yet be well!'
I ween she had no power to tell
Aught else, so mighty was the spell.

Yet he who saw this Geraldine
Had deemed her sure a thing divine,
Such sorrow with such grace she blended,
As if she feared she had offended
Sweet Christabel, that gentle maid!
And with such lowly tones she prayed
She might be sent without delay
Home to her father's mansion.
'Nay,
Nay, by my soul!' said Leoline.
'Ho! Bracy the bard, the charge be thine!
Go thou with music sweet and loud,
And take two steeds with trappings proud,
And take the youth whom thou lov'st best
To bear thy harp and learn thy song,
And clothe you both in solemn vest,
And over the mountains haste along,
Lest wand'ring folk that are abroad
Detain you on the valley road.

And when he has crossed the Irthing flood,
My merry bard, he hastes, he hastes
Up Knorren Moor, through Halegarth Wood,[41]
And reaches soon that castle good
Which stands and threatens Scotland's wastes.

Bard Bracy! Bard Bracy! Your horses are fleet,
Ye must ride up the hall, your music so sweet,
More loud than your horses' echoing feet!
And loud and loud to Lord Roland call,
"Thy daughter is safe in Langdale hall!
Thy beautiful daughter is safe and free –
Sir Leoline greets thee thus through me.
He bids thee come without delay
With all thy numerous array,

Notes

40 *The touch . . . after rest* In a MS marginal note to a copy of the 1816 printed text, Coleridge wrote: 'Christabel for a moment sees her mother's spirit.'

41 *Irthing flood . . . Halegarth Wood* In a MS marginal note to a copy of the 1816 printed text, Coleridge wrote: 'How gladly Sir Leoline repeats the names and shows how familarly he had once been acquainted with all the spots and paths in the neighbourhood of his former friend's castle and residence.'

And take thy lovely daughter home;
And he will meet thee on the way
With all his numerous array,
White with their panting palfreys' foam!"
And, by mine honour, I will say
That I repent me of the day
When I spake words of fierce disdain
To Roland de Vaux of Tryermaine!
For since that evil hour hath flown,
Many a summer's sun have shone;
Yet ne'er found I a friend again
Like Roland de Vaux of Tryermaine.'

The lady fell and clasped his knees,
Her face upraised, her eyes o'erflowing;
And Bracy replied, with faltering voice,
His gracious hail[42] on all bestowing:
'Thy words, thou sire of Christabel,
Are sweeter than my harp can tell;
Yet might I gain a boon[43] of thee,
This day my journey should not be,
So strange a dream hath come to me,
That I had vowed with music loud
To clear yon wood from thing unblessed,
Warned by a vision in my rest!

For in my sleep I saw that dove,
That gentle bird whom thou dost love,
And call'st by thy own daughter's name –
Sir Leoline! I saw the same
Fluttering and uttering fearful moan
Among the green herbs[44] in the forest alone;
Which when I saw, and when I heard,
I wondered what might ail the bird,
For nothing near it could I see
Save the grass and green herbs underneath the old tree.

And in my dream methought I went
To search out what might there be found,
And what the sweet bird's trouble meant
That thus lay fluttering on the ground.
I went, and peered, and could descry
No cause for her distressful cry;
But yet for her dear lady's sake
I stooped, methought the dove to take,
When lo! I saw a bright green snake
Coiled around its wings and neck.
Green as the herbs on which it couched,

Notes

[42] *hail* greeting.
[43] *boon* favour.
[44] *herbs* plants.

Close by the dove's its head it crouched,
And with the dove it heaves and stirs,
Swelling its neck as she swelled hers!

I woke; it was the midnight hour,
The clock was echoing in the tower;
But though my slumber was gone by,
This dream it would not pass away –
It seems to live upon my eye!
And thence I vowed this self-same day,
With music strong and saintly song,
To wander through the forest bare
Lest aught unholy loiter there.'

Thus Bracy said: the Baron the while,
Half-listening heard him with a smile,
Then turned to Lady Geraldine,
His eyes made up of wonder and love;
And said, in courtly accents fine,
'Sweet maid, Lord Roland's beauteous dove,
With arms more strong than harp or song,
Thy sire and I will crush the snake!'
He kissed her forehead as he spake,
And Geraldine, in maiden wise,
Casting down her large bright eyes,
With blushing cheek and courtesy fine
She turned her from Sir Leoline,
Softly gathering up her train
That o'er her right arm fell again,
And folded her arms across her chest,
And couched her head upon her breast,
And looked askance at Christabel –
Jesu Maria, shield her well!

A snake's small eye blinks dull and shy,
And the lady's eyes they shrunk in her head,
Each shrunk up to a serpent's eye;
And with somewhat of malice and more of dread
At Christabel she looked askance!
One moment and the sight was fled;
But Christabel, in dizzy trance,
Stumbling on the unsteady ground,
Shuddered aloud with a hissing sound;
And Geraldine again turned round
And like a thing that sought relief,
Full of wonder and full of grief,
She rolled her large bright eyes divine
Wildly on Sir Leoline.

The maid, alas! her thoughts are gone,
She nothing sees, no sight but one!
The maid, devoid of guile and sin,
I know not how, in fearful wise

So deeply had she drunken in
That look, those shrunken serpent eyes,
That all her features were resigned
To this sole image in her mind,
And passively did imitate
That look of dull and treacherous hate.
And thus she stood in dizzy trance,
Still picturing that look askance
With forced unconscious sympathy
Full before her father's view –
As far as such a look could be,
In eyes so innocent and blue!

But when the trance was o'er, the maid
Paused awhile and inly prayed,
Then falling at her father's feet,
'By my mother's soul do I entreat
That thou this woman send away!'
She said – and more she could not say,
For what she knew she could not tell,
O'er-mastered by the mighty spell.

Why is thy cheek so wan and wild,
Sir Leoline? Thy only child
Lies at thy feet, thy joy, thy pride,
So fair, so innocent, so mild –
The same for whom thy lady died!
Oh by the pangs of her dear mother,
Think thou no evil of thy child!
For her and thee, and for no other
She prayed the moment ere she died,
Prayed that the babe for whom she died
Might prove her dear lord's joy and pride!
That prayer her deadly pangs beguiled,
    Sir Leoline!
And would'st thou wrong thy only child,
    Her child and thine!

Within the Baron's heart and brain,
If thoughts like these had any share,
They only swelled his rage and pain
And did but work confusion there;
His heart was cleft with pain and rage,
His cheeks they quivered, his eyes were wild –
Dishonoured thus in his old age,
Dishonoured by his only child,
And all his hospitality
To th' insulted daughter of his friend
By more than woman's jealousy
Brought thus to a disgraceful end.
He rolled his eye with stern regard
Upon the gentle minstrel bard,

And said in tones abrupt, austere,
'Why, Bracy, dost thou loiter here?
I bade thee hence!' The bard obeyed;
And, turning from his own sweet maid,
The aged knight, Sir Leoline,
Led forth the lady Geraldine![45]

The Conclusion to Part II[46]

A little child,[47] a limber elf,
Singing, dancing to itself,
A fairy thing with red round cheeks
That always finds and never seeks,
Makes such a vision to the sight
As fills a father's eyes with light,
And pleasures flow in so thick and fast
Upon his heart, that he[48] at last
Must needs express his love's excess
With words of unmeant bitterness.
Perhaps 'tis pretty to force together
Thoughts so all unlike each other,
To mutter and mock a broken charm,
To dally with wrong that does no harm.
Perhaps 'tis tender too and pretty
At each wild word to feel within
A sweet recoil of love and pity.
And what if, in a world of sin
(Oh sorrow and shame should this be true!),
Such giddiness of heart and brain
Comes seldom save from rage and pain,
So talks as it's most used to do.

Notes

[45] The poem was never concluded, and partly for this reason was not included in *Lyrical Ballads* (1800). In later years Coleridge gave varying accounts of how it might have ended, including this, the most extensive, recorded by James Gillman: 'Over the mountains, the Bard, as directed by Sir Leoline, "hastes" with his disciple; but in consequence of one of those inundations supposed to be common in this country, the spot only where the castle once stood is discovered, the edifice itself being washed away. He determines to return. Geraldine being acquainted with all that is passing, like the Weird Sisters in *Macbeth*, vanishes. Reappearing, however, she waits the return of the Bard, exciting in the meantime, by her wily arts, all the anger she could rouse in the Baron's breast, as well as the jealousy of which he is described to have been susceptible. The old Bard and the youth at length arrive, and therefore she can no longer personate the character of Geraldine, the daughter of Lord Roland de Vaux, but changes her appearance to that of the accepted though absent lover of Christabel. Next ensues a courtship most distressing to Christabel, who feels (she knows not why) great disgust for her once favoured knight. This coldness is very painful to the Baron, who has no more conception than herself of the supernatural transformation. She at last yields to her father's entreaties, and consents to approach the altar with this hated suitor. The real lover returning, enters at this moment, and produces the ring which she once had given him in sign of her betrothment. Thus defeated, the supernatural being Geraldine disappears. As predicted, the castle bell tolls, the mother's voice is heard, and to the exceeding great joy of the parties, the rightful marriage takes place, after which follows a reconciliation and explanation between the father and daughter.'

[46] These lines were sent as a fragment to Southey in a letter of 6 May 1801 (Griggs ii 728); it is not clear whether they were at that time considered to form part of *Christabel* (quite possibly not). They appeared as the conclusion to Part II in the printed text of 1816.

[47] *A little child* Hartley Coleridge.

[48] *he* i.e. Hartley.

Letter from S. T. Coleridge to Thomas Poole, 6 April 1799[1] (extract)

My baby has not lived in vain! This life has been to him what it is to all of us – education and development! Fling yourself forward into your immortality only a few thousand years, and how small will not the difference between one year old and sixty years appear! Consciousness! It is not otherwise necessary to our conceptions of future continuance than as connecting the *present link* of our being with the one *immediately* preceding it – and *that* degree of consciousness, *that* small portion of *memory*, it would not only be arrogant, but in the highest degree absurd, to deny even to a much younger infant.

'Tis a strange assertion that the essence of identity lies in *recollective* consciousness; 'twere scarcely less ridiculous to affirm that the 8 miles from Stowey to Bridgwater consist in the 8 milestones. Death in a doting old age falls upon my feelings ever as a more hopeless phenomenon than death in infancy – but *nothing* is hopeless.

What if the vital force which I sent from my arm into the stone, as I flung it in the air and skimmed it upon the water – what if even that did not perish? It was *Life*! It was a particle of *Being*! It was *Power*! – and *how could* it perish? *Life, Power, Being*! – organization may be and probably *is* their *effect*; their *cause* it *cannot* be! I have indulged very curious fancies concerning that force, that *swarm* of motive powers which I sent out of my body into that stone – and which, one by one, left the untractable or already possessed mass, and – but the German ocean lies between us. It is all too far to send you such fancies as these! Grief indeed,

> Doth love to dally with fantastic thoughts,
> And smiling, like a sickly moralist,
> Finds some resemblance to her own concerns
> In the straws of chance, and things inanimate![2]

But I cannot truly say that I grieve. I am perplexed, I am sad – and a little thing, a very trifle, would make me weep. But for the death of the baby I have *not* wept! Oh, this strange, strange, strange scene-shifter, death! – that giddies one with insecurity, and so unsubstantiates the living things that one has grasped and handled! Some months ago Wordsworth transmitted to me a most sublime epitaph;[3] whether it had any reality, I cannot say. Most probably, in some gloomier moment he had fancied the moment in which his sister might die.

Notes

Letter from S. T. Coleridge to Thomas Poole

1 Coleridge's son, Berkeley (born 14 May 1798), died 10 February 1799 during his father's stay in Germany. At first the news was kept from Coleridge, but later Poole thought it better to let him know. This letter is Coleridge's first written response to the news, from Göttingen. Berkeley's death seems to have been a catalyst for the Infant Babe passage in *Two-Part Prelude* ii 267–310.

2 Coleridge quotes himself: *Osorio* V i 11–14.

3 *a most sublime epitaph* 'A Slumber did my Spirit Seal', p. 478.

Lines Written in the Album at Elbingerode, in the Hartz Forest (composed by 17 May 1799)[1]

From The Annual Anthology (1800)

I stood on Brocken's sovran height,[2] and saw
Woods crowding upon woods, hills over hills,
A *surging* scene,[3] and only limited
By the blue distance. Heavily my way
Homeward I dragged through fir-groves evermore,
Where bright green moss heaves in sepulchral forms,
Speckled with sunshine; and, but seldom heard,
The sweet bird's song became an hollow sound;
And the breeze murmuring indivisibly
Preserved its solemn murmur most distinct
From many a note of many a waterfall,
And the brook's chatter, mid whose islet stones
The dingy kidling with its tinkling bell
Leapt frolicsome, or old romantic goat
Sat, his white beard slow-waving. I moved on
In low and languid mood,[4] for I had found
That grandest scenes have but imperfect charms,
Where the sight vainly wanders, nor beholds
One spot with which the heart associates
Holy remembrances of friend or child,
Or gentle maid, our first and early love,
Or father, or the venerable name
Of our adored country!
Oh thou Queen,
Thou delegated deity of earth,
Oh dear, dear, England! How my longing eye
Turned westward, shaping in the steady clouds
Thy sand and high white cliffs! Oh native land,
Filled with the thought of thee, this heart was proud,
Yea, mine eye swam with tears, that all the view
From sovran Brocken, woods and woody hills,
Floated away like a departing dream,
Feeble and dim! Stranger, these impulses
Blame thou not lightly, nor will I profane

Notes

LINES WRITTEN IN THE ALBUM AT ELBINGERODE

1 Coleridge sent this poem in a letter to his wife, 17 May 1799, with the introduction: 'At the inn they brought us an Album, or Stammbuch, requesting that we would write our names and something or other as a remembrance that we had been there. I wrote the following lines, which I send to you not that they possess a grain of merit as poetry, but because they contain a true account of my journey from the Brocken to Elbinrode' (Griggs i 504).

2 *Brocken's sovran height* Coleridge notes that the Great Brocken is 'the highest mountain in the Hartz, and indeed in north Germany'.

3 *A surging scene* In Thomas Poole's copy, Coleridge substituted the phrase, 'A land of billows'.

4 *In low and languid mood* Coleridge glosses this with a quotation from Southey:

When I have gazed
From some high eminence on goodly vales,
And cots and villages embowered below,
The thought would rise that all to me was strange
Amid the scenes so fair, nor one small spot
Where my tired mind might rest, and call it 'home'.
(Southey's *Hymn to the Penates*)

With hasty judgement or injurious doubt
That man's sublimer spirit, who can feel
That God is everywhere! – the God who framed
Mankind to be one mighty family,
Himself our Father, and the world our home.

The Day-Dream (composed March 1802, published *The Morning Post* 19 October 1802; edited from MS)[1]

I

If thou wert here, these tears were 'tears of light'![2]
But from as sweet a day-dream did I start
As ever made these eyes grow idly bright;
And though I weep, yet still about the heart
A dear and playful tenderness doth linger,
Touching my heart as with a baby's finger.

2

My mouth half-open like a witless man,
I saw the couch, I saw the quiet room,
The heaving shadows and the firelight gloom;
And on my lips I know not what there ran –
On my unmoving lips a subtile[3] feeling;
I know not what, but had the same been stealing

3

Upon a sleeping mother's lips, I guess
It would have made the loving mother dream
That she was softly stooping down to kiss
Her babe, that something more than babe did seem –
An obscure presence of its darling father,
Yet still its own sweet baby self far rather!

4

Across my chest there lived a weight so warm
As if some bird had taken shelter there;
And lo, upon the couch, a woman's form! –
Thine, Sara,[4] thine! Oh joy, if thine it were!
I gazed with anxious hope, and feared to stir it –
A deeper trance ne'er rapt a yearning spirit!

Notes

THE DAY-DREAM

[1] The date of composition is conjectural, based on George Whalley's argument that the poem was written prior to 'A Letter to Sara Hutchinson', probably at Greta Hall. When published in the *Morning Post*, in somewhat revised form, it appeared under the title, 'The Day-Dream, from an Emigrant to his Absent Wife'.

[2] *tears of light* The phrase is borrowed from Wordsworth, 'Matthew' 23–4: 'The tears which came to Matthew's eyes / Were tears of light, the oil of gladness.'

[3] *subtle* delicate, fine.

[4] Sara Hutchinson (1775–1835), Coleridge's 'Asra', was Wordsworth's sister-in-law. Coleridge's unconsummated love for her lasted until his break with Wordsworth led him to reside in London.

5

And now, when I seemed *sure* my love to see,
Her very self in her own quiet home,
There came an elfish laugh, and wakened me!
'Twas Hartley,[5] who behind my chair had clomb,[6]
And with his bright eyes at my face was peeping;
I blessed him, tried to laugh – and fell a-weeping.

The Picture; or, The Lover's Resolution (composed March 1802)[1]

From The Morning Post No. 10,584 (6 September 1802)

Through weeds and thorns, and matted underwood
I force my way; now climb, and now descend
O'er rocks, or bare or mossy, with blind foot
Crushing the purple whorts;[2] while oft unseen,
Hurrying along the drifted forest leaves,
The scared snake rustles. Onward still I toil,
I know not, ask not whither. A new joy
Lovely as light, sudden as summer gust
And gladsome as the first-born of the spring,
Beckons me on, or follows from behind,
Playmate or guide.[3] The master-passion quelled,
I feel that I am free. With dun-red bark
The fir-trees and th' unfrequent slender oak
Forth from this tangle wild of bush and brake
Soar up, and form a melancholy vault
High o'er me, murm'ring like a distant sea.
No myrtle-walks are here![4] These are no groves
For Love[5] to dwell in; the low stumps would gore
His dainty feet; the briar and the thorn
Make his plumes haggard; till, like wounded bird,
Easily caught, the dusky dryads,[6]
With prickles sharper than his darts, would mock
His little godship, making him perforce
Creep through a thorn-bush on yon hedgehog's back.
This is my hour of triumph! I can now
With my own fancies play the merry fool,
And laugh away worse folly, being free.
Here will I seat myself beside this old,

Notes

[5] Hartley Coleridge (b. 1796).

[6] *clomb* climbed.

The Picture; or, The Lover's Resolution

[1] In March 1802 Coleridge made the following entry in a notebook: 'A poem on the endeavour to emancipate the soul from day-dreams and note the different attempts and the vain ones' (*Notebooks* i 1153). The poem was *The Picture.*

[2] *whorts* whortleberries.

[3] Lines 7–11 recall Wordsworth's search for a guide in the Glad Preamble (composed early 1800) (see pp. 479–81).

[4] *No myrtle-walks are here* Coleridge may be recalling the myrtle at Clevedon, mentioned at *Eolian Harp* (1795) 4–5 and *Reflections on Having Left a Place of Retirement* 5.

[5] *Love* cupid.

[6] *dryads* wood-nymphs.

Hollow, and woody oak, which ivy-twine
Clothes, as with network;[7] here will couch my limbs
Close by this river, in this silent shade,
As safe and sacred from the step of man
As an invisible world – unheard, unseen,[8]
And list'ning only to the pebbly stream
That murmurs with a dead yet bell-like sound
Tinkling, or bees, that in the neighb'ring trunk
Make honey-hoards. This breeze that visits me
Was never Love's accomplice, never raised
The tendril ringlets from the maiden's brow,
And the blue, delicate veins above her cheek;
Ne'er played the wanton, never half-disclosed
The maiden's snowy bosom, scatt'ring thence
Eye-poisons for some love-distempered youth,
Who ne'er, henceforth, may see an aspen-grove
Shiver in sunshine, but his feeble heart
Shall flow away like a dissolving thing.
Sweet breeze! thou only, if I guess aright,
Liftest the feathers of the robin's breast,
Who swells his little breast, so full of song,
Singing above me on the mountain ash.
And thou too, desert stream! No pool of thine,
Though clear as lake in latest summer eve,
Did e'er reflect the stately virgin's robe,
The face, the form divine, her downcast look
Contemplative, her cheek upon her palm
Supported; the white arm and elbow rest
On the bare branch of half-uprooted tree,
That leans towards its mirror! He, meanwhile,
Who from her count'nance turned, or looked by stealth
(For fear is true love's cruel nurse), he now,
With steadfast gaze and unoffending eye,
Worships the wat'ry idol, dreaming hopes
Delicious to the soul – but fleeting, vain
Ev'n as that phantom-world on which he gazed!
She (sportive tyrant) with her left hand plucks
The heads of tall flow'rs that behind her grow –
Lychnis, and willow-herb, and foxglove-bells;
And suddenly, as one that toys with time,
Scatters them on the pool! Then all the charm
Is broken – all that phantom world so fair
Vanishes, and a thousand circlets spread,
And each misshape the other. Stay awhile,
Poor youth, who scarcely dar'st lift up thine eyes –
The stream will soon renew its smoothness, soon

Notes

[7] *network* light fabric made of netted threads.

[8] *Close by . . . unseen* cf. Coleridge's notebook entry, March 1802: 'A river, so translucent as not to be seen – and yet murmuring – shadowy world – and these a dream / Enchanted river' (*Notebooks* i 1124).

The visions will return! And lo, he stays,
And soon the fragments dim of lovely forms
Come trembling back, unite, and now once more
The pool becomes a mirror;[9] and behold
Each wild-flow'r on the marge inverted there,
And there the half-uprooted tree – but where,
Oh where the virgin's snowy arm, that leaned
On its bare branch? He turns, and she is gone!
Homeward she steals through many a woodland maze
Which he shall seek in vain. Ill-fated youth,
Go, day by day, and waste thy manly prime
In mad love-gazing on the vacant brook,
Till sickly thoughts bewitch thine eyes, and thou
Behold'st her shadow still abiding there,
The naiad of the mirror![10]
Not to thee,
Oh wild and desert stream, belongs this tale.
Gloomy and dark art thou; the crowded firs
Tow'r from thy shores, and stretch across thy bed,
Making thee doleful as a cavern well!
Save when the shy kingfishers build their nest
On thy steep banks, no loves hast thou, wild stream!
This be my chosen haunt – emancipate[11]
From passion's dreams, a freeman, and alone,
I rise and trace its devious course. Oh lead,
Lead me to deeper shades, to lonelier glooms.
Lo! stealing through the canopy of firs,
How fair the sunshine spots that mossy rock,
Isle of the river, whose disparted[12] waters
Dart off asunder with an angry sound,
How soon to reunite! They meet, they join
In deep embrace, and open to the sun
Lie calm and smooth. Such the delicious hour
Of deep enjoyment, foll'wing love's brief quarrels!
And hark, the noise of a near waterfall!
I come out into light – I find myself
Beneath a weeping birch (most beautiful
Of forest trees, the lady of the woods)
Hard by the brink of a tall weedy rock
That overbrows the cataract. How bursts
The landscape on my sight! Two crescent hills
Fold in behind each other, and so make
A circular vale, and landlocked, as might seem,
With brook and bridge, and grey-stone cottages,
Half hid by rocks and fruit-trees. Beneath my feet
The whortleberries are bedewed with spray,

Notes

[9] Lines 69–78 are quoted by Coleridge in the introduction to the printed text of *Kubla Khan* (1816), p. 620.

[10] *naiad of the mirror* nymph of the pond.

[11] *emancipate* free (i.e. from romantic entanglement).

[12] *disparted* divided (by the rock).

Dashed upwards by the furious waterfall.
How solemnly the pendent ivy mass
Swings in its winnow![13] All the air is calm,
The smoke from cottage chimneys, tinged with light,
Rises in columns; from this house alone
Close by the waterfall, the column slants
And feels its ceaseless breeze. But what is this?
That cottage, with its slanting chimney smoke,
And close beside its porch a sleeping child,
His dear head pillowed on a sleeping dog,
One arm between its forelegs, and the hand
Holds loosely its small handful of wild-flow'rs,
Unfilletted,[14] and of unequal lengths –
A curious picture, with a master's haste
Sketched on a strip of pinky-silver skin
Peeled from the birchen bark! Divinest maid –
Yon bark her canvas, and these purple berries
Her pencil! See, the juice is scarcely dried
On the fine skin! She has been newly here,
And lo! Yon patch of heath has been her couch –
The pressure still remains! Oh blessed couch,
For this may'st thou flow'r early, and the sun
Slanting, at eve rest bright, and linger long
Upon thy purple bells! Oh Isabel,
Daughter of genius, stateliest of our maids,
More beautiful than whom Alcaeus wooed,
The Lesbian woman of immortal song,[15]
Oh child of genius, stately, beautiful,
And full of love to all, save only one,
And not ungentle ev'n to me! My heart,
Why beats it thus? Through yonder coppice-wood
Needs must the pathway turn, that leads away
On to her father's house. She is alone!
The night draws on – such ways are hard to hit –
And fit it is I should restore this sketch
Dropped unawares, no doubt. Why should I yearn
To keep the relic? 'Twill but idly feed
The passion that consumes me. Let me haste!
This picture in my hand, which she has left;
She cannot blame me, that I followed her,
And I may be her guide the long wood through!

Notes

[13] *winnow* swinging motion caused by the spray of the waterfall.

[14] *Unfilletted* i.e. the stems of the bunch of flowers are not tied up together.

[15] *whom Alcaeus . . . song* Sappho, as in Wordsworth's 'Alcaeus to Sappho', published *Morning Post* 2 October 1800 (see Griggs i 629).

A Letter to Sara Hutchinson[1]*, 4 April 1802.*[2] *Sunday Evening* (edited from MS)[3]

1

Well! if the bard was weather-wise who made
The dear old ballad of Sir Patrick Spence,[4]
This night, so tranquil now, will not go hence
Unroused by winds that ply a busier trade
Than that which moulds yon clouds in lazy flakes,
Or the dull sobbing draught that drones and rakes
Upon the strings of this Eolian lute,[5]
Which better far were mute.
For lo! the new moon, winter-bright,
And all suffused[6] with phantom light
(With swimming phantom light o'erspread,
But rimmed and circled with a silver thread);
I see the old moon in her lap, foretelling
The coming-on of rain and squally blast.
Ah Sara![7] that the gust ev'n now were swelling,
And the slant night-shower driving loud and fast.

2

A grief without a pang – void, dark, and drear;
A stifling, drowsy, unimpassioned grief
That finds no natural outlet, no relief
In word, or sigh, or tear –

Notes

A Letter to Sara Hutchinson

[1] In MS the title actually reads 'A Letter to ——', but there can be no doubt that the addressee was Sara Hutchinson. For the relation of this poem to Wordsworth's 'Ode' (the first four stanzas of which were composed at much the same time), see Lucy Newlyn, *Coleridge, Wordsworth, and the Language of Allusion* (Oxford, 1986), chapter 3.

[2] 4 April 1802 was the day before Wordsworth set out from Grasmere to propose marriage to Mary Hutchinson. Coleridge later recalled that 'I – then ill – continued talking with Wordsworth the whole night till the dawn of the day, urging him to conclude on marrying Mary Hutchinson' (*Notebooks* iii 3304) – a step he could not take with regard to her sister, Sara, even though he very much wanted to.

[3] This is the poem from which Coleridge derived *Dejection: An Ode* (published here in the 1817 text, pp. 673–7). It is a product of the depressed state in which he had been languishing for some time; as long before as March 1801 he had told Godwin that 'The Poet is dead in me; my imagination (or rather the somewhat that had been imaginative) lies, like a cold snuff on the circular rim of a brass candlestick, without even a stink of tallow to remind you that it was once clothed and mitred with flame' (Griggs ii 714). In December that year he sketched the plan of this poem in a notebook entry: 'A lively picture of a man, disappointed in marriage and endeavouring to make a compensation to himself by virtuous and tender and brotherly friendship with an amiable woman – the obstacles – the jealousies – the impossibility of it. Best advice that he should as much as possible withdraw himself from pursuits of morals etc. – and devote himself to abstract sciences' (*Notebooks* i 1065). By this time he had passed his poetic ambitions on to Wordsworth, in the form of *The Recluse*, and was hopelessly in love with Sara Hutchinson (Wordsworth's sister-in-law), who preferred Wordsworth's company to his. This poem initiated a dialogue with Wordsworth, who 'replied' with the first version of *Resolution and Independence* (3–9 May).

[4] *the bard . . . Spence* unknown; Coleridge knew *The Ballad of Sir Patrick Spens* from Thomas Percy's *Reliques of Ancient English Poetry* (1765).

[5] *Eolian lute* Aeolian harps were placed lengthways in front of open windows, where their strings were 'played' by the wind; see Coleridge's *The Eolian Harp*, pp. 600–5.

[6] *suffused* overspread.

[7] Sara Hutchinson (1775–1835), Coleridge's 'Asra', was Wordsworth's sister-in-law. Coleridge's unconsummated love for her lasted until his break with Wordsworth led him to reside in London.

This, Sara, well thou know'st,
Is that sore evil which I dread the most
And oft'nest suffer in this heartless mood,
To other thoughts by yonder throstle wooed,
That pipes within the larch-tree not unseen
(The larch which pushes out in tassels green
Its bundled leafits), wooed to mild delights
By all the tender sounds and gentle sights
Of this sweet primrose-month – and *vainly* wooed,
Oh dearest Sara, in this heartless[8] mood.

3

All this long eve so balmy and serene
Have I been gazing on the western sky
And its peculiar tint of yellow-green;
And still I gaze, and with how blank an eye!
And those thin clouds above, in flakes and bars,
That give away their motion to the stars,
Those stars that glide behind them and between,
Now sparkling, now bedimmed, but always seen;
Yon crescent moon, as fixed as if it grew
In its own cloudless, starless lake of blue –
A boat becalmed! Dear William's sky canoe![9]
I see them all, so excellently fair;
I *see*, not *feel*, how beautiful they are!

4

My genial spirits fail,[10]
And what can these avail
To lift the smoth'ring weight from off my breast?
It were a vain endeavour,
Though I should gaze forever
On that green light that lingers in the west:[11]
I may not hope from outward forms to win
The passion and the life, whose fountains are within;
These lifeless shapes, around, below, above –
Oh dearest Sara, what can they impart?
Even when the gentle thought that thou, my love,
Art gazing now like me
And see'st the heaven I see –
Sweet thought it is, yet feebly stirs my heart!

Notes

[8] *heartless* depressed, discouraged.

[9] *Dear William's sky canoe* as featured in the prologue to Wordsworth's *Peter Bell* (composed 1798, published 1819).

[10] *My genial spirits fail* an echo of Milton, 'Samson Agonistes' 594: 'my genial spirits droop.'

[11] *that green light that lingers in the west* borrowed from Southey, *Madoc* (1805) II xxxvi 260: 'The last green light that lingers in the west'.

5

Feebly, oh feebly! Yet
(I well remember it)
In my first dawn of youth, that fancy stole
With many gentle yearnings on my soul.
At eve, sky-gazing in 'ecstatic fit'[12]
(Alas, far-cloistered in a city school,[13]
The sky was all I knew of beautiful),
At the barred window often did I sit,
And often on the leaded school-roof lay,
        And to myself would say,
'There does not live the man so stripped of good affections
As not to love to see a maiden's quiet eyes
Upraised and linking on sweet dreams by dim connections
To moon, or evening star, or glorious western skies!'
While yet a boy, this thought would so pursue me,
That often it became a kind of vision to me.

6

Sweet thought, and dear of old
To hearts of finer mould![14]
Ten thousand times by friends and lovers blessed!
        I spake with rash despair,
        And ere I was aware,
The weight was somewhat lifted from my breast!
Dear Sara! in the weather-fended wood,[15]
Thy loved haunt where the stock-doves coo at noon,
        I guess that thou hast stood
And watched yon crescent and that ghost-like moon;
        And yet far rather, in my present mood,
I would that thou'dst been sitting all this while
Upon the sod-built seat of camomile,[16]
And though thy robin may have ceased to sing,
Yet needs for *my* sake must thou love to hear
The beehive murmuring near –
That ever-busy and most quiet thing
Which I have heard at midnight murmuring.

Notes

[12] Milton, 'The Passion' 42.

[13] *a city school* Christ's Hospital in the City of London; cf. 'Frost at Midnight' (1798) 26–48.

[14] *mould* form.

[15] *the weather-fended wood* The wood provides cover from wind and rain, and is therefore weather (de)fended. The phrase 'weather-fends' is from Shakespeare, *The Tempest* V i 10.

[16] *the sod-built seat of camomile* 'Sara's seat' was built by Coleridge and the Wordsworths on White Moss Common, Rydal, 10 October 1801.

7

I feel my spirit moved:
And wheresoe'er thou be,
Oh sister, oh beloved!
Thy dear mild eyes that see
The very heaven *I* see –
There is a prayer in them, it is for *me*!
And I, dear Sara, *I* am blessing *thee*![17]

8

It was as calm as this, the happy night[18]
When Mary, thou and I together were,
The low decaying fire our only light,
And listened to the stillness of the air!
Oh, that affectionate and blameless maid,
Dear Mary, on her lap my head she laid –
Her hand was on my brow
Even as my own is now,
And on my cheek I felt thy eyelash play.[19]
Such joy I had that I may truly say
My spirit was awe-stricken with the excess
And trance-like depth of its brief happiness.

9

Ah fair remembrances that so revive
My heart and fill it with a living power –
Where were they, Sara? Or did I not strive
To win them to me on the fretting hour
Then when I wrote thee that complaining scroll,[20]
Which even to bodily sickness bruised thy soul?
And yet thou blam'st thyself alone, and yet
Forbidd'st me all regret.[21]

10

And must I not *regret* that I distressed
Thee, best beloved, who lovest me the best?
My better mind had fled I know not whither –
For oh! was this an absent friend's employ,

Notes

[17] *I am blessing thee* one in a long line of benedictions; cf. those of Hartley in 'Frost at Midnight' and Charles Lamb in 'This Lime-Tree Bower My Prison'.

[18] *the happy night* the exact date is not known, but it was during Coleridge's visit to Gallow Hill, 2–13 March 1802. It is recalled also in *A Day-Dream* and *The Day-Dream* (pp. 658–9, 672–3).

[19] *And on my cheek . . . play* cf. *A Day-Dream* 31–2: 'Thine eyelash on my cheek doth play – / 'Tis Mary's hand upon my brow!'

[20] *that complaining scroll* a letter to Sara. The 'bodily sickness' of l. 116 may be the sickness into which she had fallen by 29 February 1802, which drew Coleridge back to Gallow Hill from London. He remained at Gallow Hill from 2 to 13 March, weeping aloud when he left for Keswick.

[21] Coleridge's letters not infrequently caused Sara distress. On 13 December 1801 Dorothy recorded: 'The boy brought letters from Coleridge and from Sara. Sara in bad spirits about Coleridge' (*Grasmere Journals* 48).

To send from far both pain and sorrow thither,
Where still his blessings should have called down joy?
I read thy guileless letter o'er again,
I hear thee of thy blameless self complain,
And only this I learn – and this, alas, I know –
That thou art weak and pale with sickness, grief, and pain,
And *I* – *I* made thee so!

11

Oh, *for my own sake*, I regret *perforce*
Whatever turns *thee*, Sara, from the course
Of calm well-being and a heart at rest.
When thou and, with thee, those whom thou lov'st best
Shall dwell together in one quiet home,
One home the sure *abiding* home of all,
I too will crown me with a coronal;[22]
Nor shall this heart in idle wishes roam
      Morbidly soft!
No, let me trust that I shall wear away
In no inglorious toils the manly day;
And only now and then, and not too oft,
Some dear and memorable eve shall bless,
Dreaming of all your love and happiness.

12

Be happy, and I need thee not in sight!
Peace in thy heart, and quiet in thy dwelling,
Health in thy limbs, and in thy eyes the light
Of love, and hope, and honourable feeling;
Where'er I am, I needs must be content –
Not near thee, haply shall be more content!
To all things I prefer the permanent.[23]
And better seems it for a heart like mine
Always to *know*, than sometimes to *behold*
      Their happiness and thine:
For change doth trouble me with pangs untold!
To see thee, hear thee, feel thee, then to part –
      Oh, it weighs down the heart!
To visit those I love, as I love *thee*,
Mary, William, and dear Dorothy,
It is but a temptation to repine!
The transientness is poison in the wine,
Eats out the pith of joy, makes all joy hollow,
All pleasure a dim dream of pain to follow!
My own peculiar lot, my household life,

Notes

[22] *I too . . . coronal* an allusion to Wordsworth's 'Ode': 'My heart is at your festival, / My head hath its coronal' (ll.39–40).

[23] *To all things . . . permanent* Cf. Wordsworth's reference to the 'beautiful and permanent forms of nature', Preface to *Lyrical Ballads*, p. 497.

It is (and will remain) indifference or strife;
While ye are well and happy, 'twould but wrong you
If I should fondly yearn to be among you –
Wherefore, oh wherefore, should I wish to be
A withered branch upon a blossoming tree?

13

But (let me say it, for I vainly strive
To beat away the thought) – but if thou pined,
Whate'er the cause, in body or in mind,
I were the miserablest man alive
To know it and be absent! Thy delights
Far off or near, alike shall I partake –
But oh! to mourn for thee, and to forsake
All power, all hope of giving comfort to thee;
To know that thou art weak and worn with pain
And not to hear thee, Sara, not to view thee,
Not sit beside thy bed,
Not press thy aching head,
Not bring thee health again,
At least to hope, to try
By this voice which thou lov'st, and by this earnest eye –

14

Nay, wherefore did I let it haunt my mind,
This dark distressful dream?
I turn from it and listen to the wind
Which long has howled unnoticed! What a scream
Of agony, by torture lengthened out,
That lute sent forth! Oh thou wild storm without!
Or crag, or tairn,[24] or lightning-blasted tree,
Or pine-grove whither woodman never clomb,[25]
Or lonely house long held the witches' home,
Methinks were fitter instruments for thee,
Mad lutanist, that in this month of showers,
Of dark-brown gardens and of peeping flowers,
Mak'st devil's yule,[26] with worse than wintry song,
The blooms and buds and timorous leaves among!
Thou actor, perfect in all tragic sounds,
Thou mighty poet, even to frenzy bold,
What tell'st thou now about?
'Tis of a rushing of an host[27] in rout,
And many groans from men with smarting wounds,[28]

Notes

[24] *tairn* expanse of water high among the mountains; see Coleridge's note to *Christabel* 294, p. 647.

[25] *clomb* climbed.

[26] *yule* festival; yule was the pagan festival that became Christmas. This is the devil's yule because it is April rather than December.

[27] *host* army.

[28] *an host . . . wounds* Coleridge was very conscious of the war against France, which had been going on since 1793 and which had halted (temporarily) after signing of the Treaty of Amiens, just a week before; see also *Reflections on Having Left a Place of Retirement* 43–8, *Fears in Solitude*.

That groan at once from smart, and shudder with the cold!
But hush, there is a break of deepest silence –
Again! But that dread sound, as of a rushing crowd,
And groans and tremulous shuddering – all are over.
And it has other sounds, and all less deep, less loud;
A tale of less affright,
And tempered with delight,
As William's self had made the tender lay!
'Tis of a little child
Upon a heathy wild[29]
Not far from home, but it has lost its way,
And now moans low in utter grief and fear,
And now screams loud, and hopes to make its mother hear!

15

'Tis midnight, and small thought have I of sleep –
Full seldom may my friend[30] such vigils keep –
Oh breathe she softly in her gentle sleep!
Cover her, gentle sleep, with wings of healing,
And be this tempest but a mountain birth!
May all the stars hang bright above her dwelling,
Silent, as though they watched the sleeping earth,
Like elder sisters with love-twinkling eyes!
Healthful and light, my darling, may'st thou rise,
And of the same good tidings to me send –
For oh, beloved friend!
I am not the buoyant thing I was of yore,
When like an own child, I to joy belonged;
For others mourning oft, myself oft sorely wronged,
Yet bearing all things then as if I nothing bore.

16

Ere I was wedded,[31] though my path was rough,
The joy within me dallied with distress,
And all misfortunes were but as the stuff
Whence fancy made me dreams of happiness;
For hope grew round me like the climbing vine,
And leaves and fruitage not my own, seemed mine!
But now ill tidings bow me down to earth,
Nor care I that they rob me of my mirth;
But oh! each visitation
Suspends what nature gave me at my birth –
My shaping spirit of imagination!
I speak not now of those habitual ills
That wear out life, when two unequal minds
Meet in one house, and two discordant wills –

Notes

[29] *a little child . . . wild* Coleridge has in mind Wordsworth's 'Lucy Gray', published in *Lyrical Ballads* (1800).
[30] *my friend* Sara Hutchinson.

[31] *Ere I was wedded* Before Coleridge married Sara Fricker in 1795 he had enjoyed a career as a political lecturer and pamphleteer.

This leaves me where it finds,
Past cure and past complaint – a fate austere
Too fixed and hopeless to partake of fear!

17

But thou, *dear* Sara (dear indeed thou art,
My comforter, a heart within my heart!),
Thou and the few we love, though few ye be,
Make up a world of hopes and fears for me.
And when affliction or distempering pain
Or wayward chance befall you, I complain
Not that I mourn – oh friends most dear, most true!
Methinks to weep with you
Were better far than to rejoice alone –
But that my coarse domestic life[32] has known
No griefs but such as dull and deaden me,
No habits of heart-nursing sympathy,
No mutual mild enjoyments of its own,
No hopes of its own vintage – none, oh none! –
Whence, when I mourn for you, my heart must borrow
Fair forms and living motions for its sorrow.
For not to think of what I needs must feel,
But to be still and patient all I can,
And haply by abstruse research to steal
From my own nature all the natural man –
This was my sole resource, my wisest plan;
And that which suits a part infects the whole,
And now is almost grown the temper of my soul.[33]

18

My little children[34] are a joy, a love,
A good gift from above!
But what is bliss, that ever calls up woe,
And makes it doubly keen,
Compelling me to feel what well I know –
What a most blessed lot mine *might* have been.
Those little angel children (woe is me!),
There have been hours when, feeling how they bind
And pluck out the wing-feathers of my mind,
Turning my error to necessity,
I have half-wished they never had been born![35]

Notes

[32] *my coarse domestic life* Coleridge's marriage was disintegrating. On 20 October 1802 he told Thomas Wedgwood of what he had endured at Greta Hall: 'Ill-tempered speeches sent after me when I went out of the house; ill-tempered speeches on my return; my friends received with freezing looks' (Griggs ii 876).

[33] *For not . . . soul* These lines were not included in *Dejection: An Ode* in 1802, but were readmitted to the 1817 text (see p. 676).

[34] *My little children* Hartley (b.1796) and Derwent (b.1800). Sara would be born 23 December 1802.

[35] *I have . . . born* The unsatisfactoriness of his marriage was largely the cause of these guilty feelings about his children, with whom he was spending less and less time. Cf. *The Day-Dream* 25–30, and his comment to his wife in a letter of Christmas Day 1801: 'Oh my dear Hartley, my Derwent! My children! The night before last I dreamt I saw them so vividly, that I was quite ill in the morning and wept my eyes red' (Griggs ii 776).

That, seldom; but sad thought they always bring,
And, like the poet's nightingale,[36] I sing
My love-song with my breast against a thorn.

19

With no unthankful spirit I confess
This clinging grief, too, in its turn awakes
That love and father's joy – but oh! it makes
The love the greater, and the joy far less.
These mountains too, these vales, these woods, these lakes,
Scenes full of beauty and of loftiness
Where all my life I fondly hope to live –
I were sunk low indeed, did they *no* solace give.
But oft I seem to feel, and evermore to fear,
They are not to me now the things which once they were.[37]

20

Oh Sara, we receive but what we give,
And in *our* life alone does nature live;
Ours is her wedding-garment, ours her shroud!
And would we aught behold of higher worth
Than that inanimate cold world allowed
To the poor, loveless, ever-anxious crowd –
Ah! from the soul itself must issue forth
A light, a glory,[38] and a luminous cloud
    Enveloping the earth!
And from the soul itself must there be sent
A sweet and potent voice, of its own birth,
Of all sweet sounds the life and element.
Oh pure of heart![39] thou need'st not ask of me
What this strange music in the soul may be,
What and wherein it doth exist,
This light, this glory, this fair luminous mist,
This beautiful and beauty-making power!
Joy,[40] innocent Sara! Joy that ne'er was given
Save to the pure and in their purest hour,
Joy, Sara, is the spirit and the power
That, wedding nature to us, gives in dower[41]
    A new earth and new heaven
Undreamt of by the sensual and the proud!
Joy is that sweet voice, joy that luminous cloud –

Notes

[36] *the poet's nightingale* Philomela, one of the subjects of Ovid's *Metamorphoses*. She was seduced by her brother-in-law, Tereus King of Thrace, who cut out her tongue to prevent her from incriminating him. She was finally turned into a nightingale, her sad song said to derive from the thorn in her breast

[37] *They are not . . . were* a reworking of Wordsworth, 'Ode' 9: 'The things which I have seen I now can see no more.'

[38] *glory* divine effulgence of light, as at Wordsworth, 'Ode' 18.

[39] *Oh pure of heart* Sara Hutchinson.

[40] *Joy* In a notebook entry Coleridge glossed joy as 'when the heart is full as of a deep and quiet fountain overflowing insensibly, or the gladness of joy, when the fountain becomes ebullient' (*Notebooks* ii 2279).

[41] *dower* a wedding-gift.

We, we ourselves rejoice!
And thence flows all that charms or ear or sight,
All melodies the echoes of that voice,
All colours a suffusion from that light.
Sister and friend[42] of my devoutest[43] choice!
Thou being innocent and full of love,
And nested with the darlings of thy love;
And feeling in thy soul, heart, lips, and arms
Even what the conjugal and mother dove
That borrows genial warmth from these she warms
Feels in her thrilled wings, blessedly outspread[44] –
Thou, freed awhile from cares and human dread
By the immenseness of the good and fair
Which thou seest everywhere –
Thus, thus would'st thou rejoice!
To thee would all things *live* from pole to pole,[45]
Their life the eddying of thy living soul.
Oh dear! Oh innocent! Oh full of love!
Sara, thou friend of my devoutest[46] choice,
As dear as light and impulse from above –
So may'st thou ever, evermore rejoice!

A Day-Dream (composed June 1802; published 1828)[1]

From Poetical Works (1828)

My eyes make pictures, when they are shut:
I see a fountain, large and fair,
A willow and a ruined hut,[2]
And thee,[3] and me, and Mary[4] there.
Oh Mary, make thy gentle lap our pillow!
Bend o'er us, like a bower, my beautiful green willow!

A wild rose roofs the ruined shed,
And that and summer well agree;
And lo! where Mary leans her head –

Notes

[42] *Sister and friend* i.e. Sara Hutchinson.

[43] *devoutest* most devoted, most attached.

[44] *Even what . . . outspread* Coleridge has in mind the moment of creation, *Paradise Lost* i 21–2, where the Holy Spirit 'Dove-like sat'st brooding on the vast abyss / And madest it pregnant'.

[45] *To thee . . . pole* Coleridge blesses Sara with the pantheist perception of the one life in the natural world, as he had done Charles Lamb in 'This Lime-Tree Bower My Prison'.

[46] *devoutest* most devoted, most attached.

A Day-Dream

[1] The date of composition remains conjectural, but Coleridge himself says that it was written in June (l. 16), and 1802 is a likely year because this poem appears to be closely related to 'A Letter to Sara Hutchinson' and recalls an incident that occurred during Coleridge's visit to Gallow Hill, 2–13 March 1802.

[2] *hut* cottage.

[3] *thee* Sara Hutchinson (1775–1835), Coleridge's 'Asra', was Wordsworth's sister-in-law. Coleridge's unconsummated love for her lasted until his break with Wordsworth led him to reside in London.

[4] Mary Hutchinson (1770–1859), who married Wordsworth on 4 October 1802.

Two dear names carved upon the tree!
And Mary's tears, they are not tears of sorrow:
Our sister and our friend[5] will both be here tomorrow.

'Twas day! But now few, large, and bright
The stars are round the crescent moon!
And now it is a dark warm night,
The balmiest of the month of June!
A glow-worm fallen, and on the marge remounting
Shines, and its shadow[6] shines, fit stars for our sweet fountain.

Oh ever, ever be thou blessed!
For dearly, Asra, love I thee!
This brooding warmth across my breast,[7]
This depth of tranquil bliss – ah me!
Fount, tree and shed are gone, I know not whither,
But in one quiet room we three are still together.

The shadows dance upon the wall
By the still dancing fire-flames made;
And now they slumber, moveless all,
And now they melt to one deep shade!
But not from me shall this mild darkness steal thee;
I dream thee with mine eyes, and at my heart I feel thee.

Thine eyelash on my cheek doth play –
'Tis Mary's hand upon my brow![8]
But let me check this tender lay
Which none may hear but she and thou!
Like the still hive at quiet midnight humming,
Murmur it to yourselves, ye two beloved women!

Dejection: An Ode (composed *c.* July 1802)[1]

From Sibylline Leaves (1817)

Late, late yestreen I saw the new moon
With the old moon in her arms;
And I fear, I fear, my master dear,
We shall have a deadly storm.
(Ballad of Sir Patrick Spence)[2]

Notes

[5] *Our sister and our friend* Dorothy and William Wordsworth.

[6] *shadow* reflection (in the fountain).

[7] *This brooding warmth . . . breast* Sara has become the 'the conjugal and mother dove' of 'A Letter to Sara Hutchinson' 327–9.

[8] *Thine eyelash . . . brow* Cf. 'A Letter to Sara Hutchinson' 104–7.

Dejection: An Ode

[1] Coleridge first published this poem in the *Morning Post*, 4 October 1802, as a sort of gift to Wordsworth, whose wedding-day it was (as well as being the seventh anniversary of Coleridge's own unhappy marriage). In that version he addressed it to 'Edmund'; in this text the addressee is a 'Lady'.

[2] Coleridge knew *The Ballad of Sir Patrick Spens* from Thomas Percy's *Reliques of Ancient English Poetry* (1765).

I

Well! if the bard was weather-wise who made
The grand old ballad of Sir Patrick Spence,[3]
This night, so tranquil now, will not go hence
Unroused by winds that ply a busier trade
Than those which mould yon clouds in lazy flakes,
Or the dull sobbing draught that moans and rakes
Upon the strings of this Eolian lute,[4]
Which better far were mute.
For lo! the new moon, winter-bright,
And overspread with phantom light
(With swimming phantom light o'erspread,
But rimmed and circled by a silver thread);
I see the old moon in her lap, foretelling
The coming-on of rain and squally blast.
And oh, that even now the gust were swelling,
And the slant night-shower driving loud and fast.
Those sounds which oft have raised me whilst they awed
And sent my soul abroad,
Might now perhaps their wonted[5] impulse give,
Might startle this dull pain, and make it move and live!

II

A grief without a pang – void, dark, and drear;
A stifled, drowsy, unimpassioned grief
Which finds no natural outlet, no relief
In word, or sigh, or tear –
Oh Lady![6] in this wan and heartless mood,
To other thoughts by yonder throstle wooed
All this long eve so balmy and serene,
Have I been gazing on the western sky
And its peculiar tint of yellow-green;
And still I gaze, and with how blank an eye!
And those thin clouds above, in flakes and bars,
That give away their motion to the stars,
Those stars that glide behind them or between,
Now sparkling, now bedimmed, but always seen;
Yon crescent moon, as fixed as if it grew
In its own cloudless, starless lake of blue –
I see them all, so excellently fair;
I see, not feel, how beautiful they are!

Notes

[3] *the bard . . . Spence* unknown; the ballad is anonymous.

[4] *Eolian lute* Aeolian harps were placed lengthways in front of open windows, where their strings were 'played' by the wind; see Coleridge's *The Eolian Harp*, pp. 600–5.

[5] *wonted* expected, usual.

[6] *Lady* Coleridge once again has in mind the original addressee of this work, Sara Hutchinson.

III

My genial spirits fail,[7]
And what can these avail
To lift the smoth'ring weight from off my breast?
It were a vain endeavour,
Though I should gaze for ever
On that green light that lingers in the west:
I may not hope from outward forms to win
The passion and the life, whose fountains are within!

IV

Oh Lady, we receive but what we give,
And in our life alone does nature live;
Ours is her wedding-garment, ours her shroud!
And would we aught behold of higher worth
Than that inanimate cold world allowed
To the poor loveless ever-anxious crowd –
Ah! from the soul itself must issue forth
A light, a glory,[8] a fair luminous cloud
Enveloping the earth!
And from the soul itself must there be sent
A sweet and potent voice, of its own birth,
Of all sweet sounds the life and element.

V

Oh pure of heart![9] thou need'st not ask of me
What this strong music in the soul may be,
What and wherein it doth exist,
This light, this glory, this fair luminous mist,
This beautiful and beauty-making power!
Joy, virtuous Lady! Joy that ne'er was given
Save to the pure and in their purest hour,
Life, and life's effluence,[10] cloud at once and shower,
Joy, Lady, is the spirit and the power
Which, wedding nature to us, gives in dower[11]
A new earth and new heaven
Undreamt of by the sensual and the proud!
Joy is the sweet voice, joy the luminous cloud –
We in ourselves rejoice!
And thence flows all that charms or ear or sight,
All melodies the echoes of that voice,
All colours a suffusion from that light.

Notes

[7] *My genial spirits fail* An echo of Milton, 'Samson Agonistes' 594: 'my genial spirits droop.'

[8] *glory* divine effulgence of light, as at Wordsworth, 'Ode' 18.

[9] *Oh pure of heart* the addressee of the poem, in this case, 'Lady'.

[10] *effluence* emanation, radiating energies.

[11] *dower* wedding-gift.

VI

There was a time[12] when, though my path was rough,
This joy within me dallied with distress,
And all misfortunes were but as the stuff
Whence fancy made me dreams of happiness;
For hope grew round me like the twining vine,
And fruits and foliage not my own, seemed mine!
But now afflictions bow me down to earth,
Nor care I that they rob me of my mirth;
But oh! each visitation
Suspends what nature gave me at my birth –
My shaping spirit of imagination!
For not to think of what I needs must feel,
But to be still and patient all I can,
And haply by abstruse research to steal
From my own nature all the natural man –
This was my sole resource, my only plan;
Till that which suits a part infects the whole,
And now is almost grown the habit of my soul.

VII

Hence, viper thoughts, that coil around my mind,
Reality's dark dream!
I turn from you, and listen to the wind,
Which long has raved unnoticed. What a scream
Of agony, by torture lengthened out,
That lute sent forth! Thou wind, that rav'st without!
Bare crag, or mountain tairn,[13] or blasted tree,
Or pine-grove whither woodman never clomb,[14]
Or lonely house long held the witches' home,
Methinks were fitter instruments for thee,
Mad lutanist, who in this month of show'rs,
Of dark-brown gardens and of peeping flow'rs,
Mak'st devil's yule,[15] with worse than wintry song,
The blossoms, buds, and tim'rous leaves among!
Thou actor, perfect in all tragic sounds,
Thou mighty poet,[16] e'en to frenzy bold,
What tell'st thou now about?
'Tis of the rushing of an host[17] in rout,
With groans of trampled men with smarting wounds[18] –
At once they groan with pain, and shudder with the cold!

Notes

[12] *There was a time* echoes Wordsworth, 'Ode' 1. In the 'Letter to Sara Hutchinson', this was the time 'Ere I was wedded' (l. 231).

[13] 'Tairn is a small lake, generally if not always applied to the lakes up in the mountains, and which are the feeders of those in the valleys. This address to the storm-wind will not appear extravagant to those who have heard it at night, and in a mountainous country' (Coleridge's note).

[14] *clomb* climbed.

[15] *yule* festival; yule was the pagan festival that became Christmas. This is the devil's yule because it is April rather than December.

[16] *Thou mighty poet* i.e. the wind of line 93.

[17] *host* army.

[18] *an host . . . wounds,* In 1815, Britain's long war with France (which had begun in 1793) had come to an end.

But hush, there is a pause of deepest silence!
And all that noise, as of a rushing crowd,
With groans and tremulous shudderings – all is over.
It tells another tale, with sounds less deep and loud,
A tale of less affright
And tempered with delight,
As Otway's[19] self had framed the tender lay –
'Tis of a little child
Upon a lonesome wild
Not far from home, but she hath lost her way,
And now moans low in bitter grief and fear,
And now screams loud, and hopes to make her mother hear.

VIII

'Tis midnight, but small thoughts have I of sleep;
Full seldom may my friend such vigils keep!
Visit her, gentle sleep, with wings of healing,
And may this storm be but a mountain birth;
May all the stars hang bright above his dwelling,
Silent, as though they watched the sleeping earth!
With light heart may she rise,
Gay fancy, cheerful eyes,
Joy lift her spirit, joy attune her voice:
To her may all things live, from pole to pole,
Their life the eddying of her living soul!
Oh simple spirit, guided from above;
Dear Lady, friend devoutest[20] of my choice,
Thus may'st thou ever, evermore rejoice.

Chamouny; the Hour Before Sunrise. A Hymn (composed not before 26 August 1802)[1]

From The Morning Post No.10,589 (11 September 1802)

Chamouny is one of the highest mountain valleys of the Barony of Faucigny in the Savoy Alps, and exhibits a kind of fairy world in which the wildest appearances (I had almost said horrors) of nature alternate with the softest and most beautiful. The chain of Mont Blanc is its boundary, and, besides the Arvé, it is filled with sounds from the

Notes

[19] This reference to Thomas Otway (1652–85), who, according to Johnson, died in penury after wandering across a heath in a state of near-nakedness, further veils the reference to Wordsworth, whose 'Lucy Gray' tells the story of a lost child. Coleridge would have been aware of Charlotte Smith's interest in Otway.

[20] *devoutest* most devoted, most attached.

CHAMOUNY; THE HOUR BEFORE SUNRISE

[1] On 10 September 1802 Coleridge told William Sotheby that he composed this poem 'when I was on Scafell. I involuntarily poured forth a hymn in the manner of the Psalms, though afterwards I thought the ideas etc. disproportionate to our humble mountains, and, accidentally lighting on a short note in some Swiss poems concerning the Vale of Chamouni and its mountains, I transferred myself thither, in the spirit, and adapted my former feelings to these grander external objects' (Griggs ii 864–5). However, Griggs notes that the poem could not have been composed until after 26 August 1802 – three weeks after Coleridge's Scafell ascent. He had certainly not seen Chamouni (now spelled Chamonix) when this poem was written; the main literary inspiration was Frederika Brun's 'Chamouny beym Sonnenaufgange'. Coleridge's poem is often contrasted with the religious scepticism of Shelley's poem about the same locale, *Mont Blanc* (pp. 1075–9).

Arveiron, which rushes from the melted glaciers like a giant mad with joy from a dungeon, and forms other torrents of snow-water, having their rise in the glaciers which slope down into the valley. The beautiful *gentiana major*, or greater gentian, with blossoms of the brightest blue, grows in large companies a few steps from the never-melted ice of the glaciers. I thought it an affecting emblem of the boldness of human hope, venturing near, and, as it were, leaning over, the brink of the grave. Indeed, the whole vale, its every light, its every sound, must needs impress every mind not utterly callous with the thought, Who *would* be, who *could* be an atheist in this valley of wonders? If any readers of *The Morning Post* have visited this vale in their journeys among the Alps, I am confident that they will not find the sentiments and feelings expressed, or attempted to be expressed, in the following poem, extravagant.

Hast thou a charm to stay[2] the morning star
In his steep course? So long he seems to pause
On thy bald awful head, oh Chamouny!
The Arvé and Arveiron at thy base
Rave ceaselessly; but thou, dread mountain form,
Risest from forth thy silent sea of pines
How silently! Around thee and above,
Deep is the sky, and black – transpicuous,[3] deep,
An ebon mass. Methinks thou piercest it
As with a wedge! But when I look again,
It seems thy own calm home, thy crystal shrine,
Thy habitation from eternity.
Oh dread and silent form! I gazed upon thee
Till thou, still present to my bodily eye,
Didst vanish from my thought. Entranced in pray'r,
I worshipped the Invisible alone.
Yet thou, meantime, wast working on my soul,
E'en like some deep enchanting melody,
So sweet, we know not we are list'ning to it.
But I awake, and with a busier mind
And active will self-conscious, offer now,
Not, as before, involuntary pray'r
And passive adoration.
                                        Hand and voice,
Awake, awake! And thou, my heart, awake!
Awake, ye rocks! Ye forest pines, awake!
Green fields and icy cliffs, all join my hymn!
And thou, oh silent mountain, sole and bare,
Oh blacker than the darkness, all the night,
And visited all night by troops of stars,
Or when they climb the sky, or when they sink;
Companion of the morning star at dawn,
Thyself earth's rosy star, and of the dawn
Co-herald! Wake, oh wake, and utter praise!
Who sank thy sunless pillars deep in earth?
Who filled thy countenance with rosy light?

Notes

[2] *stay* stop.

[3] *transpicuous* transparent, as at *Paradise Lost* viii 141.

Who made thee father of perpetual streams?
And you, ye five wild torrents, fiercely glad,
Who called you forth from night and utter death,
From darkness let you loose, and icy dens,
Down those precipitous, black, jagged rocks
For ever shattered, and the same for ever?
Who gave you your invulnerable life,
Your strength, your speed, your fury, and your joy,
Unceasing thunder, and eternal foam?
And who commanded (and the silence came),
'Here shall the billows stiffen, and have rest'?
  Ye ice-falls! Ye that from yon dizzy heights
Adown enormous ravines steeply slope –
Torrents, methinks, that heard a mighty voice,
And stopped at once amid their maddest plunge!
Motionless torrents! Silent cataracts!
Who made you glorious as the gates of heav'n
Beneath the keen full moon? Who bade the sun
Clothe you with rainbows? Who with lovely flow'rs
Of living blue spread garlands at your feet?
'God, God!'[4] the torrents, like a shout of nations,
Utter. The ice-plain bursts, and answers 'God!'
'God!' sing the meadow-streams with gladsome voice,
And pine-groves, with their soft and soul-like sound!
The silent snow-mass, loos'ning, thunders 'God!'
Ye dreadless flow'rs that fringe th' eternal frost!
Ye wild goats bounding by the eagle's nest!
Ye eagles, playmates of the mountain blast!
Ye lightnings, the dread arrows of the clouds!
Ye signs and wonders of the element
Utter forth 'God!' and fill the hills with praise!
  And thou, oh silent form, alone and bare,
Whom, as I lift again my head bowed low
In adoration, I again behold,
And to thy summit upward from thy base
Sweep slowly with dim eyes suffused[5] by tears,
Awake, thou mountain form! Rise like a cloud!
Rise like a cloud of incense from the earth!
Thou kingly spirit throned among the hills,
Thou dread ambassador from earth to heav'n –
Great hierarch,[6] tell thou the silent sky,
And tell the stars, and tell the rising sun,
Earth with her thousand voices calls on God!

Notes

[4] *God, God!* While climbing in the Lake District Coleridge seems to have been in the habit of shouting 'Dodd!' so as to hear the echo, as Charles Lamb pointed out: 'I have heard your own lips teaching your Cumbrian mountains to resound, Tod, Tod, meaning the unlucky doctor' (Marrs ii 74–5). Dr William Dodd was a forger hanged at Tyburn in 1777.

[5] *suffused* overspread.

[6] *hierarch* priest.

Letter from S. T. Coleridge to Robert Southey, 11 September 1803 (extract) (including early version of *The Pains of Sleep*)[1]

I have been on a wild journey – taken up for a spy and clapped into Fort Augustus – and I am afraid they may have frightened poor Sara by sending her off a scrap of a letter I was writing to her.[2] I have walked 263 miles in eight days, so I must have strength somewhere, but my spirits are dreadful, owing entirely to the horrors of every night. I truly dread to sleep; it is no shadow with me, but substantial misery foot-thick that makes me sit by my bedside of a morning and *cry*. I have abandoned all opiates except ether be one, and that only in *fits* – and that is a blessed medicine! and when you see me drink a glass of spirit and water, except by prescription of a physician, you shall despise me – but I still cannot get quiet rest –

When on my bed my limbs I lay,
It hath not been my use to pray
With moving lips or bended knees;
But silently, by slow degrees,
My spirit I to love compose,
In humble trust my eyelids close
With reverential resignation;
No wish conceived, no thought expressed!
Only a *sense* of supplication,
A *sense* o'er all my soul impressed
That I am weak, yet not unblessed –
Since *round* me, *in* me, everywhere,
Eternal strength and goodness are!

But yesternight I prayed aloud
In anguish and in agony,
Awaking from the fiendish crowd
Of shapes and thoughts that tortured me!
Desire with loathing strangely mixed,
On wild or hateful objects fixed:
Pangs of revenge, the powerless will,
Still baffled, and consuming still,
Sense of intolerable wrong,
And men whom I despised made strong
Vainglorious threats, unmanly vaunting,
Bad men my boasts and fury taunting –
Rage, sensual passion, mad'ning brawl,
And shame and terror over all!
Deeds to be hid that were not hid,

Notes

LETTER FROM S. T. COLERIDGE TO ROBERT

[1] The letter in which Coleridge enshrined this early version of *The Pains of Sleep*, and the early readings themselves, make the poem more powerful than the version published in 1816 with *Christabel* and *Kubla Khan*. Coleridge had embarked on 15 August 1803 on a tour of Scotland with the Wordsworths. Badly depressed, partly thanks to his unfulfilled love for Sara Hutchinson, partly to his opium addiction, he accompanied them as far as Loch Lomond, but departed from them at Arrochar. Attempting to withdraw from opium, he embarked on a marathon walk, covering 263 miles in eight days before reaching Perth on 11 September.

[2] Probably Sara Hutchinson, with whom Coleridge was hopelessly in love. In August 1803, shortly after setting off on the Scottish tour, he had confided to his notebook: 'Oh Asra, wherever I am, and am impressed, my heart aches for you' (*Notebooks* i 1451).

The Pains of Sleep

From Christabel; Kubla Khan: a vision; The Pains of Sleep (1816)

Ere on my bed my limbs I lay,
It hath not been my use to pray
With moving lips or bended knees;
But silently, by slow degrees,
My spirit I to love compose,
In humble trust mine eyelids close
With reverential resignation;
No wish conceived, no thought expressed!
Only a *sense* of supplication,
A sense o'er all my soul impressed
That I am weak, yet not unblessed –
Since in me, round me, everywhere,
Eternal strength and wisdom are.

But yesternight I prayed aloud
In anguish and in agony,
Upstarting from the fiendish crowd
Of shapes and thoughts that tortured me;
A lurid light, a trampling throng,
Sense of intolerable wrong,
And whom I scorned, those only strong!
Thirst of revenge, the powerless will
Still baffled, and yet burning still!
Desire with loathing strangely mixed,
On wild or hateful objects fixed.
Fantastic passions! Mad'ning brawl!
And shame and terror over all!
Deeds to be hid which were not hid,

Which all confused I might not know,
Whether I suffered or I did –
For all was horror, guilt and woe,
My own or others, still the same
Life-stifling fear, soul-stifling shame!

Thus two nights passed: the night's dismay
Saddened and stunned the boding day.
I feared to sleep – sleep seemed to be
Disease's worst malignity.
The third night when my own loud scream
Had freed me from the fiendish dream,
O'ercome with sufferings dark and wild,
I wept as I had been a child –
And having thus by tears subdued
My trouble to a milder mood,
Such punishments, I thought, were due
To natures deepliest stained with sin:
Still to be stirring up anew
The self-created hell within,
The horror of their crimes to view,
To know and loathe, yet wish and do!
With such let fiends make mockery –
But I – oh wherefore this on *me*?
Frail is my soul, yea, strengthless wholly,
Unequal, restless, melancholy,
But free from hate and sensual folly!
To live beloved is all I need,
And whom I love, I love indeed.

Which all confused I could not know,
Whether I suffered or I did –
For all seemed guilt, remorse or woe,
My own or others, still the same
Life-stifling fear, soul-stifling shame!

So two nights passed: the night's dismay
Saddened and stunned the coming day.
Sleep, the wide blessing, seemed to me
Distemper's worst calamity.
The third night when my own loud scream
Had waked me from the fiendish dream,
O'ercome with sufferings strange and wild,
I wept as I had been a child –
And having thus by tears subdued
My anguish to a milder mood,
Such punishments, I said, were due
To natures deepliest stained with sin:
For aye entempesting anew
Th' unfathomable hell within,
The horror of their deeds to view,
To know and loathe, yet wish and do!
Such griefs with such men well agree,
But wherefore, wherefore fall on me?
To be beloved is all I need,
And whom I love, I love indeed.

Epigram on Spots in the Sun, from Wernicke[1]

From The Morning Post No.10,614 (11 October 1802)

My father confessor is strict and holy,
'Mi fili', still he cries, 'peccare noli.'[2]
And yet how oft I find the pious man
At Annette's door, the lovely courtesan![3]
Her soul's deformity the good man wins,
And not her charms – he comes to hear her sins!
Good father, I would fain not do thee wrong,
But ah! I fear that they who oft and long
Stand gazing at the sun, to count each spot,
Must sometimes find the sun itself too hot.

Letter from S. T. Coleridge to Thomas Poole, 14 October 1803 (extract)[1]

Wordsworth is in good health, and all his family. He has one LARGE boy, christened John. He has made a beginning to his *Recluse*.[2] He was here on Sunday last. His wife's sister, who is on a visit at Grasmere, was in a bad hysterical way, and he rode in to consult our excellent medical men.[3] I now see very little of Wordsworth. My own health makes it inconvenient and unfit for me to go thither one third as often, as I used to do – and Wordsworth's indolence, etc., keeps him at home. Indeed, were I an irritable man (and an unthinking one), I should probably have considered myself as having been very unkindly used by him in this respect, for I was at one time confined for two months, and he never came in to see me – me, who had ever paid such unremitting attentions to him!

But we must take the good and the ill together – and by seriously and habitually reflecting on our own faults and endeavouring to amend them, we shall then find little difficulty in confining our attention (as far as it acts on our friends' characters) to their good qualities. Indeed, I owe it to truth and justice, as well as to myself, to say that the concern which I have felt in this instance (and one or two other more *crying* instances) of self-involution in Wordsworth, has been almost wholly a feeling of friendly regret and

Notes

EPIGRAM ON SPOTS IN THE SUN

1 Like Wordsworth's 'A Complaint', this poem arose out of the strains that had crept into Coleridge's relationship with Wordsworth. Christian Wernicke (1661–1725) was a German poet famous for satirical epigrams.

2 *Mi . . . noli* 'Sin not, my son.'

3 *At Annette's door, the lovely courtesan* Hardly diplomatic in view of Wordsworth's marriage just days before. Coleridge was aware of Wordsworth's abandonment of Annette Vallon and their child, Caroline, in 1792, and of his visit to Calais to see them in August 1802 (see 'It is a beauteous evening, calm and free', p. 536).

LETTER FROM S. T. COLERIDGE TO THOMAS POOLE

1 This letter, written from Greta Hall, Keswick, where Coleridge's family were now living with Southey, indicates something of the strain that had crept into the relationship with Wordsworth.

2 *The Recluse* was the epic poem planned in 1798, which Coleridge and Wordsworth believed, would help precipitate the millennium (Christ's thousand-year rule on earth predicted in the Bible, as in Revelations 20: 6). Coleridge was becoming increasingly impatient at Wordsworth's failure to get on with it.

3 Joanna Hutchinson suffered a 'hysteric and fainting fit' at Dove Cottage on the evening of 7 October 1803. Wordsworth rode to Keswick to consult Mr Edmondson about it the next day, meeting Southey and Coleridge on 9 October before returning to Grasmere that evening. Coleridge is writing from Greta Hall, Keswick, where he was staying with Southey.

disinterested apprehension. I saw him more and more benetted in hypochondriacal fancies, living wholly among *devotees*, having every the minutest thing, almost his very eating and drinking, done for him by his sister or wife – and I trembled lest a film should rise and thicken on his moral eye.

The habit too of writing such a multitude of small poems was in this instance hurtful to him – such things as that sonnet of his in Monday's *Morning Post* about Simonides and the ghost.[4] I rejoice, therefore, with a deep and true joy, that he has at length yielded to my urgent and repeated (almost unremitting) requests and remonstrances, and will go on with *The Recluse* exclusively – a great work in which he will sail on an open ocean and a steady wind, unfretted by short tacks, reefing and hauling and disentangling the ropes; great work necessarily comprehending his attention and feelings within the circle of great objects and elevated conceptions. This is his natural element. The having been out of it has been his disease; to return into it is the specific remedy – both remedy and health. It is what food is to famine.

I have seen enough positively to give me feelings of hostility towards the plan of several of the poems in the *Lyrical Ballads*, and I really consider it as a misfortune that Wordsworth ever deserted his former mountain-track to wander in lanes and alleys – though in the event it may prove to have been a great benefit to him. He will steer, I trust, the middle course.

Letter from S. T. Coleridge to Richard Sharp, 15 January 1804 (extract)[1]

Wordsworth is a poet, a most original poet. He no more resembles Milton than Milton resembles Shakespeare – no more resembles Shakespeare than Shakespeare resembles Milton: he is himself. And I dare affirm that he will hereafter be admitted as the first and greatest philosophical poet – the only man who has effected a complete and constant synthesis of thought and feeling, and combined them with poetic forms, with the music of pleasurable passion and with imagination, or the *modifying* power in that highest sense of the word in which I have ventured to oppose it to fancy, or the *aggregating* power (in that sense in which it is a dim analogue of creation – not all that we can *believe* but all that we can *conceive* of creation). Wordsworth is a poet, and I feel myself a better poet, in knowing how to honour *him*, than in all my own poetic compositions – all I have done or hope to do. And I prophesy immortality to his *Recluse*, as the first and finest philosophical poem, if only it be (as it undoubtedly will be) a faithful transcript of his own most august and innocent life, of his own habitual feelings and modes of seeing and hearing.

Notes

[4] 'I find it written of Simonides', composed by 7 October 1803, published in the *Morning Post* 10 October 1803. Coleridge may also have in mind some of the poems which were to appear in *Poems in Two Volumes* (1807).

LETTER FROM S. T. COLERIDGE TO RICHARD SHARP

[1] The euphoric tone of this letter may owe something to Coleridge's opium addiction, as well as to the fact that in the week preceding Wordsworth had read *The Two-Part Prelude* to him, and they had agreed that it would comprise part of 'The Recluse'. Wordsworth had promised Coleridge that he would begin serious work on 'The Recluse' immediately, and in return Coleridge had promised to send him his 'notes' on its contents. Unfortunately those 'notes' never arrived in Grasmere (and it may be doubted whether they ever existed). However, Coleridge's approval of *The Prelude* initiated a lengthy period of composition that would conclude just over a year later with completion of *The Thirteen-Book Prelude*.

To William Wordsworth. Lines composed, for the greater part, on the night on which he finished the recitation of his poem in Thirteen Books, concerning the growth and history of his own mind, January 1807, Coleorton, near Ashby-de-la-Zouch (composed January 1807; first published 1817; edited from MS)[2]

Oh friend! Oh teacher! God's great gift to me!
Into my heart have I received that lay
More than historic, that prophetic lay
Wherein (high theme by thee first sung aright)
Of the foundations and the building-up
Of thy own spirit, thou hast loved to tell
What may be told, to th' understanding mind
Revealable; and what within the mind
May rise enkindled. Theme as hard as high!
Of smiles spontaneous, and mysterious fear
(The first-born they of reason, and twin-birth);
Of tides obedient to external force,
And currents self-determined, as might seem,
Or by interior power; of moments awful,[3]
Now in thy hidden life, and now abroad,
Mid festive crowds, *thy* brows too garlanded,
A brother of the feast; of fancies fair,
Hyblaean[4] murmurs of poetic thought,
Industrious in its joy, by lilied streams
Native or outland, lakes and famous hills!
Of more than fancy – of the hope of man
Amid the tremor of a realm aglow,
Where France in all her towns lay vibrating,[5]
Ev'n as a bark becalmed on sultry seas
Beneath the voice from heaven, the bursting crash
Of heaven's immediate thunder, when no cloud
Is visible, or shadow on the main!
Ah, soon night rolled on night, and every cloud
Opened its eye of fire; and hope aloft
Now fluttered, and now tossed upon the storm
Floating![6] Of hope afflicted, and struck down,
Thence summoned homeward – homeward to thy heart,
Oft from the watchtower of man's absolute self,
With light unwaning on her eyes, to look
Far on – herself a glory to behold,

Notes

[2] This poem is one of the earliest literary responses to Wordsworth's great poem. Wordsworth, Dorothy, Mary, Coleridge, Hartley and Sara Hutchinson, all spent the Christmas of 1806 at Coleorton, the country seat of Sir George Beaumont, and in the New Year, 7 January 1807, Wordsworth read them the *Thirteen-Book Prelude* in its entirety. It remained unpublished until 1850.

[3] *awful* i.e. full of awe.

[4] *Hyblaean* honeyed; Hybla was a Sicilian town near Syracuse, known for honey and herbs.

[5] *of the hope . . . aglow* a reference to Books IX and X of *The Prelude*, in which Wordsworth describes his residence in France, 1791–2.

[6] *and hope aloft . . . Floating* a reference to the Reign of Terror, which led radicals in England to lose hope in the French Revolution.

The angel of the vision! Then (last strain!)
Of duty, chosen laws controlling[7] choice,
Virtue and love! An Orphic[8] tale indeed,
A tale divine of high and passionate thoughts
To their own music chaunted!
                                        Ah great bard!
Ere yet that last swell dying awed the air,
With steadfast ken[9] I viewed thee in the choir
Of ever-enduring men. The truly great
Have all one age, and from one visible space
Shed influence;[10] for they, both power and act,
Are permanent, and time is now with them,
Save as it worketh for them, they in it.
Nor less a sacred roll, than those of old,
And to be placed, as they, with gradual fame
Among the archives of mankind, thy work
Makes audible a linked song of truth,
Of truth profound a sweet continuous song
Not learnt but native, her own natural notes!
Dear shall it be to every human heart,
To me how more than dearest! Me, on whom
Comfort from thee and utterance of thy love
Came with such heights and depths of harmony,
Such sense of wings uplifting, that the storm
Scattered and whirled me, till my thoughts became
A bodily tumult! And thy faithful hopes,
Thy hopes of me, dear friend, by me unfelt
Were troublous[11] to me, almost as a voice
Familiar once and more than musical
To one cast forth, whose hope had seemed to die,
A wanderer with a worn-out heart,
Mid strangers pining with untended wounds![12]
   Oh friend, too well thou know'st, of what sad years
The long suppression had benumbed my soul,[13]
That even as life returns upon the drowned,
Th' unusual joy awoke a throng of pains –
Keen pangs of *love*, awakening, as a babe,
Turbulent, with an outcry in the heart;
And fears self-willed, that shunned the eye of hope,
And hope, that would not know itself from fear;
Sense of passed youth, and manhood come in vain;
And genius given, and knowledge won in vain;
And all which I had culled in wood-walks wild,
And all which patient toil had reared, and all

Notes

[7] In the MS Coleridge writes: 'Impelling? Directing?'

[8] *Orphic* oracular; communicated by God.

[9] *ken* gaze.

[10] *Shed influence* Coleridge is thinking of Milton's description of the Pleiades 'Shedding sweet influence' (*Paradise Lost* vii 375).

[11] *troublous* confusing (because Coleridge had lost hope in himself).

[12] *Mid strangers . . . wounds* cf. the 'Letter to Sara Hutchinson', where Coleridge compares the sound of the wind to 'many groans from men with smarting wounds' (l.202).

[13] *benumbed my soul* as at 'Letter to Sara Hutchinson' 39: 'I *see*, not *feel*, how beautiful they are!'

Commune with thee had opened out, but[14] flowers
Strewed on my corse, and borne upon my bier,
In the same coffin, for the self-same grave!
  That way no more! And ill beseems it me,
Who came a welcomer in herald's guise,
Singing of glory and futurity,
To wander back on such unhealthful road
Plucking the poisons of self-harm! And ill
Such intertwine beseems triumphal wreaths
Strewed before thy advancing! Thou too, friend!
Oh injure not the memory of that hour
Of thy communion with my nobler mind[15]
By pity or grief,[16] already felt too long!
Nor let my words import more blame than needs.
The tumult rose and ceased; for peace is nigh
Where Wisdom's voice has found a list'ning heart.
Amid the howl of more than wintry storms
The halcyon[17] hears the voice of vernal hours,
Already on the wing!
          Eve following eve,[18]
Dear tranquil time, when the sweet sense of home
Becomes most sweet! Hours for their own sake hailed,
And more desired, more precious, for thy song!
In silence list'ning, like a devout child,
My soul lay passive, by thy various strain[19]
Driven as in surges now, beneath the stars,
With momentary stars of my own birth,
Fair constellated foam still darting off
Into the darkness! – now a tranquil sea
Outspread and bright, yet swelling to the moon!
  And when, oh friend, my comforter, my guide,
Strong in thyself and powerful to give strength,
Thy long-sustained lay finally closed,
And thy deep voice had ceased (yet thou thyself
Wert still before mine eyes, and round us both
That happy vision of beloved faces,
All whom I deepliest love, in one room all!),
Scarce conscious and yet conscious of its close,
I sat, my being blended in one thought
(Thought was it? Or aspiration? Or resolve?)
Absorbed, yet hanging still upon the sound:
And when I rose, I found myself in prayer!

Notes

[14] *but* i.e. [nothing] but.

[15] *that hour . . . mind* a reference to the *annus mirabilis* of 1797–8.

[16] *pity or grief* i.e. felt for Coleridge in his present, miserable state.

[17] *halcyon* kingfisher which, according to classical legend, brought the seas and winds to a calm when it bred in a nest which floated on the ocean.

[18] *Eve following eve* the evenings when Wordsworth recited *The Thirteen-Book Prelude* to Coleridge at Coleorton.

[19] *thy various strain* 'varied in tone and subject-matter' i.e. *The Prelude*.

Letter from S. T. Coleridge to William Wordsworth, 30 May 1815 (extract)[1]

What did my criticism amount to, reduced to its full and naked sense? This: that, *comparatively* with the former poem, *The Excursion*, as far as it was new to me, had disappointed my expectations; that the excellences were so many and of so high a class, that it was impossible to attribute the inferiority (if any such really existed) to any flagging of the writer's own genius; and that I conjectured that it might have been occasioned by the influence of self-established convictions having given to certain thoughts and expressions a depth and force which they had not for readers in general. In order, therefore, to explain the *disappointment*, I must recall to your mind what my *expectations* were; and as these again were founded on the supposition that (in whatever order it might be published) the poem on the growth of your own mind[2] was as the ground-plat[3] and the roots out of which *The Recluse* was to have sprung up as the tree. As far as the same sap in both, I expected them doubtless to have formed one complete whole, but in matter, form, and product to be different, each not only a distinct but a different work. In the first I had found 'themes by thee first sung aright'[4]:

> Of smiles spontaneous, and mysterious fears
> (The first-born they of reason, and twin-birth);
> Of tides obedient to external force,
> And currents self-determined, as might seem,
> Or by some central breath; of moments awful,
> Now in thy inner life, and now abroad,
> When power streamed from thee, and thy soul received
> The light reflected as a light bestowed!
> Of fancies fair, and milder hours of youth,
> Hyblaean[5] murmurs of poetic thought,
> Industrious in its joy, in vales and glens
> Native or outland, lakes and famous hills!

Notes

Letter from S. T. Coleridge to William Wordsworth

[1] Wordsworth and Coleridge's friendship had soured in 1810, when a mutual friend, Basil Montagu, told Coleridge of a thoughtless remark Wordsworth made about his opium addiction. Despite repeated attempts to patch things up, both men were aware of a rift that would never be properly healed. Wordsworth had published *The Excursion* in 1814, for which he had high hopes, as it was supposed to be part of 'The Recluse'; unfortunately, it was greeted by some of the worst reviews he would ever receive, not least Francis Jeffrey's in the *Edinburgh Review* (see pp. 715–20). Then, on 3 April 1815, Coleridge confided to another mutual friend, Lady Beaumont, that he thought *The Excursion* less good than *The Prelude* and that its chief fault was that

> having by the conjoint operation of his own experiences, feelings, and reason *himself* convinced *himself* of truths, which the generality of persons have either taken for granted from their infancy, or at least adopted in early life, he has attached all their own depth and weight to doctrines and words, which come almost as truisms or commonplaces to others. (Griggs iv 564)

Word of this got back to Wordsworth, and on 22 May he wrote to Coleridge to say that he was more 'perplexed than enlightened by your *comparative* censure' (*MY* ii 238). On reading that, Coleridge composed this reply, explaining his disappointment in detail. As with many of Coleridge's retrospective comments on 'The Recluse', the reader should approach this letter with caution. It was written over seventeen years after 'The Recluse' was formulated, and provides a plan that may be more detailed than anything ever written by Coleridge in 1798. He had been able to develop (and perhaps embroider) his ambitions for it over the years, without necessarily communicating them to Wordsworth. Furthermore, his disappointment could be coloured by the falling-out between them. Another account of 'The Recluse' may be found at pp. 712–13, below.

[2] *the poem . . . mind* i.e. *The Prelude*.

[3] *ground-plat* plot of ground on which the edifice of *The Recluse* would be built.

[4] *themes by thee . . . aright* Coleridge's *To William Wordsworth* 4; he goes on to quote ll. 10–40.

[5] *Hyblaean* honeyed; Hybla was a Sicilian town near Syracuse known for honey and herbs.

Or on the lonely high-road, when the stars
Were rising, or by secret mountain streams,
The guides and the companions of thy way;
Of more than fancy – of the social sense
Distending wide, and man beloved as man,
Where France in all her towns lay vibrating,
Ev'n as a bark becalmed beneath the burst
Of heaven's immediate thunder, when no cloud
Is visible, or shadow on the main!
For thou wert there,[6] thy own brows garlanded
Amid the tremor of a realm aglow,
Amid a mighty nation jubilant,
When from the general heart of humankind
Hope sprang forth, like a full-born deity!
Of that dear hope afflicted, and amazed,
So homeward summoned! Thenceforth calm and sure
From the dread watchtower of man's absolute self,
With light unwaning on her eyes, to look
Far on – herself a glory[7] to behold,
The angel of the vision! Then (last strain!)
Of duty! Chosen laws controlling choice!
Action and joy! – AN ORPHIC[8] SONG INDEED,
A SONG DIVINE OF HIGH AND PASSIONATE TRUTHS
TO THEIR OWN MUSIC CHAUNTED!

Indeed through the whole of that poem *Αὔρα τις εἰσεπνὲυσε μυστικωτάτη.*[9] *This* I considered as *The Excursion*, and the second as *The Recluse* I had (from what I had at different times gathered from your conversation on the plan) anticipated as commencing with you set down and settled in an abiding home, and that with the description of that home you were to begin a *Philosophical Poem*, the result and fruits of a spirit so framed and so disciplined, as had been told in the former.

Whatever in Lucretius[10] is poetry is not philosophical; whatever is philosophical is not poetry – and in the very pride of confident hope I looked forward to *The Recluse* as the *first* and *only* true philosophical poem in existence. Of course, I expected the colours, music, imaginative life, and passion of *poetry*, but the matter and arrangement of *philosophy* – not doubting from the advantages of the subject that the totality of a system was not only capable of being harmonized with, but even calculated to aid, the unity (beginning, middle, and end) of a *poem*. Thus, whatever the length of the work might be, still it was a *determinate* length.

Of the subjects announced each would have its own appointed place and, excluding repetitions, each would relieve and rise in interest above the other. I supposed you first to have meditated the faculties of man in the abstract; in their correspondence with his sphere of action – and first, in the feeling, touch, and taste, then in the eye, and last in the ear; to have laid a solid and immovable foundation for the edifice by removing the sandy sophisms[11] of Locke and the mechanic dogmatists;[12] and demonstrating that

Notes

6 *For thou wert there* i.e. in Revolutionary France, 1791–2.

7 *a glory* an effulgent light.

8 *Orphic* oracular; communicated by God.

9 'a certain most mystical breeze blew into me' (Aristophanes, *The Frogs* 313–14).

10 Lucretius, *De rerum natura*, philosophical poem in six Books.

11 *sandy sophisms* dry and specious arguments.

12 *Locke . . . mechanic dogmatists* John Locke (1632–1704), author of the *Essay concerning Human Understanding* (1690);

the senses were living growths and developments of the mind and spirit in a much juster as well as higher sense than the mind can be said to be formed by the senses. Next I understood that you would take the human race in the concrete, have exploded the absurd notion of Pope's *Essay on Man*,[13] Darwin,[14] and all the countless believers (even, strange to say, among Christians) of man's having progressed from an orang-utan state – so contrary to all history, to all religion, nay, to all possibility; to have affirmed a fall, in some sense, as a fact the possibility of which cannot be understood from the nature of the will, but the reality of which is attested by experience and conscience; fallen men contemplated in the different ages of the world, and in the different states – savage – barbarous – civilized – the lonely cot or borderer's wigwam – the village – the manufacturing town – sea-port – city – universities – and, not disguising the sore evils under which the whole creation groans, to point out, however, a manifest scheme of redemption from this slavery, of reconciliation from this enmity with nature (What are the obstacles? The Antichrist that must be and already is); and to conclude by a grand didactic swell on the necessary identity of a true philosophy with true religion, agreeing in the results and differing only as the analytic and synthetic process, as discursive from intuitive,[15] the former chiefly useful as perfecting the latter.

In short, the necessity of a general revolution in the modes of developing and disciplining the human mind by the substitution of life and intelligence (considered in its different powers, from the plant up to that state in which the difference of degree becomes a new kind – man, self-consciousness – but yet not by essential opposition), for the philosophy of mechanism which in everything that is needworthy of the human intellect strikes *death*, and cheats itself by mistaking clear images for distinct conceptions, and which idly demands conceptions where intuitions alone are possible or adequate to the majesty of the truth. In short, facts elevated into theory, theory into laws, and laws into living and intelligent powers – true idealism necessarily perfecting itself in realism, and realism refining itself into idealism.

Such or something like this was the plan I had supposed that you were engaged on.

From Biographia Literaria (1817)

Chapter 13 (extract)[1]

The imagination then I consider either as primary or secondary. The primary imagination I hold to be the living power and prime agent of all human perception, and as a repetition in the finite mind of the eternal act of creation in the infinite I AM. The secondary imagination I consider as an echo of the former, coexisting with the conscious will, yet still as identical with the primary in the *kind* of its agency, and

Notes

other 'dogmatists' probably include Isaac Newton (1642–1727) and Francis Bacon (1561–1626).

[13] *Essay on Man* (1732–4), a philosophical poem, part of a larger work never completed by Pope, in which he seeks to vindicate the ways of God to man and prove that the universe is the best of all possible schemes.

[14] Erasmus Darwin (1731–1802), grandfather of Charles Darwin, author of *The Botanic Garden* (1789–91) and *Zoönomia* (1794–6).

[15] *discursive or intuitive* The same distinction is mentioned by Wordsworth in *Thirteen-Book Prelude* xiii 113 (p. 568). Milton had differentiated discursive reason (belonging to man), from a higher, 'intuitive' reason, to which man may aspire, and which is possessed by angels (*Paradise Lost* v 487–90).

FROM BIOGRAPHIA LITERARIA (1817) CHAPTER 13

[1] The first of the extracts from *Biographia* consists of the famous definition of the primary and secondary imagination. Coleridge began dictating the volume in July 1815, and it was intended to be a combination of autobiography, a defence of Wordsworth against reviewers such as Jeffrey, and a treatise on philosophy and religion.

differing only in *degree*, and in the *mode* of its operation. It dissolves, diffuses, dissipates, in order to recreate; or, where this process is rendered impossible, yet still at all events it struggles to idealize and to unify. It is essentially *vital*, even as all objects (*as* objects) are essentially fixed and dead.

Fancy, on the contrary, has no other counters to play with but fixities and definites. The fancy is indeed no other than a mode of memory emancipated from the order of time and space – while it is blended with, and modified by, that empirical phenomenon of the will which we express by the word 'choice'. But equally with the ordinary memory the fancy must receive all its materials ready-made from the law of association.

Chapter 14 (extracts)[1]

During the first year that Mr Wordsworth and I were neighbours,[2] our conversations turned frequently on the two cardinal points of poetry: the power of exciting the sympathy of the reader by a faithful adherence to the truth of nature, and the power of giving the interest of novelty by the modifying colours of imagination. The sudden charm which accidents of light and shade, which moonlight or sunset diffused over a known and familiar landscape, appeared to represent the practicability of combining both. These are the poetry of nature.

The thought suggested itself (to which of us I do not recollect) that a series of poems might be composed of two sorts. In the one, the incidents and agents were to be (in part at least) supernatural – and the excellence aimed at was to consist in the interesting of the affections by the dramatic truth of such emotions as would naturally accompany such situations, supposing them real. And real in this sense they have been to every human being who, from whatever source of delusion, has at any time believed himself under supernatural agency. For the second class, subjects were to be chosen from ordinary life. The characters and incidents were to be such as will be found in every village and its vicinity, where there is a meditative and feeling mind to seek after them or to notice them when they present themselves.

In this idea originated the plan of the *Lyrical Ballads*, in which it was agreed that my endeavours should be directed to persons and characters supernatural, or at least romantic – yet so as to transfer, from our inward nature, a human interest and a semblance of truth sufficient to procure for these shadows of imagination that willing suspension of disbelief for the moment, which constitutes poetic faith. Mr Wordsworth, on the other hand, was to propose to himself as his object, to give the charm of novelty to things of every day, and to excite a feeling analogous to the supernatural, by awakening the mind's attention to the lethargy of custom, and directing it to the loveliness and the wonders of the world before us – an inexhaustible treasure but for which, in consequence of the film of familiarity and selfish solicitude, we have eyes yet see not, ears that hear not, and hearts that neither feel nor understand.

With this view I wrote 'The Ancient Mariner', and was preparing (among other poems) 'The Dark Ladie' and the 'Christabel', in which I should have more nearly realised my ideal than I had done in my first attempt. But Mr Wordsworth's industry had proved so much more successful, and the number of his poems so much greater,

Notes

Chapter 14

[1] The account given by Coleridge of the evolution of *Lyrical Ballads* is important, but fictionalizes in retrospect; it differs markedly from that later given by Wordsworth (see p. 496n5, above). The facts may be found in the Introduction to *Lyrical Ballads, and Other Poems, 1797–1800* ed. James Butler and Karen Green (Ithaca, NY, 1992), pp. 3–12.

[2] *the first year . . . neighbours* July 1797–July 1798, when Wordsworth was at Alfoxden and Coleridge four miles away at Nether Stowey.

that my compositions, instead of forming a balance, appeared rather an interpolation of heterogeneous matter. Mr Wordsworth added two or three poems written in his own character, in the impassioned, lofty, and sustained diction which is characteristic of his genius. In this form the *Lyrical Ballads* were published, and were presented by him, as an 'experiment'[3] whether subjects, which from their nature rejected the usual ornaments and extra-colloquial style of poems in general, might not be so managed in the language of ordinary life as to produce the pleasurable interest which it is the peculiar business of poetry to impart.

To the second edition he added a Preface of considerable length in which (notwithstanding some passages of apparently a contrary import) he was understood to contend for the extension of this style to poetry of all kinds, and to reject as vicious and indefensible all phrases and forms of speech that were not included in what he – unfortunately, I think, adopting an equivocal expression – called the language of *real* life.[4] From this Preface, prefixed to poems in which it was impossible to deny the presence of original genius (however mistaken its direction might be deemed), arose the whole long-continued controversy.[5] For, from the conjunction of perceived power with supposed heresy, I explain the inveteracy and (in some instances, I grieve to say) the acrimonious passions with which the controversy has been conducted by the assailants.

Had Mr Wordsworth's poems been the silly, the childish things which they were for a long time described as being; had they been really distinguished from the compositions of other poets merely by meanness of language and inanity of thought; had they indeed contained nothing more than what is found in the parodies and pretended imitations of them – they must have sunk at once, a dead weight, into the slough of oblivion, and have dragged the Preface along with them. But year after year increased the number of Mr Wordsworth's admirers. They were found, too, not in the lower classes of the reading public, but chiefly among young men of strong sensibility and meditative minds,[6] and their admiration (inflamed perhaps in some degree by opposition) was distinguished by its intensity – I might almost say, by its religious fervour.

These facts, and the intellectual energy of the author (which was more or less consciously felt, where it was outwardly and even boisterously denied), meeting with sentiments of aversion to his opinions, and of alarm at their consequences, produced an eddy of criticism which would of itself have borne up the poems by the violence with which it whirled them round and round.

With many parts of this Preface in the sense attributed to them and which the words undoubtedly seem to authorize, I never concurred – but on the contrary objected to them as erroneous in principle, and as contradictory (in appearance at least) both to other parts of the same Preface, and to the author's own practice in the greater part of the poems themselves.[7] Mr Wordsworth in his recent collection[8] has, I find, degraded this prefatory disquisition to the end of his second volume, to be read or not at the reader's choice. But he has not (as far as I can discover) announced any

Notes

[3] *experiment* See the Advertisement to *Lyrical Ballads* (1798), p. 331 above. See also his remarks to Hazlitt, p. 782 below.

[4] *To the second edition . . . life* Coleridge's account of the Preface is not strictly accurate; here he distances himself from it, though it was, as he said at the time, 'half the child of my own brain'. Wordsworth referred to the 'real language of men'; see p. 495 above.

[5] *controversy* Coleridge refers to the criticism Wordsworth received particularly from the *Edinburgh Review*, culminating with Jeffrey's review of *The Excursion*, see pp. 715–20 below.

[6] *young men . . . minds* such as John Wilson and Thomas De Quincey, both of whom, as young men, wrote admiringly to Wordsworth of the *Lyrical Ballads*.

[7] *With many parts . . . themselves* Not true; Coleridge was the mastermind behind the Preface, and its fundamental principles were drawn largely from his reading.

[8] *his recent collection* Wordsworth published his first collected *Poems* in 1815.

change in his poetic creed. At all events, considering it as the source of a controversy in which I have been honoured more than I deserve by the frequent conjunction of my name with his, I think it expedient to declare once for all, in what points I coincide with the opinions supported in that Preface, and in what points I altogether differ . . .

'What is poetry?' is so nearly the same question with 'what is a poet?' that the answer to the one is involved in the solution of the other. For it is a distinction resulting from the poetic genius itself, which sustains and modifies the images, thoughts, and emotions of the poet's own mind. The poet, described in ideal perfection, brings the whole soul of man into activity, with the subordination of its faculties to each other, according to their relative worth and dignity. He diffuses a tone and spirit of unity that blends and (as it were) *fuses* each into each by that synthetic and magical power to which I would exclusively appropriate the name of imagination. This power, first put in action by the will and understanding, and retained under their irremissive, though gentle and unnoticed, control (*laxis effertur habenis*[9]), reveals itself in the balance or reconcilement of opposite or discordant qualities; of sameness with difference; of the general with the concrete; the idea with the image; the individual with the representative; the sense of novelty and freshness, with old and familiar objects; a more than usual state of emotion, with more than usual order; judgement ever awake and steady self-possession, with enthusiasm and feeling profound or vehement – and, while it blends and harmonizes the natural and the artificial, still subordinates art to nature; the manner to the matter; and our admiration of the poet to our sympathy with the poetry.

The Rime of the Ancient Mariner. In seven parts.[1]

From Sibylline Leaves (1817)

Facile credo, plures esse Naturas invisibiles quam visibiles in rerum universitate. Sed harum omnium familiam quis nobis enarrabit? et gradus et cognationes et discrimina et singularum munera? Quid agunt? quae loca habitant? Harum rerum notitiam semper ambivit ingenium humanum, nunquam attigit. Juvat, interea, non diffiteor, quandoque in animo, tanquam in Tabulâ, majoris et melioris mundi imaginem contemplari: ne mens assuefecta hodierniae vitae minutiis se contrahat nimis, et tota subsidat in pusillas cogitationes. Sed veritati interea invigilandum est, modusque servandus, ut certa ab incertis, diem a nocte, distinguamus.[2]

(Thomas Burnet, *Archaeologiae Philosophicae* [London, 1692], p. 68–9)

Notes

[9] 'carried on with slackened reins' (Petrarch, *Epistola Barbato Sulmonensi* 39); see *Notebooks* iii 4178 and n.

THE RIME OF THE ANCIENT MARINER. IN SEVEN PARTS

[1] This was the fifth published text of *The Ancient Mariner*, and the first in which Coleridge was identified as the author. It is radically different from previous texts in containing the Latin epigraph, marginal glosses, and numerous revisions to the poem itself. The earliest, 1798 version of the poem is presented in this volume with the other *Lyrical Ballads* at p. 332.

[2] This adaptation from Burnet may be translated: 'I can easily believe that there are more invisible than visible beings in the universe. But who will describe to us their families, ranks, affinities, differences, and functions? What do they do? Where do they live? The human mind has always sought knowledge of these things, but has never attained it. I admit that it is good sometimes to contemplate in thought, as in a picture, the image of a greater and better world; otherwise the mind, used to the minor concerns of daily life, may contract itself too much, and concentrate entirely on trivia. But meanwhile we must be vigilant for truth and moderation, that we may distinguish certainty from doubt, day from night.' Coleridge entered Burnet's remarks in his notebook, 1801 or 1802; see *Notebooks* i 1000H and n.

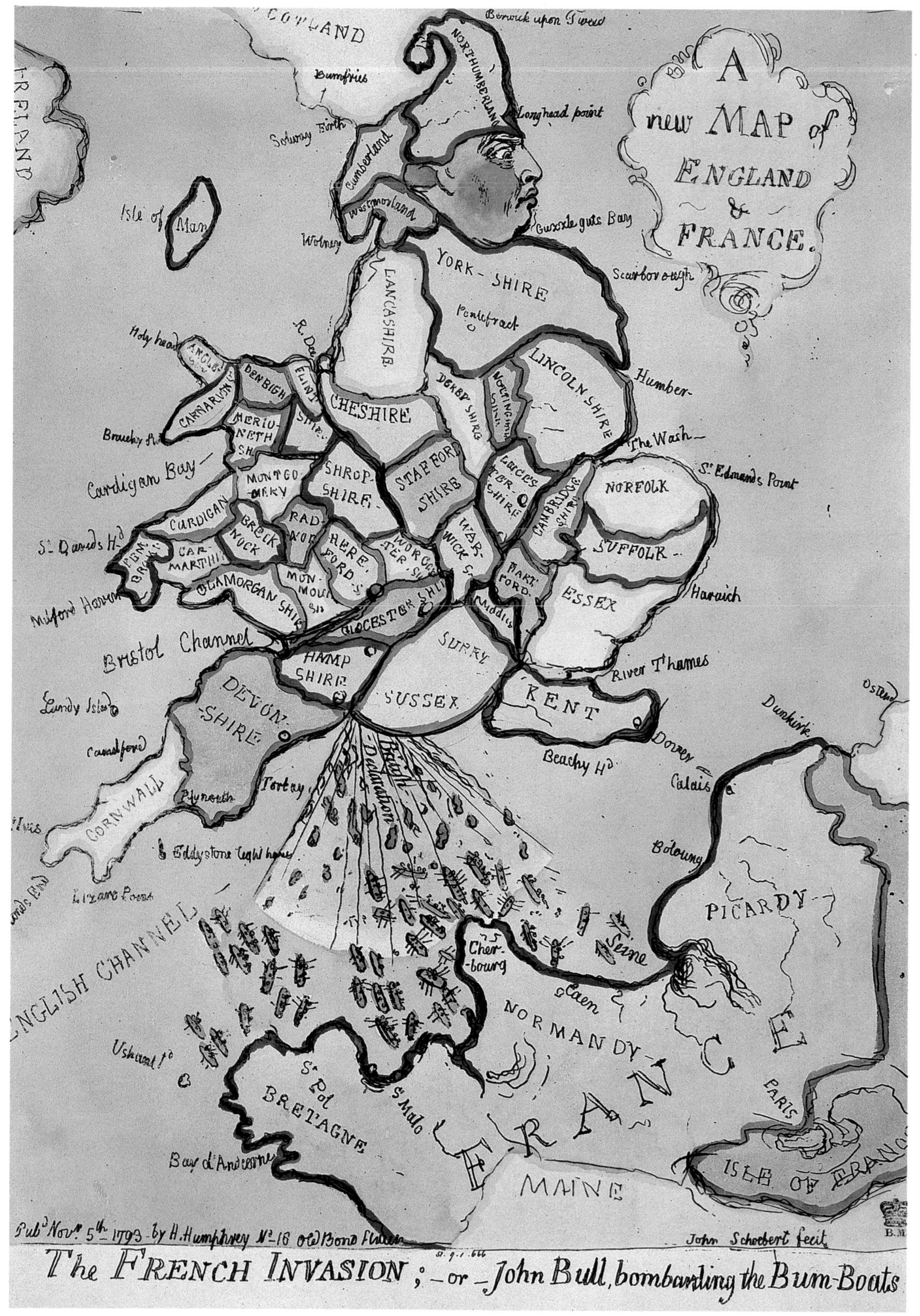

Plate 1 The French Invasion, or John Bull bombarding the Bum-boats, hand-coloured etching by James Gillray, 5 November 1793. Britain goes to war in the shape of George III, defecating gunboats onto the French coastline. The image is a gross one that aptly encapsulates British defiance in the face of a threatened French invasion. (Copyright © The British Museum.)

Plate 2 The Blood of the Murdered Crying for Vengeance, hand-coloured etching by James Gillray, published 16 February 1793. Louis XVI had been guillotined in Paris on 21 January, precipitating what was effectively a world war that would continue until the final defeat of Napoleon in 1815. Gillray depicts the King, seconds after his head has been severed; his blood rises heavenwards bearing imagined lamentations of him.
(Copyright © The British Museum.)

Plate 3 The Chelsea Pensioners reading the Waterloo Dispatch, oil on wood, by Sir David Wilkie (1785–1841). A sensation at the Royal Academy in 1822, Wilkie's masterpiece shows army veterans at a pub near the Chelsea Royal Hospital, receiving news of Wellington's victory at Waterloo. At the focal point of the picture, a man reads the Waterloo gazette aloud to his friends. The image would exercise a powerful influence on other artists, including Géricault, who saw it in Wilkie's studio. (Apsley House, The Wellington Museum, London/Bridgeman Art Library.)

Plate 4 William Cowper (1731–1800) painted by George Romney, 1792. Cowper was 61 when this was painted; it inspired a complimentary sonnet from the sitter to the artist. (National Portrait Gallery, London.)

p 5 William Blake (1757–1827) painted by Thomas Phillips, 1807. While sitting for this portrait, Blake told Phillips of a visiting angel who claimed to have been painted by Michelangelo, perhaps accounting for the rapt expression on his face. (National Portrait Gallery, London.)

Plate 6 'The Tyger', Plate 42 from Copy AA of Blake's *Songs of Experience and of Innocence*. 'Did he who made the lamb make thee?' Blake's inscrutable tiger never provides an answer. (Etching, ink and w/c by William Blake; Fitzwilliam Museum, University of Cambridge/Bridgeman Art Library.)

Plate 7 Mary Wollstonecraft (1759–97) by an unknown artist, 1791. The 'Amazon' portrait, painted when its sitter was 32, just before she wrote *A Vindication of the Rights of Woman*. (National Museums Liverpool, The Walker.)

Plate 8 The Inside of Tintern Abbey, by J. M. W. Turner, 1794. A view of the crossing, chancel and east window of the abbey, seen from the nave. Although he visited the ruins in July 1798, Wordsworth's poem was written 'a few miles above' it – that is to say, further up the Wye Valley. (Ashmolean Museum, Oxford.)

Plate 9 William Wordsworth (1770–1850) by Benjamin Robert Haydon, 1818. The 'Brigand' portrait, taken when its sitter was 48. (National Portrait Gallery, London.)

Plate 10 Charles Lamb (1775–1834) by William Hazlitt, 1804. One of Hazlitt's last works before he gave up painting, this portrait shows Lamb dressed as Velazquez's *Philip IV*. For Henry Crabb Robinson, who was a friend of both men, it was 'certainly the only painting by Hazlitt that I ever saw with pleasure'. (National Portrait Gallery, London.)

Plate 11 William Hazlitt (1778–1830) by William Hazlitt, 1802. Hazlitt is at his most intensely self-analytical in this self-portrait made when he was 23, still hoping to become an artist. (Maidstone Museum and Art Gallery/Bridgeman Art Library.)

Plate 12 George Gordon, 6th Lord Byron (1788–1824) by Thomas Phillips, 1835 (after an original of 1813). Byron in the costume he acquired in Albania in 1809, in a portrait he commissioned. 'I have some very "magnifique" Albanian dresses,' he told his mother in November 1809, 'the only expensive articles in this country'. The original, fuller length portrait is now in the British Embassy in Athens. (National Portrait Gallery, London.)

Plate 13 The Finding of Don Juan by Haidée, by Ford Madox Brown, 1873. Scenes from Byron's poems provided artists throughout the nineteenth century with provocative subject-matter. (Birmingham Museums and Art Gallery.)

Plate 14 Percy Bysshe Shelley (1792–1822) by Joseph Severn. This painting, entitled *Shelley at the Baths of Caracalla* and made after Shelley's death by Keats's friend, Joseph Severn, shows the poet at the Baths of Caracalla in Rome, where he composed much of *Prometheus Unbound*. (Keats–Shelley Memorial Association, Rome.)

Plate 15 Shelley's Funeral Rites (16 August 1822) by Louis-Edward Fournier. The figures watching Shelley's funeral pyre are, from the left, Trelawny, Leigh Hunt and Byron. The heart, as Trelawny recorded, 'would not take the flame', and it was preserved by him along with the ashes and some unconsumed bones. Leigh Hunt was given the heart, and the remainder buried in a tomb designed by Trelawny in the Protestant Cemetery in Rome, having been stored for several months in a mahogany chest in the British Consul's wine-cellar. (National Museums Liverpool, The Walker.)

Plate 16 John Clare (1793–1864) by William Hilton, 1820. This portrait was probably commissioned by Clare's publisher, John Taylor, at the height of the poet's success, shortly after publication of his *Poems Descriptive of Rural Life and Scenery*. (National Portrait Gallery, London.)

Plate 17 John Keats (1795–1821) by Benjamin Robert Haydon, signed and dated 'Nov 1816 BRH'. Keats and Haydon became close friends in 1816, having been introduced by Charles Cowden Clarke. At the bottom of the page Haydon has written: 'Keats was a spirit that in passing over the Earth came within its attraction and expired in fruitless struggles to make its dull inhabitants comprehend the beauty of its soarings -' (National Portrait Gallery, London.)

Part the First

An ancient mariner meeteth three gallants bidden to a wedding-feast, and detaineth one.

It is an ancient mariner,
And he stoppeth one of three:
'By thy long grey beard and glittering eye
Now wherefore stopp'st thou me?

The bridegroom's doors are opened wide,
And I am next of kin;
The guests are met, the feast is set –
Mayst hear the merry din.'

He holds him with his skinny hand,
'There was a ship', quoth he;
'Hold off! Unhand me, grey-beard loon!'
Eftsoons his hand dropped he.

The wedding-guest is spellbound by the eye of the old seafaring man, and constrained to hear his tale.

He holds him with his glittering eye –
The wedding-guest stood still,
And listens like a three years' child:
The mariner hath his will.

The wedding-guest sat on a stone,
He cannot choose but hear;
And thus spake on that ancient man,
The bright-eyed mariner:

'The ship was cheered, the harbour cleared,
Merrily did we drop
Below the kirk, below the hill,
Below the lighthouse top.

The mariner tells how the ship sailed southward with a good wind and fair weather till it reached the line.[3]

The sun came up upon the left,
Out of the sea came he;
And he shone bright, and on the right
Went down into the sea.

Higher and higher every day,
Till over the mast at noon –'
The wedding-guest here beat his breast,
For he heard the loud bassoon.

The wedding-guest heareth the bridal music, but the mariner continueth his tale.

The bride hath paced into the hall,
Red as a rose is she;
Nodding their heads before her goes
The merry minstrelsy.[4]

Notes

[3] *line* equator.

[4] *before her . . . minstrelsy* cf. Chaucer, *Squire's Tale* 268: 'Toforn hym gooth the louds mynstralcye'.

The wedding-guest he beat his breast,
Yet he cannot choose but hear;
And thus spake on that ancient man,
The bright-eyed mariner.

The ship drawn by a storm toward the south pole.

'And now the storm-blast came, and he
Was tyrannous and strong;
He struck with his o'ertaking wings,
And chased us south along.

With sloping masts and dipping prow,
As who pursued with yell and blow
Still treads the shadow of his foe
And forward bends his head,
The ship drove fast, loud roared the blast,
And southward aye we fled.

And now there came both mist and snow,
And it grew wondrous cold:
And ice mast-high came floating by
As green as emerald.

The land of ice, and of fearful sounds where no living thing was to be seen.

And through the drifts[5] the snowy clift[6]
Did send a dismal sheen;
Nor shapes of men nor beasts we ken –
The ice was all between.

The ice was here, the ice was there,
The ice was all around;
It cracked and growled, and roared and howled
Like noises in a swound.[7]

Till a great sea-bird, called the albatross, came through the snow-fog, and was received with great joy and hospitality.

At length did cross an albatross,
Thorough the fog it came;
As if it had been a Christian soul,[8]
We hailed it in God's name.

It ate the food it ne'er had eat,
And round and round it flew:
The ice did split with a thunder-fit;
The helmsman steered us through.

And lo! the albatross proveth a bird of good omen, and followeth the ship as it returned northward through fog and floating ice.

And a good south wind sprung up behind,
The albatross did follow;
And every day, for food or play,
Came to the mariners' hollo!

Notes

[5] *drifts* floating ice.
[6] *clift* cleft.
[7] *swound* swoon.
[8] *a Christian soul* i.e. a human being.

In mist or cloud, on mast or shroud,
It perched for vespers[9] nine,
Whiles all the night, through fogsmoke white,
Glimmered the white moonshine.'

The ancient mariner inhospitably killeth the pious bird of good omen.

'God save thee, ancient mariner,
From the fiends that plague thee thus!
Why look'st thou so?' 'With my crossbow
I shot the albatross.[10]

Part the Second

The sun now rose upon the right,
Out of the sea came he;
Still hid in mist, and on the left
Went down into the sea.

And the good south wind still blew behind,
But no sweet bird did follow,
Nor any day for food or play
Came to the mariners' hollo!

His shipmates cry out against the ancient mariner, for killing the bird of good luck.

And I had done an hellish thing
And it would work 'em woe:
For all averred[11] I had killed the bird
That made the breeze to blow.
"Ah wretch!" said they, "the bird to slay
That made the breeze to blow!"

But when the fog cleared off, they justify the same – and thus make themselves accomplices in the crime.

Nor dim nor red, like God's own head
The glorious sun uprist:
Then all averred I had killed the bird
That brought the fog and mist.
"'Twas right", said they, "such birds to slay,
That bring the fog and mist."

The fair breeze continues; the ship enters the Pacific Ocean and sails northward, even till it reaches the line.

The fair breeze blew, the white foam flew,
The furrow[12] streamed off free:
We were the first that ever burst
Into that silent sea.

The ship hath been suddenly becalmed.

Down dropped the breeze, the sails dropped down,
'Twas sad as sad could be,
And we did speak only to break
The silence of the sea.

Notes

[9] *vespers* evenings.

[10] The central event of the poem was suggested by a travel book which Wordsworth read, Shelvocke's *Voyage Round the World* (1726); see p. 334n14.

[11] *averred* maintained that.

[12] 'In the former edition the line was "The furrow followed free". But I had not been long on board a ship before I perceived that this was the image as seen by a spectator from the shore, or from another vessel. From the ship itself the wake appears like a brook flowing off from the stern' (Coleridge's note).

All in a hot and copper sky
The bloody sun at noon
Right up above the mast did stand,
No bigger than the moon.

Day after day, day after day,
We stuck, nor breath nor motion,
As idle as a painted ship
Upon a painted ocean.

And the albatross begins to be avenged.

Water, water, everywhere,
And all the boards did shrink;
Water, water, everywhere,
Nor any drop to drink.

The very deeps did rot: oh Christ,
That ever this should be!
Yea, slimy things did crawl with legs
Upon the slimy sea.

About, about, in reel and rout
The death-fires danced at night;
The water, like a witch's oils,
Burnt green and blue and white.

A spirit had followed them; one of the invisible inhabitants of this planet, neither departed souls nor angels; concerning whom the learned Jew, Josephus,[13] and the Platonic Constantinopolitan,[14] Michael Psellus,[15] may be consulted. They are very numerous, and there is no climate or element without one or more.

And some in dreams assured were
Of the spirit that plagued us so;
Nine fathom deep he had followed us
From the land of mist and snow.

And every tongue, through utter drought,
Was withered at the root;
We could not speak, no more than if
We had been choked with soot.

The shipmates in their sore distress would fain throw the whole guilt on the ancient mariner: in sign whereof they hang the dead sea-bird round his neck.

Ah wel-a-day! what evil looks
Had I from old and young!
Instead of the cross the albatross
About my neck was hung.

Notes

[13] Flavius Josephus (*c.*37–*c.*100), author of *Antiquitates Judaicae* and, more famously, *De bello Judaico*, which Coleridge read in November 1800 (*Notebooks* i 851).

[14] *Platonic Constantinopolitan* Neoplatonic philosopher from Constantinople (see next note).

[15] Michael Constantine Psellus (*c.*1018–*c.*1078), whose commentary to the *Chaldaean Oracles*, as John Livingston Lowes has pointed out, informed both this poem and *Kubla Khan*; see Lowes, *The Road to Xanadu* (1978), pp. 216–17.

Part the Third

There passed a weary time. Each throat
Was parched, and glazed each eye.
A weary time! a weary time!
How glazed each weary eye!

The ancient mariner beholdeth a sign in the element afar off.

When looking westward, I beheld
A something in the sky.

At first it seemed a little speck
And then it seemed a mist;
It moved and moved, and took at last
A certain shape, I wist.[16]

A speck, a mist, a shape, I wist!
And still it neared and neared:
And as if it dodged a water-sprite,
It plunged and tacked and veered.

At its nearer approach, it seemeth him to be a ship; and at a dear ransom he freeth his speech from the bonds of thirst.

With throat unslaked, with black lips baked,
We could nor laugh nor wail;
Through utter drought all dumb we stood!
I bit my arm, I sucked the blood,
And cried, "A sail! A sail!"

With throat unslaked, with black lips baked,
Agape they heard me call:

A flash of joy.

Gramercy![17] they for joy did grin
And all at once their breath drew in
As they were drinking all.

And horror follows. For can it be a *ship* that comes onward without wind or tide?

"See, see!" I cried, "She tacks no more,
Hither to work us weal;[18]
Without a breeze, without a tide,
She steadies with upright keel."

The western wave was all a-flame,
The day was well nigh done!
Almost upon the western wave
Rested the broad bright sun;
When that strange shape drove suddenly
Betwixt us and the sun.

It seemeth him but the skeleton of a ship.

And straight the sun was flecked with bars
(Heaven's Mother send us grace!),
As if through a dungeon-grate he peered
With broad and burning face.

Notes

[16] *wist* was aware of.

[17] *Gramercy!* mercy on us!

[18] *weal* harm.

Alas! thought I, and my heart beat loud,
How fast she nears and nears!
Are those *her* sails that glance in the sun
Like restless gossameres?

And its ribs are seen as bars on the face of the setting sun.

Are those *her* ribs through which the sun
Did peer, as through a grate?
And is that woman all her crew?
Is that a Death? And are there two?
Is Death that woman's mate?

The spectre-woman and her death-mate, and no other on board the skeleton-ship.

Her lips were red, *her* looks were free,
Her locks were yellow as gold;
Her skin was as white as leprosy,
The nightmare Life-in-Death was she
Who thicks man's blood with cold.

Like vessel, like crew!

Death and Life-in-Death have diced for the ship's crew, and she (the latter) winneth the ancient mariner.

The naked hulk alongside came,
And the twain were casting dice;
"The game is done! I've won! I've won!"
Quoth she, and whistles thrice.

The sun's rim dips, the stars rush out,
At one stride comes the dark;[19]
With far-heard whisper, o'er the sea,
Off shot the spectre-bark.

We listened and looked sideways up!
Fear at my heart, as at a cup,
My life-blood seemed to sip!
The stars were dim, and thick the night,
The steersman's face by his lamp gleamed white;
From the sails the dews did drip –
Till clomb[20] above the eastern bar
The horned moon, with one bright star
Within the nether tip.[21]

At the rising of the moon,

One after another,

One after one, by the star-dogged moon
Too quick for groan or sigh,
Each turned his face with a ghastly pang
And cursed me with his eye.

His shipmates drop down dead;

Four times fifty living men
(And I heard nor sigh nor groan)
With heavy thump, a lifeless lump,
They dropped down one by one.

Notes

[19] *The sun's rim . . . dark* Coleridge added a marginal gloss in MS in copies of *Sibylline Leaves* to explain: 'Between the tropics there is no twilight. As the sun's last segment dips down, and the evening gun is fired, the constellations appear arrayed.' Subsequent printed texts included the terser gloss: 'No twilight within the courts of the sun.'

[20] *clomb* climbed.

[21] *with one bright star . . . tip* In one copy of *Sibylline Leaves*, Coleridge noted: 'It is a common superstition among sailors "that something evil is about to happen whenever a star dogs the moon."'

But Life-in-Death begins her work on the ancient mariner.

The souls did from their bodies fly,
They fled to bliss or woe!
And every soul, it passed me by
Like the whiz of my crossbow.'

Part the Fourth

The wedding-guest feareth that a spirit is talking to him;

'I fear thee, ancient mariner,
I fear thy skinny hand;
And thou art long and lank and brown
As is the ribbed sea-sand.[22]

I fear thee and thy glittering eye,
And thy skinny hand so brown –'

But the ancient mariner assureth him of his bodily life, and proceedeth to relate his horrible penance.

'Fear not, fear not, thou wedding-guest,
This body dropped not down.

Alone, alone, all all alone,
Alone on a wide wide sea;
And never a saint took pity on
My soul in agony.

He despiseth the creatures of the calm,

The many men so beautiful,
And they all dead did lie!
And a thousand thousand slimy things
Lived on – and so did I.

And envieth that *they* should live, and so many lie dead.

I looked upon the rotting sea
And drew my eyes away;
I looked upon the rotting deck,
And there the dead men lay.

I looked to heaven and tried to pray
But or ever a prayer had gushed,
A wicked whisper came and made
My heart as dry as dust.

I closed my lids and kept them close
And the balls like pulses beat;
For the sky and the sea, and the sea and the sky
Lay like a load on my weary eye,
And the dead were at my feet.

But the curse liveth for him in the eye of the dead men.

The cold sweat melted from their limbs,
Nor rot nor reek did they;
The look with which they looked on me
Had never passed away.

Notes

[22] 'For the last two lines of this stanza I am indebted to Mr Wordsworth. It was on a delightful walk from Nether Stowey to Dulverton, with him and his sister, in the autumn of 1797, that this poem was planned and in part composed' (Coleridge's note). For Wordsworth's comment on this note, see p. 583.

An orphan's curse would drag to hell
A spirit from on high;
But oh! more horrible than that
Is the curse in a dead man's eye!
Seven days, seven nights, I saw that curse
And yet I could not die.

In his loneliness and fixedness, he yearneth towards the journeying moon, and the stars that still sojourn, yet still move onward; and everywhere the blue sky belongs to them, and is their appointed rest, and their native country, and their own natural homes, which they enter unannounced, as lords that are certainly expected, and yet there is a silent joy at their arrival.

The moving moon went up the sky
And nowhere did abide;
Softly she was going up
And a star or two beside;

Her beams bemocked the sultry main
Like April hoar-frost spread;
But where the ship's huge shadow lay
The charmed[23] water burnt alway
A still and awful red.

By the light of the moon he beholdeth God's creatures of the great calm.

Beyond the shadow of the ship
I watched the water-snakes;
They moved in tracks of shining white,
And when they reared, the elfish light
Fell off in hoary flakes.

Within the shadow of the ship
I watched their rich attire:
Blue, glossy green, and velvet black,
They coiled and swam, and every track
Was a flash of golden fire.

Their beauty and their happiness.

Oh happy living things! no tongue
Their beauty might declare:
A spring of love gushed from my heart

He blesseth them in his heart.

And I blessed them unaware!
Sure my kind saint took pity on me,
And I blessed them unaware.

The spell begins to break.

The self-same moment I could pray,
And from my neck so free
The albatross fell off and sank
Like lead into the sea.

Part the Fifth

Oh sleep, it is a gentle thing
Beloved from pole to pole!
To Mary Queen[24] the praise be given;
She sent the gentle sleep from heaven
That slid into my soul.

Notes

[23] *charmed* dead calm.

[24] *Mary Queen* the Virgin Mary.

By grace of the holy Mother, the ancient mariner is refreshed with rain.

The silly[25] buckets on the deck
That had so long remained,
I dreamt that they were filled with dew
And when I awoke it rained.

My lips were wet, my throat was cold,
My garments all were dank;
Sure I had drunken in my dreams
And still my body drank.

I moved and could not feel my limbs,
I was so light, almost
I thought that I had died in sleep
And was a blessed ghost.

He heareth sounds, and seeth strange sights and commotions in the sky and the element.

And soon I heard a roaring wind,
It did not come anear;
But with its sound it shook the sails
That were so thin and sere.[26]

The upper air bursts into life
And a hundred fire-flags sheen,[27]
To and fro they were hurried about;
And to and fro, and in and out
The wan stars danced between.[28]

And the coming wind did roar more loud,
And the sails did sigh like sedge;
And the rain poured down from one black cloud,
The moon was at its edge.

The thick black cloud was cleft, and still
The moon was at its side;
Like waters shot from some high crag,
The lightning fell with never a jag,
A river steep and wide.

The bodies of the ship's crew are inspirited,[29] and the ship moves on;

The loud wind never reached the ship,
Yet now the ship moved on!
Beneath the lightning and the moon
The dead men gave a groan.

They groaned, they stirred, they all uprose,
Nor spake, nor moved their eyes;
It had been strange, even in a dream,
To have seen those dead men rise.

The helmsman steered, the ship moved on,
Yet never a breeze up-blew;
The mariners all 'gan work the ropes

Notes

[25] *silly* plain, rustic, homely.
[26] *sere* worn.
[27] *sheen* shining.
[28] *The upper air . . . between* the aurora borealis.
[29] *inspirited* quickened, animated.

Where they were wont to do;
They raised their limbs like lifeless tools –
We were a ghastly crew.

The body of my brother's son
Stood by me, knee to knee;
The body and I pulled at one rope
But he said nought to me.'

But not by the souls of the men, nor by dæmons of earth or the middle air, but by a blessed troop of angelic spirits, sent down by the invocation of the guardian saint.

'I fear thee, ancient mariner!'
'Be calm, thou wedding-guest!
'Twas not those souls that fled in pain,
Which to their corses came again,
But a troop of spirits blessed;

For when it dawned, they dropped their arms
And clustered round the mast;
Sweet sounds rose slowly through their mouths
And from their bodies passed.

Around, around, flew each sweet sound
Then darted to the sun;
Slowly the sounds came back again,
Now mixed, now one by one.

Sometimes a-dropping from the sky
I heard the skylark sing;
Sometimes all little birds that are,
How they seemed to fill the sea and air
With their sweet jargoning![30]

And now 'twas like all instruments,
Now like a lonely flute,
And now it is an angel's song
That makes the heavens be mute.

It ceased, yet still the sails made on
A pleasant noise till noon,
A noise like of a hidden brook
In the leafy month of June,
That to the sleeping woods all night
Singeth a quiet tune.

Till noon we quietly sailed on,
Yet never a breeze did breathe;
Slowly and smoothly went the ship,
Moved onward from beneath.

Notes

[30] *jargoning* birdsong.

The lonesome spirit from the South Pole carries on the ship as far as the line, in obedience to the angelic troop, but still requireth vengeance.

Under the keel nine fathom deep,
From the land of mist and snow,
The spirit slid, and it was he
That made the ship to go.
The sails at noon left off their tune
And the ship stood still also.

The sun right up above the mast
Had fixed her to the ocean;
But in a minute she 'gan stir
With a short uneasy motion –
Backwards and forwards half her length,
With a short uneasy motion.

Then like a pawing horse let go,
She made a sudden bound;
It flung the blood into my head,
And I fell down in a swound.

The Polar Spirit's fellow dæmons, the invisible inhabitants of the element, take part in his wrong; and two of them relate, one to the other, that penance long and heavy for the ancient mariner hath been accorded to the Polar Spirit, who returneth southward.

How long in that same fit I lay,
I have not to declare;
But ere my living life returned,
I heard and in my soul discerned
Two voices in the air.

"Is it he?" quoth one, "Is this the man?
By him who died on cross,
With his cruel bow he laid full low
The harmless albatross.

The spirit who bideth by himself
In the land of mist and snow,
He loved the bird that loved the man
Who shot him with his bow."

The other was a softer voice,
As soft as honey-dew;
Quoth he, "The man hath penance done
And penance more will do." '

Part the Sixth

First Voice
But tell me, tell me! speak again,
Thy soft response renewing –
What makes that ship drive on so fast?
What is the ocean doing?

Second Voice
Still as a slave before his lord,
The ocean hath no blast;
His great bright eye most silently
Up to the moon is cast –

If he may know which way to go,
For she guides him smooth or grim.
See, brother, see – how graciously
She looketh down on him!

FIRST VOICE

The mariner hath been cast into a trance; for the angelic power causeth the vessel to drive northward, faster than human life could endure.

But why drives on that ship so fast
Without or wave or wind?

SECOND VOICE

The air is cut away before
And closes from behind.

Fly, brother, fly! more high, more high,
Or we shall be belated;
For slow and slow that ship will go
When the mariner's trance is abated.

The supernatural motion is retarded; the mariner awakes, and his penance begins anew.

'I woke, and we were sailing on
As in a gentle weather;
'Twas night, calm night, the moon was high –
The dead men stood together.

All stood together on the deck,
For a charnel-dungeon[31] fitter;
All fixed on me their stony eyes
That in the moon did glitter.

The pang, the curse, with which they died
Had never passed away;
I could not draw my eyes from theirs
Nor turn them up to pray.

The curse is finally expiated.

And now this spell was snapped; once more
I viewed the ocean green,
And looked far forth, yet little saw
Of what had else been seen –

Like one that on a lonesome road
Doth walk in fear and dread,
And having once turned round walks on
And turns no more his head,
Because he knows a frightful fiend
Doth close behind him tread.

But soon there breathed a wind on me,
Nor sound nor motion made;
Its path was not upon the sea,
In ripple or in shade.

Notes

[31] *charnel-dungeon* dungeon containing dead prisoners' bodies.

It raised my hair, it fanned my cheek,
Like a meadow-gale of spring –
It mingled strangely with my fears,
Yet it felt like a welcoming.

Swiftly, swiftly flew the ship,
Yet she sailed softly too;
Sweetly, sweetly blew the breeze –
On me alone it blew.

And the ancient mariner beholdeth his native country.

Oh dream of joy! Is this indeed
The lighthouse top I see?
Is this the hill? Is this the kirk?
Is this mine own countree?

We drifted o'er the harbour-bar,[32]
And I with sobs did pray,
"Oh let me be awake, my God!
Or let me sleep alway!"

The harbour-bay was clear as glass,
So smoothly it was strewn![33]
And on the bay the moonlight lay
And the shadow of the moon.

The rock shone bright, the kirk no less
That stands above the rock;
The moonlight steeped in silentness
The steady weathercock.

The angelic spirits leave the dead bodies,

And the bay was white with silent light,
Till rising from the same,
Full many shapes that shadows were
In crimson colours came.

And appear in their own forms of light.

A little distance from the prow
Those crimson shadows were;
I turned my eyes upon the deck –
Oh Christ! What saw I there!

Each corse lay flat, lifeless and flat,
And by the holy rood,[34]
A man all light, a seraph-man[35]
On every corse there stood.

This seraph-band, each waved his hand –
It was a heavenly sight!
They stood as signals to the land,
Each one a lovely light;

Notes

[32] *bar* bank of silt across the mouth of the harbour.

[33] *strewn* levelled.

[34] *rood* cross.

[35] *seraph-man* The seraphim were the highest order of angels, whose purpose was to glow with the love of God.

This seraph-band, each waved his hand,
No voice did they impart –
No voice, but oh! the silence sank
Like music on my heart.

But soon I heard the dash of oars,
I heard the pilot's cheer;
My head was turned perforce away
And I saw a boat appear.

The pilot and the pilot's boy,
I heard them coming fast –
Dear Lord in heaven! it was a joy
The dead men could not blast.

I saw a third, I heard his voice –
It is the hermit good!
He singeth loud his godly hymns
That he makes in the wood.
He'll shrieve my soul, he'll wash away
The albatross's blood.

Part the Seventh

The hermit of the wood

This hermit good lives in that wood
Which slopes down to the sea;
How loudly his sweet voice he rears!
He loves to talk with mariners
That come from a far countree.

He kneels at morn, and noon and eve,
He hath a cushion plump;
It is the moss that wholly hides
The rotted old oak-stump.

The skiff-boat neared, I heard them talk:
"Why, this is strange, I trow!
Where are those lights so many and fair,
That signal made but now?"

Approacheth the ship with wonder.

"Strange, by my faith!" the hermit said,
"And they answered not our cheer!
The planks look warped, and see those sails,
How thin they are and sere!
I never saw aught like to them
Unless perchance it were

The skeletons of leaves that lag
My forest brook along,
When the ivy-tod[36] is heavy with snow
And the owlet whoops to the wolf below
That eats the she-wolf's young."

"Dear Lord! it hath a fiendish look",
The pilot made reply,
"I am a-feared." "Push on, push on!"
Said the hermit cheerily.

The boat came closer to the ship
But I nor spake nor stirred;
The boat came close beneath the ship
And straight a sound was heard!

The ship suddenly sinketh.

Under the water it rumbled on,
Still louder and more dread;
It reached the ship, it split the bay –
The ship went down like lead.

The ancient mariner is saved in the pilot's boat.

Stunned by that loud and dreadful sound
Which sky and ocean smote,
Like one that hath been seven days drowned,
My body lay afloat;
But swift as dreams, myself I found
Within the pilot's boat.

Upon the whirl where sank the ship
The boat spun round and round,
And all was still, save that the hill
Was telling of the sound.

I moved my lips – the pilot shrieked
And fell down in a fit;
The holy hermit raised his eyes
And prayed where he did sit.

I took the oars; the pilot's boy,
Who now doth crazy go,
Laughed loud and long, and all the while
His eyes went to and fro:
"Ha! ha!" quoth he, "full plain I see
The Devil knows how to row."

And now all in my own countrée
I stood on the firm land!
The hermit stepped forth from the boat,
And scarcely he could stand.

Notes

[36] *ivy-tod* ivy-bush.

The ancient mariner earnestly entreateth the hermit to shrieve him; and the penance of life falls on him.

"Oh shrieve me, shrieve me, holy man!"
The hermit crossed his brow.
"Say quick", quoth he, "I bid thee say
What manner of man art thou?"

Forthwith this frame of mine was wrenched
With a woeful agony,
Which forced me to begin my tale –
And then it left me free.

And ever and anon throughout his future life an agony constraineth him to travel from land to land,

Since then, at an uncertain hour,
That agony returns,
And till my ghastly tale is told,
This heart within me burns.

I pass, like night, from land to land,
I have strange power of speech;
The moment that his face I see,
I know the man that must hear me –
To him my tale I teach.

What loud uproar bursts from that door!
The wedding-guests are there;
But in the garden bower the bride
And bridemaids singing are;
And hark, the little vesper-bell[37]
Which biddeth me to prayer.

Oh wedding-guest! this soul hath been
Alone on a wide wide sea;
So lonely 'twas, that God himself
Scarce seemed there to be.

Oh sweeter than the marriage-feast,
'Tis sweeter far to me
To walk together to the kirk
With a goodly company!

To walk together to the kirk
And all together pray,
While each to his great Father bends,
Old men, and babes, and loving friends,
And youths and maidens gay.

And to teach by his own example love and reverence to all things that God made and loveth.

Farewell, farewell! but this I tell
To thee, thou wedding-guest!
He prayeth well who loveth well
Both man and bird and beast.

Notes

[37] *vesper-bell* bell used to summon the congregation for vespers, evensong.

He prayeth best who loveth best
All things both great and small,
For the dear God who loveth us,
He made and loveth all.'

The mariner, whose eye is bright,
Whose beard with age is hoar,
Is gone; and now the wedding-guest
Turned from the bridegroom's door.

He went like one that hath been stunned
And is of sense forlorn:
A sadder and a wiser man
He rose the morrow morn.

Constancy to an Ideal Object (composed possibly in 1804; certainly by June 1825)[1]

From Poetical Works (1829)

Since all that beat about in Nature's range
Or[2] veer or vanish, why should'st thou remain
The only constant in a world of change,
Oh yearning thought, that liv'st but in the brain?
Call to the Hours that in the distance play,
The fairy people of the future day –
Fond thought! not one of all that shining swarm
Will breathe on *thee* with life-enkindling breath,
Till when, like strangers shelt'ring from a storm,
Hope and Despair meet in the porch of Death!
Yet still thou haunt'st me; and though well I see,
She is not thou, and only thou art she,
Still, still as though some dear embodied Good,
Some living Love before my eyes there stood
With answering look a ready ear to lend,
I mourn to thee and say, 'Ah, loveliest friend!
That this the meed of all my toils might be,
To have a home, an English home, and thee!'
Vain repetition! Home and Thou are one.
The peacefull'st cot, the moon shall shine upon,
Lulled by the thrush and wakened by the lark,
Without thee were but a becalmed bark[3]

Notes

CONSTANCY TO AN IDEAL OBJECT

[1] The notion of an 'ideal object' is an impossibility, as Coleridge believed objects could exist only by their being perceived by other objects. As he writes in *Biographia Literaria* chapter 12, Thesis 5: 'Each thing is what it is in consequence of some other thing. An infinite, independent thing, is no less a contradiction, than an infinite circle or sideless triangle.'

[2] *Or* Either.

[3] *bark* boat.

Whose helmsman on an ocean waste and wide
Sits mute and pale his mouldering helm beside.

And art thou nothing? Such thou art, as when
The woodman winding westward up the glen
At wintry dawn, where o'er the sheep-track's maze
The viewless[4] snow-mist weaves a glist'ning haze,
Sees full before him, gliding without tread,
An image[5] with a glory[6] round its head;
The enamoured rustic worships its fair hues,
Nor knows he *makes* the shadow he pursues![7]

From Table Talk (edited from MS)
[*On 'The Ancient Mariner'*] (dictated 30 May 1830)

The fault of 'The Ancient Mariner' consists in making the moral sentiment too apparent and bringing it in too much as a principle or cause in a work of such pure imagination.

[*The True Way for a Poet*] (dictated 19 September 1830)

Southey picked nature's pockets as a poet, instead of borrowing from her. He went out and took some particular image, for example a water-insect – and then exactly copied its make, colours and motions. This he put in a poem. The true way for a poet is to examine nature, but write from your recollection, and trust more to your imagination than your memory.

[*On 'The Recluse'*][1] (dictated 21 July 1832)

Wordsworth should have first published his Thirteen Books on the growth of an individual mind,[2] far superior to any part of *The Excursion*. Then the plan suggested and laid out by me was that he should assume the station of a man in repose, whose

Notes

[4] *viewless* invisible.

[5] 'This phenomenon, which the author has himself experienced, and of which the reader may find a description in one of the earlier volumes of the Manchester Philosophical Transactions, is applied figuratively in the following passage of the *Aids to Reflection*:

> Pindar's fine remark respecting the different effects of music on different characters holds equally true of genius: as many as are not delighted by it are disturbed, perplexed, irritated. The beholder either recognizes it as a projected form of his own being, that moves before him with a Glory round its head, or recoils from it as a spectre. (*Aids to Reflection*, 1825)' (Coleridge's note)

[6] *glory* corona of light; halo.

[7] Coleridge was fascinated by the illusion whereby people in the mountains with the sun behind them cast magnified images of themselves onto cloudscapes beyond – a natural phenomenon he had come across in Germany in 1799, known as the Brocken Spectre (see *Notebooks* i 430).

On 'The Recluse'

[1] This account of 'The Recluse' should be regarded as a supplement to Coleridge's longer and more detailed account of the poem in his letter to Wordsworth of May 1815; see pp. 689–91. As with that document, it should be approached with caution. 'The Recluse' was conceived in 1797–8, and may not have been thought out in quite the way Coleridge suggested over three decades later. For suggestions as to 'The Recluse' at the time of its conception see pp. 413–15.

[2] *The Thirteen-Book Prelude*; for Coleridge's immediate reaction to it, see *To William Wordsworth*, pp. 686–8.

mind was made up, and so prepared to deliver upon authority a system of philosophy. He was to treat man as man – a subject of eye, ear, touch, taste, in contact with external nature, informing the senses from the mind and not compounding a mind out of the senses; then the pastoral and other states, assuming a satiric or Juvenalian spirit as he approached the high civilization of cities and towns; and then opening a melancholy picture of the present state of degeneracy and vice; thence revealing the necessity for and proof of the whole state of man and society being subject to and illustrative of a redemptive process in operation, showing how this idea reconciled all the anomalies, and how it promised future glory and restoration. Something of this sort I suggested, and it was agreed on. It is what in substance I have been all my life doing in my system of philosophy.

Wordsworth spoilt many of his best poems by abandoning the contemplative position, which is alone fitted for him, and introducing the object in a dramatic way. This is seen in 'The Leech-Gatherer'[3] and 'Ruth'. Wordsworth had more materials for the great philosophic poet than any man I ever knew or (as I think) has existed in this country for a long time – but he was utterly unfitted for the epic or narrative style. His mental-internal action is always so excessively disproportionate to the actual business that the latter either goes to sleep or becomes ridiculous.[4] In his reasoning you will find no progression: it eddies, it comes round and round again, perhaps with a wider circle, but it is repetition still.

[*Keats*[1]] (dictated 11 August 1832)

A loose, not well-dressed youth, met Mr Green and me in Mansfield Lane.[2] Green knew him and spoke. It was Keats. He was introduced to me, and stayed a minute or so.[3] After he had gone a little, he came back and said, 'Let me carry away the memory, Coleridge, of having pressed your hand.' There is death in *his* hand, said I to Green when he was gone. Yet this was before the consumption showed itself.[4]

Notes

[3] i.e. 'Resolution and Independence'.

[4] Coleridge here echoes the point made by Jeffrey in his review of *The Excursion*, when he notes that its incidents are 'few and trifling'; p. 718 below.

KEATS

[1] Keats's account of this meeting may be found on pp. 1388–9; it took place probably on 11 April 1819. Joseph Henry Green (1791–1863) performed a number of services for Coleridge, including that of amanuensis, confidant, friend and literary executor. Like Keats, he had grown up close to the Swan and Hoop in Moorgate, and was one of Keats's lecturers in anatomy at Guy's Hospital.

[2] *Mansfield Lane* ran adjacent to Kenwood House on Hampstead Heath.

[3] *stayed a minute or so* Their respective accounts of the meeting differ most at this point, where according to Keats Coleridge embarked on a lengthy discourse covering a vast range of subjects during which time they walked two miles. It led Keats to regard Coleridge less as a man of imagination than as a 'consequitive reasoner'.

[4] Keats knew he was fatally infected with tuberculosis by early February 1820.

Francis, Lord Jeffrey (1773–1850)

'The severest of critics,' Hazlitt remarked of his friend, Francis Jeffrey, 'is the best-natured of men' (Wu vii 198). Jeffrey was a lawyer (and later a judge), but is best remembered as one of the founders of the *Edinburgh Review*, one of the most influential journals of the period. Having attended Glasgow, Edinburgh and Oxford Universities, he preferred the rigorous education he received in his native Scotland. By the time he was admitted to the bar in 1794 he had become a Whig, much to his father's dismay. His politics would do him no favours: as the Scottish legal system was dominated by Tories, advancement came slowly.

Jeffrey found solace among other intellectuals such as Henry Brougham, Francis Horner and Sydney Smith, who regularly met at his flat in Buccleuch Place. It was Smith who proposed that they establish a periodical to be called the *Edinburgh Review*, the first number of which appeared in October 1802. Jeffrey, who assumed the role of editor, was doubtful of success – but he turned out to be wrong. The initial printing of 750 copies did not meet demand, and a second printing was called for within the month. By the end of 1803, 2,150 copies of the first issue had been sold in Edinburgh alone, many passing through several hands. Printings of subsequent numbers were expanded, and Longman acquired publication rights in London. By 1809, 9,000 copies were being sold each quarter. Wordsworth had good reason to be irked by the bad reviews of his work that regularly appeared there: they were eagerly devoured by a large readership on both sides of the border.

Despite his reputation for severity, Jeffrey wrote appreciatively of Crabbe, Scott, Byron and, surprisingly, Keats. But he bore a grudge against Wordsworth, Coleridge and Southey, whom he lumped together as the 'Lake School', despite their differences as writers. He held them collectively responsible for the Preface to *Lyrical Ballads*, which he interpreted as an attack on Pope and his imitators. Contrary to what he claims in the review of *The Excursion*, this made him consistently and unstintingly hostile to Wordsworth: *Lyrical Ballads* suffered from 'vulgarity, affectation and silliness', while the *Poems, in Two Volumes* (1807) were 'very flat, feeble, and affected'. And even after delivering a damning review of *The Excursion* he was not finished with him. The following year he wrote a lengthy essay on *The White Doe of Rylstone* (1815) which begins:

> This, we think, has the merit of being the very worst poem we ever saw imprinted in a quarto volume; and though it was scarcely to be expected, we confess that Mr Wordsworth, with all his ambition, should so soon have attained to that distinction, the wonder may perhaps be diminished when we state that it seems to us to consist of a happy union of all the faults, without any of the beauties, which belong to his school of poetry. It is just such a work, in short, as some wicked enemy of that school might be supposed to have devised, on purpose to make it ridiculous.

As he saw it, Wordsworth was enslaved to a misguided system which it was his duty to condemn lest others be tempted to follow in his path. That system (which consisted, in Jeffrey's view, of the wrong-headed notions expounded in the Preface to *Lyrical Ballads*), combined with years of seclusion in the countryside, had made Wordsworth pompous, vain and self-regarding. Jeffrey was wrong, but his review of *The Excursion* is an important reminder of how shockingly new Wordsworth's poetry seemed even in the second decade of the nineteenth century. The idea of placing peasant folk, country vicars and village children at the centre of poems meant to be read by sophisticated metropolitan readers seemed to many an absurdity, to the point at which Wordsworth was seen as the deserving target of ridicule that set the tone for criticism of his work for decades. One of the least likeable aspects of Jeffrey was his disingenuousness. He claims to regard Wordsworth as 'great' and in later years told Henry Crabb Robinson, 'I was always among Wordsworth's admirers.' 'You had an odd way of showing it,' Robinson answered, with some justice (Morley ii 838).

Jeffrey's most notorious attack remains that on *The Excursion*, which debunks it and its author on the grounds of: (i) a perverse plainness of diction; (ii) lowly subject-matter; (iii) bogus metaphysics. The portrayal of Wordsworth as a self-obsessed, incomprehensible mystic stuck, and was repeated by generations of wags, beginning most famously with Byron in the dedication to *Don Juan* (see p. 934). In private, Wordsworth remarked that he held Jeffrey's remarks 'in entire contempt, and therefore shall not pollute my fingers with the touch of it' (*MY* ii 190). All the same, he was aware of its effects, and even if, as he claimed, he did not read it, he probably heard about its contents from others.

Unlike Scott, Jeffrey was always more dependent on his legal career than on his writing for a living. After the Whigs came to power in 1830, he gained the advancement for which he had waited. In 1832 he was elected to Parliament, and two years later was made a judge and became Lord Jeffrey. He was a friend of Carlyle and Dickens. Posterity has granted him a variable press, thanks to his merciless, and not always fair, criticisms of Wordsworth. All the same, Hazlitt, who knew him as a friend, described him as 'a Scotchman without one particle of hypocrisy, of cant, of servility, or selfishness' (Wu vii 198).

Further reading

British Romanticism and the Edinburgh Review ed. Massimiliano Demata and Duncan Wu (Basingstoke, 2002).

Philip Flynn, *Francis Jeffrey* (Canbury, NJ, 1978).

Peter Morgan, *Jeffrey's Criticism* (Edinburgh, 1983).

Review of William Wordsworth, 'The Excursion'[1] (extracts)

From Edinburgh Review (November 1814)

This will never do. It bears, no doubt, the stamp of the author's heart and fancy – but unfortunately not half so visibly as that of his peculiar system. His former poems were intended to recommend that system, and to bespeak favour for it by their individual merit, but this, we suspect, must be recommended by the system, and can only expect to succeed where it has been previously established. It is longer, weaker, and tamer, than any of Mr Wordsworth's other productions, with less boldness of originality, and less even of that extreme simplicity and lowliness of tone which wavered so prettily, in the *Lyrical Ballads*, between silliness and pathos. We have imitations of Cowper and even of Milton here, engrafted on the natural drawl of the Lakers – and all diluted into harmony by that profuse and irrepressible wordiness which deluges all the blank verse of this school of poetry, and lubricates and weakens the whole structure of their style.

Notes

Review of William Wordsworth, 'The Excursion'

[1] Wordsworth published *The Excursion* in 1814 as part of his great, never-to-be-completed epic, *The Recluse*. What Jeffrey could not have known was that it had its roots in the *annus mirabilis* of 1797–8 when Wordsworth had composed 'The Ruined Cottage', 'The Pedlar' and 'Not Useless do I Deem', all of which were incorporated into *The Excursion* in drastically revised form (see pp. 422–47). Another reader, Coleridge, was also disappointed with *The Excursion*, but for different reasons (see pp. 689–91).

Though it fairly fills four hundred and twenty good quarto pages,[2] without note, vignette, or any sort of extraneous assistance, it is stated in the title (with something of an imprudent candour) to be but 'a portion' of a larger work,[3] and in the preface – where an attempt is rather unsuccessfully made to explain the whole design – it is still more rashly disclosed that it is but 'a part of the second part of a *long* and laborious work'[4] which is to consist of three parts!

What Mr Wordsworth's ideas of length are, we have no means of accurately judging, but we cannot help suspecting that they are liberal to a degree that will alarm the weakness of most modern readers. As far as we can gather from the preface, the entire poem – or one of them (for we really are not sure whether there is to be one or two) – is of a biographical nature, and is to contain the history of the author's mind and of the origin and progress of his poetical powers up to the period when they were sufficiently matured to qualify him for the great work on which he has been so long employed. Now the quarto before us contains an account of one of his youthful rambles in the vales of Cumberland, and occupies precisely the period of three days; so that, by the use of a very powerful calculus,[5] some estimate may be formed of the probable extent of the entire biography.

This small specimen, however, and the statements with which it is prefaced, have been sufficient to set our minds at rest in one particular. The case of Mr Wordsworth, we perceive, is now manifestly hopeless, and we give him up as altogether incurable, and beyond the power of criticism. We cannot indeed altogether omit taking precautions now and then against the spreading of the malady – but for himself, though we shall watch the progress of his symptoms as a matter of professional curiosity and instruction, we really think it right not to harass him any longer with nauseous remedies, but rather to throw in cordials and lenitives, and wait in patience for the natural termination of the disorder. In order to justify this desertion of our patient, however, it is proper to state why we despair of the success of a more active practice.

A man who has been for twenty years at work on such matter as is now before us, and who comes complacently forward with a whole quarto of it after all the admonitions he has received, cannot reasonably be expected to 'change his hand, or check his pride', upon the suggestion of far weightier monitors[6] than we can pretend to be. Inveterate habit must now have given a kind of sanctity to the errors of early taste; and the very powers of which we lament the perversion, have probably become incapable of any other application. The very quantity, too, that he has written, and is at this moment working up for publication upon the old pattern, makes it almost hopeless to look for any change of it. All this is so much capital already sunk in the concern, which must be sacrificed if it be abandoned:[7] and no man likes to give up for lost the time and talent and labour which he has embodied in any permanent production. We were not previously aware of these obstacles to Mr Wordsworth's conversion; and, considering the peculiarities of his former writings merely as the result of certain wanton and capricious experiments on public taste and indulgence,[8]

Notes

[2] *four hundred and twenty good quarto pages* In fact, *The Excursion* was 447 pages long, and carries an explanatory preface of 14 pages and 20 pages of notes. The word 'quarto' refers to the format of the volume – a 'quarto' consisted of pages made from large folio-size paper folded twice (to produce four separate leaves).

[3] *a larger work* i.e. *The Recluse* (see pp. 413–15).

[4] *a long and laborious work* unfortunately these were Wordsworth's exact words, though he did not italicize 'long'.

[5] *calculus* calculation.

[6] *monitors* judges.

[7] *which must be sacrificed if it be abandoned* In fact, Wordsworth was never to complete 'The Recluse', of which *The Excursion* was part. Jeffrey's harsh words may have contributed to Wordsworth's inability to go on with it.

[8] *certain wanton and capricious experiments on public taste and indulgence* Wordsworth himself, in the Advertisement to *Lyrical Ballads* (1798), had described them as experiments (see p. 331).

conceived it to be our duty to discourage their repetition by all the means in our power. We now see clearly, however, how the case stands – and making up our minds, though with the most sincere pain and reluctance, to consider him as finally lost to the good cause of poetry, shall endeavour to be thankful for the occasional gleams of tenderness and beauty which the natural force of his imagination and affections must still shed over all his productions, and to which we shall ever turn with delight, in spite of the affectation and mysticism and prolixity with which they are so abundantly contrasted.

Long habits of seclusion, and an excessive ambition of originality, can alone account for the disproportion which seems to exist between this author's taste and his genius; or for the devotion with which he has sacrificed so many precious gifts at the shrine of those paltry idols which he has set up for himself among his lakes and mountains. Solitary musings, amidst such scenes, might no doubt be expected to nurse up[9] the mind to the majesty of poetical conception (though it is remarkable that all the greater poets lived, or had lived, in the full current of society) – but the collision of equal minds, the admonition of prevailing impressions, seems necessary to reduce its redundancies, and repress that tendency to extravagance or puerility, into which the self-indulgence and self-admiration of genius is so apt to be betrayed when it is allowed to wanton, without awe or restraint, in the triumph and delight of its own intoxication. That its flights should be graceful and glorious in the eyes of men, it seems almost to be necessary that they should be made in the consciousness that men's eyes[10] are to behold them, – and that the inward transport and vigour by which they are inspired, should be tempered by an occasional reference to what will be thought of them by those ultimate dispensers of glory. An habitual and general knowledge of the few settled and permanent maxims which form the canon of general taste in all large and polished societies – a certain tact, which informs us at once that many things which we still love and are moved by in secret, must necessarily be despised as childish, or derided as absurd, in all such societies – though it will not stand in the place of genius, seems necessary to the success of its exertions; and though it will never enable anyone to produce the higher beauties of art, can alone secure the talent which does produce them from errors that must render it useless. Those who have most of the talent, however, commonly acquire this knowledge with the greatest facility;[11] – and if Mr Wordsworth, instead of confining himself almost entirely to the society of the dalesmen and cottagers, and little children, who form the subjects of this book, had condescended to mingle a little more with the people that were to read and judge of it, we cannot help thinking that its texture would have been considerably improved: at least it appears to us to be absolutely impossible that anyone who had lived or mixed familiarly with men of literature and ordinary judgement in poetry (of course we exclude the coadjutors and disciples of his own school[12]) could ever have fallen into such gross faults, or so long mistaken them for beauties. His first essays we looked upon in a good degree as poetical paradoxes,[13] maintained experimentally in order to display talent and court notoriety; and so maintained, with no more serious belief in their truth, than is usually generated by an ingenious and animated defence of other paradoxes. But when we find that he has been for twenty years exclusively employed upon articles of this very fabric, and that

Notes

[9] *nurse up* cultivate.

[10] *mens' eyes* There may be an echo of Shakespeare, *Sonnet* 29: 'When in disgrace with fortune and men's eyes'.

[11] *facility* ease.

[12] *the coadjutors and disciples of his own school* Coleridge and Southey.

[13] *paradoxes* i.e. puzzles, conundrums.

he has still enough of raw material on hand to keep him so employed for twenty years to come, we cannot refuse him the justice of believing that he is a sincere convert to his own system, and must ascribe the peculiarities of his composition, not to any transient affectation, or accidental caprice of imagination, but to a settled perversity of taste or understanding, which has been fostered, if not altogether created, by the circumstances to which we have already alluded.

The volume before us, if we were to describe it very shortly, we should characterize as a tissue of moral and devotional ravings in which innumerable changes are rung upon a few very simple and familiar ideas – but with such an accompaniment of long words, long sentences, and unwieldy phrases, and such a hubbub of strained raptures and fantastical sublimities, that it is often extremely difficult for the most skilful and attentive student to obtain a glimpse of the author's meaning, and altogether impossible for an ordinary reader to conjecture what he is about.

Moral and religious enthusiasm,[14] though undoubtedly poetical emotions, are at the same time but dangerous inspirers of poetry, nothing being so apt to run into interminable dullness or mellifluous extravagance, without giving the unfortunate author the slightest intimation of his danger. His laudable zeal for the efficacy of his preachments,[15] he very naturally mistakes for the ardour of poetical inspiration – and, while dealing out the high words and glowing phrases which are so readily supplied by themes of this description, can scarcely avoid believing that he is eminently original and impressive. All sorts of commonplace notions and expressions are sanctified in his eyes by the sublime ends for which they are employed, and the mystical verbiage of the Methodist pulpit is repeated till the speaker entertains no doubt that he is the elected organ of divine truth and persuasion. But if such be the common hazards of seeking inspiration from those potent fountains, it may easily be conceived what chance Mr Wordsworth had of escaping their enchantment, with his natural propensities to wordiness, and his unlucky habit of debasing pathos with vulgarity.[16] The fact accordingly is that in this production he is more obscure than a Pindaric poet of the seventeenth century,[17] and more verbose 'than even himself of yore', while the wilfulness with which he persists in choosing his examples of intellectual dignity and tenderness exclusively from the lowest ranks of society will be sufficiently apparent from the circumstance of his having thought fit to make his chief prolocutor[18] in this poetical dialogue, and chief advocate of providence and virtue, *an old Scotch Pedlar*, retired indeed from business, but still rambling about in his former haunts, and gossiping among his old customers without his pack on his shoulders. The other persons of the drama are a retired military chaplain, who has grown half an atheist and half a misanthrope; the wife of an unprosperous weaver; a servant girl with her infant; a parish pauper, and one or two other personages of equal rank and dignity.

The character of the work is decidedly didactic, and more than nine-tenths of it are occupied with a species of dialogue, or rather a series of long sermons or harangues which pass between the Pedlar, the author, the old chaplain, and a worthy vicar who entertains the whole party at dinner on the last day of their excursion. The incidents which occur in the course of it are as few and trifling as can be imagined – and those which the different speakers narrate in the course of their discourses are introduced rather to illustrate their arguments or opinions than for any interest they are supposed to possess of their own. The doctrine which the work is intended to enforce, we are by

Notes

[14] *enthusiasm* fervour, rapture, perhaps even madness.

[15] *preachments* sermonizing, obtrusive or wearisome discourse.

[16] *vulgarity* the commonplace, banality.

[17] *a Pindaric poet of the seventeenth century* It is not clear why such a poet should necessarily be 'obscure'; though Coleridge may be thinking of the metaphysicals.

[18] *prolocutor* spokesman.

no means certain that we have discovered. In so far as we can collect, however, it seems to be neither more nor less than the old familiar one that a firm belief in the providence of a wise and beneficent Being must be our great stay and support[19] under all afflictions and perplexities upon earth, and that there are indications of his power and goodness in all the aspects of the visible universe, whether living or inanimate – every part of which should therefore be regarded with love and reverence, as exponents of those great attributes.

We can testify, at least, that these salutary and important truths are inculcated at far greater length, and with more repetitions, than in any ten volumes of sermons that we ever perused. It is also maintained, with equal conciseness and originality, that there is frequently much good sense, as well as much enjoyment, in the humbler conditions of life; and that, in spite of great vices and abuses, there is a reasonable allowance both of happiness and goodness in society at large. If there be any deeper or more recondite[20] doctrines in Mr Wordsworth's book, we must confess that they have escaped us – and, convinced as we are of the truth and soundness of those to which we have alluded, we cannot help thinking that they might have been better enforced with less parade and prolixity.[21] His effusions on what may be called the physiognomy[22] of external nature, or its moral and theological expression, are eminently fantastic, obscure, and affected . . .

[At this point Jeffrey summarizes *The Excursion*, followed by extracts from it, interspersed with his own critical commentary, before concluding the review as follows.]

Nobody can be more disposed to do justice to the great powers of Mr Wordsworth than we are, and, from the first time that he came before us, down to the present moment, we have uniformly testified in their favour, and assigned indeed our high sense of their value as the chief ground of the bitterness with which we resented their perversion.[23] That perversion, however, is now far more visible than their original dignity; and while we collect the fragments, it is impossible not to mourn over the ruins from which we are condemned to pick them. If anyone should doubt of the existence of such a perversion, or be disposed to dispute about the instances we have hastily brought forward, we would just beg leave to refer him to the general plan and character of the poem now before us.

Why should Mr Wordsworth have made his hero a superannuated Pedlar? What but the most wretched affectation, or provoking perversity of taste, could induce anyone to place his chosen advocate of wisdom and virtue in so absurd and fantastic[24] a condition? Did Mr Wordsworth really imagine that his favourite doctrines were likely to gain anything in point of effect or authority by being put into the mouth of a person accustomed to higgle about tape, or brass sleeve-buttons? Or is it not plain that, independent of the ridicule and disgust which such a personification[25] must excite in many of his readers, its adoption exposes his work throughout to the charge of revolting incongruity, and utter disregard of probability or nature? For, after he has thus wilfully debased his moral teacher by a low occupation, is there one word that he puts into his mouth, or one sentiment of which he makes him the organ, that has the

Notes

[19] *stay and support* Cheekily, Jeffrey echoes Wordsworth's 'Resolution and Independence' 146.

[20] *recondite* abstruse, profound.

[21] *parade and prolixity* showiness and wordiness.

[22] *physiognomy* outward form.

[23] *Nobody can . . . perversion* highly disingenuous; Jeffrey's first review of Wordsworth was of *Poems, in Two Volumes* (1807), where he described the contents as 'trash', and said that their author appeared 'like a bad imitator of the worst of his former productions'.

[24] *fantastic* fanciful; perhaps also quaint, eccentric.

[25] *personification* dramatic representation of a character; Jeffrey's language emphasizes Wordsworth's artifice.

most remote reference to that occupation? Is there anything in his learned, abstract, and logical harangues, that savours of the calling that is ascribed to him? Are any of their materials, the diction, the sentiments, in any, the very smallest degree, accommodated to a person in that condition? Or are they not eminently and conspicuously such as could not by possibility belong to it? A man who went about selling flannel and pocket-handkerchiefs in this lofty diction, would soon frighten away all his customers; and would infallibly pass either for a madman, or for some learned and affected gentleman, who, in a frolic,[26] had taken up a character which he was peculiarly ill-qualified for supporting.[27]

The absurdity in this case, we think, is palpable and glaring: but it is exactly of the same nature with that which infects the whole substance of the work – a puerile ambition of singularity[28] engrafted on an unlucky predilection for truisms;[29] and an affected passion for simplicity and humble life, most awkwardly combined with a taste for mystical refinements, and all the gorgeousness of obscure phraseology. His taste for simplicity is evinced by sprinkling up and down his interminable declamations a few descriptions of baby-houses,[30] and of old hats with wet brims;[31] and his amiable partiality for humble life, by assuring us that a wordy rhetorician, who talks about Thebes,[32] and allegorizes all the heathen mythology, was once a pedlar – and making him break in upon his magnificent orations with two or three awkward notices of something that he had seen when selling winter raiment about the country – or of the changes in the state of society, which had almost annihilated his former calling.

Robert Southey (1774–1843)

Southey was born in Bristol, 12 August 1774. He entered Westminster School in April 1788 but was expelled in April 1792 for writing a pamphlet called *The Flagellant*, attacking the use of corporal punishment. By the time he went up to Balliol College, Oxford, in November 1792, he was a fervent supporter of the French Revolution. He read Godwin's *Political Justice* as soon as it was published in February 1793, and exclaimed enthusiastically to his friend, Grosvenor Bedford, 'I am studying such a book!'[1] Soon after, he began writing an epic poem, *Joan of Arc*, which aimed to denounce church and state – the apparatus of the establishment.

On 17 June 1794 he met Coleridge, whose hero-worship of him seems to have begun immediately. Together they planned a 'pantisocracy', a sort of commune on the banks of the Susquehanna River in America, and recruited fellow-pantisocrats, including George Burnett and

Notes

[26] *frolic* fit of amusement; prank.

[27] Perhaps with these comments in mind, Wordsworth appended a note to the 1827 edition of *The Excursion*, which quoted Robert Heron's *Observations Made in a Journey through the Western Counties of Scotland* (1793) as follows: 'It is not more than twenty or thirty years, since a young man going from any part of Scotland to England, of purpose to carry the pack, was considered as going to lead the life, and acquire the fortune, of a gentleman.'

[28] *singularity* originality.

[29] *truisms* commonplace thoughts; Jeffrey's point is that Wordsworth is no philosopher.

[30] *baby-houses* See *Excursion* ii 425.

[31] *old hats with wet brims* See *Excursion* i 445, or *Ruined Cottage* 50–1 (p. 423).

[32] *Thebes* The Pedlar (or the Wanderer, as he is called in *The Excursion*) mentions 'Egyptian Thebes' at Book VIII, l. 216.

Robert Southey (1774–1843)

[1] Quoted in Nicholas Roe, 'Robert Southey, Pantisocracy, and the Poet's Myth', in *The Politics of Nature: Wordsworth and Some Contemporaries* (2nd edn, Basingstoke, 2002), pp. 43–67, 52.

Robert Lovell (Oxford friends of Southey's; for a fuller account see pp. 413–15 above). In August Coleridge met the Fricker family, who instantly became involved in the project: Lovell had just married the second daughter, Mary; Southey was courting the third, Edith; and, by the middle of the month, Coleridge was engaged to the eldest, Sara. The plan was that Coleridge, Southey and Lovell, with their new wives, would emigrate to America in March 1795.[2] The scheme failed, partly through lack of money, partly because Southey and Coleridge fell out.

Distressed to hear that Southey was contemplating marriage, and irritated at his decision not to enter the church, his uncle, Herbert Hill, invited him to stay with him in Lisbon, Portugal, in the hope of reforming him. Southey agreed to go, but secretly married Edith before departing. As they travelled through Spain and Portugal, Southey remained impervious to his uncle's attempts to persuade him to become a clergyman. For one thing, he was too contemptuous of the Church of England and its political power to want to become part of it; for another, his vocation as a writer was close to being realized.

Written in the space of six weeks, *Joan of Arc* was published in 1796, followed by two volumes of *Poems* (1797, 1799), and *Letters Written during a Short Residence in Spain and Portugal* (1797). On the basis of *Joan of Arc*, Lamb declared, 'I expect Southey one day to rival Milton. I already deem him equal to Cowper, and superior to all living poets besides' (Marrs i 16). Wordsworth disagreed: 'You were right about Southey, he is certainly a coxcomb, and has proved it completely by the preface to his *Joan of Arc*, an *epic* poem which he has just published' (*EY* 169).

Southey's poetry is variable. He had facility, but his verse was produced in copious amounts, often at low intensity. Writing to John Thelwall in December 1796, Coleridge offered a clear-sighted account of Southey's creative strengths and weaknesses:

> In language at once natural, perspicuous, and dignified, in manly pathos, in soothing and sonnet-like description, and above all, in character and dramatic dialogue, Southey is unrivalled; but as certainly he does not possess opulence of imagination, lofty-paced harmony, or that *toil* of thinking, which is necessary in order to plan *a whole*. . . . I think that an admirable poet might be made by amalgamating him and me. I think too much for a poet; he too little for a great poet. But he abjures thinking and lays the whole stress of excellence on feeling. (Griggs i 294)

This sharp assessment was made early on in Southey's career, and was borne out by what followed. Wordsworth's observation that poetry was not just the product of powerful feelings but of someone who had 'thought long and deeply' (see p. 498) was never more pertinent. Southey's poetry has many charms, but was never the fruit of the meditation everywhere to be found in Wordsworth: that is the main reason why it has fallen from favour.

That said, there was a period in 1797–9 when Southey was the closest rival to Wordsworth and Coleridge. In September 1797, Coleridge told Southey that 'Hannah' 'is to me the most affecting of all your little pieces' (Griggs i 345). It was not wholly original, influenced as it was by Cowper's 'Crazy Kate' (p. 18 above), but shows Southey thinking in ways that parallel those in which Wordsworth and Coleridge were heading. Despite the Christian ending (not a feature of Wordsworth's poetry), 'Hannah' is impressive because it is based on Southey's own observation. 'I met the funeral,' Southey wrote, 'and learnt the circumstances in a village in Hampshire' (see pp. 724–5). We cannot know for certain whether it was an influence on 'The Ruined Cottage', but scholars speculate that it might have been.

Notes

[2] This was, at least, the date given in Coleridge's letter to Charles Heath of 29 August 1794 (Griggs i 97).

Unfortunately 'Hannah' is untypical of Southey, and in early April 1797 Coleridge expressed the well-founded fear that he depended 'too much on story and event in his poems, to the neglect of those lofty imaginings that are peculiar to, and definitive of, the poet' (Griggs i 320). The truth of this can be revealed by a comparison of 'The Idiot' with 'The Idiot Boy', or by that of 'The Night' with 'Frost at Midnight'. These are two of many works imitative of Wordsworth and Coleridge that Southey composed in 1798; Christopher J. P. Smith has listed others.[3] Unfortunately, instead of learning from them, Southey's treatment of human relationships remains rooted in the eighteenth-century cult of sensibility – trite, lurid and superficial. His friend, William Taylor of Norwich, said that he had 'an imagination excessively accustomed to summon up trains of melancholy ideas, and marshal up funeral processions; a mind too fond by half, for its own comfort, of sighs and sadness, of pathetic emotions and heart-rending woe'.[4] For that reason, he is at his poorest when at his most ambitious; 'The Battle of Blenheim', perhaps his best and most anthologized work, succeeds because it aims to make a single political point (although the sharp-eyed will note its debt to Wordsworth's 'We are Seven' and 'Anecdote for Fathers').

Despite borrowing from *Lyrical Ballads*, Southey had no qualms about dismissing it in a notice he wrote for the *Critical Review*. 'The Idiot Boy' and 'The Thorn' were, he declared, 'bald in story' (see p. 731). He may genuinely have thought so, but it did not stop him summarizing 'The Idiot Boy' at length before quoting sixteen stanzas. Wordsworth was offended. 'Southey's review I have seen,' he told their mutual friend (and publisher) Joseph Cottle:

> He knew that I published those poems for money and money alone. He knew that money was of importance to me. If he could not conscientiously have spoken differently of the volume, in common delicacy he ought to have declined the task of reviewing it.
>
> The bulk of the poems he has described as destitute of merit. Am I recompensed for this by vague praises of my talents? I care little for the praise of Southey or any other professional critic but as it may help me to pudding.[5]

In September 1803, grieved by the death of his daughter, Southey settled with the Coleridges at Greta Hall, Keswick. He spent the rest of his life there, engaged in unremitting literary activity. One cause for this was Coleridge's departure for London, which meant that Southey had two families to provide for.

His growing conservatism led the establishment to think him a safe bet for the post of Poet Laureate, to which he was appointed in 1813. But at what cost? As Laureate he was aligned with a conservative government that prosecuted a ruinously expensive war for which the poorest people in Britain would continue to pay for many years after its bloody conclusion at Waterloo. The King, who suffered prolonged bouts of madness, was unpopular and out of touch, and his heir, the Prince Regent, the butt of endless ridicule for his extravagant and self-indulgent lifestyle. As it happened, Southey's personal politics were Tory: he was an opponent of revolution, Catholic emancipation, and parliamentary reform – views that colour his work, not least in such pro-government works as *Carmen Triumphale* (1814) and *The Poet's Pilgrimage to Waterloo* (1816).

As a result, virtually every noteworthy writer of the time, with the possible exceptions of Wordsworth and Coleridge (who had also drifted into a conservative middle age), were to regard him as a traitor to the views he had once espoused – and it was as such they lampooned him. Byron spurted venom at him most famously (and amusingly) in the dedication to *Don Juan* (see

Notes

[3] See Smith, *A Quest for Home: Reading Robert Southey* (Liverpool, 1997), p. 271.

[4] Quoted by Smith, *A Quest for Home*, p. 272.

[5] James A. Butler, 'Wordsworth, Cottle, and the *Lyrical Ballads*: Five Letters, 1797–1800', *JEGP* 75 (1976) 139–53, p. 145.

p. 933), while Hazlitt's *Political Essays* (1819) is festooned with attacks on him, though nothing in that volume compares with the acid observation in *The Spirit of the Age* (1825) that:

> It is indeed to be deplored, it is a stain on genius, a blow to humanity, that the author of *Joan of Arc* – that work in which the love of Liberty is exhaled like the breath of spring, mild, balmy, heaven-born, that is full of tears and virgin-sighs, and yearnings of affection after truth and good, gushing warm and crimsoned from the heart – should ever after turn to folly, or become the advocate of a rotten cause. After giving up his heart to that subject, he ought not (whatever others might do) ever to have set his foot within the threshold of a court. (Wu vii 217)

It is worth adding that both Hazlitt and Byron had personal grudges against Southey. Hazlitt somehow got wind of the fact that he had written to the Prime Minister, Lord Liverpool, demanding that radical journalists be punished with transportation to Australia (a punishment that often ended in death); while Byron resented the fact that Southey had spread rumours in London that he and Shelley had been involved in a 'league of incest' with Mary Shelley and Claire Clairmont.[6] For this he described Southey, in his letters, as 'a dirty, lying rascal',[7] among other things. When Southey published *A Vision of Judgment*, a tribute to the late King George III, in 1821, he made the mistake of referring to Byron, without naming him, as the leader of the Satanic school of writers whose works 'breathe the spirit of Belial in their lascivious parts'. This was the cue for a brilliant *tour de force* by Byron in his own *The Vision of Judgment* (1822), which satirized Southey's verses, depicting the Laureate reading his work and sending the devils howling back to hell.

He never recovered from the death of his favourite child, Herbert, in 1816, at the age of 9. Nearly two years after his wife's death in November 1837, he married the poetess Caroline Bowles. By this time he was exhausted after a lifetime of unremitting literary toil, and in summer 1839 his mind and memory failed. His remaining years were lamentable; increasingly debilitated, unable to read or write, he died on 21 March 1843 and was buried in Crosthwaite Church in Keswick, where the Brazilian government paid for his monument out of gratitude for his *History of Brazil* (1810).

Largely unread today, Southey's poetry enjoyed considerable popularity in its time: *Thalaba the Destroyer* (1801), *Madoc* (1805), *The Curse of Kehama* (1810) and *Roderick, the Last of the Goths* (1814) were all reprinted. But it is his prose works that do him most credit. His *Life of Nelson* (1813) remained compulsory reading for all schoolchildren until well into the last century.

Further reading

Robert Southey: Poetical Works 1793–1810 ed. Lynda Pratt, Tim Fulford and Daniel Roberts (5 vols, London, 2004).

Geoffrey Carnall, *Robert Southey and His Age: The Development of a Conservative Mind* (Oxford, 1960).

Nicholas Roe, 'Robert Southey, Pantisocracy, and the Poet's Myth', in *The Politics of Nature: Wordsworth and Some Contemporaries* (2nd edn, Basingstoke, 2002), pp. 43–67.

Christopher J. P. Smith, *A Quest for Home: Reading Robert Southey* (Liverpool, 1997).

Mark Storey, *Robert Southey: A Life* (Oxford, 1997).

Notes

6 See Peter Cochran, 'Robert Southey, the "Atheist" Inscription, and the "League of Incest" ', *N&Q* NS 37 (1990) 415–18.

7 Marchand vi 83.

Hannah, A Plaintive Tale (composed by 15 September 1797)[1]

From The Monthly Magazine (October 1797)

The coffin, as I crossed the common lane,
Came sudden on my view; it was not here
A sight of every day, as in the streets
Of the great city – and we paused and asked
Who to the grave was going. It was one,
A village girl; they told us she had borne
An eighteen months' strange illness, pined away
With such slow wasting as had made the hour
Of death most welcome. To the house of mirth
We held our way and, with that idle talk
That passes o'er the mind and is forgot,
We wore away the hour. But it was eve
When homewardly I went, and in the air
Was that cool freshness, that discolouring shade
That makes the eye turn inward. Then I heard,
Over the vale, the heavy toll of death[2]
Sound slow, and questioned of the dead again.
It was a very plain and simple tale.
She bore, unhusbanded, a mother's name,
And he who should have cherished her, far off
Sailed on the seas, self-exiled from his home,
For he was poor. Left thus, a wretched one,
Scorn[3] made a mock of her, and evil tongues
Were busy with her name. She had one ill
Heavier: neglect, forgetfulness from him
Whom she had loved so dearly. Once he wrote,
But only once that drop of comfort came,
To mingle with her cup of wretchedness;
And when his parents had some tidings from him
There was no mention of poor Hannah there;
Or 'twas the cold enquiry, bitterer
Than silence. So she pined and pined away,
And for herself and baby toiled and toiled,
Till she sunk with very weakness;[4] her old mother
Omitted no kind office, and she worked
Most hard, and with hard working barely earned
Enough to make life struggle. Thus she lay
On the sickbed of poverty, so worn

Notes

HANNAH, A PLAINTIVE TALE

[1] When 'Hannah' was published, revised, in Southey's *Poems* (1799), Southey noted: 'It is proper to remark that the story related in this Eclogue is strictly true. I met the funeral, and learnt the circumstances, in a village in Hampshire. The indifference of the child was mentioned to me; indeed, no addition whatever has been made to the story. I should have thought it wrong to have weakened the effect of a faithful narrative by adding anything.'

[2] *the heavy toll of death* i.e. the death-bell.

[3] *Scorn* i.e. scornful people.

[4] *So she pined . . . weakness* cf. Wordsworth's *The Ruined Cottage* 428–31.

That she could make no effort to express
Affection for her infant – and the child
Whose lisping love perhaps had solaced her,
With strangest infantine ingratitude,
Shunned her as one indifferent. She was past
That anguish, for she felt her hour draw on,
And 'twas her only comfort now to think
Upon the grave. 'Poor girl!' her mother said,
'Thou hast suffered much.' 'Aye mother; there is none
Can tell what I have suffered', she replied,
'But I shall soon be where the weary rest.'
And she did rest her soon, for it pleased God
To take her to his mercy.

The Idiot

From The Morning Post (30 June 1798)

The circumstance related in the following ballad happened some years since in Herefordshire.

It had pleased God to form poor Ned
  A thing of idiot mind,
Yet to the poor unreas'ning man
  God had not been unkind.

Old Sarah loved her helpless child
  Whom helplessness made dear,
And life was happiness to him
  Who had no hope nor fear.

She knew his wants, she understood
  Each half-artic'late call,
And he was ev'rything to her
  And she to him was all.

And so for many a year they dwelt
  Nor knew a wish beside,
But age at length on Sarah came,
  And she fell sick and died.

He tried in vain to waken her,
  And called her o'er and o'er;
They told him she was dead – the sound
  To him no import bore.

They closed her eyes and shrouded her,
  And he stood wond'ring by;
And when they bore her to the grave
  He followed silently.

They laid her in the narrow house,[1]
They sung the fun'ral stave,[2]
But when the fun'ral train dispersed
He loitered by the grave.

The rabble boys who used to jeer
Whene'er they saw poor Ned
Now stood and watched him at the grave,
And not a word they said.

They came and went and came again
Till night at last came on,
And still he loitered by the grave
Till all to rest were gone.

And when he found himself alone
He swift removed the clay,
And raised the coffin up in haste
And bore it swift away.

And when he reached his hut he laid
The coffin on the floor,
And with the eagerness of joy
He barred the cottage door.

And out he took his mother's corpse
And placed it in her chair,
And then he heaped the hearth and blew
The kindling fire with care.

He placed his mother in her chair
And in her wonted place,
And blew the kindling fire that shone
Reflected on her face.

And pausing now, her hand would feel,
And now her face behold –
'Why, mother, do you look so pale
And why are you so cold?'

It had pleased God from the poor wretch
His only friend to call,
But God was kind to him and soon
In death restored him all.[3]

Notes

THE IDIOT

[1] *narrow house* grave.

[2] *stave* i.e. hymn.

[3] When 'The Idiot' was published in *Sarah Farley's Bristol Journal* (21 July 1798), two new stanzas were substituted for the last stanza of this text:

But, hapless boy, he now found out
His efforts were in vain,
Sarah would warmth again ne'er feel,
Her eyes ne'er ope again.

Heaven pitying, saw the wretch had lost
The only friend it gave;
Then shortly had his lifeless limbs
Conveyed to Sarah's grave.

The Battle of Blenheim[1]

From The Morning Post (9 August 1798)

I

It was a summer evening,
Old Kaspar's work was done,
And he before his cottage door
Was sitting in the sun,
And by him sported on the green
His little grandchild Wilhelmine.

II

She saw her brother Peterkin
Roll something large and round
That he beside the rivulet
In playing there had found;
He came to ask what he had found
That was so large, and smooth, and round.

III

Old Kaspar took it from the boy
Who stood expectant by,
And then the old man shook his head
And with a natural sigh,
''Tis some poor fellow's skull', said he,
'Who fell in the great victory.

IV

I find them in the garden for
There's many here about,
And often when I go to plough
The ploughshare turns them out –
For many thousand men', said he,
'Were slain in the great victory.'

V

'Now tell us what 'twas all about',
Young Peterkin he cries,
And little Wilhelmine looks up
With wonder-waiting eyes,
'Now tell us all about the war
And what they killed each other for.'

Notes

THE BATTLE OF BLENHEIM

[1] The Battle of Blenheim, 13 August 1704, the most famous victory in the Wars of the Spanish Succession, was credited to John Churchill, 1st Duke of Marlborough, and Prince Eugene of Savoy; the French and Bavarians were defeated.

VI

'It was the English', Kaspar cried,
'That put the French to rout,
But what they killed each other for
I could not well make out.
But everybody said', quoth he,
'That 'twas a famous victory.

VII

My father lived at Blenheim then,
Yon little stream hard by –
They burnt his dwelling to the ground
And he was forced to fly;
So with his wife and child he fled,
Nor had he where to rest his head.

VIII

With fire and sword the country round
Was wasted far and wide,
And many a childing[2] mother then
And new-born infant died.
But things like that, you know, must be
At every famous victory.

IX

They say it was a shocking sight
After the field was won,
For many thousand bodies here
Lay rotting in the sun –
But things like that you know must be
After a famous victory.

X

Great praise the Duke of Marlbro' won,
And our good Prince Eugene.'
'Why 'twas a very wicked thing!'
Said little Wilhelmine.
'Nay, nay, my little girl', quoth he,
'It was a famous victory,

Notes

[2] *childing* pregnant.

XI

And everybody praised the Duke
  Who such a fight did win.'
'But what good came of it at last?'
  Quoth little Peterkin.
'Why that I cannot tell', said he,
'But 'twas a famous victory.'

Night[1]

From The Morning Post (26 September 1798)

How calm, how quiet all![2] still, or at times
Just interrupted by such stirring sounds
As harmonise with stillness; even the bark
Of yonder watch-dog, heard at intervals,[3]
Comes from the distance pleasantly. Where now
The lovely landscape! hill and vale and wood,[4]
Broad oak, high-tufted elm or lighter ash,
Green field and stubble meadows sapless grey,
Or brown variety of new-ploughed land?
A dim obscurity o'ermantles all,
An undistinguished greyness, save that near
The church tower seems in heavier gloom to rest
More massy, and those light-leaved poplars rise
Dark as a cypress grove. How fair at morn
It opened on the eye as the grey mists
Rolled off, how bright at noon, how beautiful
Its evening glories, when more radiant,
Of majesty more visible, the sun
Beyond the brow of yonder western hill
Blazed o'er the clustered clouds! nor charmless now
The scene so dim, nor idly wanders there
The unprofitable eye; earth, air and heaven,
Earth so o'ershadowed, air thus void of sounds,
And yonder moonless vastity[5] of heaven,
With all its countless worlds, all minister[6]
To fill with soothing thoughts the ready mind.
No dissipating objects now distract
Her calm employ; the stir of this low earth
Is silenced, and the bodily powers subdued

Notes

NIGHT

[1] This poem is strongly influenced by Coleridge's *Frost at Midnight*, which had been published shortly before 'Night' was written; Southey did not reprint the poem.

[2] *How calm, how quiet all!* cf. Coleridge, *Frost at Midnight* 8: ''Tis calm indeed!'

[3] *yonder watch-dog, heard at intervals* cf. Wordsworth, *An Evening Walk* (1793) 444: 'And at long intervals the mill-dog's howl'.

[4] *hill and vale and wood* Cf. Coleridge, *Frost at Midnight* 10: 'Sea and hill and wood'.

[5] *vastity* vastness – a 17th-century word.

[6] *minister* an obvious reference to Coleridge, *Frost at Midnight* 72: 'the secret ministry of frost'.

By the day's business, leave her tranquillized,
And aptest for such feelings as this hour
Inspires – nor light nor fruitless; for as now
The lively hues of nature all are fled,
Gone with the light that gave them; so the toys
The puppetry of life[7] have lost their glare,
Their worthless splendour. Wise is he[8] who lets
The influence of this spirit-soothing hour
Fill all his thoughts, who passively receives[9]
The calmness that descends upon his soul,
That like the sober[10] wisdom of old age,
Softens and purifies the hallowed heart.

Review of William Wordsworth and S. T. Coleridge, 'Lyrical Ballads' (1798)[1]

From Critical Review (October 1798)

The majority of these poems, we are informed in the Advertisement, are to be considered as 'experiments': 'They were written chiefly with a view to ascertain how far the language of conversation in the middle and lower classes of society is adapted to the purposes of poetic pleasure'.[2]

Of these 'experimental' poems, the most important is 'The Idiot Boy', the story of which is simply this: Betty Foy's neighbour Susan Gale is indisposed, and no one can be conveniently sent for the doctor but Betty's idiot boy. She therefore puts him upon her pony at eight o'clock in the evening, gives him proper directions, and returns to take care of her sick neighbour. Johnny is expected with the doctor by eleven, but the clock strikes eleven, and twelve, and one, without the appearance either of Johnny or the doctor. Betty's restless fears become insupportable and she now leaves her friend to look for her idiot son. She goes to the doctor's house but hears nothing of Johnny. About five o'clock, however, she finds him sitting quietly upon his feeding pony. As they go home they meet old Susan, whose apprehensions have cured her, and brought her out to seek them. And they all return merrily together. Upon this subject the author has written nearly five hundred lines. With what spirit the story is told, our extract will evince. [Southey quotes *Idiot Boy* 322–401.]

Notes

[7] *The puppetry of life* While staying with Southey in August 1797, Charles Lloyd composed 'Written at Burton', published 1798, which contains the lines:

The noble soul
Swells as the tempest thickens, and most feels
Its own sufficiencies of happiness,
Its plenitude of solitary strength,
When all the *puppetry of life's* brief day
Has done its business; when the dark night comes,
And all is vacancy, or unshaped gloom,
Big with invisible perils. (ll. 40–7)

[8] *Wise is he* The tone is highly reminiscent of the concluding passage of Wordsworth's 'Lines Left upon a Seat in a Yew-Tree' 55: 'Oh be wiser thou!'

[9] *passively receives* This proves that Southey was aware of Coleridge and Wordsworth's poetry of the preceding years, even if he did not understand it. As early as 1795 Coleridge had written, in 'The Eolian Harp', of 'my indolent and passive brain' – but from the outset, the idea was that the mind was not purely receptive; the imagination shaped the data which it received. Hence Wordsworth's concept of 'wise passiveness' ('Expostulation and Reply' 24), by which wisdom consists of imaginative engagement with the natural world.

[10] *sober* a Wordsworthian word if ever there was one. Cf. the 'sober pleasure' at 'Tintern Abbey' 140. The tone, if not the language of these lines, is highly reminiscent of 'Animal Tranquillity and Decay'.

REVIEW OF WILLIAM WORDSWORTH AND S. T. COLERIDGE

[1] Southey's review upset Coleridge and Wordsworth, whom he knew to be the authors of *Lyrical Ballads*, even though he pretends not to. For Wordsworth's response see p. 722 above.

[2] Southey quotes accurately from the Advertisement to *Lyrical Ballads*, p. 331.

No tale less deserved the labour that appears to have been bestowed upon this. It resembles a Flemish picture in the worthlessness of its design and the excellence of its execution. From Flemish artists we are satisfied with such pieces; who would not have lamented if Corregio or Raphael[3] had wasted their talents in painting Dutch boors or the humours of a Flemish wake?[4]

The other ballads of this kind are as bald in story, and are not so highly embellished in narration. With that which is entitled 'The Thorn' we were altogether displeased. The Advertisement says it is not told in the person of the author, but in that of some 'loquacious narrator'. The author should have recollected that he who personates tiresome loquacity becomes tiresome himself.[5] The story of a man who suffers the perpetual pain of cold because an old woman prayed that he never might be warm is perhaps a good story for a ballad because it is a well-known tale – but is the author certain that it is 'well-authenticated'?[6] And does not such an assertion promote the popular superstition of witchcraft?

In a very different style of poetry is 'The Rime of the Ancyent Marinere' – a ballad (says the Advertisement) 'professedly written in imitation of the *style*, as well as of the spirit, of the elder poets.' We are tolerably conversant with the early English poets and can discover no resemblance whatever, except in antiquated spelling and a few obsolete words. This piece appears to us perfectly original in style as well as in story. Many of the stanzas are laboriously beautiful, but in connection they are absurd or unintelligible. Our readers may exercise their ingenuity in attempting to unriddle what follows. [Southey quotes 'Ancient Mariner' 301–22.] We do not sufficiently understand the story to analyze it. It is a Dutch attempt at German sublimity.[7] Genius has here been employed in producing a poem of little merit.[8]

With pleasure we turn to the serious pieces, the better part of the volume. 'The Foster-Mother's Tale' is in the best style of dramatic narrative; 'The Dungeon' and the 'Lines upon the Yew-Tree Seat' are beautiful. The tale of 'The Female Vagrant' is written in the stanza, not the style, of Spenser. We extract a part of this poem. [Southey quotes 'Female Vagrant' 91–180.] Admirable as this poem is, the author seems to discover still superior powers in the 'Lines written near Tintern Abbey'. On reading this production it is impossible not to lament that he should ever have condescended to write such pieces as 'The Last of the Flock', 'The Convict', and most of the ballads. In the whole range of English poetry, we scarcely recollect anything superior to a part of the following passage. [Southey quotes 'Tintern Abbey' 65–111.]

The 'experiment', we think, has failed, not because the language of conversation is little adapted to 'the purposes of poetic pleasure', but because it has been tried upon uninteresting subjects. Yet every piece discovers genius, and, ill as the author[9] has frequently employed his talents, they certainly rank him with the best of living poets.

Notes

[3] *Corregio or Raphael* Italian Renaissance artists who specialized in Biblical subjects.

[4] This was not Southey's true opinion. In a letter to his friend Charles Wynn of December 1798, Southey remarked: 'though "The Idiot Boy" is sadly dilated, it is very well done' (Curry i 177).

[5] This remark may have prompted Wordsworth to add his Note to 'The Thorn' to the second edition of *Lyrical Ballads*; see p. 507.

[6] *well-authenticated* Southey was apparently unaware of the poem's source in Erasmus Darwin's *Zoönomia* (see p. 363n1).

[7] *a Dutch attempt at German sublimity* After reading Southey's review, Charles Lamb wrote to him to protest: 'so far from calling it, as you do, with some wit, but more severity, "A Dutch attempt", etc., I call it a right English attempt, and a successful one, to dethrone German sublimity' (Marrs i 142).

[8] These remarks may have helped instigate Wordsworth's 'apology' for Coleridge's poem in the second edition of *Lyrical Ballads*; see p. 509. In a letter to his friend Wynn in December 1798 Southey described 'The Ancient Mariner' as 'nonsense'.

[9] *the author* Southey was aware of the joint authorship of Wordsworth and Coleridge despite the fact that *Lyrical Ballads* was published anonymously.

The Sailor who had Served in the Slave-Trade[1]

From Poems (1799)

He stopped: it surely was a groan
 That from the hovel came!
He stopped and listened anxiously –
 Again it sounds the same.

It surely from the hovel comes!
 And now he hastens there,
And thence he hears the name of Christ
 Amidst a broken prayer.

He entered in the hovel now,
 A sailor there he sees,
His hands were lifted up to heaven
 And he was on his knees.

Nor did the sailor so intent
 His entering footsteps heed,
But now the Lord's prayer said, and now
 His half-forgotten creed.[2]

And often on his Saviour called
 With many a bitter groan,
In such heart-anguish as could spring
 From deepest guilt alone.

He asked the miserable man
 Why he was kneeling there,
And what the crime had been that caused
 The anguish of his prayer.

'Oh I have done a wicked thing![3]
 It haunts me night and day,
And I have sought this lonely place,
 Here undisturbed to pray.

Notes

The Sailor

[1] Southey printed this poem under the following note: 'In September 1798, a Dissenting Minister of Bristol discovered a sailor in the neighbourhood of that city, groaning and praying in a hovel. The circumstance that occasioned his agony of mind is detailed in the annexed ballad, without the slightest addition or alteration. By presenting it as a poem the story is made more public, and such stories ought to be made as public as possible.' Southey was strongly opposed to the slave trade and, like many of his contemporaries, advised friends not to put sugar in their tea, as it was the product of slave labour. His early poems include many anti-slavery poems, including a series of sonnets and a poem entitled *To the Genius of Africa*. Many efforts were made to abolish the trade during the 1790s, but complete abolition did not come until 1807. This poem is influenced by 'The Ancient Mariner', which Southey had condemned in his review of *Lyrical Ballads*; see p. 731.

[2] *creed* beliefs of the Christian church, repeated as a form of devotion.

[3] *Oh I have done a wicked thing!* strongly reminiscent of Coleridge, 'The Ancient Mariner' 89: 'And I had done a hellish thing.' See also line 54 of Southey's poem.

I have no place to pray on board
  So I came here alone,
That I might freely kneel and pray
  And call on Christ and groan.

If to the mainmast-head[4] I go,
  The wicked one[5] is there –
From place to place, from rope to rope,
  He follows everywhere.

I shut my eyes, it matters not,
  Still still the same I see;
And when I lie me down at night
  'Tis always day with me.

He follows, follows everywhere[6]
  And every place is hell!
Oh God! – and I must go with him
  In endless fire to dwell.

He follows, follows everywhere,
  He's still above, below –
Oh tell me where to fly from him!
  Oh tell me where to go!'

'But tell me', quoth the stranger then,
  'What this thy crime hath been?
So haply I may comfort give
  To one that grieves for sin.'

'Oh I have done a cursed deed'[7]
  The wretched man replies,
'And night and day and everywhere
  'Tis still before my eyes.

I sailed on board a Guinea-man[8]
  And to the slave-coast went –
Would that the sea had swallowed me
  When I was innocent!

And we took in our cargo there,
  Three hundred Negro slaves,
And we sailed homeward merrily
  Over the ocean waves.

Notes

[4] *mainmast-head* the top of the principal mast in the ship.

[5] *The wicked one* the Devil.

[6] *He follows, follows everywhere* cf. Coleridge, 'The Ancient Mariner' 115: 'Water, water everywhere'.

[7] *a cursed deed* Southey borrows the idea of a curse from 'The Ancient Mariner'. He also knew of its use in Wordsworth's 'Goody Blake and Harry Gill'.

[8] *Guinea-man* ship trading slaves from Guinea.

But some were sulky of the slaves
　And would not touch their meat,
So therefore we were forced by threats
　And blows to make them eat.

One woman sulkier than the rest
　Would still refuse her food –
Oh Jesus God! I hear her cries,
　I see her in her blood!

The Captain made me tie her up
　And flog while he stood by,
And then he cursed me if I stayed
　My hand to hear her cry.

She groaned, she shrieked – I could not spare,
　For the Captain he stood by –
Dear God! that I might rest one night
　From that poor woman's cry!

She twisted from the blows – her blood,
　Her mangled flesh I see;
And still the Captain would not spare –
　Oh, he was worse than me!

She could not be more glad than I
　When she was taken down,
A blessed minute – 'twas the last
　That I have ever known!

I did not close my eyes all night,
　Thinking what I had done;
I heard her groans and they grew faint
　About the rising sun.

She groaned and groaned, but her groans grew
　Fainter at morning tide,
Fainter and fainter still they came
　Till at the noon she died.

They flung her overboard – poor wretch,
　She rested from her pain;
But when, oh Christ! oh blessed God!
　Shall I have rest again?

I saw the sea close over her,
　Yet she was still in sight;
I see her twisting everywhere,
　I see her day and night.

Go where I will, do what I can,
The wicked one I see –
Dear Christ, have mercy on my soul,
Oh God deliver me!

Tomorrow I set sail again
Not to the Negro shore;
Wretch that I am, I will at least
Commit that sin no more.

Oh give me comfort if you can,
Oh tell me where to fly –
And bid me hope, if there be hope
For one so lost as I.'

'Poor wretch,' the stranger he replied,
'Put thou thy trust in Heaven,
And call on Him for whose dear sake
!All sins shall be forgiven.[9]

This night at least is thine – go thou
And seek the house of prayer,
There shalt thou hear the word of God
And he will help thee there!'[10]

Charles Lamb (1775–1834)

'I want individuals. I am made up of queer points and I want so many answering needles,' Lamb once said of himself – as concise and perceptive a summary of his essential nature as anyone would ever produce. He was an eccentric, a misfit, and one of the finest essayists of the age.

Charles Lamb was the youngest son of John Lamb and Elizabeth Field, born in 1775 at Crown Office Row, London, where his father was clerk to Samuel Salt, a Bencher (senior member of the Inns of Court) of the Inner Temple. He had an older brother, John (1763–1821), and a sister, Mary (1764–1847). He was educated at Christ's Hospital in Newgate Street, where he was a contemporary of Coleridge, as recalled in his essay, 'Christ's Hospital Five and Thirty Years Ago'.

Lamb spent vacations at Blakesware, a country house in Hertfordshire, where his grandmother was housekeeper. It was here that he met his first love, Ann Simmons, but her rejection of him in 1795 was such a shock that it precipitated a fit of insanity. By now he had begun a long career with the East India Company (1792–1825), which kept him in his office for nine hours a day, six days a week. He was always to

Notes

[9] This advice is similar to that given at 'The Ancient Mariner' 645–6.

[10] Charles Lamb criticized this conclusion in a letter of March 1799, shortly after the poem had been reprinted in Southey's *Poems* (1799): 'This is to convert religion into mediocre feelings, which should burn and glow and tremble. A moral should be wrought into the body and soul, the matter and tendency, of a poem, not tagged to the end, like a "God send the good ship into harbour", at the end of our bills of lading . . . The finishing of the "Sailor" is also imperfect. Any dissenting minister may say and do as much' (Marrs i 163).

Figure 12 Charles Lamb (1775–1834) reading three books at once by candlelight, as portrayed by Daniel Maclise.

regret not having gone to university, but he suffered from a stutter that made it impossible for him to pursue a career in the church (the usual destiny for men of his class and background). Instead, his 'university' would be his beloved London, where he was surrounded by his favourite things: old books, theatre, drink and good conversation.

On Thursday 22 September 1796 he came home from work to find that his sister Mary had stabbed their mother to death and wounded their father by embedding a fork in his head. He took her straight to the Islington Asylum, Fisher House, and saved her from permanent incarceration by agreeing in future to look after her at home, which he did for the rest of his life. This was the 'strange calamity' which cast its shadow over him when he was given an offstage role in Coleridge's *This Lime-Tree Bower my Prison.* He was only 21 years old, and these events determined the course of his future life. Subject to occasional relapses, his sister needed constant care, and he vowed to provide it. 'We are in a manner marked,' he would tell Coleridge.

Lamb's early literary career was promising. He became known for his poetry, much of it inspired by the Unitarian theology that underpins Coleridge's *Religious Musings.* In 1798 he published *Blank Verse* with Coleridge's pupil and acolyte Charles Lloyd, which contained his best-known poem, 'The Old Familiar Faces' (pp. 739–40). It is an inspired example of confessional verse in unrhymed stanzas derived from the Elizabethan dramatist Philip Massinger. Using this unexpected vehicle, Lamb manages to universalize his experience of the 'day of horrors' when he arrived home to find his mother dead and his sister with a carving-knife in her hand. Beginning with that, he reviews other losses he has sustained through his life, before concluding with the elegant refrain, 'All, all are gone, the old familiar faces.' Not only does it transcend the particular context out of which it comes, but it sets the tone for much of Lamb's later prose writing, which also concerns the riches taken from us by time and circumstance.

It is worth emphasizing for a moment the fact that Lamb visited Coleridge at Nether Stowey in July 1797, at the beginning of the *annus mirabilis.* He there met Wordsworth and Dorothy for the first time, with whom he would enjoy a close friendship that lasted for the rest of his life. More important, Lamb understood the way in which Wordsworth and Coleridge were thinking from the outset, providing him with the most valuable education he could have received for his burgeoning career as a writer. Their beliefs and aspirations permeate his writings.

This can be observed in 'Living without God in the World', written at the height of the fashion for atheism, popular among those who espoused radical political ideologies. Wordsworth himself had been described by Coleridge as 'a semi-atheist', partly because of his former attachment to Godwinian philosophy. Coleridge, like Lamb, was devoutly religious, and both were adherents of Priestleyan Unitarianism. When he visited Coleridge at Nether Stowey in July 1797, Lamb met Wordsworth for the first time and almost certainly heard a reading of his play, *The Borderers* (1797). By then disillusioned with Godwinism, Wordsworth critiques it through his portrait of the amoral Rivers, who champions the law of an 'independent intellect'. That phrase makes its way into Lamb's poem as part of an attack on Godwinism, atheists, 'Deists only in the name', all of whom form a Jacobinical congregation united to 'deny a God'.[1]

In 1798 he published *Rosamund Gray,* a novella whose eponymous heroine was a thinly disguised portrait of Ann Simmons, and, in 1802, a

Notes

CHARLES LAMB

[1] See Nicholas Roe, *The Politics of Nature: William Wordsworth and Some Contemporaries* (2nd edn, Basinbgstoke, 2002), pp. 78–84.

play – *John Woodvil, a Tragedy.* Although *Blank Verse* made him sufficiently well-known to be portrayed in Gillray's famous 1798 caricature of radical intellects, *New Morality,* Lamb's talents did not lie in poetry. In subsequent years he turned to prose, often in collaboration with his sister. Together they produced *Tales from Shakespear* (1807) – so popular it has remained in print ever since; *Mrs Leicester's School* and *Poetry for Children* (both 1809). These ventures helped turn him into one of the finest prose stylists of the day.

In the second decade of the nineteenth century he began to write for journals including Leigh Hunt's *Reflector, Examiner* and *Indicator.* At the same time he cultivated his skills as the author of some of the most entertaining letters of the period, which also contain much critical disquisition. Then, in 1820, came the turning-point in his career; he was asked to contribute to John Scott's *London Magazine*. Under the pseudonym 'Elia', Lamb began to publish what are now regarded as some of the finest essays in the history of English letters. In due course these were collected as *Elia* (1823) and *Last Essays of Elia* (1833). It was the glory of those essays to seek to retrieve, in fine romantic fashion, that instinct from which the adult has long been cut adrift – a sense of the numinous and magical. They are a distinctive and inimitable combination of romantic yearning for the intensity of childhood vision, combined with an underlying fear that the world may turn out to be no more than the materialist nightmare – matter in motion.

Elia's art lay to some extent in his manner; as Lamb told his publisher, John Taylor, 'The Essays want no Preface: they are *all Preface*. A Preface is nothing but a talk with the reader; and they do nothing else.'[2] Doubtless it was the persona of Elia that enabled Lamb to indulge his prejudices and whims with a freedom he would not have enjoyed otherwise. Such was his success that he was soon the highest-paid contributor to the *London Magazine*; indeed, still turning up at his office at East India House, he became a literary celebrity, being invited to dine with the Lord Mayor at the Guildhall.

For this volume two essays are presented in full: the first, 'Imperfect Sympathies', may be read as the manifesto for a philosophy applied in the second, 'Witches, and Other Night-Fears'.

In 1819 he fell in love again, with an actress, Fanny Kelly; she refused his proposal of marriage, but remained a friend. Perhaps she simply could not contemplate a life spent living with both Lamb and his sister, whose bouts of insanity continued, or perhaps she did not believe that they were suited to one another. He found consolation by entertaining groups of friends at home on Thursday evenings, riotous occasions that were mythologized by Hazlitt (see Plate 10) in one of his finest essays, 'On the Conversation of Authors':

> There was Lamb himself, the most delightful, the most provoking, the most witty and sensible of men. He always made the best pun, and the bestremark in the course of the evening. His serious conversation, like his serious writing, is his best. No one ever stammered out such fine, piquant, deep, eloquent things in half a dozen half-sentences as he does. His jests scald like tears: and he probes a question with a play upon words. What a keen, laughing, hare-brained vein of home-felt truth! What choice venom! How often did we cut into the haunch of letters, while we discussed the haunch of mutton on the table! How we skimmed the cream of criticism! How we got into the heart of controversy! How we picked out the marrow of authors! (Wu viii 32)

Lamb's eventual retirement from the East India Company was something of a disappointment, as

Notes

[2] *The Letters of Charles and Mary Lamb* ed. E. V. Lucas (3 vols, London, 1935), ii 350.

he moved to the London suburbs of Enfield and Edmonton. There he felt increasingly exiled from the excitements of the town, and Mary's occasional return visits to the asylum left him isolated and lonely. He died of erysipelas after a bad fall on 27 December 1834 and was buried in Edmonton; Mary died in 1847 and was interred alongside him.

Further reading

Charles Lamb and Elia ed. J. E. Morpurgo (Manchester, 1993).

Lamb as Critic ed. Roy Park (London, 1980).

Sarah Burton, *A Double Life: A Biography of Charles and Mary Lamb* (London, 2003).

Winifred F. Courtney, *Young Charles Lamb 1775–1802* (London, 1982).

Claude A. Prance, *Companion to Charles Lamb: A Guide to People and Places 1760–1847* (London, 1983).

Duncan Wu, 'John Scott's Death and Lamb's "Imperfect Sympathies" ', *Charles Lamb Bulletin* NS 114 (April 2001) 38–50.

A journal dedicated to Lamb and his circle, the *Charles Lamb Bulletin*, is published quarterly by the Charles Lamb Society.

The Old Familiar Faces (composed January 1798)

From Blank Verse by Charles Lloyd and Charles Lamb (1798)

Where are they gone, the old familiar faces?
I had a mother, but she died and left me,
Died prematurely in a day of horrors –
All, all are gone, the old familiar faces.

I have had playmates, I have had companions
In my days of childhood, in my joyful schooldays –
All, all are gone, the old familiar faces.

I have been laughing, I have been carousing,
Drinking late, sitting late, with my bosom cronies –
All, all are gone, the old familiar faces.

I loved a love once, fairest among women;[1]
Closed are her doors on me, I must not see her –
All, all are gone, the old familiar faces.

I have a friend,[2] a kinder friend has no man;
Like an ingrate, I left my friend abruptly,
Left him, to muse on the old familiar faces.

Ghostlike, I paced round the haunts of my childhood;
Earth seemed a desert I was bound to traverse,
Seeking to find the old familiar faces.

Friend of my bosom, thou more than a brother![3]
Why wert not thou born in my father's dwelling,
So might we talk of the old familiar faces?

Notes

THE OLD FAMILIAR FACES

[1] *a love . . . women* Ann Simmons, Lamb's sweetheart of 1792 (see headnote).

[2] *a friend* Charles Lloyd.

[3] *Friend . . . brother* Coleridge.

For some they have died, and some they have left me,
And some are taken from me[4] – all are departed,
All, all are gone, the old familiar faces.

Living without God in the World (probably composed between 1796 and 1798)[1]

From The Annual Anthology (1799)

Mystery of God! thou brave and beauteous world,
Made fair with light and shade and stars and flowers,
Made fearful and august with woods and rocks,
Jagg'd precipice, black mountain, sea in storms,
Sun over all that no co-rival owns,
But through Heaven's pavement rides as in despite
Or mockery of the littleness of man!
I see a mighty arm, by man unseen,
Resistless, not to be controlled, that guides,
In solitude of unshared energies,
All these thy ceaseless miracles, oh world!
Arm of the world, I view thee, and I muse
On Man, who trusting in his mortal strength,
Leans on a shadowy staff, a staff of dreams.
  We consecrate our total hopes and fears
To idols, flesh and blood, our love (heaven's due),
Our praise and admiration; praise bestowed
By man on man, and acts of worship done
To a kindred nature, certes[2] do reflect
Some portion of the glory and rays oblique
Upon the politic worshipper – so man
Extracts a pride from his humility.
Some braver spirits of the modern stamp
Affect a Godhead nearer: these talk loud
Of mind and independent intellect,[3]
Of energies omnipotent in man,
And man of his own fate artificer –
Yea, of his own life Lord, and of the days
Of his abode on earth, when time shall be
That life immortal shall become an art;

Notes

[4] *And some are taken from me* Shortly before this poem was written, Mary Lamb suffered a relapse and was returned to hospital.

Living without God in the World

[1] This intriguing poem is one of Lamb's most important from the 1790s. It is usefully discussed by Nicholas Roe, *The Politics of Nature* (2nd edn, Basingstoke, 2002), pp. 78–83, and David Chandler, 'A Study of Lamb's "Living Without God in the World" ', *Charles Lamb Bulletin* NS 99 (July 1997) 86–101. As Chandler points out, the title alludes to Joseph Priestley's criticism of the 'merely nominal believer' in God who 'may be a practical atheist, and worse than a mere speculative one, living as without God in the world, entirely thoughtless of his being, perfections, and providence' (*Letters to a Philosophical Unbeliever* (1780), p. x).

[2] *certes* certainly.

[3] *independent intellect* probably a borrowing from Wordsworth's play *The Borderers*, which refers to the Godwinian virtues of an 'independent intellect' (III v 33).

Or Death, by chemic practices deceived,
Forego the scent which for six thousand years,
Like a good hound he has followed, or at length,
More manners learning, and a decent sense
And reverence of a philosophic world,
Relent, and leave to prey on carcasses.
But these are fancies of a few: the rest,
Atheists, or Deists only in the name,
By word or deed deny a God. They eat
Their daily bread, and draw the breath of heaven,
Without or thought or thanks; heaven's roof to them
Is but a painted ceiling hung with lamps,
No more, that light them to their purposes.
They wander 'loose about',[4] they nothing see,
Themselves except, and creatures like themselves,
Short-lived, short-sighted, impotent to save.
So on their dissolute spirits, soon or late,
Destruction cometh 'like an armed man',[5]
Or like a dream of murder in the night,
Withering their mortal faculties, and breaking
The bones of all their pride.

Letter from Charles Lamb to William Wordsworth, 30 January 1801 (extract)

Separate from the pleasure of your company, I don't much care if I never see a mountain in my life.[1] I have passed all my days in London until I have formed as many and intense local attachments as any of you mountaineers can have done with dead nature.

The lighted shops of the Strand and Fleet Street, the innumerable trades, tradesmen and customers, coaches, wagons, playhouses, all the bustle and wickedness round about Covent Garden,[2] the very women of the town, the watchmen, drunken scenes, rattles; life awake, if you awake, at all hours of the night, the impossibility of being dull in Fleet Street, the crowds, the very dirt and mud, the sun shining upon houses and pavements, the print shops, the old book stalls,[3] parsons cheapening[4] books, coffee-houses, steams of soups from kitchens, the pantomimes[5] – London itself a pantomime and a masquerade:[6] all these things work themselves into my mind and feed me without a power of satiating me.

Notes

[4] *loose about* from Milton's damning reference to the 'common rout', *Samson Agonistes* 675.

[5] *like an armed man* Lamb alludes to the attack on the slothful and the ignorant at Proverbs 24:34.

LETTER FROM CHARLES LAMB TO WILLIAM WORDSWORTH

[1] In fact, Lamb was to visit the Lake District in August 1802, when he was to climb Skiddaw and Helvellyn.

[2] *all the bustle . . . Covent Garden* Covent Garden was the heart of a red-light district.

[3] *old book stalls* stalls selling old books.

[4] *cheapening* bargaining for.

[5] *pantomimes* dramatic entertainments in which the performers express themselves by gestures to the accompaniment of music.

[6] *a masquerade* i.e. London is as diverse, varied and fantastic as a masked ball.

The wonder of these sights impels me into night-walks about her crowded streets, and I often shed tears in the motley[7] Strand from fullness of joy at so much life. All these emotions must be strange to you; so are your rural emotions to me. But consider, what must I have been doing all my life not to have lent great portions of my heart with usury[8] to such scenes?

My attachments are all local, purely local. I have no passion (or have had none since I was in love – and then it was the spurious engendering of poetry and books) to groves and valleys. The rooms where I was born,[9] the furniture which has been before my eyes all my life, a bookcase which has followed me about like a faithful dog (only exceeding him in knowledge) wherever I have moved, old chairs, old tables, streets, squares where I have sunned myself, my old school[10] – these are my mistresses. Have I not enough, without your mountains? I do not envy you. I should pity you, did I not know that the mind will make friends of anything. Your sun and moon and skies and hills and lakes affect me no more, or scarcely come to me in more venerable characters, than as a gilded room with tapestry and tapers where I might live with handsome visible objects. I consider the clouds above me but as a roof beautifully painted, but unable to satisfy the mind, and at last, like the pictures of the apartment of a connoisseur, unable to afford him any longer a pleasure.

Letter from Charles Lamb to John Taylor,[1] *30 June 1821* (extract)

Poor Elia the real (for I am but a counterfeit) is dead. The fact is a person of that name, an Italian, was a fellow-clerk of mine at the South Sea House thirty (not forty) years ago,[2] when the characters I described there existed, but had left it like myself many years – and I having a brother[3] now there, and doubting how he might relish certain descriptions in it, I clapped down the name of Elia to it, which passed off pretty well, for Elia himself added the function of an author to that of a scrivener, like myself.

I went the other day (not having seen him for a year) to laugh over with him at my usurpation of his name, and found him, alas, no more than a name, for he died of consumption eleven months ago, and I knew not of it.

So the name has fairly devolved to me, I think, and 'tis all he has left me.

Imperfect Sympathies[1]

From Elia (1823)

I am of a constitution so general, that it consorts and sympathizeth with all things; I have no antipathy, or rather idiosyncrasy, in anything. Those national repugnancies do not touch me, nor do I behold with prejudice the French, Italian, Spaniard, or Dutch.

(Sir Thomas Browne, Religio Medici)[2]

Notes

[7] *motley* varied, diverse, unpredictable.

[8] *usury* interest, advantage.

[9] *The rooms . . . born* No. 2 Crown Office Row, Inner Temple.

[10] *my old school* Christ's Hospital, in the City of London.

Letter from Charles Lamb to John Taylor

[1] Taylor was the proprietor of the *London Magazine*, and, with his business partner, James Hessey (1785–1870), published volumes by Keats, Clare, Hazlitt, De Quincey, Coleridge and Carlyle.

[2] *thirty . . . years ago* Lamb was a clerk in the Pacific trade office of the South Sea House, 1791–2.

[3] John Lamb the younger (1763–1821).

Imperfect Sympathies

[1] First published, *London Magazine* August 1821, as 'Jews, Quakers, Scotchmen, and other Imperfect Sympathies'.

[2] Sir Thomas Browne (1605–82) was a favourite author of Lamb, Coleridge and Wordsworth.

That the author of the *Religio Medici*, mounted upon the airy stilts of abstraction, conversant about notional and conjectural essences, in whose categories of being the possible took the upper hand of the actual, should have overlooked the impertinent individualities[3] of such poor concretions[4] as mankind, is not much to be admired. It is rather to be wondered at, that in the genus of animals he should have condescended to distinguish that species at all.

For myself, earthbound and fettered to the scene of my activities, 'Standing on earth, not rapt above the sky',[5] I confess that I do feel the differences of mankind, national or individual, to an unhealthy excess. I can look with no indifferent eye upon things or persons. Whatever is, is to me a matter of taste or distaste, or, when once it becomes indifferent, it begins to be disrelishing.[6] I am, in plainer words, a bundle of prejudices made up of likings and dislikings, the veriest thrall[7] to sympathies, apathies,[8] antipathies.

In a certain sense, I hope it may be said of me that I am a lover of my species. I can feel for all indifferently,[9] but I cannot feel towards all equally. The more purely English word that expresses sympathy will better explain my meaning. I can be a friend to a worthy man who, upon another account, cannot be my mate or *fellow*. I cannot *like* all people alike.[10]

I have been trying all my life to like Scotchmen and am obliged to desist from the experiment in despair. They cannot like me and, in truth, I never knew one of that nation who attempted to do it. There is something more plain and ingenuous[11] in their mode of proceeding. We know one another at first sight. There is an order of imperfect intellects (under which mine must be content to rank) which in its constitution is essentially anti-Caledonian. The owners of the sort of faculties I allude to have minds rather suggestive[12] than comprehensive.[13] They have no pretences to much clearness or precision in their ideas, or in their manner of expressing them. Their intellectual wardrobe (to confess fairly) has few whole pieces in it. They are content with fragments and scattered pieces of Truth; she presents no full front to them – a feature or side-face at the most. Hints and glimpses, germs and crude essays at a system, is the utmost they pretend to. They beat up a little game peradventure,[14] and leave it to knottier heads, more robust constitutions, to run it down.[15] The light that lights them is not steady and polar,[16] but mutable and shifting – waxing, and again waning. Their conversation is accordingly.[17] They will throw out a random word in or out of season, and be content to let it pass for what it is worth. They cannot speak always as if they were upon their oath, but must be understood, speaking or writing, with some abatement.[18] They seldom wait to mature a proposition, but e'en bring it

Notes

[3] *impertinent individualities* trivial distinctions.

[4] *concretions* masses.

[5] *Paradise Lost* vii 23.

[6] *disrelishing* disgusting.

[7] *thrall* prisoner.

[8] *apathies* feelings of indifference.

[9] *indifferently* disinterestedly.

[10] 'I would be understood as confining myself to the subject of *imperfect sympathies*. To nations or classes of men there can be no direct *antipathy*. There may be individuals born and constellated so opposite to another individual nature, that the same sphere cannot hold them. I have met with my moral antipodes, and can believe the story of two men meeting (who never saw one another before in their lives) and instantly fighting' (Lamb's note).

[11] *ingenuous* frank, candid.

[12] *suggestive* fitted to conceive, or comprehend suggestions, rather than to reach final conclusions.

[13] *comprehensive* interested only in understanding conclusively.

[14] *They beat up . . . peradventure* i.e. they put forward an argument as it chances to occur.

[15] *run it down* i.e. dispute it.

[16] *polar* fixed; 'as fixed as the poles'.

[17] *accordingly* i.e. consistent with these tendencies.

[18] *abatement* i.e. indulgence; it is the expectation of seriousness that must be abated in the listener.

to market in the green ear.[19] They delight to impart their defective discoveries as they arise, without waiting for their full development. They are no systematizers, and would but err more by attempting it. Their minds, as I said before, are suggestive merely.

The brain of a true Caledonian (if I am not mistaken) is constituted upon quite a different plan. His Minerva is born in panoply.[20] You are never admitted to see his ideas in their growth – if indeed they do grow, and are not rather put together upon principles of clockwork. You never catch his mind in an undress. He never hints or suggests anything, but unlades[21] his stock of ideas in perfect order and completeness. He brings his total wealth into company, and gravely unpacks it. His riches are always about him. He never stoops to catch a glittering something in your presence to share it with you, before he quite[22] knows whether it be true touch[23] or not. You cannot cry *halves*[24] to anything that he finds – he does not find, but bring. You never witness his first apprehension of a thing. His understanding is always at its meridian;[25] you never see the first dawn, the early streaks. He has no falterings of self-suspicion. Surmises, guesses, misgivings, half-intuitions, semi-consciousnesses, partial illuminations, dim instincts, embryo conceptions, have no place in his brain or vocabulary. The twilight of dubiety[26] never falls upon him. Is he orthodox? He has no doubts. Is he an infidel? He has none either. Between the affirmative and the negative there is no borderland with him. You cannot hover with him upon the confines of truth, or wander in the maze of a probable argument. He always keeps the path. You cannot make excursions with him, for he sets you right. His taste never fluctuates. His morality never abates.[27] He cannot compromise, or understand middle actions. There can be but a right and a wrong. His conversation is as a book. His affirmations have the sanctity of an oath. You must speak upon the square[28] with him. He stops a metaphor like a suspected person in an enemy's country. 'A healthy[29] book!' said one of his countrymen to me, who had ventured to give that appellation to *John Buncle*,[30] 'Did I catch rightly what you said? I have heard of a man in health, and of a healthy state of body, but I do not see how that epithet can be properly applied to a book.'

Above all, you must beware of indirect expressions before a Caledonian. Clap an extinguisher upon your irony if you are unhappily blessed with a vein of it: remember you are upon your oath. I have a print of a graceful female after Leonardo da Vinci,[31] which I was showing off to Mr ****. After he had examined it minutely, I ventured to ask him how he liked 'my beauty' (a foolish name it goes by among my friends), when he very gravely assured me that he had considerable respect for my character and talents (so he was pleased to say) but had not given himself much thought about the degree of my personal pretensions. The misconception staggered me, but did not seem much to disconcert him.

Persons of this nation[32] are particularly fond of affirming a truth which nobody doubts. They do not so properly affirm, as annunciate[33] it. They do indeed appear to have such a love of truth (as if, like virtue, it were valuable for itself) that all truth

Notes

[19] *in the green ear* prematurely.
[20] *in panoply* in armour. Minerva sprang fully armed from the head of her father, Zeus.
[21] *unlades* unloads.
[22] *quite* completely.
[23] *true touch* indisputably correct.
[24] *cry halves* to claim a half share in anything found or caught by someone else.
[25] *meridian* fullest height.
[26] *dubiety* doubt.
[27] *abates* weakens.
[28] *upon the square* with extreme exactness and precision. Lamb goes on to criticize extreme literal-mindedness.
[29] *healthy* in the sense of wholesome.
[30] Thomas Amory's novel, *The Life and Opinions of John Buncle, Esq.* (1756–66), was one of Lamb's favourite books.
[31] The Virgin of the Rocks.
[32] *this nation* Scotland, though Lamb means all those of Caledonian tendencies, wherever they may come from.
[33] *annunciate* proclaim, declare.

becomes equally valuable whether the proposition that contains it be new or old, disputed, or such as is impossible to become a subject of disputation. I was present not long since at a party of north Britons[34] where a son of Burns was expected, and happened to drop a silly expression (in my south British way), that I wished it were the father instead of the son – when four of them started up at once to inform me, that 'that was impossible, because he was dead.' An impracticable wish, it seems, was more than they could conceive. Swift has hit off this part of their character (namely their love of truth) in his biting way, but with an illiberality[35] that necessarily confines the passage to the margin.[36]

The tediousness of these people is certainly provoking. I wonder if they ever tire one another? In my early life I had a passionate fondness for the poetry of Burns. I have sometimes foolishly hoped to ingratiate myself with his countrymen by expressing it. But I have always found that a true Scot resents your admiration of his compatriot even more than he would your contempt of him. The latter he imputes to your 'imperfect acquaintance with many of the words which he uses', and the same objection makes it a presumption in you to suppose that you can admire him. Thomson[37] they seem to have forgotten. Smollett they have neither forgotten nor forgiven for his delineation of Rory and his companion upon their first introduction to our metropolis.[38] Speak of Smollett as a great genius and they will retort upon you Hume's *History* compared with *his* continuation of it.[39] What if the historian had continued *Humphrey Clinker*?[40]

I have, in the abstract, no disrespect for Jews. They are a piece of stubborn antiquity compared with which Stonehenge is in its nonage.[41] They date beyond the pyramids. But I should not care to be in habits of familiar intercourse with any of that nation. I confess that I have not the nerves to enter their synagogues; old prejudices cling about me – I cannot shake off the story of Hugh of Lincoln.[42] Centuries of injury, contempt, and hate, on the one side, of cloaked revenge, dissimulation, and hate, on the other, between our and their fathers, must and ought to affect the blood of the children. I cannot believe it can run clear and kindly yet, or that a few fine words, such as candour, liberality, the light of a nineteenth century, can close up the breaches of so deadly a disunion.

A Hebrew is nowhere congenial to me. He is least distasteful on 'Change,[43] for the mercantile spirit levels all distinctions, as all are beauties in the dark. I boldly confess that I do not relish the approximation[44] of Jew and Christian which has become so fashionable. The reciprocal endearments have, to me, something hypocritical and unnatural in them. I do not like to see the Church and Synagogue kissing and

Notes

[34] *north Britons* i.e. Scots.

[35] *illiberality* rudeness, ungenerousness.

[36] *the margin* i.e. of the page. Lamb notes a passage from Swift's 'Hints towards an Essay on Conversation':

> There are some people who think they sufficiently acquit themselves, and entertain their company, with relating facts of no consequence, not at all out of the road of such common incidents as happen every day. And this I have observed more frequently among the Scots than any other nation, who are very careful not to omit the minutest circumstances of time or place – which kind of discourse, if it were not a little relieved by the uncouth terms and phrases, as well as accent and gesture peculiar to that country, would be hardly tolerable.

[37] James Thomson (1700–48), author of *The Seasons*.

[38] Rory, the eponymous hero of *Roderick Random* (1748) by Tobias Smollett, arrives in London at chapter 13.

[39] Smollett's *A Complete History of England* (1757–8) was frequently published as a continuation of David Hume's *History of Great Britain* (1754–62).

[40] *The Expedition of Humphry Clinker* (1771), the most accomplished of Smollett's novels. Lamb's point is that it is so thoroughly imaginative (and, in effect, anti-Caledonian), that no historian could have written a sequel.

[41] *nonage* infancy.

[42] *Hugh of Lincoln* a 10-year-old boy supposedly crucified and killed by Jews.

[43] *'Change* place where merchants meet for the transaction of business, an exchange.

[44] *approximation* closeness, proximity.

congeeing[45] in awkward postures of an affected civility. If *they* are converted, why do they not come over to us altogether? Why keep up a form of separation when the life of it is fled? If they can sit with us at table, why do they keck[46] at our cookery? I do not understand these half-convertites: Jews christianizing, Christians judaizing, puzzle me. I like fish or flesh. A moderate Jew is a more confounding piece of anomaly than a wet Quaker.[47] The spirit of the Synagogue is essentially *separative*.

Braham[48] would have been more in keeping if he had abided by the faith of his forefathers;[49] there is a fine scorn in his face, which nature meant to be of[50] – Christians. The Hebrew spirit is strong in him, in spite of his proselytism.[51] He cannot conquer the shibboleth.[52] How it breaks out when he sings, 'The Children of Israel passed through the Red Sea!'[53] The auditors, for the moment, are as Egyptians to him, and he rides over our necks in triumph. There is no mistaking him. Braham has a strong expression of sense[54] in his countenance, and it is confirmed by his singing. The foundation of his vocal excellence is sense. He sings with understanding, as Kemble[55] delivered dialogue. He would sing the Commandments and give an appropriate character to each prohibition.

His nation, in general, have not over-sensible countenances. How should they? But you seldom see a silly expression among them. Gain, and the pursuit of gain, sharpen a man's visage. I never heard of an idiot being born among them. Some admire the Jewish female physiognomy.[56] I admire it, but with trembling. Jael[57] had those full dark inscrutable eyes.

In the Negro countenance you will often meet with strong traits of benignity. I have felt yearnings of tenderness towards some of these faces, or rather masks, that have looked out kindly upon one in casual encounters in the streets and highways. I love what Fuller[58] beautifully calls these 'images of God cut in ebony.' But I should not like to associate with them, to share my meals and my goodnights with them – because they are black.

I love Quaker ways and Quaker worship. I venerate the Quaker principles. It does me good for the rest of the day when I meet any of their people in my path. When I am ruffled or disturbed by any occurrence, the sight, or quiet voice of a Quaker, acts upon me as a ventilator, lightening the air and taking off a load from the bosom. But I cannot like the Quakers (as Desdemona would say) 'to live with them.'[59] I am all over-sophisticated[60] – with humours,[61] fancies,[62] craving hourly sympathy. I must have books, pictures, theatres, chit-chat,[63] scandal, jokes, ambiguities, and a thousand whim-whams which their simpler taste can do without. I should starve at their primitive banquet. My appetites are too high for the salads which (according to

Notes

[45] *congeeing* bowing in courtesy.
[46] *keck* retch.
[47] *a wet Quaker* a Quaker lax in the observances of his or her sect.
[48] John Braham (1774–1856), renowned tenor of Jewish parentage who converted to Christianity.
[49] *the faith of his forefathers* Judaism (see preceding note).
[50] *of* i.e. directed towards.
[51] *proselytism* conversion.
[52] *shibboleth* accent or intonation revealing a person's racial origins.
[53] Presumably a version of Hebrews 11: 29 set to music.
[54] *sense* i.e. understanding of what he sings.
[55] John Philip Kemble (1757–1823), manager of Drury Lane theatre (1788–1802) and Covent Garden theatre (1803–17), the leading Shakespearian actor/director of his time.
[56] *physiognomy* facial cast.
[57] Judges 4: 21: 'Then Jael Heber's wife took a nail of the tent, and took an hammer in her hand, and went softly unto him, and smote the nail into his temples, and fastened it into the ground: for he was fast asleep and weary. So he died.'
[58] Thomas Fuller (1608–61), author of *History of the Worthies of England* (1662), one of Lamb's favourite books.
[59] *Othello* I iii 248.
[60] *over-sophisticated* completely and utterly lacking in the natural and simple tastes demanded of the Quaker.
[61] *humours* inclinations, likings, enthusiasms.
[62] *fancies* whims.
[63] *chit-chat* gossip.

Evelyn[64]) Eve dressed for the angel, my gusto[65] too excited 'To sit a guest with Daniel at his pulse.'[66]

The indirect answers which Quakers are often found to return to a question put to them may be explained, I think, without the vulgar[67] assumption that they are more given to evasion and equivocating than other people. They naturally look to their words more carefully, and are more cautious of committing themselves. They have a peculiar character to keep up on this head. They stand in a manner upon their veracity.[68] A Quaker is by law exempted from taking an oath. The custom of resorting to an oath in extreme cases, sanctified as it is by all religious antiquity, is apt[69] (it must be confessed) to introduce into the laxer sort of minds the notion of two kinds of truth – the one applicable to the solemn affairs of justice, and the other to the common proceedings of daily intercourse. As truth bound upon the conscience by an oath can be but truth, so in the common affirmations of the shop and the marketplace a latitude is expected and conceded upon questions wanting this solemn covenant. Something less than truth satisfies. It is common to hear a person say, 'You do not expect me to speak as if I were upon my oath.' Hence a great deal of incorrectness and inadvertency (short of falsehood) creeps into ordinary conversation, and a kind of secondary or laic-truth[70] is tolerated, where clergy-truth – oath-truth, by the nature of the circumstances – is not required. A Quaker knows none of this distinction. His simple affirmation being received upon the most sacred occasions, without any further test, stamps a value upon the words which he is to use upon the most indifferent topics of life. He looks to them, naturally, with more severity.

You can have of him no more than his word. He knows, if he is caught tripping in a casual expression,[71] he forfeits, for himself at least, his claim to the invidious exemption.[72] He knows that his syllables are weighed – and how far a consciousness of this particular watchfulness, exerted against a person, has a tendency to produce indirect answers and a diverting of the question by honest means, might be illustrated (and the practice justified) by a more sacred example than is proper to be adduced upon this occasion. The admirable presence of mind, which is notorious in Quakers upon all contingencies, might be traced to this imposed self-watchfulness, if it did not seem rather an humble and secular scion of that old stock of religious constancy which never bent or faltered in the Primitive Friends,[73] or gave way to the winds of persecution, to the violence of judge or accuser, under trials and racking examinations. 'You will never be the wiser, if I sit here answering your questions till midnight', said one of those upright Justicers[74] to Penn,[75] who had been putting law-cases with a puzzling subtlety. 'Thereafter as the answers may be', retorted the Quaker.

The astonishing composure of this people is sometimes ludicrously displayed in lighter instances. I was travelling in a stagecoach with three male Quakers, buttoned up in the straitest non-conformity of their sect. We stopped to bait[76] at Andover, where a

Notes

[64] *according to Evelyn* Lamb refers to John Evelyn, *Acetaria: A Discourse of Sallets* (1699), a short account of salad plants and dressings.

[65] *gusto* appetite for good food.

[66] *Paradise Regained* ii 278. Daniel refused to eat the food provided for the children of Jewish nobles, preferring the simple diet of 'pulse' (lentils, beans, etc.); see Daniel 1: 3–21.

[67] *vulgar* usual.

[68] *veracity* honesty.

[69] *is apt* tends.

[70] *laic-truth* the sort of honesty expected of those not under oath.

[71] *tripping in . . . expression* committing an error by using a casual expression.

[72] *exemption* i.e. as a Quaker.

[73] *the Primitive Friends* The Quakers, or Religious Society of Friends, was founded by George Fox in 1648–50, distinguished by its stress on the 'Inner Light' and rejection of sacraments, an ordained ministry and set forms of worship.

[74] *Justicers* judges.

[75] William Penn (1644–1718), an English Quaker.

[76] *bait* stop at an inn to refresh the horses.

meal (partly tea apparatus, partly supper) was set before us. My friends confined themselves to the tea-table. I in my way took supper. When the landlady brought in the bill, the eldest of my companions discovered that she had charged for both meals. This was resisted. Mine hostess was very clamorous and positive. Some mild arguments were used on the part of the Quakers, for which the heated mind of the good lady seemed by no means a fit recipient. The guard[77] came in with his usual peremptory notice. The Quakers pulled out their money and formally tendered it (so much for tea), I, in humble imitation, tendering mine for the supper which I had taken. She would not relax in her demand. So they all three quietly put up[78] their silver, as did myself, and marched out of the room, the eldest and gravest going first, with myself closing up the rear, who thought I could not do better than follow the example of such grave and warrantable personages. We got in. The steps went up. The coach drove off. The murmurs of mine hostess (not very indistinctly or ambiguously pronounced) became after a time inaudible – and now, my conscience (which the whimsical scene had for a while suspended) beginning to give some twitches, I waited in the hope that some justification would be offered by these serious persons for the seeming injustice of their conduct. To my great surprise not a syllable was dropped on the subject. They sat as mute as at a meeting. At length the eldest of them broke silence, by enquiring of his next neighbour, 'Hast thee heard how indigos[79] go at the India House?' And the question operated as a soporific[80] on my moral feeling as far as Exeter.

Witches, and Other Night-Fears[1]

From Elia (1823)

We are too hasty when we set down our ancestors in the gross for fools, for the monstrous inconsistencies (as they seem to us) involved in their creed of witchcraft. In the relations of this visible world we find them to have been as rational, and shrewd to detect an historic anomaly, as ourselves. But when once the invisible world was supposed to be opened, and the lawless agency of bad spirits assumed, what measures of probability, of decency, of fitness, or proportion of that which distinguishes the likely from the palpable absurd, could they have to guide them in the rejection or admission of any particular testimony? That maidens pined away, wasting inwardly as their waxen images consumed before a fire; that corn was lodged[2] and cattle lamed;[3] that whirlwinds uptore in diabolic revelry the oaks of the forest; or that spits and kettles only danced a fearful-innocent vagary about some rustic's kitchen when no wind was stirring – were all equally probable where no law of agency was understood. That the Prince of the powers of darkness, passing by the flower and pomp of the earth, should lay preposterous siege to the weak fantasy of indigent eld,[4] has neither likelihood nor unlikelihood *a priori*[5] to us who have no measure to guess at his policy, or standard to estimate what rate those anile[6] souls may fetch in the devil's market. Nor, when the wicked are expressly symbolized by a goat, was it to be wondered at so much, that *he* should come

Notes

[77] *guard* i.e. of the stagecoach, to warn them of its departure.

[78] *put up* i.e. put their money back in their pockets.

[79] *indigos* plants yielding blue dye, imported from India.

[80] *soporific* anaesthetic.

WITCHES, AND OTHER NIGHT-FEARS

[1] First published in the *London Magazine*, October 1821.

[2] *lodged* prematurely beaten down as if by supernatural means.

[3] *lamed* crippled.

[4] *indigent eld* needy people in olden times.

[5] *a priori* prior to investigation.

[6] *anile* imbecilic.

sometimes in that body and assert his metaphor. That the intercourse was opened at all between both worlds was perhaps the mistake – but that once assumed, I see no reason for disbelieving one attested story of this nature more than another on the score of absurdity. There is no law to judge of the lawless, or canon by which a dream may be criticized.

I have sometimes thought that I could not have existed in the days of received witchcraft, that I could not have slept in a village where one of those reputed hags dwelt. Our ancestors were bolder (or more obtuse). Amidst the universal belief that these wretches were in league with the author of all evil, holding hell tributary[7] to their muttering, no simple Justice of the Peace seems to have scrupled issuing, or silly headborough[8] serving, a warrant upon them – as if they should subpoena Satan! Prospero in his boat, with his books and wand about him, suffers himself to be conveyed away at the mercy of his enemies to an unknown island.[9] He might have raised a storm or two, we think, on the passage.[10] His acquiescence is in exact analogy to the non-resistance of witches to the constituted powers. What stops the fiend in Spenser from tearing Guyon to pieces?[11] Or who had made it a condition of his prey that Guyon must take assay of the glorious bait?[12] We have no guess; we do not know the laws of that country.

From my childhood I was extremely inquisitive about witches and witch-stories. My maid, and more legendary aunt, supplied me with good store. But I shall mention the accident which directed my curiosity originally into this channel. In my father's book-closet, the *History of the Bible* by Stackhouse[13] occupied a distinguished station. The pictures with which it abounds – one of the ark, in particular, and another of Solomon's temple, delineated with all the fidelity of ocular admeasurement,[14] as if the artist had been upon the spot – attracted my childish attention. There was a picture, too, of the witch raising up Samuel, which I wish that I had never seen. (We shall come to that hereafter.)

Stackhouse is in two huge tomes, and there was a pleasure in removing folios[15] of that magnitude, which, with infinite straining, was as much as I could manage, from the situation which they occupied upon an upper shelf. I have not met with the work from that time to this, but I remember it consisted of Old Testament stories, orderly set down, with the 'objection' appended to each story, and the 'solution' of the objection regularly tacked to that. The objection was a summary of whatever difficulties had been opposed to the credibility of the history, by the shrewdness of ancient or modern infidelity,[16] drawn up with an almost complimentary[17] excess of candour; the solution was brief, modest, and satisfactory. The bane and antidote were both before you. To doubts so put (and so quashed), there seemed to be an end for ever. The dragon lay dead, for the foot of the veriest babe to trample on.

But (like as was rather feared than realized from that slain monster in Spenser) from the womb of those crushed errors young dragonets[18] would creep, exceeding the

Notes

7 *tributary* contributory.

8 *silly headborough* rustic constable.

9 *Prospero . . . island* See *Tempest* I ii 159–68.

10 *He might . . . passage The Tempest* begins in the midst of a storm raised by Prospero.

11 *What stops . . . pieces* a reference to *Faerie Queene* II vii st.64, where Guyon is said not to have been 'rent in thousand peeces' by the 'dreadfull feend'. Bob Cummings points out to me that Lamb refers again to this episode in his essay, 'Sanity of True Genius'.

12 *Or who had . . . bait* See *Faerie Queene* II vii st.34, where Guyon is tempted by the 'glorious bayte'. The short answer to Lamb's question is, of course, Mammon.

13 Thomas Stackhouse, *New History of the Holy Bible* (1737).

14 *ocular admeasurement* proportions and size as if seen.

15 *folios* a folio is a book of the largest magnitude, made of sheets of paper folded only once.

16 *infidelity* lack of religious faith.

17 *complimentary* respectful.

18 *dragonets* baby dragons; Lamb has in mind *Faerie Queene* I xii st.10 5–6: 'some hidden nest / Of many dragonets, his fruitfull seed'.

prowess of so tender a St George as myself to vanquish. The habit of expecting objections to every passage set me upon starting more objections, for the glory of finding a solution of my own for them. I became staggered[19] and perplexed, a sceptic in long coats. The pretty Bible stories which I had read, or heard read in church, lost their purity and sincerity of impression, and were turned into so many historic or chronologic theses to be defended against whatever impugners. I was not to disbelieve them, but (the next thing to that) I was to be quite sure that someone or other would or had disbelieved them. Next to making a child an infidel is the letting him know that there are infidels at all. Credulity is the man's weakness, but the child's strength. Oh, how ugly sound scriptural doubts from the mouth of a babe and a suckling!

I should have lost myself in these mazes and have pined away, I think, with such unfit sustenance as these husks afforded, but for a fortunate piece of ill-fortune, which about this time befell me. Turning over the picture of the ark with too much haste, I unhappily made a breach in its ingenious fabric – driving my inconsiderate fingers right through the two larger quadrupeds (the elephant and the camel) that stare, as well they might, out of the two last windows next the steerage in that unique piece of naval architecture. Stackhouse was henceforth locked up, and became an interdicted[20] treasure. With the book, the objections and solutions gradually cleared out of my head, and have seldom returned since in any force to trouble me. But there was one impression which I had imbibed from Stackhouse which no lock or bar could shut out, and which was destined to try my childish nerves rather more seriously – that detestable picture!

I was dreadfully alive to nervous terrors. The night-time solitude and the dark were my hell. The sufferings I endured in this nature would justify the expression. I never laid my head on my pillow, I suppose, from the fourth to the seventh or eighth year of my life (so far as memory serves in things so long ago), without an assurance, which realized its own prophecy, of seeing some frightful spectre. Be old Stackhouse then acquitted in part, if I say that to his picture of the witch raising up Samuel[21] (oh, that old man covered with a mantle![22]) I owe not my midnight terrors, the hell of my infancy, but the shape and manner of their visitation. It was he who dressed up for me a hag that nightly sat upon my pillow – a sure bedfellow when my aunt or my maid was far from me. All day long, while the book was permitted me, I dreamed waking over his delineation,[23] and at night (if I may use so bold an expression) awoke into sleep, and found the vision true. I durst not, even in the daylight, once enter the chamber where I slept, without my face turned to the window, aversely from the bed where my witch-ridden pillow was. Parents do not know what they do when they leave tender babes alone to go to sleep in the dark. The feeling about for a friendly arm, the hoping for a familiar voice when they wake screaming and find none to soothe them – what a terrible shaking it is to their poor nerves! The keeping them up till midnight, through candlelight and the unwholesome hours (as they are called), would, I am satisfied, in a medical point of view, prove the better caution. That detestable picture, as I have said, gave the fashion[24] to my dreams – if dreams they were, for the scene of them was invariably the room in which I lay. Had I never met with the picture, the fears would have come self-pictured in some shape or other – 'Headless bear, black man, or ape'[25] – but, as it was, my imaginations took that form.

Notes

[19] *staggered* doubtful.

[20] *interdicted* forbidden.

[21] *the witch raising up Samuel* The witch of Endor brought Samuel back to life from death; see 1 Samuel 28: 7–14.

[22] *that old man . . . mantle* When the witch brought him back to life, Samuel was covered in a cloak (mantle); 1 Samuel 28: 14.

[23] *delineation* pictorial representation.

[24] *fashion* shape and substance.

[25] From 'The Author's Abstract of Melancholy' prefixed to Robert Burton, *The Anatomy of Melancholy* (1621).

It is not book, or picture, or the stories of foolish servants which create these terrors in children; they can at most but give them a direction. Dear little T.H.[26] who, of all children, has been brought up with the most scrupulous exclusion of every taint of superstition, who was never allowed to hear of goblin or apparition, or scarcely to be told of bad men, or to read or hear of any distressing story, finds all this world of fear, from which he has been so rigidly excluded *ab extra* in his own 'thick-coming fancies'[27] – and from his little midnight pillow, this nurse-child of optimism will start at shapes unborrowed of tradition, in sweats to which the reveries of the cell-damned murderer are tranquillity.

Gorgons and hydras and chimeras,[28] dire stories of Celaeno and the harpies,[29] may reproduce themselves in the brain of superstition – but they were there before. They are transcripts, types; the archetypes are in us, and eternal.[30] How else should the recital of that which we know in a waking sense to be false come to affect us at all? Or 'Names whose sense we see not, / Fray us with things that be not?'[31] Is it that we naturally conceive terror from such objects, considered in their capacity of being able to inflict upon us bodily injury? Oh, least of all! These terrors are of older standing. They date beyond body – or, without the body, they would have been the same. All the cruel, tormenting, defined devils in Dante[32] – tearing, mangling, choking, stifling, scorching demons – are they one half so fearful to the spirit of a man as the simple idea of a spirit unembodied following him?

Like one that on a lonesome road
  Doth walk in fear and dread,
And having once turned round walks on
  And turns no more his head
Because he knows a frightful fiend
  Doth close behind him tread.[33]

That the kind of fear here treated of is purely spiritual, that it is strong in proportion as it is objectless upon earth, that it predominates in the period of sinless infancy – are difficulties, the solution of which might afford some probable insight into our ante-mundane[34] condition, and a peep at least into the shadowland of pre-existence.

My night-fancies have long ceased to be afflictive. I confess an occasional night-mare, but I do not, as in early youth, keep a stud[35] of them. Fiendish faces, with the extinguished taper, will come and look at me – but I know them for mockeries, even while I cannot elude their presence, and I fight and grapple with them. For the credit of my imagination, I am almost ashamed to say how tame and prosaic my dreams are

Notes

[26] Thornton Leigh Hunt (1810–73), eldest son of Leigh Hunt, who was to become editor of the *Daily Telegraph*.

[27] *Macbeth* V iii 38.

[28] *Gorgons . . . chimeras* an echo of *Paradise Lost* ii 628: 'Gorgons and hydras and chimeras dire'.

[29] *Celaeno . . . harpies* Celaeno was the leader of the harpies in Virgil's *Aeneid* Book III.

[30] *They are transcripts . . . eternal* a considerable claim – Lamb is saying that the sense of the great and the sublime is innate; cf. *Thirteen-Book Prelude* vi 571: 'the types and symbols of eternity'. This should be seen in the context of Wordsworth's disquisition on pre-existence in his *Ode* (pp. 538–42).

[31] Spenser, *Epithalamion* 343–4.

[32] Dante was a relatively new discovery for those who did not know the language of the original; the first full English translation, by Lamb's friend, Henry Francis Cary (1772–1844), was published in 1814.

[33] 'The Ancient Mariner' 451–6.

[34] *ante-mundane* i.e. before our life on earth.

[35] *stud* as in a stud-farm; presumably the nightmares were like horses on a stud, in that they multiplied.

grown. They are never romantic, seldom even rural. They are of architecture and of buildings – cities abroad, which I have never seen, and hardly have hope to see. I have traversed, for the seeming length of a natural day, Rome, Amsterdam, Paris, Lisbon – their churches, palaces, squares, market-places, shops, suburbs, ruins, with an inexpressible sense of delight, a map-like distinctness of trace, and a daylight vividness of vision, that was all but being awake.

I have formerly travelled among the Westmorland fells (my highest Alps),[36] but they are objects too mighty for the grasp of my dreaming recognition, and I have again and again awoke with ineffectual struggles of the inner eye, to make out a shape, in any way whatever, of Helvellyn.[37] Methought I was in that country, but the mountains were gone. The poverty of my dreams mortifies me. There is Coleridge, at his will can conjure up icy domes and pleasure-houses for Kubla Khan, and Abyssinian maids, and songs of Abara, and caverns 'Where Alph, the sacred river, runs', to solace his night solitudes, when I cannot muster a fiddle. Barry Cornwall has his tritons and his nereids gambolling before him in nocturnal visions, and proclaiming sons born to Neptune,[38] when my stretch of imaginative activity can hardly, in the night season, raise up the ghost of a fishwife. To set my failures in somewhat a mortifying light, it was after reading the noble 'Dream' of this poet that my fancy ran strong upon these marine spectra[39] – and the poor plastic[40] power (such as it is) within me set to work, to humour my folly in a sort of dream that very night. Methought I was upon the ocean billows at some sea nuptials, riding and mounted high, with the customary train[41] sounding their conchs before me (I myself, you may be sure, the leading god), and jollily we went careering over the main, till, just where Ino Leucothea[42] should have greeted me (I think it was Ino) with a white embrace, the billows, gradually subsiding, fell from a sea-roughness to a sea-calm, and thence to a river-motion, and that river (as happens in the familiarization of dreams) was no other than the gentle Thames – which landed me, in the wafture of a placid wave or two, alone, safe and inglorious, somewhere at the foot of Lambeth Palace.[43]

The degree of the soul's creativeness in sleep might furnish no whimsical criterion of the quantum[44] of poetical faculty resident in the same soul waking. An old gentleman, a friend of mine, and a humorist, used to carry this notion so far that when he saw any stripling of his acquaintance ambitious of becoming a poet, his first question would be, 'Young man, what sort of dreams have you?' I have so much faith in my old friend's theory that when I feel that idle vein returning upon me, I presently subside into my proper element of prose, remembering those eluding nereids, and that inauspicious inland landing.

Notes

[36] *I have . . . Alps* Lamb and his sister visited the Lake District in August 1802. They stayed with Southey at Greta Hall in Keswick, and with Charles Lloyd at Brathay Hall, near Ambleside.

[37] Helvellyn is a large mountain (3116 ft) in the centre of the Lake District.

[38] *Barry Cornwall . . . Neptune* Bryan Waller Procter (1787–1874) wrote under the name of Barry Cornwall. Lamb refers to his poem, 'A Dream', published in *Dramatic Scenes and Other Poems* (1819).

[39] *spectra* ghosts, apparitions.

[40] *plastic* shaping.

[41] *train* wedding procession.

[42] *Ino Leucothea* girl transformed into a sea-goddess in Homer's *Odyssey*.

[43] *Lambeth Palace* official residence in London of the Archbishop of Canterbury, head of the Church of England, on Lambeth Palace Road, on the south bank of the Thames.

[44] *quantum* amount.

William Hazlitt (1778–1830)

Perhaps the most important relationship in his life was that with his father, also William Hazlitt (1737–1820), a Unitarian minister who wanted his youngest son to follow in his footsteps. When preaching at churches in America the Reverend Mr Hazlitt would take his 6-year old son to stand at his side in the pulpit as he delivered his sermon. The family spent the years 1783–7 in America, while his father struggled, and failed, to find a permanent posting first in Philadelphia, then in Boston, and finally in Maine. He was a determined Socinian of the Priestleyan stripe, uncompromising in his rejection of Trinitarianism. These were early days for the Unitarian faith in America, and his ideas were simply too radical for many of the Presbyterian congregations he addressed. In 1787, accepting defeat, he returned to England, settling in the small Shropshire village of Wem, where he continued until retirement.

His son decided against a career in the church during his student days at the Unitarian New College in Hackney, East London, where Joseph Priestley was one of his lecturers. Indeed, it was at that time that he became an atheist. His father was devastated. Correspondence testifies to the strains this generated between them, but Hazlitt remained anxious to please his father through his industry and commitment to intellectual matters.

While at the New College, Hazlitt benefited from an exemplary training in classical literature and philosophy (its educational standards closely rivalled those of either Oxford or Cambridge Universities), and continued his studies under his father's direction at Wem. It was no surprise that such an aggressively intelligent young man should have formulated his own philosophical system, and attempted to articulate it. His philosophy of disinterestedness underpins almost everything he wrote. In essence, it postulates that self-love is cognate with love of others. From this Hazlitt deduced that human beings were as capable of acting altruistically as for selfish reasons. The implications of this are more far-reaching than may at first appear. For one thing, it puts Hazlitt at loggerheads with a long and distinguished tradition of philosophers who believed humanity to be essentially selfish, and therefore given to ill motives. In broad terms, Hazlitt is aligned with radical philosophers of the 1790s who postulated mankind as a virtuous animal given to good deeds. Out of this Hazlitt constructed an aesthetic theory which understood the artist's role as being that of entering completely into other worlds, other minds or personalities. The ability to do so in a completely disinterested manner he called 'gusto' – a quality defined in one of his most important essays (pp. 756–9). It would have a powerful influence on Keats's concept of negative capability (see p. 1336).

One of Hazlitt's most formative experiences was his first encounter with the polymorphously creative fountain that was Samuel Taylor Coleridge in January 1798. Having heard that Coleridge was to take over the Unitarian congregation in Shrewsbury, he went to hear him preach. 'I could not have been more delighted if I had heard the music of the spheres,' he recalled. Years later, he was scathing of his former mentor for what he saw as the betrayal of his early beliefs – and indeed it is true that Coleridge renounced Unitarianism, radical politics, even the optimistic Hartleyan philosophy which he expounded during the 1790s – but 1798 was the perfect moment for Coleridge to initiate him into the literary and intellectual melting-pot out of which would come his own poetry and that of Wordsworth. Indeed, Coleridge invited him to Nether Stowey in the summer, where he heard Wordsworth recite the lyrical ballads prior to their publication. It would be hard to overstate the importance of this experience: it turned him into the principal interpreter of the work and lives of the first-generation

Romantics – but not immediately. Believing he wanted to pursue a career as an artist he visited the Louvre in Paris during the Peace of Amiens in 1802, and the following year went to the Lake District to paint Wordsworth, Coleridge and Southey. On that occasion Coleridge gave a detailed description of him in a letter to his friend Richard Sharp:

> William Hazlitt is a thinking, observant, original man, of great power as a painter of character portraits, and far more in the manner of the old painters than any living artist; but the object must be *before* him: he has no imaginative memory . . . His manners are to 99 in 100 singularly repulsive – brow-hanging, shoe-contemplative, *strange* . . . he is, I verily believe, kindly-natured – is very fond of, attentive to, and patient with, children. But he is jealous, gloomy, and of an irritable pride – and addicted to women as objects of sexual indulgence. With all this, there is much good in him . . . and though from habitual shyness and the outside and bearskin at least of misanthropy, he is strangely confused and dark in his conversation and delivers himself of almost all his conceptions with a forceps, yet he says more than any man I ever knew, yourself only excepted, that is his own in a way of his own – and oftentimes when he has warmed his mind, and the synovial juice has come out and spread over his joints he will gallop for half an hour together with real eloquence. (Griggs ii 990–1)

Hazlitt published his philosophy as *An Essay on the Principles of Human Actions* (1805) with Joseph Johnson, the Unitarian who had published his father's sermons in the 1780s and 1790s. The *Essay* did not sell. He continued to try to make his way as an artist (see Plate 11), but commissions tailed off and by the time he married his first wife, Sarah Stoddart, in 1808 he had begun to realize that his future lay in journalism. He made his name writing parliamentary reports and theatrical criticism for the *Morning Chronicle*. In 1812 he moved his wife and son to London, where he delivered lectures, first on philosophy and then on literature, all of which he published subsequently.

His drama reviews were collected in 1818 as *A View of the English Stage*, which provides us with vivid glimpses of such stars as Edmund Kean as Iago – 'Perhaps the accomplished hypocrite was never so finely, so adroitly portrayed – a gay, light-hearted monster, a careless, cordial, comfortable villain' (Wu iii 20) – and Othello ('He plays it like a gypsy, and not like a Moor', Wu iii 171); or of John Philip Kemble's '*intensity*, in the seizing upon some one feeling or idea, in insisting upon it, in never letting it go, and in working it up, with a certain graceful consistency, and conscious grandeur of conception, to a very high degree of pathos or sublimity' (Wu iii 213).

By the end of the second decade of the new century, Hazlitt was pre-eminent as a writer and lecturer on a range of topics – philosophy, the arts, politics, and literature. He was an all-round journalist. When John Scott was shot in a duel, he stepped in as editor of the *London Magazine* until a permanent replacement could be found. It was not just that he had one of the most delicious prose styles in literature, but that his judgements were sharp, brilliantly expressed and honest. His father had trained him always to speak as he felt, whatever the consequence, and he did so fearlessly throughout his life. It was to cost him dearly. None of his middle-aged contemporaries enjoyed being reminded of their former radicalism, especially when they accepted sinecures from the government and its supporters. Southey, for instance, cannot have been amused to find Hazlitt observing that 'he has no principles; or he does not himself know what they are' (Wu iv 85–6), any more than Coleridge can have rejoiced to read Hazlitt's judgement that 'He belongs to all parties and is of service to none' (Wu iv 110). These entirely accurate assessments were repeated time and again: typically, Hazlitt reviewed Coleridge's *Lay Sermons* not just once, but no less than three times, giving him as many opportunities to accuse his former mentor of apostasy.

For his own part, Hazlitt remained doggedly faithful to his beliefs, hero-worshipping Napoleon until the day he died because he saw him as the human embodiment of the core principles of the French Revolution. Although such a view seems absurd to us, Hazlitt's eye was on the reforms he brought about, and on the effective abolition of the monarchy and aristocracy. Such was Hazlitt's grief at Napoleon's defeat at Waterloo that he was drunk and unwashed for weeks afterwards, in the midst of what we would now recognize as a nervous breakdown. The ensuing years were his most productive; they saw publication of *Characters of Shakespeare's Plays* (1817), *The Round Table* (1817, with Leigh Hunt), *Lectures on the English Poets* (1818), *Lectures on the English Comic Writers* (1819), *Political Essays* (1819), *Lectures on the Dramatic Literature of the Age of Elizabeth* (1821), *Table-Talk* (1821–2), *Spirit of the Age* (1825) and *The Plain Speaker* (1826). Dependent on writing for his income, he was prolific almost to a fault, and yet none of his books could be said to betray the haste with which they were prepared for the printer.

He ran into trouble in 1823 with *Liber Amoris*, his confessional memoir of his thwarted infatuation with his landlady's 19-year-old daughter, Sarah Walker. The affair led him to divorce his wife – but there was no need for him to compound his miseries by publishing a blow-by-blow account, exposing not just Sarah's flirtatiousness, but his slavish obsession with her. To have done so was typical: he had been trained to observe human behaviour with the disinterestedness of a scientist, and to record what he saw as honestly as he could. In *Liber Amoris* he was no less sparing of his own foibles than of his contemporaries'. His honest rendering of male weakness earned him the contempt of literary London, not least the anonymous reviewer of the Tory newspaper *John Bull*:

> The dirty abominations of the raffs of literature are far below notice, but when to innate stupidity, grossness, vulgarity, and impudence are added the most degraded practical sensuality, the most inveterate ignorance, and the most depraved principle, it becomes necessary to take a double view of their abominable struggles against taste, decency, and morality.[1]

The onslaught continued, and it destroyed his reputation. It led him and his publishers to remove his name from the title-pages of subsequent books, for fear that his notoriety would depress sales. Eight years after his death, Wordsworth noted that 'the wreck of his morals was the ruin of him' (*LY* iii 595). Perhaps what none of his enemies understood was that *Liber Amoris* was an experiment in objectivity – an attempt to record as dispassionately as possible the twists and turns of a compulsion. And, as Hazlitt realized, that was something that could be done only at first hand.

He is represented here by four of his best essays, included here in full: 'On Gusto', 'The Fight', 'My First Acquaintance with Poets' and 'Mr Coleridge'. The first is central to any discussion of the Romantic imagination. Hazlitt defines gusto as 'power or passion defining any object', using precisely the same parameters that Wordsworth uses in his note to *The Thorn* (pp. 507–9). Passion for the Romantics was more than just emotion – it was the index of imaginative truth, the measure of the artist's imaginative sympathy with his subject, without which the artwork was worthless. Thus, Titian's paintings are remarkable to Hazlitt for their flesh tones, which appear 'not merely to have the look and texture of flesh, but the feeling in itself'; it was a theory as applicable to literature as to the visual arts, and was

Notes

[1] *John Bull* 15 June 1823, p. 188.

adapted by Keats for his theory of negative capability.

'The Fight' shows Hazlitt's discursive technique at its best. A keen amateur sportsman himself, Hazlitt was fascinated, as were other writers like Byron, by the art of pugilism – bare-knuckle fighting. There were strict laws against such fights, which meant that they were seldom advertised in advance; the news would go round by word of mouth that a certain time and place had been nominated, often outside London. Thousands of people would set out on horseback, in coaches, gigs, carts, or on foot, converging on the venue. Sometimes an officer of the law or an alderman would arrive to prohibit the fight from taking place at the spot and the entire show would move on, sometimes for miles. But that did not happen on this occasion, when Tom Hickman, the 'Gas-man', fought Bill Neate on 11 December 1821, at Hungerford, Berkshire. But the essay is not just about prize-fighting; as Tom Paulin points out, 'Hazlitt intends his readers to activate the reference to Cobbett's style, and to see the two boxers as living symbols of vehement prose in action.'[2]

'My First Acquaintance with Poets' is probably the most important first-hand testimony we have as to the *annus mirabilis* of 1797–8, and the aspirations of those involved. It is composed, of course, in the light of what was widely regarded as Coleridge's failure to live up to his early promise, something fully explored in 'Mr Coleridge', one of the most important chapters from *The Spirit of the Age* (1825). One of the arguments of that work is that intellectuals of the time could be categorized as rationalists (Godwin, Malthus) and non-rationalists (Lamb, Southey, Leigh Hunt). Coleridge cuts across such distinctions: he has an unquenchable appetite for philosophy, but is seduced into the interminable vortex of metaphysics. Besides being one of the most poignant of Hazlitt's essays, combining affection for his old mentor with a profound regret at his failure to fulfil his potential, this is also one of his funniest.

Hazlitt placed great hope in his final work, the huge four-volume *Life of Napoleon* (1826–30). It was largely quarried from the work of other biographers, but those passages by Hazlitt are written with his distinctive genius. He died in 1830 having just completed it, destitute, but with his old friend, Charles Lamb, at his side. He was 52.

Further reading

William Hazlitt ed. Harold Bloom (New York, 1986).

David Bromwich, *Hazlitt: The Mind of a Critic* (New Haven, 1999).

A. C. Grayling, *The Quarrel of the Age: The Life and Times of William Hazlitt* (London, 2000).

Stanley Jones, *Hazlitt: A Life* (Oxford, 1991).

Uttara Natarajan, *Hazlitt and the Reach of Sense* (Oxford, 1998).

Tom Paulin, *The Day-Star of Liberty: William Hazlitt's Radical Style* (London, 1998).

On Gusto[1]

From The Round Table (1817)

Gusto in art is power or passion defining any object. It is not so difficult to explain this term in what relates to expression (of which it may be said to be the highest degree), as in what relates to things without expression, to the natural appearances of objects, as mere colour or form. In one sense, however, there is hardly any object entirely devoid of expression, without some character of power belonging to it, some precise association with pleasure or pain. And it is in giving this truth of character from the

Notes

[2] *The Day-Star of Liberty* (London, 1998), p. 104.

On Gusto

[1] First published in *The Examiner*, 26 May 1816

truth of feeling, whether in the highest or the lowest degree (but always in the highest degree of which the subject is capable), that gusto consists.

There is a gusto in the colouring of Titian.[2] Not only do his heads seem to think, his bodies seem to feel. This is what the Italians mean by the *morbidezza*[3] of his flesh colour. It seems sensitive and alive all over – not merely to have the look and texture of flesh, but the feeling in itself. For example, the limbs of his female figures have a luxurious softness and delicacy, which appears conscious of the pleasure of the beholder. As the objects themselves in nature would produce an impression on the sense – distinct from every other object, and having something divine in it which the heart owns and the imagination consecrates – the objects in the picture preserve the same impression, absolute, unimpaired, stamped with all the truth of passion, the pride of the eye, and the charm of beauty. Rubens[4] makes his flesh colour like flowers; Albani's[5] is like ivory – Titian's is like flesh, and like nothing else. It is as different from that of other painters, as the skin is from a piece of white or red drapery thrown over it. The blood circulates here and there, the blue veins just appear, the rest is distinguished throughout only by that sort of tingling sensation to the eye, which the body feels within itself. This is gusto.

Van Dyck's[6] flesh colour, though it has great truth and purity, wants gusto. It has not the internal character, the living principle in it. It is a smooth surface, not a warm, moving mass. It is painted without passion, with indifference. The hand only has been concerned. The impression slides off from the eye, and does not, like the tones of Titian's pencil, leave a sting behind it in the mind of the spectator. The eye does not acquire a taste or appetite for what it sees. In a word, gusto in painting is where the impression made on one sense excites by affinity those of another.

Michelangelo's[7] forms are full of gusto. They everywhere obtrude[8] the sense of power upon the eye. His limbs convey an idea of muscular strength, of moral grandeur, and even of intellectual dignity; they are firm, commanding, broad and massy, capable of executing with ease the determined purposes of the will. His faces have no other expression than his figures, conscious power and capacity. They appear only to think what they shall do, and to know that they can do it. This is what is meant by saying that his style is hard and masculine; it is the reverse of Correggio's,[9] which is effeminate. That is, the gusto of Michelangelo consists in expressing energy of will without proportionable sensibility; Correggio's in expressing exquisite sensibility without energy of will. In Correggio's faces as well as figures we see neither bones nor muscles, but then what a soul is there, full of sweetness and of grace – pure, playful, soft, angelical! There is sentiment enough in a hand painted by Correggio to set up a school of history painters. Whenever we look at the hands of Correggio's women, or of Raphael's,[10] we always wish to touch them.

Again, Titian's landscapes have a prodigious gusto, both in the colouring and forms. We shall never forget one that we saw many years ago in the Orleans Gallery[11] of Actaeon hunting.[12] It had a brown, mellow, autumnal look. The sky was of the colour of stone.

Notes

[2] *Titian* Tiziano Vecellio (*c.*1490–1576), Venetian painter whose work Hazlitt greatly admired.

[3] *morbidezza* softness.

[4] Peter Paul Rubens (1577–1640), Flemish painter whose work Hazlitt also saw in Paris in 1802.

[5] Francesco Albani (1578–1660), painter of the school of Bologna.

[6] Sir Anthony Van Dyck (1599–1641), Flemish portraitist.

[7] Michelangelo Buonarroti (1475–1564), Italian painter, sculptor, architect.

[8] *obtrude* impose, thrust forth.

[9] Antonio Allegri da Correggio (1494–1534), eminent Italian painter.

[10] Raffaello Santi (1483–1520), Renaissance artist.

[11] *Orleans Gallery* exhibition of Italian old masters, so called because most of them came from the collection of the Duke of Orléans in Paris, and placed on sale in Pall Mall, December 1798, remaining there until July 1799.

[12] *Actaeon hunting* Titian's *Diana and Actaeon*. Actaeon was a hunter who came upon the naked Diana bathing with her

The winds seemed to sing through the rustling branches of the trees, and already you might hear the twanging of bows resound through the tangled mazes of the wood. (Mr West,[13] we understand, has this landscape; he will know if this description of it is just.)

The landscape background of the St Peter Martyr[14] is another well-known instance of the power of this great painter to give a romantic interest and an appropriate character to the objects of his pencil, where every circumstance adds to the effect of the scene: the bold trunks of the tall forest trees, the trailing ground plants, with that cold convent spire rising in the distance amidst the blue sapphire mountains and the golden sky.

Rubens has a great deal of gusto in his fauns and satyrs and in all that expresses motion, but in nothing else. Rembrandt[15] has it in everything; everything in his pictures has a tangible character. If he puts a diamond in the ear of a burgomaster's[16] wife, it is of the first water[17] – and his furs and stuffs are proof against a Russian winter. Raphael's gusto was only in expression; he had no idea of the character of anything but the human form. The dryness and poverty of his style in other respects is a phenomenon in the art. His trees are like sprigs of grass stuck in a book of botanical specimens. Was it that Raphael never had time to go beyond the walls of Rome, that he was always in the streets, at church, or in the bath? He was not one of the Society of Arcadians.[18]

Claude's[19] landscapes, perfect as they are, want gusto. This is not easy to explain. They are perfect abstractions of the visible images of things; they speak the visible language of nature truly. They resemble a mirror or a microscope. To the eye only they are more perfect than any other landscapes that ever were or will be painted. They give more of nature as cognizable by one sense alone, but they lay an equal stress on all visible impressions; they do not interpret one sense by another; they do not distinguish the character of different objects as we are taught (and can only be taught) to distinguish them by their effect on the different senses. That is, his eye wanted imagination; it did not strongly sympathize with his other faculties. He saw the atmosphere but he did not feel it. He painted the trunk of a tree or a rock in the foreground as smooth, with as complete an abstraction of the gross, tangible impression, as any other part of the picture; his trees are perfectly beautiful, but quite immovable – they have a look of enchantment. In short, his landscapes are unequalled imitations of nature, released from its subjection to the elements – as if all objects were become a delightful fairy vision, and the eye had rarefied and refined away the other senses.

Notes

train of nymphs on Mount Cithaeron; she turned him into a stag and he was devoured by his own hounds. Hazlitt is referring to Titian's 'Diana and Actaeon', which depicts Actaeon's discovery of Diana and her attendants in the forest, now at the Scottish National Gallery in Edinburgh.

[13] Benjamin West (1738–1820), historical painter born in America, who succeeded Reynolds as President of the Royal Academy in 1792.

[14] *the St Peter Martyr* Hazlitt saw this painting at the Louvre, 1802, and again in Venice in 1825. It was painted as an altarpiece for the great Venetian church, Santi Giovanni e Paolo, and was Titian's most famous and widely admired picture until being destroyed by fire in 1867.

[15] Rembrandt van Rijn (1606–69), Dutch painter.

[16] *burgomaster* chief magistrate of a Dutch town, equivalent to a mayor in England.

[17] *it is of the first water* i.e. it is so well painted that you can tell the quality of the stone. 'Water' is the measure of the quality of a diamond.

[18] *He was not . . . Arcadians* i.e. he didn't like the countryside. 'Raphael not only could not paint a landscape; he could not paint people in a landscape. He could not have painted the heads or the figures, or even the dresses of the St Peter Martyr. His figures have always an *indoor* look – that is, a set, determined, voluntary, dramatic character, arising from their own passions, or a watchfulness of those of others, and want that wild uncertainty of expression which is connected with the accidents of nature and the changes of the elements. He has nothing *romantic* about him' (Hazlitt's note).

[19] Claude Lorraine (1600–82), French landscape painter.

The gusto in the Greek statues is of a very singular kind. The sense of perfect form nearly occupies the whole mind, and hardly suffers it to dwell on any other feeling. It seems enough for them *to be*, without acting or suffering. Their forms are ideal, spiritual. Their beauty is power. By their beauty they are raised above the frailties of pain or passion; by their beauty they are deified.[20]

The infinite quantity of dramatic invention in Shakespeare takes from his gusto. The power he delights to show is not intense, but discursive. He never insists on anything as much as he might, except a quibble. Milton has great gusto. He repeats his blow twice, grapples with and exhausts his subject. His imagination has a double relish of its objects, an inveterate attachment to the things he describes, and to the words describing them:

Or where Chineses drive
With sails and wind their *cany* waggons *light* . . .
Wild above rule or art, *enormous* bliss.[21]

There is a gusto in Pope's compliments, in Dryden's satires, and Prior's tales. And among prose writers, Boccaccio and Rabelais had the most of it. We will only mention one other work which appears to us to be full of gusto, and that is *The Beggar's Opera*.[22] If it is not, we are altogether mistaken in our notions on this delicate subject.

The Fight

From The New Monthly Magazine (February 1822)

----- The fight, the fight's the thing,
Wherein I'll catch the conscience of the king.[1]

Where there's a will, there's a way. – I said so to myself, as I walked down Chancery Lane, about half-past six o'clock on Monday the 10th of December, to inquire at Jack Randall's[2] where the fight the next day was to be; and I found 'the proverb' nothing 'musty'[3] in the present instance. I was determined to see this fight, come what would, and see it I did, in great style. It was my *first fight*, yet it more than answered my expectations. Ladies! it is to you I dedicate this description; nor let it seem out of character for the fair to notice the exploits of the brave. Courage and modesty are the old English virtues; and may they never look cold and askance on one another! Think, ye fairest of the fair, loveliest of the lovely kind, ye practisers of soft enchantment, how many more ye kill with poisoned baits than ever fell in the ring; and listen with subdued air and without shuddering, to a tale tragic only in appearance, and sacred to the FANCY![4]

I was going down Chancery Lane, thinking to ask at Jack Randall's where the fight was to be, when looking through the glass door of the *Hole in the Wall*, I heard a gentleman asking the same question *at* Mrs Randall, as the author of *Waverley*[5] would

Notes

[20] *by their beauty . . . deified* Hazlitt echoes Wordsworth, *Resolution and Independence* 47: 'By our own spirits are we deified.'

[21] *Or where Chineses . . . enormous bliss* from *Paradise Lost* iii 438–9, v 297.

[22] *The Beggar's Opera* a popular musical play by John Gay (produced 1728).

THE FIGHT

[1] *The fight . . . the conscience of the king* adapted from *Hamlet* II ii 604–5.

[2] *Jack Randall's* 'The Hole in the Wall' in Chancery Lane, kept by Jack Randall, the pugilist.

[3] *the proverb . . . musty* from *Hamlet* II ii 343–4.

[4] *the FANCY* boxing aficionados.

[5] *the author of Waverley* Walter Scott.

express it. Now Mrs Randall stood answering the gentlemen's question, with the authenticity of the lady of the Champion of the Light Weights. Thinks I, I'll wait till this person comes out, and learn from him how it is. For to say a truth, I was not fond of going into this house to call for heroes and philosophers, ever since the owner of it (for Jack is no gentleman) threatened once upon a time to kick me out of doors for wanting a mutton chop at his hospitable board, when the conqueror in thirteen battles was more full of *blue ruin*[6] than of good manners. I was the more mortified at this repulse, inasmuch as I had heard Mr James Simpkins, hosier in the Strand, one day when the character of the *Hole in the Wall* was brought in question, observe, 'The house is a very good house, and the company quite genteel: I have been there myself!'

Remembering this unkind treatment of mine host, to which mine hostess was also a party, and not wishing to put her in unquiet thoughts at a time jubilant like the present, I waited at the door when who should issue forth but my friend Jo. Toms,[7] and turning suddenly up Chancery Lane with that quick jerk and impatient stride which distinguishes a lover of the Fancy, I said, 'I'll be hanged if that fellow is not going to the fight, and is on his way to get me to go with him.' So it proved in effect, and we agreed to adjourn to my lodgings to discuss measures with that cordiality which makes old friends like new, and new friends like old, on great occasions. We are cold to others only when we are dull in ourselves, and have neither thoughts nor feelings to impart to them. Give a man a topic in his head, a throb of pleasure in his heart, and he will be glad to share it with the first person he meets. Toms and I, though we seldom meet, were an *alter idem* on this memorable occasion, and had not an idea that we did not candidly impart; and 'so carelessly did we fleet the time',[8] that I wish no better, when there is another fight, than to have him for a companion on my journey down, and to return with my friend Jack Pigott,[9] talking of what was to happen or of what did happen, with a noble subject always at hand, and liberty to digress to others whenever they offered. Indeed, on my repeating the lines from Spenser in an involuntary fit of enthusiasm,

> What more felicity can fall to creature,
> Than to enjoy delight with liberty?[10]

my last-named ingenious friend stopped me by saying that this, translated into the vulgate, meant 'Going to see a fight'.

Jo. Toms and I could not settle about the method of going down. He said there was a caravan, he understood, to start from Tom Belcher's[11] at two, which would go there *right out* and back again the next day. Now I never travel all night, and said I should get a cast[12] to Newbury by one of the mails. Jo. swore the thing was impossible, and I could only answer that I had made up my mind to it. In short, he seemed to me to waver, said he only came to see if I was going, had letters to write, a cause coming on the day after, and faintly said at parting (for I was bent on setting out that moment) – 'Well, we meet at Philippi!'[13] I made the best of my way to Piccadilly. The mail-coach

Notes

6 *blue ruin* low-grade gin

7 *Joe Toms* Joseph Parkes (1796–1865), one of Hazlitt's sporting and social acquaintances. He was one of the young men who surrounded Jeremy Bentham, and at this date was articled to a London solicitor. Hazlitt calls him both 'Jo.' and 'Joe'.

8 *so carelessly did we fleet the time* from *As You Like It* I i 118.

9 *Jack Pigott* in reality, P. G. Patmore (1786–1855), journalist; friend of Hazlitt and Lamb.

10 *What more felicity . . . delight with liberty?* from Spenser, *Muiopotmos* 209–10.

11 *to start from Tom Belcher's* Tom Belcher (1783–1854), a younger brother of the better-known prize-fighter, James Belcher, kept the Castle tavern in Holborn.

12 *cast* lift, ride.

13 *Well, we meet at Philippi!* from *Julius Cæsar* IV iii 286.

stand was bare. 'They are all gone', said I – 'this is always the way with me – in the instant I lose the future – if I had not stayed to pour out that last cup of tea, I should have been just in time' – and cursing my folly and ill-luck together, without inquiring at the coach-office whether the mails were gone or not, I walked on in despite, and to punish my own dilatoriness and want of determination. At any rate, I would not turn back: I might get to Hounslow, or perhaps farther, to be on my road the next morning. I passed Hyde Park Corner (my Rubicon), and trusted to fortune.

Suddenly I heard the clattering of a Brentford stage, and the fight rushed full upon my fancy. I argued (not unwisely) that even a Brentford coachman was better company than my own thoughts (such as they were just then), and at his invitation mounted the box with him. I immediately stated my case to him – namely, my quarrel with myself for missing the Bath or Bristol mail, and my determination to get on in consequence as well as I could, without any disparagement or insulting comparison between longer or shorter stages. It is a maxim with me that stage-coaches, and consequently stage-coachmen, are respectable in proportion to the distance they have to travel: so I said nothing on that subject to my Brentford friend. Any incipient tendency to an abstract proposition, or (as he might have construed it) to a personal reflection of this kind, was however nipped in the bud; for I had no sooner declared indignantly that I had missed the mails, than he flatly denied that they were gone along, and lo! at the instant three of them drove by in rapid, provoking, orderly succession, as if they would devour the ground before them. Here again I seemed in the contradictory situation of the man in Dryden who exclaims,

> I follow Fate, which does too hard pursue![14]

If I had stopped to inquire at the White Horse Cellar, which would not have taken me a minute, I should now have been driving down the road in all the dignified unconcern and *ideal* perfection of mechanical conveyance. The Bath mail I had set my mind upon, and I had missed it, as I missed everything else, by my own absurdity, in putting the will for the deed, and aiming at ends without employing means. 'Sir', said he of the Brentford, 'the Bath mail will be up presently, my brother-in-law drives it, and I will engage to stop him if there is a place empty.' I almost doubted my good genius; but, sure enough, up it drove like lightning, and stopped directly at the call of the Brentford Jehu.[15] I would not have believed this possible, but the brother-in-law of a mail-coach driver is himself no mean man. I was transferred without loss of time from the top of one coach to that of the other, desired the guard to pay my fare to the Brentford coachman for me as I had no change, was accommodated with a great coat, put up my umbrella to keep off a drizzling mist, and we began to cut through the air like an arrow.

The milestones disappeared one after another, the rain kept off; Tom Turtle,[16] the trainer, sat before me on the coach-box, with whom I exchanged civilities as a gentleman going to the fight; the passion that had transported me an hour before

Notes

[14] *I follow Fate, which does too hard pursue* from Dryden, *The Indian Emperor* IV iii 3–5:

> As if the cares of Humane Life were few
> We seek out new:
> And follow Fate which would too fast pursue.

[15] *the Brentford Jehu* a mock-heroic reference to the fast and furious driver of the Brentford stage-coach.

[16] *Tom Turtle, the trainer* John Thurtell (1794–1824), the trainer and organizer of sporting events, who also owned a tavern, the Black Boy in Long Acre. Here Thurtell kept a mistress and entertained so many rough, brawling companions that he eventually lost his licence. By 1821, his reputation was distinctly shady. He was known for declining invitations to fight the likes of Tom Belcher, and made his living by gambling, fraud, hazard, billiards and arranging crooked fights. He was tried and executed for the murder of William Weare, one of his gambling companions, an ex-waiter, billiards sharp and expert gamester, on 9 January 1824 In the MS, Hazlitt at one point describes him as 'my friend Thirtle'.

was subdued to pensive regret and conjectural musing on the next day's battle; I was promised a place inside at Reading, and upon the whole, I thought myself a lucky fellow. Such is the force of imagination! On the outside of any other coach on the 10th of December with a Scotch mist drizzling through the cloudy moonlight air, I should have been cold, comfortless, impatient, and, no doubt, wet through; but seated on the Royal mail, I felt warm and comfortable, the air did me good, the ride did me good, I was pleased with the progress we had made, and confident that all would go well through the journey.

When I got inside at Reading, I found Turtle and a stout valetudinarian, whose costume bespoke him one of the FANCY, and who had risen from a three months' sick-bed to get into the mail to see the fight. They were intimate, and we fell into a lively discourse. My friend the trainer was confined in his topics to fighting-dogs and men, to bears and badgers; beyond this he was 'quite chap-fallen',[17] had not a word to throw at a dog, or indeed very wisely fell asleep, when any other game was started. The whole art of training (I, however, learnt from him) consists in two things, exercise and abstinence, abstinence and exercise, repeated alternately and without end. A yolk of an egg with a spoonful of rum in it is the first thing in a morning, and then a walk of six miles till breakfast. This meal consists of a plentiful supply of tea and toast and beef-steaks. Then another six or seven miles till dinner-time, and another supply of solid beef or mutton with a pint of porter, and perhaps, at the utmost, a couple of glasses of sherry. Martin trains on water,[18] but this increases his infirmity on another very dangerous side. The Gas-man takes now and then a chirping glass (under the rose) to console him, during a six weeks' probation, for the absence of Mrs Hickman – an agreeable woman, with (I understand) a pretty fortune of two hundred pounds.

How matter presses on me! What stubborn things are facts! How inexhaustible is nature and art! 'It is well', as I once heard Mr Richmond observe,[19] 'to see a variety.' He was speaking of cockfighting as an edifying spectacle. I cannot deny but that one learns more of what *is* (I do not say of what *ought to be*) in this desultory mode of practical study, than from reading the same book twice over, even though it should be a moral treatise. Where was I? I was sitting at dinner with the candidate for the honours of the ring, 'where good digestion waits on appetite, and health on both'.[20] Then follows an hour of social chat and native glee;[21] and afterwards, to another breathing over heathy hill or dale. Back to supper, and then to bed, and up by six again – Our hero

> Follows so the ever-running sun,
> With profitable ardour[22] –

to the day that brings him victory or defeat in the green fairy circle. Is not this life more sweet than mine?[23] I was going to say; but I will not libel any life by comparing it

Notes

[17] *quite chap-fallen* from *Hamlet* V i 192.

[18] *Martin trains on water* Jack Martin, a baker by trade – hence, in sporting parlance, 'The Master of the Rolls'.

[19] *I once heard Mr Richmond observe* Born in 1763, Bill Richmond was, according to Pierce Egan, 'a man of colour, and a native of America'. He came to England in 1777 with the Duke of Northumberland, and beat Tom Cribb in 1805. According to Egan, writing in 1812, he 'has given instructions to some hundreds, not only in various parts of the kingdom, but in the very zenith of competition – LONDON.' One of his pupils was Hazlitt.

[20] *where good digestion . . . and health on both* from *Macbeth*, III iv 37–8.

[21] *social chat and native glee* an echo of Burns, *Address to the Unco Guid* 33: 'See Social-life and Glee sit down'.

[22] *Follows so . . . With profitable ardour* from *Henry V* IV i 276–7:

> And follows so the ever-running year
> With profitable labor to his grave.

[23] *Is not this life more sweet than mine?* cf. *As You Like It* II i 2–3: 'Hath not old custom made this life more sweet / Than that of painted pomp?'

to mine, which is (at the date of these presents) bitter as coloquintida[24] and the dregs of aconitum!

The invalid in the Bath mail soared a pitch above the trainer, and did not sleep so sound, because he had 'more figures and more fantasies'.[25] We talked the hours away merrily. He had faith in surgery,[26] for he had had three ribs set right, that had been broken in a *turn-up* at Belcher's, but thought physicians old women, for they had no antidote in their catalogue for brandy. An indigestion is an excellent commonplace for two people that never met before. By way of ingratiating myself, I told him the story of my doctor who, on my earnestly representing to him that I thought his regimen had done me harm, assured me that the whole pharmacopeia contained nothing comparable to the prescription he had given me; and, as a proof of his undoubted efficacy, said that 'he had had one gentleman with my complaint under his hands for the last fifteen years'. This anecdote made my companion shake the rough sides of his three greatcoats with boisterous laughter; and Turtle, starting out of his sleep, swore he knew how the fight would go, for he had had a dream about it. Sure enough, the rascal told us how the three first rounds went off, but 'his dream', like others, 'denoted a foregone conclusion'.[27] He knew his men.

The moon now rose in silver state, and I ventured, with some hesitation, to point out this object of placid beauty, with the blue serene beyond, to the man of science, to which his ear he 'seriously inclined',[28] the more as it gave promise *d'un beau jour*[29] for the morrow, and showed the ring undrenched by envious showers, arrayed in sunny smiles. Just then, all going on well, I thought on my friend Toms, whom I had left behind, and said innocently, 'There was a blockhead of a fellow I left in town, who said there was no possibility of getting down by the mail, and talked of going by a caravan from Belcher's at two in the morning, after he had written some letters.' 'Why', said he of the lapels, 'I should not wonder if that was the very person we saw running about like mad from one coach-door to another, and asking if anyone had seen a friend of his, a gentleman going to the fight, whom he had missed stupidly enough by staying to write a note.' 'Pray sir', said my fellow-traveller, 'he had a plaid cloak on?' – 'Why, no', said I, 'not at the time I left him, but he very well might afterwards, for he offered to lend me one.' The plaid cloak and the letter decided the thing. Joe, sure enough, was in the Bristol mail, which preceded us by about fifty yards. This was droll enough.

We had now but a few miles to our place of destination, and the first thing I did on alighting at Newbury, both coaches stopping at the same time, was to call out, 'Pray, is there a gentleman in that mail of the name of Toms?' 'No', said Joe, borrowing something of the vein of Gilpin, 'for I have just got out.' 'Well!' says he, 'this is lucky; but you don't know how vexed I was to miss you; for', added he, lowering his voice, 'do you know when I left you I went to Belcher's to ask about the caravan, and Mrs Belcher said very obligingly, she couldn't tell about that, but there were two gentlemen who had taken places by the mail and were gone on in a landau, and she could frank us. It's a pity I didn't meet with you; we could then have got down for nothing. But *mum's the word.*' It's the devil for anyone to tell me a secret, for it is sure to come

Notes

24 *bitter as coloquintida* from *Othello,* I iii 349: 'as acerb as the coloquintida'. The colocynth or 'bitter apple' was used as an emetic.

25 *more figures and more fantasies* from *Julius Cæsar* II i 231.

26 *He had faith in surgery* an allusion to *1 Henry IV* V i 133: 'Honor hath no skill in surgery then?'

27 *his dream . . . denoted a foregone conclusion* an allusion to *Othello,* III iii 427.

28 *seriously inclined* from *Othello* I iii 146.

29 *d'un beau jour* an allusion to Burke's *Reflections on the Revolution in France,* where he attacks those in the National Assembly who supported the removal of Louis XVI from Versailles to Paris: 'Miserable king! Miserable Assembly! How must that assembly be silently scandalised with those of their members, who could call a day which seemed to blot out the sun of Heaven 'un beau jour'!

out in print. I do not care so much to gratify a friend, but the public ear is too great a temptation to me.

Our present business was to get beds and a supper at an inn; but this was no easy task. The public houses were full, and where you saw a light at a private house, and people poking their heads out of the casement to see what was going on, they instantly put them in and shut the window, the moment you seemed advancing with a suspicious overture for accommodation. Our guard and coachman thundered away at the outer gate of the Crown for some time without effect – such was the greater noise within; – and when the doors were unbarred, and we got admittance, we found a party assembled in the kitchen round a good hospitable fire, some sleeping, others drinking, others talking on politics and on the fight. A tall English yeoman (something like Matthews in the face,[30] and quite as great a wag) –

A lusty man to ben an abbot able,[31] –

was making such a prodigious noise about rent and taxes, and the price of corn now and formerly, that he had prevented us from being heard at the gate. The first thing I heard him say was to a shuffling fellow who wanted to be off a bet for a shilling glass of brandy and water – 'Confound it, man, don't be *insipid*!' Thinks I, that is a good phrase. It was a good omen. He kept it up so all night, nor flinched with the approach of morning. He was a fine fellow, with sense, wit, and spirit, a hearty body and a joyous mind, free-spoken, frank, convivial – one of that true English breed that went with Harry the Fifth to the siege of Harfleur – 'standing like greyhounds on the slips',[32] etc.

We ordered tea and eggs (beds were soon found to be out of the question) and this fellow's conversation was *sauce piquante*. It did one's heart good to see him brandish his oaken towel and to hear him talk. He made mincemeat of a drunken, stupid, red-faced, quarrelsome, *frowsy* farmer, whose nose 'he moralised into a thousand similes',[33] making it out a firebrand like Bardolph's.[34] 'I'll tell you what, my friend', says he, 'the landlady has only to keep you here to save fire and candle. If one was to touch your nose, it would go off like a piece of charcoal.' At this the other only grinned like an idiot, the sole variety in his purple face being his little peering grey eyes and yellow teeth; called for another glass, swore he would not stand it; and after many attempts to provoke his humorous antagonist to single combat, which the other turned off (after working him up to a ludicrous pitch of choler) with great adroitness, he fell quietly asleep with a glass of liquor in his hand, which he could not lift to his head. His laughing persecutor made a speech over him, and turning to the opposite side of the room, where they were all sleeping in the midst of this 'loud and furious fun',[35] said, 'There's a scene, by God, for Hogarth to paint. I think he and Shakespeare were our two best men at copying life!' This confirmed me in my good opinion of him. Hogarth, Shakespeare, and Nature, were just enough for him (indeed for any man) to know. I said, 'You read Cobbett,[36] don't you? At least', says I, 'you talk just as well as he writes.' He seemed to doubt this. But I said, 'We have an hour to spare: if you'll get pen, ink and paper, and keep on talking, I'll write down what you say; and if it doesn't make a capital *Political Register*, I'll forfeit my head. You have kept me alive tonight,

Notes

[30] *something like Matthews in the face* Hazlitt refers to Charles Mathews (1776–1835), a popular comedian.

[31] *A lusty man to ben an abbot able* from Chaucer, *General Prologue to the Canterbury Tales*, 167.

[32] *standing like greyhounds on the slips* from *Henry V* III i 31.

[33] *he moralized into a thousand similes* from *As You Like It* II i 44–5.

[34] *a firebrand like Bardolph's* Hazlitt alludes to *2 Henry IV* II iv 329–30: 'honest Bardolph, whose zeal burns in his nose'.

[35] *loud and furious fun* from Burns, *Tam o'Shanter* 144: 'The mirth and fun grew fast and furious.'

[36] William Cobbett (1763–1835), radical leader and journalist whose weekly *Political Register* strongly supported the movement for parliamentary reform.

however. I don't know what I should have done without you.' He did not dislike this view of the thing, nor my asking if he was not about the size of Jem Belcher; and told me soon afterwards, in the confidence of friendship, that 'the circumstance which had given him nearly the greatest concern in his life, was Cribb's beating Jem[37] after he had lost his eye by racket-playing.'

The morning dawns; that dim but yet clear light appears, which weighs like solid bars of metal on the sleepless eyelids; the guests drop down from their chambers one by one – but it was too late to think of going to bed now (the clock was on the stroke of seven), we had nothing for it but to find a barber's (the pole that glittered in the morning sun lighted us to his shop), and then a nine miles' march to Hungerford. The day was fine, the sky was blue, the mists were retiring from the marshy ground, the path was tolerably dry, the sitting-up all night had not done us much harm – at least the cause was good; we talked of this and that with amicable difference, roving and sipping of many subjects, but still invariably we returned to the fight. At length, a mile to the left of Hungerford, on a gentle eminence, we saw the ring surrounded by covered carts, gigs, and carriages, of which hundreds had passed us on the road; Toms gave a youthful shout, and we hastened down a narrow lane to the scene of action.

Reader! have you ever seen a fight? If not, you have a pleasure to come, at least if it is a fight like that between the Gas-man and Bill Neate. The crowd was very great when we arrived on the spot; open carriages were coming up, with streamers flying and music playing, and the country-people were pouring in over hedge and ditch in all directions, to see their hero beat or be beaten. The odds were still on Gas, but only about five to four. Gully[38] had been down to try Neate, and had backed him considerably, which was a damper to the sanguine confidence of the adverse party. About two hundred thousand pounds were pending. The Gas says, he has lost £3,000 which were promised him by different gentlemen if he had won. He had presumed too much on himself, which had made others presume on him. This spirited and formidable young fellow seems to have taken for his motto the old maxim, that 'there are three things necessary to success in life – *Impudence! Impudence! Impudence!*'[39] It is so in matters of opinion, but not in the *Fancy*, which is the most practical of all things, though even here confidence is half the battle, but only half. Our friend had vapoured and swaggered too much, as if he wanted to grin and bully his adversary out of the fight. 'Alas! the Bristol man was not so tamed!'[40] – 'This is *the grave digger*' (would Tom Hickman exclaim in the moments of intoxication from gin and success, showing his tremendous right hand), 'this will send many of them to their long homes; I haven't done with them yet!' Why should he – though he had licked four of the best men within the hour, yet why should he threaten to inflict dishonourable chastisement on my old master Richmond, a veteran going off the stage, and who has borne his sable honours meekly? Magnanimity, my dear Tom, and bravery, should be inseparable. Or why should he go up to his antagonist, the first time he ever saw him at the Fives[41] Court, and measuring him from head to foot with a glance of contempt, as Achilles

Notes

[37] *Cribb's beating Jem* Tom Cribb defeated Jem Belcher twice, in 1807 and 1809. Belcher lost an eye in 1803 through an accident when playing at rackets.

[38] *Gully* John Gully (1783–1863), prize-fighter, horse-racer, legislator and colliery proprietor. He retired from the ring in 1808 after two victories over Bob Gregson. In 1812 he became a racehorse-owner.

[39] *the old maxim . . . Impudence!* Hazlitt is recalling Danton's utterance in 1792: 'De l'audace, encore de l'audace, toujours de l'audace, et la France est sauvée.'

[40] *Alas! the Bristol man was not so tamed!* Hazlitt echoes Cowper, *The Task* ii 322: 'Alas! Leviathan is not so tamed.'

[41] *Fives* a game at which Hazlitt was expert, in which the ball is struck by the hand against the front wall of a three-sided court; a forerunner of squash. The Fives Court was a regular venue for bare-knuckle fights in London.

surveyed Hector,[42] say to him, 'What, are you Bill Neate? I'll knock more blood out of that great carcase of thine, this day fortnight, than you ever knock'd out of a bullock's!' It was not manly, 'twas not fighter-like. If he was sure of the victory (as he was not), the less said about it the better. Modesty should accompany the *Fancy* as its shadow. The best men were always the best behaved. Jem Belcher, the Game Chicken[43] (before whom the Gas-man could not have lived) were civil, silent men. So is Cribb, so is Tom Belcher, the most elegant of sparrers, and not a man for every one to take by the nose. I enlarged on this topic in the mail (while Turtle was asleep), and said very wisely (as I thought) that impertinence was a part of no profession. A boxer was bound to beat his man, but not to thrust his fist, either actually or by implication, in everyone's face. Even a highwayman, in the way of trade, may blow out your brains, but if he uses foul language at the same time, I should say he was no gentleman. A boxer, I would infer, need not be a blackguard or a coxcomb, more than another. Perhaps I press this point too much on a fallen man – Mr Thomas Hickman has by this time learnt that first of all lessons, 'That man was made to mourn'.[44] He has lost nothing by the late fight but his presumption; and that every man may do as well without! By an over-display of this quality, however, the public has been prejudiced against him, and the *knowing-ones* were taken in. Few but those who had bet on him wished Gas to win. With my own prepossessions on the subject, the result of the 11th of December appeared to me as fine a piece of poetical justice as I had ever witnessed. The difference of weight between the two combatants (14 stone to 12) was nothing to the sporting men. Great, heavy, clumsy, long-armed Bill Neate kicked the beam in the scale of the Gas-man's vanity. The amateurs were frightened at his big words, and thought that they would make up for the difference of six feet and five feet nine. Truly, the FANCY are not men of imagination. They judge of what has been, and cannot conceive of anything that is to be. The Gas-man had won hitherto; therefore he must beat a man half as big again as himself – and that to a certainty. Besides, there are as many feuds, factions, prejudices, pedantic notions in the FANCY as in the state or in the schools. Mr Gully is almost the only cool, sensible man among them, who exercises an unbiased discretion, and is not a slave to his passions in these matters. But enough of reflections, and to our tale. The day, as I have said, was fine for a December morning. The grass was wet and the ground miry, and ploughed up with multitudinous feet, except that, within the ring itself, there was a spot of virgin-green closed in and unprofaned by vulgar tread, that shone with dazzling brightness in the midday sun. For it was noon now, and we had an hour to wait. This is the trying time. It is then the heart sickens, as you think what the two champions are about, and how short a time will determine their fate. After the first blow is struck, there is no opportunity for nervous apprehensions; you are swallowed up in the immediate interest of the scene – but

> Between the acting of a dreadful thing
> And the first motion, all the interim is
> Like a phantasma, or a hideous dream.[45]

I found it so as I felt the sun's rays clinging to my back, and saw the white wintry clouds sink below the verge of the horizon. So, I thought, my fairest hopes have faded from my side! – so will the Gas-man's glory, or that of his adversary, vanish in an hour.

Notes

42 *as Achilles surveyed Hector* see Homer, *Iliad*, Book XXII.

43 *the Game Chicken* Henry Pearce (1777–1809), or 'Hen' Pearce – hence his soubriquet – was a popular boxer of the day.

44 *That man was made to mourn* an allusion to Burns's poem, 'Man was Made to Mourn'.

45 *Between the acting . . . or a hideous dream* from *Julius Cæsar* II i 63–5.

The *swells* were parading in their white box-coats, the outer ring was cleared with some bruises on the heads and shins of the rustic assembly (for the *cockneys* had been distanced by the sixty-six miles); the time drew near, I had got a good stand; a bustle, a buzz, ran through the crowd, and from the opposite side entered Neate, between his second and bottle-holder. He rolled along, swathed in his loose greatcoat, his knock-knees bending under his huge bulk; and, with a modest cheerful air, threw his hat into the ring. He then just looked round, and began quietly to undress; when from the other side there was a similar rush and an opening made, and the Gas-man came forward with a conscious air of anticipated triumph, too much like the cock-of-the-walk. He strutted about more than became a hero, sucked oranges with a supercilious air, and threw away the skin with a toss of his head, and went up and looked at Neate, which was an act of supererogation. The only sensible thing he did was, as he strode away from the modern Ajax, to fling out his arms, as if he wanted to try whether they would do their work that day. By this time they had stripped, and presented a strong contrast in appearance. If Neate was like Ajax, 'with Atlantean shoulders, fit to bear'[46] the pugilistic reputation of all Bristol, Hickman might be compared to Diomed, light, vigorous, elastic, and his back glistened in the sum, as he moved about, like a panther's hide. There was now a dead pause – attention was awestruck. Who at that moment, big with a great event, did not draw his breath short – did not feel his heart throb? All was ready. They tossed up for the sun, and the Gas-man won. They were lead up to the *scratch* – shook hands, and went at it.

In the first round everyone thought it was all over. After making play a short time, the Gas-man flew at his adversary like a tiger, struck five blows in as many seconds, three first, and then following him as he staggered back, two more, right and left, and down he fell, a mighty ruin. There was a shout, and I said, 'There is no standing this.' Neate seemed like a lifeless lump of flesh and bone, round which the Gas-man's blows played with the rapidity of electricity or lighting, and you imagined he would only be lifted up to be knocked down again. It was as if Hickman held a sword or a fire in that right hand of his, and directed it against an unarmed body. They met again, and Neate seemed not cowed but particularly cautious. I saw his teeth clenched together and his brows knit close against the sun. He held out both his arms at full length straight before him, like two sledge-hammers, and raised his left an inch or two higher. The Gas-man could not get over this guard – they struck mutually and fell, but without advantage on either side. It was the same in the next round; but the balance of power was thus restored – the fate of the battle was suspended. No one could tell how it would end. This was the only moment in which opinion was divided; for, in the next, the Gas-man aiming a mortal blow at his adversary's neck with his right hand, and failing from the length he had to reach, the other returned it with his left at full swing, planted a tremendous blow on his cheekbone and eyebrow, and made a red ruin of that side of his face. The Gas-man went down, and there was another shout – a roar of triumph as the waves of fortune rolled tumultuously from side to side. This was a settler. Hickman got up and 'grinned horrible a ghastly smile',[47] yet he was evidently dashed in his opinion of himself; it was the first time he had ever been so punished; all one side of his face was perfect scarlet, and his right eye was closed in dingy blackness, as he advanced to the fight, less confident, but still determined. After one or two rounds, not receiving another such remembrancer, he rallied and went at it with his

Notes

[46] *with Atlantean shoulders, fit to bear* from *Paradise Lost* ii 306.

[47] *grinned horrible a ghastly smile* like Death, *Paradise Lost* ii 846

former impetuosity. But in vain. His strength had been weakened – his blows could not tell at such a distance – he was obliged to fling himself at his adversary, and could not strike from his feet; and almost as regularly as he flew at him with his right hand, Neate warded the blow, or drew back out of its reach, and felled him with the return of his left. There was little cautious sparring – no half-hits – no tapping and trifling, none of the *petit-maîtreship* of the art – they were almost all knock-down blows: – the fight was a good stand-up fight.

The wonder was the half-minute-time. If there had been a minute or more allowed between each round, it would have been intelligible how they should by degrees recover strength and resolution; but to see two men smashed to the ground, smeared with gore, stunned, senseless, the breath beaten out of their bodies; and then, before you recover from the shock, to see them rise up with new strength and courage, stand steady to inflict or receive mortal offence, and rush upon each other 'like two clouds over the Caspian'[48] – this is the most astonishing thing of all: – this is the high and heroic state of man!

From this time forward the event became more certain every round; and about the twelfth it seemed as if it must have been over. Hickman generally stood with his back to me; but in the scuffle he had changed positions, and Neate just then made a tremendous lunge at him, and hit him full in the face. It was doubtful whether he would fall backwards or forwards; he hung suspended for a second or two, and then fell back, throwing his hands in the air, and with his face lifted up to the sky. I never saw anything more terrific than his aspect just before he fell. All traces of life, of natural expression, were gone from him. His face was like a human skull, a death's head, spouting blood. The eyes were filled with blood, the nose streamed with blood, the mouth gaped blood. He was not like an actual man, but like a preternatural, spectral appearance, or like one of the figures in Dante's *Inferno*. Yet he fought on after this for several rounds, still striking the first desperate blow, and Neate standing on the defensive, and using the same cautious guard to the last, as if he had still all his work to do; and it was not till the Gas-man was so stunned in the seventeenth or eighteenth round, that his senses forsook him, and he could not come to time, that the battle was declared over.[49] Ye who despise the Fancy, do something to show as much *pluck*, or as much self-possession as this, before you assume a superiority which you have never given a single proof of by any one action in the whole course of your lives! – When the Gas-man came to himself, the first words he uttered were, 'Where am I? What is the matter!' 'Nothing is the matter, Tom – you have lost the battle, but you are the bravest man alive.' And Jackson[50] whispered to him, 'I am collecting a purse for you, Tom.' – Vain sounds, and unheard at that moment! Neate instantly went up and shook him cordially by the hand, and seeing some old acquaintance, began to flourish with his fists, calling out, 'Ah! you always said I couldn't fight – What do you think now?' But

Notes

[48] *like two clouds over the Caspian* from *Paradise Lost* ii 714–16.

[49] 'Scroggins said of the Gas-man, that he thought he was a man of that courage, that if his hands were cut off, he would still fight on with the stumps – like that of Widrington, –

In doleful dumps,
Who, when his legs were smitten off,
Still fought upon his stumps.' (Hazlitt's note)

Jack Scroggins was a well-known prizefighter. In May 1817 he fought Ned Turner (1791–1826) in a field near Hayes before a crowd of 30,000. Hazlitt quotes from *The Ancient Ballad of Chevy-Chase* 119–22.

[50] *Jackson* 'Gentleman' John Jackson (1769–1845) succeeded Daniel Mendoza as champion of the sport in 1795. He set up rooms at 13 Bond Street with the aim of coaching noblemen; Byron was one of his pupils. He founded the Pugilistic Club in his rooms in 1814, and retired in 1824.

all in good humour, and without any appearance of arrogance; only it was evident Bill Neate was pleased that he had won the fight. When it was over, I asked Cribb if he did not think it was a good one? He said, '*Pretty well!*' The carrier-pigeons now mounted into the air, and one of them flew with the news of her husband's victory to the bosom of Mrs Neate. Alas, for Mrs Hickman! –

Mais au revoir, as Sir Fopling Flutter says.[51] I went down with Toms; I returned with Jack Pigott, whom I met on the ground. Toms is a rattle-brain; Pigott is a sentimentalist. Now, under favour, I am a sentimentalist too – therefore I say nothing, but that the interest of the excursion did not flag as I came back. Pigott and I marched along the causeway leading from Hungerford to Newbury, now observing the effect of a brilliant sun on the tawny meads or moss-coloured cottages, now exulting in the fight, now digressing to some topic of general and elegant literature. My friend was dressed in character for the occasion, or like one of the FANCY; that is, with a double portion of greatcoats, clogs, and overalls: and just as we had agreed with a couple of country lads to carry his superfluous wearing-apparel to the next town, we were overtaken by a return post-chaise, into which I got, Pigott preferring a seat on the bar. There were two strangers already in the chaise, and on their observing they supposed I had been to the fight, I said I had, and concluded they had done the same. They appeared, however, a little shy and sore on the subject; and it was not till after several hints dropped, and questions put, that it turned out that they had missed it. One of these friends had undertaken to drive the other there in his gig: they had set out, to make sure work, the day before at three in the afternoon. The owner of the one-horse vehicle scorned to ask his way, and drove right on to Bagshot, instead of turning off at Hounslow: there they stopped all night, and set off the next day across the country to Reading, from whence they took coach, and got down within a mile or two of Hungerford, just half an hour after the fight was over. This might be safely set down as one of the miseries of human life.

We parted with these two gentlemen who had been to see the fight, but had returned as they went, at Wolhampton, where we were promised beds (an irresistible temptation, for Pigott had passed the preceding night at Hungerford as we had done at Newbury), and we turned into an old bow-windowed parlour with a carpet and a snug fire; and after devouring a quantity of tea, toast, and eggs, sat down to consider, during an hour of philosophic leisure, what we should have for supper. In the midst of an Epicurean deliberation between a roasted fowl and mutton-chops with mashed potatoes, we were interrupted by an inroad of Goths and Vandals – *O procul este profani*[52] – not real flash-men, but interlopers, noisy pretenders, butchers from Tothill-fields, brokers from Whitechapel, who called immediately for pipes and tobacco, hoping it would not be disagreeable to the gentlemen, and began to insist that it was a *cross*. Pigott withdrew from the smoke and noise into another room, and left me to dispute the point with them for a couple of hours *sans intermission* by the dial.[53]

The next morning we rose refreshed; and on observing that Jack had a pocket volume in his hand, in which he read in the intervals of our discourse, I inquired what it was, and learned to my particular satisfaction that it was a volume of the *New Eloise*. Ladies, after this, will you contend that a love for the FANCY is incompatible with the cultivation of sentiment? – We jogged on as before, my friend setting me up in a

Notes

[51] *Mais au revoir, as Sir Fopling Flutter says* Dorimant in Etherege, *The Man of Mode* III ii 305: '*A revoir*, as Sir Fopling says.'

[52] *O procul este profani* from Virgil, *Aeneid* vi 258.

[53] *sans intermission by the dial* from *As You Like It* II vii 32–3.

genteel drab greatcoat and green silk handkerchief (which I must say became me exceedingly), and after stretching our legs for a few miles, and seeing Jack Randall, Ned Turner, and Scroggins, pass on the top of one of the Bath coaches, we engaged with the driver of the second to take us to London for the usual fee. I got inside, and found three other passengers. One of them was an old gentleman with an aquiline nose, powdered hair, and a pigtail, and who looked as if he had played many a rubber at the Bath rooms. I said to myself, he is very like Mr Windham;[54] I wish he would enter into conversation, that I might hear what fine observations would come from those finely-turned features. However, nothing passed till, stopping to dine at Reading, some inquiry was made by the company about the fight, and I gave (as the reader may believe) an eloquent and animated description of it. When we got into the coach again, the old gentleman, after a graceful exordium, said he had, when a boy, been to a fight between the famous Broughton and George Stevenson,[55] who was called the *Fighting Coachman*, in the year 1770, with the late Mr Windham. This beginning flattered the spirit of prophecy within me, and he riveted my attention. He went on – 'George Stevenson was coachman to a friend of my father's. He was an old man when I saw him some years afterwards. He took hold of his own arm and said, "There was muscle here once, but now it is no more than this young gentleman's." He added, "Well, no matter; I have been here long, I am willing to go hence, and hope I have done no more harm than another man." Once', said my unknown companion, 'I asked him if he had ever beat Broughton? He said Yes; that he had fought with him three times, and the last time he fairly beat him, though the world did not allow it. "I'll tell you how it was, master. When the seconds lifted us up in the last round, we were so exhausted that neither of us could stand, and we fell upon one another, and as Master Broughton fell uppermost, the mob gave it in his favour, and he was said to have won the battle. But," says he, "the fact was, that as his second (John Cuthbert) lifted him up, he said to him, 'I'll fight no more, I've had enough'; which", says Stevenson, "you know gave me the victory. And to prove to you that this was the case, when John Cuthbert was on his deathbed, and they asked him if there was anything on his mind which he wished to confess, he answered, 'Yes, that there was one thing he wished to set right, for that certainly Master Stevenson won that last fight with Master Broughton; for he whispered him as he lifted him up in the last round of all, that he had had enough.' " This,' said the Bath gentleman, 'was a bit of human nature;' and I have written this account of the fight on purpose that it might not be lost to the world. He also stated as a proof of the candour of mind in this class of men, that Stevenson acknowledged that Broughton could have beat him in his best day; but that he (Broughton) was getting old in their last rencounter. When we stopped in Piccadilly, I wanted to ask the gentleman some questions about the late Mr Windham, but had not courage. I got out, resigned my coat and green silk handkerchief to Pigott (loath to part with these ornaments of life), and walked home in high spirits.

P.S. Toms called upon me the next day, to ask me if I did not think the fight was a complete thing? I said I thought it was. I hope he will relish my account of it.

PHANTASTES

Notes

[54] William Windham (1750–1810), politician, Secretary for War under Pitt (1794–1801) and Grenville (1806–7).

[55] *the famous Broughton and George Stevenson* Jack Broughton (1704–1789) fought George Stevenson, 'The Coachman', in 1741. Their fight lasted forty minutes, and Broughton was victorious.

My First Acquaintance with Poets[1]

From The Liberal (April 1823)

My father was a Dissenting minister[2] at Wem in Shropshire, and in the year 1798 (the figures that compose that date are to me like the 'dreaded name of Demogorgon'[3]), Mr Coleridge came to Shrewsbury to succeed Mr Rowe in the spiritual charge of a Unitarian congregation there.

He did not come till late on the Saturday afternoon before he was to preach, and Mr Rowe, who himself went down to the coach in a state of anxiety and expectation to look for the arrival of his successor, could find no one at all answering the description but a round-faced man in a short black coat, like a shooting jacket, which hardly seemed to have been made for him, but who seemed to be talking at a great rate to his fellow-passengers. Mr Rowe had scarce returned to give an account of his disappointment, when the round-faced man in black entered, and dissipated all doubts on the subject by beginning to talk. He did not cease while he stayed – nor has he since, that I know of. He held the good town of Shrewsbury in delightful suspense for three weeks that he remained there, 'fluttering the *proud Salopians* like an eagle in a dovecot',[4] and the Welsh mountains that skirt the horizon with their tempestuous confusion agree to have heard no such mystic sounds since the days of 'High-born Hoel's harp or soft Llewellyn's lay!'[5]

As we passed along between Wem and Shrewsbury, and I eyed their blue tops seen through the wintry branches, or the red rustling leaves of the sturdy oak-trees by the roadside, a sound was in my ears as of a siren's song. I was stunned, startled with it, as from deep sleep, but I had no notion then that I should ever be able to express my admiration to others in motley imagery or quaint allusion, till the light of his genius shone into my soul, like the sun's rays glittering in the puddles of the road. I was at that time dumb, inarticulate, helpless, like a worm by the wayside,[6] crushed, bleeding, lifeless – but now, bursting from the deadly bands that 'bound them, / With Styx nine times round them',[7] my ideas float on winged words, and as they expand their plumes, catch the golden light of other years. My soul has indeed remained in its original bondage, dark, obscure, with longings infinite[8] and unsatisfied; my heart, shut up in the prison-house of this rude clay, has never found (nor will it ever find) a heart to speak to – but that my understanding also did not remain dumb and brutish, or at length found a language to express itself, I owe to Coleridge. But this is not to my purpose.

My father lived ten miles from Shrewsbury and was in the habit of exchanging visits with Mr Rowe and with Mr Jenkins of Whitchurch (nine miles farther on), according to the custom of Dissenting ministers in each other's neighbourhood. A line of communication is thus established, by which the flame of civil and religious liberty

Notes

My First Acquaintance with Poets

[1] The present text is emended by the advice of Stanley Jones in 'A Hazlitt Anomaly', *The Library* ser. 6, 7 (1985) 60–2, and 'A Hazlitt Corruption', *The Library* ser. 5, 33 (1978) 235–8.

[2] *My father . . . minister* William Hazlitt Sr was a Unitarian minister (see headnote).

[3] *dreaded name of Demogorgon* from *Paradise Lost* ii 964–5. Tom Paulin suggests that Hazlitt's reason for regarding 1798 in this light is because of the Irish uprising, which Hazlitt would have been aware of, given that his father was Irish.

[4] *fluttering the proud Salopians like an eagle in a dovecot* An allusion to *Coriolanus* V vi 114–15.

[5] *High-born Hoel's harp or soft Llewellyn's lay!* from Gray, *The Bard* 28.

[6] *like a worm by the wayside* cf. Chaucer, *The Clerk's Tale* 879–80: 'wherfore I yow preye, / Lat me nat lyk a worm go by the weye'.

[7] *bound them . . . round them* from Pope, *Ode on St Cecilia's Day* 90–1.

[8] *with longings infinite* cf. Wordsworth, 'The Affliction of Margaret' 63: 'With love and longings infinite'.

is kept alive, and nourishes its smouldering fire unquenchable, like the fires in the *Agamemnon* of Aeschylus, placed at different stations, that waited for ten long years to announce with their blazing pyramids the destruction of Troy.

Coleridge had agreed to come over to see my father, according to the courtesy of the country, as Mr Rowe's probable successor, but in the meantime I had gone to hear him preach the Sunday after his arrival. A poet and a philosopher getting up into a Unitarian pulpit to preach the gospel was a romance in these degenerate days, a sort of revival of the primitive spirit of Christianity, which was not to be resisted.

It was in January 1798 that I rose one morning before daylight, to walk ten miles in the mud, to hear this celebrated person preach. Never, the longest day I have to live, shall I have such another walk as this cold, raw, comfortless one in the winter of the year 1798. *Il y a des impressions que ni le tems ni les circonstances peuvent effacer. Dusse-je vivre des siècles entiers, le doux tems de ma jeunesse ne peut renaitre pour moi, ni s'effacer jamais dans ma mémoire.*[9]

When I got there the organ was playing the 100th Psalm, and, when it was done, Mr Coleridge rose and gave out his text: 'And he went up into the mountain to pray, HIMSELF, ALONE.'[10] As he gave out this text, his voice 'rose like a steam of rich distilled perfumes',[11] and when he came to the two last words, which he pronounced loud, deep, and distinct, it seemed to me, who was then young, as if the sounds had echoed from the bottom of the human heart, and as if that prayer might have floated in solemn silence through the universe. The idea of St John came into mind, 'of one crying in the wilderness, who had his loins girt about, and whose food was locusts and wild honey'.[12]

The preacher then launched into his subject like an eagle dallying with the wind. The sermon was upon peace and war,[13] upon church and state (not their alliance, but their separation), on the spirit of the world and the spirit of Christianity – not as the same, but as opposed to one another. He talked of those who had 'inscribed the cross of Christ on banners dripping with human gore.' He made a poetical and pastoral excursion, and, to show the fatal effects of war, drew a striking contrast between the simple shepherd boy driving his team afield, or sitting under the hawthorn piping to his flock 'as though he should never be old', and the same poor country lad, crimped,[14] kidnapped, brought into town, made drunk at an alehouse, turned into a wretched drummer-boy, with his hair sticking on end with powder and pomatum,[15] a long cue[16] at his back, and tricked out in the loathsome finery of the profession of blood – 'Such were the notes our once-loved poet sung.'[17]

And for myself I could not have been more delighted if I had heard the music of the spheres. Poetry and philosophy had met together, truth and genius had embraced under the eye and with the sanction of religion. This was even beyond my hopes. I returned home well-satisfied. The sun that was still labouring pale and wan through the sky, obscured by thick mists, seemed an emblem of the *good cause*, and the cold dank drops of dew that hung half-melted on the beard of the thistle had something genial and refreshing in them – for there was a spirit of hope and youth in all nature,

Notes

[9] 'There are impressions which neither time nor circumstance is able to efface. Were I to live entire centuries, the sweet time of my youth could never be reborn for me – nor could it ever be erased from my memory.' Hazlitt has adapted Rousseau, *Julie, ou la Nouvelle Héloïse* (6 vols, Amsterdam, 1761), vi 55–6.

[10] Matthew 14: 23 and John 6: 15.

[11] *rose like a steam of rich distilled perfumes* from Milton, *Comus* 556.

[12] Matthew 3: 3–4 and Mark 1: 3.

[13] *peace and war* Coleridge was at this time much preoccupied with the war with France, which had been in progress since 1793. Given Hazlitt's remarks here, it is evident that Coleridge's reservations about the war, fully expressed in *France: An Ode*, were brewing in January 1798

[14] *crimped* forced into the army.

[15] *pomatum* pomade, a scented ointment.

[16] *cue* pigtail.

[17] *Such were the notes our once-loved poet sung* from Pope, 'Epistle to Robert, Earl of Oxford' 1.

that turned everything into good. The face of nature had not then the brand of *jus divinum*[18] on it, 'Like to that sanguine flower inscribed with woe.'[19]

On the Tuesday following the half-inspired speaker came. I was called down into the room where he was, and went half-hoping, half-afraid. He received me very graciously, and I listened for a long time without uttering a word. I did not suffer in his opinion by my silence. 'For those two hours', he afterwards was pleased to say, 'he was conversing with W.H.'s forehead'. His appearance was different from what I had anticipated from seeing him before. At a distance, and in the dim light of the chapel, there was to me a strange wildness in his aspect, a dusky obscurity, and I thought him pitted with the smallpox. His complexion was at that time clear, and even bright, 'As are the children of yon azure sheen'.[20] His forehead was broad and high; light, as if built of ivory, with large projecting eyebrows, and his eyes rolling beneath them like a sea with darkened lustre. 'A certain tender bloom his face o'erspread',[21] a purple tinge as we see it in the pale thoughtful complexions of the Spanish portrait-painters, Murillo and Velasquez. His mouth was gross, voluptuous, open, eloquent; his chin good-humoured and round; but his nose, the rudder of the face, the index of the will, was small, feeble, nothing – like what he has done.[22] It might seem that the genius[23] of his face, as from a height, surveyed and projected him (with sufficient capacity and huge aspiration) into the world unknown of thought and imagination, with nothing to support or guide his veering purpose, as if Columbus had launched his adventurous course for the New World in a scallop, without oars or compass. So at least I comment on it after the event.

Coleridge in his person was rather above the common size, inclining to the corpulent, or like Lord Hamlet, 'somewhat fat and pursy'.[24] His hair (now, alas, grey) was then black and glossy as the raven's, and fell in smooth masses over his forehead. This long pendulous hair is peculiar to enthusiasts,[25] to those whose minds tend heavenward, and is traditionally inseparable (though of a different colour) from the pictures of Christ. It ought to belong, as a character, to all who preach Christ crucified, and Coleridge was at that time one of those.

It was curious to observe the contrast between him and my father, who was a veteran in the cause,[26] and then declining into the vale of years.[27] He had been a poor Irish lad, carefully brought up by his parents, and sent to the University of Glasgow, where he studied under Adam Smith,[28] to prepare him for his future destination. It was his mother's proudest wish to see her son a Dissenting minister. So if we look back to past generations as far as eye can reach, we see the same hopes, fears, wishes,

Notes

[18] *jus divinum* 'The divine right' of kings.

[19] *that flower . . . woe* the hyacinth; see *Lycidas* 106.

[20] *As are the children of yon azure sheen* from Thomson, *The Castle of Indolence* ii 295.

[21] *A certain tender bloom his face o'erspread* from Thomson, *The Castle of Indolence* i 507: 'A certain tender gloom o'erspread his face.'

[22] *his nose . . . like what he has done* Cf. Coleridge's description of himself two years earlier, p. 610. When this essay first appeared in *The Liberal* a number of reviewers thought that Hazlitt's comments on Coleridge's nose were in bad taste. The *Literary Register* (3 May 1823) described the essay as 'disgusting', and concluded by asking

> What does Mr Hazlitt mean by Coleridge's nose being feeble? – What does he mean by its being nothing? Does he mean to say that Coleridge has *no nose* – no rudder – no cutwater? We believe he does. . . . Now, really, is this endurable? except to laugh at for which purpose it is, as we said before, well worth the money. Is it bearable that a fool, like this Hazlitt, should make a fool of a person so amiable as Coleridge; or that a man's personal peculiarities are served up in this manner to raise money? It is as shameful and contemptible as it is improper and absurd. (p. 275)

[23] *genius* tutelary deity.

[24] *somewhat fat and pursy* from *Hamlet* III iv 153.

[25] *enthusiasts* fanatics.

[26] *the cause* i.e. of Unitarianism.

[27] *declining into the vale of years* an allusion to Cowper, *Task* ii 725–6: 'But Discipline, a faithful servant long, / Declined at length into the vale of years.' William Hazlitt Sr was 60 in January 1798.

[28] Adam Smith (1723–90), distinguished Scottish economist and man of letters, author, most notably, of *The Wealth of Nations* (1776).

followed by the same disappointments, throbbing in the human heart – and so we may see them, if we look forward, rising up forever, and disappearing, like vapourish bubbles, in the human breast. After being tossed about from congregation to congregation in the heats of the Unitarian controversy and squabbles about the American War,[29] he had been relegated to an obscure village where he was to spend the last thirty years of his life[30] far from the only converse that he loved – the talk about disputed texts of scripture, and the cause of civil and religious liberty. Here he passed his days, repining but resigned, in the study of the Bible and the perusal of the commentators[31] – huge folios not easily got through, one of which would outlast a winter. Why did he pore on these from morn to night (with the exception of a walk in the fields or a turn in the garden to gather broccoli plants or kidney beans of his own rearing, with no small degree of pride and pleasure)? Here were 'no figures nor no fantasies',[32] neither poetry nor philosophy, nothing to dazzle, nothing to excite modern curiosity – but to his lacklustre eyes there appeared, within the pages of the ponderous, unwieldy, neglected tomes, the sacred name of JEHOVAH in Hebrew capitals: pressed down by the weight of the style, worn to the last fading thinness of the understanding, there were glimpses, glimmering notions of the patriarchal wanderings, with palm-trees hovering in the horizon, and processions of camels at the distance of three thousand years; there was Moses with the burning bush, the number of the Twelve Tribes, types, shadows, glosses on the law and the prophets; there were discussions (dull enough) on the age of Methuselah[33] (a mighty speculation!); there were outlines, rude guesses at the shape of Noah's Ark and of the riches of Solomon's Temple; questions as to the date of the creation, predictions of the end of all things; the great lapses of time, the strange mutations of the globe were unfolded with the voluminous leaf, as it turned over; and though the soul might slumber with an hieroglyphic veil of inscrutable mysteries drawn over it, yet it was in a slumber ill-exchanged for all the sharpened realities of sense, wit, fancy, or reason. My father's life was comparatively a dream, but it was a dream of infinity and eternity, of death, the resurrection, and a judgement to come.

No two individuals were ever more unlike than were the host and his guest. A poet was to my father a sort of nondescript, yet whatever added grace to the Unitarian cause was to him welcome. He could hardly have been more surprised or pleased if our visitor had worn wings. Indeed, his thoughts had wings, and as the silken sounds rustled round our little wainscoted parlour, my father threw back his spectacles over his forehead, his white hairs mixing with its sanguine hue, and a smile of delight beamed across his rugged cordial face, to think that Truth had found a new ally in Fancy! Besides, Coleridge seemed to take considerable notice of me, and that of itself was enough. He talked very familiarly, but agreeably, and glanced over a variety of subjects.

At dinnertime he grew more animated, and dilated in a very edifying manner on Mary Wollstonecraft and Mackintosh.[34] The last he said he considered (on my father's

Notes

[29] *squabbles about the American War* Like other Unitarian ministers, Hazlitt's father had been a close associate of Benjamin Franklin during his second English agency, and was a staunch supporter of the American cause during the war with Britain. Typically, he and his family were on the first boat to sail to America after the war ended in 1783.

[30] *an obscure village . . . last thirty years of his life* Not quite true. The 'obscure village' is Wem, where Hazlitt's father served as pastor of the Dissenting congregation from 1787 to 1813, when he retired to Addlestone, Surrey, before moving to Bath and then Crediton, Devonshire, where he died on 16 July 1820 at the age of 83.

[31] *the commentators* i.e. Biblical interpreters.

[32] *no figures nor no fantasies* from *Julius Caesar* II i 231.

[33] *Methuselah* one of the pre-Noachian patriarchs, stated to have lived 969 years (Genesis 5: 27), hence used as a type of extreme longevity.

[34] *Mary Wollstonecraft and Mackintosh* Coleridge met James Mackintosh, a leading sympathizer with the French Revolution, only weeks before meeting Hazlitt, in December 1797; it is not known if he met Wollstonecraft.

speaking of his *Vindiciae Gallicae* as a capital performance) as a clever scholastic man, a master of the topics – or as the ready warehouseman of letters, who knew exactly where to lay his hand on what he wanted, though the goods were not his own. He thought him no match for Burke,[35] either in style or matter. Burke was a metaphysician, Mackintosh a mere logician. Burke was an orator (almost a poet) who reasoned in figures because he had an eye for nature; Mackintosh, on the other hand, was a rhetorician who had only an eye to commonplaces. On this I ventured to say that I had always entertained a great opinion of Burke, and that (as far as I could find) the speaking of him with contempt might be made the test of a vulgar democratical mind. This was the first observation I ever made to Coleridge, and he said it was a very just and striking one. I remember the leg of Welsh mutton and the turnips on the table that day had the finest flavour imaginable. Coleridge added that Mackintosh and Tom Wedgwood[36] (of whom, however, he spoke highly) had expressed a very indifferent opinion of his friend Mr Wordsworth, on which he remarked to them: 'He strides on so far before you that he dwindles in the distance!'

Godwin[37] had once boasted to him of having carried on an argument with Mackintosh for three hours with dubious success; Coleridge told him, 'If there had been a man of genius in the room, he would have settled the question in five minutes.' He asked me if I had ever seen Mary Wollstonecraft, and I said I had once for a few moments,[38] and that she seemed to me to turn off[39] Godwin's objections to something she advanced with quite a playful, easy air. He replied that 'This was only one instance of the ascendancy which people of imagination exercised over those of mere intellect'. He did not rate Godwin very high[40] (this was caprice or prejudice, real or affected), but he had a great idea of Mrs Wollstonecraft's powers of conversation, none at all of her talent for book-making.[41] We talked a little about Holcroft.[42] He had been asked if he was not much struck *with* him, and he said he thought himself in more danger of being struck *by* him. I complained that he would not let me get on at all, for he required a definition of every the commonest word, exclaiming, 'What do you mean by a *sensation*, sir? What do you mean by an *idea*?' This, Coleridge said, was barricadoing the road to truth; it was setting up a turnpike-gate at every step we took.[43]

I forget a great number of things (many more than I remember), but the day passed off pleasantly, and the next morning Mr Coleridge was to return to Shrewsbury. When I came down to breakfast I found that he had just received a letter from his friend, T. Wedgwood, making him an offer of £150 a year if he chose to waive his present pursuit and devote himself entirely to the study of poetry and philosophy. Coleridge seemed to make up his mind to close with this proposal in the act of tying on one of his shoes. It threw an additional damp on his departure. It took the wayward enthusiast quite from us to cast him into Deva's winding vales[44] or by the shores of old romance. Instead of

Notes

35 *Burke* see pp. 7–9.

36 Thomas Wedgwood (1771–1805), third surviving son of Josiah Wedgwood, the famous potter, was a good friend of Coleridge, and died of stomach cancer.

37 *Godwin* see pp. 151–2.

38 If Hazlitt met Wollstonecraft, it must have been in September or October 1796 in London; the following year he was in Wem.

39 *turn off* dismiss.

40 *He did not . . . high* cf. Coleridge's comment to Southey, 19 December 1799: 'Godwin is no great things in intellect, but in heart and manner he is all the better for having been the husband of Mary Wollstonecraft' (Griggs i 549).

41 *book-making* i.e. book-writing.

42 Thomas Holcroft (1745–1809), dramatist, novelist, man of letters, noted radical. Coleridge met him in London in December 1794, just after the Treason Trials at which he had been a defendant (see p. 317); the most notable work of Hazlitt's early career was his *Memoir of Thomas Holcroft* (1816). Hazlitt probably met Holcroft for the first time in the autumn of 1796.

43 Coleridge evidently had a trying time with Holcroft, whose atheism he found difficult to take; see Griggs i 138–9.

44 *Deva's winding vales* Hazlitt has in mind *Lycidas* 55.

living at ten miles' distance, of being the pastor of a Dissenting congregation at Shrewsbury, he was henceforth to inhabit the hill of Parnassus,[45] to be a shepherd on the Delectable Mountains.[46] Alas, I knew not the way thither, and felt very little gratitude for Mr Wedgwood's bounty! I was presently relieved from this dilemma, for Mr Coleridge, asking for a pen and ink, and going to a table to write something on a bit of card, advanced towards me with undulating step and, giving me the precious document, said that that was his address – 'Mr Coleridge, Nether Stowey, Somersetshire' – and that he should be glad to see me there in a few weeks' time, and, if I chose, would come halfway to meet me. I was not less surprised than the shepherd boy (this simile is to be found in *Cassandra*)[47] when he sees a thunderbolt fall close at his feet. I stammered out my acknowledgements and acceptance of this offer (I thought Mr Wedgwood's annuity a trifle to it) as well as I could, and, this mighty business being settled, the poet-preacher took leave, and I accompanied him six miles on the road.

It was a fine morning in the middle of winter, and he talked the whole way. The scholar in Chaucer is described as going 'Sounding on his way';[48] so Coleridge went on his. In digressing, in dilating, in passing from subject to subject, he appeared to me to float in air, to slide on ice. He told me in confidence (going along) that he should have preached two sermons before he accepted the situation at Shrewsbury, one on infant baptism, the other on the Lord's Supper, showing that he could not administer either, which would have effectually disqualified him for the object in view. I observed that he continually crossed me on the way by shifting from one side of the footpath to the other. This struck me as an odd movement, but I did not at that time connect it with any instability of purpose or involuntary change of principle, as I have done since. He seemed unable to keep on in a straight line.

He spoke slightingly of Hume,[49] whose 'Essay on Miracles' he said was stolen from an objection started in one of South's[50] sermons – *Credat Judaeus Apella*![51] I was not very much pleased at this account of Hume, for I had just been reading, with infinite relish, that completest of all metaphysical *choke-pears*,[52] his *Treatise on Human Nature*, to which the *Essays*, in point of scholastic subtlety and close reasoning, are mere elegant trifling, light summer reading. Coleridge even denied the excellence of Hume's general style, which I think betrayed a want of taste or candour.

He however made me amends by the manner in which he spoke of Berkeley. He dwelt particularly on his *Essay on Vision* as a masterpiece of analytical reasoning – so it undoubtedly is.[53] He was exceedingly angry with Dr Johnson for striking the stone with his foot, in allusion to this author's theory of matter and spirit, and saying, 'Thus I confute him, sir!'[54] Coleridge drew a parallel (I don't know how he brought about the

Notes

[45] *Parnassus* mountain sacred to the muses in classical literature.

[46] In Bunyan's *Pilgrim's Progress* Christian and Hopeful reach the Delectable Mountains after escaping from Doubting Castle and the Giant Despair.

[47] Ten-volume romance by Gauthier de Costes de la Calprenède.

[48] *Sounding on his way* probably, as P. P. Howe has suggested, a confused recollection of several lines from Chaucer and Wordsworth. In the General Prologue to *The Canterbury Tales*, the Merchant is described as 'Sownynge alwey th' encrees of his wynnyng' (l. 275), and of the Clerk Chaucer writes: 'Sownynge in moral vertu was his speche' (l. 307). Hazlitt may also be recalling Wordsworth, *Excursion* iii 701 ('Went sounding on a dim and perilous way'), to which Coleridge alludes at the end of *Biographia Literaria* chapter 5.

[49] David Hume (1711–76), Scottish sceptic and philosopher, whose publications included *Treatise of Human Nature* (1739) and *Essays Moral and Political* (1741–2); Hartley and Berkeley were more to Coleridge's taste.

[50] Robert South (1634–1716), noted divine and sermonist.

[51] 'Apella the Jew may believe it' [but I don't] (Horace, *Satires* I v 100); i.e. tell it to the marines.

[52] *choke-pear* an unanswerable objection. A choke-pear was used by robbers: it was made of iron in the shape of a pear, and would be placed into the mouths of their victims. With the turn of a key, it would enlarge so that it could not be removed.

[53] George Berkeley (1685–1753), Bishop of Cloyne, *An Essay Towards a New Theory of Vision* (1709, 1710, 1732).

[54] Related in Boswell's *Life of Johnson* (1791).

connection) between Bishop Berkeley and Tom Paine.[55] He said the one was an instance of a subtle, the other of an acute mind, than which no two things could be more distinct. The one was a shopboy's quality, the other the characteristic of a philosopher. He considered Bishop Butler[56] as a true philosopher, a profound and conscientious thinker, a genuine reader of nature and of his own mind. He did not speak of his *Analogy* but of his *Sermons at the Rolls Chapel*, of which I had never heard. Coleridge somehow always contrived to prefer the *unknown* to the *known*; in this instance he was right. The *Analogy* is a tissue of sophistry, of wire-drawn,[57] theological special pleading; the *Sermons* (with the Preface to them) are in a fine vein of deep, matured reflection, a candid appeal to our observation of human nature, without pedantry and without bias.

I told Coleridge I had written a few remarks, and was sometimes foolish enough to believe that I had made a discovery on the same subject ('The Natural Disinterestedness of the Human Mind'[58]), and I tried to explain my view of it to Coleridge, who listened with great willingness, but I did not succeed in making myself understood. I sat down to the task shortly afterwards for the twentieth time, got new pens and paper, determined to make clear work of it, wrote a few meagre sentences in the skeleton style of a mathematical demonstration, stopped halfway down the second page, and, after trying in vain to pump up any words, images, notions, apprehensions, facts or observations from that gulf of abstraction in which I had plunged myself for four or five years preceding, gave up the attempt as labour in vain, and shed tears of helpless despondency on the blank unfinished paper. I can write fast enough now. Am I better than I was then? Oh no! One truth discovered, one pang of regret at not being able to express it, is better than all the fluency and flippancy in the world. Would that I could go back to what I then was! Why can we not revive past times as we can revisit old places? If I had the quaint[59] muse of Sir Philip Sidney to assist me, I would write a 'Sonnet to the Road between Wem and Shrewsbury', and immortalize every step of it by some fond enigmatical conceit. I would swear that the very milestones had ears, and that Harmer Hill stooped with all its pines to listen to a poet as he passed!

I remember but one other topic of discourse in this walk. He mentioned Paley,[60] praised the naturalness and clearness of his style, but condemned his sentiments, thought him a mere time-serving casuist, and said that 'the fact of his work on *Moral and Political Philosophy* being made a textbook in our universities was a disgrace to the national character'.

We parted at the six-milestone and I returned homeward, pensive but much pleased. I had met with unexpected notice from a person whom I believed to have been prejudiced against me: 'Kind and affable to me had been his condescension, and should be honoured ever with suitable regard'.[61] He was the first poet I had known, and he certainly answered to that inspired name. I had heard a great deal of his powers of conversation and was not disappointed. In fact, I never met with anything at all like them, either before or since. I could easily credit the accounts which were circulated of his holding forth to a large party of ladies and gentlemen, an evening or two, before on the Berkeleian theory, when he made the whole material universe look like a transparency of

Notes

55 *Tom Paine* see p. 23.

56 Joseph Butler, Bishop of Bristol (1692–1752), whose *Fifteen Sermons* (1726) preached at the Rolls Chapel defines his moral philosophy.

57 *wire-drawn* drawn out at great length and with subtle ingenuity.

58 Published as *An Essay on the Principles of Human Action* (1805).

59 *quaint* clever, ingenious.

60 William Paley (1743–1805), theologian and philosopher, whose *Moral and Political Philosophy* (1785) was a University textbook by the time Wordsworth went up to Cambridge in 1787.

61 *Paradise Lost* viii 648–50.

fine words;[62] and another story (which I believe he has somewhere told himself) of his being asked to a party at Birmingham, of his smoking tobacco and going to sleep after dinner on a sofa, where the company found him to their no small suprise, which was increased to wonder when he started up of a sudden and, rubbing his eyes, looked about him, and launched into a three hours' description of the third heaven, of which he had had a dream, very different from Mr Southey's *Vision of Judgement*, and also from that other *Vision of Judgement* which Mr. Murray, the Secretary of the Bridge Street junto,[63] has taken into his especial keeping.[64]

On my way back I had a sound in my ears; it was the voice of fancy – I had a light before me: it was the face of Poetry. The one still lingers there, the other has not quitted my side! Coleridge in truth met me halfway on the ground of philosophy, or I should not have been won over to his imaginative creed. I had an uneasy, pleasurable sensation all the time till I was to visit him. During those months the chill breath of winter gave me a welcoming; the vernal air was balm and inspiration to me. The golden sunsets, the silver star of evening, lighted me on my way to new hopes and prospects. *I was to visit Coleridge in the spring*. This circumstance was never absent from my thoughts, and mingled with all my feelings. I wrote to him at the time proposed and received an answer postponing my intended visit for a week or two, but very cordially urging me to complete my promise then. This delay did not damp, but rather increased my ardour. In the meantime I went to Llangollen Vale by way of initiating myself in the mysteries of natural scenery, and I must say I was enchanted with it. I had been reading Coleridge's description of England in his fine *Ode on the Departing Year*,[65] and I applied it *con amore*[66] to the objects before me. That valley was to me, in a manner, the cradle of a new existence: in the river that winds through it, my spirit was baptized in the waters of Helicon![67]

I returned home and soon after set out on my journey with unworn heart and untired feet. My way lay through Worcester and Gloucester and by Upton – where I thought of Tom Jones and the adventure of the muff.[68] I remember getting completely wet through one day and stopping at an inn (I think it was at Tewkesbury) where I sat up all night to read *Paul and Virginia*.[69] Sweet were the showers in early youth that drenched my body, and sweet the drops of pity that fell upon the books I read! I recollect a remark of Coleridge's upon this very book, that nothing could show the gross indelicacy of French manners and the entire corruption of their imagination more strongly than the behaviour of the heroine in the last fatal scene, who turns away from a person on board the sinking vessel that offers to save her life, because he has thrown off his clothes to assist him in swimming. Was this a time to think of such a circumstance? I once hinted to Wordsworth,[70] as we were sailing in his boat on Grasmere lake, that I thought he had borrowed the idea of his 'Poems on the Naming of Places' from the local inscriptions of the same kind in *Paul*

Notes

[62] *he made . . . fine words* George Berkeley (1685–1753), Bishop of Cloyne, argued that the material world was no more than an idea in the mind of God.

[63] *junto* political clique, cabal.

[64] Southey's *A Vision of Judgement* (1821) describes the reception in heaven of George III; Byron's *The Vision of Judgement* (1822) was a satirical response aimed largely at Southey, though Charles Murray of Bridge Street, an officer of the Constitutional Association, prosecuted the publishers of Byron's poem on the grounds of its libellous attack on George III.

[65] Published in pamphlet form, 1796.

[66] with love.

[67] The River Dee flows through the Vale of Llangollen; the fountains of Aganippe and Hippocrene rose out of Mount Helicon, sacred to the muses.

[68] Henry Fielding, *Tom Jones* (1749), Book X, chapters 5–7.

[69] Popular novel by Jacques-Henri Bernardin de Saint-Pierre (1737–1814), disciple of Rousseau, published 1788.

[70] *I once hinted to Wordsworth* probably on his visit to the Lakes, August–September 1803.

and Virginia. He did not own the obligation, and stated some distinction without a difference in defence of his claim to originality. Any the slightest variation would be sufficient for this purpose in his mind, for whatever *he* added or omitted would inevitably be worth all that anyone else had done, and contain the marrow of the sentiment.

I was still two days before the time fixed for my arrival, for I had taken care to set out early enough. I stopped these two days at Bridgwater, and when I was tired of sauntering on the banks of its muddy river, returned to the inn and read *Camilla*.[71] So have I loitered my life away, reading books, looking at pictures, going to plays, hearing, thinking, writing on what pleased me best. I have wanted only one thing to make me happy – but wanting that, have wanted everything.

I arrived, and was well-received. The country about Nether Stowey is beautiful, green and hilly, and near the seashore. I saw it but the other day[72] after an interval of twenty years from a hill near Taunton. How was the map of my life spread out before me, as the map of the country lay at may feet! In the afternoon, Coleridge took me over to Alfoxden, a romantic old family mansion of the St Aubins, where Wordsworth lived. It was then in the possession of a friend of the poet's who gave him the free use of it.[73] Somehow that period (the time just after the French Revolution) was not a time when nothing was given for nothing. The mind opened, and a softness might be perceived coming over the heart of individuals beneath 'the scales that fence' our self-interest.

Wordsworth himself was from home, but his sister kept house, and set before us a frugal repast – and we had free access to her brother's poems, the *Lyrical Ballads*, which were still in manuscript, or in the form of sibylline leaves.[74] I dipped into a few of these with great satisfaction, and with the faith of a novice. I slept that night in an old room with blue hangings and covered with the round-faced family portraits of the age of George I and II, and from the wooded declivity of the adjoining park that overlooked my window, at the dawn of day, could 'hear the loud stag speak'.[75]

In the outset of life (and particularly at this time I felt it so) our imagination has a body to it. We are in a state between sleeping and waking, and have indistinct but glorious glimpses of strange shapes, and there is always something to come better than what we see. As in our dreams the fullness of the blood gives warmth and reality to the coinage of the brain, so in youth our ideas are clothed and fed and pampered with our good spirits; we breathe thick with thoughtless happiness, the weight of future years presses on the strong pulses of the heart, and we repose with undisturbed faith in truth and good. As we advance, we exhaust our fund of enjoyment and of hope. We are no longer wrapped in lamb's wool, lulled in Elysium. As we taste the pleasures of life, their spirit evaporates, the sense palls, and nothing is left but the phantoms, the lifeless shadows of what *has been*.

That morning, as soon as breakfast was over, we strolled out into the park and, seating ourselves on the trunk of an old ash-tree that stretched along the ground, Coleridge read aloud with a sonorous and musical voice the ballad of Betty Foy.[76] I was not critically or sceptically inclined. I saw touches of truth and nature, and took the rest for granted. But in 'The Thorn', 'The Mad Mother', and 'The Complaint of a Poor Indian Woman', I felt that deeper power and pathos which have been since

Notes

[71] Popular novel (1796) by Fanny Burney (1752–1840).

[72] *I saw it but the other day* Hazlitt visited John Hunt, the radical publisher, near Taunton in March 1820.

[73] Wordsworth paid £23 a year; see p. 612 above.

[74] *sibylline leaves* In Virgil's *Aeneid*, the Sibyl's prophecies are written on dry leaves scattered in confusion by the wind; the MS of *Lyrical Ballads* is also on scattered sheets of paper.

[75] Ben Jonson, 'To Sir Robert Wroth' 22.

[76] *the ballad of Betty Foy* 'The Idiot Boy', pp. 388–99.

acknowledged, 'In spite of pride, in erring reason's spite',[77] as the characteristics of this author; and the sense of a new style and a new spirit in poetry came over me. It had to me something of the effect that arises from the turning up of the fresh soil, or of the first welcome breath of spring 'While yet the trembling year is unconfirmed'.[78]

Coleridge and myself walked back to Stowey that evening, and his voice sounded high

> Of Providence, foreknowledge, will and fate,
> Fixed fate, free will, foreknowledge absolute,[79]

as we passed through echoing grove, by fairy stream or waterfall gleaming in the summer moonlight. He lamented that Wordsworth was not prone enough to belief in the traditional superstitions of the place, and that there was a something corporeal, a matter-of-factness, a clinging to the palpable, or often to the petty, in his poetry, in consequence. His genius was not a spirit that descended to him through the air; it sprung out of the ground like a flower, or unfolded itself from a green spray on which the goldfinch sang. He said, however (if I remember right), that this objection must be confined to his descriptive pieces, that his philosophic poetry had a grand and comprehensive spirit in it, so that his soul seemed to inhabit the universe like a palace, and to discover truth by intuition rather than by deduction.

The next day Wordsworth arrived from Bristol at Coleridge's cottage. I think I see him now. He answered in some degree to his friend's description of him, but was more gaunt and Don Quixote-like. He was quaintly dressed, according to the costume of that unconstrained period, in a brown fustian jacket and striped pantaloons.[80] There was something of a roll, a lounge in his gait, not unlike his own Peter Bell.[81]

There was a severe, worn pressure of thought about his temples; a fire in his eye, as if he saw something in objects more than the outward appearance; an intense, high, narrow forehead; a Roman nose; cheeks furrowed by strong purpose and feeling, and a convulsive inclination to laughter about the mouth, a good deal at variance with the solemn, stately expression of the rest of his face. Chantrey's bust[82] wants[83] the marking[84] traits, but he was teased into making it regular and heavy; Haydon's head of him, introduced into the 'Entrance of Christ into Jerusalem',[85] is the most like his drooping weight of thought and expression.

He sat down and talked very naturally and freely, with a mixture of clear gushing accents in his voice, a deep guttural intonation, and a strong tincture of the northern *burr*, like the crust on wine. He instantly began to make havoc of the half of a Cheshire cheese on the table, and said triumphantly that 'his marriage with experience had not been so unproductive as Mr Southey's in teaching him a knowledge of the good things of this life'. He had been to see *The Castle Spectre* by Monk Lewis,[86] while at Bristol,

Notes

[77] Pope, *An Essay on Man* i 293. Hazlitt is presumably thinking of Jeffrey's review of *The Excursion*, pp. 715–20 above.

[78] Thomson, *Spring* 18.

[79] *Paradise Lost* ii 559–60.

[80] *pantaloons* breeches.

[81] Wordsworth had completed a version of *Peter Bell* by this time, although the poem was published only in 1819.

[82] Sir Francis Leggatt Chantrey (1781–1841) exhibited his bust of Wordsworth at the Royal Academy in 1821.

[83] *wants* lacks.

[84] *marking* defining.

[85] Benjamin Robert Haydon (1786–1846), whose 'Christ's Triumphant Entry into Jerusalem' (now at Mount St Mary's Seminary, Norwood, Ohio) contains portraits of Wordsworth, Lamb, Keats and Hazlitt (among others). The pencil sketch of Wordsworth, made for the painting, which Hazlitt refers to here, is now at the Wordsworth Museum, Grasmere.

[86] Matthew Gregory Lewis (1775–1818), author of a popular Gothic novel, *The Monk* (1796), and play, *The Castle Spectre* (1798). Wordsworth attended a performance of the play at the Theatre Royal, Bristol, Monday 21 May 1798; he returned to Alfoxden the following day. Coleridge read and reviewed it for the *Critical Review* in February 1797.

and described it very well. He said 'it fitted the taste of the audience like a glove'. This *ad captandum*[87] merit was however by no means a recommendation of it according to the severe principles of the new school, which reject rather than court popular effect.

Wordsworth, looking out of the low, latticed window, said, 'How beautifully the sun sets on that yellow bank!' I thought within myself, 'With what eyes these poets see nature!' And ever after, when I saw the sunset stream upon the objects facing it, conceived I had made a discovery, or thanked Mr Wordsworth for having made one for me.

We went over to Alfoxden again the day following and Wordsworth read us the story of Peter Bell in the open air, and the comment made upon it by his face and voice was very different from that of some later critics. Whatever might be thought of the poem, 'his face was as a book where men might read strange matters',[88] and he announced the fate of his hero in prophetic tones. There is a *chaunt* in the recitation both of Coleridge and Wordsworth which acts as a spell upon the hearer, and disarms the judgement. Perhaps they have deceived themselves by making habitual use of this ambiguous accompaniment. Coleridge's manner is more full, animated, and varied; Wordsworth's more equable, sustained, and internal. The one might be termed more dramatic, the other more lyrical. Coleridge has told me that he himself liked to compose in walking over uneven ground, or breaking through the straggling branches of a copsewood, whereas Wordsworth always wrote (if he could) walking up and down a straight gravel-walk, or in some spot where the continuity of his verse met with no collateral[89] interruption.

Returning that same evening, I got into a metaphysical argument with Wordsworth while Coleridge was explaining the different notes of the nightingale to his sister, in which we neither of us succeeded in making ourselves perfectly clear and intelligible.[90] Thus I passed three weeks at Nether Stowey and in the neighbourhood generally devoting the afternoons to a delightful chat in an arbour made of bark by the poet's friend Tom Poole, sitting under two fine elm-trees, and listening to the bees humming round us while we quaffed our flip.[91] It was agreed, among other things, that we should make a jaunt down the Bristol Channel as far as Lynton.[92] We set off together on foot, Coleridge, John Chester[93] and I. This Chester was a native of Nether Stowey, one of those who were attracted to Coleridge's discourse as flies are to honey, or bees in swarming-time to the sound of a brass pan. He 'followed in the chase like a dog who hunts, not like one that made up the cry'.[94] He had on a brown cloth coat, boots, and corduroy breeches, was low in stature, bow-legged, had a drag in his walk like a drover, which he assisted by a hazel switch,[95] and kept on a sort of trot by the side of Coleridge, like a running footman by a state coach, that he might not lose a syllable or sound that fell from Coleridge's lips. He told me his private opinion that Coleridge was a wonderful man. He scarcely opened his lips, much less offered an opinion the whole way – yet, of the three, had I to choose during that journey, I would be John Chester. He afterwards followed Coleridge into Germany, where the Kantean philosophers were puzzled how to bring him under any of their categories. When he sat down at table with his idol, John's felicity was complete; Sir Walter Scott's, or Mr Blackwood's, when they sat down at the same table with the King, was not more so.[96]

Notes

[87] *ad captandum [vulgus]* [designed] to take the fancy of [the crowd].

[88] *Macbeth* I v 62–3.

[89] *collateral* accompanying.

[90] This argument seems to have inspired 'Expostulation and Reply' and 'The Tables Turned'.

[91] *flip* mixture of hot beer and spirits sweetened with sugar.

[92] *Lynton* village on the north coast of Devon.

[93] John Chester was a farmer who encouraged Coleridge in his quest for agricultural knowledge. They went to Germany together in 1798 so as to study agricultural techniques.

[94] *Othello* II iii 363–4.

[95] *switch* riding whip.

[96] William Blackwood (1776–1834), publisher, and Sir Walter Scott, were Tories; they banqueted with George IV in Edinburgh, 24 August 1822.

We passed Dunster on our right, a small town between the brow of a hill and the sea. I remember eyeing it wistfully as it lay below us; contrasted with the woody scene around, it looked as clear, as pure, as embrowned and ideal as any landscape I have seen since, of Gaspar Poussin's or Domenichino's.[97] We had a long day's march (our feet kept time to the echoes of Coleridge's tongue) through Minehead and by the Blue Anchor and on to Lynton, which we did not reach till near midnight, and where we had some difficulty in making a lodgement.[98] We however knocked the people of the house up at last, and we were repaid for our apprehensions and fatigue by some excellent rashers of fried bacon and eggs. The view in coming along had been splendid. We walked for miles and miles on dark brown heaths overlooking the Channel,[99] with the Welsh hills beyond, and at times descended into little sheltered valleys close by the seaside, with a smuggler's face scowling by us, and then had to ascend conical hills with a path winding up through a coppice to a barren top, like a monk's shaven crown, from one of which I pointed out to Coleridge's notice the bare masts of a vessel on the very edge of the horizon and within the red-orbed disk of the setting sun, like his own spectre-ship in 'The Ancient Mariner'.

At Lynton the character of the sea-coast becomes more marked and rugged. There is a place called the Valley of Rocks (I suspect this was only the poetical name for it) bedded among precipices overhanging the sea, with rocky caverns beneath, into which the waves dash, and where the seagull forever wheels its screaming flight. On the tops of these are huge stones thrown transverse, as if an earthquake had tossed them there, and behind these is a fretwork of perpendicular rocks, something like the Giant's Causeway.[100]

A thunderstorm came on while we were at the inn, and Coleridge was running out bareheaded to enjoy the commotion of the elements in the Valley of Rocks, but, as if in spite, the clouds only muttered a few angry sounds, and let fall a few refreshing drops. Coleridge told me that he and Wordsworth were to have made this place the scene of a prose tale which was to have been in the manner of, but far superior to, *The Death of Abel*,[101] but they had relinquished the design.

In the morning of the second day, we breakfasted luxuriously in an old-fashioned parlour on tea, toast, eggs, and honey, in the very sight of the beehives from which it had been taken, and a garden full of thyme and wild-flowers that had produced it. On this occasion Coleridge spoke of Virgil's *Georgics*, but not well. I do not think he had much feeling for the classical or elegant. It was in this room that we found a little worn-out copy of *The Seasons* lying in a window-seat, on which Coleridge exclaimed, '*That* is true fame!' He said Thomson was a great poet rather than a good one; his style was as meretricious as his thoughts were natural. He spoke of Cowper as the best modern poet. He said the *Lyrical Ballads* were an experiment about to be tried by him and Wordsworth, to see how far the public taste would endure poetry written in a more natural and simple style than had hitherto been attempted – totally discarding the artifices of poetical diction, and making use only of such words as had probably been common in the most ordinary language since the days of Henry II.[102]

Some comparison was introduced between Shakespeare and Milton. He said he hardly knew which to prefer. Shakespeare seemed to him a mere stripling in the art; he was as tall and as strong, with infinitely more activity, than Milton, but he never

Notes

[97] Gaspard Poussin (1615–75), landscape artist; Domenico Zampieri (1581–1641), Italian artist.

[98] *making a lodgement* i.e. finding an inn that could accommodate them.

[99] *the Channel* i.e. the Bristol Channel.

[100] *the Giant's Causeway* a beauty-spot on the west coast of Ireland.

[101] Salomon Gessner, *The Death of Abel* (1758).

[102] Henry II reigned 1154–89.

appeared to have come to man's estate – or if he had, he would not have been a man, but a monster. He spoke with contempt of Gray and with intolerance of Pope. He did not like the versification of the latter. He observed that 'the ears of these couplet-writers might be charged with having short memories, that could not retain the harmony of whole passages'. He thought little of Junius[103] as a writer, he had a dislike of Dr Johnson, and a much higher opinion of Burke as an orator and politician, than of Fox or Pitt.[104] He however thought him very inferior in richness of style and imagery to some of our elder prose writers, particularly Jeremy Taylor.[105] He liked Richardson but not Fielding, nor could I get him to enter into the merits of *Caleb Williams*.[106] In short, he was profound and discriminating with respect to those authors whom he liked, and where he gave his judgement fair play; capricious, perverse, and prejudiced in his antipathies and distastes.

We loitered on the 'ribbed sea-sands'[107] in such talk as this a whole morning, and I recollect met with a curious seaweed of which John Chester told us the country name. A fisherman gave Coleridge an account of a boy that had been drowned the day before, and that they had tried to save him at the risk of their own lives. He said he 'did not know how it was that they ventured, but, sir, we have a *nature* towards one another.' This expression, Coleridge remarked to me, was a fine illustration of that theory of disinterestedness which I (in common with Butler[108]) had adopted. I broached to him an argument of mine to prove that *likeness* was not mere association of ideas. I said that the mark in the sand put one in mind of a man's foot not because it was part of a former impression of a man's foot (for it was quite new), but because it was like the shape of a man's foot. He assented to the justness of this distinction (which I have explained at length elsewhere[109] for the benefit of the curious), and John Chester listened not from any interest in the subject, but because he was astonished that I should be able to suggest anything to Coleridge that he did not already know. We returned on the third morning, and Coleridge remarked the silent cottage-smoke curling up the valleys where, a few evenings before, we had seen the lights gleaming through the dark.

In a day or two after we arrived at Stowey, we set out, I on my return home and he for Germany. It was a Sunday morning and he was to preach that day for Dr Toulmin of Taunton. I asked him if he had prepared anything for the occasion. He said he had not even thought of the text, but should as soon as we parted. I did not go to hear him (this was a fault) but we met in the evening at Bridgwater. The next day we had a long day's walk to Bristol, and sat down, I recollect, by a well-side on the road, to cool ourselves and satisfy our thirst, when Coleridge repeated to me some descriptive lines from his tragedy of *Remorse*, which I must say became his mouth and that occasion better than they, some years after, did Mr Elliston's[110] and the Drury Lane boards:

> Oh memory, shield me from the world's poor strife
> And give those scenes thine everlasting life.[111]

Notes

[103] 'Junius' was the pseudonymous author of a series of letters published in the *Public Advertiser*, January 1769–January 1772, attacking Tory worthies.

[104] Charles James Fox (1749–1806), Whig statesman and orator; William Pitt (1759–1806), Prime Minister 1783–1801 and 1804–6.

[105] Jeremy Taylor (1613–67), prose stylist famous for *Holy Living* (1650) and *Holy Dying* (1651).

[106] Novel by Godwin (1794).

[107] *ribbed sea-sands* from 'The Ancient Mariner' (1798) 219.

[108] *Butler* see p. 787n40.

[109] *elsewhere* in his essay 'Remarks on the Systems of Hartley and Helvetius'.

[110] Robert William Elliston (1774–1831), famous actor who appeared in *Remorse* when first produced at Drury Lane theatre, 1813.

[111] The quotation is not to be found in *Remorse* or any other work by Coleridge.

I saw no more of him for a year or two, during which period he had been wandering in the Hartz Forest in Germany,[112] and his return was cometary, meteorous (unlike his setting-out). It was not till some time after that I knew his friends Lamb[113] and Southey. The last always appears to me as I first saw him, with a commonplace book under his arm;[114] and the first with a *bon mot* in his mouth. It was at Godwin's that I met him with Holcroft and Coleridge, where they were disputing fiercely which was the best – man as he was, or man as he is to be. 'Give me', says Lamb, 'man as he is *not* to be.' This saying was the beginning of a friendship between us which I believe still continues. Enough of this for the present.

> But there is matter for another rhyme,
> And I to this may add a second tale.[115]

Mr Coleridge

From The Spirit of the Age (1825)

The present is an age of talkers, and not of doers – and the reason is that the world is growing old. We are so far advanced in the arts and sciences, that we live in retrospect and dote on past achievements. The accumulation of knowledge has been so great that we are lost in wonder at the height it has reached, instead of attempting to climb or add to it; while the variety of objects distracts and dazzles the looker-on.

What niche remains unoccupied? What path untried? What is the use of doing anything unless we could do better than all those who have gone before us? What hope is there of this? We are like those who have been to see some noble monument of art, who are content to admire without thinking of rivalling it – or, like guests after a feast, who praise the hospitality of the donor 'and thank the bounteous Pan',[1] perhaps carrying away some trifling fragments – or, like the spectators of a mighty battle, who still hear its sound afar off, and the clashing of armour and the neighing of the warhorse and the shout of victory is in their ears, like the rushing of innumerable waters!

Mr. Coleridge has 'a mind reflecting ages past'.[2] His voice is like the echo of the congregated roar of the 'dark rearward and abyss'[3] of thought. He who has seen a mouldering tower by the side of a crystal lake, hid by the mist but glittering in the wave below, may conceive the dim, gleaming, uncertain intelligence of his eye; he who has marked the evening clouds uprolled (a world of vapours) has seen the picture of his mind – unearthly, unsubstantial, with gorgeous tints and ever-varying forms:

> That which was now a horse, even with a thought
> The rack dislimns, and makes it indistinct
> As water is in water.[4]

Notes

[112] *during which . . . Germany* Coleridge was in Germany from September 1798 to July 1799.

[113] Hazlitt was introduced to Lamb by Coleridge in 1804; in that year Hazlitt painted Lamb's portrait, now in the National Portrait Gallery.

[114] Hazlitt's first serious acquaintance with Southey was in the Lakes, September–November 1803.

[115] Wordsworth, *Hart-Leap Well* 95–6. Hazlitt wrote no sequel to this essay.

From The Spirit of the Age

[1] Milton, *Comus* 175. Pan, god of woods and shepherds, was the subject of festivals in ancient Rome.

[2] *a mind reflecting ages past* I.M.S., 'On Worthy Master Shakespeare and his Poems' 1, prefixed to the second Folio (1632).

[3] *dark rearward and abyss* from *The Tempest* I ii 50.

[4] *Antony and Cleopatra* IV xiv 9–11.

Our author's mind is (as he himself might express it) *tangential*. There is no subject on which he has not touched, none on which he has rested. With an understanding fertile, subtle, expansive, 'quick, forgetive,[5] apprehensive'[6] beyond all living precedent, few traces of it will perhaps remain. He lends himself to all impressions alike; he gives up his mind and liberty of thought to none. He is a general lover of art and science, and wedded to no one in particular. He pursues knowledge as a mistress, with outstretched hands and winged speed, but as he is about to embrace her, his Daphne turns – alas, not to a laurel![7] Hardly a speculation has been left on record from the earliest time, but it is loosely folded up in Mr Coleridge's memory, like a rich but somewhat tattered piece of tapestry. We might add (with more seeming than real extravagance) that scarce a thought can pass through the mind of man, but its sound has at some time or other passed over his head with rustling pinions.

On whatever question or author you speak, he is prepared to take up the theme with advantage – from Peter Abelard[8] down to Thomas Moore,[9] from the subtlest metaphysics to the politics of *The Courier*.[10] There is no man of genius in whose praise he descants,[11] but the critic seems to stand above the author, and 'what in him is weak, to strengthen; what is low, to raise and support'.[12] Nor is there any work of genius that does not come out of his hands like an illuminated missal,[13] sparkling even in its defects.

If Mr Coleridge had not been the most impressive talker of his age, he would probably have been the finest writer – but he lays down his pen to make sure of an auditor, and mortgages the admiration of posterity for the stare of an idler. If he had not been a poet, he would have been a powerful logician; if he had not dipped his wing in the Unitarian controversy, he might have soared to the very summit of fancy. But in writing verse, he is trying to subject the muse to *transcendental* theories; in his abstract reasoning, he misses his way by strewing it with flowers. All that he has done of moment, he had done twenty years ago; since then he may be said to have lived on the sounds of his own voice. Mr Coleridge is too rich in intellectual wealth to need to task himself to any drudgery – he has only to draw the sliders[14] of his imagination, and a thousand subjects expand before him, startling him with their brilliancy, or losing themselves in endless obscurity,

> And by the force of blear illusion,[15]
> They draw him on to his confusion.[16]

What is the little he could add to the stock, compared with the countless stores that lie about him, that he should stoop to pick up a name, or to polish an idle fancy? He walks abroad in the majesty of an universal understanding, eyeing the 'rich strond',[17]

Notes

[5] *forgetive* inventive.

[6] *quick, forgetive, apprehensive* from *2 Henry IV* IV iii 99.

[7] In Greek myth, Daphne was pursued by Apollo; on the point of capture, she was turned by the gods into a laurel tree.

[8] Pierre Abelard (1079–1142), medieval French theologian.

[9] *Thomas Moore* poet.

[10] *The Courier* was an evening paper to which Coleridge contributed; Hazlitt resented Coleridge's involvement with it because of its Tory sympathies.

[11] *descants* discourses.

[12] *Paradise Lost* i 22–3.

[13] *illuminated missal* book containing Roman Catholic liturgy, with hand-painted illustrations and decorations.

[14] *sliders* a figurative usage; drawn apart (like curtains), the sliders enable the imagination to take flight.

[15] *blear illusion* Milton, *Comus* 155.

[16] *Macbeth* III v 28–9.

[17] *rich strond* Spenser, *Faerie Queene* III iv st.34 2

or golden sky above him, and 'goes sounding on his way',[18] in eloquent accents, uncompelled and free!

Persons of the greatest capacity are often those who, for this reason, do the least – for, surveying themselves from the highest point of view amidst the infinite variety of the universe, their own share in it seems trifling and scarce worth a thought, and they prefer the contemplation of all that is, or has been, or can be, to the making a coil[19] about doing what (when done) is no better than vanity. It is hard to concentrate all our attention and efforts on one pursuit, except from ignorance of others, and, without this concentration of our faculties, no great progress can be made in any one thing. It is not merely that the mind is not capable of the effort; it does not think the effort worth making. Action is one, but thought is manifold. He whose restless eye glances through the wide compass of nature and art will not consent to have 'his own nothings monstered',[20] but he must do this before he can give his whole soul to them. The mind, after 'letting contemplation have its fill',[21] or

Sailing with supreme dominion
Through the azure deep of air,[22]

sinks down on the ground, breathless, exhausted, powerless, inactive, or, if it must have some vent to its feelings, seeks the most easy and obvious – is soothed by friendly flattery, lulled by the murmur of immediate applause, thinks as it were aloud, and babbles in its dreams! A scholar (so to speak) is a more disinterested and abstracted character than a mere author: the first looks at the numberless volumes of a library, and says, 'All these are mine'; the other points to a single volume (perhaps it may be an immortal one) and says, 'My name is written on the back of it'. This is a puny and grovelling ambition beneath the lofty amplitude of Mr Coleridge's mind. No, he revolves in his wayward soul, or utters to the passing wind, or discourses to his own shadow things mightier and more various! Let us draw the curtain and unlock the shrine.

Learning rocked him in his cradle, and, while yet a child, 'He lisped in numbers, for the numbers came'.[23] At sixteen he wrote his 'Ode on Chatterton',[24] and he still reverts to that period with delight, not so much as it relates to himself (for that string of his own early promise of fame rather jars than otherwise), but as exemplifying the youth of a poet. Mr Coleridge talks of himself without being an egotist, for in him the individual is always merged in the abstract and general. He distinguished himself at school and at the University[25] by his knowledge of the classics, and gained several prizes for Greek epigrams.[26] (How many men are there – great scholars, celebrated names in literature – who, having done the same thing in their youth, have no other idea all the rest of their lives but of this achievement, of a fellowship and dinner, and who, installed in academic honours, would look down on our author as a mere strolling bard!) At Christ's Hospital where he was brought up, he was the idol of those among his schoolfellows who mingled with their bookish studies the music of thought and of humanity, and he was

Notes

18 *goes sounding on his way* In the General Prologue to *The Canterbury Tales*, the Merchant is described as 'Sownynge alwey th' encrees of his wynnyng' (l.275), and of the Clerk Chaucer writes: 'Sownynge in moral vertu was his speche' (l. 307). Hazlitt may also be recalling Wordsworth, *Excursion* iii 701 ('Went sounding on a dim and perilous way'), to which Coleridge alludes at the end of *Biographia Literaria* chapter 5.

19 *coil* fuss.

20 *Coriolanus* II ii 77. *monstered* put on show.

21 John Dyer, *Grongar Hill* (1761) 26.

22 Gray, *The Progress of Poesy* 116–17.

23 Pope, *Epistle to Dr Arbuthnot* 128: 'I lisp'd in numbers, for the numbers came.'

24 Coleridge's *Monody on the Death of Chatterton* seems to date from 1790, when he was still at Christ's Hospital.

25 Coleridge attended Jesus College, Cambridge, 1791–4.

26 In June 1792 Coleridge was awarded the Browne Medal for Greek verse at Cambridge.

usually attended round the cloisters by a group of these (inspiring and inspired) whose hearts, even then, burnt within them as he talked, and where the sounds yet linger to mock Elia[27] on his way, still turning pensive to the past![28]

One of the finest and rarest parts of Mr Coleridge's conversation is when he expatiates[29] on the Greek tragedians (not that he is not well-acquainted, when he pleases, with the epic poets, or the philosophers, or orators, or historians of antiquity) – on the subtle reasonings and melting pathos of Euripides; on the harmonious gracefulness of Sophocles, tuning his love-laboured song like sweetest warblings from a sacred grove; on the high-wrought trumpet-tongued eloquence of Aeschylus, whose Prometheus, above all, is like an Ode to Fate and a pleading with Providence, his thoughts being let loose as his body is chained on his solitary rock,[30] and his afflicted will (the emblem of mortality) 'Struggling in vain with ruthless destiny'.[31] As the impassioned critic speaks and rises in his theme, you would think you heard the voice of the man hated by the gods contending with the wild winds as they roar, and his eye glitters with the spirit of antiquity!

Next he was engaged with Hartley's tribes of mind, 'ethereal braid, thought-woven',[32] and he busied himself for a year or two with vibrations and vibratiuncles and the great law of association that binds all things in its mystic chain, and the doctrine of necessity (the mild teacher of charity) and the millennium, anticipative of a life to come;[33] and he plunged deep into the controversy on matter and spirit, and, as an escape from Dr Priestley's materialism[34] (where he felt himself imprisoned by the logician's spell like Ariel in the cloven pine-tree),[35] he became suddenly enamoured of Bishop Berkeley's fairy-world,[36] and used in all companies to build the universe (like a brave poetical fiction) of fine words; and he was deep-read in Malebranche,[37] and in Cudworth's *Intellectual System*[38] (a huge pile of learning – unwieldy, enormous), and in Lord Brook's hieroglyphic theories,[39] and in Bishop Butler's *Sermons*,[40] and in the Duchess of Newcastle's fantastic folios,[41] and in Clarke and South and Tillotson,[42] and all the fine thinkers and masculine reasoners of that age – and Leibniz's *Pre-established Harmony*[43] reared its arch above his head, like the rainbow in the cloud, covenanting with the hopes of man; and then he fell plump ten thousand fathoms down (but his wings saved him harmless) into the *hortus siccus* of Dissent,[44] where he pared religion down to the standard of reason and stripped faith of mystery, and preached Christ

Notes

27 *Elia* Charles Lamb's pen-name (see p. 738).

28 Hazlitt refers to Lamb's essay, 'Christ's Hospital Five and Thirty Years Ago'.

29 *expatiates* discourses at length.

30 *chained on his solitary rock* Jupiter nailed Prometheus to a rock (the Caucasus) for 30,000 years, with an eagle incessantly devouring his liver.

31 Wordsworth, *The Excursion* vi 557.

32 Collins, *Ode to Evening* 7. In *Ode on the Poetical Character* 47, Collins refers to 'the shad'wy tribes of mind'.

33 *vibrations . . . life to come* features of Hartleian philosophy; see p. 459n86.

34 Joseph Priestley, *Disquisitions Relating to Matter and Spirit* (1777). Coleridge was for a long time a disciple of Priestleyan Unitarianism.

35 *The Tempest* I ii 277–9.

36 *Bishop Berkeley's fairy-world* George Berkeley (1685–1753), Bishop of Cloyne, argued that the material world was no more than an idea in the mind of God.

37 Nicolas Malebranche (1638–1715), *De la recherche de la vérité* (1674).

38 Ralph Cudworth (1617–88), *True Intellectual System of the Universe* (1678).

39 Robert Greville, second Baron Brooke (1608–43), *The Nature of Truth, its Union and Unity with the Soul* (1640).

40 Joseph Butler, Bishop of Bristol (1692–1752), whose *Fifteen Sermons* (1726) preached at the Rolls Chapel defines his moral philosophy.

41 Margaret Cavendish, Duchess of Newcastle (1624–74) published plays, essays and poetry in large folio volumes.

42 Samuel Clarke (1657–1729), metaphysician; Robert South (1634–1716), divine and sermonist; John Tillotson (1630–94), Archbishop of Canterbury and renowned Anglican sermonist.

43 Gottfried Wilhelm Leibniz (1646–1716) assumed a 'pre-established harmony' to exist between matter and spirit; see his *Monadology* (1714).

44 *the hortus siccus of dissent* A *hortus siccus* is a collection of dried plants. The phrase comes from Burke, *Reflections on the Revolution in France* (1790), p. 15.

crucified and the Unity of the Godhead, and so dwelt for a while in the spirit with John Huss and Jerome of Prague and Socinus and old John Zisca,[45] and ran through Neal's *History of the Puritans*, and Calamy's *Non-Conformists' Memorial*[46] (having like thoughts and passions with them); but then Spinoza[47] became his god and he took up the vast chain of being in his hand, and the round world became the centre and the soul of all things in some shadowy sense forlorn of meaning, and around him he beheld the living traces and the sky-pointing proportions of the mighty Pan; but poetry redeemed him from this spectral philosophy,[48] and he bathed his heart in beauty, and gazed at the golden light of heaven, and drank of the spirit of the universe, and wandered at eve by fairy-stream or fountain,

When he saw nought but beauty,
When he heard the voice of that Almighty One
In every breeze that blew, or wave that murmured,[49]

and wedded with truth in Plato's shade, and in the writings of Proclus and Plotinus[50] saw the ideas of things in the eternal mind, and unfolded all mysteries with the schoolmen,[51] and fathomed the depths of Duns Scotus and Thomas Aquinas, and entered the third heaven with Jacob Behmen, and walked hand in hand with Swedenborg[52] through the pavilions of the New Jerusalem, and sung his faith in the promise and in the word in his *Religious Musings*[53] – and lowering himself from that dizzy height, poised himself on Milton's wings, and spread out his thoughts in charity with the glad prose of Jeremy Taylor,[54] and wept over Bowles' sonnets,[55] and studied Cowper's blank verse,[56] and betook himself to Thomson's *Castle of Indolence*,[57] and sported with the wits of Charles the Second's days[58] and of Queen Anne,[59] and relished Swift's style and that of the *John Bull* (Arbuthnot's we mean – not Mr Croker's[60]), and dallied with the *British Essayists* and *Novelists*,[61] and knew all qualities of more modern writers with a learned spirit, Johnson and Goldsmith and Junius[62] and Burke and Godwin, and the *Sorrows of Werter*,[63] and Jean Jacques Rousseau and Voltaire and Marivaux and Crebillon,[64] and thousands more; now 'laughed with Rabelais in his easy chair'[65] or pointed to Hogarth,

Notes

45 John Huss (1369–1415), Bohemian theologian; Jerome of Prague (d. 1416), colleague of Huss; Socinus was the Latinized name of two Italian theologians, Fausto Paolo Sozzini (1539–1604) and Lelio Sozzini (1525–62); John Zisca (d. 1424), Czech soldier and religious leader.

46 Daniel Neal, *History of the Puritans* (1732–8); Edmund Calamy, *Non-Conformists' Memorial* (abridged 1775).

47 Benedict Spinoza (1632–77), Dutch philosopher.

48 *spectral philosophy* i.e. unreal philosophy.

49 Coleridge, *Remorse* IV ii 100–2.

50 Proclus (410–85) and Plotinus (204–70), Platonist philosophers.

51 *schoolmen* medieval scholars and theologians.

52 Duns Scotus (1265–1308), Scottish medieval philosopher; Thomas Aquinas (1227–74), medieval philosopher; Jacob Behmen (1575–1624), German mystic; Emanuel Swedenborg (1688–1772), Swedish mystic (for whom see p. 171).

53 Poem by Coleridge, 1794–6; see pp. 608–10.

54 Jeremy Taylor (1613–67), prose stylist famous for *Holy Living* (1650) and *Holy Dying* (1651).

55 *Bowles' sonnets* popular since being published in 1789.

56 *Cowper's blank verse* probably *The Task*; see pp. 18–21.

57 James Thomson, *The Castle of Indolence* (1748), popular poem in Spenserian stanzas.

58 Charles II reigned 1660–85.

59 Queen Anne reigned 1702–14.

60 *The History of John Bull*, collection of pamphlets by John Arbuthnot (1667–1735), issued 1712. *John Bull* was also the name of a Tory newspaper which began publishing on 17 December 1820, but there is no evidence that John Wilson Croker (1780–1857), Tory politician and man of letters, was involved in its production.

61 *British Essayists* (1817), issued in 45 volumes; *British Novelists* ed. Mrs. Barbauld (1810).

62 'Junius' was the pseudonymous author of a series of letters published in the *Public Advertiser*, January 1769–January 1772, attacking Tory worthies.

63 Novel by Goethe (1774).

64 Jean-Jacques Rousseau (1712–78), French novelist and philosopher; François-Marie Arouet (1694–1778) wrote under the pseudonym of Voltaire; Pierre Carlet de Chamblain de Marivaux (1688–1763), French novelist; Crébillon the elder (1674–1762), dramatist.

65 Pope, *Dunciad* i 20.

or afterwards dwelt on Claude's classic scenes or spoke with rapture of Raphael,[66] and compared the women at Rome[67] to figures that had walked out of his pictures, or visited the Oratory of Pisa,[68] and described the works of Giotto and Ghirlandaio and Massaccio, and gave the moral of the picture of the Triumph of Death[69] (where the beggars and the wretched invoke his dreadful dart but the rich and mighty of the earth quail and shrink before it); and in that land of siren sights and sounds saw a dance of peasant girls, and was charmed with lutes and gondolas; or wandered into Germany and lost himself in the labyrinths of the Hartz Forest[70] and of the Kantean philosophy, and amongst the cabalistic[71] names of Fichte and Schelling and Lessing[72] and God knows who – this was long after, but all the former while he had nerved his heart and filled his eyes with tears, as he hailed the rising orb of liberty (since quenched in darkness and in blood), and had kindled his affections at the blaze of the French Revolution, and sang for joy[73] when the towers of the Bastille and the proud places of the insolent and the oppressor fell,[74] and would have floated his bark, freighted with fondest fancies, across the Atlantic wave with Southey and others[75] to seek for peace and freedom, 'In Philarmonia's[76] undivided dale!'[77]

Alas! 'Frailty, thy name is *Genius*!'[78] What is become of all this mighty heap of hope, of thought, of learning, and humanity? It has ended in swallowing doses of oblivion[79] and in writing paragraphs in the *Courier*. Such, and so little, is the mind of man!

It was not to be supposed that Mr Coleridge could keep on at the rate he set off; he could not realize all he knew or thought, and less could not fix his desultory ambition. Other stimulants supplied the place, and kept up the intoxicating dream, the fever and the madness of his early impressions. Liberty (the philosopher's and the poet's bride) had fallen a victim, meanwhile, to the murderous practices of the hag Legitimacy. Proscribed by court-hirelings, too romantic for the herd of vulgar politicians, our enthusiast stood at bay, and at last turned on the pivot of a subtle casuistry to the *unclean side* – but his discursive reason would not let him trammel himself into a Poet Laureate or stamp-distributor,[80] and he stopped, ere he had quite passed that well-known 'bourne from whence no traveller returns',[81] and so has sunk into torpid, uneasy repose, tantalized by useless resources, haunted by vain imaginings, his lips idly moving but his heart forever still, or, as the shattered chords vibrate of themselves, making melancholy music to the ear of memory!

Such is the fate of genius in an age when, in the unequal contest with sovereign wrong, every man is ground to powder who is not either a born slave, or who does not willingly and at once offer up the yearnings of humanity and the dictates of reason as a welcome sacrifice to besotted prejudice and loathsome power.

Notes

66 Coleridge saw priceless sketches by Raphael at Helmstedt, 3 July 1799, and his mature works at Rome in 1806.

67 Coleridge was at Rome, January–May 1806.

68 Coleridge travelled to Pisa from Rome, June 1806.

69 *the picture . . . Death* 'The Triumph of Death', is the fresco cycle in the Campo Santo in Pisa, which Coleridge visited in June 1806.

70 *wandered into Germany . . . Forest* Coleridge visited Germany, 1798–9.

71 *cabalistic* esoteric, abstruse.

72 Johann Gottlieb Fichte (1762–1814), Friedrich Wilhelm von Schelling (1775–1854), and Gotthold Ephraim Lessing (1729–81), German philosophers.

73 *sang for joy* a reference to Coleridge's 1789 poem, *Destruction of the Bastile*, first published 1834.

74 *when the towers . . . fell* the Bastille prison, symbol of the tyranny of the *ancien regime*, was stormed by the Paris mob on 14 July 1789, and quickly demolished.

75 *across the Atlantic . . . others* a reference to pantisocracy; see p. 593.

76 *Philarmonia* love of order.

77 Coleridge's 'Monody on the Death of Chatterton' (1796) 129.

78 Compare *Hamlet* I ii 146.

79 *swallowing . . . oblivion* a reference to Coleridge's opium addiction.

80 Hazlitt swipes at Southey, who became Poet Laureate in 1813, and Wordsworth, Distributor of Stamps for Westmorland, 1813–42.

81 *Hamlet* III i 78–9.

Of all Mr Coleridge's productions, *The Ancient Mariner* is the only one that we could with confidence put into any person's hands, on whom we wished to impress a favourable idea of his extraordinary powers. Let whatever other objections be made to it, it is unquestionably a work of genius – of wild, irregular, overwhelming imagination, and has that rich, varied movement in the verse which gives a distant idea of the lofty or changeful tones of Mr Coleridge's voice. In the *Christabel*, there is one splendid passage on divided friendship. The translation of Schiller's *Wallenstein*[82] is also a masterly production in its kind, faithful and spirited. Among his smaller pieces there are occasional bursts of pathos and fancy equal to what we might expect from him, but these form the exception and not the rule; such, for instance, is his affecting sonnet to the author of *The Robbers*:[83]

Schiller! that hour I would have wished to die,
 If through the shudd'ring midnight I had sent
 From the dark dungeon of the tower time-rent
That fearful voice, a famished father's cry,
That in no after-moment aught less vast
 Might stamp me mortal! A triumphant shout
 Black horror screamed, and all her goblin rout
From the more with'ring scene diminished passed.
Ah, bard tremendous in sublimity!
 Could I behold thee in thy loftier mood,
Wand'ring at eve, with finely frenzied eye,
 Beneath some vast old tempest-swinging wood –
 Awhile, with mute awe gazing, I would brood,
Then weep aloud in a wild ecstasy.

His tragedy entitled *Remorse*[84] is full of beautiful and striking passages, but it does not place the author in the first rank of dramatic writers. But if Mr Coleridge's works do not place him in that rank, they injure instead of conveying a just idea of the man, for he himself is certainly in the first class of general intellect.

If our author's poetry is inferior to his conversation, his prose is utterly abortive. Hardly a gleam is to be found in it of the brilliancy and richness of those stores of thought and language that he pours out incessantly, when they are lost like drops of water in the ground. The principal work in which he has attempted to embody his general views of things is *The Friend*,[85] of which, though it contains some noble passages and fine trains of thought, prolixity and obscurity are the most frequent characteristics.

No two persons can be conceived more opposite in character or genius than the subject of the present and of the preceding sketch. Mr Godwin, with less natural capacity and with fewer acquired advantages, by concentrating his mind on some given object and doing what he had to do with all his might, has accomplished much and will leave more than one monument of a powerful intellect behind him; Mr Coleridge, by dissipating his and dallying with every subject by turns, has done little or nothing to justify to the world or to posterity the high opinion which all who have ever heard him converse, or known him intimately, with one accord entertain of him.

Notes

[82] Coleridge translated Johann Christoph Friedrich von Schiller (1759–1805), *The Piccolomini, or the first part of Wallenstein* and *The Death of Wallenstein*, and published them both in 1800.

[83] *The Robbers* another play by Schiller.

[84] Produced at Drury Lane theatre, 23 January 1813.

[85] Weekly periodical edited by Coleridge, 1808–10.

Mr Godwin's faculties have kept house and plied their task in the workshop of the brain, diligently and effectually; Mr Coleridge's have gossipped away their time and gadded about from house to house, as if life's business were[86] to melt the hours in listless talk. Mr Godwin is intent on a subject only as it concerns himself and his reputation; he works it out as a matter of duty, and discards from his mind whatever does not forward his main object as impertinent and vain. Mr Coleridge, on the other hand, delights in nothing but episodes and digressions, neglects whatever he undertakes to perform, and can act only on spontaneous impulses, without object or method: 'He cannot be constrained by mastery.'[87] While he should be occupied with a given pursuit, he is thinking of a thousand other things; a thousand tastes, a thousand objects tempt him and distract his mind, which keeps open house and entertains all comers and, after being fatigued and amused with morning calls from idle visitors, finds the day consumed and its business unconcluded. Mr Godwin, on the contrary, is somewhat exclusive and unsocial in his habits of mind, entertains no company but what he gives his whole time and attention to, and wisely writes over the doors of his understanding, his fancy, and his senses, 'No admittance except on business'. He has none of that fastidious refinement and false delicacy which might lead him to balance between the endless variety of modern attainments. He does not throw away his life (nor a single half-hour of it) in adjusting the claims of different accomplishments, and in choosing between them or making himself master of them all. He sets about his task, whatever it may be, and goes through it with spirit and fortitude. He has the happiness to think an author the greatest character in the world, and himself the greatest author in it. Mr Coleridge, in writing an harmonious stanza, would stop to consider whether there was not more grace and beauty in a *pas de trois*,[88] and would not proceed till he had resolved this question by a chain of metaphysical reasoning without end. Not so Mr Godwin. That is best to him which he can do best. He does not waste himself in vain aspirations and effeminate sympathies. He is blind, deaf, insensible to all but the trump of fame. Plays, operas, painting, music, ballrooms, wealth, fashion, titles, lords, ladies, touch him not: all these are no more to him than to the anchorite in his cell, and he writes on to the end of the chapter through good report and evil report. *Pingo in eternitatem*[89] is his motto. He neither envies nor admires what others are, but is contented to be what he is, and strives to do the utmost he can. Mr Coleridge has flirted with the muses as with a set of mistresses; Mr Godwin has been married twice – to Reason and to Fancy – and has to boast no short-lived progeny by each. So to speak, he has *valves* belonging to his mind to regulate the quantity of gas admitted into it, so that, like the bare, unsightly, but well-compacted steam-vessel, it cuts its liquid way, and arrives at its promised end; while Mr Coleridge's bark, 'taught with the little nautilus to sail',[90] the sport of every breath, dancing to every wave, 'Youth at its prow, and Pleasure at its helm',[91] flutters its gaudy pennons in the air, glitters in the sun, but we wait in vain to hear of its arrival in the destined harbour. Mr Godwin, with less variety and vividness, with less subtlety and susceptibility both of thought and feeling, has had firmer nerves, a more determined purpose, a more comprehensive grasp of his subject, and the results are as we find them. Each has met with his reward – for justice has, after all, been done to the pretensions of each, and we must in all cases use means to ends!

Notes

[86] *as if life's business were* an echo of Wordsworth 'Resolution and Independence' 37: 'As if life's business were a summer mood'.

[87] Chaucer, *The Franklin's Tale* 764: 'Love wol nat been constreyned by maistrye.'

[88] *pas de trois* dance for three people.

[89] 'I delineate for all time.'

[90] Pope, *Essay on Man* iii 177.

[91] Gray, *The Bard* 74.

James Henry Leigh Hunt (1784–1859)

Leigh Hunt was born on 19 October 1784 to Isaac and Mary Hunt, American Loyalists whose allegiance to George III led them to move to England shortly before their son's birth. He was educated as a charity boy at Christ's Hospital (1791–9) where he emerged as a precocious poet, publishing his youthful verse as *Juvenilia* in 1801. In 1808, with his brother John (1775–1848), he set up *The Examiner* – a reforming weekly newspaper that gained immediate popularity. Also, from 1810 to 1811 he edited *The Reflector*, which contained some of Lamb's early writings.

Hunt enjoyed his role of thorn in the government's side. There was much to criticize. A seemingly endless war against Napoleon was draining the country's resources – human and economic – and from 1811 it was waged by a government led by the Prince Regent, who was a byword for gluttony, indolence and self-indulgence. (His factotum, Sir William Knighton, called him 'The Great Beast'.) In his leading article in *The Examiner* for 22 March 1812, entitled 'The Prince on St Patrick's Day', Hunt began: 'The Prince Regent is still in everybody's mouth, and unless he is as insensible to biting as to bantering, a delicious time he has of it in that remorseless ubiquity!' Such *double entendres* were bad enough, but what really upset the Regent was the observation that:

> this *Exciter of Desire* . . . this *Adonis in Loveliness*, was a corpulent gentleman of fifty! In short, that this *delightful, blissful, wise, pleasurable, honourable, virtuous, true, and immortal* PRINCE was a violater of his word, a libertine over head and ears in debt and disgrace, a despiser of domestic ties, the companion of gamblers and demireps, a man who has just closed half a century without one single claim on the gratitude of his country or the respect of posterity!

Not surprisingly, the Regent did not take kindly to this, and the Hunts were successfully prosecuted for libel, fined £500 each (£16,500 / US$31,000 today), and imprisoned for two years. This made them martyrs to a cause widely regarded as just, and despite an uneasy start to Hunt's prison term, the governor of the Surrey Gaol soon realized that he had to make life comfortable for his new inmate. Hunt's family was allowed to move in; he wrote and edited *The Examiner* from his cell, and was permitted to receive visitors until 10 o'clock at night. Rose-trellised wallpaper adorned his cell walls along with a pianoforte, a lute, busts of the great poets and bookcases filled with the works of Chaucer, Spenser, Milton and Dryden. Charles Lamb declared that 'there was no other such room except in a fairy tale.' Besides Lamb and hissister, visitors included Byron, Hazlitt and Haydon.

After release in February 1815 Hunt moved to the Vale of Health, Hampstead, where in 1816 he completed *The Story of Rimini*, dedicated to Byron (who had given advice during composition), now regarded as the most ambitious of his poems. Its story is taken from Dante's *Inferno*. Engaged to be married to Lanciotto da Rimini against her will, Francesca falls in love with his younger brother, Paulo. When their adultery is discovered they are murdered. Hunt's reworking of the tale enjoyed considerable success, especially among his friends. 'I have read, and reread your exquisite pathetic tale,' Haydon told him, 'till my soul is cut in two – and every nerve about me pierced with trembling needles . . . it is the sweetest thing of the time.'

Hunt's notoriety as a freethinker was bound to generate controversy, and criticism of *Rimini* began in earnest with publication of the essays 'On the Cockney School of Poetry' by John Gibson Lockhart in *Blackwood's Edinburgh Magazine*. Lockhart styled Hunt the 'chief Doctor and

Figure 13 Leigh Hunt (1784–1859) striking a raffish pose during the 1830s, as portrayed by Daniel Maclise.

Professor' of the Cockney School (so-called after those born within the sound of Bow Bells in the City of London), which he defined by its irreligion (Hunt was an atheist), 'sour Jacobinism' and 'extreme moral depravity'. On this last matter, Lockhart was particularly scathing: alluding to Francesca in *Rimini*, he observed that, as far as Hunt was concerned, 'Every woman is useful only as a breeding machine, unless she is fond of reading Launcelot of the Lake, in an antique summer-house.'[1] Lockhart's attacks were spread across a number of essays written between 1817 and 1819, and alongside Hunt he would include Shelley, Byron, Hazlitt and Keats as fellow Cockneys (all of whom contributed to *The Examiner*).[2]

One of Hunt's chief tenets was that poetry was the vehicle of pleasure, and to that end he devised the concept of 'luxuries' – lush, verbally rich formulations equated with feelings of physical delight. This, as much as the subject-matter of the poem, led Lockhart to accuse him of indecency and vulgarity. The extract from Canto III of the poem, presented here, was one of those which most upset him. It begins with a description of Francesca's summerhouse, continues with a vivid catalogue of Huntian luxuries, and culminates with a summary of 'Launcelot of the Lake, a bright romance', whichshe is reading, followed by her first kiss with Paulo. Lockhart was incensed:

> The scene is in a little antique temple adorned by sculpture, and had Mr Hunt filled his friezes with funeral processions, or with the agonies of Orestes, or the despair of Oedipus, we might indeed have acknowledged that there was some propriety in his fancy. But as he has made of his temple a bagnio, so is its furniture conceived in the very spirit of the place.[3]

Lockhart then quoted lines 470–85 of the passage to illustrate his point (see p. 798 below), concluding 'that we think that poet deserving of chastisement, who prostitutes his talents in a manner that is likely to corrupt milliners and apprentice-boys, no less than him who flies at noble game, and spreads his corruption among princes'.[4] Hazlitt, by contrast, in *The Spirit of the Age* (1825), remarked that 'We will venture to oppose his Third Canto of the *Story of Rimini* for classic elegance and natural feeling to any equal number of lines from Mr Southey's Epics or from Mr Moore's Lalla Rookh' (Wu vii 228).

When Keats met Hunt in October 1816 he realized he had found a mentor when he most needed one. Hunt provided constructive criticism of his verse, and even kept a bed for him at his house in Hampstead, where Keats composed 'Sleep and Poetry'. But Keats was as aware as anyone of Hunt's vanity: 'There is no greater sin after the seven deadly than to flatter oneself into an idea of being a great poet,' he wrote, after a visit to Hampstead (Rollins i 143). And by October 1817 he had come to regard Hunt's revisions to *Endymion* as 'corrections and amputations' which would give him the 'reputation of Hunt's élève' (Rollins i 170). He was right: when Lockhart published the fourth of his articles on the Cockney School in 1818, his principal target was Keats. Their respective abilities as poets can be gauged by a comparison of their sonnets on the grasshopper and the cricket, products of a competition in December 1816 umpired by their mutual friend,

Notes

[1] J. G. Lockhart, 'On the Cockney School of Poetry. No. I', *Blackwood's Edinburgh Magazine* 2 (October 1817) 38–41, p. 40. It is worth noting that even in the Keats circle there were those who, like Richard Woodhouse, regretted Hunt's 'indecent discoursings' (*The Keats Circle* ed. H. E. Rollins (2 vols, Cambridge, Mass., 1948), i 156).

[2] For one of Lockhart's Cockney School attacks, see pp. 1327–31 below. For a more detailed examination of the aesthetics of Leigh Hunt, see my 'Keats and the "Cockney School"', in *The Cambridge Companion to Keats* ed. Susan Wolfson (Cambridge, 2001), pp. 37–52.

[3] J. G. Lockhart, 'On the Cockney School of Poets. No. II', *Blackwood's Edinburgh Magazine* 2 (November 1817) 194–201, p. 199.

[4] Ibid., p. 201.

Charles Cowden Clarke. The poems appeared side by side in *The Examiner*, 21 September 1817; Keats's is on p. 1344 of this volume.

Foliage was published in 1818, and is one of Hunt's most important collections of poetry. It contains a cluster of sonnets addressed to other members of the Cockney School, including Shelley and Keats (see p. 1332).[5] Now resident in leafy Hampstead (which at that time was in the countryside, though near London), the Hunt of *Foliage* is a bucolic writer in the Hellenic manner. 'I write to enjoy myself,' he says in its preface. 'The main features of the book are a love of sociality, of the country, and of the fine imagination of the Greeks.'

Hunt was best known in his own time as a prose writer, and the bulk of his literary output consisted of essays. He was Hazlitt's partner for *The Round Table*, an essay collection published first in *The Examiner* and then as a volume in 1817. 'A Now, Descriptive of a Hot Day' was written for *The Indicator*, another of Hunt's journals, which ran from 1819 to 1821. Hunt's *Autobiography* recalls that of all his essays it was Keats's favourite: 'He was with me while I was writing and reading it to him, and contributed one or two of the passages.'[6] Like the poetry, it is a catalogue of luxuries, exemplifying the view that literature is a vehicle of 'pleasure'.

In later years Hunt published, besides other works, *Leigh Hunt's London Journal* (1834–5), *Imagination and Fancy* (1844), *Men, Women, and Books* (1847), his *Autobiography* (1850) and *Table Talk* (1851). Like many professional writers, he was often in financial difficulty, but much assisted by the award of a Civil List pension in 1847. He died in Putney and was buried at Kensal Green cemetery, where his grave is still to be seen.

Further reading

The Autobiography of Leigh Hunt ed. J. E. Morpurgo (London, 1949).

The Examiner 1808–22 introduced by Yasuo Deguchi (15 vols, London, 1996–8).

Leigh Hunt: Life, Poetics, Politics ed. Nicholas Roe (London and New York, 2003).

Leigh Hunt: Selected Writings ed. David Jesson Dibley (Manchester, 1990).

Edmund Blunden, *Leigh Hunt: A Biography* (London, 1930).

The Cambridge Companion to Keats ed. Susan Wolfson (Cambridge, 2001).

Jeffrey N. Cox, *Poetry and Politics in the Cockney School: Keats, Shelley, Hunt and their Circle* (Cambridge, 1998).

Rodney Stenning Edgecombe, *Leigh Hunt and the Poetry of Fancy* (London and Toronto, 1994).

Nicholas Roe, *John Keats and the Culture of Dissent* (Oxford, 1997).

Nicholas Roe, *Fiery Heart: The First Life of Leigh Hunt* (London, 2005).

To Hampstead (composed 7 May 1815)[1]

From The Examiner (14 May 1815)

As one who after long and far-spent years
  Comes on his mistress in an hour of sleep,
  And half-surprised that he can silence keep
Stands smiling o'er her through a flash of tears,

Notes

[5] Jeffrey N. Cox has discussed these 'sociable sonnets' in 'Leigh Hunt's *Foliage*: A Cockney Manifesto', in *Leigh Hunt: Life, Poetics, Politics* ed. Nicholas Roe (London and New York, 2003), pp. 58–77.

[6] *The Autobiography of Leigh Hunt* ed. J. E. Morpurgo (London, 1949), p. 281.

To Hampstead

[1] Hunt wrote a series of sonnets in praise of Hampstead, which he published in *The Examiner*.

To see how sweet and self-same she appears;
Till at his touch, with little moving creep
Of joy, she wakes from out her calmness deep,
And then his heart finds voice, and dances round her ears –
So I, first coming on my haunts again,[2]
In pause and stillness of the early prime,[3]
Stood thinking of the past and present time
With earnest eyesight, scarcely crossed with pain;
Till the fresh moving leaves, and startling birds,
Loosened my long-suspended breath in words.

Canto III. The Fatal Passion (extract)

From The Story of Rimini, A Poem (1816)[1]

At times like these the princess tried to shun
The face of Paulo as too kind a one;
And shutting up her tears with resolute sigh,
Would walk into the air, and see the sky,
And feel about her all the garden green,
And hear the birds that shot the covert boughs between.
A noble range it was, of many a rood,[2]
Walled round with trees, and ending in a wood:
Indeed the whole was leafy; and it had
A winding stream about it, clear and glad,
That danced from shade to shade, and on its way
Seemed smiling with delight to feel the day.
There was the pouting rose, both red and white,
The flamy heart's-ease, flushed with purple light,
Blush-hiding strawberry, sunny-coloured box,
Hyacinth, handsome with his clustering locks,
The lady lily, looking gently down,
Pure lavender, to lay in bridal gown,
The daisy, lovely on both sides – in short,
All the sweet cups to which the bees resort,
With plots of grass, and perfumed walks between
Of citron, honeysuckle, and jessamine,[3]
With orange, whose warm leaves so finely suit,
And look as if they'd shade a golden fruit;
And midst the flowers, turfed round beneath a shade
Of circling pines, a babbling fountain played,

Notes

[2] *first coming on my haunts again* this was Hunt's first visit to Hampstead Heath since incarceration in the Surrey Gaol, 1813–15 (see headnote, p. 792).

[3] *prime* about 6 a.m.

From The Story of Rimini

[1] *Rimini* was Hunt's most important poetical work, largely written during his imprisonment in the Surrey Gaol (see headnote). This extract describes Francesca da Rimini's garden and culminates with her first kiss with Paulo, with whom she is to have an illicit affair.

[2] *rood* a measure of between 6 and 8 yards.

[3] *jessamine* jasmine. Throughout this passage Hunt alludes to Adam and Eve's 'blissful bower' which is planted with 'Iris all hues, roses, and jessamine' (*Paradise Lost* iv 698).

And 'twixt their shafts you saw the water bright,
Which through the darksome tops glimmered with showering light.
So now you walked beside an odorous bed
Of gorgeous hues, white, azure, golden red,
And now turned off into a leafy walk
Close and continuous, fit for lovers' talk;
And now pursued the stream, and as you trod
Onward and onward o'er the velvet sod,
Felt on your face an air, watery and sweet,
And a new sense in your soft-lighting feet;
And then perhaps you entered upon shades
Pillowed with dells and uplands 'twixt the glades,
Through which the distant palace, now and then,
Looked lordly forth with many-windowed ken;[4]
A land of trees, which reaching round about,
In shady blessing stretched their old arms out,
With spots of sunny opening, and with nooks
To lie and read in, sloping into brooks,
Where at her drink you started the slim deer,
Retreating lightly with a lovely fear.
And all about, the birds kept leafy house,
And sung and sparkled in and out the boughs;
And all about, a lovely sky of blue
Clearly was felt, or down the leaves laughed through;
And here and there, in every part, were seats,
Some in the open walks, some in retreats,
With bowering leaves o'erhead, to which the eye
Looked up half sweetly and half awfully –
Places of nestling green for poets made,
Where when the sunshine struck a yellow shade,
The slender trunks, to inward-peeping sight,
Thronged in dark pillars up the gold green light.
But 'twixt the wood and flowery walks, halfway,
And formed of both, the loveliest portion lay,
A spot, that struck you like enchanted ground:
It was a shallow dell, set in a mound
Of sloping shrubs, that mounted by degrees,
The birch and poplar mixed with heavier trees;
From under which, sent through a marble spout,
Betwixt the dark wet green, a rill gushed out,
Whose low sweet talking seemed as if it said
Something eternal to that happy shade.
The ground within was lawn, with plots of flowers
Heaped towards the centre, and with citron bowers;
And in the midst of all, clustered about
With bay and myrtle, and just gleaming out,
Lurked a pavilion, a delicious sight,
Small, marble, well-proportioned, mellowy white,

Notes

[4] *ken* view.

With yellow vine-leaves sprinkled – but no more –
And a young orange either side the door.
The door was to the wood, forward and square,
The rest was domed at top, and circular;
And through the dome the only light came in,
Tinged, as it entered, with the vine-leaves thin.
It was a beauteous piece of ancient skill,
Spared from the rage of war, and perfect still;
By some supposed the work of fairy hands,
Famed for luxurious taste, and choice of lands –
Alcina or Morgana, who from fights
And errant fame inveigled amorous knights,
And lived with them in a long round of blisses,
Feasts, concerts, baths, and bower-enshaded kisses.
But 'twas a temple, as its sculpture told,
Built to the nymphs that haunted there of old;
For o'er the door was carved a sacrifice
By girls and shepherds brought, with reverent eyes,
Of sylvan drinks and foods, simple and sweet,
And goats with struggling horns and planted feet:
And on a line with this ran round about
A like relief, touched exquisitely out,
That showed, in various scenes, the nymphs themselves;
Some by the water side on bowery shelves
Leaning at will – some in the water sporting
With sides half swelling forth, and looks of courting;[5]
Some in a flowery dell, hearing a swain
Play on his pipe, till the hills ring again;
Some tying up their long moist hair; some sleeping
Under the trees, with fauns and satyrs peeping,
Or, sidelong-eyed, pretending not to see,
The latter in the brakes come creepingly,
While their forgotten urns, lying about
In the green herbage, let the water out.
Never, be sure, before or since was seen
A summer-house so fine in such a nest of green.[6]
All the green garden, flowerbed, shade and plot
Francesca loved, but most of all this spot.
Whenever she walked forth, wherever went
About the grounds, to this at last she bent:
Here she had brought a lute and a few books;
Here would she lie for hours, with grateful looks,
Thanking at heart the sunshine and the leaves,
The summer raindrops counting from the eaves,
And all that promising, calm smile we see
In nature's face, when we look patiently.

Notes

[5] *the nymphs themselves . . . courting* Lockhart was particularly offended by this: 'The indecent attitudes of the nymphs on the cornice can only be equalled by the blasphemous allusion to the history of our first parents.'

[6] *A summer-house . . . green* Lockhart described this is a 'bagnio' (see headnote p. 794).

Then would she think of heaven; and you might hear
Sometimes, when everything was hushed and clear,
Her gentle voice from out those shades emerging,
Singing the evening anthem to the Virgin.
The gardeners and the rest, who served the place,
And blest whenever they beheld her face,
Knelt when they heard it, bowing and uncovered,
And felt as if in air some sainted beauty hovered.
   One day, 'twas on a summer afternoon
When airs and gurgling brooks are best in tune,
And grasshoppers are loud, and day-work done,
And shades have heavy outlines in the sun,
The princess came to her accustomed bower
To get her, if she could, a soothing hour,
Trying, as she was used, to leave her cares
Without, and slumberously enjoy the airs,
And the low-talking leaves, and that cool light
The vines let in, and all that hushing sight
Of closing wood seen through the opening door,
And distant plash of waters tumbling o'er,
And smell of citron blooms, and fifty luxuries more.
She tried, as usual, for the trial's sake,
For even that diminished her heart-ache;
And never yet, how ill soe'er at ease,
Came she for nothing midst the flowers and trees.
Yet somehow or another, on that day
She seemed to feel too lightly borne away,
Too much relieved, too much inclined to draw
A careless joy from everything she saw,
And looking round her with a new-born eye,
As if some tree of knowledge[7] had been nigh,
To taste of nature, primitive and free,
And bask at ease in her heart's liberty.
Painfully clear those rising thoughts appeared,
With something dark at bottom that she feared;
And snatching from the fields her thoughtful look,
She reached o'er-head, and took her down a book,
And fell to reading with as fixed an air,
As though she had been wrapt since morning there.
'Twas Launcelot of the Lake, a bright romance,
That like a trumpet made young pulses dance,
Yet had a softer note that shook still more;
She had begun it but the day before,
And read with a full heart, half sweet, half sad,
How old King Ban was spoiled of all he had
But one fair castle: how one summer's day
With his fair queen and child he went away
To ask the great King Arthur for assistance;

Notes

[7] *tree of knowledge* a reference to the story of Adam and Eve.

How reaching by himself a hill at distance
He turned to give his castle a last look,
And saw its far white face: and how a smoke,
As he was looking, burst in volumes forth,
And good King Ban saw all that he was worth,
And his fair castle, burning to the ground,
So that his wearied pulse felt over-wound,
And he lay down, and said a prayer apart
For those he loved, and broke his poor old heart.
Then read she of the queen with her young child,
How she came up, and nearly had gone wild,
And how in journeying on in her despair,
She reached a lake and met a lady there,
Who pitied her, and took the baby sweet
Into her arms, when lo, with closing feet
She sprang up all at once, like bird from brake,
And vanished with him underneath the lake.
The mother's feelings we as well may pass:
The fairy of the place that lady was,
And Launcelot (so the boy was called) became
Her inmate, till in search of knightly fame
He went to Arthur's court, and played his part
So rarely, and displayed so frank a heart,
That what with all his charms of look and limb,
The Queen Geneura fell in love with him:
And here, with growing interest in her reading,
The Princess, doubly fixed, was now proceeding.
  Ready she sat with one hand to turn o'er
The leaf, to which her thoughts ran on before,
The other propping her white brow, and throwing
Its ringlets out, under the skylight glowing.
So sat she fixed; and so observed was she
Of one, who at the door stood tenderly –
Paulo, who from a window seeing her
Go straight across the lawn, and guessing where,
Had thought she was in tears, and found, that day,
His usual efforts vain to keep away.
'May I come in?' said he (it made her start,
That smiling voice); she coloured, pressed her heart
A moment, as for breath, and then with free
And usual tone said, 'Oh yes, certainly.'
There's wont to be, at conscious times like these,
An affectation of a bright-eyed ease,
An air of something quite serene and sure,
As if to seem so, was to be, secure:
With this the lovers met, with this they spoke,
With this they sat down to the self-same book,
And Paulo, by degrees, gently embraced
With one permitted arm her lovely waist;
And both their cheeks, like peaches on a tree,
Leaned with a touch together, thrillingly;

And o'er the book they hung, and nothing said,
And every lingering page grew longer as they read.
As thus they sat, and felt with leaps of heart
Their colour change, they came upon the part
Where fond Geneura, with her flame long nursed,
  Smiled upon Launcelot when he kissed her first:
That touch, at last, through every fibre slid;
And Paulo turned, scarce knowing what he did,
Only he felt he could no more dissemble,
And kissed her, mouth to mouth, all in a tremble.
Sad were those hearts, and sweet was that long kiss:
Sacred be love from sight, whate'er it is.
The world was all forgot,[8] the struggle o'er,[9]
Desperate the joy. That day they read no more.[10]

On the Grasshopper and Cricket[1]

From The Examiner (21 September 1817)

Green little vaulter in the sunny grass,
Catching your heart up at the feel of June,
Sole voice left stirring midst the lazy noon,
When ev'n the bees lag at the summoning brass;
And you, warm little housekeeper, who class
With those who think the candles come too soon,
Loving the fire, and with your tricksome tune
Nick the glad silent moments as they pass; –
Oh sweet and tiny cousins, that belong
One to the fields, the other to the hearth,
Both have your sunshine; both though small are strong
At your clear hearts; and both were sent on earth
To ring in thoughtful ears this natural song,
In doors and out, summer and winter – Mirth.

December 30, 1816.

Notes

[8] *The world was all forgot* Nicholas Roe suggests an echo of the casting-out of Adam and Eve from Eden: 'The world was all before them' (*Paradise Lost* xii 646).

[9] *the struggle o'er* Nicholas Roe suggests 'a semi-blasphemous allusion to Christ's crucifixion, refiguring his martyrdom at a climax of all too human passion'; see *John Keats and the Culture of Dissent* (Oxford, 1997), p. 121.

[10] *That day they read no more* This translates the famous line in Dante, *Inferno* v 138.

On the Grasshopper and Cricket

[1] This was the product of a sonnet-writing competition with Keats. Hunt published both poems side by side in *The Examiner*. For Keats's sonnet, see p. 1344.

To Percy Shelley, on the degrading notions of deity[1]

From Foliage (1818)

What wonder, Percy, that with jealous rage
Men should defame the kindly and the wise,[2]
When in the midst of the all-beauteous skies,
And all this lovely world, that should engage
Their mutual search for the old golden age,
They seat a phantom,[3] swelled into grim size
Out of their own passions and bigotries,
And then, for fear, proclaim it meek and sage!
And this they call a light and a revealing!
Wise as the clown[4] who, plodding home at night
In autumn, turns at call of fancied elf,
And sees upon the fog, with ghastly feeling,
A giant shadow in its imminent might,
Which his own lanthorn[5] throws up from himself.

To the Same

From Foliage (1818)

Yet, Percy, not for this, should he whose eye
Sees loveliness, and the unselfish joy
Of justice, turn him, like a peevish boy,
At hindrances and thwartings, and deny
Wisdom's divinest privilege, constancy –
That which most proves him free from the alloy
Of useless earth, least prone to the decoy[1]
That clamours down weak pinions from the sky.
The Spirit of Beauty,[2] though by solemn choirs
Hourly blasphemed, stoops not from its calm end,
And forward breathing love, but ever on
Rolls the round day, and calls the starry fires
To their glad watch. Therefore, high-hearted friend,
Be still with thine own task in unison.

Notes

To Percy Shelley

[1] This poem and the one that follows should be read in the light of Shelley's comments on Hunt's atheism, 8 May 1811: 'he is a Deist despising Jesus Christ, etc., etc., yet having a high veneration for the Deity . . . with him God is neither omnipotent, omnipresent, nor identical . . . he says that God *is* comprehensible, not doubting but an adequate exertion of reason . . . would lead us from a contemplation of his works to a definite knowledge of his attributes, which are by no means limited' (Jones i 77).

[2] *the kindly and the wise* presumably themselves (i.e. Hunt and Shelley). Shelley had been expelled from Oxford for publishing a pamphlet on 'The Necessity of Atheism'.

[3] *a phantom* i.e. conventional notions of God.

[4] *clown* untutored peasant.

[5] *lanthorn* lantern.

To the Same

[1] *decoy* bird trained to lure others into the hunter's trap.

[2] *The Spirit of Beauty* an allusion to Shelley's 'Hymn to Intellectual Beauty', published by Hunt in *The Examiner* for 19 January 1817 (see pp. 1071–3), which features an address to the 'Spirit of Beauty' in stanzas 2–4.

To John Keats (composed 1 December 1816)[1]

From Foliage (1818)

'Tis well you think me truly one of those
Whose sense discerns the loveliness of things;
For surely as I feel the bird that sings
Behind the leaves, or dawn as it up grows,
Or the rich bee rejoicing as he goes,
Or the glad issue of emerging springs,
Or overhead the glide of a dove's wings,
Or turf, or trees, or, midst of all, repose;
And surely as I feel things lovelier still,
The human look, and the harmonious form
Containing woman, and the smile in ill,
And such a heart as Charles',[2] wise and warm –
As surely as all this, I see, ev'n now,
Young Keats, a flowering laurel on your brow.

A Now, Descriptive of a Hot Day[1]

From The Indicator (1820)

Now the rosy- (and lazy-) fingered Aurora, issuing from her saffron house,[2] calls up the moist vapours to surround her, and goes veiled with them as long as she can; till Phoebus,[3] coming forth in his power, looks everything out of the sky, and holds sharp uninterrupted empire from his throne of beams. Now the mower begins to make his sweeping cuts more slowly, and resorts oftener to the beer. Now the carter sleeps atop of his load of hay, or plods with double slouch of shoulder, looking out with eyes winking under his shading hat, and with a hitch upward of one side of his mouth. Now the little girl at her grandmother's cottage-door watches the coaches that go by, with her hand held up over her sunny forehead. Now labourers look well, resting in their white shirts at the doors of rural alehouses. Now an elm is fine there, with a seat under it; and horses drink out of the trough, stretching their yearning necks with loosened collars; and the traveller calls for his glass of ale, having been without one for more than ten minutes; and his horse stands wincing at the flies, giving sharp shivers of his skin, and moving to and fro his ineffectual docked tail; and now Miss Betty Wilson, the host's daughter, comes streaming forth in a flowered gown and earrings, carrying with four of her beautiful fingers the foaming glass, for which, after the

Notes

To John Keats

[1] This sonnet was written on the day Hunt published his article, 'Young Poets', in *The Examiner*, which praised Keats alongside Shelley and published 'On First Looking into Chapman's Homer' for the first time. See p. 1334.

[2] Charles Cowden Clarke (1787–1877), mutual friend of Keats and Hunt.

A Now, Descriptive of a Hot Day

[1] During the summer of 1820 Hunt was resident at Mortimer Terrace, Kentish Town, and arranged for the ailing Keats to stay in his own apartment nearby. Keats was present while this essay was being composed during that summer, and contributed to it.

[2] *Now the . . . house* an elaborate way of saying that dawn sky (Aurora) is filled with orange-yellow (saffron) light; 'rosy-fingered dawn' is a stock phrase from Homer, *Odyssey* ii 1.

traveller has drank it, she receives with an indifferent eye, looking another way, the lawful two pence: that is to say, unless the traveller, nodding his ruddy face, pays some gallant compliment to her before he drinks – such as, 'I'd rather kiss you, my dear, than the tumbler', or, 'I'll wait for you, my love, if you'll marry me' – upon which, if the man is good-looking, and the lady in good humour, she smiles and bites her lips, and says, 'Ah, men can talk fast enough', upon which the old stagecoachman, who is buckling something near her before he sets off, says in a hoarse voice, 'So can women too for that matter', and John Boots grins through his ragged red locks, and dotes on the repartee all the day after. Now grasshoppers 'fry', as Dryden says.[4] Now cattle stand in water and ducks are envied. Now boots and shoes and trees by the roadside are thick with dust; and dogs, rolling in it, after issuing out of the water into which they have been thrown to fetch sticks, come scattering horror among the legs of the spectators. Now a fellow who finds he has three miles further to go in a pair of tight shoes is in a pretty situation.[5] Now rooms with the sun upon them become intolerable; and the apothecary's apprentice,[6] with a bitterness beyond aloes,[7] thinks of the pond he used to bathe in at school. Now men with powdered heads (especially if thick) envy those that are unpowdered, and stop to wipe them uphill, with countenances that seem to expostulate with destiny. Now boys assemble round the village pump with a ladle to it, and delight to make a forbidden splash and get wet through the shoes. Now also they make suckers of leather,[8] and bathe all day long in rivers and ponds, and follow the fish into their cool corners, and say millions of 'My eyes!' at tittle-bats.[9] Now the bee, as he hums along, seems to be talking heavily of the heat. Now doors and brick walls are burning to the hand; and a walled lane, with dust and broken bottles in it, near a brick-field,[10] is a thing not to be thought of. Now a green lane, on the contrary, thick-set with hedgerow elms, and having the noise of a brook 'rumbling in pebble-stone',[11] is one of the pleasantest things in the world. Now youths and damsels walk through hayfields by chance; and if the latter say, 'Ha' done then, William', and the overseer[12] in the next field calls out to 'Let thic thear hay thear bide', the girls persist, merely to plague 'such a frumpish[13] old fellow'.

Now, in town, gossips talk more than ever to one another, in rooms, in doorways, and out of window, always beginning the conversation with saying that the heat is overpowering. Now blinds are let down and doors thrown open and flannel waistcoats left off, and cold meat preferred to hot, and wonder expressed why tea continues so refreshing, and people delight to sliver lettuces into bowls, and apprentices water doorways with tin canisters that lay several atoms of dust. Now the water-cart, jumbling along the middle of the street, and jolting the showers out of its box of water, really does something. Now boys delight to have a water-pipe let out, and see it bubbling away in a tall and frothy volume. Now fruiterers' shops and dairies look pleasant, and ices are the only things to those who can get them. Now ladies loiter in baths; and people make presents of flowers; and wine is put into ice; and the after-dinner lounger recreates[14] his head with applications of perfumed water out of long-necked bottles. Now the lounger, who cannot resist riding his new horse, feels his

Notes

[3] *Phoebus* i.e. the sun.

[4] Hunt recalls Dryden, *Virgil's Georgics* iii 510–11, although the word 'fry' is not used.

[5] *pretty situation* ironic; he's in a terrible situation.

[6] *the apothecary's apprentice* Keats trained as an apothecary.

[7] *aloes* a drug of nauseous odour, bitter taste, and purgative qualities, procured from the juice of the aloe plant.

[8] *suckers of leather* a toy, consisting of a round piece of leather with a string attached at the centre, which, laid wet upon a solid surface and drawn up by the string, adheres by reason of the vacuum created.

[9] *tittlebats* sticklebats.

[10] *brick-field* yard where bricks are made.

[11] Spenser, 'Virgil's Gnat' 163: 'caerule streame, rombling in pible stone'.

[12] *overseer* supervisor.

[13] *frumpish* ill-tempered.

[14] *recreates* revives, refreshes.

boots burn him. Now buckskins[15] are not the lawn[16] of Cos. Now jockeys, walking in greatcoats to lose flesh, curse inwardly. Now five fat people in a stagecoach hate the sixth fat one who is coming in, and think he has no right to be so large. Now clerks in offices do nothing but drink soda-water and spruce beer,[17] and read the newspaper. Now the old-clothes-man[18] drops his solitary cry more deeply into the areas on the hot and forsaken side of the street; and bakers look vicious; and cooks are aggravated; and the steam of a tavern-kitchen catches hold of one like the breath of Tartarus.[19] Now delicate skins are beset with gnats; and boys make their sleeping companion start up with playing a burning-glass[20] on his hand; and blacksmiths are super-carbonated;[21] and cobblers in their stalls almost feel a wish to be transplanted; and butter is too easy to spread; and the dragoons wonder whether the Romans liked their helmets; and old ladies, with their lappets[22] unpinned, walk along in a state of dilapidation; and the servant-maids are afraid they look vulgarly hot; and the author, who has a plate of strawberries brought him, finds that he has come to the end of his writing.

Thomas De Quincey (1785–1859)

He was born Thomas Penson Quincey in Manchester on 15 August 1785, the fourth of seven children born to Thomas Quincey, a linen merchant, and Elizabeth Penson Quincey, then resident in central Manchester. In November 1790 his father purchased three acres of land close to Moss Side, in the countryside beyond the city boundaries, where his wife designed the house in which their children were to grow up, called Greenhay. They moved into it in 1791.

De Quincey hardly knew his father, who worked in Manchester and travelled increasingly to the West Indies, where he had business interests. He died of tuberculosis at the age of 40 in 1793. By that time De Quincey had also lost his elder sister, Elizabeth, who was only 9. Her death, from meningitis, was a blow partly because a coldness between him and his mother led him to depend emotionally on his sister. It was with her that he read books and played games in the nursery. His last, affectionate tribute to her is one of the key recollections of *Suspiria De Profundis* (see pp. 825–9). He wanted to see her after a post-mortem had been performed, but fortunately for him the door of her room was locked and he was unable to enter.

Elizabeth's death caused him grief at an early age, for which he later remembered being teased, probably by his elder brother William:

> And when I was told insultingly to cease 'my girlish tears', that word *girlish* had no sting for me, except as a verbal echo to the one eternal thought in my heart – that girl was the sweetest thing I, in my short life, had known – that a girl it was who had crowned the earth with beauty, and had opened to my thirst fountains of pure celestial love, from which, in this world, I was to drink no more. (Lindop xv 148)

It is tempting to see his intense encounters with other young women as an attempt to reclaim his relationship with Elizabeth. The extent to which

Notes

[15] *buckskins* breeches made of buckskin (too warm in the summer).

[16] *lawn* fine linen, such as that made of the island of Cos in the Aegean.

[17] *spruce beer* beer made from leaves and branches of the spruce fir.

[18] *old-clothes-man* dealer in old or second-hand clothes.

[19] *Tartarus* in classical literature, the walled and dark underworld prison reserved for the punishment of the wicked.

[20] *burning-glass* lens through which the rays of the sun are concentrated so as to burn.

[21] *super-carbonated* so hot that they are completely reduced to carbon.

[22] *lappets* flaps of their dress which would normally be fastened down.

that early loss scarred him is indicated by the fact that it led to visions of sick and dying children while he gazed at the stained-glass windows in church. It must also have given rise to feelings of guilt at loving Elizabeth more than his mother.

De Quincey was tutored privately for the next three years and distinguished himself in the study of Latin and Greek. In 1796 the family sold Greenhay and moved to the fashionable North Parade in Bath; there he visited the mysterious maze in Sydney Gardens, where he played on his own. His academic progress at the Grammar School was excellent and he was soon the star pupil, capable of haranguing an Athenian mob. How perverse, then, that his mother decided, on a whim, to remove him: he protested, as did the headmaster, but she was adamant. Instead she sent him to the small Winkfield School in Wiltshire, where the comparatively unchallenging regime left him bored.

At this time the family changed its name to De Quincey on the dubious basis that they were descended from the De Quincis who came over with William the Conqueror – typical of the kind of social climbing his mother went in for. One day in 1799, while at Bath, Thomas came across a manuscript copy of Wordsworth's 'We Are Seven', published in the first edition of *Lyrical Ballads* the year before. (The poem was composed not far from Bath, at Alfoxden in Somerset.) He was immediately impressed and determined to find out more about its author.

After an eventful summer holiday in 1800, during which he met George III, he enrolled at Manchester Grammar School. One of the few consolations of his first year was the acquisition of a copy of the newly published *Lyrical Ballads* (second edition, 1800) – his first exposure to the entire volume. It was a revelation. Wordsworth and Coleridge kept their names off the title-page, but he soon found out their identities (known in social and literary circles), and from that time onwards was determined to meet them. Continuing unhappiness at school during his second year led him to run away in July 1802, his copy of *Lyrical Ballads* in his coat-pocket. His mother became aware of his plans through his uncle, but it was eventually agreed that he be allowed to continue on his way provided he remained in touch.

He walked through north Wales – sometimes sleeping rough, sometimes at inns along the road. Somewhere along the line he decided to break off contact with his family and go to London, where he arrived in late November. He was to remain there throughout a harsh winter, living on the breadline. We do not know for sure whether 'Ann of Oxford Street' was a real person; if so, it was at this time that he came to know her.

In March 1803 he was reconciled with his family. Wordsworth was his literary idol, and in May he sent a fan letter to him. 'Your name is with me forever linked to the lovely scenes of nature,' he told him:

> you will never find anyone more zealously attached to you – more full of admiration for your mental excellence and of reverential love for your moral character – more ready (I speak from my heart!) to sacrifice even his life – whenever it could have a chance of promoting your interest and happiness – than he who now bends the knee before you. And I will add that to no man on earth except yourself and *one* other (a friend of yours[1]) would I thus lowly and suppliantly prostrate myself.[2]

At a time when his poetry was still an acquired taste, Wordsworth must have found such words welcome, even though he would have known that such hero-worship might not endure, and perhaps turn sour. He wrote a gracious but cautious reply, declaring that 'it will give me great pleasure to

Notes

[1] De Quincey refers to Coleridge.

[2] John E. Jordan, *De Quincey to Wordsworth: A Biography of a Relationship* (Berkeley and Los Angeles, 1962), p. 31.

see you at Grasmere if you should ever come this way.'[3]

In December 1803 De Quincey went up to Worcester College, Oxford, as a commoner. He was unhappy there, declining to take much part in either social or educational activities, and pursued a course of private study of his own devising, concentrated on German and philosophy. In need of money, he was soon journeying to London to visit a moneylender. It was on one such trip in October 1804 that he first tried opium, to treat 'rheumatic pains' in his head stemming from toothache. It was, he later recalled, an 'abyss of divine enjoyment', 'the secret of happiness', and 'a panacea . . . for all human woes'. His addiction had begun. From now on his life would be a round of depression, euphoria and opium reveries. Indeed, he became something of a hedonist, sometimes committing what he called 'a debauch of opium'[4] before a visit to the opera, where the music was enhanced by the drug, 'its passions exalted, spiritualized, and sublimed'.[5]

He made three abortive attempts to visit Wordsworth in Grasmere, each time turning back out of anxiety. Instead, he went to Nether Stowey to meet his other hero, Coleridge. He became a good friend, particularly of Coleridge's children, and escorted Mrs Coleridge and the family to the Lake District, where they were to settle with Southey at Greta Hall in Keswick. On arrival in Cumbria they headed for Dove Cottage in Grasmere and there, finally, De Quincey met Wordsworth. He gradually gained the trust of both him and his sister, who was the more approachable. For her part, Dorothy was delighted with him, as she told her friend, Lady Beaumont:

He is a remarkable and very interesting young man; very diminutive in person, which to strangers makes him appear insignificant; and so modest, and so very shy that even now I wonder how he ever had the courage to address himself to my brother by letter. I think of this young man with extraordinary pleasure, as he is a remarkable instance of the power of my brother's poems over a lonely and contemplative mind, unwarped by any established laws of taste – a pure and innocent mind![6]

He had to return to Oxford to take his final examinations: the first day went well, but for some reason he panicked on the second and ran off, never to return. He went straight to London where he continued to meet with Coleridge, and in autumn 1808 returned to Grasmere, where the Wordsworths had moved to Allan Bank, a large house that overlooked the valley. Wordsworth was at this time exercised by the plight of the Spanish freedom-fighters, struggling to repel Napoleon's army despite the treacherous tactics of the Allies. He wrote a pamphlet in their support, entitled *The Convention of Cintra,* and entrusted De Quincey with the task of seeing it through the press. This was a bit of a disaster, as De Quincey failed to ensure that potentially libellous remarks (some of them about the Duke of Wellington) were suppressed, and was responsible for a system of punctuation of which Wordsworth disapproved. It sold badly, and Wordsworth could not help but blame De Quincey for its failure.

In October 1809 De Quincey became the new tenant of Dove Cottage, where the Wordsworths had spent some of their happiest and most productive years. Part of the attraction of this arrangement was that they could still visit it and enjoy its garden, in which they had invested so much loving care – and to begin with, they were almost daily visitors. Not surprisingly then, they took umbrage when De Quincey chopped down Wordsworth's beloved trees in the back garden, and demolished the 'moss-hut' which he had painstakingly constructed in order to provide

Notes

[3] *EY* 401.
[4] Lindop ii 47.
[5] Ibid. 48.
[6] *MY* i 180.

a view across the valley. Before lasting strains developed in the relationship, De Quincey became one of the few people to read *The Prelude* – in manuscript, as it would not be published until after Wordsworth's death in 1850, four decades later. De Quincey was highly impressed, in particular by the 'spots of time', which he adapted for his theory of involutes (see p. 826). The idea is taken to an extreme in 'Savannah-la-Mar' and 'The Palimpsest of the Human Brain'.

Catharine (Kate) Wordsworth was a mere infant when she first met De Quincey, but he took to her immediately and was appointed by her father as her sole tutor. She was a very special child. Wordsworth called her his 'little Chinese maiden', and Dorothy described her face as 'perfectly comic'. Kate was as attached to De Quincey (whom she called 'Kinsey') as he was to her; when he went away she searched every room in the cottage for him, even pulling the sheets from the bed to see if he were there. One morning in 1810, she had a fit that left her paralysed down her right side. She made a partial recovery, but the convulsions returned in June 1812 and killed her. She was in her fourth year. 'Oh that I could have died for her or with her!' De Quincey told Dorothy. 'Willingly dear friend I would have done this.' For two months after her death he slept on her grave and claimed to have visions of her walking the fells.

If that wasn't enough to distance him from the Wordsworth family, his opium addiction was. By 1816 he was consuming 320 grains a day – quite a sizeable dose, signalling that he was a confirmed addict. And the Wordsworths disapproved of his affair with Margaret Simpson, a local serving girl ten years his junior (she was 17). They thought she was beneath him in social standing, and Dorothy uncharitably described her as 'a stupid heavy girl . . . a dunce at Grasmere School'. Such was Wordsworth's feeling on the matter that he wrote to De Quincey's mother to warn her of what was afoot. De Quincey found such interference hard either to forgive or understand, and temporarily broke off contact with the Wordsworths, leading him to become depressed, on account of which he prescribed himself more opium. Margaret gave birth to a son, William Penson, in 1816, and married De Quincey the following year.

De Quincey would re-establish relations with Wordsworth, but there was little warmth left in the association. The outgrowing of his mentor proved a liberation, and his journalistic career took off when in 1818 he became editor of the *Westmorland Gazette*. Though sacked for inefficiency within the year, he drove himself hard, and under his editorship the paper began to show a profit, which it would not do again for years. Most importantly, it revealed to him his future path.

De Quincey was not out of work for long. He was almost immediately invited by John Wilson to write for *Blackwood's Edinburgh Magazine*. He fell out with the editors by failing to submit his work on time, but soon travelled to London and began submitting work to the *London Magazine*. He found himself writing a series of articles that would form his masterpiece – *Confessions of an English Opium-Eater*, published in book form a year later. The articles were hugely popular, and helped increase circulation of the *London*, and when in 1821 the book came out it was instantly famous, and has remained in print ever since. Poe and Baudelaire would hail it as a masterpiece. Coleridge was less impressed. In 1833 he would speak of it 'with absolute abhorrence', calling it 'a wicked book, a monstrous exaggeration', attacking De Quincey for 'laying open his nakedness to the world'.[7]

The series of false starts and failures that characterized his early life were due to the influence of the drug, and it set a trend against which he

Notes

[7] CC *Table Talk* i 581.

would battle for the remainder of his life. He was expected to produce a third instalment of the *Confessions* for the *London Magazine*, but never did so; he returned to Grasmere with an advance for a novel, but never wrote it. All the same, despite his addiction, he wrote a vast quantity of material for a wide variety of newspapers and periodicals, including the *London Magazine*, John Stoddart's *The New Times*, *Blackwood's*, the *Edinburgh Saturday Post*, *Edinburgh Literary Gazette* and *Tait's Edinburgh Magazine*. Foremost among his journalism was his article 'On the Knocking at the Gate in *Macbeth*' – a brilliant analysis of Macduff's knocking after the murder of King Duncan. This he thought of as 'psychological criticism', a way of thinking learnt through discussions with Wordsworth. It is something again seen in his comments 'On Wordsworth's *There was a boy*', which is extracted from the series of articles written for *Tait's*.

In order to appreciate the intellectual triumph of these essays you have first to accept that psychology as we understand it simply did not exist in De Quincey's day. He had learnt from conversations with Wordsworth and his own close reading of *The Prelude* that literary works operated on our emotions by replicating psychological processes that we recognize as true. In 'On the Knocking at the Gate in *Macbeth*' he reveals just one of those processes, analysing it in close detail, and in doing so reveals both what he had learnt from Wordsworth, and how perceptive a critic he had become. It is typical of his best work, in that it begins with an emotional effect, and shows us how that effect is obtained.

His 'Recollections of the Lake Poets' (1839–40) are among the most important of his later works, giving us intimate accounts of Southey, Wordsworth and Coleridge as he knew them. They are entertaining, memorable, and in many respects wrong. He had known both men well, but hero-worship had turned to resentment, and he could not help portraying them in a bad light. Wordsworth, he commented, was 'not a well-made man', he had 'a crooked walk', his manners were imperfect, he dressed 'slovenly' and did not read much. Dorothy had a stammer; Mary Wordsworth was plain. Not surprisingly, Wordsworth was infuriated and remained so. 'I have never read a word of his infamous production, nor ever shall,' he remarked:

> My acquaintance with him was the result of a letter of his own volunteered to me. He was 7 months an inmate of my house; and by what breach of the laws of hospitality that kindness was repaid, his performance, if rightly represented to me, sufficiently shows. A man who can set such an example, I hold to be a pest in society, and one of the most worthless of mankind.[8]

One reason why De Quincey so ruthlessly exploited his acquaintance with Wordsworth was the fact that he was in dire need of money. He suffered throughout his life from financial troubles; in 1829 he was forced to raise a second mortgage on Nab Cottage in Rydal, where he then lived; he was imprisoned for debt in 1831, was twice prosecuted two years later (when he took refuge in the debtors' sanctuary at Holyrood Palace) and thrice prosecuted in 1837. He described the extent of his poverty in May 1840:

> Having in a moment of pinching difficulty for my children about ten months since pawned every article of my dress which could produce a shilling, I have since that time had no stockings, no shoes, no neck-handkerchief, coat, waistcoat, or hat . . . But the painful result from the whole is that I am about £100 worse than I was when I began. This is terrific.[9]

Notes

[8] *Barron Field's Memoirs of Wordsworth* ed. Geoffrey Little (Sydney, 1975), p. 28.

[9] *De Quincey as Critic* ed. John E. Jordan (London, 1973), p. 17.

During these years he struggled to continue writing, when he was able, on a variety of subjects, including German metaphysics, politics, economics, classical scholarship and the opium wars. Financial pressure eased when in 1840 his eldest daughter Margaret (aged 22) took control of his accounts, but it was not until 1846, when his mother died, leaving him as estate of £200 a year (£11,000 / US$20,000 today), that his finances became manageable.

In July 1844 he began work on *Suspiria de Profundis,* serialized in *Blackwood's,* March–June 1845. This was the second of his great works, a final monument to his incredible powers, subtitled 'a Sequel to the Confessions of an English Opium-Eater'. It was designed as a series of interconnected prose poems, exploratory of the intricate relation between dream and reality. This selection contains three extracts – 'The Affliction of Childhood', 'The Palimpsest' and 'Savannah-la-Mar', which is presented in its entirety.

In spite of health problems, he came from a long-lived family (his mother died in 1846 at the age of 90) and survived to see himself sufficiently venerated to merit publication of a collected works. Interestingly, this was initiated by an American publisher – Ticknor, Reed, and Fields, of Boston, which began publication of *De Quincey's Writings* in 1850; it ran to twenty volumes, and was completed six years later. And in 1853 the Edinburgh publisher James Hogg began publication of *Selections Grave and Gay from Writings Published and Unpublished,* which ran to fourteen volumes, completed in 1860. De Quincey revised and substantially enlarged the *Confessions* for Hogg's edition, which appeared as volume 5 of *Selections Grave and Gay* (1856). He died at 42 Lothian Street, Edinburgh, on 7 December 1859.

It is one of the ironies of literary history that although De Quincey has remained an enduringly popular writer since his death, both for his 'Recollections of the Lake Poets' and *Confessions,* his work has come down to us in texts that have not always been reliable. Only in the last few years has an authoritative text of his complete works been published under the general editorship of Grevel Lindop. It is a remarkable achievement, and a fitting memorial to De Quincey's art, which students of his writings are advised to consult.

Further reading

The Works of Thomas De Quincey General Editor, Grevel Lindop (21 vols, London, 2000–3).

Thomas De Quincey, *Confessions of an English Opium-Eater and Other Writings* ed. Grevel Lindop (Oxford, 1985).

De Quincey as Critic ed. John E. Jordan (London, 1973).

Grevel Lindop, *The Opium-Eater: A Life of Thomas De Quincey* (London, 1981).

Robert Woof, *Thomas De Quincey: An English Opium-Eater* (Grasmere, 1985).

[*Ann of Oxford Street*][1]

From Confessions of an English Opium-Eater (1822)

Being myself at that time of necessity a peripatetic (or a walker of the streets), I naturally fell in more frequently with those female peripatetics who are technically called street-walkers.[2] Many of these women had occasionally taken my part against watchmen who wished to drive me off the steps of houses where I was sitting. But one

Notes

Ann of Oxford Street

[1] De Quincey recalls the period, 1802–3, when he ran away from school, aged 17, and lived rough in London; see headnote, p. 806.

[2] *street-walkers* i.e. prostitutes.

amongst them, the one on whose account I have at all introduced this subject – yet no! let me not class thee, oh noble-minded Ann, with that order of women! Let me find, if it be possible, some gentler name to designate the condition of her to whose bounty and compassion, ministering to my necessities when all the world had forsaken me, I owe it that I am at this time alive.

For many weeks I had walked at nights with this poor friendless girl up and down Oxford Street,[3] or had rested with her on steps and under the shelter of porticos.[4] She could not be so old as myself; she told me, indeed, that she had not completed her sixteenth year. By such questions as my interest about her prompted, I had gradually drawn forth her simple history. Hers was a case of ordinary occurrence (as I have since had reason to think), and one in which, if London beneficence had better adapted its arrangements to meet it, the power of the law might oftener be interposed to protect and to avenge. But the stream of London charity flows in a channel which, though deep and mighty, is yet noiseless and underground, not obvious or readily accessible to poor houseless wanderers[5] – and it cannot be denied that the outside air and framework of London society is harsh, cruel, and repulsive. In any case, however, I saw that part of her injuries might easily have been redressed, and I urged her often and earnestly to lay her complaint before a magistrate; friendless as she was, I assured her that she would meet with immediate attention, and that English justice, which was no respecter of persons, would speedily and amply avenge her on the brutal ruffian who had plundered her little property. She promised me often that she would, but she delayed taking the steps I pointed out from time to time, for she was timid and dejected to a degree which showed how deeply sorrow had taken hold of her young heart, and perhaps she thought justly that the most upright judge and the most righteous tribunals could do nothing to repair her heaviest wrongs. Something, however, would perhaps have been done, for it had been settled between us at length (but unhappily on the very last time but one that I was ever to see her) that in a day or two we should go together before a magistrate, and that I should speak on her behalf. This little service it was destined, however, that I should never realize.

Meantime, that which she rendered to me, and which was greater than I could ever had repaid her, was this. One night, when we were pacing slowly along Oxford Street, and after a day when I had felt more than usually ill and faint, I requested her to turn off with me into Soho Square.[6] Thither we went, and we sat down on the steps of a house which to this hour I never pass without a pang of grief and an inner act of homage to the spirit of that unhappy girl, in memory of the noble action which she there performed. Suddenly, as we sat, I grew much worse: I had been leaning my head against her bosom, and all at once I sank from her arms and fell backwards on the steps. From the sensations I then had, I felt an inner conviction of the liveliest kind that without some powerful and reviving stimulus I should either have died on the spot or should at least have sunk to a point of exhaustion from which all re-ascent under my friendless circumstances would soon have become hopeless.

Then it was, at this crisis of my fate, that my poor orphan companion – who had herself met with little but injuries in this world – stretched out a saving hand to me. Uttering a cry of terror, but without a moment's delay, she ran off into Oxford Street and in less time than could be imagined returned to me with a glass of port wine and

Notes

[3] *Oxford Street* central thoroughfare in the west end of London, running from St Giles' Circus to Park Lane. In 1802 its properties were mainly residential.

[4] *porticos* porchways, some of which in Oxford Street would have been quite grand.

[5] *wanderers* vagrants.

[6] *Soho Square* square of buildings just off the south side of the eastern end of Oxford Street. In 1802 its properties were the residences of professionals – doctors, lawyers, dentists and architects.

spices, that acted upon my empty stomach (which at that time would have rejected all solid food) with an instantaneous power of restoration – and for this glass the generous girl without a murmur paid out of her own humble purse at a time (be it remembered) when she had scarcely wherewithal to purchase the bare necessaries of life, and when she could have no reason to expect that I should ever be able to reimburse her.

Oh youthful benefactress! How often, in succeeding years, standing in solitary places and thinking of thee with grief of heart and perfect love – how often have I wished that, as in ancient times the curse of a father was believed to have a supernatural power, and to pursue its object with a fatal necessity of self-fulfilment, even so, the benediction of a heart oppressed with gratitude might have a like prerogative,[7] might have power given to it from above to chase, to haunt, to waylay, to overtake, to pursue thee into the central darkness of a London brothel, or (if it were possible) into the darkness of the grave, there to awaken thee with an authentic message of peace and forgiveness, and of final reconciliation!

I do not often weep, for not only do my thoughts on subjects connected with the chief interests of man daily, nay hourly, descend a thousand fathoms 'too deep for tears';[8] not only does the sternness of my habits of thought present an antagonism[9] to the feelings which prompt tears (wanting of necessity to those who, being protected usually by their levity from any tendency to meditative sorrow, would by that same levity be made incapable of resisting it on any casual access of such feelings) – but also I believe that all minds which have contemplated such objects as deeply as I have done, must for their own protection from utter despondency have early encouraged and cherished some tranquillizing belief as to the future balances[10] and the hieroglyphic[11] meanings of human sufferings. On these accounts, I am cheerful to this hour, and, as I have said, I do not often weep. Yet some feelings, though not deeper or more passionate, are more tender than others, and often, when I walk at this time in Oxford Street by dreamy lamplight, and hear those airs played on a barrel-organ which years ago solaced me and my dear companion (as I must always call her), I shed tears, and muse with myself at the mysterious dispensation[12] which so suddenly and so critically separated us for ever.

[*The Malay*]

From Confessions of an English Opium-Eater (1822)

One day a Malay knocked at my door.[1] What business a Malay could have to transact amongst English mountains I cannot conjecture, but possibly he was on his road to a seaport about forty miles distant.[2]

The servant who opened the door to him was a young girl born and bred amongst the mountains, who had never seen an Asiatic dress of any sort – his turban, therefore,

Notes

[7] *prerogative* privilege.

[8] *too deep for tears* from Wordsworth, 'Ode' 206: 'Thoughts that do often lie too deep for tears'.

[9] *antagonism* opposition.

[10] *balances* i.e. the belief that all suffering is balanced with an equal amount of happiness.

[11] *hieroglyphic* symbolic, emblematic. De Quincey is comforted by the thought that suffering is not meaningless – that it has some kind of higher significance in the making of the soul.

[12] *dispensation* ordering agency (implicitly, of God).

The Malay

[1] *my door* that of Dove Cottage, Grasmere, where De Quincey lived from 1809 to 1819. Assuming that this episode is a record of an actual event, the Malay's visit probably took place in 1816.

[2] *a seaport . . . distant* probably Whitehaven, a trading port on the north-west coast of the Lake District.

confounded her not a little – and as it turned out that his attainments in English were exactly of the same extent as hers in the Malay, there seemed to be an impassable gulf fixed between all communication of ideas (if either party had happened to possess any). In this dilemma, the girl, recollecting the reputed learning of her master (and doubtless giving me credit for a knowledge of all the languages of the earth, besides, perhaps, a few of the lunar ones), came and gave me to understand that there was a sort of demon below, whom she clearly imagined that my art could exorcise from the house.

I did not immediately go down, but when I did, the group which presented itself – arranged as it was by accident, though not very elaborate, took hold of my fancy and my eye in a way that none of the statuesque attitudes exhibited in the ballets at the Opera House, though so ostentatiously complex, had ever done. In a cottage kitchen, but panelled on the wall with dark wood that from age and rubbing resembled oak, and looking more like a rustic hall of entrance than a kitchen, stood the Malay, his turban and loose trousers of dingy white relieved upon[3] the dark panelling. He had placed himself nearer to the girl than she seemed to relish, though her native spirit of mountain intrepidity contended with the feeling of simple awe which her countenance expressed as she gazed upon the tiger-cat before her. And a more striking picture there could not be imagined, than the beautiful English face of the girl, and its exquisite fairness, together with her erect and independent attitude, contrasted with the sallow and bilious[4] skin of the Malay, enamelled or veneered with mahogany, by marine air, his small fierce restless eyes, thin lips, slavish gestures and adorations.[5] Half-hidden by the ferocious-looking Malay was a little child from a neighbouring cottage who had crept in after him and was now in the act of reverting its head, and gazing upwards at the turban and the fiery eyes beneath it, whilst with one hand he caught at the dress of the young woman for protection.

My knowledge of the oriental tongues is not remarkably extensive, being indeed confined to two words: the Arabic word for barley, and the Turkish for opium (madjoon), which I have learnt from *Anastasius*.[6] And as I had neither a Malay dictionary, nor even Adelung's *Mithridates*,[7] which might have helped me to a few words, I addressed him in some lines from the *Iliad*, considering that, of such languages as I possessed, Greek, in point of longitude, came geographically nearest to an oriental one. He worshipped me in a most devout manner, and replied in what I suppose was Malay. In this way I saved my reputation with my neighbours, for the Malay had no means of betraying the secret. He lay down upon the floor for about an hour, and then pursued his journey.

On his departure, I presented him with a piece of opium. To him, as an orientalist, I concluded that opium must be familiar, and the expression of his face convinced me that it was. Nevertheless, I was struck with some little consternation when I saw him suddenly raise his hand to his mouth and (in the schoolboy phrase) bolt[8] the whole, divided into three pieces, at one mouthful. The quantity was enough to kill three dragoons and their horses, and I felt some alarm for the poor creature – but what could be done? I had given him the opium in compassion for his solitary life, on

Notes

3 *relieved upon* i.e. standing out against.

4 *bilious* brownish-yellow (like bile, the fluid secreted from the liver).

5 *adorations* gestures of respect.

6 *Anastasius, or, Memoirs of a Greek* (1819), popular novel by Thomas Hope (1770–1831), often attributed to Byron. At one point an old man warns its hero that opium leads to madness.

7 Friedrich von Adelung, *Mithridates, oder Allegemeine Sprachenkunde* (1806), polyglot grammar and dictionary, which contains a section on Malay.

8 *bolt* swallow.

recollecting that, if he had travelled on foot from London, it must be nearly three weeks since he could have exchanged a thought with any human being. I could not think of violating the laws of hospitality by having him seized and drenched[9] with an emetic, and thus frightening him into a notion that we were going to sacrifice him to some English idol. No – there was clearly no help for it. He took his leave, and for some days I felt anxious; but as I never heard of any Malay being found dead, I became convinced that he was used to opium, and that I must have done him the service I designed, by giving him one night of respite from the pains of wandering.

This incident I have digressed to mention because this Malay (partly from the picturesque exhibition he assisted to frame, partly from the anxiety I connected with his image for some days) fastened afterwards upon my dreams,[10] and brought other Malays with him worse than himself, that ran amuck at me,[11] and led me into a world of troubles.

[*The Pains of Opium*]

From Confessions of an English Opium-Eater (1822)

I now pass to what is the main subject of these latter confessions – to the history and journal of what took place in my dreams, for these were the immediate and proximate cause of my acutest suffering.

The first notice I had of any important change going on in this part of my physical economy, was from the reawakening of a state of eye generally incident[1] to childhood or exalted states of irritability.[2] I know not whether my reader is aware that many children – perhaps most – have a power of painting, as it were, upon the darkness, all sorts of phantoms. In some, that power is simply a mechanic affection[3] of the eye; others have a voluntary or a semi-voluntary power to dismiss or to summon them – or, as a child once said to me when I questioned him on this matter, 'I can tell them to go and they go, but sometimes they come when I don't tell them to come.' Whereupon I told him that he had almost as unlimited a command over apparitions as a Roman centurion over his soldiers.[4]

In the middle of 1817, I think it was, that this faculty became positively distressing to me. At night, when I lay awake in bed, vast processions passed along in mournful pomp,[5] friezes of never-ending stories that to my feelings were as sad and solemn as if they were stories drawn from times before Oedipus or Priam[6] – before Tyre, before Memphis.[7] And at the same time a corresponding change took place in my dreams; a theatre seemed suddenly opened and lighted up within my brain, which presented

Notes

[9] *drenched* force-fed.

[10] *fastened afterwards upon my dreams* The Malay returns to haunt De Quincey; see 'Oriental Dreams', p. 816.

[11] 'See the common accounts in any eastern traveller or voyage of the frantic excesses committed by Malays who have taken opium, or are reduced to desperation by ill luck at gambling' (De Quincey's note).

THE PAINS OF OPIUM

[1] *incident* relating.

[2] *irritability* excitement, rather than annoyance.

[3] *mechanic affection* involuntary property.

[4] *as a Roman centurion . . . soldiers* a recollection of Matthew 8: 9.

[5] *At night . . . pomp* De Quincey is recalling a fragment composed by Wordsworth at the same time as the *Two-Part Prelude*, 'When in my bed I lay':

When in my bed I lay
Alone in darkness, I have seen the gloom
Peopled with shapes arrayed in hues more bright
Than flowers or gems or than the evening sky:
Processions . . . (ll.1–5)

[6] *Oedipus or Priam* Oedipus was the King of Thebes, whose remarkable story is told in *Oedipus Rex* and *Oedipus Coloneus*; Priam, King of Troy, oversaw the Trojan Wars, which were started when his son, Paris, abducted Helen.

[7] Tyre was a Phoenician seaport founded *c.*400 BC; the Egyptian city of Memphis dates from 3000 BC.

nightly spectacles of more than earthly splendour. And the four following facts may be mentioned as noticeable at this time:

1. That, as the creative state of the eye increased, a sympathy seemed to arise between the waking and the dreaming states of the brain in one point – that whatsoever I happened to call up and to trace by a voluntary act upon the darkness was very apt to transfer itself to my dreams, so that I feared to exercise this faculty, for, as Midas turned all things to gold[8] that yet baffled his hopes and defrauded his human desires, so whatsoever things capable of being visually represented I did but think of in the darkness, immediately shaped themselves into phantoms of the eye, and, by a process apparently no less inevitable, when thus once traced in faint and visionary colours, like writings in sympathetic ink, they were drawn out by the fierce chemistry of my dreams into insufferable splendour that fretted[9] my heart.

2. For this and all other changes in my dreams were accompanied by deep-seated anxiety and gloomy melancholy, such as are wholly incommunicable by words. I seemed every night to descend – not metaphorically, but literally to descend, into chasms and sunless abysses, depths below depths, from which it seemed hopeless that I could ever reascend. Nor did I, by waking, feel that I *had* reascended. This I do not dwell upon, because the state of gloom which attended these gorgeous spectacles, amounting at least to utter darkness, as of some suicidal despondency, cannot be approached by words.

3. The sense of space and, in the end, the sense of time, were both powerfully affected. Buildings, landscapes, etc., were exhibited in proportions so vast as the bodily eye is not fitted to receive. Space swelled and was amplified to an extent of unutterable infinity. This however did not disturb me so much as the vast expansion of time: I sometimes seemed to have lived for 70 or 100 years in one night – nay, sometimes had feelings representative of a millennium[10] passed in that time, or, however, of a duration far beyond the limits of any human experience.

4. The minutest incidents of childhood, or forgotten scenes of later years, were often revived. I could not be said to recollect them, for if I had been told of them when waking, I should not have been able to acknowledge them as parts of my past experience. But placed as they were before me, in dreams like intuitions, and clothed in all their evanescent circumstances and accompanying feelings, I *recognized* them instantaneously. I was once told by a near relative of mine[11] that, having in her childhood fallen into a river, and being on the very verge of death but for the critical assistance which reached her, she saw in a moment her whole life, in its minutest incidents, arrayed before her simultaneously as in a mirror, and she had a faculty developed as suddenly for comprehending the whole and every part. This, from some opium experiences of mine, I can believe; I have indeed seen the same thing asserted twice in modern books,[12] and accompanied by a remark which I am convinced is true – viz. that the dread book of account[13] which the scriptures speak of is, in fact, the mind itself of each individual. Of this at least I feel assured: that there is no such thing as *forgetting* possible to the mind; a thousand accidents may and will interpose a veil

Notes

[8] *as Midas . . . gold* mythical King of Phrygia, who asked that whatever he touched be turned to gold. He realized he had made an error when his food turned into gold, and he was cured by bathing in the River Pactolus.

[9] *fretted* tormented.

[10] *a millennium* 1,000 years.

[11] *a near relative of mine* his mother, Elizabeth Penson Quincey, who at this time was 65.

[12] *modern books* probably Swedenborg's *Arcana Coelestia* and Coleridge's *Biographia Literaria*.

[13] *the dread book of account* mentioned Revelation 13: 8: 'And all that dwell upon the earth shall worship him, whose names are not written in the book of life of the Lamb slain from the foundation of the world.'

between our present consciousness and the secret inscriptions on the mind[14] – accidents of the same sort will also rend away this veil. But alike, whether veiled or unveiled, the inscription remains for ever, just as the stars seem to withdraw before the common light of day, whereas in fact we all know that it is the light which is drawn over them as a veil, and that they are waiting to be revealed when the obscuring daylight shall have withdrawn . . .

[*The Pains of Opium: Visions of Piranesi*][1]

From Confessions of an English Opium-Eater (1822)

Many years ago, when I was looking over Piranesi's *Antiquities of Rome*, Mr Coleridge,[2] who was standing by, described to me a set of plates by that artist called his 'Dreams', and which record the scenery of his own visions during the delirium of a fever. Some of them (I describe only from memory of Mr Coleridge's account) represented vast Gothic halls: on the floor of which stood all sorts of engines and machinery, wheels, cables, pulleys, levers, catapults, etc., etc. expressive of enormous power put forth, and resistance overcome. Creeping along the sides of the walls, you perceived a staircase, and upon it, groping his way upwards, was Piranesi himself. Follow the stairs a little further, and you perceive it come to a sudden abrupt termination, without any balustrade, and allowing no step onwards to him who had reached the extremity, except into the depths below. Whatever is to become of poor Piranesi, you suppose, at least, that his labours must in some way terminate here. But raise your eyes, and behold a second flight of stairs still higher: on which again Piranesi is perceived, but this time standing on the very brink of the abyss. Again elevate your eye, and a still more aerial flight of stairs is beheld: and again is poor Piranesi busy on his aspiring labours: and so on, until the unfinished stairs and Piranesi both are lost in the upper gloom of the hall.

With the same power of endless growth and self-reproduction did my architecture proceed in dreams. In the early stage of my malady, the splendours of my dreams were indeed chiefly architectural: and I beheld such pomp of cities and palaces as was never yet beheld by the waking eye, unless in the clouds.

[*Oriental Dreams*]

From Confessions of an English Opium-Eater (1822)

May 1818

The Malay has been a fearful enemy for months. I have been every night, through his means, transported into Asiatic scenes. I know not whether others share in my feelings on this point, but I have often thought that if I were compelled to forego England and to live in China and among Chinese manners and modes of life and scenery, I should go mad.

Notes

[14] *secret inscriptions on the mind* memories impressed indelibly on the mind. De Quincey is thinking in Wordsworthian terms; cf. *Pedlar* 30–4.

THE PAINS OF OPIUM: VISIONS OF PIRANESI

[1] This passage is inspired by recollections of the engravings of Giovanni Battista Piranesi (1720–78). He was responsible for depictions of the ruins of ancient Rome, entitled *Vedute di Roma* (1748–78) as well as for the visionary, and terrifying, *Carceri d'invenzione* ('Imaginary Prisons') of 1745. Reproductions of some of these images can be found on the internet at http://users.ox.ac.uk/~scat1492/piranesi.htm.

[2] *Mr Coleridge* Coleridge sent a box 'containing the Piranesi Folios for William' [i.e. Wordsworth] to Grasmere in 1808. De Quincey probably saw them, and may have seen others in Coleridge's possession in London.

The causes of my horror lie deep, and some of them must be common to others. Southern Asia, in general, is the seat of awful images and associations. As the cradle of the human race, it would alone have a dim and reverential feeling connected with it. But there are other reasons. No man can pretend that the wild, barbarous, and capricious superstitions of Africa, or of savage tribes elsewhere, affect him in the way that he is affected by the ancient, monumental, cruel, and elaborate religions of Indostan,[1] etc. The mere antiquity of Asiatic things, of their institutions, histories, modes of faith, etc., is so impressive, that to me the vast age of the race and name overpowers the sense of youth in the individual. A young Chinese seems to me an antediluvian man[2] renewed. Even Englishmen, though not bred in any knowledge of such institutions, cannot but shudder at the mystic sublimity of castes that have flowed apart and refused to mix, through such immemorial tracts of time – nor can any man fail to be awed by the names of the Ganges or the Euphrates.

It contributes much to these feelings that southern Asia is, and has been for thousands of years, the part of the earth most swarming with human life – the great *officina gentium*.[3] Man is a weed in those regions. The vast empires also, into which the enormous population of Asia has always been cast, give a further sublimity to the feelings associated with all oriental names or images. In China, over and above what it has in common with the rest of southern Asia, I am terrified by the modes of life, by the manners, and the barrier of utter abhorrence and want of sympathy placed between us by feelings deeper than I can analyze. I could sooner live with lunatics or brute animals.[4] All this, and much more than I can say or have time to say, the reader must enter into before he can comprehend the unimaginable horror which these dreams of oriental imagery and mythological tortures impressed upon me.

Under the connecting feeling of tropical heat and vertical sunlights, I brought together all creatures, birds, beasts, reptiles, all trees and plants, usages[5] and appearances that are found in all tropical regions, and assembled them together in China or Indostan. From kindred feelings I soon brought Egypt and all her gods under the same law. I was stared at, hooted at, grinned at, chattered at, by monkeys, by parakeets, by cockatoos. I ran into pagodas and was fixed for centuries at the summit, or in secret rooms. I was the idol, I was the priest, I was worshipped, I was sacrificed. I fled from the wrath of Brahma[6] through all the forests of Asia. Vishnu hated me. Siva laid wait for me.[7] I came suddenly upon Isis and Osiris.[8] I had done a deed, they said, which the ibis[9] and the crocodile trembled at. I was buried for a thousand years in stone coffins, with mummies and sphinxes, in narrow chambers at the heart of eternal pyramids. I was kissed with cancerous kisses by crocodiles, and laid confounded with all unutterable slimy things amongst reeds and Nilotic mud.

I thus give the reader some slight abstraction of[10] my oriental dreams, which always filled me with such amazement at the monstrous[11] scenery, that horror seemed absorbed for a while in sheer astonishment. Sooner or later came a reflux[12] of feeling

Notes

Oriental Dreams

[1] *Indostan* India.

[2] *antediluvian man* man before the great flood.

[3] *officina gentium* workshop of peoples.

[4] *I am terrified . . . animals* De Quincey wrote a number of anti-Chinese articles inspired by the opium wars in 1839. It should be remembered that racist opinions were so common in his day as to be unremarkable – so common that the very concept of racism was unknown (the *OED*'s first usage is dated 1907).

[5] *usages* customs.

[6] *Brahma* supreme God of Hindu myth.

[7] Vishnu and Siva are Hindu deities.

[8] *Isis and Osiris* Egyptian deities.

[9] *ibis* The Sacred Ibis of Egypt (*Ibis religiosa*), with white and black plumage, was an object of veneration among the ancient Egyptians.

[10] *slight abstraction of* brief extract from.

[11] *monstrous* unnatural.

[12] *reflux* return.

that swallowed up the astonishment, and left me not so much in terror as in hatred and abomination of what I saw. Over every form, and threat, and punishment, and dim sightless incarceration, brooded a sense of eternity and infinity that drove me into an oppression as of madness. Into these dreams only it was (with one or two slight exceptions) that any circumstances of physical horror entered. All before had been moral and spiritual terrors, but here the main agents were ugly birds, or snakes, or crocodiles – especially the last. The cursed crocodile became to me the object of more horror than almost all the rest. I was compelled to live with him, and (as was always the case almost in my dreams) for centuries. I escaped sometimes, and found myself in Chinese houses with cane tables, etc. All the feet of the tables, sofas, etc., soon became instinct[13] with life. The abominable head of the crocodile, and his leering eyes, looked out at me, multiplied into a thousand repetitions – and I stood loathing and fascinated. And so often did this hideous reptile haunt my dreams, that many times the very same dream was broken up in the very same way: I heard gentle voices speaking to me (I hear everything when I am sleeping), and instantly I awoke.

It was broad noon, and my children were standing, hand in hand, at my bedside, come to show me their coloured shoes or new frocks, or to let me see them dressed for going out. I protest that so awful was the transition from the damned crocodile and the other unutterable monsters and abortions of my dreams to the sight of innocent *human* natures and of infancy, that, in the mighty and sudden revulsion of mind, I wept, and could not forbear it, as I kissed their faces.[14]

[*Easter Sunday*]

From Confessions of an English Opium-Eater (1822)

June 1819

I have had occasion to remark, at various periods of my life, that the deaths of those whom we love – and indeed the contemplation of death generally – is, *caeteris paribus*,[1] more affecting in summer than in any other season of the year. And the reasons are these three, I think:

First, that the visible heavens in summer appear far higher, more distant, and (if such a solecism may be excused) more infinite; the clouds, by which chiefly the eye expounds[2] the distance of the blue pavilion stretched over our heads, are in summer more voluminous, massed, and accumulated in far grander and more towering piles; secondly, the light and the appearances of the declining and the setting sun are much more fitted to be types and characters of the Infinite;[3] and thirdly (which is the main reason), the exuberant and riotous prodigality[4] of life naturally forces the mind more powerfully upon the antagonist[5] thought of death and the wintry sterility of the grave – for it may be observed generally that wherever two thoughts stand related to each

Notes

[13] *instinct* animated.

[14] De Quincey is recalling Coleridge's *The Day-Dream* (see pp. 658–9).

Easter Sunday

[1] *caeteris paribus* other things being equal.

[2] *expounds* infers.

[3] *types . . . Infinite* a phrase that reveals De Quincey's understanding of Berkeley's philosophy (imbibed, perhaps, from Coleridge), though in fact he echoes Wordsworth, *Thirteen-Book Prelude* vi 571: 'types and symbols of eternity'. Berkeley's central idea was that the material world was an idea in the mind of God, and that nature was God's 'writing' (hence 'types', as in the sense of a typeface).

[4] *prodigality* rich profusion.

[5] *antagonist* opposite.

other by a law of antagonism, and exist, as it were, by mutual repulsion, they are apt to suggest each other.

On these accounts it is that I find it impossible to banish the thought of death when I am walking alone in the endless days of summer, and any particular death, if not more affecting, at least haunts my mind more obstinately and besiegingly in that season. Perhaps this cause, and a slight incident which I omit, might have been the immediate occasions of the following dream – to which, however, a predisposition must always have existed in my mind. But having been once roused, it never left me, and split into a thousand fantastic varieties, which often suddenly reunited and composed again the original dream.

I thought that it was a Sunday morning in May, that it was Easter Sunday, and as yet very early in the morning. I was standing, as it seemed to me, at the door of my own cottage.[6] Right before me lay the very scene which could really be commanded from that situation, but exalted (as was usual) and solemnized by the power of dreams. There were the same mountains and the same lovely valley at their feet, but the mountains were raised to more than Alpine height, and there was interspace[7] far larger between them of meadows and forest lawns. The hedges were rich with white roses, and no living creature was to be seen, excepting that in the green churchyard there were cattle tranquilly reposing upon the verdant graves, and particularly round about the grave of a child[8] whom I had tenderly loved, just as I had really beheld them, a little before sunrise in the same summer, when that child died. I gazed upon the well-known scene, and I said aloud (as I thought) to myself, 'It yet wants much of sunrise; and it is Easter Sunday, and that is the day on which they celebrate the first fruits of resurrection. I will walk abroad. Old griefs shall be forgotten today, for the air is cool and still, and the hills are high, and stretch away to heaven, and the forest-glades are as quiet as the churchyard; and, with the dew, I can wash the fever from my forehead, and then I shall be unhappy no longer.'

And I turned as if to open my garden gate – and immediately I saw upon the left a scene far different, but which yet the power of dreams had reconciled into harmony with the other. The scene was an oriental one, and there also it was Easter Sunday and very early in the morning. And at a vast distance were visible, as a stain upon the horizon, the domes and cupolas of a great city – an image or faint abstraction caught perhaps in childhood from some picture of Jerusalem. And not a bowshot[9] from me, upon a stone and shaded by Judean palms, there sat a woman – and I looked – and it was – Ann! She fixed her eyes upon me earnestly, and I said to her at length, 'So then I have found you at last.' I waited, but she answered me not a word. Her face was the same as when I saw it last, and yet again how different! Seventeen years ago, when the lamplight fell upon her face, as for the last time I kissed her lips (lips, Ann, that to me were not polluted), her eyes were streaming with tears; the tears were now wiped away. She seemed more beautiful than she was at that time, but in all other points the same, and not older. Her looks were tranquil, but with unusual solemnity of expression, and I now gazed upon her with some awe.

Notes

[6] *my own cottage* Dove Cottage, Grasmere.

[7] *interspace* intervening space.

[8] *a child* Catharine Wordsworth (1808–12), the poet's daughter; De Quincey was close to Kate and devastated by her death. For more than two months after he slept on her grave; see headnote, p. 808.

[9] *a bowshot* an arrow's flight; about 300 yards.

But suddenly her countenance grew dim, and, turning to the mountains, I perceived vapours rolling between us. In a moment all had vanished; thick darkness came on, and, in the twinkling of an eye, I was far away from mountains, and by lamplight in Oxford Street, walking again with Ann – just as we walked seventeen years before when we were both children.[10]

On the Knocking at the Gate in Macbeth (first published under the pseudonym, 'X.Y.Z.')[1]

From London Magazine (October 1823)

From my boyish days I had always felt a great perplexity on one point in *Macbeth*. It was this: the knocking at the gate which succeeds to the murder of Duncan[2] produced to my feelings an effect for which I never could account. The effect was that it reflected back upon the murder a peculiar awfulness[3] and a depth of solemnity. Yet however obstinately I endeavoured with my understanding to comprehend this, for many years I never could see *why* it should produce such an effect.[4]

Here I pause for one moment to exhort the reader never to pay any attention to his understanding when it stands in opposition to any other faculty of his mind. The mere understanding, however useful and indispensable, is the meanest faculty in the human mind and the most to be distrusted – and yet the great majority of people trust to nothing else, which may do for ordinary life, but not for philosophic purposes. Of this, out of ten thousand instances that I might produce, I will cite one. Ask of any person whatsoever, who is not previously prepared for the demand by a knowledge of perspective, to draw in the rudest way the commonest appearance which depends upon the laws of that science[5] – as for instance, to represent the effect of two walls standing at right angles to each other, or the appearance of the houses on each side of a street, as seen by a person looking down the street from one extremity. Now in all cases, unless the person has happened to observe in pictures how it is that artists produce these effects, he will be utterly unable to make the smallest approximation to it. Yet why? For he has actually seen the effect every day of his life. The reason is that he allows his understanding to overrule his eyes. His understanding, which includes no intuitive[6] knowledge of the laws of vision, can furnish him with no reason why a line which is known and can be proved to be a horizontal line, should not *appear* a horizontal line; a line that made any angle with the perpendicular less than a right angle would seem to him to indicate that his houses were all tumbling down together. Accordingly he makes the line of his houses a horizontal line and fails of course to produce the effect demanded.

Here then is one instance out of many in which not only the understanding is allowed to overrule the eyes, but where the understanding is positively allowed to

Notes

[10] *both children* De Quincey had been 17, Ann 16.

On the Knocking at the Gate in Macbeth

[1] This is probably De Quincey's most important work of literary criticism. In it, he is interested by the emotional response produced by the knocking of Macduff and Lennox at the gate of Macbeth's castle, which begins at the end of Act II, scene ii, continuing into scene iii.

[2] *the murder of Duncan* Macbeth, a general in the army, kills King Duncan as a first step to taking the throne.

[3] *awfulness* feeling of awe.

[4] De Quincey is pointing out the disparity between a trivial, apparently insignificant stage direction, 'Knock within', and his response (awe and solemnity).

[5] *that science* i.e. the laws of perspective.

[6] *intuitive* Behind this lies the distinction, followed by Coleridge and Wordsworth, between discursive (belonging to man) and intuitive understanding (belonging to angels), as stated in *Paradise Lost* v 486–90. See also *Thirteen-Book Prelude* xiii 113.

obliterate the eyes as it were. For not only does the man believe the evidence of his understanding in opposition to that of his eyes, but (which is monstrous!) the idiot is not aware that his eyes ever gave such evidence. He does not know that he has seen (and therefore *quoad*[7] his consciousness has *not* seen) that which he *has* seen every day of his life.

But to return from this digression. My understanding could furnish no reason why the knocking at the gate in *Macbeth* should produce any effect direct or reflected;[8] in fact, my understanding said positively that it could *not* produce any effect. But I knew better.[9] I felt that it did, and I waited and clung to the problem until further knowledge should enable me to solve it. At length, in 1812, Mr Williams made his début on the stage of Ratcliffe Highway,[10] and executed those unparalleled murders which have procured for him such a brilliant and undying reputation.

On which murders, by the way, I must observe that in one respect they have had an ill effect, by making the connoisseur in murder very fastidious in his taste and dissatisfied with anything that has been since done in that line. All other murders look pale by the deep crimson of his – and, as an amateur once said to me in a querulous tone, 'There has been absolutely nothing *doing* since his time, or nothing that's worth speaking of.' But this is wrong, for it is unreasonable to expect all men to be great artists, and born with the genius of Mr Williams.

Now it will be remembered that in the first of these murders (that of the Marrs) the same incident (of a knocking at the door soon after the work of extermination was complete) did actually occur which the genius of Shakespeare had invented – and all good judges and the most eminent dilettanti[11] acknowledged the felicity of Shakespeare's suggestion as soon as it was actually realized. Here then was a fresh proof that I had been right in relying on my own feeling in opposition to my understanding, and again I set myself to study the problem. At length I solved it to my own satisfaction, and my solution is this. Murder in ordinary cases, where the sympathy is wholly directed to the case of the murdered person, is an incident of coarse and vulgar horror, and for this reason – that it flings the interest exclusively upon the natural but ignoble instinct by which we cleave to life (an instinct which, as being indispensable to the primal law of self-preservation, is the same in kind, though different in degree, amongst all living creatures) – this instinct therefore, because it annihilates all distinctions and degrades the greatest of men to the level of 'the poor beetle that we tread on',[12] exhibits human nature in its most abject and humiliating attitude.

Such an attitude would little suit the purposes of the poet. What then must he do? He must throw the interest on the murderer: our sympathy must be with *him* (of course I mean a sympathy of comprehension, a sympathy by which we enter into his feelings and are made to understand them – not a sympathy of pity or approbation). In the murdered person all strife of thought, all flux and reflux of passion and of purpose, are crushed by one overwhelming panic: the fear of instant death smites him 'with its

Notes

7 *quoad* with respect to.

8 *reflected* i.e. indirect.

9 *But I knew better* Discursive reason tells him that his response is nonsensical; intuitive reason tells him that it is justified.

10 *Mr Williams . . . Highway* John Williams (1784–1811) was presumed to have committed a series of murders that began on 7 December 1811. He was apprehended on Christmas Day and tried two days later, but was later found dead in his prison cell. A servant-girl sent out on an errand returned and knocked at the door while Williams, who had murdered the entire family, was still inside the house with the bodies of his victims: Timothy Marr, linen-draper; Celia Marr, his wife; Timothy Marr Jr, their infant son; and James Gowen, Marr's apprentice.

11 *dilettanti* lovers of the fine arts.

12 *the poor beetle that we tread on* from *Measure for Measure* III i 78.

petrific mace'.[13] But in the murderer, such a murderer as a poet will condescend to, there must be raging some great storm of passion – jealousy, ambition, vengeance, hatred – which will create a hell within him, and into this hell we are to look. In *Macbeth*, for the sake of gratifying his own enormous and teeming faculty of creation, Shakespeare has introduced two murderers,[14] and, as usual in his hands, they are remarkably discriminated. But though in Macbeth the strife of mind is greater than in his wife, the tiger-spirit not so awake, and his feelings caught chiefly by contagion from her – yet, as both were finally involved in the guilt of murder, the murderous mind of necessity is finally to be presumed in both. This was to be expressed; and on its own account, as well as to make it a more proportionable antagonist to the unoffending nature of their victim, 'the gracious Duncan',[15] and adequately to expound 'the deep damnation of his taking off',[16] this was to be expressed with peculiar energy. We were to be made to feel that the human nature (i.e. the divine nature of love and mercy, spread through the hearts of all creatures, and seldom utterly withdrawn from man) was gone, vanished, extinct – and that the fiendish nature had taken its place. And as this effect is marvellously accomplished in the dialogues and soliloquies themselves, so it is finally consummated[17] by the expedient under consideration[18] – and it is to this that I now solicit the reader's attention.

If the reader has ever witnessed a wife, daughter or sister in a fainting fit, he may chance to have observed that the most affecting moment in such a spectacle is that in which a sigh and a stirring announce the recommencement of suspended life. Or if the reader has ever been present in a vast metropolis on the day when some great national idol was carried in funeral pomp to his grave, and chancing to walk near to the course through which it passed, has felt powerfully, in the silence and desertion of the streets, and in the stagnation of ordinary business, the deep interest which at that moment was possessing the heart of man; if all at once he should hear the deathlike stillness broken up by the sound of wheels rattling away from the scene, and making known that the transitory vision was dissolved, he will be aware that at no moment was his sense of the complete suspension and pause in ordinary human concerns so full and affecting as at that moment when the suspension ceases, and the goings-on of human life are suddenly resumed. All action in any direction is best expounded, measured, and made apprehensible, by reaction.

Now apply this to the case in *Macbeth*. Here, as I have said, the retiring of the human heart and the entrance of the fiendish heart was to be expressed and made sensible.[19] Another world has stepped in, and the murderers are taken out of the region of human things, human purposes, human desires. They are transfigured: Lady Macbeth is 'unsexed',[20] Macbeth has forgot that he was born of woman,[21] both are conformed to the image of devils, and the world of devils is suddenly revealed. But how shall this be conveyed and made palpable? In order that a new world may step in, this world must for a time disappear. The murderers and the murder must be insulated, cut off by an immeasurable gulf from the ordinary tide and succession of human affairs, locked up and sequestered in some deep recess; we must be made sensible that the world of ordinary life is suddenly arrested, laid asleep,[22] tranced,

Notes

[13] *with its petrific mace* from *Paradise Lost* x 294.

[14] *two murderers* i.e. Macbeth and Lady Macbeth.

[15] *the gracious Duncan* from *Macbeth* III i 65.

[16] *the deep damnation of his taking off* from *Macbeth* I vii 20.

[17] *consummated* completed.

[18] *the expedient under consideration* i.e. the knocking at the gate.

[19] *sensible* perceptible.

[20] *unsexed* an allusion to *Macbeth* I v 40–1: 'Come, you spirits / That tend on mortal thoughts, unsex me here.'

[21] *born of woman* an allusion to *Macbeth* IV i 80–1: 'for none of woman born / Shall harm Macbeth'.

[22] *laid asleep* cf. *Tintern Abbey* 46–7: 'we are laid asleep / In body, and become a living soul.'

racked into a dread armistice;[23] time must be annihilated, relation to things without[24] abolished, and all must pass self-withdrawn into a deep syncope[25] and suspension of earthly passion.

Hence it is that, when the deed is done, when the work of darkness is perfect, then the world of darkness passes away like a pageantry in the clouds. The knocking at the gate is heard, and it makes known audibly that the reaction has commenced – the human has made its reflux upon the fiendish, the pulses of life are beginning to beat again, and the re-establishment of the goings-on of the world in which we live first makes us profoundly sensible of the awful parenthesis[26] that had suspended them.

Oh mighty poet![27] Thy works are not as those of other men, simply and merely great works of art, but are also like the phenomena of nature, like the sun and the sea, the stars and the flowers, like frost and snow, rain and dew, hailstorm and thunder – which are to be studied with entire submission of our own faculties, and in the perfect faith that in them there can be no too much or too little, nothing useless or inert, but that the further we press in our discoveries, the more we shall see proofs of design and self-supporting arrangement where the careless eye had seen nothing but accident.

N.B. In the above specimen of psychological criticism, I have purposely omitted to notice another use of the knocking at the gate (viz. the opposition and contrast which it produces in the porter's comments[28] to the scenes immediately preceding) because this use is tolerably obvious to all who are accustomed to reflect on what they read. A third use also, subservient to the scenical illusion, has been lately noticed by a critic in the *London Magazine*.[29] I fully agree with him, but it did not fall in my way to insist on this.

[*On Wordsworth's 'There was a boy'*][1]

From Tait's Edinburgh Magazine (February 1839)

There is amongst the poems of Wordsworth one most ludicrously misconstrued by his critics, which offers a philosophical hint upon this subject, of great instruction. I will preface it with the little incident which first led Wordsworth into a commentary upon his own meaning.

One night, as often enough happened, during the Peninsular War,[2] he and I walked up Dunmail Raise from Grasmere,[3] about midnight, in order to meet the carrier who brought the London newspapers by a circuitous course from Keswick. The case was

Notes

[23] *racked into a dread armistice* time is stretched into a fearful suspension.

[24] *things without* i.e. external reality.

[25] *syncope* cessation.

[26] *awful parenthesis* awesome interlude.

[27] *Oh mighty poet!* Shakespeare.

[28] *the porter's comments* See *Macbeth* II iii 1–21.

[29] George Darley (as John Lacy) in his 'Third Letter to the Dramatists of the Day', *London Magazine* 8 (1823) 275–83, p. 276.

On Wordsworth's 'There was a boy'

[1] De Quincey began publishing his 'Lake Reminiscences' in *Tait's* in January 1839; they remain among his popular works because they provide the most lifelike and persuasive portrait of Wordsworth by one of his circle.

[2] *the Peninsular war* war in the Spanish and Portuguese peninsula, 1808–14, between the French and the English, Spanish and Portuguese. Wordsworth's fascination with the campaign, and sympathy with the Spanish freedom fighters, led him to write *The Convention of Cintra*, which De Quincey saw through the press in 1809 (see headnote, p. 807).

[3] *from Grasmere* The Wordsworths were then living at Allan Bank, De Quincey at Dove Cottage. Dunmail Raise is on the main road leading northwards out of Grasmere to Keswick.

this. Coleridge, for many years, received a copy of *The Courier*[4] as a mark of esteem, and in acknowledgement of his many contributions to it, from one of the proprietors, Mr Daniel Stuart. This went up in any case, let Coleridge be where he might,[5] to Mrs Coleridge.[6] For a single day it stayed at Keswick for the use of Southey, and on the next it came on to Wordsworth by the slow conveyance of a carrier, plying with a long train of carts between Whitehaven and Kendal.[7] Many a time the force of storms or floods would compel the carrier to stop on his route, five miles short of Grasmere at Wythburn, or even eight miles short at Legberthwaite. But as there was always hope until one or two o'clock in the morning, often and often it would happen that, in the deadly[8] impatience for earlier intelligence, Wordsworth and I would walk off to meet him about midnight, to a distance of three or four miles.

Upon one of these occasions, when some great crisis in Spain was daily apprehended, we had waited for an hour or more, sitting upon one of the many huge blocks of stone which lie scattered over that narrow field of battle on the desolate frontier of Cumberland and Westmorland, where King Dunmail with all his peerage fell more than a thousand years ago.[9] The time had arrived, at length, that all hope for that night had left us. No sound came up through the winding valleys that stretched to the north, and the few cottage lights, gleaming at wide distances from recesses amidst the rocky hills, had long been extinct. At intervals, Wordsworth had stretched himself at length on the high road, applying his ear to the ground so as to catch any sound of wheels that might be groaning along at a distance.

Once, when he was slowly rising from this effort, his eye caught a bright star that was glittering between the brow of Seat Sandal and of the mighty Helvellyn. He gazed upon it for a minute or so, and then, upon turning away to descend into Grasmere, he made the following explanation:

'I have remarked from my earliest days that if, under any circumstances, the attention is energetically braced up to an act of steady observation or of steady expectation, then, if this intense condition of vigilance should suddenly relax, at that moment any beautiful, any impressive visual object, or collection of objects, falling upon the eye, is carried to the heart with a power not known under other circumstances. Just now, my ear was placed upon the stretch in order to catch any sound of wheels that might come down upon the lake of Wythburn from the Keswick road; at the very instant when I raised my head from the ground in final abandonment of hope for this night, at the very instant when the organs of attention were all at once relaxing from their tension, the bright star hanging in the air above those outlines of massy blackness fell suddenly upon my eye, and penetrated my capacity of apprehension with a pathos and a sense of the infinite that would not have arrested me under other circumstances.'

He then went on to illustrate the same psychological principle from another instance. It was an instance derived from that exquisite poem[10] in which he describes

Notes

[4] *The Courier* quality evening newspaper of early 19th century, to which Coleridge, Wordsworth, Lamb and Southey contributed. Its proprietor was Daniel Stuart (1766–1846), who also published *The Morning Post*, 1796–1803.

[5] *let Coleridge be where he might* Generally speaking, Coleridge spent little of the first decade of the 19th century with his family, leaving it to Southey to provide for them. He had separated from his wife by 1807.

[6] *Mrs Coleridge* Sara (née Fricker), resident, with Southey and his family, at Greta Hall in Keswick.

[7] Whitehaven is a seaport on the far north-western coast of Cumbria, Kendal a market town in the south.

[8] *deadly* excessive.

[9] Dunmail, King of Cumberland, was defeated by the Saxon King Edmund in the decisive battle at Dunmail Raise. Dunmail was buried under a pile of stones which may still be seen on the Raise today.

[10] *that exquisite poem* 'There was a boy', published in *Lyrical Ballads* (1800); see p. 474. De Quincey would have known (though his readers would not) that it had been incorporated into *Thirteen-Book Prelude* v 389–422.

a mountain boy planting himself at twilight on the margin of some solitary bay of Windermere, and provoking the owls to a contest with himself by 'mimic hootings' blown through his hands – which of itself becomes an impressive scene to anyone able to realize to his fancy the various elements of the solitary woods and waters, the solemn vesper hour,[11] the solitary bird, the solitary boy. Afterwards, the poem goes on to describe the boy as waiting amidst 'the pauses of his skill' for the answers of the birds, waiting with intensity of expectation. And then at length when, after waiting to no purpose, his attention began to relax – that is, in other words, under the giving way of one exclusive direction of his senses, began suddenly to allow an admission to other objects – then, in that instant, the scene actually before him, the visible scene, would enter unawares, 'With all its solemn imagery'. This complex scenery was – what?

> Was carried *far* into his heart
> With all its pomp, and that uncertain heav'n received
> Into the bosom of the steady lake.[12]

This very expression, 'far', by which space and its infinities are attributed to the human heart, and to its capacities of re-echoing the sublimities of nature, has always struck me as with a flash of sublime revelation.

Suspiria de Profundis: The Affliction of Childhood (extract)[1]

From Blackwood's Edinburgh Magazine (March 1845)

It was upon a Sunday evening (or so people fancied) that the spark of fatal fire fell upon that train of predispositions to a brain complaint[2] which had hitherto slumbered within her. She had been permitted to drink tea at the house of a labouring man, the father of an old female servant. The sun had set when she returned in the company of this servant through meadows reeking with exhalations after a fervent day. From that time she sickened. Happily a child in such circumstances feels no anxieties. Looking upon medical men as people whose natural commission it is to heal diseases, since it is their natural function to profess it, knowing them only as *ex officio*[3] privileged to make war upon pain and sickness, I never had a misgiving about the result. I grieved indeed that my sister should lie in bed; I grieved still more sometimes to hear her moan. But all this appeared to me no more than a night of trouble on which the dawn would soon arise.

Oh moment of darkness and delirium when a nurse awakened me from that delusion, and launched God's thunderbolt at my heart in the assurance that my sister *must* die! Rightly it is said of utter, utter misery, that it 'cannot be *remembered*';[4] itself, as a rememberable thing, is swallowed up in its own chaos. Mere anarchy and confusion

Notes

[11] *vesper hour* time at which Venus (Vesper), the evening star, and the brightest, emerges in the evening sky.

[12] De Quincey is recollecting 'There was a boy' 20–5.

SUSPIRIA DE PROFUNDIS: THE AFFLICTION OF CHILDHOOD

[1] *Suspiria de Profundis* was a sequel to De Quincey's *Confessions*; see headnote, p. 810.

[2] *a brain complaint* Elizabeth Quincey died of meningitis in 1792, at the age of 9. De Quincey was 6. See headnote, p. 805, above.

[3] *ex officio* by virtue of their office.

[4] *cannot be remembered* De Quincey is quoting Alhadra, having seen her murdered husband, from Coleridge's *Remorse* (1813): 'I stood in unimaginable trance / And agony that cannot be remembered' (IV iii 53–4). He probably knew the original version of the play, *Osorio* (1797).

of mind fell upon me. Deaf and blind I was as I reeled under the revelation. I wish not to recall the circumstances of that time, when *my* agony was at its height, and hers in another sense was approaching. Enough to say that all was soon over, and the morning of that day had at last arrived which looked down upon her innocent face, sleeping the sleep from which there is no awaking, and upon me sorrowing the sorrow for which there is no consolation.

On the day after my sister's death, whilst the sweet temple of her brain was yet unviolated by human scrutiny,[5] I formed my own scheme for seeing her once more. Not for the world would I have made this known, nor have suffered a witness to accompany me. I had never heard of feelings that take the name of 'sentimental', nor dreamed of such a possibility. But grief even in a child hates the light, and shrinks from human eyes. The house was large; there were two staircases, and by one of these I knew that about noon, when all would be quiet, I could steal up into her chamber. I imagine that it was exactly high noon when I reached the chamber door. It was locked, but the key was not taken away. Entering, I closed the door so softly that, although it opened upon a hall which ascended through all the stories, no echo ran along the silent walls. Then turning round, I sought my sister's face. But the bed had been moved, and the back was now turned. Nothing met my eyes but one large window wide open, through which the sun of midsummer at noonday was showering down torrents of splendour. The weather was dry, the sky was cloudless, the blue depths seemed the express types of infinity,[6] and it was not possible for eye to behold or for heart to conceive any symbols more pathetic[7] of life and the glory of life.

Let me pause for one instant in approaching a remembrance so affecting and revolutionary for my own mind, and one which (if any earthly remembrance) will survive for me in the hour of death, to remind some readers and to inform others that in the original *Opium Confessions*[8] I endeavoured to explain the reason why death, *caeteris paribus*,[9] is more profoundly affecting in summer than in other parts of the year – so far at least as it is liable to any modification at all from accidents of scenery or season.[10] The reason, as I there suggested, lies in the antagonism between the tropical redundancy of life in summer and the dark sterilities of the grave. The summer we see, the grave we haunt with our thoughts; the glory is around us, the darkness is within us. And, the two coming into collision, each exalts the other into stronger relief. But in my case there was even a subtler reason why the summer had this intense power of vivifying[11] the spectacle or the thoughts of death. And, recollecting it, often I have been struck with the important truth that far more of our deepest thoughts and feelings pass to us through perplexed combinations of concrete objects, pass to us as *involutes* (if I may coin that word) in compound[12] experiences incapable of being disentangled, than ever reach us directly, and in their own abstract shapes.

It had happened that amongst our nursery collection of books was the Bible illustrated with many pictures. And in long dark evenings, as my three sisters with myself sat by the firelight round the guard[13] of our nursery, no book was so much in request amongst us. It ruled us and swayed us as mysteriously as music. One young

Notes

[5] *whilst the sweet temple . . . scrutiny* The usual procedure would have been to perform an autopsy as soon as possible to confirm the cause of death.

[6] *the express types of infinity* cf. *Thirteen-Book Prelude* vi 571: 'types and symbols of eternity'.

[7] *pathetic* evocative, emotionally stirring.

[8] *in the original . . . Confessions* See 'Easter Sunday', pp. 818–20 above.

[9] *caeteris paribus* all things being equal.

[10] 'Some readers will question the *fact*, and seek no reason. But did they ever suffer grief at *any* season of the year?' (De Quincey's note).

[11] *vivifying* reviving. As De Quincey was aware, Wordsworth had used this word to describe the spots of time in early versions of *The Prelude*.

[12] *compound* i.e. compounded, mixed up.

[13] *guard* fireguard.

nurse whom we all loved, before any candle was lighted, would often strain her eyes to read it for us – and sometimes, according to her simple powers, would endeavour to explain what we found obscure. We, the children, were all constitutionally touched with pensiveness. The fitful gloom and sudden lambencies[14] of the room by firelight suited our evening state of feelings, and they suited also the divine revelations of power and mysterious beauty which awed us. Above all, the story of a just man[15] – man and yet *not* man, real above all things and yet shadowy above all things, who had suffered the passion of death in Palestine, slept upon our minds like early dawn upon the waters. The nurse knew and explained to us the chief differences in oriental climates, and all these differences (as it happens) express themselves in the great varieties of summer. The cloudless sunlights of Syria – those seemed to argue everlasting summer; the disciples plucking the ears of corn[16] – that *must* be summer; but above all the very name of Palm Sunday[17] (a festival in the English church) troubled me like an anthem. 'Sunday?' What was *that*? That was the day of peace which masked another peace deeper than the heart of man can comprehend. 'Palms?' What were they? *That* was an equivocal word: 'palms' in the sense of 'trophies' expressed the pomps of life; 'palms' as a product of nature expressed the pomps of summer. Yet still even this explanation does not suffice: it was not merely by the peace and by the summer, by the deep sound of rest below all rest and of ascending glory, that I had been haunted. It was also because Jerusalem stood near to those deep images both in time and in place. The great event of Jerusalem was at hand when Palm Sunday came, and the scene of that Sunday was near in place to Jerusalem. Yet what then was Jerusalem? Did I fancy it to be the *omphalos* (navel) of the earth? That pretension had once been made for Jerusalem, and once for Delphi[18] – and both pretensions had become ridiculous, as the figure[19] of the planet became known. Yes – but if not of the earth, for earth's tenant Jerusalem was the *omphalos* of mortality. Yet how? There on the contrary it was, as we infants understood, that mortality had been trampled underfoot.[20] True, but for that very reason there it was that mortality had opened its very gloomiest crater. There it was indeed that the human had risen on wings from the grave. But for that reason there also it was that the divine had been swallowed up by the abyss; the lesser star could not rise before the greater would submit to eclipse. Summer, therefore, had connected itself with death not merely as a mode of antagonism, but also through intricate relations to scriptural scenery and events.

Out of this digression, which was almost necessary for the purpose of showing how inextricably my feelings and images of death were entangled with those of summer, I return to the bedchamber of my sister. From the gorgeous sunlight I turned round to the corpse. There lay the sweet childish figure, there the angel face – and, as people usually fancy, it was said in the house that no features had suffered any change. Had they not? The forehead indeed, the serene and noble forehead – *that* might be the same. But the frozen eyelids, the darkness that seemed to steal from beneath them, the marble lips, the stiffening hands laid palm to palm as if repeating the supplications of closing anguish – could these be mistaken for life? Had it been so, wherefore did I not spring to those heavenly lips with tears and never-ending kisses? But so it was *not*.

Notes

14 *lambencies* lightings-up, illuminations.

15 *a just man* Christ.

16 *the disciples . . . corn* the disciples plucked ears of corn from the fields when they were hungry; see, for instance, Matthew 12: 1.

17 *Palm Sunday* Christ's followers greeted him with palm branches when he entered Jerusalem; John 12: 13.

18 *Delphi* believed in ancient times to be the centre or navel of the earth, because it was close to a ravine.

19 *figure* i.e. shape; once the earth was known to be spherical, it was no longer possible to think of it having a centre (or navel).

20 *mortality . . . underfoot* i.e. by Christ's resurrection.

I stood checked for a moment – awe, not fear, fell upon me – and whilst I stood, a solemn wind began to blow, the most mournful that ear ever heard. Mournful! That is saying nothing. It was a wind that had swept the fields of mortality for a hundred centuries. Many times since, upon a summer day, when the sun is about the hottest, I have remarked the same wind arising and uttering the same hollow, solemn, Memnonian,[21] but saintly swell; it is in this world the one sole *audible* symbol of eternity. And three times in my life I have happened to hear the same sound in the same circumstances, viz. when standing between an open window and a dead body on a summer day.

Instantly, when my ear caught this vast Aeolian intonation,[22] when my eye filled with the golden fullness of life, the pomps and glory of the heavens outside, and turning when it settled upon the frost[23] which overspread my sister's face, instantly a trance fell upon me. A vault seemed to open in the zenith of the far blue sky, a shaft which ran up for ever. I in spirit rose as if on billows that also ran up the shaft for ever, and the billows seemed to pursue the throne of God – but that also ran before us and fled away continually. The flight and the pursuit seemed to go on for ever and ever. Frost, gathering frost, some sarsar[24] wind of death, seemed to repel me. I slept, for how long I cannot say; slowly I recovered my self-possession, and found myself standing as before, close to my sister's bed.

Oh flight of the solitary child to the solitary God[25] – flight from the ruined corpse to the throne that could not be ruined! How rich wert thou in truth for after-years! Rapture of grief that, being too mighty for a child to sustain, foundest a happy oblivion in a heaven-born sleep, and within that sleep didst conceal a dream whose meanings in after-years, when slowly I deciphered, suddenly there flashed upon me new light – and even by the grief of a child, as I will show you reader hereafter, were confounded the falsehoods of philosophers.[26]

In the *Opium Confessions* I touched a little upon the extraordinary power connected with opium (after long use) of amplifying the dimensions of time.[27] Space also it amplifies by degrees that are sometimes terrific.[28] But time it is upon which the exalting and multiplying power of opium chiefly spends its operation. Time becomes infinitely elastic, stretching out to such immeasurable and vanishing termini that it seems ridiculous to compute the sense of it on waking by expressions commensurate to human life. As in starry fields one computes by diameters of the earth's orbit, or of Jupiter's, so in valuing the *virtual* time lived during some dreams, the measurement by generations is ridiculous, by millennia is ridiculous – by aeons, I should say (if aeons were more determinate), would be also ridiculous. On this single occasion, however, in my life, the very inverse phenomenon occurred. But why speak of it in connection with opium? Could a child of six years old have been under that influence? No, but simply because it so exactly reversed the operation of opium. Instead of a short interval expanding into a vast one, upon this occasion a long one had contracted into

Notes

[21] *Memnonian* i.e. sensitive to sunlight. The Romantics believed that the statue of Memnon, King of Ethiopia, which was believed to have been holding a lute, produced music when struck by the rising or setting sun.

[22] *Aeolian intonation* De Quincey probably has in mind the other-worldly sound of an Aeolian harp.

[23] *frost* coldness, though De Quincey may also be referring to the frost-like pallor of death.

[24] *sarsar* cold.

[25] 'Φυγη μν ωρσ μνν. Plotinus' (De Quincey's note). De Quincey quotes the final words of *Ennead* VI 9 11, line 51, in which Plotinus writes of 'deliverance from the things of this world, a life which takes no delight in the things of this world, *escape in solitude to the solitary*'.

[26] 'The thoughts referred to will be given in final notes, as at this point they seemed too much to interrupt the course of the narrative' (De Quincey's note). These 'notes' were never published, and may never have been written.

[27] *In the Opium Confessions . . . time* see p. 815.

[28] *terrific* terrifying.

a minute. I have reason to believe that a *very* long one had elapsed during this wandering or suspension of my perfect mind. When I returned to myself, there was a foot (or I fancied so) on the stairs. I was alarmed. For I believed that, if anybody should detect me, means would be taken to prevent my coming again. Hastily, therefore, I kissed the lips that I should kiss no more, and slunk like a guilty thing[29] with stealthy steps from the room. Thus perished the vision, loveliest amongst all the shows which earth has revealed to me; thus mutilated was the parting which should have lasted for ever; thus tainted with fear was the farewell sacred to love and grief, to perfect love and perfect grief.

Oh Ahasuerus, everlasting Jew![30] Fable or not a fable, thou when first starting on thy endless pilgrimage of woe, thou when first flying through the gates of Jerusalem and vainly yearning to leave the pursuing curse behind thee, couldst not more certainly have read thy doom of sorrow in the misgivings of thy troubled brain than I when passing for ever from my sister's room. The worm was at my heart – and, confining myself to that stage of life, I may say, the worm that could not die. For if, when standing upon the threshold of manhood, I had ceased to feel its perpetual gnawings, that was because a vast expansion of intellect, it was because new hopes, new necessities, and the frenzy of youthful blood, had translated me into a new creature. Man is doubtless *one* by some subtle nexus[31] that we cannot perceive, extending from the new-born infant to the superannuated dotard; but as regards many affections and passions incident to his nature at different stages, he is *not* one – the unity of man in this respect is coextensive[32] only with the particular stage to which the passion belongs. Some passions, as that of sexual love, are celestial by one half of their origin, animal and earthy by the other half. These will not survive their own appropriate stage. But love which is *altogether* holy, like that between two children, will revisit undoubtedly by glimpses the silence and the darkness of old age – and I repeat my belief that, unless bodily torment should forbid it, that final experience in my sister's bedroom, or some other in which her innocence was concerned, will rise again for me to illuminate the hour of death.

On the day following this which I have recorded, came a body of medical men to examine the brain, and the particular nature of the complaint, for in some of its symptoms it had shown perplexing anomalies. Such is the sanctity of death (and especially of death alighting on an innocent child), that even gossiping people do not gossip on such a subject. Consequently I knew nothing of the purpose which drew together these surgeons, nor suspected anything of the cruel changes which might have been wrought in my sister's head. Long after this I saw a similar case; I surveyed the corpse (it was that of a beautiful boy eighteen years old,[33] who had died of the same complaint) one hour *after* the surgeons had laid the skull in ruins – but the dishonours of this scrutiny were hidden by bandages, and had not disturbed the repose of the countenance. So it might have been here, but if it were *not* so, then I was happy in being spared the shock, from having that marble image of peace, icy and rigid as it was, unsettled by disfiguring images. Some hours after the strangers had withdrawn, I crept again to the room, but the door was now locked, the key was taken away, and I was shut out for ever.

Notes

[29] *like a guilty thing* compare *Hamlet* I i 148–9 and Wordsworth, 'Ode' 150.

[30] ' "Everlasting Jew!" – *der ewige Jude* – which is the common German expression for *The Wandering Jew,* and even sublimer than our own' (De Quincey's note). Because he denied rest to Christ on the way to the crucifixion, Ahasuerus was doomed to wander the earth until the Day of Judgement. This is not in the Bible, and therefore, as De Quincey admits, might well be 'fable'.

[31] *nexus* connection.

[32] *coextensive* extends over the same space and time.

[33] *a beautiful boy eighteen years old* William, De Quincey's son, died 1834.

Suspiria de Profundis: The Palimpsest (extract)[1]

From Blackwood's Edinburgh Magazine (June 1845)

What else than a natural and mighty palimpsest is the human brain? Such a palimpsest is my brain; such a palimpsest, oh reader! is yours. Everlasting layers of ideas, images, feelings, have fallen upon your brain softly as light. Each succession has seemed to bury all that went before, and yet in reality not one has been extinguished. And if, in the vellum palimpsest, lying amongst the other *diplomata*[2] of human archives or libraries, there is anything fantastic or which moves to laughter – as oftentimes there is in the grotesque collisions of those successive themes, having no natural connection, which by pure accident have consecutively occupied the roll – yet in our own heaven-created palimpsest, the deep memorial palimpsest of the brain, there are not and cannot be such incoherencies. The fleeting accidents of a man's life and its external shows may indeed be irrelate and incongruous, but the organizing principles which fuse into harmony and gather about fixed predetermined centres, whatever heterogeneous elements life may have accumulated from without, will not permit the grandeur of human unity greatly to be violated, or its ultimate repose to be troubled in the retrospect from dying moments or from other great convulsions.

Such a convulsion is the struggle of gradual suffocation, as in drowning – and in the original *Opium Confessions* I mentioned a case of that nature communicated to me by a lady from her own childish experience.[3] The lady is still living, though now of unusually great age.[4] And I may mention that amongst her faults never was numbered any levity[5] of principle, or carelessness of the most scrupulous veracity[6] – but, on the contrary, such faults as arise from austerity, too harsh perhaps, and gloomy, indulgent neither to others nor herself. And at the time of relating this incident, when already very old, she had become religious to asceticism.

According to my present belief, she had completed her ninth year when, playing by the side of a solitary brook, she fell into one of its deepest pools. Eventually (but after what lapse of time nobody ever knew) she was saved from death by a farmer who, riding in some distant lane, had seen her rise to the surface – but not until she had descended within the abyss of death, and looked into its secrets as far, perhaps, as ever human eye *can* have looked that had permission to return. At a certain stage of this descent, a blow seemed to strike her, phosphoric radiance sprang forth from her eyeballs, and immediately a mighty theatre expanded within her brain. In a moment, in the twinkling of an eye, every act, every design of her past life lived again – arraying themselves not as a succession but as parts of a coexistence. Such a light fell upon the whole path of her life backwards into the shades of infancy, as the light perhaps which wrapped the destined apostle on his road to Damascus.[7] Yet that light blinded for a season, but hers poured celestial vision upon the brain, so that her consciousness became omnipresent at one moment to every feature in the infinite review.

Notes

SUSPIRIA DE PROFUNDIS: THE PALIMPSEST

[1] This is an extract from the final part of *Suspiria*, which compares the human mind to a 'palimpsest' or parchment, in this case of vellum (sheepskin), written upon twice, the original writing having been erased or rubbed out to make place for the second. It is a remarkable essay, in which he expounds his theory concerning the way in which the conscious, subconscious and unconscious minds are interconnected. Coleridge had noted observations about this in his notebooks, and Wordsworth had speculated on it, particularly in *The Prelude*, but De Quincey was the first to refer to the subconscious in print.

[2] *diplomata* historical documents.

[3] *in the original Opium Confessions . . . experience* See p. 815.

[4] De Quincey's mother, who was 90.

[5] *levity* inconstancy, fickleness.

[6] *And I may mention . . . veracity* i.e. she was always principled and honest.

[7] *as the light perhaps . . . Damascus* St Paul, who was struck by 'a great light' on the road to Damascus; see Acts 22: 6.

This anecdote was treated sceptically at the time by some critics. But besides that it has since been confirmed by other experiences essentially the same, reported by other parties in the same circumstances who had never heard of each other. The true point for astonishment is not the *simultaneity* of arrangement under which the past events of life – though in fact successive – had formed their dread line of revelation; this was but a secondary phenomenon. The deeper lay in the resurrection itself, and the possibility of resurrection for what had so long slept in the dust. A pall deep as oblivion had been thrown by life over every trace of these experiences, and yet suddenly, at a silent command, at the signal of a blazing rocket sent up from the brain, the pall draws up and the whole depths of the theatre are exposed. Here was the greater mystery: now this mystery is liable to no doubt, for it is repeated, and ten thousand times repeated by opium, for those who are its martyrs.

Yes, reader, countless are the mysterious handwritings of grief or joy which have inscribed themselves successively upon the palimpsest of your brain – and like the annual leaves of aboriginal forests,[8] or the undissolving snows on the Himalaya, or light falling upon light, the endless strata have covered up each other in forgetfulness. But by the hour of death, but by fever, but by the searchings of opium, all these can revive in strength. They are not dead, but sleeping. In the illustration imagined by myself, from the case of some individual palimpsest, the Grecian tragedy had seemed to be displaced, but was *not* displaced, by the monkish legend – and the monkish legend had seemed to be displaced, but was *not* displaced, by the knightly romance. In some potent convulsion of the system, all wheels back into its earliest elementary stage. The bewildering romance, light tarnished with darkness, the semi-fabulous legend, truth celestial mixed with human falsehoods, these fade even of themselves as life advances. The romance has perished that the young man adored. The legend has gone that deluded the boy. But the deep, deep tragedies of infancy, as when the child's hands were unlinked for ever from his mother's neck, or his lips for ever from his sister's kisses,[9] these remain lurking below all, and these lurk to the last. Alchemy there is none of passion or disease that can scorch away these immortal impresses.

Suspiria de Profundis: Finale to Part I. Savannah-la-Mar[1]

From Blackwood's Edinburgh Magazine (July 1845)

God smote Savannah-la-Mar, and in one night, by earthquake, removed her, with all her towers standing and population sleeping, from the steadfast foundations of the shore to the coral floors of ocean. And God said, 'Pompeii did I bury and conceal from men through seventeen centuries:[2] this city I will bury, but not conceal. She shall be a monument to men of my mysterious anger, set in azure light through generations to come – for I will enshrine her in a crystal dome of my tropic seas.'

This city, therefore, like a mighty galleon with all her apparel[3] mounted, streamers flying and tackling perfect, seems floating along the noiseless depths of ocean. And oftentimes in glassy calms, through the translucid[4] atmosphere of water that now

Notes

[8] *aboriginal forests* i.e. unexplored jungles.

[9] *or his lips . . . kisses* a recollection of his sister Elizabeth.

Suspiria de Profundis: Finale to Part I

[1] *Savannah-la-Mar* Jamaican port destroyed by a tidal wave during the West Indian hurricane of 1780.

[2] *Pompeii . . . seventeen centuries* Mount Vesuvius erupted on 24 August AD 79, burying the port of Pompeii. Excavations began in 1738 and still continue.

[3] *apparel* outfit and rigging of a ship.

[4] *translucid* translucent.

stretches like an air-woven awning above the silent encampment, mariners from every clime look down into her courts and terraces, count her gates, and number the spires of her churches. She is one ample cemetery and has been for many a year, but in the mighty calms that brood for weeks over tropic latitudes, she fascinates the eye with a *fata Morgana*[5] revelation, as of human life still subsisting in submarine asylums sacred from the storms that torment our upper air.[6]

Thither lured by the loveliness of cerulean depths, by the peace of human dwellings privileged from molestation, by the gleam of marble altars sleeping in everlasting sanctity, oftentimes in dreams did I and the Dark Interpreter[7] cleave the watery veil that divided us from her streets. We looked into the belfries where the pendulous bells were waiting in vain for the summons which should awaken their marriage peals; together we touched the mighty organ keys that sang no *jubilates*[8] for the ear of Heaven, that sang no requiems for the ear of human sorrow; together we searched the silent nurseries where the children were all asleep – and *had* been asleep through five generations.

'They are waiting for the heavenly dawn', whispered the Interpreter to himself, 'and when *that* comes, the bells and the organs will utter a *jubilate* repeated by the echoes of paradise.' Then, turning to me, he said, 'This is sad, this is piteous, but less would not have sufficed for the purposes of God. Look here – put into a Roman clepsydra[9] one hundred drops of water. Let these run out as the sands in an hourglass, every drop measuring the hundredth part of a second, so that each shall represent but the three-hundred-and-sixty-thousandth part of an hour. Now count the drops as they race along, and, when the fiftieth of the hundred is passing, behold! Forty-nine are not because already they have perished, and fifty are not because they are yet to come. You see, therefore, how narrow, how incalculably narrow, is the true and actual present.

Of that time which we call the present, hardly a hundredth part but belongs either to a past which has fled, or to a future which is still on the wing. It has perished, or it is not born. It was, or it is not. Yet even this approximation to the truth is *infinitely* false. For again subdivide that solitary drop which only was found to represent the present into a lower series of similar fractions, and the actual present which you arrest measures now but the thirty-sixth millionth of an hour. And so by infinite declensions the true and very present in which only we live and enjoy, will vanish into a mote of a mote, distinguishable only by a heavenly vision. Therefore the present, which only man possesses, offers less capacity for his footing than the slenderest film that ever spider twisted from her womb. Therefore, also, even this incalculable shadow from the narrowest pencil of moonlight is more transitory than geometry can measure or thought of angel can overtake. The time which *is* contracts into a mathematic point, and even that point perishes a thousand times before we can utter its birth. All is finite in the present, and even that finite is infinite in its velocity of flight towards death. But in God there is nothing finite; but in God there is nothing transitory; but in God there *can* be nothing that tends to death. Therefore it follows that for God there can be no present. The future is the present of God, and to the future it is that he sacrifices the human present. Therefore it is that he works by earthquake. Therefore it is that he works by grief. Oh deep is the ploughing of earthquake! Oh deep' – and his voice swelled like a *sanctus*[10] rising from the choir of a cathedral – 'Oh deep is the ploughing

Notes

[5] *fata Morgana* mirage of a city, seen floating in the Straits of Messina, said to be the work of fairies.

[6] *upper air* i.e. above water level.

[7] *the Dark Interpreter* De Quincey's own interpreting angel.

[8] *jubilates* songs of rejoicing; strictly speaking, a reference to Psalm 100.

[9] *clepsydra* water-clock.

[10] *sanctus* Isaiah 6: 3, 'Holy, holy, holy . . . ', used to preface the administration of the sacrament at Holy Communion or mass.

of grief! But oftentimes less would not suffice for the agriculture of God. Upon a night of earthquake he builds a thousand years of pleasant habitations for man. Upon the sorrow of an infant, he raises oftentimes from human intellects glorious vintages that could not else have been. Less than these fierce ploughshares would not have stirred the stubborn soil. The one is needed for earth, our planet – for earth itself as the dwelling-place of man. But the other is needed yet oftener for God's mightiest intrument; yes,' (and he looked solemnly at myself) 'is needed for the mysterious children of the earth!'

Benjamin Robert Haydon (1786–1846)

Haydon was born at Plymouth on 25 January 1786. His artistic talent emerged quickly: at school he taught other pupils. Frustrated by seven years' apprenticeship to his father, a bookseller, he broke his indentures and left for London to study at the Royal Academy schools. Despite having talent and ambition, he was never successful as an artist, and suffered frequent bouts of poverty. But the patronage of the likes of Lord Mulgrave and Sir George and Lady Beaumont led to occasional commissions. In 1811 he began to keep a diary, the 'secret history of my mind', which eventually ran to over a million words. Though in many ways a difficult, prickly man, he enjoyed consorting with his contemporaries and by the end of 1812 his circle included Hazlitt, Lamb and Leigh Hunt.

One of his most important paintings, *Christ's Entry into Jerusalem* (now at St Mary's Seminary, Ohio), was begun in 1814, and was present on the evening of the immortal dinner. It was to occupy him for the next six years, and included portraits of Keats, Wordsworth, Hazlitt and Newton. He met Keats at Leigh Hunt's Hampstead cottage in October 1816, and by the time of the dinner Keats practically worshipped him, having included him as one of the three 'Great spirits' on earth in 'Addressed to Haydon' (see p. 1343). They fell out partly because Keats was disturbed by Haydon's quarrels with Leigh Hunt, and partly because of Haydon's refusal to repay a loan of £30.

On 28 December 1817 he held the 'immortal dinner' at his lodgings and studio, 22 Lisson Grove North, Paddington. Haydon's diary account of the evening is one of the most vivid portraits we have of the Romantics at play. It appeals to us not just for the social comedy of Lamb's drunkenness, or the discomfort of Wordsworth when confronted with his boss from the Stamp Office, John Kingston, but because it offers us the sense of an artistic fraternity that understood that as Romantics they were different from the generation that had preceded them; as Haydon puts it: 'I never passed a more delightful day, and I am convinced that nothing in Boswell is equal to what came out from these poets. Indeed there were no such poets in his time.'

Keats, who was among Haydon's guests, described it briefly in a letter to George and Tom Keats, written just over a week after the event:

> I forget whether I had written my last before my Sunday evening at Haydon's – no, I did not or I should have told you, Tom, of a young man you met at Paris at Scott's of the name of Richer,[1] I think. He is going to Fezzan[2] in Africa there to proceed if possible like Mungo Park. He was very polite to me and

Notes

Benjamin Robert Haydon

[1] Joseph Ritchie (1788–1819).

[2] Fezzan is the Saharan region in Libya, where in fact Ritchie was to die in November 1819.

enquired very particularly after you. Then there was Wordsworth, Lamb, Monkhouse, Landseer, Kingston and your humble sarvant. Lamb got tipsy and blew up Kingston, proceeding so far as to take the candle across the room, hold it to his face, and show us wh-a-at-sort-fellow he-waas. I astonished Kingston at supper with a pertinacity in favour of drinking, keeping my two glasses at work in a knowing way. (Rollins i 198)

Like many of the Romantics, Haydon was not appreciated in his own day, and financial difficulties led to his imprisonment for debt in 1828. For much of his career he was compelled to paint genre scenes and portraits just to make ends meet, although he did produce such exceptional pictures as *Marcus Curtius Leaping into the Gulf* (1836–42) and *Wordsworth on Helvellyn* (1842) – the subject of a sonnet by Elizabeth Barrett (p. 1467), and an icon of the period. All the same, he felt himself to have been a failure even as he hung the final exhibition of his works at the Egyptian Hall, Piccadilly, in April 1846. It closed after six weeks, losing him more than £111. Pressured by debt, persuaded of the uselessness of his life, on 22 June he first attempted unsuccessfully to shoot himself, and then slit his own throat. 'Stretch me no longer on this rough world,' he had written on the last page of his diary.

Further reading

David Blayney Brown, Robert Woof and Stephen Hebron, *Benjamin Robert Haydon 1786–1846* (Grasmere, 1996).

Alethea Hayter, *A Sultry Month: Scenes of London Literary Life in 1846* (London, 1992).

Penelope Hughes-Hallett, *The Immortal Dinner: A Famous Evening of Genius and Laughter in Literary London, 1817* (London, 2000).

[The Immortal Dinner]

28 December 1817. Wordsworth dined with me; Keats and Lamb with a friend made up the dinner party, and a very pleasant party we had. Wordsworth was in fine and powerful cue.[1] We had a glorious set-to on Homer, Shakespeare, Milton and Virgil. Lamb got excessively merry and witty, and his fun in the intervals of Wordsworth's deep and solemn intonations of oratory was the fun and wit of the fool in the intervals of Lear's passion.[2] Lamb soon gets tipsy, and tipsy he got very shortly, to our infinite amusement.

'Now, you rascally Lake Poet', said Lamb, 'you call Voltaire[3] a dull fellow.'[4] We all agreed there was a state of mind when he would appear so – and 'Well let us drink his health', said Lamb. 'Here's Voltaire, the Messiah of the French nation, and a very fit one!'

He then attacked me for putting in Newton,[5] 'a fellow who believed nothing unless it was as clear as the three sides of a triangle!' And then he and Keats agreed he had destroyed all the poetry of the rainbow by reducing it to a prism. It was impossible to resist them, and we drank 'Newton's health, and confusion to mathematics!' It was delightful to see the good humour of Wordsworth in giving in to all our frolics without affectation[6] and laughing as heartily as the best of us.

Notes

The Immortal Dinner

[1] *cue* form, condition.

[2] *the fool . . . Lear's passion* See *King Lear* III vi.

[3] François Marie Arouet de Voltaire (1694–1778), French philosopher and novelist.

[4] *you call . . . fellow* a reference to Wordsworth's criticism of *Candide* as the 'dull product of a scoffer's pen' (*Excursion* ii 484). The comment had come in for criticism from Hazlitt in his review of the *Excursion* in the *Examiner*, and Lamb had corresponded with Wordsworth about it on 19 September 1814 (Marrs iii 112).

[5] Haydon inserted the face of Sir Isaac Newton into the background of his painting, *Christ's Entry into Jerusalem*.

[6] *affectation* pretence.

By this time other visitors began to drop in, and a Mr Ritchie,[7] who is going to penetrate into the interior of Africa. I introduced him to Wordsworth as such, and the conversation got into a new train. After some time, Lamb, who had seemingly paid no attention to anyone, suddenly opened his eyes and said, alluding to the dangers of penetrating into the interior of Africa, 'And pray, who is the gentleman we are going *to lose*?' Here was a roar of laughter, the victim Ritchie joining with us.

We now retired to tea, and, among other friends, a gentleman[8] who was Comptroller of the Stamp Office came. He had been peculiarly anxious to know and see Wordsworth. The moment he was introduced he let Wordsworth know *who* he officially was.[9] This was an exquisite touch of human nature. Though Wordsworth of course would not have suffered him to speak indecently or impiously without reproof, yet he had a visible effect on Wordsworth. I felt pain at the slavery of office. In command men are despotic, and those who are dependent on others who have despotic control must and do feel affected by their presence. The Comptroller was a very mild and nice fellow, but rather weak and very fond of talking. He got into conversation with Wordsworth on poetry, and just after he had been putting forth some of his silly stuff, Lamb, who had been dozing as usual, suddenly opened his mouth and said, 'What did you say, sir?'

'Why, sir', said the Comptroller, in his milk and water insipidity, 'I was saying . . . ', etc., etc., etc.

'Do you say so, sir?' 'Yes sir', was the reply. 'Why then, sir, I say (hiccup) you are – you are a silly fellow!' This operated like thunder. The Comptroller knew nothing of his previous tipsiness and looked at him like a man bewildered. The venerable anxiety of Wordsworth to prevent the Comptroller being angry, and his expostulations with Lamb, who had sunk back again into his doze, as insensible to the confusion he had produced as a being above it; the astonishment of Landseer the engraver,[10] who was totally deaf, and with his hand to his ear and his eye was trying to catch the meaning of the gestures he saw; and the agonizing attempts of Keats, Ritchie, and I to suppress our laughter; and the smiling struggle of the Comptroller to take all in good part without losing his dignity, made up a story of comic expressions totally unrivalled in nature. I felt pain that such a poet as Wordsworth should be under the supervisorship of such a being as this Comptroller. The people of England have a horror of office, an instinct against it. They are right. A man's liberty is gone the moment he becomes official; he is the slave of superiors, and makes others slaves to him. The Comptroller went on making his profound remarks, and when anything very *deep* came forth,[11] Lamb roared out,

Notes

[7] Joseph Ritchie (1788–1819), surgeon and African traveller, who had recently returned from Paris, and was about to travel from Tripoli to Timbuktu in search of the source of the Niger. He died at Murzuk, Libya. He told his friend Richard Garnett that Keats 'is to be the great poetical luminary of the age to come'.

[8] John Kingston, Deputy Comptroller of Stamps, was Wordsworth's immediate superior at the Stamp Office.

[9] *who he officially was* Wordsworth was Distributor of Stamps for Westmorland, 1813–42, a post which carried no salary, but was expected to realize about £400 a year.

[10] John Landseer (1769–1852), painter and engraver, father of Edwin Landseer.

[11] 'Such as "Pray sir, don't you think Milton a very *great genius*?" This I really recollect. 1823' (Haydon's note).

Diddle iddle don
My son John
Went to bed with his breeches on,
One stocking off and one stocking on,
My son John.

The Comptroller laughed as if he marked it, and went on; every remark Lamb chorused with

Went to bed with his breeches on
Diddle iddle on.

There is no describing this scene adequately. There was not the restraint of refined company, nor the vulgar freedom of low, but a frank natural license such as one sees in an act of Shakespeare, every man expressing his natural emotions without fear. Into this company, a little heated with wine, a Comptroller of the Stamp Office walked, frilled, dressed, and official, with a due awe of the powers above him and a due contempt for those beneath him. His astonishment at finding where he was come cannot be conceived, and in the midst of his mild namby-pamby[12] opinions, Lamb's address deadened his views. When they separated, Wordsworth softened his feelings, but Lamb kept saying in the Painting Room, 'Who is that fellow? Let me go and hold the candle once more to his face –

My son John
Went to bed with his breeches on!'

And these were the last words of C. Lamb. The door was closed upon him. There was something interesting in seeing Wordsworth sitting, and Keats and Lamb, and my picture of Christ's entry towering up behind them, occasionally brightened by the gleams of flame that sparkled from the fire, and hearing the voice of Wordsworth repeating Milton with an intonation like the funeral bell of St Paul's[13] and the music of Handel mingled, and then Lamb's wit came sparkling in between, and Keats' rich fancy of satyrs and fauns and doves and white clouds wound up the stream of conversation. I never passed a more delightful day, and I am convinced that nothing in Boswell[14] is equal to what came out from these poets. Indeed there were no such poets in his time.[15] It was an evening worthy of the Elizabethan age, and will long flash upon 'that inward eye which is the bliss of solitude.'[16] Hail and farewell!

Notes

[12] *namby-pamby* weak, insipid.

[13] St Paul's Cathedral in the City of London.

[14] *Boswell* Haydon refers to James Boswell's *Life of Johnson* (1791).

[15] *there were no such . . . time* a comment that reveals that by 1817 the likes of Haydon were aware that they lived at a time of tremendous artistic achievement.

[16] *that inward eye . . . solitude* from Wordsworth, *Daffodils* 15–16.

George Gordon Byron, 6th Baron Byron (1788–1824)

George Gordon, Lord Byron, that most seductively attractive of poets (and one of the biggest-selling of his day), was born 22 January 1788, to Catherine Gordon and Captain John 'Mad Jack' Byron, in poor lodgings in London. He had a deformed right foot from birth and was lame for the rest of his life. His mother was abandoned by her husband (who, having spent his wife's inheritance, died in mysterious circumstances in France in 1791), and took Byron to Aberdeen in her native Scotland, where she brought him up as best she could. Here he came to love the Scottish countryside – and, at the age of 7, his cousin, Mary Duff.

He was only 10 years old when, on the death of his great-uncle in 1798, he succeeded to the barony, becoming the sixth Lord Byron. At that point he and his mother moved into Newstead Abbey in Nottinghamshire, and he began to receive private tuition in Nottingham in preparation for entrance to a public school. At this period, his nurse May Gray beat and molested him. This went on for about two years before it was discovered and she was dismissed.

At home, he fell in love with another cousin, Margaret Parker, who inspired Byron's 'first dash into poetry'. He entered Harrow School in 1801. Among his contemporaries were a future marquess, two actual and five future earls and viscounts, four other lords, four baronets, two future Prime Ministers (Lord Palmerston and Robert Peel), and the Duke of Dorset, who became Byron's fag. At the age of 15 he fell in love with yet another cousin, Mary Chaworth, refusing to go back to Harrow on account of his feelings for her. This gave way to an intense friendship with the 23-year-old Lord Grey de Ruthyn, who had taken a lease on Newstead Abbey until Byron's coming of age five years hence. Their association came to an abrupt halt in January 1804 when Grey seduced Byron, who fled back to Harrow shortly after.

He fell in love with other boys in his remaining year and a half there; Lady Caroline Lamb later claimed that he had slept with three of them. In spite of his obvious brilliance, he was never a diligent student but read widely, noting at the age of 19 that he had digested 'about four thousand novels, including the works of Cervantes, Fielding, Smollett, Richardson, Mackenzie, Sterne, Rabelais and Rousseau'. In 1805 he led a rebellion against the new headmaster, the Reverend Dr George Butler, whom he found affected, ingratiating, overbearing, boastful, pedantic and socially inadequate. He organized the dragging of Butler's desk into the middle of the School House where it was set on fire, and composed scurrilous poems about him. Other triumphs included his performance of King Lear's address to the storm at the 1805 Speech Day, followed by the scoring of eighteen runs in the Eton–Harrow cricket match – no mean feat for someone with a club foot.

He left having incurred numerous debts, and he took every opportunity, after going up to Trinity College, Cambridge, in October 1805, to live more extravagantly than ever. (By January 1808 his debts amounted to over £5,000 – £210,000 / US$378,400 today.) Cambridge brought out his lordliness: the keeping of dogs being prohibited, he kept a tame bear in a turret at the top of a staircase. He struck up a passionate friendship with the choirboy John Edleston, 'the only being

I esteem', who provided the inspiration for the 'Thyrza' poems (see pp. 846–8). In 1806 he gathered his juvenile poetry together under the title of *Fugitive Pieces* but suppressed the book at the last moment; in January 1807 he privately printed a collection of juvenilia as *Poems on Various Occasions*; and in the summer of 1807 he published a third volume, *Hours of Idleness*. It drew damning criticism from Henry Brougham (anonymously) in the *Edinburgh Review* for January 1808, whose opening remarks set the tone for what was to come: 'His effusions are spread over a dead flat, and can no more get above or below the level, than if they were so much stagnant water.' Byron was mortified. He downed three bottles of claret after dinner and contemplated suicide.

The following day he decided to take revenge with a vigorous satire on literary life, *English Bards and Scotch Reviewers* (1809), the chief butt of which was Francis Jeffrey (see pp. 714–15), editor of the *Edinburgh*, whom he held responsible for the review. He laboured over it for over a year before it was published anonymously, by which time it had grown to the point that it lambasted virtually everyone in the literary world – the 'dunces', as he put it, which included his guardian, the Earl of Carlisle, who nurtured the ambition of being a verse-dramatist: 'No muse will cheer, with renovating smile, / The paralytic puking of Carlisle.'

The only writers of whom he had anything good to say were Thomas Campbell, Thomas Moore, Samuel Rogers and William Gifford. Strange though it may seem, Byron remained true to this view of poetry throughout his life. He saw them as faithful to the 'correct' Augustan tradition of Pope, Dryden and Swift, which had been rejected by Wordsworth, Coleridge and Southey in exchange for misguided poetic and philosophical systems. That was why he sniffed at Wordsworth's *Poems in Two Volumes* when he reviewed it in 1807, dismissing its author's 'namby-pamby' weakness for 'the most commonplace ideas'. Even his own poetry failed sufficiently to conform to the Augustan tradition, as he noted in correspondence with his publisher, John Murray, in September 1817:

> With regard to poetry in general I am convinced, the more I think of it, that he [Thomas Moore] and *all* of us – Scott, Southey, Wordsworth, Moore, Campbell, I – are all in the wrong, one as much as another – that we are upon a wrong revolutionary poetical system (or systems) not worth a damn in itself – and from which none but Rogers and Crabbe are free – and that the present and next generations will finally be of this opinion. I am the more confirmed in this by having lately gone over some of our classics, particularly Pope, whom I tried[1] in this way: I took Moore's poems and my own and some others, and went over them side by side with Pope's, and I was really astonished (I ought not to have been so) and mortified at the ineffable distance in point of sense, harmony, effect, and even *Imagination*, passion, and invention, between the little Queen Anne's man [Pope] and us of the lower Empire.[2]

This was the position from which Byron attacked his contemporaries, and which was to inform his criticism of the Lake poets in *Don Juan*. Whatever the rights and wrongs of that, *English Bards and Scotch Reviewers*, a satire written in Popean couplets, enjoyed huge popularity, going through numerous editions, and attracting favourable press coverage.

Having graduated from Cambridge in July 1808, he became a man about town, known liaisons including his adolescent page, Robert Rushton; Caroline Cameron, a 16-year-old Brighton prostitute who dressed as his pageboy; 'a famous French "Entremetteuse"

Notes

[1] *tried* i.e. tested.

[2] Marchand v 265

who assisted young gentlemen in their youthful pastimes'; and at least three regular mistresses. It was as a supporter of Napoleon (who now, as Emperor, ruled most of Europe) that he took his seat in the House of Lords on 13 March 1809 on the Whig side, in opposition to the government. In July, more than £12,000 in debt (£460,000 / US$850,000 today), he eluded his creditors by embarking with his Cambridge friend Hobhouse on a tour of Portugal, Spain, Gibraltar, Malta, Albania and Greece. In the course of his travels he met the former robber baron Ali Pasha (the Turkish despot of Albania and western Greece), swam the Hellespont, saved the life of a Turkish girl condemned to death for sexual impropriety, and met the young woman he would celebrate in verse as the 'Maid of Athens'.

After two years and twelve days, he landed at Sheerness in Kent on 14 July 1811, bringing with him the manuscript of *Childe Harold's Pilgrimage*, a semi-autobiographical poem about his travels. It was published by John Murray in March 1812, and was an instant success. All 500 copies of the first edition sold out within three days of publication, and he became a celebrity. As Samuel Rogers recalled: 'The genius which the poem exhibited, the youth, the rank of the author, his romantic wanderings in Greece, – these combined to make the world stark mad about *Childe Harold* and Byron.' In a favourable notice in the *Edinburgh Review*, Francis Jeffrey described the poem as follows:

> Childe Harold is a sated epicure – sickened with the very fullness of prosperity – oppressed with ennui, and stung by occasional remorse; – his heart hardened by a long course of sensual indulgence, and his opinion of mankind degraded by his acquaintance with the baser part of them. In this state he wanders over the fairest and most interesting parts of Europe, in the vain hope of stimulating his palsied sensibility by novelty, or at least of occasionally forgetting his mental anguish in the toils and perils of his journey.

The identification of Byron with his protagonist fuelled interest in the poem and its author. Female admirers wrote him fan mail, enclosing their own verses, requesting signed copies of his works, samples of his handwriting and locks of his hair – a trend that continued unabated until his death. From this point onwards virtually everything he published would sell in thousands, making him one of the best-selling writers of the day.

He delivered his maiden speech in the House of Lords on 27 February 1812 on behalf of the stocking-weavers of Nottingham (the Luddites), in response to a vicious piece of legislation, the Tory Frame Work Bill, which proposed the death penalty as punishment for destruction of the new 'frames' that mechanized production.

> How will you carry the bill into effect? Can you commit a whole county to their own prisons? Will you erect a gibbet in every field to hang up men like scarecrows? Or will you proceed . . . by decimation, place the country under martial law, depopulate and lay waste all around you, and restore Sherwood forest as an acceptable gift to the crown in its former condition of a royal chase and an asylum for outlaws? Are these the remedies for a starving and desperate populace?[3]

Byron would never cease to feel incensed by the iniquities of his homeland, but was probably too much of a freethinker to have made a successful career within the constraints of the party system. Though welcomed into Whig circles at the highest levels, he seems not to have gained the trust of such grandees as Lord Holland, who may have suspected the relish with which Byron castigated authority figures. 'I was born for opposition,' Byron later wrote.[4]

Notes

[3] *Lord Byron: The Complete Miscellaneous Prose* ed. Andrew Nicholson (Oxford, 1991), pp. 26–7.

[4] *Don Juan* xv 176

In any case, *Childe Harold* put an end to his political ambitions, but confirmed him as a writer – and with the tidal wave of female admirers came Lady Caroline Lamb, married to the Hon. William Lamb since 1805. In February 1812, she was handed the manuscript of *Childe Harold* by Rogers, who told her to read it with the words: 'You should know the new poet.' As Lamb recalled,

> I read it, and that was enough. Rogers said, 'He has a club-foot, and bites his nails.' I said, 'If he was ugly as Aesop I must know him.' I was one night at Lady Westmoreland's; the women were all throwing their heads at him. Lady Westmoreland led me up to him. I looked earnestly at him, and turned on my heel. My opinion, in my journal was, 'mad – bad – and dangerous to know'. A day or two passed; I was sitting with Lord and Lady Holland, when he was announced. Lady Holland said, 'I must present Lord Byron to you'. Lord Byron said, 'That offer was made to you before; may I ask why you rejected it?' He begged permission to come and see me. He did so the next day. Rogers and Moore were standing by me: I was on the sofa. I had just come in from riding. I was filthy and heated. When Lord Byron was announced, I flew out of the room to wash myself. When I returned, Rogers said, 'Lord Byron, you are a happy man. Lady Caroline has been sitting here in all her dirt with us, but when you were announced, she flew to beautify herself.' Lord Byron wished to come and see me at eight o'clock, when I was alone; that was my dinner-hour. I said he might. From that moment, for more than nine months, he almost lived at Melbourne House. It was then the centre of all gaiety, at least in appearance.[5]

Her husband knew about the affair, but preferred to turn a blind eye. Perhaps he knew it would not last: it began in March and ended in November – short but intense. Byron described Caroline as a 'volcano', and encouraged her to dress as his pageboy, in which disguise she frequently gained access to his rooms. He brought it to a sudden and brutal end with a letter bearing the seal of his new conquest, Lady Oxford. But she could not let him go, and became what we would today describe as a 'stalker', following him wherever he went, loitering in the street when he was attending a party. 'You talked to me about keeping her out,' Byron told Lady Melbourne in June 1814; 'it is impossible – she comes at all times – at any time – and the moment the door is open in she walks – I can't throw her out of the window.'[6] Her revenge would take the form of a novel, *Glenarvon* (1816), which portrayed Byron as the evil and depraved Earl of Glenarvon, and reprinted, word for word, the letter with which he ended their affair.

Byron (see Plate 12) consolidated his success with Oriental romances that reworked the successful formula of *Childe Harold*, in which the dark, brooding hero found himself in exotic locations: *The Giaour* (1813), *The Bride of Abydos* (1813), *The Corsair* (1814) and *Lara* (1814). Enormously popular, they were literary fantasies for an audience eager for escape – diverting enough for both author and reader, but hardly the great poetry for which he was destined. All the same, his stock was on the rise. By 1816 he had sufficient clout to order John Murray to publish Coleridge's *Christabel; Kubla Khan: A Vision; The Pains of Sleep* for the first time. Murray knew it was unlikely to sell, but Byron was too important an author to displease.

During these years he became very close to Augusta Leigh, his half-sister, the child of his father's first marriage. Her mother had died only two days after her birth, so that she had been brought up by a grandmother and various relatives. She did not meet Byron as a child; they

Notes

5 *Lady Morgan's Memoirs: Autobiography, Diaries and Correspondence* (2 vols, London, 1852), ii 200–1.

6 Marchand iv 132

first met while he was at Harrow, and began to correspond in 1804. In 1807 she married a cousin, Colonel George Leigh, and over the next six years gave birth to three daughters. In the summer of 1813 Byron visited the Leighs near Newmarket, fell in love with her, and took her back to London, showing her off around town. An intimacy developed, and it was thanks only to the counsel of Lady Melbourne that he was dissuaded from the plan of eloping with Augusta to the Continent. He realized that he was in danger of ruining her reputation, and that it had to end – but he would always believe it to have been the most important relationship of his life, and commemorated it in his *Stanzas* and *Epistle* to her (see pp. 888–93), as well as in *Childe Harold's Pilgrimage* Canto III (stanza 55).

Partly at Augusta's bidding, he married Annabella Milbanke on 2 January 1815. The decision was made in haste, and they turned out to be disastrously ill-matched (though it is hard to conceive what sort of woman might have been happily married to him). Annabella was the opposite of her volatile husband, her enthusiasm for mathematics bespeaking a temperament that had little in common with his. Byron called her the Princess of Parallelograms. (The character of Don Juan's mother, Donna Inez, whose 'favourite science was the mathematical', is based partly on her.) Their daughter, Augusta Ada, was born on 10 December, by which time their marriage was seriously on the rocks and debt-collectors once more on the doorstep.

They separated in February 1816 amidst accusations of infidelity and outright insanity. Caroline Lamb revealed to Annabella details of Byron's homosexual affairs, and in a short time London was buzzing with talk of his private life. Ostracized from society, besieged by creditors, Byron decided once again to leave England – this time for ever. He ordered his coachmaker to manufacture a replica of Napoleon's carriage and on 25 April 1816 set out with his old Cambridge friend, John Cam Hobhouse, and a personal physician, John Polidori, on a tour that took in Bruges, Antwerp, Brussels and Waterloo (already a tourist destination thanks to the decisive battle the previous year).

The strange ménage arrived at the Hotel Angleterre in Sécheron near Geneva on 25 May, where Byron amused himself by putting his age down in the Hotel register as 100. Two days later on the hotel jetty he met Shelley, who had arrived ten days before with Mary Godwin and her half-sister Claire Clairmont (with whom Byron had had an affair in London). Geneva remained his base until the end of September, and during that summer he and Shelley saw a great deal of each other. It was an important moment in literary history, not unlike the *annus mirabilis* of 1797–8 when Wordsworth and Coleridge inspired each other to ever greater heights of poetic achievement. Shelley's influence had an immediate effect: from this time onwards one senses a seriousness and commitment in Byron's poetry that was not there before.

The Shelleys soon moved to Maison Chappuis, a small house on the far side of the lake at Montalègre, while Byron moved into Villa Diodati at Cologny, high on the bank above them. Diodati had pleasant associations because Milton stayed there with his friend Charles Diodati in 1639. Each day Byron and Shelley would sail across the lake and talk. Towards the end of June they even set out for a week-long expedition round Lac Léman in a new boat Byron had purchased, taking with them an English translation of Rousseau's novel *Julie, ou La Nouvelle Héloïse* from which Shelley read aloud. In the evenings they read each other ghost stories. This led Byron to suggest the ghost-story competition that inspired Mary Godwin's *Frankenstein*. Byron began, but did not finish, a fragment of a novel about an aristocratic vampire, Augustus Darvell. Polidori stole the idea and wrote his own story, *The Vampyre*, featuring the evil Lord Ruthven, who bore more than a passing resemblance to his employer.

This was a productive time for Byron. During the summer he composed much of *Manfred, Prometheus, Darkness* and *Childe Harold* Canto III; for his part, Shelley wrote two of his most important poems, *Hymn to Intellectual Beauty* and *Mont Blanc* (see pp. 1075–9). Complete texts of *Childe Harold* Canto III and *Manfred* are presented here. Both, in their different ways, are extraordinary; both are influenced byextraordinary; both are influenced by Wordsworth. Though for most of his life contemptuous of Wordsworth (for his rejection of Pope), Byron during the summer of 1816 listened to Shelley's recitals of Wordsworth's *Poems* (1815) and *The Excursion* (1814) – as he later told Thomas Medwin, Shelley 'used to dose me with Wordsworth physic even to nausea'.[7] That Wordsworthian influence went straight into *Childe Harold* Canto III, and was noted by Wordsworth himself, when he told Henry Taylor that Byron's 'poetical obligations to me' consisted 'not so much in particular expressions, though there is no want of these, as in the tone (*assumed* rather than natural) of enthusiastic admiration of nature, and a sensibility to her influences'.[8]

Canto III ranges across Europe, taking the same route as that followed by Byron in April–May 1816, visiting Waterloo (for melancholy reflections on war), travelling up the Rhine (for further reflections of a similar kind), into Switzerland, and finally arriving at Geneva, where Harold celebrates the work of Rousseau and Voltaire. Perhaps the most impressive stanzas are those about Napoleon:

> There sunk the greatest, nor the worst of men,
> Whose spirit antithetically mixed
> One moment of the mightiest, and again
> On little objects with like firmness fixed,
> Extreme in all things!
>
> (ll. 316–20)

There is a degree of provocation in this: back home, Napoleon was public enemy number one, and Byron knew that such comments would scandalize his readers. All the same, his admiration was genuine. To be 'a god unto thyself' was a principal Byronic ambition, and as Napoleon had achieved precisely that, it was natural that he should have regarded him as a kindred spirit. In exile Byron may have come to identify with him more than ever; both had been hurled from their former eminences – Byron by disgrace, Napoleon by fortune. He goes on to cast Napoleon as a type of overreacher, possessing 'a fever at the core, / Fatal to him who bears, to all who ever bore' (ll. 377–8): a tragic hero condemned by circumstance and the injustice of his time.[9]

You can't hold views like this and claim to subscribe to the central tenets of Christian theism, and neither Byron nor Shelley believed in God in anything like the conventional sense. In Canto III Byron goes out of his way to declare that 'I have not loved the world . . . Nor coined my cheek to smiles, nor cried aloud / In worship of an echo' (ll. 1049, 1052–3). If he believes in anything, it is his own god-like potential. Even at his most credulous, Byron is willing to admit only the bare possibility of 'the Power which gave' (l.156) – and, even then, makes the point that it is responsible for having permitted the appalling carnage of Waterloo.

If the plight of the Byronic overreacher is that of Childe Harold, so too is it that of Manfred. *Manfred* was written immediately after, inspired partly by Matthew G. Lewis's readings to Byron of Goethe's *Faust*. (Lewis was a friend who had written a popular Gothic novel, *The Monk*.) But Manfred is distinguished from other versions of the Faust character by defiance of the spirits he invokes, and passion for his dead sister, Astarte (a passion that echoes Byron's for Augusta). It is one of Byron's most serious works, in which the

Notes

[7] Medwin 237.
[8] *LY* i 237.
[9] For more on Canto III, see Michael O'Neill, *Romanticism and the Self-Conscious Poem* (Oxford, 1997), chapter 4.

eponymous hero embodies his creator's frustration at the human condition, and contempt for institutionalized religion. Although a drama, Byron claimed to have 'rendered it *quite impossible* for the stage – for which my intercourse with Drury Lane had given me the greatest contempt'.[10]

He left Switzerland at the end of August and travelled south, arriving in Venice in November. Although he would continue to tour Italy, he was to be based, for the next three years, in Venice.- Here, in 1818, he composed the fourth and final Canto of *Childe Harold*, and discovered *ottava rima*. It was a turning-point in his poetic development, as he realized immediately that it was much better suited to his purposes that the Spenserian stanza he had used up to now. Why? Because the Italian form was geared to feminine rhymes and a rapid metre – ideal for comedy. He experimented with it in *Beppo* and the *Epistle to Augusta* (pp. 890–3), and then, in 1818, began his masterpiece: *Don Juan*. This was originally to have been a single poem no longer than Canto I, but as he reached the end of it he saw that the central character had more potential than he thought at first. He began to write a second Canto. Cantos I and II were the first to appear in print, and are presented here in their entirety with the Dedication, as Byron intended. He wanted to include the Dedication in the first edition of 1819, but in the end decided against it on the grounds that he did not want 'to attack the dog [Southey] so fiercely without putting my name' – and he knew that *Don Juan* was to appear anonymously. As a result, the Dedication was not published until after Byron's death in 1832.

Byron declared, 'I *have* no plan – I *had* no plan – but I had or have materials,'[11] and indeed the manner in which *Don Juan* is written is just as important as the story – as he observed, 'I mean it for a poetical *Tristram Shandy*.'[12] He was right. It is sufficiently relaxed to contain all the waywardness, unpredictability and accumulated detritus of life as lived. 'Almost all *Don Juan* is real life,' Byron declared, 'either my own, or from people I know.'[13] He worked on it for his remaining years, leaving it unfinished at the time of his death. It would run to sixteen Cantos, and fourteen stanzas of a seventeenth.

Anxious about the content of the poem, John Murray issued Cantos I and II on 15 July 1819, omitting both his name and Byron's from the title-page. All the same, everyone knew who was responsible for it, and despite (or perhaps because of) its risqué subject-matter, it sold very well. That it was widely regarded as indecent, fit only for degraded and perverted old scoundrels like its author, was the subtext of the outraged condemnation of the shipwreck scene which appeared in the *British Critic*:

> In the scenes of confusion and agony attending a shipwreck, in the struggles for self-preservation, in the loss of so many souls, perhaps but too unprepared for their great account, in tracing the protracted sufferings of those whose lot is still to linger on in desperation drearier than death, in viewing a company of fellow-creatures on the wide ocean, devouring their last morsel, in witnessing hunger and thirst increasing upon them, the cannibal passions beginning to rise, the casting of lots for destruction, the self-immolation, the feast upon human blood, the frantic feeling of satiety – surely in bringing all these things home to our hearts, we can ill endure a full-born jest. Much less can we tolerate the mixing up of these fearful events with low doggerel and vapid absurdity.

In one sense, the reviewer was right. *Don Juan* was a calculated and gleeful affront to public taste. You could hardly argue that the shipwreck was not intended to be realistic – it was, and

Notes

10 Marchand v 170.
11 Marchand vi 207.
12 Marchand x 150.
13 Marchand viii 186.

Byron took care to base it on first-hand accounts.[14] But what really upset the reviewer (though he was too shocked to put it in this way) was the pleasure Byron took in undermining human virtue and religious faith, exposing the animalistic urges that underlie almost all social behaviour. Another poet might have had the inhabitants of the lifeboat pray for salvation and receive sustenance, but Byron takes pleasure in ensuring that it is Pedrillo, Juan's tutor, licensed to carry out religious rites, who is the first to beeaten. As if that was not enough, he then has those who have dined on Pedrillo go insane, implying that religious belief is a kind of madness.

In *Don Juan*, nothing is sacred; everything is reduced to the same materialistic level, everything is profaned. Take for instance the moment in the cave when, frying eggs for the emaciated Juan, Zoe notes that 'the best feelings must have victual'[15] – love is dependent on the state of one's stomach. Not very surprisingly, perhaps, Wordsworth did not see the joke; in late January 1820, he told Henry Crabb Robinson: 'I am persuaded that *Don Juan* will do more harm to the English character than anything of our time.'[16] That copious absence of respect for things sacred, besides being funny, has been the secret of the poem's popularity, which came only in the twentieth century.

It was one of Byron's more appalling boasts that, during his time in Venice, he made love to over 200 women. True or not, a degree of stability entered his private life when, in the year of *Juan*'s appearance, he became *cavaliere servente* (lover of a married woman) to Contessa Teresa Guiccioli, whom he encountered at a *conversazione* at the Palazzo Benzoni in Venice. Their first assignation took place the day after, and the 'essential part of the business' occupied them, according to Byron, 'four continuous days'. Their love affair would sustain him until the end of his life. He followed the Guicciolis to their home in Ravenna, and then to their palace in Bologna. It was while on that journey that he composed one of his most successful love poems, 'To the Po' (p. 1036).

In 1821 he moved to Pisa to be near Shelley who, with him and Leigh Hunt, wished to set up a new literary periodical entitled *The Liberal*. Unfortunately, before it could begin publishing, Shelley went sailing in his new boat, the *Ariel*, and drowned on 8 July. Shelley's corpse was washed up several days later, and was cremated on the beach on 16 July, with Byron in attendance. The heart, according to Byron, 'would not take the flame'. *The Liberal* struggled on for four numbers, attracting terrible reviews until it was discontinued and Hunt returned with his family to England.

Byron prided himself on consistency in his politics, and it was characteristic of him to join the fight for Greek independence. The massacre of Chios in spring 1822, in which 25,000 Greeks were slaughtered by the Turks, led to an outpouring of support for their plight. He was an eager recruit to the London Greek Committee, formed in January 1823. It was not just the cause that drew him, but identification with the Suliotes, the exiled military caste of Orthodox Christian Albanians whom he thought of as similar to a Scottish clan. He decided that he would not only donate funds, but form an elite private army to fight on the Greek side, which he would command. He parted with Teresa Guiccioli at Genoa and sailed for Cephalonia. By the time he landed at Missolonghi on 5 January 1824 he was in charge of up to 1,000 Suliote warriors. But he would never reach the battlefield. He contracted a fever in early April and, weakened by repeated bleeding (the usual treatment for fever was to apply leeches to the forehead and arms), died on 19 April. He was in his thirty-seventh year.

Notes

14 He found numerous examples in Sir John Graham Dalyell's *Shipwrecks and Disasters at Sea* (3 vols, 1812).

15 *Don Juan* ii 1153. It is a reworking of Terence, *Eunuchus* iv 5,6: 'sine Cerere et Libero friget Venus' (without Ceres (i.e. bread) and Bacchus (wine), Venus is frigid), alluded to more explicitly at *Don Juan* ii 1351–2.

16 *MY* ii 579.

He was already one of the most mythologized writers who had ever lived, thanks to his own writings; his death consolidated his popularity. When his body was shipped back to England, it lay in state for two days at 20 Great George Street in London. So hysterical with grief were those who came to view it that barriers were erected to hold them back. When the body was taken on the long journey to Hucknall Torkard churchyard in Nottinghamshire, crowds lined the streets, weeping openly as it passed. This was only the beginning. In no time at all Byron was a cult figure, a trend fuelled in part by the publication of his conversations (always lively) by such associates as Leigh Hunt, Thomas Medwin and Lady Blessington. His correspondence and journals began to trickle into print in 1826, with the first attempt at a collected edition by Thomas Moore in 1830. It was an international best-seller, and the more recent edition (1973–93) by Leslie A. Marchand remains one of the great scholarly achievements (and one of the most entertaining) of our own time. For a while it was fashionable for artists to paint Byron during his final illness – *The Death of Byron* by Joseph-Denis von Odevaere and *Lord Byron on his Deathbed* by R. C. Moore are two of the most notable depictions. His poetry attracted some of the most skilled illustrators of the day, including Thomas Stothard, Richard Westall, J. M. W. Turner, and George and I. R. Cruikshank; Ford Madox Brown produced some remarkable full-scale paintings based on *Manfred*, *Sardanapalus* and *The Prisoner of Chillon*. If anything, he was more famous on the Continent, where Delacroix depicted scenes from *The Corsair*, *Lara*, *Mazeppa* and *The Prisoner of Chillon*, while Berlioz composed music based on *Manfred* and *Childe Harold* Cantos III and IV. In Greece he remains a national hero, with streets and town squares named after him. He is perhaps the most enduringly popular personality of the Romantic period, and the one who most exemplifies the myth of the poet who lived life to the full and died in his prime.

I am grateful to Peter Cochran for advice in resolving some of the textual conundrums in Byron's texts.

Further reading

Byron ed. Jerome J. McGann. Oxford Authors (Oxford, 1986).

W. H. Auden, 'Don Juan', in *The Dyer's Hand and Other Essays* (London, 1963).

Anne Barton, *Byron: Don Juan* (Cambridge, 1992).

Bernard Beatty, *Byron's Don Juan* (Basingstoke, 1985).

Byron ed. Jane Stabler (Harlow, 1998).

Stephen Cheeke, *Byron and Place* (Basingstoke, 2003).

Caroline Franklin, *Byron's Heroines* (Oxford, 1992).

Caroline Franklin, *Byron: A Literary Life* (Basingstoke, 2000).

Malcolm Kelsall, *Byron's Politics* (Brighton, 1987).

Peter Manning, '*Don Juan* and Byron's Imperceptiveness to the English Word', in *Romanticism: A Critical Reader*, ed. Duncan Wu (Oxford, 1995) 217–42.

Leslie Marchand, *Byron: A Portrait* (London, 1971).

Fiona McCarthy, *Byron: Life and Legend* (London, 2002).

Jerome J. McGann, 'Byron and the Anonymous Lyric', in *Romanticism: A Critical Reader*, ed. Duncan Wu (Oxford, 1995) 243–60.

Jerome J. McGann, *Don Juan in Context* (London, 1976).

Jane Stabler, *Burke to Byron, Barbauld to Baillie, 1790–1830* (Basingstoke, 2002), pp. 149–55.

Jane Stabler, *Byron, Poetics and History* (Cambridge, 2002).

Susan Wolfson, *Borderlines: The Shiftings of Genders in British Romanticism* (forthcoming, 2005).

Susan Wolfson, *Formal Charges: The Shaping of Poetry in British Romanticism* (Stanford, Calif., 1997), chapter 5

Written Beneath a Picture (composed *c.* January 1812)[1]

From Childe Harold's Pilgrimage: A Romaunt (1812)[2]

1

Dear object of defeated care!
  Though now of love and thee bereft,
To reconcile me with despair
  Thine image and my tears are left.

2

'Tis said with sorrow time can cope,
  But this I feel can ne'er be true;
For by the death-blow of my hope
  My memory immortal grew.

Stanzas (composed February 1812)

From Childe Harold's Pilgrimage: A Romaunt (2nd edn., 1812)

Heu quanto minus est cum reliquis versari quam tui meminisse![1]

1

And thou art dead, as young and fair
  As aught of mortal birth;
And form so soft, and charms so rare,
  Too soon returned to earth!
Though earth received them in her bed,
And o'er the spot the crowd may tread
  In carelessness or mirth,
There is an eye which could not brook
A moment on that grave to look.

2

I will not ask where thou liest low,
  Nor gaze upon the spot;
There flowers or weeds at will may grow,
  So I behold them not;

Notes

WRITTEN BENEATH A PICTURE

[1] This poem was probably written to John Edleston, the boy chorister to whom Byron was passionately attached while at Cambridge, 1805–7. Edleston died in May 1811; Byron heard about this in October, and immediately found relief for his feelings in a series of poems about 'Thyrza'. By using a woman's name he could write freely about the relationship.

[2] *Childe Harold's Pilgrimage* (1812) contained a number of shorter poems besides the one that made his name (see headnote, p. 839).

STANZAS

[1] Shenstone's epitaph to his cousin, Mary Dolman: 'Alas, how much less it is to move among those left behind than to remember thee.'

It is enough for me to prove
That what I loved and long must love
  Like common earth can rot –
To me there needs no stone to tell
'Tis nothing that I loved so well.

3

Yet did I love thee to the last
  As fervently as thou,
Who didst not change through all the past,
  And canst not alter now.
The love where death has set his seal
Nor age can chill, nor rival steal,
  Nor falsehood disavow;
And, what were worse, thou canst not see
Or wrong, or change, or fault in me.

4

The better days of life were ours,
  The worst can be but mine;
The sun that cheers, the storm that lours,
  Shall never more be thine.
The silence of that dreamless sleep
I envy now too much to weep;
  Nor need I to repine
That all those charms have passed away
I might have watched through long decay.

5

The flower in ripened bloom unmatched
  Must fall the earliest prey,
Though by no hand untimely snatched,
  The leaves must drop away;
And yet it were a greater grief
To watch it withering leaf by leaf
  Than see it plucked today –
Since earthly eye but ill can bear
To trace the change to foul from fair.

6

I know not if I could have borne
  To see thy beauties fade;
The night that followed such a morn
  Had worn a deeper shade;
Thy day without a cloud hath passed,
And thou wert lovely to the last,
  Extinguished, not decayed –
As stars that shoot along the sky
Shine brightest as they fall from high.

7

As once I wept, if I could weep,
   My tears might well be shed,
To think I was not near to keep
   One vigil o'er thy bed,
To gaze, how fondly, on thy face,
To fold thee in a faint embrace,
   Uphold thy drooping head;
And show that love, however vain,
Nor thou nor I can feel again.

8

Yet how much less it were to gain
   (Though thou hast left me free)
The loveliest things that still remain,
   Than thus remember thee!
The all of thine that cannot die
Through dark and dread eternity
   Returns again to me,
And more thy buried love endears
Than aught, except its living years.

She Walks in Beauty (composed *c.* 12 June 1814)[1]

From Hebrew Melodies (1815)

I

She walks in beauty like the night
   Of cloudless climes and starry skies,
And all that's best of dark and bright
   Meet in her aspect and her eyes,
Thus mellowed to that tender light
   Which heaven to gaudy day denies.

II

One shade the more, one ray the less
   Had half-impaired the nameless grace
Which waves in every raven tress
   Or softly lightens o'er her face –
Where thoughts serenely sweet express
   How pure, how dear their dwelling place.

Notes

She Walks in Beauty

[1] A MS version of the poem is entitled, 'Lines written by Lord Byron after seeing Mrs Wilmot at Lansdowne House'. Byron met Anne Wilmot (1784–1871) on 11 June 1814; she was the wife of his first cousin, Robert John Wilmot.

III

And on that cheek and o'er that brow,
So soft, so calm, yet eloquent,
The smiles that win, the tints that glow,
But tell of days in goodness spent,
A mind at peace with all below,
A heart whose love is innocent.

When we two parted (composed August or September 1815)[1]

From **Poems** (1816)

1

When we two parted
In silence and tears,
Half broken-hearted,
To sever for years,
Pale grew thy cheek and cold,
Colder thy kiss –
Truly that hour foretold
Sorrow to this.

2

The dew of the morning
Sunk chill on my brow –
It felt like the warning
Of what I feel now.
Thy vows are all broken,
And light is thy fame;
I hear thy name spoken,
And share in its shame.

3

They name thee before me –
A knell to mine ear;
A shudder comes o'er me –
Why wert thou so dear?
They know not I knew thee,
Who knew thee too well;
Long, long shall I rue thee,
Too deeply to tell.[2]

Notes

WHEN WE TWO PARTED

[1] The subject of the poem is Lady Frances Wedderburn Webster, with whom Byron had a brief, 'platonic' affair late in 1813; its immediate occasion was gossip about her affair with the Duke of Wellington in Paris in 1815.

[2] Byron's original draft contains an extra stanza at this point, which refers explicitly to Lady Frances:

Then fare thee well, Fanny,
Now doubly undone,
To prove false unto many
As faithless to one.
Thou art past all recalling
Even would I recall,
For the woman once falling
Forever must fall.

4

In secret we met,
  In silence I grieve
That thy heart could forget,
  Thy spirit deceive.
If I should meet thee
  After long years,
How should I greet thee?
  With silence and tears.

Fare Thee Well! (composed 18 March 1816)[1]

From Poems (1816)

Alas! they had been friends in youth;
But whispering tongues can poison truth;
And constancy lives in realms above:
And life is thorny; and youth is vain:
And to be wroth with one we love,
Doth work like madness in the brain. . . .
But never either found another
To free the hollow heart from paining –
They stood aloof, the scars remaining,
Like cliffs which had been rent asunder;
A dreary sea now flows between,
But neither heat, nor frost, nor thunder
Shall wholly do away, I ween,
The marks of that which once hath been.[2]

Fare thee well! and if for ever –
  Still for ever, fare *thee well*! –
Even though unforgiving, never
  'Gainst thee shall my heart rebel.
Would that breast were bared before thee
  Where thy head so oft hath lain,
While that placid sleep came o'er thee
  Which thou ne'er canst know again;
Would that breast by thee glanced over,
  Every inmost thought could show!
Then thou wouldst at last discover

Notes

Fare Thee Well!

[1] This valedictory poem was addressed to Lady Byron the day after ratification of her preliminary Separation Agreement with the poet; the final agreement was signed on 21 April. The poem was sent to her in early April with a view to moving her to a reconciliation. In the event a version appeared in *The Champion* as part of an attack on Byron engineered by his wife's allies.

[2] The epigraph is from Coleridge's *Christabel* 396–414. Byron was responsible for the first publication of *Christabel* in 1816 (see headnote, p. 840).

'Twas not well to spurn it so.
Though the world for this commend thee
Though it smile upon the blow,
Even its praises must offend thee,
Founded on another's woe;
Though my many faults defaced me,
Could no other arm be found
Than the one which once embraced me
To inflict a cureless wound?
Yet, oh yet, thyself deceive not:
Love may sink by slow decay;
But by sudden wrench, believe not,
Hearts can thus be torn away.
Still thine own its life retaineth –
Still must mine, though bleeding, beat,
And the undying thought which paineth
Is – that we no more may meet.
These are words of deeper sorrow
Than the wail above the dead;
Both shall live, but every morrow
Wake us from a widowed bed.
And when thou wouldst solace gather
When our child's[3] first accents flow
Wilt thou teach her to say 'Father!'
Though his care she must forgo?
When her little hands shall press thee,
When her lip to thine is pressed,
Think of him whose prayer shall bless thee,
Think of him thy love had blessed.
Should her lineaments resemble
Those thou never more may'st see[4]
Then thy heart will softly tremble
With a pulse yet true to me.
All my faults (perchance thou knowest),
All my madness[5] – none can know;
All my hopes, where'er thou goest,
Wither – yet with *thee* they go.
Every feeling hath been shaken,
Pride (which not a world could bow)
Bows to thee – by thee forsaken

Notes

[3] Ada Augusta Byron, born 10 December 1815. After his departure from England in 1816, Byron never saw her again. Knowledge of her father was kept from her as she grew up, but her husband, Lord King, eventually weaned her from her mother's influence, and she came to revere her father's poetry and his memory. She died at the age of 35.

[4] *Those thou . . . see* i.e. Byron's.

[5] *madness* Annabella accused Byron of madness prior to their separation.

Even my soul forsakes me now.
But 'tis done, all words are idle –
Words from me are vainer still;
But the thoughts we cannot bridle
Force their way without the will.
Fare thee well! – thus disunited,
Torn from every nearer tie,
Seared in my heart – and lone – and blighted –
More than this, I scarce can die.

Childe Harold's Pilgrimage

Canto the Third (composed 25 April–4 July 1816; published 18 November 1816)[1]

Afin que cette application vous forçât à penser à autre chose. Il n'y a en vérité de remède que celui-là et le temps.
Lettre du Roi de Prusse à D'Alembert, Sept. 7, 1776[2]

1

Is thy face like thy mother's, my fair child,[3]
Ada, sole daughter of my house and heart?
When last I saw thy young blue eyes, they smiled;
And then we parted – not as now we part,
But with a hope. Awaking with a start,
The waters heave around me, and on high
The winds lift up their voices. I depart
Whither I know not, but the hour's gone by
When Albion's lessening shores could grieve or glad mine eye.[4]

2

Once more upon the waters, yet once more![5]
And the waves bound beneath me as a steed
That knows his rider – welcome to their roar!
Swift be their guidance, wheresoe'er it lead!
Though the strained mast should quiver as a reed
And the rent canvas fluttering strew the gale,
Still must I on – for I am as a weed
Flung from the rock on ocean's foam, to sail
Where'er the surge may sweep, the tempest's breath prevail.

Notes

CHILDE HAROLD'S PILGRIMAGE

[1] For a general introduction to this poem see headnote, p. 842.

[2] 'So that this work will force you to think of something else. Truly, that and time are the only remedies.'

[3] *my fair child* Byron's only legitimate daughter Ada Augusta, born 10 December 1815. After Lady Byron left him five weeks later, he never saw Ada again.

[4] *the hour's gone by . . . mine eye* Byron began writing this Canto while at sea, 25 April 1816. He felt hounded out of England by the bad publicity whipped up by his wife.

[5] *Once more . . . once more* Byron echoes *Henry V* III i 1: 'Once more unto the breach, dear friends, once more.'

3

In my youth's summer I did sing of one,[6]
The wandering outlaw of his own dark mind;
Again I seize the theme then but begun,
And bear it with me as the rushing wind
Bears the cloud onwards. In that tale I find
The furrows of long thought, and dried-up tears
Which, ebbing, leave a sterile track behind,
O'er which all heavily the journeying years
Plod the last sands of life, where not a flower appears.

4

Since my young days of passion[7] (joy or pain),
Perchance my heart and harp have lost a string
And both may jar; it may be that in vain
I would essay,[8] as I have sung, to sing.
Yet, though a dreary[9] strain, to this I cling,
So that it wean me from the weary dream
Of selfish grief or gladness; so it fling
Forgetfulness around me. It shall seem
To me (though to none else) a not ungrateful theme.

5

He, who grown aged in this world of woe
(In deeds not years), piercing the depths of life
So that no wonder waits him; nor below
Can love or sorrow, fame, ambition, strife,
Cut to his heart again with the keen knife
Of silent sharp endurance – he can tell
Why thought seeks refuge in lone caves yet[10] rife
With airy images,[11] and shapes which dwell
Still unimpaired, though old, in the soul's haunted cell.

6

'Tis to create, and in creating live
A being more intense, that we endow
With form our fancy, gaining as we give
The life we image – even as I do now.

Notes

[6] *In my youth's summer . . . one* i.e. Childe Harold. Byron began Canto I on 31 October 1809, when he was 21.

[7] *Since my young days of passion* Byron was 28 at the time of writing.

[8] *essay* attempt.

[9] *dreary* melancholy.

[10] *yet* still.

[11] *airy images* Byron is probably recalling *A Midsummer Night's Dream* V i 14–17:

> And as imagination bodies forth
> The forms of things unknown, the poet's pen
> Turns them to shapes, and gives to aery nothing
> A local habitation and a name.

What am I? Nothing. But not so art thou,
Soul of my thought,[12] with whom I traverse earth,
Invisible but gazing, as I glow
Mixed with thy spirit, blended with thy birth,
And feeling still with thee in my crushed feelings' dearth.

7

Yet must I think less wildly. I *have* thought
Too long and darkly till my brain became,
In its own eddy, boiling and o'erwrought,
A whirling gulf of fantasy and flame;
And thus, untaught in youth my heart to tame,
My springs of life were poisoned. 'Tis too late!
Yet am I changed, though still enough the same
In strength to bear what time cannot abate,
And feed on bitter fruits without accusing fate.

8

Something too much of this:[13] but now 'tis past,
And the spell closes with its silent seal.
Long absent Harold[14] reappears at last;
He of the breast which fain no more would feel,
Wrung with the wounds which kill not, but ne'er heal;
Yet Time, who changes all, had altered him
In soul and aspect as in age: years steal
Fire from the mind as vigour from the limb;
And Life's enchanted cup but sparkles near the brim.

9

His had been quaffed too quickly, and he found
The dregs were wormwood;[15] but he filled again,
And from a purer fount,[16] on holier ground,
And deemed its spring perpetual – but in vain!
Still round him clung invisibly a chain
Which galled for ever, fettering though unseen,
And heavy though it clanked not; worn with pain,
Which pined although it spoke not, and grew keen,
Entering with every step he took, through many a scene.

Notes

[12] *Soul of my thought* Byron is still thinking of his daughter.

[13] *Something too much of this* borrowed from *Hamlet* III ii 74.

[14] *Harold* A late entrance for the hero of the poem, whose character was Byron's alter ego, embodying the deepest anxieties and preoccupations of his creator.

[15] *wormwood* plant known for its bitter taste.

[16] *a purer fount* Greece, where Harold had gone in Canto II.

10

Secure in guarded coldness, he had mixed
Again in fancied safety with his kind,
And deemed his spirit now so firmly fixed
And sheathed with an invulnerable mind,
That, if no joy, no sorrow lurked behind;
And he, as one, might midst the many stand
Unheeded, searching through the crowd to find
Fit speculation – such as in strange land
He found in wonder-works of God and Nature's hand.

11

But who can view the ripened rose, nor seek
To wear it? Who can curiously behold
The smoothness and the sheen of Beauty's cheek,
Nor feel the heart can never all grow old?
Who can contemplate fame through clouds unfold
The star which rises o'er her steep, nor climb?
Harold, once more within the vortex, rolled
On with the giddy circle, chasing Time,
Yet with a nobler aim than in his Youth's fond prime.

12

But soon he knew himself the most unfit
Of men to herd with man,[17] with whom he held
Little in common; untaught to submit
His thoughts to others, though his soul was quelled
In youth by his own thoughts; still uncompelled,
He would not yield dominion of his mind
To spirits against whom his own rebelled,
Proud though in desolation – which could find
A life within itself, to breathe without mankind.

13

Where rose the mountains, there to him were friends;
Where rolled the ocean, thereon was his home;
Where a blue sky, and glowing clime, extends,
He had the passion and the power to roam;
The desert, forest, cavern, breaker's foam,

Notes

[17] *man* i.e. mankind.

Were unto him companionship; they spake
A mutual language, clearer than the tome
Of his land's tongue, which he would oft forsake
For nature's pages glassed by sunbeams on the lake.

14

Like the Chaldean,[18] he could watch the stars
Till he had peopled them with beings bright
As their own beams; and earth, and earth-born jars,[19]
And human frailties, were forgotten quite:
Could he have kept his spirit to that flight
He had been happy; but this clay will sink
Its spark immortal, envying it the light
To which it mounts, as if to break the link
That keeps us from yon heaven which woos us to its brink.

15

But in Man's dwellings he became a thing
Restless and worn, and stern and wearisome,
Drooped as a wild-born falcon with clipped wing,
To whom the boundless air alone were home:
Then came his fit again, which to o'ercome,
As eagerly the barred-up bird will beat
His breast and beak against his wiry dome
Till the blood tinge his plumage – so the heat
Of his impeded soul would through his bosom eat.

16

Self-exiled Harold wanders forth again,
With nought of hope left, but with less of gloom;
The very knowledge that he lived in vain,
That all was over on this side the tomb,[20]
Had made Despair a smilingness[21] assume,
Which, though 'twere wild (as on the plundered wreck
When mariners would madly meet their doom
With draughts intemperate on the sinking deck),
Did yet inspire a cheer, which he forbore to check.

17

Stop! For thy tread is on an Empire's dust!
An earthquake's spoil is sepulchred below![22]
Is the spot marked with no colossal bust?

Notes

[18] *Chaldean* the Chaldeans were renowned astronomers.

[19] *jars* quarrels.

[20] *That all was over . . . tomb* i.e. that there was no afterlife.

[21] *a smilingness* a smiling expression.

[22] *Stop! . . . below* Byron visited the battlefield at Waterloo on Saturday 4 May 1816. The 'earthquake's spoil' consists of thousands of people killed in battle.

Nor column trophied for triumphal show?
None; but the moral's truth tells simpler so.
As the ground was before, thus let it be;
How that red rain[23] hath made the harvest grow!
And is this all the world has gained by thee,
Thou first and last of fields, king-making Victory?[24]

18

And Harold stands upon this place of skulls,
The grave of France, the deadly Waterloo!
How in an hour the Power which gave[25] annuls
Its gifts, transferring fame as fleeting too!
In 'pride of place'[26] here last the eagle flew,
Then tore with bloody talon the rent plain,
Pierced by the shaft[27] of banded nations through;
Ambition's life and labours all were vain;
He wears the shattered links of the world's broken chain.

19

Fit retribution! Gaul[28] may champ the bit
And foam in fetters – but is earth more free?
Did nations combat to make *one*[29] submit?
Or league[30] to teach all kings true sovereignty?
What? Shall reviving thraldom[31] again be
The patched-up idol of enlightened days?
Shall we, who struck the lion down, shall we
Pay the wolf homage? Proffering lowly gaze
And servile knees to thrones? No! Prove[32] before ye praise!

20

If not, o'er one fallen despot boast no more!
In vain fair cheeks were furrowed with hot tears
For Europe's flowers long rooted up before
The trampler of her vineyards; in vain, years
Of death, depopulation, bondage, fears,
Have all been borne, and broken by the accord

Shelley influence.

Waterloo – Problematic + complex for Byron

Notes

[23] *red rain* blood shed on the fields in the battle.

[24] *king-making Victory* The Bourbon restoration of April–May 1814 strengthened monarchical power throughout Europe. In a letter written soon after his visit to Waterloo, Byron commented on the Battle: 'I detest the cause and the victors – and the victory – including Blucher and the Bourbons' (Marchand v 76).

[25] *the Power which gave* Rather than say 'God', Byron uses the term employed by Shelley in *Hymn to Intellectual Beauty* and *Mont Blanc*.

[26] ' "Pride of place" is a term of falconry, and means the highest pitch of flight. See *Macbeth*, etc.' (Byron's note). Byron refers to *Macbeth* II iv 12: 'A falcon, tow'ring in her pride of place'.

[27] *shaft* arrow.

[28] *Gaul* France.

[29] *one* Napoleon.

[30] *league* band together. The Battle of Waterloo was fought by an alliance of the British, the Dutch, the Austrians, the Swedes, and the Prussians.

[31] *thraldom* slavery. Byron was no friend to monarchy.

[32] *Prove* i.e. establish the true value of the victory.

Of roused-up millions: all that most endears
Glory, is when the myrtle wreathes a sword,
Such as Harmodius drew on Athens' tyrant lord.[33]

21

There was a sound of revelry by night,[34]
And Belgium's capital had gathered then
Her beauty and her chivalry – and bright
The lamps shone o'er fair women and brave men;
A thousand hearts beat happily; and when
Music arose with its voluptuous swell,
Soft eyes looked love to eyes which spake again,
And all went merry as a marriage bell;
But hush! hark! a deep sound strikes like a rising knell!

22

Did ye not hear it? No, 'twas but the wind,
Or the car rattling o'er the stony street;
On with the dance! Let joy be unconfined;
No sleep till morn, when Youth and Pleasure meet
To chase the glowing Hours with flying feet –
But hark! that heavy sound breaks in once more,
As if the clouds its echo would repeat;
And nearer – clearer – deadlier than before!
Arm! Arm! It is – it is – the cannon's opening roar![35]

23

Within a windowed niche of that high hall
Sate Brunswick's fated chieftain;[36] he did hear
That sound the first amidst the festival,
And caught its tone with Death's prophetic ear;
And when they smiled because he deemed it near,
His heart more truly knew that peal too well
Which stretched his father on a bloody bier,
And roused the vengeance blood alone could quell;
He rushed into the field, and, foremost fighting, fell.

Notes

[33] *Such as Harmodius . . . tyrant lord* Byron alludes to Harmodius and Aristogeiton, their daggers wreathed in myrtle branches, who in 514 BC attempted to kill Hippias and Hipparchus, tyrannical rulers of Athens. The sword wreathed in myrtle leaves is an emblem of the freedom fighter.

[34] *There was a sound . . . night* The stanza recalls the famous ball given by the Duchess of Richmond in Brussels on 15 June 1815, the night prior to the inconclusive Battle of Quatre-Bras; Waterloo was fought three days later.

[35] *the cannon's opening roar!* Wellington discovered the approach of Napoleon not from the sound of cannon but from dispatches sent by the Prussian commander, Blücher.

[36] *Brunswick's fated chieftain* Frederick, Duke of Brunswick (1771–1815), nephew of George III, killed at Quatre-Bras. His father, Charles William Ferdinand, was killed in 1806 at Auerstädt.

24

Ah! then and there was hurrying to and fro,
And gathering tears, and tremblings of distress,
And cheeks all pale, which but an hour ago
Blushed at the praise of their own loveliness –
And there were sudden partings, such as press
The life from out young hearts, and choking sighs
Which ne'er might be repeated; who could guess
If ever more should meet those mutual eyes,
Since upon nights so sweet such awful morn could rise?

25

And there was mounting in hot haste: the steed,
The mustering squadron, and the clattering car,
Went pouring forward with impetuous speed,
And swiftly forming in the ranks of war;
And the deep thunder peal on peal afar;
And near, the beat of the alarming drum[37]
Roused up the soldier ere the morning star;
While thronged the citizens with terror dumb,
Or whispering, with white lips, 'The foe! They come! They come!'

26

And wild and high the 'Cameron's gathering'[38] rose!
The war-note of Lochiel,[39] which Albyn's[40] hills
Have heard, and, heard, too, have her Saxon foes:
How in the noon of night that pibroch[41] thrills,
Savage and shrill! But with the breath which fills
Their mountain-pipe, so fill the mountaineers
With the fierce native daring which instils
The stirring memory of a thousand years,
And Evan's, Donald's fame rings in each clansman's ears![42]

27

And Ardennes[43] waves above them her green leaves,
Dewy with nature's tear-drops, as they pass,

Notes

[37] *the alarming drum* The drum sounds an alarm to the soldiers.

[38] *Cameron's gathering* rallying-cry of the Cameron clan.

[39] *Lochiel* title of the chief of the Camerons.

[40] *Albyn* Gaelic name for Scotland.

[41] *pibroch* series of martial variations for the bagpipe, on a theme called the 'urlar'.

[42] *And Evan's . . . ears* Sir Evan or Ewen Cameron (1629–1719) resisted Cromwell 1652–8 and fought at Killiecrankie for James II in 1689. His grandson Donald Cameron (1695–1748) fought to restore the Stuarts in 1745 and was wounded at Culloden the following year. Byron spent his formative years in Scotland.

[43] *Ardennes* 'The woods of Soignies is supposed to be a remnant of the "forest of Ardennes", famous in Boiardo's *Orlando*, and immortal in Shakespeare's *As You Like It*. It in also celebrated in Tacitus as being the spot of successful defence by the Germans against the Roman encroachments. I have ventured to adopt the name connected with more noble associations than those of mere slaughter' (Byron's note). A note full of errors: Soignies is between Waterloo and Brussels, Ardennes is in Luxembourg, and Arden is English.

Grieving, if aught inanimate e'er grieves,
Over the unreturning brave – alas!
Ere evening to be trodden like the grass
Which now beneath them, but above shall grow
In its next verdure, when this fiery mass
Of living valour, rolling on the foe
And burning with high hope, shall moulder cold and low.

28

Last noon beheld them full of lusty life,
Last eve in Beauty's circle proudly gay,
The midnight brought the signal-sound of strife,
The morn the marshalling in arms, the day
Battle's magnificently-stern array!
The thunder-clouds close o'er it, which when rent
The earth is covered thick with other clay,[44]
Which her own clay shall cover, heaped and pent,
Rider and horse, friend, foe, in one red burial blent![45]

29

Their praise is hymned by loftier harps than mine;[46]
Yet one I would select from that proud throng,
Partly because they blend me with his line,[47]
And partly that I did his sire some wrong,
And partly that bright names will hallow song;
And his was of the bravest, and when showered
The death-bolts deadliest the thinned files along,
Even where the thickest of war's tempest loured,
They reached no nobler breast than thine – young, gallant Howard![48]

30

There have been tears and breaking hearts for thee,
And mine were nothing, had I such to give;
But when I stood beneath the fresh green tree,
Which living waves where thou didst cease to live,[49]
And saw around me the wide field revive

Notes

[44] *other clay* corpses.

[45] *blent* blended.

[46] *loftier harps than mine* Scott's, in *The Field of Waterloo* (Edinburgh, 1815).

[47] *line* i.e. of descent.

[48] *young, gallant Howard!* The Hon. Frederick Howard (1785–1815), Byron's cousin, son of his guardian, the Earl of Carlisle, whom he had criticised in *English Bards and Scotch Reviewers* (1809) for his ambitions as a verse-dramatist: 'So dull in youth, so drivelling in his age, / His scenes alone had damned our sinking stage' (ll. 733–4).

[49] *didst cease to live* i.e. died.

With fruits and fertile promise, and the spring
Come forth her work of gladness to contrive,
With all her reckless[50] birds upon the wing,
I turned from all she brought to those she could not bring.[51]

31

I turned to thee, to thousands, of whom each
And one as all a ghastly gap did make
In his own kind and kindred, whom to teach
Forgetfulness were mercy for their sake;
The Archangel's trump, not Glory's, must awake
Those whom they thirst for; though the sound of Fame
May for a moment soothe, it cannot slake
The fever of vain longing, and the name
So honoured but assumes a stronger, bitterer claim.

32

They mourn, but smile at length – and, smiling, mourn:
The tree will wither long before it fall;
The hull drives on, though mast and sail be torn;
The roof-tree sinks, but moulders on the hall
In massy hoariness; the ruined wall
Stands when its wind-worn battlements are gone;
The bars survive the captive they enthrall;[52]
The day drags through though storms keep out the sun;
And thus the heart will break, yet brokenly live on:

33

Even as a broken mirror, which the glass
In every fragment multiplies; and makes
A thousand images of one that was,
The same, and still the more, the more it breaks;
And thus the heart will do which not forsakes,
Living in shattered guise; and still, and cold,

Notes

[50] *reckless* carefree.

[51] 'My guide from Mont St Jean over the field seemed intelligent and accurate. The place where Major Howard fell was not far from two tall and solitary trees (there was a third cut down, or shivered in the battle) which stand a few yards from each other at a pathway's side. Beneath these he died and was buried. The body has since been removed to England. A small hollow for the present marks where it lay, but will probably soon be effaced; the plough has been upon it, and the grain is.

After pointing our the different spots where Picton and other gallant men had perished, the guide said, 'Here Major Howard lay; I was near him when wounded.' I told him my relationship, and he seemed then still more anxious to point out the particular spot and circumstances. The place is one of the most marked in the field from the peculiarity of the two trees above mentioned.

I went on horseback twice over the field, comparing it with my recollection of similar scenes. As a plain, Waterloo seems marked out for the scene of some great action, though this may be mere imagination: I have viewed with attention those of Platea, Troy, Mantinea, Leuctra, Chaeronea, and Marathon; and the field around Mont St Jean and Hougoumont appears to want little but a better cause, and that undefinable but impressive halo which the lapse of ages throws around a celebrated spot, to vie in interest with any or all of these, except perhaps the last mentioned' (Byron's note).

[52] *enthrall* imprison.

And bloodless, with its sleepless sorrow aches,
Yet withers on till all without is old,
Showing no visible sign, for such things are untold.

34

There is a very life in our despair,
Vitality of poison – a quick[53] root
Which feeds these deadly branches; for it were
As nothing did we die; but Life will suit
Itself to Sorrow's most detested fruit,
Like to the apples on the Dead Sea's shore,
All ashes to the taste.[54] Did man compute
Existence by enjoyment, and count o'er
Such hours 'gainst years of life, say, would he name threescore?

35

The Psalmist numbered out the years of man:[55]
They are enough; and if thy tale[56] be *true*,
Thou, who didst grudge him even that fleeting span,
More than enough, thou fatal Waterloo!
Millions of tongues record thee, and anew
Their children's lips shall echo them, and say,
'Here, where the sword united nations drew,
Our countrymen were warring on that day!'
And this is much, and all which will not pass away.

36

There sunk the greatest, nor the worst of men,[57]
Whose spirit antithetically mixed
One moment of the mightiest, and again
On little objects with like firmness fixed,
Extreme in all things! Hadst thou been betwixt,[58]
Thy throne[59] had still been thine, or never been;
For daring made thy rise as fall: thou seek'st
Even now to reassume the imperial mien,[60]
And shake again the world, the Thunderer of the scene!

Notes

[53] *quick* living.

[54] 'The (fabled) apples on the brink of the Lake Asphaltes were said to be fair without, and within ashes. – Vide Tacitus, *Historia* [Book 5, sec.7]' (Byron's note).

[55] *The Psalmist . . . years of man* Byron refers to Psalm 90: 10: 'The days of our years are threescore years and ten; and if by reason of strength they be fourscore years, yet is their strength labour and sorrow; for it is soon cut off, and we fly away.'

[56] *tale* a pun, meaning both 'story' and 'counting'.

[57] *There sunk . . . men* Napoleon. Byron thought Napoleon had been no worse than the despots who had taken his place.

[58] *betwixt* i.e. between the mightiest and the meanest.

[59] *Thy throne* Napoleon crowned himself Emperor in December 1804.

[60] *thou seek'st . . . mien* Napoleon was at this time in exile on St Helena.

37

Conqueror and captive of the earth art thou!
She trembles at thee still, and thy wild name
Was ne'er more bruited[61] in men's minds than now
That thou art nothing, save the jest of Fame,
Who wooed thee once, thy vassal, and became
The flatterer of thy fierceness – till thou wert
A god unto thyself; nor less the same
To the astounded kingdoms all inert,
Who deemed thee for a time whate'er thou didst assert.

38

Oh, more or less than man – in high or low,
Battling with nations, flying from the field;
Now making monarchs' necks thy footstool, now
More than thy meanest soldier taught to yield;[62]
An empire thou couldst crush, command, rebuild,
But govern not thy pettiest passion, nor,
However deeply in men's spirits skilled,
Look through thine own,[63] nor curb the lust of war,
Nor learn that tempted Fate will leave the loftiest star.

39

Yet well thy soul hath brooked[64] the turning tide
With that untaught innate philosophy,
Which, be it wisdom, coldness, or deep pride,
Is gall and wormwood[65] to an enemy.
When the whole host of hatred stood hard by
To watch and mock thee shrinking, thou hast smiled
With a sedate and all-enduring eye;
When Fortune fled her spoiled and favourite child,
He stood unbowed beneath the ills upon him piled.

40

Sager than in thy fortunes; for in them
Ambition steeled thee on too far to show
That just habitual scorn, which could contemn
Men and their thoughts; 'twas wise to feel, not so
To wear it ever on thy lip and brow,
And spurn the instruments[66] thou wert to use
Till they were turned unto thine overthrow:
'Tis but a worthless world to win or lose;
So hath it proved to thee, and all such lot who choose.

Notes

[61] *bruited* celebrated.

[62] *now / More than thy meanest soldier . . . yield* Napoleon has been taught to humble himself even more than the lowest of his soldiers.

[63] *thine own* i.e. spirit.

[64] *brooked* endured.

[65] *gall and wormwood* i.e. very bitter.

[66] *the instruments* i.e. other men.

41

If, like a tower upon a headlong rock,
Thou[67] hadst been made to stand or fall alone,
Such scorn of man had helped to brave the shock;
But men's thoughts were the steps which paved thy throne,
Their admiration thy best weapon shone;
The part of Philip's son[68] was thine, not then
(Unless aside thy purple[69] had been thrown)
Like stern Diogenes[70] to mock at men:
For sceptred cynics earth were far too wide a den.[71]

42

But quiet to quick[72] bosoms is a hell,
And *there* hath been thy bane: there is a fire
And motion of the soul which will not dwell
In its own narrow being, but aspire
Beyond the fitting medium of desire,
And, but once kindled, quenchless evermore,
Preys upon high adventure, nor can tire
Of aught but rest – a fever at the core,
Fatal to him who bears, to all who ever bore.[73]

43

This makes the madmen who have made men mad
By their contagion: conquerors and kings,
Founders of sects and systems, to whom add
Sophists, bards, statesmen, all unquiet things
Which stir too strongly the soul's secret springs,
And are themselves the fools to those they fool –
Envied, yet how unenviable! What stings
Are theirs! One breast laid open were a school
Which would unteach mankind the lust to shine or rule:

Notes

67 *Thou* Napoleon, at the time of writing imprisoned on St Helena in the wake of his final defeat at Waterloo.

68 *Philip's son* Alexander the Great, son of Philip of Macedonia, who also conquered an empire.

69 *thy purple* the colour worn by emperors. Napoleon crowned himself Emperor in 1804.

70 *stern Diogenes* Greek, Cynic, philosopher of the 4th century BC, known for austere habits, and choosing to live in the open.

71 'The great error of Napoleon, "if we have writ our annals true", was a continued obtrusion on mankind of his want of all community of feeling for or with them; perhaps more offensive to human vanity than the active cruelty of more trembling and suspicious tyranny.

Such were his speeches to public assemblies as well as individuals: and the single expression which he is said to have used on returning to Paris after the Russian winter had destroyed his army, rubbing his hands over a fire, "This is pleasanter than Moscow", would probably alienate more favour from his cause than the destruction and reverses which led to the remark' (Byron's note).

72 *quick* vital, hasty.

73 Napoleon is styled here as a type of the Byronic over-reacher, not unlike Manfred.

44

Their breath is agitation, and their life
A storm whereon they ride, to sink at last;
And yet so nursed and bigoted to strife,
That, should their days (surviving perils passed)
Melt to calm twilight, they feel overcast
With sorrow and supineness, and so die;
Even as a flame unfed, which runs to waste
With its own flickering, or a sword laid by
Which eats into itself, and rusts ingloriously.

45

He who ascends to mountain-tops shall find
The loftiest peaks most wrapped in clouds and snow;
He who surpasses or subdues mankind
Must look down on the hate of those below.
Though high *above* the sun of glory glow
And far *beneath* the earth and ocean spread,
Round him are icy rocks, and loudly blow
Contending tempests on his naked head,
And thus reward the toils which to those summits led.

46

Away with these! True wisdom's world will be
Within its own creation, or in thine,
Maternal Nature![74] For who teems like thee,
Thus on the banks of thy majestic Rhine?[75]
There Harold gazes on a work divine,
A blending of all beauties; streams and dells,
Fruit, foliage, crag, wood, cornfield, mountain, vine,
And chiefless castles breathing stern farewells
From gray but leafy walls, where Ruin greenly dwells.

47

And there they[76] stand, as stands a lofty mind,
Worn, but unstooping to the baser crowd,
All tenantless, save to the crannying[77] wind,
Or holding dark communion with the cloud.
There was a day when they were young and proud;
Banners on high, and battles[78] passed below;
But they who fought are in a bloody shroud,
And those which waved[79] are shredless dust ere now,
And the bleak battlements shall bear no future blow.

Notes

[74] *Maternal Nature!* Byron's celebration of nature was uncharacteristic, and owes much to the temporary influence of Wordsworth, whose poetry Shelley read to him in Geneva in the summer of 1816, when this poem was composed.

[75] *thy majestic Rhine?* Byron travelled up the Rhine via Bonn, Koblenz and Mannheim, 10–16 May 1816

[76] *they* i.e. ruined castles.

[77] *crannying* The wind is so strong it penetrates into nooks and crannies of the ruin.

[78] *battles* a pun, meaning both battalions and military engagements.

[79] *those which waved* flags.

48

Beneath these battlements, within those walls,
Power dwelt amidst her passions; in proud state
Each robber-chief upheld his armed halls,
Doing his evil will, nor less elate[80]
Than mightier heroes of a longer date.
What want these outlaws conquerors should have[81]
But history's purchased page to call them great?[82]
A wider space? An ornamented grave?
Their hopes were not less warm, their souls were full as brave.

49

In their baronial feuds and single fields,
What deeds of prowess unrecorded died!
And Love, which lent a blazon[83] to their shields,
With emblems well devised by amorous pride,
Through all the mail of iron hearts would glide;
But still their flame was fierceness, and drew on
Keen contest and destruction near allied,
And many a tower for some fair mischief won,
Saw the discoloured[84] Rhine beneath its ruin run.

50

But thou, exulting and abounding river!
Making thy waves a blessing as they flow
Through banks whose beauty would endure for ever
Could man but leave thy bright creation so,
Nor its fair promise from the surface mow
With the sharp scythe of conflict – then to see
Thy valley of sweet waters, were to know
Earth paved like heaven, and to seem such to me,
Even now what wants thy stream? – that it should Lethe[85] be.

51

A thousand battles have assailed thy banks,
But these and half their fame have passed away,
And Slaughter heaped on high his weltering ranks:
Their very graves are gone, and what are they?
Thy tide washed down the blood of yesterday,
And all was stainless, and on thy clear stream
Glassed, with its dancing light, the sunny ray;
But o'er the blackened memory's blighting dream
Thy waves would vainly roll, all sweeping as they seem.

Notes

80 *elate* proud.

81 ' "What wants that knave / That a king should have?" was King James' question on meeting Johnny Armstrong and his followers in full accoutrements. See the ballad' (Byron's note). Johnnie Armstrong, Laird of Gilnockie, surrendered to James V in such fine attire that the king hanged him for his insolence. Byron knew the ballad of *Johnie Armstrang* from Scott's *Minstrelsy of the Scottish Border* (1802–3).

82 *What want . . . great* i.e. if they have conquerors, what else do these outlaws need, except for a historian to write up their story and call them great?

83 *a blazon* the device of a bleeding heart.

84 *discoloured* i.e. with blood.

85 *Lethe* river of forgetfulness in Hades, from which souls drank in order to forget their previous lives.

52

Thus Harold inly said,[86] and passed along,
Yet not insensible[87] to all which here
Awoke the jocund birds to early song
In glens which might have made even exile[88] dear:
Though on his brow were graven lines austere,
And tranquil sternness, which had ta'en the place
Of feelings fierier far but less severe,
Joy was not always absent from his face,
But o'er it in such scenes would steal with transient trace.

53

Nor was all love shut from him, though his days
Of passion had consumed themselves to dust.
It is in vain that we would coldly gaze
On such as smile upon us; the heart must
Leap kindly back to kindness, though disgust
Hath weaned it from all worldlings: thus he felt,
For there was soft remembrance, and sweet trust
In one fond breast,[89] to which his own would melt,
And in its tenderer hour on that his bosom dwelt.

54

And he had learned to love – I know not why,
For this in such as him seems strange of mood,
The helpless looks of blooming infancy,
Even in its earliest nurture; what subdued,
To change like this, a mind so far imbued
With scorn of man, it little boots to know –
But thus it was; and though in solitude
Small power the nipped affections have to grow,
In him this glowed when all beside had ceased to glow.

55

And there was one soft breast, as hath been said,
Which unto his was bound by stronger ties
Than the church links withal; and, though unwed,
That love was pure, and, far above disguise,
Had stood the test of mortal enmities
Still undivided, and cemented more

Notes

[86] *Thus Harold inly said* Stanzas 47–51 comprise Harold's inner thoughts.

[87] *insensible* unaware.

[88] *exile* Byron exiled himself from England permanently after separating from his wife in spring 1816 (see headnote).

[89] *one fond breast* Augusta Leigh, Byron's half-sister, to whom he was passionately attached, the subject of his 'Stanzas' and 'Epistle' (pp. 888–93).

By peril, dreaded most in female eyes;
But this was firm, and from a foreign shore
Well to that heart might his these absent greetings pour!

1

The castled crag of Drachenfels[90]
Frowns o'er the wide and winding Rhine,
Whose breast of waters broadly swells
Between the banks which bear the vine,
And hills all rich with blossomed trees,
And fields which promise corn and wine,
And scattered cities crowning these,
Whose far white walls along them shine,
Have strewed a scene, which I should see
With double joy wert *thou* with me.

2

And peasant girls, with deep blue eyes,
And hands which offer early flowers,
Walk smiling o'er this Paradise;
Above, the frequent feudal towers
Through green leaves lift their walls of gray;
And many a rock which steeply lours,
And noble arch in proud decay,
Look o'er this vale of vintage-bowers;
But one thing want these banks of Rhine –
Thy gentle hand to clasp in mine!

3

I send the lilies given to me;
Though long before thy hand they touch,
I know that they must withered be,
But yet reject them not as such;
For I have cherished them as dear,
Because they yet may meet thine eye,
And guide thy soul to mine even here,
When thou behold'st them drooping nigh,
And know'st them gathered by the Rhine,
And offered from my heart to thine!

4

The river nobly foams and flows,
The charm of this enchanted ground,
And all its thousand turns disclose
Some fresher beauty varying round;

Notes

[90] 'The castle of Drachenfels stands on the highest summit of "the Seven Mountains", over the Rhine banks; it is in ruins, and connected with some singular traditions. It is the first in view on the road from Bonn, but on the opposite side of the river; on this bank, nearly facing it, are the remains of another called the Jew's castle, and a large cross commemorative of the murder of a chief by his brother. The number of castles and cities along the course of the Rhine on both sides is very great, and their situations remarkably beautiful' (Byron's note).

The haughtiest breast its wish might bound
Through life to dwell delighted here;
Nor could on earth a spot be found
To nature and to me so dear,
Could thy dear eyes in following mine
Still sweeten more these banks of Rhine!

56

By Coblentz, on a rise of gentle ground,
There is a small and simple pyramid,[91]
Crowning the summit of the verdant mound;
Beneath its base are heroes' ashes hid –
Our enemy's[92] – but let not that forbid
Honour to Marceau![93] o'er whose early tomb
Tears, big tears, gushed from the rough soldier's lid,[94]
Lamenting and yet envying such a doom,[95]
Falling for France, whose rights he battled to resume.[96]

57

Brief, brave, and glorious was his young career,
His mourners were two hosts,[97] his friends and foes;
And fitly may the stranger lingering here
Pray for his gallant spirit's bright repose;
For he was Freedom's champion, one of those,
The few in number, who had not o'erstepped
The charter to chastise[98] which she bestows
On such as wield her weapons; he had kept
The whiteness of his soul – and thus men o'er him wept.[99]

Notes

[91] *pyramid* i.e. a memorial.

[92] *Our enemy's* i.e. those of French heroes.

[93] *Marceau* François Sévérin Desgravins Marceau (1769–96) died in a battle with the forces of the Archduke Charles of Austria.

[94] *lid* eyelid.

[95] *doom* fate.

[96] *resume* take back.

[97] *hosts* armies. Marceau was mourned by both forces: the French, retreating from Altenkirchen, had to leave him behind, and the Austrians buried him.

[98] *chastise* i.e. teach tyrants (enemies of Freedom) a lesson.

[99] 'The monument of the young and lamented General Marceau (killed by a rifle-ball at Altenkirchen on the last day of the fourth year of the French republic) still remains as described.

The inscriptions on his monument are rather too long, and not required; his name was enough. France adored, and her enemies admired; both wept over him. His funeral was attended by the generals and detachments from both armies. In the same grave General Hoche is interred, a gallant man also in every sense of the word, but though he distinguished himself greatly in battle, *he* had not the good fortune to die there; his death was attended by suspicions of poison.

A separate monument (not over his body, which is buried by Marceau's) is raised for him near Andernach, opposite to which one of his most memorable exploits was performed, in throwing a bridge to an island on the Rhine. The shape and style are different from that of Marceau's, and the inscription more simple and pleasing.

The Army of the Sambre and Meuse
to its Commander in Chief
Hoche

This is all, and as it should be. Hoche was esteemed among the first of France's earlier generals before Bonaparte monopolized her triumphs. He was the destined commander of the invading army of Ireland' (Byron's note). Lazare Hoche (1768–97) died of consumption, but the rapid deterioration of his health led to speculation that he had been poisoned.

58

Here Ehrenbreitstein,[100] with her shattered wall
Black with the miner's blast,[101] upon her height
Yet shows of what she was, when shell and ball
Rebounding idly on her strength did light;
A tower of victory! from whence the flight
Of baffled foes was watched along the plain:
But peace destroyed what war could never blight,
And laid those proud roofs bare to Summer's rain –
On which the iron shower[102] for years had poured in vain.

59

Adieu to thee, fair Rhine! How long delighted
The stranger fain would linger on his way!
Thine is a scene alike where souls united
Or lonely Contemplation thus might stray;
And could the ceaseless vultures cease to prey
On self-condemning bosoms,[103] it were here,
Where nature, nor too sombre nor too gay,
Wild but not rude, awful yet not austere,
Is to the mellow earth as autumn to the year.

60

Adieu to thee again! A vain adieu!
There can be no farewell to scene like thine;
The mind is coloured by thy every hue;
And if reluctantly the eyes resign
Their cherished gaze upon thee, lovely Rhine,
'Tis with the thankful glance of parting praise;
More mighty spots may rise – more glaring shine,
But none unite in one attaching maze
The brilliant, fair, and soft – the glories of old days,

61

The negligently grand, the fruitful bloom
Of coming ripeness, the white city's sheen,
The rolling stream, the precipice's gloom,

Notes

[100] 'Ehrenbreitstein (i.e. "the broad stone of honour"), one of the strongest fortresses in Europe, was dismantled and blown up by the French at the Truce of Leoben. It had been and could only be reduced by famine or treachery. It yielded to the former, aided by surprise. After having seen the fortifications of Gibraltar and Malta, it did not much strike by comparison, but the situation is commanding. General Marceau besieged it in vain for some time, and I slept in a room where I was shown a window at which he is said to have been standing observing the progress of the siege by moonlight, when a ball struck immediately below it' (Byron's note). Marceau unsuccessfully besieged Ehrenbreitstein in 1795–6. It was finally taken, after a long siege, in 1799. It was blown up not after the Treaty of Leoben (1797), but after the Treaty of Lunéville (1801). Byron visited the ruins in mid-May 1816.

[101] *the miner's blast* The miner would dig tunnels under the walls of the fortresses, for the detonation of explosives – to 'undermine' the building.

[102] *the iron shower* i.e. artillery fire directed against the fortress.

[103] *ceaseless vultures . . . bosoms* Jupiter had Prometheus nailed to a rock for 30,000 years, with an eagle devouring his liver.

The forest's growth, and gothic walls between,
The wild rocks shaped, as they had turrets been[104]
In mockery of man's art; and these withal
A race of faces happy as the scene,
Whose fertile bounties here extend to all,
Still springing o'er thy banks, though empires near them fall.

62

But these recede. Above me are the Alps,
The palaces of nature, whose vast walls
Have pinnacled in clouds their snowy scalps,
And throned Eternity in icy halls
Of cold sublimity, where forms and falls
The avalanche – the thunderbolt of snow!
All that expands the spirit, yet appals,
Gather around these summits, as to show
How earth may pierce to heaven, yet leave vain man below.

63

But ere these matchless heights I dare to scan,
There is a spot should not be passed in vain –
Morat,[105] the proud, the patriot field! where man
May gaze on ghastly trophies of the slain,
Nor blush for those who conquered on that plain;
Here Burgundy bequeathed his tombless host,
A bony heap, through ages to remain,
Themselves their monument; the Stygian coast
Unsepulchred they roamed, and shrieked each wandering ghost.[106]

64

While Waterloo with Cannae's carnage vies,
Morat and Marathon twin names shall stand;[107]
They were true Glory's stainless victories
Won by the unambitious heart and hand
Of a proud, brotherly, and civic band,
All unbought champions in no princely cause
Of vice-entailed Corruption;[108] they no land

Notes

[104] *as they had turrets been* as if they had been turrets.

[105] *Morat* The Battle of Morat was the bloodiest of three battles fought by the Swiss against the French (under Charles the Bold, Duke of Burgundy) in 1476.

[106] 'The chapel is destroyed, and the pyramid of bones diminished to a small number by the Burgundian legion in the service of France, who anxiously effaced this record of their ancestors' less successful invasions. A few still remain notwithstanding the pains taken by the Burgundians for ages (all who passed that way removing a bone to their own country) and the less justifiable larcenies of the Swiss postillions, who carried them off to sell for knife-handles, a purpose for which the whiteness imbibed by the bleaching of years had rendered them in great request. Of these relics I ventured to bring away as much as may have made the quarter of a hero, for which the sole excuse is, that if I had not,the next passer-by might have perverted them to worse uses than the careful preservation which I intend for them' (Byron's note).

[107] Morat and Marathon (490 BC) were victories of men fighting for their freedom; Waterloo and Cannae (216 BC) were battles between countries seeking power over each other.

[108] *vice-entailed Corruption* i.e. corruption is inseparable from vice.

Doomed to bewail the blasphemy of laws
Making kings' rights divine, by some Draconic[109] clause.[110]

65

By a lone wall a lonelier column rears
A gray and grief-worn aspect of old days;
'Tis the last remnant of the wreck of years,
And looks as with the wild-bewildered gaze
Of one to stone converted by amaze,
Yet still with consciousness; and there it stands
Making a marvel that it not decays,
When the coeval pride of human hands,
Levelled Aventicum,[111] hath strewed her subject lands.

66

And there – oh, sweet and sacred be the name! –
Julia – the daughter, the devoted – gave
Her youth to heaven; her heart, beneath a claim
Nearest to heaven's, broke o'er a father's grave.
Justice is sworn 'gainst tears, and hers would crave
The life she lived in; but the judge was just,
And then she died on him she could not save.
Their tomb was simple, and without a bust,
And held within their urn one mind, one heart, one dust.[112]

67

But these are deeds which should not pass away,
And names that must not wither, though the earth
Forgets her empires with a just decay,
The enslavers and the enslaved, their death and birth;
The high, the mountain-majesty of worth
Should be, and shall, survivor of its woe,
And from its immortality look forth
In the sun's face, like yonder Alpine snow,
Imperishably pure beyond all things below.

Notes

[109] *Draconic* harsh, cruel; after Draco, author of the notoriously severe penal code for Athens (621 BC).

[110] Like many radicals of the day, Byron disagreed heartily with the divine right of kings. 'Draco, the author of the first red book on record, was an Athenian special pleader in great business. Hippias, the Athenian Bourbon, was in the Battle of Marathon, and did not keep at the respectful distance from danger of the Ghent refugees – but the English and Prussians resembled the Medes and Persians as little as Blucher and the British General did Datis and Artaphernes and Bonaparte was still more remote in cause and character from Miltiades – and a parallel "after the manner of Plutarch" might have still existed in the fortunes of the sons of Pisistratus and the reigning doctors of right-divinity' (Byron's note). Byron offers an ironic comparison between the principals at Waterloo and those at Marathon. The sons of Pisistratus, Hippias, and Hipparchus died inglorious.

[111] 'Aventicum (near Morat) was the Roman capital of Helvetia, where Avenches now stands' (Byron's note).

[112] 'Julia Alpinula, a young Aventian priestess, died soon after a vain endeavour to save her father, condemned to death as a traitor by Aulus Caecina. Her epitaph was discovered many years ago; it is thus –

Julia Alpinula
Hic jaceo
Infelicis patris, infelix proles
Deae Aventiae Sacerdos;
Exorare patris necem non potui
Male mori in fatis ille erat.
Vixi annos XXIII.

I know of no human composition so affecting as this, nor a history of deeper interest. These are the names and actions which ought not to perish, and to which we turn with a true and healthy tenderness, from the wretched and glittering detail of a confused mass of conquests and battles, with which the mind is roused for a time to a false and feverish sympathy, from whence it recurs at length with all the nausea consequent on such intoxication' (Byron's note).

68

Lake Leman[113] woos me with its crystal face,
The mirror where the stars and mountains view
The stillness of their aspect in each trace
Its clear depth yields of their far height and hue:
There is too much of man here to look through,
With a fit mind, the might which I behold;
But soon in me shall loneliness renew
Thoughts hid, but not less cherished than of old,
Ere mingling with the herd had penned me in their fold.

69

To fly from, need not be to hate, mankind;
All are not fit with them to stir and toil,
Nor is it discontent to keep the mind
Deep in its fountain, lest it overboil
In the hot throng, where we become the spoil[114]
Of our infection, till too late and long
We may deplore and struggle with the coil[115]
In wretched interchange of wrong for wrong
Midst a contentious world, striving where none are strong.

70

There in a moment we may plunge our years
In fatal penitence, and in the blight
Of our own soul turn all our blood to tears,
And colour things to come with hues of night;
The race of life becomes a hopeless flight
To those that walk in darkness: on the sea
The boldest steer but where their ports invite,
But there are wanderers o'er eternity
Whose bark drives on and on, and anchored ne'er shall be.

71

Is it not better, then, to be alone,
And love earth only for its earthly sake?
By the blue rushing of the arrowy Rhone[116]
Or the pure bosom of its nursing lake,
Which feeds it as a mother who doth make
A fair but froward[117] infant her own care,
Kissing its cries away as these awake?
Is it not better thus our lives to wear
Than join the crushing crowd, doomed to inflict or bear?

Notes

[113] *Lake Leman* Lake Geneva.
[114] *spoil* prey.
[115] *coil* mortal coil; bustle of life.
[116] 'The colour of the Rhone at Geneva is blue, to a depth of tint which I have never seen equalled in water, salt or fresh, except in the Mediterranean and Archipelago' (Byron's note). The 'Archipelago' is the Aegean, in which he swam in May 1810.
[117] *froward* refractory.

72

I live not in myself, but I become
Portion of that around me; and to me
High mountains are a feeling, but the hum
Of human cities torture.[118] I can see
Nothing to loathe in nature, save to be
A link reluctant in a fleshly chain,
Classed among creatures, when the soul can flee,
And with the sky, the peak, the heaving plain
Of ocean, or the stars, mingle, and not in vain.

73

And thus I am absorbed, and this is life.
I look upon the peopled desert past
As on a place of agony and strife
Where for some sin to sorrow I was cast
To act and suffer, but remount at last
With a fresh pinion, which I feel to spring
(Though young, yet waxing vigorous as the blast
Which it would cope with) on delighted wing,
Spurning the clay-cold bonds which round our being cling.[119]

74

And when at length the mind shall be all free
From what it hates in this degraded form,[120]
Reft of its carnal life, save what shall be
Existent happier in the fly and worm;
When elements to elements conform
And dust is as it should be, shall I not
Feel all I see – less dazzling, but more warm?
The bodiless thought? The spirit of each spot –
Of which, even now, I share at times the immortal lot?

75

Are not the mountains, waves and skies a part
Of me and of my soul, as I of them?
Is not the love of these deep in my heart
With a pure passion? Should I not contemn
All objects if compared with these, and stem
A tide of suffering, rather than forego
Such feelings for the hard and worldly phlegm[121]

Notes

[118] Here and in succeeding lines Byron repeats attitudes he had encountered in Wordsworth's 'Tintern Abbey'.

[119] *Spurning . . . cling* the attitude of the Byronic overreacher; cf. *Manfred* I ii 39–41: 'we / Half-dust, half-deity, alike unfit / To sink or soar'.

[120] *this degraded form* The human body is inherently degraded as far as Byron is concerned.

[121] *phlegm* coldness, lack of passion.

Of those whose eyes are only turned below,
Gazing upon the ground, with thoughts which dare not glow?

76

But this is not my theme, and I return
To that which is immediate – and require
Those who find contemplation in the urn
To look on one[122] whose dust was once all fire,
A native of the land where I respire[123]
The clear air for a while, a passing guest
Where he became a being whose desire
Was to be glorious ('twas a foolish quest,
The which to gain and keep, he sacrificed all rest).

77

Here the self-torturing sophist,[124] wild Rousseau,
The apostle of affliction, he who threw
Enchantment over passion, and from woe
Wrung overwhelming eloquence – first drew
The breath which made him wretched; yet he knew
How to make madness beautiful, and cast
O'er erring deeds and thoughts a heavenly hue
Of words like sunbeams, dazzling as they passed
The eyes, which o'er them shed tears feelingly and fast.

78

His love was passion's essence, as a tree
On fire by lightning;[125] with ethereal flame[126]
Kindled he was, and blasted – for to be
Thus, and enamoured, were in him the same.
But his was not the love of living dame,
Nor of the dead who rise upon our dreams,[127]
But of ideal beauty,[128] which became
In him existence, and o'erflowing teems
Along his burning page, distempered though it seems.

79

This breathed itself to life in Julie,[129] this
Invested her with all that's wild and sweet;
This hallowed, too, the memorable kiss

Notes

[122] *one* Jean-Jacques Rousseau, born in Geneva 1712 (d. 1778) whose political, fictional and philosophical writings strongly influenced the outbreak of revolution at the end of the 18th century.

[123] *respire* inhale.

[124] *sophist* learned man.

[125] *a tree / On fire by lightning* an image used also by Shelley and Mary Shelley.

[126] *ethereal flame* fire from heaven.

[127] *But his . . . dreams* The comparison is with Dante's Beatrice and Petrarch's Laura.

[128] *ideal beauty* cf. Shelley's *Hymn to Intellectual Beauty,* which Byron would have known in manuscript as it was not yet published.

[129] *Julie* heroine of Rousseau's *Julie, ou la Nouvelle Héloïse* (1761), which Shelley and Byron read in 1816, and deals with the illicit love of Julie and her tutor Saint-Preux.

Which every morn his fevered lip would greet
From hers[130] who, but with friendship, his would meet:
But to that gentle touch, through brain and breast
Flashed the thrilled spirit's love-devouring heat –
In that absorbing sigh, perchance more blessed
Than vulgar minds may be with all they seek possessed.[131]

80

His life was one long war with self-sought foes
Or friends by him self-banished,[132] for his mind
Had grown suspicion's sanctuary, and chose,
For its own cruel sacrifice, the kind,
'Gainst whom he raged with fury strange and blind.
But he was frenzied – wherefore, who may know,
Since cause might be which skill could never find?
But he was frenzied by disease or woe
To that worst pitch of all, which wears a reasoning show.

81

For then he was inspired, and from him came,
As from the Pythian's mystic cave of yore,[133]
Those oracles[134] which set the world in flame,
Nor ceased to burn till kingdoms were no more.
Did he not this for France, which lay before
Bowed to the inborn tyranny of years?
Broken and trembling to the yoke she bore,
Till by the voice of him and his compeers
Roused up to too much wrath, which follows o'ergrown fears?

82

They made themselves a fearful monument!
The wreck of old opinions, things which grew
Breathed from the birth of time: the veil they rent,[135]
And what behind it lay, all earth shall view.
But good with ill they also overthrew,
Leaving but ruins, wherewith to rebuild

Notes

130 *hers* Rousseau describes his unrequited love of the Comtesse d'Houdetot in his *Confessions*.

131 'This refers to the account in his *Confessions* of his passion for the Comtesse d'Houdetot (the mistress of St Lambert) and his long walk every morning for the sake of the single kiss which was the common salutation of French acquaintance. Rousseau's description of his feelings on this occasion may be considered as the most passionate, yet not impure description and expression of love that ever kindled into words; which after all must be felt, from their very force, to be inadequate to the delineation: a painting can give no sufficient idea of the ocean' (Byron's note).

132 *self-sought foes . . . self-banished* including Madame de Warens, Madame d'Epinay, Diderot, Grimm, Voltaire, Hume and St Lambert.

133 *the Pythian's mystic cave of yore* The Pythian was the priestess of the oracle at Delphi; she gave utterance in a state of frenzy and sat on a three-legged stool.

134 *oracles* The *Discours* of 1750 and 1753 and *Le Contrat social* (1762) helped inspire the French Revolution.

135 *the veil they rent* cf. the moment of Christ's death: 'And, behold, the veil of the temple was rent in twain from the top to the bottom' (Matthew 27: 51).

Upon the same foundation, and renew
Dungeons[136] and thrones,[137] which the same hour refilled
As heretofore, because ambition was self-willed.

83

But this will not endure, nor be endured!
Mankind have felt their strength and made it felt.[138]
They might have used it better, but, allured
By their new vigour, sternly have they dealt
On one another; pity ceased to melt
With her once-natural charities. But they
Who in oppression's darkness caved had dwelt,
They were not eagles, nourished with the day;
What marvel then, at times, if they mistook their prey?

84

What deep wounds ever closed without a scar?
The heart's[139] bleed longest, and but heal to wear
That which disfigures it; and they who war
With their own hopes, and have been vanquished, bear
Silence but not submission. In his lair
Fixed Passion holds his breath until the hour
Which shall atone for years – none need despair:
It came, it cometh, and will come, the power
To punish or forgive; in *one* we shall be slower.

85

Clear placid Leman! thy contrasted lake,
With the wild world I dwelt in, is a thing
Which warns me, with its stillness, to forsake
Earth's troubled waters for a purer spring.
This quiet sail is as a noiseless wing
To waft me from distraction; once I loved
Torn ocean's roar, but thy soft murmuring
Sounds sweet as if a sister's voice reproved
That I with stern[140] delights should e'er have been so moved.

86

It is the hush of night, and all between
Thy margin and the mountains, dusk – yet clear,
Mellowed and mingling, yet distinctly seen

Notes

[136] *Dungeons* The Bastille prison in Paris, symbol of the *ancien régime*, was demolished soon after 14 July 1789 during the Revolution; it was not rebuilt.

[137] *thrones* Ferdinand VII of Spain and Louis XVIII of France were restored to their respective thrones in 1814 – not something that gave Byron much cheer.

[138] *Mankind have felt their strength and made it felt* this stanza picks up a subject that preoccupied all defenders of revolution: the necessity for violence in the cause of liberty.

[139] *The heart's* i.e. the heart's wounds.

[140] *stern* uncompromising.

(Save darkened Jura, whose capped heights appear
Precipitously steep); and, drawing near,
There breathes a living fragrance from the shore
Of flowers yet fresh with childhood; on the ear
Drops the light drip of the suspended oar,[141]
Or chirps the grasshopper one goodnight carol more

87

(He is an evening reveller who makes
His life an infancy, and sings his fill);
At intervals, some bird from out the brakes[142]
Starts into voice a moment, then is still.
There seems a floating whisper on the hill,
But that is fancy, for the starlight dews
All silently their tears of love instil,
Weeping themselves away, till they infuse
Deep into nature's breast the spirit of her hues.

88

Ye stars which are the poetry of heaven!
If in your bright leaves we would read the fate
Of men and empires, 'tis to be forgiven
That in our aspirations to be great,
Our destinies o'erleap their mortal state,
And claim a kindred with you – for ye are
A beauty and a mystery, and create
In us such love and reverence from afar
That fortune, fame, power, life, have named themselves a star.[143]

89

All heaven and earth are still – though not in sleep,
But breathless (as we grow when feeling most)
And silent (as we stand in thoughts too deep[144]);
All heaven and earth are still: from the high host
Of stars to the lulled lake and mountain-coast,
All is concentred in a life intense
Where not a beam, nor air, nor leaf is lost,
But hath a part of being,[145] and a sense
Of that which is of all creator and defence.

Notes

[141] *Drops the light . . . oar* an echo of Wordsworth's *Lines Written near Richmond*: 'Remembrance! as we glide along, / For him suspend the dashing oar' (ll. 33–4).

[142] *brakes* fern, bracken.

[143] *have named themselves a star* cf. Manfred's affinity with the stars, *Manfred* III iv 1–7.

[144] *thoughts too deep* Byron echoes Wordsworth, 'Ode' 206: 'Thoughts that do often lie too deep for tears'.

[145] *Where not a beam . . . part of being* The sentiment is virtually identical to the pantheism of Wordsworth's *Tintern Abbey* 96–103.

90

Then stirs the feeling infinite, so felt
In solitude, where we are least alone –
A truth which through our being then doth melt
And purifies from self; it is a tone,
The soul and source of music, which makes known
Eternal harmony, and sheds a charm
Like to the fabled Cytherea's zone,[146]
Binding all things with beauty – 'twould disarm
The spectre death, had he substantial power to harm.

91

Not vainly did the early Persian make
His altar the high places and the peak
Of earth-o'ergazing mountains,[147] and thus take
A fit and unwalled temple, there to seek
The spirit in whose honour shrines are weak,
Upreared of human hands. Come and compare
Columns and idol-dwellings, Goth[148] or Greek,
With nature's realms of worship, earth and air,[149]
Nor fix on fond[150] abodes to circumscribe thy prayer!

92

The sky is changed, and such a change![151] Oh night
And storm and darkness, ye are wondrous strong,
Yet lovely in your strength, as is the light

Notes

[146] *Cytherea's zone* Aphrodite's girdle ('zone') brought love to those wearing it.

[147] 'It is to be recollected that the most beautiful and impressive doctrines of the founder of Christianity were delivered not in the Temple, but on the mount.

To waive the question of devotion, and turn to human eloquence – the most effectual and splendid specimens were not pronounced within walls. Demosthenes addressed the public and popular assemblies. Cicero spoke in the forum. That this added to their effect on the mind of both orator and hearers, may be conceived from the difference between what we read of the emotions then and there produced, and those we ourselves experience in the perusal in the closet. It is one thing to read the *Iliad* at Sigaeum and on the tumuli, or by the springs with Mount Ida above, and the plain and rivers and Archipelago around you, and another to trim your taper over it in a snug library – *this* I know.

Were the early and rapid progress of what is called Methodism to be attributed to any cause beyond the enthusiasm excited by its vehement faith and doctrines (the truth or error of which I presume neither to canvas nor to question) I should venture to ascribe it to the practice of preaching in the *fields*, and the unstudied and extemporaneous effusions of its teachers.

The Musselmans, whose erroneous devotion (at least in the lower orders) is most sincere, and therefore impressive, are accustomed to repeat their prescribed orisons and prayers wherever they may be at the stated hours – of course frequently in the open air, kneeling upon a light mat (which they carry for the purpose of a bed or cushion as required); the ceremony lasts some minutes, during which they are totally absorbed, and only living in their supplication. Nothing can disturb them. On me the simple and entire sincerity of these men, and the spirit which appeared to be within and upon them, made a far greater impression than any general rite which was ever performed in places of worship, of which I have seen those of almost every persuasion under the sun: including most of our own sectaries, and the Greek, the Catholic, the Armenian, the Lutheran, the Jewish, and the Mahometan. Many of the negroes, of whom there are numbers in the Turkish empire, are idolators, and have free exercise of their belief and its rites. Some of these I had a distant view of at Patras, and from what I could make out of them, they appeared to be of a truly pagan description, and not very agreeable to a spectator' (Byron's note).

[148] *Goth* one of a Germanic tribe, who, in the third, fourth and fifth centuries, invaded both the Eastern and Western empires, and founded kingdoms in Italy, France, and Spain.

[149] *earth and air* Once again, Byron is thinking of the pantheistic statement of faith in *Tintern Abbey*, in which Wordsworth seeks 'a sense sublime' in 'the round ocean, and the living air, / And the blue sky, and in the mind of man' (ll. 96–100).

[150] *fond* foolish.

[151] 'The thunder-storms to which these lines refer occurred on 13 June 1816 at midnight. I have seen among the Acroceraunian mountains of Chimari several more terrible, but none more beautiful' (Byron's note).

Of a dark eye in woman! Far along
From peak to peak, the rattling crags among,
Leaps the live thunder – not from one lone cloud
But every mountain now hath found a tongue,
And Jura answers through her misty shroud
Back to the joyous Alps, who call to her aloud!

93

And this is in the night – most glorious night,
Thou wert not sent for slumber! Let me be
A sharer in thy fierce and far delight,
A portion of the tempest and of thee!
How the lit lake shines, a phosphoric sea,
And the big rain comes dancing to the earth!
And now again 'tis black, and now the glee
Of the loud hills shakes with its mountain-mirth,
As if they did rejoice o'er a young earthquake's birth.[152]

94

Now where the swift Rhone cleaves his way between
Heights which appear as lovers who have parted
In hate, whose mining depths so intervene
That they can meet no more, though broken-hearted,
Though in their souls (which thus each other thwarted)
Love was the very root of the fond rage
Which blighted their life's bloom, and then departed –
Itself expired, but leaving them an age
Of years all winters, war within themselves to wage;

95

Now where the quick Rhone thus hath cleft his way,
The mightiest of the storms hath ta'en his stand:
For here not one but many make their play,
And fling their thunderbolts from hand to hand,
Flashing and cast around; of all the band
The brightest through these parted hills hath forked
His lightnings, as if he did understand
That in such gaps as desolation worked,
There the hot shaft[153] should blast whatever therein lurked.

96

Sky, mountains, river, winds, lake, lightnings – ye
With night and clouds and thunder, and a soul
To make these felt and feeling, well may be
Things that have made me watchful; the far roll
Of your departing voices is the knoll[154]
Of what in me is sleepless – if I rest.

Notes

[152] *a young earthquake's birth* Byron is probably echoing Shelley, 'Mont Blanc' 72–3.

[153] *the hot shaft* i.e. of lightning.

[154] *knoll* summit.

But where of ye, oh tempests, is the goal?
Are ye like those within the human breast?
Or do ye find, at length, like eagles, some high nest?

97

Could I embody and unbosom now
That which is most within me! Could I wreak[155]
My thoughts upon expression, and thus throw
Soul, heart, mind, passions, feelings (strong or weak),
All that I would have sought and all I seek,
Bear, know, feel, and yet breathe – into *one* word,
And that one word were lightning, I would speak!
But as it is, I live and die unheard
With a most voiceless thought, sheathing it as a sword.

98

The morn is up again, the dewy morn
With breath all incense, and with cheek all bloom,
Laughing the clouds away with playful scorn
And living as if earth contained no tomb,
And glowing into day: we may resume
The march of our existence. And thus I,
Still on thy shores, fair Leman, may find room
And food for meditation, nor pass by
Much that may give us pause, if pondered fittingly.

99

Clarens![156] Sweet Clarens, birthplace of deep Love!
Thine air is the young breath of passionate thought;
Thy trees take root in Love; the snows above,
The very glaciers have his colours caught,
And sunset into rose hues[157] sees them wrought
By rays which sleep there lovingly: the rocks,
The permanent crags, tell here of Love, who sought

Notes

155 *wreak* vent.

156 *Clarens!* Byron and Shelley sailed to Clarens, visiting the Castle of Chillon, on 26 June 1816. Shelley had just been reading *La Nouvelle Héloïse*; Byron had read it many times before.

157 'Rousseau's Heloise, Letter 17, part 4, note. "Ces montagnes sont si hautes qu'une demi-heure après le soleil couché, leurs sommets sont encore éclairés de ses rayons; dont le rouge forme sur ces cimes blanches *une belle couleur de rose* qu'on apperçoit de fort loin."

This applies more particularly to the heights over Meillerie. "J'allai à Vévay loger à la Clef, et pendant deux jours que j'y restai sans voir personne, je pris pour cette ville un amour qui m'a suivi dans tous mes voyages, et qui m'y a fait établir enfin les héros de mon roman. Je dirois volontiers à ceux qui ont du goût et qui sont sensibles: allez à Vévay – visitez le pays, examinez les sites, promenez-vous sur le lac, et dites si la Nature n'a pas fait ce beau pays pour une Julie, pour une Claire et pour un St Preux; mais ne les y cherchez pas." *Les Confessions*, livre iv. Page 306. Lyons ed. 1796.

In July 1816, I made a voyage round the Lake of Geneva; and, as far as my own observations have led me in a not uninterested nor inattentive survey of all the scenes most celebrated by Rousseau in his *Heloise*, I can safely say, that in this there is no exaggeration. It would be difficult to see Clarens (with the scenes around it, Vevay, Chillon, Bôveret, St Gingo, Meillerie, Evian, and the entrances of the Rhone), without being forcibly struck with its peculiar adaptation to the persons and events with which it has been peopled. But this is not all; the feeling with which all around Clarens, and the opposite rocks of Meillerie is invested, is of a still higher and more comprehensive order than the mere sympathy with individual passion; it is a sense of the existence of love in its most extended and sublime capacity, and of our own participation of its good and of its glory: it is the great principle of the universe, which is there more condensed,

In them a refuge from the worldly shocks,
Which stir and sting the soul with hope that woos, then mocks.

100

Clarens! By heavenly feet thy paths are trod –
Undying Love's, who here ascends a throne
To which the steps are mountains;[158] where the god
Is a pervading life and light – so shown
Not on those summits solely, nor alone
In the still cave and forest; o'er the flower
His eye is sparkling, and his breath hath blown,
His soft and summer breath, whose tender power
Passes the strength of storms in their most desolate hour.

101

All things are here of *him*;[159] from the black pines,
Which are his shade on high, and the loud roar
Of torrents, where he listeneth, to the vines
Which slope his green path downward to the shore,
Where the bowed waters meet him, and adore,
Kissing his feet with murmurs; and the wood,
The covert of old trees, with trunks all hoar,
But light leaves, young as joy, stands where it stood,
Offering to him, and his, a populous solitude,

102

A populous solitude of bees and birds,
And fairy-formed and many-coloured things,
Who worship him with notes more sweet than words,
And innocently open their glad wings,
Fearless and full of life: the gush of springs,

Notes

but not less manifested; and of which, though knowing ourselves a part, we lose our individuality, and mingle in the beauty of the whole.

If Rousseau had never written, nor lived, the same associations would not less have belonged to such scenes. He has added to the interest of his works by their adoption; he has shown his sense of their beauty by the selection; but they have done that for him which no human being could do for them.

I had the fortune (good or evil as it might be) to sail from Meillerie (where we landed for some time), to St Gingo during a lake storm, which added to the magnificence of all around, although occasionally accompanied by danger to the boat, which was small and overloaded. It was over this very part of the lake that Rousseau has driven the boat of St Preux and Madame Wolmar to Meillerie for shelter during a tempest.

On gaining the shore at St Gingo, I found that the wind had been sufficiently strong to blow down some fine old chestnut trees on the lower part of the mountains. On the opposite height of Clarens is a chateau.

The hills are covered with vineyards, and interspersed with some small but beautiful woods; one of these was named the "Bosquet de Julie", and it is remarkable that, though long ago cut down by the brutal selfishness of the monks of St Bernard (to whom the land appertained), that the ground might be enclosed into a vineyard for the miserable drones of an execrable superstition, the inhabitants of Clarens still point out the spot where its trees stood, calling it by the name which consecrated and survived them.

Rousseau has not been particularly fortunate in the preservation of the "local habitations" he has given to "airy nothings". The Prior of Great St Bernard has cut down some of his woods for the sake of a few casks of wine, and Bonaparte has levelled part of the rocks of Meillerie in improving the road to the Simplon. The road is an excellent one, but I cannot quite agree with a remark which I heard made, that "La route vaut mieux que les souvenirs"' (Byron's note).

158 *a throne . . . mountains* This image is reworked at *Manfred* I i 60–2, and may be borrowed from Shelley, *Mont Blanc* 15–17.

159 *him* i.e. Love.

And fall of lofty fountains, and the bend
Of stirring branches, and the bud which brings
The swiftest thought of beauty, here extend
Mingling, and made by Love, unto one mighty end.

103

He who hath loved not, here would learn that lore,
And make his heart a spirit; he who knows
That tender mystery, will love the more,
For this is Love's recess, where vain men's woes,
And the world's waste, have driven him far from those,
For 'tis his nature to advance or die;
He stands not still, but or decays, or grows
Into a boundless blessing, which may vie
With the immortal lights, in its eternity!

104

'Twas not for fiction chose Rousseau this spot,
Peopling it with affections; but he found
It was the scene which passion must allot
To the mind's purified beings; 'twas the ground
Where early Love his Psyche's zone unbound,[160]
And hallowed it with loveliness: 'tis lone,
And wonderful, and deep, and hath a sound,
And sense, and sight of sweetness; here the Rhone
Hath spread himself a couch, the Alps have reared a throne.[161]

105

Lausanne, and Ferney! Ye have been the abodes
Of names[162] which unto you bequeathed a name;
Mortals who sought and found, by dangerous roads,
A path to perpetuity of fame:
They were gigantic minds, and their steep aim
Was, Titan-like, on daring doubts to pile[163]
Thoughts which should call down thunder, and the flame
Of heaven again assailed – if heaven the while
On man, and man's research, could deign do more than smile.

106

The one[164] was fire and fickleness, a child
Most mutable in wishes, but in mind
A wit as various – gay, grave, sage, or wild –

Notes

[160] *Where early Love his Psyche's zone unbound* In Apuleius, *Metamorphoses,* Love undid Psyche's girdle when he made love to her, disobeying the orders of Venus, who was jealous of Psyche's beauty. Byron's point is that Rousseau chose Clarens for setting his novel's love-scenes because he wanted to project, through the novel, his own feelings for Madame d'Houdetot (one of the mind's 'purified beings').

[161] *throne* in *Mont Blanc,* Shelley describes the mountain as the 'secret throne' of Power (l. 17).

[162] *names* 'Voltaire and Gibbon' (Byron's note). Edward Gibbon (1737–94), author of *The Decline and Fall of the Roman Empire,* lived at Lausanne 1783–93. Voltaire resided at his estate at Ferney 1758–77. Both were freethinkers.

[163] *Titan-like . . . pile* The Titans and Giants piled Pelion upon Ossa in an attempt to gain heaven and overthrow Jupiter.

[164] *The one* i.e. Voltaire.

Historian, bard, philosopher, combined;
He multiplied himself among mankind,
The Proteus[165] of their talents: but his own
Breathed most in ridicule – which, as the wind,
Blew where it listed,[166] laying all things prone –
Now to o'erthrow a fool, and now to shake a throne.[167]

107

The other,[168] deep and slow, exhausting thought,
And hiving[169] wisdom with each studious year,
In meditation dwelt, with learning wrought,[170]
And shaped his weapon with an edge severe,
Sapping a solemn creed with solemn sneer;
The lord of irony – that master-spell
Which stung his foes to wrath, which grew from fear,
And doomed him to the zealot's ready hell,
Which answers to all doubts so eloquently well.[171]

108

Yet peace be with their ashes – for by them,
If merited, the penalty is paid;
It is not ours to judge, far less condemn;
The hour must come when such things shall be made
Known unto all – or hope and dread allayed
By slumber, on one pillow, in the dust,
Which, thus much we are sure, must lie decayed;
And when it shall revive, as is our trust,
'Twill be to be forgiven, or suffer what is just.

109

But let me quit man's works, again to read
His maker's,[172] spread around me, and suspend
This page, which from my reveries[173] I feed,
Until it seems prolonging without end.
The clouds above me to the white Alps tend,
And I must pierce them, and survey whate'er
May be permitted, as my steps I bend
To their most great and growing region, where
The earth to her embrace compels the powers of air.

Notes

[165] *Proteus* sea-god with the ability to change his shape; Voltaire mastered different forms of intellectual endeavour.
[166] *listed* wanted.
[167] *now to shake a throne* Voltaire's writings helped bring about the French Revolution.
[168] *The other* i.e. Gibbon.
[169] *hiving* hoarding.
[170] *wrought* created (i.e. his history of the Roman Empire).
[171] Gibbon's work was controversial in its day, because it effectively demolished the traditional, religiously slanted views of the later Roman period. He said that his history recorded the triumph of superstition and barbarism over culture and civilization.
[172] *His maker's* i.e. nature.
[173] *reveries* i.e. his sublime experiences in the midst of natural things (which inspire him).

110

Italia too, Italia! Looking on thee,
Full flashes on the soul the light of ages,
Since the fierce Carthaginian[174] almost won thee,
To the last halo of the chiefs and sages
Who glorify thy consecrated pages;
Thou wert the throne and grave of empires;[175] still,
The fount at which the panting mind assuages
Her thirst of knowledge, quaffing there her fill,
Flows from the eternal source of Rome's imperial hill.[176]

111

Thus far have I proceeded in a theme
Renewed with no kind auspices[177] – to feel
We are not what we have been, and to deem
We are not what we should be; and to steel
The heart against itself; and to conceal,
With a proud caution, love, or hate, or aught
(Passion or feeling, purpose, grief or zeal)
Which is the tyrant spirit of our thought,
Is a stern task of soul. No matter, it is taught.

112

And for these words, thus woven into song,
It may be that they are a harmless wile,
The colouring of the scenes which fleet along,
Which I would seize, in passing, to beguile
My breast, or that of others, for a while.
Fame is the thirst of youth – but I am not
So young as to regard men's frown or smile
As loss or guerdon[178] of a glorious lot;
I stood and stand alone, remembered or forgot.

113

I have not loved the world, nor the world me;
I have not flattered its rank breath, nor bowed
To its idolatries a patient knee,
Nor coined[179] my cheek to smiles, nor cried aloud
In worship of an echo;[180] in the crowd
They could not deem me one of such.[181] I stood
Among them, but not of them, in a shroud
Of thoughts which were not their thoughts, and still could,
Had I not filed[182] my mind,[183] which thus itself subdued.

Notes

[174] *the fierce Carthaginian* Hannibal, Carthaginian general who attempted to conquer Italy in the third century BC, won many battles against the Romans, but finally failed.

[175] *Thou wert the throne and grave of empires* Rome conquered the Etruscan and Carthaginian civilizations, and incorporated the Greek and Persian empires.

[176] *Flows . . . hill* a reference to the founding of the Roman Empire.

[177] *auspices* i.e. prospect of success.

[178] *guerdon* reward.

[179] *coined* counterfeited.

[180] *In worship of an echo* To Byron, God is no more than an echo.

[181] *such* i.e. a worshipper of God.

[182] *filed* debased.

[183] *Had I not filed my mind* Byron notes the allusion to *Macbeth* III i 63–4: 'If't be so, / For Banquo's issue have I filed my mind.'

114

I have not loved the world, nor the world me,
But let us part fair foes; I do believe,
Though I have found them not, that there may be
Words which are things, hopes which will not deceive,
And virtues which are merciful, nor weave
Snares for the failing. I would also deem
O'er others' griefs that some sincerely grieve,[184]
That two, or one, are almost what they seem,
That goodness is no name, and happiness no dream.

115

My daughter! with thy name this song begun!
My daughter! with thy name thus much shall end!
I see thee not – I hear thee not – but none
Can be so wrapped in thee; thou art the friend
To whom the shadows of far years extend:
Albeit my brow thou never should'st behold,
My voice shall with thy future visions blend
And reach into thy heart – when mine is cold –
A token and a tone, even from thy father's mould.[185]

116

To aid thy mind's development, to watch
Thy dawn of little joys, to sit and see
Almost thy very growth, to view thee catch
Knowledge of objects (wonders yet to thee!),
To hold thee lightly on a gentle knee,
And print on thy soft cheek a parent's kiss –
This, it should seem, was not reserved for me,
Yet this was in my nature. As it is,
I know not what is there, yet something like to this.

117

Yet though dull hate as duty should be taught,
I know that thou wilt love me, though my name
Should be shut from thee, as a spell still fraught[186]
With desolation, and a broken claim.
Though the grave closed between us, 'twere the same,
I know that thou wilt love me, though to drain
My blood from out thy being were an aim
And an attainment, all would be in vain:
Still thou would'st love me, still that more than life retain.

Notes

[184] 'It is said by Rochfoucault that "there is *always* something in the misfortunes of men's best friends not displeasing to them"' (Byron's note).

[185] *mould* body.

[186] *fraught* loaded.

118

The child of love, though born in bitterness
And nurtured in convulsion,[187] of thy sire
These were the elements – and thine no less.
As yet such are around thee, but thy fire
Shall be more tempered, and thy hope far higher.
Sweet be thy cradled slumbers! O'er the sea
And from the mountains where I now respire,
Fain would I waft such blessing upon thee,
As, with a sigh, I deem thou might'st have been to me!

Prometheus (composed July or early August 1816)[1]

From The Prisoner of Chillon and Other Poems (1816)

I

Titan![2] to whose immortal eyes
The sufferings of mortality
Seen in their sad reality,
Were not as things that gods despise –
What was thy pity's recompense?
A silent suffering, and intense;
The rock, the vulture, and the chain,
All that the proud can feel of pain,
The agony they do not show,
The suffocating sense of woe
Which speaks but in its loneliness,
And then is jealous lest the sky
Should have a listener, nor will sigh
Until its voice is echoless.

II

Titan! to thee the strife was given
Between the suffering and the will,
Which torture where they cannot kill;
And the inexorable heaven,
And the deaf tyranny of fate,
The ruling principle of hate
Which for its pleasure doth create
The things it may annihilate,
Refused thee even the boon to die:

Notes

[187] *convulsion* i.e. Byron's rancorous separation from his wife.

PROMETHEUS

[1] When Jupiter took fire away from earth, Prometheus stole replacement fire from the chariot of the sun. In revenge, Jupiter had Prometheus nailed to a rock for 30,000 years, with an eagle incessantly devouring his liver. He was eventually freed, and the bird killed, by Hercules. Byron uses the story to reprise his concept of the overreacher. Prometheus was much on the minds of Shelley, Mary Godwin and Byron in the summer of 1816. He helped inspire Mary's *Frankenstein; or, the Modern Prometheus* (1818), and would be the subject of Shelley's *Prometheus Unbound* several years later (pp. 1091–1164).

[2] *Titan!* In classical literature, the Titans were the children of Uranus (heaven) and Ge (earth)

The wretched gift eternity
Was thine – and thou hast borne it well.
All that the thunderer[3] wrung from thee
Was but the menace which flung back
On him the torments of thy rack;[4]
The fate thou didst so well foresee
But would not to appease him tell;
And in thy silence was his sentence,
And in his soul a vain repentance,
And evil dread so ill dissembled
That in his hand the lightnings trembled.

III

Thy godlike crime was to be kind,
To render with thy precepts less
The sum of human wretchedness,
And strengthen man with his own mind;
But baffled[5] as thou wert from high,
Still in thy patient energy,
In the endurance and repulse
Of thine impenetrable spirit,
Which earth and heaven could not convulse,
A mighty lesson we inherit:
Thou art a symbol and a sign
To mortals of their fate and force;
Like thee, man is in part divine,
A troubled stream from a pure source;
And man in portions can foresee
His own funereal destiny;
His wretchedness and his resistance,
And his sad unallied existence:
To which his spirit may oppose
Itself – an equal to all woes,
And a firm will, and a deep sense,
Which even in torture can descry
Its own concentred recompense,
Triumphant where it dares defy,
And making death a victory.

Stanzas to Augusta (composed 24 July 1816)[1]

From The Prisoner of Chillon and Other Poems (1816)

I

Though the day of my destiny's over,
  And the star of my fate hath declined,

Notes

[3] *the thunderer* Jupiter, who was responsible for Prometheus' punishment, used the thunderbolt as his instrument of war.
[4] *rack* suffering.
[5] *baffled* obstructed, prevented.

Stanzas to Augusta
[1] Originally published as *Stanzas to* ———. The relationship he had with Augusta Leigh, his half-sister, was always to be one of the most highly valued in Byron's life; for more on which, see pp. 840–1.

Thy soft heart refused to discover
The faults which so many could find;
Though thy soul with my grief was acquainted,
It shrunk not to share it with me,
And the love which my spirit hath painted
It never hath found but in *thee*.

2

Then when nature around me is smiling
The last smile which answers to mine,
I do not believe it beguiling
Because it reminds me of thine;
And when winds are at war with the ocean,
As the breasts I believed in with me,
If their billows excite an emotion
It is that they bear me from *thee*.

3

Though the rock of my last hope is shivered[2]
And its fragments are sunk in the wave,
Though I feel that my soul is delivered
To pain – it shall not be its slave.
There is many a pang to pursue me –
They may crush, but they shall not contemn;
They may torture, but shall not subdue me –
'Tis of *thee* that I think, not of them.[3]

4

Though human, thou didst not deceive me;
Though woman, thou didst not forsake;
Though loved, thou forborest to grieve me;
Though slandered, thou never couldst shake;
Though trusted, thou didst not betray[4] me;
Though parted, it was not to fly;
Though watchful, 'twas not to defame me,
Nor, mute, that the world might belie.

5

Yet I blame not the world, nor despise it,
Nor the war of the many with one –
If my soul was not fitted to prize it
'Twas folly not sooner to shun:
And if dearly that error hath cost me,

Notes

[2] *shivered* shattered.

[3] At this period Byron felt persecuted by the unfavourable publicity arising from his separation from his wife; as he told Thomas Moore on 29 February 1816: 'I am at war "with all the world and his wife"; or, rather, "all the world and *my* wife" are at war with me, and have not yet crushed me – whatever they may do. I don't know that in the course of a hair-breadth existence I was ever, at home or abroad, in a situation so completely uprooting of present pleasure, or rational hope for the future, as this same' (Marchand v 35).

[4] *betray* All printed texts until McGann's Clarendon Press edition (1980–93) have 'disclaim'. McGann's emendation reinstates a reading attributable to Byron rather than his publisher.

And more than I once could foresee,
I have found that, whatever it lost me,
It could not deprive me of *thee*.

6

From the wreck of the past, which hath perished,
Thus much I at least may recall,
It hath taught me that what I most cherished
Deserved to be dearest of all:
In the desert a fountain is springing,[5]
In the wide waste there still is a tree,
And a bird in the solitude singing,
Which speaks to my spirit of *thee*.

Epistle to Augusta (composed August 1816; edited from MS)[1]

1

My sister, my sweet sister – if a name
Dearer and purer were, it should be thine.
Mountains and seas divide us,[2] but I claim
No tears, but tenderness to answer mine:
Go where I will, to me thou art the same –
A loved regret which I would not resign;
There yet are two things in my destiny:
A world to roam through,[3] and a home with thee.

2

The first were nothing – had I still the last
It were the haven of my happiness;
But other claims and other ties thou hast,[4]
And mine is not the wish to make them less.
A strange doom[5] was thy father's son's,[6] and past
Recalling, as it lies beyond redress,
Reversed for him our grandsire's fate of yore[7] –
He had no rest at sea, nor I on shore.

Notes

[5] *In the desert a fountain is springing* the ultimate source is biblical (Judges 15: 19), but Byron is probably recalling Milton, *Samson Agonistes* 581–2: 'But God who caused a fountain at thy prayer / From the dry ground to spring . . . '

EPISTLE TO AUGUSTA

[1] Originally published 1830, posthumously; this is Byron's first sustained composition in *ottava rima*.

[2] Byron was resident at the Villa Diodati on the shores of Lake Geneva (Lake Leman at l. 75).

[3] *A world to roam through* Byron had exiled himself from England in April 1816 after separating from his wife and daughter. There is a slight verbal echo of the exile of Adam and Eve from Eden in the final lines of *Paradise Lost*: 'The world was all before them . . . '; cf. line 81 and n.

[4] *But other claims . . . hast* Augusta married Colonel George Leigh in 1807, and had by now given birth to three daughters.

[5] *doom* fate.

[6] *thy father's son's* i.e. Byron. They had the same father, Captain John (Mad Jack) Byron.

[7] The rough draft of the poem contains the following note in Byron's hand: 'Admiral Byron was remarkable for never making a voyage without a tempest: "But, though it were tempest-tossed, / Still his bark could not be lost." He returned safely from the wreck of the Wager (in Anson's voyage) and subsequently circumnavigated the world many years after, as commander of a similar expedition.' The quotation reworks *Macbeth* I iii 24–5.

3

If my inheritance of storms hath been
In other elements, and on the rocks
Of perils overlooked or unforeseen,
I have sustained my share of worldly shocks;
The fault was mine – nor do I seek to screen
My errors with defensive paradox:
I have been cunning in mine overthrow,[8]
The careful pilot of my proper woe.

4

Mine were my faults, and mine be their reward;
My whole life was a contest, since the day
That gave me being gave me that which marred
The gift – a fate or will that walked astray –
And I at times have found the struggle hard,
And thought of shaking off my bonds of clay;[9]
But now I fain would for a time survive,
If but to see what next can well arrive.

5

Kingdoms and empires in my little day
I have outlived and yet I am not old;
And when I look on this, the petty spray
Of my own years of trouble, which have rolled
Like a wild bay of breakers, melts away:
Something (I know not what) does still uphold
A spirit of slight patience; not in vain,
Even for its own sake, do we purchase pain.

6

Perhaps the workings of defiance stir
Within me, or perhaps a cold despair
Brought on when ills habitually recur;
Perhaps a harder clime or purer air –
For to all such may change of soul refer,
And with light armour we may learn to bear –
Have taught me a strange quiet which was not
The chief companion of a calmer lot.

7

I feel almost at times as I have felt
In happy childhood[10] – trees and flowers and brooks,
Which do remember me of where I dwelt
Ere my young mind was sacrificed to books,
Come as of yore upon me, and can melt

Notes

[8] *overthrow* ruin; somewhat self-dramatizing, but Byron saw himself as having been ruined, at least in social terms, by his wife's campaign against him.

[9] *my bonds of clay* For the Byronic overreacher, who longs to fulfil his divine aspirations, the human body is a form of imprisonment; cf. Childe Harold, who spurns 'the clay-cold bonds which round our being cling' (*Childe Harold's Pilgrimage* iii 697).

[10] *In happy childhood* Byron did not know Augusta as a child, when he was brought up by his mother in the Scottish countryside.

My heart with recognition of their looks –
And even at moments I could think I see
Some living things to love – but none like thee.

8

Here are the Alpine landscapes, which create
A fund for contemplation – to admire
Is a brief feeling of a trivial date –
But something worthier do such scenes inspire:
Here to be lonely is not desolate,
For much I view which I could most desire,
And above all a lake I can behold –
Lovelier, not dearer, than our own of old.[11]

9

Oh that thou wert but with me! – but I grow
The fool of my own wishes, and forget;
The solitude which I have vaunted so
Has lost its praise in this but one regret –
There may be others which I less may show;
I am not of the plaintive mood – and yet
I feel an ebb in my philosophy
And the tide rising in my altered eye.

10

I did remind thee of our own dear lake
By the old Hall which may be mine no more;[12]
Leman's is fair, but think not I forsake
The sweet remembrance of a dearer shore:
Sad havoc time must with my memory make
Ere *that* or *thou* can fade these eyes before –
Though like all things which I have loved, they[13] are
Resigned[14] for ever, or divided far.

11

The world is all before me[15] – I but ask
Of Nature that with which she will comply:
It is but in her summer's sun to bask,
To mingle in the quiet of her sky,[16]
To see her gentle face without a mask
And never gaze on it with apathy.
She was my early friend, and now shall be
My sister – till I look again on thee.

Notes

[11] *than our own of old* Byron refers to the lake at Newstead Abbey, where he had frolicked with Augusta in January and late August 1814.

[12] Byron had to sell Newstead Abbey to pay off his debts. At the time of writing, however, it was still on his hands; it was sold in late 1817 to his Harrow schoolfriend Major Thomas Wildman for £94,500.

[13] *they* i.e. the lake at Newstead and Augusta.

[14] *Resigned* surrendered.

[15] A sardonic echo of the more optimistic context of Adam and Eve leaving Eden, *Paradise Lost* xii 646.

[16] *the quiet of her sky* a deliberate echo of Wordsworth, *Tintern Abbey* 8.

12

I can reduce all feelings but this one,
  And that I would not – for at length I see
Such scenes as those wherein my life begun –
  The earliest – were the only paths for me.
Had I but sooner known the crowd to shun,
  I had been better than I now can be;
The passions which have torn me would have slept –
I had not suffered, and *thou* hadst not wept.

13

With false ambition what had I to do?
  Little with love, and least of all with fame!
And yet they came unsought and with me grew,
  And made me all which they can make – a name.
Yet this was not the end I did pursue –
  Surely I once beheld a nobler aim.
But all is over – I am one the more
To baffled millions which have gone before.

14

And for the future – this world's future may
  From me demand but little from my care;
I have outlived myself by many a day,
  Having survived so many things that were;
My years have been no slumber – but the prey
  Of ceaseless vigils; for I had the share
Of life which might have filled a century
Before its fourth in time had passed me by.

15

And for the remnants which may be to come
  I am content – and for the past I feel
Not thankless, for within the crowded sum
  Of struggles happiness at times would steal;
And for the present, I would not benumb
  My feelings farther – nor shall I conceal
That with all this I still can look around
And worship nature with a thought profound.

16

For thee, my own sweet sister, in thy heart
  I know myself secure – as thou in mine
We were and are – I am – even as thou art –
  Beings who ne'er each other can resign,
It is the same together or apart:
  From life's commencement to its slow decline
We are entwined – let death come slow or fast,
The tie[17] which bound the first endures the last.

Notes

[17] *tie* Byron implicitly compares his blood tie to Augusta with the marriage tie to Annabella.

Darkness (composed between 21 July and 25 August 1816)[1]

From The Prisoner of Chillon and Other Poems (1816)

I had a dream, which was not all a dream.
The bright sun was extinguished, and the stars
Did wander darkling[2] in the eternal space,
Rayless, and pathless,[3] and the icy earth
Swung blind and blackening in the moonless air;
Morn came, and went – and came, and brought no day,
And men forgot their passions in the dread
Of this their desolation; and all hearts
Were chilled into a selfish prayer for light:
And they did live by watchfires – and the thrones,
The palaces of crowned kings – the huts,
The habitations of all things which dwell,
Were burnt for beacons;[4] cities were consumed,
And men were gathered round their blazing homes
To look once more into each other's face;
Happy were those who dwelt within the eye
Of the volcanoes, and their mountain-torch:
A fearful hope was all the world contained;
Forests were set on fire – but hour by hour
They fell and faded – and the crackling trunks
Extinguished with a crash – and all was black.
The brows of men by the despairing light
Wore an unearthly aspect, as by fits
The flashes fell upon them; some lay down
And hid their eyes and wept; and some did rest
Their chins upon their clenched hands, and smiled;
And others hurried to and fro, and fed
Their funeral piles with fuel, and looked up
With mad disquietude on the dull sky,
The pall of a past world; and then again
With curses cast them down upon the dust,
And gnashed their teeth and howled. The wild birds shrieked,
And, terrified, did flutter on the ground,[5]
And flap their useless wings; the wildest brutes

Notes

Darkness

[1] The end of the world was one of the topics discussed with Shelley and Mary Godwin in summer 1816; it is also the theme of Mary's novel *The Last Man* (1826). But the most obvious source for this poem is the weather system that prevailed across Europe in summer 1816. A series of disturbances, including the eruption of the Tambora volcano in Indonesia, caused an unusual incidence of mists, fogs and rains in Geneva. Byron is also indebted to various apocalyptic passages in the Bible, notably Jeremiah 4, Ezekiel 32 and 38, Joel 2: 31, Matthew 25, and Revelation 6: 12.

[2] *darkling* in the dark.

[3] *the stars . . . pathless* as McGann notes, there is an echo here of Milton's *Il Penseroso* (appropriately, as the poem was written at the Villa Diodati, where Milton once resided), where the moon is compared with 'one that had been led astray / Through the heaven's wide pathless way' (ll. 69–70).

[4] *beacons* signals – of continuing life.

[5] *The wild birds . . . on the ground* a recollection of Coleridge's *Christabel*, where the sweet bird in Bracy's dream 'lay fluttering on the ground' (l. 532).

Came tame and tremulous;[6] and vipers crawled
And twined themselves among the multitude,
Hissing, but stingless – they were slain for food:
And War, which for a moment was no more,
Did glut himself again; a meal was bought
With blood, and each sat sullenly apart
Gorging himself in gloom. No love was left;
All earth was but one thought – and that was death,
Immediate and inglorious; and the pang
Of famine fed upon all entrails – men
Died, and their bones were tombless as their flesh;
The meagre by the meagre were devoured,
Even dogs assailed their masters, all save one,
And he was faithful to a corpse, and kept
The birds and beasts and famished men at bay,
Till hunger clung[7] them, or the dropping dead
Lured their lank jaws; himself sought out no food,
But with a piteous and perpetual moan
And a quick desolate cry, licking the hand
Which answered not with a caress – he died.
The crowd was famished by degrees, but two
Of an enormous city did survive,
And they were enemies; they met beside
The dying embers of an altar-place
Where had been heaped a mass of holy things
For an unholy usage; they raked up,
And shivering scraped with their cold skeleton hands
The feeble ashes, and their feeble breath
Blew for a little life, and made a flame
Which was a mockery; then they lifted up
Their eyes as it grew lighter, and beheld
Each other's aspects – saw, and shrieked, and died –
Even of their mutual hideousness they died,
Unknowing who he was upon whose brow
Famine had written Fiend. The world was void,
The populous and the powerful – was a lump,
Seasonless, herbless, treeless, manless, lifeless –
A lump of death – a chaos of hard clay.
The rivers, lakes, and ocean all stood still,
And nothing stirred within their silent depths;
Ships sailorless lay rotting on the sea,
And their masts fell down piecemeal; as they dropped
They slept on the abyss without a surge –
The waves were dead; the tides were in their grave,
The moon their mistress had expired before;

Notes

[6] *The wildest brutes . . . tremulous* an allusion to the famous apocalyptic prophecy, when 'The wolf also shall dwell with the lamb, and the leopard shall lie down with the kid; and the calf and the young lion and the fatling together; and a little child shall lead them' (Isaiah 11: 6).

[7] *clung* shrivelled, as at *Macbeth* V v 39: 'Till famine cling thee'.

The winds were withered in the stagnant air,
And the clouds perished; Darkness had no need
Of aid from them – she was the universe.

Manfred, A Dramatic Poem (composed September 1816–15 February 1817; published 1817)[1]

There are more things in heaven and earth, Horatio,
Than are dreamt of in your philosophy.[2]

Dramatis Personae

Manfred
Chamois Hunter
Abbot of St Maurice
Manuel
Herman
Witch of the Alps
Arimanes
Nemesis
The Destinies
Spirits, etc.

The scene of the drama is amongst the higher Alps – partly in the Castle of Manfred, and partly in the mountains.

Act I, Scene I[1]

Manfred alone. Scene: a Gothic gallery.[2] *Time: midnight.*

MANFRED. The lamp must be replenished, but even then
It will not burn so long as I must watch;
My slumbers (if I slumber) are not sleep
But a continuance of enduring thought,
Which then I can resist not. In my heart
There is a vigil, and these eyes but close
To look within – and yet I live, and bear
The aspect and the form of breathing men.
But grief should be the instructor of the wise –
Sorrow is knowledge;[3] they who know the most

Notes

Manfred, A Dramatic Poem

[1] This verse drama is one of Byron's most explicit and earnest discussions of the concept of the overreacher; for further introductory comments see headnote, pp. 842–3.

[2] *Hamlet* I v 166–7. The epigraph underlines Byron's belief in the supernatural and metaphysical – of which he was, to put it mildly, highly sceptical by the time he published *Don Juan*, two years later.

Act I, Scene I

[1] The first scene of the play betrays its source in Goethe's *Faust*, which M. G. Lewis (author of *The Monk* (1796)) translated for Byron, aloud, in August 1816. Goethe recognized the debt, and when he read *Manfred* declared it 'a wonderful phenomenon'.

[2] *a Gothic gallery* Byron means a covered balcony designed in the Gothic manner.

[3] *But grief . . . knowledge* Ecclesiastes 1: 18: 'For in much wisdom is much grief: and he that increaseth knowledge increaseth sorrow.'

Must mourn the deepest o'er the fatal truth:
The tree of knowledge is not that of life.
Philosophy and science,[4] and the springs
Of wonder, and the wisdom of the world
I have essayed,[5] and in my mind there is
A power to make these subject to itself,
But they avail not. I have done men good,
And I have met with good even among men –
But this availed not. I have had my foes
And none have baffled,[6] many fallen before me –
But this availed not. Good or evil, life,
Powers, passions, all I see in other beings
Have been to me as rain unto the sands
Since that all-nameless hour. I have no dread,
And feel the curse to have no natural fear,
Nor fluttering throb that beats with hopes or wishes
Or lurking love of something on the earth.
Now to my task. Mysterious agency![7]
Ye spirits of the unbounded universe
Whom I have sought in darkness and in light;
Ye who do compass earth about, and dwell
In subtler[8] essence; ye to whom the tops
Of mountains inaccessible are haunts,
And earth's and ocean's caves familiar things –
I call upon ye by the written charm
Which gives me power upon you: rise, appear! (*a pause*)
They come not yet. Now by the voice of him
Who is the first among you; by this sign
Which makes you tremble; by the claims of him
Who is undying[9] – rise, appear! Appear! (*a pause*)
If it be so. Spirits of earth and air,
Ye shall not thus elude me: by a power
Deeper than all yet urged, a tyrant-spell
Which had its birthplace in a star condemned,
The burning wreck of a demolished world,
A wandering hell in the eternal space;
By the strong curse which is upon my soul,
The thought which is within me and around me,
I do compel ye to my will. Appear!

Notes

[4] *science* knowledge, although it includes subjects which today would be described as 'science' (physics, chemistry, and so forth).

[5] *essayed* attempted.

[6] *baffled* confounded.

[7] *Mysterious agency!* Significantly, Byron avoids the use of the word 'God'.

[8] *subtler* i.e. more refined than human flesh.

[9] *him / Who is undying* deliberately ambiguous – calculated to permit a reference to Satan as well as God.

A star is seen at the darker end of the gallery. It is stationary, and a voice is heard singing.

First Spirit[10]

Mortal,[11] to thy bidding bowed
From my mansion in the cloud
Which the breath of twilight builds
And the summer's sunset gilds
With the azure and vermilion
Which is mixed for my pavilion,
Though thy quest may be forbidden,
On a starbeam I have ridden,
To thine adjuration[12] bowed;
Mortal – be thy wish avowed!

Voice of the Second Spirit[13]

Mont Blanc[14] is the monarch of mountains,
They crowned him long ago
On a throne of rocks,[15] in a robe of clouds
With a diadem of snow.
Around his waist are forests braced,
The avalanche in his hand;
But ere it fall that thundering ball[16]
Must pause for my command.
The glacier's cold and restless mass
Moves onward day by day,[17]
But I am he who bids it pass
Or with its ice delay.
I am the spirit of the place,
Could make the mountain bow
And quiver to his caverned base –
And what with me wouldst *thou*?

Voice of the Third Spirit[18]

In the blue depth of the waters
Where the wave hath no strife,
Where the wind is a stranger
And the sea-snake hath life,
Where the mermaid is decking[19]
Her green hair with shells,

Notes

[10] The Spirit of the air.
[11] *Mortal* The spirit puts Manfred in his place from the start.
[12] *adjuration* appeal.
[13] The Spirit of earth.
[14] Byron visited Mont Blanc with Hobhouse in late August–September 1816.
[15] *throne of rocks* an image stemming back to *Childe Harold* iii 932–4, and picked up by Shelley in *Mont Blanc* 15–17.
[16] *that thundering ball* i.e. the rock which starts the avalanche.
[17] *The glacier's . . . day by day* an observation made by Shelley on his visit to Mont Blanc and Chamounix; see pp. 1073–4.
[18] The Spirit of water.
[19] *decking* adorning.

Like the storm on the surface
  Came the sound of thy spells;
O'er my calm hall of coral
  The deep echo rolled –
To the spirit of ocean
  Thy wishes unfold!

Fourth Spirit[20]

Where the slumbering earthquake
  Lies pillowed on fire,
And the lakes of bitumen
  Rise boilingly higher;
Where the roots of the Andes
  Strike deep in the earth,
As their summits to heaven
  Shoot soaringly forth;
I have quitted my birthplace,
  Thy bidding to bide –
Thy spell hath subdued me,
  Thy will be my guide!

Fifth Spirit

I am the rider of the wind,
  The stirrer of the storm;
The hurricane I left behind
  Is yet with lightning warm;
To speed to thee, o'er shore and sea
  I swept upon the blast;
The fleet I met sailed well and yet
  'Twill sink ere night be passed.

Sixth Spirit

My dwelling is the shadow of the night,
Why doth thy magic torture me with light?

Seventh Spirit

The star which rules thy destiny
Was ruled, ere earth began, by me;
It was a world as fresh and fair
As e'er revolved round sun in air;
Its course was free and regular,
Space bosomed not a lovelier star.
The hour arrived, and it became
A wandering mass of shapeless flame,

Notes

[20] The Spirit of fire.

A pathless comet and a curse –
The menace of the universe.
Still rolling on with innate force,
Without a sphere, without a course,
A bright deformity on high,
The monster[21] of the upper sky!
And thou beneath its influence born,
Thou worm whom I obey and scorn!
Forced by a power (which is not thine,
And lent thee but to make thee mine)
For this brief moment to descend,
Where these weak spirits round thee bend
And parley with a thing like thee –
What wouldst thou, child of clay, with me?

The Seven Spirits

Earth, ocean, air, night, mountains, winds, thy star,
Are at thy beck and bidding, child of clay!
Before thee at thy quest their spirits are –
What wouldst thou with us, son of mortals? Say!
MANFRED. Forgetfulness –
FIRST SPIRIT. Of what, of whom, and why?
MANFRED. Of that which is within me; read it there –
Ye know it, and I cannot utter it.
SPIRIT. We can but give thee that which we possess.
Ask of us subjects, sovereignty, the power
O'er earth, the whole or portion, or a sign
Which shall control the elements whereof
We are the dominators, each and all –
These shall be thine.
MANFRED. Oblivion, self-oblivion –
Can ye not wring from out the hidden realms
Ye offer so profusely what I ask?
SPIRIT. It is not in our essence, in our skill;
But – thou mayst die.
MANFRED. Will death bestow it on me?
SPIRIT. We are immortal and do not forget;
We are eternal and to us the past
Is, as the future, present. Art thou answered?
MANFRED. Ye mock me – but the power which brought ye here
Hath made you mine. Slaves, scoff not at my will!
The mind, the spirit, the Promethean spark,
The lightning of my being, is as bright,
Pervading, and far-darting as your own –
And shall not yield to yours, though cooped in clay!
Answer, or I will teach ye what I am.

Notes

[21] *monster* in the sense of an unnatural and extraordinary phenomenon.

SPIRIT. We answer as we answered; our reply
Is even in thine own words.
MANFRED. Why say ye so?
SPIRIT. If, as thou say'st, thine essence be as ours,
We have replied in telling thee, the thing
Mortals call death hath nought to do with us.
MANFRED. I then have called ye from your realms in vain;
Ye cannot, or ye will not, aid me.
SPIRIT. Say;
What we possess we offer, it is thine.
Bethink ere thou dismiss us, ask again;
Kingdom, and sway, and strength, and length of days –
MANFRED. Accursed! What have I to do with days?
They are too long already. Hence! Begone!
SPIRIT. Yet pause. Being here, our will would do thee service;
Bethink thee, is there then no other gift
Which we can make not worthless in thine eyes?
MANFRED. No, none – yet stay one moment ere we part,
I would behold ye face to face.[22] I hear
Your voices, sweet and melancholy sounds,
As music on the waters, and I see
The steady aspect of a clear large star –
But nothing more. Approach me as ye are,
Or one, or all, in your accustomed forms.
SPIRIT. We have no forms beyond the elements
Of which we are the mind and principle.
But choose a form – in that we will appear.
MANFRED. I have no choice; there is no form on earth
Hideous or beautiful to me. Let him
Who is most powerful of ye, take such aspect
As unto him may seem most fitting. Come!

SEVENTH SPIRIT (*appearing in the shape of a beautiful female figure*[23]).
Behold!
MANFRED. Oh God! If it be thus, and *thou*
Art not a madness and a mockery,
I yet might be most happy. I will clasp thee,
And we again will be – (*the figure vanishes*)
My heart is crushed!

Manfred falls senseless. A voice is heard in the incantation[24] *which follows.*

When the moon is on the wave
And the glow-worm in the grass,

Notes

[22] *face to face* Exodus 33: 11: 'And the Lord spake unto Moses face to face, as a man speaketh unto his friend.'

[23] The Spirit appears in the form of Astarte, but, as McGann observes, ll. 232–51 were written with Lady Byron in mind.

[24] The incantation (ll. 192–261) was one of the earliest parts of *Manfred* to be composed, certainly by 14 August 1816, when Byron was resident at Villa Diodati in Geneva. Most of the remainder of the play was composed during Byron's tour of the Bernese Alps the following month, and during his residence in Venice, winter 1816–17.

And the meteor on the grave
 And the wisp on the morass,[25]
When the falling stars are shooting
And the answered owls are hooting,
And the silent leaves are still
In the shadow of the hill,
Shall my soul be upon thine
With a power and with a sign.

Though thy slumber may be deep
Yet thy spirit shall not sleep;
There are shades which will not vanish,
There are thoughts thou canst not banish;
By a power to thee unknown
Thou canst never be alone;
Thou art wrapped as with a shroud,
Thou art gathered in a cloud –
And forever shalt thou dwell
In the spirit of this spell.

Though thou seest me not pass by,
Thou shalt feel me with thine eye
As a thing that, though unseen,
Must be near thee, and hath been;
And when in that secret dread
Thou hast turned around thy head,
Thou shalt marvel I am not
As thy shadow on the spot,
And the power which thou dost feel
Shall be what thou must conceal.

And a magic voice and verse
Hath baptized thee with a curse;
And a spirit of the air
Hath begirt thee with a snare;
In the wind there is a voice
Shall forbid thee to rejoice;
And to thee shall night deny
All the quiet of her sky;
And the day shall have a sun
Which shall make thee wish it done.
From thy false tears I did distill

An essence which hath strength to kill;
From thy own heart I then did wring
The black mood in its blackest spring;
From thy own smile I snatched the snake,
For there it coiled as in a brake;[26]

Notes

[25] *morass* bog, marsh. The 'wisp' is a phosphorescent light seen hovering or flitting over marshy ground, supposed to be due to the spontaneous combustion of an inflammable gas (phosphuretted hydrogen) derived from decaying organic matter; popularly called *Will-o'-the-wisp.*

[26] *brake* bracken.

From thy own lip I drew the charm
Which gave all these their chiefest harm;
In proving every poison known,
I found the strongest was thine own.

By thy cold breast and serpent smile,
By thy unfathomed gulfs of guile,
By that most seeming virtuous eye,
By thy shut soul's hypocrisy,
By the perfection of thine art
Which passed for human thine own heart,
By thy delight in others' pain,
And by thy brotherhood of Cain,[27]
I call upon thee, and compel
Thyself to be thy proper[28] hell!

And on thy head I pour the vial
Which doth devote[29] thee to this trial;
Nor to slumber, nor to die,
Shall be in thy destiny;
Though thy death shall still seem near
To thy wish, but as a fear;
Lo! the spell now works around thee
And the clankless chain hath bound thee;
O'er thy heart and brain together
Hath the word been passed: now wither!

Act I, Scene II[1]

The mountain of the Jungfrau.[2] Time: morning. Manfred alone upon the cliffs.

MANFRED. The spirits I have raised abandon me,
The spells which I have studied baffle me,
The remedy I recked[3] of tortured me;
I lean no more on superhuman aid,
It hath no power upon the past, and for
The future, till the past be gulfed in darkness,
It is not of my search. My mother earth,
And thou fresh-breaking day, and you, ye mountains –
Why are ye beautiful? I cannot love ye.
And thou, the bright eye of the universe
That openest over all, and unto all

Notes

[27] Cain murdered his brother Abel, and was cast out, a fugitive and vagabond; Genesis 4: 8–12. Manfred has been cursed in a similar manner to Cain. Byron was preoccupied with Cain's story too, and dramatised it in 1821.

[28] *proper* own.

[29] *devote* condemn.

Act I, Scene II

[1] As McGann notes, this scene reworks that of Prometheus bound on the rock of the Caucasus in Aeschylus' *Prometheus Bound*.

[2] Byron first saw the mountain of the Jungfrau 23 September 1816 (Marchand v 101–2).

[3] *recked* thought.

Art a delight – thou shin'st not on my heart.
And you, ye crags upon whose extreme edge
I stand, and on the torrent's brink beneath
Behold the tall pines dwindled as to shrubs
In dizziness of distance, when a leap,
A stir, a motion, even a breath would bring
My breast upon its rocky bosom's bed
To rest for ever – wherefore do I pause?
I feel the impulse, yet I do not plunge;
I see the peril, yet do not recede;
And my brain reels, and yet my foot is firm.
There is a power upon me which withholds
And makes it my fatality to live[4] –
If it be life to wear within myself
This barrenness of spirit, and to be
My own soul's sepulchre,[5] for I have ceased
To justify my deeds unto myself
(The last infirmity of evil[6]). (*an eagle passes*) Aye,
Thou winged and cloud-cleaving minister,
Whose happy flight is highest into heaven,
Well may'st thou swoop so near me – I should be
Thy prey, and gorge thine eaglets. Thou art gone
Where the eye cannot follow thee, but thine
Yet pierces downward, onward, or above
With a pervading vision. Beautiful!
How beautiful is all this visible world,
How glorious in its action and itself!
But we who name ourselves its sovereigns, we
Half-dust, half-deity, alike unfit
To sink or soar,[7] with our mixed essence make
A conflict of its elements, and breathe
The breath of degradation and of pride,
Contending with low wants and lofty will
Till our mortality predominates –
And men are what they name not to themselves,
And trust not to each other. (*The shepherd's pipe in the distance is heard.*)
Hark! the note,
The natural music of the mountain reed
(For here the patriarchal days are not
A pastoral fable) pipes in the liberal[8] air,
Mixed with the sweet bells of the sauntering herd!
My soul would drink those echoes. Oh that I were
The viewless spirit of a lovely sound,
A living voice, a breathing harmony,
A bodiless enjoyment, born and dying
With the blessed tone which made me!

Notes

[4] *my fatality to live* a clever paradox that echoes Hamlet, who mentions the 'calamity of so long life' (*Hamlet* III i 68).

[5] *My own soul's sepulchre* cf. Milton's *Samson Agonistes* 102: 'Myself, my sepulchre, a moving grave'.

[6] *The last infirmity of evil* an echo of *Lycidas* 71, in which fame is 'That last infirmity of noble mind'.

[7] *How beautiful . . . sink or soar* There is a general recollection here of Hamlet's famous speech, *Hamlet* II ii 293–310.

[8] *liberal* abundant.

Enter from below a Chamois Hunter

CHAMOIS HUNTER. Even so
This way the chamois[9] leapt. Her nimble feet
Have baffled me; my gains today will scarce
Repay my breakneck travail. What is here
Who seems not of my trade, and yet hath reached
A height which none even of our mountaineers,
Save our best hunters, may attain? His garb
Is goodly, his mien manly, and his air
Proud as a freeborn peasant's, at this distance.
I will approach him nearer.

MANFRED (*not perceiving the other*). To be thus;
Grey-haired with anguish like these blasted pines,
Wrecks of a single winter, barkless, branchless,
A blighted trunk upon a cursed root,
Which but supplies a feeling to decay –
And to be thus, eternally but thus,
Having been otherwise! Now furrowed o'er
With wrinkles; ploughed by moments, not by years;
And hours all tortured into ages – hours
Which I outlive! Ye toppling crags of ice,
Ye avalanches whom a breath draws down
In mountainous o'erwhelming, come and crush me!
I hear ye momently above, beneath,
Crash with a frequent conflict, but ye pass
And only fall on things which still would live –
On the young flourishing forest, or the hut
And hamlet of the harmless villager.

CHAMOIS HUNTER. The mists begin to rise from up the valley;
I'll warn him to descend, or he may chance
To lose at once his way and life together.

MANFRED. The mists boil up around the glaciers; clouds
Rise curling fast beneath me, white and sulphury
Like foam from the roused ocean of deep hell
Whose every wave breaks on a living shore,
Heaped with the damned like pebbles.[10] I am giddy.

CHAMOIS HUNTER. I must approach him cautiously; if near,
A sudden step will startle him, and he
Seems tottering already.

MANFRED. Mountains have fallen,
Leaving a gap in the clouds, and with the shock
Rocking their Alpine brethren, filling up
The ripe green valleys with destruction's splinters,
Damming the rivers with a sudden dash
Which crushed the waters into mist and made
Their fountains find another channel – thus,

Notes

[9] *chamois* antelope found in the highest parts of the Alps.

[10] *The mists . . . pebbles* Typically, Manfred sees everything in terms that reflect his sense of his own damnation.

Thus in its old age, did Mount Rosenberg;[11]
Why stood I not beneath it?
CHAMOIS HUNTER. Friend, have a care,
Your next step may be fatal! For the love
Of him who made you, stand not on that brink!
MANFRED (*not hearing him*). Such would have been for me a fitting tomb;
My bones had then been quiet in their depth;
They had not then been strewn upon the rocks
For the wind's pastime, as thus – thus they shall be,
In this one plunge. Farewell, ye opening heavens!
Look not upon me thus reproachfully,
Ye were not meant for me. Earth, take these atoms!

As Manfred is in act to spring from the cliff, the Chamois Hunter seizes and retains him with a sudden grasp.

CHAMOIS HUNTER. Hold, madman! Though aweary of thy life,
Stain not our pure vales with thy guilty[12] blood!
Away with me – I will not quit my hold.
MANFRED. I am most sick at heart – nay, grasp me not,
I am all feebleness; the mountains whirl
Spinning around me – I grow blind. What art thou?
CHAMOIS HUNTER. I'll answer that anon. Away with me;
The clouds grow thicker – there, now lean on me;
Place your foot here – here, take this staff, and cling
A moment to that shrub. Now give me your hand
And hold fast by my girdle[13] – softly, well.
The chalet will be gained within an hour;
Come on, we'll quickly find a surer footing
And something like a pathway, which the torrent
Hath washed since winter. Come, 'tis bravely done –
You should have been a hunter! Follow me.

As they descend the rocks with difficulty, the scene closes.

ACT II, SCENE I

A cottage amongst the Bernese Alps.[1] *Manfred and the Chamois Hunter.*

CHAMOIS HUNTER. No, no – yet pause, thou must not yet go forth;
Thy mind and body are alike unfit
To trust each other for some hours, at least.
When thou art better, I will be thy guide –
But whither?
MANFRED. It imports not. I do know
My route full well, and need no further guidance.
CHAMOIS HUNTER. Thy garb and gait bespeak thee of high lineage –

Notes

[11] On 2 September 1806 part of Mt Rossberg fell and buried four villages.
[12] *guilty* i.e. guilty of suicide; but there is an irony, because Manfred is guilty of other sins of which the Chamois Hunter knows nothing.
[13] *girdle* belt.

ACT II, SCENE I
[1] Byron toured the Bernese Alps with Hobhouse, 17–29 September 1816.

One of the many chiefs, whose castled crags
Look o'er the lower valleys. Which of these
May call thee lord? I only know their portals;[2]
My way of life leads me but rarely down
To bask by the huge hearths of those old halls,
Carousing with the vassals; but the paths
Which step from out our mountains to their doors
I know from childhood – which of these is thine?

MANFRED. No matter.

CHAMOIS HUNTER. Well sir, pardon me the question,
And be of better cheer. Come taste my wine,
'Tis of an ancient vintage – many a day
'T has thawed my veins among our glaciers; now
Let it do thus for thine. Come, pledge[3] me fairly.

MANFRED. Away, away! There's blood upon the brim!
Will it then never, never sink in the earth?

CHAMOIS HUNTER. What dost thou mean? Thy senses wander from thee.

MANFRED. I say 'tis blood – my blood! The pure warm stream
Which ran in the veins of my fathers, and in ours
When we were in our youth, and had one heart,
And loved each other as we should not love,
And this was shed.[4] But still it rises up,
Colouring the clouds that shut me out from heaven,
Where thou art not, and I shall never be.

CHAMOIS HUNTER. Man of strange words and some half-maddening sin
Which makes thee people vacancy, whate'er
Thy dread and sufferance be, there's comfort yet –
The aid of holy men, and heavenly patience –

MANFRED. Patience and patience hence! That word was made
For brutes of burden, not for birds of prey;
Preach it to mortals of a dust like thine,
I am not of thine order.

CHAMOIS HUNTER. Thanks to heaven!
I would not be of thine for the free fame
Of William Tell! But whatsoe'er thine ill,
It must be borne, and these wild starts are useless.

MANFRED. Do I not bear it? Look on me – I live.

CHAMOIS HUNTER. This is convulsion, and no healthful life.

MANFRED. I tell thee, man! I have lived many years,
Many long years, but they are nothing now
To those which I must number: ages, ages,
Space and eternity – and consciousness
With the fierce thirst of death – and still unslaked!

CHAMOIS HUNTER. Why, on thy brow the seal of middle age
Hath scarce been set; I am thine elder far.

MANFRED. Think'st thou existence doth depend on time?
It doth, but actions are our epochs. Mine

Notes

[2] *portals* gateways.

[3] *pledge* toast.

[4] *The pure warm stream . . . shed* The archetypal model of Manfred's sins is again Cain, who killed his brother Abel.

Have made my days and nights imperishable,
Endless, and all alike as sands on the shore,
Innumerable atoms, and one desert,
Barren and cold, on which the wild waves break
But nothing rests save carcases and wrecks,
Rocks, and salt-surf weeds of bitterness.

CHAMOIS HUNTER. Alas, he's mad – but yet I must not leave him.

MANFRED. I would I were, for then the things I see
Would be but a distempered dream.

CHAMOIS HUNTER. What is it
That thou dost see, or think thou look'st upon?

MANFRED. Myself and thee, a peasant of the Alps;
Thy humble virtues, hospitable home
And spirit patient, pious, proud and free;
Thy self-respect, grafted on innocent thoughts;
Thy days of health and nights of sleep; thy toils
By danger dignified, yet guiltless; hopes
Of cheerful old age and a quiet grave
With cross and garland over its green turf,
And thy grandchildren's love for epitaph –
This do I see, and then I look within –
It matters not; my soul was scorched already.

CHAMOIS HUNTER. And would'st thou then exchange thy lot for mine?

MANFRED. No, friend! I would not wrong thee, nor exchange
My lot with living being. I can bear –
However wretchedly, 'tis still to bear –
In life what others could not brook[5] to dream,
But perish in their slumber.

CHAMOIS HUNTER. And with this,
This cautious feeling for another's pain,
Canst thou be black with evil? Say not so.
Can one of gentle thoughts have wreaked revenge
Upon his enemies?

MANFRED. Oh no, no, no!
My injuries came down on those who loved me,
On those whom I best loved. I never quelled
An enemy, save in my just defence,
My wrongs were all on those I should have cherished,
But my embrace was fatal.

CHAMOIS HUNTER. Heaven give thee rest,
And penitence restore thee to thyself;
My prayers shall be for thee.

MANFRED. I need them not,
But can endure thy pity. I depart;
'Tis time, farewell! Here's gold, and thanks for thee –
No words, it is thy due. Follow me not.
I know my path, the mountain peril's past –
And once again I charge thee, follow not!

Exit Manfred.

Notes

[5] *brook* endure.

Act II, Scene II

A lower valley in the Alps. A cataract. Enter Manfred.

It is not noon. The sunbow's rays still arch
The torrent with the many hues of heaven,[1]
And roll the sheeted silver's waving column
O'er the crag's headlong perpendicular,
And fling its lines of foaming light along,
And to and fro, like the pale courser's tail,
The giant steed to be bestrode by death,
As told in the Apocalypse.[2] No eyes
But mine now drink this sight of loveliness;
I should be sole[3] in this sweet solitude,
And with the spirit of the place divide
The homage of these waters. I will call her.[4]

Manfred takes some of the water into the palm of his hand, and flings it in the air, muttering the adjuration. After a pause, the Witch of the Alps rises beneath the arch of the sunbow of the torrent.

Beautiful spirit, with thy hair of light
And dazzling eyes of glory, in whose form
The charms of earth's least mortal daughters grow
To an unearthly stature in an essence
Of purer elements, while the hues of youth –
Carnationed like a sleeping infant's cheek,
Rocked by the beating of her mother's heart,
Or the rose tints, which summer's twilight leaves
Upon the lofty glacier's virgin snow,
The blush of earth embracing with her heaven –
Tinge thy celestial aspect, and make tame
The beauties of the sunbow which bends o'er thee;
Beautiful spirit, in thy calm clear brow
Wherein is glassed[5] serenity of soul,
Which of itself shows immortality,
I read that thou wilt pardon to a son

Notes

Act II, Scene II

[1] 'This iris is formed by the rays of the sun over the lower part of the Alpine torrents. It is exactly like a rainbow come down to pay a visit, and so close that you may walk into it. This effect lasts until noon' (Byron's note). Byron described the effect in his journal sent to Augusta Leigh, 23 September 1816: 'Before ascending the mountain went to the torrent . . . again – the sun upon it forming a rainbow of the lower part of all colours – but principally purple and gold' (Marchand v 101).

[2] *the Apocalypse* i.e. the Book of Revelation of St John the Divine 6: 8. Lines 3–8 versify remarks made by Byron in the journal for Augusta Leigh, 22 September 1816: 'the torrent is in shape curving over the rock – like the tail of a white horse streaming in the wind – such as it might be conceived would be that of the "pale horse" on which Death is mounted in the Apocalypse' (Marchand v 101).

[3] *sole* single, alone.

[4] *her* i.e. the spirit of the place, the Witch of the Alps.

[5] *glassed* reflected.

Of earth, whom the abstruser[6] powers permit
At times to commune with them, if that he
Avail him of his spells, to call thee thus
And gaze on thee a moment.

WITCH. Son of earth!
I know thee and the powers which give thee power;
I know thee for a man of many thoughts
And deeds of good and ill (extreme in both),
Fatal and fated in thy sufferings.
I have expected this – what wouldst thou with me?

MANFRED. To look upon thy beauty, nothing further.
The face of the earth hath maddened me, and I
Take refuge in her mysteries, and pierce
To the abodes of those who govern her,
But they can nothing aid me. I have sought
From them what they could not bestow, and now
I search no further.

WITCH. What could be the quest
Which is not in the power of the most powerful,
The rulers of the invisible?

MANFRED. A boon –
But why should I repeat it? 'Twere in vain.

WITCH. I know not that; let thy lips utter it.

MANFRED. Well, though it torture me, 'tis but the same;
My pang shall find a voice. From my youth upwards
My spirit walked not with the souls of men,
Nor looked upon the earth with human eyes;
The thirst of their ambition was not mine,
The aim of their existence was not mine;
My joys, my griefs, my passions and my powers
Made me a stranger; though I wore the form,
I had no sympathy with breathing flesh,
Nor midst the creatures of clay that girded me
Was there but one[7] who – but of her anon.
I said, with men, and with the thoughts of men
I held but slight communion, but instead
My joy was in the wilderness – to breathe
The difficult air of the iced mountain's top
Where the birds dare not build, nor insect's wing
Flit o'er the herbless granite; or to plunge
Into the torrent, and to roll along
On the swift whirl of the new-breaking wave
Of river-stream or ocean in their flow.
In these my early strength exulted – or
To follow through the night the moving moon,[8]
The stars and their development; or catch

Notes

[6] *abstruser* hidden, concealed; i.e. not perceptible to the senses.

[7] *one* i.e. Astarte, his sister.

[8] *the moving moon* borrowed from Coleridge, *The Ancient Mariner* (1817) 263: 'The moving moon went up the sky.'

The dazzling lightnings till my eyes grew dim;
Or to look, list'ning, on the scattered leaves
While autumn winds were at their evening song.
These were my pastimes, and to be alone;
For if the beings of whom I was one
(Hating to be so) crossed me in my path,
I felt myself degraded back to them
And was all clay again. And then I dived
In my lone wanderings to the caves of death,
Searching its cause in its effect, and drew
From withered bones and skulls and heaped-up dust
Conclusions most forbidden.[9] Then I passed
The nights of years in sciences untaught,
Save in the old time, and with time and toil
And terrible ordeal, and such penance
As in itself hath power upon the air,
And spirits that do compass air and earth,
Space and the peopled infinite, I made
Mine eyes familiar with eternity,
Such as, before me, did the Magi[10] and
He[11] who from out their fountain dwellings raised
Eros and Anteros at Gadara,
As I do thee. And with my knowledge grew
The thirst of knowledge, and the power and joy
Of this most bright intelligence, until –

WITCH. Proceed.

MANFRED. Oh, I but thus prolonged my words,
Boasting these idle attributes,[12] because,
As I approach the core of my heart's grief –
But to my task. I have not named to thee
Father or mother, mistress, friend or being
With whom I wore the chain of human ties;
If I had such, they seemed not such to me.
Yet there was one[13] –

WITCH. Spare not thyself; proceed.

MANFRED. She was like me in lineaments – her eyes,
Her hair, her features, all, to the very tone
Even of her voice, they said were like to mine,
But softened all and tempered into beauty.
She had the same lone thoughts and wanderings,
The quest of hidden knowledge, and a mind

Notes

[9] *And then I dived . . . forbidden* Manfred's dabbling among corpses has much in common with the researches of Victor Frankenstein in Mary Godwin's novel, conceived at the same time as Byron's poem, summer 1816, though not published until 1818. Byron is probably thinking, however, of Shelley's Alastor, who 'made my bed / In charnels and on coffins' (ll. 23–4).

[10] *the Magi* the ancient Persian priestly caste.

[11] *He* 'The philosopher Iamblicus. The story of the raising of Eros and Anteros may be found in his life, by Eunapius. It is well-told' (Byron's note). Iamblicus (died *c.* AD 330) summoned by magic Love and its opposite from fountains in Syria.

[12] *attributes* achievements.

[13] *one* Astarte.

To comprehend the universe – nor these
Alone, but with them gentler powers than mine:
Pity and smiles and tears (which I had not)
And tenderness (but that I had for her),
Humility (and that I never had).
Her faults were mine; her virtues were her own –
I loved her, and destroyed her!

WITCH. With thy hand?

MANFRED. Not with my hand, but heart – which broke her heart:
It gazed on mine and withered. I have shed
Blood, but not hers, and yet her blood was shed –
I saw and could not staunch it.

WITCH. And for this,
A being of the race thou dost despise,
The order which thine own would rise above,
Mingling with us and ours, thou dost forego
The gifts of our great knowledge, and shrink'st back
To recreant mortality? Away!

MANFRED. Daughter of air, I tell thee, since that hour –
But words are breath; look on me in my sleep
Or watch my watchings – come and sit by me!
My solitude is solitude no more,
But peopled with the Furies;[14] I have gnashed
My teeth in darkness till returning morn,
Then cursed myself till sunset; I have prayed
For madness as a blessing – 'tis denied me;
I have affronted death, but in the war
Of elements the waters shrunk from me,
And fatal things passed harmless – the cold hand
Of an all-pitiless demon held me back,
Back by a single hair which would not break.
In fantasy, imagination, all
The affluence of my soul (which one day was
A Croesus in creation[15]), I plunged deep,
But like an ebbing wave, it dashed me back
Into the gulf of my unfathomed thought.
I plunged amidst mankind; forgetfulness
I sought in all save where 'tis to be found,
And that I have to learn; my sciences,
My long-pursued and superhuman art
Is mortal here. I dwell in my despair
And live – and live for ever.

WITCH. It may be
That I can aid thee.

MANFRED. To do this thy power
Must wake the dead, or lay me low with them.
Do so, in any shape, in any hour,

Notes

[14] *Furies* avenging agents of the gods.

[15] *A Croesus in creation* i.e. endlessly creative. Croesus was the last king of Lydia, of fabulous wealth; Byron may be recalling the legend that when Croesus met Solon, Solon distinguished between the imagined happiness of being Croesus and the genuine happiness of being dead.

With any torture – so it be the last.
WITCH. That is not in my province, but if thou
Wilt swear obedience to my will and do
My bidding, it may help thee to thy wishes.
MANFRED. I will not swear![16] Obey? And whom? The spirits
Whose presence I command – and be the slave
Of those who served me? Never!
WITCH. Is this all?
Hast thou no gentler answer? Yet bethink thee,
And pause ere thou rejectest.
MANFRED. I have said it.
WITCH. Enough! I may retire then – say!
MANFRED. Retire!

The Witch disappears.

MANFRED (*alone*). We are the fools of time and terror. Days
Steal on us and steal from us, yet we live,
Loathing our life, and dreading still to die.
In all the days of this detested yoke
(This heaving burden, this accursed breath,
This vital weight upon the struggling heart
Which sinks with sorrow or beats quick with pain,
Or joy that ends in agony or faintness);
In all the days of past and future – for
In life there is no present – we can number
How few, how less than few, wherein the soul
Forbears to pant for death and yet draws back
As from a stream in winter, though the chill
Be but a moment's. I have one resource
Still in my science; I can call the dead
And ask them what it is we dread to be.
The sternest answer can but be the grave,
And that is nothing; if they answer not . . .
The buried prophet answered to the hag
Of Endor,[17] and the Spartan monarch drew
From the Byzantine maid's unsleeping spirit
An answer and his destiny – he slew
That which he loved, unknowing what he slew,
And died unpardoned, though he called in aid
The Phyxian Jove, and in Phigalia roused
The Arcadian evocators[18] to compel
The indignant shadow[19] to depose[20] her wrath
Or fix her term of vengeance; she replied

Notes

16 Manfred's defiance of the supernatural powers is a distinctively Byronic departure from the *Faust* legend.

17 Samuel was raised from the dead by the Witch of Endor, 1 Samuel 28: 7.

18 *evocators* those who invoke spirits.

19 *shadow* ghost.

20 *depose* lay aside.

In words of dubious import, but fulfilled.[21]
  If I had never lived, that which I love
Had still been living; had I never loved,
That which I loved would still be beautiful,
Happy and giving happiness. What is she,
What is she now? A sufferer for my sins,
A thing I dare not think upon – or nothing.
Within few hours I shall not call in vain,
Yet in this hour I dread the thing I dare.
Until this hour I never shrunk to gaze
On spirit, good or evil; now I tremble
And feel a strange cold thaw upon my heart.
But I can act even what I most abhor
And champion human fears. The night approaches.

Exit

Act II, Scene III

The summit of the Jungfrau mountain. Enter First Destiny.

The moon is rising broad and round and bright,
And here on snows where never human foot
Of common mortal trod,[1] we nightly tread
And leave no traces. O'er the savage sea,
The glassy ocean of the mountain ice,
We skim its rugged breakers, which put on
The aspect of a tumbling tempest's foam,
Frozen in a moment – a dead whirlpool's image;
And this most steep fantastic pinnacle,
The fretwork[2] of some earthquake where the clouds
Pause to repose themselves in passing by,
Is sacred to our revels or our vigils.
Here do I wait my sisters, on our way
To the Hall of Arimanes, for tonight
Is our great festival. 'Tis strange they come not.

A VOICE WITHOUT, SINGING

The captive usurper[3]
  Hurled down from the throne,[4]
Lay buried in torpor,
  Forgotten and lone;
I broke through his slumbers,

Notes

[21] 'The story of Pausanias, King of Sparta (who commanded the Greeks in the Battle of Platea, and afterwards perished for an attempt to betray the Lacedemonians), and Cleonice, is told in Plutarch's life of Cimon, and in the Laconics of Pausanias the Sophist, in his description of Greece' (Byron's note).

Act II, Scene III

[1] The Jungfrau had been scaled in 1811.

[2] *fretwork* figurative; usually refers to carved, decorative woodwork.

[3] *The captive usurper* Napoleon Bonaparte who, at the time of writing, was in exile on St Helena. These lines should be read in the light of Byron's meditation on Napoleon, *Childe Harold* iii, stanzas 36–42 (pp. 862–4).

[4] *Hurled down from the throne* Napoleon crowned himself Emperor in 1804, and abdicated in 1814. He was 'hurled down' when the combined might of the allies defeated him at Waterloo, 1815.

I shivered[5] his chain,
I leagued him with numbers[6] –
He's tyrant again![7]
With the blood of a million he'll answer my care,
With a nation's destruction, his flight and despair.

SECOND VOICE WITHOUT

The ship sailed on, the ship sailed fast,
But I left not a sail, and I left not a mast;
There is not a plank of the hull or the deck,
And there is not a wretch to lament o'er his wreck,
Save one whom I held, as he swam, by the hair,
And he was a subject well worthy my care –
A traitor on land and a pirate at sea –
But I saved him to wreak further havoc for me!

FIRST DESTINY (*answering*)

The city lies sleeping;
The morn, to deplore it,
May dawn on it weeping;
Sullenly, slowly,
The black plague flew o'er it –
Thousands lie lowly;
Tens of thousands shall perish;
The living shall fly from
The sick they should cherish,
But nothing can vanquish
The touch that they die from.
Sorrow and anguish
And evil and dread
Envelop a nation;
The blessed are the dead
Who see not the sight
Of their own desolation.
This work of a night,
This wreck of a realm, this deed of my doing –
For ages I've done and shall still be renewing!

Enter the Second and Third Destinies

THE THREE

Our hands contain the hearts of men,
Our footsteps are their graves;
We only give to take again
The spirits of our slaves!

FIRST DESTINY. Welcome! Where's Nemesis?
SECOND DESTINY. At some great work,

Notes

[5] *shivered* shattered.
[6] *numbers* i.e. of soldiers.
[7] The Spirit prophesies the return of Napoleon from St Helena. It was not to happen.

But what I know not, for my hands were full.
THIRD DESTINY. Behold, she cometh.
Enter Nemesis
FIRST DESTINY. Say, where hast thou been?
My sisters and thyself are slow tonight.
NEMESIS. I was detained repairing shattered thrones,[8]
Marrying fools,[9] restoring dynasties,
Avenging men upon their enemies,
And making them repent their own revenge;
Goading the wise to madness, from the dull
Shaping out oracles[10] to rule the world
Afresh – for they were waxing[11] out of date
And mortals dared to ponder for themselves,
To weigh kings in the balance,[12] and to speak
Of freedom, the forbidden fruit.[13] Away!
We have outstayed the hour; mount we our clouds!

Exeunt

Act II, Scene IV

The Hall of Arimanes,[1] Arimanes on his throne, a globe of fire, surrounded by the spirits.
Hymn of the Spirits

Hail to our master, Prince of earth and air!
  Who walks the clouds and waters – in his hand
The sceptre of the elements, which tear
  Themselves to chaos at his high command!
He breatheth, and a tempest shakes the sea;
  He speaketh, and the clouds reply in thunder;
He gazeth – from his glance the sunbeams flee;
  He moveth – earthquakes rend the world asunder.
Beneath his footsteps the volcanoes rise;
  His shadow is the pestilence, his path
The comets herald through the crackling skies,
  And planets turn to ashes at his wrath.
To him war offers daily sacrifice,
  To him death pays his tribute; life is his,
With all its infinite of agonies,
  And his the spirit of whatever is!

Notes

[8] *I was detained repairing shattered thrones* Byron has in mind the Treaty of Vienna in 1815, following the restoration to power of the monarchies of Spain and France.

[9] *Marrying fools* perhaps a sardonic reference to Byron's own marriage to Annabella Milbanke, which had resulted in acrimonious separation and Byron's exile from England.

[10] *oracles* effectively, prophets and priests, empowered to utter the will of God. Byron may have in mind Joanna Southcott (1750–1814), who claimed to be pregnant by the Holy Ghost, with Shiloh, the saviour of the world. After her death the 'pregnancy' was diagnosed as dropsy.

[11] *waxing* growing.

[12] *To weigh kings in the balance* Daniel 5: 27: 'Thou art weighed in the balances, and art found wanting.'

[13] Nemesis is effectively an anti-Revolutionary force.

Act II, Scene III

[1] Arimanes derives his name from Ahriman, the principle of darkness and evil in Persian dualism.

Enter the Destinies and Nemesis

FIRST DESTINY. Glory to Arimanes! On the earth
His power increaseth; both my sisters did
His bidding, nor did I neglect my duty.
SECOND DESTINY. Glory to Arimanes! We who bow
The necks of men, bow down before his throne.
THIRD DESTINY. Glory to Arimanes! We await
His nod.
NEMESIS. Sovereign of Sovereigns! We are thine,
And all that liveth, more or less, is ours,
And most things wholly so; still to increase
Our power increasing thine, demands our care,
And we are vigilant. Thy late commands
Have been fulfilled to the utmost.

Enter Manfred

A SPIRIT What is here?
A mortal? Thou most rash and fatal wretch,
Bow down and worship!
SECOND SPIRIT. I do know the man,
A Magian[2] of great power and fearful skill.
THIRD SPIRIT. Bow down and worship, slave! What, know'st thou not
Thine and our sovereign? Tremble, and obey!
ALL THE SPIRITS. Prostrate thyself and thy condemned clay,
Child of the earth, or dread the worst!
MANFRED. I know it,
And yet ye see I kneel not.
FOURTH SPIRIT. 'Twill be taught thee.
MANFRED. 'Tis taught already; many a night on the earth,
On the bare ground have I bowed down my face
And strewed my head with ashes.[3] I have known
The fullness of humiliation, for
I sunk before my vain despair, and knelt
To my own desolation.
FIFTH SPIRIT. Dost thou dare
Refuse to Arimanes on his throne
What the whole earth accords, beholding not
The terror of his glory? Crouch, I say!
MANFRED. Bid *him* bow down to that which is above him,
The overruling Infinite, the Maker
Who made him not for worship; let him kneel,
And we will kneel together.
THE SPIRITS. Crush the worm!
Tear him in pieces!
FIRST DESTINY. Hence! Avaunt! He's mine.
Prince of the powers invisible! This man
Is of no common order, as his port[4]

Notes

[2] *Magian* magician, wizard.

[3] *strewed my head with ashes* an expression of grief and repentance.

[4] *port* bearing, deportment.

And presence here denote. His sufferings
Have been of an immortal nature like
Our own; his knowledge and his powers and will,
As far as is compatible with clay
(Which clogs the ethereal essence), have been such
As clay hath seldom borne; his aspirations
Have been beyond the dwellers of the earth,
And they have only taught him what we know –
That knowledge is not happiness, and science
But an exchange of ignorance for that
Which is another kind of ignorance.
This is not all. The passions, attributes
Of earth and heaven, from which no power nor being
Nor breath from the worm upwards is exempt,
Have pierced his heart, and in their consequence
Made him a thing which I, who pity not,
Yet pardon those who pity. He is mine,
And thine, it may be; be it so or not,
No other spirit in this region hath
A soul like his – or power upon his soul.

NEMESIS. What doth he here then?

FIRST DESTINY. Let *him* answer that.

MANFRED. Ye know what I have known, and without power
I could not be amongst ye; but there are
Powers deeper still beyond. I come in quest
Of such, to answer unto what I seek.

NEMESIS. What wouldst *thou*?

MANFRED. Thou canst not reply to me.
Call up the dead – my question is for them.

NEMESIS. Great Arimanes, doth thy will avouch
The wishes of this mortal?

ARIMANES. Yea.

NEMESIS. Whom would'st thou
Uncharnel?[5]

MANFRED. One without a tomb. Call up
Astarte.

NEMESIS.

Shadow or spirit,
Whatever thou art,
Which still doth inherit
The whole or a part
Of the form of thy birth,
Of the mould of thy clay
Which returned to the earth,
Reappear to the day!
Bear what thou borest,
The heart and the form,

Notes

[5] *Uncharnel* i.e. raise from the dead. A charnel is a cemetery.

And the aspect thou worest
   Redeem from the worm.
Appear! Appear! Appear!
Who sent thee there requires thee here!

The phantom of Astarte rises and stands in the midst.

MANFRED. Can this be death? There's bloom upon her cheek,
  But now I see it is no living hue
  But a strange hectic,[6] like the unnatural red
  Which autumn plants upon the perished leaf.
  It is the same! Oh God, that I should dread
  To look upon the same – Astarte! No,
  I cannot speak to her; but bid her speak –
  Forgive me or condemn me.

NEMESIS.
  By the power which hath broken
    The grave which enthralled[7] thee,
  Speak to him who hath spoken,
    Or those who have called thee!

MANFRED. She is silent,
  And in that silence I am more than answered.

NEMESIS. My power extends no further. Prince of air!
  It rests with thee alone; command her voice.

ARIMANES. Spirit – obey this sceptre!

NEMESIS. Silent still!
  She is not of our order, but belongs
  To the other powers. Mortal, thy quest is vain,
  And we are baffled[8] also.

MANFRED. Hear me, hear me –
  Astarte, my beloved, speak to me!
  I have so much endured, so much endure –
  Look on me! The grave hath not changed thee more
  Than I am changed for thee. Thou lovedst me
  Too much, as I loved thee; we were not made
  To torture thus each other, though it were
  The deadliest sin to love as we have loved.
  Say that thou loath'st me not, that I do bear
  This punishment for both, that thou wilt be
  One of the blessed, and that I shall die,
  For hitherto all hateful things conspire
  To bind me in existence, in a life
  Which makes me shrink from immortality –
  A future like the past. I cannot rest.
  I know not what I ask nor what I seek;
  I feel but what thou art and what I am,
  And I would hear yet once before I perish
  The voice which was my music: speak to me!
  For I have called on thee in the still night,

Notes

6 *hectic* a flush or heightened colour on the cheek, often a symptom of fever.

7 *enthralled* imprisoned.

8 *baffled* defeated.

Startled the slumbering birds from the hushed boughs,
And woke the mountain wolves, and made the caves
Acquainted with thy vainly-echoed name,
Which answered me – many things answered me,
Spirits and men, but thou wert silent all.
Yet speak to me! I have outwatched the stars
And gazed o'er heaven in vain in search of thee.
Speak to me! I have wandered o'er the earth
And never found thy likeness – speak to me!
Look on the fiends around; they feel for me.
I fear them not, and feel for thee alone –
Speak to me, though it be in wrath, but say –
I reck[9] not what – but let me hear thee once –
This once – once more!

PHANTOM OF ASTARTE. Manfred!

MANFRED. Say on, say on;
I live but in the sound – it is thy voice!

PHANTOM OF ASTARTE. Manfred! Tomorrow ends thine earthly ills.
Farewell!

MANFRED. Yet one word more: am I forgiven?

PHANTOM OF ASTARTE. Farewell!

MANFRED. Say, shall we meet again?

PHANTOM OF ASTARTE. Farewell!

MANFRED. One word for mercy; say thou lovest me.

PHANTOM OF ASTARTE. Manfred!

The spirit of Astarte disappears.

NEMESIS. She's gone and will not be recalled;
Her words will be fulfilled. Return to the earth.

A SPIRIT. He is convulsed; this is to be a mortal
And seek the things beyond mortality.

ANOTHER SPIRIT. Yet see, he mastereth himself and makes
His torture tributary to his will;
Had he been one of us, he would have made
An awful[10] spirit.

NEMESIS. Hast thou further question
Of our great sovereign or his worshippers?

MANFRED. None.

NEMESIS. Then for a time farewell.

MANFRED. We meet then –
Where? On the earth?

NEMESIS. That will be seen hereafter.

MANFRED. Even as thou wilt; and for the grace accorded
I now depart a debtor. Fare ye well!

Exit Manfred.

Notes

[9] *reck* care.

[10] *awful* awe-inspiring.

Act III, Scene I[1]

A hall in the castle of Manfred. Manfred and Herman.

MANFRED. What is the hour?
HERMAN. It wants but one till sunset,
And promises a lovely twilight.
MANFRED. Say,
Are all things so disposed of[2] in the tower
As I directed?
HERMAN. All, my lord, are ready;
Here is the key and casket.
MANFRED. It is well;
Thou mayst retire.
Exit Herman.
MANFRED (*alone*). There is a calm upon me –
Inexplicable stillness, which till now
Did not belong to what I knew of life.
If that I did not know philosophy
To be of all our vanities the motliest,[3]
The merest[4] word that ever fooled the ear
From out the schoolman's[5] jargon, I should deem
The golden secret, the sought kalon,[6] found
And seated in my soul. It will not last,
But it is well to have known it, though but once;
It hath enlarged my thoughts with a new sense,
And I within my tablets[7] would note down
That there is such a feeling. Who is there?
Re-enter Herman.
HERMAN. My lord, the Abbot of St Maurice craves
To greet your presence.
Enter the Abbot of St. Maurice.
ABBOT. Peace be with Count Manfred![8]
MANFRED. Thanks, holy father; welcome to these walls!
Thy presence honours them, and blesseth those
Who dwell within them.
ABBOT. Would it were so, Count;
But I would fain confer with thee alone.
MANFRED. Herman, retire. (*Exit Herman.*) What would my reverend guest?
ABBOT. Thus, without prelude. Age and zeal, my office,

Notes

Act III, Scene I

[1] This scene reworks Faust's meeting with an Old Man in *Faust* V i.
[2] *disposed of* arranged, prepared.
[3] *motliest* most foolish.
[4] *merest* most insignificant.
[5] *schoolman's* scholar's.
[6] *kalon* the ideal good, the morally beautiful.
[7] *tablets* research documents.
[8] An ironic greeting, given the circumstances.

And good intent, must plead my privilege;
Our near, though not acquainted neighbourhood
May also be my herald. Rumours strange
And of unholy nature are abroad
And busy with thy name – a noble name
For centuries. May he who bears it now[9]
Transmit it unimpaired!
MANFRED. Proceed, I listen.
ABBOT. 'Tis said thou holdest converse with the things
Which are forbidden to the search of man;
That with the dwellers of the dark[10] abodes,
The many evil and unheavenly spirits
Which walk the valley of the shade of death,[11]
Thou communest. I know that with mankind,
Thy fellows in creation, thou dost rarely
Exchange thy thoughts, and that thy solitude
Is as an anchorite's, were it but holy.
MANFRED. And what are they who do avouch these things?
ABBOT. My pious brethren, the scared peasantry –
Even thy own vassals, who do look on thee
With most unquiet eyes. Thy life's in peril.
MANFRED. Take it.
ABBOT. I come to save, and not destroy.[12]
I would not pry into thy secret soul,
But if these things be sooth,[13] there still is time
For penitence and pity: reconcile thee
With the true church, and through the church to heaven.
MANFRED. I hear thee. This is my reply: whate'er
I may have been, or am, doth rest between
Heaven and myself. I shall not choose a mortal
To be my mediator. Have I sinned
Against your ordinances?[14] Prove and punish!
ABBOT. My son, I did not speak of punishment,
But penitence and pardon; with thyself
The choice of such remains. And for the last,
Our institutions and our strong belief
Have given me power to smooth the path from sin
To higher hope and better thoughts; the first
I leave to heaven – 'Vengeance is mine alone!'[15]
So saith the Lord, and with all humbleness
His servant echoes back the awful word.
MANFRED. Old man! There is no power in holy men,
Nor charm in prayer, nor purifying form
Of penitence, nor outward look, nor fast,

Notes

[9] *he who bears it now* i.e. Manfred himself.

[10] *dark* means both 'lacking in light' and 'evil'.

[11] *the valley of the shade of death* Psalm 23: 4: 'Yea, though I walk through the valley of the shadow of death, I will fear no evil.'

[12] *I come to save, and not destroy* cf. Christ's words at Matthew 5: 17: 'Think not that I am come to destroy the law, or the prophets: I am not come to destroy, but to fulfil.'

[13] *sooth* true.

[14] *ordinances* laws.

[15] See Romans 12: 19.

Nor agony – nor, greater than all these,
The innate tortures of that deep despair
Which is remorse without the fear of hell
But all in all sufficient to itself
Would make a hell of heaven, can exorcise
From out the unbounded spirit the quick[16] sense
Of its own sins, wrongs, sufferance, and revenge
Upon itself. There is no future pang
Can deal that justice on the self-condemned
He deals on his own soul.

ABBOT. All this is well –
For this will pass away, and be succeeded
By an auspicious hope which shall look up
With calm assurance to that blessed place[17]
Which all who seek may win, whatever be
Their earthly errors, so they be atoned;[18]
And the commencement of atonement is
The sense of its necessity. Say on,
And all our church can teach thee shall be taught,
And all we can absolve thee shall be pardoned.

MANFRED. When Rome's sixth Emperor[19] was near his last,
The victim of a self-inflicted wound,
To shun the torments of a public death
From senates once his slaves, a certain soldier,
With show of loyal pity, would have staunched
The gushing throat with his officious[20] robe;
The dying Roman thrust him back and said
(Some empire[21] still in his expiring glance),
'It is too late – is this fidelity?'

ABBOT. And what of this?

MANFRED. I answer with the Roman,
'It is too late!'

ABBOT. It never can be so,
To reconcile thyself with thy own soul,
And thy own soul with heaven. Hast thou no hope?
'Tis strange; even those who do despair above
Yet shape themselves some fantasy on earth
To which frail twig they cling like drowning men.

MANFRED. Aye, father! I have had those earthly visions
And noble aspirations in my youth –
To make my own the mind of other men,
The enlightener[22] of nations, and to rise
I knew not whither; it might be to fall,
But fall even as the mountain-cataract
Which, having leaped from its more dazzling height,

Notes

[16] *quick* living, vital.
[17] *that blessed place* i.e. heaven.
[18] *atoned* reconciled (with God).
[19] According to Suetonius, the sixth Roman emperor was Nero. Manfred's use of his words is ironic because Nero's deeds (the burning of Rome and the first major persecution of Christians) overshadow the circumstances of his death. The line quoted here was spoken to a former soldier who had turned against him.
[20] *officious* dutiful.
[21] *empire* i.e. some sense of his emperorship.
[22] *enlightener* guide, teacher.

Even in the foaming strength of its abyss
(Which casts up misty columns that become
Clouds raining from the reascended skies)
Lies low but mighty still. But this is passed;
My thoughts mistook themselves.

ABBOT. And wherefore so?

MANFRED. I could not tame my nature down; for he
Must serve who fain would sway, and soothe, and sue,[23]
And watch all time, and pry into all place –
And be a living lie, who would become
A mighty thing amongst the mean (and such
The mass are). I disdained to mingle with
A herd, though to be leader – and of wolves.
The lion is alone, and so am I.

ABBOT. And why not live and act with other men?

MANFRED. Because my nature was averse from life,
And yet not cruel – for I would not make,
But find a desolation. Like the wind,
The red-hot breath of the most lone simoom,[24]
Which dwells but in the desert, and sweeps o'er
The barren sands which bear no shrubs to blast,
And revels o'er their wild and arid waves
And seeketh not, so that it is not sought,
But being met is deadly; such hath been
The course of my existence. But there came
Things in my path which are no more.

ABBOT. Alas,
I 'gin to fear that thou art past all aid
From me and from my calling; yet so young,
I still would –

MANFRED. Look on me! There is an order
Of mortals on the earth, who do become
Old in their youth, and die ere middle age
Without the violence of warlike death –
Some perishing of pleasure, some of study,
Some worn with toil, some of mere weariness,
Some of disease, and some insanity,
And some of withered or of broken hearts;
For this last is a malady which slays
More than are numbered in the lists of fate,
Taking all shapes, and bearing many names.
Look upon me! For even of all these things
Have I partaken, and of all these things
One were enough; then wonder not that I
Am what I am, but that I ever was,
Or, having been, that I am still on earth.

Notes

[23] *sue* follow.

[24] *simoom* a hot, dry, suffocating sand-wind which sweeps across the African deserts at intervals during the spring and summer.

ABBOT. Yet hear me still –
MANFRED. Old man! I do respect
Thine order, and revere thine years; I deem
Thy purpose pious, but it is in vain.
Think me not churlish;[25] I would spare thyself
Far more than me, in shunning at this time
All further colloquy[26] – and so farewell.

Exit Manfred

ABBOT. This should have been a noble creature; he
Hath all the energy which would have made
A goodly frame of glorious elements,[27]
Had they been wisely mingled. As it is,
It is an awful[28] chaos – light and darkness,
And mind and dust, and passions and pure thoughts,
Mixed and contending without end or order,
All dormant or destructive: he will perish,
And yet he must not. I will try once more,
For such are worth redemption, and my duty
Is to dare all things for a righteous end.
I'll follow him – but cautiously, though surely.

Exit Abbot

Act III, Scene II

Another chamber. Manfred and Herman.

HERMAN. My Lord, you bade me wait on you at sunset:
He[1] sinks behind the mountain.
MANFRED. Doth he so?
I will look on him.

Manfred advances to the window of the hall.

Glorious orb![2] The idol
Of early nature, and the vigorous race
Of undiseased mankind, the giant sons
Of the embrace of angels, with a sex
More beautiful than they, which did draw down
The erring spirits who can ne'er return;[3]
Most glorious orb, that wert a worship ere
The mystery of thy making was revealed!
Thou earliest minister of the Almighty,
Which gladdened on their mountain-tops the hearts
Of the Chaldean shepherds,[4] till they poured
Themselves in orisons![5] Thou material god

Notes

[25] *churlish* ungracious.
[26] *colloquy* conversation.
[27] *A goodly frame of glorious elements* The Abbot echoes Hamlet's description of the earth as 'this goodly frame' (II ii 298), and there is a general recollection of Hamlet's comments on man's innate nobility, II ii 303–10.
[28] *awful* awesome.

Act III, Scene II
[1] *He* the sun.
[2] This is a pagan address to the sun.
[3] See Genesis 6: 1–4.
[4] *the Chaldean shepherds* renowned astronomers; see *Childe Harold* iii 118.
[5] Compare *Childe Harold's Pilgrimage* iii stanza 91, above. *orisons* prayers.

And representative of the unknown,
Who chose thee for his shadow! Thou chief star,
Centre of many stars, which mak'st our earth
Endurable, and temperest the hues
And hearts of all who walk within thy rays!
Sire of the seasons! Monarch of the climes
And those who dwell in them (for near or far,
Our inborn spirits have a tint of thee,
Even as our outward aspects), thou dost rise
And shine and set in glory – fare thee well,
I ne'er shall see thee more! As my first glance
Of love and wonder was for thee, then take
My latest look: thou wilt not beam on one
To whom the gifts of life and warmth have been
Of a more fatal nature. He is gone;
I follow.

Exit Manfred

Act III, Scene III

The mountains. The castle of Manfred at some distance. A terrace before a tower. Time: twilight. Herman, Manuel, and other dependants of Manfred.

HERMAN. 'Tis strange enough; night after night for years
He hath pursued long vigils in this tower
Without a witness. I have been within it –
So have we all been oft-times; but from it,
Or its contents, it were impossible
To draw conclusions absolute of aught
His studies tend to. To be sure, there is
One chamber where none enter; I would give
The fee of what I have to come these three years[1]
To pore upon its mysteries.

MANUEL. 'Twere dangerous;
Content thyself with what thou knowest already.

HERMAN. Ah, Manuel! Thou art elderly and wise,
And could'st say much; thou hast dwelt within the castle –
How many years is't?

MANUEL. Ere Count Manfred's birth
I served his father, whom he nought resembles.

HERMAN. There be more sons in like predicament.
But wherein do they differ?

MANUEL. I speak not
Of features or of form, but mind and habits:
Count Sigismund was proud, but gay and free,
A warrior and a reveller; he dwelt not
With books and solitude, nor made the night

Notes

Act III, Scene III

[1] *The fee of what I have to come these three years* i.e. his next three years' salary.

A gloomy vigil, but a festal time,
Merrier than day; he did not walk the rocks
And forests like a wolf, nor turn aside
From men and their delights.

HERMAN. Beshrew the hour,
But those were jocund times! I would that such
Would visit the old walls again; they look
As if they had forgotten them.

MANUEL. These walls
Must change their chieftain first – oh, I have seen
Some strange things in them, Herman!

HERMAN. Come, be friendly,
Relate me some to while away our watch;
I've heard thee darkly speak of an event
Which happened hereabouts, by this same tower.

MANUEL. That was a night indeed. I do remember
'Twas twilight, as it may be now, and such
Another evening; yon red cloud, which rests
On Eiger's pinnacle,[2] so rested then,
So like that it might be the same; the wind
Was faint and gusty, and the mountain snows
Began to glitter with the climbing moon.
Count Manfred was, as now, within his tower,
How occupied we knew not, but with him
The sole companion of his wanderings
And watchings – her, whom of all earthly things
That lived, the only thing he seemed to love,
As he indeed by blood was bound to do,
The lady Astarte, his[3] –
Hush! Who comes here?

Enter the Abbot

ABBOT. Where is your master?

HERMAN. Yonder, in the tower.

ABBOT. I must speak with him.

MANUEL. 'Tis impossible.
He is most private, and must not be thus
Intruded on.

ABBOT. Upon myself I take
The forfeit of my fault, if fault there be;
But I must see him.

HERMAN. Thou hast seen him once
This eve already.

ABBOT. Sirrah, I command thee
Knock and apprise the Count of my approach!

HERMAN. We dare not.

Notes

[2] *Eiger's pinnacle* The Eiger is a mountain, east of the Jungfrau, which Byron first saw on 22 September 1816.

[3] *his* – This is the closest anyone in the play gets to saying that Astarte is Manfred's sister.

ABBOT. Then it seems I must be herald
Of my own purpose.
MANUEL. Reverend father, stop,
I pray you pause.
ABBOT. Why so?
MANUEL. But step this way,
And I will tell you further.
Exeunt

Act III, Scene IV

Interior of the tower. Manfred alone.

MANFRED. The stars are forth, the moon above the tops
Of the snow-shining mountains – beautiful!
I linger yet with nature, for the night
Hath been to me a more familiar face
Than that of man, and in her starry shade
Of dim and solitary loveliness
I learned the language of another world.
I do remember me that in my youth
When I was wandering, upon such a night[1]
I stood within the Colosseum's wall
Midst the chief relics of almighty Rome;[2]
The trees which grew along the broken arches
Waved dark in the blue midnight, and the stars
Shone through the rents of ruin; from afar
The watchdog bayed beyond the Tiber, and
More near from out the Caesars' palace came
The owl's long cry, and, interruptedly,
Of distant sentinels the fitful song
Begun and died upon the gentle wind.
Some cypresses beyond the time-worn breach[3]
Appeared to skirt the horizon, yet they stood
Within a bowshot,[4] where the Caesars dwelt,
And dwell the tuneless birds of night; amidst
A grove which springs through levelled battlements,
And twines its roots with the imperial hearths,
Ivy usurps the laurel's place of growth;[5]
But the gladiators' bloody circus[6] stands,
A noble wreck in ruinous perfection,[7]

Notes

Act III, Scene IV

[1] *upon such a night* There is a general recollection, throughout this speech, of the exchange between Jessica and Lorenzo, *Merchant of Venice* V i 1–22, which uses the repeated tag, 'In such a night . . . '

[2] Byron first visited Rome in April 1817. This passage may have been inspired partly by Gibbon's *Decline and Fall of the Roman Empire*; Gibbon is celebrated as a freethinker at the conclusion of *Childe Harold* iii (see pp. 883–4).

[3] *breach* break in the old city walls.

[4] *Within a bowshot* i.e. within about 300 yards.

[5] *Ivy . . . place of growth* Ivy (a plant of death) has taken over where the laurel (a plant of victory) once grew.

[6] *circus* oval arena.

[7] *A noble wreck in ruinous perfection* Manfred is effectively describing himself.

While Caesar's chambers and the Augustan halls
Grovel on earth in indistinct decay.
And thou didst shine, thou rolling moon, upon
All this, and cast a wide and tender light
Which softened down the hoar austerity
Of rugged desolation, and filled up,
As 'twere, anew, the gaps of centuries,
Leaving that beautiful which still was so,
And making that which was not, till the place
Became religion, and the heart ran o'er
With silent worship of the great of old[8] –
The dead but sceptred sovereigns who still rule
Our spirits from their urns.
'Twas such a night!
'Tis strange that I recall it at this time,
But I have found our thoughts take wildest flight
Even at the moment when they should array[9]
Themselves in pensive[10] order.

Enter the Abbot

ABBOT. My good Lord!
I crave a second grace for this approach,
But yet let not my humble zeal offend
By its abruptness; all it hath of ill
Recoils on me. Its good in the effect
May light upon your head – could I say *heart*,
Could I touch *that*, with words or prayers, I should
Recall a noble spirit which hath wandered
But is not yet all lost.

MANFRED. Thou know'st me not;
My days are numbered and my deeds recorded.
Retire, or 'twill be dangerous – away!

ABBOT. Thou dost not mean to menace me?

MANFRED. Not I;
I simply tell thee peril is at hand
And would preserve thee.

ABBOT. What dost mean?

MANFRED. Look there –
What dost thou see?

ABBOT. Nothing.

MANFRED. Look there, I say,
And steadfastly; now tell me what thou seest?

ABBOT. That which should shake me, but I fear it not;
I see a dusk and awful figure rise

Notes

[8] *till the place . . . great of old* These lines prove that, even at this late stage, Manfred might still be redeemed to the cause of orthodox religion.

[9] *array* arrange.

[10] *pensive* meditative, reflective.

Like an infernal god from out the earth,
His face wrapped in a mantle, and his form
Robed as with angry clouds. He stands between
Thyself and me, but I do fear him not.

MANFRED. Thou hast no cause; he shall not harm thee, but
His sight may shock thine old limbs into palsy.[11]
I say to thee, retire!

ABBOT. And I reply
Never, till I have battled with this fiend.
What doth he here?

MANFRED. Why, aye, what doth he here?
I did not send for him, he is unbidden.

ABBOT. Alas, lost mortal! What with guests like these
Hast thou to do? I tremble for thy sake;
Why doth he gaze on thee, and thou on him?
Ah! he unveils his aspect: on his brow
The thunder-scars are graven; from his eye
Glares forth the immortality of hell –
Avaunt!

MANFRED. Pronounce – what is thy mission?

SPIRIT. Come!

ABBOT. What art thou, unknown being? Answer! Speak!

SPIRIT. The genius[12] of this mortal. Come, 'tis time!

MANFRED. I am prepared for all things, but deny
The power which summons me. Who sent thee here?

SPIRIT. Thou'lt know anon; come, come!

MANFRED. I have commanded
Things of an essence greater far than thine,
And striven with thy masters. Get thee hence!

SPIRIT. Mortal, thine hour is come. Away, I say!

MANFRED. I knew, and know my hour is come, but not
To render up my soul to such as thee;
Away! I'll die as I have lived – alone.

SPIRIT. Then I must summon up my brethren. Rise!

Other spirits rise up

ABBOT. Avaunt, ye evil ones! Avaunt I say!
Ye have no power where piety hath power,
And I do charge ye in the name –

SPIRIT. Old man!
We know ourselves, our mission, and thine order;
Waste not thy holy words on idle uses,
It were in vain – this man is forfeited.
Once more I summon him: away, away!

MANFRED. I do defy ye, though I feel my soul
Is ebbing from me, yet I do defy ye;

Notes

[11] *palsy* paralysis.

[12] *genius* guardian spirit.

Nor will I hence, while I have earthly breath
To breathe my scorn upon ye, earthly strength
To wrestle (though with spirits): what ye take
Shall be ta'en limb by limb.

SPIRIT. Reluctant mortal!
Is this the Magian who would so pervade
The world invisible, and make himself
Almost our equal? Can it be that thou
Art thus in love with life – the very life
Which made thee wretched?

MANFRED. Thou false fiend, thou liest!
My life is in its last hour – *that* I know,
Nor would redeem a moment of that hour;
I do not combat against death, but thee
And thy surrounding angels; my past power
Was purchased by no compact with thy crew,
But by superior science, penance, daring,
And length of watching, strength of mind, and skill
In knowledge of our fathers – when the earth
Saw men and spirits walking side by side,
And gave ye no supremacy. I stand
Upon my strength: I do defy, deny,
Spurn back, and scorn ye!

SPIRIT. But thy many crimes
Have made thee –

MANFRED. What are they to such as thee?
Must crimes be punished but by other crimes
And greater criminals? Back to thy hell!
Thou hast no power upon me, *that* I feel;
Thou never shalt possess me, *that* I know.
What I have done is done; I bear within
A torture which could nothing gain from thine.
The mind which is immortal makes itself
Requital for its good or evil thoughts,[13]
Is its own origin of ill and end,
And its own place and time; its innate sense,
When stripped of this mortality, derives
No colour from the fleeting things without,
But is absorbed in sufferance or in joy,
Born from the knowledge of its own desert.
Thou didst not tempt me, and thou couldst not tempt me,
I have not been thy dupe nor am thy prey –
But was my own destroyer, and will be
My own hereafter. Back, ye baffled fiends,
The hand of death is on me – but not yours!

The demons disappear

Notes

[13] *The mind . . . thoughts* cf. *Paradise Lost* i 254–5: 'The mind is its own place, and in itself / Can make a heaven of hell, a hell of heaven.'

ABBOT. Alas, how pale thou art! Thy lips are white
And thy breast heaves, and in thy gasping throat
The accents rattle; give thy prayers to heaven;
Pray, albeit but in thought – but die not thus.
MANFRED. 'Tis over; my dull eyes can fix thee not,
But all things swim around me, and the earth
Heaves as it were beneath me. Fare thee well;
Give me thy hand.
ABBOT. Cold, cold, even to the heart;
But yet one prayer – alas, how fares it with thee?
MANFRED. Old man! 'Tis not so difficult to die.
Manfred expires
ABBOT. He's gone; his soul hath ta'en its earthless flight –
Whither, I dread to think – but he is gone.

Letter from Lord Byron to Thomas Moore, 28 February 1817 (extract; including 'So we'll go no more a-roving')[1]

I feel anxious to hear from you, even more than usual, because your last indicated that you were unwell. At present, I am on the invalid regimen myself. The Carnival – that is, the latter part of it – and sitting up late o' nights, had knocked me up a little. But it is over, and it is now Lent, with all its abstinence and Sacred Music.

The mumming[2] closed with a masked ball at the Fenice,[3] where I went, as also to most of the ridottos,[4] etc., etc. And, though I did not dissipate much upon the whole, yet I find 'the sword wearing out the scabbard', though I have but just turned the corner of twenty-nine.

So we'll go no more a-roving
So late into the night,
Though the heart be still as loving,
And the moon be still as bright.

For the sword outwears its sheath,
And the soul wears out the breast,
And the heart must pause to breathe,
And love itself have rest.

Though the night was made for loving,
And the day returns too soon,
Yet we'll go no more a-roving
By the light of the moon.

Notes

LETTER FROM LORD BYRON TO THOMAS MOORE

[1] This important letter was written from Venice, and presents Byron's famous poem, 'So we'll go no more a-roving', in the context in which it was first composed. For Moore see p. 935n23.

[2] *mumming* revelries conducted behind masks.

[3] *the Fenice* Venetian opera theatre, principal venue for the carnival, which closed on the evening of 18 February. It was destroyed by fire in summer 1996.

[4] *ridottos* entertainment or social assembly consisting of music and dancing.

Don Juan (first published 1819; edited from MS)[1]
Dedication (composed 3 July–6 September 1818; first published 1832)

1

Bob Southey! You're a poet – Poet Laureate,[2]
   And representative of all the race;[3]
Although 'tis true you turned out a Tory at
   Last, yours has lately been a common case;
And now, my epic renegade, what are ye at,
   With all the Lakers[4] in and out of place?
A nest of tuneful persons, to my eye
Like 'four and twenty blackbirds in a pie,

2

Which pie[5] being opened, they began to sing'
   (This old song and new simile holds good),
'A dainty dish to set before the King'
   Or Regent,[6] who admires such kind of food.
And Coleridge[7] too has lately taken wing,
   But like a hawk encumbered with his hood,
Explaining metaphysics to the nation;[8]
I wish he would explain his explanation.

3

You, Bob, are rather insolent, you know,
   At being disappointed in your wish
To supersede all warblers here below,

Notes

Don Juan

[1] *Don Juan* is probably Byron's finest achievement in verse. It was the epic poem he was born to write. Cantos I and II appeared first, without the Dedication, in 1819; they are published here in their entirety. See headnote, pp. 843–4.

[2] Southey was Poet Laureate 1813–43, a post that entailed the composition of occasional poems in honour of the king. For Byron and Shelley, this was conclusive proof, were any needed, that Southey had abandoned his early radicalism. In an unpublished Preface to *Don Juan*, Byron wrote that the Dedication 'may be further supposed to be produced by someone who may have a cause of aversion from the said Southey – for some personal reason – perhaps a gross calumny invented or circulated by this Pantisocratic apostle of apostasy, who is sometimes as unguarded in his assertions as atrocious in his conjectures, and feeds the cravings of his wretched vanity – disappointed in its nobler hopes, and reduced to prey upon such snatches of fame as his contributions to the *Quarterly Review*'. Byron's animus towards him was indeed personal: as he told Hobhouse on 11 November 1818, 'The son of a bitch on his return from Switzerland two years ago, said that Shelley and I "had formed a league of incest and practised our precepts with etc." He lied like a rascal, for *they were not sisters* – one being Godwin's daughter by Mary Wollstonecraft, and the other the daughter of the present Mrs Godwin by a *former* husband. The attack contains no allusion to the cause, but some good verses, and all political and poetical. He lied in another sense, for there was no promiscuous intercourse, my commerce being limited to the carnal knowledge of the Miss Clairmont' (Marchand vi 76). Having heard Byron read the Dedication, Shelley said of Southey that 'The poor wretch will writhe under the lash' (Jones ii 42).

[3] *all the race* i.e. of poets.

[4] *Lakers* i.e. Southey, Wordsworth and Coleridge, who were first lumped together as the 'Lake School' by Jeffrey (see pp. 714–15). By this time Coleridge was resident in London rather than Cumbria.

[5] *pie* There may be a pun on the name of Henry James Pye (1745–1813), arch poetaster and Laureate prior to Southey.

[6] *Regent* George, Prince of Wales, governed as Prince Regent 1811–20, during his father's insanity.

[7] As recently as 1816, Byron had given Coleridge £100 to help him through a bad patch; enmity developed because, as Byron told Murray, 'Coleridge went about repeating Southey's lie with pleasure' (Marchand v 83). The lie is, of course, the rumour about the league of incest (see note 2 above).

[8] *Explaining metaphysics to the nation* Byron is thinking of Coleridge's recent prose discourses, *The Statesman's Manual* (1816), *Biographia Literaria* and *Lay Sermon* (1817) and *The Friend* (1818).

And be the only blackbird in the dish;
And then you overstrain yourself, or so,
And tumble downward like the flying fish
Gasping on deck, because you soar too high, Bob,
And fall for lack of moisture, quite a dry-bob![9]

4

And Wordsworth, in a rather long *Excursion*
(I think the quarto holds five hundred pages[10]),
Has given a sample from the vasty[11] version
Of his new system to perplex the sages;
'Tis poetry (at least by his assertion),
And may appear so when the dog-star rages;[12]
And he who understands it would be able
To add a story[13] to the Tower of Babel.[14]

5

You gentlemen, by dint of long seclusion
From better company, have kept your own
At Keswick,[15] and, through still-continued fusion
Of one another's minds, at last have grown
To deem as a most logical conclusion
That poesy has wreaths for you alone;
There is a narrowness in such a notion
Which makes me wish you'd change your lakes for ocean.

6

I would not imitate the petty thought,
Nor coin[16] my self-love to so base a vice,
For all the glory your conversion[17] brought,
Since gold alone should not have been its price.
You have your salary – was't for that you wrought?[18]
And Wordsworth has his place in the Excise.[19]
You're shabby fellows, true – but poets still,
And duly seated on the immortal hill.[20]

Notes

[9] *a dry-bob!* sex without ejaculation.

[10] *five hundred pages* Jeffrey criticized *The Excursion* (1814) for its length; see p. 716 above.

[11] *vasty* vast, enormous.

[12] *when the dog-star rages* The star Sirius, in the constellation of the Greater Dog, the brightest of the fixed stars, has been alleged to have all kinds of bad effects when its influence rises with the sun; the joke here is that it will distort everyone's judgement so much as to make *The Excursion* appear to be poetry. Cf. Pope, *Epistle to Dr Arbuthnot* 3–4: 'The dog-star rages! Nay 'tis past a doubt, / All Bedlam, or Parnassus, is let out'.

[13] *story* floor, level.

[14] *the Tower of Babel* the cause of God's decision to confound the language of men; Genesis 11: 1–9.

[15] *At Keswick* Only Southey lived at Keswick (as Byron well knew); Coleridge lived in London, and Wordsworth in Grasmere.

[16] *coin* 'fashion', effectively, 'convert'. The implication is that Southey's vanity has led him to relinquish his ideals for the pittance he is paid as Laureate.

[17] *conversion* a pun, meaning: (i) conversion of vanity to the gold Southey is paid as Laureate, and (ii) conversion from radical to Tory.

[18] *wrought* i.e. composed poetry.

[19] An unpublished note appears in the proofs: 'Wordsworth's place may be in the Customs; it is, I think, in that of the Excise – besides another at Lord Lonsdale's table, where this poetical charlatan and political parasite picks up the crumbs with a hardened alacrity, the converted Jacobin having long subsided into the clownish sycophant of the worst prejudices of aristocracy.' William Lowther, 1st Earl of Lonsdale, was Wordsworth's patron; he procured Wordsworth's job as Distributor of Stamps and was the dedicatee of *The Excursion*.

[20] *the immortal hill* Parnassus, a mountain of Phocis (north-west of Athens), sacred to the muses.

7

Your bays[21] may hide the baldness of your brows,
  Perhaps some virtuous blushes (let them go);
To you I envy neither fruit nor boughs,
  And for the fame you would engross[22] below
The field is universal, and allows
  Scope to all such as feel the inherent glow –
Scott, Rogers, Campbell, Moore and Crabbe[23] will try
'Gainst you the question with posterity.

8

For me who, wandering with pedestrian[24] muses,
  Contend not with you on the winged steed,
I wish your fate may yield ye, when she chooses,
  The fame you envy[25] and the skill you need;[26]
And recollect a poet nothing loses
  In giving to his brethren their full meed
Of merit, and complaint of present days
Is not the *certain* path to future praise.[27]

9

He that reserves his laurels for posterity
  (Who does not often claim the bright reversion?[28])
Has generally no great crop[29] to spare it, he
  Being only injured by his own assertion;
And although here and there some glorious rarity
  Arise like Titan from the sea's immersion,[30]
The major part of such appellants[31] go
To God knows where – for no one else can know.

10

If, fallen in evil days on evil tongues,[32]
  Milton appealed to the avenger, Time;
If Time, the avenger, execrates his wrongs,
  And makes the word 'Miltonic' mean 'sublime',
He deigned not to belie his soul in songs,

Notes

[21] *bays* The leaves of the bay-tree or bay-laurel were, in classical times, the symbol of poetic excellence.

[22] *engross* monopolize. Byron was quite famous himself.

[23] *Scott, Rogers, Campbell, Moore and Crabbe* Walter Scott, Samuel Rogers, Thomas Campbell, Thomas Moore and George Crabbe were well-known and respected poets in their day. Byron saw them as working, broadly speaking, within the neoclassical tradition stemming from Pope; as such, they were vastly preferable to the Lakers; for more on this see p. 838 above.

[24] *pedestrian* by implication, less metaphysical and more down to earth.

[25] *The fame you envy* In the Proem to *Carmen Nuptiale* (1816), Southey had written: 'There was a time when all my youthful thought / Was of the muse; and of the poet's fame' (ll. 1–2).

[26] *need* i.e. lack.

[27] *And recollect . . . praise* In the Proem to *Carmen Nuptiale* (1816), Southey wrote that Fancy had told him to walk 'Far from the vain, the vicious, and the proud' (l.27). Byron seems to have taken this as a reference to himself.

[28] *the bright reversion* the right of succession (i.e. to posthumous fame).

[29] *no great crop* i.e. of praise for other poets.

[30] *Arise like Titan from the sea's immersion* Byron has in mind Helios, son of Hyperion, god of the sun.

[31] *appellants* challengers, i.e. those who reserve their laurels for posterity.

[32] *Paradise Lost* vii 25–6.

Nor turn his very talent to a crime;
He did not loathe the sire to laud the son,[33]
But closed the tyrant-hater he begun.[34]

11

Think'st thou, could he, the blind old man,[35] arise
Like Samuel from the grave,[36] to freeze once more
The blood of monarchs with his prophecies,
Or be alive again, again all hoar
With time and trials, and those helpless eyes
And heartless daughters,[37] worn and pale and poor –
Would *he* adore a sultan? – *he* obey
The intellectual eunuch Castlereagh?[38]

12

Cold-blooded, smooth-faced, placid miscreant!
Dabbling its sleek young hands in Erin's[39] gore,
And thus for wider carnage taught to pant,
Transferred to gorge upon a sister-shore;
The vulgarest tool that tyranny could want,
With just enough of talent, and no more,
To lengthen fetters by another fixed,
And offer poison long already mixed.

13

An orator of such set trash of phrase[40]
Ineffably, legitimately vile,
That even its grossest flatterers dare not praise,
Nor foes (all nations) condescend to smile;
Not even a sprightly blunder's spark can blaze
From that Ixion grindstone's[41] ceaseless toil,
That turns and turns, to give the world a notion
Of endless torments and perpetual motion.

14

A bungler even in its disgusting trade,
And botching, patching, leaving still behind
Something of which its masters are afraid,

Notes

[33] *He did not loathe . . . son* Charles I and II. Byron's point is that Southey (a former republican) hated George III (in his radical youth) but praised his son (the Prince Regent); by contrast, Milton remained a republican throughout his life.

[34] *But closed the tyrant-hater he begun* As far as Byron was concerned, both George III and the Prince Regent were tyrants. At that time, the monarch (an inherited post) had enormous political power.

[35] *the blind old man* Milton.

[36] *Like Samuel from the grave* Samuel was raised from the grave by the Witch of Endor; 1 Samuel 28: 13–14.

[37] *heartless daughters* said to have robbed Milton of his books.

[38] Robert Stewart, Viscount Castlereagh (1769–1822), Foreign Secretary 1812–22. As Secretary to the Lord Lieutenant of Ireland (1797–1801), he had been responsible for imprisoning the leaders of the United Irish rebellion.

[39] *Erin's* Ireland's.

[40] *such set trash of phrase* Castlereagh was renowned as an incompetent speaker.

[41] *Ixion grindstone's* Ixion, king of Thessaly, was banished from heaven and sentenced to be tied to a burning and spinning wheel in Hades.

States to be curbed[42] and thoughts to be confined,
Conspiracy or congress[43] to be made,
Cobbling at manacles for all mankind –
A tinkering slavemaker who mends old chains,
With God and man's abhorrence for its gains.

15

If we may judge of matter by the mind,
Emasculated to the marrow, *It*
Hath but two objects: how to serve and bind,
Deeming the chain it wears even men may fit;
Eutropius[44] of its many masters – blind
To worth as freedom, wisdom as to wit –
Fearless, because *no* feeling dwells in ice,
Its very courage stagnates to a vice.

16

Where shall I turn me not to view its bonds
(For I will never feel them)? Italy,
Thy late-reviving Roman soul desponds
Beneath the lie this state-thing[45] breathed o'er thee;
Thy clanking chain and Erin's yet green wounds
Have voices, tongues to cry aloud for me.
Europe has slaves, allies, kings, armies still –
And Southey lives to sing them very ill.[46]

17

Meantime, Sir Laureate,[47] I proceed to dedicate,
In honest, simple verse, this song to you,
And if in flattering strains I do not predicate,[48]
'Tis that I still retain my 'buff and blue'[49]
(My politics, as yet, are all to educate);
Apostasy's so fashionable too,
To keep *one* creed's a task grown quite herculean –
Is it not so, my Tory ultra-Julian?[50]

Notes

[42] *States to be curbed* i.e. France under Napoleon; Castlereagh helped negotiate the alliance with Russia, Austria, and Prussia that led to Napoleon's defeat.

[43] *congress* As Foreign Secretary, Castlereagh was instrumental in the Treaty of Paris (May 1814), which restored the Bourbon monarchy after Napoleon's abdication, and the Congress of Vienna (1814–15), which reorganized Europe after the Napoleonic Wars.

[44] *Eutropius* Roman eunuch raised to high office; see Gibbon, *Decline and Fall of the Roman Empire*, chapter 32.

[45] *this state-thing* The Congress of Vienna ('this state-thing') restored papal power.

[46] This stanza provides an overview of Castlereagh's misdeeds. In 1798 he had helped to defeat the Irish insurrection and establish the Union of 1801; as a chief negotiator of the Treaty of Vienna, 1814–15, he had been responsible for suppressing the revival of free Italian cities, instead placing Italy under Austrian rule. Southey celebrated his deeds in *Carmen Triumphale* (1814) and *The Poet's Pilgrimage to Waterloo* (1816).

[47] *Sir Laureate* Southey.

[48] *predicate* extol, commend (i.e. Southey and his poetry).

[49] *buff and blue* colours of the Whig Club. The comparison is with Southey, who has relinquished all his liberal credentials.

[50] 'I allude not to our friend Landor's hero, the traitor Count Julian, but to Gibbon's hero, vulgarly yclept "The Apostate"' (Byron's note). Julian was brought up as a Christian, but secretly worshipped Roman gods before he became Emperor in AD 361. During his brief reign he attempted to restore pagan worship (he died 363).

Canto I

1

I want a hero[1] – an uncommon want
When every year and month sends forth a new one,
Till after cloying the gazettes with cant,
The age discovers he is not the true one;
Of such as these I should not care to vaunt,
I'll therefore take our ancient friend Don Juan;[2]
We all have seen him in the pantomime[3]
Sent to the devil,[4] somewhat ere his time.

2

Vernon, the butcher Cumberland, Wolfe, Hawke,
Prince Ferdinand, Granby, Burgoyne, Keppel, Howe,[5]
Evil and good, have had their tithe of talk,
And filled their signposts then, like Wellesley now;[6]
Each in their turn like Banquo's monarchs stalk,[7]
Followers of fame, 'nine farrow' of that sow;[8]
France, too, had Buonaparté and Dumourier,[9]
Recorded in the *Moniteur* and *Courier*.[10]

3

Barnave, Brissot, Condorcet, Mirabeau,
Petion, Clootz, Danton, Marat, La Fayette
Were French, and famous people as we know;
And there were others, scarce forgotten yet –
Joubert, Hoche, Marceau, Lannes, Dessaix, Moreau,[11]
With many of the military set,
Exceedingly remarkable at times,
But not at all adapted to my rhymes.

4

Nelson[12] was once Britannia's god of war,
And still should be so, but the tide is turned;
There's no more to be said of Trafalgar –
'Tis with our hero quietly inurned

Notes

CANTO I

[1] *I want a hero* Byron's lack of a hero is a witty variation on Virgil's epic opening, 'Of arms and the man I sing . . . '

[2] *Juan* pronounced with a hard 'J', to rhyme with 'new one' and 'true one'.

[3] *pantomime* musical drama without words. In London, only Drury Lane and Covent Garden were allowed to perform 'spoken drama'; other theatres were confined to plays without words. Byron may well have seen Don Juan portrayed in Italian

[4] *Sent to the devil* by contrast, Byron's poem will humanize Juan, and redeem him from the accusations commonly levelled against him.

[5] *Vernon . . . Howe* celebrated eighteenth-century military and naval commanders.

[6] *And filled their signposts then, like Wellesley now* Wellington Street and Waterloo Bridge were opened and dedicated on the anniversary of Waterloo in 1817.

[7] *like Banquo's monarchs stalk* an allusion to the vision granted Macbeth at *Macbeth* IV ii 112–24.

[8] *'nine farrow' of that sow* an allusion to the witches' spell in *Macbeth* IV i 64–5: 'Pour in sow's blood, that hath eaten / Her nine farrow.'

[9] Charles Dumouriez (1729–1823) defeated the Austrian army in 1792 at Jemappes.

[10] *the Moniteur and Courier* French official newspapers: *Gazette Nationale; ou le moniteur universel* and *Courier Républicain*.

[11] These are politicians and military leaders involved with the French Revolution.

[12] Horatio, Lord Nelson (1758–1805), killed at the Battle of Trafalgar, with Napoleon's forces, 21 October 1805.

Because the army's grown more popular,[13]
  At which the naval people are concerned;
Besides, the Prince is all for the land-service,
Forgetting Duncan, Nelson, Howe, and Jervis.[14]

5

Brave men were living before Agamemnon[15]
  And since, exceeding valorous and sage –
A good deal like him too, though quite the same none;
  But then they shone not on the poet's page,
And so have been forgotten. I condemn none,
  But can't find any in the present age
Fit for my poem (that is, for my new one),
So as I said, I'll take my friend Don Juan.

6

Most epic poets plunge *in medias res*[16]
  (Horace makes this the heroic turnpike road[17]),
And then your hero tells, whene'er you please,
  What went before by way of episode,
While seated after dinner at his ease
  Beside his mistress in some soft abode –
Palace or garden, paradise or cavern,
Which serves the happy couple for a tavern.

7

That is the usual method, but not mine;
  My way is to begin with the beginning.
The regularity of my design
  Forbids all wandering as the worst of sinning,
And therefore I shall open with a line
  (Although it cost me half an hour in spinning)
Narrating somewhat of Don Juan's father
And also of his mother, if you'd rather.

8

In Seville was he born, a pleasant city
  Famous for oranges and women; he
Who has not seen it will be much to pity,
  So says the proverb – and I quite agree:[18]
Of all the Spanish towns is none more pretty

Notes

[13] *Because the army's grown more popular* i.e. since Waterloo.
[14] These are all distinguished admirals.
[15] Agamemnon commanded the Greeks in the Trojan wars.
[16] *in medias res* into the middle of things; i.e. start in mid-story. This is the recommendation of Horace, *Ars Poetica* 148.
[17] *the heroic turnpike road* i.e. the initial step in the writing of an epic poem. A 'turnpike road' is one on which turnpikes are or were erected for the collection of tolls; hence, a main road or highway.
[18] *and I quite agree* Byron was in Seville, 25–9 July 1809. The 'proverb' runs: 'Quien no ha visto Sevilla / No ha visto maravilla' ('Whoever has not seen Seville has not seen a marvel').

(Cadiz perhaps,[19] but that you soon may see).
Don Juan's parents lived beside the river,
A noble stream, and called the Guadalquivir.

9

His father's name was Jóse (Don, of course) –
A true hidalgo,[20] free from every stain
Of Moor or Hebrew blood, he traced his source
Through the most Gothic gentlemen of Spain;
A better cavalier ne'er mounted horse
(Or, being mounted, e'er got down again)
Than Jóse, who begot our hero, who
Begot – but that's to come. Well, to renew:

10

His mother was a learned lady famed
For every branch of every science known,[21]
In every Christian language ever named,
With virtues equalled by her wit alone;
She made the cleverest people quite ashamed,
And even the good with inward envy groan,
Finding themselves so very much exceeded
In their own way by all the things that she did.

11

Her memory was a mine – she knew by heart
All Calderon and greater part of Lopé,[22]
So that if any actor missed his part
She could have served him for the prompter's copy;
For her Feinagle's[23] were an useless art,
And he himself obliged to shut up shop – he
Could never make a memory so fine as
That which adorned the brain of Donna Inez.

12

Her favourite science was the mathematical,[24]
Her noblest virtue was her magnanimity,
Her wit (she sometimes tried at wit) was Attic[25] all,
Her serious sayings darkened to sublimity;

Notes

[19] Byron was in Cadiz, 29 July–3 August 1809.

[20] *hidalgo* a gentleman by birth, one of the lower nobility.

[21] *His mother . . . known* Byron always denied that Donna Inez was supposed to be a caricature of his wife, but friends recognized the similarities, and advised him not to publish the poem on that account. Lady Byron was renowned for her expertise at mathematics, classical literature and philosophy.

[22] *All Calderon . . . Lopé* Pedro Calderón de la Barca (1600–81) and Lopé de Vega (1562–1635) were Spanish playwrights.

[23] Gregor von Feinagle (1765–1819) devised a system of mnemonics, on which he lectured in England and Scotland in 1811.

[24] *Her favourite science . . . mathematical* Byron used to call his wife the Princess of Parallelograms.

[25] Attic wit is refined, delicate, and piquant.

In short, in all things she was fairly what I call
A prodigy – her morning dress was dimity,[26]
Her evening silk or, in the summer, muslin
(And other stuffs with which I won't stay puzzling).

13

She knew the Latin – that is, the Lord's prayer,
And Greek – the alphabet, I'm nearly sure;
She read some French romances here and there,
Although her mode of speaking was not pure;
For native Spanish she had no great care
(At least her conversation was obscure);
Her thoughts were theorems, her words a problem,
As if she deemed that mystery would ennoble 'em.

14

She liked the English and the Hebrew tongue,
And said there was analogy between 'em;
She proved it somehow out of sacred song,
But I must leave the proofs to those who've seen 'em;
But this I heard her say, and can't be wrong,
And all may think which way their judgments lean 'em,
''Tis strange; the Hebrew noun which means "I am",
The English always use to govern damn.'[27]

15

Some women use their tongues; she looked a lecture,
Each eye a sermon, and her brow a homily,
An all-in-all-sufficient self-director
Like the lamented late Sir Samuel Romilly,[28]
The law's expounder and the state's corrector[29]
Whose suicide was almost an anomaly –
One sad example more that 'All is vanity';[30]
The jury brought their verdict in: insanity.

16

In short, she was a walking calculation,
Miss Edgeworth's[31] novels stepping from their covers,
Or Mrs Trimmer's books on education,[32]

Notes

[26] *dimity* stout cotton fabric; said by Thomas Moore to have been Lady Byron's favourite dress material.

[27] *'Tis strange . . . damn* 'damn' was spelt 'd–n' in the first edition. Yahweh ('I am' in Hebrew) indicates God; see Exodus 3: 13–14.

[28] *the lamented late Sir Samuel Romilly* bitterly ironic. Romilly (1757–1818) sided with Lady Byron when she separated from her husband, earning Byron's lasting hatred. After Romilly's suicide, Byron commented: 'I still loathe him as much as we can hate dust – but that is nothing' (Marchand vi 150).

[29] *the state's corrector* Romilly had been MP for Westminster.

[30] *All is vanity* Ecclesiastes 1: 2: 'Vanity of vanities, saith the Preacher, vanity of vanities; all is vanity.'

[31] Maria Edgeworth (1767–1849) wrote educational volumes for children, including *The Parent's Assistant* (1796) and *Practical Education* (co-authored with her father, Richard Lovell Edgeworth) (1798). She was also a distinguished novelist.

[32] Sarah Trimmer (1741–1810) wrote a number of exemplary tales and moral lessons for children, including *An Easy Introduction to the Knowledge of Nature* (1790) and *Instructive Tales* (1810).

Or 'Coeleb's Wife' set out in search of lovers,[33]
Morality's prim personification
In which not envy's self a flaw discovers:
To others' share let 'female errors fall',[34]
For she had not even one – the worst of all.

17

Oh she was perfect past all parallel
Of any modern female saint's comparison;
So far beyond the cunning powers of hell,
Her guardian angel had given up his garrison;
Even her minutest motions went as well
As those of the best timepiece made by Harrison;[35]
In virtues nothing earthly could surpass her,
Save thine 'incomparable oil', Macassar![36]

18

Perfect she was, but as perfection is
Insipid in this naughty world of ours,
Where our first parents[37] never learned to kiss
Till they were exiled from their earlier bowers,[38]
Where all was peace and innocence and bliss
(I wonder how they got through the twelve hours) –
Don Jóse, like a lineal son of Eve,
Went plucking various fruit without her leave.

19

He was a mortal of the careless kind
With no great love for learning or the learned,
Who chose to go where'er he had a mind,
And never dreamed his lady was concerned;
The world, as usual, wickedly inclined
To see a kingdom or a house o'erturned,
Whispered he had a mistress, some said *two* –
But for domestic quarrels *one* will do.

Notes

[33] Hannah More was famous in 1819 as the author of a monstrously successful didactic novel, *Coelebs in Search of a Wife* (1808), which had gone to a twelfth edition by the end of 1809.

[34] *female errors fall* an allusion to Pope, *The Rape of the Lock* ii 17–18: 'If to her share some female errors fall, / Look on her face, and you'll forget 'em all.'

[35] John Harrison (1693–1776), eminent horologist of the day.

[36] *thine 'incomparable oil', Macassar* Macassar oil was a tonic for the follicles advertised in hyperbolic terms that gave Byron and his cronies much amusement; see, for example, the front page of *The Courier*, 2 January 1809: 'Macassar oil, for the growth of HAIR. The virtues of this oil, extracted from a tree in the island of Macassar, are proudly pre-eminent to anything ever produced in this or any other country, for improving and accelerating the growth of hair, preventing it falling off, or turning grey, giving it an incomparable gloss, and producing wonderful effects on children's hair. Its virtues need only the test of experience to evince its extraordinary effects.' Byron was using Macassar oil as he composed *Don Juan* (Marchand vi 137).

[37] *our first parents* Adam and Eve.

[38] Adam and Eve had children only after being cast out of Paradise.

20

Now Donna Inez had, with all her merit,
  A great opinion of her own good qualities;
Neglect, indeed, requires a saint to bear it –
  And so indeed, she was in her moralities;
But then she had a devil of a spirit,
  And sometimes mixed up fancies with realities,
And let few opportunities escape
Of getting her liege-lord into a scrape.

21

This was an easy matter with a man
  Oft in the wrong and never on his guard;
And even the wisest, do the best they can,
  Have moments, hours, and days, so unprepared
That you might 'brain them with their lady's fan',[39]
  And sometimes ladies hit exceeding hard,
And fans turn into falchions[40] in fair hands,
And why and wherefore no one understands.

22

'Tis pity learned virgins ever wed
  With persons of no sort of education,
Or gentlemen who, though well-born and bred,
  Grow tired of scientific conversation.
I don't choose to say much upon this head;
  I'm a plain man and in a single station,
But oh, ye lords of ladies intellectual,[41]
Inform us truly, have they not hen-pecked you all?

23

Don Jóse and his lady quarrelled – *why*
  Not any of the many could divine,
Though several thousand people chose to try,
  'Twas surely no concern of theirs nor mine;
I loathe that low vice curiosity,
  But if there's anything in which I shine,
'Tis in arranging all my friends' affairs –
Not having, of my own, domestic cares.

24

And so I interfered, and with the best
  Intentions, but their treatment was not kind;
I think the foolish people were possessed,
  For neither of them could I ever find,
Although their porter afterwards confessed –
  But that's no matter, and the worst's behind,
For little Juan o'er me threw, downstairs,
A pail of housemaid's water, unawares.

Notes

[39] *brain them with their lady's fan* Hotspur's comment at *1 Henry IV* II iii 22–3: 'Zounds, and I were now by this rascal, I could brain him with his lady's fan.'

[40] *falchions* broad swords.

[41] *ladies intellectual* a reference to Bluestocking circles of Byron's day, which included Lady Caroline Lamb, Lady Oxford and Annabella Milbanke.

25

A little curly-headed, good-for-nothing,
And mischief-making monkey from his birth;
His parents ne'er agreed except in doting
Upon the most unquiet imp on earth;
Instead of quarrelling, had they been but both in
Their senses, they'd have sent young master forth
To school, or had him soundly whipped at home
To teach him manners for the time to come.

26

Don Jóse and the Donna Inez led
For some time an unhappy sort of life,
Wishing each other not divorced but dead;
They lived respectably as man and wife,
Their conduct was exceedingly well-bred,
And gave no outward signs of inward strife –
Until at length the smothered fire broke out,
And put the business past all kind of doubt.

27

For Inez called some druggists and physicians[42]
And tried to prove her loving lord was mad,[43]
But as he had some lucid intermissions,
She next decided he was only bad;
Yet when they asked her for her depositions,[44]
No sort of explanation could be had,
Save that her duty both to man and God
Required this conduct (which seemed very odd).

28

She kept a journal where his faults were noted
And opened certain trunks of books and letters –
All which might, if occasion served, be quoted;
And then she had all Seville for abettors,
Besides her good old grandmother (who doted);
The hearers of her case became repeaters,
Then advocates, inquisitors, and judges –
Some for amusement, others for old grudges.[45]

29

And then this best and meekest woman bore
With such serenity her husband's woes,
Just as the Spartan ladies did of yore
Who saw their spouses killed, and nobly chose

Notes

[42] *druggists and physicians* chemists and doctors.

[43] *And tried to prove . . . was mad* Byron believed his wife had tried to prove him mad.

[44] *depositions* statements, testimony (that he was mad).

[45] This is a description of the whispering campaign conducted against Byron by his wife.

Never to say a word about them more;
Calmly she heard each calumny that rose,
And saw his agonies with such sublimity
That all the world exclaimed 'What magnanimity!'

30

No doubt this patience, when the world is damning us,
Is philosophic in our former friends;
'Tis also pleasant to be deemed magnanimous
(The more so in obtaining our own ends);
And what the lawyers call a *malus animus*,[46]
Conduct like this by no means comprehends:[47]
Revenge in person's certainly no virtue,
But then 'tis not *my* fault, if *others* hurt you.

31

And if our quarrels should rip up old stories
And help them with a lie or two additional,
I'm not to blame, as you well know, no more is
Anyone else – they were become traditional;
Besides, their resurrection aids our glories
By contrast, which is what we just were wishing all:
And science profits by this resurrection –
Dead scandals form good subjects for dissection.

32

Their friends[48] had tried at reconciliation,
Then their relations[49] who made matters worse
('Twere hard to say upon a like occasion
To whom it may be best to have recourse;
I can't say much for friend or yet relation);
The lawyers did their utmost for divorce
But scarce a fee was paid on either side
Before, unluckily, Don Jóse died.

33

He died – and most unluckily, because,
According to all hints I could collect
From counsel[50] learned in those kinds of laws
(Although their talk's obscure and circumspect),
His death contrived to spoil a charming cause:
A thousand pities also with respect
To public feeling, which on this occasion
Was manifested in a great sensation.

Notes

[46] *malus animus* bad intent.

[47] *comprehends* comprises.

[48] *friends* in Byron's case, Hobhouse, Rogers and Madame de Staël.

[49] *relations* in Byron's case, his sister Augusta, and cousin George Anson Byron (who ended up supporting Lady Byron).

[50] *counsel* body of legal advisers.

34
But ah, he died – and buried with him lay
The public feeling and the lawyers' fees;
His house was sold, his servants sent away,
A Jew took one of his two mistresses,
A priest the other (at least so they say).
I asked the doctors after his disease:
He died of the slow fever called the tertian[51]
And left his widow to her own aversion.

35
Yes, Jóse was an honourable man[52] –
That I must say, who knew him very well;
Therefore his frailties I'll no further scan
(Indeed there were not many more to tell),
And if his passions now and then outran
Discretion, and were not so peaceable
As Numa's (who was also named Pompilius),[53]
He had been ill brought up, and was born bilious.[54]

36
Whate'er might be his worthlessness or worth,
Poor fellow, he had many things to wound him,
Let's own, since it can do no good on earth;
It was a trying moment that which found him
Standing alone beside his desolate hearth
Where all his household gods lay shivered[55] round him;
No choice was left his feelings or his pride
Save death or Doctors' Commons[56] – so he died.

37
Dying intestate, Juan was sole heir
To a chancery-suit[57] and messuages[58] and lands
Which, with a long minority and care,
Promised to turn out well in proper hands;
Inez became sole guardian (which was fair)
And answered but to nature's just demands;
An only son left with an only mother
Is brought up much more wisely than another.

38
Sagest of women, even of widows, she
Resolved that Juan should be quite a paragon
And worthy of the noblest pedigree

Notes

[51] *the slow fever called the tertian* tertian fever progresses slowly because it strikes only every other day.

[52] *an honourable man* an echo of Antony's attack on Brutus and the assassins of Caesar, *Julius Caesar* III ii 82–3.

[53] The 43-year reign of Numa, second king of Rome, was known for its peaceability.

[54] *bilious* ill-tempered.

[55] *shivered* shattered.

[56] *Doctors' Commons* divorce courts.

[57] *chancery-suit* legal claim for property.

[58] *messuages* dwelling-place with adjoining lands.

(His sire was of Castile, his dam from Aragon).
Then for accomplishments of chivalry,
In case our lord the king should go to war again,
He learned the arts of riding, fencing, gunnery,
And how to scale a fortress – or a nunnery.

39

But that which Donna Inez most desired,
And saw into herself each day before all
The learned tutors whom for him she hired,
Was that his breeding should be strictly moral;
Much into all his studies she enquired,
And so they were submitted first to her, all,
Arts, sciences – no branch was made a mystery
To Juan's eyes, excepting natural history.

40

The languages (especially the dead),[59]
The sciences (and most of all the abstruse),
The arts (at least all such as could be said
To be the most remote from common use) –
In all these he was much and deeply read;
But not a page of anything that's loose[60]
Or hints continuation of the species
Was ever suffered, lest he should grow vicious.[61]

41

His classic studies made a little puzzle
Because of filthy loves of gods and goddesses
Who in the earlier ages made a bustle,
But never put on pantaloons or bodices;
His reverend tutors had at times a tussle,
And for their *Aeneids*, *Iliads*, and *Odysseys*,
Were forced to make an odd sort of apology –
For Donna Inez dreaded the mythology.

42

Ovid's a rake, as half his verses show him,
Anacreon's morals are a still worse sample,
Catullus scarcely has a decent poem,
I don't think Sappho's 'Ode' a good example,
Although Longinus tells us there is no hymn
Where the sublime soars forth on wings more ample;
But Virgil's songs are pure, except that horrid one
Beginning with *Formosum pastor Corydon*.[62]

Notes

59 *The languages (especially the dead)* i.e. Latin and Greek.

60 *loose* wanton, immoral.

61 *vicious* immoral, depraved.

62 *Ovid's a rake . . . Corydon* Byron lists erotic poets and poems, including Sappho's 'Ode to Aphrodite', Ovid's *Amores* and *Ars Amatoria*, the love-songs of Anacreon and Catullus, and Virgil's *Eclogue* ii (dealing with pederastic love).

43

Lucretius' irreligion[63] is too strong
For early stomachs, to prove wholesome food;
I can't help thinking Juvenal was wrong
(Although no doubt his real intent was good)
For speaking out so plainly in his song –
So much indeed as to be downright rude;[64]
And then what proper person can be partial
To all those nauseous epigrams of Martial?[65]

44

Juan was taught from out the best edition,
Expurgated by learned men who place
Judiciously, from out the schoolboy's vision,
The grosser parts; but fearful to deface
Too much their modest bard by this omission,
And pitying sore his mutilated case,
They only add them all in an appendix[66] –
Which saves, in fact, the trouble of an index;

45

For there we have them all at one fell swoop,
Instead of being scattered through the pages;
They stand forth marshalled in a handsome troop
To meet the ingenuous youth of future ages,
Till some less rigid editor shall stoop
To call them back into their separate cages,
Instead of standing staring altogether
Like garden gods – and not so decent either.

46

The missal[67] too (it was the family missal)
Was ornamented in a sort of way
Which ancient mass-books often are, and this all
Kinds of grotesques illumined; and how they,
Who saw those figures on the margin kiss all,
Could turn their optics[68] to the text and pray
Is more than I know – but Don Juan's mother
Kept this herself, and gave her son another.

47

Sermons he read and lectures he endured,
And homilies and lives of all the saints;
To Jerome and to Chrysostom[69] inured,

Notes

[63] *Lucretius' irreligion* In *De rerum natura*, Lucretius attempted to show that the course of world history had taken place without divine intervention.

[64] *downright rude* Juvenal portrayed the vices and depravities of Roman society.

[65] *Martial* Roman epigrammatist, witty and indecent.

[66] 'Fact. There is, or was, such an edition, with all the obnoxious epigrams of Martial placed by themselves at the end' (Byron's note).

[67] *missal* Roman Catholic prayer book containing masses for each day of the year.

[68] *optics* eyes.

[69] Jerome and Chrysostom were early Christian theologians.

He did not take such studies for restraints;
But how faith is acquired and then insured,
So well not one of the aforesaid paints
As St Augustine in his fine *Confessions* –
Which make the reader envy his transgressions.[70]

48

This too was a sealed book to little Juan –
I can't but say that his mamma was right,
If such an education was the true one.
She scarcely trusted him from out her sight;
Her maids were old, and if she took a new one
You might be sure she was a perfect fright;
She did this during even her husband's life –
I recommend as much to every wife.

49

Young Juan waxed[71] in goodliness and grace;
At six a charming child, and at eleven
With all the promise of as fine a face
As e'er to man's maturer growth was given.
He studied steadily and grew apace
And seemed, at least, in the right road to heaven –
For half his days were passed at church, the other
Between his tutors, confessor, and mother.

50

At six, I said, he was a charming child,
At twelve he was a fine but quiet boy;
Although in infancy a little wild,
They tamed him down amongst them; to destroy
His natural spirit not in vain they toiled
(At least it seemed so); and his mother's joy
Was to declare how sage and still and steady
Her young philosopher was grown already.

51

I had my doubts – perhaps I have them still,
But what I say is neither here nor there;
I knew his father well, and have some skill
In character, but it would not be fair
From sire to son to augur good or ill;
He and his wife were an ill-sorted pair –
But scandal's my aversion, I protest
Against all evil speaking, even in jest.

Notes

[70] *his transgressions* i.e. as committed in his early life.

[71] *waxed* grew. There seems to be an echo of Christ: 'And the child grew, and waxed strong in spirit, filled with wisdom: and the grace of God was upon him' (Luke 2:40).

52

For my part I say nothing – nothing – but
This I will say (my reasons are my own):
That if I had an only son to put
To school (as God be praised that I have none),
'Tis not with Donna Inez I would shut
Him up to learn his catechism alone –
No, no; I'd send him out betimes to college,
For there it was I picked up my own knowledge.

53

For there one learns – 'tis not for me to boast,
Though I acquired – but I pass over *that*,
As well as all the Greek I since have lost;
I say that there's the place – but *Verbum sat*;[72]
I think I picked up too, as well as most,
Knowledge of matters – but no matter *what* –
I never married – but I think, I know,
That sons should not be educated so.

54

Young Juan now was sixteen years of age –
Tall, handsome, slender, but well-knit; he seemed
Active, though not so sprightly, as a page,
And everybody but his mother deemed
Him almost man. But she flew in a rage
And bit her lips (for else she might have screamed)
If any said so – for to be precocious
Was in her eyes a thing the most atrocious.

55

Amongst her numerous acquaintance, all
Selected for discretion and devotion,
There was the Donna Julia, whom to call
Pretty were but to give a feeble notion
Of many charms in her as natural
As sweetness to the flower, or salt to ocean,
Her zone to Venus,[73] or his bow to Cupid
(But this last simile is trite and stupid).

56

The darkness of her oriental eye
Accorded with her Moorish origin
(Her blood was not all Spanish, by the by –
In Spain, you know, this is a sort of sin);
When proud Granada fell and, forced to fly,

Notes

72 *Verbum sat* 'a word [to the wise] is enough'.

73 Venus' girdle ('zone') would make the wearer fall in love.

Boabdil wept,[74] of Donna Julia's kin
Some went to Africa, some stayed in Spain;
Her great-great-grandmamma chose to remain.

57

She married (I forget the pedigree)
With an hidalgo, who transmitted down
His blood less noble than such blood should be;
At such alliances his sires would frown,
In that point so precise in each degree
That they bred *in and in*, as might be shown,
Marrying their cousins – nay, their aunts and nieces,
Which always spoils the breed, if it increases.

58

This heathenish cross restored the breed again,
Ruined its blood, but much improved its flesh;
For from a root the ugliest in old Spain
Sprung up a branch as beautiful as fresh –
The sons no more were short, the daughters plain
(But there's a rumour which I fain would hush:
'Tis said that Donna Julia's grandmamma
Produced her Don more heirs at love than law).

59

However this might be, the race[75] went on
Improving still through every generation
Until it centred in an only son
Who left an only daughter; my narration
May have suggested that this single one
Could be but Julia (whom on this occasion
I shall have much to speak about), and she
Was married, charming, chaste, and twenty-three.

60

Her eye (I'm very fond of handsome eyes)
Was large and dark, suppressing half its fire
Until she spoke, then through its soft disguise
Flashed an expression more of pride than ire,
And love than either; and there would arise
A something in them which was not desire,
But would have been, perhaps – but for the soul
Which struggled through and chastened down the whole.

61

Her glossy hair was clustered o'er a brow
Bright with intelligence, and fair and smooth;
Her eyebrow's shape was like the aerial bow,[76]
Her cheek all purple with the beam of youth

Notes

[74] *Boabdil wept* Mohamed XI, last Moorish king of Granada, wept when the city was besieged and surrendered to Spain, 1492.

[75] *race* family.

[76] *the aerial bow* rainbow.

Mounting, at times, to a transparent glow
   As if her veins ran lightning; she, in sooth,
Possessed an air and grace by no means common,
Her stature tall – I hate a dumpy woman.

62

Wedded she was some years, and to a man
   Of fifty – and such husbands are in plenty;
And yet, I think, instead of such a ONE
   'Twere better to have TWO of five and twenty,
Especially in countries near the sun;
   And now I think on't, 'mi vien in mente',[77]
Ladies even of the most uneasy virtue
Prefer a spouse whose age is short of thirty.

63

'Tis a sad thing, I cannot choose but say,
   And all the fault of that indecent sun
Who cannot leave alone our helpless clay,[78]
   But will keep baking, broiling, burning on,
That howsoever people fast and pray
   The flesh is frail,[79] and so the soul undone;
What men call gallantry, and gods adultery,
Is much more common where the climate's sultry.

64

Happy the nations of the moral north!
   Where all is virtue, and the winter season
Sends sin, without a rag on, shivering forth
   ('Twas snow that brought St Francis back to reason[80]);
Where juries cast up what a wife is worth
   By laying whate'er sum, in mulct,[81] they please on
The lover, who must pay a handsome price,
Because it is a marketable vice.

65

Alfonso was the name of Julia's lord –
   A man well looking for his years and who
Was neither much beloved nor yet abhorred;
   They lived together as most people do,
Suffering each other's foibles by accord,
   And not exactly either *one* or *two*;
Yet he was jealous, though he did not show it,
For jealousy dislikes the world to know it.

Notes

[77] *mi vien in mente* 'it occurs to me'.
[78] *clay* i.e. flesh.
[79] *The flesh is frail* Matthew 26: 41: 'the spirit indeed is willing, but the flesh is weak.'
[80] St Francis had a 'wife of snow', according to Jacobus de Voragine's *Golden Legend*, containing the 'Life of St Francis'.
[81] *mulct* penalty.

66

Julia was (yet I never could see why)
With Donna Inez quite a favourite friend;
Between their tastes there was small sympathy,
For not a line had Julia ever penned;
Some people whisper (but no doubt they lie,
For malice still imputes some private end)
That Inez had, ere Don Alfonso's marriage,
Forgot with him her very prudent carriage,[82]

67

And that still keeping up the old connection,
Which time had lately rendered much more chaste,
She took his lady also in affection,
And certainly this course was much the best.
She flattered Julia with her sage protection
And complimented Don Alfonso's taste,
And if she could not (who can?) silence scandal,
At least she left it a more slender handle.

68

I can't tell whether Julia saw the affair
With other people's eyes, or if her own
Discoveries made, but none could be aware
Of this; at least no symptom e'er was shown.
Perhaps she did not know, or did not care,
Indifferent from the first, or callous grown;
I'm really puzzled what to think or say –
She kept her counsel in so close a way.

69

Juan she saw and, as a pretty child,
Caressed him often – such a thing might be
Quite innocently done, and harmless styled,
When she had twenty years and thirteen he;
But I am not so sure I should have smiled
When he was sixteen, Julia twenty-three
(These few short years make wondrous alterations,
Particularly amongst sunburnt nations).

70

Whate'er the cause might be, they had become
Changed; for the dame grew distant, the youth shy,
Their looks cast down, their greetings almost dumb,

Notes

[82] *carriage* social behaviour, conduct.

  And much embarrassment in either eye.
There surely will be little doubt with some
  That Donna Julia knew the reason why;
But as for Juan, he had no more notion
Than he who never saw the sea of ocean.

71

Yet Julia's very coldness still was kind,
  And tremulously gentle her small hand
Withdrew itself from his, but left behind
  A little pressure, thrilling, and so bland[83]
And slight, so very slight, that to the mind
  'Twas but a doubt – but ne'er magician's wand
Wrought change with all Armida's[84] fairy art
Like what this light touch left on Juan's heart.

72

And if she met him, though she smiled no more,
  She looked a sadness sweeter than her smile,
As if her heart had deeper thoughts in store
  She must not own, but cherished more the while,
For that compression in its burning core;
  Even innocence itself has many a wile
And will not dare to trust itself with truth –
And love is taught hypocrisy from youth.

73

But passion most dissembles yet betrays
  Even by its darkness; as the blackest sky
Foretells the heaviest tempest, it displays
  Its workings through the vainly guarded eye,
And in whatever aspect it arrays
  Itself, 'tis still the same hypocrisy;
Coldness or anger, even disdain or hate
Are masks it often wears, and still too late.

74

Then there were sighs, the deeper for suppression,
  And stolen glances, sweeter for the theft,
And burning blushes, though for no transgression,
  Tremblings when met, and restlessness when left;
All these are little preludes to possession
  Of which young passion cannot be bereft,
And merely tend to show how greatly love is
Embarrassed at first starting with a novice.

Notes

[83] *bland* soothing.

[84] Armida is the sorceress in Tasso, *Jerusalem Delivered*, who ensnares the hero, Rinaldo.

75

Poor Julia's heart was in an awkward state –
She felt it going, and resolved to make
The noblest efforts for herself and mate,
For honour's, pride's, religion's, virtue's sake;
Her resolutions were most truly great
And almost might have made a Tarquin quake;[85]
She prayed the Virgin Mary for her grace,
As being the best judge of a lady's case.

76

She vowed she never would see Juan more
And next day paid a visit to his mother,
And looked extremely at the opening door
Which, by the Virgin's grace, let in another;
Grateful she was, and yet a little sore;
Again it opens, it can be no other,
'Tis surely Juan now – no! I'm afraid
That night the Virgin was no further prayed.

77

She now determined that a virtuous woman
Should rather face and overcome temptation,
That flight was base and dastardly, and no man
Should ever give her heart the least sensation –
That is to say, a thought beyond the common
Preference, that we must feel upon occasion
For people who are pleasanter than others,
But then they only seem so many brothers.

78

And even if by chance (and who can tell?
The Devil's so very sly) she should discover
That all within was not so very well,
And if still free, that such or such a lover
Might please perhaps, a virtuous wife can quell
Such thoughts and be the better when they're over;
And if the man should ask, 'tis but denial:
I recommend young ladies to make trial.

79

And then there are things such as love divine,
Bright and immaculate, unmixed and pure,
Such as the angels think so very fine,
And matrons who would be no less secure,

Notes

[85] *Her resolutions . . . quake* The comparison is with Lucretia, legendary heroine of ancient Rome, the beautiful and virtuous wife of the nobleman Lucius Tarquinius Collatinus. She was raped by Sextus Tarquinus, and later stabbed herself to death.

Platonic, perfect, 'just such love as mine',
Thus Julia said, and thought so, to be sure –
And so I'd have her think, were I the man
On whom her reveries celestial ran.

80

Such love is innocent, and may exist
Between young persons without any danger;
A hand may first, and then a lip be kissed –
For my part, to such doings I'm a stranger,
But *hear* these freedoms form the utmost list[86]
Of all o'er which such love may be a ranger;
If people go beyond, 'tis quite a crime
But not my fault – I tell them all in time.

81

Love then, but love within its proper limits
Was Julia's innocent determination
In young Don Juan's favour, and to him its
Exertion might be useful on occasion;
And lighted at too pure a shrine to dim its
Ethereal lustre, with what sweet persuasion
He might be taught by love and her together –
I really don't know what, nor Julia either.

82

Fraught with this fine intention, and well-fenced[87]
In mail of proof[88] – her purity of soul,
She, for the future of her strength convinced,
And that her honour was a rock, or mole,[89]
Exceeding sagely from that hour dispensed
With any kind of troublesome control;
But whether Julia to the task was equal
Is that which must be mentioned in the sequel.[90]

83

Her plan she deemed both innocent and feasible,
And surely with a stripling of sixteen
Not scandal's fangs could fix on much that's seizable,
Or if they did so, satisfied to mean
Nothing but what was good, her breast was peaceable –
A quiet conscience makes one so serene!
Christians have burnt each other, quite persuaded
That all the Apostles would have done as they did.

Notes

86 *list* territory.

87 *well-fenced* well-protected.

88 *mail of proof* good-quality chain mail; but the usage is metaphorical.

89 *mole* great immovable mass.

90 *the sequel* i.e. what follows.

84

And if in the meantime her husband died –
But heaven forbid that such a thought should cross
Her brain, though in a dream! And then she sighed;
Never could she survive that common loss,
But just suppose that moment should betide –
I only say suppose it, *inter nos*[91]
(This should be *entre nous*, for Julia thought
In French, but then the rhyme would go for nought),

85

I only say suppose this supposition:
Juan being then grown up to man's estate[92]
Would fully suit a widow of condition[93] –
Even seven years hence it would not be too late;
And in the interim (to pursue this vision)
The mischief, after all, could not be great,
For he would learn the rudiments of love
(I mean the seraph[94] way of those above).

86

So much for Julia. Now we'll turn to Juan –
Poor little fellow, he had no idea
Of his own case, and never hit the true one;
In feelings quick as Ovid's Miss Medea,[95]
He puzzled over what he found a new one,
But not as yet imagined it could be a
Thing quite in course, and not at all alarming
Which, with a little patience, might grow charming.

87

Silent and pensive, idle, restless, slow,
His home deserted for the lonely wood,
Tormented with a wound he could not know,
His, like all deep grief, plunged in solitude;
I'm fond myself of solitude or so,
But then I beg it may be understood –
By solitude I mean a sultan's, not
A hermit's, with a harem for a grot.

88

'Oh love, in such a wilderness as this,
Where transport and security entwine,
Here is the empire of thy perfect bliss,
And here thou art a god indeed divine!'[96]

Notes

[91] *inter nos* between us.

[92] *man's estate* i.e. manhood.

[93] *of condition* of quality.

[94] Seraphs are angels whose purpose is to adore God.

[95] *Ovid's Miss Medea* Medea felt a sudden, overpowering love for Jason, leader of the famous Argonauts, in Ovid, *Metamorphoses* vii 9–10.

[96] Campbell, *Gertrude of Wyoming* iii 1–4. Campbell was one of the few poets of his time that Byron admired (see headnote p. 838).

The bard I quote from does not sing amiss,
With the exception of the second line –
For that same twining 'transport and security'
Are twisted to a phrase of some obscurity.

89

The poet meant, no doubt (and thus appeals
To the good sense and senses of mankind),
The very thing which everybody feels,
As all have found on trial, or may find –
That no one likes to be disturbed at meals
Or love. I won't say more about 'entwined'
Or 'transport', as we knew all that before,
But beg 'security' will bolt the door.

90

Young Juan wandered by the glassy brooks
Thinking unutterable things; he threw
Himself at length within the leafy nooks
Where the wild branch of the cork forest grew;
There poets find materials for their books,
And every now and then we read them through
So that[97] their plan and prosody are eligible –
Unless, like Wordsworth, they prove unintelligible.[98]

91

He, Juan (and not Wordsworth[99]), so pursued
His self-communion with his own high soul,
Until his mighty heart[100] in its great mood
Had mitigated part (though not the whole)
Of its disease; he did the best he could
With things not very subject to control,
And turned, without perceiving his condition,
Like Coleridge, into a metaphysician.

92

He thought about himself, and the whole earth,
Of man the wonderful, and of the stars,
And how the deuce they ever could have birth;
And then he thought of earthquakes and of wars,
How many miles the moon might have in girth,
Of air-balloons,[101] and of the many bars[102]
To perfect knowledge of the boundless skies –
And then he thought of Donna Julia's eyes.

Notes

[97] *So that* so long as.

[98] *Unlike . . . unintelligible* another gibe at *The Excursion* (1814), mocked for incomprehensibility in the Dedication, stanza 4, above.

[99] *and not Wordsworth* somewhat disingenuous, as Byron is using Juan's love-sickness to burlesque Wordsworthian responses to nature.

[100] *mighty heart* The phrase is borrowed from Wordsworth, *Composed upon Westminster Bridge, 3 September 1802* 14: 'And all that mighty heart is lying still.'

[101] *air-balloons* Hot-air balloons were the invention of Joseph Michel Montgolfier, 1783. They were all the rage across Europe at this time.

[102] *bars* barriers.

93

In thoughts like these true wisdom may discern
Longings sublime and aspirations high,
Which some are born with, but the most part learn
To plague themselves withal, they know not why;
'Twas strange that one so young should thus concern
His brain about the action of the sky:
If you think 'twas philosophy that this did,
I can't help thinking puberty assisted.

94

He pored upon the leaves and on the flowers,
And heard a voice in all the winds; and then
He thought of wood-nymphs and immortal bowers,
And how the goddesses came down to men:
He missed the pathway, he forgot the hours,
And when he looked upon his watch again,
He found how much old Time had been a winner –
He also found that he had lost his dinner.

95

Sometimes he turned to gaze upon his book,
Boscan or Garcilasso;[103] by the wind
Even as the page is rustled while we look,
So by the poesy of his own mind
Over the mystic leaf his soul was shook,
As if 'twere one whereon magicians bind
Their spells, and give them to the passing gale,
According to some good old woman's tale.

96

Thus would he while his lonely hours away
Dissatisfied, nor knowing what he wanted;
Nor[104] glowing reverie, nor poet's lay
Could yield his spirit that for which it panted,
A bosom whereon he his head might lay,
And hear the heart beat with the love it granted,
With – several other things which I forget,
Or which, at least, I need not mention yet.

97

Those lonely walks and lengthening reveries
Could not escape the gentle Julia's eyes;
She saw that Juan was not at his ease;

Notes

[103] *Boscan or Garcilasso* Juan Boscán Almogáver (d. c.1543) and Garcilaso de la Vega, sixteenth-century Spanish poets who introduced Italian features into their literature through their imitations of Petrarch.

[104] *Nor* neither.

But that which chiefly may, and must surprise
Is that the Donna Inez did not tease
Her only son with question or surmise –
Whether it was she did not see or would not,
Or like all very clever people, could not.

98

This may seem strange, but yet 'tis very common;
For instance, gentlemen, whose ladies take
Leave to o'erstep the written rights of woman,
And break the – which commandment is't they break?[105]
I have forgot the number, and think no man
Should rashly quote, for fear of a mistake.
I say, when these same gentlemen are jealous,
They make some blunder which their ladies tell us.

99

A real husband always is suspicious,
But still no less suspects in the wrong place,
Jealous of someone who had no such wishes,[106]
Or pandering blindly to his own disgrace
By harbouring some dear friend extremely vicious[107] –
The last indeed's infallibly the case,
And when the spouse and friend are gone off wholly,[108]
He wonders at their vice, and not his folly.

100

Thus parents also are at times short-sighted;
Though watchful as the lynx, they ne'er discover
(The while the wicked world beholds delighted)
Young Hopeful's mistress or Miss Fanny's lover,
Till some confounded escapade has blighted
The plan of twenty years, and all is over;
And then the mother cries, the father swears,
And wonders why the devil he got[109] heirs.

101

But Inez was so anxious and so clear
Of sight, that I must think on this occasion
She had some other motive much more near
For leaving Juan to this new temptation;
But what that motive was I shan't say here –
Perhaps to finish Juan's education,
Perhaps to open Don Alfonso's eyes
In case he thought his wife too great a prize.

Notes

105 *which commandment is't they break* 'Thou shalt not commit adultery' (Exodus 20: 14).

106 *no such wishes* i.e. to commit adultery.

107 *vicious* immoral. The husband makes the mistake of unwittingly welcoming a friend who is having an affair with his wife.

108 *are gone off wholly* i.e. have run away together.

109 *got* conceived.

102

It was upon a day, a summer's day –
   Summer's indeed a very dangerous season,
And so is spring about the end of May;
   The sun, no doubt, is the prevailing reason;
But whatsoe'er the cause is, one may say
   (And stand convicted of more truth than treason),
That there are months which nature grows more merry in;
March has its hares, and May must have its heroine.

103

'Twas on a summer's day, the sixth of June –
   I like to be particular in dates,
Not only of the age and year, but moon;
   They are a sort of post-house[110] where the Fates[111]
Change horses, making history change its tune,
   Then spur away o'er empires and o'er states,
Leaving at last not much besides chronology,
Excepting the post-obits[112] of theology.

104

'Twas on the sixth of June, about the hour
   Of half-past six – perhaps still nearer seven,
When Julia sat within as pretty a bower
   As e'er held houri[113] in that heathenish heaven
Described by Mahomet and 'Anacreon' Moore[114] –
   To whom the lyre and laurels have been given
With all the trophies of triumphant song;
He won them well, and may he wear them long!

105

She sat, but not alone; I know not well
   How this same interview had taken place,
And even if I knew, I should not tell –
   People should hold their tongues in any case;
No matter how or why the thing befell,
   But there were she and Juan, face to face –
When two such faces are so, 'twould be wise
(But very difficult) to shut their eyes.

106

How beautiful she looked! Her conscious heart
   Glowed in her cheek, and yet she felt no wrong.
Oh love, how perfect is thy mystic art,
   Strengthening the weak, and trampling on the strong;
How self-deceitful is the sagest part

Notes

[110] *post-house* inn where horses are kept for the use of travellers.

[111] In Greek myth, the Fates were three goddesses who determined the course of human life.

[112] *post-obits* legacies.

[113] *houri* nymph of the Muslim heaven.

[114] *'Anacreon' Moore* Thomas Moore translated a set of 'anacreontic' poems (first printed in 1554) of unknown origin. It was one of his most successful publications.

Of mortals whom thy lure hath led along;
The precipice she stood on was immense –
So was her creed[115] in her own innocence.

107

She thought of her own strength,[116] and Juan's youth,
And of the folly of all prudish fears,
Victorious virtue and domestic truth –
And then of Don Alfonso's fifty years:
I wish these last had not occurred, in sooth,
Because that number rarely much endears,
And through all climes, the snowy and the sunny,
Sounds ill in love, whate'er it may in money.

108

When people say, 'I've told you *fifty* times',
They mean to scold, and very often do;
When poets say, 'I've written *fifty* rhymes',
They make you dread that they'll recite them too;
In gangs of *fifty*, thieves commit their crimes;
At *fifty* love for love is rare, 'tis true –
But then, no doubt, it equally as true is,
A good deal may be bought for *fifty* louis.[117]

109

Julia had honour, virtue, truth and love
For Don Alfonso, and she inly swore
By all the vows below to powers above
She never would disgrace the ring she wore,
Nor leave a wish which wisdom might reprove;
And while she pondered this, besides much more,
One hand on Juan's carelessly was thrown
Quite by mistake – she thought it was her own;

110

Unconsciously she leaned upon the other
Which played within the tangles of her hair;[118]
And to contend with thoughts she could not smother,
She seemed by the distraction of her air.
'Twas surely very wrong in Juan's mother
To leave together this imprudent pair,
She who for many years had watched her son so –
I'm very certain *mine* would not have done so.

Notes

115 *creed* belief.

116 *strength* i.e. moral strength.

117 *louis* gold coin issued in the reign of Louis XIII and subsequently till that of Louis XVI.

118 *Which played . . . hair* Byron is recalling *Lycidas* 68–9: 'To sport with Amaryllis in the shade, / Or with the tangles of Neaera's hair?'

111

The hand which still held Juan's, by degrees
  Gently but palpably confirmed its grasp,
As if it said 'detain me, if you please';
  Yet there's no doubt she only meant to clasp
His fingers with a pure Platonic squeeze;
  She would have shrunk as from a toad or asp
Had she imagined such a thing could rouse
A feeling dangerous to a prudent spouse.

112

I cannot know what Juan thought of this,
  But what he did is much what you would do;
His young lip thanked it with a grateful kiss,
  And then, abashed at its own joy, withdrew
In deep despair lest he had done amiss –
  Love is so very timid when 'tis new;
She blushed and frowned not, but she strove to speak
And held her tongue, her voice was grown so weak.

113

The sun set and uprose the yellow moon –
  The devil's in the moon for mischief; they
Who called her chaste, methinks began too soon
  Their nomenclature;[119] there is not a day,
The longest, not the twenty-first of June,
  Sees half the business in a wicked way
On which three single hours of moonshine smile –
And then she looks so modest all the while.

114

There is a dangerous silence in that hour,
  A stillness which leaves room for the full soul
To open all itself, without the power
  Of calling wholly back its self-control;
The silver light which, hallowing tree and tower,
  Sheds beauty and deep softness o'er the whole,
Breathes also to the heart, and o'er it throws
A loving languor which is not repose.

115

And Julia sat with Juan, half-embraced
  And half-retiring from the glowing arm,
Which trembled like the bosom where 'twas placed;
  Yet still she must have thought there was no harm,
Or else 'twere easy to withdraw her waist;
  But then the situation had its charm,
And then – God knows what next – I can't go on;
I'm almost sorry that I e'er begun.

Notes

[119] *nomenclature* act of naming things.

116

Oh Plato, Plato! You have paved the way,
With your confounded fantasies, to more
Immoral conduct by the fancied sway
Your system feigns o'er the controlless core
Of human hearts, than all the long array
Of poets and romancers – you're a bore,
A charlatan, a coxcomb, and have been
At best no better than a go-between.

117

And Julia's voice was lost except in sighs,
Until too late for useful conversation;
The tears were gushing from her gentle eyes –
I wish, indeed, they had not had occasion,
But who, alas, can love, and then be wise?
Not that remorse did not oppose temptation,
A little still she strove, and much repented,
And whispering 'I will ne'er consent' – consented.

118

'Tis said that Xerxes[120] offered a reward
To those who could invent him a new pleasure –
Methinks the requisition's rather hard
And must have cost his majesty a treasure;
For my part, I'm a moderate-minded bard,
Fond of a little love (which I call leisure);
I care not for new pleasures, as the old
Are quite enough for me, so they but hold.

119

Oh pleasure, you're indeed a pleasant thing,
Although one must be damned for you, no doubt;
I make a resolution every spring
Of reformation, ere the year run out;
But somehow, this my vestal vow[121] takes wing,
Yet still, I trust, it may be kept throughout:
I'm very sorry, very much ashamed,
And mean, next winter, to be quite reclaimed.

120

Here my chaste muse a liberty must take –
Start not, still chaster reader! She'll be nice hence-
Forward, and there is no great cause to quake;
This liberty is a poetic licence,
Which some irregularity may make

Notes

[120] Xerxes I, king who fought in the Persian Wars, 485–79 BC. Montaigne wrote that he was 'wrapped in all human pleasures . . . [and] offered a prize to anyone who would find him others' ('Of Experience').

[121] *vestal vow* i.e. of chastity.

In the design, and as I have a high sense
Of Aristotle and the rules,[122] 'tis fit
To beg his pardon when I err a bit.

121

This licence is to hope the reader will
Suppose from June the sixth (the fatal day
Without whose epoch my poetic skill
For want of facts would all be thrown away),
But keeping Julia and Don Juan still
In sight, that several months have passed; we'll say
'Twas in November, but I'm not so sure
About the day – the era's more obscure.

122

We'll talk of that anon. 'Tis sweet to hear
At midnight on the blue and moonlit deep
The song and oar of Adria's[123] gondolier
By distance mellowed, o'er the waters sweep;
'Tis sweet to see the evening star appear;
'Tis sweet to listen as the nightwinds creep
From leaf to leaf; 'tis sweet to view on high
The rainbow, based on ocean, span the sky;

123

'Tis sweet to hear the watchdog's honest bark
Bay deep-mouthed welcome as we draw near home;
'Tis sweet to know there is an eye will mark
Our coming, and look brighter when we come;
'Tis sweet to be awkened by the lark
Or lulled by falling waters; sweet the hum
Of bees, the voice of girls, the song of birds,
The lisp of children and their earliest words;

124

Sweet is the vintage, when the showering grapes
In Bacchanal profusion[124] reel to earth
Purple and gushing; sweet are our escapes
From civic revelry to rural mirth;
Sweet to the miser are his glittering heaps;
Sweet to the father is his first-born's birth;
Sweet is revenge – especially to women;
Pillage to soldiers, prize-money[125] to seamen;

Notes

[122] *the rules* Byron is thinking of the *Poetics* (the 'unities'), as suggested by stanza 121.
[123] *Adria* Venice.
[124] *Bacchanal profusion* Bacchus was the Roman name for the god of wine. The individual grapes are, by implication, like drunken revellers.
[125] *prize-money* proceeds from the sale of a captured ship, distributed among the captors.

125

Sweet is a legacy, and passing sweet
The unexpected death of some old lady
Or gentleman of seventy years complete,
Who've made 'us youth'[126] wait too too long already
For an estate or cash or country-seat,
Still breaking, but with stamina so steady,
That all the Israelites[127] are fit to mob its
Next owner for their double-damned post-obits.[128]

126

'Tis sweet to win (no matter how) one's laurels
By blood or ink; 'tis sweet to put an end
To strife; 'tis sometimes sweet to have our quarrels,
Particularly with a tiresome friend;
Sweet is old wine in bottles, ale in barrels;
Dear is the helpless creature we defend
Against the world; and dear the schoolboy spot
We ne'er forget, though there we are forgot.

127

But sweeter still than this, than these, than all,
Is first and passionate love – it stands alone
Like Adam's recollection of his fall;
The tree of knowledge has been plucked, all's known,
And life yields nothing further to recall
Worthy of this ambrosial[129] sin, so shown
No doubt in fable, as the unforgiven
Fire which Prometheus filched for us from heaven.

128

Man's a strange animal, and makes strange use
Of his own nature and the various arts,[130]
And likes particularly to produce
Some new experiment to show his parts;[131]
This is the age of oddities let loose,
Where different talents find their different marts;
You'd best begin with truth, and when you've lost your
Labour, there's a sure market for imposture.

129

What opposite discoveries we have seen
(Signs of true genius, and of empty pockets)!
One makes new noses, one a guillotine,
One breaks your bones, one sets them in their sockets;

Notes

[126] *us youth* 'They hate us youth'; Falstaff, *1 Henry IV* II ii 93.

[127] *Israelites* i.e. money-lenders.

[128] *post-obits* in this case, money owed to them by the deceased, for which the heir is liable.

[129] *ambrosial* divine; Prometheus was a demigod.

[130] *arts* skills, abilities.

[131] *parts* as McGann notes, an obscene pun.

But vaccination certainly has been
A kind antithesis to Congreve's rockets,
With which the doctor paid off an old pox
By borrowing a new one from an ox.[132]

130

Bread has been made (indifferent) from potatoes,
And galvanism has set some corpses grinning,
But has not answered like the apparatus
Of the Humane Society's beginning,
By which men are unsuffocated gratis;
What wondrous new machines have late been spinning![133]
I said the smallpox has gone out of late,
Perhaps it may be followed by the great.[134]

131

'Tis said the great came from America,
Perhaps it may set out on its return;
The population there so spreads, they say,
'Tis grown high time to thin it in its turn
With war or plague or famine, any way,
So that civilization they may learn,
And which in ravage the more loathsome evil is:
Their real lues,[135] or our pseudo-syphilis?

132

This is the patent-age of new inventions
For killing bodies and for saving souls,[136]
All propagated with the best intentions:
Sir Humphry Davy's lantern,[137] by which coals
Are safely mined for in the mode he mentions;
Tombuctoo travels, voyages to the Poles
Are ways to benefit mankind, as true,
Perhaps, as shooting them at Waterloo.

133

Man's a phenomenon, one knows not what,
And wonderful beyond all wondrous measure;
'Tis pity though, in this sublime world, that

Notes

[132] This stanza is a catalogue of recent scientific developments. The American quack doctor Benjamin Charles Perkins made new noses; Sir William Congreve (1772–1828) invented an artillery shell, first used against the French in the Battle of Leipzig (1813); Edward Jenner (1749–1823) first vaccinated against smallpox in 1796.

[133] Luigi Galvani used electricity to attempt to restore corpses to life (an inspiration for Mary Shelley's *Frankenstein*), as well as for therapeutic purposes (first described 1792); the Humane Society was founded 1774, for the rescue of drowning persons (the 'apparatus' is a resuscitator); the spinning-jenny was patented by James Hargreaves, 1770.

[134] *the great* syphilis.

[135] *lues* syphilis.

[136] *saving souls* probably a reference to the British and Foreign Bible Society, founded 1804, which published and distributed cheap bibles around the world. It is still going strong.

[137] Davy (1778–1829), friend of Wordsworth, Coleridge, Scott and Byron, not only wrote poetry but invented the miner's safety-lamp, 1815.

Pleasure's a sin, and sometimes sin's a pleasure;
Few mortals know what end[138] they would be at,
But whether glory, power, or love or treasure,
The path is through perplexing ways, and when
The goal is gained, we die, you know – and then –

134

What then? I do not know, no more do you –
And so goodnight. Return we to our story:
'Twas in November when fine days are few,
And the far mountains wax[139] a little hoary
And clap a white cape on their mantles blue;
And the sea dashes round the promontory,
And the loud breaker boils against the rock,
And sober suns must set at five o'clock.

135

'Twas, as the watchmen say, a cloudy night;
No moon, no stars, the wind was low or loud
By gusts, and many a sparkling hearth was bright
With the piled wood round which the family crowd;
There's something cheerful in that sort of light,
Even as a summer sky's without a cloud –
I'm fond of fire and crickets, and all that,
A lobster-salad, and champagne, and chat.

136

'Twas midnight; Donna Julia was in bed –
Sleeping, most probably – when at her door
Arose a clatter might awake the dead[140]
(If they had never been awoke before,
And that they have been so we all have read,
And are to be so, at the least, once more);
The door was fastened, but with voice and fist
First knocks were heard, then 'Madam, madam – hist!

137

For God's sake, madam – madam, here's my master
With more than half the city at his back;
Was ever heard of such a cursed disaster!
'Tis not my fault, I kept good watch – alack!

Notes

[138] *end* an obscene pun.
[139] *wax* become.
[140] *awake the dead* a reference to 1 Corinthians 15: 51–2, which prophesies that 'the dead shall be raised incorruptible.'

Do pray undo the bolt a little faster;
They're on the stair just now, and in a crack[141]
Will all be here – perhaps he yet may fly;
Surely the window's not so *very* high!'

138

By this time Don Alfonso was arrived
With torches, friends and servants in great number;
The major part of them had long been wived,
And therefore paused not[142] to disturb the slumber
Of any wicked woman who contrived
By stealth her husband's temples to encumber;[143]
Examples of this kind are so contagious,
Were *one* not punished, *all* would be outrageous.

139

I can't tell how or why or what suspicion
Could enter into Don Alfonso's head,
But for a cavalier of his condition[144]
It surely was exceedingly ill-bred,
Without a word of previous admonition,
To hold a levee[145] round his lady's bed
And summon lackeys armed with fire and sword,
To prove himself the thing he most abhorred.[146]

140

Poor Donna Julia! Starting as from sleep
(Mind that I do not say she had not slept)
Began at once to scream and yawn and weep;
Her maid Antonia, who was an adept,
Contrived to fling the bedclothes in a heap,
As if she had just now from out them crept –
I can't tell why she should take all this trouble
To prove her mistress had been sleeping double.

141

But Julia mistress, and Antonia maid,
Appeared like two poor harmless women who
Of goblins, but still more of men afraid,
Had thought one man might be deterred by two,
And therefore side by side were gently laid
Until the hours of absence should run through,
And truant husband should return and say,
'My dear, I was the first who came away.'

Notes

[141] *in a crack* immediately.
[142] *paused not* did not hesitate.
[143] *her husband's temples to encumber* Horns sprout on the foreheads of cuckolded husbands.
[144] *a cavalier of his condition* a gentleman of his rank.
[145] *levee* a social meeting held immediately on rising from bed; Don Alfonso has not even allowed his wife the opportunity to get up.
[146] *the thing he most abhorred* i.e. a cuckold.

142

Now Julia found at length a voice, and cried,
'In Heaven's name, Don Alfonso, what d'ye mean?
Has madness seized you? Would that I had died
Ere such a monster's victim I had been!
What may this midnight violence betide?
A sudden fit of drunkenness or spleen?
Dare you suspect me, whom the thought would kill?
Search then the room!' Alfonso said, 'I will.'

143

He searched, *they* searched, and rummaged everywhere,
Closet and clothes-press, chest and window-seat,
And found much linen, lace, and several pair
Of stockings, slippers, brushes, combs, complete
With other articles of ladies fair,
To keep them beautiful or leave them neat;
Arras they pricked,[147] and curtains with their swords,
And wounded several shutters and some boards.

144

Under the bed they searched, and there they found –
No matter what, it was not that they sought;
They opened windows, gazing if the ground
Had signs or footmarks, but the earth said nought;
And then they stared each others' faces round:
'Tis odd not one of all these seekers thought
(And seems to me almost a sort of blunder)
Of looking *in* the bed as well as under.

145

During this inquisition Julia's tongue
Was not asleep: 'Yes, search and search', she cried,
'Insult on insult heap, and wrong on wrong!
It was for this that I became a bride!
For this in silence I have suffered long
A husband like Alfonso at my side;
But now I'll bear no more, nor here remain,
If there be law or lawyers in all Spain.

146

Yes, Don Alfonso, husband now no more
(If ever you indeed deserved the name)!
Is't worthy of your years? You have threescore,
Fifty or sixty (it is all the same),
Is't wise or fitting causeless to explore
For facts against a virtuous woman's fame?
Ungrateful, perjured, barbarous Don Alfonso –
How dare you think your lady would go on so?

Notes

147 *Arras they pricked* i.e. they poked the hanging tapestry with their swords.

147

Is it for this I have disdained to hold
   The common privileges of my sex?[148] –
That I have chosen a confessor so old
   And deaf, that any other it would vex,
And never once he has had cause to scold,
   But found my very innocence perplex
So much, he always doubted I was married?
How sorry you will be when I've miscarried![149]

148

Was it for this that no cortejo ere
   I yet have chosen from out the youth of Seville?
Is it for this I scarce went anywhere
   Except to bullfights, mass, play, rout[150] and revel?
Is it for this, whate'er my suitors were,
   I favoured none – nay, was almost uncivil?
Is it for this that General Count O'Reilly,
Who took Algiers,[151] declares I used him vilely?

149

Did not the Italian musico Cazzani[152]
   Sing at my heart six months at least in vain?
Did not his countryman, Count Corniani,[153]
   Call me the only virtuous wife in Spain?
Were there not also Russians, English, many?
   The Count Strongstroganoff[154] I put in pain,
And Lord Mount Coffeehouse, the Irish peer,[155]
Who killed himself for love (with wine) last year.

150

Have I not had two bishops at my feet,
   The Duke of Ichar, and Don Fernan Nunez?
And is it thus a faithful wife you treat?
   I wonder in what quarter now the moon is;[156]
I praise your vast forbearance not to beat
   Me also, since the time so opportune is –
Oh valiant man, with sword drawn and cocked trigger,
Now tell me, don't you cut a pretty figure?

Notes

[148] *The common privileges of my sex* i.e. to take a lover (or 'cortejo').

[149] *when I've miscarried* i.e. when you've lost me.

[150] *rout* party.

[151] 'Donna Julia here made a mistake. Count O'Reilly did not take Algiers – but Algiers very nearly took him. He and his army and fleet retreated with great loss, and not much credit, from before that city in the year 1775' (Byron's note). The Irish-born Spanish general Alexander O'Reilly (?1722–94) was governor of Madrid and later Cadiz. The unsuccessful assault on Algiers was mounted in 1775.

[152] *musico* musician. Cazzani is an obscene pun on 'cazzo' (penis).

[153] Corniani derives from 'cornuto' (horned, cuckolded).

[154] *Count Strongstroganoff* Count Alexander Stroganov was a fellow-reveller of Byron's in Venice.

[155] This is a disdainful reference to the peerages created by the Act of Union between Ireland and England in 1801, for which Byron's *bête noire*, Castlereagh, had been largely responsible. The Mount was a coffeehouse near Grosvenor Square, London.

[156] *I wonder in what quarter now the moon is* i.e. because a full moon would explain why Don Alfonso is behaving like a lunatic.

151

Was it for this you took your sudden journey
 Under pretence of business indispensable
With that sublime of rascals, your attorney,
 Whom I see standing there, and looking sensible[157]
Of having played the fool? Though both I spurn, he
 Deserves the worst, his conduct's less defensible,
Because, no doubt, 'twas for his dirty fee,
And not from any love to you nor me.

152

If he comes here to take a deposition,[158]
 By all means let the gentleman proceed –
You've made the apartment in a fit condition!
 There's pen and ink for you, sir, when you need;
Let everything be noted with precision
 (I would not you for nothing should be feed[159]);
But as my maid's undressed, pray turn your spies out.'
'Oh!' sobbed Antonia, 'I could tear their eyes out!'

153

'There is the closet,[160] there the toilet,[161] there
 The antechamber[162] – search them under, over;
There is the sofa, there the great armchair,
 The chimney (which would really hold a lover).
I wish to sleep, and beg you will take care
 And make no further noise, till you discover
The secret cavern of this lurking treasure –
And when 'tis found, let me, too, have that pleasure.

154

And now, hidalgo, now that you have thrown
 Doubt upon me, confusion over all,[163]
Pray have the courtesy to make it known
 Who is the man you search for? How d'ye call
Him? What's his lineage? Let him but be shown;
 I hope he's young and handsome – is he tall?
Tell me, and be assured that since you stain
My honour thus, it shall not be in vain.

155

At least, perhaps, he has not sixty years –
 At that age he would be too old for slaughter
Or for so young a husband's jealous fears!

Notes

157 *sensible* aware.

158 *deposition* statement for use as evidence.

159 *I would not you for nothing should be feed* I would not want you to be paid ('feed') for doing nothing.

160 *closet* private apartment.

161 *toilet* table on which toilet articles are placed.

162 *antechamber* waiting-room.

163 *confusion over all* an echo of the final line of Pope's *Dunciad*: 'And universal darkness buries all.'

Antonia, let me have a glass of water;
I am ashamed of having shed these tears,
They are unworthy of my father's daughter;
My mother dreamed not in my natal hour[164]
That I should fall into a monster's power.

156

Perhaps 'tis of Antonia you are jealous –
You saw that she was sleeping by my side
When you broke in upon us with your fellows;
Look where you please, we've nothing, sir, to hide;
Only another time, I trust, you'll tell us,
Or for the sake of decency abide
A moment at the door, that we may be
Dressed to receive so much good company.

157

And now, sir, I have done, and say no more;
The little I have said may serve to show
The guileless heart in silence may grieve o'er
The wrongs to whose exposure it is slow;
I leave you to your conscience as before –
'Twill one day ask you *why* you used me so?
God grant you feel not then the bitterest grief!
Antonia, where's my pocket-handkerchief?'

158

She ceased, and turned upon her pillow; pale
She lay, her dark eyes flashing through their tears
Like skies that rain and lighten; as a veil,
Waved and o'ershading her wan cheek, appears
Her streaming hair; the black curls strive but fail
To hide the glossy shoulder, which uprears
Its snow through all; her soft lips lie apart,
And louder than her breathing beats her heart.

159

The *señor* Don Alfonso stood confused;
Antonia bustled round the ransacked room
And, turning up her nose, with looks abused
Her master and his myrmidons,[165] of whom
Not one, except the attorney, was amused;
He, like Achates,[166] faithful to the tomb,
So[167] there were quarrels, cared not for the cause,
Knowing they must be settled by the laws.

Notes

[164] *my natal hour* hour of my birth.
[165] *myrmidons* base unscrupulous henchmen.
[166] Achates was Aeneas' proverbially faithful companion.
[167] *So* if.

160

With prying snubnose and small eyes he stood,
Following Antonia's motions here and there
With much suspicion in his attitude;
For reputations he had little care,
So that a suit or action were made good;
Small pity had he for the young and fair,
And ne'er believed in negatives, till these
Were proved by competent false witnesses.

161

But Don Alfonso stood with downcast looks,
And, truth to say, he made a foolish figure –
When after searching in five hundred nooks,
And treating a young wife with so much rigour,
He gained no point except some self-rebukes,
Added to those his lady with such vigour
Had poured upon him for the last half-hour,
Quick, thick, and heavy, as a thunder-shower.

162

At first he tried to hammer an excuse
To which the sole reply were tears and sobs
And indications of hysterics, whose
Prologue is always certain throes and throbs,
Gasps and whatever else the owners choose;
Alfonso saw his wife and thought of Job's;[168]
He saw too, in perspective,[169] her relations,
And then he tried to muster all his patience.

163

He stood in act to speak, or rather stammer,
But sage Antonia cut him short before
The anvil of his speech received the hammer,
With, 'Pray sir, leave the room, and say no more,
Or madam dies.' Alfonso muttered, 'Damn her!'
But nothing else – the time of words was o'er;
He cast a rueful look or two, and did
(He knew not wherefore) that which he was bid.

164

With him retired his *posse comitatus*[170] –
The attorney last, who lingered near the door
Reluctantly, still tarrying there as late as
Antonia let him, not a little sore
At this most strange and unexplained hiatus[171]

Notes

[168] Job's wife berated him: 'Dost thou still retain thine integrity? Curse God, and die' (Job 2: 9).

[169] *in perspective* i.e. stretching into the distance.

[170] *posse comitatus* 'the force of the county'; armed posse.

[171] *hiatus* i.e. missing piece of evidence.

In Don Alfonso's facts, which just now wore
An awkward look; as he resolved the case
The door was fastened in his legal face.

165

No sooner was it bolted than – oh shame!
Oh sin! Oh sorrow! And oh womankind!
How can you do such things and keep your fame,
Unless this world (and t'other too) be blind?
Nothing so dear as an unfilched good name![172]
But to proceed, for there is more behind;
With much heartfelt reluctance be it said,
Young Juan slipped, half-smothered, from the bed.

166

He had been hid – I don't pretend to say
How, nor can I indeed describe the where;
Young, slender, and packed easily, he lay
No doubt, in little compass, round or square;
But pity him I neither must nor may
His suffocation by that pretty pair;
'Twere better, sure, to die so, than be shut
With maudlin Clarence in his Malmsey butt.[173]

167

And secondly, I pity not, because
He had no business to commit a sin
Forbid by heavenly, fined by human laws
(At least 'twas rather early to begin);
But at sixteen the conscience rarely gnaws
So much as when we call our old debts in
At sixty years, and draw the accompts of evil,
And find a deuced balance with the Devil.

168

Of his position I can give no notion;
'Tis written in the Hebrew chronicle
How the physicians, leaving pill and potion,
Prescribed by way of blister, a young belle,
When old King David's blood grew dull in motion,
And that the medicine answered very well;[174]
Perhaps 'twas in a different way applied,
For David lived, but Juan nearly died.

Notes

[172] *Nothing so dear as an unfilched good name* a lighthearted echo of *Othello* III iii 159: 'But he that filches from me my good name . . .'

[173] George, Duke of Clarence, brother of Richard III, is drowned in a barrel of malmsey wine in Shakespeare's play (*Richard III* I iv 270).

[174] *'Tis written . . . very well* see 1 Kings 1: 1–3. King David was revived by 'a young virgin'.

169

What's to be done? Alfonso will be back
The moment he has sent his fools away.
Antonia's skill was put upon the rack,
But no device could be brought into play –
And how to parry the renewed attack?
Besides, it wanted but few hours of day;
Antonia puzzled, Julia did not speak
But pressed her bloodless lip to Juan's cheek.

170

He turned his lip to hers, and with his hand
Called back the tangles of her wandering hair;
Even then their love they could not all command,
And half forgot their danger and despair.
Antonia's patience now was at a stand[175] –
'Come, come, 'tis no time now for fooling there',
She whispered in great wrath, 'I must deposit
This pretty gentleman within the closet:

171

Pray keep your nonsense for some luckier night –
Who can have put my master in this mood?
What will become on't? I'm in such a fright,
The Devil's in the urchin, and no good –
Is this a time for giggling? this a plight?
Why, don't you know that it may end in blood?
You'll lose your life, and I shall lose my place,[176]
My mistress, all, for that half-girlish face.

172

Had it but been for a stout cavalier
Of twenty-five or thirty (come, make haste!) –
But for a child, what piece of work is here![177]
I really, madam, wonder at your taste –
Come sir, get in; my master must be near.
There for the present, at the least he's fast,
And if we can but till the morning keep
Our counsel – Juan, mind, you must not sleep!'

173

Now Don Alfonso entering, but alone,
Closed the oration of the trusty maid;
She loitered, and he told her to be gone –
An order somewhat sullenly obeyed;

Notes

[175] *at a stand* i.e. at an end.

[176] *place* job.

[177] *what piece of work is here!* an ironic reworking of *Hamlet* II ii 303–4: 'What a piece of work is a man . . .'

However, present remedy was none,
  And no great good seemed answered if she stayed;
Regarding both with slow and sidelong view,
She snuffed the candle, curtsied and withdrew.

174

Alfonso paused a minute, then begun
  Some strange excuses for his late proceeding;
He would not justify what he had done –
  To say the best, it was extreme ill-breeding;
But there were ample reasons for it, none
  Of which he specified in this his pleading:
His speech was a fine sample, on the whole,
Of rhetoric which the learned call *rigmarole*.

175

Julia said nought, though all the while there rose
  A ready answer – which at once enables
A matron (who her husband's foible knows)
  By a few timely words to turn the tables,
Which, if it does not silence, still must pose,
  Even if it should comprise a pack of fables;
'Tis to retort with firmness, and when he
Suspects with *one*, do you reproach with *three*.

176

Julia in fact had tolerable grounds:
  Alfonso's loves with Inez were well-known;
But whether 'twas that one's own guilt confounds –
  But that can't be, as has been often shown,
A lady with apologies abounds;
  It might be that her silence sprang alone
From delicacy to Don Juan's ear,
To whom she knew his mother's fame was dear.

177

There might be one more motive (which makes two):
  Alfonso ne'er to Juan had alluded –
Mentioned his jealousy, but never who
  Had been the happy lover he concluded
Concealed amongst his premises; 'tis true
  His mind the more o'er this its mystery brooded;
To speak of Inez now were, one may say,
Like throwing Juan in Alfonso's way.

178

A hint, in tender cases, is enough;
  Silence is best – besides there is a *tact*[178]
(That modern phrase appears to me sad stuff,

Notes

[178] *tact* a keen faculty of perception or discrimination likened to the sense of touch.

But it will serve to keep my verse compact)
Which keeps, when pushed by questions rather rough,
A lady always distant from the fact –
The charming creatures lie with such a grace,
There's nothing so becoming to the face.

179

They blush, and we believe them – at least I
Have always done so; 'tis of no great use
In any case attempting a reply,
For then their eloquence grows quite profuse;
And when at length they're out of breath, they sigh
And cast their languid eyes down, and let loose
A tear or two, and then we make it up,
And then – and then – and then – sit down and sup.

180

Alfonso closed his speech and begged her pardon,
Which Julia half-withheld, and then half-granted,
And laid conditions, he thought, very hard on,
Denying several little things he wanted;
He stood like Adam lingering near his garden,[179]
With useless penitence perplexed and haunted,
Beseeching she no further would refuse –
When lo! he stumbled o'er a pair of shoes.

181

A pair of shoes! What then? Not much, if they
Are such as fit with lady's feet, but these
(No one can tell how much I grieve to say)
Were masculine: to see them and to seize
Was but a moment's act – ah wel-a-day![180]
My teeth begin to chatter, my veins freeze;
Alfonso first examined well their fashion,
And then flew out into another passion.

182

He left the room for his relinquished sword
And Julia instant to the closet flew,
'Fly, Juan, fly! For Heaven's sake, not a word –
The door is open, you may yet slip through
The passage you so often have explored;
Here is the garden-key – fly – fly – adieu!
Haste, haste! I hear Alfonso's hurrying feet –
Day has not broke; there's no one in the street.'

Notes

[179] *Adam lingering near his garden* While being cast out of Eden in Milton's poem, Adam and Eve lingered near the eastern gate (*Paradise Lost* xii 636–9).

[180] *ah wel-a-day* cf. Coleridge, 'Christabel' 252.

183

None can say that this was not good advice,
  The only mischief was it came too late;
Of all experience 'tis the usual price,
  A sort of income tax[181] laid on by fate:
Juan had reached the room-door in a trice
  And might have done so by the garden-gate,
But met Alfonso in his dressing-gown,
Who threatened death – so Juan knocked him down.

184

Dire was the scuffle, and out went the light,
  Antonia cried out 'Rape!' and Julia, 'Fire!'
But not a servant stirred to aid the fight.
  Alfonso, pommelled to his heart's desire,
Swore lustily he'd be revenged this night;
  And Juan too blasphemed an octave higher,
His blood was up – though young, he was a Tartar,[182]
And not at all disposed to prove a martyr.

185

Alfonso's sword had dropped ere he could draw it,
  And they continued battling hand to hand,
For Juan very luckily ne'er saw it;
  His temper not being under great command,
If at that moment he had chanced to claw it,
  Alfonso's days had not been in the land
Much longer. Think of husbands', lovers', lives,
And how ye may be doubly widows, wives!

186

Alfonso grappled to detain the foe
  And Juan throttled him to get away,
And blood ('twas from the nose) began to flow;
  At last, as they more faintly wrestling lay,
Juan contrived to give an awkward blow,
  And then his only garment quite gave way;
He fled, like Joseph,[183] leaving it – but there,
I doubt, all likeness ends between the pair.

187

Lights came at length, and men and maids who found
  An awkward spectacle their eyes before:
Antonia in hysterics, Julia swooned,
  Alfonso leaning breathless by the door;

Notes

[181] *income tax* introduced in England as a war tax in 1799.

[182] *a Tartar* i.e. a young savage.

[183] *like Joseph* When Joseph refused to commit adultery with Potiphar's wife, she claimed that he had tried to rape her, and that, 'when he heard that I lifted up my voice and cried, that he left his garment with me, and fled, and got him out' (Genesis 39: 14).

Some half-torn drapery scattered on the ground,
  Some blood and several footsteps, but no more –
Juan the gate gained, turned the key about,
And liking not the inside, locked the out.

188

Here ends this canto. Need I sing, or say,
  How Juan, naked, favoured by the night
(Who favours what she should not), found his way,
  And reached his home in an unseemly plight?
The pleasant scandal which arose next day,
  The nine days' wonder which was brought to light,
And how Alfonso sued for a divorce,
Were in the English newspapers, of course.

189

If you would like to see the whole proceedings,
  The depositions, and the cause at full,
The names of all the witnesses, the pleadings
  Of counsel to nonsuit or to annul,[184]
There's more than one edition, and the readings
  Are various, but they none of them are dull;
The best is that in shorthand ta'en by Gurney,[185]
Who to Madrid on purpose made a journey.

190

But Donna Inez, to divert the train[186]
  Of one of the most circulating scandals
That had for centuries been known in Spain
  Since Roderic's Goths or older Genseric's Vandals,[187]
First vowed (and never had she vowed in vain)
  To Virgin Mary several pounds of candles;
And then by the advice of some old ladies,
She sent her son to be embarked[188] at Cadiz.

191

She had resolved that he should travel through
  All European climes by land or sea
To mend his former morals, or get new,
  Especially in France and Italy –
At least this is the thing most people do.
  Julia was sent into a nunnery,
And there perhaps her feelings may be better
Shown in the following copy of her letter:

Notes

[184] *to nonsuit or to annul* i.e. to bring the case to an end through lack of sufficient evidence.

[185] William Brodie Gurney (1777–1855), shorthand clerk in Parliament, famous for transcripts of trials and speeches of the day.

[186] *train* progress.

[187] Don Roderick was the last of Spain's Gothic kings, and ruled in the eighth century. In the year 455 the Vandal King Genseric led a marauding expedition against Rome, which he took and completely sacked.

[188] *embarked* put on board ship.

192

'They tell me 'tis decided – you depart.
'Tis wise, 'tis well, but not the less a pain;
I have no further claim on your young heart –
Mine was the victim, and would be again;
To love too much has been the only art
I used; I write in haste, and if a stain
Be on this sheet, 'tis not what it appears –
My eyeballs burn and throb, but have no tears.

193

I loved, I love you, for that love have lost
State, station, heaven, mankind's, my own esteem,
And yet cannot regret what it hath cost,
So dear is still the memory of that dream;
Yet if I name my guilt, 'tis not to boast –
None can deem harshlier of me than I deem:
I trace this scrawl because I cannot rest,
I've nothing to reproach, nor to request.

194

Man's love is of his life a thing apart,
'Tis woman's whole existence; man may range
The court, camp, church, the vessel and the mart,
Sword, gown, gain, glory, offer in exchange
Pride, fame, ambition, to fill up his heart,
And few there are whom these cannot estrange;
Man has all these resources, we but one –
To love again, and be again undone.

195

My breast has been all weakness, is so yet;
I struggle, but cannot collect my mind;
My blood still rushes where my spirit's set
As roll the waves before the settled wind;
My brain is feminine, nor can forget –
To all, except your image, madly blind;
As turns the needle trembling to the pole
It ne'er can reach, so turns to you, my soul.

196

You will proceed in beauty and in pride,
Beloved and loving many; all is o'er
For me on earth, except some years to hide
My shame and sorrow deep in my heart's core;
These I could bear, but cannot cast aside
The passion which still rends it as before,
And so farewell; forgive me, love me – no,
That word is idle now, but let it go.

197

I have no more to say, but linger still,
And dare not set my seal upon this sheet,
And yet I may as well the task fulfil –
My misery can scarce be more complete;
I had not lived till now, could sorrow kill;
Death flies the wretch who fain the blow would meet,
And I must even survive this last adieu,
And bear with life, to love and pray for you!'

198

This note was written upon gilt-edged paper
With a neat crow-quill – rather hard, but new;
Her small white fingers scarce could reach the taper
But trembled as magnetic needles do,
And yet she did not let one tear escape her;
The seal a sunflower, 'Elle vous suit partout'[189]
The motto, cut upon a white cornelian;[190]
The wax was superfine, its hue vermilion.

199

This was Don Juan's earliest scrape – but whether
I shall proceed with his adventures is
Dependent on the public altogether;
We'll see, however, what they say to this;
Their favour in an author's cap's a feather,
And no great mischief's done by their caprice;
And if their approbation we experience,
Perhaps they'll have some more about a year hence.

200

My poem's epic, and is meant to be
Divided in twelve books, each book containing,
With love and war, a heavy gale at sea,
A list of ships and captains, and kings reigning,
New characters; the episodes are three:
A panorama view of hell's in training[191]
After the style of Virgil and of Homer,
So that my name of epic's no misnomer.

201

All these things will be specified in time
With strict regard to Aristotle's rules,
The vade-mecum[192] of the true sublime
Which makes so many poets, and some fools;

Notes

[189] 'She follows you everywhere'. Byron owned a seal bearing this motto.

[190] *cornelian* stone used for making seals (for letters).

[191] *training* preparation.

[192] *vade-mecum* handbook.

Prose poets like blank verse, I'm fond of rhyme –
Good workmen never quarrel with their tools;
I've got new mythological machinery
And very handsome supernatural scenery.

202

There's only one slight difference between
Me and my epic brethren gone before,
And here the advantage is my own, I ween[193]
(Not that I have no several merits more,
But this will more peculiarly be seen) –
They so embellish that 'tis quite a bore
Their labyrinth of fables to thread through,
Whereas this story's actually true.

203

If any person doubt it, I appeal
To history, tradition, and to facts,
To newspapers (whose truth all know and feel),
To plays in five, and operas in three acts –
All these confirm my statement a good deal,
But that which more completely faith exacts
Is that myself, and several now in Seville,
Saw Juan's last elopement with the Devil.[194]

204

If ever I should condescend to prose,
I'll write poetical commandments[195] which
Shall supersede beyond all doubt all those
That went before; in these I shall enrich
My text with many things that no one knows,
And carry precept to the highest pitch:
I'll call the work 'Longinus o'er a bottle,
Or, Every poet his *own* Aristotle'.

205

Thou shalt believe in Milton, Dryden, Pope;
Thou shalt not set up Wordsworth, Coleridge, Southey,
Because the first is crazed beyond all hope,
The second drunk,[196] the third so quaint and mouthy;[197]
With Crabbe it may be difficult to cope,

Notes

193 *ween* believe.

194 When in Seville in 1809, Byron saw a performance of *El Burlador de Sevilla o el Convidado de Piedra* ('The Trickster of Seville, or the Guest Made of Stone'), by Tirso de Molina (1583–1648).

195 *poetical commandments* The parody of the ten commandments in the following stanzas caused uproar in England when *Don Juan* was first published.

196 *drunk* stupefied by opium.

197 *quaint and mouthy* affected and bombastic (in language).

And Campbell's Hippocrene[198] is somewhat drouthy;[199]
Thou shalt not steal from Samuel Rogers, nor
Commit . . . flirtation with the muse of Moore.[200]

206

Thou shalt not covet Mr Sotheby's[201] muse,
His Pegasus,[202] nor anything that's his;
Thou shalt not bear false witness like the Blues[203]
(There's one, at least, is very fond of this);
Thou shalt not write, in short, but what I choose:
This is true criticism, and you may kiss
Exactly as you please, or not, the rod –
But if you don't, I'll lay it on, by God!

207

If any person should presume to assert
This story is not moral, first I pray
That they will not cry out before they're hurt,
Then that they'll read it o'er again, and say
(But, doubtless, nobody will be so pert)
That this is not a moral tale, though gay;
Besides, in Canto Twelfth I mean to show
The very place where wicked people go.

208

If, after all, there should be some so blind
To their own good this warning to despise,
Led by some tortuosity[204] of mind
Not to believe my verse and their own eyes,
And cry that they 'the moral cannot find',
I tell him, if a clergyman, he lies;
Should captains the remark or critics make,
They also lie too – under a mistake.

209

The public approbation I expect,
And beg they'll take my word about the moral,
Which I with their amusement will connect
(So children cutting teeth receive a coral);

Notes

[198] *Hippocrene* fountain of Mt Helicon, sacred to the muses.

[199] *drouthy* dry.

[200] Byron thought of George Crabbe, Samuel Rogers, Thomas Moore and Thomas Campbell as among the few decent poets of his own time. Byron's comment about Campbell refers to the fact that he had recently given up poetry for the writing of prose criticism.

[201] William Sotheby (1757–1833), most famous for his translation of Wieland's *Oberon* (1798), and for his plays, *The Death of Darnley* (1814) and *Ivan* (1816).

[202] Pegasus was the winged horse who created Hippocrene, the fountain of Mt Helicon, with his hoof; he is generally referred to as a symbol of poetic inspiration.

[203] *the Blues* i.e. the Bluestockings, many of whom were acquainted with Byron (Lady Blessington, Lady Oxford, Lady Caroline Lamb).

[204] *tortuosity* crookedness.

Meantime, they'll doubtless please to recollect
   My epical pretensions to the laurel:
For fear some prudish readers should grow skittish
I've bribed my grandmother's review – the *British*.[205]

210

I sent it in a letter to the editor
   Who thanked me duly by return of post –
I'm for a handsome article his creditor;
   Yet if my gentle muse he please to roast,
And break a promise after having made it her,
   Denying the receipt of what it cost
And smear his page with gall[206] instead of honey,
All I can say is – that he had the money.

211

I think that with this holy new alliance
   I may ensure the public, and defy
All other magazines of art or science –
   Daily or monthly or three-monthly; I
Have not essayed[207] to multiply their clients
   Because they tell me 'twere in vain to try,
And that the *Edinburgh Review* and *Quarterly*
Treat a dissenting author very martyrly.

212

'Non ego hoc ferrem calida juventa
   Consule Planco',[208] Horace said, and so
Say I; by which quotation there is meant a
   Hint that some six or seven good years ago
(Long ere I dreamt of dating from the Brenta[209])
   I was most ready to return a blow,
And would not brook at all this sort of thing
In my hot youth – when George the third was King.

213

But now at thirty years my hair is gray
   (I wonder what it will be like at forty?
I thought of a peruke[210] the other day),
   My heart is not much greener, and, in short, I
Have squandered my whole summer while 'twas May,
   And feel no more the spirit to retort; I
Have spent my life, both interest and principal,
And deem not what I deemed, my soul invincible.

Notes

205 The *British Review* was outraged by *Don Juan*, and particularly this line; its editor, William Roberts, in his review of the poem, solemnly denied the 'accusation', provoking Byron's 'Letter to the Editor of my Grandmother's Review' in the *Liberal* (1822).

206 *gall* i.e. bitterness.

207 *essayed* attempted.

208 *Non ego . . . Consule Planco* from Horace, *Odes* III xiv 27–8; translated (roughly) at lines 1695–6.

209 *the Brenta* The Brenta Riviera is several kilometres from Venice.

210 *peruke* wig.

214

No more, no more – oh never more on me
  The freshness of the heart can fall like dew,
Which out of all the lovely things we see
  Extracts emotions beautiful and new,
Hived[211] in our bosoms like the bag o' the bee:
  Think'st thou the honey with those objects grew?
Alas, 'twas not in them, but in thy power
To double even the sweetness of a flower.

215

No more, no more – oh never more, my heart,
  Canst thou be my sole world, my universe!
Once all in all, but now a thing apart,
  Thou canst not be my blessing or my curse;
The illusion's gone forever, and thou art
  Insensible, I trust, but none the worse,
And in thy stead I've got a deal of judgement –
Though heaven knows how it ever found a lodgement.

216

My days of love are over, me no more
  The charms of maid, wife, and still less of widow,
Can make the fool of which they made before;
  In short, I must not lead the life I did do;
The credulous hope of mutual minds is o'er,
  The copious use of claret is forbid too –
So, for a good old gentlemanly vice,
I think I must take up with avarice.

217

Ambition was my idol, which was broken
  Before the shrines of sorrow and of pleasure;
And the two last have left me many a token
  O'er which reflection may be made at leisure;
Now like Friar Bacon's brazen[212] head I've spoken,
  'Time is, time was, time's past';[213] a chemic[214] treasure
Is glittering youth, which I have spent betimes –
My heart in passion, and my head on rhymes.

218

What is the end of fame?[215] 'Tis but to fill
  A certain portion of uncertain paper;
Some liken it to climbing up a hill
  Whose summit, like all hills', is lost in vapour;

Notes

211 *Hived* stored.

212 *brazen* brass.

213 *Time is, time was, time's past* the words of the brass head in Robert Greene's play, *Friar Bacon and Friar Bungay* (1594), IV i 1584, 1595, 1604.

214 *chemic* i.e. transforming; alchemists attempted to convert base metals into gold.

215 *What is the end of fame?* Byron was disdainful of literary fame; see for instance his remarks about Southey, Dedication, l. 60.

For this men write, speak, preach, and heroes kill,
  And bards burn what they call their 'midnight taper' –
To have, when the original is dust,
A name, a wretched picture, and worse bust.[216]

219

What are the hopes of man? Old Egypt's King
  Cheops erected the first pyramid
And largest, thinking it was just the thing
  To keep his memory whole, and mummy hid;
But somebody or other rummaging,
  Burglariously broke his coffin's lid:
Let not a monument give you or me hopes,
Since not a pinch of dust remains of Cheops.

220

But I, being fond of true philosophy,
  Say very often to myself, 'Alas!
All things that have been born were born to die,
  And flesh (which death mows down to hay) is grass;[217]
You've passed your youth not so unpleasantly,
  And if you had it o'er again, 'twould pass;
So thank your stars that matters are no worse
And read your Bible, sir, and mind your purse.'

221

But for the present, gentle reader and
  Still gentler purchaser, the bard (that's I)
Must with permission shake you by the hand;
  And so your humble servant, and goodbye!
We meet again, if we should understand
  Each other – and if not, I shall not try
Your patience further than by this short sample
('Twere well if others followed my example).

222

'Go, little book, from this my solitude!
  I cast thee on the waters, go thy ways!
And if, as I believe, thy vein be good,
  The world will find thee after many days.'[218]
When Southey's read, and Wordsworth understood,
  I can't help putting in my claim to praise;
The four first rhymes are Southey's every line –
For God's sake, reader, take them not for mine!

Notes

[216] *and worse bust* Bertel Thorwaldsen, the Danish sculptor, made a bust of Byron during his stay in Rome, summer 1817. Byron found it embarrassing, and commented that 'It is not at all like me; my expression is more unhappy.'

[217] *And flesh . . . is grass* cf. Isaiah 40: 6.

[218] *Go, little book . . . many days* a cheeky recycling of Southey, 'L'Envoy', *Carmen Nuptiale* (1816).

Canto II
(composed 13 December 1818–mid January 1819)

1

Oh ye who teach the ingenuous youth of nations –
   Holland, France, England, Germany, or Spain –
I pray ye flog them upon all occasions:
   It mends their morals, never mind the pain!
The best of mothers and of educations
   In Juan's case were but employed in vain,
Since, in a way that's rather of the oddest, he
Became divested of his native modesty.[1]

2

Had he but been placed at a public school,[2]
   In the third form, or even in the fourth,
His daily task had kept his fancy cool,
   At least, had he been nurtured in the north;
Spain may prove an exception to the rule,
   But then exceptions always prove its worth –
A lad of sixteen causing a divorce
Puzzled his tutors very much, of course.

3

I can't say that it puzzles me at all,
   If all things be considered: first there was
His lady-mother, mathematical,
   A – never mind; his tutor, an old ass;
A pretty woman (that's quite natural,
   Or else the thing had hardly come to pass);
A husband rather old, not much in unity
With his young wife; a time, and opportunity.

4

Well – well, the world must turn upon its axis,
   And all mankind turn with it, heads or tails,
And live and die, make love and pay our taxes,
   And, as the veering wind shifts, shift our sails;
The king commands us, and the doctor quacks us,[3]
   The priest instructs, and so our life exhales
A little breath, love, wine, ambition, fame,
Fighting, devotion, dust, perhaps a name.

Notes

Canto II

[1] *native modesty* i.e. the modesty he was born with.

[2] *a public school* in England, one of the old-established fee-paying schools, such as Eton or Harrow (where Byron was educated).

[3] *quacks us* administers quack medicines to us.

5

I said that Juan had been sent to Cadiz –
A pretty town, I recollect it well –
'Tis there the mart of the colonial trade is
(Or was, before Peru learned to rebel[4]);
And such sweet girls – I mean, such graceful ladies,
Their very walk would make your bosom swell;
I can't describe it, though so much it strike,
Nor liken it – I never saw the like:

6

An Arab horse, a stately stag, a barb[5]
New broke, a cameleopard,[6] a gazelle –
No, none of these will do – and then their garb,
Their veil and petticoat! (Alas, to dwell
Upon such things would very near absorb
A canto!) Then their feet and ankles – well,
Thank heaven I've got no metaphor quite ready
(And so, my sober muse, come, let's be steady,

7

Chaste Muse! – Well, if you must, you must); the veil
Thrown back a moment with the glancing hand,
While the o'erpowering eye that turns you pale
Flashes into the heart. All sunny land
Of love, when I forget you, may I fail
To – say my prayers; but never was there planned
A dress through which the eyes give such a volley,
Excepting the Venetian *fazzioli*.[7]

8

But to our tale: the Donna Inez sent
Her son to Cadiz only to embark;
To stay there had not answered her intent,
But why? We leave the reader in the dark –
'Twas for a voyage that the young man was meant,
As if a Spanish ship were Noah's ark,
To wean him from the wickedness of earth
And send him like a dove of promise forth.

9

Don Juan bade his valet pack his things
According to direction, then received
A lecture and some money: for four springs

Notes

[4] *before Peru learned to rebel* The Peruvian struggle for independence had begun in 1813, and after many obstacles was won in 1824, under Bolivar's leadership.

[5] *barb* a horse from the Barbary coast.

[6] *cameleopard* giraffe.

[7] *fazzioli* white kerchiefs used as a veil by the lower ranks.

He was to travel, and though Inez grieved
(As every kind of parting has its stings),
She hoped he would improve – perhaps believed:
A letter, too, she gave (he never read it)
Of good advice – and two or three of credit.

10

In the meantime, to pass her hours away,
Brave Inez now set up a Sunday school
For naughty children, who would rather play
(Like truant rogues) the devil or the fool;
Infants of three years old were taught that day,
Dunces were whipped, or set upon a stool:
The great success of Juan's education[8]
Spurred her to teach another generation.

11

Juan embarked, the ship got under way,
The wind was fair, the water passing rough;
A devil of a sea rolls in that bay,
As I, who've crossed it oft,[9] know well enough;
And, standing upon deck, the dashing spray
Flies in one's face, and makes it weather-tough:
And there he stood to take, and take again,
His first, perhaps his last, farewell of Spain.

12

I can't but say it is an awkward sight
To see one's native land receding through
The growing waters;[10] it unmans one quite,
Especially when life is rather new.
I recollect Great Britain's coast looks white,
But almost every other country's blue,
When gazing on them, mystified by distance,
We enter on our nautical existence.

13

So Juan stood, bewildered, on the deck:
The wind sung, cordage[11] strained, and sailors swore,
And the ship creaked, the town became a speck,
From which away so fair and fast they bore.

Notes

[8] *The great success of Juan's education* ironic, of course. His education has been a complete failure.

[9] *As I, who've crossed it oft* Byron sailed from Cadiz on 3 August 1809, travelling to Gibraltar.

[10] *I can't but say . . . waters* Byron draws on his own experience of self-exile.

[11] *cordage* the ship's rigging.

The best of remedies is a beefsteak
  Against seasickness; try it, sir, before
You sneer, and I assure you this is true,
For I have found it answer – so may you.

14

Don Juan stood and, gazing from the stern,
  Beheld his native Spain receding far.
First partings form a lesson hard to learn,
  Even nations feel this when they go to war;
There is a sort of unexpressed concern,
  A kind of shock that sets one's heart ajar:[12]
At leaving even the most unpleasant people
And places, one keeps looking at the steeple.

15

But Juan had got many things to leave,
  His mother, and a mistress, and no wife,
So that he had much better cause to grieve
  Than many persons more advanced in life;
And if we now and then a sigh must heave
  At quitting even those we quit in strife,
No doubt we weep for those the heart endears –
That is, till deeper griefs congeal our tears.

16

So Juan wept, as wept the captive Jews
  By Babel's waters, still remembering Zion:[13]
I'd weep, but mine is not a weeping muse,
  And such light griefs are not a thing to die on;
Young men should travel, if but to amuse
  Themselves – and the next time their servants tie on
Behind their carriages their new portmanteau,[14]
Perhaps it may be lined with this my canto.

17

And Juan wept, and much he sighed and thought,
  While his salt tears dropped into the salt sea,
'Sweets to the sweet'[15] (I like so much to quote;
  You must excuse this extract – 'tis where she,
The Queen of Denmark, for Ophelia brought
  Flowers to the grave), and, sobbing often, he
Reflected on his present situation,
And seriously resolved on reformation.

Notes

[12] *ajar* out of harmony.

[13] *By Babel's waters . . . Zion* Byron alludes to Psalm 137: 1: 'By the rivers of Babylon, there we sat down, yea, we wept, when we remembered Zion.'

[14] *portmanteau* travelling bag.

[15] *Sweets to the sweet* from *Hamlet* V i 243.

18

'Farewell, my Spain, a long farewell!' he cried,
'Perhaps I may revisit thee no more,
But die, as many an exiled heart hath died,
Of its own thirst to see again thy shore;
Farewell, where Guadalquivir's waters glide!
Farewell, my mother! And, since all is o'er,
Farewell, too dearest Julia!' (Here he drew
Her letter out again, and read it through.)

19

'And oh, if e'er I should forget, I swear –
But that's impossible, and cannot be –
Sooner shall this blue ocean melt to air,
Sooner shall earth resolve itself to sea,
Than I resign thine image, oh my fair!
Or think of anything excepting thee;
A mind diseased no remedy can physic[16] –'
(Here the ship gave a lurch, and he grew seasick.)

20

'Sooner shall heaven kiss earth –' (Here he fell sicker)
'Oh Julia, what is every other woe?
(For God's sake let me have a glass of liquor,
Pedro, Battista,[17] help me down below!)
Julia, my love! – you rascal, Pedro, quicker –
Oh Julia! – this cursed vessel pitches so –
Beloved Julia, hear me still beseeching!'
(Here he grew inarticulate with reaching.)[18]

21

He felt that chilling heaviness of heart,
Or rather stomach – which, alas, attends,
Beyond the best apothecary's[19] art,
The loss of love, the treachery of friends,
Or death of those we dote on, when a part
Of us dies with them as each fond hope ends:
No doubt he would have been much more pathetic,
But the sea acted as a strong emetic.[20]

22

Love's a capricious power; I've known it hold
Out through a fever caused by its own heat,
But be much puzzled by a cough and cold,
And find a quinsy[21] very hard to treat;

Notes

[16] *physic* cure. The line recalls *Macbeth* V iii 40: 'Canst thou not minister to a mind diseased . . . ?'

[17] Byron's own servant was a former gondolier called Giovanni Battista Lusieri (1798–1874). He remained with him until his death at Missolonghi.

[18] *reaching* retching.

[19] *apothecary* one who prepared and sold drugs for medicinal purposes – the business now (since about 1800) conducted by a chemist.

[20] *emetic* medicine designed to induce vomiting.

[21] *a quinsy* tonsillitis.

Against all noble maladies he's bold,
  But vulgar illnesses don't like to meet –
Nor that a sneeze should interrupt his sigh,
  Nor inflammations redden his blind eye.

23

But worst of all is nausea, or a pain
  About the lower region of the bowels;
Love, who heroically breathes a vein,[22]
  Shrinks from the application of hot towels,
And purgatives are dangerous to his reign,
  Seasickness death: his love was perfect, how else
Could Juan's passion, while the billows roar,
Resist his stomach, ne'er at sea before?

24

The ship, called the most holy *Trinidada*,
  Was steering duly for the port Leghorn,
For there the Spanish family Moncada[23]
  Were settled long ere Juan's sire was born:
They were relations, and for them he had a
  Letter of introduction, which the morn
Of his departure had been sent him by
His Spanish friends for those in Italy.

25

His suite consisted of three servants and
  A tutor – the licentiate[24] Pedrillo,
Who several languages did understand,
  But now lay sick and speechless on his pillow,
And, rocking in his hammock, longed for land,
  His headache being increased by every billow;
And the waves oozing through the porthole made
His berth a little damp, and him afraid.

26

'Twas not without some reason, for the wind
  Increased at night until it blew a gale;
And though 'twas not much to a naval mind,
  Some landsmen would have looked a little pale –
For sailors are, in fact, a different kind.
  At sunset they began to take in sail,
For the sky showed it would come on to blow,
And carry away, perhaps, a mast or so.

Notes

[22] *breathes a vein* Lancing the veins was in Byron's day a frequently used method of treatment.

[23] *Moncada* A family of this name lived next door to Byron at La Mira, Venice, in 1818.

[24] *licentiate* Pedrillo was licensed in one or both of two ways: either he held a degree from the University of Salamanca (stanza 37) or he was authorized to teach and perform religious rites.

27

At one o'clock the wind with sudden shift
Threw the ship right into the trough of the sea,[25]
Which struck her aft, and made an awkward rift,
Started the stern-post,[26] also shattered the
Whole of her stern-frame, and ere she could lift
Herself from out her present jeopardy
The rudder tore away: 'twas time to sound[27]
The pumps, and there were four feet water found.

28

One gang of people instantly was put
Upon the pumps, and the remainder set
To get up part of the cargo, and what-not,
But they could not come at the leak as yet;
At last they did get at it really, but
Still their salvation was an even bet.
The water rushed through in a way quite puzzling,
While they thrust sheets, shirts, jackets, bales of muslin

29

Into the opening – but all such ingredients
Would have been vain, and they must have gone down,
Despite of all their efforts and expedients,
But for the pumps: I'm glad to make them known
To all the brother tars who may have need hence,
For fifty tons of water were upthrown
By them per hour, and they had all been undone
But for their maker, Mr Mann, of London.[28]

30

As day advanced the weather seemed to abate,
And then the leak they reckoned to reduce,
And keep the ship afloat, though three feet yet
Kept two hand- and one chain-pump[29] still in use.
The wind blew fresh again: as it grew late
A squall came on, and while some guns broke loose,
A gust, which all descriptive power transcends,
Laid with one blast the ship on her beam-ends.[30]

Notes

[25] *the trough of the sea* the hollow between waves.

[26] *Started the stern-post* displaced or loosened the upright beam at the stern of the ship, which supported the rudder.

[27] *sound* i.e. use the pumps to find out how much water the ship had taken in.

[28] *Mr Mann, of London* This detail derives from Byron's source, Sir John Graham Dalyell's *Shipwrecks and Disasters at Sea* (3 vols, 1812).

[29] *chain-pump* machine for raising water by means of an endless chain.

[30] *Laid . . . beam-ends* when the ends of a ship's beams touch the water, the vessel lies on its side, in imminent danger of capsizing.

31

There she lay, motionless, and seemed upset;
  The water left the hold, and washed the decks,
And made a scene men do not soon forget;
  For they remember battles, fires, and wrecks,
Or any other thing that brings regret,
  Or breaks their hopes, or hearts, or heads, or necks:
Thus drownings are much talked of by the divers
And swimmers who may chance to be survivors.

32

Immediately the masts were cut away,
  Both main and mizen; first the mizen went,
The mainmast followed. But the ship still lay
  Like a mere log, and baffled our intent.
Foremast and bowsprit were cut down, and they
  Eased her at last (although we never meant
To part with all till every hope was blighted),
And then with violence the old ship righted.

33

It may be easily supposed, while this
  Was going on, some people were unquiet,
That passengers would find it much amiss
  To lose their lives as well as spoil their diet;
That even the able seaman, deeming his
  Days nearly o'er, might be disposed to riot,
As upon such occasions tars will ask
For grog, and sometimes drink rum from the cask.

34

There's nought, no doubt, so much the spirit calms
  As rum and true religion; thus it was
Some plundered, some drank spirits, some sung psalms,
  The high wind made the treble, and as bass
The hoarse harsh waves kept time; fright cured the qualms
  Of all the luckless landsmen's seasick maws:
Strange sounds of wailing, blasphemy, devotion,
Clamoured in chorus to the roaring ocean.

35

Perhaps more mischief had been done, but for
  Our Juan who, with sense beyond his years,
Got to the spirit-room,[31] and stood before
  It with a pair of pistols; and their fears,
As if Death were more dreadful by his door
  Of fire than water, spite of oaths and tears,
Kept still aloof the crew who, ere they sunk,
Thought it would be becoming to die drunk.

Notes

[31] *spirit-room* cabin where alcohol was stored.

36

'Give us more grog', they cried, 'for it will be
All one an hour hence.' Juan answered, 'No!
'Tis true that death awaits both you and me,
But let us die like men, not sink below
Like brutes.' And thus his dangerous post kept he,
And none liked to anticipate the blow;
And even Pedrillo, his most reverend tutor,
Was for some rum a disappointed suitor.

37

The good old gentleman was quite aghast
And made a loud and a pious lamentation,
Repented all his sins, and made a last
Irrevocable vow of reformation;
Nothing should tempt him more (this peril past)
To quit his academic occupation
In cloisters of the classic Salamanca,[32]
To follow Juan's wake like Sancho Panza.[33]

38

But now there came a flash of hope once more:
Day broke, and the wind lulled – the masts were gone,
The leak increased; shoals round her, but no shore,
The vessel swam, yet still she held her own.
They tried the pumps again, and though before
Their desperate efforts seemed all useless grown,
A glimpse of sunshine set some hands to bale –
The stronger pumped, the weaker thrummed a sail.[34]

39

Under the vessel's keel the sail was past,
And for the moment it had some effect;
But with a leak, and not a stick of mast,
Nor rag of canvas, what could they expect?
But still 'tis best to struggle to the last,
'Tis never too late to be wholly wrecked –
And though 'tis true that man can only die once,
'Tis not so pleasant in the Gulf of Lyons.

40

There winds and waves had hurled them, and from thence,
Without their will, they carried them away;
For they were forced with steering to dispense,
And never had as yet a quiet day

Notes

[32] *the classic Salamanca* Spanish university founded in the 13th century.

[33] Sancho Panza was Don Quixote's sidekick in Cervantes's famous novel.

[34] *thrummed a sail* They fastened bunches of rope-yarn over a sail so as to produce a shaggy surface, suitable to stop the leak.

On which they might repose, or even commence
  A jury-mast[35] or rudder, or could say
The ship would swim an hour, which, by good luck,
Still swam – though not exactly like a duck.

41

The wind, in fact, perhaps, was rather less,
  But the ship laboured so, they scarce could hope
To weather out much longer; the distress
  Was also great with which they had to cope
For want of water, and their solid mess
  Was scant enough: in vain the telescope
Was used – nor sail nor shore appeared in sight,
Nought but the heavy sea, and coming night.

42

Again the weather threatened; again blew
  A gale, and in the fore- and after-hold
Water appeared – yet, though the people knew
  All this, the most were patient, and some bold,
Until the chains and leathers were worn through
  Of all our pumps: a wreck complete she rolled
At mercy of the waves, whose mercies are
Like human beings during civil war.

43

Then came the carpenter at last, with tears
  In his rough eyes, and told the captain he
Could do no more; he was a man in years,
  And long had voyaged through many a stormy sea,
And if he wept at length, they were not fears
  That made his eyelids as a woman's be,
But he, poor fellow, had a wife and children,
Two things for dying people quite bewildering.

44

The ship was evidently settling now
  Fast by the head;[36] and, all distinction gone,
Some went to prayers again, and made a vow
  Of candles to their saints – but there were none
To pay them with; and some looked o'er the bow;
  Some hoisted out the boats; and there was one
That begged Pedrillo for an absolution,
Who told him to be damned – in his confusion.

Notes

[35] *jury-mast* temporary replacement mast.

[36] *head* the fore-part of the ship, the bow.

45

Some lashed them in their hammocks, some put on
Their best clothes, as if going to a fair;
Some cursed the day on which they saw the sun,[37]
And gnashed their teeth and, howling, tore their hair;
And others went on as they had begun,
Getting the boats out, being well aware
That a tight boat will live in a rough sea,
Unless with breakers close beneath her lee.[38]

46

The worst of all was that, in their condition,
Having been several days in great distress,
'Twas difficult to get out such provision
As now might render their long suffering less –
Men, even when dying, dislike inanition.
Their stock was damaged by the weather's stress:
Two casks of biscuit and a keg of butter
Were all that could be thrown into the cutter.[39]

47

But in the longboat they contrived to stow
Some pounds of bread, though injured by the wet;
Water, a twenty gallon cask or so;
Six flasks of wine; and they contrived to get
A portion of their beef up from below,
And with a piece of pork, moreover, met,
But scarce enough to serve them for a luncheon –
Then there was rum, eight gallons in a puncheon.[40]

48

The other boats, the yawl and pinnace, had
Been stove[41] in the beginning of the gale;
And the longboat's condition was but bad,
As there were but two blankets for a sail
And one oar for a mast, which a young lad
Threw in by good luck over the ship's rail –
And two boats could not hold, far less be stored,
To save one half the people then on board.

49

'Twas twilight, and the sunless day went down
Over the waste of waters, like a veil
Which, if withdrawn, would but disclose the frown

Notes

[37] *Some cursed . . . the sun* as at Jeremiah 20: 14: 'Cursed be the day wherein I was born.'

[38] *lee* side of the boat sheltered from the wind. The line means 'unless the boat could be driven by the wind against breakers to the lee-side'.

[39] *cutter* lifeboat.

[40] *puncheon* large cask.

[41] *had / Been stove* had a hole made in the side.

Of one whose hate is masked but to assail;
Thus to their hopeless eyes the night was shown
And grimly darkled o'er their faces pale,
And the dim desolate deep; twelve days had Fear
Been their familiar, and now Death was here.

50

Some trial had been making at a raft
With little hope in such a rolling sea –
A sort of thing at which one would have laughed,
If any laughter at such times could be,
Unless with people who too much have quaffed,
And have a kind of wild and horrid glee,
Half-epileptical, and half-hysterical:
Their preservation would have been a miracle.

51

At half-past eight o'clock, booms, hencoops, spars,
And all things, for a chance, had been cast loose,
That still could keep afloat the struggling tars –
For yet[42] they strove, although of no great use.
There was no light in heaven but a few stars,
The boats put off o'ercrowded with their crews;
She gave a heel, and then a lurch to port,
And, going down head foremost – sunk, in short.

52

Then rose from sea to sky the wild farewell,
Then shrieked the timid, and stood still the brave,
Then some leaped overboard with dreadful yell,
As eager to anticipate their grave;
And the sea yawned around her like a hell,
And down she sucked with her the whirling wave,
Like one who grapples with his enemy,
And strives to strangle him before he die.

53

And first one universal shriek there rushed,
Louder than the loud ocean, like a crash
Of echoing thunder; and then all was hushed
Save the wild wind and the remorseless dash
Of billows; but at intervals there gushed,
Accompanied with a convulsive splash,
A solitary shriek, the bubbling cry
Of some strong swimmer in his agony.

Notes

[42] *yet* still.

54

The boats, as stated, had got off before,
And in them crowded several of the crew;
And yet their present hope was hardly more
Than what it had been, for so strong it blew
There was slight chance of reaching any shore;
And then they were too many, though so few –
Nine in the cutter, thirty in the boat
Were counted in them when they got afloat.

55

All the rest perished; near two hundred souls
Had left their bodies – and, what's worse, alas!
When over Catholics the ocean rolls,
They must wait several weeks before a mass
Takes off one peck[43] of purgatorial coals,
Because, till people know what's come to pass,
They won't lay out their money on the dead:
It costs three francs for every mass that's said.

56

Juan got into the longboat, and there
Contrived to help Pedrillo to a place;
It seemed as if they had exchanged their care,
For Juan wore the magisterial face
Which courage gives, while poor Pedrillo's pair
Of eyes were crying for their owner's case:
Battista, though (a name called shortly Tita),
Was lost by getting at some aqua vita.[44]

57

Pedro, his valet, too, he tried to save,
But the same cause, conducive to his loss,
Left him so drunk, he jumped into the wave
As o'er the cutter's edge he tried to cross,
And so he found a wine-and-watery grave;
They could not rescue him although so close,
Because the sea ran higher every minute,
And for the boat – the crew kept crowding in it.

58

A small old spaniel which had been Don Jóse's,
His father's, whom he loved, as ye may think
(For on such things the memory reposes
With tenderness), stood howling on the brink,

Notes

[43] *peck* small quantity (technically, the fourth part of a bushel, or two gallons).

[44] *aqua vita* spirits (probably brandy).

Knowing (dogs have such intellectual noses!),
No doubt, the vessel was about to sink;
And Juan caught him up, and ere he stepped
Off, threw him in, then after him he leapt.

59

He also stuffed his money where he could
About his person, and Pedrillo's too –
Who let him do, in fact, whate'er he would,
Not knowing what himself to say or do,
As every rising wave his dread renewed;
But Juan, trusting they might still get through,
And deeming there were remedies for any ill,
Thus re-embarked[45] his tutor and his spaniel.

60

'Twas a rough night, and blew so stiffly yet,
That the sail was becalmed between the seas,
Though on the wave's high top too much to set,
They dared not take it in for all the breeze;
Each sea curled o'er the stern, and kept them wet,
And made them bale without a moment's ease,
So that themselves as well as hopes were damped,
And the poor little cutter quickly swamped.

61

Nine souls more went in her: the longboat still
Kept above water, with an oar for mast;
Two blankets stitched together, answering ill
Instead of sail, were to the oar made fast –
Though every wave rolled menacing to fill,
And present peril all before surpassed,
They grieved for those who perished with the cutter,
And also for the biscuit casks and butter.

62

The sun rose red and fiery, a sure sign
Of the continuance of the gale: to run
Before the sea, until it should grow fine,
Was all that for the present could be done.
A few teaspoonfuls of their rum and wine
Was served out to the people, who begun
To faint, and damaged bread wet through the bags,
And most of them had little clothes but rags.

Notes

[45] *re-embarked* again put on board a boat.

63

They counted thirty, crowded in a space
Which left scarce room for motion or exertion.
They did their best to modify their case:
One half sat up, though numbed with the immersion,
While t'other half were laid down in their place
At watch and watch; thus, shivering like the tertian
Ague[46] in its cold fit, they filled their boat,
With nothing but the sky for a greatcoat.

64

'Tis very certain the desire of life
Prolongs it; this is obvious to physicians
When patients, neither plagued with friends nor wife,
Survive through very desperate conditions,
Because they still can hope, nor shines the knife
Nor shears of Atropos[47] before their visions:
Despair of all recovery spoils longevity,
And makes men's miseries of alarming brevity.

65

'Tis said that persons living on annuities
Are longer lived than others – God knows why,
Unless to plague the grantors;[48] yet so true it is,
That some, I really think, *do* never die.
Of any creditors the worst a Jew it is,
And *that's* their mode of furnishing supply:
In my young days they lent me cash that way,
Which I found very troublesome to pay.[49]

66

'Tis thus with people in an open boat,
They live upon the love of life, and bear
More than can be believed, or even thought,
And stand like rocks the tempest's wear and tear;
And hardship still has been the sailor's lot
Since Noah's ark went cruising here and there;
She had a curious crew as well as cargo,
Like the first old Greek privateer, the Argo.[50]

67

But man is a carnivorous production
And must have meals, at least one meal a day;
He cannot live, like woodcocks, upon suction,[51]

Notes

[46] *the tertian / Ague* a fever that recurs every other day.

[47] *shears of Atropos* Atropos, eldest of the three Fates, is represented blind, with a pair of scissors with which she cuts the thread of life.

[48] *the grantors* those who set up the annuity.

[49] *In my young days . . . to pay* By 1816, when he left England, Byron had amassed £30,000 in debts.

[50] *Argo* the ship (named after the city of Argos) which carried Jason and his companions to capture the golden fleece.

[51] *like woodcocks, upon suction* Woodcocks appear to be sucking as they probe with their long bills in the turf.

But, like the shark and tiger, must have prey –
Although his anatomical construction
Bears vegetables in a grumbling way,
Your labouring people think beyond all question
Beef, veal, and mutton, better for digestion.

68

And thus it was with this our hapless crew,
For on the third day there came on a calm,
And though at first their strength it might renew,
And lying on their weariness like balm,
Lulled them like turtles sleeping on the blue
Of ocean, when they woke they felt a qualm,
And fell all ravenously on their provision,
Instead of hoarding it with due precision.

69

The consequence was easily foreseen:
They ate up all they had, and drank their wine
In spite of all remonstrances, and then –
On what, in fact, next day were they to dine?
They hoped the wind would rise, these foolish men,
And carry them to shore! These hopes were fine,
But as they had but one oar, and that brittle,
It would have been more wise to save their victual.[52]

70

The fourth day came, but not a breath of air,
And ocean slumbered like an unweaned child;
The fifth day, and their boat lay floating there,
The sea and sky were blue, and clear, and mild –
With their one oar (I wish they had had a pair)
What could they do? And hunger's rage grew wild;
So Juan's spaniel, spite of his entreating,
Was killed, and portioned out for present eating.

71

On the sixth day they fed upon his hide,
And Juan, who had still refused, because
The creature was his father's dog that died,
Now feeling all the vulture[53] in his jaws,
With some remorse received (though first denied)
As a great favour one of the forepaws,
Which he divided with Pedrillo, who
Devoured it, longing for the other too.

Notes

[52] *victual* food (pronounced 'vittle').

[53] *feeling all the vulture* i.e. feeling as hungry as a vulture.

72

The seventh day, and no wind; the burning sun
 Blistered and scorched, and, stagnant on the sea,
They lay like carcasses; and hope was none,
 Save in the breeze that came not. Savagely
They glared upon each other – all was done,
 Water, and wine, and food; and you might see
The longings of the cannibal arise
(Although they spoke not) in their wolfish eyes.

73

At length one whispered his companion, who
 Whispered another, and thus it went round,
And then into a hoarser murmur grew –
 An ominous, and wild, and desperate sound;
And when his comrade's thought each sufferer knew,
 'Twas but his own, suppressed till now, he found.
And out they spoke of lots for flesh and blood,
And who should die to be his fellow's food.

74

But ere they came to this, they that day shared
 Some leathern caps, and what remained of shoes;
And then they looked around them and despaired,
 And none to be the sacrifice would choose;
At length the lots were torn up and prepared,
 But of materials that much shock the muse –
Having no paper, for the want of better,
They took by force from Juan Julia's letter.

75

The lots were made, and marked, and mixed and handed
 In silent horror, and their distribution
Lulled even the savage hunger which demanded,
 Like the Promethean vulture,[54] this pollution;[55]
None in particular had sought or planned it,
 'Twas nature gnawed them to this resolution
By which none were permitted to be neuter[56] –
And the lot fell on Juan's luckless tutor.

76

He but requested to be bled to death:
 The surgeon had his instruments, and bled
Pedrillo, and so gently ebbed his breath,
 You hardly could perceive when he was dead.

Notes

[54] *the Promethean vulture* Prometheus was nailed to the rock of the Caucasus for 3,000 years while an eagle (in some versions a vulture) feasted on his liver.

[55] *pollution* defilement (of Julia's love-letter). Nothing is sacred in the face of starvation.

[56] *neuter* exempt.

He died as born, a Catholic in faith,
  Like most in the belief in which they're bred,
And first a little crucifix he kissed,
  And then held out his jugular and wrist.

77

The surgeon, as there was no other fee,
  Had his first choice of morsels for his pains;
But being thirstiest at the moment, he
  Preferred a draught from the fast-flowing veins:
Part was divided, part thrown in the sea,
  And such things as the entrails and the brains
Regaled two sharks, who followed o'er the billow –
The sailors ate the rest of poor Pedrillo.

78

The sailors ate him, all save three or four
  Who were not quite so fond of animal food;
To these was added Juan who, before
  Refusing his own spaniel, hardly could
Feel now his appetite increased much more;
  'Twas not to be expected that he should,
Even in extremity of their disaster,
Dine with them on his pastor and his master.

79

'Twas better that he did not, for, in fact,
  The consequence was awful in the extreme;
For they who were most ravenous in the act
  Went raging mad – Lord, how they did blaspheme,
And foam and roll, with strange convulsions racked,
  Drinking salt-water like a mountain-stream,
Tearing and grinning, howling, screeching, swearing,
And, with hyena laughter, died despairing.

80

Their numbers were much thinned by this infliction,
  And all the rest were thin enough, Heaven knows;
And some of them had lost their recollection,
  Happier than they who still perceived their woes;
But others pondered on a new dissection,
  As if not warned sufficiently by those
Who had already perished, suffering madly,
For having used their appetites so sadly.

81

And next they thought upon the master's mate
  As fattest – but he saved himself because,
Besides being much averse from such a fate,
  There were some other reasons: the first was
He had been rather indisposed of late;

And that which chiefly proved his saving clause
Was a small present made to him at Cadiz,
By general subscription of the ladies.[57]

82

Of poor Pedrillo something still remained,
But was used sparingly – some were afraid,
And others still their appetites constrained,
Or but at times a little supper made;
All except Juan, who throughout abstained,
Chewing a piece of bamboo, and some lead:
At length they caught two boobies and a noddy,[58]
And then they left off eating the dead body.

83

And if Pedrillo's fate should shocking be,
Remember Ugolino condescends
To eat the head of his arch-enemy
The moment after he politely ends
His tale;[59] if foes be food in hell, at sea
'Tis surely fair to dine upon our friends
When shipwreck's short allowance grows too scanty,
Without being much more horrible than Dante.

84

And the same night there fell a shower of rain
For which their mouths gaped, like the cracks of earth
When dried to summer dust; till taught by pain,
Men really know not what good water's worth:
If you had been in Turkey or in Spain,
Or with a famished boat's-crew had your berth,
Or in the desert heard the camel's bell,
You'd wish yourself where Truth is – in a well.

85

It poured down torrents, but they were no richer
Until they found a ragged piece of sheet
Which served them as a sort of spongy pitcher,
And when they deemed its moisture was complete,
They wrung it out, and though a thirsty ditcher[60]
Might not have thought the scanty draught so sweet
As a full pot of porter, to their thinking
They ne'er till now had known the joys of drinking.

Notes

[57] *a small present . . . ladies* i.e. he was suffering from syphilis.

[58] *boobies . . . noddy* species of sea-bird.

[59] *Remember Ugolino . . . His tale* In his *Inferno*, Dante relates how Count Ugolino was imprisoned with his two sons and two grandsons and starved to death with them. In Hell, Ugolino is seen chewing on the skull of the man responsible for the atrocity (*Inferno* xxxiii 76–8).

[60] *ditcher* one who makes and repairs ditches.

86

And their baked lips,[61] with many a bloody crack,
  Sucked in the moisture, which like nectar streamed;
Their throats were ovens, their swoln tongues were black
  As the rich man's in hell,[62] who vainly screamed
To beg the beggar, who could not rain back
  A drop of dew, when every drop had seemed
To taste of heaven (if this be true, indeed,
Some Christians have a comfortable creed).

87

There were two fathers in this ghastly crew,
  And with them their two sons, of whom the one
Was more robust and hardy to the view,
  But he died early; and when he was gone,
His nearest messmate[63] told his sire, who threw
  One glance on him, and said, 'Heaven's will be done!
I can do nothing', and he saw him thrown
Into the deep without a tear or groan.

88

The other father had a weaklier child,
  Of a soft cheek, and aspect delicate;
But the boy bore up long, and with a mild
  And patient spirit held aloof his fate;
Little he said, and now and then he smiled,
  As if to win a part from off the weight
He saw increasing on his father's heart,
With the deep deadly thought that they must part.

89

And o'er him bent his sire, and never raised
  His eyes from off his face, but wiped the foam
From his pale lips, and ever on him gazed,
  And when the wished-for shower at length was come,
And the boy's eyes, which the dull film half glazed,
  Brightened, and for a moment seemed to roam,
He squeezed from out a rag some drops of rain
Into his dying child's mouth – but in vain.

90

The boy expired; the father held the clay,[64]
  And looked upon it long, and when at last
Death left no doubt, and the dead burden lay
  Stiff on his heart, and pulse and hope were past,

Notes

[61] *baked lips* apparently an echo of Coleridge, *Ancient Mariner* (1817) 157: 'With throat unslaked, with black lips baked'.

[62] *As the rich man's in hell* an allusion to the parable of Dives and Lazarus, Luke 16: 19–26.

[63] *messmate* companion at mealtimes; a sardonic joke.

[64] *clay* body.

He watched it wistfully, until away
'Twas borne by the rude wave wherein 'twas cast.
Then he himself sunk down all dumb and shivering,
And gave no sign of life, save his limbs quivering.

91

Now overhead a rainbow, bursting through
The scattering clouds, shone, spanning the dark sea,
Resting its bright base on the quivering blue;
And all within its arch appeared to be
Clearer than that without, and its wide hue
Waxed[65] broad and waving, like a banner free,
Then changed like to a bow that's bent, and then
Forsook the dim eyes of these shipwrecked men.

92

It changed, of course; a heavenly chameleon,
The airy child of vapour and the sun,
Brought forth in purple, cradled in vermilion,
Baptized in molten gold, and swathed in dun,[66]
Glittering like crescents o'er a Turk's pavilion,
And blending every colour into one,
Just like a black eye in a recent scuffle[67]
(For sometimes we must box without the muffle[68]).

93

Our shipwrecked seamen thought it a good omen –
It is as well to think so, now and then;
'Twas an old custom of the Greek and Roman,
And may become of great advantage when
Folks are discouraged; and most surely no men
Had greater need to nerve themselves again
Than these, and so this rainbow looked like hope –
Quite a celestial kaleidoscope.[69]

94

About this time a beautiful white bird,
Webfooted, not unlike a dove in size
And plumage (probably it might have erred
Upon its course), passed oft before their eyes
And tried to perch, although it saw and heard
The men within the boat, and in this guise
It came and went, and fluttered round them till
Night fell – this seemed a better omen still.

Notes

[65] *Waxed* became.

[66] *dun* dull brown.

[67] Byron is deliberately profaning the image celebrated in Wordsworth's *The Rainbow.*

[68] *muffle* boxing-glove. Bare-knuckle boxing was fashionable in the early 19th century; Byron himself trained with 'Gentleman' Jackson.

[69] *kaleidoscope* invented as recently as 1817 by Sir David Brewster; Byron was sent one by John Murray in November 1818.

95

But in this case I also must remark
 'Twas well this bird of promise did not perch,
Because the tackle of our shattered bark
 Was not so safe for roosting as a church;
And had it been the dove from Noah's ark,
 Returning there from her successful search,
Which in their way that moment chanced to fall,
They would have eat[70] her, olive-branch and all.[71]

96

With twilight it again came on to blow,
 But not with violence; the stars shone out,
The boat made way; yet now they were so low,
 They knew not where nor what they were about;
Some fancied they saw land, and some said 'No!'
 The frequent fog-banks gave them cause to doubt –
Some swore that they heard breakers,[72] others guns,
And all mistook about the latter once.

97

As morning broke the light wind died away,
 When he who had the watch sung out and swore
If 'twas not land that rose with the sun's ray,
 He wished that land he never might see more;
And the rest rubbed their eyes, and saw a bay,
 Or thought they saw, and shaped their course for shore –
For shore it was,[73] and gradually grew
Distinct, and high, and palpable to view.

98

And then of these some part burst into tears,
 And others, looking with a stupid stare,
Could not yet separate their hopes from fears,
 And seemed as if they had no further care;
While a few prayed (the first time for some years),
 And at the bottom of the boat three were
Asleep; they shook them by the hand and head,
And tried to awaken them, but found them dead.

99

The day before, fast sleeping on the water,
 They found a turtle of the hawk's-bill kind,
And by good fortune gliding softly, caught her,

Notes

[70] *eat* pronounced 'ett' by Byron.

[71] See Genesis 8: 6–11. In a useful note, Peter Cochran suggests that Byron has in mind a narrative of the shipwreck of the *Medusa*; see 'Byron's *Don Juan*, Canto II, Stanza 95: A Previously Unnoted Source in the *Medusa* Narrative', *N&Q* NS 39 (1992) 172–3.

[72] *breakers* waves breaking against the shore.

[73] *For shore it was* that of one of the smaller Cyclades (l. 1010); as the *Trinidada* went down near the Golfe du Lion, that would mean that the survivors had drifted an improbable 2,000 kilometres.

Which yielded a day's life, and to their mind
Proved even still a more nutritious matter
Because it left encouragement behind:
They thought that in such perils, more than chance
Had sent them this for their deliverance.

100

The land appeared a high and rocky coast,
And higher grew the mountains as they drew,
Set by a current, toward it: they were lost
In various conjectures, for none knew
To what part of the earth they had been tossed,
So changeable had been the winds that blew;
Some thought it was Mount Etna, some the highlands
Of Candia,[74] Cyprus, Rhodes, or other islands.

101

Meantime the current, with a rising gale,
Still set them onwards to the welcome shore
Like Charon's bark of spectres,[75] dull and pale.
Their living freight was now reduced to four,
And three dead, whom their strength could not avail
To heave into the deep with those before –
Though the two sharks still followed them, and dashed
The spray into their faces as they splashed.

102

Famine, despair, cold, thirst and heat, had done
Their work on them by turns, and thinned them to
Such things a mother had not known her son
Amidst the skeletons of that gaunt crew;
By night chilled, by day scorched – thus one by one
They perished, until withered to these few,
But chiefly by a species of self-slaughter,
In washing down Pedrillo with salt water.

103

As they drew nigh the land, which now was seen
Unequal in its aspect here and there,
They felt the freshness of its growing green
That waved in forest-tops and smoothed the air,
And fell upon their glazed eyes like a screen
From glistening waves, and skies so hot and bare –
Lovely seemed any object that should sweep
Away the vast, salt, dread, eternal deep.

Notes

[74] *Candia* Crete.

[75] *Like Charon's bark of spectres* The grim ferryman Charon took the ghosts of the dead across the rivers of the underworld.

104

The shore looked wild, without a trace of man,
And girt by formidable waves; but they
Were mad for land, and thus their course they ran,
Though right ahead the roaring breakers lay:
A reef between them also now began
To show its boiling surf and bounding spray –
But finding no place for their landing better,
They ran the boat for shore, and overset[76] her.

105

But in his native stream, the Guadalquivir,
Juan to lave his youthful limbs was wont;
And having learnt to swim in that sweet river,
Had often turned the art to some account:
A better swimmer you could scarce see ever,
He could, perhaps, have passed the Hellespont,
As once (a feat on which ourselves we prided)
Leander, Mr Ekenhead, and I did.[77]

106

So here, though faint, emaciated, and stark,
He buoyed his boyish limbs, and strove to ply
With the quick wave, and gain, ere it was dark,
The beach which lay before him, high and dry:
The greatest danger here was from a shark
That carried off his neighbour by the thigh;
As for the other two they could not swim,
So nobody arrived on shore but him.

107

Nor yet had he arrived but for the oar,
Which, providentially for him, was washed
Just as his feeble arms could strike no more,
And the hard wave o'erwhelmed him as 'twas dashed
Within his grasp; he clung to it, and sore
The waters beat while he thereto was lashed;
At last, with swimming, wading, scrambling, he
Rolled on the beach, half-senseless, from the sea.

108

There, breathless, with his digging nails he clung
Fast to the sand, lest the returning wave,
From whose reluctant[78] roar his life he wrung,
Should suck him back to her insatiate grave:

Notes

[76] *overset* capsized.

[77] A MS note by Byron reads: 'Mr Ekenhead, Lieutenant of Marines on board of the Salsette (then commanded by Capt Bathurst) swam across the Dardanelles May 10th (I think) 1810. See the account in Hobhouse's travels.' Byron actually swam the Hellespont on 3 May 1810, and it was described in detail in 'Extract from Lord Byron's Journal', *London Magazine* 1 (1820) 295–6.

[78] *reluctant* opposing; Byron is also punning on the Latin root, *reluctari*, 'to struggle against'.

And there he lay, full-length, where he was flung,
  Before the entrance of a cliff-worn cave,
With just enough of life to feel its pain,
  And deem that it was saved, perhaps, in vain.

109

With slow and staggering effort he arose,
  But sunk again upon his bleeding knee
And quivering hand; and then he looked for those
  Who long had been his mates upon the sea,
But none of them appeared to share his woes
  Save one, a corpse from out the famished three,
Who died two days before, and now had found
An unknown barren beach for burial ground.

110

And as he gazed, his dizzy brain spun fast,
  And down he sunk; and as he sunk, the sand
Swam round and round, and all his senses passed:
  He fell upon his side, and his stretched hand
Drooped dripping on the oar (their jury-mast),[79]
  And, like a withered lily, on the land
His slender frame and pallid aspect lay,
As fair a thing as e'er was formed of clay.[80]

111

How long in his damp trance young Juan lay[81]
  He knew not, for the earth was gone for him,
And Time had nothing more of night nor day
  For his congealing blood, and senses dim;
And how this heavy faintness passed away
  He knew not, till each painful pulse and limb
And tingling vein seemed throbbing back to life –
For Death, though vanquished, still retired with strife.

112

His eyes he opened, shut, again unclosed,
  For all was doubt and dizziness; methought
He still was in the boat, and had but dozed,
  And felt again with his despair o'erwrought,
And wished it death in which he had reposed,
  And then once more his feelings back were brought;
And slowly by his swimming eyes was seen
A lovely female face of seventeen.

Notes

[79] *jury-mast* replacement mast.

[80] *clay* flesh.

[81] *How long in his damp trance young Juan lay* an echo of Coleridge, *Ancient Mariner* (1817) 393–4: 'How long in that same fit I lay, / I have not to declare.'

113

'Twas bending close o'er his, and the small mouth
Seemed almost prying into his for breath;
And chafing him, the soft warm hand of youth
Recalled his answering spirits back from death;
And, bathing his chill temples, tried to soothe
Each pulse to animation, till beneath
Its gentle touch and trembling care, a sigh
To these kind efforts made a low reply.

114

Then was the cordial poured, and mantle flung
Around his scarce-clad limbs; and the fair arm
Raised higher the faint head which o'er it hung;
And her transparent cheek, all pure and warm,
Pillowed his death-like forehead; then she wrung
His dewy curls, long drenched by every storm;
And watched with eagerness each throb that drew
A sigh from his heaved bosom – and hers too.

115

And lifting him with care into the cave,
The gentle girl, and her attendant – one
Young, yet her elder, and of brow less grave,
And more robust of figure – then begun
To kindle fire, and as the new flames gave
Light to the rocks that roofed them, which the sun
Had never seen, the maid, or whatsoe'er
She was, appeared distinct, and tall, and fair.

116

Her brow was overhung with coins of gold
That sparkled o'er the auburn of her hair,
Her clustering hair, whose longer locks were rolled
In braids behind, and though her stature were
Even of the highest for a female mould,
They nearly reached her heel; and in her air
There was a something which bespoke command,
As one who was a lady in the land.

117

Her hair, I said, was auburn; but her eyes
Were black as death, their lashes the same hue,
Of downcast length, in whose silk shadow lies
Deepest attraction – for when to the view
Forth from its raven fringe the full glance flies,
Ne'er with such force the swiftest arrow flew;
'Tis as the snake late coiled, who pours his length,
And hurls at once his venom and his strength.

118

Her brow was white and low, her cheek's pure dye
Like twilight rosy still with the set sun;
Short upper lip, sweet lips! – that make us sigh
Ever to have seen such, for she was one
Fit for the model of a statuary
(A race of mere impostors, when all's done;
I've seen much finer women, ripe and real,
Than all the nonsense of their stone[82] ideal).

119

I'll tell you why I say so, for 'tis just
One should not rail without a decent cause:
There was an Irish lady,[83] to whose bust
I ne'er saw justice done, and yet she was
A frequent model; and if e'er she must
Yield to stern Time and Nature's wrinkling laws,
They will destroy a face which mortal thought
Ne'er compassed, nor less mortal chisel wrought.

120

And such was she, the lady of the cave:
Her dress was very different from the Spanish –
Simpler, and yet of colours not so grave;
For, as you know, the Spanish women banish
Bright hues when out of doors, and yet, while wave
Around them (what I hope will never vanish)
The basquiña[84] and the mantilla,[85] they
Seem at the same time mystical[86] and gay.

121

But with our damsel this was not the case:
Her dress was many-coloured, finely spun;
Her locks curled negligently round her face,
But through them gold and gems profusely shone;
Her girdle sparkled, and the richest lace
Flowed in her veil, and many a precious stone
Flashed on her little hand; but, what was shocking,
Her small snow feet had slippers, but no stocking.
[see Plate 13]

122

The other female's dress was not unlike,
But of inferior materials; she
Had not so many ornaments to strike[87] –

Notes

[82] *stone* an early MS reading is 'damned'.

[83] *an Irish lady* probably, as commentators have noted, Lady Adelaide Forbes (1789–1858); 'The Apollo Belvidere is the image of Lady Adelaide Forbes,' he told Moore, 12 May 1817 (Marchand v 227).

[84] *basquiña* an outer skirt placed over indoor dress when going out.

[85] *mantilla* light cloak.

[86] *mystical* solemn.

[87] *strike* remove, take off.

Her hair had silver only, bound to be
Her dowry; and her veil, in form alike,
Was coarser; and her air, though firm, less free;
Her hair was thicker, but less long; her eyes
As black, but quicker, and of smaller size.

123

And these two tended him, and cheered him both
With food and raiment, and those soft attentions
Which are (as I must own) of female growth,
And have ten thousand delicate inventions:
They made a most superior mess of broth,
A thing which poesy but seldom mentions,
But the best dish that e'er was cooked since Homer's
Achilles ordered dinner for newcomers.[88]

124

I'll tell you who they were, this female pair,
Lest they should seem princesses in disguise;
Besides, I hate all mystery, and that air
Of claptrap, which your recent poets prize;
And so, in short, the girls they really were
They shall appear before your curious eyes –
Mistress and maid; the first was only daughter
Of an old man, who lived upon the water.

125

A fisherman he had been in his youth,
And still a sort of fisherman was he;
But other speculations were, in sooth,
Added to his connection with the sea –
Perhaps not so respectable, in truth:
A little smuggling, and some piracy
Left him, at last, the sole of many masters
Of an ill-gotten million of piastres.[89]

126

A fisher, therefore, was he – though of men,
Like Peter the Apostle[90] – and he fished
For wandering merchant vessels, now and then,
And sometimes caught as many as he wished;
The cargoes he confiscated, and gain
He sought in the slave-market too, and dished
Full many a morsel for that Turkish trade,
By which, no doubt, a good deal may be made.

Notes

[88] *But the best dish . . . newcomers* Homer describes in the *Iliad* ix how Patroclus, Achilles and Automedon ate a sheep, a goat and a pig.

[89] *piastres* small Turkish coins.

[90] *though of men . . . Apostle* see Matthew 4: 18–19.

127

He was a Greek, and on his isle had built
(One of the wild and smaller Cyclades)[91]
A very handsome house from out his guilt,
And there he lived exceedingly at ease;
Heaven knows what cash he got, or blood he spilt –
A sad[92] old fellow was he, if you please,
But this I know: it was a spacious building,
Full of barbaric carving, paint, and gilding.

128

He had an only daughter called Haidee,[93]
The greatest heiress of the Eastern Isles;
Besides, so very beautiful was she,
Her dowry was as nothing to her smiles:
Still in her teens, and like a lovely tree
She grew to womanhood, and between whiles
Rejected several suitors, just to learn
How to accept a better in his turn.

129

And walking out upon the beach below
The cliff, towards sunset, on that day she found,
Insensible – not dead, but nearly so –
Don Juan, almost famished, and half-drowned;
But being naked, she was shocked, you know,
Yet deemed herself in common pity bound,
As far as in her lay, 'to take him in,
A stranger',[94] dying, with so white a skin.

130

But taking him into her father's house
Was not exactly the best way to save,
But like conveying to the cat the mouse,
Or people in a trance into their grave;
Because the good old man had so much νοῦς,[95]
Unlike the honest Arab thieves so brave,
He would have hospitably cured the stranger,
And sold him instantly when out of danger.

131

And therefore, with her maid, she thought it best
(A virgin always on her maid relies)
To place him in the cave for present rest;
And when, at last, he opened his black eyes,

Notes

[91] *Cyclades* group of islands in the Aegean between the Peloponnese and the Dodecanese.

[92] *sad* appallingly bad.

[93] *Haidee* 'a caress' or 'the caressed one'; Byron would have encountered the name in popular Greek songs of the time. (See Plate 13.)

[94] Matthew 25: 35.

[95] νοῦς pronounced 'nouse' (rhyme with 'mouse'); sense, intelligence.

Their charity increased about their guest,
And their compassion grew to such a size,
It opened half the turnpike-gates to heaven
(St Paul says 'tis the toll which must be given).[96]

132

They made a fire, but such a fire as they
Upon the moment could contrive with such
Materials as were cast up round the bay –
Some broken planks, and oars, that to the touch
Were nearly tinder, since so long they lay,
A mast was almost crumbled to a crutch;
But, by God's grace, here wrecks were in such plenty,
That there was fuel to have furnished twenty.

133

He had a bed of furs, and a pelisse,[97]
For Haidee stripped her sables off to make
His couch; and, that he might be more at ease
And warm, in case by chance he should awake,
They also gave a petticoat apiece,
She and her maid, and promised by daybreak
To pay him a fresh visit, with a dish
For breakfast, of eggs, coffee, bread, and fish.

134

And thus they left him to his lone repose.
Juan slept like a top,[98] or like the dead
Who sleep at last, perhaps (God only knows),
Just for the present; and in his lulled head
Not even a vision of his former woes
Throbbed in accursed dreams, which sometimes spread
Unwelcome visions of our former years,
Till the eye, cheated, opens thick with tears.

135

Young Juan slept all dreamless, but the maid
Who smoothed his pillow as she left the den
Looked back upon him, and a moment stayed,
And turned, believing that he called again.
He slumbered; yet she thought, at least she said
(The heart will slip even as the tongue and pen),
He had pronounced her name – but she forgot
That at this moment Juan knew it not.

Notes

[96] 'And above all these things put on charity, which is the bond of perfectness' (Colossians 3: 14).

[97] *pelisse* long cloak reaching the ankles, with sleeves or armholes.

[98] *Juan slept like a top* a reference to the apparent stillness of a spinning top when its axis of rotation is vertical.

136

And pensive to her father's house she went,
    Enjoining silence strict to Zoe,[99] who
Better than her knew what, in fact, she meant,
    She being wiser by a year or two:
A year or two's an age when rightly spent,
    And Zoe spent hers, as most women do,
In gaining all that useful sort of knowledge
Which is acquired in nature's good old college.

137

The morn broke, and found Juan slumbering still
    Fast in his cave, and nothing clashed upon
His rest; the rushing of the neighbouring rill
    And the young beams of the excluded sun
Troubled him not, and he might sleep his fill;
    And need he had of slumber yet, for none
Had suffered more – his hardships were comparative
To those related in my granddad's *Narrative*.[100]

138

Not so Haidee: she sadly tossed and tumbled,
    And started from her sleep, and, turning o'er,
Dreamed of a thousand wrecks o'er which she stumbled,
    And handsome corpses strewed upon the shore;
And woke her maid so early that she grumbled,
    And called her father's old slaves up, who swore
In several oaths – Armenian, Turk, and Greek;
They knew not what to think of such a freak.[101]

139

But up she got, and up she made them get
    With some pretence about the sun, that makes
Sweet skies just when he rises, or is set;
    And 'tis, no doubt, a sight to see when breaks
Bright Phoebus, while the mountains still are wet
    With mist, and every bird with him awakes,
And night is flung off like a mourning suit
Worn for a husband, or some other brute.

140

I say, the sun is a most glorious sight;
    I've seen him rise full oft, indeed of late
I have sat up on purpose all the night,
    Which hastens, as physicians say, one's fate –
And so all ye, who would be in the right

Notes

[99] *Zoe* 'life'.

[100] *my granddad's Narrative* i.e. *A Narrative of the Hon. John Byron, containing an account of the great distress suffered by himself and his companions on the coast of Patagonia, from the year 1740, till their arrival in England, 1746* (1768) – a popular volume which went through eleven editions before 1825, reprinted intermittently until 1925.

[101] *a freak* i.e. freakish behaviour.

In health and purse, begin your day to date
From daybreak, and when coffined at fourscore,[102]
Engrave upon the plate, you rose at four.

141

And Haidee met the morning face to face;
  Her own was freshest, though a feverish flush
Had dyed it with the headlong blood, whose race
  From heart to cheek is curbed into a blush,
Like to a torrent which a mountain's base,
  That overpowers some alpine river's rush,
Checks to a lake, whose waves in circles spread,
Or the Red Sea – but the sea is not red.

142

And down the cliff the island virgin came,
  And near the cave her quick light footsteps drew,
While the sun smiled on her with his first flame,
  And young Aurora[103] kissed her lips with dew,
Taking her for a sister; just the same
  Mistake you would have made on seeing the two,
Although the mortal, quite as fresh and fair,
Had all the advantage too of not being air.

143

And when into the cavern Haidee stepped
  All timidly, yet rapidly, she saw
That like an infant Juan sweetly slept;
  And then she stopped, and stood as if in awe
(For sleep is awful[104]), and on tiptoe crept
  And wrapped him closer, lest the air, too raw,
Should reach his blood, then o'er him still as death
Bent, with hushed lips, that drank his scarce-drawn breath.

144

And thus like to an angel o'er the dying
  Who die in righteousness,[105] she leaned; and there
All tranquilly the shipwrecked boy was lying,
  As o'er him lay the calm and stirless air.
But Zoe the meantime some eggs was frying,
  Since, after all, no doubt the youthful pair
Must breakfast, and betimes; lest they should ask it,
She drew out her provision from the basket.

145

She knew that the best feelings must have victual
  And that a shipwrecked youth would hungry be;
Besides, being less in love, she yawned a little,

Notes

[102] *fourscore* eighty.

[103] *Aurora* goddess of dawn and morning.

[104] *awful* awe-inspiring.

[105] *the dying . . . righteousness* a profane reference to Matthew 25: 46.

And felt her veins chilled by the neighbouring sea.
And so she cooked their breakfast to a tittle;[106]
I can't say that she gave them any tea,
But there were eggs, fruit, coffee, bread, fish, honey,
With Scio[107] wine – and all for love, not money.

146

And Zoe, when the eggs were ready, and
The coffee made, would fain have wakened Juan,
But Haidee stopped her with her quick small hand,
And without a word, a sign her finger drew on
Her lip, which Zoe needs must understand;
And, the first breakfast spoilt, prepared a new one,
Because her mistress would not let her break
That sleep which seemed as it would ne'er awake.

147

For still he lay, and on his thin worn cheek
A purple hectic[108] played like dying day
On the snow-tops of distant hills; the streak
Of sufferance yet upon his forehead lay,
Where the blue veins looked shadowy, shrunk, and weak;
And his black curls were dewy with the spray
Which weighed upon them yet, all damp and salt,
Mixed with the stony vapours of the vault.

148

And she bent o'er him, and he lay beneath,
Hushed as the babe upon its mother's breast,
Drooped as the willow when no winds can breathe,
Lulled like the depth of ocean when at rest,
Fair as the crowning rose of the whole wreath,
Soft as the callow cygnet[109] in its nest;
In short, he was a very pretty fellow,
Although his woes had turned him rather yellow.

149

He woke and gazed, and would have slept again,
But the fair face which met his eyes forbade
Those eyes to close, though weariness and pain
Had further sleep a further pleasure made;
For woman's face was never formed in vain
For Juan, so that, even when he prayed,
He turned from grisly saints and martyrs hairy
To the sweet portraits of the Virgin Mary.

Notes

[106] *to a tittle* with minute exactness.

[107] *Scio* Italian form of Chios (island off the Ionian coast between Lesbos and Samos, known for the high quality of its wines).

[108] *purple hectic* purple flush.

[109] *cygnet* young swan.

150

And thus upon his elbow he arose,
And looked upon the lady, in whose cheek
The pale contended with the purple rose,
As with an effort she began to speak;
Her eyes were eloquent, her words would pose,[110]
Although she told him, in good modern Greek,
With an Ionian accent, low and sweet,
That he was faint, and must not talk, but eat.

151

Now Juan could not understand a word,
Being no Grecian; but he had an ear,
And her voice was the warble of a bird,
So soft, so sweet, so delicately clear,
That finer, simpler music ne'er was heard;
The sort of sound we echo with a tear
Without knowing why – an overpowering tone
Whence melody descends as from a throne.

152

And Juan gazed as one who is awoke
By a distant organ, doubting if he be
Not yet a dreamer, till the spell is broke
By the watchman, or some such reality,
Or by one's early valet's cursed knock –
At least it is a heavy sound to me
Who like a morning slumber, for the night
Shows stars and women in a better light.

153

And Juan, too, was helped out from his dream
Or sleep, or whatsoe'er it was, by feeling
A most prodigious appetite: the steam
Of Zoe's cookery no doubt was stealing
Upon his senses, and the kindling beam
Of the new fire, which Zoe kept up, kneeling,
To stir her viands, made him quite awake
And long for food, but chiefly a beefsteak.

154

But beef is rare within these oxless isles;
Goat's flesh there is, no doubt, and kid, and mutton;
And, when a holiday upon them smiles,
A joint upon their barbarous spits they put on:
But this occurs but seldom, between whiles,
For some of these are rocks with scarce a hut on;
Others are fair and fertile, among which
This, though not large, was one of the most rich.

Notes

[110] *pose* puzzle, confuse.

155

I say that beef is rare, and can't help thinking
  That the old fable of the Minotaur –
From which our modern morals, rightly shrinking,
  Condemn the royal lady's taste who wore
A cow's shape for a mask – was only (sinking
  The allegory) a mere type, no more;
That Pasiphae promoted breeding cattle
To make the Cretans bloodier in battle.[111]

156

For we all know that English people are
  Fed upon beef (I won't say much of beer
Because 'tis liquor only, and being far
  From this my subject, has no business here);
We know, too, they are very fond of war,
  A pleasure (like all pleasures) rather dear;
So were the Cretans – from which I infer
That beef and battles both were owing to her.[112]

157

But to resume. The languid Juan raised
  His head upon his elbow, and he saw
A sight on which he had not lately gazed,
  As all his latter meals had been quite raw –
Three or four things, for which the Lord he praised,
  And, feeling still the famished vulture gnaw,
He fell upon whate'er was offered, like
A priest, a shark, an alderman,[113] or pike.

158

He ate, and he was well supplied; and she
  Who watched him like a mother, would have fed
Him past all bounds, because she smiled to see
  Such an appetite in one she had deemed dead:
But Zoe, being older than Haidee,
  Knew (by tradition, for she ne'er had read)
That famished people must be slowly nursed,
And fed by spoonfuls, else they always burst.

Notes

[111] Minos of Crete challenged Poseidon, god of the sea, to produce a bull from the ocean. So beautiful was it, that he could not sacrifice it, and substituted another, incurring Poseidon's wrath. After Minos' marriage to Pasiphaë, Poseidon made her fall in love with the bull, with which she had intercourse, giving birth to the Minotaur – half bull, half man. It became a scourge, devouring the Cretans, until Daedalus built a labyrinth to contain it.

[112] *her* Pasiphaë. As a result of the imprisonment of the Minotaur in the labyrinth, Minos waged war on Athens; having defeated it, he fed the Minotaur a yearly tribute of seven young men and seven maidens.

[113] *alderman* in London, the chief officer of a ward. They were a byword for greed in their levying of fines.

159

And so she took the liberty to state,
Rather by deeds than words, because the case
Was urgent, that the gentleman whose fate
Had made her mistress quit her bed to trace[114]
The seashore at this hour, must leave his plate
Unless he wished to die upon the place –
She snatched it and refused another morsel,
Saying he had gorged enough to make a horse ill.

160

Next they – he being naked, save a tattered
Pair of scarce decent trousers – went to work,
And in the fire his recent rags they scattered
And dressed him, for the present, like a Turk
Or Greek; that is (although it not much mattered),
Omitting turban, slippers, pistols, dirk,[115]
They furnished him, entire except some stitches,
With a clean shirt and very spacious breeches.

161

And then fair Haidee tried her tongue at speaking,
But not a word could Juan comprehend,
Although he listened so that the young Greek in
Her earnestness would ne'er have made an end;
And, as he interrupted not, went ekeing
Her speech out to her protégé and friend,
Till pausing at the last her breath to take,
She saw he did not understand Romaic.[116]

162

And then she had recourse to nods and signs,
And smiles, and sparkles of the speaking eye,
And read (the only book she could) the lines
Of his fair face, and found, by sympathy,
The answer eloquent, where the soul shines
And darts in one quick glance a long reply;
And thus in every look she saw expressed
A world of words, and things at which she guessed.

163

And now, by dint of fingers and of eyes,
And words repeated after her, he took
A lesson in her tongue – but by surmise,
No doubt, less of her language than her look;

Notes

[114] *trace* tread.
[115] *dirk* dagger.
[116] *Romaic* modern Greek vernacular, some of which Byron learnt on his visit to Athens in 1810–11.

As he who studies fervently the skies
   Turns oftener to the stars than to his book,
Thus Juan learned his alpha beta better
From Haidee's glance than any graven letter.

164

'Tis pleasing to be schooled in a strange tongue
   By female lips and eyes;[117] that is, I mean,
When both the teacher and the taught are young,
   As was the case, at least, where I have been;
They smile so when one's right, and when one's wrong
   They smile still more, and then there intervene
Pressure of hands, perhaps even a chaste kiss;
I learned the little that I know by this –

165

That is, some words of Spanish, Turk, and Greek,
   Italian not at all, having no teachers;
Much English I cannot pretend to speak,
   Learning that language chiefly from its preachers,
Barrow, South, Tillotson, whom every week
   I study, also Blair[118] – the highest reachers
Of eloquence in piety and prose;
I hate your poets, so read none of those.[119]

166

As for the ladies, I have nought to say,
   A wanderer from the British world of fashion,[120]
Where I, like other 'dogs, have had my day';[121]
   Like other men too, may have had my passion –
But that, like other things, has passed away,
   And all her fools whom I *could* lay the lash on:
Foes, friends, men, women, now are nought to me
But dreams of what has been, no more to be.

167

Return we to Don Juan. He begun
   To hear new words, and to repeat them, but
Some feelings, universal as the sun,
   Were such as could not in his breast be shut
More than within the bosom of a nun;
   He was in love – as you would be, no doubt,
With a young benefactress; so was she,
Just in the way we very often see.

Notes

[117] *'Tis pleasing . . . eyes* Byron learned Spanish in Seville from a female tutor, Greek from Teresa Macri in Athens, and Italian from Marianna Segati in Venice.

[118] Isaac Barrow (1630–77), Robert South (1634–1716), John Tillotson (1630–94) and Hugh Blair (1718–1800), distinguished sermonists.

[119] *I hate your poets, so read none of those* an overstatement designed to emphasize Byron's dislike of the Lake poets and admiration of Pope (see p. 838).

[120] *the British world of fashion* in which Byron had been a very big fish, 1812–16.

[121] *Hamlet* V i 292: 'The cat will mew, and dog will have his day.'

168

And every day by daybreak – rather early
For Juan, who was somewhat fond of rest,
She came into the cave, but it was merely
To see her bird reposing in his nest;
And she would softly stir his locks so curly,
Without disturbing her yet-slumbering guest,
Breathing all gently o'er his cheek and mouth,
As o'er a bed of roses the sweet south.[122]

169

And every morn his colour freshlier came,
And every day helped on his convalescence;
'Twas well, because health in the human frame
Is pleasant, besides being true love's essence;
For health and idleness to passion's flame
Are oil and gunpowder, and some good lessons
Are also learnt from Ceres and from Bacchus,[123]
Without whom Venus will not long attack us.[124]

170

While Venus fills the heart (without heart really
Love, though good always, is not quite so good),
Ceres presents a plate of vermicelli;[125]
For love must be sustained like flesh and blood,
While Bacchus pours out wine, or hands a jelly.[126]
Eggs, oysters too, are amatory food;[127]
But who is their purveyor from above
Heaven knows – it may be Neptune, Pan, or Jove.

171

When Juan woke he found some good things ready;
A bath, a breakfast, and the finest eyes
That ever made a youthful heart less steady,
Besides her maid's, as pretty for their size –
But I have spoken of all this already,
And repetition's tiresome and unwise;
Well, Juan, after bathing in the sea,
Came always back to coffee and Haidee.

172

Both were so young, and one so innocent,
That bathing passed for nothing; Juan seemed
To her, as 'twere, the kind of being sent,
Of whom these two years she had nightly dreamed:

Notes

[122] *the sweet south* i.e. the warm south wind.

[123] *Ceres . . . Bacchus* corn (bread) and wine. Ceres is the goddess of corn and harvest; Bacchus the god of wine.

[124] *Are also learnt . . . attack us* a reworking of Terence, *Eunuchus* iv 56: 'sine Cerere et Libero friget Venus' (without Ceres and Bacchus, Venus freezes).

[125] *vermicelli* pasta is made of wheat.

[126] *a jelly* partly made of wine.

[127] *amatory food* aphrodisiacs (containing protein).

A something to be loved, a creature meant
To be her happiness, and whom she deemed
To render happy; all who joy would win
Must share it – Happiness was born a twin.

173

It was such pleasure to behold him, such
Enlargement of existence to partake
Nature with him, to thrill beneath his touch,
To watch him slumbering, and to see him wake:
To live with him for ever were too much,
But then the thought of parting made her quake;
He was her own, her ocean-treasure, cast
Like a rich wreck – her first love, and her last.[128]

174

And thus a moon rolled on, and fair Haidee
Paid daily visits to her boy, and took
Such plentiful precautions, that still he
Remained unknown within his craggy nook;
At last her father's prows put out to sea,
For certain merchantmen upon the look,
Not as of yore to carry off an Io,[129]
But three Ragusan[130] vessels, bound for Scio.

175

Then came her freedom, for she had no mother,
So that, her father being at sea, she was
Free as a married woman, or such other
Female, as where she likes may freely pass,
Without even the encumbrance of a brother –
The freest she that ever gazed on glass
(I speak of Christian lands in this comparison,
Where wives, at least, are seldom kept in garrison).

176

Now she prolonged her visits and her talk
(For they must talk), and he had learnt to say
So much as to propose to take a walk –
For little had he wandered since the day
On which, like a young flower snapped from the stalk,
Drooping and dewy on the beach he lay;
And thus they walked out in the afternoon,
And saw the sun set opposite the moon.

Notes

[128] *her first love, and her last* a claim Byron himself made in a letter to Countess Teresa Guiccioli on 22 April 1819: 'You who are my only and last love, who are my only joy.'

[129] *Io* Io, a priestess at Argos, was kidnapped by Phoenicians (Herodotus I i 4–5).

[130] Ragusa was in Byron's day the name for Dubrovnik, an ancient seaport still flourishing on the Adriatic coast of Croatia.

177

It was a wild and breaker-beaten coast,
With cliffs above, and a broad sandy shore
Guarded by shoals and rocks as by an host,[131]
With here and there a creek whose aspect wore
A better welcome to the tempest-tossed;
And rarely ceased the haughty billow's roar,
Save on the dead long summer days, which make
The outstretched ocean glitter like a lake.

178

And the small ripple spilt upon the beach
Scarcely o'erpassed the cream of your champagne,
When o'er the brim the sparkling bumpers reach,
That spring-dew of the spirit, the heart's rain!
Few things surpass old wine – and they may preach
Who please (the more because they preach in vain) –
Let us have wine and woman, mirth and laughter,
Sermons and soda-water the day after.

179

Man, being reasonable, must get drunk;
The best of life is but intoxication:
Glory, the grape, love, gold – in these are sunk
The hopes of all men, and of every nation;
Without their sap, how branchless were the trunk
Of life's strange tree, so fruitful on occasion.
But to return; get very drunk, and when
You wake with headache, you shall see what then.

180

Ring for your valet, bid him quickly bring
Some hock[132] and soda-water[133] – then you'll know
A pleasure worthy Xerxes the great king;[134]
For not the blessed sherbet, sublimed[135] with snow,
Nor the first sparkle of the desert-spring,
Nor Burgundy in all its sunset glow,
After long travel, ennui,[136] love, or slaughter,
Vie with that draught of hock and soda-water.

Notes

[131] *host* army.

[132] *hock* white German wine.

[133] *hock and soda-water* cf. the stanza used as a headpiece to the poem in editions from 1832 onwards. Byron never intended it as a headpiece, and in fact scribbled it in MS and then deleted it:

I would to Heaven that I were so much clay –
As I am blood – bone – marrow, passion – feeling –
Because at least the past were past away –
And for the future (but I write this reeling,
Having got drunk exceedingly today
So that I seem to stand upon the ceiling)
I say, the future is a serious matter –
And so, for godsake, hock and soda-water.

[134] Xerxes I, Persian king who in 480 BC assembled a great navy and army to avenge his father Darius for the loss of the Battle of Marathon in 490 BC. He was eventually defeated at Salamis.

[135] *sublimed* chilled.

[136] *ennui* feeling of mental weariness and dissatisfaction produced by want of occupation.

181

The coast (I think it was the coast that I
Was just describing; yes, it *was* the coast)
Lay at this period quiet as the sky,
The sands untumbled, the blue waves untossed,
And all was stillness save the sea-bird's cry
And dolphin's leap, and little billow crossed
By some low rock or shelf, that made it fret[137]
Against the boundary it scarcely wet.

182

And forth they wandered, her sire being gone,
As I have said, upon an expedition;
And mother, brother, guardian, she had none,
Save Zoe, who, although with due precision
She waited on her lady with the sun,
Thought daily service was her only mission,
Bringing warm water, wreathing her long tresses,
And asking now and then for cast-off dresses.

183

It was the cooling hour, just when the rounded
Red sun sinks down behind the azure hill,
Which then seems as if the whole earth it bounded,
Circling all nature, hushed, and dim, and still,
With the far mountain-crescent half surrounded
On one side, and the deep sea calm and chill
Upon the other, and the rosy sky,
With one star sparkling through it like an eye.

184

And thus they wandered forth, and, hand in hand,
Over the shining pebbles and the shells
Glided along the smooth and hardened sand,
And in the worn and wild receptacles
Worked by the storms, yet worked as it were planned,
In hollow halls, with sparry[138] roofs and cells,
They turned to rest; and, each clasped by an arm,
Yielded to the deep twilight's purple charm.

185

They looked up to the sky, whose floating glow
Spread like a rosy ocean, vast and bright;
They gazed upon the glittering sea below,
Whence the broad moon rose circling into sight;
They heard the wave's splash, and the wind so low,

Notes

[137] *fret* chafe.

[138] *spar* an opaque crystalline mineral, which is embedded in the roofs and cells of the rocks.

And saw each other's dark eyes darting light
Into each other; and, beholding this,
Their lips drew near, and clung into a kiss –

186

A long, long kiss, a kiss of youth and love
And beauty, all concentrating like rays
Into one focus, kindled from above;
Such kisses as belong to early days
Where heart and soul and sense in concert[139] move,
And the blood's lava, and the pulse ablaze,
Each kiss a heartquake – for a kiss's strength,
I think, it must be reckoned by its length.

187

By length I mean duration; theirs endured
Heaven knows how long – no doubt they never reckoned,
And if they had, they could not have secured
The sum of their sensations to a second:
They had not spoken, but they felt allured
As if their souls and lips each other beckoned,
Which, being joined, like swarming bees they clung,
Their hearts the flowers from whence the honey sprung.

188

They were alone, but not alone as they
Who shut in chambers think it loneliness;
The silent ocean, and the starlight bay,
The twilight glow, which momently grew less,
The voiceless sands, and dropping caves that lay
Around them, made them to each other press,
As if there were no life beneath the sky
Save theirs, and that their life could never die.

189

They feared no eyes nor ears on that lone beach,
They felt no terrors from the night,[140] they were
All in all to each other; though their speech
Was broken words, they *thought* a language there,
And all the burning tongues the passions teach
Found in one sigh the best interpreter
Of nature's oracle – first love, that all
Which Eve has left her daughters since her fall.

190

Haidee spoke not of scruples, asked no vows,
Nor offered any; she had never heard
Of plight and promises to be a spouse,
Or perils by a loving maid incurred;

Notes

[139] *concert* unison.

[140] *They felt no terrors from the night* a profane allusion to Psalm 91: 5, where the godly are told: 'Thou shalt not be afraid for the terror by night.'

She was all which pure ignorance allows,
And flew to her young mate like a young bird;
And, never having dreamt of falsehood, she
Had not one word to say of constancy.

191

She loved, and was beloved; she adored,
And she was worshipped; after nature's fashion,
Their intense souls, into each other poured,
If souls could die, had perished in that passion;
But by degrees their senses were restored,
Again to be o'ercome, again to dash on;
And, beating 'gainst *his* bosom, Haidee's heart
Felt as if never more to beat apart.

192

Alas, they were so young, so beautiful,
So lonely, loving, helpless, and the hour
Was that in which the heart is always full,
And, having o'er itself no further power,
Prompts deeds eternity cannot annul,
But pays off moments in an endless shower
Of hellfire – all prepared for people giving
Pleasure or pain to one another living.

193

Alas for Juan and Haidee! They were
So loving and so lovely – till then never,
Excepting our first parents, such a pair
Had run the risk of being damned for ever;
And Haidee, being devout as well as fair,
Had doubtless heard about the Stygian river,[141]
And hell and purgatory – but forgot
Just in the very crisis she should not.

194

They look upon each other, and their eyes
Gleam in the moonlight; and her white arm clasps
Round Juan's head, and his around hers lies
Half-buried in the tresses which it grasps;
She sits upon his knee, and drinks his sighs,
He hers, until they end in broken gasps;
And thus they form a group that's quite antique –
Half-naked, loving, natural, and Greek.

Notes

[141] *the Stygian river* The river Styx circled Hades nine times; those seeking to enter Hades had to be ferried across it by Charon.

195

And when those deep and burning moments passed,
  And Juan sunk to sleep within her arms,
She slept not, but all tenderly, though fast,
  Sustained his head upon her bosom's charms;
And now and then her eye to heaven is cast,
  And then on the pale cheek her breast now warms,
Pillowed on her o'erflowing heart, which pants
With all it granted, and with all it grants.

196

An infant when it gazes on a light,
  A child the moment when it drains the breast,
A devotee when soars the Host[142] in sight,
  An Arab with a stranger for a guest,
A sailor when the prize has struck in fight,[143]
  A miser filling his most hoarded chest,
Feel rapture; but not such true joy are reaping
As they who watch o'er what they love while sleeping.

197

For there it lies so tranquil, so beloved,
  All that it hath of life with us is living;
So gentle, stirless, helpless, and unmoved,
  And all unconscious of the joy 'tis giving;
All it hath felt, inflicted, passed, and proved,
  Hushed into depths beyond the watcher's diving;
There lies the thing we love with all its errors
And all its charms, like death without its terrors.

198

The lady watched her lover, and that hour
  Of love's, and night's, and ocean's solitude
O'erflowed her soul with their united power;
  Amidst the barren sand and rocks so rude
She and her wave-worn love had made their bower
  Where nought upon their passion could intrude,
And all the stars that crowded the blue space
Saw nothing happier than her glowing face.

199

Alas, the love of women! It is known
  To be a lovely and a fearful thing;
For all of theirs upon that die[144] is thrown,
  And if 'tis lost, life hath no more to bring
To them but mockeries of the past alone,

Notes

[142] *Host* eucharistic wafer. The word 'soars' is distinctly comic.

[143] *when the prize has struck in fight* i.e. when the prize-ship (being attacked) has surrendered ('struck'). At this point it and its contents became booty, to be divided among the crew.

[144] *die* dice.

And their revenge is as the tiger's spring,
Deadly, and quick, and crushing; yet as real
Torture is theirs – what they inflict they feel.

200

They are right; for man, to man so oft unjust,
Is always so to women; one sole bond
Awaits them, treachery is all their trust;
Taught to conceal, their bursting hearts despond
Over their idol, till some wealthier lust
Buys them in marriage – and what rests beyond?
A thankless husband, next a faithless lover,
Then dressing, nursing, praying, and all's over.

201

Some take a lover, some take drams[145] or prayers,
Some mind their household, others dissipation,
Some run away and but exchange their cares,
Losing the advantage of a virtuous station;
Few changes e'er can better their affairs,
Theirs being an unnatural situation
From the dull palace to the dirty hovel:
Some play the devil, and then write a novel.[146]

202

Haidee was Nature's bride, and knew not this;[147]
Haidee was Passion's child, born where the sun
Showers triple light, and scorches even the kiss
Of his gazelle-eyed daughters; she was one
Made but to love, to feel that she was his
Who was her chosen: what was said or done
Elsewhere was nothing – she had nought to fear,
Hope, care, nor love beyond, her heart beat *here*.

203

And oh, that quickening of the heart, that beat!
How much it costs us! Yet each rising throb
Is in its cause as its effect so sweet,
That Wisdom, ever on the watch to rob
Joy of its alchemy,[148] and to repeat
Fine truths, even Conscience, too, has a tough job
To make us understand each good old maxim,
So good – I wonder Castlereagh don't tax 'em.

Notes

[145] *drams* A dram is a measure – in this case, of alcohol.

[146] *Some play the devil, and then write a novel* Lady Caroline Lamb, unceremoniously dumped by Byron after an affair of several months in 1812, took her revenge by fictionalizing their relationship in *Glenarvon* (1816). See headnote, p. 840.

[147] *this* i.e. the sufferings of the woman of the world, related in the previous three stanzas.

[148] *alchemy* magic.

204

And now 'twas done – on the lone shore were plighted
  Their hearts; the stars, their nuptial torches, shed
Beauty upon the beautiful they lighted;
  Ocean their witness, and the cave their bed,
By their own feelings hallowed and united,
  Their priest was Solitude, and they were wed:
And they were happy, for to their young eyes
Each was an angel, and earth paradise.

205

Oh love, of whom great Caesar was the suitor,
  Titus the master, Antony the slave,[149]
Horace, Catullus scholars, Ovid tutor,[150]
  Sappho the sage bluestocking, in whose grave
All those may leap who rather would be neuter
  (Leucadia's rock still overlooks the wave[151]);
Oh love, thou art the very god of evil –
For, after all, we cannot call thee devil.

206

Thou mak'st the chaste connubial[152] state precarious,
  And jestest with the brows of mightiest men:
Caesar and Pompey, Mahomet, Belisarius,[153]
  Have much employed the muse of history's pen;
Their lives and fortunes were extremely various,
  Such worthies Time will never see again;
Yet to these four in three things the same luck holds –
They all were heroes, conquerors, and cuckolds.

207

Thou mak'st philosophers; there's Epicurus
  And Aristippus,[154] a material crew!
Who to immoral courses would allure us
  By theories quite practicable too;
If only from the devil they would insure us,
  How pleasant were the maxim (not quite new),
'Eat, drink, and love, what can the rest avail us?' –
So said the royal sage Sardanapalus.[155]

Notes

[149] Julius Caesar was Cleopatra's suitor; Mark Antony was her slave. Titus 'mastered' his love of Berenice and sent her away.

[150] Horace, Catullus and Ovid wrote about love. Ovid's *Ars Amatoria* is a textbook of lovemaking.

[151] Sappho was said to have thrown herself off the Leucadian rock into the sea when her love for Phaon was unrequited.

[152] *connubial* married.

[153] *Caesar and Pompey, Mahomet, Belisarius* famous cuckolds: Caesar was cuckolded by his first wife, Pompeia; Pompey by his wife Mucia (who 'played the wanton' with Caesar); Mahomet by his wife Ayesha; and Belisarius (famous Byzantine general) by his wife Antonina (who seduced their adopted son).

[154] Aristippus (*c.*370 BC) founded a hedonistic philosophy that offered pleasure as the goal of life; he lived luxuriously. Epicurus (342–270 BC) said that happiness was the aim of life, achieved through virtuous living. Epicureanism was quickly devalued and became associated with sensual pleasures.

[155] Sardanapalus was an Assyrian of uncertain historical origin and character, renowned for being effeminate, slothful, and immersed in luxury and debauchery. He was the subject of a tragedy written by Byron in 1821.

208

But Juan! Had he quite forgotten Julia?
   And should he have forgotten her so soon?
I can't but say it seems to me most truly a
   Perplexing question; but, no doubt, the moon
Does these things for us, and whenever newly a
   Strong palpitation rises, 'tis her boon;
Else how the devil is it that fresh features
Have such a charm for us poor human creatures?

209

I hate inconstancy – I loathe, detest,
   Abhor, condemn, abjure the mortal made
Of such quicksilver[156] clay that in his breast
   No permanent foundation can be laid;
Love, constant love, has been my constant guest,
   And yet last night, being at a masquerade,
I saw the prettiest creature, fresh from Milan,
Which gave me some sensations like a villain.

210

But soon Philosophy came to my aid
   And whispered, 'Think of every sacred tie!'
'I will, my dear Philosophy!' I said,
   'But then her teeth, and then, oh heaven, her eye!
I'll just enquire if she be wife or maid,
   Or neither, out of curiosity.'
'Stop!' cried Philosophy, with air so Grecian
(Though she was masked then as a fair Venetian).

211

'Stop!' So I stopped. But to return: that which
   Men call inconstancy is nothing more
Than admiration due where nature's rich
   Profusion with young beauty covers o'er
Some favoured object; and as in the niche
   A lovely statue we almost adore,
This sort of adoration of the real
Is but a heightening of the *beau-ideal*.[157]

212

'Tis the perception of the beautiful,
   A fine extension of the faculties,
Platonic, universal, wonderful,
   Drawn from the stars, and filtered through the skies,
Without which life would be extremely dull;

Notes

[156] *quicksilver* fast-changing.
[157] *beau-ideal* ideal beauty. Byron's argument (deliberately specious) is that admiration of a beautiful woman is no different from that of a beautiful work of art.

In short, it is the use of our own eyes,
With one or two small senses added, just
To hint that flesh is formed of fiery dust.

213

Yet 'tis a painful feeling, and unwilling,
For surely if we always could perceive
In the same object graces quite as killing[158]
As when she rose upon us like an Eve,
'Twould save us many a heartache, many a shilling[159]
(For we must get them anyhow, or grieve),
Whereas if one sole lady pleased for ever,
How pleasant for the heart, as well as liver![160]

214

The heart is like the sky, a part of heaven,
But changes night and day too, like the sky;
Now o'er it clouds and thunder must be driven,
And darkness and destruction as on high:
But when it hath been scorched, and pierced, and riven,
Its storms expire in water-drops; the eye
Pours forth at last the heart's-blood turned to tears,
Which make the English climate of our years.

215

The liver is the lazaret[161] of bile,[162]
But very rarely executes its function,
For the first passion stays there such a while,
That all the rest creep in and form a junction
Like knots of vipers on a dunghill's soil –
Rage, fear, hate, jealousy, revenge, compunction –
So that all mischiefs spring up from this entrail[163]
Like earthquakes from the hidden fire called 'central'.

216

In the meantime, without proceeding more
In this anatomy, I've finished now
Two hundred and odd stanzas as before,
That being about the number I'll allow
Each canto of the twelve, or twenty-four;
And laying down my pen, I make my bow,
Leaving Don Juan and Haidee to plead
For them and theirs with all who deign to read.

Notes

[158] *killing* overpoweringly beautiful.

[159] *many a shilling* a typically Byronic twist, reducing everything to material terms. His point is that if he had loved only one woman, he would have saved the money he has spent on the many he has known in his life.

[160] *liver* seat of intense passion.

[161] *lazaret* lazaretto, hospital.

[162] *bile* intense passion, anger.

[163] *entrail* organ (i.e. the liver).

To the Po. 2 June 1819 (composed 1 or 2 June 1819; first published 1824; edited from MS)[1]

River that rollest by the ancient walls
  Where dwells the lady of my love,[2] when she
Walks by thy brink and there perchance recalls
  A faint and fleeting memory of me –
What if thy deep and ample stream should be
  A mirror of my heart, where she may read
The thousand thoughts I now betray[3] to thee,
  Wild as thy wave and headlong as thy speed?
What do I say? 'A mirror of my heart'?
  Are not thy waters sweeping, dark and strong?
Such as my feelings were and are, thou art,
  And such as thou art were my passions long;
Time may have somewhat tamed them – not forever
  Thou overflow'st thy banks, and not for aye
The bosom overboils, congenial river!
  Thy floods subside, and mine have sunk away,
But left long wrecks behind us; yet again
  Borne on our old career unchanged we move,
Thou tendest wildly to the wilder main
  And I to loving one I should not love.
The current I behold will sweep beneath
  Her palace walls, and murmur at her feet,
Her eyes will look on thee when she shall breathe
  The twilight air unchained from summer's heat.
She will look on thee; I have looked on thee
  Full of that thought, and from this moment ne'er
Thy waters could I name, hear named, or see
  Without the inseparable sigh for her.
Her bright eyes will be imaged in thy stream –
  Yes, they will meet the wave I gaze on now,
But mine cannot even witness in a dream
  That happy wave repass me in its flow;
The wave that bears my tear returns no more –
  Will she return by whom that wave shall sweep?
Both tread thy bank, both wander by thy shore,
  I near thy source,[4] and she by the blue deep;
But that which keepeth us apart is not
  Distance, nor depth of wave, nor space of earth,

Notes

TO THE PO. 2 JUNE 1819

[1] This is one of Byron's finest love poems. It was written in honour of Contessa Teresa Guiccioli, with whom Byron began an affair in spring 1819. He had travelled south to be with her and her husband, who had left Venice for their home town of Ravenna.

[2] *the lady of my love* Teresa Guiccioli.

[3] *betray* reveal.

[4] *near thy source* the Po, Italy's major river, rises at Mt Viso in Piedmont.

But the distractions of a various lot –
  Ah, various as the climates of our birth!
A stranger loves a lady of the land
  Born far beyond the mountains, but his blood
Is all meridian,[5] as if never fanned
  By the bleak wind that chills the polar flood.
My heart is all meridian; were it not,
  I had not suffered now, nor should I be,
Despite of tortures ne'er to be forgot,
  The slave again, oh love, at least of thee!
'Tis vain to struggle – I have struggled long
  To love again no more as once I loved.
Oh time, why leave this earliest passion strong? –
  To tear a heart which pants to be unmoved?

Letter from Lord Byron to Douglas Kinnaird, 26 October 1819 (extract)

As to *Don Juan*, confess – confess, you dog (and be candid), that it is the sublime of *that there* sort of writing. It may be bawdy, but is it not good English? It may be profligate, but is it not *life*, is it not *the thing*? Could any man have written it who has not lived in the world? – and tooled in a post-chaise? In a hackney coach? In a gondola? Against a wall? In a court carriage? In a vis-à-vis?[1] On a table – and under it? I have written about a hundred stanzas of a third Canto, but it is damned modest – the outcry has frightened me.[2] I had such projects for the Don, but the *cant* is so much stronger than *cunt* nowadays, that the benefit of experience in a man who had well weighed the worth of both monosyllables must be lost to despairing posterity.[3]

Messalonghi, 22 January 1824. On this day I complete my thirty-sixth year (first published 1824; edited from MS)

I

'Tis time this heart should be unmoved,
  Since others it hath ceased to move;
Yet though I cannot be beloved,
    Still let me love.

Notes

[5] *meridian* noon; at its most passionate.

Letter from Lord Byron to Douglas Kinnaird

[1] *vis-à-vis* a light carriage for two people sitting face to face.

[2] *Don Juan* I–II was strongly attacked for 'degrading debauchery' and 'shameless indecency'.

[3] All the same, *Don Juan* III–V was published in August 1821.

2

My days are in the yellow leaf,
   The flowers and fruits of love are gone,
The worm, the canker and the grief
         Are mine alone.

3

The fire that on my bosom preys
   Is lone as some volcanic isle,
No torch is kindled at its blaze –
         A funeral pile!

4

The hope, the fear, the jealous care,
   The exalted portion of the pain,
And power of love I cannot share
         But wear the chain.

5

But 'tis not thus, and 'tis not here
   Such thoughts should shake my soul, nor now
Where glory decks the hero's bier
         Or binds his brow.

6

The sword, the banner, and the field,
   Glory and Greece about us see –
The Spartan borne upon his shield[1]
         Was not more free!

7

Awake (not Greece – she *is* awake),[2]
   Awake my spirit – think through whom
Thy life-blood tracks its parent lake
         And then strike home!

8

Tread those reviving passions down,
   Unworthy manhood; unto thee
Indifferent should the smile or frown
         Of beauty be.

Notes

MESSALONGHI, 22 JANUARY 1824

[1] 'The slain were borne upon their shields' (Byron's MS note).

[2] The Greeks were waging a war of Independence against the Turks (see headnote).

9

If thou regret'st thy youth, why live?
The land of honourable death
Is here: up to the field, and give
Away thy breath!

10

Seek out (less often sought than found)
A soldier's grave, for thee the best,
Then look around and choose thy ground
And take thy rest.

Richard Woodhouse, Jr (1788–1834)

Woodhouse was neither a poet, a playwright nor a novelist. He was, in fact, the legal adviser to Keats's publishers, Taylor and Hessey, and one of the most far-sighted and perceptive of Keats's friends.

He was born in Bath, 11 December 1788, the eldest in a family of fourteen children. After being educated at Eton, he went to Spain and Portugal; when he returned, he decided not to go to university (although he was capable of doing so), instead turning to the law. He met the publishers John Taylor and James Augustus Hessey in March 1811 while working as a conveyancer, and quickly entered their intellectual circle. Taylor regarded him at this time as erudite, hard-working, self-effacing and strictly religious.

Woodhouse met Keats at 93 Fleet Street soon after Keats himself had been introduced to Taylor and Hessey by John Hamilton Reynolds. He realized that there were faults in Keats's diction, but at the same time regarded him as potentially a great poet: 'Such a genius, I very much believe, has not appeared since Shakespeare and Milton.'[1] With equal shrewdness he realized that one day all 'Keatsiana' (a term he himself uses at least twice) would be invaluable. Thus, he copied every Keats manuscript, poem and letter on which he could lay his hands, with the result that today a number of texts are known only through his transcriptions. The letters below reveal Woodhouse's skill as an interpreter and critic of Keats. The first outlines Keats's concept of the poetical character and negative capability; the second discusses his revision of 'The Eve of St Agnes'.

After Keats's death, Woodhouse increased his efforts to gather materials that would be of use to scholars and biographers. He sought out acquaintances of the poet and spoke to them, jotting down detailed accounts of their conversations; he encouraged John Taylor to write a biography; he commissioned a portrait of the poet by Hilton, and a medallion by Giuseppe Girometti.

In due course, Woodhouse developed tuberculosis, the disease that had killed Keats. Like the poet, he went south in search of improved health, visiting Madeira in 1829–30 and Italy two years later. Back in London, his health declined rapidly, and he died on 3 September 1834.

Notes

[1] *The Keats Circle* ed. Hyder E. Rollins (2 vols, Cambridge, Mass., 1965), i p. cxlv.

Letter from Richard Woodhouse to John Taylor, c. 27 October 1818

I believe him to be right with regard to his own poetical character, and I perceive clearly the distinction he draws between himself and those of the Wordsworth school.[1]

There are gradations in poetry and in poets. One is purely descriptive, confining himself to external nature and visible objects; another describes, in addition, the effects of the thoughts of which he is conscious, and which others are affected by. Another will soar so far into the regions of imagination as to conceive of beings and substances in situations different from what he has ever seen them, but still such as either have actually occurred or may possibly occur. Another will reason in poetry; another be witty; another will imagine things that never did nor probably ever will occur, or such as cannot in nature occur, and yet he will describe them so that you recognize nothing very unnatural in the descriptions when certain principles or powers or conditions are admitted. Another will throw himself into various characters and make them speak as the passions would naturally incite them to do.

The highest order of poet will not only possess all the above powers but will have as high an imagination that he will be able to throw his own soul into any object he sees or imagines, so as to see, feel, be sensible of, and express all that the object itself would see, feel, be sensible of, or express – and he will speak out of that object, so that his own self will, with the exception of the mechanical part, be 'annihilated'.[2] And it is the excess of this power that I suppose Keats to speak, when he says he has no identity. As a poet, and when the fit is upon him, this is true. And it is a fact that he does by the power of his imagination create ideal personages, substances, and powers – that he lives for a time in their souls or essences or ideas – and that occasionally so intensely as to lose consciousness of what is round him. We all do the same in a degree, when we fall into a reverie.[3]

If, then, his imagination has such power, and he is continually cultivating it and giving it play, it will acquire strength by the indulgence and exercise. This in excess is the case of mad persons. And this may be carried to that extent that he may lose sight of his identity so far as to give him a habit of speaking generally in an assumed character. So that what he says shall be tinged with the sentiments proper to the character which, at the time, has possessed itself of his imagination.

This being his idea of the poetical character, he may well say that a poet has no identity. As a man he must have identity, but as a poet he need not. And in this sense a poet is 'the most unpoetical of God's creatures',[4] for his soul has no distinctive characteristic – it cannot be itself made the subject of poetry that is another person's soul, cannot be thrown into the poet's, for there is no identity (separatedness, distinctiveness) or personal impulse to be acted upon.

Notes

1 For Keats's comments on Wordsworth, see pp. 1352–3.

2 *annihilated* Woodhouse is discussing negative capability; for Keats's account see p. 1375.

3 'The power of his imagination is apparent in every page of his *Endymion*. And he has affirmed that he can conceive of a billiard ball – that it may have a sense of delight from its own roundness, smoothness, volubility, and the rapidity of its motion' (Woodhouse's note).

4 Woodhouse is quoting from a letter Keats had sent him that day; see p. 1375.

Shakespeare was a poet of the kind above mentioned, and he was perhaps the only one besides Keats who possessed this power in an extraordinary degree, so as to be a feature in his works. He gives a description of his idea of a poet:

> The poet's eye, in a fine frenzy rolling,
> Doth glance from heaven to earth, from earth to heaven;
> And as imagination bodies forth
> The forms of things unknown, the poet's pen
> Turns them to shapes, and gives to airy nothing
> A local habitation and a name.[5]

Lord Byron does not come up to this character. He can certainly conceive and describe a dark accomplished villain in love, and a female tender and kind who loves him; or a sated and palled sensualist, misanthrope, and deist[6] – but here his power ends. The true poet cannot only conceive this, but can assume any character, essence, idea, or substance at pleasure. And he has this imaginative faculty not in a limited manner, but in full universality.

Let us pursue speculation on these matters, and we shall soon be brought to believe in the truth of every syllable of Keats' letter, taken as a description of himself and his own ideas and feelings.

Letter from Richard Woodhouse to John Taylor, 19 September 1819

He had 'The Eve of St Agnes' copied fair.[1] He has made trifling alterations, inserted an additional stanza early in the poem to make the *legend* more intelligible,[2] and correspondent[3] with what afterwards takes place, particularly with respect to the supper and the playing on the lute. He retains the name of Porphyro, has altered the last three lines to leave on the reader a sense of pettish disgust, by bringing Old Angela in (only) dead, stiff and ugly.[4] He says he likes that the poem should leave off with this change of sentiment – it was what he aimed at, and was glad to find from my objections to it that he had succeeded. I apprehend he had a fancy for trying his hand at an attempt to play with his reader, and fling him off[5] at last. I should have thought he affected the 'Don Juan'[6] style of mingling up sentiment and sneering, but that he had before asked Hessey[7] if he could procure him a sight of that work, as he

Notes

[5] *A Midsummer Night's Dream* V i 12–17.

[6] Woodhouse has in mind a range of works by Byron. The hit of the moment was *Beppo*, published in the summer of 1818. Woodhouse seems also to be referring to *Manfred* (1816) and *Childe Harold's Pilgrimage*, the final Canto of which was published in April 1818.

Letter from Richard Woodhouse to John Taylor

[1] 'The Eve of St Agnes' was composed 18 January–2 February 1819, and revised the following September. Woodhouse is discussing Keats's revisions, not all of which were published in the 1820 text.

[2] *inserted . . . intelligible* The stanza was not included in the published text; I include it in a note, p. 1378n10.

[3] *correspondent* consistent.

[4] See *The Eve of St Agnes* 375–8.

[5] *fling him off* i.e. Keats is trying deliberately to disgust the reader at the end of the poem.

[6] Byron's poem had been published anonymously on 15 July 1819.

[7] James Augustus Hessey (1785–1870), business partner of John Taylor (1781–1864); together they published Keats, Clare, Hazlitt and Lamb.

had not met with it – and if 'The Eve of St Agnes' had not, in all probability, been altered before his Lordship[8] had thus flown in the face of the public.

There was another alteration, which I abused for 'a full hour by the Temple clock'.[9] You know, if a thing has a decent side, I generally look no further. As the poem was originally written, *we* innocent ones (ladies and myself) might very well have supposed that Porphyro, when acquainted with Madeline's love for him, and when 'he arose, / Ethereal, flushed'[10] etc. etc. (turn to it), set himself at once to persuade her to go off with him, and succeeded and went over the 'Dartmoor black' (now changed for some other place[11]) to be married, in right honest, chaste, and sober wise.[12] But as it is now altered, as soon as Madeline has confessed her love, Porphyro winds by degrees his arm round her, presses breast to breast, and acts all the acts of a bona fide husband, while she fancies she is only playing the part of a wife in a dream.[13]

This alteration is of about three stanzas, and though there are no improper expressions, but all is left to inference; and though, profanely speaking, the interest on the reader's imagination is greatly heightened – yet I do apprehend it will render the poem unfit for ladies, and indeed scarcely to be mentioned to them among the 'things that are'.[14] He says he does not want ladies to read his poetry; that he writes for men,[15] and that if in the former poem there was an opening for doubt what took place, it was his fault for not writing clearly and comprehensibly; that he should despise a man who would be such an eunuch in sentiment as to leave a maid, with that character about her, in such a situation;[16] and should despise himself to write about it, etc., etc., etc. – and all this sort of Keats-like rodomontade.[17]

Notes

8 *his Lordship* i.e. Byron.

9 *1 Henry IV* V iv 148: 'fought a long hour by Shrewsbury clock'.

10 'The Eve of St Agnes' 317–18.

11 *now changed . . . place* 'the southern moors' (line 351).

12 *wise* manner.

13 *But as it is now altered . . . dream* see stanzas 35–6. The revised stanza did not appear in the 1820 text; I include it in a footnote, p. 1386n66.

14 *things that are* An allusion that demonstrates how well-read Woodhouse was; the quotation is from Shelley, *The Revolt of Islam* (1818), ix st.29: 'let sense and thought / Pass from our being, or be numbered not / Among the things that are' (ll. 4–6).

15 *that he writes for men* this extraordinary statement may have been suggested by Keats's desire to resist the 'effeminate' influence of Leigh Hunt, and imitate the more 'manly' poetry of Byron.

16 *in such a situation* i.e. in bed, 'entoiled in woofed fantasies'.

17 *rodomontade* bragging.

Percy Bysshe Shelley (1792–1822)

According to Hazlitt, Percy Bysshe Shelley

> has a fire in his eye, a fever in his blood, a maggot in his brain, a hectic flutter in his speech, which mark out the philosophic fanatic. He is sanguine complexioned, and shrill-voiced . . . He is clogged by no dull system of realities, no earth-bound feelings, no rooted prejudices, by nothing that belongs to the mighty trunk and hard husk of nature and habit, but is drawn up by irresistible levity to the regions of mere speculation and fancy, to the sphere of air and fire, where his delighted spirit floats in 'seas of pearl and clouds of amber'. (Howe viii 148–9)

Some of Shelley's friends, such as Leigh Hunt, thought this too near the knuckle for comfort, and reprimanded Hazlitt for writing it. The problem was that it was all too true. Few descriptions are more evocative of the visionary, proselytizing energies of one of the greatest Romantic poets.

Shelley was born on 4 August 1792 at Field Place, near Horsham in Sussex, the eldest child and only son of a baronet and Whig Member of Parliament. After two years at Syon House Academy in London, where he met his lifelong friend Thomas Medwin, he went to Eton, 1804–10. There he received a thorough grounding in the classics, became interested in science and radical politics, and wrote two Gothic novels – *Zastrozzi* and *St Irvyne* (both published in 1810).

Such promise was expected to blossom at University College, Oxford, where he matriculated in October 1810 – and, in a sense, it did. His formal education came to an abrupt halt when he was expelled in March 1811 for refusing to answer questions concerning a pamphlet, *The Necessity of Atheism*, which he had written with his friend, Thomas Jefferson Hogg. It argued that God's existence could be proved only by reference to the senses, reason, and testimony of others. Having denied their validity, it concluded: 'Truth has always been found to promote the best interests of mankind. Every reflecting mind must allow that there is no proof of the existence of a Deity. Q.E.D.'[1] A contemporary, C. J. Ridley, who witnessed their sending down, recorded: 'The aforesaid two had made themselves as conspicuous as possible by great singularity of dress, and by walking up and down the centre of the quadrangle, as if proud of their anticipated fate. I believe no one regretted their departure, for there are but few, if any, who are not afraid of Shelley's strange and fantastic pranks, and the still stranger opinions he was known to entertain.'[2]

Shelley's father, Sir Timothy, was horrified, not least by the probability of legal action for blasphemous libel. He began communicating with his son through his solicitor in order 'to guard my character and honour in case of any prosecutions in the courts'. Shelley reacted by requesting that he be disinherited – the first step in the process of self-exile that dominated the rest of his life.

Isolation from family and friends led to closeness with the 16-year-old Harriet Westbrook, daughter of a retired merchant and coffee-house proprietor, with whom in August 1811 he eloped to Edinburgh, where they married before settling for a while in Keswick in the Lake District. Shelley hoped to meet Wordsworth and Coleridge there but instead met Southey. Southey was 37, Shelley 19. They got on well, Shelley going so far as to describe the older poet as 'an advocate of liberty and equality', a deist and 'a great man'.[3]

Notes

[1] P. B. Shelley (with T. J. Hogg), *The Necessity of Atheism* (1811), p. 13. Critics were particularly enraged by the final 'Q.E.D.'

[2] Quoted by Richard Holmes, *Shelley: The Pursuit* (London, 1974), p. 55.

[3] Jones i 211–12.

After one of their conversations, he noted that 'Southey says I am not an atheist but a pantheist.'[4] But he became disillusioned with Southey when he realized how conservative he was in his politics. Shelley's time in Keswick culminated with an attempted housebreaking and robbery in which he was physically attacked. This kind of thing would happen again, almost as if he attracted violence.

In February 1812 he and Harriet sailed to Ireland, where he wanted to start a revolution. On arrival in Dublin he published and distributed his *Address to the Irish People*, arguing for Catholic emancipation and repeal of the Act of Union. He distributed all 1,500 copies, mailing some to prominent liberals such as John Philpot Curran; sending a servant to give some away at public houses, while he threw others into passing carriages and open windows, or gave them to beggars, drunks and prostitutes. 'Are you slaves, or are you men?' the pamphlet asked its readers, 'a real man is free.'[5]

Invited to speak at the Fishamble Street Theatre by the Catholic Committee, Shelley came to the attention of Home Office spies, just as Wordsworth and Coleridge had done in Somerset in 1797–8. But the most important thing Shelley was to learn from his visit to Ireland was that revolution then was unlikely to come from the oppressed majority. 'The poor of Dublin are assuredly the meanest and most miserable of all,' he told Godwin, 'In their narrow streets thousands seem huddled together – one mass of animated filth! . . . These were the persons to whom in my fancy I had addressed myself.'[6]

By now William Godwin was his hero. Godwin's philosophy, first articulated in *Political Justice* (1793), envisaged a utopian society governed entirely by reason. Human property and corrupt institutions such as 'government' and 'marriage' would wither away, leaving human beings free to do as they pleased, governed only by innate rationality. Such theories had an undeniable attraction for young radicals (in the early 1790s Wordsworth had subscribed to them) and by the time he arrived in Ireland Shelley was in correspondence with their creator.

After returning to Wales in April, the Shelleys moved from one place to the next until settling in Lynmouth in Devon, where he founded a sort of commune consisting mainly of females – Harriet, her sister Eliza, and his friend Elizabeth Hitchener. He wrote to Godwin inviting Fanny Imlay (Mary Wollstonecraft's daughter by the traveller Gilbert Imlay), but he would not allow it. From here Shelley distributed revolutionary propaganda, putting messages in bottles and floating them out to sea, or sending them up in miniature hot-air balloons. This led the Home Office, under Viscount Sidmouth, to step up their surveillance of him. Then, on 19 August, his servant was caught pasting subversive handbills up in Barnstaple and arrested. It was time for Shelley to move on.

They went to Wales and, after a visit to London in early October 1812, where Shelley finally met the 56-year-old William Godwin, returned to Wales, settling for a while at Tremadoc, where he continued to distribute revolutionary propaganda. There, on 26 February 1813, he was assaulted late in the evening by an 'assassin'. Shots were fired. A henchman returned early in the morning and there was another skirmish. Shelley survived both attacks, but the experience changed him. From now on he would no longer be an activist for revolution – instead, he would be a mouthpiece for it.

Back in London in July 1813, Shelley published his first major poem, *Queen Mab* (1813), which denounced the monarchy and religion while arguing for free love: 'Love is free: to promise for ever to love the same woman is not less absurd

Notes

[4] Ibid., 219.

[5] *Shelley's Prose* ed. David Lee Clark (London, 1988), p. 54.

[6] Jones i 268.

than to promise to believe the same creed: such a vow in both cases excludes us from all enquiry.'[7] As it happened, relations with his wife were deteriorating, and despite remarriage in March 1814 they separated the following month. 'I felt as if a dead and living body had been linked together in loathsome and horrible communion,'[8] he later told Hogg.

He met the 16-year-old Mary Godwin in May or June 1814, and arranged clandestine meetings with her and her half-sister Jane (later called Claire) at Mary Wollstonecraft's grave in St Pancras churchyard. 'I am thine, exclusively thine,' Mary wrote in a copy of *Queen Mab*, 'I have pledged myself to thee and sacred is the gift.'[9] When Godwin found out he banned further meetings. Shelley threatened suicide, brandishing a small pistol and a bottle of laudanum. 'His eyes were bloodshot, his hair and dress disordered,' recalled his friend Thomas Love Peacock, 'He caught up a bottle of laudanum, and said: "I never part from this."'[10]

On 28 July he eloped with Mary and Jane to the Continent. It was typical of him that he should have written to Harriet from France, inviting her to join them in Switzerland. Needless to add, she didn't – and after a whirlwind tour of France, Switzerland and Germany shortage of funds compelled them to return to England in September.

On their return the *ménage à trois* settled in St Pancras, close to what is now the Euston Road in central London, where they set off fireworks in the fields, discussed another Irish trip, and devised a plan to kidnap Shelley's two younger sisters from their school in Hackney. In the following months Jane changed her name to Claire, and Wordsworth's *The Excursion* was published. Wordsworth was one of Shelley's favourite poets, but though Shelley continued to admire his spiritual aspirations, it was clear with this latest publication that Wordsworth had abandoned his earlier radicalism. 'He is a slave,' Mary wrote in her journal on 14 September 1814, adding that they were 'much disappointed' with *The Excursion*.[11] Shelley may not have composed his sonnet 'To Wordsworth' as early as this (a more likely date being September–October 1815), but it marks the point at which he grew disillusioned with the Lake Poets generally.

In August 1815, after giving birth to a premature baby who died shortly after, Mary moved with Shelley to Bishopsgate, Old Windsor. Shelley's first major poem, *Alastor*, was composed there after a lengthy expedition up the Thames, and the river is a constant presence in the poem. It seems often to be driving him on, just as the Poet is driven by the spirit of solitude which Shelley thought selfish and leads the Poet to his death. That visionary spirit, conjured up by the Poet from within, compels him to reject the Arab maiden, and instead to feast on her visionary counterpart, the 'veiled maid' (l. 151) who dances through his dreams. Shelley's preoccupation with the Poet's unhealthy state of mind derives partly from his reading of Wordsworth's 'Lines left upon a Seat in a Yew-Tree' (see p. 352), also in blank verse.

Publication of *Alastor* coincided roughly with the birth of a second child, William, in January 1816. Shortly after, Claire Clairmont had an affair with Byron in April and, pregnant by him, joined Percy and Mary for a second foray to the Continent in the summer. Journeying through Switzerland, Shelley amused himself by writing the word 'atheist' after his name in at least four hotel registers, thus fuelling the outrage of such tourists as Southey, who would go home with tales about Shelley's obscene 'league of incest' with Mary and her half-sister.[12]

Notes

[7] *The Poems of Shelley* ed. Geoffrey Matthews and Kelvin Everest (2 vols, London, 1989–2000), i 370.

[8] Jones i 402.

[9] Quoted Richard Holmes, *Shelley: The Pursuit* (London, 1974), p. 230.

[10] Newman Ivey White, *Shelley* (2 vols, London, 1947), i 344.

[11] *Shelley Journals* i 25.

[12] For scholarly discussion see Peter Cochran, 'Robert Southey, the "Atheist" Inscription, and the "League of Incest" ', *N&Q* NS 37 (1990) 415–18.

In truth, Percy's attitude to God was more complex than the word 'atheist' suggests. It is hardly surprising that the concept appealed to someone opposed to an established church deeply implicated in the social and political oppression by which England was dominated. On the other hand, he was tremendously attracted to the pantheist life-force of *Tintern Abbey*,

> A motion and a spirit that impels
> All thinking things, all objects of all thought,
> And rolls through all things.
> (*Tintern Abbey* 101–3)

Rather than reject a benevolent deity outright, Shelley's poems prefer to argue for the existence of a 'Power' similar to Wordsworth's motion and spirit – at times identified with the tyrannical Jupiter in *Prometheus Unbound*, at others, closer to Demogorgon. Writing approvingly of Leigh Hunt's spiritual beliefs in 1811, Shelley noted his conviction of a God 'by no means perfect, but composed of good and evil like man' (Jones i 77). From time to time this is what Shelley thought too, but he could also contemplate the possibility of a universe without any creator. If any phrase were to be used to encapsulate his position, it might be 'awful doubt'[13] – awe for the natural world, mixed with scepticism as to a divine creator in the Christian sense.

Shelley was introduced to Byron for the first time on the jetty of the Hotel d'Angleterre on the shore of Lake Geneva, 27 May 1816. It was the start of a stimulating and productive summer, reminiscent of the *annus mirabilis* of 1797–8, when Wordsworth, Dorothy and Coleridge had enjoyed a year of intellectual and creative collaboration. During its course, Shelley remained an enthusiastic, if critical, reader of Wordsworth, eagerly devouring the collected *Poems* of 1815, especially *Tintern Abbey* and the *Ode*.[14] Byron later told Thomas Medwin that Shelley 'used to dose me with Wordsworth physic even to nausea'.[15] As a result, Byron composed most of *Childe Harold's Pilgrimage* Canto III, affecting (not always convincingly) a Wordsworthian enthusiasm for nature, and would go on, towards the end of the summer, to write *Manfred*, which also shows Wordsworth's influence.

As for Shelley, he composed two of his most important shorter poems in response to *Tintern Abbey* – *Mont Blanc* and the *Hymn to Intellectual Beauty*. What he enjoyed about it was its refusal to subscribe to conventional notions of the deity: Wordsworth's 'sense sublime / Of something far more deeply interfused'[16] flows straight into his poetry. But Shelley is capable of pulling back even from that, suggesting that it might be illusory – that, as he suggests in the *Hymn*, the grave is not the gateway to life everlasting but, 'Like life and fear, a dark reality' (l. 48).

Mont Blanc may be Shelley's masterpiece. It is an attempt to explain the function of poetry, where it comes from, and how it relates to the cosmos. It questions not just his vocation, but his entire belief-system. Its argument is that the poet is inspired by the same forces that produced the precipitous, violent landscape before him; they move him to speak ultimate truths capable of repealing 'Large codes of fraud and woe' – the casual injustices of repressive governments such as those who had recently defeated Napoleon at Waterloo.

One evening Shelley heard Byron recite the section of Coleridge's *Christabel* (recently published by John Murray at Byron's request) dealing with Geraldine's deformed side. He stared at Mary in the silence, shrieked, pressed his hands over his head, seized a candle and ran out of the room. He later said that the sight of Mary put him in mind of a woman with eyes for nipples. As a result, Byron proposed that they have a

Notes

13 'Mont Blanc' 77.

14 Neither Shelley, Byron nor Keats knew *The Prelude*, which remained unpublished until 1850, long after they had died.

15 Medwin 237.

16 *Tintern Abbey* 96–7.

AFTER TERM.
Thursday . . . . Feb. 13 | Friday . . . . . . Feb. 14

ORIGINAL POETRY.

[The following Ode, originally announced under the signature of the *Elfin Knight*, we have since found to be from the pen of the author, whose name was mentioned among others a week or two back in an article entitled "Young Poets." The reader will think with us, that it is alone sufficient to justify what was there observed;—but we shall say more on this subject in a review of the book we mentioned:—]

HYMN TO INTELLECTUAL BEAUTY.

1.

THE awful shadow of some unseen Power
Floats tho' unseen amongst us,—visiting
This various world with as inconstant wing
As summer winds that creep from flower to flower.—
Like moonbeams that behind some piny mountain shower,
It visits with inconstant glance
Each human heart and countenance;
Like hues and harmonies of evening,—
Like clouds in starlight widely spread,—
Like memory of music fled,—
Like aught that for its grace may be
Dear, and yet dearer for its mystery.

2.

Spirit of BEAUTY, that doth consecrate
With thine own hues all thou dost shine upon
Of human thought or form,—where art thou gone?

Figure 14 Shelley's 'Hymn to Intellectual Beauty' as it was first published, in the pages of Leigh Hunt's *Examiner*

ghost-story competition, as a result of which Mary began her masterpiece, *Frankenstein*.

A week later, Shelley and Byron set out on a boating expedition across Lake Leman, heading eastwards towards Evian. They visited places associated with Rousseau and Gibbon, freethinkers whom they admired, as Byron mentions in *Childe Harold's Pilgrimage* Canto III, on which he was then working (see pp. 883–4). They were nearly drowned when caught in a squall off the rocks of St Gingoux; in contrast with Byron, Shelley could not swim and sat tight in the boat until they were safe.

The summer with Byron came to an end, and having agreed to meet him again in Italy, Shelley returned to London with Mary and Claire. There followed two suicides – first that of Mary's half-sister Fanny Imlay, who may have recently discovered that her parents had not been married, followed by that of Shelley's wife Harriet in November. Believing that they would be able to assume custody of his two children by Harriet, Shelley married Mary Godwin on 30 December. Much to his distress, it would make no difference. Harriet's family disputed his suitability as a parent on the grounds of his being a revolutionary and an atheist, and the children were farmed out to foster-parents. The outcome was a disastrous one for Shelley, who would never again see his children by Harriet.

At this period Shelley and Mary socialized with other writers in London, particularly Leigh Hunt, Hazlitt, Haydon, Keats, and Charles and Mary Lamb. Meeting Shelley in January 1817, Haydon recorded that:

> he could not bear the inhumanity of Wordsworth in talking about the beauty of the shining trout as they lay after being caught, that he had such a horror of torturing animals it was impossible to express it. Ah, thought I, you have more horror at putting a hook into a fish's mouth than giving a pang to a mother's bosom. He had seduced Mary Wollstonecraft's daughter and enticed away Mrs Godwin's own daughter, to her great misery.[17]

Keats was wary of him too, and declined an invitation to visit him at Marlow in Buckinghamshire, where the Shelleys were now living. With the failure of his longest and most ambitious poem to date, *The Revolt of Islam*, he decided to travel to Italy. Passing through London, he engaged in a last sonnet-writing competition with Keats and Leigh Hunt, and after a visit to the British Museum with the stockbroker poet Horace Smith, wrote *Ozymandias* (see pp. 1079–80).

In March 1818 he set out across the Continent with Mary, William, Clara (their son and daughter), Claire, Allegra (Claire's daughter by Byron), their Swiss maid Elise and Milly Shields, their servant-girl from Marlow. They lived a nomadic life, travelling from Milan to Livorno, Venice, Rome, Naples, Livorno again, Florence and Pisa. Shelley was reunited with Byron in Venice in August 1818, where he was treated to a recitation of *Childe Harold* Canto IV. Just over a month later he was seriously ill with dysentery and his daughter Clara died, partly through his own negligence. 'Stanzas written in Dejection, near Naples' and 'Lines written among the Euganean Hills' (pp. 1081–91) speak powerfully of his mood at the time.

They arrived in Rome on 5 March 1819 and took rooms on the Corso. Each day Shelley visited the Baths of Caracalla, majestic ruins that in their heyday housed 1,500 people, and continued work on *Prometheus Unbound* (p. 1091), begun in Venice the previous year. It was finished in Rome in early April. (Joseph Severn's painting of Shelley writing at the Baths, now at the Keats Memorial House in Rome, is one of the great icons of the Romantic period.)

The Prometheus figure reverberates through the writings of Shelley and Byron partly because they saw him as symbolic of political defiance (see Plate 14). According to classical sources, Prometheus was the son of Iapetus and Asia, renowned for his cunning, which led to his theft of fire from heaven for the benefit of mankind. When Jupiter took fire away from the earth, Prometheus stole replacement fire from the chariot of the sun. Enraged, Jupiter nailed him to the rock of the Caucasus for 3,000 years, an eagle incessantly devouring his liver. He was freed, and the bird slaughtered, by Hercules.

Byron once recalled how, at Harrow, he had read Aeschylus' *Prometheus Bound*, commenting that 'The Prometheus – if not exactly in my plan – has always been so much in my head – that I can easily conceive its influence over all or anything that I have written.'[18] Prometheus was a topic of discussion when Shelley met Byron at Geneva in 1816; one of Byron's poems of that moment was *Prometheus* (see p. 887), and *Frankenstein* reinvents the myth (its subtitle being 'The Modern Prometheus'). With *Prometheus Unbound*, Shelley gives it a twist of his own. His Prometheus is a recognizable reworking of the poet-figure who in turn is an echo of Christ. The rebirth foreseen in the *Ode to the West Wind* is also much in evidence here, a logical consequence of Prometheus' Christ-like speech to Jupiter: 'Disdain? Ah no, I pity thee' (I 53). Shelley's Prometheus redeems the world from post-lapsarian hostilities, leading to the 'diviner day' of the millennium:

Notes

[17] *The Diary of Benjamin Robert Haydon* ed. Willard Bissell Pope (5 vols, Cambridge, Mass., 1960–3), ii 89.

[18] Marchand v 268.

Beyond the glassy gulfs we flee
Of shadow-peopled Infancy,
Through death and birth to a diviner day –
A paradise of vaulted bowers
Lit by downward-gazing flowers.
(II v 101–5)

He called *Prometheus Unbound* 'the most perfect of my productions' (Jones ii 127). Its most percipient and helpful critic was his wife, who encapsulated its central theme when she said that 'The prominent feature of Shelley's theory of the destiny of the human species was that evil is not inherent in the system of the creation, but an accident that might be expelled' (see p. 1440).

By now he was a controversial and despised figure among the English, and one day at the post office in Rome a man, hearing his name, approached him exclaiming, 'What, are you that damned atheist Shelley?' before striking him to the ground. In June the Shelleys prepared to head northwards to Livorno, but before their departure their beloved son William, 4 years old, died. He was buried in the Protestant Cemetery where, two years later, he would be joined by Keats.

Shelley had been travelling for a year in Italy when a political event in England inspired a burst of intense creative activity that would produce some of his finest works. On 16 August 1819, at St Peter's Field, on the outskirts of Manchester, 60,000 working men and women met to listen to the orator Henry Hunt declare the need for universal suffrage, liberty and political rights; all came from a region of fifty miles radius in orderly groups. The response of the local magistrates was to send in the Manchester and Salford yeomanry to arrest Hunt as he addressed the crowd. As they did so, they knocked down a woman and trampled her child to death. When the crowd surged, mounted hussars charged, sabres drawn, to disperse them. The result was that eleven people were killed and over 400 seriously injured, mainly as a result of sabre wounds. These included more than a hundred women and children. Unofficial figures were higher. Lord Sidmouth, Lord Liverpool (the Prime Minister) and the Prince Regent publicly endorsed the action. This was widely reported, and news reached Shelley within the week. A fortnight later he told his publisher, Charles Ollier, that 'the torrent of my indignation has not yet done boiling in my veins. I wait anxiously to hear how the country will express its sense of this bloody murderous oppression of its destroyers' (Jones ii 117).

Shelley's response was swift: within twelve days he composed the greatest poem of political protest in the language. *The Mask of Anarchy* begins as satire, depicting the ministers of Lord Liverpool's government riding the horses which trample the crowd; then, from stanzas 34 to 63, a maid who has risen up to halt Anarchy (the idol of both the government and the people) addresses the crowd, telling them of false freedom and then of true freedom; and in the concluding section she tells them to stand up for their rights using passive, non-violent demonstration:

Rise like lions after slumber
In unvanquishable number;
Shake your chains to earth like dew
Which in sleep had fallen on you –
Ye are many, they are few.
(ll. 368–72)

The poem warns against Anarchy – it recognizes the appetite of the people for revenge, but warns them that were they to take it, the government would use it as the excuse for far more violent suppression.

Shelley posted the poem to Leigh Hunt for *The Examiner* but he decided against publication, choosing to retain it until 1832, well after Shelley's death, when he brought it out to coincide with the passing of the first Parliamentary Reform Bill. Had it been published in 1819, it would have made Shelley's name. It was designed for mass consumption, and would have had an immediate impact. But it would also have led, inevitably, to Hunt's imprisonment for sedition – there were over seventy-five such prosecutions that year – and he had no wish to return to prison (where he had already been sent for libelling the Prince Regent in 1813 – see p. 792). He was also less of a radical than Shelley, and genuinely thought this a bad time to inflame the populace.

This was bad luck for Shelley, and typical of the fate of much of his best writing during his lifetime. Absence from England meant that he was unlikely to get his work into print in the form he would have wished, if at all. He could not speak to publishers to argue his case, and on the rare occasions when it was published it was ridiculed and attacked, because he was too radical for his time. Shortly after completing *The Mask of Anarchy* he happened to read a review of *The Revolt of Islam* (1818) in the Tory *Quarterly Review*, which characterized him as someone who 'would overthrow the constitution . . . he would pull down our churches, level our Establishment, and burn our bibles . . . marriage he cannot endure.' It went on to attack him on personal grounds and mock his poem.

This kind of criticism must have hurt, but it further clarified his response to the Peterloo Massacre. He began to understand better his poetical aims and ambitions, and in order to articulate that renewed sense of purpose he composed *Ode to the West Wind* (in *terza rima*) around 25 October 1819. Like the *Mask*, it is a statement of faith in the ability of human beings to resist the oppression of church and state, and realize their power of self-determination; thus, the 'Pestilence-stricken multitudes' are bidden to participate in the millennial vision of 'a new birth'. But the poem goes further than that. It insists on the primacy of the poet as the central agency, the saviour-like prophet, 'tameless, and swift, and proud', who will awaken the masses to their potential: 'Drive my dead thoughts over the universe / Like withered leaves to quicken a new birth!' (ll. 63–4).

In the essay 'On Love' he observed, 'I have found my language misunderstood like one in a distant and savage land' (see p. 1080), and in a letter of April 1819 he expressed his cynicism as to the reviewers' opinion of *Rosalind and Helen* (1819): 'As to the reviews, I suppose there is nothing but abuse' (Jones ii 94). It is moving to consider that a poet who during his lifetime was compelled to accept failure should have continued to believe in the power of his words to change the world for the better. What he could not know was that, for decades after his death, working-class people across the world would take inspiration from his poems in their struggle for their rights.

Mary Shelley's fourth child was born in November 1819 – Percy Florence (named after the city of his birth) was the only one that would survive. This was a period of remarkable artistic productivity for Shelley, and besides much else he composed *England in 1819*, a sonnet that glances back at the events of the past autumn. In a spirit of resignation, he sent it to Leigh Hunt for *The Examiner*, adding wisely, 'I do not expect you to publish it, but you may show it to whom you please' (Jones ii 167). Hunt decided not to publish.

The Shelleys moved to Pisa, where by 20 January 1821 he had read an article by his old friend Thomas Love Peacock entitled 'The Four Ages of Poetry', in the first number of Ollier's *Literary Miscellany*, arguing that English poetry was in terminal decline. He decided to respond. The result was his *Defence of Poetry*, of which extracts are presented here, an amplification of many of the ideas found elsewhere in his writing. At its heart is a belief that the poet, a participant in 'the eternal, the infinite, and the one' – that is to say, a kind of priest or prophet – is the mouthpiece for cosmic, moral and political truths. It is Shelley's most important prose utterance, and was sent to Ollier for the next number of his *Literary Miscellany*; it was not published.

In April 1821 Shelley heard of Keats's death. They had met at Hunt's in 1817, and he had become an admirer of his work, particularly *Hyperion*. During his frequent boating expeditions

Shelley devised a poem on Keats's death entitled *Adonais*. Its starting-point was the belief that a 'savage criticism' of *Endymion* in the *Quarterly Review* had exacerbated Keats's incipient tuberculosis, contracted while nursing his brother Tom. This had not been so, but Shelley became convinced of it. It turned Keats into yet another version of the prophet in the wilderness, which was how he saw himself. *Adonais* is the occasion for some of the most persuasive Neoplatonic poetry Shelley was to compose:

> He is made one with Nature: there is heard
> His voice in all her music, from the moan
> Of thunder, to the song of night's sweet bird;
> He is a presence to be felt and known
> In darkness and in light, from herb and stone,
> Spreading itself where'er that Power may move
> Which has withdrawn his being to its own,
> Which wields the world with never-wearied love,
> Sustains it from beneath, and kindles it above.
>
> (ll. 370–8)

This is akin to the pantheist passages in *Tintern Abbey* (ll. 94–103); both poems speak of the indefinable 'presence' that transcends the limitations of the human condition, coexistent with a universal consciousness that runs through nature. Shelley saw Keats as absorbed into that larger entity, just as the nameless woman of Wordsworth's 'A Slumber did my Spirit Seal' was incorporated into the 'earth's diurnal course / With rocks and stones and trees!' (ll. 7–8).

By now, strains had appeared in Mary and Percy's marriage, due partly to mutual despondency at their children's deaths, and partly to an unfounded allegation that Claire had given birth to Shelley's child. In a letter of March 1820 Shelley complained that 'Mary considers me a portion of herself, and feels no more remorse in torturing me than in torturing her own mind. Could she suddenly know a person in every way my equal, and hold close and perpetual communion with him, as a distinct being from herself, as a friend instead of a husband, she would obtain empire over herself that she might not make him miserable.'[19] There would be scant respite from these tensions during their last years together. In fact, the arrival in Pisa of Edward and Jane Williams brought another woman into Shelley's life. According to Mary, Jane 'has a very pretty voice, and a taste and ear for music which is almost miraculous. The harp is her favourite instrument; but we have none, and a very bad piano.' Little wonder, then, that Shelley should have given Jane a guitar, enclosing the fair copy of 'With a Guitar, To Jane' (p. 1220) – as undisguised a love poem as he would ever write. The Shelleys moved to San Terenzo near Lerici in April 1822, where he received his boat, the *Ariel*, on 22 May. He sailed to Livorno with Edward Williams, but on the way back a storm blew up and the boat went down under full sail. Ten days later his body was washed up along the beach between Massa and Viareggio, the flesh of his arms and face entirely eaten away. The corpse was identified by the copy of Keats's poems in his jacket pocket, and burnt on the beach in Byron's presence (see Plate 15).

Shelley's literary reputation has risen comparatively slowly, thanks in part to the deplorable state of his texts. Most of his poems were printed incorrectly, often because he was unable to supervise their production. Alongside her remarkable novels, one of Mary Shelley's greatest creative achievements was to edit the first collected edition of her husband's poetry in 1839, which remained the critical standard well into the late twentieth century. The works presented here are edited for this anthology from early printed texts and Shelley's manuscripts.

Further reading

Two scholarly editions of Shelley's poetry are now in production: the Longman Annotated Poets edition, by Geoffrey Matthews, Kelvin Everest et al. (two volumes so far, 1989–) and the Johns Hopkins

Notes

[19] B. C. Barker-Benfield, *Shelley's Guitar* (Oxford 1992), p. 131.

University Press edition by Neil Freistat and Donald H. Reiman (one volume so far, 2000–).

Stephen C. Behrendt, *Shelley and His Audiences* (Lincoln, Neb., 1989).
Judith Chernaik, *The Lyrics of Shelley* (Cleveland, Ohio, and London, 1972).
Richard Cronin, *Shelley's Poetic Thoughts* (London, 1981).
David Duff, *Romance and Revolution: Shelley and the Politics of a Genre* (Cambridge, 1994).
Richard Holmes, *Shelley: The Pursuit* (London, 1974).
William Keach, *Shelley's Style* (London, 1984).
Michael O'Neill, *The Human Mind's Imaginings: Conflict and Achievement in Shelley's Poetry* (Oxford, 1989).
Michael O'Neill, *Romanticism and the Self-Conscious Poem* (Oxford, 1997), chapters 5 and 6.
Michael O'Neill, *Shelley* (London, 1993).
Donald H. Reiman, *Percy Bysshe Shelley* (2nd edn, Boston, 1990).
Neville Rogers, *Shelley at Work: A Critical Inquiry* (2nd edn, Oxford, 1967).
Shelley Revalued: Essays from the Gregynog Conference ed. Kelvin Everest (Leicester, 1983).
Timothy Webb, *Shelley: A Voice not Understood* (Manchester, 1977).
Susan J. Wolfson, 'Social Form: Shelley and the Determination of Reading', in *Formal Charges: The Shaping of Poetry in British Romanticism* (Stanford, Calif., 1997), pp. 193–226.

To Wordsworth (composed probably September–October 1815)[1]

From Alastor; or, The Spirit of Solitude, and Other Poems (1816)

Poet of nature, thou hast wept to know
That things depart which never may return;
Childhood and youth, friendship and love's first glow
Have fled like sweet dreams,[2] leaving thee to mourn.
These common woes I feel. One loss is mine
Which thou too feel'st, yet I alone deplore.[3]
Thou wert as a lone star,[4] whose light did shine
On some frail bark in winter's midnight roar;
Thou hast like to a rock-built refuge stood
Above the blind and battling multitude;
In honoured poverty[5] thy voice did weave
Songs consecrate to truth and liberty –
Deserting these, thou leavest me to grieve,
Thus having been, that thou shouldst cease to be.

Notes

To Wordsworth

[1] Shelley admired *Tintern Abbey* and the *Ode*, but was disappointed by *The Excursion* (1814), and despised Wordsworth for the conservatism of his middle age. He did not know *The Prelude*. See headnote, pp. 1045–6, for further discussion.

[2] *Poet of nature . . . dreams* a reference to Wordsworth's lament for the loss of his earlier intensity of vision in the *Ode* (p. 538).

[3] *deplore* lament.

[4] *Thou wert as a lone star* cf. Wordsworth's praise of Milton, 'London 1802' 9: 'Thy soul was like a star and dwelt apart.'

[5] *In honoured poverty* it cannot be said that Wordsworth was ever truly poor (although he and his siblings had known hard times after they were orphaned in 1783). Shelley is lamenting Wordsworth's acceptance of the job of Distributor for Stamps in Westmorland, which brought him a yearly salary of £400 (£15,000 / US$27,000 today).

Alastor; or, The Spirit of Solitude (composed 10 September and 14 December 1815)[1]

From Alastor; or, The Spirit of Solitude, and Other Poems (1816)

Preface

The poem entitled 'Alastor' may be considered as allegorical of one of the most interesting situations of the human mind. It represents a youth[2] of uncorrupted feelings and adventurous genius led forth by an imagination inflamed and purified through familiarity with all that is excellent and majestic, to the contemplation of the universe. He drinks deep of the fountains of knowledge and is still insatiate. The magnificence and beauty of the external world sinks profoundly into the frame of his conceptions, and affords to their modifications a variety not to be exhausted. So long as it is possible for his desires to point towards objects thus infinite and unmeasured, he is joyous and tranquil and self-possessed. But the period arrives when these objects cease to suffice. His mind is at length suddenly awakened and thirsts for intercourse with an intelligence similar to itself. He images to himself the being whom he loves. Conversant with speculations of the sublimest and most perfect natures, the vision in which he embodies his own imaginations unites all of wonderful, or wise, or beautiful, which the poet, the philosopher, or the lover could depicture. The intellectual faculties, the imagination, the functions of sense, have their respective requisitions[3] on the sympathy of corresponding powers in other human beings. The poet is represented as uniting these requisitions, and attaching them to a single image. He seeks in vain for a prototype of his conception.[4] Blasted by his disappointment, he descends to an untimely grave.

The picture is not barren of instruction to actual men. The poet's self-centred seclusion was avenged by the furies of an irresistible passion pursuing him to speedy ruin. But that power which strikes the luminaries of the world with sudden darkness and extinction, by awakening them to too exquisite a perception of its influences, dooms to a slow and poisonous decay those meaner spirits that dare to abjure its dominion. Their destiny is more abject and inglorious as their delinquency is more contemptible and pernicious. They who, deluded by no generous error, instigated by no sacred thirst of doubtful knowledge, duped by no illustrious superstition, loving nothing on this earth, and cherishing no hopes beyond, yet keep aloof from sympathies with their kind, rejoicing neither in human joy nor mourning with human grief; these, and such as they, have their apportioned curse. They languish because none feel with them their common nature. They are morally dead. They are neither friends, nor lovers, nor fathers, nor citizens of the world, nor benefactors of their country. Among

Notes

ALASTOR; OR, THE SPIRIT OF SOLITUDE

[1] For introductory remarks on this poem see p. 1045. Thomas Love Peacock recalled, in his *Memoirs of Shelley*: 'I proposed that [title] which he adopted: *Alastor; or, the Spirit of Solitude.* The Greek word 'Ἀλάστωρ is an evil genius, A κακοδαίμων . . . The poem treated the spirit of solitude as a spirit of evil. I mention the true meaning of the word because many have supposed *Alastor* to be the name of the hero of the poem.'

[2] *a youth* not named in the poem, though obviously a version of Shelley himself.

[3] *requisitions* claims.

[4] *a prototype of his conception* an ideal embodiment of his imaginings. The essay 'On Love' refers to 'the ideal prototype of everything excellent or lovely that we are capable of conceiving as belonging to the nature of man'; see p. 1080. See also Shelley's letter to John Gisborne, 18 June 1822: 'I think one is always in love with something or other; the error (and I confess it is not easy for spirits cased in flesh and blood to avoid it) consists in seeking in a mortal image the likeness of what is perhaps eternal' (Jones ii 434). For more on ideal prototypes, see 'On Love', pp. 1080–1.

those who attempt to exist without human sympathy, the pure and tender-hearted perish through the intensity and passion of their search after its communities, when the vacancy of their spirit suddenly makes itself felt. All else,[5] selfish, blind, and torpid, are those unforeseeing multitudes who constitute, together with their own, the lasting misery and loneliness of the world. Those who love not their fellow-beings live unfruitful lives, and prepare for their old age a miserable grave.

The good die first,
And those whose hearts are dry as summer dust,
Burn to the socket![6]

14 December 1815

Nondum amabam, et amare amabam, quaerebam quid amarem, amans amare.[7]

Earth, ocean, air, beloved brotherhood!
If our great mother[8] has imbued my soul
With aught of natural piety[9] to feel
Your love, and recompense the boon with mine;
If dewy morn, and odorous noon, and even,
With sunset and its gorgeous ministers,
And solemn midnight's tingling silentness;
If autumn's hollow sighs in the sere[10] wood,
And winter robing with pure snow and crowns
Of starry ice the grey grass and bare boughs;
If spring's voluptuous pantings when she breathes
Her first sweet kisses, have been dear to me;
If no bright bird, insect, or gentle beast
I consciously[11] have injured, but still loved
And cherished these my kindred – then forgive
This boast, beloved brethren, and withdraw
No portion of your wonted favour now.
 Mother of this unfathomable world![12]
Favour my solemn song, for I have loved
Thee ever, and thee only; I have watched
Thy shadow and the darkness of thy steps,
And my heart ever gazes on the depth
Of thy deep mysteries. I have made my bed
In charnels[13] and on coffins, where black death
Keeps record of the trophies won from thee,
Hoping to still these obstinate questionings[14]

Notes

[5] *All else* completely different.

[6] Shelley quoted these lines from Wordsworth, *The Excursion* i 500–2, but they had originally been composed as *Ruined Cottage* 96-8 (p. 424).

[7] 'I was not yet in love, and I loved to be in love, I sought what I might love, in love with loving,' St Augustine, *Confessions* III i.

[8] *our great mother* Cybele, goddess of the powers of nature.

[9] *natural piety* Wordsworth, 'The Rainbow' 8–9: 'And I could wish my days to be / Bound each to each by natural piety.'

[10] *sere* dry, withered.

[11] *consciously* i.e. conscious of his culpability. Shelley used to go shooting, but became a vegetarian at the age of 19.

[12] *Mother of this unfathomable world* Nature, as well as Necessity; compare *Queen Mab* vi 198: 'Necessity! Thou mother of the world!'

[13] *charnels* graveyards.

[14] *obstinate questionings* an allusion to Wordsworth, 'Ode' 144–5: 'those obstinate questionings / Of sense and outward things'.

Of thee and thine, by forcing some lone ghost,
Thy messenger, to render up the tale
Of what we are.[15] In lone and silent hours,
When night makes a weird sound of its own stillness,
Like an inspired and desperate alchemist[16]
Staking his very life on some dark hope,
Have I mixed awful talk[17] and asking looks
With my most innocent love, until strange tears,
Uniting with those breathless kisses, made
Such magic as compels the charmed night
To render up thy charge – and though ne'er yet
Thou hast unveiled thy inmost sanctuary,
Enough from incommunicable dream,
And twilight phantasms, and deep noonday thought,
Has shone within me, that serenely now
And moveless, as a long-forgotten lyre[18]
Suspended in the solitary dome
Of some mysterious and deserted fane,[19]
I wait thy breath, Great Parent, that my strain
May modulate with murmurs of the air
And motions of the forests and the sea,
And voice of living beings, and woven hymns
Of night and day, and the deep heart of man.
There was a poet whose untimely tomb
No human hands with pious reverence reared,
But the charmed eddies of autumnal winds
Built o'er his mouldering bones a pyramid
Of mouldering leaves in the waste wilderness;
A lovely youth – no mourning maiden decked
With weeping flowers or votive cypress[20] wreath
The lone couch of his everlasting sleep;
Gentle and brave and generous – no lorn[21] bard
Breathed o'er his dark fate one melodious sigh;
He lived, he died, he sung, in solitude.
Strangers have wept to hear his passionate notes,
And virgins, as unknown he passed, have pined
And wasted for fond love of his wild eyes.
The fire of those soft orbs has ceased to burn,
And silence, too enamoured of that voice,
Locks its mute music in her rugged cell.
By solemn vision and bright silver dream
His infancy was nurtured;[22] every sight
And sound from the vast earth and ambient[23] air

Notes

[15] *I have made . . . what we are* Thomas Jefferson Hogg recalled that Shelley had, as a boy, frequented graveyards in the hope of meeting ghosts.

[16] *alchemist* Alchemists sought to turn base metals to gold – an impossibility.

[17] *awful talk* awe-inspired discussion.

[18] *a long-forgotten lyre* an Aeolian harp; with lines 42–9 compare Coleridge, 'Eolian Harp' 36–40.

[19] *fane* temple.

[20] *cypress* symbol of death and mourning.

[21] *lorn* lonesome.

[22] *By solemn vision . . . nurtured* Shelley catches the tone of Wordsworth's account of the Wanderer's natural education in *The Excursion*, originally composed as *The Pedlar* in 1798 (see pp. 435–44).

[23] *ambient* surrounding.

Sent to his heart its choicest impulses.
The fountains of divine philosophy[24]
Fled not his thirsting lips, and all of great
Or good or lovely, which the sacred past
In truth or fable consecrates, he felt
And knew. When early youth had passed, he left
His cold fireside and alienated home[25]
To seek strange truths in undiscovered lands:
Many a wide waste and tangled wilderness
Has lured his fearless steps, and he has bought
With his sweet voice and eyes, from savage men,
His rest and food. Nature's most secret steps
He like her shadow has pursued, where'er
The red volcano overcanopies
Its fields of snow and pinnacles of ice
With burning smoke, or where bitumen lakes[26]
On black bare pointed islets ever beat
With sluggish surge, or where the secret caves
Rugged and dark, winding among the springs
Of fire and poison, inaccessible
To avarice or pride, their starry domes
Of diamond and of gold expand above
Numberless and immeasurable halls,
Frequent[27] with crystal column, and clear shrines
Of pearl, and thrones radiant with chrysolite.[28]
Nor had that scene of ampler majesty
Than gems or gold, the varying roof of heaven
And the green earth lost in his heart its claims
To love and wonder; he would linger long
In lonesome vales, making the wild his home,
Until the doves and squirrels would partake
From his innocuous hand his bloodless food,[29]
Lured by the gentle meaning of his looks,
And the wild antelope that starts whene'er
The dry leaf rustles in the brake, suspend
Her timid steps to gaze upon a form
More graceful than her own.
His wandering step,[30]
Obedient to high thoughts, has visited
The awful ruins of the days of old:
Athens, and Tyre, and Balbec,[31] and the waste

Notes

[24] *divine philosophy* cf. Milton, *Comus* 475: 'How charming is divine philosophy!'.

[25] *alienated home* Like Victor Frankenstein, the poet alienates his family. Shelley's relationship with his own father became strained during his undergraduate years and ended with a complete break in January 1812

[26] *bitumen lakes* lakes of mineral pitch, used in ancient times as mortar. Cf. the 'lakes of bitumen' in Byron's *Manfred* I i 90.

[27] *Frequent* crowded.

[28] *chrysolite* olivine, a silicate of magnesia and iron found in lava. Its colour varies from pale yellowish-green (the precious stone) to dark bottle-green.

[29] *his bloodless food* Shelley was a vegetarian; see his 'Essay on the Vegetable System of Diet'.

[30] The poet's journey takes him back through human history to the birth of time (l. 128).

[31] *Tyre, and Balbec* ancient cities in the present-day Lebanon.

Where stood Jerusalem,[32] the fallen towers
Of Babylon,[33] the eternal pyramids,
Memphis and Thebes,[34] and whatsoe'er of strange
Sculptured on alabaster obelisk
Or jasper tomb, or mutilated sphinx,
Dark Ethiopia in her desert hills
Conceals. Among the ruined temples there,
Stupendous columns and wild images
Of more than man, where marble demons[35] watch
The Zodiac's brazen mystery[36] and dead men
Hang their mute thoughts on the mute walls around,
He lingered, poring on memorials
Of the world's youth, through the long burning day
Gazed on those speechless shapes, nor, when the moon
Filled the mysterious halls with floating shades,
Suspended he that task, but ever gazed
And gazed, till meaning on his vacant mind
Flashed[37] like strong inspiration, and he saw
The thrilling secrets of the birth of time.
  Meanwhile an Arab maiden brought his food,
Her daily portion, from her father's tent,
And spread her matting for his couch, and stole
From duties and repose to tend his steps –
Enamoured, yet not daring for deep awe
To speak her love – and watched his nightly sleep,
Sleepless herself, to gaze upon his lips
Parted in slumber, whence the regular breath
Of innocent dreams arose. Then when red morn
Made paler the pale moon, to her cold home
Wildered, and wan, and panting, she returned.
  The poet wandering on, through Arabie
And Persia and the wild Carmanian waste,
And o'er the aerial mountains which pour down
Indus and Oxus from their icy caves,
In joy and exultation held his way;
Till in the Vale of Kashmir,[38] far within
Its loneliest dell, where odorous plants entwine
Beneath the hollow rocks a natural bower,
Beside a sparkling rivulet he stretched
His languid limbs.[39] A vision on his sleep

Notes

[32] Jerusalem was destroyed by the Emperor Titus in AD 70; in 1867 it had a population of only 16,000.

[33] The ancient city of Babylon, home of the hanging gardens (one of the seven wonders of the ancient world), was in modern Iraq, south of Baghdad.

[34] *Memphis and Thebes* The youth goes up the Nile; these are ancient Egyptian cities.

[35] *demons* spirits, genii.

[36] *The Zodiac's brazen mystery* The Zodiac in the temple of Denderah, Upper Egypt, was renowned; mythological figures were arranged around the ceiling of its portico. The Zodiac was taken to Paris in 1822 and is now in the Bibliothèque Nationale de France.

[37] *on his vacant mind / Flashed* as in Wordsworth's *Daffodils* 15–16: 'They flash upon that inward eye / Which is the bliss of solitude.'

[38] *through Arabie . . . Kashmir* the poet's journey takes him through Arabia, Persia (modern Iran), through the Kerman desert in eastern Persia, over the Hindu Kush mountains (the 'Indian Caucasus'), and into Kashmir in north-west India.

[39] *he stretched . . . limbs* a recollection of Gray, *Elegy* 103–4: 'His listless length at noontide would he stretch / And pore upon the brook that babbles by.'

There came, a dream of hopes that never yet
Had flushed his cheek: he dreamed a veiled maid
Sat near him, talking in low solemn tones.
Her voice was like the voice of his own soul
Heard in the calm of thought;[40] its music long,[41]
Like woven sounds of streams and breezes, held
His inmost sense suspended in its web
Of many-coloured woof and shifting hues.
Knowledge and truth and virtue were her theme,
And lofty hopes of divine liberty,
Thoughts the most dear to him, and poesy,
Herself a poet. Soon the solemn mood
Of her pure mind kindled through all her frame
A permeating fire – wild numbers[42] then
She raised, with voice stifled in tremulous sobs
Subdued by its own pathos;[43] her fair hands
Were bare alone, sweeping from some strange harp
Strange symphony,[44] and in their branching veins
The eloquent blood told an ineffable tale.
The beating of her heart was heard to fill
The pauses of her music, and her breath
Tumultuously accorded with those fits
Of intermitted song. Sudden she rose,
As if her heart impatiently endured
Its bursting burden: at the sound he turned,
And saw by the warm light of their own life
Her glowing limbs beneath the sinuous veil
Of woven wind, her outspread arms now bare,
Her dark locks floating in the breath of night,
Her beamy bending eyes, her parted lips
Outstretched and pale, and quivering eagerly.
His strong heart sunk and sickened with excess
Of love. He reared his shuddering limbs and quelled
His gasping breath, and spread his arms to meet
Her panting bosom; she drew back awhile,
Then, yielding to the irresistible joy,
With frantic gesture and short breathless cry
Folded his frame in her dissolving arms.
Now blackness veiled his dizzy eyes, and night
Involved[45] and swallowed up the vision; sleep,
Like a dark flood suspended in its course,
Rolled back its impulse on his vacant brain.
    Roused by the shock he started from his trance –
The cold white light of morning, the blue moon
Low in the west, the clear and garish[46] hills,

Notes

[40] 'His mind . . . thirsts for intercourse with an intelligence similar to itself. He images to himself the being whom he loves', p. 1053 above; see also 'On Love', pp. 1080–1 below.

[41] *long* for a long time.

[42] *numbers* a song, with the accompaniment of a lute.

[43] *pathos* emotion.

[44] *Strange symphony* There is possibly an echo here of Coleridge's *Kubla Khan* 42–3: 'Could I revive within me / Her symphony and song'.

[45] *Involved* wrapped around.

[46] *garish* glaring.

The distinct valley and the vacant woods,
Spread round him where he stood. Whither have fled
The hues of heaven that canopied his bower
Of yesternight? The sounds that soothed his sleep,
The mystery and the majesty of earth,
The joy, the exultation? His wan eyes
Gaze on the empty scene as vacantly
As ocean's moon looks on the moon in heaven.
The spirit of sweet human love has sent
A vision to the sleep of him who spurned
Her choicest gifts. He eagerly pursues
Beyond the realms of dream that fleeting shade;
He overleaps the bounds.[47] Alas, alas!
Were limbs and breath and being intertwined
Thus treacherously? Lost, lost, forever lost
In the wide pathless desert of dim sleep,
That beautiful shape! Does the dark gate of death
Conduct to thy mysterious paradise,
Oh sleep? Does the bright arch of rainbow clouds
And pendent[48] mountains seen in the calm lake
Lead only to a black and watery depth,
While death's blue vault with loathliest[49] vapours hung,
Where every shade which the foul grave exhales
Hides its dead eye from the detested day,
Conducts, oh sleep, to thy delightful realms?[50]
This doubt with sudden tide flowed on his heart;
The insatiate hope which it awakened stung
His brain even like despair.[51]
While daylight held
The sky, the poet kept mute conference[52]
With his still soul. At night the passion came
Like the fierce fiend of a distempered dream,
And shook him from his rest, and led him forth
Into the darkness. As an eagle grasped
In folds of the green serpent, feels her breast
Burn with the poison, and precipitates[53]
Through night and day, tempest and calm and cloud,
Frantic with dizzying anguish, her blind flight
O'er the wide airy wilderness; thus driven
By the bright shadow[54] of that lovely dream,
Beneath the cold glare of the desolate night,

Notes

[47] *the bounds* i.e. between illusion and reality, in trying to pursue the dream-image into the real world. As Peter Butter suggests, there is a divergence here from the essay 'On Love' (pp. 1080–1). There, the desire for love draws us to nature; here, the natural world appears vacant and dead to the poet, whose love is narcissistic, directed to an ideal conceived within his own mind.

[48] *pendent* overhanging.

[49] *loathliest* obnoxious.

[50] *Does the bright arch . . . delightful realms?* i.e. can it be that nature in all its beauty leads to nothing, while death, in all its horror, leads to the paradise revealed to the poet in sleep? The question is not answered.

[51] *despair* i.e. of ever being united with the ideal he has been allowed to see.

[52] *conference* communion; part of his inner being was at repose.

[53] *precipitates* hurries.

[54] *shadow* memory.

Through tangled swamps and deep precipitous dells,
Startling with careless step the moonlight snake,
He fled. Red morning dawned upon his flight,
Shedding the mockery of its vital hues
Upon his cheek of death. He wandered on
Till vast Aornos seen from Petra's steep[55]
Hung o'er the low horizon like a cloud;
Through Balk[56] and where the desolated tombs
Of Parthian kings scatter to every wind
Their wasting dust, wildly he wandered on
Day after day, a weary waste of hours,
Bearing within his life the brooding care
That ever fed on its decaying flame.
And now his limbs were lean: his scattered hair
Sered[57] by the autumn of strange suffering
Sung dirges in the wind; his listless hand
Hung like dead bone within its withered skin;
Life, and the lustre that consumed it, shone
As in a furnace burning secretly
From his dark eyes alone. The cottagers,
Who ministered with human charity
His human wants, beheld with wondering awe
Their fleeting visitant. The mountaineer,
Encountering on some dizzy precipice
That spectral form, deemed that the spirit of wind
With lightning eyes, and eager breath, and feet
Disturbing not the drifted snow, had paused
In its career; the infant would conceal
His troubled visage in his mother's robe
In terror at the glare of those wild eyes,
To remember their strange light in many a dream
Of after-times; but youthful maidens, taught
By nature, would interpret half the woe[58]
That wasted him, would call him with false names
Brother and friend, would press his pallid hand
At parting, and watch, dim through tears, the path
Of his departure from their father's door.
At length upon the lone Chorasmian shore[59]
He paused, a wide and melancholy waste
Of putrid marshes. A strong impulse urged
His steps to the seashore; a swan[60] was there,
Beside a sluggish stream among the reeds.
It rose as he approached, and with strong wings
Scaling the upward sky, bent its bright course

Notes

[55] *vast Aornos seen from Petra's steep* The poet returns from India, where the great rock Aornos stands by the Indus. There is no place called Petra in this area.

[56] The ancient city of Balkh was in modern-day Afghanistan. He is travelling through the area south-east of the Caspian Sea, where the Parthian kingdom used to be.

[57] *Sered* thinned, faded.

[58] *would interpret half the woe* i.e. they would guess that he was in love, but not that he was in love with an ideal.

[59] *Chorasmian shore* eastern shore of the Caspian Sea.

[60] *a swan* sacred to Apollo, god of poetry; it sang before dying.

High over the immeasurable main.
His eyes pursued its flight. 'Thou hast a home,
Beautiful bird; thou voyagest to thine home,
Where thy sweet mate will twine her downy neck
With thine, and welcome thy return with eyes
Bright in the lustre of their own fond joy.
And what am I that I should linger here,
With voice far sweeter than thy dying notes,
Spirit more vast than thine, frame more attuned
To beauty, wasting these surpassing powers
In the deaf air, to the blind earth, and heaven
That echoes not my thoughts?' A gloomy smile
Of desperate hope wrinkled his quivering lips –
For sleep, he knew, kept[61] most relentlessly
Its precious charge, and silent death exposed,
Faithless perhaps as sleep, a shadowy lure,[62]
With doubtful smile mocking its own strange charms.[63]
Startled by his own thoughts he looked around.
There was no fair fiend near him, not a sight
Or sound of awe but in his own deep mind.
A little shallop[64] floating near the shore
Caught the impatient wandering of his gaze.
It had been long abandoned, for its sides
Gaped wide with many a rift, and its frail joints
Swayed with the undulations of the tide.
A restless impulse urged him to embark
And meet lone death on the drear ocean's waste,
For well he knew that mighty shadow loves
The slimy caverns of the populous deep.
The day was fair and sunny, sea and sky
Drank its inspiring radiance, and the wind
Swept strongly from the shore, blackening the waves.
Following his eager soul, the wanderer
Leaped in the boat, he spread his cloak aloft
On the bare mast and took his lonely seat,
And felt the boat speed o'er the tranquil sea
Like a torn cloud before the hurricane.
As one that in a silver vision floats
Obedient to the sweep of odorous winds
Upon resplendent clouds, so rapidly
Along the dark and ruffled waters fled
The straining boat. A whirlwind swept it on
With fierce gusts and precipitating force
Through the white ridges of the chafed sea.
The waves arose; higher and higher still
Their fierce necks writhed beneath the tempest's scourge
Like serpents struggling in a vulture's grasp.

Notes

[61] *kept* concealed, kept to itself.

[62] *lure* temptation.

[63] *For sleep . . . charms* The poet has not seen his vision in sleep; perhaps he will not see her in death.

[64] *shallop* small open boat.

Calm and rejoicing in the fearful war
Of wave ruining[65] on wave, and blast on blast
Descending, and black flood on whirlpool driven
With dark obliterating course, he sat:
As if their genii were the ministers
Appointed to conduct him to the light
Of those beloved eyes, the poet sat
Holding the steady helm. Evening came on,
The beams of sunset hung their rainbow hues[66]
High mid the shifting domes of sheeted spray
That canopied his path o'er the waste deep;
Twilight, ascending slowly from the east,
Entwined in duskier wreaths her braided locks
O'er the fair front and radiant eyes of day;
Night followed, clad with stars. On every side
More horribly the multitudinous streams
Of ocean's mountainous waste to mutual war
Rushed in dark tumult thundering, as to mock
The calm and spangled sky. The little boat
Still fled before the storm, still fled like foam
Down the steep cataract of a wintry river –
Now pausing on the edge of the riven[67] wave,
Now leaving far behind the bursting mass
That fell, convulsing ocean; safely fled –
As if that frail and wasted human form
Had been an elemental god.[68]
At midnight
The moon arose – and lo! the ethereal cliffs[69]
Of Caucasus,[70] whose icy summits shone
Among the stars like sunlight, and around
Whose caverned base the whirlpools and the waves,
Bursting and eddying irresistibly,
Rage and resound forever. Who shall save?
The boat fled on, the boiling torrent drove,
The crags closed round with black and jagged arms,
The shattered mountain overhung the sea,
And faster still, beyond all human speed,
Suspended on the sweep of the smooth wave,
The little boat was driven. A cavern there
Yawned, and amid its slant and winding depths
Engulfed the rushing sea. The boat fled on
With unrelaxing speed. 'Vision and love!'
The poet cried aloud, 'I have beheld
The path of thy departure. Sleep and death
Shall not divide us long!'

Notes

[65] *ruining* tumbling.
[66] *hung their rainbow hues* i.e. made rainbows in the spray.
[67] *riven* split, torn asunder.
[68] *an elemental god* a god of the elements.
[69] *the ethereal cliffs* the cliffs reach into the ether.
[70] The boat has crossed the Caspian Sea to the mountains of the Caucasus, now in Georgia and Russia, on the western shore. Prometheus was nailed to the Caucasus by Jupiter.

The boat pursued
The windings of the cavern. Daylight shone
At length upon that gloomy river's flow;
Now, where the fiercest war among the waves
Is calm, on the unfathomable stream
The boat moved slowly. Where the mountain, riven,
Exposed those black depths to the azure sky,
Ere yet the flood's enormous volume fell
Even to the base of Caucasus, with sound
That shook the everlasting rocks, the mass
Filled with one whirlpool all that ample chasm;
Stair above stair the eddying waters rose,[71]
Circling immeasurably fast, and laved
With alternating dash the gnarled roots
Of mighty trees that stretched their giant arms
In darkness over it. I' the midst was left,
Reflecting yet distorting every cloud,
A pool of treacherous and tremendous calm.
Seized by the sway of the ascending stream,
With dizzy swiftness, round and round and round,
Ridge after ridge the straining boat arose,
Till on the verge of the extremest curve,
Where, through an opening of the rocky bank,
The waters overflow, and a smooth spot
Of glassy quiet mid those battling tides
Is left, the boat paused shuddering. Shall it sink
Down the abyss? Shall the reverting stress
Of that resistless gulf embosom it?
Now shall it fall? A wandering stream of wind,
Breathed from the west, has caught the expanded sail,
And lo! with gentle motion, between banks
Of mossy slope, and on a placid stream,
Beneath a woven grove it sails – and hark!
The ghastly torrent mingles its far roar
With the breeze murmuring in the musical woods.
Where the embowering trees recede, and leave
A little space of green expanse, the cove
Is closed by meeting banks, whose yellow flowers[72]
Forever gaze on their own drooping eyes,
Reflected in the crystal calm. The wave
Of the boat's motion marred their pensive task
Which nought but vagrant bird, or wanton wind,
Or falling spear-grass, or their own decay
Had e'er disturbed before. The poet longed
To deck with their bright hues his withered hair,
But on his heart its solitude returned
And he forbore. Not the strong impulse hid

Notes

[71] *Stair above stair the eddying waters rose* As it spins, the whirlpool lifts the boat up at its outer edge higher and higher ('Stair above stair').

[72] *yellow flowers* Narcissus was a beautiful youth who mistook his own image, reflected in the water, for a nymph. He fell in love with it, committed suicide, and was changed into the flower today named after him.

In those flushed cheeks, bent eyes, and shadowy frame
Had yet performed its ministry;[73] it hung
Upon his life, as lightning in a cloud
Gleams, hovering ere it vanish, ere the floods
Of night close over it.
The noonday sun
Now shone upon the forest, one vast mass
Of mingling shade whose brown[74] magnificence
A narrow vale embosoms; there huge caves,
Scooped in the dark base of their airy[75] rocks,
Mocking its moans,[76] respond and roar forever.
The meeting boughs and implicated[77] leaves
Wove twilight o'er the poet's path as, led
By love, or dream, or god, or mightier death,
He sought in nature's dearest haunt some bank,
Her cradle,[78] and his sepulchre. More dark
And dark the shades accumulate. The oak,
Expanding its immense and knotty arms,
Embraces the light beech. The pyramids
Of the tall cedar overarching, frame
Most solemn domes within, and far below,
Like clouds suspended in an emerald sky,
The ash and the acacia floating hang
Tremulous and pale. Like restless serpents clothed
In rainbow and in fire, the parasites,[79]
Starred with ten thousand blossoms, flow around
The grey trunks, and, as gamesome[80] infants' eyes
With gentle meanings and most innocent wiles
Fold their beams round the hearts of those that love,
These twine their tendrils with the wedded boughs
Uniting their close union; the woven leaves
Make network of the dark blue light of day[81]
And the night's noontide clearness, mutable
As shapes in the weird clouds. Soft mossy lawns[82]
Beneath these canopies extend their swells,
Fragrant with perfumed herbs, and eyed with blooms
Minute yet beautiful. One darkest glen
Sends from its woods of musk-rose, twined with jasmine,
A soul-dissolving odour, to invite
To some more lovely mystery. Through the dell,
Silence and Twilight here, twin-sisters, keep
Their noonday watch, and sail among the shades
Like vaporous shapes half-seen; beyond, a well,

Notes

[73] *performed its ministry* an allusion to Coleridge, *Frost at Midnight* 1: 'The frost performs its secret ministry.'
[74] *brown* dark.
[75] *airy* lofty, high.
[76] *Mocking its moans* echoing the moans of the wind in the forest.
[77] *implicated* intertwining.
[78] *Her cradle* The poet travels back to the source of life.
[79] *parasites* climbing plants.
[80] *gamesome* playful.
[81] *Make network of the dark blue light of day* Daylight is seen as if through netted threads.
[82] *lawns* grassy clearings.

Dark, gleaming, and of most translucent wave,
Images[83] all the woven boughs above,
And each depending[84] leaf, and every speck
Of azure sky, darting between their chasms;
Nor aught else in the liquid mirror laves
Its portraiture,[85] but some inconstant star
Between one foliaged lattice[86] twinkling fair,
Or painted bird, sleeping beneath the moon,
Or gorgeous insect floating motionless,
Unconscious of the day ere yet his wings
Have spread their glories to the gaze of noon.[87]
  Hither the poet came. His eyes beheld
Their own wan light through the reflected lines
Of his thin hair, distinct in the dark depth
Of that still fountain; as the human heart,
Gazing in dreams over the gloomy grave,
Sees its own treacherous likeness there.[88] He heard
The motion of the leaves, the grass that sprung
Startled and glanced and trembled even to feel
An unaccustomed presence, and the sound
Of the sweet brook that from the secret springs
Of the dark fountain rose. A spirit[89] seemed
To stand beside him, clothed in no bright robes
Of shadowy silver or enshrining light
Borrowed from aught the visible world affords
Of grace, or majesty, or mystery –
But, undulating woods and silent well,
And leaping rivulet and evening gloom
Now deepening the dark shades, for speech assuming[90]
Held commune with him, as if he and it
Were all that was – only, when his regard
Was raised by intense pensiveness, two eyes,
Two starry eyes, hung in the gloom of thought
And seemed with their serene and azure smiles
To beckon him.
                        Obedient to the light
That shone within his soul, he went pursuing
The windings of the dell. The rivulet
Wanton and wild, through many a green ravine
Beneath the forest flowed. Sometimes it fell
Among the moss with hollow harmony
Dark and profound; now on the polished stones
It danced, like childhood laughing as it went;

Notes

83 *Images* reflects.
84 *depending* hanging.
85 *laves / Its portraiture* There is nothing else reflected in the well.
86 *one foliaged lattice* a mass of interlaced leaves.
87 *Or gorgeous insect . . . noon* The butterfly is unaware that outside the forest it is noon.
88 *Gazing in dreams . . . there* i.e. imagines its continued but uncertain (treacherous) life after death.
89 *A spirit* probably nature.
90 *for speech assuming* Nature used woods, well, rivulet and gloom as a means of communication.

Then through the plain in tranquil wanderings crept,
Reflecting every herb and drooping bud
That overhung its quietness. 'Oh stream!
Whose source is inaccessibly profound,
Whither do thy mysterious waters tend?
Thou imagest my life: thy darksome stillness,
Thy dazzling waves, thy loud and hollow gulfs,
Thy searchless fountain[91] and invisible course
Have each their type[92] in me. And the wide sky
And measureless ocean may declare as soon
What oozy[93] cavern or what wandering cloud
Contains thy waters, as the universe
Tell where these living thoughts reside, when stretched
Upon thy flowers my bloodless limbs shall waste
I' the passing wind!'
Beside the grassy shore
Of the small stream he went; he did impress
On the green moss his tremulous step that caught
Strong shuddering from his burning limbs. As one
Roused by some joyous madness from the couch
Of fever, he did move, yet not like him
Forgetful of the grave,[94] where, when the flame
Of his frail exultation shall be spent,
He must descend. With rapid steps he went
Beneath the shade of trees, beside the flow
Of the wild babbling rivulet – and now
The forest's solemn canopies were changed
For the uniform and lightsome[95] evening sky.
Grey rocks did peep from the spare moss, and stemmed
The struggling brook; tall spires of windlestrae[96]
Threw their thin shadows down the rugged slope,
And nought but gnarled roots of ancient pines
Branchless and blasted, clenched with grasping roots
The unwilling soil. A gradual change was here,
Yet ghastly. For, as fast years flow away,
The smooth brow gathers, and the hair grows thin
And white, and where irradiate[97] dewy eyes
Had shone, gleam stony orbs: so from his steps
Bright flowers departed, and the beautiful shade
Of the green groves, with all their odorous winds
And musical motions. Calm, he still pursued
The stream, that with a larger volume[98] now
Rolled through the labyrinthine dell; and there
Fretted[99] a path through its descending curves

Notes

91 *searchless fountain* undiscoverable source.
92 *type* i.e. corresponding idealized version.
93 *oozy* damp.
94 *Forgetful of the grave* It is the fever-stricken man who, in his delirium, forgets the grave; the poet is all too mindful of death.
95 *lightsome* illuminated.
96 *windlestrae* dry stalks left by dead or dying plants.
97 *irradiate* shining.
98 *volume* of water.
99 *Fretted* wore, ground.

With its wintry speed. On every side now rose
Rocks which, in unimaginable forms,
Lifted their black and barren pinnacles
In the light of evening, and, its precipice
Obscuring, the ravine disclosed above,
Mid toppling stones, black gulfs and yawning caves,
Whose windings gave ten thousand various tongues
To the loud stream. Lo! where the pass expands
Its stony jaws, the abrupt mountain breaks
And seems, with its accumulated crags,
To overhang the world – for wide expand,
Beneath the wan stars and descending moon,
Islanded seas, blue mountains, mighty streams,
Dim tracts and vast, robed in the lustrous gloom
Of leaden-coloured[100] even, and fiery hills
Mingling their flames with twilight, on the verge
Of the remote horizon. The near scene,
In naked and severe simplicity,
Made contrast with the universe. A pine,
Rock-rooted, stretched athwart the vacancy
Its swinging boughs, to each inconstant blast
Yielding one only response, at each pause
In most familiar cadence, with the howl,
The thunder and the hiss of homeless streams
Mingling its solemn song, whilst the broad river,
Foaming and hurrying o'er its rugged path,
Fell into that immeasurable void,
Scattering its waters to the passing winds.
  Yet the grey precipice and solemn pine
And torrent were not all; one silent nook
Was there. Even on the edge of that vast mountain,
Upheld by knotty roots and fallen rocks,
It overlooked in its serenity
The dark earth and the bending vault of stars.
It was a tranquil spot that seemed to smile
Even in the lap of horror. Ivy clasped
The fissured stones with its entwining arms,
And did embower with leaves forever green,
And berries dark, the smooth and even space
Of its inviolated floor; and here
The children of the autumnal whirlwind[101] bore,
In wanton sport, those bright leaves whose decay,
Red, yellow, or ethereally pale,
Rivals the pride of summer. 'Tis the haunt
Of every gentle wind whose breath can teach
The wilds to love tranquillity. One step,[102]
One human step alone, has ever broken

Notes

[100] *leaden-coloured* dark grey.

[101] *The children of the autumnal whirlwind* i.e. gusts of wind.

[102] *One step* i.e. that of the poet.

The stillness of its solitude; one voice
Alone[103] inspired its echoes – even that voice
Which hither came floating among the winds,
And led the loveliest among human forms[104]
To make their[105] wild haunts the depository
Of all the grace and beauty that endued[106]
Its motions, render up its majesty,
Scatter its music on the unfeeling storm,
And to the damp leaves and blue cavern mould,
Nurses of rainbow flowers and branching moss,
Commit[107] the colours of that varying cheek,
That snowy breast, those dark and drooping eyes.
The dim and horned moon hung low, and poured
A sea of lustre on the horizon's verge
That overflowed its mountains. Yellow mist
Filled the unbounded atmosphere, and drank
Wan moonlight even to fullness: not a star
Shone, not a sound was heard; the very winds,
Danger's grim playmates, on that precipice
Slept, clasped in his embrace. Oh storm of Death,
Whose sightless speed divides this sullen night,
And thou, colossal skeleton,[108] that, still
Guiding its irresistible career
In thy devastating omnipotence,
Art king of this frail world – from the red field
Of slaughter, from the reeking hospital,
The patriot's sacred couch, the snowy bed
Of innocence, the scaffold and the throne,
A mighty voice invokes thee: Ruin calls
His brother Death. A rare and regal prey[109]
He hath prepared, prowling around the world –
Glutted with which thou mayst repose, and men
Go to their graves like flowers or creeping worms,
Nor ever more offer at thy dark shrine
The unheeded tribute of a broken heart.
When on the threshold of the green recess
The wanderer's footsteps fell, he knew that death
Was on him. Yet a little, ere it fled,
Did he resign his high and holy soul
To images of the majestic past
That paused within his passive[110] being now,
Like winds that bear sweet music when they breathe
Through some dim latticed chamber. He did place
His pale lean hand upon the rugged trunk

Notes

103 *one voice / Alone* i.e. that of the vision.
104 *the loveliest among human forms* the poet.
105 *their* i.e. the winds'.
106 *endued* invested.
107 *Commit* entrust.
108 *colossal skeleton* Death.
109 *A rare and regal prey* i.e. the world's rulers, who will glut Death, so that their victims may die according to their worth. It is worth remembering that this poem was written just after Napoleon's defeat at Waterloo.
110 *passive* an important detail; compare 'Mont Blanc' 37–8.

Of the old pine; upon an ivied stone
Reclined his languid head; his limbs did rest,
Diffused and motionless, on the smooth brink
Of that obscurest chasm – and thus he lay,
Surrendering to their final impulses
The hovering powers of life. Hope and despair,
The torturers, slept;[111] no mortal pain or fear
Marred his repose, the influxes of sense[112]
And his own being unalloyed by pain,
Yet feebler and more feeble, calmly fed
The stream of thought, till he lay breathing there
At peace, and faintly smiling. His last sight
Was the great moon, which o'er the western line
Of the wide world her mighty horn suspended,
With those dun beams inwoven darkness seemed
To mingle. Now upon the jagged hills
It rests, and still as[113] the divided frame
Of the vast meteor[114] sunk, the poet's blood,
That ever beat in mystic sympathy
With nature's ebb and flow, grew feebler still;
And when two lessening points of light[115] alone
Gleamed through the darkness, the alternate gasp
Of his faint respiration scarce did stir
The stagnate[116] night – till the minutest ray
Was quenched, the pulse yet lingered in his heart.
It paused, it fluttered. But when heaven remained
Utterly black, the murky shades involved
An image, silent, cold, and motionless,
As their own voiceless earth and vacant air.
Even as a vapour[117] fed with golden beams
That ministered on sunlight ere the west
Eclipses it, was now that wondrous frame –
No sense, no motion,[118] no divinity –
A fragile lute[119] on whose harmonious strings
The breath of heaven did wander, a bright stream
Once fed with many-voiced[120] waves, a dream
Of youth, which night and time have quenched for ever –
Still, dark, and dry, and unremembered now.
Oh for Medea's wondrous alchemy,
Which wheresoe'er it fell made the earth gleam
With bright flowers, and the wintry boughs exhale

Notes

[111] *Hope and despair . . . slept* cf. Percy's journal entry for 28 July 1814: 'I hope – but my hopes are not unmixed with fear for what will befall this inestimable spirit when we appear to die' (*Shelley Journals* i 7).

[112] *the influxes of sense* his perceptions.

[113] *still as* i.e. as still as.

[114] *meteor* at this period, a reference to any atmospheric occurrence.

[115] *two lessening points of light* tips of the setting moon's crescent.

[116] *stagnate* stagnant.

[117] *vapour* cloud.

[118] *No sense, no motion* echoes Wordsworth, 'A Slumber did my Spirit Seal' 5: 'No motion has she now, no force.'

[119] *A fragile lute* Once again, Shelley has in mind an Aeolian harp.

[120] *many-voiced* Compare 'Mont Blanc' 13.

From vernal blooms fresh fragrance![121] Oh that God,
Profuse[122] of poisons, would concede the chalice
Which but one living man[123] has drained – who now,
Vessel of deathless wrath, a slave that feels
No proud exemption in the blighting curse
He bears, over the world wanders for ever,
Lone as incarnate death! Oh that the dream
Of dark magician[124] in his visioned cave,
Raking the cinders of a crucible
For life and power, even when his feeble hand
Shakes in its last decay, were the true law
Of this so lovely world! But thou art fled
Like some frail exhalation which the dawn
Robes in its golden beams – ah, thou hast fled! –
The brave, the gentle, and the beautiful,
The child of grace and genius. Heartless things
Are done and said i' the world, and many worms
And beasts and men live on, and mighty earth
From sea and mountain, city and wilderness,
In vesper low or joyous orison,[125]
Lifts still its solemn voice – but thou art fled;
Thou canst no longer know or love the shapes
Of this phantasmal scene,[126] who have to thee
Been purest ministers – who are, alas,
Now thou art not! Upon those pallid lips,
So sweet even in their silence, on those eyes
That image sleep in death, upon that form
Yet safe from the worm's outrage, let no tear
Be shed, not even in thought; nor – when those hues
Are gone, and those divinest lineaments
Worn by the senseless[127] wind – shall live alone
In the frail pauses of this simple strain.
Let not high verse, mourning the memory
Of that which is no more, or painting's woe
Or sculpture, speak in feeble imagery
Their own cold powers. Art and eloquence
And all the shows o' the world are frail and vain
To weep a loss that turns their lights to shade.
It is a woe too 'deep for tears',[128] when all
Is reft at once, when some surpassing spirit,
Whose light adorned the world around it, leaves
Those who remain behind not sobs or groans,

Notes

[121] *Oh for . . . fragrance* Medea, an enchantress in Greek mythology, brewed a potion to restore youth to Aeson, the father of her lover Jason; when spilt on the ground it had the effects described here.

[122] *Profuse* productive.

[123] *one living man* Ahasuerus, the wandering Jew, doomed to eternal life.

[124] *dark magician* the alchemist who, besides seeking to turn base metals into gold, seeks the elixir of eternal life.

[125] *vesper . . . orison* evensong . . . prayer – uttered, figuratively, by the earth.

[126] *this phantasmal scene* i.e. the transcendent, visionary world.

[127] *senseless* unfeeling.

[128] *It is a woe too 'deep for tears'* Wordsworth, 'Ode' 206: 'Thoughts that do often lie too deep for tears'.

The passionate tumult of a clinging hope,
But pale despair and cold tranquillity,
Nature's vast frame, the web of human things,
Birth and the grave, that are not as they were.[129]

Atheist?

Hymn to Intellectual Beauty (composed between 22 June and 29 August 1816; edited from printed text corrected by Shelley)[1]

From The Examiner (19 January 1817)

Asking where the spirit of beauty has gone

1

The awful[2] shadow of some unseen Power
Floats though unseen amongst us, visiting
This various world with as inconstant wing[3]
As summer winds that creep from flower to flower;
Like moonbeams that behind some piny mountain shower,[4]
It visits with inconstant glance
Each human heart and countenance;
Like hues and harmonies of evening,
Like clouds in starlight widely spread,
Like memory of music fled,
Like aught that for its grace may be
Dear, and yet dearer for its mystery.

2

Spirit of Beauty, that doth consecrate
With thine own hues all thou dost shine upon
Of human thought or form – where art thou gone?
Why dost thou pass away and leave our state,
This dim vast vale of tears, vacant and desolate?
Ask why the sunlight not forever
Weaves rainbows o'er yon mountain river,
Why aught should fail and fade that once is shown,
Why fear and dream, and death and birth
Cast on the daylight of this earth
Such gloom, why man has such a scope
For love and hate, despondency and hope?

Notes

[129] *that are not as they were* cf. Wordsworth, 'Ode' 6: 'It is not now as it has been of yore.'

Hymn to Intellectual Beauty

[1] This poem should be read in the light of Wordsworth's 'Ode' (p. 538), by which it was inspired, which is also about the 'inconstancy' of the kind of intense vision that Shelley celebrates.

[2] *awful* awesome.

[3] *with as inconstant wing* Shelley's point is that the 'awful Power' is not always perceptible.

[4] *some piny mountain shower* rainfall among the pine trees on a mountain-slope. This poem was composed during Shelley's residence on the banks of Lake Geneva.

3

No voice from some sublimer world hath ever
To sage or poet these responses given;
Therefore the name of God, and ghosts, and heaven[5]
Remain the records of their vain endeavour,
Frail spells, whose uttered charm might not avail to sever,
From all we hear and all we see,
Doubt, chance, and mutability.
Thy light alone, like mist o'er mountains driven,
Or music by the night wind sent
Through strings of some still instrument,[6]
Or moonlight on a midnight stream,
Gives grace and truth to life's unquiet dream.

4

Love, hope, and self-esteem, like clouds depart
And come, for some uncertain moments lent.
Man were immortal and omnipotent,
Didst thou,[7] unknown and awful as thou art,
Keep with thy glorious train firm state within his heart.
Thou messenger of sympathies
That wax and wane in lovers' eyes;
Thou that to human thought art nourishment,
Like darkness to a dying flame![8]
Depart not as thy shadow came,
Depart not lest the grave should be,
Like life and fear, a dark reality.

5

While yet a boy I sought for ghosts, and sped
Through many a listening chamber, cave and ruin
And starlight wood, with fearful steps pursuing
Hopes of high talk with the departed dead.[9]
I called on poisonous names[10] with which our youth is fed –
I was not heard, I saw them not
When musing deeply on the lot
Of life, at that sweet time when winds are wooing
All vital things that wake to bring

Notes

[5] *Therefore the name of God, and ghosts, and heaven* The original *Examiner* printed text reads: 'Therefore the names of Demon, Ghost, and Heaven'.

[6] *some still instrument* an Aeolian harp.

[7] *Man were . . . Didst thou* man would be . . . if thou didst . . .

[8] *nourishment, / Like darkness to a dying flame* Strong light was believed to stifle candlelight; conversely, darkness would feed it.

[9] As a boy, Shelley did go to cemeteries and woods at night, in the hope of meeting ghosts.

[10] *poisonous names* presumably those of God and Christ. In earlier years Shelley did try prayer.

News of buds and blossoming.
Sudden thy shadow fell on me –
I shrieked, and clasped my hands in ecstasy!

6

I vowed that I would dedicate my powers
To thee and thine; have I not kept the vow?
With beating heart and streaming eyes, even now
I call the phantoms of a thousand hours
Each from his voiceless grave: they have in visioned bowers
Of studious zeal or love's delight
Outwatched with me the envious night;
They know that never joy illumed my brow
Unlinked with hope that thou wouldst free
This world from its dark slavery,
That thou, oh awful loveliness,
Wouldst give whate'er these words cannot express.

7

The day becomes more solemn and serene
When noon is past; there is a harmony
In autumn, and a lustre in its sky,
Which through the summer is not heard or seen,
As if it could not be, as if it had not been!
Thus let thy power, which like the truth
Of nature on my passive youth
Descended,[11] to my onward life supply
Its calm – to one who worships thee,
And every form containing thee,
Whom, spirit fair, thy spells did bind
To fear[12] himself, and love all humankind.

Journal-Letter from Percy Bysshe Shelley to Thomas Love Peacock, 22 July to 2 August 1816 (extract)[1]

22 July 1816. From Servox, three leagues remain to Chamounix. Mont Blanc was before us. The Alps with their innumerable glaciers on high, all around, closing in the complicated windings of the single vale; forests inexpressibly beautiful, but majestic in their beauty; interwoven beech and pine and oak overshadowed our road or receded whilst lawns of such verdure as I had never seen before occupied these openings, and, extending gradually, becoming darker into their recesses.

Notes

[11] *the truth / Of nature . . . Descended* The passivity of the mind is equivalent to the psychological relaxation mentioned by De Quincey in his discussion of Wordsworth's 'There was a boy' (pp. 823–5). Shelley discusses it in his 'Essay on Christianity', written between 1813 and 1819: 'All that it [i.e. human life] contains of pure or of divine visits the passive mind in some serenest mood' (*Shelley's Prose* 205).

[12] *fear* revere.

Journal-Letter from Percy Bysshe Shelley

[1] This important letter describes Shelley's initial response to the landscape which later provided an important setting for *Mont Blanc* and *Frankenstein*. He had set off, with Mary Godwin and Claire Clairmont, on a tour of the vale of Chamounix, on 21 July; they would return to Maison Chappuis a week later.

Mont Blanc was before us but was covered with cloud, and its base furrowed with dreadful gaps was seen alone. Pinnacles of snow, intolerably bright, part of the chain connected with Mont Blanc, shone though the clouds at intervals on high. I never knew I never imagined what mountains were before. The immensity of these aerial[2] summits excited, when they suddenly burst upon the sight, a sentiment of ecstatic wonder not unallied to madness. And remember this was all one scene. It all pressed home to our regard and to our imagination. Though it embraced a great number of miles, the snowy pyramids which shot into the bright blue sky seemed to overhang our path; the ravine, clothed with gigantic pines and black with its depth below (so deep that the very roaring of the untameable Arve which rolled through it could not be heard above), was close to our very footsteps. All was as much our own as if we had been the creators of such impressions in the minds of others, as now occupied our own. Nature was the poet whose harmony held our spirits more breathless than that of the divinest.

25 July 1816. We have returned from visiting this glacier – a scene, in truth, of dizzying wonder. The path that winds to it along the side of a mountain, now clothed with pines, now intersected with snowy hollows, is wide and steep. The cabin of Montanvert is three leagues from Chamounix, half of which distance is performed on mules – not so sure-footed but that, on the first day, the one which I rode fell in what the guides call a 'mauvais pas', so that I narrowly escaped being precipitated down the mountain. The guide continually held that which Mary rode.

We passed over a hollow covered with snow down which vast stones, detached from the rock above, are accustomed to roll. One had fallen the preceding day, a little time after we had returned. The guides desired us to pass quickly, for it is said that sometimes the least sound will accelerate their fall. We arrived at Montanvert, however, safe.

On all sides precipitous mountains, the abodes of unrelenting frost, surround this vale. Their sides are banked up with ice and snow, broken and heaped-up, and exhibiting terrific chasms. The summits are sharp and naked pinnacles whose overhanging steepness will not even permit snow to rest there. They pierce the clouds like things not belonging to this earth. The vale itself is filled with a mass of undulating ice, and has an ascent sufficiently gradual even to the remotest abysses of these horrible deserts. It is only half a league (about two miles) in breadth, and seems much less. It exhibits an appearance as if frost had suddenly bound up the waves and whirlpools of a mighty torrent.

We walked to some distance upon its surface. The waves are elevated about 12 or 15 feet from the surface of the mass, which is intersected with long gaps of unfathomable depth, the ice of whose sides is more beautifully azure than the sky. In these regions, everything changes and is in motion. This vast mass of ice has one general progress which ceases neither day nor night. It breaks and rises forever; its undulations sink whilst others rise. From the precipices which surround it, the echo of rocks which fall from their aerial summits, or of the ice and snow, scarcely ceases for one moment. One would think that Mont Blanc was a living being, and that the frozen blood forever circulated slowly through his stony veins.

Notes

[2] *aerial* lofty.

Mont Blanc. Lines written in the Vale of Chamouni (composed between 22 July and 29 August 1816)[1]

From History of a Six Weeks' Tour through a Part of France, Switzerland, Germany and Holland by Percy Bysshe and Mary Shelley (1817)

I

The everlasting universe of things
Flows through the mind, and rolls its rapid waves,
Now dark, now glittering, now reflecting gloom,
Now lending splendour, where from secret springs
The source of human thought its tribute[2] brings
Of waters, with a sound but half its own,[3]
Such as a feeble brook will oft assume
In the wild woods, among the mountains lone,
Where waterfalls around it leap forever,
Where woods and winds contend, and a vast river
Over its rocks ceaselessly bursts and raves.

II

Thus thou, ravine of Arve – dark, deep ravine –
Thou many-coloured, many-voicéd vale,
Over whose pines, and crags, and caverns sail
Fast cloud-shadows and sunbeams: awful[4] scene,
Where Power in likeness of the Arve comes down
From the ice gulfs that gird his secret throne,
Bursting through these dark mountains like the flame
Of lightning through the tempest; thou dost lie,
Thy giant brood of pines around thee clinging,
Children of elder time, in whose devotion
The chainless winds still come and ever came
To drink their odours, and their mighty swinging
To hear – an old and solemn harmony;
Thine earthly rainbows stretched across the sweep

Notes

MONT BLANC. LINES WRITTEN IN THE VALE OF CHAMOUNI

[1] This is Shelley's exploration of the nature of imaginative thought, and its relation to the natural world; as such, it should be read in the light of Wordsworth's *Tintern Abbey*, to which it is a response (see pp. 407–11). It has been seen as a defiant reaction to the religious certainties of Coleridge's *Chamouny; the Hour Before Sunrise. A Hymn* (pp. 677–9), which Shelley may have read in *The Friend* (1809). Mary Shelley wrote that the poem 'was composed under the immediate impression of the deep and powerful feelings excited by the objects which it attempts to describe; and, as an undisciplined overflowing of the soul, rests its claim to approbation on an attempt to imitate the untamable wilderness and inaccessible solemnity from which those feelings sprang.'

[2] *tribute* tributary. In Shelley's metaphor the human mind is like a mountain spring feeding into a large river (the 'everlasting universe of things' – effectively, the perceived world).

[3] *with a sound but half its own* cf. *Tintern Abbey*, in which Wordsworth refers to 'what they [the senses] half-create / And what perceive' (ll. 107–8).

[4] *awful* awe-inspiring.

Of the ethereal waterfall, whose veil
Robes some unsculptured image;[5] the strange sleep
Which, when the voices of the desert fail,
Wraps all in its own deep eternity;
Thy caverns echoing to the Arve's commotion –
A loud, lone sound no other sound can tame;
Thou art pervaded with that ceaseless motion,
Thou art the path of that unresting sound,
Dizzy ravine! – and when I gaze on thee
I seem as in a trance sublime and strange
To muse on my own separate fantasy,
My own, my human mind, which passively[6]
Now renders and receives fast influencings,
Holding an unremitting interchange[7]
With the clear universe of things around;
One legion of wild thoughts, whose wandering wings
Now float above thy darkness, and now rest
Where that[8] or thou[9] art no unbidden guest,
In the still cave of the witch Poesy,
Seeking among the shadows that pass by,
Ghosts of all things that are, some shade of thee,
Some phantom, some faint image;[10] till the breast
From which they[11] fled recalls them, thou art there![12]

III

Some say that gleams of a remoter world
Visit the soul in sleep, that death is slumber,
And that its shapes the busy thoughts outnumber
Of those who wake and live.[13] I look on high;
Has some unknown omnipotence unfurled[14]
The veil of life and death? Or do I lie
In dream, and does the mightier world of sleep
Spread far around and inaccessibly
Its circles?[15] For the very spirit fails,

Notes

[5] *some unsculptured image* artistic potential.

[6] *passively* The mind is receptive to outside stimuli, not willing itself to do, or be, anything.

[7] *an unremitting interchange* the 'interchange' takes place because the mind does not merely perceive; it works on its perceptions, transforming them imaginatively.

[8] *that* the darkness of line 42.

[9] *thou* the ravine.

[10] Shelley claims that his art bears the same relation to truth as do the shadows, in Plato's allegory of the cave, to a metaphysical reality; see Plato, *Republic* vii, summarized by Rogers, *Shelley at Work* (Oxford, 1967), pp. 148–7.

[11] *they* the 'legion of wild thoughts' (l. 41).

[12] Until Shelley recalls the 'wild thoughts' (line 41) by coming out of his reverie, the ravine he has been addressing, and the mystery that surrounds it, are to be found within Poesy's cave (i.e. subject to the imagination, and perhaps half-created by it).

[13] *Some say . . . live* Some say (i) that the soul is visited in sleep by 'gleams' of otherworldly truth; (ii) that death is an extreme form of this visionary sleep; and (iii) that it is more active and imaginative than anything experienced by the living mind. Shelley has in mind Wordsworth's 'Ode': 'The winds come to me from the fields of sleep' (l. 28).

[14] *unfurled* drawn aside.

[15] *Or do I lie . . . circles* Shelley suggests that the ecstatic vision he enjoys is a kind of sleep.

Driven like a homeless cloud from steep to steep
That vanishes among the viewless gales!
Far, far above, piercing the infinite sky,
Mont Blanc appears, still, snowy, and serene.
Its subject mountains their unearthly forms
Pile around it, ice and rock; broad vales between
Of frozen floods, unfathomable deeps
Blue as the overhanging heaven, that spread
And wind among the accumulated steeps;
A desert peopled by the storms alone,
Save when the eagle brings some hunter's bone,
And the wolf tracks her there. How hideously
Its shapes are heaped around! – rude, bare, and high,
Ghastly, and scarred, and riven. Is this the scene
Where the old earthquake-demon[16] taught her young
Ruin? Were these their toys?[17] Or did a sea
Of fire envelop once this silent snow?
None can reply – all seems eternal now.
The wilderness has a mysterious tongue
Which teaches awful doubt,[18] or faith so mild,
So solemn, so serene, that man may be
But for such faith with nature reconciled.[19]
Thou hast a voice, great mountain, to repeal
Large codes[20] of fraud and woe – not understood
By all, but which the wise, and great, and good
Interpret, or make felt, or deeply feel.[21]

IV

The fields, the lakes, the forests, and the streams,
Ocean, and all the living things that dwell
Within the daedal[22] earth; lightning, and rain,
Earthquake, and fiery flood, and hurricane,
The torpor of the year[23] when feeble dreams
Visit the hidden buds, or dreamless sleep
Holds every future leaf and flower; the bound
With which from that detested trance they leap;

Notes

[16] *earthquake-demon* spirit of earthquake, which gives rise to destructive tremors (its 'young').

[17] Shelley replaces Christian theology with pagan caprice. With the children of the old earthquake-demon, compare Byron, *Childe Harold's Pilgrimage* iii 877.

[18] *awful doubt* awe-inspired scepticism – effectively Shelley's own position.

[19] *But for . . . reconciled* Only by ('But for') a Wordsworthian faith in nature can man be reconciled to the mysterious indifference and violence of nature; otherwise, one must adopt Shelley's respectful open-mindedness ('awful doubt').

[20] *codes* laws.

[21] *Thou hast a voice . . . feel* Enlightened witnesses to nature's Power will defy the codes of fraud and woe made by the church and the state. The imaginative perception of nature therefore has the ability to liberate the individual from political oppression. Shelley's argument that the voice of the mountain is deeply felt is highly Wordsworthian; cf. *Pedlar* 217–18 (which Shelley knew from *The Excursion*): 'in all things / He saw one life, and felt that it was joy.'

[22] *daedal* variously adorned.

[23] *The torpor of the year* i.e. winter.

The works and ways of man, their death and birth,
And that of him and all that his may be;
All things that move and breathe[24] with toil and sound
Are born and die; revolve, subside and swell.
Power dwells apart in its tranquillity
Remote, serene, and inaccessible:[25]
And *this*, the naked countenance of earth
On which I gaze, even these primeval mountains
Teach the adverting[26] mind. The glaciers creep
Like snakes that watch their prey, from their far fountains
Slow rolling on; there, many a precipice,
Frost and the sun in scorn of mortal power
Have piled: dome, pyramid, and pinnacle,
A city of death, distinct[27] with many a tower
And wall impregnable of beaming ice.
Yet not a city, but a flood of ruin
Is there, that from the boundaries of the sky
Rolls its perpetual stream; vast pines are strewing
Its destined path, or in the mangled soil
Branchless and shattered stand; the rocks, drawn down
From yon remotest waste, have overthrown
The limits of the dead and living world,
Never to be reclaimed. The dwelling-place
Of insects, beasts, and birds, becomes its spoil;
Their food and their retreat for ever gone,
So much of life and joy is lost. The race
Of man flies far in dread; his work and dwelling
Vanish like smoke before the tempest's stream,
And their place is not known. Below, vast caves
Shine in the rushing torrents' restless gleam,
Which from those secret chasms in tumult welling[28]
Meet in the vale; and one majestic river,
The breath and blood of distant lands, forever
Rolls its loud waters to the ocean waves,[29]
Breathes its swift vapours to the circling air.

Notes

[24] *All things that move and breathe* an echo of Wordsworth's pantheist statement of faith (much admired by Shelley) in *Tintern Abbey* 101–3:

> A motion and a spirit that impels
> All thinking things, all objects of all thought,
> And rolls through all things.

[25] *inaccessible* At 4,810 metres, Mont Blanc is the highest mountain in Europe; it had been climbed only three times by 1816.

[26] *adverting* heedful, observant, thoughtful.

[27] *distinct* adorned.

[28] *Which from those secret chasms in tumult welling* an echo of Coleridge's recently published *Kubla Khan* 17: 'And from this chasm, with ceaseless turmoil seething'. Shelley had seen Byron's copy of the printed text, brought from England in April 1816.

[29] *one majestic river* The Rhône, fed by Lake Geneva, into which flows the Arve.

V

Mont Blanc yet gleams on high: the Power is there,
The still and solemn Power of many sights
And many sounds, and much of life and death.
In the calm darkness of the moonless nights,
In the lone glare of day, the snows descend
Upon that mountain; none beholds them there,
Nor when the flakes burn in the sinking sun,
Or the starbeams dart through them; winds contend
Silently there, and heap the snow with breath
Rapid and strong, but silently! Its home
The voiceless lightning in these solitudes
Keeps innocently, and like vapour broods
Over the snow. The secret strength of things
Which governs thought, and to the infinite dome
Of heaven is as a law, inhabits thee!
And what were thou, and earth, and stars, and sea,
If to the human mind's imaginings
Silence and solitude were vacancy?[30]

Ozymandias (composed 26–28 December 1817)[1]

From The Examiner (11 January 1818)

I met a traveller from an antique land
Who said, 'Two vast and trunkless legs of stone
Stand in the desert. Near them, on the sand
Half-sunk, a shattered visage lies, whose frown
And wrinkled lip, and sneer of cold command,
Tell that its sculptor well those passions read
Which yet survive, stamped on these lifeless things,
The hand that mocked them, and the heart that fed;
And on the pedestal these words appear:
"My name is Ozymandias, King of Kings,

Notes

[30] Shelley's concluding expression of doubt stands in stark contrast to the certainty of Coleridge's *Chamouny; the Hour Before Sunrise. A Hymn* (see p. 677).

Ozymandias

[1] Horace Smith (1779–1849), a banker and writer of light verse, met Shelley in London in December 1816. Shelley and Smith visited the British Museum together, and their admiration of the newly acquired statue of Rameses II (13th century BC, also known as Ozymandias) in 1817 prompted Smith to propose a sonnet competition on the subject. Smith's sonnet was published on 1 February 1818 in *The Examiner*, and reads as follows:

In Egypt's sandy silence, all alone,
Stands a gigantic leg, which far off throws
The only shadow that the desert knows.
'I am great Ozymandias', saith the stone,
'The King of Kings; this mighty city shows
The wonders of my hand.' The city's gone;
Nought but the leg remaining to disclose
The site of this forgotten Babylon.
We wonder, and some hunter may express
Wonder like ours, when through the wilderness
Where London stood, holding the wolf in chase,
He meets some fragment huge, and stops to guess
What powerful but unrecorded race
Once dwelt in that annihilated place.

Look on my works, ye mighty, and despair!"
Nothing beside remains. Round the decay
Of that colossal wreck, boundless and bare,
The lone and level sands stretch far away.'

On Love (composed probably 20–25 July 1818; edited from MS)[1]

What is love? Ask him who lives, what is life; ask him who adores, what is God.

I know not the internal constitution of other men, or even of thine whom I now address. I see that in some external attributes they resemble me, but, when misled by that appearance I have thought to appeal to something in common and unburden my inmost soul to them, I have found my language misunderstood like one in a distant and savage land. The more opportunities they have afforded me for experience, the wider has appeared the interval between us, and to a greater distance have the points of sympathy been withdrawn. With a spirit ill-fitted to sustain such proof,[2] trembling and feeble through its tenderness, I have everywhere sought, and have found only repulse and disappointment.

Thou demandest what is love. It is that powerful attraction towards all that we conceive, or fear, or hope beyond ourselves, when we find within our own thoughts the chasm of an insufficient void, and seek to awaken in all things that are, a community with what we experience within ourselves. If we reason, we would be understood; if we imagine, we would that the airy children of our brain were born anew within another's; if we feel, we would that another's nerves should vibrate to our own, that the beams of their eyes should kindle at once and mix and melt into our own, that lips of motionless ice should not reply to lips quivering and burning with the heart's best blood. This is love. This is the bond and the sanction which connects not only man with man, but with everything which exists. We are born into the world and there is something within us which, from the instant that we live and move, thirsts after its likeness; it is probably in correspondence with this law that the infant drains milk from the bosom of its mother. This propensity develops itself with the development of our nature.

We see dimly[3] within our intellectual nature a miniature, as it were, of our entire self, yet deprived of all that we condemn or despise: the ideal prototype of everything excellent or lovely that we are capable of conceiving as belonging to the nature of man – not only the portrait of our external being, but an assemblage of the minutest particulars of which our nature is composed; a mirror whose surface reflects only the forms of purity and brightness; a soul within our soul that describes a circle around its proper Paradise which pain and sorrow and evil dare not overleap.[4] To this we eagerly refer all sensations, thirsting that they should resemble or correspond with it.

The discovery of its antitype – the meeting with an understanding capable of clearly estimating the deductions of our own, an imagination which should enter into and seize upon the subtle and delicate peculiarities which we have delighted to cherish and unfold in secret, with a frame whose nerves, like the chords of two exquisite lyres strung to the accompaniment of one delightful voice, vibrate with the vibrations of

Notes

On Love

[1] This essay, Reiman suggests, is 'Shelley's response to Plato's *Symposium* and may possibly be the false start of an essay introductory to his translation' (*SC* vi 639). Shelley translated the *Symposium* 7–20 July 1818.

[2] *proof* trial.

[3] 'These words inefficient and metaphorical. Most words so. No help' (Shelley's note).

[4] *Paradise . . . overleap* Shelley recalls *Paradise Lost* iv 181–2, where Satan 'overleaped all bound / Of hill or highest wall' in order to enter Eden.

our own, and of a combination of all these in such proportion as the type within demands: this is the invisible and unattainable point to which love tends, and to attain which it urges forth the powers of man to arrest the faintest shadow of that without the possession of which there is no rest or respite to the heart over which it rules.

Hence in solitude, or in that deserted state when we are surrounded by human beings and yet they sympathize not with us, we love the flowers, the grass, and the waters and the sky. In the motion of the very leaves of spring in the blue air there is then found a secret correspondence with our heart. There is eloquence in the tongueless wind and a melody in the flowing of brooks and the rustling of the reeds beside them, which by their inconceivable relation to something within the soul, awaken the spirits to a dance of breathless rapture, and bring tears of mysterious tenderness to the eyes like the enthusiasm of patriotic success or the voice of one beloved singing to you alone. Sterne says that if he were in a desert he would love some cypress[5] . . . So soon as this want or power is dead, man becomes the living sepulchre of himself, and what yet survives is the mere husk of what once he was.

Lines written among the Euganean Hills, October 1818[1]

From Rosalind and Helen (1819)

Many a green isle[2] needs must be
In the deep wide sea of misery,
Or the mariner, worn and wan,
Never thus could voyage on
Day and night, and night and day,
Drifting on his dreary way,
With the solid darkness black
Closing round his vessel's track;
Whilst above, the sunless sky,
Big with clouds, hangs heavily,
And behind the tempest fleet
Hurries on with lightning feet,
Riving[3] sail and cord and plank

Notes

[5] 'I declare, said I, clapping my hands cheerily together, that was I in a desert, I would find out wherewith in it to call forth my affections. If I could not do better, I would fasten them upon some sweet myrtle, or seek some melancholy cypress to connect myself to' (Sterne, *A Sentimental Journey* ed. Gardner D. Stout, Jr (Berkeley, Calif., 1967), pp. 115–16).

LINES WRITTEN AMONG THE EUGANEAN HILLS

[1] This meditative poem was written at a difficult moment in Shelley's life. His baby daughter Clara had died at Venice in late September (barely a year old), and on their return to Byron's villa at Este, I Capuccini, a deep gloom had pervaded the household. Clara's death depressed Mary, and Percy found himself in bad health. He sent this poem with a number of others to his publisher, prefacing them with this: 'I do not know which of the few scattered poems I left in England will be selected by my bookseller, to add to this collection. One, which I sent from Italy, was written after a day's excursion among those lovely mountains which surround what was once the retreat, and where is now the sepulchre, of Petrarch. If anyone is inclined to condemn the insertion of the introductory lines, which image forth the sudden relief of a state of deep despondency by the radiant visions disclosed by the sudden burst of an Italian sunrise in autumn on the highest peak of those delightful mountains, I can only offer as my excuse, that they were not erased at the request of a dear friend, with whom added years of intercourse only add to my apprehension of its value, and who would have had more right than anyone to complain, that she has not been able to extinguish in me the very power of delineating sadness.' The 'dear friend' is Mary Shelley.

[2] *a green isle* the Euganean hills stand in the midst of a plain to the west of Padua.

[3] *Riving* tearing.

Till the ship has almost drank
Death from the o'er-brimming deep,
And sinks down, down, like that sleep
When the dreamer seems to be
Weltering[4] through eternity;
And the dim low line before
Of a dark and distant shore
Still recedes, as ever still
Longing with divided will,
But no power to seek or shun,
He is ever drifted on
O'er the unreposing wave
To the haven of the grave.
What if there no friends will greet?[5]
What if there no heart will meet
His with love's impatient beat?
Wander wheresoe'er he may,
Can he dream before that day
To find refuge from distress
In friendship's smile, in love's caress?
Then 'twill wreak[6] him little woe
Whether such there be or no:
Senseless[7] is the breast, and cold,
Which relenting love would fold;
Bloodless are the veins and chill
Which the pulse of pain did fill;
Every little living nerve
That from bitter words did swerve
Round the tortured lips and brow,
Are like sapless leaflets now
Frozen upon December's bough.

On the beach of a northern sea[8]
Which tempests shake eternally,
As once the wretch there lay to sleep,
Lies a solitary heap:
One white skull and seven dry bones,
On the margin of the stones
Where a few grey rushes stand,
Boundaries of the sea and land.
Nor is heard one voice of wail
But the sea-mews,[9] as they sail
O'er the billows of the gale;
Or the whirlwind up and down
Howling like a slaughtered town,
When a king in glory rides

Notes

[4] *Weltering* tumbling.
[5] *What if there no friends will greet?* In Greek myth, friends were supposed to be reunited after death in the Elysian fields, where they would revel for eternity.
[6] *wreak* give.
[7] *Senseless* i.e. unperceiving (because dead).
[8] Shelley's daughter Clara was buried on the Lido, by the northern Adriatic.
[9] *sea-mews* seagulls.

Through the pomp of fratricides.[10]
Those unburied bones around
There is many a mournful sound;
There is no lament for him
Like a sunless vapour, dim,
Who once clothed with life and thought
What now moves nor murmurs not.

Aye, many flowering islands lie
In the waters of wide agony;
To such a one this morn was led
My bark, by soft winds piloted.
Mid the mountains Euganean[11]
I stood listening to the paean
With which the legioned rooks[12] did hail
The sun's uprise majestical;
Gathering round with wings all hoar,
Through the dewy mist they soar
Like grey shades, till th' eastern heaven
Bursts,[13] and then, as clouds of even[14]
Flecked with fire and azure lie
In the unfathomable sky,
So their plumes of purple grain,[15]
Starred with drops of golden rain,
Gleam above the sunlight woods,
As in silent multitudes
On the morning's fitful gale
Through the broken mist they sail,
And the vapours cloven and gleaming
Follow down the dark steep streaming,
Till all is bright and clear and still
Round the solitary hill.

Beneath is spread like a green sea
The waveless plain of Lombardy,[16]
Bounded by the vaporous air,
Islanded by cities fair;
Underneath day's azure eyes
Ocean's nursling, Venice,[17] lies,
A peopled labyrinth of walls,
Amphitrite's[18] destined halls

Notes

[10] *a slaughtered town . . . fratricides* a reference to the mass slaughter of the Danish King Christian II after he entered Stockholm, 1520.

[11] *Euganean* stressed on the third syllable, like 'Caribbean'.

[12] *rooks* Shelley may be referring to jackdaws, as there are no rooks in Italy. He may be thinking favourably of them because Coleridge had done so in *This Lime-Tree Bower My Prison* (p. 617).

[13] *Bursts* i.e. into light – the sun rises in the east.

[14] *even* i.e. night.

[15] *their plumes of purple grain* their feathers were dyed purple by the light of the rising sun.

[16] *Beneath . . . Lombardy* in a letter to Peacock of 8 October 1818 Shelley described the view from his villa in the Euganean Hills: 'We see before us the wide flat plains of Lombardy, in which we see the sun and moon rise and set, and the evening star, and all the golden magnificence of autumnal clouds' (Jones ii 43).

[17] Shelley was at Venice for a few days at the end of September 1818.

[18] Amphitrite was the daughter of Oceanus, god of the sea (her 'sire', line 98), and the wife of Poseidon. She will inherit the halls of Venice when they are swamped by the sea.

Which her hoary sire now paves
With his blue and beaming waves!
Lo! the sun upsprings behind,[19]
Broad, red, radiant, half-reclined
On the level quivering line
Of the waters crystalline;
And before that chasm of light,
As within a furnace bright,
Column, tower, and dome, and spire,
Shine like obelisks of fire,
Pointing with inconstant motion
From the altar of dark ocean
To the sapphire-tinted skies;
As the flames of sacrifice
From the marble shrines did rise,
As to pierce the dome of gold[20]
Where Apollo spoke of old.

Sun-girt city, thou hast been
Ocean's child, and then his queen;
Now is come a darker day,[21]
And thou soon must be his prey,
If the power that raised thee here
Hallow so thy watery bier.
A less drear ruin then than now,
With thy conquest-branded brow
Stooping to the slave of slaves
From thy throne, among the waves
Wilt thou be, when the sea-mew
Flies, as once before it flew,
O'er thine isles depopulate,[22]
And all is in its ancient state,
Save where many a palace gate
With green sea-flowers overgrown
Like a rock of ocean's own,
Topples o'er the abandoned sea
As the tides change sullenly.
The fisher on his watery way,
Wandering at the close of day,
Will spread his sail and seize his oar
Till he pass the gloomy shore,
Lest thy dead should, from their sleep
Bursting o'er the starlight[23] deep,
Lead a rapid masque[24] of death
O'er the waters of his path.

Notes

[19] *behind* i.e. behind Venice.

[20] *dome of gold* the Delphic oracle, through which Apollo (god of youth, poetry, and music) was believed to speak.

[21] *Now is come a darker day* Shelley's sorrow for Venice was due partly to the fact that, by the terms of the Congress of Vienna, 1815, it had been handed over to Austria; as he told Peacock on 8 October 1818: 'Venice, which was once a tyrant, is now the next worse thing – a slave' (Jones ii 43).

[22] *depopulate* laid waste.

[23] *starlight* i.e. starlit (an adjective).

[24] *masque* procession.

Those who alone thy towers behold
Quivering through aerial gold,
As I now behold them here,
Would imagine not they were
Sepulchres where human forms,
Like pollution-nourished worms,
To the corpse of greatness cling,
Murdered and now mouldering;[25]
But if Freedom should awake
In her omnipotence, and shake
From the Celtic Anarch's[26] hold
All the keys of dungeons[27] cold,
Where a hundred cities lie
Chained like thee, ingloriously,
Thou and all thy sister band
Might adorn this sunny land,
Twining memories of old time
With new virtues more sublime:
If not, perish thou and they! –
Clouds which stain truth's rising day
By her sun consumed away,
Earth can spare ye, while like flowers
In the waste of years and hours,
From your dust new nations spring
With more kindly blossoming.

Perish! let there only be
Floating o'er thy hearthless sea,
As the garment of thy sky
Clothes the world immortally,
One remembrance more sublime
Than the tattered pall of time,
Which scarce hides thy visage wan –
That a tempest-cleaving swan[28]
Of the songs of Albion,[29]
Driven from his ancestral streams
By the might of evil dreams,[30]
Found a nest in thee; and Ocean
Welcomed him with such emotion
That its joy grew his,[31] and sprung

Notes

[25] Shelley was shocked by the degraded state of Venice under Austrian occupation: 'I had no conception of the excess to which avarice, cowardice, superstition, ignorance, passionless lust, and all the inexpressible brutalities which degrade human nature could be carried, until I had lived a few days among the Venetians' (Jones ii 43).

[26] *Celtic Anarch* Austrian tyrant, as at line 223.

[27] *dungeons* On his visit to Venice in September 1818 Shelley visited the dungeons in the Doges' palace 'where the prisoners were confined sometimes half up to their middles in stinking water' (Jones ii 43).

[28] *a tempest-cleaving swan* Byron, then living at the Palazzo Mocenigo, Venice, where Shelley had met him the previous month.

[29] *Albion* England.

[30] *Driven . . . dreams* Byron was in self-exile, having been driven out of England by his wife's campaign against him after their separation.

[31] *its joy grew his* As Shelley reported to Peacock on 8 October 1818: '[Byron] is changed into the liveliest, and happiest looking man I ever met' (Jones ii 42).

From his lips[32] like music flung
O'er a mighty thunder-fit,
Chastening terror. What though yet
Poesy's unfailing river,
Which through Albion winds forever,
Lashing with melodious wave
Many a sacred poet's grave,
Mourn its latest nursling fled?
What though thou with all thy dead
Scarce can for this fame repay
Aught thine own?[33] Oh rather say,
Though[34] thy sins and slaveries foul
Overcloud a sunlike soul?
As the ghost of Homer clings
Round Scamander's[35] wasting springs;
As divinest Shakespeare's might
Fills Avon and the world with light,
Like omniscient power which he
Imaged mid mortality;
As the love from Petrarch's urn
Yet amid yon hills doth burn,[36]
A quenchless lamp by which the heart
Sees things unearthly – so thou art,
Mighty spirit;[37] so shall be
The city that did refuge thee.

Lo, the sun floats up the sky
Like thought-winged liberty,
Till the universal light
Seems to level plain and height;
From the sea a mist has spread,
And the beams of morn lie dead
On the towers of Venice now,
Like its glory long ago.
By the skirts of that grey cloud
Many-domed Padua[38] proud
Stands, a peopled solitude
Mid the harvest-shining plain,
Where the peasant heaps his grain
In the garner of his foe,[39]
And the milk-white oxen slow
With the purple vintage strain,
Heaped upon the creaking wain,

Notes

[32] *sprung / From his lips* a reference to *Don Juan* Canto I, which Byron had read to Shelley in late September 1818.

[33] *What though . . . own* Venice lacks a poet of its own as famous as Byron.

[34] *Though* i.e. '[What] Though thy sins . . . ?'

[35] Scamander, a river near Troy, site of the wars described by Homer in the *Iliad*, but now neglected by poets (and therefore wasted).

[36] *As the love . . . burn* The house and grave of the great Italian poet Petrarch (1304–74) are at Arqua in the Euganean Hills.

[37] *Mighty spirit* Byron.

[38] Shelley was in Padua August 1818.

[39] *the garner of his foe* the granary of the Austrians. Shelley told Peacock, 'The Austrians take sixty percent in taxes' (Jones ii 43).

That the brutal Celt[40] may swill
Drunken sleep with savage will;
And the sickle to the sword
Lies unchanged, though many a lord,
Like a weed whose shade is poison,
Overgrows this region's foison,[41]
Sheaves of whom are ripe to come
To destruction's harvest home:
Men must reap the things they sow,
Force from force must ever flow
Or worse – but 'tis a bitter woe
That love or reason cannot change
The despot's rage, the slave's revenge.

Padua, thou within whose walls
Those mute guests at festivals,
Son and mother, Death and Sin,
Played at dice for Ezzelin,[42]
Till Death cried, 'I win, I win!'
And Sin cursed to lose the wager,
But Death promised, to assuage her,
That he would petition for
Her to be made Vice-Emperor,
When the destined years were o'er,
Over all between the Po
And the eastern Alpine snow,
Under the mighty Austrian.
Sin smiled so as Sin only can,
And since that time, aye, long before,
Both have ruled from shore to shore –
That incestuous pair who follow
Tyrants as the sun the swallow,
As repentance follows crime,
And as changes follow time.

In thine halls the lamp of learning,
Padua, now no more is burning;[43]
Like a meteor, whose wild way
Is lost over the grave of day,
It gleams betrayed and to betray.
Once remotest nations came
To adore that sacred flame,
When it lit not many a hearth
On this cold and gloomy earth;
Now new fires from antique light

Notes

[40] *Celt* Austrian.

[41] *foison* harvest.

[42] Ezzelino da Romano (1194–1259), despot of Padua. Shelley is probably recalling Coleridge's *Ancient Mariner*, where Death and Life-in-Death cast dice for the mariner's soul.

[43] *In thine halls . . . burning* Padua University is one of the oldest in Europe, as it was founded in the 11th century.

Spring beneath the wide world's might,
But their spark lies dead in thee,
Trampled out by tyranny.
As the Norway woodman quells,
In the depth of piny dells,[44]
One light flame among the brakes,[45]
While the boundless forest shakes,
And its mighty trunks are torn
By the fire thus lowly born;
The spark beneath his feet is dead,
He starts to see the flames it fed
Howling through the darkened sky
With a myriad tongues victoriously,
And sinks down in fear: so thou,
Oh tyranny, beholdest now
Light around thee, and thou hearest
The loud flames ascend, and fearest –
Grovel on the earth! Aye, hide
In the dust thy purple[46] pride!

Noon descends around me now;
'Tis the noon of autumn's glow
When a soft and purple mist,
Like a vaporous amethyst,
Or an air-dissolved star[47]
Mingling light and fragrance, far
From the curved horizon's bound
To the point of heaven's profound,
Fills the overflowing sky;
And the plains that silent lie
Underneath, the leaves unsodden
Where the infant frost has trodden
With his morning-winged feet,
Whose bright print is gleaming yet;
And the red and golden vines,
Piercing with their trellised lines
The rough, dark-skirted wilderness;
The dun and bladed grass no less,
Pointing from this hoary tower[48]
In the windless air; the flower
Glimmering at my feet; the line
Of the olive-sandalled Apennine[49]
In the south dimly islanded;
And the Alps, whose snows are spread
High between the clouds and sun;

Notes

[44] *piny dells* dells of pine trees.

[45] *brakes* ferns.

[46] *purple* colour of imperial triumph.

[47] *an air-dissolved star* the star's light is diffused by the atmosphere.

[48] *this hoary tower* of the Benedictine monastery of the Olivetani on Monte Venda, the highest point in the Euganean Hills.

[49] *olive-sandalled Apennine* olive trees grow in the Apennines.

And of living things each one;
And my spirit which so long
Darkened this swift stream of song –
Interpenetrated lie
By the glory of the sky:
Be it love, light, harmony,
Odour, or the soul of all
Which from heaven like dew doth fall,
Or the mind which feeds this verse
Peopling the lone universe.

Noon descends, and after noon
Autumn's evening meets me soon,
Leading the infantine moon
And that one star,[50] which to her
Almost seems to minister
Half the crimson light she brings
From the sunset's radiant springs;
And the soft dreams of the morn
(Which like winged winds had borne
To that silent isle, which lies
Mid remembered agonies,
The frail bark of this lone being)
Pass, to other sufferers fleeing,
And its ancient pilot, Pain,
Sits beside the helm again.

Other flowering isles must be
In the sea of life and agony;
Other spirits float and flee
O'er that gulf – even now, perhaps,
On some rock the wild wave wraps,
With folding wings they waiting sit
For my bark, to pilot it
To some calm and blooming cove,
Where for me and those I love,
May a windless bower be built
Far from passion, pain, and guilt,[51]
In a dell mid lawny hills
Which the wild sea-murmur fills,
And soft sunshine, and the sound
Of old forests echoing round,
And the light and smell divine
Of all flowers that breathe and shine.
We may live so happy there
That the spirits of the air,
Envying us, may even entice

Notes

[50] *that one star* Hesper, the evening star.

[51] *guilt* this poem is inspired partly by guilt at the death of Shelley's baby daughter, Clara, due in part to his negligence.

To our healing paradise
The polluting multitude;
But their rage would be subdued
By that clime divine and calm,
And the winds whose wings rain balm
On the uplifted soul, and leaves
Under which the bright sea heaves;
While each breathless interval
In their whisperings musical
The inspired soul supplies
With its own deep melodies,
And the love which heals all strife
Circling like the breath of life,
All things in that sweet abode
With its own mild brotherhood:
They, not it, would change, and soon
Every sprite beneath the moon
Would repent its envy vain,
And the earth grow young again.

Stanzas written in Dejection, near Naples (composed December 1818)[1]

From Posthumous Poems (1824)

The sun is warm, the sky is clear,
The waves are dancing fast and bright,
Blue isles and snowy mountains wear
The purple noon's transparent light:
The breath of the moist air is light
Around its unexpanded buds;
Like many a voice of one delight
The winds, the birds, the ocean floods,
The City's voice itself is soft like Solitude's.

I see the Deep's untrampled floor
With green and purple seaweeds strown;
I see the waves upon the shore,
Like light dissolved in star-showers, thrown:
I sit upon the sands alone,
The lightning of the noontide ocean
Is flashing round me, and a tone
Arises from its measured motion,
How sweet! did any heart now share in my emotion.

Notes

Stanzas written in Dejection

[1] For the background to this poem see headnote, p. 1048. Shelley had brought his family to Naples at the end of November 1818. Key influences on the poem include Wordsworth's 'Resolution and Independence' and Coleridge's 'Dejection: An Ode'.

Alas! I have nor hope nor health,[2]
Nor peace within nor calm around,
Nor that content surpassing wealth
The sage in meditation found,
And walked with inward glory crowned –
Nor fame, nor power, nor love, nor leisure.
Others I see whom these surround –
Smiling they live, and call life pleasure;
To me that cup has been dealt in another measure.

Yet now despair itself is mild,
Even as the winds and waters are;
I could lie down like a tired child,
And weep away the life of care
Which I have borne and yet must bear,
Till death like sleep might steal on me,
And I might feel in the warm air
My cheek grow cold, and hear the sea
Breathe o'er my dying brain its last monotony.

Some might lament that I were cold,
As I when this sweet day is gone,
Which my lost heart, too soon grown old,
Insults with this untimely moan;
They might lament – for I am one
Whom men love not – and yet regret,
Unlike this day, which, when the sun
Shall on its stainless glory set,
Will linger, though enjoyed, like joy in memory yet.

Prometheus Unbound A Lyrical Drama in Four Acts (composed September 1818–December 1819; edited from printed and MS sources)[1]

Audisne haec Amphiarae, sub terram abdite?[2]

Preface

The Greek tragic writers, in selecting as their subject any portion of their national history or mythology, employed in their treatment of it a certain arbitrary discretion. They by no means conceived themselves bound to adhere to the common interpret-

Notes

[2] *health* Mary Shelley recalled: 'At this time Shelley suffered greatly in health. He put himself under the care of a medical man, who promised great things, and made him endure severe bodily pain, without any good results. Constant and poignant physical pain exhausted him; and though he preserved the appearance of cheerfulness, and often greatly enjoyed our wanderings in the environs of Naples, and our excursions on the sunny sea, yet many hours were passed when his thoughts, shadowed by illness, became gloomy, and then he escaped to solitude, and in verses, which he hid from fear of wounding me, poured forth morbid but too natural bursts of discontent and sadness.'

Prometheus Unbound

[1] This work should be read in the light of Mary Shelley's note, p. 1440; for introductory remarks see headnote, p. 1048. See also M. H. Abrams, 'Shelley's "Prometheus Unbound" ', in *Natural Supernaturalism: Tradition and Revolution in Romantic Literature* (New York, 1971), pp. 299–307.

[2] 'Do you hear this, Amphiaraus, in your home beneath the earth?' (Cicero, *Tusculan Disputations* II xxv 59). Amphiaraus was a prophet, saved by Jupiter from pursuers by being miraculously swallowed by the earth, after which he became an oracular god. Shelley directs the comment to

ation, or to imitate in story (as in title) their rivals and predecessors. Such a system would have amounted to a resignation of those claims to preference over their competitors which incited the composition: the Agamemnonian story[3] was exhibited on the Athenian theatre with as many variations as dramas.

I have presumed to employ a similar licence. The *Prometheus Unbound* of Aeschylus supposed the reconciliation of Jupiter with his victim[4] as the price of the disclosure of the danger threatened to his empire by the consummation of his marriage with Thetis. Thetis, according to this view of the subject, was given in marriage to Peleus;[5] and Prometheus, by the permission of Jupiter, delivered from his captivity by Hercules. Had I framed my story on this model, I should have done no more than have attempted to restore the lost drama of Aeschylus[6] – an ambition which, if my preference to this mode of treating the subject had incited me to cherish, the recollection of the high comparison such an attempt would challenge might well abate. But in truth, I was averse from a catastrophe so feeble as that of reconciling the champion with the oppressor of mankind. The moral interest of the fable, which is so powerfully sustained by the sufferings and endurance of Prometheus, would be annihilated if we could conceive of him as unsaying his high language and quailing before his successful and perfidious adversary.[7] The only imaginary being resembling in any degree Prometheus, is Satan; and Prometheus is, in my judgement, a more poetical character than Satan, because, in addition to courage and majesty, and firm and patient opposition to omnipotent force, he is susceptible of being described as exempt from the taints of ambition, envy, revenge, and a desire for personal aggrandizement[8] – which, in the hero of *Paradise Lost*, interfere with the interest. The character of Satan engenders in the mind a pernicious casuistry which leads us to weigh his faults with his wrongs, and to excuse the former because the latter exceed all measure. In the minds of those who consider that magnificent fiction with a religious feeling, it engenders something worse. But Prometheus is, as it were, the type of the highest perfection of moral and intellectual nature, impelled by the purest and the truest motives to the best and noblest ends.

This poem was chiefly written upon the mountainous ruins of the Baths of Caracalla,[9] among the flowery glades, and thickets of odoriferous blossoming trees, which are extended in ever-winding labyrinths upon its immense platforms and dizzy arches suspended in the air. The bright blue sky of Rome, and the effect of the vigorous awakening spring in that divinest climate, and the new life with which it drenches the spirits even to intoxication, were the inspiration of this drama.

The imagery which I have employed will be found, in many instances, to have been drawn from the operations of the human mind, or from those external actions by

Notes

Aeschylus, asking him to hear this reworking of the Prometheus myth.

[3] *the Agamemnonian story* famously related by Aeschylus in the *Oresteia* (458 BC), a trilogy of plays that tells of the tragic homecoming of the Greek commander Agamemnon from the Trojan war and its consequences.

[4] *his victim* Prometheus, whom he nailed to the rock of the Caucasus for 30,000 years.

[5] Thetis, a goddess of the sea, married Peleus, King of Thessaly, after a long courtship.

[6] *the lost drama of Aeschylus* i.e. Aeschylus' *Prometheus Unbound*, the lost sequel to *Prometheus Bound*. It is not known how Aeschylus effected the reconciliation between Prometheus and Jupiter. Fragments show that it opened with Prometheus restored to light after 3,000 years, and that the chorus was composed of Titans. In Greek myth, the Titans were a god-like race expelled from heaven by Jupiter.

[7] Shelley points to a crucial distinction between his work and Aeschylus'. He refused to accept the idea of Prometheus' submission to Jupiter; in his poem it is Jupiter who succumbs.

[8] *Prometheus is . . . aggrandizement* Prometheus returned fire to man after it was taken away by Jupiter.

[9] *the Baths of Caracalla* ancient baths in Rome, named after Emperor Caracalla (AD 211–217). Shelley began *Prometheus Unbound* in Este near Padua, September 1818, and completed it in Rome, December 1819.

which they are expressed. This is unusual in modern poetry, although Dante and Shakespeare are full of instances of the same kind – Dante indeed more than any other poet, and with greater success. But the Greek poets, as writers to whom no resource of awakening the sympathy of their contemporaries was unknown, were in the habitual use of this power; and it is the study of their works (since a higher merit would probably be denied me) to which I am willing that my readers should impute this singularity.

One word is due in candour to the degree in which the study of contemporary writings may have tinged my composition, for such has been a topic of censure with regard to poems far more popular (and indeed more deservedly popular) than mine.[10] It is impossible that anyone who inhabits the same age with such writers[11] as those who stand in the foremost ranks of our own, can conscientiously assure himself that his language and tone of thought may not have been modified by the study of the productions of those extraordinary intellects. It is true that, not the spirit of their genius, but the forms in which it has manifested itself, are due less to the peculiarities of their own minds than to the peculiarity of the moral and intellectual condition of the minds among which they have been produced. Thus a number of writers possess the form, whilst they want the spirit, of those whom (it is alleged) they imitate; because the former is the endowment of the age in which they live, and the latter must be the uncommunicated lightning of their own mind.

The peculiar style of intense and comprehensive imagery which distinguishes the modern literature of England has not been, as a general power, the product of the imitation of any particular writer. The mass of capabilities remains at every period materially the same; the circumstances which awaken it to action perpetually change. If England were divided into forty republics, each equal in population and extent to Athens, there is no reason to suppose but that, under institutions not more perfect than those of Athens, each would produce philosophers and poets equal to those who (if we except Shakespeare) have never been surpassed. We owe the great writers of the golden age of our literature[12] to that fervid awakening of the public mind which shook to dust the oldest and most oppressive form of the Christian religion.[13] We owe Milton to the progress and development of the same spirit – the sacred Milton was, let it ever be remembered, a republican, and a bold enquirer into morals and religion. The great writers of our own age are, we have reason to suppose, the companions and forerunners of some unimagined change in our social condition, or the opinions which cement it. The cloud of mind is discharging its collected lightning, and the equilibrium between institutions and opinions is now restoring, or is about to be restored.

As to imitation, poetry is a mimetic art. It creates, but it creates by combination and representation. Poetical abstractions are beautiful and new, not because the portions of which they are composed had no previous existence in the mind of man or in nature, but because the whole produced by their combination has some intelligible and beautiful analogy with those sources of emotion and thought, and with the

Notes

10 *One word . . . than mine* The remainder of the Preface is a response to John Taylor Coleridge who, in an anonymous review of *The Revolt of Islam* (1818) in the *Quarterly Review* 21 (1819) 460–71, described Shelley as 'an unsparing imitator' of Wordsworth, 'to whose religious mind it must be matter, we think, of perpetual sorrow to see the philosophy which comes pure and holy from his pen, degraded and perverted, as it continually is, by this miserable crew of atheists or pantheists'. Shelley thought that the review was by Southey.

11 *such writers* identified in the MS as Wordsworth, Coleridge and Byron. It is worth bearing in mind that Shelley's works, when published, enjoyed virtually no sale and were widely attacked; that's why he writes from the standpoint of someone whose writings were less popular than theirs.

12 *the golden age of our literature* Shelley means the Elizabethan age – that of Spenser and Sidney.

13 *the oldest and most oppressive form of the Christian religion* Roman Catholicism.

contemporary condition of them. One great poet is a masterpiece of nature which another not only ought to study but must study. He might as wisely and as easily determine that his mind should no longer be the mirror of all that is lovely in the visible universe, as exclude from his contemplation the beautiful which exists in the writings of a great contemporary. The pretence of doing it would be a presumption in any but the greatest; the effect, even in him, would be strained, unnatural, and ineffectual. A poet is the combined product of such internal powers as modify the nature of others, and of such external influences as excite and sustain these powers; he is not one, but both. Every man's mind is, in this respect, modified by all the objects of nature and art; by every word and every suggestion which he ever admitted to act upon his consciousness; it is the mirror upon which all forms are reflected, and in which they compose one form. Poets, not otherwise than philosophers, painters, sculptors and musicians, are in one sense the creators, and in another the creations, of their age. From this subjection the loftiest do not escape. There is a similarity between Homer and Hesiod, between Aeschylus and Euripides, between Virgil and Horace, between Dante and Petrarch, between Shakespeare and Fletcher, between Dryden and Pope: each has a generic resemblance under which their specific distinctions are arranged. If this similarity be the result of imitation, I am willing to confess that I have imitated.

Let this opportunity be conceded to me of acknowledging that I have what a Scotch philosopher[14] characteristically terms, 'a passion for reforming the world'. What passion incited him to write and publish his book, he omits to explain. For my part, I had rather be damned with Plato and Lord Bacon,[15] than go to heaven with Paley and Malthus.[16] But it is a mistake to suppose that I dedicate my poetical compositions solely to the direct enforcement of reform, or that I consider them in any degree as containing a reasoned system on the theory of human life. Didactic poetry is my abhorrence; nothing can be equally well expressed in prose that is not tedious and supererogatory in verse. My purpose has hitherto been simply to familiarize the highly-refined imagination of the more select classes of poetical readers with beautiful idealisms of moral excellence, aware that until the mind can love, and admire, and trust, and hope, and endure, reasoned principles of moral conduct are seeds cast upon the highway of life, which the unconscious passenger tramples into dust although they would bear the harvest of his happiness. Should I live to accomplish what I purpose (that is, produce a systematical history of what appear to me to be the genuine elements of human society), let not the advocates of injustice and superstition flatter themselves that I should take Aeschylus rather than Plato as my model.[17]

The having spoken of myself with unaffected freedom will need little apology with the candid, and let the uncandid consider that they injure me less than their own hearts and minds by misrepresentation. Whatever talents a person may possess to amuse and instruct others (be they ever so inconsiderable), he is yet bound to exert them. If his attempt be ineffectual, let the punishment of an unaccomplished purpose have been sufficient; let none trouble themselves to heap the dust of oblivion upon his efforts. The pile they raise will betray his grave which might otherwise have been unknown.

Notes

[14] *a Scotch philosopher* Robert Forsyth in *The Principles of Moral Science* (1805).

[15] *Plato and Lord Bacon* in the MS, Shelley adds Rousseau and Milton to this group. Francis Bacon (1561–1626), Lord Chancellor of England, philosopher and essayist, appealed to Shelley because he was a Neoplatonist.

[16] William Paley (1743–1805) argued the usefulness of hell as a means of controlling morals; Thomas Robert Malthus (1776–1834) argued that famine, war and disease were necessary as means of controlling population growth. Shelley regarded them as conservative and utilitarian.

[17] Plato's hero is a man leading others towards the light.

Dramatis Personae

Prometheus
Demogorgon
Jupiter
The Earth
Ocean
Apollo
Mercury
Hercules
Asia, Panthea, Ione } Oceanides
The Phantasm of Jupiter
The Spirit of the Earth
The Spirit of the Moon
Spirits of the Hours
Echoes
Fauns
Furies
Spirits

Act I

Scene: a ravine of icy rocks in the Indian Caucasus.[1] Prometheus[2] *is discovered bound to the precipice. Panthea and Ione are seated at his feet. Time: night. During the scene, morning slowly breaks.*

PROMETHEUS. Monarch of Gods and Daemons,[3] and all spirits
But One,[4] who throng those bright and rolling worlds
Which thou and I alone of living things
Behold with sleepless eyes! Regard this earth
Made multitudinous with thy slaves, whom thou
Requitest for knee-worship, prayer, and praise,
And toil, and hecatombs[5] of broken hearts,
With fear and self-contempt and barren hope;
Whilst me, who am thy foe, eyeless in hate,[6]
Hast thou made reign and triumph, to thy scorn,
O'er mine own misery and thy vain revenge.
Three thousand years of sleep-unsheltered hours
And moments, aye[7] divided by keen pangs

Notes

Act I

[1] Shelley moves the location from the Caucasus mountains near the Caspian to the Indian Caucasus, the Hindu Kush mountains in north India and Afghanistan. It was believed to have been the original home of the human race, and associated with the golden age; it was thus appropriate as the location for universal rebirth.

[2] *Prometheus* 'forethinker' in Greek.

[3] *Monarch of Gods and Daemons* Jupiter (Jove). In Shelley's terms, a symbol of political and religious tyranny. Daemons are capable of mediating between humanity and the gods.

[4] *One* Prometheus, who is in much the same position that Shelley felt himself to be.

[5] *hecatombs* numerous sacrifices.

[6] *eyeless in hate* blind with hatred; for a moment Prometheus becomes Samson, 'Eyeless in Gaza at the mill with slaves' (Milton, *Samson Agonistes* 41).

[7] *aye* continually.

Till they seemed years, torture and solitude,
Scorn and despair – these are mine empire:
More glorious far than that which thou surveyest
From thine unenvied throne, oh mighty God!
Almighty, had I deigned to share the shame
Of thine ill tyranny, and hung not here
Nailed to this wall of eagle-baffling mountain,
Black, wintry, dead, unmeasured; without herb,
Insect, or beast, or shape or sound of life –
Ah me, alas! Pain, pain ever, forever!
    No change, no pause, no hope; yet I endure.
I ask the Earth, have not the mountains felt?
I ask yon Heaven, the all-beholding Sun,
Has it not seen? The Sea, in storm or calm,
Heaven's ever-changing shadow, spread below,
Have its deaf waves not heard my agony?
Ah me, alas! Pain, pain ever, forever!
    The crawling glaciers[8] pierce me with the spears
Of their moon-freezing crystals; the bright chains
Eat with their burning cold into my bones;
Heaven's winged hound,[9] polluting from thy lips
His beak in poison not his own, tears up
My heart; and shapeless sights come wandering by,
The ghastly people of the realm of dream,
Mocking me; and the Earthquake-fiends are charged
To wrench the rivets from my quivering wounds
When the rocks split and close again behind;
While from their loud abysses howling throng
The genii of the storm, urging the rage
Of whirlwind, and afflict me with keen hail.
    And yet to me welcome is Day and Night,
Whether one breaks the hoar-frost of the morn,
Or starry, dim, and slow, the other climbs
The leaden-coloured east – for then they lead
The wingless, crawling Hours,[10] one among whom
(As some dark priest hales[11] the reluctant victim)
Shall drag thee, cruel King, to kiss the blood
From these pale feet, which then might trample thee
If they disdained not such a prostrate slave.
Disdain? Ah no, I pity thee.[12] What Ruin
Will hunt thee undefended through wide Heaven!
How will thy soul, cloven to its depth with terror,
Gape like a hell within! I speak in grief,
Not exultation, for I hate no more

Notes

[8] *crawling glaciers* Observed by Shelley in Switzerland; see his letter to Peacock (p. 1074), and the creeping glaciers at 'Mont Blanc' 100.

[9] Heaven's winged hound the eagle or vulture that incessantly devoured Prometheus' liver over a 3,000-year period.

[10] *Hours* Latin 'Horae', female divinities that preside over the changing of the seasons.

[11] *hales* drags.

[12] *Ah no, I pity thee* the pivotal statement of the play. Prometheus' Christ-like pity for his torturer marks the beginning of his redemption.

As then, ere misery made me wise. The curse
Once breathed on thee I would recall.[13] Ye Mountains,
Whose many-voiced Echoes, through the mist
Of cataracts, flung the thunder of that spell;
Ye icy Springs, stagnant with wrinkling frost,
Which vibrated to hear me, and then crept
Shuddering through India; thou serenest Air,
Through which the Sun walks burning without beams;
And ye swift Whirlwinds, who on poised wings
Hung mute and moveless o'er yon hushed abyss,
As thunder, louder than your own, made rock
The orbed world – if then my words had power
(Though I am changed so that aught evil wish
Is dead within, although no memory be
Of what is hate), let them not lose it now!
What was that curse, for ye all heard me speak?

FIRST VOICE (*from the mountains*)
Thrice three hundred thousand years[14]
O'er the Earthquake's couch we stood;
Oft, as men convulsed with fears,
We trembled in our multitude.

SECOND VOICE (*from the springs*)
Thunderbolts had parched our water,
We had been stained with bitter blood,
And had run mute, mid shrieks of slaughter,
Through a city and a solitude.

THIRD VOICE (*from the air*)
I had clothed, since Earth uprose,
Its wastes in colours not their own,
And oft had my serene repose
Been cloven by many a rending groan.

FOURTH VOICE (*from the whirlwinds*)
We had soared beneath these mountains
Unresting ages; nor had thunder,
Nor yon volcano's flaming fountains,
Nor any power above or under
Ever made us mute with wonder.

Notes

[13] *recall* revoke.

[14] Lines 74–106 describe the effects of the curse of Prometheus on Jupiter, which he has now revoked.

FIRST VOICE
But never bowed our snowy crest
As at the voice of thine unrest.[15]

SECOND VOICE
Never such a sound before
To the Indian waves we bore.
A pilot asleep on the howling sea
Leaped up from the deck in agony,
And heard, and cried, 'Ah, woe is me!'
And died as mad as the wild waves be.

THIRD VOICE
By such dread words from Earth to Heaven
My still realm was never riven;
When its wound was closed, there stood
Darkness o'er the day like blood.

FOURTH VOICE
And we shrank back; for dreams of ruin
To frozen caves our flight pursuing
Made us keep silence thus, and thus,
Though silence is as hell to us.

THE EARTH
The tongueless caverns of the craggy hills
Cried, 'Misery!' then; the hollow Heaven replied
'Misery!' And the Ocean's purple waves,
Climbing the land, howled to the lashing winds,
And the pale nations heard it, 'Misery!'

PROMETHEUS. I heard a sound of voices – not the voice
Which I gave forth. Mother,[16] thy sons and thou
Scorn him, without whose all-enduring will
Beneath the fierce omnipotence of Jove
Both they and thou had vanished, like thin mist
Unrolled on the morning wind. Know ye not me,
The Titan?[17] He who made his agony
The barrier to your else all-conquering foe?
Oh rock-embosomed lawns and snow-fed streams
Now seen athwart frore[18] vapours, deep below,
Through whose o'ershadowing woods I wandered once
With Asia,[19] drinking life from her loved eyes,

Notes

[15] *the voice of thine unrest* i.e. Prometheus' curse.
[16] *Mother* Earth, mother of the Titans and of all things that spring from the earth.
[17] *The Titan* Prometheus was one of the Titans.
[18] *frore* frosty.
[19] *Asia* daughter of Oceanus and bride of Prometheus, from whom she is now separated.

Why scorns the spirit which informs ye, now
To commune with me? Me alone, who checked,
As one who checks a fiend-drawn charioteer,
The falsehood and the force of him who reigns
Supreme, and with the groans of pining slaves
Fills your dim glens and liquid wildernesses?
Why answer ye not still, brethren?[20]

THE EARTH. They dare not.

PROMETHEUS. Who dares? For I would hear that curse again. . . .
Ha, what an awful whisper rises up!
'Tis scarce like sound; it tingles through the frame
As lightning tingles, hovering ere it strike.
Speak, Spirit! From thine inorganic voice
I only know that thou art moving near
And love. How cursed I him?

THE EARTH. How canst thou hear,
Who knowest not the language of the dead?

PROMETHEUS. Thou art a living spirit; speak as they.

THE EARTH. I dare not speak like life, lest Heaven's fell King
Should hear, and link me to some wheel of pain[21]
More torturing than the one whereon I roll.
Subtle thou art and good, and though the Gods
Hear not this voice, yet thou art more than God,
Being wise and kind. Earnestly hearken now.

PROMETHEUS. Obscurely through my brain, like shadows dim,
Sweep awful[22] thoughts, rapid and thick. I feel
Faint, like one mingled in entwining love;
Yet 'tis not pleasure.

THE EARTH. No, thou canst not hear;
Thou art immortal, and this tongue is known
Only to those who die.

PROMETHEUS. And what art thou,
Oh melancholy Voice?

THE EARTH. I am the Earth,
Thy mother; she within whose stony veins,[23]
To the last fibre of the loftiest tree
Whose thin leaves trembled in the frozen air,
Joy ran, as blood within a living frame,
When thou didst from her bosom, like a cloud
Of glory,[24] arise – a spirit of keen joy![25]

Notes

[20] *brethren* Prometheus is the sibling of forests and streams, as they are all children of Earth.

[21] *some wheel of pain* Ixion's punishment was to be banished from heaven and tied to a burning and spinning wheel in Hades.

[22] *awful* awesome.

[23] *stony veins* In his letter to Peacock, Shelley had referred to the blood circulating through the 'stony veins' of Mont Blanc (see p. 1074).

[24] *a cloud / Of glory* compare Wordsworth, 'Ode': 'But trailing clouds of glory do we come / From God, who is our home' (ll. 64–5).

[25] This refers to Prometheus' rebellion against Jupiter.

And at thy voice her pining sons uplifted
Their prostrate brows from the polluting dust,
And our almighty Tyrant[26] with fierce dread
Grew pale, until his thunder chained thee here.
Then – see those million worlds which burn and roll
Around us; their inhabitants beheld
My sphered light wane in wide heaven; the sea
Was lifted by strange tempest, and new fire
From earthquake-rifted mountains of bright snow
Shook its portentous hair beneath Heaven's frown;
Lightning and inundation vexed the plains;
Blue thistles bloomed in cities; foodless toads
Within voluptuous chambers panting crawled,
When plague had fallen on man and beast and worm,
And famine and black blight on herb and tree;
And in the corn and vines and meadow-grass
Teemed ineradicable poisonous weeds
Draining their growth – for my wan breast was dry
With grief, and the thin air, my breath, was stained
With the contagion of a mother's hate
Breathed on her child's destroyer. Aye, I heard
Thy curse, the which, if thou rememberest not,
Yet my innumerable seas and streams,
Mountains, and caves, and winds, and yon wide air,
And the inarticulate people of the dead,
Preserve, a treasured spell. We meditate
In secret joy and hope those dreadful words,
But dare not speak them.

PROMETHEUS. Venerable mother!
All else who live and suffer take from thee
Some comfort: flowers, and fruits, and happy sounds,
And love, though fleeting. These may not be mine;
But mine own words, I pray, deny me not.

THE EARTH. They shall be told. Ere Babylon was dust,
The magus Zoroaster,[27] my dead child,
Met his own image walking in the garden;
That apparition, sole of men, he saw.
For know there are two worlds of life and death;
One that which thou beholdest – but the other
Is underneath the grave, where do inhabit
The shadows of all forms that think and live
Till death unite them and they part no more,
Dreams and the light imaginings of men,
And all that faith creates or love desires,

Notes

[26] *our almighty Tyrant* Jupiter.

[27] *Zoroaster* Persian religious leader, King of Bactria (6th or 7th century BC), who taught that the universe is ruled by two powers, but that the eventual victory of the good spirit (Ahura Mazda or Ormuzd) over the evil (Ahriman) is guaranteed. The encounter with his double is apocryphal; Shelley apparently has in mind Zoroaster's formative meeting with the angel Vohu Manah ('good thought'), who introduced him to Ahura Mazda.

Terrible, strange, sublime and beauteous shapes.
There thou art, and dost hang, a writhing shade
Mid whirlwind-peopled mountains; all the gods
Are there, and all the powers of nameless worlds –
Vast, sceptred phantoms, heroes, men, and beasts,
And Demogorgon,[28] a tremendous gloom –
And he, the supreme Tyrant,[29] on his throne
Of burning gold. Son, one of these shall utter
The curse which all remember. Call at will
Thine own ghost, or the ghost of Jupiter,
Hades or Typhon,[30] or what mightier Gods
From all-prolific Evil since thy ruin
Have sprung and trampled on my prostrate sons.
Ask, and they must reply; so the revenge
Of the Supreme may sweep through vacant shades,
As rainy wind through the abandoned gate
Of a fallen palace.

PROMETHEUS. Mother, let not aught
Of that which may be evil pass again
My lips, or those of aught resembling me.
Phantasm of Jupiter, arise, appear!

IONE.[31]
My wings are folded o'er mine ears;
My wings are crossed over mine eyes;
Yet through their silver shade appears,
And through their lulling plumes arise
A shape, a throng of sounds:
May it be no ill to thee,
Oh thou of many wounds,[32]
Near whom, for our sweet sister's[33] sake,
Ever thus we watch and wake.

PANTHEA.
The sound is of whirlwind underground,
Earthquake, and fire, and mountains cloven;[34]
The shape is awful like the sound,
Clothed in dark purple, star-inwoven.
A sceptre of pale gold,
To stay[35] steps proud, o'er the slow cloud
His veined hand doth hold.[36]
Cruel he looks, but calm and strong,
Like one who does, not suffers wrong.

Notes

[28] *Demogorgon* important deity described by Mary Shelley as 'the primal power of the world'.
[29] *the supreme Tyrant* Jupiter.
[30] *Hades or Typhon* In Greek myth, Hades was the brother of Jupiter, king of the underworld; Typhon was a monster with a hundred serpentine heads, each of which emitted flames.
[31] Ione and Panthea are daughters of Oceanus and younger sisters of Asia. They are a chorus, describing and commenting on the events.
[32] *Oh thou of many wounds* Prometheus.
[33] *sweet sister* Asia.
[34] *cloven* split asunder.
[35] *stay* steady.
[36] *A sceptre . . . hold* The Phantasm of Jupiter holds a sceptre as he approaches over the cloud.

PHANTASM OF JUPITER. Why have the secret powers of this strange world
Driven me, a frail and empty phantom, hither
On direst storms? What unaccustomed sounds
Are hovering on my lips, unlike the voice
With which our pallid race hold ghastly talk
In darkness? And, proud sufferer, who art thou?

PROMETHEUS. Tremendous Image, as thou art must be
He whom thou shadowest forth. I am his foe,
The Titan. Speak the words which I would hear
Although no thought inform thine empty voice.

THE EARTH. Listen, and though your echoes must be mute,
Grey mountains, and old woods, and haunted springs,
Prophetic caves, and isle-surrounding streams,
Rejoice to hear what yet ye cannot speak.

PHANTASM. A spirit seizes me and speaks within:
It tears me as fire tears a thunder-cloud!

PANTHEA. See how he lifts his mighty looks; the heaven
Darkens above.

IONE. He speaks; oh shelter me!

PROMETHEUS. I see the curse on gestures proud and cold,
And looks of firm defiance and calm hate,
And such despair as mocks itself with smiles,
Written as on a scroll – yet speak, oh speak!

PHANTASM.
Fiend, I defy thee! With a calm, fixed mind,
All that thou canst inflict I bid thee do;
Foul tyrant both of Gods and humankind,
One only being shalt thou not subdue.
Rain then thy plagues upon me here,
Ghastly disease, and frenzying fear;
And let alternate frost and fire
Eat into me, and be thine ire
Lightning, and cutting hail, and legioned forms
Of furies, driving by upon the wounding storms.

Aye, do thy worst. Thou art omnipotent.
O'er all things but thyself I gave thee power,
And my own will.[37] Be thy swift mischiefs sent
To blast mankind, from yon ethereal tower.
Let thy malignant spirit move
Its darkness over those I love;

Notes

[37] *O'er all things . . . will* Prometheus empowered Jupiter; in the same way, we empower the tyrants who rule over us.

On me and mine I imprecate[38]
The utmost torture of thy hate,
And thus devote[39] to sleepless agony
This undeclining head, while thou must reign on high.

But thou, who art the God and Lord – oh thou
Who fillest with thy soul this world of woe;
To whom all things of Earth and Heaven do bow
In fear and worship; all-prevailing foe!
I curse thee! Let a sufferer's curse
Clasp thee, his torturer, like remorse;
Till thine infinity shall be
A robe of envenomed agony,[40]
And thine omnipotence a crown of pain
To cling like burning gold round thy dissolving brain.

Heap on thy soul, by virtue of this curse,
Ill deeds; then be thou damned, beholding good,
Both infinite as is the universe,
And thou, and thy self-torturing solitude.[41]
An awful image of calm power
Though now thou sittest, let the hour
Come when thou must appear to be
That which thou art internally;
And after many a false and fruitless crime
Scorn track thy lagging fall through boundless space and time.
The Phantasm vanishes.

PROMETHEUS. Were these my words, oh Parent?

THE EARTH. They were thine.

PROMETHEUS. It doth repent me; words are quick and vain –
Grief for awhile is blind, and so was mine.
I wish no living thing to suffer pain.[42]

THE EARTH.
Misery, oh misery to me,
That Jove at length should vanquish thee.
Wail, howl aloud, Land and Sea;
The Earth's rent heart shall answer ye.
Howl, spirits of the living and the dead,
Your refuge, your defence lies fallen and vanquished.

Notes

[38] *imprecate* invoke, call down.

[39] *devote* condemn, doom.

[40] *A robe of envenomed agony* There is a recollection of Nessus' poisoned shirt which, when worn by Hercules, burned his skin and tore off his flesh when he attempted to remove it.

[41] *Both infinite . . . solitude* ' . . . both good and evil being infinite as the universe is, and as thou art, and as thy solitude is.'

[42] A deleted stage-direction in the MS reveals at this point that Prometheus 'bends his head as in pain'.

FIRST ECHO. Lies fallen and vanquished?

SECOND ECHO. Fallen and vanquished!

IONE.
Fear not, 'tis but some passing spasm –
The Titan is unvanquished still.
But see, where through the azure chasm
Of yon forked and snowy hill,
Trampling the slant winds on high
With golden-sandalled feet that glow
Under plumes of purple dye
Like rose-ensanguined ivory –
A shape comes now,
Stretching on high from his right hand
A serpent-cinctured[43] wand.

PANTHEA. 'Tis Jove's world-wandering herald, Mercury.[44]

IONE.
And who are those with hydra tresses[45]
And iron wings that climb the wind,
Whom the frowning God represses
Like vapours steaming up behind,
Clanging loud, an endless crowd?

PANTHEA.
These are Jove's tempest-walking hounds[46]
Whom he gluts with groans and blood,
When charioted on sulphurous cloud
He bursts Heaven's bounds.

IONE.
Are they now led from the thin dead
On new pangs to be fed?

PANTHEA. The Titan looks as ever – firm, not proud.

FIRST FURY. Ha! I scent life!

SECOND FURY. Let me but look into his eyes.

THIRD FURY. The hope of torturing him smells like a heap
Of corpses to a death-bird after battle.

FIRST FURY. Darest thou delay, oh Herald? Take cheer, hounds
Of hell; what if the Son of Maia[47] soon
Should make us food and sport? Who can please long
The Omnipotent?

Notes

[43] *cinctured* entwined.
[44] *Mercury* son of Maia and Zeus, messenger of the gods. He is the unwilling servant of tyranny.
[45] *hydra tresses* hair of snakes.
[46] *Jove's tempest-walking hounds* i.e. the Furies, avenging spirits.
[47] *the Son of Maia* Mercury.

MERCURY. Back to your towers of iron
And gnash, beside the streams of fire and wail,
Your foodless teeth![48] Geryon, arise! And Gorgon,
Chimera, and thou Sphinx,[49] subtlest of fiends,
Who ministered to Thebes Heaven's poisoned wine:
Unnatural love and more unnatural hate[50] –
These shall perform your task.

FIRST FURY. Oh mercy, mercy!
We die with our desire; drive us not back.

MERCURY. Crouch then in silence.
Awful sufferer!
To thee unwilling, most unwillingly
I come, by the great Father's will driven down,
To execute a doom[51] of new revenge.
Alas, I pity thee, and hate myself
That I can do no more. Aye from thy sight
Returning, for a season, Heaven seems Hell,
So thy worn form pursues me night and day,
Smiling reproach. Wise art thou, firm and good,
But vainly wouldst stand forth alone in strife
Against the Omnipotent, as yon clear lamps
That measure and divide the weary years
From which there is no refuge, long have taught
And long must teach. Even now thy torturer arms
With the strange might of unimagined pains
The powers who scheme slow agonies in Hell,
And my commission is to lead them here,
Or what more subtle, foul or savage fiends
People the abyss, and leave them to their task.
Be it not so! There is a secret[52] known
To thee, and to none else of living things,
Which may transfer the sceptre of wide Heaven,
The fear of which perplexes the Supreme.
Clothe it in words, and bid it clasp his throne
In intercession; bend thy soul in prayer,
And like a suppliant in some gorgeous fane
Let the will kneel within thy haughty heart;
For benefits and meek submission tame
The fiercest and the mightiest.

Notes

[48] *Back to your towers . . . teeth* Mercury threatens to drive the Furies back to Hades, where flow the rivers Phlegethon and Cocytus ('streams of fire and wail' – 'wail' is a noun).

[49] Geryon, Gorgon, Chimera and Sphinx are all monsters of classical legend.

[50] *Unnatural love and more unnatural hate* Before solving the riddle of the Sphinx, Oedipus was led to an 'Unnatural love' for his mother, and (unwittingly) to kill his father ('more unnatural hate').

[51] *doom* judgement.

[52] *a secret* i.e. that the children of Thetis (a sea-goddess) will be greater than their father, so that if Jupiter unites with her he will be overthrown by his own son.

PROMETHEUS. Evil minds
Change good to their own nature. I gave all
He has, and in return he chains me here
Years, ages, night and day – whether the sun
Split my parched skin, or in the moony night
The crystal-winged snow cling round my hair –
Whilst my beloved race is trampled down
By his thought-executing[53] ministers.
Such is the Tyrant's recompense – 'tis just;
He who is evil can receive no good;
And for a world bestowed, or a friend lost,
He can feel hate, fear, shame – not gratitude.
He but requites me for his own misdeed.
Kindness to such is keen reproach, which breaks
With bitter stings the light sleep of Revenge.
Submission, thou dost know I cannot try;
For what submission but that fatal word,
The death-seal of mankind's captivity –
Like the Sicilian's hair-suspended sword
Which trembles o'er his crown[54] – would he accept;
Or could I yield? Which yet I will not yield.
Let others flatter Crime, where it sits throned
In brief omnipotence; secure are they,
For Justice, when triumphant, will weep down
Pity, not punishment, on her own wrongs,
Too much avenged by those who err.[55] I wait,
Enduring thus the retributive hour
Which since we spake is even nearer now.
But hark, the hell-hounds clamour; fear delay!
Behold – Heaven lours under thy Father's frown!

MERCURY. Oh that we might be spared – I to inflict
And thou to suffer. Once more answer me:
Thou knowest not the period[56] of Jove's power?

PROMETHEUS. I know but this, that it must come.

MERCURY. Alas!
Thou canst not count thy years to come of pain?

PROMETHEUS. They last while Jove must reign – nor more nor less
Do I desire or fear.

MERCURY. Yet pause, and plunge
Into eternity, where recorded time,

Notes

[53] *thought-executing* i.e. acting out one's will as quickly as it is conceived; cf. *King Lear* III ii 4: 'Yon sulph'rous and thought-executing fires'.

[54] *Like the Sicilian's . . . crown* Damocles was a court flatterer exposed by Dionysius I of Syracuse who, to show him the precariousness of monarchy, seated him on a throne beneath a sword suspended by a hair.

[55] *For Justice . . . err* Justice will take pity on those who commit crimes against her, evil-doers having already punished themselves by the misery of being what they are.

[56] *period* end.

Even all that we imagine, age on age,
Seems but a point, and the reluctant mind
Flags wearily in its unending flight,
Till it sink, dizzy, blind, lost, shelterless.
Perchance it has not numbered the slow years
Which thou must spend in torture, unreprieved.

PROMETHEUS. Perchance no thought can count them – yet they pass.

MERCURY. If thou might'st dwell among the Gods the while,
Lapped in voluptuous joy?

PROMETHEUS. I would not quit
This bleak ravine, these unrepentant pains.

MERCURY. Alas! I wonder at, yet pity thee.

PROMETHEUS. Pity the self-despising slaves of Heaven –
Not me, within whose mind sits peace serene
As light in the sun, throned. How vain is talk!
Call up the fiends.

IONE. Oh sister, look! White fire
Has cloven to the roots yon huge snow-loaded cedar;
How fearfully God's thunder howls behind!

MERCURY. I must obey his words and thine, alas;
Most heavily remorse hangs at my heart.[57]

PANTHEA. See where the child of Heaven,[58] with winged feet
Runs down the slanted sunlight of the dawn.

IONE. Dear sister, close thy plumes over thine eyes
Lest thou behold and die; they come – they come
Blackening the birth of day with countless wings,
And hollow underneath, like death.

FIRST FURY. Prometheus!

SECOND FURY. Immortal Titan!

THIRD FURY. Champion of Heaven's slaves!

PROMETHEUS. He whom some dreadful voice invokes is here –
Prometheus, the chained Titan. Horrible forms,
What and who are ye? Never yet there came
Phantasms so foul through monster-teeming Hell
From the all-miscreative[59] brain of Jove.
Whilst I behold such execrable shapes,
Methinks I grow like what I contemplate,
And laugh and stare in loathsome sympathy.

Notes

[57] Shelley is implicitly critical of Mercury. Although he sympathizes with Prometheus, he continues to obey Jupiter. He is like those who detest the tyrants who govern them, but do nothing to bring them down.

[58] *the child of Heaven* Mercury.

[59] *all-miscreative* Jupiter is infinitely capable of creating bad or horrible things – like the Furies. Shelley may be recalling Byron, *Childe Harold's Pilgrimage* iv 1122–3: 'And Circumstance, that unspiritual god / And miscreator'.

FIRST FURY. We are the ministers of pain and fear,
And disappointment, and mistrust, and hate,
And clinging crime; and as lean dogs pursue
Through wood and lake some struck and sobbing fawn,[60]
We track all things that weep and bleed and live,
When the great King betrays them to our will.

PROMETHEUS. Oh many fearful natures in one name,
I know ye; and these lakes and echoes know
The darkness and the clangour of your wings.
But why more hideous than your loathed selves
Gather ye up in legions from the deep?

SECOND FURY. We knew not that; sisters, rejoice, rejoice!

PROMETHEUS. Can aught exult in its deformity?

SECOND FURY. The beauty of delight makes lovers glad,
Gazing on one another; so are we.[61]
As from the rose which the pale priestess kneels
To gather for her festal crown of flowers
The aerial crimson falls, flushing her cheek –
So from our victim's destined agony
The shade which is our form invests us round,
Else are we shapeless as our mother Night.

PROMETHEUS. I laugh your power, and his who sent you here,
To lowest scorn. Pour forth the cup of pain.

FIRST FURY. Thou thinkest we will rend thee bone from bone,
And nerve from nerve, working like fire within?

PROMETHEUS. Pain is my element, as hate is thine;
Ye rend me now – I care not.

SECOND FURY. Dost imagine
We will but laugh into thy lidless[62] eyes?

PROMETHEUS. I weigh not what ye do, but what ye suffer,
Being evil. Cruel was the Power which called
You, or aught else so wretched, into light.

THIRD FURY. Thou think'st we will live through thee, one by one,
Like animal life, and though we can obscure not
The soul which burns within, that we will dwell
Beside it, like a vain loud multitude
Vexing the self-content of wisest men;
That we will be dread thought beneath thy brain,
And foul desire round thine astonished heart,

Notes

[60] *as lean dogs . . . fawn* cf. Wordsworth's 'Hart-Leap Well' and *Twelfth Night* I i 21–2: 'And my desires, like fell and cruel hounds, / E'er since pursue me.'

[61] *so are we* i.e. glad.

[62] *lidless* unclosing.

And blood within thy labyrinthine veins
Crawling like agony.[63]

PROMETHEUS. Why, ye are thus now;
Yet am I king over myself, and rule
The torturing and conflicting throngs within,
As Jove rules you when Hell grows mutinous.

CHORUS OF FURIES.
From the ends of the earth, from the ends of the earth,
Where the night has its grave and the morning its birth,
Come, come, come!
Oh ye who shake hills with the scream of your mirth
When cities sink howling in ruin, and ye
Who with wingless footsteps trample the sea,
And close upon shipwreck and famine's track
Sit chattering with joy on the foodless wreck –
Come, come, come!
Leave the bed, low, cold, and red,
Strewed beneath a nation dead;
Leave the hatred, as in ashes
Fire is left for future burning:
It will burst in bloodier flashes
When ye stir it, soon returning;
Leave the self-contempt implanted
In young spirits, sense-enchanted,
Misery's yet unkindled fuel;
Leave Hell's secrets half unchanted
To the maniac dreamer – cruel
More than ye can be with hate,
Is he with fear.
Come, come, come!
We are steaming up from Hell's wide gate,
And we burden the blasts of the atmosphere,
But vainly we toil till ye come here.

IONE. Sister, I hear the thunder of new wings.[64]

PANTHEA. These solid mountains quiver with the sound
Even as the tremulous air; their shadows make
The space within my plumes more black than night.

FIRST FURY.
Your call was as a winged car
Driven on whirlwinds fast and far;
It rapt[65] us from red gulfs of war;

Notes

[63] *That we will . . . like agony* Evil thoughts and desires will be as intimately present to Prometheus as the blood in his body.

[64] *new wings* a second group of Furies which are to show Prometheus visions of external evils (the first have shown him internal ones).

[65] *rapt* carried.

SECOND FURY.
From wide cities, famine-wasted;

THIRD FURY.
Groans half-heard, and blood untasted;

FOURTH FURY.
Kingly conclaves[66] stern and cold,
Where blood with gold is bought and sold;

FIFTH FURY.
From the furnace, white and hot,
In which –

A FURY.
Speak not, whisper not!
I know all that ye would tell,
But to speak might break the spell[67]
Which must bend the Invincible,
The stern of thought;
He yet defies the deepest power of Hell.

A FURY. Tear the veil![68]

ANOTHER FURY. It is torn!

CHORUS. The pale stars of the morn
Shine on a misery dire to be borne.
Dost thou faint, mighty Titan? We laugh thee to scorn.
Dost thou boast the clear knowledge thou wakenedst for man?
Then was kindled within him a thirst which outran
Those perishing waters; a thirst of fierce fever,
Hope, love, doubt, desire – which consume him forever.
One[69] came forth of gentle worth
Smiling on the sanguine earth;
His words outlived him, like swift poison
Withering up truth, peace, and pity.
Look, where round the wide horizon
Many a million-peopled city
Vomits smoke in the bright air.
Hark that outcry of despair!
'Tis his mild and gentle ghost
Wailing for the faith he kindled.
Look again, the flames almost
To a glow-worm's lamp have dwindled;
The survivors round the embers
Gather in dread.
Joy, joy, joy!

Notes

[66] *Kingly conclaves* secret meetings where important decisions of state are taken.

[67] *to speak might break the spell* To speak might weaken the force of that which is shown.

[68] A deleted stage-direction in the MS reveals that at this point 'The Furies, having mingled in a strange dance, divide, and in the background is seen a plain covered with burning cities.' The events Prometheus is shown are in the past: the Crucifixion, the French Revolution and their consequences.

[69] *One* Jesus Christ.

Past ages crowd on thee,[70] but each one remembers,
And the future is dark, and the present is spread
Like a pillow of thorns for thy slumberless head.

SEMICHORUS I.
Drops of bloody agony flow
From his white and quivering brow.[71]
Grant a little respite now –
See, a disenchanted nation[72]
Springs like day from desolation;
To Truth its state is dedicate,
And Freedom leads it forth, her mate;
A legioned band of linked brothers
Whom Love calls children –

SEMICHORUS II.
'Tis another's:[73]
See how kindred murder kin![74]
'Tis the vintage-time for Death and Sin;
Blood, like new wine, bubbles within,
Till Despair smothers
The struggling world, which slaves and tyrants win.

All the Furies vanish, except one.

IONE. Hark, sister! What a low yet dreadful groan
Quite unsuppressed is tearing up the heart
Of the good Titan, as storms tear the deep,
And beasts hear the sea moan in inland caves.
Darest thou observe how the fiends torture him?

PANTHEA. Alas, I looked forth twice, but will no more.

IONE. What didst thou see?

PANTHEA. A woeful sight; a youth[75]
With patient looks nailed to a crucifix.

IONE. What next?

PANTHEA. The Heaven around, the earth below
Was peopled with thick shapes of human death,
All horrible, and wrought by human hands;
And some appeared the work of human hearts,
For men were slowly killed by frowns and smiles.
And other sights too foul to speak and live
Were wandering by. Let us not tempt worse fear
By looking forth; those groans are grief enough.

Notes

[70] *thee* Prometheus, rather than Christ.

[71] Lines 564–5 describe Prometheus as if he were Christ.

[72] *a disenchanted nation* France during the Revolution. Shelley borrows the phrase from Coleridge, 'France: An Ode' 28.

[73] *'Tis another's* The Revolutionaries are no longer Love's, but children of Hatred.

[74] *See how kindred murder kin!* During the Reign of Terror (July 1793–July 1794), Robespierre and his associates were responsible for the guillotining of many innocent people.

[75] *a youth* Christ.

FURY. Behold an emblem: those who do endure
Deep wrongs for man, and scorn, and chains, but heap
Thousandfold torment on themselves and him.

PROMETHEUS. Remit the anguish of that lighted stare;
Close those wan lips; let that thorn-wounded brow
Stream not with blood – it mingles with thy tears!
Fix, fix those tortured orbs[76] in peace and death,
So thy sick throes shake not that crucifix,
So those pale fingers play not with thy gore.
Oh horrible! Thy name I will not speak –
It hath become a curse. I see, I see
The wise, the mild, the lofty, and the just,
Whom thy slaves hate for being like to thee;[77]
Some hunted by foul lies from their heart's home,
An early-chosen, late-lamented home,
As hooded ounces[78] cling to the driven hind;[79]
Some linked to corpses in unwholesome cells;
Some (hear I not the multitude laugh loud?)
Impaled in lingering fire. And mighty realms
Float by my feet, like sea-uprooted isles,
Whose sons are kneaded down in common blood
By the red light of their own burning homes.

FURY. Blood thou canst see, and fire – and canst hear groans;
Worse things, unheard, unseen, remain behind.

PROMETHEUS. Worse?

FURY. In each human heart terror survives
The ravin[80] it has gorged; the loftiest fear
All that they would disdain to think were true.[81]
Hypocrisy and custom make their minds
The fanes of many a worship, now outworn.
They dare not devise good for man's estate,
And yet they know not that they do not dare.
The good want power, but to weep barren tears;
The powerful goodness want – worse need for them;
The wise want love, and those who love want wisdom;
And all best things are thus confused to ill.
Many are strong and rich, and would be just,
But live among their suffering fellow-men
As if none felt: they know not what they do.[82]

Notes

[76] *tortured orbs* eyes, tormented by the appalling sights they have witnessed.

[77] *Whom thy slaves hate for being like to thee* cf. Shelley's note to *Hellas* 1090–1: 'The sublime human character of Jesus Christ was deformed by an imputed identification with a Power, who tempted, betrayed, and punished the innocent beings who were called into existence by His sole will; and for the period of a thousand years, the spirit of this most just, wise, and benevolent of men has been propitiated with myriads of hecatombs of those who approached the nearest to His innocence and wisdom.'

[78] *hooded ounces* hunting leopards, hooded until released at their prey.

[79] *hind* female deer.

[80] *ravin* prey.

[81] *In each human heart . . . true* 'Superstitious fear lingers in every man's mind after he has stopped believing in the cause of it.'

[82] Lines 618–31 comprise the climax of the temptation. The temptation is to despair, because it seems impossible to improve things. Prometheus silences the Fury by saying that he would prefer any amount of suffering to acquiescence.

PROMETHEUS. Thy words are like a cloud of winged snakes;
And yet I pity those they torture not.[83]

FURY. Thou pitiest them? I speak no more. (*vanishes*)

PROMETHEUS. Ah woe!
Ah woe! Alas, pain, pain ever, forever!
I close my tearless eyes, but see more clear
Thy works within my woe-illumed mind,
Thou subtle[84] Tyrant! Peace is in the grave.
The grave hides all things beautiful and good:
I am a God and cannot find it there –
Nor would I seek it. For, though dread revenge,
This is defeat, fierce King, not victory.
The sights with which thou torturest gird my soul
With new endurance, till the hour arrives
When they shall be no types of things which are.

PANTHEA. Alas! What sawest thou more?

PROMETHEUS. There are two woes:
To speak, and to behold; thou spare me one.
Names are there, nature's sacred watchwords: they
Were borne aloft in bright emblazonry.
The nations thronged around, and cried aloud
As with one voice, 'Truth, Liberty, and Love!'[85]
Suddenly fierce confusion fell from Heaven
Among them – there was strife, deceit, and fear;
Tyrants rushed in, and did divide the spoil.
This was the shadow[86] of the truth I saw.

THE EARTH. I felt thy torture, son, with such mixed joy
As pain and virtue give. To cheer thy state
I bid ascend[87] those subtle and fair spirits
Whose homes are the dim caves of human thought,
And who inhabit, as birds wing the wind,
Its world-surrounding ether; they behold
Beyond that twilight realm, as in a glass,[88]
The future: may they speak comfort to thee!

PANTHEA. Look, sister, where a troop of spirits gather,
Like flocks of clouds in spring's delightful weather,
Thronging in the blue air!

IONE. And see, more come,
Like fountain-vapours when the winds are dumb,

Notes

they know not what they do an allusion to Christ on the cross, Luke 23: 34: 'Father, forgive them; for they know not what they do.'

[83] *And yet I pity those they torture not* a transcendental act of pity; Prometheus pities those who do not recognize the miseries of the world for what they are.

[84] *subtle* cunning.

[85] *Truth, Liberty, and Love!* A reference to the motto of the French Revolution: *liberté, egalité, fraternité*.

[86] *shadow* image.

[87] *ascend* The spirits, which are like angels, ascend from within, rather than descend from without.

[88] *glass* a fortune-teller's glass ball.

That climb up the ravine in scattered lines.
And hark – is it the music of the pines?
Is it the lake? Is it the waterfall?

PANTHEA. 'Tis something sadder, sweeter far than all.

CHORUS OF SPIRITS.

From unremembered ages we
Gentle guides and guardians be
Of Heaven-oppressed mortality;
And we breathe, and sicken not,
The atmosphere of human thought:
Be it dim, and dank, and grey,
Like a storm-extinguished day
Travelled o'er by dying gleams;
  Be it bright as all between
Cloudless skies and windless streams,
  Silent, liquid, and serene;
As the birds within the wind,
  As the fish within the wave,
As the thoughts of man's own mind
  Float through all above the grave,
We make there our liquid lair,
Voyaging cloudlike and unpent[89]
Through the boundless element:
Thence we bear the prophecy
Which begins and ends in thee.

IONE. More yet come, one by one: the air around them
Looks radiant as the air around a star.

FIRST SPIRIT.

On a battle-trumpet's blast
I fled hither, fast, fast, fast,
Mid the darkness upward cast.
From the dust of creeds outworn,[90]
From the tyrant's banner torn,
Gathering round me, onward borne,
There was mingled many a cry –
'Freedom! Hope! Death! Victory!'
Till they faded through the sky;
And one sound above, around,
One sound beneath, around, above,
Was moving – 'twas the soul of love;
'Twas the hope, the prophecy
Which begins and ends in thee.

Notes

89 *unpent* free, unconfined.

90 *creeds outworn* Wordsworth, 'The world is too much with us' 10.

SECOND SPIRIT.

A rainbow's arch stood on the sea,
Which rocked beneath, immovably;
And the triumphant storm did flee,
Like a conqueror swift and proud,
Between, with many a captive cloud,
A shapeless, dark and rapid crowd,
Each by lightning riven in half.
I heard the thunder hoarsely laugh.
Mighty fleets were strewn like chaff
And spread beneath a hell of death[91]
O'er the white waters. I alit
On a great ship lightning-split,
And speeded hither on the sigh
Of one who gave an enemy
His plank, then plunged aside to die.

THIRD SPIRIT.

I sat beside a sage's bed,
And the lamp was burning red
Near the book where he had fed,[92]
When a dream with plumes of flame
To his pillow hovering came,
And I knew it was the same
Which had kindled long ago
Pity, eloquence, and woe;
And the world awhile below
Wore the shade its lustre made.
It has borne me here as fleet
As Desire's lightning feet:
I must ride it back ere morrow,
Or the sage will wake in sorrow.

FOURTH SPIRIT.

On a poet's lips I slept
Dreaming like a love-adept[93]
In the sound his breathing kept;
Nor seeks nor finds he mortal blisses,
But feeds on the aerial kisses
Of shapes that haunt thought's wildernesses.
He will watch from dawn to gloom
The lake-reflected sun illume
The yellow bees in the ivy-bloom,
Nor heed nor see what things they be;
But from these create he can
Forms more real than living man,

Notes

[91] *Mighty fleets . . . death* Spread beneath the wrecked fleets was a hell of death.

[92] *where he had fed* i.e. his mind.

[93] *love-adept* one skilled in love.

Nurslings of immortality!
One of these awakened me,
And I sped to succour thee.

IONE. Behold'st thou not two shapes from the east and west
Come, as two doves to one beloved nest,
Twin nurslings of the all-sustaining air
On swift still wings glide down the atmosphere?
And hark, their sweet, sad voices! 'Tis despair
Mingled with love, and then dissolved in sound.

PANTHEA. Canst thou speak, sister? All my words are drowned.

IONE. Their beauty gives me voice. See how they float
On their sustaining wings of skyey grain,[94]
Orange and azure deepening into gold;
Their soft smiles light the air like a star's fire.

CHORUS OF SPIRITS. Hast thou beheld the form of Love?

FIFTH SPIRIT. As over wide dominions
I sped, like some swift cloud that wings the wide air's wildernesses,
That planet-crested shape[95] swept by on lightning-braided pinions,[96]
Scattering the liquid joy of life[97] from his ambrosial[98] tresses:
His footsteps paved the world with light, but as I passed 'twas fading,
And hollow Ruin yawned behind. Great sages bound in madness,
And headless patriots and pale youths who perished, unupbraiding,
Gleamed in the night I wandered o'er; till thou, oh King of sadness,
Turned by thy smile the worst I saw to recollected gladness.

SIXTH SPIRIT. Ah sister! Desolation is a delicate thing:
It walks not on the earth, it floats not on the air,
But treads with lulling footstep, and fans with silent wing
The tender hopes which in their hearts the best and gentlest bear,
Who, soothed to false repose by the fanning plumes above,
And the music-stirring motion of its soft and busy feet,
Dream visions of aerial joy, and call the monster, Love,
And wake, and find the shadow Pain, as he whom now we greet.

CHORUS.
Though Ruin now Love's shadow be,
Following him destroyingly
  On Death's white and winged steed,[99]
Which the fleetest cannot flee –
  Trampling down both flower and weed,
Man and beast, and foul and fair,

Notes

[94] *skyey grain* the colour of the sky.

[95] *planet-crested shape* Love wears the crest of Venus.

[96] *lightning-braided pinions* electric wings.

[97] *the liquid joy of life* love; for Shelley, love is a liquid energy (just as electricity, heat and light were believed to be forms of liquid energy in his day).

[98] *ambrosial* divine, celestial.

[99] *On Death's white and winged steed* Revelation 6: 8: 'And I looked, and behold a pale horse: and his name that sat on him was Death, and Hell followed with him.'

Like a tempest through the air;
Thou shalt quell this horseman grim,
Woundless though in heart or limb.

PROMETHEUS. Spirits, how know ye this shall be?

CHORUS.
In the atmosphere we breathe –
As buds grow red when snowstorms flee
From spring gathering up beneath,
Whose mild winds shake the elder brake,[100]
And the wandering herdsmen know
That the whitethorn[101] soon will blow –
Wisdom, Justice, Love, and Peace,
When they struggle to increase,
Are to us as soft winds be
To shepherd-boys – the prophecy
Which begins and ends in thee.

IONE. Where are the spirits fled?

PANTHEA. Only a sense
Remains of them, like the omnipotence
Of music, when the inspired voice and lute
Languish, ere yet the responses are mute
Which, through the deep and labyrinthine soul,
Like echoes through long caverns, wind and roll.

PROMETHEUS. How fair these air-born[102] shapes! And yet I feel
Most vain all hope but love – and thou art far,
Asia, who, when my being overflowed,
Wert like a golden chalice to bright wine
Which else had sunk into the thirsty dust.
All things are still. Alas, how heavily
This quiet morning weighs upon my heart.
Though I should dream, I could even sleep with grief
If slumber were denied not. I would fain
Be what it is my destiny to be,
The saviour and the strength of suffering man,
Or sink into the original gulf of things.
There is no agony and no solace left;
Earth can console, Heaven can torment no more.

PANTHEA. Hast thou forgotten one who watches thee
The cold dark night, and never sleeps but when
The shadow of thy spirit falls on her?

PROMETHEUS. I said all hope was vain but love; thou lovest.

PANTHEA. Deeply in truth; but the eastern star looks white,
And Asia waits in that far Indian vale,

Notes

[100] *brake* braken.

[101] *whitethorn* hawthorn; compare Milton, *Lycidas* 48.

[102] *air-born* born in air; imaginary.

The scene of her sad exile – rugged once,
And desolate and frozen, like this ravine,
But now invested with fair flowers and herbs,
And haunted by sweet airs and sounds, which flow
Among the woods and waters, from the ether[103]
Of her transforming presence, which would fade
If it were mingled not with thine. Farewell!

ACT II, SCENE I

Morning. A lovely vale in the Indian Caucasus. Asia[1] alone.

ASIA. From all the blasts of Heaven thou hast descended –
Yes, like a spirit, like a thought which makes
Unwonted tears throng to the horny eyes,[2]
And beatings haunt the desolated heart
Which should have learnt repose; thou hast descended
Cradled in tempests; thou dost wake, oh Spring,
Oh child of many winds! As suddenly
Thou comest as the memory of a dream,
Which now is sad because it hath been sweet;
Like genius, or like joy which riseth up
As from the earth, clothing with golden clouds
The desert of our life.
This is the season, this the day, the hour;
At sunrise thou shouldst come, sweet sister mine,
Too long desired, too long delaying, come!
How like death-worms the wingless moments crawl!
The point of one white star[3] is quivering still
Deep in the orange light of widening morn
Beyond the purple mountains; through a chasm
Of wind-divided mist the darker lake
Reflects it: now it wanes – it gleams again
As the waves fade, and as the burning threads
Of woven cloud unravel in pale air.
'Tis lost! And through yon peaks of cloudlike snow
The roseate sunlight quivers – hear I not
The Aeolian music of her[4] sea-green plumes
Winnowing the crimson dawn? (*Panthea enters*)
I feel, I see
Those eyes which burn through smiles that fade in tears,
Like stars half-quenched in mists of silver dew.

Notes

[103] *ether* a more refined substance than air, believed in the 19th century to be the medium which transmitted heat, light and electricity.

ACT II, SCENE I

[1] *Asia* daughter of Oceanus and bride of Prometheus.

[2] *horny eyes* the eyes have the appearance of horn.

[3] *one white star* Venus, the morning star.

[4] *her* i.e. Panthea's.

Beloved and most beautiful, who wearest
The shadow of that soul by which I live,
How late thou art! The sphered sun had climbed
The sea, my heart was sick with hope, before
The printless air felt thy belated plumes.

PANTHEA. Pardon, great sister; but my wings were faint
With the delight of a remembered dream,
As are the noontide plumes of summer winds
Satiate with sweet flowers. I was wont to sleep
Peacefully, and awake refreshed and calm
Before the sacred Titan's fall and thy
Unhappy love had made, through use and pity,
Both love and woe familiar to my heart
As they had grown to thine. Erewhile[5] I slept
Under the glaucous[6] caverns of old Ocean
Within dim bowers of green and purple moss,
Our young Ione's soft and milky arms
Locked then, as now, behind my dark moist hair,
While my shut eyes and cheek were pressed within
The folded depth of her life-breathing bosom –
But not as now, since I am made the wind
Which fails beneath the music that I bear
Of thy most wordless converse; since dissolved
Into the sense with which love talks, my rest
Was troubled and yet sweet, my waking hours
Too full of care and pain.

ASIA. Lift up thine eyes
And let me read thy dream.

PANTHEA. As I have said,
With our sea-sister at his feet I slept.[7]
The mountain mists, condensing at our voice
Under the moon, had spread their snowy flakes,
From the keen ice shielding our linked sleep.
Then two dreams came.[8] One I remember not.
But in the other his pale, wound-worn limbs
Fell from Prometheus, and the azure night
Grew radiant with the glory of that form
Which lives unchanged within, and his voice fell
Like music which makes giddy the dim brain,
Faint with intoxication of keen joy:
'Sister of her whose footsteps pave the world
With loveliness – more fair than aught but her,
Whose shadow thou art – lift thine eyes on me!'

Notes

[5] *Erewhile* before Prometheus' fall.

[6] *glaucous* pale green.

[7] *I slept* In Act I, we saw Panthea leaving Prometheus after seeing his ordeal and sympathizing with it. Now we hear of her sleep and dreams before departing for Asia.

[8] The relation of the dreams is the main action of the scene.

I lifted them: the overpowering light
Of that immortal shape was shadowed o'er
By love, which, from his soft and flowing limbs,
And passion-parted lips, and keen, faint eyes,
Steamed forth like vaporous fire – an atmosphere
Which wrapped me in its all-dissolving power
As the warm ether of the morning sun
Wraps ere it drinks some cloud of wandering dew.
I saw not, heard not, moved not, only felt
His presence flow and mingle through my blood
Till it became his life, and his grew mine,
And I was thus absorbed until it passed,
And like the vapours when the sun sinks down,
Gathering again in drops upon the pines,
And tremulous as they, in the deep night
My being was condensed; and as the rays
Of thought were slowly gathered, I could hear
His voice, whose accents lingered ere they died
Like footsteps of far melody. Thy name
Among the many sounds, alone I heard
Of what might be articulate; though still
I listened through the night when sound was none.
Ione wakened then, and said to me,
'Canst thou divine what troubles me tonight?
I always knew what I desired before,
Nor ever found delight to wish in vain.
But now I cannot tell thee what I seek,
I know not – something sweet, since it is sweet
Even to desire. It is thy sport, false sister;
Thou hast discovered some enchantment old,
Whose spells have stolen my spirit as I slept
And mingled it with thine[9] – for when just now
We kissed, I felt within thy parted lips
The sweet air that sustained me, and the warmth
Of the life-blood, for loss of which I faint,
Quivered between our intertwining arms.'
I answered not, for the eastern star grew pale,
But fled to thee.

ASIA. Thou speakest, but thy words
Are as the air; I feel them not. Oh lift
Thine eyes, that I may read his written soul!

PANTHEA. I lift them, though they droop beneath the load
Of that they would express: what canst thou see
But thine own fairest shadow imaged there?

Notes

[9] *Whose spells . . . thine* Both Ione and Panthea have experienced a loss of their sense of separate identity, in favour of a spiritual commingling.

ASIA. Thine eyes are like the deep, blue, boundless Heaven
Contracted to two circles underneath
Their long, fine lashes; dark, far, measureless,
Orb within orb, and line through line inwoven.

PANTHEA. Why lookest thou as if a spirit passed?

ASIA. There is a change; beyond their inmost depth
I see a shade, a shape – 'tis he, arrayed
In the soft light of his own smiles, which spread
Like radiance from the cloud-surrounded moon.
Prometheus, it is thou – depart not yet!
Say not those smiles that we shall meet again
Within that bright pavilion which their beams
Shall build o'er the waste world? The dream is told.
What shape is that between us?[10] Its rude hair
Roughens the wind that lifts it, its regard
Is wild and quick, yet 'tis a thing of air –
For through its grey robe gleams the golden dew
Whose stars the noon has quenched not.

DREAM. Follow, follow!

PANTHEA. It is mine other dream.

ASIA. It disappears.

PANTHEA. It passes now into my mind. Methought
As we sat here, the flower-enfolding buds
Burst[11] on yon lightning-blasted almond tree,
When swift from the white Scythian wilderness
A wind swept forth, wrinkling the earth with frost.
I looked, and all the blossoms were blown down;[12]
But on each leaf was stamped – as the blue-bells
Of Hyacinth tell Apollo's written grief[13] –
'Oh follow, follow!'

ASIA. As you speak, your words
Fill, pause by pause, my own forgotten sleep
With shapes. Methought among these lawns together
We wandered, underneath the young grey dawn,
And multitudes of dense white fleecy clouds
Were wandering in thick flocks along the mountains,
Shepherded by the slow, unwilling wind;
And the white dew on the new-bladed grass,

Notes

10 *What shape is that between us?* It is the second dream.

11 *Burst* blossomed.

12 The almond tree blossoms early, in anticipation of the spring. Panthea and Asia must not be discouraged by the fall of the blossoms, but must follow the dream.

13 *as the blue-bells . . . grief* After Hyacinthus was killed by Zephyrus, Apollo changed his blood into a flower and wrote his lament, 'Ai', on the petals.

Just piercing the dark earth, hung silently.
And there was more which I remember not,
But on the shadows of the morning clouds,
Athwart the purple mountain slope, was written
'Follow, oh follow!' as they vanished by;
And on each herb from which heaven's dew had fallen
The like was stamped, as with a withering fire.
A wind arose among the pines; it shook
The clinging music from their boughs, and then
Low, sweet, faint sounds like the farewell of ghosts,
Were heard: 'Oh follow, follow, follow me!'
And then I said, 'Panthea, look on me.'
But in the depth of those beloved eyes
Still I saw, 'Follow, follow!'

ECHO. Follow, follow!

PANTHEA. The crags, this clear spring morning, mock our voices
As they were spirit-tongued.

ASIA. It is some being
Around the crags. What fine clear sounds, oh list!

ECHOES (*unseen*)

Echoes we; listen!
 We cannot stay:
As dew-stars glisten
 Then fade away,
Child of Ocean![14]

ASIA. Hark! Spirits speak! The liquid responses
Of their aerial tongues yet sound.

PANTHEA. I hear.

ECHOES.

Oh follow, follow,
 As our voice recedeth
Through the caverns hollow
 Where the forest spreadeth; (*more distant*)
Oh follow, follow,
Through the caverns hollow;
As the song floats, thou pursue,
Where the wild bee never flew,
Through the noontide darkness deep,
By the odour-breathing sleep
Of faint night-flowers, and the waves
At the fountain-lighted caves,
While our music, wild and sweet,
Mocks thy gently-falling feet,
 Child of Ocean!

Notes

[14] *Child of Ocean* Asia, Panthea and Ione are daughters of Ocean.

ASIA. Shall we pursue the sound? It grows more faint
And distant.

PANTHEA. List, the strain floats nearer now.

ECHOES.

In the world unknown
Sleeps a voice unspoken;
By thy step alone
Can its rest be broken,
Child of Ocean!

ASIA. How the notes sink upon the ebbing wind!

ECHOES.

Oh follow, follow,
Through the caverns hollow;
As the song floats thou pursue,
By the woodland noontide dew,
By the forest, lakes, and fountains,
Through the many-folded mountains,
To the rents, and gulfs, and chasms,
Where the Earth reposed from spasms,
On the day when he and thou
Parted, to commingle now,
Child of Ocean!

ASIA. Come, sweet Panthea, link thy hand in mine,
And follow ere the voices fade away.

Act II, Scene II

A forest, intermingled with rocks and caverns. Asia and Panthea pass into it. Two young fauns[1] *are sitting on a rock, listening.*

SEMICHORUS I OF SPIRITS.

The path through which that lovely twain[2]
Have passed, by cedar, pine, and yew,
And each dark tree that ever grew,
Is curtained out from Heaven's wide blue;
Nor sun, nor moon, nor wind, nor rain,
Can pierce its interwoven bowers;
Nor aught, save when some cloud of dew,
Drifted along the earth-creeping breeze
Between the trunks of the hoar trees,
Hangs each a pearl in the pale flowers[3]
Of the green laurel, blown anew,
And bends, and then fades silently,

Notes

[1] *fauns* minor Roman deities, usually depicted as men with the ears, horns, tail and feet of goats.

[2] *that lovely twain* Asia and Panthea.

[3] *Hangs each a pearl in the pale flowers* hangs a pearl in each pale flower.

One frail and fair anemone;
Or when some star of many a one
That climbs and wanders through steep night,
Has found the cleft through which alone
Beams fall from high those depths upon,
Ere it is borne away, away,
By the swift Heavens that cannot stay –
It[4] scatters drops of golden light,
Like lines of rain that ne'er unite;
And the gloom divine is all around,
And underneath is the mossy ground.

SEMICHORUS II.

There the voluptuous nightingales
Are awake through all the broad noonday.
When one with bliss or sadness fails
(And through the windless ivy-boughs,
Sick with sweet love, droops dying away
On its mate's music-panting bosom),
Another from the swinging blossom,
Watching to catch the languid close
Of the last strain, then lifts on high
The wings of the weak melody,
Till some new strain of feeling bear
The song, and all the woods are mute;
When there is heard through the dim air
The rush of wings, and rising there
Like many a lake-surrounded flute,
Sounds overflow the listener's brain
So sweet that joy is almost pain.

SEMICHORUS I.

There those enchanted eddies play
Of echoes, music-tongued, which draw,
By Demogorgon's mighty law,
With melting rapture or deep awe,
All spirits on that secret way,
As inland boats are driven to ocean
Down streams made strong with mountain-thaw;
And first there comes a gentle sound
To those in talk or slumber bound,
And wakes the destined; soft emotion
Attracts, impels them. Those who saw
Say from the breathing earth behind
There steams a plume-uplifting wind
Which drives them on their path, while they
Believe their own swift wings and feet
The sweet desires within obey;

Notes

[4] *It* the star of line 14.

And so they float upon their way
Until, still sweet, but loud and strong,
The storm of sound is driven along,
  Sucked up and hurrying – as they fleet
  Behind, its gathering billows meet
And to the fatal mountain bear[5]
Like clouds amid the yielding air.

FIRST FAUN. Canst thou imagine where those spirits live
Which make such delicate music in the woods?
We haunt within the least frequented caves
And closest coverts, and we know these wilds,
Yet never meet them, though we hear them oft:
Where may they hide themselves?

SECOND FAUN. 'Tis hard to tell.
I have heard those more skilled in spirits[6] say,
The bubbles, which the enchantment of the sun
Sucks from the pale faint water-flowers that pave
The oozy bottom of clear lakes and pools,
Are the pavilions where such dwell and float
Under the green and golden atmosphere
Which noontide kindles through the woven leaves;
And when these burst, and the thin fiery air,
The which they breathed within those lucent[7] domes,
Ascends to flow like meteors through the night,
They ride on it, and rein their headlong speed,
And bow their burning crests, and glide in fire
Under the waters of the earth again.[8]

FIRST FAUN. If such live thus, have others other lives,
Under pink blossoms or within the bells
Of meadow flowers, or folded violets deep,
Or on their dying odours, when they die,
Or in the sunlight of the sphered dew?

SECOND FAUN. Aye, many more which we may well divine.
But should we stay to speak, noontide would come,
And thwart[9] Silenus find his goats undrawn,[10]
And grudge to sing those wise and lovely songs
Of fate, and chance, and God, and Chaos old,
And love, and the chained Titan's woeful doom,
And how he shall be loosed, and make the earth
One brotherhood: delightful strains which cheer
Our solitary twilights, and which charm
To silence the unenvying nightingales.

Notes

[5] The 'destined' spirits (Asia and Panthea) are borne by the gathering 'storm of sound' to the 'fatal' (i.e. fated, destined) mountain of Demogorgon.

[6] *those more skilled in spirits* scientists.

[7] *lucent* shining.

[8] *I have heard those . . . again* In Shelley's day it was believed that hydrogen was released by pond-plants in hot weather, and that it ascended to the upper atmosphere, where it became charged with electricity, ignited, and appeared as meteors or falling stars. Lines 81–2 describe the return of atmospheric electricity to the earth.

[9] *thwart* obstinate, difficult.

[10] *undrawn* unmilked; Silenus was a demigod and attendant of Bacchus.

Act II, Scene III

A pinnacle of rock among mountains. Asia and Panthea.

PANTHEA. Hither the sound has borne us – to the realm
Of Demogorgon, and the mighty portal,[1]
Like a volcano's meteor-breathing[2] chasm,
Whence the oracular vapour[3] is hurled up
Which lonely men drink wandering in their youth,
And call truth, virtue, love, genius, or joy;
That maddening wine of life, whose dregs they drain
To deep intoxication, and uplift,
Like maenads[4] who cry loud, 'Evoe! Evoe!' –
The voice which is contagion to the world.
ASIA. Fit throne for such a Power – magnificent!
How glorious art thou, Earth! And if thou be
The shadow of some spirit lovelier still,[5]
Though evil stain its work, and it should be
Like its creation, weak yet beautiful,
I could fall down and worship that and thee.
Even now my heart adoreth – wonderful!
Look, sister, ere the vapour dim thy brain:
Beneath is a wide plain of billowy mist,
As a lake, paving in the morning sky,
With azure waves which burst in silver light,
Some Indian vale. Behold it, rolling on
Under the curdling winds, and islanding
The peak whereon we stand; midway, around,
Encinctured[6] by the dark and blooming forests,
Dim twilight-lawns, and stream-illumed caves,
And wind-enchanted shapes of wandering mist;
And far on high the keen sky-cleaving mountains
From icy spires of sunlike radiance fling
The dawn, as lifted Ocean's dazzling spray,
From some Atlantic islet scattered up,
Spangles the wind with lamp-like water-drops.
The vale is girdled with their walls; a howl
Of cataracts from their thaw-cloven ravines
Satiates the listening wind, continuous, vast,
Awful as silence. Hark, the rushing snow!
The sun-awakened avalanche! whose mass,
Thrice sifted by the storm, had gathered there
Flake after flake, in Heaven-defying minds

Notes

Act II, Scene III

[1] *portal* gateway.

[2] *meteor-breathing* Meteors were believed to be exhalations from the earth.

[3] *the oracular vapour* Anyone inhaling the vapour of Demogorgon's volcano-like residence is likely to be inspired with the power of prophecy.

[4] *maenads* drunken female worshippers of Bacchus.

[5] *And if thou be . . . still* A similar thought occurs in *Paradise Lost* v 574–6: 'though what if earth / Be but the shadow of heaven, and things therein / Each to other like, more than on earth is thought?'

[6] *Encinctured* surrounded.

As thought by thought is piled, till some great truth
Is loosened, and the nations echo round,
Shaken to their roots, as do the mountains now.

PANTHEA. Look how the gusty sea of mist is breaking
In crimson foam, even at our feet! It rises
As Ocean at the enchantment of the moon
Round foodless men wrecked on some oozy isle.

ASIA. The fragments of the cloud are scattered up;
The wind that lifts them disentwines my hair;
Its billows now sweep o'er mine eyes; my brain
Grows dizzy; seest those shapes within the mist?

PANTHEA. A countenance with beckoning smiles: there burns
An azure fire within its golden locks!
Another and another – hark, they speak!

SONG OF SPIRITS.

To the deep, to the deep,
Down, down!
Through the shade of sleep,
Through the cloudy strife
Of Death and of Life;
Through the veil and the bar[7]
Of things which seem and are,
Even to the steps of the remotest throne,
Down, down!

While the sound whirls around,
Down, down!
As the fawn draws the hound,
As the lightning the vapour,
As a weak moth the taper;
Death, despair; love, sorrow;
Time both; today, tomorrow;
As steel obeys the spirit of the stone,[8]
Down, down!

Through the grey, void abysm,
Down, down!
Where the air is no prism,[9]
And the moon and stars are not,
And the cavern-crags wear not
The radiance of Heaven,
Nor the gloom to Earth given;
Where there is One pervading, One alone,
Down, down!

Notes

[7] *bar* barrier. Asia and Panthea are passing through the barrier dividing earthly appearance from the higher, transcendental reality.

[8] *the stone* i.e. a magnet.

[9] *Where the air is no prism* Shelley believed that white light in its purest form was that of heaven, and that its breaking down into different colours was characteristic of the fallen world.

In the depth of the deep,
  Down, down!
Like veiled lightning asleep,
Like that spark nursed in embers,
The last look Love remembers,
Like a diamond which shines
On the dark wealth of mines,[10]
A spell is treasured but for thee alone.
  Down, down!

We have bound thee, we guide thee
  Down, down![11]
With the bright form beside thee;
Resist not the weakness;
Such strength is in meekness,
That the Eternal, the Immortal,
Must unloose through life's portal
The snake-like Doom coiled underneath his throne
  By that alone.

Act II, Scene IV

The Cave of Demogorgon. Asia and Panthea.

PANTHEA. What veiled form sits on that ebon throne?

ASIA. The veil has fallen.

PANTHEA. I see a mighty darkness
Filling the seat of power, and rays of gloom
Dart round, as light from the meridian sun,[1]
Ungazed upon and shapeless; neither limb,
Nor form, nor outline[2] – yet we feel it is
A living spirit.

DEMOGORGON. Ask what thou wouldst know.

ASIA. What canst thou tell?

DEMOGORGON. All things thou dar'st demand.

ASIA. Who made the living world?

DEMOGORGON. God.

ASIA. Who made all
That it contains – thought, passion, reason, will, Imagination?

Notes

[10] *Like a diamond . . . mines* It was believed that diamonds glowed in the dark.

[11] *We have bound thee . . . down* Asia and Panthea have been bound, and are being led by the spirits. Asia has to submit so that Demogorgon (the Eternal) can permit the destined downfall of Jupiter.

Act II, Scene IV

[1] *the meridian sun* the noonday sun.

[2] *neither limb . . . outline* cf. Milton's description of Death, *Paradise Lost* ii 668–9.

DEMOGORGON. God. Almighty God.

ASIA. Who made that sense which, when the winds of spring
In rarest visitation, or the voice
Of one beloved heard in youth alone,
Fills the faint eyes with falling tears which dim
The radiant looks of unbewailing flowers,
And leaves this peopled earth a solitude
When it returns no more?

DEMOGORGON. Merciful God.

ASIA. And who made terror, madness, crime, remorse,
Which from the links of the great chain of things,
To every thought within the mind of man
Sway and drag heavily, and each one reels
Under the load towards the pit of death;[3]
Abandoned hope, and love that turns to hate;
And self-contempt, bitterer to drink than blood;
Pain, whose unheeded and familiar speech
Is howling, and keen shrieks, day after day;
And Hell, or the sharp fear of Hell?

DEMOGORGON. He reigns.[4]

ASIA. Utter his name. A world pining in pain
Asks but his name; curses shall drag him down.

DEMOGORGON. He reigns.

ASIA. I feel, I know it – who?

DEMOGORGON. He reigns.

ASIA. Who reigns? There was the Heaven and Earth[5] at first,
And Light and Love; then Saturn, from whose throne
Time fell, an envious shadow;[6] such the state
Of the earth's primal spirits beneath his sway,
As the calm joy of flowers and living leaves
Before the wind or sun has withered them,
And semivital worms; but he[7] refused
The birthright of their being – knowledge, power,
The skill which wields the elements, the thought

Notes

[3] *Which from the links . . . death* Shelley refers to the doctrine of the great chain of being by which England justified its monarchy and its rigidly hierarchical social system for centuries. As Peter Butter suggests, the image may be suggested by the sight of convicts chained together in Rome, which Shelley described to Peacock on 6 April 1819: 'In the square of St Peter's there are about 300 fettered criminals at work, hoeing out the weeds that grow between the stones of the pavement. Their legs are heavily ironed, and some are chained two by two. They sit in long rows hoeing out the weeds. . . . Near them sit or saunter groups of soldiers armed with loaded muskets' (Jones ii 93).

[4] *He reigns* a statement that fails to identify the force that has taken over a world created by a benevolent deity. It could be Jupiter, or 'Almighty God', or some other force. Matthews suggests that Asia is interrogating herself, and the answers therefore reveal only what she already knows.

[5] *Heaven and Earth* Ouranos and Gaia, parents of Saturn and the other giants.

[6] *Saturn . . . envious shadow* The Greek name for Saturn was Kronos (time), which was therefore Saturn's 'shadow'.

[7] *he* Saturn.

Which pierces this dim universe like light,
Self-empire and the majesty of love –
For thirst of which they fainted. Then Prometheus
Gave wisdom, which is strength, to Jupiter,
And with this law alone, 'Let man be free',
Clothed him with the dominion of wide Heaven.
To know nor faith, nor love, nor law; to be
Omnipotent but friendless is to reign –
And Jove now reigned; for on the race of man
First famine, and then toil, and then disease,
Strife, wounds, and ghastly death unseen before,
Fell; and the unseasonable seasons[8] drove,
With alternating shafts of frost and fire,
Their shelterless, pale tribes to mountain caves;
And in their desert[9] hearts fierce wants[10] he sent,
And mad disquietudes, and shadows idle
Of unreal good, which levied[11] mutual war,
So ruining the lair wherein they raged.
Prometheus saw, and waked the legioned hopes
Which sleep within folded Elysian[12] flowers,
Nepenthe, moly, amaranth,[13] fadeless blooms,
That they might hide with thin and rainbow wings
The shape of Death; and Love he sent to bind
The disunited tendrils of that vine
Which bears the wine of life, the human heart;
And he tamed fire which, like some beast of chase
Most terrible, but lovely, played beneath
The frown of man; and tortured to his will
Iron and gold, the slaves and signs of power,
And gems and poisons, and all subtlest forms
Hidden beneath the mountains and the waves.
He gave man speech, and speech created thought,
Which is the measure of the universe;
And Science struck the thrones of Earth and Heaven,
Which shook but fell not; and the harmonious mind
Poured itself forth in all-prophetic song,
And music lifted up the listening spirit
Until it walked, exempt from mortal care,
Godlike, o'er the clear billows of sweet sound;
And human hands first mimicked and then mocked,[14]
With moulded limbs more lovely than its own,
The human form, till marble grew divine,
And mothers, gazing, drank the love men see

Notes

[8] *unseasonable seasons* In the golden age perpetual spring reigned.

[9] *desert* abandoned, desolate.

[10] *fierce wants* desperate needs.

[11] *levied* undertook.

[12] *Elysian* heavenly; from the Elysian fields, where Greek heroes were believed to spend an afterlife in revelry.

[13] Nepenthe is a grief-banishing drug; moly is the magic herb given by Hermes to Odysseus to counteract the poison of Circe; amaranth is an unfading flower.

[14] *mimicked . . . mocked* imitated . . . created forms more beautiful than the merely natural (i.e. idealized).

Reflected in their race,[15] behold, and perish.
He told the hidden power of herbs and springs,
And Disease drank and slept. Death grew like sleep.
He taught the implicated[16] orbits woven
Of the wide-wandering stars,[17] and how the sun
Changes his lair,[18] and by what secret spell
The pale moon is transformed, when her broad eye
Gazes not on the interlunar[19] sea.
He taught to rule, as life directs the limbs,
The tempest-winged chariots of the Ocean,[20]
And the Celt knew the Indian. Cities then
Were built, and through their snow-like columns flowed
The warm winds, and the azure ether shone,
And the blue sea and shadowy hills were seen.
Such the alleviations of his state
Prometheus gave to man, for which he hangs
Withering in destined pain; but who rains down
Evil, the immedicable plague, which, while
Man looks on his creation like a God
And sees that it is glorious, drives him on,
The wreck of his own will, the scorn of earth,
The outcast, the abandoned, the alone?
Not Jove; while yet his frown shook Heaven – aye, when
His adversary from adamantine chains
Cursed him – he trembled like a slave. Declare
Who is his master? Is he too a slave?

DEMOGORGON. All spirits are enslaved which serve things evil;
Thou knowest if Jupiter be such or no.

ASIA. Whom calledst thou God?

DEMOGORGON. I spoke but as ye speak,
For Jove is the supreme of living things.

ASIA. Who is the master of the slave?

DEMOGORGON. If the abysm
Could vomit forth its secrets – but a voice
Is wanting, the deep truth is imageless;[21]
For what would it avail to bid thee gaze
On the revolving world? What to bid speak
Fate, Time, Occasion, Chance, and Change? To these
All things are subject but eternal Love.

Notes

[15] *And mothers . . . race* Pregnant women, gazing at the statues, gave birth to children like them, whose features reflect the passion with which the statues were made. Yeats reworks this idea in his poem, 'The Statues'.

[16] *implicated* intertwined.

[17] *stars* planets or comets.

[18] *lair* position in the Zodiac.

[19] *interlunar* between the old and the new moon.

[20] *chariots of the ocean* boats.

[21] *the deep truth is imageless* Neville Rogers offers a useful Platonic reading; *Shelley at Work* (2nd edn, Oxford, 1967), pp. 160–1.

ASIA. So much I asked before, and my heart gave
The response thou hast given; and of such truths
Each to itself must be the oracle.
One more demand; and do thou answer me
As my own soul would answer, did it know
That which I ask. Prometheus shall arise
Henceforth the Sun of this rejoicing world:
When shall the destined hour arrive?

DEMOGORGON. Behold![22]

ASIA. The rocks are cloven,[23] and through the purple night
I see cars drawn by rainbow-winged steeds
Which trample the dim winds; in each there stands
A wild-eyed charioteer urging their flight.
Some look behind, as fiends pursued them there,
And yet I see no shapes but the keen stars;
Others, with burning eyes, lean forth, and drink
With eager lips the wind of their own speed,
As if the thing they loved fled on before,
And now, even now, they clasped it. Their bright locks
Stream like a comet's flashing hair – they all
Sweep onward.

DEMOGORGON. These are the immortal Hours,
Of whom thou didst demand. One waits for thee.

ASIA. A spirit with a dreadful countenance
Checks its dark chariot by the craggy gulf.
Unlike thy brethren, ghastly charioteer,
What art thou? Whither wouldst thou bear me? Speak!

SPIRIT. I am the shadow of a destiny
More dread than is my aspect; ere yon planet
Has set, the Darkness which ascends with me
Shall wrap in lasting night Heaven's kingless throne.

ASIA. What meanest thou?

PANTHEA. The terrible shadow[24] floats
Up from its throne, as may the lurid smoke
Of earthquake-ruined cities o'er the sea.
Lo! it ascends the car; the coursers fly
Terrified. Watch its path among the stars
Blackening the night!

ASIA. Thus I am answered; strange!

PANTHEA. See, near the verge,[25] another chariot stays;
An ivory shell inlaid with crimson fire
Which comes and goes within its sculptured rim

Notes

[22] *Behold* i.e. the destined hour *has* arrived.

[23] *The rocks are cloven* volcanic eruption caused by the meeting of Demogorgon and the sea-sisters.

[24] *The terrible shadow* Demogorgon.

[25] *verge* horizon.

Of delicate strange tracery; the young spirit
That guides it has the dove-like eyes of hope;
How its soft smiles attract the soul! as light
Lures winged insects through the lampless air.

SPIRIT.
My coursers are fed with the lightning,[26]
They drink of the whirlwind's stream,
And when the red morning is bright'ning
They bathe in the fresh sunbeam;
They have strength for their swiftness, I deem –
Then ascend with me, Daughter of Ocean.

I desire – and their speed makes night kindle;
I fear – they outstrip the typhoon;
Ere the cloud piled on Atlas can dwindle
We encircle the earth and the moon;
We shall rest from long labours ere noon –
Then ascend with me, Daughter of Ocean.

Act II, Scene V

The car pauses within a cloud on the top of a snowy mountain. Asia, Panthea, and the Spirit of the Hour.

SPIRIT.
On the brink of the night and the morning
My coursers are wont to respire;[1]
But the Earth has just whispered a warning
That their flight must be swifter than fire –
They shall drink the hot speed of desire!

ASIA. Thou breathest on their nostrils, but my breath
Would give them swifter speed.

SPIRIT. Alas, it could not.

PANTHEA. Oh Spirit, pause and tell whence is the light
Which fills the cloud? The sun is yet unrisen.

SPIRIT. The sun will rise not until noon.[2] Apollo
Is held in Heaven by wonder; and the light
Which fills this vapour, as the aerial hue
Of fountain-gazing roses fills the water,
Flows from thy mighty sister.[3]

Notes

[26] *My coursers . . . lightning* The chariot is fuelled by electricity from the sun.

Act II, Scene V

[1] *respire* rest.

[2] *The sun . . . until noon* All morning the sun is obscured by volcanic ash thrown into the atmosphere.

[3] *the light . . . sister* Asia emanates light, as a revelation of what she essentially is.

PANTHEA. Yes, I feel –
ASIA. What is it with thee, sister? Thou art pale.

PANTHEA. How thou art changed! I dare not look on thee;
I feel, but see thee not. I scarce endure
The radiance of thy beauty. Some good change
Is working in the elements, which suffer
Thy presence thus unveiled. The Nereids[4] tell
That on the day when the clear hyaline[5]
Was cloven at thine uprise, and thou didst stand
Within a veined shell,[6] which floated on
Over the calm floor of the crystal sea,
Among the Aegean isles, and by the shores
Which bear thy name – love, like the atmosphere
Of the sun's fire filling the living world,
Burst from thee, and illumined Earth and Heaven
And the deep Ocean and the sunless caves
And all that dwells within them; till grief cast
Eclipse upon the soul from which it came:
Such art thou now; nor is it I alone,
Thy sister, thy companion, thine own chosen one,
But the whole world which seeks thy sympathy.
Hearest thou not sounds i' the air which speak the love
Of all articulate beings? Feelest thou not
The inanimate winds enamoured of thee? List!

(*Music*)

ASIA. Thy words are sweeter than aught else but his
Whose echoes they are – yet all love is sweet,
Given or returned. Common as light is love,
And its familiar voice wearies not ever.
Like the wide Heaven, the all-sustaining air,
It makes the reptile equal to the God:
They who inspire it most are fortunate,
As I am now; but those who feel it most
Are happier still, after long sufferings,
As I shall soon become.

PANTHEA. List! Spirits speak.

VOICE (*in the air, singing*)[7]
Life of Life! thy lips enkindle
With their love the breath between them;
And thy smiles before they dwindle
Make the cold air fire; then screen them
In those looks, where whoso gazes
Faints, entangled in their mazes.

Notes

[4] *Nereids* sea-nymphs, daughters of Nereus.
[5] *hyaline* glassy, transparent sea.
[6] *thou didst stand . . . shell* Asia is identified with Aphrodite, the goddess of love, who came floating on a shell to land on the island of Cythera.
[7] This is the voice of Prometheus.

Child of Light! thy limbs are burning
   Through the vest which seems to hide them,
As the radiant lines of morning
   Through the clouds ere they divide them;
And this atmosphere divinest
Shrouds thee wheresoe'er thou shinest.

Fair are others; none beholds thee,
   But thy voice sounds low and tender
Like the fairest, for it folds thee
   From the sight, that liquid splendour,
And all feel, yet see thee never,
As I feel now, lost forever!

Lamp of Earth! where'er thou movest
   Its dim shapes are clad with brightness,
And the souls of whom thou lovest
   Walk upon the winds with lightness,
Till they fail, as I am failing,
Dizzy, lost, yet unbewailing!

ASIA.

My soul is an enchanted boat,
Which, like a sleeping swan, doth float
Upon the silver waves of thy sweet singing;
And thine doth like an angel sit
Beside the helm conducting it,
Whilst all the winds with melody are ringing.
It seems to float ever, forever,
Upon that many-winding river,
Between mountains, woods, abysses,
A paradise of wildernesses!
Till, like one in slumber bound,
Borne to the ocean, I float down, around,
Into a sea profound of ever-spreading sound.

Meanwhile thy spirit lifts its pinions
In music's most serene dominions,
Catching the winds that fan that happy Heaven.
And we sail on, away, afar,
Without a course, without a star,
But by the instinct of sweet music driven,
Till through Elysian garden islets
By thee, most beautiful of pilots,
Where never mortal pinnace glided,
The boat of my desire is guided:
Realms where the air we breathe is love,
Which in the winds and on the waves doth move,
Harmonizing this earth with what we feel above.

We have passed Age's icy caves,
And Manhood's dark and tossing waves,
And Youth's smooth ocean, smiling to betray:

Beyond the glassy gulfs we flee
Of shadow-peopled Infancy,
Through death and birth to a diviner day[8] –
A paradise of vaulted bowers
Lit by downward-gazing flowers,
And watery paths that wind between
Wildernesses calm and green,
Peopled by shapes too bright to see,
And rest, having beheld – somewhat like thee,
Which walk upon the sea and chaunt melodiously![9]

Act III, Scene I

Heaven. Jupiter on his throne; Thetis and the other deities assembled.

JUPITER. Ye congregated powers of Heaven, who share
The glory and the strength of him ye serve,
Rejoice! Henceforth I am omnipotent.
All else had been subdued to me; alone
The soul of man, like unextinguished fire,
Yet burns towards Heaven with fierce reproach, and doubt,
And lamentation, and reluctant prayer –
Hurling up insurrection, which might make
Our antique empire insecure, though built
On eldest faith, and Hell's coeval,[1] fear.
And though my curses through the pendulous air,[2]
Like snow on herbless peaks, fall flake by flake
And cling to it;[3] though under my wrath's night
It climb the crags of life, step after step,
Which wound it, as ice wounds unsandalled feet,
It yet remains supreme o'er misery,
Aspiring, unrepressed, yet soon to fall.
Even now have I begotten a strange wonder,
That fatal child, the terror of the earth,[4]
Who waits but till the destined Hour arrive,
Bearing from Demogorgon's vacant throne
The dreadful might of ever-living limbs
Which clothed that awful spirit unbeheld,
To redescend and trample out the spark.

Notes

[8] *Beyond the glassy gulfs . . . day* Asia and Prometheus travel into the world of pre-existence, described by Wordsworth in his 'Ode' (p. 538).

[9] *Peopled by shapes . . . melodiously* The inhabitants of the realm of pre-existence are too bright to see at first, but now that Asia and Prometheus have got used to it, Asia sees that Prometheus is the same kind of being as the others, and that they both belong there.

Act III, Scene I

[1] *coeval* contemporary. Fear and faith enable Jupiter to retain power.

[2] *pendulous air* The air hangs; cf. *King Lear* III iv 69.

[3] *it* i.e. the soul of man, as in line 16.

[4] *That fatal child, the terror of the earth* Jupiter's rape of Thetis produced Demogorgon.

Pour forth Heaven's wine, Idaean Ganymede,[5]
And let it fill the daedal[6] cups like fire;
And from the flower-inwoven soil divine
Ye all-triumphant harmonies arise,
As dew from earth under the twilight stars.
Drink! Be the nectar circling through your veins
The soul of joy, ye ever-living Gods,
Till exultation burst in one wide voice
Like music from Elysian winds!
And thou
Ascend beside me, veiled in the light
Of the desire which makes thee one with me,
Thetis,[7] bright image of eternity!
When thou didst cry, 'Insufferable might!
God! Spare me! I sustain not the quick flames,
The penetrating presence;[8] all my being
(Like him whom the Numidian seps did thaw
Into a dew with poison[9]) is dissolved,
Sinking through its foundations' – even then
Two mighty spirits, mingling, made a third
Mightier than either, which unbodied now
Between us floats, felt although unbeheld,
Waiting the incarnation which ascends
(Hear ye the thunder of the fiery wheels
Griding[10] the winds?) from Demogorgon's throne.
Victory! Victory! Feel'st thou not, oh World,
The earthquake of his chariot thundering up
Olympus?

(The car of the Hour arrives. Demogorgon descends, and moves towards the throne of Jupiter.)

Awful shape, what art thou? Speak!

DEMOGORGON. Eternity. Demand no direr name.
Descend, and follow me down the abyss.
I am thy child, as thou wert Saturn's child,
Mightier than thee: and we must dwell together
Henceforth in darkness. Lift thy lightnings not.
The tyranny of Heaven none may retain,
Or reassume, or hold, succeeding thee;
Yet if thou wilt (as 'tis the destiny
Of trodden worms to writhe till they are dead),
Put forth thy might.

JUPITER. Detested prodigy!
Even thus beneath the deep Titanian prisons[11]
I trample thee! Thou lingerest?

Notes

[5] A shepherd-boy from Mt Ida, Ganymede was abducted to satisfy Jupiter's lust and be his cup-bearer.

[6] *daedal* beautifully crafted.

[7] Thetis was the daughter of Nereus, a sea-god.

[8] Semele was consumed by fire when she tricked Jupiter into appearing in his own undisguised form.

[9] Sabellus dissolved when bitten by a seps (a legendary snake) in the Numidian desert.

[10] *Griding* grating against.

[11] *the deep Titanian prisons* after their overthrow by Jupiter, the Titans were imprisoned in Tartarus, far below the earth.

Mercy! Mercy!
No pity, no release, no respite! Oh,
That thou wouldst make mine enemy my judge,
Even where he hangs, seared by my long revenge,
On Caucasus! He would not doom me thus.
Gentle, and just, and dreadless, is he not
The monarch of the world? What then art thou?
No refuge! No appeal!
Sink with me then;
We two will sink on the wide waves of ruin,
Even as a vulture and a snake outspent
Drop, twisted in inextricable fight,
Into a shoreless sea. Let Hell unlock
Its mounded oceans of tempestuous fire,
And whelm[12] on them into the bottomless void
The desolated world, and thee, and me,
The conqueror and the conquered, and the wreck
Of that for which they combated.
Ai! Ai!
The elements obey me not. I sink
Dizzily down – ever, forever, down –
And, like a cloud, mine enemy above
Darkens my fall with victory! Ai! Ai!

Act III, Scene II

The mouth of a great river in the island Atlantis.[1] *Ocean*[2] *is discovered reclining near the shore; Apollo stands beside him.*

OCEAN. He fell, thou sayest, beneath his conqueror's frown?

APOLLO. Aye, when the strife was ended which made dim
The orb I rule,[3] and shook the solid stars.[4]
The terrors of his eye illumined Heaven
With sanguine light through the thick ragged skirts
Of the victorious Darkness, as he fell,
Like the last glare of day's red agony,
Which from a rent among the fiery clouds
Burns far along the tempest-wrinkled deep.

OCEAN. He sunk to the abyss? To the dark void?

APOLLO. An eagle so,[5] caught in some bursting cloud
On Caucasus, his thunder-baffled wings
Entangled in the whirlwind, and his eyes,

Notes

[12] *whelm* throw violently.

Act III, Scene II

[1] *Atlantis* legendary sunken city west of the Straits of Gibraltar, believed by Plato to be the home of an ideal commonwealth.

[2] Ocean was god of the sea.

[3] *The orb I rule* Apollo was the Greek god of the sun.

[4] *solid stars* fixed stars.

[5] *An eagle so* i.e. 'Yes, he sank like an eagle . . .'

Which gazed on the undazzling sun, now blinded
By the white lightning, while the ponderous hail
Beats on his struggling form, which sinks at length
Prone, and the aerial ice clings over it.

OCEAN. Henceforth the fields of Heaven-reflecting sea
Which are my realm, will heave, unstained with blood,
Beneath the uplifting winds, like plains of corn
Swayed by the summer air; my streams will flow
Round many-peopled continents, and round
Fortunate isles; and from their glassy thrones
Blue Proteus[6] and his humid nymphs shall mark
The shadow of fair ships – as mortals see
The floating bark of the light-laden moon[7]
With that white star,[8] its sightless pilot's crest,
Borne down the rapid sunset's ebbing sea –
Tracking their path no more by blood and groans,
And desolation, and the mingled voice
Of slavery and command, but by the light
Of wave-reflected flowers, and floating odours,
And music soft, and mild, free, gentle voices,
That sweetest music, such as spirits love.

APOLLO. And I shall gaze not on the deeds which make
My mind obscure with sorrow, as eclipse
Darkens the sphere I guide; but list, I hear
The small, clear, silver lute of the young spirit
That sits in the morning star.[9]

OCEAN. Thou must away?
Thy steeds will pause at even, till when farewell.
The loud deep calls me home even now, to feed it
With azure calm out of the emerald urns
Which stand forever full beside my throne.
Behold the Nereids under the green sea –
Their wavering limbs borne on the wind-like streams,
Their white arms lifted o'er their streaming hair
With garlands pied and starry sea-flower crowns –
Hastening to grace their mighty sister's joy.
(*a sound of waves is heard*)
It is the unpastured[10] sea hungering for calm.
Peace, monster; I come now. Farewell.

APOLLO. Farewell.

Notes

[6] *Blue Proteus* elusive sea-god, able to change his shape at will.

[7] *the light-laden moon* the new moon (full of light).

[8] *that white star* Venus, the evening star.

[9] *I hear . . . star* It is time for the sun to rise. All the events thus far have taken place during a single dawn.

[10] *unpastured* unfed.

Act III, Scene III

Caucasus. Prometheus, Hercules, Ione, the Earth, Spirits, Asia, and Panthea, borne in the car with the Spirit of the Hour. Hercules unbinds Prometheus, who descends.[1]

HERCULES. Most glorious among spirits, thus doth strength
To wisdom, courage, and long-suffering love,
And thee, who art the form they animate,
Minister like a slave.

PROMETHEUS. Thy gentle words
Are sweeter even than freedom long desired
And long delayed.
Asia, thou light of life,
Shadow of beauty unbeheld; and ye,
Fair sister nymphs, who made long years of pain
Sweet to remember, through your love and care –
Henceforth we will not part. There is a cave,
All overgrown with trailing odorous[2] plants
Which curtain out the day with leaves and flowers,
And paved with veined emerald; and a fountain
Leaps in the midst with an awakening sound.
From its curved roof the mountain's frozen tears,
Like snow, or silver, or long diamond spires,
Hang downward, raining forth a doubtful light;
And there is heard the ever-moving air
Whispering without from tree to tree, and birds
And bees; and all around are mossy seats,
And the rough walls are clothed with long soft grass –
A simple dwelling which shall be our own,
Where we will sit and talk of time and change
As the world ebbs and flows, ourselves unchanged.
What can hide man from mutability?
And if ye sigh, then I will smile; and thou,
Ione, shall chant fragments of sea-music
Until I weep, when ye shall smile away
The tears she brought, which yet were sweet to shed.
We will entangle buds and flowers and beams
Which twinkle on the fountain's brim, and make
Strange combinations out of common things,
Like human babes in their brief innocence;
And we will search, with looks and words of love,
For hidden thoughts, each lovelier than the last,
Our unexhausted spirits, and, like lutes
Touched by the skill of the enamoured wind,
Weave harmonies divine, yet ever new,

Notes

Act III, Scene III

[1] According to legend, Hercules killed the eagle torturing Prometheus and freed him after Prometheus had made his peace with Jupiter.

[2] *odorous* fragrant.

From difference sweet where discord cannot be.
And hither come – sped on the charmed winds
Which meet from all the points of Heaven, as bees
From every flower aerial Enna[3] feeds
At their known island-homes in Himera[4] –
The echoes of the human world, which tell
Of the low voice of love, almost unheard,
And dove-eyed pity's murmured pain, and music,
Itself the echo of the heart, and all
That tempers or improves man's life, now free.
And lovely apparitions, dim at first,
Then radiant – as the mind, arising bright
From the embrace of beauty (whence the forms
Of which these are the phantoms) casts on them
The gathered rays which are reality –
Shall visit us, the progeny immortal
Of Painting, Sculpture, and rapt Poesy,
And arts, though unimagined, yet to be.
The wandering voices and the shadows these
Of all that man becomes, the mediators[5]
Of that best worship, Love, by him and us
Given and returned; swift shapes and sounds which grow
More fair and soft as man grows wise and kind,
And veil by veil, evil and error fall:[6]
Such virtue has the cave and place around. (*Turning to the Spirit of the Hour*)
For thee, fair Spirit, one toil remains. Ione,
Give her that curved shell which Proteus old
Made Asia's nuptial boon, breathing within it
A voice to be accomplished, and which thou
Didst hide in grass under the hollow rock.

IONE. Thou most desired Hour, more loved and lovely
Than all thy sisters, this is the mystic shell;
See the pale azure fading into silver,
Lining it with a soft yet glowing light –
Looks it not like lulled music sleeping there?

SPIRIT. It seems in truth the fairest shell of Ocean;
Its sound must be at once both sweet and strange.

PROMETHEUS. Go, borne over the cities of mankind
On whirlwind-footed coursers – once again
Outspeed the sun around the orbed world;
And as thy chariot cleaves the kindling air,
Thou breathe into the many-folded shell,
Loosening its mighty music; it shall be
As thunder mingled with clear echoes. Then

Notes

[3] *Enna* town in the middle of Sicily, an emblem of fertility. Shelley recalls *Paradise Lost* iv 269.

[4] *Himera* town on the north coast of Sicily.

[5] *mediators* Man's works of art are the mediators of love between him and Prometheus.

[6] *evil and error fall* Shelley regards human nature as progressive.

Return, and thou shalt dwell beside our cave.
And thou, oh Mother Earth –

THE EARTH. I hear, I feel;
Thy lips are on me, and their touch runs down
Even to the adamantine central gloom
Along these marble nerves – 'tis life, 'tis joy,
And through my withered, old, and icy frame
The warmth of an immortal youth shoots down,
Circling. Henceforth the many children fair
Folded in my sustaining arms – all plants
And creeping forms, and insects rainbow-winged,
And birds, and beasts, and fish, and human shapes,
Which drew disease and pain from my wan bosom,
Draining the poison of despair – shall take
And interchange sweet nutriment; to me
Shall they become like sister-antelopes
By one fair dam, snow-white and swift as wind,
Nursed among lilies near a brimming stream.
The dew-mists of my sunless sleep shall float
Under the stars like balm; night-folded flowers
Shall suck unwithering hues in their repose;
And men and beasts in happy dreams shall gather
Strength for the coming day and all its joy;
And death shall be the last embrace of her
Who takes the life she gave, even as a mother
Folding her child, says, 'Leave me not again.'

ASIA. Oh mother, wherefore speak the name of death?
Cease they to love, and move, and breathe, and speak,
Who die?

THE EARTH. It would avail not to reply:
Thou art immortal, and this tongue is known
But to the uncommunicating dead.
Death is the veil which those who live call life:
They sleep, and it is lifted;[7] and meanwhile
In mild variety the seasons mild –
With rainbow-skirted showers, and odorous winds,
And long blue meteors cleansing the dull night,
And the life-kindling shafts of the keen sun's
All-piercing bow, and the dew-mingled rain
Of the calm moonbeams, a soft influence mild –
Shall clothe the forests and the fields, aye, even
The crag-built deserts of the barren deep
With ever-living leaves, and fruits, and flowers.
And thou![8] There is a cavern where my spirit
Was panted forth in anguish whilst thy pain
Made my heart mad, and those who did inhale it

Notes

[7] *They sleep . . . lifted* cf. 'Mont Blanc' 50: 'death is slumber.'

[8] *And thou!* Earth turns from Asia to Prometheus.

Became mad too, and built a temple there,
And spoke, and were oracular,[9] and lured
The erring nations round to mutual war
And faithless faith, such as Jove kept with thee –
Which breath now rises, as among tall weeds
A violet's exhalation, and it fills
With a serener light and crimson air
Intense, yet soft, the rocks and woods around;
It feeds the quick growth of the serpent vine,
And the dark linked ivy tangling wild,
And budding, blown, or odour-faded blooms
Which star the winds with points of coloured light
As they rain through them, and bright golden globes
Of fruit, suspended in their own green heaven,
And, through their veined leaves and amber stems
The flowers whose purple and translucid bowls
Stand ever mantling with aerial dew,
The drink of spirits. And it circles round,
Like the soft waving wings of noonday dreams,
Inspiring calm and happy thoughts like mine,
Now thou art thus restored. This cave is thine.
Arise, appear! (*A spirit rises in the likeness of a winged child.*)
    This is my torch-bearer,
Who let his lamp out in old time with gazing
On eyes from which he kindled it anew
With love, which is as fire, sweet daughter mine,
For such is that within thine own. Run, wayward!
And guide this company beyond the peak
Of Bacchic Nysa,[10] maenad-haunted mountain,
And beyond Indus and its tribute rivers,
Trampling the torrent streams and glassy lakes
With feet unwet, unwearied, undelaying;
And up the green ravine, across the vale,
Beside the windless and crystalline pool,
Where ever lies, on unerasing waves,
The image of a temple,[11] built above,
Distinct with column, arch, and architrave,
And palm-like capital, and over-wrought,
And populous with most living imagery –
Praxitelean shapes,[12] whose marble smiles
Fill the hushed air with everlasting love.
It is deserted now, but once it bore

Notes

[9] *a temple . . . oracular* perhaps the temple at Delphi, where the priestess uttered prophecies in a state of ecstasy – although Shelley's meaning could be metaphorical.

[10] They are to be guided from the Indian Caucasus to Greece, passing Nysa (a city in India), where Bacchus was born.

[11] *a temple* the Academy outside Athens where Plato once taught.

[12] *Praxitelean shapes* i.e. statues carved by Praxiteles, Greek sculptor of the fourth century BC, famous for his depictions of Artemis and Aphrodite. In Rome, March 1819, Shelley saw the statues of Castor and Pollux believed to have been made by Praxiteles: 'These figures combine the irresistible energy with the sublime and perfect loveliness supposed to have belonged to the divine nature' (Jones ii 88–9).

Thy name, Prometheus; there the emulous youths
Bore to thy honour through the divine gloom
The lamp which was thine emblem[13] – even as those
Who bear the untransmitted torch of hope
Into the grave, across the night of life,
As thou hast borne it most triumphantly
To this far goal of time. Depart – farewell.
Beside that temple is the destined cave.

Act III, Scene IV

A forest. In the background a cave. Prometheus, Asia, Panthea, Ione, and the Spirit of the Earth.

IONE. Sister, it is not earthly: how it glides
Under the leaves! How on its head there burns
A light, like a green star whose emerald beams
Are twined with its fair hair! How, as it moves,
The splendour drops in flakes upon the grass!
Knowest thou it?

PANTHEA. It is the delicate spirit
That guides the earth through Heaven. From afar
The populous constellations call that light
The loveliest of the planets; and sometimes
It floats along the spray of the salt sea,
Or makes its chariot of a foggy cloud,
Or walks through fields or cities while men sleep,
Or o'er the mountain-tops, or down the rivers,
Or through the green waste wilderness, as now,
Wondering at all it sees. Before Jove reigned
It loved our sister Asia, and it came
Each leisure hour to drink the liquid light
Out of her eyes, for which it said it thirsted
As one bit by a dipsas;[1] and with her
It made its childish confidence, and told her
All it had known or seen, for it saw much,
Yet idly reasoned what it saw; and called her
(For whence it sprung it knew not, nor do I)
'Mother, dear mother'.

THE SPIRIT OF THE EARTH (*running to Asia*) Mother, dearest mother;
May I then talk with thee as I was wont?
May I then hide my eyes in thy soft arms
After thy looks have made them tired of joy?
May I then play beside thee the long noons
When work is none in the bright silent air?

Notes

[13] *there the . . . emblem* In the Athenian festival in honour of the fire-gods, young men raced from the altar of Prometheus to the city, carrying lighted torches, without letting them go out.

Act III, Scene IV

[1] *dipsas* serpent which induced an unquenchable thirst in those it bit.

ASIA. I love thee, gentlest being, and henceforth
Can cherish thee unenvied; speak, I pray –
Thy simple talk once solaced, now delights.

SPIRIT OF THE EARTH. Mother, I am grown wiser, though a child
Cannot be wise like thee, within this day,
And happier too – happier and wiser both.
Thou knowest that toads, and snakes, and loathly worms,
And venomous and malicious beasts, and boughs
That bore ill berries in the woods, were ever
An hindrance to my walks o'er the green world;
And that, among the haunts of humankind,
Hard-featured men, or with proud, angry looks,
Or cold, staid gait, or false and hollow smiles,
Or the dull sneer of self-loved ignorance,
Or other such foul masks, with which ill thoughts
Hide that fair being whom we spirits call man;
And women too, ugliest of all things evil
(Though fair, even in a world where thou art fair
When good and kind, free and sincere like thee),
When false or frowning made me sick at heart
To pass them, though they slept, and I unseen.
Well, my path lately lay through a great city
Into the woody hills surrounding it.
A sentinel was sleeping at the gate,
When there was heard a sound so loud, it shook
The towers amid the moonlight, yet more sweet
Than any voice but thine, sweetest of all;
A long, long sound, as it would never end –
And all the inhabitants leapt suddenly
Out of their rest, and gathered in the streets,
Looking in wonder up to Heaven, while yet
The music pealed along. I hid myself
Within a fountain in the public square,
Where I lay like the reflex[2] of the moon
Seen in a wave under green leaves – and soon
Those ugly human shapes and visages
Of which I spoke as having wrought me pain,
Passed floating through the air, and fading still
Into the winds that scattered them; and those
From whom they passed seemed mild and lovely forms
After some foul disguise had fallen, and all
Were somewhat changed, and after brief surprise
And greetings of delighted wonder, all
Went to their sleep again; and when the dawn
Came – wouldst thou think that toads, and snakes, and efts,[3]
Could e'er be beautiful? Yet so they were,
And that with little change of shape or hue:

Notes

[2] *reflex* reflection.

[3] *efts* small lizards. Everything is returning to a prelapsarian state.

All things had put their evil nature off.
I cannot tell my joy, when o'er a lake,
Upon a drooping bough with nightshade twined,
I saw two azure halcyons clinging downward
And thinning one bright bunch of amber berries
With quick long beaks,[4] and in the deep there lay
Those lovely forms imaged as in a sky.
So with my thoughts full of these happy changes,
We meet again, the happiest change of all.

ASIA. And never will we part, till thy chaste sister[5]
Who guides the frozen and inconstant moon,
Will look on thy more warm and equal light
Till her heart thaw like flakes of April snow,
And love thee.

SPIRIT OF THE EARTH. What? As Asia loves Prometheus?

ASIA. Peace, wanton![6] Thou are yet not old enough.
Think ye by gazing on each other's eyes
To multiply your lovely selves, and fill
With sphered fires the interlunar air?

SPIRIT OF THE EARTH. Nay, mother, while my sister trims her lamp[7]
'Tis hard I should go darkling.[8]

ASIA. Listen, look! (*The Spirit of the Hour enters.*)

PROMETHEUS. We feel what thou hast heard and seen – yet speak.

SPIRIT OF THE HOUR. Soon as the sound had ceased whose thunder filled
The abysses of the sky and the wide earth
There was a change: the impalpable thin air
And the all-circling sunlight were transformed,
As if the sense of love dissolved in them
Had folded itself round the sphered world.
My vision then grew clear, and I could see
Into the mysteries of the universe:
Dizzy as with delight I floated down;
Winnowing[9] the lightsome air with languid plumes
My coursers sought their birthplace in the sun,
Where they henceforth will live exempt from toil,
Pasturing flowers of vegetable fire,
And where my moonlike car[10] will stand within
A temple – gazed upon by Phidian forms[11]
Of thee, and Asia, and the Earth, and me,

Notes

[4] *Upon a drooping bough . . . beaks* In the regenerated, purified world, deadly nightshade is no longer poisonous, and kingfishers turn vegetarian rather than eat fish. (Shelley was a vegetarian.)

[5] *thy chaste sister* Selene, Greek goddess of the moon.

[6] *wanton* spoiled child.

[7] *trims her lamp* When trimming a lamp, one prepares the wick for fresh burning.

[8] *darkling* in the dark.

[9] *Winnowing* beating.

[10] *car* chariot.

[11] *Phidian forms* statues carved by Phidias, Greek sculptor of the 5th century BC, famous for his portrayal of Jupiter at Olympia.

And you fair nymphs, looking the love we feel,
In memory of the tidings it has borne –
Beneath a dome fretted[12] with graven flowers,[13]
Poised on twelve columns of resplendent stone,
And open to the bright and liquid sky.
Yoked to it by an amphisbaenic snake
The likeness of those winged steeds will mock
The flight from which they find repose. Alas!
Whither has wandered now my partial tongue
When all remains untold which ye would hear?
As I have said, I floated to the earth:
It was, as it is still, the pain of bliss
To move, to breathe, to be; I wandering went
Among the haunts and dwellings of mankind,
And first was disappointed not to see
Such mighty change as I had felt within
Expressed in outward things. But soon I looked,
And behold! thrones were kingless, and men walked
One with the other even as spirits do –
None fawned, none trampled; hate, disdain, or fear,
Self-love or self-contempt, on human brows
No more inscribed, as o'er the gate of Hell,
'All hope abandon, ye who enter here';[14]
None frowned, none trembled, none with eager fear
Gazed on another's eye of cold command
Until the subject of a tyrant's will
Became, worse fate, the abject of his own,[15]
Which spurred him, like an outspent horse, to death;
None wrought his lips in truth-entangling lines
Which smiled the lie his tongue disdained to speak;
None, with firm sneer, trod out in his own heart
The sparks of love and hope, till there remained
Those bitter ashes, a soul self-consumed,
And the wretch crept, a vampire among men,
Infecting all with his own hideous ill;
None talked that common, false, cold, hollow talk
Which makes the heart deny the 'yes' it breathes,
Yet question that unmeant hypocrisy
Which such a self-mistrust as has no name.
And women, too – frank, beautiful, and kind
As the free Heaven which rains fresh light and dew
On the wide earth, passed – gentle radiant forms,
From custom's evil taint exempt and pure,
Speaking the wisdom once they could not think,
Looking emotions once they feared to feel,

Notes

[12] *fretted* decorated.

[13] The scene described is based on the Pantheon at Rome and the Sala della Biga in the Vatican, both of which Shelley visited. The Biga is a two-horse chariot, the emblem of the moon. Its yoke was a snake with a head at both ends, the amphisbaena.

[14] *All hope abandon, ye who enter here* The inscription above the gate leading to hell in Dante, *Inferno* iii 9.

[15] *the abject of his own* the outcast of his own will.

And changed to all which once they dared not be,
Yet being now, made earth like Heaven; nor pride,
Nor jealousy, nor envy, nor ill shame,
The bitterest of those drops of treasured gall,
Spoilt the sweet taste of the nepenthe,[16] love.
   Thrones, altars, judgement-seats[17] and prisons (wherein,
And beside which, by wretched men were borne
Sceptres, tiaras, swords and chains, and tomes
Of reasoned wrong glozed on[18] by ignorance)
Were like those monstrous and barbaric shapes,[19]
The ghosts of a no more remembered fame
Which, from their unworn obelisks,[20] look forth
In triumph o'er the palaces and tombs
Of those who were their conquerors, mouldering round.
These[21] imaged to the pride of kings and priests
A dark yet mighty faith, a power as wide
As is the world it wasted, and are now
But an astonishment; even so the tools
And emblems of its last captivity,
Amid the dwellings of the peopled earth,
Stand, not o'erthrown, but unregarded now.
And those foul shapes,[22] abhorred by God and man –
Which, under many a name and many a form
Strange, savage, ghastly, dark and execrable,
Were Jupiter, the tyrant of the world;
And which the nations, panic-stricken, served
With blood, and hearts broken by long hope, and love
Dragged to his altars soiled and garlandless,
And slain amid men's unreclaiming tears,
Flattering the thing they feared, which fear was hate –
Frown,[23] mouldering fast, o'er their abandoned shrines.
The painted veil, by those who were, called life,
Which mimicked, as with colours idly spread,
All men believed and hoped, is torn aside;
The loathsome mask has fallen, the man remains
Sceptreless, free, uncircumscribed – but man:
Equal, unclassed, tribeless, and nationless,
Exempt from awe, worship, degree; the king
Over himself; just, gentle, wise – but man.
Passionless? No, yet free from guilt or pain,
Which were, for his will made, or suffered them;
Nor yet exempt, though ruling them like slaves,

Notes

[16] *nepenthe* grief-banishing drink.

[17] *judgement-seats* tribunals.

[18] *glozed on* explained, glossed.

[19] *monstrous and barbaric shapes* i.e. of Egyptian deities, carved into the obelisks. In Shelley's day hieroglyphics seemed monstrous and barbarous because they had not then been deciphered.

[20] *obelisks* Egyptian obelisks had been brought to Rome in ancient times and erected in the main piazzas, where Shelley saw them.

[21] *These* i.e. the 'monstrous and barbaric shapes' (l. 168).

[22] *those foul shapes* i.e. of religions that rule by fear.

[23] *Frown* the subject governing this verb is 'shapes' (l. 180).

From chance, and death, and mutability,
The clogs[24] of that which else might oversoar
The loftiest star of unascended Heaven,
Pinnacled dim in the intense inane.[25]

Act IV

Scene: a part of the forest near the Cave of Prometheus. Panthea and Ione are sleeping; they awaken gradually during the first song.

VOICE OF UNSEEN SPIRITS.
The pale stars are gone!
For the sun, their swift shepherd,
To their folds them compelling
In the depths of the dawn,
Hastes, in meteor-eclipsing array, and they flee
Beyond his blue dwelling,
As fawns flee the leopard.
But where are ye?

(*A train of dark forms and shadows passes by confusedly, singing.*)

Here, oh, here;
We bear the bier
Of the father of many a cancelled year!
Spectres we
Of the dead Hours be,
We bear Time to his tomb in eternity.

Strew, oh strew
Hair, not yew!
Wet the dusty pall with tears, not dew!
Be the faded flowers
Of Death's bare bowers
Spread on the corpse of the King of Hours!

Haste, oh haste!
As shades are chased,
Trembling, by day, from heaven's blue waste,
We melt away,
Like dissolving spray,
From the children of a diviner day,
With the lullaby
Of winds that die
On the bosom of their own harmony.

IONE. What dark forms were they?

PANTHEA. The past Hours weak and grey,
With the spoil which their toil
Raked together
From the conquest but One[1] could foil.

Notes

[24] *clogs* hindrances.
[25] *intense inane* deep space.

Act IV
[1] *One* Prometheus.

IONE. Have they passed?

PANTHEA. They have passed;
They outspeeded the blast,
While 'tis said, they are fled –

IONE. Whither, oh whither?

PANTHEA. To the dark, to the past, to the dead.

VOICE OF UNSEEN SPIRITS.
Bright clouds float in Heaven,
Dew-stars gleam on earth,
Waves assemble on ocean –
They are gathered and driven
By the storm of delight, by the panic of glee!
They shake with emotion,
They dance in their mirth –
But where are ye?[2]
The pine boughs are singing
Old songs with new gladness,
The billows and fountains
Fresh music are flinging,
Like the notes of a spirit from land and from sea;
The storms mock the mountains
With the thunder of gladness –
But where are ye?

IONE. What charioteers are these?

PANTHEA. Where are their chariots?

SEMICHORUS OF HOURS I.
The voice of the Spirits of Air and of Earth
Has drawn back the figured[3] curtain of sleep
Which covered our being and darkened our birth
In the deep –

A VOICE.
In the deep?

SEMICHORUS II.
Oh, below the deep.

SEMICHORUS I.
A hundred ages[4] we had been kept
Cradled in visions of hate and care,
And each one who waked as his brother slept,
Found the truth –

SEMICHORUS II.
Worse than his visions were!

Notes

[2] *ye* the new Hours.
[3] *figured* patterned.
[4] *A hundred ages* i.e. for the duration of Saturn's long reign.

SEMICHORUS I.
We have heard the lute of Hope in sleep;
We have known the voice of Love in dreams;
We have felt the wand of Power, and leap –

SEMICHORUS II.
As the billows leap in the morning beams!

CHORUS.
Weave the dance on the floor of the breeze,
Pierce with song heaven's silent light,
Enchant the Day that too swiftly flees,
To check its flight ere the cave of Night.

Once the hungry Hours were hounds
Which chased the Day like a bleeding deer,
And it limped and stumbled with many wounds
Through the nightly dells of the desert year.

But now, oh weave the mystic measure
Of music and dance and shapes of light;
Let the Hours, and the spirits of might and pleasure,
Like the clouds and sunbeams, unite.

A VOICE. Unite!

PANTHEA. See, where the Spirits of the human mind[5]
Wrapped in sweet sounds, as in bright veils, approach.

CHORUS OF SPIRITS.
We join the throng
Of the dance and the song,
By the whirlwind of gladness borne along –
As the flying-fish leap
From the Indian deep,
And mix with the sea-birds, half asleep.

CHORUS OF HOURS.
Whence come ye, so wild and so fleet,
For sandals of lightning are on your feet,
And your wings are soft and swift as thought,
And your eyes are as love which is veiled not?

CHORUS OF SPIRITS.
We come from the mind
Of humankind,
Which was late so dusk,[6] and obscene, and blind;
Now 'tis an ocean
Of clear emotion,
A Heaven of serene and mighty motion;

Notes

[5] *the Spirits of the human mind* presumably the same spirits who comforted Prometheus in Act I.

[6] *dusk* gloomy.

From that deep abyss
Of wonder and bliss,
Whose caverns are crystal palaces;
From those skyey towers
Where Thought's crowned powers
Sit watching your dance, ye happy Hours;

From the dim recesses
Of woven caresses,
Where lovers catch ye by your loose tresses;
From the azure isles
Where sweet Wisdom smiles,
Delaying your ships with her siren wiles;

From the temples high
Of man's ear and eye,
Roofed over Sculpture and Poesy;
From the murmurings
Of the unsealed springs,
Where Science[7] bedews her daedal[8] wings.

Years after years,
Through blood and tears
And a thick hell of hatreds, and hopes, and fears,
We waded and flew,
And the islets were few
Where the bud-blighted flowers of happiness grew.

Our feet now, every palm,[9]
Are sandalled with calm,
And the dew of our wings is a rain of balm;
And beyond our eyes[10]
The human love lies
Which makes all it gazes on paradise.

CHORUS OF SPIRITS AND HOURS.

Then weave the web of the mystic measure;
From the depths of the sky and the ends of the earth,
Come, swift Spirits of might and of pleasure,
Fill the dance and the music of mirth –
As the waves of a thousand streams rush by
To an ocean of splendour and harmony!

CHORUS OF SPIRITS.

Our spoil is won,
Our task is done,
We are free to dive, or soar, or run

Notes

7 *Science* knowledge.
8 *daedal* skilful.
9 *palm* sole of the foot.
10 *beyond our eyes* beyond our range of vision.

Beyond and around,
Or within the bound[11]
Which clips[12] the world with darkness round.

We'll pass the eyes
Of the starry skies
Into the hoar deep to colonize;
Death, Chaos, and Night,
From the sound of our flight
Shall flee, like mist from a tempest's might;

And Earth, Air, and Light,
And the Spirit of Might
Which drives round the stars in their fiery flight;
And Love, Thought, and Breath,
The powers that quell Death,
Wherever we soar shall assemble beneath;

And our singing shall build,
In the void's loose field,
A world for the Spirit of Wisdom to wield;
We will take our plan
From the new world of man,
And our work shall be called the Promethean.

CHORUS OF HOURS.
Break the dance, and scatter the song;
Let some depart and some remain.

SEMICHORUS I.
We, beyond Heaven, are driven along –

SEMICHORUS II.
Us the enchantments of earth retain –

SEMICHORUS I.
Ceaseless, and rapid, and fierce, and free,
With the Spirits which build a new earth and sea,
And a Heaven where yet Heaven could never be –

SEMICHORUS II.
Solemn, and slow, and serene, and bright,
Leading the Day and outspeeding the Night
With the powers of a world of perfect light –

SEMICHORUS I.
We whirl, singing loud, round the gathering sphere,
Till the trees, and the beasts, and the clouds appear
From its chaos made calm by love, not fear –

Notes

[11] *the bound* i.e. of the earth's atmosphere.

[12] *clips* embraces.

SEMICHORUS II.
We encircle the oceans and mountains of earth,
And the happy forms of its death and birth
Change to the music of our sweet mirth.

CHORUS OF HOURS AND SPIRITS.
Break the dance, and scatter the song;
Let some depart, and some remain;
Wherever we fly we lead along
In leashes, like starbeams, soft yet strong,
The clouds that are heavy with love's sweet rain.

PANTHEA. Ha! They are gone!

IONE. Yet feel you no delight
From the past sweetness?

PANTHEA. As the bare green hill
When some soft cloud vanishes into rain,
Laughs with a thousand drops of sunny water
To the unpavilioned sky![13]

IONE. Even whilst we speak
New notes arise. What is that awful sound?

PANTHEA. 'Tis the deep music of the rolling world,
Kindling within the strings of the waved air
Aeolian modulations.

IONE. Listen too,
How every pause is filled with under-notes,
Clear, silver, icy, keen, awakening tones,
Which pierce the sense, and live within the soul,
As the sharp stars pierce winter's crystal air
And gaze upon themselves within the sea.

PANTHEA. But see where, through two openings in the forest
Which hanging branches overcanopy,
And where two runnels[14] of a rivulet,
Between the close moss, violet-inwoven,
Have made their path of melody – like sisters
Who part with sighs that they may meet in smiles,
Turning their dear disunion to an isle
Of lovely grief, a wood of sweet sad thoughts –
Two visions of strange radiance float upon
The ocean-like enchantment of strong sound,
Which flows intenser, keener, deeper yet
Under the ground and through the windless air.

IONE. I see a chariot – like that thinnest boat
In which the Mother of the Months[15] is borne
By ebbing light into her western cave

Notes

[13] *the unpavilioned sky* The sky is not separated from the earth by a pavilion.

[14] *runnels* streamlets.

[15] *the Mother of the Months* the moon.

When she upsprings from interlunar dreams –
O'er which is curved an orblike canopy
Of gentle darkness, and the hills and woods,
Distinctly seen through that dusk[16] airy veil,
Regard[17] like shapes in an enchanter's glass;
Its wheels are solid clouds, azure and gold,
Such as the genii of the thunderstorm
Pile on the floor of the illumined sea
When the sun rushes under it; they roll
And move and grow as with an inward wind.
Within it sits a winged infant: white
Its countenance, like the whiteness of bright snow;
Its plumes are as feathers of sunny frost;
Its limbs gleam white through the wind-flowing folds
Of its white robe, woof of ethereal pearl;
Its hair is white – the brightness of white light[18]
Scattered in strings; yet its two eyes are heavens
Of liquid darkness, which the Deity
Within seems pouring, as a storm is poured
From jagged clouds, out of their arrowy lashes,
Tempering the cold and radiant air around
With fire that is not brightness;[19] in its hand
It sways a quivering moonbeam, from whose point
A guiding power directs the chariot's prow
Over its wheeled clouds, which, as they roll
Over the grass, and flowers, and waves, wake sounds
Sweet as a singing rain of silver dew.

PANTHEA. And from the other opening in the wood
Rushes, with loud and whirlwind harmony,
A sphere, which is as many thousand spheres,
Solid as crystal, yet through all its mass
Flow, as through empty space, music and light:
Ten thousand orbs involving and involved,[20]
Purple and azure, white, and green, and golden,
Sphere within sphere; and every space between
Peopled with unimaginable shapes,
Such as ghosts dream dwell in the lampless deep,
Yet each intertranspicuous;[21] and they whirl
Over each other with a thousand motions,
Upon a thousand sightless[22] axles spinning,
And, with the force of self-destroying swiftness,

Notes

[16] *dusk* dark, dusk-like.

[17] *Regard* appear.

[18] *the brightness of white light* in other words, the brilliant, unrefracted light of 'pure', transcendental vision.

[19] *fire that is not brightness* Contemporary scientific thought indicated that there were 'dark rays' – infrared emanations that produced heat but no light. Humphry Davy suggested that they were emitted by the moon.

[20] *involving and involved* entwined and entwining; inextricably intertwined.

[21] *intertranspicuous* transparent between and through each other.

[22] *sightless* invisible.

Intensely, slowly, solemnly roll on,
Kindling with mingled sounds, and many tones,
Intelligible words and music wild.
With mighty whirl the multitudinous[23] orb
Grinds the bright brook into an azure mist
Of elemental subtlety, like light;
And the wild odour of the forest flowers,
The music of the living grass and air,
The emerald light of leaf-entangled beams
Round its intense yet self-conflicting speed,
Seem kneaded into one aerial mass
Which drowns the sense. Within the orb itself,
Pillowed upon its alabaster arms
Like to a child o'erwearied with sweet toil,
On its own folded wings and wavy hair
The Spirit of the Earth is laid asleep,
And you can see its little lips are moving
Amid the changing light of their own smiles,
Like one who talks of what he loves in dream –

IONE. 'Tis only mocking[24] the orb's harmony.

PANTHEA. And from a star upon its forehead, shoot –
Like swords of azure fire, or golden spears
With tyrant-quelling myrtle[25] overtwined,
Embleming Heaven and Earth united now –
Vast beams like spokes of some invisible wheel
Which whirl as the orb whirls, swifter than thought,
Filling the abyss with sunlike lightenings;
And perpendicular now, and now transverse,
Pierce the dark soil, and, as they pierce and pass,
Make bare the secrets of the earth's deep heart:
Infinite mines of adamant[26] and gold,
Valueless[27] stones, and unimagined gems,
And caverns on crystalline columns poised
With vegetable silver[28] overspread;
Wells of unfathomed fire, and water-springs
Whence the great sea, even as a child, is fed,
Whose vapours clothe earth's monarch mountain-tops
With kingly, ermine snow. The beams flash on
And make appear the melancholy ruins
Of cancelled cycles[29] – anchors, beaks of ships,
Planks turned to marble, quivers, helms,[30] and spears,
And gorgon-headed targes,[31] and the wheels

Notes

[23] *multitudinous* thronging with multitudes.

[24] *mocking* imitating.

[25] *tyrant-quelling myrtle* Greek warriors were sometimes crowned with myrtle, a symbol of love.

[26] *adamant* diamonds.

[27] *Valueless* precious beyond price.

[28] *vegetable silver* silver crafted to appear in organic form; Shelley is recalling the fruit of the tree of life in Milton's Eden, which was 'Of vegetable gold' (*Paradise Lost* iv 220).

[29] *cycles* i.e. eras of time.

[30] *helms* helmets.

[31] *targes* shields.

Of scythed chariots,[32] and the emblazonry
Of trophies, standards, and armorial beasts –
Round which Death laughed: sepulchred emblems
Of dead Destruction, ruin within ruin!
The wrecks beside of many a city vast,
Whose population which the earth grew over
Was mortal, but not human – see, they lie,
Their monstrous works and uncouth skeletons,
Their statues, homes and fanes;[33] prodigious[34] shapes
Huddled in grey annihilation, split,
Jammed in the hard black deep; and over[35] these
The anatomies[36] of unknown winged things,
And fishes which were isles of living scale,
And serpents, bony chains, twisted around
The iron crags, or within heaps of dust
To which the tortuous strength of their last pangs
Had crushed the iron crags; and over[37] these
The jagged alligator, and the might
Of earth-convulsing behemoth,[38] which once
Were monarch beasts, and on the slimy shores
And weed-overgrown continents of earth
Increased and multiplied like summer worms
On an abandoned corpse, till the blue globe
Wrapped deluge round it like a cloak, and they
Yelled, gasped, and were abolished – or some God
Whose throne was in a comet, passed, and cried,
'Be not!' – and like my words they were no more.

THE EARTH.[39]

The joy, the triumph, the delight, the madness!
The boundless, overflowing, bursting gladness!
The vaporous exultation not to be confined!
  Ha! Ha! the animation of delight
  Which wraps me, like an atmosphere of light,
And bears me as a cloud is borne by its own wind!

THE MOON.

  Brother mine, calm wanderer,
  Happy globe of land and air,
Some spirit is darted like a beam from thee,
  Which penetrates my frozen frame,
  And passes with the warmth of flame,
With love, and odour, and deep melody
    Through me, through me!

Notes

[32] *scythed chariots* The ancient British queen Boudicca used to put blades on the axles of her chariot-wheels.

[33] *fanes* temples.

[34] *prodigious* fantastic.

[35] *over* i.e. under. Shelley is burrowing ever further into the mists of time.

[36] *anatomies* skeletons.

[37] *over* i.e. under.

[38] *behemoth* either the elephant or the hippopotamus – probably, as in Milton, the former: 'Behemoth biggest born of earth upheaved / His vastness' (*Paradise Lost* vii 471–2).

[39] Where the Earth of Act I and III iv was a Hellenic goddess and earth-mother, that which appears here is brother and lover of the moon.

THE EARTH.

Ha! Ha! the caverns of my hollow mountains,
My cloven fire-crags,[40] sound-exulting fountains,
Laugh with a vast and inextinguishable laughter:
The oceans, and the deserts, and the abysses
Of the deep air's unmeasured wildernesses,
Answer from all their clouds and billows, echoing after.

They cry aloud as I do: 'Sceptred Curse,[41]
Who all our green and azure universe
Threatenedst to muffle round with black destruction, sending
A solid cloud to rain hot thunderstones,
And splinter and knead down my children's bones,
All I bring forth, to one void mass battering and blending;

Until each crag-like tower, and storied column,
Palace, and obelisk, and temple solemn,
My imperial mountains crowned with cloud, and snow, and fire,
My sea-like forests, every blade and blossom
Which finds a grave or cradle in my bosom,
Were stamped by thy strong hate into a lifeless mire:

How art thou sunk, withdrawn, covered, drunk up
By thirsty nothing, as the brackish cup[42]
Drained by a desert-troop, a little drop for all;
And from beneath, around, within, above,
Filling thy void annihilation, love
Burst in like light on caves cloven by the thunderball.

THE MOON.

The snow upon my lifeless mountains
Is loosened into living fountains,
My solid oceans flow, and sing, and shine;
A spirit from my heart bursts forth,
It clothes with unexpected birth
My cold bare bosom – oh, it must be thine
On mine, on mine!

Gazing on thee I feel, I know
Green stalks burst forth, and bright flowers grow,
And living shapes upon my bosom move;
Music is in the sea and air,
Winged clouds soar here and there,
Dark with the rain new buds are dreaming of –
'Tis love, all love!

THE EARTH.

It interpenetrates my granite mass,
Through tangled roots and trodden clay doth pass
Into the utmost leaves and delicatest flowers;

Notes

[40] *My cloven fire-crags* volcanoes.

[41] *Sceptred Curse* Jupiter.

[42] *the brackish cup* i.e. the salty water in the cup.

Upon the winds, among the clouds 'tis spread;
It wakes a life in the forgotten dead –
They breathe a spirit up from their obscurest bowers –

And like a storm, bursting its cloudy prison
With thunder and with whirlwind, has arisen[43]
Out of the lampless caves of unimagined being,
With earthquake shock and swiftness making shiver
Thought's stagnant chaos, unremoved for ever,[44]
Till hate, and fear, and pain, light-vanquished shadows, fleeing,

Leave Man – who was a many-sided mirror
Which could distort to many a shape of error
This true fair world of things – a sea reflecting love;
Which[45] over all his kind,[46] as the sun's Heaven
Gliding o'er ocean, smooth, serene, and even,
Darting from starry depths radiance and life, doth move:

Leave Man, even as a leprous child is left
Who follows a sick beast to some warm cleft
Of rocks, through which the might of healing springs is poured;
Then when it wanders home with rosy smile,
Unconscious, and its mother fears awhile
It is a spirit, then weeps on her child restored:[47]

Man, oh not men! a chain of linked thought,
Of love and might to be divided not,
Compelling the elements with adamantine stress,
As the sun rules, even with a tyrant's gaze,
The unquiet republic of the maze
Of planets, struggling fierce toward Heaven's free wilderness:

Man, one harmonious soul of many a soul,
Whose nature is its own divine control,
Where all things flow to all, as rivers to the sea;
Familiar acts are beautiful through love;
Labour, and Pain, and Grief, in life's green grove
Sport like tame beasts – none knew how gentle they could be!

His will – with all mean passions, bad delights,
And selfish cares, its trembling satellites,
A spirit ill to guide, but mighty to obey –
Is as a tempest-winged ship, whose helm
Love rules through waves which dare not overwhelm,
Forcing life's wildest shores to own its sovereign sway:

Notes

43 *has arisen* 'Love' is the subject that governs this verb.

44 *unremoved for ever* i.e. hitherto not removed.

45 *Which* i.e. Love.

46 *his kind* i.e. mankind.

47 *Leave man . . . restored* Shelley refers to the legend of King Bladud of Britain, a leper who followed a lost pig to the hot springs of Bath, by which he was cured.

All things confess his strength. Through the cold mass
Of marble and of colour his dreams pass –
Bright threads whence mothers weave the robes their children wear;
Language is a perpetual Orphic song,[48]
Which rules with Daedal harmony[49] a throng
Of thoughts and forms, which else senseless and shapeless were:

The lightning is his slave;[50] Heaven's utmost deep
Gives up her stars, and like a flock of sheep
They pass before his eye, are numbered, and roll on!
The tempest is his steed, he strides the air;[51]
And the abyss shouts from her depth laid bare,
'Heaven, hast thou secrets? Man unveils me; I have none.'

THE MOON.
The shadow of white Death has passed
From my path in heaven at last,
A clinging shroud of solid frost and sleep;
And through my newly-woven bowers
Wander happy paramours
Less mighty, but as mild as those who keep
Thy vales more deep.

THE EARTH.
As the dissolving warmth of dawn may fold
A half-unfrozen dew-globe, green and gold
And crystalline, till it becomes a winged mist,
And wanders up the vault of the blue day,
Outlives the noon, and on the sun's last ray
Hangs o'er the sea, a fleece of fire and amethyst –

THE MOON.
Thou art folded, thou art lying
In the light which is undying
Of thine own joy, and Heaven's smile divine;
All suns and constellations shower
On thee a light, a life, a power
Which doth array thy sphere; thou pourest thine
On mine, on mine!

THE EARTH.
I spin beneath my pyramid of night,[52]
Which points into the heavens, dreaming delight,

Notes

[48] Language is a perpetual Orphic song i.e. it governs our morals and actions. Orpheus tamed wild beasts and stopped the tortures of Hades with his music.

[49] *Daedal harmony* Shelley is thinking of Daedalus, the Greek inventor and craftsman, who devised the labyrinth in which the minotaur was kept. His name is a byword for intricacy and skill.

[50] The lightning is his slave in the sense that man was discovering how electricity could be harnessed to his purposes.

[51] *he strides the air* Ballooning was all the rage in London after the Montgolfier brothers made their first flight in 1783. Shelley had used balloons as a means of distributing his broadside, 'A Declaration of Rights', in the summer of 1812.

[52] *my pyramid of night* As with the 'shadowy cone' at *Paradise Lost* iv 776, Shelley refers to the idea that the earth's shadow is a cone or pyramid of darkness in diametrical opposition to the sun.

Murmuring victorious joy in my enchanted sleep –
As a youth lulled in love-dreams, faintly sighing,
Under the shadow of his beauty lying,[53]
Which round his rest a watch of light and warmth doth keep.

THE MOON.
As in the soft and sweet eclipse
When soul meets soul on lovers' lips,
High hearts are calm, and brightest eyes are dull –
So when thy shadow falls on me,
Then am I mute and still, by thee
Covered; of thy love, Orb most beautiful,
Full, oh too full! –

Thou art speeding round the sun,
Brightest world of many a one,
Green and azure sphere, which shinest
With a light which is divinest
Among all the lamps of Heaven
To whom life and light is given;
I, thy crystal paramour
Borne beside thee by a power
Like the polar paradise,
Magnet-like, of lovers' eyes;
I, a most enamoured maiden,
Whose weak brain is overladen
With the pleasure of her love,
Maniac-like around thee move,
Gazing, an insatiate bride,
On thy form from every side
Like a maenad round the cup
Which Agave lifted up
In the weird Cadmaean forest.[54]
Brother, wheresoe'er thou soarest
I must hurry, whirl and follow
Through the heavens wide and hollow,
Sheltered, by the warm embrace
Of thy soul, from hungry space;
Drinking from thy sense and sight
Beauty, majesty, and might,
As a lover or chameleon
Grows like what it looks upon;
As a violet's gentle eye
Gazes on the azure sky
Until its hue grows like what it beholds;
As a grey and watery mist
Glows like solid amethyst

Notes

[53] *As a youth . . . lying* The youth lies under the halo ('shadow') cast by the light of his beauty into the air above him.

[54] *Like a maenad . . . forest* Agave, daughter of Cadmus, became a maenad and killed her own son, Pentheus.

Athwart the western mountain it enfolds,
When the sunset sleeps
Upon its snow –

THE EARTH.
And the weak day weeps
That it should be so.
Oh gentle Moon, the voice of thy delight
Falls on me like thy clear and tender light
Soothing the seaman, borne the summer night
Through isles forever calm;
Oh gentle Moon, thy crystal accents pierce
The caverns of my pride's deep universe,
Charming the tiger joy, whose tramplings fierce
Made wounds which need thy balm.

PANTHEA. I rise as from a bath of sparkling water,
A bath of azure light, among dark rocks,
Out of the stream of sound.

IONE. Ah me! sweet sister,
The stream of sound has ebbed away from us,
And you pretend to rise out of its wave
Because your words fall like the clear soft dew
Shaken from a bathing wood-nymph's limbs and hair.

PANTHEA. Peace, peace! A mighty Power, which is as darkness,
Is rising out of Earth, and from the sky
Is showered like night, and from within the air
Bursts, like eclipse which had been gathered up
Into the pores of sunlight:[55] the bright visions,
Wherein the singing spirits rode and shone,
Gleam like pale meteors through a watery night.

IONE. There is a sense of words upon mine ear –

PANTHEA. A universal sound like words – oh list!

DEMOGORGON.
Thou Earth, calm empire of a happy soul,
Sphere of divinest shapes and harmonies;
Beautiful orb! gathering as thou dost roll
The love which paves thy path along the skies:

THE EARTH.
I hear! I am as a drop of dew that dies.

DEMOGORGON.
Thou Moon, which gazest on the nightly Earth
With wonder, as it gazes upon thee,
Whilst each to men, and beasts, and the swift birth[56]
Of birds, is beauty, love, calm, harmony:

Notes

[55] *the pores of sunlight* It was believed in the 18th century that there were minute gaps (or pores) between light particles.

[56] *birth* race.

THE MOON.
I hear! I am a leaf shaken by thee.

DEMOGORGON.
Ye kings of suns and stars, Daemons and Gods,
Ethereal Dominations,[57] who possess
Elysian, windless, fortunate abodes
Beyond Heaven's constellated wilderness:

A VOICE (*from above*)
Our great Republic hears: we are blessed, and bless.

DEMOGORGON.
Ye happy dead, whom beams of brightest verse
Are clouds to hide, not colours to portray,
Whether your nature is that universe
Which once ye saw and suffered –

A VOICE (*from beneath*)
Or as they
Whom we have left, we change and pass away.

DEMOGORGON.
Ye elemental Genii,[58] who have homes
From man's high mind even to the central stone
Of sullen lead; from Heaven's star-fretted domes
To the dull weed some sea-worm battens[59] on:

A CONFUSED VOICE.
We hear: thy words waken Oblivion.

DEMOGORGON.
Spirits, whose homes are flesh; ye beasts and birds;
Ye worms and fish; ye living leaves and buds;
Lightning and wind; and ye untameable herds,
Meteors and mists, which throng air's solitudes:

A VOICE.
Thy voice to us is wind among still woods.

DEMOGORGON.
Man, who wert once a despot and a slave;
A dupe and a deceiver; a decay;
A traveller from the cradle to the grave
Through the dim night[60] of this immortal day:

ALL.
Speak: thy strong words may never pass away.

DEMOGORGON.
This is the day, which down the void abysm
At the Earth-born's spell[61] yawns for Heaven's despotism,

Notes

[57] *Dominations* the fourth of the nine orders of angels, as at *Paradise Lost* iii 392.

[58] *elemental Genii* animating spirits of the elements.

[59] *battens* feeds gluttonously.

[60] *the dim night* i.e. the period preceding the eternal day.

[61] *the Earth-born's spell* i.e. Prometheus' revocation of his curse.

And Conquest is dragged captive through the deep:
Love, from its awful throne of patient power
In the wise heart, from the last giddy hour
Of dread endurance, from the slippery, steep,
And narrow verge of crag-like agony, springs
And folds over the world its healing wings.

Gentleness, Virtue, Wisdom, and Endurance:
These are the seals of that most firm assurance
Which bars the pit over Destruction's strength;
And if, with infirm hand, Eternity,
Mother of many acts and hours, should free
The serpent that would clasp her with his length,
These are the spells by which to reassume
An empire o'er the disentangled Doom.

To suffer woes which Hope thinks infinite;
To forgive wrongs darker than death or night;
To defy Power which seems omnipotent;
To love, and bear; to hope, till Hope creates
From its own wreck the thing it contemplates;
Neither to change, nor falter, nor repent:
This, like thy glory, Titan, is to be
Good, great and joyous, beautiful and free;
This is alone Life, Joy, Empire, and Victory.

The Mask of Anarchy Written on the Occasion of the Massacre at Manchester (composed 5–23 September 1819; edited from MS; published 1832)[1]

As I lay asleep in Italy[2]
There came a voice from over the Sea,
And with great power it forth led me
To walk in the visions of Poesy.

I met Murder on the way –
He had a mask like Castlereagh[3] –
Very smooth he looked, yet grim;
Seven bloodhounds followed him.[4]

Notes

THE MASK OF ANARCHY

[1] On 16 August 1819, at St Peter's Field, on the outskirts of Manchester, a political meeting of 60,000 working men and women was dispersed by mounted dragoons, with a brutality that left eleven people dead and 421 cases of serious injury. The news reached Shelley within about a week, and he began meditating this poetic response to the event. See headnote, p. 1049.

[2] Shelley was in Livorno when he heard of the Peterloo Massacre, 'and the torrent of my indignation has not yet done boiling in my veins,' as he told Charles Ollier on 5 September 1819 (Jones ii 117).

[3] Robert Stewart, Viscount Castlereagh (1769–1822), Foreign Secretary 1812–22. As Secretary to the Lord Lieutenant of Ireland (1797–1801), he had been responsible for imprisoning the leaders of the United Irish rebellion. Shelley would have been aware of Byron's stanzas attacking him, *Don Juan* Dedication, stanzas 12–15 (pp. 936–7).

[4] In 1815, Britain joined an alliance of seven other nations (Austria, France, Russia, Prussia, Portugal, Spain and Sweden) in an agreement to postpone final abolition of the slave trade.

Figure 15 *The Peterloo Massacre*, by an unknown artist, published by Richard Carlile, 1 October 1819. On 16 August 1819, at St Peter's Field, on the outskirts of Manchester, a peaceful public meeting was dispersed by armed dragoons with a brutality that left eleven people dead and 421 cases of serious injury. The news reached Shelley within about a week, and inspired 'The Mask of Anarchy'. (Dove Cottage, The Wordsworth Trust, Grasmere.)

All were fat; and well they might
Be in admirable plight,
For one by one, and two by two,
He tossed them human hearts to chew,
Which from his wide cloak he drew.

Next came Fraud, and he had on,
Like Eldon,[5] an ermined gown;
His big tears, for he wept well,
Turned to millstones as they fell.

And the little children, who
Round his feet played to and fro,
Thinking every tear a gem,
Had their brains knocked out by them.

Notes

[5] John Scott, Baron Eldon, Lord Chancellor, who, on 27 March 1817, was responsible for depriving Shelley of access to his children (Ianthe and Charles) by Harriet Westbrook. Shelley did not see Ianthe again, and Charles he never saw.

Clothed with the Bible, as with light,
And the shadows of the night,
Like Sidmouth,[6] next Hypocrisy
On a crocodile[7] rode by.

And many more Destructions played
In this ghastly masquerade,
All disguised, even to the eyes,
Like Bishops, lawyers, peers, or spies.

Last came Anarchy:[8] he rode
On a white horse, splashed with blood;
He was pale even to the lips,
Like Death in the Apocalypse.[9]

And he wore a kingly crown,
And in his grasp a sceptre shone;
On his brow this mark I saw –
'I am God, and King, and Law.'[10]

With a pace stately and fast,
Over English land he passed,
Trampling to a mire of blood
The adoring multitude.[11]

And a mighty troop around,
With their trampling shook the ground,
Waving each a bloody sword,
For the service of their Lord.[12]

And with glorious triumph, they
Rode through England proud and gay,
Drunk as with intoxication
Of the wine of desolation.

O'er fields and towns, from sea to sea,
Passed the Pageant[13] swift and free,
Tearing up, and trampling down,
Till they came to London town.

Notes

[6] Henry Addington (1757–1844), created Viscount Sidmouth in 1805, had been Prime Minister and Chancellor of the Exchequer, and was in 1819 Home Secretary. He applauded the Peterloo Massacre in the House of Commons, as reported by Hazlitt (Howe xx 142).

[7] *a crocodile* Crocodiles were believed to weep as they devoured their prey, and 'crocodile tears' remain a byword for hypocrisy.

[8] *Anarchy* For more on Anarchy see headnote, p. 1049. Shelley refers to the breakdown of order such as that which led to the Peterloo Massacre. He did not regard it as a good thing either for the government or for the victims.

[9] *He was pale . . . Apocalypse* Revelation 6: 8: 'And I looked, and behold a pale horse: and his name that sat on him was Death, and Hell followed with him.'

[10] *On his brow . . . Law* a parody of the inscription borne by the messianic rider of Revelation: 'And he hath on his vesture and on his thigh a name written, KING OF KINGS, AND LORD OF LORDS' (Revelation 19: 16).

[11] *The adoring multitude* The people admire Anarchy. Shelley's point is that to resort to violence is to justify the government's equally violent means of suppression.

[12] *their Lord* George III, the 'old, mad, blind, despised, and dying king' of *England in 1819* (p. 1180), although the term could also apply to the Christian God of the Church of England, part of what Shelley regarded as the corrupt political system responsible for the Peterloo Massacre.

[13] *Pageant* tableau, allegorical procession.

And each dweller, panic-stricken,
Felt his heart with terror sicken
Hearing the tempestuous cry
Of the triumph of Anarchy.

For with pomp to meet him came
Clothed in arms like blood and flame,
The hired murderers, who did sing
'Thou art God, and Law, and King.

We have waited, weak and lone,
For thy coming, Mighty One!
Our purses are empty, our swords are cold,
Give us glory, and blood, and gold.'

Lawyers and priests, a motley crowd,
To the earth their pale brows bowed;
Like a bad prayer, not overloud,
Whispering, 'Thou art Law and God.'

Then all cried with one accord,
'Thou art King, and God, and Lord;
Anarchy, to thee we bow,
By thy name made holy now!'

And Anarchy, the Skeleton,
Bowed and grinned to everyone,
As well as if his education
Had cost ten millions to the nation.

For he knew the Palaces
Of our Kings were rightly his;
His the sceptre, crown, and globe,[14]
And the gold-inwoven robe.

So he sent his slaves before
To seize upon the Bank and Tower,[15]
And was proceeding with intent
To meet his pensioned Parliament;[16]

When one fled past, a maniac maid,
And her name was Hope, she said;
But she looked more like Despair,
And she cried out in the air:

Notes

[14] *globe* golden orb, symbol of kingly power.

[15] *the Bank and Tower* strongholds of power: the Bank of England, in Threadneedle Street since 1734, and the Tower of London, the most perfect medieval fortress in Britain, on Tower Hill since around 1066. They had been the objects of an alleged plot in 1817, providing an excuse for the suspension of habeas corpus.

[16] *his pensioned Parliament* The politicians are in the pay of Anarchy, because his violent means enable them to retain power.

'My father Time is weak and grey
With waiting for a better day;
See how idiot-like he stands,
Fumbling with his palsied hands!

He has had child after child
And the dust of death is piled
Over everyone but me –
Misery, oh, misery!'

Then she lay down in the street,
Right before the horses' feet,
Expecting, with a patient eye,
Murder, Fraud and Anarchy.

When between her and her foes
A mist, a light, an image rose,
Small at first, and weak, and frail,
Like the vapour of a vale;

Till as clouds grow on the blast,
Like tower-crowned giants striding fast,
And glare with lightnings as they fly,
And speak in thunder to the sky,

It grew – a Shape arrayed in mail
Brighter than the viper's scale,
And upborne on wings whose grain[17]
Was as the light of sunny rain.

On its helm,[18] seen far away,
A planet, like the morning's,[19] lay;
And those plumes[20] its light rained through
Like a shower of crimson dew.

With step as soft as wind it passed
O'er the heads of men – so fast
That they knew the presence there,
And looked – and all was empty air.

As flowers beneath May's footstep waken,
As stars from night's loose hair are shaken,
As waves arise when loud winds call,
Thoughts sprung where'er that step did fall.

And the prostrate multitude
Looked – and ankle-deep in blood,
Hope, that maiden most serene,
Was walking with a quiet mien.

Notes

[17] *grain* colour.
[18] *helm* helmet.
[19] *A planet, like the morning's* i.e. a star, like Venus (the morning star).
[20] *plumes* feathers in the helmet.

And Anarchy, the ghastly birth,
Lay dead earth upon the earth;
The Horse of Death, tameless as wind,
Fled, and with his hoofs did grind
To dust the murderers thronged behind.

A rushing light of clouds and splendour,
A sense awakening and yet tender,
Was heard and felt – and at its close
These words of joy and fear arose

(As if their own indignant Earth
Which gave the sons of England birth
Had felt their blood upon her brow,
And shuddering with a mother's throe

Had turned every drop of blood
By which her face had been bedewed
To an accent unwithstood;
As if her heart had cried aloud):

'Men of England, heirs of Glory,
Heroes of unwritten story,
Nurslings of one mighty Mother,
Hopes of her, and one another,

Rise like lions after slumber
In unvanquishable number,
Shake your chains to Earth like dew
Which in sleep had fallen on you –
Ye are many; they are few.

What is Freedom? Ye can tell
That which slavery is, too well –
For its very name has grown
To an echo of your own.

'Tis to work and have such pay
As just keeps life from day to day
In your limbs, as in a cell
For the tyrants' use to dwell.

So that ye for them are made
Loom, and plough, and sword, and spade,
With or without your own will bent
To their defence and nourishment.

'Tis to see your children weak
With their mothers pine and peak,[21]
When the winter winds are bleak –
They are dying whilst I speak.

Notes

[21] *pine and peak* grow thin and emaciated; cf. *Macbeth* I iii 23.

'Tis to hunger for such diet
As the rich man in his riot[22]
Casts to the fat dogs that lie
Surfeiting beneath his eye.

'Tis to let the Ghost of Gold[23]
Take from toil a thousandfold –
More than ere its substance could
In the tyrannies of old.

Paper coin – that forgery
Of the title-deeds, which ye
Hold to something of the worth
Of the inheritance of Earth.

'Tis to be a slave in soul
And to hold no strong control
Over your own wills, but be
All that others make of ye.

And at length when ye complain
With a murmur weak and vain,
'Tis to see the Tyrant's crew
Ride over your wives and you –
Blood is on the grass like dew.

Then it is to feel revenge
Fiercely thirsting to exchange
Blood for blood and wrong for wrong –
Do not thus when ye are strong.

Birds find rest in narrow nest
When weary of their winged quest;
Beasts find fare in woody lair
When storm and snow are in the air.

Asses, swine, have litter spread
And with fitting food are fed;
All things have a home but one –
Thou, oh, Englishman, hast none![24]

This is slavery – savage men
Or wild beasts within a den
Would endure not as ye do;
But such ills they never knew.

Notes

[22] *riot* extravagance.

[23] *the Ghost of Gold* paper money, which Shelley regarded as a trick to inflate the currency and depress the cost of labour.

[24] *Asses, swine . . . hast none* a reworking of Christ's words: 'The foxes have holes, and the birds of the air have nests; but the Son of man hath not where to lay his head' (Matthew 8: 20).

What art thou Freedom? Oh, could slaves
Answer from their living graves
This demand, tyrants would flee
Like a dream's dim imagery.

Thou art not, as impostors say,
A shadow soon to pass away,
A superstition, and a name
Echoing from the cave of Fame.[25]

For the labourer thou art bread,
And a comely table spread
From his daily labour come
To a neat and happy home.

Thou art clothes, and fire, and food
For the trampled multitude;
No – in countries that are free
Such starvation cannot be
As in England now we see.

To the rich thou art a check,
When his foot is on the neck
Of his victim, thou dost make
That he treads upon a snake.

Thou art Justice; ne'er for gold
May thy righteous laws be sold
As laws are in England – thou
Shieldst alike the high and low.

Thou art Wisdom – Freemen never
Dream that God will damn for ever
All who think those things untrue
Of which Priests make such ado.

Thou art Peace – never by thee
Would blood and treasure wasted be,
As tyrants wasted them, when all
Leagued to quench thy flame in Gaul.[26]

What if English toil and blood
Was poured forth, even as a flood?
It availed, oh Liberty!
To dim, but not extinguish thee.

Notes

[25] *Fame* rumour, gossip.

[26] *Gaul* Revolutionary France. England formed an alliance with Prussia and Austria in 1793, against France, following the execution of Louis XVI.

Thou art Love – the rich[27] have kissed
Thy feet, and like him following Christ,[28]
Give their substance to the free
And through the rough world follow thee;

Or turn their wealth to arms, and make
War for thy beloved sake
On wealth, and war, and fraud – whence they
Drew the power which is their prey.

Science,[29] Poetry, and Thought
Are thy lamps; they make the lot
Of the dwellers in a cot[30]
So serene, they curse it not.

Spirit, Patience, Gentleness,
All that can adorn and bless
Art thou – let deeds, not words, express
Thine exceeding loveliness.

Let a great Assembly be
Of the fearless and the free
On some spot of English ground
Where the plains stretch wide around.

Let the blue sky overhead
The green earth on which ye tread,
All that must eternal be
Witness the solemnity.

From the corners uttermost
Of the bounds of English coast;
From every hut, village and town
Where those who live and suffer moan
For others' misery or their own;

From the workhouse and the prison
Where pale as corpses newly risen,
Women, children, young and old,
Groan for pain, and weep for cold;

From the haunts of daily life
Where is waged the daily strife
With common wants and common cares
Which sows the human heart with tares;[31]

Notes

[27] *the rich* i.e. those dedicated to liberty, such as Shelley.
[28] *like him following Christ* Shelley appears to have in mind the three disciples of Christ described at Luke 9: 57–62.
[29] *Science* knowledge.
[30] *cot* cottage.
[31] *tares* weeds – i.e. anxieties.

Lastly from the palaces
Where the murmur of distress
Echoes, like the distant sound
Of a wind alive around,

Those prison halls of wealth and fashion,
Where some few feel such compassion
For those who groan, and toil, and wail
As must make their brethren pale –

Ye who suffer woes untold,
Or to feel, or[32] to behold
Your lost country bought and sold
With a price of blood and gold –

Let a vast Assembly be,
And with great solemnity
Declare with measured words that ye
Are, as God has made ye, free.

Be your strong and simple words
Keen to wound as sharpened swords,
And wide as targes[33] let them be
With their shade to cover ye.

Let the tyrants pour around
With a quick and startling sound,
Like the loosening of a sea,
Troops of armed emblazonry.

Let the charged artillery drive
Till the dead air seems alive
With the clash of clanging wheels,
And the tramp of horses' heels.

Let the fixed bayonet
Gleam with sharp desire to wet
Its bright point in English blood,
Looking keen as one for food.

Let the horsemen's scimitars[34]
Wheel and flash, like sphereless stars
Thirsting to eclipse their burning
In a sea of death and mourning.

Stand ye calm and resolute,
Like a forest close and mute,
With folded arms and looks which are
Weapons of an unvanquished war;

Notes

[32] *Or . . . or* either . . . or.

[33] *targes* shields.

[34] *the horsemen's scimitars* Most of the wounded at Peterloo suffered sabre cuts.

And let Panic, who outspeeds
The career of armed steeds
Pass, a disregarded shade
Through your phalanx undismayed.

Let the laws of your own land,
Good or ill, between ye stand
Hand to hand, and foot to foot,
Arbiters of the dispute,

The old laws of England – they
Whose reverend heads with age are grey,
Children of a wiser day;
And whose solemn voice must be
Thine own echo – Liberty!

On those who first should violate
Such sacred heralds in their state,
Rest the blood that must ensue,
And it will not rest on you.

And if then the tyrants dare,
Let them ride among you there,
Slash, and stab, and maim, and hew –
What they like, that let them do.

With folded arms and steady eyes,
And little fear, and less surprise,
Look upon them as they slay,
Till their rage has died away.

Then they will return with shame
To the place from which they came,
And the blood thus shed will speak
In hot blushes on their cheek.

Every woman in the land
Will point at them as they stand –
They will hardly dare to greet
Their acquaintance in the Street.

And the bold, true warriors
Who have hugged Danger in wars
Will turn to those who would be free,
Ashamed of such base company.

And that slaughter to the nation
Shall steam up like inspiration,
Eloquent, oracular –
A volcano heard afar.[35]

Notes

[35] *And that slaughter . . . afar* This image of revolution is comparable to the image of 'a volcano's meteor-breathing chasm, / Whence the oracular vapour is hurled up' (*Prometheus Unbound* II iii 3–4).

And these words shall then become
Like oppression's thundered doom
Ringing through each heart and brain,
Heard again – again – again.

Rise like lions after slumber
In unvanquishable number;
Shake your chains to earth like dew
Which in sleep had fallen on you –
Ye are many, they are few.'

Ode to the West Wind (composed *c.* 25 October 1819)[1]

From Prometheus Unbound (1820)[2]

I

Oh wild west wind, thou breath of autumn's being;
Thou from whose unseen presence the leaves dead
Are driven, like ghosts from an enchanter fleeing,

Yellow, and black, and pale, and hectic[3] red,
Pestilence-stricken multitudes; oh thou
Who chariotest to their dark wintry bed

The winged seeds, where they lie cold and low,
Each like a corpse within its grave, until
Thine azure sister of the spring shall blow

Her clarion[4] o'er the dreaming earth, and fill
(Driving sweet buds like flocks to feed in air)
With living hues and odours plain and hill –

Wild spirit, which art moving everywhere,
Destroyer and preserver, hear, oh hear!

II

Thou on whose stream, mid the steep sky's commotion,
Loose clouds like earth's decaying leaves are shed,
Shook from the tangled boughs of heaven and ocean,

Notes

Ode to the West Wind

[1] 'This poem was conceived and chiefly written in a wood that skirts the Arno, near Florence, and on a day when that tempestuous wind, whose temperature is at once mild and animating, was collecting the vapours which pour down the autumnal rains. They began, as I foresaw, at sunset, with a violent tempest of hail and rain, attended by that magnificent thunder and lightning peculiar to the Cisalpine regions' (Shelley's note). This is Shelley's most powerful account of the poet's function, in the light of the Peterloo Massacre; see headnote, p. 1049.

[2] In addition to *Prometheus Unbound*, Shelley's 1820 volume contained a number of shorter works composed in Italy.

[3] *hectic* Shelley is thinking of the 'hectic' flush of a fever.

[4] *clarion* war-trumpet.

Angels[5] of rain and lightning; there are spread
On the blue surface of thine airy surge,
Like the bright hair uplifted from the head

Of some fierce maenad,[6] even from the dim verge
Of the horizon to the zenith's height,
The locks of the approaching storm. Thou dirge[7]

Of the dying year, to which this closing night
Will be the dome of a vast sepulchre,
Vaulted with all thy congregated might

Of vapours, from whose solid atmosphere
Black rain, and fire, and hail will burst[8] – oh hear!

III

Thou who didst waken from his summer dreams
The blue Mediterranean, where he lay,
Lulled by the coil of his crystalline streams,

Beside a pumice isle in Baiae's bay,
And saw in sleep old palaces and towers
Quivering within the wave's intenser day,[9]

All overgrown with azure moss and flowers
So sweet, the sense faints picturing them! Thou
For whose path the Atlantic's level powers

Cleave themselves into chasms, while far below
The sea-blooms and the oozy woods which wear
The sapless foliage of the ocean, know

Thy voice, and suddenly grow grey with fear,
And tremble and despoil themselves[10] – oh hear!

IV

If I were a dead leaf thou mightest bear;
If I were a swift cloud to fly with thee;
A wave to pant beneath thy power, and share

Notes

[5] *Angels* messengers.

[6] *maenad* Bacchante, an inspired votary of Bacchus, god of wine.

[7] *dirge* lament for the dead.

[8] *Black rain, and fire, and hail will burst* millennial weather conditions, but also those which prevailed on the day this poem was conceived; see p. 1175n1, above.

[9] *Beside a pumice isle . . . day* In a letter to Peacock of 17 or 18 December 1818, Shelley described 'passing the Bay of Baiae and observing the ruins of its antique grandeur standing like rocks in the transparent sea under our boat' (Jones ii 61). In Roman times Baiae was the resort of emperors and the rich.

[10] 'The phenomenon alluded to at the conclusion of the third stanza is well known to naturalists. The vegetation at the bottom of the sea, of rivers, and of lakes, sympathizes with that of the land in the change of seasons, and is consequently influenced by the winds which announce it' (Shelley's note).

The impulse of thy strength, only less free
Than thou, oh uncontrollable! If even
I were as in my boyhood, and could be

The comrade of thy wanderings over heaven,
As then, when to outstrip thy skyey speed
Scarce seemed a vision; I would ne'er have striven

As thus with thee in prayer in my sore need.
Oh lift me as a wave, a leaf, a cloud!
I fall upon the thorns of life! I bleed!

A heavy weight of hours has chained and bowed
One too like thee[11] – tameless, and swift, and proud.

V

Make me thy lyre, even as the forest is:
What if my leaves are falling like its own?[12]
The tumult of thy mighty harmonies

Will take from both a deep autumnal tone,
Sweet though in sadness. Be thou, spirit fierce,
My spirit! Be thou me, impetuous one!

Drive my dead thoughts over the universe
Like withered leaves to quicken a new birth!
And, by the incantation of this verse,

Scatter, as from an unextinguished hearth
Ashes and sparks, my words among mankind!
Be through my lips to unawakened earth

The trumpet of a prophecy! Oh wind,
If winter comes, can spring be far behind?

On Life (composed late 1819)

From Essays, Letters from Abroad, Translations and Fragments (2 vols, Philadelphia, 1840)

Life and the world, or whatever we call that which we are and feel, is an astonishing thing. The mist of familiarity[1] obscures from us the wonder of our being. We are struck with admiration at some of its transient modifications, but it is itself the great miracle. What are changes of empires, the wreck of dynasties, with the opinions

Notes

[11] *One too like thee* i.e. the poet.

[12] *What if my leaves are falling like its own?* Shelley was only 27, but he had just noticed that had some premature strands of grey hair.

On Life

[1] *mist of familiarity* compare Coleridge's 'film of familiarity', *Biographia Literaria*, p. 692, above.

which supported them; what is the birth and the extinction of religious and of political systems, to life? What are the revolutions of the globe which we inhabit, and the operations of the elements of which it is composed, compared with life? What is the universe of stars and suns (of which this inhabited earth is one), and their motions and their destiny, compared with life? Life, the great miracle, we admire not because it is so miraculous. It is well that we are so shielded by the familiarity of what is at once so certain and so unfathomable, from an astonishment which would otherwise absorb and overawe the functions of that which is its object.

If any artist, I do not say had executed, but had merely conceived in his mind the system of the sun, and the stars and planets, they not existing, and had painted to us in words or upon canvas the spectacle now afforded by the nightly cope of heaven, and illustrated it by the wisdom of astronomy, great would be our admiration. Or had he imagined the scenery of this earth, the mountains, the seas and the rivers, the grass and the flowers, and the variety of the forms and masses of the leaves of the woods, and the colours which attend the setting and the rising sun, and the hues of the atmosphere, turbid or serene, these things not before existing, truly we should have been astonished – and it would not have been a vain boast to have said of such a man, 'Non merita nome di creatore, sennon Iddio ed il Poeta'.[2] But now these things are looked on with little wonder, and to be conscious of them with intense delight is esteemed to be the distinguishing mark of a refined and extraordinary person. The multitude of men care not for them; it is thus with life – that which includes all.

What is life? Thoughts and feelings arise, with or without our will, and we employ words to express them. We are born, and our birth is unremembered, and our infancy remembered but in fragments. We live on, and in living we lose the apprehension of life. How vain is it to think that words can penetrate the mystery of our being! Rightly used they may make evident our ignorance to ourselves, and this is much. For what are we? Whence do we come, and whither do we go? Is birth the commencement, is death the conclusion of our being? What is birth and death?

The most refined abstractions of logic conduct to a view of life which, though startling to the apprehension, is in fact that which the habitual sense of its repeated combinations has extinguished in us. It strips, as it were, the painted curtain from this scene of things. I confess that I am one of those who am unable to refuse my assent to the conclusions of those philosophers who assert that nothing exists but as it is perceived.

It is a decision against which all our persuasions struggle, and we must be long convicted before we can be convinced that the solid universe of external things is 'such stuff as dreams are made of'.[3] The shocking absurdities of the popular philosophy of mind and matter, and its fatal consequences in morals, their violent dogmatism concerning the source of all things, had early conducted me to materialism.[4] This materialism is a seducing system to young and superficial minds; it allows its disciples to talk, and dispenses them from thinking. But I was discontented with such a view of things as it afforded; man is a being of high aspirations 'looking both before and after',[5] whose 'thoughts wander through eternity',[6] disclaiming alliance with transience and decay, incapable of imagining to himself annihilation, existing but in the future and the past, being not what he is, but what he has been and shall be. Whatever

Notes

[2] 'None deserves the name of creator except God and the poet'; from Pierantonio Serassi's *Life of Torquato Tasso* (1785).

[3] *such stuff as dreams are made of* from *The Tempest* IV i 156–7.

[4] *materialism* i.e. the philosophy of Locke, Hartley, Priestley, and of the French Enlightenment, particularly Holbach.

[5] *looking both before and after* from *Hamlet* IV iv 37.

[6] *thoughts wander through eternity* from *Paradise Lost* ii 148: 'Those thoughts that wander through eternity'.

may be his true and final destination, there is a spirit within him at enmity with nothingness and dissolution. This is the character of all life and being. Each is at once the centre and the circumference, the point to which all things are referred, and the line in which all things are contained. Such contemplations as these, materialism and the popular philosophy of mind and matter alike forbid; they are only consistent with the intellectual system.

It is absurd to enter into a long recapitulation of arguments sufficiently familiar to those enquiring minds whom alone a writer on abstruse subjects can be conceived to address. Perhaps the most clear and vigorous statement of the intellectual system is to be found in Sir William Drummond's *Academical Questions*; after such an exposition it would be idle to translate into other words what could only lose its energy and fitness by the change. Examined point by point and word by word, the most discriminating intellects have been able to discern no train of thoughts in the process of reasoning, which does not conduct inevitably to the conclusion which has been stated.

What follows from the admission? It establishes no new truth, it gives us no additional insight into our hidden nature, neither its action, nor itself. Philosophy, impatient as it may be to build, has much work yet remaining as pioneer for the overgrowth of ages. It makes one step towards this object; it destroys error and the roots of error. It leaves what is too often the duty of the reformer in political and ethical questions to leave – a vacancy. It reduces the mind to that freedom in which it would have acted, but for the misuse of words and signs, the instruments of its own creation. By signs, I would be understood in a wide sense, including what is properly meant by that term, and what I peculiarly mean. In this latter sense, almost all familiar objects are signs, standing not for themselves but for others, in their capacity of suggesting one thought which shall lead to a train of thoughts. Our whole life is thus an education of error.

Let us recollect our sensations as children. What a distinct and intense apprehension had we of the world and of ourselves. Many of the circumstances of social life were then important to us, which are now no longer so. But that is not the point of comparison on which I mean to insist. We less habitually distinguished all that we saw and felt from ourselves. They seemed as it were to constitute one mass. There are some persons who in this respect are always children. Those who are subject to the state called reverie feel as if their nature were dissolved into the surrounding universe, or as if the surrounding universe were absorbed into their being.[7] They are conscious of no distinction. And these are states which precede or accompany or follow an unusually intense and vivid apprehension of life. As men grow up, this power commonly decays, and they become mechanical and habitual agents. Thus feelings and then reasonings are the combined result of a multitude of entangled thoughts, and of a series of what are called impressions, planted by reiteration.

The view of life presented by the most refined deductions of the intellectual philosophy, is that of unity. Nothing exists but as it is perceived. The difference is merely nominal between those two classes of thought which are vulgarly distinguished by the names of ideas and of external objects.[8] Pursuing the same thread of reasoning, the existence of distinct individual minds, similar to that which is employed in now questioning its own nature, is likewise found to be a delusion. The words, *I*,

Notes

[7] *as if . . . being* Compare Wordsworth's 'abyss of idealism', p. 582 above. This paragraph is reminiscent of the 'Ode'.

[8] This is essentially the argument put forward by George Berkeley, to whose ideas the young Coleridge subscribed (see p. 614n17); it was a means of justifying Coleridge's hope that thoughts and things were essentially the same – that they were 'Parts and proportions of one wondrous whole' (*Religious Musings* 142).

you, they are not signs of any actual difference subsisting between the assemblage of thoughts thus indicated, but are merely marks employed to denote the different modifications of the one mind.

Let it not be supposed that this doctrine conducts to the monstrous presumption that I, the person who now write and think, am that one mind. I am but a portion of it. The words *I*, and *you* and *they* are grammatical devices invented simply for arrangement and totally devoid of the intense and exclusive sense usually attached to them. It is difficult to find terms adequate to express so subtle a conception as that to which the intellectual philosophy has conducted us. We are on that verge where words abandon us, and what wonder if we grow dizzy to look down the dark abyss of how little we know!

The relations of *things* remain unchanged by whatever system. By the word *things* is to be understood any object of thought; that is, any thought upon which any other thought is employed, with an apprehension of distinction. The relations of these remain unchanged – and such is the material of our knowledge.

What is the cause of life? That is, how was it produced, or what agencies distinct from life, have acted or act upon life? All recorded generations of mankind have wearily busied themselves in inventing answers to this question. And the result has been religion. Yet that the basis of all things cannot be (as the popular philosophy alleges) mind, is sufficiently evident. Mind (as far as we have any experience of its properties, and, beyond that, experience how vain is argument) cannot create, it can only perceive. It is said also to be the cause; but cause is only a word expressing a certain state of the human mind with regard to the manner in which two thoughts are apprehended to be related to each other. If anyone desires to know how unsatisfactorily the popular philosophy employs itself upon this great question, they need only impartially reflect upon the manner in which thoughts develop themselves in their minds. It is infinitely improbable that the cause of mind – that is, of existence – is similar to mind.

England in 1819 (composed by 23 December 1819; published 1839; edited from MS)[1]

An old, mad, blind, despised, and dying king;[2]
Princes,[3] the dregs of their dull race, who flow
Through public scorn – mud from a muddy spring;
Rulers who neither see, nor feel, nor know,
But leech-like to their fainting country cling,
Till they drop, blind in blood, without a blow.
A people starved and stabbed in th' untilled field;[4]
An army, which liberticide[5] and prey
Makes as a two-edged sword to all who wield;[6]

Notes

England in 1819

[1] Shelley sent this sonnet to Leigh Hunt for *The Examiner* on 23 December 1819. By now, he was becoming resigned to the fact that no one wanted to publish his poems. He sounds almost impatient in the letter to Hunt: 'What a state England is in! But you will never write politics. I don't wonder; but I wish then that you would write a paper in the *Examiner* on the actual state of the country, and what, under all the circumstances of the conflicting passions and interests of men, we are to expect' (Jones ii 166).

[2] George III, on the throne since 1760, was old and ill, and had been insane for years. He died on 29 January 1820.

[3] *Princes* George III's sons were prodigal, profligate and unstable to the point of madness.

[4] *A people . . . field* a reference to the Peterloo Massacre, 16 August 1819 (see p. 1049).

[5] *liberticide* the killing of liberty.

[6] *Makes . . . wield* the soldiers destroy their own freedom as they cut down the crowd.

Golden and sanguine[7] laws which tempt and slay;
Religion Christless, Godless – a book sealed;
A senate, time's worst statute, unrepealed[8] –
Are graves from which a glorious phantom may
Burst, to illumine our tempestuous day.

'Lift not the painted veil' (composed 1819;[1] first published 1824; edited from MS)

Lift not the painted veil which those who live
Call Life; though unreal shapes be pictured there
And it but mimic all we would believe
With colours idly spread – behind lurk Fear
And Hope, twin destinies, who ever weave
Their shadows o'er the chasm, sightless and drear.[2]
I knew one who had lifted it. He sought,
For his lost heart was tender, things to love
But found them not, alas; nor was there aught
The world contains, the which he could approve.
Through the unheeding many[3] he did move,
A splendour among shadows, a bright blot
Upon this gloomy scene, a Spirit that strove
For truth, and like the Preacher,[4] found it not.

To a Skylark (composed late June 1820)[1]

From Prometheus Unbound (1820)[2]

Hail to thee, blithe spirit!
 Bird thou never wert –
That from heaven, or near it,
 Pourest thy full heart
In profuse strains of unpremeditated art.

Notes

[7] *Golden and sanguine* gold and blood are associated with tyranny.

[8] An early, deleted version of this line in MS reads: 'A cloak of lies worn on Power's holiday'. The 'senate', or Houses of Parliament, was woefully unrepresentative in Shelley's day.

'LIFT NOT THE PAINTED VEIL'

[1] The dating of this sonnet is disputed; Mary Shelley placed it in 1818. Its mood of isolation and dejection may be due in part to an attack on Shelley in the *Quarterly Review,* news of which reached him in July that year. Some editors suggest it might have been composed as late as spring 1820.

[2] *sightless and drear* invisible and dark.

[3] *many* i.e. crowds, multitudes.

[4] *the Preacher* a reference to the Preacher in Ecclesiastes, who 'applied mine heart to know, and to search, and to seek out wisdom, and the reason of things, and to know the wickedness of folly, even of foolishness and madness . . . but I find not' (Ecclesiastes 7: 25, 28).

TO A SKYLARK

[1] As Mary Shelley recalled, this poem was written at the Gisbornes' house at Livorno, probably on 22 June: 'It was on a beautiful summer evening, while wandering among the lanes whose myrtle hedges were the bowers of the fireflies, that we heard the carolling of the skylark which inspired one of the most beautiful of his poems.'

[2] In addition to *Prometheus Unbound*, Shelley's 1820 volume contained a number of shorter works composed in Italy.

Higher still and higher
From the earth thou springest
Like a cloud of fire;
The blue deep thou wingest,
And singing still dost soar, and soaring ever singest.

In the golden lightning
Of the sunken sun
O'er which clouds are brightning,
Thou dost float and run
Like an unbodied joy whose race is just begun.

The pale purple even
Melts around thy flight;
Like a star of heaven
In the broad daylight
Thou art unseen[3] – but yet I hear thy shrill delight,

Keen as are the arrows
Of that silver sphere,[4]
Whose intense lamp narrows
In the white dawn clear,
Until we hardly see – we feel that it is there.

All the earth and air
With thy voice is loud,
As when night is bare
From one lonely cloud
The moon rains out her beams – and heaven is overflowed.

What thou art we know not;
What is most like thee?
From rainbow clouds there flow not
Drops so bright to see
As from thy presence showers a rain of melody.

Like a poet hidden
In the light of thought,
Singing hymns unbidden,[5]
Till the world is wrought
To sympathy with hopes and fears it heeded not;

Like a high-born maiden
In a palace-tower,
Soothing her love-laden
Soul in secret hour,
With music sweet as love, which overflows her bower;

Notes

[3] *Thou art unseen* John Gisborne recalled how he and Shelley used to listen to the skylarks, which flew 'to a height at which the straining eye could scarcely ken the stationary and diminutive specks into which their soft and still receding forms had at length vanished' (journal of John Gisborne, 20 October 1827).

[4] *that silver sphere* The morning star (Venus) is so bright that it can be seen even after sunrise.

[5] *hymns unbidden* i.e. poems that are the direct result of inspiration.

Like a glow-worm golden
  In a dell of dew,
Scattering unbeholden
  Its aerial hue
Among the flowers and grass which screen it from the view;

Like a rose embowered
  In its own green leaves,
By warm winds deflowered
  Till the scent it gives
Makes faint with too much sweet these heavy-winged thieves;

Sound of vernal showers
  On the twinkling grass,
Rain-awakened flowers,
  All that ever was
Joyous and clear and fresh, thy music doth surpass.

Teach us, sprite or bird,
  What sweet thoughts are thine;
I have never heard
  Praise of love or wine
That panted forth a flood of rapture so divine:

Chorus Hymeneal[6]
  Or triumphal chaunt
Matched with thine would be all
  But an empty vaunt,[7]
A thing wherein we feel there is some hidden want.

What objects are the fountains
  Of thy happy strain?[8]
What fields or waves or mountains?
  What shapes of sky or plain?
What love of thine own kind? What ignorance of pain?

With thy clear keen joyance
  Languor cannot be –
Shadow of annoyance
  Never came near thee;
Thou lovest, but ne'er knew love's sad satiety.

Waking or asleep,
  Thou of death must deem
Things more true and deep
  Than we mortals dream,
Or how could thy notes flow in such a crystal stream?

Notes

[6] *Chorus Hymeneal* wedding-song. Hymen was the Greek god of marriage.

[7] *vaunt* boast.

[8] *strain* song.

We look before and after,[9]
And pine for what is not;
Our sincerest laughter
With some pain is fraught –
Our sweetest songs are those that tell of saddest thought.

Yet if we could scorn
Hate and pride and fear;
If we were things born
Not to shed a tear,
I know not how thy joy we ever should come near.

Better than all measures
Of delightful sound;
Better than all treasures
That in books are found –
Thy skill to poet were, thou scorner of the ground!

Teach me half the gladness
That thy brain must know,
Such harmonious madness[10]
From my lips would flow
The world should listen then, as I am listening now.

A Defence of Poetry; or, Remarks Suggested by an Essay Entitled 'The Four Ages of Poetry' (extracts) (composed February–March 1821; first published 1840; edited from MS)[1]

According to one mode of regarding those two classes of mental action which are called reason and imagination, the former may be considered as mind contemplating the relations borne by one thought to another, however produced; and the latter, as mind acting upon those thoughts so as to colour them with its own light, and composing from them, as from elements, other thoughts, each containing within itself the principle of its own integrity. The one is the *to poiein*,[2] or the principle of synthesis, and has for its objects those forms which are common to universal nature

Notes

[9] *We look before and after* Hamlet speaks of how human beings were created 'with such large discourse, / Looking before and after' (*Hamlet* IV iv 36–7).

[10] *harmonious madness* inspiration to write beautiful poetry.

A DEFENCE OF POETRY

[1] Inspired by Thomas Love Peacock's essay, 'The Four Ages of Poetry', published in *Ollier's Literary Miscellany* (1820). Peacock's argument was that classical poetry passed through four ages: (1) an iron age of warriors, heroes and gods; (2) a golden age of recollection (Homeric); (3) a silver age in which poetry took new forms and recreated itself (Virgilian); and (4) the brass age, a second childhood in which it regressed to the crudities of the iron age. Then came the dark ages, and then the 'four ages' of modern poetry. The romantic age, Peacock argued, is that of brass, in which the poet is half-barbarian, living in the past, with an outmoded way of thinking. Shelley had read it by 20 January 1821, and told Ollier (his and Peacock's publisher) that it 'has excited my polemical faculties so violently, that the moment I get rid of ophthalmia I mean to set about an answer to it, which I will send you, if you please. It is very clever, but, I think, very false' (Jones ii 258). Shelley began his response in late February; Part I was finished by 20 March. He sent it to Ollier, promising another two Parts after its publication. Unfortunately, the *Literary Miscellany* failed, and Part I of the 'Defence' did not appear; Shelley was drowned in 1822 without completing it or seeing Part I into print. It was published in 1840. Of the various influences on it, the two most obvious are Wordsworth's Preface to *Lyrical Ballads* and Sir Philip Sidney's *Apologie for Poetrie*.

[2] *to poiein* 'making' – the source of the word 'poet'.

and existence itself; the other is the *to logizein*,[3] or principle of analysis, and its action regards the relations of things simply as relations, considering thoughts not in their integral unity but as the algebraical representations which conduct to certain general results. Reason is the enumeration of quantities already known; imagination the perception of the value of those quantities, both separately and as a whole. Reason respects the differences, and imagination the similitudes of things. Reason is to imagination as the instrument to the agent, as the body to the spirit, as the shadow to the substance.

Poetry, in a general sense, may be defined to be 'the expression of the imagination'; and poetry is connate[4] with the origin of man. Man is an instrument over which a series of external and internal impressions are driven, like the alternations of an ever-changing wind over an Aeolian lyre, which move it, by their motion, to ever-changing melody.[5] But there is a principle within the human being (and perhaps within all sentient beings) which acts otherwise than in the lyre, and produces not melody alone, but harmony, by an internal adjustment of the sounds or motions thus excited to the impressions which excite them. It is as if the lyre could accommodate its chords to the motions of that which strikes them, in a determined proportion of sound – even as the musician can accommodate his voice to the sound of the lyre. A child at play by itself will express its delight by its voice and motions, and every inflection of tone and every gesture will bear exact relation to a corresponding antitype[6] in the pleasurable impressions which awakened it. It will be the reflected image of that impression – and as the lyre trembles and sounds after the wind has died away, so the child seeks, by prolonging in its voice and motions the duration of the effect, to prolong also a consciousness of the cause. In relation to the objects which delight a child, these expressions are what poetry is to higher objects.

The savage (for the savage is to ages what the child is to years) expresses the emotions produced in him by surrounding objects in a similar manner – and language and gesture, together with plastic or pictorial imitation, become the image of the combined effect of those objects, and of his apprehension of them. Man in society, with all his passions and his pleasures, next becomes the object of the passions and pleasures of man; an additional class of emotions produces an augmented treasure of expressions; and language, gesture, and the imitative arts become at once the representation and the medium, the pencil and the picture, the chisel and the statue, the chord and the harmony. The social sympathies (or those laws from which as from its elements society results) begin to develop themselves from the moment that two human beings coexist; the future is contained within the present as the plant within the seed; and equality, diversity, unity, contrast, mutual dependence, become the principles alone capable of affording the motives according to which the will of a social being is determined to action (inasmuch as he is social), and constitute pleasure in sensation, virtue in sentiment, beauty in art, truth in reasoning, and love in the intercourse of kind. Hence men, even in the infancy of society, observe a certain order in their words and actions distinct from that of the objects and the impressions represented by them, all expression being subject to the laws of that from which it proceeds.

Notes

[3] *to logizein* 'reasoning', 'calculating'.

[4] *connate* coeval, as old as.

[5] *Man is an instrument . . . melody* cf. Shelley's 'Essay on Christianity': 'There is a power by which we are surrounded, like the atmosphere in which some motionless lyre is suspended, which visits with its breath our silent chords at will.'

[6] *antitype* 'that which is shadowed forth or represented by the "type" or symbol' (*OED*).

But let us dismiss those more general considerations which might involve an enquiry into the principles of society itself, and restrict our view to the manner in which the imagination is expressed upon its forms.

In the youth of the world, men dance and sing and imitate natural objects, observing in these actions (as in all others) a certain rhythm or order. And although all men observe a similar, they observe not the same order in the motions of the dance, in the melody of the song, in the combinations of language, in the series of their imitations of natural objects. For there is a certain order or rhythm belonging to each of these classes of mimetic representation, from which the hearer and the spectator receive an intenser and a purer pleasure than from any other. The sense of an approximation to this order has been called taste by modern writers.[7] Every man in the infancy of art observes an order which approximates more or less closely to that from which this highest delight results. But the diversity is not sufficiently marked as that its gradations should be sensible,[8] except in those instances where the predominance of this faculty of approximation to the beautiful (for so we may be permitted to name the relation between this highest pleasure and its cause) is very great. Those in whom it exists in excess are poets, in the most universal sense of the word – and the pleasure resulting from the manner in which they express the influence of society or nature upon their own minds, communicates itself to others, and gathers a sort of reduplication from that community. Their language is vitally metaphorical; that is, it marks the before unapprehended relations of things, and perpetuates their apprehension, until the words which represent them become through time signs for portions or classes of thoughts, instead of pictures of integral thoughts; and then if no new poets should arise to create afresh the associations which have been thus disorganized, language will be dead to all the nobler purposes of human intercourse.

These similitudes or relations are finely said by Lord Bacon[9] to be 'the same footsteps of nature impressed upon the various subjects of the world'[10] – and he considers the faculty which perceives them as the storehouse of axioms common to all knowledge. In the infancy of society every author is necessarily a poet, because language itself is poetry; and to be a poet is to apprehend the true and the beautiful, in a word the good which exists in the relation subsisting first between existence and perception, and secondly between perception and expression. Every original language near to its source is in itself the chaos of a cyclic poem: the copiousness of lexicography and the distinctions of grammar are the works of a later age, and are merely the catalogue and the form of the creations of poetry.

But poets, or those who imagine and express this indestructible order, are not only the authors of language and of music, of the dance and architecture and statuary and painting; they are the institutors of laws, and the founders of civil society, and the inventors of the arts of life, and the teachers who draw into a certain propinquity with

Notes

7 *has been called taste by modern writers* most notably Hazlitt, who, in his 'Essay on Taste' (1818), wrote: 'Genius is the power of producing excellence: taste is the power of perceiving the excellence thus produced in its several sorts and degrees, with all their force, refinement, distinctions, and connections' (Howe xvii 57). Other writers on the subject include Coleridge (in *Biographia Literaria*), Burke and Hume.

8 *sensible* perceptible.

9 Francis Bacon, Baron Verulam, Viscount St Albans (1561–1626), Lord Chancellor of England, philosopher and essayist. His work appealed to Shelley because he was a Neoplatonist.

10 *Of the Advancement of Learning* (1605), Book II, Chapter 5: 'Are not the organs of the senses of one kind with the organs of reflection, the eye with a glass . . . ? Neither are these only similitudes, as men of narrow observation may conceive them to be, but the same footsteps of Nature, treading or printing upon several subjects or matters.'

the beautiful and the true that partial apprehension of the agencies of the invisible world which is called religion. Hence all original religions are allegorical, or susceptible of allegory, and like Janus have a double face of false and true. Poets, according to the circumstances of the age and nation in which they appeared, were called in the earlier epochs of the world legislators or prophets.[11] A poet essentially comprises and unites both these characters. For he not only beholds intensely the present as it is, and discovers those laws according to which present things ought to be ordered, but he beholds the future in the present, and his thoughts are the germs of the flower and the fruit of latest time. Not that I assert poets to be prophets in the gross sense of the word, or that they can foretell the form as surely as they foreknow the spirit of events – such is the pretence of superstition which would make poetry an attribute of prophecy, rather than prophecy an attribute of poetry.

A poet participates in the eternal, the infinite, and the one; as far as relates to his conceptions, time and place and number are not. The grammatical forms which express the moods of time, and the difference of persons and the distinction of place are convertible with respect to the highest poetry without injuring it as poetry, and the choruses of Aeschylus, and the Book of Job, and Dante's *Paradise* would afford, more than any other writings, examples of this fact, if the limits of this paper did not forbid citation. The creations of sculpture, painting, and music, are illustrations still more decisive.

Language, colour, form, and religious and civil habits of action are all the instruments and the materials of poetry; they may be called poetry by that figure of speech which considers the effect as a synonym of the cause. But poetry in a more restricted sense expresses those arrangements of language, and especially metrical language, which are created by that imperial faculty whose throne is curtained within the invisible nature of man. And this springs from the nature itself of language, which is a more direct representation of the actions and passions of our internal being, and is susceptible of more various and delicate combinations, than colour, form, or motion, and is more plastic[12] and obedient to the control of that faculty of which it is the creation. For language is arbitrarily produced by the imagination and has relation to thoughts alone; but all other materials, instruments and conditions of art, have relations among each other which limit and interpose between conception and expression. The former is as a mirror which reflects, the latter as a cloud which enfeebles, the light of which both are mediums of communication. Hence the fame of sculptors, painters and musicians (although the intrinsic powers of the great masters of these arts may yield in no degree to that of those who have employed language as the hieroglyphic of their thoughts) has never equalled that of poets in the restricted sense of the term, as two performers of equal skill will produce unequal effects from a guitar and a harp. The fame of legislators and founders of religions (so long as their institutions last) alone seems to exceed that of poets in the restricted sense – but it can scarcely be a question whether, if we deduct the celebrity which their flattery of the gross opinions of the vulgar usually conciliates, together with that which belonged to them in their higher character of poets, any excess will remain.

We have thus circumscribed the word 'poetry' within the limits of that art which is the most familiar and the most perfect expression of the faculty itself. It is necessary however to make the circle still narrower, and to determine the distinction between

Notes

[11] *prophets* In his *Apologie for Poetrie*, Sir Philip Sidney had observed: 'Among the Romans a poet was called "Vates", which is as much as a diviner, foreseer, or prophet . . . so heavenly a title did that excellent people bestow upon this heart-ravishing knowledge.'

[12] *plastic* susceptible to the artist's creative power.

measured and unmeasured language,[13] for the popular division into prose and verse is inadmissible in accurate philosophy.

Sounds as well as thoughts have relation both between each other and towards that which they represent, and a perception of the order of those relations has always been found connected with a perception of the order of the relations of thoughts. Hence the language of poets has ever affected a certain uniform and harmonious recurrence of sound, without which it were not poetry, and which is scarcely less indispensable to the communication of its influence than the words themselves, without reference to that peculiar order. Hence the vanity of translation: it were as wise to cast a violet into a crucible that you might discover the formal principle of its colour and odour, as seek to transfuse from one language into another the creations of a poet. The plant must spring again from its seed or it will bear no flower – and this is the burden of the curse of Babel.

An observation of the regular mode of the recurrence of this harmony in the language of poetical minds, together with its relation to music, produced metre, or a certain system of traditional forms of harmony and language. Yet it is by no means essential that a poet should accommodate his language to this traditional form, so that the harmony which is its spirit be observed. The practice is indeed convenient and popular, and to be preferred, especially in such composition as includes much action: but every great poet must inevitably innovate upon the example of his predecessors in the exact structure of his peculiar versification.

The distinction between poets and prose writers is a vulgar error. The distinction between philosophers and poets has been anticipated. Plato was essentially a poet[14] – the truth and splendour of his imagery and the melody of his language is the most intense that it is possible to conceive. He rejected the measure of the epic, dramatic, and lyrical forms, because he sought to kindle a harmony in thoughts divested of shape and action, and he forbore to invent any regular plan of rhythm which would include, under determinate forms, the varied pauses of his style. Cicero[15] sought to imitate the cadence of his periods but with little success. Lord Bacon was a poet.[16] His language has a sweet and majestic rhythm which satisfies the sense no less than the almost superhuman wisdom of his philosophy satisfies the intellect; it is a strain which distends,[17] and then bursts the circumference of the reader's mind, and pours itself forth together with it into the universal element with which it has perpetual sympathy. All the authors of revolutions in opinion are not only necessarily poets as they are inventors, nor even as their words unveil the permanent analogy of things by images which participate in the life of truth – but as their periods[18] are harmonious and rhythmical and contain in themselves the elements of verse, being the echo of the eternal music. Nor are those supreme poets who have employed traditional forms of rhythm on account of the form and action of their subjects, less capable of perceiving and teaching the truth of things, than those who have omitted that form. Shakespeare, Dante and Milton (to confine ourselves to modern writers) are philosophers of the very loftiest power.

A poem is the very image of life expressed in its eternal truth. There is this difference between a story and a poem: that a story is a catalogue of detached facts

Notes

[13] *measured and unmeasured language* Shelley is looking for a more accurate definition of poetry and prose than that popularly conceived.

[14] *Plato was essentially a poet* again, Shelley follows Sidney, who wrote in his *Apologie*: 'Of all philosophers he [Plato] is the most poetical.'

[15] Marcus Tullius Cicero (106–43 BC), Roman statesman and man of letters.

[16] 'See the Filium Labyrinthi, and the Essay on Death particularly' (Shelley's note).

[17] *distends* expands.

[18] *periods* sentences.

which have no other bond of connection than time, place, circumstance, cause and effect; the other is the creation of actions according to the unchangeable forms of human nature, as existing in the mind of the creator, which is itself the image of all other minds. The one is partial, and applies only to a definite period of time, and a certain combination of events which can never again recur; the other is universal, and contains within itself the germ of a relation to whatever motives or actions have place in the possible varieties of human nature. Time, which destroys the beauty and the use of the story of particular facts, stripped of the poetry which should invest them, augments that of poetry, and forever develops new and wonderful applications of the eternal truth which it contains. Hence epitomes[19] have been called the moths of just history;[20] they eat out the poetry of it. The story of particular facts is as a mirror which obscures and distorts that which should be beautiful: poetry is a mirror which makes beautiful that which is distorted.

The parts of a composition may be poetical, without the composition as a whole being a poem. A single sentence may be considered as a whole though it may be found in the midst of a series of unassimilated portions; a single word even may be a spark of inextinguishable thought. And thus all the great historians – Herodotus, Plutarch, Livy[21] – were poets; and although the plan of these writers, especially that of Livy, restrained them from developing this faculty in its highest degree, they make copious and ample amends for their subjection, by filling all the interstices of their subject with living images.

Having determined what is poetry and who are poets, let us proceed to estimate its effects upon society.

Poetry is ever accompanied with pleasure: all spirits on which it falls, open themselves to receive the wisdom which is mingled with its delight.[22] In the infancy of the world, neither poets themselves nor their auditors are fully aware of the excellency of poetry, for it acts in a divine and unapprehended manner, beyond and above consciousness – and it is reserved for future generations to contemplate and measure the mighty cause and effect in all the strength and splendour of their union. Even in modern times, no living poet ever arrived at the fullness of his fame. The jury which sits in judgement upon a poet, belonging as he does to all time, must be composed of his peers; it must be impanelled[23] by Time from the selectest of the wise of many generations. A poet is a nightingale who sits in darkness and sings to cheer its own solitude with sweet sounds; his auditors are as men entranced by the melody of an unseen musician, who feel that they are moved and softened, yet know not whence or why.[24] The poems of Homer and his contemporaries were the delight of infant Greece; they were the elements of that social system which is the column upon which all succeeding civilization has reposed. Homer embodied the ideal perfection of his age in human character – nor can we doubt

Notes

[19] *epitomes* summary accounts.

[20] Bacon, *Of the Advancement of Learning* Book II, Chapter 2: 'As for the corruptions and moths of history, which are epitomes, the use of them deserveth to be banished, as all men of sound judgment have confessed, as those that have fretted and corroded the sound bodies of many excellent histories, and wrought them into base and unprofitable dregs.'

[21] *Herodotus, Plutarch, Livy* historians of ancient Greece and Rome: Herodotus (*c.*480–*c.*425 BC) wrote the first Greek history in nine books about the struggle between Asia and Greece, from Croesus to Xerxes; Plutarch (*c.* AD 46–*c.*120) wrote the *Parallel Lives* of eminent Romans and Greeks; Titus Livius (59 BC–AD 17) wrote a history of Rome in 142 books, 35 of which are extant.

[22] *Poetry . . . delight* Shelley echoes Sidney's remark that the poet 'cometh to you with words set in delightful proportion, either accompanied with, or prepared for the well enchanting skill of music; and with a tale forsooth he cometh unto you, with a tale which holdeth children from play, and old men from the chimney corner; and, pretending no more, doth intend the winning of the mind from wickedness to virtue'.

[23] *impanelled* summoned, chosen.

[24] *A poet . . . or why* cf. 'To a Skylark' 36–40.

that those who read his verses were awakened to an ambition of becoming like to Achilles, Hector and Ulysses.[25] The truth and beauty of friendship, patriotism and persevering devotion to an object, were unveiled to the depths in these immortal creations; the sentiments of the auditors must have been refined and enlarged by a sympathy with such great and lovely impersonations, until from admiring they imitated, and from imitation they identified themselves with the objects of their admiration. Nor let it be objected that these characters are remote from moral perfection, and that they can by no means be considered as edifying patterns for general imitation. Every epoch under names more or less specious has deified its peculiar errors; revenge is the naked idol of the worship of a semi-barbarous age, and self-deceit is the veiled image of unknown evil before which luxury and satiety[26] lie prostrate.

But a poet considers the vices of his contemporaries as the temporary dress in which his creations must be arrayed, and which cover without concealing the eternal proportions of their beauty.[27] An epic or dramatic personage is understood to wear them around his soul, as he may the ancient armour or the modern uniform around his body – whilst it is easy to conceive a dress more graceful than either. The beauty of the internal nature cannot be so far concealed by its accidental vesture,[28] but that the spirit of its form shall communicate itself to the very disguise, and indicate the shape it hides from the manner in which it is worn. A majestic form and graceful motions will express themselves through the most barbarous and tasteless costume. Few poets of the highest class have chosen to exhibit the beauty of their conceptions in its naked truth and splendour, and it is doubtful whether the alloy of costume, habit, etc., be not necessary to temper this planetary music for mortal ears.

The whole objection however of the immorality of poetry rests upon a misconception of the manner in which poetry acts to produce the moral improvement of man. Ethical science[29] arranges the elements which poetry has created, and propounds schemes and proposes examples of civil and domestic life. Nor is it for want of admirable doctrines that men hate, and despise, and censure, and deceive, and subjugate one another. But poetry acts in another and a diviner manner. It awakens and enlarges the mind itself by rendering it the receptacle of a thousand unapprehended combinations of thought. Poetry lifts the veil from the hidden beauty of the world, and makes familiar objects be as if they were not familiar; it re-produces all that it represents, and the impersonations clothed in its Elysian[30] light stand thenceforward in the minds of those who have once contemplated them as memorials of that gentle and exalted content which extends itself over all thoughts and actions with which it coexists. The great secret of morals is love, or a going out of our own nature, and an identification of ourselves with the beautiful which exists in thought, action, or person not our own. A man, to be greatly good, must imagine intensely and comprehensively; he must put himself in the place of another and of many others; the pains and pleasures of his species must become his own. The great instrument of moral good is the imagination – and poetry administers to the effect by acting upon the cause.[31]

Notes

[25] *Achilles, Hector and Ulysses* heroes in the Trojan war.

[26] *luxury and satiety* lust and excessive gratification.

[27] *But a poet . . . beauty* cf. Shelley's remark in a letter to the Gisbornes of 13 July 1821: 'Poets, the best of them, are a very chameleonic race: they take the colour not only of what they feed on, but of the very leaves under which they pass' (Jones ii 308). This is close to Keats's notion of negative capability, which also uses the metaphor of a chameleon; see his letter to Woodhouse of 27 October 1818 (p. 1375).

[28] *accidental vesture* i.e. outward appearance.

[29] *Ethical science* the science (or philosophy) of ethics.

[30] *Elysian* divine.

[31] *A man . . . upon the cause* a fundamental principal in Shelley's philosophy.

Poetry enlarges the circumference of the imagination by replenishing it with thoughts of ever-new delight which have the power of attracting and assimilating to their own nature all other thoughts, and which form new intervals and interstices whose void forever craves fresh food. Poetry strengthens the faculty which is the organ of the moral nature of man, in the same manner as exercise strengthens a limb. A poet therefore would do ill to embody his own conceptions of right and wrong (which are usually those of his place and time) in his poetical creations (which participate in neither). By this assumption of the inferior office of interpreting the effect, in which perhaps after all he might acquit himself but imperfectly, he would resign a glory in a participation in the cause. There was little danger that Homer, or any of the eternal poets, should have so far misunderstood themselves as to have abdicated this throne of their widest dominion. Those in whom the poetical faculty, though great, is less intense (as Euripides, Lucan, Tasso, Spenser[32]) have frequently affected a moral aim, and the effect of their poetry is diminished in exact proportion to the degree in which they compel us to advert to[33] this purpose. . . .

The poetry of Dante[34] may be considered as the bridge thrown over the stream of time, which unites the modern and the ancient world. The distorted notions of invisible things which Dante and his rival Milton have idealized, are merely the mask and the mantle in which these great poets walk through eternity enveloped and disguised. It is a difficult question to determine how far they were conscious of the distinction which must have subsisted[35] in their minds between their own creed and that of the people. Dante at least appears to wish to mark the full extent of it by placing Riphaeus (whom Virgil calls 'justissimus unus'[36]) in Paradise, and observing a most heretical caprice in his distribution of rewards and punishments. And Milton's poem contains within itself a philosophical refutation of that system of which, by a strange but natural antithesis, it has been a chief popular support.

Nothing can exceed the energy and magnificence of the character of Satan as expressed in *Paradise Lost*. It is a mistake to suppose that he could ever have been intended for the popular personification of evil. Implacable hate, patient cunning, and a sleepless refinement of device to inflict the extremest anguish on an enemy – these things are evil; and, although venial[37] in a slave, are not to be forgiven in a tyrant; although redeemed by much that ennobles his defeat in one subdued, are marked by all that dishonours his conquest in the victor. Milton's Devil as a moral being is as far superior to his God as one who perseveres in some purpose which he has conceived to be excellent in spite of adversity and torture, is to one who in the cold security of undoubted triumph inflicts the most horrible revenge upon his enemy, not from any mistaken notion of inducing him to repent of a perseverance in enmity, but with the alleged design of exasperating him to deserve new torments. Milton has so far violated the popular creed (if this shall be judged to be a violation) as to have alleged no superiority of moral virtue to his God over his Devil. And this bold neglect of a direct moral purpose is the most decisive proof of the supremacy of Milton's genius. He mingled, as it were, the elements of human nature as colours upon a single palette,

Notes

[32] *Euripides, Lucan, Tasso, Spenser* Euripides (*c*.480–406 BC), one of the three great Attic tragedians, author of *Orestes*, *Medea*, *Bacchae*, among others; Marcus Annaeus Lucanus (AD 39–65), whose one surviving poem is the *Pharsalia*, the greatest Latin epic after the *Aeneid*; Torquato Tasso (1544–95) was the author of the epic *Gerusalemme Liberata* (1575).

[33] *advert to* take notice of.

[34] *The poetry of Dante* Shelley read Dante in the original and in the blank verse translation of H. F. Cary (1775–1844), which began with the *Inferno* (1805), and continued in 1812 with *Purgatorio* and *Paradiso*. He visited Dante's tomb at Ravenna in August 1821 (Jones ii 335).

[35] *subsisted* existed.

[36] 'The one man who was most just' (*Aeneid* ii 426). Dante places the Trojan Rhipheus in Paradise, even though he died before Christ's birth (*Paradiso* xx).

[37] *venial* pardonable.

and arranged them into the composition of his great picture according to the laws of epic truth; that is, according to the laws of that principle by which a series of actions of the external universe and of intelligent and ethical beings is calculated to excite the sympathy of succeeding generations of mankind. The *Divina Commedia* and *Paradise Lost* have conferred upon modern mythology a systematic form; and when change and time shall have added one more superstition to the mass of those which have arisen and decayed upon the earth, commentators will be learnedly employed in elucidating the religion of ancestral Europe, only not utterly forgotten because it will have been stamped with the eternity of genius.

Homer was the first, and Dante the second, epic poet – that is, the second poet the series of whose creations bore a defined and intelligible relation to the knowledge, and sentiment, and religion, and political conditions of the age in which he lived, and of the ages which followed it, developing itself in correspondence with their development. For Lucretius had limed[38] the wings of his swift spirit in the dregs of the sensible[39] world; and Virgil, with a modesty which ill became his genius, had affected the fame of an imitator even whilst he created anew all that he copied; and none among the flock of mock-birds, though their notes were sweet (Apollonius Rhodius, Quintus Calaber Smyrnaeus, Nonnus, Lucan, Statius, or Claudian[40]), have sought even to fulfil a single condition of epic truth. Milton was the third epic poet. For, if the title of epic in its highest sense is to be refused to the *Aeneid*, still less can it be conceded to the *Orlando Furioso*,[41] the *Gerusalemme Liberata*, *The Lusiad*,[42] or *The Faerie Queene*.

Dante and Milton were both deeply penetrated with the ancient religion of the civilized world – and its spirit exists in their poetry probably in the same proportion as its forms survived in the unreformed worship of modern Europe.[43] The one preceded and the other followed the Reformation at almost equal intervals. Dante was the first religious reformer, and Luther surpassed him rather in the rudeness and acrimony, than in the boldness of his censures of papal usurpation.[44] Dante was the first awakener of entranced Europe; he created a language in itself music and persuasion out of a chaos of inharmonious barbarisms; he was the congregator of those great spirits who presided over the resurrection of learning, the Lucifer[45] of that starry flock which in the thirteenth century shone forth from republican Italy, as from a heaven, into the darkness of the benighted world. His very words are instinct[46] with spirit – each is as a spark, a burning atom of inextinguishable thought, and many yet lie covered in the ashes of their birth, and pregnant with a lightning which has yet found no conductor. All high poetry is infinite; it is as the first acorn, which contained all oaks potentially. Veil after veil may be undrawn, and the inmost naked beauty of the meaning never exposed. A great poem is a fountain forever overflowing with the waters of wisdom and delight – and after one person or one age has exhausted all its

Notes

[38] *limed* birds were caught by smearing bird-lime, a sticky substance, on twigs where they perched.

[39] *sensible* perceived.

[40] *Apollonius Rhodius . . . Claudian* minor classical poets: Apollonius Rhodius (*c.* 295–15 BC), author of *Argonautica*; Quintus Smyrnaeus (fourth century AD), called Calaber because of the discovery in Calabria of the only known MS of his *Posthomerica*, a 14-book sequel to Homer; Nonnus (*c.* AD 400), author of a Greek epic in 48 books on the adventures of the god Dionysus, *Dionysiaca*; Publius Papinius Statius (*c.* AD 40–*c.*96), author of the *Thebaid*; Claudius Claudianus, Roman poet of the 4th century AD, author of the epic *Rape of Proserpine*. For Lucan see p. 1191n32.

[41] *Orlando Furioso* epic by Ariosto.

[42] *The Lusiad* epic by Luiz de Camoëns.

[43] *the unreformed worship of modern Europe* i.e. the domination of the Roman Catholic Church.

[44] *papal usurpation* wrongful assumption of supreme authority of the Pope.

[45] *Lucifer* i.e. light-bearer.

[46] *instinct* imbued.

divine effluence[47] which its peculiar relations enable them to share, another and yet another succeeds, and new relations are ever developed, the source of an unforeseen and an unconceived delight.

The age immediately succeeding to that of Dante, Petrarch, and Boccaccio, was characterized by a revival of painting, sculpture, music, and architecture. Chaucer caught the sacred inspiration, and the superstructure of English literature is based upon the materials of Italian invention.

But let us not be betrayed from a defence into a critical history of poetry and its influence on society. Be it enough to have pointed out the effects of poetry (in the large and true sense of the word) upon their own and all succeeding times, and to revert to the partial instances cited as illustrations of an opinion the reverse of that attempted to be established by the author of 'The Four Ages of Poetry'.[48]

But poets have been challenged to resign the civic crown[49] to reasoners and mechanists on another plea. It is admitted that the exercise of the imagination is more delightful, but it is alleged that that of the reason is more useful. Let us examine as the grounds of this distinction what is here meant by utility. Pleasure or good in a general sense is that which the consciousness of a sensitive and intelligent being seeks, and in which, when found, it acquiesces. There are two modes or degrees of pleasure – one durable, universal, and permanent; the other transitory and particular. Utility may either express the means of producing the former or the latter. In the former sense, whatever strengthens and purifies the affections, enlarges the imagination, and adds a spirit to sense, is useful. But the meaning in which the author of 'The Four Ages of Poetry' seems to have employed the word utility is the narrower one of banishing the importunity of the wants of our animal nature, the surrounding men with security of life, the dispersing the grosser delusions of superstition, and the conciliating such a degree of mutual forbearance among men as may consist with the motives of personal advantage.

Undoubtedly the promoters of utility in this limited sense have their appointed office in society. They follow the footsteps of poets, and copy the sketches of their creations into the book of common life. They make space, and give time. Their exertions are of the highest value so long as they confine their administration of the concerns of the inferior powers of our nature within the limits of what is due to the superior ones. But whilst the sceptic destroys gross superstitions, let him spare to deface, as some of the French writers have defaced, the eternal truths charactered[50] upon the imaginations of men. Whilst the mechanist abridges,[51] and the political economist combines labour,[52] let them beware that their speculations, for want of a correspondence with those first principles which belong to the imagination, do not tend, as they have in modern England, to exasperate at once the extremes of luxury[53] and want. They have exemplified the saying, 'To him that hath, more shall be given; and from him that hath not, the little that he hath shall be taken away'.[54] The rich have become richer, and the poor have become poorer; and the vessel of the state is driven between the Scylla and Charybdis[55] of anarchy and despotism. Such are the effects which must ever flow from an unmitigated exercise of the calculating faculty.

Notes

47 *effluence* emanations.

48 *the author of 'The Four Ages of Poetry'* Thomas Love Peacock (see p. 1184n1).

49 *civic crown* (*corona civica*) a garland of oak leaves and acorns, bestowed as a much-prized distinction upon one who saved the life of a fellow-citizen in war, here meant as the emblem of public utility.

50 *charactered* represented.

51 *the mechanist abridges* by inventing machines that reduce the need for labour.

52 *the political economist combines labour* by organizing workers in the most efficient manner.

53 *luxury and want* excessive overindulgence and desperate poverty.

54 Matthew 25: 29.

55 *Scylla and Charybdis* dangerous cave of the monster Scylla, and a whirlpool, which demolished part of Ulysses' fleet in the *Odyssey*.

It is difficult to define pleasure in its highest sense, the definition involving a number of apparent paradoxes. For, from an inexplicable defect of harmony in the constitution of human nature, the pain of the inferior is frequently connected with the pleasure of the superior portions of our being. Sorrow, terror, anguish, despair itself are often the chosen expressions of an approximation to the highest good. Our sympathy in tragic fiction depends on this principle; tragedy delights by affording a shadow of the pleasure which exists in pain. This is the source also of the melancholy which is inseparable from the sweetest melody.[56] The pleasure that is in sorrow is sweeter than the pleasure of pleasure itself – and hence the saying, 'It is better to go to the house of mourning than to the house of mirth'.[57] Not that this highest species of pleasure is necessarily linked with pain. The delight of love and friendship, the ecstacy of the admiration of nature, the joy of the perception and still more of the creation of poetry is often wholly unalloyed.

The production and assurance of pleasure in this highest sense is true utility; those who produce and preserve this pleasure are poets or poetical philosophers.

The exertions of Locke, Hume, Gibbon, Voltaire, Rousseau,[58] and their disciples, in favour of oppressed and deluded humanity, are entitled to the gratitude of mankind. Yet it is easy to calculate the degree of moral and intellectual improvement which the world would have exhibited had they never lived. A little more nonsense would have been talked for a century or two, and perhaps a few more men, women and children burnt as heretics. We might not at this moment have been congratulating each other on the abolition of the Inquisition in Spain.[59] But it exceeds all imagination to conceive what would have been the moral condition of the world if neither Dante, Petrarch, Boccaccio, Chaucer, Shakespeare, Calderón,[60] Lord Bacon, nor Milton, had ever existed; if Raphael and Michelangelo had never been born; if the Hebrew poetry had never been translated; if a revival of a study of Greek literature had never taken place; if no monuments of ancient sculpture had been handed down to us; and if the poetry of the religion of the ancient world had been extinguished together with its belief. The human mind could never, except by the intervention of these excitements, have been awakened to the invention of those grosser[61] sciences, and that application of analytical reasoning to the aberrations of society, which it is now attempted to exalt over the direct expression of the inventive and creative faculty itself.

We have more moral, political and historical wisdom than we know how to reduce into practice; we have more scientific and economical knowledge than can be accommodated to the just distribution of the produce which they multiply. The poetry in these systems of thought is concealed by the accumulation of facts and calculating processes. There is no want of knowledge respecting what is wisest and best in morals, government, and political economy – or at least, what is wiser and better than what men now practise and endure. But we let '*I dare not* wait upon *I would*, like the poor cat i' the adage.'[62] We want the creative faculty to imagine that

Notes

[56] *This is the source . . . melody* cf. 'To a Skylark' 90: 'Our sweetest songs are those that tell of saddest thought.'

[57] Ecclesiastes 7: 2.

[58] 'I follow the classification adopted by the author of "The Four Ages of Poetry", but Rousseau was essentially a poet. The others, even Voltaire, were mere reasoners' (Shelley's note).

[59] *We might not . . . Spain* The Spanish Inquisition was suppressed in 1820, restored in 1823, and abolished finally in 1834.

[60] Pedro Calderón de la Barca (1600–81), whose plays Shelley was reading in Spanish in August 1819; as he told Peacock: 'A kind of Shakespeare is this Calderon, and I have some thoughts, if I find that I cannot do anything better, of translating some of his plays' (Jones ii 115).

[61] *grosser* more materialistic, to do with the physical world.

[62] *Macbeth* I vii 44–5.

which we know; we want the generous impulse to act that which we imagine; we want the poetry of life – our calculations have outrun conception; we have eaten more than we can digest. The cultivation of those sciences which have enlarged the limits of the empire of man over the external world, has, for want of the poetical faculty, proportionally circumscribed those of the internal world – and man, having enslaved the elements, remains himself a slave. To what but to a cultivation of the mechanical arts in a degree disproportioned to the presence of the creative faculty (which is the basis of all knowledge) is to be attributed the abuse of all inventions for abridging and combining labour, to the exasperation of the inequality of mankind? From what other cause has it arisen that these inventions which should have lightened, have added a weight to the curse imposed on Adam?[63] Thus, poetry, and the principle of self (of which money is the visible incarnation) are the God and the Mammon of the world.[64]

The functions of the poetical faculty are twofold: by one it creates new materials for knowledge and power and pleasure; by the other it engenders in the mind a desire to reproduce and arrange them according to a certain rhythm and order which may be called the beautiful and the good. The cultivation of poetry is never more to be desired than at periods when, from an excess of the selfish and calculating principle, the accumulation of the materials of external life exceed the quantity of the power of assimilating them to the internal laws of human nature. The body has then become too unwieldy for that which animates it.

Poetry is indeed something divine. It is at once the centre and the circumference of knowledge; it is that which comprehends all science, and that to which all science must be referred. It is at the same time the root and the blossom of all other systems of thought. It is that from which all spring, and that which adorns all – and that which, if blighted, denies the fruit and the seed, and withholds from the barren world the nourishment and the succession of the scions[65] of the tree of life. It is the perfect and consummate[66] surface and bloom of things; it is as the odour and the colour of the rose to the texture of the elements which compose it, as the form and the splendour of unfaded beauty to the secrets of anatomy and corruption. What were virtue, love, patriotism, friendship etc.; what were the scenery of this beautiful universe which we inhabit; what were our consolations on this side of the grave; and what were our aspirations beyond it – if poetry did not ascend to bring light and fire from those eternal regions where the owl-winged faculty of calculation dare not ever soar? Poetry is not like reasoning, a power to be exerted according to the determination of the will. A man cannot say, 'I will compose poetry'. The greatest poet even cannot say it: for the mind in creation is as a fading coal which some invisible influence, like an inconstant wind, awakens to transitory brightness. This power arises from within, like the colour of a flower which fades and changes as it is developed, and the conscious portions of our natures are unprophetic either of its approach or its departure. Could this influence be durable in its original purity and force, it is impossible to predict the greatness of the results – but when composition begins, inspiration is already on the decline, and the most glorious poetry that has ever been communicated to the world is probably a feeble shadow of the original conception of the poet. I appeal to the greatest poets of the present day, whether it be not an error to

Notes

[63] *the curse imposed on Adam* at Genesis 3: 17–19.

[64] *the God and the Mammon of the world* 'No man can serve two masters: for either he will hate the one, and love the other; or else he will hold to the one, and despise the other. Ye cannot serve God and mammon' (Matthew 6: 24).

[65] *scions* shoots, buds.

[66] *consummate* complete.

assert that the finest passages of poetry are produced by labour and study. The toil and the delay recommended by critics can be justly interpreted to mean no more than a careful observation of the inspired moments, and an artificial connection of the spaces between them by the intertexture of conventional expressions; a necessity only imposed by a limitedness of the poetical faculty itself. For Milton conceived the *Paradise Lost* as a whole before he executed it in portions. We have his own authority also for the muse having 'dictated' to him the 'unpremeditated song',[67] and let this be an answer to those who would allege the fifty-six various readings of the first line of the *Orlando Furioso*. Compositions so produced are to poetry what mosaic is to painting. This instinct and intuition of the poetical faculty is still more observable in the plastic and pictorial arts:[68] a great statue or picture grows under the power of the artist as a child in the mother's womb, and the very mind which directs the hands in formation is incapable of accounting to itself for the origin, the gradations, or the media of the process.

Poetry is the record of the best and happiest moments of the happiest and best minds. We are aware of evanescent visitations of thought and feeling sometimes associated with place or person, sometimes regarding our own mind alone, and always arising unforeseen and departing unbidden, but elevating and delightful beyond all expression – so that even in the desire and the regret they leave, there cannot but be pleasure, participating as it does in the nature of its object. It is, as it were, the interpenetration of a diviner nature through our own, but its footsteps are like those of a wind over a sea, which the coming calm erases, and whose traces remain only as on the wrinkled sand which paves it.

These, and corresponding conditions of being, are experienced principally by those of the most delicate sensibility and the most enlarged imagination – and the state of mind produced by them is at war with every base desire. The enthusiasm of virtue, love, patriotism and friendship, is essentially linked with these emotions; and whilst they last, self appears as what it is – an atom to a universe. Poets are not only subject to these experiences as spirits of the most refined organization, but they can colour all that they combine with the evanescent hues of this ethereal world; a word or a trait in the representation of a scene or a passion, will touch the enchanted chord, and reanimate, in those who have ever experienced these emotions, the sleeping, the cold, the buried image of the past. Poetry thus makes immortal all that which is best and most beautiful in the world; it arrests the vanishing apparitions which haunt the interlunations[69] of life, and veiling them in language or in form sends them forth among mankind, bearing sweet news of kindred joy to those with whom their sisters abide – abide, because there is no portal of expression from the caverns of the spirit which they inhabit, into the universe of things. Poetry redeems from decay the visitations of the divinity in man.

Poetry turns all things to loveliness: it exalts the beauty of that which is most beautiful, and it adds beauty to that which is most deformed; it marries exultation and horror, grief and pleasure, eternity and change; it subdues to union under its light yoke all irreconcilable things. It transmutes all that it touches, and every form moving within the radiance of its presence is changed by wondrous sympathy to an incarnation of the spirit which it breathes; its secret alchemy turns to potable gold[70] the poisonous

Notes

[67] *We have . . . song* a reference to *Paradise Lost* ix 21–4, where Milton says that Urania, his 'celestial patroness', 'dictates to me slumbering, or inspires / Easy my unpremeditated verse'.

[68] *the plastic and pictorial arts* sculpture and painting.

[69] *interlunations* dark intervals.

[70] *potable gold* the elixir of life, potable (drinkable) gold, was the goal of the alchemist. There are rivers of it at *Paradise Lost* iii 608–9.

waters which flow from death through life; it strips the veil of familiarity from the world, and lays bare the naked and sleeping beauty which is the spirit of its forms.[71]

All things exist as they are perceived, at least in relation to the percipient: 'The mind is its own place, and of itself can make a heaven of hell, a hell of heaven'.[72] But poetry defeats the curse which binds us to be subjected to the accident of surrounding impressions. And whether it spreads its own figured[73] curtain or withdraws life's dark veil from before the scene of things, it equally creates for us a being within our being. It makes us the inhabitants of a world to which the familiar world is a chaos. It reproduces the common universe of which we are portions and percipients, and it purges from our inward sight the film of familiarity which obscures from us the wonder of our being. It compels us to feel that which we perceive, and to imagine that which we know. It creates anew the universe after it has been annihilated in our minds by the recurrence of impressions blunted by reiteration. It justifies that bold and true word of Tasso: 'Non merita nome di creatore, sennon Iddio ed il Poeta'.[74]

A poet, as he is the author to others of the highest wisdom, pleasure, virtue and glory, so he ought personally to be the happiest, the best, the wisest, and the most illustrious of men. As to his glory, let time be challenged to declare whether the fame of any other institutor of human life be comparable to that of a poet. That he is the wisest, the happiest, and the best, inasmuch as he is a poet, is equally incontrovertible: the greatest poets have been men of the most spotless virtue, of the most consummate prudence, and (if we could look into the interior of their lives) the most fortunate of men. And the exceptions, as they regard those who possessed the imaginative faculty in a high yet an inferior degree, will be found on consideration to confirm rather than destroy the rule. Let us for a moment stoop to the arbitration[75] of popular breath, and usurping and uniting in our own persons the incompatible characters of accuser, witness, judge and executioner, let us without trial, testimony, or form, determine that certain motives of those who are 'there sitting where we dare not soar'[76] are reprehensible. Let us assume that Homer was a drunkard, that Virgil was a flatterer, that Horace was a coward, that Tasso was a madman, that Lord Bacon was a peculator,[77] that Raphael was a libertine, that Spenser was a Poet Laureate.[78] It is inconsistent with this division of our subject to cite living poets, but posterity has done ample justice to the great names now referred to. Their errors have been weighed and have been found as dust in the balance – if their sins 'were as scarlet, they are now white as snow';[79] they have been washed in the blood of the mediator and the redeemer Time. Observe in what a ludicrous chaos the imputations of real and of fictitious crime have been confused in the contemporary calumnies against poetry and poets; consider how little is as it appears – or appears as it is; look to your own motives, and judge not lest ye be judged.[80]

Poetry, as has been said, in this respect differs from logic: that it is not subject to the control of the active powers of the mind, and that its birth and recurrence has no necessary connection with consciousness or will. It is presumptuous to determine that

Notes

[71] *it strips . . . forms* probably a recollection of *Biographia Literaria* chapter 14, where Coleridge says that Wordsworth aimed to remove 'the film of familiarity' from 'the wonders of the world before us' (see p. 692).

[72] *Paradise Lost* i 254–5.

[73] *figured* patterned.

[74] 'None deserves the name of creator except God and the poet'; from Pierantonio Serassi's *Life of Torquato Tasso* (1785).

[75] *arbitration* judgement.

[76] *Paradise Lost* iv 829.

[77] *peculator* embezzler of public money.

[78] *Poet Laureate* Although he liked him when he met him (see headnote), Shelley thought that Southey's acceptance of the Laureateship marked his total abandonment of his youthful radicalism.

[79] A paraphrase of Isaiah 1: 18.

[80] *judge not lest ye be judged* There are a number of scriptural echoes; see Daniel 5: 27; Isaiah 40: 15; Revelation 7: 14; Hebrews 9: 15; and Matthew 7: 1.

these are the necessary conditions of all mental causation, when mental effects are experienced insusceptible of being referred to them. The frequent recurrence of the poetical power, it is obvious to suppose, may produce in the mind an habit of order and harmony correlative with its own nature and with its effects upon other minds. But in the intervals of inspiration (and they may be frequent without being durable) a poet becomes a man, and is abandoned to the sudden reflux[81] of the influences under which others habitually live. But as he is more delicately organized than other men, and sensible to pain and pleasure (both his own and that of others) in a degree unknown to them, he will avoid the one and pursue the other with an ardour proportioned to this difference. And he renders himself obnoxious to calumny, when he neglects to observe the circumstances under which these objects of universal pursuit and flight have disguised themselves in one another's garments.

But there is nothing necessarily evil in this error, and thus cruelty, envy, revenge, avarice, and the passions purely evil, have never formed any portion of the popular imputations on the lives of poets.

I have thought it most favourable to the cause of truth to set down these remarks according to the order in which they were suggested to my mind by a consideration of the subject itself, instead of following that of the treatise which excited me to make them public. Thus, although devoid of the formality of a polemical reply, if the views which they contain be just, they will be found to involve a refutation of the doctrines of 'The Four Ages of Poetry', so far at least as regards the first division of the subject. I can readily conjecture what should have moved the gall[82] of the learned and intelligent author of that paper; I confess myself, like him, unwilling to be stunned by the *Theseids* of the hoarse Codri of the day.[83] Bavius and Maevius undoubtedly are, as they ever were, insufferable persons.[84] But it belongs to a philosophical critic to distinguish rather than confound.

The first part of these remarks has related to poetry in its elements and principles; and it has been shown, as well as the narrow limits assigned them would permit, that what is called poetry in a restricted sense has a common source with all other forms of order and of beauty according to which the materials of human life are susceptible of being arranged, and which is poetry in an universal sense.

The second part[85] will have for its object an application of these principles to the present state of the cultivation of poetry, and a defence of the attempt to idealize the modern forms of manners and opinion, and compel them into a subordination to the imaginative and creative faculty. For the literature of England, an energetic development of which has ever preceded or accompanied a great and free development of the national will, has arisen, as it were, from a new birth. In spite of the low-thoughted envy which would undervalue contemporary merit, our own will be a memorable age in intellectual achievements, and we live among such philosophers and poets as surpass beyond comparison any who have appeared since the last national struggle for civil and religious liberty. The most unfailing herald, companion, or follower of the awakening of a great people to work a beneficial change in opinion

Notes

[81] *reflux* flowing back.

[82] *gall* bitterness. Peacock had argued that the poets of the present day were barbarians.

[83] *unwilling to be stunned . . . day* Codrus was the name applied by Roman poets to bad writers who annoyed others by reading aloud their feeble outpourings. Juvenal had criticized Codrus' *Theseid* in the first of his satires.

[84] *Bavius and Maevius . . . persons* Bavius and Maevius were mediocre poets mocked by Virgil (*Eclogues* iii 90–1) and (Maevius only) Horace (*Epode* x). William Gifford was the author of *The Baviad* (1794) and *The Maeviad* (1795) in which he lampooned the Della Cruscans (mannered poetasters of the 1780s and 1790s) and their ilk. Shelley refers to the proliferation of bad poetry in his own day; as he told Peacock, 21 March 1821: 'The Bavii and Maevii of the day are very fertile' (Jones ii 276).

[85] *The second part* never written by Shelley (see p. 1184n1).

or institution, is poetry. At such periods there is an accumulation of the power of communicating and receiving intense and impassioned conceptions respecting man and nature. The persons in whom this power resides may often (as far as regards many portions of their nature) have little apparent correspondence with that spirit of good of which they are the ministers.[86] But even whilst they deny and abjure,[87] they are yet compelled to serve the power which is seated upon the throne of their own soul. It is impossible to read the compositions of the most celebrated writers of the present day without being startled with the electric life which burns within their words. They measure the circumference and sound the depths of human nature with a comprehensive and all-penetrating spirit, and they are themselves perhaps the most sincerely astonished at its manifestations, for it is less their own spirit than the spirit of the age. Poets are the hierophants[88] of an unapprehended inspiration, the mirrors of the gigantic shadows which futurity casts upon the present, the words which express what they understand not; the trumpets which sing to battle, and feel not what they inspire; the influence which is moved not, but moves. Poets are the unacknowledged legislators of the world.

Adonais: An Elegy on the Death of John Keats, author of Endymion, Hyperion, etc. (1821; composed between 11 April and 8 June 1821)[1]

Ἀστὴρ πρὶν μὲν ἔλαμπες ἐνὶ ζωοῖσιν Ἑῷος.
νῦν δὲ θανὼν, λάμπεις Ἕσπερος ἐν φθιμένοις. (Plato)[2]

Preface

Φάρμακον ἦλθε, Βίων, ποτὶ σὸν στόμα, φάρμακον εἶδες.
πῶς τευ τοῖς χείλεσσι ποτέδραμε, κοὐκ; ἐγλυκάνθη;
τίς δὲ βροτὸς τοσσοῦτον ἀνάμερος, ἢ κεράσαι τοι,
ἢ δοῦναι λαλέοντι τὸ φάρμακον; ἔκφυγεν ᾠδάν.
(Moschus, *Lament for Bion*)[3]

It is my intention to subjoin to the London edition of this poem,[4] a criticism upon the claims of its lamented object to be classed among the writers of the highest genius who have adorned our age. My known repugnance to the narrow principles of taste

Notes

[86] *The persons . . . ministers* Shelley may be thinking of Southey and Wordsworth, who had both, in Shelley's eyes, betrayed the cause of 'civil and religious liberty'; like Byron, he regarded both as traitors to the radical cause.
[87] *abjure* recant.
[88] *hierophants* expounders.

ADONAIS: AN ELEGY ON THE DEATH OF JOHN KEATS
[1] For introductory comments, see headnote, pp. 1050–1. See also James A. W. Heffernan, '*Adonais*: Shelley's Consumption of Keats', in *Romanticism: A Critical Reader*, ed. Duncan Wu (Oxford, 1995) 173–91. Shelley adapted the name from Adonis, the beautiful youth with whom Aphrodite, the Greek goddess of fertility, fell in love. He was killed by a wild boar, and from his blood sprang the rose, or from Aphrodite's tears the anemone. The poem was completed by 11 June 1821, and five days later Shelley told John Gisborne: 'this day I send it to the press at Pisa . . . I think it will please you: I have dipped my pen in consuming fire for his destroyers, otherwise the style is calm and solemn' (Jones ii 300).
[2] Shortly before composing *Adonais*, Shelley translated Plato's 'Epigram on Aster':

Thou wert the morning star among the living,
Ere thy fair light had fled;
Now, having died, thou art as Hesperus, giving
New splendour to the dead.

[3] 'Poison came, Bion, to thy mouth, thou didst know poison. To such lips as thine did it come, and was not sweetened? What mortal was so cruel that could mix poison for thee, or who could give thee the venom that heard thy voice? Surely, he had not music in his soul.'
[4] *the London edition of this poem* Shelley supervised the first publication of this poem in Pisa, 1821, but died before it could appear in London. The first English edition was published at Cambridge, 1829.

on which several of his earlier compositions were modelled, prove at least that I am an impartial judge. I consider the fragment of *Hyperion*[5] as second to nothing that was ever produced by a writer of the same years.

John Keats died at Rome of a consumption in his twenty-fourth year, on the ___ of ___ 1821,[6] and was buried in the romantic and lonely cemetery of the protestants in that city, under the pyramid which is the tomb of Cestius, and the massy walls and towers, now mouldering and desolate, which formed the circuit of ancient Rome. The cemetery is an open space among the ruins covered in winter with violets and daisies. It might make one in love with death[7] to think that one should be buried in so sweet a place.[8]

The genius[9] of the lamented person to whose memory I have dedicated these unworthy verses was not less delicate and fragile than it was beautiful; and where canker-worms abound, what wonder if its young flower was blighted in the bud? The savage criticism on his *Endymion*, which appeared in the *Quarterly Review*, produced the most violent effect on his susceptible mind; the agitation thus originated ended in the rupture of a blood-vessel in the lungs; a rapid consumption ensued, and the succeeding acknowledgements from more candid critics of the true greatness of his powers, were ineffectual to heal the wound thus wantonly inflicted.[10]

It may be well said that these wretched men know not what they do.[11] They scatter their insults and their slanders without heed as to whether the poisoned shaft lights on a heart made callous by many blows, or one like Keats', composed of more penetrable stuff.[12] One of their associates is, to my knowledge, a most base and unprincipled calumniator.[13] As to *Endymion* – was it a poem (whatever might be its defects) to be treated contemptuously by those who had celebrated with various degrees of complacency and panegyric, *Paris*, and *Woman*, and *A Syrian Tale*, and Mrs. Lefanu, and Mr. Barrett, and Mr Howard Payne,[14] and a long list of the illustrious obscure? Are these the men who, in their venal good nature, presumed to draw a parallel between the Revd. Mr Milman and Lord Byron?[15] What gnat did they strain at here, after having swallowed all those camels?[16] Against what woman taken in adultery, dares the foremost of these literary prostitutes to cast his opprobrious stone?[17] Miserable man! You, one of the meanest, have wantonly defaced one of the noblest specimens of the workmanship of

Notes

[5] *the fragment of Hyperion* i.e. *Hyperion: A Fragment*, published 1820 (see p. 1354), rather than *The Fall of Hyperion* (p. 1420), not published during Shelley's lifetime. When Shelley first received Keats's 1820 volume, he commented: 'the fragment called Hyperion promises for him that he is destined to become one of the first writers of the age' (letter of 29 October 1820, Jones ii 239).

[6] Keats died 23 February 1821, aged 25.

[7] *in love with death* Compare Keats, 'Ode to a Nightingale' 52.

[8] Shelley visited the Protestant (or, more correctly, the non-Catholic) Cemetery in Rome in late November 1818; his son William was buried there in 1819.

[9] *genius* spirit.

[10] *The savage criticism . . . inflicted* This helped perpetuate the myth that Keats was 'killed' by a review – that of *Endymion* in the *Quarterly* for April 1818, by Croker.

[11] *these wretched men know not what they do* an echo of Christ's comment on those who crucified him: 'Father, forgive them; for they know not what they do' (Luke 23: 34).

[12] *penetrable stuff* cf. *Hamlet* III iv 35–6: 'And let me wring your heart, for so I shall / If it be made of penetrable stuff'.

[13] *One of their associates . . . calumniator* Robert Southey, who Shelley thought had attacked his poem, *The Revolt of Islam*, in the *Quarterly* in 1817; the actual author was John Taylor Coleridge. Shelley has in mind Southey's part in the spreading of rumours about the 'league of incest'; see p. 933n2.

[14] Revd George Croly, *Paris in 1815* (1817); Eaton Stannard Barrett, *Woman* (1810); H. Galley Knight, *Ilderim: A Syrian Tale* (1816): all these works were reviewed in the *Quarterly*, 1817–20. Mrs Alicia Lefanu (*c*.1795–*c*.1826) was the author of *The Flowers* (1809). John Howard Payne was an American dramatist, whose *Brutus* was reviewed harshly by the *Quarterly*.

[15] Revd Henry Hart Milman's *Saviour, Lord of the Bright City* and *Fall of Jerusalem* were praised by the *Quarterly*, 1818–20.

[16] *What gnat . . . camels* cf. Christ's criticism of the Pharisees, Matthew 23: 24: 'Ye blind guides, which strain at a gnat, and swallow a camel.'

[17] *Against what woman . . . stone* see John 8: 7.

God. Nor shall it be your excuse that, murderer as you are, you have spoken daggers but used none.[18]

The circumstances of the closing scene of poor Keats' life were not made known to me until the *Elegy* was ready for the press. I am given to understand that the wound which his sensitive spirit had received from the criticism of *Endymion*, was exasperated by the bitter sense of unrequited benefits; the poor fellow seems to have been hooted from the stage of life, no less by those on whom he had wasted the promise of his genius, than those on whom he had lavished his fortune and his care. He was accompanied to Rome, and attended in his last illness by Mr Severn,[19] a young artist of the highest promise, who, I have been informed, 'almost risked his own life, and sacrificed every prospect to unwearied attendance upon his dying friend.'[20] Had I known these circumstances before the completion of my poem, I should have been tempted to add my feeble tribute of applause to the more solid recompense which the virtuous man finds in the recollection of his own motives. Mr Severn can dispense with a reward from 'such stuff as dreams are made of'.[21] His conduct is a golden augury of the success of his future career; may the unextinguished spirit of his illustrious friend animate the creations of his pencil, and plead against oblivion for his name!

I

I weep for Adonais – he is dead!
Oh weep for Adonais, though our tears
Thaw not the frost which binds so dear a head!
And thou, sad Hour, selected from all years
To mourn our loss, rouse thy obscure compeers,
And teach them thine own sorrow, say: 'With me
Died Adonais; till the Future dares
Forget the Past, his fate and fame shall be
An echo and a light unto eternity!'

II

Where wert thou, mighty Mother,[1] when he lay,
When thy Son lay, pierced by the shaft[2] which flies
In darkness?[3] Where was lorn Urania
When Adonais died? With veiled eyes,
Mid listening Echoes, in her Paradise
She sat, while one,[4] with soft enamoured breath,

Notes

[18] *you have spoken daggers but used none* cf. *Hamlet* III ii 396: 'I will speak daggers to her, but use none.'

[19] Joseph Severn (1793–1879), a young artist who accompanied Keats to Rome, and nursed him until his death. Severn remained in Rome, became British Consul there in 1860, and was buried next to Keats.

[20] This information was in a letter from the Revd Robert Finch to John Gisborne, and was passed on to Shelley on 13 June 1821.

[21] *such stuff as dreams are made of* from *The Tempest* IV i 156–7.

[1] *mighty Mother* Urania, muse of astronomy, whom Shelley makes the mother of Adonais. She is forsaken ('lorn') in line 12.

[2] *the shaft* i.e. of an arrow. Shelley is writing figuratively of Croker's hostile review of *Endymion* in the *Quarterly*. He is also recalling Psalm 91: 5: 'Thou shalt not be afraid for the terror by night; nor for the arrow that flieth by day.'

[3] *Where wert thou . . . darkness* the appeal is an essential part of formal elegy; cf. *Lycidas* 50–1: 'Where were ye nymphs when the remorseless deep / Closed o'er the head of your loved Lycidas?'

[4] *one* i.e. an Echo.

Rekindled all the fading melodies,
With which, like flowers that mock the corpse beneath,
He had adorned and hid the coming bulk of death.

III

Oh weep for Adonais – he is dead!
Wake, melancholy Mother, wake and weep!
Yet wherefore? Quench within their burning bed
Thy fiery tears, and let thy loud heart keep,
Like his, a mute and uncomplaining sleep;
For he is gone, where all things wise and fair
Descend. Oh dream not that the amorous Deep
Will yet restore him to the vital air –
Death feeds on his mute voice, and laughs at our despair.

IV

Most musical of mourners, weep again!
Lament anew, Urania! He died,[5]
Who was the Sire of an immortal strain,
Blind, old, and lonely, when his country's pride,
The priest, the slave, and the liberticide,[6]
Trampled and mocked with many a loathed rite
Of lust and blood;[7] he went, unterrified,
Into the gulf of death, but his clear Sprite[8]
Yet reigns o'er earth – the third among the sons of light.[9]

V

Most musical of mourners, weep anew!
Not all to that bright station dared to climb –
And happier they their happiness who knew,
Whose tapers yet burn through that night of time
In which suns perished;[10] others more sublime,
Struck by the envious wrath of man or God,
Have sunk, extinct in their refulgent[11] prime;
And some yet live, treading the thorny road
Which leads, through toil and hate, to Fame's serene abode.

Notes

[5] *He died* Milton, whose muse was also Urania. He died on 8 November 1674 in Bunhill House, London.

[6] *liberticide* destroyer of liberty.

[7] When the Stuart monarchy was restored with Charles II in 1660, some of those responsible for the execution of Charles I were beheaded. Milton escaped punishment, partly through the efforts of his friend and former colleague, Andrew Marvell.

[8] *Sprite* spirit.

[9] *the third among the sons of light* a reference to Shelley's discussion of epic poets in 'A Defence of Poetry', where Milton is ranked alongside Homer and Dante. In a MS note, Shelley lists the poets who would mourn Keats: 'It is difficult to assign any order of precedence except that founded on fame; thence, why (the Scriptures excepted), Virgil, Anacreon, Petrarch, Homer, Sophocles, Aeschylus, Dante, Petrarch, Lucretius, Virgil, Calderon, Shakespeare, Milton.'

[10] *And happier they . . . perished* minor poets ('tapers') whose works survive are happier than major poets ('suns') whose work is lost.

[11] *refulgent* glorious, radiant.

VI

But now, thy youngest, dearest one, has perished
The nursling of thy widowhood,[12] who grew,
Like a pale flower by some sad maiden cherished,
And fed with true love tears instead of dew[13] –
Most musical of mourners, weep anew!
Thy extreme hope, the loveliest and the last,
The bloom, whose petals nipped before they blew[14]
Died on the promise of the fruit, is waste;
The broken lily lies – the storm is overpast.

VII

To that high Capital,[15] where kingly Death
Keeps his pale court[16] in beauty and decay,
He came; and bought, with price of purest breath,
A grave among the eternal.[17] Come away![18]
Haste, while the vault of blue Italian day
Is yet his fitting charnel-roof![19] while still
He lies, as if in dewy sleep he lay;
Awake him not! surely he takes his fill
Of deep and liquid[20] rest, forgetful of all ill.

VIII

He will awake no more, oh never more!
Within the twilight chamber spreads apace
The shadow of white Death, and at the door
Invisible Corruption waits to trace
His extreme way to her dim dwelling-place;
The eternal Hunger sits, but pity and awe
Soothe her pale rage, nor dares she to deface
So fair a prey, till darkness, and the law
Of mortal change, shall fill the grave which is her maw.

Notes

[12] *The nursling of thy widowhood* Keats is presented as Milton's heir. Shelley was an admirer of Keats's Miltonic 'Hyperion'; see p. 1200n5.

[13] Lines 48–9 recall Keats' *Isabella* 424.

[14] *blew* blossomed.

[15] *that high Capital* Rome; Keats died at 26, Piazza di Spagna, today a museum devoted to him, Shelley and Byron.

[16] *Death . . . court* an echo of *Richard II* III ii 160–2:

> for within the hollow crown
> That rounds the mortal temples of a king
> Keeps Death his court . . .

[17] *the eternal* i.e. both Rome, the eternal city, and the many illustrious people buried there.

[18] *Come away!* addressed to those gathered round the body of Adonais.

[19] *charnel-roof* the roof of a tomb.

[20] *liquid* undisturbed, perfect.

IX

Oh weep for Adonais! The quick Dreams,[21]
The passion-wingèd Ministers of thought
Who were his flocks, whom near the living streams
Of his young spirit he fed, and whom he taught
The love which was its music, wander not –
Wander no more from kindling brain to brain,
But droop there, whence they sprung; and mourn their lot
Round the cold heart, where, after their sweet pain,[22]
They ne'er will gather strength, or find a home again.

X

And one with trembling hands clasps his cold head,
And fans him with his moonlight wings, and cries,
'Our love, our hope, our sorrow, is not dead;[23]
See, on the silken fringe of his faint eyes,
Like dew upon a sleeping flower, there lies
A tear some Dream has loosened from his brain.'
Lost Angel of a ruined Paradise![24]
She knew not 'twas her own; as with no stain
She faded, like a cloud which had outwept its rain.[25]

XI

One from a lucid urn of starry dew
Washed his light limbs as if embalming them;
Another clipped her profuse locks, and threw
The wreath upon him, like an anadem,[26]
Which frozen tears instead of pearls begem;
Another in her wilful grief would break
Her bow and wingèd reeds,[27] as if to stem
A greater loss with one which was more weak,
And dull the barbèd fire[28] against his frozen cheek.

Notes

[21] *quick Dreams* Keats's living ('quick') poems, which grieve for him.

[22] *sweet pain* Curiously, this appears in Keats's manuscript draft of 'Hyperion: A Fragment' Book III (starting at line 125 of the published text):

> Soon wild commotions shook him, and made flush
> All the immortal fairness of his limbs
> Into a hue more roseate than sweet pain
> Gives to a ravish'd Nymph when her warm tears
> Gush luscious with no sob . . .

It seems unlikely that Shelley knew Keats's unpublished manuscript; 'sweet pain' is just a very typical Keatsian formulation.

[23] *our sorrow, is not dead* cf. *Lycidas* 166: 'For Lycidas your sorrow is not dead.'

[24] *a ruined Paradise* Adonais' creative imagination.

[25] *like a cloud that had outwept its rain* i.e. like a cloud that had more grief than it could express through its available moisture.

[26] *anadem* garland of flowers.

[27] *wingèd reeds* arrows.

[28] *barbèd fire* a peculiar image that refers to the hooks or barbs on arrows that makes them difficult to remove from the wound. Shelley is almost certainly thinking of the 'storm of arrows barbed with fire' at *Paradise Lost* vi 546.

XII

Another Splendour on his mouth alit[29] –
That mouth, whence it was wont to draw the breath
Which gave it strength to pierce the guarded wit,
And pass into the panting heart beneath
With lightning and with music: the damp death
Quenched its caress upon his icy lips,
And, as a dying meteor stains a wreath
Of moonlight vapour, which the cold night clips,[30]
It flushed through his pale limbs, and passed to its eclipse.

XIII

And others came – Desires and Adorations,
Winged Persuasions and veiled Destinies,
Splendours, and Glooms, and glimmering Incarnations
Of hopes and fears, and twilight Fantasies;
And Sorrow, with her family of Sighs,
And Pleasure, blind with tears, led by the gleam
Of her own dying smile instead of eyes,
Came in slow pomp – the moving pomp might seem
Like pageantry of mist on an autumnal stream.[31]

XIV

All he had loved, and moulded into thought,
From shape, and hue, and odour, and sweet sound,
Lamented Adonais. Morning sought
Her eastern watchtower, and her hair unbound,
Wet with the tears which should adorn the ground,
Dimmed the aerial eyes that kindle day;
Afar the melancholy thunder moaned,
Pale Ocean in unquiet slumber lay,
And the wild winds flew round, sobbing in their dismay.

XV

Lost Echo[32] sits amid the voiceless mountains
And feeds her grief with his remembered lay,[33]
And will no more reply to winds or fountains,
Or amorous birds perched on the young green spray,
Or herdsman's horn, or bell at closing day;

Notes

29 *alit* alighted.

30 *clips* means both 'embraces' and 'cuts off'.

31 *the moving pomp . . . autumnal stream* Shelley has in mind Keats's 'Season of mists and mellow fruitfulness' ('To Autumn' 1).

32 The nymph Echo faded into an echo of sound when Narcissus rejected her; Narcissus fell in love with his own reflection and was transformed into a flower.

33 *lay* Keats's poetry.

Since she can mimic not his lips, more dear
Than those for whose disdain she pined away
Into a shadow of all sounds – a drear
Murmur, between their songs, is all the woodmen hear.

XVI

Grief made the young Spring wild, and she threw down
Her kindling buds, as if she Autumn were,
Or they dead leaves; since her delight is flown
For whom should she have waked the sullen year?
To Phoebus was not Hyacinth so dear[34]
Nor to himself Narcissus, as to both
Thou Adonais: wan they stand and sere[35]
Amid the drooping comrades of their youth,
With dew all turned to tears; odour, to sighing ruth.[36]

XVII

Thy spirit's sister, the lorn nightingale,[37]
Mourns not her mate with such melodious pain;
Not so the eagle, who like thee could scale
Heaven, and could nourish in the sun's domain
Her mighty youth with morning,[38] doth complain,
Soaring and screaming round her empty nest,
As Albion[39] wails for thee: the curse of Cain[40]
Light on his head[41] who pierced thy innocent breast,
And scared the angel soul that was its earthly guest!

XVIII

Ah woe is me! Winter is come and gone,
But grief returns with the revolving year;
The airs and streams renew their joyous tone;
The ants, the bees, the swallows reappear;
Fresh leaves and flowers deck the dead Seasons' bier;
The amorous birds now pair in every brake,[42]
And build their mossy homes in field and brere;[43]
And the green lizard, and the golden snake,
Like unimprisoned flames, out of their trance awake.

Notes

[34] Hyacinth, loved by Phoebus Apollo, was killed out of jealousy by Zephyrus and then turned into a flower by Apollo.

[35] *sere* withered.

[36] *ruth* pity.

[37] *the lorn nightingale* a reference to Keats's 'Ode to a Nightingale'.

[38] The eagle was believed to be able to replenish its youthful vision by flying into the sun and then diving into a fountain.

[39] *Albion* England.

[40] *the curse of Cain* Cain, who killed his brother Abel and brought murder into the world, was cursed as 'a fugitive and a vagabond . . . in the earth' (Genesis 4: 12, 14).

[41] *his head* i.e. that of the critic held responsible by Shelley for Keats's death – John Wilson Croker (although Shelley was unaware of his identity, the review having been published anonymously).

[42] *brake* thicket.

[43] *brere* archaic spelling of 'briar'.

XIX

Through wood and stream and field and hill and Ocean
A quickening life from the Earth's heart has burst
As it has ever done, with change and motion,
From the great morning of the world when first
God dawned on Chaos; in its steam immersed
The lamps of Heaven flash with a softer light;
All baser things pant with life's sacred thirst,
Diffuse themselves, and spend in love's delight,
The beauty and the joy of their renewed might.

XX

The leprous corpse touched by this spirit tender
Exhales itself in flowers of gentle breath;[44]
Like incarnations of the stars, when splendour
Is changed to fragrance, they illumine death
And mock the merry worm that wakes beneath;
Nought we know, dies. Shall that alone which knows[45]
Be as a sword consumed before the sheath[46]
By sightless[47] lightning? – th' intense atom glows
A moment, then is quenched in a most cold repose.

XXI

Alas! that all we loved of him should be,
But for our grief, as if it had not been,
And grief itself be mortal! Woe is me!
Whence are we, and why are we? Of what scene
The actors or spectators? Great and mean
Meet massed in death, who lends what life must borrow.
As long as skies are blue, and fields are green,
Evening must usher night, night urge the morrow,
Month follow month with woe, and year wake year to sorrow.

XXII

He will awake no more, oh never more!
'Wake thou,' cried Misery, 'childless Mother, rise
Out of thy sleep, and slake,[48] in thy heart's core,
A wound more fierce than his with tears and sighs.'
And all the Dreams that watched Urania's eyes,
And all the Echoes whom their sister's song[49]

Notes

[44] *flowers of gentle breath* anemones, thought to have sprung from Adonis' blood when he was killed by a boar.

[45] *that alone which knows* the human mind.

[46] *a sword consumed before the sheath* Shelley would have known Byron's variations on this image: *Childe Harold's Pilgrimage* iii 913, and 'So we'll go no more a-roving' 5: 'For the sword outwears its sheath.'

[47] *sightless* invisible.

[48] *slake* soothe.

[49] *And all the Echoes . . . song* Echo repeated Keats's poem at line 15.

Had held in holy silence, cried: 'Arise!'
Swift as a Thought by the snake Memory stung,
From her ambrosial[50] rest the fading Splendour sprung.[51]

XXIII

She rose like an autumnal Night, that springs
Out of the East, and follows wild and drear
The golden Day, which, on eternal wings,
Even as a ghost abandoning a bier,
Had left the Earth a corpse. Sorrow and fear
So struck, so roused, so rapt[52] Urania;
So saddened round her like an atmosphere
Of stormy mist; so swept her on her way
Even to the mournful place where Adonais lay.

XXIV

Out of her secret Paradise she sped,
Through camps and cities rough with stone, and steel,
And human hearts, which to her airy tread
Yielding not, wounded the invisible
Palms[53] of her tender feet where'er they fell:
And barbed tongues,[54] and thoughts more sharp than they
Rent the soft Form they never could repel,
Whose sacred blood, like the young tears of May,
Paved with eternal flowers that undeserving way.

XXV

In the death-chamber for a moment Death,
Shamed by the presence of that living Might,
Blushed to annihilation, and the breath
Revisited those lips, and life's pale light
Flashed through those limbs, so late her dear delight.
'Leave me not wild and drear and comfortless,
As silent lightning leaves the starless night!
Leave me not!' cried Urania. Her distress
Roused Death: Death rose and smiled, and met her vain caress.

XXVI

'Stay yet awhile! speak to me once again;
Kiss me, so long but as a kiss may live;
And in my heartless[55] breast and burning brain

Notes

50 *ambrosial* heavenly.
51 *the fading Splendour sprung* the Splendour was fading from grief.
52 *rapt* enchanted.
53 *Palms* soles.
54 *barbed tongues* i.e. hostile critics.
55 *heartless* disheartened, dejected.

That word, that kiss shall all thoughts else survive,
With food of saddest memory kept alive,
Now thou art dead, as if it were a part
Of thee, my Adonais! I would give
All that I am to be as thou now art!
But I am chained to Time, and cannot thence depart!

XXVII

Oh gentle child, beautiful as thou wert,
Why didst thou leave the trodden paths of men
Too soon, and with weak hands[56] though mighty heart
Dare the unpastured dragon[57] in his den?
Defenceless as thou wert, oh where was then
Wisdom the mirrored shield,[58] or scorn the spear?
Or hadst thou waited the full cycle, when
Thy spirit should have filled its crescent sphere,
The monsters of life's waste had fled from thee like deer.

XXVIII

The herded wolves, bold only to pursue;
The obscene ravens, clamorous o'er the dead;
The vultures to the conqueror's banner true
Who feed where Desolation first has fed,
And whose wings rain contagion – how they fled,
When, like Apollo, from his golden bow,
The Pythian of the age one arrow sped
And smiled![59] The spoilers[60] tempt no second blow,
They fawn on the proud feet that spurn them lying low.

XXIX

The sun comes forth, and many reptiles spawn;
He sets, and each ephemeral insect then
Is gathered into death without a dawn,
And the immortal stars awake again;[61]
So is it in the world of living men:
A godlike mind soars forth, in its delight
Making earth bare and veiling heaven, and when
It sinks, the swarms that dimmed or shared its light
Leave to its kindred lamps[62] the spirit's awful night.'

Notes

56 *with weak hands* a reference to the weakness of Keats's early verse. Keats wrote to Shelley, 16 August 1820: 'I remember you advising me not to publish my first-blights, on Hampstead Heath' (Rollins ii 323). In fact, Keats's first volume, *Poems* (1817) received generally favourable reviews; it was *Endymion* (1818) that attracted criticism.

57 *the unpastured dragon* the critic blamed by Shelley for Keats's death.

58 *the mirrored shield* Perseus used a mirrored shield to slay the Medusa.

59 *The Pythian . . . smiled* Byron's *English Bards and Scotch Reviewers* (1809) attacked those responsible for the harsh review of his *Hours of Idleness*; see p. 838. Apollo killed a python with an arrow and established the Pythian games in celebration.

60 *spoilers* ravagers, barbarians (i.e. the reviewers).

61 *The sun . . . awake again* in Shelley's metaphor, the sun is the great poet during his lifetime; the reptiles are the critics; the ephemeral insects imitate the great poet's works; the stars are great poets of the past.

62 *its kindred lamps* stars (i.e. other creative spirits).

XXX

Thus ceased she: and the mountain shepherds came
Their garlands sere, their magic mantles rent;
The Pilgrim of Eternity[63] (whose fame
Over his living head like Heaven is bent,
An early but enduring monument)
Came, veiling all the lightnings of his song
In sorrow; from her wilds Ierne sent
The sweetest lyrist[64] of her saddest wrong,
And love taught grief to fall like music from his tongue.

XXXI

Midst others of less note came one frail Form,[65]
A phantom among men, companionless
As the last cloud of an expiring storm
Whose thunder is its knell. He, as I guess,
Had gazed on Nature's naked loveliness,
Actaeon-like,[66] and now he fled astray
With feeble steps o'er the world's wilderness,
And his own thoughts, along that rugged way,
Pursued, like raging hounds, their father and their prey.

XXXII

A pardlike[67] Spirit beautiful and swift,
A Love in desolation masked, a Power
Girt round with weakness – it can scarce uplift
The weight of the superincumbent hour:[68]
It is a dying lamp, a falling shower,
A breaking billow; even whilst we speak,
Is it not broken? On the withering flower
The killing sun smiles brightly: on a cheek
The life can burn in blood, even while the heart may break.

XXXIII

His head was bound with pansies overblown,
And faded violets, white, and pied, and blue;
And a light spear topped with a cypress cone,

Notes

[63] *The Pilgrim of Eternity* Byron; the reference is to *Childe Harold's Pilgrimage*.

[64] *Ierne sent . . . lyrist* Thomas Moore, from Ireland (Ierne) – popular poet, author of ballads and songs. Shelley forwarded a copy of *Adonais* to Moore through Horace Smith, who reported, 3 October 1821: 'I gave Moore your copy of *Adonais* and he was very much pleased with it, particularly with the allusion to himself' (Jones ii 351).

[65] *one frail Form* Shelley.

[66] Actaeon, seeing Diana bathing, was turned into a stag and torn to pieces by his own dogs.

[67] *pardlike* A pard is a leopard or panther; in an early draft, Shelley has 'Pantherlike'.

[68] *the superincumbent hour* The overhanging ('superincumbent') hour is that of Adonais' death.

Round whose rude shaft dark ivy tresses grew[69]
Yet dripping with the forest's noonday dew,
Vibrated, as the ever-beating heart
Shook the weak hand that grasped it: of that crew
He came the last, neglected and apart –
A herd-abandoned deer struck by the hunter's dart.

XXXIV

All stood aloof, and at his partial moan
Smiled through their tears; well knew that gentle band
Who in another's fate now wept his own;
As in the accents of an unknown land,
He sung new sorrow; sad Urania scanned
The Stranger's mien, and murmured, 'Who art thou?'
He answered not, but with a sudden hand
Made bare his branded and ensanguined brow,
Which was like Cain's or Christ's[70] – oh that it should be so!

XXXV

What softer voice is hushed over the dead?
Athwart what brow is that dark mantle thrown?
What form leans sadly o'er the white deathbed
In mockery[71] of monumental stone,
The heavy heart heaving without a moan?
If it be He[72] who, gentlest of the wise,
Taught, soothed, loved, honoured the departed one,
Let me not vex, with inharmonious sighs,
The silence of that heart's accepted sacrifice.

XXXVI

Our Adonais has drunk poison – oh!
What deaf and viperous murderer could crown
Life's early cup with such a draught of woe?[73]
The nameless worm would now itself disown:
It felt, yet could escape the magic tone
Whose prelude held all envy, hate, and wrong,

Notes

[69] *a light spear . . . grew* A thyrsus, a staff or spear tipped with an ornament like a pine-cone, and sometimes wreathed with ivy or vine branches, was carried, in Greek myth, by Dionysus (Bacchus) and his votaries. Ivy was the emblem of the poet in Latin poetry.

[70] Shelley's comparison of himself with Christ enraged early reviewers, although it had already been made, implicitly at least, in *Prometheus Unbound* and 'Ode to the West Wind'. In particular, the Revd George Croly, in *Blackwood's Edinburgh Magazine* (December 1821), quoted this line and remarked: 'We have heard it mentioned as the only apology for the predominant irreligion and nonsense of this person's works, that his understanding is unsettled.'

[71] *mockery* imitation; the 'form' is alive, but is so still it appears to be a statue.

[72] *He* Leigh Hunt, a crucial influence on Keats (p. 794).

[73] *What deaf . . . woe* Stanzas 36–7 attack the reviewer responsible for Keats's death. Shelley thought him to be Southey, though the actual culprit was John Wilson Croker.

But what was howling in one breast alone,
Silent with expectation of the song,
Whose master's hand is cold, whose silver lyre unstrung.

XXXVII

Live thou whose infamy is not thy fame!
Live! Fear no heavier chastisement from me,
Thou noteless[74] blot on a remembered name!
But be thyself, and know thyself to be!
And ever at thy season[75] be thou free
To spill the venom when thy fangs o'erflow –
Remorse and self-contempt shall cling to thee;
Hot Shame shall burn upon thy secret brow,
And like a beaten hound tremble thou shalt – as now.

XXXVIII

Nor let us weep that our delight is fled
Far from these carrion kites that scream below –
He wakes or sleeps with the enduring dead;
Thou canst not soar where he is sitting now.
Dust to the dust! But the pure spirit shall flow
Back to the burning fountain whence it came,
A portion of the Eternal, which must glow
Through time and change, unquenchably the same,
Whilst thy cold embers choke the sordid hearth of shame.

XXXIX

Peace, peace! He is not dead, he doth not sleep –
He hath awakened from the dream of life –
'Tis we who, lost in stormy visions, keep
With phantoms an unprofitable strife,
And in mad trance, strike with our spirit's knife
Invulnerable nothings. *We* decay
Like corpses in a charnel;[76] fear and grief
Convulse us and consume us day by day,
And cold hopes swarm like worms within our living clay.

XL

He has outsoared the shadow of our night;[77]
Envy and calumny and hate and pain,
And that unrest which men miscall delight,

Notes

[74] *noteless* not worth noting, undistinguished.

[75] *at thy season* every quarter, when the *Quarterly Review* was published.

[76] *charnel* tomb.

[77] *the shadow of our night* The shadow cast by the earth away from the sun.

Can touch him not and torture not again;
From the contagion of the world's slow stain
He is secure, and now can never mourn
A heart grown cold, a head grown grey in vain;
Nor, when the spirit's self has ceased to burn,
With sparkless ashes load an unlamented urn.

XLI

He lives, he wakes – 'tis Death is dead, not he;
Mourn not for Adonais. Thou young Dawn
Turn all thy dew to splendour, for from thee
The spirit thou lamentest is not gone;
Ye caverns and ye forests, cease to moan!
Cease ye faint flowers and fountains, and thou Air
Which like a mourning veil thy scarf hadst thrown
O'er the abandoned Earth, now leave it bare
Even to the joyous stars which smile on its despair!

XLII

He is made one with Nature: there is heard
His voice in all her music, from the moan
Of thunder, to the song of night's sweet bird;[78]
He is a presence to be felt and known
In darkness and in light, from herb and stone,
Spreading itself where'er that Power[79] may move
Which has withdrawn his being to its own,
Which wields the world with never-wearied love,
Sustains it from beneath, and kindles it above.[80]

XLIII

He is a portion of the loveliness
Which once he made more lovely: he doth bear
His part, while the one Spirit's plastic stress[81]
Sweeps through the dull dense world, compelling there
All new successions to the forms they wear;
Torturing th' unwilling dross that checks its flight
To its own likeness, as each mass may bear;
And bursting in its beauty and its might
From trees and beasts and men into the Heaven's light.

Notes

78 *night's sweet bird* the nightingale. Shelley refers, again, to Keats's 'Ode to a Nightingale'.

79 *Power* cf. *Mont Blanc* and *Hymn to Intellectual Beauty.*

80 On the Neoplatonism of this stanza see headnote, p. 1051.

81 *plastic stress* shaping, moulding power. Shelley is almost certainly thinking of the pantheism of Coleridge's *Eolian Harp*, where the divine 'intellectual breeze' is 'Plastic and vast' (l. 39).

XLIV

The splendours of the firmament of time[82]
May be eclipsed, but are extinguished not;
Like stars to their appointed height they climb,
And death is a low mist which cannot blot
The brightness it may veil. When lofty thought
Lifts a young heart above its mortal lair,
And love and life contend in it for what
Shall be its earthly doom,[83] the dead live there
And move like winds of light on dark and stormy air.[84]

XLV

The inheritors of unfulfilled renown[85]
Rose from their thrones, built beyond mortal thought,
Far in the Unapparent. Chatterton
Rose pale, his solemn agony had not
Yet faded from him; Sidney, as he fought
And as he fell and as he lived and loved
Sublimely mild, a Spirit without spot,
Arose; and Lucan, by his death approved:
Oblivion as they rose shrank like a thing reproved.

XLVI

And many more whose names on Earth are dark,
But whose transmitted effluence[86] cannot die
So long as fire outlives the parent spark,
Rose, robed in dazzling immortality.
'Thou art become as one of us', they cry,
'It was for thee yon kingless sphere has long
Swung blind in unascended majesty,
Silent alone amid an Heaven of song.
Assume thy winged throne, thou Vesper of our throng!'[87]

Notes

[82] *The splendours . . . time* i.e. Keats and other poets.

[83] *doom* destiny.

[84] *When lofty thought . . . air* The creative minds of the dead influence the hearts of the young.

[85] *inheritors of unfulfilled renown* poets who died before they could realize their full potential. Shelley goes on to specify Thomas Chatterton, who committed suicide at the age of 17 in 1770; Sir Philip Sidney, who died in 1586 at the age of 32, from a wound sustained in the Netherlands in their fight against Spain; and Lucan, who committed suicide in AD 65 at the age of 25. (Having been a flatterer of Nero, Lucan joined a conspiracy against him; his suicide served to redeem his reputation.)

[86] *effluence* i.e. power.

[87] In the Ptolemaic system of astronomy, the songs of concentric whirling spheres around the earth blended into a harmony. Adonais is to be the genius of the third sphere of Venus.

XLVII

Who mourns for Adonais? Oh come forth
Fond[88] wretch, and know thyself and him aright!
Clasp with thy panting soul the pendulous Earth;[89]
As from a centre, dart thy spirit's light
Beyond all worlds, until its spacious might
Satiate the void circumference; then shrink
Even to a point within our day and night –
And keep thy heart light lest it make thee sink
When hope has kindled hope, and lured thee to the brink.[90]

XLVIII

Or go to Rome, which is the sepulchre
Oh not of him, but of our joy: 'tis nought
That ages, empires, and religions there
Lie buried in the ravage they have wrought;
For such as he[91] can lend – they[92] borrow not
Glory from those who made the world their prey;[93]
And he is gathered to the kings of thought[94]
Who waged contention with their time's decay,
And of the past are all that cannot pass away.

XLIX

Go thou to Rome – at once the Paradise,
The grave, the city, and the wilderness;
And where its wrecks like shattered mountains rise,
And flowering weeds, and fragrant copses dress
The bones of Desolation's nakedness,
Pass, till the Spirit of the spot shall lead
Thy footsteps to a slope of green access[95]
Where, like an infant's smile,[96] over the dead,
A light of laughing flowers along the grass is spread.

Notes

88 *Fond* It is foolish ('Fond') to mourn Adonais.

89 *the pendulous Earth* an allusion to 'The pendulous round earth' of *Paradise Lost* iv 1000, where 'pendulous' means 'suspended' (i.e. in space).

90 *And keep . . . brink* Shelley tells the 'Fond wretch' to keep his heart light so that when death is near, he has not built too much hope on immortality.

91 *he* Adonais.

92 *they* 'such as he'; creative spirits like Keats.

93 *they borrow not . . . prey* Adonais lends his glory to his Roman surroundings; the ruins of empires pass away, while the influence of creative minds endures. Those who have made the world their prey would include the likes of Ozymandias (see p. 1079).

94 *kings of thought* including Chatterton, Sidney and Lucan.

95 *a slope of green access* the Protestant Cemetery in Rome, where Keats was buried.

96 *like an infant's smile* Shelley's son William died suddenly at the age of 3 in June 1819; he was also buried in the Protestant Cemetery in Rome.

L

And grey walls[97] moulder round, on which dull Time
Feeds, like slow fire upon a hoary brand;[98]
And one keen pyramid with wedge sublime,[99]
Pavilioning the dust of him who planned
This refuge for his memory, doth stand
Like flame transformed to marble; and beneath,
A field is spread, on which a newer band
Have pitched in Heaven's smile their camp of death
Welcoming him we lose with scarce extinguished breath.

LI

Here pause: these graves are all too young as yet
To have outgrown the sorrow which consigned
Its charge to each; and if the seal is set,
Here, on one fountain of a mourning mind,
Break it not thou![100] Too surely shalt thou find
Thine own well full, if thou returnest home,
Of tears and gall.[101] From the world's bitter wind[102]
Seek shelter in the shadow of the tomb.
What Adonais is, why fear we to become?

LII

The One remains, the many change and pass;
Heaven's light forever shines, Earth's shadows fly;
Life, like a dome of many-coloured glass,
Stains the white radiance of Eternity,[103]
Until Death tramples it to fragments. Die,
If thou wouldst be with that which thou dost seek!
Follow where all is fled! Rome's azure sky,
Flowers, ruins, statues, music, words, are weak
The glory they transfuse with fitting truth to speak.

LIII

Why linger, why turn back, why shrink, my Heart?[104]
Thy hopes are gone before: from all things here
They have departed – thou shouldst now depart!
A light is passed from the revolving year,

Notes

[97] *grey walls* of Rome, begun by Aurelian (emperor, 270–5), which bound one side of the cemetery.
[98] *a hoary brand* a log in the fireplace, nearly burnt up.
[99] The pyramid is a monument to a Roman tribune, Gaius Cestius, who died about 12 BC, incorporated into the city walls.
[100] *on one fountain . . . thou* The mourner is told not to break the seal on the fountain of Shelley's grief for his son William.
[101] *gall* bitter grief.
[102] *bitter wind* a wry pun on 'malaria', the disease from which William Shelley died (meaning 'bad air' in Italian).
[103] *Life . . . Eternity* Just as sunlight shining through stained glass separates into different colours, so eternal unity is distributed among different people and things on earth.
[104] Shelley is addressing himself.

And man, and woman; and what still is dear
Attracts to crush, repels to make thee wither.
The soft sky smiles, the low wind whispers near:
'Tis Adonais calls! Oh, hasten thither,
No more let Life divide what Death can join together.

LIV

That Light whose smile kindles the Universe,
That Beauty in which all things work and move,
That Benediction which the eclipsing Curse
Of birth can quench not, that sustaining Love
Which through the web of being blindly wove
By man and beast and earth and air and sea,
Burns bright or dim, as each are mirrors of
The fire for which all thirst – now beams on me,
Consuming the last clouds of cold mortality.

LV

The breath whose might I have invoked in song
Descends on me; my spirit's bark is driven
Far from the shore, far from the trembling throng
Whose sails were never to the tempest given;
The massy earth and sphered skies are riven!
I am borne darkly, fearfully, afar;
Whilst burning through the inmost veil of Heaven,
The soul of Adonais, like a star,
Beacons from the abode where the Eternal are.[105]

Music, when soft voices die

From Posthumous Poems (1824)

Music, when soft voices die,
Vibrates in the memory –
Odours, when sweet violets sicken,
Live within the sense they quicken.
Rose leaves, when the rose is dead,
Are heaped for the beloved's bed;
And so thy thoughts, when thou art gone,
Love itself shall slumber on.

Notes

105 *The soul of Adonais . . . are* an allusion to Plato's epigram (p. 1199).

When passion's trance is overpast (composed 1821)[1]

From Posthumous Poems (1824)

When passion's trance is overpast,
If tenderness and truth could last
Or live, whilst all wild feelings keep
Some mortal slumber, dark and deep,
I should not weep, I should not weep!

It were enough to feel, to see
Thy soft eyes gazing tenderly,
And dream the rest – and burn and be
The secret food of fires unseen,
Couldst thou but be as thou hast been.

After the slumber of the year
The woodland violets reappear;
All things revive in field or grove,
And sky and sea; but two, which move,
And for all others, life and love.

To Edward Williams (composed 26 January 1822; edited from MS)[1]

I

The serpent[2] is shut out from Paradise –
The wounded deer must seek the herb no more
In which its heart's cure lies;
The widowed dove must cease to haunt a bower
Like that from which its mate with feigned sighs
Fled in the April hour;
I too must seldom seek again
Near happy friends a mitigated pain.

Notes

WHEN PASSION'S TRANCE IS OVERPAST

[1] Strains had formed within the Shelleys' marriage during the months prior to composition of this poem.

TO EDWARD WILLIAMS

[1] Edward and Jane Williams were friends of Thomas Medwin, Shelley's boyhood friend, who brought them to meet the Shelleys in Pisa in January 1821. By January 1822 Shelley had become somewhat estranged from Mary and had developed strong feelings for Jane. He gave a copy of this poem to Edward Williams on 26 January 1822, saying: 'If any of these stanzas should please you, you may read them to Jane, but to no one else – and yet on second thoughts I had rather you would not' (Jones ii 384). On the same day, Williams recorded in his journal that 'Shelley sent us some beautiful but too melancholy lines.'

[2] *The serpent* Byron's nickname for Shelley was 'The Snake'.

2

Of hatred I am proud; with scorn, content;
Indifference, which once hurt me, is now grown
Itself indifferent.
But not to speak of love, Pity alone
Can break a spirit already more than bent.
The miserable one
Turns the mind's poison into food:
Its medicine is tears, its evil, good.[3]

3

Therefore if now I see you seldomer
Dear friends, dear *friend*,[4] know that I only fly
Yours looks, because they stir
Griefs that should sleep, and hopes that cannot die.
The very comfort which they minister
I scarce can bear; yet I
(So deeply is the arrow gone)
Should quickly perish if it were withdrawn.

4

When I return to my cold home,[5] you ask
Why I am not as I have lately been?
You spoil me for the task
Of acting a forced part in life's dull scene.
Of wearing on my brow the idle mask
Of author, great or mean,
In the world's carnival. I sought
Peace thus, and but in you I found it not.

5

Full half an hour today I tried my lot
With various flowers, and every one still said
'She loves me, loves me not'.
And if this meant a vision long since fled –
If it meant Fortune, Fame, or Peace of thought,
If it meant – (but I dread
To speak what you may know too well);
Still there was truth in the sad oracle.

Notes

[3] *its evil good* Shelley is recalling Satan: 'Evil be thou my good' (*Paradise Lost* iv 110).

[4] *dear friend* presumably a reference to Jane Williams.

[5] *my cold home* a reference to his strained marriage.

6

The crane o'er seas and forests seeks her home.
No bird so wild but has its quiet nest
When it no more would roam.
The sleepless billows on the ocean's breast
Break like a bursting heart, and die in foam
And thus, at length, find rest.
Doubtless there is a place of peace
Where *my* weak heart and all its throbs will cease.

7

I asked her yesterday if she believed
That I had resolution; one who *had*
Would ne'er have thus relieved
His heart with words, but what his judgement bad
Would do, and leave the scorner unrelieved.
These verses were too sad
To send to you, but that I know,
Happy yourself you feel another's woe.

With a Guitar, to Jane (composed April 1822; edited from MS)[1]

Ariel to *Miranda* – Take
This slave of music for the sake
Of him who is the slave of thee;
And teach it all the harmony
In which thou canst, and only thou,
Make the delighted spirit glow,
Till joy denies itself again
And, too intense, is turned to pain;
For by permission and command
Of thine own Prince Ferdinand[2]
Poor Ariel[3] sends this silent token
Of more than ever can be spoken;
Your guardian spirit Ariel, who
From life to life must still pursue
Your happiness, for thus alone
Can Ariel ever find his own;
From Prospero's enchanted cell,
As the mighty verses tell,

Notes

WITH A GUITAR, TO JANE

[1] By the time this poem was written, the Shelleys' relationship had more or less broken down, and Shelley was becoming strongly attached to Jane Williams. He bought her a beautiful guitar in April 1822 and gave it to her with a fair copy draft of this poem, from which my text is taken. Both the guitar and the manuscript survive today in the Bodleian Library, Oxford.

[2] *Ferdinand* a reference to Edward Williams. By coincidence, the maker of the guitar given to Jane was Ferdinando Bottari.

[3] *Poor Ariel* Shelley casts himself in the role of Jane's guardian spirit.

To the throne of Naples he
Lit you o'er the trackless sea,[4]
Flitting on, your prow before,
Like a living meteor.
When you die, the silent moon
In her interlunar swoon[5]
Is not sadder in her cell
Than deserted Ariel;
When you live again on earth[6]
Like an unseen star of birth[7]
Ariel guides you o'er the sea
Of life from your nativity.
Many changes have been run
Since Ferdinand and you begun
Your course of love, and Ariel still
Has tracked your steps and served your will;
Now in humbler, happier lot
This is all remembered not;
And now, alas! the poor sprite[8] is
Imprisoned for some fault of his
In a body like a grave –
From you he only dares to crave,
For his service and his sorrow,
A smile today, a song tomorrow.

The artist who this idol[9] wrought
To echo all harmonious thought
Felled a tree, while on the steep
The woods were in their winter sleep,
Rocked in that repose divine
On the windswept Apennine;
And dreaming, some of autumn past,
And some of spring approaching fast,
And some of April buds and showers,
And some of songs in July bowers,
And all of love; and so this tree –
Oh that such our death may be –
Died in sleep, and felt no pain,
To live in happier form again,
From which, beneath Heaven's fairest star,[10]
The artist wrought this loved guitar
And taught it justly to reply

Notes

[4] *To the throne . . . sea* In Shakespeare's play, Ariel conducts Prospero and Miranda back to Naples, from where they were once banished.

[5] *In her interlunar swoon* a recollection of Milton's *Samson Agonistes*:

> The sun to me is dark
> And silent as the moon,
> When she deserts the night
> Hid in her vacant interlunar cave. (ll. 86–9)

Pliny writes that the time when the moon is in conjunction with the sun is called the interlunar day.

[6] *When you live again on earth* a reference to reincarnation.

[7] *star of birth* Astrologers believe that we are born under particular stars that govern our fates.

[8] *the poor sprite* Ariel (Shelley).

[9] *this idol* the guitar, made by Ferdinando Bottari in Pisa.

[10] *Heaven's fairest star* Venus, which is the brightest 'star' in the sky, and that of love.

To all who question skilfully
In language gentle as thine own;
Whispering in enamoured tone
Sweet oracles of woods and dells
And summer winds in sylvan cells;
For it had learnt all harmonies
Of the plains and of the skies,
Of the forests and the mountains,
And the many-voiced fountains,
The clearest echoes of the hills,
The softest notes of falling rills,
The melodies of birds and bees,
The murmuring of summer seas,
And pattering rain and breathing dew,
And airs of evening; and it knew
That seldom-heard mysterious sound[11]
Which, driven on its diurnal round[12]
As it floats through boundless day,
Our world enkindles on its way –
All this it knows, but will not tell
To those who cannot question well
The Spirit that inhabits it;
It talks according to the wit
Of its companions; and no more
Is heard than has been felt before
By those who tempt it to betray
These secrets of an elder day.
But, sweetly as its answers will
Flatter hands of perfect skill,
It keeps its highest holiest tone
For one beloved Jane alone.

Notes

[11] *mysterious sound* the music of the spheres.

[12] *its diurnal round* Shelley's phrasing is Wordsworthian, recalling Lucy: 'Rolled round in earth's diurnal course' ('A slumber did my spirit seal' 7). 'Diurnal' means 'daily'.

John Clare (1793–1864)

Clare was born on 13 July 1793 in the village of Helpston, Northamptonshire. His father, Parker Clare, was a thresher, but, as the illegitimate son of a Scottish schoolmaster, he wanted to give his son the best education he could, and sent him to school for at least three months a year until he was 12. At school John met Mary Joyce, who was four years younger; she was his girlfriend until their relationship ended at around the time of her father's death. She would be the subject of many of his later poems; in later life he believed that she was his wife.

He became a labourer while still a boy, and began to write poetry for pleasure, scribbling on any scrap of paper he could find. With the encouragement of Edward Drury, a local businessman, he found a supporter (and editor[1]) in the London publisher, John Taylor. *Poems Descriptive of Rural Life and Scenery* went into print in January 1820; its success made him a literary celebrity, the 'Northamptonshire Peasant Poet', and on his visits to London he mixed with Lamb,[2] Hazlitt, De Quincey and Coleridge.[3] Another volume, *The Village Minstrel*, was published in 1821, but sales were disappointing; by 1830 it had sold only 1,250 copies. Clare was forced to continue working as a labourer, and suffered increasing bouts of ill health; it was six years before he published *The Shepherd's Calendar* (1827), which sold only 425 copies in the next two years. When he asked for an accounting of the proceeds from his publications in 1829, Clare learnt that he was actually £140 (£7000 / US$13,800 today) in debt.

His attempt to set himself up as an independent farmer at Northborough in 1831 was blighted by bouts of bad physical and mental health. In June 1837 he was committed by John Taylor to Matthew Allen's asylum, from which he escaped in 1841, believing that when he returned to Northborough he would find his childhood sweetheart, Mary Joyce, waiting for him. Six months later he was taken to the General Lunatic Asylum at Northampton, where he remained until his death on 20 May 1864.

Clare appears to have written incessantly throughout his life, even during his insanity. Obsessed with Byron, and believing that he was the noble Lord, he composed two poems, 'Child Harold' and 'Don Juan', which adapt the Byronic manner to his own idiosyncratic purposes. In the selection that follows I have concentrated on Clare's lyrics – of which 'First Love', 'I am', 'Oh could I be as I have been', 'The Flitting' and 'Silent Love' are among his finest (see Plate 16).

Further reading

John Clare: A Bicentenary Celebration ed. Richard Foulkes (Leicester, 1994).

John Clare in Context ed. Hugh Haughton, Adam Phillips and Geoffrey Summerfield (Cambridge, 1994).

John Clare: New Approaches ed. John Goodridge and Simon Kovesi (Helpston, 2000).

Jonathan Bate, *John Clare: A Biography* (London, 2003).

Notes

1 Much has been written about Clare's relationship with Taylor; for different viewpoints, see Tim Chilcott, *A Publisher and his Circle: The Life and Work of John Taylor, Keats's Publisher* (London, 1972), and Zachary Leader, 'John Taylor and the Poems of Clare', in *Revision and Romantic Authorship* (Oxford, 1996), pp. 206–61.

2 See Scott McEathron, 'John Clare and Charles Lamb: Friends in the Past', *Charles Lamb Bulletin* NS 95 (1996) 98–109.

3 For more on Clare and London, see James C. McKusick, 'John Clare's London Journal: A Peasant Poet Encounters the Metropolis', *TWC* 23 (1992) 172–5.

George Deacon, *John Clare and the Folk Tradition* (London, 2002).

The Independent Spirit: John Clare and the Self-Taught Tradition ed. John Goodridge (n.p., 1994).

Simon Kovesi, 'John Clare's "I" and "eye": Egotism and Ecologism', in *Green and Pleasant Land: English Culture and the Romantic Countryside* ed. Amanda Gilroy (Groningen, 2004).

John Lucas, *John Clare* (Plymouth, 1994).

John Lucas, 'Peasants and Outlaws: John Clare', in *England and Englishness* (London, 1990), pp. 135–60.

Tom Paulin, 'John Clare in Babylon', in *Romanticism: A Critical Reader*, ed. Duncan Wu (Oxford, 1995), pp. 401–7.

Roger Sales, *John Clare: A Literary Life* (Basingstoke, 2001).

Alan Vardy, *John Clare: Politics and Poetry* (Basingstoke, 2003).

The *John Clare Journal* is published annually by the John Clare Society.

To Elia (unsigned)[1]

From The London Magazine (1822)

Elia, thy reveries and visioned themes
To care's lorn heart a luscious pleaure prove,
Wild as the mystery of delightful dreams,
Soft as the anguish of remembered love;
Like records of past days their memory dances
Mid the cool feelings manhood's reason brings,
As the unearthly visions of romances
Peopled with sweet and uncreated things;
And yet thy themes thy gentle worth enhances!
Then wake again thy wild harp's tenderest strings –
Sing on, sweet bard, let fairy loves again
Smile in thy dreams with angel ecstasies;
Bright o'er our souls will break the heavenly strain
Through the dull gloom of earth's realities.

Sonnet (first published *London Magazine* 6 (1822) 272; edited from MS)

Ere I had known the world and understood
Those many follys wisdom names its own
Distinguishing things evil from things good
The dreads of sin and death ere I had known
Knowledge the root of evil – had I been
Left in some lone place where the world is wild
And trace of troubling man was never seen
Brought up by nature as her favoured child
As born for nought but joy where all rejoice
Emparadised in ignorance of sin
Where nature trys with never chiding voice
Like tender nurse nought but our smiles to win
The future dreamless – beautiful would be
The present – foretaste of eternity

Notes

To Elia

[1] Elia was the pen-name of Charles Lamb (pp. 735–9).

January (A Cottage Evening) (extract)

From The Shepherd's Calendar (first published 1827; edited from MS)

Oh spirit of the days gone bye
Sweet childhoods fearful extacy
The witching[1] spells of winter nights
Where are they fled wi their delights
When listning on the corner seat
The winter evenings length to cheat
I heard my mothers memory tell
Tales superstition loves so well
Things said or sung a thousand times
In simple prose or simpler ryhmes
Ah where is page of poesy
So sweet as theirs was wont to be
The majic wonders that decievd
When fictions were as truths believd
The fairey feats that once prevaild
Told to delight and never faild
Where are they now their fears and sighs
And tears from founts of happy eyes
Breathless suspense and all their crew
To what wild dwelling have they flew
I read in books but find them not
For poesy hath its youth forgot
I hear them told to childern still
But fear ne'er numbs my spirits chill
I still see faces pale wi dread
While mine coud laugh at what is said
See tears imagind woes supply
While mine wi real cares are dry
Where are they gone the joys and fears
The links the life of other years
I thought they bound around my heart
So close that we coud never part
Till reason like a winters day
Nipt childhoods visions all away
Nor left behind one withering flower
To cherish in a lonly hour
Memory may yet the themes repeat
But childhoods heart doth cease to beat
At storys reasons sterner lore
Turneth like gossips from her door

Notes

January

[1] *witching* bewitching.

June (extract)

From The Shepherd's Calendar

And now when sheering of the flocks are done
Some ancient customs mixd wi harmless fun
Crowns the swains merry toils – the timid maid
Pleasd to be praisd and yet of praise affraid
Seeks her best flowers not those of woods and fields
But such as every farmers garden yields
Fine cabbage roses[1] painted like her face
And shining pansys trimd in golden lace
And tall tuft larkheels[2] featherd thick wi flowers
And woodbines[3] climbing oer the door in bowers
And London tufts[4] of many a mottld hue
And pale pink pea and monkshood[5] darkly blue
And white and purple jiliflowers[6] that stay
Lingering in blossom summer half away
And single blood walls[7] of a lucious smell
Old fashiond flowers which hus wives love so well
And columbines stone blue or deep night brown
Their honey-comb-like blossoms hanging down
Each cottage-gardens fond adopted child
Tho heaths still claim them where they yet grow wild
Mong their old wild companions summer blooms
Furze brake and mozzling ling[8] and golden broom
Snap dragons gaping like to sleeping clowns[9]
And 'clipping pinks'[10] (which maidens sunday gowns
Full often wear catched at by toying chaps)
Pink as the ribbons round their snowy caps
'Bess in her bravery'[11] too of glowing dyes
As deep as sunsets crimson pillowd skyes
And marjoram notts sweet briar and ribbon grass
And lavender the choice of every lass
And sprigs of lads love[12] all familiar names
Which every garden thro the village claims
These the maid gathers wi a coy delight
And tyes them up in readiness for night
Giving to every swain tween love and shame
Her 'clipping poseys'[13] as their yearly claim
And turning as he claims the custom kiss
Wi stifld smiles half ankering after bliss
She shrinks away and blushing calls it rude

Notes

JUNE

[1] *cabbage rose* the Provins rose, *Rosa centifolia*.

[2] *larkheels* larkspurs, *Delphinium ambiguum*.

[3] *woodbines* honeysuckles, *Lonicera periclymenum*.

[4] *London tuft* London pride, *Saxifraga umbrosa*.

[5] *monkshood* poisonous plant, *Aconitum napelius*.

[6] *jiliflowers* gillyflowers, wallflowers, *Cheiranthus cheiri*.

[7] *blood walls* dark, double wallflower.

[8] *mozzling ling* mottled heather.

[9] *clowns* peasants.

[10] *clipping pinks* common garden carnation.

[11] *Bess in her bravery* probably the double-flowered garden daisy.

[12] *lads love* southernwood, *Artemisia abrotanum*.

[13] *clipping poseys* nosegays given to sheep-shearers.

But turns to smile and hopes to be pursued
While one to whom the seeming hint applied
Follows to claim it and is not denyd
No doubt a lover for within his coat
His nosgay owns each flower of better sort
And when the envious mutter oer their beer
And nodd the secret to his neighbor near
Raising the laugh to make the matter known
She blushes silent and will not disown
And ale and songs and healths and merry ways
Keeps up a shadow of old farmers days
But the old beachen bowl that once supplyd
Its feast of frumity[14] is thrown aside
And the old freedom that was living then
When masters made them merry wi their men
Whose coat was like his neighbors russet brown
And whose rude speech was vulgar as his clown[15]
Who in the same hour drank the rest among
And joind the chorus while a labourer sung
All this is past – and soon may pass away
The time torn remnant of the holiday
As proud distinction makes a wider space
Between the genteel and the vulgar race
Then must they fade as pride oer custom showers
Its blighting mildew on her feeble flowers

To the Snipe (composed before 1831; edited from MS)

Lover of swamps
The quagmire[1] overgrown
With hassock[2] tufts of sedge – where fear encamps
Around thy home alone

The trembling grass
Quakes from the human foot
Nor bears the weight of man to let him pass
Where he alone and mute

Sitteth at rest
In safety neath[3] the clump
Of hugh flag-forrest[4] that thy haunts invest
Or some old sallow[5] stump

Notes

[14] *frumity* frumenty, a dish of hulled wheat boiled in milk, seasoned with cinnamon and sugar.

[15] *clown* peasant.

To the Snipe

[1] *quagmire* bog, marsh. Clare is thinking of Whittlesey Mere, the habitat of snipe and other water-birds, which extended to 2,000 acres; it was drained in 1850.

[2] *hassock* firm tuft or clump of matted vegetation, especially of coarse grass or sedge, such as occurs in boggy ground.

[3] *neath* underneath.

[4] *hugh flag-forrest* a forest of huge marsh-reeds.

[5] *sallow* willow.

Thriving on seams
That tiney islands swell
Just hilling from the mud and rancid streams
Suiting thy nature well

For here thy bill
Suited by wisdom good
Of rude unseemly length doth delve and drill
The gelid mass for food

And here may hap
When summer suns hath drest
The moors rude desolate and spungy lap
May hide thy mystic nest

Mystic indeed
For isles that ocean make
Are scarcely more secure for birds to build
Then this flag-hidden lake

Boys thread the woods
To their remotest shades
But in these marshy flats these stagnant floods
Security pervades

From year to year
Places untrodden lye
Where man nor boy nor stock[6] hath ventured near
– Nought gazed on but the sky

And fowl that dread
The very breath of man
Hiding in spots that never knew his tread
A wild and timid clan

Wigeon and teal[7]
And wild duck – restless lot
That from mans dreaded sight will ever steal
To the most dreary spot

Here tempests howl
Around each flaggy plot
Where they who dread mans sight the water fowl
Hide and are frighted not

Tis power divine
That heartens them to brave
The roughest tempest and at ease recline
On marshes or the wave

Notes

6 *stock* livestock, cattle.

7 *Wigeon and teal* wigeon is a species of duck; teal is a small freshwater bird.

Yet instinct knows
Not safetys bounds to shun
The firmer ground where skulking fowler goes
With searching dogs and gun

By tepid springs
Scarcely one stride across
Though brambles from its edge a shelter flings
Thy safety is at loss

And never chuse
The little sinky foss[8]
Streaking the moores whence spa-red water[9] spews
From puddles fringed with moss

Free booters[10] there
Intent to kill and slay
Startle with cracking guns the trepid[11] air
And dogs thy haunts betray

From dangers reach
Here thou art safe to roam
Far as these washy flag-worn marshes stretch
A still and quiet home

In these thy haunts
Ive gleaned habitual love
From the vague world where pride and folly taunts
I muse and look above

Thy solitudes
The unbounded heaven esteems
And here my heart warms into higher moods
And dignifying dreams

I see the sky
Smile on the meanest spot
Giving to all that creep or walk or flye
A calm and cordial lot

Thine teaches me
Right feelings to employ
That in the dreariest places peace will be
A dweller and a joy

Notes

8 *sinky foss* yielding ditch.
9 *spa-red water* the water is red with iron oxide.
10 *Free booters* plunderers, poachers.
11 *trepid* agitated, fearful.

The Flitting (composed 1832; edited from MS)[1]

Ive left my own old home of homes
Green fields and every pleasant place
The summer like a stranger comes
I pause and hardly know her face
I miss the hazels happy green
The blue bells quiet hanging blooms
Where envys sneer was never seen
Where staring malice never comes

I miss the heath its yellow furze
Molehills and rabbit tracks that lead
Through beesom ling[2] and teazel burrs
That spread a wilderness indeed
The woodland oaks and all below
That their white powdered branches shield
The mossy pads[3] – the very crow
Croaked music in my native fields

I sit me in my corner chair
That seems to feel itself from home
I hear bird music here and there
From awthorn hedge and orchard come
I hear but all is strange and new
– I sat on my old bench in June
The sailing puddocks[4] shrill 'peelew'
Oer royce wood[5] seemed a sweeter tune

I walk adown the narrow lane
The nightingale is singing now
But like to me she seems at loss
For royce wood and its shielding bough
I lean upon the window sill
The trees and summer happy seem
Green sunny green they shine – but still
My heart goes far away to dream

Of happiness and thoughts arise
With home bred pictures many a one
Green lanes that shut out burning skies
And old crooked stiles to rest upon
Above them hangs the maple tree

Notes

THE FLITTING

[1] The valedictory tone of this remarkable poem owes much to the fact that it was composed shortly after Clare had moved to a cottage in Northborough from Helpston. Clare was born in Helpston in 1793, and although Northborough was only a few miles away it felt as if he had been exiled to a different country.

[2] *beesom ling* besom (heath and broom), and heather ('ling').

[3] *pads* paths.

[4] *puddocks* kite's.

[5] *royce wood* Royce Wood was a favourite haunt of Clare's, a home to many nightingales.

Below grass swells a velvet hill
And little footpads[6] sweet to see
Goes seeking sweeter places still

With bye and bye a brook to cross
Oer which a little arch is thrown
No brook is here I feel the loss
From home and friends and all alone
– The stone pit with its shelvey sides
Seemed hanging rocks in my esteem
I miss the prospect far and wide
From Langley bush[7] and so I seem

Alone and in a stranger scene
Far far from spots my heart esteems
The closen with their ancient green
Heath woods and pastures sunny streams
The hawthorns here were hung with may
But still they seem in deader green
The sun e'en seems to loose its way
Nor knows the quarter[8] it is in

I dwell on trifles like a child
I feel as ill becomes a man
And still my thoughts like weedlings wild
Grow up to blossom where they can
They turn to places known so long
And feel that joy was dwelling there
So homebred pleasure fills the song
That has no present joys to heir

I read in books for happiness
But books mistake the way to joy
They change as well give age the glass
To hunt its visage when a boy
For books they follow fashions new
And throw all old esteems away
In crowded streets flowers never grew
But many there hath died away

Some sing the pomps of chivalry[9]
As legends of the ancient time
Where gold and pearls and mystery
Are shadows painted for sublime
But passions of sublimity
Belong to plain and simpler things
And David underneath a tree
Sought when a shepherd Salems[10] springs[11]

Notes

[6] *footpads* footpaths.

[7] *Langley bush* an old whitethorn bush that was a favourite spot for gypsies in Clare's youth. Clare's journal records its destruction in 1823.

[8] *the quarter* i.e. which part of the sky.

[9] *Some sing the pomps of chivalry* John Lucas, *John Clare* (1994), p. 61, suggests that Clare has Byron in mind.

[10] *Salems* Jerusalem's.

[11] *And David . . . springs* Clare could have any number of the Psalms in mind.

Where moss did unto cushions spring
Forming a seat of velvet hue
A small unnoticed trifling thing
To all but heavens daily dew
And Davids crown hath passed away
Yet poesy breaths his shepherd-skill
His palace lost – and to this day
The little moss is blooming still[12]

Strange scenes mere shadows are to me
Vague unpersonifying things
I love with my old haunts to be
By quiet woods and gravel springs
Where little pebbles wear as smooth
As hermits beads by gentle floods
Whose noises doth my spirits sooth
And warms them into singing moods

Here every tree is strange to me
All foreign things where ere I go
Theres none where boyhood made a swee[13]
Or clambered up to rob a crow
No hollow tree or woodland bower
Well known when joy was beating high
Where beauty ran to shun a shower
And love took pains to keep her dry

And laid the shoaf[14] upon the ground
To keep her from the dripping grass
And ran for stowks[15] and set them round
Till scarse a drop of rain could pass
Through – where the maidens they reclined
And sung sweet ballads now forgot
Which brought sweet memorys to the mind
But here a memory knows them not

There have I sat by many a tree
And leaned oer many a rural stile
And conned[16] my thoughts as joys to me
Nought heeding who might frown or smile
Twas natures beautys that inspired
My heart with rapture not its own
And shes a fame that never tires
How could I feel myself alone

Notes

[12] John Lucas comments on lines 79–88: 'Clare is saying not merely that true poetry is "nature" poetry, but that it has its roots in ordinary living, the lives of commoners. "Salems springs" can after all be linked not merely to the life of the fields but to the sermons of the radical Methodists who spoke to and for the people. . . . Methodist chapels were often named "Salem"' (*John Clare* (1994), p. 61).

[13] *swee* swing.

[14] *shoaf* sheaf.

[15] *stowk* stook (of wheat or barley).

[16] *conned* examined.

No – pasture molehills used to lie
And talk to me of sunny days
And then the glad sheep listing bye
And still in ruminating praise
Of summer and the pleasant place
And every weed and blossom too
Was looking upward in my face
With friendships welcome 'how do ye do'

All tennants of an ancient place
And heirs of noble heritage
Coeval they with adams race
And blest with more substantial age
For when the world first saw the sun
These little flowers beheld him too
And when his love for earth begun
They were the first his smiles to woo

These little lambtoe[17] bunches springs
In red tinged and begolden dye
For ever and like china kings
They come but never seem to die
These may-blooms with its little threads
Still comes upon the thorny bowers
And ne'er forgets those pinky heads
Like fairy pins amid the flowers

And still they bloom as in the day
They first crowned wilderness and rock
When abel haply crowned with may
The firstlings of his little flock
And Eve might from the matted thorn
To deck her lone and lovely brow
Reach that same rose that heedless scorn
Misnames as the dog rosey[18] now

Give me no high flown fangled things
No haughty pomp in marching chime
Where muses play on golden strings
And splendour passes for sublime
Where citys stretch as far as fame
And fancys straining eye can go
And piled untill the sky for shame
Is stooping far away below

I love the verse that mild and bland
Breaths of green fields and open sky[19]
I love the muse that in her hand

Notes

[17] *lambtoe* common bird's-foot trefoil.

[18] *dog rosey* dog-rose, a common species of wild rose (*Rosa canina*), with pale red flowers, frequent in hedges.

[19] *green fields and open sky* possibly an echo of Wordsworth, 'Composed upon Westminster Bridge, 3 September 1802' 6–7: 'Ships, towers, domes, theatres, and temples lie / Open unto the fields, and to the sky.'

Bears wreaths of native poesy
Who walks nor skips the pasture brook
In scorn – but by the drinking horse
Leans oer its little brig[20] to look
How far the sallows[21] lean accross

And feels a rapture in her breast
Upon their root-fringed grains to mark
A hermit morehens sedgy nest
Just like a naiads[22] summer bark
She counts the eggs she cannot reach
Admires the spot and loves it well
And yearns so natures lessons teach
Amid such neighbourhoods to dwell

I love the muse who sits her down
Upon the molehills little lap
Who feels no fear to stain her gown
And pauses by the hedgerow gap
Not with that affectation praise
Of song to sing and never see
A field flower grown in all her days
Or e'en a forests aged tree

E'en here my simple feelings nurse
A love for every simple weed
And e'en this little shepherds purse[23]
Grieves me to cut it up – Indeed
I feel at times a love and joy
For every weed and every thing
A feeling kindred from a boy
A feeling brought with every spring

And why – this 'shepherds purse' that grows
In this strange spot in days gone bye
Grew in the little garden rows
Of that old hut[24] now left – and I
Feel what I never felt before
This weed an ancient neighbour here
And though I own the spot no more
Its every trifle makes it dear

The ivy at the parlour end
The woodbine[25] at the garden gate
Are all and each affections friend

Notes

[20] *brig* bridge.
[21] *sallows* willows.
[22] *naiad* water-nymph.
[23] *shepherds purse* a common cruciferous weed, *Capsella bursa-pastoris.*
[24] *hut* cottage – presumably the one he had just moved out of in Helpston.
[25] *woodbine* honeysuckle.

That renders parting desolate
But times will change and friends must part
And nature still can make amends
Their memory lingers round the heart
Like life whose essence is its friends

Time looks on pomp with careless moods
Or killing apathys disdain
– So where old marble citys stood
Poor persecuted weeds remain
She feels a love for little things
That very few can feel beside
And still the grass eternal springs
Where castles stood and grandeur died[26]

The Badger (composed between 1835 and 1837; edited from MS)

The badger grunting on his woodland track
With shaggy hide and sharp nose scrowed[1] with black
Roots in the bushes and the woods and makes
A great hugh[2] burrow in the ferns and brakes[3]
With nose on ground he runs a awkard pace
And anything will beat him in the race
The shepherds dog will run him to his den
Followed and hooted by the dogs and men
The woodman when the hunting comes about
Go round at night to stop the foxes out
And hurrying through the bushes ferns and brakes
Nor sees the many holes the badger makes
And often through the bushes to the chin
Breaks the old holes and tumbles headlong in

When midnight comes a host of dogs and men
Go out and track the badger to his den
And put a sack within the hole and lye
Till the old grunting badger passes bye
He comes and hears they let the strongest loose
The old fox hears the noise and drops the goose
The poacher shoots and hurrys from the cry
And the old hare half wounded buzzes bye
They get a forked stick to bear him down
And clapt[4] the dogs and bore him to the town
And bait him all the day with many dogs
And laugh and shout and fright the scampering hogs

Notes

[26] The poem ends on a note of defiance: the grass is like the poor because no matter how often you cut it down it grows back up. Lucas commends Clare's 'exultant insistence on the "grass eternal" as an invading army which will finally overwhelm its apparently irresistible enemies' (*John Clare* (1994), p. 62).

THE BADGER

[1] *scrowed* marked.

[2] *hugh* huge.

[3] *brakes* bracken.

[4] *clapt* set on.

He runs along and bites at all he meets
They shout and hollo down the noisey streets
He turns about to face the loud uproar
And drives the rebels to their very doors
The frequent stone is hurled where ere they go
When badgers fight and every ones a foe
The dogs are clapt and urged to join the fray
The badger turns and drives them all away
Though scarcely half as big dimute[5] and small
He fights with dogs for hours and beats them all
The heavy mastiff savage in the fray
Lies down and licks his feet and turns away
The bull dog knows his match and waxes[6] cold
The badger grins and never leaves his hold
He drives the crowd and follows at their heels
And bites them through the drunkard swears and reels

The frighted women takes the boys away
The blackguard laughs and hurrys on the fray
He trys to reach the woods a awkard race
But sticks and cudgels quickly stop the chace
He turns agen and drives the noisey crowd
And beats the many dogs in noises loud
He drives away and beats them every one
And then they loose them all and set them on
He falls as dead and kicked by boys and men
Then starts and grins and drives the crowd agen
Till kicked and torn and beaten out he lies
And leaves his hold and cackles groans and dies

Some keep a baited badger tame as hog
And tame him till he follows like the dog
They urge him on like dogs and show fair play
He beats and scarcely wounded goes away
Lapt[7] up as if asleep he scorns to fly
And siezes any dog that ventures nigh
Clapt like a dog he never bites the men
But worrys dogs and hurrys to his den
They let him out and turn a barrow down
And there he fights the pack of all the town
He licks the patting hand and trys to play
And never trys to bite or run away
And runs away from noise in hollow trees
Burnt by the boys to get a swarm of bees

Notes

5 *dimute* diminutive.

6 *waxes* becomes.

7 *Lapt* curled.

A Vision (composed 2 August 1844; edited from MS)

1

I lost the love, of heaven above;
I spurn'd the lust, of earth below;
I felt the sweets of fancied love, –
And hell itself my only foe.

2

I lost earths joys, but felt the glow,
Of heaven's flame abound in me:
'Till loveliness, and I did grow,
The bard of immortality.

3

I loved, but woman fell away;
I hid me, from her faded fame:
I snatched the sun's eternal ray, –
And wrote 'till earth was but a name.

4

In every language upon earth,
On every shore, o'er every sea;
I gave my name immortal birth,
And kep't my spirit with the free.

'I am' (composed by 20 December 1846; edited from MS)

1

I am – yet what I am, none cares or knows;
  My friends forsake me like a memory lost: –
I am the self-consumer of my woes; –
  They rise and vanish in oblivion's host,
Like shadows in love's frenzied stifled throes: –
And yet I am, and live – like vapours tost

2

Into the nothingness of scorn and noise, –
  Into the living sea of waking dreams,
Where there is neither sense of life or joys,
  But the vast shipwreck of my lifes esteems;
Even the dearest, that I love the best
Are strange – nay, rather stranger than the rest.

3

I long for scenes where man hath never trod
  A place where woman never smiled or wept
There to abide with my Creator, God;

And sleep as I in childhood, sweetly slept,
Untroubling, and untroubled where I lie,
The grass below – above the vaulted sky.

An Invite to Eternity (composed by July 1847; edited from MS)

1

Wilt thou go with me sweet maid
Say maiden wilt thou go with me
Through the valley depths of shade
Of night and dark obscurity
Where the path hath lost its way
Where the sun forgets the day
Where there's nor life nor light to see
Sweet maiden wilt thou go with me

2

Where stones will turn to flooding streams
Where plains will rise like ocean waves
Where life will fade like visioned dreams
And mountains darken into caves
Say maiden wilt thou go with me
Through this sad non-identity
Where parents live and are forgot
And sisters live and know us not

3

Say maiden wilt thou go with me
In this strange death of life to be
To live in death and be the same
Without this life, or home, or name
At once to be, and not to be
That was, and is not – yet to see
Things pass like shadows – and the sky
Above, below, around us lie

4

The land of shadows wilt thou trace
And look – nor know each others face
The present mixed with reasons gone
And past, and present all as one
Say maiden can thy life be led
To join the living with the dead
Then trace thy footsteps on with me
We're wed to one eternity

Little Trotty Wagtail (composed 9 August 1849; edited from MS)

1

Little trotty wagtail he went in the rain
And tittering tottering sideways he near got straight again
He stooped to get a worm and look'd up to catch a fly
And then he flew away e're his feathers they were dry

2

Little trotty wagtail he waddled in the mud
And left his little foot marks trample where he would
He waddled in the water pudge and waggle went his tail
And chirrupt up his wings to dry upon the garden rail

3

Little trotty wagtail you nimble all about
And in the dimpling water pudge you waddle in and out
Your home is nigh at hand and in the warm pigsty
So little Master Wagtail I'll bid you a 'Good bye'

Silent Love (composed between 1842 and 1864; edited from MS)

1

The dew it trembles on the thorn
Then vanishes so love is born
Young love that speaks in silent thought
'Till scorned, then withers and is nought

2

The pleasure of a single hour
The blooming of a single flower
The glitter of the morning dew
Such is young love when it is new

3

The twitter of the wild birds wing
The murmur of the bees
Lays of hay crickets when they sing
Or other things more frail than these

4

Such is young love when silence speaks
Till weary with the joy it seeks
Then fancy shapes supplies
'Till sick of its own heart it dies

5

The dew drop falls at mornings hour
When none are standing by
And noiseless fades the broken flower
So lovers in their silence die

[*'O could I be as I have been'*] (composed between 1842 and 1864; edited from MS)

1

O could I be as I have been
And ne'er can be no more
A harmless thing in meadows green
Or on the wild sea shore

2

Oh could I be what once I was
In heaths and valleys green
A dweller in the summer grass
Green fields and places green

3

A tennant of the happy fields
By grounds of wheat and beans
By gipseys' camps and milking bield[1]
Where lussious woodbine[2] leans

4

To sit on the deserted plough
Left when the corn was sown
In corn and wild weeds buried now
In quiet peace unknown

5

The harrows resting by the hedge
The roll[3] within the Dyke[4]
Hid in the Ariff[5] and the sedge[6]
Are things I used to like.

6

I used to tread through fallow lands
And wade through paths of grain
When wheat ears pattered on the hands
And head-aches[7] left a stain

Notes

'O could I be as I have been'

1 *bield* shelter.

2 *woodbine* honeysuckle.

3 *roll* large wooden roller for breaking clods of earth.

4 *Dyke* ditch.

5 *Ariff* goose-grass.

6 *sedge* various coarse grassy, rush-like plants growing in wet places.

7 *head-aches* poppies.

7

I wish I was what I have been
  And what I was could be
As when I roved in shadows green
  And loved my willow tree

8

To gaze upon the starry sky
  And higher fancies build
And make in solitary joy
  Loves temple in the field

Felicia Dorothea Hemans (*née* Browne) (1793–1835)

Felicia Dorothea Browne was born at 118 Duke Street, Liverpool, on 25 September 1793,[1] the daughter of George Browne, merchant, and Felicity Wagner (of mingled German, Italian and Lancashire descent). She had three brothers: Sir Thomas Henry Browne, KCH, distinguished in the Peninsular Wars; Lieutenant-Colonel George Baxter Browne, CB, also distinguished in the Peninsular Wars, later chief commissioner of police in Ireland; and Claude Scott Browne, Deputy Assistant Commissary-General in Upper Canada. Her father suffered business problems in 1800 and moved his family to Gwyrch (pronounced 'Gooerch'), near Abergele, North Wales, where Felicia was largely brought up, her education being supervised by her mother, who taught her French, Portuguese, Spanish and Italian. Her sister recalled that 'She could repeat pages of poetry from her favourite authors, after having read them but once over . . . . One of her earliest tastes was a passion for Shakespeare, which she read, as her choicest recreation, at six years old.'[2]

She began writing poetry, and published her first volume of poems by subscription when she was 14, in 1808. Subscribers included John Wilson Croker, Reginald Heber and William Roscoe. According to her biographer, the reviews were so harsh 'as to confine her to her bed for several days'.[3] In fact, the critics were fair; they were certainly firm, but all found encouraging words for the author. Anna Laetitia Barbauld in the *Monthly Review* commented, not unfairly, that some of the poems were 'jejune', and that they 'contain some erroneous and some pitiable lines', but concluded by remarking that, 'if the youthful author were to content herself for some years with reading instead of writing, we should open any future work from her pen with an expectation of pleasure, founded on our recollection of this publication.'[4] And the *Poetical Register* found in

Notes

Felicia Dorothea Hemans

[1] The year of her birth is variously given as 1793, 1794 and 1795. I have followed the dating given by her sister, Harriet Hughes, in her memoir, *The Works of Mrs Hemans* (7 vols, Edinburgh and London, 1839), i 4.

[2] *The Works of Mrs Hemans* (7 vols, Edinburgh and London, 1839), i 6.

[3] Henry F. Chorley, *Memorials of Mrs Hemans* (2 vols, London, 1836), i 37.

[4] *Monthly Review* 60 (1809) 323.

the poems 'promise of something better in future . . . They are pretty, and not devoid of poetical ideas.'[5] Hemans cannot have been too much discouraged, because within the year she would publish her second volume, *England and Spain; or, Valour and Patriotism*, inspired by her brothers' involvement in the Peninsular campaign.

One of the subscribers to *Poems* (1808) was young Thomas Medwin, who had met its author in North Wales. He showed the book to his friend, Percy Bysshe Shelley, who in turn wrote to Thomas Jefferson Hogg, 28 July 1811: 'Now there is Miss F. D. Browne (certainly a tyger); yet she surpasses my sister in poetical talents, this your dispassionate criticism *must* allow.'[6] Shelley scholarship has it that he bombarded Miss Browne with letters but that, recognizing trouble when she saw it, her mother forbade her from responding.[7]

Her father left for Canada in 1810, looking for fresh opportunities, but he was to die there two years later. The following year Captain Alfred Hemans returned to England, a veteran of the Peninsular campaign, and one of the subscribers to the 1808 volume. While still Felicia Browne, she published *The Domestic Affections* in 1812, shortly before marrying him. For a while they lived at Daventry, a dull Midlands town which she detested, before returning to her maternal home in Wales. The pair were ill-suited; her husband is reported to have said that 'it was the curse of having a literary wife that he could never get a pair of stockings mended.'[8] It is interesting to find this corroborated by none other than Wordsworth, who noted: 'She was totally ignorant of housewifery and could as easily have managed the spear of Minerva as her needle.'[9]

Literary success came with publication of *The Restoration of the Works of Art to Italy* in 1816, which was snapped up for a second edition by Byron's publisher, John Murray. 'It is a good poem – very,' Byron told him.[10] By now Hemans had four children (all boys), and just before the birth of a fifth, her husband abandoned his wife for Italy, never to return.

Although her mother and sister helped raise her children, the need to provide meant that she had to keep writing. It was a trap from which she was not to escape. 'Her poetry was often written with a readiness approaching improvisation,' W. M. Rossetti wrote; 'this she felt as in some degree a blemish, and towards the close of her life she regretted having often had to write in a haphazard way, so as to supply means for the education of her sons.'[11] The swiftness with which her poems were composed may be seen in her manuscripts; few carry corrections, revisions or even deletions.[12] Her working life was one of furious productivity, undertaken in spare moments from household chores. A stream of books flowed from her pen: *Tales, and Historic Scenes in Verse* (1819); *Stanzas to the Memory of the Late King* (1820); *Welsh Melodies* (1822); *The Siege of Valencia, and Other Poems* (1823); *The Forest Sanctuary* (1825); *Lays of Many Lands* (1826); *Records of Woman* (1828); and *Songs of the Affections* (1830). She also contributed poems and essays to a wide range of periodicals and magazines, becoming a regular contributor to the *New Monthly Magazine* in 1823. Her usual practice was to publish poems first in periodicals, and then collect them in volume form. By this

Notes

5 *Poetical Register* 7 (1808) 550.

6 Jones i 129.

7 See Newman Ivey White, *Shelley* (2 vols, London, 1947), i 61.

8 *A Short Sketch of the Life of Mrs Hemans* (London, 1835), p. 32.

9 *FN* 60.

10 Marchand v 108. It should be added that Byron would not always be so complimentary; in 1820 he criticized her 'false stilted trashy style [which] . . . is neither English nor poetry' (Marchand vii 182).

11 *The Poetical Works of Mrs Felicia Hemans* ed. W. M. Rossetti (London, 1873), p. xxv.

12 See for instance the manuscript of 'The Spirit's Mysteries' in the British Library.

means she maximized her income and became known to a range of different audiences.

She was on a treadmill, but there were rewards: her work enjoyed widespread popularity and sold in large quantities, sometimes outselling even Byron. It was the kind of success that Shelley and Keats could only dream about. As early as 1819, the *Edinburgh Monthly Review* commented: 'The more we become acquainted with Mrs Hemans as a poet, the more we are delighted with her productions, and astonished by her powers.'[13] The reviewer then became quite rapturous: 'With an exquisite airiness and spirit, with an imagery which quite sparkles, are touched her lighter delineations; with a rich and glowing pencil her descriptions of visible nature: a sublime eloquence is the charm of her sentiments of magnanimity; while she melts into tenderness with a grace in which she has few equals.'[14] Reviewing *The Siege of Valencia* in 1823, the *British Critic* remarked: 'When a woman can write like this, she *ought* to write. Her mind is national property. In the grand scheme of a popular literature, there are many departments which can alone be filled by the emanations of female genius.'[15] In 1826 the *Literary Chronicle* described her as, quite simply, 'the first poetess of the day'.[16]

Perhaps the most influential of her many reviews was that by Francis Jeffrey for the second editions of *Records of Woman* and *The Forest Sanctuary*. He praised her work because

> It is infinitely sweet, elegant, and tender – touching, perhaps, and contemplative, rather than vehement and overpowering; and not only finished throughout with an exquisite delicacy, and even serenity of execution, but informed with a purity and loftiness of feeling, and a certain sober and humble tone of indulgence and piety, which must satisfy all judgements, and allay the apprehensions of those who are most afraid of the passionate exaggerations of poetry.[17]

This was not meant to be as patronizing as it sounds. Not only was Jeffrey a genuine admirer of her work, he was a personal friend, and sought to promote her poetry for what he saw as its virtues. If his comments betray a gendered view of literature, they are representative of their time and place.

By now, successive reprints of her poetry in America meant that she was among the foremost internationally acclaimed poets of the day. Fan mail arrived for her on every boat that crossed the Atlantic, bringing correspondence from such distinguished readers as Ellery Channing. The first collected edition of her poems, edited by Professor Andrews Norton, was published in America in 1825, to widespread acclaim. At about this time Ann Grant wrote, telling her that she was 'Praised by all that read you, loved by all that praise you, and known, in some degree, wherever our language is spoken.'[18] At the height of her fame, Bishop Reginald Heber, friend and literary adviser, encouraged her to write a five-act tragedy, *The Vespers of Palermo*, staged at Covent Garden on 12 December 1823 – about the 'Sicilian Vespers' insurrection against French rule in 1282; it was, alas, a failure, though staged the following year in Edinburgh, with an epilogue by Sir Walter Scott, with some success.

There were darker hours ahead. Her eldest brother died in 1826, followed by her mother the following year. It was a terrible blow, by which time her own health, ravaged by years of unrelenting hard work, was beginning to fail. She moved to Wavertree, a village near Liverpool, where she continued to write. Hoping that it would reinvigorate her, she toured Scotland and the Lakes in 1830, meeting Wordsworth along the way.

Notes

13 *Edinburgh Monthly Review* 2 (1819) 194–209, p. 194.
14 Ibid., p. 207.
15 *British Critic* 20 (1823) 50–61, p. 53.
16 *Literary Chronicle* 379 (19 August 1826) 518–19, p. 518.
17 *Edinburgh Review* 50 (1829) 32–47, p. 34.
18 *The Works of Mrs Hemans* (7 vols, Edinburgh and London, 1839), i 120.

Figure 16 Felicia Dorothea Hemans (1793–1835), bust by Angus Fletcher, 1829. Hemans was pleased with Fletcher's bust, remarking that 'it is so graceful that I cannot but accuse the artist of flattery'. (National Portrait Gallery, London.)

Hemans was always an admirer of Wordsworth. His poems, she once wrote, 'quite haunt me, and I have a strange feeling as if I must have known them in my childhood, they come over me so like old melodies'.[19] She loved the Lake District, partly because she viewed it through the lens of his poetry.

> I seem to be writing to you almost from the spirit-land; all is here so brightly still, so remote from everyday cares and tumults, that I sometimes can scarcely persuade myself I am not dreaming. It scarcely seems to be 'the light of common day' that is clothing the woody mountain before me; there is something almost *visionary* in its soft gleams and ever-changing shadows. I am charmed with Mr Wordsworth, whose kindness to me has been quite a soothing influence over my spirits.[20]

Wordsworth enjoyed her company; he spent a morning with her, 'reading to me a great deal from Spenser, and afterwards his own *Laodamia*, my favourite *Tintern Abbey*, and many of his noble sonnets'.[21] That evening he helped her onto a horse and led her on a ride along a mountain-path overlooking Grasmere valley.

Perhaps feeling the draw of her Celtic roots, she said farewell to England and moved to Ireland in April 1831, to be closer to her brother, George Browne, Commissioner of the Dublin City Police, then residing at the Hermitage near Kilkenny. She was able to make a pilgrimage to the home of Mary Tighe, the author of the remarkable poem *Psyche* (1805), written in Spenserian stanzas, whom she had celebrated in 'The Grave of a Poetess' (see pp. 1306–8). She was embarrassed to find that, such was her fame, 'I found myself the object of quite a reception. There was no help for it, though I never felt so much as if I wanted a large leaf to wrap me up and shelter me.'[22]

She moved to Dublin in the autumn and made friends with such liberal Anglicans as Archbishop Whateley and Joseph Blanco White. On occasion she attended concerts, and heard Paganini: 'he is certainly singular-looking, pale, slight, and with long, neglected hair . . . I thought the expression of his countenance rather that of good-natured and mild *enjouement*, than of anything else.'[23] Her health continued to deteriorate. A tour of the Wicklow mountains in search of fresh air ended prematurely when she stayed, unwittingly, at an inn at which the proprietor and his family were infected with scarlet fever, which she then contracted.

While recovering she visited the gardens of the Dublin Society, but on a visit in November 1834 became so immersed in the book she was reading

Notes

19 Henry F. Chorley, *Memorials of Mrs Hemans* (2 vols, London, 1836), i 175.

20 *A Short Sketch of the Life of Mrs Hemans* (London, 1835), p. 26.

21 *The Works of Mrs Hemans* (7 vols, London, 1839), i 209.

22 Ibid., i 238.

23 Ibid., i 245.

that before she knew it she found herself in the midst of an autumnal fog. She went home immediately but was 'attacked by a fit of ague', as her sister described it.[24] This was no passing illness; it was the final *coup de grâce* that would precipitate her death the following year. Her remaining time was short, but the habit of writing was so deeply ingrained that she could not stop, regardless of her physical state. It was at this moment that she composed her last great work, *Despondency and Aspiration* (p. 1319), in which she takes the reader on that most Wordsworthian of quests – to the roots of her poetic talent.

And then a glorious mountain-chain uprose,
 Height above spiry height!
A soaring solitude of woods and snows,
 All steeped in golden light!
While as it passed, those regal peaks unveiling,
 I heard, methought, a waving of dread wings
And mighty sounds, as if the vision hailing,
 From lyres that quivered through ten thousand strings.[25]

The 'glorious mountain-chain' is Welsh, and the lyres those of Druidic bards. The vision is morally and ideologically loaded. The mountain range exemplifies the virtues of steadfastness and fidelity she celebrates in her poetry, and which comprise:

The deep religion, which hath dwelt from yore,
Silently brooding by lone cliff and lake,
 And wildest river shore![26]

Hemans's Welshness is often overlooked by critics, but it is worth bearing in mind that Wales was her adoptive home, and a profound attachment to it runs through her work. In *The Rock of Cader Idris* (pp. 1247–8), that famous mountain, like the bards who once thronged its summits, is freighted with a Welshness felt to the core of her being, a symbol of heroic independence against the incursions of Roman and Saxon invaders.

Having completed *Despondency and Aspiration,* she might have been expected to put down her pen for good, but she could not stop. In a final expression of heroic energy of the kind she had often written about, she composed a final series of sonnets under the rubric, *Thoughts During Sickness.* The second of these, *Sickness like Night* (p. 1323), moves us because of its determination to convert something terrifying – the darkness of impending death – into the promise of 'starry, spiritual night'.

She lingered on for several months, confessing that she felt 'as if hovering between heaven and earth'.[27] For some time her condition stabilized, but tuberculosis had not left her. One day in April it tightened its grip, she went into a decline and died on Saturday 16 May 1835. She was buried in St Anne's Church, Dublin.

There were to be many tributes to her, some of them in verse. Indeed, poems inspired by her life and death comprise an intriguing sub-genre in themselves – notably Letitia Landon's *Felicia Hemans, Stanzas on the Death of Mrs Hemans* and Elizabeth Barrett's *Stanzas Addressed to Miss Landon, and suggested by her 'Stanzas on the Death of Mrs Hemans'*, all included in this volume (see pp. 1450, 1453, 1464 below). But the finest may be Wordsworth's lament for her in his *Extempore Effusion on the Death of James Hogg*:

Mourn rather for that holy spirit,
Sweet as the spring, as ocean deep;
For her who, ere her summer faded,
Has sunk into a breathless sleep.

Hemans was deeply Wordsworthian in that she shared his sense of the numinous, vividly real in the discussion of second sight in her poem of 1830 (p. 1318). No doubt her Welshness had much to do with this, as well as the close contact she enjoyed with the natural world as a child (her

Notes

[24] Ibid., i 287.

[25] *Despondency and Aspiration* 75–82.

[26] Ibid., ll. 141–3.

[27] *The Works of Mrs Hemans* (7 vols, London, 1839), i 306.

hatred of Daventry stemmed partly from its lack of green spaces).

She spent the first two decades of her life in a country obsessed with the threat of invasion – from France. There were two ways of reacting to this: you could denounce the war, like Anna Laetitia Barbauld in *Eighteen Hundred and Eleven*; or, if your brothers and husband had seen service (as was true of Hemans), you could strike a more patriotic attitude. Her readiness to do this was partly the cause of her popularity, and explains why she was acceptable to Tory critics like Croker, who attacked Barbauld for her scepticism. But this doesn't do Hemans full justice, as even her early work is concerned with more than love of her country. Pride, defiance, courage in the face of inevitable defeat, even love: these are the virtues that pervade her poems.

Her work is best represented by *Records of Woman* (1828), the complete sequence of which is included here (alongside some of the accompanying 'Miscellaneous Pieces'). The volume was published by William Blackwood, the Edinburgh publisher, in May 1828, on a profit-sharing plan. 'I have put my heart and individual feelings into it more than anything else I have written,' she told Mary Russell Mitford, 'but whether it will interest my friends more for this reason remains to be seen.'[28] It was her masterpiece, and an instant commercial success. By August all 1,000 copies were sold, and Blackwood was able to remit her share of the profits – £75 (£3,870 / US$7,000 today). A second edition was in print by October. (A third edition was out in June the following year.)

Hemans described it as 'a series of poetic tales . . . illustrative of the female character, affections, and fate'.[29] Its theme is the hardship and duties of womanhood, ranging from Joan of Arc to 'ordinary' women like Edith. It was something she knew much about, having been under pressure to support her family from the moment her husband left. 'My life after eighteen became so painfully, laboriously domestic, that it was an absolute duty to crush intellectual tastes,' she once confided; 'I could neither read nor write legitimately till the day was over.'[30] Many of the *Records of Woman* are concerned with the plight of those shackled to feckless, unreliable, weak or ineffectual men. The first four poems ('Arabella Stuart', 'The Bride of the Greek Isle', 'The Switzer's Wife' and 'Properzia Rossi') seem to praise the constancy of their heroines. The poems that follow, however, temper their commitment with bleaker lessons drawn from such characters as the Indian Woman, 'driven to despair by her husband's desertion of her for another wife', or Constanza, the nun who nurses the warrior who once betrayed her. Although the Indian Woman ends by committing suicide, other heroines have the pleasure of witnessing the deaths of the men who abandoned or deceived them, and there is a strong sense, throughout the volume, that their fate is merited. As Adam Roberts has observed, men die bloodily, and seem to deserve it: 'Physical frailty is transformed to the masculine, and women adopt heroism in a more than metaphorical sense.'[31]

On the other hand, Hemans celebrates the love of mother and child, most obviously in such works as 'Madeline', 'The Memorial Pillar' and 'The Grave of a Poetess'. The volume thus moves away from heterosexual love towards that between mothers and (usually) daughters, away from betrayal to fidelity.

In editing these poems afresh, including the complete *Records of Woman*, I have benefited greatly

Notes

[28] *Felicia Hemans: Selected Poems, Letters, Reception Materials* ed. Susan J. Wolfson (Princeton, NJ, 2000), p. 498.

[29] Ibid., p. 495.

[30] Henry F. Chorley, *Memorials of Mrs Hemans* (2 vols, London, 1836), i 166, 175.

[31] Adam Roberts, 'Felicia Hemans, *Records of Woman*', in *A Companion to Romanticism*, ed. Duncan Wu (Oxford, 1997), pp. 313–19, p. 319.

from the labours of two of Hemans's most diligent and insightful editors – Paula R. Feldman and Susan J. Wolfson. Professor Wolfson has been particularly generous in response to requests for information of various kinds.

Further reading

Felicia Hemans: Selected Poems, Letters, Reception Materials ed. Susan J. Wolfson (Princeton, NJ, 2000).

Felicia Hemans, *Records of Woman with Other Poems* ed. Paula Feldman (Lexington, Ky., 1999).

Felicia Hemans: The Siege of Valencia (A Parallel Text Edition) ed. Susan J. Wolfson and Elizabeth Fay (Peterborough, Ontario, 2002).

Felicia Hemans: Reimagining Poetry in the Nineteenth Century ed. Nanora Sweet and Julie Melnyk (Basingstoke, 2000).

Paula R. Feldman, 'The Poet and the Profits: Felicia Hemans and the Literary Marketplace', *Keats-Shelley Journal* 46 (1997) 148–76.

Angela Leighton, *Victorian Women Poets: Writing Against the Heart* (London, 1992), pp. 8–44.

Tricia Lootens, 'Hemans and Home: Victorianism, Feminine "Internal Enemies" and the Domestication of National Identity', *PMLA* 109 (1994) 238–53.

Jerome J. McGann, *The Poetics of Sensibility: A Revolution in Literary Style* (Oxford, 1996), pp. 174–94.

Anne K. Mellor, *Romanticism and Gender* (London, 1992), pp. 123–43.

Marlon B. Ross, *The Contours of Masculine Desire* (Oxford, 1989), pp. 232–310.

Diego Saglia, *Poetic Castles in Spain: British Romanticism and Figurations of Iberia* (Amsterdam, 2000).

Nanora Sweet, 'History, Imperialism, and the Aesthetics of the Beautiful: Hemans and the Post-Napoleonic Moment', in *At the Limits of Romanticism*, ed. Mary Favret and Nicola Watson (Bloomington, Ind., 1994), pp. 170–84.

Nanora Sweet, *Hemans and the Shaping of History* (forthcoming, 2007).

Patrick Vincent, *The Romantic Poetess* (Lebanon, NH, 2004).

Susan J. Wolfson, *Borderlines: The Shiftings of Gender in British Romanticism* (forthcoming, 2006).

Written on the Sea-Shore

From Poems (1808)

How awful, how sublime this view,
Each day presenting something new;
Hark! now the seas majestic roar,
And now the birds their warblings pour;
Now yonder lark's sweet notes resound,
And now an awful stillness reigns around.

F.D.B. aged 10

The Rock of Cader Idris[1]

From Welsh Melodies (1822)[2]

It is an old tradition of the Welsh bards that, on the summit of the mountain Cader Idris, is an excavation resembling a couch, and that whoever should pass a night in that hollow would be found in the morning either dead, in a state of frenzy, or endowed with the highest poetical inspiration.

I lay on that rock where the storms have their dwelling,
The birthplace of phantoms, the home of the cloud;

Notes

The Rock of Cader Idris

[1] *Cader Idris* (Chair of Idris), a long mountain ridge, reaching a height of 2,927 ft at Pen-y-Gader.

[2] Though born in Liverpool, Hemans identified strongly with the Welsh, and poetry celebrating Welsh cultural identity forms a small but significant part of her output. This is probably the most famous of those works.

Around it for ever deep music is swelling,
The voice of the mountain wind, solemn and loud.
'Twas a midnight of shadows all fitfully streaming,
Of wild waves and breezes that mingled their moan,
Of dim shrouded stars, as from gulfs faintly gleaming,
And I met the dread gloom of its grandeur alone.

I lay there in silence — a spirit came o'er me;
Man's tongue hath no language to speak what I saw:
Things glorious, unearthly, passed floating before me,
And my heart almost fainted with rapture and awe.
I viewed the dread beings around us that hover,
Though veiled by the mists of mortality's breath;
And I called upon darkness the vision to cover,
For a strife was within me of madness and death.

I saw them — the powers of the wind and the ocean,
The rush of whose pinion bears onward the storms;
Like the sweep of the white-rolling wave was their motion,
I *felt* their dim presence, but knew not their forms!
I saw them — the mighty of ages departed —
The dead were around me that night on the hill:
From their eyes, as they passed, a cold radiance they darted —
There was light on my soul, but my heart's blood was chill.

I saw what man looks on, and dies – but my spirit
Was strong, and triumphantly lived through that hour;
And as from the grave, I awoke to inherit
A flame all immortal, a voice, and a power!
Day burst on that rock with the purple cloud crested,
And high Cader Idris rejoiced in the sun —
But oh, what new glory all nature invested,
When the sense which gives soul to her beauty was won!

Manuscript fragments in prose (composed *c.* 1827)

From The Works of Mrs Hemans (1839)[1]

Oh, that we could but fix upon one eternal and unchangeable Being, the affections which here we pour forth, a wasted treasure, upon the dust! But they are 'of the earth, earthy';[2] they cling with vain devotedness to mortal idols; how often to be thrown back upon our own hearts, and to press them down with a weight of 'voiceless thoughts',[3] and of feelings which find no answer in the world!

Oh, that the mind could throw from it the burden of the past for ever! Why is it that voices and tones and looks, which have passed away, come over us with a suddenness and intenseness of remembrance which make the heart die within us, and the eyes overflow with fruitless tears? Who shall explain the mysteries of the world within?

Notes

MANUSCRIPT FRAGMENTS IN PROSE

[1] This is a brief selection of some of the fragments published in 1839 in the collected edition of Hemans's poetry. It is introduced by her sister with the comment: 'A few original fragments found after Mrs Hemans's death in one of her MS. books, may here be given as belonging to this date.'

[2] *of the earth, earthy* from 1 Corinthians 15: 47.

[3] *voiceless thoughts* from Byron, *Childe Harold's Pilgrimage* iii 912–13: 'I live and die unheard, / With a most voiceless thought, sheathing it as a sword.'

How the name of love is profaned in this world! Truly does Lord Byron call 'circumstance' an 'unspiritual God'.[4] What strange, coarse ties – coarse but not strong – one daily sees him forming! – not of the 'silver cords'[5] of the heart, but of the homely housewifely worsted of interest – convenience – economical consideration. One wonders how they are to resist the wear and tear of life, or how those whom they link together are to be held side by side through sorrow, difficulty, disappointment, without the strong affection which 'overcometh all things',[6] and ennobles all things – even the humblest offices performed in attendance at the sick-bed of one we love. What work, what sacrifice is there which a deep, true, powerful feeling cannot dignify!

What is fame to a heart yearning for affection, and finding it not? Is it not as a triumphal crown to the brow of one parched with fever, and asking for one fresh healthful draught – the 'cup of cold water'?[7]

Is it real affliction – ill health – disappointment – or the 'craving void that aches within the breast'[8] for sympathies which perhaps earth does not afford – that weans us most from life? I think the latter. If we could only lie down to die as to sleep, how few would not willingly throw off what Wordsworth calls

the weight
Of all this unintelligible world![9]

and 'flee away, and be at rest.'[10]

Records of Woman: With Other Poems (1828)
(complete *Records of Woman* sequence included here, with some of the 'Miscellaneous Poems'; edited from the first edition)

Mightier far
Than strength of nerve and sinew, or the sway
Of magic potent over sun and star,
Is love, though oft to agony distressed,
And though his favourite seat be feeble woman's breast.
(Wordsworth)[1]

Das ist das Los des Schönen auf der Erde!
(Schiller)[2]

Notes

[4] *Truly does Lord Byron . . . unspiritual God* Hemans refers to Byron, *Childe Harold's Pilgrimage* iv 1122: 'And Circumstance, that unspiritual god'.

[5] *silver cords* a frequently used image in poetry, deriving from Ecclesiastes 12: 6: 'Or ever the silver cord be loosed, or the golden bowl be broken . . . '

[6] *overcometh all things* interestingly, a recollection of Sir Thomas Browne's 'Fragment on Mummies', which discusses poetry, observing that 'Time sadly overcometh all things.'

[7] *cup of cold water* Hemans is recalling Matthew 10: 42: 'And whosoever shall give to drink unto one of these little ones a cup of cold water only in the name of a disciple, verily I say unto you, he shall in no wise lose his reward.'

[8] *craving void that aches within the breast* an echo of Pope, 'Eloisa to Abelard' 94: 'No craving void left aching in the breast.'

[9] *the weight . . . world* from Wordsworth, *Tintern Abbey* 40–1.

[10] *flee away, and be at rest* the memorable final line of Byron's *Stanzas* ('I would I were a careless child').

Records of Woman

[1] Wordsworth, 'Laodamia' 86–90. Hemans's epigraph is from Laodamia's speech about the power and agony of love – a running theme of *Records of Woman*. For Hemans's friendship with Wordsworth, see headnote, p. 1244.

[2] 'That is the lot of the beautiful on earth!' From Schiller, *Wallenstein* IV xii. Thekla is speaking, having just learnt that her lover, Max Piccolomini, has been slaughtered in battle, and insists on visiting his grave. In June 1830 Hemans read Schiller with Wordsworth.

Dedication

To
Mrs Joanna Baillie,[3]
this volume,
as a slight token of
grateful respect and admiration,
is affectionately inscribed
by
THE AUTHOR.

Arabella Stuart[1]

'The Lady Arabella' (as she has been frequently entitled) was descended from Margaret, eldest daughter of Henry VII, and consequently allied by birth to Elizabeth, as well as James I. This affinity to the throne proved the misfortune of her life, as the jealousies which it constantly excited in her royal relatives, who were anxious to prevent her marrying, shut her out from the enjoyment of that domestic happiness which her heart appears to have so fervently desired. By a secret, but early discovered union with William Seymour, son of Lord Beauchamp, she alarmed the cabinet of James, and the wedded lovers were immediately placed in separate confinement. From this they found means to concert a romantic plan of escape and, having won over a female attendant, by whose assistance she was disguised in male attire, Arabella, though faint from recent sickness and suffering, stole out in the night, and at last reached an appointed spot where a boat and servants were in waiting. She embarked and, at break of day, a French vessel, engaged to receive her, was discovered and gained. As Seymour, however, had not yet arrived, she was desirous that the vessel should lie at anchor for him; but this wish was overruled by her companions who, contrary to her entreaties, hoisted sail, 'which', says Disraeli,

> occasioned so fatal a termination to this romantic adventure. Seymour, indeed, had escaped from the Tower; he reached the wharf, and found his confidential man[2] waiting with a boat, and arrived at Lee.[3] The time passed; the waves were rising; Arabella was not there; but in the distance he descried a vessel. Hiring a fisherman to take him on board, he discovered, to his grief, on hailing it, that it was not the French ship charged with his Arabella; in depair and confusion he found another ship from Newcastle which, for a large sum, altered its course and landed him in Flanders.

Arabella, meantime, whilst imploring her attendants to linger, and earnestly looking out for the expected boat of her husband, was overtaken in Calais Roads[4] by a vessel in the King's service, and brought back to a captivity, under the suffering of which her mind and constitution gradually sank.

Notes

[3] Hemans never met Baillie, but they enjoyed a cordial correspondence. Shortly after Hemans's death, the 73-year-old Baillie told Andrews Norton that, of all the poets she knew, 'there is not one of them all whose lyre emitted sweeter or more touching sounds than her own' (*Felicia Hemans* ed. Susan J. Wolfson (Princeton, NJ, 2000), p. 576).

Arabella Stuart

[1] Arabella Stuart (1575–1615) was imprisoned by Elizabeth I for her liaison with Edward Seymour; she was released with the accession of James I in 1603. Against his wishes, she married William Seymour in June 1610. Both were interrogated and arrested; Seymour imprisoned in the Tower of London, Stuart held in private custody. In June 1611, disguised as a man, Stuart escaped with Seymour. While Seymour went to Ostend, Stuart was recaptured and imprisoned in the Tower. In Hemans's time it was thought that Stuart went mad in prison, but today it is believed that she remained sane and was party to several escape plots. But to no avail: she died in the Tower, 25 September 1615.

[2] *confidential man* servant entrusted with a confidential task.

[3] *Lee* a town in Kent, six miles south-east of London.

[4] *Roads* sheltered piece of water near the shore where vessels lie at anchor.

What passed in that dreadful imprisonment cannot perhaps be recovered for authentic history, but enough is known; that her mind grew impaired, that she finally lost her reason, and, if the duration of her imprisonment was short, that it was only terminated by her death. Some effusions, often begun and never ended, written and erased, incoherent and rational, yet remain among her papers.

(Disraeli's *Curiosities of Literature*)[5]

The following poem, meant as some record of her fate, and the imagined fluctuations of her thoughts and feelings, is supposed to commence during the time of her first imprisonment, whilst her mind was yet buoyed up by the consciousness of Seymour's affection, and the cherished hope of eventual deliverance.

And is not love in vain
Torture enough without a living tomb?[1]
(Byron)

Fermossi al fin il cor che balzò tanto.
(Pindemonte)[2]

I

'Twas but a dream! I saw the stag leap free
Under the boughs where early birds were singing;
I stood o'ershadowed by the greenwood tree,[3]
And heard, it seemed, a sudden bugle ringing
Far through a royal forest: then the fawn
Shot, like a gleam of light, from grassy lawn
To secret covert; and the smooth turf shook,
And lilies quivered by the glade's lone brook,
And young leaves trembled as, in fleet career,
A princely band with horn and hound and spear,
Like a rich masque swept forth. I saw the dance
Of their white plumes[4] that bore a silvery glance
Into the deep wood's heart, and all passed by
Save one – I met the smile of *one* clear eye,
Flashing out joy to mine. Yes, *thou* wert there,
Seymour! A soft wind blew the clustering hair
Back from thy gallant brow, as thou didst rein
Thy courser, turning from that gorgeous train,
And fling, methought, thy hunting-spear away
And, lightly graceful in thy green array,
Bound to my side; and we, that met and parted,
Ever in dread of some dark watchful power,
Won back to childhood's trust and, fearless-hearted,
Blent the glad fullness of our thoughts that hour,
Even like the mingling of sweet streams beneath
Dim woven leaves, and midst the floating breath
Of hidden forest flowers.

Notes

[5] Isaac Disraeli (1766–1848) published his *Curiosities of Literature* in 1791.

[1] *The Prophecy of Dante* iii 147–8.

[2] 'The heart that beat so strongly has finally stopped', Ippolito Pindemonte, *Clizia* 55.

[3] *the greenwood tree* Hemans probably has in mind the sylvan setting of *As You Like It* II v 1.

[4] *white plumes* in their hats.

II

'Tis past! I wake
A captive, and alone, and far from thee,
My love and friend! Yet fostering, for thy sake,
A quenchless hope of happiness to be,
And feeling still my woman's spirit strong,
In the deep faith which lifts from earthly wrong
A heavenward glance. I know, I know our love
Shall yet call gentle angels from above
By its undying fervour; and prevail,
Sending a breath as of the spring's first gale
Through hearts now cold; and, raising its bright face,
With a free gush of sunny tears, erase
The characters of anguish. In this trust
I bear, I strive, I bow not to the dust,
That I may bring thee back no faded form,
No bosom chilled and blighted by the storm,
But all my youth's first treasures, when we meet,
Making past sorrow, by communion, sweet.

III

And thou too art in bonds! Yet droop thou not,
Oh, my beloved! There is *one* hopeless lot,
But one, and that not ours. Beside the dead
There sits the grief that mantles up its head,
Loathing the laughter and proud pomp of light,
When darkness, from the vainly-doting sight,
Covers its beautiful![5] If thou wert gone
To the grave's bosom with thy radiant brow;
If thy deep-thrilling voice, with that low tone
Of earnest tenderness, which now, ev'n now,
Seems floating through my soul, were music taken
For ever from this world – oh thus forsaken
Could I bear on? Thou liv'st, thou liv'st, thou'rt mine!
With this glad thought I make my heart a shrine
And, by the lamp which quenchless there shall burn,
Sit, a lone watcher for the day's return.

IV

And lo! the joy that cometh with the morning,
Brightly victorious o'er the hours of care!
I have not watched in vain, serenely scorning
The wild and busy whispers of despair!
Thou hast sent tidings, as of heaven. I wait
The hour, the sign, for blessed flight to thee.
Oh for the skylark's wing that seeks its mate

Notes

[5] '"Wheresoever you are, or in what state soever you be, it sufficeth me you are mine. *Rachel wept, and would not be comforted, because her children were no more.* And that, indeed, is the remediless sorrow, and none else!" From a letter of Arabella Stuart's to her husband. See *Curiosities of Literature*' (Hemans's note; her italics).

As a star shoots! But on the breezy sea
We shall meet soon. To think of such an hour!
Will not my heart, o'erburdened by its bliss,
Faint and give way within me, as a flower
Borne down and perishing by noontide's kiss?
Yet shall I *fear* that lot, the perfect rest,
The full deep joy of dying on thy breast
After long-suffering won? So rich a close
Too seldom crowns with peace affection's woes.

V

Sunset! I tell each moment – from the skies
The last red splendour floats along my wall
Like a king's banner! Now it melts, it dies!
I see one star – I hear – 'twas not the call,
Th' expected voice; my quick heart throbbed too soon.
I must keep vigil till yon rising moon
Shower down less golden light. Beneath her beam,
Through my lone lattice[6] poured, I sit and dream
Of summer lands afar, where holy love,
Under the vine or in the citron-grove,
May breathe from terror.
Now the night grows deep
And silent as its clouds, and full of sleep.
I hear my veins beat. Hark, a bell's slow chime!
My heart strikes with it. Yet again – 'tis time!
A step! A voice! Or but a rising breeze?
Hark, haste – I come to meet thee on the seas!

* * * * * * * *

VI

Now never more, oh never, in the worth
Of its pure cause, let sorrowing love on earth
Trust fondly – never more! The hope is crushed
That lit my life, the voice within me hushed
That spoke sweet oracles, and I return
To lay my youth, as in a burial-urn,
Where sunshine may not find it. All is lost!
No tempest met our barks, no billow tossed;
Yet were they severed, ev'n as we must be
That so have loved, so striven our hearts to free
From their close-coiling fate! In vain, in vain –
The dark links meet and clasp themselves again,
And press out life. Upon the deck I stood,
And a white sail came gliding o'er the flood
Like some proud bird of ocean; then mine eye
Strained out, one moment earlier to descry

Notes

[6] *lattice* window.

The form it ached for, and the bark's career
Seemed slow to that fond yearning. It drew near,
Fraught with our foes! What boots it[7] to recall
The strife, the tears? Once more a prison-wall
Shuts the green hills and woodlands from my sight,
And joyous glance of waters to the light,
And thee, my Seymour, thee!
I will not sink!
Thou, *thou* hast rent the heavy chain that bound thee,
And this shall be my strength – the joy to think
That thou mayst wander with heaven's breath around thee,
And all the laughing sky! This thought shall yet
Shine o'er my heart, a radiant amulet
Guarding it from despair. Thy bonds are broken,
And unto me, I know, thy true love's token
Shall one day be deliverance, though the years
Lie dim between, o'erhung with mists of tears.

VII

My friend, my friend, where art thou? Day by day,
Gliding, like some dark mournful stream, away
My silent youth flows from me. Spring the while
Comes and rains beauty on the kindling boughs
Round hall and hamlet; summer, with her smile,
Fills the green forest; young hearts breathe their vows;
Brothers long parted meet; fair children rise
Round the glad board; Hope laughs from loving eyes –
All this is in the world! These joys lie sown,
The dew of every path; on *one* alone
Their freshness may not fall – the stricken deer,[8]
Dying of thirst with all the waters near.

VIII

Ye are from dingle and fresh glade, ye flowers,
By some kind hand to cheer my dungeon sent!
O'er you the oak shed down the summer showers,
And the lark's nest was where your bright cups bent,
Quivering to breeze and raindrop like the sheen
Of twilight stars. On you heaven's eye[9] hath been,
Through the leaves pouring its dark sultry blue
Into your glowing hearts; the bee to you
Hath murmured, and the rill. My soul grows faint
With passionate yearning, as its quick dreams paint
Your haunts by dell and stream – the green, the free,
The full of all sweet sound, the shut from me!

Notes

[7] *What boots it* 'What good is it . . . ?'

[8] *the stricken deer* borrowed from Cowper's description of himself as 'a stricken deer that left the herd / Long since' (*Task* iii 108–9).

[9] *heaven's eye* the sun.

IX

There went a swift bird singing past my cell –
   Oh love and freedom, ye are lovely things!
With you the peasant on the hills may dwell,
   And by the streams, but I – the blood of kings,
A proud unmingling river, through my veins
Flows in lone brightness, and its gifts are chains!
Kings! I had silent visions of deep bliss,
Leaving their thrones far distant, and for this
I am cast under their triumphal car,[10]
An insect to be crushed. Oh, heaven is far –
Earth pitiless!

Dost thou forget me, Seymour? I am proved[11]
So long, so sternly! Seymour, my beloved!
There are such tales of holy marvels done
By strong affection, of deliverance won
Through its prevailing power! Are these things told
Till the young weep with rapture, and the old
Wonder, yet dare not doubt – and thou, oh thou,
   Dost thou forget me in my hope's decay?
Thou canst not! Through the silent night, ev'n now,
   I that need prayer so much, awake and pray
Still first for thee. Oh gentle, gentle friend!
How shall I bear this anguish to the end?

Aid! Comes there yet no aid? The voice of blood
Passes heaven's gate, ev'n ere the crimson flood
Sinks through the greensward! Is there not a cry
From the wrung heart, of power, through agony,
To pierce the clouds? Hear, Mercy, hear me! None
That bleed and weep beneath the smiling sun
Have heavier cause – yet hear! My soul grows dark –
Who hears the last shriek from the sinking bark[12]
On the mid seas, and with the storm alone,
And bearing to th' abyss, unseen, unknown,
Its freight of human hearts? Th' o'ermastering wave!
Who shall tell how it rushed – and none to save?

Thou hast forsaken me![13] I feel, I know,
There would be rescue if this were not so.
Thou'rt at the chase, thou'rt at the festive board,
Thou'rt where the red wine free and high is poured,
Thou'rt where the dancers meet! A magic glass
Is set within my soul, and proud shapes pass,
Flushing it o'er with pomp from bower and hall;
I see one shadow, stateliest there of all –

Notes

[10] *car* chariot.
[11] *proved* tested.
[12] *bark* ship.
[13] *Thou hast forsaken me* an echo of Christ's words on the cross: 'My God, my God, why hast thou forsaken me?' (Matthew 27: 46).

Thine! What dost *thou* amidst the bright and fair,
Whispering light words, and mocking my despair?
It is not well of thee! My love was more
Than fiery song may breathe, deep thought explore;
And there thou smilest while my heart is dying,
With all its blighted hopes around it lying;
Ev'n thou, on whom they hung their last green leaf –
Yet smile, smile on – too bright art thou for grief!
Death! What, is death a locked and treasured thing
Guarded by swords of fire?[14] A hidden spring,
A fabled fruit, that I should thus endure
As if the world within me held no cure?
Wherefore not spread free wings – Heaven, Heaven control
These thoughts – they rush – I look into my soul
As down a gulf, and tremble at th' array
Of fierce forms crowding it! Give strength to pray,
So shall their dark host pass.

The storm is stilled.
Father in heaven, thou, only thou canst sound
The heart's great deep, with floods of anguish filled,
For human line too fearfully profound.
Therefore forgive, my Father, if thy child,
Rocked on its heaving darkness, hath grown wild
And sinned in her despair! It well may be
That thou wouldst lead my spirit back to thee,
By the crushed hope too long on this world poured,
The stricken love which hath perchance adored
A mortal in thy place! Now let me strive
With thy strong arm no more! Forgive, forgive –
Take me to peace!

And peace at last is nigh.
A sign is on my brow, a token sent
Th' o'erwearied dust from home: no breeze flits by,
But calls me with a strange sweet whisper blent
Of many mysteries.

Hark! The warning tone
Deepens – its word is *Death*. Alone, alone,
And sad in youth, but chastened, I depart,
Bowing to Heaven. Yet, yet my woman's heart
Shall wake a spirit and a power to bless,
Ev'n in this hour's o'ershadowing fearfulness –
Thee, its first love! Oh tender still, and true!
Be it forgotten if mine anguish threw
Drops from its bitter fountain on thy name,

Notes

[14] ' "And if you remember of old, *I dare die*. Consider what the world would conceive, if I should be violently enforced to do it." *Fragments of her Letters*' (Hemans's note; her italics).

Though but a moment.
Now, with fainting frame,
With soul just lingering on the flight begun,
To bind for thee its last dim thoughts in one,
I bless thee! Peace be on thy noble head,
Years of bright fame, when I am with the dead!
I bid this prayer survive me, and retain
Its might, again to bless thee, and again!
Thou hast been gathered into my dark fate
Too much; too long, for my sake, desolate
Hath been thine exiled youth; but now take back,
From dying hands, thy freedom, and retrack
(After a few kind tears for her whose days
Went out in dreams of thee) the sunny ways
Of hope, and find thou happiness! Yet send,
Ev'n then in silent hours, a thought, dear friend,
Down to my voiceless chamber; for thy love
Hath been to me all gifts of earth above,
Though bought with burning tears! It is the sting
Of death to leave that vainly-precious thing
In this cold world! What were it then, if thou,
With thy fond eyes, were gazing on me now?
Too keen a pang! Farewell, and yet once more,
Farewell! The passion of long years I pour
Into that word: thou hear'st not, but the woe
And fervour of its tones may one day flow
To thy heart's holy place; there let them dwell –
We shall o'ersweep the grave to meet – farewell!

The Bride of the Greek Isle[1]

Fear! I'm a Greek, and how should I fear death?
A slave, and wherefore should I dread my freedom?
. . . I will not live degraded.[2] (*Sardanapalus*)

Come from the woods with the citron-flowers,
Come with your lyres for the festal hours,
Maids of bright Scio![3] They came, and the breeze
Bore their sweet songs o'er the Grecian seas;
They came, and Eudora stood robed and crowned,
The bride of the morn, with her train around.
Jewels flashed out from her braided hair
Like starry dews midst the roses there;
Pearls on her bosom quivering shone,
Heaved by her heart through its golden zone;

Notes

THE BRIDE OF THE GREEK ISLE

[1] 'Founded on a circumstance related in the Second Series of the *Curiosities of Literature*, and forming part of a picture in the *Painted Biography*, there described' (Hemans's note).

[2] Byron, *Sardanapalus* I ii 479–80, 629.

[3] *Scio* Greek island now known as Chios in the Aegean.

But a brow, as those gems of the ocean pale,
Gleamed from beneath her transparent veil;
Changeful and faint was her fair cheek's hue,
Though clear as a flower which the light looks through;
And the glance of her dark resplendent eye,
For the aspect of woman at times too high,
Lay floating in mists, which the troubled stream
Of the soul sent up o'er its fervid beam.
    She looked on the vine at her father's door
Like one that is leaving his native shore;
She hung o'er the myrtle once called her own,
As it greenly waved by the threshold stone;
She turned – and her mother's gaze brought back
Each hue of her childhood's faded track.
Oh hush the song, and let her tears
Flow to the dream of her early years!
Holy and pure are the drops that fall
When the young bride goes from her father's hall;
She goes unto love yet untried and new,
She parts from love which hath still been true;
Mute be the song and the choral strain
Till her heart's deep wellspring is clear again!
She wept on her mother's faithful breast
Like a babe that sobs itself to rest;
She wept – yet laid her hand awhile
In *his* that waited her dawning smile,
Her soul's affianced, nor cherished less
For the gush of nature's tenderness!
She lifted her graceful head at last –
The choking swell of her heart was past;
And her lovely thoughts from their cells found way
In the sudden flow of a plaintive lay.[4]

The Bride's Farewell

Why do I weep? To leave the vine
    Whose clusters o'er me bend,
The myrtle (yet, oh call it mine!),
    The flowers I loved to tend;
A thousand thoughts of all things dear
    Like shadows o'er me sweep,
I leave my sunny childhood here –
    Oh therefore let me weep!

I leave thee, sister, we have played
    Through many a joyous hour,
Where the silvery green of the olive shade
    Hung dim o'er fount and bower.

Notes

[4] 'A Greek bride, on leaving her father's house, take leave of her friends and relatives frequently in extemporaneous verse. See Fauriel's *Chants Populaires de la Grèce Moderne*' (Hemans's note). Claude Fauriel (1772–1844) published his *Chants* 1824–5.

Yes, thou and I, by stream, by shore,
In song, in prayer, in sleep,
Have been as we may be no more –
Kind sister, let me weep!

I leave thee, father! Eve's bright moon
Must now light other feet,
With the gathered grapes and the lyre in tune,
Thy homeward step to greet.
Thou in whose voice, to bless thy child,
Lay tones of love so deep,
Whose eye o'er all my youth hath smiled –
I leave thee! Let me weep!

Mother, I leave thee! On thy breast,
Pouring out joy and woe,
I have found that holy place of rest
Still changeless – yet I go!
Lips that have lulled me with your strain,
Eyes that have watched my sleep!
Will earth give love like *yours* again?
Sweet mother, let me weep!

And like a slight young tree that throws
The weight of rain from its drooping boughs,
Once more she wept. But a changeful thing
Is the human heart, as a mountain spring
That works its way through the torrent's foam,
To the bright pool near it, the lily's home!
It is well! The cloud on her soul that lay
Hath melted in glittering drops away.
Wake again, mingle, sweet flute and lyre!
She turns to her lover, she leaves her sire.
Mother, on earth it must still be so,
Thou rearest the lovely to see them go!
They are moving onward, the bridal throng,
Ye may track their way by the swells of song;
Ye may catch through the foliage their white robes' gleam
Like a swan midst the reeds of a shadowy stream.
Their arms bear up garlands, their gliding tread
Is over the deep-veined violet's bed;
They have light leaves around them, blue skies above,
An arch for the triumph of youth and love!

II

Still and sweet was the home that stood
In the flowering depths of a Grecian wood,
With the soft green light o'er its low roof spread,
As if from the flow of an emerald shed,
Pouring through lime-leaves that mingled on high,
Asleep in the silence of noon's clear sky.

Citrons amidst their dark foliage glowed,
Making a gleam round the lone abode;
Laurels o'erhung it, whose faintest shiver
Scattered out rays like a glancing river;
Stars of the jasmine its pillars crowned,
Vine-stalks its lattice and walls had bound,
And brightly before it a fountain's play
Flung showers through a thicket of glossy bay
To a cypress[5] which rose in that flashing rain,
Like one tall shaft of some fallen fane.
  And thither Ianthis had brought his bride,
And the guests were met by that fountain-side;
They lifted the veil from Eudora's face,
It smiled out softly in pensive grace
With lips of love and a brow serene,
Meet for the soul of the deep wood-scene.
Bring wine, bring odours, the board is spread!
Bring roses, a chaplet for every head!
The wine-cups foamed, and the rose was showered
On the young and fair from the world embowered;
The sun looked not on them in that sweet shade,
The winds amid scented boughs were laid;
But there came by fits, through some wavy tree,
A sound and a gleam of the moaning sea.

  Hush, be still! Was that no more
  Than the murmur from the shore?
  Silence! Did thick raindrops beat
  On the grass like trampling feet?
  Fling down the goblet and draw the sword –
  The groves are filled with a pirate-horde!
  Through the dim olives their sabres shine;
  Now must the red blood stream for wine!

The youths from the banquet to battle sprang,
The woods with the shriek of the maidens rang;
Under the golden-fruited boughs
There were flashing poniards and dark'ning brows,
Footsteps o'er garland and lyre that fled,
And the dying soon on a greensward bed.
  Eudora, Eudora! *Thou* dost not fly!
She saw but Ianthis before her lie,
With the blood from his breast in a gushing flow,
Like a child's large tears in its hour of woe,
And a gathering film in his lifted eye,
That sought his young bride out mournfully.
She knelt down beside him, her arms she wound
Like tendrils his drooping neck around,

Notes

[5] *cypress* rather a portentous sight, as it is associated with death.

As if the passion of that fond grasp
Might chain in life with its ivy-clasp.
But they tore her thence in her wild despair,
The sea's fierce rovers, they left him there;
They left to the fountain a dark-red vein,
And on the wet violets a pile of slain,
And a hush of fear through the summer-grove –
So closed the triumph of youth and love!

III

Gloomy lay the shore that night
When the moon, with sleeping light,
Bathed each purple Sciote hill –
Gloomy lay the shore, and still.
O'er the wave no gay guitar
Sent its floating music far;
No glad sound of dancing feet
Woke, the starry hours to greet.
But a voice of mortal woe
In its changes wild or low
Through the midnight's blue repose,
From the sea-beat rocks arose,
As Eudora's mother stood
Gazing o'er th' Aegean flood
With a fixed and straining eye –
Oh, was the spoilers' vessel nigh?
Yes, there becalmed in silent sleep,
Dark and alone on a breathless deep,
On a sea of molten silver, dark,
Brooding – it frowned, that evil bark!
There its broad pennon a shadow cast,
Moveless and black from the tall still mast,
And the heavy sound of its flapping sail
Idly and vainly wooed the gale.
Hushed was all else; had ocean's breast
Rocked e'en Eudora that hour to rest?

To rest? The waves tremble! What piercing cry
Bursts from the heart of the ship on high?
What light through the heavens, in a sudden spire,
Shoots from the deck up? Fire, 'tis fire!
There are wild forms hurrying to and fro,
Seen darkly clear on that lurid glow;
There are shout, and signal-gun, and call,
And the dashing of water, but fruitless all!
Man may not fetter, nor ocean tame
The might and wrath of the rushing flame!
It hath twined the mast like a glittering snake
That coils up a tree from a dusky brake;
It hath touched the sails, and their canvas rolls
Away from its breath into shrivelled scrolls;

It hath taken the flag's high place in air,
And reddened the stars with its wavy glare,
And sent out bright arrows, and soared in glee
To a burning mount midst the moonlight sea.
The swimmers are plunging from stern and prow –
Eudora, Eudora – where, where art thou?
The slave and his master alike are gone;
Mother, who stands on the deck alone?
The child of thy bosom! And lo, a brand
Blazing up high in her lifted hand!
And her veil flung back, and her free dark hair
Swayed by the flames as they rock and flare;
And her fragile form to its loftiest height
Dilated, as if by the spirit's might,
And her eye with an eagle-gladness fraught –
Oh, could this work be of woman wrought?
Yes, 'twas her deed! By that haughty smile
It was hers – she hath kindled her funeral pile![6]
Never might shame on that bright head be –
Her blood was the Greek's, and hath made her free.
   Proudly she stands, like an Indian bride
On the pyre with the holy dead beside;
But a shriek from her mother hath caught her ear,
As the flames to her marriage-robe draw near,
And starting, she spreads her pale arms in vain
To the form they must never enfold again.
   One moment more, and her hands are clasped,
Fallen is the torch they had wildly grasped,
Her sinking knee unto Heaven is bowed,
And her last look raised through the smoke's dim shroud,
And her lips as in prayer for her pardon move –
Now the night gathers o'er youth and love![7]

The Switzer's Wife

Werner Stauffacher, one of the three confederates of the field of Grutli, had been alarmed by the envy with which the Austrian bailiff,[1] Landenberg, had noticed the appearance of wealth and comfort which distinguished his dwelling. It was not, however, until roused by the entreaties of his wife, a woman who seems to have been of an heroic spirit, that he was induced to deliberate with his friends upon the measures by which Switzerland was finally delivered.

Nor look nor tone revealeth aught
Save woman's quietness of thought;

Notes

[6] *she hath kindled her funeral pile* In India it was customary for a widow to throw herself on her husband's funeral pyre.

[7] 'Originally published, as well as several other of these *Records*, in the *New Monthly Magazine*' (Hemans's note). This poem appeared in the *New Monthly* for October 1825.

THE SWITZER'S WIFE

[1] *bailiff* law officer.

And yet around her is a light
Of inward majesty and might.
(M.J.J.)[2]

Wer solch ein Herz an seinen Busen drückt,
Der kann fur Herd und Hof mit Freuden fechten.
(*Wilhelm Tell*)[3]

It was the time when children bound to meet
Their father's homeward step from field or hill,
And when the herd's returning bells are sweet
In the Swiss valleys, and the lakes grow still,
And the last note of that wild horn swells by
Which haunts the exile's heart with melody.

And lovely smiled full many an Alpine home,
Touched with the crimson of the dying hour,
Which lit its low roof by the torrent's foam,
And pierced its lattice through the vine-hung bower;
But one, the loveliest o'er the land that rose,
Then first looked mournful in its green repose.

For Werner sat beneath the linden tree
That sent its lulling whispers through his door,
Ev'n as man sits, whose heart alone would be
With some deep care, and thus can find no more
Th' accustomed joy in all which evening brings,
Gathering a household with her quiet wings.

His wife stood hushed before him – sad, yet mild
In her beseeching mien; he marked it not.
The silvery laughter of his bright-haired child
Rang from the greensward round the sheltered spot,
But seemed unheard; until at last the boy
Raised from his heaped-up flowers a glance of joy,

And met his father's face: but then a change
Passed swiftly o'er the brow of infant glee,
And a quick sense of something dimly strange
Brought him from play to stand beside the knee
So often climbed, and lift his loving eyes
That shone through clouds of sorrowful surprise.

Then the proud bosom of the strong man shook;
But tenderly his babe's fair mother laid
Her hand on his, and with a pleading look,
Through tears half-quivering, o'er him bent, and said,

Notes

[2] Maria Jane Jewsbury, *Arria* 5–8, which Hemans knew from Jewsbury's *Phantasmagoria* (1825). Jewsbury (1800–33) was a friend and correspondent of Hemans, and they saw a good deal of each other when Jewsbury visited Wales in the summer of 1828. Many of the poems which she wrote that summer appeared in her *Lays of the Leisure Hours* (1829), dedicated to Hemans 'in remembrance of the summer passed in her society'.

[3] 'Whoever presses such a heart to his bosom can with joy fight for hearth and home.' Schiller's *Wilhelm Tell* was first published in 1804, and first translated into English in 1825.

'What grief, dear friend, hath made thy heart its prey,
That thou shouldst turn thee from our love away?

It is too sad to see thee thus, my friend!
  Mark'st thou the wonder on thy boy's fair brow,
Missing the smile from thine? Oh cheer thee! Bend
  To his soft arms, unseal thy thoughts e'en now!
Thou dost not kindly to withhold the share
Of tried affection in thy secret care.'

He looked up into that sweet earnest face,
  But sternly, mournfully; not yet the band
Was loosened from his soul, its inmost place
  Not yet unveiled by love's o'ermastering hand.
'Speak low!' he cried, and pointed where on high
The white Alps glittered through the solemn sky.

'We must speak low amidst our ancient hills
  And their free torrents, for the days are come
When tyranny lies couched by forest rills
  And meets the shepherd in his mountain-home.
Go pour the wine of our own grapes in fear,
Keep silence by the hearth – its foes are near.

The envy of th' oppressor's eye hath been
  Upon my heritage.[4] I sit tonight
Under my household tree, if not serene,
  Yet with the faces best beloved in sight;
Tomorrow eve may find me chained, and thee –
How can I bear the boy's young smiles to see?'

The bright blood left that youthful mother's cheek;
  Back on the linden-stem she leaned her form,
And her lip trembled, as it strove to speak,
  Like a frail harp-string, shaken by the storm.
'Twas but a moment, and the faintness passed,
And the free Alpine spirit woke at last.

And she, that ever through her home had moved
  With the meek thoughtfulness and quiet smile
Of woman, calmly loving and beloved,
  And timid in her happiness the while,
Stood brightly forth, and steadfastly, that hour,
Her clear glance kindling into sudden power.

Aye, pale she stood, but with an eye of light,
  And took her fair child to her holy breast,
And lifted her soft voice, that gathered might
  As it found language. 'Are we thus oppressed?
Then must we rise upon our mountain-sod,
And man must arm, and woman call on God!

Notes

[4] *heritage* inherited property.

I know what thou wouldst do – and be it done!
Thy soul is darkened with its fears for me.
Trust me to Heaven, my husband! This, thy son,
The babe whom I have borne thee, must be free!
And the sweet memory of our pleasant hearth
May well give strength – if aught be strong on earth.

Thou hast been brooding o'er the silent dread
Of my desponding tears; now lift once more,
My hunter of the hills, thy stately head,
And let thine eagle-glance my joy restore!
I can bear all, but seeing *thee* subdued –
Take to thee back thine own undaunted mood.

Go forth beside the waters, and along
The chamois-paths, and through the forests go;
And tell, in burning words, thy tale of wrong
To the brave hearts that midst the hamlets glow.
God shall be with thee, my beloved, away!
Bless but thy child, and leave me – I can pray!'

He sprang up like a warrior-youth awaking
To clarion-sounds upon the ringing air;
He caught her to his breast, while proud tears breaking
From his dark eyes, fell o'er her braided hair,
And 'Worthy art thou' was his joyous cry,
'That man for thee should gird himself to die.

My bride, my wife, the mother of my child!
Now shall thy name be armour to my heart;
And this our land, by chains no more defiled,
Be taught of thee to choose the better part!
I go – thy spirit on my words shall dwell,
Thy gentle voice shall stir the Alps – farewell!'

And thus they parted, by the quiet lake,
In the clear starlight: he, the strength to rouse
Of the free hills; she, thoughtful for his sake,
To rock her child beneath the whispering boughs,
Singing its blue, half-curtained eyes to sleep,
With a low hymn amidst the stillness deep.

Properzia Rossi

Properzia Rossi, a celebrated female sculptor of Bologna,[1] possessed also of talents for poetry and music, died in consequence of an unrequited attachment. A painting by

Notes

Properzia Rossi

[1] Properzia de' Rossi (?1490–1530) of Bologna, was an accomplished musician and sculptor who specialized in bas-relief sculptures, usually in stone or wood. She is believed to have loved, unrequitedly, Anton Galeazzo di Napoleone Malvasia who, in response to a lawsuit, was compelled to say that she was not his mistress. Persecuted by Amico Aspertini, another artist, her stock fell, and she died in poverty.

Ducis[2] represents her showing her last work, a basso-relievo of Ariadne,[3] to a Roman knight, the object of her affection, who regards it with indifference.

Tell me no more, no more
Of my soul's lofty gifts! Are they not vain
To quench its haunting thirst for happiness?
Have I not loved, and striven, and failed to bind
One true heart unto me, whereon my own
Might find a resting-place, a home for all
Its burden of affections? I depart
Unknown, though Fame goes with me; I must leave
The earth unknown. Yet it may be that death
Shall give my name a power to win such tears
As would have made life precious.[4]

I

One dream of passion and of beauty more,
And in its bright fulfilment let me pour
My soul away! Let earth retain a trace
Of that which lit my being, though its race
Might have been loftier far – yet one more dream!
From my deep spirit one victorious gleam
Ere I depart – for thee alone, for thee!
May this last work, this farewell triumph be –
Thou, loved so vainly! I would leave enshrined
Something immortal of my heart and mind
That yet may speak to thee when I am gone,
Shaking thine inmost bosom with a tone
Of lost affection – something that may prove
What she hath been whose melancholy love
On thee was lavished; silent pang and tear,
And fervent song that gushed when none were near,
And dream by night, and weary thought by day,
Stealing the brightness from her life away,
While thou – awake, not yet within me die
Under the burden and the agony
Of this vain tenderness; my spirit, wake!
Ev'n for thy sorrowful affection's sake,
Live! In thy work breathe out, that he may yet,
Feeling sad mastery there, perchance regret
Thine unrequited gift.

II

It comes – the power
Within me born, flows back; my fruitless dower

Notes

[2] Louis Ducis (1775–1847), painter of historical subjects and portraits.

[3] An appropriate subject: Ariadne helped Theseus to escape the Minotaur's labyrinth. Afterwards she married him and had his child, but he abandoned her at Naxos and later married her sister, Phaedra.

[4] This epigraph, like many of those in Hemans's later poems, was composed for its appearance here by Hemans herself.

That could not win me love. Yet once again
I greet it proudly, with its rushing train
Of glorious images: they throng, they press;
A sudden joy lights up my loneliness –
I shall not perish all!
The bright work grows
Beneath my hand, unfolding, as a rose,
Leaf after leaf, to beauty; line by line
I fix my thought, heart, soul, to burn, to shine
Through the pale marble's veins. It grows – and now
I give my own life's history to thy brow,
Forsaken Ariadne! Thou shalt wear
My form, my lineaments – but oh, more fair,
Touched into lovelier being by the glow
Which in me dwells, as by the summer light
All things are glorified! From thee my woe
Shall yet look beautiful to meet his sight
When I am passed away. Thou art the mould
Wherein I pour the fervent thoughts, th' untold,
The self-consuming! Speak to him of me,
Thou, the deserted by the lonely sea,
With the soft sadness of thine earnest eye;
Speak to him, lorn one, deeply, mournfully,
Of all my love and grief! Oh could I throw
Into thy frame a voice, a sweet and low
And thrilling voice of song – when he came nigh,
To send the passion of its melody
Through his pierced bosom – on its tones to bear
My life's deep feeling, as the southern air
Wafts the faint myrtle's breath – to rise, to swell,
To sink away in accents of farewell,
Winning but one, *one* gush of tears, whose flow
Surely my parted spirit yet might know,
If love be strong as death!

III

Now fair thou art,
Thou form whose life is of my burning heart!
Yet all the vision that within me wrought,
I cannot make thee! Oh, I might have given
Birth to creations of far nobler thought;
I might have kindled, with the fire of heaven,
Things not of such as die! But I have been
Too much alone; a heart whereon to lean,
With all these deep affections that o'erflow
My aching soul, and find no shore below,
An eye to be my star, a voice to bring
Hope o'er my path, like sounds that breathe of spring,
These are denied me – dreamt of still in vain,
Therefore my brief aspirings from the chain
Are ever but as some wild fitful song,

Rising triumphantly to die erelong
In dirge-like echoes.

IV

Yet the world will see
Little of this, my parting work, in thee;
Thou shalt have fame – oh mockery! Give the reed
From storms a shelter, give the drooping vine
Something round which its tendrils may entwine;
Give the parched flower a raindrop, and the meed
Of love's kind words to woman! Worthless fame,
That in *his* bosom wins not for my name
Th' abiding place it asked! Yet how my heart,
In its own fairy world of song and art,
Once beat for praise! Are those high longings o'er?
That which I have been can I be no more?
Never, oh never more – though still thy sky
Be blue as then, my glorious Italy!
And though the music, whose rich breathings fill
Thine air with soul, be wandering past me still,
And though the mantle of thy sunlight streams
Unchanged on forms instinct with poet-dreams –
Never, oh never more! Where'er I move,
The shadow of this broken-hearted love
Is on me and around! Too well *they* know,
Whose life is all within, too soon and well,
When there the blight hath settled – but I go
Under the silent wings of peace to dwell;
From the slow wasting, from the lonely pain,
The inward burning of those words 'in vain'
Seared on the heart – I go. 'Twill soon be past.
Sunshine, and song, and bright Italian heaven,
And thou, oh thou on whom my spirit cast
Unvalued wealth, who know'st not what was given
In that devotedness – the sad and deep
And unrepaid, farewell! If I could weep
Once, only once, beloved one, on thy breast,
Pouring my heart forth ere I sink to rest!
But that were happiness, and unto me
Earth's gift is *fame*. Yet I was formed to be
So richly blessed! With thee to watch the sky,
Speaking not, feeling but that thou wert nigh;
With thee to listen, while the tones of song
Swept ev'n as part of our sweet air along,
To listen silently – with thee to gaze
On forms, the deified of olden days –
This had been joy enough, and hour by hour,
From its glad wellsprings drinking life and power,
How had my spirit soared, and made its fame

A glory for thy brow. Dreams, dreams! The fire
Burns faint within me. Yet I leave my name –
As a deep thrill may linger on the lyre
When its full chords are hushed – awhile to live,
And one day haply in thy heart revive
Sad thoughts of me; I leave it with a sound,
A spell o'er memory, mournfully profound,
I leave it on my country's air to dwell –
Say proudly yet, ''Twas hers who loved me well!'

Gertrude, or Fidelity till Death

The Baron Von Der Wart,[1] accused, though it is believed unjustly, as an accomplice in the assassination of the Emperor Albert, was bound alive on the wheel, and attended by his wife Gertrude throughout his last agonizing hours, with the most heroic devotedness. Her own sufferings, with those of her unfortunate husband, are most affectingly described in a letter which she afterwards addressed to a female friend, and which was published some years ago, at Haarlem, in a book entitled *Gertrude Von Der Wart, or Fidelity unto Death*.[2]

Dark lours our fate,
And terrible the storm that gathers o'er us;
But nothing, till that latest agony
Which severs thee from nature, shall unloose
This fixed and sacred hold. In thy dark prison-house,
In the terrific face of armed law –
Yea, on the scaffold, if it needs must be,
I never will forsake thee.

(Joanna Baillie)[3]

Her hands were clasped, her dark eyes raised,
The breeze threw back her hair;
Up to the fearful wheel she gazed –
All that she loved was there.
The night was round her clear and cold,
The holy heaven above,
Its pale stars watching to behold
The might of earthly love.

'And bid me not depart', she cried,
'My Rudolph, say not so!
This is no time to quit thy side –
Peace, peace, I cannot go!

Notes

GERTRUDE, OR FIDELITY TILL DEATH

[1] *Baron Von Der Wart* Rudolph von Wart was one of four conspirators who assassinated the Emperor Albert I (1250–1308), King of Germany and ruler of the Holy Roman Empire. He was the only conspirator who was captured and was tortured before being killed.

[2] Johann Konrad Appenzeller, *Gertrude de Wart; or, Fidelity unto Death* (London, 1826).

[3] *De Monfort* V iv 66–73.

Hath the world aught for *me* to fear
   When death is on thy brow?
The world – what means it? *Mine* is *here* –
   I will not leave thee now.

I have been with thee in thine hour
   Of glory and of bliss;
Doubt not its memory's living power
   To strengthen me through *this*!
And thou, mine honoured love and true,
   Bear on, bear nobly on!
We have the blessed heaven in view,
   Whose rest shall soon be won.'

And were not these high words to flow
   From woman's breaking heart?
Through all that night of bitterest woe
   She bore her lofty part;
But oh, with such a glazing eye,
   With such a curdling cheek –
Love, love, of mortal agony,
   Thou, only *thou* shouldst speak!

The wind rose high, but with it rose
   Her voice, that he might hear.
Perchance that dark hour brought repose
   To happy bosoms near,
While she sat striving with despair
   Beside his tortured form,
And pouring her deep soul in prayer
   Forth on the rushing storm.

She wiped the death-damps from his brow
   With her pale hands and soft,
Whose touch upon the lute-chords low
   Had stilled his heart so oft.
She spread her mantle o'er his breast,
   She bathed his lips with dew,
And on his cheek such kisses pressed
   As hope and joy ne'er knew.

Oh lovely are ye, love and faith
   Enduring to the last!
She had her meed – one smile in death –
   And his worn spirit passed,
While ev'n as o'er a martyr's grave
   She knelt on that sad spot,
And weeping blessed the God who gave
   Strength to forsake it not!

Imelda

Sometimes
The young forgot the lessions they had learnt
And loved when they should hate – like thee, Imelda![1]
(Italy, a Poem)[2]

Passa la bella Donna, e par che dorma.[3]
(Tasso)

We have the myrtle's breath around us here,
Amidst the fallen pillars; this hath been
Some naiad's fane of old. How brightly clear,
Flinging a vein of silver o'er the scene,
Up through the shadowy grass, the fountain wells,
And music with it, gushing from beneath
The ivied altar – that sweet murmur tells
The rich wildflowers no tale of woe or death;
Yet once the wave was darkened, and a stain
Lay deep, and heavy drops (but not of rain)
On the dim violets by its marble bed,
And the pale shining water-lily's head.

Sad is that legend's truth. A fair girl met
One whom she loved by this lone temple's spring,
Just as the sun behind the pine-grove set,
And eve's low voice in whispers woke to bring
All wanderers home. They stood, that gentle pair,
With the blue heaven of Italy above,
And citron-odours dying on the air,
And light leaves trembling round, and early love
Deep in each breast. What recked *their* souls of strife
Between their fathers? Unto them young life
Spread out the treasures of its vernal years,
And if they wept, they wept far other tears
Than the cold world wrings forth. They stood that hour
Speaking of hope, while tree, and fount, and flower,
And star, just gleaming through the cypress boughs,[4]
Seemed holy things, as records of their vows.

Notes

IMELDA

[1] 'The tale of Imelda is related in Sismondi's *Histoire des Republiques Italiennes*, Vol. 3, p. 443' (Hemans's note). She refers to Jean Charles Léonard Simonde de Sismondi (1773–1842), *Histoire des républiques italiennes du moyen âge* (16 vols, Paris, 1809–26). The story is essentially that of Romeo and Juliet. Imelda's family, the Lambertazzis, are Ghibellines, the imperial and aristocratic party; Boniface is from the Giérémei family, associated with the Guelphs, the Papal faction. Boniface's murder led to forty days' battle, and reconciliation did not come for another six years.

[2] Samuel Rogers (1763–1855), poet and banker, published *Italy* as a series of discrete poems in two parts in 1822 and 1828, before publishing the entire thing in 1830. It was one of the biggest best-sellers of its time. These lines are from *The Campagna of Florence* 228–30.

[3] 'The beautiful lady dies, and appears to sleep.' From Tasso, *Gerusalemme Liberata* xii 69. The reference is to Clorinda, accidentally killed in battle by her lover, Tancred, who bends over her as she dies, attempting to forgive him.

[4] *the cypress boughs* emblematic of grief.

But change came o'er the scene. A hurrying tread
   Broke on the whispery shades. Imelda knew
The footstep of her brother's wrath, and fled
   Up where the cedars make yon avenue
Dim with green twilight; pausing there, she caught –
Was it the clash of swords? A swift dark thought
   Struck down her lip's rich crimson as it passed,
And from her eye the sunny sparkle took
One moment with its fearfulness, and shook
   Her slight frame fiercely, as a stormy blast
Might rock the rose. Once more, and yet once more,[5]
She stilled her heart to listen – all was o'er;
Sweet summer winds alone were heard to sigh,
Bearing the nightingale's deep spirit[6] by.

That night Imelda's voice was in the song,
Lovely it floated through the festive throng,
Peopling her father's halls. That fatal night
Her eye looked starry in its dazzling light,
And her cheek glowed with beauty's flushing dyes,
Like a rich cloud of eve in southern skies –
A burning ruby cloud. There were[7] whose gaze
Followed her form beneath the clear lamp's blaze,
And marvelled at its radiance. But a few
Beheld the brightness of that feverish hue
With something of dim fear, and in that glance
   Found strange and sudden tokens of unrest,
Startling to meet amidst the mazy dance
   Where thought, if present, an unbidden guest,
Comes not unmasked. Howe'er this were, the time
Sped as it speeds with joy, and grief, and crime
Alike, and when the banquet's hall was left
Unto its garlands of their bloom bereft,
When trembling stars looked silvery in their wane,
And heavy flowers yet slumbered, once again
There stole a footstep, fleet and light and lone,
Through the dim cedar shade – the step of one
That started at a leaf, of one that fled,
Of one that panted with some secret dread:
What did Imelda there? She sought the scene
Where love so late with youth and hope had been;
Bodings were on her soul – a shuddering thrill
Ran through each vein, when first the naiad's rill
Met her with melody – sweet sounds and low;
We hear them yet – they live along its flow –
Her voice is music lost! The fountain-side
She gained – the wave flashed forth – 'twas darkly dyed
Ev'n as from warrior-hearts, and on its edge,

Notes

[5] *Once more, and yet once more* an allusion to the opening of Milton's *Lycidas*: 'Yet once more, oh ye laurels, and once more . . . '

[6] *the nightingale's deep spirit* The nightingale's sad song was said to be caused by a thorn in its breast.

[7] *There were* i.e. there were [those] . . .

Amidst the fern, and flowers, and moss-tufts deep,
There lay, as lulled by stream and rustling sedge,
A youth, a graceful youth. 'Oh, dost thou sleep,
Azzo?' she cried, 'My Azzo, is this rest?'
But then her low tones faltered. 'On thy breast
Is the stain – yes, 'tis blood! And that cold cheek,
That moveless lip! Thou dost not slumber? Speak,
Speak, Azzo, my beloved! No sound – no breath –
What hath come thus between our spirits? Death!
Death? I but dream – I dream!' And there she stood,
A faint, frail trembler, gazing first on blood,
With her fair arm around yon cypress[8] thrown,
Her form sustained by that dark stem alone,
And fading fast, like spell-struck maid of old,
Into white waves dissolving, clear and cold,
When from the grass her dimmed eye caught a gleam –
'Twas where a sword lay shivered[9] by the stream,
Her brother's sword! She knew it, and she knew
'Twas with a venomed point that weapon slew!
Woe for young love! But love is strong. There came
Strength upon woman's fragile heart and frame,
There came swift courage! On the dewy ground
She knelt, with all her dark hair floating round,
Like a long silken stole; she knelt and pressed
Her lips of glowing life to Azzo's breast,
Drawing the poison forth – a strange, sad sight!
Pale death, and fearless love, and solemn night:
So the moon saw them last.
The morn came singing
Through the green forests of the Appenines,
With all her joyous birds their free flight winging,
And steps and voices out amongst the vines.
What found that dayspring *here*? Two fair forms laid
Like sculptured sleepers, from the myrtle shade
Casting a gleam of beauty o'er the wave –
Still, mournful, sweet. Were such things for the grave?
Could it be so indeed? That radiant girl,
Decked as for bridal hours – long braids of pearl
Amidst her shadowy locks were faintly shining,
As tears might shine, with melancholy light;
And there was gold her slender waist entwining,
And her pale graceful arms – how sadly bright!
And fiery gems upon her breast were lying,
And round her marble brow red roses dying.
But she died first! The violet's hue had spread
O'er her sweet eyelids with repose oppressed,
She had bowed heavily her gentle head,
And, on the youth's hushed bosom, sunk to rest.
So slept they well – the poison's work was done;
Love with true heart had striven, but Death had won.

Notes

[8] *cypress* a symbol of grief.

[9] *shivered* splintered.

Edith, a Tale of the Woods[1]

Du Heilige! rufe dein Kind zurück!
Ich habe genossen das irdische Glück,
Ich habe gelebt und geliebet.
(*Wallenstein*)[2]

The woods – oh, solemn are the boundless woods
  Of the great western world when day declines,
And louder sounds the roll of distant floods,
  More deep[3] the rustling of the ancient pines;
When dimness gathers on the stilly air,
  And mystery seems o'er every leaf to brood,
Awful it is for human heart to bear
  The might and burden of the solitude!
Yet in that hour, midst those green wastes, there sate
One young and fair – and oh, how desolate
But undismayed; while sank the crimson light,
And the high cedars darkened with the night,
Alone she sate; though many lay around,
They, pale and silent on the bloody ground,
Were severed from her need and from her woe,
  Far as death severs life. O'er that wild spot
Combat had raged and brought the valiant low,
  And left them with the history of their lot
Unto the forest oaks. A fearful scene
For her whose home of other days had been
Midst the fair halls of England! But the love
  Which filled her soul was strong to cast out fear,
And by its might upborne all else above,
  She shrank not – marked not that the dead were near.
Of him alone she thought, whose languid head
  Faintly upon her wedded bosom fell;
Memory of aught but him on earth was fled,
  While heavily she felt his life-blood well
Fast o'er her garments forth, and vainly bound
With her torn robe and hair the streaming wound,
Yet hoped, still hoped! Oh from such hope how long

Notes

EDITH, A TALE OF THE WOODS

[1] 'Founded on incidents related in an American work, *Sketches of Connecticut*' (Hemans's note). Hemans refers to Lydia Sigourney's *Sketches of Connecticut, Forty Years Since* (1824), which tells how the Englishwoman Oriana Selden is adopted by Zachary and Martha, a Mohegan Indian couple, after witnessing her husband's death at Yorktown in 1781. Sigourney's poetry was so influenced by Hemans that she was often referred to as 'The American Hemans'.

[2] 'Thou holy one! Call thy child back! I have enjoyed earthly pleasure; I have lived and loved.' Johann Christoph Friedrich Schiller (1759–1805) composed *Wallenstein* in 1797–8; it was performed in 1799 and translated into English by Coleridge the following year. Hemans knew the play both in the original and in Coleridge's rendering. The quotation is from Thekla's song, after her lover Max has left her.

[3] *More deep* i.e. More deep [than] . . .

Affection woos the whispers that deceive,
Ev'n when the pressure of dismay grows strong,
And we that weep, watch, tremble, ne'er believe
The blow indeed can fall! So bowed she there
Over the dying, while unconscious prayer
Filled all her soul. Now poured the moonlight down,
Veining the pine-stems through the foliage brown,
And fireflies, kindling up the leafy place,
Cast fitful radiance o'er the warrior's face
Whereby she caught its changes: to her eye
The eye that faded looked through gathering haze
Whence love, o'ermastering mortal agony,
Lifted a long, deep, melancholy gaze
When voice was not: that fond sad meaning passed –
She knew the fullness of her woe at last!
One shriek the forests heard, and mute she lay,
And cold, yet clasping still the precious clay
To her scarce-heaving breast. Oh love and death,
Ye have sad meetings on this changeful earth,
Many and sad! But airs of heavenly breath
Shall melt the links which bind you, for your birth
Is far apart.
Now light of richer hue
Than the moon sheds came flushing mist and dew;
The pines grew red with morning; fresh winds played,
Bright-coloured birds with splendour crossed the shade,
Flitting on flower-like wings; glad murmurs broke
From reed and spray and leaf, the living strings
Of Earth's Aeolian lyre,[4] whose music woke
Into young life and joy all happy things.
And she too woke from that long dreamless trance
The widowed Edith: fearfully her glance
Fell, as in doubt, on faces dark and strange,
And dusky forms. A sudden sense of change
Flashed o'er her spirit, ev'n ere memory swept
The tide of anguish back with thoughts that slept;
Yet half instinctively she rose and spread
Her arms, as 'twere for something lost or fled,
Then faintly sank again. The forest bough,
With all its whispers waved not o'er her now –
Where was she? Midst the people of the wild,
By the red hunter's fire: an aged chief
Whose home looked sad (for therein played no child)
Had borne her, in the stillness of her grief,
To that lone cabin of the woods, and there,
Won by a form so desolately fair,
Or touched with thoughts from some past sorrow sprung,

Notes

[4] *Aeolian lyre* Hemans has Coleridge's poem of 1795 in mind (p. 600), and seems even to be thinking of his pantheist vision.

O'er her low couch an Indian matron hung,
While in grave silence, yet with earnest eye,
The ancient warrior of the waste stood by,
Bending in watchfulness his proud grey head
And leaning on his bow.
And life returned –
Life, but with all its memories of the dead,
To Edith's heart; and well the sufferer learned
Her task of meek endurance, well she wore
The chastened grief that humbly can adore
Midst blinding tears. But unto that old pair,
Ev'n as a breath of spring's awakening air
Her presence was, or as a sweet wild tune
Bringing back tender thoughts, which all too soon
Depart with childhood. Sadly they had seen
A daughter to the land of spirits go,
And ever from that time her fading mien
And voice, like winds of summer, soft and low,
Had haunted their dim years; but Edith's face
Now looked in holy sweetness from her place,
And they again seemed parents. Oh the joy,
The rich, deep blessedness (though earth's alloy,
Fear that still bodes, be there) of pouring forth
The heart's whole power of love, its wealth and worth
Of strong affection, in one healthful flow,
On something all its own! – that kindly glow,
Which to shut inward is consuming pain,
Gives the glad soul its flowering time again
When, like the sunshine, freed. And gentle cares
Th' adopted Edith meekly gave for theirs
Who loved her thus: her spirit dwelt the while
With the departed, and her patient smile
Spoke of farewells to earth – yet still she prayed,
Ev'n o'er her soldier's lowly grave, for aid
One purpose to fulfil, to leave one trace
Brightly recording that her dwelling-place
Had been among the wilds, for well she knew
The secret whisper of her bosom true,
Which warned her hence.
And now by many a word
Linked unto moments when the heart was stirred,
By the sweet mournfulness of many a hymn
Sung when the woods at eve grew hushed and dim,
By the persuasion of her fervent eye,
All eloquent with childlike piety,
By the still beauty of her life, she strove
To win for heaven, and heaven-born truth, the love
Poured out on her so freely. Nor in vain
Was that soft-breathing influence to enchain
The soul in gentle bonds: by slow degrees
Light followed on, as when a summer breeze

Parts the deep masses of the forest shade
And lets the sunbeam through. Her voice was made
Ev'n such a breeze, and she, a lowly guide,
By faith and sorrow raised and purified,
So to the cross her Indian fosterers led,
Until their prayers were one. When morning spread
O'er the blue lake, and when the sunset's glow
Touched into golden bronze the cypress bough,
And when the quiet of the Sabbath time
Sank on her heart, though no melodious chime
Wakened the wilderness, their prayers were one.
Now might she pass in hope, her work was done.
And she *was* passing from the woods away;
The broken flower of England might not stay
Amidst those alien shades; her eye was bright
Ev'n yet with something of a starry light,
But her form wasted, and her fair young cheek
Wore oft and patiently a fatal streak,
A rose whose root was death. The parting sigh
Of autumn through the forests had gone by,
And the rich maple o'er her wanderings lone
Its crimson leaves in many a shower had strewn,
Flushing[5] the air; and winter's blast had been
Amidst the pines; and now a softer green
Fringed their dark boughs, for spring again had come,
The sunny spring! But Edith to her home
Was journeying fast. 'Alas, we think it sad
To part with life when all the earth looks glad
In her young lovely things, when voices break
Into sweet sounds, and leaves and blossoms wake.
Is it not brighter then, in that far clime
Where graves are not, nor blights of changeful time,[6]
If *here* such glory dwell with passing blooms,
Such golden sunshine rest around the tombs?'
So thought the dying one. 'Twas early day,
And sounds and odours with the breezes' play,
Whispering of springtime, through the cabin-door
Unto her couch life's farewell sweetness bore;
Then with a look where all her hope awoke,
'My father!' – to the grey-haired chief she spoke –
'Know'st thou that I depart?' 'I know, I know',
He answered mournfully, 'that thou must go
To thy beloved, my daughter!' 'Sorrow not
   For me, kind mother!' With meek smiles once more
She murmured in low tones; 'one happy lot
   Awaits us, friends, upon the better shore;
For we have prayed together in one trust,

Notes

[5] *Flushing* reddening.

[6] *blights of changeful time* disease that comes with the passage of time.

And lifted our frail spirits from the dust
To God who gave them. Lay me by mine own
Under the cedar-shade: where he is gone
Thither I go. There will my sisters be,
And the dead parents, lisping at whose knee
My childhood's prayer was learned – the Saviour's prayer
Which now *ye* know, and I shall meet you there,
Father and gentle mother! Ye have bound
The bruised reed, and mercy shall be found
By Mercy's children.' From the matron's eye
Dropped tears, her sole and passionate reply,
But Edith felt them not; for now a sleep,
Solemnly beautiful, a stillness deep,
Fell on her settled face. Then, sad and slow,
And mantling up his stately head in woe,
'Thou'rt passing hence', he sang, that warrior old,
In sounds like those by plaintive waters rolled.

Thou'rt passing from the lake's green side
  And the hunter's hearth away;
For the time of flowers, for the summer's pride,
  Daughter, thou canst not stay!

Thou'rt journeying to thy spirit's home,
  Where the skies are ever clear!
The corn-month's golden hours will come,
  But they shall not find thee here.

And we shall miss thy voice, my bird,
  Under our whispering pine!
Music shall midst the leaves be heard,
  But not a song like thine.

A breeze that roves o'er stream and hill
  Telling of winter gone
Hath such sweet falls – yet caught we still
  A farewell in its tone.

But thou, my bright one, thou shalt be
  Where farewell sounds are o'er;
Thou, in the eyes thou lov'st, shalt see
  No fear of parting more.

The mossy grave thy tears have wet,
  And the wind's wild moanings by,
Thou with thy kindred shalt forget,
  Midst flowers – not such as die.

The shadow from thy brow shall melt,
  The sorrow from thy strain,[7]
But where thine earthly smile hath dwelt,
  Our hearts shall thirst in vain.

Notes

[7] *strain* song.

Dim will our cabin be, and lone,
  When thou, its light, art fled;
Yet hath thy step the pathway shown
  Unto the happy dead.

And we will follow thee, our guide,
  And join that shining band;
Thou'rt passing from the lake's green side –
  Go to the better land!

The song had ceased – the listeners caught no breath;
That lovely sleep had melted into death.

The Indian City[1]

What deep wounds ever closed without a scar?
The heart's bleed longest, and but heal to wear
That which disfigures it.

(*Childe Harold*)[2]

I

Royal in splendour went down the day
On the plain where an Indian city lay,
With its crown of domes o'er the forest high,
Red as if fused in the burning sky,
And its deep groves pierced by the rays which made
A bright stream's way through each long arcade,
Till the pillared vaults of the banyan[3] stood
Like torch-lit aisles midst the solemn wood,
And the plantain[4] glittered with leaves of gold,
As a tree midst the genii-gardens old,
And the cypress lifted a blazing spire,
And the stems of the cocoas were shafts of fire.
Many a white pagoda's gleam
Slept lovely round upon lake and stream,
Broken alone by the lotus-flowers,
As they caught the glow of the sun's last hours
Like rosy wine in their cups, and shed
Its glory forth on their crystal bed.
Many a graceful Hindu maid
With the water-vase from the palmy shade

Notes

The Indian City

[1] 'From a tale in Forbes' *Oriental Memoirs'* (Hemans's note). James Forbes (1749–1819) published his *Oriental Memoirs* in 1813. He tells how Sciad Ballah and his mother Mamah-Doocre, Muslims journeying to Mecca, passed the gates of Dhuboy, a Hindu city in Guzerat, western India, from which Muslims were banned. Sciad entered nonetheless and bathed illegally in the city's sacred lake. He was punished by having his hands cut off, and died just after returning to his mother. Having returned home she asked her sovereign for revenge. He besieged Dhuboy for years before eventually destroying it.

[2] Byron, *Childe Harold's Pilgrimage* iii 788–90.

[3] *banyan* East Indian fig tree.

[4] *plantain* tree with banana-like fruit.

Came gliding light as the desert's roe,[5]
Down marble steps to the tanks below;
And a cool sweet plashing was ever heard,
As the molten glass of the wave was stirred;
And a murmur, thrilling the scented air,
Told where the Brahmin[6] bowed in prayer.
  There wandered a noble Muslim boy
Through the scene of beauty in breathless joy;
He gazed where the stately city rose
Like a pageant of clouds in its red repose;
He turned where birds through the gorgeous gloom
Of the woods went glancing on starry plume;
He tracked the brink of the shining lake
By the tall canes feathered in tuft and brake,
Till the path he chose, in its mazes wound
To the very heart of the holy ground.
  And there lay the water, as if enshrined
In a rocky urn from the sun and wind,
Bearing the hues of the grove on high,
Far down through its dark still purity.
The flood beyond, to the fiery west
Spread out like a metal mirror's[7] breast,
But that lone bay, in its dimness deep,
Seemed made for the swimmer's joyous leap,
For the stag athirst from the noontide chase,
For all free things of the wildwood's race.
  Like a falcon's glance on the wide blue sky
Was the kindling flash of the boy's glad eye,
Like a sea-bird's flight to the foaming wave
From the shadowy bank was the bound he gave;
Dashing the spray-drops, cold and white,
O'er the glossy leaves in his young delight,
And bowing his locks to the waters clear –
Alas, he dreamt not that fate was near!
  His mother looked from her tent the while
O'er heaven and earth with a quiet smile;
She, on her way unto Mecca's fane,
Had stayed[8] the march of her pilgrim-train
Calmly to linger a few brief hours
In the Bramin city's glorious bowers,
For the pomp of the forest, the wave's bright fall,
The red gold of sunset – she loved them all.

II

The moon rose clear in the splendour given
To the deep blue night of an Indian heaven;

Notes

[5] *roe* small deer.

[6] *Brahmin* highest priestly caste among the Hindus.

[7] *metal mirror* Some mirrors were at this time made of highly polished metal.

[8] *stayed* halted.

The boy from the high-arched woods came back –
Oh, what had he met in his lonely track?
The serpent's glance, through the long reeds bright?
The arrowy spring of the tiger's might?
No! Yet as one by a conflict worn,
With his graceful hair all soiled and torn,
And a gloom on the lids of his darkened eye,
And a gash on his bosom – he came to die!
He looked for the face to his young heart sweet,
And found it, and sank at his mother's feet.
'Speak to me! Whence doth the swift blood run?
What hath befall'n thee, my child, my son?'
The mist of death on his brow lay pale,
But his voice just lingered to breathe the tale,
Murmuring faintly of wrongs and scorn,
And wounds from the children of Brahma[9] born.
This was the doom[10] for a Muslim found
With foot profane on their holy ground;
This was for sullying the pure waves free
Unto them alone – 'twas their God's decree.
A change came o'er his wandering look –
The mother shrieked not then, nor shook;
Breathless she knelt in her son's young blood,
Rending her mantle to staunch its flood,
But it rushed like a river which none may stay,
Bearing a flower to the deep away.
That which our love to the earth would chain,
Fearfully striving with Heaven in vain,
That which fades from us while yet we hold,
Clasped to our bosoms, its mortal mould,
Was fleeting before her, afar and fast;
One moment – the soul from the face had passed!
Are there no words for that common woe?
Ask of the thousands, its depths that know!
The boy had breathed, in his dreaming rest,
Like a low-voiced dove on her gentle breast;
He had stood, when she sorrowed, beside her knee,
Painfully stilling his quick heart's glee;
He had kissed from her cheek the widow's tears
With the loving lip of his infant years;
He had smiled o'er her path like a bright spring day –
Now in his blood on the earth he lay
Murdered! Alas, and we love so well
In a world where anguish like this can dwell!
She bowed down mutely o'er her dead –
They that stood round her watched in dread;
They watched – she knew not they were by;
Her soul sat veiled in its agony.
On the silent lip she pressed no kiss,

Notes

[9] *Brahma* God in Hindu myth.

[10] *doom* law.

Too stern was the grasp of her pangs for this;
She shed no tear as her face bent low
O'er the shining hair of the lifeless brow;
She looked but into the half-shut eye
With a gaze that found there no reply
And, shrieking, mantled her head from sight
And fell, struck down by her sorrow's might!
  And what deep change, what work of power,
Was wrought on her secret soul that hour?
How rose the lonely one? She rose
Like a prophetess from dark repose,
And proudly flung from her face the veil,
And shook the hair from her forehead pale,
And midst her wondering handmaids stood
With the sudden glance of a dauntless mood.
Aye, lifting up to the midnight sky
A brow in its regal passion high,
With a close and rigid grasp she pressed
The bloodstained robe to her heaving breast,
And said, 'Not yet, not yet I weep,
Not yet my spirit shall sink or sleep,
Not till yon city, in ruins rent,
Be piled for its victim's monument.
Cover his dust, bear it on before –
It shall visit those temple-gates once more!'
  And away in the train of the dead she turned,
The strength of her step was the heart that burned;
And the Brahmin groves in the starlight smiled
As the mother passed with her slaughtered child.

III

Hark, a wild sound of the desert's horn
Through the woods round the Indian city borne!
A peal of the cymbal and tambour[11] afar –
War, 'tis the gathering of Muslim war!
The Bramin looked from the leaguered[12] towers –
He saw the wild archer amidst his bowers,
And the lake that flashed through the plantain shade
As the light of the lances along it played,
And the canes that shook as if winds were high
When the fiery steed of the waste swept by,
And the camp as it lay, like a billowy sea,
Wide round the sheltering banyan tree.
  There stood one tent from the rest apart –
That was the place of a wounded heart.
Oh, deep is a wounded heart, and strong

Notes

[11] *tambour* drum.

[12] *leaguered* beleaguered, besieged; as in Byron, *Siege of Corinth* 30–1: 'The tent is pitched, the crescent shines / Along the Muslim's leaguering lines.'

A voice that cries against mighty wrong,
And full of death as a hot wind's blight[13]
Doth the ire of a crushed affection light!
  Maimuna from realm to realm had passed,
And her tale had rung like a trumpet's blast;
There had been words from her pale lips poured,
Each one a spell to unsheath the sword.
The Tartar had sprung from his steed to hear,
And the dark chief of Araby grasped his spear
Till a chain of long lances begirt[14] the wall,
And a vow was recorded that doomed its fall.
  Back with the dust of her son she came,
When her voice had kindled that lightning flame;
She came in the might of a queenly foe –
Banner, and javelin, and bended bow;
But a deeper power on her forehead sate –
There sought the warrior his star of fate;
Her eye's wild flash through the tented line
Was hailed as a spirit and a sign,
And the faintest tone from her lip was caught
As a Sybil's breath of prophetic thought.
  Vain, bitter glory! The gift of grief
That lights up vengeance to find relief,
Transient and faithless – it cannot fill
So the deep void of the heart, nor still
The yearning left by a broken tie,
That haunted fever of which we die!
  Sickening she turned from her sad renown,
As a king in death might reject his crown;
Slowly the strength of the walls gave way –
She withered faster from day to day.
All the proud sounds of that bannered plain
To stay the flight of her soul were vain;
Like an eagle caged, it had striven, and worn
The frail dust ne'er for such conflicts born,
Till the bars were rent, and the hour was come
For its fearful rushing through darkness home.
  The bright sun set in his pomp and pride,
As on that eve when the fair boy died;
She gazed from her couch, and a softness fell
O'er her weary heart with the day's farewell;
She spoke, and her voice in its dying tone
Had an echo of feelings that long seemed flown.
She murmured a low sweet cradle song,
Strange midst the din of a warrior throng,
A song of the time when her boy's young cheek
Had glowed on her breast in its slumber meek;
But something which breathed from that mournful strain

Notes

[13] *full of death as a hot wind's blight* Winds were believed to be carriers of disease.

[14] *begirt* surrounded.

Sent a fitful gust o'er her soul again,
And starting as if from a dream, she cried,
'Give him proud burial at my side!
There, by yon lake, where the palm-boughs wave,
When the temples are fallen, make there our grave.'
 And the temples fell, though the spirit passed
That stayed not for victory's voice at last,
When the day was won for the martyr-dead,
For the broken heart, and the bright blood shed.
 Through the gates of the vanquished the Tartar steed
Bore in the avenger with foaming speed;
Free swept the flame through the idol-fanes
And the streams flowed red, as from warrior-veins,
And the sword of the Muslim, let loose to slay,
Like the panther leapt on its flying prey,
Till a city of ruin begirt the shade
Where the boy and his mother at rest were laid.
 Palace and tower on that plain were left
Like fallen trees by the lightning cleft;
The wild vine mantled the stately square,
The Rajah's throne was the serpent's lair,
And the jungle grass o'er the altar sprung –
This was the work of one deep heart wrung!

The Peasant Girl of the Rhône[1]

There is but one place in the world –
Thither, where he lies buried! . . .
There, there is all that still remains of him,
That single spot is the whole earth to me.
(Coleridge's *Wallenstein*)[2]

Alas, our young affections run to waste,
Or water but the desert.
(*Childe Harold*)[3]

There went a warrior's funeral through the night,
A waving of tall plumes, a ruddy light
Of torches, fitfully and wildly thrown
From the high woods along the sweeping Rhône,
Far down the waters. Heavily and dead,
Under the moaning trees the horse-hoof's tread
In muffled sounds upon the greensward fell
As chieftains passed, and solemnly the swell
Of the deep requiem, o'er the gleaming river
Borne with the gale, and with the leaves' low shiver,

Notes

THE PEASANT GIRL OF THE RHÔNE

[1] This poem was first published in the *Literary Souvenir* for 1826 under the title 'Aymer's Tomb'.

[2] Coleridge, *The Death of Wallenstein* (1800), IV v 5–6, 9–10. Thekla speaks these lines to Lady Neubrunn after she hears of the death of her lover, Max Piccolomini, and of the site of his grave.

[3] Byron, *Childe Harold's Pilgrimage* iv 1072–3.

Floated and died. Proud mourners there, yet pale,
 Wore man's mute anguish sternly – but of *one*,
Oh who shall speak? What words *his* brow unveil?
 A father following to the grave his son –
That is no grief to picture! Sad and slow,
 Through the wood-shadows moved the knightly train
With youth's fair form upon the bier laid low,
 Fair even when found, amidst the bloody slain,
Stretched by its broken lance. They reached the lone
 Baronial chapel, where the forest gloom
Fell heaviest, for the massy boughs had grown
 Into thick archways, as to vault the tomb.
Stately they trod the hollow ringing aisle,
A strange deep echo shuddered through the pile
Till crested heads at last, in silence bent
Round the De Coucis' antique monument,
When dust to dust was given, and Aymer slept
 Beneath the drooping banners of his line,
Whose broidered folds the Syrian wind had swept
 Proudly and oft o'er fields of Palestine.
So the sad rite was closed. The sculptor gave
Trophies erelong, to deck that lordly grave,
And the pale image of a youth arrayed
As warriors are for fight, but calmly laid
 In slumber on his shield. Then all was done,
All still around the dead. His name was heard
Perchance when wine-cups flowed, and hearts were stirred
 By some old song, or tale of battle won,
Told round the hearth; but in his father's breast
Manhood's high passions woke again, and pressed
On to their mark, and in his friend's clear eye
There dwelt no shadow of a dream gone by,
And with the brethren of his fields, the feast
Was gay as when the voice whose sounds had ceased
Mingled with theirs. Ev'n thus life's rushing tide
Bears back affection from the grave's dark side;
Alas, to think of this! The heart's void place
 Filled up so soon – so like a summer-cloud,
All that we loved to pass and leave no trace!
 He lay forgotten in his early shroud.
Forgotten? Not of all! The sunny smile
Glancing in play o'er that proud lip erewhile,
And the dark locks whose breezy waving threw
A gladness round, whene'er their shade withdrew
From the bright brow, and all the sweetness lying
 Within that eagle-eye's jet radiance deep,
And all the music with that young voice dying,
 Whose joyous echoes made the quick heart leap
As at a hunter's bugle – these things lived
Still in one breast whose silent love survived
The pomps of kindred sorrow. Day by day

On Aymer's tomb fresh flowers in garlands lay,
Through the dim fane soft summer-odours breathing,
And all the pale sepulchral trophies wreathing,
And with a flush of deeper brilliance glowing
In the rich light, like molten rubies flowing
Through storied windows down. The violet there
Might speak of love, a secret love and lowly,
And the rose image all things fleet and fair,
And the faint passion-flower, the sad and holy,
Tell of diviner hopes. But whose light hand,
As for an altar, wove the radiant band?
Whose gentle nurture brought, from hidden dells
That gem-like wealth of blossoms and sweet bells,
To blush through every season? Blight and chill
Might touch the changing woods, but duly still
For years those gorgeous coronals renewed,
  And brightly clasping marble spear and helm,
Even through midwinter, filled the solitude
  With a strange smile, a glow of summer's realm.
Surely some fond and fervent heart was pouring
Its youth's vain worship on the dust, adoring
In lone devotedness!
        One spring morn rose,
  And found, within that tomb's proud shadow laid
(Oh, not as midst the vineyards, to repose
  From the fierce noon) a dark-haired peasant maid:
Who could reveal her story? That still face
  Had once been fair; for on the clear arched brow
And the curved lip, there lingered yet such grace
  As sculpture gives its dreams; and long and low
The deep black lashes o'er the half-shut eye
(For death was on its lids) fell mournfully.
But the cold cheek was sunk, the raven hair
Dimmed, the slight form all wasted as by care.
Whence came that early blight? *Her* kindred's place
Was not amidst the high De Couci race,
Yet there her shrine had been! She grasped a wreath,
The tomb's last garland – this was love in death!

Indian Woman's Death Song

An Indian woman, driven to despair by her husband's desertion of her for another wife, entered a canoe with her children, and rowed it down the Mississippi towards a cataract. Her voice was heard from the shore singing a mournful death-song until overpowered by the sound of the waters in which she perished. The tale is related in Long's *Expedition to the Source of St. Peter's River.*[1]

Notes

INDIAN WOMAN'S DEATH SONG

[1] William H. Keating, *Narrative of an Expedition to the Source of the St Peter's River . . . under the command of S. H. Long* was first published in two volumes in Philadelphia, 1824; it was published in London the following year.

Non, je ne puis vivre avec un coeur brisé. Il faut que je retrouve la joie, et que je m'unisse aux esprits libres de l'air.

(*Bride of Messina*, translated by Madame de Staël)[2]

Let not my child be a girl, for very sad is the life of a woman.

(*The Prairie*)[3]

Down a broad river of the western wilds,
Piercing thick forest glooms, a light canoe
Swept with the current: fearful was the speed
Of the frail bark, as by a tempest's wing
Borne leaf-like on to where the mist of spray
Rose with the cataract's thunder. Yet within,
Proudly, and dauntlessly, and all alone,
Save that a babe lay sleeping at her breast,
A woman stood. Upon her Indian brow
Sat a strange gladness, and her dark hair waved
As if triumphantly. She pressed her child,
In its bright slumber, to her beating heart,
And lifted her sweet voice that rose awhile
Above the sound of waters, high and clear,
Wafting a wild proud strain, her song of death.

Roll swiftly to the spirit's land, thou mighty stream and free!
Father of ancient waters,[4] roll, and bear our lives with thee!
The weary bird that storms have tossed would seek the sunshine's calm,
And the deer that hath the arrow's hurt flies to the woods of balm.

Roll on![5] My warrior's eye hath looked upon another's face,
And mine hath faded from his soul, as fades a moonbeam's trace;
My shadow comes not o'er his path, my whisper to his dream,
He flings away the broken reed – roll swifter yet, thou stream!

The voice that spoke of other days is hushed within *his* breast,
But *mine* its lonely music haunts, and will not let me rest;
It sings a low and mournful song of gladness that is gone;
I cannot live without that light – father of waves, roll on!

Will he not miss the bounding step that met him from the chase?
The heart of love that made his home an ever-sunny place?
The hand that spread the hunter's board, and decked his couch of yore?
He will not! Roll, dark foaming stream, on to the better shore!

Notes

[2] 'No, I can't live with a broken heart. I must retrieve my happiness, and be reunited with the spirits of the air.' Schiller's *Die Braut von Messina* was first published in 1803, but not translated into English until 1837. The play was summarized in Madame de Staël's *De l'Allemagne* (1813).

[3] James Fenimore Cooper's popular novel was published in London, 1827. This remark is made by the third wife of a Sioux chief who feels betrayed when she finds out that her husband is to marry a fourth wife – a captured Mexican woman.

[4] *Father of ancient waters* 'The Indian name for the Mississippi' (Hemans's note).

[5] *Roll on!* Hemans is recalling Byron, *Childe Harold's Pilgrimage* iv 1603: 'Roll on, thou deep and dark blue ocean – roll!'

Some blessed fount amidst the woods of that bright land must flow
Whose waters from my soul may lave the memory of this woe;
Some gentle wind must whisper there, whose breath may waft away
The burden of the heavy night, the sadness of the day.

And thou, my babe, though born, like me, for woman's weary lot,
Smile – to that wasting of the heart, my own! I leave thee not;
Too bright a thing art *thou* to pine in aching love away,
Thy mother bears thee far, young fawn, from sorrow and decay.

She bears thee to the glorious bowers where none are heard to weep,
And where th' unkind one hath no power again to trouble sleep;
And where the soul shall find its youth, as wakening from a dream –
One moment, and that realm is ours: on, on, dark rolling stream!

Joan of Arc, in Rheims

Jeanne d'Arc avait eu la joie de voir à Chalons quelques amis de son enfance. Une joie plus ineffable encore l'attendait à Rheims, au sein de son triomphe: Jacques d'Arc, son père, y se trouva, aussitot que les troupes de Charles VII y furent entrées; et comme les deux frères de notre Héroine l'avaient accompagnés, elle se vit, pour un instant au milieu de sa famille, dans les bras d'un père vertueux.

(*Vie de Jeanne d'Arc*)[1]

Thou hast a charmed cup, oh fame,
A draught that mantles high,
And seems to lift this earth-born frame
Above mortality;
Away! To me, a woman, bring
Sweet waters from affection's spring.[2]

That was a joyous day in Rheims of old,
When peal on peal of mighty music rolled
Forth from her thronged cathedral, while around
A multitude whose billows[3] made no sound,
Chained to a hush of wonder, though elate
With victory, listened at their temple's gate.
And what was done within? Within, the light
Through the rich gloom of pictured windows flowing,
Tinged with soft awfulness a stately sight –
The chivalry of France, their proud heads bowing
In martial vassalage – while midst that ring,
And shadowed by ancestral tombs, a king
Received his birthright's crown. For this the hymn
Swelled out like rushing waters, and the day
With the sweet censer's misty breath grew dim,

Notes

JOAN OF ARC, IN RHEIMS

[1] 'Joan of Arc had had the pleasure of seeing some childhood friends at Châlons. A yet more sublime joy awaited her at Rheims, at the peak of her triumph. Jacques d'Arc, her father, had arrived there as soon as the troops of Charles VII had entered the city, and as our heroine's two brothers had accompanied him, she found herself momentarily amidst her family, and in the arms of a virtuous father.' There were many lives of Joan of Arc in French; Hemans is probably using Jean-Baptiste Prosper Jollois, *Histoire abrégée de la vie et des exploits de Jeanne d'Arc* (Paris, 1821).

[2] This epigraph is stanza 1 of Hemans's *Woman and Fame*, published in *The Amulet* (1829).

[3] *billows* movements.

As through long aisles it floated o'er th' array
Of arms and sweeping stoles. But who, alone
And unapproached, beside the altar-stone,
With the white banner, forth like sunshine streaming,
And the gold helm,[4] through clouds of fragrance gleaming,
Silent and radiant stood? The helm was raised,
And the fair face revealed that upward gazed,
Intensely worshipping – a still, clear face,
Youthful, but brightly solemn! Woman's cheek
And brow were there, in deep devotion meek,
Yet glorified with inspiration's trace
On its pure paleness, while, enthroned above,
The pictured Virgin with her smile of love
Seemed bending o'er her votaress[5] – that slight form!
Was that the leader through the battle storm?
Had the soft light in that adoring eye
Guided the warrior where the swords flashed high?
'Twas so, even so, and thou, the shepherd's child,
Joanne, the lowly dreamer of the wild!
Never before, and never since that hour,
Hath woman, mantled with victorious power,
Stood forth as *thou* beside the shrine didst stand,
Holy amidst the knighthood of the land,
And beautiful with joy and with renown,
Lift thy white banner o'er the olden crown
Ransomed for France by thee!

The rites are done.
Now let the dome with trumpet-notes be shaken,
And bid the echoes of the tombs awaken,
And come thou forth, that Heaven's rejoicing sun
May give thee welcome from thine own blue skies,
Daughter of Victory! A triumphant strain,
A proud rich stream of warlike melodies,
Gushed through the portals of the antique fane
And forth she came. Then rose a nation's sound –
Oh, what a power to bid the quick heart bound
The wind bears onward with the stormy cheer
Man gives to glory on her high career!
Is there indeed such power? Far deeper dwells
In one kind household voice, to reach the cells
Whence happiness flows forth! The shouts that filled
The hollow heaven tempestuously were stilled
One moment, and in that brief pause the tone,
As of a breeze that o'er her home had blown,
Sank on the bright maid's heart – 'Joanne!'

Notes

[4] *helm* helmet.

[5] *votaress* female worshipper.

Who spoke
Like those whose childhood with *her* childhood grew
Under one roof? 'Joanne!' – *that* murmur broke
With sounds of weeping forth! She turned – she knew
Beside her, marked from all the thousands there,
In the calm beauty of his silver hair,
The stately shepherd; and the youth whose joy
From his dark eye flashed proudly; and the boy,
The youngest-born, that ever loved her best –
'Father! And ye, my brothers!' On the breast
Of that grey sire she sank – and swiftly back,
Ev'n in an instant, to their native track
Her free thoughts flowed. She saw the pomp no more –
The plumes, the banners; to her cabin-door,
And to the fairy's fountain in the glade,[6]
Where her young sisters by her side had played,
And to her hamlet's chapel, where it rose
Hallowing the forest unto deep repose,
Her spirit turned. The very woodnote sung
In early springtime by the bird which dwelt
Where o'er her father's roof the beech-leaves hung
Was in her heart; a music heard and felt,
Winning her back to nature.[7] She unbound
The helm of many battles from her head,
And, with her bright locks bowed to sweep the ground,
Lifting her voice up, wept for joy, and said,
'Bless me, my father, bless me! And with thee,
To the still cabin and the beechen-tree,
Let me return!'

Oh, never did thine eye
Through the green haunts of happy infancy
Wander again, Joanne! Too much of fame
Had shed its radiance on thy peasant name,
And bought alone by gifts beyond all price,
The trusting heart's repose, the paradise
Of home with all its loves, doth fate allow
The crown of glory unto woman's brow.

Notes

[6] 'A beautiful fountain near Domremi, believed to be haunted by fairies, and a favourite resort of Jeanne d'Arc in her childhood' (Hemans's note). Domrémy La Pucelle, a village in the department of Meuse, was Joan's birthplace.

[7] *nature* Wolfson suggests that this is a reference not just to the natural world but to Joan's 'deepest female "nature"'.

Pauline[1]

To die for what we love! Oh there is power
In the true heart, and pride, and joy, for this;
It is to live without the vanished light
That strength is needed.[2]

Così trapassa al trapassar d'un giorno
Della vita mortal il fiore e'l verde.
(Tasso)[3]

Along the starlit Seine[4] went music swelling,
Till the air thrilled with its exulting mirth;
Proudly it floated, even as if no dwelling
For cares or stricken hearts were found on earth;
And a glad sound the measure lightly beat,
A happy chime of many dancing feet.

For in a palace of the land that night,
Lamps, and fresh roses, and green leaves were hung,
And from the painted walls a stream of light
On flying forms beneath soft splendour flung;
But loveliest far amidst the revel's pride
Was one, the lady from the Danube-side.[5]

Pauline, the meekly bright! Though now no more
Her clear eye flashed with youth's all tameless glee,
Yet something holier than its dayspring wore,
There in soft rest lay beautiful to see –
A charm with graver, tenderer sweetness fraught,
The blending of deep love and matron thought.[6]

Through the gay throng she moved, serenely fair,
And such calm joy as fills a moonlight sky
Sate on her brow beneath its graceful hair,
As her young daughter in the dance went by
With the fleet step of one that yet hath known
Smiles and kind voices in this world alone.

Notes

PAULINE

[1] When first published in the *New Monthly Magazine* (February 1827), this poem was given an epigraph from Wordsworth's *Excursion* iv 10–17:

One adequate support
For the calamities of mortal life
Exists, one only; an assured belief
That the procession of our fate, howe'er
Sad or disturbed, is ordered by a Being
Of infinite benevolence and power,
Whose everlasting purposes embrace
All accidents, converting them to Good.

[2] This epigraph was composed by Hemans for this poem.

[3] 'Thus the flower and the green of the mortal life fade as the day fades.' Torquato Tasso, *Gerusalemme Liberata* canto 16, st. 15, 1–2. The lines are from a bird's song in the garden of the enchantress Armida, where the Crusader, Rinaldo, is imprisoned.

[4] *Seine* river of Paris and northern France, flowing into the English Channel.

[5] 'The Princess Pauline Schwartzenberg. The story of her fate is beautifully related in *L'Allemagne*, Vol. 3, p. 336' (Hemans's note). Anne-Louise-Germaine Necker, Madame de Staël (1766–1817), *De l'Allemagne*, was published as *Germany*, by John Murray, in 1813. Pauline's story is told in vol. 3, pp. 337–9.

[6] Hemans is close to her source: Staël says that Pauline 'still united the charm of perfect beauty to all the dignity of the maternal character' (*Germany* iii 337).

Lurked there no secret boding in her breast?
  Did no faint whisper warn of evil nigh?
Such oft awake when most the heart seems blessed
  Midst the light laughter of festivity –
Whence come those tones! Alas, enough we know,
To mingle fear with all triumphal show!

Who spoke of evil when young feet were flying
  In fairy-rings around the echoing hall?
Soft airs through braided locks in perfume sighing,
  Glad pulses beating unto music's call?
Silence! The minstrels pause – and hark, a sound,
A strange quick rustling which their notes had drowned!

And lo, a light upon the dancers breaking –
  Not such their clear and silvery lamps had shed!
From the gay dream of revelry awaking,
  One moment holds them still in breathless dread;
The wild, fierce lustre grows – then bursts a cry –
Fire! Through the hall and round it gathering – fly![7]

And forth they rush as chased by sword and spear –
  To the green coverts of the garden-bowers,
A gorgeous masque of pageantry and fear
  Startling the birds and trampling down the flowers,
While from the dome behind, red sparkles driven
Pierce the dark stillness of the midnight heaven.

And where is she, Pauline? The hurrying throng
  Have swept her onward, as a stormy blast
Might sweep some faint o'erwearied bird along –
  Till now the threshold of that death is passed,
And free she stands beneath the starry skies
Calling her child – but no sweet voice replies.

'Bertha, where art thou? Speak, oh speak, my own!'
  Alas, unconscious of her pangs the while,
The gentle girl, in fear's cold grasp alone,
  Powerless hath sunk within the blazing pile –
A young bright form, decked gloriously for death,
With flowers all shrinking from the flame's fierce breath!

But oh, thy strength, deep love! There is no power
  To stay the mother from that rolling grave,
Though fast on high the fiery volumes tower,
  And forth, like banners, from each lattice[8] wave.
Back, back she rushes through a host combined –
Mighty is anguish, with affection twined!

And what bold step may follow midst the roar
  Of the red billows, o'er their prey that rise?

Notes

[7] 'On a sudden the numberless torches, which restored the splendour of the day, are about to be changed into devouring flames' (Staël, *Germany* iii 337).

[8] *lattice* window.

None! Courage there stood still – and never more
  Did those fair forms emerge on human eyes!
Was one brief meeting theirs, one wild farewell?
  And died they heart to heart? Oh, who can tell?

Freshly and cloudlessly the morning broke
  On that sad palace, midst its pleasure-shades;
Its painted roofs had sunk – yet black with smoke
  And lonely stood its marble colonnades;
But yestereve their shafts with wreaths were bound –
Now lay the scene one shrivelled scroll[9] around!

And bore the ruins no recording trace
  Of all that woman's heart had dared and done?
Yes, there were gems to mark its mortal place,
  That forth from dust and ashes dimly shone!
Those had the mother on her gentle breast
Worn round her child's fair image, there at rest.[10]

And they were all! The tender and the true
  Left this alone her sacrifice to prove,
Hallowing the spot where mirth once lightly flew
  To deep, lone, chastened thoughts of grief and love.
Oh, we have need of patient faith below,
To clear away the mysteries of such woe!

Juana[1]

Juana, mother of the Emperor Charles V,[2] upon the death of her husband, Philip the Handsome of Austria, who had treated her with uniform neglect, had his body laid upon a bed of state in a magnificent dress and, being possessed with the idea that it would revive, watched it for a length of time incessantly, waiting for the moment of returning life.

It is but dust thou look'st upon. This love,
This wild and passionate idolatry,
What doth it in the shadow of the grave?
Gather it back within thy lonely heart,
So must it ever end: too much we give
Unto the things that perish.[3]

Notes

[9] *scroll* spiral ornament at the top of a pillar.

[10] 'A woman braved them; her hand seized that of her daughter, her hand saved her daughter; and although the fatal blow then struck her, her last act was maternal; her last act preserved the object of her affection; it was at this sublime instant that she appeared before God; and it was impossible to recognize what remained of her upon earth except by the impression on a medal, given by her children, which also marked the place where this angel perished' (Staël, *Germany* iii 338–9).

JUANA

[1] Juana of Aragon, Queen of Castile (1479–1555) was married to Philip, Duke of Burgundy (1478–1506), as part of her father's policy in linking the Spanish with the Austrian, Portuguese and English royal families so as to surround France. Philip was not only neglectful; he was openly unfaithful to her, and supported France. His death in September 1506, from a fever, intensified her depression, and she refused to be separated from his embalmed body, precipitating accusations of insanity. Her father assumed the Regency, and she was effectively imprisoned in Spain for the rest of her life.

[2] Charles V (1500–1558), Holy Roman Emperor, 1519–56.

[3] This epigraph is by Hemans.

The night-wind shook the tapestry round an ancient palace-room,
And torches, as it rose and fell, waved through the gorgeous gloom,
And o'er a shadowy regal couch threw fitful gleams and red,
Where a woman with long raven hair sat watching by the dead.

Pale shone the features of the dead, yet glorious still to see,
Like a hunter or a chief struck down while his heart and step were free;
No shroud he wore, no robe of death, but there majestic lay,
Proudly and sadly glittering in royalty's array.

But she that with the dark hair watched by the cold slumberer's side,
On *her* wan cheek no beauty dwelt, and in her garb no pride;
Only her full impassioned eyes as o'er that clay she bent,
A wildness and a tenderness in strange resplendence blent.

And as the swift thoughts crossed her soul, like shadows of a cloud,
Amidst the silent room of death, the dreamer spoke aloud;
She spoke to him who could not hear, and cried, 'Thou yet wilt wake,
And learn my watchings and my tears, beloved one, for thy sake.

They told me this was death, but well I knew it could not be;
Fairest and stateliest of the earth, who spoke of death for *thee*?
They would have wrapped the funeral shroud thy gallant form around,
But I forbade, and there thou art – a monarch, robed and crowned!

With all thy bright locks gleaming still, their coronal beneath,
And thy brow so proudly beautiful – who said that this was death?
Silence hath been upon thy lips, and stillness round thee long,
But the hopeful spirit in my breast is all undimmed and strong.

I know thou hast not loved me yet; I am not fair like thee,
The very glance of whose clear eye threw round a light of glee!
A frail and drooping form is mine – a cold unsmiling cheek,
Oh, I have but a woman's heart, wherewith *thy* heart to seek.

But when thou wak'st, my prince, my lord, and hear'st how I have kept
A lonely vigil by thy side, and o'er thee prayed and wept;
How in one long, deep dream of thee my nights and days have passed,
Surely that humble, patient love *must* win back love at last!

And thou wilt smile – my own, my own, shall be the sunny smile
Which brightly fell, and joyously, on all *but* me erewhile!
No more in vain affection's thirst my weary soul shall pine –
Oh, years of hope deferred were paid by one fond glance of thine!

Thou'lt meet me with that radiant look when thou com'st from the chase,
For me, for me, in festal halls it shall kindle o'er thy face!
Thou'lt reck no more though beauty's gift mine aspect may not bless;
In thy kind eyes this deep, deep love shall give me loveliness.

But wake! My heart within me burns yet once more to rejoice
In the sound to which it ever leaped – the music of thy voice;

Awake! I sit in solitude, that thy first look and tone,
And the gladness of thine opening eyes may all be mine alone.'

In the still chambers of the dust thus poured forth day by day
The passion of that loving dream from a troubled soul found way,
Until the shadows of the grave had swept o'er every grace
Left midst the awfulness of death on the princely form and face.

And slowly broke the fearful truth upon the watcher's breast,
And they bore away the royal dead with requiems to his rest,
With banners and with knightly plumes all waving in the wind –
But a woman's broken heart was left in its lone despair behind.

The American Forest Girl[1]

A fearful gift upon thy heart is laid,
Woman – a power to suffer and to love,
Therefore thou so canst pity.[2]

Wildly and mournfully the Indian drum
  On the deep hush of moonlight forests broke;
'Sing us a death-song, for thine hour is come',
  So the red warriors to their captive spoke.
Still, and amidst those dusky forms alone,
  A youth, a fair-haired youth of England stood
Like a king's son, though from his cheek had flown
  The mantling crimson of the island-blood,
And his pressed lips looked marble. Fiercely bright
And high around him blazed the fires of night,
Rocking beneath the cedars to and fro
As the wind passed, and with a fitful glow
Lighting the victim's face. But who could tell
Of what within his secret heart befell,
Known but to heaven that hour? Perchance a thought
Of his far home then so intensely wrought,
That its full image, pictured to his eye
On the dark ground of mortal agony,
Rose clear as day – and he might *see* the band,
Of his young sisters wandering hand in hand
Where the laburnums drooped, or haply binding
The jasmine, up the door's low pillars winding,
Or, as day closed upon their gentle mirth,
Gathering with braided hair around the hearth
Where sat their mother – and that mother's face,
Its grave sweet smile yet wearing in the place

Notes

The American Forest Girl

[1] Wolfson observes that this is a 'captivity narrative', a primary genre in the literature of New World encounters – more so than 'Edith'.

[2] The epigraph is composed by Hemans.

Where so it ever smiled! Perchance the prayer
Learned at her knee came back on his despair,
The blessing from her voice, the very tone
Of her 'Goodnight!' might breathe from boyhood gone.
He started and looked up; thick cypress boughs,
   Full of strange sound, waved o'er him, darkly red
In the broad stormy firelight; savage brows
   With tall plumes crested and wild hues o'erspread,
Girt him like feverish phantoms, and pale stars
Looked through the branches as through dungeon bars,
Shedding no hope. He knew, he felt his doom –
Oh, what a tale to shadow with its gloom
That happy hall in England! Idle fear!
Would the winds tell it? Who might dream or hear
The secret of the forests? To the stake
   They bound him, and that proud young soldier strove
His father's spirit in his breast to wake,
   Trusting to die in silence! He, the love
Of many hearts, the fondly reared, the fair,
Gladdening all eyes to see! And fettered there
He stood beside his death-pyre, and the brand
Flamed up to light it in the chieftain's hand.
He thought upon his God. Hush, hark! A cry
Breaks on the stern and dread solemnity –
A step hath pierced the ring! Who dares intrude
On the dark hunters in their vengeful mood?
A girl, a young slight girl, a fawn-like child
Of green savannahs[3] and the leafy wild,
Springing unmarked till then, as some lone flower,
Happy because the sunshine is its dower,
Yet one that knew how early tears are shed,
For *hers* had mourned a playmate brother dead.

She had sat gazing on the victim long
Until the pity of her soul grew strong
And, by its passion's deep'ning fervour swayed,
Ev'n to the stake she rushed, and gently laid
His bright head on her bosom, and around
His form her slender arms to shield it wound
Like close liannes,[4] then raised her glittering eye
And clear-toned voice that said, 'He shall not die!'
'He shall not die!' – the gloomy forest thrilled
   To that sweet sound. A sudden wonder fell
On the fierce throng, and heart and hand were stilled,
   Struck down as by the whisper of a spell.
They gazed – their dark souls bowed before the maid,
She of the dancing step in wood and glade!
And as her cheek flushed through its olive hue,

Notes

[3] *savannahs* treeless plains.

[4] *liannes* lianas, climbing plants that grow in the tropics.

As her black tresses to the night-wind flew,
Something o'ermastered them from that young mien,
Something of heaven, in silence felt and seen,
And seeming, to their childlike faith, a token
That the Great Spirit by her voice had spoken.

They loosed the bonds that held their captive's breath;
From his pale lips they took the cup of death;
They quenched the brand beneath the cypress tree;
'Away', they cried, 'young stranger, thou art free!'

Costanza[1]

Art thou then desolate?
Of friends, of hopes forsaken? Come to me,
I am thine own! Have trusted hearts proved false?
Flatterers deceived thee? Wanderer, come to me!
Why didst thou ever leave me? Know'st thou all
I would have borne, and called it joy to bear
For thy sake? Know'st thou that thy voice had power
To shake me with a thrill of happiness
By one kind tone, to fill mine eyes with tears
Of yearning love? And thou – oh, thou didst throw
That crushed affection back upon my heart –
Yet come to me! It died not.[2]

She knelt in prayer. A stream of sunset fell
Through the stained window of her lonely cell,
And with its rich, deep, melancholy glow
Flushing her cheek and pale Madonna brow,
While o'er her long hair's flowing jet it threw
Bright waves of gold – the autumn forest's hue –
Seemed all a vision's mist of glory spread
By painting's touch around some holy head,
Virgin's or fairest martyr's. In her eye,
Which glanced as dark clear water to the sky,
What solemn fervour lived! And yet what woe
Lay like some buried thing, still seen below
The glassy tide! Oh, he that could reveal
What life had taught that chastened heart to feel
Might speak indeed of woman's blighted years,
And wasted love, and vainly bitter tears!
But she had told her griefs to heaven alone,
And of the gentle saint no more was known
Than that she fled the world's cold breath, and made
A temple of the pine and chestnut shade,
Filling its depths with soul, whene'er her hymn

Notes

COSTANZA

[1] Costanza is a feminine Italian noun meaning 'constancy, loyalty'.

[2] The epigraph is by Hemans.

Rose through each murmur of the green and dim
And ancient solitude; where hidden streams
Went moaning through the grass like sounds in dreams,
Music for weary hearts! Midst leaves and flowers
She dwelt, and knew all secrets of their powers,
All nature's balms, wherewith her gliding tread
To the sick peasant on his lowly bed
Came and brought hope; while scarce of mortal birth
He deemed the pale fair form, that held on earth
Communion but with grief.

Erelong a cell,
A rock-hewn chapel rose, a cross of stone
Gleamed through the dark trees o'er a sparkling well,
And a sweet voice of rich yet mournful tone
Told the Calabrian wilds that duly there
Costanza lifted her sad heart in prayer.
And now 'twas prayer's own hour. That voice again
Through the dim foliage sent its heavenly strain
That made the cypress quiver where it stood
In day's last crimson soaring from the wood
Like spiry flame. But as the bright sun set,
Other and wilder sounds in tumult met
The floating song. Strange sounds! The trumpet's peal
Made hollow by the rocks, the clash of steel,
The rallying war-cry. In the mountain-pass
There had been combat; blood was on the grass;
Banners had strewn the waters; chiefs lay dying,
And the pine-branches crashed before the flying.
And all was changed within the still retreat,
Costanza's home – there entered hurrying feet,
Dark looks of shame and sorrow; mail-clad men,
Stern fugitives from that wild battle-glen,
Scaring the ringdoves from the porch-roof, bore
A wounded warrior in. The rocky floor
Gave back deep echoes to his clanging sword
As there they laid their leader and implored
The sweet saint's prayers to heal him; then for flight,
Through the wide forest and the mantling night,
Sped breathlessly again. They passed – but he,
The stateliest of a host – alas, to see
What mother's eyes have watched in rosy sleep
Till joy, for very fullness, turned to weep,
Thus changed – a fearful thing! His golden crest
Was shivered, and the bright scarf on his breast
(Some costly love-gift) rent – but what of these?
There were the clustering raven-locks – the breeze
As it came in through lime and myrtle flowers
Might scarcely lift them – steeped in bloody showers
So heavily upon the pallid clay
Of the damp cheek they hung! The eyes' dark ray,

Where was it? And the lips – they gasped apart
With their light curve, as from the chisel's art,
Still proudly beautiful! But that white hue –
Was it not death's? That stillness, that cold dew
On the scarred forehead? No! His spirit broke
From its deep trance erelong, yet but awoke
To wander in wild dreams, and there he lay,
By the fierce fever as a green reed shaken,
The haughty chief of thousands, the forsaken
Of all save one! *She* fled not. Day by day
(Such hours are woman's birthright), she, unknown,
Kept watch beside him, fearless and alone,
Binding his wounds, and oft in silence laving
His brow with tears that mourned the strong man's raving.
He felt them not, nor marked the light veiled form
Still hovering nigh, yet sometimes when that storm
    Of frenzy sank, her voice, in tones as low
As a young mother's by the cradle singing,
Would soothe him with sweet *aves*, gently bringing
    Moments of slumber, when the fiery glow
Ebbed from his hollow cheek.
                                        At last faint gleams
Of memory dawned upon the cloud of dreams,
And feebly lifting, as a child, his head,
And gazing round him from his leafy bed,
He murmured forth, 'Where am I? What soft strain
Passed like a breeze across my burning brain?
Back from my youth it floated, with a tone
Of life's first music, and a thought of one –
Where is she now? And where the gauds of pride[3]
Whose hollow splendour lured me from her side?
All lost – and this is death! I *cannot* die
Without forgiveness from that mournful eye!
Away – the earth hath lost her! Was *she* born
To brook abandonment, to strive with scorn?
My first, my holiest love! Her broken heart
Lies low, and I – unpardoned, I depart.'
    But then Costanza raised the shadowy veil
From her dark locks and features brightly pale,
And stood before him with a smile – oh, ne'er
Did aught that *smiled* so much of sadness wear –
And said, 'Cesario, look on me; I live
To say my heart hath bled, and can forgive.
I loved thee with such worship, such deep trust
As should be Heaven's alone – and Heaven is just!
I bless thee – be at peace!'
                                        But o'er his frame
Too fast the strong tide rushed – the sudden shame,

Notes

[3] *gauds of pride* medals.

The joy, th' amaze! He bowed his head – it fell
On the wronged bosom which had loved so well,
And love still perfect gave him refuge there –
His last faint breath just waved her floating hair.

Madeline, a Domestic Tale[1]

Who should it be? Where shouldst thou look for kindness?
When we are sick where can we turn for succour?
When we are wretched where can we complain?
And when the world looks cold and surly on us,
Where can we go to meet a warmer eye
With such sure confidence as to a mother?
(Joanna Baillie)[2]

'My child, my child, thou leav'st me! I shall hear
The gentle voice no more that blessed mine ear
With its first utterance; I shall miss the sound
Of thy light step amidst the flowers around,
And thy soft-breathing hymn at twilight's close,
And thy 'Goodnight' at parting for repose.
Under the vine-leaves I shall sit alone,
And the low breeze will have a mournful tone
Amidst their tendrils, while I think of thee,
My child; and thou, along the moonlight sea,
With a soft sadness haply in thy glance,
Shalt watch thine own, thy pleasant land of France,
Fading to air. Yet blessings with thee go;
Love guard thee, gentlest, and the exile's woe
From thy young heart be far! And sorrow not
For me, sweet daughter; in my lonely lot
God shall be with me. Now farewell, farewell!
Thou that hast been what words may never tell
Unto thy mother's bosom, since the days
When thou wert pillowed there, and wont to raise
In sudden laughter thence thy loving eye
That still sought mine – those moments are gone by,
Thou too must go, my flower! Yet with thee dwell
The peace of God! One, one more gaze – farewell!'
  This was a mother's parting with her child,
A young meek bride on whom fair fortune smiled
And wooed her with a voice of love away
From childhood's home; yet there, with fond delay,
She lingered on the threshold, heard the note
Of her caged bird through trellised rose-leaves float,

Notes

MADELINE, A DOMESTIC TALE

[1] 'Originally published in the *Literary Souvenir* for 1828' (Hemans's note). The genre of the domestic tale attracted many female novelists and poets during the eighteenth century. Wordsworth's *Michael* and *The Brothers* are well-known examples.

[2] *Rayner* IV ii 15–20. This is from the Countess Zaterloo's speech to her son after she has removed her mask, revealing her identity.

And fell upon her mother's neck and wept,
Whilst old remembrances that long had slept
Gushed o'er her soul, and many a vanished day,
As in one picture traced, before her lay.
  But the farewell was said, and on the deep,
When its breast heaved in sunset's golden sleep,
With a calmed heart young Madeline erelong
Poured forth her own sweet solemn vesper song,[3]
Breathing of home; through stillness heard afar,
And duly rising with the first pale star,
That voice was on the waters, till at last
The sounding ocean-solitudes were passed
And the bright land was reached, the youthful world
That glows along the west.[4] The sails were furled
In its clear sunshine, and the gentle bride
Looked on the home that promised hearts untried
A bower of bliss[5] to come. Alas, we trace
The map of our own paths, and long ere years
With their dull steps the brilliant lines efface,
On sweeps the storm, and blots them out with tears.
That home was darkened soon: the summer breeze
Welcomed with death the wanderers from the seas,[6]
Death unto one, and anguish (how forlorn!)
To her that, widowed in her marriage-morn,
Sat in her voiceless dwelling, whence with him
  Her bosom's first beloved, her friend and guide,
Joy had gone forth, and left the green earth dim,
  As from the sun shut out on every side
By the close veil of misery! Oh, but ill,
  When with rich hopes o'erfraught, the young high heart
Bears its first blow! It knows not yet the part
Which life will teach: to suffer and be still,
And with submissive love to count the flowers
Which yet are spared, and through the future hour
To send no busy dream! *She* had not learned
Of sorrow till that hour, and therefore turned
In weariness from life; then came th' unrest,
The heart-sick yearning of the exile's breast,
The haunting sounds of voices far away
And household steps, until at last she lay
On her lone couch of sickness, lost in dreams
Of the gay vineyards and blue-rushing streams
In her own sunny land, and murmuring oft
Familiar names in accents wild yet soft
To strangers round that bed, who knew not aught
Of the deep spells wherewith each word was fraught.

Notes

[3] *vesper song* evening song, a phrase used by Scott, *Lady of the Lake* iii st.23 7.

[4] *the youthful world / That glows along the west* America or, possibly, Canada.

[5] *bower of bliss* The phrase is borrowed from Spenser, *Faerie Queene* II i st.51 9.

[6] *the summer breeze . . . the seas* the wind was believed to carry disease.

To strangers? Oh, could strangers raise the head
Gently as *hers* was raised? Did strangers shed
The kindly tears which bathed that feverish brow
And wasted cheek with half-unconscious flow?
Something was there that through the lingering night
Outwatches patiently the taper's light,
Something that faints not through the day's distress,
That fears not toil, that knows not weariness –
Love, true and perfect love! Whence came that power
Uprearing through the storm the drooping flower?
Whence? Who can ask? The wild delirium passed,
And from her eyes the spirit looked at last
Into her *mother's* face, and wakening knew
The brow's calm grace, the hair's dear silvery hue,
The kind sweet smile of old – and had *she* come,
Thus in life's evening, from her distant home,
To save her child? Ev'n so, nor yet in vain:
In that young heart a light sprung up again,
And lovely still, with so much love to give,
Seemed this fair world, though faded; still to live
Was not to pine forsaken. On the breast
That rocked her childhood, sinking in soft rest,
'Sweet mother, gentlest mother! Can it be?'
The lorn one cried, 'and do I look on thee?
Take back thy wanderer from this fatal shore,[7]
Peace shall be ours beneath our vines once more.'

The Queen of Prussia's Tomb[1]

This tomb is in the garden of Charlottenburgh, near Berlin. It was not without surprise that I came suddenly, among trees, upon a fair white Doric temple. I might, and should have deemed it a mere adornment of the grounds, but the cypress and the willow declare it a habitation of the dead. Upon a sarcophagus of white marble lay a sheet, and the outline of the human form was plainly visible beneath its folds. The person with me reverently turned it back and displayed the statue of his Queen. It is a portrait-statue recumbent, said to be a perfect resemblance – not as in death, but when she lived to bless and be blessed. Nothing can be more calm and kind than the expression of her features. The hands are folded on the bosom, the limbs are sufficiently crossed to show the repose of life. Here the King brings her children annually to offer garlands at her grave.[2] These hang in withered mournfulness above this living image of their departed mother.

(Sherer's *Notes and Reflections during a Ramble in Germany*)[3]

Notes

[7] *this fatal shore* probably a recollection of Wordsworth, 'Laodamia' 52, where Laodamia refers to the courage that took her husband Protesilaus to the 'fatal shore' of Troy.

The Queen of Prussia's Tomb

[1] The tomb is that of Queen Louise of Mecklenburg-Strelitz (1776–1810), who is buried in the mausoleum in the palace park of Charlottenburg, a district in Berlin, which also contains the grave of her husband, Frederick William III of Prussia (1770–1840). Severely damaged in World War II, it is still to be seen. Although in modern terms Hemans's sympathy for Prussia may now seem odd, the Germans were at the time of writing recent allies of Britain in the fight against Napoleon. Louise had come to represent libertarian hopes and patriotic spirit, and her grave was a popular destination for pilgrims.

[2] Louise had no less than ten children.

[3] Joseph Moyle Sherer (1789–1869), traveller, published his *Notes and Reflections During a Ramble in Germany* in 1826. The passage to which Hemans refers is on pp. 391–5.

In sweet pride upon that insult keen
She smiled; then drooping mute and broken-hearted,
To the cold comfort of the grave departed.
(Milman)[4]

It stands where northern willows weep,
  A temple fair and lone;
Soft shadows o'er its marble sweep,
  From cypress-branches[5] thrown,
While silently around it spread,
Thou feel'st the presence of the dead.

And what within is richly shrined?
  A sculptured woman's form,
Lovely in perfect rest reclined
  As one beyond the storm –
Yet not of death but slumber lies
The solemn sweetness on those eyes.[6]

The folded hands, the calm pure face,
  The mantle's quiet flow,
The gentle yet majestic grace
  Throned on the matron brow;
These, in that scene of tender gloom,
With a still glory robe the tomb.

There stands an eagle at the feet
  Of the fair image wrought;
A kingly emblem nor unmeet
  To wake yet deeper thought;
She whose high heart finds rest below
Was royal in her birth and woe.

There are pale garlands hung above
  Of dying scent and hue;
She was a mother – in her love
  How sorrowfully true!
Oh, hallowed long be every leaf,
The records of her children's grief!

She saw their birthright's warrior-crown
  Of olden glory spoiled,[7]
The standard of their sires borne down,

Notes

[4] Henry Hart Milman (1791–1868), *Judicium Regale, An Ode* 74–6. The poem describes a dream in which Napoleon, Queen Louise and others are judged. Milman was highly sympathetic to Louise; he was also a friend to Hemans, helping her revise *The Vespers of Palermo* for production on the London stage.

[5] *cypress-branches* symbolic of grief.

[6] 'The character of this monumental statue is that of the deepest serenity; the repose, however, of sleep – not the grave. See the description in Russell's *Germany*' (Hemans's note). Hemans refers to John Russell, *A Tour in Germany, and some of the Southern Provinces of the Austrian Empire* (1824), pp. 263–4.

[7] Louise accompanied her husband to the battlefield in the Jena campaign, when Prussia and its ally, Russia, attempted to repulse Napoleon, October 1806. The result was defeat for the Prussians; Napoleon entered Berlin on 25 October, and ten days later the Prussian rearguard capitulated.

The shield's bright blazon soiled;
She met the tempest meekly brave,
Then turned o'erwearied to the grave.[8]

She slumbered, but it came – it came,
Her land's redeeming hour,[9]
With the glad shout and signal flame
Sent on from tower to tower![10]
Fast through the realm a spirit moved –
'Twas hers, the lofty and the loved.

Then was her name a note that rung
To rouse bold hearts from sleep,
Her memory as a banner flung
Forth by the Baltic deep;
Her grief, a bitter vial poured
To sanctify th' avenger's sword.

And the crowned eagle[11] spread again
His pinion to the sun,
And the strong land shook off its chain –
So was the triumph won!
But woe for earth, where sorrow's tone
Still blends with victory's – *she* was gone![12]

The Memorial Pillar

On the roadside between Penrith and Appleby stands a small pillar with this inscription: 'This pillar was erected in the year 1656 by Ann, Countess Dowager of Pembroke, for a memorial of her last parting, in this place, with her good and pious mother, Margaret, Countess Dowager of Cumberland, on 2 April 1616'. See notes to the *Pleasures of Memory.*[1]

Hast thou, through Eden's wildwood vales, pursued
Each mountain-scene, magnificently rude,
Nor with attention's lifted eye, revered

Notes

[8] Louise did not die immediately. She worked hard to maintain the alliance with Russia, and damaged her health in doing so; she died 18 July 1810.

[9] Prussia began the fight back against Napoleon in 1813, with their allies – Russia, Austria and Britain. Napoleon's final defeat came with abdication on 22 June 1815, after the battle of Waterloo.

[10] Before telephones or indeed telegraphs, the most rapid means of communication was the chain of beacons (or, as here, towers) that stretched across the country, on hills, in which fires could be lit so as to signal important events.

[11] *the crowned eagle* symbol of Prussia.

[12] 'Originally published in the *Monthly Magazine*' (Hemans's note). The poem appeared in the issue for December 1826.

THE MEMORIAL PILLAR

[1] Samuel Rogers (1763–1855), *The Pleasures of Memory* (1792); most of Hemans's note is quoted from page 69 of Rogers's volume. The poem concerns Anne, Countess of Pembroke (1590–1676), and her mother, Margaret Russell Clifford, Countess of Cumberland (1560–1616), who was one of the pall-bearers of Elizabeth I. Forty years after her mother's death, Lady Pembroke consecrated the spot where she and her mother parted with a memorial which became known as the 'Countess's Pillar', still to be seen on the road to Appleby, not far from Brougham Castle. Wordsworth would publish a sonnet on this subject, 'Countess's Pillar', in *Yarrow Revisited and Other Poems* (1835).

That modest stone, by pious Pembroke reared,
Which still records, beyond the pencil's power,
The silent sorrows of a parting hour?
(*Rogers*)[2]

Mother and child, whose blending tears
Have sanctified the place,
Where, to the love of many years,
Was given one last embrace,
Oh ye have shrined[3] a spell of power,
Deep in your record of that hour!

A spell to waken solemn thought,
A still small undertone[4]
That calls back days of childhood fraught
With many a treasure gone,
And smites, perchance, the hidden source
(Though long untroubled) of remorse.

For who that gazes on the stone
Which marks your parting spot,
Who but a mother's love hath known,
The *one* love changing not?
Alas, and haply learned its worth
First with the sound of 'earth to earth?'

But thou, high-hearted daughter, thou
O'er whose bright honoured head
Blessings and tears of holiest flow
Ev'n here were fondly shed –
Thou from the passion of thy grief,
In its full burst, couldst draw relief.

For oh, though painful be th' excess,
The might wherewith it swells,
In nature's fount no bitterness
Of nature's mingling dwells;
And thou hadst not, by wrong or pride,
Poisoned the free and healthful tide.

But didst thou meet the face no more
Which thy young heart first knew?
And all – was all in this world o'er,
With ties thus close and true?
It was! On earth no other eye
Could give thee back thine infancy.

Notes

[2] *The Pleasures of Memory* ii 173–4, 177–80. The River Eden flows through Cumbria.

[3] *shrined* enshrined.

[4] *A still small undertone* Hemans echoes 1 Kings 19: 12: 'And after the earthquake a fire; but the Lord was not in the fire: and after the fire a *still small voice*.'

No other voice could pierce the maze
  Where deep within thy breast
The sounds and dreams of other days
  With memory lay at rest;
No other smile to thee could bring
A gladd'ning like the breath of spring.

Yet while thy place of weeping still
  Its lone memorial keeps,
While on thy name, midst wood and hill,
  The quiet sunshine sleeps
And touches in each graven line
Of reverential thought a sign,

Can I, while yet these tokens wear
  The impress of the dead,
Think of the love embodied there,
  As of a vision fled?
A perished thing, the joy and flower
And glory of one earthly hour?[5]

Not so; I will not bow me so
  To thoughts that breathe despair!
A loftier faith we need below,
  Life's farewell words to bear.
Mother and child, your tears are past –
Surely your hearts have met at last!

The Grave of a Poetess[1]

Ne me plaignez pas – si vous saviez
Combien de peines ce tombeau m'a epargnées![2]

Notes

[5] *joy and flower . . . hour* an echo of Wordsworth, *Ode* 180–1: 'Though nothing can bring back the hour / Of splendour in the grass, of glory in the flower'.

The Grave of a Poetess

[1] 'Extrinsic interest has lately attached to the fine scenery of Woodstock, near Kilkenny, on account of its having been the last residence of the author of *Psyche* [Mary Tighe]. Her grave is one of many in the churchyard of the village. The river runs smoothly by. The ruins of an ancient abbey that have been partially converted into a church reverently throw their mantle of tender shadow over it. (*Tales by the O'Hara Family*)' (Hemans's note). John Banim (1798–1842) and Michael Banim (1796–1874) published *Tales by the O'Hara Family* in 1825–7. Felicia managed to visit Mary Tighe's grave only in April 1831, when she described it as follows: 'We went to the tomb, "the grave of a poetess", where there is a monument by Flaxman. It consists of a recumbent female figure, with much of the repose, the mysterious sweetness of happy death, which is to me so affecting in monumental sculpture. There is, however, a very small Titania-looking sort of figure with wings, sitting at the head of the sleeper, which I thought interfered with the singleness of effect which the tomb would have produced. Unfortunately, too, the monument is carved in very rough stone, which allows no delicacy of touch. That place of rest made me very thoughtful; I could not but reflect on the many changes which had brought me to the spot I had commemorated three years since, without the slightest idea of ever visiting it; and, though surrounded by attention and the appearance of interest, my heart was envying the repose of her who slept there' (*The Works of Mrs Hemans* (7 vols, Edinburgh and London, 1839), i 238–9).

[2] 'Don't pity me; if only you knew how much suffering this tomb has spared me!' From Madame de Staël, *Corinne, ou L'Italie* (1807), Book 18, chapter 3, last paragraph. Corinne is in a graveyard in Florence and is reading an epitaph. It is worth adding that *Corinne* was one of Hemans's favourite novels; she said that 'it has a power over me that is quite indescribable. Some passages seem to give me back my own thoughts and feelings, my whole inner being, with a mirror more true than ever friend could hold up' (*Works* (1839) i 160).

I stood beside thy lowly grave,
  Spring odours breathed around,
And music in the river-wave
  Passed with a lulling sound.

All happy things that love the sun[3]
  In the bright air glanced by,
And a glad murmur seemed to run
  Through the soft azure sky.

Fresh leaves were on the ivy-bough
  That fringed the ruins near;
Young voices were abroad, but thou
  Their sweetness couldst not hear.

And mournful grew my heart for thee,
  Thou in whose woman's mind
The ray that brightens earth and sea,
  The light of song was shrined;[4]

Mournful that thou wert slumbering low
  With a dread curtain drawn
Between thee and the golden glow
  Of this world's vernal dawn.

Parted from all the song and bloom
  Thou wouldst have loved so well,
To thee the sunshine round thy tomb
  Was but a broken spell.

The bird, the insect on the wing,
  In their bright reckless play,
Might feel the flush and life of spring,
  And thou wert passed away!

But then, ev'n then, a nobler thought
  O'er my vain sadness came;
Th' immortal spirit woke, and wrought
  Within my thrilling frame.

Surely on lovelier things, I said,
  Thou must have looked ere now,
Than all that round our pathway shed
  Odours and hues below,

The shadows of the tomb are here,
  Yet beautiful is earth!
What seest thou then where no dim fear,
  No haunting dream hath birth?

Notes

[3] *All happy things that love the sun* an echo of Wordsworth, *Resolution and Independence* 8: 'All things that love the sun are out of doors.'

[4] *shrined* enshrined.

Here a vain love to passing flowers
 Thou gav'st, but where thou art
The sway is not with changeful hours –
 There love and death must part.

Thou hast left sorrow in thy song,
 A voice not loud, but deep!
The glorious bowers of earth among,
 How often didst thou weep!

Where couldst thou fix on mortal ground
 Thy tender thoughts and high?
Now peace the woman's heart hath found,
 And joy the poet's eye.

Miscellaneous Pieces

The Homes of England[1]

Where's the coward that would not dare
To fight for such a land?
(*Marmion*)[2]

The stately homes of England,
 How beautiful they stand!
Amidst their tall ancestral trees,
 O'er all the pleasant land.
The deer across their greensward bound
 Through shade and sunny gleam,
And the swan glides past them with the sound
 Of some rejoicing stream.

The merry homes of England!
 Around their hearths by night,
What gladsome looks of household love
 Meet in the ruddy light!
There woman's voice flows forth in song
 Or childhood's tale is told,
Or lips move tunefully along
 Some glorious page of old.

Notes

THE HOMES OF ENGLAND

[1] For extended discussion see Fiona Stafford, *Starting Lines in Scottish, Irish, and English Poetry: From Burns to Heaney* (Oxford, 2000), chapter 5.

[2] Walter Scott (1771–1832), *Marmion* (1808), iv st. 30 34–5. It may be significant, in view of the uncertainty over Hemans's intentions for this poem (see preceding note), that these lines are completely *un*ironic. They are spoken by Fitz-Eustace as he and Marmion see the Scots army massing across the landscape of Scotland.

The blessed homes of England!
How softly on their bowers
Is laid the holy quietness
That breathes from Sabbath hours!
Solemn yet sweet, the church-bell's chime
Floats through their woods at morn;
All other sounds, in that still time,
Of breeze and leaf are born.

The cottage homes of England!
By thousands on her plains,
They are smiling o'er the silvery brooks
And round the hamlet fanes.[3]
Through glowing orchards forth they peep,
Each from its nook of leaves,
And fearless there the lowly sleep,
As the bird beneath their eaves.

The free, fair homes of England!
Long, long, in hut and hall,
May hearts of native proof be reared
To guard each hallowed wall!
And green for ever be the groves
And bright the flowery sod,
Where first the child's glad spirit loves
Its country and its God![4]

The Sicilian Captive

I have dreamt thou wert
A captive in thy hopelessness; afar
From the sweet home of thy young infancy,
Whose image unto thee is as a dream
Of fire and slaughter; I can see thee wasting,
Sick for thy native air. (L.E.L.)[1]

The champions had come from their fields of war,
Over the crests of the billows far,
They had brought back the spoils of a hundred shores,
Where the deep had foamed to their flashing oars.

They sat at their feast round the Norse-king's board;
By the glare of the torch-light the mead was pour'd;
The hearth was heaped with the pine-boughs high,
And it flung a red radiance on shields thrown by.

Notes

[3] *fanes* churches.

[4] 'Originally published in *Blackwood's Magazine*' (Hemans's note). The poem first appeared in *Blackwood's*, April 1827. In view of the uncertainty over its interpretation (see note 1, above), it is worth noting that readers of *Blackwood's* would not have been inclined to read the poem ironically.

The Sicilian Captive

[1] Letitia Landon, 'Unknown Female Head' 14–19.

The Scalds[2] had chaunted in Runic rhyme,
Their songs of the Sword and the olden time,
And a solemn thrill, as the harp-chords rung,
Had breathed from the walls where the bright spears hung.

But the swell was gone from the quivering string,
They had summoned a softer voice to sing,
And a captive girl, at the warriors' call,
Stood forth in the midst of that frowning hall.

Lonely she stood: in her mournful eyes
Lay the clear midnight of southern skies,
And the drooping fringe of their lashes low,
Half-veiled a depth of unfathomed woe.

Stately she stood, though her fragile frame
Seemed struck with the blight of some inward flame,
And her proud pale brow had a shade of scorn,
Under the waves of her dark hair worn.

And a deep flush passed, like a crimson haze,
O'er her marble cheek by the pine-fire's blaze;
No soft hue caught from the south-wind's breath,
But a token of fever, at strife with death.

She had been torn from her home away,
With her long locks crowned for her bridal day,
And brought to die of the burning dreams
That haunt the exile by foreign streams.

They bade her sing of her distant land –
She held its lyre with a trembling hand,
Till the spirit its blue skies had given her, woke,
And the stream of her voice into music broke.

Faint was the strain, in its first wild flow;
Troubled its murmur, and sad, and low;
But it swelled into deeper power ere long,
As the breeze that swept over her soul grew strong.

They bid me sing of thee, mine own, my sunny land! of thee!
Am I not parted from thy shores by the mournful-sounding sea?
Doth not thy shadow wrap my soul? In silence let me die,
In a voiceless dream of thy silvery founts, and thy pure, deep sapphire sky;
How should thy lyre give here its wealth of buried sweetness forth?

Notes

[2] *Scalds* Icelandic poets of the ninth to thirteenth centuries. They used the runic alphabet.

Its tones of summer's breathings born, to the wild winds of the north?
Yet thus it shall be once, once more! – my spirit shall awake,
And through the mists of death shine out, my country, for thy sake!
That I may make thee known, with all the beauty and the light,
And the glory never more to bless thy daughter's yearning sight!
Thy woods shall whisper in my song, thy bright streams warble by,
Thy soul flow o'er my lips again – yet once, my Sicily!
There are blue heavens – far hence, far hence! but oh! their glorious blue!
Its very night is beautiful, with the hyacinth's deep hue!
It is above my own fair land, and round my laughing home,
And arching o'er my vintage-hills, they hang their cloudless dome;
And making all the waves as gems, that melt along the shore,
And steeping happy hearts in joy – that now is mine no more.
And there are haunts in that green land – oh! who may dream or tell,
Of all the shaded loveliness it hides in grot and dell!
By fountains flinging rainbow-spray on dark and glossy leaves,
And bowers wherein the forest-dove her nest untroubled weaves;
The myrtle dwells there, sending round the richness of its breath,
And the violets gleam like amethysts, from the dewy moss beneath.

And there are floating sounds that fill the skies through night and day,
Sweet sounds! the soul to hear them faints in dreams of heaven away!
They wander through the olive-woods, and o'er the shining seas,
They mingle with the orange-scents that load the sleepy breeze;
Lute, voice, and bird, are blending there; it were a bliss to die,
As dies a leaf, thy groves among, my flowery Sicily!

I may not thus depart – farewell! yet no, my country! no!
Is not love stronger than the grave? I feel it must be so!
My fleeting spirit shall o'ersweep the mountains and the main,
And in thy tender starlight rove, and through thy woods again.
Its passion deepens – it prevails! – I break my chain – I come
To dwell a viewless thing, yet blest – in thy sweet air, my home!

And her pale arms dropped the ringing lyre,
There came a mist o'er her eye's wild fire,
And her dark rich tresses, in many a fold,
Loosed from their braids, down her bosom rolled.

For her head sank back on the rugged wall,
A silence fell o'er the warriors' hall;
She had poured out her soul with her song's last tone;
The lyre was broken, the minstrel gone!

To Wordsworth[1]

Thine is a strain to read among the hills,
  The old and full of voices; by the source
Of some free stream, whose gladdening presence fills
  The solitude with sound, for in its course
Even such is thy deep song, that seems a part
Of those high scenes, a fountain from their heart.

Or its calm spirit fitly may be taken
  To the still breast in sunny garden bowers,
Where vernal winds each tree's low tones awaken,
  And bud and bell with changes mark the hours.
There let thy thoughts be with me, while the day
Sinks with a golden and serene decay.

Or by some hearth where happy faces meet,
  When night hath hushed the woods with all their birds,
There, from some gentle voice, that lay were sweet
  As antique music, linked with household words,
While, in pleased murmurs, woman's lip might move,
And the raised eye of childhood shine in love.

Or where the shadows of dark solemn yews
  Brood silently o'er some lone burial-ground,
Thy verse hath power that brightly might diffuse
  A breath, a kindling as of spring, around
From its own glow of hope and courage high,
And steadfast faith's victorious constancy.

True bard, and holy! Thou art ev'n as one
  Who, by some secret gift of soul or eye,
In every spot beneath the smiling sun,
  Sees where the springs of living waters lie;
Unseen awhile they sleep – till, touched by thee,
Bright healthful waves flow forth to each glad wanderer free.

The Spirit's Mysteries

And slight, withal, may be the things which bring
Back on the heart the weight which it would fling
  Aside for ever; it may be a sound –
A tone of music – summer's breath, or spring –

Notes

TO WORDSWORTH

[1] Hemans was both an admirer and a friend of Wordsworth, whom she visited in the Lakes, and with whom she maintained a friendly correspondence; see headnote, p. 1244. This poem was inspired by Wordsworth's *Miscellaneous Poems* (1820), lent to Hemans by Maria Jane Jewsbury, a mutual friend. As Hemans told her, 'I . . . really *studied* these poems, and they have been the daily food of my mind ever since I borrowed them . . . This author is the true *Poet of Home*, and of all the lofty feelings which have their root in the soil of home affections' (*Felicia Hemans: Selected Poems, Letters, Reception Materials* ed. Susan J. Wolfson (Princeton, NJ, 2000), p. 492).

A flower – a leaf – the ocean – which may wound –
Striking th' electric chain wherewith we are darkly bound.
(Childe Harold)[1]

The power that dwelleth in sweet sounds to waken
Vague yearnings, like the sailor's for the shore,
And dim remembrances, whose hue seems taken
From some bright former state, our own no more –
Is not this all a mystery? Who shall say
Whence are those thoughts, and whither tends their way?

The sudden images of vanished things
That o'er the spirit flash, we know not why;
Tones from some broken harp's deserted strings,
Warm sunset hues of summers long gone by,
A rippling wave – the dashing of an oar –
A flower scent floating past our parents' door;

A word scarce noted in its hour perchance,
Yet back returning with a plaintive tone;
A smile – a sunny or a mournful glance,
Full of sweet meanings now from this world flown –
Are not these mysteries when to life they start,
And press vain tears in gushes from the heart?

And the far wanderings of the soul in dreams,
Calling up shrouded faces from the dead,
And with them bringing soft or solemn gleams,
Familiar objects brightly to o'erspread,
And wakening buried love, or joy, or fear:
These are night's mysteries – who shall make them clear?

And the strange inborn sense of coming ill
That ofttimes whispers to the haunted breast
In a low tone which nought can drown or still,
Midst feasts and melodies a secret guest;
Whence doth that murmur wake, that shadow fall?
Why shakes the spirit thus? 'Tis mystery all!

Darkly we move – we press upon the brink
Haply of viewless[2] worlds, and know it not;
Yes, it may be that nearer than we think
Are those whom death has parted from our lot!
Fearfully, wondrously, our souls are made –
Let us walk humbly on,[3] but undismayed!

Humbly – for knowledge strives in vain to feel
Her way amidst these marvels of the mind –

Notes

THE SPIRIT'S MYSTERIES

[1] Byron, *Childe Harold's Pilgrimage* iv 202–7.

[2] *viewless* unseen.

[3] *Let us walk humbly on* an echo of Micah 6: 8: 'what doth the Lord require of thee, but to do justly, and to love mercy, and to walk humbly with thy God?'

Yet undismayed; for do they not reveal
  Th' immortal being with our dust entwined?
So let us deem, and e'en the tears they wake
Shall then be blessed, for that high nature's sake!

The Graves of a Household[1]

They grew in beauty, side by side,
  They filled one home with glee;
Their graves are severed far and wide,
  By mount and stream and sea.

The same fond mother bent at night
  O'er each fair sleeping brow;
She had each folded flower in sight –
  Where are those dreamers now?

One midst the forests of the west[2]
  By a dark stream is laid –
The Indian knows his place of rest
  Far in the cedar shade.

The sea, the blue lone sea hath one,
  He lies where pearls lie deep;
He was the loved of all, yet none
  O'er his low bed may weep.

One sleeps where southern vines are dressed
  Above the noble slain;
He wrapped his colours round his breast
  On a blood-red field of Spain.[3]

And one – o'er *her* the myrtle showers
  Its leaves, by soft winds fanned;
She faded midst Italian flowers,
  The last of that bright band.

And parted thus they rest, who played
  Beneath the same green tree;
Whose voices mingled as they prayed
  Around one parent knee![4]

They that with smiles lit up the hall
  And cheered with song the hearth –
Alas, for love, if *thou* wert all,
  And nought beyond, oh earth!

Notes

The Graves of a Household

[1] In its preoccupation with the dispersal of siblings and use of the ballad stanza, this poem bears comparison with Wordsworth's 'We Are Seven', Wolfson suggests.

[2] Hemans was thinking in this stanza of her brother Claude Scott Browne, one year younger than her, who died in Kingston, Canada, in 1821.

[3] *Spain* Hemans's husband and two of her brothers served in the Peninsular Wars in Spain.

[4] Hemans's mother died in January 1827.

The Land of Dreams

From Songs of the Affections, with Other Poems (1830)

And dreams, in their development, have breath
And tears, and tortures, and the touch of joy;
They leave a weight upon our waking thoughts . . .
They make us what we were not – what they will,
And shake us with the vision that's gone by . . . [1]

Oh spirit land, thou land of dreams!
A world thou art of mysterious gleams,
Of startling voices, and sounds at strife –
A world of the dead in the hues of life.

Like a wizard's magic-glass thou art
When the wavy shadows float by, and part –
Visions of aspects, now loved, now strange,
Glimmering and mingling in ceaseless change.

Thou art like a city of the past
With its gorgeous halls into fragments cast,
Amidst whose ruins there glide and play
Familiar forms of the world's today.

Thou art like the depths where the seas have birth,
Rich with the wealth that is lost from earth –
All the sere flowers of our days gone by,
And the buried gems in thy bosom lie.

Yes, thou art like those dim sea-caves,
A realm of treasures, a realm of graves!
And the shapes through thy mysteries that come and go,
Are of beauty and terror, of power and woe.

But for *me*, oh thou picture-land of sleep,
Thou art all one world of affections deep –
And wrung from my heart is each flushing dye
That sweeps o'er thy chambers of imagery.

And thy bowers are fair – even as Eden fair;
All the beloved of my soul are there!
The forms my spirit most pines to see,
The eyes whose love hath been life to me –

They are there, and each blessed voice I hear,
Kindly, and joyous, and silvery clear;
But undertones are in each, that say,
'It is but a dream; it will melt away!'

Notes

THE LAND OF DREAMS

[1] Byron, 'The Dream' 5–7, 15–16.

I walk with sweet friends in the sunset's glow;
I listen to music of long ago;
But one thought, like an omen, breathes faint through the lay –
'It is but a dream; it will melt away!'

I sit by the hearth of my early days;
All the home-faces are met by the blaze,
And the eyes of the mother shine soft, yet say,
'It is but a dream; it will melt away!'

And away, like a flower's passing breath, 'tis gone,
And I wake more sadly, more deeply lone –
Oh, a haunted heart is a weight to bear!
Bright faces, kind voices, where are ye, where?

Shadow not forth, oh thou land of dreams,
The past, as it fled by my own blue streams!
Make not my spirit within me burn
For the scenes and the hours that may ne'er return!

Call out from the *future* thy visions bright,
From the world o'er the grave, take thy solemn light,
And oh! with the loved, whom no more I see,
Show me my home as it yet may be!

As it yet may be in some purer sphere –
No cloud, no parting, no sleepless fear;
So my soul may bear on through the long, long day,
Till I go where the beautiful melts not away!

Nature's Farewell

From Songs of the Affections, with Other Poems (1830)

The beautiful is vanished, and returns not.[1]

A youth rode forth from his childhood's home,
Through the crowded paths of the world to roam,
And the green leaves whispered as he passed:
'Wherefore, thou dreamer, away so fast?

Knew'st thou with what thou art parting here,
Long wouldst thou linger in doubt and fear;
Thy heart's light laughter, thy sunny hours,
Thou hast left in our shades with the spring's wild-flowers.

Notes

Nature's Farewell

[1] Coleridge, *The Death of Wallenstein*, V i 68.

Under the arch by our mingling made,
Thou and thy brother have gaily played;
Ye may meet again where ye roved of yore,
But as ye *have* met there – oh, never more!'

On rode the youth – and the boughs among,
Thus the free birds o'er his pathway sung:
'Wherefore so fast unto life away?
Thou art leaving for ever thy joy in our lay![2]

Thou mayst come to the summer woods again,
And thy heart have no echo to greet their strain;
Afar from the foliage its love will dwell –
A change must pass o'er thee – farewell, farewell!'

On rode the youth, and the founts and streams
Thus mingled a voice with his joyous dreams:
'We have been thy playmates through many a day,
Wherefore thus leave us? Oh yet delay!

Listen but once to the sound of our mirth!
For thee 'tis a melody passing from earth.[3]
Never again wilt thou find in its flow
The peace it could once on thy heart bestow.

Thou wilt visit the scenes of thy childhood's glee
With the breath of the world on thy spirit free;
Passion and sorrow its depth will have stirred,
And the singing of waters be vainly heard.

Thou wilt bear in our gladsome laugh no part –
What should it do for a burning heart?
Thou wilt bring to the banks of our freshest rill
Thirst which no fountain on earth may still.

Farewell! When thou comest again to thine own,
Thou wilt miss from our music its loveliest tone;
Mournfully true is the tale we tell –
Yet on, fiery dreamer! Farewell, farewell!'

And a something of gloom on his spirit weighed
As he caught the last sounds of his native shade;
But he knew not, till many a bright spell broke,
How deep were the oracles nature spoke!

Notes

[2] *lay* song.

[3] *'tis a melody passing from earth* an echo of Wordsworth, 'Ode' 18: 'there hath passed away a glory from the earth.'

Second Sight

From Songs of the Affections, with Other Poems (1830)

Ne'er erred the prophet heart that grief inspired,
Though joy's illusions mock their votarist.
(*Maturin*)[1]

A mournful gift is mine, oh friends,
A mournful gift is mine!
A murmur of the soul which blends
With the flow of song and wine.

An eye that through the triumph's hour
Beholds the coming woe,
And dwells upon the faded flower
Midst the rich summer's glow.

Ye smile to view fair faces bloom
Where the father's board is spread;
I see the stillness and the gloom
Of a home whence all are fled.

I see the withered garlands lie
Forsaken on the earth,
While the lamps yet burn and the dancers fly
Through the ringing hall of mirth.

I see the blood-red future stain
On the warrior's gorgeous crest,
And the bier amidst the bridal train
When they come with roses dressed.

I hear the still small moan of time[2]
Through the ivy branches made,
Where the palace in its glory's prime
With the sunshine stands arrayed.

The thunder of the seas I hear,
The shriek along the wave,
When the bark sweeps forth, and song and cheer
Salute the parting brave.

With every breeze a spirit sends
To me some warning sign –
A mournful gift is mine, oh friends,
A mournful gift is mine!

Notes

Second Sight

[1] Charles Robert Maturin (1782–1824), *Bertram* IV ii 144–5. Maturin's play was produced by Kean at Drury Lane in 1816, with great success.

[2] *the still small moan of time* an echo of 1 Kings 19: 12: 'And after the earthquake a fire; but the Lord was not in the fire: and after the fire a *still small voice*.'

Oh, prophet heart, thy grief, thy power
 To all deep souls belong;
The shadow in the sunny hour,
 The wail in the mirthful song.

Their sight is all too sadly clear –
 For them a veil is riven;
Their piercing thoughts repose not here,
 Their home is but in heaven.

Despondency and Aspiration[1] (composed November 1834)

From The Works of Mrs Hemans (1839)

Per correr miglior acqua alza le vele,
Omai la navicella del mio intelletto.[2]
(*Dante*)

My soul was mantled with dark shadows born
 Of lonely fear, disquieted in vain;
Its phantoms hung around the star of morn,
 A cloud-like weeping train;
Through the long day they dimmed the autumn gold
On all the glistening leaves, and wildly rolled,
 When the last farewell flush of light was glowing
 Across the sunset sky,
 O'er its rich isles of vaporous glory throwing
 One melancholy dye.

 And when the solemn night
 Came rushing with her might
 Of stormy oracles from caves unknown,
 Then with each fitful blast
 Prophetic murmurs passed,
 Wakening or answering some deep sybil tone
 Far buried in my breast, yet prompt to rise
With every gusty wail that o'er the wind-harp flies.

'Fold, fold thy wings', they cried, 'and strive no more,
Faint spirit, strive no more! For thee too strong
 Are outward ill and wrong,
And inward wasting fires! Thou canst not soar
 Free on a starry way
 Beyond their blighting sway,
At Heaven's high gate serenely to adore!
How shouldst *thou* hope earth's fetters to unbind?
Oh passionate yet weak, oh trembler to the wind!

Notes

Despondency and Aspiration

[1] 'Partly composed during the Author's last illness' (editorial note in 1839 text). For commentary on this poem see p. 1245.

[2] Dante, *Purgatorio* i 1–2: 'This ship of my mind by now unfurls the sails to navigate more quickly.'

Never shall aught but broken music flow
From joy of thine, deep love, or tearful woe;
Such homeless notes as through the forest sigh,
From the reeds hollow shaken
When sudden breezes waken
Their vague wild symphony:
No power is theirs, and no abiding-place
In human hearts; their sweetness leaves no trace –
Born only so to die!

Never shall aught but perfume, faint and vain,
On the fleet pinion of the changeful hour,
From thy bruised life again
A moment's essence breathe;
Thy life, whose trampled flower
Into the blessed wreath
Of household charities[3] no longer bound,
Lies pale and withering on the barren ground.

So fade, fade on! Thy gift of love shall cling,
A coiling sadness round thy heart and brain,
A silent, fruitless, yet undying thing
All sensitive to pain!
And still the shadow of vain dreams shall fall
O'er thy mind's world, a daily darkening pall.
Fold, then, thy wounded wing, and sink subdued
In cold and unrepining quietude!'

Then my soul yielded; spells of numbing breath
Crept o'er it heavy with a dew of death,
Its powers, like leaves before the night rain, closing;
And, as by conflict of wild sea-waves tossed
On the chill bosom of some desert coast,
Mutely and hopelessly I lay reposing.

When silently it seemed
As if a soft mist gleamed
Before my passive sight, and, slowly curling,
To many a shape and hue
Of visioned beauty grew,
Like a wrought banner, fold by fold unfurling.
Oh, the rich scenes that o'er mine inward eye[4]
Unrolling then swept by
With dreamy motion! Silvery seas were there
Lit by large dazzling stars, and arched by skies
Of southern midnight's most transparent dyes,
And gemmed with many an island, wildly fair,
Which floated past me into orient day

Notes

[3] *charities* affections; by this time Hemans's mother was dead.

[4] *inward eye* an echo of Wordsworth, *Daffodils* 15–16, where the memory of daffodils 'flash upon that inward eye / Which is the bliss of solitude'.

Still gathering lustre on th' illumined way,
Till its high groves of wondrous flowering trees
Coloured the silvery seas.

And then a glorious mountain-chain uprose,
Height above spiry height!
A soaring solitude of woods and snows
All steeped in golden light!
While as it passed, those regal peaks unveiling,
I heard, methought, a waving of dread wings
And mighty sounds, as if the vision hailing,
From lyres that quivered through ten thousand strings;
Or as if waters forth to music leaping,
From many a cave, the Alpine Echo's hall,
On their bold way victoriously were sweeping,
Linked in majestic anthems, while through all
That billowy swell and fall
Voices, like ringing crystal, filled the air
With inarticulate melody that stirred
My being's core, then, moulding into word
Their piercing sweetness, bade me rise and bear
In that great choral strain my trembling part
Of tones, by love and faith struck from a human heart.

Return no more, vain bodings of the night!
A happier oracle within my soul
Hath swelled to power – a clear unwavering light
Mounts through the battling clouds that round me roll,
And to a new control
Nature's full harp gives forth rejoicing tones,
Wherein my glad sense owns
The accordant rush of elemental sound
To one consummate harmony profound,
One grand creation hymn
Whose notes the seraphim
Lift to the glorious height of music winged and crowned.

Shall not those notes find echoes in my lyre,
Faithful though faint? Shall not my spirit's fire,
If slowly, yet unswervingly, ascend
Now to its fount and end?
Shall not my earthly love, all purified,
Shine forth a heavenward guide,
An angel of bright power, and strongly bear
My being upward into holier air,
Where fiery passion-clouds have no abode,
And the sky's temple-arch o'erflows with God?

The radiant hope new-born
Expands like rising morn
In my life's life and, as a ripening rose,
The crimson shadow of its glory throws

More vivid, hour by hour, on some pure stream,
So from that hope are spreading
Rich hues, o'er nature shedding,
Each day, a clearer, spiritual gleam.

Let not those rays fade from me – once enjoyed,
Father of spirits, let them not depart!
Leaving the chilled earth, without form and void,
Darkened by mine own heart!
Lift, aid, sustain me! Thou by whom alone
All lovely gifts and pure
In the soul's grasp endure;
Thou, to the steps of whose eternal throne
All knowledge flows – a sea for evermore
Breaking its crested waves on that sole shore[5] –
Oh consecrate my life, that I may sing
Of Thee with joy that hath a living spring
In a full heart of music! Let my lays
Through the resounding mountains waft thy praise,
And with that theme the wood's green cloisters fill,
And make their quivering leafy dimness thrill
To the rich breeze of song! Oh let me wake
The deep religion, which hath dwelt from yore,
Silently brooding by lone cliff and lake,
And wildest river shore,
And let me summon all the voices dwelling
Where eagles build, and caverned rills are welling,
And where the cataract's organ-peal is swelling,
In that one spirit gathered to adore!

Forgive, oh Father, if presumptuous thought
Too daringly in aspiration rise!
Let not thy child all vainly have been taught
By weakness, and by wanderings, and by sighs
Of sad confession! Lowly be my heart,
And on its penitential altar spread
The offerings worthless, till Thy grace impart
The fire from heaven, whose touch alone can shed
Life, radiance, virtue! Let that vital spark
Pierce my whole being, wildered else and dark!

Thine are all holy things – oh make *me* Thine,
So shall I, too, be pure – a living shrine
Unto that spirit which goes forth from Thee,
Strong and divinely free,
Bearing thy gifts of wisdom on its flight,
And brooding o'er them with a dove-like wing,[6]
Till thought, word, song, to Thee in worship spring,
Immortally endowed for liberty and light.

Notes

[5] *a sea for evermore . . . shore* a reminiscence of Wordsworth, *Ode* 169–70: 'And see the children sport upon the shore, / And hear the mighty waters rolling evermore'.

[6] *brooding o'er them with a dove-like wing* an allusion to *Paradise Lost* i 21–2, where the Holy Spirit 'Dove-like sat'st brooding on the vast abyss / And madest it pregnant'.

Thoughts During Sickness: II. Sickness Like Night (composed late 1834)

From The New Monthly Magazine (1835)

Thou art like night, oh sickness, deeply stilling
Within my heart the world's disturbing sound,
And the dim quiet of my chamber filling
With low, sweet voices, by life's tumult drowned.
Thou art like awful night! Thou gatherest round
The things that are unseen, though close they lie,
And with a truth, clear, startling, and profound,
Giv'st their dread presence to our mortal eye.
Thou art like starry, spiritual night!
High and immortal thoughts attend thy way,
And revelations, which the common light
Brings not, though wakening with its rosy ray
All outward life: be welcome, then, thy rod,
Before whose touch my soul unfolds itself to God!

John Gibson Lockhart (1794–1854)

A graduate of the University of Glasgow, Lockhart also attended Balliol College, Oxford, where he graduated in 1813. He became a lawyer in Edinburgh, but always nurtured literary ambitions, which found an outlet in *Blackwood's Edinburgh Magazine*, of which he and John Wilson were appointed editors in 1817. The magazine had floundered under the editorship of James Cleghorn and Thomas Pringle; in Wilson and Lockhart, Blackwood saw two likely prospects who could rejuvenate it, for which he paid £500 a year (£20,000/US$36,500 today) to be divided between them.

His instincts were right. *Blackwood's* soon established itself as one of the most important magazines of the day in opposition to the Whiggish tendencies of Jeffrey's *Edinburgh Review*. 'Toryism is an innate principle o' human nature; Whiggism but an evil habit,' says the Ettrick Shepherd (James Hogg) in the twenty-third episode of 'Noctes Ambrosianae'[1] in December 1825 – a political stance taken for granted from the outset. It could only be a matter of time before they targeted Leigh Hunt and his circle.

A former inmate of the Horsemonger Lane Gaol (where he was incarcerated for libelling the Prince Regent), still liberal in his politics, and now a poet as well as editor of *The Examiner* weekly newspaper, Hunt was a prominent cultural figure and political commentator – the ideal subject for Lockhart's envenomed pen.[2] And Lockhart was clever. Just as Jeffrey had used the idea that Wordsworth, Coleridge and Southey comprised a 'School' as a vehicle for criticising their work *en masse*, so Lockhart realized that were he to place Hunt at the centre of a coterie, his criticisms might in future be applied to others whose politics he disliked. Those lumped with

Notes

John Gibson Lockhart

[1] The 'Noctes' was a kind of running soap-opera in *Blackwood's*, featuring the various members of its editorial board in various guises, including Blackwood himself.

[2] For further details concerning Hunt, see the headnote on him, p. 792 above.

him as fellow-members of the Cockney School would include Shelley (who wasn't a Londoner, but had contributed to *The Examiner*), Byron (co-editor of *The Liberal* with Hunt), Hazlitt (not a Londoner by birth, but certainly a denizen of the city, and a contributor to *The Examiner*), Lamb (a contributor to Hunt's journals *The Reflector, The Examiner* and *The Indicator*) and Keats.

Lockhart and Wilson's attacks were virulent and recurrent, spanning years. In the cases of Keats and Hazlitt, the Cockney label stuck, conditioning the reception accorded their work elsewhere. In a letter of late 1818 to John Murray, Lockhart and Wilson congratulated themselves on the fact that:

> the articles on the Cockney School are little if at all more severe than those in the *Quarterly Review,* and that they give more offence to the objects of their severity, only on account of their superior keenness – above all that happy name which you and all the reviews are now borrowing – *the Cockney School* – a thorn which will stick to them and madden them and finally damn them.[3]

From the outset, Lockhart's chief ploy was to disguise his true motives by referring to as many non-political (or at least, politically neutral) factors as possible – personal (im)morality, literary (bad) taste, social climbing, lack of self-awareness and the like.

> Every man is, according to Mr Hunt, a dull potato-eating blockhead – of no greater value to God or man than any ox or dray-horse – who is not an admirer of Voltaire's *romans*, a worshipper of Lord Holland and Mr Haydon, and a quoter of *John Buncle* and Chaucer's *Flower and Leaf.* Every woman is useful only as a breeding machine, unless she is fond of reading Launcelot of the Lake, in an antique summer-house.[4]
>
> How such a profligate creature as Mr Hunt can pretend to be an admirer of Mr Wordsworth, is to us a thing altogether inexplicable. One great charm of Wordsworth's noble compositions consists in the dignified purity of thought, and the patriarchal simplicity of feeling, with which they are throughout penetrated and imbued. We can conceive a vicious man admiring with distant awe the spectacle of virtue and purity; but if he does so sincerely, he must also do so with the profoundest feeling of the error of his own ways, and the resolution to amend them. His admiration must be humble and silent, not pert and loquacious. Mr Hunt praises the purity of Wordsworth as if he himself were pure, his dignity as if he also were dignified.[5]

Although he appears to discuss everything except politics, this is nothing if not ideological. The adjectives used to describe Hunt – 'profligate', 'vicious' – are designed to appeal to the prejudices of *Blackwood's* Tory readership; by contrast, Wordsworth's 'patriarchal' simplicity of feeling elevates him to the same level as those whose fear of revolution led to the Peterloo Massacre.[6] The paragraph enacts an anxiety of the age – that of patrician poet besieged by a dissolute and jumped-up member of the lower orders, clamouring for fame and wealth. Even Hunt's worship of Lord Holland[7] is motivated by the same self-interest, it is implied. All of which is confirmed by Lockhart's attack on Hunt's pantheon: Voltaire (French, and therefore renowned for licentiousness), Chaucer (whose

Notes

[3] Quoted in Nicholas Roe, *John Keats and the Culture of Dissent* (Oxford, 1997), p. 12.

[4] This is a reference to Hunt's *Rimini*, Canto III (see p. 796).

[5] Z. [J. G. Lockhart], 'On the Cockney School of Poetry No.1', *Blackwood's Edinburgh Magazine* 2 (October 1817) 38–41, p. 40.

[6] It is worth noting that Wordsworth's immediate response to the Peterloo Massacre was not one of sympathy with its victims. In correspondence with Lord Lonsdale in August 1819, he expressed sadness that 'several special constables were cut down or trampled', and described a paper in support of the reformers as 'a mischievous publication!' (*MY* ii 554).

[7] Henry Richard Vassall Fox, third Baron Holland (1773–1840), statesman and man of letters, nephew of Charles James Fox, and Whig grandee.

work was full of ruderies), *John Buncle* (the story of an amorous Unitarian) and *Launcelot of the Lake* (about a morally questionable liaison).

And why should *The Flower and the Leaf* be included – at the time thought to have been written by Chaucer, but now ascribed to an anonymous female poet of the last quarter of the fifteenth century? Because, months before, on 16 March 1817, *The Examiner* published Keats's sonnet *Written on a Blank Space at the end of Chaucer's Tale of 'The Floure and the Lefe'* under a brief introductory note: 'The following exquisite Sonnet, as well as one or two others that have lately appeared under the same signature, is from the pen of the young poet (KEATS), who was mentioned not long since in this paper, and who may already lay true claim to that title: – "The youngest he, / That sits in shadow of Apollo's tree." '[8] Mention of *The Flower and the Leaf* suggests that, as early as this first attack, Keats was in Lockhart's sights. Such was Keats's own interpretation when reporting it to his friend Benjamin Bailey on 3 November: 'There has been a flaming attack upon Hunt in [*Blackwood's*] *Edinburgh Magazine* – I never read anything so virulent – accusing him of the greatest crimes . . . I have no doubt that the second Number was intended for me.'[9] Even then, he realized that as the recipient of Hunt's patronage he was in the firing line, and fretted that 'I shall have the reputation of Hunt's élève.'[10]

Hunt also objected, and in *The Examiner* for 16 November challenged 'Z.' (Lockhart's pen-name) to 'avow himself; which he cannot fail to do, unless to an utter disregard of all *Truth* and Decency, he adds the height of Meanness and COWARDICE.'[11] He published no less than three such demands, none of which was heeded.

Keats was correct to suppose that Lockhart would soon mount a similar assault on him. For the moment, however, Lockhart's problem was that he did not have sufficient information: that would soon change. In July 1818, Bailey happened to meet Lockhart at his father-in-law's house and had the unpleasant experience of hearing him attack Keats. His response was to tell him that Keats:

> was of a respectable family; and though he and his brothers and sister were orphans, they were left with a small but independent patrimony. He had been brought up to the profession of medicine which he had abandoned for the pursuit of literature.[12]

Lockhart then promised Bailey that he would not criticize Keats in print – a promise which, even after Keats's death, Bailey continued to believe. But he did not count on Lockhart's ruthlessness. Far from dissuading him, Bailey had inadvertently provided him with precisely the ammunition he required.[13] Lockhart went straight to his office and drafted the fourth of the Cockney School essays, which appeared in the next available issue of *Blackwood's*, August 1818.[14] His sneers at Keats's lack of classical learning and social class could now be backed up by factual evidence. It was worse than Croker's review of *Endymion* in the *Quarterly* (April 1818) which Shelley thought precipitated Keats' demise (see p. 1200n10). (Shelley apparently did not see Lockhart's essay – he was in Italy when it appeared.)

Keats may have been disappointed by some of his reviews, but there is nothing to suggest that they seriously depressed him, or that they ruined

Notes

[8] *The Examiner*, 16 March 1817, p. 173.

[9] Rollins i 180.

[10] Ibid., i 170.

[11] Leigh Hunt, 'To Z.', *The Examiner*, 16 November 1817, p. 729.

[12] *Keats Circle* i 246.

[13] When he saw Lockhart's essay Bailey realized how foolish he had been, and was always to regret that he was now 'under suspicion that he furnished materials to one of his coadjutors with a view to the nefarious purpose of making that shameless attack, so full of contempt and scorn' (*Keats Circle* i 246).

[14] I have followed Alan Lang Strout's attribution of the essay to Lockhart. See Alan Lang Strout, *A Bibliography of Articles in Blackwood's Magazine* (Lubbock, Tex., 1959), p. 43.

his health. In a letter to his publisher of October 1818, he said that 'My own domestic criticism has given me pain without comparison beyond what *Blackwood* or the *Quarterly* could possibly inflict.'[15] His brother Tom was, at this point, seriously ill with tuberculosis, and that would have placed Lockhart's article in its proper context. In correspondence, Keats took revenge by referring to 'the ignorant malevolence of cold lying Scotchmen and stupid Englishmen'.[16] And in a letter to George and Georgiana Keats on 19 February 1819, he remarked that:

> I have no doubt of success in a course of years if I persevere. But it must be patience, for the reviews have enervated and made indolent men's minds; few think for themselves. These reviews too are getting more and more powerful and especially the *Quarterly*. They are like a superstition which, the more it prostrates the crowd, and the longer it continues, the more powerful it becomes just in proportion to their increasing weakness. (Rollins ii 65)

Keats's friends and colleagues were not so relaxed, especially when they knew he was dying. John Taylor, his publisher, fulminated in a letter to James Hessey of August 1820:

> Did they not speak of him in ridicule as 'Johnny Keats', describe his appearance while addressing a sonnet [to] Ailsa Crag, and compare him as a Friesland hen to Shelley as a bird of paradise?[17] Besides, what can you say to that cold-blooded passage where they say they will take care he shall never get £50 again for a volume of his poems?[18] What had he done to cause such attacks as these? 'Oh, it was all a joke, the writer meant nothing more than to be witty; he certainly thought there was much affectation in his poetry, and he expressed his opinion only, it was done in the fair spirit of criticism.' – It was done in the spirit of this Devil, Mr Blackwood. So, if a young man is guilty of affectation while he is walking the streets, it is fair in another person, because he dislikes it, to come and knock him down? . . .
>
> I feel regard for Mr Keats as a man of real genius, a gentleman, nay more – as one of *the gentlest of human beings*. He does not resent these things himself, he merely says of his opponents, 'They don't know me'. Now, this mildness makes those who are his friends feel the more warmly when they see him ill-used.[19]

Taylor's judgements, though influenced by his love of Keats, are compelling. Lockhart and Wilson were brief-less advocates with time on their hands – amateur journalists who despised paid hacks like Hazlitt and Hunt. As they saw it, they wrote from a position of social, economic and moral superiority as much as from one of political opposition. Furthermore, they were in the employ of a hard-nosed Edinburgh bookseller with 'the instincts of the small-town bully, ready to force a passage and crush competition with his fists if necessary'.[20] And that was the ethos by which Blackwood's journal was run. He encouraged Lockhart and Wilson to use spies to gather information about their victims, and to use their knowledge of the law to write articles that stopped short of what might be actionable in court. All the same, they were arrogant enough sometimes to overstep the mark. In August 1818 John Wilson was responsible for a scorching attack, 'Hazlitt Cross-Questioned', for which Hazlitt sued Blackwood. When it became clear that Hazlitt was

Notes

[15] Rollins i 374.

[16] Ibid., i 376. There is reason to think that Lamb's criticism of the Scots in 'Imperfect Sympathies' is related to the depredations of the *Blackwood's* journalists.

[17] In December 1819, John Wilson in *Blackwood's* had ridiculed 'Mister John Keates standing on the sea-shore at Dunbar, without a neckcloth, according to the custom of Cockaigne, and cross-questioning the Craig of Ailsa!' He goes on to remark that 'A bird of paradise and a Friezeland fowl would not look more absurdly, on the same perch' than Shelley and 'Johnny Keates' in company.

[18] See Lockhart's fourth Cockney School attack, p. 1331 below.

[19] *Keats Circle* i 135–6.

[20] Stanley Jones, *Hazlitt: A Life* (Oxford, 1991), p. 288.

likely to win, the case was settled out of court. More importantly, an attack on *Blackwood's* by John Scott, the editor of the *London Magazine* (and friend of Hunt, Hazlitt, Lamb and De Quincey), led to his fighting a duel with Lockhart's friend Jonathan Christie. He was fatally wounded, and died a painful and drawn-out death in February 1821. (Walter Scott, Lockhart's father-in-law, often said to have been a restraining influence, commented: 'It would be great hypocrisy in me to say I am sorry for John Scott. He has got exactly what he was long fishing for.'[21])

It was proof, were any needed, that words can kill, particularly when wielded by those as reckless as Lockhart and Wilson. The fourth of the Cockney School attacks, directed at Keats, is typical. Given its obviously partisan nature, it is regrettable that it set the tone of much Keats criticism until well into the twentieth century. In the short term it depressed sales of his books to the extent that Taylor and Hessey were compelled to remainder *Endymion*. Had he not succumbed to tuberculosis, Keats would probably not have been able to live by his pen.

In Lockhart's defence, it is often remarked that marriage and his illustrious father-in-law mellowed him – and that is probably true. His significance for students of the Romantic period, however, is less for *Peter's Letters to his Kinsfolk* (1819, a study of Edinburgh life and letters) or his seven-volume *Memoirs of the Life of Sir Walter Scott* (1837–8), but for his reputation as 'The Scorpion which delighteth to sting men's faces'.

Further reading

Jeffrey N. Cox, *Poetry and Politics in the Cockney School: Keats, Shelley, Hunt and their Circle* (Cambridge, 1998).

Andrew Lang, *The Life and Letters of John Gibson Lockhart* (2 vols, London, 1897).

John O. Hayden, *The Romantic Reviewers 1802–1824* (London, 1969), chapter 5.

Nicholas Roe, *John Keats and the Culture of Dissent* (Oxford, 1997).

Duncan Wu, 'Keats and the "Cockney School" ', in *The Cambridge Companion to Keats* ed. Susan Wolfson (Cambridge, 2001), pp. 37–52.

The Cockney School of Poetry No. IV (signed 'Z.') (extracts)

From Blackwood's Edinburgh Magazine (August 1818)

Of Keats,
The muses' son of promise, and what feats
He yet may do, etc.

(*Cornelius Webb*[1])

Of all the manias of this mad age, the most incurable, as well as the most common, seems to be no other than the *metromanie*.[2] The just celebrity of Robert Burns and Miss Baillie[3] has had the melancholy effect of turning the heads of we know not how many farm-servants and unmarried ladies; our very footmen compose tragedies, and there is scarcely a superannuated governess in the island that does not leave a roll of lyrics behind her in her bandbox.[4]

Notes

[21] *The Letters of Sir Walter Scott* ed. H. J. C. Grierson (12 vols, London, 1932–79), vi 374.

THE COCKNEY SCHOOL OF POETRY NO. IV

[1] Probably from Cornelius 'Corny' Webb's 'Epistle to a Friend', sent to William Blackwood in September 1817, for publication. In addition, Webb sent three sonnets in manuscript, edited by Nicholas Roe, *John Keats and the Culture of Dissent* (Oxford, 1997), pp. 269–70. Webb's phrase, 'The muses' son of promise', was quoted in ridicule of Keats for years.

[2] *metromanie* mania for writing poetry.

[3] Joanna Baillie (1762–1851), dramatist; see p. 307.

[4] *bandbox* cardboard box for caps, hats, millinery.

To witness the disease of any human understanding, however feeble, is distressing – but the spectacle of an able mind reduced to a state of insanity is of course ten times more afflicting. It is with such sorrow as this that we have contemplated the case of Mr John Keats. This young man appears to have received from nature talents of an excellent, perhaps even of a superior order – talents which, devoted to the purposes of any useful profession, must have rendered him a respectable, if not an eminent citizen. His friends, we understand, destined him to the career of medicine, and he was bound apprentice some years ago to a worthy apothecary in town.[5]

But all has been undone by a sudden attack of the malady to which we have alluded. Whether Mr John had been sent home with a diuretic or composing draught[6] to some patient far gone in the poetical mania, we have not heard. This much is certain: that he has caught the infection, and that thoroughly. For some time we were in hopes that he might get off with a violent fit or two, but of late the symptoms are terrible. The frenzy of the *Poems* was bad enough in its way,[7] but it did not alarm us half so seriously as the calm, settled, imperturbable drivelling idiocy of *Endymion*.[8] We hope, however, that in so young a person, and with a constitution originally so good, even now the disease is not utterly incurable. Time, firm treatment, and rational restraint, do much for many apparently hopeless invalids – and if Mr Keats should happen, at some interval of reason, to cast his eye upon our pages, he may perhaps be convinced of the existence of his malady, which in such cases is often all that is necessary to put the patient in a fair way of being cured.

The readers of the *Examiner* newspaper were informed, some time ago, by a solemn paragraph, in Mr Hunt's best style, of the appearance of two new stars of glorious magnitude and splendour in the poetical horizon of the land of Cockaigne.[9] One of these turned out, by and by, to be no other than Mr John Keats. This precocious adulation confirmed the wavering apprentice in his desire to quit the gallipots, and at the same time excited in his too susceptible mind a fatal admiration for the character and talents of the most worthless and affected[10] of all the versifiers of our time. One of his first productions was the following sonnet, 'written on the day when Mr Leigh Hunt left prison'. It will be recollected that the cause of Hunt's confinement was a series of libels against his sovereign, and that its fruit was the odious and incestuous *Story of Rimini*.[11]

[Quotes all of Keats's 'Written on the Day that Mr Leigh Hunt left Prison' ('What though, for showing truth to flattered state'), published *Poems* (1817). Lockhart italicizes the phrases 'Kind Hunt', 'In Spenser's walls' and 'With daring Milton'.]

Notes

5 *His friends . . . town* Keats was apprenticed to the Edmonton physician Thomas Hammond from summer 1811, when he left Enfield School, until October 1815, when he began his formal training at Guy's Hospital. He qualified at Apothecaries' Hall in July 1816. Apothecaries were forerunners of the modern-day chemist. Lockhart got this information from one of Keats's best friends, Benjamin Bailey; see headnote, p. 1325 above.

6 *a diuretic or composing draught* a diuretic is a drug designed to promote production of urine; a 'composing draught' is a sedative.

7 *The frenzy . . . way* Keats's *Poems* (1817) had a reasonable press from the reviewers; of the six notices, three were by friends, and the remainder were favourable.

8 *the calm, settled . . . Endymion* By the time Lockhart's essay appeared, *Endymion* (1818) had been given short shrift by a number of reviewers, including the *British Critic* and the *Quarterly Review*.

9 *The readers . . . Cockaigne* Lockhart refers to Hunt's article, 'Young Poets', in the *Examiner* for 1 December 1817, in which he presented to his readers the work of Shelley, John Hamilton Reynolds and Keats. It is true that this article confirmed Keats in his desire to be a poet. 'Cockaigne' is Lockhart's view of literary London – characterized by effeminacy, bad taste and loose morals.

10 *affected* mannered.

11 Leigh Hunt composed *Rimini* largely in prison, having been successfully prosecuted for libelling the Prince Regent. For more detail, and an extract from *Rimini*, see pp. 792, 796.

The absurdity of the thought in this sonnet is, however, if possible, surpassed in another, 'addressed to Haydon'[12] the painter – that clever but most affected artist, who as little resembles Raphael[13] in genius as he does in person, notwithstanding the foppery of having his hair curled over his shoulders in the old Italian fashion. In this exquisite piece it will be observed that Mr Keats classes together Wordsworth, Hunt, and Haydon as the three greatest spirits of the age, and that he alludes to himself, and some others of the rising brood of Cockneys, as likely to attain hereafter an equally honourable elevation.[14] Wordsworth and Hunt! What a juxtaposition! The purest, the loftiest, and, we do not fear to say it, the most classical of living English poets, joined together in the same compliment with the meanest, the filthiest, and the most vulgar of Cockney poetasters. No wonder that he who could be guilty of this should class Haydon with Raphael, and himself with Spenser.[15]

[Quotes 'Addressed to Haydon' (see p. 1343), italicizing ll. 5–6 and 13–15.]

The nations are to listen and be dumb! And why, good Johnny Keats? Because Leigh Hunt is editor of the *Examiner*, and Haydon has painted the judgement of Solomon,[16] and you and Cornelius Webb, and a few more city sparks, are pleased to look upon yourselves as so many future Shakespeares and Miltons! The world has really some reason to look to its foundations! Here is a *tempestas in matulâ*[17] with a vengeance. At the period when these sonnets were published, Mr Keats had no hesitation in saying that he looked on himself as 'not yet a glorious denizen of the wide heaven of poetry',[18] but he had many fine soothing visions of coming greatness, and many rare plans of study to prepare him for it. The following we think is very pretty raving.

[Quotes ll. 98–121 of 'Sleep and Poetry'.]

Having cooled a little from this 'fine passion', our youthful poet passes very naturally into a long strain of foaming abuse against a certain class of English poets, whom, with Pope at their head, it is much the fashion with the ignorant unsettled pretenders of the present time to undervalue.[19] Begging these gentlemen's pardon, although Pope was not a poet of the same high order with some who are now living, yet, to deny his genius, is just about as absurd as to dispute that of Wordsworth, or to believe in that of Hunt. Above all things, it is pitiably ridiculous to hear men, of whom their country will always have reason to be proud, reviled by uneducated and flimsy striplings, who are not capable of understanding either merits, or those of any other *men of power* – fanciful dreaming tea-drinkers who, without logic enough to analyse a single idea, or imagination enough to form one original image, or learning enough to distinguish between

Notes

[12] See p. 1343.

[13] *resembles Raphael* a mean-spirited reference to 'Addressed to Haydon' 8, which mentions 'Raphael's whispering'.

[14] *alludes to himself . . . honourable elevation* Lockhart refers to 'Addressed to Haydon' 9–10: 'And other spirits there are standing apart / Upon the forehead of the age to come.' In fairness, Keats does not say that one of them is himself.

[15] *himself with Spenser* probably a reference to Keats's 'Specimen of an Induction to a Poem' 55–7:

> Therefore, great bard, I not so fearfully
> Call on thy gentle spirit to hover nigh
> My daring steps . . .

[16] Haydon painted 'The Judgement of Solomon' 1812–14, now at Plymouth Museum and Art Gallery.

[17] *tempestas in matulâ* storm in a pisspot.

[18] *not yet . . . of poetry* a paraphrase of Keats's 'Sleep and Poetry' 47–9:

> O Poesy! For thee I hold my pen
> That am not yet a glorious denizen
> Of thy wide heaven.

[19] Lockhart refers to 'Sleep and Poetry' 181–206, which criticizes use of the heroic couplet by eighteenth-century poets, but does not single out Pope:

> with a puling infant's force
> They swayed about upon a rocking horse
> And thought it Pegasus. (ll. 185–7)

the written language of Englishmen and the spoken jargon of Cockneys, presume to talk with contempt of some of the most exquisite spirits the world ever produced, merely because they did not happen to exert their faculties in laborious affected descriptions of flowers seen in window-pots, or cascades heard at Vauxhall;[20] in short, because they chose to be wits, philosophers, patriots, and poets, rather than to found the Cockney school of versification, morality, and politics, a century before its time. . . .

So much for the opening bud; now for the expanded flower. It is time to pass from the juvenile *Poems* to the mature and elaborate *Endymion: A Poetic Romance*. The old story of the moon falling in love with a shepherd, so prettily told by a Roman classic,[21] and so exquisitely enlarged and adorned by one of the most elegant of German poets,[22] has been seized upon by Mr John Keats, to be done with as might seem good unto the sickly fancy of one who never read a single line either of Ovid or of Wieland. If the quantity, not the quality, of the verses dedicated to the story is to be taken into account, there can be no doubt that Mr John Keats may now claim Endymion entirely to himself.

To say the truth, we do not suppose either the Latin or the German poet would be very anxious to dispute about the property of the hero of the 'Poetic Romance'. Mr Keats has thoroughly appropriated the character, if not the name. His Endymion is not a Greek shepherd loved by a Grecian goddess; he is merely a young Cockney[23] rhymester dreaming a fantastic dream at the full of the moon. Costume, were it worthwhile to notice such a trifle, is violated in every page of this goodly octavo.[24] From his prototype Hunt,[25] John Keats has acquired a sort of vague idea that the Greeks were a most tasteful people, and that no mythology can be so finely adapted for the purposes of poetry as theirs. It is amusing to see what a hand the two Cockneys make of this mythology: the one confesses that he never read the Greek tragedians, and the other knows Homer only from Chapman[26] – and both of them write about Apollo, Pan, nymphs, muses and mysteries as might be expected from persons of their education. We shall not, however, enlarge at present upon this subject, as we mean to dedicate an entire paper to the classical attainments and attempts of the Cockney poets.

As for Mr Keats' *Endymion*, it has just as much to do with Greece as it has with 'old Tartary the fierce'.[27] No man whose mind has ever been imbued with the smallest knowledge or feeling of classical poetry or classical history, could have stooped to profane and vulgarize every association in the manner which has been adopted by this 'son of promise'. Before giving any extracts, we must inform our readers that this romance is meant to be written in English heroic rhyme. To those who have read any of Hunt's poems, this hint might indeed be needless; Mr Keats has adopted the loose, nerveless versification and Cockney rhymes of the poet of *Rimini*.[28] But in fairness to that gentleman, we must add that the defects of the system are tenfold more

Notes

[20] The Vauxhall pleasure-gardens on the south bank of the Thames contained ruins, arches, statues, a cascade, a music-room, Chinese pavilions and a Gothic orchestra space accommodating fifty musicians.

[21] *The old story . . . classic* Endymion was a shepherd king of Elis who asked Jupiter to make him ever young. Diana, virgin goddess of the moon, saw him lying naked on Mt Latmus and fell in love with him. In time she bore him fifty daughters. His story had been told by the Greek writers Apollodorus and Pausanias, but Lockhart seems to have in mind the retelling by Ovid, who was in fact one of Keats's sources.

[22] Christoph Martin Wieland (1733–1813), whose *Oberon* incorporated the story of Endymion and gained popularity in England through William Sotheby's translation (1798).

[23] *Cockney* usually applied to anyone born within the sound of Bow Bells, but Lockhart and Wilson redefined it to apply to lower-middle-class vulgarity (as they saw it), lasciviousness, radicalism and aesthetic lack of taste (among other things).

[24] *octavo* the format in which the book was published, taken from the fact that its pages were made from a folio sheet folded three times, so as to create eight leaves.

[25] *his prototype Hunt* Lockhart's point is that Keats is a pale imitation of Hunt.

[26] *know Homer only from Chapman* a sarcastic reference to Keats's 'On First Looking into Chapman's Homer' (p. 1342).

[27] *old Tartary the fierce* a quotation from *Endymion* iv 262

[28] Leigh Hunt, *The Story of Rimini* was published in February 1816

conspicuous in his disciple's work than in his own. Mr Hunt is a small poet, but he is a clever man. Mr Keats is a still smaller poet, and he is only a boy of pretty[29] abilities, which he has done everything in his power to spoil. . . .

We had almost forgot to mention that Keats belongs to the Cockney School of Politics, as well as the Cockney School of Poetry.

It is fit that he who holds *Rimini* to be the first poem should believe *The Examiner*[30] to be the first politician of the day. We admire consistency, even in folly. Hear how their bantling[31] has already learned to lisp sedition.

[Quotes *Endymion* iii 1–23.]

And now good morrow to 'the muses' son of promise'; as for 'the feats he yet may do', as we do not pretend to say, like himself, 'Muse of my native land am I inspired',[32] we shall adhere to the safe old rule of *pauca verba*.[33] We venture to make one small prophecy: that his bookseller will not a second time venture £50 upon anything he can write.[34] It is a better and a wiser thing to be a starved apothecary than a starved poet; so back to the shop Mr John, back to 'plasters, pills, and ointment boxes',[35] etc. But for heaven's sake, young Sangrado,[36] be a little more sparing of extenuatives and soporifics[37] in your practice than you have been in your poetry.

Notes

[29] *pretty* satisfactory. Not a compliment.

[30] A radical journal edited by Leigh Hunt and his brother John, 1808–21 (see p. 792).

[31] *bantling* bastard.

[32] *Muse of . . . inspired* from Keats, *Endymion* iv 354 But the line is much more tentative in context: it concludes with a question mark, which Lockhart deliberately omits.

[33] *pauca verba* few words.

[34] *bookseller . . . he can write* Keats's publishers were John Taylor (1781–1864) and James Augustus Hessey (1785–1870). They strongly resented this imputation, although reviews such as this one depressed Keats's sales; see headnote, p. 1327.

[35] *plasters . . . boxes* Nicholas Roe points out that this is a mocking allusion to the Apothecaries Act of 1815, in which 'the art and mystery of apothecaries' was defined as extending to 'medicines simple or compound, wares, drugs, receipts, distilled waters, chemical oils, syrups, conserves, lohocks, electuaries, pills, powders, lozenges, oils, ointments, plaisters'. Roe concludes that in this light Lockhart's attack 'was directed more broadly at the new professionalism of medicine, codified by the Act, and the enhanced social status which was thus acquired by medical practitioners' (*John Keats and the Culture of Dissent* (Oxford, 1997), p. 162).

[36] *Sangrado* in Le Sage's *Gil Blas*, a physician whose sole remedies were bleeding and the drinking of hot water; often applied to quack doctors of any kind.

[37] *extenuatives and soporifics* diet and sleeping pills.

John Keats (1795–1821)

> Mr Keats is also dead. He gave the greatest promise of genius of any poet of his day. He displayed extreme tenderness, beauty, originality and delicacy of fancy; all he wanted was manly strength and fortitude to reject the temptations of singularity in sentiment and expression. Some of his shorter and later pieces are, however, as free from faults as they are full of beauties. (Hazlitt, *Select British Poets*, 1824)

Of the major Romantic poets, Keats was the last to be born and the first to die, at the early age of 25. Had any of the other writers in this volume died at such an early age, we would regard them as little more than promising – for the simple fact that poets mature late, often around the age of 30. In achieving what he did, in terms of both magnitude and quality, Keats demonstrated almost unparalleled precocity. Fearing that he did not have long to live, he laboured furiously, developed with abnormal rapidity and, in what time he had, produced some of the finest poetry of the period (see Plate 17).

He was born on 31 October 1795, in Finsbury, north London, the eldest child of Thomas Keats, head ostler at the Swan and Hoop, Moorgate, and Frances Jennings. They were not working-class, as is sometimes suggested, but a fairly well-to-do, respectable, middle-class family. From the very beginning Keats knew he wanted to be a poet, declaring as much from the time he could speak.[1] Brothers George and Tom were born in 1797 and 1799, his sister Fanny in 1803. But like many of their time, they were soon orphaned, for in 1804 their father died after falling from his horse, and in 1810 their mother died from consumption.

From 1803 Keats attended the Enfield school run by the Revd John Clarke, whose son, Charles Cowden Clarke, became a lifelong friend. Clarke later remembered him as having a highly retentive memory, and as reading the entire contents of the school library, 'which consisted principally of abridgements of all the voyages and travels of any note; Mavor's collection, also his "Universal History"; Robertson's histories of Scotland, America, and Charles the Fifth; all Miss Edgeworth's productions, together with many other works equally well calculated for youth'.[2] Nicholas Roe suggests that a number of republican authors were also in the school library, which together with Leigh Hunt's liberal newspaper, *The Examiner* (which Clarke says Keats read at Enfield), exerted a strong influence on his political opinions.[3]

With the deaths of his parents it became imperative that Keats find a trade, and in summer 1811 he left school to become a physician. He began as apprentice to Thomas Hammond, a doctor in Edmonton (two miles to the south of Enfield), who taught him how to give vaccinations for smallpox, bleed patients with a lancet or leeches, dress wounds, set bones, pull teeth, diagnose illnesses, make up pills, ointments, poultices and other medicines. He did well enough to register as a student at Guy's Hospital in October 1815, a month short of his twentieth birthday. He made rapid progress: four weeks into his studies he was appointed dresser to Mr Lucas, one of the hospital surgeons, and in July 1816 he was awarded a licence to practise by the Court of Apothecaries. During this period he continued to write; a fellow-student at Guy's recalled that in

Notes

John Keats

[1] According to Benjamin Robert Haydon, *The Diary of Benjamin Robert Haydon* ed. Willard Bissell Pope (5 vols, Cambridge, Mass., 1960–3), ii 107.

[2] Charles and Mary Cowden Clarke, *Recollections of Writers* (Fontwell, 1969), pp. 123–4.

[3] See Nicholas Roe, *Keats and the Culture of Dissent* (Oxford, 1997), chapter 1.

Figure 17 A View of Cheapside in the City of London, by T. M. Baynes after W. Duryer, published 11 December 1823. A view known to all of the Romantics. Keats lived at 76 Cheapside before moving to Hampstead with his brothers in March 1817. (Guildhall Library, Corporation of London.)

the lecture room 'I have seen Keats in a deep poetic dream: his mind was on Parnassus with the muses.'[4]

In mid-October 1816, he began the long climb up Parnassus when he was introduced to Leigh Hunt on the gentle slopes of Hampstead Heath. It was an encounter that changed his life. 'We became intimate on the spot,' Hunt recalled, 'and I found the young poet's heart as warm as his imagination.'[5] More than a decade older than Keats, Hunt was an established writer eager to form a coterie of like-minded souls with shared ideological convictions, prepared to engage in intellectual and cultural discourse, both in person and in print. For his part, Keats had reached the point at which he needed a mentor, someone to help him refine, develop and promote his talent. Hunt would give Keats access to a host of cultural arbiters – Shelley, Lamb, Hazlitt, John Scott (who would become editor of the *London Magazine*), Charles and James Ollier (who would publish Keats's first book of poems) and Benjamin Robert Haydon, among others.

Hunt lived in the Vale of Health in Hampstead, in a white cottage full of music, pictures, busts of poets, flowers and books. Keats was soon a 'familiar of the household, and was always welcomed'.[6] He fell into the habit of sleeping on the sofa in Hunt's library where, awakening one morning, he began to compose 'Sleep and Poetry', probably in October or November 1816:

> What is more gentle than a wind in summer?
> What is more soothing than the pretty hummer
> That stays one moment in an open flower
> And buzzes cheerily from bower to bower?
> (ll. 1–4)

It is worth comparing these lines with Hunt's *Rimini* (pp. 796–801); the feminine rhymes, fey diction (the 'hummer' is a 'bee') and unashamed use of such adjectives as 'pretty' conform to what critics termed Hunt's 'namby-pamby' poetics. Hunt believed that poetry was the vehicle of pleasure – or, to use his term, 'luxury'. 'We should consider ourselves as what we really are: creatures made to enjoy more than to know,' he wrote in *Foliage* (1818), adding, 'I write to enjoy myself.'[7] This belief in the ornamental, pleasure-giving function of poetry was at first a powerful influence on Keats. Although it has often been the occasion of criticism, Hunt's patronage enabled him to develop with unprecedented speed.

Not long afterwards, Keats relinquished his medical studies in order to devote himself to poetry. Towards the end of 1816 he broke the news to his guardian, Richard Abbey. 'Not intend to be a surgeon!' said Abbey, 'Why, what do you mean to be?' 'I mean to rely on my abilities as a poet.' 'John, you are either mad or a fool to talk in so absurd a manner.' 'My mind is made up. I know that I possess abilities greater than most men, and therefore I am determined to gain my living by exercising them.'[8] Abbey is said to have called him a 'Silly Boy', and prophesied a 'speedy termination to his inconsiderate enterprise'.

But there was encouragement too. On 1 December *The Examiner* published an article by Hunt entitled 'Young Poets', which praised Keats alongside Shelley: 'He has not yet published any thing except in a newspaper; but a set of his manuscripts was handed us the other day, and fairly surprised us with the truth of their ambition, and ardent grappling with Nature.' It concluded with the complete text of 'On First Looking into Chapman's Homer'.[9] While reading it on the day of its appearance Hunt was inspired to compose 'To John Keats' (p. 803).

Keats met Shelley at Hunt's cottage in December 1816, and shortly after read his 'Hymn to Intellectual Beauty' in manuscript, which Hunt

Notes

[4] W. C. Dendy, *The Philosophy of Mystery* (1841), p. 99.

[5] Leigh Hunt, *Lord Byron and Some of his Contemporaries* (2 vols, London, 1828), i 410.

[6] Charles and Mary Cowden Clarke, *Recollections of Writers* (Fontwell, 1969), p. 133.

[7] Leigh Hunt, *Foliage* (1818), pp. 16, 18.

[8] *Keats Circle* i 307–8.

[9] [Leigh Hunt], 'Young Poets', *The Examiner* 1 December 1816, p. 761.

was to publish in *The Examiner* early the following year (for text see p. 1071). At this point, Shelley was living in Bath with Mary Godwin, in the wake of the death of his first wife, Harriet Westbrook. When he moved to Marlow in Buckinghamshire in February 1817, he invited Keats to visit, but Keats declined in order that 'I might have my own unfettered scope.'[10] Evidently, he feared that Shelley might prove too overbearing an influence, perhaps because he felt that one mentor was enough. Keats would engage in a last sonnet-writing competition with him, shortly before Shelley left for the Continent in February 1818.

Hunt and Keats celebrated the publication of Keats's *Poems* on 1 March 1817 by breaking open a bottle of wine in Hunt's garden and crowning each other with garlands of ivy (Hunt) and laurel (Keats). They then wrote commemorative sonnets upon the occasion; Hunt was sufficiently unashamed to publish them in *Foliage*. But first, his own critical opinion on Keats's first book was called for, and in June and July he published a three-part review in *The Examiner*, which began by hailing Keats as 'a young poet indeed' before pointing out his faults ('a tendency to notice everything too indiscriminately and without an eye to natural proportion and effect; and second, a sense of the proper variety of versification without a due consideration of its principles') and 'beauties', to which the third instalment was dedicated. 'Happy Poetry Preferred', reads the heading given by Hunt to an extract from 'Sleep and Poetry'. It was hugely patronizing. Perhaps the most insulting stroke was his use of Keats's 'smiling Muse' as a means of criticizing 'the morbidity that taints the productions of the Lake Poets'.[11]

By then the friendship had begun to cool. A month before, Keats said in a letter that Hunt had flattered himself 'into an idea of being a great poet'.[12] The use of his poems as ammunition for an attack on Wordsworth must have enraged him. Keats was an admirer of Wordsworth: he loved 'Tintern Abbey', and despite reservations about *The Excursion* (1814) was awestruck by it. For him, Wordsworth succeeded in incorporating the hardships and vicissitudes of the world into a transcendent vision, as he told John Hamilton Reynolds on 3 May 1818:

> We no sooner get into the second chamber, which I shall call the chamber of maiden thought, than we become intoxicated with the light and the atmosphere, we see nothing but pleasant wonders, and think of delaying there forever in delight. However, among the effects this breathing is father of, is that tremendous one of sharpening one's vision into the heart and nature of man, of convincing one's nerves that the world is full of misery and heartbreak, pain, sickness, and oppression – whereby this chamber of maiden thought becomes gradually darkened and, at the same time, on all sides of it many doors are set open – but all dark, all leading to dark passages. We see not the balance of good and evil. We are in a mist. *We* are now in that state. We feel the 'burden of the mystery'. To this point was Wordsworth come, as far as I can conceive, when he wrote 'Tintern Abbey', and it seems to me that his genius is explorative of those dark passages. (See p. 1353)

'Tintern Abbey' marks Wordsworth's artistic coming of age. It looks back to the time when nature 'To me was all in all', in favour of the present of July 1798, when that love is qualified by 'The still sad music of humanity'. At its heart is a definition of artistic maturity, one tempered by 'misery and heartbreak, pain, sickness, and oppression', to which Keats was always to aspire.[13] If this was 'morbidity', he

Notes

[10] Rollins i 170.

[11] [Leigh Hunt], *The Examiner* 1 June, 6 July, 13 July 1817, pp. 345, 428–9, 443–4.

[12] Rollins i 143.

[13] For more on Keats's reading of Wordsworth, see Beth Lau, *Keats's Reading of the Romantic Poets* (Ann Arbor, Mich., 1991), chapter 1.

recognized it as the key to Wordsworth's poetic achievement.

Wordsworth's influence is evident in *Endymion* (see p. 1344), on which Keats worked throughout the spring and summer of 1817, particularly in its 'Hymn to Pan', composed on 26 April. It shows him exploring the possibility of the heroic couplet in ways that reveal a new concentration and power derived from Wordsworth and Shakespeare. The 'Hymn' was the strongest evidence thus far that Keats would turn into the author of the 1819 Odes. Shelley was among those who recognized its quality, but not Wordsworth, who expressed his opinion of it when introduced to Keats in London, as Haydon recalled:

> Wordsworth received him kindly, and after a few minutes Wordsworth asked him what he had been lately doing. I said, 'He has just finished an exquisite Ode to Pan', and as he had not a copy I begged Keats to repeat it, which he did in his usual half-chant (most touching), walking up and down the room. When he had done I felt, really, as if I had heard a young Apollo. Wordsworth drily said, 'a very pretty piece of Paganism'.[14]

Biographers continue to dispute Keats's reaction to this. He saw a good deal of Wordsworth at this period, and it seems unlikely that he took it to heart. Their encounter at the 'immortal dinner' at the end of the year seems to have been friendly and cordial (see pp. 834–5).

While working on *Endymion,* Keats continued to develop his ideas about creativity, which were influenced by Hazlitt's essay 'On Gusto', reprinted from *The Examiner* in Hazlitt and Hunt's *The Round Table* (1817). 'How is Hazlitt?' he asked Reynolds in September 1817, 'We were reading his *Table* last night. I know he thinks himself not estimated by ten people in the world. I wish he knew he is.'[15]

Hazlitt's starting-point is that 'Gusto in art is power or passion defining any object.' For him, works of art are ratified by the emotional conviction of their creators; indeed, their success depends on it. Hazlittian gusto is what Keats terms 'imagination': for Keats, it gave the artist access to a heightened reality which he called 'truth'. That reality was intensified beyond the level of everyday experience – idealized and exemplary (or 'true'). Where he differed from Hazlitt was in his belief that the artist had to be a kind of chameleon, capable of abnegating the self and assuming the emotions and character of any other thing or person. Hazlitt, who was a great believer in the egotistical sublime of Wordsworth – in 'genius' – does not license this. In fact he thought of genius and gusto as identical. Keats's problem with it must have had something to do with his increasing tendency to reject Hunt, whose claims to genius he found irritating and absurd. For Keats, the imagination worked where the self was submerged in an act of what he called 'negative capability'.

> A poet is the most unpoetical of any thing in existence, because he has no identity, he is continually in for – and filling – some other body. The sun, the moon, the sea, and men and women who are creatures of impulse, are poetical, and have about them an unchangeable attribute; the poet has none, no identity – he is certainly the most unpoetical of all God's creatures. (See p. 1375)

It is crucial to Keats that the poet lose all sense of self in imaginative engagement with his subject. And he goes further:

> What the imagination seizes as beauty must be truth, whether it existed before or not. For I have the same idea of all our passions as of love: they are all in their sublime, creative of essential beauty . . . The imagination may be compared to Adam's dream: he awoke and found it truth. (See p. 1349)

Emerging from an imaginative experience in which he has 'lost' awareness of the self, the

Notes

[14] *Keats Circle* ii 143–4.

[15] Rollins i 166.

poet 'awakens' to an apprehension he would not otherwise have been granted – the reality ('essential beauty') of the thing created by his negatively capable imagination. The point about that 'essential beauty' (equivalent to 'truth') is that it derives from the otherness of something distinct and separate from the artist's ego. Even so, it may not be external to the poet, having the same relation to him as Eve did to Adam.

Keats states that the artist who negates himself in the creation of something other is 'capable of being in uncertainties, mysteries, doubts, without any irritable reaching after fact and reason'.[16] Coleridge had once been such a poet, but the middle-aged man Keats once encountered on Hampstead Heath seemed to be following rational, logical trains of thought ('consequitive reasoning', in Keats's words), discoursing at length on 'a thousand things' with barely a glance in his direction: 'I heard his voice as he came towards me – I heard it as he moved away – I had heard it all the interval' (see p. 1389).

By the time Keats finished *Endymion* the Cockney School attacks were under way, and he knew that he would soon be their chief target. Rather than brood on it, he set out on a walking tour of the Lake District and Scotland with his friend Charles Brown in the summer of 1818. One of his aims was to visit Wordsworth at Rydal Mount, but he was shaken to discover that Wordsworth was not at home because there was a general election under way, and he was campaigning on behalf of the Tory Lord Lowther. It was a disappointing reminder of how the middle-aged poet had sold out to the conservative establishment.

Keats and Brown walked round Derwentwater and climbed Skiddaw before crossing the border into Dumfries, then headed north to Inverary, and then Oban, towards the western Highlands, where the dominant language was Gaelic. But the weather was variable, and after climbing Ben Nevis on 2 August Keats realized that he was suffering from tonsillitis and decided to return home. He arrived in London to find his brother Tom suffering from tuberculosis in its advanced stages, and would nurse him until his death. That gave him a perspective from which to view Lockhart's Cockney School attack on him when it appeared in early September (see pp. 1327–31). It was the kind of onslaught that might have finished off a lesser talent, but instead it galvanized Keats into further composition, this time 'Hyperion: A Fragment', on which he worked until Tom's death on 1 December.

The new poem aspired, Keats said, to 'a more naked and grecian manner' (Rollins i 207). By this he meant he wanted to purge his poetry of Huntian sentimentality, which he now saw as the main flaw in *Endymion*. Instead, his new theme was loss and suffering, which he hoped would draw him closer to Wordsworth and Milton. 'Hyperion' follows the exile of the Titans, pre-Hellenic gods, by their children, led by Jupiter. As the poem opens Saturn and the Titans are already defeated and in despair, except for Hyperion, god of the sun, who is still in power and in Books I and II attempts to rouse them to action. In Book III Apollo enters, in the midst of being transformed into the god of the sun, music, healing and prophecy, by the Titan goddess, Mnemosyne (who has changed sides): 'Knowledge enormous makes a god of me,' Apollo tells her (iii 113). Keats's friend Richard Woodhouse noted that 'The poem, if completed, would have treated of the dethronement of Hyperion, the former god of the sun, by Apollo (and incidentally of those of Oceanus by Neptune, of Saturn by Jupiter, etc., and of the war of the giants for Saturn's reestablishment), with other events of which we have but very dark hints in the mythological poets of Greece and Rome. In fact, the incidents would have been pure creations of the poet's brain.'[17] For Keats, the appeal of the story was

Notes

[16] See his letter to George and Tom Keats, 21 December 1817, pp. 1350–1.

[17] Written in Woodhouse's copy of *Endymion* (1818).

that Apollo's painful emergence and the despondency of the fallen Titans illustrated aspects of his artistic self.

Shelley, always a sensitive reader of his work, recognized its achievement as soon as he read it. He would have enjoyed the way in which it appeared to rewrite *Paradise Lost* in non-Christian terms: on 29 October 1820 he told Marianne Hunt that 'the fragment called "Hyperion" promises for him that he is destined to become one of the first writers of the age' (Jones ii 239). Never one of Keats's admirers, Byron moderated his usual severity when assessing 'Hyperion', partly because Keats had just died, and partly because he was writing to Shelley: 'The impression of "Hyperion" upon my mind was that it was the best of his works.'[18]

In late September 1818 the Tory *Quarterly Review* published a highly critical review of *Endymion* by John Wilson Croker. It was a meticulous and destructive analysis of Keats's diction and style, which began by arguing that he was 'a copyist of Mr Hunt, but he is more unintelligible, almost as rugged, twice as diffuse, and ten times more tiresome and absurd than his prototype who, though he impudently presumed to seat himself in the chair of criticism, and to measure his own poetry by his own standard, yet generally had a meaning.' Croker went on to suggest that Keats had mindlessly imbibed Hunt's aesthetic system, which had stifled what little native talent he possessed. As with the Cockney School attacks, Keats cannot have been pleased that he had been aligned with Hunt, but it would not be long before he dismissed the critics' animus with the calm certainty that 'I shall be among the English Poets after my death.'[19] This was in stark opposition to Shelley's belief that Croker's review led directly to the disease from which Keats was to die. Although Keats must have been hurt, he had the confidence to rise above it.

At this period he met the 18-year-old Fanny Brawne, who later recalled that 'His conversation was in the highest degree interesting, and his spirits good, excepting at moments when anxiety regarding his brother's health dejected them.' He must have felt both relieved and guilty when his brother Tom died less than two weeks after his nineteenth birthday on 1 December 1818. Work on 'Hyperion' came to an abrupt halt, but he was soon able to give attention to the rest of his life, on hold since he began nursing Tom. He spent Christmas with Fanny Brawne and her family, before going away to Chichester for a break in January 1819. Its medieval cathedral inspired a poem he had just begun – 'The Eve of St Agnes'. Although it was complete by 2 February, he revised it in September: few episodes illustrate so vividly the speed with which he was developing. The problem with the first version, as Keats saw it, was its 'smokeability' – in other words, the Huntian qualities singled out for attack by reviewers. He wanted to make it less obviously a vehicle of 'luxuries' by emphasizing the sense of suffering, death and the intensity of love. To that end he revised the last stanza so as to kill off Angela – 'dead, stiff and ugly' (as Woodhouse complained), and added a stanza to the bedroom scene so that 'as soon as Madeline has confessed her love, Porphyro winds by degrees his arm round her, presses breast to breast, and acts all the acts of a *bona fide* husband, while she fancies she is only playing the part of a wife in a dream.'

His publishers balked at the indecency, and dropped the new stanza for the 1820 printed text (though readers of this volume will find it in a footnote on p. 1386). Woodhouse says he challenged Keats over these alterations, saying that ladies would not wish to read such things (an

Notes

[18] Marchand viii 163. Byron had earlier attacked the 1820 volume, in correspondence with Murray, as 'Johnny Keats's *piss a bed* poetry' and 'the *Onanism* of poetry – something like the pleasure an Italian fiddler extracted out of being suspended daily by a streetwalker in Drury Lane' (Marchand vii 200, 217).

[19] Rollins i 394.

important matter, as the vast majority of poetry-readers were women); his response was that he wrote only for men.[20] (Manliness is one of the virtues emphasized by Hazlitt in the quotation with which this headnote begins.) It was not that he sought to be offensive for its own sake, but he was striving to emerge from under Hunt's shadow, to take his poetry into the world – one filled with death as well as ecstasy, the two often side by side.

Love and death-like suffering converge in 'La Belle Dame Sans Merci: A Ballad', a poem of April 1819 that may reflect Keats's increasingly frustrated feeling for Fanny Brawne, not to mention his reaction to the letters sent to his dying brother by a friend, Charles Wells, under the fictitious identity of a woman, Amena. Writing as Amena, Wells had tantalized Tom with thoughts that he, as her Knight, might be soothed and lulled by her. It was a horrible conceit that, Keats believed, hastened Tom's death, and so helped to shape the nightmarish view of love in 'La Belle Dame'. In the end the Knight is trapped forever on the cold hill's side in a landscape that speaks of sterility and unfulfilled desire.

The darkness of 'La Belle Dame' was symptomatic not merely of the distance he had travelled since the start of Hunt's patronage eighteen months before; it speaks of an awareness of the proximity of death, which suffused the great poetry on which he was about to embark. 'Ode to Psyche' was written in the days following its completion. Keats said that it:

> is the first and the only one with which I have taken even moderate pains. I have for the most part dashed off my lines in a hurry; this I have done leisurely. I think it reads the more richly for it, and will I hope encourage me to write other things in even a more peaceable and healthy spirit. You must recollect that Psyche was not embodied as a goddess before the time of Apuleius the Platonist, who lived after the Augustan age, and consequently the goddess was never worshipped or sacrificed to with any of the ancient fervour, and perhaps never thought of in the old religion. I am more orthodox than to let a heathen goddess be so neglected. (Rollins ii 105–6)

This 'Ode' is usually read in the light of Keats's statements of 21 April 1819 in the journal letter to the George Keatses (see pp. 1389–90). His reaction to Psyche's tribulations when he comes across her and Cupid is to wish to celebrate her 'experience' by establishing a temple to her in his mind. In that sense, his journal-letter entry for 21 April 1819 usefully explicates some of his concerns; just as the religions of the world have their gods, so he has Psyche. In some ways the poem's most significant achievement is its stanzaic structure, derived from experiments with the sonnet, used throughout the remaining Odes.

It is not certain which poem Keats composed next. 'Ode to a Nightingale' is usually placed before 'Ode on a Grecian Urn' (as here), but John Barnard has argued for the reverse order. The 'Ode to a Nightingale' (written at Charles Brown's house in Hampstead) turns to the nature of artistic endeavour, which while aspiring to the immortal status of the bird's song is seen as limited by human mortality. And yet, the intensity of the poet's response, as he is swept into a 'vision, or a waking dream', reminds us that it exemplifies the 'essential beauty' to which his art aspires. It comprises the ultimate model of the creative process.

'Ode on a Grecian Urn' declares its preoccupation with artistic endeavour in its title, taking as its conceit the idea that the figures and places depicted on the vase are painted with such gusto that they have lives of their own. Keats is thus able to write of the lovers 'For ever panting and for ever young', and of the heifer with its 'silken flanks with garlands dressed'. It is not merely a matter of acknowledging the illusory nature of great art; Keats admits us into the vision of the negatively capable artist who leaves no trace of

Notes

[20] For Woodhouse's important account see pp. 1041–2.

himself, his ego submerged within the vitality of the objects he depicted.

There is a dark potency about the 'Ode on Melancholy', in which Keats is reminded of the presence of death behind even the 'peerless' beauty of his 'mistress', and which paves the way for the 'Ode on Indolence', in which he turns to himself, and meditates on the unsettling visitation of 'three ghosts' – Love, Ambition and Poesy.

By the end of June 1819, Keats had reached some kind of understanding with Fanny Brawne – not an engagement, exactly, more an expression of intent – before leaving for the Isle of Wight, where he began 'Lamia', which he would complete at Winchester in early autumn. Based on a story he had come across in Burton's *Anatomy of Melancholy*, it heralded a renewed attempt to escape the mawkishness and 'smokeability' of Cockney School aesthetics. In particular, he aspired to an objectivity lacking from earlier poems – a more negatively capable work. The defect of 'The Eve of St Agnes', he feared, was his identification with its characters. In 'Lamia' he would strive to tell the story as clearly and objectively as he could.

He knew Coleridge's 'Christabel' (published in 1816), as well as the definition of the lamia from Lemprière's classical dictionary: 'Certain monsters of Africa, who had the face and breast of a woman, and the rest of the body like that of a serpent. They allured strangers to them, that they might devour them, and though they were not endowed with the faculty of speech, yet their hissings were pleasing and agreeable.' Keats makes his lamia more sympathetic; she does not devour small children (as Lemprière advised), and possesses something of the glamour of Coleridge's Geraldine. The appeal of the narrative borrowed from Burton (quoted p. 1403n1) lay in the fact that it permitted Keats further to explore the difference between the 'consequitive' reasoner, and the artist or lover – in this case, Apollonius the philosopher, and Lycius. Apollonius is therefore less agreeable than in Burton, where he is the instigator of a successful witch-hunt. Furthermore, Keats adds Lycius' death which makes his fatal passion more than merely poignant; it is nearly tragic. He was fairly satisfied with 'Lamia', as he wrote in September 1819: 'I am certain there is that sort of fire in it which must take hold of people in some way – give them either pleasant or unpleasant sensation. What they want is a sensation of some sort.'[21] Keats's friend Woodhouse admired 'Lamia' when he heard it, as he told John Taylor: 'You may suppose all these events have given Keats scope for some beautiful poetry which, even in this cursory hearing of it, came every now and then upon me, and made me "start, as though a sea-nymph quired".'[22] Of all the various reactions, the most appreciative was that of Charles Lamb, whose review appeared in the *New Times*:

> More exuberantly rich in imagery and painting is the story of the Lamia. It is of as gorgeous stuff as ever romance was composed of. Her first appearance in serpentine form –
>
> a beauteous wreath with melancholy eyes[23] –
>
> her dialogue with Hermes, the *Star of Lethe*, as he is called by one of those prodigal phrases which Mr Keats abounds in, which are each a poem in a word, and which in this instance lays upon to us at once, like a picture, all the dim regions and their inhabitants, and the sudden coming of a celestial among them; the charming of her into woman's shape again by the God; her marriage with the beautiful Lycius; her magic palace, which those who knew the street, and remembered it complete from childhood, never

Notes

[21] Rollins ii 189.

[22] Rollins ii 165; Woodhouse quotes from the conclusion of Keats's sonnet 'On the Sea': 'Sit ye near some old cavern's mouth and brood / Until ye start, as if the sea-nymphs quired!'

[23] 'Lamia' i 84.

remembered to have seen before; the few Persian mutes, her attendants,

> – who that same year
> Were seen about the markets: none knew where
> They could inhabit;[24] –

the high-wrought splendours of the nuptial bower, with the fading of the whole pageantry, Lamia, and all, away, before the glance of Apollonius, – are all that fairy land can do for us. They are for younger impressibilities.[25]

Keats's last great ode, 'To Autumn', was written in mid-September in Winchester, shortly after completion of 'Lamia'. A day or two after, he told Reynolds:

> How beautiful the season is now, how fine the air. A temperate sharpness about it. Really, without joking, chaste weather – Dian skies. I never liked stubble fields so much as now. Aye better than the chilly green of the spring. Somehow a stubble plain looks warm – in the same way that some pictures look warm. This struck me so much in my Sunday's walk that I composed upon it. (Rollins ii 167)

'To Autumn' reveals Keats's talent at its most fully realized. He seems, without effort, to take us through the season, beginning with pre-harvest ripeness, moving to the repletion of harvest, before concluding with the following emptiness prior to the onset of winter. It progresses also through the senses, and the times of day.

In recent years the poem has generated controversy. Jerome J. McGann has criticized it for ignoring the political turmoil in English society and devoting himself to the idealized world of nature. It is, he argues, 'politically reactionary'.[26] This initiated a series of historicized readings of the poem, which repudiated McGann by reading it as a thinly veiled political statement – most notably by Andrew Bennett, Nicholas Roe and Andrew Motion.[27]

The two parts of 'Lamia' were interrupted so that Keats could work on a revised version of 'Hyperion', influenced by Milton (*Paradise Lost*) and Dante (*Inferno*). This time it was framed within a dream-vision, whereby Moneta would relate the Titans' fall, picking up the original narrative at line 294 of Canto I with the entrance of Saturn and Thea. 'The Fall of Hyperion' would not be published until 1857, and during the nineteenth century it had few admirers – but it is now recognized that the passages written for it show the fruits of his development over the preceding year. They show how critical Keats had become of the self-indulgent dreamer, instead favouring the poet for whom 'the miseries of the world / Are misery' (i 148–9). This was part of an increasing disillusionment with Byron, who falls into the category of 'mock lyrists, large self-worshippers / And careless hectorers in proud bad verse' (i 207–8).

Keats would write more, but nothing that would surpass the achievements of 1818–19. His enemy was time. In early February 1820, he collapsed on arrival at Wentworth Place in Hampstead, with a haemorrhage of the lungs. 'I know the colour of that blood,' he told Charles Brown, 'it is arterial blood. I cannot be deceived in that colour. That drop of blood is my death-warrant. I must die.' The story of what happened next is well known. He would release Fanny Brawne from their understanding and commence a long-drawn-out physical decline. His last lifetime volume, *Lamia, Isabella, The Eve of St Agnes, and Other Poems*, was published in July 1820. In September he travelled to Italy with his friend Joseph Severn in search of a warmer climate, only to die a few months after their arrival

Notes

24 'Lamia' i 390–2.

25 [Charles Lamb], *New Times* 19 July 1820; reprinted in *The Examiner*, 30 July 1820.

26 'Keats and the Historical Method in Literary Criticism', in *The Beauty of Inflections* (Oxford, 1979), pp. 51–62.

27 See Andrew Bennett, *Keats, Narrative, and Audience* (Cambridge, 1994), pp. 162–4; Nicholas Roe, *John Keats and the Culture of Dissent* (Oxford, 1997), pp. 254–67; Andrew Motion, *Keats* (London, 1997), pp. 460–2.

in Rome, 23 February 1821.[28] He was buried in the non-Catholic cemetery there three days later.- Unaware that his old friend was already dead, Leigh Hunt wrote to Severn at Rome, with a last request:

> Tell him – tell that great poet and noble-hearted man – that we shall all bear his memory in the most precious part of our hearts, and that the world shall bow their heads to it, as our loves do. Or if this, again, will trouble his spirit, tell him that we shall never cease to remember and love him; and that the most sceptical of us has faith enough in the high things that nature puts into our heads to think all who are of one accord in mind or heart are journeying to one and the same place, and shall unite somewhere or other again, face to face, mutually conscious, mutually delighted. Tell him he is only before us on the road, as he was in everything else; or whether you tell him the latter or no, tell him the former, and add that we shall never forget that he was so, and that we are coming after . . .

Within three years both Shelley and Byron would follow; the next thirteen years saw the deaths of Hazlitt, Lamb and Coleridge. Keats's death marked the beginning of the end of Romanticism.

Further reading

The standard scholarly edition of Keats's poems is that produced by Jack Stillinger in 1978, republished in revised form as a reading text in 1982. Miriam Allott's Longman Annotated Poets edition (1970) remains useful to students of Keats for its annotations, as does John Barnard's Penguin English Poets edition (1988).

John Barnard, *John Keats* (Cambridge, 1987).

Walter Jackson Bate, *John Keats* (London, 1979).

Andrew Bennett, *Keats, Narrative and Audience: The Posthumous Life of Writing* (Cambridge, 1994).

Cleanth Brooks, 'History Without Footnotes: An Account of Keats' Urn', in *The Well Wrought Urn* (New York, 1947).

The Cambridge Companion to Keats ed. Susan J. Wolfson (Cambridge, 2001).

John Jones, *John Keats's Dream of Truth* (London, 1969).

Keats and History ed. Nicholas Roe (Cambridge, 1995).

Christopher Ricks, *Keats and Embarrassment* (Oxford, 1974).

Nicholas Roe, *John Keats and the Culture of Dissent* (Oxford, 1997).

A Routledge Literary Sourcebook on the Poems of John Keats ed. John Strachan (London, 2003).

Stuart M. Sperry, *Keats the Poet* (Princeton, NJ, 1974).

Jack Stillinger, *The Hoodwinking of Madeline and Other Essays on Keats's Poetry* (Urbana, Ill., 1971).

Helen Vendler, *The Odes of John Keats* (Cambridge, Mass., 1983).

Robert Woof and Stephen Hebron, *John Keats* (Grasmere, 1995).

On First Looking into Chapman's Homer (composed October 1816)[1]

From Poems (1817)

Much have I travelled in the realms of gold,
    And many goodly states and kingdoms seen;
    Round many western islands have I been
Which bards in fealty to Apollo[2] hold.
Oft of one wide expanse had I been told

Notes

[28] The house where Keats died, 26 Piazza di Spagna, is now a museum preserved by the Keats-Shelley Memorial Association.

On First Looking into Chapman's Homer

[1] George Chapman (1559–1634) translated *The Whole Works of Homer* (1614). In October 1816 Charles Cowden Clarke was lent a copy and read through it with Keats one night. Keats returned to his lodgings in Dean Street at dawn the following morning, and had composed this poem by 10 o'clock. It was first published in *The Examiner*, 1 December 1816 (see headnote, p. 1334).

[2] Apollo is the god of poetry; bards are therefore bound in fealty to him.

That deep-browed Homer ruled as his demesne,[3]
Yet did I never breathe its pure serene[4]
Till I heard Chapman speak out loud and bold:
Then felt I like some watcher of the skies
When a new planet swims into his ken;
Or like stout Cortez[5] when with eagle eyes
He stared at the Pacific, and all his men
Looked at each other with a wild surmise –
Silent, upon a peak in Darien.[6]

Addressed to Haydon[1] (composed 19 November 1816)

From Poems (1817)

Great spirits now on earth are sojourning:[2]
He of the cloud, the cataract, the lake,
Who on Helvellyn's[3] summit, wide awake,
Catches his freshness from archangel's wing;
He of the rose, the violet, the spring,
The social smile, the chain for freedom's sake;[4]
And lo! whose steadfastness would never take
A meaner sound than Raphael's whispering.[5]
And other spirits there are standing apart
Upon the forehead of the age to come;
These, these will give the world another heart
And other pulses: hear ye not the hum
Of mighty workings?[6] ——
Listen awhile ye nations, and be dumb.

Notes

[3] *demesne* domain, kingdom.

[4] *serene* clear, bright sky (Latin *serenum* means a clear or bright sky).

[5] *Cortez* It was in fact Vasco Nuñez de Balboa (1475–1519) who was the first European to stand, in 1513, on that peak and see the Pacific (which he claimed for Spain). In 1519 Hernán Cortés (1485–1547) conquered Mexico for Spain and entered Mexico City for the first time.

[6] *Darien* is the region that connects Panama to Colombia.

On the Grasshopper and the Cricket

[1] *Haydon* the artist Benjamin Robert Haydon, for whom see pp. 833–4. Keats sent this poem to him in a letter, 20 November 1816, having dined with him the previous evening.

[2] Keats celebrates the achievement of Wordsworth (lines 2–4), Leigh Hunt (lines 5–6) and Haydon (lines 7–8). For Lockhart's criticism of this sonnet, see p. 1329.

[3] Helvellyn mountain towers over Grasmere (3,116 ft).

[4] *the chain for freedom's sake* a reference to Hunt's spell in jail for libelling the Prince Regent (p. 792).

[5] *whose steadfastness . . . Raphael's whispering* Obscurity is an element of Keats's early manner, and this is far from clear, as editors have observed. The overall meaning seems to be that Haydon's artistic ability rivals that of Raphael.

[6] The incompleteness of the line is deliberate, and was suggested by Haydon. It originally read: 'Of mighty workings in a distant mart?'

On the Grasshopper and the Cricket (composed 30 December 1816)[1]

From Poems (1817)

The poetry of earth is never dead:[2]
When all the birds are faint with the hot sun,
And hide in cooling trees, a voice will run
From hedge to hedge about the new-mown mead;
That is the Grasshopper's – he takes the lead
In summer luxury, he has never done
With his delights; for when tired out with fun
He rests at ease beneath some pleasant weed.
The poetry of earth is ceasing never:
On a lone winter evening, when the frost
Has wrought a silence,[3] from the stove there shrills
The Cricket's song, in warmth increasing ever,
And seems to one in drowsiness half lost,
The Grasshopper's among some grassy hills.

From *Endymion: A Poetic Romance, Book I* (extracts) (composed April–November 1817; published 1818)[1]

[*'A thing of beauty is a joy for ever'*]

A thing of beauty is a joy for ever:[2]
Its loveliness increases; it will never
Pass into nothingness, but still will keep
A bower quiet for us, and a sleep
Full of sweet dreams, and health, and quiet breathing.
Therefore, on every morrow, are we wreathing
A flowery band to bind us to the earth,
Spite of despondence, of the inhuman dearth
Of noble natures, of the gloomy days,
Of all the unhealthy and o'er-darkened ways
Made for our searching – yes, in spite of all,

Notes

ON THE GRASSHOPPER AND THE CRICKET

[1] This poem was the product of a sonnet-writing competition with Leigh Hunt; both sonnets were published in *The Examiner*, 21 September 1817; Hunt's can be seen on p. 801. Charles Cowden Clarke, who umpired the competition, said that 'Keats won as to time.'

[2] According to Charles Cowden Clarke, Leigh Hunt thought the first line was 'a preposterous opening'.

[3] *On a lone winter . . . a silence* When he first heard this line and a half, Hunt exclaimed 'Ah! That's perfect! Bravo Keats!' It is reminiscent of the opening of Coleridge's 'Frost at Midnight' (p. 624).

'A THING OF BEAUTY IS A JOY FOR EVER'

[1] Keats's mythological romance has attracted few supporters since its first publication. It is interesting both for the way in which it reveals Hunt's influence, and the indications it provides of Keats's development. See headnote, p. 1336.

[2] *A thing of beauty is a joy for ever* Keats's fellow-student at Guy's Hospital, Henry Stephens, who was present when this line was composed, recalled that it originally read: 'A thing of beauty is a constant joy.'

Some shape of beauty moves away the pall
From our dark spirits. Such the sun, the moon,
Trees old and young, sprouting a shady boon
For simple sheep; and such are daffodils
With the green world they live in; and clear rills
That for themselves a cooling covert make
'Gainst the hot season; the mid-forest brake,
Rich with a sprinkling of fair musk-rose[3] blooms;
And such too is the grandeur of the dooms[4]
We have imagined for the mighty dead,
All lovely tales that we have heard or read –
An endless fountain of immortal drink,
Pouring unto us from the heaven's brink.

[*Hymn to Pan*[1]]

Oh thou, whose mighty palace roof doth hang
From jagged trunks, and overshadoweth
Eternal whispers, glooms, the birth, life, death
Of unseen flowers in heavy peacefulness;
Who lov'st to see the hamadryads[2] dress
Their ruffled locks where meeting hazels darken,
And through whole solemn hours dost sit, and hearken
The dreary melody of bedded reeds
In desolate places, where dank moisture breeds
The pipy hemlock[3] to strange overgrowth;
Bethinking thee, how melancholy loath
Thou wast to lose fair Syrinx[4] – do thou now,
By thy love's milky brow,
By all the trembling mazes that she ran,
Hear us, great Pan!

Oh thou, for whose soul-soothing quiet, turtles[5]
Passion their voices[6] cooingly 'mong myrtles,[7]
What time thou wanderest at eventide
Through sunny meadows that outskirt the side
Of thine enmossed realms; oh thou, to whom

Notes

[3] *musk-rose* a rambling rose with white flowers and a characteristic scent.

[4] *dooms* destinies.

Hymn to Pan

[1] In spite of the fact that Wordsworth disparagingly told Keats that the 'Hymn to Pan' was 'a very pretty piece of Paganism', it looks forward to the mature style of the major 1819 odes; see headnote, p. 1336 above. Pan is the god of universal nature. The 'Hymn' was composed on 26 April 1817.

[2] *hamadryads* wood-nymphs fabled to live and die with the trees they inhabited.

[3] *pipy hemlock* poison hemlock has tall hollow stems.

[4] When Pan pursued Syrinx, she was changed into a reed.

[5] *turtles* turtle-doves.

[6] *Passion their voices* fill their voices with passion. The use of 'passion' as a verb follows Spenser's *Faerie Queene*, but was taken by reviewers to be a prime example of Cockney affectation.

[7] *myrtles* shrubs with shiny evergreen leaves and white sweet-scented flowers, sacred to Venus and used as an emblem of love.

Broad-leaved fig trees even now foredoom[8]
Their ripened fruitage, yellow-girted bees
Their golden honeycombs, our village leas
Their fairest-blossomed beans and poppied corn,
The chuckling[9] linnet its five young unborn
To sing for thee, low-creeping strawberries
Their summer coolness, pent-up butterflies[10]
Their freckled wings – yea, the fresh-budding year
All its completions; be quickly near,
By every wind that nods the mountain pine,[11]
Oh forester divine!

Thou, to whom every faun and satyr flies
For willing service, whether to surprise
The squatted hare[12] while in half-sleeping fit;
Or upward ragged precipices flit
To save poor lambkins from the eagle's maw;
Or by mysterious enticement draw
Bewildered shepherds to their path again;
Or to tread breathless round the frothy main,
And gather up all fancifullest shells
For thee to tumble into naiads'[13] cells,
And, being hidden, laugh at their out-peeping;
Or to delight thee with fantastic leaping,
The while they pelt each other on the crown
With silvery oak-apples, and fir-cones brown –
By all the echoes that about thee ring,
Hear us, oh satyr king!

Oh hearkener to the loud-clapping shears,
While ever and anon to his shorn peers
A ram goes bleating; winder of the horn,[14]
When snouted wild-boars routing[15] tender corn
Anger our huntsmen; breather round our farms,
To keep off mildews and all weather harms;
Strange ministrant of undescribed sounds,
That come a-swooning over hollow grounds
And wither drearily on barren moors;
Dread opener of the mysterious doors
Leading to universal knowledge – see,
Great son of Dryope,[16]
The many that are come to pay their vows
With leaves about their brows!

Be still the unimaginable lodge
For solitary thinkings; such as dodge

Notes

8 *foredoom* anticipate.
9 *chuckling* clucking.
10 *pent-up butterflies* butterflies still in chrysalis form.
11 *pine* emblem of Pan.
12 *squatted hare* the hare in its form.
13 *naiad* water-nymph.
14 *winder of the horn* one who blows the horn.
15 *routing* digging up (with the snout).
16 Keats follows Chapman's 'Hymn to Pan' which represents Pan as the son of Dryope and Hermes.

Conception to the very bourne[17] of heaven,
Then leave the naked brain; be still the leaven
That spreading in this dull and clodded earth
Gives it a touch ethereal,[18] a new birth;[19]
Be still a symbol of immensity,
A firmament reflected in a sea,
An element filling the space between,
An unknown – but no more. We humbly screen
With uplift hands our foreheads, lowly bending,
And giving out a shout most heaven-rending,
Conjure thee to receive our humble paean,[20]
Upon thy Mount Lycean![21]

[*The Pleasure Thermometer*[1]]

Wherein lies happiness? In that which becks[2]
Our ready minds to fellowship divine,
A fellowship with essence,[3] till we shine
Full alchemized,[4] and free of space. Behold
The clear religion[5] of heaven! Fold
A rose-leaf round thy finger's taperness
And soothe thy lips; hist, when the airy stress
Of music's kiss impregnates the free winds,
And with a sympathetic touch unbinds
Aeolian magic from their lucid wombs;[6]
Then old songs waken from enclouded[7] tombs,
Old ditties sigh above their father's grave,
Ghosts of melodious prophecyings rave
Round every spot where trod Apollo's foot;
Bronze clarions awake and faintly bruit[8]
Where long ago a giant battle[9] was;
And from the turf, a lullaby doth pass
In every place where infant Orpheus[10] slept.

Notes

[17] *bourne* boundary.

[18] *ethereal* divine.

[19] *Be still the unimaginable lodge . . . new birth* In his hostile review of *Endymion* in the *Quarterly Review* (April 1818), John Wilson Croker quoted these lines to support his charge that Keats 'seems to us to write a line at random, and then he follows not the thought excited by this line, but that suggested by the *rhyme* with which it concludes. . . . *Lodge, dodge – heaven, leaven – earth, birth*; such, in six words, is the sum and substance of six lines'.

[20] *paean* hymn of praise.

[21] Lycaeus was a mountain of Arcadia sacred to Pan.

The Pleasure Thermometer

[1] The 'thermometer' measures happiness by its intensity and selfless involvement; the four 'degrees', in ascending order, are (i) sensual enjoyment of nature (line 782); (ii) music (lines 783–94); (iii) friendship (lines 803–5); passion (lines 805–42). This passage is spoken by Endymion. Keats commented on it in his letter to John Taylor of 30 January 1818: 'The whole thing must, I think, have appeared to you, who are a consequitive man, as a thing almost of mere words. But I assure you that when I wrote it, it was a regular stepping of the Imagination towards a Truth. My having written that argument will perhaps be of the greatest service to me of anything I ever did. It set before me at once the gradations of happiness even like a kind of Pleasure Thermometer' (Rollins i 218).

[2] *becks* beckons.

[3] *essence* used as a synonym for 'a thing of beauty'.

[4] *alchemized* transformed, spiritualized.

[5] *religion* pronounced as four syllables.

[6] *when the airy stress . . . wombs* Keats is thinking of an Aeolian harp.

[7] *enclouded* dim, obscure.

[8] *bruit* proclaim.

[9] *a giant battle* between the Titans and the gods of Olympus, the background to 'Hyperion'.

[10] Orpheus was taught to play the lyre by Apollo, his father, and reached such skill that he could influence animate and inanimate nature by his music.

Feel we these things? That moment have we stepped
Into a sort of oneness, and our state
Is like a floating spirit's. But there are
Richer entanglements, enthralments far
More self-destroying,[11] leading, by degrees,
To the chief intensity: the crown of these
Is made of love and friendship, and sits high
Upon the forehead of humanity.
All its more ponderous and bulky worth
Is friendship, whence there ever issues forth
A steady splendour; but at the tip-top
There hangs by unseen film an orbed drop
Of light, and that is love. Its influence,
Thrown in our eyes, genders[12] a novel sense
At which we start and fret; till in the end,
Melting into its radiance, we blend,
Mingle, and so become a part of it –
Nor with aught else can our souls interknit
So wingedly. When we combine therewith,
Life's self is nourished by its proper pith,[13]
And we are nurtured like a pelican brood.[14]
Aye, so delicious is the unsating[15] food,
That men who might have towered in the van[16]
Of all the congregated world, to fan
And winnow from the coming step of time
All chaff of custom, wipe away all slime
Left by men-slugs and human serpentry,
Have been content to let occasion[17] die
Whilst they did sleep in love's Elysium.
And truly, I would rather be struck dumb
Than speak against this ardent listlessness;[18]
For I have ever thought that it might bless
The world with benefits unknowingly,
As does the nightingale, up-perched high,
And cloistered among cool and bunched leaves –
She sings but to her love, nor e'er conceives
How tiptoe night holds back her dark-grey hood.
Just so may love, although 'tis understood
The mere commingling[19] of passionate breath,
Produce more than our searching witnesseth:
What I know not – but who of men can tell
That flowers would bloom, or that green fruit would swell
To melting pulp, that fish would have bright mail,[20]

Notes

[11] *self-destroying* capable of negating our sense of self (a good thing in Keats; see headnote, p. 1336).

[12] *genders* creates.

[13] *proper pith* own substance.

[14] *a pelican brood* the pelican was said to feed its young with its own blood.

[15] *unsating* uncloying.

[16] *towered in the van* a military metaphor; had been foremost at the front of an attacking army.

[17] *occasion* ephemeral circumstance.

[18] *ardent listlessness* passionate suspension of self-consciousness, mystic trance.

[19] *commingling* intermingling.

[20] *bright mail* i.e. scales.

The earth its dower[21] of river, wood, and vale,
The meadows runnels,[22] runnels pebble-stones,
The seed its harvest, or the lute its tones,
Tones ravishment, or ravishment its sweet,
If human souls did never kiss and greet?

Letter from John Keats to Benjamin Bailey, 22 November 1817 (extract)[1]

I wish you knew all that I think about genius and the heart – and yet I think you are thoroughly acquainted with my innermost breast in that respect, or you could not have known me even thus long and still hold me worthy to be your dear friend. In passing, however, I must say of one thing that has pressed upon me lately and increased my humility and capability of submission, and that is this truth: men of genius are great as certain ethereal chemicals operating on the mass of neutral intellect – but they have not any individuality, any determined character. I would call the top and head of those who have a proper self, men of power.

But I am running my head into a subject which I am certain I could not do justice to under five years' study and 3 vols. octavo – and moreover long to be talking about the imagination. So, my dear Bailey, do not think of this unpleasant affair if possible – do not – I defy any harm to come of it – I defy – I shall write to Crips this week and request him to tell me all his goings-on from time to time by letter wherever I may be – it will all go on well. So don't, because you have suddenly discovered a coldness in Haydon,[2] suffer yourself to be teased. Do not, my dear fellow.

Oh, I wish I was as certain of the end of all your troubles as that of your momentary start about the authenticity of the imagination. I am certain of nothing but of the holiness of the heart's affections[3] and the truth of imagination. What the imagination seizes as beauty must be truth, whether it existed before or not. For I have the same idea of all our passions as of love: they are all, in their sublime, creative of essential beauty.[4] In a word, you may know my favourite speculation by my first book and the little song I sent in my last – which is a representation from the fancy of the probable mode of operating in these matters. The imagination may be compared to Adam's dream: he awoke and found it truth.[5] I am the more zealous in this affair because I have never yet been able to perceive how anything can be known for truth by consequitive[6] reasoning – and yet it must be. Can it be that even the greatest philosopher ever arrived at his goal without putting aside numerous objections? However it may be, oh for a life of sensations rather than of thoughts! It is 'a vision in the form of youth', a shadow of reality to come. And this consideration has further convinced me, for it has come as auxiliary to another favourite speculation of mine – that we shall enjoy ourselves hereafter by having what we called happiness on earth

Notes

[21] *dower* gift.

[22] *runnels* streams.

LETTER FROM JOHN KEATS TO BENJAMIN BAILEY

[1] This letter contains one of Keats's earliest, and most important, statements on the imagination. Benjamin Bailey (1791–1853) was an undergraduate at Oxford when John Hamilton Reynolds introduced him to Keats in spring 1817. Throughout September 1817 Keats shared Bailey's college quarters, and composed *Endymion* Book III there.

[2] Benjamin Robert Haydon, artist and friend of Keats; see pp. 833–4.

[3] *affections* feelings.

[4] *For I have . . . beauty* at their most sublime (i.e. intense and powerful), human emotions ('passions') apprehend the inherent beauty of the 'essences' they perceive.

[5] *The imagination . . . truth* Genesis 2: 21–2: 'And the Lord God caused a deep sleep to fall upon Adam, and he slept: and he took one of his ribs, and closed up the flesh instead thereof; And the rib, which the Lord God had taken from man, made he a woman, and brought her unto the man.' This episode was reworked in one of the most impressive passages of *Paradise Lost* viii 452–86.

[6] *consequitive* consecutive, logical, rational.

repeated in a finer tone and so repeated. And yet such a fate can only befall those who delight in sensation, rather than hunger as you do after truth; Adam's dream will do here, and seems to be a conviction that imagination and its empyreal reflection is the same as human life and its spiritual repetition. But as I was saying, the simple imaginative mind may have its rewards in the repetition of its own silent working coming continually on the spirit with a fine suddenness. To compare great things with small, have you never, by being surprised with an old melody in a delicious place by a delicious voice, felt over again your very speculations and surmises at the time it first operated on your soul? Do you not remember forming to yourself the singer's face more beautiful than it was possible, and yet with the elevation of the moment you did not think so? Even then, you were mounted on the wings of imagination so high that the prototype must be hereafter – that delicious face you will see! What a time!

I am continually running away from the subject. Sure this cannot be exactly the case with a complex mind, one that is imaginative and at the same time careful of its fruits, who would exist partly on sensation, partly on thought – to whom it is necessary that years should bring the philosophic mind.[7] Such an one I consider yours and therefore it is necessary to your eternal happiness that you not only drink this old wine of heaven, which I shall call the redigestion of our most ethereal musings on earth, but also increase in knowledge and know all things.

Letter from John Keats to George and Tom Keats, 21 December 1817 (extract)

I spent Friday evening with Wells[1] and went the next morning to see 'Death on the Pale Horse'.[2] It is a wonderful picture when West's age is considered, but there is nothing to be intense upon – no women one feels mad to kiss, no face swelling into reality.[3] The excellence of every art is its intensity, capable of making all disagreeables evaporate, from their being in close relationship with beauty and truth. Examine *King Lear* and you will find this exemplified throughout, but in this picture we have unpleasantness without any momentous depth of speculation excited, in which to bury its repulsiveness. The picture is larger than 'Christ Rejected'.[4]

I dined with Haydon the Sunday after you left, and had a very pleasant day. I dined too (for I have been out too much lately) with Horace Smith, and met his two brothers[5] with Hill and Kingston and one Dubois. They only served to convince me how superior humour is to wit in respect to enjoyment. These men say things which make one start without making one feel. They are all alike; their manners are alike; they all know fashionables; they have a mannerism in their very eating and drinking, in their mere handling a decanter. They talked of Kean[6] and his low company. Would I were with that company instead of yours, said I to myself! I know suchlike acquaintance will never do for me, and yet I am going to Reynolds[7] on Wednesday.

Notes

[7] *the philosophic mind* Wordsworth, 'Ode' 189.

Letter from John Keats to George and Tom Keats

[1] Charles Jeremiah Wells (1800–79), a schoolfriend of Tom Keats.

[2] Painting by Benjamin West (1738–1820), President of the Royal Academy. His exhibition was at 125 Pall Mall.

[3] *It is . . . reality* Keats follows the opinions expressed by Hazlitt in his article, 'West's Picture of Death on the Pale Horse', in the *Edinburgh Magazine* for December 1817: 'There is no gusto, no imagination in Mr West's colouring' (Howe xviii 138).

[4] West painted *Christ Rejected* 1812–14; it had been exhibited in the autumn of 1814 in Pall Mall, and attracted almost a quarter of a million visitors.

[5] Horace (1779–1849) and James Smith (1775–1839) were responsible for the parodic *Rejected Addresses* (1812). Their brother was Leonard Smith (1778–1837).

[6] Edmund Kean (1787–1833), after Kemble the most celebrated Shakespearean actor of his day.

[7] John Hamilton Reynolds (1794–1852), friend of Keats and poet.

Brown and Dilke[8] walked with me and back from the Christmas pantomime. I had not a dispute but a disquisition with Dilke, on various subjects. Several things dovetailed in my mind, and at once it struck me what quality went to form a man of achievement, especially in literature, and which Shakespeare possessed so enormously. I mean *negative capability*; that is, when man is capable of being in uncertainties, mysteries, doubts, without any irritable reaching after fact and reason. Coleridge, for instance, would let go by a fine isolated verisimilitude[9] caught from the penetralium[10] of mystery, from being incapable of remaining content with half-knowledge. This pursued through volumes would perhaps take us no further than this: that with a great poet the sense of beauty overcomes every other consideration, or rather obliterates all consideration.

On Sitting Down to Read King Lear *Once Again* (composed 22 January 1818; published 1838; edited from MS)

Oh golden-tongued Romance, with serene lute!
  Fair plumèd siren,[1] queen of far away!
Leave melodizing on this wintry day,
Shut up thine olden pages, and be mute.
Adieu! for, once again, the fierce dispute
  Betwixt damnation and impassioned clay[2]
  Must I burn through; once more humbly assay[3]
The bitter-sweet of this Shakespearian fruit.
Chief poet, and ye clouds of Albion,[4]
  Begetters of our deep eternal theme!
When through the old oak forest I am gone,[5]
  Let me not wander in a barren dream;
But when I am consumed in the fire,
Give me new phoenix wings to fly at my desire.

Sonnet: 'When I have fears that I may cease to be' (composed 22–31 January 1818; edited from MS)

When I have fears that I may cease to be
Before my pen has gleaned my teeming brain,
Before high-piled books, in charact'ry,[1]
Hold like rich garners[2] the full-ripened grain;
When I behold, upon the night's starred face,

Notes

[8] Charles Armitage Brown (1786–1842), one of Keats's closest friends; Charles Wentworth Dilke (1789–1864), with whose family Keats was close, and who introduced Keats to the love of his life, Fanny Brawne.
[9] *verisimilitude* revelation.
[10] *penetralium* interior, depth.

On Sitting Down to Read *King Lear* Once Again
[1] *Fair plumèd siren* Romance is imagined as a fair-haired, Spenserian heroine.
[2] *clay* i.e. flesh.
[3] *assay* test.
[4] *Albion* England.
[5] *When through the old oak forest I am gone* i.e. when I have finished reading this play . . .

Sonnet
[1] *charact'ry* words.
[2] *garners* storehouses for grain.

Huge cloudy symbols of a high romance,
And think that I may never live to trace
Their shadows, with the magic hand of chance;
And when I feel, fair creature of an hour,[3]
That I shall never look upon thee more,
Never have relish in the fairy power
Of unreflecting love – then on the shore
Of the wide world I stand alone and think,
Till love and fame to nothingness do sink.

Letter from John Keats to John Hamilton Reynolds, 3 February 1818 (extract)

It may be said that we ought to read our contemporaries, that Wordsworth etc. should have their due from us. But, for the sake of a few fine imaginative or domestic passages, are we to be bullied into a certain philosophy engendered in the whims of an egotist?[1] Every man has his speculations, but every man does not brood and peacock[2] over them till he makes a false coinage and deceives himself. Many a man can travel to the very bourne of heaven,[3] and yet want confidence to put down his half-seeing. Sancho[4] will invent a journey heavenward as well as anybody. We hate poetry that has a palpable design upon us – and if we do not agree, seems to put its hand in its breeches' pocket.[5] Poetry should be great and unobtrusive, a thing which enters into one's soul, and does not startle it or amaze it with itself but with its subject. How beautiful are the retired flowers! How would they lose their beauty were they to throng into the highway crying out, 'Admire me, I am a violet!', 'Dote upon me, I am a primrose!' Modern poets differ from the Elizabethans in this: each of the moderns, like an Elector[6] of Hanover, governs his petty state, and knows how many straws are swept daily from the causeways in all his dominions, and has a continual itching that all the housewives should have their coppers[7] well-scoured. The ancients were emperors of vast provinces – they had only heard of the remote ones and scarcely cared to visit them. I will cut all this – I will have no more of Wordsworth or Hunt in particular. Why should we be of the tribe of Manasseh, when we can wander with Esau?[8] Why should we kick against the pricks,[9] when we can walk on roses? Why should we be owls, when we can be eagles? Why be teased with 'nice-eyed wagtails',[10] when we have in sight 'The cherub Contemplation'?[11] Why with Wordsworth's Matthew, 'with a bough of wilding in his

Notes

3 *fair creature of an hour* According to Woodhouse, Keats was remembering a beautiful woman he had seen at Vauxhall pleasure-garden.

LETTER FROM JOHN KEATS TO JOHN HAMILTON REYNOLDS

1 Keats, like Hazlitt, regarded Wordsworth as too preoccupied with the workings of his own mind.

2 *peacock* preen himself.

3 *the very bourne of heaven* the gateway to heaven; Keats alludes to himself, *Endymion* i 295.

4 Sancho Panza, the comic buffoon who accompanies Don Quixote on his adventures.

5 *seems to put its hand . . . pocket* apparently a gesture of defiant hostility.

6 *Elector* one of the princes of Germany formerly entitled to take part in the election of the emperor.

7 *coppers* copper fittings (on their front doors, etc.).

8 *Why should we . . . Esau* Keats may be thinking of Gideon's comment, 'my family is poor in Manasseh, and I am the least in my father's house' (Judges 6: 15). The point is that Manasseh's lands are small, while Esau was a nomad, free to go where he liked. See also Genesis 48: 5–20.

9 *Why should we . . . pricks* Keats alludes to Acts 9: 5: 'I am Jesus whom thou persecutest: it is hard for thee to kick against the pricks.'

10 *nice-eyed wagtails* an allusion to Leigh Hunt, 'The Nymphs' (1818) ii 169–71:

Little ponds that hold the rains,
Where the nice-eyed wagtails glance,
Sipping 'twixt their jerking dance.

11 *The cherub Contemplation* from Milton, 'Il Penseroso' 54.

hand',[12] when we can have Jaques 'under an oak',[13] etc. The secret of the bough of wilding will run through your head faster than I can write it. Old Matthew spoke to him some years ago on some nothing, and because he happens in an evening walk to imagine the figure of the old man, he must stamp it down in black and white, and it is henceforth sacred. I don't mean to deny Wordsworth's grandeur and Hunt's merit, but I mean to say we need not be teased with grandeur and merit, when we can have them uncontaminated and unobtrusive. Let us have the old poets and Robin Hood!

Letter from John Keats to John Hamilton Reynolds, 3 May 1818 (extract)

I will return to Wordsworth, whether or no he has an extended vision or a circumscribed grandeur, whether he is an eagle in his nest or on the wing. And to be more explicit and to show you how tall I stand by the giant, I will put down a simile of human life as far as I now perceive it – that is, to the point to which I say we both have arrived at. Well, I compare human life to a large mansion of many apartments,[1] two of which I can only describe, the doors of the rest being as yet shut upon me. The first we step into we call the infant or thoughtless chamber, in which we remain as long as we do not think. We remain there a long while, and, notwithstanding the doors of the second chamber remain wide open, showing a bright appearance, we care not to hasten to it, but are at length imperceptibly impelled by the awakening of the thinking principle within us. We no sooner get into the second chamber, which I shall call the chamber of maiden thought, than we become intoxicated with the light and the atmosphere, we see nothing but pleasant wonders, and think of delaying there forever in delight. However, among the effects this breathing[2] is father of, is that tremendous one of sharpening one's vision into the heart and nature of man, of convincing one's nerves that the world is full of misery and heartbreak, pain, sickness, and oppression – whereby this chamber of maiden thought becomes gradually darkened and, at the same time, on all sides of it many doors are set open – but all dark, all leading to dark passages. We see not the balance of good and evil. We are in a mist. *We* are now in that state. We feel the 'burden of the mystery'.[3] To this point was Wordsworth come, as far as I can conceive, when he wrote 'Tintern Abbey', and it seems to me that his genius is explorative of those dark passages. Now if we live, and go on thinking, we too shall explore them. He is a genius and superior to us, insofar as he can, more than we, make discoveries, and shed a light in them. Here I must think Wordsworth is deeper than Milton, though I think it has depended more upon the general and gregarious advance of intellect, than individual greatness of mind. From the *Paradise Lost* and the other works of Milton, I hope it is not too presuming (even between ourselves) to say, his philosophy, human and divine, may be tolerably understood by one not much advanced in years. In his time, Englishmen were just emancipated from a great superstition[4] – and men had got hold of certain points and resting-places in reasoning which were too newly born to be doubted, and too much opposed by the mass of Europe not to be thought ethereal and authentically divine. Who could gainsay his ideas on virtue, vice, and chastity in *Comus*, just at the time of the dismissal of

Notes

[12] *with a bough of wilding in his hand!* an allusion to Wordsworth, 'The Two April Mornings' 59–60.

[13] *under an oak* Keats alludes to *As You Like It*, where Jaques is described 'Under an oak, whose antique root peeps out / Upon the brook that brawls along this wood' (II i 31–2).

LETTER FROM JOHN KEATS TO JOHN HAMILTON REYNOLDS

[1] *a large mansion . . . apartments* cf. John 14: 2: 'In my Father's house are many mansions.'

[2] *breathing* influence.

[3] *burden of the mystery* from 'Tintern Abbey' 39.

[4] *a great superstition* the Roman Catholic Church.

codpieces,[5] and a hundred other disgraces? Who would not rest satisfied with his hintings at good and evil in the *Paradise Lost*, when just free from the Inquisition[6] and burning in Smithfield?[7] The Reformation produced such immediate and great benefits, that Protestantism was considered under the immediate eye of heaven, and its own remaining dogmas and superstitions then, as it were, regenerated, constituted those resting-places and seeming sure points of reasoning. From that I have mentioned, Milton, whatever he may have thought in the sequel, appears to have been content with these by his writings. He did not think into the human heart, as Wordsworth has done; yet Milton as a philosopher had sure as great powers as Wordsworth. What is then to be inferred? Oh, many things. It proves there is really a grand march of intellect; it proves that a mighty providence subdues the mightiest minds to the service of the time being, whether it be in human knowledge or religion . . .

Hyperion: A Fragment (composed late September–1 December 1818; abandoned April 1819)[1]

From Lamia, Isabella, The Eve of St Agnes, and Other Poems (1820)

Book I

Deep in the shady sadness of a vale
Far sunken from the healthy breath of morn,
Far from the fiery noon, and eve's one star,
Sat grey-haired Saturn,[2] quiet as a stone,
Still as the silence round about his lair;
Forest on forest hung about his head
Like cloud on cloud. No stir of air was there,
Not so much life as on a summer's day
Robs not one light seed from the feathered grass,

Notes

[5] *the dismissal of codpieces* Codpieces (bagged appendages, often highly ornamented, worn by men on the front of breeches), went out of fashion in the last half of the 17th century. Milton's *Comus* was written in 1634.

[6] *the Inquisition* ecclesiastical tribunal (officially styled the Holy Office) for the suppression of heresy and punishment of heretics, organized in the 13th century under Pope Innocent III, with a central governing body at Rome called the Congregation of the Holy Office. The Inquisition existed in Italy, France, the Netherlands, Spain, Portugal, and the Spanish and Portuguese colonies. The Spanish Inquisition, reorganized 1478–83, became notorious in the 16th century for its severities. It was abolished in France in 1772, and in Spain finally in 1834. The Congregation of the Holy Office still exists, but is chiefly concerned with heretical literature.

[7] *burning in Smithfield* many Protestants were burned, roasted or boiled alive in Smithfield in the City of London during Mary's reign.

HYPERION

[1] 'I recollect at this moment the origin of the *Hyperion*,' Severn wrote in 1845. 'Keats was abusing Milton to me, and a friend whose name I forget, but who was rather stern. I had expressed my great admiration and delight in Milton, when this friend, turning to Keats, said "Keats, I think it great reproach to you that Severn should admire and appreciate Milton, and you a poet should know nothing of him, for you confess never to have read him, therefore your dislike goes for nothing." After this, Keats took up Milton and became an ardent admirer and soon began the *Hyperion*. I mention this to show that his likings and dislikings were extraordinary' (*Keats Circle* ii 132–3). When it first appeared, Leigh Hunt hailed it as 'a fragment – a gigantic one, like a ruin in the desert, or the bones of a mastodon. It is truly of a piece with its subject, which is the downfall of the elder gods' (*The Indicator*, 2 and 9 August 1820). Keats never finished this attempt to recast *Paradise Lost* in pagan terms. For introductory remarks see headnote, pp. 1337–80.

[2] *grey-haired Saturn* Hyperion's brother, leader of the Titans and father of the rebellious Jupiter. As the poem opens Saturn and the Titans are defeated. The Titans were a god-like race expelled from heaven by Jupiter in Greek myth.

But where the dead leaf fell, there did it rest.
A stream went voiceless by, still deadened more
By reason of his fallen divinity
Spreading a shade; the naiad[3] mid her reeds
Pressed her cold finger closer to her lips.
  Along the margin-sand large footmarks went,
No further than to where his feet had strayed,
And slept there since. Upon the sodden ground
His old right hand lay nerveless,[4] listless, dead,
Unsceptred; and his realmless eyes were closed,
While his bowed head seemed list'ning to the earth,
His ancient mother, for some comfort yet.
  It seemed no force could wake him from his place;
But there came one who, with a kindred hand
Touched his wide shoulders, after bending low
With reverence, though to one who knew it not.
She was a goddess of the infant world;
By her in stature the tall Amazon
Had stood a pigmy's height – she would have ta'en
Achilles by the hair and bent his neck,
Or with a finger stayed Ixion's wheel.[5]
Her face was large as that of Memphian sphinx,[6]
Pedestalled haply in a palace court
When sages looked to Egypt for their lore.
But oh, how unlike marble was that face!
How beautiful, if sorrow had not made
Sorrow more beautiful than Beauty's self.
There was a listening fear in her regard,
As if calamity had but begun;
As if the vanward clouds of evil days
Had spent their malice, and the sullen rear
Was with its stored thunder labouring up.[7]
One hand she pressed upon that aching spot
Where beats the human heart, as if just there,
Though an immortal, she felt cruel pain;
The other upon Saturn's bended neck
She laid, and to the level of his ear
Leaning with parted lips, some words she spake
In solemn tenor and deep organ tone,
Some mourning words which in our feeble tongue
Would come in these like accents (oh how frail
To[8] that large utterance of the early gods!),

Notes

[3] *naiad* water-nymph.

[4] *nerveless* weak.

[5] *Ixion's wheel* Ixion was banished from heaven and sentenced to be tied to a burning and spinning wheel in Hades for eternity.

[6] *Memphian sphinx* Memphis was a city in Egypt. Keats saw a sphinx in the British Museum, early in 1819.

[7] *As if the vanward clouds . . . up* Calamity is compared to clouds building up before a storm, followed by the cloud mass; the storm itself is compared to the artillery moving in the wake of advancing troops.

[8] *To* i.e. compared with.

'Saturn, look up! – though wherefore, poor old King?
I have no comfort for thee, no, not one;
I cannot say, "Oh wherefore sleepest thou?"
For heaven is parted from thee, and the earth
Knows thee not, thus afflicted, for a god;
And ocean too, with all its solemn noise,
Has from thy sceptre passed, and all the air
Is emptied of thine hoary majesty.
Thy thunder, conscious of the new command,[9]
Rumbles reluctant o'er our fallen house,
And thy sharp lightning in unpractised hands
Scorches and burns our once serene domain.[10]
Oh aching time! Oh moments big as years!
All as ye pass swell out the monstrous truth,
And press it so upon our weary griefs
That unbelief has not a space to breathe.
Saturn, sleep on! Oh thoughtless, why did I
Thus violate thy slumbrous solitude?
Why should I ope thy melancholy eyes?
Saturn, sleep on, while at thy feet I weep!'
  As when, upon a tranced summer night,
Those green-robed senators of mighty woods,
Tall oaks, branch-charmed by the earnest stars,
Dream, and so dream all night without a stir,
Save from one gradual solitary gust
Which comes upon the silence, and dies off
As if the ebbing air had but one wave;
So came these words and went, the while in tears
She touched her fair large forehead to the ground,
Just where her falling hair might be outspread,
A soft and silken mat for Saturn's feet.
One moon, with alteration slow, had shed
Her silver seasons four upon the night,
And still these two were postured motionless,
Like natural sculpture in cathedral cavern[11] –
The frozen god still couchant[12] on the earth,
And the sad goddess weeping at his feet.
Until at length old Saturn lifted up
His faded eyes, and saw his kingdom gone,
And all the gloom and sorrow of the place,
And that fair kneeling goddess, and then spake
As with a palsied[13] tongue, and while his beard
Shook horrid[14] with such aspen[15] malady:
'Oh tender spouse of gold Hyperion,[16]

Notes

[9] *conscious of the new command* Jupiter is the new thunderer.

[10] *our once serene domain* the Saturnian golden age.

[11] *Like natural sculpture in cathedral cavern* The motionless gods are compared to huge rock formations.

[12] *couchant* lying down.

[13] *palsied* trembling.

[14] *horrid* bristling.

[15] *aspen* the leaves of the aspen tremble in the slightest breeze.

[16] *tender spouse of gold Hyperion* Thea is the sister and third wife of Hyperion.

Thea, I feel thee ere I see thy face;
Look up, and let me see our doom in it,
Look up, and tell me if this feeble shape
Is Saturn's; tell me if thou hear'st the voice
Of Saturn; tell me if this wrinkling brow,
Naked and bare of its great diadem,[17]
Peers like the front[18] of Saturn. Who had power
To make me desolate? Whence came the strength?
How was it nurtured to such bursting forth,
While Fate seemed strangled in my nervous[19] grasp?
But it is so, and I am smothered up
And buried from all godlike exercise
Of influence benign on planets pale,[20]
Of admonitions to the winds and seas,
Of peaceful sway above man's harvesting,
And all those acts which deity supreme
Doth ease its heart of love in. I am gone
Away from my own bosom; I have left
My strong identity, my real self,[21]
Somewhere between the throne and where I sit
Here on this spot of earth. Search, Thea, search!
Open thine eyes eterne,[22] and sphere them round
Upon all space – space starred, and lorn of light;
Space regioned with life-air, and barren void;
Spaces of fire, and all the yawn of hell.
Search, Thea, search! And tell me if thou seest
A certain shape or shadow, making way
With wings or chariot fierce to repossess
A heaven he lost erewhile: it must – it must
Be of ripe progress; Saturn must be King.
Yes, there must be a golden victory;
There must be gods thrown down, and trumpets blown
Of triumph calm, and hymns of festival
Upon the gold clouds metropolitan,[23]
Voices of soft proclaim, and silver stir
Of strings in hollow shells; and there shall be
Beautiful things made new, for the surprise
Of the sky-children. I will give command:
Thea! Thea! Thea! Where is Saturn?'
  This passion lifted him upon his feet,
And made his hands to struggle in the air,
His Druid locks[24] to shake and ooze with sweat,
His eyes to fever out, his voice to cease.
He stood, and heard not Thea's sobbing deep;

Notes

[17] *diadem* crown.
[18] *front* forehead.
[19] *nervous* muscular.
[20] *And buried . . . pale* Jupiter has taken control of the planets.
[21] *My strong identity, my real self* Titans depend on their identity for their power.
[22] *eterne* eternal.
[23] *the gold clouds metropolitan* The clouds are the gods' metropolis.
[24] *Druid locks* i.e. long-haired.

A little time, and then again he snatched
Utterance thus: 'But cannot I create?
Cannot I form? Cannot I fashion forth
Another world, another universe,
To overbear and crumble this to naught?
Where is another chaos? Where?' That word
Found way unto Olympus,[25] and made quake
The rebel three.[26] Thea was startled up,
And in her bearing was a sort of hope
As thus she quick-voiced spake, yet full of awe:
'This cheers our fallen house; come to our friends,[27]
Oh Saturn, come away and give them heart!
I know the covert,[28] for thence came I hither.'
Thus brief, then with beseeching eyes she went
With backward footing through the shade a space;
He followed, and she turned to lead the way
Through aged boughs that yielded like the mist
Which eagles cleave upmounting from their nest.
  Meanwhile in other realms big tears were shed,
More sorrow like to this, and suchlike woe
Too huge for mortal tongue or pen of scribe.
The Titans fierce, self-hid, or prison-bound,
Groaned for the old allegiance once more,
And listened in sharp pain for Saturn's voice.
But one of the whole mammoth-brood still kept
His sov'reignty, and rule, and majesty:
Blazing Hyperion on his orbed fire[29]
Still sat, still snuffed the incense, teeming up
From man to the sun's god – yet unsecure.
For as among us mortals omens drear
Fright and perplex, so also shuddered he –
Not at dog's howl, or gloom-bird's[30] hated screech,
Or the familiar visiting of one
Upon the first toll of his passing-bell,[31]
Or prophesyings of the midnight lamp,
But horrors portioned[32] to a giant nerve
Oft made Hyperion ache. His palace bright,
Bastioned with pyramids of glowing gold,
And touched with shade of bronzed obelisks,
Glared a blood-red through all its thousand courts,
Arches, and domes, and fiery galleries;
And all its curtains of aurorean[33] clouds
Flushed angerly,[34] while sometimes eagle's wings

Notes

[25] *Olympus* the mountain that provided Jupiter with his seat of power.
[26] *The rebel three* Saturn's sons – Jupiter, Neptune and Pluto.
[27] *our friends* the rest of the Titans.
[28] *covert* hiding-place.
[29] *orbed fire* the sun, of which Hyperion is god.
[30] *gloom-bird* owl.
[31] *passing-bell* death-bell.
[32] *portioned* proportioned.
[33] *aurorean* roseate.
[34] *His palace . . . angerly* Hyperion's palace is part-Roman and part-Egyptian.

(Unseen before by gods or wondering men)
Darkened the place; and neighing steeds were heard,
Not heard before by gods or wondering men.
Also, when he would taste the spicy wreaths
Of incense, breathed aloft from sacred hills,
Instead of sweets, his ample palate took
Savour of poisonous brass and metal sick.
And so, when harboured in the sleepy west
After the full completion of fair day,
For rest divine upon exalted couch
And slumber in the arms of melody,
He paced away the pleasant hours of ease
With stride colossal on from hall to hall;
While far within each aisle and deep recess
His winged minions in close clusters stood,
Amazed and full of fear, like anxious men
Who on wide plains gather in panting troops
When earthquakes jar their battlements and towers.
Even now, while Saturn, roused from icy trance,
Went step for step with Thea through the woods,
Hyperion, leaving twilight in the rear,
Came slope[35] upon the threshold of the west;
Then, as was wont, his palace-door flew ope
In smoothest silence, save what solemn tubes[36]
Blown by the serious zephyrs[37] gave of sweet
And wandering sounds, slow-breathed melodies;
And like a rose in vermeil[38] tint and shape,
In fragrance soft, and coolness to the eye,
That inlet to severe magnificence
Stood full-blown, for the god to enter in.
He entered, but he entered full of wrath;
His flaming robes streamed out beyond his heels
And gave a roar as if of earthly fire,
That scared away the meek ethereal Hours[39]
And made their dove-wings tremble. On he flared,
From stately nave to nave, from vault to vault,
Through bowers of fragrant and enwreathed light
And diamond-paved lustrous long arcades,
Until he reached the great main cupola.[40]
There standing fierce beneath, he stamped his foot,
And from the basements deep to the high towers
Jarred his own golden region; and before
The quavering thunder thereupon had ceased,
His voice leaped out, despite of godlike curb,
To this result: 'Oh dreams of day and night!
Oh monstrous forms! Oh effigies of pain!

Notes

[35] *slope* sloping downward.
[36] *solemn tubes* of a musical instrument, such as an organ.
[37] *zephyrs* breezes.
[38] *vermeil* scarlet.
[39] *Hours* 'Horae', attendant nymphs of the sun.
[40] *cupola* dome.

Oh spectres busy in a cold, cold gloom!
Oh lank-eared phantoms of black-weeded pools!
Why do I know ye? Why have I seen ye? Why
Is my eternal essence[41] thus distraught
To see and to behold these horrors new?
Saturn is fallen, am I too to fall?
Am I to leave this haven of my rest,
This cradle of my glory, this soft clime,
This calm luxuriance of blissful light,
These crystalline pavilions and pure fanes[42]
Of all my lucent[43] empire? It is left
Deserted, void, nor any haunt of mine.
The blaze, the splendour, and the symmetry,
I cannot see – but darkness, death and darkness.
Even here, into my centre of repose,
The shady visions come to domineer,
Insult, and blind, and stifle up my pomp.
Fall? No, by Tellus[44] and her briny robes!
Over the fiery frontier of my realms
I will advance a terrible right arm
Shall scare that infant thunderer, rebel Jove,
And bid old Saturn take his throne again.'
He spake, and ceased, the while a heavier threat
Held struggle with his throat but came not forth;
For as in theatres of crowded men
Hubbub increases more they call out 'Hush!'
So at Hyperion's words the phantoms pale
Bestirred themselves, thrice horrible and cold,
And from the mirrored level where he stood
A mist arose as from a scummy marsh.
At this, through all his bulk an agony
Crept gradual from the feet unto the crown,
Like a lithe serpent vast and muscular
Making slow way, with head and neck convulsed
From over-strained might. Released, he fled
To the eastern gates, and full six dewy hours
Before the dawn in season due should blush,
He breathed fierce breath against the sleepy portals,[45]
Cleared them of heavy vapours, burst them wide
Suddenly on the ocean's chilly streams.
The planet orb of fire whereon he rode
Each day from east to west the heavens through,
Spun round in sable curtaining of clouds;
Not therefore veiled quite, blindfold and hid,
But ever and anon the glancing spheres,
Circles, and arcs, and broad-belting colure,[46]

Notes

41 *essence* being.
42 *fanes* temples.
43 *lucent* shining.
44 *Tellus* mother of the Titans, married to her brother Saturn.
45 *portals* gateways.
46 *colure* technical term for 'each of two great circles which intersect each other at right angles at the poles, and divide the equinoctial and the ecliptic into four equal parts' (*OED*).

Glowed through, and wrought upon the muffling dark
Sweet-shaped lightnings from the nadir deep
Up to the zenith – hieroglyphics old[47]
Which sages and keen-eyed astrologers
Then living on the earth, with labouring thought
Won from the gaze of many centuries –
Now lost, save what we find on remnants huge
Of stone, or marble swart,[48] their import gone,
Their wisdom long since fled. Two wings this orb
Possessed for glory, two fair argent[49] wings
Ever exalted at the god's approach;
And now from forth the gloom their plumes immense
Rose one by one, till all outspreaded were,
While still the dazzling globe maintained eclipse,
Awaiting for Hyperion's command.
Fain would he have commanded, fain took throne
And bid the day begin, if but for change.
He might not – no, though a primeval god;
The sacred seasons might not be disturbed.
Therefore the operations of the dawn
Stayed in their birth, even as here 'tis told.
Those silver wings expanded sisterly,
Eager to sail their orb; the porches wide
Opened upon the dusk demesnes[50] of night;
And the bright Titan, frenzied with new woes,
Unused to bend, by hard compulsion bent
His spirit to the sorrow of the time;
And all along a dismal rack of clouds,[51]
Upon the boundaries of day and night,
He stretched himself in grief and radiance faint.
There as he lay, the heaven with its stars
Looked down on him with pity, and the voice
Of Coelus,[52] from the universal space,
Thus whispered low and solemn in his ear:
'Oh brightest of my children dear, earth-born
And sky-engendered, son of mysteries
All unrevealed even to the powers[53]
Which met at thy creating; at whose joys
And palpitations sweet, and pleasures soft,
I, Coelus, wonder how they came and whence,
And at the fruits thereof what shapes they be,
Distinct and visible – symbols divine,
Manifestations of that beauteous life
Diffused unseen throughout eternal space.

Notes

[47] *hieroglyphics old* signs of the zodiac.
[48] *swart* black.
[49] *argent* silver.
[50] *demesnes* domains, regions.
[51] *rack of clouds* cloud-mass.
[52] *Coelus* father of the Titans.
[53] *the powers* Coelus and Terra (parents of the Titans).

Of these new-formed art thou, oh brightest child!
Of these, thy brethren and the goddesses!
There is sad feud among ye, and rebellion
Of son against his sire.[54] I saw him fall,
I saw my first-born[55] tumbled from his throne!
To me his arms were spread, to me his voice
Found way from forth the thunders round his head!
Pale wox[56] I, and in vapours hid my face.
Art thou, too, near such doom? Vague fear there is,
For I have seen my sons most unlike gods.
Divine ye were created, and divine
In sad demeanour, solemn, undisturbed,
Unruffled, like high gods, ye lived and ruled.
Now I behold in you fear, hope, and wrath,
Actions of rage and passion – even as
I see them on the mortal world beneath,
In men who die. This is the grief, oh son;
Sad sign of ruin, sudden dismay, and fall!
Yet do thou strive; as thou art capable,
As thou canst move about, an evident god,[57]
And canst oppose to each malignant hour
Ethereal presence. I am but a voice;
My life is but the life of winds and tides,
No more than winds and tides can I avail –
But thou canst. Be thou therefore in the van
Of circumstance;[58] yea, seize the arrow's barb
Before the tense string murmur.[59] To the earth!
For there thou wilt find Saturn and his woes.
Meantime I will keep watch on thy bright sun,
And of thy seasons be a careful nurse.'
Ere half this region-whisper had come down,
Hyperion arose, and on the stars
Lifted his curved lids, and kept them wide
Until it ceased, and still he kept them wide,
And still they were the same bright, patient stars.
Then with a slow incline of his broad breast,
Like to a diver in the pearly seas,
Forward he stooped over the airy shore
And plunged all noiseless into the deep night.

Book II

Just at the self-same beat of Time's wide wings
Hyperion slid into the rustled air,
And Saturn gained with Thea that sad place
Where Cybele and the bruised Titans mourned.

Notes

54 *son against his sire* i.e. Jupiter's rebellion against Saturn.

55 *my first-born* Saturn.

56 *wox* became.

57 *an evident god* Saturn has being; Coelus is the sky, and is just a place – he cannot move around and has no 'essence'.

58 *the van / Of circumstance* i.e. act, take the initiative.

59 *seize . . . murmur* i.e. shoot your arrow before someone shoots at you.

It was a den where no insulting[1] light
Could glimmer on their tears; where their own groans
They felt, but heard not, for the solid roar
Of thunderous waterfalls and torrents hoarse,
Pouring a constant bulk, uncertain where.[2]
Crag jutting forth to crag, and rocks that seemed
Ever as if just rising from a sleep,
Forehead to forehead held their monstrous horns;
And thus in thousand hugest fantasies
Made a fit roofing to this nest of woe.
Instead of thrones, hard flint they sat upon,
Couches of rugged stone, and slaty ridge
Stubborned with iron. All were not assembled,
Some chained in torture and some wandering.
Coeus, and Gyges, and Briareus,
Typhon, and Dolor, and Porphyrion,
With many more, the brawniest in assault,
Were pent in regions of laborious breath,
Dungeoned in opaque element to keep
Their clenched teeth still clenched, and all their limbs
Locked up like veins of metal, cramped and screwed;
Without a motion, save of their big hearts
Heaving in pain, and horribly convulsed
With sanguine feverous boiling gurge[3] of pulse.[4]
Mnemosyne[5] was straying in the world;
Far from her moon had Phoebe[6] wandered;
And many else were free to roam abroad,
But for the main, here found they covert[7] drear.
Scarce images of life, one here, one there,
Lay vast and edgeways; like a dismal cirque
Of Druid stones upon a forlorn moor,[8]
When the chill rain begins at shut of eve
In dull November, and their chancel vault,[9]
The heaven itself, is blinded throughout night.
Each one kept shroud,[10] nor to his neighbour gave
Or word, or look, or action of despair.
Creus was one; his ponderous iron mace
Lay by him, and a shattered rib of rock
Told of his rage ere he thus sank and pined.
Iapetus another – in his grasp
A serpent's plashy[11] neck, its barbed tongue

Notes

BOOK II

[1] *insulting* The light would be an insulting reminder of their loss of power.

[2] *for the solid roar . . . where* Keats recollects the waterfalls he had
seen on his walking tour of the Lake District and Scotland, summer 1818.

[3] *gurge* whirlpool.

[4] *pulse* i.e. that of blood in the heart.

[5] *Mnemosyne* mother of the muses by Jupiter, included among the Titans. She is seeking Apollo.

[6] *Phoebe* goddess of the moon.

[7] *covert* shelter.

[8] *Druid stones upon a forlorn moor* Keats visited the Castlerigg stone circle near Keswick in June 1818.

[9] *their chancel vault* The stones and the darkness evoke the atmosphere of a church.

[10] *shroud* shrouded.

[11] *plashy* marked as if splashed with colour.

Squeezed from the gorge,[12] and all its uncurled length
Dead, and because[13] the creature could not spit
Its poison in the eyes of conquering Jove.
Next Cottus; prone he lay, chin uppermost
As though in pain, for still upon the flint
He ground severe his skull, with open mouth
And eyes at horrid working.[14] Nearest him
Asia, born of most enormous Caf,
Who cost her mother Tellus keener pangs,
Though feminine, than any of her sons.
More thought than woe was in her dusky face,
For she was prophesying of her glory,
And in her wide imagination stood
Palm-shaded temples and high rival fanes
By Oxus or in Ganges' sacred isles.[15]
Even as Hope upon her anchor[16] leans,
So leant she, not so fair, upon a tusk
Shed from the broadest of her elephants.
Above her, on a crag's uneasy shelve,[17]
Upon his elbow raised, all prostrate else,
Shadowed Enceladus – once tame and mild
As grazing ox unworried in the meads,
Now tiger-passioned, lion-thoughted, wroth,
He meditated, plotted, and even now[18]
Was hurling mountains in that second war[19]
Not long delayed, that scared the younger gods
To hide themselves in forms of beast and bird.
Not far hence Atlas; and beside him prone
Phorcus, the sire of Gorgons. Neighboured close
Oceanus, and Tethys, in whose lap
Sobbed Clymene among her tangled hair.[20]
In midst of all lay Themis, at the feet
Of Ops the queen, all clouded round from sight;
No shape distinguishable, more than when
Thick night confounds the pine-tops with the clouds:
And many else whose names may not be told.
For when the muse's wings are air-ward spread
Who shall delay her flight? And she must chaunt
Of Saturn and his guide, who now had climbed
With damp and slippery footing from a depth
More horrid[21] still. Above a sombre cliff
Their heads appeared, and up their stature grew
Till on the level height their steps found ease;

Notes

[12] *gorge* throat.
[13] *and because* i.e. and all this because.
[14] *at horrid working* looking round in a frightening manner.
[15] *For she was . . . sacred isles* Asia will become the goddess of a future cult.
[16] *anchor* traditional emblem of hope; see Hebrews 6: 19.
[17] *shelve* slope.
[18] *even now* i.e. in his imagination.
[19] *that second war* presumably to have been the subject of a further book of the poem, never written.
[20] *her tangled hair* a recollection of *Lycidas* 69: 'the tangles of Neaera's hair'.
[21] *horrid* frightening.

Then Thea spread abroad her trembling arms
Upon the precincts of this nest of pain,
And sidelong fixed her eye on Saturn's face.
There saw she direst strife, the supreme god
At war with all the frailty of grief,
Of rage, of fear, anxiety, revenge,
Remorse, spleen, hope, but most of all despair.
Against these plagues he strove in vain, for Fate
Had poured a mortal oil upon his head,
A disanointing poison,[22] so that Thea,
Affrighted, kept her still, and let him pass
First onwards in, among the fallen tribe.
As with us mortal men, the laden heart
Is persecuted more, and fevered more,
When it is nighing to the mournful house
Where other hearts are sick of the same bruise;
So Saturn, as he walked into the midst,
Felt faint, and would have sunk among the rest,
But that he met Enceladus' eye,
Whose mightiness and awe of him, at once
Came like an inspiration – and he shouted,
'Titans, behold your god!' At which some groaned,
Some started on their feet, some also shouted,
Some wept, some wailed, all bowed with reverence;
And Ops, uplifting her black folded veil,
Showed her pale cheeks and all her forehead wan,
Her eyebrows thin and jet, and hollow eyes.
There is a roaring in the bleak-grown pines
When winter lifts his voice; there is a noise
Among immortals when a god gives sign,
With hushing finger, how he means to load
His tongue with the full weight of utterless[23] thought,
With thunder, and with music, and with pomp:
Such noise is like the roar of bleak-grown pines,
Which, when it ceases in this mountained world,
No other sound succeeds; but ceasing here,
Among these fallen, Saturn's voice therefrom
Grew up like organ, that begins anew
Its strain, when other harmonies, stopped short,
Leave the dinned air vibrating silverly.[24]
Thus grew it up: 'Not in my own sad breast,
Which is its own great judge and searcher-out,
Can I find reason why ye should be thus;
Not in the legends of the first of days,
Studied from that old spirit-leaved book[25]
Which starry Uranus with finger bright

Notes

[22] *A disanointing poison* the ointment deprives Saturn of his godhead.
[23] *utterless* unutterable.
[24] *silverly* with a silvery sound.
[25] *that old spirit-leaved book* an imaginary book dating from the beginning of time, recording the first stages of the evolution of the world.

Saved from the shores of darkness, when the waves
Low-ebbed still hid it up in shallow gloom,
And the which book ye know I ever kept
For my firm-based footstool – ah, infirm!
Not there, nor in sign, symbol, or portent
Of element, earth, water, air, and fire,
At war, at peace, or inter-quarrelling
One against one, or two, or three, or all
Each several one against the other three,
As fire with air loud warring when rainfloods
Drown both, and press them both against earth's face,
Where, finding sulphur, a quadruple wrath
Unhinges the poor world – not in that strife,
Wherefrom I take strange lore and read it deep,
Can I find reason why ye should be thus.
No, nowhere can unriddle, though I search
And pore on nature's universal scroll
Even to swooning, why ye divinities,
The first-born of all shaped and palpable gods,
Should cower beneath what, in comparison,
Is untremendous might. Yet ye are here,
O'erwhelmed, and spurned, and battered – ye are here!
Oh Titans, shall I say "Arise"? Ye groan;
Shall I say "Crouch"? Ye groan. What can I then?
Oh heaven wide! Oh unseen parent dear!
What can I? Tell me, all ye brethren gods,
How we can war, how engine our great wrath;[26]
Oh speak your counsel now, for Saturn's ear
Is all a-hungered. Thou, Oceanus,
Ponderest high and deep, and in thy face
I see, astonied,[27] that severe content
Which comes of thought and musing – give us help!'
 So ended Saturn, and the god of the sea,[28]
Sophist and sage from no Athenian grove,[29]
But cogitation in his watery shades,
Arose, with locks not oozy,[30] and began,
In murmurs, which his first-endeavouring tongue
Caught infant-like from the far-foamed sands:
'Oh ye, whom wrath consumes, who, passion-stung,
Writhe at defeat, and nurse your agonies!
Shut up your senses, stifle up your ears,
My voice is not a bellows unto ire.
Yet listen, ye who will, whilst I bring proof

Notes

[26] *engine our great wrath* turn our wrath into an instrument of war.

[27] *astonied* astonished; an archaism used by Spenser and Milton.

[28] *the god of the sea* Oceanus, father of all the gods.

[29] *no Athenian grove* Oceanus did not gain his wisdom from an academy in Athens. Plato established his 'Academia' (academy) in Academus's grove.

[30] *locks not oozy* Oceanus is not in the sea; Keats is also alluding to *Lycidas* 175: 'With nectar pure his oozy locks he laves.'

How ye, perforce, must be content to stoop;
And in the proof much comfort will I give,
If ye will take that comfort in its truth.
We fall by course of nature's law, not force
Of thunder, or of Jove. Great Saturn, thou
Hast sifted well the atom-universe;[31]
But for this reason, that thou art the King,
And only blind from sheer supremacy,
One avenue was shaded from thine eyes
Through which I wandered to eternal truth.
And first, as thou wast not the first of powers,
So art thou not the last; it cannot be.
Thou art not the beginning nor the end.[32]
From chaos and parental darkness came
Light, the first fruits of that intestine broil,[33]
That sullen ferment which for wondrous ends
Was ripening in itself. The ripe hour came,
And with it light, and light, engendering
Upon its own producer,[34] forthwith touched
The whole enormous matter into life.
Upon that very hour, our parentage,
The heavens and the earth, were manifest;
Then thou first-born, and we the giant-race,
Found ourselves ruling new and beauteous realms.
Now comes the pain of truth, to whom 'tis pain;[35]
Oh folly! for to bear all naked truths,
And to envisage circumstance, all calm,
That is the top of sovereignty. Mark well!
As heaven and earth are fairer, fairer far
Than chaos and blank darkness, though once chiefs;
And as we show beyond[36] that heaven and earth
In form and shape compact and beautiful,
In will, in action free, companionship,
And thousand other signs of purer life –
So on our heels a fresh perfection treads,
A power more strong in beauty, born of us
And fated to excel us, as we pass
In glory that old darkness. Nor are we
Thereby more conquered than by us the rule
Of shapeless chaos. Say, doth the dull soil
Quarrel with the proud forests it hath fed,
And feedeth still, more comely than itself?

Notes

[31] *atom-universe* Although Keats may be echoing Milton (*Paradise Lost* ii 900), he was aware that John Dalton (1766–1844) had proposed in 1801 that all elements are composed of fundamental units, or 'atoms', that are specific to that element.

[32] *Thou art not the beginning nor the end* Revelation 1: 8: 'I am Alpha and Omega, the beginning and the ending, saith the Lord.'

[33] *intestine broil* civil war.

[34] *its own producer* the darkness of chaos.

[35] *to whom 'tis pain* for those to whom it is pain.

[36] *show beyond* are manifestly superior to.

Can it deny the chiefdom of green groves?
Or shall the tree be envious of the dove
Because it cooeth, and hath snowy wings
To wander wherewithal and find its joys?
We are such forest trees, and our fair boughs
Have bred forth not pale solitary doves
But eagles golden-feathered, who do tower
Above us in their beauty, and must reign
In right thereof; for 'tis the eternal law
That first in beauty should be first in might –
Yea, by that law another race may drive
Our conquerors to mourn as we do now.
Have ye beheld the young god of the seas,[37]
My dispossessor? Have ye seen his face?
Have ye beheld his chariot, foamed along
By noble winged creatures he hath made?
I saw him on the calmed waters scud,
With such a glow of beauty in his eyes
That it enforced me to bid sad farewell
To all my empire; farewell sad I took,
And hither came to see how dolorous fate
Had wrought upon ye, and how I might best
Give consolation in this woe extreme.
Receive the truth, and let it be your balm.'
　Whether through posed[38] conviction, or disdain,
They guarded silence when Oceanus
Left murmuring, what deepest thought can tell?
But so it was; none answered for a space,
Save one whom none regarded, Clymene.[39]
And yet she answered not, only complained
With hectic[40] lips, and eyes up-looking mild,
Thus wording timidly among the fierce:
'Oh father, I am here the simplest voice,
And all my knowledge is that joy is gone,
And this thing woe crept in among our hearts,
There to remain for ever, as I fear.
I would not bode of evil, if I thought
So weak a creature could turn off the help
Which by just right should come of mighty gods;
Yet let me tell my sorrow, let me tell
Of what I heard, and how it made we weep,
And know that we had parted from all hope.
I stood upon a shore, a pleasant shore
Where a sweet clime was breathed from a land
Of fragrance, quietness, and trees, and flowers.
Full of calm joy it was, as I of grief,
Too full of joy and soft delicious warmth –

Notes

[37] *the young god of the seas* Neptune, traditionally depicted as riding a chariot over the sea.
[38] *posed* feigned.
[39] *Clymene* daughter of Oceanus and Tethys.
[40] *hectic* feverish.

So that I felt a movement in my heart
To chide, and to reproach that solitude
With songs of misery, music of our woes;
And sat me down, and took a mouthed shell
And murmured into it, and made melody.
Oh melody no more! For while I sang,
And with poor skill let pass into the breeze
The dull shell's echo, from a bowery strand[41]
Just opposite, an island of the sea,
There came enchantment with the shifting wind,
That did both drown and keep alive my ears.
I threw my shell away upon the sand
And a wave filled it, as my sense was filled
With that new blissful golden melody.
A living death was in each gush of sounds,
Each family of rapturous hurried notes
That fell, one after one, yet all at once,
Like pearl beads dropping sudden from their string;
And then another, then another strain,
Each like a dove leaving its olive perch,
With music winged instead of silent plumes,
To hover round my head, and make me sick
Of joy and grief at once.[42] Grief overcame,
And I was stopping up my frantic ears,
When, past all hindrance of my trembling hands,
A voice came sweeter, sweeter than all tune,
And still it cried, "Apollo! Young Apollo!
The morning-bright Apollo! Young Apollo!"
I fled, it followed me, and cried "Apollo!"
Oh father and oh brethren, had ye felt
Those pains of mine – oh Saturn, hadst thou felt,
Ye would not call this too indulged tongue
Presumptous in thus venturing to be heard.'
 So far her voice flowed on, like timorous brook
That, lingering along[43] a pebbled coast,
Doth fear to meet the sea – but sea it met
And shuddered; for the overwhelming voice
Of huge Enceladus[44] swallowed it in wrath –
The ponderous syllables, like sullen waves
In the half-glutted[45] hollows of reef-rocks,
Came booming thus, while still upon his arm
He leaned (not rising, from supreme contempt):
'Or shall we listen to the over-wise,
Or to the over-foolish, giant gods?
Not thunderbolt on thunderbolt, till all
That rebel Jove's whole armoury were spent,

Notes

[41] *bowery strand* sheltered seashore.

[42] *Of joy and grief at once* joy at the music; grief that her music is surpassed.

[43] *lingering along* meandering towards.

[44] *Enceladus* one of the most powerful of the Titans.

[45] *half-glutted* half-filled.

Not world on world upon these shoulders piled
Could agonize me more than baby-words
In midst of this dethronement horrible.
Speak! Roar! Shout! Yell, ye sleepy Titans all!
Do ye forget the blows, the buffets vile?
Are ye not smitten by a youngling arm?[46]
Dost thou forget, sham monarch of the waves,
Thy scalding in the seas? What, have I roused
Your spleens with so few simple words as these?
Oh joy, for now I see ye are not lost!
Oh joy, for now I see a thousand eyes
Wide glaring for revenge!' As this he said,
He lifted up his stature vast, and stood,
Still without intermission speaking thus:
'Now ye are flames, I'll tell you how to burn
And purge the ether of our enemies;[47]
How to feed fierce the crooked stings of fire[48]
And singe away the swollen clouds of Jove,
Stifling that puny essence in its tent.
Oh let him feel the evil he hath done –
For though I scorn Oceanus' lore,
Much pain have I for more than loss of realms.
The days of peace and slumberous calm are fled;
Those days, all innocent of scathing war,
When all the fair Existences of heaven
Came open-eyed to guess what we would speak –
That was before our brows were taught to frown,
Before our lips knew else but solemn sounds;
That was before we knew the winged thing,
Victory, might be lost, or might be won.
And be ye mindful that Hyperion,
Our brightest brother, still is undisgraced –
Hyperion, lo! His radiance is here!'
    All eyes were on Enceladus' face,
And they beheld, while still Hyperion's name
Flew from his lips up to the vaulted rocks,[49]
A pallid gleam across his features stern –
Not savage, for he saw full many a god
Wroth as himself. He looked upon them all,
And in each face he saw a gleam of light,
But splendider in Saturn's, whose hoar locks
Shone like the bubbling foam about a keel
When the prow sweeps into a midnight cove.
In pale and silver silence they remained,
Till suddenly a splendour, like the morn,
Pervaded all the beetling[50] gloomy steeps,
All the sad spaces of oblivion,

Notes

[46] *youngling arm* inexperienced arm.
[47] *the ether of our enemies* the air our enemies breathe.
[48] *the crooked stings of fire* flashes of lightning.
[49] *the vaulted rocks* The rocks form a roof above them.
[50] *beetling* overhanging.

And every gulf, and every chasm old,
And every height, and every sullen depth,
Voiceless, or hoarse with loud tormented streams,
And all the everlasting cataracts,
And all the headlong torrents far and near,
Mantled[51] before in darkness and huge shade,
Now saw the light and made it terrible.
It was Hyperion: a granite peak
His bright feet touched, and there he stayed to view
The misery his brillance had betrayed
To the most hateful seeing of itself.[52]
Golden his hair of short Numidian curl,
Regal his shape majestic, a vast shade
In midst of his own brightness, like the bulk
Of Memnon's image at the set of sun
To one who travels from the dusking east;[53]
Sighs, too, as mournful as that Memnon's harp
He uttered, while his hands contemplative
He pressed together, and in silence stood.
Despondence seized again the fallen gods
At sight of the dejected King of Day,
And many hid their faces from the light.
But fierce Enceladus sent forth his eyes
Among the brotherhood, and at their glare
Uprose Iapetus, and Creus too,
And Phorcus, sea-born, and together strode
To where he towered on his eminence.[54]
There those four shouted forth old Saturn's name;
Hyperion from the peak loud answered, 'Saturn!'
Saturn sat near the mother of the gods,
In whose face was no joy, though all the gods
Gave from their hollow throats the name of 'Saturn!'

Book III

Thus in alternate uproar and sad peace,
Amazed were those Titans utterly.
Oh leave them, muse! Oh leave them to their woes,
For thou art weak to sing such tumults dire;
A solitary sorrow best befits
Thy lips, and antheming a lonely grief.
Leave them, oh muse! For thou anon wilt find
Many a fallen old divinity[1]

Notes

[51] *Mantled* cloaked, obscured.
[52] *The misery . . . itself* Hyperion's radiance throws the misery of the Titans into sharper relief.
[53] *Memnon's image . . . east* The statue was in fact one of a pair representing the Egyptian King Amenhotep III, outside his funerary temple on the west bank at Thebes, mentioned by Juvenal in his fifteenth satire. The eighteenth- and early nineteenth-century English poets believed that the statue held a lyre which, when struck by the sun at dawn or sunset, sounded forth.
[54] *eminence* mountain.

Book III
[1] *divinity* god.

Wandering in vain about bewildered shores.
Meantime touch piously the Delphic harp,[2]
And not a wind of heaven but will breathe
In aid soft warble from the Dorian flute;[3]
For lo! 'tis for the father of all verse.[4]
Flush everything that hath a vermeil[5] hue,
Let the rose glow intense and warm the air,
And let the clouds of even and of morn
Float in voluptuous fleeces o'er the hills;
Let the red wine within the goblet boil,
Cold as a bubbling well; let faint-lipped shells
On sands or in great deeps, vermilion turn
Through all their labyrinths; and let the maid
Blush keenly, as with some warm kiss surprised.
Chief isle of the embowered Cyclades,[6]
Rejoice, oh Delos,[7] with thine olives green,
And poplars, and lawn-shading palms, and beech
In which the zephyr breathes the loudest song,
And hazels thick, dark-stemmed beneath the shade.
Apollo is once more the golden theme!
Where was he when the giant of the sun[8]
Stood bright amid the sorrow of his peers?
Together had he left his mother fair
And his twin-sister[9] sleeping in their bower,
And in the morning twilight wandered forth
Beside the osiers of a rivulet,
Full ankle-deep in lilies of the vale.
The nightingale had ceased, and a few stars
Were lingering in the heavens, while the thrush
Began calm-throated. Throughout all the isle
There was no covert,[10] no retired cave
Unhaunted by the murmurous noise of waves,
Though scarcely heard in many a green recess.
He listened and he wept, and his bright tears
Went trickling down the golden bow he held.
Thus with half-shut suffused[11] eyes he stood,
While from beneath some cumbrous boughs hard by
With solemn step an awful goddess[12] came,
And there was purport in her looks for him,
Which he with eager guess began to read
Perplexed, the while melodiously he said:

Notes

[2] *the Delphic harp* i.e. the divinely inspired harp.

[3] *the Dorian flute* flute of classical Greece. Keats echoes *Paradise Lost* i 550–1: 'the Dorian mood / Of flutes and soft recorders'. He marked the lines in his copy of Milton with the comment: 'The light and shade . . . the sorrow, the pain, the sad-sweet melody'.

[4] *the father of all verse* Apollo, god of the sun and poetry.

[5] *vermeil* bright scarlet.

[6] *Cyclades* a cluster of islands in the Aegean.

[7] *Delos* island in the centre of the Cyclades, sacred to Apollo as it was his birthplace.

[8] *the giant of the sun* Hyperion.

[9] *mother . . . twin-sister* Latona and Diana.

[10] *covert* hiding-place.

[11] *suffused* tearful.

[12] *an awful goddess* The awe-inspiring goddess is Mnemosyne, mother of the Muses by Jupiter, and another Titan. She has abandoned the Titans and joined Apollo.

'How cam'st thou over the unfooted sea?
Or hath that antique mien and robed form
Moved in these vales invisible till now?
Sure I have heard those vestments[13] sweeping o'er
The fallen leaves, when I have sat alone
In cool mid-forest. Surely I have traced
The rustle of those ample skirts about
These grassy solitudes, and seen the flowers
Lift up their heads, as still the whisper passed.
Goddess! I have beheld those eyes before,
And their eternal calm, and all that face,
Or I have dreamed.' 'Yes', said the supreme shape,
'Thou hast dreamed of me; and awaking up
Didst find a lyre all golden by thy side,
Whose strings touched by thy fingers, all the vast
Unwearied ear of the whole universe
Listened in pain and pleasure at the birth
Of such new tuneful wonder. Is't not strange
That thou shouldst weep, so gifted? Tell me, youth,
What sorrow thou canst feel – for I am sad
When thou dost shed a tear. Explain thy griefs
To one who in this lonely isle hath been
The watcher of thy sleep and hours of life,
From the young day when first thy infant hand
Plucked witless the weak flowers, till thine arm
Could bend that bow heroic to all times.
Show thy heart's secret to an ancient power
Who hath forsaken old and sacred thrones
For prophecies of thee, and for the sake
Of loveliness new born.' Apollo then,
With sudden scrutiny and gloomless eyes,[14]
Thus answered, while his white melodious throat
Throbbed with the syllables: 'Mnemosyne!
Thy name is on my tongue I know not how;
Why should I tell thee what thou so well seest?
Why should I strive to show what from thy lips
Would come no mystery? For me, dark, dark
And painful, vile oblivion seals my eyes.
I strive to search wherefore I am so sad
Until a melancholy numbs my limbs;
And then upon the grass I sit and moan
Like one who once had wings. Oh why should I
Feel cursed and thwarted, when the liegeless air[15]
Yields to my step aspirant? Why should I
Spurn the green turf as hateful to my feet?
Goddess benign, point forth some unknown thing.
Are there not other regions than this isle?
What are the stars? There is the sun, the sun!

Notes

[13] *vestments* clothes.

[14] *gloomless eyes* Apollo's gloom lifts at hearing Mnemosyne.

[15] *the liegeless air* the air has no master ('liege').

And the most patient brilliance of the moon!
And stars by thousands! Point me out the way
To any one particular beauteous star,
And I will flit into it with my lyre
And make its silvery splendour pant with bliss.
I have heard the cloudy thunder. Where is power?
Whose hand, whose essence, what divinity
Makes this alarum[16] in the elements
While I here idle listen on the shores
In fearless yet in aching[17] ignorance?
Oh tell me, lonely goddess, by thy harp
That waileth every morn and eventide,
Tell me why thus I rave about these groves!
Mute thou remainest, mute! Yet I can read
A wondrous lesson in thy silent face:
Knowledge enormous[18] makes a god of me.
Names, deeds, grey legends, dire events, rebellions,
Majesties, sovran[19] voices, agonies,
Creations and destroyings, all at once
Pour into the wide hollows of my brain
And deify me, as if some blithe wine
Or bright elixir peerless I had drunk,
And so become immortal.' Thus the god,
While his enkindled eyes, with level glance
Beneath his white soft temples, steadfast kept
Trembling with light upon Mnemosyne.
Soon wild commotions shook him, and made flush
All the immortal fairness of his limbs,
Most like the struggle at the gate of death;
Or liker still to one who should take leave
Of pale immortal death, and with a pang
As hot as death's is chill, with fierce convulse[20]
Die into life. So young Apollo anguished;
His very hair, his golden tresses famed
Kept undulation round his eager neck.
During the pain Mnemosyne upheld
Her arms as one who prophesied. At length
Apollo shrieked – and lo! from all his limbs
Celestial[21] . . .

Notes

[16] *alarum* turmoil.

[17] *aching* longing.

[18] *Knowledge enormous* Knowledge of suffering has made a god of Apollo. See Keats's admiring comments on Wordsworth for his ability to portray a world 'full of misery and heartbreak, pain, sickness, and oppression' (p. 1353).

[19] *sovran* sovereign.

[20] *convulse* convulsion.

[21] In his annotated copy of *Endymion* (1818), Woodhouse recorded that this poem, 'if completed, would have treated of the dethronement of Hyperion, the former god of the sun, by Apollo (and incidentally of those of Oceanus by Neptune, of Saturn by Jupiter, etc., and of the war of the giants for Saturn's re-establishment), with other events of which we have but very dark hints in the mythological poets of Greece and Rome. In fact, the incidents would have been pure creations of the poet's brain.' Reviewing the poem, Leigh Hunt remarked: 'If any living poet could finish this fragment, we believe it is the author himself. But perhaps he feels that he ought not' (*The Indicator*, 2 and 9 August 1820). By the time those comments were published Keats was suffering frequent episodes of blood-spitting, and was preparing his final departure for Italy.

Letter from John Keats to Richard Woodhouse, 27 October 1818[1]

My dear Woodhouse,

Your letter gave me a great satisfaction, more on account of its friendliness than any relish of that matter in it which is accounted so acceptable in the 'genus irritabile'.[2] The best answer I can give you is, in a clerk-like manner, to make some observations on two principal points, which seem to point like indices into the midst of the whole pro and con, about genius, and views, and achievements, and ambition, etc.

First: as to the poetical character itself (I mean that sort of which, if I am anything, I am a member – that sort distinguished from the Wordsworthian or egotistical sublime, which is a thing *per se* and stands alone[3]), it is not itself – it has no self – it is everything and nothing – it has no character – it enjoys light and shade – it lives in gusto,[4] be it foul or fair, high or low, rich or poor, mean or elevated. It has as much delight in conceiving an Iago as an Imogen.[5] What shocks the virtuous philosopher delights the chameleon poet. It does no harm from its relish of the dark side of things, any more than from its taste for the bright one – because they both end in speculation. A poet is the most unpoetical of any thing in existence, because he has no identity, he is continually in for – and filling – some other body. The sun, the moon, the sea, and men and women who are creatures of impulse, are poetical, and have about them an unchangeable attribute; the poet has none, no identity – he is certainly the most unpoetical of all God's creatures. If, then, he has no self, and if I am a poet, where is the wonder that I should say I would write no more? Might I not at that very instant have been cogitating on the characters of Saturn and Ops?[6] It is a wretched thing to confess, but is a very fact that not one word I ever utter can be taken for granted as an opinion growing out of my identical nature – how can it, when I have no nature? When I am in a room with people, if I ever am free from speculating on creations of my own brain, then not myself goes home to myself: but the identity of everyone in the room begins so to press upon me, that I am, in a very little time, annihilated – not only among men; it would be the same in a nursery of children. I know not whether I make myself wholly understood. I hope enough so to let you see that no dependence is to be placed on what I said that day.

In the second place I will speak of my views, and of the life I purpose to myself. I am ambitious of doing the world some good – if I should be spared, that may be the work of maturer years. In the interval I will assay to reach to as high a summit in poetry as the nerve bestowed upon me will suffer. The faint conceptions I have of poems to come brings the blood frequently into my forehead. All I hope is that I may not lose all interest in human affairs, that the solitary indifference I feel for applause, even from the finest spirits, will not blunt any acuteness of vision I may have. I do not think it will – I feel assured I should write from the mere yearning and fondness I have for the beautiful, even if my night's labours should be burnt every morning and no eye ever shine upon them.

Notes

LETTER FROM JOHN KEATS TO RICHARD WOODHOUSE

[1] This important letter about negative capability was the occasion for Woodhouse's equally important summary of it in correspondence with John Taylor on the same day; see pp. 1040–1.

[2] *genus irritabile* from Horace, *Epistles* II ii 102.

[3] *Troilus and Cressida* I ii 15–16: 'he is a very man *per se*, / And stands alone.'

[4] *gusto* as an admirer of Hazlitt, Keats uses this word in its Hazlittian sense (see p. 1336).

[5] Iago is the villain of *Othello*, Imogen the daughter to Cymbeline by a former Queen in *Cymbeline*.

[6] Saturn and Ops are characters in 'Hyperion'. Ops is usually identified with Cybele, wife of Saturn.

But even now I am perhaps not speaking from myself, but from some character in whose soul I now live. I am sure, however, that this next sentence is from myself. I feel your anxiety, good opinion, and friendliness, in the highest degree, and am

Yours most sincerely
John Keats

The Eve of St Agnes (composed 18 January–2 February 1819)[1]

From Lamia, Isabella, The Eve of St Agnes, and Other Poems (1820)

I

St. Agnes' Eve – ah, bitter chill it was!
The owl, for all his feathers, was a-cold;
The hare limped trembling through the frozen grass,
And silent was the flock in woolly fold.
Numb were the beadsman's[2] fingers, while he told[3]
His rosary, and while his frosted breath,
Like pious incense from a censer old,
Seemed taking flight for heaven, without a death,
Past the sweet Virgin's picture, while his prayer he saith.

II

His prayer he saith, this patient, holy man;
Then takes his lamp and riseth from his knees,
And back returneth, meagre,[4] barefoot, wan,
Along the chapel aisle by slow degrees.
The sculptured dead on each side seem to freeze,
Imprisoned in black, purgatorial rails;
Knights, ladies, praying in dumb orat'ries,[5]
He passeth by; and his weak spirit fails
To think how they may ache in icy hoods and mails.

Notes

The Eve of St Agnes

[1] The inspiration for this poem was the superstition that on St Agnes' Eve (20 January) virgins might use various means of divination to conjure up an image of their future husbands. Keats originally composed the poem between 18 January and 2 February 1819; he revised it in September, much to the dismay of Woodhouse, who communicated his feelings to Keats's publishers, Taylor and Hessey (see pp. 1041–2). Although Woodhouse later noted that 'Keats left it to his publishers to adopt which [alterations] they pleased,' Keats went through the proofs of the poem as printed in 1820, and insisted that some of the revisions be allowed to stand. Some of the more controversial revisions, not included in 1820, are given in footnotes.

[2] *beadsman* one paid to pray for others.

[3] *told* counted.

[4] *meagre* thin.

[5] *Knights . . . orat'ries* Keats probably saw the sculptured effigies on the tombstones in Chichester Cathedral, January 1819. An oratory is a small chapel.

III

Northward he turneth through a little door,
And scarce three steps ere music's golden tongue
Flattered to tears this aged man and poor;
But no – already had his deathbell rung,
The joys of all his life were said and sung –
His was harsh penance on St Agnes' Eve:
Another way he went, and soon among
Rough ashes sat he for his soul's reprieve,[6]
And all night kept awake, for sinners' sake to grieve.

IV

That ancient beadsman heard the prelude[7] soft,
And so it chanced, for many a door was wide
From hurry to and fro. Soon, up aloft,
The silver, snarling trumpets 'gan to chide;
The level chambers, ready with their pride,
Were glowing to receive a thousand guests;
The carved angels, ever eager-eyed,
Stared, where upon their heads the cornice[8] rests,
With hair blown back, and wings put crosswise on their breasts.

V

At length burst in the argent[9] revelry,
With plume, tiara, and all rich array,
Numerous as shadows haunting fairily
The brain, new stuffed in youth, with triumphs gay
Of old romance. These let us wish away,
And turn, sole-thoughted, to one lady there,
Whose heart had brooded all that wintry day
On love, and winged St Agnes' saintly care,
As she had heard old dames full many times declare.

VI

They told her how, upon St Agnes' Eve,
Young virgins might have visions of delight,
And soft adorings from their loves receive
Upon the honeyed middle of the night,
If ceremonies due they did aright –
As, supperless to bed they must retire,

Notes

[6] *reprieve* redemption.

[7] *prelude* introductory music.

[8] *cornice* ornamental moulding between the wall and ceiling.

[9] *argent* silver.

And couch supine their beauties, lily-white;
Nor look behind, nor sideways, but require
Of heaven with upward eyes for all that they desire.[10]

VII

Full of this whim was thoughtful Madeline.
The music, yearning like a god in pain,
She scarcely heard; her maiden eyes divine,
Fixed on the floor, saw many a sweeping train[11]
Pass by – she heeded not at all; in vain
Came many a tiptoe, amorous cavalier,
And back retired, not cooled by high disdain,
But she saw not; her heart was otherwhere.
She sighed for Agnes' dreams, the sweetest of the year.

VIII

She danced along with vague, regardless eyes;
Anxious her lips, her breathing quick and short.
The hallowed hour was near at hand: she sighs
Amid the timbrels[12] and the thronged resort
Of whisperers in anger, or in sport,
Mid looks of love, defiance, hate, and scorn,
Hoodwinked with fairy fancy – all amort,[13]
Save to St Agnes and her lambs unshorn,[14]
And all the bliss to be before tomorrow morn.

IX

So, purposing each moment to retire,
She lingered still. Meantime, across the moors
Had come young Porphyro, with heart on fire
For Madeline. Beside the portal doors,
Buttressed from moonlight,[15] stands he, and implores
All saints to give him sight of Madeline

Notes

[10] At this point in a MS version of the poem, Keats inserted an additional stanza, intended to clarify the narrative:

> 'Twas said her future lord would there appear
> Offering, as sacrifice (all in the dream),
> Delicious food, even to her lips brought near,
> Viands, and wine, and fruit, and sugared cream,
> To touch her palate with the fine extreme
> Of relish; then soft music heard, and then
> More pleasures followed in a dizzy stream,
> Palpable almost; then to wake again
> Warm in the virgin morn, no weeping Magdalen.

[11] *train* long skirts and robes sweeping along the floor.

[12] *timbrels* tambourines.

[13] *amort* listless, inanimate.

[14] *her lambs unshorn* The Feast of St Agnes is celebrated, 21 January, at Sant' Agnese fuori le Mura in Rome by the presentation and blessing of two unshorn lambs. See Margaret Visser, *The Geometry of Love: Space, Time, Mystery and Meaning in an Ordinary Church* (London, 2001), pp.119–21.

[15] *Buttressed from moonlight* Porphyro stands in the shade of a buttress.

But for one moment in the tedious hours,
That he might gaze and worship all unseen,
Perchance speak, kneel, touch, kiss – in sooth such things have been.

X

He ventures in – let no buzzed whisper tell;
All eyes be muffled, or a hundred swords
Will storm his heart, love's fev'rous citadel.
For him those chambers held barbarian hordes,[16]
Hyena foemen, and hot-blooded lords
Whose very dogs would execrations howl
Against his lineage;[17] not one breast affords
Him any mercy in that mansion foul,
Save one old beldame,[18] weak in body and in soul.

XI

Ah, happy chance! The aged creature came,
Shuffling along with ivory-headed wand
To where he stood, hid from the torch's flame
Behind a broad hall-pillar, far beyond
The sound of merriment and chorus bland.[19]
He startled her; but soon she knew his face,
And grasped his fingers in her palsied hand,
Saying, 'Mercy, Porphyro! Hie thee from this place;
They are all here tonight, the whole bloodthirsty race!

XII

Get hence! Get hence! There's dwarfish Hildebrand –
He had a fever late, and in the fit
He cursed thee and thine, both house and land;
Then there's that old Lord Maurice, not a whit
More tame for his grey hairs. Alas me! Flit,
Flit like a ghost away!' 'Ah, gossip[20] dear,
We're safe enough; here in this armchair sit
And tell me how –' 'Good Saints! Not here, not here;
Follow me, child, or else these stones will be thy bier.'

Notes

[16] *barbarian hordes* the barbarians who attacked Rome.

[17] *Against his lineage* Madeline's and Porphyro's families are at war.

[18] *beldame* old lady.

[19] *bland* soothing.

[20] *gossip* talkative old lady.

XIII

He followed through a lowly arched way,
Brushing the cobwebs with his lofty plume,
And as she muttered, 'Wel-a – wel-a-day!'[21]
He found him in a little moonlight room,
Pale, latticed, chill, and silent as a tomb.
'Now tell me where is Madeline', said he,
'Oh tell me, Angela, by the holy loom
Which none but secret sisterhood may see,
When they St Agnes' wool are weaving piously.'[22]

XIV

'St Agnes! Ah! It is St Agnes' Eve –
Yet men will murder upon holy days!
Thou must hold water in a witch's sieve
And be liege-lord[23] of all the elves and fays
To venture so; it fills me with amaze
To see thee, Porphyro! St Agnes' Eve!
God's help! My lady fair the conjuror plays[24]
This very night. Good angels her deceive![25]
But let me laugh awhile, I've mickle[26] time to grieve.'

XV

Feebly she laugheth in the languid moon,
While Porphyro upon her face doth look
Like puzzled urchin on an aged crone
Who keepeth closed a wondrous riddle-book,
As spectacled she sits in chimney nook.
But soon his eyes grew brilliant, when she told
His lady's purpose; and he scarce could brook[27]
Tears, at the thought of those enchantments cold,[28]
And Madeline asleep in lap of legends old.

Notes

[21] *Wel-a – wel-a-day* Keats is probably recalling Coleridge, *Christabel* 252. It was a fairly recent publication, having been issued at Byron's request in 1816, eighteen years after Coleridge began to write it.

[22] *by the holy loom . . . piously* The Feast of St Agnes is celebrated by the presentation and blessing of two unshorn sheep, whose wool is spun and woven by nuns.

[23] *liege-lord* master.

[24] *the conjuror plays* Madeline is attempting to conjure visions of her future husband.

[25] *Good angels her deceive* Let angels send her instead good dreams.

[26] *mickle* much.

[27] *brook* restrain.

[28] *enchantments cold* If Madeline is successful she will see only cold visions, not a living being.

XVI

Sudden a thought came like a full-blown rose,
Flushing his brow, and in his pained heart
Made purple riot;[29] then doth he propose
A stratagem that makes the beldame start:
'A cruel man and impious thou art –
Sweet lady, let her pray, and sleep, and dream
Alone with her good angels, far apart
From wicked men like thee. Go, go! I deem
Thou canst not surely be the same that thou didst seem.'

XVII

'I will not harm her, by all saints I swear',
Quoth Porphyro, 'Oh may I ne'er find grace
When my weak voice shall whisper its last prayer,
If one of her soft ringlets I displace,
Or look with ruffian passion in her face;
Good Angela, believe me by these tears,
Or I will, even in a moment's space,
Awake, with horrid shout, my foemen's ears,
And beard[30] them, though they be more fanged than wolves and bears.'

XVIII

'Ah, why wilt thou affright a feeble soul?
A poor, weak, palsy-stricken, churchyard thing,
Whose passing-bell[31] may ere the midnight toll;
Whose prayers for thee, each morn and evening,
Were never missed!' Thus plaining, doth she bring
A gentler speech from burning Porphyro;
So woeful, and of such deep sorrowing,
That Angela gives promise she will do
Whatever he shall wish, betide her weal or woe[32] –

XIX

Which was to lead him, in close secrecy,
Even to Madeline's chamber, and there hide
Him in a closet, of such privacy
That he might see her beauty unespied,
And win perhaps that night a peerless bride,
While legioned fairies paced the coverlet

Notes

[29] *Made purple riot* i.e. made his heart beat excitedly.
[30] *beard* defy.
[31] *passing-bell* death-bell.
[32] *betide her weal or woe* whether good or ill befalls her.

And pale enchantment held her sleepy-eyed.
Never on such a night have lovers met,
Since Merlin paid his Demon all the monstrous debt.[33]

XX

'It shall be as thou wishest', said the Dame,
'All cates[34] and dainties shall be stored there
Quickly on this feast-night; by the tambour frame[35]
Her own lute thou wilt see. No time to spare,
For I am slow and feeble, and scarce dare
On such a catering trust my dizzy head.
Wait here, my child, with patience; kneel in prayer
The while. Ah! Thou must needs the lady wed,
Or may I never leave my grave among the dead.'

XXI

So saying, she hobbled off with busy fear.
The lover's endless minutes slowly passed;
The dame returned, and whispered in his ear
To follow her, with aged eyes aghast
From fright of dim espial.[36] Safe at last,
Through many a dusky gallery, they gain
The maiden's chamber, silken, hushed, and chaste,
Where Porphyro took covert,[37] pleased amain.
His poor guide hurried back with agues in her brain.

XXII

Her falt'ring hand upon the balustrade,
Old Angela was feeling for the stair,
When Madeline, St Agnes' charmed maid,[38]
Rose, like a missioned spirit, unaware.
With silver taper's light, and pious care,
She turned, and down the aged gossip led
To a safe level matting. Now prepare,
Young Porphyro, for gazing on that bed:
She comes, she comes again, like ring-dove frayed[39] and fled.

Notes

33 *Since Merlin paid his Demon all the monstrous debt* The precise reference of this line has puzzled commentators. Merlin was the son of a Welsh princess and a demon-father, from whom he inherited his magical powers.

34 *cates* delicacies.

35 *tambour frame* embroidery frame.

36 *aghast . . . dim espial* terrified of not being able to see the dangers around them.

37 *took covert* hid himself.

38 *maid* maiden.

39 *frayed* frightened.

XXIII

Out went the taper as she hurried in;
Its little smoke, in pallid moonshine, died.
She closed the door, she panted, all akin
To spirits of the air, and visions wide –
No uttered syllable, or woe betide![40]
But to her heart, her heart was voluble,[41]
Paining with eloquence her balmy[42] side,
As though a tongueless nightingale should swell
Her throat in vain, and die, heart-stifled, in her dell.

XXIV

A casement high and triple-arched there was,
All garlanded with carven imag'ries[43]
Of fruits, and flowers, and bunches of knot-grass,
And diamonded with panes of quaint device,
Innumerable of stains and splendid dyes,
As are the tiger-moth's deep-damasked wings;
And in the midst, 'mong thousand heraldries,
And twilight saints, and dim emblazonings,
A shielded scutcheon[44] blushed with blood of queens and kings.

XXV

Full on this casement[45] shone the wintry moon,
And threw warm gules[46] on Madeline's fair breast,
As down she knelt for heaven's grace and boon;[47]
Rose-bloom fell on her hands, together pressed,
And on her silver cross soft amethyst,
And on her hair a glory,[48] like a saint:
She seemed a splendid angel, newly dressed,
Save wings, for heaven. Porphyro grew faint;
She knelt, so pure a thing, so free from mortal taint.

XXVI

Anon his heart revives; her vespers[49] done,
Of all its wreathed pearls her hair she frees,
Unclasps her warmed jewels one by one,

Notes

[40] *No uttered syllable, or woe betide* If she speaks she will break the spell.
[41] *voluble* beating fast with excitement.
[42] *balmy* soft and fragrant.
[43] *imag'ries* designs.
[44] *shielded scutcheon* coat-of-arms with royal quarterings on a field of gules.
[45] *casement* window.
[46] *gules* red light.
[47] *boon* blessing.
[48] *glory* halo.
[49] *vespers* evening prayers.

Loosens her fragrant bodice – by degrees
Her rich attire creeps rustling to her knees.
Half-hidden, like a mermaid in seaweed,
Pensive awhile she dreams awake, and sees
In fancy, fair St Agnes in her bed,
But dares not look behind, or all the charm is fled.

XXVII

Soon, trembling in her soft and chilly nest,
In sort of wakeful swoon, perplexed she lay,
Until the poppied warmth of sleep oppressed
Her soothed limbs, and soul fatigued away –
Flown like a thought, until the morrow-day,
Blissfully havened both from joy and pain,
Clasped like a missal where swart paynims pray;[50]
Blinded alike from sunshine and from rain,
As though a rose should shut, and be a bud again.

XXVIII

Stol'n to this paradise, and so entranced,
Porphyro gazed upon her empty dress,
And listened to her breathing, if it chanced
To wake into a slumberous tenderness;
Which when he heard, that minute did he bless,
And breathed himself, then from the closet crept,
Noiseless as fear in a wide wilderness –
And over the hushed carpet, silent stepped
And 'tween the curtains peeped, where lo! – how fast she slept.

XXIX

Then by the bedside, where the faded moon
Made a dim, silver twilight, soft he set
A table, and, half anguished, threw thereon
A cloth of woven crimson, gold, and jet.
Oh for some drowsy Morphean amulet![51]
The boisterous, midnight, festive clarion,[52]
The kettle-drum, and far-heard clarionet,
Affray his ears, though but in dying tone;
The hall door shuts again, and all the noise is gone.

Notes

[50] *Clasped like a missal where swart paynims pray* clasped like a prayer-book carried by a believer through a pagan country.

[51] *Morphean amulet* sleeping pill.

[52] *clarion* trumpet.

XXX

And still she slept an azure-lidded sleep
In blanched linen, smooth and lavendered,
While he from forth the closet brought a heap
Of candied apple, quince, and plum, and gourd;[53]
With jellies soother[54] than the creamy curd,
And lucent syrups tinct with cinnamon;[55]
Manna[56] and dates, in argosy[57] transferred
From Fez;[58] and spiced dainties, every one
From silken Samarcand to cedared Lebanon.

XXXI

These delicates he heaped with glowing hand
On golden dishes and in baskets bright
Of wreathed silver; sumptuous they stand
In the retired quiet of the night,
Filling the chilly room with perfume light.
'And now, my love, my seraph fair, awake!
Thou art my heaven, and I thine eremite.[59]
Open thine eyes, for meek St Agnes' sake,
Or I shall drowse beside thee, so my soul doth ache.'

XXXII

Thus whispering, his warm, unnerved[60] arm
Sank in her pillow. Shaded was her dream
By the dusk curtains; 'twas a midnight charm
Impossible to melt as iced stream.
The lustrous salvers in the moonlight gleam,
Broad golden fringe[61] upon the carpet lies;
It seemed he never, never could redeem
From such a steadfast spell his lady's eyes;
So mused awhile, entoiled in woofed[62] fantasies.

XXXIII

Awakening up, he took her hollow lute;
Tumultuous, and, in chords that tenderest be,
He played an ancient ditty, long since mute,

Notes

[53] *gourd* melon.
[54] *soother* more soothing.
[55] *lucent syrups tinct with cinnamon* clear syrups tinged with cinnamon.
[56] *Manna* probably an exotic fruit.
[57] *argosy* large merchant ship.
[58] *Fez* in northern Morocco.
[59] *eremite* hermit.
[60] *unnerved* weak.
[61] *golden fringe* of the tablecloth.
[62] *woofed* woven.

In Provence called, 'La belle dame sans mercy',[63]
Close to her ear touching the melody –
Wherewith disturbed, she uttered a soft moan.
He ceased – she panted quick – and suddenly
Her blue affrayed[64] eyes wide open shone;
Upon his knees he sank, pale as smooth-sculptured stone.

XXXIV

Her eyes were open, but she still beheld,
Now wide awake, the vision of her sleep –
There was a painful change, that nigh expelled
The blisses of her dream so pure and deep.
At which fair Madeline began to weep
And moan forth witless words with many a sigh,
While still her gaze on Porphyro would keep;
Who knelt, with joined hands and piteous eye,
Fearing to move or speak, she looked so dreamingly.

XXXV

'Ah, Porphyro!' said she, 'but even now
Thy voice was at sweet tremble in mine ear,
Made tuneable with every sweetest vow,
And those sad eyes were spiritual[65] and clear.
How changed thou art! How pallid, chill, and drear!
Give me that voice again, my Porphyro,
Those looks immortal, those complainings dear!
Oh leave me not in this eternal woe,
For if thou diest, my love, I know not where to go.'

XXXVI

Beyond a mortal man impassioned far
At these voluptuous accents, he arose
Ethereal, flushed, and like a throbbing star
Seen mid the sapphire heaven's deep repose;
Into her dream he melted, as the rose
Blendeth its odour with the violet –
Solution sweet.[66] Meantime the frost-wind blows
Like love's alarum pattering the sharp sleet
Against the window-panes; St Agnes' moon hath set.

Notes

[63] *La belle dame sans mercy* title of a poem by Alain Chartier, 1424 – as well as one by Keats (p. 1390n1).

[64] *affrayed* startled.

[65] *spiritual* lacking bodily substance.

[66] The revised version of lines 314–22 reads:

See, while she speaks, his arms encroaching slow,
Have zoned her, heart to heart – loud, loud the dark winds blow!

For on the midnight came a tempest fell;
More sooth, for that his quick rejoinder flows
Into her burning ear – and still the spell
Unbroken guards her in serene repose.
With her wild dream he mingled, as a rose
Marryeth its odour to a violet.
Still, still she dreams; louder the frost-wind blows . . .

For Woodhouse's comment on the stanza, see p. 1042 above.

XXXVII

'Tis dark; quick pattereth the flaw-blown sleet.[67]
'This is no dream, my bride, my Madeline!'
'Tis dark; the iced gusts still rave and beat.
'No dream, alas! Alas, and woe is mine!
Porphyro will leave me here to fade and pine.
Cruel! What traitor could thee hither bring?
I curse not, for my heart is lost in thine,
Though thou forsakest a deceived thing,
A dove forlorn and lost with sick unpruned[68] wing.'

XXXVIII

'My Madeline! Sweet dreamer! Lovely bride!
Say, may I be for aye thy vassal blessed?
Thy beauty's shield, heart-shaped and vermeil dyed?
Ah, silver shrine, here will I take my rest
After so many hours of toil and quest,
A famished pilgrim, saved by miracle.
Though I have found, I will not rob thy nest,
Saving of thy sweet self – if thou think'st well
To trust, fair Madeline, to no rude infidel.

XXXIX

Hark! 'Tis an elfin-storm from fairy land,
Of haggard seeming,[69] but a boon[70] indeed.
Arise, arise! The morning is at hand;
The bloated wassaillers will never heed.
Let us away, my love, with happy speed;
There are no ears to hear, or eyes to see,
Drowned all in Rhenish[71] and the sleepy mead.
Awake! Arise, my love, and fearless be,
For o'er the southern moors I have a home for thee.'

XL

She hurried at his words, beset with fears,
For there were sleeping dragons[72] all around,
At glaring watch, perhaps, with ready spears;
Down the wide stairs a darkling[73] way they found.

Notes

[67] *flaw-blown sleet* sleet blown by a sudden, tempestuous gust of wind.

[68] *unpruned* unpreened.

[69] *haggard seeming* wild appearance.

[70] *boon* blessing.

[71] *Rhenish* wine from the Rhine valley.

[72] *dragons* dragoons.

[73] *darkling* dark.

In all the house was heard no human sound;
A chain-drooped lamp was flickering by each door;
The arras,[74] rich with horseman, hawk, and hound
Fluttered in the besieging wind's uproar,
And the long carpets rose along the gusty floor.

XLI

They glide, like phantoms, into the wide hall;
Like phantoms to the iron porch they glide,
Where lay the porter, in uneasy sprawl,
With a huge empty flagon by his side;
The wakeful bloodhound rose and shook his hide,
But his sagacious eye an inmate owns.
By one, and one, the bolts full easy slide,
The chains lie silent on the footworn stones –
The key turns, and the door upon its hinges groans.

XLII

And they are gone – aye, ages long ago
These lovers fled away into the storm.
That night the Baron dreamt of many a woe,
And all his warrior-guests, with shade and form
Of witch and demon, and large coffin-worm,
Were long be-nightmared. Angela the old
Died palsy-twitched,[75] with meagre face deform;
The beadsman, after thousand aves told,
For aye unsought for, slept among his ashes cold.

Journal-Letter from John Keats to George and Georgiana Keats, 14 February–3 May 1819 (extracts)[1]

[16 April 1819] Last Sunday I took a walk towards Highgate and, in the lane that winds by the side of Lord Mansfield's park, I met Mr Green, our demonstrator at Guy's, in conversation with Coleridge.[2] I joined them, after enquiring by a look whether it would be agreeable. I walked with him at his alderman[3]-after-dinner pace for near two miles, I suppose. In those two miles he broached a thousand things; let me see if I can give you a list. Nightingales, poetry – on poetical sensation – metaphysics – different genera and species of dreams – nightmare – a dream accompanied by a sense of touch

Notes

[74] *arras* tapestry.

[75] *Angela . . . palsy-twitched* for Woodhouse's view of this, see pp. 1041–2.

Journal-Letter from John Keats

[1] The lengthy journal-letter from which these two extracts are taken is one of Keats's most entertaining and illuminating.

[2] Coleridge's account of this meeting can be found on p. 713. It took place in the grounds of Kenwood House, seat of William Murray, Lord Mansfield (1705–93). Joseph Henry Green (1791–1863) was Coleridge's literary executor, and had been Keats's demonstrator at Guy's Hospital, 1815–16.

[3] *alderman* '[portly, elderly] dignitary'.

– single and double touch – a dream related – first and second consciousness – the difference explained between will and volition – so many metaphysicians from a want of smoking – the second consciousness – monsters – the kraken[4] – mermaids – Southey believes in them – Southey's belief too much diluted – a ghost story – Good morning – I heard his voice as he came towards me – I heard it as he moved away – I had heard it all the interval (if it may be called so). He was civil enough to ask me to call on him at Highgate[5] goodnight! It looks so much like rain I shall not go to town to day, but put it off till tomorrow . . . .

[21 April 1819[1]] The common cognomen[2] of this world among the misguided and superstitious is 'a vale of tears', from which we are to be redeemed by a certain arbitrary interposition of God and taken to Heaven. What a little, circumscribed, straitened notion! Call the world, if you please, 'the Vale of Soul-Making'. Then you will find out the use of the world. (I am speaking now in the highest terms for human nature, admitting it to be immortal – which I will here take for granted for the purpose of showing a thought which has struck me concerning it.) I say 'Soul-Making' soul, as distinguished from an intelligence – there may be intelligences or sparks of the divinity in millions, but they are not souls till they acquire identities, till each one is personality itself.

Intelligences are atoms of perception. They know and they see and they are pure – in short, they are God. How then are souls to be made? How then are these sparks which are God to have identity[3] given them – so as ever to possess a bliss peculiar to each one's individual existence? How, but by the medium of a world like this? This point I sincerely wish to consider because I think it a grander system of salvation than the Christian religion – or rather it is a system of spirit-creation. This is effected by three grand materials acting the one upon the other for a series of years. These three materials are the intelligence; the human heart (as distinguished from intelligence or mind); and the world or elemental space suited for the proper action of mind and heart on each other for the purpose of forming the soul or intelligence destined to possess the sense of identity. I can scarcely express what I but dimly perceive, and yet I think I perceive it. That you may judge the more clearly I will put it in the most homely form possible: I will call the *world* a school instituted for the purpose of teaching little children to read; I will call the *human heart* the hornbook[4] used in that school; and I will call the *child able to read it* the soul made from that school and its hornbook.

Do you not see how necessary a world of pains and troubles is to school an intelligence and make it a soul, a place where the heart must feel and suffer in a thousand diverse ways? Not merely is the heart a hornbook, it is the mind's Bible, it is the mind's experience, it is the teat from which the mind or intelligence sucks its identity. As various as the lives of men are, so various become their souls, and thus does God make individual beings, souls, identical souls of the sparks of his own essence. This appears to me a faint sketch of a system of salvation which does not

Notes

[4] *kraken* mythical sea-monster of enormous size.

[5] Coleridge was at this time resident at Highgate in north London, at the home of Dr James Gillman.

21 April 1819

[1] For useful comment on this important letter see John Barnard, *John Keats* (Cambridge, 1987), pp. 134–5. Keats's remarks relate to his 'Ode to Psyche', which was copied out later in this letter.

[2] *cognomen* nickname.

[3] *identity* Rollins suggests that Keats must have been reading John Locke's *Essay Concerning Human Understanding* (1690), Book II, chapter 27, 'Of Identity or Diversity'.

[4] *hornbook* In Keats's day children learned the alphabet from a leaf of paper mounted on a piece of wood with a handle. The paper was protected by a thin piece of horn.

affront our reason and humanity; I am convinced that many difficulties which Christians labour under would vanish before it.

There is one which even now strikes me: the salvation of children. In them the spark or intelligence returns to God without any identity, it having had no time to learn of, and be altered by, the heart – or seat of the human passions. It is pretty generally suspected that the Christian scheme has been copied from the ancient Persian and Greek philosophers. Why may they not have made this simple thing even more simple for common apprehension, by introducing mediators and personages in the same manner as in the heathen mythology abstractions are personified? Seriously, I think it probable that this system of soul-making may have been the parent of all the more palpable and personal schemes of redemption, among the Zoroastrians,[5] the Christians, and the Hindus.[6] For as one part of the human species must have their carved Jupiter, so another part must have the palpable and named mediator and saviour – their Christ, their Oromanes,[7] and their Vishnu.[8]

If what I have said should not be plain enough, as I fear it may not be, I will put you in the place where I began in this series of thoughts. I mean, I began by seeing how man was formed by circumstances – and what are circumstances, but touchstones[9] of his heart? And what are touchstones, but provings of his heart? And what are provings of his heart, but fortifiers or alterers of his nature? And what is his altered nature, but his soul? And what was his soul before it came into the world and had these provings and alterations and perfectionings? An intelligence without identity – and how is this identity to be made? Through the medium of the heart? And how is the heart to become this medium, but in a world of circumstances?

La Belle Dame Sans Merci: A Ballad (composed 21 April 1819; edited from MS)[1]

I

Oh what can ail thee, knight-at-arms,
Alone and palely loitering?
The sedge has withered from the lake,
And no birds sing.

Notes

[5] *Zoroastrians* followers of the Zoroastrian religion, which originated in India and spread to Persia (modern-day Iran).

[6] For Keats, Christianity derives from ancient philosophies, offering a redemptive scheme which is as valid as Hinduism and Zoroastrianism.

[7] *Oromanes* Oromanes or Ahriman is the evil spirit in the dualistic doctrine of Zoroastrianism, who is opposed to Ormuzd, the deity of light. Keats is thus mistaken in thinking of him as a 'mediator and saviour'. Numerous sources for Keats's knowledge of Oromanes are suggested. Rollins suggests that he was probably an admirer of J. R. Planché's *Abudah, or the Talisman of Oromanes*, performed during Easter 1819 in London. Ronald Tetreault points out to me (via the NASSR-List) that in 1813–16 Thomas Love Peacock projected (and wrote part of) a twelve-Book epic poem entitled *Ahrimanes*, about which Keats may have known (see *Shelley and his Circle* ed. Kenneth Neil Cameron, vol. 3 (1970), pp. 211–44).

[8] *Vishnu* preserver of the universe in Hindu mythology.

[9] *touchstone* anything that can be used to test the authenticity of something else.

La Belle Dame Sans Merci

[1] The poem's title derives from Alain Chartier's poem of 1424, which existed in a translation believed in Keats's day to be by Chaucer. For other possible sources, see headnote, p. 1339. Keats's poem, believed to be one of his finest, was published in a revised version in Hunt's magazine *The Indicator*, 10 May 1820, over the signature, 'Caviare'. It is widely agreed that the manuscript version, published here, is the better of the two.

2

Oh what can ail thee, knight-at-arms,
So haggard and so woe-begone?
The squirrel's granary is full,
And the harvest's done.

3

I see a lily on thy brow
With anguish moist and fever dew,
And on thy cheeks a fading rose
Fast withereth too.

4

I met a lady in the meads,
Full beautiful – a fairy's child;
Her hair was long, her foot was light,
And her eyes were wild.

5

I made a garland for her head,
And bracelets too, and fragrant zone;[2]
She looked at me as she did love,
And made sweet moan.

6

I set her on my pacing steed,
And nothing else saw all day long,
For sidelong would she bend, and sing
A fairy's song.

7

She found me roots of relish sweet,
And honey wild and manna dew,[3]
And sure in language strange she said,
'I love thee true'.

Notes

[2] *fragrant zone* belt made out of flowers.

[3] *honey wild and manna dew* Keats is recalling the conclusion of Coleridge's 'Kubla Khan': 'For he on honey-dew hath fed / And drank the milk of paradise.'

8

She took me to her elfin grot
And there she wept, and sighed full sore,
And there I shut her wild wild eyes
With kisses four.[4]

9

And there she lulled me asleep,
And there I dreamed – ah, woe betide! –
The latest dream I ever dreamed
On the cold hill's side.

10

I saw pale kings and princes too,
Pale warriors, death-pale were they all;
They cried, 'La belle dame sans merci
Hath thee in thrall!'

11

I saw their starved lips in the gloam[5]
With horrid warning gaped wide,
And I awoke and found me here
On the cold hill's side.

12

And this is why I sojourn here,
Alone and palely loitering,
Though the sedge is withered from the lake,
And no birds sing.

Notes

[4] *kisses four* Sending this poem to his brother George, Keats wrote: 'Why four kisses? you will say. Why four? Because I wish to restrain the headlong impetuosity of my Muse. She would have fain said "score" without hurting the rhyme – but we temper the imagination (as the critics say) with judgment. I was obliged to choose an even number, that both eyes might have fair play: and to speak truly I think two a piece quite sufficient. Suppose I had said "seven"? There would have been three and a half apiece, a very awkward affair' (Rollins ii 97).

[5] *gloam* twilight.

Ode to Psyche (composed 21–30 April 1819)[1]

From Lamia, Isabella, The Eve of St. Agnes, and Other Poems (1820)

Oh goddess! Hear these tuneless numbers,[2] wrung
By sweet enforcement and remembrance dear,
And pardon that thy secrets should be sung
Even into thine own soft-conched[3] ear.
Surely I dreamt today, or did I see
The winged Psyche with awakened eyes?
I wandered in a forest thoughtlessly,[4]
And, on the sudden, fainting with surprise,
Saw two fair creatures, couched side by side
In deepest grass, beneath the whisp'ring roof
Of leaves and trembled blossoms, where there ran
A brooklet, scarce espied.[5]
Mid hushed, cool-rooted flowers, fragrant-eyed,
Blue, silver-white, and budded Tyrian,[6]
They lay calm-breathing on the bedded grass;
Their arms embraced, and their pinions[7] too;
Their lips touched not, but had not bade adieu,
As if disjoined by soft-handed slumber,
And ready still past kisses to outnumber
At tender eye-dawn of aurorean[8] love.
The winged boy[9] I knew;
But who wast thou, oh happy, happy dove?
His Psyche true!

Oh latest born and loveliest vision far
Of all Olympus' faded hierarchy![10]
Fairer than Phoebe's sapphire-regioned star,[11]
Or Vesper,[12] amorous glow-worm of the sky;
Fairer than these, though temple thou hast none,
Nor altar heaped with flowers;
Nor virgin-choir to make delicious moan
Upon the midnight hours;

Notes

ODE TO PSYCHE

[1] According to Keats's source, Lemprière's *Bibliotheca Classica* (1788), Psyche was 'a nymph whom Cupid [Eros] married and carried to a place of bliss, where he long enjoyed her company. Venus put her to death because she had robbed the world of her son; but Jupiter, at the request of Cupid, granted immortality to Psyche. The word signifies *the soul*, and this personification of Psyche is posterior to the Augustan age, though still it is connected with ancient mythology. Psyche is generally represented with the wings of a butterfly, to intimate the lightness of the soul, of which the butterfly is the symbol, and on that account, among the ancients, when a man has just expired, a butterfly appeared fluttering above, as if rising from the mouth of the deceased.' Keats was an admirer of Mary Tighe's *Psyche* (1805), and Claude Lorrain's famous painting, *Landscape with Psyche outside the Palace of Cupid* (1664, now at the National Gallery, London). For more commentary, see headnote p. 1339.

[2] *tuneless numbers* his poetry.

[3] *soft-conched* her ear is shaped like a conch-shell.

[4] *thoughtlessly* without an anxious thought.

[5] *scarce espied* seen only with difficulty.

[6] *Tyrian* purple, after the dye made at Tyre.

[7] *pinions* wings.

[8] *aurorean* roseate.

[9] *The winged boy* Cupid.

[10] *Olympus' faded hierarchy* The gods of Olympus are faded by comparison with the beauty of Psyche.

[11] *Phoebe's sapphire-regioned star* the moon, of which Phoebe is goddess.

[12] *Vesper* evening star.

No voice, no lute, no pipe, no incense sweet
From chain-swung censer teeming;
No shrine, no grove, no oracle, no heat
Of pale-mouthed prophet dreaming.[13]

Oh brightest! though too late for antique vows,
Too, too late for the fond believing lyre,[14]
When holy were the haunted forest boughs,
Holy the air, the water and the fire;
Yet even in these days so far retired
From happy pieties, thy lucent fans,[15]
Fluttering among the faint Olympians,
I see, and sing, by my own eyes inspired.
So let me be thy choir, and make a moan
Upon the midnight hours;
Thy voice, thy lute, thy pipe, thy incense sweet
From swinged censer teeming;
Thy shrine, thy grove, thy oracle, thy heat
Of pale-mouthed prophet dreaming.

Yes, I will be thy priest, and build a fane[16]
In some untrodden region of my mind,
Where branched thoughts, new grown with pleasant pain,
Instead of pines shall murmur in the wind;
Far, far around shall those dark-clustered trees
Fledge the wild-ridged mountains steep by steep;
And there by zephyrs, streams, and birds, and bees,
The moss-lain dryads[17] shall be lulled to sleep;
And in the midst of this wide quietness
A rosy sanctuary will I dress
With the wreathed trellis of a working brain,
With buds, and bells, and stars without a name,
With all the gardener Fancy e'er could feign,[18]
Who, breeding flowers, will never breed the same:
And there shall be for thee all soft delight
That shadowy thought can win –
A bright torch, and a casement[19] ope at night,
To let the warm love in!

Notes

[13] *No heat . . . dreaming* There are no prophets inspired to speak on Psyche's behalf.

[14] *fond believing lyre* hymns sung by the unquestioningly devoted.

[15] *lucent fans* shining wings.

[16] *fane* temple.

[17] *dryads* wood-nymphs.

[18] *feign* invent.

[19] *casement* window.

Ode to a Nightingale (composed May 1819)[1]

From Lamia, Isabella, The Eve of St. Agnes, and Other Poems (1820)

1

My heart aches, and a drowsy numbness pains
My sense, as though of hemlock[2] I had drunk,
Or emptied some dull opiate to the drains[3]
One minute past,[4] and Lethe-wards[5] had sunk;
'Tis not through envy of thy happy lot,
But being too happy in thine happiness,
That thou, light-winged dryad[6] of the trees,
In some melodious plot
Of beechen green, and shadows numberless,
Singest of summer in full-throated ease.

2

Oh for a draught of vintage![7] that hath been
Cooled a long age in the deep-delved earth,
Tasting of flora and the country green,
Dance, and Provençal song, and sunburnt mirth!
Oh for a beaker full of the warm south,[8]
Full of the true, the blushful Hippocrene,[9]
With beaded bubbles winking at the brim,
And purple-stained mouth;
That I might drink, and leave the world unseen,
And with thee fade away into the forest dim –

3

Fade far away, dissolve, and quite forget
What thou among the leaves hast never known,
The weariness,[10] the fever, and the fret
Here, where men sit and hear each other groan;

Notes

Ode to a Nightingale

[1] Twenty years after the event Keats's friend Charles Brown recorded how this poem was composed: 'In the spring of 1819 a nightingale had built her nest near my house. Keats felt a tranquil and continual joy in her song; and one morning he took his chair from the breakfast-table to the grass-plot under a plum-tree, where he sat for two or three hours. When he came into the house, I perceived he had some scraps of paper in his hand, and these he was quietly thrusting behind the books. On enquiry, I found those scraps, four or five in number, contained his poetic feeling on the song of our nightingale. The writing was not well legible; and it was difficult to arrange the stanzas on so many scraps. With his assistance I succeeded, and this was his "Ode to a Nightingale", a poem which has been the delight of everyone' (*Keats Circle* ii 65). See also headnote, p. 1339.

[2] *hemlock* can be used as a sedative; it should be noted that Keats is not saying that he has actually taken hemlock.

[3] *drains* dregs.

[4] *past* ago.

[5] *Lethe-wards* towards Lethe, river of forgetfulness in Hades, from which souls drank to forget their past lives.

[6] *dryad* wood-nymph.

[7] *vintage* wine.

[8] *warm south* wine from the Mediterranean.

[9] *Hippocrene* spring sacred to the muses on Mt Helicon. Keats means wine.

[10] *weariness* Wordsworth had written of 'hours of weariness' amid the 'din / Of towns and cities' in *Tintern Abbey* 26–8.

Where palsy shakes a few, sad, last grey hairs,
  Where youth grows pale, and spectre-thin, and dies;[11]
    Where but to think is to be full of sorrow
      And leaden-eyed despairs;
  Where Beauty cannot keep her lustrous eyes,
    Or new Love pine at them beyond tomorrow.

4

Away! Away! For I will fly to thee,
  Not charioted by Bacchus and his pards,[12]
But on the viewless[13] wings of Poesy,
  Though the dull brain perplexes and retards;
Already with thee! Tender is the night,
  And haply[14] the Queen Moon is on her throne,
    Clustered around by all her starry fays;[15]
      But here there is no light
  Save what from heaven is with the breezes blown
    Through verdurous glooms and winding mossy ways.

5

I cannot see what flowers are at my feet,
  Nor what soft incense hangs upon the boughs,
But, in embalmed darkness,[16] guess each sweet
  Wherewith the seasonable month[17] endows
The grass, the thicket, and the fruit-tree wild,
  White hawthorn, and the pastoral eglantine,
    Fast-fading violets covered up in leaves,
      And mid-May's eldest child,
  The coming musk-rose,[18] full of dewy wine,
    The murmurous haunt of flies on summer eves.

6

Darkling[19] I listen; and for many a time
  I have been half in love with easeful Death,
Called him soft names in many a mused rhyme,
  To take into the air my quiet breath;
Now more than ever seems it rich to die,
  To cease upon the midnight with no pain,

Notes

[11] *Where youth . . . dies* often taken to refer to the death of Tom Keats from consumption, 1 December 1818. Cf. Wordsworth, *Excursion* iv 760: 'While man grows old, and dwindles, and decays'.

[12] *Not charioted by Bacchus and his pards* Keats' source, Lemprière's *Bibliotheca Classica* (1788), recorded that when Bacchus (god of wine) travelled east, he 'was drawn in a chariot by a lion and a tyger and was accompanied by Pan and Silenus and all the satyrs'.

[13] *viewless* invisible.

[14] *haply* perhaps.

[15] *fays* fairies.

[16] *embalmed darkness* The night is full of the scent of plants.

[17] *the seasonable month* May.

[18] *The coming musk-rose* usually flowers in June.

[19] *Darkling* in darkness.

While thou art pouring forth thy soul abroad
In such an ecstasy!
Still wouldst thou sing, and I have ears in vain –
To thy high requiem become a sod.

7

Thou wast not born for death, immortal bird!
No hungry generations tread thee down;
The voice I hear this passing night was heard
In ancient days by emperor and clown:[20]
Perhaps the self-same song that found a path
Through the sad heart of Ruth, when, sick for home,
She stood in tears amid the alien corn;[21]
The same that oft-times hath
Charmed magic casements, opening on the foam
Of perilous seas, in fairy lands forlorn.

8

Forlorn! The very word is like a bell
To toll me back from thee to my sole self!
Adieu! The fancy cannot cheat so well
As she is famed to do, deceiving elf.
Adieu! Adieu! Thy plaintive anthem fades
Past the near meadows, over the still stream,
Up the hillside, and now 'tis buried deep
In the next valley-glades:
Was it a vision, or a waking dream?
Fled is that music – do I wake or sleep?

Ode on a Grecian Urn (composed *c.* May 1819)[1]

From Lamia, Isabella, The Eve of St Agnes, and Other Poems (1820)

1

Thou still unravished bride of quietness,
Thou foster-child of silence and slow time,[2]
Sylvan historian,[3] who canst thus express
A flowery tale more sweetly than our rhyme –

Notes

[20] *clown* peasant.

[21] *Through the . . . corn* Ruth was forced, by famine, to leave home and labour in the fields of her kinsman, Boaz (Ruth 2: 1–2).

Ode on a Grecian Urn

[1] The inspiration for this poem came from a variety of sources, including the Townley Vase at the British Museum and the Elgin Marbles (reproduced in Woof and Hebron, *John Keats* (Grasmere, 1995), pp. 128–30). See also headnote, pp. 1339–40.

[2] *foster-child of silence and slow time* The potter who made the vase is dead, leaving it to be fostered by time and silence.

[3] *Sylvan historian* The vase is a historian because it tells a story; 'sylvan' refers to the pastoral scenes it depicts.

What leaf-fringed legend haunts about thy shape
Of deities or mortals, or of both,
In Tempe or the dales of Arcady?[4]
What men or gods are these? What maidens loath?
What mad pursuit? What struggle to escape?
What pipes and timbrels?[5] What wild ecstasy?

2

Heard melodies are sweet, but those unheard
Are sweeter; therefore, ye soft pipes, play on –
Not to the sensual[6] ear, but, more endeared,
Pipe to the spirit ditties of no tone:
Fair youth, beneath the trees, thou canst not leave
Thy song, nor ever can those trees be bare;
Bold lover, never, never canst thou kiss,
Though winning near the goal – yet do not grieve;
She cannot fade, though thou hast not thy bliss,
For ever wilt thou love, and she be fair!

3

Ah, happy, happy boughs! that cannot shed
Your leaves, nor ever bid the spring adieu;
And, happy melodist, unwearied,
For ever piping songs for ever new;
More happy love, more happy, happy love!
For ever warm and still to be enjoyed,
For ever panting and for ever young;
All breathing human passion far above,[7]
That leaves a heart high-sorrowful and cloyed,
A burning forehead, and a parching tongue.

4

Who are these coming to the sacrifice?
To what green altar, oh mysterious priest,
Lead'st thou that heifer lowing at the skies,
And all her silken flanks with garlands dressed?
What little town by river or seashore,
Or mountain-built with peaceful citadel,
Is emptied of this folk, this pious morn?
And, little town, thy streets for evermore
Will silent be, and not a soul to tell
Why thou art desolate, can e'er return.

Notes

[4] Tempe and Arcadia, places known in classical times for their beauty and the happiness of their inhabitants.

[5] *timbrels* tambourines.

[6] *sensual* of sense.

[7] *All breathing . . . above* Compare Hazlitt's remarks on Greek statuary, 'On Gusto', p. 759.

Figure 18 This tracing of an engraving of the Sosibios Vase in the Louvre, attributed to Keats, is thought to be one of the influences on his 'Ode on a Grecian Urn'. (Keats–Shelley Memorial Association, Rome.)

5

Oh Attic[8] shape! Fair attitude! With brede[9]
   Of marble men and maidens overwrought,[10]
With forest branches and the trodden weed;
   Thou, silent form, dost tease us out of thought
As doth eternity. Cold Pastoral!
   When old age shall this generation waste,
      Thou shalt remain, in midst of other woe
Than ours, a friend to man, to whom thou say'st,
   'Beauty is truth, truth beauty'; that is all
      Ye know on earth, and all ye need to know.

Notes

[8] *Attic* Grecian.

[9] *brede* braid.

[10] *overwrought* fashioned over the surface of the urn.

Ode on Melancholy (composed *c.* May 1819)[1]

From Lamia, Isabella, The Eve of St Agnes, and Other Poems (1820)

1

No, no, go not to Lethe, neither twist
Wolfsbane,[2] tight-rooted, for its poisonous wine;
Nor suffer thy pale forehead to be kissed
By nightshade,[3] ruby grape of Proserpine;[4]
Make not your rosary of yew-berries,[5]
Nor let the beetle, nor the death-moth[6] be
Your mournful Psyche, nor the downy owl
A partner in your sorrow's mysteries;
For shade to shade will come too drowsily,
And drown the wakeful anguish of the soul.

2

But when the melancholy fit shall fall
Sudden from heaven like a weeping cloud,
That fosters the droop-headed flowers all,
And hides the green hill in an April shroud;
Then glut thy sorrow on[7] a morning rose,
Or on the rainbow of the salt sand-wave,
Or on the wealth of globed peonies;
Or if thy mistress some rich anger shows,
Imprison her soft hand, and let her rave,
And feed deep, deep upon her peerless eyes.

3

She dwells with Beauty – Beauty that must die;
And Joy, whose hand is ever at his lips
Bidding adieu; and aching Pleasure nigh,
Turning to poison while the bee-mouth sips.
Aye, in the very temple of Delight

Notes

Ode on Melancholy

[1] Miriam Allott remarks: 'The poem is a characteristic Keatsian statement about the necessary relationship between joy and sorrow. True Melancholy is not to be found among thoughts of oblivion, death and gloom (stanza 1); it descends suddenly and is linked with the perception of beauty and its transience (stanza 2); it is associated with beauty, joy, pleasure and delight and is felt only by those who can experience these intensely (stanza 3).' A cancelled opening stanza in MS reads:

> Though you should build a bark of dead men's bones,
> And rear a phantom gibbet for a mast,
> Stitch creeds together for a sail, with groans
> To fill it out, bloodstained and aghast;
> Although your rudder be a dragon's tail,
> Long severed, yet still hard with agony,
> Your cordage large uprootings from the skull
> Of bald Medusa, certes you would fail
> To find the Melancholy – whether she
> Dreameth in any isle of Lethe dull.

[2] *Wolfsbane* aconite, a poisonous plant.

[3] *nightshade* a poisonous plant with bright red berries.

[4] *Proserpine* Queen of the Underworld.

[5] *yew-berries* Yew-trees have small red berries which are poisonous.

[6] *death-moth* The death's head moth has markings which resemble a human skull.

[7] *glut . . . on* enjoy to the full . . . by thinking of.

Veiled Melancholy has her sovran shrine,
Though seen of none save him whose strenuous tongue
Can burst Joy's grape against his palate fine;
His soul shall taste the sadness of her might,
And be among her cloudy trophies hung.

Ode on Indolence (composed between 19 March and 9 June 1819; edited from MS)[1]

They toil not, neither do they spin.[2]

1

One morn before me were three figures seen,
With bowed necks and joined hands, side-faced;
And one behind the other stepped serene,
In placid sandals and in white robes graced;
They passed, like figures on a marble urn,
When shifted round to see the other side;
They came again, as when the urn once more
Is shifted round, the first-seen shades return –
And they were strange to me, as may betide
With vases, to one deep in Phidian lore.[3]

2

How is it, shadows, that I knew ye not?
How came ye muffled in so hush[4] a masque?[5]
Was it a silent deep-disguised plot
To steal away, and leave without a task
My idle days? Ripe was the drowsy hour;
The blissful cloud of summer indolence
Benumbed my eyes; my pulse grew less and less;
Pain had no sting, and pleasure's wreath no flower –
Oh why did ye not melt, and leave my sense
Unhaunted quite of all but – nothingness?

3

A third time passed they by, and, passing, turned
Each one the face a moment whiles to me;
Then faded, and to follow them I burned
And ached for wings, because I knew the three:
The first was a fair maid, and Love her name;

Notes

Ode on Indolence

[1] This poem was not included in Keats's 1820 volume.

[2] Matthew 6: 28: 'Consider the lilies of the field, how they grow; they toil not, neither do they spin.'

[3] *Phidian lore* scupture; Phidias (born *c.*500 BC) may have designed and probably supervised construction of the Elgin marbles.

[4] *hush* silent.

[5] *masque* procession.

The second was Ambition, pale of cheek
  And ever watchful with fatigued eye;
The last, whom I love more, the more of blame
  Is heaped upon her, maiden most unmeek,
    I knew to be my demon Poesy.

4

They faded, and, forsooth, I wanted wings!
  Oh folly! What is love? And where is it?
And, for that poor ambition – it springs
  From a man's little heart's short fever-fit;[6]
For Poesy! No, she has not a joy –
  At least for me – so sweet as drowsy noons,
    And evenings steeped in honeyed indolence.
Oh for an age so sheltered from annoy,[7]
  That I may never know how change the moons,
    Or hear the voice of busy common sense!

5

A third time came they by – alas, wherefore?
  My sleep had been embroidered with dim dreams;
My soul had been a lawn besprinkled o'er
  With flowers, and stirring shades, and baffled beams;
The morn was clouded, but no shower fell,
  Though in her lids hung the sweet tears of May;
    The open casement pressed a new-leaved vine,
Let in the budding warmth and throstle's lay –
  Oh shadows, 'twas a time to bid farewell!
    Upon your skirts had fallen no tears of mine.

6

So ye three ghosts, adieu! Ye cannot raise
  My head cool-bedded in the flowery grass,
For I would not be dieted with praise –
  A pet-lamb in a sentimental farce![8]
Fade softly from my eyes, and be once more
  In masque-like figures on the dreamy urn;
    Farewell! I yet have visions for the night,
And for the day faint visions there is store.
  Vanish, ye phantoms, from my idle sprite,
    Into the clouds, and never more return!

Notes

[6] *fever-fit* an echo of *Macbeth* III ii 23: 'After life's fitful fever he sleeps well.'

[7] *annoy* harm.

[8] *For I would not . . . farce* Keats is saying that praise from reviewers is worthless, as it is as patronizing as the stroking of a lamb.

Lamia (Part I written c.28 June and 11 July 1819, completed 12 August and *c*.5 September 1819, revised March 1820)[1]

From Lamia, Isabella, The Eve of St Agnes, and Other Poems (1820)

Part I

Upon a time, before the fairy broods
Drove nymph and satyr from the prosperous woods,[2]
Before King Oberon's bright diadem,
Sceptre, and mantle, clasped with dewy gem,
Frighted away the dryads[3] and the fauns
From rushes green, and brakes, and cowslipped lawns,[4]
The ever-smitten Hermes[5] empty left
His golden throne, bent warm on amorous theft.
From high Olympus had he stolen light
On this side of Jove's clouds, to escape the sight
Of his great summoner, and made retreat
Into a forest on the shores of Crete,
For somewhere in that sacred island[6] dwelt
A nymph to whom all hoofed satyrs knelt,
At whose white feet the languid Tritons[7] poured
Pearls, while on land they withered and adored.
Fast by the springs where she to bathe was wont,
And in those meads where sometime she might haunt,
Were strewn rich gifts, unknown to any muse,[8]
Though fancy's casket were unlocked to choose.
'Ah, what a world of love was at her feet!'
So Hermes thought, and a celestial heat
Burnt from his winged heels to either ear,

Notes

LAMIA

[1] When the poem was published in 1820, Keats added a note providing the source for this poem: ' "Philostratus, in his fourth book *de Vita Apollonii*, hath a memorable instance in this kind, which I may not omit, of one Menippus Lycius, a young man twenty-five years of age, that going betwixt Cenchreas and Corinth, met such a phantasm in the habit of a fair gentlewoman, which taking him by the hand, carried him home to her house in the suburbs of Corinth, and told him she was a Phoenician by birth, and if he would tarry with her, he should hear her sing and play, and drink such wine as never any drank, and no man should molest him; but she, being fair and lovely, would live and die with him, that was fair and lovely to behold. The young man, a philosopher, otherwise staid and discreet, able to moderate his passions, though not this of love, tarried with her a while to his great content, and at last married her, to whose wedding, amongst other guests, came Apollonius; who, by some probable conjectures, found her out to be a serpent, a lamia; and that all her furniture was, like Tantalus' gold, described by Homer, no substance but mere illusions. When she saw herself descried, she wept, and desired Apollonius to be silent, but he would not be moved, and thereupon she, plate, house, and all that was in it, vanished in an instant: many thousands took notice of this fact, for it was done in the midst of Greece." Burton's *Anatomy of Melancholy* Part 3. Sect. 2. Memb. 1. Subs. 1.' As Gittings has observed, Keats was reading extensively in Burton throughout the spring and summer of 1819; see Robert Gittings, *John Keats: The Living Year* (1954). As soon as he saw it, Keats knew that the lamia story would fascinate his readers: 'I am certain there is that sort of fire in it which must take hold of people in some way – give them either pleasant or unpleasant sensation. What they want is a sensation of some sort' (Rollins ii 189). For more comment see headnote, p. 1340.

[2] *prosperous woods* the woods were more widespread than now.

[3] *dryads* wood-nymphs.

[4] *before the fairy broods . . . lawns* i.e. before medieval fairy-lore had superseded classical myth.

[5] *The ever-smitten Hermes* or Mercury, messenger of the gods, celebrated for his numerous love affairs.

[6] *sacred island* Crete was sacred as the birthplace of Zeus.

[7] *Tritons* sea-gods – half-man, half-fish.

[8] *unknown to any muse* beyond the imagination of any poet.

That from a whiteness, as the lily clear,
Blushed into roses mid his golden hair,
Fallen in jealous curls about his shoulders bare.
  From vale to vale, from wood to wood, he flew,
Breathing upon the flowers his passion new,
And wound with many a river to its head
To find where this sweet nymph prepared her secret bed –
In vain; the sweet nymph might nowhere be found.
And so he rested on the lonely ground,
Pensive, and full of painful jealousies
Of the wood-gods, and even the very trees.
There as he stood, he heard a mournful voice,
Such as once heard, in gentle heart, destroys
All pain but pity. Thus the lone voice spake:
'When from this wreathed tomb shall I awake?
When move in a sweet body fit for life
And love and pleasure, and the ruddy strife
Of hearts and lips? Ah, miserable me!'
The god, dove-footed, glided silently
Round bush and tree, soft-brushing, in his speed,
The taller grasses and full-flowering weed,
Until he found a palpitating snake,
Bright, and cirque-couchant[9] in a dusky brake.
  She was a gordian[10] shape of dazzling hue,
Vermilion-spotted, golden, green, and blue;
Striped like a zebra, freckled like a pard,[11]
Eyed like a peacock, and all crimson barred;
And full of silver moons that, as she breathed,
Dissolved, or brighter shone, or interwreathed
Their lustres with the gloomier tapestries –
So rainbow-sided, touched with miseries,
She seemed at once some penanced lady elf,
Some demon's mistress, or the demon's self.
Upon her crest she wore a wannish fire
Sprinkled with stars, like Ariadne's tiar;[12]
Her head was serpent but – ah, bitter-sweet! –
She had a woman's mouth with all its pearls complete.
And for her eyes: what could such eyes do there
But weep and weep, that they were born so fair? –
As Proserpine[13] still weeps for her Sicilian air.
Her throat was serpent, but the words she spake
Came, as through bubbling honey, for love's sake,
And thus; while Hermes on his pinions lay,
Like a stooped falcon ere he takes his prey.

Notes

[9] *cirque-couchant* lying in circular coils.
[10] *gordian* intricately knotted.
[11] *pard* leopard.
[12] *Ariadne's tiar* Ariadne was loved by Bacchus, god of wine. He gave her a crown of seven stars which, after her death, was made into a constellation. Keats probably has in mind Titian's painting, *Bacchus and Ariadne*, now in the National Gallery, London.
[13] Proserpine, gathering flowers in the Vale of Enna in Sicily, was carried off by Pluto, king of the underworld, to be his queen.

'Fair Hermes, crowned with feathers, fluttering light,
I had a splendid dream of thee last night:
I saw thee sitting on a throne of gold
Among the gods upon Olympus old,
The only sad one – for thou didst not hear
The soft, lute-fingered Muses chaunting clear,
Nor even Apollo when he sang alone,
Deaf to his throbbing throat's long, long melodious moan.
I dreamt I saw thee, robed in purple flakes,[14]
Break amorous through the clouds, as morning breaks,
And, swiftly as a bright Phoebean dart,[15]
Strike for the Cretan isle – and here thou art!
Too gentle Hermes, hast thou found the maid?'
Whereat the star of Lethe[16] not delayed
His rosy eloquence, and thus enquired:
'Thou smooth-lipped serpent, surely high inspired!
Thou beauteous wreath, with melancholy eyes,
Possess whatever bliss thou canst devise,
Telling me only where my nymph is fled –
Where she doth breathe!' 'Bright planet, thou hast said',
Returned the snake, 'but seal with oaths, fair God!'
'I swear', said Hermes, 'by my serpent rod,
And by thine eyes, and by thy starry crown!'
Light flew his earnest words among the blossoms blown.
Then thus again the brilliance feminine:
'Too frail of heart! for this lost nymph of thine,
Free as the air, invisibly she strays
About these thornless wilds; her pleasant days
She tastes unseen; unseen her nimble feet
Leave traces in the grass and flowers sweet;
From weary tendrils and bowed branches green
She plucks the fruit unseen, she bathes unseen:
And by my power is her beauty veiled
To keep it unaffronted, unassailed
By the love-glances of unlovely eyes,
Of satyrs, fauns, and bleared Silenus'[17] sighs.
Pale grew her immortality, for woe
Of all these lovers, and she grieved so
I took compassion on her, bade her steep
Her hair in weird syrups that would keep
Her loveliness invisible, yet free
To wander as she loves, in liberty.
Thou shalt behold her, Hermes, thou alone,
If thou wilt, as thou swearest, grant my boon!'

Notes

[14] *purple flakes* fleecy clouds, coloured by the sun.

[15] *Phoebean dart* a ray of the sun, Phoebus being god of the sun.

[16] *the star of Lethe* Hermes, so-called because he led the souls of the dead to Hades over Lethe, the river of forgetfulness.

[17] Silenus, a demi-god of the woods, was foster-father of Bacchus.

Then once again, the charmed god began
An oath, and through the serpent's ears it ran
Warm, tremulous, devout, psalterian.[18]
Ravished, she lifted her Circean[19] head,
Blushed a live damask, and swift-lisping said:
'I was a woman, let me have once more
A woman's shape, and charming as before.
I love a youth of Corinth – oh the bliss!
Give me my woman's form, and place me where he is.
Stoop, Hermes, let me breathe upon thy brow,
And thou shalt see thy sweet nymph even now.'
The god on half-shut feathers sank serene,
She breathed upon his eyes, and swift was seen
Of both the guarded nymph near-smiling[20] on the green.
It was no dream – or say a dream it was,
Real are the dreams of gods, and smoothly pass
Their pleasures in a long immortal dream.
One warm, flushed moment, hovering, it might seem
Dashed by the wood-nymph's beauty, so he burned;
Then, lighting on the printless verdure, turned
To the swooned[21] serpent, and with languid arm
Delicate, put to proof the lithe caducean charm.[22]
So done, upon the nymph his eyes he bent
Full of adoring tears and blandishment,
And towards her stepped; she, like a moon in wane,
Faded before him, cowered, nor could restrain
Her fearful sobs, self-folding like a flower
That faints into itself at evening hour.
But the god fostering her chilled hand,
She felt the warmth, her eyelids opened bland,
And, like new flowers at morning song of bees,
Bloomed, and gave up her honey to the lees;[23]
Into the green-recessed woods they flew,
Nor grew they pale, as mortal lovers do.
Left to herself, the serpent now began
To change; her elfin blood in madness ran,
Her mouth foamed, and the grass, therewith besprent,[24]
Withered at dew so sweet and virulent.
Her eyes in torture fixed, and anguish drear,
Hot, glazed, and wide, with lid-lashes all sear,[25]
Flashed phosphor and sharp sparks, without one cooling tear.
The colours all inflamed throughout her train,
She writhed about, convulsed with scarlet pain;
A deep volcanian yellow took the place

Notes

[18] *psalterian* like the sound of a psaltery, an antique stringed instrument.

[19] *Circean* Circe was the enchantress who was capable of turning men into animals.

[20] *near-smiling* smiling nearby.

[21] *swooned* with love.

[22] *lithe caducean charm* an olive staff wound about with two intertwined ('lithe') snakes at one end.

[23] *gave up her honey to the lees* surrendered totally.

[24] *besprent* sprinkled – an archaism even in Keats' day.

[25] *sear* scorched.

Of all her milder-mooned body's grace,
And, as the lava ravishes the mead,[26]
Spoilt all her silver mail, and golden brede,
Made gloom of all her frecklings, streaks and bars,
Eclipsed her crescents, and licked up her stars.
So that in moments few she was undressed
Of all her sapphires, greens, and amethyst,
And rubious-argent;[27] of all these bereft,
Nothing but pain and ugliness were left.
Still shone her crown – that vanished, also she
Melted and disappeared as suddenly,
And in the air, her new voice luting soft,
Cried, 'Lycius! Gentle Lycius!' Borne aloft
With the bright mists about the mountains hoar
These words dissolved – Crete's forests heard no more.
   Whither fled Lamia, now a lady bright,
A full-born beauty new and exquisite?
She fled into that valley they pass o'er
Who go to Corinth from Cenchreas' shore,
And rested at the foot of those wild hills,
The rugged founts of the Peraean rills,
And of that other ridge whose barren back
Stretches, with all its mist and cloudy rack,
South-westward to Cleone. There she stood
About a young bird's flutter from a wood,
Fair on a sloping green of mossy tread,
By a clear pool, wherein she passioned
To see herself escaped from so sore ills,
While her robes flaunted[28] with the daffodils.
   Ah, happy Lycius! For she was a maid
More beautiful than ever twisted braid,
Or sighed, or blushed, or on spring-flowered lea
Spread a green kirtle[29] to the minstrelsy –
A virgin purest lipped, yet in the lore
Of love deep learned to the red heart's core;
Not one hour old, yet of sciential[30] brain
To unperplex bliss from its neighbour pain;
Define their pettish limits, and estrange
Their points of contact, and swift counterchange;
Intrigue with the specious chaos, and dispart
Its most ambiguous atoms with sure art,
As though in Cupid's college she had spent
Sweet days a lovely graduate, still unshent,[31]
And kept his rosy terms in idle languishment.

Notes

[26] *lava ravishes the mead* lava buries and burns the grass.
[27] *rubious-argent* silver embedded with rubies.
[28] *flaunted* waved vigorously.
[29] *kirtle* woman's gown.
[30] *sciential* wise.
[31] *unshent* unspoilt.

Why this fair creature chose so fairily
By the wayside to linger, we shall see;
But first 'tis fit to tell how she could muse
And dream, when in the serpent prison-house,
Of all she list, strange or magnificent;
How, ever, where she willed, her spirit went –
Whether to faint Elysium,[32] or where
Down through tress-lifting waves the nereids[33] fair
Wind into Thetis'[34] bower by many a pearly stair,
Or where god Bacchus drains his cups divine,
Stretched out at ease beneath a glutinous[35] pine,
Or where in Pluto's[36] gardens palatine[37]
Mulciber's columns gleam in far piazzian line.[38]
And sometimes into cities she would send
Her dream, with feast and rioting to blend;
And once, while among mortals dreaming thus,
She saw the young Corinthian Lycius
Charioting foremost in the envious race
Like a young Jove with calm uneager face
And fell into a swooning love of him.
Now on the moth-time[39] of that evening dim
He would return that way, as well she knew,
To Corinth from the shore – for freshly blew
The eastern soft wind, and his galley now
Grated the quaystones with her brazen prow
In port Cenchreas, from Egina isle
Fresh anchored, whither he had been awhile
To sacrifice to Jove, whose temple there
Waits with high marble doors for blood and incense rare.
Jove heard his vows, and bettered his desire;
For by some freakful chance he made retire
From his companions, and set forth to walk,
Perhaps grown wearied of their Corinth talk.
Over the solitary hills he fared,
Thoughtless at first, but ere eve's star appeared
His fantasy was lost where reason fades,
In the calmed twilight of Platonic shades.[40]
Lamia beheld him coming, near, more near –
Close to her passing, in indifference drear,
His silent sandals swept the mossy green;
So neighboured to him, and yet so unseen
She stood. He passed, shut up in mysteries,
His mind wrapped like his mantle, while her eyes

Notes

[32] *Elysium* paradisal place of rest where Greek heroes were believed to spend an afterlife revelling and sporting in the sunshine.

[33] *nereids* water-nymphs.

[34] *Thetis* sea-deity, the daughter of Nereus and Doris.

[35] *glutinous* resinous.

[36] Pluto was king of the underworld.

[37] *palatine* palatial.

[38] *in far piazzian line* the construction resembles a piazza – a square or colonnaded walkway surrounded by buildings. Keats is recalling the construction of Pandemonium by Mulciber (Vulcan) in *Paradise Lost* i 713–15.

[39] *moth-time* early evening.

[40] *In the calm . . . shades* Lycius begins his walk unthinkingly, but starts to meditate on Plato's mystic philosophy.

Followed his steps, and her neck regal white
Turned, syllabling thus: 'Ah, Lycius bright,
And will you leave me on the hills alone?
Lycius, look back, and be some pity shown!'
He did, not with cold wonder fearingly,
But Orpheus-like at an Eurydice[41] –
For so delicious were the words she sung,
It seemed he had loved them a whole summer long.
And soon his eyes had drunk her beauty up,
Leaving no drop in the bewildering cup,
And still the cup was full – while he, afraid
Lest she should vanish ere his lip had paid
Due adoration, thus began to adore;
Her soft look growing coy, she saw his chain[42] so sure.
'Leave thee alone! Look back! Ah, goddess, see
Whether my eyes can ever turn from thee!
For pity do not this sad heart belie –
Even as thou vanishest so I shall die.
Stay, though a Naiad of the rivers, stay!
To thy far wishes will thy streams obey;
Stay, though the greenest woods be thy domain,
Alone they can drink up the morning rain!
Though a descended Pleiad,[43] will not one
Of thine harmonious sisters keep in tune
Thy spheres,[44] and as thy silver proxy shine?
So sweetly to these ravished ears of mine
Came thy sweet greeting, that if thou shouldst fade
Thy memory will waste me to a shade:
For pity do not melt!'
'If I should stay',
Said Lamia, 'here, upon this floor of clay,
And pain my steps upon these flowers too rough,
What canst thou say or do of charm enough
To dull the nice remembrance of my home?
Thou canst not ask me with thee here to roam
Over these hills and vales, where no joy is –
Empty of immortality and bliss!
Thou art a scholar, Lycius, and must know
That finer spirits cannot breathe below
In human climes, and live. Alas, poor youth,
What taste of purer air hast thou to soothe
My essence? What serener palaces,
Where I may all my many senses please,
And by mysterious sleights a hundred thirsts appease?
It cannot be. Adieu!'

Notes

[41] Orpheus nearly managed to reclaim his wife, Eurydice, from Hades, but lost her forever when he looked back at her out of curiosity.

[42] *chain* the metaphorical 'chain' of love.

[43] The Pleiades were the seven daughters of Atlas, who became a constellation after death.

[44] *Thy spheres* reference to the music which the heavenly bodies were believed to make as they circled the earth.

So said, she rose
Tiptoe with white arms spread. He, sick to lose
The amorous promise of her lone complain,[45]
Swooned, murmuring of love, and pale with pain.
The cruel lady, without any show
Of sorrow for her tender favourite's woe –
But rather, if her eyes could brighter be,
With brighter eyes and slow amenity,
Put her new lips to his, and gave afresh
The life she had so tangled in her mesh;
And as he from one trance was wakening
Into another, she began to sing,
Happy in beauty, life, and love, and everything,
A song of love, too sweet for earthly lyres,
While, like held breath, the stars drew in their panting fires.
 And then she whispered in such trembling tone,
As those who, safe together met alone
For the first time through many anguished days,
Use other speech than looks – bidding him raise
His drooping head, and clear his soul of doubt,
For that she was a woman, and without
Any more subtle[46] fluid in her veins
Than throbbing blood, and that the self-same pains
Inhabited her frail-strung heart as his.
And next she wondered how his eyes could miss
Her face so long in Corinth, where, she said,
She dwelt but half retired, and there had led
Days happy as the gold coin could invent
Without the aid of love – yet in content
Till she saw him, as once she passed him by,
Where 'gainst a column he leant thoughtfully
At Venus' temple porch, mid baskets heaped
Of amorous herbs and flowers, newly reaped
Late on that eve, as 'twas the night before
The Adonian feast;[47] whereof she saw no more,
But wept alone those days, for why should she adore?
 Lycius from death awoke into amaze
To see her still, and singing so sweet lays;
Then from amaze into delight he fell
To hear her whisper woman's lore so well;
And every word she spake enticed him on
To unperplexed delight and pleasure known.
Let the mad poets say whate'er they please
Of the sweets of fairies, peris,[48] goddesses;
There is not such a treat among them all,

Notes

[45] *complain* complaint.
[46] *subtle* rarefied.
[47] *The Adonian feast* a fertility ritual held annually in Venus' temple. Adonis was the beautiful young man in love with Venus, killed by a boar while hunting.
[48] *peris* superhuman beings or good genii from Persian myth.

Haunters of cavern, lake, and waterfall,
As a real woman, lineal indeed
From Pyrrha's pebbles[49] or old Adam's seed.
Thus gentle Lamia judged, and judged aright,
That Lycius could not love in half a fright,
So threw the goddess off, and won his heart
More pleasantly by playing woman's part
With no more awe than what her beauty gave,
That, while it smote, still guaranteed to save.
Lycius to all made eloquent reply,
Marrying to every word a twinborn sigh;
And last, pointing to Corinth, asked her sweet,
If 'twas too far that night for her soft feet.
The way was short, for Lamia's eagerness
Made, by a spell, the triple league decrease
To a few paces – not at all surmised
By blinded Lycius, so in her comprised.[50]
They passed the city gates, he knew not how,
So noiseless, and he never thought to know.
   As men talk in a dream, so Corinth all,
Throughout her palaces imperial,
And all her populous streets and temples lewd[51]
Muttered like tempest in the distance brewed
To the wide-spreaded night above her towers.
Men, women, rich and poor, in the cool hours,
Shuffled their sandals o'er the pavement white,
Companioned or alone, while many a light
Flared here and there from wealthy festivals,
And threw their moving shadows on the walls,
Or found them clustered in the corniced shade
Of some arched temple door or dusky colonnade.
   Muffling his face, of greeting friends in fear,
Her fingers he pressed hard, as one came near
With curled gray beard, sharp eyes, and smooth bald crown,
Slow-stepped, and robed in philosophic gown.
Lycius shrank closer as they met and passed
Into his mantle, adding wings to haste,
While hurried Lamia trembled. 'Ah', said he,
'Why do you shudder, love, so ruefully?
Why does your tender palm dissolve in dew?'
'I'm wearied', said fair Lamia. 'Tell me who
Is that old man? I cannot bring to mind

Notes

[49] Exasperated by the crimes of humanity, Jupiter is said to have sent a flood that covered the world. The only ones to be saved, Deucalion and Pyrrha, repopulated the world by throwing stones behind them which turned into men and women.

[50] *comprised* absorbed.

[51] *lewd* Keats is thinking of Robert Burton's description of Corinth: 'It was plenty of all things, which made Corinth so infamous of old, and the opportunity of the place to entertain those foreign comers, every day strangers came in, at each gate, from all quarters. In that one temple of Venus a thousand whores did prostitute themselves . . . all nations resorted thither as to a school of Venus' (*Anatomy of Melancholy* III 2 ii 1).

His features. Lycius, wherefore did you blind
Yourself from his quick eyes?' Lycius replied,
''Tis Apollonius[52] sage, my trusty guide
And good instructor. But tonight he seems
The ghost of folly haunting my sweet dreams.'
While yet he spake they had arrived before
A pillared porch with lofty portal door,
Where hung a silver lamp, whose phosphor[53] glow
Reflected in the slabbed steps below,
Mild as a star in water – for so new
And so unsullied was the marble hue,
So through the crystal polish, liquid fine,
Ran the dark veins, that none but feet divine
Could e'er have touched there. Sounds Aeolian[54]
Breathed from the hinges, as the ample span
Of the wide doors disclosed a place unknown
Some time to any, but those two alone,
And a few Persian mutes, who that same year
Were seen about the markets; none knew where
They could inhabit – the most curious
Were foiled, who watched to trace them to their house.
And but the flitter-winged verse must tell,
For truth's sake, what woe afterwards befell;
'Twould humour many a heart to leave them thus,
Shut from the busy world of more incredulous.

Part II

Love in a hut,[1] with water and a crust,
Is (Love forgive us!) cinders, ashes, dust;
Love in a palace is perhaps at last
More grievous torment than a hermit's fast:
That is a doubtful tale from fairyland,
Hard for the non-elect to understand.
Had Lycius lived to hand his story down
He might have given the moral a fresh frown
Or clenched it quite[2] – but too short was their bliss
To breed distrust and hate, that make the soft voice hiss.
Besides, there, nightly, with terrific glare,
Love, jealous[3] grown of so complete a pair,
Hovered and buzzed his wings with fearful roar
Above the lintel of their chamber door,
And down the passage cast a glow upon the floor.[4]

Notes

[52] Apollonius of Tyana, philosopher of the first century AD, whose life was recorded by Philostratus. He advocated strict moral and religious reform, and was credited with magic powers.

[53] *phosphor* phosphorescent.

[54] *Sounds Aeolian* i.e. like the sounds of an Aeolian harp.

PART II

[1] *hut* cottage.

[2] *clenched it quite* proved it conclusively.

[3] *jealous* protective.

[4] *Love . . . floor* Cupid guards perfect love from intrusion.

For all[5] this came a ruin: side by side
They were enthroned in the eventide,
Upon a couch, near to a curtaining
Whose airy texture, from a golden string,
Floated into the room, and let appear
Unveiled the summer heaven, blue and clear,
Betwixt two marble shafts.[6] There they reposed
Where use had made it sweet, with eyelids closed,
Saving a tithe[7] which love still open kept,
That they might see each other while they almost slept –
When, from the slope side of a suburb hill,
Deafening the swallow's twitter, came a thrill
Of trumpets. Lycius started – the sounds fled,
But left a thought, a buzzing in his head.
For the first time, since first he harboured in
That purple-lined palace of sweet sin,
His spirit passed beyond its golden bourn[8]
Into the noisy world almost forsworn.
The lady, ever watchful, penetrant,[9]
Saw this with pain, so arguing a want
Of something more, more than her empery[10]
Of joys; and she began to moan and sigh
Because he mused beyond her, knowing well
That but a moment's thought is passion's passing-bell.
'Why do you sigh, fair creature?' whispered he.
'Why do you think?' returned she tenderly;
'You have deserted me; where am I now?
Not in your heart while care weighs on your brow.
No, no, you have dismissed me, and I go
From your breast houseless – aye, it must be so.'
He answered, bending to her open eyes,
Where he was mirrored small in paradise:
'My silver planet,[11] both of eve and morn!
Why will you plead yourself so sad forlorn
While I am striving how to fill my heart
With deeper crimson and a double smart?
How to entangle, trammel up[12] and snare
Your soul in mine, and labyrinth you there
Like the hid scent in an unbudded rose?
Aye, a sweet kiss – you see your mighty woes.
My thoughts! Shall I unveil them? Listen then!
What mortal hath a prize, that other men
May be confounded and abashed withal,
But lets it sometimes pace abroad majestical
And triumph, as in thee I should rejoice
Amid the hoarse alarm of Corinth's voice?
Let my foes choke, and my friends shout afar,

Notes

[5] *For all* in spite of.
[6] *marble shafts* two marble pillars supporting the lintel of the window.
[7] *tithe* a small part.
[8] *bourn* realm, domain.
[9] *penetrant* perceptive, acute.
[10] *empery* empire.
[11] *silver planet* Venus, star of morning and evening.
[12] *trammel up* enmesh.

While through the thronged streets your bridal car
Wheels round its dazzling spokes!'
The lady's cheek
Trembled; she nothing said but, pale and meek,
Arose and knelt before him, wept a rain
Of sorrows at his words; at last with pain
Beseeching him, the while his hand she wrung
To change his purpose. He thereat was stung,
Perverse, with stronger fancy to reclaim
Her wild and timid nature to his aim –
Besides, for all his love, in self-despite,
Against his better self, he took delight
Luxurious in her sorrows, soft and new.
His passion, cruel grown, took on a hue
Fierce and sanguineous[13] as 'twas possible
In one whose brow had no dark veins to swell.
Fine was the mitigated[14] fury, like
Apollo's presence when in act to strike
The serpent[15] – ha, the serpent! Certes[16] she
Was none. She burnt, she loved the tyranny,
And, all subdued, consented to the hour
When to the bridal he should lead his paramour.
Whispering in midnight silence, said the youth:
'Sure some sweet name thou hast, though, by my truth,
I have not asked it, ever thinking thee
Not mortal, but of heavenly progeny,
As still I do. Hast any mortal name,
Fit appellation for this dazzling frame?
Or friends or kinsfolk on the citied earth,
To share our marriage feast and nuptial mirth?'
'I have no friends', said Lamia, 'no, not one;
My presence in wide Corinth hardly known.
My parents' bones are in their dusty urns
Sepulchred, where no kindled incense burns,
Seeing all their luckless race are dead, save me –
And I neglect the holy rite for thee.
Even as you list invite your many guests;
But if, as now it seems, your vision rests
With any pleasure on me, do not bid
Old Apollonius – from him keep me hid.'
Lycius, perplexed at words so blind and blank,
Made close enquiry, from whose touch she shrank,
Feigning a sleep – and he to the dull shade
Of deep sleep in a moment was betrayed.[17]
It was the custom then to bring away
The bride from home at blushing shut of day

Notes

[13] *sanguineous* red with anger.
[14] *mitigated* moderated.
[15] Apollo killed a huge dragon (called Python) at Delphi, where he established his shrine.
[16] *Certes* certainly.
[17] *to the dull shade . . . betrayed* Lycius is tricked into a deep sleep by Lamia's magic spell.

Veiled in a chariot, heralded along
By strewn flowers, torches, and a marriage song,
With other pageants – but this fair unknown
Had not a friend. So being left alone
(Lycius was gone to summon all his kin)
And knowing surely she could never win
His foolish heart from its mad pompousness,[18]
She set herself, high-thoughted, how to dress
The misery in fit magnificence.
She did so, but 'tis doubtful how and whence
Came, and who were her subtle[19] servitors.
About the halls, and to and from the doors
There was a noise of wings, till in short space
The glowing banquet-room shone with wide-arched grace.
A haunting music, sole perhaps and lone
Supportress of the fairy-roof, made moan
Throughout, as fearful the whole charm might fade.
Fresh carved cedar, mimicking a glade
Of palm and plantain,[20] met from either side
High in the midst, in honour of the bride –
Two palms and then two plantains, and so on,
From either side their stems branched one to one
All down the aisled place; and beneath all
There ran a stream of lamps straight on from wall to wall.
So canopied, lay an untasted feast
Teeming with odours. Lamia, regal dressed,
Silently paced about, and as she went,
In pale contented sort of discontent,
Missioned her viewless[21] servants to enrich
The fretted[22] splendour of each nook and niche.
Between the tree-stems, marbled plain at first,
Came jasper panels; then anon there burst
Forth creeping imagery of slighter trees,
And with the larger wove in small intricacies.
Approving all, she faded[23] at self-will,
And shut the chamber up, close, hushed and still,
Complete and ready for the revels rude,
When dreadful guests would come to spoil her solitude.
The day appeared, and all the gossip rout.
Oh senseless Lycius! Madman! Wherefore flout
The silent-blessing fate, warm cloistered hours,
And show to common eyes these secret bowers?
The herd approached – each guest, with busy brain,
Arriving at the portal, gazed amain,
And entered marvelling, for they knew the street,
Remembered it from childhood all complete
Without a gap, yet ne'er before had seen

Notes

[18] *pompousness* love of display.
[19] *subtle* invisible.
[20] *plantain* a tropical tree-like plant.
[21] *viewless* invisible.
[22] *fretted* carved.
[23] *faded* disappeared, as if by magic.

That royal porch, that high-built fair demesne.[24]
So in they hurried all, mazed, curious and keen,
Save one who looked thereon with eye severe,
And with calm-planted steps walked in austere;
'Twas Apollonius; something too he laughed,
As though some knotty problem, that had daffed[25]
His patient thought, had now begun to thaw
And solve and melt – 'twas just as he foresaw.
  He met within the murmurous vestibule
His young disciple. ''Tis no common rule,
Lycius', said he, 'for uninvited guest
To force himself upon you, and infest
With an unbidden presence the bright throng
Of younger friends – yet must I do this wrong,
And you forgive me.' Lycius blushed, and led
The old man through the inner doors broad-spread;
With reconciling words and courteous mien
Turning into sweet milk the sophist's[26] spleen.
  Of wealthy lustre was the banquet-room,
Filled with pervading brilliance and perfume;
Before each lucid[27] panel fuming stood
A censer fed with myrrh and spiced wood,
Each by a sacred tripod held aloft
Whose slender feet wide-swerved upon the soft
Wool-woofed carpets; fifty wreaths of smoke
From fifty censers their light voyage took
To the high roof, still mimicked as they rose
Along the mirrored walls by twin-clouds odorous.
Twelve sphered tables, by silk seats ensphered,
High as the level of a man's breast reared
On libbard's[28] paws, upheld the heavy gold
Of cups and goblets, and the store thrice told
Of Ceres' horn,[29] and, in huge vessels, wine
Come from the gloomy tun[30] with merry shine.
Thus loaded with a feast the tables stood,
Each shrining in the midst the image of a god.
  When in an ante-chamber every guest
Had felt the cold full sponge to pleasure pressed
By minist'ring slaves upon his hands and feet,
And fragrant oils with ceremony meet
Poured on his hair, they all moved to the feast
In white robes, and themselves in order placed
Around the silken couches, wondering
Whence all this mighty cost and blaze of wealth could spring.
  Soft went the music the soft air along,
While fluent Greek a vowelled undersong

Notes

[24] *demesne* palace.
[25] *daffed* toyed with, baffled.
[26] *sophist* philosopher.
[27] *lucid* shining.
[28] *libbard's* leopard's.
[29] *Ceres' horn* the horn of plenty.
[30] *tun* cask.

Kept up among the guests, discoursing low
At first, for scarcely was the wine at flow;
But when the happy vintage touched their brains,
Louder they talk, and louder come the strains
Of powerful instruments. The gorgeous dyes,
The space, the splendour of the draperies,
The roof of awful richness, nectarous cheer,
Beautiful slaves and Lamia's self appear,
Now, when the wine has done its rosy deed,
And every soul from human trammels freed,
No more so strange – for merry wine, sweet wine,
Will make Elysian shades not too fair, too divine.[31]
  Soon was god Bacchus at meridian height;
Flushed were their cheeks, and bright eyes double bright.
Garlands of every green, and every scent
From vales deflowered, or forest-trees branch-rent,
In baskets of bright osiered[32] gold were brought
High as the handles heaped, to suit the thought
Of every guest – that each, as he did please,
Might fancy-fit his brows, silk-pillowed at his ease.
  What wreath for Lamia? What for Lycius?
What for the sage, old Apollonius?
Upon her aching forehead be there hung
The leaves of willow and of adder's tongue;[33]
And for the youth – quick, let us strip for him
The thyrsus,[34] that his watching eyes may swim
Into forgetfulness; and, for the sage,
Let spear-grass and the spiteful thistle wage
War on his temples. Do not all charms fly
At the mere touch of cold philosophy?
There was an awful[35] rainbow once in heaven:
We know her woof, her texture – she is given
In the dull catalogue of common things.
Philosophy will clip an angel's wings,
Conquer all mysteries by rule and line,
Empty the haunted air, and gnomed mine,
Unweave a rainbow, as it erewhile made
The tender-personed Lamia melt into a shade.
  By her glad Lycius sitting in chief place
Scarce saw in all the room another face
Till, checking his love trance, a cup he took
Full brimmed, and opposite sent forth a look
'Cross the broad table, to beseech a glance
From his old teacher's wrinkled countenance,

Notes

[31] Wine makes the idyllic world of the Elysian fields seem less remote.

[32] *osiered* woven.

[33] *The leaves of willow and of adder's tongue* emblems of grief; adder's tongue is a fern once used as a medicine for its soothing properties.

[34] Lycius' wreath is made from the ivy and vine-leaves wrapped round Bacchus' thyrsus (wand).

[35] *awful* awesome, awe-inspiring.

And pledge him. The bald-head philosopher
Had fixed his eye without a twinkle or stir
Full on the alarmed beauty of the bride,
Brow-beating her fair form, and troubling her sweet pride.
Lycius then pressed her hand, with devout touch,
As pale it lay upon the rosy couch:
'Twas icy, and the cold ran through his veins –
Then sudden it grew hot, and all the pains
Of an unnatural heat shot to his heart.
'Lamia, what means this? Wherefore dost thou start?
Know'st thou that man?' Poor Lamia answered not.
He gazed into her eyes, and not a jot
Owned they the lovelorn piteous appeal;
More, more he gazed; his human senses reel;
Some hungry spell that loveliness absorbs –
There was no recognition in those orbs.
'Lamia!' he cried – and no soft-toned reply.
The many heard, and the loud revelry
Grew hush; the stately music no more breathes;
The myrtle sickened in a thousand wreaths.
By faint degrees, voice, lute, and pleasure ceased;
A deadly silence step by step increased
Until it seemed a horrid presence there,
And not a man but felt the terror in his hair.
'Lamia!' he shrieked – and nothing but the shriek
With its sad echo did the silence break.
'Begone, foul dream!' he cried, gazing again
In the bride's face, where now no azure vein
Wandered on fair-spaced temples; no soft bloom
Misted the cheek; no passion to illume
The deep-recessed vision – all was blight.
Lamia, no longer fair, there sat a deadly white.
    'Shut, shut those juggling[36] eyes, thou ruthless man!
Turn them aside, wretch, or the righteous ban
Of all the gods, whose dreadful images
Here represent their shadowy presences,
May pierce them on the sudden with the thorn
Of painful blindness – leaving thee forlorn,
In trembling dotage to the feeblest fright
Of conscience, for their long offended might,
For all thine impious proud-heart sophistries,
Unlawful magic, and enticing lies.
Corinthians, look upon that gray-beard wretch!
Mark how, possessed, his lashless eyelids stretch
Around his demon eyes! Corinthians, see!
My sweet bride withers at their potency.'
    'Fool!' said the sophist, in an undertone
Gruff with contempt; which a death-nighing moan

Notes

[36] *juggling* conjuring.

From Lycius answered, as heart-struck and lost,
He sank supine beside the aching ghost.
'Fool! Fool!' repeated he, while his eyes still
Relented not, nor moved. 'From every ill
Of life have I preserved thee to this day,
And shall I see thee made a serpent's prey?'
Then Lamia breathed death breath; the sophist's eye,
Like a sharp spear, went through her utterly,
Keen, cruel, perceant,[37] stinging; she, as well
As her weak hand could any meaning tell,
Motioned him to be silent – vainly so,
He looked and looked again a level 'No!'
  'A serpent!' echoed he – no sooner said,
Than with a frightful scream she vanished,
And Lycius' arms were empty of delight,
As were his limbs of life from that same night.[38]
On the high couch he lay – his friends came round,
Supported him; no pulse or breath they found,
And, in its marriage robe, the heavy body wound.

To Autumn (composed *c.* 19 September 1819)[1]

From Lamia, Isabella, The Eve of St Agnes, and Other Poems (1820)

1

Season of mists and mellow fruitfulness,
  Close bosom-friend of the maturing sun,
Conspiring with him how to load and bless
  With fruit the vines that round the thatch-eaves run;
To bend with apples the mossed cottage-trees,
  And fill all fruit with ripeness to the core;
    To swell the gourd,[2] and plump the hazel shells
With a sweet kernel; to set budding more,
  And still more, later flowers for the bees,
  Until they think warm days will never cease,
    For summer has o'er-brimmed their clammy cells.

2

Who hath not seen thee oft amid thy store?
  Sometimes whoever seeks abroad may find
Thee sitting careless[3] on a granary floor,
  Thy hair soft-lifted by the winnowing wind;

Notes

[37] *perceant* piercing.

[38] Apollonius saves Lycius from Lamia, killing her in the process.

To Autumn

[1] For commentary on the poem see headnote, p. 1341.

[2] *gourd* melon.

[3] *careless* without care.

Or on a half-reaped furrow sound asleep,
Drowsed with the fume of poppies,[4] while thy hook[5]
Spares the next swath[6] and all its twined flowers;
And sometimes like a gleaner[7] thou dost keep
Steady thy laden head across a brook;
Or by a cider-press, with patient look,
Thou watchest the last oozings hours by hours.

3

Where are the songs of spring? Aye, where are they?
Think not of them, thou hast thy music too –
While barred clouds bloom the soft-dying day,
And touch the stubble-plains with rosy hue;
Then in a wailful choir the small gnats mourn
Among the river sallows,[8] borne aloft
Or sinking as the light wind lives or dies;
And full-grown lambs loud bleat from hilly bourn,
Hedge-crickets sing, and now with treble soft
The redbreast whistles from a garden-croft,
And gathering swallows twitter in the skies.

The Fall of Hyperion: A Dream
(composed between late July and 21 September 1819; edited from MS)[1]

Canto I

Fanatics[2] have their dreams, wherewith they weave
A paradise for a sect; the savage too
From forth the loftiest fashion of his sleep[3]
Guesses at heaven; pity these have not
Traced upon vellum or wild Indian leaf
The shadows of melodious utterance.
But bare of laurel they live, dream and die;
For Poesy alone can tell her dreams,
With the fine spell of words alone can save
Imagination from the sable charm
And dumb enchantment. Who alive can say

Notes

[4] *Drowsed . . . poppies* poppies are associated with sleep.
[5] *hook* blade for reaping corn.
[6] *swath* width of corn cut by a scythe.
[7] *gleaner* one who gathers stray ears of corn missed by the reapers.
[8] *sallows* willows.

The Fall of Hyperion
[1] This much revised version of 'Hyperion' was first published in 1857. Keats gave it up because 'there were too many Miltonic inversions in it. Miltonic verse cannot be written but in an artful or rather artist's humour. I wish to give myself up to other sensations. English ought to be kept up. It may be interesting to you to pick out some lines from Hyperion and put a mark X to the false beauty proceeding from art, and one || to the true voice of feeling. Upon my soul 'twas imagination; I cannot make the distinction. Every now and then there is a Miltonic intonation – but I cannot make the division properly' (Rollins ii 167). For further comment see headnote, p. 1341.
[2] *Fanatics* religious fanatics.
[3] *the loftiest fashion of his sleep* the depths of his dreams.

'Thou art no poet; may'st not tell thy dreams'?
Since every man whose soul is not a clod
Hath visions, and would speak, if he had loved
And been well nurtured in his mother tongue.
Whether the dream now purposed to rehearse
Be poet's or fanatic's will be known
When this warm scribe my hand is in the grave.
   Methought I stood where trees of every clime,
Palm, myrtle, oak, and sycamore, and beech,
With plantain,[4] and spice-blossoms, made a screen;
In neighbourhood of fountains, by the noise
Soft-showering in mine ears, and, by the touch
Of scent, not far from roses. Turning round,
I saw an arbour with a drooping roof
Of trellis vines, and bells, and larger blooms,
Like floral censers swinging light in air;
Before its wreathed doorway, on a mound
Of moss, was spread a feast of summer fruits,
Which nearer seen, seemed refuse of a meal
By angel tasted, or our mother Eve;
For empty shells were scattered on the grass,
And grape-stalks but half bare, and remnants more,
Sweet smelling, whose pure kinds I could not know.
Still was more plenty than the fabled horn[5]
Thrice emptied could pour forth, at banqueting
For Proserpine[6] returned to her own fields,
Where the white heifers low. And appetite
More yearning than on earth I ever felt
Growing within, I ate deliciously;
And, after not long, thirsted, for thereby
Stood a cool vessel of transparent juice
Sipped by the wandered bee, the which I took,
And, pledging all the mortals of the world,
And all the dead whose names are in our lips,
Drank. That full draught is parent of my theme.
No Asian poppy nor elixir fine
Of the soon-fading jealous Caliphat,[7]
No poison gendered in close monkish cell
To thin the scarlet conclave of old men,[8]
Could so have rapt[9] unwilling life away.
Among the fragrant husks and berries crushed,
Upon the grass I struggled hard against
The domineering potion, but in vain –
The cloudy swoon came on, and down I sunk

Notes

[4] *plantain* tropical tree-like plant.

[5] *the fabled horn* the cornucopia of plenty.

[6] Proserpine was Ceres' daughter; she was carried off to hell by Pluto. To soothe Ceres' grief, Jupiter decided that Proserpine should spend half the year in hell, and the other half on earth.

[7] *No Asian poppy . . . Caliphat* the Caliphs ruled the Muslim world after the death of Mohammed. They were believed to use poison as a means of political intrigue.

[8] *the scarlet conclave of old men* Cardinals elect a Pope in 'scarlet conclave'.

[9] *rapt* taken.

Like a Silenus[10] on an antique vase.
How long I slumbered 'tis a chance to guess.
When sense of life returned, I started up
As if with wings; but the fair trees were gone,
The mossy mound and arbour were no more.
I looked around upon the carved sides
Of an old sanctuary with roof august,
Builded so high, it seemed that filmed clouds
Might spread beneath, as o'er the stars of heaven.
So old the place was, I remembered none
The like upon the earth – what I had seen
Of grey cathedrals, buttressed walls, rent towers,
The superannuations[11] of sunk realms,
Or nature's rocks toiled hard in waves and winds,
Seemed but the faulture[12] of decrepit things
To that eternal domed monument.
Upon the marble at my feet there lay
Store of strange vessels, and large draperies
Which needs had been of dyed asbestos wove,
Or in that place the moth could not corrupt,[13]
So white the linen; so, in some, distinct
Ran imageries[14] from a sombre loom.
All in a mingled heap confused there lay
Robes, golden tongs, censer and chafing-dish,[15]
Girdles, and chains, and holy jewelleries.
  Turning from these with awe, once more I raised
My eyes to fathom the space every way;
The embossed roof, the silent massy range
Of columns north and south, ending in mist
Of nothing; then to eastward, where black gates
Were shut against the sunrise evermore.
Then to the west I looked, and saw far off
An image,[16] huge of feature as a cloud,
At level of whose feet an altar slept,
To be approached on either side by steps,
And marble balustrade, and patient travail
To count with toil the innumerable degrees.
Towards the altar sober-paced I went,
Repressing haste as too unholy there;
And, coming nearer, saw beside the shrine
One minist'ring;[17] and there arose a flame.
When in mid-May the sickening east wind
Shifts sudden to the south, the small warm rain

Notes

[10] *Silenus* attendant of Bacchus, who would sink down in a drunken stupor.

[11] *superannuations* ruins, obsolete remains.

[12] *faulture* weakness.

[13] *Or in . . . corrupt* heaven; Matthew 6: 19–20: 'Lay not up for yourselves treasures upon earth, where moth and rust doth corrupt and where thieves break through and steal.'

[14] *imageries* patterns in the cloth, embroidered designs.

[15] *chafing-dish* censer. This is a list of items used in religious rites.

[16] *An image* of Saturn.

[17] *One minist'ring* Moneta, the priestess of the temple.

Melts out the frozen incense from all flowers,
And fills the air with so much pleasant health
That even the dying man forgets his shroud;
Even so that lofty sacrificial fire,
Sending forth Maian incense,[18] spread around
Forgetfulness of everything but bliss,
And clouded all the altar with soft smoke,
From whose white fragrant curtains thus I heard
Language pronounced: 'If thou canst not ascend
These steps, die on that marble where thou art.
Thy flesh, near cousin to the common dust,
Will parch for lack of nutriment; thy bones
Will wither in few years, and vanish so
That not the quickest eye could find a grain
Of what thou now art on that pavement cold.
The sands of thy short life are spent this hour,
And no hand in the universe can turn
Thy hourglass, if these gummed leaves[19] be burnt
Ere thou canst mount up these immortal steps.'
    I heard, I looked – two senses both at once,
So fine, so subtle, felt the tyranny
Of that fierce threat and the hard task proposed.
Prodigious seemed the toil; the leaves were yet
Burning, when suddenly a palsied chill
Struck from the paved level up my limbs,
And was ascending quick to put cold grasp
Upon those streams that pulse beside the throat.[20]
I shrieked, and the sharp anguish of my shriek
Stung my own ears – I strove hard to escape
The numbness, strove to gain the lowest step.
Slow, heavy, deadly was my pace; the cold
Grew stifling, suffocating, at the heart;
And when I clasped my hands I felt them not.
One minute before death, my iced foot touched
The lowest stair; and as it touched, life seemed
To pour in at the toes. I mounted up,
As once fair angels on a ladder flew
From the green turf to heaven. 'Holy Power',
Cried I, approaching near the hornèd shrine,[21]
'What am I that should so be saved from death?
What am I, that another death come not
To choke my utterance sacrilegious here?'
Then said the veiled shadow:[22] 'Thou hast felt
What 'tis to die and live again before
Thy fated hour. That thou hadst power to do so

Notes

[18] *Maian incense* flowery scent.

[19] *gummed leaves* leaves of aromatic trees.

[20] *those streams . . . throat* Having had a medical training, Keats would have known that he was referring to the carotid arteries which carry blood to the neck.

[21] *the hornèd shrine* It was believed that altars in ancient times were adorned with animal horns.

[22] *veiled shadow* Moneta, as at l. 211 below.

Is thy own safety; thou hast dated on
Thy doom.'[23] 'High Prophetess', said I, 'purge off
Benign, if so it please thee, my mind's film.'[24]
'None can usurp this height', returned that shade,
'But those to whom the miseries of the world
Are misery, and will not let them rest.
All else who find a haven in the world,
Where they may thoughtless sleep away their days,
If by a chance into this fane[25] they come,
Rot on the pavement where thou rotted'st half.'
'Are there not thousands in the world', said I,
Encouraged by the sooth[26] voice of the shade,
'Who love their fellows even to the death;
Who feel the giant agony of the world;
And more, like slaves to poor humanity,
Labour for mortal good? I sure should see
Other men here – but I am here alone.'
'They whom thou spak'st of are no vision'ries,'
Rejoined that voice, 'They are no dreamers weak,
They seek no wonder but the human face,[27]
No music but a happy-noted voice,
They come not here, they have no thought to come –
And thou art here, for thou art less than they.
What benefit canst thou do, or all thy tribe,
To the great world? Thou art a dreaming thing,
A fever of thyself.[28] Think of the earth;
What bliss even in hope is there for thee?
What haven? Every creature hath its home;
Every sole[29] man hath days of joy and pain,
Whether his labours be sublime or low –
The pain alone; the joy alone; distinct.
Only the dreamer venoms all his days,[30]
Bearing more woe than all his sins deserve.
Therefore, that happiness be somewhat shared,
Such things as thou art are admitted oft
Into like gardens thou didst pass erewhile,
And suffered in[31] these temples; for that cause
Thou standest safe beneath this statue's knees.'
'That I am favoured for unworthiness,
By such propitious parley medicined
In sickness not ignoble, I rejoice –
Aye, and could weep for love of such award.'

Notes

[23] *dated on / Thy doom* postponed your death.

[24] *purge off . . . film* help me to understand clearly.

[25] *fane* temple.

[26] *sooth* smooth.

[27] *They seek no wonder but the human face* Miriam Allott suggests comparison with Keats's letter to John Taylor, 17 November 1819: 'Wonders are no wonders to me. I am more at home amongst men and women. I would rather read Chaucer than Ariosto' (Rollins ii 234).

[28] *A fever of thyself* i.e. he is prone to feverish fits of poetic inspiration. This kind of fever is healthy.

[29] *sole* single.

[30] *Only the dreamer venoms all his days* with the awareness of human misery.

[31] *suffered in* allowed to enter.

So answered I, continuing, 'If it please,
Majestic shadow, tell me – sure not all
Those melodies sung into the world's ear
Are useless? Sure a poet is a sage,
A humanist,[32] physician to all men.
That I am none I feel, as vultures feel
They are no birds when eagles are abroad.
What am I then? Thou spakest of my tribe –
What tribe?' The tall shade veiled in drooping white
Then spake, so much more earnest, that the breath
Moved the thin linen folds that drooping hung
About a golden censer from the hand
Pendent: 'Art thou not of the dreamer tribe?
The poet and the dreamer are distinct,
Diverse, sheer opposite, antipodes.
The one pours out a balm upon the world,
The other vexes it.' Then shouted I
Spite of myself, and with a Pythia's spleen:[33]
'Apollo![34] Faded, far-flown Apollo!
Where is thy misty pestilence[35] to creep
Into the dwellings, through the door crannies,
Of all mock lyrists, large self-worshippers,
And careless hectorers in proud bad verse?[36]
Though I breathe death with them it will be life
To see them sprawl before me into graves.
Majestic shadow, tell me where I am;
Whose altar this; for whom this incense curls;
What image this, whose face I cannot see,
For the broad marble knees; and who thou art,
Of accent feminine, so courteous.'
Then the tall shade, in drooping linens veiled,
Spake out, so much more earnest, that her breath
Stirred the thin folds of gauze that drooping hung
About a golden censer from her hand
Pendent – and by her voice I knew she shed
Long-treasured tears: 'This temple sad and lone
Is all spared[37] from the thunder of a war[38]
Foughten long since by giant hierarchy
Against rebellion. This old image here,
Whose carved features wrinkled as he fell,
Is Saturn's; I, Moneta,[39] left supreme,

Notes

[32] *humanist* humanitarian.

[33] *a Pythia's spleen* Oracles in the temple of Apollo, god of poetry and prophecy, at Delphi were delivered by a priestess called 'the Pythia', whose wild and incoherent speeches were transcribed.

[34] *Apollo!* Son of Jupiter.

[35] *thy misty pestilence* Apollo was associated with plagues and diseases.

[36] *careless hectorers in proud bad verse* suggested candidates include Byron, Wordsworth and Moore. In September 1819 Keats referred to *Don Juan* as 'Lord Byron's last flash poem' (Rollins ii 192).

[37] *Is all spared* is all that is spared.

[38] *war* that of the Titans against the Olympians.

[39] *Moneta* Mnemosyne, mother of the muses.

Sole priestess of his desolation.'
I had no words to answer, for my tongue,
Useless, could find about its roofed home
No syllable of a fit majesty
To make rejoinder to Moneta's mourn.
There was a silence while the altar's blaze
Was fainting for sweet food. I looked thereon,
And on the paved floor, where nigh were piled
Faggots of cinnamon, and many heaps
Of other crisped spice-wood – then again
I looked upon the altar, and its horns
Whitened with ashes, and its lang'rous flame,
And then upon the offerings again;
And so by turns, till sad Moneta cried,
'The sacrifice is done, but not the less
Will I be kind to thee for thy goodwill.
My power, which to me is still a curse,
Shall be to thee a wonder; for the scenes
Still swooning vivid through my globed brain[40]
With an electral[41] changing misery,
Thou shalt with those dull mortal eyes behold,
Free from all pain, if wonder pain thee not.'
As near as an immortal's sphered words
Could to a mother's soften, were these last.
But yet I had a terror of her robes,
And chiefly of the veils, that from her brow
Hung pale, and curtained her in mysteries,
That made my heart too small to hold its blood.
This saw that goddess, and with sacred hand
Parted the veils. Then saw I a wan face,
Not pined[42] by human sorrows, but bright-blanched
By an immortal sickness which kills not;
It works a constant change, which happy death
Can put no end to; deathwards progressing
To no death was that visage; it had passed
The lily and the snow; and beyond these
I must not think now, though I saw that face –
But for her eyes I should have fled away.
They held me back with a benignant light,
Soft-mitigated by divinest lids
Half-closed, and visionless[43] entire they seemed
Of all external things – they saw me not,
But in blank splendour beamed like the mild moon,
Who comforts those she sees not, who knows not
What eyes are upward cast. As I had found
A grain of gold upon a mountain's side,

Notes

[40] *the scenes . . . brain* The scenes are vivid enough in her memory to make her swoon.
[41] *electral* charged as if by electricity.
[42] *pined* wasted.
[43] *visionless* The eyes do not see the outside world, but are directed on inner visions.

And twinged with avarice strained out my eyes
To search its sullen[44] entrails rich with ore,
So at the view of sad Moneta's brow
I ached to see what things the hollow brain
Behind enwombed, what high tragedy
In the dark secret chambers of her skull
Was acting, that could give so dread a stress
To her cold lips, and fill with such a light
Her planetary eyes, and touch her voice
With such a sorrow. 'Shade of Memory!'[45]
Cried I, with act adorant at her feet,
'By all the gloom hung round thy fallen house,
By this last temple, by the golden age,[46]
By great Apollo, thy dear foster child,[47]
And by thyself, forlorn divinity,
The pale omega[48] of a withered race,
Let me behold, according as thou said'st,
What in thy brain so ferments to and fro.'
No sooner had this conjuration passed
My devout lips, than side by side we stood,
Like a stunt bramble by a solemn pine,
Deep in the shady sadness of a vale,
Far sunken from the healthy breath of morn,
Far from the fiery noon and eve's one star.
Onward I looked beneath the gloomy boughs,
And saw what first I thought an image huge,
Like to the image pedestalled so high
In Saturn's temple. Then Moneta's voice
Came brief upon mine ear: 'So Saturn sat
When he had lost his realms.' Whereon there grew
A power within me of enormous ken[49]
To see as a god sees, and take the depth
Of things as nimbly as the outward eye
Can size and shape pervade. The lofty theme
At those few words hung vast before my mind,
With half-unravelled web. I set myself
Upon an eagle's watch, that I might see,
And seeing ne'er forget. No stir of life
Was in this shrouded vale, not so much air
As in the zoning[50] of a summer's day
Robs not one light seed from the feathered grass,
But where the dead leaf fell there did it rest.
A stream went voiceless by, still deadened more
By reason of the fallen divinity

Notes

[44] *sullen* gloomy.

[45] *Shade of Memory* Moneta, whose other name, Mnemosyne, means 'memory'.

[46] *the golden age* of Saturn's rule.

[47] *Apollo, thy dear foster child* Apollo was the son of Jupiter by Latona. Moneta was Jupiter's wife at the time.

[48] *omega* survivor (omega is the final letter of the Greek alphabet).

[49] *ken* sight.

[50] *zoning* duration.

Spreading more shade; the naiad[51] mid her reeds
Pressed her cold finger closer to her lips.
Along the margin sand large footmarks went
No farther than to where old Saturn's feet
Had rested, and there slept – how long a sleep!
Degraded, cold, upon the sodden ground
His old right hand lay nerveless,[52] listless, dead,
Unsceptred; and his realmless eyes were closed,
While his bowed head seemed listening to the earth,
His ancient mother,[53] for some comfort yet.
It seemed no force could wake him from his place;
But there came one who, with a kindred hand
Touched his wide shoulders, after bending low
With reverence, though to one who knew it not.
Then came the grieved voice of Mnemosyne,
And grieved I hearkened: 'That divinity
Whom thou saw'st step from yon forlornest wood,
And with slow pace approach our fallen King,
Is Thea,[54] softest-natured of our brood.'
I marked the goddess in fair statuary[55]
Surpassing wan Moneta by the head,
And in her sorrow nearer woman's tears.
There was a listening fear in her regard,
As if calamity had but begun;
As if the vanward clouds of evil days
Had spent their malice, and the sullen rear
Was with its stored thunder labouring up.[56]
One hand she pressed upon that aching spot
Where beats the human heart, as if just there,
Though an immortal, she felt cruel pain;
The other upon Saturn's bended neck
She laid, and to the level of his hollow ear,
Leaning with parted lips, some words she spake
In solemn tenor and deep organ tune –
Some mourning words, which in our feeble tongue
Would come in this-like accenting (how frail
To that large utterance of the early gods!):
'Saturn, look up! And for what, poor lost King?
I have no comfort for thee – no, not one;
I cannot cry, "Wherefore thus sleepest thou?"
For heaven is parted from thee, and the earth
Knows thee not, so afflicted, for a god;
And ocean too, with all its solemn noise,
Has from thy sceptre passed, and all the air
Is emptied of thine hoary majesty.

Notes

51 *naiad* water-nymph.

52 *nerveless* weak.

53 *His ancient mother* Tellus (earth).

54 *Thea* daughter of Uranus and Terra.

55 *statuary* stature.

56 *As if the vanward clouds . . . up* Calamity is compared with clouds building up before a storm, followed by the cloud mass; the storm itself is compared with artillery moving in the wake of advancing troops.

Thy thunder, captious[57] at the new command,
Rumbles reluctant o'er our fallen house;
And thy sharp lightning in unpractised hands
Scorches and burns our once serene domain.[58]
With such remorseless speed still come new woes
That unbelief has not a space to breathe.
Saturn, sleep on. Me thoughtless, why should I
Thus violate thy slumbrous solitude?
Why should I ope thy melancholy eyes?
Saturn, sleep on, while at thy feet I weep.'
    As when, upon a tranced summer night,
Forests, branch-charmed by the earnest stars,
Dream, and so dream all night, without a noise,
Save from one gradual solitary gust
Swelling upon the silence, dying off,
As if the ebbing air had but one wave;
So came these words, and went, the while in tears
She pressed her fair large forehead to the earth,
Just where her fallen hair might spread in curls,
A soft and silken mat for Saturn's feet.
Long, long those two were postured motionless,
Like sculpture builded up upon the grave
Of their own power. A long awful time
I looked upon them; still they were the same,
The frozen god still bending to the earth,
And the sad goddess weeping at his feet;
Moneta silent. Without stay or prop
But my own weak mortality, I bore
The load of this eternal quietude,
The unchanging gloom, and the three fixed shapes
Ponderous upon my senses a whole moon.
For by my burning brain I measured sure
Her silver seasons shedded on the night,
And every day by day methought I grew
More gaunt and ghostly; oftentimes I prayed
Intense, that death would take me from the vale
And all its burdens; gasping with despair
Of change, hour after hour I cursed myself –
Until old Saturn raised his faded eyes,
And looked around and saw his kingdom gone,
And all the gloom and sorrow of the place,
And that fair kneeling goddess at his feet.
As the moist scent of flowers, and grass, and leaves
Fills forest dells with a pervading air
Known to the woodland nostril, so the words
Of Saturn filled the mossy glooms around,

Notes

[57] *captious* objecting querulously.

[58] *our once serene domain* the Saturnian golden age.

Even to the hollows of time-eaten oaks,
And to the windings in the foxes' hole,
With sad low tones, while thus he spake, and sent
Strange musings to the solitary Pan:[59]
'Moan, brethren, moan, for we are swallowed up
And buried from all godlike exercise
Of influence benign on planets pale,
And peaceful sway above man's harvesting,
And all those acts which deity supreme
Doth ease its heart of love in. Moan and wail.
Moan, brethren, moan, for lo! the rebel spheres
Spin round, the stars their ancient courses keep,
Clouds still with shadowy moisture haunt the earth,
Still suck their fill of light from sun and moon,
Still buds the tree, and still the seashores murmur.
There is no death in all the universe,
No smell of death – there shall be death. Moan, moan,
Moan, Cybele,[60] moan, for thy pernicious babes
Have changed a god into a shaking palsy.
Moan, brethren, moan, for I have no strength left,
Weak as the reed – weak – feeble as my voice –
Oh, oh, the pain, the pain of feebleness.
Moan, moan, for still I thaw – or give me help:
Throw down those imps,[61] and give me victory.
Let me hear other groans, and trumpets blown
Of triumph calm, and hymns of festival
From the gold peaks of heaven's high-piled clouds;
Voices of soft proclaim, and silver stir
Of strings in hollow shells; and let there be
Beautiful things made new, for the surprise
Of the sky-children.' So he feebly ceased,
With such a poor and sickly sounding pause,
Methought I heard some old man of the earth
Bewailing earthly loss; nor could my eyes
And ears act with that pleasant unison of sense
Which marries sweet sound with the grace of form,
And dolorous accent from a tragic harp
With large-limbed visions. More I scrutinized:
Still fixed he sat beneath the sable trees,
Whose arms spread straggling in wild serpent forms,
With leaves all hushed; his awful presence there
Now all was silent, gave a deadly lie
To what I erewhile heard – only his lips
Trembled amid the white curls of his beard.
They told the truth, though, round the snowy locks

Notes

[59] Pan is the natural world, solitary after the passing of the golden age.

[60] *Cybele* mother of all the gods.

[61] *those imps* his own children, the Olympians, by whom he has been usurped.

Hung nobly, as upon the face of heaven
A midday fleece of clouds. Thea arose
And stretched her white arm through the hollow dark,
Pointing some whither, whereat he too rose
Like a vast giant seen by men at sea
To grow pale from the waves at dull midnight.
They melted from my sight into the woods;
Ere I could turn, Moneta cried, 'These twain
Are speeding to the families of grief,
Where roofed in by black rocks they waste in pain
And darkness for no hope.' And she spake on,
As ye may read who can unwearied pass
Onward from the antechamber of this dream,
Where even at the open doors awhile
I must delay, and glean my memory
Of her high phrase – perhaps no further dare.

Canto II

'Mortal, that thou may'st understand aright,
I humanize my sayings to thine ear,
Making comparisons of earthly things;
Or thou might'st better listen to the wind,
Whose language is to thee a barren noise,
Though it blows legend-laden through the trees.
In melancholy realms big tears are shed,
More sorrow like to this, and suchlike woe
Too huge for mortal tongue, or pen of scribe.
The Titans[1] fierce, self-hid or prison-bound,
Groan for the old allegiance once more,
Listening in their doom for Saturn's voice.
But one of our whole eagle-brood still keeps
His sov'reignty, and rule, and majesty;
Blazing Hyperion on his orbed fire[2]
Still sits, still snuffs the incense teeming up
From man to the sun's god – yet unsecure.
For as upon the earth dire prodigies[3]
Fright and perplex, so also shudders he;
Nor at dog's howl, or gloom-bird's even screech,[4]
Or the familiar visitings of one
Upon the first toll of his passing-bell,[5]
But horrors, portioned[6] to a giant nerve,
Make great Hyperion ache. His palace bright,

Notes

CANTO II

[1] *The Titans* a god-like race expelled from heaven by Jupiter in Greek myth.

[2] *orbed fire* the sun; Hyperion is god of the sun.

[3] *prodigies* unnatural events.

[4] *gloom-bird's even screech* owl's hooting in the evening.

[5] *passing-bell* death-bell.

[6] *portioned* proportioned.

Bastioned with pyramids of glowing gold,
And touched with shade of bronzed obelisks,
Glares a blood-red through all the thousand courts,
Arches, and domes, and fiery galleries;
And all its curtains of aurorean[7] clouds
Flush angerly[8] – when he would taste the wreaths
Of incense breathed aloft from sacred hills,
Instead of sweets, his ample palate takes
Savour of poisonous brass and metals sick.
Wherefore, when harboured in the sleepy west,
After the full completion of fair day,
For rest divine upon exalted couch
And slumber in the arms of melody,
He paces through the pleasant hours of ease
With strides colossal, on from hall to hall,
While far within each aisle and deep recess
His winged minions in close clusters stand
Amazed, and full of fear; like anxious men
Who on a wide plain gather in sad troops
When earthquakes jar their battlements and towers.
Even now, while Saturn, roused from icy trance,
Goes step for step with Thea from yon woods,
Hyperion, leaving twilight in the rear,
Is sloping to the threshold of the west.
Thither we tend.' Now in clear light I stood,
Relieved from the dusk vale. Mnemosyne
Was sitting on a square-edged polished stone,
That in its lucid depth reflected pure
Her priestess-garments. My quick eyes ran on
From stately nave to nave, from vault to vault,
Through bowers of fragrant and enwreathed light
And diamond-paved lustrous long arcades.
Anon rushed by the bright Hyperion;
His flaming robes streamed out beyond his heels,
And gave a roar, as if of earthly fire,
That scared away the meek ethereal hours[9]
And made their dove-wings tremble. On he flared . . .

Notes

[7] *aurorean* roseate.

[8] *His palace . . . angerly* Hyperion's palace is part Greek, part Byzantine and part Egyptian.

[9] *hours* Latin 'Horae', attendant nymphs of the sun.

[*Bright star, would I were steadfast as thou art*] (composed October-December 1819; edited from MS)[1]

Bright star, would I were steadfast as thou art –
Not in lone splendour hung aloft the night
And watching, with eternal lids apart,
Like nature's patient, sleepless eremite,[2]
The moving waters[3] at their priestlike task
Of pure ablution[4] round earth's human shores,
Or gazing on the new soft-fallen mask
Of snow upon the mountains and the moors;
No – yet still steadfast, still unchangeable,
Pillowed upon my fair love's ripening breast,
To feel for ever its soft swell and fall,
Awake for ever in a sweet unrest,
Still, still to hear her tender-taken breath,
And so live ever – or else swoon to death.

[*This living hand, now warm and capable*] (composed towards the end of 1819)[1]

This living hand, now warm and capable
Of earnest grasping, would, if it were cold
And in the icy silence of the tomb,
So haunt thy days and chill thy dreaming nights
That thou would wish thine own heart dry of blood,
So in my veins red life might stream again,
And thou be conscience-calmed. See, here it is –
I hold it towards you.

Notes

BRIGHT STAR, WOULD I WERE STEADFAST AS THOU ART

[1] This sonnet was published first in 1838. It has traditionally been thought of as Keats's last poem, but editors now place it in late 1819.

[2] *eremite* anchorite, hermit.

[3] *The moving waters* cf. Wordsworth, *The Excursion* ix 9: 'The moving waters and the invisible air'.

[4] *ablution* cleansing. The ebb and flow of the waters are like a religious ritual.

THIS LIVING HAND, NOW WARM AND CAPABLE

[1] First published 1898. This is probably a jotting for use in a play or poem.

Hartley Coleridge (1796–1849)

Thoroughly mythologized by some of the greatest poetry of the age (see Coleridge's 'The Nightingale', 'Frost at Midnight', the conclusion to 'Christabel' and Wordsworth's 'To H. C., Six Years Old' and 'Ode'), Hartley no doubt felt he had a great deal to live up to. Born on 19 September 1796, he was gifted with a prodigious intelligence, but, thanks partly to his father's abandonment of his family, his early education was erratic and irregular. He was elected to a Fellowship at Oriel College, Oxford, 16 April 1819, but his academic career was blighted from the start by his drunkenness. After the College Dean found him lying in the gutter of Oriel Lane one evening, Hartley was asked to resign.

He went to London to pursue a journalistic career, but his best works were his poems. His first published verses appeared in the *London Magazine* in 1823. As a journalist his main problem was that he was unproductive. By the summer of 1823 he was in Ambleside, working as a schoolteacher. That lasted only a short time, and he moved to Leeds, where he published *Biographia Borealis; or, Lives of Distinguished Northerns* in 1833. In the same year he published a volume of *Poems*. In 'Long time a child', he addressed the mythologized self of 'Frost at Midnight'; there is pathos in the reckoning, more pronounced in 'When I review the course that I have run', posthumously published in 1851. 'To Wordsworth', however, is a moving tribute to the poet who first described him as a 'Seer blessed' ('Ode' 114).

Further reading

Bricks without Mortar: The Selected Poems of Hartley Coleridge ed. Lisa Gee (London, 2000).

Letters of Hartley Coleridge ed. Grace Evelyn Griggs and Earl Leslie Griggs (Oxford, 1937).

Herbert Hartman, *Hartley Coleridge: Poet's Son and Poet* (Oxford, 1931).

Sister Mary Joseph Pomeroy, *The Poetry of Hartley Coleridge* (Washington, DC, 1927).

Sonnet IX

***From* Poems (1833)**

Long time a child, and still a child, when years
Had painted manhood on my cheek, was I;
For yet I lived like one not born to die;
A thriftless prodigal of smiles and tears,
No hope I needed, and I knew no fears.
But sleep, though sweet, is only sleep, and waking,
I waked to sleep no more, at once o'ertaking
The vanguard of my age, with all arrears
Of duty on my back. Nor child, nor man,
Nor youth, nor sage, I find my head is grey,
For I have lost the race I never ran,
A rathe[1] December blights my lagging May;
And still I am a child, though I be old –
Time is my debtor for my years untold.

Notes

[1] *rathe* early.

Sonnet: 'When I review the course that I have run'

***From* Essays and Marginalia (1851)**

When I review the course that I have run,
And count the loss of all my wasted days,
I find no argument for joy or praise
In whatsoe'er my soul hath thought or done.
I am a desert, and the kindly sun
On me hath vainly spent his fertile rays.
Then wherefore do I tune my idle lays,
Or dream that haply I may be the one
Of the vain thousands, that shall win a place
Among the poets – that a single rhyme
Of my poor wit's devising may find grace
To breed high memories in the womb of time?
But to confound the time the muse I woo;
Then 'tis but just that time confound me too.

To Wordsworth

***From* Essays and Marginalia (1851)**

There have been poets that in verse display
The elemental forms of human passions;
Poets have been, to whom the fickle fashions
And all the wilful humours of the day
Have furnished matter for a polished lay;
And many are the smooth elaborate tribe
Who, emulous of thee, the shape describe,
And fain would every shifting hue portray
Of restless nature. But, thou mighty seer!
'Tis thine to celebrate the thoughts that make
The life of souls, the truths for whose sweet sake
We to ourselves and to our God are dear.
Of nature's inner shrine thou art the priest,
Where most she works when we perceive her least.

Mary Wollstonecraft Shelley (*née* Godwin) (1797–1851)

Born 30 August 1797, Mary Wollstonecraft Godwin could hardly have had two more distinguished parents – William Godwin (p. 151) and Mary Wollstonecraft (p. 276). Her mother died of post-natal septicaemia ten days later. She was raised by her father and stepmother, Mary Jane Clairmont, who had two children, Charles and Jane (later known as Claire).

Her father had been conducting a mutually admiring correspondence with the young Percy Bysshe Shelley for almost two years when she met him at dinner on 11 November 1812. Shelley was married to Harriet Westbrook at the time, but over the next eighteen months unresolvable strains developed; Mary and Percy began seeing a good deal of each other in June and July 1814, and the emotional pressure culminated in their flight to the continent, with Claire Clairmont on 28 July. They toured France and Switzerland, returning to England in the autumn. In 1816 they set out for the continent again, with Claire again in tow, and spent the summer in Geneva, where they made the acquaintance of Byron. This was one of those remarkable moments in literary history where the unique chemistry of the various personalities was conducive to the production of great literature: under Shelley's influence, Byron composed *Childe Harold's Pilgrimage* III (pp. 852–87) and *Manfred*, and Shelley composed two of his greatest poems, *Mont Blanc* and *Hymn to Intellectual Beauty* (pp. 1071–3, 1075–9). But perhaps the most enduringly popular work of that summer was Mary's great novel *Frankenstein*, inspired by a ghost-story competition. Something of the flavour of the summer of 1816 is captured in the first of the journal entries below.

In November 1816 Harriet Shelley committed suicide, and Percy and Mary were married on 30 December. She completed *Frankenstein* in May 1817, and it was published the following year. The Shelleys lived a nomadic and difficult life, residing successively in Venice, Rome, Naples, Florence and Pisa. In May 1822 they settled in Lerici, and Percy was drowned in July when sailing in a storm in a dangerously unstable boat. She was almost as devastated by Byron's death two years later, as her journal entry, reproduced below, shows.

She published more novels, including *Mathilda* (1819), *Valperga* (1823), *The Last Man* (1826), *Perkin Warbeck* (1830), *Lodore* (1835) and *Falkner* (1837). And in 1839 she supervised the production of what remains the definitive edition of her husband's *Poetical Works*, which included her own commentary. It was an extraordinary act of scholarship, and her note on *Prometheus Unbound*, below, remains an essential tool in the study of that challenging work.

Her life after Percy's death was difficult. She was often impoverished, ostracized from society, and encountered much opposition from her late husband's father over the maintenance and custody of Percy Florence Shelley (her only surviving child). However, she persevered and established herself, at least in Bohemian circles, as a novelist and reviewer. Her health was never good, and in 1846 she fell seriously ill. She died on 1 February 1851 at the age of 53.

Further reading

The Mary Shelley Reader ed. Betty T. Bennett and Charles E. Robinson (New York, 1990).

The Novels and Selected Works of Mary Shelley, General Editor, Nora Crook with Pamela Clemit (8 vols, London, 1996).

R. Glynn Grylls, *Mary Shelley: A Biography* (London, 1938).

A Routledge Literary Sourcebook on Mary Shelley's Frankenstein ed. Tim Morton (London, 2002).

Muriel Spark, *Mary Shelley* (London, 1988).

From Journals (edited from MS)

28 May 1817. I am melancholy with reading the third Canto of *Childe Harold*. Do you not remember, Shelley, when you first read it to me, one evening after returning from Diodati?[1] It was in our little room at Chapuis;[2] the lake was before us and the mighty Jura. That time is past and this will also pass, when I may weep to read these words and again moralize on the flight of time.

Dear Lake! I shall ever love thee. How a powerful mind[3] can sanctify past scenes and recollections! His is a powerful mind, one that fills me with melancholy yet mixed with pleasure, as is always the case when intellectual energy is displayed. To think of our excursions on the Lake; how we saw him when he came down to us or welcomed our arrival with a good-humoured smile.[4] How very vividly does each verse of his poem recall some scene of this kind to my memory.

This time will soon also be a recollection. We may see him again and again, enjoy his society, but the time will also arrive when that which is now an anticipation will be only in the memory. Death will at length come and in the last moment all will be a dream.

15 May 1824. This then was the 'coming event' that cast its shadow on my last night's miserable thoughts. Byron has become one of the people of the grave[1] – that innumerable conclave to which the beings I best loved belong. I knew him in the bright days of youth, when neither care or fear had visited me; before death had made me feel my mortality and the earth was the scene of my hopes. Can I forget our evening visits to Diodati, our excursions of the lake when he sang the Tyrolese hymn, and his voice was harmonized with winds and waves? Can I forget his attentions and consolations to me during my deepest misery? Never. Beauty sat on his countenance and power beamed from his eye; his faults being for the most part weaknesses, induced one readily to pardon them. Albe,[2] the dear capricious fascinating Albe has left this desert world.

What do I do here? Why am I doomed to live on seeing all expire before me? God grant I may die young. A new race is springing about me. At the age of twenty six I am in the condition of an aged person. All my friends are gone; I have no wish to form new. I cling to the few remaining, but they slide away and my heart fails when I think by how few ties I hold to the world. Albe, dearest Albe, was knit by long associations. Each day I repeat with bitterer feelings, 'Life is the desert and the solitude, how populous the grave'[3] – and that region, to the dearer and best beloved beings which it has torn from me, now adds that resplendent spirit, whose departure leaves the dull earth dark as midnight.

Notes

FROM JOURNALS

[1] Byron was resident at Villa Diodati, on the shores of Lake Geneva, during the summer of 1816.

[2] On 3 June 1816 the Shelleys moved into a small cottage near Cologny in the region of Montalègre, known as Campagne Chappuis; they moved out on 29 August. Their reading of *Childe Harold* III is likely to have taken place between *c.*14 August (when Claire Clairmont produced a fair copy) and the end of the month. Percy took a copy of the poem to Byron's publisher in London the following month.

[3] *a powerful mind* She is thinking of Byron's comments on Lake Geneva in *Childe Harold* III st.68ff.

[4] Shelley's cottage was a mere eight-minute walk down the slope from Diodati.

15 MAY 1824

[1] *Byron . . . grave* news of Byron's death on 19 April 1824 at Missolonghi reached England on 14 May.

[2] *Albe* i.e. 'LB', a familiar name for Byron in the Shelley circle.

[3] *Life is the desert . . . the grave* from Edward Young, *Night Thoughts* i 115–16.

On Reading Wordsworth's Lines on Peele Castle (composed 8 December 1825; edited from MS)

It is with me, as erst with you,
Oh poet, nature's chronicler,
The summer seas have lost their hue
And storm sits brooding everywhere.

The gentlest rustling of the deep
Is but the dirge of him I lost,
And when waves raise their furrows steep,
And bring foam in which is tossed.

A voice I hear upon the wind
Which bids me haste to join him there,
And woo the tempest's breath unkind
Which gives to me a kindred bier.

And when all smooth are ocean's plains
And sails afar are glittering,
The fairest skiff his form contains
To my poor heart's fond picturing.

Then wildly to the beach I rush,
And fain would seize the frailest boat,
And from dull earth the slight hull push,
On dancing waves towards him to float.

'Nor may I e'er again behold
The sea, and be as I have been;
My bitter grief will ne'er grow old,
Nor say I this with mind serene.'[1]

For oft I weep in solitude
And shed so many bitter tears,
While on past joys I vainly brood
And shrink in fear from coming years.

Notes

On Reading Wordsworth's Lines on Peele Castle

[1] See Wordsworth, 'Elegiac Stanzas Suggested by a Picture of Peele Castle' 37–40.

A Dirge (composed November 1827; edited from MS)

To the air of 'My Phillida, adieu, love!'

This morn thy gallant bark, love,
  Sailed on a sunny sea;
'Tis noon, and tempests dark, love,
  Have wrecked it on the lee.
    Ah woe! Ah woe! Ah woe!
  By spirits of the deep
  He's cradled on the billow
  To his unwaking sleep.

Thou liest upon the shore, love,
  Beside the knelling surge,
But sea-nymphs evermore, love,
  Shall sadly chaunt thy dirge.
    Oh come! Oh come! Oh come!
  Ye spirits of the deep,
  While near his seaweed pillow
  My lonely watch I keep.

From far across the sea, love,
  I hear a wild lament,
By Echo's voice for thee, love,
  From ocean's caverns sent:
    Oh list! Oh list! Oh list!
  The spirits of the deep –
  Loud sounds their wail of sorrow,
  While I for ever weep.

[*Oh listen while I sing to thee*] (composed 12 March 1838; edited from MS)

Oh listen while I sing to thee,
  My song is meant for thee alone;
My thought imparts its melody,
  And gives the soft impassioned tone.

I sing of joy, and see thy smile
  That to the swelling note replies;
I sing of love, and feel the while
  The gaze of thy love-beaming eyes.

If thou wert far, my voice would die
  In murmurs faint and sorrowing;
If thou wert fake – in agony
  My heart would break, I could not sing.

Then listen while I sing to thee,
My song is meant for thee alone;
And now that thou art near to me
I pour a full impassioned tone.

Note on the 'Prometheus Unbound' (extracts)

From The Poetical Works of Percy Bysshe Shelley ed. Mary Shelley (4 vols, 1839)

The prominent feature of Shelley's theory of the destiny of the human species was that evil is not inherent in the system of the creation, but an accident that might be expelled. This also forms a portion of Christianity: God made earth and man perfect, till he, by his fall, 'Brought death into the world, and all our woe'.[1] Shelley believed that mankind had only to will that there should be no evil, and there would be none. It is not my part in these notes to notice the arguments that have been urged against this opinion, but to mention the fact that he entertained it, and was indeed attached to it with fervent enthusiasm. That man could be so perfectionized as to be able to expel evil from his own nature and from the greater part of the creation, was the cardinal point of his system. And the subject he loved best to dwell on, was the image of One warring with the Evil Principle, oppressed not only by it, but by all – even the good who were deluded into considering evil a necessary portion of humanity.

A victim full of fortitude and hope, and the spirit of triumph emanating from a reliance in the ultimate omnipotence of good: such he had depicted in his last poem,[2] when he made Laon the enemy and the victim of tyrants. He now took a more idealized image of the same subject. He followed certain classical authorities in figuring Saturn as the good principle, Jupiter the usurping evil one, and Prometheus as the regenerator, who, unable to bring mankind back to primitive innocence, used knowledge as a weapon to defeat evil, by leading mankind beyond the state wherein they are sinless through ignorance, to that in which they are virtuous through wisdom. Jupiter punished the temerity of the Titan by chaining him to a rock of Caucasus, and causing a vulture to devour his still renewed heart. There was a prophecy afloat in heaven portending the fall of Jove, the secret of averting which was known only to Prometheus – and the god offered freedom from torture on condition of its being communicated to him. According to the mythological story, this referred to the offspring of Thetis, who was destined to be greater than his father. Prometheus at last bought pardon for his crime of enriching mankind with his gifts, by revealing the prophecy. Hercules killed the vulture and set him free, and Thetis was married to Peleus, the father of Achilles.

Shelley adapted the catastrophe of this story to his peculiar views. The son, greater than his father, born of the nuptials of Jupiter and Thetis, was to dethrone Evil, and bring back a happier reign than that of Saturn. Prometheus defies the power of his enemy, and endures centuries of torture till the hour arrives when Jove, blind to the real event, but darkly guessing that some great good to himself will flow, espouses Thetis. At the moment, the primal power of the world drives him from his usurped throne, and strength, in the person of Hercules, liberates humanity, typified in Prometheus, from the tortures generated by evil done or suffered. Asia, one of the

Notes

Note on the 'Prometheus Unbound'

[1] *Brought death . . . our woe* from Milton, *Paradise Lost* i 3.

[2] *his last poem* i.e. his previous poem, *Laon and Cythna*, later retitled *The Revolt of Islam*, composed March–September 1817, published December 1817.

Oceanides, is the wife of Prometheus (she was, according to other mythological interpretations, the same as Venus and nature). When the benefactor of mankind is liberated, nature resumes the beauty of her prime, and is united to her husband, the emblem of the human race, in perfect and happy union. In the fourth Act, the poet gives further scope to his imagination and idealizes the forms of creation, such as we know them, instead of such as they appeared to the Greeks. Maternal Earth, the mighty parent, is superseded by the Spirit of the Earth – the guide of our planet through the realms of sky – while his fair and weaker companion and attendant, the Spirit of the Moon, receives bliss from the annihilation of Evil in the superior sphere.

Shelley develops (more particularly in the lyrics of this drama) his abstruse and imaginative theories with regard to the creation. It requires a mind as subtle and penetrating as his own to understand the mystic meanings scattered throughout the poem. They elude the ordinary reader by their abstraction and delicacy of distinction, but they are far from vague.

It was his design to write prose metaphysical essays on the nature of man, which would have served to explain much of what is obscure in his poetry; a few scattered fragments of observations and remarks alone remain. He considered these philosophical views of mind and nature to be instinct with the intensest spirit of poetry.

More popular poets clothe the ideal with familiar and sensible imagery. Shelley loved to idealize the real – to gift the mechanism of the material universe with a soul and a voice, and to bestow such also on the most delicate and abstract emotions and thoughts of the mind. Sophocles was his great master in this species of imagery. . . .

In the 'Prometheus Unbound', Shelley fulfils the promise quoted from a letter in the note on *The Revolt of Islam*. The tone of the composition is calmer and more majestic, the poetry more perfect as a whole, and the imagination displayed at once more pleasingly beautiful and more varied and daring. The description of the Hours as they are seen in the cave of Demogorgon, is an instance of this – it fills the mind as the most charming picture; we long to see an artist at work to bring to our view the

cars drawn by rainbow-winged steeds
Which trample the dim winds; in each there stands
A wild-eyed charioteer urging their flight.
Some look behind, as fiends pursued them there,
And yet I see no shapes but the keen stars;
Others, with burning eyes, lean forth, and drink
With eager lips the wind of their own speed,
As if the thing they loved fled on before,
And now, even now, they clasped it. Their bright locks
Stream like a comet's flashing hair – they all
Sweep onward.

(*Prometheus Unbound* II iv 130–40)

Through the whole poem there reigns a sort of calm and holy spirit of love; it soothes the tortured, and is hope to the expectant, till the prophecy is fulfilled, and love, untainted by any evil, becomes the law of the world.

England had been rendered a painful residence to Shelley, as much by the sort of persecution with which in those days all men of liberal opinions were visited, and by the injustice he had lately endured in the Court of Chancery,[3] as by the symptoms of

Notes

[3] *the injustice . . . Chancery* Shelley lost his battle for custody of Charles and Ianthe, his two children by his first wife, Harriet Westbrook, on 17 March 1816. Shelley departed for the continent on 3 May.

disease which made him regard a visit to Italy as necessary to prolong his life. An exile, and strongly impressed with the feeling that the majority of his countrymen regarded him with sentiments of aversion (such as his own heart could experience towards none), he sheltered himself from such disgusting and painful thoughts in the calm retreats of poetry, and built up a world of his own, with the more pleasure, since he hoped to induce some one or two to believe that the earth might become such, did mankind themselves consent. The charm of the Roman climate helped to clothe his thoughts in greater beauty than they had ever worn before. And as he wandered among the ruins, made one with nature in their decay, or gazed on the Praxitelean shapes[4] that throng the Vatican, the Capitol, and the palaces of Rome, his soul imbibed forms of loveliness which became a portion of itself.[5] There are many passages in the 'Prometheus' which show the intense delight he received from such studies, and give back the impression with a beauty of poetical description peculiarly his own. He felt this, as a poet must feel when he satisfies himself by the result of his labours, and he wrote from Rome: 'My "Prometheus Unbound" is just finished, and in a month or two I shall send it. It is a drama, with characters and mechanism of a kind yet unattempted, and I think the execution is better than any of my former attempts.'

Letitia Elizabeth Landon (1802–1838)

Letitia Elizabeth Landon was born on 14 August 1802 at 25 Hans Place, Chelsea. Catherine Jane Bishop, her mother, was of Welsh ancestry; her father, John Landon, had been an explorer in Africa, and had returned to London to become a partner in Adair's army agency in Pall Mall. Her education was fragmented and unsystematic; she was taught to read by an invalid neighbour, and at 5 sent for a few months to Miss Rowden's Chelsea school where Lady Caroline Lamb and Mary Russell Mitford had been pupils.

She was 7 when her family moved to Coventry Farm, an ill-advised investment by her father at East Barnet, and the source of his later financial difficulties. Here she was educated by her cousin Elizabeth, who by her own admission was less well-informed than her pupil: 'When I asked Letitia any question relating either to history, geography, grammar – to Plutarch's Lives, or to any book we had been reading, I was pretty certain her answers would be perfectly correct; still, not exactly recollecting, and unwilling she should find out just then that I was less learned than herself, I used thus to question her: "Are you quite certain?" . . . I never knew her to be wrong.'[1]

Landon was a voracious reader, at an early age devouring between 100 and 150 volumes of Cooke's *Poets and Novelists*, in addition to 'Rollin's Ancient History, Hume and Smollett; then come Plutarch's Lives, the Fables of Gay and Aesop, Life of Josephus, Montesquieu's Spirit of the Laws, Dobson's Life of Petrarch, and many

Notes

[4] *Praxitelean shapes* statues like those by Praxiteles, one of the most famous Greek sculptors, born at Athens, *c.*390 BC. Mary is recalling *Prometheus Unbound* III iii 165 (p. 1143).

[5] See Shelley's letter of 23 March 1819 to Peacock: 'Rome is yet the capital of the world. It is a city of palaces and temples more glorious than those which any other city contains, and of ruins more glorious than they' (Jones ii 87).

LETITIA ELIZABETH LANDON

[1] Laman Blanchard, *Life and Literary Remains of L.E.L.* (2 vols, London, 1841), i 9.

Figure 19 Letitia Elizabeth Landon (1802–1838) as portrayed by Daniel Maclise, *c.*1830–5

others, more or less adapted to the young reader'.[2] Also by this time she was composing poetry. 'I cannot remember the time when composition in some shape or other was not a habit,' she later told S. C. Hall. 'I used to invent long stories, which I was only too glad if I could get my mother to hear. These soon took a metrical form, and I used to walk about the grounds and lie awake half the night, reciting my verses aloud.'[3]

When she was 13 the family moved back to Fulham and then to Old Brompton, largely because of her father's troubled finances. It was there, while still a teenager, that she came to the notice of William Jerdan, editor of the *Literary Gazette*: 'My first recollection of the future poetess is that of a plump girl, grown enough to be almost mistaken for a woman, bowling a hoop round the walks, with the hoop-stick in one hand and a book in the other, reading as she ran, and as well as she could manage both exercise and instruction at the same time.'[4]

At the age of 18 she began contributing to the *Literary Gazette* under the initials 'L.E.L.', and soon attracted a following. The intrigue that surrounded her enigmatic initials was evoked in a poem of February 1822 by the Quaker poet, Bernard Barton:

I know not who or what thou art,
　　Nor do I seek to know thee,
Whilst thou, performing thus thy part,
　Such banquets can bestow me.
Then be, as long as thou shalt list,
My viewless, nameless, melodist.

At first she had great difficulty finding a publisher for a long poem she had written, *The Improvisatrice*; it was, she later recalled, rejected by every publisher in London. But as the *Literary Gazette* brought her recognition it became comparatively easy to find a publisher for it in 1824. She later told Alaric Watts that 'I wrote the *Improvisatrice* in less than five weeks, and during that time I often was for two or three days without touching it. I never saw the MS till in proof-sheets a year afterwards, and I made no additions, only verbal alterations.'[5] Her publishers paid her £300 for it, and it was an instant success, going through six editions within the year. Reviews were generally favourable, including an outrageous puff by Jerdan in the *Literary Gazette*; it began by describing Letitia as 'the English Sappho', and went on: 'If true poetry consist in originality of conception, fineness of imagination, beautiful fitness and glow of expression, genuine feeling, and the outpourings of fresh and natural thoughts in all the force of fresh and natural language, it is pre-eminently conspicuous in the writings of L.E.L. Neither are her subjects nor mode of treating them, borrowed from others; but simplicity, gracefulness, fancy and pathos seem to gush forth in spontaneous and sweet union, whatever may be the theme.'[6] Jerdan wanted to present Letitia as an improvisatrice herself, gifted with spontaneous poetic utterance: 'What may spring from the continued cultivation of such promise, it is not easy to predicate; but if the author never excels what she has already done, we can confidently give her the assurance of what the possessor of such talents must most earnestly covet – *Immortality*.'[7]

Jerdan was hardly a disinterested party, and the puff attracted the attentions of other reviewers. Alaric Watts in the *Literary Magnet* ridiculed him at length before reminding his readers of a recent hoax in which Jerdan was implicated: 'We remember that some time since, a report was spread of the premature death of this same interesting young lady, and the *Literary Gazette* joined in the

Notes

[2] Ibid., i 10.
[3] S. C. Hall, *A Book of Memories of Great Men and Women of the Age, from Personal Acquaintance* (1871), p. 267.
[4] *The Autobiography of William Jerdan* (4 vols, London, 1853), iii 174.
[5] Alaric Alfred Watts, *Alaric Watts: A Narrative of his Life* (2 vols, London, 1884), ii 21.
[6] *Literary Gazette* 389–90 (3–10 July 1824) 417–20, 436–7, p. 417.
[7] Ibid., p. 420.

solemn foolery, lamenting her timeless decease as if it really happened.'[8] Despite this, Watts contributed his share of praise to the new star on the literary horizon: 'We are no hermits, nor have we reached that sober decline of life, when the hey-day of the blood attends upon the judgement; and, indeed, if we had, the verses of our "English Sappho" would go far in heating us again. Her descriptions are sufficiently warm and luxurious: she appears to be the very creature of passionate inspiration; and the wild and romantic being whom she describes as the Improvisatrice seems to be the very counterpart of her sentimental self. Her poetical breathing appears to proceed from a soul whose very essence is love; and seared hearts – withered hopes – broken lutes – blighted flowers – music and moonlight, sing their melancholy changes through all her verses.'[9]

Jerdan's encomium also drew fire from the *Westminster Review*, which commented: 'If we are to trust the *Literary Gazette* and common gossip, authorities pretty much on a par on this subject, poets are as plenty as mushrooms, and start up, in the present day, as rapidly as they do after a shower. We cannot walk the streets of London without jostling a poet; and our provincial towns and country places equally abound in them.'[10] Although the reviewer had praise for the poem, it nonetheless contained 'much that is mere verbiage, and pages filled with puny and sickly thoughts clothed in glittering language that draws the eye off from their real character and value'.[11] Others had kinder words and fewer reservations: the *Gentleman's Magazine* claimed seldom to have 'seen a volume more conspicuous for vivid imagination, felicity of diction, vigorous condensation of language, and passionate intensity of sentiment'.[12] In rather a patronizing account of the work, *Blackwood's Edinburgh Magazine* conceded that 'Miss L. has a good command of language, and a fair store of poetical ideas, with a great deal of taste in arrangement, and an ear tuned to the varied melodies of the language.'[13] And the *New Monthly Magazine* commented: 'There is scarcely a line which does not glow with some ray of warm or bright feeling; scarcely an image which is not connected with the heart by some fine and secret association . . . in ardent and impassioned feeling, clothed in language most befitting, *The Improvisatrice* and the poems which follow it have been seldom surpassed.'[14]

This was, of course, business. By 1824 women poets were not just acceptable to the literary marketplace – they were positively fashionable. Hungry for new talent, publishers were willing to take anything saleable and feed it to the ever-open maw of the reading public. Felicia Hemans had colluded with the process because, as a single parent with five children, she had little choice; she burned herself out and died young. Landon may have been unaware of the pressure of the publishing machine that was about to chew her into a pulp, and Alaric Watts sounded an appropriately admonitory note when, in his review, he remarked that 'She possesses taste, sweetness, and a high poetical feeling; and we only regret she should have fallen into interested hands, by which her talents are prematurely thrust upon the world, and rated so far beyond their merits.'[15] That shrewd observation is amplified by Germaine Greer: 'The reality of her life was daily work, endless deadlines, poor pay and no power whatsoever, even to express what she really believed. Grub Street destroyed her personal integrity, worked her to exhaustion and then turned on

Notes

[8] *Literary Magnet* 2 (1824) 106–9, p. 108.

[9] Ibid., p. 106.

[10] *Westminster Review* 3 (1825) 537–9, p. 538.

[11] Ibid., p. 539.

[12] *Gentleman's Magazine* 94 (1824) 61–3, pp. 61–2.

[13] *Blackwood's Edinburgh Magazine* 16 (1824) 189–93, p. 191.

[14] *New Monthly Magazine* 12 (1824) 365–6, p. 365.

[15] *Literary Magnet* 2 (1824) 106–9, p. 109.

her.'[16] To some extent, Landon's own testimony to S. C. Hall corroborates this, although she seems to have been grateful for the opportunity to make a living from her writing:

> I certainly am not one of the authors who complain of the booksellers. My whole life has been one of constant labour. My contributions to various periodicals – whether tales, poetry, or criticism – amount to far more than my published volumes. I have been urged to this by the necessity of aiding those nearly connected with me, whom my father's death left entirely destitute.[17]

Jerdan calculated that Landon earned £2,585 in total from her work, about £250 a year.[18] That made her one of the highest-earning poetesses of her day, partly because of her furious rate of productivity: besides *The Improvisatrice*, she published *The Troubadour* (1825), *The Golden Violet* (1827) and *The Venetian Bracelet* (1829), among many other titles.

The real hardship in her literary life was embroilment in scandal – first through association with the dissolute William Maginn, and then through friendship with Daniel Maclise, the artist. Despite the fuss that surrounded her private life, Germaine Greer is right to observe that 'There is no proof that L.E.L. ever had a lover by day or night, let alone several.'[19] All the same, her vulnerability as an object of scandal intensified the desire for domestic stability, and on 7 June 1838, at St Mary's, Bryanston Square, she married George Maclean, governor of Cape Coast Castle in Africa who, according to S. C. Hall, 'neither knew, felt, nor estimated her value. He wedded her, I am sure, only because he was vain of her celebrity.'[20]

Landon sailed for Africa on 5 July, and arrived on 15 August. Life on the Gold Coast was not what she expected; she found herself cut off from the metropolitan society to which she was accustomed, and on 15 October wrote to Anna Maria Hall, 'I do not wish to form new friends, and never does a day pass without thinking most affectionately of my old ones.'[21] Later that day she was found dead, a bottle of prussic acid in her hand. She was only 36. Suspicions about her husband, and the failure of the coroner to perform a post-mortem, led to much speculation about the causes and means of her death: 'The wildest rumours were immediately set afloat by the hapless lady's female friends in England – each pretending to have been in her confidence, and each affecting to know the facts of the case better than anybody else. One averred that a cup of coffee had been given her by a black boy, which had been drugged by a native woman who had lived with the Governor as his mistress; others denied that she had ever employed hydrocyanic acid, or taken any poison with her; and the rest accused Mr Maclean of cruelty and adultery, and even of being accessory to the murder of his wife.'[22]

It would be difficult, today, to claim Letitia as a neglected genius; she had talent and facility, and the best of her poems contain energy and charm, but her work was wildly variable, even within single works. *The Improvisatrice* remains her quintessential poem, featuring Lorenzo, its Byronic hero, who pursues its thwarted heroine, dark and passionate (like its author), doomed to be jilted for a vacuous blonde. But even her admirers tend to agree that she worked too rapidly for there to have been much polish to her work:

> The injury that resulted from the rule of rapidity – breathless and reckless rapidity – is shown throughout the various poems that compose the overwrought richness, the beautiful excess,

Notes

[16] *Slip-Shod Sibyls* (London, 1995), p. 259.

[17] S. C. Hall, *A Book of Memories of Great Men and Women of the Age, from Personal Acquaintance* (1871), p. 268.

[18] *The Autobiography of William Jerdan* (4 vols, London, 1853), iii 185.

[19] *Slip-Shod Sibyls* (1995), p. 311.

[20] S. C. Hall, *A Book of Memories of Great Men and Women of the Age, from Personal Acquaintance* (1871), p. 274.

[21] Anna Maria Hall, 'The Last Letters of L.E.L.', *Gentleman's Magazine* 11 (1839) 150–2, p. 152.

[22] The Hon. Grantley F. Berkeley, *My Life and Recollections* (4 vols, London, 1865–6), iii 192.

the melodious confusion of the *Improvisatrice*. If the superfluities, amounting to at least one third of the poem had been cut away, all that is obscure would have been clear – all that is languid, strong – all that is incongruous, harmonised.[23]

It is easier to value her verse for precisely the qualities Laman Blanchard singled out – its 'breathless rapidity', richness, and, indeed, confusion. Letitia had, as she rightly observed, 'a soul of romance', but if she represented in any sense the spirit of romanticism, it was of a transitional, even decadent, kind. True, she is capable of writing about Lake District beauty spots, such as Airey Force and Scale Force, in a decidedly Wordsworthian manner, and even her poem about Piccadilly Circus is reminiscent of *Composed upon Westminster Bridge, 3 September 1802*.[24] She is, after all, strongly influenced by Wordsworth, as she admits in her tribute, *On Wordsworth's Cottage, near Grasmere Lake*. But the truth was that the kind of subject-matter that appealed most to her was romantic not in the sense of the sublime set-pieces of *The Prelude*, but in its melancholy preoccupation with thwarted or deceived love.

Sappho's Song from *The Improvisatrice*, which many critics singled out for praise, is a good example. For Landon, Sappho was the exemplar not just of the female poet, but of the jilted lover. Though no more than twenty lines long, Landon's poem is cleverly evocative of the compulsive intensity of love. That fascination is the distinctive preoccupation that drives Letitia's poetic vision. Even when writing about Airey Force, it is to imagine herself as a hermit no longer susceptible to such betrayals.[25]

In content, she is an inheritor of the romantic tradition of Hemans, Scott and Byron; in manner, she is one of the first Victorians: 'Her imaginary tableaux are dense and dramatic, all the space crowded like a Pre-Raphaelite painting with flowers and luxury effects.'[26] Less pronounced in the poems and extracts selected here, the profusion of descriptive detail in the entirely imaginary account of Florence in *The Improvisatrice* is decadent by the standards of high Romanticism. Her attitudes presaged those of the Victorian era in another sense: unlike many of the poets here, she was one of the first truly urban poets. 'I have lived almost wholly in London,' she told S. C. Hall, 'and though very susceptible to the impressions produced by the beauty of the country, certainly never felt at home but on the pavement.'[27] In a letter to Laman Blanchard she was even more emphatic: 'I have such a horror of living in the country: hawthorn hedges and unhappy attachments always go together in my mind.'[28]

She looks forward, quite literally, in *The Princess Victoria*, to the era that was about to dawn – one divorced from the depravity and indolence in which George IV had wallowed. The poem is a curious one, in that it features a heroine – the future Queen and Empress – who is not doomed in the manner of the heroines in the poems of Felicia Hemans. Instead, her 'fair young face' gazes fearlessly into a future in which her throne will be the source of 'knowledge, power, and liberty'. To describe such sentiments as conservative is to miss the point; for Landon it is important that the next monarch is a woman whose status is such that she is not just preserved from the disappointment to which her other heroines are subject, but capable of redeeming others. It is a form of transcendence – and if we are looking for some way of defining what is romantic in Letitia's poetry, that is as good as any.

Notes

23 Laman Blanchard, *Life and Literary Remains of L.E.L.* (2 vols, London, 1841), i 42.

24 See *Romanticism: A Critical Reader*, ed. Duncan Wu (1995), p. 276.

25 See *Airey Force* 9–16.

26 Germaine Greer, *Slip-Shod Sibyls* (1995), pp. 264–5.

27 S. C. Hall, *A Book of Memories of Great Men and Women of the Age, from Personal Acquaintance* (1871), p. 268.

28 Laman Blanchard, *Life and Literary Remains of L.E.L.* (2 vols, London, 1841), i 269.

Her most impressive single work may be her lament, *Felicia Hemans*. Like much of her writing, it was composed to order, for *Fisher's Drawing Room Scrap Book*. The idea behind this annual publication was that Letitia would compose verses to accompany engravings – the main reason for buying the volume. Three years before, she had composed her elegiac *Stanzas on the Death of Mrs Hemans* for the periodical to which both had contributed, the *New Monthly Magazine*. In 1838, she still had much to say about her former colleague. 'Thy name was lovely and thy song was dear', she wrote:

> Was not this purchased all too dearly? – never
> Can fame atone for all that fame hath cost.
> We see the goal but know not the endeavour,
> Nor what fond hopes have on the way been lost.
> What do we know of the unquiet pillow
> By the worn cheek and tearful eyelids pressed,
> When thoughts chase thoughts like the tumultuous billow
> Whose very light and foam reveal unrest?
> We say the song is sorrowful, but know not
> What may have left that sorrow on the song.
> (ll. 33–42)

The verse is moving because Letitia identifies so strongly with her subject, and it indicates how drastically things had changed since Hannah More had first been admitted into the male-dominated world of letters back in the 1770s. By force of numbers, women now had the right to be accepted as poets, providing they stuck to certain 'feminine' themes – but only at a price: in finding an audience for their work, they were sucked into an industry that exploited them mercilessly before destroying them.

'Was not this purchased all too dearly?' Letitia poses the question she must already have been asking about her own career. Within months of publishing this tribute, she was dead. As the years passed, a host of writers would pay tribute to her in verse, including John Greenleaf Whittier, Elizabeth Barrett (see p. 1462), Christina Rossetti and Walter Savage Landor.

Further reading

Letitia Elizabeth Landon: Selected Writings ed. Jerome McGann and Daniel Riess (Peterborough, Ontario, 1997).

Adriana Craciun, *Fatal Women of Romanticism* (Cambridge, 2003), chapter 6.

Germaine Greer, *Slip-Shod Sibyls: Recognition, Rejection and the Woman Poet* (1995), chapter 10.

Glennis Stephenson, *Letitia Landon: The Woman Behind L.E.L.* (Manchester, 1995).

The Improvisatrice: Introduction

From The Improvisatrice; and Other Poems (1824)

I am a daughter of that land
Where the poet's lip and the painter's hand
Are most divine, where the earth and sky
Are picture both and poetry –
I am of Florence. Mid the chill
Of hope and feeling – oh, I still
Am proud to think to where I owe
My birth, though but the dawn of woe!
My childhood passed mid radiant things,
Glorious as hope's imaginings;
Statues but known from shapes of the earth

By being too lovely for mortal birth;[1]
Paintings whose colours of life were caught
From the fairy tints in the rainbow wrought;
Music whose sighs had a spell like those
That float on the sea at the evening's close;
Language so silvery that every word
Was like the lute's awakening chord;
Skies half sunshine and half starlight,
Flowers whose lives were a breath of delight,
Leaves whose green pomp knew no withering,
Fountains bright as the skies of our spring,
And songs whose wild and passionate line
Suited a soul of romance like mine.
    My power was but a woman's power,
Yet in that great and glorious dower
Which genius gives, I had my part;
I poured my full and burning heart
In song, and on the canvas made
    My dreams of beauty visible;
I knew not which I loved the most –
    Pencil or lute, both loved so well.

[*Sappho's Song*]

From The Improvisatrice; and Other Poems (1824)

Farewell, my lute, and would that I
    Had never waked thy burning chords!
Poison has been upon thy sigh,
    And fever has breathed in thy words.

Yet wherefore, wherefore should I blame
    Thy power, thy spell, my gentlest lute?
I should have been the wretch I am
    Had every chord of thine been mute.

It was my evil star above,
    Not my sweet lute that wrought me wrong;
It was not song that taught me love,
    But it was love that taught me song.

If song be past, and hope undone,
    And pulse, and head, and heart, are flame;
It is thy work, thou faithless one –
    But no, I will not name thy name![1]

Notes

The Improvisatrice: Introduction

[1] Lines 9–12 bear a general resemblance to Wordsworth's *Ode*, including the use of the birth/earth rhyme from *Ode* 16–18.

Sappho's Song

[1] *thou faithless one* Phaon.

Sun-god, lute, wreath are vowed to thee!
Long be their light upon my grave,
My glorious grave – yon deep blue sea;
I shall sleep calm beneath its wave![2]

Stanzas on the Death of Mrs Hemans

From New Monthly Magazine (1835)[1]

The rose – the glorious rose is gone.
(Felicia Hemans, Lays of Many Lands)[2]

Bring flowers to crown the cup and lute,
Bring flowers, the bride is near;
Bring flowers to soothe the captive's cell,
Bring flowers to strew the bier!
Bring flowers! – thus said the lovely song;[3]
And shall they not be brought
To her who linked the offering
With feeling and with thought?

Bring flowers, the perfumed and the pure,
Those with the morning dew,
A sigh in every fragrant leaf,
A tear on every hue.
So pure, so sweet thy life has been,
So filling earth and air
With odours and with loveliness
Till common scenes grew fair.

Thy song around our daily path
Flung beauty born of dreams,
That shadows on the actual world
The spirit's sunny gleams.
Mysterious influence, that to earth
Brings down the heaven above,
And fills the universal heart
With universal love.

Notes

[2] Sappho committed suicide by jumping into the sea from the Leucadian rock.

STANZAS ON THE DEATH OF MRS HEMANS

[1] Later in 1835, Landon would contribute an essay 'On the Character of Mrs Hemans's Writings' to the *New Monthly*, in which she commented on Hemans's poetry: 'Nothing can be more pure, more feminine and exalted, than the spirit which pervades the whole: it is the intuitive sense of right, elevated and strengthened into a principle. It is a glorious and a beautiful memory to bequeath; but she who left it is little to be envied. Open the volumes which she has left, legacies from many various hours, and what a record of wasted feelings and disappointed hopes may be traced in their sad and sweet complainings!'

[2] The quotation is from 'The Nightingale's Death-Song' 3–4: 'The rose, the glorious rose is gone, / And I, too, will depart.'

[3] *thus said the lovely song* 'Bring Flowers' was one of the miscellaneous poems included in Hemans's *Lays of Many Lands* (1825).

Such gifts were thine – as from the block,
The unformed and the cold,
The sculptor calls to breathing life
Some shape of perfect mould;
So thou from common thoughts and things
Didst call a charmed song,
Which on a sweet and swelling tide
Bore the full soul along.

And thou from far and foreign lands
Didst bring back many a tone,
And giving such new music still,
A music of thine own.
A lofty strain of generous thoughts,
And yet subdued and sweet –
An angel's song, who sings of earth,
Whose cares are at his feet.

And yet thy song is sorrowful,
Its beauty is not bloom;
The hopes of which it breathes are hopes
That look beyond the tomb.
Thy song is sorrowful as winds
That wander o'er the plain,
And ask for summer's vanished flowers,
And ask for them in vain.

Ah, dearly purchased is the gift,
The gift of song like thine;
A fated doom is hers who stands
The priestess of the shrine.
The crowd – they only see the crown,
They only hear the hymn –
They mark not that the cheek is pale,
And that the eye is dim.

Wound to a pitch too exquisite,
The soul's fine chords are wrung;
With misery and melody
They are too highly strung.
The heart is made too sensitive
Life's daily pain to bear;
It beats in music, but it beats
Beneath a deep despair.

It never meets the love it paints,
The love for which it pines;
Too much of heaven is in the faith
That such a heart enshrines.

The meteor wreath the poet wears
  Must make a lonely lot;
It dazzles only to divide
  From those who wear it not.

Didst thou not tremble at thy fame
  And loathe its bitter prize,
While what to others triumph seemed,
  To thee was sacrifice?
Oh flower brought from paradise
  To this cold world of ours,
Shadows of beauty such as thine
  Recall thy native bowers.

Let others thank thee – 'twas for them
  Thy soft leaves thou didst wreathe;
The red rose wastes itself in sighs
  Whose sweetness others breathe!
And they have thanked thee – many a lip
  Has asked of thine for words,
When thoughts, life's finer thoughts, have touched
  The spirit's inmost chords.

How many loved and honoured thee
  Who only knew thy name;
Which o'er the weary working world
  Like starry music came!
With what still hours of calm delight
  Thy songs and image blend;
I cannot choose but think thou wert
  An old familiar friend.

The charm that dwelt in songs of thine
  My inmost spirit moved;
And yet I feel as thou hadst been
  Not half enough beloved.
They say that thou wert faint and worn
  With suffering and with care;
What music must have filled the soul
  That had so much to spare!

Oh weary one! since thou art laid
  Within thy mother's breast –
The green, the quiet mother earth –
  Thrice blessed be thy rest!
Thy heart is left within our hearts
  Although life's pang is o'er;
But the quick tears are in my eyes,
  And I can write no more.

Felicia Hemans

From Fisher's Drawing Room Scrap-book (1838)[1]

No more, no more, oh never more returning
Will thy beloved presence gladden earth;
No more wilt thou with sad, yet anxious, yearning
Cling to those hopes which have no mortal birth.
Thou art gone from us, and with thee departed
How many lovely things have vanished too;
Deep thoughts[2] that at thy will to being started,
And feelings, teaching us our own were true.
Thou hast been round us like a viewless spirit
Known only by the music on the air;
The leaf or flowers which thou hast named inherit
A beauty known but from thy breathing there,
For thou didst on them fling thy strong emotion,
The likeness from itself the fond heart gave,
As planets from afar look down on ocean
And give their own sweet image to the wave.[3]

And thou didst bring from foreign lands their treasures,[4]
As floats thy various melody along;
We know the softness of Italian measures,[5]
And the grave cadence of Castilian song.
A general bond of union is the poet,
By its immortal verse is language known,
And for the sake of song do others know it –
One glorious poet makes the world his own.
And thou, how far thy gentle sway extended –
The heart's sweet empire over land and sea;
Many a stranger and far flower was blended
In the soft wreath that glory bound for thee.
The echoes of the Susquehanna's waters
Paused in the pine-woods, words of thine to hear,[6]
And to the wide Atlantic's younger daughters[7]
Thy name was lovely and thy song was dear.

Was not this purchased all too dearly? – never
Can fame atone for all that fame hath cost.
We see the goal but know not the endeavour,[8]
Nor what fond hopes have on the way been lost.

Notes

FELICIA HEMANS

[1] This poem appears opposite an engraving of Felicia Hemans taken from a portrait by W. E. West. Hemans died 16 May 1835, of tuberculosis (see pp. 1244–5).

[2] *Deep thoughts* possibly an echo of Wordsworth's 'Thoughts that do often lie too deep for tears' (*Ode* 206).

[3] *The leaf or flowers . . . to the wave* Felicia Hemans conferred beauty on the natural world through her emotional portrayal of it, just as the stars, by their reflection, beautify the sea.

[4] Hemans produced a volume of translations, *Translations from Camoens, and Other Poets, with Original Poetry* (1818), and experimented with foreign metres, subjects, and verse forms, in *Lays of Many Lands* (1826).

[5] *measures* metres.

[6] Landon alludes to Hemans's popularity with American readers.Collected editions of her poetry appeared there before publication in England.

[7] *the wide Atlantic's younger daughters* American women.

[8] *endeavour* effort, pains.

What do we know of the unquiet pillow
By the worn cheek and tearful eyelid pressed,
When thoughts chase thoughts like the tumultuous billow
Whose very light and foam reveals unrest?
We say the song is sorrowful, but know not
What may have left that sorrow on the song;
However mournful words may be, they show not
The whole extent of wretchedness and wrong.
They cannot paint the long sad hours passed only
In vain regrets o'er what we feel we are.[9]
Alas, the kingdom of the lute is lonely –
Cold is the worship coming from afar.

Yet what is mind in woman but revealing
In sweet clear light the hidden world below,
By quicker fancies and a keener feeling
Than those around, the cold and careless, know?
What is to feed such feeling, but to culture[10]
A soil whence pain will never more depart?
The fable of Prometheus and the vulture[11]
Reveals the poet's and the woman's heart.
Unkindly are they judged, unkindly treated
By careless tongues and by ungenerous words,[12]
While cruel sneer and hard reproach repeated
Jar the fine music of the spirit's chords.
Wert thou not weary, thou whose soothing numbers[13]
Gave other lips the joy thine own had not?
Didst thou not welcome thankfully the slumbers
Which closed around thy mourning human lot?

What on this earth could answer thy requiring,
For earnest faith – for love, the deep and true,
The beautiful, which was thy soul's desiring,
But only from thyself its being drew!
How is the warm and loving heart requited
In this harsh world, where it awhile must dwell;
Its best affections wronged, betrayed and slighted –
Such is the doom of those who love too well.
Better the weary dove should close its pinion,
Fold up its golden wings and be at peace;
Enter, oh ladye, that serene dominion
Where earthly cares and earthly sorrows cease.

Notes

[9] *what we feel we are* perhaps an echo of Wordsworth, *Duddon Afterthought* 14: 'We feel that we are greater than we know.'

[10] *culture* cultivate.

[11] *The fable of Prometheus and the vulture* apparently a reference to the story of how Jupiter nailed Prometheus to a rock where, for 3,000 years, an eagle incessantly devoured his liver. Hercules finally freed him and killed the bird. Landon means that woman's fate is, like Prometheus, forever to have her passions exposed and tormented.

[12] *By careless tongues and by ungenerous words* Landon certainly experienced this in the wake of her scandalous associations with William Maginn and Daniel Maclise (see headnote).

[13] *numbers* poetry.

Fame's troubled hour has cleared, and now replying,
A thousand hearts their music ask of thine;
Sleep with a light, the lovely and undying,
Around thy grave – a grave which is a shrine.

Scenes in London: Piccadilly

From The Works of L. E. Landon (Philadelphia, 1838)

The sun is on the crowded street,
It kindles those old towers
Where England's noblest memories meet
Of old historic hours.

Vast, shadowy, dark and indistinct,
Tradition's giant fane
Whereto a thousand years are linked
In one electric chain.

So stands it when the morning light
First steals upon the skies,
And shadowed by the fallen night
The sleeping city lies.

It stands with darkness round it cast,
Touched by the first cold shine;
Vast, vague, and mighty as the past
Of which it is the shrine.

'Tis lovely when the moonlight falls
Around the sculptured stone,
Giving a softness to the walls
Like love that mourns the gone.

Then comes the gentlest influence
The human heart can know,
The mourning over those gone hence
To the still dust below.

The smoke, the noise, the dust of day
Have vanished from the scene;
The pale lamps[1] gleam with spirit ray
O'er the park's sweeping green.

Notes

Scenes in London: Piccadilly

[1] *lamps* Gas lighting was commonly used to illuminate public places by 1820.

Sad shining on her lonely path,
The moon's calm smile above
Seems as it lulled life's toil and wrath
With universal love.

Past that still hour, and its pale moon,
The city is alive;
It is the busy hour of noon
When man must seek and strive.

The pressure of our actual life
Is on the waking brow;
Labour and care, endurance, strife,
These are around him now.

How wonderful the common street,
Its tumult and its throng,
The hurrying of the thousand feet
That bear life's cares along.

How strongly is the present felt
With such a scene beside;
All sounds in one vast murmur melt
The thunder of the tide.

All hurry on – none pause to look
Upon another's face;
The present is an open book
None read, yet all must trace.

The poor man hurries on his race,
His daily bread to find;
The rich man has yet wearier chase,
For pleasure's hard to bind.[2]

All hurry, though it is to pass
For which they live so fast –
What doth the present but amass
The wealth that makes the past?

The past is round us, those old spires
That glimmer o'er our head;
Not from the present are their fires,
Their light is from the dead.

But for the past, the present's powers
Were waste of toil and mind,
But for those long and glorious hours
Which leave themselves behind.

Notes

[2] *bind* retain, keep.

The Princess Victoria[1]

From The Works of L. E. Landon (Philadelphia, 1838)

A fair young face o'er which is only cast
The delicate hues of spring,
Though round her is the presence of the past,
And the stern future gathers darkly fast;
As yet no heavy shadow loads their wing.

A little while hast thou to be a child,
Thy lot is all too high;
Thy face is very fair, thine eyes are mild,
But duties on thine arduous path are piled –
A nation's hopes and fears blend with thy destiny.

Change is upon thy world – it may be thine
To soothe its troubled way,
To make thy throne a beacon and a shrine
Whence knowledge, power, and liberty may shine,
As yet they have not shone on mortal day.

There is much misery on this worn earth,
But much that may be spared;
Of great and generous thought there is no dearth,
And highest hopes of late have had their birth,
Hopes for the many, what the few have shared.[2]

The wind that bears our flag[3] from soil to soil
Teaches us as it flies;
It carries in its breath a summer spoil,[4]
And seeds spring up to stimulate man's toil –
So should our mind spread round its rich supplies.

Thou royal child, the future is thine own,
May it be blessed in thee!
May peace that smiles on all be round thy throne,
And universal truth, whose light alone
Gives golden records unto history.

Notes

THE PRINCESS VICTORIA

[1] Princess Victoria (1819–1901) became Queen of the United Kingdom of Great Britain and Ireland, 1837–1901. By 1837 the monarchy had been brought into disrepute; her reign was to restore its dignity, and may even have saved the institution of the monarchy from oblivion.

[2] *And highest hopes . . . have shared* A reference to the reforms of the 1830s, e.g. Factory Act (1833).

[3] *The wind that bears our flag* Ships were the primary means of international trade.

[4] *spoil* reward, booty; Letitia is probably recalling *Paradise Lost* iv 156–8: 'now gentle gales dispense / Native perfumes, and whisper whence they stole / Those balmy spoils.'

On Wordsworth's Cottage, near Grasmere Lake

From **The Zenana, and Minor Poems of L.E.L. (1839)**

Not for the glory on their heads
  Those stately hilltops wear,
Although the summer sunset sheds
  Its constant crimson there;
Not for the gleaming lights that break
The purple of the twilight lake,
  Half dusky and half fair,
Does that sweet valley seem to be
A sacred place on earth to me.

The influence of a moral spell
  Is found around the scene,
Giving new shadows to the dell,
  New verdure to the green.
With every mountain-top is wrought
The presence of associate thought,
  A music that has been;
Calling that loveliness to life,
With which the inward world is rife.

His home, our English poet's home,
  Amid these hills is made;
Here with the morning hath he come,
  There, with the night delayed.
On all things is his memory cast,
For every place wherein he passed
  Is with his mind arrayed –
That, wandering in a summer hour,
Asked wisdom of the leaf and flower.

Great poet, if I dare to throw
  My homage at thy feet,
'Tis thankfulness for hours which thou
  Hast made serene and sweet;
As wayfarers have incense thrown
Upon some mighty altar-stone
  Unworthy, and yet meet –
The human spirit longs to prove
The truth of its uplooking love.

Until thy hand unlocked its store,
  What glorious music slept!
Music that can be hushed no more
  Was from our knowledge kept.

But the great Mother[1] gave to thee
The poet's universal key,
And forth the fountains swept –
A gushing melody for ever,
The witness of thy high endeavour.

Rough is the road which we are sent,
Rough with long toil and pain;
And when upon the steep ascent,
A little way we gain,
Vexed with our own perpetual care,
Little we heed what sweet things are
Around our pathway blent;
With anxious steps we hurry on,
The very sense of pleasure gone.

But thou dost in this feverish dream
Awake a better mood,
With voices from the mountain stream,
With voices from the wood.
And with their music dost impart
Their freshness to the world-worn heart,
Whose fever is subdued
By memories sweet with other years,
By gentle hopes, and soothing tears.

A solemn creed is thine, and high,
Yet simple as a child,
Who looketh hopeful to yon sky
With eyes yet undefiled
By all the glitter and the glare
This life's deceits and follies wear,
Exalted, and yet mild,
Conscious of those diviner powers
Brought from a better world than ours.

Thou hast not chosen to rehearse
The old heroic themes;
Thou hast not given to thy verse
The heart's impassioned dreams.
Forth flows thy song as waters flow,
So bright above – so calm below,
Wherein the heaven seems
Eternal as the golden shade
Its sunshine on the stream hath laid.

The glory which thy spirit hath
Is round life's common things,
And flingeth round our common path,

Notes

On Wordsworth's Cottage, near Grasmere Lake

[1] *the great Mother* earth.

As from an angel's wings,
A light that is not of our sphere,
Yet lovelier for being here,
Beneath whose presence springs
A beauty never marked before,
Yet once known, vanishing no more.

How often with the present sad,
And weary with the past,
A sunny respite have we had,
By but a chance look cast
Upon some word of thine that made
The sullenness forsake the shade,
Till shade itself was past:
For hope divine, serene and strong,
Perpetual lives within thy song.

Eternal as the hills thy name,
Eternal as thy strain;
So long as ministers of fame
Shall love and hope remain.
The crowded city in its streets,
The valley, in its green retreats,
Alike thy words retain.
What need hast thou of sculptured stone?
Thy temple is thy name alone.

The Poet's Lot

From Life and Literary Remains of L.E.L. (1841)

The poet's lovely faith creates
The beauty he believes;
The light which on his footsteps waits,
He from himself receives.

His lot may be a weary lot,
His thrall a heavy thrall,
And cares and griefs the crowd know not,
His heart may know them all.

But still he hath a mighty dower,
The loveliness that throws
Over the common thought and hour
The beauty of the rose.[1]

Notes

The Poet's Lot

[1] There seems to be a general reminiscence of Wordsworth's *Ode*, and perhaps an echo of ll. 10–11: 'The rainbow comes and goes / And lovely is the rose.'

Death in the Flower

From Life and Literary Remains of L.E.L. (1841)

'Tis a fair tree, the almond tree; there spring[1]
Shows the first promise of her rosy wreath,
Or ere the green leaves venture from the bud,
Those fragile blossoms light the winter bough
With delicate colours heralding the rose,
Whose own aurora[2] they might seem to be.
What lurks beneath their faint and lovely red?
What the dark spirit in those fairy flowers?
'Tis death!

Experience Too Late

From Life and Literary Remains of L.E.L. (1841)

It is the past that maketh my despair;
The dark, the sad, the irrevocable past.
Alas, why should our lot in life be made
Before we know that life? Experience comes,
But comes too late. If I could now recall[1]
All that I now regret, how different
Would be my choice – at best a choice of ill,
But better than my miserable past.
Loathed yet despised, why must I think of it?

The Farewell

From Life and Literary Remains of L.E.L. (1841)

Farewell,
Shadows and scenes that have, for many hours,
Been my companions; I part from ye like friends –
Dear and familiar ones – with deep sad thoughts,
And hopes, almost misgivings!

Notes

DEATH IN THE FLOWER

[1] The almond tree flowers in April.

[2] *aurora* dawn.

EXPERIENCE TOO LATE

[1] *recall* bring back, as at *Paradise Lost* ix 926: 'But past who can recall, or done, undo?'

Elizabeth Barrett Browning (1806–1861)

Elizabeth Barrett was the eldest of eleven children born to Edward and Mary Moulton Barrett, at Coxhoe Hall, Durham, 6 March 1806. As a child, she was a precocious scholar, sharing her brother's lessons and overtaking him in Greek and Latin. She later taught herself Hebrew. An illness in her teens (still not adequately explained) left her a semi-invalid for the rest of her life, and led to dependence on laudanum.

She was composing poetry by 11, when she wrote *The Battle of Marathon*, privately printed three years later. Her first published poem appeared in a magazine when she was 15, and in 1826 she published a second volume, *An Essay on Mind, with Other Poems*. *Prometheus Bound* (1833) and *The Seraphim, and Other Poems* (1838) were fairly well received and led to a volume of collected poems in 1844. Her courtship with Robert Browning began a year later, and they married clandestinely, against her father's wishes, on 12 September 1845. A week later they eloped to Italy.

For most of her life she remained there, returning to London for occasional visits. Her major poetical works are *Casa Guidi Windows* (1851) and *Aurora Leigh* (1857). She died in Florence on 29 June 1861, and was buried in the Protestant Cemetery in Florence.

Although Barrett's most important work marks her as a Victorian, she grew up a Romantic. One of her first idols was Byron, and as a teenager she enjoyed dressing as his page. Her 'Stanzas on the Death of Lord Byron', among her earliest published poems, shows a deft control of the Spenserian stanza, the essentially slow tempo of which was suited to elegy (more so, perhaps, than to *Childe Harold's Pilgrimage*). It can be read as a farewell to Romanticism itself. Another elegy, 'Stanzas Addressed to Miss Landon', responds to Landon's lament for Felicia Hemans, advising her to take comfort from Christian consolation. It is underpinned in part by Barrett's reservations about Landon's verse; as she told Lady Margaret Cocks on 9 December 1835, Landon 'is deficient in energy and condensation, as well as in variety . . . There is a vividness and a naturalness, both in the ideas and the expression of them – yes! And a pathos too! She is like a bird of few notes. They are few – but nature gave them!'[1] Barrett's concerns are sharply focused in the elegy she composed a year later for Landon, 'L.E.L.'s Last Question', which deals with Landon's mysterious death, apparently by prussic acid poisoning. Barrett's best work was yet to come, but her originality and unique abilities are evident even here.

Further reading

Alethea Hayter, *Mrs Browning: A Poet's Work and its Setting* (London, 1962).

Angela Leighton, *Elizabeth Barrett Browning* (Brighton, 1986).

Notes

[1] *The Brownings' Correspondence* ed. Philip Kelley, Ronald Hudson and Scott Lewis (14 vols, Winfield, Kans., 1984–), iii 159.

Stanzas on the Death of Lord Byron (composed shortly after 14 May 1824)

From The Globe and Traveller No. 6733 (30 June 1824)

λέγε πᾶσιν ἀπώλετο.[1]

I am not what I have been.[2]

He *was*, and *is* not! Graecia's trembling shore,
Sighing through all her palmy groves, shall tell
That Harold's pilgrimage at last is o'er;
Mute the impassioned tongue, and tuneful shell,
That erst was wont in noblest strains to swell!
Hushed the proud shouts that rode th' Aegean wave,
For lo! the great deliv'rer breathes farewell!
Gives to the world his mem'ry, and a grave –
And dies amidst the land he lived and fought to save!

Mourn, Hellas,[3] mourn! and o'er thy widowed brow,
For aye the cypress wreath of sorrow twine;
And in thy new-formed beauty, desolate, throw
The fresh-culled flowers on *his* sepulchral shrine.
Yes, let that heart, whose fervour was all thine,
In consecrated urn lamented be!
That generous heart whose genius thrilled divine
Hath spent its last most glorious throb for thee –
Then sank amidst the storm that made thy children free.

Britannia's poet, Graecia's hero, sleeps!
And Freedom, bending o'er the breathless clay,
Lifts up her voice, and in her wildness weeps!
For *us*, a night hath clouded o'er our day
And hushed the lips that breathed our fairest lay.
Alas! and must the British lyre resound
A requiem, while the spirit wings away
Of *him* who on her strings such music found,
And taught her startling chords to breathe so sweet a sound?

The theme grows sadder – and my soul shall find
A language in these tears. No more, no more!
Soon, midst the shrieking of the tossing wind,
The 'dark blue depths'[4] he sang of shall have bore
Our *all* of Byron to his native shore![5]
His grave is thick with voices, murm'ring here
The awful tale of greatness swiftly o'er;
But mem'ry strives with death and, ling'ring near,
Shall consecrate the dust of Harold's lonely bier!

Notes

Stanzas on the Death of Lord Byron

1 Bion, *Lament for Adonis* 5: '. . . tell everyone he is dead . . .'

2 Byron, *Childe Harold's Pilgrimage* iv 1662–3.

3 *Hellas* Greece.

4 Byron *Manfred* I i 76.

5 Byron's remains arrived in London 5 July 1824

Stanzas Addressed to Miss Landon, and suggested by her 'Stanzas on the Death of Mrs Hemans' (signed 'B.')[1]

***From* New Monthly Magazine (1835)**

Thou bay-crowned living one,[2] who o'er
The bay-crowned dead[3] art bowing,
And o'er the shadeless, moveless brow
Thy human shadow throwing;
And o'er the sighless, songless lips
The wail and music wedding,
Dropping o'er the tranquil eyes
Tears not of *their* shedding[4] –

Go take thy music from the dead,
Whose silentness is sweeter;
Reserve thy tears for living brows,
For whom such tears are meeter;
And leave the violets in the grass
To brighten where thou treadest –
No flowers for her – oh, bring no flowers,
Albeit 'Bring flowers',[5] thou saidest.

But bring not near her solemn corse
A type of human seeming;
Lay only dust's stern verity
Upon her dust undreaming.
And while the calm perpetual stars
Shall look upon it solely,
Her sphered soul shall look on *them*
With eyes more bright and holy.

Nor mourn, oh living one, because
Her part in life was mourning:
Would she have lost the poet's flame
For anguish of the burning?
The minstrel harp, for the strained string?
The tripod,[6] for th' afflated[7]
Woe? Or the vision, for those tears
Through which it shone dilated?

Notes

Stanzas Addressed to Miss Landon, and suggested

[1] In a letter to Mary Russell Mitford of 23 November 1842, Barrett wrote of Hemans: 'I admire her genius, love her memory, respect her piety and high moral tone. But she always does seem to me a lady rather than a woman, and so, much rather than a poetess – her refinement, like the prisoner's iron, enters into her soul. She is polished all over to one smoothness and one level, and is monotonous in her best qualities' (*Felicia Hemans* ed. Susan J. Wolfson (Princeton, NJ, 2000), p. 590).

[2] Letitia Landon, who died in the year in which this poem was published. Bay (laurel) was used to crown distinguished poets in Renaissance Italy.

[3] Felicia Hemans.

[4] See Landon, 'Stanzas on the Death of Mrs. Hemans' 111.

[5] See Landon, 'Stanzas on the Death of Mrs Hemans' 1–5.

[6] *tripod* the priestess at Delphi usually sat on a three-legged stool when delivering her prophecies.

[7] *afflated* inspired.

Perhaps she shuddered while the world's
Cold hand her brow was wreathing,
But wronged she ne'er that mystic breath
Which breathed in all her breathing;
Which drew from rocky earth and man
Abstractions high and moving –
Beauty, if not the beautiful,
And love, if not the loving.

Such visionings have paled in sight
The Saviour she descrieth,
And little recks who wreathed the brow
That on His bosom lieth.
The whiteness of His innocence
O'er all her garments flowing –
There learneth she that sweet 'new song'
She will not mourn in knowing.

Be blessed, crowned and living one,
And when thy dust decayeth,
May thine own England say for thee
What now for her it sayeth –
'Albeit softly in our ears
Her silver song was ringing,
The footsteps of her parting soul
Were softer than her singing.'

L.E.L.'s Last Question

From The Athenaeum (26 January 1839)

'Do you think of me as I think of you,
My friends, my friends?'[1] She said it from the sea,
The English minstrel in her minstrelsy,
While under brighter skies than erst she knew[2]
Her heart grew dark, and gropèd as the blind,
To touch, across the waves, friends left behind –
'Do you think of me as I think of you?'

It seemed not much to ask – 'as I of you?'
We all do ask the same – no eyelids cover
Within the meekest eyes that question over;
And little in this world the loving do

Notes

L.E.L.'s Last Question

[1] Barrett's sister, Arabella, explained to Hugh Stuart Boyd on 28 January 1839: 'I daresay you heard of Miss Landon's last letter that she wrote to some friend in England, a day or two before her death . . . the question upon which these lines are written were the last words of her letter.'

[2] *under brighter skies . . . knew* Landon died on the Gold Coast, where she resided with her husband, George Maclean, Governor of Cape Coast Castle.

But sit (among the rocks?) and listen for
The echo of their own love evermore;
Do you think of me as I think of you?

Love-learned, she had sung of only love,
And as a child asleep (with weary head
Dropped on the fairy book he lately read),
Whatever household noises round him move,
Hears in his dream some elfin turbulence –
Even so, suggestive to her inward sense,
All sounds of life assumed one tune of love.

And when the glory of her dream withdrew,
When knightly gestes[3] and courtly pageantries
Were broken in her visionary eyes
By tears, the solemn seas attested true –
Forgetting that sweet lute beside her hand,
She asked not, 'Do you praise me, oh my land?'
But 'Think ye of me, friends, as I of you?'

True heart to love, that pourèd many a year
Love's oracles for England, smooth and well –
Would God thou hadst an inward oracle
In that lone moment, to confirm thee dear!
For when thy questioned friends in agony
Made passionate response, 'We think of thee',
Thy place was in the dust – too deep to hear!

Could she not wait to catch the answering breath?
Was she content with that drear ocean's sound,
Dashing his mocking infinite around
The craver of a little love, beneath
Those stars, content – where last her song had gone?
They, mute and cold in radiant life, as soon
Their singer was to be, in darksome death!

Bring your vain answers, cry, 'We think of thee!'
How think ye of her? In the long ago
Delights, or crowned by new bays? Not so;
None smile, and none are crowned where lyeth she,
With all her visions unfulfilled – save one,
Her childhood's, of the palm-trees in the sun:
And lo, their shadow on her sepulchre!

Do you think of me as I think of you?
Oh friends, oh kindred, oh dear brotherhood
Of the whole world, what are we that we should
For covenants of long affection sue?

Notes

[3] *gestes* brave deeds.

Why press so near each other, when the touch
Is barred by graves? Not much, and yet too much,
This 'Think upon me as I think of you.'

But while on mortal lips I shape anew
A sigh to mortal issues, verily
Above th' unshaken stars that see us die,
A vocal pathos rolls – and He who drew
All life from dust, and *for* all tasted death,
By death, and life, and love appealing, saith,
'Do you think of me as I think of you?'

Sonnet on Mr Haydon's Portrait of Mr Wordsworth[1]

From The Athenaeum (29 October 1842)

Wordsworth upon Helvellyn! Let the cloud
Ebb audibly along the mountain wind,
Then break against the rock, and show behind
The lowland valleys floating up to crowd
The sense with beauty. *He* with forehead bowed
And humble-lidded eyes, as one inclined
Before the sovran thoughts of his own mind,
And very meek with inspirations proud,
Takes here his rightful place as poet-priest,
By the high altar, singing prayer and prayer
To the yet higher heav'ns. A vision free
And noble, Haydon, hath thine art released[2] –
No portrait this, with academic air!
This is the poet and his poetry.

Notes

Sonnet on Mr Haydon's Portrait of Mr Wordsworth

[1] Haydon's painting, *Wordsworth on Helvellyn*, was completed in 1842 and is now at the National Gallery, London. It is reproduced by Gill, *William Wordsworth: A Life* (Oxford, 1989), Plate 17. Haydon and Barrett enjoyed a warm and friendly correspondence, but never met; they were brought together by a mutual admiration for Wordsworth.

[2] Haydon forwarded a copy of the sonnet to Wordsworth on 19 October 1842. In an appreciative letter to her of 26 October, Wordsworth suggested a revision to lines 11–12: 'By a vision free / And noble, Haydon, is thine art released' (*LY* iv 384–5).

Index of First Lines

This index list first lines of verse only.

Index to Headnotes and Notes